MW01041511

UNIVERSITY CASEBOOK SERIES

CASES AND COMMENTS

CRIMINAL PROCEDURE

SEVENTH EDITION

by

JAMES B. HADDAD
Late Professor of Law
Northwestern University

ELIZABETH P. MARSH
Professor of Law
Quinnipiac College of Law

JAMES B. ZAGEL
Judge, United States District Court for the
Northern District of Illinois

LINDA R. MEYER
Professor of Law
Quinnipiac College of Law

GARY L. STARKMAN
Attorney-at-Law, Chicago, Illinois
Former Assistant United States Attorney
Northern District of Illinois

WILLIAM J. BAUER
Judge, United States Court of Appeals
for the Seventh Circuit

FOUNDATION PRESS

395 Hudson Street
New York, NY 10014
Phone Toll Free 1–877–888–1330
Fax (212) 367–6799
foundation–press.com

Printed in the United States of America

ISBN 978–1–59941–250–4

DEDICATION

This edition of Cases and Comments on Criminal Procedure is dedicated to the memory of Professor Fred E. Inbau who died a decade ago at the age of eighty-nine. At his death he was still reading and writing in the law. It was Professor Inbau who served as the first senior author of the first edition of this casebook. He served for many years as the Wigmore Professor of Law at Northwestern University. He was a superior scholar and an exceptionally fair man. His scholarship in the fields of criminal law, criminal procedure and evidence would alone place him among the pre-eminent figures of American law. To this he added pivotal work in the reformation of criminology and police science. He led the drive to implement the use of scientific methods of evidence gathering and analysis and served as President of the American Academy of Forensic Sciences. He led the reform of coercive police practices in the interrogation of criminal suspects. Along with John Reid, he wrote the definitive text on Criminal Interrogation and Confessions. This master work is likely to be studied for as long as police question suspects, in other words, as long-lived as it is possible for a law book to be.

Professor Inbau was a decent, forthright man deeply committed to truth, to the law, to his school, to his family, and his community. He was respected even by those true scholars who strongly disagreed with him. He inspired countless men and women to do important work. He will be missed both for himself and for the contributions he might yet have made to the administration of justice.

*

PREFACE

This seventh edition continues with the same approach that the series began in 1968 by Professor Fred Inbau, Claude Sowle and James R. Thompson. We continue to use both the case study method and our own summaries drawn from extensive research of state and federal cases. We believe these summaries serve to remind the student that criminal procedure does not begin and end with the decisions of the Supreme Court.

As with prior editions, the text begins with a treatment of limitations of law enforcement investigative procedures. And also, like prior editions, we stress the newer decisions (which manifest a clear trend of judicial caution) with reliance upon summaries of older decisions to trace the development of the law in various areas. We provide materials related to problems in the context of trial procedure to remind the student that criminal procedure does not begin and end with police conduct and pre-trial motions.

We continue the practice of extensive notes and comments which allows each teacher to choose the particular constellation of issues to be explored in each course.

Every chapter has been revised, updated and contracted or expanded as the law has developed.

One person largely responsible for this edition, as well as the last six, was the late Professor James Haddad who died in 1992 at the age of forty-nine. From 1969, he served on the faculty of the Northwestern University School of Law. He also served as First Assistant State's Attorney, appointed by defense attorney in scores of criminal cases, board member of the Illinois State appellate Defender's Office, and as a lawyer for the Northwestern Legal Assistance Clinic.

Elizabeth Phillips Marsh is a Professor of Law at Quinnipiac University School of Law. She teaches Criminal Procedure, Evidence, Federal Criminal Law, Computer Crime and Constitutional Law. She earned her J.D. from New York University School of Law after completing her undergraduate degree at Harvard University (Radcliffe College). As an assistant district attorney in the office of Robert M. Morgenthau, she handled numerous trial cases, including homicides. She was also a liaison member of the Career Criminal Division which focused on cases against defendants with extensive criminal records. In addition, she has taught at the University of Alabama School of Law and Washington and Lee University School of Law. She served for many years as the chair of the Committee on the Rules of Evidence and Criminal Procedure for the Criminal Justice Section of the American Bar Association. Her writings focus on the Fourth Amendment, the exclusionary rule, the litigation of motions to suppress, the Federal Rules of

Evidence, the investigation and prosecution of cybercrime, and the intersection of criminal law and the Internet.

James Zagel is a Judge of the United States District Court for the Northern District of Illinois. He holds undergraduate and graduate degrees in philosophy from the University of Chicago. At Harvard Law School he was an officer of the Harvard Voluntary Defenders. Later, as a prosecutor, Zagel argued several cases before the United States Supreme Court, including *Witherspoon v. Illinois, Lego v. Twomey, and Kirby v. Illinois*. He has been lead trial prosecutor in numerous major homicide cases. He has lectured extensively to lawyers and judges, specializing in the law of confessions, eye-witness identification, discovery, evidentiary privileges, and psychiatric defenses. He has served as Director of the Illinois State Police. He is a published novelist writing on legal themes.

Linda Ross Meyer is a Professor of Law at Quinnipiac Law School. She teaches Criminal Procedure, Criminal Law, Theories of Punishment, Jurisprudence, Torts, Animal Law, Professional Responsibility, Wills and Trusts, and a Supreme Court Seminar. She holds a J.D. and Ph.D. from the University of California, Berkeley, and spent three years clerking for federal judges at the district, appellate, and Supreme Court levels. She currently writes in the areas of habeas corpus, qualified immunity, punishment theory, mercy, and jurisprudence.

Gary Starkman is in private practice in Chicago. As a trial lawyer, he has participated in a significant number of federal criminal cases. He has had extensive federal appellate practice. He headed the Appellate Division of the office of the United States Attorney for the Northern District of Illinois, serving in that role under former co-author James R. Thompson, during a period of innovative uses of long existing federal penal laws.

William J. Bauer is a Judge of the United States Court of Appeals for the Seventh Circuit and now serves as a senior circuit judge. Judge Bauer practiced criminal law as a State's Attorney, United States Attorney, and criminal defense lawyer in state and federal courts. He had extensive experience as a trial judge in criminal cases in both the state and the federal systems. He has served as a federal judge for over twenty-five years. Judge Bauer has regularly taught criminal procedure courses to law students.

July, 2008

SUMMARY OF CONTENTS

TABLE OF CONTENTS

CHAPTER 4. Wiretapping and Electronic Surveillance 337

TABLE OF CASES

Principal cases are in bold type. Non-principal cases are in roman type. References are to Pages.

Powers v. Ohio, 499 U.S. 400, 111 S.Ct. 1364, 113 L.Ed.2d 411 (1991), 1408
Poyner v. Murray, 964 F.2d 1404 (4th Cir. 1992), 168
Pozo, People v., 746 P.2d 523 (Colo.1987), 1321
Pozzy, United States v., 902 F.2d 133 (1st Cir.1990), 1972
Pratt v. Chicago Housing Authority, 848 F.Supp. 792 (N.D.Ill.1994), 672
Pratt v. State, 9 Md.App. 220, 263 A.2d 247 (Md.App.1970), 187
Pratt, United States v., 913 F.2d 982 (1st Cir.1990), 1563
Presley, United States v., 52 F.3d 64 (4th Cir.1995), 1092
Pressel, State v., 2 Or.App. 477, 468 P.2d 915 (Or.App.1970), 164
Press–Enterprise Co. v. Superior Court, 464 U.S. 501, 104 S.Ct. 819, 78 L.Ed.2d 629 (1984), 1200
Preston v. United States, 376 U.S. 364, 84 S.Ct. 881, 11 L.Ed.2d 777 (1964), 560
Price v. Georgia, 398 U.S. 323, 90 S.Ct. 1757, 26 L.Ed.2d 300 (1970), 1114
Prieskorn, United States v., 658 F.2d 631 (8th Cir.1981), 1732
Priestley v. State, 446 P.2d 405 (Wyo.1968), 121
Probasco, People v., 795 P.2d 1330 (Colo. 1990), 119
Procopio, United States v., 88 F.3d 21 (1st Cir.1996), 826
Procter & Gamble, United States v., 356 U.S. 677, 78 S.Ct. 983, 2 L.Ed.2d 1077 (1958), 1030
Proctor v. United States, 404 F.2d 819 (D.C.Cir.1968), 139
Prosser, State v., 235 So.2d 740 (Fla.App. 1 Dist.1970), 167
Provo v. Warden, 844 P.2d 360 (Utah App. 1992), 590
Provost, State v., 490 N.W.2d 93 (Minn. 1992), 147
Pruitt, State v., 286 N.C. 442, 212 S.E.2d 92 (N.C.1975), 43
Pugh v. Rainwater, 572 F.2d 1053 (5th Cir. 1978), 1093
Pugh, United States ex rel. v. Pate, 401 F.2d 6 (7th Cir.1968), 444
Pugliese, People v., 311 N.Y.S.2d 851, 260 N.E.2d 499 (N.Y.1970), 117
Puglisi, United States v., 723 F.2d 779 (11th Cir.1984), 637
Pulido, United States v., 69 F.3d 192 (7th Cir.1995), 1661
Pulliam v. Allen, 466 U.S. 522, 104 S.Ct. 1970, 80 L.Ed.2d 565 (1984), 985
Pungitore, United States v., 910 F.2d 1084 (3rd Cir.1990), 1140
Pupo, United States v., 841 F.2d 1235 (4th Cir.1988), 1071
Purkett v. Elem, 514 U.S. 765, 115 S.Ct. 1769, 131 L.Ed.2d 834 (1995), 1411

Quartermaine, United States v., 913 F.2d 910 (11th Cir.1990), 1092
Query, United States v., 928 F.2d 383 (11th Cir.1991), 1848
Quinn, People v., 183 Colo. 245, 516 P.2d 420 (Colo.1973), 992
Quinn, United States v., 365 F.2d 256 (7th Cir.1966), 1188
Quinones, People v., 61 A.D.2d 765, 402 N.Y.S.2d 196 (N.Y.A.D. 1 Dept.1978), 613

Raibon, People v., 843 P.2d 46 (Colo.App. 1992), 39
Rainwater, Commonwealth v., 425 Mass. 540, 681 N.E.2d 1218 (Mass.1997), 183
Rakas v. Illinois, 439 U.S. 128, 99 S.Ct. 421, 58 L.Ed.2d 387 (1978), 398, **788**
Ralls v. United States, 52 F.3d 223 (9th Cir.1995), **1049**
Ramirez, State v., 817 P.2d 774 (Utah 1991), 314
Ramirez–Encarnacion, United States v., 291 F.3d 1219 (10th Cir.2002), 361
Ramirez–Rizo, United States v., 809 F.2d 1069 (5th Cir.1987), 1784
Ramirez–Sandoval, United States v., 872 F.2d 1392 (9th Cir.1989), 826
Ramjit, People v., 203 A.D.2d 488, 612 N.Y.S.2d 600 (N.Y.A.D. 2 Dept.1994), 1057
Ramsey, United States v., 431 U.S. 606, 97 S.Ct. 1972, 52 L.Ed.2d 617 (1977), 690
Randall, People v., 83 Cal.Rptr. 658, 464 P.2d 114 (Cal.1970), 175
Randazzo, United States v., 80 F.3d 623 (1st Cir.1996), 1187
Ransom, State v., 182 Neb. 243, 153 N.W.2d 916 (Neb.1967), 166
Raper, United States v., 676 F.2d 841 (D.C.Cir.1982), 1780
Rastelli, United States v., 870 F.2d 822 (2nd Cir.1989), 1818
Rasul v. Bush, 542 U.S. 466, 124 S.Ct. 2686, 159 L.Ed.2d 548 (2004), 1999
Rawlings v. Kentucky, 448 U.S. 98, 100 S.Ct. 2556, 65 L.Ed.2d 633 (1980), 797
Ray, People v., 105 A.D.2d 988, 482 N.Y.S.2d 133 (N.Y.A.D. 3 Dept.1984), 186
Reagan v. United States, 157 U.S. 301, 15 S.Ct. 610, 39 L.Ed. 709 (1895), **1778**
Recio et al., United States v., 537 U.S. 270, 123 S.Ct. 819, 154 L.Ed.2d 744 (2003), 881
Reck v. Pate, 367 U.S. 433, 81 S.Ct. 1541, 6 L.Ed.2d 948 (1961), 26
Redd v. Sowders, 809 F.2d 1266 (6th Cir. 1987), 1157
Redding v. State, 10 Md.App. 601, 272 A.2d 70 (Md.App.1971), 287
Redinger, People v., 906 P.2d 81 (Colo.1995), 659
Redmond, Commonwealth v., 357 Mass. 333, 258 N.E.2d 287 (Mass.1970), 315
Redondo–Lemos, United States v., 27 F.3d 439 (9th Cir.1994), 936
Redondo–Lemos, United States v., 955 F.2d 1296 (9th Cir.1992), 936
Reed v. Ross, 468 U.S. 1, 104 S.Ct. 2901, 82 L.Ed.2d 1 (1984), 1732

CASES AND COMMENTS

CRIMINAL PROCEDURE

*

CHAPTER 1

INTRODUCTION: OUTLINE OF CRIMINAL PROCEDURE

The procedure followed in a criminal case is not the same for all states, but the differences are slight as regards basic concepts and principles. In essential respects there is also little difference between the procedure of the state courts and that which exists in federal courts. This similarity stems, at least in part, from the application of constitutional principles to the criminal justice process. The federal system and most state systems also rely on a statutory system for guiding criminal procedure. The Federal Rules of Criminal Procedure govern federal prosecutions.

The following outline of criminal procedure is presented to familiarize the law student with basic procedures involved or referred to in the case reports he or she will encounter in subsequent chapters.

PRE-ARREST PROCEDURES

In state jurisdictions most prosecutions are initiated by an arrest made before a formal criminal charge has been brought. Sometimes the arrest is made "on the scene," as in a domestic disturbance or a burglary where the offender has been caught within the premises. In other situations, a police investigation precedes the arrest. Sometimes, particularly in the case of crimes without complaining witnesses, such as narcotics and gambling, officers may obtain a search warrant to aid their pre-arrest investigation. More frequently, however, no legal "process" (e.g., a search warrant, or a grand jury subpoena) is used in the pre-arrest investigation conducted by local authorities.

Even when an investigation has preceded an arrest, the typical arrest by state or local authorities, at least in felony cases, is made without an arrest warrant. Because of constitutional limitations upon non-emergency warrantless entries to arrest, police are more likely to obtain an arrest warrant when they contemplate making a non-consensual entry into a suspect's home to arrest him or her. Once the arrest has been effected, the police often engage in investigative procedures before bringing the arrestee before a judge or magistrate. Generally, they search the suspect's person for evidence and for weapons. In some cases they may interrogate the arrestee in an effort to obtain a confession or an admission. In serious cases, such as armed robbery, the police may present the suspect to witnesses for possible identification, either alone (in a "show-up") or with others (in a "line-up"). Many of the legal issues discussed in Part I of this book arise from police procedures utilized between the arrest and the defendant's first judicial appearance.

In local and state prosecutions, the law enforcement is generally more reactive. Often an arrest is made before an investigation is completed. If the police decide to go forward with a prosecution, they will seek to formally charge the suspect. Depending upon law and practice in a jurisdiction, sometimes a prosecutor will participate in the decision to charge. In fact, he or she may have final authority. In other jurisdictions, particularly in less serious cases, the police, unassisted by the prosecutor, may decide what charges, if any, are to be made against the arrestee. Typically, where charges are to be filed, an officer or the victim will sign a preliminary hearing felony complaint or a misdemeanor complaint. In some jurisdictions prosecution is initiated when a prosecutor signs a similar document known as an "information."

Another mode of initiating prosecution is used ordinarily in federal prosecutions and occasionally in state prosecutions. Federal prosecutions are generally more proactive. A United States Attorney conducts an investigation, sometimes utilizing the power of a grand jury to compel testimony and to issue subpoenas *duces tecum* for books and records. The prosecutor also may issue directions to investigators from his or her office or, as in the federal system, to investigators from other agencies such as the Federal Bureau of Investigation, the Treasury Department, or the Drug Enforcement Administration. In cases of that type, prosecution is initiated by indictment. An arrest warrant or a summons then issues for the defendant.

PROCEDURE BETWEEN ARREST AND TRIAL

In most states, by statute or court rule, an arrested person must be taken without unnecessary delay before the nearest judge or magistrate. What happens after presentation to the judge or magistrate will depend upon whether the arrested person is accused of a felony or a misdemeanor. If the charge is a misdemeanor, the judge or magistrate will sometimes have the power and authority to hear the case, and he or she may proceed with the trial unless the accused demands trial by jury or a continuance is ordered for some reason. If the offense is a felony, the judge or magistrate before whom the accused is brought will ordinarily lack the constitutional or legislative authority to conduct trials for crimes of that degree of seriousness, and in such instances conducts what is known as a "preliminary examination." The first judicial appearance of an arrestee is often known as the "arraignment."

The Right to Bail

After arrest, the first decision made by a court frequently is whether the accused is entitled to release on bail. Subject to some exceptions for persons charged with death penalty offenses, persons on parole and others, and persons subject to special preventive detention procedures, an accused is entitled to have the court set bail. Bail is fixed at a specific dollar amount. If the accused places cash or property worth that amount with the clerk of court, he or she will be at liberty pending his trial. If the accused appears at the required proceedings, bail is refunded but failure to appear results in forfeiture of bail. In some states, professional bail bondsmen will, in effect, deposit bail in exchange for a non-refundable fee from the defendant. In other states, a defendant is allowed to deposit a portion of his bail (usually equivalent to the bondsman's fee, i.e., 10%), most of which is refunded if the defendant honors the obligation to appear. Moreover, courts generally have the power to allow release without any deposit—merely accepting the defendant's signature on a bond which makes him or her liable for the amount of bail if he or she fails to appear. Such defendants, usually thought to be highly likely to appear for trial, are said to be released on "recognizance," "signature," or "individual bond." A number of defendants fail to "make" bail and remain in jail pending trial.

In some jurisdictions, defendants charged with certain offenses may be "preventively detained" without bail upon a showing of the likelihood that they will flee or upon a showing of their dangerousness to others. Usually special procedural safeguards must be satisfied before such a defendant can be held without bail.

Probable Cause to Detain

After a person has been arrested as a suspect by the police or upon authorization of a prosecutor, and remains deprived of liberty, he or she is entitled, as a constitutional right, to a prompt, though limited judicial hearing on the question of probable cause *to detain*, usually within forty-eight hours of arrest. At this kind of hearing, normal rules of evidence are not applicable and counsel for the accused is not required. This procedure is akin to that used when, prior to arrest, the prosecutor seeks an arrest warrant from a court. The accused does not have this right, however, when prosecution has been initiated by arrest warrant or indictment. In such instances an *ex parte* probable cause determination has already been made.

The Right to an Attorney

The Sixth Amendment of the Constitution of the United States provides that "in all criminal prosecutions, the accused shall enjoy the right ... to have the assistance of Counsel for his defense." And the Supreme Court of the United States has held that a defendant cannot be sentenced to any period of incarceration unless he or she has been afforded this right. The right includes the appointment of counsel for the indigent accused. A "preliminary hearing", of course, is a part of the "criminal prosecution."

Preliminary Hearing

A preliminary hearing is a relatively informal proceeding by means of which a determination is made as to whether there are reasonable grounds for believing the accused person committed the offense—as to whether it is fair, under the circumstances, to require the accused to stand a regular trial. If after such a hearing the judge or magistrate decides that the accusation is without probable cause, the accused will be discharged. This discharge, however, will not bar a grand jury indictment if subsequently developed evidence (or the same evidence presented on the preliminary hearing) satisfies the grand jury that the accusation is well founded.

If the preliminary hearing judge or magistrate decides that the accusation is a reasonable one, the accused will be "bound over" to the grand jury—that is, held in jail, or subject to bond or recognizance, until the charge against him is presented for grand jury consideration. (The nature and composition of a "grand jury" and the difference between it and a "petit" or "trial jury" are described later in this outline.)

In some jurisdictions, as subsequently detailed, once the magistrate has found probable cause, the prosecutor may bypass the grand jury and file a felony "information" upon which the accused will be tried.

Preliminary hearings are not held if the *initial* charge was by way of indictment. In many federal and in some state jurisdictions, even if the original charge is a preliminary complaint or an information, the prosecution will pre-empt the defendant's right to a preliminary hearing by promptly obtaining a grand jury indictment before the preliminary is conducted.

The Grand Jury

Misdemeanors are usually prosecuted upon an "information" filed by the prosecuting attorney after he or she has received and considered the sworn complaint of the victim or of some other person with knowledge of the facts. As regards felonies, however, in about half of the states and in the federal system, absent waiver by the accused, the matter must first be submitted to a "grand jury." Then, after hearing the alleged facts related by the victim or other persons, the grand jury determines whether there are reasonable grounds for proceeding to an actual trial of the person charged.

A grand jury is often composed of 23 citizens, 16 of whom constitute a quorum. The votes of 12 members are necessary to the return of an "indictment." Some jurisdictions use smaller grand juries.

The Constitution of the United States does not require that *state* prosecutors use a grand jury to charge felony offenses[1], and there is an increasing tendency to enact statutes permitting the prosecution to charge felonies by filing an "information." Ordinarily a person charged by information must have a preliminary hearing before he or she can be tried for the charge. A defendant charged by a grand jury, however, may not have a right to a preliminary hearing since it is thought that rights are adequately safeguarded by fellow citizens who serve on the grand jury.

One highly significant purpose of the grand jury is to investigate complex crimes. The grand jury has the right to subpoena witnesses, to ask them questions, and to require the production of books and records. It may exercise these rights before any charge is filed and before the specific crime or its perpetrator is known. Police agencies usually do not possess this authority to compel the production of evidence, and it is generally conceded that such a right is required for effective investigation of much financial crime, official corruption, and organized crime.

The consideration of a felony charge by a grand jury is in no sense a trial. Only the state's evidence is presented and considered; the suspected offender is usually not even heard, nor is his or her lawyer present to offer evidence. However, some state laws now provide that the suspect has a

1. The Grand Jury process is one of the few criminal procedure rights in the Constitution that has not been incorporated through the Fourteenth Amendment to apply to the states.

right to appear before the grand jury if he or she elects to do so, but very few suspects exercise that option. Other laws provide that a "target" of the grand jury investigation has the right to have counsel present when summoned to appear before the grand jury.

The Arraignment and Plea

Following an indictment, the next step in felony cases is the appearance of the accused person before a judge who is empowered to try felony cases. The indictment is read to the defendant or the essence of its contents is made known to him; in other words, he is advised of the criminal charges made against him. If he pleads guilty, the judge can sentence him immediately or take the matter under advisement for a decision at an early date. If the accused pleads "not guilty," a date is then set for his actual trial. This appearance is sometimes called an "arraignment," but it should not be confused with an arrestee's first appearance before a judge following his or her arrest.

In some states, and in the federal system, the defendant may sometimes enter a plea of "nolo contendere," a plea which has the same effect as a plea of guilty, except that the admission thereby made cannot be used as evidence in a civil action.

Usually the initial plea is not guilty. Most defendants who plead guilty to felony charges do so after completion of pre-trial discovery procedures.

Pre-trial Motions

After the formal charge has been made against the accused, he or she may, in advance of trial, seek to terminate the prosecution's case, or at least seek to better prepare his defense, by utilizing a procedure known as making or filing a "motion." A motion is merely a request for a court ruling or order that will afford the defendant the assistance or remedy sought. Some of the more frequently used motions are the following:

Motion to Quash the Indictment. With this motion the defendant may question the legal sufficiency of the indictment. If the court decides that the indictment adequately charges a criminal offense, and that it was obtained in accordance with the prescribed legal procedures, the motion will be overruled; otherwise the indictment will be considered invalid and "quashed." Even after an indictment has been thus rejected and set aside, the prosecutor may nevertheless proceed to obtain another and proper indictment. Moreover, the prosecution is entitled to appeal from a court order quashing an indictment, since at this stage of the proceedings, the defendant has not been placed in jeopardy and consequently a subsequent indictment and trial would not constitute a violation of the constitutional privilege against "double jeopardy."

Motions to dismiss indictments are also sometimes based upon claims of denial of a speedy trial, former jeopardy, or grand jury abuse. When granted, prosecutors may usually appeal these decisions just as they may appeal orders that quash an indictment.

Motion for a Bill of Particulars. Although the indictment, if valid, will ordinarily contain all the allegations of fact necessary to set forth the offense, the defendant may, by a motion for a "bill of particulars," obtain further details respecting the accusation.

In addition to the motion for a bill of particulars, there now exists an expanded right, accorded to both the prosecution and the defense, to learn what evidence the other side intends to use. It is known as a *Motion for Discovery*, whereby both parties seek to learn not only the details of the crime but also the names of the other side's witnesses and what they are expected to say.

Motion for a Change of Venue. A defendant may attempt to avoid trial before a particular judge or in the city, county, or district where the crime occurred by seeking a "change of venue." In instances where this appears to be necessary in order that the defendant may receive a fair trial, the motion for a change of venue will be granted.

Motion to Suppress Evidence. A defendant may file with the court, normally in advance of trial, a "motion to suppress" evidence which he or she contends has been obtained in an unconstitutional manner. The evidence in question may be, on the one hand, a tangible item such as a gun, narcotics, or stolen property or, on the other hand, an intangible item such as a confession or the testimony of eyewitnesses who are expected to identify the accused as the offender. If the court is satisfied that the evidence has been obtained in violation of the defendant's rights, it will order the evidence suppressed, which means that it cannot be used at the trial. If the court decides that the evidence was lawfully obtained, it is usable against the defendant at the trial in the prosecutor's direct case.

THE TRIAL

In all states, and in the federal system, the accused is entitled to "a speedy trial." This right to an early trial is guaranteed by the various state constitutions, and the constitutional provisions are generally supplemented by legislative enactments particularizing and specifically limiting the pretrial detention period. The federal courts are governed by the Speedy Trial Act of 1974, which is a statutory scheme providing time periods within which federal trials must begin. Subject to exceptions, a federal trial must commence within one hundred days from arrest. Not more than seventy days may pass between indictment, or a first judicial appearance, and the commencement of trial. Even under this act, some circumstances permit the accused to waive his right to a trial within the statutory period. Some periods of delay are excluded from the statutory period.

Jury Trial—Trial by Judge Alone

A person accused of a "serious crime", which is considered to be one for which there may be incarceration beyond six months, is entitled to trial by jury, as a matter of constitutional right. By statute or rule, the right to trial by jury has been extended to even more minor cases in many jurisdictions. However, the accused may waive this right and elect a bench trial, a trial by a judge alone. In some jurisdictions the defendant has an absolute right to this waiver; in others (e.g., the federal system) waiver is conditioned upon the concurrence of the judge and the prosecution.

If the case is tried without a jury, the judge hears the evidence and decides whether the defendant is guilty or not guilty. Where the trial is by a jury, the jury determines the facts and the judge serves more as an umpire or referee; it is his or her function to determine what testimony or evidence is legally "admissible," that is, to decide what should be heard or considered by the jury. But the ultimate decision as to guilt or innocence is made by the jury alone.

Jury Selection

In the selection of the jurors, usually twelve in number, who hear the defendant's case, many states permit the defense as well as the prosecuting attorney to question a larger number who have been chosen for jury service from the list of registered voters. In the federal system and a growing number of states, however, most trial judges will do practically all of the questioning, with very little opportunity for questioning accorded the prosecutor and defense counsel. Nevertheless, each lawyer has a certain number of "peremptory challenges" which means that he or she can arbitrarily refuse to accept as jurors a certain number of those who appear as prospective jurors. And in all cases, if any prospective juror's answers to the questions of either attorney reveal a prejudice or bias which prevents him or her from being a fair and impartial juror, the judge, either sua sponte or at the suggestion of either counsel, will dismiss that person from jury service. Although the desired result is not always achieved, the avowed purpose of this practice of permitting lawyers to question prospective jurors is to obtain twelve jurors who will be fair to both sides of the case.

Opening Statements

After the jury is selected, both the prosecuting attorney and the defense lawyer are entitled to make "opening statements" in which each outlines what he or she intends to prove. The purpose is to acquaint the jurors with each side of the case, so that it will be easier for them to follow the evidence as it is presented.

The Prosecution's Evidence

After the opening statements the prosecuting attorney produces the prosecution's testimony and evidence. He or she has the burden of proving the state's case "beyond a reasonable doubt." If at the close of the prosecution's case the judge is of the opinion that reasonable jurors could not conclude that the charge against the defendant has been proved, the judge will "direct a verdict" of acquittal. That ends the matter and the defendant goes free—forever immune from further prosecution for the crime, just the same as if a jury had heard all the evidence and found him or her "not guilty."

The Defendant's Evidence

If the court does not direct the jury, at the close of the prosecution's case, to find the defendant not guilty, the defendant may present evidence in refutation. The defendant may or may not testify, and if he or she chooses not to appear as a witness, the prosecuting attorney is not permitted to comment upon that fact to the jury.

The prosecution is given an opportunity to rebut the defendant's evidence, if any, and the presentation of testimony usually ends at that point. Then, once more, defense counsel will try to persuade the court to "direct a verdict" in favor of the defendant. If the court decides to let the case go to the jury, the prosecuting attorney and defense counsel make their "closing arguments."

The defense and the prosecution have the right to subpoena witnesses and require them to testify at trial or to produce records if such evidence would be of value at trial. It is possible in certain case situations to enforce subpoenas against out-of-state witnesses and, in some instances, against American witnesses in foreign countries.

The prosecution has the obligation to notify the defense of any evidence which would be of significance in exculpating the accused or in mitigating the sentence if the prosecution is aware of this evidence.

Closing Arguments

In their closing arguments the prosecutor and defense counsel review and analyze the evidence and attempt to persuade the jury to render a favorable verdict.

Instructions of the Court to the Jury

After or before closing arguments, the judge will read to the jury certain written instructions as to the legal principles which should be applied to the facts of the case as determined by the jury. The judge in some jurisdictions gives the jury copies of the written instructions. He or she also gives the jury certain written forms of possible verdicts. The jurors then retire to the jury room where they are given an adequate opportunity to deliberate upon the matter, away from everyone, including the judge.

The Verdict of the Jury

When the jurors have reached a decision, they advise the bailiff and then return to the court room. The foreperson, usually selected by the jurors themselves to serve as their leader and spokesperson, announces the verdict of the jury. Insofar as jury participation is concerned, the case is then at an end.

If the verdict is "not guilty" the defendant is free forever from any further prosecution by that particular state or jurisdiction for the crime for which he or she was tried. If the jury finds the defendant "guilty," then, in most types of cases and in most jurisdictions, it becomes the function of the trial judge to fix the sentence within the legislatively prescribed limitations.

In the event the jurors are unable to agree upon a verdict—and it must be unanimous in most states—the jury, commonly referred to as a "hung jury," is discharged and a new trial date may be set for a retrial of the case before another jury. The retrial does not constitute a violation of the constitutional protection against double jeopardy.

The Motion for a New Trial

After a verdict of "guilty" there are still certain opportunities provided the defendant to obtain freedom. He or she may file a "motion for a new trial," which alleges certain "errors" committed in the course of trial; and if the trial judge agrees, the conviction is set aside and the defendant may be tried again by a new jury and usually before a different judge. Where this motion for a new trial is "overruled" or "denied," the judge will then sentence the defendant.

The defendant may also seek a new trial on the grounds of newly discovered evidence favorable to him or her. Such motions are rarely granted. The defendant must establish that he or she was not aware of the evidence and could not have discovered the evidence by exercising due diligence, and that the evidence would probably change the result of the trial.

The Sentence

In cases tried without a jury, the judge, of course, will determine the sentence to be imposed except in a few states where a jury is selected to fix punishment. In jury cases the practice varies among the states, with most of them following the practice of confining the jury function to a determination of guilt or innocence and permitting the judge to fix the penalty. Where death is a possible punishment, however, most of the states place both responsibilities upon the jury.

In some states there are statutory provisions which prescribe that upon conviction of a felony the defendant must be sentenced for a specified minimum-maximum term in the penitentiary—for example, 1 year to 10 years for burglary—and the determination of the appropriate time of release within that period is to be made by a "parole board," whose judgment in that respect is based upon the extent of the convict's rehabilitation, the security risk involved, and similar factors. In many states a judge is permitted to set a minimum-maximum period anywhere within the minimum-maximum term prescribed by the legislature. In other words, the sentence given for grand larceny may be one to ten years, the statutory range, or 1 to 2, 9 to 10, or any other combination between 1 to 10. This minimum-maximum term means that he or she cannot be released before serving the minimum period, less "time off for good behavior," nor can he or she be kept in the penitentiary longer than the maximum period, less "time off for good behavior." In between this minimum-maximum period the convict is eligible for "parole," a procedure to be subsequently described.

In instances where imprisonment is fixed at a specified number of years, rather than for an indeterminate period, the law usually provides that the convicted person must serve some specified period, such as one half or one third, of the sentence before becoming eligible for parole.

Some states and the federal government have adopted a plan which limits the sentencing discretion of judges and the release powers of parole boards, or even abolishes parole boards. Under this system the judge is required to set a specific term according to guidelines. Although the federal sentencing guidelines are no longer mandatory, they still guide the sentences that federal judges impose. The sentence may be reduced by "good time" allowance (for "good behavior") in prison, which is calculated by a set formula. When the inmate serves the sentence less "good time" he or she is released.

In recent years there has been an increase in two new forms of incarceration. "Work release" allows an inmate to work at a job and return to custody during non-working hours. "Periodic imprisonment" allows an inmate freedom except for certain specified periods, e.g., weekends.

PROBATION

In certain cases, a judge is empowered, by statute, to grant "probation" to a convicted person. This means that instead of sending the defendant to the penitentiary the court permits him or her to remain at liberty but upon certain conditions prescribed by law and by the judge. His or her background must first be investigated by a probation officer for the purpose of determining whether the defendant is the kind of person who may have "learned his lesson" by the mere fact of being caught and convicted, or whether he or she could be rehabilitated outside of prison better than behind prison walls. In other words, would any useful purpose be served for the defendant or society by sending the defendant to prison?

Among the conditions of a defendant's probation, the court may require restitution of money stolen, or reparations to a person physically injured. Some state statutes provide that for a period of up to six months in misdemeanor cases, and up to five years in felony cases, a defendant on probation will be subjected to the supervision of a probation officer and, in general, must remain on "good behavior" during the period fixed by the court. A failure to abide by the conditions prescribed by the court will subject the defendant to a sentence in the same manner and form as though he or she had been denied probation and sentenced immediately after conviction for the offense.

PAROLE

A penitentiary sentence of a specified term or number of years does not necessarily mean that a convicted person will remain in the penitentiary for that particular period of time. Under certain conditions and circumstances he or she may be released earlier "on parole," which means a release under supervision until the expiration of the sentence or until the expiration of a period otherwise specified by law. For instance, a person sentenced "for life" is, in some states, eligible for release "on parole" at the end of twenty years, with a subsequent five year period of parole supervision. One sentenced for a fixed number of years, for example 14 years for murder, may be eligible for parole in some states after he has served one-third that period of time. And a person who has been given an indeterminate minimum-maximum sentence, such as to 5 to 10 years for grand larceny, may be eligible for a parole after he has served the 5 year minimum, less time off for good behavior.

A violation of the conditions of the parole will subject the parolee to possible return to prison for the remainder of the unexpired sentence.

In most states with determinate sentences, prisoners are released before the end of their term, if they have obtained "good behavior" time, but they are still subject to parole-like conditions and the possibility of further incarceration if they violate those terms.

In states maintaining the conventional parole system, revocation of probation or parole cannot be arbitrary. In either case there must be a hearing. The hearing need not be like a full scale trial, i.e., there is no jury, but it must be a fair determination of whether the conditions of probation and parole were violated.

POST-CONVICTION REMEDIES

The Appeal

After sentence has been pronounced, the defendant may appeal the conviction to a reviewing court. The reviewing court will examine all or part of the written record of what happened at the trial, and consider the arguments of both the defense attorney and the prosecutor. It will then render a written decision and opinion which will either reverse or affirm the trial court conviction and state the reasons for the decision. If the trial court's decision is "reversed and remanded", it means that the defendant's conviction is nullified, although he may be tried over again by another jury. The Double Jeopardy Clause of the Fifth Amendment does not prevent a second trial when the conviction has been reversed "for error." A decision of "reversed" ordinarily means that there appears to be insufficient competent evidence upon which to try the defendant again, and consequently the prosecuting attorney may not make a second attempt to win a conviction. In a jurisdiction which has an intermediate court of review, the losing party can seek discretionary review from the jurisdiction's highest court.

A decision of the state's highest court affirming a conviction is, in nearly all instances, a final disposition of the case, and there is nothing else the convicted person can do but submit to the judgment of the trial court. But if the appeal involved a *federal* constitutional question or issue the defendant is entitled to seek a review of the state appellate court decision by the Supreme Court of the United States. Such requests, known as petitions for a *writ of certiorari*, are rarely granted, however.

The courts may allow the defendant to remain free on bail pending appeal or they may increase the amount of bail or revoke bail entirely while the case is on appeal. In the federal system, release on bail pending appeal is increasingly rare.

Collateral Attacks

In addition to the appeal itself, nearly all states in recent years have provided additional post-conviction remedies by which a defendant may attack the conviction. Such "collateral" remedies are known, variously, as proceedings in habeas corpus, post-conviction petitions, or by other titles. A defendant may thereby seek a re-litigation, in a trial court, of an issue that had been considered and decided on the direct appeal or may attempt to raise an entirely new issue. Moreover, the decision with respect to a collateral attack may be the subject of an appeal to a reviewing court.

Even after a conviction is upheld against collateral attack in the state courts, if a federal constitutional question had been presented, the convicted person has yet another remedy available—the *federal* writ of habeas corpus. The Supreme Court of the United States has held that a state court judgment of conviction resulting from a trial which involved a substantial error of federal constitutional dimension is void, and a prisoner held pursuant to a void judgment is unlawfully confined and subject to release by a federal court upon a writ of habeas corpus. However, the Court has imposed some limitations upon this right. A state prisoner who claims that evidence used against him at trial was obtained in violation of constitutional rules governing arrest, search and seizure cannot present those claims in a federal habeas corpus proceeding if he had the opportunity to make them in the state court.

In considering a petition for habeas corpus, a federal district court judge may order another "evidentiary hearing." And she has the power to remand the case to the state court for a new trial or for the outright release of the defendant, depending upon the kind of error committed and the evidence still available to the state. But this decision is appealable to higher federal courts.

APPEALS BY THE PROSECUTION

Only the defendant has a right to appeal the result of a trial; to permit the prosecution to appeal from a verdict of acquittal or a trial judge's finding of not guilty has been held to violate the constitutional protection against double jeopardy.

In a growing number of jurisdictions, however, the prosecution is being accorded the right to appeal certain decisions of a pre-trial nature.

Although only a minority of jurisdictions provide for such an appeal, the United States Supreme Court has upheld the validity of a particular statutory scheme which provides the prosecution an opportunity to seek an increase of the defendant's sentence through appellate review under limited circumstances.

NOTES

This volume encompasses cases and comments which, in no small part, concern the efforts of courts to govern the process of criminal adjudication by using mandates embedded in the federal constitution. Many of these decisions prohibit the prosecution from introducing certain forms of evidence or using certain tactics. The major phase of constitutional criminal procedure decisions began in 1961 when the Supreme Court said that no state could allow into evidence that which was seized in violation of the Fourth Amendment (Mapp v. Ohio) and continued in 1963 when states were required to provide free defense counsel to defendants who could not afford an attorney (Gideon v. Wainwright). The "revolution," as some called it, reached its apex in 1965–67 when the Court imposed constitutional bans upon prosecutorial comment on a failure of a defendant to testify (Griffin v. California) upon custodial confessions made without warnings of the rights to silence and to counsel (Miranda v. Arizona) and upon certain eyewitness testimony (Wade–Gilbert–Stovall). These rulings have been controversial; critics said the Court went too far here or not far enough there. In the twenty or so years after 1967, the pace of change slowed and some retrenchment occurred. In the 1990s, critics began to question the entire enterprise. See Craig M. Bradley, The Failure of the Criminal Procedure Revolution (1993).

Consider excerpts from two articles, one by a scholar who largely supports the decisions of the "revolution" (Stuntz) and one who does not (Amar).

(a) William J. Stuntz, the Uneasy Relationship Between Criminal Justice and Criminal Procedure, 107 Yale L.J. 1 (1997).

... For the past thirty-five years, the legal system's discussion of criminal defendants' rights has suffered from an air of unreality, a sense the all goals can be satisfied and all values honored—that we can, for example, have the jury selection process we want at no cost to anything else we might want. A sense of rank ordering, of assigning priority to some constitutional norms rather than treating all as equally deserving of regulatory attention, is absent.

That should change. It is time to acknowledge the tradeoffs, to take seriously the nature of the system the law of criminal procedure regulates and the ways in which that system can evade or undermine the regulation. In a regime like ours, countermajoritarian restraints on the criminal process can succeed only at a cost, the cost is probably substantial, and it is disproportionately imposed on those who least deserve to bear it. Leaving more of the process to majoritarian institutions might be better, not least for some of the defendants the process is designed to protect.

That need not mean leaving defendants to the mercies of state legislatures and local prosecutors. If constitutional law's response to criminal justice has failed, it has failed not just from too much intervention but from too little as well. Making *Gideon* a formal right only, without any ancillary funding requirements, has produced a criminal process that is, for poor defendants, a scandal. Courts' reluctance to police legislatures' criminalization and sentencing decisions—coupled with the way those legislative decisions can be used in a system that gives prosecutors blanket authority to choose whom to go after and for what—has produced its own scandals. Defendants' interests might best be protected by less procedure, coupled with a much more activist judicial posture toward funding, the definition of crime, and sentencing—all areas where judges have been loath to take dramatic stands.

This judicial reticence seems to have been motivated by a desire not to trench on the prerogatives of the politicians, a desire to stick to the more law-like and presumably less contentious ground of process. That the 1960s produced a revolution in criminal *procedure* may testify to the underrated conservatism of Warren Court constitution thought, to that radical court's willingness to confine its intervention to conventional categories. If so, in this area these conservative instincts may have been misplaced—as, perhaps, was the Court's reformist (procedural) zeal. The system might be better off today had Warren and his colleagues worried less about criminal procedure, and more about criminal justice.

(b) Akhil Reed Amar, The Future of Constitutional Criminal Procedure, 33 Am. Crim. L. Rev. 1123 (1996).

... The Constitution seeks to protect the innocent. The guilty, in general, receive procedural protection only as an incidental and unavoidable byproduct of protecting the innocent *because* of their innocence. Law breaking, *as such*, is entitled to no legitimate expectation of privacy, and so if a search can detect only law breaking as such, it poses little threat to Fourth Amendment values. By the same token, the exclusionary rule is wrong, as a constitutional rule, precisely because it creates huge windfalls for guilty defendants but givens no direct remedy to the innocent woman wrongly searched. The guiltier you are, the more evidence the police will find, the bigger the exclusionary rule windfall, but if the police know you are innocent, and just want to hassle you (because of your race, or politics, or whatever) the exclusionary rule offers exactly zero compensation or deterrence.

Truth and accuracy are vital values. A procedural system that cannot sort the innocent from the guilty will confound any set of substantive laws, however just. And so to throw out highly reliable evidence that can indeed help us separate the innocent from the guilty—and to throw it out by pointing to the Constitution, no less—is constitutional madness. A Constitution proclaimed in the name of We the People should be rooted in enduring values that Americans can recognize as *our* values. Truth and the protection of innocence are such values. Virtually everything in the Fourth, Fifth, and Sixth Amendments, properly read, promotes, or at least does not betray, these values.

PART 1

LIMITATIONS UPON LAW ENFORCEMENT PRACTICES AND PROCEDURES

CHAPTER 2

CONFESSIONS AND INTERROGATIONS

A. VOLUNTARINESS OF CONFESSIONS

1. STANDARDS OF VOLUNTARINESS

Brown v. Mississippi

Supreme Court of the United States, 1936.
297 U.S. 278, 56 S.Ct. 461.

■ MR. CHIEF JUSTICE HUGHES delivered the opinion of the Court.

* * *

The question in this case is whether convictions, which rest solely upon confessions shown to have been extorted by officers of the state by brutality and violence, are consistent with the due process of law required by the Fourteenth Amendment of the Constitution of the United States.

Petitioners were indicted for the murder of one Raymond Stewart, whose death occurred on March 30, 1934. They were indicted on April 4, 1934, and were then arraigned and pleaded not guilty. Counsel were appointed by the court to defend them. Trial was begun the next morning and was concluded on the following day, when they were found guilty and sentenced to death.

Aside from the confessions, there was no evidence sufficient to warrant the submission of the case to the jury. After a preliminary inquiry, testimony as to the confessions was received over the objection of defendants' counsel. Defendants then testified that the confessions were false and had been procured by physical torture. The case went to the jury with instructions, upon the request of defendants' counsel, that if the jury had reasonable doubt as to the confessions having resulted from coercion, and that they were not true, they were not to be considered as evidence. On their appeal to the Supreme Court of the State, defendants assigned as error the inadmissibility of the confessions. The judgment was affirmed....

... The state court [then] considered the federal question, and decided it against defendants' contentions. ...Two judges dissented.... We granted a writ of certiorari....

The grounds of the decision were (1) that immunity from self-incrimination is not essential to due process of law; and (2) that the failure of the trial court to exclude the confessions after the introduction of evidence showing their incompetency, in the absence of a request for such exclusion, did not deprive the defendants of life or liberty without due process of law; and that even if the trial court had erroneously overruled a motion to exclude the confessions, the ruling would have been mere error reversible on appeal, but not a violation of constitutional right....

[Editor's Note: The Supreme Court agreed that the Fifth Amendment's prohibition against compelled self-incrimination was not applicable to the States. It overruled that declaration in 1964.]

The opinion of the state court did not set forth the evidence as to the circumstances in which the confessions were procured. That the evidence established that they were procured by coercion was not questioned. The state court said: "After the state closed its case on the merits, the appellants, for the first time, introduced evidence from which it appears that the confessions were not made voluntarily but were coerced." ... There is no dispute as to the facts upon this point, and as they are clearly and adequately stated in the dissenting opinion of Judge Griffith (with whom Judge Anderson concurred), showing both the extreme brutality of the measures to extort the confessions and the participation of the state authorities, we quote this part of his opinion in full, as follows ...:

"The crime with which these defendants, all ignorant negroes, are charged, was discovered about 1 o'clock p.m. on Friday, March 30, 1934. On that night one Dial, a deputy sheriff, accompanied by others, came to the home of Ellington, one of the defendants, and requested him to accompany them to the house of the deceased, and there a number of white men were gathered, who began to accuse the defendant of the crime. Upon his denial they seized him, and with the participation of the deputy they hanged him by a rope to the limb of a tree, and, having let him down, they hung him again, and when he was let down the second time, and he still protested his innocence, he was tied to a tree and whipped, and, still declining to accede to the demands that he confess, he was finally released, and he returned with some difficulty to his home, suffering intense pain and agony. The record of the testimony shows that the signs of the rope on his neck were plainly visible during the so-called trial. A day or two thereafter the said deputy, accompanied by another, returned to the home of the said defendant and arrested him, and departed with the prisoner towards the jail in an adjoining county, but went by a route which led into the state of Alabama; and while on the way, in that state, the deputy stopped and again severely whipped the defendant, declaring that he would continue the whipping until he confessed, and the defendant then agreed to confess to such a statement as the deputy would dictate, and he did so, after which he was delivered to jail.

"The other two defendants, Ed Brown and Henry Shields, were also arrested and taken to the same jail. On Sunday night, April 1, 1934, the same deputy, accompanied by a number of white men, one of whom was also an officer, and by the jailer, came to the jail, and the two last named defendants were made to strip and they were laid over chairs and their backs were cut to pieces with a leather strap with buckles on it, and they were likewise made by the said deputy definitely to understand that the whipping would be continued unless and until they confessed, and not only confessed, but confessed in every matter of detail as demanded by those present; and in this manner the defendants confessed the crime, and, as the whippings progressed and were repeated, they changed or adjusted their confession in all particulars of detail so as to conform to the demands of their torturers. When the confessions had been obtained in the exact form and contents as desired by the mob, they left with the parting admonition and warning that, if the defendants changed their story at any time in any respect from that last stated, the perpetrators of the outrage would administer the same or equally effective treatment.

"Further details of the brutal treatment to which these helpless prisoners were subjected need not be pursued. It is sufficient to say that in pertinent respects the transcript reads more like pages torn from some medieval account than a record made within the confines of a modern civilization which aspires to an enlightened constitutional government.

"All this having been accomplished, on the next day, that is, on Monday, April 2, when the defendants had been given time to recuperate somewhat from the tortures to which they had been subjected, the two sheriffs, one of the county where the crime was committed, and the other of the county of the jail in which the prisoners were confined, came to the jail, accompanied by eight other persons, some of them deputies, there to hear the free and voluntary confession of these miserable and abject defendants. The sheriff of the county of the crime admitted that he had heard of the whipping, but averred that he had no personal knowledge of it. He admitted that one of the defendants, when brought before him to confess, was limping and did not sit down, and that this particular defendant then and there stated that he had been strapped so severely that he could not sit down, and, as already stated, the signs of the rope on the neck of another of the defendants were plainly visible to all. Nevertheless the solemn farce of hearing the free and voluntary confessions was gone through with, and these two sheriffs and one other person then present were the three witnesses used in court to establish the so-called confessions, which were received by the court and admitted in evidence over the objections of the defendants duly entered of record as each of the said three witnesses delivered their alleged testimony. There was thus enough before the court when these confessions were first offered to make known to the court that they were not, beyond all reasonable doubt, free and voluntary; and the failure of the court then to exclude the confessions is sufficient to reverse the judgment, under every rule of procedure that has heretofore been prescribed, and hence it was not necessary subsequently to renew the objections by motion or otherwise.

"The spurious confessions having been obtained—and the farce last mentioned having been gone through with on Monday, April 2d—the court, then in session, on the following day, Tuesday, April 3, 1934, ordered the grand jury to reassemble on the succeeding day, April 4, 1934, at 9 o'clock, and on the morning of the day last mentioned the grand jury returned an indictment against the defendants for murder. Late that afternoon the defendants were brought from the jail in the adjoining county and arraigned, when one or more of them offered to plead guilty, which the court declined to accept, and, upon inquiry whether they had or desired counsel, they stated that they had none, and did not suppose that counsel could be of any assistance to them. The court thereupon appointed counsel, and set the case for trial for the following morning at 9 o'clock, and the defendants were returned to the jail in the adjoining county about thirty miles away.

"The defendants were brought to the courthouse of the county on the following morning, April 5th, and the so-called trial was opened, and was concluded on the next day, April 6, 1934, and resulted in a pretended conviction with death sentences. The evidence upon which the conviction was obtained was the so-called confessions. Without this evidence, a peremptory instruction to find for the defendants would have been inescapable. The defendants were put on the stand, and by their testimony the facts and the details thereof as to the manner by which the confessions were extorted from them were fully developed, and it is further disclosed by the record that the same deputy, Dial, under whose guiding hand and active participation the tortures to coerce the confessions were administered, was actively in the performance of the supposed duties of a court deputy in the courthouse and in the presence of the prisoners during what is denominated, in complimentary terms, the trial of these defendants. This deputy was put on the stand by the state in rebuttal, and admitted the whippings. It is interesting to note that in his testimony with reference to the whipping of the defendant Ellington, and in response to the inquiry as to how severely he was whipped, the deputy stated, 'Not too much for a negro; not as much as I would have done if it were left to me.' Two others who had participated in these whippings were introduced and admitted it—not a single witness was introduced who denied it. The facts are not only undisputed, they are admitted, and admitted to have been done by officers of the state, in conjunction with other participants, and all this was definitely well known to everybody connected with the trial, and during the trial, including the state's prosecuting attorney and the trial judge presiding."

* * *

The State is free to regulate the procedure of its courts in accordance with its own conceptions of policy, unless in so doing it "offends some principle of justice so rooted in the traditions and conscience of our people as to be ranked as fundamental." ... But the freedom of the State in establishing its policy is the freedom of constitutional government and is limited by the requirement of due process of law. Because a State may dispense with a jury trial, it does not follow that it may substitute trial by ordeal. The rack and torture chamber may not be substituted for the witness stand. The State may not permit an accused to be hurried to conviction under mob domination—where the whole proceeding is but a mask—without supplying corrective process. Moore v. Dempsey, 261 U.S. 86, 91, 43 S.Ct. 265. The State may not deny to the accused the aid of counsel. Powell v. Alabama, 287 U.S. 45, 53 S.Ct. 55. Nor may a State, through the action of its officers, contrive a conviction through the pretense of a trial which in truth is "but used as a means of depriving a defendant of liberty through a deliberate deception of court and jury by the presentation of testimony known to be perjured." Mooney v. Holohan, 294 U.S. 103, 112, 55 S.Ct. 340. And the trial equally is a mere pretense where the state authorities have contrived a conviction resting solely upon confessions obtained by violence. The due process clause requires "that state action, whether through one agency or another, shall be consistent with the fundamental principles of liberty and justice which lie at the base of all our civil and political institutions." Hebert v. Louisiana, 272 U.S. 312, 316, 47 S.Ct. 103. It would be difficult to conceive of methods more revolting to the sense of justice than those taken to procure the confessions of these petitioners, and the use of the confessions thus obtained as the basis for conviction and sentence was clear denial of due process.

* * *

In the instant case, the trial court was fully advised by the undisputed evidence of the way in which the confessions had been procured. The trial court knew that there was no other evidence upon which conviction and sentence could be based. Yet it proceeded to permit conviction and to pronounce sentence. The conviction and sentence were void for want of the essential elements of due process, and the proceeding thus vitiated could be challenged in any appropriate manner. Mooney v. Holohan, supra. It was challenged before the Supreme Court of the State by the express invocation of the Fourteenth Amendment. That court entertained the challenge, considered the federal question thus presented, but declined to enforce petitioners' constitutional right. The court thus denied a federal right fully established and specially set up and claimed and the judgment must be

Reversed.

Watts v. Indiana

Supreme Court of the United States, 1949.
338 U.S. 49, 69 S.Ct. 1347.

■ MR. JUSTICE FRANKFURTER announced the judgment of the Court and an opinion in which MR. JUSTICE MURPHY and MR. JUSTICE RUTLEDGE join.

Although the Constitution puts protection against crime predominantly in the keeping of the States, the Fourteenth Amendment severely restricted the States in their administration of criminal justice. Thus, while the State courts have the responsibility for securing the rudimentary requirements of a civilized order, in discharging that responsibility there hangs over them the reviewing power of this Court.

* * *

This case is here because the Supreme Court of Indiana rejected petitioner's claim that confessions elicited from him were procured under circumstances rendering their admission as evidence against him a denial of due process of law.[1]

* * *

1. In the petitioner's statements there was acknowledgment of the possession of an incriminating gun, the existence of which the police independently established. But a coerced confession is inadmissible under the Due Process Clause even though statements in it may be independently established as true. See Lisenba v. California, 314 U.S. 219, 236–237.

On review here of State convictions, all those matters which are usually termed issues of fact are for conclusive determination by the State courts and are not open for reconsideration by this Court. Observance of this restriction in our review of State courts calls for the utmost scruple. But "issue of fact" is a coat of many colors. It does not cover a conclusion drawn from uncontroverted happenings, when that conclusion incorporates standards of conduct or criteria for judgment which in themselves are decisive of constitutional rights. Such standards and criteria, measured against the requirements drawn from constitutional provisions, and their proper applications, are issues for this Court's adjudication.

* * *

[In all the cases where] it was claimed that the admission of coerced confessions vitiated convictions for murder, there has been complete agreement that any conflict in testimony as to what actually led to a contested confession is not this Court's concern. Such conflict comes here authoritatively resolved by the State's adjudication. Therefore only those elements of the events and circumstances in which a confession was involved that are unquestioned in the State's version of what happened are relevant to the constitutional issue here. But if force has been applied, this Court does not leave to local determination whether or not the confession was voluntary. There is torture of mind as well as body; the will is as much affected by fear as by force. And there comes a point where this Court should not be ignorant as judges of what we know as men.

This brings us to the undisputed circumstances which must determine the issue of due process in this case. Thanks to the forthrightness of counsel for Indiana, these circumstances may be briefly stated.

On November 12, 1947, a Wednesday, petitioner was arrested and held as the suspected perpetrator of an alleged criminal assault earlier in the day. Later the same day, in the vicinity of this occurrence, a woman was found dead under conditions suggesting murder in the course of an attempted criminal assault. Suspicion of murder quickly turned towards petitioner and the police began to question him. They took him from the county jail to State Police Headquarters, where he was questioned by officers in relays from about 11:30 that night until sometime between 2:30 and 3 o'clock the following morning. The same procedure of persistent interrogation from about 5:30 in the afternoon until about 3 o'clock the following morning, by a relay of six to eight officers, was pursued on Thursday the 13th, Friday the 14th, Saturday the 15th, Monday the 17th. Sunday was a day of rest from interrogation. About 3 o'clock on Tuesday morning, November 18, the petitioner made an incriminating statement after continuous questioning since 6 o'clock of the preceding evening. The statement did not satisfy the prosecutor who had been called in and he then took petitioner in hand. Petitioner, questioned by an interrogator of twenty years' experience as lawyer, judge and prosecutor, yielded a more incriminating document.

Until his inculpatory statements were secured, the petitioner was a prisoner in the exclusive control of the prosecuting authorities. He was kept for the first two days in solitary confinement in a cell aptly enough called "the hole" in view of its physical conditions as described by the State's witnesses. Apart from the five night sessions, the police intermittently interrogated Watts during the day and on three days drove him around town, hours at a time, with a view to eliciting identifications and other disclosures. Although the law of Indiana required that petitioner be given a prompt preliminary hearing before a magistrate, with all the protection a hearing was intended to give him, the petitioner was not only given no hearing during the entire period of interrogation but was without friendly or professional aid and without advice as to his constitutional rights. Disregard of rudimentary needs of life—opportunities for sleep and a decent allowance of food—are also relevant, not as aggravating elements of petitioner's treatment, but as part of the total situation out of which his confessions came and which stamped their character.

A confession by which life becomes forfeit must be the expression of free choice. A statement to be voluntary of course need not be volunteered. But if it is the product of sustained pressure by the police it does not issue from a free choice. When a suspect speaks because he is overborne, it is immaterial whether he has been subjected to a physical or a mental ordeal. Eventual yielding to questioning under such circumstances is plainly the product of the suction process of interrogation and therefore the reverse of voluntary. We would have to shut our minds to the plain significance of what here transpired to deny that this was a calculated endeavor to secure a confession through the pressure of unrelenting interrogation. The very relentlessness of such interrogation implies that it is better for the prisoner to answer than to persist in the refusal of disclosure which is his constitutional right. To turn the detention of an accused into a process of wrenching from him evidence which could not be extorted in open court with all its safeguards, is so grave an abuse of the power of arrest as to offend the procedural standards of due process.

This is so because it violates the underlying principle in our enforcement of the criminal law. Ours is the accusatorial as opposed to the inquisitorial system. Such has been the characteristic of Anglo–American criminal justice since it freed itself from practices borrowed by the Star Chamber from the Continent whereby an accused was interrogated in secret for hours on end. Under our system society carries the burden of proving its charge against the accused not out of his own mouth. It must establish its case, not by interrogation of the accused even under judicial safeguards, but by evidence independently secured through skillful investigation. "The law will not suffer a prisoner to be made the deluded instrument of his own conviction." The requirement of specific charges, their proof beyond a reasonable doubt, the protection of the accused from confessions extorted through whatever form of police pressures, the right to a prompt hearing before a magistrate, the right to assistance of counsel, to be supplied by government when circumstances make it necessary, the duty to advise an accused of his constitutional rights—these are all characteristics of the accusatorial system and manifestations of its demands. Protracted, systematic and uncontrolled subjection of an accused to interrogation by the police for the purpose of eliciting disclosures or confessions is subversive of the accusatorial system. It is the inquisitorial system without its safeguards. For while under that system the accused is subjected to judicial interrogation, he is protected by the disinterestedness of the judge in the presence of counsel.

In holding that the Due Process Clause bars police procedure which violates the basic notions of our accusatorial mode of prosecuting crime and vitiates a conviction based on the fruits of such procedure, we apply the Due Process Clause to its historic function of assuring appropriate procedure before liberty is curtailed or life is taken. We are deeply mindful of the anguishing problems which the incidence of crime presents to the States. But the history of the criminal law proves overwhelmingly that brutal methods of law enforcement are essentially self-defeating, whatever may be their effect in a particular case. Law triumphs when the natural impulses aroused by a shocking crime yield to the safeguards which our civilization has evolved for an administration of criminal justice at once rational and effective.

We have examined petitioner's other contentions and do not sustain them.

Reversed.

■ MR. JUSTICE BLACK concurs in the judgment of the Court on the authority of Chambers v. Florida, 309 U.S. 227, 60 S.Ct. 472; Ashcraft v. Tennessee, 322 U.S. 143, 64 S.Ct. 921.

On the record before us and in view of the consideration given to the evidence by the state courts and the conclusion reached, THE CHIEF JUSTICE, MR. JUSTICE REED and MR. JUSTICE BURTON believe that the judgment should be affirmed.

■ MR. JUSTICE DOUGLAS, concurring.

It would be naive to think that this protective custody was less than the inquisition. The man was held until he broke. Then and only then was he arraigned and given the protection which the law provides all accused. Detention without arraignment is a time-honored method for keeping an accused under the exclusive control of the police. They can then operate at their leisure. The accused is wholly at their mercy. He is without the aid of counsel or friends; and he is denied the protection of the magistrate. We should unequivocally condemn the procedure and stand ready to outlaw, as we did in Malinski v. New York, 324 U.S. 401, 65 S.Ct. 781, and Haley v. Ohio, 332 U.S. 596, 68 S.Ct. 302, any confession obtained during the period of the unlawful detention. The procedure breeds coerced confessions. It is the root of the evil. It is the procedure without which the inquisition could not flourish in the country.

■ MR. JUSTICE JACKSON concurring in the result [of the Watts case, but dissenting in the other two companion cases of Harris v. South Carolina and Turner v. Pennsylvania].

These three cases, from widely separated states, present essentially the same problem. Its recurrence suggests that it has roots in some condition fundamental and general to our criminal system.

In each case police were confronted with one or more brutal murders which the authorities were under the highest duty to solve. Each of these murders was unwitnessed, and the only positive knowledge on which a solution could be based was possessed by the killer. In each there was reasonable ground to *suspect* an individual but not enough legal evidence to *charge* him with guilt. In each the police attempted to meet the situation by taking the suspect into custody and interrogating him. This extended over varying periods. In each, confessions were made and received in evidence at the trial. Checked with external evidence, they are inherently believable, and were not shaken as to truth by anything that occurred at the trial. Each confessor was convicted by a jury and state courts affirmed. This Court sets all three convictions aside.

The seriousness of the Court's judgment is that no one suggests that any course held promise of solution of these murders other than to take the suspect into custody for questioning. The alternative was to close the books on the crime and forget it, with the suspect at large. This is a grave choice for a society in which two-thirds of the murders already are closed out as insoluble.

A concurring opinion, however, goes to the very limit and seems to declare for outlawing any confession, however freely given, if obtained during a period of custody between arrest and arraignment—which, in practice, means all of them.

Others would strike down these confessions because of conditions which they say make them "involuntary." In this, on only a printed record, they pit their judgment against that of the trial judge and the jury. Both, with the great advantage of hearing and seeing the confessor and also the officers whose conduct and bearing toward him is in question, have found that the confessions were voluntary. In addition, the majority overrule in each case one or more state appellate courts, which have the same limited opportunity to know the truth that we do.

Amid much that is irrelevant or trivial, one serious situation seems to me to stand out in these cases. The suspect neither had nor was advised of his right to get counsel. This presents a real dilemma in a free society. To subject one without counsel to questioning which may and is intended to convict him, is a real peril to individual freedom. To bring in a lawyer means a real peril to solution of the crime, because, under our adversary system, he deems that his sole duty is to protect his client—guilty or innocent—and that in such a capacity he owes no duty whatever to help society solve its crime problem. Under this conception of criminal procedure, any lawyer worth his salt will tell the suspect in no uncertain terms to make no statement to police under any circumstances.

If the State may arrest on suspicion and interrogate without counsel, there is no denying the fact that it largely negates the benefits of the constitutional guaranty of the right to assistance of counsel. Any lawyer who has ever been called into a case after his client has "told all" and turned any evidence he has over to the Government, knows how helpless he is to protect his client against the facts thus disclosed.

I suppose the view one takes will turn on what one thinks should be the right of an accused person against the State. Is it his right to have the judgment on the facts? Or is it his right to have a judgment based on only such evidence as he cannot conceal from the authorities, who cannot compel him to testify in court and also cannot question him before? Our system comes close to the latter by any interpretation, for the defendant is shielded by such safeguards as no system of law except the Anglo–American concedes to him.

Of course, no confession that has been obtained by any form of physical violence to the person is reliable and hence no conviction should rest upon one obtained in that manner. Such treatment not only breaks the will to conceal or lie, but may even break the will to stand by the truth. Nor is it questioned that the same result can sometimes be achieved by threats, promises, or inducements which torture the mind but put no scar on the body. If the opinion of Mr. Justice Frankfurter in the *Watts* case were based solely on the State's admissions as to the treatment of Watts, I should not disagree. But if ultimate quest in a criminal trial is the truth and if the circumstances indicate no violence or threats of it, should society be deprived of the suspect's help in solving a crime merely because he was confined and questioned when uncounseled?

We must not overlook that, in these as in some previous cases, once a confession is obtained it supplies ways of verifying its trustworthiness. In these cases before us the verification is sufficient to leave me in no doubt that the admissions of guilt were genuine and truthful. Such corroboration consists in one case of finding a weapon where the accused has said he hid it, and in others that conditions which could only have been known to one who was implicated correspond with his story. It is possible, but it is rare, that a confession, if repudiated on the trial, standing alone will convict unless there is external proof of its verity.

In all such cases, along with other conditions criticized, the continuity and duration of the questioning is invoked and it is called an "inquiry," "inquest" or "inquisition," depending mainly on the emotional state of the writer. But as in some of the cases here, if interrogation is permissible at all, there are sound reasons for prolonging it—which the opinions here ignore. The suspect at first perhaps makes an effort to exculpate himself by alibis or other statements. These are verified, found false, and he is then confronted with his falsehood. Sometimes (though such cases do not reach us) verification proves them true or credible and the suspect is released. Sometimes, as here, more than one crime is involved. The duration of an interrogation may well depend on the temperament, shrewdness and cunning of the accused and the competence of the examiner. But, assuming a right to examine at all, the right must include what is made reasonably necessary by the facts of the particular case.

If the right of interrogation be admitted, then it seems to me that we must leave it to trial judges and juries and state appellate courts to decide individual cases, unless they show some want of proper standards of decision. I find nothing to indicate that any of the courts below in these cases did not have a correct understanding of the Fourteenth Amendment, unless this Court thinks it means absolute prohibition of interrogation while in custody before arraignment.

I suppose no one would doubt that our Constitution and Bill of Rights, grounded in revolt against the arbitrary measures of George III and in the philosophy of the French Revolution, represent the maximum restrictions upon the power of organized society over the individual that are compatible with the maintenance of organized society itself. They were so intended and should be so interpreted. It cannot be denied that, even if construed as these provisions traditionally have been, they contain an aggregate of restrictions which seriously limit the power of society to solve such crimes as confront us in these cases. Those restrictions we should not for that reason cast aside, but that is good reason for indulging in no unnecessary expansion of them.

I doubt very much if they require us to hold that the State may not take into custody and question one suspected reasonably of an unwitnessed murder. If it does, the people of this country must discipline themselves to seeing their police stand by helplessly while those suspected of murder prowl about unmolested. Is it a necessary price to pay for the fairness which we know as "due process of law"? And if not a necessary one, should it be demanded by this Court? I do not know the ultimate answer to these questions; but, for the present, I should not increase the handicap on society.

NOTE

The United States Supreme Court has weighed many factors in determining whether a statement is voluntary. In any given case one factor may have nearly decisive weight (e.g., sustained physical violence). But the weight of most factors cannot be determined outside the facts of the individual case. Consequently, the Court has criticized any procedure which simply compares the factors found in reported cases with the factors present in the case to be decided—a practice called "color matching." The importance of each factor must be carefully evaluated. Reck v. Pate, 367 U.S. 433, 81 S.Ct. 1541 (1961); Mincey v. Arizona, 437 U.S. 385, 98 S.Ct. 2408 (1978). The principal factors are related either to the condition of the suspect, (i.e., age, mental capacity, education, experience, physical and mental state) or to the conditions of the interrogation (lengthy detention, deprivation of food and drink or contact with outside world, denial of sleep, etc.) or the tactics of the interrogators (relay questioning, lengthy interrogation, use or threat of force).

Colorado v. Connelly

Supreme Court of the United States, 1986.
479 U.S. 157, 107 S.Ct. 515.

■ CHIEF JUSTICE REHNQUIST delivered the opinion of the Court.

* * *

I

On August 18, 1983, Officer Patrick Anderson of the Denver Police Department was in uniform, working in an off-duty capacity in downtown

Denver. Respondent Francis Connelly approached Officer Anderson and, without any prompting, stated that he had murdered someone and wanted to talk about it. Anderson immediately advised respondent that he had the right to remain silent, that anything he said could be used against him in court, and that he had the right to an attorney prior to any police questioning. Respondent stated that he understood these rights but he still wanted to talk about the murder. Understandably bewildered by this confession, Officer Anderson asked respondent several questions. Connelly denied that he had been drinking, denied that he had been taking any drugs, and stated that, in the past, he had been a patient in several mental hospitals. Officer Anderson again told Connelly that he was under no obligation to say anything. Connelly replied that it was "all right," and that he would talk to Officer Anderson because his conscience had been bothering him. To Officer Anderson, respondent appeared to understand fully the nature of his acts.

Shortly thereafter, Homicide Detective Stephen Antuna arrived. Respondent was again advised of his rights, and Detective Antuna asked him "what he had on his mind." Respondent answered that he had come all the way from Boston to confess to the murder of Mary Ann Junta, a young girl whom he had killed in Denver sometime during November 1982. Respondent was taken to police headquarters, and a search of police records revealed that the body of an unidentified female had been found in April 1983. Respondent openly detailed his story to Detective Antuna and Sergeant Thomas Haney, and readily agreed to take the officers to the scene of the killing. Under Connelly's sole direction, the two officers and respondent proceeded in a police vehicle to the location of the crime. Respondent pointed out the exact location of the murder. Throughout this episode, Detective Antuna perceived no indication whatsoever that respondent was suffering from any kind of mental illness.

Respondent was held overnight. During an interview with the public defender's office the following morning, he became visibly disoriented. He began giving confused answers to questions, and for the first time, stated that "voices" had told him to come to Denver and that he had followed the directions of these voices in confessing. Respondent was sent to a state hospital for evaluation. He was initially found incompetent to assist in his own defense. By March 1984, however, the doctors evaluating respondent determined that he was competent to proceed to trial.

At a preliminary hearing, respondent moved to suppress all of his statements. Dr. Jeffrey Metzner, a psychiatrist employed by the state hospital, testified that respondent was suffering from chronic schizophrenia and was in a psychotic state at least as of August 17, 1983, the day before he confessed. Metzner's interviews with respondent revealed that respondent was following the "voice of God." This voice instructed respondent to withdraw money from the bank, to buy an airplane ticket, and to fly from Boston to Denver. When respondent arrived from Boston, God's voice became stronger and told respondent either to confess to the killing or to commit suicide. Reluctantly following the command of the voices, respondent approached Officer Anderson and confessed.

Dr. Metzner testified that, in his expert opinion, respondent was experiencing "command hallucinations." This condition interfered with respondent's "volitional abilities; that is, his ability to make free and rational choices." Dr. Metzner further testified that Connelly's illness did not significantly impair his cognitive abilities. Thus, respondent understood the rights he had when Officer Anderson and Detective Antuna advised him that he need not speak. Dr. Metzner admitted that the "voices" could in reality be Connelly's interpretation of his own guilt, but explained that in his opinion, Connelly's psychosis motivated his confession.

On the basis of this evidence the Colorado trial court decided that respondent's statements must be suppressed because they were "involuntary."

The Colorado Supreme Court affirmed. 702 P.2d 722 (1985). In that court's view, the proper test for admissibility is whether the statements are "the product of a rational intellect and a free will." Indeed, "the absence of police coercion or duress does not foreclose a finding of involuntariness. One's capacity for rational judgment and free choice may be overborne as much by certain forms of severe mental illness as by external pressure." The court found that the very admission of the evidence in a court of law was sufficient state action to implicate the Due Process Clause of the Fourteenth Amendment to the United States Constitution. The evidence fully supported the conclusion that respondent's initial statement was not the product of a rational intellect and a free will. . . .

II

The Due Process Clause of the Fourteenth Amendment provides that no State shall "deprive any person of life, liberty, or property, without due process of law." Just last Term, in *Miller v. Fenton* (1985), we held that by virtue of the Due Process Clause "certain interrogation techniques, either in isolation or as applied to the unique characteristics of a particular suspect, are so offensive to a civilized system of justice that they must be condemned."

Indeed, coercive government misconduct was the catalyst for this Court's seminal confession case, *Brown v. Mississippi* (1936). . . .

[T]he cases considered by this Court over the 50 years since *Brown v. Mississippi* have focused upon the crucial element of police overreaching.[1] While each confession case has turned on its own set of factors justifying

1. E.g., *Mincey v. Arizona* (1978) (defendant subjected to 4–hour interrogation while incapacitated and sedated in intensive-care unit); *Greenwald v. Wisconsin* (1968) (defendant, on medication, interrogated for over 18 hours without food or sleep); *Beecher v. Alabama* (1967) (police officers held gun to the head of wounded confessant to extract confession); *Davis v. North Carolina* (1966) (16 days of incommunicado interrogation in closed cell without windows, limited food, and coercive tactics); *Reck v. Pate* (1961) (defendant held for four days with inadequate food and medical attention until confession obtained); *Culombe v. Connecticut* (1961) (defendant held for five days of repeated questioning during which police employed coercive tactics); *Payne v. Arkansas* (1958) (defendant held incommunicado for three days with little food; confession obtained when officers informed defendant that Chief of Police was preparing to admit lynch mob into jail); *Ashcraft v. Tennessee* (1944) (defendant questioned by relays of officers for 36 hours without an opportunity for sleep).

the conclusion that police conduct was oppressive, all have contained a substantial element of coercive police conduct. Absent police conduct causally related to the confession, there is simply no basis for concluding that any state actor has deprived a criminal defendant of due process of law. Respondent correctly notes that as interrogators have turned to more subtle forms of psychological persuasion, courts have found the mental condition of the defendant a more significant factor in the "voluntariness" calculus. See *Spano v. New York* (1959). But this fact does not justify a conclusion that a defendant's mental condition, by itself and apart from its relation to official coercion, should ever dispose of the inquiry into constitutional "voluntariness."

Respondent relies on *Blackburn v. Alabama* (1960), and *Townsend v. Sain* (1963), for the proposition that the "deficient mental condition of the defendants in those cases was sufficient to render their confessions involuntary." But respondent's reading of *Blackburn* and *Townsend* ignores the integral element of police overreaching present in both cases. In *Blackburn*, the Court found that the petitioner was probably insane at the time of his confession and the police learned during the interrogation that he had a history of mental problems. The police exploited this weakness with coercive tactics: "the eight- to nine-hour sustained interrogation in a tiny room which was upon occasion literally filled with police officers; the absence of Blackburn's friends, relatives, or legal counsel; [and] the composition of the confession by the Deputy Sheriff rather than by Blackburn." These tactics supported a finding that the confession was involuntary. ...*Townsend* presented a similar instance of police wrongdoing. In that case, a police physician had given Townsend a drug with truth-serum properties. The subsequent confession, obtained by officers who knew that Townsend had been given drugs, was held involuntary. These two cases demonstrate that while mental condition is surely relevant to an individual's susceptibility to police coercion, mere examination of the confessant's state of mind can never conclude the due process inquiry.

Our "involuntary confession" jurisprudence is entirely consistent with the settled law requiring some sort of "state action" to support a claim of violation of the Due Process Clause of the Fourteenth Amendment. ...[T]he Supreme Court of Colorado concluded that sufficient state action was present by virtue of the admission of the confession into evidence in a court of the State.

The difficulty with the approach of the Supreme Court of Colorado is that it fails to recognize the essential link between coercive activity of the State, on the one hand, and a resulting confession by a defendant, on the other. The flaw in respondent's constitutional argument is that it would expand our previous line of "voluntariness" cases into a far-ranging requirement that courts must divine a defendant's motivation for speaking or acting as he did even though there be no claim that governmental conduct coerced his decision.

The most outrageous behavior by a private party seeking to secure evidence against a defendant does not make that evidence inadmissible under the Due Process Clause. See *Walter v. United States* (1980); *Coolidge v. New Hampshire* (1971); *Burdeau v. McDowell* (1921). We have also observed that "[j]urists and scholars uniformly have recognized that the exclusionary rule imposes a substantial cost on the societal interest in law enforcement by its proscription of what concededly is relevant evidence." *United States v. Janis* (1976). Moreover, suppressing respondent's statements would serve absolutely no purpose in enforcing constitutional guarantees. The purpose of excluding evidence seized in violation of the Constitution is to substantially deter future violations of the Constitution. Only if we were to establish a brand new constitutional right—the right of a criminal defendant to confess to his crime only when totally rational and properly motivated—could respondent's present claim be sustained.

We have previously cautioned against expanding "currently applicable exclusionary rules by erecting additional barriers to placing truthful and probative evidence before state juries...." *Lego v. Twomey* (1972). We abide by that counsel now. "[T]he central purpose of a criminal trial is to decide the factual question of the defendant's guilt or innocence," *Delaware v. Van Arsdall* (1986), and while we have previously held that exclusion of evidence may be necessary to protect constitutional guarantees, both the necessity for the collateral inquiry and the exclusion of evidence deflect a criminal trial from its basic purpose. Respondent would now have us require sweeping inquiries into the state of mind of a criminal defendant who has confessed, inquiries quite divorced from any coercion brought to bear on the defendant by the State. We think the Constitution rightly leaves this sort of inquiry to be resolved by state laws governing the admission of evidence and erects no standard of its own in this area. A statement rendered by one in the condition of respondent might be proved to be quite unreliable, but this is a matter to be governed by the evidentiary laws of the forum, and not by the Due Process Clause of the Fourteenth Amendment. "The aim of the requirement of due process is not to exclude presumptively false evidence, but to prevent fundamental unfairness in the use of evidence, whether true or false." *Lisenba v. California* (1941).

We hold that coercive police activity is a necessary predicate to the finding that a confession is not "voluntary" within the meaning of the Due Process Clause of the Fourteenth Amendment. We also conclude that the taking of respondent's statements, and their admission into evidence, constitute no violation of that Clause.

* * *

It is so ordered.

■ JUSTICE BLACKMUN, concurring in part and concurring in the judgment.

[OMITTED]

■ JUSTICE STEVENS, concurring in the judgment in part and dissenting in part.

[OMITTED]

■ JUSTICE BRENNAN, with whom JUSTICE MARSHALL joins, dissenting.

Today the Court denies Mr. Connelly his fundamental right to make a vital choice with a sane mind, involving a determination that could allow the State to deprive him of liberty or even life. This holding is unprecedented: "Surely in the present stage of our civilization a most basic sense of justice is affronted by the spectacle of incarcerating a human being upon the basis of a statement he made while insane...." *Blackburn v. Alabama* (1960). Because I believe that the use of a mentally ill person's involuntary confession is antithetical to the notion of fundamental fairness embodied in the Due Process Clause, I dissent.

* * *

The absence of police wrongdoing should not, by itself, determine the voluntariness of a confession by a mentally ill person. The requirement that a confession be voluntary reflects a recognition of the importance of free will and of reliability in determining the admissibility of a confession, and thus demands an inquiry into the totality of the circumstances surrounding the confession.

... The Court's failure to recognize all forms of involuntariness or coercion as antithetical to due process reflects a refusal to acknowledge free will as a value of constitutional consequence. But due process derives much of its meaning from a conception of fundamental fairness that emphasizes the right to make vital choices voluntarily....

This Court's assertion that we would be required "to establish a brand new constitutional right" to recognize the respondent's claim, ignores 200 years of constitutional jurisprudence. As we stated in *Culombe v. Connecticut* (1961):

> "The ultimate test remains that which has been the only clearly established test in Anglo–American courts for two hundred years: the test of voluntariness. Is the confession the product of an essentially free and unconstrained choice by its maker? ... The line of distinction is that at which governing self-direction is lost *and compulsion, of whatever nature or however infused*, propels or helps to propel the confession." (emphasis added).

A true commitment to fundamental fairness requires that the inquiry be "not whether the conduct of state officers in obtaining the confession is shocking, but whether the confession was 'free and voluntary'...." Malloy v. Hogan, supra, 378 U.S., at 7, 84 S.Ct., at 1493.

... While it is true that police overreaching has been an element of every confession case to date, it is also true that in every case the Court has made clear that ensuring that a confession is a product of free will is an independent concern. The fact that involuntary confessions have always been excluded in part because of police overreaching signifies only that this is a case of first impression. Until today, we have never upheld the admission of a confession that does not reflect the exercise of free will.

The Court cites *Townsend v. Sain* (1963), and *Blackburn* in support of its view that police wrongdoing should be the central focus of inquiry. In *Townsend*, we overturned a murder conviction because the defendant's conviction was determined to be involuntary. The defendant suffered from stomach pains induced by heroin withdrawal. The police properly contacted a physician who administered medications alleviating the withdrawal symptoms. The defendant then confessed. Although the physician denied that he purposely administered "truth serum," there was an indication that the medications could have had such a side effect upon a narcotic addict.

The *Townsend* Court examined "many relevant circumstances": "Among these are [the defendant's] lack of counsel at the time, his drug addiction, the fact that he was a 'near mental defective,' and his youth and inexperience." According to today's Court, the police wrongdoing in *Townsend* was that the police physician had allegedly given the defendant a drug with truth-serum properties, and that the confession was obtained by officers who knew that the defendant had been given drugs. But, in fact, "the police . . . did not know what [medications] the doctor had given [the defendant]." And the *Townsend* Court expressly states that police wrongdoing was not an essential factor:

> "It is not significant that the drug may have been administered and the questions asked by persons unfamiliar with hyoscine's properties as a 'truth serum,' if these properties exist. Any questioning by police officers which *in fact* produces a confession which is not the product of a free intellect renders that confession inadmissible. The Court has usually so stated the test."

Furthermore, in prescient refutation of this Court's "police wrongdoing" theory, the *Townsend* Court analyzed *Blackburn*, the other case relied upon by this Court to "demonstrate" that police wrongdoing was a more important factor than the defendant's state of mind. The Court in *Townsend* stated:

> "[I]n Blackburn v. Alabama, 361 U.S. 199 [80 S.Ct. 274, 4 L.Ed.2d 242] we held *irrelevant* the absence of evidence of improper purpose on the part of the questioning officers. There the evidence indicated that the interrogating officers thought the defendant sane when he confessed, but we judged the confession inadmissible because the probability was that the defendant was *in fact* insane at the time."

Thus the *Townsend* Court interpreted *Blackburn* as a case involving a confession by a mentally ill defendant in which the police harbored no improper purpose.

This Court abandons this precedent in favor of the view that only confessions rendered involuntary by some state action are inadmissible, and that the only relevant form of state action is police conduct. But even if state action is required, police overreaching is not its only relevant form. The Colorado Supreme Court held that the trial court's admission of the involuntary confession into evidence is also state action. The state court's analysis is consistent with *Brown v. Mississippi* (1936), on which this Court so heavily relies. *Brown*, a case involving the use of confessions at trial, makes clear that "[t]he due process clause requires 'that state action, *whether through one agency or another*, shall be consistent with the fundamental principles of liberty and justice which lie at the base of all our civil and political institutions.' ". . . .

* * *

Since the Court redefines voluntary confessions to include confessions by mentally ill individuals, the reliability of these confessions becomes a central concern. A concern for reliability is inherent in our criminal justice system, which relies upon accusatorial rather than inquisitorial practices....

Our interpretation of the Due Process Clause has been shaped by this preference for accusatorial practices.

Our distrust for reliance on confessions is due, in part, to their decisive impact upon the adversarial process. Triers of fact accord confessions such heavy weight in their determinations that "the introduction of a confession makes the other aspects of a trial in court superfluous, and the real trial, for all practical purposes, occurs when the confession is obtained." E. Cleary, McCormick on Evidence 316 (2d ed. 1972)....

Because the admission of a confession so strongly tips the balance against the defendant in the adversarial process, we must be especially careful about a confession's reliability. We have to date not required a finding of reliability for involuntary confessions only because *all* such confessions have been excluded upon a finding of involuntariness, regardless of reliability. The Court's adoption today of a restrictive definition of an "involuntary" confession will require heightened scrutiny of a confession's reliability.

The instant case starkly highlights the danger of admitting a confession by a person with a severe mental illness. The trial court made no findings concerning the reliability of Mr. Connelly's involuntary confession, since it believed that the confession was excludable on the basis of involuntariness. However, the overwhelming evidence in the record points to the unreliability of Mr. Connelly's delusional mind. Mr. Connelly was found incompetent to stand trial because he was unable to relate accurate information, and the court-appointed psychiatrist indicated that Mr. Connelly was actively hallucinating and exhibited delusional thinking at the time of his confession. The Court, in fact, concedes that "[a] statement rendered by one in the condition of respondent might be proved to be quite unreliable...."

Moreover, the record is barren of any corroboration of the mentally ill defendant's confession. No physical evidence links the defendant to the alleged crime. Police did not identify the alleged victim's body as the woman named by the defendant. Mr. Connelly identified the alleged scene of the crime, but it has not been verified that the unidentified body was found there or that a crime actually occurred there. There is not a shred of competent evidence in this record linking the defendant to the charged homicide. There is only Mr. Connelly's confession.

Minimum standards of due process should require that the trial court find substantial indicia of reliability, on the basis of evidence extrinsic to the confession itself, before admitting the confession of a mentally ill person into evidence. I would require the trial court to make such a finding on remand. To hold otherwise allows the State to imprison and possibly to execute a mentally ill defendant based solely upon an inherently unreliable confession.

* * *

NOTES

1. In Arizona v. Fulminante, 499 U.S. 279, 111 S.Ct. 1246 (1991), the Court sustained a finding by a state judge that a confession was involuntary.

Fulminante was incarcerated in the Ray Brook Federal Correctional Institution in New York. There he became friends with another inmate, Anthony Sarivola. The two men came to spend several hours a day together. Sarivola, a former police officer, had been involved in loansharking for organized crime but then became a paid informant for the Federal Bureau of Investigation. While at Ray Brook, he masqueraded as an organized crime figure. After becoming friends with Fulminante, Sarivola heard a rumor that Fulminante was suspected of killing a child in Arizona. Sarivola then raised the subject with Fulminante in several conversations, but Fulminante repeatedly denied any involvement in Jeneane's death. During one conversation, he told Sarivola that Jeneane had been killed by bikers looking for drugs; on another occasion, he said he did not know what had happened. Sarivola passed this information on to an agent of the Federal Bureau of Investigation, who instructed Sarivola to find out more.

Sarivola learned more one evening in October 1983, as he and Fulminante walked together around the prison track. Sarivola said that he knew Fulminante was "starting to get some tough treatment and whatnot" from other inmates because of the rumor. Sarivola offered to protect Fulminante from his fellow inmates, but told him, " 'You have to tell me about it,' you know. I mean, in other words, 'For me to give you any help.' " Fulminante then admitted to Sarivola that he had driven Jeneane to the desert on his motorcycle, where he choked her, sexually assaulted her, and made her beg for her life, before shooting her twice in the head.

Calling the case a close one, and giving deference to state court findings, five justices found "a credible threat of physical violence unless Fulminante confessed such as to overbear [his] will". Four dissenters found the conversations short and said Fulminante "was free at all times to leave Sarivola's company." Fulminante "was an experienced habitue of prisons, and presumably able to fend for himself."

2. An interesting case involving the issue of coercive conduct on the part of a private group of citizens in seeking a confession from a young male college student suspected of murdering a female student is Commonwealth v. Mahnke, 368 Mass. 662, 335 N.E.2d 660 (1975). Following unsuccessful police efforts to locate the missing student and their futile efforts to obtain any helpful information from her suspected boyfriend, several citizens abducted the suspect, took him to a cabin in the woods where he was threatened and interrogated for about twenty hours. He ultimately admitted killing the missing girl and told where he had buried the body. Thereupon, all abusive conduct was abandoned, and he willingly directed the police to the location of the body.

Although the statements made in the cabin were considered involuntary, the court held that the subsequent ones as the group proceeded to the grave site were held voluntary and admissible.

3. See State v. Phelps, 235 Neb. 569, 456 N.W.2d 290 (1990) (confession involuntary where officers indicated that lack of cooperation could lead to a painful penile swab procedure); United States v. Anderson, 929 F.2d 96 (2d Cir.1991) (confession involuntary where officers said that a request for a lawyer would foreclose any future chance of defendant to cooperate with the government as part of a plea bargain); United States v. Macklin, 900 F.2d 948 (6th Cir.1990) (confession by defendant with an I.Q. of 60 is voluntary; any per se rule to the contrary stigmatizes the retarded); United States v. Yunis, 859 F.2d 953 (D.C.Cir.1988) (reversing suppression of confession of hijacker who blew up airplane in Beirut; he was lured into United States custody and when he was arrested both wrists were fractured; he was questioned during a boat trip where he became seasick and stayed in a poorly ventilated area. He did agree to answer questions, his requests to cease questioning were honored, and efforts were made to relieve his discomfort).

4. Consider United States v. Rutledge, 900 F.2d 1127 (7th Cir.1990), where the defendant asked if his cooperation would be helpful. He was told it, in good faith, would be helpful. This statement revealed that he dealt in much larger drug quantities than those charged against him and much larger than the government knew or suspected of him. By virtue of federal sentence guidelines this "helped" him to a sentence 4 to 6 times longer than he would have received if he had kept mum. The Court found the statements voluntary:

> POSNER, J. ... whether a confession is voluntary is not really a fact, but a characterization. There is indeed no "faculty of will" inside our heads that has two states, on and off, such that through careful reconstruction of events the observer can determine whether the switch was on when the defendant was confessing. * * * courts have not been successful in devising a standard that will determine in a consistent fashion when confessions should be excluded on grounds of involuntariness. Of course if the confession is *unreliable*, it should go out, along with other unreliable evidence. It is on this basis that confessions extracted by torture are excluded. But in most cases in which a confession is sought to be excluded because involuntary, there is little likelihood that the inducements placed before the defendant were so overpowering as to induce an untrue confession. The courts in such cases retreat to the proposition that a confession, to be admissible, must be the product of a free choice. *Watts v. Indiana* (1949) (plurality opinion), illustrates the approach, but it is just the faculty of will approach, and, as the courts are beginning to suspect, *Colorado v. Connelly*, it leads nowhere. Taken seriously it would require the exclusion of virtually all fruits of custodial interrogation, since few choices to confess can be thought truly "free" when made by a person who is incarcerated and is being questioned by armed officers without the presence of counsel or anyone else to give him moral support. The formula is not taken seriously. *Connelly* may have driven the stake through its heart by holding that a confession which is not a product of the defendant's free choice—maybe he was so crazy, retarded, high on drugs, or intoxicated that he did not even know he was being interrogated—is admissible so long as whatever it was that destroyed the defendant's power of choice was not police conduct. In any event, very few incriminating statements, custodial or otherwise, are held to be involuntary, though few are the product of a choice that the interrogators left completely free.
>
> An alternative approach, which is implied by *Connelly* and may well describe the courts' actual as distinct from articulated standard, is to ask whether the government has made it impossible for the defendant to make a *rational* choice as to whether to confess—has made it in other words impossible for him to weigh the pros and cons of confessing and go with the balance as it appears at the time. This approach, implies, for example, that if the government feeds the defendant false information that seriously distorts his choice, by promising him that if he confesses he will be set free,

or if the government drugs him so that he cannot make a conscious choice at all, then the confession must go out. Rutledge appeals to this standard in contending that he could not make a rational choice whether to confess unless he knew whether the confession would expose him to a heavier sentence; that the government interfered with his choice by falsely stating that cooperation could only help, and not hurt, him; that in short the false statement destroyed the information that he required for a rational choice.

If the officers, fully intending to use anything Rutledge said against him, had said to him, "Tell us all you know about the drug trade, and we promise you that nothing you tell us will be used against you," then he would have a strong argument that any ensuing confession had been extracted by fraud and was involuntary. For in our hypothetical case the officers would have deflected Rutledge from weighing the pros and cons of confessing and going in the direction that the balance leaned. Alternatively, Rutledge could in our hypothetical case hold the government to its promise, and could do so whether or not the promise was fraudulent.

At the other extreme, if the officers had merely promised Rutledge to inform the prosecutors of his cooperation, or had stated that, other things being equal, cooperation is helpful to an accused, or had reminded him that while cooperation might help him the government would not hesitate to use anything he said against him, there could be no serious argument that he had been coerced to confess. Our case is in between. The challenged statement was not quite a promise not to use anything Rutledge said against him; at the same time, as the judge found, it was not quite truthful.

... When moments after signing his waiver of *Miranda* rights Rutledge asked whether cooperation would help him, he could not have meant by this—having just been told that anything he said could be used against him—to be asking whether he could confess with impunity to mass murder. He could not have meant to be asking whether, if he confessed to being the head of a Colombian drug cartel, the government would do its best to get him a lighter sentence for the crimes for which he had been indicted. He may have been asking just whether the *fact* of his confessing would receive consideration as cooperation. The officers said it would. This was not, so far as appears, a lie when made (which means, it was not a lie at all). The government later agreed to drop one of the charges against Rutledge and it informed the judge of his cooperation. Government is not forbidden to "buy" information with honest promises of consideration. Fare v. Michael C., 442 U.S. 707, 727, 99 S.Ct. 2560, 2573 (1979). Such an offer requires the accused to weigh the cost in giving the government information about his criminal activity that it might otherwise not discover against the benefit in possibly receiving brownie points for cooperation. Rutledge may have thought that the government would discover the incriminating information anyway; if so, he would rationally rate the cost of cooperation as slight and the benefit as larger even though small in absolute terms, and he would confess. The government was not required to tell him that if he was wise he would shut up because it had no other source of information about the extent of his illegal activities. The policeman is not a fiduciary of the suspect. The police are allowed to play on a suspect's ignorance, his anxieties, his fears, and his uncertainties; they just are not allowed to magnify those fears, uncertainties, and so forth to the point where rational decision becomes impossible.

An alternative interpretation of the officer's statement, however, is that it promised Rutledge a *net* benefit from spilling the beans. If this was the promise, it is unlikely that the officer intended to keep it; and if he did not, then the statement was fraudulent. But it was the sort of minor fraud that the cases allow. Far from making the police a fiduciary of the suspect, the law permits the police to pressure and cajole, conceal material facts, and actively mislead—all up to limits not exceeded here. United States v. Guerrero, 847 F.2d 1363, 1366–67 (9th Cir.1988).

There was no net benefit to Rutledge, clearly; was there *any* benefit? We have said there was, yet against this it can be argued that the agreement to drop one of the charges against Rutledge and to bring his cooperation to the judge's attention was in exchange not for his confessing to a larger role in the drug trade but simply for his forgoing his right to a trial. If so, then it can be argued that the confession helped him not at all—the government had reneged on its promise that his cooperating would help him. The defendant's forgoing his right to trial is an important consideration in virtually every plea bargain, because the government does not have the resources to try every criminal defendant. But cooperation in the investigation of other offenders is also an important consideration in plea bargaining, and there is no reason to doubt that it was important here. A better argument is that the written plea agreement recites as the consideration for dropping the charge that was dropped Rutledge's cooperation in testifying against and otherwise helping the government bring his accomplices to justice; the agreement makes no mention of the confession. But the confession was the beginning of the cooperation, for it was the confession that revealed that Rutledge was involved in more than bush-league drug dealing. Had Rutledge not revealed his part in a larger drug operation his cooperation would have been less valuable—would not have commanded as high a "price" in the plea-bargaining market.

* * *

5. In United States v. Roark, 753 F.2d 991 (11th Cir.1985), the defendant sought to persuade the jury that a confession was unreliable because it was involuntary. The trial court barred the testimony of a physician-psychologist called by the defense to explain to the jury that the accused might have falsely confessed to please her interrogators. The reviewing court, under the particular circumstances, held that the exclusion was an abuse of discretion. As *Roark* indicates, ordinarily evidence which has a bearing on the voluntariness issue is also relevant to a jury determination of the weight to be accorded a confession. The Supreme Court so held in Crane v. Kentucky, 476 U.S. 683, 106 S.Ct. 2142 (1986). There have been several cases dealing with admissibility of the use of an expert on the issue of whether a confession is false. See e.g., Miller v. State, 770 N.E.2d 763 (Ind.2002).

6. An accused is constitutionally entitled to have the trial court rule on the question of the voluntariness before it is submitted to a jury. If a confession is found to be involuntary, it may not be presented to the jury. See Jackson v. Denno, infra, Ch. 13, Sec. H.

7. Among the certainties in the law on confessions is that the use of actual physical force, or the threat of physical force, will nullify a confession. The reasoning behind such a rule is one that is readily appreciated by all reasonable persons—the protection of the innocent from the use against them of a coerced confession. No other single factor dictates a conclusion about voluntariness. State v. Knight, 183 N.J. 449, 874 A.2d 546 (2005) (length of interrogation) The only possible exception that could arise is in a case where force or threat of force to obtain a confession seems absolutely necessary in order to save the life of a kidnaped person or some other innocent person. However, that issue has not been squarely resolved. One of the nearest approaches is Leon v. State, 410 So.2d 201

(Fla.Dist.Ct.App.1982), in which the threat of force and the use of force were used to obtain information about the location of a kidnap victim. In *Leon* the court held that the admissions made by the defendant, which the prosecutor refrained from offering in evidence, did not taint or render inadmissible a subsequent confession. In cases of this nature, however, the state has a heavy burden of establishing that when the subsequent confession is made the confessor was no longer dominated or affected by the influence of the prior events. State v. Henry, 196 La. 217, 198 So. 910 (1940); People v. La Coco, 406 Ill. 303, 94 N.E.2d 178 (1950); People v. Brommel, 56 Cal.2d 629, 15 Cal.Rptr. 909, 364 P.2d 845 (1961). That requirement prevails even where the earlier mistreatment had been administered by private persons rather than police personnel. People v. Berve, 51 Cal.2d 286, 332 P.2d 97 (1958). See United States v. Murphy, 763 F.2d 202 (6th Cir.1985) (Statements made while under attack by police dog are involuntary even though it is clear the use of dog was proper and not motivated by desire to provoke statements).

8. In State v. James, 237 Conn. 390, 678 A.2d 1338 (1996) a divided court addressed two related issues arising when the voluntariness of a confession is challenged. The court adopted (after extensive analysis) the rule which requires voluntariness to be proved by a preponderance of the evidence. The court also decided that there was no constitutional requirement that confession be electronically recorded, where feasible, as a precondition for admissibility. After considering the precedents of the fourteen states which had ruled on the question, the court said:

> "[E]lectronic recording 'would, in many cases, be a helpful tool in evaluating the voluntariness of confessions' [but].... recording would not in all circumstances be a foolproof mechanism for accurately resolving disputes between an accused and the police.... [e.g.] disputes concerning what transpired before the recording began or during breaks ... or on occasions when the tape may be inaudible. More importantly,.... [w]e are not persuaded that determinations of admissibility traditionally made by courts are inherently untrustworthy or that independent corroboration of otherwise competent testimonial or documentary evidence ... is necessary.... Finally.... the costs [of having and maintaining recording equipment] might be substantial, there are also other 'costs'.... Requiring the police to record all confessions ... might severely inhibit the police in pursuing, by constitutionally valid methods, confession evidence. Moreover, a criminal suspect's knowledge that an interview with the police will be recorded might limit his or her willingness to speak. We have noted that it is 'a common experience of life that ... persons are willing to convey information orally but are reluctant to put the same thing in writing' [citation omitted].... the cost of noncompliance with a recordation requirement.... due to negligence or for other reasons, is the loss of otherwise admissible, probative evidence of guilt."

In a lone dissent, Berdon, Associate Justice said:

> "In my view, as a matter of public policy the police should, from the time a citizen is first taken into the police station for investigative purposes, whether voluntarily or involuntarily, electronically record all that transpires with respect to the person as long as he or she is there. Such a procedure would benefit the police by dispelling any claims of coercion.... Equally important, the suspect and the public would perceive that justice had been done. Lacking such independent verification, it strains credulity that the defendant would voluntarily go to the police station as 1:30 a.m. at the 'invitation' of the police and voluntarily remain there for fourteen hours. We cannot ignore as judges what we know as men and women."

How would recording work? Would it be enough to record the confession or would "all that transpires with respect to the defendant" be necessary. No jurisdiction has found recordation to be constitutionally required.

Some statutes require recordation in some classes of cases e.g., crimes of violence and enact a rebuttable presumption of involuntariness or an exclusion rule for unrecorded confessions. See 725 ILCS 5/103–2.1 (Illinois) and D.C. St. Ann. § 5–133.20; Tex.Code Crim. Proc. art. 38.22 § 3(a)(1) (2002)

Many state courts have found recording was not required under their state due process clause: Colorado, Georgia, Idaho, Illinois, Maine, Mississippi, Nevada, Utah, Vermont, Washington, and West Virginia. People v. Raibon, 843 P.2d 46, 49 (Colo.Ct.App.1992); Coleman v. State, 189 Ga.App. 366, 375 S.E.2d 663, 664 (1988); State v. Rhoades, 120 Idaho 795, 820 P.2d 665, 674–75 (1991); People v. Everette, 187 Ill.App.3d 1063, 135 Ill.Dec. 472, 543 N.E.2d 1040, 1047 (1989), rev'd on other grounds, 141 Ill.2d 147, 152 Ill.Dec. 377, 565 N.E.2d 1295 (1990); State v. Buzzell, 617 A.2d 1016, 1018 (Me.1992); Williams v. State, 522 So.2d 201, 208 (Miss.1988); Jimenez v. State, 105 Nev. 337, 775 P.2d 694, 696–97 (1989); State v. James, 858 P.2d 1012, 1018 (Utah Ct.App.1993); State v. Gorton, 149 Vt. 602, 548 A.2d 419, 422 (1988); State v. Spurgeon, 63 Wash.App. 503, 820 P.2d 960, 963 (1991); State v. Kilmer, 190 W.Va. 617, 439 S.E.2d 881, 893 (1993); People v. Holt, 15 Cal.4th 619, 63 Cal.Rptr.2d 782, 937 P.2d 213, 242–43 (1997); State v. James, 237 Conn. 390, 678 A.2d 1338, 1360 (1996); State v. Kekona, 77 Hawai'i 403, 886 P.2d 740, 745–46 (1994); Stoker v. State, 692 N.E.2d 1386, 1390 (Ind.Ct.App.1998); Commonwealth v. Diaz, 422 Mass. 269, 661 N.E.2d 1326, 1328–29 (1996); People v. Fike, 228 Mich.App. 178, 577 N.W.2d 903, 906–07 (1998); State v. Barnett, 147 N.H. 334, 789 A.2d 629, 632 (2001); Commonwealth v. Craft, 447 Pa.Super. 371, 669 A.2d 394, 394–98 (1995); State v. Godsey, 60 S.W.3d 759, 771–72 (Tenn.2001).

Minnesota and Alaska exclude statements based on a failure to record. State v. Scales, 518 N.W.2d 587, 592 (Minn.1994); Stephan v. State, 711 P.2d 1156, 1162 (Alaska 1985). New Hampshire opted for a middle ground, holding that "immediately following the valid waiver of a defendant's Miranda rights, a tape recorded interrogation will not be admitted into evidence unless the statement is recorded in its entirety." Barnett, 789 A.2d at 632. A number of courts have recognized the merits of recording, but have refused to require the practice.

9. An interesting article analyzing the debate over confessions as a product of three separate rhetorics in check and balance is Sherwin, "Dialects and Dominance", 136 U.Pa.L.Rev. 729 (1988).

There are also several studies suggesting that a significant number of persons exonerated by DNA evidence made false confessions although the most common factor in exonerations cases is mistaken identification. R. Leo, S. Drizin & P. Neufeld, et al., "Bringing Reliability Back In: False Confessions and Legal Safeguards in the Twenty–First Century," 2006 Wis.L.Rev. 479 (2006); S. Drizin & R.Leo, "The Problem of False Confessions in the Post–DNA World," 82 N.C. L.Rev. 891 (2004) and "Exonerations in the United States 1989 through 2003" 95 J.Crim.L. & Criminology (2005)

A case for the necessity of increased gatekeeping by courts in the face of claims of false confessions is found in Sharon L. Davies, "The Reality of False Confessions—Lessons of the Central Park Jogger Case," 30 N.Y.U. Rev. L. & Soc. Change 209 (2006). See also Miriam S. Gohara, "A Lie for a Lie: False Confessions and the Case for Reconsidering the Legality of Deceptive Interrogation Techniques," 33 Fordham Urb. L.J. 791 (2006).

2. PERMISSIBLE INTERROGATION TACTICS AND TECHNIQUES

(a) TRICKERY, DECEIT, PROMISES?

Frazier v. Cupp

Supreme Court of the United States, 1969.
394 U.S. 731, 89 S.Ct. 1420.

■ MR. JUSTICE MARSHALL delivered the opinion of the Court.

* * *

Petitioner's second argument concerns the admission into evidence of his own confession. The circumstances under which the confession was obtained can be summarized briefly. Petitioner was arrested about 4:15 p.m. on September 24, 1964. He was taken to headquarters where questioning began at about 5 p.m. The interrogation, which was tape-recorded, ended slightly more than an hour later, and by 6:45 p.m. petitioner had signed a written version of his confession.

After the questioning had begun and after a few routine facts were ascertained, petitioner was questioned briefly about the location of his Marine uniform. He was next asked where he was on the night in question. Although he admitted that he was with his cousin Rawls, he denied being with any third person. Then petitioner was given a somewhat abbreviated description of his constitutional rights. He was told that he could have an attorney if he wanted one and that anything he said could be used against him at trial. Questioning thereafter became somewhat more vigorous, but petitioner continued to deny being with anyone but Rawls. At this point, the officer questioning petitioner told him, falsely, that Rawls had been brought in and that he had confessed. Petitioner still was reluctant to talk, but after the officer sympathetically suggested that the victim had started a fight by making homosexual advances, petitioner began to spill out his story. Shortly after he began he again showed signs of reluctance and said, "I think I had better get a lawyer before I talk any more. I am going to get into trouble more than I am in now." The officer replied simply, "You can't be in any more trouble than you are in now," and the questioning session proceeded. A full confession was obtained and, after further warnings, a written version was signed.

* * *

Petitioner also presses the alternative argument that his confession was involuntary and that it should have been excluded for that reason. The trial judge, after an evidentiary hearing during which the tape recording was played, could not agree with this contention, and our reading of the record does not lead us to a contrary conclusion. Before petitioner made any incriminating statements, he received partial warnings of his constitutional rights; this is, of course, a circumstance quite relevant to a finding of voluntariness. Davis v. North Carolina, 384 U.S. 737, 740, 741, 86 S.Ct. 1761 (1966). The questioning was of short duration, and petitioner was a mature individual of normal intelligence. The fact that the police misrepresented the statements that Rawls had made is, while relevant, insufficient in our view to make this otherwise voluntary confession inadmissible. These cases must be decided by viewing the "totality of the circumstances," see, e.g., Clewis v. Texas, 386 U.S. 707, 708, 87 S.Ct. 1338 (1967), and on the facts of this case we can find no error in the admission of petitioner's confession.

* * *

Because we find none of petitioner's contentions meritorious, we affirm the judgment of the Court of Appeals.

Affirmed.

■ MR. CHIEF JUSTICE WARREN and MR. JUSTICE DOUGLAS concur in the result.

■ MR. JUSTICE FORTAS took no part in the consideration or decision of this case.

NOTES

1. The result reached in *Frazier* is echoed in many other cases. See People v. Guerra, 37 Cal.4th 1067, 40 Cal.Rptr.3d 118, 129 P.3d 321 (2006) People v. Martin, 102 Ill.2d 412, 80 Ill.Dec. 776, 466 N.E.2d 228 (1984); People v. Boone, 22 N.Y.2d 476, 293 N.Y.S.2d 287, 239 N.E.2d 885 (1968); United States ex rel. Caminito v. Murphy, 222 F.2d 698 (2d Cir.1955) (officers pretended to be witnesses to the crime and then "identified" the accused). See also State v. Manning, 506 So.2d 1094 (Fla.App.1987) (suspect falsely told his records showed venereal disease of the same sort diagnosed in five year old victim—deception unlikely to induce false confession); State v. Carrillo, 156 Ariz. 125, 750 P.2d 883 (1988) (proper for police to use a ruse to get defendant to station and then surprise him with accusation; "the police are not forbidden to outsmart, they are forbidden to compel"). Compare Edwards v. State, 274 Ind. 387, 412 N.E.2d 223 (1980) (disapproving confession made after a police female clerk, posing as a witness, had walked to a door where the police were holding the suspect, a mental patient on furlough from a state hospital, and said to him: "That's the man"); Woods v. Clusen, 794 F.2d 293 (7th Cir.1986) (false statements that fingerprints of suspect were found on stolen property), and State v. Cayward, 552 So.2d 971 (Fla.App.1989) (use of falsified scientific report to prompt a confession violates due process rights). State v. Ritter, 268 Ga. 108, 485 S.E.2d 492 (1997) (False statement that victim was alive and well renders confession involuntarily).

In State v. Kelekolio, 74 Haw. 479, 849 P.2d 58 (1993) the Supreme Court of Hawaii restated the law governing deception:

> "... In our view, the relevant case law and scholarly authority, including that cited above, is amenable to the formulation of a rule by which to measure the legitimacy of the use of 'deception' by the police in eliciting confessions or inculpatory statements from suspects and arrestees. That rule, which we now adapt, is that employment by the police of deliberate falsehoods intrinsic to the facts of the alleged offense in question will be treated as one of the totality of circumstances surrounding the confession or statement to be considered in assessing its voluntariness; on the other hand, deliberate falsehoods extrinsic to the facts of the alleged offense, which are of a type reasonably likely to procure an untrue statement or to influence an accused to make a confession regardless of guilt, will be regarded as coercive per se, thus obviating the need for a 'totality of circumstances' analysis or voluntariness.

Although the foregoing rule will, of course, have to be applied on a case-by-case basis, some examples of intrinsic falsehoods would include such misrepresentations regarding the existence of incriminating evidence as (1) placement of the defendant's vehicle at the crime scene, ... (2) physical evidence linked to the victim found in the defendant's car, ... (3) discovery of the murder weapon, ... (4) a claim that the murder victim is still alive, ... (5) presence of the defendant's fingerprints on the getaway car or at the crime scene, ... (6) positive identification of the defendant by reliable witnesses, ... and (7) discovery of a nonexistent witness.... Some examples of extrinsic falsehoods—of a type reasonably likely to procure an untrue statement or to influence an accused to make a confession regardless of guilt—would include (1) assurances of divine salvation upon confession, see *Nelson*, (2) promises of mental health treatment in exchange for a confession, see *Hogan*, (3) assurances of treatment in a 'nice hospital' (in which the defendant could have his personal belongings and be visited by his girlfriend) in lieu of incarceration, in exchange for a confession, (4) promises of more favorable treatment in the event of a confession, see *Meehan*, (5) misrepresentations of legal principles, such as (a) suggesting that the defendant would have the burden of convincing a judge and jury at trial that he was 'perfectly innocent' and had nothing to do with the offense, ... (b) misrepresenting the consequences of a 'habitual offender' conviction, and (c) holding out that the defendant's confession cannot be used against him at trial, ... and (6) misrepresentations by an interrogating police officer, who is a close friend of the defendant, that the defendant's failure to confess will get the officer into trouble with his superiors and jeopardize the well-being of the officer's pregnant wife and children."

2. In the Canadian Supreme Court case of Rothman v. The Queen, 59 C.C.C.2d 30 (1981), the following appeared in the concurring opinion of Justice Lamar:

"The Judge, in determining whether under the circumstances the use of the statement in the proceedings would bring the administration of justice into disrepute, should consider all of the circumstances of the proceedings, the manner in which the statement was obtained, the degree to which there was a breach of social values, the seriousness of the charge, the effect the exclusion would have on the result of the proceedings. It must also be borne in mind that the investigation of crime and the detection of criminals is not a game to be governed by the Marquess of Queensbury rules. The authorities, in dealing with shrewd and often sophisticated criminals, must sometimes of necessity resort to tricks or other forms of deceit and should not through the rule be hampered in their work. What should be repressed vigorously is conduct on their part that shocks the community. That a police officer pretend to be a lock-up chaplain and hear a suspect's confession is conduct that shocks the community; so is pretending to be the duty legal aid lawyer eliciting in that way incriminating statements from suspects or accused; injecting pentothal into a diabetic suspect pretending it is his daily shot of insulin and using his statement in evidence would also shock the community; but generally speaking, pretending to be a hard drug addict to break a drug ring would not shock the community; nor would, as in this case, pretending to be a truck driver to secure the conviction of a trafficker; in fact, what would shock the community would be preventing the police from resorting to such a trick."

3. For a viewpoint in opposition to the employment of trickery in the interrogation of criminal suspects, see White, "Police Trickery in Inducing Confessions," 127 U.Pa.L.Rev. 581 (1979). Following are excerpts from Professor White's conclusion:

"The protections provided by the *Miranda* warnings, the sixth amendment right to an attorney, and the modern version of the 'voluntariness' test limit the types of deceptive practices that the police may employ.... effective protection of these constitutional rights can only be achieved through the formulation of per se rules—that is, whenever the practice under scrutiny creates an unacceptable risk that the ordinary suspect's constitutional rights will be infringed, the practice should be proscribed. Application of this analysis to several widely employed interrogation tactics results in a finding that they should be absolutely prohibited."

4. Some of the most troublesome cases for the courts are those where the issue concerns promises or suggestions by an interrogator of some benefit to the suspect as an inducement to confess. The following cases illustrate the problem:

In Bram v. United States, 168 U.S. 532, 554, 18 S.Ct. 183, 191 (1897), the Court suggested that any inducement "however slight" may be improper. This rule was never strictly applied. More recently promises of leniency have been treated as just one factor in the "totality of the circumstances." See Lynumn v. Illinois, 372 U.S. 528, 83 S.Ct. 917 (1963) ("It will go lighter if you cooperate"). And in Arizona v. Fulminante, 499 U.S. 279, 111 S.Ct. 1246 (1991) the Court rejected an absolute rule that any promise invalidates a confession.

The decided cases on the question of what is a fatal promise of leniency are not to be reconciled. An exhortation to tell the truth is proper. Crooker v. California, 357 U.S. 433, 437, 78 S.Ct. 1287 (1958). But what of suggestions, even general ones, that things will go better or easier if the truth is told. Compare State v. Pruitt, 286 N.C. 442, 212 S.E.2d 92 (1975) (statement inadmissible where suspect was told it would be better for him if he got it off his chest and would be harder if he did not cooperate) and Dorsciak v. Gladden, 246 Or. 233, 425 P.2d 177 (1967) (improper to say that judge "would be easier on you"), with People v. Hartgraves, 31 Ill.2d 375, 202 N.E.2d 33 (1964) (confession admissible despite statement that "It would go easier in court for you if you made a statement") and Brooks v. State, 229 A.2d 833 (Del.1967) (proper to admit confession where officers said they would see what they could do to help the accused but could not promise anything). Courts sometimes say the proper line is between holding out hope as opposed to making a commitment. Commonwealth v. O'Brian, 445 Mass. 720, 840 N.E.2d 500 (2006).

Specific promises not to prosecute or not to impose a specific sentence generally render confessions invalid Grades v. Boles, 398 F.2d 409 (4th Cir.1968) and State v. Whitsel, 339 N.W.2d 149 (Iowa 1983) (offer to recommend to prosecutor that he secure psychiatric help for a sex offender and to tell of suspect's cooperation while stating that they could not promise or guarantee that the prosecutor would agree does not invalidate confession) (review of cases).

Threats to take actions within the law may not cause a confession to be involuntary. United States v. Johnson, 351 F.3d 254 (6th Cir.2003) (prosecution of a guilty relative) State v. Davison, 280 Ga. 84, 623 S.E.2d 500 (2005) (lawful arrest). Threats of illegal action are not allowable. People v. Medina, 25 P.3d 1216 (Colo. 2001) In United States v. Alvarado, 882 F.2d 645 (2d Cir.1989), a law enforcement agent told a suspect that she had best cooperate because she had a daughter, promised to tell the judge and the prosecutor of the suspect's cooperation if it was forthcoming, and indicated that she would get ten years if she did not cooperate. The court upheld a finding of voluntariness.

In United States v. Harrison, 34 F.3d 886 (9th Cir.1994) the Court noted its rule that offering to tell a prosecutor about cooperation and suggesting this increases the likelihood of leniency is permissible while threatening to tell the prosecutor of the failure to cooperate is not. The Court then found involuntary a confession which occurred after an agent told Harrison she might get twenty years and *asking* her whether she thought it would be better if the judge were told that she had cooperated or had not cooperated. She responded it would be better if she talked to the agents and they told the judge she cooperated.

A promise kept—leniency was given—is still an improper inducement when made by officer who had no authority to make it. People v. Vasila, 38 Cal.App.4th 865, 45 Cal.Rptr.2d 355 (1995) ("if we get the guns back today, I'll release you [and not prosecute in federal court"]). Some courts have said that even an authorized (and honored) promise is improper because it is the equivalent of a plea bargain with an unrepresented defendant. State v. Rezk, 150 N.H. 483, 840 A.2d 758 (2004) but this is not the common rule.

5. In Welch v. Butler, 835 F.2d 92 (5th Cir.1988), a confession was held voluntary although it seemingly was induced by a lengthy prayer session conducted by a born-again Christian police officer who talked to the suspect about the nature of divine forgiveness and salvation. The court noted that the suspect had been concerned about salvation and forgiveness, and that he made an informed choice to confess of his own free will. "What coercion that existed was sacred, not profane," said the court. Would it have made a difference if the interrogator was a non-believer who privately ridiculed notions of a deity, salvation, and an afterlife? The answer to that question might depend on how much the concept of voluntariness turns upon subjective free choice and how much turns upon objective standards of decency in police practices. See United States v. Crowder, 62 F.3d 782 (6th Cir.1995) (subjective fears of defendant not caused by police). See State v. Amaya–Ruiz, 166 Ariz. 152, 800 P.2d 1260 (1990) (Confession upheld where officer said:

> "We can forgive your lies, but the United States court system will not forgive your lies;" "If you want any forgiveness, you should tell the truth;" and "If you lie to us now it will be on the record for the rest of your life that you lied, and then you'll never be able to say you are sorry.")

6. The exchange of a confession for some consideration is analogous to the plea bargaining process where pleas may be exchanged for rather specific promises not to prosecute or to impose certain sentences. Presumably the difference in judicial tolerance of the guilty plea practice stems from the fact that defendant is represented by counsel who participates in the bargaining. United States v. Long, 852 F.2d 975 (7th Cir.1988) (Confession pursuant to plea agreement admissible despite unforeseen use in another jurisdiction).

7. Consider the idea that voluntariness of confessions is enhanced if the accused is fully apprised of the probable consequences of his confession and of the legal significance of each of the facts he admits. The courts have never required such awareness, but where it exists it clearly supports a claim of voluntariness. If this rule is applied, why preclude the police from telling an accused that the fact he has confessed will mitigate his punishment if, in fact, it will? Is the basis for objecting to such police statements that they can never be based on certainty but only probability? Is the basis for objection the belief that the practice may cause an innocent person to confess? See Wigmore, Evidence §§ 824–826, 831–841 (Chadbourn Rev. 1970). Consider United States v. Rutledge, supra, p. 35.

8. Over dissent, an en banc Court of Appeals reversed a trial court's finding of involuntariness arising from a statement that "If you're not coming clean . . . you can get five, you know, you can do five years because you're not coming clean." The majority held that, in a non-custodial interrogation where the suspect is answering questions, it is a truthful (and thus non-coercive) statement of the consequences of making a false statement to law enforcement officers, an admonition that, if you speak, speak only the truth because lying is a punishable offense. The dissent argued that the statement told the suspect that he would get five years if he did not come clean. See United States v. Braxton, 112 F.3d 777 (4th Cir.1997) (en banc). In cases like these, should the court decide how a reasonable person might interpret the "come clean" statement or how the particular suspect would interpret it? If there is more than one interpretation, who should bear the burden of proving the correct interpretation? Is it significant that Braxton did not ask what the officer meant by five years for not coming clean? Is it significant that the officer did not specifically say that he could get five years for lying during the interview?

9. Consider the following circumstances and decide whether the confession is voluntary:

On October 11, 1993, Seward Police Officer Todd McGillivray received information that Cole had sexually abused C.C., Cole's sixteen-year-old adopted daughter. Upon being interviewed at the police station, C.C. confirmed the report.

C.C. told McGillivray that in September of 1993 her father (Cole) caught her smoking. Cole offered C.C. a deal: C.C. could continue to smoke if she would let him teach her "the ways of the Ninja." C.C. agreed to the deal. Cole told her not to discuss the Ninja training with anyone, including her mother. At first, the training consisted of ordinary calisthenics such as sit-ups, leg bends, and the like. However, after the first "session," Cole insisted that C.C. exercise in only her underwear. On October 10, 1993, Cole instructed C.C. to completely disrobe for the Ninja training. Cole was also nude during the session; at some point, acting on the pretext of checking C.C.'s muscular development, he lifted up her breasts with his hands. C.C. asked Cole to stop touching her, and he did. Cole then asked C.C. to touch him, but she refused. The next day, C.C. reported the incident to the mother of one of her friends, who, in turn, notified the police.

While C.C. was describing the incident to McGillivray, Cole called the police station to report C.C. as a runaway. That evening, Cole called again, and spoke to the police dispatcher, saying that he had located his daughter and had heard that she was accusing him of molesting her. The dispatcher notified McGillivray, who asked the dispatcher to have Cole meet him at the police station, ostensibly to file a runaway report. Cole soon arrived at the station and met with McGillivray.

In actuality, McGillivray planned to interrogate Cole about C.C.'s report that Cole had sexually touched her on October 10.

The interview began at approximately 9:30 p.m. and continued for seventy-two minutes. At the outset, McGillivray twice assured Cole that "no matter what we talk about here tonight, you will not be arrested." After listening to Cole explain why he had reported C.C. as a runaway, McGillivray assured Cole that C.C. was safe; McGillivray said he had spoken with C.C. earlier that night and that she was presently a ward of the state.

McGillivray then informed Cole that "we're going to talk about ... some accusations that she made to me," and that "this is serious." McGillivray told Cole that "it's very important that you're completely honest with me[.]" He explained that complete honesty was important "because if there is a problem, whether it's on your side or her side, our main objective is to get help for whoever needs it and get the problem solved." McGillivray reassured Cole that it was this desire to help that enabled him to promise that Cole would not be arrested: "That's why I want to set you at ease that no matter what we talk about tonight, you're free to leave here tonight. Ok? I mean, it's very important that you understand that." McGillivray repeated that he was motivated solely by the desire to provide help. "Like I say, our objective is to just, you know, we need to get help for whoever needs it. Ok?" Cole responded, "Ok."

This explanation brought McGillivray to his formal interrogation. He asked Cole a series of general questions about the background circumstances C.C. had reported. Gradually, McGillivray focused on C.C.'s report of the sexual touching itself. Cole consistently denied knowledge and involvement in any of the kinds of conduct C.C. had reported. McGillivray ultimately asked, point blank, "have you ever had any sexual contact with your daughter?" Cole responded, "No, absolutely not."

At this point, McGillivray abruptly shifted course. He falsely told Cole that the police had been involved in investigating C.C.'s report of abuse for "[a] week or so," that "we've known this for awhile," and that "[t]his just isn't something that cropped up tonight." He then began to talk about a polygraph test, saying, again falsely, that the district attorney had authorized the police to give Cole a polygraph examination.

> (OM): Uh, I've talked to the District Attorney on it. Uh, one thing that we do have at our disposal that, that they're to spend the money on and that is, that is real helpful to both you and me ... is what they call a polygraph examination.

After making sure that Cole knew what a polygraph examination was, McGillivray asked if Cole was willing to submit to one. When Cole expressed his distrust of lie detector tests, McGillivray falsely proclaimed that he had extensive experience with such tests, that he had never known the tests to be inaccurate, and that he was prepared to obtain a court order requiring Cole to submit to polygraph questioning.

> (OM): Ok. Would you be willing to take a polygraph examination [in] reference to these allegations? (GC): Um I, I don't know at this time. I don't ... (OM): And why would that be? (GC): I, I'm scared of them. (OM): Why is that? (GC): I don't know. I've seen so many things on TV where [they] had these lie detectors ... (OM): Well ... I'll tell you right now ... I've dealt with polygraphs a lot over the last couple of years. Ok ... I find them to be very helpful and very accurate. Ok. I've never had one false positive and I've never had one negative. Ok. And I've had a lot of people through polygraphs ... if you know going in that you're going to pass the polygraph, you will pass the polygraph. (GC): Yeah. (OM): Ok. If there is nothing there. If not I need to know about it now. Ok? (GC): Ok. What will happen[?] (OM): Because we will, we will do a polygraph. Ok? (GC): By a court order? (OM): Well if I have to.

McGillivray made no effort to actually arrange a polygraph test. Saying that he wanted to avoid wasting time on a test if Cole would simply fail it, and reminding Cole that his objective was to get help for Cole and his family as soon as possible, McGillivray declared that he needed to know immediately whether Cole would fail. Cole answered that he did not think a test would be a waste of time and that, although he was still "scared of the machines," he was willing to take a test, "if you're going to get a court order and all this stuff[.]"

But McGillivray immediately deflected Cole away from an actual test and steered him into a series of hypothetical polygraph questions about the sexual touching incident. As to each hypothetical question, McGillivray asked Cole to tell him how Cole would respond when the polygraph examiner asked the question and what Cole thought the polygraph machine would reveal about the truthfulness of his answer.

> For example: (OM): ... one of the questions is going to be: have you ever exercised with your daughter while she's been in her underwear? (GC): Ok. (OM): How would you answer that question? (GC): Uh, I, uh, given a statement and I, I'm confused. (OM): Well I'm not trying to confuse you, sir. I'm, I'm trying to ... (GC): You're trying, you're trying to say that, that I did this. (OM): Well, I'm tryin' to find out whether you did or you didn't[.] ... How do you think the polygraph would say? (GC): I don't know. Because I'm scared

of 'em. (OM): Okay, well, in your own mind, how would you say the polygraph would say that (both talking) (GC): I don't, I don't want to speculate. Please? I really don't want to speculate, because, I don't know what that machine w' say. (OM): Well, if you're truthful, the machine would say you're truthful. If you're not, the machine's gonna say that you're not truthful, that you're being deceptive. (GC): Okay. (OM): If a polygraph examiner ever asked you if you've ever touched your daughter's breast, how would you answer that question? (GC): I, again, I don't know. (OM): Well, Mr. Cole, I, I'm gonna answer those questions for you. (GC): Okay. (OM): Okay? On the answer to both those questions, I think you would fail the polygraph.

As McGillivray pressed on with the mock polygraph interrogation, he alternated between accusations of dishonesty and assurances that he just wanted to "get help for the right person."

McGillivray also suggested that confessing would make things easier on Cole and that failure to confess might be held against him:

(OM): . . . it's just gonna be easier on the both of us, and I think would look better for you too, if you were truthful with me. Because I will get to the truth. And if I have to go digging to get to the truth, and I do find out that, you know, you weren't telling me everything that you could have tonight, it's not gonna look real good. Can you understand that? Don't you think that it would look better if you were honest with me from the get go then . . . (GC): But I have been honest with you from the get go! Why, why . . . (OM): Are you sure? (GC): Yes, I'm sure.

Cole steadfastly denied ever touching C.C.'s breasts or exercising with her while she was in only her underwear.

Eventually it became clear that the mock polygraph technique was fruitless; McGillivray turned to a new tactic by confronting Cole with evidence that did not actually exist. McGillivray falsely informed Cole that the police had already obtained a "Glass" warrant authorizing electronic monitoring of Cole's home and that, pursuant to the warrant, they had recorded the previous night's "exercise" session with C.C. McGillivray demanded to know what Cole had to say in light of this revelation.

(OM): . . . If, if I told you that your daughter came to me with this days ago, what would you say? (GC): I don't know. I'm just shocked. I'm surprised. (OM): What would you say if I had a Glass warrant. (GC): A what? (OM): . . . a Glass warrant, which is an electronic surveillance warrant, which means I can record another person's conversations, without them knowing it. (GC): Uh huh. (OM): What would you say if I had one of those in my possession right now? To record the conversations of you? (GC): Do you? (OM): Now do you think I would bring it up if I didn't? (GC): I don't know. I'm just asking. (OM): And would you say if I had this electronic surveillance device in your home last night when you and your daughter exercised? (GC): Did you? (OM): Would I know about it if I didn't? Last night she wasn't even wearing clothes. Because you changed the deal on her.

Cole's resistance cracked: he told McGillivray, "I need help." He then specified that the help he needed was "mental." McGillivray pursued this opening and pressed Cole for details, emphasizing that the "only reason" he wanted to hear the details was "so we know which kind of help we need to get."

(OM): What kind of help? (GC): Mental. (OM): You agree with me then? (GC): Yes. (OM): Why don't you tell me the problem that we've got goin' at home? The only reason I do that is just, I wanna hear it from you, an' I wanna know your side of the story so we know which kind a help we need to get.

But despite persistent questioning, Cole was reluctant to reveal more. Faced with Cole's reluctance, McGillivray insisted that Cole would get no help unless he told McGillivray "what happened with your daughter."

> (GC): I need psychological help. (OM): And why is that? (GC): I should never have put my daughter through (inaudible). It's not right. (OM): Tell me about it. (GC): I don't know what to say. (OM): Tell me what happened a month and a half ago when you caught her smoking. (GC): I'll remember the best that I can. (OM): Tell me about the deal that you made with her. And I know this is hard, George. I mean, I understand, an' that's why I'm here, is you know, like I say, we need to get to the truth so that we can get it corrected. Okay. (GC): I just. I need help. (OM): But to do that, you need to tell me what happened. (GC): I just. I need help. (OM): But to do that, you need to tell me what happened. (GC): (sighs) Uh. (OM): Okay, George. (GC): I, I need help.... [interruption as tape changed] (OM): ... Uh, e', George, you were just, you know, like I was telling you before, I need, I need you to tell me what happened. An' I know it's tough, an' I know it's hard, and you know, you've told me that you needed help and I'd like to see you get the help. And, but for you to do that, I need you to tell me what happened with your daughter, [C.C.]. An', uh, did you make a deal with her that day when you caught her smoking?

Upon hearing this, Cole acknowledged making a deal to teach C.C. "The ways of the Ninja" but declined to divulge what this entailed, professing a "code of silence."

Under McGillivray's persistent interrogation, however, Cole gradually began to reveal more information. He admitted that he had exercised with C.C. while she was nude and had touched her breasts.

But Cole continued to deny that sexual intercourse was the "final goal" of the Ninja training. When asked to explain why he had touched C.C., Cole said that it "was ... to help her overcome the fear of being touched." Cole also admitted that he had told C.C. "she had the freedom" to touch him during the sessions "if she wanted to."

Cole still insisted that this conduct was integral to "Ninja training." McGillivray pressed for details about the Ninja "code of silence," but Cole said he was fearful that the tape of his interview with McGillivray would be played publicly, in "a public courtroom, an' stuff like that." McGillivray falsely assured Cole, "that won't happen" and that "[t]hese type of cases are very confidential."

Upon receiving these assurances, Cole asserted that nudity and exercising with offspring were part of Japanese custom. But he continued to be evasive about precisely why the touching had taken place. McGillivray, proclaiming that "I don't feel like I'm getting the whole truth here," then resurrected the mock polygraph technique. This quickly yielded Cole's ultimate admission—that he had touched C.C. for his own sexual gratification.

> (OM): Why do you feel you have to make a deal with her to get her to do this. (GC): I don't know. (OM): Are you sure you don't know. (GC): Unless I ... (OM): I wish that you'd get back, again I'll go back to the polygraph. (GC): Uh huh. (OM): Okay. If a polygraph operator asked you which we may still do. (GC): Okay. (OM): Because I don't feel like I'm getting the whole truth here. (GC): Okay.... (OM): Alright, just let me finish, if a polygraph operator asked you, when you made the deal with [C.C.] for her to partake in this type of training. Was it for Ninja purposes or your own personal pleasure. How would you answer that? (GC): I'll probably truthfully have to say my own personal pleasure. (OM): So in reality the training had nothing to do with all of this.

(Inaudible—both speaking.) (OM): Right. (GC): Yeah cos I probably used that as an excuse.

See Cole v. State, 923 P.2d 820 (Alaska App.1996).

10. Consider the en banc decision in United States v. LeBrun, 363 F.3d 715 (8th Cir.2004).

■ HANSEN, CIRCUIT JUDGE.

After thirty-three minutes of questioning, Michael LeBrun confessed to naval investigators that in 1968, while he was enlisted in the United States Navy, he strangled to death his superior officer, Ensign Andrew Muns, on board the U.S.S. Cacapon after Ensign Muns caught LeBrun robbing the safe in the ship's disbursing office....

Muns and LeBrun served as shipmates during the Vietnam War aboard the U.S.S. Cacapon. Ensign Muns served as the disbursing officer, and LeBrun served as the disbursing clerk. On January 16 or 17, 1968, while the U.S.S. Cacapon was moored in the Subic Bay, Muns disappeared. After conducting an investigation into Muns' disappearance, the Navy concluded that Muns had stolen $8600 from the disbursing office and had deserted. Thirty years later, still unconvinced of her brother's wrong-doing, Muns' sister convinced Special Agent Peter Hughes of the Naval Criminal Investigative Service ("NCIS") Cold Case Homicide Unit to reopen the investigation.

In the fall of 1999, NCIS agents conducted four interviews with LeBrun. On each of these four occasions, LeBrun cooperated with the investigators and voluntarily answered questions regarding Muns' disappearance. On three of these occasions, he was given his *Miranda* warnings by the interviewers. During an interview conducted on November 20, 1999, LeBrun told NCIS agents that he realized that he may have been involved in the death and disappearance of Ensign Muns. LeBrun also told the agents that he felt that he had repressed memories, and he asked Agent Hughes if he knew of a therapist who could help LeBrun recover those memories. After completing the first round of interviews, the NCIS agents did not have any further significant contact with LeBrun for approximately ten months as they continued to investigate other leads. By September of 2000, however, the NCIS had focused on LeBrun as the lead suspect in the case. At that time, NCIS agents decided to interview LeBrun again.

On September 21, 2000, NCIS Special Agent Early and Corporal Hunter of the Missouri Highway Patrol arrived unexpectedly at LeBrun's place of employment. Hunter told LeBrun that he and Early were conducting an investigation and requested that LeBrun accompany them to the Missouri Highway Patrol office to participate in an interview. Although the officers did not tell LeBrun the subject of their investigation, LeBrun agreed to accompany the officers because he thought that the officers might be investigating certain criminal allegations concerning LeBrun's employer. At the officers' suggestion, LeBrun rode in the front seat of an unmarked patrol car to the station house. The door was unlocked during the trip, and LeBrun was not restrained in any manner.

After they arrived at the patrol office, but before they went inside, Agent Early told LeBrun that he was not under arrest, that he was free to terminate the impending interview at any time, and that he was free to leave at any time. He was also told that he was subject to audio and visual recording anywhere inside the building. The officers then took LeBrun inside the office to a windowless interview room. The authorities had prepared the room prior to LeBrun's arrival, adorning the interview room walls with enlarged photographs of scenes from LeBrun's life. After LeBrun took a seat, NCIS Agents Early and Grebas identified themselves and initiated the interview. At no point immediately prior to or during the September 21, 2000, interview did the agents recite to LeBrun the *Miranda* warnings. The district court found that the decision not to warn was a conscious one made by the interviewers. Special Agent Early testified that no warning was thought necessary because it was not an under arrest custodial situation.

Despite the agents' failure to recite the *Miranda* warnings, LeBrun testified at the suppression hearing that at the time of the interview he understood what his *Miranda* rights were. LeBrun also testified that at the time the interview commenced he believed that he was not in custody and that he was free to leave at any time. The government concedes that the officers used psychological ploys during the course of the interview to facilitate a confession. For example, the agents told LeBrun that he was the prime suspect in Muns' death and that they had significant evidence establishing that LeBrun was the killer. The agents also told LeBrun that a protracted trial in a distant district would drain his financial resources and would ruin his family's reputation. At no point, however, did the agents shout at LeBrun or use physical force against him. After approximately thirty-three minutes of questioning, LeBrun confessed to the crime. LeBrun explained that while he was robbing the safe, Ensign Muns walked into the disbursing office. He confessed that he rushed Muns and killed him by strangling him and then smashing his head against the deck of the disbursing office. At the agents' urging, LeBrun then physically reenacted the robbery and attack. He also explained how he had dumped Muns' body and the missing money into a tank of caustic fuel oil to dispose of the evidence.

After LeBrun confessed to the killing, Agents Early and Grebas asked whether he wanted to apologize to Muns' sister, Mary Lou Taylor, who had flown in from Milwaukee to assist in the interrogation if it became necessary. He indicated that he did. Dr. Taylor, accompanied by Agent Billington, who was posing as Muns' brother and whom the agents had told LeBrun was stricken with cancer, then entered the interview room. LeBrun acknowledged to Taylor and Billington that he was responsible for Muns' death, and he apologized. After the agents had completed their questioning, LeBrun consented to having his house searched. LeBrun then withdrew a cellular telephone from his pocket and called his spouse. The agents drove LeBrun to his house and searched it. After conducting their search, the officers left LeBrun at home. They did not arrest him that day.

LeBrun was charged with felony murder....

* * *

The government concedes that it used psychological pressure to facilitate a confession. The district court correctly recognized that the type of psychological pressure Agents Grebas and Early exerted on LeBrun here did not alone render his confession involuntary. *See Astello*, 241 F.3d at 967–68 (holding that tactics such as subjecting a suspect to psychological pressure, making false promises, playing on a suspect's emotions, and using his family against him did not render a confession involuntary). The district court concluded, however, that these tactics, when coupled with certain statements that Agents Early and Grebas made concerning nonprosecution, rendered LeBrun's confession involuntary. The critical exchange occurred as follows:

LEBRUN: So, am I hearing that I won't be prosecuted?

GREBAS: That's what you are hearing.

LEBRUN: Is that what I am hearing?

GREBAS: That's what you are hearing.

EARLY: If it's [the killing of Ensign Muns] spontaneous and that's the truth, you will not be prosecuted.

GREBAS: That's absolutely right.

LEBRUN: I am here to tell you there was no premeditation.

EARLY: All right.

LEBRUN: It was spontaneous.

EARLY: Okay.

GREBAS: So it was, let me get this clear. It was spontaneous?

LEBRUN: Correct.

GREBAS: If this is true, then you killed him and it was over, it was over the money; is that right?

LEBRUN: I don't know what it was over.

The district court noted that the agents qualified their representations by stating to LeBrun that it was only "possible" that LeBrun would not be prosecuted. The district court explicitly did not "make any findings as to what-if any-promise was actually made, or what the legal effect of any promise [was]." Instead, the district court found only that "LeBrun *believed* he would not be prosecuted if he confessed to a 'spontaneous' murder."

[W]e conclude that LeBrun's confession was not compelled because a defendant's mistaken *belief* that he could not be prosecuted does not render a confession involuntary. *See United States v. Kilgore*, 58 F.3d 350, 353 (8th Cir.1995) (stating that defendant's mistaken belief that he had been promised leniency would not render confession involuntary); *Winfrey v. Wyrick*, 836 F.2d 406, 411–12 (8th Cir.1987) (concluding that defendant's murder confession was voluntary even though defendant was encouraged to talk because of erroneous *belief* that if the shooting was accidental it would negate an element of the offense).

Even assuming that a reasonable person would view the Agents' statements as a promise, a promise made by law enforcement "does not render a confession involuntary per se." ... *Tippitt v. Lockhart*, 859 F.2d 595, 598 (8th Cir.1988) (concluding that defendant's confession was voluntary despite officers' promise). A promise is merely one factor in the totality of the circumstances... Whatever the facts of an individual case, our polestar always must be to determine whether or not the authorities overbore the defendant's will and critically impaired his capacity for self-determination. Thus, it is not enough to show that the authorities' representations were the but-for cause of a confession. *See Schneckloth v. Bustamonte*, (1973) (concluding that a but-for type analysis is inadequate because "[u]nder such a test, virtually no statement would be voluntary because very few people give incriminating statements in the absence of official action of some kind"). Therefore, even assuming that the agents' statements could be construed as a promise and that the statements induced LeBrun's confession, our inquiry remains the same: whether the facts surrounding this interview demonstrate that the authorities overbore LeBrun's will and capacity for self-determination. This is a very demanding standard, and we are of the view that the facts of this case do not rise to that level.

We have previously concluded that a promise not to seek execution or a promise not to prosecute failed to render the confessions of similarly situated defendants involuntary. For example, in *Tippitt*, we held that the government's promise to a defendant not to prosecute him for capital murder in exchange for a confession did not render the confession involuntary in light of other facts showing that the interrogation was brief and that the defendant possessed an eleventh grade education...

We place substantial weight on the fact that LeBrun confessed after a mere thirty-three minutes. Thus, this is not a situation where the officers wore down a defendant's will with persistent questioning over a considerable length of time. We also place significant weight on the fact that LeBrun testified that he had a subjective understanding of his *Miranda* rights at the time of the interview ... We also place substantial weight on the fact that LeBrun was a sophisticated individual with legal training. LeBrun was fifty years old at the time of the interview. He has served in the military, attended five years of college and one year of law school, and worked as a manager in a real estate office ... Generally, we have concluded that where the defendant possessed at least average intelligence, then his inculpatory statements were not compelled...

In addition to possessing average intelligence, LeBrun did not display any unique sensitivity that would indicate that the agents might overbear his will. LeBrun had met with NCIS investigators on four prior occasions. The videotape of the interview demonstrates that LeBrun was composed and aware of his surroundings and the circumstances confronting him. In fact, as LeBrun and the Agents discussed the potential statute of limitations problems, LeBrun became more animated and much more interested in the interview. After watching the videotape, it is apparent that LeBrun is an intelligent, calculating person who erroneously perceived a potential loophole in the prosecution's case and tried to take advantage of it by confessing to "spontaneous" murder. Whatever his motivation, it is clear to us that LeBrun's capacity for self-determination was not impaired. Thus, the district court erred in concluding that LeBrun's confession was involuntary.

* * *

MORRIS SHEPPARD ARNOLD, CIRCUIT JUDGE, with whom MCMILLIAN, BYE, and SMITH, CIRCUIT JUDGES, join, dissenting.

... Our panel opinion in this case, *see United States v. LeBrun*, 306 F.3d 545, 548–50, 552–56 (8th Cir.2002), very effectively rehearsed the tactics used to bring Mr. LeBrun to the point of confessing, which included threatening to ruin him financially, preying on fears related to his cancer, and vividly limning the effects that protracted civil and criminal litigation in a faraway place would have on his family, on its reputation, and in particular on his pregnant wife. I will therefore content myself with some observations on the court's opinion....

While, as the court notes, the agents never shouted at Mr. LeBrun or threatened him physically, the district court found on ample evidence that the atmosphere at the interrogation was police-dominated and that the agents frequently raised their voices and changed their tone when doing so. They also interrupted Mr. LeBrun in a bullying manner and demonstrated a threatening kind of impatience with him....

The court ... adverts to the fact that the district court made no findings as to what promises the interrogators actually made, but instead found only that Mr. LeBrun reasonably believed that he was promised that he would not be prosecuted if he would say that he had killed Mr. Muns "spontaneously." The court then looks for support in cases that hold that a mistaken belief as to what the law is will not render a confession involuntary. But in at least one of those, *Winfrey v. Wyrick*, 836 F.2d 406, 411–12 (8th Cir.1987), it was crucial to the holding that the defendant's mistaken belief that he would not be prosecuted was not induced by anything that his interviewers told him; it was based entirely on his own ideas about what the law was. I agree that that kind of mistake cannot possibly render a confession inadmissible. But the clear purport of what the agents said in this case was that Mr. LeBrun would not be prosecuted if he said what the agents wanted him to say, and they even assured Mr. LeBrun that Mr. Muns's family approved of the deal. Indeed, they said that the family would not pursue civil remedies if he confessed and apologized. What the family wanted, the interrogators said, was simply to clear Mr. Muns's name.

In addition to the part of the interview that the court quotes in its opinion, the record reveals that, both before and after the exchange that the court isolates, the interviewers made reference to an alleged statute of limitations difficulty that would prevent prosecution for a "spontaneous" murder; and the officers intimated, moreover, that if Mr. LeBrun would simply admit to a spontaneous killing, they would call the United States Attorney in charge of the prosecution and tell him that there was no case against Mr. LeBrun. In addition, I respectfully suggest that the district court did not, as the court maintains, note that the agents qualified their representations by telling Mr. LeBrun that it was "only 'possible' " that he would not be prosecuted. In relevant part, the transcript of the interview reveals only that one of the agents said at one point that "it was possible, beyond possible" that no prosecution would take place if Mr. LeBrun would cooperate, which is significantly different from what the court asserts was said. Taken in their entirety, the agents' assurances, which operated both as representations of what the law was and as promises, were categorical.

The district court shrank from holding that an absolute promise not to prosecute was made, not because of this part of the exchange between Mr. LeBrun and his interrogators, but because the promise not to prosecute was fleetingly qualified at one point, by one agent, by the condition that Mr. LeBrun must be telling the truth that the killing was spontaneous before the government would refrain from prosecution. This transitory allusion to truth-telling does nothing to undermine the district court's factual finding that Mr. LeBrun believed that he would not be prosecuted. My own examination of the transcript and the video tape leaves little room for doubt that the agents were in fact making such a representation about the law and a promise that Mr. LeBrun would not be prosecuted, and indeed it appears that the entire interview was deliberately structured around this stratagem. But nothing in particular really turns on this point: The coercive effect, if any, of a reasonably perceived promise is exactly the same as that of an actual promise.

In addition to the coercive tactics that the court briefly rehearses, among the enlarged pictures displayed prominently on the wall of the small interrogation room was a picture of Mr. Muns's family at his gravesite. The agents, moreover, did not merely invent generic phantom witnesses to the killing; they contrived a bizarre tale of a suicide note implicating Mr. LeBrun, and even claimed that there were other witnesses to the killing who were so haunted that their lives had been ruined by what they had seen. These were all knowing falsehoods. None of this finds a place in the court's opinion. Finally, and perhaps most importantly, the court fails altogether to mention the district court's finding that, despite the agents' assurances, Mr. LeBrun did not feel free to leave as the interview progressed. This is a finding of fact that is supported by Mr. LeBrun's testimony and cannot be reasonably rejected as clearly erroneous. It is also a finding that weighs heavily in favor of the district court's conclusion that Mr. LeBrun's confession was involuntary.

This is probably the right juncture to observe that it is not immediately apparent why statements by interrogators that are untrue, and known to be false, are more "coercive" than statements that are true. Such techniques may be reprehensible, but that fact would not seem to contribute to their propensity to overwhelm the will. Perhaps it is enough simply to note that the Supreme Court has said that "[t]he fact that the police misrepresented the statements that [a witness] had made is ... relevant," *Frazier v. Cupp*, 394 U.S. 731, 739, 89 S.Ct. 1420, 22 L.Ed.2d 684 (1969), in circumstances like the present ones. But we need also to consider the possibility that what lies at the bottom of these kinds of cases is not merely an aversion to something called coercion, but a general uneasiness about the fairness of admitting confessions that were induced by knowing, lurid falsehoods and unfulfilled promises, whether "coercive" or not. In fact, the Supreme Court has specifically said that "the admissibility of a confession turns as much on whether the techniques for extracting the statements ... are compatible with a system that presumes innocence and assures that a conviction will not be secured by inquisitorial means as on whether the defendant's will was in fact overborne." *Miller v. Fenton*, 474 U.S. 104, 116, 106 S.Ct. 445, 88 L.Ed.2d 405 (1985).

In sum, a consideration of the evidence in this case, including the kinds of pressure that were brought to bear on Mr. LeBrun, the assurances of leniency that went unfulfilled, and the deceit that the interrogators practiced, leads me to the conclusion that his confession was illegally obtained and should have been suppressed. At the very least, it seems to me relatively plain that the government has not carried its burden, *see Lego v. Twomey*, 404 U.S. 477, 489, 92 S.Ct. 619, 30 L.Ed.2d 618 (1972), of showing that the relevant statements were voluntary.

I therefore respectfully dissent and would affirm the judgment of the district court....

(b) A SUMMARY OF INTERROGATION PRACTICES

Consider the following from a Summary Card and the Table of Contents of Inbau, Reid and Buckley, CRIMINAL INTERROGATION AND CONFESSIONS (3d Ed.1986):

THE 9 STEPS OF INTERROGATION—IN BRIEF

Step One: Direct Positive Confrontation

A. Fact synopsis is presented to suspect.

B. Suspect is told that he is involved in the crime.

C. Suspect's behavioral symptoms are observed.

D. Confrontation statement is restated.

Step Two: Theme Development

Emotional Offenders

A. Transitional phrases from confrontation occur.

B. Reasons that will psychologically justify or excuse the commission of the crime are proposed by interrogator.

C. Blame is placed on someone else or some set of circumstances beyond the suspect's control.

D. A sympathetic and understanding attitude is displayed.

Theme 1: Sympathize with Suspect by Saying Anyone Else Might Have Done Same Thing

Theme 2: Reduce Suspect's Feeling of Guilt by Minimizing Moral Seriousness of Offense

Theme 3: Suggest a Less Revolting and More Morally Acceptable Motivation or Reason for the Offense than That Which Is Known or Presumed

Theme 4: Sympathize with Suspect by Condemning Others

Condemning the Victim

Condemning the Accomplice

Condemning Anyone Else Upon Whom Some Degree of Moral Responsibility Might be Placed

Theme 5: Appeal to Suspect's Pride by Well–Selected Flattery

Theme 6: Point Out Possibility of Exaggeration on Part of Accuser or Victim, or Exaggerate Nature and Seriousness of Event Itself

Theme 7: Point out to Suspect Grave Consequences and Futility of Continuation of Criminal Behavior

Nonemotional Offenders

Theme 1: Seek Admission of Lying about Some Incidental Aspect of Occurrence

Theme 2: Have Suspect Place Himself at Scene of Crime or in Contact with Victim or Occurrence

Theme 3: Point out Futility of Resistance to Telling the Truth

Theme 4: When Co–Offenders are Being Interrogated and Previously Described Themes Have Been Ineffective, "Play One Against the Other"

Step Three: Handling Denials

A. Both guilty and innocent deny the crime at issue.

B. Interrogator recognizes and stops the deceptive suspect's denial before it is completed.

C. Progress is indicated by cessation or weakening of denials.

D. Innocent suspects never move past denials; become stronger and more sincere.

Step Four: Overcoming Objections

A. Suspect proposes a reason why accusation is wrong.

B. Objections normally offered by only the guilty, and indicate progress in the interrogation if given *after* denials.

C. Interrogator's statements of agreement or understanding are made.

D. Interrogator reverses meaning of the objection.

Step Five: Procurement and Retention of Suspect's Attention

A. Suspect is on defensive and is withdrawn and confused.

B. The themes will work only if suspect is listening.

C. Interrogator reaches peak of sincerity in his speech.

D. Physical closeness and use of verbal techniques are used to retain attention and to establish attitude of understanding.

Step Six: Handling Suspect's Passive Mood

A. The physical signs of remorse begin to appear.

B. The themes are shortened and lead toward the alternative question.

C. Establishment of eye contact is most important at this point by verbal and physical techniques.

D. Tears at this stage indicate possible guilt.

Step Seven: Presenting an Alternative Question

A. Question asked to have suspect tacitly acknowledge involvement in crime.

B. Choice is given between acceptable reason and unacceptable reason for committing the crime.

C. One alternative is stressed to encourage the suspect to choose the positive alternative.

D. Either choice is an admission of guilt.

Step Eight: Having Suspect Orally Relate the Various Details of the Offense

A. The acceptance of one alternative is reinforced by the interrogator.

B. The suspect is encouraged to talk about aspects of the crime.

C. The use of realistic words is introduced by the interrogator.

D. Initial corroboration of the confession is begun.

E. Admissions are orally witnessed by two persons.

Step Nine: Converting an Oral Confession into a Written Confession

A. Oral statements are reduced into written, typed, or electronically recorded form.

B. Voluntariness of statement is established along with corroboration of details.

C. Suspect's signing of statement is witnessed by two or more persons.

The use of these techniques in the case of a person in custody presupposes the giving of warnings and the waiver of rights mandated by Miranda v. Arizona, infra.

NOTES

1. Inbau, Reid, Buckley and Jayne suggest:

A guideline that an interrogator may use in any case situation ... is to ask himself the following question: "Is what I am about to do, or say, apt to make an innocent person confess"? If the answer to the question is "no," the interrogator should go ahead and do or say what was contemplated. On the other hand, if the answer is "yes," the interrogator should refrain from doing or saying what he had in mind. This is the only understandable test of any practical value for interrogators to follow. Moreover, it is the only test that is fair both to the public and to the accused or suspected individual. Criminal Interrogations and Confessions (4th Ed.2001), p. 486–87.

Contrast the foregoing guideline with the rule expressed in Rogers v. Richmond, 365 U.S. 534, 81 S.Ct. 735 (1961), which was decided, of course, prior to the Supreme Court's decision in Frazier v. Cupp, supra:

> "Our decisions have made clear that convictions following the admission into evidence of confessions which are involuntary, i.e., the product of coercion, either physical or psychological, cannot stand. This is so not because such confessions are unlikely to be true but because the methods used to extract them offend an underlying principle in the enforcement of our criminal law: that ours is an accusatorial and not an inquisitorial system—a system in which the State must establish guilt by evidence independently and freely secured and may not by coercion prove its charge against an accused out of his own mouth. To be sure, confessions cruelly extorted may be and have been, to an unascertained extent, found to be untrustworthy. But the constitutional principle of excluding confessions that are not voluntary does not rest on this consideration. Indeed, in many of the cases in which the command of the Due Process Clause has compelled us to reverse state convictions involving the use of confessions obtained by impermissible methods, independent corroborating evidence left little doubt of the truth of what the defendant had confessed. Despite such verification, confessions were found to be the product of constitutionally impermissible methods in their inducement. Since a defendant had been subjected to pressures to which, under our accusatorial system, an accused should not be subjected, we were constrained to find that the procedures leading to his conviction had failed to afford him that due process of law which the Fourteenth Amendment guarantees.

"In the present case, while the trial judge ruled that each of petitioner's confessions was 'freely and voluntarily made and accordingly was admissible in evidence,' he reached that conclusion on the basis of considerations that undermine its validity. He found that the pretense of bringing petitioner's wife in for questioning 'had no tendency to produce a confession that was not in accord with the truth.'

* * *

"We cannot but conclude that the question whether Rogers' confessions were admissible into evidence was answered by reference to a legal standard which took into account the circumstance of probable truth or falsity. And this is not a permissible standard under the Due Process Clause of the Fourteenth Amendment. The attention of the trial judge should have been focused, for purposes of the Federal Constitution, on the question whether the behavior of the State's law enforcement officials was such as to overbear petitioner's will to resist and bring about confessions not freely self-determined—a question to be answered with complete disregard of whether or not petitioner in fact spoke the truth."

Is the interrogator's ban on anything "apt to make an innocent person confess" inconsistent with the ban on looking to truth in judging the voluntariness of confessions? Is the interrogator's guideline a useful rule of thumb for police? Can there or should there be a real difference between the standard for interrogation tactics and the standard for admissibility of confessions? See Gisli Gudjenson, The Psychology of Interrogation Confessions and Testimony (1992).

2. The Inbau, Reid and Buckley text in its several editions is widely used and its specific techniques have been the subject of several opinions. In People v. Sickley, 114 Ill.App.3d 167, 69 Ill.Dec. 894, 448 N.E.2d 612 (1983), a private polygraph examiner used some of the interrogation techniques espoused in the previous section (as well as one or two not so approved). The trial judge originally denied a motion to suppress. He denied a motion to reconsider after viewing videotapes. Eventually, however, he changed his mind and suppressed the evidence. He concluded that after "much soul searching," he was "appalled at the tactics" which, he said, amounted to "psychological brainwashing." The reviewing court affirmed the suppression order after viewing the tapes of the interrogation. See People v. Freeman, 668 P.2d 1371 (Colo.1983), which held a confession involuntary, in part because of police use of trickery, false suggestions of what the police knew, and a "Mutt and Jeff" routine. The trickery was among the factors which the court cited in applying a totality of the circumstances test. People v. Hogan, 31 Cal.3d 815, 183 Cal.Rptr. 817, 647 P.2d 93 (1982) (Confession excluded where officers suggested suspect acted unknowingly, needed mental help and falsely told him he had been seen at the crime). Compare Rodgers v. Commonwealth, 227 Va. 605, 318 S.E.2d 298 (1984) (appealing to suspect's religion, falsely stating evidence against him and claiming confession would be submitted to prosecutor for decision does not invalidate confession—trial court found defendant to be "the subject of skillful tactics, almost mesmerizing interrogation by an experienced investigator,") State v. Waugh, 238 Kan. 537, 712 P.2d 1243 (1986) (Confession voluntary despite deliberate "goodguy" approach of detective who exhorted the suspect to serve his own best interest by confessing and getting treatment for alcoholism) Barrera v. Young, 794 F.2d 1264 (7th Cir.1986) (approves giving accurate information about adverse evidence and appeals to religious beliefs) Bryant v. Vose, 785 F.2d 364 (1st Cir.1986)

("even if . . . confession were an emotional response to the thought of alienating the family he loved it was not . . . the product of coercion or . . . improper tactics")

An interesting interrogation using a variety of tactics is set out in full (it was taped) and analyzed thoroughly in both majority and dissenting opinions in Miller v. Fenton, 796 F.2d 598 (3d Cir.1986). See also People v. Montano, 226 Cal.App.3d 914, 277 Cal.Rptr. 327 (1991).

3. On commentator has argued that the techniques suggested by Inbau, Reid and Buckley may well lead to false (or least untrustworthy) confessions by persons who are mentally retarded or who possess compliant personalities. See Welsh S. White, False Confession and The Constitutional Safeguard Against Untrustworthy confessions, 32 Harv. C.R.–C.L. L.Rev. 105 (1996). White argues that there be an absolute ban on using false forensic evidence to trick a confession, and on saying that a suspect could help himself by confession. Interrogations should not last more than five hours and should be videotaped.

(c) THE PRACTICAL NECESSITY FOR INTERROGATION

Consider the views of Inbau, Reid, Buckley and Jayne.

There is a gross misconception, generated and perpetuated by fiction writers, movies, and TV, that if criminal investigators carefully examine a crime scene, they will almost always find a clue that will lead them to the offender; and that, furthermore, once the criminal is located, he will readily confess or otherwise reveal guilt, as by attempting to escape. This, however, is pure fiction. As a matter of fact, the art and science of criminal investigation have not developed to a point where the search for and the examination of physical evidence will always, or even in most cases, reveal a clue to the identity of the perpetrator or provide the necessary legal proof of guilt. In criminal investigations, even the most efficient type, there are many, many instances where physical clues are entirely absent, and the only approach to a possible solution of the crime is the interrogation of the criminal suspect himself, as well as of others who may possess significant information.

* * *

1. MANY CRIMINAL CASES, EVEN WHEN INVESTIGATED BY THE BEST QUALIFIED POLICE DEPARTMENTS, ARE CAPABLE OF SOLUTION ONLY BY MEANS OF AN ADMISSION OR CONFESSION FROM THE GUILTY INDIVIDUAL OR UPON THE BASIS OF INFORMATION OBTAINED FROM THE QUESTIONING OF OTHER CRIMINAL SUSPECTS.

As to the validity of this statement, we suggest that consideration be given to the situations presented by cases such as the following ones. A man is hit on the head while walking home late at night. He does not see his assailant, nor does anyone else. A careful and thorough search of the crime scene reveals no physical clues. Or, a woman is grabbed on the street at night and dragged into an alley and raped. Here, too, the assailant was accommodating enough to avoid leaving his wallet or other means of identification at the crime scene, and there are no physical clues. All the police have to work on is the description of the assailant given by the victim herself. She describes him as about 6 feet tall, white, and wearing a dark suit. Or consider this case, an actual one in Illinois. Three women are vacationing in a wooded resort area. They are found dead, the result of physical violence, alongside a foot trail, and no physical clues are present.

* * *

2. CRIMINAL OFFENDERS, EXCEPT, OF COURSE, THOSE CAUGHT IN THE COMMISSION OF THEIR CRIMES, ORDINARILY WILL NOT ADMIT THEIR GUILT UNLESS QUESTIONED UNDER CONDITIONS OF PRIVACY, AND FOR A PERIOD OF PERHAPS SEVERAL HOURS.

This point is one that should be readily apparent not only to any person with the least amount of criminal investigative experience, but also to anyone who will reflect momentarily upon the behavior of ordinary law-abiding persons when suspected or accused of nothing more than simple social indiscretions. Self-condemnation and self-destruction not being normal behavior characteristics, human beings ordinarily do not utter unsolicited, spontaneous confessions. They must first be questioned regarding the offense. In some instances, a little bit of information inadvertently given to a competent interrogator by the suspect may suffice to start a line of investigation that might ultimately establish guilt. On other occasions, a full confession, with a revelation of details regarding a body, loot, or instruments used in the crime, may be required to prove the case. Whatever the possible consequences may be, it is impractical to expect any but a very few confessions to result from a guilty conscience unprovoked by an interrogation. It is also impractical to expect admissions or confessions to be obtained under circumstances other than privacy. Here again, recourse to our everyday experience will support the basic validity of this requirement. For instance, in asking a personal friend to divulge a secret, or embarrassing information, we carefully avoid making the request in the presence of other persons, and seek a time and place when the matter can be discussed in private. The same psychological factors are involved in a criminal interrogation, and even to a greater extent. For related psychological considerations, if an interrogation is to be had at all, it must be one based upon an unhurried interview, the necessary length of which will in many instances extend to several hours, depending upon various factors, such as the nature of the case situation and the personality of the suspect.

CRIMINAL INTERROGATION AND CONFESSIONS pp. xiii–xv (4th Ed.2001).

NOTE

Conceding the necessity for confessions does not end the argument about whether they ought to be admitted at all. See Rosenberg & Rosenberg, A Modest Proposal for the Abolition of Custodial Confessions, 68 N.C.L.Rev. 69 (1989).

3. REMEDIES FOR ABUSIVE INTERROGATIONS

It is unmistakably clear that an improperly obtained confession is inadmissible as substantive evidence. As with the exclusion of illegally seized tangible evidence, however, this provides little consolation for the innocent person who is never brought to trial (and hence does not benefit by a suppressed confession), but whose rights and personal dignity were nevertheless violated. There are remedies to which this person can turn, as well as supplemental remedies available to the individual who has already benefited by suppression of illegally obtained evidence. They are discussed in the following sections (a) and (b).

(a) CIVIL REMEDIES

A federal civil rights action may lie for a person who has been the victim of a coerced confession or even an abusive interrogation. The pertinent federal statute (42 U.S.C. § 1983) reads:

> Every person who, under color of any statute, ordinance, regulation, custom, or usage, of any State or Territory, subjects, or causes to be subjected, any citizen of the United States or other person within the jurisdiction thereof to the deprivation of any rights, privileges, or immunities secured by the Constitution and laws, shall be liable to the party injured in an action at law, suit in equity, or other proper proceeding for redress.

... In Kerr v. City of Chicago, 424 F.2d 1134 (7th Cir.1970), cert. denied 400 U.S. 833, 91 S.Ct. 66 (1970) (see casenote, 20 De Paul L.Rev. 984 (1971)), a complainant alleged that he was illegally detained for 18 hours and a confession was coerced from him through force, threats, and deprivation of food and other necessities of life. The reviewing court reversed the lower court's refusal to admit evidence of the circumstances surrounding the interrogation. The court wrote:

> ... the jury was entitled to hear the testimony surrounding all the events from the moment Kerr was taken from his home until his indictment by the Grand Jury. All of the acts of commission and omission—the totality of all the circumstances—are of great importance in determining whether plaintiff's confession was coerced in violation of his civil rights and thereby cognizable under 42 U.S.C. § 1983....

The court further stated:

> ... in a civil rights action alleging the extraction of an involuntary confession, the issue of guilt or innocence is irrelevant....

Since this is an emerging body of law, there are as yet no concrete guidelines to define the kind and quality of constitutional infringement that must be alleged in order to state a cause of action. Consider the court's opinion in Duncan v. Nelson, 466 F.2d 939 (7th Cir.1972), cert. denied 409 U.S. 894, 93 S.Ct. 116 (1972):

> There is no indication from ... any other case that physical violence need be present to produce the coercion necessary to constitute an involuntary confession cognizable under § 1983 [citation omitted]. In fact, Mr. Justice Harlan in his concurrence in Monroe v. Pape ... recognized the possibility that psychological coercion leading to a confession would constitute damages under § 1983....

In Cooper v. Dupnik, 963 F.2d 1220 (9th Cir.1992), (en banc) (8–3) the plaintiff was a suspect in a case of serial rapes, robberies and kidnappings. Officers investigating the case decided they would ignore any assertion of rights by a suspect and persist in interrogation. The purpose was to pin cooper down to a single story which he could not later change. They did so with Cooper for four hours, invoking Cooper's religion and making false and true statements about the evidence against him. Eventually a mistake in a fingerprint identification was discovered and Cooper was released. He did not confess to the crimes. The Court of Appeals accepted his claim that he could collect damages for the violation of his *Miranda* rights and for the use of coercive tactics even in the absence of a confession.

Other courts have reached an opposite conclusion. See Warren v. Lincoln, 864 F.2d 1436 (8th Cir.1989).

(b) CRIMINAL SANCTIONS

A civil rights violation which gives rise to a civil suit under 42 U.S.C. § 1983, may also precipitate a criminal indictment against the offending officer(s) under 18 U.S.C. § 242. That provision reads as follows:

> Whoever, under color of any law, statute, ordinance, regulation, or custom, willfully subjects any inhabitant of any State, Territory, or District to the deprivation of any rights, privileges, or immunities secured or protected by the Constitution or laws of the United States, or to different punishments, pains, or penalties, on account of such inhabitant being an alien, or by reason of his color, or race, than are prescribed for the punishment of citizens, shall be fined not more than $1,000 or imprisoned not more than one year, or both; and if death results shall be subject to imprisonment for any term of years or for life.

If two or more persons are involved, the civil rights conspiracy statute may be invoked (18 U.S.C. § 242). That statute provides for a 10 year penalty and a $10,000 fine.

A criminal sanction specifically drafted to encompass the problems under discussion here is the Illinois provision, 720 ILCS 5/12–7.

Compelling Confession or Information by Force or Threat

(a) A person who, with intent to obtain a confession, statement or information regarding any offense, inflicts or threatens to inflict physical harm upon the person threatened or upon any other person commits the offense of compelling a confession or information by force or threat.

(b) Sentence.

Compelling a confession or information is a Class 4 felony.

While criminal prosecutions alleging improper interrogation are not requiring prosecutors to work overtime, the recent expansion of the civil side of this question may well lead to an accompanying increase in criminal indictments. One prosecution occurred in United States v. Lee, 744 F.2d 1124 (5th Cir.1984).

B. MIRANDA V. ARIZONA AND THE INTERPRETATION OF ITS REQUIREMENTS

1. MIRANDA V. ARIZONA

Miranda v. Arizona
Vignera v. New York
Westover v. United States
California v. Stewart

Supreme Court of the United States, 1966.
384 U.S. 436, 86 S.Ct. 1602.

■ MR. CHIEF JUSTICE WARREN delivered the opinion of the Court.

The cases before us raise questions which go to the roots of our concepts of American criminal jurisprudence: the restraints society must observe consistent with the Federal Constitution in prosecuting individuals for crime. More specifically, we deal with the admissibility of statements obtained from an individual who is subjected to custodial police interrogation and the necessity for procedures which assure that the individual is accorded his privilege under the Fifth Amendment to the Constitution not to be compelled to incriminate himself.

* * *

I.

These cases all share salient features—incommunicado interrogation of individuals in a police-dominated atmosphere, resulting in self-incriminating statements without full warnings of constitutional rights.

An understanding of the nature and setting of this in-custody interrogation is essential to our decisions today. The difficulty in depicting what transpires at such interrogations stems from the fact that in this country they have largely taken place incommunicado. From extensive factual studies undertaken in the early 1930's, ... it is clear that police violence and the "third degree" flourished at that time. ...The Commission on Civil Rights in 1961 found much evidence to indicate that "some policemen still resort to physical force to obtain confessions." The use of physical brutality and violence is not, unfortunately, relegated to the past or to any part of the country. Only recently in Kings County, New York, the police brutally beat, kicked and placed lighted cigarette butts on the back of a potential witness under interrogation for the purpose of securing a statement incriminating a third party.

The examples given above are undoubtedly the exception now, but they are sufficiently widespread to be the object of concern. Unless a proper limitation upon custodial interrogation is achieved—such as these decisions will advance—there can be no assurance that practices of this nature will be eradicated in the foreseeable future. . . .

* * *

Again we stress that the modern practice of in-custody interrogation is psychologically rather than physically oriented. As we have stated before, . . . "this Court has recognized that coercion can be mental as well as physical, and that the blood of the accused is not the only hallmark of an unconstitutional inquisition." Interrogation still takes place in privacy. Privacy results in secrecy and this in turn results in a gap in our knowledge as to what in fact goes on in the interrogation rooms. A valuable source of information about present police practices, however, may be found in various police manuals and texts which document procedures employed with success in the past, and which recommended various other effective tactics. These texts are used by law enforcement agencies themselves as guides.[2] It should be noted that these texts professedly present the most enlightened and effective means presently used to obtain statements through custodial interrogation. By considering these texts and other data, it is possible to describe procedures observed and noted around the country.

The officers are told by the manuals that the "principal psychological factor contributing to a successful interrogation is privacy—being alone with the person under interrogation." [Inbau and Reid] The efficacy of this tactic has been explained as follows:

> "In his own home he may be confident, indignant, or recalcitrant. In his office, the investigator possesses all the advantages. The atmosphere suggests the invincibility of the forces of the law." [O'Hara]

To highlight the isolation and unfamiliar surroundings, the manuals instruct the police to display an air of confidence in the suspect's guilt and from outward appearance to maintain only an interest in confirming certain details. The guilt of the subject is to be posited as a fact. The interrogator should direct his comments toward the reasons why the subject committed the act, rather than court failure by asking the subject whether he did it. Like other men, perhaps the subject has had a bad family life, had an unhappy childhood, had too much to drink, had an unrequited

2. The methods described in Inbau & Reid, Criminal Interrogation and Confessions (1962), are a revision and enlargement of material presented in three prior editions of a predecessor text, Lie Detection and Criminal Interrogation (3d ed. 1953). The authors and their associates are officers of the Chicago Police Scientific Crime Detection Laboratory and have had extensive experience in writing, lecturing and speaking to law enforcement authorities over a 20-year period. They say that the techniques portrayed in their manuals reflect their experiences and are the most effective psychological stratagems to employ during interrogations. Similarly, the techniques described in O'Hara, Fundamentals of Criminal Investigation (1956), were gleaned from long service as observer, lecturer in police science, and work as a federal criminal investigator. All these texts have had rather extensive use among law enforcement agencies and among students of police science, with total sales and circulation of over 44,000.

[Editors' note: Inbau was Director of the Laboratory from 1938–1941; he has had no official connection with it since then. Reid was on the Laboratory staff from 1938 to 1947; he too has had no official connection with it since that time.]

desire for women. The officers are instructed to minimize the moral seriousness of the offense, to cast blame on the victim or on society. These tactics are designed to put the subject in a psychological state where his story is but an elaboration of what the police purport to know already—that he is guilty. Explanations to the contrary are dismissed and discouraged.

The texts thus stress that the major qualities an interrogator should possess are patience and perseverance. One writer describes the efficacy of these characteristics in this manner:

> "In the preceding paragraphs emphasis has been placed on kindness and stratagems. The investigator will, however, encounter many situations where the sheer weight of his personality will be the deciding factor. Where emotional appeals and tricks are employed to no avail, he must rely on an oppressive atmosphere of dogged persistence.... In a serious case, the interrogation may continue for days, with the required intervals for food and sleep, but with no respite from the atmosphere of domination. It is possible in this way to induce the subject to talk without resorting to duress or coercion. The method should be used only when the guilt of the subject appears highly probable." [O'Hara]

The manuals suggest that the suspect be offered legal excuses for his actions in order to obtain an initial admission of guilt. Where there is a suspected revenge-killing, for example, the interrogator may say:

> "Joe, you probably didn't go out looking for this fellow with the purpose of shooting him. My guess is, however, that you expected something from him and that's why you carried a gun—for your own protection. You knew him for what he was, no good. Then when you met him he probably started using foul, abusive language and he gave some indication that he was about to pull a gun on you, and that's when you had to act to save your own life. That's about it, isn't it, Joe?" [Inbau & Reid]

Having then obtained the admission of shooting, the interrogator is advised to refer to circumstantial evidence which negates the self-defense explanation. This should enable him to secure the entire story. One text notes that "Even if he fails to do so, the inconsistency between the subject's original denial of the shooting and his present admission of at least doing the shooting will serve to deprive him of a self-defense 'out' at the time of trial." [Inbau & Reid]

When the techniques described above prove unavailing, the texts recommend they be alternated with a show of some hostility. One ploy often used has been termed the "friendly-unfriendly" or the "Mutt and Jeff" act:

> "... In this technique, two agents are employed. Mutt, the relentless investigator, who knows the subject is guilty and is not going to waste any time. He's sent a dozen men away for this crime and he's going to send the subject away for the full term. Jeff, on the other hand, is obviously a kindhearted man. He has a family himself. He has a brother who was involved in a little

> scrape like this. He disapproves of Mutt and his tactics and will arrange to get him off the case if the subject will cooperate. He can't hold Mutt off for very long. The subject would be wise to make a quick decision. The technique is applied by having both investigators present while Mutt acts out his role. Jeff may stand by quietly and demur at some of Mutt's tactics. When Jeff makes his plea for cooperation, Mutt is not present in the room." [O'Hara]

The interrogators sometimes are instructed to induce a confession out of trickery. The technique here is quite effective in crimes which require identification or which run in series. In the identification situation, the interrogator may take a break in his questioning to place the subject among a group of men in a line-up. "The witness or complainant (previously coached if necessary) studies the line-up and confidently points out the subject as the guilty party." [O'Hara] Then the questioning resumes "as though there were now no doubt about the guilt of the subject." A variation on this technique is called the "reverse line-up":

> "The accused is placed in a line-up, but this time he is identified by several fictitious witnesses or victims who associated him with different offenses. It is expected that the subject will become desperate and confess to the offense under investigation in order to escape from the false accusations." [O'Hara]

The manuals also contain instructions for police on how to handle the individual who refuses to discuss the matter entirely, or who asks for an attorney or relatives. The examiner is to concede him the right to remain silent. "This usually has a very undermining effect. First of all, he is disappointed in his expectation of an unfavorable reaction on the part of the interrogator. Secondly, a concession of this right to remain silent impresses the subject with the apparent fairness of his interrogator." [Inbau & Reid] After this psychological conditioning, however, the officer is told to point out the incriminating significance of the suspect's refusal to talk:

> "Joe, you have a right to remain silent. That's your privilege and I'm the last person in the world who'll try to take it away from you. If that's the way you want to leave this, O.K. But let me ask you this. Suppose you were in my shoes and I were in yours and you called me in to ask me about this and I told you, 'I don't want to answer any of your questions.' You'd think I had something to hide, and you'd probably be right in thinking that. That's exactly what I'll have to think about you, and so will everybody else. So let's sit here and talk this whole thing over." [Inbau & Reid]

Few will persist in their initial refusal to talk, it is said, if this monologue is employed correctly.

In the event that the subject wishes to speak to a relative or an attorney, the following advice is tendered:

> "[T]he interrogator should respond by suggesting that the subject first tell the truth to the interrogator himself rather than get

anyone else involved in the matter. If the request is for an attorney, the interrogator may suggest that the subject save himself or his family the expense of any such professional service, particularly if he is innocent of the offense under investigation. The interrogator may also add, 'Joe, I'm only looking for the truth, and if you're telling the truth, that's it. You can handle this by yourself.' " [Inbau & Reid]

* * *

Even without employing brutality, the "third degree" or the specific stratagems described above, the very fact of custodial interrogation exacts a heavy toll on individual liberty and trades on the weakness of individuals. . . .

. . . In Miranda v. Arizona, the police arrested the defendant and took him to a special interrogation room where they secured a confession. In Vignera v. New York, the defendant made oral admissions to the police after interrogation in the afternoon, and then signed an inculpatory statement upon being questioned by an assistant district attorney later the same evening. In Westover v. United States, the defendant was handed over to the Federal Bureau of Investigation by local authorities after they had detained and interrogated him for a lengthy period, both at night and the following morning. After some two hours of questioning, the federal officers had obtained signed statements from the defendant. Lastly, in California v. Stewart, the local police held the defendant five days in the station and interrogated him on nine separate occasions before they secured his inculpatory statement.

In these cases, we might not find the defendants' statements to have been involuntary in traditional terms. Our concern for adequate safeguards to protect precious Fifth Amendment rights is, of course, not lessened in the slightest. In each of the cases, the defendant was thrust into an unfamiliar atmosphere and run through menacing police interrogation procedures. The potentiality for compulsion is forcefully apparent, for example, in *Miranda*, where the indigent Mexican defendant was a seriously disturbed individual with pronounced sexual fantasies, and in *Stewart*, in which the defendant was an indigent Los Angeles Negro who had dropped out of school in the sixth grade. To be sure the records do not evince over physical coercion or patent psychological ploys. The fact remains that in none of these cases did the officers undertake to afford appropriate safeguards at the outset of the interrogation to insure that the statements were truly the product of free choice.

It is obvious that such an interrogation environment is created for no purpose other than to subjugate the individual to the will of his examiner. This atmosphere carries its own badge of intimidation. To be sure, this is not physical intimidation, but it is equally destructive of human dignity. The current practice of incommunicado interrogation is at odds with one of our Nation's most cherished principles—that the individual may not be compelled to incriminate himself. Unless adequate protective devices are employed to dispel the compulsion inherent in custodial surroundings, no statement obtained from the defendant can truly be the product of his free choice.

From the foregoing, we can readily perceive an intimate connection between the privilege against self-incrimination and police custodial questioning. It is fitting to turn to the Self–Incrimination Clause to determine its applicability in this situation.

II.

* * *

The question in these cases is whether the privilege is fully applicable during a period of custodial interrogation. In this Court, the privilege has consistently been accorded liberal construction. . . . We are satisfied that all the principles embodied in the privilege apply to informal compulsion exerted by law-enforcement officers during in-custody questioning. An individual swept from familiar surroundings into police custody, surrounded by antagonistic forces, and subjected to the techniques of persuasion described above cannot be otherwise than under compulsion to speak. . . .

* * *

Our decision in Malloy v. Hogan (1964) necessitates an examination of the scope of the privilege in state cases as well. In *Malloy*, we squarely held the privilege applicable to the States, and held that the substantive standards underlying the privilege applied with full force to state court proceedings. . . . the reasoning in *Malloy* made clear what had already become apparent—that the substantive and procedural safeguards surrounding admissibility of confessions in state cases had become exceedingly exacting, reflecting all the policies embedded in the privilege. The voluntariness doctrine in the state cases, as *Malloy* indicates, encompasses all interrogation practices which are likely to exert such pressure upon an individual as to disable him from making a free and rational choice.

* * *

III.

Today, then, there can be no doubt that the Fifth Amendment privilege is available outside of criminal court proceedings and serves to protect persons in all settings in which their freedom of action is curtailed in any significant way from being compelled to incriminate themselves.

* * *

At the outset, if a person in custody is to be subjected to interrogation, he must first be informed in clear and unequivocal terms that he has the right to remain silent. For those unaware of the privilege, the warning is needed simply to make them aware of it—the threshold requirement for an intelligent decision as to its exercise. More important, such a warning is an absolute prerequisite in overcoming the inherent pressures of the interrogation atmosphere. It is not just the subnormal or woefully ignorant who succumb to an interrogator's imprecations, whether implied or expressly stated, that the interrogation will continue until a confession is obtained or that silence in the face of accusation is itself damning and will bode ill when presented to a jury. Further, the warning will show the individual that his interrogators are prepared to recognize his privilege should he choose to exercise it.

The Fifth Amendment privilege is so fundamental to our system of constitutional rule and the expedient of giving an adequate warning as to the availability of the privilege so simple, we will not pause to inquire in individual cases whether the defendant was aware of his rights without a warning being given. Assessments of the knowledge the defendant possessed, based on information as to his age, education, intelligence, or prior contact with authorities, can never be more than speculation; a warning is a clearcut fact. More important, whatever the background of the person interrogated, a warning at the time of the interrogation is indispensable to overcome its pressures and to insure that the individual knows he is free to exercise the privilege at that point in time.

The warning of the right to remain silent must be accompanied by the explanation that anything said can and will be used against the individual in court. This warning is needed in order to make him aware not only of the privilege, but also of the consequences of foregoing it. It is only through an awareness of these consequences that there can be any assurance of real understanding and intelligent exercise of the privilege. Moreover, this warning may serve to make the individual more acutely aware that he is faced with a phase of the adversary system—that he is not in the presence of persons acting solely in his interest.

The circumstances surrounding in-custody interrogation can operate very quickly to overbear the will of one merely made aware of his privilege by his interrogators. Therefore, the right to have counsel present at the interrogation is indispensable to the protection of the Fifth Amendment privilege under the system we delineate today. Our aim is to assure that the individual's right to choose between silence and speech remains unfettered throughout the interrogation process. A once-stated warning, delivered by those who will conduct the interrogation, cannot itself suffice to that end among those who most require knowledge of their rights. A mere warning given by the interrogators is not alone sufficient to accomplish that end. Prosecutors themselves claim that the admonishment of the right to remain silent without more "will benefit only the recidivist and the professional." Brief for the National District Attorneys Association as *amicus curiae*, p. 14. Even preliminary advice given to the accused by his own attorney can be swiftly overcome by the secret interrogation process. Thus, the need for counsel to protect the Fifth Amendment privilege comprehends not merely a right to consult with counsel prior to questioning, but also to have counsel present during any questioning if the defendant so desires.

The presence of counsel at the interrogation may serve several significant subsidiary functions as well. If the accused decides to talk to his interrogators, the assistance of counsel can mitigate the dangers of untrustworthiness. With a lawyer present the likelihood that the police will practice coercion is reduced, and if coercion is nevertheless exercised the lawyer can testify to it in court. The presence of a lawyer can also help to guarantee that the accused gives a fully accurate statement to the police and that the statement is rightly reported by the prosecution at trial....

An individual need not make a pre-interrogation request for a lawyer. While such request affirmatively secures his right to have one, his failure to ask for a lawyer does not constitute a waiver. No effective waiver of the right to counsel during interrogation can be recognized unless specifically made after the warnings we here delineate have been given. The accused who does not know his rights and therefore does not make a request may be the person who most needs counsel.

* * *

Accordingly we hold that an individual held for interrogation must be clearly informed that he has the right to consult with a lawyer and to have the lawyer with him during interrogation under the system for protecting the privilege we delineate today. As with the warnings of the right to remain silent and that anything stated can be used in evidence against him, this warning is an absolute prerequisite to interrogation. No amount of circumstantial evidence that the person may have been aware of this right will suffice to stand in its stead. Only through such a warning is there ascertainable assurance that the accused was aware of this right.

If an individual indicates that he wishes the assistance of counsel before any interrogation occurs, the authorities cannot rationally ignore or deny his request on the basis that the individual does not have or cannot afford a retained attorney. The financial ability of the individual has no relationship to the scope of the rights involved here....

In order fully to apprise a person interrogated of the extent of his rights under this system then, it is necessary to warn him not only that he has the right to consult with an attorney, but also that if he is indigent a lawyer will be appointed to represent him....

Once warnings have been given, the subsequent procedure is clear. If the individual indicates in any manner, at any time prior to or during questioning, that he wishes to remain silent, the interrogation must cease. At this point he has shown that he intends to exercise his Fifth Amendment privilege; any statement taken after the person invokes his privilege cannot be other than the product of compulsion, subtle or otherwise. Without the right to cut off questioning, the setting of in-custody interrogation operates on the individual to overcome free choice in producing a statement after the privilege has been once invoked. If the individual states that he wants an attorney, the interrogation must cease until an attorney is present. At that time, the individual must have an opportunity to confer with the attorney and to have him present during any subsequent questioning. If the individual cannot obtain an attorney and he indicates that he wants one before speaking to police, they must respect his decision to remain silent.

This does not mean, as some have suggested, that each police station must have a "station house lawyer" present at all times to advise prisoners. It does mean, however, that if police propose to interrogate a person they must make known to him that he is entitled to a lawyer and that if he cannot afford one, a lawyer will be provided for him prior to any interrogation. If authorities conclude that they will not provide counsel during a reasonable period of time in which investigation in the field is carried out, they may refrain from doing so without violating the person's Fifth Amendment privilege so long as they do not question him during that time.

If the interrogation continues without the presence of an attorney and a statement is taken, a heavy burden rests on the government to demonstrate that the defendant knowingly and intelligently waived his privilege against self-incrimination and his right to retained or appointed counsel.... Since the State is responsible for establishing the isolated circumstances under which the interrogation takes place and has the only means of making available corroborated evidence of warnings given during incommunicado interrogation, the burden is rightly on its shoulders.

An express statement that the individual is willing to make a statement and does not want an attorney followed closely by a statement could constitute a waiver. But a valid waiver will not be presumed simply from the silence of the accused after warnings are given or simply from the fact that a confession was in fact eventually obtained.... Moreover, where in-custody interrogation is involved, there is no room for the contention that the privilege is waived if the individual answers some questions or gives some information on his own prior to invoking his right to remain silent when interrogated....

Whatever the testimony of the authorities as to waiver of rights by an accused, the fact of lengthy interrogation or incommunicado incarceration before a statement is made is strong evidence that the accused did not validly waive his rights. In these circumstances the fact that the individual eventually made a statement is consistent with the conclusion that the compelling influence of the interrogation finally forced him to do so. It is inconsistent with any notion of a voluntary relinquishment of the privilege. Moreover, any evidence that the accused was threatened, tricked, or cajoled into a waiver will, of course, show that the defendant did not voluntarily waive his privilege. The requirement of warnings and waiver of rights is a fundamental with respect to the Fifth Amendment privilege and not simply a preliminary ritual to existing methods of interrogation.

The warnings required and the waiver necessary in accordance with our opinion today are, in the absence of a fully effective equivalent, prerequisites to the admissibility of any statement made by a defendant. No distinction can be drawn between statements which are direct confessions and statements which amount to "admissions" of part or all of an offense.... Similarly, for precisely the same reason, no distinction may be drawn between inculpatory statements and statements alleged to be merely "exculpatory." If a statement made were in fact truly exculpatory it would, of course, never be used by the prosecution. In fact, statements merely intended to be exculpatory by the defendant are often used to impeach his testimony at trial or to demonstrate untruths in the statement given under interrogation and thus to prove guilt by implication. These statements are incriminating in any meaningful sense of the word and may not be used without the full warnings and effective waiver required for any other statement....

The principles announced today deal with the protection which must be given to the privilege against self-incrimination when the individual is first subjected to police interrogation while in custody at the station or otherwise deprived of his freedom of action in any significant way. It is at this point that our adversary system of criminal proceedings commences, distinguishing itself at the outset from the inquisitorial system recognized in some countries. Under the system of warnings we delineate today or under any other system which may be devised and found effective, the safeguards to be erected about the privilege must come into play at this point.

Our decision is not intended to hamper the traditional function of police officers in investigating crime. When an individual is in custody on probable cause, the police may, of course, seek out evidence in the field to be used at trial against him. Such investigation may include inquiry of persons not under restraint. General on-the-scene questioning as to facts surrounding a crime or other general questioning of citizens in the fact-finding process is not affected by our holding. It is an act of responsible citizenship for individuals to give whatever information they may have to aid in law enforcement. In such situations the compelling atmosphere inherent in the process of in-custody interrogation is not necessarily present.[3]

In dealing with statements obtained through interrogation, we do not purport to find all confessions inadmissible. Confessions remain a proper element in law enforcement. Any statement given freely and voluntarily without any compelling influences is, of course, admissible in evidence. The fundamental import of the privilege while an individual is in custody is not whether he is allowed to talk to the police without the benefit of warnings and counsel, but whether he can be interrogated. There is no requirement that police stop a person who enters a police station and states that he wishes to confess to a crime, or a person who calls the police to offer a confession or any other statement he desires to make. Volunteered statements of any kind are not barred by the Fifth Amendment and their admissibility is not affected by our holding today.

To summarize, we hold that when an individual is taken into custody or otherwise deprived of his freedom by the authorities in any significant way and is subjected to questioning, the privilege against self-incrimination is jeopardized. Procedural safeguards must be employed to protect the privilege and unless other fully effective means are adopted to notify the person of his right of silence and to assure that the exercise of the right will be scrupulously honored, the following measures are required. He must be warned prior to any questioning that he has the right to remain silent, that anything he says can be used against him in a court of law, that he has the

3. The distinction and its significance has been aptly described in the opinion of a Scottish court:

"In former times such questioning, if undertaken would be conducted by police officers visiting the house or place of business of the suspect and there questioning him, probably in the presence of a relation or friend. However convenient the modern practice may be, it must normally create a situation very unfavorable to the suspect." Chalmers v. H.M. Advocate, [1954] Sess.Cas. 66, 78 (J.C.).

right to the presence of an attorney, and that if he cannot afford an attorney one will be appointed for him prior to any questioning if he so desires. Opportunity to exercise these rights must be afforded to him throughout the interrogation. After such warnings have been given, and such opportunity afforded him, the individual may knowingly and intelligently waive these rights and agree to answer questions or make a statement. But unless and until such warnings and waiver are demonstrated by the prosecution at trial, no evidence obtained as a result of interrogation can be used against him.

IV.

A recurrent argument made in these cases is that society's need for interrogation outweighs the privilege....

* * *

In announcing these principles, we are not unmindful of the burdens which law enforcement officials must bear, often under trying circumstances. We also fully recognize the obligation of all citizens to aid in enforcing the criminal laws. This Court, while protecting individual rights, has always given ample latitude to law enforcement agencies in the legitimate exercise of their duties. The limits we have placed on the interrogation process should not constitute an undue interference with a proper system of law enforcement. As we have noted, our decision does not in any way preclude police from carrying out their traditional investigatory functions. Although confessions may play an important role in some convictions, the cases before us present graphic examples of the overstatement of the "need" for confessions. In each case authorities conducted interrogations ranging up to five days in duration despite the presence, through standard investigating practices, of considerable evidence against each defendant.[4]

* * *

Over the years the Federal Bureau of Investigation has compiled an exemplary record of effective law enforcement while advising any suspect or arrested person at the outset of an interview, that he is not required to make a statement, that any statement may be used against him in court, that the individual may obtain the services of an attorney of his own choice and, more recently, that he has a right to free counsel if he is unable to pay....

The practice of the FBI can readily be emulated by state and local enforcement agencies. The argument that the FBI deals with different crimes than are dealt with by state authorities does not mitigate the significance of the FBI experience.

The experience in some other countries also suggests that the danger to law enforcement in curbs on interrogation is overplayed. ...

4. Miranda, Vignera, and Westover were identified by eyewitnesses. Marked bills from the bank robbed were found in Westover's car. Articles stolen from the victim as well as from several other robbery victims were found in Stewart's home at the outset of the investigation.

The English procedure since 1912 under the Judges' Rules is significant. As recently strengthened, the Rules require that a cautionary warning be given an accused by a police officer as soon as he has evidence that affords reasonable grounds for suspicion; they also require that any statement made be given by the accused without questioning by police.

The right of the individual to consult with an attorney during this period is expressly recognized.

The safeguards present under Scottish law may be even greater than in England. Scottish judicial decisions bar use in evidence of most confessions obtained through police interrogation. In India, confessions made to police not in the presence of a magistrate have been excluded by rule of evidence since 1872, at a time when it operated under British law. Identical provisions appear in the Evidence Ordinance of Ceylon, enacted in 1895.... There appears to have been no marked detrimental effect on criminal law enforcement in these jurisdictions as a result of these rules. ...

It is also urged upon us that we withhold decision on this issue until state legislative bodies and advisory groups have had an opportunity to deal with these problems by rule making.... We have already pointed out that the Constitution does not require any specific code of procedures for protecting the privilege against self-incrimination during custodial interrogation. Congress and the States are free to develop their own safeguards for the privilege, so long as they are fully as effective as those described above in informing accused persons of their right of silence and in affording a continuous opportunity to exercise it. In any event, however, the issues presented are of constitutional dimensions and must be determined by the courts. The admissibility of a statement in the face of a claim that it was obtained in violation of the defendant's constitutional rights is an issue the resolution of which has long since been undertaken by this Court.... Where rights secured by the Constitution are involved, there can be no rule making or legislation which would abrogate them.

* * *

[Miranda reversed; Vignera reversed; Westover reversed; Stewart (state appellate court reversal of conviction) affirmed.]

■ MR. JUSTICE CLARK, dissenting in Nos. 759, 760, and 761, and concurring in the result in No. 584.

* * *

The *ipse dixit* of the majority has no support in our cases. ...Such a strict constitutional specific [as the warnings required by the majority] inserted at the nerve center of crime detection may well kill the patient.[5]

5. The Court points to England, Scotland, Ceylon and India as having equally rigid rules. As my Brother Harlan points out, post, ... the Court is mistaken in this regard, for it overlooks counterbalancing prosecutorial advantages. Moreover, the requirements of the Federal Bureau of Investigation do not appear ... to be as strict as those imposed today in at least two respects: (1) The offer of counsel is articulated only as "a right to counsel"; nothing is said about a right to have counsel present at the custodial interrogation ...; [and (2) the warning issued by the FBI does not indicate that the agent "will secure counsel"].

Since there is at this time a paucity of information and an almost total lack of empirical knowledge on the practical operation of requirements truly comparable to those announced by the majority, I would be more restrained lest we go too far too fast.

* * *

The rule prior to today ... depended upon "a totality of circumstances evidencing an involuntary ... admission of guilt." ...

I would continue to follow that rule. Under the "totality of circumstances" rule ... I would consider in each case whether the police officer prior to custodial interrogation added the warning that the suspect might have counsel present at the interrogation and, further, that a court would appoint one at his request if he was too poor to employ counsel. In the absence of warnings, the burden would be on the State to prove that counsel was knowingly and intelligently waived or that in the totality of the circumstances, including the failure to give the necessary warnings, the confession was clearly voluntary.

... In this way we would not be acting in the dark nor in one full sweep changing the traditional rules of custodial interrogation which this Court has for so long recognized as a justifiable and proper tool in balancing individual rights against the rights of society. It will be soon enough to go further when we are able to appraise with somewhat better accuracy the effect of such a holding.

* * *

■ MR. JUSTICE HARLAN, whom MR. JUSTICE STEWART and MR. JUSTICE WHITE join, dissenting.

I believe the decision of the Court represents poor constitutional law and entails harmful consequences for the country at large. How serious these consequences may prove to be only time can tell. ...

I. INTRODUCTION

* * *

... The new rules are not designed to guard against police brutality or other unmistakably banned forms of coercion. Those who use third-degree tactics and deny them in court are equally able and destined to lie as skillfully about warnings and waivers. Rather, the thrust of the new rules is to negate all pressures, to reinforce the nervous or ignorant suspect, and ultimately to discourage any confession at all. The aim in short is toward "voluntariness" in a utopian sense, or to view it from a different angle, voluntariness with a vengeance.

* * *

II. CONSTITUTIONAL PREMISES

It is most fitting to begin an inquiry into the constitutional precedents by surveying the limits on confessions the Court has evolved under the Due

Process Clause ... because these cases show that there exists a workable and effective means of dealing with confessions in a judicial manner; because the cases are the baseline from which the Court now departs and so serve to measure the actual as opposed to the professed distance it travels....

The earliest confession cases in this Court emerged from federal prosecutions and were settled on a nonconstitutional basis, the Court adopting the common-law rule that the absence of inducements, promises, and threats made a confession voluntary and admissible. Hopt v. People of Territory of Utah [1884]; Pierce v. United States [1896]. While a later case said the Fifth Amendment privilege controlled admissibility, this proposition was not itself developed in subsequent decisions. The Court did, however, heighten the test of admissibility in federal trials to one of voluntariness "in fact," Ziang Sung Wan v. United States [1921], and then by and large left federal judges to apply the same standards the Court began to derive in a string of state court cases.

This new line of decisions, testing admissibility by the Due Process Clause, began in 1936 with Brown v. State of Mississippi, ... While the voluntariness rubric was repeated ..., the Court never pinned it down to a single meaning ... To travel quickly over the main themes, there was an initial emphasis on reliability, e.g., Ward v. State of Texas [1942], supplemented by concern over the legality and fairness of the police practices, e.g., Ashcraft v. State of Tennessee [1944], in an "accusatorial" system of law enforcement, Watts v. State of Indiana [1949], and eventually by close attention to the individual's state of mind and capacity for effective choice, e.g., Gallegos v. State of Colorado [1962] ... The outcome was a continuing re-evaluation on the facts of each case of *how much* pressure on the suspect was permissible.

Among the criteria often taken into account were threats or imminent danger, e.g., Payne v. State of Arkansas [1958], physical deprivations such as lack of sleep or food, e.g., Reck v. Pate [1961], repeated or extended interrogation, e.g., Chambers v. State of Florida [1940], limits on access to counsel or friends, Crooker v. State of California [1958]; Cicenia v. La Gay [1958], length and illegality of detention under state law, e.g., Haynes v. State of Washington [1963], an individual weakness or incapacities, Lynumn v. State of Illinois [1963]. Apart from direct physical coercion, however, no single default or fixed combination of defaults guaranteed exclusion, and synopses of the cases would serve little use because the overall gauge has been steadily changing, usually in the direction of restricting admissibility. ...

There are several relevant lessons to be drawn from this constitutional history. The first is that with over 25 years of precedent the Court has developed an elaborate, sophisticated, and sensitive approach to admissibility of confessions. It is "judicial" in its treatment of one case at a time, flexible in its ability to respond to the endless mutations of fact presented, and ever more familiar to the lower courts. Of course, strict certainty is not obtained in this developing process, but this is often so with constitutional principles, and disagreement is usually confined to that borderland of close cases where it matters least.

. . . In practice and from time to time in principle, the Court has given ample recognition to society's interest in suspect questioning as an instrument of law enforcement. Cases countenancing quite significant pressures can be cited without difficulty, and the lower courts may often have been yet more tolerant. Of course the limitations imposed today were rejected by necessary implication in case after case, the right to warnings having been explicitly rebuffed in this Court many years ago. . . .

Finally, the cases disclose that the language in many of the opinions overstates the actual course of decision. It has been said, for example, that an admissible confession must be made by the suspect "in the unfettered exercise of his own will," Malloy v. Hogan [1964], and that "a prisoner is not 'to be made the deluded instrument of his own conviction,' " Culombe v. Connecticut [1961]. Though often repeated, such principles are rarely observed in full measure. Even the word "voluntary" may be deemed somewhat misleading, especially when one considers many of the confessions that have been brought under its umbrella. The tendency to overstate may be laid in part to the flagrant facts often before the Court; but in any event one must recognize how it has tempered attitudes and lent some color of authority to the approach now taken by the Court.

I turn now to the Court's asserted reliance on the Fifth Amendment, an approach which I frankly regard as a *trompe l'oeil*. . . .

The Court's opening contention, that the Fifth Amendment governs police station confessions, is perhaps not an impermissible extension of the law but it has little to commend itself in the present circumstances. Historically, the privilege against self-incrimination did not bear at all on the use of extra-legal confessions, for which distinct standards evolved; indeed, "the *history* of the two principles is wide apart, differing by one hundred years in origin, and derived through separate lines of precedents. . . ." . . . Even those who would readily enlarge the privilege must concede some linguistic difficulties since the Fifth Amendment in terms proscribes only compelling any person "in any criminal case to be a witness against himself." . . .

. . . Certainly the privilege does represent a protective concern for the accused and an emphasis upon accusatorial rather than inquisitorial values in law enforcement, although this is similarly true of other limitations such as the grand jury requirement and the reasonable doubt standard. Accusatorial values, however, have openly been absorbed into the due process standard governing confessions; this indeed is why at present "the kinship of the two rules [governing confessions and self-incrimination] is too apparent for denial." . . . Since extension of the general principle has already occurred, to insist that the privilege applies as such serves only to carry over inapposite historical details and engaging rhetoric and to obscure the policy choices to be made in regulating confessions.

Having decided that the Fifth Amendment privilege does apply in the police station, the Court reveals that the privilege imposes more exacting restrictions than does the Fourteenth Amendment's voluntariness test. It then emerges . . . that the Fifth Amendment requires for an admissible confession that it be given by one distinctly aware of his right not to speak and shielded from "the compelling atmosphere" of interrogation. From these key premises, the Court finally develops the safeguards of warning, counsel, and so forth. I do not believe these premises are sustained by precedents under the Fifth Amendment.

The more important premise is that pressure on the suspect must be eliminated though it be only the subtle influence of the atmosphere and surroundings. The Fifth Amendment, however, has never been thought to forbid *all* pressure to incriminate one's self in the situations covered by it. On the contrary, it has been held that failure to incriminate one's self can result in denial of removal of one's case from state to federal court; in refusal of a military commission; in denial of a discharge in bankruptcy; and in numerous other adverse consequences. This is not to say that short of jail or torture any sanction is permissible in any case; policy and history alike may impose sharp limits. However, the Court's unspoken assumption that *any* pressure violates the privilege is not supported by the precedents and it has failed to show why the Fifth Amendment prohibits that relatively mild pressure the Due Process Clause permits.

The Court appears similarly wrong in thinking that precise knowledge of one's rights is a settled prerequisite under the Fifth Amendment to the loss of its protections. A number of lower federal court cases have held that grand jury witnesses need not always be warned of their privilege, ... and Wigmore states this to be the better rule for trial witnesses.... No Fifth Amendment precedent is cited for the Court's contrary view....

* * *

III. POLICY CONSIDERATIONS

... Legal history has been stretched before to satisfy deep needs of society. In this instance, however, the Court has not and cannot make the powerful showing that its new rules are plainly desirable in the context of our society, something which is surely demanded before those rules are engrafted onto the Constitution and imposed on every State and county in the land.

Without at all subscribing to the generally black picture of police conduct painted by the Court, I think it must be frankly recognized at the outset that police questioning allowable under due process precedents may inherently entail some pressure on the suspect and may seek advantage in his ignorance or weaknesses. The atmosphere and questioning techniques, proper and fair though they be, can in themselves exert a tug on the suspect to confess, and in this light "[t]o speak of any confessions of crime made after arrest as being 'voluntary' or 'uncoerced' is somewhat inaccurate, although traditional. A confession is wholly and incontestably voluntary only if a guilty person gives himself up to the law and become his own accuser." ... Until today, the role of the Constitution has been only to sift out *undue* pressure, not to assure spontaneous confessions. ...

The Court's new rules aim to offset these minor pressures and disadvantages intrinsic to any kind of police interrogation. The rules do not serve due process interests in preventing blatant coercion since, as I noted earlier, they do nothing to contain the policeman who is prepared to lie from the start. The rules work for reliability in confessions almost only in the Pickwickian sense that they can prevent some from being given at all.[6] . . .

What the Court largely ignores is that its rules impair, if they will not eventually serve wholly to frustrate, an instrument of law enforcement that has long and quite reasonably been thought worth the price paid for it. There can be little doubt that the Court's new code would markedly decrease the number of confessions. To warn the suspect that he may remain silent and remind him that his confession be may used in court are minor obstructions. To require also an express waiver by the suspect and an end to questioning whenever he demurs must heavily handicap questioning. And to suggest or provide counsel for the suspect simply invites the end of the interrogation.

How much harm this decision will inflict on law enforcement cannot fairly be predicted with accuracy. Evidence on the role of confessions is notoriously incomplete, and little is added by the Court's reference to the FBI experience and the resources believed wasted in interrogation. We do know that some crimes cannot be solved without confessions, that ample expert testimony attests to their importance in crime control, and that the Court is taking a real risk with society's welfare in imposing its new regime on the country. The social costs of crime are too great to call the new rules anything but a hazardous experimentation.

While passing over the costs and risks of its experiment, the Court portrays the evils of normal police questioning in terms which I think are exaggerated. Albeit stringently confined by the due process standards interrogation is no doubt often inconvenient and unpleasant for the suspect. However, it is no less so for a man to be arrested and jailed, to have his house searched, or to stand trial in court, yet all this may properly happen to the most innocent given probable cause, a warrant, or an indictment. Society has always paid a stiff price for law and order, and peaceful interrogation is not one of the dark moments of the law.

. . . it may make the analysis more graphic to consider the actual facts of one of the four cases reversed by the Court. Miranda v. Arizona serves best, being neither the hardest nor easiest of the four under the Court's standards.

On March 3, 1963, an 18–year–old girl was kidnaped and forcibly raped near Phoenix, Arizona. Ten days later, on the morning of March 13, petitioner Miranda was arrested and taken to the police station. At this time Miranda was 23 years old, indigent, and educated to the extent of completing half the ninth grade. He had "an emotional illness" of the schizophrenic type, according to the doctor who eventually examined him; the doctor's report also stated that Miranda was "alert and oriented as to time, place, and person," intelligent within normal limits, competent to stand trial, and came within the legal definition. At the police station, the

6. The Court's vision of a lawyer "mitigat[ing] the dangers of untrustworthiness" by witnessing coercion and assisting accuracy in the confession is largely a fancy; for if counsel arrives, there is rarely going to be a police station confession. Watts v. State of Indiana [1949] (separate opinion of Jackson, J.): "[A]ny lawyer worth his salt will tell the suspect in no uncertain terms to make no statement to police under any circumstances." . . .

victim picked Miranda out of a lineup, and two officers then took him into a separate room to interrogate him, starting about 11:30 a.m. Though at first denying his guilt, within a short time Miranda gave a detailed oral confession and then wrote out in his own hand and signed a brief statement admitting and describing the crime. All this was accomplished in two hours or less without any force, threats or promises and—I will assume this though the record is uncertain, without any effective warnings at all.

Miranda's oral and written confessions are now held inadmissible under the Court's new rules. One is entitled to feel astonished that the Constitution can be read to produce this result. These confessions were obtained during brief, daytime questioning conducted by two officers and unmarked by any of the traditional indicia of coercion. They assured a conviction for a brutal and unsettling crime, for which the police had and quite possibly could obtain little evidence other than the victim's identifications, evidence which is frequently unreliable. There was, in sum, a legitimate purpose, no perceptible unfairness, and certainly little risk of injustice in the interrogation.

* * *

The Court in closing its general discussion invokes the practice in federal and foreign jurisdictions as lending weight to its new curbs on confessions for all the States. A brief résumé will suffice to show that none of these jurisdictions has struck so one-sided a balance as the Court does today. Heaviest reliance is placed on the FBI practice. Differing circumstances may make this comparison quite untrustworthy, but in any event the FBI falls sensibly short of the Court's formalistic rules. For example, there is no indication that FBI agents must obtain an affirmative "waiver" before they pursue their questioning. Nor is it clear that one invoking his right to silence may not be prevailed upon to change his mind. And the warning as to appointed counsel apparently indicates only that one will be assigned by the judge when the suspect appears before him; the thrust of the Court's rules is to induce the suspect to obtain appointed counsel before continuing the interview. Apparently American military practice, briefly mentioned by the Court, has these same limits and is still less favorable to the suspect than the FBI warning, making no mention of appointed counsel.

The law of the foreign countries described by the Court also reflects a more moderate conception of the rights of the accused as against those of society when other data are considered. Concededly, the English experience is most relevant. In that country, a caution as to silence but not counsel has long been mandated by the "Judges' Rules," which also place other somewhat imprecise limits on police cross-examination suspects. However, in the court's discretion confessions can be and apparently quite frequently are admitted in evidence despite disregard of the Judges' Rules, so long as they are found voluntary under the common-law test. Moreover, the check that exists on the use of pretrial statements is counterbalanced by the evident admissibility of fruits of an illegal confession and by the judge's often-used authority to comment adversely on the defendant's failure to testify.

India, Ceylon and Scotland are the other examples chosen by the Court. In India and Ceylon the general ban on police-adduced confessions cited by the Court is subject to a major exception: if evidence is uncovered by police questioning, it is fully admissible at trial along with the confession itself, so far as it relates to the evidence and is not blatantly coerced. Scotland's limits on interrogation do measure up to the Court's; however, restrained comment at trial on the defendant's failure to take the stand is allowed the judge, and in many other respects Scotch law redresses the prosecutor's disadvantage in ways not permitted in this country. The Court ends its survey by imputing added strength to our privilege against self-incrimination since, by contrast to other countries, it is embodied in a written Constitution. Considering the liberties the Court has today taken with constitutional history and precedent, few will find this emphasis persuasive.

* * *

... Despite the Court's disclaimer, the practical effect of the decision made today must inevitably be to handicap seriously sound efforts at reform, not least by removing options necessary to a just compromise of competing interests. Of course legislative reform is rarely speedy or unanimous, though this Court has been more patient in the past. But the legislative reforms when they come would have the vast advantage of empirical data and comprehensive study, they would allow experimentation and use of solutions not open to the courts, and they would restore the initiative in criminal law reform to those forums where it truly belongs.

* * *

In conclusion: Nothing in the letter or the spirit of the Constitution or in the precedents squares with the heavy-handed and one-sided action that is so precipitously taken by the Court in the name of fulfilling its constitutional responsibilities. The foray which the Court makes today brings to mind the wise and far-sighted words of Mr. Justice Jackson: "This Court is forever adding new stories to the temples of constitutional law, and the temples have a way of collapsing when one story too many is added."

■ MR. JUSTICE WHITE, with whom MR. JUSTICE HARLAN and MR. JUSTICE STEWART join, dissenting.

* * *

... To reach the result announced on the grounds it does, the Court must stay within the confines of the Fifth Amendment, which forbids self-incrimination only if *compelled*. Hence the core of the Court's opinion is that because of the "compulsion inherent in custodial surroundings, no statement obtained from [a] defendant [in custody] can truly be the product of his free choice," absent the use of adequate protective devices as described by the Court. However, the Court does not point to any sudden in-rush of new knowledge requiring the rejection of 70 years' experience. ... Rather than asserting new knowledge, the Court concedes that it cannot truly know what occurs during custodial questioning, because of the innate secrecy of such proceedings. It extrapolates a picture of what it conceives to be the norm from police investigatorial manuals, published in 1959 and

1962 or earlier, without any attempt to allow for adjustments in police practices that may have occurred in the wake of more recent decisions of state appellate tribunals or this Court. But even if the relentless application of the described procedures could lead to involuntary confessions, it most assuredly does not follow that each and every case will disclose this kind of interrogation or this kind of consequence.[7] Insofar as appears from the Court's opinion, it has not examined a single transcript of any police interrogation, let alone the interrogation that took place in any one of these cases which it decides today. Judged by any of the standards for empirical investigation utilized in the social sciences the factual basis for the Court's premise is patently inadequate.

* * *

... Even if one were to postulate that the Court's concern is not that all confessions induced by police interrogation are coerced but rather that some such confessions are coerced and present judicial procedures are believed to be inadequate to identify the confessions that are coerced and those that are not, it would still not be essential to impose the rule that the Court has now fashioned. Transcripts or observers could be required, specific time limits, tailored to fit the cause, could be imposed, or other devices could be utilized to reduce the chances that otherwise indiscernible coercion will produce an inadmissible confession.

On the other hand, even if one assumed that there was an adequate factual basis for the conclusion that all confessions obtained during in-custody interrogation are the product of compulsion, the rule propounded by the Court will still be irrational, for, apparently, it is only if the accused is also warned of his right to counsel and waives both that right and the right against self-incrimination that the inherent compulsiveness of interrogation disappears. But if the defendant may not answer without a warning a question such as "Where were you last night?" without having his answer be a compelled one, how can the Court ever accept his negative answer to the question of whether he wants to consult his retained counsel or counsel whom the court will appoint? And why if counsel is present and the accused nevertheless confesses, or counsel tells the accused to tell the truth, and that is what the accused does, is the situation any less coercive insofar as the accused is concerned?

* * *

... The Court's duty to assess the consequences of its action is not satisfied by the utterance of the truth that a value of our system of criminal justice is "to respect the inviolability of the human personality"

7. In fact, the type of sustained interrogation described by the Court appears to be the exception rather than the rule. A survey of 399 cases in one city found that in almost half of the cases the interrogation lasted less than 30 minutes. Barrett, Police Practices and the Law—From Arrest to Release or Charge, 50 Calif.L.Rev. 11, 41–45 (1962). Questioning tends to be confused and sporadic and is usually concentrated on confrontations with witnesses or new items of evidence, as these are obtained by officers conducting the investigation. See generally LaFave, Arrest: The Decision to Take a Suspect into Custody 386 (1965); ALI, A Model Code of Pre–Arraignment Procedure, Commentary § 5.01, at 170, n. 4 (Tent.Draft No. 1, 1966).

and to require government to produce the evidence against the accused by its own independent labors. More than the human dignity of the accused is involved; the human personality of others in the society must also be preserved. Thus the values reflected by the privilege are not the sole desideratum; society's interest in the general security is of equal weight.

The obvious underpinning of the Court's decision is a deep-seated distrust of all confessions. . . . This is the not so subtle overtone of the opinion—that it is inherently wrong for the police to gather evidence from the accused himself. And this is precisely the nub of this dissent. I see nothing wrong or immoral, and certainly nothing unconstitutional, in the police's asking a suspect whom they have reasonable cause to arrest whether or not he killed his wife or in confronting him with the evidence on which the arrest was based, at least where he has been plainly advised that he may remain completely silent. Until today, "the admissions or confessions of the prisoner, when voluntarily and freely made, have always ranked high in the scale of incriminating evidence." . . . Particularly when corroborated, as where the police have confirmed the accused's disclosure of the hiding place of implements or fruits of the crime, such confessions have the highest reliability and significantly contribute to the certitude with which we may believe the accused is guilty. Moreover, it is by no means certain that the process of confessing is injurious to the accused. To the contrary it may provide psychological relief and enhance the prospects for rehabilitation.

* * *

The most basic function of any government is to provide for the security of the individual and of his property. These ends of society are served by the criminal laws which for the most part are aimed at the prevention of crime. Without the reasonably effective performance of the task of preventing private violence and retaliation, it is idle to talk about human dignity and civilized values.

* * *

. . . Criminal trials, no matter how efficient the police are, are not sure bets for the prosecution, nor should they be if the evidence is not forthcoming. Under the present law, the prosecution fails to prove its case in about 30% of the criminal cases actually tried in the federal courts. But it is something else again to remove from the ordinary criminal case all those confessions which heretofore have been held to be free and voluntary acts of the accused and to thus establish a new constitutional barrier to the ascertainment of truth by the judicial process. There is, in my view, every reason to believe that a good many criminal defendants who otherwise would have been convicted on what this Court has previously thought to be the most satisfactory kind of evidence will now under this new version of the Fifth Amendment, either not be tried at all or will be acquitted if the State's evidence, minus the confession, is put to the test of litigation.

I have no desire whatsoever to share the responsibility for any such impact on the present criminal process.

In some unknown number of cases the Court's rule will return a killer, a rapist or other criminal to the streets and to the environment which produced him, to repeat his crime whenever it pleases him. As a consequence, there will not be a gain, but a loss, in human dignity. The real concern is not the unfortunate consequences of this new decision on the criminal law as an abstract, disembodied series of authoritative proscriptions, but the impact on those who rely on the public authority for protection and who without it can only engage in violent self-help with guns, knives and the help of their neighbors similarly inclined. There is, of course, a saving factor: the next victims are uncertain, unnamed and unrepresented in this case.

* * *

And what about the accused who has confessed or would confess in response to simple, noncoercive questioning and whose guilt could not otherwise be proved? Is it so clear that release is the best thing for him in every case? Has it so unquestionably been resolved that in each and every case it would be better for him not to confess and to return to his environment with no attempt whatsoever to help him? I think not. It may well be that in many cases it will be no less than a callous disregard for his own welfare as well as for the interests of his next victim.

There is another aspect to the effect of the Court's rule on the person whom the police have arrested on probable cause. The fact is that he may not be guilty at all and may be able to extricate himself quickly and simply if he were told the circumstances of his arrest and were asked to explain. This effort, and his release, must now await the hiring of a lawyer or his appointment by the court, consultation with counsel and then a session with the police or the prosecutor. Similarly, where probable cause exists to arrest several suspects, as where the body of the victim is discovered in a house having several residents, it will often be true that a suspect may be cleared only through the results of interrogation of other suspects. Here too the release of the innocent may be delayed by the Court's rule.

Much of the trouble with the Court's new rule is that it will operate indiscriminately in all criminal cases, regardless of the severity of the crime or the circumstances involved. It applies to every defendant, whether the professional criminal or one committing a crime of momentary passion who is not part and parcel of organized crime. It will slow down the investigation and the apprehension of confederates in those cases where time is of the essence, such as kidnapping, ... those involving national security ... and some of those involving organized crime. In the latter context the lawyer who arrives may also be the lawyer for the defendant's colleagues and can be relied upon to insure that no breach of the organization's security takes place even though the accused may feel that the best thing he can do is to cooperate.

At the same time, the Court's *per se* approach may not be justified on the ground that it provides a "bright line" permitting the authorities to judge in advance whether interrogation may safely be pursued without jeopardizing the admissibility of any information obtained as a consequence. Nor can it be claimed that judicial time and effort, assuming that is a relevant consideration, will be conserved because of the ease of application of the new rule. Today's decision leaves open such questions as whether the accused was in custody, whether his statements were spontaneous or the product of interrogation, whether the accused has effectively waived his rights, and whether nontestimonial evidence introduced at trial is the fruit of statements made during a prohibited interrogation, all of which are certain to prove productive of uncertainty during investigation and litigation during prosecution. For all these reasons, if further restrictions on police interrogation are desirable at this time, a more flexible approach makes much more sense than the Court's constitutional straitjacket which forecloses more discriminating treatment by legislative or rule-making pronouncements.

NOTES

1. Statements elicited by custodial interrogation in the absence of warnings and waiver are inadmissible under *Miranda*. Are all such statements actually "compelled" within the meaning of *Miranda?* Or does *Miranda* require warnings and waiver as a means of deterring compulsion, while excluding statements whether they have in fact been compelled if they were elicited by custodial interrogation without warnings and waiver? A decade and a half after *Miranda*, a Supreme Court with a very different membership, expressed itself on this subject. Oregon v. Elstad, Chapter 6, Section E. The *Elstad* Court indicated that not all statements excluded by *Miranda* are compelled within the meaning of the fifth amendment, but that *Miranda* creates an irrefutable presumption of compulsion. See also one view of whether the Supreme Court can properly exercise the power to invoke the fifth amendment to exclude statements that are not actually compelled. Joseph D. Grano, Confessions, Truth and The Law (1993). It is difficult to describe (in a short paragraph) the upheaval in attitudes and procedures caused by Miranda. The notion that police must give advice of rights before custodial interrogation is now part the established legal landscape, indeed part of the cultural landscape since the warning procedure is portrayed repeatedly in popular entertainments. No jurisdiction in the United States required the exact warnings prescribed by Miranda. Few required any warnings. The impact of the decision was heightened by the poor communications technology of the day. The decision was announced and covered in the media on a day in June but the text of the opinion was not available until some hours or (in some cases) days after it was announced. Some police officers were interrupting ongoing interrogations to seek advice which prosecutors could not give. Prosecutors near Washington, D.C. sent assistants to the Supreme Court to read the opinion and phone in a report. Prosecutors in the Midwest went to the Commerce Clearing House which had telex or wire copies of the opinion after a few hours had passed. Defense counsel were making objections to admissibility and citing radio news reports. For those who practiced in the field, Miranda was the most memorable decision of its generation because, unlike other decisions, it applied to a huge number of investigations and altered the rules in every state and federal jurisdiction.

In some jurisdictions Miranda type doctrines had been endorsed or at least their seeds planted. See Wesley W. Horton & Brendon P. Levesque, "The Wheeler Court," 24 Quinnipiac L. Rev. 301, 306 (2006).

Despite the change in police procedure engendered by Miranda, there is no clear assessment of the costs and benefits of the decision. This question was essentially ignored until quite recently. See George Thomas III, Is Miranda a Real World Failure? A Plea for More (and Better) Empirical Evidence, 43 U.C.L.A. L.

Rev. 821 (1996). Paul G. Cassell and Bret s. Hayman, Police Interrogation in the 1990's: An Empirical Study of the Effect of Miranda, 43 U.C.L.A. L. Rev. 839 (1996). A spirited debate on the subject appears in a series of four articles. Paul G. Cassell, Miranda's Social Costs: An Empirical Reassessment, 90 N.W. U. L. Rev. 387 (1996) Stephen J. Schulhofer, Miranda's Practical Effect, Substantial Benefits and Vanishing Social Costs, 90 NW. U. L. Rev. 500 (1996), Paul G. Cassell, All Benefits, No Costs: The Grand Illusion of Miranda's Defenders, 90 NW. U. L. Rev. 1084 (1996), Stephen J. Schulhofer, Miranda and Clearance Rates, 91 NW. U. L. Rev. 278 (1996). The difficulty faced by Miranda's defenders is that even a very small effect of losing a confession in one-half percent of cases may mean thousands of violent criminals and many thousands of other offenders will escape justice. The difficulty faced by Miranda's opponents is that while crime rates have risen, law enforcement resources have not risen nearly as fast and this may well be the reason that so many criminals avoid conviction.

In a striking article Professor Ronald Allen makes the point that both the traditional test of voluntariness and the Miranda warnings rest on the foundation that a confession ought to be an act of free will. He notes that free will is, at best, a troublesome concept since one always has a choice whether to confess or not even under torture, to choose between continued pain or confessing. This is inherent within the concept of free will even if we disregard all the environmental and genetic constraints that many believe limit or destroy free will in humans. What in fact we decide in confession cases is not whether a confession was "voluntary" but rather whether the interrogators went too far. All this "leads us back to the common law's focus on coercion and its evolution into a rule about police practices. As Professor Alschuler has argued: The Court should define the term coerced confessions to mean a confession caused by offensive governmental conduct period ... shifting their attention almost entirely from the minds of suspects to the conduct of government officers, courts should abandon the search for 'overborne wills' and attempts to assess the quality of individual choices. [citing Albert W. Alschuler, 'Constraint and Confession,' 74 Denver U.L.Rev. 957, 964–67 (1997)]... The obvious progression from Miranda was the elimination of confessions, but instead the Court's cases have led to a near-return of the previous equilibrium. Notwithstanding the ambiguity of the test [of voluntariness], that prior equilibrium was largely informed by a set of concerns that reduced to the question of what is too much pressure to be brought to bear on a suspect. [I]f the prior equilibrium had settled at an approximately appropriate level, then the consequence of Miranda should be small rather than large." Ronald J. Allen, "Miranda's Hollow Core", 100 Nw.U.L.Rev 71 (2006)

2. Assuming the continued employment of the exclusionary rule as a device by which police conduct is conformed to the requirements of substantive law, the question remains, how far should a court—particularly the Supreme Court—go in laying down *specific* rules of police conduct? See Friendly, The Bill of Rights as a Code of Criminal Procedure, 53 Calif.L.Rev. 929 (1965). What form should such "rules" take? Between the decision in *Escobedo* and that in *Miranda*, one writer suggested that the Supreme Court ought to promulgate rules outside the vehicle of an adjudicated case, and that the Congress, under its power to enforce the Fourteenth Amendment, ought to enact a code of criminal procedure to govern state law enforcement officers. Consider the following materials from Dowling, Escobedo and Beyond: The Need for a Fourteenth Amendment Code of Criminal Procedure, 56 J.Crim.L., C. & P.S. 143, 153–57 (1965).

"The readily traceable reason for the inaction of Congress and the absence of court rules specially promulgated by the Supreme Court for the area of state-federal criminal procedure is the division of powers between the states and the federal government inherent in our history and emphasized in the ninth and tenth amendments. The reason rested on bedrock when that division existed and where it legitimately continues to exist. But when the reservation of powers of the states in the criminal area is brought into the penumbra of the federal system, it is inefficient, foolhardy and contrary to our form of government to permit the federal-fourteenth amendment part of state-federal criminal procedure to drift forward, backward, or stand still, exclusively on the pages of the *Supreme Court Reports*. Moreover, it is a disservice to make state law enforcement officials and state courts flounder in their duties upon a sea of doubt over which they have no navigable control. If the states are to operate the state-federal criminal system, they ought to be allowed to participate in the full panoply of governmental processes which control that system—which means legislative participation as well as judicial imposition. The resolution of the demands and challenges of the fourteenth amendment to afford fair criminal proceedings against the citizen and on behalf of the state should not be exclusively reposited in the Supreme Court.

"It is, of course, true that the states are left to their own devices in meeting the dictates of the Supreme Court. But obedience, even when it is willing and eager, can be misguided and—when it comes to operating a system of criminal justice within a state—grossly inefficient.... I do not suggest that we need to find a way to curb the Court. On the contrary, as to the Court, I suggest that to supplement its present role in making state-federal criminal law on a case-by-case basis, it be encouraged to perform the further function of promulgating rules which would be helpful to the states and lead to greater efficiency in the administration of the state-federal law. The scope of these rules would be within the range of power generally conceded to appellate courts administering laws over which they have jurisdiction.

"Professor Allen's point is sound that many of the problems of fair and decent criminal procedure are, apart from those of the limits of constitutional power, ones of policy and common sense. And legislative initiative on the local level should not preclude legislation *for* the local level by a conglomerate legislature representing thousands of localities and fifty states with *common* local problems under the fourteenth amendment. If the Congress is intelligently advised, perhaps through a Committee on State–Federal Criminal Law with local sub-groups, legislation meeting the demands of decency and efficiency to the citizens prosecuted and the state as law-enforcer could be passed and included in a title to the United States code recognizing and implementing the existing, growing body of state-federal case law under the fourteenth amendment.

"The relationship of the states to the federal government in this area has understandably, but needlessly, been a touchy subject. Fourteenth amendment doctrine has been developed by the Court under a tip-toe method which the states have found leaves the scuff-marks of the big boot. The Supreme Court, while reassuring the states of exclusive jurisdiction in procedural matters concerning the operation of state systems of criminal justice, at the same time dictates requirements under the fourteenth amendment which generally affect the most important aspects of criminal procedure followed within the states. Consider the then thought to be reassuring language of Mr. Justice Burton in Bute v. Illinois, a 1948 decision following the now discarded rule of Betts v. Brady:

> " 'The Fourteenth Amendment ... does not say that no state shall deprive any person of liberty without following the *federal* process of law as prescribed for the federal courts in comparable federal cases.... This *due* process is not an equivalent for the process of the federal courts or for the process of any particular state. It has reference rather to a standard of process that may cover many varieties of processes that are expressive of differing combinations of historical or modern, local or other judicial standards, provided they do not conflict with the 'fundamental principles of

liberty and justice which lie at the base of all our civil and political institutions' . . .

"Can it really be said that the problems confronting the California, Oregon, Rhode Island and Illinois Supreme Courts, the New York trial judge, the one from Tennessee and, no doubt, hundreds of other trial judges, are 'local' problems? Are there 'varieties of processes' open to the state courts to be divined out of their own local, historical or modern settings—the fifty separate precincts—to comport with 'this *due* process' which, it is said, is not an equivalent for federal process or the process of any given state? Is the question whether a man charged with misdemeanor is entitled to appointment of counsel, a question left over from *Gideon*, a 'local' question, assuming the man's indigency? Is whether a man suspected of, say, murder entitled to be provided with a free lawyer if he is poor and wants one during police interrogation, a 'local' question? . . . Or whether we should do away with the voluntary confession altogether? Or what rights a man ought to be told he has before we elicit a confession from him? Or just how to go about 'effectively' telling him about those rights? These questions could be posed for quite some time before one got down to the really 'local' issues: how to charge an offense, as long as one is intelligibly charged; how to provide counsel, as long as counsel is provided; how to provide appellate review of convictions, as long as it is open to all; how to conduct a post-conviction hearing, as long as there is a hearing; and how to conduct a criminal trial, as long as it is conducted fairly. The local and the national procedures can be sorted out for quite some time, and this is the hub of what I propose we do; not just by a majority, but by the fifty states through the Congress.

". . . There is no mysterious process at arriving at the answers that makes the Supreme Court more fit to articulate them than the Congress. There is nothing inherent in our system, other than Congressional lethargy, some lack of imagination, the force of legislative inertia at rest, and the willingness to pass the buck to judicial interpolation, that restricts Congress from legislating fourteenth amendment requirements for state criminal processes.

"We do not have to nationalize the criminal procedure of the several States. But we do have to 'fourteenth amendmentize' their procedure. And the code of fourteenth amendment criminal procedure that we have to start thinking about cannot be thought about in terms of traditional procedural codes. For the code that will have to be worked out with all of the originality that went into drafting the Constitution does not now exist. To be sure, the Congress will have to draw on the best talent in this nation to do the sorting-out and, indeed, the drafting. . . .

"We do not have to search very far for the answer to the question: does the Congress have authority to enact legislation for the federal part of the state-federal trial that the states are now administering? Section five of the fourteenth amendment states: 'The Congress shall have power to enforce, by appropriate legislation, the provisions of this article.' . . .

* * *

"Assuming Congressional authority to enact a code of fourteenth amendment criminal procedure applicable to state criminal cases, and further assuming a desire on the part of Congress to legislate with a genuine sensitivity to concepts of fairness developed by the Supreme Court and those still being debated in chambers, such a code could contribute substantially to the efficient and sound administration of criminal justice in the United States. Congressional participation potentially offers a greater degree of certainty and predictability for state systems of criminal justice. It offers a wider forum for resolution of important problems confronting the administration of criminal justice, including the opportunity for Congress to solicit the reasoned judgment of members of the state judiciary on important constitutional problems confronting the nation—not just the judiciary.

"Justice Walter V. Schaefer of the Supreme Court of Illinois has said that '[s]uperimposed upon the recency of many of our procedural safeguards is the novelty of federal intervention in the field.' Since Justice Schaefer made that statement in 1956 the 'novelty' has begun to wear off. Nevertheless we remain lulled by the sense of transiency that goes with novelty. The Supreme Court, standing at the summit of our constitutional system, will continue to intervene on a case-by-case basis so long as we—through our Congress—continue to default in our responsibilities to provide uniform machinery to meet the ever-evolving demands and challenges of the fourteenth amendment. But if we use it, there is reason to believe the Court will heed our common sense."

In contrast to judicial rulemaking the experience of other nations is described in "The Emerging International Consensus As to Criminal Procedure Rules", 14 Mich. J. of International Law 171 (1993) a survey of criminal procedure of England, Australia, Canada, France, Germany and Italy, Professor Craig Bradley, concludes:

> Four trends emerge from the comparative analysis in this article. First, every country examined here except the United States agrees that the declaration of criminal procedure rules is, at least primarily, the province of the *legislative*, not the judicial branch. The legislature enacts rules in a code that the police can learn and obey, rather than in a series of court opinions. Second, most countries require *Miranda*-type warnings prior to interrogation. If the requirement of such warnings in the United States was once aberrational, that is no longer the case. Third, exclusionary remedies are finding increasing favor as a means of deterring police breaches of the rules, even though the courts of two countries, Canada and Germany, continue to maintain that deterrence of police misconduct is *not* the purpose of the exclusionary rule. Fourth, these exclusionary remedies tend, except in the case of coerced confessions, to be discretionary, rather than mandatory as in the United States. Nonetheless, they tend to be enforced often enough to have an impact on the police, at least in Canada and England, increasingly in Germany, and perhaps in Italy and Australia as well.
>
> It seems that these countries, influenced by U.S. developments, may have the right idea: develop, either directly through the legislature or by means of a legislatively appointed body, a comprehensive code of rules, all of which *may* be enforced with the exclusionary remedy so that the police are encouraged to obey them. Then, use that remedy often, but only when, on balance, the use of the evidence would be unfair or would bring the administration of justice into dispute. The clearer the rules that the police are supposed to follow, the more likely that their failure to follow them will cause the public to lose confidence in the justice system. Thus, on the admittedly frequent (but far *less* frequent than is currently the case) occasions when the statutory rules would not give the police clear guidance, evidentiary exclusion would ordinarily be inappropriate. But, when the rules are clear, evidentiary exclusion would be the norm, at least for violations of non-technical rules. However, other factors, such as the seriousness of the crime, the quantum of evidence possessed by the police, the willfulness of the violation, and the importance of the evidence to the government's case, could also figure into the equation.

3. One week after the decision in *Miranda*, the Court held that neither *Escobedo* nor *Miranda* were to apply to cases in which the *trials* were commenced prior to the dates of decision in those cases. Johnson v. New Jersey, 384 U.S. 719, 86 S.Ct. 1772

(1966). In 1969 the Court further limited the effect of *Miranda* by declaring it inapplicable on re-trial of any case where the original trial occurred before *Miranda*, Jenkins v. Delaware, 395 U.S. 213, 89 S.Ct. 1677 (1969).

4. The Supreme Court found that Miranda was based on the Constitution and could not be overturned by an Act of Congress. Dickerson v. United States, 530 U.S. 428, 120 S.Ct. 2326 (2000).

> "Rehnquist, C.J.
>
> "The law in this area is clear. This Court has supervisory authority over the federal courts, and we may use that authority to prescribe rules of evidence and procedure that are binding in those tribunals. Carlisle v. United States (1996). However, the power to judicially create and enforce nonconstitutional 'rules of procedure and evidence for the federal courts exists only in the absence of a relevant Act of Congress.' Palermo v. United States. [citations omitted] ... Congress retains the ultimate authority to modify or set aside any judicially created rules of evidence and procedure that are not required by the Constitution.... But Congress may not legislatively supersede our decisions interpreting and applying the Constitution.... Relying on the fact that we have created several exceptions to Miranda's warnings requirement and that we have repeatedly referred to the Miranda warnings as 'prophylactic,' New York v. Quarles (1984), and 'not themselves rights protected by the Constitution,' Michigan v. Tucker (1974), the Court of Appeals concluded that the protections announced in Miranda are not constitutionally required. [citations omitted] ... We disagree with the Court of Appeals' conclusion, although we concede that there is language in some of our opinions that supports the view taken by that court. But first and foremost of the factors on the other side that Miranda is a constitutional decision is that both Miranda and two of its companion cases applied the rule to proceedings in state courts to wit, Arizona, California, and New York. Since that time, we have consistently applied Miranda's rule to prosecutions arising in state courts. [citations omitted] ... It is beyond dispute that we do not hold a supervisory power over the courts of the several States.... The Miranda opinion itself begins by stating that the Court granted certiorari 'to explore some facets of the problems ... of applying the privilege against self-incrimination to in-custody interrogation, and to give concrete constitutional guidelines for law enforcement agencies and courts to follow.' ... In fact, the majority opinion is replete with statements indicating that the majority thought it was announcing a constitutional rule. Indeed, the Court's ultimate conclusion was that the unwarned confessions obtained in the four cases before the Court in Miranda 'were obtained from the defendant under circumstances that did not meet constitutional standards for protection of the privilege.' ... The Court of Appeals also relied on the fact that we have, after our Miranda decision, made exceptions from its rule in cases. But we have also broadened the application of the Miranda doctrine in cases such as Doyle v. Ohio (1988). These decisions illustrate the principle not that Miranda is not a constitutional rule but that no constitutional rule is immutable. No court laying down a general rule can possibly foresee the various circumstances in which counsel will seek to apply it, and the sort of modifications represented by these cases are as much a normal part of constitutional law as the original decision. [citations omitted] ... The dissent argues that it is judicial overreaching for this Court to hold 3501 unconstitutional unless we hold that the Miranda warnings are required by the Constitution, in the sense that nothing else will suffice to satisfy constitutional requirements. But we need not go farther than Miranda to

decide this case. In Miranda, the Court noted that reliance on the traditional totality-of-the-circumstances test raised a risk of overlooking an involuntary custodial confession, a risk that the Court found unacceptably great when the confession is offered in the case in chief to prove guilt. The Court therefore concluded that something more than the totality test was necessary. As discussed above, 3501 reinstates the totality test as sufficient. Section 3501 therefore cannot be sustained if Miranda is to remain the law. [citations omitted] Whether or not we would agree with Miranda's reasoning and its resulting rule, were we addressing the issue in the first instance, the principles of stare decisis weigh heavily against overruling it now.... We do not think there is such justification for overruling Miranda. Miranda has become embedded in routine police practice to the point where the warnings have become part of our national culture.... While we have overruled our precedents when subsequent cases have undermined their doctrinal underpinnings, we do not believe that this has happened to the Miranda decision. If anything, our subsequent cases have reduced the impact of the Miranda rule on legitimate law enforcement while reaffirming the decision's core ruling that unwarned statements may not be used as evidence in the prosecution's case in chief. The disadvantage of the Miranda rule is that statements which may be by no means involuntary, made by a defendant who is aware of his 'rights,' may nonetheless be excluded and a guilty defendant go free as a result. But experience suggests that the totality-of-the-circumstances test which 3501 seeks to revive is more difficult than Miranda for law enforcement officers to conform to, and for courts to apply in a consistent manner. [citations omitted] ... In sum, we conclude that Miranda announced a constitutional rule that Congress may not supersede legislatively. Following the rule of stare decisis, we decline to overrule Miranda ourselves."

"Justice Scalia, with whom Justice Thomas joins, dissenting.

... It was once possible to characterize the so-called Miranda rule as resting (however implausibly) upon the proposition that what the statute here before us permits the admission at trial of un-Mirandized confessions violates the Constitution. That is the fairest reading of the Miranda case itself. The Court began by announcing that the Fifth Amendment privilege against self-incrimination applied in the context of extrajudicial custodial interrogation. Having extended the privilege into the confines of the station house, the Court liberally sprinkled throughout its sprawling 60 page opinion suggestions that, because of the compulsion inherent in custodial interrogation, the privilege was violated by any statement thus obtained that did not conform to the rules set forth in Miranda, or some functional equivalent. [citations omitted] ... So understood, Miranda was objectionable for innumerable reasons, not least the fact that cases spanning more than 70 years had rejected its core premise that, absent the warnings and an effective waiver of the right to remain silent and of the (hitherto unknown) right to have an attorney present, a statement obtained pursuant to custodial interrogation was necessarily the product of compulsion.... Moreover, history and precedent aside, the decision in Miranda, if read as an explication of what the Constitution requires, is preposterous. There is, for example, simply no basis in reason for concluding that a response to the very first question asked, by a suspect who already knows all of the rights described in the Miranda warning, is anything other than a volitional act.... And even if one assumes that the elimination of compulsion absolutely requires informing even the most knowledgeable suspect of his right to remain silent, it cannot conceivably require the right to have counsel present. There is a world of difference, which the Court recognized under the traditional voluntariness test but ignored in Miranda, between compelling a suspect to incriminate himself and preventing him from foolishly doing so of his own accord. Only the latter (which is not required by the Constitution) could explain the Court's inclusion of a right to counsel and the requirement that it, too, be knowingly and intelligently waived. Counsel's presence is not required to tell the suspect that he need not speak; the interrogators can do that. The only good reason for having counsel there is that he can be counted on to advise the suspect that he should not speak.... Preventing foolish (rather than compelled) confessions is likewise the only conceivable basis for the rules that courts must exclude any confession elicited by questioning conducted, without interruption, after the suspect has indicated a desire to stand on his right to remain silent, or initiated by police after the suspect has expressed a desire to have counsel present. Nonthreatening attempts to persuade the suspect to reconsider that initial decision are not, without more, enough to render a change of heart the product of anything other than the suspect's free will. Thus, what is most remarkable about the Miranda decision and what made it unacceptable as a matter of straightforward constitutional interpretation in the Marbury tradition is its palpable hostility toward the act of confession per se, rather than toward what the Constitution abhors, compelled confession. [citations omitted] ... For these reasons, and others more than adequately developed in the Miranda dissents and in the subsequent works of the decision's many critics, any conclusion that a violation of the Miranda rules necessarily amounts to a violation of the privilege against compelled self-incrimination can claim no support in history, precedent, or common sense, and as a result would at least presumptively be worth reconsidering even at this late date. But that is unnecessary, since the Court has (thankfully) long since abandoned the notion that failure to comply with Miranda's rules is itself a violation of the Constitution.... As the Court today acknowledges, since Miranda we have explicitly, and repeatedly, interpreted that decision as having announced, not the circumstances in which custodial interrogation runs afoul of the Fifth or Fourteenth Amendment, but rather only 'prophylactic' rules that go beyond the right against compelled self-incrimination.... Michigan v. Tucker. It held that exclusion of the "fruits" of a Miranda violation the statement of a witness whose identity the defendant had revealed while in custody was not required. The opinion explained that the question whether the "police conduct complained of directly infringed upon respondent's right against compulsory self-incrimination" was a "separate question" from "whether it instead violated only the prophylactic rules developed to protect that right." The "procedural safeguards" adopted in Miranda, the Court said, "were not themselves rights protected by the Constitution but were instead measures to insure that the right against compulsory self-incrimination was protected," and to "provide practical reinforcement for the right." Comparing the particular facts of the custodial interrogation with the "historical circumstances underlying the privilege," the Court concluded, unequivocally, that the defendant's statement could not be termed "involuntary as that term has been defined in the decisions of this Court," and thus that there had been no constitutional violation, notwithstanding the clear violation of the "procedural rules later established in Miranda." [citations omitted] ... The next year, in Oregon v. Hass, the Court held that a defendant's statement taken in violation of Miranda that was nonetheless voluntary could be used at trial for impeachment purposes. This holding turned upon the recognition that violation of Miranda is not unconstitutional compulsion, since statements obtained in actual violation of the privilege against compelled self-incrimination, "as opposed to . . . taken in violation of Miranda," quite simply "may not be put to any testimonial use whatever against [the defendant] in a criminal trial," including as impeachment evidence. [citations omitted] . . . Nearly a decade later, in New York v. Quarles, (1984), the Court relied upon the fact that '[t]he prophylactic Miranda warnings . . . are "not themselves rights protected by the Constitution," "to create a 'public safety' exception. In that case, police apprehended, after a chase in a grocery store, a rape suspect known to be carrying a gun. After handcuffing and searching him (and finding no gun)but before reading him his Miranda warnings the police demanded to know where the gun was. The defendant nodded in the direction of some empty cartons and responded that 'the gun is over there.' The Court held that both the unwarned statement 'the gun is over there' and the recovered weapon were admissible in the prosecution's case in chief under a 'public safety exception' to the 'prophylactic rules enunciated in Miranda.' The next year, the Court again declined to apply the 'fruit of the poisonous tree' doctrine to a Miranda violation, this time allowing the admission of a suspect's properly warned statement even though it had been preceded (and, arguably, induced) by an earlier inculpatory statement taken in violation of Miranda. Oregon v. Elstad (1985). . . . The Court seeks to avoid this conclusion by misdescribing these post-Miranda cases as mere dicta. The Court concedes only 'that there is language in some of our opinions that supports the view' that Miranda's protections are not 'constitutionally required.' It is not a matter of language; it is a matter of holdings. The proposition that failure to comply with Miranda's rules does not establish a constitutional violation was central to the holdings of Tucker, Hass, Quarles, and Elstad. [citations omitted] . . . Finally, the Court asserts that Miranda must be a 'constitutional decision' announcing a 'constitutional rule,' and thus immune to congressional modification, because we have since its inception applied it to the States. If this argument is meant as an invocation of stare decisis, it fails because, though it is true that our cases applying Miranda against the States must be reconsidered if Miranda is not required by the Constitution, it is likewise true that our cases (discussed above) based on the principle that Miranda is not required by the Constitution will have to be reconsidered if it is. So the stare decisis argument is a wash. If, on the other hand, the argument is meant as an appeal to logic rather than stare decisis, it is a classic example of begging the question: Congress's attempt to set aside Miranda, since it represents an assertion that violation of Miranda is not a violation of the Constitution, also represents an assertion that the Court has no power to impose Miranda on the States. To answer this assertion not by showing why violation of Miranda is a violation of the Constitution but by asserting that Miranda does apply against the States, is to assume precisely the point at issue. In my view, our continued application of the Miranda code to the States despite our consistent statements that running afoul of its dictates does not necessarily or even usually result in an actual constitutional violation, represents not the source of Miranda's salvation but rather evidence of its ultimate illegitimacy. . . . Thus, while I agree with the Court that 3501 cannot be upheld without also concluding that Miranda represents an illegitimate exercise of our authority to review state-court judgments, I do not share the Court's hesitation in reaching that conclusion. For while the Court is also correct that the doctrine of stare decisis demands some 'special justification' for a departure from longstanding precedent even precedent of the constitutional variety that criterion is more than met here.... The Court cites Patterson v. McLean Credit Union, (1989), as accurately reflecting our standard for overruling, I am pleased to accept, even though Patterson was speaking of overruling statutory cases and the standard for constitutional decisions is somewhat more lenient. What is set forth there reads as though it was written precisely with the current status of Miranda in mind "In cases where statutory precedents have been overruled, the primary reason for the Court's shift in position has been the intervening development of the law, through either the growth of judicial doctrine or further action taken by Congress. Where such changes have removed or weakened the conceptual underpinnings from the prior decision, ... or where the later law has rendered the decision irreconcilable with competing legal doctrines or policies, ... the Court has not hesitated to overrule an earlier decision." [citations omitted] ...

Neither am I persuaded by the argument for retaining Miranda that touts its supposed workability as compared with the totality-of-the-circumstances test it purported to replace. Miranda's proponents cite ad nauseam the fact that the Court was called upon to make difficult and subtle distinctions in applying the "voluntariness" test in some 30 odd due process "coerced confessions" cases in the 30 years between Brown v. Mississippi, 297 U.S. 278, 56 S.Ct. 461, 80 L.Ed. 682 (1936), and Miranda. It is not immediately apparent, however, that the judicial burden has been eased by the "bright-line" rules adopted in Miranda. In fact, in the 34 years since Miranda was decided, this Court has been called upon to decide nearly 60 cases involving a host of Miranda issues, most of them predicted with remarkable prescience by Justice White in his Miranda dissent. 384 U.S., at 545, 86 S.Ct. 1602.... But even were I to agree that the old totality-of-the-circumstances test was more cumbersome, it is simply not true that Miranda has banished it from the law and replaced it with a new test. Under the current regime, which the Court today retains in its entirety, courts are frequently called upon to undertake both inquiries. That is because, as explained earlier, voluntariness remains the constitutional standard, and as such continues to govern the admissibility for impeachment purposes of statements taken in violation of Miranda, the admissibility of the "fruits" of such statements, and the admissibility of statements challenged as unconstitutionally obtained despite the interrogator's compliance with Miranda.

5. The seeds of Miranda were, it is well argued, planted in some earlier state cases. See Wesley W. Horton & Brendon P. Levesque, "The Wheeler Court," 24 Quinnipiac L. Rev. 301, 306 (2006).

2. INTERPRETATION OF THE MIRANDA REQUIREMENTS

(a) THE MEANING OF "CUSTODY" AND "DEPRIVATION OF FREEDOM OF ACTION IN ANY SIGNIFICANT WAY"

Beckwith v. United States

Supreme Court of the United States, 1976.
425 U.S. 341, 96 S.Ct. 1612.

■ MR. CHIEF JUSTICE BURGER delivered the opinion of the Court.

The important issue presented in this case is whether a special agent of the Internal Revenue Service, investigating potential criminal income tax violations, must, in an interview with a taxpayer, not in custody, give the warnings called for by this Court's decision in Miranda v. Arizona.... After a considerable amount of investigation, two special agents of the Intelligence Division of the Internal Revenue Service met with petitioner in a private home where petitioner occasionally stayed. The senior agent testified that they went to see petitioner at this private residence at 8 a.m. in order to spare petitioner the possible embarrassment of being interviewed at his place of employment which opened at 10 a.m. Upon their arrival, they identified themselves to the person answering the door and asked to speak to petitioner. The agents were invited into the house and, when petitioner entered the room where they were waiting, they introduced themselves and, according to the testimony of the senior agent, Beckwith then excused himself for a period in excess of five minutes, to finish dressing. Petitioner then sat down at the dining room table with the agents; they presented their credentials and stated they were attached to the Intelligence Division and that one of their functions was to investigate the possibility of criminal tax fraud. They then informed petitioner that they were assigned to investigate his federal income tax liability for the years 1966 through 1971. The senior agent then read to petitioner from a printed card the following:

> "As a special agent, one of my functions is to investigate the possibility of criminal violations of the Internal Revenue laws, and related offenses.
>
> "Under the Fifth Amendment to the Constitution of the United States, I cannot compel you to answer any questions or to submit any information if such answers or information might tend to incriminate you in any way. I also advise you that anything which you say and any information which you submit may be used against you in any criminal proceeding which may be undertaken. I advise you further that you may, if you wish, seek the assistance of an attorney before responding."

Petitioner acknowledged that he understood his rights. The agents then interviewed him until about 11 o'clock. The agents described the conversation as "friendly" and "relaxed." The petitioner noted that the agents did not "press" him on any question he could not or chose not to answer.

Prior to the conclusion of the interview, the senior agent requested that petitioner permit the agents to inspect certain records. Petitioner indicated that they were at his place of employment. The agents asked if they could meet him there later. Traveling separately from petitioner the agents met petitioner approximately 45 minutes later and the senior agent advised the petitioner that he was not required to furnish any books or records; petitioner, however, supplied the books to the agents....

... The Court of Appeals affirmed the judgment of conviction. 510 F.2d 741 (1975). It noted that the reasoning of *Miranda* was based "in crucial part" on whether the suspect " 'has been taken into custody or otherwise deprived of his freedom in any significant way.' ", and agreed with the District Court that "Beckwith was neither arrested nor detained against his will." We agree with the analysis of the Court of Appeals and, therefore, affirm its judgment.

Petitioner contends that the "entire starting point" for the criminal prosecution brought against him secured from his own statements and disclosures during the interview with the Internal Revenue Agents from the Intelligence Division. He correctly points out that cases are assigned to the Intelligence Division only when there is some indication of criminal fraud and that, especially since tax offenses rarely result in pretrial custody, the taxpayer is clearly the "focus" of a criminal investigation when a matter is assigned to the Intelligence Division. Given the complexity of the tax structure and the confusion on the part of taxpayers between the civil and criminal function of the Internal Revenue Service, such a confrontation, argues petitioner, places the taxpayer under "psychological restraints" which are the functional, and, therefore, the legal equivalent of custody. In short we agree with Chief Judge Bazelon speaking for a unanimous Court of Appeals, that:

> "[t]he major thrust of Beckwith's argument is that the principle of *Miranda* should be extended to cover interrogation in non-custodial circumstances after a police investigation has focused on the suspect."

With the Court of Appeals, we "are not impressed with this argument in the abstract nor as applied to the particular facts of Beckwith's interrogation." It goes far beyond the reasons for that holding and such an extension of the *Miranda* requirements would cut this Court's holding in that case completely loose from its own explicitly stated rationale. The narrow issue before the Court in *Miranda* was presented very precisely in the opening paragraph of that opinion—"the admissibility of statements obtained from an individual who is subjected to *custodial* police interrogation." (Emphasis supplied.) The Court concluded that compulsion "is inherent in custodial surroundings," and, consequently, that special safeguards were required in the case of "incommunicado interrogation of individuals in a police-dominated atmosphere, resulting in self-incrimination statements without full warnings of constitutional rights." In subsequent decisions, the Court specifically stressed that it was the *custodial* nature of the interrogation which triggered the necessity for adherence in the specific requirements of its *Miranda* holding. Orozco v. Texas (1968).

Petitioner's argument that he was placed in the functional and, therefore, legal equivalent of the *Miranda* situation asks us now to ignore completely that *Miranda* was grounded squarely in the Court's explicit and detailed assessment of the peculiar "nature and setting of ... in-custody interrogation." That courts of appeals have so read *Miranda* is suggested by Chief Judge Lumbard in United States v. Caiello, 420 F.2d 471, 473 (C.A.2 1969):

> "It was the compulsive aspect of custodial interrogation, and not the strength or content of the government's suspicions at the time the questioning was conducted, which led the court to impose the *Miranda* requirements with regard to custodial questioning."

* * *

An interview with government agents in a situation such as the one shown by this record simply does not present the elements which the

Miranda Court found so inherently coercive as to require its holding. Although the "focus" of an investigation may indeed have been on Beckwith at the time of the interview in the sense that it was his tax liability which was under scrutiny, he hardly found himself in the custodial situation described by the *Miranda* Court as the basis for its holding. *Miranda* specifically defined "focus," for its purposes, as "questioning initiated by law enforcement officers *after* a person has been taken into custody or otherwise deprived of his freedom of action in any significant way." It may well be true, as petitioner contends that the "starting point" for the criminal prosecution was the information obtained from petitioner and the records exhibited by him. But this amounts to no more than saying that a tax return signed by a taxpayer can be the "starting point" for a prosecution.

We recognize, of course, that non-custodial interrogation might possibly in some situations, by virtue of some special circumstances, be characterized as one where "the behavior of ... law enforcement officials was such as to overbear petitioner's will to resist and bring about confessions not freely self-determined...." When such a claim is raised, it is the duty of an appellate court, including this Court, "to examine the entire record and make an independent determination of the ultimate issue of voluntariness." Proof that some kind of warnings were given or that none were given would be relevant evidence only on the issue of whether the questioning was in fact coercive. In the present case, however, as Chief Judge Bazelon noted, "[t]he entire interview was free of coercion."

■ Mr. Justice Stevens took no part in the consideration or decision of this case.

■ Mr. Justice Marshall, concurring in the judgment.

While the Internal Revenue Service agents in this case did not give petitioner the full warnings prescribed in *Miranda* they did give him [some] warning before questioning him.

* * *

Under the circumstances of this case, in which petitioner was not under arrest and the interview took place in a private home where petitioner occasionally stayed, the warning recited above satisfied the requirements of the Fifth Amendment. If this warning had not been given, however, I would not join the judgment of the Court.

■ Mr. Justice Brennan, dissenting.

I respectfully dissent. ...The fact that Beckwith had not been taken into formal "custody" is not determinative of the question whether the agents were required to give him the *Miranda* warnings ... the warnings are also mandated when the taxpayer is, as here, interrogated by Intelligence Division agents of the Internal Revenue Service in the surroundings where, as in the case of the subject in "custody," the practical compulsion to respond to questions about his tax returns is comparable to the psychological pressures described in *Miranda*. United States v. Oliver, 505 F.2d 301 (1974). Interrogation under conditions that have the practical consequence of compelling the taxpayer to make disclosures, and interrogation in "custody" having the same consequence, are in my view peas from the same pod. *Oliver* states the analysis with which I agree and required suppression of Beckwith's statements:

"... The fact of custody is emphasized in the [*Miranda*] opinion as having the practical consequence of compelling the accused to make disclosures. But the test also differentiates between the questioning of a mere witness and the interrogation of an accused for the purpose of securing his conviction; the test serves the purpose 'of determining when the adversary process has begun, i.e., when the investigative machinery of the government is directed toward the ultimate conviction of a particular individual and when, therefore, a suspect should be advised of his rights.'

* * *

"The requirement of warnings set forth in *Dickerson* rests on the same underlying rationale. While the commencement of adversary proceedings against Dickerson had not been marked by taking him into custody, the I.R.S., by assigning the matter to the Intelligence Division, had commenced the preparation of its criminal case. When the agents questioned him about his tax return, without clearly explaining their mission, the dual criminal-civil nature of an I.R.S. interrogation created three key misapprehensions for the taxpayer.

" 'Incriminating statements elicited in reliance upon the taxpayer's misapprehension as to *the nature of the inquiry, his obligation to respond*, and *the possible consequences of doing so* must be regarded as equally violative of constitutional protections as a custodial confession extracted without proper warnings.' 413 F.2d at 1116 (emphasis added).

"The practical effect of these misapprehensions during questioning of a taxpayer was to 'compel' him to provide information that could be used to obtain his conviction in a criminal tax fraud proceeding, in much the same way that placing a suspect under physical restraint leads to psychological compulsion. Thus, the misapprehensions are tantamount to the deprivation of the suspect's 'freedom of action in any significant way,' repeatedly referred to in *Miranda*."

I would reverse the judgment of conviction and remand to the District Court for a new trial.

Oregon v. Mathiason

Supreme Court of the United States, 1977.
429 U.S. 492, 97 S.Ct. 711.

■ PER CURIAM:

Carl Mathiason was convicted of first-degree burglary after a bench trial in which his confession was critical to the State's case. At trial he moved to suppress the confession as the fruit of questioning by the police not preceded by the warnings required in Miranda v. Arizona (1966). The trial court refused to exclude the confession because it found that Mathiason was not in custody at the time of the confession.

The ... Supreme Court of Oregon that court by a divided vote reversed the conviction. It found that although Mathiason had not been arrested or otherwise formally detained, "the interrogation took place in a 'coercive environment' " of the sort to which Miranda was intended to apply. The court conceded that its holding was contrary to decisions in other jurisdictions, and referred in particular to People v. Yukl, 25 N.Y.2d 585, 256 N.E.2d 172 (1969). We think that court has read Miranda too broadly, and we therefore reverse its judgment.

The Supreme Court of Oregon described the factual situation surrounding the confession as follows:

> "An officer of the State Police investigated a theft at a residence near Pendleton. He asked the lady of the house which had been burglarized if she suspected anyone. She replied that the defendant was the only one she could think of. The defendant was a parolee and a 'close associate' of her son. The officer tried to contact defendant on three or four occasions with no success. Finally, about 25 days after the burglary, the officer left his card at defendant's apartment with a note asking him to call because 'I'd like to discuss something with you.' The next afternoon the defendant did call. The officer asked where it would be convenient to meet. The defendant had no preference; so the officer asked if the defendant could meet him at the state patrol office in about an hour and a half, about 5:00 p.m. The patrol office was about two blocks from defendant's apartment. The building housed several state agencies.
>
> "The officer met defendant in the hallway, shook hands and took him into an office. The defendant was told he was not under arrest. The door was closed. The two sat across a desk. The police radio in another room could be heard. The officer told defendant he wanted to talk to him about a burglary and that his truthfulness would possibly be considered by the district attorney or judge. The officer further advised that the police believed defendant was involved in the burglary and [falsely stated that] defendant's fingerprints were found at the scene. The defendant sat for a few minutes and then said he had taken the property. This occurred within five minutes after defendant had come to the office. The officer then advised defendant of his Miranda rights and took a taped confession.
>
> "At the end of the taped conversation the officer told defendant he was not arresting him at this time; he was released to go about his job and return to his family. The officer said he was referring the case to the district attorney for him to determine whether criminal charges would be brought. It was 5:30 p.m. when the defendant left the office.
>
> "The officer gave all the testimony relevant to this issue. The defendant did not take the stand either at the hearing on the motion to suppress or at the trial."

The Supreme Court of Oregon reasoned from these facts that:

> "We hold the interrogation took place in a 'coercive environment.' The parties were in the offices of the State Police; they were alone behind closed doors; the officer informed the defendant he was a suspect in a theft and the authorities had evidence incriminating him in the crime; and the defendant was a parolee under supervision. We are of the opinion that this evidence is not overcome by the evidence that the defendant came to the office in response to a request and was told he was not under arrest."

Our decision in Miranda set forth rules of police procedure applicable to "custodial interrogation." "By custodial interrogation, we mean questioning initiated by law enforcement officers after a person has been taken into custody or otherwise deprived of his freedom of action in any significant way." Subsequently we have found the Miranda principle applicable to questioning which takes place in a prison setting during a suspect's term of imprisonment on a separate offense. Mathis v. United States (1968), and to questioning taking place in a suspect's home, after he has been arrested and is no longer free to go where he pleases, Orozco v. Texas (1969).

In the present case, however, there is no indication that the questioning took place in a context where respondent's freedom to depart was restricted in any way. He came voluntarily to the police station, where he was immediately informed that he was not under arrest. At the close of a one half-hour interview respondent did in fact leave the police station without hindrance. It is clear from these facts that Mathiason was not in custody "or otherwise deprived of his freedom of action in any significant way."

Such a noncustodial situation is not converted to one in which Miranda applies simply because a reviewing court concludes that, even in the absence of any formal arrest or restraint on freedom of movement, the questioning took place in a "coercive environment." Any interview of one suspected of a crime by a police officer will have coercive aspects to it, simply by virtue of the fact that the police officer is part of a law enforcement system which may ultimately cause the suspect to be charged with a crime. But police officers are not required to administer Miranda warnings to everyone whom they question. Nor is the requirement of warnings to be imposed simply because the questioning takes place in the station house, or because the questioned person is one whom the police suspect. Miranda warnings are required only where there has been such a restriction on a person's freedom as to render him "in custody." It was that sort of coercive environment to which Miranda by its terms was made applicable, and to which it is limited.

The officer's false statement about having discovered Mathiason's fingerprints at the scene was found by the Supreme Court of Oregon to be another circumstance contributing to the coercive environment which makes the Miranda rationale applicable. Whatever relevance this fact may have to other issues in the case, it has nothing to do with whether respondent was in custody for purposes of the Miranda rule.

The petition for certiorari is granted, the judgment of the Oregon Supreme Court is reversed, and the case is remanded for proceedings not inconsistent with this opinion.

Mr. Justice Brennan would grant the writ but dissents from the summary disposition and would set the case for oral argument.

■ MR. JUSTICE MARSHALL, dissenting.

* * *

... I recognize that Miranda is limited to custodial interrogations, but that is because, as we noted last Term, the facts in the Miranda cases raised only this "narrow issue." Beckwith v. United States. The rationale of Miranda, however, is not so easily cabined.

Miranda requires warnings to "combat" a situation in which there are "inherently compelling pressures which work to undermine the individual's will to resist and to compel him to speak where he would not otherwise do so freely." It is of course true, as the Court notes, that "[a]ny interview of one suspected of a crime by a police officer will have coercive aspects to it." But it does not follow that because police "are not required to administer Miranda warnings to everyone whom they question," that they need not administer warnings to *anyone*, unless the factual setting of the Miranda cases is replicated. Rather, faithfulness to Miranda requires us to distinguish situations that resemble the "coercive aspects" of custodial interrogation from those that more nearly resemble "[g]eneral on-the-scene questioning ... or other general questioning of citizens in the fact-finding process" which Miranda states usually can take place without warnings.

In my view, even if respondent were not in custody, the coercive elements in the instant case were so pervasive as to require Miranda-type warnings.[1] Respondent was interrogated in "privacy" and in "unfamiliar surroundings," factors on which Miranda places great stress. The investigation had focused on respondent. And respondent was subjected to some of the "deceptive stratagems" which called forth the Miranda decision. I therefore agree with the Oregon Supreme Court that to excuse the absence of warnings given these facts is "contrary to the rationale expressed in Miranda."

The privilege against self-incrimination "has always been as 'broad as the mischief against which it seeks to guard.' " Miranda v. Arizona, quoting Counselman v. Hitchcock (1892). Today's decision means, however, that the Fifth Amendment privilege does not provide full protection against mischiefs equivalent to, but different from custodial interrogation. It is therefore important to note that the state courts remain free, in interpreting state constitutions, to guard against the evil clearly identified by this case.

■ (Dissent of MR. JUSTICE STEVENS omitted.)

1. I do not rule out the possibility that lesser warnings would suffice when a suspect is not in custody but is subjected to a highly coercive atmosphere. See, e.g., Beckwith v. United States, 425 U.S. 341, 348–349, 96 S.Ct. 1612 (1976) (Marshall, J., concurring in judgment); ALI, Model Code of Pre–Arraignment Procedure § 110.1(2) (Approved Draft 1975) (suspects interrogated at police station must be advised of their right to leave and right to consult with counsel, relatives, or friends).

NOTES

1. The Supreme Court resolved all doubt on the question in Stansbury v. California, 511 U.S. 318, 114 S.Ct. 1526 (1994). In that case the state court considered "whether the investigation had focused on the subject" and concluded that it had not and, for that and other reasons, found no custody. A unanimous Court reversed and remanded, holding:

"It is well settled, then that a police officer's subjective view that the individual under questioning is a suspect, if undisclosed, does not bear upon the question whether the individual is in custody for purposes of Miranda. See F. Inbau, J. Reid, & J. Buckley, Criminal Interrogation and Confessions, 232, 236, 297–298 (3d ed. 1986). The same principle obtains if an officer's undisclosed assessment is that the person being questioned is not a suspect. In either instance, one cannot expect the person under interrogation to probe the officer's innermost thoughts. Save as they are communicated or otherwise manifested to the person being questioned, an officer's evolving but unarticulated suspicions do not affect the objective circumstances of an interrogation or interview, and thus cannot affect the Miranda custody inquiry.

"An officer's knowledge or beliefs may bear upon the custody issue if they are conveyed, by word or deed, to the individual being questioned. Those beliefs are relevant only to the extent they would affect how a reasonable person in the position of the individual being questioned would gauge the breadth of his or her 'freedom of action.' Even a clear statement from an officer that a person under interrogation is a prime suspect is not, in itself, dispositive of the custody issue, for some suspects are free to come and go until the police decide to make an arrest. The weight and pertinence of any communications regarding the officer's degree of suspicion will depend upon the facts and circumstances of the particular case. In sum, an officer's views concerning the nature of an interrogation, or beliefs concerning the potential culpability of the individual being questioned, may be one among many factors that bear upon the assessment whether that individual was in custody, but only if the officer's views or beliefs were somehow manifested to the individual under interrogation and would have affected how a reasonable person in that position would perceive his or her freedom to leave. (Of course, instances may arise in which the officer's undisclosed views are relevant in testing the credibility of his or her account of what happened during an interrogation; but it is the objective surroundings, and not any undisclosed views, that control the Miranda custody inquiry)."

What the suspect says may matter as well. One court has held that a suspect, not in custody, who says, "I put my hands on his throat and tried to suffocate him," may reasonably believe that he is not free to leave. An ordinary Miranda warning and waiver will be sufficient to permit continued interrogation—no special procedure is required because the "cat is out of the bag." State v. Champion, 533 N.W.2d 40 (Minn.1995).

2. One of the central issues of *Miranda* is the scope of the phrase "custodial interrogation". It is a complex issue simply because the determination of whether interrogation is "custodial" depends upon a consideration of many circumstances. It was the first issue explored by the courts because many interrogations conducted prior to *Miranda* were being judged against *Miranda* standards. Since adequate warnings were rarely given, the only matter for decision was whether the interrogation was custodial. In time, as the police established a practice of warning, the issues shifted to the adequacy of warning and waiver. Arguments over custody will never disappear; as often as the police may give warnings, they will not, nor can they be expected to invoke a warning and waiver process lasting from thirty seconds to a minute or more every time and every place they ask a citizen a question.

3. The intermesh of notions of focus and custody prior to the decision in *Beckwith* and *Mathiason* was a substantial issue. The majority of courts had generally held early on that (1) the fact an officer knows the suspect committed the crime, or (2) intends to arrest the suspect at the end of the interview, or (3) would not allow the suspect to leave if he tried, does *not* require that *Miranda* warnings be given if the interview is not otherwise custodial. People v. Hazel, 252 Cal.App.2d 412, 60 Cal.Rptr. 437 (1967). The most striking example of this interpretation of *Miranda* is People v. Allen, 28 A.D.2d 724, 281 N.Y.S.2d 602 (1967). There an officer with probable cause to arrest and an intention to arrest went to the suspect's home and questioned him in the presence of his family without telling him he was under arrest. After the conversation the suspect was arrested. The court held that warnings were not required.

These courts formulated an "objective" test of custody, i.e., whether under the circumstances of the case, a reasonable man would believe himself to be in custody. The key phrase is a "reasonable" belief on the part of the "reasonable" suspect. The mere subjective assertion of a suspect that he considered himself under arrest is not enough. Freije v. United States, 408 F.2d 100 (1st Cir.1969). Extraordinary frailties and sensitivities of the individual are not relevant. People v. Rodney P., 21 N.Y.2d 1, 286 N.Y.S.2d 225, 233 N.E.2d 255 (1967) holds that the issue is "not what the defendant thought but rather what a *reasonable man, innocent of any crime*, would have thought had he been in the defendant's position."

At the other end of the spectrum were those courts which have used focus as the definitive test. Those courts reasoned that custody arose at the latest when the officer has probable cause to arrest. See Campbell v. Superior Court, 106 Ariz. 542, 479 P.2d 685 (1971) (when officer determines arrest is to be made); People v. Orf, 172 Colo. 253, 472 P.2d 123 (1970) (little doubt in the officer's mind that they had the offender); State v. Kinn, 288 Minn. 31, 178 N.W.2d 888 (1970) (when the officer determines to take the suspect into custody).

Nearly all jurisdictions which initially decided some cases on focus tests have abandoned or modified them with the passage of time. See State v. Anderson, 937 S.W.2d 851 (Tenn.1996); People v. Hill, 429 Mich. 382, 415 N.W.2d 193 (1987); United States v. Bengivenga, 845 F.2d 593 (5th Cir.1988) (en banc);

The focus cases have also been criticized for ignoring the implication in Hoffa v. United States, 385 U.S. 293, 309–10, 87 S.Ct. 408 (1966), that whether the police have probable cause has no relevance to when the right of a suspect to receive warnings attaches. In *Hoffa*, an informer in Hoffa's group recorded several conversations in which the informer participated and which constituted evidence of jury tampering. In answer to the contention that when the informer and the Government had probable cause to arrest Hoffa, they should have done so instead of continuing to participate in additional conversations, the Court said:

> "Law enforcement officers are under no constitutional duty to call a halt to a criminal investigation the moment they have the minimum evidence to establish probable cause, a quantum of evidence which may fall short of the amount necessary to support a criminal conviction."

4. Does the custody test (and a fair reading of *Miranda*) permit what has been termed a "tactical" interrogation? This is a "designed" noncustodial interview conducted with an individual who is known or suspected of having committed a crime. The purpose of the interview is to secure damaging evidence. Consider the words of Chief Justice Weintraub in dealing with a *Miranda* problem, in State v. McKnight, 52 N.J. 35, 52–53, 243 A.2d 240 (1968):

> "There is no right to escape detection. There is no right to commit a perfect crime or to an equal opportunity to that end. The Constitution is

> not at all offended when a guilty man stubs his toe. On the contrary, it is decent to hope that he will. Nor is it dirty business to use evidence a defendant himself may furnish in the detectional stage.... As to the culprit who reveals his guilt unwittingly with no intent to shed his inner burden, it is no more unfair to use the evidence he thereby reveals than it is to turn against him clues at the scene of the crime which a brighter, better informed or more gifted criminal would not have left. ...It is consonant with good morals and the Constitution to exploit a criminal's ignorance or stupidity in the detectional process."

See People v. Robles, 72 N.Y.2d 689, 536 N.Y.S.2d 401, 533 N.E.2d 240 (1988) (police may consciously delay interrogation until other charges are resolved in order to avoid New York rule barring interrogation of one who has counsel on any charge).

A NOTE ON TACTICAL INTERROGATION

From the time Miranda was decided in 1966 there was always the issue of whether the police would be able to avoid giving the warnings by structuring the encounter with the suspect as non-custodial or as non-interrogation. There seemed to be little disagreement that the police could escape the strictures of Miranda by conducting interviews in settings which would objectively appear to be non-custodial or even by conducting interviews in police stations after telling the suspect that he or she was free to go. So too, courts agreed that volunteered statements made by persons in custody were admissible even in the absence of Miranda warnings although courts applied Miranda to practices which might not be interrogation but were the functional equivalent of interrogation. As time passed, the Supreme Court decided that non-compliance with Miranda would not bar use of a defendant's statement used solely to impeach the defendant's testimony in cases where the defendant took the stand at trial. (See Casebook pp. 809–812. Harris v. New York). The Supreme Court also held that an initial confession secured in violation of Miranda would not render a subsequent Miranda compliant confession inadmissible, if the initial confession was voluntary. (See Casebook p. 846. Oregon v. Elstad). The Court has been far less accepting of tactical decisions to omit the warning when interrogating a person *who is clearly in custody* in the expectation that an inadmissible confession will be repeated after warnings are given in a second interrogation after some passage of time. (See Missouri v. Seibert, 542 U.S. 600, 124 S.Ct. 2601 (2004))

In all of these circumstances—non-custody, non-interrogation, impeachment, subsequent confession—it is possible for the police to act deliberately to take advantage of these rules. Of course, in some cases the police conduct may not be chosen for purposes of avoiding Miranda. Most courts assumed that in the custody and interrogation cases, the police were often acting with the explicit purpose of avoiding the giving of warnings or of getting statements from suspects who were unwilling to answer direct questions. There was rarely direct evidence of the police purpose.

In recent years there have been some decisions in cases in which the police officers testified that they adopted a particular tactic because they wanted to take advantage of specific rules which limit the application of Miranda. In State v. Edrozo, 578 N.W.2d 719 (Minn.Sup.Ct.1998) an officer arrested a man who had been identified by five young men as someone who had attempted to run them over with his vehicle. Eventually the suspect was put into a squad car which contained a hidden tape recorder. The officer activated the recorder, asked some questions and elicited an exculpatory tale and then left the suspect and his companion alone in the squad car. It is clear from the act of turning on the recording device that the officer created a situation in which he hoped or expected that some damaging conversation would be recorded. The two men spoke with each other about threats to the people who complained against them and about how the police would not find any evidence that the suspect's car was involved in a collision. The Court found the recorded conversation to be admissible. It said:

"The only distinguishing feature of this case is that Edrozo was unaware that the police would later have access to his statements by means of the hidden tape recorder. Although it may be true ... that 'human nature' would inevitably encourage an individual in custody in a squad care to relieve his tension by speaking to a companion, that human tendency is not sufficient to transform this set of circumstances into the equivalent of interrogation. No active or coercive police conduct was involved; no subtle psychological ploys were used; no questions were asked at all."

Consider the opinions in Drury v. State, 368 Md. 331, 793 A.2d 567 (2002) in what might be characterized as the equivalent of a tactical interrogation designed to avoid custody in order to avoid giving warnings. In this case, there may have been an attempt to avoid interrogation.

RAKER, Judge.

On July, 14, 1996, Corporal Whaley went to the Hillside Market in response to a report of a break-in and theft at the market. The owner of the market told Corporal Whaley that he had found a tire iron behind the counter near the cash register. The officer looked around and saw that the rear door of the building had been pried open; it appeared to him that the tire iron had possibly been used to gain entry. Further investigation revealed that some property was missing, including several adult magazines, several cartons of cigarettes, bottles of liquor, and numerous Maryland Instant Scratch–Off Lottery tickets.

Later that evening, a deputy sheriff told Corporal Whaley that he had seen two men acting suspiciously near an alleyway close to the market. Corporal Whaley went to that location, looked through the trash, and found several adult magazines and a liquor bottle. The officer interviewed Karl Kirby, a suspect in the case, who led him to petitioner. Corporal Whaley went to petitioner's home, brought him to the police station, and sat him down "within the department" for questioning. Before advising petitioner of his rights pursuant to Miranda, Corporal Whaley placed the tire iron and the trash bag containing the magazines on a desk in front of petitioner. Petitioner made some statements about the tire iron and the magazines.

Corporal Whaley testified as follows:

Q: After you talked with Mr. Kirby, did you go visit Mr. Drury?

A: Yes. I picked Mr. Drury up for questioning, at which time I proceeded to show Mr. Drury the evidence which was retrieved. In showing Mr. Drury the tire iron that was retrieved from the actual incident area, Mr. Drury said, well, my fingerprints could be on that and are on hundreds of tire irons around Centreville, okay, and picking up the trash bag in which the magazines were located in, Mr. Drury proceeded to tell me the contents of the bag prior to me even stating what was in the bag myself.

Q: What did he tell you?

A: He said that he had touched the magazines that were in that bag.

On cross-examination, the officer testified as follows:

Q: So you took the evidence out and put it in front of Mr. Drury?

A: I put it up on the desk in front of myself.

* * * *

Q: And did you tell Mr. Drury that you were going to send this evidence off for fingerprints?

A: As I recall, yes sir.

Q: You told him all that before you Mirandized him?

A: Yes sir.

Q: And that's when you claim that he made some statement about his fingerprints possibly being on these physical items?

A: Yes sir.

Q: And then once he was Mirandized, he didn't want to talk to you?

A: No sir

Petitioner had been brought to the police station for the express purpose of questioning and, in fact, had been told so by Corporal Whaley. The police were not engaged in routine booking procedures; they were not required by any Maryland rule or procedure to read any document (other than the Miranda rights) to petitioner. Nonetheless, the officer placed the tire iron and the trash bag containing the stolen magazines on the table before petitioner before advising him of his Miranda rights. The officer told petitioner that he was going to send the evidence to be examined for fingerprints. Moreover, the officer testified that he "was presenting the evidence that was going to be used for questioning."

It appears to us that the only reasonable conclusion that can be drawn from the foregoing facts is that the officer should have known, in light of his having told petitioner that he was being brought in for questioning, that putting the evidence before petitioner and telling him that the items were going to be fingerprinted was reasonably likely to evoke an incriminating response from him. The only plausible explanation for the officer's conduct is that he expected to elicit a statement from petitioner.

Corporal Whaley had reason to know that his conduct was reasonably likely to elicit an incriminating response; indeed, there is no explanation for his conduct but that he expected to elicit such statements. In stark contrast to the cases relied on by the State, this is not a case where a suspect incriminated himself while police officers merely conducted routine arrest procedures. Accordingly, we hold that the trial court should have suppressed the statements that petitioner made before he was given his Miranda warnings.

CATHELL and BATTAGLIA, JJ., dissent.

Corporal Whaley went to Drury's residence from whence he and Drury traveled to the Centreville Police Department to discuss the matter.

The situation presented does not differ significantly from the scenario that arises when a suspect is in custody and is expressly questioned while being "booked," when Miranda warnings are not required.

From the majority's perspective, being brought by police officers to, and crossing the threshold of, the police station creates an environment which is instantaneously infused with coercive and compelling elements for a suspect. In their view, being taken to the police station itself could be sufficient to trigger the administration of Miranda warnings.

In the present case, Drury was not confronted with a situation in which he was questioned at all or asked for a response to which he would have to decide among truthfulness, falsity or silence ... Rather, he blurted out an explanation about his fingerprints and the trash bag, which he intended to be exculpatory and explanatory.

Furthermore, Corporal Whaley posed no question to Drury, which would call for an answer or expression of an opinion; the officer simply informed Drury that the evidence would be sent off for fingerprinting. See United States v. Allen, 247 F.3d 741, 765 (8th Cir.2001), ("Informing a suspect that he has been identified in a lineup contributes to the intelligent exercise of his judgment and may likely make firm his resolve to refuse to talk to the police without counsel."); United States v. Jackson, 863 F.2d 1168, 1172 (4th Cir.1989) (DEA agent's statement which was in the form of a declaration, not a question, was not the functional equivalent of an interrogation where defendant responded to hearing the agent's declaration by making a false exculpatory statement which was used against him at trial);

A practice that the police should know is reasonably likely to evoke an incriminating response from a suspect thus amounts to interrogation. But, since the police surely cannot be held accountable for the unforeseeable results of their words or actions, the definition of interrogation can extend only to words or actions on the part of police officers that they should have known were reasonably likely to elicit an incriminating response.

Ascertaining whether a particular situation involved an interrogation or the functional equivalent of an interrogation depends on the facts and circumstances of each case ... I believe that Corporal Whaley's direct factual statement that the items would be processed for fingerprinting does not rise to the level of coercion or compulsion contemplated in Innis as being the functional equivalent of an interrogation.

Although one could opine that Corporal Whaley was being deceptive in his placement of the evidence on the desk in front of Drury simultaneously with his declaration that the items would be processed for fingerprints, that opinion is not enough of a basis to require suppression of Drury's statement. It is not improper to confront a suspect with the factual or physical evidence of his or her allegedly criminal act. Numerous federal and state jurisdictions have rejected what Drury asserts when they have considered a wide range of factual scenarios which involved confronting a suspect with physical evidence of the crime or a verbal recitation to the suspect of the evidence against him.

It is also important to note that Drury was not arrested on July 15, 1996, after he gave his explanation. He was arrested on July 26, 1996, after additional investigation.

Thus, my analysis reveals that Drury's pre-Miranda custodial statements concerning the physical evidence of his crime were the product of his own free will and consciousness, rather than the result of an interrogation. I believe the majority stretches the holding of Innis to conclude that under the circumstances present in this case, of having the defendant view physical evidence of the crime and of having a police officer state that the evidence will be processed for fingerprints, is tantamount to an interrogation.

Yarborough v. Alvarado

United States Supreme Court.
541 U.S. 652, 124 S.Ct. 2140 (2004).

■ OPINION: JUSTICE KENNEDY delivered the opinion of the Court.

... The United States Court of Appeals for the Ninth Circuit ruled that a state court unreasonably applied clearly established law when it held that the respondent was not in custody for *Miranda* purposes. *Alvarado v. Hickman*, 316 F.3d 841 (2002). We disagree and reverse.

I

Paul Soto and respondent Michael Alvarado attempted to steal a truck in the parking lot of a shopping mall in Santa Fe Springs, California. Soto and Alvarado were part of a larger group of teenagers at the mall that night. Soto decided to steal the truck, and Alvarado agreed to help. Soto pulled out a .357 Magnum and approached the driver, Francisco Castaneda, who was standing near the truck emptying trash into a dumpster. Soto demanded money and the ignition keys from Castaneda. Alvarado, then five months short of his 18th birthday, approached the passenger side door of the truck and crouched down. When Castaneda refused to comply with Soto's demands, Soto shot Castaneda, killing him. Alvarado then helped hide Soto's gun.

Los Angeles County Sheriff's detective Cheryl Comstock led the investigation into the circumstances of Castaneda's death. About a month after the shooting, Comstock left word at Alvarado's house and also contacted Alvarado's mother at work with the message that she wished to speak with Alvarado. Alvarado's parents brought him to the Pico Rivera Sheriff's Station to be interviewed around lunchtime. They waited in the lobby while Alvarado went with Comstock to be interviewed. Alvarado contends that his parents asked to be present during the interview but were rebuffed.

Comstock brought Alvarado to a small interview room and began interviewing him at about 12:30 pm. The interview lasted about two hours, and was recorded by Comstock with Alvarado's knowledge. Only Comstock and Alvarado were present. Alvarado was not given a warning under *Miranda v. Arizona*, 384 U.S. 436 (1965). Comstock began the interview by asking Alvarado to recount the events on the night of the shooting. On that night, Alvarado explained, he had been drinking alcohol at a friend's house with some other friends and acquaintances. After a few hours, part of the group went home and the rest walked to a nearby mall to use its public telephones. In Alvarado's initial telling, that was the end of it. The group went back to the friend's home and "just went to bed."

Unpersuaded, Comstock pressed on:

"Q. Okay. We did real good up until this point and everything you've said it's pretty accurate till this point, except for you left out the shooting.

"A. The shooting?

"Q. Uh huh, the shooting.

"A. Well I had never seen no shooting.

"Q. Well I'm afraid you did.

"A. I had never seen no shooting.

"Q. Well I beg to differ with you. I've been told quite the opposite and we have witnesses that are saying quite the opposite.

"A. That I had seen the shooting?

"Q. So why don't you take a deep breath, like I told you before, the very best thing is to be honest.... You can't have that many people get involved in a murder and expect that some of them aren't going to tell the truth, okay? Now granted if it was maybe one person, you might be able to keep your fingers crossed and say, god I hope he doesn't tell the truth, but the problem is is that they have to tell the truth, okay? Now all I'm simply doing is giving you the opportunity to tell the truth and when we got that many people telling a story and all of a sudden you tell something way far fetched different."

At this point, Alvarado slowly began to change his story. First he acknowledged being present when the carjacking occurred but claimed that he did not know what happened or who had a gun. When he hesitated to say more, Comstock tried to encourage Alvarado to discuss what happened by appealing to his sense of honesty and the need to bring the man who shot Castaneda to justice. ("[W]hat I'm looking for is to see if you'll tell the truth"); ("I know it's very difficult when it comes time to 'drop the dime' on somebody[,] ... [but] if that had been your parent, your mother, or your brother, or your sister, you would darn well want [the killer] to go to jail 'cause no one has the right to take someone's life like that ..."). Alvarado then admitted he had helped the other man try to steal the truck by standing near the passenger side door. Next he admitted that the other man was Paul Soto, that he knew Soto was armed, and that he had helped hide the gun after the murder. Alvarado explained that he had expected Soto to scare the driver with the gun, but that he did not expect Soto to kill anyone. Toward the end of the interview, Comstock twice asked Alvarado if he needed to take a break. Alvarado declined. When the interview was over, Comstock returned with Alvarado to the lobby of the sheriff's station where his parents were waiting. Alvarado's father drove him home. (Cites omitted)

In few months later, the State of California charged Soto and Alvarado with first-degree murder and attempted robbery. Alvarado moved to suppress his statements from the Comstock interview. The trial court denied the motion on the ground that the interview was noncustodial. Alvarado and Soto were tried together, and Alvarado testified in his own defense. He offered an innocent explanation for his conduct, testifying that he happened to be standing in the parking lot of the mall when a gun went off nearby. The government's cross-examination relied on Alvarado's statement to Comstock. Alvarado admitted having made some of the statements but denied others. When Alvarado denied particular statements, the prosecution countered by playing excerpts from the audio recording of the interview.

During cross-examination, Alvarado agreed that the interview with Comstock "was a pretty friendly conversation," that there was "sort of a free flow between [Alvarado] and Detective Comstock," and that Alvarado did not "feel coerced or threatened in any way" during the interview, (cites omitted). The jury convicted Soto and Alvarado of first-degree murder and attempted robbery. The trial judge later reduced Alvarado's conviction to second-degree murder for his comparatively minor role in the offense. The judge sentenced Soto to life in prison and Alvarado to 15–years–to–life.

On direct appeal, the Second Appellate District Court of Appeal (hereinafter state court) affirmed.

The Court of Appeals for the Ninth Circuit reversed [on habeas corpus review]. *Alvarado* v. *Hickman*, 316 F.3d 841 (2002). First, the Court of Appeals held that the state court erred in failing to account for Alvarado's youth and inexperience when evaluating whether a reasonable person in his position would have felt free to leave... A minor with no criminal record would be more likely to feel coerced by police tactics and conclude he is under arrest than would an experienced adult, the Court of Appeals reasoned. This required extra "safeguards ... commensurate with the age and circumstances of a juvenile defendant." According to the Court of Appeals, the effect of Alvarado's age and inexperience was so substantial that it turned the interview into a custodial interrogation.

We granted certiorari.

II

. . .

Our more recent cases instruct that custody must be determined based on how a reasonable person in the suspect's situation would perceive his circumstances. In *Berkemer v. McCarty*, 468 U.S. 420 (1984), a police officer stopped a suspected drunk driver and asked him some questions. Although the officer reached the decision to arrest the driver at the beginning of the traffic stop, he did not do so until the driver failed a sobriety test and acknowledged that he had been drinking beer and smoking marijuana. The Court held the traffic stop noncustodial despite the officer's intent to arrest because he had not communicated that intent to the driver. "A policeman's unarticulated plan has no bearing on the question whether a suspect was 'in custody' at a particular time," the Court explained. "[T]he only relevant inquiry is how a reasonable man in the suspect's position would have understood his situation." In a footnote, the Court cited a New York state case for the view that an objective test was preferable to a subjective test in part because it does not " 'place upon the police the burden of anticipating the frailties or idiosyncrasies of every person whom they question.' " (quoting *People* v. *P.*, 21 N.Y. 2d 1, 9–10 (1967)).

. . .

Finally, in *Thompson v. Keohane*, 516 U.S. 99 (1995), the Court offered the following description of the *Miranda* custody test:

> "Two discrete inquiries are essential to the determination: first, what were the circumstances surrounding the interrogation; and second, given those circumstances, would a reasonable person have felt he or she was not at liberty to terminate the interrogation and leave. Once

the scene is set and the players' lines and actions are reconstructed, the court must apply an objective test to resolve the ultimate inquiry: was there a formal arrest or restraint on freedom of movement of the degree associated with a formal arrest." 516 U.S., at 112. (internal quotation marks omitted).

We turn now to the case before us and ask if the state-court adjudication of the claim "involved an unreasonable application" of clearly established law when it concluded that Alvarado was not in custody.... we conclude that the state court's application of our clearly established law was reasonable. Ignoring the deferential standard of § 2254(d)(1) for the moment, it can be said that fair-minded jurists could disagree over whether Alvarado was in custody. On one hand, certain facts weigh against a finding that Alvarado was in custody. The police did not transport Alvarado to the station or require him to appear at a particular time ... They did not threaten him or suggest he would be placed under arrest. Alvarado's parents remained in the lobby during the interview, suggesting that the interview would be brief. In fact, according to trial counsel for Alvarado, he and his parents were told that the interview was " 'not going to be long.' " ... During the interview, Comstock focused on Soto's crimes rather than Alvarado's. Instead of pressuring Alvarado with the threat of arrest and prosecution, she appealed to his interest in telling the truth and being helpful to a police officer. In addition, Comstock twice asked Alvarado if he wanted to take a break. At the end of the interview, Alvarado went home. All of these objective facts are consistent with an interrogation environment in which a reasonable person would have felt free to terminate the interview and leave. Indeed, a number of the facts echo those of *Mathiason*, a *per curiam* summary reversal in which we found it "clear from these facts" that the suspect was not in custody.

Other facts point in the opposite direction. Comstock interviewed Alvarado at the police station. The interview lasted two hours, four times longer than the 30–minute interview in *Mathiason*. Unlike the officer in *Mathiason*, Comstock did not tell Alvarado that he was free to leave. Alvarado was brought to the police station by his legal guardians rather than arriving on his own accord, making the extent of his control over his presence unclear. Counsel for Alvarado alleges that Alvarado's parents asked to be present at the interview but were rebuffed, a fact that—if known to Alvarado—might reasonably have led someone in Alvarado's position to feel more restricted than otherwise. These facts weigh in favor of the view that Alvarado was in custody.

These differing indications lead us to hold that the state court's application of our custody standard was reasonable. The Court of Appeals was nowhere close to the mark when it concluded otherwise. Although the question of what is an "unreasonable application" of law might be difficult in some cases, it is not difficult here. The custody test is general, and the state court's application of our law fits within the matrix of our prior decisions. We cannot grant relief under [habeas corpus law] by conducting our own independent inquiry into whether the state court was correct as a *de novo* matter. "[A] federal habeas court may not issue the writ simply because that court concludes in its independent judgment that the state-court decision applied [the law] incorrectly." *Woodford v. Visciotti*, 537 U.S. 19, 24–25 (2002) *(per curiam)*. Relief is available under § 2254(d)(1) only if the state court's decision is objectively unreasonable ... Under that standard, relief cannot be granted.

III

The Court of Appeals reached the opposite result by placing considerable reliance on Alvarado's age and inexperience with law enforcement. Our Court has not stated that a suspect's age or experience is relevant to the *Miranda* custody analysis, and counsel for Alvarado did not press the importance of either factor on direct appeal or in habeas proceedings. According to the Court of Appeals, however, our Court's emphasis on juvenile status in other contexts demanded consideration of Alvarado's age and inexperience here. The Court of Appeals viewed the state court's failure to "extend a clearly established legal principle [of the relevance of juvenile status] to a new context" as objectively unreasonable in this case, requiring issuance of the writ.

. . .

There is an important conceptual difference between the *Miranda* custody test and the line of cases from other contexts considering age and experience. The *Miranda* custody inquiry is an objective test. As we stated in *Keohane*, "[o]nce the scene is set and the players' lines and actions are reconstructed, the court must apply an objective test to resolve the ultimate inquiry." The objective test furthers "the clarity of [Miranda's] rule," ensuring that the police do not need "to make guesses as to [the circumstances] at issue before deciding how they may interrogate the suspect." To be sure, the line between permissible objective facts and impermissible subjective experiences can be indistinct in some cases. It is possible to subsume a subjective factor into an objective test by making the latter more specific in its formulation. Thus the Court of Appeals styled its inquiry as an objective test by considering what a "reasonable 17-year-old, with no prior history of arrest or police interviews' would perceive."

At the same time, the objective *Miranda* custody inquiry could reasonably be viewed as different from doctrinal tests that depend on the actual mindset of a particular suspect, where we do consider a suspect's age and experience. For example, the voluntariness of a statement is often said to depend on whether "the defendant's will was overborne," *Lynumn v. Illinois*, 372 U.S. 528, 534 (1963), a question that logically can depend on "the characteristics of the accused." *Schneckloth v. Bustamonte*, 412 U.S. 218, 226 (1973). The characteristics of the accused can include the suspect's age, education, and intelligence, see *ibid.*, as well as a suspect's prior experience with law enforcement, see *Lynumn*, *supra*, at 534, 9 L. Ed. 2d 922. In concluding that there was "no principled reason" why such factors should not also apply to the *Miranda* custody inquiry ... the Court of Appeals ignored the argument that the custody inquiry states an objective rule designed to give clear guidance to the police, while consideration of a suspect's individual characteristics—including his age—could be viewed as creating a subjective inquiry. Cf. *Mathiason*, 429 U.S., at 495–496 (noting that facts arguably relevant to whether an environment is coercive may have "nothing to do with whether respondent was in custody for purposes of the *Miranda* rule"). For these reasons, the state court's failure to consider Alvarado's age does not provide a proper basis for finding that the state court's decision was an unreasonable application of clearly established law.

Indeed, reliance on Alvarado's prior history with law enforcement was improper not only under the deferential standard of 28 U.S.C. § 2254(d)(1), but also as a *de novo* matter. In most cases, police officers will not know a suspect's interrogation history. Even if they do, the relationship between a suspect's past experiences and the likelihood a reasonable person with that experience would feel free to leave often will be speculative. True, suspects with prior law enforcement experience may understand police procedures and reasonably feel free to leave unless told otherwise. On the other hand, they may view past as prologue and expect another in a string of arrests. We do not ask police officers to consider these contingent psychological factors when deciding when suspects should be advised of their *Miranda* rights. The inquiry turns too much on the suspect's subjective state of mind and not enough on the "objective circumstances of the interrogation."

The state court considered the proper factors and reached a reasonable conclusion. The judgment of the Court of Appeals is reversed.

■ JUSTICE O'CONNOR, concurring.

[Omitted]

■ JUSTICE BREYER, with whom JUSTICE STEVENS, JUSTICE SOUTER, and JUSTICE GINSBURG join, dissenting.

... To put the question in terms of federal law's well-established legal standards: Would a "reasonable person" in Alvarado's "position" have felt he was "at liberty to terminate the interrogation and leave"? ... A court must answer this question in light of "all of the circumstances surrounding the interrogation." And the obvious answer here is "no."

A

The law in this case asks judges to apply, not arcane or complex legal directives, but ordinary common sense. Would a reasonable person in Alvarado's position have felt free simply to get up and walk out of the small room in the station house at will during his 2–hour police interrogation? I ask the reader to put himself, or herself, in Alvarado's circumstances and then answer that question: Alvarado hears from his parents that he is needed for police questioning. His parents take him to the station. On arrival, a police officer separates him from his parents. His parents ask to come along, but the officer says they may not. Another officer says, " 'What do we have here; we are going to question a suspect.' "

The police take Alvarado to a small interrogation room, away from the station's public area. A single officer begins to question him, making clear in the process that the police have evidence that he participated in an attempted carjacking connected with a murder. When he says that he never saw any shooting, the officer suggests that he is lying, while adding that she is "giving [him] the opportunity to tell the truth" and "tak[e] care of [him]self." Toward the end of the questioning, the officer gives him permission to take a bathroom or water break. After two hours, by which time he has admitted he was involved in the attempted theft, knew about the gun, and helped to hide it, the questioning ends.

What reasonable person in the circumstances—brought to a police station by his parents at police request, put in a small interrogation room, questioned for a solid two hours, and confronted with claims that there is strong evidence that he participated in a serious crime, could have thought to himself, "Well, anytime I want to leave I can just get up and walk out"? If the person harbored any doubts, would he still think he might be free to leave once he recalls that the police officer has just refused to let his parents remain with him during questioning? Would he still think that he, rather than the officer, controls the situation?

There is only one possible answer to these questions. A reasonable person would *not* have thought he was free simply to pick up and leave in the middle of the interrogation. I believe the California courts were clearly wrong to hold the contrary, and the Ninth Circuit was right in concluding that those state courts unreasonably applied clearly established federal law.

B

What about the majority's view that "fair-minded jurists could disagree over whether Alvarado was in custody"? Consider each of the facts it says "weigh against a finding" of custody:

> (1) "*The police did not transport Alvarado to the station or require him to appear at a particular time.*" True. His parents brought him to the station at police request. But why does that matter? The relevant question is whether Alvarado came to the station of his own free will or submitted to questioning voluntarily . . . And the involvement of Alvarado's parents suggests *in*voluntary, not voluntary, behavior on Alvarado's part.
>
> (2) "*Alvarado's parents remained in the lobby during the interview, suggesting that the interview would be brief. In fact, [Alvarado] and his parents were told that the interview 'was not going to be long.'*" Whatever was communicated to Alvarado *before* the questioning began, the fact is that the interview was not brief, nor, after the first half hour or so, would Alvarado have expected it to be brief. And those are the relevant considerations.
>
> (3) "*At the end of the interview, Alvarado went home.*" As the majority acknowledges, our recent case law makes clear that the relevant question is how a reasonable person would have gauged his freedom to leave *during*, not *after*, the interview.
>
> (4) "*During the interview, [Officer] Comstock focused on Soto's crimes rather than Alvarado's.*" In fact, the police officer characterized Soto as the ringleader, while making clear that she knew Alvarado had participated in the attempted carjacking during which Castaneda was killed. Her questioning would have reinforced, not diminished, Alvarado's fear that he was not simply a witness, but also suspected of having been involved in a serious crime.

(5) "[The officer did not] pressur[e] Alvarado with the threat of arrest and prosecution . . . [but instead] appealed to his interest in telling the truth and being helpful to a police officer." This factor might be highly significant were the question one of "coercion." But it is not. The question is whether Alvarado would have felt free to terminate the interrogation and leave. In respect to that question, police politeness, while commendable, does not significantly help the majority.

(6) "*Comstock twice asked Alvarado if he wanted to take a break.*" This circumstance, emphasizing the officer's control of Alvarado's movements, makes it *less* likely, not *more* likely, that Alvarado would have thought he was free to leave at will.

The facts to which the majority points make clear what the police did *not* do, for example, come to Alvarado's house, tell him he was under arrest, handcuff him, place him in a locked cell, threaten him, or tell him explicitly that he was not free to leave. But what is important here is what the police *did* do—namely, have Alvarado's parents bring him to the station, put him with a single officer in a small room, keep his parents out, let him know that he was a suspect, and question him for two hours. These latter facts compel a single conclusion: A reasonable person in Alvarado's circumstances would *not* have felt free to terminate the interrogation and leave.

C

What about Alvarado's youth? The fact that Alvarado was 17 helps to show that he was unlikely to have felt free to ignore his parents' request to come to the station. See *Schall v. Martin*, 467 U.S. 253, 265 (1984) (juveniles assumed "to be subject to the control of their parents"). And a 17–year–old is more likely than, say, a 35–year–old, to take a police officer's assertion of authority to keep parents outside the room as an assertion of authority to keep their child inside as well.

The majority suggests that the law might *prevent* a judge from taking account of the fact that Alvarado was 17. I can find nothing in the law that supports that conclusion. Our cases do instruct lower courts to apply a "reasonable person" standard. But the "reasonable person" standard does not require a court to pretend that Alvarado was a 35–year–old with aging parents whose middle-aged children do what their parents ask only out of respect. Nor does it say that a court should pretend that Alvarado was the statistically determined "average person"—a working, married, 35–year–old white female with a high school degree. See U.S. Dept. of Commerce, Bureau of Census, Statistical Abstract of the United States: 2003 (123d ed.).

. . .

In the present context, that of *Miranda*'s "in custody" inquiry, the law has introduced the concept of a "reasonable person" to avoid judicial inquiry into subjective states of mind, and to focus the inquiry instead upon objective circumstances that are known to both the officer and the suspect and that are likely relevant to the way a person would understand his situation.... This focus helps to keep *Miranda* a workable rule....

In this case, Alvarado's youth is an objective circumstance that was known to the police. It is not a special quality, but rather a widely shared characteristic that generates commonsense conclusions about behavior and perception. To focus on the circumstance of age in a case like this does not complicate the "in custody" inquiry. And to say that courts should ignore widely shared, objective characteristics, like age, on the ground that only a (large) *minority* of the population possesses them would produce absurd results, the present instance being a case in point. I am not surprised that the majority points to no case suggesting any such limitation ...

Nor am I surprised that the majority makes no real argument at all explaining *why* any court would believe that the objective fact of a suspect's age could *never* be relevant. But see *ante* (O'Connor, J., concurring) ("There may be cases in which a suspect's age will be relevant to the *Miranda* 'custody' inquiry"). The majority does discuss a suspect's "history with law enforcement," *ante*—a bright red herring in the present context where Alvarado's youth (an objective fact) simply helps to show (with the help of a legal presumption) that his appearance at the police station was not voluntary.

. . .

As I have said, the law in this case is clear. This Court's cases establish that, even if the police do not tell a suspect he is under arrest, do not handcuff him, do not lock him in a cell, and do not threaten him, he may nonetheless reasonably believe he is not free to leave the place of questioning—and thus be in custody for *Miranda* purposes. [cites omitted]

Our cases also make clear that to determine how a suspect would have "gaug[ed]" his "freedom of movement," a court must carefully examine all of the circumstances surrounding the interrogation, including, for example, how long the interrogation lasted (brief and routine or protracted?), how the suspect came to be questioned (voluntarily or against his will?); where the questioning took place (at a police station or in public?); and what the officer communicated to the individual during the interrogation (that he was a suspect? that he was under arrest? that he was free to leave at will?). In the present case, every one of these factors argues—and argues strongly—that Alvarado was in custody for *Miranda* purposes when the police questioned him. [*cites omitted*]

Common sense, and an understanding of the law's basic purpose in this area, are enough to make clear that Alvarado's age—an objective, widely shared characteristic about which the police plainly knew—is also relevant to the inquiry. Unless one is prepared to pretend that Alvarado is someone he is not, a middle-aged gentleman, well-versed in police practices, it seems to me clear that the California courts made a serious mistake. I agree with the Ninth Circuit's similar conclusions. Consequently, I dissent.

NOTES

1. How are facts and circumstances defined and weighed by the courts in determining custody? A summary of the rules follows.

(a) Place of Interrogation

The place of interrogation is a vital, but not conclusive factor. Usually the cases evince a concern with the location of the interrogation but the physical circumstances of the room in which the interrogation takes place may be significant. United States v. Lackey, 413 F.2d 655 (7th Cir.1969) (small room); People v. Bryant, 87 Ill.App.2d 238, 231 N.E.2d 4 (1967) (closed room); United States v. Gravens, 129 F.3d 974 (7th Cir.1997) (back of police car).

In all three of the cases decided along with *Miranda*, the suspect was questioned in a police station after arrest, and usually police station interrogation is custodial.

Oregon v. Mathiason found a station house interrogation to be non-custodial as did earlier cases. Clark v. United States, 400 F.2d 83 (9th Cir.1968) (two drivers in an accident; both brought into station for report); People v. Pugliese, 26 N.Y.2d 478, 311 N.Y.S.2d 851, 260 N.E.2d 499 (1970) (defendant was a complainant of whom police were suspicious and who was asked to report under oath).

There are cases in which the defendant walks into the station essentially on his own initiative. In People v. Hill, 70 Cal.2d 678, 76 Cal.Rptr. 225, 452 P.2d 329 (1969), the defendant called the police station and volunteered some information concerning a crime; he then offered to and did come to the police station and gave a statement. The questioning was held to be non-custodial. Questioning in police vehicles is also common and where the presence of the person interrogated is clearly a result of invitation the questioning has been held non-custodial. Wussow v. State, 507 S.W.2d 792 (Tex.Crim.App.1974) (a request to sit in a police car does not create custody when the alternative is to stand in a heavy rain). Police car questioning, however, has usually been characterized as custodial. State v. Saunders, 102 Ariz. 565, 435 P.2d 39 (1967); Myers v. State, 3 Md.App. 534, 240 A.2d 288 (1968).

In Mathis v. United States, 391 U.S. 1, 88 S.Ct. 1503 (1968), the Court, by a vote of 5–3, reversed the Fifth Circuit Court and held that one who was incarcerated in a penitentiary for one offense was in custody for purposes of interrogation conducted by I.R.S. agents with respect to another offense. Indeed the general rule is that if the suspect is in jail he is in custody for purposes of any interrogation. But some persons doubt that *Mathis* would be decided the same way today, or that there is a per se rule deeming a person to be in custody for *Miranda* purposes if he or she is incarcerated on other charges. Mathis is not applied to investigations of crimes in prison. People v. Alls, 83 N.Y.2d 94, 629 N.E.2d 1018, 608 N.Y.S.2d 139 (1993).

In Commonwealth v. O'Toole, 351 Mass. 627, 223 N.E.2d 87 (1967) the City Manager of Revere, Massachusetts was (and knew he was) the principal suspect in a rather large series of misappropriations of city funds. He was asked to come to the prosecutor's office where he was asked for an explanation of certain records and disbursements. His explanations were used against him at his trial on grounds he was not in custody in the prosecutor's office nor brought there under arrest. The courts have regarded interrogations in prosecutor's office with a fair degree of willingness to find them non-custodial. United States v. Micieli, 594 F.2d 102 (5th Cir.1979).

Ordinarily interrogation in a suspect's home is not custodial, but this principle is not absolute. Avery v. State, 122 Nev. 278, 129 P.3d 664 (2006) In Orozco v. Texas, 394 U.S. 324, 89 S.Ct. 1095 (1969), a suspect was questioned at 4 a.m. in his bedroom by four officers, one of whom testified that the suspect was under arrest. The Court held that the suspect was the subject of custodial interrogation even though the questioning was brief and took place in his own bedroom. The key factors were the time of the interrogation (at 4 a.m., and after the officers were told defendant was asleep), the number of officers, and the evidence of formal arrest (though this is unclear). See United States v. Mittel–Carey, 493 F.3d 36 (1st Cir.2007) (Custody found where eight officers entered to execute search warrant, refused to allow defendant to move about and questioned him in a hostile manner for two hours)

Most cases of interrogation at homes involve less severe circumstances, and generally the holding is that questioning a suspect in his own home without arrest is not custodial interrogation. United States v. Axsom, 289 F.3d, 496 (8th Cir.2002) (questioned in home during search by nine officers); People v. Rodney P., 21 N.Y.2d 1, 286 N.Y.S.2d 225, 233 N.E.2d 255 (1967) (defendant was questioned in his back yard); People v. Miller, 71 Cal.2d 459, 78 Cal.Rptr. 449, 455 P.2d 377 (1969) (the questioning of defendant in his front yard was non-custodial although the officer suspected the defendant to be involved in what turned out to be a homicide); Virgin Islands v. Berne, 412 F.2d 1055 (3d Cir.1969) (officers questioned a man who they strongly suspected committed rape—he was questioned at his home and surrendered some clothes from the trunk of his car. Questioning of a person at his friend's or relative's home is also generally ruled non-custodial). Steigler v. Superior Court, 252 A.2d 300 (Del.1969) (neighbor's home); People v. Rogers, 14 Mich.App. 207, 165 N.W.2d 337 (1968) (grandmother's house). There have been a few, but very few cases in which custodial interrogation was held to have occurred in the suspect's home.

Interrogation of a suspect in his place of business is usually considered non-custodial. As in the case of homes, the place of business represents a familiar surrounding. United States v. Gallagher, 430 F.2d 1222 (7th Cir.1970) (suspect's law office);United States v. Courtney, 463 F.3d 333 (5th Cir.2006); United States v. Dockery, 736 F.2d 1232 (8th Cir.1984) (bank employee ordered by superior to report to manager's office where she is questioned is not in custody); but see United States v. Nash, 563 F.2d 1166 (5th Cir.1977) (bank clerk interrogated in bank security office).

The rationale of familiar surroundings applicable to questioning in homes and offices does not invariably apply when the interrogation occurs in a restaurant or other public place. However, the usual view in such cases is that the interrogation is not custodial. Owens v. State, 399 Md. 388, 924 A.2d 1072 (2007) This result is due to the fact that the suspect is, if not in a completely familiar place, at least in a place of his own choosing. Another significant factor is the lack of isolation from the outside world and the distinct absence of police station atmosphere. See Lucas v. United States, 408 F.2d 835 (9th Cir.1969) (night club); United States v. Messina, 388 F.2d 393 (2d Cir.1968) (park bench and restaurant). Compare United States v. Ward, 961 F.2d 1526 (10th Cir.1992) (train compartment).

Questioning of a suspect who is confined in a hospital as a patient, but who is not under arrest, is often held not to be custodial interrogation. State v. Zucconi, 50 N.J. 361, 235 A.2d 193 (1967) (defendant involved in a fatal auto accident and the principal evidence against him were his admissions on two separate occasions to an interrogating State Trooper that he was driving the car; the court said, "defendant never was in the custody of the police nor was he deprived of his freedom by authorities). The questioning here took place in defendant's hospital room and at his home, surroundings totally lacking in the compelling atmosphere inherent in the process of in-custody interrogation". On the other hand hospital interviews have often been held custodial in nature. See Shedrick v. State, 10 Md.App. 579, 271 A.2d 773 (1970) (suspect at hospital is considered in custody when, aware of the victim's poor condition, he was questioned in a small room by two officers). In a dispute over whether a person was in custody when transported to a hospital in a police car, a divided court found custody where an officer said to a driver, who had been in a crash, "I've got to investigate the accident. Why don't you just get into my car and

I'll take you to [a nearby hospital]". The court relied upon the fact that the driver had wanted to go to a different hospital and the officer's statement followed on the heels of a request to leave and go to another hospital. See, State v. Veiman, 249 Neb. 875, 546 N.W.2d 785 (1996).

In *Miranda* the Court said that its decision was "not intended to hamper the traditional function of police officers in investigating crime ... General on-the-scene questioning as to facts surrounding a crime or other general questioning of citizens in the fact finding process is not affected by our holding. It is an act of responsible citizenship for individuals to give whatever information they may have to aid in law enforcement. In such situations the compelling atmosphere inherent in the process of in-custody interrogation is not necessarily present." Accordingly, it was decided early on that questioning of a suspect prior to arrest near the scene of crime is not custodial interrogation: Laury v. State, 260 A.2d 907 (Del.1969) (accosting suspect at robbery scene); Nevels v. State, 216 So.2d 529 (Miss.1968) (at the end of chase and search); State v. Largo, 24 Utah 2d 430, 473 P.2d 895 (1970) (interrogation at school of sixty boys concerning incident where some boys invaded a girl's dormitory and raped one girl); The most commonly reported instance of on-the-scene questioning involves homicides: People v. Probasco, 795 P.2d 1330 (Colo. 1990) (inquiry made of police officer who had shot a person during traffic stop); Tate v. State, 219 Tenn. 698, 413 S.W.2d 366 (1967) (the defendant shot his boss at the office and his defense at trial was self-defense). Officers testified that they arrived on the scene and asked who did the shooting. In the presence of others, defendant said that he did. The officers asked why and he said because the boss was firing him from his job. See also Bell v. State, 442 S.W.2d 716 (Tex.Crim.App.1969) ("what happened?").

Can it be argued that, even if the officer at the scene of a crime asks one or more persons to remain at the scene, this should not be thought to establish custody? The Court in *Miranda* referred to deprivation "of freedom of action in any significant way" and declared that its opinion did not apply to "general on-the-scene" interviews, and that "it is an act of responsible citizenship" for persons to give information to the police. Did the Court envision the brief retention of all potential witnesses at the scene of a crime and exclude this kind of interviewing from *Miranda?* Would an ordinary innocent person directed by an officer not to leave the scene of a crime consider himself in custody or under arrest? See Commonwealth v. Podlaski, 377 Mass. 339, 385 N.E.2d 1379 (1979) (non-custodial).

Another form of general on-the-scene questioning occurs when an officer makes inquiries of persons on the public ways under suspicious circumstances. See United States v. Thomas, 396 F.2d 310 (2d Cir.1968) (suspect prowling in railroad yard); United States v. Diaz, 427 F.2d 636 (1st Cir.1970) (request for identification from a hitchhiker); United States v. Owens, 431 F.2d 349 (5th Cir.1970) (where an officer simply finds someone he is seeking on the street and there makes inquiries of him; the incident is non-custodial in nature); State v. Webster, 20 Wash.App. 128, 579 P.2d 985 (1978). The basic premise underlying these decisions is that the officers were confronted with suspicious circumstances which could have been resolved with an explanation from the person questioned. The absence of a custodial atmosphere is significant but the investigative nature of the encounter is foremost. Of course, under certain circumstances street and scene encounters may be deemed custodial. See United States v. Ward, 488 F.2d 162 (9th Cir.1973) (en banc).

(b) Time of Interrogation

The intrusion of police in the early morning hours to make inquiries would create serious doubts as to whether an ordinary man would consider himself in custody. (Consider Orozco v. Texas, 394 U.S. 324, 89 S.Ct. 1095 (1969).) Of course, on the scene questioning shortly after the commission of a crime may permissibly take place at odd hours, but seeking out someone some distance away from the scene, as was done in *Orozco*, may create a custodial situation.

(c) The Persons Present at the Interrogation

The language of *Miranda* evinces concern for a suspect "cut off from the outside world". It follows that the presence of friends or neutrals at an interview is a fact of some relevance. Accordingly, several courts have considered the presence of friends as indicative of non-custody. Archer v. United States, 393 F.2d 124 (5th Cir.1968) (suspect's husband); People v. Butterfield, 258 Cal.App.2d 586, 65 Cal. Rptr. 765 (1968) (suspect's mother). By the same token the deliberate removal of a suspect from the presence of his family and friends tends to support a finding of custody. Commonwealth v. Sites, 427 Pa. 486, 235 A.2d 387 (1967). The "balance of power" may also be significant in cases where the sheer number of police is inferential of police dominated atmosphere. Wass v. Commonwealth, 5 Va.App. 27, 359 S.E.2d 836 (1987) (presence of twelve armed officers during a search overcomes statement to defendant that he was free to leave). Presumably the reverse is true and the officer who is significantly outnumbered by suspects or a suspect's friends may be found to have conducted a non-custodial interview. See People v. Robinson, 22 Mich.App. 124, 177 N.W.2d 234 (1970) (single officer). The fact that the interviewer is a uniformed policeman does not render the interview, per se, custodial. State v. Hall, 12 Ariz.App. 147, 468 P.2d 598 (1970)

Miranda claims usually arise when police conduct an interrogation. Does Miranda apply when other public employees, such as teachers and principals, question a suspect? The Fourth Amendment applies to searches of student in high school by principals. New Jersey v. T.L.O., 469 U.S. 325, 105 S.Ct. 733 (1985). Does the Fifth Amendment? See Meg Penrose, "Miranda, Please Report to the Principal's Office," 33 Fordham Urb. L.J. 775 (2006).

(d) Indicia of Arrest

The courts have generally recognized that the existence of physical restraint is a significant factor in determining questions of custody. The absence of physical restraint has led several courts to the conclusion that the defendant was not under arrest or in custody. United States v. Fiorillo, 376 F.2d 180 (2d Cir.1967) (telephone conversation with suspect); People v. Merchant, 260 Cal.App.2d 875, 67 Cal.Rptr. 459 (1968) (police asked questions from outside locked screen door). But the absence of physical restraint does not automatically require a finding of non-custody. United States v. Bekowies, 432 F.2d 8 (9th Cir.1970). The existence of physical restraint has almost invariably led to a finding of custody. State v. Rodriguez, 272 Neb. 930, 726 N.W.2d 157 (2007) (handcuffing); State v. Saunders, 102 Ariz. 565, 435 P.2d 39 (1967) (officer placed his hand on suspect's arm and led him to patrol car). But see United States v. Bautista, 684 F.2d 1286 (9th Cir.1982) (no custody where cuffing was used on an investigatory stop).

The courts also recognize that in certain cases restraint may be non-physical in nature, but the drawing of lines is not simple. Defendant was asked to go to the police station, agreed to do so and was transported without handcuffs; during interrogation he began to implicate himself, the officers told him they were only interested in who actually fired the fatal shots, but he was not forthcoming so the officer said, in effect, tell us what went down so we can check it out or we're simply going to charge you and lock you up. The "lock you up" statement established custody. See Withrow v. Williams, 507 U.S. 680, 113 S.Ct. 1745 (1993). In People v.

Gilbert, 21 Mich.App. 442, 175 N.W.2d 547 (1970), a suspect was asked to come to a police car and there informed of an accusation of rape. The court found custody. In Priestley v. State, 446 P.2d 405 (Wyo.1968), custody was found where the officer told the suspect to get into his car. On the other hand, the mere request of an officer to a suspect to step aside does not create a custodial situation. Arnold v. United States, 382 F.2d 4 (9th Cir.1967). Nor does a request to step outside a cafe for routine questions create custody. United States v. Gibson, 392 F.2d 373 (4th Cir.1968). See People v. Pantoja, 28 Mich.App. 681, 184 N.W.2d 762 (1970) (request to step into separate room at tavern did not establish custody). Holding a gun on a suspect clearly creates a custodial situation. Fleming v. Collins, 917 F.2d 850 (5th Cir.1990). The fact that a suspect is himself armed should be weighed strongly against a finding of custody. Yates v. United States, 384 F.2d 586 (5th Cir.1967); State v. Paz, 31 Or.App. 851, 572 P.2d 1036 (1977) (en banc) (handcuffs). This sort of situation is not rare; armed felons often make damaging admissions when holding off police. See People v. Tahl, 65 Cal.2d 719, 56 Cal.Rptr. 318, 423 P.2d 246 (1967); United States v. Mesa, 638 F.2d 582 (3d Cir.1980).

It has been recognized in the earliest cases that the absence of fingerprinting, photographing, and other booking procedures are indicative of the non-custodial interview. Hicks v. United States, 382 F.2d 158 (D.C.Cir.1967). The use of booking procedures, however, leads to the contrary conclusion. People v. Ellingsen, 258 Cal.App.2d 535, 65 Cal.Rptr. 744 (1968) (fingerprinting and removal of clothes). Similarly, the absence of frisk or search helps to show absence of custody. United States v. Thomas, 396 F.2d 310 (2d Cir.1968).

A related problem arises when a suspect is interviewed on premises where the officer is executing a search warrant. A single question to a suspect whose apartment was being searched was held permissible in People v. Cerrato, 24 N.Y.2d 1, 298 N.Y.S.2d 688, 246 N.E.2d 501 (1969), and People v. Fischetti, 47 Ill.2d 92, 264 N.E.2d 191 (1970). Contra: People v. Wilson, 268 Cal.App.2d 581, 74 Cal.Rptr. 131 (1968); United States v. Bekowies, 432 F.2d 8 (9th Cir.1970).

The officer who tells a suspect that he is not under arrest and is free to leave at any time has fairly definitely established that the interview is non-custodial. Lucas v. United States, 408 F.2d 835 (9th Cir.1969); United States v. Williamson, 437 F.3d 354 (3d Cir.2006). Exceptions to this rule are rare. See United States v. Ceballos, 812 F.2d 42 (2d Cir.1987) (suspect was refused the right to drive his own car to station); United States v. DiGiacomo, 579 F.2d 1211 (10th Cir.1978) (suspect given choice between arrest and voluntary appearance next day).

If a suspect is told he is under arrest then, of course, there is custody for *Miranda* purposes. In all such cases a reasonable man would reasonably conclude that he is in custody. It is also clear that custody exists in all cases after formal arrest.

Finally, the demeanor of the officer may be significant. The higher the level of courtesy and deference toward the suspect, the more likely a court is to find that the suspect did not reasonably believe he was in custody: State v. Bode, 108 N.J.Super. 363, 261 A.2d 396 (1970) (police chief questioning subordinate with the aim of protecting his fellow officer); Commonwealth v. Willman, 434 Pa. 489, 255 A.2d 534 (1969) (friendly attitude of officers). Where, however, the officer is accusatory and insistently confronts the suspect with evidence of his guilt, the argument that custody existed is strengthened. People v. Arnold, 66 Cal.2d 438, 58 Cal.Rptr. 115, 426 P.2d 515 (1967).

One rather incongruous problem is whether *the giving* of gratuitous warnings establishes the existence of custody. Gratuitous warnings may be given when an individual officer incorrectly believes that warnings are necessary under *Miranda*. Some courts have held that the fact that warnings are given does not establish the existence of custody. United States v. Owens, 431 F.2d 349 (5th Cir.1970); State v. Robinson, 496 A.2d 1067 (Me.1985).

(e) The Length and Form of Questions

The length and nature of the interrogation is of considerable significance. Almost all of the cases approving crime scene and street interrogations conducted without warnings rely upon the additional fact that questioning was brief, consuming little time and involving a few, very general inquiries. Brief, routine police inquiries are indicative of a non-custodial interview designed to clarify a questionable situation. In Allen v. United States, 390 F.2d 476 (D.C.Cir.1968), modified in 404 F.2d 1335 (1968), an officer stopped a car driven by defendant. There was a passenger in the car who was bleeding and injured. The driver gave some suspicious answers to the officer's questions and the officer asked the passenger if he had been beaten or by whom he had been beaten. The passenger mumbled incoherently and pointed at the driver. The officer asked the driver if he had done it and the driver said "yes". The court held that the officer had to clarify the situation and that he did so properly by asking routine questions. The court found that such questioning was permissible under *Miranda* and pointed out that warnings demean routine police investigation and make cooperative citizens nervous. The courts have generally reached the same result where short, neutral (non-accusatory) inquiries were put, i.e., Who are you?; Where do you live?; What are you doing here?; Where do you come from?; Is this car (or other item) yours?; Where did you get it?; etc. Compare State v. Countryman, 572 N.W.2d 553 (Iowa 1997) (suspect appeared to be in need of rescue and three hour conversation was not custodial).

The existence of lengthy interrogations indicates custody. Commonwealth v. Magee, 423 Mass. 381, 668 N.E.2d 339 (1996); United States v. Kennedy, 573 F.2d 657 (9th Cir.1978). The use of relay questioning or repeated interviews is highly damaging to a contention of no custody. Commonwealth v. Banks, 429 Pa. 53, 239 A.2d 416 (1968). The use of accusatory and leading questions, close and persistent questioning, confronting the suspect with evidence against him, and discounting the suspect's denials, are all indicative of custody. United States v. Little, 60 F.3d 708 (10th Cir.1995). The logic behind the latter cases is fairly sound; confrontation and accusation by the police in many situations would give rise to a reasonable belief of a suspect that he is in custody. Finally those courts that use the concept of focus may approve routine interrogation on the additional grounds that the routine nature of the inquiry tends to show lack of focus.

(f) Seeking Police Aid and Initiating the Interviews

The fact that a suspect summons the police and/or initiates the interview supports the premise that the interview was non-custodial. The rationale is similar to that underlying the admission of volunteered statements; the element of compulsion is lacking and the statements are not solely the result of police action. It may also be thought that where the suspect initiates contact with the police the police are likely not to assume, at least in the beginning, that he is a guilty party. State v. Huson, 73 Wash.2d 660, 440 P.2d 192 (1968) (the defendant arranged for an officer to pick him up at an agreed place; the conversation at the agreed place was held not custodial). Hunt v. State, 687 So.2d 1154 (Miss.1996) (defendant went to police station to give a false "missing person" report).

(g) The Lack of Arrest After the Interview

The fact that a suspect was arrested immediately following an interview does not mean the interview was necessarily custodial. In nearly every case dealing with non-custodial interviews the suspect was, in fact, promptly arrested thereafter.

However, the case where a suspect is allowed to go free after the interview is almost certainly one in which the interrogation was non-custodial.; United States v. Scully, 415 F.2d 680 (2d Cir.1969); Adkins v. Commonwealth, 218 Va. 945, 243 S.E.2d 205 (1978); State v. Jones, 283 Kan. 186, 151 P.3d 22 (2007).

(h) Statements Constituting the Crime and Statements to Undercover Agents

Where a suspect in custody attempts to bribe an officer, his statement constitutes a crime in itself and should be admissible even though he may make the bribe offer during a period of custodial interrogation without having received warnings. People v. Ricketson, 129 Ill.App.2d 365, 264 N.E.2d 220 (1970) ("you take the stuff and let us go"—a bribe offer not within *Miranda*).

If a suspect does not know he is speaking to a policeman he can hardly be said to have a reasonable belief that he is in custody. Nevertheless, it has been argued that undercover police should give warnings when the investigation focuses on the particular suspect, but this argument clearly conflicts with Hoffa v. United States, 385 U.S. 293, 87 S.Ct. 408 (1966), and has been rejected by every court that has considered it. United States v. Baker, 373 F.2d 28 (6th Cir.1967). The ordinary situation involving an undercover agent is clearly non-custodial in all respects. United States v. Viviano, 437 F.2d 295 (2d Cir.1971) (no "police compulsion" to meet with supposedly corrupt inspector). Miranda does not apply when a jailed suspect makes a statement to his cellmate who conveys the information to the police. See Illinois v. Perkins, infra p. 127, Note 4.

(i) Statements After Traffic Stops

Questioning of the driver of a vehicle stopped for traffic violations is usually non-custodial. See Berkemer v. McCarty, 468 U.S. 420, 104 S.Ct. 3138 (1984) infra, Note 5.

(j) Statements During the Course of Stop-and-Frisk

In most jurisdictions having stop-and-frisk procedures, the officer is usually authorized to ask a few simple questions, i.e., name, address, and explanation of actions. People v. Rosemond, 26 N.Y.2d 101, 308 N.Y.S.2d 836, 257 N.E.2d 23 (1970). In Berkemer v. McCarty, 468 U.S. 420, 433, 104 S.Ct. 3138, 3151 (1984), infra note 5, the Court indicated that a stop and frisk may or may not trigger *Miranda* rights dependent on whether the person is "subjected to restraints comparable to those of a formal arrest". It must be emphasized that the courts sustaining stop-and-frisk inquiries rely heavily on the brevity and neutrality of the questions. This suggests that what underlies the opinions is not only the belief that the situation is not "custodial", but also the belief that what takes place does not constitute "interrogation" as the Court in *Miranda* used the word. The line is not always easy to draw. See United States v. Martinez, 462 F.3d 903 (8th Cir.2006) (Court divided over whether request to explain a wad of cash is interrogation) In recent years courts have approved as stops (rather than arrests) incidents in which police weapons are drawn and handcuffs are used. One court has reasoned that when such stops occur, one cannot mechanically apply the rule that stops do not require *Miranda* warnings. United States v. Perdue, 8 F.3d 1455 (10th Cir.1993) (stopping a car at gunpoint, ordering driver to get out and lie face down on the ground while police weapons were drawn is custody for *Miranda* purposes). Compare United Commonwealth v. Pakacki, 587 Pa. 511, 901 A.2d 983 (2006).

(k) Public Safety Exception

In New York v. Quarles, 467 U.S. 649, 104 S.Ct. 2626 (1984), infra, p. 128 the Supreme Court held that a police officer need not recite the warnings required by

Miranda before asking a custodial suspect questions that could reasonably be said to have been prompted by a concern for public safety. This narrow "public safety" exception to Miranda justified an officer's failure to advise a handcuffed suspect of his rights before questioning him, in the public place where he had just been taken into custody, as to the location of a gun the officer had been told he possessed.

An officer, called to the scene by a bank alarm, sees one man on his knees and another pointing a gun at him. The police did not know the kneeling man was a bank robber and the other man a witness who helped apprehend him although the fact that the witness was not involved in crime soon became apparent. The officer testified that the kneeling man said he was shot and:

> A: I asked him, "Who shot you?" because I didn't know if it was the man holding the gun. I didn't know who he was or anything and he said, "The man at the bank."
>
> Q: He said that the man at the bank had shot him?
>
> A: Yes.
>
> Q: Did you ask him anything else?
>
> A: I asked him several questions. I said, "Who was with you?" And he said, "I was alone," and I asked him his name and he told me, "Johnny Ray Powers" was the name he gave us.
>
> Q: Okay.
>
> A: I asked him, "Where is the gun?" and he said, "I dropped it." And he said, "I didn't get any money," and that was the first couple of minutes conversation—

No Miranda warnings had been given and the kneeling man was in custody. The officer was pointing her weapon at him. Does the public safety exception excuse warnings. See Fleming v. Collins, 954 F.2d 1109 (5th Cir.1992) (en banc).

2. In Berkemer v. McCarty, 468 U.S. 420, 104 S.Ct. 3138 (1984), McCarty was stopped for erratic driving. Upon observing that McCarty was having difficulty standing, the officer decided he would charge McCarty and was not going to allow him to leave, but the officer did not state this to him. The officer administered a field sobriety test which McCarty failed and then asked McCarty if he had been using intoxicants. McCarty admitted, in slurred speech, that he had two beers and some marijuana. The officer then arrested McCarty and took him to jail where, without *Miranda* warnings, he asked McCarty more questions and McCarty gave incriminating replies. The Supreme Court found McCarty's admissions at the scene of the traffic stop admissible despite the absence of warnings, but found the statements at the jail to be inadmissible. The opinion of the Court which was without dissent on the merits addressed several issues discussed in prior notes:

* * *

> It must be acknowledged at the outset that a traffic stop significantly curtails the "freedom of action" of the driver and the passengers, if any, of the detained vehicle. Under the law of most States, it is a crime either to ignore a policeman's signal to stop one's car or, once having stopped, to drive away without permission. Certainly few motorists would feel free either to disobey a directive to pull over or to leave the scene of a traffic stop without being told they might do so. Partly for these reasons, we have long acknowledged that "stopping an automobile and detaining its occupants constitute a 'seizure' within the meaning of [the Fourth] Amendmen[t], even though the purpose of the stop is limited and the resulting detention quite brief." Delaware v. Prouse. (1979).

However, we decline to accord talismanic power to the phrase in the *Miranda* opinion emphasized by respondent. Fidelity to the doctrine announced in *Miranda* requires that it be enforced strictly, but only in those types of situations in which the concerns that powered the decision are implicated. Thus, we must decide whether a traffic stop exerts upon a detained person pressures that sufficiently impair his free exercise of his privilege against self-incrimination to require that he be warned of his constitutional rights.

Two features of an ordinary traffic stop mitigate the danger that a person questioned will be induced "to speak where he would not otherwise do so freely," Miranda v. Arizona. First, detention of a motorist pursuant to a traffic stop is presumptively temporary and brief. The vast majority of roadside detentions last only a few minutes. A motorist's expectations, when he sees a policeman's light flashing behind him, are that he will be obliged to spend a short period of time answering questions and waiting while the officer checks his license and registration, that he may then be given a citation, but that in the end he most likely will be allowed to continue on his way. In this respect, questioning incident to an ordinary traffic stop is quite different from stationhouse interrogation, which frequently is prolonged, and in which the detainee often is aware that questioning will continue until he provides his interrogators the answers they seek.

Second, circumstances associated with the typical traffic stop are not such that the motorist feels completely at the mercy of the police. To be sure, the aura of authority surrounding an armed, uniformed officer and the knowledge that the officer has some discretion in deciding whether to issue a citation, in combination, exert some pressure on the detainee to respond to questions. But other aspects of the situation substantially offset these forces. Perhaps most importantly, the typical traffic stop is public, at least to some degree. Passersby, on foot or in other cars, witness the interaction of officer and motorist. This exposure to public view both reduces the ability of an unscrupulous policeman to use illegitimate means to elicit self-incriminating statements and diminishes the motorist's fear that, if he does not cooperate, he will be subjected to abuse. The fact that the detained motorist typically is confronted by only one or at most two policemen further mutes his sense of vulnerability. In short, the atmosphere surrounding an ordinary traffic stop is substantially less "police dominated" than that surrounding the kinds of interrogation at issue in *Miranda* itself, and in the subsequent cases in which we have applied *Miranda*.

In both of these respects, the usual traffic stop is more analogous to a so-called "*Terry* stop," see Terry v. Ohio, (1968), than to a formal arrest. Under the Fourth Amendment, we have held, a policeman who lacks probable cause but whose "observations lead him reasonably to suspect" that a particular person has committed, is committing, or is about to commit a crime, may detain that person briefly in order to "investigate the circumstances that provoke suspicion." United States v. Brignoni–Ponce, (1975). "[T]he stop and inquiry must be 'reasonably related in scope to the justification for their initiation.' " Ibid. Typically, this means that the officer may ask the detainee a moderate number of questions to determine his identity and to try to obtain information confirming or dispelling the officer's suspicions. But the detainee is not obliged to respond. And, unless the detainee's answers provide the officer with probable cause to arrest him, he must then be released. The comparatively nonthreatening character of detentions of this sort explains the absence of any suggestion in our opinions that *Terry* stops are subject to the dictates of *Miranda*. The similarly noncoercive aspect of ordinary traffic stops prompts us to hold that persons temporarily detained pursuant to such stops are not "in custody" for the purposes of *Miranda*.

Respondent contends that to "exempt" traffic stops from the coverage of *Miranda* will open the way to widespread abuse. Policemen will simply delay formally arresting detained motorists, and will subject them to sustained and intimidating interrogation at the scene of their initial detention. The net result, respondent contends, will be a serious threat to the rights that the *Miranda* doctrine is designed to protect.

We are confident that the state of affairs projected by respondent will not come to pass. It is settled that the safeguards prescribed by *Miranda* become applicable as soon as a suspect's freedom of action is curtailed to a "degree associated with formal arrest." California v. Beheler (1983). If a motorist who has been detained pursuant to a traffic stop thereafter is subjected to treatment that renders him "in custody" for practical purposes, he will be entitled to the full panoply of protections prescribed by *Miranda*.

Admittedly, our adherence to the doctrine just recounted will mean that the police and lower courts will continue occasionally to have difficulty deciding exactly when a suspect has been taken into custody. Either a rule that *Miranda* applies to all traffic stops or a rule that a suspect need not be advised of his rights until he is formally placed under arrest would provide a clearer, more easily administered line. However, each of these two alternatives has drawbacks that make it unacceptable. The first would substantially impede the enforcement of the nation's traffic laws—by compelling the police either to take the time to warn all detained motorists of their constitutional rights or to forgo use of self-incriminating statements made by those motorists—while doing little to protect citizens' Fifth Amendment rights. The second would enable the police to circumvent the constraints on custodial interrogations established by *Miranda*.

Turning to the case before us, we find nothing in the record that indicates that respondent should have been given *Miranda* warnings at any point prior to the time Trooper Williams placed him under arrest. For the reasons indicated above, we reject the contention that the initial stop of respondent's car, by itself, rendered him "in custody." And respondent has failed to demonstrate that, at any time between the initial stop and the arrest, he was subjected to restraints comparable to those associated with a formal arrest. Only a short period of time elapsed between the stop and the arrest. At no point during that interval was respondent informed that his detention would not be temporary. Although Trooper Williams apparently decided as soon as respondent stepped out of his car that respondent would be taken into custody and charged with a traffic offense, Williams never communicated his intention to respondent. A policeman's unarticulated plan has no bearing on the question whether a suspect was "in custody" at a particular time; the only relevant inquiry is how a reasonable man in the suspect's position would have understood his situation.[35] Nor do other

35. Cf. Beckwith v. United States, (1976) ("'It was the compulsive aspect of custodial interrogation, and not the strength or content of the government's suspicions at the time the questioning was conducted, which led the Court to impose the *Miranda* requirements with regard to custodial questioning'") People v. P., 21 N.Y.2d 1, 286

aspects of the interaction of Williams and respondent support the contention that respondent was exposed to "custodial interrogation" at the scene of the stop. From aught that appears in the stipulation of facts, a single police officer asked respondent a modest number of questions and requested him to perform a simple balancing test at a location visible to passing motorists. Treatment of this sort cannot fairly be characterized as the functional equivalent of formal arrest.

We conclude, in short, that respondent was not taken into custody for the purposes of *Miranda* until Williams arrested him. Consequently, the statements respondent made prior to that point were admissible against him.

Berkemer was applied to find the absence of custody at a drunk driving stop. Pennsylvania v. Bruder, 488 U.S. 9, 109 S.Ct. 205 (1988).

* * *

3. Members of the United States military in some respects have broader rights than civilian suspects. In investigations conducted under Article 31 of the United States Uniform Code of Military Justice, interrogators must provide warnings to suspects even if the suspects are not in custody. See, e.g., United States v. Baird, 851 F.2d 376 (D.C.Cir.1988).

4. In Illinois v. Perkins, 496 U.S. 292, 110 S.Ct. 2394 (1990), the Court expounded upon the interplay between custody and interrogation which the *Miranda* Court had said created "compulsion" within the meaning of the Fifth Amendment. Perkins was incarcerated in a county jail awaiting trial on an aggravated battery charge. The police had received a tip that he had been involved in a previous unrelated homicide. They placed in the same cellblock with Perkins undercover agent Parisi, who posed as a recent arrestee, and Charlton, the prisoner who had supplied the police with the information linking Perkins to the murder.

Perkins was charged with murder, but the state trial and appellate courts ruled that *Miranda* required the exclusion of the cellblock admission. Eight justices of the United States Supreme Court disagreed. The majority stated:

> ... *Miranda* warnings are not required when the suspect is unaware that he is speaking to a law enforcement officer and gives a voluntary statement.
>
> * * *
>
> Conversations between suspects and undercover agents do not implicate the concerns underlying *Miranda*. The essential ingredients of a "police-dominated atmosphere" and compulsion are not present when an incarcerated person speaks freely to someone that he believes to be a fellow inmate. Coercion is determined from the perspective of the suspect. When a suspect considers himself in the company of cellmates and not officers, the coercive atmosphere is lacking.
>
> * * *
>
> It is the premise of *Miranda* that the danger of coercion results from the interaction of custody and official interrogation. We reject the argu-

N.Y.S.2d 225, 232, 233 N.E.2d 255 (1967) (an objective, reasonable-man test is appropriate because, unlike a subjective test, it "is not solely dependent either on the self-serving declarations of the police officers or the defendant nor does it place upon the police the burden of anticipating the frailties or idiosyncracies of every person whom they question").

ment that *Miranda* warnings are required whenever a suspect is in custody in a technical sense and converses with someone who happens to be a government agent. Questioning by captors, who appear to control the suspect's fate, may create mutually reinforcing pressures that the Court has assumed will weaken the suspect's will, but where a suspect does not know that he is conversing with a government agent, these pressures do not exist. The State Court here mistakenly assumed that because the suspect was in custody, no undercover questioning could take place. When the suspect has no reason to think that the listeners have official power over him, it should not be assumed that his words are motivated by the reaction he expects from his listeners. "[W]hen the agent carries neither badge nor gun and wears not 'police blue,' but the same prison gray" as the suspect, there is no "*interplay* between police interrogation and police custody." Kamisar, *Brewer v. Williams, Massiah* and *Miranda:* What is "Interrogation"? When Does it Matter?, 67 Geo.L.J. 1, 63, 67 (1978).

Miranda forbids coercion, not mere strategic deception by taking advantage of a suspect's misplaced trust in one he supposes to be a fellow prisoner.

Justice Marshall dissented. He observed that the case involved both custody and interrogation, which is all that *Miranda* required in order to create the necessity for warnings in order to dispel the coercive atmosphere. He also asserted that "the compulsion proscribed by *Miranda* includes deception by the police."

In a concurring opinion, while finding no *Miranda* violation, Justice Brennan suggested that the police tactics could render the cellblock statement involuntary and therefore inadmissible under the Fourteenth Amendment.

Is this another form of custodial interrogation which does not constitute compulsion within the meaning of the Fifth Amendment?

In State v. Ybarra, 111 N.M. 234, 804 P.2d 1053 (1990), a suspect was in police custody at a hospital. With officers in the room where the suspect had been brought for treatment of a knee injury suffered in a fight with a man whom he had killed, a nurse asked the suspect questions which elicited incriminating responses. The State argued that the case did not involve custodial interrogation for *Miranda* purposes. A majority of the Court, without citing *Perkins*, disagreed. The dissent contended that, unless the nurse was acting as the agent of the police, *Miranda* had no application. Is the atmosphere in *Ybarra* manifestly different than in *Perkins?* Should a known police presence make the difference no matter who is doing the questioning?

The Court in *Perkins* might have chosen to overrule *Mathis* (supra, p. 117) and to declare that incarceration on one charge does not automatically convert to custody for all purposes. It chose not to expressly do so in the context of a situation where the defendant had been in a local jail awaiting trial.

Mathis-type cases typically involve a suspect who is incarcerated in a penitentiary under a felony conviction. While recognizing that some courts now reject *Mathis* as compelling the conclusion that that setting is always custodial for *Miranda* purposes, the court in People v. Patterson, 207 Ill.App.3d 104, 151 Ill.Dec. 699, 564 N.E.2d 1361 (1990), found impermissible custodial interrogation. There Department of Correction employees placed a prisoner in segregation after they found a shank in his cell. Later they brought him to their office and questioned him. The court, over a strong dissent, held that the fruits of such questioning were inadmissible in a criminal proceeding, as distinguished from an administrative proceeding to revoke good time or to impose some other penalty within the correctional setting.

(b) THE MEANING OF "INTERROGATION"

Rhode Island v. Innis

Supreme Court of the United States, 1980.
446 U.S. 291, 100 S.Ct. 1682.

■ MR. JUSTICE STEWART delivered the opinion of the Court.

In *Miranda v. Arizona* the Court held that, once a defendant in custody asks to speak with a lawyer, all interrogation must cease until a lawyer is present. The issue in this case is whether the respondent was "interrogated" in violation of the standards promulgated in the *Miranda* opinion.

On the night of January 12, 1975, John Mulvaney, a Providence, R.I., taxicab driver, disappeared after being dispatched to pick up a customer. His body was discovered four days later buried in a shallow grave in Coventry, R.I. He had died from a shotgun blast aimed at the back of his head.

On January 17, 1975, shortly after midnight, the Providence police received a telephone call from Gerald Aubin, also a taxicab driver, who reported that he had just been robbed by a man wielding a sawed-off shotgun. Aubin further reported that he had dropped off his assailant near Rhode Island College in a section of Providence known as Mount Pleasant. While at the Providence police station waiting to give a statement, Aubin noticed a picture of his assailant on a bulletin board. Aubin so informed one of the police officers present. The officer prepared a photo array, and again Aubin identified a picture of the same person. That person was the respondent. Shortly thereafter, the Providence police began a search of the Mount Pleasant area.

At approximately 4:30 a.m. on the same date, Patrolman Lovell, while cruising the streets of Mount Pleasant in a patrol car, spotted the respondent standing in the street facing him. When Patrolman Lovell stopped his car, the respondent walked towards it. Patrolman Lovell then arrested the respondent, who was unarmed, and advised him of his so-called *Miranda* rights. While the two men waited in the patrol car for other police officers to arrive, Patrolman Lovell did not converse with the respondent other than to respond to the latter's request for a cigarette.

Within minutes, Sergeant Sears arrived at the scene of the arrest, and he also gave the respondent the *Miranda* warnings. Immediately thereafter, Captain Leyden and other police officers arrived. Captain Leyden advised the respondent of his *Miranda* rights. The respondent stated that he understood those rights and wanted to speak with a lawyer. Captain Leyden then directed that the respondent be placed in a "caged wagon," a four-door police car with a wire screen mesh between the front and rear seats, and be driven to the central police station. Three officers, Patrolmen Gleckman, Williams, and McKenna, were assigned to accompany the respondent to the central station. They placed the respondent in the vehicle and shut the doors. Captain Leyden then instructed the officers not to question the respondent or intimidate or coerce him in any way. The three officers then entered the vehicle, and it departed.

While en route to the central station, Patrolman Gleckman initiated a conversation with Patrolman McKenna concerning the missing shotgun. As Patrolman Gleckman later testified:

> "A. At this point, I was talking back and forth with Patrolman McKenna stating that I frequent this area while on patrol and [that because a school for handicapped children is located nearby,] there's a lot of handicapped children running around in this area, and God forbid one of them might find a weapon with shells and they might hurt themselves."

Patrolman McKenna apparently shared his fellow officer's concern:

> "A. I more or less concurred with him [Gleckman] that it was a safety factor and that we should, you know, continue to search for the weapon and try to find it."

While Patrolman Williams said nothing, he overheard the conversation between the two officers:

> "A. He [Gleckman] said it would be too bad if the little—I believe he said girl—would pick up the gun, maybe kill herself."

The respondent then interrupted the conversation, stating that the officers should turn the car around so he could show them where the gun was located. At this point, Patrolman McKenna radioed back to Captain Leyden that they were returning to the scene of the arrest and that the respondent would inform them of the location of the gun. At the time the respondent indicated that the officers should turn back, they had traveled no more than a mile, a trip encompassing only a few minutes.

The police vehicle then returned to the scene of the arrest where a search for the shotgun was in progress. There, Captain Leyden again advised the respondent of his *Miranda* rights. The respondent replied that he understood those rights but that he "wanted to get the gun out of the way because of the kids in the area in the school." The respondent then led the police to a nearby field, where he pointed out the shotgun under some rocks by the side of the road.

* * *

In the present case, the parties are in agreement that the respondent was fully informed of his *Miranda* rights and that he invoked his *Miranda* right to counsel when he told Captain Leyden that he wished to consult with a lawyer. It is also uncontested that the respondent was "in custody" while being transported to the police station.

The issue, therefore, is whether the respondent was "interrogated" by the police officers in violation of the respondent's undisputed right under *Miranda* to remain silent until he had consulted with a lawyer.[2] In resolving this issue, we first define the term "interrogation" under *Miranda* before turning to a consideration of the facts of this case.

2. Since we conclude that the respondent was not "interrogated" for *Miranda* purposes, we do not reach the question whether the respondent waived his right under *Miranda* to be free from interrogation until counsel was present.

The starting point for defining "interrogation" in this context is, of course, the Court's *Miranda* opinion. There the Court observed that "[b]y custodial interrogation, we mean *questioning* initiated by law enforcement officers after a person has been taken into custody or otherwise deprived of his freedom of action in any significant way" (emphasis added). This passage and other references throughout the opinion to "questioning" might suggest that the *Miranda* rules were to apply only to those police interrogation practices that involve express questioning of a defendant while in custody.

We do not, however, construe the *Miranda* opinion so narrowly. The concern of the Court in *Miranda* was that the "interrogation environment" created by the interplay of interrogation and custody would "subjugate the individual to the will of his examiner" and thereby undermine the privilege against compulsory self-incrimination. The police practices that evoked this concern included several that did not involve express questioning. For example, one of the practices discussed in *Miranda* was the use of line-ups in which a coached witness would pick the defendant as the perpetrator. This was designed to establish that the defendant was in fact guilty as a predicate for further interrogation. A variation on this theme discussed in *Miranda* was the so-called "reverse line-up" in which a defendant would be identified by coached witnesses as the perpetrator of a fictitious crime, with the object of inducing him to confess to the actual crime of which he was suspected in order to escape the false prosecution. The Court in *Miranda* also included in its survey of interrogation practices the use of psychological ploys, such as to "posit [ ]" "the guilt of the subject," to "minimize the moral seriousness of the offense," and "to cast blame on the victim or on society." It is clear that these techniques of persuasion, no less than express questioning, were thought, in a custodial setting, to amount to interrogation.[3]

This is not to say, however, that all statements obtained by the police after a person has been taken into custody are to be considered the product of interrogation. As the Court in *Miranda* noted:

> "Confessions remain a proper element in law enforcement. Any statement given freely and voluntarily without any compelling influences is, of course, admissible in evidence. *The fundamental import of the privilege while an individual is in custody is not whether he is allowed to talk with the police without the benefit of warnings and counsel, but whether he can be interrogated.* ... Volunteered statements of any kind are not barred by the Fifth Amendment and their admissibility is not affected by our holding today (emphasis added)."

It is clear therefore that the special procedural safeguards outlined in *Miranda* are required not where a suspect is simply taken into custody, but rather where a suspect in custody is subjected to interrogation. "Interroga-

3. To limit the ambit of *Miranda* to express questioning would "place a premium on the ingenuity of the police to devise methods of indirect interrogation, rather than to implement the plain mandate of *Miranda*." Commonwealth v. Hamilton, 445 Pa. 292, 297, 285 A.2d 172, 175.

tion," as conceptualized in the *Miranda* opinion, must reflect a measure of compulsion above and beyond that inherent in custody itself.

We conclude that the *Miranda* safeguards come into play whenever a person in custody is subjected to either express questioning or its functional equivalent. That is to say, the term "interrogation" under *Miranda* refers not only to express questioning, but also to any words or actions on the part of the police (other than those normally attendant to arrest and custody) that the police should know are reasonably likely to elicit an incriminating response from the suspect.[6] The latter portion of this definition focuses primarily upon the perceptions of the suspect, rather than the intent of the police. This focus reflects the fact that the *Miranda* safeguards were designed to vest a suspect in custody with an added measure of protection against coercive police practices, without regard to objective proof of the underlying intent of the police. A practice that the police should know is reasonably likely to evoke an incriminating response from a suspect thus amounts to interrogation.[7] But, since the police surely cannot be held accountable for the unforeseeable results of their words or actions, the definition of interrogation can extend only to words or actions on the part of police officers that they *should have known* were reasonably likely to elicit an incriminating response.[8]

Turning to the facts of the present case, we conclude that the respondent was not "interrogated" within the meaning of *Miranda*. It is undisputed that the first prong of the definition of "interrogation" was not satisfied, for the conversation between Patrolmen Gleckman and McKenna included no express questioning of the respondent. Rather, that conversation was, at least in form, nothing more than a dialogue between the two officers to which no response from the respondent was invited.

Moreover, it cannot be fairly concluded that the respondent was subjected to the "functional equivalent" of questioning. It cannot be said, in short, that Patrolmen Gleckman and McKenna should have known that their conversation was reasonably likely to elicit an incriminating response from the respondent. There is nothing in the record to suggest that the officers were aware that the respondent was peculiarly susceptible to an appeal to his conscience concerning the safety of handicapped children. Nor is there anything in the record to suggest that the police knew that the respondent was unusually disoriented or upset at the time of his arrest.[9]

6. One of the dissenting opinions seems totally to misapprehend this definition in suggesting that it "will almost certainly exclude every statement [of the police] that is not punctuated with a question mark."

7. This is not to say that the intent of the police is irrelevant, for it may well have a bearing on whether the police should have known that their words or actions were reasonably likely to evoke an incriminating response. In particular, where a police practice is designed to elicit an incriminating response from the accused, it is unlikely that the practice will not also be one which the police should have known was reasonably likely to have that effect.

8. Any knowledge the police may have had concerning the unusual susceptibility of a defendant to a particular form of persuasion might be an important factor in determining whether the police should have known that their words or actions were reasonably likely to elicit an incriminating response from the suspect.

9. The record in no way suggests that the officers' remarks were *designed* to elicit a response. It is significant that the trial judge, after hearing the officers' testimony, conclud-

The case thus boils down to whether, in the context of a brief conversation, the officers should have known that the respondent would suddenly be moved to make a self-incriminating response. Given the fact that the entire conversation appears to have consisted of no more than a few off-hand remarks, we cannot say that the officers should have known that it was reasonably likely that Innis would so respond. This is not a case where the police carried on a lengthy harangue in the presence of the suspect. Nor does the record support the respondent's contention that, under the circumstances, the officers' comments were particularly "evocative." It is our view, therefore, that the respondent was not subjected by the police to words or actions that the police should have known were reasonably likely to elicit an incriminating response from him.

[In reversing the conviction] the Rhode Island Supreme Court erred, in short, in equating "subtle compulsion" with interrogation. That the officers' comments struck a responsive cord is readily apparent. Thus, it may be said, as the Rhode Island Supreme Court did say, that the respondent was subjected to "subtle compulsion." But that is not the end of the inquiry. It must also be established that a suspect's incriminating response was the product of words or actions on the part of the police that they should have known were reasonably likely to elicit an incriminating response.[10] This was not established in the present case.

For the reasons stated, the judgment of the Supreme Court of Rhode Island is vacated, and the case is remanded to that court for further proceedings not inconsistent with this opinion.

■ MR. JUSTICE WHITE, concurring.

[OMITTED]

■ MR. CHIEF JUSTICE BURGER, concurring in the judgment.

Since the result is not inconsistent with *Miranda*, I concur in the judgment.

The meaning of *Miranda* has become reasonably clear and law enforcement practices have adjusted to its strictures; I would neither overrule *Miranda*, disparage it, nor extend it at this late date. I fear, however, that the Court's opinion may introduce new elements of uncertainty; under the Court's test, a police officer in the brief time available, apparently must evaluate the suggestibility and susceptibility of an accused. Few, if any, police officers are competent to make the kind of evaluation seemingly contemplated; even a psychiatrist asked to express an expert opinion on these aspects of a suspect in custody would very likely employ extensive questioning and observation to make the judgment now charged to police officers.

ed that it was "entirely understandable that [the officers] would voice their concern [for the safety of the handicapped children] to each other."

10. By way of example, if the police had done no more than to drive past the site of the concealed weapon while taking the most direct route to the police station, and if the respondent, upon noticing for the first time the proximity of the school for handicapped children, had blurted out that he would show the officers where the gun was located, it could not seriously be argued that this "subtle compulsion" would have constituted "interrogation" within the meaning of the *Miranda* opinion.

Trial judges have enough difficulty discerning the boundaries and nuances flowing from post-*Miranda* opinions, and we do not clarify that situation today.

■ MR. JUSTICE MARSHALL, with whom MR. JUSTICE BRENNAN joins, dissenting.

I am substantially in agreement with the Court's definition of "interrogation" within the meaning of *Miranda*. . . .

I am utterly at a loss, however, to understand how this objective standard as applied to the facts before us can rationally lead to the conclusion that there was no interrogation.

* * *

One can scarcely imagine a stronger appeal to the conscience of a suspect—*any* suspect—than the assertion that if the weapon is not found an innocent person will be hurt or killed. And not just any innocent person, but an innocent child—a little girl—a helpless, handicapped little girl on her way to school. The notion that such an appeal could not be expected to have any effect unless the suspect were known to have some special interest in handicapped children verges on the ludicrous. As a matter of fact, the appeal to a suspect to confess for the sake of others, to "display some evidence of decency and honor," is a classic interrogation technique. See, e.g., F. Inbau & J. Reid, Criminal Interrogation and Confessions 60–62 (2d ed. 1967).

Gleckman's remarks would obviously have constituted interrogation if they had been explicitly directed to petitioner, and the result should not be different because they were nominally addressed to McKenna. This is not a case where police officers speaking among themselves are accidentally overheard by a suspect. These officers were "talking back and forth" in close quarters with the handcuffed suspect, traveling past the very place where they believed the weapon was located. They knew petitioner would hear and attend to their conversation, and they are chargeable with knowledge of and responsibility for the pressures to speak which they created.

■ MR. JUSTICE STEVENS, dissenting.

* * *

In my view any statement that would normally be understood by the average listener as calling for a response is the functional equivalent of a direct question, whether or not it is punctuated by a question mark. The Court, however, takes a much narrower view. It holds that police conduct is not the "functional equivalent" of direct questioning unless the police should have known that what they were saying or doing was likely to elicit an incriminating response from the suspect. This holding represents a plain departure from the principles set forth in *Miranda*.

* * *

[I]f after being told that he has a right to have an attorney present during interrogation, a suspect chooses to cut off questioning until counsel can be obtained, his choice must be "scrupulously honored" by the police. At the least this must mean that the police are prohibited from making deliberate attempts to elicit statements from the suspect. Yet the Court is unwilling to characterize all such attempts as "interrogation," noting only that "where a police practice is designed to elicit an incriminating response from the accused, it is unlikely that the practice will not also be one which the police should have known was reasonably likely to have that effect."[8]

From the suspect's point of view, the effectiveness of the warnings depends on whether it appears that the police are scrupulously honoring his rights. Apparent attempts to elicit information from a suspect after he has invoked his right to cut off questioning necessarily demean that right and tend to reinstate the imbalance between police and suspect that the *Miranda* warnings are designed to correct. Thus, if the rationale for requiring those warnings in the first place is to be respected, any police conduct or statements that would appear to a reasonable person in the suspect's position to call for a response must be considered "interrogation."

In short, in order to give full protection to a suspect's right to be free from any interrogation at all, the definition of "interrogation" must include any police statement or conduct that has the same purpose or effect as a direct question. Statements that appear to call for a response from the suspect, as well as those that are designed to do so, should be considered interrogation.

In any event, I think the Court is clearly wrong in holding, as a matter of law, that Officer Gleckman should not have realized that his statement was likely to elicit an incriminating response.

* * *

[E]ven if I were to agree with the Court's much narrower standard, I would disagree with its disposition of this particular case because the Rhode Island courts should be given an opportunity to apply the new standard to the facts of this case.

NOTES

1. The decided cases can be divided roughly into two categories:

(a) Confronting the Suspect With the Evidence Against Him

The first state court rulings before *Innis* held that showing the suspect the evidence against him was not interrogation and might even help the accused decide intelligently whether to waive his rights. People v. Sunday, 275 Cal.App.2d 473, 79 Cal.Rptr. 752 (1969); People v. Doss, 44 Ill.2d 541, 256 N.E.2d 753 (1970); Combs v. Commonwealth, 438 S.W.2d 82 (Ky.1969). The procedure was to show the suspect a copy of an accomplice's confession or a ballistics report without asking any further questions.

A later set of federal opinions still prior to *Innis* found fault with this practice but it was not clear whether this was so because it was the equivalent of interrogation or because the conduct did not adequately defer to the suspect's assertion of his right to silence. Nearly every case involved the use of confrontation

8. This factual assumption is extremely dubious. I would assume that police often interrogate suspects without any reason to believe that their efforts are likely to be successful in the hope that a statement will nevertheless be forthcoming.

after the suspect refused to be interrogated. See United States ex rel. Doss v. Bensinger, 463 F.2d 576 (7th Cir.1972); Combs v. Wingo, 465 F.2d 96 (6th Cir.1972). It was rare to encounter a case where an arrestee is neither warned nor questioned but simply shown a copy of a report identifying his fingerprint on the murder weapon in response to which he said, "I did it." See State v. McLean, 294 N.C. 623, 242 S.E.2d 814 (1978) (admissible). Would *Innis* bar this response from evidence? Suppose the arrestee says nothing but an hour later asks to see an officer and then makes a statement as the officer enters the room.

After *Innis* in State v. Grisby, 97 Wash.2d 493, 647 P.2d 6 (1982), an officer was sorting physical evidence in front of the suspect who asked a question about it and then volunteered an incriminating statement which was admitted because the Court found the officer was engaged in a routine action without intent to provoke a response. See State v. Conover, 312 Md. 33, 537 A.2d 1167 (1988) (Proper to show the statement of charges to suspect and say "read them, look at them, if you have any questions, ask them.") Compare United States v. Vazquez, 857 F.2d 857 (1st Cir.1988) (placing two suspects in a room together is not interrogation even though they had told differing stories), *with* Nelson v. Fulcomer, 911 F.2d 928 (3d Cir.1990) (informing suspect that his partner in crime confessed and then putting the two together was interrogation—"How much did you tell them? I told it all.")

The opinion in State v. Grisby supra, suggests that *Innis* will not change the status of rulings which admit volunteered responses to routine police procedures which do not ordinarily elicit statements. Camacho v. United States, 407 F.2d 39 (9th Cir.1969) (after identification in line-up); United States v. Godfrey, 409 F.2d 1338 (10th Cir.1969) (after being told a stolen car inquiry was being made); People v. Torres, 21 N.Y.2d 49, 286 N.Y.S.2d 264, 233 N.E.2d 282 (1967) (after being shown a search warrant).

(b) Statements in Response to Statements by Others

Confronting a suspect with incriminating evidence is always at least arguably intended to elicit a statement. A comment by an officer may not be. Prior to *Innis*, most courts found no interrogation to have occurred. Commonwealth v. Boone, 467 Pa. 168, 354 A.2d 898 (1975) ("Where are we going?" "To the homicide bureau." "Then the girl I stabbed must have died."); But see People v. Paulin, 25 N.Y.2d 445, 306 N.Y.S.2d 929, 255 N.E.2d 164 (1969) (comments about a "terrible tragedy" and "funeral arrangements" were subtle interrogation);

The cases after *Innis* have usually found no interrogation. United States v. Thierman, 678 F.2d 1331 (9th Cir.1982) (after refusal to speak suspect was told police would have to contact his family and friends and that it was too bad his girl friend would become involved—no violation of *Innis* even though officer "guessed" he was trying to elicit a response); State v. Ingold, 450 N.W.2d 344 (Minn.App.1990) (officer overhears inmate say to others "I was arrested only because I had a record"; officer says "must have been more", inmate responds with damaging admission); State v. Jones, 386 So.2d 1363 (La.1980) (comment that "God takes care of little babies, the baby is already in heaven" was consolation, not interrogation); Howard v. United States, 452 A.2d 966 (D.C.App.1982) (rape suspect repeatedly asked for the name of the victim despite the officer's refusal to give it—officer finally gave a fictitious name and suspect responded, "That bitch, I didn't think she'd go that far"). Contra State v. Finehout, 136 Ariz. 226, 665 P.2d 570 (1983) (comments about the value of telling the truth were interrogation); United States v. Gomez, 927 F.2d 1530 (11th Cir.1991) (advice that, absent cooperation, a stiff sentence awaits violates *Innis*).

In Arizona v. Mauro, 481 U.S. 520, 107 S.Ct. 1931 (1987), William Mauro, having admitted killing his son, invoked his right to a lawyer after being taken to a police station and being warned a second time of his rights under *Miranda*. Police were questioning Mauro's wife in a separate room at the police station. Mrs. Mauro asked to speak to her husband. After initially declining this request, the police told her she could speak to Mauro only if the police were present to "observe and hear what was going on." An officer then brought Mrs. Mauro into the room, where the officer sat at a desk and placed a tape recorder in plain sight on the desk.

When Mrs. Mauro began to talk, Mr. Mauro told his wife to shut up until she had an attorney. He reminded her that she had done her best to stop him from killing their child. At trial the prosecution introduced Mauro's statements to his wife in rebuttal of an insanity defense.

A majority of the Court held that the police conduct in allowing Mrs. Mauro to speak to her husband was not the functional equivalent of interrogation for *Miranda* purposes. The Court stated that there was "no evidence that the officer sent Mrs. Mauro in to see her husband for the purpose of eliciting incriminating statements." It acknowledged that the officers were aware of the possibility that Mauro would incriminate himself if his wife were allowed to speak with him. It emphasized, however, that Mauro was not subject to psychological ploys or compelling influences. It said that the husband would not have felt compelled to incriminate himself in any way.

The Court concluded by saying that it did not wish to adopt a rule that would discourage the police from allowing suspects to visit with their spouses. Nor did it wish to mandate the police "ignore legitimate security concerns by allowing spouses to meet in *private*."

Four justices dissented. They concluded that because the police "allowed respondent's conversation with his wife to commence at a time when they knew it was reasonably likely to produce an incriminating statement, the police interrogated him," [and] argued that the *Innis* test does not require explicit police subterfuge. Justice Stevens added that, in his opinion, it was highly probable that one of the suspects would make a statement that the prosecutor might seek to introduce at trial. Because the police had exclusive control over whether Mrs. Mauro could speak to her husband, it made no difference that Mrs. Mauro had initiated the request for the visit, according to the dissenters.

2. In cases deciding whether there is custody, the courts generally look to the objective circumstances rather than the state of mind of either interrogator or suspect. Is the officer's intent relevant in determining whether questioning occurs. *Rhode Island v. Innis*, says interrogation includes any words or actions that the police "should know are reasonably likely to elicit an incriminating response from the suspect." This standard could mean words or actions that, on their face, were likely to elicit a response regardless of what the officer knew or intended. Or the rule could take such intent or knowledge into account. The question is important because courts do allow police deliberately to avoid placing someone in custody in order to avoid warnings. Could a police officer similarly avoid interrogating or does any deliberate act which the officer hopes will get a response constitute interrogation? What if that act has one chance in ten of drawing a response? Two courts recently reached their conclusions after considering the officer's state of mind. In United States v. Taylor, 985 F.2d 3 (1st Cir.1993), an arrestee was being driven to the county jail after officers seized a lot of marijuana growing on her property. She was unwarned because no interrogation was intended. During the ride she said "Why is this happening to me?" The officer replied "You can't be growing dope on your property like that?" She said "If you had waited and come next week you'd have only gotten half the plants you did ... the way you do is you pull the male plants early." The officer said nothing but did write down what she said. The Court noted the standard was whether the police conduct would be perceived as interrogation by a reasonable person in the same circumstance but the Court declined to decide the result if the conduct had been deliberate. Here the officer was aware that defendant might say something but her opening question was abrupt and he did not even think before responding, and there was nothing about the response which was particularly inviting of a further remark.

In United States v. Henley, 984 F.2d 1040 (9th Cir.1993) the F.B.I. suspected Henley of being involved in a bank robbery, the getaway car was a 1974 Plymouth Duster. The F.B.I. found the car and arrested Henley; they asked him if he owned the car. The court said, "When a police officer has reason to know that a suspect's answer may incriminate him, however, even routine questioning may amount to interrogation.... An officer investigating a bank robbery who has the getaway car but isn't sure who owns it should well know that asking a suspect if he's the owner of the vehicle is reasonably likely to elicit an incriminating answer." The Court grounded its opinion on the premise that the routine booking question exception to interrogation did not apply. What if there had not been a question, rather one agent said to another (in Henley's hearing) "That car is going to be ticketed and towed by the city, unless the guy who owns it comes and moves it away" at which time Henley says "It's mine, will you let me park it in a legal space?" Is this interrogation?

3. Consider the following case: A missing man last seen in the company of Haire's wife who is arrested and quickly confesses that she and her husband killed the man. She says the body is in a field on the right side of a road where an unsuccessful search is made. Haire who has been arrested but not warned is brought to the scene. When the officer asked his wife whether she had said the body was on the right side, he did not wait for her to answer. He said "No Honey, on the left side." His wife was asked where the gun was, she replied "under the bed" but he said it was in the fireplace. The body was found on the left side and a gun which proved to be the murder weapon was found in the fireplace.

Was Haire interrogated? See Haire v. Sarver, 437 F.2d 1262 (8th Cir.1971).

4. In *Miranda* the Court stated that "volunteered statements of any kind are not barred by the Fifth Amendment and their admissibility is not affected by our holding today." A volunteered statement is one that is *not* made in response to questioning by an officer. The relative simplicity of this concept makes the determination of whether a statement is volunteered a much easier issue than the question of custody.

Volunteered statements occur when a person simply walks into a police station or talked to a policeman and makes a damaging admission. See Taylor v. Page, 381 F.2d 717 (10th Cir.1967); People v. Hines, 66 Cal.2d 348, 57 Cal.Rptr. 757, 425 P.2d 557 (1967). These sorts of volunteered statements are probably also admissible as non-custodial in nature.

Volunteered statements most frequently occur after a suspect has been taken into custody. Such statements may occur before, during or after actual interrogation so long as they are clearly volunteered. See Anderson v. United States, 399 F.2d 753 (10th Cir.1968) (suspect told police that his companion had nothing to do with it); United States v. Maret, 433 F.2d 1064 (8th Cir.1970) (volunteered during warnings); United States v. McNeil, 433 F.2d 1109 (D.C.Cir.1969) (volunteered after warnings).

Volunteered statements also occur during interrogation when the suspect makes a damaging admission that is not responsive to the officer's question. For example, an officer may ask "What is your name?" and the response may be "I'm sorry I killed her". See Parson v. United States, 387 F.2d 944 (10th Cir.1968); DeHart v. State, 468 S.W.2d 435 (Tex.Crim.App.1971) ("Do you know your father is dead?" "I know, I only wish it had been my mother."); State v. Armstrong, 344 A.2d 42 (Me.1975) ("Do you understand your rights?"C"I killed her and I want to get her out of there.")

On occasion conversations among co-defendants are overheard as are conversations of defendants with relatives, victims and friends. Admissions made during these conversations are not the product of *Miranda* interrogation. Soolook v. State, 447 P.2d 55 (Alaska 1968) (parents); Edington v. State, 243 Ark. 10, 418 S.W.2d 637 (1967) (girl friend); Chancellor v. Commonwealth, 438 S.W.2d 783 (Ky.1969) (offer of restitution to victim).

The police have no duty to interrupt a volunteered statement in order to warn a suspect of his rights. Taylor v. Page, 381 F.2d 717 (10th Cir.1967).

Finally, a volunteered statement is admissible regardless of when it was made, i.e., while in custody, after indictment, after counsel is retained, etc. People v. Smith, 173 Colo. 10, 475 P.2d 627 (1970) (after request for counsel); Dempsey v. State, 238 So.2d 446 (Fla.App.1970) (after request for counsel); Graybeal v. State, 13 Md.App. 557, 284 A.2d 37 (1971) (after assertion of right to silence); State v. Robinson, 198 Neb. 785, 255 N.W.2d 835 (1977) ("The dude died at the hospital, eh?")

5. Apart from the purely volunteered statement the courts have recognized a category which, for want of a better term, may be called noninterrogation questioning. There are four basic types of such questions.

(a) Threshold and Clarifying Questions

The problem of threshold questioning arises because most volunteered admissions are not very detailed. In People v. Savage, 102 Ill.App.2d 477, 242 N.E.2d 446 (1968) a man walked into a police station and said "I done it. I done it. Arrest me. Arrest me." Naturally the officer asked him what he did and when the man said he killed his wife the officer asked him how and he replied, "With an axe, that's all I had." The Court held that this was "threshold questioning" and was permitted by *Miranda*.

The rule is stated in People v. Sunday, 76 Cal.Rptr. 668 and 275 Cal.App.2d 473, 79 Cal.Rptr. 752 (1969), where the defendant, who was in custody, initiated an interview with the police. His statement was largely a monologue but some routine questions were asked. The Court held that a statement is volunteered even if some questions are asked, as long as the questions are neutral, intended to clarify and are not designed to expand the scope of the statement the witness wants to make. See also People v. Superior Court, 3 Cal.App.3d 476, 83 Cal.Rptr. 771 (1970) ("I did it, I am sorry" "What happened?" "Where is the knife?"); Campbell v. State, 4 Md.App. 448, 243 A.2d 642 (1968) ("How much time can I get for this" "For what?" "For robbing that old lady"). But see, People v. Matthews, 264 Cal.App.2d 557, 70 Cal.Rptr. 756 (1968) (exceeded permissible scope of clarification); People v. Connor, 270 Cal.App.2d 630, 75 Cal.Rptr. 905 (1969) (same—32 page transcript of "clarifying" questions).

(b) Routine Questions and Booking Procedures

The questions asked during booking of suspects by the booking officer are usually held to be non-interrogative. See Toohey v. United States, 404 F.2d 907 (9th Cir.1968) (information secured in normal booking process is admissible); United States v. Schipani, 414 F.2d 1262 (2d Cir.1969) (routine personal history survey in prison is admissible); United States v. Taylor, 799 F.2d 126 (4th Cir.1986) (name); People v. Hernandez, 263 Cal.App.2d 242, 69 Cal.Rptr. 448 (1968) (age); Clarke v. State, 3 Md.App. 447, 240 A.2d 291 (1968) (name, address, employment); Contra,

Proctor v. United States, 404 F.2d 819 (D.C.Cir.1968) (routine question about employment inadmissible under *Miranda*). See United States v. Webb, 755 F.2d 382 (5th Cir.1985) (question about what did "you get yourself into" answered with an admission of murder served no legitimate jail administration purpose, was not part of normal procedure and was asked by a guard, who stated he was trying to help the F.B.I., produced inadmissible statement). Franks v. State, 268 Ga. 238, 486 S.E.2d 594 (question how defendant got a bandage on his arm).

The rationale that brief, routine questions are not interrogation extends to cases beyond the booking procedure. The courts seem to read *Miranda* as directed toward the combination of custody coupled with a series of authoritative demands for answers. See State v. Travis, 250 Or. 213, 441 P.2d 597 (1968). And from this it is concluded that the simple run-of-the-mill question does not constitute interrogation. Further, courts rely heavily in such situations on the lack of focus or intent to incriminate on the part of the officer asking the question. See People v. Ashford, 265 Cal.App.2d 673, 71 Cal.Rptr. 619 (1968) (question from bailiff "How's it going, Ashford?"); Rubey v. City of Fairbanks, 456 P.2d 470 (Alaska 1969) (request for marked money made after arrest).

In Pennsylvania v. Muniz, 496 U.S. 582, 110 S.Ct. 2638 (1990), questioning occurred at a police "booking center," where an officer had transported the driver after the driver had failed roadside sobriety tests.

> Officer Hosterman first asked Muniz his name, address, height, weight, eye color, date of birth, and current age. He responded to each of these questions, stumbling over his address and age. The officer then asked Muniz, "Do you know what the date was of your sixth birthday?" After Muniz offered an inaudible reply, the officer repeated, "When you turned six years old, do you remember what the date was?" Muniz responded, "No, I don't."
>
> Officer Hosterman next requested Muniz to perform each of the three sobriety tests that Muniz had been asked to perform earlier during the initial roadside stop. The videotape reveals that his eyes jerked noticeably during the gaze test, that he did not walk a very straight line, and that he could not balance himself on one leg for more than several seconds. During the latter two tests, he did not complete the requested verbal counts from one to nine and from one to thirty. Moreover, while performing these tests, Muniz "attempted to explain his difficulties in performing the various tasks, and often requested further clarification of the tasks he was to perform."
>
> Finally, Officer Deyo asked Muniz to submit to a breathalyzer test designed to measure the alcohol content of his expelled breath. Officer Deyo read to Muniz the Commonwealth's Implied Consent Law and explained that under the law his refusal to take the test would result in automatic suspension of his drivers' license for one year. Muniz asked a number of questions about the law, commenting in the process about his state of inebriation. Muniz ultimately refused to take the breath test. At this point, Muniz was for the first time advised of his *Miranda* rights. Muniz then signed a statement waiving his rights and admitted in response to further questioning that he had been driving while intoxicated.

For the Court, Justice Brennan wrote:

> * * *
>
> When Officer Hosterman asked Muniz if he knew the date of his sixth birthday and Muniz, for whatever reason, could not remember or calculate that date, he was confronted with the trilemma. By hypothesis, the

inherently coercive environment created by the custodial interrogation precluded the option of remaining silent. Muniz was left with the choice of incriminating himself by admitting that he did not then know the date of his sixth birthday, or answering untruthfully by reporting a date that he did not then believe to be accurate (an incorrect guess would be incriminating as well as untruthful). The content of his truthful answer supported an inference that his mental faculties were impaired, because his assertion (he did not know the date of his sixth birthday) was different from the assertion (he knew the date was [correct date]) that the trier of fact might reasonably have expected a lucid person to provide. Hence, the incriminating inference of impaired mental faculties stemmed, not just from the fact that Muniz slurred his response, but also from a testimonial aspect of that response.

Eight of the justices agreed that the responses to the seven "booking" questions were admissible. Speaking for himself and three other justices, Justice Brennan wrote:

> We disagree with the Commonwealth's contention that Officer Hosterman's first seven questions regarding Muniz's name, address, height, weight, eye color, date of birth, and current age do not qualify as custodial interrogation as we defined the term in *Innis*, supra, merely because the questions were not intended to elicit information for investigatory purposes. As explained above, the *Innis* test focuses primarily upon "the perspective of the suspect." Perkins (1990). We agree however, that Muniz's answers to these first seven questions are nonetheless admissible because the questions fall within a "routine booking question" exception which exempts from *Miranda's* coverage questions to secure the "biographical data necessary to complete booking or pretrial services."

Chief Justice Rehnquist, writing for himself and three other justices wrote:

> The sixth birthday question here was an effort on the part of the police to check how well Muniz was able to do a simple mathematical exercise. Indeed, had the question related only to the date of his birth, it presumably would have come under the "booking exception" to Miranda v. Arizona, 384 U.S. 436, 86 S.Ct. 1602 (1966), to which the Court refers elsewhere in its opinion. The Court holds in this very case that Muniz may be required to perform a "horizontal gaze nystagmus" test, the "walk and turn" test, and the "one leg stand" test, all of which are designed to test a suspect's physical coordination. If the police may require Muniz to use his body in order to demonstrate the level of his physical coordination, there is no reason why they should not be able to require him to speak or write in order to determine his mental coordination. That was all that was sought here. Since it was permissible for the police to extract and examine a sample of blood to determine how much that part of his system had been affected by alcohol, I see no reason why they may not examine the functioning of Muniz' mental processes for the same purpose.
>
> For substantially the same reasons, Muniz' responses to the videotaped "booking" questions were not testimonial and do not warrant application of the privilege. Thus, it is unnecessary to determine whether the questions fall within the "routine booking question" exception to *Miranda* Justice Brennan recognizes.
>
> * * *

Justice Marshall joined with the Brennan four in ruling inadmissible the responses concerning the defendant's sixth birthday. He wrote a lone dissent, arguing that there is no exception to *Miranda* for routine booking questions if such questions are reasonably likely to elicit an incriminating response, as, he said, they were in the case of an apparently intoxicated arrestee.

(c) Spontaneous Questions

In People v. Morse, 70 Cal.2d 711, 76 Cal.Rptr. 391, 452 P.2d 607 (1969), a jailer and a guard were called to a cell area where they found one prisoner garroted near death. While tending to this prisoner they asked the defendant, who was also a prisoner, questions about what happened and received incriminating replies. The Court upheld this questioning as not a deliberate effort to elicit damaging evidence but rather general on-the-scene questioning by an "astonished" jailer.

The spontaneity or impulsive nature of questioning depends upon the circumstances in which the question is asked. Though very few courts, of the courts which rely upon the brevity of questions in sustaining the admissibility of the answers explicitly mention the spontaneous nature of the questions, it can be persuasively argued that spontaneity is at least a subliminal factor supporting those judgments. In United States v. Castro, 723 F.2d 1527 (11th Cir.1984) an officer having custody of the accused at a scene where narcotics were obviously present asked "What is going on here?" The response was a bribe offer, "You want money? We got money." Over a dissent the bribe offer was held admissible as not the product of interrogation. See also Dennis v. Commonwealth, 464 S.W.2d 253 (Ky.1971) (after arrest for intoxication defendant who had blood on his arm was asked "What happened?"); Bugg v. State, 267 Ind. 614, 372 N.E.2d 1156 (1978) (police officer went to home of a friend and asked questions out of concern for her health); People v. Huffman, 41 N.Y.2d 29, 390 N.Y.S.2d 843, 359 N.E.2d 353 (1976) (man comes out of the bushes and startled police by asking "What are you doing here?"). But see, Harryman v. Estelle, 616 F.2d 870 (5th Cir.1980) (en banc) (no *Miranda* exception for question of officer surprised by what he had found). In the Interest of D.F.L., 931 P.2d 448 (Colo.1997) (where four individuals were in custody and officer said "whose purse is this?" the answer "That's mine" is a response to interrogation).

(d) Emergency Questions

(1) Consider the decision in New York v. Quarles, 467 U.S. 649, 104 S.Ct. 2626 (1984):

> JUSTICE REHNQUIST delivered the opinion of the Court.
>
> Respondent Benjamin Quarles was charged in the New York trial court with criminal possession of a weapon. . . .
>
> On September 11, 1980, at approximately 12:30 a.m., Officer Frank Kraft and Officer Sal Scarring were on road patrol in Queens, New York, when a young woman approached their car. She told them that she had just been raped by a black male, approximately six feet tall, who was wearing a black jacket with the name "Big Ben" printed in yellow letters on the back. She told the officers that the man had just entered an A & P supermarket located nearby and that the man was carrying a gun.
>
> The officers drove the woman to the supermarket, and Officer Kraft entered the store while Officer Scarring radioed for assistance. Officer Kraft quickly spotted respondent, who matched the description given by the woman, approaching a check-out counter. Apparently upon seeing the officer, respondent turned and ran toward the rear of the store, and Officer Kraft pursued him with a drawn gun. When respondent turned the corner at the end of an aisle, Officer Kraft lost sight of him for several seconds,

and upon regaining sight of respondent, ordered him to stop and put his hands over his head.

Although more than three other officers had arrived on the scene by that time, Officer Kraft was the first to reach respondent. He frisked him and discovered that he was wearing a shoulder holster which was then empty. After handcuffing him, Officer Kraft asked him where the gun was. Respondent nodded in the direction of some empty cartons and responded, "the gun is over there." Officer Kraft thereafter retrieved a loaded .38 caliber revolver from one of the cartons, formally placed respondent under arrest, and read him his *Miranda* rights from a printed card. Respondent indicated that he would be willing to answer questions without an attorney present. Officer Kraft then asked respondent if he owned the gun and where he had purchased it. Respondent answered that he did own it and that he had purchased it in Miami, Florida.

In the subsequent prosecution of respondent for criminal possession of a weapon, the judge excluded the statement, "the gun is over there," and the gun because the officer had not given respondent the warnings required by our decision in *Miranda* before asking him where the gun was located. . . .

In this case we have before us no claim that respondent's statements were actually compelled by police conduct which overcame his will to resist. Thus the only issue before us is whether Officer Kraft was justified in failing to make available to respondent the procedural safeguards associated with the privilege against compulsory self-incrimination since *Miranda*.

The New York Court of Appeals was undoubtedly correct in deciding that the facts of this case come within the ambit of the *Miranda* decision. We agree that respondent was in police custody . . . Quarles was surrounded by at least four police officers and was handcuffed when the questioning at issue took place. As the New York Court of Appeals observed, there was nothing to suggest that any of the officers were any longer concerned for their own physical safety. The . . . majority declined to express an opinion as to whether there might be an exception to the *Miranda* rule if the police had been acting to protect the public, because the lower courts in New York had made no factual determination that the police had acted with that motive.

We hold that on these facts there is a "public safety" exception to the requirement that *Miranda* warnings be given before a suspect's answers may be admitted into evidence, and that the availability of that exception does not depend upon the motivation of the individual officers involved. In a kaleidoscopic situation such as the one confronting these officers, where spontaneity rather than adherence to a police manual is necessarily the order of the day, the application of the exception which we recognize today should not be made to depend on *post hoc* findings at a suppression hearing concerning the subjective motivation of the arresting officer. Undoubtedly most police officers, if placed in Officer Kraft's position, would act out of a host of different, instinctive, and largely unverifiable motives—their own safety, the safety of others, and perhaps as well the desire to obtain incriminating evidence from the suspect.

Whatever the motivation of individual officers in such a situation, we do not believe that the doctrinal underpinnings of *Miranda* require that it be applied in all its rigor to a situation in which police officers ask questions reasonably prompted by a concern for the public safety. The *Miranda* decision was based in large part on this Court's view that the warnings which it required police to give to suspects in custody would reduce the likelihood that the suspects would fall victim to constitutionally impermissible practices of police interrogation in the presumptively coercive environment of the station house.

* * *

The police in this case, in the very act of apprehending a suspect, were confronted with the immediate necessity of ascertaining the whereabouts of a gun which they had every reason to believe the suspect had just removed from his empty holster and discarded in the supermarket. So long as the gun was concealed somewhere in the supermarket, with its actual whereabouts unknown, it obviously posed more than one danger to the public safety: an accomplice might make use of it, a customer or employee might later come upon it.

In such a situation, if the police are required to recite the familiar *Miranda* warnings before asking the whereabouts of the gun, suspects in Quarles' position might well be deterred from responding. Procedural safeguards which deter a suspect from responding were deemed acceptable in *Miranda* in order to protect the Fifth Amendment privilege; when the primary social cost of those added protections is the possibility of fewer convictions, the *Miranda* majority was willing to bear that cost. Here, had *Miranda* warnings deterred Quarles from responding to Officer Kraft's question about the whereabouts of the gun, the cost would have been something more than merely the failure to obtain evidence useful in convicting Quarles. Officer Kraft needed an answer to his question not simply to make his case against Quarles but to insure that further danger to the public did not result from the concealment of the gun in a public area.

We conclude that the need for answers to questions in a situation posing a threat to the public safety outweighs the need for the prophylactic rule protecting the Fifth Amendment's privilege against self-incrimination. We decline to place officers such as Officer Kraft in the untenable position of having to consider, often in a matter of seconds, whether it best serves society for them to ask the necessary questions without the *Miranda* warnings and render whatever probative evidence they uncover inadmissible, or for them to give the warnings in order to preserve the admissibility of evidence they might uncover but possibly damage or destroy their ability to obtain that evidence and neutralize the volatile situation confronting them.[7]

In recognizing a narrow exception to the *Miranda* rule in this case, we acknowledge that to some degree we lessen the desirable clarity of that rule.

* * *

7. The dissent argues that a public safety exception to *Miranda* is unnecessary because in every case an officer can simply ask the necessary questions to protect himself or the public, and then the prosecution can decline to introduce any incriminating responses at a subsequent trial. But absent actual coercion by the officer, there is no constitutional imperative requiring the exclusion of the evidence that results from police inquiry of this kind; and we do not believe that the doctrinal underpinnings of *Miranda* require us to exclude the evidence, thus penalizing officers for asking the very questions which are the most crucial to their efforts to protect themselves and the public.

... But ... we believe that the exception which we recognize today lessens the necessity of that on-the-scene balancing process. The exception will not be difficult for police officers to apply because in each case it will be circumscribed by the exigency which justifies it. We think police officers can and will distinguish almost instinctively between questions necessary to secure their own safety or the safety of the public and questions designed solely to elicit testimonial evidence from a suspect.

The facts of this case clearly demonstrate that distinction and an officer's ability to recognize it. Officer Kraft asked only the question necessary to locate the missing gun before advising respondent of his rights. It was only after securing the loaded revolver and giving the warnings that he continued with investigatory questions about the ownership and place of purchase of the gun. The exception which we recognize today, far from complicating the thought processes and the on-the-scene judgments of police officers, will simply free them to follow their legitimate instincts when confronting situations presenting a danger to the public safety.

We hold that the Court of Appeals in this case erred in excluding the statement, "the gun is over there," and the gun because of the officer's failure to read respondent his *Miranda* rights before attempting to locate the weapon. Accordingly we hold that it also erred in excluding the subsequent statements as illegal fruits of a *Miranda* violation. We therefore reverse and remand for further proceedings not inconsistent with this opinion.

JUSTICE O'CONNOR, concurring in part in the judgment and dissenting in part.

* * *

Were the Court writing from a clean slate, I could agree with its holding. But *Miranda* is now the law and, in my view, the Court has not provided sufficient justification for departing from it or for blurring its now clear strictures. ...

* * *

In my view, a "public safety" exception unnecessarily blurs the edges of the clear line heretofore established and makes *Miranda's* requirements more difficult to understand. In some cases, police will benefit because a reviewing court will find that an exigency excused their failure to administer the required warnings. But in other cases, police will suffer because, though they thought an exigency excused their noncompliance, a reviewing court will view the "objective" circumstances differently and require exclusion of admissions thereby obtained. The end result will be a finespun new doctrine on public safety exigencies incident to custodial interrogation, complete with the hair-splitting distinctions that currently plague our Fourth Amendment jurisprudence. ...

The justification the Court provides for upsetting the equilibrium that has finally been achieved—that police cannot and should not balance considerations of public safety against the individual's interest in avoiding compulsory testimonial self-incrimination—really misses the critical question to be decided. *Miranda* has never been read to prohibit the police from asking questions to secure the public safety. Rather, the critical question *Miranda* addresses is who shall bear the cost of securing the public safety when such questions are asked and answered: the defendant or the State.

Miranda, for better or worse, found the resolution of that question implicit in the prohibition against compulsory self-incrimination and placed the burden on the State. When police ask custodial questions without administering the required warnings, *Miranda* quite clearly requires that the answers received be presumed compelled and that they be excluded from evidence at trial.

. . . In my view, since there is nothing about an exigency that makes custodial interrogation any less compelling, a principled application of *Miranda* requires that respondent's statement be suppressed.

* * *

JUSTICE MARSHALL, with whom JUSTICE BRENNAN and JUSTICE STEVENS join, dissenting.

* * *

The majority's entire analysis rests on the factual assumption that the public was at risk during Quarles' interrogation. This assumption is completely in conflict with the facts as found by New York's highest court. Before the interrogation began, Quarles had been "reduced to a condition of physical powerlessness." Contrary to the majority's speculations, Quarles was not believed to have, nor did he in fact have, an accomplice to come to his rescue. When the questioning began, the arresting officers were sufficiently confident of their safety to put away their guns. As Officer Kraft acknowledged at the suppression hearing, "the situation was under control."

* * *

No customers or employees were wandering about the store in danger of coming across Quarles' discarded weapon. Although the supermarket was open to the public, Quarles' arrest took place during the middle of the night when the store was apparently deserted except for the clerks at the checkout counter. The police could easily have cordoned off the store and searched for the missing gun. Had they done so, they would have found the gun forthwith. The police were well aware that Quarles had discarded his weapon somewhere near the scene of the arrest. As the State acknowledged before the New York Court of Appeals: "After Officer Kraft had handcuffed and frisked the defendant in the supermarket, *he knew with a high degree of certainty that the defendant's gun was within the immediate vicinity of the encounter*. He undoubtedly would have searched for it in the carton a few feet away without the defendant having looked in that direction and saying that it was there."

* * *

The majority implies that *Miranda* consisted of no more than a judicial balancing act in which the benefits of "enlarged protection for the Fifth Amendment privilege" were weighed against "the cost to society in terms of fewer convictions of guilty suspects." Supposedly because the scales tipped in favor of the privilege against self-incrimination, the *Miranda* Court erected a prophylactic barrier around statements made during custodial interrogations. The majority now proposes to return to the scales of social utility to calculate whether *Miranda's* prophylactic rule remains cost-effective when threats to public's safety are added to the balance. The results of the majority's "test" are announced with pseudoscientific precision:

> "We conclude that the need for answers to questions in a situation posing a threat to the public safety outweighs the need for the prophylactic rule protecting the Fifth Amendment's privilege against self-incrimination."

The majority misreads *Miranda.* * * * Whether society would be better off if the police warned suspects of their rights before beginning an interrogation or whether the advantages of giving such warnings would outweigh their costs did not inform the *Miranda* decision. On the contrary, the *Miranda* Court was concerned with the proscriptions of the Fifth Amendment, and, in particular, whether the Self–Incrimination Clause permits the government to prosecute individuals based on statements made in the course of custodial interrogations.

* * *

In fashioning its "public-safety" exception to *Miranda*, the majority makes no attempt to deal with the constitutional presumption established by that case. The majority does not argue that police questioning about issues of public safety is any less coercive than custodial interrogations into other matters. The majority's only contention is that police officers could more easily protect the public if *Miranda* did not apply to custodial interrogations concerning the public's safety. But *Miranda* was not a decision about public safety; it was a decision about coerced confessions. Without establishing that interrogations concerning the public's safety are less likely to be coercive than other interrogations, the majority cannot endorse the "public-safety" exception and remain faithful to the logic of Miranda v. Arizona.

* * *

The irony of the majority's decision is that the public's safety can be perfectly well protected without abridging the Fifth Amendment. If a bomb is about to explode or the public is otherwise imminently imperiled, the police are free to interrogate suspects without advising them of their constitutional rights. Such unconsented questioning may take place not only when police officers act on instinct but also when higher faculties lead them to believe that advising a suspect of his constitutional rights might decrease the likelihood that the suspect would reveal life-saving information. If trickery is necessary to protect the public, then the police may trick a suspect into confessing. While the Fourteenth Amendment sets limits on such behavior, nothing in the Fifth Amendment or our decision in Miranda v. Arizona proscribes this sort of emergency questioning. All the Fifth Amendment forbids is the introduction of coerced statements at trial. ...

* * *

(2) Prior to *Quarles*, other courts had applied a public safety exception to Miranda in a few contexts. Negotiations between barricaded suspect and police negotiator is not interrogation. United States v. Mesa, 638 F.2d 582 (3d Cir.1980). Similarly, where the interest of the police is justifiable self-protection they may ask if the suspect is armed or where his weapon is.

Where the officer asks the defendant a question about what happened in order to aid the medical treatment or the rescue of the victim or the suspect, this has been considered non-interrogative. Where the need is strong even lengthy questioning may be justified without warnings. State v. Provost, 490 N.W.2d 93 (Minn.1992) (man with singed hair and an odor of gasoline walks into a police station saying he has burned his wife, he is questioned about where she is); People v. Panah, 35

Cal.4th, 25 Cal.Rptr.3d 672, 107 P.3d 790 (2005) (rescue of injured 8 year old child); People v. Krom, 61 N.Y.2d 187, 473 N.Y.S.2d 139, 461 N.E.2d 276 (1984) (it is proper for police to forego *Miranda* warning in order to ascertain the location of a kidnap victim). Benson v. State, 698 So.2d 333 (Fla.App.1997) (How much crack cocaine did you swallow?)

6. Consider the following conversation between a trooper and an arrestee:

Defendant: "Is there a doctor at the jail?"

Trooper: "Well, do you want to go to the hospital?"

Defendant: "No. But I am going to need to see somebody."

Trooper: "Why?"

Defendant: "Well, I am going to be coming down in a few hours, and I am going to need something."

Trooper: "Well, what are you coming down from?"

Defendant: "Coke. What do you think?"

Trooper Quinn then asked the defendant how much cocaine he had ingested. The defendant responded by saying that he had "freebased" an "eightball" (eighth of an ounce) of cocaine earlier in the day. The conversation continued:

Trooper: "Oh.... Well, do you have any more drugs on you?"

Defendant: "No. I am not stupid enough to get caught carrying it."

Trooper: "Well, where do you do your drugs?"

Defendant: "I do everything in my bedroom."

What part, if any, of this conversation is admissible in the absence of a *Miranda* waiver? See State v. Gravel, 135 N.H. 172, 601 A.2d 678 (1991) (concerning use of admissions to secure warrant to search the bedroom).

Consider also the case of a man arrested with a bag of a controlled substance (the exact nature of which was not known) in the trunk of his car. A booking sergeant inventoried the man's possessions and saw a photograph of the arrestee's wife and child. The sergeant exclaimed, "What are you doing with crap like that when you have these two waiting for you at home?" The arrestee said, "That's not my coke." The substance turned out to be cocaine. See United States v. Soto, 953 F.2d 263 (6th Cir.1992).

Consider finally whether the following is interrogation of a suspect arrested for the third time in one month:

Officer: You need to find something else to do with your life.

Arrestee: No, I'll not stop selling dope because then you all would not have anything to do.

See State v. Goseland, 256 Kan. 729, 887 P.2d 1109 (1994).

(c) THE REQUIRED WARNINGS

Duckworth v. Eagan

Supreme Court of the United States, 1989.
492 U.S. 195, 109 S.Ct. 2875.

■ CHIEF JUSTICE REHNQUIST delivered the opinion of the Court.

Respondent confessed to stabbing a woman nine times after she refused to have sexual relations with him, and he was convicted of attempted murder. Before confessing, respondent was given warnings by the police, which included the advice that a lawyer would be appointed "if and when you go to court. . . ."

Late on May 16, 1982, respondent contacted a Chicago police officer he knew to report that he had seen the naked body of a dead woman lying on a Lake Michigan beach. Respondent denied any involvement in criminal activity. He then took several Chicago police officers to the beach, where the woman was crying for help. When she saw respondent, the woman exclaimed: "Why did you stab me? Why did you stab me?" Respondent told the officers that he had been with the woman earlier that night, but that they had been attacked by several men who abducted the woman in a van.

The next morning, after realizing that the crime had been committed in Indiana, the Chicago police turned the investigation over to the Hammond, Indiana, Police Department. Respondent repeated to the Hammond police officers his story that he had been attacked on the lakefront, and that the woman had been abducted by several men. After he filled out a battery complaint at a local police station, respondent agreed to go to the Hammond police headquarters for further questioning.

At about 11 a.m., the Hammond police questioned respondent. Before doing so, the police read to respondent a waiver form, entitled "Voluntary Appearance; Advice of Rights," and they asked him to sign it. The form provided:

> "Before we ask you any questions, you must understand your rights. You have the right to remain silent. Anything you say can be used against you in court. *You have a right to talk to a lawyer for advice before we ask you any questions, and to have him with you during questioning.* You have this right to the advice and presence of a lawyer even if you cannot afford to hire one. *We have no way of giving you a lawyer, but one will be appointed for you, if you wish, if and when you go to court.* If you wish to answer questions now without a lawyer present, you have the right to stop answering questions at any time. You also have the right to stop answering at any time until you've talked to a lawyer."

Respondent signed the form and repeated his exculpatory explanation for his activities of the previous evening.

Respondent was then placed in the "lock up" at the Hammond police headquarters. Some 29 hours later, at about 4 p.m. on May 18, the police again interviewed respondent. Before this questioning, one of the officers read the following waiver form to respondent:

> "1. Before making this statement, I was advised that I have the right to remain silent and that anything I might say may or will be used against me in a court of law.
>
> "2. That I have the right to consult with an attorney of my own choice before saying anything, and that an attorney may be present while I am making any statement or throughout the course of any conversation with any police officer if I so choose.

"3. That I can stop and request an attorney at any time during the course of the taking of any statement or during the course of any such conversation.

"4. That in the course of any conversation I can refuse to answer any further questions and remain silent, thereby terminating the conversation.

"5. That if I do not hire an attorney, one will be provided for me."

Respondent read the form back to the officers and signed it. He proceeded to confess to stabbing the woman. The next morning, respondent led the officers to the Lake Michigan beach where they recovered the knife he had used in the stabbing and several items of clothing.

At trial, over respondent's objection, the state court admitted his confession, his first statement denying any involvement in the crime, the knife, and the clothing. The jury found respondent guilty of attempted murder, but acquitted him of rape. He was sentenced to 35 years' imprisonment....

* * *

... We then granted certiorari to resolve a conflict among the lower courts as to whether informing a suspect that an attorney would be appointed for him "if and when you go court" renders *Miranda* warnings inadequate.[2] We agree with the majority of the lower courts that it does not.

2. The majority of federal and state courts to consider the issue have held that warnings that contained "if and when you go to court" language satisfied *Miranda*. See Wright v. North Carolina, 483 F.2d 405, 406–407 (C.A.4 1973), cert. denied, 415 U.S. 936, 94 S.Ct. 1452, 39 L.Ed.2d 494 (1974); Massimo v. United States, 463 F.2d 1171, 1174 (C.A.2 1972), cert. denied, 409 U.S. 1117, 93 S.Ct. 920, 34 L.Ed.2d 700 (1973); United States v. Lacy, 446 F.2d 511, 513 (C.A.5 1971); State v. Sterling, 377 So.2d 58, 62–63 (La.1979); Harrell v. State, 357 So.2d 643, 645–646 (Miss.1978); Rowbotham v. State, 542 P.2d 610, 618–619 (Okla.Crim.App.1975); Grennier v. State, 70 Wis.2d 204, 213–215, 234 N.W.2d 316, 321–322 (1975); Schade v. State, 512 P.2d 907, 915–916 (Alaska 1973); State v. Mumbaugh, 107 Ariz. 589, 596–597, 491 P.2d 443, 450–451 (1971); People v. Campbell, 26 Mich.App. 196, 201–202, 182 N.W.2d 4, 6–7 (1970), cert. denied, 401 U.S. 945, 91 S.Ct. 960, 28 L.Ed.2d 228 (1971); People v. Swift, 32 App.Div.2d 183, 186–187, 300 N.Y.S.2d 639, 643–644 (1969), cert. denied, 396 U.S. 1018, 90 S.Ct. 584, 24 L.Ed.2d 510 (1970). Other courts, although not using the precise "if and when you go to court" language, have held *Miranda* was satisfied by a warning that an attorney could not be appointed for a suspect until he appeared in court. See United States v. Contreras, 667 F.2d 976, 979 (C.A.11), cert. denied, 459 U.S. 849, 103 S.Ct. 109, 74 L.Ed.2d 97 (1982); Coyote v. United States, 380 F.2d 305, 308 (C.A.10), cert. denied, 389 U.S. 992, 88 S.Ct. 489, 19 L.Ed.2d 484 (1967); State v. Maluia, 56 Haw. 428, 431–435, 539 P.2d 1200, 1205–1207 (1975); Emler v. State, 259 Ind. 241, 243–244, 286 N.E.2d 408, 410–411 (1972); Jones v. State, 69 Wis.2d 337, 343–345, 230 N.W.2d 677, 682–683 (1975).

On the other hand, a minority of federal and state courts, including the Seventh Circuit in this case, have held that "if and when you go to court" language did not satisfy *Miranda*. See United States ex rel. Williams v. Twomey, 467 F.2d 1248, 1249–1250 (C.A.7 1972); Gilpin v. United States, 415 F.2d 638, 641 (C.A.5 1969); State v. Dess, 184 Mont. 116, 120–122, 602 P.2d 142, 144–145 (1979); Commonwealth v. Johnson, 484 Pa. 349, 352–357, 399 A.2d 111, 112–114 (1979); Square v. State, 283 Ala. 548, 550, 219 So.2d 377, 378–379 (1969).

In *Miranda v. Arizona* ... the Court said that the suspect must be told that "he has the right to remain silent, that anything he says can be used against him in a court of law, that he has the right to the presence of an attorney, and that if he cannot afford an attorney one will be appointed for him prior to any questioning if he so desires." ...

We have never insisted that *Miranda* warnings be given in the exact form described in that decision. ...In *California v. Prysock* (1981), we stated that "the 'rigidity' of *Miranda* [does not] exten[d] to the precise formulation of the warnings given a criminal defendant," and that "no talismanic incantation [is] required to satisfy its strictures."

Miranda has not been limited to stationhouse questioning, and the officer in the field may not always have access to printed *Miranda* warnings, or he may inadvertently depart from routine practice, particularly if a suspect requests an elaboration of the warnings. The prophylactic *Miranda* warnings are "not themselves rights protected by the Constitution but [are] instead measures to insure that the right against compulsory self-incrimination [is] protected." *Michigan v. Tucker* (1974). Reviewing courts therefore need not examine *Miranda* warnings as if construing a will or defining the terms of an easement. The inquiry is simply whether the warnings reasonably "conve[y] to [a suspect] his rights as required by *Miranda*." *Prysock*.

We think the initial warnings given to respondent touched all of the bases required by *Miranda*. ... The Court of Appeals thought this "if and when you go to court" language suggested that "only those accused who can afford an attorney have the right to have one present before answering any questions," and "implie[d] that if the accused does not 'go to court,' *i.e.[,]* the government does not file charges, the accused is not entitled to [counsel] at all."

In our view, the Court of Appeals misapprehended the effect of the inclusion of "if and when you go to court" language in *Miranda* warnings. First, this instruction accurately described the procedure for the appointment of counsel in Indiana.... We think it must be relatively commonplace for a suspect, after receiving *Miranda* warnings, to ask *when* he will obtain counsel. The "if and when you go to court" advice simply anticipates that question. Second, *Miranda* does not require that attorneys be producible on call, but only that the suspect be informed, as here, that he has the right to an attorney before and during questioning, and that an attorney would be appointed for him if he could not afford one. The Court in *Miranda* emphasized that it was not suggesting that "each police station must have a 'station house lawyer' present at all times to advise prisoners." If the police cannot provide appointed counsel, *Miranda* requires only that the police not question a suspect unless he waives his right to counsel. Here, respondent did just that.

Respondent relies on language in *California v. Prysock*, where we suggested that *Miranda* warnings would not be sufficient "if the reference to the right to appointed counsel was linked [to a] future point in time *after* the police interrogation." ... But the vice referred to in *Prysock* was that such warnings would not apprise the accused of his right to have an attorney present if he chose to answer questions. The warnings in this case did not suffer from that defect. Of the eight sentences in the initial warnings, one described respondent's right to counsel "before [the police] ask[ed] [him] questions," while another stated his right to "stop answering at any time until [he] talk[ed] to a lawyer." We hold that the initial warnings given to respondent, in their totality, satisfied *Miranda*, and therefore that his first statement denying his involvement in the crime, as well as the knife and the clothing were all properly admitted into evidence.

... The judgment of the Court of Appeals is accordingly reversed, and the case is remanded for further proceedings not inconsistent with our decision.

It is so ordered.

■ JUSTICE O'CONNOR, with whom JUSTICE SCALIA joins, concurring.

[OMITTED]

■ JUSTICE MARSHALL, with whom JUSTICE BRENNAN joins, and with whom JUSTICE BLACKMUN and JUSTICE STEVENS join, dissenting.

* * *

Miranda mandated no specific verbal formulation that police must use, but the Court, speaking through Chief Justice Warren, emphasized repeatedly that the offer of appointed counsel must be "effective and express." ... A clear and unequivocal offer to provide appointed counsel prior to questioning is, in short, an "absolute prerequisite to interrogation."

... As the Court of Appeals found, Eagan could easily have concluded from the "if and when" caveat that only "those accused who can afford an attorney have the right to have one present before answering any questions; those who are not so fortunate must wait." Eagan was, after all, never told that questioning would be *delayed* until a lawyer was appointed "if and when" Eagan did, in fact, go to court. Thus, the "if and when" caveat may well have had the effect of negating the initial promise that counsel could be present. At best, a suspect like Eagan "would not know ... whether or not he had a right to the services of a lawyer." *Emler v. State*, 259 Ind. 241 (1972) (DeBruler, J., dissenting).

In lawyer-like fashion, The Chief Justice parses the initial warnings given Eagan and finds that the most plausible interpretation is that Eagan would not be questioned until a lawyer was appointed when he later appeared in court. What goes wholly overlooked in The Chief Justice's analysis is that the recipients of police warnings are often frightened suspects unlettered in the law, not lawyers or judges or others schooled in interpreting legal or semantic nuance. Such suspects can hardly be expected to interpret, in as facile a manner as The Chief Justice, "the pretzel-like warnings here—intertwining, contradictory, and ambiguous as they are." Commonwealth v. Johnson, 484 Pa. 349, 356 (1979) (citation omitted) (finding inadequate a similar "if and when" caveat). ...

Even if the typical suspect could draw the inference the majority does—that questioning will not commence until a lawyer is provided at a later court appearance—a warning qualified by an "if and when" caveat still fails to give a suspect any indication of *when* he will be taken to court. Upon hearing the warnings given in this case, a suspect would likely conclude that no lawyer would be provided until trial. In common parlance, "going to court" is synonymous with "going to trial." Furthermore, the negative implication of the caveat is that, if the suspect is never taken to court, he "is not entitled to an attorney at all." An unwitting suspect harboring uncertainty on this score is precisely the sort of person who may feel compelled to talk "voluntarily" to the police, without the presence of counsel, in an effort to extricate himself from his predicament:

... That the warning given to Eagan "accurately described the procedure for the appointment of counsel in Indiana," does nothing to mitigate the possibility that he would feel coerced into talking to the police. *Miranda*, it is true, does not require the police to have a "station house lawyer" ready at all times to counsel suspects taken into custody. But if a suspect does not understand that a lawyer will be made available within a reasonable period of time after he has been taken into custody and advised of his rights, the suspect may decide to talk to the police *for that reason alone*. The threat of an indefinite deferral of interrogation, in a system like Indiana's, thus constitutes an effective means by which the police can pressure a suspect to speak without the presence of counsel. Sanctioning such police practices simply because the warnings given do not misrepresent state law does nothing more than let the state-law tail wag the federal constitutional dog.

NOTES

1. The warnings required under *Miranda* are these: (1) Right to silence: "At the outset, if a person in custody is to be subjected to interrogation, he must first be informed in clear and unequivocal terms that he has the right to remain silent." The Court's reasoning is that this warning is needed (a) to assist the uninformed to exercise intelligently this right, (b) to overcome the "inherent pressures of the interrogation atmosphere", and (c) to assure the accused that his interrogators will recognize this right; (2) Courtroom use of the statement: The accused must be given to understand "that anything said can and will be used against the individual in court." In this way the Court states, (a) the accused is made aware of the right that he has to refuse to talk and he is alerted to the consequences that he faces in waiving this right, and (b) he is made to realize "that he is not in the presence of persons acting solely in his interest"; (3) Right to assistance of counsel during interrogation: "An individual held for interrogation must be clearly informed that he has the right to consult with a lawyer and to have the lawyer with him during interrogation under the system for protecting the privilege we delineate today". The accused must be warned "not only that he has the right to consult with an attorney, but also that if he is indigent a lawyer will be appointed to represent him". The Court specifically holds the interrogator to this measure: "If an individual indicates that he wishes the assistance of counsel before any interrogation occurs, the authorities cannot rationally ignore or deny his request on the basis that the individual does not have or cannot afford a retained attorney".

There has been almost no dispute concerning the substance of the *Miranda* warnings. The only contention made with any frequency at all is that the suspect must be warned that anything he says "can and will" be used against him. Warning a suspect about adverse use of his statements is "perhaps the most critical" of the Miranda admonitions. United States v. Tillman, 963 F.2d 137, 141 (6th Cir.1992). However, the courts have uniformly rejected the argument holding that it is enough to warn the suspect that what he says "might", "can", or "could" be used against him. Davis v. United States, 425 F.2d 673 (9th Cir.1970). Peterson v. State, 562 P.2d 1350 (Alaska 1977). Courts have held that the warning that a statement could be used "for or against you" is misleading. See Commonwealth v. Singleton, 439 Pa. 185, 266 A.2d 753 (1970). Creager v. State, 952 S.W.2d 852 (Tex.Crim.App.1997).

There has been some dispute as to whether additional warnings other than those mentioned should be given. Although suspects are often warned of their right to stop answering questions at any time, Sanchez v. State, 454 S.W.2d 210 (Tex.Crim.App.1970), it has been held that such a warning is not necessary; Commonwealth v. White, 374 Mass. 132, 371 N.E.2d 777 (1977) (reviews decided cases). It is also held that a suspect need not be warned that his refusal to answer questions cannot be used against him nor need he be informed of certain applicable legal rules, i.e., felony murder. State v. McRae, 276 N.C. 308, 172 S.E.2d 37 (1970); Harris v. Riddle, 551 F.2d 936 (4th Cir.1977) (police need not explain legal rules), State v. Norfolk, 221 Neb. 810, 381 N.W.2d 120 (1986) (suspect not entitled to a legal education). State v. Jones, 566 N.W.2d 317 (Minn.1997) (need not warn juvenile of possible prosecution as an adult). The suspect need not be told that he needs or could use the help of a lawyer in deciding to waive his rights. United States v. Hall, 396 F.2d 841 (4th Cir.1968).

In Colorado v. Spring, 479 U.S. 564, 107 S.Ct. 851 (1987), federal Alcohol, Tobacco, and Firearms agents had received information that Spring was involved in illegal weapons transactions and had killed a man in Colorado. They set up an undercover operation and purchased a weapon from Spring in Kansas City, Missouri. They then arrested Spring and provided him with *Miranda* warnings without telling him what they wished to question him about. Spring agreed to talk and signed a written waiver form. The ATF agents questioned him about firearms violations, then shifted to his past record. When Spring said he had a juvenile record from age ten when he had shot his aunt, the agents asked whether he had ever shot anyone else. He mumbled that he shot another guy once. Specific questions about the Colorado killing brought denials. Months later Colorado officials questioned Spring while he was held in jail in Kansas City on the gun charge. They gave him *Miranda* warnings and told him that they wanted to question him about the Colorado homicide. Spring agreed to talk, indicated that "he wanted to get it off his chest," and confessed to the murder.

The Colorado trial judge excluded the statement given to the ATF agents in which Spring had admitted that he had shot another guy once. The judge deemed the statement irrelevant because there was no indication that the admission related to the Colorado homicide. The defendant, however, theorized that the statement to the ATF agents had been *Miranda*-violative, and that the confession given to the Colorado police must be viewed as derived from the earlier *Miranda* violation.

Applying Oregon v. Elstad (Casebook 560), the Court rejected this derivative evidence theory, finding the confession secured by Colorado authorities to be voluntary. Beyond this, however, the Court rejected the claim that the ATF agents had violated *Miranda* by failing to warn Spring that they wished to question him about a homicide.

While acknowledging that the suspect had been warned that *anything* he said could be used against him, two dissenters argued that awareness of the scope and seriousness of the matters under investigation is relevant under a totality of the circumstances test for judging the validity of *Miranda* waivers. They went on to say that the suspect's ignorance on this subject may be a determinative factor, arguing that in the case at hand it was reasonable to conclude that Spring would not have consented to the interrogation in the absence of counsel if he had known that the ATF officials were going to question him about a homicide.

Prior to *Spring* most courts had refused to require a warning concerning the nature of the investigation. United States v. Campbell, 431 F.2d 97 (9th Cir.1970) (suspect need not be warned that he was being investigated for Dyer Act violations); State v. Wilbur, 186 Neb. 306, 182 N.W.2d 906 (1971) (suspect need not be informed of the charges where investigation was in progress); State v. Clough, 259 Iowa 1351, 147 N.W.2d 847 (1967) (suspect need not be informed of charge). Collins v. Brierly, 492 F.2d 735 (3d Cir.1974) (en banc). See also Riddick v. Edmiston, 894 F.2d 586 (3d Cir.1990) (fact of indictment). People v. Pease, 934 P.2d 1374 (Colo.1997) (need not inform of arrest warrant.) In any event the issue will not arise often because a suspect generally knows the nature of the charge and because local statutes and police procedures usually require such admonishments. There are analogous precedents approving interrogation in homicide cases where the police do not inform the suspect that the victim has died. See Satterfield v. Boles, 297 F.Supp. 609 (N.D.W.Va.1967), affirmed 408 F.2d 1029 (4th Cir.1969); Sanchez v. State, 454 S.W.2d 210 (Tex.Crim.App.1970).

2. Two recent Supreme Court decisions support the view that warnings beyond those explicitly required in *Miranda* are not necessary. In Moran v. Burbine, 475 U.S. 412, 106 S.Ct. 1135 (1986), the Court held police need not advise a suspect that a lawyer had called to ask about his status. The Court refused "to require that the police supply a suspect with a flow of information to help him calibrate his self interest in deciding whether to speak. . . ." The Court found that standard warnings in all cases preserved the ease and clarity of applying *Miranda*. Several state courts reject Moran on state law grounds. See People v. Bender, 452 Mich. 594, 551 N.W.2d 71 (1996) (4–3) (review of cases) State v. Roache, 148 N.H. 45, 803 A.2d 572 (2002).

In Oregon v. Elstad, 470 U.S. 298, 105 S.Ct. 1285 (1985) Elstad was arrested at his home, but not warned, told he was suspected of involvement in a burglary and stated, "Yes, I was there." He was then taken to a police station, warned of his rights and questioned. He admitted, in detail, his involvement in the crime. The Court found the statement at the police station to be admissible. It refused to preclude a proper interrogation in cases where the only error in the first interrogation was the failure to warn and the product of the first interrogation was a voluntary, albeit unwarned, admission. The Court dealt with the claim that more than a simple *Miranda* warning is required in this type of case.

"Respondent, however, has argued that he was unable to give a fully *informed* waiver of his rights because he was unaware that his prior statement could not be used against him. Respondent suggests that Deputy McAllister, to cure this deficiency, should have added an additional warning to those given him at the Sheriff's office. Such a requirement is neither practicable nor constitutionally necessary. In many cases, a breach of *Miranda* procedures may not be identified as such until long after full *Miranda* warnings are administered and a valid confession obtained . . . This Court has never embraced the theory that a defendant's ignorance of the full consequences of his decisions vitiates their voluntariness. . . .the Court has refused to find that a defendant who confesses, after being falsely told that his codefendant has turned state's evidence, does so involuntarily. Frazier v. Cupp (1969). The Court has also rejected the argument that a defendant's ignorance that a prior coerced confession could not be admitted in evidence compromised the voluntariness of his guilty plea. McMann v. Richardson (1970). Likewise, in California v. Beheler, the Court declined to accept defendant's contention that, because he was unaware of the potential adverse consequences of statements he made to the police, his participation in the interview was involuntary. Thus we have not held that the *sine qua non* for a knowing and voluntary waiver of the right to remain silent is a full and complete appreciation of all of the consequences flowing from the nature and the quality of the evidence in the case."

The dissenting Justices argued that the decision gave too much leeway to the police to ignore *Miranda* in initial interrogations and then use the admissions of that interrogation to secure further or repeated admissions at a second, fully warned interrogation. They argued that even if the police do not refer to the original admissions they have gained a substantial advantage because the suspect's internal psychological resistance to confession is dissipated.

3. One court has sanctioned a less rigorous form of warning for "field interrogation" in two tandem decisions. In both cases the defendants were arrested on the street and given warnings with respect to counsel that were inadequate. In one case defendant was told he had a "right to an attorney"; in the other, that he had a "right to an attorney while making a statement". The court held that both warnings were proper in context and held that they were adequate for on the street interrogation. The court indicated that a more careful warning procedure would be required for a station-house interrogation. The dichotomy between street warning and station-house warnings was based on the practical differences between the two situations both in terms of police security and custodial atmosphere. See United States v. Lamia, 429 F.2d 373 (2d Cir.1970) (cited with favor in Prysock); United States v. Cusumano, 429 F.2d 378 (2d Cir.1970). There have been no further cases applying this rule, perhaps because police give full warnings as a matter of routine.

4. *Miranda* warnings must be given in a clear, unhurried manner—in such a way that the individual would feel free to claim his rights without fear. The warnings should not be given in a perfunctory fashion. United States v. Vanterpool, 394 F.2d 697 (2d Cir.1968); Lathers v. United States, 396 F.2d 524 (5th Cir.1968). But, "*Miranda* does not require law enforcement officials to insist upon or to suggest the refusal of cooperation. As long as the suspect is clearly told and clearly understands that he need not talk, that he may consult a lawyer before deciding whether or not to talk, and that he may have one present when he talks, if he decides to talk, all the requirements of *Miranda* are met". United States v. Duke, 409 F.2d 669 (4th Cir.1969).

When warnings are given to an illiterate or subnormal person, "Miranda requires meaningful advice ... in language which he can comprehend and on which he can knowingly act. The crucial test is whether the words used by the officers, in view of the age, intelligence and demeanor of the individual being interrogated (conveyed) a clear understanding of all his rights." Jenkins v. State, 214 So.2d 470 (Miss.1968). For an example of great care in warning one of subnormal intelligence, see Anderson v. State, 6 Md.App. 688, 253 A.2d 387 (1969).

In dealing with suspects who do not speak English, the warnings, of course, must be given in a language they understand. United States v. Hernandez, 93 F.3d 1493 (10th Cir.1996). Warnings may be read from a card (Hammond v. State, 244 Ark. 1113, 428 S.W.2d 639 (1968)) and written warnings are sufficient where the suspect is literate. United States v. Lucarz, 430 F.2d 1051 (9th Cir.1970). See United States v. Cazares, 112 F.3d 1391 (9th Cir.1997) (oral warnings in English followed by reading of Spanish language warning card).

It seems clear that claims arising from an improper manner of admonishment will be settled in trial courts. If the required warnings are fully stated it is impossible for anyone but a trier of fact to determine whether admittedly proper warnings were given in an improper manner. It is doubtful that a court of review can effectively deal with such claims. See State v. Lay, 427 S.W.2d 394 (Mo.1968) (hollow recitation); People v. McCottrell, 117 Ill.App.2d 1, 254 N.E.2d 284 (1969) (hurried recitation); State v. Ortega, 95 Idaho 239, 506 P.2d 466 (1973) (15–20 second warning is not per se improper).

5. The warnings must be given at the very beginning of the interrogation, but need not be repeated as the questioning moves from one crime to another, State v. Jennings, 104 Ariz. 6, 448 P.2d 62 (1968); State v. Davidson, 252 Or. 617, 451 P.2d 481 (1969), or after a short break, Davis v. State, 698 So.2d 1182 (Fla.1997); United States v. Hopkins, 433 F.2d 1041 (5th Cir.1970) (no need to rewarn where there was no significant interval between state and federal interrogations); Mitchell v. State, 3 Tenn.Crim.App. 153, 458 S.W.2d 630 (1970) (where warnings with respect to first interrogation concerning one crime are clearly adequate, interrogation with respect to another crime the next day need not begin with warnings). When the questioning is taken over by a new officer, he does not have to rewarn. Commonwealth v. Bradley, 449 Pa. 19, 295 A.2d 842 (1972). It has been held that the warnings must precede only the incriminating question and answer; it need not precede all questions. Commonwealth v. Bartlett, 446 Pa. 392, 288 A.2d 796 (1972). But see People v. Honeycutt, 20 Cal.3d 150, 141 Cal.Rptr. 698, 570 P.2d 1050 (1977) (improper to discuss waiver before giving warnings even where warnings preceded interrogation).

In Wyrick v. Fields, 459 U.S. 42, 103 S.Ct. 394 (1982), a suspect and his lawyer consented to the suspect's submission to a polygraph examination out of the presence of the lawyer. Authorities warned the suspect of his *Miranda* rights before the test commenced. After the exam, they told him that the test indicated deception. They continued to interrogate him without further warnings. The Supreme Court, per curiam, rejected the claim that, absent renewed warnings, there could be no valid *Miranda* waiver. The accused had previously sought the polygraph exam and had clearly agreed to questioning. The Court pointed out that even if the accused had believed that the polygraph examiner's opinion would be inadmissible at trial, he had no reason to believe that his answers to questions would be excluded. It found no significance in the fact that some of the questions were asked after the machine had been disconnected.

6. The testimony of an officer that he gave the warnings is sufficient. It need not be corroborated even if contradicted by defendant. State v. Bower, 73 Wash.2d 634, 440 P.2d 167 (1968); Bridges v. State, 255 Ind. 201, 263 N.E.2d 368 (1970); Cf. Madkins v. State, 50 Wis.2d 347, 184 N.W.2d 144 (1971) (testimony of two officers not exactly the same). But see Williams v. State, 220 So.2d 325 (Miss.1969) (fact of warnings contradicted, prosecution failed to prove warnings when it did not call second interrogating officer).

The precise nature of the warnings given must be clearly shown in the record. Conclusory testimony that defendant "was given his rights and agreed to talk" is insufficient. (State v. Graham, 240 So.2d 486 (Fla.App.1970); State v. Seefeldt, 51 N.J. 472, 242 A.2d 322 (1968)). However, it is not necessary to tape record warnings, or to have them stenographically reported. State v. Cassell, 280 Mont. 397, 932 P.2d 478 (1996).

The decision in almost all cases is for the trier of fact, and disputes as to the giving of warnings are rarely considered on the merits in a court of review. United States v. Hensley, 374 F.2d 341 (6th Cir.1967); United States v. Abigando, 439 F.2d 827 (5th Cir.1971). Often, officers read warnings from a card to be certain they omit nothing. If so, it is essential to either introduce the card into evidence or have it read into evidence. Moll v. United States, 413 F.2d 1233 (5th Cir.1969); Contra: Tudela v. State, 212 So.2d 387 (Fla.App.1968) (court took judicial notice of the text of the warning card).

Where written or oral warnings are given and one is defective and the other not, the courts have considered the correct warning as reparative of the inadequate one. Brooks v. State, 229 A.2d 833 (Del.1967) (inadequate written warnings); State v. Taggert, 443 S.W.2d 168 (Mo.1969) (inadequate written warnings); People v.

Swift, 32 A.D.2d 183, 300 N.Y.S.2d 639 (1969) (inadequate oral warning). But see United States v. Garcia, 431 F.2d 134 (9th Cir.1970) (conflict between two different warnings serves only to confuse.)

7. Some police officers go beyond the requirements of *Miranda* by adding to the four necessary admonitions, specifying, for example, the right to cut off questioning at any time. Even "standard" *Miranda* cards in some jurisdictions go beyond the four warnings required by the Supreme Court. Some officers also repeat the litany of warnings several times over a short period, another practice not mandated by *Miranda*. These practices are exemplified by reference to specific cases, including the John Hinckley interrogation, in Inbau, Over–Reaction—The Mischief of Miranda v. Arizona, 73 J.Crim.L. & Criminology 101 (1982). Professor Inbau criticizes the practices and suggests that officers often go beyond securing a valid waiver of rights and effectively draw out an invocation of rights from a suspect who was willing to make a statement.

A variation of this theme is found in Smith v. United States, 529 A.2d 312 (D.C.App.1987), where a written waiver form concluded with four questions 1) Have you read warnings? 2) Do you understand rights? 3) Do you wish to answer? 4) Are you willing to do so without an attorney? Defendant answered yes to all questions except the last (and unnecessary question)—the statement was suppressed because in the words of Judge Terry "Detective Corboy asked one question too many."

(d) THE ADEQUACY OF WAIVER

North Carolina v. Butler

Supreme Court of the United States, 1979.
441 U.S. 369, 99 S.Ct. 1755.

■ MR. JUSTICE STEWART delivered the opinion of the Court.

In evident conflict with the present view of every other court that has considered the issue, the North Carolina Supreme Court, has held that Miranda v. Arizona requires that no statement of a person under custodial interrogation may be admitted in evidence against him unless, at the time the statement was made, he explicitly waived the right to the presence of a lawyer. We granted certiorari to consider whether this *per se* rule reflects a proper understanding of the *Miranda* decision.

The respondent was convicted in a North Carolina trial court of kidnapping, armed robbery, and felonious assault. The evidence at his trial showed that he and a man named Elmer Lee had robbed a gas station in Goldsboro, N.C., in December 1976, and had shot the station attendant as he was attempting to escape. The attendant was paralyzed, but survived to testify against the respondent.

The prosecution also produced evidence of incriminating statements made by the respondent shortly after his arrest by FBI agents in the Bronx, N.Y. on the basis of a North Carolina fugitive warrant. Outside the presence of the jury, FBI Agent Martinez testified that at the time of the arrest he fully advised the respondent of the rights delineated in the *Miranda* case. According to the uncontroverted testimony of Martinez, the agents then took the respondent to the FBI office in nearby New Rochelle, N.Y. There, after the agents determined that the respondent had an 11th grade education and was literate, he was given the Bureau's "Advice of Rights" form which he read. When asked if he understood his rights, he replied that he did. The respondent refused to sign the waiver at the bottom of the form. He was told that he need neither speak nor sign the form, but that the agents would like him to talk to them. The respondent replied, "I will talk to you but I am not signing any form." He then made inculpatory statements. Agent Martinez testified that the respondent said nothing when advised of his right to the assistance of a lawyer. At no time did the respondent request counsel or attempt to terminate the agents' questioning.

At the conclusion of this testimony the respondent moved to suppress the evidence of his incriminating statements on the ground that he had not waived his right to the assistance of counsel at the time the statements were made. The court denied the motion, finding that

> "the statement made by the defendant, William Thomas Butler, to Agent David C. Martinez, was made freely and voluntarily to said agent after having been advised of his rights as required by the Miranda ruling, including his right to an attorney being present at the time of the inquiry and that the defendant, Butler, understood his rights; [and] that he effectively waived his rights, including the right to have an attorney present during the questioning by his indication that he was willing to answer questions, having read the rights form together with the Waiver of Rights. . . ."

The respondent's statements were then admitted into evidence, and the jury ultimately found the respondent guilty of each offense charged.

On appeal, the North Carolina Supreme Court reversed the convictions and ordered a new trial. It found that the statements had been admitted in violation of the requirements of the *Miranda* decision, noting that the respondent had refused to waive in writing his right to have counsel present and that there had not been a *specific* oral waiver. As it had in at least two earlier cases, the court read the *Miranda* opinion as

> "provid[ing] in plain language that waiver of the right to counsel during interrogation will not be recognized unless such waiver is 'specifically made' after the *Miranda* warnings have been given."

We conclude that the North Carolina Supreme Court erred in its reading of the *Miranda* opinion. There, this Court said that

> "If the interrogation continues without the presence of an attorney and a statement is taken, a heavy burden rests on the government to demonstrate that the defendant knowingly and intelligently waived his privilege against self-incrimination and his right to retained or appointed counsel."

The Court's opinion went on to say that

> "An express statement that the individual is willing to make a statement and does not want an attorney followed closely by a statement could constitute a waiver. But a valid waiver will not be presumed simply from the silence of the accused after warnings are given or simply from the fact that a confession was in fact eventually obtained."

Thus the Court held that an express statement can constitute a waiver, and that silence alone after such warnings cannot do so. But the Court did not hold that such an express statement is indispensable to a finding of waiver.

An express written or oral statement of waiver of the right to remain silent or of the right to counsel is usually strong proof of the validity of that waiver, but is not inevitably either necessary or sufficient to establish waiver. The question is not one of form, but rather whether the defendant in fact knowingly and voluntarily waived the rights delineated in the *Miranda* case. As was unequivocally said in *Miranda*, mere silence is not enough. That does not mean that the defendant's silence, coupled with an understanding of his rights and a course of conduct indicating waiver, may never support a conclusion that a defendant has waived his rights. The courts must presume that a defendant did not waive his rights; the prosecution's burden is great; but in at least some cases waiver can be clearly inferred from the actions and words of the person interrogated.[4]

The Court's opinion in *Miranda* explained the reasons for the prophylactic rules it created:

> "We have concluded that without proper safeguards the process of in-custody interrogation of persons suspected or accused of crime contains inherently compelling pressures which work to undermine the individual's will to resist and to compel him to speak where he would not otherwise do so freely. In order to combat these pressures and to permit a full opportunity to exercise the privilege against self-incrimination, the accused must be adequately and effectively apprised of his rights and the exercise of those rights must be fully honored."

The *per se* rule that the North Carolina Supreme Court has found in *Miranda* does not speak to these concerns. There is no doubt that this respondent was adequately and effectively apprised of his rights. The only question is whether he waived the exercise of one of those rights, the right to the presence of a lawyer. Neither the state court, nor the respondent has offered any reason why there must be a negative answer to that question in the absence of an *express* waiver. This is not the first criminal case to question whether a defendant waived his constitutional rights. It is an issue with which courts must repeatedly deal. Even when the right so fundamental as that to counsel at trial is involved, the question of waiver must be determined on "the particular facts and circumstances surround-

4. We do not today even remotely question the holding in Carnley v. Cochran, 369 U.S. 506, 82 S.Ct. 884, which was specifically approved in the *Miranda* opinion. In that case, decided before Gideon v. Wainwright, 372 U.S. 335, 83 S.Ct. 792, the Court held that the defendant had a constitutional right to counsel under the Fourteenth Amendment. The Florida Supreme Court had presumed that his right had been waived because there was no evidence in the record that he had requested counsel. The Court refused to allow a presumption of waiver from a silent record. It said "the record must show, or there must be an allegation and evidence which show, that an accused was offered counsel but intelligently and understandingly rejected the offer." This statement is consistent with our decision today, which is merely that a court *may* find an intelligent and understanding rejection of counsel in situations where the defendant did not *expressly* state as much.

ing that case, including the background, experience, and conduct of the accused."

We see no reason to discard that standard and replace it with an inflexible *per se* rule in a case such as this. As stated at the outset of this opinion, it appears that every court that has considered this question has now reached the same conclusion. Ten of the 11 United States Courts of Appeals and the courts of at least 17 States[6] have held that an explicit statement of waiver is not invariably necessary to support a finding that the defendant waived the right to remain silent or the right to counsel guaranteed by the *Miranda* case. By creating an inflexible rule that no implicit waiver can ever suffice, the North Carolina Supreme Court has gone beyond the requirements of federal organic law. . . .

■ MR. JUSTICE POWELL took no part in the consideration or decision of this case.

■ [MR. JUSTICE BLACKMUN's concurring opinion is omitted.]

■ MR. JUSTICE BRENNAN, with whom MR. JUSTICE MARSHALL and MR. JUSTICE STEVENS joins, dissenting.

Miranda v. Arizona, held that "[n]o effective waiver of the right to counsel during interrogation can be recognized unless *specifically* made after the warnings we here delineate have been given." (Emphasis added.) Support for this holding was found in Carnley v. Cochran, 369 U.S. 506, 516, 82 S.Ct. 884, 890 (1962), which held that in the absence of an allegation of an "*affirmative* waiver . . . there is no disputed fact question requiring a hearing." (Emphasis added.)

There is no allegation of an affirmative waiver in this case. As the Court concedes, the respondent here refused to sign the waiver form, and "said nothing when advised of his right to the assistance of a lawyer." Thus, there was no "disputed fact question requiring a hearing," and the trial Court erred in holding one. In the absence of an "affirmative waiver" in the form of an express written or oral statement, the Supreme Court of North Carolina correctly granted a new trial. I would, therefore, affirm its decision.

The rule announced by the Court today allows a finding of waiver based upon "inference from the actions and words of the person interroga-

6. Sullivan v. State, 351 So.2d 659 (Ala. Cr.App.), cert. denied, 351 So.2d 665 (Ala.Cr. App.1977); State v. Pineda, 110 Ariz. 342, 519 P.2d 41 (1974); State ex rel. Berger v. Superior Court, 109 Ariz. 506, 513 P.2d 935 (1973); People v. Johnson, 70 Cal.2d 541, 75 Cal.Rptr. 401, 450 P.2d 865 (1969) (reversed on other grounds); People v. Weaver, 179 Colo. 331, 500 P.2d 980 (1972); Reed v. People, 171 Colo. 421, 467 P.2d 809 (1970); State v. Craig, 237 So.2d 737 (Fla.1970); Peek v. State, 239 Ga. 422, 238 S.E.2d 12 (1977); People v. Brooks, 51 Ill.2d 156, 281 N.E.2d 326 (1972); State v. Wilson, 215 Kan. 28, 523 P.2d 337 (1974); State v. Hazelton, 330 A.2d 919 (Me.1975); Miller v. State, 251 Md. 362, 247 A.2d 530 (1968); Commonwealth v. Murray, 359 Mass. 541, 269 N.E.2d 641 (1971); State v. Alewine, 474 S.W.2d 848 (Mo.1972); Burnside v. State, 473 S.W.2d 697 (Mo.1971); Shirey v. State, 520 P.2d 701 (Okl.Cr.App. 1974); State v. Davidson, 252 Or. 617, 451 P.2d 481 (1969); Commonwealth v. Garnett, 458 Pa. 4, 326 A.2d 335 (1974); Bowling v. State, 3 Tenn.Cr.App. 176, 458 S.W.2d 639 (1970); State v. Young, 89 Wash.2d 613, 574 P.2d 1171 (1978). See also Aaron v. State, 275 A.2d 791 (Del.1971); State v. Nelson, Minn., 257 N.W.2d 356 (1977); Land v. Commonwealth, 211 Va. 223, 176 S.E.2d 586 (1970) (reversed on other grounds).

ted." The Court thus shrouds in half-light the question of waiver, allowing courts to construct inferences from ambiguous words and gestures. But the very premise of *Miranda* requires that ambiguity be interpreted against the interrogator. That premise is the recognition of the "compulsion inherent in custodial" interrogation, and of its purpose "to subjugate the individual to the will of [the] examiner." Under such conditions, only the most explicit waivers of rights can be considered knowingly and freely given.

The instant case presents a clear example of the need for an express waiver requirement. As the Court acknowledges, there is a disagreement over whether respondent was orally advised of his rights at the time he made his statement. The fact that Butler received a written copy of his rights is deemed by the Court to be sufficient basis to resolve the disagreement. But, unfortunately, there is also a dispute over whether Butler could read. And, obviously, if Butler did not have his rights read to him, and could not read them himself, there could be no basis upon which to conclude that he knowingly waived them. Indeed, even if Butler could read there is no reason to believe that his oral statements, which followed a refusal to sign a written waiver form were intended to signify relinquishment of his rights.

Faced with "actions and words" of uncertain meaning, some judges may find waivers where none occurred. Others may fail to find them where they did. In the former case, the defendant's rights will have been violated; in the latter, society's interest in effective law enforcement will have been frustrated. A simple prophylactic rule requiring the police to obtain an express waiver of the right to counsel before proceeding with interrogation eliminates these difficulties. And since the Court agrees that *Miranda* requires the police to obtain some kind of waiver—whether express or implied—the requirement of an express waiver would impose no burden on the police not imposed by the Court's interpretation. It would merely make that burden explicit. Had Agent Martinez simply elicited a clear answer from Willie Butler to the question, "Do you waive your right to a lawyer?," this journey through three courts would not have been necessary.

NOTES

1. The issue of waiver under *Miranda* has become the most dominant issue. And the resolution of waiver issues, as is the case with custody issues, is complex. Where once there were claims of coerced confession there now arise claims of coerced waiver. See Miranda v. Arizona, 384 U.S. at 476, 86 S.Ct. at 1628, 1629; Coyote v. United States, 380 F.2d 305 (10th Cir.1967); State v. LaFernier, 37 Wis.2d 365, 155 N.W.2d 93 (1967). Indeed, debates over the existence of waiver parallel the old debates over voluntariness because voluntariness of waiver must be determined by the same "totality of the circumstances" that once determined voluntariness of confession. See People v. Hill, 39 Ill.2d 125, 233 N.E.2d 367 (1968).

Some commentators believe the Court erred in permitting waiver of *Miranda* rights—the rights ought to be nonwaivable and custodial confessions inadmissible if the result of interrogation. Others agree that waivers are untrustworthy but the conclusion drawn is that *Miranda* ought not to have imposed its rule on police interrogation. See Caplan, Questioning Miranda, 38 Vand.L.Rev. 1417 (1985) Ogletree, Are Confessions Really Good for the Soul?: A Proposal to Mirandize *Miranda*,

100 Harv.L.Rev. 1826 (1987); Schulhofer, Reconsidering Miranda, 54 U.Chi.L.Rev. 435 (1987); White, Defending Miranda: A Reply to Professor Caplan, 39 Vand.L.Rev. 1 (1986). One scholar suggests the use of courtroom questioning along with some curtailment of privilege (refusal to answer may be used adversely) and a ban on custodial police interrogation, Dripps, Against Police Interrogation, 78 J.Crim.L. & C. 699 (1988).

The courts have singled out certain facts which particularly support findings of waiver. The selective exercise of certain rights, i.e., refusal to answer some questions, tends to show the existence of a deliberate waiver with respect to the questions answered. United States v. Marchildon, 519 F.2d 337 (8th Cir.1975); People v. McReavy, 436 Mich. 197, 462 N.W.2d 1 (1990); Mitchell v. United States, 434 F.2d 483 (D.C.Cir.1970) (request for counsel immediately after statement); The existence of a motive to make a statement is supportive of a conscious waiver. State v. Collins, 74 Wash.2d 729, 446 P.2d 325 (1968) (attempt to secure deal for providing evidence); State v. LaFernier, 37 Wis.2d 365, 155 N.W.2d 93 (1967) (desire to avoid publicity). A suspect's extensive criminal experience will also serve to substantiate existence of a knowing waiver. Mingo v. People, 171 Colo. 474, 468 P.2d 849 (1970).

In Colorado v. Connelly, 479 U.S. 157, 107 S.Ct. 515 (1986), supra, p. 26, the Court held (notwithstanding the "heavy burden" language in *Miranda*) that compliance with *Miranda* is to be proved by a preponderance of the evidence.

2. Even if there are adequate warnings the question may arise as to whether the suspect was mentally competent to waive his rights. A leading case sustaining waiver is People v. Lara, 67 Cal.2d 365, 62 Cal.Rptr. 586, 432 P.2d 202 (1967). In Dover v. State, 227 So.2d 296 (Miss.1969) a suspect with an I.Q. of 60 with lowered ability in stress situations was held incompetent to waive his right. The question of competency to waive will normally deal with the effect of youth, mental capacity, insanity, drug, alcohol and injury upon the ability to comprehend the rights involved and the gravity of the decision to waive. The decisions on these questions are voluminous.

a. On the subject of youth, consider: In re David C., 116 Md.App. 580, 698 A.2d 1155 (1997) (waiver by 10–year–old is invalid; age of suspect also a factor in deciding custody question); Commonwealth v. Darden, 441 Pa. 41, 271 A.2d 257 (1970) (waiver by 15 year old, mild retarded juvenile upheld); In re P., 7 Cal.3d 801, 103 Cal.Rptr. 425, 500 P.2d 1 (1972) (waiver by 14 year old retarded shortly after he was wakened is invalid). There is no per se rule restricting a juvenile's waiver. Fare v. Michael C., 442 U.S. 707, 99 S.Ct. 2560 (1979).

b. Insanity or Retardation: See United States v. Bush, 466 F.2d 236 (5th Cir.1972) (waiver by suspect with I.Q. of 68 and mental age of 6 upheld) and Moore v. Dugger, 856 F.2d 129 (11th Cir.1988) (62 I.Q., 11 mental age, valid waiver). Low intelligence does not by itself invalidate a waiver. Commonwealth v. White, 362 Mass. 193, 285 N.E.2d 110 (1972); State v. Smith, 7 Or.App. 485, 492 P.2d 317 (1971) (waiver upheld where psychiatrist testified that *Miranda* warnings were simply and easily understood); See also Criswell v. State, 86 Nev. 573, 472 P.2d 342 (1970) (waiver by paranoid schizophrenic). People v. Bernasco, 138 Ill.2d 349, 150 Ill.Dec. 155, 562 N.E.2d 958 (1990), upheld a trial judge's decision to suppress, on *Miranda*-waiver grounds, the confession of a seventeen-year-old who had an IQ of 80. An expert testified that the youngster would not have understood many of the terms used and would have readily acquiesced to police wishes. The court said that even after *Connelly*, supra, the lack of police misconduct does not eliminate the possibility of a constitutional violation. The prosecution still must demonstrate a knowing waiver of *Miranda* rights.

c. Intoxication: State v. Pease, 129 Vt. 70, 271 A.2d 835 (1970) (intoxication does not invalidate a waiver per se); People v. Moore, 20 Cal.App.3d 444, 97

Cal.Rptr. 601 (1971) (blood alcohol reading of .21 is not sufficient to invalidate waiver); People v. Roy, 49 Ill.2d 113, 273 N.E.2d 363 (1971) (intoxication voids waiver); People v. Gurley, 23 Cal.App.3d 536, 100 Cal.Rptr. 407 (1972) (influence of heroin voids waiver); State v. Hoskins, 292 Minn. 111, 193 N.W.2d 802 (1972) (suspect using tranquilizing medication may validly waive his rights).

d. Injury: See State v. Pressel, 2 Or.App. 477, 468 P.2d 915 (1970) (wounded suspect may make a valid waiver); State v. Parker, 55 Wis.2d 131, 197 N.W.2d 742 (1972) (suspect with a minor wound may validly waive rights even though wound was thought to be major).

Compare Young v. Walls, 311 F.3d, 846 (7th Cir.2002).

> Dan Young, whose IQ has been measured at 56, has slight comprehension of abstract concepts. He is also uncontrollably violent when left to his own devices and has accumulated a lengthy criminal record. The convictions now under review are for the rape and exceptionally brutal murder of Kathy Morgan. His detailed confession was corroborated by a confederate plus a match between Young's dental pattern and a bite mark on Morgan's body. He was sentenced to life imprisonment, which is essential to incapacitate Young (who appears to be undeterrable) and protect society. According to Young, however, his mental shortcomings prevent him from making effective confessions and require him to be freed, because he can't understand the legal significance of Miranda warnings.
>
> The police who took the confession testified that they simplified the warnings for Young and that he appeared to understand the advice. Before the confession was signed, an assistant state's attorney gave Young another set of amplified warnings and concluded that he understood his entitlement to stop the questioning and have counsel. The psychiatrists agreed that this degree of comprehension is possible for someone with a low IQ, if the warnings are made sufficiently simple and the suspect's responses are elicited with care.
>
> Young's lawyers reply that comprehension of Miranda and the consequences of waiver requires abstract intelligence. Yet Young cannot count backward. He does not know which direction is "east" and thus cannot tell where the sun appears. Asked to name the Presidents since 1950, he answered "Washington" and "Lincoln." He knows that winter means cold and snow but cannot explain what "seasons" are. He cannot describe a ship (which of course he does not encounter in daily life). His command of analogies and categories is poor; he can't explain in what respects a dog is similar to a lion. But he knows that a "PD" in Illinois is a public defender, and he knows what a trial is for even though he cannot describe how the jury works. In other words, he has concrete knowledge suited to his occupation as a career criminal, but poor verbal skills, a low fund of general knowledge, and an inability to reason (or talk) abstractly.
>
> Do these deficiencies mean that a person such as Young is unable to confess to a crime? If entitlement to talk to the police depends on capacity to reason abstractly about the legal system and understand the long-term consequences of one's acts (such as the effect that a confession will have at trial), then the answer must be yes. See Morgan Cloud, George B. Shepherd, Alison Nodvin Barkoff & Justin V. Shur, Words Without Meaning: The Constitution, Confessions, and Mentally Retarded Suspects, 69 U. Chi. L.Rev. 495 (2002) (concluding that retarded suspects do not understand the legal significance of Miranda warnings or the consequences of confessions).

Yet Miranda is not about abstract understanding, nor does the Constitution protect suspects against confessions that are made for reasons other than official coercion. See Colorado v. Connelly, 479 U.S. 157, 107 S.Ct. 515, 93 L.Ed.2d 473 (1986) (a confession given by a suspect who believed that God had instructed him to confess, and who therefore did not care about the legal system's agents such as lawyers, is nonetheless admissible). Recall the point of the warnings: to protect the suspect's privilege against compulsory self-incrimination. Miranda scuttled the rationale of Escobedo v. Illinois, 378 U.S. 478, 84 S.Ct. 1758, 12 L.Ed.2d 977 (1964), which had relied on the sixth amendment. There is scant risk that Young was being compelled to be a witness against himself; he confessed because he wanted to talk. This may have been an uninformed, self-destructive decision, but it was not the result of the third degree. Custodial interrogation played no role; the psychiatrists believe that Young would have confessed in any setting. Miranda is simply beside the point for persons who confess because they don't think that their words will harm them—the position in which, according to his lawyers, Young found himself following his arrest. Young had enough awareness (the state court found) to understand what a lawyer is and his entitlement to direct the police to stop asking questions. This is all the fifth amendment demands. See Moran v. Burbine, 475 U.S. 412, 421, 106 S.Ct. 1135, 89 L.Ed.2d 410 (1986).

That Young may have been unable to understand why a lawyer's assistance might be important, as one of the psychiatrists concluded, is not legally material. Suspects need not know how legal skills could be employed to best advantage. That's asking too much and is too far removed from the goal that Miranda warnings are designed to implement. It is sufficient if the suspect has enough mental capacity to make decisions in daily life. An infant, or a person so incompetent that a guardian had been appointed, would be a different matter; the legal system generally does not allow such persons to form contracts or otherwise bind themselves. Young, though, is among the great majority of adults who can live independent lives, and as part of those lives can make choices with effects both good and bad.

Perhaps the legal system should adopt additional rules to deal with suspects of limited intellectual abilities. But they are not now in place, nor has the Supreme Court concluded that rules of this kind are to be found in the Constitution.

3. What if a suspect is mentally competent to understand the warnings but does not; in fact, understand them? In State v. Norfolk, 221 Neb. 810, 381 N.W.2d 120 (1986) a valid warning was given but the suspect believed oral statements were not admissible. The Court held that actual comprehension is not required—the mentally competent suspect who receives a proper warning is presumed, probably conclusively, to understand it.

4. A difficult issue concerns when waiver may be implied where there is no specific verbal waiver. In State v. Kremens, 52 N.J. 303, 245 A.2d 313 (1968) the court held: "Any clear manifestation of a desire to waive is sufficient. The test is the showing of a knowing intent, not the utterance of a shibboleth. The criterion is not solely the language employed but a combination of that articulation and the surrounding facts and circumstances."

In United States v. Hayes, 385 F.2d 375 (4th Cir.1967), waiver was implied when after warnings defendant made no acknowledgment but asked to use a phone. He was allowed to do so. After the call he returned to the room and answered questions for a half an hour. He then stopped, asked for a lawyer, and no further questions were put.

In Brown v. State, 3 Md.App. 313, 239 A.2d 761 (1968), a suspect turned himself in and volunteered information. He was warned and made no explicit waiver but promptly answered questions. The Court construed his actions prior to warning as supporting a conclusion of implied waiver. See Commonwealth v. Fisher, 354 Mass. 549, 238 N.E.2d 525 (1968) (Suspect declines use of phone, says he wants to talk, agrees to polygraph test); People v. Matthews, 22 Mich.App. 619, 178 N.W.2d 94 (1970) (waiver is implied from defendant's initiating conversation).

By the same token a claim of privilege need not be formal in nature, i.e., Coppola v. Powell, 878 F.2d 1562 (1st Cir.1989) ("I'm not going to confess, you can't get it out of me"). "Don't bother me" is an assertion of the right to remain silent. State v. Klimczak, 159 Conn. 608, 268 A.2d 372 (1970). But see Reeves v. State, 241 Ga. 44, 243 S.E.2d 24 (1978) ("I ain't saying nothing" is not, in context, an assertion of rights). Taylor v. Riddle, 563 F.2d 133 (4th Cir.1977) ("You done asked me a question I can't answer" is not assertion of right to silence). United States v. Eaton, 890 F.2d 511 (1st Cir.1989) ("depends on the question"—does not assert rights); Owen v. State, 560 So.2d 207 (Fla.1990) ("I'd rather not talk about it" may be assertion and must be clarified).

People v. Hayes, 38 Cal.3d 780, 214 Cal.Rptr. 652, 699 P.2d 1259 (1985) (suspect admits crime and then asks, "Do I gotta still tell you after I admit it?"—held not an assertion of the right to silence but merely an understandable discomfort in going into details of a heinous crime).

In People v. Jennings, 46 Cal.3d 963, 251 Cal.Rptr. 278, 760 P.2d 475 (1988), the Court found the video record of interrogation made it clear, from demeanor and context, that silence was not asserted when defendant said "I don't like you. You're scaring me. That's it. I shut up."

5. The courts have rarely dealt with a model *Miranda* waiver, i.e., State v. Ransom, 182 Neb. 243, 153 N.W.2d 916 (1967). The area of waiver is one where "problems do exist". United States v. Corbbins, 397 F.2d 790 (7th Cir.1968). Not the least problem is the indecisive suspect who seems never to quite get to the point of waiving or claiming his rights. State v. Phillips, 563 S.W.2d 47 (Mo.1978). See especially People v. Hiles, 172 Colo. 463, 474 P.2d 153 (1970) (upholding waiver of suspect who refused to acknowledge understanding his rights and refused to waive them but insisted for half an hour that he wanted to talk), and Bliss v. United States, 445 A.2d 625 (D.C.App.1982) (suspect simply made no response of any kind to warnings, then finally nodded his head). Of course, some act of waiver must occur; waiver can not be inferred from complete silence unrelieved by any coherent gesture. See Tague v. Louisiana, 444 U.S. 469, 100 S.Ct. 652 (1980).

The courts have coped with the problems in the following ways:

When it is clear that a defendant has been fully informed of his rights any reasonable verbal acknowledgment of understanding or willingness to speak is acceptable. United States v. Gordon, 895 F.2d 932 (4th Cir.1990) ("What do you want to know?"); United States v. Boykin, 398 F.2d 483 (3d Cir.1968) (after warnings, suspect said "I might as well tell you about it"); Patrick v. State, 203 So.2d 62 (Fla.App.1967) (after warnings suspect said "I don't need a lawyer"); State v. Brown, 250 La. 1125, 202 So.2d 274 (1967) (after warning, suspect said "I know all that"); State v. Kremens, 52 N.J. 303, 245 A.2d 313 (1968) (after warnings, suspect said "I'll tell you"); State v. Montoya, 78 N.M. 294, 430 P.2d 865 (1967) ("I don't need an attorney. I want to straighten it out"); People v. Ruiz, 34 A.D.2d 908, 311 N.Y.S.2d 336 (1970) ("I know what you said and I'll take you to the car"—adequate waiver).

The most commonly encountered form of waiver is the acknowledgment that the suspect understands, followed by a statement. It is usually held that once the defendant has been informed of his rights and indicates that he understands those rights, it would seem that his choosing to speak and not requesting a lawyer is sufficient evidence that he knows of his rights and chooses not to exercise them. People v. Whitson, 17 Cal.4th 229, 70 Cal.Rptr.2d 321, 949 P.2d 18 (1998). This rule is probably valid only if the statement of the defendant follows immediately after he says he understands the warnings. Billings v. People, 171 Colo. 236, 466 P.2d 474 (1970). The cases upholding this rule are legion; e.g., State v. Trostle, 191 Ariz. 4, 951 P.2d 869 (1997); United States v. Osterburg, 423 F.2d 704 (9th Cir.1970).

In addition, the courts have also approved non-verbal waivers such as nods and shrugs. State v. Flores, 9 Ariz.App. 502, 454 P.2d 172 (1969) (nodding head); State v. Brammeier, 1 Or.App. 612, 464 P.2d 717 (1970) (shrug); People v. Hurlic, 14 Cal.App.3d 122, 92 Cal.Rptr. 55 (1971) (head shake).

The signing of a written waiver is usually sufficient if the suspect is literate; e.g. Brooks v. United States, 416 F.2d 1044 (5th Cir.1969); United States v. Chapman, 448 F.2d 1381 (3d Cir.1971). The fact that the written acknowledgment of waiver was not made until confession was completed after oral warning and waiver is not crucial. State v. Jones, 257 La. 966, 244 So.2d 849 (1971). Written waivers are not legally necessary. United States v. Crisp, 435 F.2d 354 (7th Cir.1970); United States v. McNeil, 433 F.2d 1109 (D.C.Cir.1969). A written waiver may not always be sufficient. United States v. Hall, 396 F.2d 841 (4th Cir.1968).

6. A suspect who says that he would talk to an attorney later but presently would answer questions without counsel has waived his right to counsel. State v. Green, 51 Haw. 260, 457 P.2d 505 (1969) (would retain counsel upon release); State v. Capitan, 2 Or.App. 338, 468 P.2d 533 (1970) (wanted no lawyer "at this time"); but see State v. Prosser, 235 So.2d 740 (Fla.App.1970) (sustaining trial court's finding that such language was a request for counsel). A request for counsel made by a suspect to a friend or relative does not have the effect of a request made upon the police even if the police are aware that such a request was made. People v. Smith, 108 Ill.App.2d 172, 246 N.E.2d 689 (1969).

There is a conflict over whether comments such as "maybe I should see a lawyer" is an assertion of a right to counsel and therefore inconsistent with waiver. Cases holding such statements are not assertions are: People v. Thompson, 50 Cal.3d 134, 266 Cal.Rptr. 309, 785 P.2d 857 (1990) (recital of lawyer's advice not to talk is not an assertion of right when defendant insisted on talking); United States v. Lame, 716 F.2d 515 (8th Cir.1983) ("maybe I should get a lawyer"—police responded by saying nothing); Cannady v. State, 427 So.2d 723 (Fla.1983) ("I think I should call my lawyer"); State v. Robtoy, 98 Wash.2d 30, 653 P.2d 284 (1982) ("maybe I should call my lawyer"—officer may inquire to clarify whether this is a request). Cases to the contrary are: Smith v. Endell, 860 F.2d 1528 (9th Cir.1988) ("If I am a suspect I should have counsel"—since he was a suspect this is an assertion; dissent on grounds that he was told he was a suspect and went on answering); Robinson v. Borg, 918 F.2d 1387 (9th Cir.1990) ("I got to get me a good lawyer man, can I make a call" is assertion of right to counsel; vigorous dissent); State v. Robinson, 427 N.W.2d 217 (Minn.1988) ("Should I speak to an attorney" is assertion—full review of cases). One court has held that a suspect who says he "might want to have a lawyer" has not invoked his right to counsel but the police must then clarify whether the suspect wants counsel—they may not simply ignore the statement and proceed with the interrogation. United States v. Fouche, 776 F.2d 1398 (9th Cir.1985). Compare United States v. Gotay, 844 F.2d 971 (2d Cir.1988) (concern about counsel is not an assertion of the right to counsel).

For cases dealing with the effect of an unsuccessful attempt to reach an attorney, see Rouse v. State, 255 Ind. 670, 266 N.E.2d 209 (1971) (valid waiver after failure to reach an attorney); State v. Slobodian, 57 N.J. 18, 268 A.2d 849 (1970) (no right to question after unsuccessful attempt to secure a lawyer); United States v. Coleman, 322 F.Supp. 550 (E.D.Pa.1971) (the fact that after waiver suspect asked to and was allowed to call a lawyer did not operate to retract the waiver); State v. Lamp, 322 N.W.2d 48 (Iowa 1982) (accused decided not to wake his lawyer); Grimsley v. State, 251 So.2d 671 (Fla.App.1971) (answer to question concerning counsel—"I don't know"—does not vitiate written waiver).

A suspect is arrested, warned of his rights and questioning began when two detectives told him they were aware of his possession of a murder victim's car. He responded "Didn't you say I have a right to an attorney?" The detectives said "Yes, you do, that is correct." Believing the suspect had intended to invoke his right to counsel, the detectives began to rise from their chairs to end the interrogation. As they rose, the suspect said, "Let me tell you about the car." The detectives sat back down and listened to the suspect say he had been in the area where witnesses had seen him. One detective asked "Did you kill her?" The suspect said "Yes." In response to further questions, he gave a detailed description of the crime. Did the suspect invoke his right to counsel? See Poyner v. Murray, 964 F.2d 1404 (4th Cir.1992).

7. An issue which has arisen with some frequency concerns the validity of a waiver, for Miranda purposes, when, *unknown* to the suspect, a lawyer (typically one obtained by the family) has sought to make contact with the suspect or has asked the police not to question the suspect in the absence of the lawyer. How would you construct the argument for the defense in contending that something unknown to the suspect has a bearing on the validity of a waiver where he has been accorded the usual four warnings? See also Weber v. State, 457 A.2d 674 (Del.1983) (review of cases).

While the majority of decided cases held that the suspect must be advised of a lawyer's attempt to contact him, the Supreme Court decided to the contrary in Moran v. Burbine, 475 U.S. 412, 106 S.Ct. 1135 (1986), holding that "Events occurring outside of the presence of the suspect and entirely unknown to him surely can have no bearing on the capacity to comprehend and knowingly relinquish a constitutional right." Accord Harvey v. State, 529 So.2d 1083 (Fla.1988) (unretained attorney); State v. Earls, 116 Wash.2d 364, 805 P.2d 211 (1991) (same). Several states have rejected Moran v. Burbine on state law grounds. People v. Bender, 452 Mich. 594, 551 N.W.2d 71 (1996) (review of cases).

8. A suspect who requests to see someone other than a lawyer has not asserted his rights under *Miranda*. Fare v. Michael C., 439 U.S. 1310, 99 S.Ct. 3 (1978) (request to talk to probation officer). State v. Jones, 566 N.W.2d 317 (Minn.1997) (request to see parent). Note, The Right to Non–Legal Counsel During Police Interrogation, 70 Colum.L.Rev. 757 (1970). However, a denial of such a request may lead to a valid challenge on the issue of voluntariness. See Haynes v. Washington, 373 U.S. 503, 83 S.Ct. 1336 (1963).

9. In Frazier v. United States, 419 F.2d 1161 (D.C.Cir.1969), the suspect objected to the taking of notes. The court held that this inveighed against a finding of waiver because it implied that the suspect thought oral statements could not be used against him. This ruling was made despite the existence of a written waiver.

The *Frazier* decision has run contrary to the majority rule. In Connecticut v. Barrett, 479 U.S. 523, 107 S.Ct. 828 (1987), a suspect said he would speak but give no written statement and then later said he would not give a written statement without a lawyer but would talk about the incident. The Court held there was an unambiguous agreement to speak to police without a lawyer and police did nothing to frustrate a desire to see a lawyer. Waiver was adequate even though one could infer defendant was ignorant of the full consequences of his decision to talk.

The general rule is that refusal to sign a written statement does not impeach the validity of the suspect's waiver with respect to oral statements. Pettyjohn v.

United States, 419 F.2d 651 (D.C.Cir.1969) (refusal to sign acknowledgment of warnings does not constitute non-comprehension of the warnings and such a written acknowledgment is not legally required); United States v. Jenkins, 440 F.2d 574 (7th Cir.1971) (must be a clear oral waiver after a refusal to sign a written waiver); United States v. Ellis, 457 F.2d 1204 (8th Cir.1972) (willing to give oral statements but not to sign without lawyer); United States v. Gardner, 516 F.2d 334 (7th Cir.1975); State v. Graham, 135 Ariz. 209, 660 P.2d 460 (1983) (a request to turn off a tape recorder is not an assertion of right to silence).

The refusal to answer some particular questions is the right of the suspect; however, a suspect who generally answers some questions, but refuses to answer others and does not indicate that all questioning cease, has not asserted his right to remain silent in the sense that the police must stop all questioning. State v. Adams, 76 Wash.2d 650, 458 P.2d 558 (1969); United States v. Soliz, 129 F.3d 499 (9th Cir.1997); State v. House, 54 Ohio St.2d 297, 376 N.E.2d 588, 8 Ohio Op.3d 292 (1978).

* * *

3. INTERROGATION AFTER INVOCATION OF RIGHTS

Edwards v. Arizona

Supreme Court of the United States, 1981.
451 U.S. 477, 101 S.Ct. 1880.

■ JUSTICE WHITE delivered the opinion of the Court.

On January 19, 1976, a sworn complaint was filed against Edwards in Arizona state court charging him with robbery, burglary, and first-degree murder. An arrest warrant was issued pursuant to the complaint, and Edwards was arrested at his home later that same day. At the police station, he was informed of his rights as required by Miranda v. Arizona. Petitioner stated that he understood his rights, and was willing to submit to questioning. After being told that another suspect already in custody had implicated him in the crime, Edwards denied involvement and gave a taped statement presenting an alibi defense. He then sought to "make a deal." The interrogating officer told him that he wanted a statement, but that he did not have the authority to negotiate a deal. The officer provided Edwards with the number of a county attorney. Petitioner made the call, but hung up after a few moments. Edwards then said, "I want an attorney before making a deal." At that point, questioning ceased and Edwards was taken to county jail.

At 9:15 the next morning, two detectives, colleagues of the officer who had interrogated Edwards the previous night, came to the jail and asked to see Edwards. When the detention officer informed Edwards that the detectives wished to speak with him, he replied that he did not want to talk to anyone. The guard told him that "he had" to talk and then took him to meet with the detectives. The officers identified themselves, stated they wanted to talk to him, and informed him of his *Miranda* rights. Edwards was willing to talk, but he first wanted to hear the taped statement of the alleged accomplice who had implicated him. After listening to the tape for several minutes, petitioner said that he would make a statement so long as it was not tape recorded. The detectives informed him that the recording was irrelevant since they could testify in court concerning whatever he said. Edwards replied "I'll tell you anything you want to know, but I don't want it on tape." He thereupon implicated himself in the crime.

* * *

On appeal, the Arizona Supreme Court held that Edwards had invoked both his right to remain silent and his right to counsel during the interrogation conducted on the night of January 19. The court then went on to determine, however, that Edwards had waived both rights during the January 20 meeting when he voluntarily gave his statement to the detectives after again being informed that he need not answer questions and that he need not answer without the advice of counsel: "The trial court's finding that the waiver and confession were voluntarily and knowingly made is upheld."[1]

* * *

1. We need not decide Edwards' claim that the State deprived him of his right to counsel under the Sixth and Fourteenth Amendments as construed and applied in Massiah v. United States (1964). In that case, the Court held that the Sixth Amendment right to counsel arises whenever an accused has been indicted or adversary criminal proceedings have otherwise begun and that this right is violated when admissions are subsequently elicited from the accused in the absence of counsel. While initially conceding in its opening brief on the merits that Edwards' right to counsel under *Massiah* attached immediately after he was formally charged, the State in its supplemental brief and during oral argument took the position that under Kirby v. Illinois (1972), and Moore v. Illinois (1977), the filing of the formal complaint did not constitute the "adversary judicial criminal proceedings" necessary to trigger the Sixth Amendment right to counsel. Under the state constitution, "no person shall be prosecuted criminally in any court of record for felony or misdemeanor, otherwise than by information or indictment; no person shall be prosecuted for felony by information without having had a preliminary examination before a magistrate or having waived such preliminary examination." Ariz. Const., Art. 2, § 30. The State contends that the Sixth Amendment right to counsel does not attach until either the constitutionally required indictment or information is filed or at least no earlier than the preliminary hearing to which a defendant is entitled if the matter proceeds by complaint. Under Arizona law, a felony prosecution may be commenced by way of a complaint, 17 Ariz.Rev.Stat.Ann.Rules of Criminal Procedure, Rule 2.2. The complaint is a "written statement of the essential facts constituting a public offense, made upon oath before a magistrate," Rule 2.3, upon which the magistrate either issues an arrest warrant or dismisses the complaint. Rule 2.4. Once arrested, the accused must be taken before the magistrate for a hearing. Rule 4.1. At that hearing, the magistrate ascertains the accused's true name and address, and informs him of the charges against him, his right to counsel, his right to remain silent, and his right to a preliminary hearing if charged via complaint. Rule 4.2. Unless waived, the preliminary hearing must take place no later than 10 days after the defendant is placed in custody. Rule 5.1. The purpose of the hearing is to determine whether probable cause exists to hold the defendant for trial. Rule 5.3. Against this background and in support of its position, the State relies on Moore v. Illinois, supra, where after recognizing that under Illinois law "the prosecution in this case was commenced ... when the victim's complaint was filed in court," we noted that "adversary judicial criminal proceedings" were initiated when the ensuing preliminary hearing occurred. *Moore*, supra. Compare United States v. Duvall, 537 F.2d 15, 20–22 (CA2) (the filing of a complaint and the issuance of an arrest warrant does not trigger the right to counsel under the Sixth Amendment, that right accruing only upon further proceedings), cert. denied 426 U.S. 950 (1976). The Arizona Supreme Court did not address the Sixth Amendment question, nor do we.

... It is reasonably clear under our cases that waivers of counsel must not only be voluntary, but constitute a knowing and intelligent relinquishment or abandonment of a known right or privilege, a matter which depends in each case "upon the particular facts and circumstances surrounding that case, including the background, experience and conduct of the accused." Johnson v. Zerbst (1938).

* * *

... Here, however sound the conclusion of the state courts as to the voluntariness of Edwards' admission may be, neither the trial court nor the Arizona Supreme Court undertook to focus on whether Edwards understood his right to counsel and intelligently and knowingly relinquished it. It is thus apparent that the decision below misunderstood the requirement for finding a valid waiver of the right to counsel, once invoked.

[A]lthough we have held that after initially being advised of his *Miranda* rights, the accused may himself validly waive his rights and respond to interrogation, the Court has strongly indicated that additional safeguards are necessary when the accused asks for counsel; and we now hold that when an accused has invoked his right to have counsel present during custodial interrogation, a valid waiver of that right cannot be established by showing only that he responded to further police-initiated custodial interrogation even if he has been advised of his rights. We further hold that an accused, such as Edwards, having expressed his desire to deal with the police only through counsel, is not subject to further interrogation by the authorities until counsel has been made available to him, unless the accused himself initiates further communication, exchanges or conversations with the police.

Miranda itself indicated that the assertion of the right to counsel was a significant event and that once exercised by the accused, "the interrogation must cease until an attorney is present." Our later cases have not abandoned that view.

* * *

In concluding that the fruits of the interrogation initiated by the police on January 20 could not be used against Edwards, we do not hold or imply that Edwards was powerless to countermand his election or that the authorities could in no event use any incriminating statements made by Edwards prior to his having access to counsel. Had Edwards initiated the meeting on January 20, nothing in the Fifth and Fourteenth Amendments would prohibit the police from merely listening to his voluntary, volunteered statements and using them against him at the trial. The Fifth Amendment right identified in *Miranda* is the right to have counsel present at any custodial interrogation. Absent such interrogation, there would have been no infringement of the right that Edwards invoked and there would be no occasion to determine whether there had been a valid waiver. Rhode Island v. Innis makes this sufficiently clear.

But this is not what the facts of this case show. Here, the officers conducting the interrogation on the evening of January 19, ceased interrogation when Edwards requested counsel as he had been advised he had the right to do. The Arizona Supreme Court was of the opinion that this was a sufficient invocation of his *Miranda* rights, and we are in accord. It is also clear that without making counsel available to Edwards, the police returned to him the next day. This was not at his suggestion or request. Indeed, Edwards informed the detention officer that he did not want to talk to anyone. At the meeting, the detectives told Edwards that they wanted to talk to him and again advised him of his *Miranda* rights. Edwards stated that he would talk, but what prompted this action does not appear. He listened at his own request to part of the taped statement made by one of his alleged accomplices and then made an incriminating statement, which was used against him at his trial. We think it is clear that Edwards was subjected to custodial interrogation on January 20 within the meaning of Rhode Island v. Innis, supra, and that this occurred at the instance of the authorities. His statement, made without having had access to counsel, did not amount to a valid waiver and hence was inadmissible.

Accordingly, the holding of the Arizona Supreme Court that Edwards had waived his right to counsel was infirm and the judgment of that court is reversed.

■ CHIEF JUSTICE BURGER, concurring in the judgment.

[Opinion omitted]

■ JUSTICE POWELL, with whom JUSTICE REHNQUIST joins, concurring in the result.

* * *

I hesitate to join the opinion only because of what appears to be an undue, and undefined, emphasis on a single element: "initiation." As Justice White has noted, the Court in Miranda v. Arizona imposed a general prophylactic rule that is not manifestly required by anything in the text of the Constitution. 384 U.S., at 526 (White, J., dissenting). *Miranda* itself recognized, moreover, that counsel's assistance can be waived. Waiver always has been evaluated under the general formulation at the *Zerbst* standard quoted above. My concern is that the Court's opinion today may be read as "constitutionalizing" not the generalized *Zerbst* standard but a *single element of fact* among the various facts that may be relevant to determining whether there has been a valid waiver.*

NOTES

1. In Oregon v. Bradshaw, 462 U.S. 1039, 103 S.Ct. 2830 (1983) the suspect, undergoing questioning, said "I do want an attorney before it goes very much further." The interrogation was terminated. Later as he was being transferred from police station to jail he said to a police officer, "Well, what is going to happen to me now." The officer said, "You do not have to talk to me. You have requested an attorney and I don't want you talking to me unless you so desire because anything you say—because—since you have requested an attorney, you know, it has to be at your own free will." The suspect said he understood and then the two discussed

* (Ed. Note) *Edwards* was held to apply to all pending cases including those on direct appeal but not to cases on collateral review. See Solem v. Stumes, 465 U.S. 638, 104 S.Ct. 1338 (1984).

where the suspect was being taken and what offense would be charged. The officer suggested a polygraph. The suspect agreed, saying he would do whatever he could to clear up the matter. The next day he was rewarned, waived his rights and was polygraphed. When the examiner told the suspect he was not telling the truth, the suspect recanted the earlier story and confessed. Four justices said that the "initiation" required by Edwards need not by itself waive his rights or specifically indicate that he desires to answer questions. In this case the suspect evinced willingness and a desire for a generalized discussion about the investigation. Once initiation occurs then the police may secure the necessary waiver and the court must decide whether the waiver was valid as it was in this case after the polygrapher's warnings.

Justice Powell objected to the mechanism of a two-stage inquiry—was there initiation and, if so, was there waiver and argued the facts and circumstances should be viewed in their entirety to determine initiation and waiver. He concurred that these facts clearly established waiver. The dissenters agreed with the two-stage analysis but not its application to this case:

> The safeguards identified in *Edwards* hardly pose an insurmountable obstacle to an accused who truly wishes to waive his rights after invoking his right to counsel. A waiver can be established, however, only when the accused himself reopens the dialogue about the subject matter of the criminal investigation. Since our decision in *Edwards*, the lower courts have had no difficulty in identifying such situations. See, e.g., McCree v. Housewright, 689 F.2d 797 (8th Cir.1982) (defendant initiated reinterrogation by knocking on cell door and telling police officer that he wanted to make a statement); United States v. Gordon, 655 F.2d 478 (C.A.2 1981) (defendant reopened dialogue by expressing a desire to provide information about someone else who should also be arrested); State v. Brezee, 66 Haw. 162, 657 P.2d 1044 (1983) (defendant asked detective to come back to his cell and then expressed desire to make a statement); Payne v. State, 424 So.2d 722 (Ala.Crim.App.1982) (defendant asked for a meeting with police at which statements were made); People v. Thomas, 98 Ill.App.3d 852, 54 Ill.Dec. 235, 424 N.E.2d 985 (1981), cert. denied 456 U.S. 993, 102 S.Ct. 2276 (1982) (defendant initiated further communication by inquiring about accomplice's statements linking him to the crime); State v. Pittman, 210 Neb. 117, 313 N.W.2d 252 (1981) (defendant initiated further conversation by stating that he was being "railroaded" by his codefendants).
>
> I agree with the plurality that, in order to constitute "initiation" under *Edwards*, an accused's inquiry must demonstrate a desire to discuss the subject matter of the criminal investigation. I am baffled, however, at the plurality's application of that standard to the facts of this case. The plurality asserts that respondent's question, "What is going to happen to me now?", evinced both "a willingness and a desire for a generalized discussion about the investigation." If respondent's question had been posed by Jean–Paul Sartre before a class of philosophy students, it might well have evinced a desire for a "generalized" discussion. But under the circumstances of this case, it is plain that respondent's only "desire" was to find out where the police were going to take him. As the Oregon Court of Appeals stated, respondent's query came only minutes after his invocation of the right to counsel and was simply "a normal reaction to being taken from the police station and placed in a police car, obviously for transport to some destination." 54 Or.App., at 949, 636 P.2d, at 1013. On these facts, I fail to see how respondent's question can be considered "initiation" of a conversation about the subject matter of the criminal investigation.

2. In Michigan v. Mosley, 423 U.S. 96, 96 S.Ct. 321 (1975), the Court approved a second interrogation after the suspect had invoked his right to silence but not his right to counsel. Mosley's assertion of rights was honored but a few hours later he was brought back to the police station from his cell, rewarned and asked about another offense for which he had not been arrested or interrogated. He waived his rights and answered questions for about fifteen minutes implicating himself in a homicide. Unlike the later holding in *Edwards*, the Court sustained the second interrogation even though it was not initiated by the suspect. It was sufficient, the Court said, that the original refusal to speak was honored and that a significant period elapsed before a second attempt to interrogate was made.

In *Mosley*, the second interrogation concerned a different crime and different interrogators, but other courts have not found these two factors to be essential. Several courts have simply approved second attempts to interview after an initial refusal with a caveat that successive attempts to interview will be viewed with caution. United States v. Collins, 462 F.2d 792 (2d Cir.1972) (suspect must be rewarned of *Miranda* rights); State v. Harvey, 121 N.J. 407, 581 A.2d 483 (1990) (must be rewarned); People v. Gary, 31 N.Y.2d 68, 334 N.Y.S.2d 883, 286 N.E.2d 263 (1972) (must be given second warning of *Miranda* rights). . . .

In United States v. Hsu, 852 F.2d 407 (9th Cir.1988), while being questioned by a federal agent, a suspect invoked his right to silence. Thirty minutes later another agent, unaware of the earlier invocation, warned the suspect of his rights, obtained a purported waiver, and elicited a statement from the suspect about the same offense. The questioning took place a few blocks from where the suspect had earlier invoked his rights. The court found that *Mosley* permitted admission of the statement. In finding that the agents "scrupulously honored" the right to cut off questioning, the court placed great emphasis upon the fresh set of warnings and the polite demeanor of the agents. A dissent declared that the majority had removed "all force from the rule it purports to apply."

A few courts have noted that *Edwards v. Arizona* established a bright line rule that one who asserts the right to counsel during interrogation may not be questioned again without the presence of counsel, while *Michigan v. Mosley* established a more lenient rule where the right to silence is asserted; if that right has been "scrupulously honored" when asserted, a subsequent attempt to interrogate is permissible. There is disagreement over how big is the difference between *Mosley* and *Edwards*. In United States v. Barone, 968 F.2d 1378 (1st Cir.1992) the Court held that "the officers spoke repeatedly to Barone for the purpose of changing his mind, failed to provide new Miranda warnings, applied pressure by emphasizing the danger he would face in Boston if he did not cooperate, and took advantage of a long delay in arraignment ... that the statements were voluntary [is] irrelevant." The dissent noted that the Supreme Court "has lost few opportunities to remind us that the real purpose of Miranda ... is neither to discourage voluntary confessions nor to preclude their use ... [after each assertion of silence] questioning anent the murder stopped and was not resumed for several hours ... the officers reminded Barone he was not obligated to speak to them and confirmed that he had his rights in mind, I do not believe Mosley requires ... suppression. . . ."

All courts tend to approve interrogation after refusal to talk when some of the initiative comes from the defendant. People v. Brockman, 2 Cal.App.3d 1002, 83 Cal.Rptr. 70 (1969) (defendant refused to talk but said he might like to talk about it in a couple of days and police questioned him two days later); State v. Lucia, 74 Wash.2d 819, 447 P.2d 606 (1968) (defendant initiated the second interview); United States v. Velasquez, 885 F.2d 1076 (3d Cir.1989) ("What is going to happen?"—initiates).

3. Even before Edwards v. Arizona most states did not permit a second interrogation after the accused asserted his right to counsel, Commonwealth v. Nathan, 445 Pa. 470, 285 A.2d 175 (1971) but ruled that initiation by the suspect allowed reinterrogation. People v. Randall, 1 Cal.3d 948, 83 Cal.Rptr. 658, 464 P.2d 114 (1970).

In United States v. Skinner, 667 F.2d 1306 (9th Cir.1982), a suspect not in custody asserted his right to counsel and left the scene. *Edwards* did not preclude interrogation after he was arrested some days later. Accord, McNeil v. Wisconsin, 501 U.S. 171, 111 S.Ct. 2204 (1991) (footnote 3).

Where a police officer needs to discover the location of a gun he may, in the interests of public safety, ask for the weapon even after the suspect has asserted his rights, United States v. DeSantis, 870 F.2d 536 (9th Cir.1989).

4. In some cases, the suspect may waive his rights and submit to interrogation, and after an interval of time he may, of course, be interrogated a second time. A few cases require the repetition of warnings. Brown v. State, 6 Md.App. 564, 252 A.2d 272 (1969). It is probably the better practice to re-warn. United States v. Thomas, 396 F.2d 310 (2d Cir.1968). But it is the general rule that the warnings need not be repeated. See Wyrick v. Fields, 459 U.S. 42, 103 S.Ct. 394 (1982); State v. Fuller, 118 N.J. 75, 570 A.2d 429 (1990).

5. In Smith v. Illinois, 469 U.S. 91, 105 S.Ct. 490 (1984) the question was what constitutes a request for counsel for *Edwards'* purposes. The Court stated the facts:

Shortly after his arrest, 18–year–old Steven Smith was taken to an interrogation room at the Logan County Safety Complex for questioning by two police detectives. The session began as follows:

"Q. Steve, I want to talk with you in reference to the armed robbery that took place at McDonald's restaurant on the morning of the 19th. Are you familiar with this?

"A. Yeah. My cousin Greg was.

"Q. Okay. But before I do that I must advise you of your rights. Okay? You have a right to remain silent. You do not have to talk to me unless you want to do so. Do you understand that?

"A. Uh. She told me to get my lawyer. She said you guys would railroad me.

"Q. Do you understand that as I gave it to you, Steve?

"A. Yeah.

"Q. If you do want to talk to me I must advise you that whatever you say can and will be used against you in court. Do you understand that?

"A. Yeah.

"Q. You have a right to consult with a lawyer and to have a lawyer present with you when you're being questioned. Do you understand that?

"A. *Uh, yeah. I'd like to do that.*

"Q. Okay."

Instead of terminating the questioning at this point, the interrogating officers proceeded to finish reading Smith his *Miranda* rights and then pressed him again to answer their questions:

"Q. . . . If you want a lawyer and you're unable to pay for one a lawyer will be appointed to represent you free of cost, do you understand that?

"A. Okay.

"Q. Do you wish to talk to me at this time without a lawyer being present?

"A. *Yeah and no, uh, I don't know what's what, really.*

"Q. *Well. You either have to talk to me this time without a lawyer being present* and if you do agree to talk with me without a lawyer being present you can stop at any time you want to.

"Q. All right. I'll talk to you then."

The Court found that the *Edwards* rule was violated because questioning continued after the right to counsel was invoked. While the Court conceded that overall the assertion of the right to counsel may have been ambiguous (and therefore not clearly sufficient to invoke *Edwards*) the initial comments of the accused were clear. As soon as the police heard the statement, "Uh, yeah. I'd like to do that [consult with counsel]," the rule in *Edwards* applied. Smith's request for counsel could not be deemed ambiguous based on statements made in response to questions *after* the initial request for counsel. The Court did not decide whether an ambiguous reference to counsel is an invocation of a *Miranda* right. It did say that such ambiguities or hesitations are relevant only if they precede the request for counsel or are a part of the request itself. Three Justices dissented arguing that Smith's original statement was not all that clear a request and that considering the very short period of the discussion between Smith and the officers it was proper to look at all Smith's statements to decide whether he really wanted counsel.

In Davis v. United States, 512 U.S. 452, 114 S.Ct. 2350 (1994) the Court was unanimous as to the result but severely divided on its rationale. After an initial *Miranda* waiver and an hour and a half interview defendant said "maybe I should talk to a lawyer." The interrogators inquired if he was asking for a lawyer and he said no. After a short break he was reminded of his rights and the interview continued for an hour until he specifically asked for a lawyer. A five judge majority said that "maybe I should talk to a lawyer" is not a request for an attorney, and a reasonable officer would have understood only that the suspect might be invoking the right to counsel. Under such circumstances the interrogators may simply proceed with the interrogation. The Court noted that it would be good practice to clarify whether a suspect really wants an attorney, but they are not required to ask clarifying questions. The Court said:

> We recognize that requiring a clear assertion of the right to counsel might disadvantage some suspects who—because of fear, intimidation, lack of linguistic skills, or a variety of other reasons—will not clearly articulate their right to counsel although they actually want to have a lawyer present. But the primary protection afforded suspects subject to custodial interrogation is the *Miranda* warnings themselves. "[F]ull comprehension of the rights to remain silent and request an attorney [is] sufficient to dispel whatever coercion is inherent in the interrogation process." *Moran v. Burbine*. A suspect who knowingly and voluntarily waives his right to counsel after having that right explained to him has indicated his willingness to deal with the police unassisted. Although *Edwards* provides an additional protection—if a suspect subsequently requests an attorney, questioning must cease—it is one that must be affirmatively invoked by the suspect.
>
> In considering how a suspect must invoke the right to counsel, we must consider the other side of the *Miranda* equation: the need for effective law enforcement. Although the courts ensure compliance with the *Miranda* requirements through the exclusionary rule, it is police officers who must actually decide whether or not they can question a suspect. The *Edwards* rule—questioning must cease if the suspect asks for a lawyer—provides a bright line

that can be applied by officers in the real world of investigation and interrogation without unduly hampering the gathering of information. But if we were to require questioning to cease if a suspect makes a statement that *might* be a request for an attorney, this clarity and ease of application would be lost. Police officers would be forced to make difficult judgment calls about whether the suspect in fact wants a lawyer even though he hasn't said so, with the threat of suppression if they guess wrong. We therefore hold that, after a knowing and voluntary waiver of the *Miranda* rights, law enforcement officers may continue questioning until and unless the suspect clearly requests an attorney.

Of course, when a suspect makes an ambiguous or equivocal statement it will often be good police practice for the interviewing officers to clarify whether or not he actually wants an attorney. That was the procedure followed by the NIS agents in this case. Clarifying questions help protect the rights of the suspect by ensuring that he gets an attorney if he wants one, and will minimize the chance of a confession being suppressed due to subsequent judicial second-guessing as to the meaning of the suspect's statement regarding counsel. But we decline to adopt a rule requiring officers to ask clarifying questions. If the suspect's statement is not an unambiguous or unequivocal request for counsel, the officers have no obligation to stop questioning him.

Four justices concurred with the result but only because clarifying questions had been asked and the suspect had said that he wasn't evoking his right to counsel.

Indeed, it is easy, amidst the discussion of layers of protection, to lose sight of a real risk in the majority's approach, going close to the core of what the Court has held that the Fifth Amendment provides. The experience of the timid or verbally inept suspect (whose existence the Court acknowledges) may not always closely follow that of the defendant in *Edwards v. Arizona* (whose purported waiver of his right to counsel made after having invoked the right was held ineffective, lest police be tempted to "badge[r]") others like him, *see Michigan v. Harvey* (1990). Indeed, it may be more like that of the defendant in *Escobedo v. Illinois* whose sense of dilemma was heightened by his interrogators' denial of his requests to talk to a lawyer. When a suspect understands his (expressed) wishes to have been ignored (and by hypothesis, he has said something that an objective listener could "reasonably," although not necessarily, take to be a request), in contravention of the "rights" just read to him by his interrogator, he may well see further objection as futile and confession (true or not) as the only way to end his interrogation.

Nor is it enough to say that a "statement either is . . . an assertion of the right to counsel or it is not." While it might be fair to say that every statement is meant either to deal with police through counsel or not, this fact does not dictate the rule that interrogators who hear a statement consistent with either possibility may presume the latter and forge ahead; on the contrary, clarification is the intuitively sensible course.

The other justifications offered for the "requisite level of clarity" rule, are that, whatever it costs, it will further society's strong interest in "effective law enforcement," and maintain the "ease of application," that has long been a concern of our *Miranda* jurisprudence. With respect to the first point, the margin of difference between the clarification approach advocated here and the one the Court adopts is defined by the class of cases in which a suspect, if asked, would make it plain that he meant to request counsel (at which point questioning would cease). While these lost confessions do extract a real price from society, it is one that *Miranda* itself determined should be borne.

As for practical application, while every approach including the majority's, will involve some "difficult judgment calls," the rule argued for here would relieve the officer of any responsibility for guessing "whether the suspect in fact wants a lawyer even though he hasn't said so." To the contrary, it would assure that the "judgment call" will be made by the party most competent to resolve the ambiguity, who our case law has always assumed should make it; the individual suspect.

6. Consider whether the right to silence was invoked in State v. Williams, 535 N.W.2d 277 (Minn.1995) where Williams was arrested in a car stolen from a home where a mother and her three old daughter had been murdered. A four year old boy had been stabbed, but survived.

"At approximately 5:20 a.m., Williams was taken from his detention cell to an interview room located across the hall. The interview room measured 10 feet, 8 inches long by 7 feet, 5 inches wide. The room had no exterior windows. Two banks of lights, each containing three 48–inch tube fluorescent bulbs, illuminated the room's only furniture: one table, measuring 48 inches long by 30 inches wide, and three chairs.

Detectives Bozovsky and Christensen were waiting in the interview room when Williams arrived. They introduced themselves and sat at opposite ends of the table, while Williams sat between them with his back to the door. Although the police did not test Williams's blood-alcohol level, Williams reportedly walked without difficulty, did not smell of alcohol, and spoke clearly without slurring. Williams was not wearing handcuffs.

After Williams sat down, Detective Bozovsky orally recited a full *Miranda* warning and asked Williams if he understood the rights of which he had just been advised. Williams responded affirmatively. Bozovsky then asked Williams if he was willing to talk with them. Williams responded that he was willing to talk.

Williams had not yet been informed about the homicide investigation. Instead, he was questioned about being in a stolen car. Williams initially maintained that he had stolen the car from a black man who had left the keys in its ignition while parked outside of a south Minneapolis liquor store. Responding to preliminary questions, Williams told the detectives his mother had kicked him out of the house, he did not know her phone number, and he had not seen his father in a long time. Williams reported that he had been staying with friends, and he reported staying with a friend at an address on Park Avenue in Anoka, Minnesota, the night before. Later, in a car parked at that address, police found a sawed-off shotgun, wrapped in a plaid bloodstained shirt.

Approximately 45 minutes into the interview, Detective Bozovsky informed Williams that the car he had been riding in had been stolen from the home of people who had been murdered. Bozovsky stated that he suspected Williams had injured his hand during the murders. Bozovsky next said that he wanted Williams's side of the story because if he didn't explain 'how it happened people would believe the worst about what had happened * * *.' Williams denied any involvement in the homicides. When Detective Christensen explained that the homicide scene would be processed for fingerprints and blood analysis, Williams responded that neither his fingerprints nor his blood would be found at the homicide scene.

Detective Christensen continued to hypothesize about the homicides and explained to Williams that if the adult female victim had been sexually assaulted, physical evidence, such as semen, could be traced back to the assailant. Williams emphatically denied that anything like that had happened, and Christensen accused him of lying. Williams then lost his composure, stood up from his chair, turned towards Christensen and said, 'I don't have to take any more of your bullshit.' Then Williams walked out of the interrogation room, into the hall, and back to his detention cell, where he was placed by the detention officer. This episode occurred approximately one hour into the interview. Williams never said that he wanted to stop answering questions. Christensen testified that he was shocked by Williams's behavior because, in over 17 years of police experience, a suspect had never stood up and simply walked out of the interview room. Christensen interpreted Williams's behavior to be a 'temper tantrum.'

To allow Williams some time to 'cool off,' Detectives Christensen and Bozovsky left the detention center area of the police department. After a few minutes, another officer informed them that Mathew Hage was being treated at the hospital and was expected to survive. After discussing the status of the interrogation, the two detectives decided to return to Williams's detention cell. On cross-examination at the Rasmussen hearing, Christensen explained that he and Bozovsky could not know whether Williams wanted to talk with them 'unless we went back in and informed him of [the] new development in the case.'

Approximately five minutes after leaving the detention center area, Detective Bozovsky entered Williams's detention cell. Bozovsky, who 'never got the impression [Williams] didn't want to talk to me,' sat down next to Williams, who was calmly lying on his bed. Detective Christensen did not enter the cell, because Williams's earlier behavior indicated that he was angry at Christensen for calling him a liar. Instead, Christensen stood on the door threshold, attempting to avoid creating hostility towards Williams.

Detective Bozovsky informed Williams that Mathew was expected to survive. Bozovsky then told Williams that Mathew would be able to identify him, an assertion that Bozovsky admitted was 'pure speculation.' Bozovsky then asked Williams if he would like to tell his side of the story. At that point, Williams nodded affirmatively, and while tears welled up in his eyes, he admitted that he had been in the house. Detective Christensen then entered Williams's cell and, in an attempt to comfort Williams, addressed Williams in a calm, soft tone, 'You understand that I was just doing my job.' Williams nodded that he understood and shook hands with Christensen. Bozovsky then asked Williams whether he wanted to talk with them further in the detention cell or whether he wanted to return to the interview room. Williams chose to return to the interview room.

Williams and the two detectives returned to the same interview room they had previously been in and resumed their prior seating arrangements. Williams had regained his composure, and Bozovsky fully advised him of his *Miranda* rights for the second time. Williams again said he understood his rights, and when the detectives asked whether he was willing to talk with them, Williams responded affirmatively."

In another case a suspect was being questioned about the killing of the suspect's uncle whose unclothed body was found in his home; the uncle's wallet was missing. Did the suspect assert his right to silence in the following interrogation?

Q: Tell us what happened. We know what happened, we just need to hear it from you, we need to clear it up. You were there, did Danny make advances toward you? Is that what happened?

A. No.

Q: Was he pushing you? Trying to have sex with you? Is that what happened?

A: He never did.

Q: Something happened, what happened? Did you guys get into an argument over money?

A: We never have got into an argument.

Q: What happened, what happened to Danny?

A: I don't know what happened to him.

Q: Yes you do, you were there, what happened, tell what happened?

A: No I wasn't, what happened to him?

Q: He was killed. You know he was killed.

A: How?

Q: You tell me. You tell me what happened, you were there.

A: I don't know what happened.

Q: You were there.

A: I'm through with this.

Q: Listen to me, listen....

A: I'm tired of listening to this. I'm through with it.

Q: List, just listen to me. We've got Harold over there. Harold's going to tell us about the stuff. He's going to tell us about the knife. He's going to tell us about the clothes, he's going to tell us about everything, you know? I'd rather hear it from you.

A: I'm through with this.

Q: You want to get this off your chest or not?

A: I'm through with this.

Q: [What do you mean, you're through with this]. It's going to eat at you forever until you tell somebody.

A: I said I'm through with it. I didn't kill nobody, you keep insisting I did and I didn't.

Q: I'm trying to find out what happened. I'm here to listen.

A: I wouldn't kill or hurt no one.

Q: Well I realize that you wouldn't normally kill or hurt anybody, but I think something happened. I think all this is building up in you. I think, well, we've talked to other people that you don't like homosexuals. I think something happened. Did something happen between you and Danny that made you blow up? You just lost control, you couldn't take it anymore?

A: No.

Q: Is that what it is?

A: I loved Danny, I mean I'd never do nothing to hurt him.

Q: I'm here to listen to you.

A: I'd never do nothing to hurt him.

Q: Something happened, something happened between you two. You were there, something happened, was Danny pushing himself on you?

A: No I wasn't, he never did.

Q: Was he trying to get your clothes off of you?

A: I'm through with this.

Q: What happened? Something happened between you two.

A: I said I'm through. I don't want to hear it no more.

Q: Well you have to hear it, we have to get to the bottom of it. This is not something you just....

A: I done told you everything I know.

Q: This is not something you turn off and on, you've not been in Martinsville the past two weeks, you've been in Martinsville the past few days.

The videotaped interrogation lasted approximately an hour and thirty-nine minutes.

7. May a suspect foreclose interrogation by demanding his right to counsel well before Miranda warnings are given or interrogation is commenced? Could someone write a letter to the police saying "in the event of my arrest on any charge I assert my right to counsel" and thus prevent any uncounseled interview? In a 4–3 decision the Supreme Court of Florida said no. In Sapp v. State, 690 So.2d 581 (Fla.1997) Sapp had been arrested for a robbery and talked to the police. The next day his attorney had him sign a "claim of rights form" asserting a right to counsel. A copy was sent to the prosecutor and one was stapled to Sapp's jail papers. A week later Sapp (still in jail) was taken to a police office and questioned about another crime, a homicide. He waived his rights and incriminated himself. The majority wrote:

> The closest the Supreme Court has come to addressing this issue is in McNeil v. Wisconsin (1991). In McNeil, the Court held that an accused's request for counsel at his initial appearance on a charged offense, while effective to invoke his Sixth Amendment right to counsel, did not constitute an invocation of his Miranda right to counsel that would preclude police interrogation on unrelated, uncharged offenses under Edwards. In so holding, the Court refused to merge the Sixth Amendment right to counsel, which is offense-specific, with the non-offense-specific Miranda right to counsel during interrogation.
>
> The portion of McNeil that is relevant to this case appears in the majority's response to Justice Stevens' dissent, in which he criticized the majority for maintaining a distinction between the right to counsel under the Fifth and Sixth Amendments. Justice Stevens predicted that a competent attorney could easily avoid the consequences of the majority holding by having clients in future preliminary hearings make a statement on the record invoking the right to counsel under both the Fifth and the Sixth Amendments. In a footnote, the majority responded:
>
>> We have in fact never held that a person can invoke his Miranda rights anticipatorily, in a context other than "custodial interrogation"—which a preliminary hearing will not always, or even usually, involve. If the Miranda right to counsel can be invoked at a preliminary hearing, it could be argued, there is no logical reason why it could not be invoked by a letter prior to arrest, or indeed even prior to identification as a suspect. Most rights must be asserted when the government seeks to take the action they protect against. The fact that we have allowed the Miranda right to counsel, once asserted, to be effective with respect to future custodial interrogation does not necessarily mean that we will allow it to be asserted initially outside the context of custodial interrogation, with similar future effect.

> Although this statement constitutes dictum, at least three federal courts of appeal agree in the wake of McNeil that the Supreme Court, if presented with the issue, would not permit an individual to invoke the Miranda right to counsel before custodial interrogation has begun or is imminent. United States v. LaGrone, 43 F.3d 332 (7th Cir.1994); Alston v. Redman, 34 F.3d 1237 (3d Cir.1994), United States v. Wright, 962 F.2d 953 (9th Cir.1992). * * * We must keep in mind that the reason for informing individuals of their rights before questioning is to ensure that statements made during custodial interrogation are given voluntarily, not to prevent individuals from ever making these statements without first consulting counsel. Traylor, 596 So.2d at 964. As we recognized in Traylor, freely given, voluntary confessions are an unqualified good. Id. at 965. A rule allowing one to invoke the right to counsel for custodial interrogation before it is even imminent (whether it be through a claim of rights form or by any other means) would provide little additional protection against involuntary confessions but would unnecessarily hinder lawful efforts by police to obtain voluntary confessions. We believe that requiring the invocation to occur either during custodial interrogation or when it is imminent strikes a healthier balance between the protection of the individual from police coercion on the one hand and the State's need to conduct criminal investigations on the other.

The dissenters said:

> In this case, petitioner did not "anticipate" that he might be questioned and preemptively invoke his rights. Instead, petitioner explicitly invoked his Fifth Amendment rights precisely in the context of and after having been subjected to "custodial interrogation." Petitioner first directly experienced the inherent pressures of adversarial police questioning and then, in its wake, signed a written declaration of his rights to ensure that he would not be approached and questioned again except by his own choosing. He then reasserted these rights in open court. These actions clearly meet the McNeil standard.
>
> The majority finds that under its "imminency" standard, a defendant like Sapp, who is in custody with the adversarial powers of the State mounted against him, is severely limited to invoking his Fifth Amendment right to counsel only until he is actually sitting across the table from a police officer in an interview room and facing interrogation. Further, in my view, the majority gets it wrong even under its own standard. Surely, a defendant sitting in jail facing criminal charges likely believes—and reasonably so especially once he has already been interrogated by the police—that he will be questioned by police again in the very near future, i.e., "imminently." That immediate past experience of actual interrogation conclusively establishes the reasonableness of a defendant's expectation of continued interrogation.

Some public defenders advise their incarcerated clients to sign a form letter refusing to be interviewed by law enforcement officers absent counsel and expressing a desire not to meet with law enforcement officers to discuss waiver. The form letter is delivered or made known to the jailer. Can this, or any, anticipatory invocation of rights be effective for offenses with which defendant has neither been arrested nor charged? Relying on *McNeil*, the Court said no in Alston v. Redman, 34 F.3d 1237 (3d Cir.1994). Are Sapp and Alston correctly decided?

8. To what extent did it make a difference to the analysis in Rhode Island v. Innis (supra), that the suspect had previously invoked his right to counsel? Is this factor irrelevant to the question of whether police actions in *Innis* constituted interrogation for *Miranda* purposes? In general, should the dispute about whether police conduct constituted interrogation be resolved without regard to whether the suspect previously invoked his right to counsel or to silence? If not, how should that factor be entered into the calculation in a case where the prosecution asserts that police conduct did not amount to interrogation?

9. In Arizona v. Roberson, 486 U.S. 675, 108 S.Ct. 2093 (1988), the Court laid down a "bright-line" test, prohibiting police-initiated questioning once a defendant has invoked the right to counsel under *Miranda*—even when a different officer seeks to question the suspect about a different crime without knowing that the suspect has previously requested counsel. The Court reasoned that once a suspect requests counsel, he is indicating that he does "not feel sufficiently comfortable with the pressures of custodial interrogation to answer questions without an attorney." It added that "there is no reason to assume that a suspect's state of mind is in any way investigative-specific."

The *Roberson* majority distinguished two other situations: (1) Where the suspect in custodial interrogation has invoked his Fifth Amendment right to *silence* under *Miranda*. Under *Mosley* (supra, p. 173), police-initiated questioning, especially about a separate crime, sometimes can be consistent with the police obligation to "scrupulously honor" a suspect's right to cut off questioning. (2) Where a suspect's *Sixth Amendment* right to counsel has attached upon the initiation of the formal adversary process, but where a suspect's Fifth Amendment right to counsel under *Miranda* has not attached because the suspect is not in custody (e.g., in *Massiah*, supra, p. 189). There the police can elicit information from the defendant concerning crimes other than those as to which the formal criminal process has commenced. *Roberson* limited its holding to situations where a suspect in custody has invoked what the Court has come to call a Fifth Amendment right to counsel under *Miranda*.

10. When the formal adversary process has not commenced, and when the suspect is not in custody, no right to counsel attaches under either the Fifth or the Sixth Amendment. Thus authorities during non-custodial questioning need not heed the suspect's request for counsel. United States v. Lennick, 917 F.2d 974 (7th Cir.1990); and if the suspect is later taken into custody, the prior request may have no legal effect. State v. Lavoie, 562 A.2d 146 (Me.1989). But see People v. Spivey, 209 Ill.App.3d 584, 154 Ill.Dec. 327, 568 N.E.2d 327 (1991).

The question of what is an "unrelated offense" is debated in Commonwealth v. Rainwater, 425 Mass. 540, 681 N.E.2d 1218 (1997) (4–3) (Is the offense inextricably intertwined or is it closely connected?)

11. In Minnick v. Mississippi, 498 U.S. 146, 111 S.Ct. 486 (1990), while in custody on Saturday, August 23, 1986, following an arrest for murder, after answering some questions, Minnick invoked his right to counsel under *Miranda* by stating "Come back Monday when I have a lawyer," and by asserting that he would make a more complete statement then with his lawyer present. The F.B.I. interview ended at that point.

Over the week-end, Minnick spoke to an appointed attorney two or three times. The record before the Supreme Court did not indicate whether these conversations were in person or by phone.

On Monday, August 25, local authorities re-initiated interrogation of Minnick, who was still in custody. They obtained a purported waiver of *Miranda* rights in the absence of counsel for Minnick. The suspect then admitted his participation in two murders. The Supreme Court held that Edwards v. Arizona (Casebook 139) barred admission of Minnick's August 25 statement even though Minnick had consulted counsel after he had invoked his right to counsel on August 23. The Court stated:

> The Mississippi Supreme Court relied on our statement in *Edwards* that an accused who invokes his right to counsel "is not subject to further interrogation by the authorities until counsel has been made available to

him. . . ." We do not interpret this language to mean, as the Mississippi court thought, that the protection of *Edwards* terminates once counsel has consulted with the suspect. In context, the requirement that counsel be "made available" to the accused refers to more than an opportunity to consult with an attorney outside the interrogation room.

In *Edwards*, we focused on *Miranda's* instruction that when the accused invokes his right to counsel, "the interrogation must cease until an attorney is *present*," agreeing with Edwards' contention that he had not waived his right "to have counsel *present* during custodial interrogation." In the sentence preceding the language quoted by the Mississippi Supreme Court, we referred to the "right to have counsel *present* during custodial interrogation," and in the sentence following, we again quoted the phrase " 'interrogation must cease until an attorney is *present*' " from *Miranda*. The full sentence relied on by the Mississippi Supreme Court, moreover, says: "We further hold that an accused, such as Edwards, *having expressed his desire to deal with the police only through counsel*, is not subject to further interrogation by the authorities until counsel has been made available to him, unless the accused himself initiates further communication, exchanges, or conversations with the police."

Our emphasis on counsel's *presence* at interrogation is not unique to *Edwards*. It derives from *Miranda*, where we said that in the cases before us "[t]he presence of counsel . . . would be the adequate protective device necessary to make the process of police interrogation conform to the dictates of the [Fifth Amendment] privilege. . . ." Writing for a plurality of the Court, for instance, then-Justice Rehnquist described the holding of *Edwards* to be "that subsequent incriminating statements made *without [Edwards'] attorney present* violated the rights secured to the defendant by the Fifth and Fourteenth Amendments to the United States Constitution." *Oregon v. Bradshaw* (1983). See also *Arizona v. Roberson*, ("The rule of the *Edwards* case came as a corollary to *Miranda*'s admonition that '[i]f the individual states that he wants an attorney, the interrogation must cease until an attorney is present' "); *Shea v. Louisiana* (1985) ("In *Edwards v. Arizona*, . . . this Court ruled that a criminal defendant's rights under the Fifth and Fourteenth Amendments were violated by the use of his confession obtained by police-instigated interrogation—without counsel present—after he requested an attorney"). . . . Whatever the ambiguities of our earlier cases on this point, we now hold that when counsel is requested, interrogation must cease, and officials may not reinitiate interrogation without counsel present, whether or not the accused has consulted with his attorney.

We consider our ruling to be an appropriate and necessary application of the *Edwards* rule. A single consultation with an attorney does not remove the suspect from persistent attempts by officials to persuade him to waive his rights, or from the coercive pressures that accompany custody and that may increase as custody is prolonged. The case before us well illustrates the pressures, and abuses, that may be concomitants of custody. Petitioner testified that though he resisted, he was required to submit to both the FBI and the Denham interviews. In the latter instance, the compulsion to submit to interrogation followed petitioner's unequivocal request during the FBI interview that questioning cease until counsel was present. The case illustrates also that consultation is not always effective in instructing the suspect of his rights. One plausible interpretation of the record is that petitioner thought he could keep his admissions out of evidence by refusing to sign a formal waiver of rights.

In dissent, Justice Scalia, joined by Chief Justice Rehnquist, after generally criticizing the *Edwards* rule, observed that a suspect who invoked the right to counsel is interrogated without his ever having consulted with counsel is different from a suspect who has spoken to counsel:

> [Once a] suspect has seen his request for an attorney honored, however, and has actually spoken with that attorney, the probabilities change. The suspect then knows that he has an advocate on his side, and that the police will permit him to consult that advocate. He almost certainly also has a heightened awareness (above what the *Miranda* warning itself will provide) of his right to remain silent—since at the earliest opportunity "any lawyer worth his salt will tell the suspect in no uncertain terms to make no statement to the police under any circumstances." Watts v. Indiana (1949) (Opinion of Jackson, J.).

Justice Scalia noted that Minnick himself testified that his appointed counsel had admonished Minnick not to speak to anyone and not to sign a waiver. Scalia added:

> Today's ruling, that the invocation of a right to counsel permanently prevents a police-initiated waiver, makes it largely impossible for the police to urge a prisoner who has initially declined to confess to change his mind—or indeed, even to ask whether he has changed his mind. Many persons in custody will invoke the *Miranda* right to counsel during the first interrogation, so that the permanent prohibition will attach at once. Those who do not do so will almost certainly request or obtain counsel at arraignment. We have held that a general request for counsel, after the Sixth Amendment right has attached, also triggers the *Edwards* prohibition of police-solicited confessions, see Michigan v. Jackson (1986), and I presume that the perpetuality of prohibition announced in today's opinion applies in that context as well. "Perpetuality" is not too strong a term, since, although the Court rejects one logical moment at which the *Edwards* presumption might end, it suggests no alternative. In this case Minnick was reapproached by the police three days after he requested counsel, but the result would presumably be the same if it had been three months, or three years, or even three decades. This perpetual irrebuttable presumption will apply, I might add, not merely to interrogations involving the original crime but to those involving other subjects as well.

4. MIRANDA WARNINGS IN MISDEMEANORS AND TO JUVENILES

(a) MISDEMEANORS

In Berkemer v. McCarty, 468 U.S. 420, 104 S.Ct. 3138 (1984), the Supreme Court held that statements secured through custodial interrogation without warnings and waiver must be excluded even in the trial of minor criminal cases, including those involving traffic offenses. Through Justice Marshall the Court noted that a suspect may not know whether he faces a misdemeanor charge or a felony charge and that frequently a minor traffic stop may lead to evidence of a more serious crime. The Court saw no reason to create complexity by carving out a "minor offense" exceptions to *Miranda*. It avoided the issue of whether officers must give the fourth warning—the right of the indigent to appointed counsel before interrogation—in cases where, if tried, the accused under Scott v. Illinois would not be entitled to appointed counsel.

The Court added that in routine traffic stop cases *Miranda* warnings will not be required because the detention is not custodial. There is no *significant* deprivation of freedom. The Court characterized the situation as "non-threatening" and said it was ordinarily a public event. It likened the detention to a *Terry* stop and, in significant dictum, indicated that the *Terry* stop, although a detention for Fourth Amendment purposes, did not involve custody so as to trigger *Miranda* rights.

The Court acknowledged that some traffic detentions will present close questions of whether the suspect was in custody. Whenever custody attaches—and certainly after formal arrest—officers must comply with *Miranda* if they engage in further interrogation and wish to use the suspect's responses as evidence. The Court mentioned but did not resolve the troublesome waiver issue in the case of an intoxicated driver. See Wright v. State, 288 Ark. 209, 703 S.W.2d 850 (1986) (Miranda warnings may have mislead driver into believing he could refuse intoxilyzer test without loss of license).

(b) JUVENILES

Miranda's application to juvenile proceedings is still in some doubt. See In re Gault, 387 U.S. 1, 87 S.Ct. 1428 (1967). The Supreme Court has shown a wavering reluctance to require full constitutional protections in juvenile proceedings because it is "reluctant to disallow the States to experiment . . . and to seek in new and different ways the elusive answers to the problems of the young." McKeiver v. Pennsylvania, 403 U.S. 528, 547, 91 S.Ct. 1976, 1987 (1971).

Some state jurisdictions have required all or part of the warnings in juvenile cases, either by statute—see Cal.Welf. & Inst.Code, § 625 (West 1972); Colo.Rev.Stat.Ann. § 19–2–102(3)(c)(I) (1974); N.M.Stat.Ann. § 32–1–27 (1978); Okl.Stat.Ann., Tit. 10, § 1109 (Supp.1979); Tex.Fam.Code, § 51.09(b) (Supp.1979); or by court decision—People v. Horton, 126 Ill. App.2d 401, 261 N.E.2d 693 (1970); State v. Loyd, 297 Minn. 442, 212 N.W.2d 671 (1973); Forest v. State, 76 Wash.2d 84, 455 P.2d 368 (1969); Theriault v. State, 66 Wis.2d 33, 223 N.W.2d 850 (1974).

5. MIRANDA AND INTERROGATIONS BY PERSONS OTHER THAN LAW ENFORCEMENT OFFICERS

The case law is very clear that the *Miranda* decision was directed at law enforcement officers, and is not applicable to private citizens, even when questioning persons they have restrained by virtue of a "citizen's arrest." For instance, a store security agent need not give the *Miranda* warnings to a person arrested for shoplifting or an employee arrested for thievery. See In re Deborah C., 30 Cal.3d 125, 177 Cal.Rptr. 852, 635 P.2d 446 (1981) (under ordinary circumstances, store security guards need not give *Miranda* warnings). See generally F. Inbau, B. Farley, D. Arnold, Protective Security Law Second Edition (Butterworth Heineman 1996). But see People v. Ray, 105 A.D.2d 988, 482 N.Y.S.2d 133 (1984). That decision prohibited a system in which store security guards routinely questioned suspects without providing warnings and then turned the suspects over to police officers who gave the warnings and got the suspects to repeat their admissions.

In dealing with private citizen cases, the courts have kept to a precise technical definition of the interrogator's status. In Pratt v. State, 9 Md. App. 220, 263 A.2d 247 (1970) it was held that a private security guard who had been commissioned as a special officer by the Governor was required to give *Miranda* warnings. The same result was reached in a state where parole officers have statutory police powers, State v. Lekas, 201 Kan. 579, 442 P.2d 11 (1968). The mere fact that the private citizen is employed by the state does not require him to give *Miranda* warnings. People v. Wright, 249 Cal.App.2d 692, 57 Cal.Rptr. 781 (1967). The reliance upon the technical status of the interrogator also requires the holding that *Miranda* is inapplicable even if a private citizen falsely represents himself to be a law officer when he questions a suspect. See People v. Vlcek, 114 Ill.App.2d 74, 252 N.E.2d 377 (1969).

Police officers from foreign jurisdictions are not required to give *Miranda* warnings. The theory is that suppression of statements taken in violation of *Miranda* serves to deter future violation by police, but when the police are from Mexico or Canada the deterrent effect is nil. See State v. Medlock, 86 Wash.App. 89, 935 P.2d 693 (1997); State v. Ford, 108 Ariz. 404, 499 P.2d 699 (1972) (Canadian); United States v. Welch, 455 F.2d 211 (2d Cir.1972) (Bahamian); and *Miranda* is inapplicable to American officers in foreign countries—State v. Cranford, 83 N.M. 294, 491 P.2d 511 (1971). But see Cranford v. Rodriguez, 512 F.2d 860 (10th Cir.1975) (disapproving State v. Cranford).

These generally recognized rules are subject to one universally recognized qualification. That is, the police are forbidden to use private citizens or foreign officers as their agents in order to escape the *Miranda* rule. Nearly every case cited for the proposition that private citizens are not governed by *Miranda* also states that the police may not use the private citizen as an agent. There are cases illustrative of the agency concept.

In State v. Kelly, 439 S.W.2d 487 (Mo.1969), the Court found that while *Miranda* generally was inapplicable to private witnesses it did apply in a case where the defendant was in police custody and has indicated his desire to remain silent. The defendant was in a room with the interrogating officer and the victim. The officer did not question him further but the victim did and soon after the officer joined in the interrogation. The court held that the victim's interrogation was merely a continuation of the police interrogation. In Commonwealth v. Bordner, 432 Pa. 405, 247 A.2d 612 (1968), it was held that the police used the suspect's parents as their agents. Accord: People v. Baugh, 19 Ill.App.3d 448, 311 N.E.2d 607 (1974) (victim's attorney); People v. Jones, 61 A.D.2d 264, 402 N.Y.S.2d 28 (1978) (security officer). Where the suspect asked to speak to the victim and the victim agreed if the suspect were behind bars and the conversation taped, the victim was not a police agent where no questions were suggested by police. People v. Holzer, 25 Cal.App.3d 456, 102 Cal.Rptr. 11 (1972). See Wilcher v. State, 697 So.2d 1087 (Miss.1997) (News Reporter).

See also Chapter 6, Section G.

6. MIRANDA AND THE SUSPECT WHO DOES NOT NEED THE WARNINGS

In one case where the questioning apparently occurred before *Miranda* but the case was tried thereafter, a defendant complained about lack of warnings at his interrogation. The court brushed his complaint aside because the defendant was a judge. Commonwealth v. Schwartz, 210 Pa.Super. 360, 233 A.2d 904 (1967). What of the defendant who is a lawyer or a policeman? The *Miranda* opinion was very clear on this point:

> "We will not pause to inquire in individual cases whether the defendant was aware of his rights without a warning" (on the basis of his education, intelligence and experience); "a warning is a clearcut fact" ... "More important, whatever the background of the person interrogated, a warning at the time of interrogation is indispensible to overcome its pressures and to insure that the individual knows he is free to exercise his privilege at that point in time".

The opposing principle is occasionally argued, United States v. Longbehn, 850 F.2d 450 (8th Cir.1988).

In Dupont v. United States, 259 A.2d 355 (D.C.App.1969), a defendant was about to be warned when he said, "I know my rights". The court held that his statement was taken in violation of *Miranda.* When the suspect states that he knows his rights the officer should insist on continuing the warnings. State v. Thomas, 16 Wash.App. 1, 553 P.2d 1357 (1976) (court found that one who twice refused to hear warnings had "waived his right to be informed"). One reasonable deviation from the absolute rule is found in Kear v. United States, 369 F.2d 78 (9th Cir.1966), where it was held unnecessary to warn a defendant of his right to remain silent when he said "I know I don't have to make a statement".

The prior criminal experience of the defendant can be used to help establish that the warnings given in the interrogation were understood because they had been given before in other cases. Jordan v. United States, 421 F.2d 493 (9th Cir.1970). And prior experience may serve to support the validity of a waiver of rights, Heard v. State, 244 Ark. 44, 424 S.W.2d 179 (1968).

A different problem is presented by the wealthy defendant. To warn him of his right to the services of a lawyer seems to be enough; the right is made no more meaningful to him if he is told that a lawyer will be appointed if he cannot afford one. For purposes of making a decision to waive his rights, it is enough for him to know he can see a lawyer before interrogation. In essence, the warning concerning appointed counsel is not itself a basic *Miranda* right; rather, it is a safety device designed to protect what is a basic *Miranda* right, the right to counsel. This conclusion is supported by implication in *Miranda*, 384 U.S. at 473 n. 43, 86 S.Ct. at 1627 n. 43. Some courts have required the prosecution to show non-indigency or require that it be apparent to the interrogators that the suspect is not indigent. See, for example, United States v. Messina, 388 F.2d 393 (2d Cir.1968).

Do warnings need be given where the attorney for the defendant contacted the police and said his client wished to make a statement? Can the court assume that counsel knew of the interview and did not wish to be present. Dempsey v. State, 225 Ga. 208, 166 S.E.2d 884 (1969) (yes); Jones v. State, 47 Wis.2d 642, 178 N.W.2d 42 (1970) (yes). But see Commonwealth v. Goldsmith, 438 Pa. 83, 263 A.2d 322 (1970) (cannot assume suspect knew of his rights because he came to the station with a lawyer).

C. INTERROGATION OF SUSPECTS AFTER INITIATION OF FORMAL PROCEEDINGS: THE SIXTH AMENDMENT RIGHT

Massiah v. United States

Supreme Court of the United States, 1964.
377 U.S. 201, 84 S.Ct. 1199.

■ MR. JUSTICE STEWART delivered the opinion of the Court.

The petitioner, a merchant seaman, was in 1958 a member of the crew of the S.S. *Santa Maria*. In April of that year federal customs officials in New York received information that he was going to transport a quantity of narcotics aboard that ship from South America to the United States. As a result of this and other information, the agents searched the *Santa Maria* upon its arrival in New York and found in the afterpeak of the vessel five packages containing about three and a half pounds of cocaine. They also learned of circumstances, not here relevant, tending to connect the petitioner with the cocaine. He was arrested, promptly arraigned, and subsequently indicted for possession of narcotics aboard a United States vessel. In July a superseding indictment was returned, charging the petitioner and a man named Colson with the same substantive offense, and in separate counts charging the petitioner, Colson, and others with having conspired to possess narcotics aboard a United States vessel, and to import, conceal, and facilitate the sale of narcotics. The petitioner, who had retained a lawyer, pleaded not guilty and was released on bail, along with Colson.

A few days later, and quite without the petitioner's knowledge, Colson decided to cooperate with the government agents in their continuing investigation of the narcotics activities in which the petitioner, Colson, and others had allegedly been engaged. Colson permitted an agent named Murphy to install a Schmidt radio transmitter under the front seat of Colson's automobile, by means of which Murphy, equipped with an appropriate receiving device, could overhear from some distance away conversations carried on in Colson's car.

On the evening of November 19, 1959, Colson and the petitioner held a lengthy conversation while sitting in Colson's automobile, parked on a New York street. By prearrangement with Colson, and totally unbeknown to the petitioner, the agent Murphy sat in a car parked out of sight down the street and listened over the radio to the entire conversation. The petitioner made several incriminating statements during the course of this conversation. At the petitioner's trial these incriminating statements were brought before the jury through Murphy's testimony, despite the insistent objection of defense counsel.

* * *

In Spano v. New York, 360 U.S. 315, 79 S.Ct. 1202 (1959), this Court reversed a state criminal conviction because a confession had been wrongly admitted into evidence against the defendant at his trial. In that case the defendant had already been indicted for first-degree murder at the time he confessed. The Court held that the defendant's conviction could not stand under the Fourteenth Amendment. While the Court's opinion relied upon the totality of the circumstances under which the confession had been obtained, four concurring Justices pointed out that the Constitution required reversal of the conviction upon the sole and specific ground that the confession had been deliberately elicited by the police after the defendant had been indicted, and therefore at a time when he was clearly entitled to a lawyer's help. It was pointed out that under our system of justice the most elemental concepts of due process of law contemplate that an indictment be followed by a trial, "in an orderly courtroom, presided over by a judge, open to the public, and protected by all the procedural safeguards of the law." It was said that a Constitution which guarantees a defendant the aid of counsel at such a trial could surely vouchsafe no less to an indicted defendant under interrogation by the police in a completely extrajudicial proceeding. Anything less, it was said, might deny a defendant "effective representation by counsel at the only stage when legal aid and advice would help him."

Ever since this Court's decision in the *Spano* case, the New York courts have unequivocally followed this constitutional rule. "Any secret interrogation of the defendant, from and after the finding of the indictment, without the protection afforded by the presence of counsel, contravenes the basic dictates of fairness in the conduct of criminal causes and the fundamental rights of persons charged with crime." People v. Waterman, 9 N.Y.2d 561, 565, 175 N.E.2d 445, 448.

This view no more than reflects a constitutional principle established as long ago as Powell v. Alabama, 287 U.S. 45, 53 S.Ct. 55 (1932), where the Court noted that "... during perhaps the most critical period of the proceedings ... that is to say, from the time of their arraignment until the beginning of their trial, when consultation, thorough-going investigation and preparation [are] vitally important, the defendants ... [are] as much entitled to such aid [of counsel] during that period as at the trial itself."

Here we deal not with a state court conviction, but with a federal case, where the specific guarantee of the Sixth Amendment directly applies. We hold that the petitioner was denied the basic protections of that guarantee when there was used against him at his trial evidence of his own incriminating words, which federal agents had deliberately elicited from him after he had been indicted and in the absence of his counsel. It is true that in the *Spano* case the defendant was interrogated in a police station, while here the damaging testimony was elicited from the defendant without his knowledge while he was free on bail. But, as Judge Hays pointed out in his dissent in the Court of Appeals, "if such a rule is to have any efficacy it must apply to indirect and surreptitious interrogations as well as those conducted in the jailhouse. In this case, Massiah was more seriously imposed upon ... because he did not even know that he was under interrogation by a government agent."

The Solicitor General, in his brief and oral argument, has strenuously contended that the federal law enforcement agents had the right, if not indeed the duty, to continue their investigation of the petitioner and his alleged criminal associates even though the petitioner had been indicted. He points out that the Government was continuing its investigation in order to uncover not only the source of narcotics found on the S.S. *Santa Maria*, but also their intended buyer. He says that the quantity of narcotics involved was such as to suggest that the petitioner was part of a large and well-organized ring, and indeed that the continuing investigation confirmed this suspicion, since it resulted in criminal charges against many defendants. Under these circumstances the Solicitor General concludes that the government agents were completely "justified in making use of Colson's cooperation by having Colson continue his normal associations and by surveilling them."

We may accept and, at least for present purposes, completely approve all that this argument implies, Fourth Amendment problems to one side. We do not question that in this case, as in many cases, it was entirely proper to continue an investigation of the suspected criminal activities of the defendant and his alleged confederates, even though the defendant had already been indicted. All that we hold is that the defendant's own incriminating statements, obtained by federal agents under the circumstances here disclosed, could not constitutionally be used by the prosecution as evidence against *him* at his trial.

Reversed.

■ MR. JUSTICE WHITE, with whom MR. JUSTICE CLARK and MR. JUSTICE HARLAN join, dissenting.

* * *

... I am unable to see how this case presents an unconstitutional interference with Massiah's right to counsel. Massiah was not prevented from consulting with counsel as often as he wished. No meetings with counsel were disturbed or spied upon. Preparation for trial was in no way obstructed. It is only a sterile syllogism—an unsound one, besides—to say that because Massiah had a right to counsel's aid before and during the trial, his out-of-court conversations and admissions must be excluded if obtained without counsel's consent or presence....

* * *

[The] Court's newly fashioned exclusionary principle goes far beyond the constitutional privilege against self-incrimination, which neither requires nor suggests the barring of voluntary pretrial admissions. The Fifth Amendment states that no person "shall be compelled in any criminal case to be a witness against himself...." The defendant may thus not be compelled to testify at his trial, but he may if he wishes. Likewise he may not be compelled or coerced into saying anything before trial; but until today he could if he wished to, and if he did, it could be used against him. Whether as a matter of self incrimination or of due process, the proscription is against compulsion—coerced incrimination. Under the prior law, announced in countless cases in this Court, the defendant's pretrial statements were admissible evidence if voluntarily made; inadmissible if not the product of his free will. Hardly any constitutional area has been more carefully patrolled by this Court, and until now the Court has expressly rejected the argument that admissions are to be deemed involuntary if made outside the presence of counsel.

The Court presents no facts, no objective evidence, no reasons to warrant scrapping the voluntary-involuntary test for admissibility in this area. Without such evidence I would retain it in its present form.

This case cannot be analogized to the American Bar Association's rule forbidding an attorney to talk to the opposing party litigant outside the presence of his counsel. Aside from the fact that the Association's canons are not of constitutional dimensions, the specific canon argued is inapposite because it deals with the conduct of lawyers and not with the conduct of investigators. Lawyers are forbidden to interview the opposing party because of the supposed imbalance of legal skill and acumen between the lawyer and the party litigant; the reason for the rule does not apply to nonlawyers and certainly not to Colson, Massiah's codefendant.

Applying the new exclusionary rule is peculiarly inappropriate in this case. At the time of the conversation in question, petitioner was not in custody but free on bail. He was not questioned in what anyone could call an atmosphere of official coercion. What he said was said to his partner in crime who had also been indicted. There was no suggestion or any possibility of coercion. What petitioner did not know was that Colson had decided to report the conversation to the police. Had there been no prior arrangements between Colson and the police, had Colson simply gone to the police after the conversation had occurred, his testimony relating Massiah's statements would be readily admissible at the trial, as would a recording which he might have made of the conversation. In such event, it would simply be said that Massiah risked talking to a friend who decided to disclose what he knew of Massiah's criminal activities. But if, as occurred here, Colson had been cooperating with the police prior to his meeting with Massiah, both his evidence and the recorded conversation are somehow transformed into inadmissible evidence despite the fact that the hazard to Massiah remains precisely the same—the defection of a confederate in crime.

Reporting criminal behavior is expected or even demanded of the ordinary citizen. Friends may be subpoenaed to testify about friends, relatives about relatives and partners about partners. I therefore question the soundness of insulating Massiah from the apostasy of his partner in crime and of furnishing constitutional sanctions for the strict secrecy and discipline of criminal organizations. Neither the ordinary citizen nor the confessed criminal should be discouraged from reporting what he knows to the authorities and from lending his aid to secure evidence of crime. More narrowly, and posed by the precise situation involved here, the question is this: when the police have arrested and released on bail one member of a criminal ring and another member, a confederate, is cooperating with the police, can the confederate be allowed to continue his association with the ring or must he somehow be withdrawn to avoid challenge to trial evidence on the ground that it was acquired after rather than before the arrest, after rather than before the indictment?

Defendants who are out on bail have been known to continue their illicit operations. That an attorney is advising them should not constitutionally immunize their statements made in furtherance of these operations and relevant to the question of their guilt at the pending prosecution. In this very case there is evidence that after indictment defendant Aiken tried to persuade Agent Murphy to go into the narcotics business with him. Under today's decision, Murphy may neither testify as to the content of this conversation nor seize for introduction in evidence any narcotics whose location Aiken may have made known.

Undoubtedly, the evidence excluded in this case would not have been available but for the conduct of Colson in cooperation with Agent Murphy, but is it this kind of conduct which should be forbidden to those charged with law enforcement? ... Massiah was not being interrogated in a police station, was not surrounded by numerous officers or questioned in relays, and was not forbidden access to others. Law enforcement may have the elements of a contest about it, but it is not a game. Massiah and those like him receive ample protection from the long line of precedents in this Court holding that confessions may not be introduced unless they are voluntary.

Brewer v. Williams

Supreme Court of the United States, 1977.
430 U.S. 387, 97 S.Ct. 1232.

■ MR. JUSTICE STEWART delivered the opinion of the Court.

I.

On the afternoon of December 24, 1968, a 10–year–old girl named Pamela Powers went with her family to the YMCA in Des Moines, Iowa, to watch a wrestling tournament in which her brother was participating. When she failed to return from a trip to the washroom, a search for her began. The search was unsuccessful.

Robert Williams, who had recently escaped from a mental hospital, was a resident of the YMCA. Soon after the girl's disappearance Williams was seen in the YMCA lobby carrying some clothing and a large bundle wrapped in a blanket. He obtained help from a 14–year–old boy in opening the street door of the YMCA and the door to his automobile parked outside. When Williams placed the bundle in the front seat of his car the boy "saw two legs in it and they were skinny and white." Before anyone could see what was in the bundle Williams drove away. His abandoned car was found the following day in Davenport, Iowa, roughly 160 miles east of Des Moines. A warrant was then issued in Des Moines for his arrest on a charge of abduction.

On the morning of December 26, a Des Moines lawyer named Henry McKnight went to the Des Moines police station and informed the officers present that he had just received a long distance call from Williams, and that he had advised Williams to turn himself in to the Davenport police. Williams did surrender that morning to the police in Davenport, and they booked him on the charge specified in the arrest warrant and gave him the warnings required by Miranda v. Arizona, 384 U.S. 436, 86 S.Ct. 1602 (1966). The Davenport police then telephoned their counterparts in Des Moines to inform them that Williams had surrendered. McKnight, the lawyer, was still at the Des Moines police headquarters, and Williams conversed with McKnight on the telephone. In the presence of the Des Moines Chief of Police and a Police Detective named Leaming, McKnight advised Williams that Des Moines police officers would be driving to Davenport to pick him up, that the officers would not interrogate him or mistreat him, and that Williams was not to talk to the officers about Pamela Powers until after consulting with McKnight upon his return to Des Moines. As a result of these conversations, it was agreed between McKnight and the Des Moines police officials that Detective Leaming and a fellow officer would drive to Davenport to pick up Williams, that they would bring him directly back to Des Moines, and that they would not question him during the trip.

In the meantime Williams was arraigned before a judge in Davenport on the outstanding arrest warrant. The judge advised him of his *Miranda* rights and committed him to jail. Before leaving the courtroom, Williams conferred with a lawyer named Kelly, who advised him not to make any statements until consulting with McKnight back in Des Moines.

Detective Leaming and his fellow officer arrived in Davenport about noon to pick up Williams and return him to Des Moines. Soon after their arrival they met with Williams and Kelly, who, they understood, was acting as Williams' lawyer. Detective Leaming repeated the *Miranda* warnings, and told Williams:

> "... we both know that you're being represented here by Mr. Kelly and you're being represented by Mr. McKnight in Des Moines, and ... I want you to remember this because we'll be visiting between here and Des Moines."

Williams then conferred again with Kelly alone, and after this conference Kelly reiterated to Detective Leaming that Williams was not to be questioned about the disappearance of Pamela Powers until after he had consulted with McKnight back in Des Moines. When Leaming expressed some reservations, Kelly firmly stated that the agreement with McKnight was to be carried out—that there was to be no interrogation of Williams during the automobile journey to Des Moines. Kelly was denied permission to ride in the police car back to Des Moines with Williams and the two officers.

The two Detectives, with Williams in their charge, then set out on the 160–mile drive. At no time during the trip did Williams express a willingness to be interrogated in the absence of an attorney. Instead, he stated several times that "[w]hen I get to Des Moines and see Mr. McKnight, I am going to tell you the whole story." Detective Leaming knew that Williams was a former mental patient, and knew also that he was deeply religious.

The Detective and his prisoner soon embarked on a wide-ranging conversation covering a variety of topics, including the subject of religion. Then, not long after leaving Davenport and reaching the interstate highway, Detective Leaming delivered what has been referred to in the briefs and oral arguments as the "Christian burial speech." Addressing Williams as "Reverend," the Detective said:

> "I want to give you something to think about while we're traveling down the road.... Number one, I want you to observe the weather conditions, it's raining, it's sleeting, it's freezing, driving is very treacherous, visibility is poor, it's going to be dark early this evening. They are predicting several inches of snow for tonight, and I feel that you yourself are the only person that knows where this little girl's body is, that you yourself have only been there once, and if you get a snow on top of it you yourself may be unable to find it. And, since we will be going right past the area on the way into Des Moines, I feel that we could stop and locate the body, that the parents of this little girl should be entitled to a Christian burial for the little girl who was snatched away from them on Christmas Eve and murdered. And I feel we should stop and locate it on the way in rather than waiting until morning and trying to come back out after a snow storm and possibly not being able to find it at all."

Williams asked Detective Leaming why he thought their route to Des Moines would be taking them past the girl's body, and Leaming responded that he knew the body was in the area of Mitchellville—a town they would be passing on the way to Des Moines.[1] Leaming then stated: "I do not want you to answer me. I don't want to discuss it further. Just think about it as we're riding down the road."

As the car approached Grinnell, a town approximately 100 miles west of Davenport, Williams asked whether the police had found the victim's shoes. When Detective Leaming replied that he was unsure, Williams directed the officers to a service station where he said he had left the shoes; a search for them proved unsuccessful. As they continued towards Des Moines, Williams asked whether the police had found the blanket, and directed the officers to a rest area where he said he had disposed of the blanket. Nothing was found. The car continued towards Des Moines, and as it approached Mitchellville, Williams said that he would show the officers where the body was. He then directed the police to the body of Pamela Powers.

Williams was indicted for first-degree murder. Before trial, his counsel moved to suppress all evidence relating to or resulting from any statements Williams had made during the automobile ride from Davenport to Des Moines. After an evidentiary hearing the trial judge denied the motion. He

1. The fact of the matter, of course, was that Detective Leaming possessed no such knowledge.

found that "an agreement was made between defense counsel and the police officials to the effect that the Defendant was not to be questioned on the return trip to Des Moines," and that the evidence in question had been elicited from Williams during "a critical stage in the proceedings requiring the presence of counsel on his request." The judge ruled, however, that Williams had "waived his right to have an attorney present during the giving of such information."

The evidence in question was introduced over counsel's continuing objection at the subsequent trial. The jury found Williams guilty of murder, and the judgment of conviction was affirmed by the Iowa Supreme Court, a bare majority of whose members agreed with the trial court that Williams had "waived his right to the presence of his counsel" on the automobile ride from Davenport to Des Moines. The four dissenting justices expressed the view that "when counsel and police have agreed defendant is not to be questioned until counsel is present and defendant has been advised not to talk and repeatedly has stated he will tell the whole story after he talks with counsel, the state should be required to make a stronger showing of intentional voluntary waiver than was made here."

Williams then petitioned for a writ of habeas corpus in the United States District Court for the Southern District of Iowa. ...The District Court concluded as a matter of law that the evidence in question had been wrongly admitted at Williams' trial. ...

The Court of Appeals for the Eighth Circuit, with one judge dissenting, affirmed this judgment.

* * *

Specifically, there is no need to review in this case the doctrine of Miranda v. Arizona, [nor] the ruling of the District Court that Williams' self-incriminating statements were, indeed, involuntarily made. For it is clear that the judgment before us must in any event be affirmed upon the ground that Williams was deprived of a different constitutional right—the right to the assistance of counsel.

* * *

... Whatever else it may mean, the right to counsel granted by the Sixth and Fourteenth Amendments means at least that a person is entitled to the help of a lawyer at or after the time that judicial proceedings have been initiated against him—"whether by way of formal charge, preliminary hearing, indictment, information, or arraignment." Kirby v. Illinois.

There can be no doubt in the present case that judicial proceedings had been initiated against Williams before the start of the automobile ride from Davenport to Des Moines. A warrant had been issued for his arrest, he had been arraigned on that warrant before a judge and he had been committed by the court to confinement in jail.

There can be no serious doubt, either, that Detective Leaming deliberately and designedly set out to elicit information from Williams just as surely as—and perhaps more effectively than—if he had formally interrogated him. Detective Leaming was fully aware before departing for Des

Moines that Williams was being represented in Davenport by Kelly and in Des Moines by McKnight. . . . Detective Leaming testified at Williams' trial:

"Q. In fact, Captain, whether he was a mental patient or not, you were trying to get all the information you could before he got to his lawyer, weren't you?

"A. I was sure hoping to find out where that little girl was, yes, sir.

* * *

"Q. Well, I'll put it this way: You was hoping to get all the information you could before Williams got back to McKnight, weren't you?

"A. Yes, sir."

The state courts clearly proceeded upon the hypothesis that Detective Leaming's "Christian burial speech" had been tantamount to interrogation. Both courts recognized that Williams had been entitled to the assistance of counsel at the time he made the incriminating statements. Yet no such constitutional protection would have come into play if there had been no interrogation.

The circumstances of this case are thus constitutionally indistinguishable from those presented in Massiah v. United States. . . .

That the incriminating statements were elicited surreptitiously in the *Massiah* case, and otherwise here, is constitutionally irrelevant. Rather, the clear rule of *Massiah* is that once adversary proceedings have commenced against an individual, he has a right to legal representation when the government interrogates him. . . .

* * *

In the federal habeas corpus proceeding the District Court . . . concluded:

"[U]nder the proper standards for determining waiver, there simply is no evidence to support a waiver. . . . [T]here is no affirmative indication . . . that [Williams] did waive his rights. . . . [T]he state courts' emphasis on the absence of a demand for counsel was not only legally inappropriate, but factually unsupportable as well, since Detective Leaming himself testified that [Williams], on several occasions during the trip, indicated that he would talk *after* he saw Mr. McKnight. Both these statements and Mr. Kelly's statement to Detective Leaming that [Williams] would talk only after seeing Mr. McKnight in Des Moines certainly were assertions of [Williams'] right or desire not to give information absent the presence of his attorney. . . . Moreover, the statements were obtained only after Detective Leaming's use of psychology on a person whom he knew to be deeply religious and an escapee from a mental hospital—with the specific intent to elicit incriminating statements."

* * *

The District Court and the Court of Appeals were correct in their understanding that it was incumbent upon the State to prove "an intentional relinquishment or abandonment of a known right or privilege." Johnson v. Zerbst.

* * *

We conclude, finally, that the Court of Appeals was correct in holding that, judged by these standards, the record in this case falls far short of sustaining the State's burden. It is true that Williams had been informed of and appeared to understand his right to counsel. But waiver requires not merely comprehension but relinquishment, and Williams' consistent reliance upon the advice of counsel in dealing with the authorities refutes any suggestion that he waived that right. He consulted McKnight by long distance telephone before turning himself in. He spoke with McKnight by telephone again shortly after being booked. After he was arraigned, Williams sought out and obtained legal advice from Kelly. Williams again consulted with Kelly after Detective Leaming and his fellow officer arrived in Davenport. Throughout, Williams was advised not to make any statements before seeing McKnight in Des Moines, and was assured that the police had agreed not to question him. His statements while in the car that he would tell the whole story *after* seeing McKnight in Des Moines were the clearest expressions by Williams himself that he desired the presence of an attorney before any interrogation took place. But even before making these statements, Williams had effectively asserted his right to counsel by having secured attorneys at both ends of the automobile trip, both of whom, acting as his agents, had made clear to the police that no interrogation was to occur during the journey. Williams knew of that agreement and particularly in view of his consistent reliance on counsel, there is no basis for concluding that he disavowed it.

Despite Williams' express and implicit assertions of his right to counsel, Detective Leaming proceeded to elicit incriminating statements from Williams. Leaming did not preface this effort by telling Williams that he had a right to the presence of a lawyer, and made no effort at all to ascertain whether Williams wished to relinquish that right. The circumstances of record in this case thus provide no reasonable basis for finding that Williams waived his right to the assistance of counsel.

The Court of Appeals did not hold, nor do we, that under the circumstances of this case Williams *could not*, without notice to counsel, have waived his rights under the Sixth and Fourteenth Amendments. It only held, as do we, that he did not.

IV.

The crime of which Williams was convicted was senseless and brutal, calling for swift and energetic action by the police to apprehend the perpetrator and gather evidence with which he could be convicted. No mission of law enforcement officials is more important. Yet "[d]isinterested zeal for the public good does not assure either wisdom or right in the methods it pursues." Haley v. Ohio, 332 U.S. 596, 605, 68 S.Ct. 302. (Frankfurter, J., concurring in the judgment). Although we do not lightly affirm the issuance of a writ of habeas corpus in this case, so clear a violation of the Sixth and Fourteenth Amendments as here occurred cannot be condoned. The pressures on state executive and judicial officers charged with the administration of the criminal law are great, especially when the crime is murder and the victim a small child. But it is precisely the predictability of those pressures that makes imperative a resolute loyalty to the guarantees that the Constitution extends to us all.

The judgment of the Court of Appeals is affirmed.[12]

■ MR. JUSTICE MARSHALL, concurring. [Opinion omitted.]

■ MR. JUSTICE POWELL, concurring.

* * *

The critical factual issue is whether there had been a voluntary waiver, and this turns in large part upon whether there was interrogation....

* * *

I join the opinion of the Court which also finds that the efforts of Detective Leaming "to elicit information from Williams," as conceded by counsel for the State at oral argument, were a skillful and effective form of interrogation. Moreover, the entire setting was conducive to the psychological coercion that was successfully exploited. Williams was known by the police to be a young man with quixotic religious convictions and a history of mental disorders. The date was Christmas eve, the weather was ominous, and the setting appropriate for Detective Leaming's talk of snow concealing the body and preventing a "Christian burial." Williams was alone in the automobile with two police officers for several hours. It is clear from the record, as both of the federal courts below found, that there was no evidence of a knowing and voluntary waiver of the right to have counsel present beyond the fact that Williams ultimately confessed. It is settled law that an inferred waiver of a constitutional right is disfavored. I find no basis in the record of this case—or in the dissenting opinions—for disagreeing with the conclusion of the District Court that "the State has produced no affirmative evidence whatever to support its claim of waiver."

The dissenting opinion of The Chief Justice states that the Court's holding today "conclusively presumes a suspect is legally incompetent to change his mind and tell the truth until an attorney is present." I find no justification for this view. On the contrary, the opinion of the Court is

12. The District Court stated that its decision "does not touch upon the issue of what evidence, if any, beyond the incriminating statements themselves must be excluded as 'fruit of the poisonous tree.'" 375 F.Supp., at 185. We too have no occasion to address this issue, and in the present posture of the case there is no basis for the view of our dissenting Brethen that any attempt to retry the respondent would probably be futile. While neither Williams' incriminating statements themselves nor any testimony describing his having led the police to the victim's body can constitutionally be admitted into evidence, evidence of where the body was found and of its condition might well be admissible on the theory that the body would have been discovered in any event, even had incriminating statements not been elicited from Williams. Cf. Killough v. United States, 336 F.2d 929 (1964). In the event that a retrial is instituted, it will be for the state courts in the first instance to determine whether particular items of evidence may be admitted.

explicitly clear that the right to assistance of counsel may be waived, after it has attached, without notice to or consultation with counsel. We would have such a case here if the State had proved that the police officers refrained from coercion and interrogation, as they have agreed, and that Williams freely on his own initiative had confessed the crime.

* * *

■ MR. JUSTICE STEVENS, concurring.

... The strong language in the dissenting opinions prompts me to add this brief comment about the Court's function in a case such as this.

Nothing that we write, no matter how well reasoned or forcefully expressed, can bring back the victim of this tragedy or undo the consequences of the official neglect which led to the respondent's escape from a State mental institution. The emotional aspects of the case make it difficult to decide dispassionately, but do not qualify our obligation to apply the law with an eye to the future as well as with concern for the result in the particular case before us.

Underlying the surface issues in this case is the question whether a fugitive from justice can rely on his lawyer's advice given in connection with a decision to surrender voluntarily. The defendant placed his trust in an experienced Iowa trial lawyer who in turn trusted the Iowa law enforcement authorities to honor a commitment made during negotiations which led to the apprehension of a potentially dangerous person. Under any analysis, this was a critical stage of the proceeding in which the participation of an independent professional was of vital importance to the accused and to society. At this stage—as in countless others in which the law profoundly affects the life of the individual—the lawyer is the essential medium through which the demands and commitments of the sovereign are communicated to the citizen. If, in the long run, we are seriously concerned about the individual's effective representation by counsel, the State cannot be permitted to dishonor its promise to this lawyer.

■ MR. CHIEF JUSTICE BURGER, dissenting.

The result reached by the Court in this case ought to be intolerable in any society which purports to call itself an organized society. It continues the court—by the narrowest margin—on the much criticized course of punishing the public for the mistakes and misdeeds of law enforcement officers, instead of punishing the officer directly, if in fact he is guilty of wrongdoing. It mechanically and blindly keeps reliable evidence from juries whether the claimed constitutional violation involves gross police misconduct or honest human error. Williams is guilty of the savage murder of a small child; no Member of the Court contends he is not. While in custody, and after no fewer than *five* warnings of his rights to silence and to counsel, he led police to the place where he had buried the body of his victim. The Court now holds the jury must not be told how the police found the body.

The Court concedes Williams was not threatened or coerced and that he acted voluntarily and with full awareness of his constitutional rights when he guided police to the body. In the face of all this, the Court now holds that because Williams was prompted by the detective's statement—not interrogation but a statement—his disclosure cannot be given to the jury.

The effect of this is to fulfill Justice Cardozo's grim prophecy that someday some court might carry the exclusionary rule to the absurd extent that its operative effect would exclude evidence relating to the body of a murder victim because of the means by which it was found.[1] In so doing the Court regresses to playing a grisly game of "hide and seek," once more exalting the sporting theory of criminal justice which has been experiencing a decline in our jurisprudence. With Justices White and Blackmun, I categorically reject the remarkable notion that the police in this case were guilty of unconstitutional misconduct, or any conduct justifying the bizarre result reached by the Court. Apart from a brief comment on the merits, however, I wish to focus on the irrationality of applying the increasingly discredited exclusionary rule to this case.

* * *

The evidence is uncontradicted that Williams had abundant knowledge of his right to have counsel present and of his right to silence. Since the Court does not question Williams' mental competence, it boggles the mind to suggest that he could not understand that leading police to the child's body would have other than the most serious consequences. All of the elements necessary to make out a valid waiver are shown by the record and, paradoxically, acknowledged by the Court; we thus are left to guess how the Court reached its holding.

One plausible but unarticulated basis for the result reached is that once a suspect has asserted his right not to talk without the presence of an attorney, it becomes legally impossible to waive that right until the suspect has seen an attorney. But constitutional rights are *personal*, and an otherwise valid waiver should not be brushed aside by judges simply because an attorney was not present. The Court's holding operates to "imprison a man in his privileges," Adams v. United States ex rel. McCann, 317 U.S. 269, 280, 63 S.Ct. 236 (1942); it conclusively presumes a suspect is legally incompetent to change his mind and tell the truth until an attorney is present. It denigrates an individual to some sort of nonperson whose free will has become hostage to a lawyer so that until a lawyer consents, the suspect is deprived of any legal right or power to decide for himself that he wishes to make a disclosure. It denies that the rights to counsel and silence are *personal*, nondelegable, and subject to a waiver only by that individual.

1. "The criminal is to go free because the constable has blundered. . . .A room is searched against the law, and the body of a murdered man is found. . . . The privacy of the home has been infringed, and the murderer goes free." People v. Defore, 242 N.Y. 13, 21, 23–24, 150 N.E. 585, 587, 588 (1926).

* * *

The opinions in support of the Court's judgment do not enlighten us as to why police conduct—whether good or bad—should operate to suspend Williams' right to change his mind and "tell all" at once rather than waiting until he reached Des Moines.

In his concurring opinion Mr. Justice Powell suggests that the result in this case turns on whether Detective Leaming's remarks constituted "interrogation," as he views them, or whether they were "statements" intended to prick the conscience of the accused. I find it most remarkable that a murder case should turn on judicial interpretation that a statement becomes a question simply because it is followed by an incriminating disclosure from the suspect. The Court seems to be saying that since Williams said he would "tell the whole story" at Des Moines, the police should have been content and waited; of course, that would have been the wiser course, especially in light of the nuances of constitutional jurisprudence applied by the Court, but a murder case ought not turn on such tenuous strands.

In any case, the Court assures us, this is not at all what it intends, and that a valid waiver was *possible* in these circumstances, but was not quite made. Here of course Williams did not confess to the murder in so many words; it was his conduct in guiding police to the body, not his words, which incriminated him. And the record is replete with evidence that Williams knew precisely what he was doing when he guided police to the body. The human urge to confess wrongdoing is, of course, normal in all save hardened, professional criminals, as psychiatrists and analysts have demonstrated. T. Reik, The Compulsion to Confess.

* * *

... In this case, where the evidence of how the child's body was found is of unquestioned reliability, and since the Court accepts Williams' disclosures as voluntary and uncoerced, there is no issue either of fairness or evidentiary reliability to justify suppression of truth. It appears suppression is mandated here for no other reason than the Court's general impression that it may have a beneficial effect on future police conduct; indeed, the Court fails to say even that much in defense of its holding.

* * *

■ MR. JUSTICE WHITE, with whom MR. JUSTICE BLACKMUN and MR. JUSTICE REHNQUIST join, dissenting.

The respondent in this case killed a 10–year–old child. The majority sets aside his conviction, holding that certain statements of unquestioned reliability were unconstitutionally obtained from him, and under the circumstances probably makes it impossible to retry him. Because there is nothing in the Constitution or in our previous cases which requires the Court's action, I dissent.

* * *

... The majority creates no new rule preventing an accused who has retained a lawyer from waiving his right to the lawyer's presence during questioning. The majority simply finds that no waiver was *proved* in this case. I disagree. That respondent knew of his right not to say anything to the officers without advice and presence of counsel is established on this record to a moral certainty. He was advised of the right by three officials of the State—telling at least one that he understood the right—and by two lawyers. Finally, he further demonstrated his knowledge of the right by informing the police that he would tell them the story in the presence of McKnight when they arrived in Des Moines. The issue in this case, then, is whether respondent relinquished that right intentionally.

Respondent relinquished his right not to talk to the police about his crime when the car approached the place where he had hidden the victim's clothes. Men usually intend to do what they do and there is nothing in the record to support the proposition that respondent's decision to talk was anything but an exercise of his own free will. Apparently, without any prodding from the officers, respondent—who had earlier said that he would tell the whole story when he arrived in Des Moines—spontaneously changed his mind about the timing of his disclosures when the car approached the places where he had hidden the evidence. However, even if his statements were influenced by Detective Leaming's statement, respondent's decision to talk in the absence of counsel can hardly be viewed as the product of an overborn will. The statement by Leaming was not coercive; it was accompanied by a request that respondent not respond to it; and it was delivered hours before respondent decided to make any statement. Respondent's waiver was thus knowing and intentional.

* * *

The majority's contrary conclusion seems to rest on the fact that respondent "asserted" his right to counsel by retaining and consulting with one lawyer and by consulting with another. How this supports the conclusion that respondent's later relinquishment of his right not to talk in the absence of counsel was unintentional is a mystery. The fact that respondent consulted with counsel on the question whether he should talk to the police in counsel's absence makes his later decision to talk in counsel's absence *better* informed and, if anything, more intelligent.

The majority recognizes that even after this "assertion" of his right to counsel, it would have found that respondent waived his right not to talk in counsel's absence if his waiver had been expressed—i.e., if the officers had asked him in the car whether he would be willing to answer questions in counsel's absence and if he had answered "yes." But waiver is not a formalistic concept. Waiver is shown whenever the facts establish that an accused knew of a right and intended to relinquish it. Such waiver, even if not express,[5] was plainly shown here. The only other conceivable basis for

5. The Court of Appeals, in administering the rule of Miranda v. Arizona, have not required an express waiver of the rights to silence and to counsel which an accused must be advised about under that case. Waiver has been found where the accused is informed of those rights, understands them, and then proceeds voluntarily to answer questions in the absence of counsel. United States v. Marchildon, 519 F.2d 337, 343 (C.A.8 1975) ("Waiver depends on no form of words, written or oral. It is to be determined from all of the surrounding circumstances. Addressing ourselves to this issue we held in Hughes v. Swenson, 452 F.2d 866, 867–868 (C.A.8 1971), that: 'The thrust of appellant's claim is that a valid waiver cannot be effective absent an expressed declaration to that effect. We are cited to no case which supports appellant's thesis and independent research

the majority's holding is the implicit suggestion that the right involved in Massiah v. United States, as distinguished from the right involved in Miranda v. Arizona, is a right not to be *asked* any questions in counsel's absence rather than a right not to *answer* any questions in counsel's absence, and that the right not to be *asked* questions must be waived *before* the questions are asked. Such wafer-thin distinctions cannot determine whether a guilty murderer should go free. The only conceivable purpose for the presence of counsel during questioning is to protect an accused from making incriminating *answers*. Questions, unanswered, have no significance at all. Absent coercion—no matter how the right involved is defined—an accused is amply protected by a rule requiring waiver before or simultaneously with the giving by him of an answer or the making by him of a statement.

■ MR. JUSTICE BLACKMUN, with whom MR. JUSTICE WHITE and MR. JUSTICE REHNQUIST join, dissenting.

* * *

... The Court rules that the Sixth Amendment was violated because Detective Leaming "purposely sought during Williams' isolation from his lawyers to obtain as much incriminating information as possible." I cannot regard that as unconstitutional *per se*.

First, the police did not deliberately seek to isolate Williams from his lawyers so as to deprive him of the assistance of counsel. The isolation in this case was a necessary incident of transporting Williams to the county where the crime was committed.

Second, Leaming's purpose was not solely to obtain incriminating evidence. The victim had been missing for only two days, and the police could not be certain that she was dead. Leaming, of course, and in accord with his duty, was "hoping to find out where that little girl was," but such motivation does not equate with an intention to evade the Sixth Amend-

discloses none. To the contrary, the Fifth, Seventh, Ninth, and Tenth Circuits have held in effect that if the defendant is effectively advised of his rights and intelligently and understandingly declines to exercise them, the waiver is valid' "); United States v. Ganter, 436 F.2d 364, 370 (C.A.7 1970) ("[A]n express statement that the individual does not want a lawyer is not required if it appears that the defendant was effectively advised of his rights and he then intelligently and understandingly declined to exercise them"); United States v. James, 528 F.2d 999, 1019 (C.A.5 1976) (" 'All that the prosecution must show is that the defendant was effectively advised of his rights and that he then intelligently and understandingly declined to exercise them' "); Blackmon v. Blackledge, 541 F.2d 1070, 1072 (C.A.4 1976) ("[H]e was reasonably questioned only after having been fully informed of his rights and permitted to make a telephone call. Under such circumstances, a suspect's submission to questioning without objection and without requesting a lawyer is clearly a waiver of his right to counsel, if, indeed, he understands his rights").

There is absolutely no reason to require an additional question to the already cumbersome Miranda litany just because the majority finds another case—Massiah v. United States—providing exactly the same right to counsel as that involved in Miranda. In either event, the issue is, as the majority recognizes, one of the proofs necessary to establish waiver. If an intentional relinquishment of the right to counsel under Miranda is established by proof that the accused was informed of his right and then voluntarily answered questions in counsel's absence, then similar proof establishes an intentional relinquishment of the Massiah right to counsel.

ment. Moreover, the Court seems to me to place on undue emphasis, and aspersion on what it and the lower courts have chosen to call the "Christian burial speech," and on Williams' "deeply religious" convictions.

Third, not every attempt to elicit information should be regarded as "tantamount to interrogation." I am not persuaded that Leaming's observations and comments, made as the police car traversed the snowy and slippery miles between Davenport and Des Moines that winter afternoon, were an interrogation, direct or subtle, of Williams. Contrary to this Court's statement, the Iowa Supreme Court appears to me to have thought and held otherwise, and I agree. Williams, after all, was counseled by lawyers, and warned by the arraigning judge in Davenport and by the police, and yet it was he who started the travel conversations and brought up the subject of the criminal investigation. Without further reviewing the circumstances of the trip, I would say it is clear there was no interrogation....

In summary, it seems to me that the Court is holding that *Massiah* is violated whenever police engage in any conduct, in the absence of counsel, with the subjective desire to obtain information from a suspect after arraignment. Such a rule is far too broad. Persons in custody frequently volunteer statements in response to stimuli other than interrogation....

... When there is no interrogation, such statements should be admissible as long as they are truly voluntary.

* * *

One final word: I can understand the discomfiture the Court obviously suffers and expresses in Part IV of its opinion, and the like discomfiture expressed by Justice (now United States District Judge) Stuart of the Iowa Court in the dissent he felt compelled to make by this Court's precedents, 182 N.W.2d, at 406. This was a brutal, tragic, and heinous crime inflicted upon a young girl on the afternoon of the day before Christmas. With the exclusionary rule operating as the Court effectuates it, the decision today probably means that, as a practical matter, no new trial will be possible at this date eight years after the crime, and that this respondent necessarily will go free.* That, of course, is not the standard by which a case of this kind strictly is to be judged. But, as Judge Webster in dissent below observed, 509 F.2d, at 237, placing the case in sensible and proper perspective: "The evidence of Williams' guilt was overwhelming. No challenge is made to the reliability of the fact-finding process." I am in full agreement with that observation.

Maine v. Moulton

Supreme Court of the United States, 1985.
474 U.S. 159, 106 S.Ct. 477.

■ JUSTICE BRENNAN delivered the opinion of the Court.

* * *

On the night of January 15, 1981, police officers in Belfast, Maine, responded to a fire call in the vicinity of the Belfast Dodge automobile

* [Ed. Note. See Nix v. Williams, infra, p. 826, for the subsequent history of *Williams*.]

dealership. Arriving at the scene, the officers discovered a burning Chevrolet dump truck which they recognized as a vehicle that had been reported stolen. After examining the burning truck, the officers searched a building located on the Belfast Dodge property. This building was not part of the dealership, but was leased to respondent Perley Moulton and his codefendant Gary Colson who were using the space to restore and sell old Ford Mustangs. Inside, the officers discovered evidence of several recent automobile and automobile-related thefts.

On April 7, 1981, a Waldo County grand jury returned indictments charging Moulton and Colson with four counts of theft by receiving.... On April 9, Moulton and Colson, represented by retained counsel, appeared before the Maine Superior Court for Waldo County and entered pleas of not guilty. Both were enlarged on bail pending trial.

On November 4, 1982, Colson complained by telephone to Robert Keating, Chief of the Belfast Police Department, that he had received anonymous threatening telephone calls regarding the charges pending against him and Moulton, and indicated that he wished to talk to the police about the charges. Keating told Colson to speak with his lawyer and to call back.

On November 6, Colson met with Moulton at a Belfast restaurant to plan for their upcoming trial. According to Colson, Moulton suggested the possibility of killing Gary Elwell, a State's witness, and they discussed how to commit the murder.

On November 9 and 10, Colson, accompanied by his lawyer, met with Police Chief Keating and State Police Detective Rexford Kelley. At these meetings, Colson gave full confessions of his participation with Moulton in committing the crimes for which they had been indicted. In addition, Colson admitted that he and Moulton had not merely received stolen automotive parts, but also had broken into the local Ford dealership to steal the parts. Colson also stated that he and Moulton had set fire to the dump truck and had committed other thefts. The officers offered Colson a deal: no further charges would be brought against him if he would testify against Moulton and otherwise cooperate in the prosecution of Moulton on the pending charges. Colson agreed to cooperate.

Colson also discussed with Keating and Kelley the anonymous threats he had received and Moulton's inchoate plan to kill Gary Elwell. Keating requested, and Colson consented, to have a recording device placed on Colson's telephone. Colson was instructed to turn the recording device on whenever he received a telephone call, but to turn it off immediately unless it was a threat from the anonymous caller or a call from Moulton.

The recording device was on Colson's telephone for over a month. Although he received no threats, Colson spoke to Moulton three times during this period, and the tapes of these calls were turned over to the police. The first conversation, on November 22, concerned primarily personal matters. The only reference to the pending criminal charges was Colson's question whether Moulton had "heard anything from the lawyer," and Moulton's response that he had not, but that he had "come up with a method," that he "ha[d] to work out the details on," and that "[s]ome day [he'd] like to get together and talk to [Colson] about it." Moulton, then living in New Hampshire, said that he was planning to visit Belfast around Christmas.

The second telephone conversation, on December 2, was prompted by Moulton's receipt of copies of statements of three of the State's witnesses, including Elwell; Colson had not yet received copies of the statements. Most of their talk (on Moulton's side particularly) was about the statements of Elwell and Elwell's brother, which accused Moulton and Colson of being guilty of the pending charges and which Moulton complained were an attempt to frame him and Colson. After reading Colson a statement by Elwell that he had received a threatening phone call, Moulton commented "[t]his is a big joke, man." When Colson jokingly suggested that they flee to Acapulco, Moulton vehemently rejected the suggestion, stating: "No, I'm gonna stay here and I'm gonna fight it man. I'm gonna fight it man. I ain't gonna get framed for nothing." Colson assented to this and suggested, "we'll have to get together sometime...." Moulton reminded Colson that he would be visiting at Christmas, and the conversation ended without Moulton having said anything that incriminated him.

The third telephone conversation, which took place on December 14, was similar to the second one. Most of the conversation concerned the pending charges, but Moulton said nothing inculpatory and continued to insist that he and Colson were being framed. Moulton asked Colson to set aside an entire day so that the two of them could meet and plan their defense. They agreed to meet on Sunday, December 26.

After learning from the telephone recordings about the meeting planned for December 26, the police obtained Colson's consent to be equipped with a body wire transmitter to record what was said at the meeting. Chief Keating later testified that he did this for Colson's safety in case Moulton realized that Colson was cooperating with the police, and to record any further conversation concerning threats to witnesses. Keating also testified that he was aware that Moulton and Colson were meeting to discuss the charges for which Moulton was already under indictment. Colson was instructed "not to attempt to question Perley Moulton, just be himself in his conversation...."

The December 26 meeting, as was to be expected from the recorded telephone conversations, consisted of a prolonged discussion of the pending charges—what actually had occurred, what the State's evidence would show, and what Moulton and Colson should do to obtain a verdict of acquittal. The idea of eliminating witnesses was briefly mentioned early in the conversation. After a short discussion, encouraged by Colson,[4] Moulton

4. The exchange went as follows:

"[Moulton:] You know I thought of a way to eliminate them. Remember we were talking about it before?

"[Colson:] Yes, you thought of a way?

"[Moulton:] Yeah, but ... I don't think we ought to go for it.

"[Colson:] Is it foolproof?

"[Moulton:] No.

"[Colson:] Is it, is it fairly foolproof?

concluded that he did not think the plan would work. The remainder of the lengthy meeting was spent discussing the case. Moulton and Colson decided to create false alibis as their defense at trial. Because they sought to conform these alibis as closely as possible to what really happened, much of their discussion involved recounting the crimes. Although Colson had described what had happened in detail when he confessed to the police a month earlier, he now frequently professed to be unable to recall the events. Apologizing for his poor memory, he repeatedly asked Moulton to remind him about the details of what had happened, and this technique caused Moulton to make numerous incriminating statements.[5] Nor were all of Colson's memory lapses related to events that required discussion to fabricate convincing alibis. Colson also "reminisced" about events surrounding the various thefts, and this technique too elicited additional incriminating statements from Moulton. For example, Colson asked Moulton how many locks they had drilled to steal a truck, a fact obviously not relevant to developing an alibi. Similarly, Colson questioned Moulton about whether it was the Mustang or the pick-up truck that did not have a heater. Later, Colson jokingly drew forth admissions from Moulton concerning the dumping of a stolen truck into a pond after it had been scavenged for parts, and the dumping of a load of potatoes from another stolen truck onto the road. Each of these statements was later admitted into evidence against Moulton at trial.

* * *

Moulton [claims] that the admission into evidence of his statements to Colson violated his Sixth Amendment right to the assistance of counsel. . . .

* * *

[In] Massiah v. United States (1964), Massiah was indicted, along with a man named Colson,[8] . . . Colson, meanwhile, decided to cooperate with Government agents in their continuing investigation of the narcotics activity in which Massiah and others were thought to be engaged. . . .We reversed Massiah's conviction on the ground that the incriminating statements were obtained in violation of Massiah's rights under the Sixth Amendment. . . .

* * *

"[Moulton:] I like it. I think its just for the . . .

"[Colson:] Well let me [hear it]."

Moulton explained that he had considered using air rifles to shoot poisoned darts and the conversation then turned to joking about a magazine that instructed readers how to build bombs to kill large numbers of people.

5. Colson began doing this immediately after Moulton vetoed the plan to eliminate witnesses. Colson indicated that he did not have copies of all the discovery materials, and Moulton went outside to his car to get his copies. While Moulton was gone, Colson sighed heavily and whispered "[o]h boy, I just hope I can make it through this" into the microphone. Then, when Moulton returned moments later, Colson immediately stated, slowly and deliberately, "I want you to help me with some dates. One date I cannot remember Caps [Moulton's nickname], just can't remember, I know it was in December, what night did we break into Lothrop Ford? What date?"

8. The parties have taken pains to assure us that Massiah's friend Colson and Moulton's friend Colson are unrelated.

We applied this principle most recently in United States v. Henry, 447 U.S. 264, 100 S.Ct. 2183 (1980). Henry was arrested and indicted for bank robbery. Counsel was appointed, and Henry was held in jail pending trial. Nichols, an inmate at the same jail and a paid informant for the Federal Bureau of Investigation, told a Government agent that he was housed in the same cellblock as several federal prisoners, including Henry. The agent told Nichols to pay attention to statements made by these prisoners, but expressly instructed Nichols not to initiate any conversations and not to question Henry regarding the bank robbery. Nichols and Henry subsequently engaged in some conversations during which Henry told Nichols about the robbery. Nichols testified about these conversations at Henry's trial, and Henry was convicted.

This Court reversed, finding that the Government had " 'deliberately elicited' incriminating statements from Henry within the meaning of *Massiah.*" Several facts were emphasized in the opinion for the Court: that Nichols was acting as an informant for the Government and therefore had an incentive to produce useful information; that Henry was unaware of Nichols' role as a Government informant; and, finally, that Henry and Nichols were incarcerated together at the time the conversations took place. With respect to this last fact, the Court reasoned that "confinement may bring into play subtle influences that will make [an individual] particularly susceptible to the ploys of undercover Government agents," influences that were facilitated by Nichols' "apparent status as a person sharing a common plight." Considering Nichols' conversations with Henry in light of these circumstances, the Court concluded that Nichols "deliberately used his position to secure incriminating information from Henry when counsel was not present ..." in violation of the Sixth Amendment. The Government argued that it should not be held responsible for Nichols' conduct because its agent had instructed Nichols not to question Henry and had not intended that Nichols take affirmative steps to obtain incriminating statements. We rejected this argument, finding that, under the circumstances, the agent "must have known" that Nichols would take affirmative steps to secure incriminating information. Consequently, the Court held, "[b]y intentionally creating a situation likely to induce Henry to make incriminating statements without the assistance of counsel, the Government violated Henry's Sixth Amendment right to counsel."

The State contends that the decisive fact in *Massiah* and *Henry* was that the police set up the confrontation between the accused and a police agent at which incriminating statements were elicited.... Because Moulton rather than Colson initiated the recorded telephone conversations and requested the December 26 meeting, the State concludes that Moulton's Sixth Amendment rights were not violated here.

In the first place, the identity of the party who instigated the meeting at which the Government obtained incriminating statements was not decisive or even important to our decisions in *Massiah* or *Henry*.... Moreover, four years after *Massiah*, the Court summarily reversed a conviction where the defendant requested the meeting and initiated and led the conversation in which incriminating statements were made to an undercover informant. Beatty v. United States, 389 U.S. 45, 88 S.Ct. 234

(1967) (*per curiam*). . . .Finally, in *Henry*, we deemed it "irrelevant that in *Massiah* the agent had to arrange the meeting between Massiah and his codefendant while here the agents were fortunate enough to have an undercover informant already in close proximity to the accused."

Beyond this, the State's attempt to limit our holdings in *Massiah* and *Henry* fundamentally misunderstands the nature of the right we recognized in those cases. The Sixth Amendment guarantees the accused, at least after the initiation of formal charges, the right to rely on counsel as a "medium" between him and the State. As noted above, this guarantee includes the State's affirmative obligation not to act in a manner that circumvents the protections accorded the accused by invoking this right. The determination whether particular action by state agents violates the accused's right to the assistance of counsel must be made in light of this obligation. Thus, the Sixth Amendment is not violated whenever—by luck or happenstance—the State obtains incriminating statements from the accused after the right to counsel has attached. However, knowing exploitation by the State of an opportunity to confront the accused without counsel being present is as much a breach of the State's obligation not to circumvent the right to the assistance of counsel as is the intentional creation of such an opportunity. Accordingly, the Sixth Amendment is violated when the State obtains incriminating statements by knowingly circumventing the accused's right to have counsel present in a confrontation between the accused and a state agent.[12]

Applying this principle to the case at hand, it is clear that the State violated Moulton's Sixth Amendment right when it arranged to record conversations between Moulton and its undercover informant, Colson. It was the police who suggested to Colson that he record his telephone conversations with Moulton. Having learned from these recordings that Moulton and Colson were going to meet, the police asked Colson to let them put a body wire transmitter on him to record what was said. Police Chief Keating admitted that, when they made this request, the police knew—as they must have known from the recorded telephone conversations—that Moulton and Colson were meeting for the express purpose of discussing the pending charges and planning a defense for the trial.[13] The police thus knew that Moulton would make statements that he had a constitutional right not to make to their agent prior to consulting with

12. Direct proof of the State's knowledge will seldom be available to the accused. However, as *Henry* makes clear, proof that the State "must have known" that its agent was likely to obtain incriminating statements from the accused in the absence of counsel suffices to establish a Sixth Amendment violation.

13. Because Moulton thought of Colson only as his codefendant, Colson's engaging Moulton in active conversation about their upcoming trial was certain to elicit statements that Moulton would not intentionally reveal—and had a constitutional right not to reveal—to persons known to be police agents. Under these circumstances, Colson's merely participating in this conversation was "the functional equivalent of interrogation." *Henry*, 447 U.S., at 277, 100 S.Ct., at 2190 (POWELL, J., concurring). In addition, the tapes disclose and the Supreme Judicial Court of Maine found that Colson "frequently pressed Moulton for details of various thefts and in so doing elicited much incriminating information that the State later used at trial." Thus, as in *Henry*, id., we need not reach the situation where the "listening post" cannot or does not participate in active conversation and prompt particular replies.

counsel. As in *Henry*, the fact that the police were "fortunate enough to have an undercover agent already in close proximity to the accused" does not excuse their conduct under these circumstances. By concealing the fact that Colson was an agent of the State, the police denied Moulton the opportunity to consult with counsel and thus denied him the assistance of counsel guaranteed by the Sixth Amendment.[14]

It is argued that the incriminating statements obtained by the Maine police nevertheless should not be suppressed because the police had other, legitimate reasons for listening to Moulton's conversations with Colson, namely, to investigate Moulton's alleged plan to kill Gary Elwell and to insure Colson's safety. In *Massiah*, the Government also contended that incriminating statements obtained as a result of its deliberate efforts should not be excluded because law enforcement agents had "the right, if not indeed the duty, to continue their investigation of [Massiah] and his alleged criminal associates. . . ." There, as here, the Government argued that this circumstance justified its surveillance and cured any improper acts or purposes. We rejected this argument, and held:

> "We do not question that in this case, as in many cases, it was entirely proper to continue an investigation of the suspected criminal activities of the defendant and his alleged confederates, even though the defendant had already been indicted. All that we hold is that the defendant's own incriminating statements, obtained by federal agents under the circumstances here disclosed, could not constitutionally be used by the prosecution as evidence against him at his trial."

We reaffirm this holding, which states a sensible solution to a difficult problem. The police have an interest in the thorough investigation of crimes for which formal charges have already been filed. They also have an

14. The State argues that it took steps to prevent Colson from inducing Moulton to make incriminating admissions by instructing Colson to "be himself," "act normal," and "not interrogate" Moulton. In *Henry*, we rejected this same argument although the likelihood that the accused would talk about the pending charges to a cellmate was less than here, where the accused invited his co-defendant to discuss the upcoming trial, and although the instructions to the agent were far more explicit. More importantly, under the circumstances of this case, the instructions given to Colson were necessarily inadequate. The Sixth Amendment protects the right of the accused not to be confronted by an agent of the State regarding matters as to which the right to counsel has attached without counsel being present. This right was violated as soon as the State's agent engaged Moulton in conversation about the charges pending against him. Because these charges were the only subject to be discussed at Colson's December 26 meeting with Moulton, a Sixth Amendment violation was inevitable once Colson agreed to this meeting with Moulton.

In any event, we reject the State's suggestion that these instructions were designed to protect Moulton's constitutional rights. The instructions were obviously motivated by the police's concern that Colson, who had never before served as an undercover agent, might behave unnaturally or ask too many questions, thereby tipping Moulton off to the fact that Colson was cooperating with the police. Thus, rather than explain to Colson that actively questioning Moulton might taint any evidence obtained, the police simply told Colson to "be himself," and to "act normal." In addition, the instructions were not limited to questions concerning the pending charges, the only matters as to which active questioning might create problems. On the contrary, according to Chief Keating, Colson was instructed that he could engage Moulton in a conversation but should not try to draw him out on "elimination of witnesses or anything."

interest in investigating new or additional crimes. Investigations of either type of crime may require surveillance of individuals already under indictment. Moreover, law enforcement officials investigating an individual suspected of committing one crime and formally charged with having committed another crime obviously seek to discover evidence useful at a trial of either crime. In seeking evidence pertaining to pending charges, however, the Government's investigative powers are limited by the Sixth Amendment rights of the accused. To allow the admission of evidence obtained from the accused in violation of his Sixth Amendment rights whenever the police assert an alternative, legitimate reason for their surveillance invites abuse by law enforcement personnel in the form of fabricated investigations and risks the evisceration of the Sixth Amendment right recognized in *Massiah*. On the other hand, to exclude evidence pertaining to charges as to which the Sixth Amendment right to counsel had not attached at the time the evidence was obtained, simply because other charges were pending at that time, would unnecessarily frustrate the public's interest in the investigation of criminal activities. Consequently, incriminating statements pertaining to pending charges are inadmissible at the trial of those charges, notwithstanding the fact that the police were also investigating other crimes, if, in obtaining this evidence, the State violated the Sixth Amendment by knowingly circumventing the accused's right to the assistance of counsel.[16]

Because we hold that the Maine police knowingly circumvented Moulton's right to have counsel present at a confrontation between Moulton and a police agent, the fact that the police had additional reasons for recording Moulton's meeting with Colson is irrelevant. The decision of the Supreme Judicial Court of Maine is affirmed.

■ CHIEF JUSTICE BURGER, with whom JUSTICE WHITE and JUSTICE REHNQUIST join, and with whom JUSTICE O'CONNOR joins as to Parts I and III, dissenting.

* * *

I

Before reaching the legal issues, it is important that the factual basis on which the State acted here be clearly understood. Since the Court's opinion glosses over some of the more relevant facts, I review them here briefly.

* * *

When Colson and respondent met, respondent spoke of "[g]etting rid of a couple of witnesses," including Gary Elwell, a key prosecution witness in the upcoming trial of Colson and respondent. Respondent had formulated a general plan for the murder; Colson's role was to pick up a car to be used in that endeavor.

16. Incriminating statements pertaining to other crimes, as to which the Sixth Amendment right has not yet attached, are, of course, admissible at a trial of those offenses.

On November 9 and 10, Colson met with Chief Keating and Officer Rex Kelley of the Maine State Police at the office of Colson's attorney. At these meetings, Colson revealed to the police respondent's plan to kill Elwell. Keating was aware that several witnesses connected with the case had received threats. One witness, Duke Ducaster, had been threatened personally by respondent. Another witness, Herman Peasley, "had been told ... that a cup of acid could be thrown in his face" if he talked to the police. Colson then consented to having the police place a recording device on his home telephone. Keating testified that he placed the device on the telephone because respondent was to call Colson back when plans to eliminate Elwell had been finalized and because Colson himself had been receiving anonymous threatening telephone calls.

Three telephone calls initiated by respondent were subsequently recorded. In the first, on November 22, 1982, respondent, in an apparent reference to the plan to do away with Elwell, told Colson that he had "come up with a method" and that he wanted to get together with Colson to talk about it after he had "work[ed] out the details on it." In the second recorded conversation, respondent reviewed with Colson the extent of the evidence against them and made several incriminating statements. In the last of the recorded conversations, respondent again incriminated himself and referred to statements by witnesses that they had been threatened. Finally, respondent told Colson that he wanted to meet to "review the whole plan."

Chief Keating and Detective Kelley, then arranged for Colson to wear a body recorder/transmitter during this meeting. Both officers testified that the recorder was intended to protect Colson's safety, since respondent might have learned that Colson was cooperating with the police, as well as to record any information concerning threats to other witnesses. Colson himself testified that his understanding of the reasons for using the recorder were "number 1 ... my safety" and "number 2 ... for any other plans to do away with any of the witnesses." When asked if there was a "number 3," Colson testified "no." The police instructed Colson "to act like himself, converse normally, and avoid trying to draw information out of Moulton."

During the meeting with Colson, respondent without any prompting brought up the possibility of killing Gary Elwell, by means of an air gun with hollow-tipped darts or explosives. Respondent also suggested developing false testimony for presentation at trial. These portions of the transcript were not admitted into evidence at trial. In addition, there was direct discussion of the thefts for which respondent had been indicted; these portions of the transcript were admitted. The trial court refused to suppress these portions since the State had recorded the conversations "for legitimate purposes not related to the gathering of evidence concerning the crime for which [respondent] had been indicted—*i.e.*, in order to gather information concerning the anonymous threats that Mr. Colson had been receiving, to protect Mr. Colson and to gather information concerning [respondent's] plans to kill Gary Elwell." The Maine Supreme Court in a careful opinion found "ample evidence" to support this factual finding.

II

The Court today concludes that "[t]o allow the admission of evidence obtained from an accused in violation of his Sixth Amendment rights whenever the police assert an alternative, legitimate reason for their surveillance ... risks the evisceration of the Sixth Amendment right recognized in *Massiah*." With all deference I am bound to state that this conclusion turns the Sixth Amendment on its head by first positing a constitutional violation and then asking whether "alternative, legitimate reasons" for the police surveillance are sufficient to justify that constitutional violation. As I see it, if "alternative, legitimate reasons" motivated the surveillance, then no Sixth Amendment violation has occurred. Indeed, if the police had failed to take the steps they took here knowing that Colson was endangering his life by talking to them, in my view they would be subject to censure.

* * *

Courts ought to applaud the kind of careful and diligent efforts of the police shown by this record. Indeed, the Court's opinion does not suggest that the police should have—or could have—conducted their investigation in any other way. Yet, inexplicably, the Court holds that the highly probative and reliable evidence produced by this wholly legitimate investigation must be excluded from respondent's trial for theft. The anomaly of this position, then, is that the evidence at issue in this case should have been excluded from respondent's theft trial even though the *same evidence* could have been introduced against *respondent himself* at a trial for separate crimes. Far from being "a sensible solution to a difficult problem," as the Court modestly suggests, it is a judicial aberration conferring a windfall benefit to those who are the subject of criminal investigations for one set of crimes while already under indictment for another. ...

* * *

The Court's opinion seems to rest on the notion that the evidence here is excludable because "the State 'must have known' that its agent was likely to obtain incriminating statements from the accused," with respect to the crimes for which he was already indicted. But the inquiry mandated by our holdings is whether the State recorded the statements not merely *in spite of*, but *because of* that consequence. If the State is not seeking to elicit information with respect to the crime for which the defendant is already indicted, it cannot rationally be said that the State has "planned an impermissible interference with the right to the assistance of counsel."

This case is a particularly inappropriate one for invoking the right to counsel. The right to counsel recognized in *Massiah* was designed to preserve the integrity of the trial. Here respondent was under investigation because of his plans to obstruct justice by killing an essential witness. There is no right to consult an attorney for advice on committing crimes. See United States v. Merritts, 527 F.2d 713, 716 (C.A.7 1975). Indeed, any attorney who undertook to offer such advice would undoubtedly be subject to sanction. Disciplinary Rule 7–102(A)(7) of the Code of Professional Responsibility, for example, states "a lawyer shall not ... [c]ounsel or assist his client in conduct that the lawyer knows to be illegal or fraudulent." Thus there is no warrant for vindicating respondent's right to consult counsel. An observation of this Court in connection with the attorney-client evidentiary privilege bears mention here: "The privilege takes flight if the relation is abused. A client who consults an attorney for advice that will serve him in the commission of a fraud will have no help from the law. He must let the truth be told." Clark v. United States, 289 U.S. 1, 15, 53 S.Ct. 465, 469 (1933). I would let the truth be told in this case rather than exclude evidence that was the product of this police investigation into activities designed to thwart the judicial process.

Even though the *Massiah* rule is inapplicable to situations where the government is gathering information related to a separate crime, police misconduct need not be countenanced. Accordingly, evidence obtained through a separate crimes investigation should be admitted only "so long as investigating officers show no bad faith and do not institute the investigation of the separate offense as a pretext for avoiding the dictates of *Massiah*." United States v. Darwin, 757 F.2d 1193, 1199 (C.A.11). Here the careful actions of Chief Keating and Detective Kelley steered well clear of these prohibitions.

Until today, the clearly prevailing view in the federal and state courts was that *Massiah* and its successors did not protect a defendant from the introduction of postindictment statements deliberately elicited when the police undertook an investigation of separate crimes.

* * *

III

Even if I were prepared to join the Court in this enlargement of the protections of the Sixth Amendment, I would have serious doubts about also extending the reach of the exclusionary rule to cover this case. ...

* * *

The application of the exclusionary rule here must be premised on deterrence of certain types of conduct by the police. We have explained, however, that "[t]he deterrent purpose of the exclusionary rule necessarily assumes that the police have engaged in willful, or at the very least negligent, conduct which has deprived the defendant of some right." United States v. Peltier (1975). Here the trial court found that the State obtained statements from respondent "for legitimate purposes not related to the gathering of evidence concerning the crime for which [respondent] had been indicted." Since the State was not trying to build its theft case against respondent in obtaining the evidence, excluding the evidence from the theft trial will not affect police behavior at all. The exclusion of evidence "cannot be expected, and should not be applied, to deter objectively reasonable law enforcement activity." Indeed, as noted above, it is impossible to identify any police "misconduct" to deter in this case. In fact, if anything, actions by the police of the type at issue here should be encouraged. The diligent investigation of the police in this case may have saved the lives of several potential witnesses and certainly led to the prosecution of respondent for additional serious crimes.

Texas v. Cobb

Supreme Court of the United States, 2001.
532 U.S. 162, 121 S.Ct. 1335.

■ CHIEF JUSTICE REHNQUIST delivered the opinion of the Court.

In December 1993, Lindsey Owings reported to the Walker County, Texas, Sheriff's Office that the home he shared with his wife, Margaret, and their 16–month–old daughter, Kori Rae, had been burglarized. He also informed police that his wife and daughter were missing. Respondent Raymond Levi Cobb lived across the street from the Owings. Acting on an anonymous tip that respondent was involved in the burglary, Walker County investigators questioned him about the events. He denied involvement. In July 1994, while under arrest for an unrelated offense, respondent was again questioned about the incident. Respondent then gave a written statement confessing to the burglary, but he denied knowledge relating to the disappearances. Respondent was subsequently indicted for the burglary, and Hal Ridley was appointed in August 1994 to represent respondent on that charge.

Shortly after Ridley's appointment, investigators asked and received his permission to question respondent about the disappearances. Respondent continued to deny involvement. Investigators repeated this process in September 1995, again with Ridley's permission and again with the same result.

In November 1995, respondent, free on bond in the burglary case, was living with his father in Odessa, Texas. At that time, respondent's father contacted the Walker County Sheriff's Office to report that respondent had confessed to him that he killed Margaret Owings in the course of the burglary. Walker County investigators directed respondent's father to the Odessa police station, where he gave a statement. Odessa police then faxed the statement to Walker County, where investigators secured a warrant for respondent's arrest and faxed it back to Odessa. Shortly thereafter, Odessa police took respondent into custody and administered warnings pursuant to Miranda. Respondent waived these rights.

After a short time, respondent confessed to murdering both Margaret and Kori Rae. Respondent explained that when Margaret confronted him as he was attempting to remove the Owings' stereo, he stabbed her in the stomach with a knife he was carrying. Respondent told police that he dragged her body to a wooded area a few hundred yards from the house. Respondent then stated: "I went back to her house and I saw the baby laying on its bed. I took the baby out there and it was sleeping the whole time. I laid the baby down on the ground four or five feet away from its mother. I went back to my house and got a flat edge shovel. That's all I could find. Then I went back over to where they were and I started digging a hole between them. After I got the hole dug, the baby was awake. It started going toward its mom and it fell in the hole. I put the lady in the hole and I covered them up. I remember stabbing a different knife I had in the ground where they were. I was crying right then." App. to Pet. for Cert. A–9 to A–10. [citations omitted]

Respondent later led police to the location where he had buried the victims' bodies....

The Court of Criminal Appeals reversed respondent's conviction by a divided vote and remanded for a new trial. The court held that "once the right to counsel attaches to the offense charged, it also attaches to any other offense that is very closely related factually to the offense charged." Finding the capital murder charge to be "factually interwoven with the burglary," the court concluded that respondent's Sixth Amendment right to counsel had attached on the capital murder charge even though respondent had not yet been charged with that offense. The court further found that respondent had asserted that right by accepting Ridley's appointment in the burglary case. Accordingly, it deemed the confession inadmissible and found that its introduction had not been harmless error. Three justices dissented, finding Michigan v. Jackson to be distinguishable and concluding that respondent had made a valid unilateral waiver of his right to counsel before confessing....

In McNeil v. Wisconsin, (1991), we explained when this right arises:

"The Sixth Amendment right [to counsel] ... is offense specific. It cannot be invoked once for all future prosecutions, for it does not attach until a prosecution is commenced, that is, at or after the initiation of adversary judicial criminal proceedings—whether by way of formal charge, preliminary hearing, indictment, information, or arraignment." Id., at 175, 111 S.Ct. 2204 (citations and internal quotation marks omitted).

Accordingly, we held that a defendant's statements regarding offenses for which he had not been charged were admissible notwithstanding the attachment of his Sixth Amendment right to counsel on other charged offenses.... [citations omitted]

Some state courts and Federal Courts of Appeals, however, have read into McNeil's offense-specific definition an exception for crimes that are "factually related" to a charged offense. Several of these courts have interpreted Brewer v. Williams (1977), and Maine v. Moulton (1985)—both of which were decided well before McNeil—to support this view, which respondent now invites us to approve. We decline to do so....

In Brewer, a suspect in the abduction and murder of a 10–year–old girl had fled from the scene of the crime in Des Moines, Iowa, some 160 miles east to Davenport, Iowa, where he surrendered to police. An arrest warrant was issued in Des Moines on a charge of abduction, and the suspect was arraigned on that warrant before a Davenport judge. Des Moines police traveled to Davenport, took the man into custody, and began the drive back to Des Moines. Along the way, one of the officers persuaded the suspect to lead police to the victim's body. The suspect ultimately was convicted of the girl's murder. This Court upheld the federal habeas court's conclusion that police had violated the suspect's Sixth Amendment right to counsel. We held that the officer's comments to the suspect constituted interrogation and that the suspect had not validly waived his right to counsel by responding to the officer....

The Court's opinion, however, simply did not address the significance of the fact that the suspect had been arraigned only on the abduction charge, nor did the parties in any way argue this question. Constitutional rights are not defined by inferences from opinions which did not address the question at issue. . . .

Moulton is similarly unhelpful to respondent. That case involved two individuals indicted for a series of thefts, one of whom had secretly agreed to cooperate with the police investigation of his codefendant, Moulton. At the suggestion of police, the informant recorded several telephone calls and one face-to-face conversation he had with Moulton during which the two discussed their criminal exploits and possible alibis. In the course of those conversations, Moulton made various incriminating statements regarding both the thefts for which he had been charged and additional crimes. In a superseding indictment, Moulton was charged with the original crimes as well as burglary, arson, and three additional thefts. At trial, the State introduced portions of the recorded face-to-face conversation, and Moulton ultimately was convicted of three of the originally charged thefts plus one count of burglary. Moulton appealed his convictions to the Supreme Judicial Court of Maine, arguing that introduction of the recorded conversation violated his Sixth Amendment right to counsel. That court agreed, holding:

" 'Those statements may be admissible in the investigation or prosecution of charges for which, at the time the recordings were made, adversary proceedings had not yet commenced. But as to the charges for which Moulton's right to counsel had already attached, his incriminating statements should have been ruled inadmissible at trial, given the circumstances in which they were acquired.' " . . .

But the Moulton Court did not address the question now before us, and to the extent Moulton spoke to the matter at all, it expressly referred to the offense-specific nature of the Sixth Amendment right to counsel. . . .

Respondent predicts that the offense-specific rule will prove "disastrous" to suspects' constitutional rights and will "permit law enforcement officers almost complete and total license to conduct unwanted and uncounseled interrogations." Besides offering no evidence that such a parade of horribles has occurred in those jurisdictions that have not enlarged upon McNeil, he fails to appreciate the significance of two critical considerations. First, there can be no doubt that a suspect must be apprised of his rights against compulsory self-incrimination and to consult with an attorney before authorities may conduct custodial interrogation. Second, it is critical to recognize that the Constitution does not negate society's interest in the ability of police to talk to witnesses and suspects, even those who have been charged with other offenses. . . . [citations omitted]

Although it is clear that the Sixth Amendment right to counsel attaches only to charged offenses, we have recognized in other contexts that the definition of an "offense" is not necessarily limited to the four corners of a charging instrument. In Blockburger v. United States (1932), we explained that "where the same act or transaction constitutes a violation of two distinct statutory provisions, the test to be applied to determine whether there are two offenses or only one, is whether each provision requires proof of a fact which the other does not." We have since applied the Blockburger test to delineate the scope of the Fifth Amendment's Double Jeopardy Clause, which prevents multiple or successive prosecutions for the "same offence." We see no constitutional difference between the meaning of the term "offense" in the contexts of double jeopardy and of the right to counsel. Accordingly, we hold that when the Sixth Amendment right to counsel attaches, it does encompass offenses that, even if not formally charged, would be considered the same offense under the Blockburger test.... [citations omitted]

While simultaneously conceding that its own test "lacks the precision for which police officers may hope," the dissent suggests that adopting Blockburger's definition of "offense" will prove difficult to administer. But it is the dissent's vague iterations of the " 'closely related to' " or " 'inextricably intertwined with' " test, that would defy simple application. The dissent seems to presuppose that officers will possess complete knowledge of the circumstances surrounding an incident, such that the officers will be able to tailor their investigation to avoid addressing factually related offenses. Such an assumption, however, ignores the reality that police often are not yet aware of the exact sequence and scope of events they are investigating—indeed, that is why police must investigate in the first place.

Deterred by the possibility of violating the Sixth Amendment, police likely would refrain from questioning certain defendants altogether.

It remains only to apply these principles to the facts at hand. At the time he confessed to Odessa police, respondent had been indicted for burglary of the Owings residence, but he had not been charged in the murders of Margaret and Kori Rae. As defined by Texas law, burglary and capital murder are not the same offense under Blockburger. Compare Texas Penal Code Ann. § 30.02(a) (1994) (requiring entry into or continued concealment in a habitation or building) with § 19.03(a)(7)(A) (requiring murder of more than one person during a single criminal transaction). Accordingly, the Sixth Amendment right to counsel did not bar police from interrogating respondent regarding the murders, and respondent's confession was therefore admissible....

■ KENNEDY, J., concurring.

The Court's opinion is altogether sufficient to explain why the decision of the Texas Court of Criminal Appeals should be reversed for failure to recognize the offense-specific nature of the Sixth Amendment right to counsel. It seems advisable, however, to observe that the Court has reached its conclusion without the necessity to reaffirm or give approval to the decision in Michigan v. Jackson (1986). This course is wise, in my view, for the underlying theory of Jackson seems questionable ...

The parallel rule announced in Jackson, however, supersedes the suspect's voluntary choice to speak with investigators....

The Sixth Amendment right to counsel attaches quite without reference to the suspect's choice to speak with investigators after a Miranda warning. It is the commencement of a formal prosecution, indicated by the initiation of adversary judicial proceedings, that marks the beginning of the Sixth Amendment right. These events may be quite independent of the suspect's election to remain silent, the interest which the Edwards rule serves to protect with respect to Miranda and the Fifth Amendment, and it thus makes little sense for a protective rule to attach absent such an election by the suspect. We ought to question the wisdom of a judge-made preventative rule to protect a suspect's desire not to speak when it cannot be shown that he had that intent.... [citations omitted]

Justice Breyer defends Jackson by arguing that, once a suspect has accepted counsel at the commencement of adversarial proceedings, he should not be forced to confront the police during interrogation without the assistance of counsel. But the acceptance of counsel at an arraignment or similar proceeding only begs the question: acceptance of counsel for what? It is quite unremarkable that a suspect might want the assistance of an expert in the law to guide him through hearings and trial, and the attendant complex legal matters that might arise, but nonetheless might choose to give on his own a forthright account of the events that occurred. A court-made rule that prevents a suspect from even making this choice serves little purpose, especially given the regime of Miranda and Edwards.... [citations omitted]

■ BREYER, J., dissenting, with JUSTICES STEVENS, SOUTER, and GINSBURG.

First, the Sixth Amendment right to counsel plays a central role in ensuring the fairness of criminal proceedings in our system of justice....

Second, the right attaches when adversary proceedings, triggered by the government's formal accusation of a crime, begin....

Third, once this right attaches, law enforcement officials are required, in most circumstances, to deal with the defendant through counsel rather than directly, even if the defendant has waived his Fifth Amendment rights. Michigan v. Jackson (1986) (waiver of right to presence of counsel is assumed invalid unless accused initiates communication)....

Recognizing the need for law enforcement officials to investigate "new or additional crimes" not the subject of current proceedings, Maine v. Moulton, supra, this Court has made clear that the right to counsel does not attach to any and every crime that an accused may commit or have committed, see McNeil v. Wisconsin, The right "cannot be invoked once for all future prosecutions," and it does not forbid "interrogation unrelated to the charge." ... [citations omitted]

The Court today decides that "offense" means the crime set forth within "the four corners of a charging instrument," along with other crimes that "would be considered the same offense" under the test established by Blockburger v. United States, (1932). Ante, at 1343. In my view, this unnecessarily technical definition undermines Sixth Amendment protections while doing nothing to further effective law enforcement.

For one thing, the majority's rule, while leaving the Fifth Amendment's protections in place, threatens to diminish severely the additional protection that, under this Court's rulings, the Sixth Amendment provides when it grants the right to counsel to defendants who have been charged with a crime and insists that law enforcement officers thereafter communicate with them through that counsel. See, e.g., Michigan v. Jackson (1980) (Fifth Amendment right, unlike Sixth, applies only in custodial interrogation)....

Jackson focuses upon a suspect—perhaps a frightened or uneducated suspect—who, hesitant to rely upon his own unaided judgment in his dealings with the police, has invoked his constitutional right to legal assistance in such matters. Jackson says that, once such a request has been made, the police may not simply throw that suspect—who does not trust his own unaided judgment—back upon his own devices by requiring him to rely for protection upon that same unaided judgment that he previously rejected as inadequate. In a word, the police may not force a suspect who has asked for legal counsel to make a critical legal choice without the legal assistance that he has requested and that the Constitution guarantees.... [citations omitted]

The Constitution does not take away with one hand what it gives with the other....

Justice Kennedy ... criticizes Jackson on the ground that it prevents a suspect "from ... making th[e] choice" to "give ... a forthright account of the events that occurred." But that is not so. A suspect may initiate communication with the police, thereby avoiding the risk that the police induced him to make, unaided, the kind of critical legal decision best made with the help of counsel, whom he has requested.

Unlike Justice Kennedy, the majority does not call Jackson itself into question. But the majority would undermine that case by significantly diminishing the Sixth Amendment protections that the case provides. That is because criminal codes are lengthy and highly detailed, often proliferating "overlapping and related statutory offenses" to the point where prosecutors can easily "spin out a startlingly numerous series of offenses from a single ... criminal transaction." Ashe v. Swenson (1970). Thus, an armed robber who reaches across a store counter, grabs the cashier, and demands "your money or your life," may through that single instance of conduct have committed several "offenses," in the majority's sense of the term, including armed robbery, assault, battery, trespass, use of a firearm to commit a felony, and perhaps possession of a firearm by a felon, as well. A person who is using and selling drugs on a single occasion might be guilty of possessing various drugs, conspiring to sell drugs, being under the influence of illegal drugs, possessing drug paraphernalia, possessing a gun in relation to the drug sale, and, depending upon circumstances, violating various gun laws as well. A protester blocking an entrance to a federal building might also be trespassing, failing to disperse, unlawfully assembling, and obstructing Government administration all at one and the same time.

The majority's rule permits law enforcement officials to question those charged with a crime without first approaching counsel, through the simple device of asking questions about any other related crime not actually charged in the indictment. Thus, the police could ask the individual charged with robbery about, say, the assault of the cashier not yet charged, or about any other uncharged offense (unless under Blockburger's definition it counts as the "same crime"), all without notifying counsel. Indeed, the majority's rule would permit law enforcement officials to question anyone charged with any crime in any one of the examples just given about his or her conduct on the single relevant occasion without notifying counsel unless the prosecutor has charged every possible crime arising out of that same brief course of conduct. What Sixth Amendment sense—what common sense—does such a rule make? What is left of the "communicate through counsel" rule? The majority's approach is inconsistent with any common understanding of the scope of counsel's representation. It will undermine the lawyer's role as " 'medium' " between the defendant and the government. Maine v. Moulton. And it will, on a random basis, remove a significant portion of the protection that this Court has found inherent in the Sixth Amendment....

The majority's rule threatens the legal clarity necessary for effective law enforcement. That is because the majority, aware that the word "offense" ought to encompass something beyond "the four corners of the charging instrument," imports into Sixth Amendment law the definition of "offense" set forth in Blockburger v. United States (1932), a case interpreting the Double Jeopardy Clause of the Fifth Amendment, which Clause uses the word "offence" but otherwise has no relevance here. Whatever Fifth Amendment virtues Blockburger may have, to import it into this Sixth Amendment context will work havoc.

In theory, the test says that two offenses are the "same offense" unless each requires proof of a fact that the other does not. See ante, at 1343 (majority opinion). That means that most of the different crimes mentioned above are not the "same offense." Under many States' laws, for example, the statute defining assault and the statute defining robbery each requires proof of a fact that the other does not. Compare, e.g., Cal.Penal Code Ann. § 211 (West 1999) (robbery) (requiring taking of personal property of another) with § 240 (assault) (requiring attempt to commit violent injury). Hence the extension of the definition of "offense" that is accomplished by the use of the Blockburger test does nothing to address the substantial concerns about the circumvention of the Sixth Amendment right that are raised by the majority's rule.

But, more to the point, the simple-sounding Blockburger test has proved extraordinarily difficult to administer in practice. Judges, lawyers, and law professors often disagree about how to apply it.... The test has emerged as a tool in an area of our jurisprudence that THE CHIEF JUSTICE has described as "a veritable Sargasso Sea which could not fail to challenge the most intrepid judicial navigator." Albernaz v. United States (1981). Yet the Court now asks, not the lawyers and judges who ordinarily work with double jeopardy law, but police officers in the field, to navigate Blockburger when they question suspects.... Some will apply the test successfully; some will not. Legal challenges are inevitable. The result, I believe, will resemble not so much the Sargasso Sea as the criminal law equivalent of Milton's "Serbonian Bog ... Where Armies whole have sunk."

There is, of course, an alternative. We can, and should, define "offense" in terms of the conduct that constitutes the crime that the offender committed on a particular occasion, including criminal acts that are "closely related to" or "inextricably intertwined with" the particular crime set forth in the charging instrument. This alternative is not perfect. The language used lacks the precision for which police officers may hope; and it requires lower courts to specify its meaning further as they apply it in individual cases. Yet virtually every lower court in the United States to consider the issue has defined "offense" in the Sixth Amendment context to encompass such closely related acts.... They have found offenses unrelated where time, location, or factual circumstances significantly separated the one from the other.... One cannot say in favor of this commonly followed approach that it is perfectly clear—only that, because it comports with common sense, it is far easier to apply than that of the majority....

The Texas Court of Criminal Appeals, following this commonly accepted approach, found that the charged burglary and the uncharged murders were "closely related." All occurred during a short period of time on the same day in the same basic location. The victims of the murders were also victims of the burglary. Cobb committed one of the murders in furtherance of the robbery, the other to cover up the crimes. The police, when questioning Cobb, knew that he already had a lawyer representing him on the burglary charges and had demonstrated their belief that this lawyer also represented Cobb in respect to the murders by asking his permission to question Cobb about the murders on previous occasions. The relatedness of the crimes is well illustrated by the impossibility of questioning Cobb about the murders without eliciting admissions about the burglary.... [citations omitted] The police officers ought to have spoken to Cobb's counsel before questioning Cobb. I would affirm the decision of the Texas court.

Consequently, I dissent.

NOTES

1. In Patterson v. Illinois, 487 U.S. 285, 108 S.Ct. 2389 (1988), the Supreme Court for the first time addressed the issue of "*Massiah* waiver" in a case where a defendant neither had counsel nor requested counsel. There the police took a suspect into custody and questioned him after *Miranda* warnings. The grand jury indicted him on the second day after his arrest. The police and later a prosecutor questioned him again after the indictment and before he had been taken before a judge. They gave him standard *Miranda* warnings and also informed him that he had been indicted for murder. Patterson, who neither had counsel nor requested counsel, agreed to talk without the presence of a lawyer. The last questioning was forty-four hours after Patterson had been taken into custody.

Under these circumstances, in a 5–4 decision, the Supreme Court upheld the waiver of counsel. The Court noted that it was dealing only with a situation where the defendant had been informed of his indictment:

> [W]e do not address the question of whether or not an accused must be told that he had been indicted before a postindictment Sixth Amendment waiver will be valid. Nor do we even pass on the desirability of so informing the accused—a matter that can be reasonably debated.

In this context, the majority held that *Miranda* warnings administered by law enforcement officials sufficed to support a waiver of the Sixth Amendment right to counsel for post-indictment interrogation. It emphasized that *Miranda* warnings make the defendant aware of his right to counsel and of the possible consequences of responding to questions after giving up the right to counsel. This satisfies the test of *Johnson v. Zerbst* (1938), namely "an intentional relinquishment or abandonment of a known right or privilege," for the warnings allow an arrestee to choose with "eyes open."

The majority stressed that advocates of the opposite position had not been concrete in suggesting the content of a proposed *Massiah* waiver form that would do more than *Miranda* warnings. It rejected the argument that only a judicial officer can administer warnings after the Sixth Amendment right to counsel has attached.

The Court acknowledged that it was not saying that under all circumstances *Miranda* compliance would *ipso facto* constitute *Massiah* compliance. For example, it said that if counsel were trying to reach the defendant, and the police did not tell the defendant this, Moran v. Burbine (Casebook 138) would not necessarily apply where the Sixth Amendment right to counsel had attached.

The *Patterson* majority also rejected an argument that no police-initiated questioning can occur after the Sixth Amendment right to counsel has attached. It refused to equate the mere attachment of that Sixth Amendment right with the *invocation* of the Fifth Amendment right to counsel under *Miranda* and *Edwards* (Casebook 139).

In the primary dissenting opinion, Justice Stevens, joined by Justices Brennan and Marshall, argued that *Miranda* warnings are inadequate. More important, he said, was that an adversary party cannot adequately provide legal advice to a defendant after the initiation of formal adversary proceedings. He argued that cases like *Massiah* and *Kirby* (Casebook 250) put critical emphasis upon the point at which the formal criminal process begins with the initiation of the adversary process: "Today, however, in reaching a decision similarly favorable to the interest in law enforcement unfettered by process concerns, the Court backs away from the significance previously attributed to the initiation of formal proceedings." The majority had stressed that the waiver at issue covered only the limited period of interrogation, and it had argued that counsel's function at a post-indictment interrogation was no different than counsel's function at interrogation that occurs before the initiation of the formal criminal process.

Justice Blackmun dissented, contending that "after formal adversary proceedings" have begun, the defendant cannot be subject to interrogation until counsel has actually been made available to the defendant unless the defendant initiates further communication with authorities. In his view, "the Sixth Amendment does not allow the prosecution to take undue advantage of any gap between the commencement of the adversary process and the time at which counsel is appointed for a defendant."

Some subsequent lower court decisions have held that a valid waiver of *Massiah* rights is possible even when the authorities have not informed the suspect that they have charged him with an offense. See Riddick v. Edmiston, 894 F.2d 586 (3d Cir.1990). See also United States v. Charria, 919 F.2d 842 (2d Cir.1990) (even without being told of charge, standard warnings adequately explain danger of self-representation); State v. Hamons, 248 Kan. 51, 805 P.2d 6 (1991).

2. In Michigan v. Jackson, 475 U.S. 625, 106 S.Ct. 1404 (1986), it was held that a person who is formally charged and who requests counsel at his arraignment is immune from police attempts to interrogate him unless he initiates contacts with the police. The *Jackson* rule is analogous to that established in the fifth amendment case of Edwards v. Arizona (Chapter 2, Section B(3)).

The *Jackson* dissent argued that *Edwards* made sense in the fifth amendment context. It asserted that in such context the right to counsel arose because the suspect affirmatively requested counsel. On the other hand, the *Jackson* dissent asserted that the sixth amendment right to counsel in a *Massiah* post-arraignment situation does not depend upon a request. Is the dissent's premise about the right to counsel under *Miranda* and *Edwards* accurate? Does its conclusion necessarily follow?

Brewer v. Williams rather clearly indicates that *Massiah* applies as soon as adversary judicial proceedings have begun and, in *Williams*, that point was the issuance of an arrest warrant and Williams appearance in court. There are few post-*Williams* cases on the question. See People v. Booker, 69 Cal.App.3d 654, 138 Cal.Rptr. 347 (1977) (*Massiah* inapplicable where arrest occurred on out-of-state charges and there was no warrant nor extradition paper). United States v. Brown, 569 F.2d 236 (5th Cir.1978) (*Massiah* inapplicable to interrogation by federal officers where only state charges had been filed). Moran v. Burbine, 475 U.S. 412, 106 S.Ct. 1135, 1145 (1986) ("first formal charging proceeding").

The fact that the accused has counsel and has expressed a desire not to be questioned out of the presence of counsel will not prevent non-custodial elicitation of a statement from a suspect in the absence of his counsel, as long as there has not been an initiation of the formal criminal process. See United States v. Burton, 724 F.2d 1283 (7th Cir.1984); United States v. Mitlo, 714 F.2d 294 (3d Cir.1983).

For further discussion of precisely when the right to counsel attaches, see United States v. Muzychka, 725 F.2d 1061 (3d Cir.1984) (excellent discussion). The Supreme Court also addressed the issue in United States v. Gouveia, 467 U.S. 180, 104 S.Ct. 2292 (1984). In Michigan v. Jackson, 475 U.S. 625, 106 S.Ct. 1404 (1986), the Court said, "The arraignment signals 'the initiation of adversary judicial proceedings' and thus the attachment of the Sixth Amendment."

In Meadows v. Kuhlmann, 812 F.2d 72 (2d Cir.1987), the court in dictum stated that the filing of a criminal complaint and the issuance of an arrest warrant under New York law triggers the Sixth Amendment right to counsel even where the suspect has not appeared in court. It reasoned that because a criminal accusation commences with the filing of an accusatory instrument (the felony complaint), *Massiah* rights attach at that point.

Contrast People v. Wilson, 116 Ill.2d 29, 106 Ill.Dec. 771, 506 N.E.2d 571 (1987), where the Illinois Supreme Court held that the right to counsel did not attach even though authorities had presented a criminal complaint to a judge and had obtained an arrest warrant. The Illinois case stressed that the record did not indicate that the prosecutor, as distinguished from the police, was a party to the procedure. Nor was the criminal complaint filed in court until after the investigative procedures had been completed. Nevertheless the document presented to the judge was an instrument charging an offense and not merely a document in support of the application for a warrant.

United States v. Pace, 833 F.2d 1307 (9th Cir.1987), is about as favorable to the prosecution as any decision on the issue of when the Sixth Amendment right to counsel attaches. There an F.B.I. agent filed a complaint charging Pace with a robbery in violation of 18 U.S.C. 2113. A magistrate issued an arrest warrant based upon that complaint and an accompanying affidavit. Nevada authorities arrested Pace a week later on unrelated local charges, and the federal warrant surfaced. While local authorities held Pace in jail, federal authorities allegedly used a cellmate to elicit a confession from Pace. Pace claimed a *Massiah* violation.

The Ninth Circuit noted that the filing of a complaint charging a crime is not essential to the issuance of a federal arrest warrant. It reasoned that the filing of a criminal complaint should make no difference in determining whether the right to counsel attaches; and it determined that the issuance of an arrest warrant by itself does not constitute the initiation of adversary criminal proceedings. The court noted that, under the Fifth Amendment, a federal felony prosecution may not go forward until after an indictment (absent a waiver), and it held that the return of an indictment is the point at which the adversary criminal prosecution commences. The broad language in *Pace* is limited by the fact that the defendant there had not been to court on the federal charges. Presumably if he had appeared for a preliminary hearing on the felony complaint, a different situation would have been presented. See Moore v. Illinois (Casebook p. 294).

What factors should really determine whether the right to counsel attaches? Should it make a difference that the defendant has never appeared in court? Should factors unknown to the accused, such as whether he has been formally charged, make a difference to whether he should be afforded the right to counsel at a line-up? For interrogation? On the theory that a district attorney's filing of a charging document commits the district attorney to going forward with a prosecution, should it make a difference whether the prosecutor or merely the police file the charging document? Should it make a difference whether a charging document accompanies the application for an arrest warrant or whether the warrant issues based solely upon an affidavit or upon sworn oral testimony? What ultimate values or concerns should guide a court's formulation as to when the right to counsel attaches for purposes of the Sixth Amendment?

3. *Massiah* and *Miranda* doctrines become intertwined when, prior to charge, a suspect, who is represented by counsel, is questioned.

Technically, *Massiah* is not violated because there has been no adversary judicial proceeding, but it can be argued that the Fifth Amendment rights have been violated. On the other hand, the fact that defendant has retained counsel should make his waiver under *Miranda* of his right to counsel much more persuasive, since he could secure the assistance of counsel with one phone call. Further, if he had the advice of counsel, his decision to waive his rights may be said to be more fully informed. White, J. dissenting in Brewer v. Williams.

In Moran v. Burbine, 475 U.S. 412, 106 S.Ct. 1135, 1145–47 (1986), the Court stated the accused's assertion and its response:

> "The right to non-interference with an attorney's dealings with a criminal suspect, he asserts, arises the moment that the relationship is formed, or, at the very least, once the defendant is placed in custodial interrogation.
>
> "We are not persuaded."

* * *

Does *Massiah* apply where the adversary judicial process has commenced, but where the accused has not yet obtained counsel? To what extent is *Massiah* based upon interference with an existing attorney-client relationship? In Edwards v. Arizona, 451 U.S. 477, 101 S.Ct. 1880 (1981), footnote 8, the Court wrote: "In *Massiah* and *Brewer*, counsel had been engaged or appointed and the admissions in question were elicited in his absence. But in McLeod v. Ohio, 381 U.S. 356, 85 S.Ct. 1556 (1965), we summarily affirmed a decision that the police could not elicit information after indictment even though counsel had not yet been appointed." The relationship between Sixth Amendment *Massiah* rights and Fifth Amendment *Miranda* rights is set out in McNeil v. Wisconsin. A well-known rule in New York precludes interrogation about counsel if defendant is represented on any pending matter. See People v. Burdo, 91 N.Y.2d 146, 667 N.Y.S.2d 970, 690 N.E.2d 854 (1997). The rule has little currency outside New York. See State v. Piorkowski, 243 Conn. 205, 700 A.2d 1146 (1997).

4. Courts have not extended *Massiah* to exclude volunteered statements—this perhaps is what the Court in Moulton referred to when it said "Thus, the Sixth Amendment is not violated whenever—by luck or happenstance—the State obtains incriminating statements." See State v. Blizzard, 278 Md. 556, 366 A.2d 1026 (1976) (thorough review of decisions admitting post indictment statements where defendant initiates the interview with a known agent of law enforcement); United States v. Garcia, 377 F.2d 321 (2d Cir.1967) (volunteered admissions). When a counseled and indicted defendant called the victim to threaten and to bribe her, she called the police who gave her a tape recorder and instructions on how to use it. She recorded several damaging statements by defendant. The Court of Appeals assumed without deciding that the victim was a state agent who deliberately elicited incriminating statements which were still admissible because defendant, experienced in the criminal justice system, made the statements to someone he knew was cooperating with the police in a conversation which he initiated to serve his own ends and for which he would not want counsel present because the conversations were themselves arguably criminal acts. This constituted waiver. Jenkins v. Leonardo, 991 F.2d 1033 (2d Cir.1993).

5. Similarly the Court in *Moulton* condemned only "knowing exploitation ... of an opportunity to confront the accused". Thus *Massiah* does not apply when an indictee makes admissions to one who becomes an informer only *after* the admissions are made. United States ex rel. Milani v. Pate, 425 F.2d 6 (7th Cir.1970). See People v. Smith, 5 Ill.App.3d 642, 283 N.E.2d 736 (1972) (admissions to private citizen not precluded by *Massiah*). On the question of whether informer was an agent of the police, see United States v. Hicks, 798 F.2d 446 (11th Cir.1986) (personal motivation of informer) and Gammel v. State, 259 Ark. 96, 531 S.W.2d 474 (1976) (State need not prove absence of agency).

Sometimes a person who has reached an agreement with the Government still is not deemed its agent for *Massiah* purposes. See United States v. Panza, 750 F.2d 1141 (2d Cir.1984). The issues posed in such cases occur typically where the informer is acting on his own or perhaps even against instructions.

6. *Massiah* may be viewed as a use-exclusion rule. The *Massiah* court did not flatly forbid interrogation of counseled suspects or eliciting of incriminating responses from such suspects. It merely prohibited use of statements so elicited in the case where prosecution had already been commenced. The Court left open the possibility that such statements, if they constituted evidence of further criminal activity, could be used in prosecution charging such further criminal conduct. Thus, for example, the statements could be used in a prosecution for bribery of a witness or a prosecution of new narcotic violations. See Maine v. Moulton, supra.

* * *

... Generally, exclusionary rules do not operate to prohibit proof of words or deeds which themselves are the substance of a new crime. Compare Casebook p. 123, note h. See also Commonwealth v. Saia, 372 Mass. 53, 360 N.E.2d 329 (1977) (proof of assault on officer occurring after illegal entry); People v. Pagliara, 47 Ill.App.3d 708, 7 Ill.Dec. 787, 365 N.E.2d 72 (1977) (proof of attempt bribery after alleged fourth amendment violation).

* * *

7. In Kuhlmann v. Wilson, 477 U.S. 436, 106 S.Ct. 2616 (1986), a majority of the Court held that authorities do not violate the dictates of *Massiah* or *Henry* when they merely use a "listening post" informant to hear, and later repeat in court, incriminating statements made by a defendant after the initiation of the formal judicial proceeding. The majority premised its decision upon state court findings of fact. The state court had found that although authorities had arranged with an informant-prisoner for the informant to report any incriminating statement made by the defendant, they had instructed him merely to listen and not to ask the defendant any questions. According to the state court findings, the informant had obeyed the instructions, asking no questions but only listening and later making notes. Accordingly the Supreme Court majority found that there was no violation of the "deliberate eliciting" standard of *Massiah* nor of the holding of *Henry*. Dissenting justices did not confront the "listening post" issue. They noted that the informant had encouraged the defendant to talk further by commenting that the defendant's initial exculpatory statement did not "sound too good" and that he had better come up with a better one. The dissenters claimed the informer violated the deliberate elicitation standard by encouraging defendant to talk about his crime.

8. Although a *Massiah* violation may be viewed as interference with the attorney-client relationship, it does not impede the defense lawyer's function in the same way as would, for example, prosecutorial overhearing of conversations between attorney and client. Accordingly, except under most unusual circumstances, dismissal of charges (as distinguished from suppression of evidence) will be viewed as too drastic a remedy for a *Massiah* violation. See United States v. Morrison, 449 U.S. 361, 101 S.Ct. 665 (1981).

9. In Estelle v. Smith, 451 U.S. 454, 101 S.Ct. 1866 (1981), upon order of the court, the prosecution arranged for a psychiatrist to interview an indicted defendant for purpose of determining the defendant's competency to stand trial. Later the psychiatrist, in a death penalty sentencing hearing, gave damaging testimony about the defendant's dangerousness. The Court held that the interview was a critical stage and that, as in *Massiah*, the right to counsel had attached. Because there had been no waiver of this right, the Court found a Sixth Amendment violation. It also found a *Miranda* violation in that no warnings had preceded the doctor's interview with the incarcerated defendant.

The *Estelle* Court seemingly limited its holding to a case where the defendant had sought no psychiatric examination and where he had neither raised a defense of insanity nor introduced psychiatric evidence as mitigation at the sentencing phase of the case. Does this mean that by raising a psychiatric defense, a defendant who insists that his lawyer be present at an interview with the prosecution's psychiatrist, nevertheless, waives the right to have counsel present at such session? Or does it mean that the right to counsel does not attach at a psychiatric interview under such circumstances?

10. When a suspect is represented by counsel before the initiation of the formal criminal process, he has no right to counsel under the Sixth Amendment. However, a prosecutor may violate an ethical standard by questioning the suspect out of the presence of his counsel. In United States v. Hammad, 846 F.2d 854 (2d Cir.1988), the "questioning" occurred through the prosecutor's use of a fellow suspect who was secretly cooperating with the prosecution. DR 7–104(A)(1) of the Code of Professional Responsibility had been adopted in the particular federal district, prohibiting a lawyer from communicating with a party whom he or she knows to be represented by counsel regarding the subject matter of that representation.

The Second Circuit in *Hammad* refused to hold that DR 7–104(A)(1) is inapplicable in a criminal matter until the right to counsel attaches under the Sixth Amendment. Of equal significance, it suggested that district courts should sometimes exclude incriminating statements made to the prosecutor's informer when DR 7–104(a) has been violated. On the facts of the case, the Second Circuit ruled that it would not order suppression because at the time of the prosecutorial conduct the reach of DR 7–104(a) in criminal investigations had not been settled.

The *Hammad* court later modified its opinion. See 858 F.2d 834 (1988). It indicated that generally the use of undercover informants to elicit incriminating information from an uncharged suspect who is represented by counsel would not violate DR 7–104 absent other governmental misconduct, such as the use of a spurious grand jury subpoena.

Several Attorneys General of the United States announced views that Justice Department attorneys, conducting investigative activities before the bringing of a formal charge, were not prohibited by DR 7–104(A)(1) from questioning individuals who were represented by counsel where such counsel was not present. (Attorney General Reno adopted a regulation to that effect 28 C.F.R. 77.10 Ca). The regulation was found void in O'Keefe v. McDonnell Douglas Corp., 132 F.3d 1252 (8th Cir.1998). Segments of the defense bar raised a cry that the Attorney General was placing his lawyers above the law. However, the Attorney General's position (if not the regulation) found support in United States v. Ryans, 903 F.2d 731 (10th Cir.1990). This decision permits the Government's use of undercover agents to elicit information from targets who are represented by counsel. The court rejected the *Hammad* decision. It viewed DR–7–104 as protecting "adversaries" and chose to view the relationship which exists between the Government and an uncharged suspect as non-adversarial. Hammod now stands alone among the federal circuit. United States v. Balter, 91 F.3d 427 (3d Cir.1996).

In People v. White, 209 Ill.App.3d 844, 153 Ill.Dec. 910, 567 N.E.2d 1368 (1991), the court conducted a thorough review of the federal cases, with the exception of *Ryans*. It declared that the disciplinary rule applies to criminal investigations even before the attachment of the Sixth Amendment right to counsel. It also noted that the rule applies to prosecutors, but not to investigators. While noting that prosecutors could be deemed in violation of the rule through the conduct of their non-attorney agents, the court adopted a rather narrow view of when police officers should be viewed as the agents of prosecutors. New Mexico found the rule was violated despite the opinion of the Attorney General that such contacts were authorized by law. In re Howes 123 N.M., 311, 940 P.2d 159 (1997).

11. One commentator argues that the right to counsel is a poor device for the protection of defendants questioned by undercover agents, affording too much protection in some cases and too little in others depending on the stage of the proceedings. Instead police ought to secure a warrant before using undercover agents. See Uviller, Evidence From the Mind of the Criminal Suspect: A Reconsideration of the Current Rules of Access and Restraint, 87 Colum.L.Rev. 1137 (1987).

D. VALIDITY OF INTERROGATIONS AFTER AN ILLEGAL ARREST OR DURING "UNNECESSARY DELAY" IN TAKING ARRESTEE BEFORE COMMITTING MAGISTRATE

NOTES

1. In 1943, and again in 1957, the Supreme Court of the United States held, in McNabb v. United States, 318 U.S. 332, 63 S.Ct. 608 (1943), and Mallory v. United States, 354 U.S. 449, 77 S.Ct. 1356 (1957), that where *federal officers* interrogated an arrested person instead of taking him "without unnecessary delay" before a United States commissioner or a federal judge, as required by law, any confession obtained during the period of delay was inadmissible in evidence, regardless of its voluntariness or trustworthiness. This the Court did in the exercise of its "supervisory power" over lower federal courts.

Since the *McNabb–Mallory* rule was not based upon constitutional "due process" considerations, or upon any other provision of the Bill of Rights, the rule was not binding upon the states. Of all the states, Michigan was the first, and for a while the only one, that was inclined to adopt a similar rule. See People v. Hamilton, 359 Mich. 410, 102 N.W.2d 738 (1960), and People v. McCager, 367 Mich.

116, 116 N.W.2d 205 (1962), in which the Michigan Supreme Court said that Michigan was "the first state to adopt the exclusionary rule principle announced in McNabb v. United States". (In *McCager* the confession was made four days after the defendant's arrest.) But within a short time Michigan qualified the application of the rule to such an extent as to effectively discard it. In People v. Farmer, 380 Mich. 198, 156 N.W.2d 504 (1968), the court held that the rule was applicable only where the delay in taking an arrestee before a magistrate was "for the purpose of coercing a confession". In *Farmer* the court found that there were "no circumstances to support a claim of involuntariness" such as appeared in the *Hamilton* case or in the subsequent one of People v. Ubbes, 374 Mich. 571, 132 N.W.2d 669 (1965). The Michigan Courts finally discarded *McNabb* as a per se ruling; arraignment delay is to be one factor among many to consider in deciding admissibility. People v. Cipriano, 431 Mich. 315, 429 N.W.2d 781 (1988).

During the last several years, Pennsylvania has been one of the few jurisdictions (until 1977 perhaps the only one) to apply a *per se* rule of inadmissibility to such statements. See Commonwealth v. Williams, 455 Pa. 569, 319 A.2d 419 (1974). Like other states (e.g., Michigan) which once utilized such a rule, Pennsylvania appears to be emasculating the unlawful detention principle. See Commonwealth v. Davenport, 471 Pa. 278, 370 A.2d 301 (1977) (delay less than six hours does not give rise to *per se* exclusion).

For an excellent summary of the history (and often the evisceration) of the rule in each state which has employed it, see Comment, The Ill–Advised Revival of the McNabb–Mallory Rule, 72 J.Crim.L. & Criminology 204 (1981). After that comment was published, Maryland by statute abolished its version of the rule. See Ann.Code Md., Courts and Judicial Proceedings, § 10–912 (1981 Supp.).

2. In 1968 Congress enacted 18 U.S.C. § 3501. Section (a) of that provision seemingly abolished the *McNabb–Mallory* rule by providing that voluntary confessions shall be admissible. Section (d), however, says that if a statement is admissible if it is voluntary and *if* it is taken within a period of six hours of the arrest or detention (or a greater period if there are reasonable transportation delays requiring more than six hours before arraignment). No doubt Congress could have abolished *McNabb–Mallory* because that rule was not of constitutional dimension. Some courts, however, have indicated that there is still a rule of per se exclusion where the delay exceeded six hours and was not justified by transportation problems. They reason that the particular rule of section (d) controls over the general rule of section (a). See United States v. Wilson, 838 F.2d 1081 (9th Cir.1988). The issue is debated in United States v. Yunis, 859 F.2d 953 (D.C.Cir.1988). The division over whether McNabb–Mallory was abolished by 18 U.S.C. § 3501 is noted but not resolved in United States v. Alvarez–Sanchez, 511 U.S. 350, 114 S.Ct. 1599 (1994) (holding that interviews by federal officers of persons in state custody are not covered by federal statutes prohibiting delay in presentment to court, except in "presumably rare" cases of collusion designed to avoid 18 U.S.C. § 3501).

E. OTHER FIFTH AMENDMENT ISSUES

1. NON-TESTIMONIAL EVIDENCE

United States v. Dionisio

Supreme Court of the United States, 1973.
410 U.S. 1, 93 S.Ct. 764.

■ MR. JUSTICE STEWART delivered the opinion of the Court.

A special grand jury was convened in the Northern District of Illinois in February 1971, to investigate possible violations of federal criminal statutes relating to gambling. In the course of its investigation the grand jury received in evidence certain voice recordings that had been obtained pursuant to court orders.[1]

The grand jury subpoenaed approximately 20 persons, including the respondent Dionisio, seeking to obtain from them voice exemplars for comparison with the recorded conversations that had been received in evidence. Each witness was advised that he was a potential defendant in a criminal prosecution. Each was asked to examine a transcript of an intercepted conversation, and to go to a nearby office of the United States Attorney to read the transcript into a recording device. The witnesses were advised that they would be allowed to have their attorneys present when they read the transcripts. Dionisio and other witnesses refused to furnish the voice exemplars, asserting that these disclosures would violate their rights under the Fourth and Fifth Amendments.

The Government then filed separate petitions in the United States District Court to compel Dionisio and the other witnesses to furnish the voice exemplars to the grand jury. The petitions stated that the exemplars were "essential and necessary" to the grand jury investigation, and that they would "be used solely as a standard of comparison in order to determine whether or not the witness is the person whose voice was intercepted. . . ."

Following a hearing, the district judge rejected the witnesses' constitutional arguments and ordered them to comply with the grand jury's request.

* * *

When Dionisio persisted in his refusal to respond to the grand jury's directive, the District Court adjudged him in civil contempt and ordered him committed to custody until he obeyed the court order, or until the expiration of 18 months.[3]

* * *

I.

The Court of Appeals correctly rejected the contention that the compelled production of the voice exemplars would violate the Fifth Amend-

1. The court orders were issued pursuant to 18 U.S.C. § 2518, a statute authorizing the interception of wire communications upon a judicial determination that "(a) there is probable cause for belief that an individual is committing, has committed, or is about to commit a particular offense enumerated in section 2516 of this chapter [including the transmission of wagering information]; (b) there is probable cause for belief that particular communications concerning that offense will be obtained through such interception; (c) normal investigative procedures have been tried and have failed or reasonably appear to be unlikely to succeed if tried or to be too dangerous; (d) there is probable cause for belief that the facilities from which, or the place where, the wire or oral communications are to be intercepted are being used, or are about to be used, in connection with the commission of such offense, or are leased to, listed in the name of, or commonly used by such person."

3. The life of the special grand jury was 18 months, but could be extended for an additional 18 months. 18 U.S.C. § 3331.

ment. It has long been held that the compelled display of identifiable physical characteristics infringes no interest protected by the privilege against compulsory self-incrimination. In Holt v. United States, 218 U.S. 245, 252, 31 S.Ct. 2, 6, Mr. Justice Holmes, writing for the Court, dismissed as an "extravagant extension of the Fifth Amendment" the argument that it violated the privilege to require a defendant to put on a blouse for identification purposes. He explained that "the prohibition of compelling a man in a criminal court to be witness against himself is a prohibition of the use of physical or moral compulsion to extort communications from him, not an exclusion of his body as evidence when it may be material."

More recently, in Schmerber v. California, 384 U.S. 757, 86 S.Ct. 1826, we relied on *Holt*, and noted that "both federal and state courts have usually held that [the privilege] offers no protection against compulsion to submit to fingerprinting, photographing, or measurements, to write or speak for identification, to appear in court, to stand, to assume a stance, to walk, or to make a particular gesture. The distinction which has emerged often expressed in different ways, is that the privilege is a bar against compelling 'communications' or 'testimony,' but that compulsion which makes a suspect or accused the source of 'real or physical evidence' does not violate it."

The Court held that the extraction and chemical analysis of a blood sample involved no "shadow of testimonial compulsion upon or enforced communication by the accused."

These cases led us to conclude in Gilbert v. California, 388 U.S. 263, 87 S.Ct. 1951, that handwriting exemplars were not protected by the privilege against compulsory self-incrimination. While "[o]ne's voice and handwriting are, of course, means of communication," we held that a "mere handwriting exemplar, in contrast to the content of what is written, like the voice or body itself, is an identifying physical characteristic outside its protection." And similarly in United States v. Wade, 388 U.S. 218, 87 S.Ct. 1926, we found no error in compelling a defendant accused of bank robbery to utter in a line-up words that had allegedly been spoken by the robber. The accused there was "required to use his voice as an identifying physical characteristic, not to speak his guilt."

Wade and *Gilbert* definitively refute any contention that the compelled production of the voice exemplars in this case would violate the Fifth Amendment. The voice recordings were to be used solely to measure the physical properties of the witnesses' voices, not for the testimonial or communicative content of what was to be said.

II.

The Court of Appeals held that the Fourth Amendment required a preliminary showing of reasonableness before a grand jury witness could be compelled to furnish a voice exemplar, and that in this case the proposed "seizures" of the voice exemplars would be unreasonable because of the large number of witnesses summoned by the grand jury and directed to produce such exemplars. We disagree.

The Fourth Amendment guarantees that all people shall be "secure in their persons, houses, papers, and effects, against unreasonable searches and seizures...." Any Fourth Amendment violation in the present setting must rest on a lawless governmental intrusion upon the privacy of "persons" rather than on interference with "property relationships or private papers." Schmerber v. California, 384 U.S. 757, 767, 86 S.Ct. 1826, 1833; see United States v. Doe (Schwartz), 2 Cir., 457 F.2d 895, 897. In Terry v. Ohio, 392 U.S. 1, 88 S.Ct. 1868, the Court explained the protection afforded to "persons" in terms of the statement in Katz v. United States, 389 U.S. 347, 88 S.Ct. 507, that "the Fourth Amendment protects people, not places," and concluded that "wherever an individual may harbor a reasonable 'expectation of privacy,' ... he is entitled to be free from unreasonable governmental intrusion."

As the Court made clear in *Schmerber*, supra, the obtaining of physical evidence from a person involves a potential Fourth Amendment violation at two different levels—the "seizure" of the "person" necessary to bring him into contact with government agents, see Davis v. Mississippi, 394 U.S. 721, 89 S.Ct. 1394, and the subsequent search for and seizure of the evidence. In *Schmerber* we found the initial seizure of the accused justified as a lawful arrest, and the subsequent seizure of the blood sample from his body reasonable in light of the exigent circumstances. And in *Terry*, we concluded that neither the initial seizure of the person, an investigatory "stop" by a policeman, nor the subsequent search, a pat down of his outer clothing for weapons, constituted a violation of the Fourth and Fourteenth Amendments. The constitutionality of the compulsory production of exemplars from a grand jury witness necessarily turns on the same dual inquiry—whether either the initial compulsion of the person to appear before the grand jury, or the subsequent directive to make a voice recording is an unreasonable "seizure" within the meaning of the Fourth Amendment.

It is clear that a subpoena to appear before a grand jury is not a "seizure" in the Fourth Amendment sense, even though that summons may be inconvenient or burdensome....

* * *

This is not to say that a grand jury subpoena is some talisman that dissolves all constitutional protections. The grand jury cannot require a witness to testify against himself. It cannot require the production by a person of private books and records that would incriminate him. The Fourth Amendment provides protection against a grand jury subpoena *duces tecum* too sweeping in its terms "to be regarded as reasonable."

But we are here faced with no such constitutional infirmities in the subpoena to appear before the grand jury or in the order to make the voice recordings. There is, as we have said, no valid Fifth Amendment claim. There was no order to produce private books and papers, and no sweeping subpoena *duces tecum*. And ... there is still no indication in this case of the kind of harassment ...

But the conclusion that Dionisio's compulsory appearance before the grand jury was not an unreasonable "seizure" is the answer to only the first part of the Fourth Amendment inquiry here. Dionisio argues that the grand jury's subsequent directive to make the voice recording was itself an infringement of his rights under the Fourth Amendment. We cannot accept that argument.

In Katz v. United States, supra, we said that the Fourth Amendment provides no protection for what "a person knowingly exposes to the public, even in his own home or office. . . ." The physical characteristics of a person's voice, its tone and manner, as opposed to the content of a specific conversation, are constantly exposed to the public. Like a man's facial characteristics, or handwriting, his voice is repeatedly produced for others to hear. No person can have a reasonable expectation that others will not know the sound of his voice, any more than he can reasonably expect that his face will be a mystery to the world. As the Court of Appeals for the Second Circuit stated:

> "Except for the rare recluse who chooses to live his life in complete solitude, in our daily lives we constantly speak and write, and while the content of a communication is entitled to Fourth Amendment protection, . . . the underlying identifying characteristics—the constant factor throughout both public and private communications—are open for all to see or hear. There is no basis for constructing a wall of privacy against the grand jury which does not exist in casual contacts with strangers. Hence no intrusion into an individual's privacy results from compelled execution of handwriting or voice exemplars; nothing is being exposed to the grand jury that has not previously been exposed to the public at large." United States v. Doe (Schwartz), 2 Cir., 457 F.2d 895, 898–899.

The required disclosure of a person's voice is thus immeasurably further removed from the Fourth Amendment protection than was the intrusion into the body effected by the blood extraction in *Schmerber*. "The interests in human dignity and privacy which the Fourth Amendment protects forbid any such intrusions on the mere chance that desired evidence might be obtained." Schmerber v. California, 384 U.S. 757, 769–770, 86 S.Ct. 1826, 1835. Similarly, a seizure of voice exemplars does not involve the "severe, though brief, intrusion upon cherished personal security," effected by the "pat down" in *Terry*—"surely . . . an annoying, frightening, and perhaps humiliating experience." Terry v. Ohio, 392 U.S. 1, 24–25, 88 S.Ct. 1868, 1882. Rather, this is like the fingerprinting in *Davis*, where, though the initial dragnet detentions were constitutionally impermissible, we noted that the fingerprinting itself, "involves none of the probing into an individual's private life and thoughts that marks an interrogation or search."

Since neither the summons to appear before the grand jury, nor its directive to make a voice recording infringed upon any interest protected by the Fourth Amendment, there was no justification for requiring the grand jury to satisfy even the minimal requirement of "reasonableness" imposed by the Court of Appeals. A grand jury has broad investigative powers to determine whether a crime has been committed and who has committed it. The jurors may act on tips, rumors, evidence offered by the prosecutor, or their own personal knowledge. No grand jury witness is "entitled to set limits to the investigation that the grand jury may conduct." And a sufficient basis for an indictment may only emerge at the end of the investigation when all the evidence has been received.... Since Dionisio raised no valid Fourth Amendment claim, there is no more reason to require a preliminary showing of reasonableness here than there would be in the case of any witness who, despite the lack of any constitutional or statutory privilege, declined to answer a question or comply with a grand jury request. Neither the Constitution nor our prior cases justify any such interference with grand jury proceedings.

The Fifth Amendment guarantees that no civilian may be brought to trial for an infamous crime "unless on a presentment or indictment of a Grand Jury." This constitutional guarantee presupposes an investigative body "acting independently of either prosecuting attorney or judge," Stirone v. United States, 361 U.S. 212, 218, 80 S.Ct. 270, 273, whose mission is to clear the innocent, no less than to bring to trial those who may be guilty. Any holding that would saddle a grand jury with mini-trials and preliminary showings would assuredly impede its investigation and frustrate the public's interest in the fair and expeditious administration of the criminal laws. The grand jury may not always serve its historic role as a protective bulwark standing solidly between the ordinary citizen and an overzealous prosecutor, but if it is even to approach the proper performance of its constitutional mission, it must be free to pursue its investigations unhindered by external influence or supervision so long as it does not trench upon the legitimate rights of any witness called before it.

Since the Court of Appeals found an unreasonable search and seizure where none existed, and imposed a preliminary showing of reasonableness where none was required, its judgment is reversed and this case is remanded to that Court for further proceedings consistent with this opinion.

It is so ordered.

Judgment reversed and case remanded.

[The opinion of Justice Brennan (concurring and dissenting) and the dissenting opinions of Justices Douglas and Marshall are omitted.]

NOTES

1. In United States v. Wade, 388 U.S. 218, 87 S.Ct. 1926 (1967), discussed more fully in Chapter 3, the Court held that compulsory participation in a post-indictment lineup did not violate a defendant's Fifth Amendment rights even though he was required to repeat words allegedly spoken during the course of a bank robbery. The Court held:

> Neither the lineup itself nor anything shown by this record that Wade was required to do in the lineup violated his privilege against self-incrimination. We have only recently reaffirmed that the privilege "protects an accused only from being compelled to testify against himself, or otherwise provide the State with evidence of a testimonial or communicative nature...." Schmerber v. California, 384 U.S. 757, 86 S.Ct. 1826. We there held that compelling a suspect to submit to a withdrawal of a sample of his blood for analysis for alcohol content and the admission in evidence of the analysis report was not compulsion to those ends. That holding was

supported by the opinion in Holt v. United States ... in which case a question arose as to whether a blouse belonged to the defendant. A witness testified at trial that the defendant put on the blouse and it had fit him. The defendant argued that the admission of the testimony was error because compelling him to put on the blouse was a violation of his privilege. The Court rejected the claim as "an extravagant extension of the Fifth Amendment," Mr. Justice Holmes saying for the Court:

> "[T]he prohibition of compelling a man in a criminal court to be witness against himself is a prohibition of the use of physical or moral compulsion to extort communications from him, not an exclusion of his body as evidence when it may be material."

* * *

We have no doubt that compelling the accused merely to exhibit his person for observation by a prosecution witness prior to trial involves no compulsion of the accused to give evidence having testimonial significance. It is compulsion of the accused to exhibit his physical characteristics, not compulsion to disclose any knowledge he might have. It is no different from compelling Schmerber to provide a blood sample or Holt to wear the blouse, and, as in those instances, is not within the cover of the privilege. Similarly, compelling Wade to speak within hearing distance of the witnesses, even to utter words purportedly uttered by the robber, was not compulsion to utter statements of a "testimonial" nature; he was required to use his voice as an identifying physical characteristic, not to speak his guilt. We held in Schmerber, supra, that the distinction to be drawn under the Fifth Amendment privilege against self-incrimination is one between an accused's "communications" in whatever form, vocal or physical, and "compulsion which makes a suspect or accused the source of 'real or physical evidence,' ". We recognized that "both federal and state courts have usually held that ... [the privilege] offers no protection against compulsion to submit to fingerprinting, photography, or measurements, to write or speak for identification, to appear in court, to stand, to assume a stance, to walk, or to make a particular gesture." None of these activities becomes testimonial within the scope of the privilege because required of the accused in a pretrial lineup.

Moreover, it deserves emphasis, that this case presents no question of the admissibility in evidence of anything Wade said or did at the lineup which implicates his privilege. The Government offered no such evidence as part of its case, and what came out about the lineup proceedings on Wade's cross-examination of the bank employees involved no violation of Wade's privilege.

JUSTICE BLACK dissented:

In rejecting Wade's claim that his privilege against self-incrimination was violated by compelling him to appear in the lineup wearing the tape and uttering the words given him by the police, the Court relies on the recent holding in Schmerber v. State of California. In that case the Court held that taking blood from a man's body against his will in order to convict him of a crime did not compel him to be a witness against himself. I dissented from that holding, and still dissent. The Court's reason for its holding was that the sample of Schmerber's blood taken in order to convict him of crime was neither "testimonial" nor "communicative" evidence. I think it was both. It seems quite plain to me that the Fifth Amendment's Self-incrimination Clause was designed to bar the Government from forcing any person to supply proof of his own crime, precisely what Schmerber was forced to do when he was forced to supply his blood. The Government simply took his blood against his will and over his counsel's protest for the purpose of convicting him of crime. So here, having Wade in its custody awaiting trial to see if he could or would be convicted of crime, the Government forced him to stand in a lineup, wear strips on his face, and speak certain words, in order to make it possible for government witnesses to identify him as a criminal. Had Wade been compelled to utter these or any other words in open court, it is plain that he would have been entitled to a new trial because of having been compelled to be a witness against himself. Being forced by Government to help convict himself and to supply evidence against himself by talking outside the courtroom is equally violative of his constitutional right not to be compelled to be a witness against himself. Consequently, because of this violation of the Fifth Amendment, and not because of my own personal view that the Government's conduct was "unfair," "prejudicial," or "improper," I would prohibit the prosecution's use of lineup identification at trial.

JUSTICE FORTAS, joined by CHIEF JUSTICE WARREN and JUSTICE DOUGLAS, took a middle ground:

I agree with the Court that the exhibition of the person of the accused at a lineup is not itself a violation of the privilege against self-incrimination. In itself, it is no more subject to constitutional objection than the exhibition of the person of the accused in the courtroom for identification purposes. It is an incident of the State's power to arrest, and a reasonable and justifiable aspect of the State's custody resulting from arrest. It does not require that the accused take affirmative, volitional action, but only that, having been duly arrested he may be seen for identification purposes.

* * *

In my view, however, the accused may not be compelled in a lineup to speak the words uttered by the person who committed the crime. I am confident that it could not be compelled in court. It cannot be compelled in a lineup. It is more than passive, mute assistance to the eyes of the victim or of witnesses. It is the kind of volitional act—the kind of forced cooperation by the accused—which is within the historical perimeter of the privilege against compelled self-incrimination.

Our history and tradition teach and command that an accused may stand mute. The privilege means just that; not less than that. According to the Court, an accused may be jailed—indefinitely—until he is willing to say, for an identifying audience, whatever was said in the course of the commission of the crime. Presumably this would include, "Your money or your life"Cor perhaps, words of assault in a rape case. This is intolerable under our constitutional system.

* * *

An accused cannot be compelled to utter the words spoken by the criminal in the course of the crime. I thoroughly disagree with the Court's statement that such compulsion does not violate the Fifth Amendment. The Court relies upon Schmerber v. State of California to support this.... But *Schmerber* which authorized the forced extraction of blood from the veins of an unwilling human being, did not compel the person actively to cooperate—to accuse himself by a volitional act which differs only in degree from compelling him to act out the crime, which, I assume, would be rebuffed by the Court....

> To permit *Schmerber* to apply in any respect beyond its holding is, in my opinion, indefensible. To permit its insidious doctrine to extend beyond the invasion of the body, which it permits, to compulsion of the will of a man, is to deny and defy a precious part of our historical faith and to discard one of the most profoundly cherished instruments by which we have established the freedom and dignity of the individual. We should not so alter the balance between the rights of the individual and of the state, achieved over centuries of conflict.

2. In addition to compulsory voice exemplars, as evidenced by *Dionisio*, and participation in a line-up, certain acts may be compelled because they have been found to be noncommunicative in nature. See Schmerber v. California, 384 U.S. 757, 86 S.Ct. 1826 (1966) (blood sample); Gilbert v. California, 388 U.S. 263, 87 S.Ct. 1951 (1967) (handwriting exemplar); Holt v. United States, 218 U.S. 245, 31 S.Ct. 2 (1910) (wearing of particular clothing). The compulsory conduct is justified on the ground that the suspect was not required to disclose any knowledge he might have or "to speak his guilt."

3. Are there any limits upon the grand jury's power to compel "nontestimonial" evidence without a showing of probable cause? Can a grand jury order a suspect to stand in a lineup? See In re Maguire, 571 F.2d 675 (1st Cir.1978); In re Melvin, 546 F.2d 1 (1st Cir.1976). Could a grand jury order a suspect to yield a hair sample? See In re Grand Jury Proceeding (Mills), 686 F.2d 135 (3d Cir.1982). Provide handwriting exemplars? See United States v. Mara, 410 U.S. 19, 93 S.Ct. 774 (1973); United States v. Antill, 601 F.2d 1049 (9th Cir.1979). What about a blood specimen? Presumably, the greater the intrusion, the weaker is the argument that *Dionisio* is the controlling precedent.

4. Some state courts, under their own Constitutions, are more restrictive in allowing the prosecution access to nontestimonial evidence. Thus, In re May 1991 Will County Grand Jury, 152 Ill.2d 381, 178 Ill.Dec. 406, 604 N.E.2d 929 (1992), held that the protection against invasion of privacy in the state constitution required that "some showing of individualized suspicion as well as relevance must be made before physical evidence of a noninvasive nature, such as an in-person appearance in a line-up or fingerprinting is demanded of a witness."

5. In Doe v. United States, 487 U.S. 201, 108 S.Ct. 2341 (1988), the Government sought to obtain from a foreign government bank records pertaining to accounts controlled by "John Doe," the target of a federal grand jury investigation. Under the law of the Cayman Islands and Bermuda, the United States could obtain these records only if John Doe consented. Pursuant to a Government motion, a federal district court refused to order Doe to execute the consent forms. The Supreme Court rejected a Fifth Amendment challenge to the proposed order. It held that the execution of the consent form would be non-testimonial in that the form made no reference to any specific account, but only authorized disclosure of whatever accounts, if any, Doe might have in the foreign banks. "By signing the form, Doe makes no statement, explicit or implicit regarding the existence of a foreign bank account." The Court noted that any records obtained from the bank would not be within the scope of Doe's Fifth Amendment privilege.

Justice Stevens dissented. He argued that a defendant "cannot be compelled to use his mind to assist the prosecution" in convicting him of a crime. He asserted that signing the consent form was not like yielding fingerprints: "He may in some cases be forced to surrender a key to a strong box containing incriminating documents, but I do not believe he can be compelled to reveal the combination to his wall safe—by word or deed."

6. In South Dakota v. Neville, 459 U.S. 553, 103 S.Ct. 916 (1983), the Supreme Court considered whether the fifth amendment prohibits prosecution comment upon a driver's refusal to take a blood-alcohol test. The Court decided that such comment is permissible; but it did not rest its holding upon the ground that the refusal of the test, like the yielding of blood, is non-testimonial. Instead it held that no impermissible compulsion occurs when the choice is presented to take the test or suffer comment upon the refusal. Compare Griffin v. California, Chapter 19 G.2.

7. In Baltimore City Department of Social Services v. Bouknight, 493 U.S. 549, 110 S.Ct. 900 (1990), the Court phrased the issue as whether "a mother, the custodian of a child pursuant to a court order, may invoke the Fifth Amendment privilege against self-incrimination to resist an order of the Juvenile Court to produce the child." The city social services agency feared for the safety of the child, and relatives claimed that they had not seen the child for a period of time.

For the majority, Justice O'Connor wrote:

* * *

The Court has on several occasions recognized that the Fifth Amendment privilege may not be invoked to resist compliance with a regulatory regime constructed to effect the State's public purposes unrelated to the enforcement of its criminal laws. In *Shapiro v. United States* (1948), the Court considered an application of the Emergency Price Control Act and a regulation issued thereunder which required licensed businesses to maintain records and make them available for inspection by administrators. The Court indicated that no Fifth Amendment protection attached to production of the "required records," which the "'defendant was required to keep, not for his private uses, but for the benefit of the public, and for public inspection.'" The Court's discussion of the constitutional implications of the scheme focused upon the relation between the Government's regulatory objectives and the Government's interest in gaining access to the records in Shapiro's possession:

> "It may be assumed at the outset that there are limits which the Government cannot constitutionally exceed in requiring the keeping of records which may be inspected by an administrative agency and may be used in prosecuting statutory violations committed by the record-keeper himself. But no serious misgiving that those bounds have been overstepped would appear to be evoked when there is a sufficient relation between the activity sought to be regulated and the public concern so that the Government can constitutionally regulate or forbid the basic activity concerned, and can constitutionally require the keeping of particular records, subject to inspection by the Administrator."

* * *

When a person assumes control over items that are the legitimate object of the government's non-criminal regulatory powers, the ability to invoke the privilege is reduced.

* * *

These principles readily apply to this case. Once Maurice was adjudicated a child in need of assistance, his care and safety became the particular object of the State's regulatory interests.

* * *

> Persons who care for children pursuant to a custody order, and who may be subject to a request for access to the child, are hardly a " 'selective group inherently suspect of criminal activities.' "
>
> We are not called upon to define the precise limitations that may exist upon the State's ability to use the testimonial aspects of Bouknight's act of production in subsequent criminal proceedings. But we note that imposition of such limitations is not foreclosed. The same custodial role that limited the ability to resist the production order may give rise to corresponding limitations upon the direct and indirect use of that testimony. The State's regulatory requirement in the usual case may neither compel incriminating testimony nor aid a criminal prosecution, but the Fifth Amendment protections are not thereby necessarily unavailable to the person who complies with the regulatory requirement after invoking the privilege and subsequently faces prosecution.

Justice Marshall, joined by Justice Brennan, dissented, arguing that the act of producing the child would be both testimonial "because it would amount to an admission of Bouknight's physical control of her son", and incriminating, leading perhaps to criminal abuse charges, or if the child were dead, to homicide charges.

2. IMMUNIZED TESTIMONY

Kastigar v. United States

Supreme Court of the United States, 1972.
406 U.S. 441, 92 S.Ct. 1653.

■ MR. JUSTICE POWELL delivered the opinion of the Court.

* * *

Petitioners were subpoenaed to appear before a United States grand jury in the Central District of California on February 4, 1971. The Government believed that petitioners were likely to assert their Fifth Amendment privilege. Prior to the scheduled appearances, the Government applied to the District Court for an order directing petitioners to answer questions and produce evidence before the grand jury under a grant of immunity conferred pursuant to 18 U.S.C. §§ 6002, 6003. Petitioners opposed issuance of the order, contending primarily that the scope of the immunity provided by the statute was not coextensive with the scope of the privilege against self-incrimination, and therefore was not sufficient to supplant the privilege and compel their testimony. The District Court rejected this contention, and ordered petitioners to appear before the grand jury and answer its questions under the grant of immunity.

Petitioners appeared but refused to answer questions, asserting their privilege against compulsory self-incrimination. They were brought before the District Court, and each persisted in his refusal to answer the grand jury's questions, notwithstanding the grant of immunity. The court found both in contempt, and committed them to the custody of the Attorney General until either they answered the grand jury's questions or the term of the grand jury expired. The Court of Appeals for the Ninth Circuit affirmed. This Court granted certiorari to resolve the important question whether testimony may be compelled by granting immunity from the use of the compelled testimony and evidence derived therefrom ("use and derivative use" immunity), or whether it is necessary to grant immunity from prosecution for offenses to which compelled testimony relates ("transactional" immunity).

I.

The power of government to compel persons to testify in court or before grand juries and other governmental agencies is firmly established in Anglo–American jurisprudence. The power with respect to courts was established by statute in England as early as 1562, and Lord Bacon observed in 1612 that all subjects owed the King their "knowledge and discovery." While it is not clear when grand juries first resorted to compulsory process to secure the attendance and testimony of witnesses, the general common law principle that "the public has a right to every man's evidence" was considered an "indubitable certainty" which "cannot be denied" by 1742. The power to compel testimony, and the corresponding duty to testify, are recognized in the Sixth Amendment requirements that an accused be confronted with the witnesses against him, and have compulsory process for obtaining witnesses in his favor. The first Congress recognized the testimonial duty in the Judiciary Act of 1789, which provided for compulsory attendance of witnesses in the federal courts. Mr. Justice White noted the importance of this essential power of government in his concurring opinion in Murphy v. Waterfront Comm'n (1964):

> "Among the necessary and most important of the powers of the States as well as the Federal Government to assure the effective functioning of government in an ordered society is the broad power to compel residents to testify in court or before grand juries or agencies. Such testimony constitutes one of the Government's primary sources of information."

But the power to compel testimony is not absolute. There are a number of exemptions from the testimonial duty, the most important of which is the Fifth Amendment privilege against compulsory self-incrimination. The privilege reflects a complex of our fundamental values and aspirations, and marks an important advance in the development of our liberty. It can be asserted in any proceeding, civil or criminal, administrative or judicial, investigatory or adjudicatory; and it protects against any disclosures which the witness reasonably believes could be used in a criminal prosecution or could lead to other evidence that might be so used. This Court has been zealous to safeguard the values which underlie the privilege.

Immunity statutes, which have historical roots deep in Anglo–American jurisprudence, are not incompatible with these values. Rather they seek a rational accommodation between the imperatives of the privilege and the legitimate demands of government to compel citizens to testify. The existence of these statutes reflects the importance of testimony, and the fact that many offenses are of such a character that the only persons capable of giving useful testimony are those implicated in the crime. Indeed, their origins were in the context of such offenses, and their primary use has been to investigate such offenses. Congress included immunity statutes in many of the regulatory measures adopted in the first half of this century. Indeed, prior to the enactment of the statute under consideration in this case, there were in force over 50 federal immunity statutes. In addition, every State in the Union, as well as the District of Columbia and Puerto Rico, has one or more such statutes. The commentators, and this Court on several occasions, have characterized immunity statutes as essential to the effective enforcement of various criminal statutes. As Mr. Justice Frankfurter observed, such statutes have "become part of our constitutional fabric."

II.

Petitioners contend first that the Fifth Amendment's privilege against compulsory self-incrimination, which is that "no person ... shall be compelled in any criminal case to be a witness against himself," deprives Congress of power to enact laws which compel self-incrimination, even if complete immunity from prosecution is granted prior to the compulsion of the incriminatory testimony. In other words, petitioners assert that no immunity statute, however drawn, can afford a lawful basis for compelling incriminatory testimony. They ask us to reconsider and overrule Brown v. Walker (1896), and Ullmann v. United States (1956), decisions which uphold the constitutionality of immunity statutes. We find no merit to this contention and reaffirm the decisions in *Brown* and *Ullmann*.

III.

Petitioners' second contention is that the scope of immunity provided by the federal witness immunity statute, 18 U.S.C. § 6002, is not coextensive with the scope of the Fifth Amendment privilege against compulsory self-incrimination, and therefore is not sufficient to supplant the privilege and compel testimony over a claim of the privilege. The statute provides that when a witness is compelled by district court order to testify over a claim of the privilege:

> "the witness may not refuse to comply with the order on the basis of his privilege against self-incrimination; but no testimony or other information compelled under the order (or any information directly or indirectly derived from such testimony or other information) may be used against the witness in any criminal case, except a prosecution for perjury, giving a false statement, or otherwise failing to comply with the order."

The constitutional inquiry, rooted in logic and history, as well as in the decisions of this Court, is whether the immunity granted under this statute is coextensive with the scope of the privilege. If so, petitioners' refusals to answer based on the privilege were unjustified, and the judgments of contempt were proper, for the grant of immunity has removed the dangers against which the privilege protects. If, on the other hand, the immunity granted is not as comprehensive as the protection afforded by the privilege, petitioners were justified in refusing to answer, and the judgments of contempt must be vacated.

Petitioners draw a distinction between statutes which provide transactional immunity and those which provide, as does the statute before us, immunity from use and derivative use. They contend that a statute must at a minimum grant full transactional immunity in order to be coextensive with the scope of the privilege. In support of this contention, they rely on Counselman v. Hitchcock, 142 U.S. 547, 12 S.Ct. 195 (1892), the first case in which this Court considered a constitutional challenge to an immunity statute. The statute provided that no "evidence obtained from a party or witness by means of a judicial proceeding ... shall be given in evidence, or in any manner used against him ... in any court of the United States...." This Court construed the statute as affording a witness protection only against the use of the specific testimony compelled from him under the grant of immunity. This construction meant that the statute "could not, and would not, prevent the use of his testimony to search out other testimony to be used in evidence against him." Since the revised 1868 Act, as construed by the Court, would permit the use against the immunized witness of evidence derived from his compelled testimony, it did not protect the witness to the same extent that a claim of the privilege would protect him. Accordingly, under the principle that a grant of immunity cannot supplant the privilege, and is not sufficient to compel testimony over a claim of the privilege, unless the scope of the grant of immunity is coextensive with the scope of the privilege, the witness' refusal to testify was held proper. In the course of its opinion, the Court made the following statement, on which petitioners heavily rely:

> "We are clearly of opinion that no statute which leaves the party or witness subject to prosecution after he answers the criminating question put to him, can have the effect of supplanting the privilege conferred by the Constitution of the United States.... In view of the constitutional provision, a statutory enactment, to be valid, must afford absolute immunity against future prosecution for the offence to which the question relates."

Sixteen days after the *Counselman* decision, a new immunity bill was introduced by Senator Cullom, who urged that enforcement of the Interstate Commerce Act would be impossible in the absence of an effective immunity statute. The bill, which became the Compulsory Testimony Act of 1893, was drafted specifically to meet the broad language in *Counselman* set forth above. The new Act removed the privilege against self-incrimination in hearings before the Interstate Commerce Commission and provided that:

> "no person shall be prosecuted or subjected to any penalty or forfeiture for or on account of any transaction, matter or thing, concerning which he may testify, or produce evidence, documentary or otherwise...."

This transactional immunity statute became the basic form for the numerous federal immunity statutes until 1970, when, after re-examining applicable constitutional principles and the adequacy of existing law, Congress enacted the statute here under consideration....

The statute's explicit proscription of the use in any criminal case of "testimony or other information compelled under the order (or any information directly or indirectly derived from such testimony or other information)" is consonant with Fifth Amendment standards. We hold that such immunity from use and derivative use is coextensive with the scope of the privilege against self-incrimination, and therefore is sufficient to compel testimony over a claim of the privilege. While a grant of immunity must afford protection commensurate with that afforded by the privilege, it need not be broader. Transactional immunity, which accords full immunity from prosecution for the offense to which the compelled testimony relates, affords the witness considerably broader protection than does the Fifth Amendment privilege. The privilege has never been construed to mean that one who invokes it cannot subsequently be prosecuted. Its sole concern is to afford protection against being "forced to give testimony leading to the infliction of 'penalties affixed to ... criminal acts.'" Immunity from the use of compelled testimony and evidence derived directly and indirectly therefrom affords this protection. It prohibits the prosecutorial authorities from using the compelled testimony in *any* respect, and it therefore insures that the testimony cannot lead to the infliction of criminal penalties on the witness.

Our holding is consistent with the conceptual basis of *Counselman*. The *Counselman* statute, as construed by the Court, was plainly deficient in its failure to prohibit the use against the immunized witness of evidence derived from his compelled testimony. The Court repeatedly emphasized this deficiency, noting that the statute:

> "could not, and would not, prevent the use of his testimony to search out other testimony to be used in evidence against him or his property, in a criminal proceeding ...",

> that it:

> "could not prevent the obtaining and the use of witnesses and evidence which should be attributable directly to the testimony he might give under compulsion and on which he might be convicted, when otherwise, and if he had refused to answer, he could not possibly have been convicted",

and that it:

> "affords no protection against that use of compelled testimony which consists in gaining therefrom a knowledge of the details of a crime, and of sources of information which may supply other means of convicting the witness or party".

The basis of the Court's decision was recognized in Ullmann v. United States (1956), in which the Court reiterated that the *Counselman* statute was insufficient:

> "because the immunity granted was incomplete, in that it merely forbade the use of the testimony given and failed to protect a witness from future prosecution *based on knowledge and sources of information obtained from the compelled testimony*." (Emphasis supplied.)

The broad language in *Counselman* relied upon by petitioners was unnecessary to the Court's decision, and cannot be considered binding authority.

In Murphy v. Waterfront Comm'n, (1964), ... petitioners were subpoenaed to testify at a hearing conducted by the Waterfront Commission of New York Harbor ... [and] were granted immunity from prosecution under the laws of New Jersey and New York. They continued to refuse to testify, however, on the ground that their answers might tend to incriminate them under federal law, to which the immunity did not purport to extend. They were adjudged in civil contempt, and that judgment was affirmed by the New Jersey Supreme Court.

... Since New Jersey and New York had not purported to confer immunity from federal prosecution, the Court was faced with the question what limitations the Fifth Amendment privilege imposed on the prosecutorial powers of the Federal Government, a nonimmunizing sovereign. After undertaking an examination of the policies and purposes of the privilege, the Court overturned the rule that one jurisdiction within our federal structure may compel a witness to give testimony which could be used to convict him of a crime in another jurisdiction. The Court held that the privilege protects state witnesses against incrimination under federal as well as state law, and federal witnesses against incrimination under state as well as federal law. Applying this principle to the state immunity legislation before it, the Court held the constitutional rule to be that:

> "a state witness may not be compelled to give testimony which may be incriminating under federal law unless the compelled testimony and its fruits cannot be used in any manner by federal officials in connection with a criminal prosecution against him. We conclude, moreover, that in order to implement this constitutional rule and accommodate the interests of the State and Federal Government in investigating and prosecuting crime, the Federal Government must be prohibited from making any such use of compelled testimony and its fruits."

The Court emphasized that this rule left the state witness and the Federal Government, against which the witness had immunity only from the *use* of the compelled testimony and evidence derived therefrom, "in substantially the same position as if the witness had claimed his privilege in the absence of a state grant of immunity."

* * *

IV.

Petitioners argue that use and derivative use immunity will not adequately protect a witness from various possible incriminating uses of the compelled testimony: for example, the prosecutor or other law enforcement officials may obtain leads, names of witnesses, or other information not otherwise available which might result in a prosecution. It will be difficult and perhaps impossible, the argument goes, to identify, by testimony or cross-examination the subtle ways in which the compelled testimony may disadvantage a witness, especially in the jurisdiction granting the immunity.

This argument presupposes that the statute's prohibition will prove impossible to enforce. The statute provides a sweeping proscription of any use, direct or indirect, of the compelled testimony and any information derived therefrom:

> "no testimony or other information, compelled under the order (or any information directly or indirectly derived from such testimony or other information) may be used against the witness in any criminal case. . . ." 18 U.S.C. § 6002.

This total prohibition on use provides a comprehensive safeguard barring the use of compelled testimony as an "investigatory lead," and also barring the use of any evidence obtained by focusing investigation on a witness as a result of his compelled disclosures.

A person accorded this immunity . . ., and subsequently prosecuted, is not dependent for the preservation of his rights upon the integrity and good faith of the prosecuting authorities. As stated in *Murphy:*

> "Once a defendant demonstrates that he has testified, under a state grant of immunity, to matters related to the federal prosecution, the federal authorities have the burden of showing that their evidence is not tainted by establishing that they had an independent, legitimate source for the disputed evidence."

This burden of proof, which we reaffirm as appropriate, is not limited to a negation of taint; rather, it imposes on the prosecution the affirmative duty to prove that the evidence it proposes to use is derived from a legitimate source wholly independent of the compelled testimony.

This is very substantial protection, commensurate with that resulting from invoking the privilege itself. The privilege assures that a citizen is not compelled to incriminate himself by his own testimony. It usually operates to allow a citizen to remain silent when asked a question requiring an incriminatory answer. This statute, which operates after a witness has given incriminatory testimony, affords the same protection by assuring that the compelled testimony can in no way lead to the infliction of criminal penalties. The statute, like the Fifth Amendment, grants neither pardon nor amnesty. Both the statute and the Fifth Amendment allow the government to prosecute using evidence from legitimate independent sources.

The statutory proscription is analogous to the Fifth Amendment requirement in cases of coerced confessions. A coerced confession, as revealing of leads as testimony given in exchange for immunity, is inadmissible in a criminal trial, but it does not bar prosecution. Moreover, a defendant against whom incriminating evidence has been obtained through a grant of immunity may be in a stronger position at trial than a defendant who asserts a Fifth Amendment coerced confession claim. One raising a claim under this statute need only show that he testified under a grant of immunity in order to shift to the government the heavy burden of proving that all of the evidence it proposes to use was derived from legitimate independent sources. On the other hand, a defendant raising a coerced confession claim under the Fifth Amendment must first prevail in a voluntariness hearing before his confession and evidence derived from it become inadmissible.

There can be no justification in reason or policy for holding that the Constitution requires an amnesty grant where, acting pursuant to statute and accompanying safeguards, testimony is compelled in exchange for immunity from use and derivative use when no such amnesty is required where the government, acting without colorable right, coerces a defendant into incriminating himself.

We conclude that the immunity provided by 18 U.S.C. § 6002 leaves the witness and the prosecutorial authorities in substantially the same position as if the witness had claimed the Fifth Amendment privilege. The immunity therefore is coextensive with the privilege and suffices to supplant it....

Affirmed.

■ MR. JUSTICE BRENNAN and MR. JUSTICE REHNQUIST took no part in the consideration or decision of this case.

■ MR. JUSTICE DOUGLAS, dissenting.

The Self–Incrimination Clause says "No person ... shall be compelled in any criminal case to be a witness against himself." I see no answer to the proposition that he is such a witness when only "use" immunity is granted.

* * *

This Court, however, apparently believes that *Counselman* and its progeny were overruled, *sub silentio*, in Murphy v. Waterfront Commission.

I would adhere to Counselman v. Hitchcock and hold that this attempt to dilute the Self–Incrimination Clause is unconstitutional.

■ MR. JUSTICE MARSHALL, dissenting.

* * *

... I cannot agree that a ban on use will in practice be total, if it remains open for the Government to convict the witness on the basis of evidence derived from a legitimate independent source. The Court asserts that the witness is adequately protected by a rule imposing on the Government a heavy burden of proof if it would establish the independent character of evidence to be used against the witness. But in light of the inevitable uncertainties of the fact-finding process, a greater margin of protection is required in order to provide a reliable guarantee that the witness is in exactly the same position as if he had not testified. That margin can be provided only by immunity from prosecution for the offenses to which the testimony relates, i.e., transactional immunity.

I do not see how it can suffice merely to put the burden of proof on the Government. First, contrary to the Court's assertion, the Court's rule does leave the witness "dependent for the preservation of his rights upon the integrity and good faith of the prosecuting authorities." For the information relevant to the question of taint is uniquely within the knowledge of the prosecuting authorities. They alone are in a position to trace the chains of information and investigation that lead to the evidence to be used in a criminal prosecution. A witness who suspects that his compelled testimony was used to develop a lead will be hard pressed indeed to ferret out the evidence necessary to prove it. And of course it is no answer to say he need not prove it, for though the Court puts the burden of proof on the Government, the Government will have no difficulty in meeting its burden by mere assertion if the witness produces no contrary evidence. The good faith of the prosecuting authorities is thus the sole safeguard of the witness' rights. Second, even their good faith is not a sufficient safeguard. For the paths of information through the investigative bureaucracy may well be long and winding, and even a prosecutor acting in the best of faith cannot be certain that somewhere in the depths of his investigative apparatus, often including hundreds of employees, there was not some prohibited use of the compelled testimony. The Court today sets out a loose net to trap tainted evidence and prevent its use against the witness, but it accepts an intolerably great risk that tainted evidence will in fact slip through that net.

In my view the Court turns reason on its head when it compares a statutory grant of immunity to the "immunity" that is inadvertently conferred by an unconstitutional interrogation. The exclusionary rule of evidence that applies in that situation has nothing whatever to do with this case. Evidence obtained through a coercive interrogation, like evidence obtained through an illegal search, is excluded at trial because the Constitution prohibits such methods of gathering evidence. The exclusionary rules provide a partial and inadequate remedy to some victims of illegal police conduct, and a similarly partial and inadequate deterrent to police officers. An immunity statute, on the other hand, is much more ambitious than any exclusionary rule. It does not merely attempt to provide a remedy for past police misconduct, which never should have occurred. An immunity statute operates in advance of the event, and it authorizes—even encourages—interrogation which would otherwise be prohibited by the Fifth Amendment. An immunity statute thus differs from an exclusionary rule of evidence in at least two critical respects.

First, because an immunity statute gives constitutional approval to the resulting interrogation, the Government is under an obligation here to remove the danger of incrimination completely and absolutely, whereas in the case of the exclusionary rules it may be sufficient to shield the witness from the fruits of the illegal search or interrogation in a partial and reasonably adequate manner. For when illegal police conduct has occurred, the exclusion of evidence does not purport to purge the conduct of its unconstitutional character. The constitutional violation remains, and may provide the basis for other relief, such as a damage action, or a criminal prosecution of the responsible officers. The Constitution does not authorize police officers to coerce confessions or to invade privacy without cause, so long as no use is made of the evidence they obtain. But this Court has held that the Constitution does authorize the Government to compel a witness to give potentially incriminating testimony, so long as no incriminating use is made of the resulting evidence. Before the Government puts its seal of approval on such an interrogation, it must provide an absolutely reliable guarantee that it will not use the testimony in any way at all in aid of prosecution of the witness. The only way to provide that guarantee is to give the witness immunity from prosecution for crimes to which his testimony relates.

Second, because an immunity statute operates in advance of the interrogation, there is room to require a broad grant of transactional immunity without imperiling large numbers of otherwise valid convictions.

An exclusionary rule comes into play after the interrogation or search has occurred; and the decision to question or to search is often made in haste, under pressure, by an officer who is not a lawyer. If an unconstitutional interrogation or search were held to create transactional immunity, that might well be regarded as an excessively high price to pay for the "constable's blunder." An immunity statute, on the other hand, creates a framework in which the prosecuting attorney can make a calm and reasoned decision whether to compel testimony and suffer the resulting ban on prosecution, or to forgo the testimony.

For both these reasons it is clear to me that an immunity statute must be tested by a standard far more demanding than that appropriate for an exclusionary rule fashioned to deal with past constitutional violations. Measured by that standard, the statute approved today by the Court fails miserably. I respectfully dissent.

NOTES

1. In the companion case to *Kastigar*, Zicarelli v. New Jersey State Commission of Investigation, 406 U.S. 472, 92 S.Ct. 1670 (1972), the Supreme Court upheld the validity of the New Jersey use immunity statute. The Court also held that the statutory condition of a "responsive answer" (inserted as a safeguard against a witness giving himself a complete "immunity bath" beyond the subject matter of the investigation) was not unconstitutionally vague since the phrase "responsive answer" has a clearly understood meaning, and, moreover, the person examined has the right to counsel before the Commission who could "secure clarification of vague and ambiguous questions in advance of a response by the witness."

2. Some persons, particularly prosecutors, say that there is little difference between use immunity and transactional, except where multiple jurisdictions are interested in the same matter. This is because of the difficulty of demonstrating that a prosecution is based entirely upon evidence derived independently of the immunized testimony.

In United States v. North, 920 F.2d 940 (D.C.Cir.1990), Congress granted Col. Oliver North use immunity for his testimony at a nationally-televised hearing. The trial judge at North's criminal trial upheld the special prosecutor's claim that none of the evidence presented was derived from the immunized testimony. The reviewing court remanded for further proceedings, directing the trial judge to go through the testimony witness-by-witness, and line-by-line to determine whether this was true. A dissenting opinion expressed the view that the prosecutor had adequately met his burden the first time around. In the majority in *North*, favoring an expansive interpretation of the self-incrimination privilege, were conservative members of the D.C. Circuit. In the dissent, favoring a less expansive view of the constitutional protection, was a liberal member of the court. For other examples of prosecutions of defendants who received use immunity, see United States v. Harvey, 869 F.2d 1439 (11th Cir.1989); United States v. Gallo, 863 F.2d 185 (2d Cir.1988).

In United States v. Poindexter, 951 F.2d 369 (D.C.Cir.1991) the Court reversed a conviction because Oliver North had heard Poindexter's immunized testimony and could not state what were the effects of such knowledge of his other memories of the events in question. The issues are explored in lengthy opinions both in majority and dissent.

If the prosecutor intends to indict at the time use immunity is granted, and if he has foreknowledge of the immunity order, he can "seal" his evidence, as was done by the special prosecutor to preserve evidence against John Dean in the Watergate case.

3. Consider the following scenario: The government, fully aware that it has enough evidence to indict a suspect, presents all of its evidence to the grand jury. Instead of seeking an indictment, the government subpoenas the suspect to the grand jury. When the suspect refuses to testify on fifth amendment grounds, the government "seals" its evidence—to protect it from becoming tainted by immunized testimony—and obtains an order immunizing the suspect. At this point, the suspect has three choices: he can refuse to testify and be jailed for contempt; he can confess; or he can testify in a manner that is inconsistent with the government's evidence. If he takes the latter course, the government can continue to use the grand jury to learn the suspect's story, add a perjury count to his indictment, or do both. Under circumstances such as this, is use immunity consistent with the fifth amendment privilege? Does *Kastigar* authorize the government to use immunity in this manner? In United States v. Hinton, 543 F.2d 1002 (2d Cir.1976), the court held that a nonperjury indictment cannot be returned against a person who testifies before it under a grant of immunity. Compare United States v. Anzalone, 560 F.2d 492 (2d Cir.1977).

4. In United States v. Bartel, 19 F.3d 1105 (6th Cir.1994), an immunized witness who was subsequently indicted by the same grand jury before which he had testified sought a per se rule prohibiting such a practice. The court found that no absolute rule was necessary because a *Kastigar* hearing, requiring the government to prove that its evidence emanated from independent sources, was sufficient to protect the integrity of the process. Judge Merritt dissented:

> The simple fact that there was other independent uncompelled testimony upon which the same grand jury could indict the defendant does not, as the Court seems to think, show that the grand jury did not also use against him the compelled testimony. Not only must the government show that there was independent testimony upon which the grand jury could have acted; it must also demonstrate that the grand jury did not use any of the compelled testimony against the defendant. The court summarily dismisses the latter requirement and fails to negate the defendant's argument that members of the grand jury would naturally have used that part of his testimony which corroborated the government's case against him. Both the Fifth Amendment and the use immunity statute assure "that the compelled testimony *can in no way lead* to the infliction of criminal penalties."
>
> * * *
>
> By presenting incriminating evidence to the same grand jurors who previously heard defendant's compelled corroborative testimony, the defendant's right not to incriminate himself is presumptively violated.

5. While the court must issue the immunity order, this function has been described as "ministerial". The court may not review the prosecutor's decision to grant immunity; the primary purpose of a hearing on the question is to permit technical objections to compliance requirements. See In re Lochiatto, 497 F.2d 803 (1st Cir.1974). For an argument that the judge should have a meaningful role in the decision, see Wolfson, Immunity: How it Works in Real Life, 69 J.Crim.L. & Crim. 322 (1978). Moreover, a defendant has no standing to object to the granting of immunity to a witness against him. United States v. Braasch, 505 F.2d 139, 146 (7th Cir.1974); United States v. Neal, 743 F.2d 1441 (10th Cir.1984).

6. A corporation has no Fifth Amendment privilege against self-incrimination. Therefore, it cannot invoke the privilege as a defense to a subpoena for corporate records. Is there ever a justification, then, for granting a corporation immunity?

What practical considerations might lead a prosecutor to apply for such an immunity order? Should the law deem such reasons legitimate?

7. May a witness refuse to provide grand jury testimony under a grant of immunity, given by a United States District Court or by a state court, upon the ground that his testimony might be used against him in a criminal prosecution in a foreign country? A number of courts have suggested in dictum that they would recognize foreign incrimination possibilities as a defense to a contempt petition. Generally, however, the immunized witness is unsuccessful. In this context, courts seem to demand a showing of a *realistic* risk of foreign prosecution. Some also rely upon grand jury secrecy as a guard against disclosure to foreign officials of immunized testimony, recognizing that the accused's claim would be stronger if the testimony was to be given in open court. With respect to whether fear of foreign prosecution entitles a witness to invoke the fifth amendment at all, see United States v. Balsys, 119 F.3d 122 (2d Cir.1997), cert. granted, 522 U.S. 1072, 118 S.Ct. 751 (1998).

8. In Pillsbury Co. v. Conboy, 459 U.S. 248, 103 S.Ct. 608 (1983), the Court held that a witness in civil litigation can claim the fifth amendment privilege in response to questions which he answered under a grant of immunity during a criminal investigation. The Court did not reach the issue of whether it would be proper for a prosecutor to apply for a fresh grant of immunity for the witness in order to aid a civil litigant. Of course, if the previous immunized testimony had been given in open court subject to cross-examination by a criminal defendant, it is likely that the transcript would be admissible against that same defendant in a civil suit if the witness claimed the fifth amendment privilege during the civil litigation. See Fed.R.Evid. 804(a), (b)(1). In *Pillsbury* the immunized testimony had been given before a grand jury and not subject to cross-examination. Therefore the transcript could not be used in the civil litigation under the former testimony exception to the rule against hearsay.

Moreover, the hearsay rule does not prevent the use of a prior statement against one who is a party to a litigation. Thus if an individual receives a formal grant of immunity, or if he acquires use immunity by yielding to governmental requirements that he cooperate in an investigation, his protection extends only to criminal prosecution. His immunized testimony can be used against him in a civil matter. See In re Schwarz, 51 Ill.2d 334, 282 N.E.2d 689 (1972), where a lawyer testified against a defendant in a criminal trial and then was disbarred on the basis of the testimony which he had given under a grant of immunity. Sometimes prosecutors claim that immunity from prosecution is not enough to persuade certain witnesses to cooperate in an investigation. Should a judge be permitted to enter an order protecting a witness from loss of a liquor license or disbarment in return for testimony? Would this infringe upon the authority of other agencies? See In re Daley, 549 F.2d 469 (7th Cir.1977), where the reviewing court held that federal immunity statutes do not authorize entry of an order protecting an immunized attorney from use of his immunized testimony against him in a disbarment proceeding.

9. Sometimes persons who have acquired use plus derivative-use immunity complain about non-evidentiary uses of immunized testimony. For example, a defendant might argue that a prosecutor decided to launch a tax investigation against him only after reading the defendant's immunized testimony in which the defendant admitted commission of some wholly unrelated non-financial crime.

Concerning complaints about non-evidentiary use of immunized testimony, see United States v. Mariani, 851 F.2d 595 (2d Cir.1988), where a defendant claimed that the prosecutor's thought processes were shaped by the realization, arising from the nature of the immunized testimony, that the defendant strategically would be unable to testify in his own behalf at trial. While rejecting the Fifth Amendment claim, the court mentioned United States v. McDaniel, 482 F.2d 305 (8th Cir.1973), which raised the possibility that a defendant would be protected against some non-evidentiary uses of immunized testimony.

See also United States v. Rivieccio, 919 F.2d 812 (2d Cir.1990) (rejecting claim that Fifth Amendment prohibits use of immunized testimony to benefit the thought process of prosecutors, for example in calculating whether the defendant will testify at trial).

10. Witnesses sometimes refuse to testify under a grant of immunity because they allegedly fear for their safety or for the lives of their loved ones. Very few persons have avoided a contempt citation on that basis. Some cases, however, call for an evidentiary hearing concerning the genuineness of the alleged danger. See Matter of Grand Jury Proceedings Empanelled May 1988, 894 F.2d 881 (7th Cir.1989):

> We may assume also, without having to decide, that the government is not permitted to force a witness to risk his own life or the lives of his family by testifying if the government can obtain the same evidence from a safer source or wants this witness's testimony not for its evidentiary value but to terrify or endanger him, perhaps because it thinks he has not been punished enough by his criminal sentence. But we do not want to encourage contemnors to believe that it is easy to establish improper governmental purpose; it is not. Institutional purpose is an elusive concept, and contempt proceedings should not be side-tracked into investigations of prosecutorial motive.

11. In use-immunity jurisdictions, as, for example, the federal courts, a prosecutor can obtain use-immunity for a convicted defendant while that defendant's appeal is pending. United States v. Schwimmer, 882 F.2d 22 (2d Cir.1989); Garcia–Rosell v. United States, 889 F.2d 220 (9th Cir.1989). Prosecutors in transactional-immunity jurisdictions would not ordinarily immunize someone whose conviction is on appeal for fear of wiping out the conviction, although few decisions touch on that subject.

12. When an immunized witness breaches his immunity agreement by failing to testify truthfully, he is subject to prosecution for the underlying offense. See United States v. Crawford, 20 F.3d 933 (8th Cir.1994):

> It is well settled that immunity agreements are analogous to plea agreements and therefore may be enforced under the principles of contract law, within the context of constitutional safeguards for due process. Only a material breach is sufficient to excuse the government of its performance. "In determining whether a failure to render ... performance is material, the following circumstances are significant: ... the extent to which the injured party will be deprived of the benefit which he reasonably expected; ... the likelihood that the party failing to perform ... will cure his failure, taking account of all the circumstances; [and] ... the extent to which the behavior of the party failing to perform ... comports with standards of good faith and fair dealing."

Witnesses caught lying under immunity have raised the defense of materiality, claiming that the extent of the misrepresentation (usually by minimizing their own role) did not materially deceive the government. Compare United States v. Reed, 272 F.3d 950 (7th Cir.2001) with United States v. Fitch, 964 F.2d 571 (6th Cir.1992).

Garrity v. New Jersey

Supreme Court of the United States, 1967.
385 U.S. 493, 87 S.Ct. 616.

■ MR. JUSTICE DOUGLAS delivered the opinion of the Court.

Appellants were police officers in certain New Jersey boroughs. The Supreme Court of New Jersey ordered that alleged irregularities in handling cases in the municipal courts of those boroughs be investigated by the Attorney General, invested him with broad powers of inquiry and investigation, and directed him to make a report to the court. The matters investigated concerned alleged fixing of traffic tickets.

Before being questioned each appellant was warned (1) that anything he said might be used against him in any state criminal proceeding; (2) that he had the privilege to refuse to answer if the disclosure would tend to incriminate him; but (3) that if he refused to answer he would be subject to removal from office.[1]

Appellants answered the questions. No immunity was granted, as there is no immunity statute applicable in these circumstances. Over their objections, some of the answers given were used in a subsequent prosecution for conspiracy to obstruct the administration of the traffic laws. Appellants were convicted and their conviction was sustained over their protests that their statements were coerced, by reason of the fact that, if they refused to answer, they could lose their positions with the police department.

* * *

We agree with the New Jersey Supreme Court that the forfeiture of office statute is relevant here only for the bearing it has on the voluntary character of the statements used to convict appellants in their criminal prosecutions.

The choice imposed on appellants was one between self-incrimination or job forfeiture. Coercion that vitiates a confession . . . can be "mental as well as physical"; "the blood of the accused is not the only hallmark of an unconstitutional inquisition." Subtle pressures may be as telling as coarse and vulgar ones. The question is whether the accused was deprived of his "free choice to admit, to deny, or to refuse to answer."

We adhere to Boyd v. United States, 116 U.S. 616, 6 S.Ct. 524, a civil forfeiture action against property. A statute offered the owner an election

1. "Any person holding or who has held any elective or appointive public office, position or employment (whether State, county, or municipal), who refuses to testify upon matters relating to the office, position or employment in any criminal proceeding wherein he is a defendant or is called as a witness on behalf of the prosecution, upon the ground that his answer may tend to incriminate him or compel him to be a witness against himself or refuses to waive immunity when called by a grand jury to testify thereon or who willfully refuses or fails to appear before any court, commission or body of this state which has the right to inquire under oath upon matters relating to the office, position or employment of such person or who, having been sworn, refuses to testify or to answer any material question upon the ground that his answer may tend to incriminate him or compel him to be a witness against himself, shall, if holding elective or public office, position or employment, be removed therefrom or shall thereby forfeit his office, position or employment and any vested or future right of tenure or pension granted to him by any law of this State provided the inquiry relates to a matter which occurred or arose within the preceding five years. Any person so forfeiting his office, position or employment shall not thereafter be eligible for election or appointment to any public office, position or employment in this State." N.J.Rev.Stat. § 2A:81–17.1 (Supp.1965), N.J.S.A.

between producing a document or forfeiture of the goods at issue in the proceeding. This was held to be a form of compulsion in violation of both the Fifth Amendment and the Fourth Amendment.

The choice given appellants was either to forfeit their jobs or to incriminate themselves. The option to lose their means of livelihood or to pay the penalty of self-incrimination is the antithesis of free choice to speak out or to remain silent. That practice, like interrogation practices we reviewed in Miranda v. State of Arizona, is "likely to exert such pressure upon an individual as to disable him from making a free and rational choice." We think the confessions were infected by the coercion inherent in this scheme of questioning and cannot be sustained as voluntary under our prior decisions.

It is said that there was a "waiver." That, however, is a federal question for us to decide....

Where the choice is "between the rock and the whirlpool," duress is inherent in deciding to "waive" one or the other....

Mr. Justice Holmes, in McAuliffe v. New Bedford, 155 Mass. 216, 29 N.E. 517, stated a dictum on which New Jersey heavily relies:

> "The petitioner may have a constitutional right to talk politics, but he has no constitutional right to be a policeman. There are few employments for hire in which the servant does not agree to suspend his constitutional right of free speech as well as of idleness by the implied terms of his contract. The servant cannot complain, as he takes the employment on the terms which are offered him. On the same principle the city may impose any reasonable condition upon holding offices within its control."

The question in this case, however, is not cognizable in those terms. Our question is whether the Government, contrary to the requirement of the Fourteenth Amendment, can use the threat of discharge to secure incriminatory evidence against an employee.

We held in Slochower v. Board of Education, 350 U.S. 551, 76 S.Ct. 637, that a public school teacher could not be discharged merely because he had invoked the Fifth Amendment privilege against self-incrimination when questioned by a congressional committee:

> "The privilege against self-incrimination would be reduced to a hollow mockery if its exercise could be taken as equivalent either to a confession of guilt or a conclusive presumption of perjury.... The privilege serves to protect the innocent who otherwise might be ensnared by ambiguous circumstances."

We conclude that policemen, like teachers and lawyers, are not relegated to a watered-down version of constitutional rights.

There are rights of constitutional stature whose exercise a State may not condition by the exaction of a price.... We now hold the protection of the individual under the Fourteenth Amendment against coerced confessions prohibits use in subsequent criminal proceedings of confessions obtained under threat of removal from office, and that it extends to all, whether they are policemen or other members of our body politic.

Reversed.

■ MR. JUSTICE HARLAN, whom MR. JUSTICE CLARK and MR. JUSTICE STEWART join, dissenting.

* * *

I.

I turn first to the suggestion that these statements were involuntary in fact....

* * *

... The statements of the Bellmawr petitioners were taken in a room in the local firehouse, for which Chief Garrity himself had made arrangements. None of the petitioners were in custody before or after the depositions were taken; each apparently continued to pursue his ordinary duties as a public official of the community. The statements were recorded by a court stenographer, who testified that he witnessed no indications of unwillingness or even significant hesitation on the part of any of the petitioners. The Bellmawr petitioners did not have counsel present, but the Deputy Attorney General testified without contradiction that Garrity had informed him as they strolled between Garrity's office and the firehouse that he had arranged for counsel, but thought that none would be required at that stage. The interrogations were not excessively lengthy, and reasonable efforts were made to assure the physical comfort of the witnesses. Mrs. Naglee, the clerk of the Bellmawr municipal court, who was known to suffer from a heart ailment, was assured that questioning would cease if she felt any discomfort.

The circumstances in which the depositions of the Barrington petitioners were taken are less certain, for the New Jersey Supreme Court found that there was an informal agreement at the Barrington trial that the defendants would argue simply that the possibility of dismissal made the statements "involuntary as a matter of law." The defense did not contend that the statements were the result of physical or mental coercion, or that the wills of the Barrington petitioners were overborne. Accordingly, the State was never obliged to offer evidence of the voluntariness in fact of the statements. We are, however, informed that the three Barrington petitioners had counsel present as their depositions were taken....

As interrogation commenced, each of the petitioners was sworn, carefully informed that he need not give any information, reminded that any information given might be used in a subsequent criminal prosecution, and warned that as a police officer he was subject to a proceeding to discharge him if he failed to provide information relevant to his public responsibilities....

* * *

All of the petitioners testified at trial, and gave evidence essentially consistent with the statements taken from them. At a preliminary hearing conducted at the Bellmawr trial to determine the voluntariness of the statements, the Bellmawr petitioners offered no evidence beyond proof of the warning given them.

The standards employed by the Court to assess the voluntariness of an accused's statements have reflected a number of values, and thus have emphasized a variety of factual criteria. The criteria employed have included threats of imminent danger, physical deprivations, repeated or extended interrogation, limits on access to counsel or friends, length and illegality of detention under state law, individual weakness or incapacities, and the adequacy of warnings of constitutional rights. Whatever the criteria employed, the duty of the Court has been "to examine the entire record," and thereby to determine whether the accused's will "was overborne by the sustained pressures upon him."

It would be difficult to imagine interrogations to which these criteria of duress were more completely inapplicable, or in which the requirements which have subsequently been imposed by this Court on police questioning were more thoroughly satisfied. Each of the petitioners received a complete and explicit reminder of his constitutional privilege. Three of the petitioners had counsel present; at least a fourth had consulted counsel but freely determined that his presence was unnecessary. These petitioners were not in any fashion "swept from familiar surroundings into police custody, surrounded by antagonistic forces, and subjected to the techniques of persuasion...." Miranda v. State of Arizona. I think it manifest that, under the standards developed by this Court to assess voluntariness, there is no basis for saying that any of these statements were made involuntarily.

The issue remaining is whether the statements were inadmissible because they were "involuntary as a matter of law," in that they were given after a warning that New Jersey policemen may be discharged for failure to provide information pertinent to their public responsibilities. What is really involved on this score, however, is not in truth a question of "voluntariness" at all, but rather whether the condition imposed by the State on the exercise of the privilege against self-incrimination, namely dismissal from office, in this instance serves in itself to render the statements inadmissible. Absent evidence of involuntariness in fact, the admissibility of these statements thus hinges on the validity of the consequence which the State acknowledged might have resulted if the statements had not been given. If the consequence is constitutionally permissible, there can surely be no objection if the State cautions the witness that it may follow if he remains silent. If both the consequence and the warning are constitutionally permissible, a witness is obliged, in order to prevent the use of his statements against him in a criminal prosecution, to prove under the standards established since Brown v. State of Mississippi that as a matter of fact the statements were involuntarily made. The central issues here are therefore identical to those presented in Spevack v. Klein, whether consequences may properly be permitted to result to a claimant after his invocation of the constitutional privilege, and if so, whether the consequence in question is permissible. For reasons which I have stated in Spevack v. Klein, in my view nothing in the logic or purposes of the privilege demands that all consequences which may result from a witness' silence be forbidden merely because that silence is privileged. The validity of a consequence depends both upon the hazards, if any, it presents to the integrity of the privilege and upon the urgency of the public interests it is designed to protect.

* * *

I would affirm the judgments of the Supreme Court of New Jersey.

NOTE

In Clymer, Compelled Statements from Police Officers and Garrity Immunity, 76 N.Y.U.L. Rev 1309 (2001), Professor Clymer argues that the importance of internal investigations in police departments should lead the courts to relax prohibitions on the collateral uses of compelled statements:

> Absent judicial limitations on the scope of Garrity, legislatures and police departments can and should modify policies and practices surrounding the acquisition and use of compelled statements in internal affairs investigations. Instead of compelling statements by threatening job loss, statutes and departmental policies should encourage cooperation by notifying suspect police officers that a refusal to answer questions will have evidentiary significance in administrative adjudicatory proceedings. This should permit prosecutors to make full use of any resulting statements. Alternatively, legislatures and police departments can and should impose constraints on dissemination of compelled statements.

Will these policy changes comply with the fifth amendment protections afforded by Garrity?

Gardner v. Broderick

Supreme Court of the United States, 1968.
392 U.S. 273, 88 S.Ct. 1913.

■ MR. JUSTICE FORTAS delivered the opinion of the Court.

Appellant brought this action in the Supreme Court of the State of New York seeking reinstatement as a New York City patrolman and back pay. He claimed he was unlawfully dismissed because he refused to waive his privilege against self-incrimination. In August 1965, pursuant to subpoena, appellant appeared before a New York County grand jury which was investigating alleged bribery and corruption of police officers in connection with unlawful gambling operations. He was advised that the grand jury proposed to examine him concerning the performance of his official duties. He was advised of his privilege against self-incrimination[1] but he was asked to sign a "waiver of immunity" after being told that he would be fired if he did not sign.[2] Following his refusal, he was given an administrative hearing

1. The Assistant District Attorney said to appellant:

> "You understand ... that under the Constitution of the United States, as well as the Constitution of New York, no one can be compelled to testify against himself, and that he has a right, the absolute right to refuse to answer any questions that would tend to incriminate him?"

2. Appellant was told:

> "You understand ... that under the Constitution of the United States, as the Charter of the City of New York, ... a public officer, which includes a police

and was discharged solely for this refusal, pursuant to § 1123 of the New York City Charter.

* * *

Our decisions establish beyond dispute the breadth of the privilege to refuse to respond to questions when the result may be self-incriminatory and the need fully to implement its guaranty.... The privilege is applicable to state as well as federal proceedings.... The privilege may be waived in appropriate circumstances if the waiver is knowingly and voluntarily made. Answers may be compelled regardless of the privilege if there is immunity from federal and state use of the compelled testimony or its fruits in connection with a criminal prosecution against the person testifying....

The question presented in the present case is whether a policeman who refuses to waive the protections which the privilege gives him may be dismissed from office because of that refusal.

About a year and a half after New York City discharged petitioner for his refusal to waive this immunity, we decided Garrity v. State of New Jersey (1967)....

The New York Court of Appeals considered that *Garrity* did not control the present case. It is true that *Garrity* related to the attempted use of compelled testimony. It did not involve the precise question which is presented here: namely, whether a State may discharge an officer for refusing to waive a right which the Constitution guarantees to him. The New York Court of Appeals also distinguished our post-*Garrity* decision in Spevack v. Klein. In *Spevack*, we ruled that a lawyer could not be disbarred solely because he refused to testify at a disciplinary proceeding on the ground that his testimony would tend to incriminate him. The Court of Appeals concluded that *Spevack* does not control the present case because different considerations apply in the case of a public official such as a policeman. A lawyer, it stated, although licensed by the state is not an employee. This distinction is now urged upon us. It is argued that although a lawyer could not constitutionally be confronted with Hobson's choice between self-incrimination and forfeiting his means of livelihood, the same principle should not protect a policeman. Unlike the lawyer, he is directly, immediately, and entirely responsible to the city or State which is his employer. He owes his entire loyalty to it. He has no other "client" or

officer, when called before a Grand Jury to answer questions concerning the conduct of his public office and the performance of his duties is required to sign a waiver of immunity if he wishes to retain that public office?"

The document appellant was asked to sign was phrased as follows:

"I ... do hereby waive all benefits, privileges, rights and immunity which I would otherwise obtain from indictment, prosecution, and punishment for or on account of, regarding or relating to any matter, transaction or things, concerning the conduct of my office or the performance of my official duties, or the property, government or affairs of the State of New York or of any county included within its territorial limits, or the nomination, election, appointment or official conduct of any officer of the city or of any such county, concerning any of which matters, transactions or things I may testify or produce evidence documentary or otherwise, before the [blank] Grand Jury in the County of New York in the investigation being conducted by said Grand Jury."

principal. He is a trustee of the public interest, bearing the burden of great and total responsibility to his public employer. Unlike the lawyer who is directly responsible to his client, the policeman is either responsible to the State or to no one.

We agree that these factors differentiate the situations. If appellant, a policeman, had refused to answer questions specifically, directly, and narrowly relating to the performance of his official duties, without being required to waive his immunity with respect to the use of his answers or the fruits thereof in a criminal prosecution of himself, ... the privilege against self-incrimination would not have been a bar to his dismissal.

The facts of this case, however, do not present this issue. Here, petitioner was summoned to testify before a grand jury in an investigation of alleged criminal conduct. He was discharged from office, not for failure to answer relevant questions about his official duties, but for refusal to waive a constitutional right. He was dismissed for failure to relinquish the protections of the privilege against self-incrimination. The Constitution of New York State and the City Charter both expressly provided that his failure to do so, as well as his failure to testify, would result in dismissal from his job. He was dismissed solely for his refusal to waive the immunity to which he is entitled if he is required to testify despite his constitutional privilege.

We need not speculate whether, if appellant had executed the waiver of immunity in the circumstances, the effect of our subsequent decision in Garrity v. State of New Jersey, supra, would have been to nullify the effect of the waiver. New York City discharged him for refusal to execute a document purporting to waive his constitutional rights and to permit prosecution of himself on the basis of his compelled testimony. Petitioner could not have assumed—and certainly he was not required to assume—that he was being asked to do an idle act of no legal effect. In any event, the mandate of the great privilege against self-incrimination does not tolerate the attempt, regardless of its ultimate effectiveness, to coerce a waiver of the immunity it confers on penalty of the loss of employment. It is clear that petitioner's testimony was demanded before the grand jury in part so that it might be used to prosecute him, and not solely for the purpose of securing an accounting of his performance of his public trust. If the latter had been the only purpose, there would have been no reason to seek to compel petitioner to waive his immunity. Proper regard for the history and meaning of the privilege against self-incrimination, ... dictate the conclusion that the provision of the New York City Charter pursuant to which petitioner was dismissed cannot stand. Accordingly, the judgment is reversed.

Reversed.

■ MR. JUSTICE BLACK concurs in the result.

NOTES

1. The meaning of Garrity was debated in Minnesota v. Murphy, 465 U.S. 420, 104 S.Ct. 1136 (1984). Under terms of his probation following conviction of criminal sexual conduct, Murphy was required to report to his probation officer as directed and to be truthful to the probation officer in all matters. The probation officer learned of admissions made by Murphy concerning an earlier murder. She asked that he contact her concerning the remainder of his probationary period. When they met in a non-custodial setting, she questioned him about the murder, intending to report any admissions to the police. He made statements to her which were used in a subsequent murder prosecution.

Through Justice White, the Court held that ordinarily questioning in a non-custodial setting does not violate the Fifth Amendment unless the individual expressly invokes the privilege and is nevertheless directed to answer. The Court emphasized that the Minnesota probation scheme did not expressly or by implication provide that probation would be revoked if the probationer refused to answer (as distinguished from answering falsely). It added that Murphy was not told orally before questioning that refusal to answer would result in the revocation of probation. Justice White noted that Garrity had been informed of the "penalty" for refusal to answer immediately before he was questioned. The majority also emphasized that Murphy did not establish that the actual (subjective) reason he answered the probation officer was because of fear of the penalty of revocation if he refused.

Led by Justice Marshall, the three dissenting justices asserted that, as in *Garrity*, the individual should not be required to prove why he answered the questions. Government cannot put the citizen to the impermissible choice of suffering a penalty if he refuses to respond to incriminating questions. Marshall focused upon the majority's claim that the admonition to be truthful in all matters did not tell the suspect that he must answer all questions. He called this interpretation "simply incredible."

2. Does Gardner v. Broderick permit a police department to immunize its officers from criminal prosecution by requiring them to answer questions concerning their conduct while on duty—for instance, a case involving the questionable shooting of a citizen? Granted that after *Kastigar* the immunity provided in such a situation would probably be use immunity rather than transactional immunity, the burden would still be on the prosecution to show that none of its evidence is derived from the "compelled" testimony given by the officer under threat of loss of job if the self-incrimination privilege is invoked in an official police internal investigation. Would the prosecution do better to refuse to examine the internal investigation reports for fear of tainting a criminal prosecution? Is this solution practical?

Ward v. City of Portland, 857 F.2d 1373 (9th Cir.1988), involved a police department regulation which required officers involved in a fatal shooting to prepare an incident report before consulting counsel. In the course of upholding the regulation, the court noted that an officer's incident report could not be used against the officer in any criminal prosecution of the officer.

An excellent example of the way a government employee may maneuver in order to get use-immunity and possibly taint an investigation is found in Benjamin v. Montgomery, 785 F.2d 959 (11th Cir.1986). The employee who is more concerned about a possible criminal prosecution than about his or her government job may actually wish to disclose information under a grant of immunity. The employee will refuse to do so until he or she is ordered by the employer to make disclosures. The employee will note, at the time of the disclosure, that the information is being divulged under the compulsion of the directive from the government employer. If prosecutors subsequently charge the employee, they will bear the burden of showing that prosecution evidence was not derived from the compelled disclosures.

3. The *Gardner* solution to a difficult Fifth Amendment problem, permitting the compulsion of testimony upon the promise that it may not be used, is one example of the "use exclusion" doctrine which had its origins in Murphy v. Waterfront Commission, 378 U.S. 52, 84 S.Ct. 1594 (1964). There a state investigative agency granted a witness immunity from state prosecution. The witness claimed that he still had a right to invoke the Fifth Amendment because his answers could subject him to prosecution under federal law. In upholding the statute, the Court prohibited the subsequent use by federal authorities of the testimony thus compelled.

In *Murphy* a state authority was, in effect, permitted to give use-immunity in federal prosecutions. In *Gardner* police administrators were empowered to give police officers use-immunity by requiring the officers to cooperate with internal investigations. Carried to absurdity, the use-exclusion doctrine would permit any judge to order a witness to testify over Fifth Amendment objections on the theory that testimony given under such an order, and evidence derived from such testimony, could not be used against him in any future prosecution. The fallacy is that the procedure would permit a grant of immunity without specific statutory authorization and, in many instances, without any prosecutorial participation in the decision to grant immunity. See Ellis v. United States, 416 F.2d 791 (D.C.Cir.1969), where the reviewing court held that a district judge who compelled testimony using such reasoning created "a circular self-fulfilling prophecy." The Court said that such compulsion "can only be viewed as a grant of immunity." It further declared that, absent a statute authorizing immunity and absent a prosecutorial request, the district court's order compelling testimony was "outside the scope of judicial authority."

4. Historically grants of immunity have been given only where (1) a statute specifically authorizing immunity exists, and (2) the prosecutor of the jurisdiction in question has exercised his discretion to seek judicial approval of a grant of immunity.

Use-exclusion is often proposed as a method of upholding statutory schemes which arguably compel a person to give testimony against himself. In California v. Byers, 402 U.S. 424, 91 S.Ct. 1535 (1971), a "stop and report" law applicable to motorists involved in auto accidents was challenged. One possible solution was to uphold enforcement of the statute but to prohibit use in any criminal case of evidence derived from compliance by a motorist. The Supreme Court rejected this solution, finding no Fifth Amendment violation. Nothing in the statute suggested that the California legislature had intended to make enforcement of penal provisions of its traffic code more difficult by granting use immunity to motorists who complied with the "stop and report" provision. See also Marchetti v. United States, 390 U.S. 39, 88 S.Ct. 697 (1968), where, in striking down certain gambling registration requirements, the Court refused to "save" the federal statute by creating a use immunity doctrine which would have made state gambling prosecutions more difficult. The statute was intended to do just the opposite. Thus in both *Byers*, where the statute was upheld, and in *Marchetti*, where the statute was struck down, the Court avoided the tempting middle ground of use-immunity and made the hard decision whether the statute violated the Fifth Amendment privilege. To have done otherwise would have been to create a situation where use immunity might be acquired absent specific statutory authority and absent any prosecutorial participation in the decision to grant immunity.

Generally the Court has condemned statutes requiring disclosures only when the disclosures have been extracted from a highly selective group inherently suspect of criminal activities. Moreover, it has upheld the claim of privilege only in areas permeated with criminal statutes.

5. In Lefkowitz v. Turley, 414 U.S. 70, 94 S.Ct. 316 (1973), the Supreme Court voided a statute which prohibited any person who refused to waive immunity in a grand jury investigation from obtaining public contracts for a period of five years. A majority of the court suggested that the statute would have been proper if it provided use immunity for the contractor who raised a Fifth Amendment claim before the grand jury.

How is a statute like the one in *Turley* affected by the proposition that a corporation has no protection against self-incrimination under the Fifth and Fourteenth Amendments?

In Lefkowitz v. Cunningham, 431 U.S. 801, 97 S.Ct. 2132 (1977), the Supreme Court invalidated a New York statute which provided for forfeiture of political party office by officeholders who invoked the fifth amendment privilege during a grand jury investigation related to their conduct in office. Again the Court suggested that such forfeiture would be permissible if the statutory scheme provided use-immunity for the party officeholder who is compelled to testify.

6. In Selective Service System v. Minnesota Public Interest Research Group, 468 U.S. 841, 104 S.Ct. 3348 (1984), the Court sustained a statute which denied federal education funds to those who had not registered for the draft. The Court found no evidence of a penalty invoked for assertion of privilege nor of a refusal to grant immunity at such time as the students sought to register for the draft. Nor did *Marchetti* apply because failure to register was not necessarily criminal—a knowing failure had to be proved. Dissenters argued that while the statute does not require an admission of non-registration it did coerce registration and, thereby, a concession of previous non-registration; because the statute did not provide immunity it was invalid. Justice Marshall claimed that the right of a student to claim privilege about incriminating facts, e.g., date of birth, when seeking a late registration was of no value. "It would be just as incriminating ... to exercise their privilege ... when they registered as it would be to fill out the [draft] form without exercising the privilege."

Does this argument make sense? The assertion of the self-incrimination privilege may well be an admission that someone has something to hide and the probative value of an assertion of the privilege is subject to debate. At the least it may alert the government that the claimant ought to be investigated. On the other hand, courts have always required that grounds for privilege be asserted to prevent abuse of privilege and it is difficult to conceive how one could assert a self-incrimination privilege without saying so—"I refuse to answer because of a privilege and I refuse to say why because of that same privilege." If such an answer could be asserted for all privileges then abuse of privilege would be beyond control. If it could be asserted only for self-incrimination then the cat is still let out of the bag. Would it be proper to preclude the government from ever investigating anyone who claimed self-incrimination privileges unless they had, prior to assertion, been subjects of investigation or at least known to the government?

7. In McKune v. Lile, 536 U.S. 24, 122 S.Ct. 2017 (2002), a convicted sex offender was required to disclose his sexual history, regardless of whether it involves uncharged offenses, in order to be admitted to a mandatory sexual abuse treatment program. Failure to disclose would result in the loss of certain privileges, including visitation rights, earnings and work opportunities. In a 5–4 decision, the Court held that a prison clinical rehabilitation program which bears a rational relationship to a legitimate penological objective does not violate the privilege against compelled self incrimination if the adverse consequences an inmate faces for not participating are related to the program objectives and do not impose atypical hardships in the context of prison life. Justice O'Connor, who supplied the pivotal vote, noted that the penalty imposed for compelled incrimination was the determining factor and, unlike the loss of employment, loss of livelihood and loss of right to participate in political associations, as in prior case, the restrictions on prison living conditions are minor. Justice Stevens, for the four dissenters, argued that the practical consequences to the inmate were far more serious than the plurality acknowledged and concluded that inmates should not be compelled to forfeit the privilege because the ends of the rehabilitative program are legitimate.

3. BOOKS AND RECORDS

Braswell v. United States

Supreme Court of the United States, 1988.
487 U.S. 99, 108 S.Ct. 2284.

■ CHIEF JUSTICE REHNQUIST delivered the opinion of the Court.

[A federal grand jury issued a subpoena to the president of two corporations, requiring him to produce the corporations' books and records. The president was the sole shareholder of one corporation, which he had funded with his 100 percent interest in the other corporation. The district court denied the president's motion to quash the subpoenas, ruling that the "collective entity doctrine," under which corporations and other collective entities are treated differently from individuals for purposes of the Fifth Amendment, prevented the president from asserting that his act of producing the corporations' records was protected by the Fifth Amendment.]

* * *

There is no question but that the contents of the subpoenaed business records are not privileged. Similarly, petitioner asserts no self-incrimination claim on behalf of the corporations; it is well established that such artificial entities are not protected by the Fifth Amendment. Petitioner instead relies solely upon the argument that his act of producing the documents has independent testimonial significance, which would incriminate him individually, and that the Fifth Amendment prohibits Government compulsion of that act. The bases for this argument are extrapolated from the decisions of this Court in [Fisher v. United States (1976) and United States v. Doe (1984).]

In Fisher, the Court was presented with the question whether an attorney may resist a subpoena demanding that he produce tax records which had been entrusted to him by his client. The records in question had been prepared by the client's accountants. In analyzing the Fifth Amendment claim forwarded by the attorney, the Court considered whether the client-taxpayer would have had a valid Fifth Amendment claim had he retained the records and the subpoena been issued to him. After explaining that the Fifth Amendment prohibits "compelling a person to give 'testimony' that incriminates him," the Court rejected the argument that the contents of the records were protected. The Court, however, went on to observe:

> "The act of producing evidence in response to a subpoena nevertheless has communicative aspects of its own, wholly aside from the contents of the papers produced. Compliance with the subpoena tacitly concedes the existence of the papers demanded and their possession or control by the taxpayer. It also would indicate the taxpayer's belief that the papers are those described in the subpoena. The elements of compulsion are clearly present, but the more difficult issues are whether the tacit averments of the

> taxpayer are both 'testimonial' and 'incriminating' for purposes of applying the Fifth Amendment. These questions perhaps do not lend themselves to categorical answers; their resolution may instead depend on the facts and circumstances of particular cases or classes thereof."

The Court concluded that under the "facts and circumstances" there presented, the act of producing the accountants' papers would not "involve testimonial self-incrimination."

Eight years later, in United States v. Doe, supra, the Court revisited the question, this time in the context of a claim by a sole proprietor that the compelled production of business records would run afoul of the Fifth Amendment. After rejecting the contention that the contents of the records were themselves protected, the Court proceeded to address whether respondent's act of producing the records would constitute protected testimonial incrimination. The Court concluded that respondent had established a valid Fifth Amendment claim. It deferred to the lower courts, which had found that enforcing the subpoenas at issue would provide the Government valuable information: By producing the records, respondent would admit that the records existed, were in his possession, and were authentic.

Had petitioner conducted his business as a sole proprietorship, Doe would require that he be provided the opportunity to show that his act of production would entail testimonial self-incrimination. But petitioner has operated his business through the corporate form, and we have long recognized that, for purposes of the Fifth Amendment, corporations and other collective entities are treated differently from individuals. This doctrine—known as the collective entity rule—has a lengthy and distinguished pedigree.

The rule was first articulated by the Court in the case of Hale v. Henkel (1906). Hale, a corporate officer, had been served with a subpoena ordering him to produce corporate records and to testify concerning certain corporate transactions. Although Hale was protected by personal immunity, he sought to resist the demand for the records by interposing a Fifth Amendment privilege on behalf of the corporation. The Court rejected that argument: "[W]e are of the opinion that there is a clear distinction ... between an individual and a corporation, and ... the latter has no right to refuse to submit its books and papers for an examination at the suit of the State." The Court explained that the corporation "is a creature of the State," with powers limited by the State. As such, the State may, in the exercise of its right to oversee the corporation, demand the production of corporate records.

The ruling in Hale represented a limitation on the prior holding in Boyd v. United States (1886), which involved a court order directing partners to produce an invoice received by the partnership. The partners had produced the invoice, but steadfastly maintained that the court order ran afoul of the Fifth Amendment. This Court agreed.... "[A] compulsory production of the *private* books and papers of the owner of goods sought to be forfeited ... is compelling him to be a witness against himself, within the meaning of the Fifth Amendment to the Constitution...." Hale carved an exception out of Boyd by establishing that corporate books and records are not "private papers" protected by the Fifth Amendment.

Although Hale settled that a corporation has no Fifth Amendment privilege, the Court did not address whether a corporate officer could resist a subpoena for corporate records by invoking his personal privilege—Hale had been protected by immunity. In Wilson v. United States (1911), the Court answered that question in the negative. There, a grand jury investigating Wilson had issued a subpoena to a corporation demanding the production of corporate letterpress copy books, which Wilson, the corporation's president, possessed. Wilson refused to produce the books, arguing that the Fifth Amendment prohibited compulsory production of personally incriminating books that he held and controlled. The Court rejected this argument, observing first that the records sought were not private or personal, but rather belonged to the corporation. The Court continued:

> "[Wilson] held the corporate books subject to the corporate duty. If the corporation were guilty of misconduct, he could not withhold its books to save it; and if he were implicated in the violations of law, he could not withhold the books to protect himself from the effect of their disclosures."

* * *

The next significant step in the development of the collective entity rule occurred in United States v. White (1944), in which the Court held that a labor union is a collective entity unprotected by the Fifth Amendment. There, a grand jury had issued a subpoena addressed to a union requiring the production of certain union records. White, an assistant supervisor of the union, appeared before the grand jury and declined to produce the documents " 'upon the ground that they might tend to incriminate [the union], myself as an officer thereof, or individually.' "

We upheld an order of contempt against White, reasoning first that the Fifth Amendment privilege applies only to natural individuals and protects only private papers. Representatives of a "collective group" act as agents "[a]nd the official records and documents of the organization that are held by them in a representative rather than in a personal capacity cannot be the subject of the personal privilege against self-incrimination, even though production of the papers might tend to incriminate them personally."

* * *

In applying the collective entity rule to unincorporated associations such as unions, the Court jettisoned reliance on the visitatorial powers of the State over corporations owing their existence to the State—one of the bases for earlier decisions.

The frontiers of the collective entity rule were expanded even further in Bellis v. United States, (1974), in which the Court ruled that a partner in a small partnership could not properly refuse to produce partnership records.

* * *

The plain mandate of these decisions is that without regard to whether the subpoena is addressed to the corporation, or as here, to the individual in his capacity as a custodian, a corporate custodian such as petitioner may not resist a subpoena for corporate records on Fifth Amendment grounds. Petitioner argues, however, that this rule falls in the wake of Fisher. In essence, petitioner's argument is as follows: In response to Boyd with its privacy rationale shielding personal books and records, the Court developed the collective entity rule, which declares simply that corporate records are not private and therefore are not protected by the Fifth Amendment. The collective entity decisions were concerned with the contents of the documents subpoenaed, however, and not with the act of production. In Fisher and Doe, the Court moved away from the privacy-based collective entity rule, replacing it with a compelled-testimony standard under which the contents of business documents are never privileged but the act of producing the documents may be. Under this new regime, the act of production privilege is available without regard to the entity whose records are being sought.

* * *

To be sure, the holding in Fisher—later reaffirmed in Doe—embarked upon a new course of Fifth Amendment analysis. We cannot agree, however, that it rendered the collective entity rule obsolete. The agency rationale undergirding the collective entity decisions, in which custodians asserted that production of entity records would incriminate them personally, survives. The Court has consistently recognized that the custodian of corporate or entity records holds those documents in a representative rather than a personal capacity. Artificial entities such as corporations may act only through their agents and a custodian's assumption of his representative capacity leads to certain obligations, including the duty to produce corporate records on proper demand by the Government. Under those circumstances, the custodian's act of production is not deemed a personal act, but rather an act of the corporation. Any claim of Fifth Amendment privilege asserted by the agent would be tantamount to a claim of privilege by the corporation—which of course possesses no such privilege.

* * *

Thus, whether one concludes ... that a custodian's production of corporate records is deemed not to constitute testimonial self-incrimination, or instead that a custodian waives the right to exercise the privilege, the lesson of Fisher is clear: A custodian may not resist a subpoena for corporate records on Fifth Amendment grounds.

* * *

We note further that recognizing a Fifth Amendment privilege on behalf of the records custodians of collective entities would have a detrimental impact on the Government's efforts to prosecute "white-collar crime," one of the most serious problems confronting law enforcement authorities. "The greater portion of evidence of wrongdoing by an organization or its representatives is usually found in the official records and documents of that organization. Were the cloak of the privilege to be thrown around these impersonal records and documents, effective enforcement of many federal and state laws would be impossible." If custodians could assert a privilege, authorities would be stymied not only in their enforcement efforts against those individuals but also in their prosecutions of organizations.

* * *

Petitioner suggests, however, that these concerns can be minimized by the simple expedient of either granting the custodian statutory immunity as to the act of production, or addressing the subpoena to the corporation and allowing it to choose an agent to produce the records who can do so without incriminating himself. We think neither proposal satisfactorily addresses these concerns. Taking the last first, it is no doubt true that if a subpoena is addressed to a corporation, the corporation "must find some means by which to comply because no Fifth Amendment defense is available to it." The means most commonly used to comply is the appointment of an alternate custodian. But petitioner insists he cannot be required to aid the appointed custodian in his search for the demanded records, for any statement to the surrogate would itself be testimonial and incriminating. If this is correct, then petitioner's "solution" is a chimera. In situations such as this—where the corporate custodian is likely the only person with knowledge about the demanded documents—the appointment of a surrogate will simply not ensure that the documents sought will ever reach the grand jury room; the appointed custodian will essentially be sent on an unguided search.

This problem is eliminated if the Government grants the subpoenaed custodian statutory immunity for the testimonial aspects of his act of production. But that "solution" also entails a significant drawback. All of the evidence obtained under a grant of immunity to the custodian may of course be used freely against the corporation, but if the Government has any thought of prosecuting the custodian, a grant of act of production immunity can have serious consequences. Testimony obtained pursuant to a grant of statutory use immunity may be used neither directly nor derivatively. And "[o]ne raising a claim under [the federal immunity] statute need only show that he testified under a grant of immunity in order to shift to the government the heavy burden of proving that all of the evidence it proposes to use was derived from legitimate independent sources." Even in cases where the Government does not employ the immunized testimony for any purpose—direct or derivative—against the witness, the Government's inability to meet the "heavy burden" it bears may result in the preclusion of crucial evidence that was obtained legitimately.

Although a corporate custodian is not entitled to resist a subpoena on the ground that his act of production will be personally incriminating, we do think certain consequences flow from the fact that the custodian's act of production is one in his representative rather than personal capacity. Because the custodian acts as a representative, the act is deemed one of the corporation and not the individual. Therefore, the Government concedes, as it must, that it may make no evidentiary use of the "individual act" against the individual. For example, in a criminal prosecution against the custodian, the Government may not introduce into evidence before the jury the fact that the subpoena was served upon and the corporation's documents were delivered by one particular individual, the custodian. The Government has the right, however, to use the corporation's act of production against the custodian. The Government may offer testimony—for example, from the process server who delivered the subpoena and from the individual who received the records—establishing that the corporation produced the records subpoenaed. The jury may draw from the corporation's act of production the conclusion that the records in question are authentic corporate records, which the corporation possessed, and which it produced in response to the subpoena. And if the defendant held a prominent position within the corporation that produced the records, the jury may, just as it would had someone else produced the documents, reasonably infer that he had possession of the documents or knowledge of their contents. Because the jury is not told that the defendant produced the records, any nexus between the defendant and the documents results solely from the corporation's act of production and other evidence in the case.

* * *

The judgment is therefore affirmed.

■ JUSTICE KENNEDY, with whom JUSTICE BRENNAN, JUSTICE MARSHALL, and JUSTICE SCALIA join, dissenting.

Our long course of decisions concerning artificial entities and the Fifth Amendment served us well. It illuminated two of the critical foundations for the constitutional guarantee against self-incrimination: first, that it is an explicit right of a natural person, protecting the realm of human thought and expression; second, that it is confined to governmental compulsion.

The Court today denies an individual his Fifth Amendment privilege against self-incrimination in order to vindicate the rule that a collective entity which employs him has no such privilege itself. To reach this ironic conclusion, the majority must blur an analytic clarity in Fifth Amendment doctrine that has taken almost a century to emerge. After holding that corporate employment strips the individual of his privilege, the Court then attempts to restore some measure of protection by its judicial creation of a new zone of immunity in some vaguely defined circumstances. This exercise admits what the Court denied in the first place, namely, that compelled compliance with the subpoena implicates the Fifth Amendment self-incrimination privilege.

The majority's apparent reasoning is that collective entities have no privilege and so their employees must have none either. The Court holds that a corporate agent must incriminate himself even when he is named in the subpoena and is a target of the investigation, and even when it is conceded that compliance requires compelled, personal, testimonial, incriminating assertions. I disagree with that conclusion; find no precedent for it; maintain that if there is a likelihood of personal self-incrimination the narrow use immunity permitted by statute can be granted without frustrating the investigation of collective entities; and submit that basic Fifth

Amendment principles should not be avoided and manipulated, which is the necessary effect of this decision.

There is some common ground in this case. All accept the longstanding rule that labor unions, corporations, partnerships, and other collective entities have no Fifth Amendment self-incrimination privilege; that a natural person cannot assert such a privilege on their behalf; and that the contents of business records prepared without compulsion can be used to incriminate even a natural person without implicating Fifth Amendment concerns. Further, all appear to concede or at least submit the case to us on the assumption that the act of producing the subpoenaed documents will effect personal incrimination of Randy Braswell, the individual to whom the subpoena is directed.

* * *

While a custodian has no necessary relation to the contents of documents within his control, the act of production is inescapably his own. Production is the precise act compelled by the subpoena, and obedience, in some cases, will require the custodian's own testimonial assertions.

* * *

The question before us is not the existence of the collective entity rule, but whether it contains any principle which overrides the personal Fifth Amendment privilege of someone compelled to give incriminating testimony. Our precedents establish a firm basis for assertion of the privilege. Randy Braswell, like the respondent in Doe I, is being asked to draw upon his personal knowledge to identify and to deliver documents which are responsive to the Government's subpoena. Once the Government concedes there are testimonial consequences implicit in the act of production, it cannot escape the conclusion that compliance with the subpoena is indisputably Braswell's own act. To suggest otherwise "is to confuse metaphor with reality."

* * *

The law is not captive to its own fictions. Yet, in the matter before us the Court employs the fiction that personal incrimination of the employee is neither sought by the Government nor cognizable by the law. That is a regrettable holding, for the conclusion is factually unsound, unnecessary for legitimate regulation, and a violation of the Self–Incrimination Clause of the Fifth Amendment of the Constitution. For these reasons, I dissent.

NOTES

1. In Fisher v. United States, 425 U.S. 391, 96 S.Ct. 1569 (1976), a taxpayer had turned over to his attorney certain papers which had been prepared by the taxpayer's accountant. A subpoena issued to compel the attorney to produce the papers. The Supreme Court declared that a subpoena which does not compel the client (as distinguished from his or her attorney) to do anything does not violate the client's Fifth Amendment rights. The Court went on to determine whether the subpoena violated the attorney-client privilege. It recognized that if papers which were protected by the Fifth Amendment in the hands of the client were turned over to the attorney within the scope of the attorney-client relationship, a subpoena against the attorney could violate the attorney-client privilege. On the other hand, the Court reasoned, if the papers were not privileged in the hands of the client (and therefore could be reached by a subpoena to the client), the attorney-client privilege was not violated. The Court then considered whether the papers would have been privileged in the hands of the taxpayer. It held that the papers would not have been protected by the Fifth Amendment if a subpoena had issued against the taxpayer himself while the papers were still in his hands, reasoning that the taxpayer had not been compelled to create the papers in the first instance but rather did so voluntarily. It added that the papers were actually created by the accountant and not by the client.

The Court reserved the question of whether a different result would follow if the records had been personal writings or other documents personally created by the taxpayer. Finally, the Court noted that although the act of producing papers in response to a subpoena in a sense has testimonial aspects (in that the taxpayer is admitting the existence of the papers), those aspects do not seem to be significant enough to be within the Fifth Amendment protection against testimonial compulsion. The Court especially noted that the government did not intend to rely upon the act of producing the records as a means of "authenticating" the records for use at trial.

Fisher was significant because it expressly rejected broad language in Boyd v. United States, 116 U.S. 616, 6 S.Ct. 524 (1886), which has provided a Fifth Amendment defense to the production of records in response to a subpoena duces tecum. The Court left for another day the issue of what records or other writings, if any, will remain protected by the Fifth Amendment. See, Gerstein, The Demise of Boyd: Self–Incrimination and Private Papers in the Burger Court, 27 U.C.L.A.L.Rev. 343 (1979). Note, The Rights of Criminal Defendants and the Subpoena Duces Tecum: The Aftermath of Fisher v. United States, 95 Harv.L.Rev. 683, 692–94 (1982). Note, Formalism, Legal Realism, and Constitutionally Protected Privacy Under the Fourth and Fifth Amendments, 90 Harv.L.Rev. 945 (1977).

2. A defendant in a domestic dispute was required, by a family court order, to surrender all weapons in his possession. When he did so, he was charged with possession of an unlicensed weapon. On appeal the weapons were excluded from evidence under the Fifth Amendment. "[S]urrender of the gun was testimonial because it revealed defendant's subjective thought processes—that he knowlingly possessed a weapon—and, absent this revelation, the information would not have come to the attention of the police." People v. Havrish, 8 N.Y.3d 389, 834 N.Y.S.2d 681, 866 N.E.2d 1009 (2007)

3. In United States v. Doe, 465 U.S. 605, 104 S.Ct. 1237 (1984), the Court was faced with a situation in which an individual claimed a Fifth Amendment privilege not to produce his business records, some of which he had created himself long before the issuance of a subpoena. The government represented to the trial court that it would not use the act of production either to authenticate the records or to prove that the individual had possessed these documents. The Supreme Court stated that, absent an effective grant of immunity, the act of production could be incriminating. It then held that absent a *formal* grant of immunity pursuant to statute, the individual could properly invoke the Fifth Amendment privilege.

In broad dictum a majority of the Court held that pre-existing business records were not themselves protected by the privilege and that *Fisher* had overruled *Boyd* if *Boyd* be construed to the contrary. The Court stated that if the act of production were properly immunized, an individual could be required to produce incriminating documents which he himself had created. Concurring, Justice O'Connor proclaimed that the decision logically embraced all documents (presumably including private papers such as diaries) and not just business records. Another concurring opinion, however, sharply criticized O'Connor's construction of the majority's dictum, noting that only business records were before the Court.

4. In Andresen v. Maryland, 427 U.S. 463, 96 S.Ct. 2737 (1976), decided shortly after *Fisher*, the Supreme Court held that authorities could seize records through a valid search warrant even if those same records would be protected by the Fifth Amendment if a subpoena duces tecum had been issued. Again the Court reasoned that testimonial compulsion was not present under such circumstances. When records are seized under a search warrant, their owner is not compelled to do anything of an affirmative nature. He is "not asked to do or say anything," and, therefore, is not testimonially compelled.

5. In United States v. Miller, 425 U.S. 435, 96 S.Ct. 1619 (1976), a federal prosecutor utilized the grand jury to subpoena records from two banks pertaining to Miller's accounts. Without utilizing the word, the Court, in effect, held that Miller had no "standing" to complain about alleged irregularities in the issuance of the subpoena. The Court stated that one who engages in commercial transactions utilizing banking facilities has no reasonable expectation of privacy in the papers, so that he can make no claim under the Fourth Amendment. The "depositor takes the risk, in revealing his affairs to another, that the information will be conveyed by that person to the government." The Court attributed no legal significance to the fact that it is the government itself, under the Bank Secrecy Act, upheld in California Bankers Assn. v. Shultz, 416 U.S. 21, 94 S.Ct. 1494 (1974), which requires the bank to keep the records. "Many banks traditionally kept permanent records of their depositors' accounts" even before the Bank Secrecy Act compelled that practice.

The result in *Miller* is in accord with the result in the typical state case where the target of an investigation seeks to quash a grand jury subpoena duces tecum issued to his bank or some other third party. Such a person typically is told that he has no standing to complain about the breadth of the subpoena or any other alleged irregularity.

CHAPTER 3

EYE-WITNESS IDENTIFICATION PROCEDURES

A. THE RIGHT TO PRESENCE OF COUNSEL

United States v. Wade

Supreme Court of the United States, 1967.
388 U.S. 218, 87 S.Ct. 1926.

■ MR. JUSTICE BRENNAN delivered the opinion of the Court.

The question here is whether courtroom identifications of an accused at trial are to be excluded from evidence because the accused was exhibited to the witnesses before trial at a post-indictment lineup conducted for identification purposes without notice to and in the absence of the accused's appointed counsel.

The federally insured bank in Eustace, Texas, was robbed on September 21, 1964. A man with a small strip of tape on each side of his face entered the bank, pointed a pistol at the female cashier and the vice president, the only persons in the bank at the time, and forced them to fill a pillowcase with the bank's money. The man then drove away with an accomplice waiting in a stolen car outside the bank. On March 23, 1965, an indictment was returned against respondent Wade and two others for conspiring to rob the bank, and against Wade and the accomplice for the robbery itself. Wade was arrested on April 2, and counsel was appointed to represent him on April 26. Fifteen days later an FBI agent, without notice to Wade's lawyer, arranged to have the two bank employees observe a lineup made up of Wade and five or six other prisoners and conducted in a courtroom of the local county courthouse. Each person in the line wore strips of tape such as allegedly worn by the robber and upon direction each said something like "put the money in the bag," the words allegedly uttered by the robber. Both bank employees identified Wade in the lineup as the bank robber.

At trial the two employees, when asked on direct examination if the robber was in the courtroom, pointed to Wade. The prior lineup identification was then elicited from both employees on cross-examination. At the close of testimony, Wade's counsel moved for a judgment of acquittal or, alternatively, to strike the bank officials' courtroom identifications on the ground that conduct of the lineup, without notice to and in the absence of his appointed counsel, violated his Fifth Amendment privilege against self-incrimination and his Sixth Amendment right to the assistance of counsel. The motion was denied, and Wade was convicted. The Court of Appeals for the Fifth Circuit reversed the conviction and ordered a new trial at which the in-court identification evidence was to be excluded, holding that, though the lineup did not violate Wade's Fifth Amendment rights, "the lineup, held as it was, in the absence of counsel, already chosen to represent appellant, was a violation of his Sixth Amendment rights. ..." We granted certiorari and set the case for oral argument with Gilbert v. State of California, and Stovall v. Denno, which present similar questions. We reverse the judgment of the Court of Appeals and remand to that court with direction to enter a new judgment vacating the conviction and remanding the case to the District Court for further proceedings consistent with this opinion.

I.

Neither the lineup itself nor anything shown by this record that Wade was required to do in the lineup violated his privilege against self-incrimination.

[Editors' Note: See Casebook, Chapter 2, Section E1.]

II.

* * *

... When the Bill of Rights was adopted, there were no organized police forces as we know them today. The accused confronted the prosecutor and the witnesses against him, and the evidence was marshalled, largely at the trial itself. In contrast, today's law enforcement machinery involves critical confrontations of the accused by the prosecution at pretrial proceedings where the results might well settle the accused's fate and reduce the trial itself to a mere formality. In recognition of these realities of modern criminal prosecution, our cases have construed the Sixth Amendment guarantee to apply to "critical" stages of the proceedings....

... It is central to that principle that in addition to counsel's presence at trial, the accused is guaranteed that he need not stand alone against the State at any stage of the prosecution, formal or informal, in court or out, where counsel's absence might derogate the accused's right to a fair trial.... The presence of counsel at such critical confrontations, as at the trial itself, operates to assure that the accused's interests will be protected consistently with our adversary theory of criminal prosecution.

In sum, the principle of Powell v. Alabama and succeeding cases requires that we scrutinize *any* pretrial confrontation of the accused to determine whether the presence of his counsel is necessary to preserve the defendant's basic right to a fair trial as affected by his right meaningfully to cross-examine the witnesses against him and to have effective assistance of counsel at the trial itself. It calls upon us to analyze whether potential substantial prejudice to defendant's rights inheres in the particular confrontation and the ability of counsel to help avoid that prejudice.

III.

The Government characterizes the lineup as a mere preparatory step in the gathering of the prosecution's evidence, not different—for Sixth Amendment purposes—from various other preparatory steps, such as systematized or scientific analyses of the accused's fingerprints, blood sample, clothing, hair, and the like. We think there are differences which preclude such stages being characterized as critical stages at which the accused has the right to the presence of his counsel. Knowledge of the techniques of science and technology is sufficiently available, and the variables in techniques few enough, that the accused has the opportunity for a meaningful confrontation of the Government's case at trial through the ordinary processes of cross-examination of the Government's expert witnesses and the presentation of the evidence of his own experts. The denial of a right to have his counsel present at such analyses does not therefore violate the Sixth Amendment; they are not critical stages since there is minimal risk that his counsel's absence at such stages might derogate his right to a fair trial.

IV.

But the confrontation compelled by the State between the accused and the victim or witnesses to a crime to elicit identification evidence is peculiarly riddled with innumerable dangers and variable factors which might seriously, even crucially, derogate from a fair trial. The vagaries of eyewitness identification are well-known; the annals of criminal law are rife with instances of mistaken identification.[6] Mr. Justice Frankfurter once said: "What is the worth of identification testimony even when uncontradicted? The identification of strangers is proverbially untrustworthy. The hazards of such testimony are established by a formidable number of instances in the records of English and American trials. These instances are recent—not due to the brutalities of ancient criminal procedure." The Case of Sacco and Vanzetti 30 (1927). A major factor contributing to the high incidence of miscarriage of justice from mistaken identification has been the degree of suggestion inherent in the manner in which the prosecution presents the suspect to witnesses for pretrial identification. A commentator has observed that "the influence of improper suggestion upon identifying witnesses probably accounts for more miscarriages of justice than any other single factor—perhaps it is responsible for more such errors than all other factors combined." Wall, Eyewitness Identification in Criminal Cases 26. Suggestion can be created intentionally or unintentionally in many subtle ways. And the dangers for the suspect are particularly grave when the witness' opportunity for observation was insubstantial, and thus his susceptibility to suggestion the greatest.

Moreover, "it is a matter of common experience that, once a witness has picked out the accused at the line-up, he is not likely to go back on his word later on, so that in practice the issue of identity may (in the absence of other relevant evidence) for all practical purposes be determined there and then, before the trial."[8]

6. Borchard, Convicting the Innocent; Frank & Frank, Not Guilty; Wall, Eyewitness Identification in Criminal Cases, 3 Wigmore, Evidence § 786(a) (3d ed. 1940); Rolph, Personal Identity; Gross, Criminal Investigation 47–54 (Jackson ed. 1962); Williams, Proof of Guilt 83–98 (1952); Wills, Circumstantial Evidence 192–205 (7th ed. 1937); Wigmore, The Science of Judicial Proof §§ 250–253.

8. Williams & Hammelmann, Identification Parades, Part I, [1963] Crim.L.Rev. 479, 482.

The pretrial confrontation for purpose of identification may take the form of a lineup, also known as an "identification parade" or "showup," as in the present case, or presentation of the suspect alone to the witness, as in Stovall v. Denno, post. It is obvious that risks of suggestion attend either form of confrontation and increase the dangers inhering in eyewitness identification. But as is the case with secret interrogations, there is serious difficulty in depicting what transpires at lineups and other forms of identification confrontations. "Privacy results in secrecy and this in turn results in a gap in our knowledge as to what in fact goes on...." Miranda v. State of Arizona, supra. For the same reasons, the defense can seldom reconstruct the manner and mode of lineup identification for judge or jury at trial. Those participating in a lineup with the accused may often be police officers; in any event, the participants' names are rarely recorded or divulged at trial.[11] The impediments to an objective observation are increased when the victim is the witness. Lineups are prevalent in rape and robbery prosecutions and present a particular hazard that a victim's understandable outrage may excite vengeful or spiteful motives. In any event, neither witnesses nor lineup participants are apt to be alert for conditions prejudicial to the suspect and if they were it would likely be of scant benefit to the suspect since neither witnesses nor lineup participants are likely to be schooled in the detection of suggestive influences.[13] Improper influences may go undetected by a suspect, guilty or not, who experiences the emotional tension which we might expect in one being confronted with potential accusers. Even when he does observe abuse, if he has a criminal record he may be reluctant to take the stand and open up the admission of prior convictions. Moreover any protestations by the suspect of the fairness of the lineup made at trial are likely to be in vain;[15] the jury's choice is between the accused's unsupported version and that of the police officers present.[16] In short, the accused's inability effectively to

11. See Rolph, Personal Identity 50; "The bright burden of identity, at these parades, is lifted from the innocent participants to hover about the suspects, leaving the rest featureless and unknown and without interest."

13. An additional impediment to the detection of such influences by participants, including the suspect, is the physical conditions often surrounding the conduct of the lineup. In many, lights shine on the stage in such a way that the suspect cannot see the witness. In some a one-way mirror is used and what is said on the witness' side cannot be heard.

15. See In re Groban, 352 U.S. 330, 340, 77 S.Ct. 510, 516 (Black, J., dissenting). The difficult position of defendants in attempting to protest the manner of pretrial identification is illustrated by the many state court cases in which contentions of blatant abuse rested on their unsupportable allegations, usually controverted by the police officers present.... For a striking case in which hardly anyone agreed upon what occurred at the lineup, including who identified whom, see Johnson v. State, 237 Md. 283, 206 A.2d 138 (1965).

16. An instructive example of the defendant's predicament may be found in Proctor v. State, 223 Md. 394, 164 A.2d 708 (1960). A prior identification is admissible in Maryland only under the salutary rule that it cannot have been made "under conditions of unfairness or unreliability." Against the defendant's contention that these conditions had not been met, the Court stated:

> "In the instant case, there are no such facts as, in our judgment, would call for a finding that the identification ... was made under conditions of unfairness or unreliability. The relatively large number of persons put into the room together for [the victim] to look at is one circumstance indicating fairness, and the fact that the police officer was unable to remember the appearances of the others

reconstruct at trial any unfairness that occurred at the lineup may deprive him of his only opportunity meaningfully to attack the credibility of the witness' courtroom identification.

What facts have been disclosed in specific cases about the conduct of pretrial confrontations for identification illustrate both the potential for substantial prejudice to the accused at that stage and the need for its revelation at trial. A commentator provides some striking examples:

> "In a Canadian case ... the defendant had been picked out of a lineup of six men, of which he was the only Oriental. In other cases, a blackhaired suspect was placed among a group of light-haired persons, tall suspects have been made to stand with short nonsuspects, and, in a case where the perpetrator of the crime was known to be a youth, a suspect under twenty was placed in a lineup with five other persons, all of whom were forty or over."

Similarly state reports, in the course of describing prior identifications admitted as evidence of guilt, reveal numerous instances of suggestive procedures, for example, that all in the lineup but the suspect were known to the identifying witness, that the other participants in a lineup were grossly dissimilar in appearance from the suspect, that only the suspect was required to wear distinctive clothing which the culprit allegedly wore, that the witness is told by the police that they have caught the culprit after which the defendant is brought before the witness alone or is viewed in jail, that the suspect is pointed out before or during a lineup, and that the participants in the lineup are asked to try on an article of clothing which fits only the suspect.[1]

The potential for improper influence is illustrated by the circumstances, insofar as they appear, surrounding the prior identifications in the three cases we decide today. In the present case, the testimony of the identifying witnesses elicited on cross-examination revealed that those witnesses were taken to the courthouse and seated in the courtroom to await assembly of the lineup. The courtroom faced on a hallway observable to the witnesses through an open door. The cashier testified that she saw Wade "standing in the hall" within sight of an FBI agent. Five or six other prisoners later appeared in the hall. The vice president testified that he saw a person in the hall in the custody of the agent who "resembled the person that we identified as the one that entered the bank."[24]

and could not recall if they had physical characteristics similar to [the defendant's] or not is at least suggestive that they were not of any one type or that they all differed markedly in looks from the defendant. There is no evidence that the Police Sergeant gave the complaining witness any indication as to which of the thirteen men was the defendant; the Sergeant's testimony is simply that he asked [the victim] if he could identify [the defendant] after having put the thirteen men in the courtroom."

1. [For case citations supporting the foregoing statements, consult original footnotes 18 through 21.]

24. See Wall, supra, n. 6, at 48; Napley, Problems of Effecting the Presentation of the Case for a Defendant, 66 Col.L.Rev. 94, 99 (1966): "[W]hile many identification parades are conducted by the police with scrupulous regard for fairness, it is not unknown for the identifying witness to be placed in a position where he can see the suspect before the parade forms. . . ."

The lineup in *Gilbert* was conducted in an auditorium in which some 100 witnesses to several alleged state and federal robberies charged to Gilbert made wholesale identifications of Gilbert as the robber in each others' presence, a procedure said to run counter to the most elemental precepts of the psychology of suggestion. And the vice of suggestion created by the identification in *Stovall* was the presentation to the witness of the suspect alone handcuffed to police officers. It is hard to imagine a situation more clearly conveying the suggestion to the witness that the one presented is believed guilty by the police.

The few cases that have surfaced therefore reveal the existence of a process attended with hazards of serious unfairness to the criminal accused and strongly suggest the plight of the more numerous defendants who are unable to ferret out suggestive influences in the secrecy of the confrontation. We do not assume that these risks are the result of police procedures intentionally designed to prejudice an accused. Rather we assume they derive from the dangers inherent in eyewitness identification and the suggestibility inherent in the context of the pretrial identification. Glanville Williams, in one of the most comprehensive studies of such forms of identification, said "[T]he fact that the police themselves have, in a given case, little or no doubt that the man put up for identification has committed the offense, and that their chief preoccupation is with the problem of getting sufficient proof, because he has not 'come clean,' involves a danger that this persuasion may communicate itself even in a doubtful case to the witness in some way...." Williams & Hammelmann, Identification Parades, Part I, [1963] Crim.L.Rev. 479, 483.

Insofar as the accused's conviction may rest on a courtroom identification in fact the fruit of a suspect pretrial identification which the accused is helpless to subject to effective scrutiny at trial, the accused is deprived of that right of cross-examination which is an essential safeguard to his right to confront the witnesses against him. ... And even though cross-examination is a precious safeguard to a fair trial, it cannot be viewed as an absolute assurance of accuracy and reliability. Thus in the present context, where so many variables and pitfalls exist, the first line of defense must be the prevention of unfairness and the lessening of the hazards of eyewitness identification at the lineup itself. The trial which might determine the accused's fate may well not be that in the courtroom but that at the pretrial confrontation, with the State aligned against the accused, the witness the sole jury, and the accused unprotected against the overreaching, intentional or unintentional, and with little or no effective appeal from the judgment there rendered by the witness—"that's the man."

Since it appears that there is grave potential for prejudice, intentional or not, in the pretrial lineup, which may not be capable of reconstruction at trial, and since presence of counsel itself can often avert prejudice and assure a meaningful confrontation at trial,[26] there can be little doubt that

26. One commentator proposes a model statute providing not only for counsel, but other safeguards as well:

"Most if not all, of the attacks on the lineup process could be averted by a uniform statute modeled upon the best features of the civilian codes. Any proposed

for Wade the post-indictment lineup was a critical stage of the prosecution at which he was "as much entitled to such aid [of counsel] ... as at the trial itself." ... Thus both Wade and his counsel should have been notified of the impending lineup, and counsel's presence should have been a requisite to conduct of the lineup, absent an "intelligent waiver." ... No substantial countervailing policy considerations have been advanced against the requirement of the presence of counsel. Concern is expressed that the requirement will forestall prompt identifications and result in obstruction of the confrontations. As for the first, we note that in the two cases in which the right to counsel is today held to apply, counsel had already been appointed and no argument is made in either case that notice to counsel would have prejudicially delayed the confrontations. Moreover, we leave open the question whether the presence of substitute counsel might not suffice where notification and presence of the suspect's own counsel would result in prejudicial delay.[27] And to refuse to recognize the right to counsel for fear that counsel will obstruct the course of justice is contrary to the basic assumptions upon which this Court has operated in Sixth Amendment cases. We rejected similar logic in Miranda v. State of Arizona, concerning presence of counsel during custodial interrogation:

statute should provide for the right to counsel during any lineup or during any confrontation. Provision should be made that any person, whether a victim or a witness, must give a description of the suspect before he views any arrested person. A written record of this description should be required, and the witness should be made to sign it. This written record would be available for inspection by defense counsel for copying before the trial and for use at the trial in testing the accuracy of the identification made during the lineup and during the trial.

"This ideal statute would require at least six persons in addition to the accused in a lineup, and these persons would have to be of approximately the same height, weight, coloration of hair and skin, and bodily types as the suspect. In addition, all of these men should, as nearly as possible, be dressed alike. If distinctive garb was used during the crime, the suspect should not be forced to wear similar clothing in the lineup unless all of the other persons are similarly garbed. A complete written report of the names, addresses, descriptive details of the other persons in the lineup, and of everything which transpired during the identification would be mandatory. This report would include everything stated by the identifying witness during this step, including any reasons given by him as to what features, etc., have sparked his recognition.

"This statute should permit voice identification tests by having each person in the lineup repeat identical innocuous phrases, and it would be impermissible to force the use of words allegedly used during a criminal act.

"The statute would enjoin the police from suggesting to any viewer that one or more persons in the lineup had been arrested as a suspect. If more than one witness is to make an identification, each witness should be required to do so separately and should be forbidden to speak to another witness until all of them have completed the process.

"The statute could require the use of movie cameras and tape recorders to record the lineup process in those states which are financially able to afford these devices. Finally, the statute should provide that any evidence obtained as the result of a violation of this statute would be inadmissible." Murray, The Criminal Lineup at Home and Abroad, 1966 Utah L.Rev. 610, 627–628.

27. Although the right to counsel usually means a right to the suspect's own counsel, provision for substitute counsel may be justified on the ground that the substitute counsel's presence may eliminate the hazards which render the lineup a critical stage for the presence of the suspect's *own* counsel.

> "[A]n attorney is merely exercising the good professional judgment he has been taught. This is not cause for considering the attorney a menace to law enforcement. He is merely carrying out what he is sworn to do under his oath—to protect to the extent of his ability the rights of his client. In fulfilling this responsibility the attorney plays a vital role in the administration of criminal justice under our Constitution."

In our view counsel can hardly impede legitimate law enforcement; on the contrary, for the reasons expressed, law enforcement may be assisted by preventing the infiltration of taint in the prosecution's identification evidence.[28] That result cannot help the guilty avoid conviction but can only help assure that the right man has been brought to justice.[29]

Legislative or other regulations, such as those of local police departments, which eliminate the risks of abuse and unintentional suggestion at lineup proceedings and the impediments to meaningful confrontation at trial may also remove the basis for regarding the stage as "critical."[30] But neither Congress nor the federal authorities has seen fit to provide a solution. What we hold today "in no way creates a constitutional straitjacket which will handicap sound efforts at reform, nor is it intended to have this effect." . . .

V.

We come now to the question whether the denial of Wade's motion to strike the courtroom identification by the bank witnesses at trial because of the absence of his counsel at the lineup required, as the Court of Appeals held, the grant of a new trial at which such evidence is to be excluded. We do not think this disposition can be justified without first giving the

28. Concern is also expressed that the presence of counsel will force divulgence of the identity of government witnesses whose identity the Government may want to conceal. To the extent that this is a valid or significant state interest there are police practices commonly used to effect concealment, for example, masking the face.

29. Many other nations surround the lineup with safeguards against prejudice to the suspect. In England the suspect must be allowed the presence of his solicitor or a friend, Napley, supra, at 98–99; Germany requires the presence of retained counsel; France forbids the confrontation of the suspect in the absence of his counsel; Spain, Mexico, and Italy provide detailed procedures prescribing the conditions under which confrontation must occur under the supervision of a judicial officer who sees to it that the proceedings are officially recorded to assure adequate scrutiny at trial. Murray, The Criminal Lineup at Home and Abroad, 1966 Utah L.Rev. 610, 621–627.

30. Thirty years ago Wigmore suggested a "scientific method" of pretrial identification "to reduce the risk of error hitherto inherent in such proceedings." Wigmore, The Science of Judicial Proof 541 (3d ed. 1937). Under this approach, at least 100 talking films would be prepared of men from various occupations, races, etc. Each would be photographed in a number of stock movements, with and without hat and coat, and would read aloud a standard passage. The suspect would be filmed in the same manner. Some 25 of the films would be shown in succession in a special projection room in which each witness would be provided an electric button which would activate a board backstage when pressed to indicate that the witness had identified a given person. Provision would be made for the degree of hesitancy in the identification to be indicated by the number of presses. Of course, the more systematic and scientific a process or proceeding, including one for purposes of identification, the less the impediment to reconstruction of the conditions bearing upon the reliability of that process or proceeding at trial. . . .

Government the opportunity to establish by clear and convincing evidence that the in-court identifications were based upon observations of the suspect other than the lineup identification.... Where, as here, the admissibility of evidence of the lineup identification itself is not involved, a per se rule of exclusion of courtroom identification would be unjustified.... A rule limited solely to the exclusion of testimony concerning identification at the lineup itself, without regard to admissibility of the courtroom identification, would render the right to counsel an empty one. The lineup is most often used, as in the present case, to crystallize the witnesses' identification of the defendant for future reference. We have already noted that the lineup identification will have that effect. The State may then rest upon the witnesses' unequivocal courtroom identification, and not mention the pretrial identification as part of the State's case at trial. Counsel is then in the predicament in which Wade's counsel found himself—realizing that possible unfairness at the lineup may be the sole means of attack upon the unequivocal courtroom identification, and having to probe in the dark in an attempt to discover and reveal unfairness, while bolstering the government witness' courtroom identification by bringing out and dwelling upon his prior identification. Since counsel's presence at the lineup would equip him to attack not only the lineup identification but the courtroom identification as well, limiting the impact of violation of the right to counsel to exclusion of evidence only of identification at the lineup itself disregards a critical element of that right.

We think it follows that the proper test to be applied in these situations is that quoted in Wong Sun v. United States, 371 U.S. 471, 488, 83 S.Ct. 407, 417, "Whether, granting establishment of the primary illegality, the evidence to which instant objection is made has been come at by exploitation of that illegality or instead by means sufficiently distinguishable to be purged of the primary taint." ... Application of this test in the present context requires consideration of various factors; for example, the prior opportunity to observe the alleged criminal act, the existence of any discrepancy between any pre-lineup description and the defendant's actual description, any identification prior to lineup of another person, the identification by picture of the defendant prior to the lineup, failure to identify the defendant on a prior occasion, and the lapse of time between the alleged act and the lineup identification. It is also relevant to consider those facts which, despite the absence of counsel, are disclosed concerning the conduct of the lineup.

We doubt that the Court of Appeals applied the proper test for exclusion of the in-court identification of the two witnesses. The court stated that "it cannot be said with any certainty that they would have recognized appellant at the time of trial if this intervening lineup had not occurred," and that the testimony of the two witnesses "may well have been colored by the illegal procedure [and] was prejudicial." Moreover, the court was persuaded, in part, by the "compulsory verbal responses made by Wade at the instance of the Special Agent." This implies the erroneous holding that Wade's privilege against self-incrimination was violated so that the denial of counsel required exclusion.

On the record now before us we cannot make the determination whether the in-court identifications had an independent origin. This was not an issue at trial, although there is some evidence relevant to a determination. That inquiry is most properly made in the District Court. We therefore think the appropriate procedure to be followed is to vacate the conviction pending a hearing to determine whether the in-court identifications had an independent source, or whether, in any event, the introduction of the evidence was harmless error, and for the District Court to reinstate the conviction or order a new trial, as may be proper. See United States v. Shotwell Mfg. Co., 355 U.S. 233, 245–246, 78 S.Ct. 245, 253.

The judgment of the Court of Appeals is vacated and the case is remanded to that court with direction to enter a new judgment vacating the conviction and remanding the case to the District Court for further proceedings consistent with this opinion. It is so ordered.

Judgment of Court of Appeals vacated and case remanded with direction.

* * *

■ Mr. Justice Clark, concurring.

[OMITTED]

■ Mr. Justice Black, dissenting in part and concurring in part.

* * *

I agree with the Court, in large part because of the reasons it gives, that failure to notify Wade's counsel that Wade was to be put in a lineup by government officers and to be forced to talk and wear tape on his face denied Wade the right to counsel in violation of the Sixth Amendment. Once again, my reason for this conclusion is solely the Sixth Amendment's guarantee that "the accused shall enjoy the right . . . to have the assistance of counsel for his defence." As this Court's opinion points out, "[t]he plain wording of this guarantee thus encompasses counsel's assistance whenever necessary to assure a meaningful 'defence.' " . . .

. . . But there are implications in the Court's opinion that by a "fair trial" the Court means a trial which a majority of this Court deems to be "fair" and that a lineup is a "critical stage" only because the Court, now assessing the "innumerable dangers" which inhere in it, thinks it is such. That these implications are justified is evidenced by the Court's suggestion that "legislative or other regulations . . . which eliminate the abuse . . . at lineup proceedings . . . may also remove the basis for regarding the stage as 'critical.' " . . . I am wholly unwilling to make the specific constitutional right of counsel dependent on judges' vague and transitory notions of fairness and their equally transitory, though "practical," assessment of the "risk that . . . counsel's absence . . . might derogate from a fair trial." . . .

I would reverse Wade's conviction without further ado had the prosecution at trial made use of his lineup identification either in place of courtroom identification or to bolster in a harmful manner crucial courtroom identification. But the prosecution here did neither of these things. After prosecution witnesses under oath identified Wade in the courtroom, it was the defense, and not the prosecution, which brought out the prior lineup identification. While stating that "a *per se* rule of exclusion of courtroom identification would be unjustified," the Court, nevertheless remands this case for "a hearing to determine whether the in-court identifications had an independent source," or were the tainted fruits of the invalidly conducted lineup. From this holding I dissent.

In the first place, even if this Court has power to establish such a rule of evidence I think the rule fashioned by the Court is unsound. The "taint"-"fruit" determination required by the Court involves more than considerable difficulty. I think it is practically impossible. How is a witness capable of probing the recesses of his mind to draw a sharp line between a courtroom identification due exclusively to an earlier lineup and a courtroom identification due to memory not based on the lineup? What kind of "clear and convincing evidence" can the prosecution offer to prove upon what particular events memories resulting in an in-court identification rest? How long will trials be delayed while judges turn psychologists to probe the subconscious minds of witnesses? All these questions are posed but not answered by the Court's opinion. In my view, the Fifth and Sixth Amendments are satisfied if the prosecution is precluded from using lineup identification as either an alternative to or corroboration of courtroom identification. If the prosecution does neither and its witnesses under oath identify the defendant in the courtroom, then I can find no justification for stopping the trial in midstream to hold a lengthy "taint"-"fruit" hearing. The fact of and circumstances surrounding a prior lineup identification might be used by the defense to impeach the credibility of the in-court identifications, but not to exclude them completely.

But more important, there is no constitutional provision upon which I can rely that directly or by implication gives this Court power to establish what amounts to a constitutional rule of evidence to govern, not only the Federal Government, but the States in their trial of state crimes under state laws in state courts. See Gilbert v. California, post. The Constitution deliberately reposed in States very broad power to create and to try crimes according to their own rules and policies.... Before being deprived of this power, the least that they can ask is that we should be able to point to a federal constitutional provision that either by express language or by necessary implication grants us the power to fashion this novel rule of evidence to govern their criminal trials....

... Suffice it for me to say briefly that I find no such authority in the Due Process Clause. It undoubtedly provides that a person must be tried in accordance with the "Law of the Land." Consequently, it violates due process to try a person in a way prohibited by the Fourth, Fifth, or Sixth Amendments of our written Constitution. But I have never been able to subscribe to the dogma that the Due Process Clause empowers this Court to declare any law, including a rule of evidence, unconstitutional which it believes is contrary to tradition, decency, fundamental justice, or any of the other wide-meaning words used by judges to claim power under the Due Process Clause.... I have an abiding idea that if the Framers had wanted to let judges write the Constitution on any such day-to-day beliefs of theirs, they would have said so instead of so carefully defining their grants and prohibitions in a written constitution. . . .

I would affirm Wade's conviction.

■ MR. JUSTICE WHITE, whom MR. JUSTICE HARLAN and MR. JUSTICE STEWART join, dissenting in part and concurring in part.

* * *

The Court's opinion is far reaching. It proceeds first by creating a new *per se* rule of constitutional law: a criminal suspect cannot be subjected to a pretrial identification process in the absence of his counsel without violating the Sixth Amendment. If he is, the State may not buttress a later courtroom identification of the witness by any reference to the previous identification. Furthermore, the courtroom identification is not admissible at all unless the State can establish by clear and convincing proof that the testimony is not the fruit of the earlier identification made in the absence of defendant's counsel—admittedly a heavy burden for the State and probably an impossible one. For all intents and purposes, courtroom identifications are barred if pretrial identifications have occurred without counsel being present.

The rule applies to any lineup, to any other techniques employed to produce an identification and *a fortiori* to a face-to-face encounter between the witness and the suspect alone, regardless of when the identification occurs, in time or place, and whether before or after indictment or information. It matters not how well the witness knows the suspect, whether the witness is the suspect's mother, brother, or long-time associate, and no matter how long or well the witness observed the perpetrator at the scene of the crime. The kidnap victim who has lived for days with his abductor is in the same category as the witness who had had only a fleeting glimpse of the criminal. Neither may identify the suspect without defendant's counsel being present. The same strictures apply regardless of the number of other witnesses who positively identify the defendant and regardless of the corroborative evidence showing that it was the defendant who has committed the crime.

The premise for the Court's rule is not the general unreliability of eyewitness identifications nor the difficulties inherent in observation, recall, and recognition. The Court assumes a narrower evil as the basis for its rule—improper police suggestion which contributes to erroneous identifications. The Court apparently believes that improper police procedures are so widespread that a broad prophylactic rule must be laid down, requiring the presence of counsel at all pretrial identifications, in order to detect recurring instances of police misconduct.[1] I do not share this pervasive distrust of all official investigations. None of the materials the Court relies upon supports it.[2] Certainly, I would bow to solid fact, but the Court quite

1. Yet in Stovall v. Denno, 388 U.S. 293, 87 S.Ct. 1967, the Court recognizes that improper police conduct in the identification process has not been so widespread as to justify full retroactivity for its new rule.

2. In Miranda v. State of Arizona, the Court noted that O'Hara, Fundamentals of Criminal Investigation (1956) is a text that has enjoyed extensive use among law enforcement agencies and among students of

obviously does not have before it any reliable, comprehensive survey of current police practices on which to base its new rule. Until it does, the Court should avoid excluding relevant evidence from state criminal trials.

The Court goes beyond assuming that a great majority of the country's police departments are following improper practices at pretrial identifications. To find the lineup a "critical" stage of the proceeding and to exclude identifications made in the absence of counsel, the Court must also assume that police "suggestion," if it occurs at all, leads to erroneous rather than accurate identifications and that reprehensible police conduct will have an unavoidable and largely undiscoverable impact on the trial. This in turn assumes that there is now no adequate source from which defense counsel can learn about the circumstances of the pretrial identification in order to place before the jury all of the considerations which should enter into an appraisal of courtroom identification evidence. But these are treacherous and unsupported assumptions resting as they do on the notion that the defendant will not be aware, that the police and the witnesses will forget or prevaricate, that defense counsel will be unable to bring out the truth and that neither jury, judge, nor appellate court is a sufficient safeguard against unacceptable police conduct occurring at a pretrial identification procedure. I am unable to share the Court's view of the willingness of the police and the ordinary citizen-witness to dissemble, either with respect to the identification of the defendant or with respect to the circumstances surrounding a pretrial identification.

There are several striking aspects to the Court's holding. First, the rule does not bar courtroom identifications where there have been no previous identifications in the presence of the police, although when identified in the courtroom, the defendant is known to be in custody and charged with the commission of a crime. Second, the Court seems to say that if suitable legislative standards were adopted for the conduct of pretrial identifications, thereby lessening the hazards in such confrontations, it would not insist on the presence of counsel. But if this is true, why does not the Court simply fashion what it deems to be constitutionally acceptable procedures for the authorities to follow? Certainly the Court is correct in suggesting that the new rule will be wholly inapplicable where police departments themselves have established suitable safeguards.

Third, courtroom identification may be barred, absent counsel at a prior identification, regardless of the extent of counsel's information concerning the circumstances of the previous confrontation between witness and defendant—apparently even if there were recordings or sound-movies of the events as they occurred. But if the rule is premised on the defendant's right to have his counsel know, there seems little basis for not accepting other means to inform. A disinterested observer, recordings, photographs—any one of them would seem adequate to furnish the basis

police science. The quality of the work was said to rest on the author's long service as observer, lecturer in police science, and work as a federal crime investigator. O'Hara does not suggest that the police should or do use identification machinery improperly; instead he argues for techniques that would increase the reliability of eyewitness identifications, and there is no reason to suggest that O'Hara's views are not shared and practiced by the majority of police departments throughout the land.

for a meaningful cross-examination of the eyewitness who identifies the defendant in the courtroom.

I share the Court's view that the criminal trial, at the very least, should aim at truthful factfinding, including accurate eyewitness identifications. I doubt, however, on the basis of our present information, that the tragic mistakes which have occurred in criminal trials are as much the product of improper police conduct as they are the consequence of the difficulties inherent in eyewitness testimony and in resolving evidentiary conflicts by court or jury. I doubt that the Court's new rule will obviate these difficulties, or that the situation will be measurably improved by inserting defense counsel into the investigative processes of police departments everywhere.

But, it may be asked, what possible state interest militates against requiring the presence of defense counsel at lineups? After all, the argument goes, he *may* do some good, he *may* upgrade the quality of identification evidence in state courts and he can scarcely do any harm. Even if true, this is a feeble foundation for fastening an ironclad constitutional rule upon state criminal procedures. Absent some reliably established constitutional violation, the processes by which the States enforce their criminal laws are their own prerogative. The States *do* have an interest in conducting their own affairs, an interest which cannot be displaced simply by saying that there are no valid arguments with respect to the merits of a federal rule emanating from this Court.

Beyond this, however, requiring counsel at pretrial identifications as an invariable rule trenches on other valid state interests. One of them is its concern with the prompt and efficient enforcement of its criminal laws. Identifications frequently take place after arrest but before indictment or information is filed. The police may have arrested a suspect on probable cause but may still have the wrong man. Both the suspect and the State have every interest in a prompt identification at that stage, the suspect in order to secure his immediate release and the State because prompt and early identification enhances *accurate* identification and because it must know whether it is on the right investigative track. Unavoidably, however, the absolute rule requiring the presence of counsel will cause significant delay and it may very well result in no pretrial identification at all. Counsel must be appointed and a time arranged convenient for him and the witnesses. Meanwhile, it may be necessary to file charges against the suspect who may then be released on bail, in the federal system very often on his own recognizance, with neither the State nor the defendant having the benefit of a properly conducted identification procedure.

Nor do I think the witnesses themselves can be ignored. They will now be required to be present at the convenience of counsel rather than their own. Many may be much less willing to participate if the identification stage is transformed into an adversary proceeding not under the control of a judge. Others may fear for their own safety if their identity is known at an early date, especially when there is no way of knowing until the lineup occurs whether or not the police really have the right man.[4]

4. I would not have thought that the State's interest regarding its sources of identification is any less than its interest in protecting informants, especially those who may aid in identification but who will not be used as witnesses.

Finally, I think the Court's new rule is vulnerable in terms of its own unimpeachable purpose of increasing the reliability of identification testimony.

Law enforcement officers have the obligation to convict the guilty and to make sure they do not convict the innocent. They must be dedicated to making the criminal trial a procedure for the ascertainment of the true facts surrounding the commission of the crime. To this extent, our so-called adversary system is not adversary at all; nor should it be. But defense counsel has no comparable obligation to ascertain or present the truth. Our system assigns him a different mission. He must be and is interested in not convicting the innocent, but, absent a voluntary plea of guilty, we also insist that he defend his client whether he is innocent or guilty. The State has the obligation to present the evidence. Defense counsel need present nothing, even if he knows what the truth is. He need furnish no witnesses to the police, reveal any confidences of his client, nor furnish any other information to help the prosecution's case. If he can confuse a witness, even a truthful one, or make him appear at a disadvantage, unsure or indecisive, that will be his normal course. Our interest in not convicting the innocent permits counsel to put the State to its proof, to put the State's case in the worst possible light regardless of what he thinks or knows to be the truth. Undoubtedly there are some limits which defense counsel must observe but more often than not, defense counsel will cross-examine a prosecution witness, and impeach him if he can, even if he thinks the witness is telling the truth, just as he will attempt to destroy a witness who he thinks is lying. In this respect, as part of our modified adversary system and as part of the duty imposed on the most honorable defense counsel, we countenance or require conduct which in many instances has little, if any, relation to the search for truth.

I would not extend this system, at least as it presently operates, to police investigations and would not require counsel's presence at pretrial identification procedures. Counsel's interest is in not having his client placed at the scene of the crime, regardless of his whereabouts. Some counsel may advise their clients to refuse to make any movements or to speak any words in a lineup or even to appear in one. To that extent the impact on truthful factfinding is quite obvious. Others will not only observe what occurs and develop possibilities for later cross-examination but will hover over witnesses and begin their cross-examination then, menacing truthful factfinding as thoroughly as the Court fears the police now do. Certainly there is an implicit invitation to counsel to suggest rules for the lineup and to manage and produce it as best he can. I therefore doubt that the Court's new rule, at least absent some clearly defined limits on counsel's role, will measurably contribute to more reliable pretrial identifications. My fears are that it will have precisely the opposite result. It may well produce fewer convictions, but that is hardly a proper measure of its long-run acceptability. In my view, the State is entitled to investigate and develop its case outside the presence of defense counsel. This includes the right to have private conversations with identification witnesses, just as defense counsel may have his own consultations with these and other witnesses without having the prosecutor present.

Whether today's judgment would be an acceptable exercise of supervisory power over federal courts is another question. But as a constitutional matter, the judgment in this case is erroneous and ... I respectfully register this dissent.

■ MR. JUSTICE FORTAS, with whom THE CHIEF JUSTICE and MR. JUSTICE DOUGLAS join, concurring in part and dissenting in part.

[OMITTED]

NOTES

1. In Gilbert v. California, 388 U.S. 263, 87 S.Ct. 1951 (1967), the Court elaborated on its several holdings in *Wade*. The Court held that requiring a suspect to give handwriting exemplars in the absence of counsel violated neither Fifth nor Sixth Amendment rights. The Court further held that a lineup conducted without notice to Gilbert's counsel some sixteen days after indictment violated Gilbert's right to counsel. With respect to those witnesses who identified Gilbert at trial, the Court held that Gilbert was entitled to a hearing whether their courtroom identification was untainted by their observations of Gilbert at the illegal lineup. The Court finally held that testimony concerning the pre-trial confrontation introduced by the prosecution was erroneously admitted. Such testimony, according to the Court, was the direct product of illegal law-enforcement conduct and "only a per se exclusionary rule as to such testimony can be an effective sanction to assure that law enforcement authorities will respect the accused's constitutional right to the presence of his counsel at the critical lineup."

2. Can the right to counsel at lineups be waived? Every court that has considered the question has answered in the affirmative. A waiver must be voluntary. Compare Redding v. State, 10 Md.App. 601, 272 A.2d 70 (1971), with Chambers v. State, 46 Ala.App. 247, 240 So.2d 370 (1970) (waiver voluntary when suspect was told he could go home if he was not identified). Warnings of the right to counsel *at the lineup* must be given. The mere giving of Miranda warnings is not sufficient (United States v. Ayers, 426 F.2d 524 (2d Cir.1970)) but such warnings may be considered as supplementing other warnings specifically concerning the lineup. See People v. Evans, 16 Cal.App.3d 510, 94 Cal.Rptr. 88 (1971). There is no definitive answer on the question of whether the Constitution requires that counsel be provided if the suspect requests one or whether the lineup must be delayed until counsel is present. See People v. Mitchell, 2 N.Y.3d 272, N.Y.S.2d 810 N.E.2d 879 (2004) (police must allow the suspect a reasonable time to secure counsel)

3. Fourth amendment and related issues concerning the right of authorities to place an individual in a lineup are touched upon in the Casebook, Ch. 5, K.

4. In Gross, Loss of Innocence, Eyewitness Identification and Proof of Guilt, 16 J. Legal Studies 395 (1987), Professor Gross concluded his study of the field with these words:

> The Supreme Court probably overstated the case when it said in *Wade* that "the trial which might determine the accused's fate may well not be that in the courtroom but that at the [initial] pretrial confrontation" with the eyewitness. It is no doubt true that courtroom trials are a poor remedy for identification errors, but the pretrial process of identification usually includes quite a bit more than the confrontation with the eyewitness, and

it is the overall accuracy of this process that makes erroneous convictions rare.

Rare, however, does not mean unimportant. Airline crashes are exceedingly rare, yet we go to great lengths to maintain that fact and to make them even less likely. I have argued that the best way to reduce the number of convictions based on misidentifications is to improve the quality of pretrial determinations of identity and to tighten the standards for prosecution in cases in which identity is in dispute. Some reforms in trial procedure might be useful, but primarily those designed to force the police and prosecutors to improve their investigations rather than those aimed at improving the accuracy of courtroom judgments. The major impetus for change, however, must come from the law enforcement community itself.

This conclusion leaves me uneasy. Like most American lawyers of my age and background, I was brought up to see the criminal justice system from a due process perspective. It cuts against the grain to argue that prosecutors and police officers should have primary responsibility for protecting innocent defendants. But reality, it seems, is at odds with the due process heritage, at least in this context. In fact, prosecutors and police officers already fill this protective function to some extent, and they have more power to make identifications safe than any other actors in the system. How they will use that power is another matter.

Compare Hoffheimer, Requiring Jury Instructions On Eyewitness Identification, 80 J.Crim.L. & Crim. 585 (1989).

Kirby v. Illinois

Supreme Court of the United States, 1972.
406 U.S. 682, 92 S.Ct. 1877.

■ Mr. Justice Stewart announced the judgment of the Court in an opinion in which The Chief Justice, Mr. Justice Blackmun, and Mr. Justice Rehnquist join.

. . . In the present case we are asked to extend the *Wade–Gilbert per se* exclusionary rule to identification testimony based upon a police station showup that took place *before* the defendant had been indicted or otherwise formally charged with any criminal offense.

On February 21, 1968, a man named Willie Shard reported to the Chicago police that the previous day two men had robbed him on a Chicago street of a wallet containing, among other things, travellers checks and a Social Security card. On February 22, two police officers stopped the petitioner and a companion, Ralph Bean, on West Madison Street in Chicago. When asked for identification, the petitioner produced a wallet that contained three travellers checks and a Social Security card, all bearing the name of Willie Shard. Papers with Shard's name on them were also found in Bean's possession. When asked to explain his possession of Shard's property, the petitioner first said that the travellers checks were "play money," and then told the officers that he had won them in a crap game. The officers then arrested the petitioner and Bean and took them to a police station.

Only after arriving at the police station, and checking the records there, did the arresting officers learn of the Shard robbery. A police car was then dispatched to Shard's place of employment, where it picked up Shard and brought him to the police station. Immediately upon entering the room in the police station where the petitioner and Bean were seated at a table, Shard positively identified them as the men who had robbed him two days earlier. No lawyer was present in the room, and neither the petitioner nor Bean had asked for legal assistance, or been advised of any right to the presence of counsel.

... A pretrial motion to suppress Shard's identification testimony was denied, and at the trial Shard testified as a witness for the prosecution. In his testimony he described his identification of the two men at the police station on February 22, and identified them again in the courtroom as the men who had robbed him on February 20. He was cross-examined at length regarding the circumstances of his identification of the two defendants. The jury found both defendants guilty....

I.

We note at the outset that the constitutional privilege against compulsory self-incrimination is in no way implicated here....

It follows that the doctrine of Miranda v. Arizona has no applicability whatever to the issue before us. For the *Miranda* decision was based exclusively upon the Fifth and Fourteenth Amendment privilege against compulsory self-incrimination, upon the theory that custodial *interrogation* is inherently coercive.

The *Wade–Gilbert* exclusionary rule, by contrast, stems from a quite different constitutional guarantee—the guarantee of the right to counsel contained in the Sixth and Fourteenth Amendments. Unless all semblance of principled constitutional adjudication is to be abandoned, therefore, it is to the decisions construing that guarantee that we must look in determining the present controversy.

In a line of constitutional cases in this Court stemming back to the Court's landmark opinion in Powell v. Alabama, 287 U.S. 45, 53 S.Ct. 55, it has been firmly established that a person's Sixth and Fourteenth Amendment right to counsel attaches only at or after the time that adversary judicial proceedings have been initiated against him.

This is not to say that a defendant in a criminal case has a constitutional right to counsel only at the trial itself. The *Powell* case makes clear that the right attaches at the time of arraignment, and the Court has recently held that it exists also at the time of a preliminary hearing. But the point is that, while members of the Court have differed as to existence of the right to counsel in the contexts of some of the above cases, *all* of those cases have involved points of time at or after the initiation of adversary judicial criminal proceedings—whether by way of formal charge, preliminary hearing, indictment, information, or arraignment.

* * *

The initiation of judicial criminal proceedings is far from a mere formalism. It is the starting point of our whole system of adversary criminal justice. For it is only then that the Government has committed itself to prosecute, and only then that the adverse positions of Government and defendant have solidified. It is then that a defendant finds himself faced with the prosecutorial forces of organized society, and immersed in the intricacies of substantive and procedural criminal law. It is this point, therefore, that marks the commencement of the "criminal prosecutions" to which alone the explicit guarantees of the Sixth Amendment are applicable.

In this case we are asked to import into a routine police investigation an absolute constitutional guarantee historically and rationally applicable only after the onset of formal prosecutorial proceedings. We decline to do so. Less than a year after *Wade* and *Gilbert* were decided, the Court explained the rule of those decisions as follows: "The rationale of those cases was that an accused is entitled to counsel at any 'critical stage of the *prosecution*,' and that a post-indictment lineup is such a 'critical stage.' " (Emphasis supplied.) Simmons v. United States, 390 U.S. 377, 382–383, 88 S.Ct. 967, 970. We decline to depart from that rationale today by imposing a *per se* exclusionary rule upon testimony concerning an identification that took place long before the commencement of any prosecution whatever.

II.

What has been said is not to suggest that there may not be occasions during the course of a criminal investigation when the police do abuse identification procedures. Such abuses are not beyond the reach of the Constitution. As the Court pointed out in *Wade* itself, it is always necessary to "scrutinize *any* pretrial confrontation...." The Due Process Clause of the Fifth and Fourteenth Amendments forbids a lineup that is unnecessarily suggestive and conducive to irreparable mistaken identification. When a person has not been formally charged with a criminal offense, *Stovall* strikes the appropriate constitutional balance between the right of a suspect to be protected from prejudicial procedures and the interest of society in the prompt and purposeful investigation of an unsolved crime.

The judgment is affirmed.

■ MR. CHIEF JUSTICE BURGER, concurring.

I agree that the right to counsel attaches as soon as criminal charges are formally made against an accused and he becomes the subject of a "criminal prosecution." Therefore, I join in the Court's opinion and holding.

■ MR. JUSTICE POWELL, concurring in the result.

As I would not extend the *Wade–Gilbert per se* exclusionary rule, I concur in the result reached by the Court.

■ MR. JUSTICE BRENNAN, with whom MR. JUSTICE DOUGLAS and MR. JUSTICE MARSHALL join, dissenting....

* * *

In view of *Wade*, it is plain, and the plurality today does not attempt to dispute it, that there inhere in a confrontation for identification conducted after arrest* the identical hazards to a fair trial that inhere in such a

* This case does not require me to consider confrontations that take place before custody, see e.g., Bratten v. Delaware, 307 F.Supp. 643 (Del.1969); nor accidental con-

confrontation conducted "after the onset of formal prosecutorial proceedings." The plurality apparently considers an arrest, which for present purposes we must assume to be based upon probable cause to be nothing more than part of "a routine police investigation," and thus not "the starting point of our whole system of adversary criminal justice,". An arrest, according to the plurality, does not face the accused "with the prosecutorial forces of organized society," nor immerse him "in the intricacies of substantive and procedural criminal law." Those consequences ensue, says the plurality, only with "[t]he initiation of judicial criminal proceedings," "[f]or it is only then that the Government has committed itself to prosecute, and only then that the adverse positions of Government and defendant have solidified." If these propositions do not amount to "mere formalism," it is difficult to know how to characterize them. An arrest evidences the belief of the police that the perpetrator of a crime has been caught. A post-arrest confrontation for identification is not "a mere preparatory step in the gathering of the prosecution's evidence." A primary, and frequently sole, purpose of the confrontation for identification at that stage is to accumulate proof to buttress the conclusion of the police that they have the offender in hand. The plurality offers no reason, and I can think of none, for concluding that a post-arrest confrontation for identification, unlike a post-charge confrontation is not among those "critical confrontations of the accused by the prosecution at pretrial proceedings where the results might well settle the accused's fate and reduce the trial itself to a mere formality."

The highly suggestive form of confrontation employed in this case underscores the point. This showup was particularly fraught with the peril of mistaken identification. In the setting of a police station squad room where all present except petitioner and Bean were police officers, the danger was quite real that Shard's understandable resentment might lead him too readily to agree with the police that the pair under arrest, and the only persons exhibited to him were indeed the robbers.... Shard's testimony itself demonstrates the necessity for such safeguards. On direct examination, Shard identified petitioner and Bean not as the alleged robbers on trial in the courtroom, but as the pair he saw at the police station....

* * *

Wade and *Gilbert*, of course, happened to involve post-indictment confrontations. Yet even a cursory perusal of the opinions in those cases reveals that nothing at all turned upon that particular circumstance. In short, it is fair to conclude that rather than "declin[ing] to depart from [the] rationale" of *Wade* and *Gilbert*, the plurality today, albeit purporting to be engaged in "principled constitutional adjudication," refuses even to recognize that "rationale." For my part, I do not agree that we "extend" *Wade* and *Gilbert*, by holding that the principles of those cases apply to confrontations for identification conducted after arrest. Because Shard

frontations not arranged by the police, see, e.g., United States v. Pollack, 427 F.2d 1168 (C.A.5 1970); nor on-the-scene encounters shortly after the crime, see, e.g., Russell v. United States, 408 F.2d 1280 (D.C.Cir.1969).

testified at trial about his identification of petitioner at the police station showup, the exclusionary rule of *Gilbert*, requires reversal.

■ MR. JUSTICE WHITE, dissenting.

United States v. Wade, and Gilbert v. California, govern this case and compel reversal of the judgment of the Illinois Supreme Court.

NOTES

1. Prior to the *Kirby* decision there were several lines of demarcation. It was held that the right to counsel did not apply to confrontations occurring shortly after the crimes, to accidental confrontations or to confrontations occurring when the suspect was not in custody. Some courts had restricted right to counsel to post-indictment lineups. People v. Palmer, 41 Ill.2d 571, 244 N.E.2d 173 (1969), but most rejected this limitation, People v. Fowler, 1 Cal.3d 335, 82 Cal.Rptr. 363, 461 P.2d 643 (1969).

Some courts which applied right to counsel more broadly than required by *Kirby* did reduce the scope of their rules to bring them into conformity with *Kirby*. Commonwealth v. Lopes, 362 Mass. 448, 287 N.E.2d 118 (1972). Compare Blue v. State, 558 P.2d 636 (Alaska 1977), holding, as a matter of state constitutional law, the existence of the right to counsel at a lineup or showup conducted before the initiation of judicial proceedings—at least where no exigent circumstances are present. People v. Coates, 74 N.Y.2d 244, 544 N.Y.S.2d 992, 543 N.E.2d 440 (1989) (No such right under N.Y. Constitution).

2. Two serious questions arise with reference to the scope of *Kirby*. First, in some jurisdictions a suspect is brought to a "bond" court shortly after arrest. Does this court appearance, which is limited solely to the setting of bail, represent the onset of formal prosecutorial proceedings? Does it make a difference whether a prosecutor appears at the hearing or the police appear without a prosecutor? Second, if the police get an arrest warrant from a court, does this signify the commencement of prosecution? Some courts have answered in the affirmative. United States ex rel. Robinson v. Zelker, 468 F.2d 159 (2d Cir.1972), the court said:

> "The first question we have is whether 'adversary judicial proceedings' had been 'initiated' within Kirby v. Illinois....
>
> * * *
>
> "Here the arrest warrant itself commanded that appellant be brought forthwith before the Criminal Court 'to answer the said charge, and to be dealt with according to law.' These were formal criminal proceedings, for the warrant had been signed by a judge based on an 'information upon oath' that appellant did commit the crimes of assault, robbery and possession of a dangerous weapon. This being true, *Wade* required counsel at the show-up, for we see no distinction based on the chance fact that the identifying witness was also a police officer. Time was not of the essence, a lineup could have been arranged and there appeared to be no 'substantial countervailing policy considerations' against requiring the presence of counsel as suggested in *Wade*."

In dissent Judge Hayes said:

> "I cannot agree with the majority's conclusion that 'adversary judicial criminal proceedings,' within the meaning of Kirby v. Illinois, had been begun in this case at the time of the pre-trial show-up, entitling Robinson to counsel at that show-up. In *Kirby* the Court said:

> 'The initiation of judicial criminal proceedings is far from a mere formalism. It is the starting point of our whole system of adversary criminal justice. *For it is only then that the Government has committed itself to prosecute, and only then that the adverse positions of Government and defendant have solidified.* It is this point, therefore, that marks the commencement of the "criminal prosecutions" to which alone the explicit guarantees of the Sixth Amendment are applicable.'
>
> 'Here the only judicial action taken against Robinson was the issuance of a warrant of arrest. He was not even arraigned until the day after the show-up.... It seems clear that such a warrant is not a point at which "the Government has committed itself to prosecute, and ... the adverse positions of Government and defendant have solidified." ' "

Does the answer to the question depend on whether, under local law, a complaint for an arrest warrant, which may only state the facts showing probable cause, is sufficient to meet the formal requirements for complaints charging a crime, i.e., affirmative allegations of each of the elements of the crime, citation to the statute violated, etc.?

Consider the following comments in United States v. Duvall, 537 F.2d 15, 21–22 (2d Cir.1976):

> "We see no reason in principle why the filing of a complaint should be deemed to give rise to a right to counsel immediately upon arrest pursuant to warrant. As said in 8 Moore, Federal Practice & 3.02 (Cipes, 1975 rev.), 'The principal function of a complaint "is as a basis for an application for an arrest warrant." ' See Gaither v. United States, 134 U.S.App.D.C. 154, 413 F.2d 1061, 1076 (1969). There is no reason in the nature of things why an arrest warrant should need to be predicated on a complaint rather than simply an affidavit as in the case of a search warrant, F.R.Cr.P. 41; indeed Rule 4 permits the showing of probable cause for arrest to be made either in the complaint or in an affidavit or affidavits filed with the complaint. The requirements of Rule 5 bear equally on 'an officer making an arrest under a warrant issued upon a complaint or any person making an arrest without a warrant.' We perceive no reason why Sixth Amendment rights should accrue sooner in the former instance than in the latter. Furthermore to hold that the accrual of the right to counsel is accelerated by use of the warrant procedure would tend to discourage this whereas the policy should be to encourage it."

The argument that fewer arrest warrants will be issued if the issuance of a warrant creates a right to counsel is not merely puff in an appellate brief. This is precisely what happened in Cook County, Illinois, where prosecutors are most reluctant to seek an arrest warrant if they know that a lineup will be held after the suspect is captured and if they believe that the suspect will be apprehended within a short period of time.

The issue is of increasing importance because of the more frequent use of arrest warrants mandated by Payton v. New York, 445 U.S. 573, 100 S.Ct. 1371 (1980), and by earlier state and federal decisions which before *Payton* had reached the "*Payton* result." See Tarpley v. Estelle, 703 F.2d 157 (5th Cir.1983), which indicates that an arrest followed by a judicial appearance may not always trigger the right to counsel; the Court reasoned that the taking of a suspect before a judge or magistrate does not always signify a commitment to prosecution.

Can the authorities prevent attachment of the right to counsel by declaring on the face of the arrest warrant that issuance of the warrant does not commit the district attorney to going forward with a criminal prosecution? Consider the propriety of this use of an arrest warrant. Such declarations are made on the face of arrest warrants in some California jurisdictions. See footnote 1 of Edwards v. Arizona in Chapter 2 of this text, p. 170.

3. An accused who is represented by counsel on another charge does not, for that reason alone, have the right to the presence of that attorney at a lineup conducted for another offense. Boyd v. Henderson, 555 F.2d 56 (2d Cir.1977), except under New York law. People v. Wilson, 89 N.Y.2d 754, 658 N.Y.S.2d 225, 680 N.E.2d 598 (1997).

4. If the first post-crime confrontation between a witness and the defendant occurs at a preliminary hearing, do *Wade* and *Kirby* require counsel? Must counsel know that this is the first time that the witness has viewed the defendant for the purpose of possible identification? Moore v. Illinois, 434 U.S. 220, 98 S.Ct. 458 (1977), dealt with the issue in the following way:

> "MR. JUSTICE POWELL delivered the opinion of the Court.
>
> "The Court of Appeals ... read *Kirby* as holding that evidence of a corporeal identification conducted in the absence of defense counsel must be excluded only if the identification is made after the defendant is *indicted*. Such a reading cannot be squared with *Kirby* itself, which held that an accused's rights under *Wade* and *Gilbert* attach to identifications conducted 'at or after the initiation of adversary judicial criminal proceedings,' including proceedings instituted 'by way of formal charge [or] preliminary hearing.' The prosecution in this case was commenced under Illinois law when the victim's complaint was filed in court. See Ill.Rev.Stat. Ch. 38, § 111 (1970). The purpose of the preliminary hearing was to determine whether there was probable cause to bind petitioner over to the grand jury and to set bail. Petitioner had the right to oppose the prosecution at that hearing by moving to dismiss the charges and to suppress the evidence against him. He faced counsel for the State, who elicited the victim's identification, summarized the State's other evidence against petitioner, and urged that the State be given more time to marshal its evidence. It is plain that '[t]he government ha[d] committed itself to prosecute,' and that petitioner found 'himself faced with the prosecutorial forces of organized society, and immersed in the intricacies of substantive and procedural criminal law.' The State candidly concedes that this preliminary hearing marked the 'initiation of adversary judicial criminal proceedings' against petitioner, and it hardly could contend otherwise. The Court of Appeals therefore erred in holding that petitioner's rights under *Wade* and *Gilbert* had not yet attached at the time of the preliminary hearing.
>
> * * *
>
> "If the court believed that petitioner did not have a right to counsel at this identification procedure because it was conducted in the course of a judicial proceeding, we do not agree. The reasons supporting Wade's holding that a corporeal identification is a critical stage of a criminal prosecution for Sixth Amendment purposes apply with equal force to this identification. It is difficult to imagine a more suggestive manner in which to present a suspect to a witness for their critical first confrontation than was employed in this case. The victim, who had seen her assailant for only 10 to 15 seconds, was asked to make her identification after she was told that she was going to view a suspect, after she was told his name and heard

it called as he was led before the bench, and after she heard the prosecutor recite the evidence believed to implicate petitioner. Had petitioner been represented by counsel, some or all of this suggestiveness could have been avoided.* Here, petitioner's Sixth Amendment rights were violated by a corporeal identification conducted after the initiation of adversary judicial criminal proceedings and in the absence of counsel. The courts below thought that the victim's testimony at trial that she had identified petitioner at an uncounseled pretrial confrontation was admissible even if petitioner's rights had been violated, because there was an 'independent source' for the victim's identification at the uncounseled confrontation. But Gilbert held that the prosecution cannot buttress its case-in-chief by introducing evidence of a pretrial identification made in violation of the accused's Sixth Amendment rights, even if it can prove that the pretrial identification had an independent source....

"In view of the violation of petitioner's Sixth and Fourteenth Amendment right to counsel at the pretrial corporeal identification, and of the prosecution's exploitation at trial of evidence derived directly from that violation, we reverse the judgment of the Court of Appeals and remand for a determination of whether the failure to exclude that evidence was harmless constitutional error."

5. The question of right to counsel has also arisen in connection with identification from photographs. Without exception every court considering the question has held that there is no right to counsel when police show photographs of suspects who are not in custody. What is the basis for this holding? The same result has been reached by the majority of courts when the Sixth Amendment claim was made on behalf of a suspect in custody.

In United States v. Ash, 413 U.S. 300, 93 S.Ct. 2568 (1973), the Court resolved the question, as appears in the following excerpts from the opinion.

"MR. JUSTICE BLACKMUN delivered the opinion of the Court.

* * *

"Trial was finally set for May 1968, almost three years after the crime. In preparing for trial, the prosecutor decided to use a photographic display to determine whether the witnesses he planned to call would be able to make in-court identifications. Shortly before the trial, an FBI agent and the prosecutor showed five color photographs to the four witnesses who previously had tentatively identified the black-and-white photograph of Ash. Three of the witnesses selected the picture of Ash, but one was unable to make any selection. None of the witnesses

* For example, counsel could have requested that the hearing be postponed until a lineup could be arranged at which the victim would view petitioner in a less suggestive setting. See, e.g., United States v. Ravich, 421 F.2d 1196, 1202–1203 (CA2), Mason v. United States, 134 U.S.App.D.C. 280, 283, 414 F.2d 1176, 1179 n. 19 (1969). Short of that, counsel could have asked that the victim be excused from the courtroom while the charges were read and the evidence against petitioner was recited, and that petitioner be seated with other people in the audience when the victim attempted an identification. See Allen v. Rhay, 431 F.2d 1160, 1165 (C.A.9 1970). Counsel might have sought to cross-examine the victim to test her identification before it hardened. Cf. Haberstroh v. Montanye, 493 F.2d 483, 485 (C.A.2 1974); United States ex rel. Riffert v. Rundle, 464 F.2d 1348, 1351 (C.A.3 1972). Because it is in the prosecution's interest as well as the accused's that witnesses' identifications remain untainted we cannot assume that such requests would have been in vain. Such requests ordinarily are addressed to the sound discretion of the court, see United States v. Ravich, supra, at 1203; we express no opinion as to whether the preliminary hearing court would have been required to grant any such requests.

selected the picture of Bailey which was in the group. This post-indictment identification provides the basis for respondent Ash's claim that he was denied the right to counsel at a 'critical stage' of the prosecution. . . .

"At trial, the three witnesses who had been inside the bank identified Ash as the gunman, but they were unwilling to state that they were certain of their identifications. None of these made an in-court identification of Bailey. The fourth witness, who had been in a car outside the bank and who had seen the fleeing robbers after they had removed their masks, made positive in-court identifications of both Ash and Bailey. Bailey's counsel then sought to impeach this in-court identification by calling the FBI agent who had shown the color photographs to the witnesses immediately before trial. Bailey's counsel demonstrated that the witness who had identified Bailey in court had failed to identify a color photograph of Bailey. During the course of the examination, Bailey's counsel also, before the jury, brought out the fact that this witness had selected another man as one of the robbers. At this point the prosecutor became concerned that the jury might believe that the witness had selected a third person when, in fact, the witness had selected a photograph of Ash. After a conference at the bench, the trial judge ruled that all five color photographs would be admitted into evidence. . . .

"McFarland testified as a Government witness. He said he had discussed plans for the robbery with Ash before the event and, later, had discussed the results of the robbery with Ash in the presence of Bailey. McFarland was shown to possess an extensive criminal record and a history as an informer.

"The jury convicted Ash on all counts. It was unable to reach a verdict on the charges against Bailey and his motion for acquittal was granted. . . ."

* * *

"[A] review of the history and expansion of the Sixth Amendment counsel guarantee demonstrates that the test utilized by the Court has called for examination of the event in order to determine whether the accused required aid in coping with legal problems or assistance in meeting his adversary. . . .

* * *

"The structure of *Wade*, viewed in light of the careful limitation of the Court's language to 'confrontations,' makes it clear that lack of scientific precision and inability to reconstruct an event are not the tests for requiring counsel in the first instance. These are, instead, the tests to determine whether confrontation with counsel at trial can serve as a substitute for counsel at the pretrial confrontation. If accurate reconstruction is possible, the risks inherent in any confrontation still remain, but the opportunity to cure defects at trial causes the confrontation to cease to be 'critical.' . . ."

* * *

"A substantial departure from the historical test would be necessary if the Sixth Amendment were interpreted to give Ash a right to counsel at the photographic identification in this case. Since the accused himself is not present at the time of the photographic display, and asserts no right to be present, no possibility arises that the accused might be misled by his lack of familiarity with the law or overpowered by his professional adversary. Similarly, the counsel guarantee would not be used to produce equality in a trial-like adversary confrontation. . . .

"Even if we were willing to view the counsel guarantee in broad terms as a generalized protection of the adversary process, we would be unwilling to go so far as to extend the right to a portion of the prosecutor's trial-preparation interviews with witnesses. . . . The traditional counterbalance in the American adversary system for these interviews arises from the equal ability of defense counsel to seek and interview witnesses himself.

"That adversary mechanism remains as effective for a photographic display as for other parts of pretrial interviews. No greater limitations are placed on defense counsel in constructing displays, seeking witnesses, and conducting photographic identifications than those applicable to the prosecution. Selection of the picture of a person other than the accused, or the inability of a witness to make any selection, will be useful to the defense in precisely the same manner that the selection of a picture of the defendant would be useful to the prosecution. In this very case, for example, the initial tender of the photographic display was by Bailey's counsel, who sought to demonstrate that the witness had failed to make a photographic identification. Although we do not suggest that equality of access to photographs removes all potential for abuse, it does remove any inequality in the adversary process itself and thereby fully satisfies the historical spirit of the Sixth Amendment's counsel guarantee.

* * *

"Pretrial photographic identifications, however, are hardly unique in offering possibilities for the actions of the prosecutor unfairly to prejudice the accused. Evidence favorable to the accused may be withheld; testimony of witnesses may be manipulated; the results of laboratory tests may be contrived. In many ways the prosecutor, by accident or by design, may improperly subvert the trial. The primary safeguard against abuses of this kind is the ethical responsibility of the prosecutor, who, as so often has been said, may 'strike hard blows' but not 'foul ones.' If that safeguard fails, review remains available under due process standards. These same safeguards apply to misuse of photographs.

"We are not persuaded that the risks inherent in the use of photographic displays are so pernicious that an extraordinary system of safeguards is required.

"We hold, then, that the Sixth Amendment does not grant the right to counsel at photographic displays conducted by the Government for the purpose of allowing a witness to attempt an identification of the offender....

"Mr. Justice Stewart concurring in the judgment.

* * *

"A photographic identification is quite different from a lineup, for there are substantially fewer possibilities of impermissible suggestion when photographs are used, and those unfair influences can be readily reconstructed at trial....

"Preparing witnesses for trial by checking their identification testimony against a photographic display is little different, in my view, from the prosecutor's other interviews with the victim or other witnesses before trial. While these procedures can be improperly conducted, the possibility of irretrievable prejudice is remote, since any unfairness that does occur can usually be flushed out at trial through cross-examination of the prosecution witnesses....

"Mr. Justice Brennan, with whom Mr. Justice Douglas and Mr. Justice Marshall join, dissenting.

* * *

"Indeed, in reality, preservation of the photographs affords little protection to the unrepresented accused. For although retention of the photographs may mitigate the dangers of misidentification due to the suggestiveness of the photographs themselves, it cannot in any sense reveal to defense counsel the more subtle, and therefore more dangerous, suggestiveness that might derive from the manner in which the photographs were displayed or any accompanying comments or gestures.

"Finally, and *unlike* the lineup situation, the accused himself is not even present at the photographic identification, thereby reducing the likelihood that irregularities in the procedures will ever come to light....

* * *

"The fundamental premise underlying *all* of this Court's decisions holding the right to counsel applicable at 'critical' pretrial proceedings, is that a 'stage' of the prosecution must be deemed 'critical' for the purposes of the Sixth Amendment if it is one at which the presence of counsel is necessary to protect the fairness of *the trial itself.*

"This established conception of the Sixth Amendment guarantee is, of course, in no sense dependent upon the physical 'presence of the accused,' at a 'trial-like confrontation' with the Government, at which the accused requires the 'guiding hand of counsel.' ...

* * *

"There is something ironic about the Court's conclusion today that a pretrial lineup identification is a 'critical stage' of the prosecution because counsel's presence can help to compensate for the accused's deficiencies as an observer, but that a pretrial photographic identification is not a 'critical stage' of the prosecution because the accused is not able to observe at all. In my view, there simply is no meaningful difference, in terms of the need for attendance of counsel, between corporeal and photographic identifications...."

May the police, after the initiation of a formal criminal proceeding, videotape a lineup in the absence of defense counsel and then display the tape to witnesses, again in the absence of defense counsel? Is the policy argument for the right to counsel stronger or weaker under these circumstances than in *Ash?* Does the *Ash* language about the "assistance" of counsel apply so as to exclude the right to counsel as it does in a situation where the suspect himself is not present at the photographic identification procedure. See United States v. Amrine, 724 F.2d 84 (8th Cir.1983).

6. Assuming that counsel has no right to be present when the police talk to a witness shortly before a lineup, must counsel be permitted to be present when the police interview the witness immediately after the witness views the lineup? The courts have said no. United States v. Jones, 907 F.2d 456 (4th Cir.1990); People v. Carpenter, 15 Cal.4th 312, 63 Cal.Rptr.2d 1, 935 P.2d 708 (1997) Consider United States v. Tolliver, 569 F.2d 724 (2d Cir.1978):

"The Line–Up Procedure

"... the exclusion of counsel from the room where Zima made his identification an unconstitutional deprivation of appellant's right to counsel at a 'crucial stage of the proceeding'.

"... In *Wade,* the Court held that a post-indictment line-up was a 'critical' stage in a criminal proceeding and that the Sixth Amendment right of confrontation required the presence of counsel at the line-up. The Court said nothing about when a line-up ends, so that counsel need no longer be present. It can be argued that a line-up is not finished until the witness has declared whether or not he can identify a particular person as the perpetrator of the crime. People v. Williams, 3 Cal.3d 853, 856, 92 Cal.Rptr. 6, 8–9, 478 P.2d 942, 944–45 (1971) (4 to 3). On the other hand, it can be maintained that the purpose for which counsel must be present is essentially to see that the line-up procedure is itself adequate to avoid improper suggestion, such as the wearing of differentiating clothes, or a disparity in appearance between the other persons in the line-up and the suspect himself.

"The Fourth, Fifth and Ninth Circuits have held that the 'confrontation' ends when the defendant is no longer in the presence of the identifying witness, and that his identification may, therefore, be revealed in private to the prosecution, at least in the first instance, without the presence of defense counsel.

"In [the Fourth Circuit case of United States v. Cunningham, 423 F.2d 1269 (1970)], Judge Winter reasoned that '[t]he rationale of these cases is the potential intentional or unintentional suggestion inherent in the actual confrontation and the difficulty of establishing at trial by objective evidence the circumstances under which the line-up proceeded.'

"We now join our sister circuits in holding that the actual identification from a *line-up* (as well as a photographic spread), if made outside the presence of the defendant, is constitutionally valid, since the actual confrontation is the only 'critical stage' requiring the presence of counsel.

"We note, however, that the verbatim recording of the identification or failure of identification is so easy to achieve that it should be considered as an extension of the line-up, even though the 'confrontation' feature ends when the defendant no longer faces the witness. There is no reason why the statement of the witness, even if not made immediately available to the defendant, should not be preserved and made available to defense counsel in time for a pretrial suppression hearing. And even when videotape is not available, a tape recording machine is generally procurable without difficulty.

"No recording was made here. We think this was error, but, in the circumstances of this case, harmless error.

"Our problem on this appeal goes beyond the problem faced by the Fourth, Fifth and Ninth Circuits. Those cases did not deal with a refusal by the prosecution to let the defense know who the identifying witness was, nor did they involve a denial of access to him for pretrial interview, as was the case here.

"On the contrary, part of the rationale for holding that defense counsel need not be present at the moment of identification has been thought to be that the witness was made available to defense counsel for interview thereafter and, in any event, before the trial began. In this case, the opposite procedure was followed. The witness was told not to say anything during the line-up while defense counsel was present, and defense counsel was not permitted to learn the identity of the witness until it was flushed out by means of the motion to suppress.

"Discovery of evidence in criminal prosecutions is, inevitably, more restricted than discovery in civil cases.... In strict logic one may, of course, ask why, if the object of discovery is truth, it is not even more important to allow full discovery to a criminal defendant whose liberty is at stake. The conventional answers, which have stood the test of time, are that there is more likelihood of the subornation of perjury by bribery or threat in criminal cases, and that where certain defendants who have been committed to a life of violence are involved, the danger to the safety of the witness outweighs total discovery as a *preliminary* requirement of fair trial. Cross-examination at the trial assisted by such modern aids as the Jencks

Act, 18 U.S.C. § 3500, and the limited discovery provided by the Federal Rules of Criminal Procedure, have been thought to be weapons strong enough to prevent miscarriages of justice.

"There is, to be sure, no way to prove the thesis. We may in fact, admit that the prevalence of violence in our social order has led to some weakening of the procedures available to defendants charged with crimes. In consequence, the pervasive fear for the safety of witnesses must, in some respects, adversely affect even the docile type of criminal defendant who would harm no one by physical violence....

* * *

"Even if a constitutional principle were involved, however, we could hardly suggest a neutral principle that separates the potentially violent defendant from others. It has always been the burden of the non-violent criminal to suffer from some of the restrictions imposed for fear of harm from the violent. Here the defendant was a participant in an armed robbery and escape. The third man was unapprehended and at large. We can make no special rule for such a case, but the wisdom, indeed the necessity, for protecting identifying witnesses from harm must be a paramount consideration. We, accordingly, hold that the prosecution may withhold the identity of witnesses on identification, subject to the rules applicable to disclosure of prosecutorial evidence, and, generally, only if the interview after the line-up is recorded and preserved. We believe, moreover, that, before such withholding of identity by the prosecution upon a post-indictment line-up, a direction to permit such procedure should be obtained from the judge *ex parte* as a means of resolving the conflict between a defendant's need for evidence and the Government's claim of privilege based on a finding that the public security requires the withholding. While such a direction was not obtained from Judge Dooling, and the identification interviews were not recorded, the error was harmless here. There can be no doubt that Tolliver was, indeed, the driver of the Cadillac, and the only exculpating evidence presented was defendant's pretrial statement that he was not involved in the robbery, which the jury declined to credit. There was no constitutional or other error in the line-up procedure followed, and even if the refusal to disclose the identity of Zima should be held to be error of constitutional magnitude, it would be 'harmless constitutional error.' "

7. The cases decided after *Wade* and *Gilbert* have held the essential purpose served by counsel at the lineup is that of a witness or observer. Counsel cannot stop a lineup simply by walking away. See Vernon v. State, 12 Md.App. 430, 278 A.2d 609 (1971). There are some inherent problems for defense counsel who appears at a lineup for his client. Does he have a duty to make suggestions about how to make the lineup fairer? If he does make suggestions, should they be designed to produce a fair lineup or one weighted as heavily as possible in favor of his client? A searching criticism of the use of counsel to correct lineup abuses is found in Read, Lawyers at Lineups, Constitutional Necessity or Avoidable Extravagance?, 17 UCLA L.Rev. 339 (1969). Consider these excerpts:

"(a) *Those Participating May Be Police Officers*. How will a lawyer's presence change this and is this an evil in and of itself? It must be remembered that the purpose of a lineup is to aid the police in investigating a crime. Certainly it must be conceded that police should be able to participate in their own investigative techniques.

"(b) *The Participants' Names Are Rarely Divulged*. The obvious remedy is to require the names to be divulged. In the District of Columbia a 'sheet' is routinely kept, listing the names of those participating in the lineup and the names of the conducting officers. The sheet is available to the defense.

"(c) *The Victim Is Not an Effective Witness as to What Occurred.* Neither is the defendant's lawyer. Audio and visual recording devices, photographs, and the like are much more effective. Even a lay observer, in the absence of such devices, would probably make a better witness than the defendant's lawyer. It is my view the jury would be much more likely to believe an independent observer than an accused's own attorney testifying on behalf of his client.

"(d) *The Victim's Outrage May Excite 'Vengeful or Spiteful Motives' and the Victim Will Not Be Alert to Conditions Prejudicial to the Suspect.* A lawyer's presence will not change this. Only regularized lineup procedures that are faithfully followed can minimize suggestive procedures that may point the victim's outrage at the wrong person.

"(e) *Neither Witnesses Nor Lineup Participants Are Alert for Conditions 'Prejudicial' to the Suspect or Schooled in the Detection of Suggestive Influence.* A lawyer is not necessarily 'schooled' in detecting suggestive influences either. A psychologist might be better equipped for the task. Even assuming the lawyer spots such conditions, what can he do about them except prepare himself to be a witness at trial? Certainly any impartial observer, acquainted with the problem and given examples of what to look for, could do as well as any lawyer. Better yet, since the purpose of a lawyer's presence is to acquaint judge and jury with what occurred, photographs, videotapes, or recordings would do this much more vividly. And adoption of regularized procedures might avoid suggestive conditions in the first place.

"(f) *Jury Will Not Believe a Suspect's Version of What Occurred.* Will it be much more likely to believe the suspect's lawyer's version of what occurred? Probably not. Therefore, objective reproduction by mechanical devices again will better counter this evil."

Professor Read studied one jurisdiction (District of Columbia) in which efforts were made to provide counsel at lineups. His finding:

"Legal Aid seems to concede that under present conditions there is no real reason for defense counsel to appear at the lineup. First, except for minor alterations, the police will not change their set procedures. Second, there is no one there to record any objection that might be made. Legal Aid personnel seem generally to be of the opinion that the presence of an attorney at a lineup is simply not necessary if the attorney is to take a limited role.

* * *

"Experienced police officers and prosecuting attorneys are convinced that any discovery of a witness' name by some defense attorneys is tantamount to disclosure of that name to that lawyer's client. These same police officers and prosecuting attorneys feel that many prospective witnesses are refusing to participate in lineup procedures because of real fear of retaliation from the accused or friends of the accused once a witness' identity is discovered. A particularly sensitive situation evidently exists in the District of Columbia. It was reported that fear of physical intimidation seems especially acute among many Negro witnesses and victims of crime who are asked to cooperate with the police. Police officers charged that the real problem with the lineups is not that witnesses are too susceptible to suggestion but, on the contrary, witnesses are too reluctant to participate freely in the process. Several defense attorneys conceded that a serious problem of witness intimidation does exist and that Wade's command that a lawyer be present at lineups may have exacerbated the situation.

"Another vigorously raised complaint of police and prosecution attorneys relates to the conduct of defense counsel in altering the appearance of their clients prior to their client's participation in a lineup. For example, a young defendant may be arrested while sporting a mustache, an 'Afro haircut' and very bright clothing. When he shows up for the lineup, his Afro haircut is removed, his mustache is shaved off, and he is wearing a suit and tie. An extreme example of this occurred when a female impersonator was arrested in his feminine disguise and then showed up for the lineup in typical male attire. The United States Attorney's Office thus feels that intimidation and disguise of suspects by defense lawyers is the 'other side of the coin' from the suggestive influence problem."

[Ed. Note. The incident of changed appearance cited by Professor Read is quite similar to that which occurred in United States v. Jackson, 476 F.2d 249 (7th Cir.1973)].

"My observations and conversations with police, prosecuting attorneys and defense attorneys have convinced me that the lineup is a necessary tool in the arsenal of investigatory techniques available to the police. However, it is also my view that the presence of defense counsel at a lineup is simply not necessary to insure the fairness of the procedure. His passive role renders him basically impotent; he is unable to change the slightest detail in any way unless the police decide to cooperate; he is unable to make and have recorded any objections he may have; and he has no way of preserving what occurred except through his own notes and memory.

"Not only is the defense lawyer's presence only minimally effective in preventing unfairness and preserving a record of what occurred, his presence, in certain cases, can actually hinder the administration of criminal justice. Some lawyers have turned the lineup, a police investigatory technique, into a discovery proceeding. A serious danger of intimidation exists in many cases when the identity of witnesses is discovered and disclosed to defendants. Furthermore, by drastically altering the appearance of defendants, defense counsel can actually nullify the usefulness of the lineup process as an investigatory tool. Wade was intended to protect an accused from suggestive lineup procedures; however, in certain cases, the real effect of the Wade remedy is to destroy the utility of the lineup procedure and to make intimidation of witnesses easier."

8. In *Wade* it was suggested that "Legislative or other regulations, such as those of local police departments, which eliminate the risk of abuse and unintentional suggestion at lineup proceedings and the impediments to meaningful confrontation at trial may also remove the basis for regarding the stage as 'critical' ", United States v. Wade, 388 U.S. at 239, 87 S.Ct. at 1938. Yet, that language was explicitly disavowed by four of six Justices joining in the opinion. (Black, J. and Fortas, J. joined by Warren, C.J., and Douglas, J.). A fifth Justice implicitly rejected the proposition. (Clark, J.).

The only attempt to rely on the suggestion that regulations might obviate the right to counsel has been rebuffed with the reasoning that such regulations would be adequate only if they succeeded in elevating eyewitness identification procedures to the level of reliability present in procedures for analyzing fingerprints, blood samples and hair. See People v. Fowler, 1 Cal.3d 335, 82 Cal.Rptr. 363, 461 P.2d 643, 652 (1969). If this is the standard to be met by legislation or regulation, then is acceptable regulation possible? Is this the appropriate standard by which to judge lineup regulations?

B. SUGGESTIVENESS IN IDENTIFICATION PROCEDURES

Manson v. Brathwaite

Supreme Court of the United States, 1977.
432 U.S. 98, 97 S.Ct. 2243.

■ MR. JUSTICE BLACKMUN delivered the opinion of the Court.

* * *

I.

Jimmy D. Glover, a full-time trooper of the Connecticut State Police, in 1970 was assigned to the Narcotics Division in an undercover capacity. On May 5 of that year, about 7:45 p.m. E.D.T. and while there was still daylight, Glover and Henry Alton Brown, an informant, went to an apartment building at 201 Westland, in Hartford, for the purpose of purchasing narcotics from "Dickie Boy" Cicero, a known narcotics dealer. Cicero, it was thought, lived on the third floor of that apartment building. Glover and Brown entered the building, observed by back-up Officers D'Onofrio and Gaffey, and proceeded by stairs to the third floor. Glover knocked at the door of one of the two apartments served by the stairway. The area was illuminated by natural light from a window in the third floor hallway. The door was opened 12 to 18 inches in response to the knock. Glover observed a man standing at the door and, behind him, a woman. Brown identified himself. Glover then asked for "two things" of narcotics. The man at the door held out his hand, and Glover gave him two $10 bills. The door closed. Soon the man returned and handed Glover two glassine bags. While the door was open Glover stood within two feet of the person from whom he made the purchase and observed his face. Five to seven minutes elapsed from the time the door first opened until it closed the second time.

Glover and Brown then left the building. This was about eight minutes after their arrival. Glover drove to headquarters where he described the seller to D'Onofrio and Gaffey. Glover at that time did not know the identity of the seller. He described him as being "a colored man, approximately five feet eleven inches tall, dark complexion, black hair, short Afro style, and having high cheekbones, and of heavy build. He was wearing at the time blue pants and a plaid shirt." D'Onofrio, suspecting from this description that respondent might be the seller, obtained a photograph of respondent from the Records Division of the Hartford Police Department. He left it at Glover's office. D'Onofrio was not acquainted with respondent personally, but did know him by sight and had seen him "[s]everal times" prior to May 5. Glover, when alone, viewed the photograph for the first time upon his return to headquarters on May 7; he identified the person shown as the one from whom he had purchased the narcotics.

The toxicological report on the contents of the glassine bags revealed the presence of heroin. The report was dated July 16, 1970.

Respondent was arrested on July 27 while visiting at the apartment of a Mrs. Ramsey on the third floor of 201 Westland, This was the apartment at which the narcotics sale had taken place on May 5.

Respondent was charged, in a two-count information, with possession and sale of heroin. At his trial in January 1971, the photograph from which Glover had identified respondent was received in evidence. ... Glover also testified that, although he had not seen respondent in the eight months that had elapsed since the sale, "there [was] no doubt whatsoever" in his mind that the person shown on the photograph was respondent. Glover made a positive in-court identification without objection.

No explanation was offered by the prosecution for the failure to utilize a photographic array or to conduct a lineup....

The jury found respondent guilty on both counts of the information. He received a sentence of not less than six nor more than nine years....

* * *

II.

Stovall v. Denno [1967] concerned a petitioner who had been convicted in a New York court of murder. He was arrested the day following the crime and was taken by the police to a hospital where the victim's wife, also wounded in the assault, was a patient. After observing Stovall and hearing him speak, she identified him as the murderer. She later made an in-court identification. ... This Court affirmed. On the identification issue, the Court reviewed the practice of showing a suspect singly for purposes of identification, and the claim that this was so unnecessarily suggestive and conducive to irreparable mistaken identification that it constituted a denial of due process of law. The Court noted that the practice "has been widely condemned," but it concluded that "a claimed violation of due process of law in the conduct of a confrontation depends on the totality of the circumstances surrounding it." In that case, showing Stovall to the victim's spouse "was imperative." The Court then quoted the observations of the Court of Appeals, to the effect that the spouse was the only person who could possibly exonerate the accused; that the hospital was not far from the courthouse and jail; that no one knew how long she might live; that she was not able to visit the jail; and that taking Stovall to the hospital room was the only feasible procedure, and, under the circumstances, " 'the usual police station line-up ... was out of the question.' "

Neil v. Biggers [1972] concerned a respondent who had been convicted in a Tennessee court of rape, on evidence consisting in part of the victim's visual and voice identification of Biggers at a stationhouse showup seven months after the crime. The victim had been in her assailant's presence for some time and had directly observed him indoors and under a full moon outdoors. She testified that she had "no doubt" that Biggers was her assailant. She previously had given the police a description of the assailant. She had made no identification of others presented at previous showups, lineups, or through photographs. ... held that the evidence properly had been allowed to go to the jury. The Court reviewed Stovall and certain later cases where it had considered the scope of due process protection against the admission of evidence derived from suggestive identification procedures, namely, Simmons v. United States (1968); Foster v. California (1969); and Coleman v. Alabama (1970).[8] The Court concluded that general guidelines emerged from these cases "as to the relationship between suggestiveness and misidentification." The "admission of evidence of a showup without more does not violate due process." The Court expressed concern about the lapse of seven months between the crime and the confrontation and observed that this "would be a seriously negative factor in most cases." The "central question," however, was "whether under the 'totality of the circumstances' the identification was reliable even though the confrontation procedure was suggestive." Applying that test, the Court found "no substantial likelihood of misidentification. The evidence was properly allowed to go to the jury."

* * *

Biggers well might be seen to provide an unambiguous answer to the question before us: the admission of testimony concerning a suggestive and unnecessary identification procedure does not violate due process so long as the identification possesses sufficient aspects of reliability.[9] In one passage,

8. Simmons involved photographs, mostly group ones, shown to bank-teller victims who made in-court identifications. The Court discussed the "chance of misidentification," declined to prohibit the procedure "either in the exercise of our supervisory power or, still less, as a matter of constitutional requirement," and held that each case must be considered on its facts and that a conviction would be set aside only if the identification procedure "was so impermissibly suggestive as to give rise to a very substantial likelihood of irreparable misidentification." The out-of-court identification was not offered. Mr. Justice Black would have denied Simmons' due process claim as frivolous.

Foster concerned repeated confrontations between a suspect and the manager of an office that had been robbed. At a second lineup, but not at the first and not at a personal one-to-one confrontation, the manager identified the suspect. At trial he testified as to this and made an in-court identification. The Court reaffirmed the Stovall standard and then concluded that the repeated confrontations were so suggestive as to violate due process. The case was remanded for the state courts to consider the question of harmless error.

In Coleman a plurality of the Court was of the view that the trial court did not err when it found that the victim's in-court identifications did not stem from a lineup procedure so impermissibly suggestive as to give rise to a substantial likelihood of misidentification.

9. Mr. Justice Marshall argues in dissent that our cases have "established two different due process tests for two very different situations." Pretrial identifications are to be covered by Stovall, which is said to require exclusion of evidence concerning unnecessarily suggestive pretrial identifications without regard to reliability. In-court identifications, on the other hand, are to be governed by Simmons and admissibility turns on reliability. The Court's cases are sorted into one category or the other. Biggers, which clearly adopts the reliability of the identification as the guiding factor in the admissibility of both pre-trial and in-court identifications, is condemned for mixing the two lines and for adopting a uniform rule.

Although it must be acknowledged that our cases are not uniform in their emphasis, they hardly suggest the formal structure the dissent would impose on them. If our cases truly established two different rules, one might expect at some point at least passing reference to the fact. There is none. And if Biggers departed so grievously from the past cases, it is surprising that there was not at least some mention of the point in Mr. Justice Brennan's dissent. In fact, the cases are not so readily sorted as the dissent suggests. Although Foster involved both in-court and

however, the Court observed that the challenged procedure occurred pre-*Stovall* and that a strict rule would make little sense with regard to a confrontation that preceded the Court's first indication that a suggestive procedure might lead to the exclusion of evidence. One perhaps might argue that, by implication, the Court suggested that a different rule could apply post-*Stovall*. The question before us, then, is simply whether the *Biggers* analysis applies to post-*Stovall* confrontations as well as to those pre-*Stovall*.

III.

In the present case ... the "sole evidence tying Brathwaite to the possession and sale of the heroin consisted in his identifications by the police undercover agent, Jimmy Glover."

* * *

IV.

The State at the outset acknowledges that "the procedure in the instant case was suggestive [because only one photograph was used] and unnecessary" [because there was no emergency or exigent circumstance]. The respondent, ... proposes a *per se* rule of exclusion that he claims is dictated by the demands of the Fourteenth Amendment's guarantee of due process. He rightly observes that this is the first case in which this Court has had occasion to rule upon strictly post-*Stovall* out-of-court identification evidence of the challenged kind.

Since the decision in *Biggers*, the courts of appeals appear to have developed at least two approaches to such evidence. The first, or *per se* approach, employed by the Second Circuit in the present case, focuses on the procedures employed and requires exclusion of the out-of-court identification evidence, without regard to reliability, whenever it has been obtained through unnecessarily suggested confrontation procedures.[10] The justifications advanced are the elimination of evidence of uncertain reliability, deterrence of the police and prosecutors, and the stated "fair assurance against the awful risks of misidentification."

The second, or more lenient, approach is one that continues to rely on the totality of the circumstances. It permits the admission of the confrontation evidence if, despite the suggestive aspect, the out-of-court identification possesses certain features of reliability. Its adherents feel that the *per se* approach is not mandated by the Due Process Clause of the Fourteenth

out-of-court identifications, the Court seemed to apply only a single standard for both. And although Coleman involved only an in-court identification, the plurality cited Stovall for the guiding rule that the claim was to be assessed on the "totality of the surrounding circumstances." Thus, Biggers is not properly seen as a departure from the past cases, but as a synthesis of them.

10. Although the *per se* approach demands the exclusion of testimony concerning unnecessarily suggestive identifications, it does permit the admission of testimony concerning a subsequent identification, including an in-court identification, if the subsequent identification is determined to be reliable. The totality approach, in contrast, is simpler: if the challenged identification is reliable, then testimony as to it and any identification in its wake is admissible.

Amendment. This second approach, in contrast to the other, is *ad hoc* and serves to limit the societal costs imposed by a sanction that excludes relevant evidence from consideration and evaluation by the trier of fact.

The respondent here stresses the need for deterrence of improper identification practice, a factor he regards as pre-eminent. Photographic identification, it is said, continues to be needlessly employed. He notes that the legislative regulation "the Court hoped *Wade* would engender" has not been forthcoming. He argues that a totality rule cannot be expected to have a significant deterrent impact; only a strict rule of exclusion will have direct and immediate impact on law enforcement agents. Identification evidence is so convincing to the jury that sweeping exclusionary rules are required. Fairness of the trial is threatened by suggestive confrontation evidence, and thus, it is said, an exclusionary rule has an established constitutional predicate.

There are, of course, several interests to be considered and taken into account.... *Wade* and its companion cases reflect the concern that the jury not hear eyewitness testimony unless that evidence has aspects of reliability. It must be observed that both approaches before us are responsive to this concern. The *per se* rule, however, goes too far since its application automatically and peremptorily, and without consideration of alleviating factors, keeps evidence from the jury that is reliable and relevant.

The second factor is deterrence. Although the *per se* approach has the more significant deterrent effect, the totality approach also has an influence on police behavior. The police will guard against unnecessarily suggestive procedures under the totality rule, as well as the *per se* one, for fear that their actions will lead to the exclusion of identifications as unreliable.

The third factor is the effect on the administration of justice. Here the *per se* approach suffers serious drawbacks. Since it denies the trier reliable evidence, it may result, on occasion, in the guilty going free. Also, because of its rigidity, the *per se* approach may make error by the trial judge more likely than the totality approach. And in those cases in which the admission of identification evidence is error under the *per se* approach but not under the totality approach—cases in which the identification is reliable despite an unnecessarily suggestive identification procedure—reversal is a draconian sanction. Certainly, inflexible rules of exclusion, that may frustrate rather than promote justice, have not been viewed recently by this Court with unlimited enthusiasm.

* * *

The standard, after all, is that of fairness as required by the Due Process Clause of the Fourteenth Amendment.

We therefore conclude that reliability is the linchpin in determining the admissibility of identification testimony for both pre- and post-*Stovall* confrontations. The factors to be considered are set out in *Biggers*. These include the opportunity of the witness to view the criminal at the time of the crime, the witness' degree of attention, the accuracy of his prior description of the criminal, the level of certainty demonstrated at the confrontation, and the time between the crime and the confrontation.

Against these factors is to be weighed the corrupting effect of the suggestive identification itself.

V.

We turn, then, to the facts of this case and apply the analysis:

1. The opportunity to view. Glover testified that for two to three minutes he stood at the apartment door, within two feet of the respondent. The door opened twice, and each time the man stood at the door. The moments passed, the conversation took place, and payment was made. Glover looked directly at his vendor. It was near sunset, to be sure, but the sun had not yet set, so it was not dark or even dusk or twilight. Natural light from outside entered the hallway through a window. There was natural light, as well, from inside the apartment.

2. The degree of attention. Glover was not a casual or passing observer, as is so often the case with eyewitness identification. Trooper Glover was a trained police officer on duty—and specialized in dangerous duty—when he called at the third floor of 201 Westland in Hartford on May 5, 1970. Glover himself was a Negro and unlikely to perceive only general features of "hundreds of Hartford black males," as the Court of Appeals stated. It is true that Glover's duty was that of ferreting out narcotics offenders and that he would be expected in his work to produce results. But it is also true that, as a specially trained, assigned, and experienced officer, he could be expected to pay scrupulous attention to detail, for he knew that subsequently he would have to find and arrest his vendor. In addition, he knew that his claimed observations would be subject later to close scrutiny and examination at any trial.

3. The accuracy of the description. Glover's description was given to D'Onofrio within minutes after the transaction. It included the vendor's race, his height, his build, the color and style of his hair, and the high cheekbone facial feature. It also included clothing the vendor wore. No claim has been made that respondent did not possess the physical characteristics so described. D'Onofrio reacted positively at once. Two days later, when Glover was alone, he viewed the photograph D'Onofrio produced and identified its subject as the narcotics seller.

4. The witness' level of certainty. There is no dispute that the photograph in question was that of respondent. Glover, in response to a question whether the photograph was that of the person from whom he made the purchase, testified: "There is no question whatsoever." This positive assurance was repeated.

5. The time between the crime and the confrontation. Glover's description of his vendor was given to D'Onofrio within minutes of the crime. The photographic identification took place only two days later. We do not have here the passage of weeks or months between the crime and the viewing of the photograph.

These indicators of Glover's ability to make an accurate identification are hardly outweighed by the corrupting effect of the challenged identification itself. Although identifications arising from single-photograph displays may be viewed in general with suspicion, we find in the instant case little pressure on the witness to acquiesce in the suggestion that such a display entails. D'Onofrio had left the photograph at Glover's office and was not present when Glover first viewed it two days after the event. There thus was little urgency and Glover could view the photograph at his leisure. And since Glover examined the photograph alone, there was no coercive pressure to make an identification arising from the presence of another. The identification was made in circumstances allowing care and reflection.

* * *

Surely, we cannot say that under all the circumstances of this case there is "a very substantial likelihood of irreparable misidentification." Simmons v. United States. Short of that point, such evidence is for the jury to weigh. We are content to rely upon the good sense and judgment of American juries, for evidence with some element of untrustworthiness is customary gist for the jury mill. Juries are not so susceptible that they cannot measure intelligently the weight of identification testimony that has some questionable feature.

We conclude that the criteria laid down in *Biggers* are to be applied in determining the admissibility of evidence offered by the prosecution concerning a post-*Stovall* identification, and that those criteria are satisfactorily met and complied with here.

The judgment of the Court of Appeals is reversed.

■ MR. JUSTICE STEVENS, concurring.

While I join the Court's opinion, I would emphasize two points.

First, as I indicated in my opinion in United States ex rel. Kirby v. Sturges, 510 F.2d 397, 405–406 (7th Cir.1975), the arguments in favor of fashioning new rules to minimize the danger of convicting the innocent on the basis of unreliable eyewitness testimony carry substantial force. Nevertheless, for the reasons stated in that opinion, as well as those stated by the Court today, I am persuaded that this rulemaking function can be performed "more effectively by the legislative process than by a somewhat clumsy judicial fiat," and that the Federal Constitution does not foreclose experimentation by the States in the development of such rules.

Second, in evaluating the admissibility of particular identification testimony it is sometimes difficult to put other evidence of guilt entirely to one side.*

* In this case, for example, the fact that the defendant was a regular visitor to the apartment where the drug transaction occurred tends to confirm his guilt. In the *Kirby* case, supra, where the conviction was for robbery, the fact that papers from the victim's wallet were found in the possession of the defendant made it difficult to question the reliability of the identification. These facts should not, however, be considered to support the admissibility of eyewitness testimony when applying the criteria identified in *Biggers*. Properly analyzed, however, such facts would be relevant to a question whether error, if any, in admitting identification testimony was harmless.

■ MR. JUSTICE BLACKMUN's opinion for the Court carefully avoids this pitfall and correctly relies only on appropriate indicia of the reliability of the identification itself. Although I consider the factual question in this case extremely close, I am persuaded that the Court has resolved it properly.

■ MR. JUSTICE MARSHALL, with whom MR. JUSTICE BRENNAN joins, dissenting.

Today's decision can come as no surprise to those who have been watching the Court dismantle the protections against mistaken eyewitness testimony erected a decade ago in *Wade*, *Gilbert*, and Stovall v. Denno. But it is still distressing to see the Court virtually ignore the teaching of experience embodied in those decisions and blindly uphold the conviction of a defendant who may well be innocent.

The development of due process protections against mistaken identification evidence, begun in *Stovall*, was continued in Simmons v. United States (1968). There, the Court developed a different rule to deal with the admission of in-court identification testimony that the accused claimed had been fatally tainted by a previous suggestive confrontation. In *Simmons*, the exclusionary effect of *Stovall* had already been accomplished, since the prosecution made no use of the suggestive confrontation. *Simmons*, therefore, did not deal with the constitutionality of the pretrial identification procedure. The only question was the impact of the Due Process Clause on an in-court identification that was not itself unnecessarily suggestive. *Simmons* held that due process was violated by the later identification if the pretrial procedure had been "so impermissibly suggestive as to give rise to a very substantial likelihood of irreparable misidentification." This test focused not on the necessity for the challenged pretrial procedure, but on the degree of suggestiveness that it entailed. In applying this test, the Court understandably considered the circumstances surrounding the witnesses' initial opportunity to view the crime. Finding that any suggestion in the pretrial confrontation had not affected the fairness of the in-court identification, *Simmons* rejected petitioner's due process attack on his conviction.

Again, comparison with the *Wade* cases is instructive. The inquiry mandated by *Simmons* is similar to the independent source test used in *Wade* where an in-court identification is sought following an uncounseled lineup. In both cases, the issue is whether the witness is identifying the defendant solely on the basis of his memory of events at the time of the crime, or whether he is merely remembering the person he picked out in a pretrial procedure. Accordingly, in both situations, the relevant inquiry includes factors bearing on the accuracy of the witness' identification, including his opportunity to view the crime.

Thus, *Stovall* and *Simmons* established two different due process tests for two very different situations. Where the prosecution sought to use evidence of a questionable pretrial identification, *Stovall* required its exclusion, because due process had been violated by the confrontation, unless the necessity for the unduly suggestive procedure outweighed its potential for generating an irreparably mistaken identification. The *Simmons* test, on the other hand, was directed to ascertaining due process violations in the introduction of in-court identification testimony that the defendant claimed was tainted by pretrial procedures. In the latter situation, a court could consider the reliability of the identification under all the circumstances.

* * *

The Court inexplicably seemed to erase the distinction between *Stovall* and *Simmons* situations in Neil v. Biggers.

* * *

Apparently, the Court does not consider *Biggers* controlling in this case. I entirely agree, since I believe that *Biggers* was wrongly decided. The Court, however, concludes that *Biggers* is distinguishable because it, like the identification decisions that preceded it, involved a pre-*Stovall* confrontation, and because a paragraph in *Biggers* itself seems to distinguish between pre- and post-*Stovall* confrontations. Accordingly, in determining the admissibility of the post-*Stovall* identification in this case, the Court considers two alternatives, a *per se* exclusionary rule and a totality of the circumstances approach. The Court weighs three factors in deciding that the totality approach, which is essentially the test used in *Biggers*, should be applied. In my view, the Court wrongly evaluates the impact of these factors.

First, the Court acknowledges that one of the factors, deterrence of police use of unnecessarily suggestive identification procedures, favors the *per se* rule. Indeed, it does so heavily, for such a rule would make it unquestionably clear to the police they must never use a suggestive procedure when a fairer alternative is available. I have no doubt that conduct would quickly conform to the rule.

Second, the Court gives passing consideration to the dangers of eyewitness identification recognized in the *Wade* trilogy. It concludes, however, that the grave risk of error does not justify adoption of the *per se* approach because that would too often result in exclusion of relevant evidence. In my view, this conclusion totally ignores the lessons of *Wade*. The dangers of mistaken identification are, as *Stovall* held, simply too great to permit unnecessarily suggestive identifications. Neither *Biggers* nor the Court's opinion today point to any contrary empirical evidence. Studies since *Wade* have only reinforced the validity of its assessment of the dangers of identification testimony. While the Court is "content to rely on the good sense and judgment of American juries," the impetus for *Stovall* and *Wade* was repeated miscarriages of justice resulting from juries' willingness to credit inaccurate eyewitness testimony.

Finally, the Court errs in its assessment of the relative impact of the two approaches on the administration of justice. The Court relies most heavily on this factor finding that "reversal is a draconian sanction" in cases where the identification is reliable despite an unnecessarily suggestive procedure used to obtain it. Relying on little more than a strong distaste for "inflexible rules of exclusion," the Court rejects the *per se* test. In so doing, the Court disregards two significant distinctions between the *per se* rule advocated in this case and the exclusionary remedies for certain other constitutional violations.

First, the *per se* rule here is not "inflexible." Where evidence is suppressed, for example, as the fruit of an unlawful search, it may well be forever lost to the prosecution. Identification evidence, however, can by its very nature be readily and effectively reproduced. The in-court identification, permitted under *Wade* and *Simmons* if it has a source independent of an uncounseled or suggestive procedure, is one example. Similarly, when a prosecuting attorney learns that there has been a suggestive confrontation, he can easily arrange another lineup conducted under scrupulously fair conditions. Since the same factors are evaluated in applying both the Court's totality test and the *Wade–Simmons* independent source inquiry, any identification which is "reliable" under the Court's test will support admission of evidence concerning such a fairly conducted lineup. The evidence of an additional, properly conducted confrontation will be more persuasive to a jury, thereby increasing the chance of a justified conviction where a reliable identification was tainted by a suggestive confrontation. At the same time, however, the effect of an unnecessarily suggestive identification—which has no value whatsoever in the law enforcement process—will be completely eliminated.

Second, other exclusionary rules have been criticized for preventing jury consideration of relevant and usually reliable evidence in order to serve interests unrelated to guilt or innocence, such as discouraging illegal searches or denial of counsel. Suggestively obtained eyewitness testimony is excluded, in contrast, precisely because of its unreliability and concomitant irrelevance. Its exclusion both protects the integrity of the truth-seeking function of the trial and discourages police use of needlessly inaccurate and ineffective investigatory methods.

Indeed, impermissibly suggestive identifications are not merely worthless law enforcement tools. They pose a grave threat to society at large in a more direct way than most governmental disobedience of the law. For if the police and the public erroneously conclude, on the basis of an unnecessarily suggestive confrontation, that the right man has been caught and convicted, the real outlaw must still remain at large. Law enforcement has failed in its primary function and has left society unprotected from the depredations of an active criminal.

For these reasons, I conclude that adoption of the *per se* rule would enhance, rather than detract from, the effective administration of justice. In my view, the Court's totality test will allow seriously unreliable and misleading evidence to be put before juries. Equally important, it will allow dangerous criminals to remain on the streets while citizens assume that police action has given them protection. According to my calculus, all three of the factors upon which the Court relies point to acceptance of the *per se* approach.

Even more disturbing than the Court's reliance on the totality test, however, is the analysis it uses, which suggests a reinterpretation of the concept of due process of law in criminal cases. The decision suggests that due process violations in identification procedures may not be measured by whether the Government employed procedures violating standards of fundamental fairness. By relying on the probable accuracy of a challenged identification, instead of the necessity for its use, the Court seems to be ascertaining whether the defendant was probably guilty. Until today, I had thought that "Equal justice under law" meant that the existence of constitutional violations did not depend on the race, sex, religion, nationality or likely guilt of the accused. The Due Process Clause requires adherence to the same high standard of fundamental fairness in dealing with every criminal defendant, whatever his personal characteristics and irrespective of the strength of the State's case against him. Strong evidence that the defendant is guilty should be relevant only to the determination whether an error of constitutional magnitude was nevertheless harmless beyond a reasonable doubt. See Chapman v. California (1967). By importing the question of guilt into the initial determination of whether there was a constitutional violation, the apparent effect of the Court's decision is to undermine the protection afforded by the Due Process Clause. It is therefore important to note that the state courts remain free, in interpreting state constitutions, to guard against the evil clearly identified by this case.

* * *

Despite my strong disagreement with the Court over the proper standards to be applied in this case, I am pleased that its application of the totality test does recognize the continuing vitality of *Stovall*. In assessing the reliability of the identification, the Court mandates weighing "the corrupting effect of the challenged identification itself" against the "indicators of [a witness'] ability to make an accurate identification." The Court holds, as Neil v. Biggers failed to, that a due process identification inquiry must take account of the suggestiveness of a confrontation and the likelihood that it led to misidentification, as recognized in *Stovall* and *Wade*. Thus, even if a witness did have an otherwise adequate opportunity to view a criminal, the later use of a highly suggestive identification procedure can render his testimony inadmissible. Indeed, it is my view that, assuming applicability of the totality test enunciated by the Court, the facts of the present case require that result.

* * *

NOTES

* * *

1. In determining whether there was an independent source of an in-court identification, several factors are considered. The most common of these are:

> (1) prior opportunity of witnesses to observe the criminal act, (2) existence of a discrepancy between any pre-lineup description and the actual appearance of the accused, (3) any identification of another person prior to the lineup, (4) failure to identify the accused on a prior occasion, (5) lapse of time between the criminal act and the lineup identification, (6) prior photographic identification from a large group of photographs, (7) the presence of distinctive physical characteristics in defendant, (8) prior acquaintance of witness with the suspect, (9) ability and training at identification, (10) the exercise of unusual care to make observations, (11) prompt identification at first confrontation.

See United States ex rel. Geralds v. Deegan, 292 F.Supp. 968 (S.D.N.Y.1968), and 307 F.Supp. 56 (S.D.N.Y.1969), and People v. Kachar, 400 Mich. 78, 252 N.W.2d 807 (1977).

In State v. Ramirez, 817 P.2d 774 (Utah 1991), the Court criticized *Manson* for considering the certainty of identification to be a factor supporting its reliability as "scientifically unsound". The Utah Court said the factors should be:

> "(1) The opportunity of the witness to view the actor during the event; (2) the witness's degree of attention to the actor at the time of the event; (3) the witness's capacity to observe the event, including his or her physical and mental acuity; (4) whether the witness's identification was made spontaneously and remained consistent thereafter, or whether it was the product of suggestion; and (5) the nature of the event being observed and the likelihood that the witness would perceive, remember and relate it correctly. This last area includes such factors as whether the event was an ordinary one in the mind of the observer during the time it was observed, and whether the race of the actor was the same as the observer's."

The Utah court's rejection of witness certainty as a factor to be considered (at least in support of admissibility) has been adopted in Brodes v. State, 279 Ga. 435, 614 S.E.2d 766 (2005) as well as Kansas, and Massachusetts. It has been rejected in State v. Ledbetter, 275 Conn.2d 534, 881 A.2d 290 (2005)

There are still other courts that suppress all evidence of pretrial identifications made at unnecessarily suggestive identification procedures even when they have determined there is an independent basis which would permit an identification made at trial. See State v. Dubose, 285 Wis.2d 143, 699 N.W.2d 582 (2005) (citing Massachusetts and New York practice).

There are few cases where courtroom identifications are suppressed. See United States v. Concepcion, 983 F.2d 369 (2d Cir.1992), United States v. Emanuele, 51 F.3d 1123 (3d Cir.1995). In Commonwealth v. Bonnoyer, 25 Mass.App.Ct. 444, 519 N.E.2d 791 (1988), the Court suppressed identification testimony where the witness had a poor opportunity to observe the robber, gave a vague description and hesitated before making identification. After identification she expressed doubts to a police officer who told her not to worry—an accomplice had confessed and named defendant. The trial judge found that her present recognition of defendant was based upon seeing Bonnoyer at court appearances. On appeal the Court said:

> The Commonwealth, convinced of Bonnoyer's guilt, views as disproportionate a remedy that may enable him to escape prosecution. There is no certainty, however, that he was in fact the second robber, as there sometimes is when a perpetrator is apprehended at the scene, or is known to an eyewitness, or is found shortly thereafter with identifiable stolen articles. It does not threaten the integrity of the truth-finding process to force the prosecution to rely (to the extent that it can) on what so far as now appears is the only genuinely solid evidence that it has implicating Bonnoyer: namely, the testimony of Jensen, the confessed robber.
>
> In affirming the judge's ruling as a proper exercise of his discretion, we stress the unique configuration of facts this case presents. Surely there will be many instances in which a witness to a crime will identify a perpetrator and then learn of facts confirming the correctness of his identification: that the person he had identified has confessed, for example, or has been found in possession of loot or a distinctive weapon, or has been independently identified by another witness. No problem of admissibility will arise, either under the independent source test of *Commonwealth v. Botelho* or the reliability test of *Neil v. Biggers* (1972), so long as the initial identification

and its later repetitions are found to be based on the witness's observations at the scene of the crime. The factors which make this case distinctive are that Haber's initial identification was unreliable; her ability to identify Bonnoyer now is the product not of her observations at the time of the robbery but of the confirmatory evidence of an accomplice's confession; the confession, insofar as it implicates Bonnoyer, is not self-evidently reliable; it will not be admissible (unless Jensen testifies); Haber learned of it only after expressing her doubts as to the correctness of her identification; and the source of her information was a police officer who divulged it for the purpose of putting her doubts to rest.

If the trial court decides to suppress evidence of pre-trial confrontation but refuses to suppress evidence of in-court identification, the defense has the option to bring the pre-trial confrontation out at trial if it is thought helpful to a defense attack on the courtroom identification. Davis v. State, 467 P.2d 521 (Okl.1970). If the defense brings out some of the facts concerning the pre-trial confrontation, the state may bring out the rest of the circumstances. Commonwealth v. Redmond, 357 Mass. 333, 258 N.E.2d 287 (1970).

2. There are two important questions about the functional effect of the exclusion rules:

(a) Can it be said from the point of view of the prosecutor that *Stovall* and *Brathwaite* are far more significant than *Wade* because, as a practical matter, only the application of *Stovall* and *Brathwaite* can cause the loss of the entire testimony of a witness, and that the worst consequence of a violation of *Wade–Gilbert* is the suppression of evidence of a pre-trial identification by a witness?

Assume a case arising where a defendant is placed in a post-indictment lineup without waiving counsel. *Wade–Gilbert* has been violated. But assume that the lineup is perfectly fair, consisting of seven men of the same height, hair color, race and general appearance, all similarly dressed. If the victim identifies the defendant, the victim will not be able to testify concerning the lineup. But the witness will be able to make a courtroom identification because it is clear that a perfectly fair lineup could not have tainted the courtroom identification. See Nielssen v. State, 456 S.W.2d 928 (Tex.1970). Indeed, the fairness of the lineup itself, coupled with a positive identification, is clear and convincing evidence that the witness had a strong basis for identification prior to the lineup. A *Stovall–Brathwaite* violation is of far greater potential consequence than a *Wade–Gilbert* violation. The former tends to impugn the integrity of the witness' courtroom identification while the latter does not. In those jurisdictions where the prosecution is prohibited from showing that a witness made a prior identification the effect of *Wade–Gilbert* alone is negligible. See 4 Wigmore, Evidence, Sec. 1130 (Chadbourn Rev. 1972); 71 A.L.R.2d 449.

In those jurisdictions where evidence of pre-trial identification is admissible what value does this evidence have? See United States v. Williams, 421 F.2d 1166 (D.C.Cir.1970). In an urban jurisdiction a jury may hear evidence of an in-court identification a year or more after the date of the crime. Could the absence of evidence of pre-trial identification affect their verdict?

(b) Again, as a practical matter, will there be a case where a pre-trial confrontation is deemed unreliable under *Brathwaite* but the in-court identification is properly admitted as untainted? When a court determines reliability of a pre-trial confrontation under the guidelines announced in *Brathwaite*, is it not considering precisely the same factors it must consider when determining whether an in-court identification has a source independent of a pre-trial confrontation?

3. As an alternative to exclusionary rules, would a careful jury instruction on the subject of eye-witness identification strike directly at the problem? Jurisdictions vary widely with respect to their jury-instruction policy in this area. The Supreme Court of Tennessee has drafted a standard instruction to be given in all cases in which eyewitness testimony is challenged by defendant *or* is uncorroborated. The instruction must be requested by defendant. It reads:

> One of the issues in this case is the identification of the defendant as the person who committed the crime. The state has the burden of proving identity beyond a reasonable doubt. Identification testimony is an expression of belief or impression by the witness, and its value may depend upon your consideration of several factors. Some of the factors which you may consider are:
>
> (1) The witness' capacity and opportunity to observe the offender. This includes, among other things, the length of time available for observation, the distance from which the witness observed, the lighting, and whether the person who committed the crime was a prior acquaintance of the witness;
>
> (2) The degree of certainty expressed by the witness regarding the identification and the circumstances under which it was made, including whether it is the product of the witness' own recollection:
>
> (3) The occasions, if any, on which the witness failed to make an identification of the defendant, or made an identification that was inconsistent with the identification at trial; and
>
> (4) The occasions, if any, on which the witness made an identification that was consistent with the identification at trial, and the circumstances surrounding such identifications.
>
> Again, the state has the burden of proving every element of the crime charged, and this burden specifically includes the identity of the defendant as the person who committed the crime for which he or she is on trial. If after considering the identification testimony in light of all the proof you have a reasonable doubt that the defendant is the person who committed the crime, you must find the defendant not guilty.

See State v. Dyle, 899 S.W.2d 607 (Tenn.1995). Compare the instruction advocated in United States v. Telfaire, 469 F.2d 552 (D.C.Cir.1972).

If the Utah Court in Ramirez (supra n.1) is correct that a witness' confidence in the identification should never be considered, then do the Tennessee instruction or those in Telaire actually make things worse for the defendant. One prominent defense counsel thinks so. James M. Doyle, No Confidence: A Step Toward Accuracy In Eyewitness Trials, The Champion, Jan.BFeb. 1998, page 12.

4. The due process clause condemns confrontations which are "unnecessarily suggestive and conducive to irreparable mistaken identification." Stovall v. Denno, supra, which announced this rule, also upheld a confrontation with a witness thought to be near death because the procedure was *necessarily* suggestive.

Are there any other forms of necessarily suggestive confrontations? Consider the 6 10 or the 4 10 suspect, or the suspect with prominent scars or tattoos. Consider also the suspect who engages in conduct which attracts attention, i.e., protests his arrest, buries his head in his hands, etc. See What value has the notion that in difficult cases the police ought to use photographic identification procedures? Is the notion based on the assumption that eyewitness identification is based exclusively on facial characteristics? If so, is that a valid assumption? Is photographic identification as reliable as corporeal identification? In the last analysis does the presence of unusual physical characteristics make identification more or less reliable? If a suspect is so unusual that he cannot be placed in an adequate line-up, is it fairer to use a one to one "showup"? The only general principle on which there seems to be consensus is that general similarity of persons in a display is required but there is no duty to create a lineup of look-alikes. United States v. Rose, 362 F.3d 1059 (8th Cir.2004)

5. The first test by which a line-up or a photographic display is judged is whether it is suggestive. The question of necessity need be reached only if there is suggestiveness. The suggestiveness must be the result of police actions if a motion to suppress is to succeed. Green v. State, 279 Ga. 455, 614 S.E.2d 751 (2005) (majority rule) but see the often disregarded case of Thigpen v. Cory, 804 F.2d 893 (6th Cir.1986) (holding that it is not police misconduct but reliability that is the concern that motivated the holding in *Manson*)

Suggestiveness is tested by looking at what the witness sees and then asking which of the persons in the line-up stands out. A line-up must also be weighed in terms of the individual witnesses. For example, a line-up may include several fairly similar men all wearing eyeglasses only one of which has horn rim frames. If the witness described the criminal as wearing eyeglasses, the line-up may be perfectly valid. If the witness specifically described the criminal's glasses as horn-rimmed, a different view of the line-up might be taken. Generally speaking, a few objective standards for fair line-ups can be definitely established but the courts have not had great difficulty making the determination on a case by case basis. Sometimes, however, the judgment is difficult to make at the trial level. Both court and counsel are familiar with what the defendant looks like, and in a line-up photograph, the defendant will stand out. Whether the defendant would stand out to the eyes of a witness who had observed only the crime is another question and, of course, the only question that has to be answered.

One interesting method to test suggestiveness would be to form a street corner poll, by presenting a picture of a line-up to a group of strangers and inquiring whether they can tell which person is the one suspected by the police. This was tried in People v. Suleski, 58 A.D.2d 1023, 397 N.Y.S.2d 280 (1977), but the results (seven out of ten picked the defendant) did not persuade the court to condemn the line-up. See, Reed, Eyewitness Identification of An Armed Robber Within a Biased Police Lineup, 12 J.Pol.Sci. 310 (1984). In People v. Edmonson, 75 N.Y.2d 672, 555 N.Y.S.2d 666, 554 N.E.2d 1254 (1990), a woman was attacked on the street by a man she had seen in a certain neighborhood. Police went there and videotaped persons in that area. The victim made an identification from the tape of many persons who passed by the camera. The Court found the procedure to be very fair when used with complete randomness. The Court said:

> "In short, just as there can be no objection to permitting a victim to canvass an area for her attacker, there can be none to a videotaping procedure, such as that used here, which simply permits her to do the same without actually being on the streets."

6. Suggestiveness may also inhere in circumstances occurring outside the limited sphere of what the witness sees at a line-up. The police may indirectly tell a witness that a particular man is their candidate for prosecution, i.e., "Take a good look at the third man from the left." The fact that the police say that they have a suspect in custody does not constitute a suggestive practice so long as no particular suspect is pointed out by police. See People v. Wooley, 127 Ill.App.2d 249, 262 N.E.2d 237 (1970); State v. McClure, 107 Ariz. 351, 488 P.2d 971 (1971). The reasoning of these courts is that any witness who is asked to view a line-up will obviously conclude that the police have a suspect. See Coleman v. Alabama, 399 U.S. 1, 6, 90 S.Ct. 1999, 2001 (1970).

7. In *Stovall* the Supreme Court specifically noted that "The practice of showing suspects singly to persons for the purpose of identification, and not as part of a line-up has been widely condemned."

In People v. Riley, 70 N.Y.2d 523, 522 N.Y.S.2d 842, 517 N.E.2d 520 (1987), the New York Court of Appeals strongly condemned the practice of displaying a single suspect to a witness in a non-emergency station-house showup. Where police have employed an unnecessarily suggestive procedure, *Riley* holds that the prosecution bears the "heavy" burden of showing "independent source reliability" to justify admission of any subsequent identification including the in-court identification. *Riley* seems to suggest that, even after Manson v. Brathwaite (Casebook, p. 303), sometimes the trial court should exclude an out-of-court identification on due process grounds while admitting the in-court identification. The United States Supreme Court has not resolved either the burden issue as to reliability or the question of whether once the out-of-court identification is deemed unreliable, the in-court identification also must be deemed unreliable.

Yet an exception to this rule has been found in cases involving confrontations occurring shortly after the crime. In Bates v. United States, 405 F.2d 1104 (D.C.Cir.1968), the Court (Burger, C.J.) said:

> "There is no prohibition against a view of a suspect alone in what is called a 'one-man show-up' when this occurs near the time of the alleged criminal act; such a course does not tend to bring about misidentification but rather tends under some circumstances to insure accuracy. The rationale underlying this is in some respects not unlike that which the law relies on to make an exception to the hearsay rule, allowing spontaneous utterances a standing which they would not be given if uttered at a later point in time. An early identification is not in error. Of course, proof of infirmities and subjective factors, such as hysteria of a witness, can be explored on cross-examination and in argument. Prudent police work would confine these on-the-spot identifications to situations in which possible doubts as to identification needed to be resolved promptly; absent such need the conventional line-up viewing is the appropriate procedure.
>
> "... [T]he police action in returning the suspect to the vicinity of the crime for immediate identification fosters the desirable objective of fresh, accurate identification which in some instances may lead to the immediate release of an innocent suspect and at the same time enable the police to resume the search for the fleeing culprit while the trial is fresh".

How prompt must a confrontation be in order to come within this exception? The usual case involves an identification made no more than two or three hours after the offense. People v. Duuvon, 77 N.Y.2d 541, 569 N.Y.S.2d 346, 571 N.E.2d 654 (1991); United States v. Watson, 76 F.3d 4 (1st Cir.1996).

A similar doctrine has arisen when a witness accidentally encounters a suspect as in the case where both are injured and brought to the same emergency room. In such a case *Stovall* is not likely to affect admissibility. This conclusion rests on two factors: (a) there is no deliberate misconduct by the police, see Coleman v. Alabama, 399 U.S. 1, 90 S.Ct. 1999 (1970), and, (b) if the confrontation is truly accidental then there is likely to have been no suggestive aspect leading to an unreliable identification. United States v. Pollack, 427 F.2d 1168 (5th Cir.1970) (court building); State v. Dutton, 112 N.J.Super. 402, 271 A.2d 593 (1970) (at hospital—victim on a stretcher). A victim of a mugging promptly reported the crime to police who then drove him around the vicinity to search for the muggers. During the drive the victim pointed to Dixon on the street and said he was one of the muggers. The Court held that the canvass of the neighborhood was a police sponsored procedure and not an accidental encounter and thus a hearing was required to determine whether the identification was "spontaneous" or "suggested." Two dissenters argued the hearing was pointless since it was a prompt identification procedure with no evidence of suggestion, simply because the police arranged the procedure is not enough to require inquiry into suggestiveness. People v. Dixon, 85 N.Y.2d 218, 623 N.Y.S.2d 813, 647 N.E.2d 1321 (1995).

8. The exclusionary rule of *Stovall* and *Brathwaite* has not been thought to affect the validity of normal courtroom identification procedures. It is usually within the discretion of the trial court whether to grant a defense or prosecution request for a lineup in the courtroom to test witness identification. See United States v. Meyer, 359 F.3d 820 (6th Cir.2004) People ex rel. Blassick v. Callahan, 50 Ill.2d 330, 279 N.E.2d 1 (1972) (thorough citation of cases on point). Consider the comments of the court in United States v. Hamilton, 469 F.2d 880 (9th Cir.1972):

> "It might well be argued that the deeply-rooted practice of allowing witnesses to identify the defendant in open court is no less a suggestive show-up than those condemned by *Stovall* and *Foster*. But we decline to take the giant step of holding in-court identifications inadmissible. It is sufficient safeguard that the accused be allowed to question the weight to be given the 'in-court' identification considering the length of time the witness saw the perpetrator of the crime, the elapsed time between the act and the trial, and the fact that the witness had made no other identification of the defendant."

In Moore v. Illinois, note 4 following Kirby v. Illinois, Section A, supra, the Supreme Court took note of some procedures designed to diminish courtroom suggestiveness but did not assert that they were required. Perhaps the basis for accepting a traditional courtroom identification rests on the assumption that it will have been preceded by a less suggestive identification procedure. One court has rejected the argument that an in court lineup is required where there has been no pre-trial identification procedure. United States v. Domina, 784 F.2d 1361 (9th Cir.1986) (review of prior decisions). But a few courts hold that it may be an abuse of discretion to deny a court ordered lineup in certain cases. See United States v. Archibald, 734 F.2d 938 (2d Cir.1984) and 756 F.2d 223 (2d Cir.1984); State in Interest of W.C., 85 N.J. 469, 427 A.2d 566 (1980).

The broader question of the significance of a suggestive procedure which follows a valid identification is discussed in Patterson v. United States, 384 A.2d 663 (D.C.App.1978):

> FERREN, ASSOCIATE JUDGE:
>
> "Just after 11:00 p.m. on September 6, 1975, Raymond Holmes set out for a local bar.... As he approached the corner ... Mr. Holmes spotted two men standing on the opposite side of the street. As he was waiting at the corner for a vehicle to pass, one of the men approached him, grabbed him from behind, and, pressing a hard object into his back, demanded his money. When Mr. Holmes turned and discovered that he was being threatened at 'Coke-bottle-point,' he started to scuffle with the assailant. At that point the second individual whom he had observed across the street approached, struck him on the head with a bottle, and removed his watch. After some further scuffling, during the course of which Mr. Holmes observed the facial features of the attackers, the robbers took flight amidst a shower of hard objects (stones, bottles, etc.) thrown by Mr. Holmes. The entire incident lasted approximately five minutes.
>
> "Mr. Holmes hailed a passing policewoman and reported the incident; she summoned another officer by radio. The police transported Mr. Holmes around the vicinity for a while, hoping that he might spot the attackers.

After approximately one-half hour of unsuccessful searching, they returned him to his home.

"Before long, Mr. Holmes set out once again for the bar. Sometime between 12:30 and 12:45 a.m. on September 7, as he neared the same corner at which he was robbed, he saw the individual who had first grabbed him coming down Buchanan Street. Mr. Holmes called the police, pointed out the assailant to Officer Belisle (who had responded to the call), and rode with the officer down the block to the robber's location. As he observed Officer Belisle arresting the first attacker (later identified as appellant Witherspoon), Mr. Holmes saw the other assailant (appellant Patterson) standing among the onlookers. He apprised Officer Thornes who was standing nearby, whereupon Officer Thornes arrested Mr. Patterson.

"On the morning set for trial, April 1, 1976, the [prosecutor] displayed "mug shot" photographs of the defendants to Mr. Holmes to be certain that he could identify them at trial. To the prosecutor's surprise, Mr. Holmes first stated that the individuals in the photographs did not look like his assailants—that the men in the pictures looked older, more mature. Only after more viewing and reflection did Mr. Holmes decide that the photographs depicted the likenesses of the robbers.

"The prosecutor informed defense counsel and the court about these events. The court then entertained defense motions to suppress prospective in-court identifications.

"In the present case, the trial judge implicitly found suggestiveness; he then ... found ... a basis for identification that makes it nonetheless reliable. His suggestiveness determination unquestionably was correct. ... [T]he prosecutor's single-photo displays are inherently suggestive.

"Ordinarily, once unnecessary suggestiveness is found, its conduciveness to 'irreparable misidentification' is obvious. The court accordingly proceeds ... to ... the assessment of whether the identification is nonetheless reliable, based on the various factors enumerated in *Manson*.... The present case is of a rare breed, however, for although the single-photo displays were unnecessarily suggestive, they were not conducive to irreparable misidentification. Thus ... we do not leave the first stage of the inquiry; reliability does not become an issue in the same sense that it typically does following a suggested identification.

"In the more common case of a challenged identification, a suspect is apprehended based on a police lookout, after which a complaining witness is asked to identify the suspect at a highly suggestive showup or at an arguably skewed or otherwise suggestive photographic array or lineup. From the very first identification, therefore, suggestiveness is inherent in the process; there is a risk of initial misidentification. Here, however, the first identifications occurred when Mr. Holmes sighted the suspects (who had robbed him merely an hour and a half before) and pointed them out to the officers. He led the police to the appellants; the police did not bring them to Mr. Holmes. Thus, the initial identifications to the authorities unmistakably were based on observation without suggestion.

"It may well be true that the lapse of time between robbery and trial dimmed Mr. Holmes' memory of the suspects and that the single-photo displays helped bring his memory back. Nevertheless, as recent Supreme Court cases have made clear, these suggestive showings could not have created a 'very substantial likelihood of irreparable *misidentification*.' At worst, the 'refresher' photos produced a misleadingly current, positive identification derived from a previously untainted one. Just as a procedure devoid of suggestion cannot yield the 'primary evil' of misidentification, id., a procedure that includes suggestive elements *subsequent* to an unequivocal, unsuggested identification does not pose an unconstitutional risk of misidentification—of trying and convicting the wrong person.

"In the present case, the circumstances surrounding the refresher photograph, line-up, and in-court identifications were thoroughly examined at trial. Defense counsel relied heavily on the suggestiveness of the photo display, on Mr. Holmes' unexpected, initially negative responses, and on the various contradictions and confusion betrayed by his testimony describing the assailants. In the circumstances of this case, where positive on-sight identifications were made, the ambiguity and confusion which followed the photographic showing could only redound to the defendant's benefit. The credibility of Mr. Holmes' on-the-scene identifications could well have been damaged and his subsequent identifications devalued by his hesitation and inaccuracy at the photographic display. Appellants took full advantage of this development in their presentations before the jury.

"On the facts of this case, therefore, we hold, after making the first-stage inquiry, that the unnecessarily suggestive single-photo displays were *not* conducive to irreparable misidentification, because there had been a prior unequivocal, unsuggested, and otherwise constitutionally acceptable identification. No further inquiry is required. We affirm appellants' convictions."

9. Another possible basis for excluding eye-witness identifications, either out-of-court or in-court, might be that the initial identification took place after an unlawful arrest or during an unlawful detention. This topic is discussed further in Chapter 6, Section E, infra, See United States v. Crews, 445 U.S. 463, 100 S.Ct. 1244 (1980)and Johnson v. Louisiana, 406 U.S. 356, 92 S.Ct. 1620 (1972), where the Court found that a suspect's appearance before a magistrate, after an alleged unlawful arrest but before a lineup, purged the lineup of the taint of Fourth Amendment illegality.

10. Several works by psychologists may be of assistance to attorneys in preparing for cases involving eye-witness identification. See E. Loftus, Eye–Witness Testimony (1979); A.D. Yarmee, The Psychology of Eye Witness Testimony (1980). There is disagreement among psychologists about the validity of such testimony. The conflict of views is aired in McCloskey & Egeth, Eyewitness Identification: What Can A Psychologist Tell A Jury, 38 Am.Psych. 550 (1983) and Loftus, Silence is Not Golden, 38 Am.Psych. 564 (1983). Some courts say it is within the discretion of the trial judge whether to permit expert psychological testimony concerning eye-witness identification to be presented to the jury which is deciding innocence or guilt. For a review of the cases, see State v. Helterbridle, 301 N.W.2d 545 (Minn.1980). The federal courts are hostile to its admission. United States v. Smith, 122 F.3d 1355 (11th Cir.1997).

Experimental studies have continued. Most of them are cited in recent papers that followed a federally funded study of comparative procedures in three Illinois municipal police departments. Beginning in late 2004 and lasting for a year, the Illinois State Police, pursuant to legislation, conducted a pilot program designed "to test the effectiveness of the sequential, double-blind procedure" in real life. See Report to the Legislature of the State of Illinois: The Illinois Pilot Program on Sequential Double–Blind Identification Procedures. (Sheri H. Mecklenburg, Program Director) *available at* www.chicagopolice.org.

In three separate police departments of varying sizes, Chicago, Joliet and Evanston, the police used the traditional methods of having an officer who knew the identity of the suspect showing the witness the suspect and the fillers together in a simultaneous display, i.e. the traditional line-up, in 319 cases. In 229 cases, using a widely recommended method, the suspects were shown one-at-a-time and the procedure was conducted by an officer who did not know which person was the suspect. In evaluating the results, the testers presumed that the suspect was the offender which is ordinarily but not overwhelmingly true.

The results surprised more than a few people. The rate of correct identification was nearly 60% in the simultaneous procedure and 45% in the sequential one. Moreover, the false identification rate in simultaneous viewing was a bit less than 3% and rose to slightly more than 9% with the sequential procedure. The failure of any identification was nearly 37% in simultaneous and 47% in sequential.

The results were surprising because most reported laboratory research experiments had led to the expectation that the results would demonstrate the opposite result. There were other field studies of the methods, at least one of which favored, to some degree, sequential, double-blind methods. See Klobuchar, Steblay and Caligiuri, Protecting the Innocent/Convicting the Guilty: Hennepin County's Pilot Project in Blind Sequential Eyewitness Identification, 32 Wm. Mitchell L.Rev. 1 (2005) The Minnesota experiment, though, used a variant of the laboratory sanctioned method by showing the witness all photographs before allowing the witness to make an identification. Academic studies concluded that the witness should be asked to decide on each individual photograph as it is shown thus avoiding an identification based on a kind of relative judgment, in other words, to avoid a witness definitively picking the person who, of all presented, simply looks most like the offender. This is based on the unstated assumption that the offender is in the line-up.

When the results of the Illinois Pilot program were released, it was observed that "prosecutors are happy with the results and defenders are not. Why? Because they are in the adversarial mind set which is not the way to view these results and future results. What we ought to be after is accuracy of identification and what should please us is improvement in accuracy, not an improvement in the conviction or acquittal rate." James B. Zagel, Getting to Truth Before It Falls Into the Hands of the Lawyers: Pursuing Accuracy in Criminal Cases. 11 Loyola School of Law (Chicago) Public Interest Law Reporter Vol. 2 pp. 17, 34 (2006)

The results were criticized, for a variety of reasons. The study left open the question of whether it was simultaneous or sequential procedures that made a difference or whether it was the double-blind administration or whether it was the timing of the witness's decision. Moreover, the use of suspect as a proxy for actual guilt is, under the circumstances, justifiable but with the advent of extensive use of DNA evidence future experiments may be able to utilize a more reliable measure of actual guilt. DNA based experiments, though, might require, a few years to complete. And the field is not limited to the particular sequential double-blind method, so many different field tests will have to be run. The value of the pilot program should not be discounted, though. It was a comparison of one method which many had predicted would be superior against a specific method in common use by police. It did not prove to be superior and, even if we cannot know precisely why this is so, we do know that stronger evidence is required lest courts or legislatures or police reform their practices for the worse not the better.

The study is the subject of a series of articles in 11Loyola School of Law (Chicago) Public Interest Law Reporter Vol. 2 (2006) See especially Ebbe B. Ebbesen and Kristin M. Finklea, "In Response to the Illinois Pilot Program on

Simultaneous v. Sequential Lineups'' Roy S. Malpass, Notes on the Illinois Pilot Program on Sequential Double–Blind Identification Procedures.

A forthcoming issue of Law and Human Behavior rehearses the debate about the Illinois field study. See Gary L. Wells, Field Experiments on Eyewitness Identification: Towards a Better Understanding of Pitfalls and Prospects. (critical of the design of the study) See also Sheri H. Mecklenburg, Patricia J. Bailey, and Mark R. Larson, The Illinois Field Study: A Significant Contribution To Understanding Real World Eyewitness Identification Issues (asserting that the study had limited goals and achieved them). Finally there is an article signed by seven authors, six of whom are distinguished scientists. See Daniel L Schacter, et al., Policy Forum: Studying Eyewitness Investigations in the Field. This latter article concludes with this sentence:

''If the Illinois study was not designed to address the question of what happens in a blind/simultaneous line-up, given its centrality to the issue, then our assessment is that the Illinois study addressed a question . . . that is not worth answering because the results do not inform everyday practice in a useful manner.''

To a psychologist and, perhaps, to a police investigator, this is an understandable thesis, but everyday practice includes the decisions of courts. For the last decade or two or three, courts and policy makers have been urged to mandate the use of ''better'' methods of identification. The sequential double-blind procedure has been urged upon courts (and police administrators) as conclusively proven to have been superior. It is true that this claim is made by lawyers but the tone of some of the scientific papers reflects this premature claim of certainty. One court had to resolve an argument that the United States Constitution required a sequential procedure. See United States v. Lawrence, 349 F.3d 109 (3d Cir.2003).

The value of the Illinois study is found in the red flag it raises in the minds of judges who are asked to adopt definitive rules before there is definitive proof and in the minds of police administrators. There are enough examples of judicial and police acceptance of plausible, but bad, science to warrant caution. This is the ''everyday practice'' which the study informs in a useful manner.

The Seventh Circuit reiterated its rule that the admission of expert testimony about eyewitness identifications lies within the discretion of the trial judge. United States v. Hall, 165 F.3d 1095 (7th Cir.1999) In concurrence, Judge Easterbrook offered the following:

EASTERBROOK, CIRCUIT JUDGE, Concurring.

At Hall's first trial, the district court excluded expert testimony that Hall is especially vulnerable to suggestive interrogation. The judge thought that jurors have experience with questioning and can figure this subject out for themselves, but we observed: ''Because the fields of psychology and psychiatry deal with human behavior and mental disorders, it may be more difficult at times to distinguish between testimony that reflects genuine expertise—a reliable body of genuine specialized knowledge—and something that is nothing more than fancy phrases for common sense. It is nevertheless true that disorders exist, and the very fact that a layperson will not always be aware of the disorder, its symptoms, or its consequences, means that expert testimony may be particularly important when the facts suggest a person is suffering from a psychological disorder. . . . The court indicated that it saw no potential usefulness in the evidence, because it was within the jury's knowledge. This ruling overlooked the utility of valid social science. Even though the jury may have had beliefs about the subject, the question is whether those beliefs were correct. Properly conducted social science research often shows that commonly held beliefs are in error." 93 F.3d 1337, 1343, 1345 (7th Cir.1996). On remand, the district court inquired whether the testimony would be scientifically valid and reliable, see Daubert v. Merrell Dow Pharmaceuticals, Inc., 509 U.S. 579, 113 S.Ct. 2786 (1993), answered "yes," and admitted the evidence. 974 F.Supp. 1198 (C.D.Ill.1997). But the district court excluded expert testimony about eyewitness identification, observing that jurors have experience with observation and memory and can figure this subject out for themselves. Hall contends that the court has committed the same error a second time.

The district judge relied on United States v. Daniels, 64 F.3d 311 (7th Cir.1995), and its predecessors. Daniels states that "[e]xpert testimony regarding the potential hazards of eyewitness identifications ... will not aid the jury because it addresses an issue of which the jury already generally is aware, and it will not contribute to their understanding of the particular factual issues posed." 64 F.3d at 315. [but this does] not address the point the prior panel in this case made: "Properly conducted social science research often shows that commonly held beliefs are in error." Jurors who think they understand how memory works may be mistaken, and if these mistakes influence their evaluation of testimony then they may convict innocent persons. A court should not dismiss scientific knowledge about everyday subjects. Science investigates the mundane as well as the exotic. That a subject is within daily experience does not mean that jurors know it correctly. A major conclusion of the social sciences is that many beliefs based on personal experience are mistaken. The lessons of social science thus may be especially valuable when jurors are sure that they understand something, for these beliefs may be hard for lawyers to overcome with mere argument and assertion.

Another line of cases in this circuit ...is more open to the possibility that expert testimony may be especially valuable when the subject is "common knowledge." In Carroll v. Otis Elevator Co., 896 F.2d 210 (7th Cir.1990), for example, the court held it proper to admit the testimony of a psychologist about how colors influence children's behavior. A concurring opinion in Carroll elaborated: "In principle, a product could be unreasonably dangerous because its designers neglected to consider how children see things. A specialist in vision, illusion, and reaction is just the sort of person to assist on such questions. The manufacturer observes that expert testimony is inappropriate when the subject lies within the ken of laymen and insists that 'everyone knows' red is attractive. Maybe, but much of the science of experimental psychology consists in demonstrating that what 'everybody knows' is false." 896 F.2d at 215 ...

The only warrant for them is our certitude, and certitude is not a reliable test of certainty. Many people are certain that God exists. Many are certain that He does not exist. The believer and the nonbeliever are equally certain, but they cannot both be correct. Similarly, the mere fact that we remember something with great confidence is not a powerful warrant for thinking it true. It therefore becomes an empirical question whether and in what circumstances memory is accurate.... See Elizabeth F. Loftus & James M. Doyle, Eyewitness Testimony: Civil and Criminal (3d ed.1997)....

My colleagues finesse the subject by concluding that a district judge has discretion to assess the utility of evidence under Rules 403 and 702, and to admit or exclude it as circumstances require. I agree with this conclusion and join the opinion. But I am inclined to think that Daniels is right to suggest that evidence of this kind should not be admitted though not for the reason Daniels gives.

Much of the adversarial system rests on empirical propositions that may be investigated, and sometimes refuted, through scientific means. Consider, for example, the proposition—fundamental to any system that relies on lay adjudicators—that jurors understand and follow the instructions given by the court. It may be that jurors don't understand legalese, or if they understand the instructions don't follow them. See ... Neil Vidmar, The Performance of the American Civil Jury: An Empirical Perspective, 40 Ariz. L. Rev. 849 (1998) (recapitulating evidence about this issue). Or consider cross-examination. Jurors may believe that witnesses who hesitate, perspire, or fidget during cross-examination are hiding the truth. This is the view that underlies polygraph examinations, but without the precision of measurement. Is it true? Calm and collected liars deceive polygraph examiners (and thus jurors too); other witnesses grow restless or testy although they have nothing to hide. Suppose one of the litigants offers an expert in physiology to explain to jurors the (weak) correlation between lying and the appearance of discomfort on the stand. Or an expert in group dynamics to explain to a potential dissenter on the jury how to resist the pressure of the majority to go along—or for that matter how to see through lawyers' rhetorical tricks. Because trials rest on so many contestable empirical propositions, including those about eyewitness recollection, it always would be possible to offer expert evidence along these and related lines.

Yet a trial about the process of trials not only would divert attention from the main question (did Hall kill Jessica Roach?) and substantially lengthen the process but also would not do much to improve the accuracy of the outcome. Social science evidence is difficult to absorb; the idea of hypothesis formulation and testing is alien to most persons. That's one reason why the training of social scientists is so extended. Delivering a graduate level statistical-methods course to jurors is impractical, yet without it a barrage of expert testimony may leave the jurors more befuddled than enlightened. Many lawyers think that experts neutralize each other, leaving the jurors where they were before the process began. Many lawyers think that the best (= most persuasive) experts are those who have taken acting lessons and have deep voices, rather than those who have done the best research. Perhaps that is too pessimistic a view; but then the effect of experts is itself a question open to empirical inquiry, which might be added to the agenda for trial.

Instead of using the trial process to assess trials at retail, judges can and should employ social science to improve the trial process. Lessons about how jurors respond to jury instructions can be used to draft better instructions. (The Federal Judicial Center's pattern instructions were drafted with the aid of social scientists; so were this circuit's pattern criminal instructions.) Recognition that jurors cannot (and do not) always heed judges' instructions to disregard what they have heard, or to consider evidence against one litigant but not another, leads courts to prevent the use of certain kinds of evidence or to sever the proceedings. E.g., Gray v. Maryland, 523 U.S. 185, 118 S.Ct. 1151, 140 L.Ed.2d 294 (1998). Linguists and other experts could help jurors to interpret statutes, but judges do that task instead and give the results to the jury. Similarly a judge, recognizing the main conclusions of the scholarly study of memory—that "accuracy of recollection decreases at a geometric rather than arithmetic rate (so passage of time has a highly distorting effect on recollection); accuracy of recollection is not highly correlated with the recollector's confidence; and memory is highly suggestible—people are easily 'reminded' of events that never happened, and having been 'reminded' may thereafter hold the false recollection as tenaciously as they would a true one",—could block a lawyer from arguing that a given witness is sure of his recollection, and therefore is more likely to be right. The judge could inform jurors of the rapid decrease of accurate recollection, and the problem of suggestibility, without encountering the delay and pitfalls of expert testimony. Jurors are more likely to accept that information coming from a judge than from a scholar, whose skills do not lie in the ability to persuade lay jurors (and whose fidgeting on the stand, an unusual place for a genuine scholar, is apt to be misunderstood). Altogether it is much better for judges to incorporate scientific knowledge about the trial process into that process, rather than to make the subject a debatable issue in every case. There remains a question about where judges acquire scientific knowledge, for they too may be mistaken in what they think they know. Still, professional adjudicators who attend continuing judicial education programs and read the scholarly literature are more likely to absorb the lessons of science than are jurors force fed a little information during a trial.

Hall did not ask the judge to pass scientific knowledge on to the jury. His lawyers did not appreciate the big difference between the expert evidence considered on the first appeal and the evidence offered on remand.

The evidence we dealt with the last time around was evidence about Hall, suggesting that his psychological makeup was abnormal, not evidence about how ordinary witnesses interact with the trial process itself. Or, to put this in the language of administrative law, the expert testimony in the first trial was about an adjudicative fact; the proposed expert testimony in the second trial would have concerned a legislative fact. Hall did not object to any line of questioning or argument as incompatible with the lessons of science. So the possibilities I have been exploring are not presented in this case. But the subject is vital to a judicial system that seeks to improve the accuracy of the trial process, and thus as time passes more of the findings of modern social science research should be incorporated into legal rules about proper trial tactics and arguments.

11. Normally a motion to suppress identification testimony because of unnecessary suggestiveness is heard and resolved by the judge outside the presence of the jury, frequently before trial. The Constitution does not mandate such a procedure, however. See Watkins v. Sowders, 449 U.S. 341, 101 S.Ct. 654 (1981).

12. Where a witness has not made a previous identification of the defendant but is going to be called upon to make a courtroom identification, the defense may be concerned about the suggestiveness present in the courtroom setting. Justice White, dissenting in *Wade*, commented that *Wade* does not bar such courtroom identifications. Colorado held that the law does not require a pre-trial identification for a courtroom identification. People v. Monroe, 925 P.2d 767 (Colo.1996). However, defense lawyers sometimes ask the trial judge to order authorities to conduct a lineup before the in-court identification procedures take place. Most cases reject the argument that a defendant has the right to a lineup. But see Garcia v. Superior Court, 1 Cal.App.4th 979, 2 Cal.Rptr.2d 707 (1991) (may be special need for a voice only identification procedure) and see the dictum in Sims v. Sullivan, 867 F.2d 142 (2d Cir.1989):

> [F]ailure to grant a lineup may constitute a denial of fundamental fairness where the in-court identification is so unreliable that a very substantial likelihood of irreparable mistaken identification occurs.

13. In Johnson v. Ross, 955 F.2d 178 (2d Cir.1992) a witness identified defendant and his clothing. A trial court found the identification procedure to be suggestive and suppressed the identification of the defendant while permitting the witness to say the hat and jacket were those worn by the robber after which it was proven that the hat and jacket were worn by defendant when he was arrested. The Court said:

> Johnson's claim is flawed because the special dangers attendant to the identification of suspects do not exist with equal strength where the identification of clothing is concerned. Of course, the procedures used to obtain an identification of clothing can be suggestive. But it is the notorious inaccuracy of eyewitness identifications of *suspects* that gave the initial impetus to scholarly concern and judicial remedies. *See* Felice J. Levine, The Psychology of Criminal Identification: The Gap from *Wade* to *Kirby*, 121 U.Pa.L.Rev. 1079, 1081 (1973) ("Erroneous identification of suspects has long been recognized by commentators as a crucial problem in the administration of justice."); *United States v. Wade* (1967) ("The identification of strangers is proverbially untrustworthy.") Moreover, the unfairness that results from a potentially inaccurate, confrontational identification of a suspect is compounded by the persuasiveness with which juries regard this evidence. Levine, *supra*, at 1081–82. As the Supreme Court explained in *Wade*: "The trial which might determine the accused's fate may well not be that in the courtroom but that at the pretrial confrontation, with ... the witness the sole jury ... and with little or no effective appeal from the judgment there rendered by the witness—'that's the man.'" We have no basis to believe that a witness's identification of clothing is either as susceptible to error or as persuasive to a jury as a witness's identification of a suspect. Indeed, a clothing identification is—particularly in this day and age of mass-marketing—often open to the argument that someone other than the perpetrator may have worn the same clothing. Thus, we find that identification of clothing is not a procedure so inherently "conducive to irreparable mistaken identification," as to provide the basis for a denial of due process. Any suggestiveness is of course a proper matter for cross-examination as well as argument. Therefore, Johnson's claim must fail.

14. A small number of state courts (two) have rejected the rule which permits introduction of evidence of suggestive showups if the evidence is otherwise reliable. In Massachusetts and New York, an identification made at a suggestive procedure is per se inadmissible. Both rulings are based on state constitutions. Commonwealth v. Johnson, 420 Mass. 458, 650 N.E.2d 1257 (1995); People v. Adams, 53 N.Y.2d 241, 440 N.Y.S.2d 902, 423 N.E.2d 379 (1981).

15. Finally, consider the decisions of the Court in State v. McMorris, 213 Wis.2d 156, 570 N.W.2d 384 (1997) decided by a vote of 4–3.

> SHIRLEY S. ABRAHAMSON, CHIEF JUSTICE.
>
> On December 3, 1994, Patricia Jordan, a 67–year–old white woman, was robbed at knife-point as she was working alone at a grocery store in Mt. Pleasant, WI.
>
> According to Jordan, a man entered the store, walked up to the cash register where she was working and asked her for some change. Jordan was standing behind the counter, and the man was standing a couple of feet across from her on the other side. When Jordan opened the cash register to provide the change, the man pointed a knife at her, told her to leave the cash drawer open and took money from the drawer. As the robber

removed the cash from the drawer, Jordan backed away about 10 feet from the cash register and hid behind a meat slicer, while continuing to watch the robber. Jordan was wearing her eyeglasses at the time of the robbery, and the store was well lit. After the robber left the store, Jordan called the police.

About 15 to 20 minutes after the robbery, Officer Jason Wortock of the Mt. Pleasant Police Department arrived at the store. He interviewed Jordan and took down the physical description she gave of the robber. Jordan testified that the robber was an African–American male, at least six feet tall, wearing a white golfer's cap and a tan jacket. She said that she had never seen the robber before. She described the knife he used as a tapered, single-edged knife about 12 inches long. The police never recovered, by search warrant or otherwise, the knife, cap or jacket of the robber.

Later on the day of the robbery Officer Fulton Bell and Investigator Jayn Long showed the eyewitness six photographs of potential suspects, including one of the defendant. All the photographs were of African–American men, some with facial hair, some without. Apparently the police were uncertain at this time whether the robber had facial hair. The eyewitness did not identify the defendant or anyone else from the photo array as the robber.

A store surveillance camera taped the robbery which lasted approximately 25 seconds. The eyewitness viewed the videotape shortly after the robbery and turned it over to Officer Wortock who viewed the videotape with several other officers, including Officer Bell and Investigator Long.

After seeing the videotape, Officer Bell concluded that the robber looked like the defendant with whom Bell was familiar because they had grown up in the same neighborhood. Officer Bell testified that he had seen the defendant on November 29, 1994, four days before the robbery while responding to a civil disturbance call, and had observed that at that time the defendant had full facial hair and was wearing a tan jacket and a cap. (The defendant was not involved in the civil disturbance.)

Based upon her observation of the videotape and her subsequent in-person observation of the defendant at the Racine County Jail where he was incarcerated on an unrelated charge, Investigator Long concluded that the defendant was the robber. Prior to the robbery, Investigator Long had not been acquainted with the defendant.

On January 4, 1995, the defendant was charged with armed robbery, and a public defender was appointed the defendant's counsel. Five days later on January 9, 1995, Investigator Long, with the assistance of Corporal James Stratman, staged a lineup with five African–American males, including the defendant, all of whom were approximately the same weight and age as the defendant and all of whom had facial hair. Apparently the police at this time were operating on the premise that the robber had facial hair. After initially asking another man in the lineup to step forward, the eyewitness identified the defendant as the robber.

The defendant's counsel did not attend the lineup, and at no time did the defendant waive his right to have his counsel present. Investigator Long and Corporal Stratman failed to notify the defendant's counsel about the lineup, saying they were unaware that the defendant was entitled to have counsel present at a post-indictment lineup procedure. The officers did not photograph the lineup, either by video or still camera.

The eyewitness subsequently identified the defendant at the preliminary hearing on January 24, 1995, when he was wearing an orange jail uniform and was seated next to an attorney at a table. At the preliminary hearing the eyewitness testified that she knew the robber had long sideburns but was not sure if he had a mustache or beard. When asked at the preliminary hearing why she had selected the defendant at the lineup, the eyewitness testified that she chose him, in part, because he was tall.

The circuit court refused to suppress the lineup identification, concluding that the police had acted in good faith and that the lineup procedure was not otherwise impermissibly suggestive. The circuit court ruled that the jury would be instructed that the defendant had been deprived of his right to counsel at the lineup.

The Wade test places on the State the heavy burden of producing clear and convincing evidence for admission of in-court identification after identification in a lineup in which an accused's counsel was not present and no waiver of counsel occurred.

According to the Wade Court, to determine whether the in-court identification is " 'sufficiently distinguishable to be purged of the primary taint,' " a court should consider various factors including the following: (1) the prior opportunity the witness had to observe the alleged criminal activity; (2) the existence of any discrepancy between any pre-lineup description and the accused's actual description; (3) any identification of another person prior to the lineup; (4) any identification by picture of the accused prior to the lineup; (5) failure to identify the accused on a prior occasion; (6) the lapse of time between the alleged crime and the lineup identification; and (7) the facts disclosed concerning the conduct of the lineup.

[first] In this case, it is arguable that the eyewitness had sufficient opportunity to observe the robber. The store was adequately lighted to permit the eyewitness a clear view of the robber; the eyewitness was wearing her eyeglasses at the time of the robbery; when the robber first approached the eyewitness, he was standing only a couple of feet away from her, directly across the counter.

On the other hand, the eyewitness's opportunity to observe the robber was limited. The entire incident lasted a mere 25 seconds. While a court cannot specify a minimum amount of time necessary to demonstrate a sufficient opportunity to observe, the length of time for observation of the perpetrator is important. Moreover, as the robber took the money out of the cash register, the eyewitness moved back about 10 feet and hid behind a meat slicer while still observing him. The eyewitness, therefore, was not directly facing the robber throughout the entire 25-second incident. After reviewing the surveillance videotape, the circuit court found that the eyewitness's opportunity to observe the robber lasted approximately 20 seconds.

The court has also viewed the surveillance videotape, and it is difficult to determine from the tape how much time the eyewitness spent looking at the knife or the robber's face. At the suppression hearing, the eyewitness acknowledged that she concentrated on the knife during the robbery. She was able to give a detailed description of the knife. Furthermore, in this case, the usual dangers inherent in eyewitness identification may have been exacerbated because this was a cross-race identification.

Under these circumstances, 25 seconds may not have provided sufficient time for the eyewitness to observe the robber's features so that she could make an in-court identification independent of the unconstitutional lineup.

[second] The eyewitness testified that shortly after the robbery, she gave the police the following description of the robber: African–American male, at least six feet tall, wearing a white golfer's cap and tan jacket. This description was presumably given at a time when the eyewitness would have retained the sharpest image of the robber. The description offered no detail about the robber's facial features, coloring, build, age or other distinguishing characteristics. The description could fit many African–American men.

Although the eyewitness testified that she told Officer Wortock that the robber was at least six feel tall, Officer Wortock testified that the eyewitness merely told him that the robber was taller than she. The eyewitness is five feet tall. Thus the eyewitness and Officer Wortock offered conflicting accounts of her description of the robber's height.

Testimony about the eyewitness's recollection of the robber's facial hair varied. The eyewitness first testified that she knew the robber had long sideburns but was not sure if he had a mustache or beard; she later testified that she did not notice any facial hair on the robber. Officer Wortock first testified that the eyewitness informed him that the robber did not have facial hair; Wortock then testified that she did not say one way or another whether the robber had facial hair; still later, Wortock testified that he did not recall whether he had specifically asked her if the robber had facial hair. The defendant's niece testified that the defendant, on or around the date of the robbery, had a goatee and full mustache. Officer Bell saw the defendant four days before the robbery and at that time the defendant had full facial hair.

Thus the eyewitness's descriptions of the robber varied, and a significant discrepancy exists between the eyewitness's initial description of the robber and the defendant's actual appearance. The eyewitness's inconsistent statements about the robber's facial hair, the discrepancy between the initial description of the robber and the defendant's actual appearance, together with the minimal description furnished by the eyewitness, cast doubt on the eyewitness's ability to make an in-court identification independent of the unconstitutional lineup.

[third] The defendant argues that the eyewitness's request that another man in the lineup step forward constitutes a prior identification. This argument, however, is untenable. The eyewitness testified that she asked the other man to step forward so she could get a better look at him. She never identified him as the robber. Witnesses participating in a lineup identification should be encouraged to examine carefully all participants to ensure an accurate identification. The fact that the eyewitness did not identify any other person as the robber supports the conclusion that the eyewitness's observation of the robber at the robbery would enable her to identify the defendant independent of the unconstitutional lineup.

In this case, the [fourth and fifth] factors are interrelated. The eyewitness failed to identify the defendant in photographs she viewed on the day of the robbery. Ordinarily, a witness's failure to identify an accused from a photograph only hours after the crime might demonstrate that the witness's in-court identification of the accused was not independent of an illegal lineup. However, in this case, the eyewitness's failure to identify the defendant's photo is of limited significance. The eyewitness testified that looking at a photograph is different from looking at the person. Furthermore, the circuit court found that the defendant's photograph did not bear a reasonable resemblance to his appearance in the courtroom and was therefore misleading enough to preclude the eyewitness from accurately identifying him as the robber.

[sixth] The longer the time between the initial observation and the lineup, the greater the likelihood that the initial observation at the crime will have dimmed and that the second image from the lineup will play an important role at the in-court identification. The robbery in the present case occurred on December 3, 1994, and the lineup identification occurred about five weeks later on January 9, 1995. The five-week period between the robbery and the lineup was arguably long enough to obscure the eyewitness's memory of her brief encounter with the robber at the time of the robbery and to increase the importance of her having seen the defendant in the lineup.

[seventh] The conduct of the lineup may have a bearing upon whether the in-court identification is independent of the lineup or tainted by it. In this case, the police failed to take a photograph or a video of the lineup. The record contains photographs of the men in the lineup but does not disclose when the photographs were taken. Thus, the only information we have about the physical staging of the lineup comes from the testimony of Long, Stratman and the eyewitness.

The law enforcement officers testified that all the men in the lineup were similar to the defendant in terms of race, size, height, age and facial hair. The State asserts that using men who had facial hair demonstrates the fairness of the lineup. The defendant argues that staging the lineup using only men with facial hair suggested to the eyewitness that the robber had facial hair.

Although both the State's and the defendant's interpretations of the lineup are reasonable and the circuit court found that the lineup was not unduly suggestive, we conclude that the physical staging of the lineup may have affected the eyewitness's memory of the robber by adding the detail of facial hair, a detail not present in her initial description. As the Court stated in Wade, "[s]uggestion can be created intentionally or unintentionally in many subtle ways ... and increase[s] the dangers inhering in eyewitness identification." Wade, 388 U.S. at 229, 87 S.Ct. at 1933. The lineup in this case could have crystallized the eyewitness's identification of the defendant for future reference.

The eyewitness's opportunity to observe the robber was limited to, at most, 25 seconds; she had never seen the robber prior to the robbery; she gave a general description of the robber; there was a discrepancy between her description of the robber immediately after the robbery and the defendant's actual physical appearance; there was a lapse of five weeks between the robbery and lineup identification.

The State asks the court to consider another factor in addition to the seven Wade factors, namely the witness's level of certainty in making the in-court identification. The eyewitness in this case said at the suppression hearing that she was positive the defendant was the robber and that she would be able to identify him even if he had not been in the lineup and she had seen him on the street.

This "certainty" factor is not mentioned in Wade but is set forth in Neil v. Biggers, 409 U.S. 188, 199, 93 S.Ct. 375, 382, 34 L.Ed.2d 401 (1972). The Biggers Court promulgated a "totality of circumstances" test for trial courts to apply in evaluating the reliability of pre-trial, out-of-court identifications.

The "totality of circumstances" test includes five factors: (1) the opportunity of the witness to view the criminal at the time of the crime; (2) the witness's degree of attention; (3) the accuracy of the witness's prior description of the criminal; (4) the level of certainty demonstrated by the witness at the confrontation; and (5) the length of time between the crime and the confrontation. Thus the Biggers "totality of circumstances" test overlaps to a large extent with the factors set forth in the Wade "independent origin" test.

Judges differ about whether to treat the Wade and Biggers tests as functionally equivalent. We conclude that notwithstanding the similarity of the two tests, they are not functionally equivalent, and the Biggers "certainty" factor should not be included in the Wade test.

The Wade and Biggers tests are derived from different constitutional amendments and are intended to achieve different purposes. The Wade test focuses on the Sixth Amendment right to counsel at post-indictment lineups and on the exclusionary remedy for a constitutional violation of the Sixth Amendment. The Wade test is used to exclude evidence tainted by an unconstitutional lineup. Exclusion of derivative evidence is intended to deter unlawful police conduct and preserve judicial integrity.

The inquiry in Biggers, on the other hand, evaluates the reliability of a pre-trial identification when it is claimed that the pre-trial identification was made under impermissibly suggestive circumstances. Biggers uses a witness's certainty at a suggestive pre-trial identification procedure to measure the reliability of the witness's identification in that procedure. Biggers is based on due process considerations, not on a Sixth Amendment violation or the Wong Sun exception to the fruit of the poisonous tree doctrine. Under Biggers, the "totality of the circumstances" test is applied to determine whether a pre-trial out-of-court identification was unreliable as a matter of law.

The case at bar is a Wade case. The issue is not whether a witness's observation of a perpetrator of a crime or an in-court identification of an accused was reliable. The issue is whether a witness's observation of a perpetrator of a crime constitutes an independent source for that witness's in-court identification of an accused.

The primary concern in a Wade case is whether an unconstitutional lineup tainted a subsequent in-court identification. In a Wade case, the degree of certainty displayed by a witness at an in-court identification is not relevant in determining whether the in-court identification is independent of a tainted lineup. As the Wade court stated, " '[I]t is a matter of common experience that, once a witness has picked out the accused at the line-up, he is not likely to go back on his word later on, so that in practice the issue of identity may (in the absence of other relevant evidence) for all practical purposes be determined there and then, before the trial.' "

Considering all the evidence, we hold that the eyewitness's in-court identification in the case at bar should be suppressed because the State has not shown by clear and convincing evidence that the eyewitness's in-court identification of the defendant had an "independent origin," that is, that the source of the in-court identification was the eyewitness's observation of the robber during the robbery and was independent of a lineup that violated the defendant's Sixth Amendment right to counsel.

Accordingly, we reverse that part of the decision of the court of appeals admitting the in-court identification and remand the cause to the circuit court for further proceedings not inconsistent with this opinion.

N. Patrick Crooks dissenting.

[first] In this case, the robbery occurred in a well-lit environment, and the eyewitness was wearing her eyeglasses at the time. The video tape indicates that the eyewitness was within a few feet of and directly facing the robber. The cash register was on the counter directly between the eyewitness and the robber; therefore, the eyewitness did not turn away from the robber to retrieve the requested change. In fact, at no time did the eyewitness turn away from the robber, even when she eventually backed away from him. There was nothing obstructing the eyewitness's view, and the robber made no attempt to conceal his face. The robber was the only individual in the store at the time of the robbery, and there is no evidence that the eyewitness was otherwise distracted.

Although the confrontation lasted approximately twenty seconds, courts have concluded that similar periods of time have provided witnesses with a sufficient opportunity to observe. See United States v. Goodman, 797 F.2d 468, 470 (7th Cir.1986) (fifteen to twenty second observation); United States v. Jarrad, 754 F.2d 1451, 1455 (9th Cir.1985) (three to four second observation), Government of the Canal Zone v. Waldron, 574 F.2d 283, 285 (5th Cir.1978) (opportunity to view assailant twice, for two to three seconds on each occasion); United States ex rel Phipps v. Follette, 428 F.2d 912, 916 (2d Cir.1970) (twenty to thirty second observation). Furthermore, the time period is not the only element to consider in assessing whether the witness had a sufficient opportunity to observe. Rather, the time period must be considered within the context of the additional circumstances surrounding the confrontation. Based on the circumstances as they exist in this case, I conclude that the eyewitness had a sufficient opportunity to observe the robber.

[second] In this case, there is no significant variance in the eyewitness's statements, and there is no discrepancy between her statements and the defendant's actual appearance.

The eyewitness initially stated the robber had sideburns, but later testified she did not notice or did not know if the robber had facial hair. The significance of this factor is lessened when viewed in light of the circumstances. In the video tape of the robbery, it is not apparent whether the robber did or did not have facial hair. It is apparent, however, that even if the robber had facial hair, it was neither voluminous nor lengthy.

Officer Wortock's testimony demonstrates no significant variance in the eyewitness's description of the robber's facial hair either. Officer Wortock consistently indicated that the eyewitness did not tell him whether or not the robber had facial hair. There may be some confusion because Office Wortock's initial testimony at the suppression hearing seemingly indicated that the eyewitness stated the robber did not have facial hair. However, Officer Wortock later clarified his testimony:

Q . . . the victim in this case, indicated that the assailant did not have facial hair, correct . . .?

A She did not say one way or the other.

Q In your report ... it indicates the following: The assailant in this incident did not have any facial hair. Was that not told to you by the [eyewitness]?

A She did not say that to me. That was my personal observation from the video tape.

Q And was it not, didn't you testify earlier today that she informed you that there was no facial hair on this [sic] assailant?

Q When she gave me a description of the party?

Q Yes.

A She did not say that the party had or had not any facial hair.

Furthermore, Officer Wortock's failure to recall whether he directly asked the eyewitness if the robber had facial hair provides no support for the contention that there is any variance in her description.

There is also no significant variation in the eyewitness's statements regarding the robber's height. The eyewitness testified that she described the robber as "at least six feet tall." Officer Wortock testified that the eyewitness described the robber as "taller than her." These statements vary somewhat but are consistent because the eyewitness is five feet tall. Thus, an individual who is taller than five feet could also be at least six feet tall. Furthermore, although the defendant's actual height is not noted in the record, there is no evidence that the eyewitness's statements create a discrepancy with the defendant's actual appearance.

Just as there is no significant variance in the description, there is no discrepancy between the description and the defendant's actual appearance. The majority finds compelling the testimony of the defendant's niece indicating the defendant had a goatee and full mustache on or about the date of the robbery, as well as Officer Bell's testimony that the defendant had facial hair approximately four days prior to the date of the robbery. This testimony does not evince a discrepancy.

The trial court made no findings of fact regarding the defendant's actual appearance on the date of the robbery. Facial hair is an easily modifiable physical feature, and the defendant may or may not have had facial hair on the date of the robbery. The majority's conclusion that a discrepancy exists assumes as true the defendant's niece's testimony that the defendant had facial hair on or about the date of the robbery. This is an improper assumption, as any issues surrounding inconsistent witness statements implicate considerations of credibility and are issues to be resolved by the trier of fact. Even assuming arguendo that the defendant's niece's statements are true, it does not create a discrepancy because the eyewitness did not specifically state that the robber did not have facial hair.

[third] The eyewitness in this case has not identified anyone other than the defendant as the robber.

[fourth] As the majority notes, in this case the fourth Wade factor is closely related to the fifth Wade factor, which considers whether the witness failed to identify the accused prior to the in-court identification. The eyewitness did fail to identify the defendant from a photo array; however, the circuit court found the photo presented to the eyewitness was not a reasonable resemblance of the defendant.

[sixth] I conclude the five-week period did not obscure the eyewitness's recollection. Courts have held that even a two-month lapse of time does not require suppression of an in-court identification where the witness does not identify an individual other than the defendant in the interim. See United States v. Monks, 774 F.2d 945, 957 (9th Cir.1985); United States v. Barron, 575 F.2d 752, 755 (9th Cir.1978).

[seventh] The line-up procedures were not suggestive in this case. The defendant was the suspect, and the defendant had facial hair at the time of the line-up. The additional men included in the line-up also had facial hair, just as they were also the same race and approximately the same size, height, and age as the defendant. It is reasonable that individuals with physical features similar to that of the defendant were included, so that attention was not inappropriately drawn to the defendant, and such procedures were not unduly suggestive. See Messer v. Roberts, 74 F.3d 1009, 1016 (10th Cir.1996) ("men shown possessed sufficient similarities in size, coloration, height, complexion, hair color, full mustaches, somewhat receding hairlines, dress and weight to pass constitutional muster."). It is also not unduly suggestive that all individuals in the line-up had facial hair, even though the eyewitness's description did not include facial hair. See United States v. Shoels, 685 F.2d 379, 385 (10th Cir.1982) (photo array of seven black men, all with noticeable facial hair, not unduly suggestive even though eyewitness described criminal as clean-shaven). In addition, after reviewing the facts surrounding the line-up, the trial court determined the line-up procedures were not unduly suggestive.

[I] conclude that there is clear and convincing evidence that the eyewitness's in-court identification has an independent origin apart from the line-up identification.

I also conclude that the certainty of a witness is a proper factor to consider in determining whether the in-court identification is independent of a tainted line-up identification. The "independent basis" test and the "totality of circumstances" test are derived from different constitutional amendments; however, they are both premised on concerns of accurate and reliable witness identification.

The Court's primary concern in Wade was not, as the majority argues, deterring unlawful police conduct and preserving judicial integrity. In fact, the Wade Court noted that "[w]e do not assume that these risks are the result of police procedures intentionally designed to prejudice an accused. Rather we assume they derive from the dangers inherent in eyewitness identification and the suggestibility inherent in the context of the pretrial identification." Wade, 388 U.S. at 235, 87 S.Ct. at 1936.

In assessing eyewitness identification, "[i]t is the reliability of identification evidence that primarily determines its admissibility." Watkins v. Sowders, 449 U.S. 341, 347, 101 S.Ct. 654, 658, 66 L.Ed.2d 549 (1981).

The witness's certainty is particularly relevant where, as here, it is expressed within the context of the observations at the time of the crime. At the preliminary hearing in this case, the eyewitness identified the defendant during the prosecution's examination regarding the crime itself. Without waiver, the eyewitness positively identified the defendant as the man who asked her for change, pointed the knife at her, and robbed her. Even more convincing was the eyewitness's testimony at the suppression hearing, wherein she stated she was "positive" and "one hundred percent" certain that the defendant was the armed robber. The eyewitness additionally testified at the suppression hearing that she would be able to identify the defendant as the robber even if she saw him on the street, irrespective of the line-up.

Undoubtedly, the majority would argue that the eyewitness's certainty at the preliminary hearing and the suppression hearing was irreparably tainted by the line-up identification. Yet, "[t]his difficulty has not prevented courts from finding sufficient certainty even when the evidence of certainty comes from confrontations that took place after the invocation of suggestive procedures." United States ex rel Kosik v. Napoli, 814 F.2d 1151, 1159 (7th Cir.1987).

The majority emphasizes the unreliable nature of eyewitness identification; however, the Wade test is utilized to remedy such concerns and combat any inherent unreliability. It cannot be discounted that eyewitness identification is relevant and extremely valuable to criminal convictions. Therefore, such identification evidence should not be hastily suppressed.

The language of Wade indicates the factors enumerated were proffered as a guideline—not an all-inclusive list of factors to be utilized to the exclusion of any other relevant considerations. See Wade, 388 U.S. at 241, 87 S.Ct. at 1939. The extent of the witness's certainty would not be dispositive in a Wade analysis. Rather, it would merely be a factor to be considered in addition to those outlined in Wade. See Biggers, 409 U.S. at 199, 93 S.Ct. at 382.

For these reasons, I respectfully dissent.

CHAPTER 4

WIRETAPPING AND ELECTRONIC SURVEILLANCE

A. AN OVERVIEW

This chapter concerns electronic surveillance and recording of conversations by government agents. Sometimes agents eavesdrop on conversations without the knowledge or permission of any of the parties. In other instances, agents obtain the consent of at least one party to the conversation. Courts treat these two situations differently.

Wiretapping is the prime example of electronic surveillance conducted without the consent of any party to the conversation. Historically, this required a physical connection to property and/or a hard wired phone line. More recently, agents will make an entry to place a "bug" or monitoring device on the telephone itself. Such a device can also be placed in a home or a business to effectuate the non-consensual overhearing and recording of non-telephonic conversations within the premises. Such non-consensual interception of communications sometimes is accomplished without a trespass against the property of any party to the conversation. Katz v. United States (Section B, infra), provides an example of non-consensual electronic surveillance. This seminal case is notable for its expansion of Fourth Amendment coverage (as discussed in chapter 5, infra) as well as its lessons on eavesdropping.

Distinguished from non-consensual surveillance is the electronic auditing and recording of a conversation with the consent of one party to the conversation, typified by United States v. White (Section C, supra). Usually the consenting party is "wired for sound," so that the conversation can be overheard and recorded by third-parties (often by law enforcement agents with whom the consenting party is working). Sometimes the consenting party carries the transmitter, hidden on his or her person, onto the property of the suspect and there activates the device to broadcast or record conversations between himself and the suspect.

In Olmstead v. United States, 277 U.S. 438, 48 S.Ct. 564 (1928), a prohibition era case, federal agents employed a telephone company lineman to tap a series of phone wires at the street connection without trespassing on the defendant's property. The Supreme Court held that wiretapping which was accomplished without entry was neither a search nor a seizure within the meaning of the Fourth Amendment. Over a strong, and now famous, dissent of Justice Brandeis,[1] the five-man majority refused to

1. "Decency, security and liberty alike demand that government officials shall be subjected to the same rules of conduct that are commands to the citizen. In a government of

exclude the fruits of such federal non-trespassory wiretapping from a federal prosecution even though it assumed that such wiretapping violated state penal laws. (If federal agents, pursuing a federal investigation, violate neither the Constitution nor federal law, an issue arises under the Supremacy Clause as to whether state law can restrict their investigative activities.) Thereafter, the fruits of non-consensual overhearing were excluded on Fourth Amendment grounds only if effectuated by a trespass (however slight) against property.

Through the Federal Communications Act of 1934, in 47 U.S.C. § 605, Congress prohibited interception and divulgence of certain communications. The statute was interpreted to apply to both interstate and intrastate telephonic communications. The Supreme Court engrafted upon it an exclusionary rule so as to prevent use of such communications as evidence in federal courts. Not until 1968, however, did violation of this federal statute by state agents result in the exclusion of evidence in state courts. The history of this statute is told in Lee v. Florida, 392 U.S. 378, 88 S.Ct. 2096 (1968), and in Carr, The Law of Electronic Surveillance § 1.3 (1997).

In the decades before the adoption of Title III of the Omnibus Crime Control and Safe Streets Act of 1968 (section B2, supra), a number of states had adopted statutes governing wiretaps. Many states prohibited wiretapping, and some utilized an exclusionary rule to enforce this state prohibition. New York prohibited wiretapping except by court order. In Berger v. New York, 388 U.S. 41, 87 S.Ct. 1873 (1967), a case which involved trespassory wiretapping, (and, therefore, was within the ambit of the Fourth Amendment even before the *Katz* revolution), the United States Supreme Court invalidated the New York statute. As Congress was on the eve of undertaking consideration of the issues addressed in the 1968 Title III legislation, the Court was able to send a message to the legislators through their examination of the New York statutory scheme. The Court noted several defects in the New York statute: (1) The statute did not require a showing that any particular offense was being committed and it did not mandate that the conversation to be seized must be described with specificity. (2) There were inadequate limits upon the duration of the execution of the warrant. On a single showing of probable cause, conversations could be seized, within the discretion of the officer, over a sixty-day period, without even a requirement that the wiretapping cease after the evidence sought had been obtained. (3) The warrant could be renewed without a showing that probable cause still existed. (4) The statute did not require that notice be given to the monitored party even after the conversation was seized, and it did not require a showing as to why the decision not to give notice in an individual case was justified. (5) The statute did not

laws, existence of the government will be imperilled if it fails to observe the law scrupulously. Our Government is the potent, the omnipresent teacher. For good or for ill, it teaches the whole people by its example. Crime is contagious. If the Government becomes a lawbreaker, it breeds contempt for law; it invites every man to become a law unto himself; it invites anarchy. To declare that in the administration of the criminal law the end justifies the means—to declare that the Government may commit crimes in order to secure the conviction of a private criminal—would bring terrible retribution. Against that pernicious doctrine this Court should resolutely set its face." Olmstead v. United States, 277 U.S. 438, 485, 48 S.Ct. 564, 575 (Brandeis, J., dissenting) (1928).

provide for the filing of a "return" with the court indicating what conversations had been overheard.

Although *Berger* was soon eclipsed by *Katz* and by new federal wiretapping legislation (Section B2, infra) it remains important in so far as courts must judge claimed deficiencies of the 1968 federal legislation against the standards articulated in *Berger*. Much of the debate over proposed statutes which provided for court-authorized wiretapping focused upon the experience in the State of New York. Until *Berger*, supra, invalidated the New York law, court-authorized electronic surveillance was used in New York for many years.

Consider the following comment by Mr. Edward S. Silver, District Attorney, Kings County, N.Y., in his article "Wiretapping and Electronic Surveillance" in 55 J. Crim. L., Criminology & Police Sci. 114 (1964):

> In Olmstead, the "great dissenter," Justice Holmes, was absolutely right when he said that officers of the law should not violate the law in fighting crime. Nobody should dispute this. But the principle announced in Olmstead has no bearing on a situation such as exists under the laws of New York State and other similar statutes of other states, as well as in proposed federal legislation presently under consideration by Congress. Olmstead has no application where a state constitution or a state statute authorizes district attorneys and high ranking police officials to tap wires under specified conditions and with meaningful safeguards to our liberties.

The question remains today: what are the meaningful safeguards to our liberties when we consider wiretapping and electronic surveillance, particularly in today's context in which the need for surveillance has taken on even greater importance and the ability of law enforcement to obtain information through new forms of technology has increased dramatically.

As you read the materials in this chapter, consider the following questions: Should nonconsensual eavesdropping by government agents be constitutionally prohibited in the absence of some judicial oversight? Why or why not? What types of protection should judicial oversight serve? Assuming you advocate banning the use of such evidence, or at the very least, making the requirements the government must meet stringent, should exclusion of the evidence obtained through the nonconsensual eavesdropping during the prosecution's case be the remedy for the violation? If you support an exclusionary rule approach, should there be exceptions to the application of the exclusionary rule? What values would exclusion of the illegally seized evidence serve? Would these same values be served by excluding eavesdropping evidence obtained when one party consented? What is the appropriate relation between statutory requirements and constitutional norms? If the legislature prohibits the gathering of such evidence, would the seizure of such evidence then be unconstitutional? Or would it only violate the statute? Conversely, if the legislature permits the gathering of such evidence by law enforcement agents, has it placed the constitutional imprimatur of approval on such a process so that courts should admit the evidence?

B. NON-CONSENSUAL WIRETAPPING AND ELECTRONIC SURVEILLANCE

1. THE CONSTITUTION

Katz v. United States

Supreme Court of the United States, 1967.
389 U.S. 347, 88 S.Ct. 507.

■ MR. JUSTICE STEWART delivered the opinion of the Court.

The petitioner was convicted in the District Court for the Southern District of California under an eight-count indictment charging him with transmitting wagering information by telephone from Los Angeles to Miami and Boston in violation of a federal statute. At trial the Government was permitted, over the petitioner's objection, to introduce evidence of the petitioner's end of telephone conversations, overheard by FBI agents who had attached an electronic listening and recording device to the outside of the public telephone booth from which he had placed his calls. In affirming his conviction, the Court of Appeals rejected the contention that the recordings had been obtained in violation of the Fourth Amendment, because "[t]here was no physical entrance into the area occupied by, [t]he petitioned." We granted certiorari in order to consider the constitutional questions thus presented.

The petitioner has phrased those questions as follows:

A. Whether a public telephone booth is a constitutionally protected area so that evidence obtained by attaching an electronic listening recording device to the top of such a booth is obtained in violation of the right to privacy of the user of the booth.

B. Whether physical penetration of a constitutionally protected area is necessary before a search and seizure can be said to be violative of the Fourth Amendment to the United States Constitution.

We decline to adopt this formulation of the issues. In the first place the correct solution of Fourth Amendment problems is not necessarily promoted by incantation of the phrase "constitutionally protected area." Secondly, the Fourth Amendment cannot be translated into a general constitutional "right to privacy." That Amendment protects individual privacy against certain kinds of governmental intrusion, but its protections go further, and often have nothing to do with privacy at all. Other provisions of the Constitution protect personal privacy from other forms of governmental invasion. But the protection of a person's general right to privacy "his right to be let alone by other people" is, like the protection of his property and of his very life, left largely to the law of the individual States....

Because of the misleading way the issues have been formulated, the parties have attached great significance to the characterization of the telephone booth from which the petitioner placed his calls. The petitioner has strenuously argued that the booth was a "constitutionally protected area." The Government has maintained with equal vigor that it was not. But this effort to decide whether or not a given "area," viewed in the abstract, is "constitutionally protected" deflects attention from the problem presented by this case. For the Fourth Amendment protects people, not places. What a person knowingly exposes to the public, even in his own home or office, is not a subject of Fourth Amendment protection. But what he seeks to preserve as private, even in an area accessible to the public may be constitutionally protected.

The Government stresses the fact that the telephone booth from which the petitioner made his calls was constructed partly of glass, so that he was as visible after he entered it as he would have been if he had remained outside. But what he sought to exclude when he entered the booth was not the intruding eye—it was the uninvited ear. He did not shed his right to do so simply because he made his calls from a place where he might be seen. No less than an individual in a business office, in a friend's apartment, or in a taxicab, a person in a telephone booth may rely upon the protection of the Fourth Amendment. One who occupies it, shuts the door behind him, and pays the toll that permits him to place a call, is surely entitled to assume that the word she utters into the mouthpiece will not be broadcast to the world. To read the Constitution more narrowly is to ignore the vital role that the public telephone has come to play in private communication.

The Government contends, however, that the activities of its agents in this case should not be tested by Fourth Amendment requirements, for the surveillance technique they employed involved no physical penetration of the telephone booth from which the petitioner placed his calls. It is true that the absence of such penetration was at one time thought to foreclose further Fourth Amendment inquiry, *Olmstead*, *Goldman*, for that Amendment was thought to limit only seizures of tangible property. But the premise that property interests control the right of the Government to search and seize has been discredited. Warden v. Hayden, 387 U.S. 294, 304. Thus, although a closely divided Court supposed in Olmstead v. United States, 277 U.S. 438, 48 S.Ct. 564 (1928) that surveillance without any trespass and without the seizure of any material object fell outside the ambit of the Constitution, we have since departed from the narrow view on which that decision rested ...

* * *

We conclude that the underpinnings of Olmstead v. United States, 277 U.S. 438, 48 S.Ct. 564 (1928) and Goldman v. United States, 316 U.S. 129, 62 S.Ct. 993 (1942) have been so eroded by our subsequent decisions that the "trespass" doctrine there enunciated can no longer be regarded as controlling. The Government's activities in electronically listening to and recording the petitioner's words violated the privacy upon which he justifiably relied while using the telephone booth and thus constituted a "search and seizure" within the meaning of the Fourth Amendment. The fact that the electronic device employed to achieve that end did not happen to penetrate the wall of the booth can have no constitutional significance.

The question remaining for decision, then, is whether the search and seizure conducted in this case complied with constitutional standards. In that regard, the Government's position is that its agents acted in an entirely defensible manner: They did not begin their electronic surveillance until investigation of the petitioner's activities had established a strong probability that he was using the telephone in question to transmit gambling information to persons in other States, in violation of federal law. Moreover, the surveillance was limited, both in scope and in duration, to the specific purpose of establishing the contents of the petitioner's unlawful telephonic communications. The agents confined their surveillance to the brief periods during which he used the telephone booth, and they took great care to overhear only the conversations of the petitioner himself.

Accepting this account of the Government's actions as accurate, it is clear that this surveillance was so narrowly circumscribed that a duly authorized magistrate, properly notified of the need for such investigation, specifically informed of the basis on which it was to proceed, and clearly apprised of the precise intrusion it would entail, could constitutionally have authorized, with appropriate safeguards, the very limited search and seizure that the Government asserts in fact took place. Only last Term we sustained the validity of such an authorization, holding that, under sufficiently "precise and discriminate circumstances," a federal court may empower government agents to employ a concealed electronic device "for the narrow and particularized purpose of ascertaining the truth of the ... allegations" of a "detailed factual affidavit alleging the commission of a specific criminal offense." Osborn v. United States, 385 U.S. 323, 87 S.Ct. 429 (1966). Discussing that holding, the Court in Berger v. State of New York, ... said that "the order authorizing the use of the electronic device" in *Osborn* "afforded similar protections to those ... of conventional warrants authorizing the seizure of tangible evidence." Through those protections, "no greater invasion of privacy was permitted than was necessary under the circumstances." Here, too, a similar judicial order could have accommodated "the legitimate needs of law enforcement" by authorizing the carefully limited use of electronic surveillance.

The Government urges that, because its agents relied upon the decisions in *Olmstead* and *Goldman*, and because they did no more here than they might properly have done with prior judicial sanction, we should retroactively validate their conduct. That we cannot do. It is apparent that the agents in this case acted with restraint. Yet the inescapable fact is that this restraint was imposed by the agents themselves, not by a judicial officer. They were not required, before commencing the search, to present their estimate of probable cause for detached scrutiny by a neutral magistrate. They were not compelled, during the conduct of the search itself, to observe precise limits established in advance by a specific court order. Nor were they directed, after the search had been completed, to notify the authorizing magistrate in detail of all that had been seized. In the absence of such safeguards, this Court has never sustained a search upon the sole ground that officers reasonably expected to find evidence of a particular crime and voluntarily confined their activities to the least intrusive means consistent with that end....

[The government argues that] surveillance of a telephone booth should be exempted from the usual requirement of advance authorization by a magistrate upon a showing of probable cause. We cannot agree. Omission of such authorization bypasses the safeguards provided by an objective predetermination of probable cause, and substitutes instead the far less reliable procedure of an after-the-event justification for the ... search, too likely to be subtly influenced by the familiar shortcomings of hindsight judgment. Beck v. Ohio, 379 U.S. 89, 96. And bypassing a neutral predetermination of the *scope* of a search leaves individuals secure from Fourth Amendment violations "only in the discretion of the police."

These considerations do not vanish when the search in question is transferred from the setting of a home, an office, or a hotel room, to that of a telephone booth. Wherever a man may be, he is entitled to know that he will remain free from unreasonable searches and seizures. The government agents here ignored "the procedure of antecedent justification ... that is central to the Fourth Amendment," a procedure that we hold to be a constitutional precondition of the kind of electronic surveillance involved in this case. Because the surveillance here failed to meet that condition, and because it led to the petitioner's conviction, the judgment must be reversed.

It is so ordered.

Judgment reversed.

■ MR. JUSTICE MARSHALL took no part in the consideration or decision of this case.

■ MR. JUSTICE DOUGLAS, with whom MR. JUSTICE BRENNAN joins, concurring. [OMITTED]

■ MR. JUSTICE HARLAN, concurring.

I join the opinion of the Court, which I read to hold only (a) that an enclosed telephone booth is an area where, like a home, a person has a constitutionally protected reasonable expectation of privacy; (b) that electronic as well as physical intrusion into a place that is in this sense private may constitute a violation of the Fourth Amendment; and (c) that the invasion of a constitutionally protected area by federal authorities is, as the Court has long held, presumptively unreasonable in the absence of a search warrant.

As the Court's opinion states, "The Fourth Amendment protects people, not places." The question, however, is what protection it affords to those people. Generally, as here, the answer to that question requires reference to "place." My understanding of the rule that has emerged from prior decisions is that there is a twofold requirement, first that a person have exhibited an actual (subjective) expectation of privacy, and, second, that the expectation be one that society is prepared to recognize as "reasonable." Thus a man's home is, for most purposes, a place where he expects privacy, but objects, activities, or statements that he exposes to the "plain view" of outsiders are not "protected" because no intention to keep them to himself has been exhibited. On the other hand, conversations in the open would not be protected against being overheard, for the expectation of privacy under the circumstances would be unreasonable.

The critical fact in this case is that "[o]ne who occupies it, [a telephone booth] shuts the door behind him, and pays the toll that permits him to place a call, is surely entitled to assume" that his conversation is not being intercepted. The point is not that the booth is "accessible to the public" at other times, but that it is a temporarily private place whose momentary occupants' expectations of freedom from intrusion are recognized as reasonable.

* * *

... This case requires us to reconsider *Goldman*, and I agree that it should now be overruled. Its limitation on Fourth Amendment protection is, in the present day, bad physics as well as bad law, for reasonable expectations of privacy may be defeated by electronic as well as physical invasion.

Finally, I do not read the Court's opinion to declare that no interception of conversation one-half of which occurs in a public telephone booth can be reasonable in the absence of a warrant. As elsewhere under the Fourth Amendment, warrants are the general rule, to which the legitimate needs of law enforcement may demand specific expectations. It will be time enough to consider any such exceptions when an appropriate occasion presents itself, and agree with the Court that this is not one.

■ MR. JUSTICE WHITE, concurring.

I agree that the official surveillance of petitioner's telephone conversations in a public booth must be subjected to the test of reasonableness under the Fourth Amendment and that on the record now before us the particular surveillance undertaken was unreasonable absent a warrant properly authorizing it. This application of the Fourth Amendment need not interfere with legitimate needs of law enforcement.[1]

In joining the Court's opinion, I note the Court's acknowledgement that there are circumstances in which it is reasonable to search without a warrant. In this connection, the Court points out that today's decision does not reach national security cases. Wiretapping to protect the security of the Nation has been authorized by successive Presidents. The present Administration would apparently save national security cases from restrictions against wiretapping. We should not require the warrant procedure and the

1. In previous cases, which are undisturbed by today's decision, the Court has upheld, as reasonable under the Fourth Amendment, admission at trial of evidence obtained (1) by an undercover police agent to whom a defendant speaks without knowledge that he is in the employ of the police, Hoffa v. United States, (2) by a recording device hidden on the person of such an informant, Lopez v. United States, Osborn v. United States, and (3) by a policeman listening to the secret micro-wave transmissions of an agent conversing with the defendant in another location, On Lee v. United States. When one man speaks to another he takes all the risks ordinarily inherent in so doing, including the risk that the man to whom he speaks will make public what he has heard. The Fourth Amendment does not protect against unreliable (or law-abiding) associates. Hoffa v. United States, supra. It is but a logical and reasonable extension of this principle that a man take the risk that his hearer, free to memorize what he hears for later verbatim repetitions, is instead recording it or transmitting it to another. The present case deal with an entirely different situation, for as the Court emphasizes the petitioner "sought to exclude ... the uninvited ear," and spoke under circumstances in which a reasonable person would assume that uninvited ears were not listening.

magistrate's judgment if the President of the United States or his chief legal officer, the Attorney General, has considered the requirements of national security and authorized electronic surveillance as reasonable.

■ MR. JUSTICE BLACK, dissenting.

* * *

My basic objection is twofold: (1) I do not believe that the words of the Amendment will bear the meaning given them by today's decision, and (2) I do not believe that it is the proper role of this Court to rewrite the Amendment in order "to bring it into harmony with the times" and thus reach a result that many people believe to be desirable.

While I realize that an argument based on the meaning of words lacks the scope, and no doubt the appeal, of broad policy discussions and philosophical discourses on such nebulous subjects as privacy, for me the language of the Amendment is the crucial place to look in construing a written document such as our Constitution. The Fourth Amendment says that

> "The right of the people to be secure in their persons, houses, papers, and effects, against unreasonable searches and seizures, shall not be violated, and no Warrants shall issue, but upon probable cause, supported by Oath or affirmation, and particularly describing the place to be searched, and the persons or things to be seized."

The first clause protects "persons, houses, papers, and effects, against unreasonable searches and seizures ..." These words connote the idea of tangible things with size, form, and weight, things capable of being searched, seized, or both. The second clause of the Amendment still further establishes its Framers' purpose to limit its protection to tangible things by providing that no warrants shall issue but those "particularly describing the place to be searched and the person or things to be seized." A conversation overheard by eavesdropping whether by plain snooping or wiretapping, is not tangible and, under the normally accepted meanings of the words, can neither be searched nor seized. In addition the language of the second clause indicates that the Amendment refers to something not only tangible so it can be seized but to something already in existence so it can be described. Yet the Court's interpretation would have the Amendment apply to overhearing future conversations which by their very nature are nonexistent until they take place. How can one "describe" a future conversation, and if not, how can a magistrate issue a warrant to eavesdrop one in the future? It is argued that information showing what is expected to be said is sufficient to limit the boundaries of what later can be admitted into evidence; but does such general information really meet the specific language of the Amendment which says "particularly describing"? Rather than using language in a completely artificial way, I must conclude that the Fourth Amendment simply does not apply to eavesdropping.

Tapping telephone wires, of course, was an unknown possibility at the time the Fourth Amendment was adopted. But eavesdropping (and wiretapping is nothing more than eavesdropping by telephone) was, as even the majority opinion in *Berger*, supra, recognized, "an ancient practice which at common law was condemned as a nuisance. W Blackstone, Commentaries 168". In those days the eavesdropper listened by naked ear under the eaves of houses or their windows, or beyond their walls seeking out private discourse. *Berger*, 388 U.S. 41, at 45, 87 S.Ct. 1873, at 1876. There can be no doubt that the Framers were aware of this practice, and if they had desired to outlaw or restrict the use of evidence obtained by eavesdropping, I believe that they would have used the appropriate language to do so in the Fourth Amendment. They certainly would not have left such a task to the ingenuity of language-stretching judges. No one, it seems to me, can read the debates on the Bill of Rights without reaching the conclusion that its Framers and critics well knew the meaning of the words they used, what they would be understood to mean by others, their scope and their limitations. Under these circumstances it strikes me as a charge against their scholarship, their common sense and their candor to give to the Fourth Amendment's language the eavesdropping meaning the Court imputes to it today.

I do not deny that common sense requires and that this Court often has said that the Bill of Rights' safeguards should be given a liberal construction. This principle, however, does not justify construing the search and seizure amendment as applying to eavesdropping or the "seizure" of conversations. The Fourth Amendment was aimed directly at the abhorred practice of breaking in, ransacking and searching homes and other buildings and seizing peoples' personal belongings without warrants issued by magistrates. The Amendment deserves, and this Court has given it, a liberal construction in order to protect against warrantless searches of buildings and seizures of tangible personal effects. But until today this Court has refused to say that eavesdropping comes within the ambit of Fourth Amendment restrictions . . .

* * *

Goldman v. United States, 316 U.S. 129, 62 S.Ct. 993 (1942) is an . . . example of this Court's traditional refusal to consider eavesdropping as being covered by the Fourth Amendment. There federal agents used a detectaphone, which was placed on the wall of an adjoining room, to listen to the conversation of a defendant carried on in his private office and intended to be confined within the four walls of the room. This Court, referring to *Olmstead*, found no Fourth Amendment violation.

* * *

Since I see no way in which the words of the Fourth Amendment can be construed to apply to eavesdropping, that closes the matter for me. In interpreting the Bill of Rights, I willingly go as far as a liberal construction of the language takes me, but I simply cannot in good conscience give a meaning to words which they have never before been thought to have and which they certainly do not have in common ordinary usage. I will not distort the words of the Amendment in order to "keep the Constitution up to date" or "to bring it into harmony with the times." It was never meant for this Court to have such power, which in effect would make us a continuously functioning constitutional convention.

* * *

The Fourth Amendment protects privacy only to the extent that it prohibits unreasonable searches and seizures of "persons, houses, papers and effects." No general right is created by the Amendment so as to give this Court the unlimited power to hold unconstitutional everything which affects privacy. Certainly the Framers, well acquainted as they were with the excesses of governmental power, did not intend to grant this Court such omnipotent lawmaking authority as that. The history of governments proves that it is dangerous to freedom to repose such powers in courts.

* * *

NOTES

1. Many courts have used Justice Harlan's concurring opinion in *Katz* as if it expressed the majority viewpoint. Thus they have stated that the Fourth Amendment offers protection when an individual has (1) an actual (subjective) expectation of privacy, and when (2) that expectation is "reasonable." Even Justice Stewart, who wrote the *Katz* majority opinion, occasionally paraphrased the *Katz* analysis by referring to Harlan's formulation. Today the Supreme Court sometimes substitutes the word "legitimate" in place of the word "reasonable" to indicate that the Fourth Amendment is implicated only if society makes a value judgment that an expectation of privacy is worthy of protection.

Note, that in United States v. White, 401 U.S. 745, 794–95, 91 S.Ct. 1122, 1147 (1971) (Section C, supra), Justice Harlan, writing in dissent, expresses some reservations about this two-pronged test that determines when the Fourth Amendment applies.

2. To say that government has intruded upon a reasonable expectation of privacy is not to say that it has violated the Fourth Amendment. Rather it is merely to say that the government has engaged in a search or a seizure within the meaning of the amendment. The remaining issue, then, is whether such conduct was reasonable. Sometimes, however, courts will use the term "violation of a reasonable expectation of privacy" to indicate that the government has engaged in a search or seizure *and* that such Fourth Amendment activity was unreasonable.

3. It may seem strange that Justice Stewart declined to adopt the formulation of the two questions as phrased by the petitioner in *Katz*. In fact he even characterizes these questions as "formulated" in a "misleading way." These questions assumed that there is no "search" for Fourth Amendment purposes unless there is a constitutionally protected area or a physical penetration/trespass into a constitutionally protected area. Rather than being misleading, these inquiries reflect the mainstream status quo of Fourth Amendment analysis prior to *Katz*. For a discussion of shifting Fourth Amendment terrain prior to *Katz*, see David A. Sklansky, "Katz v. United States: The Limits of Aphorism," in Criminal Procedure Stories, pages 223 et. seq. Carol S. Steiker and Pamela S. Karlan, eds. (Foundation Press, 2006).

4. The question "What is a search?" is treated more extensively in Chapter 5, Section B supra. Some surveillance methods, such as "trap and trace" devices (which captures the numbers of phones from which incoming calls are received) or pen registers (which reveal the numbers dialed from a given phone and the times the number was dialed), are not characterized as a "search" and thus, law enforcement authorities are not bound by the constitutional requirements of the Fourth Amendment when they use such surveillance tactics. Smith v. Maryland, 442 U.S. 735, 99 S.Ct. 2577 (1979).

Although the Court permitted this type of surveillance without a warrant or judicial oversight, Congress later prohibited the installation of a pen register without a court order for either domestic surveillance or foreign surveillance under the Foreign Intelligence Surveillance Act of 1978. 18 U.S.C. § 3121(a). Evidence obtained through the illegal installation of a pen register is still admissible in a criminal trial, however, since the seized evidence is seized in violation of a statute and not in violation of the Fourth Amendment constitutional provisions. United States v. Thompson, 936 F.2d 1249 (11th Cir.1991), *cert. denied*, Thompson v. United States, 502 U.S. 1075, 112 S.Ct. 975 (1992). For further discussion, see infra.

In the past this statute authorized a judge in a court with jurisdiction over the crime to enter an order to permit a pen register or a trap and trace device that could be used only in that jurisdiction. 18 U.S.C. § 3123 (2000 ed.). Now, the Patriot Act permits the government to apply to a court with jurisdiction over the crime for an order that may be used anywhere in the United States 18 U.S.C. §§ 3123 (a)(1), 3127(2).

5. The emphasis in *Katz* shifts fourth amendment analysis away from property rights and towards privacy rights. With some types of surveillance, for example, internet surveillance, does the paradigm of property rights work more efficiently? See Pamela Samuelson, "Cyberspace and Privacy: A New Legal Paradigm? Privacy As Intellectual Property," 52 Stan. L. Rev. 1125 (2000). Some internet uses, such as the social sites Myspace.com and Facebook.com, create additional questions about expectations of privacy when users of the sites are unclear about who has access to their profiles. Matthew J. Hodge, (Comment) "The Fourth Amendment and Privacy Issues on the 'New' Internet: Facebook.com and MySpace.com," 31 S. Ill. U.L.J. 95 (2006).

Professor Orin Kerr has written about the survival of the property paradigm after *Katz*. Orin S. Kerr, "The Fourth Amendment in New Technologies: Constitutional Myths and the Case for Caution," 102 Michigan L. Rev. 801 (2004). See also Swire, Peter P. "*Katz* is Dead, Long Live *Katz*," 102 Mich. L. Rev. 904 (2004).

2. THE FEDERAL STATUTES

(a) TITLE III OF THE OMNIBUS CRIME CONTROL AND SAFE STREETS ACT OF 1968

Although Congress attempted to regulate some wiretapping in § 605 of the 1934 Federal Communications Act, the "Omnibus Crime Control and Safe Streets Act of 1968" was the first Congressional attempt to regulate private and governmental wiretapping and electronic surveillance beyond that of tapping telephones. (18 U.S.C. §§ 2510–2522, also referred to as Title III). With the cold war and the advent of newer technology, the possibility of eavesdropping emerged as a topic in popular culture, see *The Conversation* (Paramount Studio, 1974). Interestingly, the star of this movie, Gene Hackman, also played a major role in the film *Enemy of the State* (Touchstone Pictures), a 1998 film that also has a plot which centers on the abuse of surveillance technology. The public perception fueled by movies such as these may have affected the outcome of some of the early Supreme Court cases in this area. Some have suggested that the Supreme Court itself was worried about being a target of illegal surveillance. Charnes, Cloak and Gavel: FBI Wiretaps, Bugs, Informers, and the Supreme Court (U. Ill. Press. 1992). With the passage of Title III, Congress prohibited these surveillance activities in the absence of judicial authorization and provided fines, imprisonment, and a statutory exclusionary rule remedy for violation of the prohibitions.

Before a judge issues a Title III order, he or she must determine if normal surveillance techniques would suffice. If so, no order should issue. If not, then assuming probable cause, an enumerated crime to be investigated, a proper authority seeking the order, and a description of the Facilities and places where interception will occur, the judge may issue the order. The order should specify the facilities and/or the places that will be "tapped," who will conduct the surveillance, and set forth minimization requirements. The order is only good for thirty days 18 U.S.C. § 2518 (5), but is often renewed upon application to the issuing court.

Notwithstanding the issue of an order authorizing a Title III surveillance, a defendant may challenge the legality of the tap in a subsequent motion to suppress in the criminal action. The question arises whether the statutory exclusionary remedy of § 2515 of the act is of the same scope as the constitutional exclusionary remedy. The statute has its own good faith defense in § 2520 (2) (d), but to the extent that the exclusionary remedy is based on constitutional grounds, at least one circuit has extended the "good faith" exception to the exclusionary rule created by United States v. Leon, 468 U.S. 897, 104 S.Ct. 3405 (1984) to wiretap applications premised on evidence illegally obtained. United States v. Malekzadeh, 855 F.2d 1492, 1496–97 (11th Cir.1988). Other aspects of the statutory exclusionary remedy are just that—statutory, but not constitutional. See Scott v. United States, 436 U.S. 128, 98 S.Ct. 1717 (1978) where the trial court had suppressed because of the agents failure to abide by the minimization requirements of § 2518(5) of Title III. The Court of Appeals reversed this ruling. Ultimately, the defendants were convicted. At the United States Supreme Court, the Justices rejected the defendant's arguments and held that even in the absence of good faith efforts to minimize the intrusion, there was no need to exclude the evidence as a matter of constitutional or statutory law. Good faith efforts at minimization will also fulfill the requirements of the Foreign Intelligence Surveillance Act. United States v. Mubayyid, 521 F. Supp. 2d 125 (D. Mass. 2007).

Law enforcement officials sued for monetary damages for an alleged violation of Title III are entitled to claim qualified immunity under appropriate conditions. Blake v. Wright, 179 F.3d 1003 (6th Cir.1999), cert. denied 528 U.S. 1136, 120 S.Ct. 980 (2000).

Although the Fourth Amendment exclusionary rule does not apply in the absence of government action, the statutory exclusionary rule of § 2515 of Title III does apply to private interceptions, though damages are the more usual remedy in private actions. Desilets v. Wal–Mart Stores, Inc., 171 F.3d 711 (1st Cir.1999). For an argument that the state action/private action dichotomy might leave the technological environment of cyberspace untouched by constitutive constitutionalist values and norms, see Paul Schiff Berman, "How (If at All) to Regulate the Internet: Cyberspace and the State Action Debate: The Cultural Value of Applying Constitutional Norms to 'Private' Regulation," 71 U. Colo. L. Rev. 1263 (2000).

What happens if a private individual taps a phone or tapes a telephone conversation and then supplies it to the government for use in a criminal prosecution? When a private party taped business calls of a spouse/business party, the court determined that the tapes were illegally made. Since they were made by a private party, however, without government involvement, the government had "clean hands" and could use the tapes in a criminal prosecution for tax evasion. United States v. Murdock, 63 F.3d 1391 (6th Cir.) cert. denied, 517 U.S. 1187, 116 S.Ct. 1672 (1996). See also Forsyth v. Barr, 19 F.3d 1527 (5th Cir.1994). See Shaun T. Olsen (Note), "Reading Between the Lines: Why a Qualified 'Clean Hands' Exception Should Preclude Suppression of Wiretap Evidence Under Title III of the Omnibus Crime Control and Safe Streets Act of 1968," 36 Val. U. L. Rev. 719 (2002). In contrast, the First Circuit suppressed a taped conversation that was excluded on the basis that it violated Title III even though the government played no part in the illegal surveillance. United States v. Vest, 813 F.2d 477 (1st Cir.1987), cert. denied 488 U.S. 965, 109 S.Ct. 489 (1988). Other cases that reject the clean hands doctrine include Chandler v. United States Army, 125 F.3d 1296 (9th Cir.1997), Spetalieri v. Kavanaugh, 36 F.Supp.2d 92 (N.D.N.Y.1998).

Courts may "overlook" a Title III anomaly violation in the face of a First Amendment claim. In Bartnicki v. Vopper, 532 U.S. 514, 121 S.Ct. 1753 (2001), there was a contentious union negotiation with the local school board. The union negotiator phoned the president of the teacher's union on her cell phone. An unidentified person intercepted and recorded the entire conversation and Vopper, a radio commentator, played the tape on air. Plaintiffs contended that he did so knowing the tape was illegally obtained. The Supreme Court held that the broadcast of the tape would not be actionable in a case seeking damages. When the recipient acquired the tape legally and the tape deals with a matter of great public interest, then this case presents a situation in which the First Amendment and the Title III prohibitions clash and the enforcement of Title III would be unconstitutional. *Bartnicki*, 532 U.S. 514, 121 S.Ct. 1753 (2001). See James M. Hilmert (Note), "The Supreme Court Takes On the First Amendment Privacy Conflict and Stumbles: Bartnicki v. Vopper, the Wiretapping Act, and the Notion of Unlawfully Obtained Information," 77 Ind. L. J. 639 (2002).

Of course the private party who illegally obtained the telephone conversations without consent and without a valid Title III order may be subject to criminal prosecution as well as a suit for damages. For example, Linda Tripp was indicted under Maryland state law (which requires the consent of all parties to eavesdropping to excuse the Title III requirement) for taping her conversations with Monica Lewinsky without consent. Efforts of Ms. Lewinsky to exclude the taped conversations from the Grand Jury, however, failed. See In re Sealed Case, 162 F.3d 670 (D.C.Cir.1998) Also in Maryland, a private citizen recorded a cell phone call made by the defendant to his wife. The individual gave the tape to the police who used the information to obtain a search warrant in connection with a homicide. At trial, the conversation was suppressed as violative of the state wiretapping law, Md. Code Ann., Cts. & Jud. Proc. § 10–402(a) of the Maryland

Wiretapping and Electronic Surveillance Act. Miles v. Maryland, 365 Md. 488, 781 A.2d 787 (2001), cert. denied 534 U.S. 1163, 122 S.Ct. 1175 (2002).

When one spouse illegally obtains conversations of the other spouse, a spousal immunity doctrine to criminal liability under Title III has arisen. See discussion and cases collected Note (Mitchell), Sex, Lies, and Spyware: Balancing the Right to Privacy Against the Right to Know in the Marital Relationship, 9 J.L. Fam. Stud 171 (2007).

Title III exempts from its prohibitions the interception or surveillance of communications when one party to the conversation consents to the recording or overhearing. Title III is not the only legislation that purports to govern government surveillance activities. Other representative statutes are discussed infra.

Title III of the Omnibus Crime Control and Safe Streets Act of 1968 specifically provides, in part, as follows:

§ 2510. Definitions

(1) "wire communication" means any aural transfer made in whole or in part through the use of facilities for the transmission of communications by the aid of wire, cable, or other like connection between the point of origin and the point of reception (including the use of such connection in a switching station) furnished or operated by any person engaged in providing or operating such facilities for the transmission of interstate or foreign communications or communications affecting interstate or foreign commerce;

(2) "oral communication" means any oral communication uttered by a person exhibiting an expectation that such communication is not subject to interception under circumstances justifying such expectation, but such term does not include any electronic communication;

* * *

(12) "electronic communication" means any transfer of signs, signals, writing, images, sounds, data, or intelligence of any nature transmitted in whole or in part by a wire, radio, electromagnetic, photoelectronic or photooptical system that affects interstate or foreign commerce, but does not include

(A) any wire or oral communication;

(B) any communication made through a tone-only paging device;

(C) any communication from a tracking device (as defined in section 3117 of this title); or

(D) electronic funds transfer information stored by a financial institution in a communications system used for the electronic storage and transfer of funds;

* * *

(17) "electronic storage" means

(A) any temporary, intermediate storage of a wire or electronic communication incidental to the electronic transmission thereof; and

(B) any storage of such communication by an electronic communication service for purposes of backup protection of such communication;

(18) "aural transfer" means a transfer containing the human voice at any point between and including the point of origin and the point of reception;

(19) "foreign intelligence information", for purposes of section 2517(6) of this title, means

(A) information, whether or not concerning a United States person, that relates to the ability of the United States to protect against—

(i) actual or potential attack or other grave hostile acts of a foreign power or an agent of a foreign power;

(ii) sabotage or international terrorism by a foreign power or an agent of a foreign power; or

(iii) clandestine intelligence activities by an intelligence service or network of a foreign power or by an agent of a foreign power; or

(B) information, whether or not concerning a United States person, with respect to a foreign power or foreign territory that relates to

(i) the national defense or the security of the United States; or

(ii) the conduct of the foreign affairs of the United States;

(20) "protected computer" has the meaning set forth in section 1030; and

(21) "computer trespasser"

(A) means a person who accesses a protected computer without authorization and thus has no reasonable expectation of privacy in any communication transmitted to, through, or from the protected computer; and

(B) does not include a person known by the owner or operator of the protected computer to have an existing contractual relationship with the owner or operator of the protected computer for access to all or part of the protected computer.

§ 2511. Interception and disclosure of wire, oral or electronic communications prohibited

[Text omitted.]

§ 2512. Manufacture, distribution, possession, and advertising of wire, oral, or electronic communication intercepting devices prohibited

[Text omitted.]

§ 2513. Confiscation of wire, oral, or electronic communication intercepting devices

[Text omitted.]

§ 2514. Immunity of witnesses [Repealed.]

§ 2515. Prohibition of use as evidence of intercepted wire or oral communications

Whenever any wire or oral communication has been intercepted, no part of the contents of such communication and no evidence derived therefrom may be received in evidence in any trial, hearing, or other proceeding in or before any court, grand jury, department, officer, agency, regulatory body, legislative committee, or other authority of the United States, a State, or a political subdivision thereof if the disclosure of that information would be in violation of this chapter.

§ 2516. Authorization for interception of wire, oral or electronic communications

(1) The Attorney General, Deputy Attorney General, Associate Attorney General, or any Assistant Attorney General, any acting Assistant Attorney General, or any Deputy Assistant Attorney General or acting Deputy Assistant Attorney General in the Criminal Division specially designated by the Attorney General, may authorize an application to a Federal judge of competent jurisdiction for, and such judge may grant in conformity with section 2518 of this chapter an order authorizing or approving the interception of wire or oral communications by the Federal Bureau of Investigation, or a Federal agency having responsibility for the investigation of the offense as to which the application is made, when such interception may provide or has provided evidence of [the statute then specifies the offenses for which interception may be ordered; "electronic communications" may be intercepted for "any felony" upon application by any attorney for the Government as that term is defined in the Federal Rules of Criminal Procedure.].

* * *

§ 2517. Authorization for disclosure and use of intercepted wire, oral, or electronic communications

(1) Any investigative or law enforcement officer who, by any means authorized by this chapter has obtained knowledge of the contents of any wire, oral, or electronic communication, or evidence derived therefrom, may disclose such contents to another investigative or law enforcement officer to the extent that such disclosure is appropriate to the proper performance of the official duties of the officer making or receiving the disclosure.

(2) Any investigative or law enforcement officer who, by any means authorized by this chapter, has obtained knowledge of the contents of any wire, oral, or electronic communication or evidence derived therefrom may use such contents to the extent such use is appropriate to the proper performance of his official duties.

(3) Any person who has received, by any means authorized by this chapter, any information concerning a wire, oral, or electronic communication, or evidence derived therefrom intercepted in accordance with the provisions of this chapter may disclose the contents of that communication or such derivative evidence while giving testimony under oath or affirma-

tion in any proceeding held under the authority of the United States or of any State or political subdivision thereof.

(4) No otherwise privileged wire, oral, or electronic communication intercepted in accordance with, or in violation of, the provisions of this chapter shall lose its privileged character.

(5) When an investigative or law enforcement officer, while engaged in intercepting wire, oral, or electronic communications in the manner authorized herein, intercepts wire, oral, or electronic communications relating to offenses other than those specified in the order of authorization or approval, the contents thereof, and evidence derived therefrom, may be disclosed or used as provided in subsections (1) and (2) of this section. Such contents and any evidence derived therefrom may be used under subsection (3) of this section when authorized or approved by a judge of competent jurisdiction where such judge finds on subsequent application that the contents were otherwise intercepted in accordance with the provisions of this chapter. Such application shall be made as soon as practicable.

(6) Any investigative or law enforcement officer, or attorney for the Government, who by any means authorized by this chapter, has obtained knowledge of the contents of any wire, oral, or electronic communication, or evidence derived therefrom, may disclose such contents to any other Federal law enforcement, intelligence, protective, immigration, national defense, or national security official to the extent that such contents include foreign intelligence or counterintelligence (as defined in section 3 of the National Security Act of 1947), or foreign intelligence information (as defined in subsection (19) of section 2510 of this title), to assist the official who is to receive that information in the performance of his official duties. Any Federal official who receives information pursuant to this provision may use that information only as necessary in the conduct of that person's official duties subject to any limitations on the unauthorized disclosure of such information.

(7) Any investigative or law enforcement officer, or other Federal official in carrying out official duties as such Federal official, who by any means authorized by this chapter, has obtained knowledge of the contents of any wire, oral, or electronic communication, or evidence derived therefrom, may disclose such contents or derivative evidence to a foreign investigative or law enforcement officer to the extent that such disclosure is appropriate to the proper performance of the official duties of the officer making or receiving the disclosure, and foreign investigative or law enforcement officers may use or disclose such contents or derivative evidence to the extent such use or disclosure is appropriate to the proper performance of their official duties.

(8) Any investigative or law enforcement officer, or other Federal official in carrying out official duties as such Federal official, who by any means authorized by this chapter, has obtained knowledge of the contents of any wire, oral, or electronic communication, or evidence derived therefrom, may disclose such contents or derivative evidence to any appropriate Federal, State, local, or foreign government official to the extent that such contents or derivative evidence reveals a threat of actual or potential attack or other grave hostile acts of a foreign power or an agent of a foreign

power, domestic or international sabotage, domestic or international terrorism, or clandestine intelligence gathering activities by an intelligence service or network of a foreign power or by an agent of a foreign power, within the United States or elsewhere, for the purpose of preventing or responding to such a threat. Any official who receives information pursuant to this provision may use that information only as necessary in the conduct of that person's official duties subject to any limitations on the unauthorized disclosure of such information, and any State, local, or foreign official who receives information pursuant to this provision may use that information only consistent with such guidelines as the Attorney General and Director of Central Intelligence shall jointly issue.

§ 2518. Procedure for interception of wire, oral, or electronic communications

(1) Each application for an order authorizing or approving the interception of wire, oral or electronic communication shall be made in writing upon oath or affirmation to a judge of competent jurisdiction and shall state the applicant's authority to make such application. Each application shall include the following information:

(a) the identity of the investigative or law enforcement officer making the application, and the officer authorizing the application;

(b) a full and complete statement of facts and circumstances relied upon by the applicant, to justify his belief that an order should be issued, including (i) details as to the particular offense that has been, is being, or is about to be committed, (ii) except as provided in subsection (11) a particular description of the nature and location of the facilities from which or the place where the communication is to be intercepted, (iii) a particular description of the type of communications sought to be intercepted, (iv) the identity of the person, if known, committing the offense and whose communications are to be intercepted;

(c) a full and complete statement as to whether or not other investigative procedures have been tried and failed or why they reasonably appear to be unlikely to succeed if tried or to be too dangerous;

(d) a statement of the period of time for which the interception is required to be maintained. If the nature of the investigation is such that the authorization for interception should not automatically terminate when the described type of communication has been first obtained, a particular description of facts establishing probable cause to believe that additional communications of the same type will occur thereafter;

(e) a full and complete statement of the facts concerning all previous applications known to the individual authorizing and making the application, made to any judge for authorization to intercept, or for approval of interceptions of, wire, oral, or electronic communications involving any of the same persons, facilities or places specified in the application, and the action taken by the judge on each such application; and

(f) where the application is for the extension of an order, a statement setting forth the results thus far obtained from the interception, or a reasonable explanation of the failure to obtain such results.

(2) The judge may require the applicant to furnish additional testimony or documentary evidence in support of the application.

(3) Upon such application the judge may enter an ex parte order, as requested or as modified, authorizing or approving interception of wire, oral, or electronic communications within the territorial jurisdiction of the court in which the judge is sitting, . . . if the judge determines on the basis of the facts submitted by the applicant that

(a) there is probable cause for belief that an individual is committing, has committed, or is about to commit a particular offense enumerated in section 2516 of this chapter;

(b) there is probable cause for belief that particular communications concerning that offense will be obtained through such interception;

(c) normal investigative procedures have been tried and have failed or reasonably appear to be unlikely to succeed if tried or to be too dangerous;

(d) except as provided in subsection (11) there is probable cause for belief that the facilities from which, or the place where, the wire or oral communications are to be intercepted are being used, or are about to be used, in connection with the commission of such offense, or are leased to, listed in the name of, or commonly used by such person.

(4) Each order authorizing or approving the interception of any wire or oral communication shall specify

(a) the identity of the person, if known, whose communications are to be intercepted;

(b) the nature and location of the communications facilities as to which, or the place where, authority to intercept is granted;

(c) a particular description of the type of communication sought to be intercepted, and a statement of the particular offense to which it relates;

(d) the identity of the agency authorized to intercept the communications, and of the person authorizing the application; and

(e) the period of time during which such interception is authorized, including a statement as to whether or not the interception shall automatically terminate when the described communication has been first obtained.

An order authorizing the interception of a wire or oral communication under this chapter shall, upon request of the applicant, direct that a provider of wire or electronic communication service, landlord, custodian or other person shall furnish the applicant forthwith all information, facilities, and technical assistance necessary to accomplish the interception unobtrusively and with a minimum of interference with the services that such service provider, landlord, custodian, or person is according the person whose communications are to be intercepted. any provider of wire or electronic communication service, landlord, custodian or other person furnishing such facilities or technical assistance shall be compensated therefore by the applicant for reasonable expense incurred in providing such facilities or assistance . . .

(5) No order entered under this section may authorize or approve the interception of any wire, oral, or electronic communication for any period longer than is necessary to achieve the objective of the authorization, nor in any event longer than thirty days. . . . Extensions of an order may be granted, but only upon application for an extension made in accordance with subsection (1) of this section and the court making the findings required by subsection (3) of this section. The period of extension shall be no longer than the authorizing judge deems necessary to achieve the purposes for which it was granted and in no event for longer than thirty days. Every order and extension thereof shall contain a provision that the authorization to intercept shall be executed as soon as practicable, shall be conducted in such a way as to minimize the interception of communications not otherwise subject to interception under this chapter, and must terminate upon attainment of the authorized objective, or in any event in thirty days. . . .

(6) Whenever an order authorizing interception is entered pursuant to this chapter, the order may require reports to be made to the judge who issued the order showing what progress has been made toward achievement of the authorized objective and the need for continued interception. Such reports shall be made at such intervals as the judge may require.

(7) Notwithstanding any other provision of this chapter, any investigative or law enforcement officer, specially designated by the Attorney General, the Deputy Attorney General, the Associate Attorney General or by the principal prosecuting attorney of any State or subdivision thereof acting pursuant to a statute of that State, who reasonably determines that

(a) an emergency situation exists that involves—

(i) immediate danger of death or serious physical injury to any person,

(ii) conspiratorial activities threatening the national security interest, or

(iii) conspiratorial activities characteristic of organized crime,

that requires a wire, oral, or electronic communication to be intercepted before an order authorizing such interception can, with due diligence, be obtained, and

there are grounds upon which an order could be entered under this chapter to authorize such interception, may intercept such wire, oral, or electronic communication if an application for an order approving the interception is made in accordance with this section within forty-eight hours after the interception has occurred, or begins to occur. In the absence of an order, such interception shall immediately terminate when the communication sought is obtained or when the application for the order is denied, whichever is earlier. In the event such application for approval is denied, or in any other case where the interception is terminated without an order having been issued, the contents of any wire, oral, or electronic communication intercepted shall be treated as having been obtained in violation of this chapter, and an inventory shall be served as provided for in subsection (d) of this section on the person named in the application.

(8)(a) The contents of any wire, oral, or electronic communication intercepted by any means authorized by this chapter shall, if possible, be recorded on tape or wire or other comparable device. The recording of the contents of any wire or oral communication under this subsection shall be done in such way as will protect the recording from editing or other alterations. Immediately upon the expiration of the period of the order, or extensions thereof, such recordings shall be made available to the judge issuing such order and sealed under his directions. Custody of the recordings shall be wherever the judge orders. They shall not be destroyed except upon an order of the issuing or denying judge and in any event shall be kept for ten years. Duplicate recordings may be made for use or disclosure pursuant to the provisions of subsections (1) and (2) of section 2517 of this chapter for investigations. The presence of the seal provided for by this subsection, or a satisfactory explanation for the absence thereof, shall be a prerequisite for the use or disclosure of the contents of any wire or oral communication or evidence derived therefrom under subsection (3) of section 2517.

(b) Applications made and orders granted under this chapter shall be sealed by the judge. Custody of the applications and orders shall be wherever the judge directs. Such applications and orders shall be disclosed only upon a showing of good cause before a judge of competent jurisdiction and shall not be destroyed except on order of the issuing or denying judge, and in any event shall be kept for ten years.

(c) Any violation of the provisions of this subsection may be punished as contempt of the issuing or denying judge.

(d) Within a reasonable time but not later than ninety days after the filing of an application for an order of approval under section 2518(7)(b) which is denied or the termination of the period of an order or extensions thereof, the issuing or denying judge shall cause to be served, on the persons named in the order or the application, and such other parties to intercepted communications as the judge may determine in his discretion that is in the interest of justice, an inventory which shall include notice of

(1) the fact of the entry of the order or the application;

(2) the date of the entry and the period of authorized, approved or disapproved interception, or the denial of the application; and

(3) the fact that during the period wire, oral, or electronic communications were or were not intercepted.

The judge, upon the filing of a motion, may in his discretion make available to such person or his counsel for inspection such portions of the intercepted communications, applications and orders as the judge determines to be in the interest of justice. On an ex parte showing of good cause to a judge of competent jurisdiction the serving of the inventory required by this subsection may be postponed.

(9) The contents of any wire, oral, or electronic communication intercepted pursuant to this chapter or evidence derived therefrom shall not be received in evidence or otherwise disclosed in any trial, hearing, or other proceeding in a Federal or State court unless each party, not less than ten days before the trial, hearing, or proceeding, has been furnished with a copy of the court order, and accompanying application, under which the interception was authorized or approved. This ten-day period may be waived by the judge if he finds that it was not possible to furnish the party with the above information ten days before the trial, hearing, or proceeding and that the party will not be prejudiced by the delay in receiving such information.

(10)(a) Any aggrieved person in any trial, hearing, or proceeding in or before any court, department, officer, agency, regulatory body, or other authority of the United States, a State, or a political subdivision thereof, may move to suppress the contents of any wire or oral communication intercepted pursuant to this chapter, or evidence derived therefrom, on the grounds that—

(i) the communication was unlawfully intercepted;

(ii) the order of authorization or approval under which it was intercepted is insufficient on its face; or

(iii) the interception was not made in conformity with the order of authorization or approval.

Such motion shall be made before the trial, hearing, or proceeding unless there was no opportunity to make such motion or the person was not aware of the grounds of the motion. If the motion is granted, the contents of the intercepted wire or oral communication, or evidence derived therefrom, shall be treated as having been obtained in violation of this chapter. The judge, upon the filing of such motion by the aggrieved person, may in his discretion make available to the aggrieved person or his counsel for inspection such portions of the intercepted communication or evidence derived therefrom as the judge determines to be in the interests of justice.

(b) In addition to any other right to appeal, the United States shall have the right to appeal from an order granting a motion to suppress made under paragraph (a) of this subsection, or the denial of an application for an order of approval, if the United States attorney shall certify to the judge or other official granting such motion or denying such application that the appeal is not taken for purposes of delay. such appeal shall be taken within thirty days after the date the order was entered and shall be diligently prosecuted.

* * *

The rest of the statute provides for civil damages and criminal penalties for violations, a mechanism for gathering appropriate statistical information on both state and federal overhearings, and penalties for service providers who fail to make their digitally encoded systems accessible to law enforcement "taps."

NOTE

Relation to State Statutes. State statutes allowing court-ordered wiretaps must conform to the federal statute. For example, wiretap orders must be based upon probable cause related to certain categories of offenses enumerated in Section 2516 of the federal statute. A state statute cannot authorize a wiretap in search of evidence for a less serious offense. See People v. Shapiro, 50 N.Y.2d 747, 431 N.Y.S.2d 422, 409 N.E.2d 897 (1980) (New York statute invalidated when it provided for tap in connection with non-forceful sexual crime against a child). But see State v. Otte, 887 So.2d 1186 (Fla. 2004). A state may not apply lower standards, but a state statute may impose more stringent requirements than the federal statute requires. United States v. Mora, 821 F.2d 860, 863 n. 3 (1st Cir.1987). Even if a state statute prohibits eavesdropping, a federal statute may preempt state law and authorize it. United States v. Hall, 543 F.2d 1229 (9th Cir.), cert. denied 429 U.S. 1075, 97 S.Ct. 814 (1977). And see Bansal v. Russ, 513 F.Supp. 2d 264 (E.D. Pa. 2007).

(b) REQUIREMENTS FOR OBTAINING A VALID TITLE III ORDER AND FOR EXECUTING THE ORDER TO CONDUCT SURVEILLANCE

1. *Who May Seek a Title III Order?* Prior to amendments, an earlier version of Title III required that authorization to seek a wiretap had to have come from the attorney general or an assistant attorney general specially designated by the attorney general. In the absence of an emergency, if the order was not sought by one of these designated officials or the government misidentified such an official, suppression was the appropriate remedy. United States v. Giordano, 416 U.S. 505, 94 S.Ct. 1820 (1974). Now, § 2516, greatly expands the list of government officials authorized to seek a Title III order.

2. *Requirements for a Valid Title III Order.* Section 2518 sets forth the requirements for a Title III application. They include a sworn statement that sets forth probable cause. In addition, there must be a specific description of who and what will be under surveillance and for how long. Unlike search warrants, however, Title III requires a statement that, on the face of it, is more stringent than the Fourth Amendment would require. An applicant must make a sufficient showing as to whether or not "other investigative procedures have been tried and failed or why they reasonably appear to be unlikely to succeed if tried or to be too dangerous." § 2518(3)(c).

3. *Proof of Lack of Alternative Means of Investigation as a Required Showing for a Title III Order.* Although many defense lawyers and some commentators suggest that boilerplate allegations ordinarily suffice to convince a court that authorities have exhausted traditional means of investigation, so as to meet the statutory prerequisite for submitting a wiretap application, occasionally a warrant is suppressed because of an inadequate showing that "normal investigative procedures have been tried and have failed or reasonably appear to be unlikely to succeed if tried or to be too dangerous." For a detailed discussion of how courts apply this standard with attention given to the standard to be applied on appeal, see United States v. Ramirez–Encarnacion, 291 F.3d 1219 (10th Cir.2002) [resolving split in circuit]. See also e.g. United States v. Simpson, 813 F.2d 1462 (9th Cir.), cert. denied 484 U.S. 898, 108 S.Ct. 233 (1987). For an example of a failure by law enforcement to demonstrate a lack of alternative means where this led to suppression of evidence seized pursuant to the wiretap order, see United States v. Arrington, 46 Fed.Appx. 935, cert. denied 539 U.S. 921, 123 S.Ct. 2290 (2003).

4. *Covert Entry for Installation.* In Dalia v. United States, 441 U.S. 238, 99 S.Ct. 1682 (1979), the Court held that a judge or magistrate who issues a wiretap authorization can also authorize covert entry upon a person's property for the purpose of installing the monitoring device. The Court also held that explicit authorization for such entry need not appear in the wiretap order: "(W)e would promote empty formalism were we to require magistrates to make explicit what unquestionably is implicit in bugging authorizations: that a covert entry, with its attendant interference with Fourth Amendment interest, may be necessary for the installation of surveillance equipment." Four justices dissented. (Today the Justice Department usually seeks express authorization for covert entries necessary for installation of surveillance equipment.)

5. *Minimizing Overhearing.* One other question of great concern is the extent to which authorities must "minimize" the overhearing and recording of conversations "not otherwise subject to interception." 18 U.S.C. § 2518(5). In Scott v. United States, 436 U.S. 128, 98 S.Ct. 1717 (1978), the government received authorization for a wiretap in connection with a narcotics investigation. Of the conversations intercepted, only "40% of them were shown to be narcotics related." The Court held that the agents actions, not their motives nor their good faith or bad faith, were relevant to the minimization issue. The percentage of innocent calls is not dispositive. The Court commented:

> ... when the investigation is focusing on what is thought to be a widespread conspiracy more extensive surveillance may be justified in an attempt to determine the precise scope of the enterprise. And it is possible that many more of the conversations will be permissibly interceptable because they will involve one or more of the coconspirators. The type of use to which the telephone is normally put may also have some bearing on the extent of minimization required. For example, if the agents are permitted to tap a public telephone because one individual is thought to be placing bets over the phone, substantial doubts as to minimization may arise if the agents listen to every call which goes out over that phone regardless of who places the call. On the other hand, if the phone is located in the residence of a person who is thought to be the head of a major drug ring, a contrary conclusion may be indicated.
>
> Other factors may also play a significant part in a particular case. For example, it may be important to determine at exactly what point during the authorized period the interception was made. During the early stages of surveillance the agents may be

> forced to intercept all calls to establish categories of nonpertinent calls which will not be intercepted thereafter. Interception of those same types of calls might be unreasonable later on, however, once the nonpertinent categories have been established and it is clear that this particular conversation is of that type. Other situations may arise where patterns of nonpertinent calls do not appear. In these circumstances it may not be unreasonable to intercept almost every short conversation because the determination of relevancy cannot be made before the call is completed.

Applying these standards, the Court held that the requirement of minimization had not been violated. Justices Brennan and Marshall dissented, noting that the agents had monitored every call and had made no effort to "minimize" the interception of innocent conversations.

6. ***Who May Monitor?*** Usually law enforcement personnel monitor the phone calls on the tapped line. The use of civilians, however, to monitor the conversations intercepted under a Title III order is not barred. United States v. Lopez, 300 F.3d 46 (1st Cir.2002).

7. ***Can Judicial Authorization Be Broader than the Act?*** In United States v. Torres, 751 F.2d 875 (7th Cir.1984), the court reviewed an order that had suppressed court-authorized videotapes of activities within "safe houses" of the Fuerzas Armadas de Liberation Nacional Puertorrequena. Chief District Judge McGarr had authorized surreptitious entry and placing of video cameras within the safe houses, acting under the purported authority of the federal wiretap act. (The government had not invoked the Foreign Intelligence Surveillance Act and had not sought an order from the special court set up under that act.) In a thoughtful opinion reported at 583 F.Supp. 86 (N.D.Ill.1984), District Judge Leighton ruled that the wiretap act does not authorize a judge to issue an authorization for video recordings, as distinguished from aural recordings. The opinion concluded that, in the absence of such statutory authorization, the videotaping violated the Fourth Amendment. The opinion was in accord with three other state and federal district court rulings.

On appeal the Government was confronted with a difficult legal challenge. The pen register case of Smith v. Maryland, 442 U.S. 735, 99 S.Ct. 2577 (1979), had specifically declared that Title III governed only "aural" interceptions. Moreover, Congress in the Foreign Intelligence Surveillance Act specifically provided for video interceptions, but Congress had not yet amended the 1968 act to provide for video interceptions under Title III.

The Government, however, knew it was in good shape when the reviewing court phrased the issue as "whether there was a right to be let alone while assembling bombs in safe houses," and when the court drew on a New York Times article describing FALN terrorist tactics. It prevailed in Judge Richard Posner's opinion for the majority. The majority agreed that there was no statutory authorization for Judge McGarr's order, but it declared that none was needed. It said that federal judges have the inherent power to issue warrants and to authorize electronic surveillance.

Their warrants and surveillance orders need only comport with the probable cause and reasonableness limitations of the Fourth Amendment and need not be pursuant to a statute setting forth such limitations.

Posner's opinion did not discuss Berger v. New York (page 338, infra). There the Supreme Court ruled wiretapping illegal because the New York wiretap statute (prior to the passage of Title III) on its face did not embody sufficient safeguards. The Berger Court ruled without commenting on the specifics of the safeguards actually employed by the New York judge who had issued the authorization.

In Torres the majority concluded that Judge McGarr's procedures had comported with the Fourth Amendment and therefore the videotaping was lawful. McGarr had adhered to the (nonapplicable) procedures outlined in Title III.

Concurring Judge Richard Cudahy concluded that it was possible to construe Title III as authorizing videotape surveillance orders. He declared that the court must pay attention to the spirit as well as the letter of statute so as to imagine how Congress would have wanted to apply it to situations which it had not foreseen, citing Posner, "Statutory Interpretation in the Classroom and in the Courtroom," 50 U. Chi. L. Rev. 800 (1983).

The Second Circuit has reached the same result as did the Torres court. See United States v. Biasucci, 786 F.2d 504 (2d Cir.1986). The Biasucci court declared that although before 1968 "there was no specific statutory authorization, ... the Supreme Court had approved the court-ordered use of concealed electronic devices to record conversations, holding that the government had satisfied Fourth Amendment requirements. See, e.g., Katz and Berger (citations omitted)." Is this a proper reading of Katz and Berger?

The Ninth Circuit took a similar view in United States v. Koyomejian, 970 F.2d 536 (9th Cir.1992) (en banc). Rejecting the argument that silent video surveillance fell within the protections given "electronic communications" under the 1986 amendments, the court nonetheless required more than probable cause. In addition, the government must show that (1) normal investigation won't work; (2) the surveillance will be as minimal and short as it can be, and (3) it is directed toward a particular, described activity which is related to a particular offense.

8. *Notification of Illegal Taps.* All records arising from illegal eavesdropping or wiretapping concerning which a criminal defendant has standing to object must be disclosed to him or her. Neither grounds of national security nor the protection of third parties justifies the withholding of such materials, although the court may place defendants and counsel under protective orders against unwarranted disclosure of the records. See Alderman v. United States, 394 U.S. 165, 89 S.Ct. 961 (1969). The Justice Department, on several occasions more than two decades ago, where illegal wiretapping occurred, dismissed prosecutions rather than disclose wiretap materials to defendants. (It is difficult to know how many of these dismissals were truly based upon "national security." It has been suggested that some were dismissed to keep from public light either gross illegalities or other conduct which might prove embarrassing to law enforcement officials or to other members of the executive branch.)

A defendant is not entitled to disclosure until after it is established that he was a victim of illegal wiretapping. To make such a determination, a judge may conduct an in camera inspection of wiretap tapes and logs without disclosing such data to the accused. See Taglianetti v. United States, 394 U.S. 316, 89 S.Ct. 1099 (1969).Thus, an in camera inspection (without defendant's participation) is thought adequate to determine whether he was the victim of illegal wiretapping; but once that is shown, the accused must be allowed to inspect the materials to determine what part, if any, the illegality may have played in the building of the case against him.

9. ***Extent of Use of Title III orders.*** Reports concerning wiretap orders are required by law unless there an order is granted with the consent of one of the parties (i.e. intercepts with police informants involved, investigation of obscene phone calls, or body wires). Surveillance not covered by Title III, such as pen registers, are not included in the reports. The wiretaps are reported only after the investigation is concluded. In 2006 reports indicated that courts issued 1,839 authorizations for intercept orders as a result of 461 federal applications (down 26% from 2005) and 1,378 state applications (up 20% from 2005) with 23 states providing reports. Report of the Director of the Administrative Office of the United States Courts on Applications for Orders Authorizing or Approving the Interception of Wire, Oral, or Electronic Communications. (hereinafter, Director's Report) http://www.uscourts.gov/wiretap06/2006WT.pdf. Of these, 48 orders were for private residences, 13 were for businesses, 1,685 were for portable devices, 15 were roving orders, 53 were "combination" orders, 24 were for "other" devices, and 1 was not specified. Director's Report, http://www.uscourts.gov/wiretap06/Table22006.pdf. The average percentage of intercepted communications that were incriminating was 20 percent in 2006, compared to 22 percent in 2005. The law requires reports to reflect the number of wiretap applications granted in which encryption was encountered. The reports must also indicate whether any such encryption prevented law enforcement officials from obtaining plain text of communications intercepted pursuant to court orders. No such encryption was reported during any state or federal wiretap in 2006. Director's Report, http://www.uscourts.gov/wiretap06/2006WT.pdf.

Wiretap applications in California (430 applications), New York (377 applications), New Jersey (189 applications), and Florida (98 applications) accounted for 79 percent of all applications approved by state judges. Director's Report, http://www.uscourts.gov/wiretap06/2006WT.pdf. The main categories of cases for which wiretaps were sought were for drug trafficking (1,473 of 1,839), homicides and assaults (119 of 1,839), and racketeering (90 of 1,839). Director's Report, http://www.uscourts.gov/wiretap06/Table32006.pdf. The average cost of per wiretap order was $52,552, though the costs varied greatly: the lowest average cost per order was $100 reported by the State Attorney General of South Carolina; the 8th Judicial Circuit of Florida (Alachua) reported the highest average cost per order of $500,040. Director's Report, http://www.uscourts.gov/wiretap06/Table

32006.pdf. Almost all applications are granted. From 1996 through 2006, government agents have sought 15,822 intercept orders. According to required reports, only five applications have been denied in this decade. Director's Report, http://www.uscourts.gov/wiretap06/2006WT.pdf. Why are so few applications rejected? Perhaps law enforcement officers exercise extraordinary care in drafting applications for wiretap orders, especially since they are often sought in only the highest priority cases. Perhaps oversight by agency attorneys and/or prosecutors enhances the quality of the applications. Perhaps the fact that judges have the authority to modify applications brought before them leads to applications that are more likely to be granted. Perhaps judges are willing to issue orders knowing that any subsequent motion to suppress will address any earlier mistakes in the investigatory stage, but may not necessarily lead to suppression due to the possibility that the good faith doctrine may apply.

10. ***Exclusionary Remedy.*** In United States v. Donovan, 429 U.S. 413, 97 S.Ct. 658 (1977), the Court held that the statutory exclusionary remedy only applied to "central" features of the Wiretap Act, not, for example, the failure to identify all the potential callers (besides the phone owner) in an intercept application. The Court distinguished its prior opinions in United States v. Giordano, 416 U.S. 505, 94 S.Ct. 1820 (1974), and United States v. Chavez, 416 U.S. 562, 94 S.Ct. 1849 (1974): "This case is unlike Giordano, where failure to satisfy the statutory requirement of prior approval by specified Justice Department officials bypassed a congressionally imposed limitation on the use of the intercept procedure. The Court there noted that it was reasonable to believe that requiring prior approval from senior officials in the Justice Department" would inevitably foreclose resort to wiretapping in various situations where investigative personnel would otherwise seek intercept authority from the court and the court would very likely authorize its use. "Here, however, the statutorily imposed preconditions to judicial authorization were satisfied, and the issuing judge was simply unaware that additional persons might be overheard engaging in incriminating conversations. In no meaningful sense can it be said that the presence of that information as to additional targets would have precluded judicial authorization of the intercept. Rather, this case resembles Chavez, where we held that a wiretap was not unlawful simply because the issuing judge was incorrectly informed as to which designated official had authorized the application. The Chavez intercept was lawful because the Justice Department had performed its task of prior approval, and the instant intercept is lawful because the application provided sufficient information to enable the issuing judge to determine that the statutory preconditions were satisfied." Justices Marshall and Brennan dissented, believing that the Court frustrated Congressional intent by applying the statutory exclusionary rule only to those provisions it deemed important.

11. ***Does the Good Faith Exception of Leon Apply to Title III Orders?*** There is a statutory good faith exception to civil or criminal liability arising from wiretapping found at 18 U.S.C. § 2520(d) (as amended by the Homeland Security Act of 2002). The question has arisen, however, as to whether a "good faith" exception should be judicially engrafted onto the exclusionary rule of the Wiretap Act. If so, evidence obtained would be admissible notwithstanding a constitutional or statutory violation. See discussion in Michael S. Leib, "E–Mail and the Wiretap Laws: Why Congress Should Add Electronic Communication to Title III's Statutory Exclusionary Rule and Expressly Reject a 'Good Faith' Exception," 34 Harv. J. on Legis. 393. Some circuits have adopted the good faith exception of United States v. Leon, 468 U.S. 897, 104 S.Ct. 3405 (1984) in the wiretap context. United States v. Moore, 41 F.3d 370, 376–77 (8th Cir.) cert. denied 514 U.S. 1121, 115 S.Ct. 1985 (1995). United States v. Malekzadeh, 855 F.2d 1492 (11th Cir.1988), cert. denied, 489 U.S. 1024, 109 S.Ct. 1149 (1989); United States v. McGuinness, 764 F.Supp. 888 (S.D.N.Y.1991). Other courts resolve challenges to Title III orders assuming arguendo that the good faith exception applies. See e.g. United States v. Jones, 493 F. Supp. 2d 611 (D.N.Y. 2006).

The good faith exception was rejected by the trial judge in United States v. Castillo–Garcia and the Court of Appeals declined to reach the issue on the basis that the issue had not be raised in a timely fashion in the district court. United States v. Castillo–Garcia, 117 F.3d 1179, 1184 (10th Cir.), cert. denied sub nom Armendariz–Amaya v. United States, 522 U.S. 962, 118 S.Ct. 395, 139 L.Ed.2d 309 (1997) and Avila v. United States, 522 U.S. 974, 118 S.Ct. 428 (1997).

12. ***Sealing the Tapes.*** Section 2518(8)(a) requires the sealing of the tapes immediately upon the expiration of the order or any extension of the order. In United States v. Ojeda Rios, 495 U.S. 257, 110 S.Ct. 1845 (1990), the Supreme Court indicated that it would apply an exclusionary remedy if the failure to immediately seal the tapes was not satisfactorily explained, even if the Government could prove that no one tampered with the tapes before they were sealed. It rejected the Government's contention that any seal, even one that was delayed without satisfactory explanation, would satisfy the language of § 2518(a), which states that the "presence of the seal provided for by this subsection, or a satisfactory explanation for the absence thereof," shall be a "prerequisite for the use or disclosure" of the contents of the oral communication.

(c) OTHER FEDERAL STATUTES AND TECHNOLOGIES: BEYOND THE TELEPHONE AND BUGS AND ONTO COMPUTERS, THE INTERNET, AND INDIVIDUAL COMMUNICATION DEVICES

In the aftermath of the September 11, 2001 crisis in which America was traumatized by hijacked planes being flown into the World Trade Center Towers in New York City and the Pentagon in Washington, D.C., there has been a flurry of new legislative initiatives to aid law enforcement in the fight against terrorism. These have also given government agencies additional arrows in their quiver to combat crime. In some instances, changes have been made in existing legislation; in others, new laws have been enacted. The rapid changes in technological capabilities have further complicated efforts to monitor government surveillance. See Schulhofer and McKay, The Enemy Within: Intelligence Gathering, Law Enforcement and Civil Liberties in the Wake of September 11. (Twentieth Century Fund, 2002) What follows does not serve as a comprehensive list of statutes that regulate surveillance, but instead attempts to alert the reader to a sampling of some of the laws and the emerging technology.

If you wish to read further in this quickly changing area, look for statements by law enforcement officials before Congressional committees and at the Department of Justice website. (http://www.usdoj.gov). In addition, there are a number of long-standing "watch dog" organizations that provide information on developing legislation and technology. These include the American Civil Liberties Union (Privacy and Technology–Government Surveillance) (http://www.aclu.org/Privacy/PrivacyMain.cfm); the Center for Democracy and Technology (http://www.cdt.org); and the Electronic Privacy Information Center (http://www.epic.org).

Overarching consideration of these issues requires some inquiry as to whether existing law can simply be carried over to the cyber territory so that they are treated akin to "real space" transactions with governments exercising territorial control. Jack L. Goldsmith, "Against Cyberanarchy," 65 U. Chicago L. Rev. 1199 (1998) or whether cyberspace is "different" and requires new approaches, David Post, "Against 'Against Cyberanarchy,' " 17 Berkeley Technology Law Journal 1365 (2003). At least one author has urged a cyber architecture that is more transparent (i.e. more easily subject to surveillance) as a method of crime control. Neil Katyal, "Digital Architecture as Crime Control," 112 Yale L. J. 2261 (2003).

A Sampling of Other Legislation

1. *FISA: FOREIGN INTELLIGENCE SECURITY ACT*

a. Is there a National Security Exception to the Fourth Amendment?

Before the Omnibus Crimes and Safe Streets Act of 1968 was amended in late 1978, the power of the President to authorize warrantless wiretapping for national security was left for the courts to decide. Section 2511(3) stated that the "constitutional power of the president" to take such measures was not limited by the Act. In United States v. United States District Court, 407 U.S. 297, 92 S.Ct. 2125 (1972), the Court addressed "the delicate question of the President's power, acting through the Attorney General, to authorize electronic surveillance in internal security matters without prior judicial approval." The government sought to justify warrantless eavesdropping on the grounds that domestic security was involved. The government relied on the Communications Act of 1934 which stated:

> Nothing contained in this chapter or in section 605 of the Communications Act of 1934 . . . shall limit the constitutional power of the President to take such measures as he deems necessary to protect the Nation against actual or potential attack or other hostile acts of a foreign power, to obtain foreign intelligence information deemed essential to the security of the United States, or to protect national security information against foreign intelligence activities. *Nor shall anything contained in this chapter be deemed to limit the constitutional power of the President to take such measures as he deems necessary to protect the United States against the*

> *overthrow of the Government by force or other unlawful means, or against any other clear and present danger to the structure or existence of the Government.* The contents of any wire or oral communication intercepted by authority of the President in the exercise of the foregoing powers may be received in evidence in any trial hearing, or other proceeding only where such interception was reasonable, and shall not be otherwise used or disclosed except as is necessary to implement that power. 18 U.S.C. § 2511(3) (1976 ed.) as quoted in United States v. United States District Court, 407 U.S. at 302. [This provision was originally enacted as part of Title III of the Omnibus Crime Control and Save Streets Act of was repealed in 1978 by § 201(c) of the Foreign Intelligence Surveillance Act.]

Based on this, the government argued that there was a national security exception that permitted the president to authorize surveillances without prior judicial approval. The Court rejected such a broad "domestic security" exception to the requirement of a Title III order.

The Court also rejected the argument that internal security matters are too subtle and complex for judicial evaluation.

The Court emphasized the scope of its decision by pointing out it has expressed no opinion with respect to surveillance of activities of foreign powers or their agents. The Court noted that Congress could provide a different set of standards for national security cases. "Different standards may be compatible with the Fourth Amendment if they are reasonable both in relation to the legitimate need of Government for intelligence information and the protected rights of our citizens." United States v. United States District Court, 407 U.S. at 322–23.

b. The Enactment of The Foreign Intelligence Surveillance Act.

Congress subsequently passed and President Carter signed the Foreign Intelligence Surveillance Act (FISA) of 1978, 50 U.S.C. §§ 1801–1811. A special warrant procedure was established for the interception, within the United States, of conversations to which a "United States person" is a party, where there is a probability that foreign intelligence, not available through other means, can be obtained. The act created a special court composed of three judges, each appointed by the Chief Justice of the Supreme Court Executive certification of the necessity for such a wiretap is required. The special panel of judges, selected by the Chief Justice, is available to rule on requests for such wiretaps.

A number of cases have upheld the Foreign Intelligence Surveillance Act against a variety of challenges. See e. g. United States v. Cavanagh, 807 F.2d 787 (9th Cir.1987); United States v. Duggan, 743 F.2d 59 (2d Cir. 1984); United States v. Abu–Jihaad, 531 F.Supp.2d 289 (D.Conn.2008); United States v. Marzook, 435 F.Supp.2d 778 (N.D.Ill.2006) (FISA procedures comport with fourth amendment including the 1994 legislative extension of FISA to physical searches to obtain foreign intelligence); United States v. Mubayyid, 512 F.Supp. 521 F. Supp. 2d 125 (D.Mass.2007) (FISA is constitutional since it satisfies the fourth amendment requirements of judicial review, probable cause, particularity, and notice requirements.

Minimization requirements do not apply to non-American citizens). For an in-depth discussion of the FISA provisions, see Hall, "Constitutional Regulation of National Security Investigation: Minimizing the Use of Unrelated Evidence", 41 Wake Forest L. Rev. 61 (2006).

c. Basis for a FISA Order in Contrast to a Title III Order.

Initially, FISA required that the government applicant for a warrant under the act must certify that the primary purpose of the surveillance is to gather foreign intelligence information. The United States Patriot Act amended FISA so that now, the applicant need only assert is that foreign intelligence "a significant purpose" for the surveillance rather than the primary purpose. Uniting and Strengthening America by Providing Appropriate Tools Required to Intercept and Obstruct Terrorism (USA PATRIOT ACT) Act of 2001, 50 U.S.C. § 1823.

It is not common for the decisions of the Foreign Surveillance Court are not published and they are seldom reviewed. James Risen, "Surveillance Court Declines to Release Opinions," New York Times, December 17, 2007.

In a rare glimpse of the operations of the specialized Foreign Surveillance Court, created to oversee intelligence wiretaps within the United States, the appellate court overruled the lower court and issued an unusual exceedingly rare opinion. At issue was the question of government powers under FISA. Before the passage of the Patriot Act (see below) any agent who sought surveillance must choose between seeking information for national security reasons or information to use in a criminal prosecution. Prior to the Patriot Act, these two purposes were clearly separated and the standards were perceived as more lax for a national security tap. In addition, the subject of a FISA surveillance did not need to be notified of the surveillance. After the Patriot Act, the lower FISA court ordered the Department of Justice to meet additional requirements before tapping the phone of an individual identified as "a resident of the United States who is working as an agent of a foreign power." In addition, it ordered that the government must show that the primary purpose of the order was for intelligence gathering and not criminal prosecution. In re All Matters Submitted to the Foreign Intelligence Surveillance Court, 218 F.Supp.2d 611 (2002).

The three-judge Court of Review, meeting for the first time, reversed the lower court and held that the passage of the Patriot Act removed the stark distinction between the criminal and intelligence sides of national security operations. The appellate court also discounted the argument that the standards of Title III (that there is probable cause to believe the subject is involved in one of the listed crimes) is constitutionally different from the FISA requirement (that there is probable cause that the subject is the agent of a foreign power). United States Foreign Intelligence Surveillance Court of Review, 310 F.3d 717 (2002). See also Neil A. Lewis, "Threats and Responses: The Search for Terrorists; Court Overturns Limits on Wiretaps to Combat Terror," New York Times, November 19, 2002, Sec. A, page 1, col. 6. See also, Jeffrey Tobin, "Annals of Law: Crackdown—Should We Be

Worried About the New Anti-terrorism Legislation?" The New Yorker, p. 56, November 5, 2001.

As technology improved, criminals began using a variety of phones for communication purposes. For example, they would switch to various cell phones or move from phone to phone. This complicated efforts by law enforcement agents to comply with Title III. Courts interpreted § 2518 of the Omnibus Crime Control and Safe Streets Act to be satisfied when a Title III wiretap order names and describes one cell phone, but the defendant shifts to another. As long as the government could prove the link between the first phone and the second, the order was sufficient. United States v. Duran, 189 F.3d 1071 (9th Cir.1999) The Patriot Act (see supra) addressed this problem. It authorizes the issuance of "roving wiretap" orders so that law enforcement may legally eavesdrop on an individual using different phones rather than be required to obtain a different wiretap order for each phone. 18 U.S.C. § 2518.

The Homeland Security Act of 2002 amends FISA 50 U.S.C. § 1806 to allow federal law enforcement officers to confer and coordinate with law enforcement personnel of a State or political subdivision of a State (including the chief executive officer of that State or subdivision who has the authority to appoint or direct the chief law enforcement officer of that State or political subdivision.). § 898

d. Executive Resistance to the Need for Judicial Approval to Obtain a FISA Order When National Security and the War on Terror is Involved.

The nation learned that George W. Bush had ordered the National Security Agency (NSA) to tap domestic phones and internet connections without the aid of judicial orders under either Title III or FISA. Administration officials turned whistleblowers revealed this news to the New York Times. At the request of President Bush, the New York Times delayed revelation for a year, but then published the news on December 16, 2005. Risen and Lichtblau, "Bush Lets U.S. Spy on Callers Without Courts," New York Times, A1, December 16, 2005.

Congress considered presidential censure when it learned that the Bush administration was circumventing the FISA warrant procedure and it was revealed that the National Security Agency (NSA), the government agency that "coordinates, directs, and performs highly specialized activities to protect U.S. government information systems and produce foreign signals intelligence information" (http:// www.nsa.gov/about) had conducted surveillance on millions of phone users in the United States and in foreign countries without any judicial oversight whatsoever. See Senate Resolution 398 (2006).

The White House and Attorney General Alberto Gonzalez defended these warrantless surveillances and came under heavy criticism. A clash of power between the President and Congress ensued. The Office of Legal Counsel defended the executive power to order the surveillance. John Yoo, The Powers of War and Peace, (Univ. of Chicago 2006). Executive branch officials were subpoenaed to testify before Congress and the White House claimed executive privilege to prevent their appearance. The President maintained it was within his executive powers to unilaterally authorize surveillance for foreign intelligence purposes without the approval of courts. Finally, the White House entered into an agreement with Congress and promised to seek FISA approval for all surveillance covered by the act.

The administration sought unsuccessfully to limit the scope of FISA. See Editorial, Fixing FISA; The rules for domestic electronic surveillance need a careful updating, Washington Post, A18, May 7, 2007.

In the winter of 2007–08, the administration sought to renew the Protect America Act for surveillance and to add provisions that would indemnify telephone companies who permit government authorities access to their equipment and subscriber accounts for purposes of surveillance. Text of the State of the Union Address, New York Times, 1/29/08 and analysis of Tom Gjelten, NPR commentary after the State of the Union Address, 1/28/07.

A constitutional challenge by the American Civil Liberties Union to the National Security Agency's surveillance was sustained in District Court, but later vacated. ACLU v. National Sec. Agency/Central Sec. Serv., 438 F. Supp. 2d 754 (D. Mich. 2006), stay granted, ACLU v. NSA, 467 F.3d 590 (6th Cir.2006), vacated and remanded 493 F.3d 644 (6th Cir.2007). The Supreme Court denied a writ of certiorari. ACLU v. NSA, 128 S.Ct. 1334 February 19, 2008 (No. 07–468).

2. *ECPA: ELECTRONIC COMMUNICATIONS PRIVACY ACT OF 1986*

As new technology developed, the Omnibus Crime Control and Safe Streets Act of 1968 was expanded in the Electronic Communications Privacy Act of 1986 to include all "electronic communication," including email and other new technologies. Congress did not include statutory suppression remedies for nonconstitutional violations (note the different treatment of "oral and wire" communication from "electronic" communication below). In a separate statute, Congress also proscribed intentional access, without authorization, to stored electronic communication, 18 U.S.C. §§ 2701–2711, but required only a search warrant, § 2703, not a court order as in § 2518 of Title III.[1]

The ECPA does not include a suppression remedy. Efforts to convince a court to suppress internet information have failed. United States v. Kennedy, 81 F.Supp.2d 1103 (D.Kan.2000). This case has been cited for the proposition that there is no Fourth Amendment privacy interest in subscriber information given to an Internet Service Provider. United States v. Cox, 190 F.Supp.2d 330 (N.D.N.Y.2002).

At least one commentator has called for a suppression remedy. "While very generous civil remedies exist against violations of a maze of statutes that on paper offer significant privacy protection for Internet users, and

1. Confusingly, the cases often refer to the original wiretap provisions 18 U.S.C. §§ 2510–2522 as "Title III," since that was their denomination in the Omnibus Crime Control and Safe Streets Act, but the same provisions are sometimes called "Title I," since that was their denomination in the Electronic Communications Privacy Act. The "stored communications" requirements of §§ 2701–2711 are referred to as "Title II" of the ECPA.

violations of the electronic surveillance statutes are also federal crimes, the statutory Internet surveillance laws lack a suppression remedy." Orin S. Kerr, "Lifting the 'Fog' of Internet Surveillance: How a Suppression Remedy Would Change Computer Crime Law," 54 Hastings Law Journal 805 (2003).

3. *ENSURING GOVERNMENT ACCESS TO COMMUNICATIONS*

a. CALEA: Communications Assistance for Law Enforcement Act

CALEA (Communications Assistance for Law Enforcement Act), 47 U.S.C. §§ 1001 et seq. requires communications providers to allow access and to modify equipment to permit access to law enforcement.

In very simplified form, CALEA sets up the following regime as to capacity, involving three key phases: (1) The Attorney General issues "notices" of what capacity is needed. The Attorney General, in fact, has delegated his duties to the FBI (2) Each carrier responds with a "statement" of the modifications any of its systems or services will need to provide the required capacity. (3) A carrier is deemed in compliance with the FBI's capacity notices, without having made the specified modifications, until the FBI agrees to reimburse the carrier for those modifications. United States Telecom Ass'n v. Federal Bureau of Investigation, 276 F.3d 620, 625 (D.C.Cir.2002). Susan Freiwald, Uncertain Privacy: Communications Attributes After the Digital Telephony Act, 69 S. CAL. L. REV. 949 (1996) (discussing the history and provisions of CALEA).

The CALEA requirements are especially hard fought when they touch on obtaining information from digital "packet mode" communications. United States Telecom Ass'n v. F.C.C., 227 F.3d 450 (D.C.Cir.2000). It will be interesting to see how the CALEA requirements are implemented with the compound devices such as iPhones that provide telephones, internet, and picture capacities.

Some technologies, such as VoIP (Voice Over Internet Protocol) such as Skype, raise questions as to whether CALEA applies or not. Comment (Linda Rushnak), 17 Alb. L.J. Sci. & Tech. 213, 230 (2007).

At least one writer has suggested that CALEA could be expanded to cover other technologies. See Note (Constance L. Martin), "Exalted Technology: Should CALEA be Expanded to Authorize Internet Wiretapping?", 32 Rutgers Computer & Tech. L. J. 140 (2005).

b. Digital Telephony Act

In the 1994 Digital Telephony Act, Congress gave protection to cordless phones by deleting an earlier exemption, and, in the Communication Assistance for Law Enforcement Act, Congress required telephone companies to make sure their facilities are capable of allowing the government to intercept and decode digitally-encoded transmissions and to use pen registers. See Note, "Uncertain Privacy: Communication Attributes After the Digital Telephony Act," 69 S. Cal. L. Rev. 949 (1996).

c. Clipper Chip and Encryption Controls

Users of the internet and of digital communications who seek to impose privacy will often use encryption. Initially, the government response to encryption programs was to limit the export of the more powerful encoding programs. This was replaced by an effort to insure that law enforcement would have access to encrypted materials when needed through a key escrow system. A description of these developments can be found in A. Michael Froomkin, "It Came from Planet Clipper: The Battle Over Cryptographic Key 'Escrow'," 1996 U. Chi. L. F 15. See also A. Michael Froomkin, "The Metaphor is the Key: Cryptography, the Clipper Chip, and the Constitution," 143 U. Pa. L. Rev. 709 (1995), A. Michael Froomkin, "The Constitution and Encryption Regulation: Do We Need a 'New Privacy'?" 3 N.Y.U. J. Legis. & Pub. Pol'y 25 (1999) and A. Michael Froomkin, "Cyberspace and Privacy: A New Legal Paradigm? The Death of Privacy?" 52 Stan. L. Rev. 1461 (2000).

4. *USA PATRIOT ACT: UNITING AND STRENGTHENING AMERICA BY PROVIDING APPROPRIATE TOOLS REQUIRED TO INTERCEPT AND OBSTRUCT TERRORISM*

The Patriot Act includes far-reaching provisions that altered existing statutes governing wire and electronic eavesdropping, but commentators disagree on the impact this will have on surveillance law.

For an overview approach, see Nathan C. Henderson, (Note), "The Patriot Act's Impact on the Government's Ability to Conduct Electronic Surveillance of Ongoing Domestic Communications,"52 Duke L. J. 179 (2002). For a views critical of the Patriot Act, see John W. Whitehead & Steven H. Aden, "Forfeiting 'Enduring Freedom' for 'Homeland Security': A Constitutional Analysis of the USA Patriot Act and the Justice Department's Anti–Terrorism Initiatives," 51 Am. U.L. Rev. 1081 (2002); Jennifer C. Evans, "Hijacking Civil Liberties: The USA Patriot Act," 33 Loy. U. Chi. L. J. 933 (2002); Sharon H. Rackow, "How the USA Patriot Act will Permit Governmental Infringement Upon the Privacy of Americans in the Name of 'Intelligence' Investigations," 150 U. Pa. L. Rev. 1651 (2002). For a view that the impact is much less drastic than initially feared, see Orin Kerr, "Internet Surveillance Law After the Patriot Act: The Big Brother that Isn't," in 97 Northwestern Univ. L. Rev. 607 (2003); Aaron Nance (Note), "Taking the Fear Out of Electronic Surveillance in the New Age of Terror," 70 UMKC L. Rev. 751 (2002).

Several changes wrought by the Patriot Act have been discussed elsewhere in this chapter. For example, the Patriot Act expanded the scope and lowered the threshold requirements for FISA warrants. It treats stored wire communications in the same manner as stored electronic communications. These provisions survived the sunset provisions of the Patriot Act.

In addition, it permits limited "sneak and peak" warrants that would affect entries to place monitoring devices.

5. *HOMELAND SECURITY ACT*

The Homeland Security Act, signed into law on November 25, 2002, created the Department of Homeland Security, but it also included a number of changes that affect surveillance.

The Act permits a wide scale sharing of information between agencies, between federal and state entities, and between branches of government that was previously not allowed because of grand jury secrecy, agency rules, and security clearance procedures. 6 U.S.C. § 481.

The Homeland Security Act provides that the Department of Justice will have an Office of Science and Technology with one mission to "carry out programs that, through the provision of equipment, training and technical assistance, improve the safety and effectiveness of law enforcement technology and improve access to such technology by Federal, State, and local law enforcement agencies." 6 U.S.C. § 232(a)(2).

One such change requires Internet Service Providers (ISPs) to voluntarily disclose information about subscribers to government agents. The contents of e-mails and instant messages may be disclosed in the event of an emergency, but no factual showing needs to be made and there is no requirement of imminent danger.

(d) SOME EXAMPLES OF OTHER TYPES OF SURVEILLANCE

Technological surveillance has changed dramatically from the days when F.B.I. agents were placing the crude listening device and recorder on top of the phone booth from which Charles Katz was placing his bets. Now, law enforcement agents seek to gather information from many other formats, including digital communication, computers, and the internet.

1. *PEN REGISTERS AND TRAP AND TRACE DEVICES*

Traditionally, pen registers are devices which record the telephone numbers which are dialed from a particular phone. They do not overhear or record conversations and do not indicate whether a call was completed.

Their use ordinarily does not involve any physical trespass against the property of the subscriber. A trap and trace device identifies the phone numbers which are dialed to a particular phone. According to the Supreme Court, governmental employment of a pen register, without a warrant, violates neither Title III nor the Fourth Amendment. In Smith v. Maryland, 442 U.S. 735, 99 S.Ct. 2577 (1979), the Court held that a subscriber can have no "reasonable" or "legitimate" expectation of privacy as to the numbers dialed. Great emphasis was placed upon the widely known fact that telephone companies have and utilize devices which indicate what numbers are dialed from specified telephones. The majority reasoned that subscribers voluntarily expose to the telephone company the numbers dialed, just as they did in former days when they had to tell an operator what number to dial. They have "assumed the risk" that the telephone company will convey this information to the government. Justices Stewart, Marshall, and Brennan dissented in Smith. In United States v. New York Telephone Co., 434 U.S. 159, 98 S.Ct. 364 (1977), the Court held that a telephone company could be compelled to assist the government in the installation of pen registers, and also held that use of such devices does not violate Title III.

Congress provided for statutory oversight of pen registers and trap and trace devices notwithstanding the fact that the United States Supreme

Court held they did not constitute fourth amendments searches and seizures nor was the use of such devices governed by Title III.

Under the 1986 Electronic Communication Privacy Act, 18 U.S.C. § 3121, installation of a pen register must first be court-approved, although it is not subject to all the safeguards surrounding the issuance of a search warrant or a Title III order. Violations of the requirement of the Pen Register Act "being" mere "statutory violations" do not give rise to the use of an exclusionary rule. See, e.g., United States v. Thompson, 936 F.2d 1249 (11th Cir.1991). In 18 U.S.C. §§ 3121, Congress provided fines and imprisonment for knowing violations of the Act, but did not provide an exclusionary remedy.

The Patriot Act of 2001 expanded the definitions of the permissible use of these devices. These surveillance techniques are now used for Internet addresses and e-mail accounts and they are governed by these same statutes. In re Application of the United States of America for an Order Authorizing the Installation and Use of a Pen Register and a Trap and Trace Device on E–Mail Account, 416 F. Supp. 2d 13 (D.D.C. 2006). The statute also governs pen registers and trap and trace methods for cell phones. In re Application of the United States for an Order Authorizing the Use of a Pen Register, 384 F. Supp. 2d 562 (E.D.N.Y. 2005); In re Application of the United States of America for an Order Authorizing the Release of Prospective Cell Site Info., 407 F. Supp. 2d 134 (D.D.C. 2006).

2. *COMPUTERIZED AND INTERNET RELATED INFORMATION*

a. Computer Searches

The Justice Department now has a Computer Crime & Intellectual Property Section. Unofficial guidelines for computer searches are available on line. Searching and Seizing Computers and Obtaining Electronic Evidence in Criminal Investigations (2001), http://www.usdoj.gov/criminal/cybercrime/s&smanual2002.html.

For other issues regarding computer searches, see Justice Department, Federal Guidelines for Searching and Seizing Computers, 56 Crim. L. Rptr. 2023 (1994); Thomas R. Greenberg, "E–Mail and Voice Mail: Employee Privacy and Federal Wiretap Statute," 44 Am. U. L. Rev. 219 (1994); Raphael Winick, "Searches and Seizures of Computers and Computer Data," 8 Harv. J. L. & Tech. 75 (1994); Lawrence Lessig, "Reading the Constitution in Cyberspace," 45 Emory L.J. 869 (1996).

Probable cause is necessary for a valid computer search under the fourth amendment. The good faith exception of United States v. Leon applies, however, when probable cause is deficient. United States v. Harrist, 2007 WL 4982688 (5th Cir.2007). As to the particularity requirement, however, computer searches may cover a great deal of territory. Huang, Radkowski III, and Roman, "Computer Crimes," 44 Am. Crim. L. Rev. 285, 322–23 (2007). The scope of permissible searches vary, but most allow the search and seizure of the computer's entire drive. See Orin S. Kerr, Searches and Seizures in a Digital World, 119 HARV. L. REV. 531, 533 (2005).

b. E-mail

The content of e-mail is protected while it is in transmission and before it is received. See Steve Jackson Games, Inc. v. United States Secret Service, 36 F.3d 457 (5th Cir.1994). See also, Davis v. Gracey, 111 F.3d 1472 (10th Cir.1997). Questions arise, however, when the e-mail is stored. Should stored e-mail communications be treated the same as stored wire communications? Should law enforcement be required to obtain a Title III wiretap order to obtain both? One, but not the other? Neither? Would a court order suffice? A search warrant? Why should e-mail and voice mail be treated differently? For one view, see Michael S. Leib, "E–Mail and the Wiretap Laws: Why Congress Should Add Electronic Communication to Title III's Statutory Exclusionary Rule and Expressly Reject a 'Good Faith' Exception," 34 Harv. J. on Legis. 393 (1997).

The distinction between the definitions of electronic and wired communications caused interpretive difficulties for the courts. The Ninth Circuit and several commentators have disagreed with the position that the Wiretap Act should be read to exclude stored e-mail from protection. See Konop v. Hawaiian Airlines, 236 F.3d 1035 (9th Cir.2001) See also, Tatsuya Akamine, "Proposal for a Fair Statutory Interpretation: E–Mail Stored in a Service Provider Computer Is Subject to an Interception Under the Federal Wiretap Act," 7 J. L. & Pol'y 519 (1999).

Konop, however, was closely distinguished by Fraser v. Nationwide Mutual Ins. Co., 135 F.Supp.2d 623 (E.D.Pa.2001), on the ground that information stored on websites is different from stored e-mail. According to Fraser, interception occurs when a third party acquires transmitted information before the intended recipient does, as when an unauthorized person downloads information from a website. The court held that an employer's retrieval of its employee's stored e-mail was not "interception" within the meaning of the Wiretap Act because the employer did not read it until after it was sent and received. See also, Eagle Inv. Sys. Corp. v. Tamm, 146 F.Supp.2d 105 (D.Mass.2001) (finding Konop's statutory analysis unpersuasive because it would make the Wiretap Act and the Stored Communications Act duplicative).

The Department of Justice argued both voice mail and e-mail should be covered by search warrants and not by wiretap orders. Government agents noted that the difference in treatment arguably led to "large and unnecessary burdens for criminal investigations. Stored voice communications possess few of the sensitivities associated with the real-time interception of telephones, making the extremely burdensome process of obtaining a wiretap order unreasonable." Computer Crime and Intellectual Property Section, "Field Guidance on New Authorities Enacted in the 2001 Anti–Terrorist Legislation," Comment to Section 209 of the Patriot Act, found at http://www.usdoj.gov/criminal/cybercrime/PatriotAct.htm.

Under the Patriot Act, the distinction was removed. Now stored electronic communications and stored wire communications are treated identically. The amendment to Title III, 18 U.S.C. § 2510 deletes "electronic storage" of wire communications from the definition of wire communication and inserts the language in 18 U.S.C. § 2703 of the Electronic

Communications Privacy Act. Thus, stored electronic communications and stored wire communications are treated the same. Now law enforcement may obtain both of these under the procedures set out in section 2703, including search warrants.

In addition, the Patriot Act amended section 2703 to permit law enforcement to subpoena records of session times and duration, internet protocol addresses, and records pertaining to means of payment to the internet service provider.

c. Carnivore

"Carnivore," started out as "Omnivore," but the government renamed the program to the more benign DCS1000. It refers to a packet sniffer program that the government may attach to an internet service provider (ISP) through a one-way tap into an Ethernet data stream. In one context, it serves as a trap and trace system to scan e-mails seeking the e-mail addresses of a senders and/or recipients, but it also may reveal the text of the e-mail headers traveling through the ISP system. Presumably it is limited to a particular sender and/or recipient, but the program does not provide audit trails. See "Independent Technical Review of the Carnivore System: Final Report 8 December 2000" available at http://www.usdoj.gov/jmd/publications/carniv_final.pdf. Alternatively, it is also capable of scanning all e-mails, including the textual content, in real time In the first mode, as a trap and trace device the government maintains that Carnivore is no more intrusive than a pen register, although the government gains access to all e-mail on a particular ISP system. The F.B.I. analogizes the filtering of e-mail headers, however, to pen registers that do not require a warrant. In the second mode when the government uses the Carnivore program to scan entire e-mails, the F.B.I. acknowledges it must have a Title III court order. The permissible scope of surveillance is sometimes unclear and a lack of consensus about what may be properly viewed may hamper government investigations. See Jonathan Schwartz, "Bin Laden Inquiry Was Hindered by F.B.I. E–Mail Tapping," New York Times, May 29, 2002, Sec. A, page 16, col. 1. See also, Griffin S. Dunham, "Carnivore, the FBI's E–Mail Surveillance System: Devouring Criminals, Not Privacy," 54 Fed. Comm. L. J. 543 (2002); Todd Heflin, "Who's Afraid of the Big Bad Wolf: Why the Fear of Carnivore is an Irrational Product of the Digital Age," 107 Dick. L. Rev. 343 (2002); Gina Tufaro (Note) "Will Carnivore Devour the Fourth? An Exploration of the Constitutionality of the FBI Created Software," 18 N.Y.L. Sch. J. Hum. Rts. 305 (2002); Stephen W. Tountas (Note), "Carnivore: Is the Regulation of Wireless Technology a Legally Viable Option to Curtail the Growth of Cybercrime?" 11 Wash. U. J. L. & Pol'y 2003.

The Patriot Act amended the trap and trace provisions of 18 U.S.C. §§ 3121, 3123, 3124, and 3127 to cover all internet user accounts or e-mail addresses; an Internet Protocol address, port number, or similar computer network address or range of addresses. It clarifies that the pen register and trap and trace devices may be used without a court order, but is limited to noncontent information, such as ISP addresses and port numbers and the "to" and "from" lines of e-mail. In addition, the amendment authorizes the installation of a pen registers or trap and trace devices on a nationwide basis.

The Carnivore program has faded into the background. One report noted "FBI surveillance experts have put their controversial Carnivore internet surveillance tool out to pasture, preferring instead to use commercial products to eavesdrop on network traffic. Two reports to Congress obtained under the Freedom of Information Act reveal that the FBI didn't use Carnivore, or its rebranded version DCS–1000, during 2002 and 2003." "Carnivore Eaten Alive," Spy Games, Melbourne, Australia (January 18, 2005)

d. Echelon

Echelon refers to a world-wide system for the interception of private and commercial communications that is run by United States, the United Kingdom, Canada, Australia and New Zealand. The existence of this system has been recognized. Report on the Existence of a Global System for the Interception of Private and Commercial Communications (ECHELON interception system) (2001/2098 (INI)), European Parliament Session Document A5–0264/2001 Rapporteur: Gerhard Schmid at page 11. It has been asserted that the system uses satellite receiver systems that have the capability of monitoring all telephone, fax, internet or e-mail messages. Id. at 23. Others indicate that the Echelon system works in a manner much more consistent with Carnivore, but on an international level. See Lawrence D. Sloan, "Echelon and the Legal Restraints on Signals Intelligence: A Need for Reevaluation," 50 Duke L J. 1467 (2001); Erin L. Brown (Comment), "Echelon: The National Security Agency's Compliance with Applicable Legal Guidelines in Light of the Need for Tighter National Security," 11 CommLaw Conspectus 185 (2003). See also, Bedan, Echelon's Effect: The Obsolescence Of The U.S. Foreign Intelligence Legal Regime, 59 U.C.L.A. Fed'l Communications L.J. 425 (2007).

e. Key Logger Systems and Magic Lantern Technology

The FBI has used a key logger system which allows them to duplicate the key strokes a computer user makes on the computer key board. This allows them, inter alia, to obtain passwords to encrypted files when the holder accesses the files. Ultimately, it allows the government access to those same files as well. In United States v. Scarfo, 180 F.Supp.2d 572 (D.N.J.2001), federal agents discovered a file that they suspected contained records of loansharking and illegal gambling activities. They obtained a search warrant and entered the defendant's house to install a key logger system of the defendant's computer. This allowed them to "capture" the pass phrase used to gain access to this encrypted file as Scarfo communicated through the phone modem connecting his computer to his AOL account. The defendant moved to suppress the evidence obtained in this manner on the theory that because it involved wire transmissions, the FBI surveillance violated Title III. The District Court rejected this argument and denied the motion to suppress. See Nathan E. Carrell (Note), "Spying on the Mob: United States v. Scarfo—A Constitutional Analysis," 2002 J. L. Tech. & Pol'y; 193.

Law enforcement agencies are also working on a more sophisticated method of obtaining and recording information about key strokes at the computer. The "Magic Lantern" system, sometimes known as a "sniffer key logger" system, differs from the more usual Key Logger System in that it can be installed without physically entering the space where the computer to be monitored is located. Instead, the Magic Lantern can be sent like a virus, trojan horse, and/or e-mail attachment to a suspect's computer and record information about the keystrokes through silent internet communications to another computer at another location operated by law enforcement. Thus physical entry (and a warrant to enter the premises) is not necessary. See "FBI Runs Trojan Horse Fed's E-mail Virus Reads Key Strokes to Bypass Encryption," Financial Times Information 11/21/2001, Nat Hentoff, "The FBI's Magic Lantern," The Village Voice, p. 35, June 4, 2002. Neal Hartzog, "The 'Magic Lantern' Revealed: A report of the FBI's New 'Key Logging' Trojan and Analysis of its Possible Treatment in a Dynamic Legal Landscape," 20 J. Marshall J. Computer & Info. L. 287 (2002); Christopher Woo Miranda So, "The Case for Magic Lantern: September 11 Highlights the Need for Increased Surveillance," 15 Harv. J. L. & Tech. 521 (2002).

3. *INFORMATION SHARING*

The Homeland Security Act allows the collection and sharing of information among various agencies, including the FBI, the CIA, and the Department of Homeland Security. Some initiatives explored data mining to collect, in one location, information culled from domestic surveillance and international intelligence. In his State of the Union address in 2003, President Bush announced that he was instructing the leaders of the F.B.I., the C.I.A., the Department of Homeland Security, and the Department of Defense "to develop a Terrorist Threat Integration Center, to merge and analyze all threat information in a single location." President George Bush, "State of the Union Message to Congress and the Nation," New York Times, January 29, 2003, sec. A, page 12, col. 1. The Department of Defense, through the Defense Advanced Research Projects Agency, is involved in this effort. See the DARPA Information Awareness Office (IA0) site at http://www.darpa.mil/iao. Now the Total Information Awareness Program seems to appear only in archived files of the DARPA site.

Congress approved funds for the Total Information Awareness Program, but indicated that it was the sense of Congress that: "the Total Information Awareness program should not be used to develop technologies for use in conducting intelligence activities or law enforcement activities against United States persons without appropriate consultation with Congress or without clear adherence to principles to protect civil liberties and privacy." Sec. 111(d)(1) 108 P.L. 7; 117 Stat. 11; 2003 Enacted H.J. Res. 2; 108 Enacted H.J. Res. 2 (2003). Ultimately, Congress derailed the Operation Total Information Awareness. Senator Wyden, Hearing Of The Senate Select Intelligence Committee; Subject: The Nomination Of Michael McConnell To Be Director Of National Intelligence; Witness: The Nominee; Chaired By: Senator Jay Rockefeller IV (D–Wv); Location: 106 Dirksen Senate Office Building, Washington, D.C. Federal News Service February 1,

2007 Thursday. Some are skeptical, however, that Congress is apprised of all data mining projects. "High Tech Data Mining; Is Your Privacy At Risk?" ABC News Now January 17, 2007 Wednesday,

See, Daniel J. Solove, "Digital Dossiers and the Dissipation of Fourth Amendment Privacy," 75 S. Cal. L. Rev. 1083 (2002), Joseph S. Fulda, "Data Mining and Privacy," 11 Alb. L. J. Sci. & Tech. 105 (2000).

4. *PAGERS*

a. Tone–Only Pagers

Should pagers be protected? Tone-only pagers are not covered by the Omnibus Crime Control and Safe Streets Act. 18 U.S.C. § 2510(12)(B). Should more sophisticated pagers be considered "electronic communication" or "oral communications"? The Court in United States v. Reyes, 922 F.Supp. 818 (S.D.N.Y.1996), held that retrieving numbers from the memory of a pager does not constitute "interception" within meaning of the Federal Wiretap Act, but is merely "accessing stored electronic communications" under 18 U.S.C. § 2701 et seq., requiring only a conventional search warrant, not a court order. See also, United States v. Meriwether, 917 F.2d 955 (6th Cir.1990) (holding that an officer who obtained a pager pursuant to a search conducted under the authority of a warrant became a party to the conversation and could therefore retrieve drug client's phone numbers from the pager's memory without further authorization); United States v. Lynch, 908 F.Supp. 284 (1995) (holding that seizing a pager and pushing a button to retrieve numbers stored therein was a valid search pursuant to a legal arrest.)

b. Display Pagers, and Voice Pagers

In some circuits, display pagers, and voice pagers are protected by Title III. 18 U.S.C. §§ 2510(1), 2510(12); see also S. REP. NO. 541, 99th Cong., 2d Sess. 10, 11, 15 (1986), reprinted in 1986 U.S.C.C.A.N. 3555, 3564–65, 3569; Brown v. Waddell, 50 F.3d 285, 289 (4th Cir.1995) (Title III covers tapping of defendant's digital display pager, while tapping of tone-only pager is not covered); U.S. v. Carrazana, 921 F.2d 1557, 1562–63 (11th Cir.1991) cert. denied sub nom Plasencia v. United States, 502 U.S. 865, 112 S.Ct. 191 (1991) and sub nom Diaz v. United States, 502 U.S. 896, 112 S.Ct. 269 (1991). (Title III covers interception of cellular mobile telephone communications without prior judicial approval).

When Congress passed the Electronic Communications Privacy Act in 1986 to amend Title III, it protected cellular communications from interception without prior judicial approval. A special rule accompanied the ECPA to afford those states with wiretap statutes an opportunity to conform to the amendments. Thus if state law authorized interception without judicial approval within two years of the passage of the ECPA, it would be valid. United States v. Carrazana, 921 F.2d 1557 (11th Cir., 1991) cert. denied sub nom Plasencia v. United States, 502 U.S. 865, 112 S.Ct. 191 (1991) and sub nom Diaz v. United States, 502 U.S. 896, 112 S.Ct. 269, 116 L.Ed.2d 221 (1991).

Elsewhere, courts have held that judicial approval is required for surveillance of cell phones, digital display pagers and voice pagers, but since the Electronic Communications Privacy Act applies, the remedy is not suppression, but rather an action for damages against government actors. Tucker v. Waddell, 83 F.3d 688 (4th Cir.1996). United States v. Wells, 2000 WL 1231722 (S.D.Ind.2000).

Some courts have held, however, that after legally seizing a display pager, police officers may attempt to activate it by using phone numbers known to belong to persons suspected of criminal activity. See, e.g., United States v. Diaz–Lizaraza, 981 F.2d 1216, 1217 (11th Cir.1993) (evidence gained when an officer who lawfully seized a display beeper and "called himself" to get information; officer was party to the conversation, and no interception occurred; furthermore, defendant had no Fourth Amendment reasonable expectation that beeper would not be called).

If police try to use a clone digital display pager to intercept numeric transmissions (with the goal of learning the names and numbers of persons calling the suspect) their actions create a cause of action under the Electronic Communications Privacy Act. Suppression of the evidence, however, may not be the remedy the court applies. Brown v. Waddell, 50 F.3d 285 (4th Cir.1995) See Jennifer Gruda, "Investigation and Police Practices in Electronic Surveillance," 88 Geo. L. J. 990 (2000).

5. *BEEPERS*

Locational beepers are not governed by Title III or other electronic surveillance legislation. The Court has drawn some fine lines. Two cases, often compared, help illustrate some of the parameters. In both cases, drug enforcement administration agents attached beepers to monitor the location of the suspect. In one, the beeper was attached to the car and signaled the location of the vehicle to law enforcement agents. United States v. Knotts, 460 U.S. 276, 103 S.Ct. 1081 (1983) In the other, the beeper gave information concerning the location of an object within the suspect's home. United States v. Karo, 468 U.S. 705, 104 S.Ct. 3296 (1984). So long as a beeper indicates a position of a person or thing in a public place, they are akin to a mechanical means of observing something that could have been properly observed by a law enforcement officer. Knotts. Once the beeper gives information from within a protected area that is not readily available, then the Fourth Amendment covers the use of the beeper. Karo.

6. *DESCRAMBLERS*

Descrambler cases often focus on cases involving copyright and cable theft. In a small number of cases, defendants have been charged with a violation of wiretap laws because of their use of descramblers. The circuits are split as to whether federal wiretap laws apply to devices which descramble satellite television signals. United States v. One Macom Video Cipher II, 985 F.2d 258 (6th Cir.1993). See also, United States v. Herring, 993 F.2d 784 (11th Cir.1993); United States v. Shriver, 989 F.2d 898 (7th Cir.1992).

7. *"INTERCEPTION"*

The Seventh Circuit held that a police officer did not intercept a telephone conversation, as defined by Section 2510(4), simply by listening in on the same telephone receiver as one of the participants in the conversation. United States v. Chiavola, 744 F.2d 1271 (7th Cir.1984). The court further held that a telephone was not an intercepting device within the meaning of Section 2510(5) where the officer listened in on an ordinary phone which was used to place the call.

8. *VIDEO CAMERA SURVEILLANCE*

Video surveillance in a public locale is arguably not a search since the camera is only picking up images that an officer's eyes could pick up in plain view. For a critique of this view, see Christopher Slobogin, "Public Privacy: Camera Surveillance of Public Places and the Right to Anonymity," 72 Miss. L. J. 213 (2002). Courts may be reluctant to approve any conceivable use of video surveillance. "There may be circumstances under which video camera surveillance, even in a public place, may constitute an unconstitutional intrusion violative of our state constitution's guarantee against unreasonable searches, seizures, and invasions of privacy. We do not believe that the facts of this case present us with such circumstances." State v. Augafa, 992 P.2d 723, 92 Haw. 454, 468 n.14 (1999). Video surveillance may provide an all-encompassing view of public activities, especially as technology continues to improve.

Efforts to regulate public video surveillance by law enforcement of demonstrations have been challenged under first amendment grounds as well as fourth. Although the procedural history is long and tangled, a class action in New York City ultimately permitted police video surveillance of protesters in public. Handschu v. Special Servs. Div, 2007 WL 1711775 (S.D.N.Y.2007).

The use of video surveillance over employees is governed by federal labor legislation which preempts state law. See Barbo v. Kroger Co., 2007 WL 2350181 (W.D.Ky.2007).

When the camera is in a private locale, however, the situation changes. The legislation governing surveillance for criminal investigation focuses primarily on oral eavesdropping, not visual. Thus, if the government seeks to pick up video images with sound recording, Title III applies. If no sound recording is involved, then the electronic surveillance statutes do not apply.

In People v. Teicher, the New York County District Attorney's office obtained a warrant to place a video camera in the defendant's office. They obtained camera images of the defendant, a dentist, sexually fondling patients. The sound was obtained, not from the camera, but from hidden microphones worn by one of the victims sent in as part of a police investigation. The evidence was held to be admissible. 52 N.Y.2d 638, 439 N.Y.S.2d 846, 422 N.E.2d 506 (1981).

After the Electronic Privacy Act was passed in 1986, the audio portion of a videotape is governed by the act. The Foreign Intelligence Security Act (FISA) now defines "electronic surveillance" which is defined to include:

"the installation or use of an electronic, mechanical, or other surveillance device in the United States for monitoring to acquire information, other than from a wire or radio communication, under circumstances in which a person has a reasonable expectation of privacy and a warrant would be required for law enforcement purposes." 50 U.S.C. § 1802(a). This would include closed-circuit or other video surveillance. United States v. Koyomejian, 970 F.2d 536 (9th Cir.1992), cert. denied, Koyomejian v. United States, 506 U.S. 1005, 113 S.Ct. 617 (1992).

9. *BIOMETRICS*

Using the law enforcement store of data that include photographs and fingerprints of individuals,[2] information, law enforcement can match individuals through a computer search. The Integrated Automated Fingerprint Identification System of the FBI allows quick electronic matching and identification. In addition, the facial features can be computer analyzed and close matches identified. This method of identification received a great deal of publicity when it was used at the 2001 Super Bowl game. Since then The USA Patriot Act allows the National Crime Information Center to retain this information in an individual's record. 8 U.S.C. § 1105.

Some governments, such as Germany, require biometric information to be embedded in their country's passports.

In the United States, challenges have been made to requiring immigrants to pay fees for the taking and storage of biometric data. Bautista–Perez v. Mukasey, 2008 WL 314486 (N.D.Cal.2008).

Currently, law enforcement is also turning to biometric surveillance For a description of changing technology in this area and the impact of the Patriot Act on biometric scanning, see Sean O'Connor, Biometrics and Identification after 9/11, 7 Bender's Immigration Bulletin 150 (2002). Biometric information is collected from air passengers[3] and they are a key part of our border security.

10. *OTHER TECHNOLOGICALLY ENHANCED SURVEILLANCE*

New technologies continue to proliferate and transmute. For example, most of the legal analysis concerning cell phones focuses on intercepting conversations. Now, many cell phones are also equipped with global positioning systems. Thus, if law enforcement locates a suspect through their cell phone without intercepting any conversations, does the Fourth Amend-

2. Since 1924, The FBI has been the repository for fingerprint records and related criminal history data in the United States. During fiscal year 2003, the FBI received a total of 17,736,541 fingerprint submissions. Testimony of Michael D. Kirkpatrick, Assistant Director in Charge, Criminal Justice Information Services Division, FBI Before the Judiciary Committee, United States House of Representatives, Subcommittee on Crime, Terrorism, and Homeland Security March 30, 2004. http://www.fbi.gov/congress/congress04/033004kirkpatrick.htm. To give you an idea of how many fingerprints are on file, in 2004, the FBI's master criminal fingerprint file contained the records of approximately 47 million individuals, while their civil file contained the prints of approximately 30.7 million individuals. Id.

3. Testimony of Secretary Michael Chertoff before Senate Committee on Homeland Security: "Confronting Terrorist Threat to Homeland: Six Years after 9/11" September 10, 2007.

ment apply? See Matthew Mickle Werdegar (Note), "Lost? The Government Knows Where you Are: Cellular Telephone Call Location Technology and the Expectation of Privacy," 10 Stan. L. & Pol'y Rev. 103 (1998).

Many cars are now equipped with global positioning systems (GPS). While these systems help drivers by giving directions, they also broadcast the location of the driver. If law enforcement intercepts these signals without a warrant, is it a violation of the fourth amendment? Renee McDonald Hutchins, "Tied Up in Knotts? GPS Technology and the Fourth Amendment," 55 UCLA L. Rev. 409 (2007); Note (Eva Marie Dowdell), "You Are Here!—Mapping the Boundaries of the Fourth Amendment with GPS Technology," 32 Rutgers Computer & Tech. L. Journal 109 (2005).

The Federal Communications Commission requires that 911 operators be able to ascertain the GPS location of callers from cell phones.[4] Critics concerns include:

> Business or government could certainly use this system, designed for emergencies, for very different purposes. A principal fear of privacy groups is that once GPS and other tracking systems are common in mobile phones, the information gathered about individuals will be stored and possibly sold without their knowledge. Once personal information has been stored, it could possibly be used by police for law enforcement purposes, unearthed by a private investigator digging up dirt on a cheating spouse, or perhaps even become the consumer equivalent of the airlines' "black boxes," used to verify a driver's actions after an automobile accident.[5]

Arguably the government could ascertain the location of any cell phone holder using this system.

As wireless payment systems abound, is the information available from them protected by the fourth amendment? For example, must law enforcement get a warrant before it intercepts information that a particular vehicle paid a toll at a given time and location using an E–Z pass system?

Similarly, are RFID chips embedded in government issued identification documents such as passports or in consumer goods worthy of fourth amendment protection? Suppose the RFID chip is the basis for a payment system? Smith, Gone in a Blink: The Overlooked Privacy Problems Caused by Contactless Payment Systems (Winner of the Computer Law Association 2006 Information Technology Law Writing Competition), 11 Marq. Intell. Prop. L. Rev. 213 (2007).

As the Court confronts new technologies, the ease of access to these new developments will play a role in determining whether constitutional and/or statutory protection will regulate government use. For example, the United States Supreme Court disallowed the warrantless use of thermal imaging, at least in part, because the technology was not widely available

4. FTC, Public Workshop: The Mobile Wireless Web, Data Services and Beyond: Emerging Technologies and Consumer Issues 9 (2002).

5. James C. White, "People, Not Places: A Policy Framework for Analyzing Location Privacy," (Duke Masters Memo prepared for Electronic Privacy Information Center citing "Privacy Foundation, E911: Big Brother's Tracking System, Tipsheet," at https://www.privacyfoundation.org (last modified Dec 04, 2000)).

except to government actors. Kyllo v. United States, 533 U.S. 27, 121 S.Ct. 2038 (2001). See David Sklansky, "Back to the Future: Kyllo, Katz, and the Common Law," 72 Miss. L. J. 143 (2002); Jeffrey W. Childers (Comment), "Kyllo v. United States: A Temporary Reprieve from Technology-Enhanced Surveillance of the Home," 81 N.C.L. Rev. 728 (2003); Courtney Dashiell (comment) "Thermal Imaging: Creating a 'Virtual Space'," 34 U. Tol. L. Rev 351 (2003); Comment, "Thermal Imaging and the Fourth Amendment: The role of the Katz Test in the Aftermath of Kyllo v. United States," 46 N.Y.L. Sch. L. Rev. 319 (2003).

C. INTERCEPTIONS WITH ONE-PARTY CONSENT

United States v. White

Supreme Court of the United States, 1971.
401 U.S. 745, 91 S.Ct. 1122.

■ MR. JUSTICE WHITE announced the judgment of the Court and an opinion in which THE CHIEF JUSTICE, MR. JUSTICE STEWART, and MR. JUSTICE BLACKMUN join.

In 1966, respondent James A. White was tried and convicted under two consolidated indictments charging various illegal transactions in narcotics violative of 26 U.S.C. § 4705(a) and 21 U.S.C. § 174. He was fined and sentenced as a second offender to 25 year concurrent sentences. The issue before us is whether the Fourth Amendment bars from evidence the testimony of governmental agents who related certain conversations which had occurred between defendant White and a government informant, Harvey Jackson, and which the agents overheard by monitoring the frequency of a radio transmitter carried by Jackson and concealed on his person. On four occasions the conversations took place in Jackson's home; each of these conversations was overheard by an agent concealed in a kitchen closet with Jackson's consent and by a second agent outside the house using a radio receiver. Four other conversations one in respondent's home, one in a restaurant, and two in Jackson's car were overheard by the use of radio equipment. The prosecution was unable to locate and produce Jackson at the trial and the trial court overruled objections to the testimony of the agents who conducted the electronic surveillance. The jury returned a guilty verdict and defendant appealed.

The Court of Appeals read Katz v. United States, 389 U.S. 347, 88 S.Ct. 507 (1967), as overruling On Lee v. United States, 343 U.S. 747, 7'Z S.Ct. 967 (1952), and interpreting the Fourth Amendment to forbid the introduction of the agents' testimony in the circumstances of this case. Accordingly, the court reversed but without adverting to the fact that the transactions at issue here had occurred before Katz was decided in this Court. In our view, the Court of Appeals misinterpreted both the Katz case and the Fourth Amendment and in any event erred in applying the Katz case to events that occurred before that decision was rendered by this Court.

* * *

The Court of Appeals understood Katz to render inadmissible against White the agents' testimony concerning conversations that Jackson broadcast to them. We cannot agree. Katz involved no revelation to the government by a party to conversations with the defendant nor did the Court indicate in any way that a defendant has a justifiable and constitutionally protected expectation that a person with whom he is conversing will not then or later reveal the conversation to the police.

* * *

To reach this result it was necessary for the Court of Appeals to hold that On Lee v. United States was no longer good law. In that case, which involved facts very similar to the case before us, the Court first rejected claims of a Fourth Amendment violation because the informer had not trespassed when he entered the defendant's premises and conversed with him. To this extent the Court's rationale cannot survive Katz. But the Court announced a second and independent ground for its decision; for it went on to say that overruling Olmstead and Goldman would be of no aid to On Lee since he "was talking confidentially and indiscreetly with one he trusted, and he was overheard.... It would be dubious service to the genuine liberties protected by the Fourth Amendment to make them bedfellows with spurious liberties improvised by farfetched analogies which would liken eavesdropping on a conversation, with the connivance of one of the parties, to an unreasonable search or seizure. We find no violation of the Fourth Amendment here." We see no indication in Katz that the Court meant to disturb that understanding of the Fourth Amendment or to disturb the result reached in the On Lee case, nor are we now inclined to overturn this view of the Fourth Amendment.

Concededly a police agent who conceals his police connections may write down for official use his conversations with a defendant and testify concerning them, without a warrant authorizing his encounters with the defendant and without otherwise violating the latter's Fourth Amendment rights. Hoffa v. United States, 385 U.S. 293, 87 S.Ct. 408 (1966). For constitutional purposes, no different result is required if the agent instead of immediately reporting and transcribing his conversations with defendant, either (1) simultaneously records them with electronic equipment which he is carrying on his person, Lopez v. United States, supra, 373 U.S. 427, 83 S.Ct. 1381 (1963); (2) or carries radio equipment which simultaneously transmits the conversations either to recording equipment located elsewhere or to other agents monitoring the transmitting frequency. If the conduct and revelations of an agent operating without electronic equipment do not invade the defendant's constitutionally justifiable expectations of privacy, neither does a simultaneous recording of the same conversations made by the agent or by others from transmissions received from the agent to whom the defendant is talking and whose trustworthiness the defendant necessarily risks.

Our problem is not what the privacy expectations of particular defendants in particular situations may be or the extent to which they may in fact have relied on the discretion of their companions. Very probably, individual defendants neither know nor suspect that their colleagues have gone or will go to the police or are carrying recorders or transmitters.

Otherwise, conversation would cease and our problem with these encounters would be nonexistent or far different from those now before us. Our problem, in terms of the principles announced in Katz, is what expectations of privacy are constitutionally "justifiable" what expectations the Fourth Amendment will protect in the absence of a warrant. So far, the law permits the frustration of actual expectations of privacy by permitting authorities to use the testimony of those associates who for one reason or another have determined to turn to the police, as well as by authorizing the use of informants in the manner exemplified by Hoffa and Lewis. If the law gives no protection to the wrongdoer whose trusted accomplice is or becomes a police agent, neither should it protect him when that same agent has recorded or transmitted the conversations which are later offered in evidence to prove the State's case. See Lopez v. United States (1963).

Inescapably, one contemplating illegal activities must realize the risk that his companions may be reporting to the police. If he sufficiently doubts their trustworthiness, the association will very probably end or never materialize. But if he has no doubts, or allays them, or risks what doubt he has, the risk is his. In terms of what his course will be, what he will or will not do or say, we are unpersuaded that he would distinguish between probable informers on the one hand and probable informers with transmitters on the other. Given the possibility or probability that one of his colleagues is cooperating with he police, it is only speculation to assert that the defendant's utterances would be substantially different or his sense of security any less if he also thought it possible that the suspected colleague is wired for sound. At least there is no persuasive evidence that the difference in this respect between the electronically equipped and the unequipped agent is substantial enough to require discrete constitutional recognition, particularly under the Fourth Amendment which is ruled by fluid concepts of "reasonableness."

Nor should we be too ready to erect constitutional barriers to relevant and probative evidence which is also accurate and reliable. An electronic recording will many times produce a more reliable rendition of what a defendant has said than will the unaided memory of a police agent. It may also be that with the recording in existence it is less likely that the informant will change his mind, less chance that threat or injury will suppress unfavorable evidence and less chance that cross-examination will confound the testimony. Considerations like these obviously do not favor the defendant, but we are not prepared to hold that a defendant who has no constitutional right to exclude the informer's unaided testimony nevertheless has a Fourth Amendment privilege against a more accurate version of the events in question.

It is thus untenable to consider the activities and reports of the police agent himself, though acting without a warrant, to be a "reasonable" investigative effort and lawful under the Fourth Amendment but to view the same agent with a recorder or transmitter as conducting an "unreasonable" and unconstitutional search and seizure. Our opinion is currently shared by Congress and the Executive Branch, Title III, Omnibus Crime Control and Safe Streets Act of 1968, 82 Stat. 212, 18 U.S.C. §§ 2510 et seq. (1964 ed. Supp.), and the American Bar Association. Project on

Standards for Criminal Justice, Electronics Surveillance § 4.1 (Approved Draft 1971). It is also the result reached by prior cases in this Court.

* * *

Hoffa v. United States (1966), which was left undisturbed by Katz, held that however strongly a defendant may trust an apparent colleague, his expectations in this respect are not protected by the Fourth Amendment when it turns out that the colleague is a government agent regularly communicating with the authorities. In these circumstances, "no interest legitimately protected by the Fourth Amendment is involved," for that amendment affords no protection to "a wrongdoer's misplaced belief that a person to whom he voluntarily confides his wrongdoing will not reveal it." No warrant to "search and seize" is required in such circumstances, nor is it when the Government sends to defendant's home a secret agent who conceals his identity and makes a purchase of narcotics from the accused, Lewis v. United States (1966), or when the same agent, unbeknown to the defendant, carries electronic equipment to record the defendant's words and the evidence so gathered is later offered in evidence. Lopez v. United States (1963).

Conceding that Hoffa, Lewis, and Lopez remained unaffected by Katz, the Court of Appeals nevertheless read both Katz and the Fourth Amendment to require a different result if the agent not only records his conversations with the defendant but instantaneously transmits them electronically to other agents equipped with radio receivers. Where this occurs, the Court of Appeals held, the Fourth Amendment is violated and the testimony of the listening agents must be excluded from evidence.

* * *

No different result should obtain where, as in On Lee and the instant case, the informer disappears and is unavailable at trial; for the issue of whether specified events on a certain day violate the Fourth Amendment should not be determinedly what later happens to the informer. His unavailability at trial and proffering the testimony of other agents may raise evidentiary problems or pose issues of prosecutorial misconduct with respect to the informer's disappearance, but they do not appear critical to deciding whether prior events invaded the defendant's Fourth Amendment rights.

II.

The Court of Appeals was in error for another reason. In Desist v. United States, 394 U.S. 244, 89 S.Ct. 1030 (1969), we held that our decision in Katz v. United States applied only to those electronic surveillance that occurred subsequent to the date of that decision. Here the events in question took place in late 1965 and early 1966, long prior to Katz. The court should have judged this case by the pre-Katz law and under that law, as On Lee clearly holds, the electronic surveillance here involved did not violate White's rights to be free from unreasonable searches and seizures.

* * *

[The brief concurring opinion of Justice Black is omitted, and so is the "concurrence in the result" of Justice Brennan, and the dissenting opinion of Justice Douglas.]

NOTES

1. Justice Black, citing his views in Katz, provided the fifth vote needed by the Government for reversal of the Court of Appeals in White. Justice Brennan concurred because of his view that Katz should not be applied retroactively. He argued, however, that Katz would require a different result if the challenged conduct took place after the date of the Katz decision: "(I)t is my view that current Fourth Amendment jurisprudence interposes a warrant requirement not only in cases of third-party electronic monitoring (the situation in On Lee and in this case) but also in cases of electronic recording by a government agent of a face-to-face conversation with a criminal suspect, which was the situation in Lopez."

Justice Douglas dissented. He argued that On Lee and Lopez were "of a vintage opposed to Berger and Katz ... products of the old common-law notions of trespass." He contended that monitoring "kills free disclosure" and suggested that the practice may run afoul of the First and Fifth Amendment, as well as the Fourth. Douglas reasserted his view that Katz and every other decision of federal constitutional dimension should be applied retroactively.

Justice Harlan also dissented, arguing that affirmance of the Court of Appeals was proper even if Katz be denied retroactive effect (a decision with which he disagreed as to cases still pending on direct review at the time Katz was announced).

Justice Marshall wrote a short dissent expressing agreement with the positions of Justices Douglas and Harlan.

2. In United States v. Caceres, 440 U.S. 741, 99 S.Ct. 1465 (1979), the Court was confronted with violation of certain internal administrative regulations of the Internal Revenue Service concerning the use of one-party consensual electronic surveillance. Even though the agent who recorded the conversation had not secured the approval of Justice Department officials as required by the regulations, the Court refused to utilize an exclusionary sanction to exclude the recordings from use as evidence in a criminal prosecution. Caceres also implicitly upheld White and Lopez, with only Justices Brennan and Marshall dissenting.

3. In the aftermath of the "Nixon tapes" episode, various Congressional proposals to limit one-party consensual recordings were made. To date, none has passed. How should that experience be interpreted? Was the value of having accurate versions of important conversations for use in criminal prosecutions against Watergate coconspirators outweighed by the invasion of privacy involved in recording conversations without the knowledge or the consent of the co-conspirators and of innocent persons as well?

4. Some states have passed statutes that require the consent of both parties before telephone calls can be intercepted and taped. For example, Linda Trip, who taped her phone calls with Monica Lewinsky made her call.[6]

6. States which require all parties to a phone call to consent before taping the call include: California (Cal. Penal Code § 631); Delaware (11 Del. C. § 2402), Florida (Fla. Stat. § 934.03 and § 934.06); Georgia (OCGA § 16–11–62); Illinois (§ 720 ILCS 5/14–2); Maryland [Md. Courts and Judicial Proceedings Code Ann. § 10–402(c)(3)]; Massachusetts (ALM GL ch. 272 § 99); Michigan (MCLS § 750.539c); Montana (Mont. Code Ann § 45–8–213); New Hampshire (58 RSA 570–A:2); Pennsylvania (18 Pa. C.S. §§ 5703–04); Washington (Rev. Code Wash. § 9–73.030).

5. Justice Harlan stated that the choice in White was not between recording and not recording, but between recording with a warrant and recording without a warrant. Often this is true. A probable cause requirement, however, will decrease the use of one-party consensual recordings. Such has been the case in Cook County, Illinois since the adoption of a probable cause requirement. Many "wired" informers are individuals from the criminal milieu whose credibility might not suffice to establish probable cause for the issuance of a warrant.

6. On state constitutional grounds some state high courts have rejected the result reached in White. See, For example, State v. Blow, 157 Vt. 513, 602 A.2d 552 (1991) (electronic monitoring within the home requires warrant).

7. Under White the electronic overhearing of a conversation with the consent of one party does not offend the Constitution. Similarly a consensual overhearing does not offend the federal wiretap statute. See 18 U.S.C. §§ 2511(2)(c). Must the consent be voluntary in order to be valid in the same sense as must be a consent to search someone's property? (See Chapter 5, Section Q.) Often when A agrees to the recording of a conversation between A and B, A does so to avoid prosecution or to get some sort of benefit in his or her dealing with government authorities. B will argue that A's consent was not voluntary but rather was the product of a governmental threat against A. Typically courts agree that the consent must be voluntary to be valid, but they reject the claim that A's efforts to avoid punishment render involuntary his or her consent to search. See, e.g., United States v. Antoon, 933 F.2d 200 (3d Cir.1991).

8. Is the videotaping of parties to a private transaction with the consent of one party controlled by White? Is such a procedure more intrusive or less intrusive than what took place in White? For one view see State v. Jennings, 101 Idaho 265, 611 P.2d 1050 (1980). See also, United States v. Laetividal–Gonzalez, 939 F.2d 1455 (11th Cir.1991). See also People v. Teicher, 52 N.Y.2d 638, 439 N.Y.S.2d 846, 422 N.E.2d 506 (1981).

CHAPTER 5

THE LAW OF ARREST, SEARCH AND SEIZURE

A. INTRODUCTION: THE THEORETICAL FRAMEWORK

The Fourth Amendment,[1] part of the original Bill of Rights, is one of the key constitutional restraints on the exercise of police power. It regulates governmental searches and seizures.

> *The right of the people to be secure in their persons, houses, papers, and effects, against unreasonable searches and seizures, shall not be violated, and no Warrants shall issue, but upon probable cause, supported by Oath or affirmation, and particularly describing the place to be searched, and the person or things to be seized.*

Although the Amendment does not use the word "arrest," arrests and other involuntary detentions of the person are seizures within the meaning of the Fourth Amendment.

The Amendment has two clauses. The first requires that governmental searches and seizures be reasonable: "*The right of the people to be secure in their persons, houses, papers, and effects, against unreasonable searches and seizures, shall not be violated. ...*" The second, the warrant clause, sets forth the requirements for a valid warrant: "*and no Warrants shall issue, but upon probable cause, supported by Oath or affirmation, and particularly describing the place to be searched, and the person or things to be seized.*" A reader trying to find the correct relationship between these two clauses could find at least three possible interpretations: (1) one might read the Fourth Amendment to allow only reasonable searches and/or seizures and the only reasonable search or seizure would be that done pursuant to a warrant [Warrant = reasonable][2]; (2) one might read the Fourth amendment to allow only searches and seizures conducted pursuant to a warrant

1. For a history of the Fourth Amendment see: Nelson B. Lasson, *The History and Development of the Fourth Amendment to the United States Constitution* (1937); Jacob Landynski, *Search and Seizure in the Supreme Court* (1966). It is commonly asserted that our Fourth Amendment has its roots in the colonial practice of General Warrants (a warrant to search that was valid for the life of the monarch who issued it without specifying who or what was to be searched) and Writs of Assistance (allowing the colonial government to impress colonists to assist in the execution of searches and seizures). See Boyd v. United States, 116 U.S. 616, 6 S.Ct. 524 (1886). Tracey Maclin, The Central Meaning of the Fourth Amendment, 35 Wm. & Mary L. Rev. 197, 223–38 (1993). Others challenge this premise. See Akhil Reed Amar, Fourth Amendment First Principles, 107 Harv. L. Rev. 757, 772 (1994).

2. Justice Frankfurter was a strong advocate of the view that a search or seizure is unreasonable unless made pursuant to a warrant.

and, in addition, the search and seizure must be reasonable [Warrant AND reasonable]; or (3) the amendment can be read in the disjunctive so that the police conduct of a search and/or seizure must be either pursuant to a warrant OR reasonable—in other words, a warrant is required, but in some instances it is reasonable to dispense with the warrant for a legitimate search and seizure [Warrant OR reasonable].[3] As you study these cases, ask yourself which view of the Fourth Amendment underlies the Court's decisions and what difference it makes.

In any Fourth Amendment analysis, the preliminary questions are whether the Fourth Amendment applies at all and if it does, does this party have standing[4] to raise the issue(s). Once those hurdles are cleared, however, we turn to merits of the Fourth Amendment claim. Courts usually adjudicate Fourth Amendment claims in the form of a motion to suppress evidence in a criminal prosecution prior to trial.[5] The defendant will move to exclude evidence on the basis that it was obtained unconstitutionally.[6] The judge may grant a hearing on the motion to suppress and if a Fourth Amendment violation is found, the judge applies the exclusionary rule to suppress the evidence. If suppression is granted, the prosecution is barred from using the evidence during its case-in-chief. The exclusionary principle, which coexists with other alternative remedies, is discussed in greater depth in Chapter 6.

In all constitutional analysis, there is another strand the reader needs to keep in mind: that of state constitutional law. A full discussion is beyond the scope of this text, but the student should know that so long as a state court relies on a state constitution to grant more, rather than less, protection given by the federal constitution and so long as the state court uses "independent and adequate state grounds," a holding based on state constitutional law is not reviewable by the United States Supreme Court. Michigan v. Long, 463 U.S. 1032, 103 S.Ct. 3469 (1983). The inclusion of state constitutional analysis in this forum is meant to suggest to the student that there are, at times, multiple approaches to the same problem. Also, state opinions shed considerable light on the pros and cons of the federal rule of law.

As noted, the "reasonableness clause" is at the heart of the merits of many Fourth Amendment claims and this clause is the source of many Fourth Amendment doctrines. Among the most important questions that call for an interpretation of the reasonableness requirement are:

3. See the discussion of this view in the classic work, Telford Taylor, Two Studies in Constitutional Interpretation (1969).

4. The concept of standing is discussed in Chapter 6.

5. Federal Rule of Criminal Procedure 12. The reader may wish to refer back to chapter 1 for an overview of where a motion to suppress evidence and a hearing on that motion fit into the overall pattern of the prosecution of a criminal case. Chapter 13 contains a more thorough discussion of pretrial motions to suppress evidence. See discussion of alternative remedies in Chapter 6. Another forum in which parties commonly litigate Fourth Amendment claims are civil actions seeking damages for constitutional violations, 42 U.S.C. § 1983 if the claim is against state actors, and a *Bivens* action if the claim is against federal actors. Bivens v. Six Unknown Named Agents, 403 U.S. 388, 91 S.Ct. 1999 (1971).

6. See Fed.R.Crim. P. 41(h) and 12.

(1) What kind and what quantum of data is necessary to make a particular search or seizure "reasonable"? (commonly addressed as whether there is sufficient evidence to establish probable cause, or in a different, less intrusive context, whether there is sufficient evidence to establish articulable or reasonable suspicion), and

(2) Is a warrant essential to make reasonable a particular search or seizure?

The second clause of the Fourth Amendment specifies that "... no warrant shall issue, but upon probable cause, supported by oath or affirmation, and particularly describing the place to be searched, and the persons or things to be seized." The warrant clause does not govern the question of when a warrant is essential to satisfy the Fourth Amendment. That issue requires an interpretation of the reasonableness clause. The Fourth Amendment's warrant clause, however, specifies certain requirements for the warrant to be valid if a warrant is utilized: probable cause, oath or affirmation, and specificity of the person or place to be searched and the items to be seized.

Although the term "probable cause" appears only in the warrant clause, the requirements of probable cause are important to an interpretation of both clauses of the Fourth Amendment. Some (though not all) warrantless actions, for example, warrantless arrests in public places, are deemed reasonable only if supported by probable cause. Thus we must know the meaning of "probable cause" to determine whether the reasonableness clause of the Fourth Amendment was satisfied in a particular case. In addition, the method by which the arrest is made must be reasonable—a statute that authorizes deadly force to arrest any felon in all circumstances, even when no danger is present, is not reasonable.[7] The meaning of probable cause also determines whether a particular search warrant conformed to the dictates of the warrant clause of the Fourth Amendment.

This chapter begins in part B with a discussion of whether the Fourth Amendment applies at all. In our treatment of "The Borderlands of the Fourth Amendment" we inquire "What is a search or a seizure?" and "What constitutes Fourth Amendment activity?" If there is no search and no seizure, the Fourth Amendment provides no limits upon governmental activity. Once we determine that the Fourth amendment applies, we then turn to what requirements must be met. In part C, the text turns to a treatment of the probable cause concept because of its central importance to litigation under both clauses of the Amendment. Next it turns in parts D and E to discuss the issuance and execution of search warrants.

In practice, warrantless searches and seizures occur more frequently than searches and seizures occur under the command of a warrant. Nevertheless, the Supreme Court has frequently interpreted the reasonableness clause of the Fourth Amendment so as to seemingly prefer searches under warrants and to make warrantless searches the exception; in other words, "searches conducted outside the judicial process, without prior judicial approval, are per se unreasonable under the Fourth Amendment subject only to a few specially established and well delineated excep-

7. Tennessee v. Garner, 471 U.S. 1, 105 S.Ct. 1694 (1985).

tions."[8] The Court has expressed a preference for warrants, whenever possible.[9] In more recent times, however, some members of the Court have suggested that the exceptions are diverse and flexible, and they have hinted that a warrantless search can be reasonable even if it does not fit within a well-delineated exception.[10]

The validity of the issuance of warrants turns largely upon the requirements of the warrant clause: probable cause, oath or affirmation, and specificity. In theory, however, a search warrant which satisfied these requirements of the warrant clause could still fail to satisfy the reasonableness requirements of the Fourth Amendment. For example, a warrant commanding the seizure of a bullet from the body of an innocent third party (or even a suspect) through a life-endangering operation might satisfy the warrant clause but still fail to satisfy the reasonableness clause absent certain additional safeguards.[11] Questions surrounding the method of seizure are discussed in part F of this chapter.

Requirements for the execution of search warrants arise from the reasonableness clause of the Fourth Amendment. For example, this chapter treats questions concerning notice of authority and purpose, and the use of force and trickery, in the execution of search warrants. So, also, the question of when a search warrant may constitutionally be executed requires an interpretation of the reasonableness clause.

The chapter then turns to the major exceptions to the requirement that searches and seizures be made under the authority of a warrant. The United States Supreme Court has recognized an increasing number of exceptions over time. In addition, the scope of these exceptions have broadened, allowing police more latitude in which to search for and seize evidence. At times, the parameters of the exceptions blur at the edges of the doctrines. One is reminded of Professor Amsterdam's quip in his classic Holmes lecture. He was trying to illustrate the growth of exceptions to the Fourth Amendment warrant requirement. He recounted to his audience

> "the progress of the apocryphal author of the celebrated treatise called Jones on Easements. The first sentence of the first edition began:

8. Katz v. United States, 389 U.S. 347, 357, 88 S.Ct. 507, 514 (1967).

9. "Although in a particular case it may not be easy to determine when an affidavit demonstrates the existence of probable cause, the resolution of doubtful or marginal cases in this area should be largely determined by the preference to be accorded to warrants." United States v. Ventresca, 380 U.S. 102, 107, 85 S.Ct. 741 (1965) (cites omitted).

10. See especially Justice Scalia's concurring opinion in California v. Acevedo, 500 U.S. 565, 111 S.Ct. 1982 (1991). See also Justice Rehnquist's opinion in Texas v. Brown, 460 U.S. 730, 103 S.Ct. 1535 (1983), and his dissent in Florida v. Royer, 460 U.S. 491, 103 S.Ct. 1319 (1983). For discussion of the tension between the well-delineated exceptions approach and the "reasonableness" approach, see Stuntz, Warrants and Fourth Amendment Remedies, 77 Va. L. Rev. 881 (1991); Wasserstrom, The Court's Turn Toward a General Reasonableness Interpretation of the Fourth Amendment, 27 Am. Crim. L. Rev. 119 (1989); Bloom, Warrant Requirement "The Burger Court Approach," 53 U. Colo. L. Rev. 691 (1982); Haddad, Well–Delineated Exceptions, Claims of Sham, and Fourfold Probable Cause, 68 J.Crim.L. & Crim. 198, 199–204 (1977). See also, Akhil Reed Amar, The Constitution and Criminal Procedure 31–45 (1997) (advocating that all warrantless searches and seizures are constitutional if reasonable); Steiker, Second Thoughts About First Principles, 107 Harv. L. Rev. 820 (1994) (disagreeing with Amar).

11. Winston v. Lee, 470 U.S. 753, 105 S.Ct. 1611 (1985).

'There are fourteen kinds of easements recognized by the law of England.' But the work was well received, and the author labored to produce a second edition, in two volumes, which necessarily began:

"There are thirty-nine kinds of easements." After the author's death, the treatise was scrupulously updated by his literary scions and now appears in a solid 12–volume sixth edition beginning with the sentence: "It is impossible to say how many kinds of easements are recognized by the law of England."[12]

This highlights the notion that the jurisprudence of the Fourth Amendment, which must be applied in a kaleidoscopic variety of factual scenarios, will sometimes morph into many different types of categories and analyses, separated by very fine distinctions.

As you consider each exception to the warrant requirement, ask yourself:

1) What is the rationale underlying this exception?

2) Is it a bright-line rule or does it employ a balancing approach? Which approach better supports the theory underlying the doctrine? Which approach is more effective in deterring police misconduct?

3) What role, if any, does the officer's state of mind or the officer's motivation play in determining the applicability of the exception to the warrant requirement?

4) Does the exception apply only in the presence of probable cause? Or may some lower standard justify the police action?

5) What is the scope of the exception?

6) Has the scope of the exception changed since its inception?

7) What is the relation of this exception to other exceptions considered by the Court?

Chronologically, the United States Supreme Court recognized the automobile exception as the first federal exception to the warrant requirement.[13] Perhaps the most commonly used exception, however, is the doctrine which permits a warrantless arrest and the concommitant search incident to a valid arrest.

When we turn to the exceptions to the warrant requirement, we turn first to the more commonly used exceptions. In part G, we consider what constitutes a valid arrest. The litigation about the legality of an arrest arises most frequently during a motion to suppress evidence seized without a search warrant in cases in which the prosecutor argues the seizure was made during the search of the defendant incident to his valid arrest. Because an essential predicate for this exception is a valid arrest, the chapter turns in section G to a discussion of the exceptions to the warrant requirement with an examination of what constitutes a valid arrest and then turns to examine what constitutes a valid search incident to arrest. We will differentiate between searches incident to arrest inside and outside constitutionally protected areas. From there, we turn to the plain view

12. Anthony Amsterdam, "Perspectives on the Fourth Amendment," 58 Minn. L. Rev. 349, 374–75 (1974).

13. Carroll v. United States, 267 U.S. 132, 45 S.Ct. 280 (1925).

doctrine in part H. Next, we focus on police actions based on exigency, such as hot pursuit in part I. After that, in part J, we will discuss the constitutional parameters of the automobile search; in part K, we examine whether a warrant is needed to discover evidence in open fields.

The Supreme Court has also recognized exceptions to the warrant requirement based on a standard that differs from probable cause. In essence, these police actions operate on a somewhat lower tier. They include "stop and frisk" discussed in part M of this chapter and the so-called administrative searches, or "special needs" searches discussed in part N. Stop and frisk frees police to engage in an intrusion that is less than an arrest and an action that is less than a search on the basis of something less than probable cause. One way to think of this is a "lower tier" of law enforcement interaction with criminal suspects. From there, we turn to "special needs" searches which are cousins to the stop and frisk doctrine. These "special needs" searches have as their main justification something other than the catching of criminals and the seizure of criminal evidence. They are considered near the end of the chapter because they require a rethinking of Fourth Amendment theory. Absent an emergency or consent, some administrative searches, such as governmental health and safety inspections of homes or of the workplace, are deemed reasonable only if authorized in advance by a judicial officer. Others are reasonable if they are part of a larger scheme for the enforcement of non-criminal law enforcement objectives. They are valid even though they are based on a showing of something other than the traditional probable cause needed for the issuance of a valid search warrant in quest of criminal evidence.

Two other categories that have evolved and been treated somewhat differently are border searches, discussed in part O, and inventory searches, discussed in part P.

Then, the text examines consent searches in part Q. Even though law enforcement officials have acted without probable cause or without any justification, a search and seizure may nevertheless be valid if it is done with the consent of the party searched. The question then arises as to what is the appropriate standard we should use to measure the validity of the consent.

One last note: when trying to list exceptions to the Fourth Amendment warrant requirement, some authors include the so-called "good faith exception" of United States v. Leon, 468 U.S. 897, 104 S.Ct. 3405 (1984) and its progeny. We have included this case, instead, in Chapter 6 on the theory that *Leon* modified bedrock principles underlying the application of the exclusionary rule rather than a true exception to the warrant requirement. As you reflect on these materials, however, ask yourself what, if any, impact *Leon* may have had on the exceptions discussed here in Chapter 5.

B. FOURTH AMENDMENT BORDERLANDS: WHEN DOES THE FOURTH AMENDMENT APPLY—WHAT CONSTITUTES A SEARCH OR SEIZURE

We now consider borderline cases where the essential preliminary question is whether the governmental conduct constitutes Fourth Amendment activity. If the answer is negative, the Fourth Amendment analysis need go no further. There can be no unreasonable search or seizure unless, to begin with, there is a search and/or a seizure. In the absence of a search or a seizure, those who would limit governmental intrusions upon liberty and privacy must look elsewhere in the law, beyond the Fourth Amendment, for a source of protection.

Katz v. United States

Supreme Court of the United States, 1967.
389 U.S. 347, 88 S.Ct. 507.

(Please return and read this opinion which appears in chapter 4)

* * *

NOTES

1. *Activities Exposed to the Public.* Assume for a moment a police officer observes an individual standing out in the open on a public street while holding an illegal machine gun. This observation would not constitute a search for purposes of the Fourth Amendment. The individual would have no privacy interest in a contraband weapon displayed in this fashion. If the officer were to arrest the individual and take the gun, then we would have a seizure. The seizure, however, would be based on probable cause and as we shall see later, an arrest in a public place based on probable cause may be executed without a warrant.

2. *"Search" as Invasion of Privacy.* There is a trend in which courts avoid the necessity of fitting governmental conduct into one of the "well-delineated" exceptions to the warrant requirement. They do so by finding that the conduct did not constitute a "search." The basis for that finding is that there was no legitimate expectation of privacy, a determination which involves a value judgment made by the court. See the concurring opinion of Justice Scalia. California v. Acevedo, 500 U.S. 565, 111 S.Ct. 1982 (1991).

Illinois v. Andreas, 463 U.S. 765, 103 S.Ct. 3319 (1983), provides an example of how intrusions which almost certainly would have been classified as searches before *Katz* now may be deemed not to be searches because they do not intrude upon a reasonable expectation of privacy. In *Andreas*, Customs agents lawfully inspected a large shipping container which contained a large table. Marijuana was concealed within the table. They resealed the package and permitted Chicago police officers, posing as delivery men, to deliver it to the consignee. Andreas accepted the package and took it into his apartment for thirty-five or forty minutes. Officers did not keep continuous watch during this period. Andreas then dragged the package into the hallway. Officers seized Andreas and the package. The police searched the package at the police station and seized the marijuana therein.

The Court held that once the package had been lawfully inspected by Customs agents, the consignee no longer had a reasonable expectation of privacy as long as there was no "substantial likelihood" that the contents have been changed during the gap in surveillance.

In dissent Justice Brennan said, "We have, to my knowledge, never [before] held that the physical opening and examination of a container in the possession of an individual was anything other than a 'search.' " Brennan also disagreed, on the facts of Andreas, with the majority's conclusion that there was no substantial likelihood that the contraband had been removed from the package during the gap in surveillance.

The Court seemingly has departed from literalism in its understanding of the term "search". What would we say about a police officer who had spent half an hour or more in unwrapping a package and taking apart its contents looking for drugs if he denied that he had engaged in a "search"? Compare the literalism adhered to by the Court in *Oliver*, the "open fields" case noted in Section K of this chapter.

With the demise of a "trespass" as an essential element of a search or a seizure, new challenges to government conduct may now be brought under the Fourth Amendment. Consider again *Katz*-inspired claims for modification of the doctrines of plain view (Section H), abandoned property (Section L) and open fields (Section K).

Conversely, with emphasis upon privacy rather than property, government lawyers sometimes argue that no search or seizure has occurred in cases in which, before *Katz*, all would have characterized the government's actions as a search or a seizure and the only issue would have been its reasonableness. Thus in Marshall v. Barlow's, Inc. (Section M) the government argued that its inspection of factories and other workplaces—including places closed to the general public—did not constitute a search because the employer knowingly exposed to its employees the areas which were to be inspected. The Barlow Court rejected the argument, reasoning that vis--vis members of the public and inspectors, the employer retained a reasonable expectation of privacy. See also note 1, supra.

3. *Transactional Records and the* Katz *reasonable expectation of privacy test.* In United States v. Miller, 425 U.S. 435, 96 S.Ct. 1619 (1976), a federal prosecutor utilized the grand jury to subpoena records from two banks pertaining to Miller's accounts. The Court stated that one who engages in commercial transactions utilizing banking facilities has no reasonable expectation of privacy in the papers, so that he can make no claim under the Fourth Amendment. The "depositor takes the risk, in revealing his affairs to another, that the information will be conveyed by that person to the government." The Court attributed no legal significance to the fact that it is the government itself, under the Bank Secrecy Act, upheld in California Bankers Assn. v. Shultz, 416 U.S. 21, 94 S.Ct. 1494 (1974), which requires the bank to keep the records. "Many banks traditionally kept permanent records of their depositors' accounts" even before the Bank Secrecy Act compelled that practice.

The result in *Miller* is in accord with the result in the typical state case where the target of an investigation seeks to quash a grand jury *subpoena duces tecum* issued to his bank or some other third party. Such a person typically is told that he has no standing to complain about the breadth of the subpoena or any other alleged irregularity.

In Rakas v. Illinois, 439 U.S. 128, 99 S.Ct. 421 (1978) (discussed in Chapter 6) the Court emphasized that whether a person has "standing" depends upon whether he has a reasonable expectation of privacy. Under this view the *Miller* approach to the bank records issue is not different from a "standing to object" approach.

What of credit card records? Records concerning location gleaned from EZ–Pass transactions? Although we often like to think that what we check out from libraries or Video/DVD stores is confidential, does the government conduct a "search" for Fourth Amendment purposes if they obtain these records? Using "data mining," the government can compile a whole series of transactions (credit, medical treatments, travel) that will reveal a great deal about someone's life. Does the Fourth

Amendment offer protection against government efforts of this type, including the Total Information Awareness program discussed in Chapter 4?

4. ***Surveillance and the* Katz *reasonable expectation of privacy test.*** Consider the application of the *Katz* formulation to the following situations to determine whether a search or a seizure has taken place. Remember that in doing so, an affirmative response does not necessarily mean that either prior judicial approval or full probable cause or both is required. Some Fourth Amendment intrusions may be so minimal, and the benefit to society so great, that the intrusion could be deemed reasonable without prior judicial approval and upon a relatively small quantity of data.

(a) Is it a search when an officer "tails" a suspect, either on foot or in an unmarked vehicle, and keeps the suspect under visual surveillance? Is that a search?

(b) Is it a search when an officer places a "tracking beeper" on the underside of a car and is thus able to electronically monitor the whereabouts of the vehicle, without overhearing or recording any conversation?

In United States v. Knotts, 460 U.S. 276, 103 S.Ct. 1081 (1983), the Court considered a "beeper case." The device had been implanted by government agents in a drum containing chloroform before certain suspects took possession of the container. The officers then used the beeper to monitor movement of the drum in a vehicle which eventually was driven onto private property. Noting that the accused had not challenged the implanting of the device, the Court considered only whether the subsequent monitoring constituted a fourth amendment violation. It concluded that the monitoring was no different from visual surveillance and that it did not constitute a search or seizure within the meaning of the fourth amendment.

In United States v. Karo, 468 U.S. 705, 104 S.Ct. 3296 (1984), the Court considered another tracking beeper case. A majority of justices agreed that monitoring a beeper in a private residence, not open to visual surveillance, constitutes a search. Like any search of a home, ordinarily the use of such a device to acquire information must be first authorized by a search warrant. Under the peculiar facts of the case, however, the Court held that no information derived from monitoring was used against any defendant with standing to complain about the intrusion.

In an interesting twist, the Fourth Circuit distinguished *Karo* by upholding the use of a tracking beeper planted in U.S. mail that defendant later stole and placed in his van. Though admitting that the defendant had a reasonable expectation of privacy in his van, and that the beeper allowed officers to get information they would not have been able to get by visual surveillance, the majority nonetheless upheld the search: The beeper had been placed inside a mail pouch belonging to the government in which the defendant had no expectation of privacy. The dissenting judge asserted that *Karo* controlled. United States v. Jones, 31 F.3d 1304 (4th Cir.1994). An interesting discussion of the issues in *Jones*, and the general tension in Fourth Amendment jurisprudence between procedural and substantive goals, can be found in Sherry F. Colb, Innocence, Privacy, and Targeting in Fourth Amendment Jurisprudence, 96 Colum.L.Rev. 1456 (1996).

(c) Suppose the tracking takes place through an RFID chip?

Radio Frequency Identification Chips are gaining in popularity as a way to speed commerce. They also, however, track objects. They are extremely small (the size of a grain of sand) and can be embedded in many objects, including vehicles, currency, bearer bonds, driver's licenses, medical information smart cards, etc. Currently, many are familiar with RFID chips as contactless forms of payment for tolls (EZ Pass etc.) or for gasoline (the fobs used for payment at Exxon stations). Shane L. Smith, Gone in a Blink: The Overlooked Privacy Problems Caused by

Contactless Payment Systems (Winner of the computer Law Association 2006 Information Technology Law Writing Competition), 11 Marq. Intell. Prop. L. Rev. 213 (2006) If the government uses this information, is it a search or seizure? Or by using this device for convenience has the consumer waived any privacy interest?

(d) Consider these scenarios of visual surveillance: An officer conducts an aerial surveillance of a suspect's yard.

> In California v. Ciraolo, 476 U.S. 207, 106 S.Ct. 1809 (1986), a closely divided Court approved aerial surveillance to ascertain if the homeowner was growing marijuana. *Ciraolo* involved observations of land within the cartilage of a home from a height of about 1000. The property owner had taken steps to make sure that the property was not visible from the public way. Nevertheless the Court concluded that the owner had no reasonable expectation of privacy since the land was visible from a vantage point of ordinary air traffic.

(e) Would aerial surveillance constitute a search if it was conducted using a helicopter that was more intrusive to the privacy interests of the suspect?

In Florida v. Riley, 488 U.S. 445, 109 S.Ct. 693 (1989), an investigator could not see the contents of a greenhouse from a public road. He then conducted aerial surveillance and

> [c]ircled twice over respondent's property in a helicopter at the height of 400 feet. With the naked eye, he was able to see through the openings of the roof and ... the sides of the greenhouse and to identify what he thought was marijuana growing in the structure.

The investigator used these observations to obtain a search warrant. A four-person plurality declared that this conduct was not a "search" within the meaning of the Fourth Amendment. It stressed that, under applicable Federal Aviation Administration Regulations, "any member of the public could legally have been flying over Riley's property in a helicopter at the altitude of 400 feet and could have observed Riley's greenhouse." The plurality added that nothing suggests "that helicopters flying at 400 feet are sufficiently rare in this country to lend substance to respondent's claim that he reasonably anticipated that his greenhouse would not be subject to observation from that altitude."

Justice O'Connor concurred in the judgment, stressing less the fact that F.A.A. regulations were not violated, but instead emphasizing that the defendant has the burden of showing that a search occurred and noting that he failed to show that there is not "considerable public use of airspace" at an altitude of 400 feet.

Three justices dissented, finding that Riley had a reasonable expectation of privacy from low-level helicopter surveillance of enclosed curtilage areas. Justice Blackmun also dissented, arguing that the prosecution, under the circumstances, should have had the burden of proving that helicopters fly over curtilage at an altitude of 400 feet often enough to negate a reasonable expectation of privacy.

How low can you go? See People v. Pollock, 796 P.2d 63 (Colo.App.1990) (hovering over a backyard at 200 feet constitutes a search); Commonwealth v. Oglialoro, 525 Pa. 250, 579 A.2d 1288 (1990) (hovering at 50 feet constitutes a search, with court emphasizing the noise and the danger more than the intrusion upon informational privacy).

In contrast, at least one court has relied on state constitutional law to conclude an aerial search does constitute a search within the reasonable expectations of *Katz*. State v. Bryant, 2008 Vt. 39, 2008 WL 820197 (2008).

(f) Suppose law enforcement authorities conduct an aerial surveillance using technological enhancement?

In Dow Chemical Co. v. United States, 476 U.S. 227, 106 S.Ct. 1819 (1986), the government conducted aerial surveillance of a Dow Chemical plant when Dow refused to volunteer for an inspection by the Environmental Protection Agency. They used a precision aerial mapping camera and took pictures from various heights. This was before such pictures were readily available on the internet. The Court concluded this was not a breach of reasonable expectations of privacy. It emphasized that in neither case was very highly sophisticated equipment used to aid the observations.

(g) What role, if any, should the use of technologically enhanced equipment play in determining if there is a search? At least one commentator has suggested that greater protections are needed with increased sophistication of law enforcement technology. Robert C. Power, "Technology and the Fourth Amendment: A Proposed Formulation for Visual Searches," 80 J. Crim. L. & Criminology 1 (1989).

(h) Suppose law enforcement agents use a specially trained dog to sniff luggage in order to detect the presence of marijuana. Is a sniff a search?

In United States v. Place, 462 U.S. 696, 103 S.Ct. 2637 (1983), a majority of the Court, in clear dictum, declared that the use of a "sniffing dog" to detect the presence or absence of contraband in luggage is not a "search" within the meaning of the fourth amendment. Saying "the canine sniff is sui generis," the Court declared it was much less intrusive than a typical search, yields limited information, and does not, by itself, subject the owner to embarrassment and inconvenience. The main issues in Place were first, the right of officers to seize the luggage without a warrant and without probable cause so that the luggage would be available to be sniffed and second, the legality of a ninety minute detention of the luggage under such circumstances.

In Illinois v. Caballes, 543 U.S. 405, 125 S.Ct. 834 (2005), the Court again held that a dog sniff of the exterior of a car was not a search. Here, the dog sniff that revealed heroin in the trunk of the car following a car stop for speeding was conducted by a second officer. Citing Place, the Court held that since the sniff does not expose noncontraband items, it does not implicate legitimate privacy interests.

(i) Suppose an officer takes a small paint scraping from a car parked on a public street. Does the Fourth Amendment apply? *See* Cardwell v. Lewis, 417 U.S. 583, 94 S.Ct. 2464 (1974).

(j) Suppose postal authorities, before delivering a citizen's mail, copy return addresses, postmarks, and other identifying features?

(k) As part of an investigation, an officer places a key in the lock of a door and turns the key to determine that it fits. He then withdraws the key without pushing the door open. See United States v. Portillo–Reyes, 529 F.2d 844 (9th Cir.1975) *cert. denied* 429 U.S. 899, 97 S.Ct. 267 (1976). Compare Thomas v. State, 145 Ga.App. 69, 243 S.E.2d 250 (1978); People v. Trull, 64 Ill.App.3d 385, 20 Ill.Dec. 960, 380 N.E.2d 1169 (1978).

(*l*) An undercover agent attends a meeting, held in a private home, but open to the public, the subject of which is police spying.

(m) Agents read e-mail, after getting a warrant for the computer. See Raphael Winick, Searches and seizures of computers and computer data, 8 Harv.J.L. & Tech. 75 (1994); United States v. Lamb, 945 F.Supp. 441, 455 (N.D.N.Y.1996) (upholding search of records, files and e-mail stored at aol office); Steve Jackson Games, Inc. v. U.S. Secret Service, 36 F.3d 457 (5th Cir.1994) (search of e-mail after computer seized not an "intercept" under the terms of Title I of the Electronic Privacy Act because not contemporaneous with transmission); Davis v. Gracey, 111 F.3d 1472 (10th Cir.1997) (when officers with search warrant for business premises of pornography seller discovered that the pornography could be accessed through a computer bulletin board the seller operated, officers were justified in seizing computer that operated bulletin board and as a result, seizing 150,000 e-mail messages, some not yet read, that had been posted to the board).

An agent enters a private "chat room" conversation on the Internet and copies the conversations of others. See United States v. Charbonneau, 979 F.Supp. 1177 (1997) ("the transmitter of an e-mail message enjoys a reasonable expectation that police officials will not intercept the transmission without probable cause and a search warrant. However, once the transmissions are received by another person, the transmitter no longer controls its destiny.")

(n) Federal agents send a "worm" out over the internet which is designed to search for certain classified documents. if the "worm" locates such a document, it reports its location to authorities. If the "worm" enters a computer with no classified documents, it searches through them but causes no harm and sends back no message. A computer user would never know that his or her computer had been searched. For discussion of this and other fourth amendment issues concerning computer searches, see Michael Adler, Cyberspace and the Fourth Amendment, 105 Yale L.J. 1093 (1996), Lawrence Lessig, Reading the Constitution in Cyberspace, 45 Emory L.J. 869 (1996).

For decisions on these and related topics, consult Volume 1 of LaFave, Search and Seizure (4th ed. 2007), particularly §§ 2.2 and 2.7.

5. The question of whether electronic recording of a conversation with one-party consent is a search or seizure is treated in Chapter 4 and United States v. White, 401 U.S. 745, 91 S.Ct. 1122 (1971).

6. In Wyman v. James, 400 U.S. 309, 91 S.Ct. 381; five Justices concluded that a mandatory home visit to a welfare recipient did not constitute a search. Now, the Court might adhere to an alternate conclusion by six Justices in that case that if it was a search, it was justified by appropriate administrative purposes. Over a strong dissent, the Court suggested that the purpose of the governmental conduct is relevant to the threshold question, "What is a search?" Does it make sense that certain non-consensual governmental entries into a home do not constitute government activity which is subject to the Fourth Amendment requirement of reasonableness?

7. A California court ruled that a homeless person had no "objectively reasonable" expectation of privacy in his shelter on a public sidewalk. The shelter was made of cardboard boxes and wooden pallets, and the defendant testified he had lived there for a year and a half. The court stated: "a person who occupies a temporary shelter on public property without permission and in violation of an ordinance prohibiting sidewalk blockages is a trespasser subject to immediate ejectment and, therefore, a person without a reasonable expectation that his shelter will remain undisturbed.... Viewed from a practical perspective, it borders on the absurd to suggest the police should have to get a warrant before searching a transient's temporary shelter. By the time the warrant issued, the odds are the shelter would be long gone." People v. Thomas, 38 Cal.App.4th 1331, 1335 & n. 2, 45 Cal.Rptr.2d 610, 613 & n. 2 (1995).

In contrast, Connecticut has recognized an expectation of privacy in a homeless person's temporary cardboard box shelter. See State v. Mooney, 588 A.2d 145, 218 Conn. 85, cert. denied, 502 U.S. 919, 112 S.Ct. 330 (1991).

Clearly, the "expectation of privacy" approach leads to giving the wealthy more protection from government investigation than the poor. Compare, for example, the expansive definition of "curtilage" in the estate discussed in United States v. Reilly, 76 F.3d 1271 (2d Cir.1996), with the much more limited privacy allowed apartment dwellers in United States v. Fields, 113 F.3d 313 (2d Cir.1997), in which a government trespass of a sideyard to peek through a gap in a window blind was held not to violate the defendants' "expectation of privacy," since other occupants of the apartment building could have been at that vantage point and seen through the window. For an argument that the shelterless should have protected privacy rights even though they may live within the public domain, Comment (Michael D. Granston), From Private Places to Private Activities: Toward a New Fourth Amendment House for the Shelterless, 101 Yale L.J. 1305 (1992).

8. How does the situation in which the fourth amendment does not apply contrast with the plain view doctrine?

9. The availability of technologically enhanced surveillance techniques continue to place the focus on what constitutes a search. For example, questions have arisen about thermal imaging. Police use thermal imaging devices to observe heat emanating from a building. If abnormal heating patterns are found, especially after police have checked for high electricity usage and blacked out windows, the police will seek to search the interior of the building. Is the thermal imaging a search? Or is it simply observing something about a building that is in plain view? Circuit courts originally split on this issue, but the Supreme Court has now ruled.

Kyllo v. United States

Supreme Court of the United States, 2001.
533 U.S. 27, 121 S.Ct. 2038.

■ JUSTICE SCALIA delivered the opinion of the Court.

This case presents the question whether the use of a thermal-imaging device aimed at a private home from a public street to detect relative amounts of heat within the home constitutes a "search" within the meaning of the Fourth Amendment.

I

In 1991 Agent William Elliott of the United States Department of the Interior came to suspect that marijuana was being grown in the home belonging to petitioner Danny Kyllo, part of a triplex on Rhododendron Drive in Florence, Oregon. Indoor marijuana growth typically requires high-intensity lamps. In order to determine whether an amount of heat was emanating from petitioner's home consistent with the use of such lamps, at 3:20 a.m. on January 16, 1992, Agent Elliott and Dan Haas used an Agema Thermovision 210 thermal imager to scan the triplex. Thermal imagers detect infrared radiation, which virtually all objects emit but which is not visible to the naked eye. The imager converts radiation into images based on relative warmth—black is cool, white is hot, shades of gray connote relative differences; in that respect, it operates somewhat like a video camera showing heat images. The scan of Kyllo's home took only a few minutes and was performed from the passenger seat of Agent Elliott's vehicle across the street from the front of the house and also from the street in back of the house. The scan showed that the roof over the garage and a side wall of petitioner's home were relatively hot compared to the rest of the home and substantially warmer than neighboring homes in the triplex. Agent Elliott concluded that petitioner was using halide lights to grow marijuana in his house, which indeed he was. Based on tips from informants, utility bills, and the thermal imaging, a Federal Magistrate

Judge issued a warrant authorizing a search of petitioner's home, and the agents found an indoor growing operation involving more than 100 plants. Petitioner was indicted on one count of manufacturing marijuana, in violation of 21 U.S.C. § 841(a)(1). He unsuccessfully moved to suppress the evidence seized from his home and then entered a conditional guilty plea. The Ninth Circuit ultimately affirmed, upholding the thermal imaging on the ground that Kyllo had shown no subjective expectation of privacy because he had made no attempt to conceal the heat escaping from his home. Even if he had, ruled the court, there was no objectively reasonable expectation of privacy because the thermal imager did not expose any intimate details of Kyllo's life, only amorphous hot spots on the roof and exterior walls.

II

The Fourth Amendment provides that "the right of the people to be secure in their persons, houses, papers, and effects, against unreasonable searches and seizures, shall not be violated." "At the very core" of the Fourth Amendment "stands the right of a man to retreat into his own home and there be free from unreasonable governmental intrusion." Silverman v. United States (1961). With few exceptions, the question whether a warrantless search of a home is reasonable and hence constitutional must be answered no. See Illinois v. Rodriguez (1990); Payton v. New York (1980).

On the other hand, the antecedent question of whether or not a Fourth Amendment "search" has occurred is not so simple under our precedent. The permissibility of ordinary visual surveillance of a home used to be clear because, well into the 20th century, our Fourth Amendment jurisprudence was tied to common-law trespass. See, e.g., Goldman v. United States (1942); Olmstead v. United States (1928). Cf. Silverman v. United States. (technical trespass not necessary for Fourth Amendment violation; it suffices if there is "actual intrusion into a constitutionally protected area"). Visual surveillance was unquestionably lawful because " 'the eye cannot by the laws of England be guilty of a trespass.' " Boyd v. United States (1886) (quoting Entick v. Carrington, 19 How. St. Tr. 1029, 95 Eng. Rep. 807 (K. B. 1765)). We have since decoupled violation of a person's Fourth Amendment rights from trespassory violation of his property, see Rakas v. Illinois (1978), but the lawfulness of warrantless visual surveillance of a home has still been preserved. As we observed in California v. Ciraolo (1986), "the Fourth Amendment protection of the home has never been extended to require law enforcement officers to shield their eyes when passing by a home on public thoroughfares."

One might think that the new validating rationale would be that examining the portion of a house that is in plain public view, while it is a "search"[1] despite the absence of trespass, is not an "unreasonable" one

1. When the Fourth Amendment was adopted, as now, to "search" meant "to look over or through for the purpose of finding something; to explore; to examine by inspection; as, to *search* the house for a book; to *search* the wood for a thief." N. Webster, An American Dictionary of the English Language 66 (1828) (reprint 6th ed. 1989).

The present case involves officers on a public street engaged in more than naked-eye

under the Fourth Amendment. See Minnesota v. Carter (1998) (BREYER, J., concurring in judgment). But in fact we have held that visual observation is no "search" at all—perhaps in order to preserve somewhat more intact our doctrine that warrantless searches are presumptively unconstitutional. See Dow Chemical Co. v. United States (1986). In assessing when a search is not a search, we have applied somewhat in reverse the principle first enunciated in Katz v. United States (1967). *Katz* involved eavesdropping by means of an electronic listening device placed on the outside of a telephone booth—a location not within the catalog ("persons, houses, papers, and effects") that the Fourth Amendment protects against unreasonable searches. We held that the Fourth Amendment nonetheless protected *Katz* from the warrantless eavesdropping because he "justifiably relied" upon the privacy of the telephone booth. Id. at 353. As Justice Harlan's oft-quoted concurrence described it, a Fourth Amendment search occurs when the government violates a subjective expectation of privacy that society recognizes as reasonable. We have subsequently applied this principle to hold that a Fourth Amendment search does *not* occur—even when the explicitly protected location of a *house* is concerned—unless "the individual manifested a subjective expectation of privacy in the object of the challenged search," and "society [is] willing to recognize that expectation as reasonable." We have applied this test in holding that it is not a search for the police to use a pen register at the phone company to determine what numbers were dialed in a private home, Smith v. Maryland (1979), and we have applied the test on two different occasions in holding that aerial surveillance of private homes and surrounding areas does not constitute a search, Ciraolo; Florida v. Riley (1989).

III

It would be foolish to contend that the degree of privacy secured to citizens by the Fourth Amendment has been entirely unaffected by the advance of technology. For example, as the cases discussed above make clear, the technology enabling human flight has exposed to public view (and hence, we have said, to official observation) uncovered portions of the house and its curtilage that once were private. The question we confront today is what limits there are upon this power of technology to shrink the realm of guaranteed privacy.

The *Katz* test—whether the individual has an expectation of privacy that society is prepared to recognize as reasonable—has often been criticized as circular, and hence subjective and unpredictable. See 1 W. LaFave, Search and Seizure § 2.1(d), pp. 393–394 (3d ed. 1996); Posner, The Uncertain Protection of Privacy by the Supreme Court, 1979 S. Ct. Rev. 173, 188; *Carter* at 97 (Scalia, J., concurring). But see *Rakas*. While it may be difficult to refine *Katz* when the search of areas such as telephone booths, automobiles, or even the curtilage and uncovered portions of

surveillance of a home. We have previously reserved judgment as to how much technological enhancement of ordinary perception from such a vantage point, if any, is too much. While we upheld enhanced aerial photography of an industrial complex in *Dow Chemical*, we noted that we found "it important that this is *not* an area immediately adjacent to a private home, where privacy expectations are most heightened," 476 U.S. at 237, n. 4 (emphasis in original).

residences are at issue, in the case of the search of the interior of homes—the prototypical and hence most commonly litigated area of protected privacy—there is a ready criterion, with roots deep in the common law, of the minimal expectation of privacy that *exists*, and that is acknowledged to be *reasonable*. To withdraw protection of this minimum expectation would be to permit police technology to erode the privacy guaranteed by the Fourth Amendment. We think that obtaining by sense-enhancing technology any information regarding the interior of the home that could not otherwise have been obtained without physical "intrusion into a constitutionally protected area," lain *Silverman*, 365 U.S. at 512, constitutes a search—at least where (as here) the technology in question is not in general public use. This assures preservation of that degree of privacy against government that existed when the Fourth Amendment was adopted. On the basis of this criterion, the information obtained by the thermal imager in this case was the product of a search.[2]

The Government maintains, however, that the thermal imaging must be upheld because it detected "only heat radiating from the external surface of the house," Brief for United States 26. The dissent makes this its leading point, contending that there is a fundamental difference between what it calls "off-the-wall" observations and "through-the-wall surveillance." But just as a thermal imager captures only heat emanating from a house, so also a powerful directional microphone picks up only sound emanating from a house-and a satellite capable of scanning from many miles away would pick up only visible light emanating from a house. We rejected such a mechanical interpretation of the Fourth Amendment in *Katz*, where the eavesdropping device picked up only sound waves that reached the exterior of the phone booth. Reversing that approach would leave the homeowner at the mercy of advancing technology—including imaging technology that could discern all human activity in the home. While the technology used in the present case was relatively crude, the rule we adopt must take account of more sophisticated systems that are already in use or in development.[3] The dissent's reliance on the distinction between

2. The dissent's repeated assertion that the thermal imaging did not obtain information regarding the interior of the home, *post*, at 3, 4 (opinion of STEVENS, J.), is simply inaccurate. A thermal imager reveals the relative heat of various rooms in the home. The dissent may not find that information particularly private or important, see *post*, at 4, 5, 10, but there is no basis for saying it is not information regarding the interior of the home. The dissent's comparison of the thermal imaging to various circumstances in which outside observers might be able to perceive, without technology, the heat of the home—for example, by observing snowmelt on the roof, *post*, at 3—is quite irrelevant. The fact that equivalent information could sometimes be obtained by other means does not make lawful the use of means that violate the Fourth Amendment. The police might, for example, learn how many people are in a particular house by setting up year-round surveillance; but that does not make breaking and entering to find out the same information lawful. In any event, on the night of January 16, 1992, no outside observer could have discerned the relative heat of Kyllo's home without thermal imaging.

3. The ability to "see" through walls and other opaque barriers is a clear, and scientifically feasible, goal of law enforcement research and development. The National Law Enforcement and Corrections Technology Center, a program within the United States Department of Justice, features on its Internet Website projects that include a "Radar-Based Through-the-Wall Surveillance System," "Handheld Ultrasound Through the Wall Surveillance," and a "Radar Flashlight" that "will enable law officers to detect indi-

"off-the-wall" and "through-the-wall" observation is entirely incompatible with the dissent's belief, which we discuss below, that thermal-imaging observations of the intimate details of a home are impermissible. The most sophisticated thermal imaging devices continue to measure heat "off-the-wall" rather than "through-the-wall"; the dissent's disapproval of those more sophisticated thermal-imaging devices ... is an acknowledgement that there is no substance to this distinction. As for the dissent's extraordinary assertion that anything learned through "an inference" cannot be a search ... that would validate even the "through-the-wall" technologies that the dissent purports to disapprove. Surely the dissent does not believe that the through-the-wall radar or ultrasound technology produces an 8–by–10 Kodak glossy that needs no analysis (*i.e.*, the making of inferences). And, of course, the novel proposition that inference insulates a search is blatantly contrary to United States v. Karo (1984), where the police "inferred" from the activation of a beeper that a certain can of ether was in the home. The police activity was held to be a search, and the search was held unlawful.[4]

The Government also contends that the thermal imaging was constitutional because it did not "detect private activities occurring in private areas," It points out that in *Dow Chemical* we observed that the enhanced aerial photography did not reveal any "intimate details." *Dow Chemical*, however, involved enhanced aerial photography of an industrial complex, which does not share the Fourth Amendment sanctity of the home. The Fourth Amendment's protection of the home has never been tied to measurement of the quality or quantity of information obtained.... there is certainly no exception to the warrant requirement for the officer who barely cracks open the front door and sees nothing but the nonintimate rug on the vestibule floor. In the home, our cases show, *all* details are intimate details, because the entire area is held safe from prying government eyes. Thus, in *Karo*, the only thing detected was a can of ether in the home; and in Arizona v. Hicks (1987), the only thing detected by a physical search that went beyond what officers lawfully present could observe in "plain view" was the registration number of a phonograph turntable. These were intimate details because they were details of the home, just as was the detail of

viduals through interior building walls." www.nlectc.org/techproj/ (visited May 3, 2001). Some devices may emit low levels of radiation that travel "through-the-wall," but others, such as more sophisticated thermal imaging devices, are entirely passive, or "off-the-wall" as the dissent puts it.

4. The dissent asserts that we have misunderstood its point, which is not that inference *insulates* a search, but that inference alone is *not* a search. If we misunderstood the point, it was only in a good-faith effort to render the point germane to the case at hand. The issue in this case is not the police's allegedly unlawful inferencing, but their allegedly unlawful thermal-imaging measurement of the emanations from a house. We say such measurement is a search; the dissent says it is not, because an inference is not a search. We took that to mean that, since the technologically enhanced emanations had to be the basis of inferences before anything inside the house could be known, the use of the emanations could not be a search. But the dissent certainly knows better than we what it intends. And if it means only that an inference is not a search, we certainly agree. That has no bearing, however, upon whether hi-tech measurement of emanations from a house is a search.

how warm—or even how relatively warm—Kyllo was heating his residence.[5]

Limiting the prohibition of thermal imaging to "intimate details" would not only be wrong in principle; it would be impractical in application, failing to provide "a workable accommodation between the needs of law enforcement and the interests protected by the Fourth Amendment," Oliver v. United States (1984). To begin with, there is no necessary connection between the sophistication of the surveillance equipment and the "intimacy" of the details that it observes—which means that one cannot say (and the police cannot be assured) that use of the relatively crude equipment at issue here will always be lawful. The Agema Thermovision 210 might disclose, for example, at what hour each night the lady of the house takes her daily sauna and bath—a detail that many would consider "intimate"; and a much more sophisticated system might detect nothing more intimate than the fact that someone left a closet light on. We could not, in other words, develop a rule approving only that through-the-wall surveillance which identifies objects no smaller than 36 by 36 inches, but would have to develop a jurisprudence specifying which home activities are "intimate" and which are not. And even when (if ever) that jurisprudence were fully developed, no police officer would be able to know *in advance* whether his through-the-wall surveillance picks up "intimate" details—and thus would be unable to know in advance whether it is constitutional.

The dissent's proposed standard—whether the technology offers the "functional equivalent of actual presence in the area being searched,"—would seem quite similar to our own at first blush. The dissent concludes that *Katz* was such a case, but then inexplicably asserts that if the same listening device only revealed the volume of the conversation, the surveillance would be permissible. Yet if, without technology, the police could not discern volume without being actually present in the phone booth, Justice Stevens should conclude a search has occurred. Cf. *Karo* (Stevens, J., concurring in part and dissenting in part) ("I find little comfort in the Court's notion that no invasion of privacy occurs until a listener obtains some significant information by use of the device.... A bathtub is a less private area when the plumber is present even if his back is turned"). The same should hold for the interior heat of the home if only a person present in the home could discern the heat. Thus the driving force of the dissent, despite its recitation of the above standard, appears to be a distinction among different types of information—whether the "homeowner would even care if anybody noticed." The dissent offers no practical guidance for the application of this standard, and for reasons already discussed, we

5. The Government cites our statement in *California v. Ciraolo* (1986), noting apparent agreement with the State of California that aerial surveillance of a house's curtilage could become " 'invasive' " if " 'modern technology' " revealed " 'those intimate associations, objects or activities otherwise imperceptible to police or fellow citizens.' " (quoting brief of the State of California). We think the Court's focus in this second-hand dictum was not upon intimacy but upon otherwise-imperceptibility, which is precisely the principle we vindicate today.

believe there can be none. The people in their houses, as well as the police, deserve more precision.[6]

We have said that the Fourth Amendment draws "a firm line at the entrance to the house," *Payton*. That line, we think, must be not only firm but also bright—which requires clear specification of those methods of surveillance that require a warrant. While it is certainly possible to conclude from the videotape of the thermal imaging that occurred in this case that no "significant" compromise of the homeowner's privacy has occurred, we must take the long view, from the original meaning of the Fourth Amendment forward.

"The Fourth Amendment is to be construed in the light of what was deemed an unreasonable search and seizure when it was adopted, and in a manner which will conserve public interests as well as the interests and rights of individual citizens." Carroll v. United States (1925).

Where, as here, the Government uses a device that is not in general public use, to explore details of the home that would previously have been unknowable without physical intrusion, the surveillance is a "search" and is presumptively unreasonable without a warrant.

Since we hold the Thermovision imaging to have been an unlawful search, it will remain for the District Court to determine whether, without the evidence it provided, the search warrant issued in this case was supported by probable cause—and if not, whether there is any other basis for supporting admission of the evidence that the search pursuant to the warrant produced.

The judgment of the Court of Appeals is reversed; the case is remanded for further proceedings consistent with this opinion.

It is so ordered.

■ JUSTICE STEVENS, with whom THE CHIEF JUSTICE, JUSTICE O'CONNOR, and JUSTICE KENNEDY join, dissenting.

There is, in my judgment, a distinction of constitutional magnitude between "through-the-wall surveillance" that gives the observer or listener direct access to information in a private area, on the one hand, and the thought processes used to draw inferences from information in the public domain, on the other hand. The Court has crafted a rule that purports to deal with direct observations of the inside of the home, but the case before us merely involves indirect deductions from "off-the-wall" surveillance, that is, observations of the exterior of the home. Those observations were made with a fairly primitive thermal imager that gathered data exposed on the outside of petitioner's home but did not invade any constitutionally

6. The dissent argues that we have injected potential uncertainty into the constitutional analysis by noting that whether or not the technology is in general public use may be a factor. That quarrel, however, is not with us but with this Court's precedent. See *Ciraolo*, *supra*, at 215 ("In an age where private and commercial flight in the public airways is routine, it is unreasonable for respondent to expect that his marijuana plants were constitutionally protected from being observed with the naked eye from an altitude of 1,000 feet"). Given that we can quite confidently say that thermal imaging is not "routine," we decline in this case to reexamine that factor.

protected interest in privacy.[1] Moreover, I believe that the supposedly "bright-line" rule the Court has created in response to its concerns about future technological developments is unnecessary, unwise, and inconsistent with the Fourth Amendment.

I

There is no need for the Court to craft a new rule to decide this case, as it is controlled by established principles from our Fourth Amendment jurisprudence. One of those core principles, of course, is that "searches and seizures *inside a home* without a warrant are presumptively unreasonable." Payton v. New York (1980) (emphasis added). But it is equally well settled that searches and seizures of property in plain view are presumptively reasonable. See id. at 586–587.[2] Whether that property is residential or commercial, the basic principle is the same: " 'What a person knowingly exposes to the public, even in his own home or office, is not a subject of Fourth Amendment protection.' " California v. Ciraolo (1986) (quoting Katz v. United States (1967)); see Florida v. Riley (1989); California v. Greenwood (1988); Dow Chemical Co. v. United States (1986); Air Pollution Variance Bd. of Colo. v. Western Alfalfa Corp. (1974). That is the principle implicated here.

While the Court "takes the long view" and decides this case based largely on the potential of yet-to-be-developed technology that might allow "through-the-wall surveillance," this case involves nothing more than off-the-wall surveillance by law enforcement officers to gather information exposed to the general public from the outside of petitioner's home. All that the infrared camera did in this case was passively measure heat emitted from the exterior surfaces of petitioner's home; all that those measurements showed were relative differences in emission levels, vaguely indicating that some areas of the roof and outside walls were warmer than others. As still images from the infrared scans show, no details regarding the interior of petitioner's home were revealed. Unlike an x-ray scan, or other possible "through-the-wall" techniques, the detection of infrared radiation emanating from the home did not accomplish "an unauthorized physical penetration into the premises," Silverman v. United States (1961), nor did

1. After an evidentiary hearing, the District Court found:

"The use of the thermal imaging device here was not an intrusion into Kyllo's home. No intimate details of the home were observed, and there was no intrusion upon the privacy of the individuals within the home. The device used cannot penetrate walls or windows to reveal conversations or human activities. The device recorded only the heat being emitted from the home." Supp. App. to Pet. for Cert. 40.

2. Thus, for example, we have found consistent with the Fourth Amendment, even absent a warrant, the search and seizure of garbage left for collection outside the curtilage of a home, California v. *Greenwood*, 486 U.S. 35, 108 S. Ct. 1625 (1988); the aerial surveillance of a fenced-in backyard from an altitude of 1,000 feet, *California v. Ciraolo* (1986); the aerial observation of a partially exposed interior of a residential greenhouse from 400 feet above, *Florida v. Riley*, 488 U.S. 445, 109 S. Ct. 693 (1989); the aerial photography of an industrial complex from several thousand feet above, *Dow Chemical Co.* v. *United States*, 476 U.S. 227, 106 S. Ct. 1819 (1986); and the observation of smoke emanating from chimney stacks, *Air Pollution Variance Bd. of Colo. v. Western Alfalfa Corp.*, 416 U.S. 861, 94 S. Ct. 2114 (1974).

it "obtain information that it could not have obtained by observation from outside the curtilage of the house," United States v. Karo (1984).

Indeed, the ordinary use of the senses might enable a neighbor or passerby to notice the heat emanating from a building, particularly if it is vented, as was the case here. Additionally, any member of the public might notice that one part of a house is warmer than another part or a nearby building if, for example, rainwater evaporates or snow melts at different rates across its surfaces. Such use of the senses would not convert into an unreasonable search if, instead, an adjoining neighbor allowed an officer onto her property to verify her perceptions with a sensitive thermometer. Nor, in my view, does such observation become an unreasonable search if made from a distance with the aid of a device that merely discloses that the exterior of one house, or one area of the house, is much warmer than another. Nothing more occurred in this case.

Thus, the notion that heat emissions from the outside of a dwelling is a private matter implicating the protections of the Fourth Amendment (the text of which guarantees the right of people "to be secure *in* their ... houses" against unreasonable searches and seizures (emphasis added)) is not only unprecedented but also quite difficult to take seriously. Heat waves, like aromas that are generated in a kitchen, or in a laboratory or opium den, enter the public domain if and when they leave a building. A subjective expectation that they would remain private is not only implausible but also surely not "one that society is prepared to recognize as 'reasonable.' " *Katz*, 389 U.S. at 361 (Harlan, J., concurring).

To be sure, the homeowner has a reasonable expectation of privacy concerning what takes place within the home, and the Fourth Amendment's protection against physical invasions of the home should apply to their functional equivalent. But the equipment in this case did not penetrate the walls of petitioner's home, and while it did pick up "details of the home" that were exposed to the public, it did not obtain "any information regarding the *interior* of the home," (emphasis added). In the Court's own words, based on what the thermal imager "showed" regarding the outside of petitioner's home, the officers "concluded" that petitioner was engaging in illegal activity inside the home. It would be quite absurd to characterize their thought processes as "searches," regardless of whether they inferred (rightly) that petitioner was growing marijuana in his house, or (wrongly) that "the lady of the house [was taking] her daily sauna and bath." In either case, the only conclusions the officers reached concerning the interior of the home were at least as indirect as those that might have been inferred from the contents of discarded garbage, see California v. Greenwood (1988), or pen register data, see Smith v. Maryland (1979), or, as in this case, subpoenaed utility records, see 190 F.3d 1041, 1043 (C.A.9 1999). For the first time in its history, the Court assumes that an inference can amount to a Fourth Amendment violation.[3]

3. Although the Court credits us with the "novel proposition that inference insulates a search," our point simply is that an inference cannot *be* a search, contrary to the Court's reasoning. Thus, the Court's use of United States v. Karo, 468 U.S. 705, 104 S. Ct. 3296 (1984), to refute a point we do not make underscores the fact that the Court has no real answer (either in logic or in law) to the point we do make. Of course, *Karo* itself

Notwithstanding the implications of today's decision, there is a strong public interest in avoiding constitutional litigation over the monitoring of emissions from homes, and over the inferences drawn from such monitoring. Just as "the police cannot reasonably be expected to avert their eyes from evidence of criminal activity that could have been observed by any member of the public," *Greenwood*, so too public officials should not have to avert their senses or their equipment from detecting emissions in the public domain such as excessive heat, traces of smoke, suspicious odors, odorless gases, airborne particulates, or radioactive emissions, any of which could identify hazards to the community. In my judgment, monitoring such emissions with "sense-enhancing technology," and drawing useful conclusions from such monitoring, is an entirely reasonable public service.

On the other hand, the countervailing privacy interest is at best trivial. After all, homes generally are insulated to keep heat in, rather than to prevent the detection of heat going out, and it does not seem to me that society will suffer from a rule requiring the rare homeowner who both intends to engage in uncommon activities that produce extraordinary amounts of heat, and wishes to conceal that production from outsiders, to make sure that the surrounding area is well insulated.... The interest in concealing the heat escaping from one's house pales in significance to the "the chief evil against which the wording of the Fourth Amendment is directed," the "physical entry of the home," and it is hard to believe that it is an interest the Framers sought to protect in our Constitution.

Since what was involved in this case was nothing more than drawing inferences from off-the-wall surveillance, rather than any "through-the-wall" surveillance, the officers' conduct did not amount to a search and was perfectly reasonable.

II

Instead of trying to answer the question whether the use of the thermal imager in this case was even arguably unreasonable, the Court has fashioned a rule that is intended to provide essential guidance for the day when "more sophisticated systems" gain the "ability to 'see' through walls and other opaque barriers." The newly minted rule encompasses "obtaining [1] by sense-enhancing technology [2] any information regarding the interior of the home [3] that could not otherwise have been obtained without physical intrusion into a constitutionally protected area ... [4] at least where (as here) the technology in question is not in general public use." In my judgment, the Court's new rule is at once too broad and too narrow, and is not justified by the Court's explanation for its adoption. As I have suggested, I would not erect a constitutional impediment to the use of sense-enhancing technology unless it provides its user with the functional equivalent of actual presence in the area being searched.

does not provide any support for the Court's view that inferences can amount to unconstitutional searches. The illegality in that case was "the monitoring of a beeper in a private residence" to obtain information that "could not have been obtained by observation from outside," id. at 714–715, rather than any thought processes that flowed from such monitoring.

Despite the Court's attempt to draw a line that is "not only firm but also bright," the contours of its new rule are uncertain because its protection apparently dissipates as soon as the relevant technology is "in general public use". Yet how much use is general public use is not even hinted at by the Court's opinion, which makes the somewhat doubtful assumption that the thermal imager used in this case does not satisfy that criterion.[5] In any event, putting aside its lack of clarity, this criterion is somewhat perverse because it seems likely that the threat to privacy will grow, rather than recede, as the use of intrusive equipment becomes more readily available.

It is clear, however, that the category of "sense-enhancing technology" covered by the new rule, is far too broad. It would, for example, embrace potential mechanical substitutes for dogs trained to react when they sniff narcotics. But in United States v. Place (1983), we held that a dog sniff that "discloses only the presence or absence of narcotics" does "not constitute a 'search' within the meaning of the Fourth Amendment," and it must follow that sense-enhancing equipment that identifies nothing but illegal activity is not a search either. Nevertheless, the use of such a device would be unconstitutional under the Court's rule, as would the use of other new devices that might detect the odor of deadly bacteria or chemicals for making a new type of high explosive, even if the devices (like the dog sniffs) are "so limited in both the manner in which" they obtain information and "in the content of the information" they reveal. If nothing more than that sort of information could be obtained by using the devices in a public place to monitor emissions from a house, then their use would be no more objectionable than the use of the thermal imager in this case.

The application of the Court's new rule to "any information regarding the interior of the home," is also unnecessarily broad. If it takes sensitive equipment to detect an odor that identifies criminal conduct and nothing else, the fact that the odor emanates from the interior of a home should not provide it with constitutional protection. The criterion, moreover, is too sweeping in that information "regarding" the interior of a home apparently is not just information obtained through its walls, but also information concerning the outside of the building that could lead to (however many) inferences "regarding" what might be inside. Under that expansive view, I suppose, an officer using an infrared camera to observe a man silently entering the side door of a house at night carrying a pizza might conclude that its interior is now occupied by someone who likes pizza, and by doing so the officer would be guilty of conducting an unconstitutional "search" of the home.

Because the new rule applies to information regarding the "interior" of the home, it is too narrow as well as too broad. Clearly, a rule that is

5. The record describes a device that numbers close to a thousand manufactured units; that has a predecessor numbering in the neighborhood of 4,000 to 5,000 units; that competes with a similar product numbering from 5,000 to 6,000 units; and that is "readily available to the public" for commercial, personal, or law enforcement purposes, and is just an 800–number away from being rented from "half a dozen national companies" by anyone who wants one. App. 18. Since, by virtue of the Court's new rule, the issue is one of first impression, perhaps it should order an evidentiary hearing to determine whether these facts suffice to establish "general public use."

designed to protect individuals from the overly intrusive use of sense-enhancing equipment should not be limited to a home. If such equipment did provide its user with the functional equivalent of access to a private place—such as, for example, the telephone booth involved in *Katz*, or an office building—then the rule should apply to such an area as well as to a home. See *Katz*, 389 U.S. at 351 ("The Fourth Amendment protects people, not places").

The final requirement of the Court's new rule, that the information "could not otherwise have been obtained without physical intrusion into a constitutionally protected area," also extends too far as the Court applies it. As noted, the Court effectively treats the mental process of analyzing data obtained from external sources as the equivalent of a physical intrusion into the home. As I have explained, however, the process of drawing inferences from data in the public domain should not be characterized as a search.

The two reasons advanced by the Court as justifications for the adoption of its new rule are both unpersuasive. First, the Court suggests that its rule is compelled by our holding in *Katz*, because in that case, as in this, the surveillance consisted of nothing more than the monitoring of waves emanating from a private area into the public domain. Yet there are critical differences between the cases. In *Katz*, the electronic listening device attached to the outside of the phone booth allowed the officers to pick up the content of the conversation inside the booth, making them the functional equivalent of intruders because they gathered information that was otherwise available only to someone inside the private area; it would be as if, in this case, the thermal imager presented a view of the heat-generating activity inside petitioner's home. By contrast, the thermal imager here disclosed only the relative amounts of heat radiating from the house; it would be as if, in *Katz*, the listening device disclosed only the relative volume of sound leaving the booth, which presumably was discernible in the public domain.[6] Surely, there is a significant difference between the general and well-settled expectation that strangers will not have direct access to the contents of private communications, on the one hand, and the rather theoretical expectation that an occasional homeowner would even care if anybody noticed the relative amounts of heat emanating from the walls of his house, on the other. It is pure hyperbole for the Court to suggest that refusing to extend the holding of *Katz* to this case would leave the homeowner at the mercy of "technology that could discern all human activity in the home."

Second, the Court argues that the permissibility of "through-the-wall surveillance" cannot depend on a distinction between observing "intimate details" such as "the lady of the house [taking] her daily sauna and bath," and noticing only "the nonintimate rug on the vestibule floor" or "objects no smaller than 36 by 36 inches." This entire argument assumes, of course, that the thermal imager in this case could or did perform "through-the-

6. The use of the latter device would be constitutional given *Smith v. Maryland*, 442 U.S. 735, 741, 99 S. Ct. 2577 (1979), which upheld the use of pen registers to record numbers dialed on a phone because, unlike "the listening device employed in *Katz* … pen registers do not acquire the *contents* of communications."

wall surveillance" that could identify any detail "that would previously have been unknowable without physical intrusion." In fact, the device could not and did not, enable its user to identify either the lady of the house, the rug on the vestibule floor, or anything else inside the house, whether smaller or larger than 36 by 36 inches. Indeed, the vague thermal images of petitioner's home that are reproduced in the Appendix were submitted by him to the District Court as part of an expert report raising the question whether the device could even take "accurate, consistent infrared images" of the *outside* of his house. Defendant's Exhibit 107, p. 4. But even if the device could reliably show extraordinary differences in the amounts of heat leaving his home, drawing the inference that there was something suspicious occurring inside the residence—a conclusion that officers far less gifted than Sherlock Holmes would readily draw—does not qualify as "through-the-wall surveillance," much less a Fourth Amendment violation.

III

Although the Court is properly and commendably concerned about the threats to privacy that may flow from advances in the technology available to the law enforcement profession, it has unfortunately failed to heed the tried and true counsel of judicial restraint. Instead of concentrating on the rather mundane issue that is actually presented by the case before it, the Court has endeavored to craft an all-encompassing rule for the future. It would be far wiser to give legislators an unimpeded opportunity to grapple with these emerging issues rather than to shackle them with prematurely devised constitutional constraints.

I respectfully dissent.

C. PROBABLE CAUSE

Generally, probable cause is a prerequisite for a search or seizure to be valid. For a warrant to be valid, it must be based upon probable cause. This is part of the Fourth Amendment itself. The standard is also used as a measure for the validity of a number of permissible warrantless police actions and it is the standard a Grand Jury uses to issue an indictment.

A precise definition of probable cause is hard to come by. Probable cause requires a finding that "a crime has been committed and this person committed it." But who is the person by which we measure probable cause? A reasonable person? A prudent person? A reasonable police officer? Is the test "whether these historical facts, viewed from the standpoint of an objectively reasonable police officer, amount to probable cause."[1] The definition necessarily focuses on probabilities. "In dealing with probable cause, however, as the very name implies, we deal with probabilities. These are not technical; they are the factual and practical considerations of everyday life on which reasonable and prudent men, not legal technicians, act. The standard of proof is accordingly correlative to what must be

1. Ornelas v. United States, 517 U.S. 690, 696, 116 S.Ct. 1657 (1996).

proved."[2] How much probability is required? Probable cause certainly requires more than a reasonable suspicion, but it need not rise to the standard of beyond a reasonable doubt.

The content of probable cause has gained more elasticity over the years.[3] The *Aguilar–Spinelli* test set by the Warren Court required a two prong inquiry: the basis of knowledge and veracity.[4] The Supreme Court has since rejected that standard and adopted a totality of the circumstances test in Illinois v. Gates.[5] Several states, however, relied on their state constitutions to retain the *Aguilar-Spinelli* standard. As you read the following materials, ask yourself which test is better suited to guiding the police and insuring that their actions are proper? Which test makes it easier for law enforcement to act within the confines of the Constitution? Herbert Packer once posited two theoretical models for the criminal justice system: the crime control model, which emphasizes maintaining societal order, and the due process model, which emphasizes protecting individual rights.[6]

Aguilar v. Texas

Supreme Court of the United States, 1964.
378 U.S. 108, 84 S.Ct. 1509.

■ JUSTICE GOLDBERG delivered the opinion of the Court:

This case presents questions concerning the constitutional requirements for obtaining a state search warrant.

Two Houston police officers applied to a local Justice of the Peace for a warrant to search for narcotics in petitioner's home. In support of their application, the officers submitted an affidavit which, in relevant part, recited that:

> "Affiants have received reliable information from a credible person and do believe that heroin, marijuana, barbiturates and other narcotics and narcotic paraphernalia are being kept at the above described premises for the purpose of sale and use contrary to the provisions of the law."[1]

2. Brinegar v. United States, 338 U.S. 160, 69 S.Ct. 1302 (1949).

3. A brief history of the probable cause concept may be found at Joseph D. Grano, "Probable Cause and Common Sense: A Reply to the Critics of Illinois v. Gates," 17 U. Mich. J.L. Reform 465 (1984).

4. Put simply, how did the informant know what he says he knows and can we believe him.

5. Some commentators viewed the totality of circumstances test of Gates as "nothing new." See Joseph D. Grano, "Probable Cause and Common Sense, A Reply to Critics of Illinois v. Gates," 17 U.Mich.J.L. Reform 465 (1984).

6. *See* HERBERT L. PACKER, THE LIMITS OF THE CRIMINAL SANCTION 149–246 (1968); Herbert L. Packer, *Two Models of the Criminal Process*, 113 U. PA. L. REV. 1 (1964). This dichotomy has been questioned. See e.g. Mirjan Damaska, *Structures of Authority and Comparative Criminal Procedure*, 84 YALE L.J. 480 (1975); Mirjan Damaska, *Evidentiary Barriers to Conviction and Two Models of Criminal Procedure: A Comparative Study*, 121 U. PA. L. REV. 506 (1973).

1. The record does not reveal, nor is it claimed, that any other information was brought to the attention of the Justice of the Peace. It is elementary that in passing on the validity of a warrant, the reviewing court may consider *only* information brought to the magistrate's attention.

* * *

The search warrant was issued. . . .

At his trial in the state court, petitioner, through his attorney, objected to the introduction of evidence obtained as a result of the execution of the warrant. The objections were overruled and the evidence admitted. Petitioner was convicted of illegal possession of heroin and sentenced to serve 20 years in the state penitentiary. . . .

An evaluation of the constitutionality of a search warrant should begin with the rule that "the informed and deliberate determinations of magistrates empowered to issue warrants ... are to be preferred over the hurried action of officers ... who may happen to make arrests." [cite omitted] The reasons for this rule go to the foundations of the Fourth Amendment. A contrary rule "that evidence sufficient to support a magistrate's disinterested determination to issue a search warrant will justify the officers in making a search without a warrant would reduce the Amendment to a nullity and leave the people's homes secure only in the discretion of police officers." [cite omitted] Under such a rule "resort to [warrants] would ultimately be discouraged." [cite omitted] Thus, when a search is based upon a magistrate's, rather than a police officer's, determination of probable cause, the reviewing courts will accept evidence of a less "judicially competent or persuasive character than would have justified an officer in acting on his own without a warrant," [cite omitted], and will sustain the judicial determination so long as "there was substantial basis for [the magistrate] to conclude that narcotics were probably present. . . ." [cite omitted]. As so well stated by Mr. Justice Jackson: "The point of the Fourth Amendment, which often is not grasped by zealous officers, is not that it denies law enforcement the support of the usual inferences which reasonable men draw from evidence. Its protection consists in requiring that those inferences be drawn by a neutral and detached magistrate instead of being judged by the officer engaged in the often competitive enterprise of ferreting out crime." Johnson v. United States(1948). Although the reviewing court will pay substantial deference to judicial determinations of probable cause, the court must still insist that the magistrate perform his "neutral and detached" function and not serve merely as a rubber stamp for the police.

In Nathanson v. United States (1933), a warrant was issued upon the sworn allegation that the affiant "has cause to suspect and does believe" that certain merchandise was in a specified location. The Court, noting that the affidavit "went upon a mere affirmation of suspicion and belief *without any statement of adequate supporting facts*," (emphasis added) announced the following rule:

> Under the Fourth Amendment, an officer may not properly issue a warrant to search a private dwelling unless he can find probable cause therefor from facts or circumstances presented to him under oath or affirmation. Mere affirmance of belief or suspicion is not enough.

The Court, in Giordenello v. United States (1958), applied this rule to an affidavit similar to that relied upon here. Affiant in that case swore that petitioner "did receive, conceal, etc., narcotic drugs ... with knowledge of unlawful importation...." The Court announced the guiding principles to be:

> that the inferences from the facts which lead to the complaint "[must] be drawn by a neutral and detached magistrate instead of being judged by the officer engaged in the often competitive enterprise of ferreting out crime." Johnson v. United States, 333 U.S. 10, 14, 68 S.Ct. 367, 369. The purpose of the complaint, then, is to enable the appropriate magistrate ... to determine whether the "probable cause" required to support a warrant exists. The Commissioner must judge for himself the persuasiveness of the facts relied on by a complaining officer to show probable cause. He should not accept without question the complainant's mere conclusion....

The Court, applying these principles to the complaint in that case, stated that:

> it is clear that it does not pass muster because it does not provide any basis for the Commissioner's determination ... that probable cause existed. The complaint contains no affirmative allegation that the affiant spoke with personal knowledge of the matters contained therein; it does not indicate any sources for the complainant's belief; and it does not set forth any other sufficient basis upon which a finding of probable cause could be made.

The vice in the present affidavit is at least as great as in Nathanson and Giordenello. Here the "mere conclusion" that petitioner possessed narcotics was not even that of the affiant himself; it was that of an unidentified informant. The affidavit here not only "contains no affirmative allegation that the affiant spoke with personal knowledge of the matters contained therein," it does not even contain an "affirmative allegation" that the affiant's unidentified source "spoke with personal knowledge." For all that appears, the source here merely suspected, believed or concluded that there were narcotics in petitioner's possession.[2] The magistrate here certainly could not "judge for himself the persuasiveness of the facts relied on ... to show probable cause." He necessarily accepted—without question—the informant's "suspicion," "belief" or "mere conclusion."

Although an affidavit may be based on hearsay information and need not reflect the direct personal observations of the affiant (cites omitted), the magistrate must be informed of some of the underlying circumstances from which the informant concluded that the narcotics were where he claimed they were, and some of the underlying circumstances from which the officer concluded that the informant, whose identity need not be disclosed was "credible" or his information "reliable." Otherwise, "the inferences from the facts which lead to the complaint" will be drawn not

2. To approve this affidavit would open the door to easy circumvention of the rule announced in Nathanson and Giordenello. A police officer who arrived at the "suspicion," "belief" or "mere conclusion" that narcotics were in someone's possession could not obtain a warrant. But he could convey this conclusion to another police officer, who could then secure the warrant by swearing that he had "received reliable information from a credible person" that the narcotics were in someone's possession.

"by a neutral and detached magistrate," as the Constitution requires, but instead, by a police officer "engaged in the often competitive enterprise of ferreting out crime," Giordenello v. United States; or, as in this case, by an unidentified informant.

We conclude, therefore, that the search warrant should not have been issued because the affidavit did not provide a sufficient basis for a finding of probable cause and that the evidence obtained as a result of the search warrant was inadmissible in petitioner's trial.

* * *

Spinelli v. United States

Supreme Court of the United States, 1969.
393 U.S. 410, 89 S.Ct. 584.

■ JUSTICE HARLAN delivered the opinion of the Court.

William Spinelli was convicted under 18 U.S.C. § 1952 of traveling to St. Louis, Missouri, from a nearby Illinois suburb with the intention of conducting gambling activities proscribed by Missouri law.... At every appropriate stage in the proceedings in the lower courts, the petitioner challenged the constitutionality of the warrant which authorized the FBI search that uncovered the evidence necessary for his conviction....

In *Aguilar*, a search warrant had issued upon an affidavit of police officers who swore only that they had "received reliable information from a credible person and do believe" that narcotics were being illegally stored on the described premises. While recognizing that the constitutional requirement of probable cause can be satisfied by hearsay information, this Court held the affidavit inadequate for two reasons. First, the application failed to set forth any of the "underlying circumstances" necessary to enable the magistrate independently to judge of the validity of the informant's conclusion that the narcotics were where he said they were. Second, the affiant-officers did not attempt to support their claim that their informant was " 'credible' or his information 'reliable.' " ...

In essence, the affidavit ... contained the following allegations:

1. The FBI had kept track of Spinelli's movements on five days during the month of August 1965. On four of these occasions, Spinelli was seen crossing one of two bridges leading from Illinois into St. Louis, Missouri, between 11 a.m. and 12:15 p.m. On four of the five days, Spinelli was also seen parking his car in a lot used by residents of an apartment house at 1108 Indian Circle Drive in St. Louis, between 3:30 p.m. and 4:45 p.m. On one day, Spinelli was followed further and seen to enter a particular apartment in the building.

2. An FBI check with the telephone company revealed that this apartment contained two telephones listed under the name of Grace P. Hagen, and carrying the numbers WYdown 4–0029 and WYdown 4–0136.

3. The application stated that "William Spinelli is known to this affiant and to federal law enforcement agents and local law enforcement agents as a bookmaker, an associate of bookmakers, a gambler, and an associate of gamblers."

4. Finally it was stated that the FBI "has been informed by a confidential reliable informant that William Spinelli is operating a handbook and accepting wagers and disseminating wagering information by means of the telephones which have been assigned the numbers WYdown 4–0029 and WYdown 4–0136."

There can be no question that the last item mentioned, detailing the informant's tip, has a fundamental place in this warrant application. Without it, probable cause could not be established. The first two items reflect only innocent-seeming activity and data. Spinelli's travels to and from the apartment building and his entry into a particular apartment on one occasion could hardly be taken as bespeaking gambling activity; and there is surely nothing unusual about an apartment containing two separate telephones. Many a householder indulges himself in this petty luxury. Finally, the allegation that Spinelli was "known" to the affiant and to other federal and local law enforcement officers as a gambler and an associate of gamblers is but a bald and unilluminating assertion of suspicion that is entitled to no weight in appraising the magistrate's decision. Nathanson v. United States (1933).

So much indeed the Government does not deny. Rather, following the reasoning of the Court of Appeals, the Government claims that the informant's tip gives a suspicious color to the FBI's reports detailing Spinelli's innocent-seeming conduct and that, conversely, the FBI's surveillance corroborates the informant's tip, thereby entitling it to more weight. It is true, of course, that the magistrate is obligated to render a judgment based upon a commonsense reading of the entire affidavit. United States v. Ventresca, 380 U.S. 102, 85 S.Ct. 741 (1964). We believe, however, that the "totality of circumstances" approach taken by the Court of Appeals paints with too broad a brush. Where, as here, the informer's tip is a necessary element in a finding of probable cause its proper weight must be determined by a more precise analysis.

The informer's report must first be measured against *Aguilar*'s standards so that its probative value can be assessed. If the tip is found inadequate under *Aguilar*, the other allegations which corroborate the information contained in the hearsay report should then be considered. At this stage as well, however, the standards enunciated in *Aguilar* must inform the magistrate's decision. He must ask: Can it fairly be said that the tip, even when certain parts of it have been corroborated by independent sources, is as trustworthy as a tip which would pass *Aguilar*'s tests without independent corroboration? *Aguilar* is relevant at this stage of the inquiry as well because the tests it establishes were designed to implement the long-standing principle that probable cause must be determined by a "neutral and detached magistrate," and not by "the officer engaged in the often competitive enterprise of ferreting out crime." A magistrate cannot be said to have properly discharged his constitutional duty if he relies on an informer's tip which "even when partially corroborated" is not as reliable as one which passes *Aguilar*'s requirements when standing alone.

Applying these principles to the present case, we first consider the weight to be given the informer's tip when it is considered apart from the rest of the affidavit. It is clear that a Commissioner could not credit it without abdicating his constitutional function. Though the affiant swore that his confidant was "reliable," he offered the magistrate no reason in support of this conclusion. Perhaps even more important is the fact that *Aguilar*'s other test has not been satisfied. The tip does not contain a sufficient statement of the underlying circumstances from which the informer concluded that Spinelli was running a bookmaking operation. We are not told how the FBI's source received his information—it is not alleged that the informant personally observed Spinelli at work or that he had ever placed a bet with him. Moreover, if the informant came by the information indirectly, he did not explain why his sources were reliable. In the absence of a statement detailing the manner in which the information was gathered, it is especially important that the tip describe the accused's criminal activity in sufficient detail so that the magistrate may know that he is relying on something more substantial than a casual rumor circulating in the underworld or an accusation based merely on an individual's general reputation.

Nor do we believe that the patent doubts *Aguilar* raises as to the report's reliability are adequately resolved by a consideration of the allegations detailing the FBI's independent investigative efforts. At most, these allegations indicated that Spinelli could have used the telephones specified by the informant for some purpose. This cannot by itself be said to support both the inference that the informer was generally trustworthy and that he had made his charge against Spinelli on the basis of information obtained in a reliable way. Once again, *Draper* provides a relevant comparison. Independent police work in that case corroborated much more than one small detail that had been provided by the informant. There, the police, upon greeting the inbound Denver train on the second morning specified by informer Hereford, saw a man whose dress corresponded precisely to Hereford's detailed description. It was then apparent that the informant had not been fabricating his report out of whole cloth; since the report was of the sort which in common experience may be recognized as having been obtained in a reliable way, it was perfectly clear that probable cause had been established.

We conclude, then, that in the present case the informant's tip—even when corroborated to the extent indicated—was not sufficient to provide the basis for a finding of probable cause. This is not to say that the tip was so insubstantial that it could not properly have counted in the magistrate's determination. Rather, it needed some further support. When we look to the other parts of the application, however, we find nothing alleged which would permit the suspicions engendered by the informant's report to ripen into a judgment that a crime was probably being committed. As we have already seen, the allegations detailing the FBI's surveillance of Spinelli and its investigation of the telephone company records contain no suggestion of criminal conduct when taken by themselves—and they are not endowed with an aura of suspicion by virtue of the informer's tip. Nor do we find that the FBI's reports take on a sinister color when read in light of common knowledge that bookmaking is often carried on over the telephone and from premises ostensibly used by others for perfectly normal purposes. Such an argument would carry weight in a situation in which the premises contain an unusual number of telephones or abnormal activity is observed but it does not fit this case where neither of these factors is present. All that remains to be considered is the flat statement that Spinelli was "known" to the FBI and others as a gambler. But just as a simple assertion of police suspicion is not itself a sufficient basis for a magistrate's finding of probable cause, we do not believe it may be used to give additional weight to allegations that would otherwise be insufficient.

The affidavit, then, falls short of the standards set forth in *Aguilar*, *Draper*, and our other decisions that give content to the notion of probable cause.... But we cannot sustain this warrant without diluting important safeguards that assure that the judgment of a disinterested judicial officer will interpose itself between the police and the citizenry ...

■ JUSTICE MARSHALL took no part in the consideration or decision of this case.

■ JUSTICE WHITE, concurring.

.... What is missing in Nathanson and like cases is a statement of the basis for the affiant's believing the facts contained in the affidavit "the good cause" which the officer in Nathanson said he had. If an officer swears that there is gambling equipment at a certain address, the possibilities are (1) that he has seen the equipment; (2) that he has observed or perceived facts from which the presence of the equipment may reasonably be inferred; and (3) that he has obtained the information from someone else. If (1) is true, the affidavit is good. But in (2), the affidavit is insufficient unless the perceived facts are given, for it is the magistrate, not the officer, who is to judge the existence of probable cause. With respect to (3), where the officer's information is hearsay, no warrant should issue absent good cause for crediting that hearsay. Because an affidavit asserting, without more, the location of gambling equipment at a particular address does not claim personal observation of any of the facts by the officer, and because of the likelihood that the information came from an unidentified third party, affidavits of this type are unacceptable.

Neither should the warrant issue if the officer states that there is gambling equipment in a particular apartment and that his information comes from an informant, named or unnamed, since the honesty of the informant and the basis for his report are unknown. Nor would the missing elements be completely supplied by the officer's oath that the informant has often furnished reliable information in the past. This attests to the honesty of the informant, but Aguilar v. Texas requires something more—did the information come from observation, or did the informant in turn receive it from another? Absent additional facts for believing the informant's report, his assertion stands no better than the oath of the officer to the same effect. Indeed, if the affidavit of an officer, known by the magistrate to be honest and experienced, stating that gambling equipment is located in a certain building is unacceptable, it would be quixotic if a similar statement from an honest informant were found to furnish probable cause. A strong argument can be made that both should be acceptable under the Fourth Amendment, but under our cases neither is. The past reliability of the informant can no more furnish probable cause for believing his current report than can previous experience with the officer himself.

If the affidavit rests on hearsay—an informant's report—what is necessary under *Aguilar* is one of two things: the informant must declare either (1) that he has himself seen or perceived the fact or facts asserted; or (2) that his information is hearsay, but there is good reason for believing it—perhaps one of the usual grounds for crediting hearsay information. The first presents few problems: since the report, although hearsay, purports to be first-hand observation, remaining doubt centers on the honesty of the informant, and that worry is dissipated by the officer's previous experience with the informant. The other basis for accepting the informant's report is more complicated. But if, for example, the informer's hearsay comes from one of the actors in the crime in the nature of admission against interest, the affidavit giving this information should be held sufficient.

I am inclined to agree with the majority that there are limited special circumstances in which an "honest" informant's report, if sufficiently detailed, will in effect verify itself—that is, the magistrate when confronted with such detail could reasonably infer that the informant had gained his information in a reliable way. Detailed information may sometimes imply that the informant himself has observed the facts. Suppose an informant with whom an officer has had satisfactory experience states that there is gambling equipment in the living room of a specified apartment and describes in detail not only the equipment itself but the appointments and furnishments in the apartment. Detail like this, if true at all must rest on personal observation of either the informant or of someone else. If the latter, we know nothing of the third person's honesty or sources; he may be fabricating a wholly false report. But it is arguable that on these facts it was the informant himself who has perceived the facts, for the information reported is not usually the subject of casual day-to-day conversation. Because the informant is honest and it is probable that he has viewed the facts, there is probable cause for the issuance of a warrant....

■ Justice Black, dissenting (joined by Stewart and Fortas)

In my view, this Court's decision in Aguilar v. Texas (1964), was bad enough. That decision went very far toward elevating the magistrate's hearing for issuance of a search warrant to a full-fledged trial, where witnesses must be brought forward to attest personally to all the facts alleged. But not content with this, the Court today expands *Aguilar* to almost unbelievable proportions. Of course, it would strengthen the probable-cause presentation if eyewitnesses could testify that they saw the defendant commit the crime. It would be stronger still if these witnesses could explain in detail the nature of the sensual perceptions on which they based their "conclusion" that the person they had seen was the defendant and that he was responsible for the events they observed. Nothing in our Constitution, however, requires that the facts be established with that degree of certainty and with such elaborate specificity before a policeman can be authorized by a disinterested magistrate to conduct a carefully limited search.

The Fourth Amendment provides that "no Warrants shall issue, but upon probable cause, supported by Oath or affirmation, and particularly describing the place to be searched, and the persons or things to be seized." In this case a search warrant was issued supported by an oath and particularly describing the place to be searched and the things to be seized. The supporting oath was three printed pages and the full text of it is included in an Appendix to the Court's opinion. The magistrate, I think properly, held the information set forth sufficient facts to show "probable cause" that the defendant was violating the law. Six members of the Court of Appeals also agreed that the affidavit was sufficient to show probable cause. A majority of this Court today holds, however, that the magistrate and all of these judges were wrong. In doing so, they substitute their own opinion for that of the local magistrate and the circuit judges, and reject the *en banc* factual conclusion of the Eighth Circuit and reverse the judgment based upon that factual conclusion. I cannot join in any such disposition of an issue so vital to the administration of justice, and dissent as vigorously as I can.

I repeat my belief that the affidavit given the magistrate was more than ample to show probable cause of the petitioner's guilt. The affidavit meticulously set out facts sufficient to show the following:

1. The petitioner had been shown going to and coming from a room in an apartment which contained two telephones listed under the name of another person. Nothing in the record indicates that the apartment was of that large and luxurious type which could only be occupied by a person to whom it would be a "petty luxury" to have two separate telephones, with different numbers, both listed under the name of a person who did not live there.

2. The petitioner's car had been observed parked in the apartment's parking lot. This fact was, of course, highly relevant in showing that the petitioner was extremely interested in some enterprise which was located in the apartment.

3. The FBI had been informed by a reliable informant that the petitioner was accepting wagering information by telephones—the particular telephones located in the apartment the defendant had been repeatedly visiting. Unless the Court, going beyond the requirements of the Fourth Amendment, wishes to require magistrates to hold trials before issuing warrants, it is not necessary—as the Court holds—to have the affiant explain "the underlying circumstances from which the informer concluded that Spinelli was running a bookmaking operation."

4. The petitioner was known by federal and local law enforcement agents as a bookmaker and an associate of gamblers. I cannot agree with the Court that this knowledge was only a "bald and unilluminating assertion of suspicion that is entitled to no weight in appraising the magistrate's decision." Although the

> statement is hearsay that might not be admissible in a regular trial, everyone knows, unless he shuts his eyes to the realities of life, that this is a relevant fact which, together with other circumstances, might indicate a factual probability that gambling is taking place.

The foregoing facts should be enough to constitute probable cause for anyone who does not believe that the only way to obtain a search warrant is to prove beyond a reasonable doubt that a defendant is guilty. Even *Aguilar*, on which the Court relies, cannot support the contrary result, at least as that decision was written before today's massive escalation of it. In *Aguilar* the Court dealt with an affidavit that stated only:

> "Affiants have received reliable information from a credible person and do believe that heroin. and other narcotics and narcotic paraphernalia are being kept at the above described premises for the purpose of sale and use contrary to the provisions of the law." 378 U.S., at 109. The Court held, over the dissent of Mr. Justice Clark, Mr. Justice Stewart, and myself, that this unsupported conclusion of an unidentified informant provided no basis for the magistrate to make an independent judgment as to the persuasiveness of the facts relied upon to show probable cause. Here, of course, we have much more, and the Court in *Aguilar* was careful to point out that additional information of the kind presented in the affidavit before us now would be highly relevant:
>
> "If the fact and results of such a surveillance had been appropriately presented to the magistrate, this would, of course, present an entirely different case." 378 U.S., at 109, n. 1.

In the present case even the two-judge minority of the court below recognized, as this Court seems to recognize today, that this additional information took the case beyond the rule of *Aguilar*. Six of the other circuit judges disagreed with the two dissenting judges, finding that all the circumstances considered together could support a reasonable judgment that gambling probably was taking place. I fully agree with this carefully considered opinion of the court below.

I regret to say I consider today's decision an indefensible departure from the principles of our former cases. Less than four years ago we reaffirmed these principles in United States v. Ventresca, 380 U.S. 102, 108 (1965): "If the teachings of the Court's cases are to be followed and the constitutional policy served, affidavits for search warrants ... must be tested and interpreted by magistrates and courts in a commonsense and realistic fashion.... Technical requirements of elaborate specificity once exacted under common law pleadings have no proper place in this area." See also *Husty v. United States*, 282 U.S. 694, 700–701 (1931).

Departures of this kind are responsible for considerable uneasiness in our lower courts, and I must say I am deeply troubled by the statements of Judge Gibson in the court below:

> I am, indeed, disturbed by decision after decision of our courts which place increasingly technical burdens upon law enforcement officials. I am disturbed by these decisions that appear to relent-

lessly chip away at the ever narrowing area of effective police operation. I believe the holdings in *Aguilar*, and *Rugendorf v. United States*, 376 U.S. 528 (1964) are sufficient to protect the privacy of individuals from hastily conceived intrusions, and I do not think the limitations and requirements on the issuance of search warrants should be expanded by setting up over-technical requirements approaching the now discarded pitfalls of common law pleadings. Moreover, if we become increasingly technical and rigid in our demands upon police officers, I fear we make it increasingly easy for criminals to operate, detected but unpunished. I feel the significant movement of the law beyond its present state is unwarranted, unneeded, and dangerous to law enforcement efficiency.' (Dissenting from panel opinion.)

The Court of Appeals in this case took a sensible view of the Fourth Amendment, and I would wholeheartedly affirm its decision.

Mapp v. Ohio, decided in 1961, held for the first time that the Fourth Amendment and the exclusionary rule of *Weeks v. United States* (1914) are now applicable to the States. That Amendment provides that search warrants shall not be issued without probable cause. The existence of probable cause is a factual matter that calls for the determination of a factual question. While no statistics are immediately available, questions of probable cause to issue search warrants and to make arrests are doubtless involved in many thousands of cases in state courts. All of those probable-cause state cases are now potentially reviewable by this Court. It is, of course, physically impossible for this Court to review the evidence in all or even a substantial percentage of those cases. Consequently, whether desirable or not, we must inevitably accept most of the fact findings of the state courts, particularly when, as here in a federal case, both the trial and appellate courts have decided the facts the same way. It cannot be said that the trial judge and six members of the Court of Appeals committed flagrant error in finding from evidence that the magistrate had probable cause to issue the search warrant here. It seems to me that this Court would best serve itself and the administration of justice by accepting the judgment of the two courts below. After all, they too are lawyers and judges, and much closer to the practical, everyday affairs of life than we are.

Notwithstanding the Court's belief to the contrary, I think that in holding as it does, the Court does:

> retreat from the established propositions that only the probability, and not a prima facie showing, of criminal activity is the standard of probable cause, *Beck v. Ohio*, 379 U.S. 89, 96 (1964); that affidavits of probable cause are tested by much less rigorous standards than those governing the admissibility of evidence at trial, *McCray v. Illinois*, 386 U.S. 300, 311 (1967); that in judging probable cause issuing magistrates are not to be confined by niggardly limitations or by restrictions on the use of their common sense, *United States v. Ventresca*, 380 U.S. 102, 108 (1965); and that their determination of probable cause should be paid great deference by reviewing courts, *Jones v. United States*, 362 U.S. 257, 270–271 (1960).

In fact, I believe the Court is moving rapidly, through complex analyses and obfuscatory language, toward the holding that no magistrate can issue a warrant unless according to some unknown standard of proof he can be persuaded that the suspect defendant is actually guilty of a crime. I would affirm this conviction.

The separate dissenting opinions by Justices Stewart and Fortas are omitted.

* * *

NOTE

In upholding a search warrant for gambling paraphernalia, Judge Charles Moylan of the Maryland Court of Special Appeals set forth in Dawson v. State, 11 Md.App. 694, 276 A.2d 680 (1971), a thoughtful analysis of probable cause doctrine in the aftermath of *Aguilar* and *Spinelli*:

Moylan, Judge.

* * *

The Dual Analysis of Probable Cause

The existence of probable cause to justify the issuance of either a search and seizure warrant or an arrest warrant may be predicated upon either or both of two broad categories of information—1) the direct observation of the affiant applying for the warrant (or of the affiants on supporting affidavits ... or 2) hearsay information furnished to the affiant by someone else and then recited by the affiant in his affidavit. It is axiomatic that probable cause may be based upon the direct observation of the affiant himself.... It is equally well-established that probable cause may be based upon hearsay information alone and need not reflect the direct personal observation of the affiant.... It follows that probable cause may also be based upon a combination of direct observation and hearsay information.

Confusion somehow manages to creep into the cases, however, where the affidavit offered to support probable cause is based upon the mixed predicate of both direct observation and hearsay information. That confusion is engendered by the failure to grasp the unifying principle—to appreciate that both of the broad categories of information are evaluated by the same general standards of measurement. The apparent difference in the standards is simply one of surface application and not of theoretical significance.

Whether the information being evaluated is the direct observation of the affiant or is hearsay information, the issuing magistrate is required to perform the same intellectual surgery. In determining the existence vel non of probable cause, the magistrate must make two distinct determinations.... He must:

(1) Evaluate the truthfulness of the source of the information; and

(2) Evaluate the adequacy of the factual premises furnished by that source, to support the validity of the source's conclusion.

In the first instance, he is judging the integrity of a person. In the second instance, he is judging the logic of a proposition....

In evaluating the truthfulness of the source of the information, the magistrate is presented with no problem in dealing with the affiant-observer. "The oath affirms the honesty of the statement and negatives the lie or imagination." *Spinelli* (concurring opinion by White, J.). The oath, as a trustworthiness device, establishes, *per se*, the credibility of the affiant-source and, thereby, the reliability of his directly observed information. Where the source of the information, however, is an absent, non-swearing declarant (an informant), the pathway to the establishment of that source's credibility is more circuitous. The issuing magistrate must have, as a substitute for the oath, some other reason to be persuaded of the credibility of the source of the information....

In evaluating the credibility of different types of sources, the practical applications may vary, but the common denominator of all such decisions is that the issuing magistrate must have before him enough circumstances to be able to judge for himself the honesty of the source of the information, whether that source be an affiant, a named non-swearing informant or an unnamed non-swearing informant. The magistrate may no more accept an affiant's assertion that his source (named or unnamed) is credible in lieu of a recitation of facts from which the magistrate may draw that conclusion for himself than he may accept an affiant's assertion that the affiant himself is credible as a substitute for the affiant's taking of the oath. The concluding, in either case, is only for the magistrate.

Once the magistrate has decided that the information is trustworthy, he has still only half completed his ultimate determination. He must still decide what the information is worth. He has decided that the source is not lying; but he has not yet decided whether the source is mistaken. The magistrate's second function is now to evaluate the information which he is accepting as true and to see what probabilities emerge from that available data. Again, he may not accept the conclusion of either the affiant-observer or then on-swearing informant. He must take from either of those sources his facts and then arrive at his own conclusion as to the significance of those facts....

In the case of the affiant-observer, the magistrate cannot accept the affiant's mere conclusion that "A probably committed a crime" or that "B probably contains contraband." The magistrate needs to know what the observations were so that he can conclude for himself whether that observed data persuades him that "A probably committed a crime" or that "B probably contains contraband." ... By the same logic, the magistrate may not accept the nonsworn hearsay conclusion of even a credible informant any more than he may accept the sworn conclusion of a credible affiant-observer.... Again, he needs to know just what the informant saw and just what the informant heard to warrant the informant's conclusion.[3]

3. If the informant himself is offering not direct observation but hearsay twice compounded, the entire evaluation process must begin again at a second level of remoteness. The primary informant must then pass along sufficient data in sufficient detail so that the magistrate may again judge for himself (1) the credibility of the secondary informant and (2) the worth of that secondary informant's information. If, in some extreme hypothetical situation, the secondary informant should be a mere conduit for hearsay thrice compounded from a tertiary informant, the evaluation process is escalated to yet another level of remoteness and so on ad infinitum. Ultimately, the magistrate must have the benefit of someone's firsthand observation in order to evaluate the worth of the information and must have also satisfactory proof of the credibility of every person involved in the chain of transmission of the information from the initial observer to the magistrate himself.

At issue here is not the informant's credibility but the informant's thinking process—not his integrity but his ratiocination. In applying then these tools of analysis to an application based upon a mixed predicate of direct observation and hearsay information, the issuing magistrate may, after evaluating both the trustworthiness of the source of the information and the weight and worth of the information itself, reach one of four conclusions:

(1) That the direct observation is adequate unto itself to establish probable cause; . . .

(2) That the hearsay information is adequate unto itself to establish probable cause; . . .

(3) That neither the direct observation nor the hearsay information, standing alone, is adequate to establish probable cause but that the two combined do add up to the establishment of such probable cause; . . .

(4) That even the sum total of the direct observation plus the hearsay information does not establish probable cause.

The most logical procedure to follow in evaluating a warrant application is to look first at the hearsay information. If the affiant has furnished the issuing magistrate enough of the underlying circumstances to persuade the magistrate (1) that the informant is credible or his information otherwise reliable and (2) that the informant's conclusion was validly arrived at, probable cause is established. What *Spinelli* refers to as "*Aguilar's* two-pronged test" has been met. If, on the other hand, the information furnished about the informant and the information furnished from the informant fail to pass muster by either or both of *Aguilar's* prongs, the informant's information is still not rendered valueless. "Rather, it need[s] some further support."

In search of that "further support," the magistrate may then look to the direct observation recounted by the affiant. That direct observation may serve a dual function. As substance in its own right, it bears directly on the question of probable cause. It may also serve the ancillary and concomitant function of corroborating or verifying the hearsay information. . . .

The necessary trustworthiness may then be established extrinsically by the independent verification of the affiant's direct observation. If some of the significant details of the informant's story are shown to be, in fact, true that encourages the magistrate to believe that all of the story is probably true.

* * *

Later Judge Moylan in Stanley v. State, 19 Md.App. 507, 313 A.2d 847 (1974), set forth a much more sophisticated and elaborate intellectualization of the so-called "two-pronged" standard of probable cause. That analysis was also reflected in his article, "Hearsay and Probable Cause: An *Aguilar* and *Spinelli* Primer," 25 Mercer L.Rev.741 (1974). To some extent, the United States Supreme Court's opinion in Illinois v. Gates, infra, may be viewed as a reaction to the elaborate nature of probable cause analysis as reflected in *Stanley*. See references to Judge Moylan's analysis in the Gates opinion that follows:

Illinois v. Gates

Supreme Court of the United States, 1983.
462 U.S. 213, 103 S.Ct. 2317.

■ JUSTICE REHNQUIST delivered the opinion of the Court.

.... Bloomingdale, Ill. is a suburb of Chicago located in DuPage County. On May 3, 1978, the Bloomingdale Police Department received by mail an anonymous handwritten letter which read as follows:

> "This letter is to inform you that you have a couple in your town who strictly make their living on selling drugs. They are Sue and Lance Gates, they live on Greenway, off Bloomingdale Rd. in the condominiums. Most of their buys are done in Florida. Sue his wife drives their car to Florida, where she leaves it to be loaded up with drugs, then Lance flys down and drives it back. Sue flys back after she drops the car off in Florida. May 3 she is driving down there again and Lance will be flying down in a few days to drive it back. At the time Lance drives the car back he has the trunk loaded with over $100,000.00 in drugs. Presently they have over $100,000.00 worth of drugs in their basement.
>
> They brag about the fact they never have to work, and make their entire living on pushers.
>
> I guarantee if you watch them carefully you will make a big catch. They are friends with some big drugs dealers, who visit their house often.
>
> Lance & Susan Gates
>
> Greenway
>
> in Condominiums"

The letter was referred by the Chief of Police of the Bloomingdale Police Department to Detective Mader, who decided to pursue the tip. Mader learned, from the office of the Illinois Secretary of State, that an Illinois driver's license had been issued to one Lance Gates, residing at a stated address in Bloomingdale. He contacted a confidential informant, whose examination of certain financial records revealed a more recent address for the Gates, and he also learned from a police officer assigned to O'Hare Airport that "L.Gates" had made a reservation on Eastern Airlines flight 245 to West Palm Beach, Fla., scheduled to depart from Chicago on May 5 at 4:15 p.m.

Mader then made arrangements with an agent of the Drug Enforcement Administration for surveillance of the May 5 Eastern Airlines flight. The agent later reported to Mader that Gates had boarded the flight, and that federal agents in Florida had observed him arrive in West Palm Beach and take a taxi to the nearby Holiday Inn. They also reported that Gates went to a room registered to one Susan Gates and that, at 7:00 a.m. the next morning, Gates and an unidentified woman left the motel in a Mercury bearing Illinois license plates and drove northbound on an interstate frequently used by travelers to the Chicago area. In addition, the DEA agent informed Mader that the license plate number on the Mercury registered to a Hornet station wagon owned by Gates. The agent also advised Mader that the driving time between West Palm Beach and Bloomingdale was approximately 22 to 24 hours.

Mader signed an affidavit setting forth the foregoing facts, and submitted it to a judge of the Circuit Court of Du Page County, together with a copy of the anonymous letter. The judge of that court thereupon issued a search warrant for the Gates' residence and for their automobile. The judge, in deciding to issue the warrant, could have determined that the modus operandi of the Gates had been substantially corroborated. As the anonymous letter predicted, Lance Gates had flown from Chicago to West Palm Beach late in the afternoon of May 5th, had checked into a hotel room registered in the name of his wife, and, at 7:00 a.m. the following morning, had headed north, accompanied by an unidentified woman, out of West Palm Beach on an interstate highway used by travelers from South Florida to Chicago in an automobile bearing a license plate issued to him.

At 5:15 a.m. on March 7th, only 36 hours after he had flown out of Chicago, Lance Gates, and his wife, returned to their home in Bloomingdale, driving the car in which they had left West Palm Beach some 22 hours earlier. The Bloomingdale police were awaiting them, searched the trunk of the Mercury, and uncovered approximately 350 pounds of marijuana. A search of the Gates' home revealed marijuana, weapons, and other contraband. The Illinois Circuit Court ordered suppression of all these items, on the ground that the affidavit submitted to the Circuit Judge failed to support the necessary determination of probable cause to believe that the Gates' automobile and home contained the contraband in question. This decision was affirmed in turn by the Illinois Appellate Court and by a divided vote of the Supreme Court of Illinois.

The Illinois Supreme Court concluded—and we are inclined to agree—that, standing alone, the anonymous letter sent to the Bloomingdale Police Department would not provide the basis for a magistrate's determination that there was probable cause to believe contraband would be found in the Gates' car and home. The letter provides virtually nothing from which one might conclude that its author is either honest or his information reliable; likewise, the letter gives absolutely no indication of the basis for the writer's predictions regarding the Gates' criminal activities. Something more was required, then, before a magistrate could conclude that there was probable cause to believe that contraband would be found in the Gates' home and car.

The Illinois Supreme Court also properly recognized that Detective Mader's affidavit might be capable of supplementing the anonymous letter with information sufficient to permit a determination of probable cause. In holding that the affidavit in fact did not contain sufficient additional information to sustain a determination of probable cause, the Illinois court applied a "two-pronged test," derived from our decision in Spinelli v. United States, 393 U.S. 410, 89 S.Ct. 584 (1969). The Illinois Supreme Court, like some others, apparently understood *Spinelli* as requiring that the anonymous letter satisfy each of two independent requirements before it could be relied on. According to this view, the letter, as supplemented by Mader's affidavit, first had to adequately reveal the "basis of knowledge" of the letter writer—the particular means by which he came by the information given in his report. Second, it had to provide facts sufficiently establishing either the "veracity" of the affiant's informant, or, alternatively, the "reliability" of the informant's report in this particular case.

The Illinois court, alluding to an elaborate set of legal rules that have developed among various lower courts to enforce the "two-pronged test,"[1] found that the test had not been satisfied. First, the "veracity" prong was not satisfied because, "there was simply no basis [for] . . . conclud[ing] that the anonymous person [who wrote the letter to the Bloomingdale Police Department] was credible." The court indicated that corroboration by police of details contained in the letter might never satisfy the "veracity" prong, and in any event, could not do so if, as in the present case, only "innocent" details are corroborated. In addition, the letter gave no indication of the basis of its writer's knowledge of the Gates' activities. The Illinois court understood *Spinelli* as permitting the detail contained in a tip to be used to infer that the informant had a reliable basis for his statements, but it thought that the anonymous letter failed to provide sufficient detail to permit such an inference. Thus, it concluded that no showing of probable cause had been made.

We agree with the Illinois Supreme Court that an informant's "veracity," "reliability" and "basis of knowledge" are all highly relevant in determining the value of his report. We do not agree, however, that these elements should be understood as entirely separate and independent requirements to be rigidly exacted in every case,[2] which the opinion of the Supreme Court of Illinois would imply. Rather, as detailed below, they should be understood simply as closely intertwined issues that may usefully illuminate the common-sense, practical question whether there is "probable cause" to believe that contraband or evidence is located in a particular place.

1. See, e.g., Stanley v. State, 19 Md. App. 507, 313 A.2d 847 (Md.App.1974). In summary, these rules posit that the "veracity" prong of the Spinelli test has two "spurs" "the informant's 'credibility' " and the "reliability" of his information. Various interpretations are advanced for the meaning of the "reliability" spur of the "veracity" prong. Both the "basis of knowledge" prong and the "veracity" prong are treated as entirely separate requirements, which must be independently satisfied in every case in order to sustain a determination of probable cause. Some ancillary doctrines are relied on to satisfy certain of the foregoing requirements. For example, the "self-verifying detail" of a tip may satisfy the "basis of knowledge" requirement, although not the "credibility" spur of the "veracity" prong. Conversely, corroboration would seem not capable of supporting the "basis of knowledge" prong, but only the "veracity" prong.

The decision in *Stanley*, while expressly approving and conscientiously attempting to apply the "two-pronged test" observes that "[t]he built-in subtleties [of the test] are such, however, that a slipshod application calls down upon us the fury of Murphy's Law." The decision also suggested that it is necessary "to evolve analogous guidelines [to hearsay rules employed in trial settings] for the reception of hearsay in a probable cause setting."

2. The entirely independent character that the *Spinelli* prongs have assumed is indicated both by the opinion of the Illinois Supreme Court in this case, and by decisions of other courts. One frequently cited decision, Stanley v. State, 19 Md.App. 507, 313 A.2d 847, 861 (Md.App.1974), remarks that "the dual requirements represented by the 'two-pronged test' are 'analytically severable' and an 'overkill' on one prong will not carry over to make up for a deficit on the other prong."

This totality of the circumstances approach is far more consistent with our prior treatment of probable cause[3] than is any rigid demand that specific "tests" be satisfied by every informant's tip. Perhaps the central teaching of our decisions bearing on the probable cause standard is that it is a "practical, nontechnical conception." Brinegar v. United States (1949). "In dealing with probable cause, . . . as the very name implies, we deal with probabilities. These are not technical; they are the factual and practical considerations of everyday life on which reasonable and prudent men, not legal technicians, act."

* * *

As these comments illustrate, probable cause is a fluid concept—turning on the assessment of probabilities in particular factual contexts—not readily, or even usefully, reduced to a neat set of legal rules. Informants' tips doubtless come in many shapes and sizes from many different types of persons. As we said in Adams v. Williams (1972), "Informants' tips, like all other clues and evidence coming to a policeman on the scene may vary greatly in their value and reliability." Rigid legal rules are ill-suited to an area of such diversity. "One simple rule will not cover every situation."

Moreover, the "two-pronged test" directs analysis into two largely independent channels "the informant's 'veracity' or 'reliability' and his 'basis of knowledge.' " There are persuasive arguments against according these two elements such independent status. Instead, they are better understood as relevant considerations in the totality of circumstances analysis that traditionally has guided probable cause determinations: a deficiency in one may be compensated for, in determining the overall reliability of a tip, by a strong showing as to the other, or by some other indicia of reliability.

If, for example, a particular informant is known for the unusual reliability of his predictions of certain types of criminal activities in a locality, his failure, in a particular case, to thoroughly set forth the basis of his knowledge surely should not serve as an absolute bar to a finding of probable cause based on his tip. See United States v. Sellers, 483 F.2d 37 (C.A.5 1973).[4] Likewise, if an unquestionably honest citizen comes forward

3. Our original phrasing of the so-called "two-pronged test" in Aguilar v. Texas (1969), suggests that the two prongs were intended simply as guides to a magistrate's determination of probable cause, not as inflexible, independent requirements applicable in every case. In *Aguilar*, we required only that:

> "the magistrate must be informed of *some of the underlying circumstances* from which the informant concluded that . . . narcotics were where he claimed they were, and *some of the underlying circumstances* from which the officer concluded that the informant . . . was 'credible' or his information 'reliable.' "

As our language indicates, we intended neither a rigid compartmentalization of the inquiries into an informant's "veracity," "reliability" and "basis of knowledge," nor that these inquiries be elaborate exegeses of an informant's tip. Rather, we required only that *some* facts bearing on two particular issues be provided to the magistrate. . . .

4. Compare Stanley v. State, 19 Md. App. 507, 313 A.2d 847, 861 (Md.App.1974), reasoning that "Even assuming 'credibility' amounting to sainthood, the judge still may not accept the bare conclusion of a sworn and known and trusted police-affiant."

with a report of criminal activity—which if fabricated would subject him to criminal liability—we have found rigorous scrutiny of the basis of his knowledge unnecessary. Adams v. Williams. Conversely, even if we entertain some doubt as to an informant's motives, his explicit and detailed description of alleged wrong doing, along with a statement that the event was observed first-hand, entitles his tip to greater weight than might otherwise be the case. Unlike a totality of circumstances analysis, which permits a balanced assessment of the relative weights of all the various indicia of reliability (and unreliability) attending an informant's tip, the "two-pronged test" has encouraged an excessively technical dissection of informants' tips,[5] with undue attention being focused on isolated issues that cannot sensibly be divorced from the other facts presented to the magistrate.

* * *

We also have recognized that affidavits "are normally drafted by nonlawyers in the midst and haste of a criminal investigation. Technical requirements of elaborate specificity once exacted under common law pleading have no proper place in this area." *Ventresca.* Likewise, search and arrest warrants long have been issued by persons who are neither lawyers nor judges, and who certainly do not remain abreast of each judicial refinement of the nature of "probable cause." See Shadwick v. City of Tampa (1972). The rigorous inquiry into the *Spinelli* prongs and the complex superstructure of evidentiary and analytical rules that some have seen implicit in our *Spinelli* decision, cannot be reconciled with the fact that many warrants are—quite properly—issued on the basis of nontechnical, common-sense judgments of laymen applying a standard less demanding than those used in more formal legal proceedings. Likewise, given the informal, often hurried context in which it must be applied, the "built-in

5. Some lower court decisions, brought to our attention by the State, reflect a rigid application of such rules. In Bridger v. State, 503 S.W.2d 801 (Tex.Crim.App.1974), the affiant had received a confession of armed robbery from one of two suspects in the robbery; in addition, the suspect had given the officer $800 in cash stolen during the robbery. The suspect also told the officer that the gun used in the robbery was hidden in the other suspect's apartment. A warrant issued on the basis of this was invalidated on the ground that the affidavit did not satisfactorily describe how the accomplice had obtained his information regarding the gun.

Likewise, in People v. Palanza, 55 Ill. App.3d 1028, 13 Ill.Dec. 752, 371 N.E.2d 687 (Ill.App.1978), the affidavit submitted in support of an application for a search warrant stated that an informant of proven and uncontested reliability had seen, in specifically described premises, "a quantity of a white crystalline substance which was represented to the informant by a white male occupant of the premises to be cocaine. Informant has observed co caine on numerous occasions in the past and is thoroughly familiar with its appearance. The informant states that the white crystalline powder he observed in the above described premises appeared to him to be cocaine." The warrant issued on the basis of the affidavit was invalidated because "There is no indication as to how the informant or for that matter any other person could tell whether a white substance was cocaine and not some other substance such as sugar or salt."

Finally, in People v. Brethauer, 174 Colo. 29, 482 P.2d 369 (Colo.1971), an informant, stated to have supplied reliable information in the past, claimed that L.S.D. and marijuana were located on certain premises. The affiant supplied police with drugs, which were tested by police and confirmed to be illegal substances. The affidavit setting forth these, and other, facts was found defective under both prongs of *Spinelli.*

subtleties," Stanley v. State, 19 Md.App.507, 313 A.2d 847, 860 (Md.App. 1974), of the"two-pronged test" are particularly unlikely to assist magistrates in determining probable cause.

Similarly, we have repeatedly said that after-the-fact scrutiny by courts of the sufficiency of an affidavit should not take the form of *de novo* review. A magistrate's "determination of probable cause should be paid great deference by reviewing courts." *Spinelli.* "A grudging or negative attitude by reviewing courts toward warrants," *Ventresca*, is inconsistent with the Fourth Amendment's strong preference for searches conducted pursuant to a warrant. "Courts should not invalidate ... warrant[s] by interpreting affidavit[s] in a hypertechnical, rather than a commonsense, manner."

If the affidavits submitted by police officers are subjected to the type of scrutiny some courts have deemed appropriate, police might well resort to warrantless searches, with the hope of relying on consent or some other exception to the warrant clause that might develop at the time of the search. In addition, the possession of a warrant by officers conducting an arrest or search greatly reduces the perception of unlawful or intrusive police conduct, by assuring "the individual whose property is searched or seized of the lawful authority of the executing officer, his need to search, and the limits of his power to search." United States v. Chadwick (1977). Reflecting this preference for the warrant process, the traditional standard for review of an issuing magistrate's probable cause determination has been that so long as the magistrate had a "substantial basis for ... conclud[ing]" that a search would uncover evidence of wrongdoing, the Fourth Amendment requires no more. Jones v. United States (1960). We think reaffirmation of this standard better serves the purpose of encouraging recourse to the warrant procedure and is more consistent with our traditional deference to the probable cause determinations of magistrates than is the "two-pronged test."

Finally, the direction taken by decisions following *Spinelli* poorly serves "the most basic function of any government": "to provide for the security of the individual and of his property." Miranda v. Arizona (1966) (White, J., dissenting). The strictures that inevitably accompany the "two-pronged test" cannot avoid seriously impeding the task of law enforcement. If, as the Illinois Supreme Court apparently thought, that test must be rigorously applied in every case, anonymous tips would be of greatly diminished value in police work. Ordinary citizens, like ordinary witnesses, see Federal Rules of Evidence 701, Advisory Committee Note (1976), generally do not provide extensive recitations of the basis of their everyday observations. Likewise, as the Illinois Supreme Court observed in this case, the veracity of persons supplying anonymous tips is by hypothesis largely unknown, and unknowable. As a result, anonymous tips seldom could survive a rigorous application of either of the *Spinelli* prongs. Yet, such tips, particularly when supplemented by independent police investigation, frequently contribute to the solution of otherwise "perfect crimes." While a conscientious assessment of the basis for crediting such tips is required by the Fourth Amendment, a standard that leaves virtually no place for anonymous citizen informants is not.

For all these reasons, we conclude that it is wiser to abandon the "two-pronged test" established by our decisions in *Aguilar* and *Spinelli*. In its place we reaffirm the totality of the circumstances analysis that traditionally has informed probable cause determinations. The task of the issuing magistrate is simply to make a practical, common-sense decision whether, given all the circumstances set forth in the affidavit before him, including the "veracity" and "basis of knowledge" of persons supplying hearsay information, there is a fair probability that contraband or evidence of a crime will be found in a particular place. And the duty of a reviewing court is simply to ensure that the magistrate had a "substantial basis for ... conclud[ing]" that probable cause existed. Jones v. United States. We are convinced that this flexible, easily applied standard will better achieve the accommodation of public and private interests that the Fourth Amendment requires than does the approach that has developed from *Aguilar* and *Spinelli*.

* * *

... Even standing alone, the facts obtained through the independent investigation of Mader and the DEA at least suggested that the Gates were involved in drug trafficking. In addition to being a popular vacation site, Florida is well-known as a source of narcotics and other illegal drugs. See United States v. Mendenhall (1980) (Powell, J., concurring); DEA, Narcotics Intelligence Estimate, The Supply of Drugs to the U.S. Illicit Market From Foreign and Domestic Sources 10 (1979). Lance Gates' flight to Palm Beach, his brief, overnight stay in a motel, and apparent immediate return north to Chicago in the family car, conveniently awaiting him in West Palm Beach, is as suggestive of a pre-arranged drug run, as it is of an ordinary vacation trip.

In addition, the magistrate could rely on the anonymous letter, which had been corroborated in major part by Mader's efforts just as had occurred in *Draper*. The Supreme Court of Illinois reasoned that *Draper* involved an informant who had given reliable information on previous occasions, while the honesty and reliability of the anonymous informant in this case were unknown to the Bloomingdale police. While this distinction might be an apt one at the time the police department received the anonymous letter, it became far less significant after Mader's independent investigative work occurred. The corroboration of the letter's predictions that the Gates' car would be in Florida, that Lance Gates would fly to Florida in the next day or so, and that he would drive the car north toward Bloomingdale all indicated, albeit not with certainty, that the informant's other assertions also were true. "Because an informant is right about some things, he is more probably right about other facts." *Spinelli* (White, J., concurring) "including the claim regarding the Gates' illegal activity. This may well not be the type of 'reliability' or 'veracity' necessary to satisfy some views of the 'veracity prong' of Spinelli, but we think it suffices for the practical, common-sense judgment called for in making a probable cause determination. It is enough, for purposes of assessing probable cause, that 'corroboration through other sources of information reduced the chances of a reckless or prevaricating tale,' thus providing 'a substantial basis for crediting the hearsay.' " Jones v. United States.[7]

Finally, the anonymous letter contained a range of details relating not just to easily obtained facts and conditions existing at the time of the tip, but to future actions of third parties ordinarily not easily predicted. The letter writer's accurate information as to the travel plans of each of the Gates was of a character likely obtained only from the Gates themselves, or from someone familiar with their not entirely ordinary travel plans. If the informant had access to accurate information of this type a magistrate could properly conclude that it was not unlikely that he also had access to reliable information of the Gates' alleged illegal activities.[8] Of course, the Gates' travel plans might have been learned from a talkative neighbor or travel agent; under the "two-pronged test" developed from *Spinelli*, the

7. The Illinois Supreme Court thought that the verification of details contained in the anonymous letter in this case amounted only to "the corroboration of innocent activity," and that this was insufficient to support a finding of probable cause. We are inclined to agree, however, with the observation of Justice Moran in his dissenting opinion that "In this case, just as in *Draper*, seemingly innocent activity became suspicious in the light of the initial tip." And it bears "noting that *all* of the corroborating detail established in *Draper*, supra, was of entirely innocent activity—a fact later pointed out by the Court in both Jones v. United States (1960), and Ker v. California, 374 U.S. 23, 36, 83 S.Ct. 1623, 1631 (1963).

This is perfectly reasonable. As discussed previously, probable cause requires only a probability or substantial chance of criminal activity, not an actual showing of such activity. By hypothesis, therefore, innocent behavior frequently will provide the basis for a showing of probable cause; to require otherwise would be to *sub silentio* impose a drastically more rigorous definition of probable cause than the security of our citizens demands. We think the Illinois court attempted a too rigid classification of the types of conduct that may be relied upon in seeking to demonstrate probable cause. See Brown v. Texas (1979). In making a determination of probable cause the relevant inquiry is not whether particular conduct is "innocent" or "guilty," but the degree of suspicion that attaches to particular types of non-criminal acts.

8. The dissent seizes on one inaccuracy in the anonymous informant's letter—its statement that Sue Gates would fly from Florida to Illinois, when in fact she drove—and argues that the probative value of the entire tip was undermined by this allegedly "material mistake." We have never required that informants used by the police be infallible, and can see no reason to impose such a requirement in this case. Probable cause, particularly when police have obtained a warrant, simply does not require the perfection the dissent finds necessary.

Likewise, there is no force to the dissent's argument that the Gates' action in leaving their home unguarded undercut the informant's claim that drugs were hidden there. Indeed, the line-by-line scrutiny that the dissent applies to the anonymous letter is akin to that we find inappropriate in reviewing magistrate's decisions. The dissent apparently attributes to the magistrate who issued the warrant in this case the rather implausible notion that persons dealing in drugs always stay at home, apparently out of fear that to leave might risk intrusion by criminals. If accurate, one could not help sympathizing with the self-imposed isolation of people so situated. In reality, however, it is scarcely likely that the magistrate ever thought that the anonymous tip "kept one spouse" at home, much less that he relied on the theory advanced by the dissent. The letter simply says that Sue would fly from Florida to Illinois, without indicating whether the Gates' made the bitter choice of leaving the drugs in their house, or those in their car, unguarded. The magistrate's determination that there might be drugs or evidence of criminal activity in the Gates' home was well-supported by the less speculative theory, noted in text, that if the informant could predict with considerable accuracy the somewhat unusual travel plans of the Gates, he probably also had a reliable basis for his statements that the Gates' kept a large quantity of drugs in their home and frequently were visited by other drug traffickers there.

character of the details in the anonymous letter might well not permit a sufficiently clear inference regarding the letter writer's "basis of knowledge." But, as discussed previously, probable cause does not demand the certainty we associate with formal trials. It is enough that there was a fair probability that the writer of the anonymous letter had obtained his entire story either from the Gates or someone they trusted. And corroboration of major portions of the letter's predictions provides just this probability. It is apparent, therefore, that the judge issuing the warrant had a "substantial basis for . . . conclud[ing]" that probable cause to search the Gates' home and car existed.The judgment of the Supreme Court of Illinois therefore must be

Reversed.

■ JUSTICE WHITE, concurring in the judgment.

In my view, the question regarding modification of the exclusionary rule framed in our order of November 29, 1982, 459 U.S. 1028 (1982), is properly before us and should be addressed. I continue to believe that the exclusionary rule is an inappropriate remedy where law enforcement officials act in the reasonable belief that a search and seizure was consistent with the Fourth Amendment—a position I set forth in Stone v. Powell, 428 U.S. 465, 537–539 (1976). . . .

■ JUSTICE STEVENS, with whom JUSTICE BRENNAN joins, dissenting.

The fact that Lance and Sue Gates made a 22–hour nonstop drive from West Palm Beach, Florida, to Bloomingdale, Illinois, only a few hours after Lance had flown to Florida provided persuasive evidence that they were engaged in illicit activity. That fact, however, was not known to the judge when he issued the warrant to search their home.

What the judge did know at that time was that the anonymous informant had not been completely accurate in his or her predictions. The informant had indicated that " 'Sue . . . drives their car to Florida *where she leaves it to be loaded up with drugs . . . . Sue [flies] back after she drops the car off in Florida.'* " 85 Ill. 2d 376, 379, 423 N. E. 2d 887, 888 (1981) (emphasis added). Yet Detective Mader's affidavit reported that she " 'left the West Palm Beach area driving the Mercury northbound.' " 82 Ill. App. 3d 749, 757, 403 N. E. 2d 77, 82 (1980).

The discrepancy between the informant's predictions and the facts known to Detective Mader is significant for three reasons. First, it cast doubt on the informant's hypothesis that the Gates already had " 'over [$100,000] worth of drugs in their basement,' " 85 Ill. 2d, at 379, 423 N. E. 2d, at 888. The informant had predicted an itinerary that always kept one spouse in Bloomingdale, suggesting that the Gates did not want to leave their home unguarded because something valuable was hidden within. That inference obviously could not be drawn when it was known that the pair was actually together over a thousand miles from home.

Second, the discrepancy made the Gates' conduct seem substantially less unusual than the informant had predicted it would be. It would have been odd if, as predicted, Sue had driven down to Florida on Wednesday, left the car, and flown right back to Illinois. But the mere facts that Sue was in West Palm Beach with the car,[1] that she was joined by her husband at the Holiday Inn on Friday,[2] and that the couple drove north together the next morning[3] are neither unusual nor probative of criminal activity.

Third, the fact that the anonymous letter contained a material mistake undermines the reasonableness of relying on it as a basis for making a forcible entry into a private home.[4] Of course, the activities in this case did not stop when the judge issued the warrant. The Gates drove all night to Bloomingdale, the officers searched the car and found 400 pounds of marihuana, and then they searched the house.[5] However, none of these subsequent events may be considered in evaluating the warrant,[6] and the search of the house was legal only if the warrant was valid. *Vale v. Louisiana*, 399 U.S. 30, 33–35 (1970). I cannot accept the Court's casual conclusion that, *before the Gates arrived in Bloomingdale*, there was probable cause to justify a valid entry and search of a private home. No one knows who the informant in this case was, or what motivated him or her to write the note. Given that the note's predictions were faulty in one

1. The anonymous note suggested that she was going down on Wednesday, 85 Ill. 2d, at 379, 423 N. E. 2d, at 888, but for all the officers knew she had been in Florida for a month. 82 Ill. App. 3d, at 755–757, 403 N. E. 2d, at 82–83.

2. Lance does not appear to have behaved suspiciously in flying down to Florida. He made a reservation in his own name and gave an accurate home phone number to the airlines. Cf. *Florida v. Royer*, 460 U.S. 491, 493, n. 2 (1983); *United States v. Mendenhall*, 446 U.S. 544, 548 (1980) (Stewart, J., announcing the judgment). And Detective Mader's affidavit does not report that he did any of the other things drug couriers are notorious for doing, such as paying for the ticket in cash, *Royer*, 460 U.S., at 493, n. 2, dressing casually, *ibid.*, looking pale and nervous, ibid.; *Mendenhall, supra*, at 548, improperly filling out baggage tags, *Royer*, 460 U.S., at 493, n. 2, carrying American Tourister luggage, *ibid.*, not carrying any luggage, *Mendenhall*, 446 U.S., at 564–565 (POWELL, J., concurring in part and concurring in judgment), or changing airlines en route, *ibid.*

3. Detective Mader's affidavit hinted darkly that the couple had set out upon "that interstate highway commonly used by travelers to the Chicago area." But the same highway is also commonly used by travelers to Disney World, Sea World, and Ringling Brothers and Barnum and Bailey Circus World. It is also the road to Cocoa Beach, Cape Canaveral, and Washington, D.C. I would venture that each year dozens of perfectly innocent people fly to Florida, meet a waiting spouse, and drive off together in the family car.

4. The Court purports to rely on the proposition that "if the [anonymous] informant could predict with *considerable accuracy* the *somewhat unusual travel plans* of the Gates, he probably also had a reliable basis for his statements that the Gates kept a large quantity of drugs in their home." *Ante*, at 245–246, n. 14 (emphasis added). Even if this syllogism were sound, but see *Spinelli v. United States*, 393 U.S. 410, 427 (1969) (WHITE, J., concurring), its premises are not met in this case.

5. The officers did not enter the unoccupied house as soon as the warrant issued; instead, they waited until the Gates returned. It is unclear whether they waited because they wanted to execute the warrant without unnecessary property damage or because they had doubts about whether the informant's tip was really valid. In either event their judgment is to be commended.

6. It is a truism that "a search warrant is valid only if probable cause has been shown to the magistrate and that an inadequate showing may not be rescued by post-search testimony on information known to the searching officers at the time of the search." *Rice v. Wolff*, 513 F.2d 1280, 1287 (C.A.8 1975). See *Coolidge v. New Hampshire*, 403 U.S. 443, 450–451 (1971); *Whiteley v. Warden*, 401 U.S. 560, 565, n. 8 (1971); *Aguilar v. Texas*, 378 U.S. 108, 109, n. 1 (1964); *Jones v. United States*, 357 U.S. 493, 497–498 (1958); *Giordenello v. United States*, 357 U.S. 480, 486 (1958); *Taylor v. United States*, 286 U.S. 1, 6 (1932); *Agnello v. United States*, 269 U.S. 20, 33 (1925).

significant respect, and were corroborated by nothing except ordinary innocent activity, I must surmise that the Court's evaluation of the warrant's validity has been colored by subsequent events.[7]

Although the foregoing analysis is determinative as to the house search, the car search raises additional issues because "there is a constitutional difference between houses and cars." *Chambers v. Maroney*, 399 U.S. 42, 52 (1970). Cf. Payton v. New York, 445 U.S. 573, 589–590 (1980). An officer who has probable cause to suspect that a highly movable automobile contains contraband does not need a valid warrant in order to search it. This point was developed in our opinion in *United States v. Ross*, 456 U.S. 798 (1982), which was not decided until after the Illinois Supreme Court rendered its decision in this case. Under *Ross*, the car search may have been valid if the officers had probable cause *after* the Gates arrived.

In apologizing for its belated realization that we should not have ordered reargument in this case,the Court today shows high regard for the appropriate relationship of this Court to state courts. When the Court discusses the merits, however, it attaches no weight to the conclusions of the Circuit Judge of DuPage County, Illinois, of the three judges of the Second District of the Illinois Appellate Court, or of the five justices of the Illinois Supreme Court, all of whom concluded that the warrant was not based on probable cause. In a fact-bound inquiry of this sort, the judgment of three levels of state courts, all of which are better able to evaluate the probable reliability of anonymous informants in Bloomingdale, Illinois, than we are, should be entitled to at least a presumption of accuracy.[8] I would simply vacate the judgment of the Illinois Supreme Court and remand the case for reconsideration in the light of our intervening decision in *United States v. Ross*.

■ JUSTICE BRENNAN, with whom JUSTICE MARSHALL joins, dissenting:

* * *

. . . Findings of probable cause, and attendant intrusions, should not be authorized unless there is some assurance that the information on which they are based has been obtained in a reliable way by an honest or credible person. As applied to police officers, the rules focus on the way in which the information was acquired. As applied to informants, the rules focus both on the honesty or credibility of the informant and on the reliability of the way

7. *Draper v. United States*, 358 U.S. 307 (1959), affords no support for today's holding. That case did not involve an anonymous informant. On the contrary, as the Court twice noted, Mr. Hereford was "employed for that purpose and [his] information had always been found accurate and reliable." *Id.*, at 313; see *id.*, at 309. In this case, the police had no prior experience with the informant, and some of his or her information in this case was unreliable and inaccurate.

8. The Court holds that what were heretofore considered two independent "prongs"—"veracity" and "basis of knowledge"—are now to be considered together as circumstances whose totality must be appraised. *Ante*, at 233. "[A] deficiency in one may be compensated for, in determining the overall reliability of a tip, by a strong showing as to the other, or by some other indicia of reliability." *Ibid.* Yet in this case, the lower courts found *neither* factor present. 85 Ill. 2d, at 390, 423 N. E. 2d, at 893. And the supposed "other indicia" in the affidavit take the form of activity that is not particularly remarkable. I do not understand how the Court can find that the "totality" so far exceeds the sum of its "circumstances."

in which the information was acquired. Insofar as it is more complicated, an evaluation of affidavits based on hearsay involves a more difficult inquiry. This suggests a need to structure the inquiry in an effort to insure greater accuracy. The standards announced in *Aguilar*, as refined by Spinelli, fulfill that need. The standards inform the police of what information they have to provide and magistrates of what information they should demand. The standards also inform magistrates of the subsidiary findings they must make in order to arrive at an ultimate finding of probable cause. Spinelli, properly understood, directs the magistrate's attention to the possibility that the presence of self-verifying detail might satisfy *Aguilar*'s basis of knowledge prong and that corroboration of the details of a tip might satisfy *Aguilar*'s veracity prong. By requiring police to provide certain crucial information to magistrates and by structuring magistrates' probable cause inquiries, *Aguilar* and *Spinelli* assure the magistrate's role as an independent arbiter of probable cause, insure greater accuracy in probable cause determinations, and advance the substantive value identified above.

* * *

At the heart of the Court's decision to abandon *Aguilar* and *Spinelli* appears to be its belief that "the direction taken by decisions following *Spinelli* poorly serves 'the most basic function of any government: to provide for the security of the individual and of his property.'" This conclusion rests on the judgment that *Aguilar* and *Spinelli* "seriously imped[e] the task of law enforcement," and render anonymous tips valueless in police work. Surely, the Court overstates its case. But of particular concern to all Americans must be that the Court gives virtually no consideration to the value of insuring that findings of probable cause are based on information that a magistrate can reasonably say has been obtained in a reliable way by an honest or credible person. I share Justice White's fear that the Court's rejection of *Aguilar* and *Spinelli* and its adoption of a new totality of the circumstances test, "may foretell an evisceration of the probable cause standard...." (White, J., concurring in the judgment)....

Rights secured by the Fourth Amendment are particularly difficult to protect because their "advocates are usually criminals." Draper v. United States (1959) (Douglas, J., dissenting). But the rules "we fashion [are] for the innocent and guilty alike." By replacing *Aguilar* and *Spinelli* with a test that provides no assurance that magistrates, rather than the police, or informants, will make determinations of probable cause; imposes no structure on magistrates' probable cause inquiries; and invites the possibility that intrusions may be justified on less than reliable information from an honest or credible person, today's decision threatens to "obliterate one of the most fundamental distinctions between our form of government, where officers are under the law, and the police-state where they are the law." Johnson v. United States (1948).

NOTES

1. ***The Heart of Gates.*** Gates has two main aspects: (1) the rejection of the *Aguilar–Spinelli* test, at least where the application for a warrant is not based solely upon the assertions of a hearsay source; and (2) deference to the issuing magistrate in subsequent review of a warrant.

Once a trial court or reviewing court defers to the magistrate's assessment of the affiant's credibility, why is not the remaining issue purely a question of law involving what Judge Moylan has called "the logic of a proposition"? Is the magistrate in any better position to correctly assess the data in an affidavit than is a reviewing court viewing the same affidavit? What is the significance of the fact that the magistrate need not be a lawyer? What is the significance of the fact that the magistrate makes the decision *ex parte* without hearing arguments from defense counsel? Or of the fact that in many jurisdictions law enforcement officials can pick the magistrate to whom they choose to apply for the warrant? Or of the fact that in many jurisdictions magistrates approve warrant applications in the overwhelming percentage of cases?

On the other hand, in arguing that warrants are usually required, and that warrantless searches must be the exception, defense lawyers exalt the role of the "neutral judicial officer" and the Supreme Court, in words, if not in deeds, has accepted the importance of the magistrate. Is it not consistent then for the Court to continue to exalt the magistrate and to reward the officer who seeks prior judicial approval of a Fourth Amendment intrusion?

2. *States Rejecting Gates as a Matter of State Constitutional Law.* A number of states, relying on state constitutional law, have rejected the Gates standard and have continued to apply the *Aguilar–Spinelli* test to evaluate probable cause. These include: State v. Jones, 706 P.2d 317 (Alaska 1985); State v. Cordova, 109 N.M. 211, 784 P.2d 30 (N.M.1989); People v. Griminger, 71 N.Y.2d 635, 529 N.Y.S.2d 55, 524 N.E.2d 409 (1988); State v. Jacumin, 778 S.W.2d 430 (Tenn.1989); State v. Jackson, 102 Wash.2d 432, 688 P.2d 136 (1984). Other states initially rejected Gates on the basis of state constitutional law, but later shifted to adopt the Gates standard for probable cause. See e.g., State v. Barton, 219 Conn. 529, 594 A.2d 917 (1991) [overruling State v. Kimbro, 197 Conn. 219, 496 A.2d 498 (1985)].

3. *Is There a Relationship Between the* Gates *Test and the Good Faith Exception in* Leon*?* Although initially, the Gates case was before the Court on a state's petition for certiorari on the question of whether the defendants' fourth Amendment rights had been violated, the Court, sua sponte, asked the parties to brief additionally the question of whether the exclusionary rule should be modified to permit a good faith exception. The Court later decided not to reach this issue. Chief Justice Rehnquist wrote: "[a] wise exercise of the powers confided in this Court dictates that we reserve for another day the question whether the exclusionary rule should be modified." In the following year, the Court decided the *Leon* case which you may find in of Chapter 6.

4. *How Much Deference Does the* Gates *Standard Require?* Under Gates, how deferential must a trial or appellate judge be to a magistrate's decision to issue a warrant? According to Judge Moylan, the required deference must be even greater than that applicable under a "clearly erroneous" standard. State v. Amerman, 84 Md.App. 461, 581 A.2d 19 (1990).

5. *How Much Deference Does the Gates Standard Require After Some Information is Excluded From Consideration?* Sometimes a suppression judge will have to excise certain probable cause data from a warrant application before reviewing the magistrate's probable cause decision. For example, the judge cannot consider statements made by the officer-affiant which were perjurious or which were made in reckless disregard of the truth. See Franks v. Delaware. Additionally, probable cause data acquired in violation of the Fourth Amendment cannot be considered. Once the suppression hearing judge has disregarded such data, is there any room left for deference? How do we know what the magistrate would have done absent the improper data? According to State v. Buccini, 167 Ariz. 550, 810 P.2d 178 (1991) no deference is owed in the Franks situation once the false statements have been set aside.

6. *Boiler Plate Probable Cause?* The law of probable cause has, since Aguilar–Spinelli (and even after *Gates*), given rise to the practice of using tried and true formulations to establish probable cause. Some police departments have put standard warrant language on word processors from which an officer can select appropriate formulae. Should this practice affect the validity of the warrant? See Coleman v. State, 308 Ark. 631, 826 S.W.2d 273 (1992) (Practice unwise where officer knew more than was implied by the verbal formula he selected from the memory bank). In Overton v. Ohio, the defendant alleged that the Toledo police simply inserted her name and address into a previously prepared "form complaint" or affidavit which contained a general description of the crime and then submitted this "form complaint" to the Magistrate as the sole evidence supporting the issuance of the warrant. She argues that the warrant therefore failed to meet minimal constitutional standards. While the majority denied her petition for certiorari, Justice Breyer dissented with three other members of the Court, noting "I agree with Overton and would summarily reverse the judgment below on the ground that the warrant is clearly inadequate under well-established Supreme Court case law." 534 U.S. 982, 122 S.Ct. 389 (2001) (Breyer, J., dissenting from denial of certiorari).

For an arrest warrant or a search warrant to be valid under the Fourth Amendment, data establishing probable cause must appear within the four corners of the warrant or, at least, must be communicated under oath to the magistrate before issuance of the warrant. Data known to the police but not communicated to the magistrate is "wasted" for the purposes of establishing the warrant's validity. Some jurisdictions, as a matter of state law, will not even accept sworn oral data, but insist upon the use of affidavits. Others require that any oral testimony presented to the issuing magistrate be contemporaneously recorded, lest a dispute later arise as to what was communicated under oath to the issuing magistrate.

In a case where a valid warrant was not essential to establish the reasonableness of the police conduct (e.g., where the police made a warrantless felony arrest in a public place), probable cause may be established at a hearing on a motion to suppress. The student may be helped by thinking of the testimony presented at such a hearing in a warrantless arrest case (as in *Draper*) as akin to an affidavit for a search warrant or for an arrest warrant. Probable cause must be established through sworn testimony at such a hearing. The probable cause determination in a warrantless arrest hearing looks back to what was known at the moment of arrest. Just as it is possible for an ineptly drawn affidavit to omit known information which could establish probable cause, so also poorly presented testimony at a motion to suppress in a warrantless arrest case may omit facts which were known to the officer and which, if brought out at the hearing, would establish that probable cause existed.

Sources of Information to Support Probable Cause: Non-hearsay and Hearsay Bases. In many instances, the information used to support probable cause comes from the officers' first hand, direct observations. More frequently, however, in a large percentage of warrant cases, and in many warrantless arrest cases, the officer must derive the information from secondary or hearsay sources. These sources could be other law enforcement officers, plain citizen informants, or tipsters. Frequently, these sources are professional tipsters from the criminal milieu, particularly in areas such as gambling and narcotics, where citizen-complaints are not likely to come forward with information (as in *Draper*, *Spinelli*, and *Dawson*). Sometimes they are anonymous tipsters (as in *Gates*). Information from other officers and citizen informants are accorded a presumptive validity not attributed to professional tipsters.

(a) Non–hearsay Sources

In a warrant situation, the issuing magistrate may be asked to conclude that probable cause exists based entirely upon the claimed personal observations of the affiant. Similarly, in warrantless arrest cases, the judge may be asked to conclude that probable cause existed, based solely on observations made by the arresting officer and later recounted in his courtroom testimony.

In either of the foregoing non-hearsay situations, the reliability of the person who made the observations and tells of them under oath need not be established mechanically. The judicial officer can assess the credibility of this person who appears before him under oath.

The judge's opportunity to personally evaluate the credibility of the source who claims he or she made the observations distinguishes non-hearsay cases from hearsay situations. Even if the affiant is a professional tipster, it is unnecessary that the affidavit contain data establishing a record of reliability. The issuing magistrate can assess credibility by scrutinizing the demeanor of the affiant and, if he chooses, by requiring the affiant orally respond to questions under oath before determining whether to issue the warrant.

Once the magistrate decides that the affiant is credible, then he or she need only decide whether the non-hearsay affiant's observations add up to probable cause. In the words of Dawson, what is left to evaluate is the "logic of a proposition." Case opinions which explain the difference between hearsay probable cause and non-hearsay probable cause include People v. O'Neal, 40 Ill.App.3d 448, 352 N.E.2d 282 (1976); State v. Collins, 317 So.2d 846 (Fla.App.1975) cert.denied 330 So.2d 16 (Fla.1976), and Skelton v. Superior Court, 1 Cal.3d 144, 81 Cal.Rptr. 613, 460 P.2d 485 (1969).

Suppose that a professional tipster contacts the police and alleges that he saw certain specified occurrences which, if they really happened, would provide probable cause. Suppose further that the tipster has no past record of reliability. To avoid problems with one prong of the Aguilar test, the officers avoid the use of hearsay, have the tipster sign the affidavit, and allow the issuing magistrate to decide whether the tipster is credible. See, for example, Latham v. State, 790 P.2d 717 (Alaska App.1990). Suppose, however that to protect the source's identity, the tipster merely signs the affidavit "John Doe." Is there anything constitutionally impermissible about this? Compare United States ex rel. Pugh v. Pate, 401 F.2d 6 (7th Cir.1968), with People v. Stansberry, 47 Ill.2d 541, 268 N.E.2d 431 (1971). Is use of the "John Doe" affidavit "where the source personally appears before the magistrate" a greater threat to liberty and privacy than the use of unnamed hearsay sources in affidavits? Do any dangers exist in the latter case that do not exist in the former?

(b) Hearsay Sources

Although the *Gates* Court disavowed mechanical application of the two-pronged test, that test remains a valuable guideline in the assessment of probable cause, especially as a mode of promoting a degree of uniformity in decision-making. For this reason even pre-*Gates* decisions generalizing about the reliability of various sorts of hearsay sources remain important.

The Professional Tipster. If a police officer is to make an arrest based upon the claimed observations of a professional tipster, such as an a addict-informant, facts known to the police must establish the reliability of the tipster. Similarly, if a warrant is to issue based upon such a tipster's alleged firsthand information, and if the tipster is not the affiant but rather is a hearsay declarant, facts made known to the magistrate must demonstrate the tipster's reliability. Granted that the affiant's sworn declaration that the tipster is "reliable" will not suffice, how much more is necessary? Will an assertion that the source "gave reliable information in the past" suffice? Compare People v. Parker, 42 Ill.2d 42, 245 N.E.2d 487 (1968), with State v. Ebron, 61 N.J. 207, 294 A.2d 1 (1972).

Reliability of a tipster is often established by an allegation in the affidavit that on a specified number of occasions the tipster gave information to the police about criminal activity, which information the police investigated and found to be true. Is a source who has proved his or her reliability in one area of criminal activity reliable for probable cause purposes when he gives information in another area? See State v. Comeau, 114 N.H. 431, 321 A.2d 590 (1974). It can also be established if the tipster provides information that is a declaration against interest, as discussed below.

The Citizen Informant. A different rationale exists for establishing the reliability of named "citizen-informers" as opposed to the traditional idea of unnamed police contacts or informers who usually themselves are criminals. Information supplied to officers by the traditional police informer is not given in the spirit of a concerned citizen, but often is given in exchange for some concession, payment, or simply out of revenge against the subject. The nature of these persons and the information which they supply convey a certain impression of unreliability, and it is proper to demand that some evidence of their credibility and reliability be shown. One practical way of making such a showing is to point to accurate information which they have supplied in the past.

However, an ordinary citizen who reports a crime which has been committed in his presence, or that a crime is being or will be committed, stands on much different ground than a police informer. She is a witness to criminal activity who acts with an intent to aid the police in law enforcement because of her concern for society or for her own safety. She does not expect any gain or concession in exchange for her information. Is this always the case however? Consider a citizen informant who is reporting a burglary and mistakes the value of the goods taken? Would that cast doubt on this person's reliability as to the identity of the perpetrator, if known? Or consider a witness who is part of the action. For example, suppose a witness witnessed an assault, but became an active participant when the witness intervened with force to save the victim. An informer of this type, however, usually would not have more than one opportunity to supply information to the police, thereby precluding proof of her reliability by pointing to previous accurate information which she has supplied.

It would be unreasonable to demand the same showing of prior reliability in the case of such an informer as in the case of a "traditional police informer." Rather, the reliability of such a person should be evaluated from the nature of her report, her opportunity to hear and see the matters reported, and the extent to which it can be verified by independent police investigation.

Named and Anonymous Sources. In *Dawson*, Judge Moylan distinguished named hearsay sources from unnamed sources and noted that naming a source may go along way toward establishing reliability. Actually there may be several categories of sources in such a classification system. *A* source's identity maybe unknown to the police, as in the case of an anonymous telephone caller. Such a person's word is not presumed reliable. Nevertheless, after the *Gates* decision police departments began soliciting anonymous tips because in the correct circumstances they could be part of the basis for probable cause. Billboards were erected with the message "Dial 1–800–777–TIPS" What are some of the dangers if the source's identity is not known? Of course, an anonymous tip alone is ordinarily insufficient to establish probable cause alone, but if it is corroborated by other evidence, even evidence of non-criminal activity, it can form the basis of probable cause.

Information may be personally conveyed to an officer by someone whose name is unknown to the officer and who quickly disappears. Alternatively, the name of a source may be known to the officer but kept secret from the judicial officer, as in the typical unnamed hearsay-declarant affidavit, or in a hearing following a warrantless arrest where the prosecutor invokes the informer privilege. Finally, the identity of the hearsay source may be revealed in the affidavit or, following a warrantless arrest, may be revealed at the motion to suppress. The presumption of reliability is increased in this progression of examples.

If the name of the hearsay source is to be revealed in the affidavit, would it make more sense if the police had the source serve as the affiant so as to eliminate the need to establish the reliability of a hearsay source?

The Fellow Officer. Officer X is safe in relying upon the claimed personal observations of Officer Y as long as those observations, if true, add up to probable cause. When the hearsay source is a fellow officer, there is a presumption of reliability.

The Declarant Against Interest. If *A* confesses to a known burglary and states that the proceeds are in his own garage, the police may relate A's confession to a magistrate through an officer's affidavit and thereby establish probable cause. The law presumes that *A* will not falsely make declarations against his own interest. Many cases extend the presumption of reliability to the portion of A's confession which implicates an alleged accomplice. Thus *B* may be arrested based upon A's unsworn confession implicating both *A* and *B* in an offense. See United States v. Long, 449 F.2d 288 (8th Cir.1971). The Supreme Court gave support to the declaration-against-interest theory of reliability in probable cause determinations when, in United States v. Harris, 403 U.S. 573, 91 S.Ct. 2075 (1971), it extended the concept quite far. See also United States v. Matlock, 415 U.S. 164, 94 S.Ct. 988 (1974). Consider such decisions in light of the Supreme Court's declaration, in the context of the right of confrontation at the trial of innocence or guilt, that what a confessing defendant says in his post-arrest statement is presumptively unreliable inso far as it implicates another. Lee v. Illinois, 476 U.S. 530, 106 S.Ct. 2056 (1986), infra.

3. Additional Probable Cause Issues

(a) Probable Cause for What?

"Probable cause for arrest" refers to the probability that a crime has been committed—crime probable cause—and the probability that the particular suspect committed it—*offender probable cause*. "Probable cause for a search warrant" refers to the probability that a crime has been committed (crime probable cause) and the probability that evidence of that crime is located at the place to be searched—*search probable cause*. In other situations, probable cause refers to the probability that an item to be seized is either contraband or constitutes evidence of a crime—*seizure probable cause*.

Probable cause for an offense defined by a statute that is subsequently held to be unconstitutional nevertheless will suffice to establish probable cause. The officer's good faith belief in the validity of the ordinance at the time of the arrest suffices as a predicate for the arrest. Michigan v. DeFillippo, 443 U.S. 31, 99 S.Ct. 2627 (1979).

(b) Special Problems Concerning "Search Probable Cause"—Staleness

For a valid search warrant to issue, there must be probable cause to believe that evidence named in the warrant is present at the place to be searched.

Similarly, because search probable cause is required under the warrantless vehicle search doctrine (treated subsequently in Section J of this chapter), there must be a probability that contraband or evidence of the crime will be discovered. The probabilities will vary from factual situation to factual situation, but some patterns recur.

An affidavit may recite facts that demonstrate the reliability of a hearsay source and then recite the source's claimed personal observations but neglect to say when the source claimed that these observations occurred. If the source saw certain criminal evidence in an apartment an hour before the affidavit was presented to the magistrate, search probable cause will exist. If the observations were three years ago, there most likely is no probable cause to believe that the items are now in the place to be searched. The affidavit just does not say.

Ordinarily the date of the observations will be stated in the affidavit. Then the question is whether the passage of time between the observation of the criminal evidence and the issuance of the warrant will raise the question as to whether probable cause still existed at the time of issuance. This may depend on a variety of factors. Obviously, a single observation of a small quantity of marijuana in an apartment will be insufficient to create a probability that marijuana will be there a month later. On the other hand, repeated observations of the use in a business of certain stolen machines may create a probability that such machines are still in the same place many months after the latest observation. Staleness is judged on a case-by-case basis; evidence of child pornography possession six and a half years earlier was not stale data because studies show that pedophiles preserve child pornography collections for years. People v. Russo, 439 Mich. 584, 487 N.W.2d 698 (1992).

Sometimes no source will have claimed that he or she saw criminal evidence in the place to be searched. The issue then is whether circumstantial evidence creates probable cause. For example, police officers may have probable cause to believe that *A* committed a burglary, that several valuable pieces of jewelry were taken and that *A* resides at a certain address. Do they have probable cause to believe that the stolen articles are hidden or kept in A's home?

Sometimes the facts will include both (1) a passage of time between the reported criminal activity, and (2) no claim that anyone ever actually saw the particular evidence in the known offender's home. Again the ultimate test is whether at the time of the issuance of the warrant (or, if no warrant is required, at the time of the search) there was probable cause to believe that evidence was at the place to be searched.

(c) *Probable cause to search when the person whose privacy will be invaded is not suspected to be a criminal offender*

Offender probable cause is not essential for the issuance of a search warrant. A person not suspected of a crime may have his privacy invaded if there is probable cause to believe that a crime has been committed and that evidence of that crime is on his property. Zurcher v. Stanford Daily, 436 U.S. 547, 98 S.Ct. 1970 (1978).

(d) Imputed Knowledge

Sometimes Officer A will act at the direction of Officer B without pausing to learn what data B has in his or her possession. The classic example is a patrol officer's response to a directive received over a police radio. From A's point of view, it may seem reasonable to do what he is told without pausing to learn of the underlying data. However, when the matter is litigated, as for example at a hearing on a motion to suppress following a warrantless arrest by A, the prosecution must prove that within the knowledge of someone in the police department were data personally observed by an officer or information from a credible source which added up to probable cause. Sometimes courts say that what is known to one officer is, for probable cause purposes, known by all under the doctrine of "imputed knowledge."

If Officer C happens to know something which would help establish probable cause to arrest X but never communicates that information to anyone and never directs or requests any action, can such data be used to support probable cause following Officer D's warrantless arrest of X? Should C's knowledge be imputed to D in such a case?

Sometimes the imputed knowledge doctrine is invoked where an officer in one jurisdiction acts at the direction of an officer in another jurisdiction. But, again, the underlying probable cause data must be brought out at the hearing on the motion to suppress. Police Department #1 cannot insulate an arrest from probable cause scrutiny by asserting that it acted at the direction of Department #2. Whiteley v. Warden, 401 U.S. 560, 91 S.Ct. 1031 (1971), may be viewed an example of the failure to prove up probable cause data in an imputed knowledge case, although that issue was not the focus of the decision.

* * *

How specific does the probable cause have to be? Suppose officers have clear probable cause to believe a crime has been committed, but it is unclear which, if any of multiple suspects committed it?

Maryland v. Pringle

Supreme Court of the United States, 2003.
540 U.S. 366, 124 S.Ct. 795.

■ CHIEF JUSTICE REHNQUIST delivered the opinion of the Court.

In the early morning hours a passenger car occupied by three men was stopped for speeding by a police officer. The officer, upon searching the car, seized $763 of rolled-up cash from the glove compartment and five glassine baggies of cocaine from between the back-seat armrest and the back seat. After all three men denied ownership of the cocaine and money, the officer arrested each of them. We hold that the officer had probable cause to arrest Pringle—one of the three men.

At 3:16 a.m. on August 7, 1999, a Baltimore County Police officer stopped a Nissan Maxima for speeding. There were three occupants in the car: Donte Partlow, the driver and owner, respondent Pringle, the front-seat passenger, and Otis Smith, the back-seat passenger. The officer asked Partlow for his license and registration. When Partlow opened the glove compartment to retrieve the vehicle registration, the officer observed a large amount of rolled-up money in the glove compartment. The officer returned to his patrol car with Partlow's license and registration to check the computer system for outstanding violations. The computer check did not reveal any violations. The officer returned to the stopped car, had Partlow get out, and issued him an oral warning.

After a second patrol car arrived, the officer asked Partlow if he had any weapons or narcotics in the vehicle. Partlow indicated that he did not. Partlow then consented to a search of the vehicle. The search yielded $763 from the glove compartment and five plastic glassine baggies containing cocaine from behind the back-seat armrest. When the officer began the search the armrest was in the upright position flat against the rear seat.

The officer pulled down the armrest and found the drugs, which had been placed between the armrest and the back seat of the car.

The officer questioned all three men about the ownership of the drugs and money, and told them that if no one admitted to ownership of the drugs he was going to arrest them all. The men offered no information regarding the ownership of the drugs or money. All three were placed under arrest and transported to the police station.

Later that morning, Pringle waived his rights under Miranda v. Arizona, and gave an oral and written confession in which he acknowledged that the cocaine belonged to him, that he and his friends were going to a party, and that he intended to sell the cocaine or "[u]se it for sex.". Pringle maintained that the other occupants of the car did not know about the drugs, and they were released.

The trial court denied Pringle's motion to suppress his confession as the fruit of an illegal arrest, holding that the officer had probable cause to arrest Pringle. A jury convicted Pringle of possession with intent to distribute cocaine and possession of cocaine. He was sentenced to 10 years' incarceration without the possibility of parole. The Court of Special Appeals of Maryland affirmed. The Court of Appeals of Maryland, by divided vote, reversed, holding that, absent specific facts tending to show Pringle's knowledge and dominion or control over the drugs, "the mere finding of cocaine in the back armrest when [Pringle] was a front seat passenger in a car being driven by its owner is insufficient to establish probable cause for an arrest for possession." We granted certiorari,and now reverse.

Under the Fourth Amendment, made applicable to the States by the Fourteenth Amendment (cite omitted), the people are "to be secure in their persons, houses, papers, and effects, against unreasonable searches and seizures, ... and no Warrants shall issue, but upon probable cause...." U.S. Const., Amdt. 4. Maryland law authorizes police officers to execute warrantless arrests, *inter alia*, for felonies committed in an officer's presence or where an officer has probable cause to believe that a felony has been committed or is being committed in the officer's presence. Md. Ann. Code, Art. 27, § 594B (1996) (repealed 2001). A warrantless arrest of an individual in a public place for a felony, or a misdemeanor committed in the officer's presence, is consistent with the Fourth Amendment if the arrest is supported by probable cause....

It is uncontested in the present case that the officer, upon recovering the five plastic glassine baggies containing suspected cocaine, had probable cause to believe a felony had been committed. Md. Ann. Code, Art. 27, § 287 (1996) (repealed 2002) (prohibiting possession of controlled dangerous substances). The sole question is whether the officer had probable cause to believe that Pringle committed that crime.[1]

The long-prevailing standard of probable cause protects "citizens from rash and unreasonable interferences with privacy and from unfounded charges of crime," while giving "fair leeway for enforcing the law in the

1. Maryland law defines "possession" as "the exercise of actual or constructive dominion or control over a thing by one or more persons." Md. Ann. Code, Art. 27, § 277(s) (1996) (repealed 2002).

community's protection." Brinegar v. United States. On many occasions, we have reiterated that the probable-cause standard is a " 'practical, nontechnical conception' " that deals with " 'the factual and practical considerations of everyday life on which reasonable and prudent men, not legal technicians, act.' " Illinois v. Gates (quoting Brinegar) . . . "[P]robable cause is a fluid concept—turning on the assessment of probabilities in particular factual contexts—not readily, or even usefully, reduced to a neat set of legal rules." *Gates*.

The probable-cause standard is incapable of precise definition or quantification into percentages because it deals with probabilities and depends on the totality of the circumstances. We have stated, however, that "[t]he substance of all the definitions of probable cause is a reasonable ground for belief of guilt," and that the belief of guilt must be particularized with respect to the person to be searched or seized, Ybarra v. Illinois (1979). In Illinois v. Gates, we noted:

> As early as Locke v. United States, 11 U.S. 339, 7 Cranch 339, 348, [3 L. Ed. 364] (1813), Chief Justice Marshall observed, in a closely related context: "[T]he term 'probable cause,' according to its usual acceptation, means less than evidence which would justify condemnation.... It imports a seizure made under circumstances which warrant suspicion. More recently, we said that 'the quanta ... of proof' appropriate in ordinary judicial proceedings are inapplicable to the decision to issue a warrant. Brinegar, 338 U.S., at 173 [69 S. Ct. 1302]. Finely tuned standards such as proof beyond a reasonable doubt or by a preponderance of the evidence, useful in formal trials, have no place in the [probable-cause] decision." 462 U.S., at 235, 103 S. Ct. 2317.

To determine whether an officer had probable cause to arrest an individual, we examine the events leading up to the arrest, and then decide "whether these historical facts, viewed from the standpoint of an objectively reasonable police officer, amount to" probable cause, *Ornelas*.

In this case, Pringle was one of three men riding in a Nissan Maxima at 3:16 a.m. There was $763 of rolled-up cash the glove compartment directly in front of Pringle.[2] Five plastic glassine baggies of cocaine were behind the back-seat armrest and accessible to all three men. Upon questioning, the three men failed to offer any information with respect to the ownership of the cocaine or the money.

2. The Court of Appeals of Maryland dismissed the $763 seized from the glove compartment as a factor in the probable-cause determination, stating that "[m]oney, without more, is innocuous." 370 Md. 524, 546, 805 A.2d 1016, 1028 (2002). The court's consideration of the money in isolation, rather than as a factor in the totality of the circumstances, is mistaken in light of our precedents. See, e.g., Illinois v. Gates (1983) (opining that the totality of the circumstances approach is consistent with our prior treatment of probable cause); Brinegar v. United States (1949) ("Probable cause exists where 'the facts and circumstances within their [the officers'] knowledge and of which they had reasonably trustworthy information [are] sufficient in themselves to warrant a man of reasonable caution in the belief that "an offense has been or is being committed"). We think it is abundantly clear from the facts that this case involves more than money alone.

We think it an entirely reasonable inference from these facts that any or all three of the occupants had knowledge of, and exercised dominion and control over, the cocaine. Thus a reasonable officer could conclude that there was probable cause to believe Pringle committed the crime of possession of cocaine, either solely or jointly.

Pringle's attempt to characterize this case as a guilt-by-association case is unavailing. His reliance on Ybarra v. Illinois and United States v. Di Reis misplaced. In *Ybarra*, police officers obtained a warrant to search a tavern and its bartender for evidence of possession of a controlled substance. Upon entering the tavern, the officers conducted patdown searches of the customers present in the tavern, including Ybarra. Inside a cigarette pack retrieved from Ybarra's pocket, an officer found six tinfoil packets containing heroin. We stated:

> "[A] person's mere propinquity to others independently suspected of criminal activity does not, without more, give rise to probable cause to search that person. Sibron v. New York. Where the standard is probable cause, a search or seizure of a person must be supported by probable cause particularized with respect to that person. This requirement cannot be undercut or avoided by simply pointing to the fact that coincidentally there exists probable cause to search or seize another or to search the premises where the person may happen to be." *444 U.S., at 91, 100 S. Ct. 338.*

We held that the search warrant did not permit body searches of all of the tavern's patrons and that the police could not pat down the patrons for weapons, absent individualized suspicion.

This case is quite different from *Ybarra* Pringle and his two companions were in a relatively small automobile, not a public tavern. In Wyoming v. Houghton (1999), we noted that "a car passenger—unlike the unwitting tavern patron in *Ybarra*—will often be engaged in a common enterprise with the driver, and have the same interest in concealing the fruits or the evidence of their wrongdoing." Here we think it was reasonable for the officer to infer a common enterprise among the three men. The quantity of drugs and cash in the car indicated the likelihood of drug dealing, an enterprise to which a dealer would be unlikely to admit an innocent person with the potential to furnish evidence against him.

In *Di Re*, a federal investigator had been told by an informant, Reed, that he was to receive counterfeit gasoline ration coupons from a certain Buttitta at a particular place. The investigator went to the appointed place and saw Reed, the sole occupant of the rear seat of the car, holding gasoline ration coupons. There were two other occupants in the car: Buttitta in the driver's seat and Di Re in the front passenger's seat. Reed informed the investigator that Buttitta had given him counterfeit coupons. Thereupon, all three men were arrested and searched. After noting that the officers had no information implicating Di Re and no information pointing to Di Re's possession of coupons, unless presence in the car warranted that inference, we concluded that the officer lacked probable cause to believe that Di Re was involved in the crime. We said "[a]ny inference that everyone on the scene of a crime is a party to it must disappear if the Government informer singles out the guilty person." No such singling out occurred in this case;

none of the three men provided information with respect to the ownership of the cocaine or money.

We hold that the officer had probable cause to believe that Pringle had committed the crime of possession of a controlled substance. Pringle's arrest therefore did not contravene the Fourth and Fourteenth Amendments. Accordingly, the judgment of the Court of Appeals of Maryland is reversed, and the case is remanded for further proceedings not inconsistent with this opinion.

It is so ordered.

D. THE ISSUANCE OF WARRANTS

For a warrant to be valid there must be compliance with the second clause of the Fourth Amendment: "... no warrants shall issue, but upon probable cause, supported by oath or affirmation and particularly describing the place to be searched, and the person or things to be seized." Most doctrines governing the issuance of warrants are derived from this clause, although occasionally the requirement of "reasonableness" from the Amendment's first clause might be invoked to limit the issuance of search warrants.

Under the rules of Federal Rules of Criminal Procedure, Rule 41 governs warrants:

Rule 41. Search and Seizure

(a) Scope and Definitions.

(1) *Scope.* This rule does not modify any statute regulating search or seizure, or the issuance and execution of a search warrant in special circumstances.

(2) *Definitions.* The following definitions apply under this rule:

(A) "Property" includes documents, books, papers, any other tangible objects, and information.

(B) "Daytime" means the hours between 6:00 a.m. and 10:00 p.m. according to local time.

(C) "Federal law enforcement officer" means a government agent (other than an attorney for the government) who is engaged in enforcing the criminal laws and is within any category of officers authorized by the Attorney General to request a search warrant.

(D) "Domestic terrorism" and "international terrorism" have the meanings set out in 18 U.S.C. § 2331.

(E) "Tracking device" has the meaning set out in 18 U.S.C. § 3117(b).

(b) Authority to Issue a Warrant. At the request of a federal law enforcement officer or an attorney for the government:

(1) a magistrate judge with authority in the district—or if none is reasonably available, a judge of a state court of record in the district—has

authority to issue a warrant to search for and seize a person or property located within the district;

(2) a magistrate judge with authority in the district has authority to issue a warrant for a person or property outside the district if the person or property is located within the district when the warrant is issued but might move or be moved outside the district before the warrant is executed;

(3) a magistrate judge—in an investigation of domestic terrorism or international terrorism—with authority in any district in which activities related to the terrorism may have occurred has authority to issue a warrant for a person or property within or outside that district; and

(4) a magistrate judge with authority in the district has authority to issue a warrant to install within the district a tracking device; the warrant may authorize use of the device to track the movement of a person or property located within the district, outside the district, or both.

(c) Persons or Property Subject to Search or Seizure. A warrant may be issued for any of the following:

(1) evidence of a crime;

(2) contraband, fruits of crime, or other items illegally possessed;

(3) property designed for use, intended for use, or used in committing a crime; or

(4) a person to be arrested or a person who is unlawfully restrained.

(d) Obtaining a Warrant.

(1) *In General.* After receiving an affidavit or other information, a magistrate judge—or if authorized by Rule 41(b), a judge of a state court of record—must issue the warrant if here is probable cause to search for and seize a person or property or to install and use a tracking device.

(2) *Requesting a Warrant in the Presence of a Judge.*

(A) *Warrant on an Affidavit.* When a federal law enforcement officer or an attorney for the government presents an affidavit in support of a warrant, the judge may require the affiant to appear personally and may examine under oath the affiant and any witness the affiant produces.

(B) *Warrant on Sworn Testimony.* The judge may wholly warrant on sworn testimony if doing so is reasonable under the circumstances.

(C) *Recording Testimony.* Testimony taken in support of a warrant must be recorded by a court reporter or by a suitable recording device, and the judge must file the transcript or recording with the clerk, along with any affidavit.

(3) *Requesting a Warrant by Telephonic or Other Means.*

(A) *In General.* A magistrate judge may issue a warrant based on information communicated by telephone or other reliable electronic means.

(B) *Recording Testimony.* Upon learning that an applicant is requesting a warrant under Rule 41(d)(3)(A), a magistrate judge must:

(i) place under oath the applicant and any person on whose testimony the application is based; and

(ii) make a verbatim record of the conversation with a suitable recording device, if available, or by a court reporter, or in writing.

(C) *Certifying Testimony.* The magistrate judge must have any recording or court reporter's notes transcribed, certify the transcription's accuracy, and file a copy of the record and the transcription with the clerk. Any written verbatim record must be signed by the magistrate judge and filed with the clerk.

(D) *Suppression Limited.* Absent a finding of bad faith, evidence obtained from a warrant issued under Rule 41(d)(3)(A) is not subject to suppression on the ground that issuing the warrant in that manner was unreasonable under the circumstances.

(e) Issuing the Warrant.

(1) *In General.* The magistrate judge or a judge of a state court of record must issue the warrant to an officer authorized to execute it.

(2) *Contents of the Warrant.*

(A) *Warrant to Search for and Seize a Person or Property.*

Except for a tracking-device warrant, the warrant must identify the person or property to be searched, identify any person or property to be seized, and designate the magistrate judge to whom it must be returned. The warrant must command the officer to:

(i) execute the warrant within a specified time no longer than 10 days;

(ii) execute the warrant during the daytime, unless the judge for good cause expressly authorizes execution at another time; and

(iii) return the warrant to the magistrate judge designated in the warrant.

(B) *Warrant for a Tracking Device.* A tracking-device warrant must identify the person or property to be tracked, designate the magistrate judge to whom it must be returned, and specify a reasonable length of time that the device may be used. The time must not exceed 45 days from the date the warrant was issued. The court may, for good cause, grant one or more extensions for a reasonable period not to exceed 45 days each. The warrant must command the officer to:

(i) complete any installation authorized by the warrant within a specified time no longer than 10 calendar days;

(ii) perform any installation authorized by the warrant during the daytime, unless the judge for good cause expressly authorizes installation at another time; and

(iii) return the warrant to the judge designated in the warrant.

(3) *Warrant by Telephonic or Other Means.* If a magistrate judge decides to proceed under Rule 41(d)(3)(A), the following additional procedures apply:

(A) *Preparing a Proposed Duplicate Original Warrant.* The applicant must prepare a "proposed duplicate original warrant" and must read or otherwise transmit the contents of that document verbatim to the magistrate judge.

(B) *Preparing an Original Warrant.* If the applicant reads the contents of the proposed duplicate original warrant, the magistrate judge must enter those contents into an original warrant. If the applicant transmits the contents by reliable electronic means, that transmission may serve as the original warrant.

(C) *Modification.* The magistrate judge may modify the original warrant. The judge must transmit any modified warrant to the applicant by reliable electronic means under Rule 41(e)(3)(D) or direct the applicant to modify the proposed duplicate original warrant accordingly.

(D) *Signing the Warrant.* Upon determining to issue the warrant, the magistrate judge must immediately sign the original warrant, enter on its face the exact date and time it is issued, and transmit it by reliable electronic means to the applicant or direct the applicant to sign the judge's name on the duplicate original warrant.

(f) Executing and Returning the Warrant.

(1) *Warrant to Search for and Seize a Person or Property.*

(A) *Noting the Time.* The officer executing the warrant must enter on it the exact date and time it was executed.

(B) *Inventory.* An officer present during the execution of the warrant must prepare and verify an inventory of any property seized. The officer must do so in the presence of another officer and the person from whom, or from whose premises, the property was taken. If either one is not present, the officer must prepare and verify the inventory in the presence of at least one other credible person.

(C) *Receipt.* The officer executing the warrant must give a copy of the warrant and a receipt for the property taken to the person from whom, or from whose premises, the property was taken or leave a copy of the warrant and receipt at the place where the officer took the property.

(D) *Return.* The officer executing the warrant must promptly return it—together with a copy of the inventory—to the magistrate judge designated on the warrant. The judge must, on request, give a copy of the inventory to the person from whom, or from whose premises, the property was taken and to the applicant for the warrant.

(2) *Warrant for a Tracking Device.*

(A) *Noting the Time.* The officer executing a tracking-device warrant must enter on it the exact date and time the device was installed and the period during which it was used.

(B) *Return.* Within 10 calendar days after the use of the tracking device has ended, the officer executing the warrant must return it to the judge designated in the warrant.

(C) *Service.* Within 10 calendar days after the use of the tracking device has ended, the officer executing a tracking-device warrant must serve a copy of the warrant on the person who was tracked or whose property was tracked. Service may be accomplished by delivering a copy to the person who, or whose property, was tracked; or by leaving a copy at the person's residence or usual place of abode with an individual of suitable age and discretion who resides at that location and by mailing a copy to the person's last known address. Upon request of the government, the judge may delay notice as provided in Rule 41(f)(3).

(3) *Delayed Notice.* Upon the government's request, a magistrate judge—or if authorized by Rule 41(b), a judge of a state court of record—may delay any notice required by this rule if the delay is authorized by statute.

(g) Motion to Return Property. A person aggrieved by an unlawful search and seizure of property or by the deprivation of property may move for the property's return. The motion must be filed in the district where the property was seized. The court must receive evidence on any factual issue necessary to decide the motion. If it grants the motion, the court must return the property to the movant, but may impose reasonable conditions to protect access to the property and its use in later proceedings.

(h) Motion to Suppress. A defendant may move to suppress evidence in the court where the trial will occur, as Rule 12 provides.

(i) Forwarding Papers to the Clerk. The magistrate judge to whom the warrant is returned must attach to the warrant a copy of the return, of the inventory, and of all other related papers and must deliver them to the clerk in the district where the property was seized.

* * *

We have already considered the probable cause requirement in the preceding Section C; now we shall consider some of the other requirements and limitations upon the issuance of search warrants.

NOTES

1. *The Issuance Requirements*

(a) Neutral Judicial Officer

Warrants may be issued only by neutral judicial officers. The centrality of the warrant requirement is premised upon the belief that the right of citizens to be free from unreasonable searches will be better protected if the assessment of probable cause is made by a judicial officer who is not in the competitive business of enforcing the criminal law. "Judges and magistrates are not adjuncts to the law enforcement team; as neutral judicial officers, they have no stake in the outcome of particular criminal prosecutions." United States v. Leon, 468 U.S. 897, 917, 104 S.Ct. 3405, 3417 (1984). Thus, in Coolidge v. New Hampshire, 403 U.S. 443, 91 S.Ct. 2022 (1971) the Court invalidated a warrant issued by the state Attorney

General (in his capacity as an ex officio justice of the peace), in a case where the Attorney General himself had directed the investigation. Similarly in Lo–Ji Sales, Inc. v. New York, 442 U.S. 319, 99 S.Ct. 2319 (1979), a magistrate signed an open-ended warrant and then went to the scene of the search and performed as if he were the supervising investigative officer was held not to be sufficiently detached. The problem often arises in the armed services, where company commanders have the power to issue warrants. If such commanders play the role of "police officer" in the investigation, they are not sufficiently neutral. United States v. Ezell, 6 M.J. 307 (C.M.A.1979). On the other hand, if neutrality is preserved, the "judicial officer" need not be a judge or magistrate, at least to issue arrest warrants. He or she can be a court clerk. Shadwick v. City of Tampa, 407 U.S. 345, 92 S.Ct. 2119 (1972). The latter case, contrasted with Coolidge, demonstrates that "detachment," not learnedness in the law, underlies the neutral judicial officer requirement. See also Connally v. Georgia, 429 U.S. 245, 97 S.Ct. 546 (1977), where neutrality was lacking because the officer received a fee if he issued the warrant, received no fee if he issued no warrant, and he had issued thousands of warrants without ever refusing to issue one.

A major premise of the neutrality requirement (and of the law's preference for the use of warrants) is that the judicial officer will not simply defer to the judgment of the law enforcement officer who presents the complaint for a warrant, together with the proposed warrant for the magistrate's signature. Rather, the magistrate will carefully review the affidavits or sworn oral testimony and will make an independent assessment of probable cause.

Perhaps because there are few empirical studies, little about actual practice is reflected in reported cases, even though many lawyers believe that the magistrate who carefully reviews a warrant application is the exception rather than the rule. Occasionally claims are raised that in the particular case the magistrate did not even read the supporting affidavits. See State v. Dudick, 158 W.Va. 629, 213 S.E.2d 458 (1975); Rooker v. Commonwealth, 508 S.W.2d 570 (Ky.1974), both of which suggest that the warrant is invalid if such an allegation is proved. Compare Clodfelter v. Commonwealth, 218 Va. 98, 235 S.E.2d 340 (1977), which suggested that a two-minute review is not presumptively inadequate. Usually the only witnesses to the issuance of a search warrant are a law enforcement officer and the issuing magistrate. (A few empirical studies are cited in LaFave, Search and Seizure, § 4.2(c) (3rd ed.1996).)

In many jurisdictions the police and the district attorney are free to select the magistrate from whom they seek a warrant although in some jurisdictions a specific judicial officer, perhaps on a rotating basis, is assigned to consider warrant applications. What happens when a magistrate declines to issue a warrant, and the authorities take the very same application to another judge? United States v. Savides, 658 F.Supp. 1399 (N.D.Ill.1987), upheld the practice, noting that the second magistrate had been informed of the first one's declination. *Savides* also suggested that two or more declinations might lead to a prohibition against further forum shopping. See also LaFave, Search and Seizure, § 4.2(e) (3rd ed. 1996), agreeing with result in *Savides*, but noting some contrary authority.

(b) Oral or Written Sworn Probable Cause Data: Personal Appearance of Affiant?

As indicated in the preceding Section C, probable cause data must be presented under oath to the issuing magistrate before issuance of a warrant. Although the Fourth Amendment has been interpreted to allow the use of sworn oral data, the normal practice is to use affidavits in applying for a search warrant. Some jurisdictions require that affidavits or recorded oral testimony be used in search warrant applications. For a review of law and policy, see Linton, Unrecorded Oral Testimony in Support of a Search Warrant: Is It Admissible? Is It Advisable? 14 Loy.U. (Chi.) L.J. 57 (1982).

Some jurisdictions have special procedures for the use of telephonic applications for search warrants. Although federal judges may compel the personal appearance of any affiant whose statement appears in an application for a warrant, they may also excuse the personal appearance. Fed.R.Crim.P. 41 now allows for telephonic applications, but requires that the application be supported by sworn testimony and that the testimony be recorded. When considering other means, the 1993 Advisory Committee "considered, but rejected ... use of computer modems. In its view facsimile transmissions provide some method of assuring the authenticity of the writing transmitted by the affiant." Notes to the 1993 Amendments. Now, Rule 41 is written in a way that does not foreclose other means: "A magistrate judge may issue a warrant based on information communicated by telephone *or other appropriate means*, including facsimile transmission." Fed.R.Crim.P. 41(d)(3)(A). (Emphasis added).

When affidavits are used, the magistrate must make a judgment about the credibility of the affiant, as pointed out in the preceding Section C. This suggests that the affiant must appear before the issuing magistrate (or at least communicate telephonically with the magistrate). Nevertheless, Federal Rule 41 allows, but does not require, the magistrate to insist upon the appearance of the affiant. Suppose that the police use a professional tipster as the affiant rather than a hearsay source, thus avoiding the need to establish within the affidavit itself the reliability of the tipster. How can the magistrate make a credibility judgment in such a situation without the opportunity to scrutinize the demeanor of the tipster-affiant?

(c) Fictitious Name Signatures

Reconsider the problem, already discussed in the preceding Section C, of the affiant who uses an admittedly fictitious signature.

(d) "Sneak and Peak" Warrants

In recent years, law enforcement have used "sneak and peak" warrants that authorize entry to survey a location, perhaps take pictures, and leave without seizing any items. The proposed amendments to the Federal Rules of Criminal Procedure in 2002 included authorization for these types of warrants. Several groups spoke out against them and ultimately, the provision was tabled. The Patriot Act, however, authorized a sneak and peak warrant in limited circumstances. The United States Supreme Court has not yet ruled on their constitutionality.

(e) Anticipatory Warrants

When reliable information indicates that contraband or criminal evidence is likely to be transported to a particular place in the near future, officers may wish to secure a search warrant for that place, to be executed after arrival of the evidence. To wait until the goods arrive may be too late, particularly if the criminals plan to quickly transport the goods elsewhere (as would be true in a common narcotics transaction). The law's preference for prior judicial evaluation of probable cause data has led some jurisdictions to approve use of anticipatory warrants based upon a kind of "future" search probable cause: a probability that evidence of a crime will soon be in the place to be searched. See Fed.R.Crim.P. 41. The United States Supreme Court has held that anticipatory warrants are not categorically invalid.

United States v. Jeffrey Grubbs

Supreme Court of the United States, 2006.
547 U.S. 90, 126 S.Ct. 1494.

■ JUSTICE SCALIA delivered the opinion of the Court.

Federal law enforcement officers obtained a search warrant for respondent's house on the basis of an affidavit explaining that tLast saved by XP XP2 Imagehe warrant would be executed only after a controlled delivery of contraband to that location. We address two challenges to the constitutionality of this anticipatory warrant.

I

Respondent Jeffrey Grubbs purchased a videotape containing child pornography from a Web site operated by an undercover postal inspector. Officers from the Postal Inspection Service arranged a controlled delivery of a package containing the videotape to Grubbs' residence. A postal inspector submitted a search warrant application to a Magistrate Judge for the Eastern District of California, accompanied by an affidavit describing the proposed operation in detail. The affidavit stated:

> "Execution of this search warrant will not occur unless and until the parcel has been received by a person(s) and has been physically taken into the residence.... At that time, and not before, this search warrant will be executed by me and other United States Postal inspectors, with appropriate assistance from other law enforcement officers in accordance with this warrant's command." App. to Pet. for Cert. 72a.

In addition to describing this triggering condition, the affidavit referred to two attachments, which described Grubbs' residence and the items officers would seize. These attachments, but not the body of the affidavit, were incorporated into the requested warrant. The affidavit concluded:

> "Based upon the foregoing facts, I respectfully submit there exists probable cause to believe that the items set forth in Attachment B to this affidavit and the search warrant, will be found [at Grubbs' residence], which residence is further described at Attachment A"

The Magistrate Judge issued the warrant as requested. Two days later, an undercover postal inspector delivered the package. Grubbs' wife signed for it and took the unopened package inside. The inspectors detained Grubbs as he left his home a few minutes later, then entered the house and commenced the search. Roughly 30 minutes into the search, Grubbs was provided with a copy of the warrant, which included both attachments but not the supporting affidavit that explained when the warrant would be executed. Grubbs consented to interrogation by the postal inspectors and admitted ordering the videotape. He was placed under arrest, and various items were seized, including the videotape.

A grand jury for the Eastern District of California indicted Grubbs on one count of receiving a visual depiction of a minor engaged in sexually explicit conduct. He moved to suppress the evidence seized during the search of his residence, arguing as relevant here that the warrant was invalid because it failed to list the triggering condition. After an evidentiary hearing, the District Court denied the motion. Grubbs pleaded guilty, but reserved his right to appeal the denial of his motion to suppress.

The Court of Appeals for the Ninth Circuit reversed. Relying on Circuit precedent, it held that "the particularity requirement of the Fourth Amendment applies with full force to the conditions precedent to an anticipatory search warrant." An anticipatory warrant defective for that reason may be "cur[ed]" if the conditions precedent are set forth in an affidavit that is incorporated in the warrant and "presented to the person whose property is being searched." Because the postal inspectors "failed to present the affidavit—the only document in which the triggering conditions were listed"—to Grubbs or his wife, the "warrant was . . . inoperative, and the search was illegal." We granted certiorari.

II

Before turning to the Ninth Circuit's conclusion that the warrant at issue here ran afoul of the Fourth Amendment's particularity requirement, we address the antecedent question whether anticipatory search warrants are categorically unconstitutional. An anticipatory warrant is "a warrant based upon an affidavit showing probable cause that at some future time (but not presently) certain evidence of crime will be located at a specified place." 2 W. LaFave, Search and Seizure § 3.7(c), p 398 (4th ed. 2004). Most anticipatory warrants subject their execution to some condition precedent other than the mere passage of time—a so-called "triggering condition." The affidavit at issue here, for instance, explained that "[e]xecution of th[e] search warrant will not occur unless and until the parcel [containing child pornography] has been received by a person(s) and has been physically taken into the residence." If the government were to execute an anticipatory warrant before the triggering condition occurred, there would be no reason to believe the item described in the warrant could be found at the searched location; by definition, the triggering condition which establishes probable cause has not yet been satisfied when the warrant is issued. Grubbs argues that for this reason anticipatory warrants contravene the Fourth Amendment's provision that "no Warrants shall issue, but upon probable cause."

We reject this view, as has every Court of Appeals to confront the issue. Probable cause exists when "there is a fair probability that contraband or evidence of a crime will be found in a particular place." Illinois v. Gates (1983). Because the probable-cause requirement looks to whether evidence will be found *when the search is conducted*, all warrants are, in a sense, "anticipatory." In the typical case where the police seek permission to search a house for an item they believe is already located there, the magistrate's determination that there is probable cause for the search amounts to a prediction that the item will still be there when the warrant is executed. . . .

Anticipatory warrants are, therefore, no different in principle from ordinary warrants. They require the magistrate to determine (1) that it is *now probable* that (2) contraband, evidence of a crime, or a fugitive *will be* on the described premises (3) when the warrant is executed. It should be noted, however, that where the anticipatory warrant places a condition (other than the mere passage of time) upon its execution, the first of these determinations goes not merely to what will probably be found *if* the condition is met. (If that were the extent of the probability determination, an anticipatory warrant could be issued for every house in the country, authorizing search and seizure *if* contraband should be delivered—though for any single location there is no likelihood that contraband will be delivered.) Rather, the probability determination for a conditioned anticipatory warrant looks also to the likelihood that the condition will occur, and thus that a proper object of seizure will be on the described premises. In other words, for a conditioned anticipatory warrant to comply with the Fourth Amendment's requirement of probable cause, two prerequisites of probability must be satisfied. It must be true not only that *if* the triggering condition occurs "there is a fair probability that contraband or evidence of a crime will be found in a particular place," ... but also that there is probable cause to believe the triggering condition *will occur*. The supporting affidavit must provide the magistrate with sufficient information to evaluate both aspects of the probable-cause determination.

In this case, the occurrence of the triggering condition—successful delivery of the videotape to Grubbs' residence—would plainly establish probable cause for the search. In addition, the affidavit established probable cause to believe the triggering condition would be satisfied. Although it is possible that Grubbs could have refused delivery of the videotape he had ordered, that was unlikely. The Magistrate therefore "had a 'substantial basis for ... conclud[ing]' that probable cause existed." *Gates*

III

The Ninth Circuit invalidated the anticipatory search warrant at issue here because the warrant failed to specify the triggering condition. The Fourth Amendment's particularity requirement, it held, "applies with full force to the conditions precedent to an anticipatory search warrant."

The Fourth Amendment, however, does not set forth some general "particularity requirement." It specifies only two matters that must be "particularly describ[ed]" in the warrant: "the place to be searched" and "the persons or things to be seized." We have previously rejected efforts to expand the scope of this provision to embrace unenumerated matters ...

Respondent, drawing upon the Ninth Circuit's analysis below, relies primarily on two related policy rationales. First, he argues, setting forth the triggering condition in the warrant itself is necessary "to delineate the limits of the executing officer's power." Brief for Respondent 20. This is an application, respondent asserts, of the following principle: "[I]f there is a precondition to the valid exercise of executive power, that precondition must be particularly identified on the face of the warrant." That principle is not to be found in the Constitution. The Fourth Amendment does not require that the warrant set forth the magistrate's basis for finding probable cause, even though probable cause is the quintessential "precondition to the valid exercise of executive power." Much less does it require description of a triggering condition.

Second, respondent argues that listing the triggering condition in the warrant is necessary to " 'assur[e] the individual whose property is searched or seized of the lawful authority of the executing officer, his need to search, and the limits of his power to search.' " The Ninth Circuit went even further, asserting that if the property owner were not informed of the triggering condition, he "would 'stand [no] real chance of policing the officers' conduct.' " This argument assumes that the executing officer must present the property owner with a copy of the warrant before conducting his search. In fact, however, neither the Fourth Amendment nor Federal Rule of Criminal Procedure 41 imposes such a requirement. The absence of a constitutional requirement that the warrant be exhibited at the outset of the search, or indeed until the search has ended, is . . . evidence that the requirement of particular description does not protect an interest in monitoring searches. The Constitution protects property owners not by giving them license to engage the police in a debate over the basis for the warrant, but by interposing, *ex ante*, the "deliberate, impartial judgment of a judicial officer . . . between the citizen and the police," and by providing, *ex post*, a right to suppress evidence improperly obtained and a cause of action for damages.

* * *

Because the Fourth Amendment does not require that the triggering condition for an anticipatory search warrant be set forth in the warrant itself, the Court of Appeals erred in invalidating the warrant at issue here. The judgment of the Court of Appeals is reversed, and the case is remanded for further proceedings consistent with this opinion.

It is so ordered.

■ JUSTICE ALITO took no part in the consideration or decision of this case.

■ JUSTICE SOUTER, with whom JUSTICE STEVENS and JUSTICE GINSBURG join, concurring in part and concurring in the judgment.

I agree with the Court that anticipatory warrants are constitutional for the reasons stated in Part II of the Court's opinion, and I join in the disposition of this case. But I would qualify some points made in Part III.

The Court notes that a warrant's failure to specify the place to be searched and the objects sought violates an express textual requirement of the Fourth Amendment, whereas the text says nothing about a condition placed by the issuing magistrate on the authorization to search (here, delivery of the package of contraband). That textual difference is, however, no authority for neglecting to specify the point or contingency intended by the magistrate to trigger authorization, and the government should beware of banking on the terms of a warrant without such specification. The notation of a starting date was an established feature even of the objectionable 18th-century writs of assistance, see, *e.g.*, Massachusetts Writs of Assistance Bill, 1762, reprinted in M. Smith, The Writs of Assistance Case 567–568 (1978); Writ of Assistance (English) of George III, 1761, reprinted in *id.*, at 524–527. And it is fair to say that the very word "warrant" in the

Fourth Amendment means a statement of authority that sets out the time at which (or, in the case of anticipatory warrants, the condition on which) the authorization begins.

An issuing magistrate's failure to mention that condition can lead to several untoward consequences with constitutional significance. To begin with, a warrant that fails to tell the truth about what a magistrate authorized cannot inform the police officer's responsibility to respect the limits of authorization, a failing assuming real significance when the warrant is not executed by the official who applied for it and happens to know the unstated condition. The peril is that if an officer simply takes such a warrant on its face and makes the ostensibly authorized search before the unstated condition has been met, the search will be held unreasonable. It is true that we have declined to apply the exclusionary rule when a police officer reasonably relies on the product of a magistrate's faulty judgment or sloppy practice, see Massachusetts v. Sheppard (1984). But when a government officer obtains what the magistrate says is an anticipatory warrant, he must know or should realize when it omits the condition on which authorization depends, and it is hard to see why the government should not be held to the condition despite the unconditional face of the warrant. Groh v. Ramirez (declaring unconstitutional a search conducted pursuant to a warrant failing to specify the items the government asked the magistrate permission to seize in part because "officers leading a search team must 'make sure that they have a proper warrant that in fact authorizes the search and seizure they are about to conduct.' ")

Nor does an incomplete anticipatory warrant address an owner's interest in an accurate statement of the government's authority to search property. To be sure, the extent of that interest is yet to be settled . . . the Court was careful to note that the right of an owner to demand to see a copy of the warrant before making way for the police had not been determined . . . and it remains undetermined today. But regardless of any right on the owner's part, showing an accurate warrant reliably "assures the individual whose property is searched or seized of the lawful authority of the executing officer, his need to search, and the limits of his power to search." And if a later case holds that the homeowner has a right to inspect the warrant on request, a statement of the condition of authorization would give the owner a right to correct any misapprehension on the police's part that the condition had been met when in fact it had not been. If the police were then to enter anyway without a reasonable (albeit incorrect) justification, the search would certainly be open to serious challenge as unreasonable within the meaning of the Fourth Amendment.

2. ***Form of Warrant.*** Whenever law enforcement obtains a warrant, there are two parts: the warrant itself and the supporting affidavit. Even when telephonic applications are used, the warrant itself is almost always a written instrument, which can serve as a notice to a property owner of the authority under which a search is to be made. It will also describe the location to be searched. A warrant may command a search to be made by a particular law enforcement agency or officer or, under different state law or custom it may be directed to all peace officers in the county or state.

The affidavit is not served at the time the warrant is executed. It becomes important at the time of a motion to suppress.

Most jurisdictions have forms for warrants. An example of one can be found at http://www.uscourts.gov/forms/AO093.pdf.

Then after the execution of the warrant, law enforcement officers must make a return to the court, detailing any item seized.

3. ***Specificity as to Place to Be Searched and Items to Be Seized.*** The place to be searched must be described with particularity. The adequacy of the detail is determined by context. In the case of a single family residence this is usually done by giving the street address. In rural areas a rural route address may be given. In some cases a map may be incorporated into the warrant or a legal description (which is the surveyor's official description) of the property may be given. Problems arise in cases involving multiple dwellings at a specific address. Often apartments do not have numbers and they must be described by location.

Occasionally deficiencies occur in warrant descriptions. When the affidavit or complaint for the warrant contains a complete description the courts sometimes construe the warrant and the affidavit together as one document and sustain the warrant. Moore v. United States, 461 F.2d 1236 (D.C.Cir.1972) (warrant for entire second floor with several apartments is saved by the affidavit which mentioned a specific apartment). Where a search warrant was for a third floor apartment, but police, when they arrived, found the third floor divided into two apartments, evidence obtained from the second apartment not named in the warrant was held to be admissible. Maryland v. Garrison, 480 U.S. 79, 107 S.Ct. 1013. But see Giles v. State, 10 Md.App. 593, 271 A.2d 766 (1970). Some law enforcement officers will draft a warrant adding the specific statement that the material contained in the affidavit is incorporated in the warrant and made a part of the warrant.

Minor errors in street address are not always fatal, if the court can conclude that only one particular place is obviously referred to in the warrant and that the officers (who may well have conducted a surveillance of the place) could not have possibly been confused about the place to be searched.

A warrant must specifically describe the items to be seized. A general warrant is constitutionally prohibited and a warrant which simply authorizes a search of a certain premises without specifying what is to be seized is invalid.

In determining what kind of description is sufficient, a rule of reason applies. "Gaming apparatus" may be sufficient, while "stolen tires" may be insufficient, because the tires clearly can be described by reference to a brand name or perhaps even serial number. "Narcotics paraphernalia" is generally good enough. Contraband generally need not be described in great detail. Steele v. United States, 267 U.S. 498, 45 S.Ct. 414 (1925).

On the other hand, when a case has First Amendment overtones, e.g., when allegedly obscene magazines are to be seized, a high degree of specificity is required. Marcus v. Search Warrants, 367 U.S. 717, 81 S.Ct. 1708 (1961).

Warrants commanding the seizure of personal or business documents, in the absence of enforcement of a stringent specificity requirement, may allow for a complete rummaging through papers. See McKenna, The Constitutional Protection of Private Papers: The Role of the Hierarchical Fourth Amendment, 53 Ind.L.J.55 (1977). Nevertheless, in Andresen v. Maryland, the Court refused to require particular exactitude in a warrant commanding the seizure of certain business records.

The specificity requirement is related to the probable cause requirement: there must be probable cause to believe that the particularly described item (not just some unspecified evidence of a particular crime) is at the place to be searched. This can be a problem in a case where the police have reason to believe that some clues, they know not what, may be found at the scene of a homicide. People ex rel. Carey v. Covelli, 61 Ill.2d 394, 336 N.E.2d 759 (1975). In upholding the search of a safe at the home of the victim in quest of unspecified clues to his murder (over the objections of his survivors) seemed to read the specificity requirement out of the Fourth Amendment. It treated the more general question of whether it was "reasonable" to search the safe under all of the known circumstances.

4. *Consequences of Overbreadth; Severability.* Sometimes the command of the warrant clause may be divisible. For instance, the warrant commands the search of the house (for which there is probable cause) and the barn (for which there is not probable cause); or the warrant specifies designated items (which is proper) and then adds "and other items too numerous to mention." Does the overbreadth invalidate the entire warrant in such a case, or are searches and seizures within the confines of the "good" part of the warrant valid?

According to one decision, a warrant is severable unless the valid portion of the warrant is "relatively" insignificant. In re Grand Jury Subpoenas Dated December 10, 1987, 926 F.2d 847 (9th Cir.1991) (upholding portion of warrant even though warrant was invalid as to nine of the persons or entities designated to be searched).

For a review of "severability" of warrant decisions, see United States v. Christine, 687 F.2d 749 (3d Cir.1982). See also United States v. Fitzgerald, 724 F.2d 633 (8th Cir.1983). That decision follows a familiar pattern. The overly broad part of the warrant is stricken and the remaining part is deemed valid. Then, the entry is declared lawful under the tailored warrant and seizures of items not named in the "revised" warrant are declared proper under plain view principles. The court reasons that, looking in a place where the officers had a right to look under the revised warrant, the officer came upon additional items, the incriminating nature of which was apparent, justifying seizure under plain view principles. (See Section H).

5. *Items Which May Be Named for Seizure.* Older warrant statutes sometimes specify items which can be named for seizure if there is probable cause, e.g., guns, narcotic paraphernalia, gambling instruments, etc. More modern statutes merely state that any evidence of a crime may be seized. Sometimes even under modern statutes a question arises as to whether a search warrant statute is broad enough to permit a search of a place in quest of a kidnap victim or an illegal alien. These are questions of state law without federal constitutional overtones. Nevertheless, from time to time certain constitutional issues have arisen concerning what may be named for seizure.

Once courts recognized a constitutional principle which prohibited the use of search warrants to seize "mere evidence"—items which were neither contraband, nor fruits of a crime, nor an instrumentality of a crime. The limitation was severely criticized by academic writers and, in actual practice, was eviscerated by courts which stretched the concept of "instrumentality" to great lengths in order to avoid the "mere evidence" prohibition. This limitation was eliminated in Warden v. Hayden, 387 U.S. 294, 87 S.Ct. 1642 (1967). Now "mere evidence" can be seized except in those jurisdictions whose warrant statutes are not broad enough to allow such seizures.

Occasionally a search warrant will issue for something even "lower" in status than "mere evidence." Exemplars (e.g., handwriting samples) may have no connection with a crime and yet could serve as evidence of guilt. See, e.g., United States v. Gomez–Soto, 723 F.2d 649 (9th Cir.1984). Many search warrant statutes would appear to authorize their seizure. If authorities had made no effort to secure exemplars through other channels, however, would it be reasonable to issue a search warrant for a home upon a showing that such items, with potential evidentiary value, probably could be located in a suspect's home? If so, in a vast number of cases, under the guise of seeking exemplars, a prosecutor under a warrant could search many a suspect's home at almost any time.

Before Andresen v. Maryland, 427 U.S. 463, 96 S.Ct. 2737 (1976), courts were divided over whether documents could be seized under a search warrant if those same documents would be protected by a Fifth Amendment claim in the event that a subpoena duces tecum issued. The question was phrased: can the government get by warrant what it cannot get by subpoena? In *Andresen* the Supreme Court answered "Yes." The Fifth Amendment protection is not violated because no testimonial compulsion takes place when a search warrant issues. The documents in Andresen were not personal, such as a diary. This distinction was once deemed important by some courts. See Romanelli v. C.I.R., 466 F.2d 872 (7th Cir.1972). The rationale of *Andresen*, however, is not easily limited to business documents. Some courts have applied *Andresen* in cases involving personal papers. See People v. Superior Court, 68 Cal.App.3d 845, 137 Cal.Rptr. 391 (Cal.App.1977) directed by California Supreme Court not to be published in bound volume. 140 Cal.Rptr. 442, 567 P.2d 1162.

In Zurcher v. Stanford Daily, 436 U.S. 547, 98 S.Ct. 1970 (1978), the court held that there is no blanket immunity from seizure under a warrant for photographs (or presumably reporters' notes or other records) in the possession of a newspaper. Of course, the requirements of probable cause and specificity must be met. The court noted that the reasonableness requirement of the Fourth Amendment still might set some limits upon the issuance of such warrants. The Zurcher decision did not resolve the question of what effect a state shield law would have on the issuance of such a warrant. Under many shield laws, probable cause to believe that the material constitutes evidence of a crime will leave the material unprotected. Does a shield law, however, with its procedural safeguards, provide the exclusive means of securing evidence in a newspaper's possession?

Congress later enacted a statute which requires that ordinarily a subpoena be utilized, rather than a search warrant, as a means of obtaining physical or documentary evidence of a criminal offense when that evidence is in the possession of a media member, as defined in the statute. The Privacy Protection Act of 1980 restricts local, state, and federal law enforcement officers' efforts to obtain a search warrant in such cases. See 42 U.S.C. §§ 2000aa to 2000aa–12 (Supp.1980).

Sometimes authorities, during an ongoing investigation, might wish to enter a place, take photographs or just look around, and then leave without disturbing anything. However, most search warrant statutes speak in terms of descriptions of the item to be *seized*. Still, some courts have approved "sneak and peek" warrants. See United States v. Villegas, 899 F.2d 1324 (2d Cir.1990). *Villegas* approved the procedure, relying upon the assertion that, even without a search warrant statute, federal courts have the inherent authority to issue warrants.

6. ***Docketing the Warrant.*** Sometimes it is suggested that there should be a system of keeping track of unproductive warrants. One way of developing insights into our probable cause standards is to study statistics reflecting success and failure in the execution of search warrants. Some persons assert that the statutory obligation of the officer to file a "return" will not be enough to accomplish the purpose. An officer may have little incentive to file a return if the search proves fruitless. Thus it is suggested that some system be used which would account for all warrants within a fixed period of time after execution. The federal wiretap statute provides for such a system. See 18 U.S.C. §§ 2518(8)(b), (d), 2519. One court has rejected an argument that the reasonableness requirement of the Fourth Amendment requires such a system of docketing search warrants. See People v. Stansberry, 47 Ill.2d 541, 268 N.E.2d 431 (1971).

E. THE EXECUTION OF SEARCH WARRANTS

The prohibition against unreasonable searches and seizures contained in the first clause of the Fourth Amendment places limits upon the manner of execution of search warrants. Added restrictions are sometimes found in the statutes or court rules of a particular jurisdiction. One of the key questions is whether any such further restrictions should be enforced as constitutional mandates or as statutory requirements only without constitutional force.

NOTES

1. ***Time Limits for Execution.*** A search warrant itself will usually not contain specific requirements that a warrant be executed at any particular time. There are time limits applicable to warrants, but these limits are usually prescribed by statute or court rule and vary from jurisdiction to jurisdiction. See Rule 41(c), Fed. R.Crim.P. (10 days); N.Y.Crim.Pro.Law, § 690.30 (10 days); Ill.Rev.Stats., ch. 725, § 5/108–6 (96 hours).

Some jurisdictions have no express time limit other than a period which is "reasonable" under all the circumstances. Whether the named items can be expected to still be at the place to be searched is a factor in deciding whether a delay is reasonable. (Note the similarity to the "search probable cause" issue when a warrant is issued based upon dated information.) Such factors as weather or road conditions and the need to prevent danger to an undercover agent, however, have also been cited as relevant to the calculation of the reasonableness of the delay.

In theory a delay that does not exceed an express statutory period could still be unreasonable for Fourth Amendment purposes.

2. ***Nighttime Execution.*** Some jurisdictions require that warrants be executed only in daylight hours unless special procedures are followed and the warrant specifies that nighttime execution is permissible. Among the special procedures are requirements of securing the signatures of two magistrates, of showing a need for prompt execution of the warrant, or of producing "positive" affidavits. The restrictive nighttime search rule is purely a matter of local or statutory law. In his dissent in Gooding v. United States, 416 U.S. 430, 94 S.Ct. 1780 (1974), however, Justice Marshall suggested that the reasonableness requirement of the Fourth Amendment should be read to place limits upon the execution of warrants at night.

3. ***Trickery and Force.*** Most jurisdictions provide that all necessary force can be used in the execution of a search warrant or an arrest warrant. Where the police have the right to enter under the authority of a warrant (and thus do not need consent), entering through use of a passkey or by means of trickery (avoiding actual force) is also permitted.

In one instance, officers accompanied a pizza delivery person to the suspect's door, and then seized the occupants when they answered the door to get their pizza. The arrests were ultimately upheld. United States v. Gori, 230 F.3d 44 (2d Cir.2000).

4. ***Places Subject to Search, and Seizable Items***. The executing officers can search any place which falls within the description in the warrant. Thus when the search of an apartment is authorized for a small item, a purse in the apartment may be searched. State v. White, 13 Wash.App. 949, 538 P.2d 860 (1975). They cannot,

however, go beyond the described area. A further limitation upon a search is that once on property to be searched, an officer can look only in a place where the item could possibly turn up. Thus, if the named item is a gun, the pages of a diary could not be perused under the authority of the warrant. If the item is a piano a search of a drawer would be improper, unless some other theory (e.g., search incident to arrest of suspect standing near drawer) is available. Nor can one look for a television in a small drawer. State v. James, 91 N.M. 690, 579 P.2d 1257 (N.M.App. 1978) (dictum). Nor is a search for wheels and tires on a closet shelf proper when the items are obviously not there. United States v. Chadwell, 427 F.Supp. 692 (D.Del.1977).

An officer can seize any item named in the warrant. Under normal plain view principles (and subject to limitations on plain view principles), he or she may also seize items not named in the warrant if the officer discovers such items while looking in a place where the officer has a right to search under the warrant and if there is probable cause to believe that such items constitute evidence of a crime. (See infra Section H).

5. *Persons to be Searched*

If an individual is specifically named by the warrant as a person to be searched (not just as the occupant of the place to be searched), then obviously that person can be searched. There are limits, however, on the scope and intensity of the permitted search. A warrant to search the "person" of a drug suspect is not sufficiently specific to authorize a body cavity search, the Eighth Circuit held. United States v. Nelson, 36 F.3d 758 (8th Cir.1994). Police, with a search warrant, detained a suspected drug courier, made a visual inspection of his rectum, had a doctor attempt a rectal examination, x-rayed him, and then used an endoscopic procedure to remove an object from his stomach.

A much more difficult question is whether a person who is found on the premises during the execution of a warrant, or one who arrives during the execution, can be detained and/or searched even though he or she is not named in the warrant as a person to be searched.

In Ybarra v. Illinois, 444 U.S. 85, 100 S.Ct. 338 (1979), the Supreme Court considered execution of an Illinois warrant which commanded the search of a certain tavern in quest of narcotics. Officers obtained a search warrant to search the bar, the Aurora Tap Tavern, and the bartender, Greg (with a physical description) for drugs. Although the officers did not have probable cause, they frisked thirteen patrons of the tavern without any particular reason to believe that any one of them was armed or dangerous. They found drugs in the shirt pocket of one patron, Ybarra The Court held that absent an indication that a patron was armed and dangerous within the meaning of Terry v. Ohio, Section F infra, the frisk was unlawful. There was an Illinois statute in place that provided "In the execution of the warrant the person executing the same may reasonably detain and search any person in the place at the time.... to prevent the disposal or concealment of any instruments, articles or things particularly described in the warrant." Ill. Rev. Stat., ch. 38, § 108–9 (1975).

The Court further stated that the quest for evidence named in a warrant does not justify either a search or a frisk of any person who happens to be in a public place which is named in a warrant. The Court did not say what quantum of evidence would be required to justify such a search of the person. Nor did it consider whether the case would be different if the place searched was a private home or if the person had a greater nexus with the place, as for example, as lessee. Several lower courts, however, have extended Ybarra's analysis to home settings. See, e.g., United States v. Robertson, 833 F.2d 777 (9th Cir.1987); United States v. Ward, 682 F.2d 876 (10th Cir.1982); State v. Lambert, 238 Kan. 444, 710 P.2d 693

(1985). But see, United States v. Young, 909 F.2d 442 (11th Cir.1990) (search of suspect's wife reasonable when seen "sneaking" out of the house with a bulging purse just before officers arrived with search warrant for the house).

Assume police have probable cause to search a home, but have not yet obtained a warrant? May police prevent the occupant from entering the home until a warrant is obtained? The Court answered this question in the affirmative in Illinois v. McArthur, 531 U.S. 326, 121 S.Ct. 946 (2001). In this case, a wife who was leaving her husband asked the police to accompany her to the trailer where the couple lived in order to recover her belongings. Two officers remained outside while she entered the trailer. When she came out, she told the officers that her husband had slid "dope" underneath a couch in the home. The husband came out of the trailer. One officer went to obtain a warrant while the other officer prevented the husband from reentering the trailer unless the police accompanied him. The husband argued that had he been allowed to enter, he would have destroyed the marijuana before the other officer returned with a warrant. Characterizing the two hour delay as a minimal intrusion, the Court indicated that the exclusion of the defendant was a reasonable accommodation when law enforcement needs were balanced with the intrusion into the defendant's privacy interests.

In Michigan v. Summers, 452 U.S. 692, 101 S.Ct. 2587 (1981), the Court considered the validity of the detention of an individual who was leaving a house as police approached the house to seek entry to execute a search warrant. This raised the question of whether he was illegally seized. The Court held that a search warrant carries with it the "limited" authority to detain persons who are associated with the premises. The Court referred to this as a mild intrusion, one not likely to be exploited, which minimized risk, warded off flight, and provided for an orderly search. It insisted that it was not calling for police officers to balance the intrusiveness of a detention against the governmental interest in order to determine on an ad hoc basis whether a particular seizure of the person is reasonable under the Fourth Amendment. Rather the Court said it was carving out a flat rule (subject to possible exceptions) concerning the authority of an officer who is executing a search warrant. In dissent, Justice Stewart declared that seizures of the person on less than probable cause are proper only upon the quantum of data necessary under *Terry* (in part M). He further noted that detention of a person during the execution of a search warrant, under some circumstances, might last for several hours.

The Supreme Court revisited the issues presented in Michigan v. Summers in the case that follows:

Muehler v. Mena

Supreme Court of the United States, 2005.
544 U.S. 93, 125 S.Ct. 1465.

■ JUDGES: REHNQUIST, C.J., delivered the opinion of the Court, in which O'CONNOR, SCALIA, KENNEDY, and THOMAS, JJ., joined. KENNEDY, J., filed a concurring opinion. STEVENS, J., filed an opinion concurring in the judgment, in which SOUTER, GINSBURG, and BREYER, JJ., joined.

■ CHIEF JUSTICE REHNQUIST delivered the opinion of the Court.

Respondent Iris Mena was detained in handcuffs during a search of the premises that she and several others occupied. Petitioners were lead members of a police detachment executing a search warrant of these premises. She sued the officers under Rev Stat § 1979, 42 U.S.C. § 1983 [42 USCS § 1983], and the District Court found in her favor. The Court of

Appeals affirmed the judgment, holding that the use of handcuffs to detain Mena during the search violated the Fourth Amendment and that the officers' questioning of Mena about her immigration status during the detention constituted an independent Fourth Amendment violation. *Mena v. Simi Valley*, 332 F.3d 1255 (CA9 2003). We hold that Mena's detention in handcuffs for the length of the search was consistent with our opinion in *Michigan* v. *Summers*, 452 U.S. 692, 69 L. Ed. 2d 340, 101 S. Ct. 2587 (1981), and that the officers' questioning during that detention did not violate her Fourth Amendment rights.

* * *

Based on information gleaned from the investigation of a gang-related, driveby shooting, petitioners Muehler and Brill had reason to believe at least one member of a gang—the West Side Locos—lived at 1363 Patricia Avenue. They also suspected that the individual was armed and dangerous, since he had recently been involved in the driveby shooting. As a result, Muehler obtained a search warrant for 1363 Patricia Avenue that authorized a broad search of the house and premises for, among other things, deadly weapons and evidence of gang membership. In light of the high degree of risk involved in searching a house suspected of housing at least one, and perhaps multiple, armed gang members, a Special Weapons and Tactics (SWAT) team was used to secure the residence and grounds before the search.

At 7 a.m. on February 3, 1998, petitioners, along with the SWAT team and other officers, executed the warrant. Mena was asleep in her bed when the SWAT team, clad in helmets and black vests adorned with badges and the word "POLICE," entered her bedroom and placed her in handcuffs at gunpoint. The SWAT team also handcuffed three other individuals found on the property. The SWAT team then took those individuals and Mena into a converted garage, which contained several beds and some other bedroom furniture. While the search proceeded, one or two officers guarded the four detainees, who were allowed to move around the garage but remained in handcuffs.

Aware that the West Side Locos gang was composed primarily of illegal immigrants, the officers had notified the Immigration and Naturalization Service (INS) that they would be conducting the search, and an INS officer accompanied the officers executing the warrant. During their detention in the garage, an officer asked for each detainee's name, date of birth, place of birth, and immigration status. The INS officer later asked the detainees for their immigration documentation. Mena's status as a permanent resident was confirmed by her papers.

The search of the premises yielded a .22 caliber handgun with .22 caliber ammunition, a box of .25 caliber ammunition, several baseball bats with gang writing, various additional gang paraphernalia, and a bag of marijuana. Before the officers left the area, Mena was released.

In her § 1983 suit against the officers she alleged that she was detained "for an unreasonable time and in an unreasonable manner" in violation of the Fourth Amendment. In addition, she claimed that the warrant and its execution were overbroad, that the officers failed to comply with the "knock and announce" rule, and that the officers had needlessly destroyed property during the search. The officers moved for summary judgment, asserting that they were entitled to qualified immunity, but the District Court denied their motion. The Court of Appeals affirmed that denial, *except* for Mena's claim that the warrant was overbroad; on this claim the Court of Appeals held that the officers were entitled to qualified immunity. *Mena v. Simi Valley*, 226 F.3d 1031 (CA9 2000). After a trial, a jury, pursuant to a special verdict form, found that Officers Muehler and Brill violated Mena's Fourth Amendment right to be free from unreasonable seizures by detaining her both with force greater than that which was reasonable and for a longer period than that which was reasonable. The jury awarded Mena $10,000 in actual damages and $20,000 in punitive damages against each petitioner for a total of $60,000.

The Court of Appeals affirmed the judgment on two grounds. Reviewing the denial of qualified immunity *de novo*, it first held that the officers' detention of Mena violated the Fourth Amendment because it was objectively unreasonable to confine her in the converted garage and keep her in handcuffs during the search. In the Court of Appeals' view, the officers should have released Mena as soon as it became clear that she posed no immediate threat. The court additionally held that the questioning of Mena about her immigration status constituted an independent Fourth Amendment violation. The Court of Appeals went on to hold that those rights were clearly established at the time of Mena's questioning, and thus the officers were not entitled to qualified immunity. We granted certiorari, and now vacate and remand.

* * *

In *Michigan v. Summers* (1981), we held that officers executing a search warrant for contraband have the authority "to detain the occupants of the premises while a proper search is conducted." Such detentions are appropriate, we explained, because the character of the additional intrusion caused by detention is slight and because the justifications for detention are substantial. We made clear that the detention of an occupant is "surely less intrusive than the search itself," and the presence of a warrant assures that a neutral magistrate has determined that probable cause exists to search the home. Against this incremental intrusion, we posited three legitimate law enforcement interests that provide substantial justification for detaining an occupant: "preventing flight in the event that incriminating evidence is found"; "minimizing the risk of harm to the officers"; and facilitating "the orderly completion of the search," as detainees' "self-interest may induce them to open locked doors or locked containers to avoid the use of force."

Mena's detention was, under *Summers*, plainly permissible. 1An officer's authority to detain incident to a search is categorical; it does not depend on the "quantum of proof justifying detention or the extent of the intrusion to be imposed by the seizure." Thus, Mena's detention for the duration of the search was reasonable under *Summers* because a warrant existed to search 1363 Patricia Avenue and she was an occupant of that address at the time of the search.

1

In determining whether a Fourth Amendment violation occurred we draw all reasonable factual inferences in favor of the jury verdict, but as we made clear in Ornelas v. United States (1996), we do not defer to the jury's legal conclusion that those facts violate the Constitution.

Inherent in *Summers'* authorization to detain an occupant of the place to be searched is the authority to use reasonable force to effectuate the detention. See *Graham v. Connor* (1989) ("Fourth Amendment jurisprudence has long recognized that the right to make an arrest or investigatory stop necessarily carries with it the right to use some degree of physical coercion or threat thereof to effect it"). Indeed, *Summers* itself stressed that the risk of harm to officers and occupants is minimized "if the officers routinely exercise unquestioned command of the situation."

The officers' use of force in the form of handcuffs to effectuate Mena's detention in the garage, as well as the detention of the three other occupants, was reasonable because the governmental interests outweigh the marginal intrusion. The imposition of correctly applied handcuffs on Mena, who was already being lawfully detained during a search of the house, was undoubtedly a separate intrusion in addition to detention in the converted garage.[2] The detention was thus more intrusive than that which we upheld in *Summers*. (concluding that the additional intrusion in the form of a detention was less than that of the warrant-sanctioned search); Maryland v. Wilson (1997) (concluding that the additional intrusion from ordering passengers out of a car, which was already stopped, was minimal).

But this was no ordinary search. The governmental interests in not only detaining, but using handcuffs, are at their maximum when, as here, a warrant authorizes a search for weapons and a wanted gang member resides on the premises. In such inherently dangerous situations, the use of handcuffs minimizes the risk of harm to both officers and occupants.... Though this safety risk inherent in executing a search warrant for weapons was sufficient to justify the use of handcuffs, the need to detain multiple occupants made the use of handcuffs all the more reasonable.

Mena argues that, even if the use of handcuffs to detain her in the garage was reasonable as an initial matter, the duration of the use of handcuffs made the detention unreasonable. The duration of a detention can, of course, affect the balance of interests under *Graham*. However, the 2–to 3–hour detention in handcuffs in this case does not outweigh the government's continuing safety interests. As we have noted, this case

2. In finding the officers should have released Mena from the handcuffs, the Court of Appeals improperly relied upon the fact that the warrant did not include Mena as a suspect. The warrant was concerned not with individuals but with locations and property. In particular, the warrant in this case authorized the search of 1363 Patricia Avenue and its surrounding grounds for, among other things, deadly weapons and evidence of street gang membership. In this respect, the warrant here resembles that at issue in Michigan v. Summers (1981), which allowed the search of a residence for drugs without mentioning any individual, including the owner of the home whom police ultimately arrested. Summers makes clear that when a neutral magistrate has determined police have probable cause to believe contraband exists, "[t]he connection of an occupant to [a] home" alone "justifies a detention of that occupant."

involved the detention of four detainees by two officers during a search of a gang house for dangerous weapons. We conclude that the detention of Mena in handcuffs during the search was reasonable.

The Court of Appeals also determined that the officers violated Mena's Fourth Amendment rights by questioning her about her immigration status during the detention. This holding, it appears, was premised on the assumption that the officers were required to have independent reasonable suspicion in order to question Mena concerning her immigration status because the questioning constituted a discrete Fourth Amendment event. But the premise is faulty. We have "held repeatedly that mere police questioning does not constitute a seizure." *Florida v. Bostick* (1991) "[E]ven when officers have no basis for suspecting a particular individual, they may generally ask questions of that individual; ask to examine the individual's identification; and request consent to search his or her luggage." As the Court of Appeals did not hold that the detention was prolonged by the questioning, there was no additional seizure within the meaning of the Fourth Amendment. Hence, the officers did not need reasonable suspicion to ask Mena for her name, date and place of birth, or immigration status.

Our recent opinion in Illinois v. Caballes (2005) is instructive. There, we held that a dog sniff performed during a traffic stop does not violate the Fourth Amendment. We noted that a lawful seizure "can become unlawful if it is prolonged beyond the time reasonably required to complete that mission," but accepted the state court's determination that the duration of the stop was not extended by the dog sniff. Because we held that a dog sniff was not a search subject to the Fourth Amendment, we rejected the notion that "the shift in purpose" "from a lawful traffic stop into a drug investigation" was unlawful because it "was not supported by any reasonable suspicion." Likewise here, the initial *Summers* detention was lawful; the Court of Appeals did not find that the questioning extended the time Mena was detained. Thus no additional Fourth Amendment justification for inquiring about Mena's immigration status was required.[3]

In summary, the officers' detention of Mena in handcuffs during the execution of the search warrant was reasonable and did not violate the Fourth Amendment. Additionally, the officers' questioning of Mena did not constitute an independent Fourth Amendment violation. Mena has advanced in this Court, as she did before the Court of Appeals, an alternative argument for affirming the judgment below. She asserts that her detention extended beyond the time the police completed the tasks incident to the search. Because the Court of Appeals did not address this contention, we too decline to address it.

3. The Court of Appeals' reliance on United States v. Brignoni–Ponce (1975), is misplaced. *Brignoni-Ponce* held that stops by roving patrols near the border "may be justified on facts that do not amount to the probable cause require[ment] for an arrest." *Id.*, We considered only whether the patrols had the "authority to *stop* automobiles in areas near the Mexican border," and expressed no opinion as to the appropriateness of questioning when an individual was already seized. We certainly did not, as the Court of Appeals suggested, create a "requirement of particularized reasonable suspicion for purposes of inquiry into citizenship status."

The judgment of the Court of Appeals is therefore vacated, and the case is remanded for further proceedings consistent with this opinion.

It is so ordered.

■ JUSTICE KENNEDY, concurring.

I concur in the judgment and in the opinion of the Court. It does seem important to add this brief statement to help ensure that police handcuffing during searches becomes neither routine nor unduly prolonged.

The safety of the officers and the efficacy of the search are matters of first concern, but so too is it a matter of first concern that excessive force is not used on the persons detained, especially when these persons, though lawfully detained under Michigan v. Summers (1981), are not themselves suspected of any involvement in criminal activity. The use of handcuffs is the use of force, and such force must be objectively reasonable under the circumstances.

The reasonableness calculation under *Graham* is in part a function of the expected and actual duration of the search. If the search extends to the point when the handcuffs can cause real pain or serious discomfort, provision must be made to alter the conditions of detention at least long enough to attend to the needs of the detainee. This is so even if there is no question that the initial handcuffing was objectively reasonable. The restraint should also be removed if, at any point during the search, it would be readily apparent to any objectively reasonable officer that removing the handcuffs would not compromise the officers' safety or risk interference or substantial delay in the execution of the search. The time spent in the search here, some two to three hours, certainly approaches, and may well exceed, the time beyond which a detainee's Fourth Amendment interests require revisiting the necessity of handcuffing in order to ensure the restraint, even if permissible as an initial matter, has not become excessive.

That said, under these circumstances I do not think handcuffing the detainees for the duration of the search was objectively unreasonable. As I understand the record, during much of this search 2 armed officers were available to watch over the 4 unarmed detainees, while the other 16 officers on the scene conducted an extensive search of a suspected gang safe house. Even if we accept as true—as we must—the factual assertions that these detainees posed no readily apparent danger and that keeping them handcuffed deviated from standard police procedure, it does not follow that the handcuffs were unreasonable. Where the detainees outnumber those supervising them, and this situation could not be remedied without diverting officers from an extensive, complex, and time-consuming search, the continued use of handcuffs after the initial sweep may be justified, subject to adjustments or temporary release under supervision to avoid pain or excessive physical discomfort. Because on this record it does not appear the restraints were excessive, I join the opinion of the Court.

■ JUSTICE STEVENS, with whom JUSTICE SOUTER, JUSTICE GINSBURG, and JUSTICE BREYER join, concurring in the judgment.

The jury in this case found that the two petitioners violated Iris Mena's Fourth Amendment right to be free from unreasonable seizure by detaining her with greater force and for a longer period of time than was reasonable under the circumstances. In their post-trial motion in the District Court, petitioners advanced three legal arguments: (1) They were entitled to qualified immunity because the unconstitutionality of their conduct was not clearly established;[1] (2) the judge's instruction to the jury was erroneous;[2] and (3) the evidence was not sufficient to support the jury's award of punitive damages. The trial judge's thoughtful explanation of his reasons for denying the motion does not address either of the issues the Court discusses today.

In its opinion affirming the judgment, the Court of Appeals made two mistakes. First, as the Court explains, it erroneously held that the immigration officers' questioning of Mena about her immigration status was an independent violation of the Fourth Amendment. Second, instead of merely deciding whether there was sufficient evidence in the record to support the jury's verdict, the Court of Appeals appears to have ruled as a matter of law that the officers should have released her from the handcuffs sooner than they did. I agree that it is appropriate to remand the case to enable the Court of Appeals to consider whether the evidence supports Mena's contention that she was held longer than the search actually lasted. In doing so, the Court of Appeals must of course accord appropriate deference to the jury's reasonable factual findings, while applying the correct legal standard.

In my judgment, however, the Court's discussion of the amount of force used to detain Mena pursuant to Michigan v. Summers (1981), is analytically unsound. Although the Court correctly purports to apply the "objective reasonableness" test announced in Graham v. Connor (1989), it misapplies that test. Given the facts of this case—and the presumption that a reviewing court must draw all reasonable inferences in favor of supporting the verdict—I think it clear that the jury could properly have found that this 5–foot–2–inch young lady posed no threat to the officers at the scene, and that they used excessive force in keeping her in handcuffs for up to three hours. Although *Summers* authorizes the detention of any individual who is present when a valid search warrant is being executed, that case does not give officers *carte blanche* to keep individuals who pose no threat in handcuffs throughout a search, no matter how long it may last. On remand, I would therefore instruct the Court of Appeals to consider

1. The Court of Appeals' conclusion that the officers were not entitled to qualified immunity was not challenged in the petition for certiorari and is therefore waived

2. The trial judge instructed the jury as follows:

> " 'Generally, a police officer carrying out a search authorized by a warrant may detain occupants of the residence during the search, so long as the detention is reasonable.
>
> " 'In determining the reasonableness of a detention conducted in connection with a search, you may look to all the circumstances, including the severity of the suspected crime, whether the person being detained is the subject of the investigation, whether such person poses an immediate threat to the security of the police or others or to the ability of the police to conduct the search, and whether such person is actively resisting arrest or attempting to flee. A detention may be unreasonable if it is unnecessarily painful, degrading, prolonged or if it involves an undue invasion of privacy. A police officer is required to release an individual detained in connection with a lawful search as soon as the officers' right to conduct the search ends or the search itself is concluded, whichever is sooner.' "

whether the evidence supports Mena's contention that the petitioners used excessive force in detaining her when it considers the length of the *Summers* detention.

I

As the Court notes, the warrant in this case authorized the police to enter the Mena home to search for a gun belonging to Raymond Romero that may have been used in a gang-related driveby shooting. Romero, a known member of the West Side Locos gang, rented a room from the Mena family. The house, described as a " 'poor house,' " was home to several unrelated individuals who rented from the Menas. Each resident had his or her own bedroom, which could be locked with a padlock on the outside, and each had access to the living room and kitchen. In addition, several individuals lived in trailers in the back yard and also had access to the common spaces in the Mena home.

In addition to Romero, police had reason to believe that at least one other West Side Locos gang member had lived at the residence, although Romero's brother told police that the individual had returned to Mexico. The officers in charge of the search, petitioners Muehler and Brill, had been at the same residence a few months earlier on an unrelated domestic violence call, but did not see any other individuals they believed to be gang members inside the home on that occasion.

In light of the fact that the police believed that Romero possessed a gun and that there might be other gang members at the residence, petitioner Muehler decided to use a Special Weapons and Tactics (SWAT) team to execute the warrant. As described in the majority opinion, eight members of the SWAT team forcefully entered the home at 7 a.m. In fact, Mena was the only occupant of the house, and she was asleep in her bedroom. The police woke her up at gunpoint, and immediately handcuffed her. At the same time, officers served another search warrant at the home of Romero's mother, where Romero was known to stay several nights each week. In part because Romero's mother had previously cooperated with police officers, they did not use a SWAT team to serve that warrant. Romero was found at his mother's house; after being cited for possession of a small amount of marijuana, he was released.

Meanwhile, after the SWAT team secured the Mena residence and gave the "all clear," police officers transferred Mena and three other individuals (who had been in trailers in the back yard) to a converted garage.[4] To get to the garage, Mena, who was still in her bedclothes, was forced to walk barefoot through the pouring rain. The officers kept her and the other three individuals in the garage for up to three hours while they searched the home. Although she requested them to remove the handcuffs, they refused to do so. For the duration of the search, two officers guarded Mena and the other three detainees. A .22 caliber handgun, ammunition, and gang-related paraphernalia were found in Romero's bedroom, and other

4. The other individuals were a 55-year-old Latina female, a 40-year-old Latino male who was removed from the scene by the Immigration and Naturalization Service (INS), and a white male who appears to be in his early 30's and who was cited for possession of a small amount of marijuana.

gang-related paraphernalia was found in the living room. Officers found nothing of significance in Mena's bedroom.

II

In analyzing the quantum of force used to effectuate the *Summers* detention, the Court rightly employs the "objective reasonableness" test of *Graham*. Under *Graham*, the trier of fact must balance " 'the nature and quality of the intrusion on the individual's Fourth Amendment interests' against the countervailing governmental interests at stake." The District Court correctly instructed the jury to take into consideration such factors as " 'the severity of the suspected crime, whether the person being detained is the subject of the investigation, whether such person poses an immediate threat to the security of the police or others or to the ability of the police to conduct the search, and whether such person is actively resisting arrest or attempting to flee.' " The District Court also correctly instructed the jury to consider whether the detention was prolonged and whether Mena was detained in handcuffs after the search had ended. Many of these factors are taken from *Graham* itself, and the jury instruction reflects an entirely reasonable construction of the objective reasonableness test in the *Summers* context.

Considering those factors, it is clear that the SWAT team's initial actions were reasonable. When officers undertake a dangerous assignment to execute a warrant to search property that is presumably occupied by violence-prone gang members, it may well be appropriate to use both overwhelming force and surprise in order to secure the premises as promptly as possible. In this case the decision to use a SWAT team of eight heavily armed officers and to execute the warrant at 7 a.m. gave the officers maximum protection against the anticipated risk. As it turned out, there was only one person in the house—Mena—and she was sound asleep. Nevertheless, "[t]he 'reasonableness' of a particular use of force must be judged from the perspective of a reasonable officer on the scene, rather than with the 20/20 vision of hindsight." At the time they first encountered Mena, the officers had no way of knowing her relation to Romero, whether she was affiliated with the West Side Locos, or whether she had any weapons on her person. Further, the officers needed to use overwhelming force to immediately take command of the situation; by handcuffing Mena they could more quickly secure her room and join the other officers. It would be unreasonable to expect officers, who are entering what they believe to be a high risk situation, to spend the time necessary to determine whether Mena was a threat before they handcuffed her. To the extent that the Court of Appeals relied on the initial actions of the SWAT team to find that there was sufficient evidence to support the jury's verdict, it was in error.

Whether the well-founded fears that justified the extraordinary entry into the house should also justify a prolonged interruption of the morning routine of a presumptively innocent person, however, is a separate question and one that depends on the specific facts of the case. This is true with respect both to how the handcuffs were used, and to the totality of the circumstances surrounding the detention, including whether Mena was detained in handcuffs after the search had concluded. With regard to the handcuffs, police may use them in different ways.[6] Here, the cuffs kept Mena's arms behind her for two to three hours. She testified that they were " 'real uncomfortable' " and that she had asked the officers to remove them, but that they had refused. Moreover, she was continuously guarded by two police officers who obviously made flight virtually impossible even if the cuffs had been removed.

A jury could reasonably have found a number of facts supporting a conclusion that the prolonged handcuffing was unreasonable. No contraband was found in Mena's room or on her person. There were no indications suggesting she was or ever had been a gang member, which was consistent with the fact that during the police officers' last visit to the home, no gang members were present. She fully cooperated with the officers and the INS agent, answering all their questions. She was unarmed, and given her small size, was clearly no match for either of the two armed officers who were guarding her. In sum, there was no evidence that Mena posed any threat to the officers or anyone else.

The justifications offered by the officers are not persuasive. They have argued that at least six armed officers were required to guard the four detainees, even though all of them had been searched for weapons. Since there were 18 officers at the scene, and since at least 1 officer who at one point guarded Mena and the other three residents was sent home after offering to assist in the search, it seems unlikely that lack of resources was really a problem. While a court should not ordinarily question the allocation of police officers or resources, a jury could have reasonably found that this is a case where ample resources were available.

The Court suggests that officers are under "no duty to divert resources from the search to make a predictive judgment about whether a particular occupant can be freed from handcuffs." In reality, the officers *did* make such an inquiry when they filled out the field identification cards, the use of which is standard police practice and takes less than five minutes. Further, the armed officers who guarded Mena had, of course, already been diverted from other search activities. It is therefore difficult to see what additional resources would have been required to determine that she posed no threat to the officers that would justify handcuffing her for two to three hours.

The jury may also have been skeptical of testimony that the officers in fact feared for their safety given that the actual suspect of the shooting had been found at the other location and promptly released. Additionally, while the officers testified that as a general matter they would not release an individual from handcuffs while searching a residence, the SWAT team's tactical plan for this particular search arguably called for them to do just that, since it directed that "[a]ny subjects encountered will be handcuffed and detained until they can be patted down, their location noted, and

6. For instance, a suspect may be handcuffed to a fixed object, to a custodian, or her hands may simply be linked to one another. The cuffs may join the wrists either in the front or the back of the torso. They can be so tight that they are painful, particularly when applied for prolonged periods. While they restrict movement, they do not necessarily preclude flight if the prisoner is not kept under constant surveillance.

released by Office Muehler or Officer R. Brill." The tactical plan suggests that they can, and often do, release individuals who are not related to the search. The SWAT team leader testified that handcuffs are not always required when executing a search.

In short, under the factors listed in *Graham* and those validly presented to the jury in the jury instructions, a jury could have reasonably found from the evidence that there was no apparent need to handcuff Mena for the entire duration of the search and that she was detained for an unreasonably prolonged period. She posed no threat whatsoever to the officers at the scene. She was not suspected of any crime and was not a person targeted by the search warrant. She had no reason to flee the scene and gave no indication that she desired to do so. Viewing the facts in the light most favorable to the jury's verdict, as we are required to do, there is certainly no obvious factual basis for rejecting the jury's verdict that the officers acted unreasonably, and no obvious basis for rejecting the conclusion that, on these facts, the quantum of force used was unreasonable as a matter of law.

III

Police officers' legitimate concern for their own safety is always a factor that should weigh heavily in balancing the relevant *Graham* factors. But, as Officer Brill admitted at trial, if that justification were always sufficient, it would authorize the handcuffing of every occupant of the premises for the duration of every *Summers* detention. Nothing in either the *Summers* or the *Graham* opinion provides any support for such a result. Rather, the decision of what force to use must be made on a case-by-case basis. There is evidence in this record that may well support the conclusion that it was unreasonable to handcuff Mena throughout the search. On remand, therefore, I would instruct the Ninth Circuit to consider that evidence, as well as the possibility that Mena was detained after the search was completed, when deciding whether the evidence in the record is sufficient to support the jury's verdict.

* * *

6. *Who may accompany police on the execution of a warrant?* A search warrant also does not give police the right to invite the media. The Second Circuit held that the warrant to search the home of credit card fraud suspects did not authorize police to invite along a CBS television news crew from "Street Stories," a weekly news magazine program. Ayeni v. Mottola, 35 F.3d 680 (2d Cir.1994). Similarly, if police may invite the media to come on a "ride along" to execute an arrest warrant in a private home, it violates the Fourth Amendment. Wilson v. Layne, 526 U.S. 603, 119 S.Ct. 1692 (1999).

7. *Notice and "No-Knock".* The Supreme Court decided in Wilson v. Arkansas, 514 U.S. 927, 115 S.Ct. 1914 (1995) that the Fourth Amendment does require police officers to knock and announce themselves before entering to execute a warrant, unless "law enforcement interests ... establish the reasonableness of an unannounced entry." The Court remanded the case to determine the reasonableness of the entry.

Eleven years after holding the Fourth Amendment required police officers to knock and announce themselves before entering to execute a warrant, the United States Supreme court reversed Wilson v. Arkansas.

Hudson v. Michigan

Supreme Court of the United States, 2006.
547 U.S. 586, 126 S.Ct. 2159.

■ JUSTICE SCALIA delivered the opinion of the Court, except as to Part IV.

We decide whether violation of the "knock-and-announce" rule requires the suppression of all evidence found in the search.

I

Police obtained a warrant authorizing a search for drugs and firearms at the home of petitioner Booker Hudson. They discovered both. Large quantities of drugs were found, including cocaine rocks in Hudson's pocket. A loaded gun was lodged between the cushion and armrest of the chair in which he was sitting. Hudson was charged under Michigan law with unlawful drug and firearm possession.

This case is before us only because of the method of entry into the house. When the police arrived to execute the warrant, they announced their presence, but waited only a short time—perhaps "three to five seconds," App. 15—before turning the knob of the unlocked front door and entering Hudson's home. Hudson moved to suppress all the inculpatory evidence, arguing that the premature entry violated his Fourth Amendment rights.

The Michigan trial court granted his motion. On interlocutory review, the Michigan Court of Appeals reversed, relying on Michigan Supreme Court cases holding that suppression is inappropriate when entry is made pursuant to warrant but without proper " 'knock and announce.' " The Michigan Supreme Court denied leave to appeal. Hudson was convicted of drug possession. He renewed his Fourth Amendment claim on appeal, but the Court of Appeals rejected it and affirmed the conviction. The Michigan Supreme Court again declined review. We granted certiorari

II

The common-law principle that law enforcement officers must announce their presence and provide residents an opportunity to open the door is an ancient one. See Wilson v. Arkansas (1995). ... Finally, in *Wilson*, we were asked whether the rule was also a command of the Fourth Amendment. Tracing its origins in our English legal heritage, we concluded that it was.

We recognized that the new constitutional rule we had announced is not easily applied. *Wilson* and cases following it have noted the many situations in which it is not necessary to knock and announce. It is not necessary when "circumstances presen[t] a threat of physical violence," or if there is "reason to believe that evidence would likely be destroyed if advance notice were given" or if knocking and announcing would be "futile." We require only that police "have a reasonable suspicion ... under the particular circumstances" that one of these grounds for failing to knock and announce exists, and we have acknowledged that "[t]his showing is not high."

When the knock-and-announce rule does apply, it is not easy to determine precisely what officers must do. How many seconds' wait are too few? Our "reasonable wait time" standard ... is necessarily vague. *Banks* (a drug case, like this one) held that the proper measure was not how long it would take the resident to reach the door, but how long it would take to dispose of the suspected drugs—but that such a time (15 to 20 seconds in that case) would necessarily be extended when, for instance, the suspected contraband was not easily concealed. If our *ex post* evaluation is subject to such calculations, it is unsurprising that, *ex ante*, police officers about to encounter someone who may try to harm them will be uncertain how long to wait.

Happily, these issues do not confront us here. From the trial level onward, Michigan has conceded that the entry was a knock-and-announce violation. The issue here is remedy. *Wilson* specifically declined to decide whether the exclusionary rule is appropriate for violation of the knock-and-announce requirement. That question is squarely before us now.

III

A

In Weeks v. United States (1914), we adopted the federal exclusionary rule for evidence that was unlawfully seized from a home without a warrant in violation of the Fourth Amendment. We began applying the same rule to the States, through the Fourteenth Amendment, in Mapp v. Ohio (1961).

Suppression of evidence, however, has always been our last resort, not our first impulse. The exclusionary rule generates "substantial social costs," United States v. Leon (1984), which sometimes include setting the guilty free and the dangerous at large.... We have rejected "[i]ndiscriminate application" of the rule, *Leon* and have held it to be applicable only "where its remedial objectives are thought most efficaciously served," United States v. Calandra (1974),—that is, "where its deterrence benefits outweigh its 'substantial social costs,'" *Scott* (quoting *Leon*).

We did not always speak so guardedly. Expansive dicta in *Mapp*, for example, suggested wide scope for the exclusionary rule. ("[A]ll evidence obtained by searches and seizures in violation of the Constitution is, by that same authority, inadmissible in a state court"). But we have long since rejected that approach. As explained in Arizona v. Evans (1995): "In *Whiteley*, the Court treated identification of a Fourth Amendment violation as synonymous with application of the exclusionary rule to evidence secured incident to that violation. Subsequent case law has rejected this reflexive application of the exclusionary rule." We had said as much in *Leon*, a decade earlier, when we explained that "[w]hether the exclusionary sanction is appropriately imposed in a particular case, ... is 'an issue separate from the question whether the Fourth Amendment rights of the party seeking to invoke the rule were violated by police conduct.' "

In other words, exclusion may not be premised on the mere fact that a constitutional violation was a "but-for" cause of obtaining evidence. Our cases show that but-for causality is only a necessary, not a sufficient, condition for suppression. In this case, of course to f. 1182, the constitutional violation of an illegal *manner* of entry was *not* a but-for cause of obtaining the evidence. Whether that preliminary misstep had occurred *or not*, the police would have executed the warrant they had obtained, and would have discovered the gun and drugs inside the house. But even if the illegal entry here could be characterized as a but-for cause of discovering what was inside, we have "never held that evidence is 'fruit of the poisonous tree' simply because 'it would not have come to light but for the illegal actions of the police.' " Segura v. United States (1984).... Even in the early days of the exclusionary rule, we declined to

> hold that all evidence is "fruit of the poisonous tree" simply because it would not have come to light *but for* the illegal actions of the police. Rather, the more apt question in such a case is "whether, granting establishment of the primary illegality, the evidence to which instant objection is made has been come at by exploitation of that illegality or instead by means sufficiently distinguishable to be purged of the primary taint." Wong Sun v. United States (1963) (emphasis added).

... For this reason, cases excluding the fruits of unlawful warrantless searches, say nothing about the appropriateness of exclusion to vindicate the interests protected by the knock-and-announce requirement. Until a valid warrant has issued, citizens are entitled to shield "their persons, houses, papers, and effects," U.S. Const., Amdt. 4, from the government's scrutiny. Exclusion of the evidence obtained by a warrantless search vindicates that entitlement. The interests protected by the knock-and-announce requirement are quite different—and do not include the shielding of potential evidence from the government's eyes.

One of those interests is the protection of human life and limb, because an unannounced entry may provoke violence in supposed self-defense by the surprised resident. Another interest is the protection of property. Breaking a house (as the old cases typically put it) absent an announcement would penalize someone who " 'did not know of the process, of which, if he had notice, it is to be presumed that he would obey it....' " The knock-and-announce rule gives individuals "the opportunity to comply with the law and to avoid the destruction of property occasioned by a forcible entry." And thirdly, the knock-and-announce rule protects those elements of privacy and dignity that can be destroyed by a sudden entrance. It gives residents the "opportunity to prepare themselves for" the entry of the police "The brief interlude between announcement and entry with a warrant may be the opportunity that an individual has to pull on clothes or get out of bed." In other words, it assures the opportunity to collect oneself before answering the door.

What the knock-and-announce rule has never protected, however, is one's interest in preventing the government from seeing or taking evidence described in a warrant. Since the interests that *were* violated in this case have nothing to do with the seizure of the evidence, the exclusionary rule is inapplicable.

B

Quite apart from the requirement of unattenuated causation, the exclusionary rule has never been applied except "where its deterrence benefits outweigh its 'substantial social costs,' " The costs here are considerable. In addition to the grave adverse consequence that exclusion of relevant incriminating evidence always entails (viz., the risk of releasing dangerous criminals into society), imposing that massive remedy for a knock-and-announce violation would generate a constant flood of alleged failures to observe the rule, and claims that any asserted *Richards* justification for a no-knock entry, had inadequate support. The cost of entering this lottery would be small, but the jackpot enormous: suppression of all evidence, amounting in many cases to a get-out-of-jail-free card. Courts would experience as never before the reality that "[t]he exclusionary rule frequently requires extensive litigation to determine whether particular evidence must be excluded." Unlike the warrant or *Miranda* requirements, compliance with which is readily determined (either there was or was not a warrant; either the *Miranda* warning was given, or it was not), what constituted a "reasonable wait time" in a particular case, (or, for that matter, how many seconds the police in fact waited), or whether there was "reasonable suspicion" of the sort that would invoke the *Richards* exceptions, is difficult for the trial court to determine and even more difficult for an appellate court to review.

Another consequence of the incongruent remedy Hudson proposes would be police officers' refraining from timely entry after knocking and announcing. As we have observed, the amount of time they must wait is necessarily uncertain. If the consequences of running afoul of the rule were so massive, officers would be inclined to wait longer than the law requires—producing preventable violence against officers in some cases, and the destruction of evidence in many others. We deemed these consequences severe enough to produce our unanimous agreement that a mere "reasonable suspicion" that knocking and announcing "under the particular circumstances, would be dangerous or futile, or that it would inhibit the effective investigation of the crime," will cause the requirement to yield.

Next to these "substantial social costs" we must consider the deterrence benefits, existence of which is a necessary condition for exclusion. It is not, of course, a sufficient condition: "[I]t does not follow that the Fourth Amendment requires adoption of every proposal that might deter police misconduct." To begin with, the value of deterrence depends upon the strength of the incentive to commit the forbidden act. Viewed from this perspective, deterrence of knock-and-announce violations is not worth a lot. Violation of the warrant requirement sometimes produces incriminating evidence that could not otherwise be obtained. But ignoring knock-and-announce can realistically be expected to achieve absolutely nothing except the prevention of destruction of evidence and the avoidance of life-threatening resistance by occupants of the premises—dangers which, if there is even "reasonable suspicion" of their existence, *suspend the knock-and-announce requirement anyway*. Massive deterrence is hardly required.

It seems to us not even true, as Hudson contends, that without suppression there will be no deterrence of knock-and-announce violations at all. Of course even if this assertion were accurate, it would not necessarily justify suppression. Assuming (as the assertion must) that civil suit is not an effective deterrent, one can think of many forms of police misconduct that are similarly "undeterred." When, for example, a confessed suspect in the killing of a police officer, arrested (along with incriminating evidence) in a lawful warranted search, is subjected to physical abuse at the station house, would it seriously be suggested that the evidence must be excluded, since that is the only "effective deterrent"? And what, other than civil suit, is the "effective deterrent" of police violation of an already-confessed suspect's Sixth Amendment rights by denying him prompt access to counsel? Many would regard these violated rights as more significant than the right not to be intruded upon in one's nightclothes—and yet nothing but "ineffective" civil suit is available as a deterrent. And the police incentive for those violations is arguably greater than the incentive for disregarding the knock-and-announce rule . . .

In sum, the social costs of applying the exclusionary rule to knock-and-announce violations are considerable; the incentive to such violations is minimal to begin with, and the extant deterrences against them are substantial—incomparably greater than the factors deterring warrantless entries when *Mapp* was decided. Resort to the massive remedy of suppressing evidence of guilt is unjustified.

IV

A trio of cases—Segura v. United States (1984); New York v. Harris (1990); and United States v. Ramirez (1998)—confirms our conclusion that suppression is unwarranted in this case.

Like today's case, *Segura* involved a concededly illegal entry. Police conducting a drug crime investigation waited for Segura outside an apartment building; when he arrived, he denied living there. The police arrested him and brought him to the apartment where they suspected illegal activity. An officer knocked. When someone inside opened the door, the police entered, taking Segura with them. They had neither a warrant nor consent to enter, and they did not announce themselves as police—an entry as illegal as can be. Officers then stayed in the apartment for *19 hours* awaiting a search warrant. Once alerted that the search warrant had been obtained, the police—still inside, having secured the premises so that no evidence could be removed—conducted a search. We refused to exclude the resulting evidence. We recognized that only the evidence gained from the particular violation could be excluded, and therefore distinguished the effects of the illegal entry from the effects of the legal search: "None of the information on which the warrant was secured was derived from or related in any way to the initial entry into petitioners' apartment. . . ." It was therefore "beyond dispute that the information possessed by the agents before they entered the apartment constituted an independent source for the discovery and seizure of the evidence now challenged."

If the search in *Segura* could be "wholly unrelated to the prior entry," when the only entry was warrantless, it would be bizarre to treat more harshly the actions in this case, where the only entry was *with* a warrant. If the probable cause backing a warrant that was issued *later in time* could be an "independent source" for a search that proceeded after the officers illegally entered and waited, a search warrant obtained *before* going in must have at least this much effect.[1]

In the second case, *Harris*, the police violated the defendant's Fourth Amendment rights by arresting him at home without a warrant, contrary to Payton v. New York (1980). Once taken to the station house, he gave an incriminating statement. We refused to exclude it. Like the illegal entry which led to discovery of the evidence in today's case, the illegal arrest in *Harris* began a process that culminated in acquisition of the evidence sought to be excluded. While Harris's statement was "the product of an arrest and being in custody," it "was not the fruit of the fact that the arrest was made in the house rather than someplace else." Likewise here: While acquisition of the gun and drugs was the product of a search pursuant to warrant, it was not the fruit of the fact that the entry was not preceded by knock and announce.[2]

United States v. Ramirez involved a claim that police entry violated the Fourth Amendment because it was effected by breaking a window. We ultimately concluded that the property destruction was, under all the circumstances, reasonable, but in the course of our discussion we unanimously said the following: "[D]estruction of property in the course of a search may violate the Fourth Amendment, even though the entry itself is lawful and the fruits of the search are not subject to suppression." Had the breaking of the window been unreasonable, the Court said, it would have been necessary to determine whether there had been a "sufficient causal relationship between the breaking of the window and the discovery of the guns to warrant suppression of the evidence." What clearer expression

1. Justice Breyer's insistence that the warrant in *Segura* was "obtained independently without use of any information found during the illegal entry," (dissenting opinion), entirely fails to distinguish it from the warrant in the present case. Similarly inapposite is his appeal to Justice Frankfurter's statement in *Wolf v. Colorado* (1949), that the " 'knock at the door, . . . as a prelude to a search, without authority of law . . . [is] inconsistent with the conception of human rights enshrined in [our] history,' ". "How much the more offensive," Justice Breyer asserts, "when the search takes place without any knock at all," But a no-knock entry "without authority of law" (*i.e.*, without a search warrant) describes not this case, but *Segura*—where the evidence was admitted anyway. Justice Breyer's assertion that *Segura*, unlike our decision in the present case, had no effect on deterrence, does not comport with the views of the *Segura* dissent. ("The Court's disposition, I fear, will provide government agents with an affirmative incentive to engage in unconstitutional violations of the privacy of the home").

2. *Harris* undermines two key points of the dissent. First, the claim that "whether the interests underlying the knock-and-announce rule are implicated in any given case is, in a sense, beside the point," This is flatly refuted by *Harris'* plain statement that the reason for a rule must govern the sanctions for the rule's violation. Second, the dissent's attempt to turn *Harris* into a vindication of the sanctity of the home. The whole point of the case was that a confession that police obtained by illegally removing a man from the sanctity of his home was admissible against him.

could there be of the proposition that an impermissible manner of entry does not necessarily trigger the exclusionary rule?

* * *

For the foregoing reasons we affirm the judgment of the Michigan Court of Appeals.

It is so ordered.

■ JUSTICE KENNEDY, concurring in part and concurring in the judgment.

Two points should be underscored with respect to today's decision. First, the knock-and-announce requirement protects rights and expectations linked to ancient principles in our constitutional order. See Wilson v. Arkansas. The Court's decision should not be interpreted as suggesting that violations of the requirement are trivial or beyond the law's concern. Second, the continued operation of the exclusionary rule, as settled and defined by our precedents, is not in doubt. Today's decision determines only that in the specific context of the knock-and-announce requirement, a violation is not sufficiently related to the later discovery of evidence to justify suppression.

As to the basic right in question, privacy and security in the home are central to the Fourth Amendment's guarantees as explained in our decisions and as understood since the beginnings of the Republic. This common understanding ensures respect for the law and allegiance to our institutions, and it is an instrument for transmitting our Constitution to later generations undiminished in meaning and force. It bears repeating that it is a serious matter if law enforcement officers violate the sanctity of the home by ignoring the requisites of lawful entry. Security must not be subject to erosion by indifference or contempt.

Our system, as the Court explains, has developed procedures for training police officers and imposing discipline for failures to act competently and lawfully. If those measures prove ineffective, they can be fortified with more detailed regulations or legislation. Supplementing these safeguards are civil remedies, such as those available under 42 U.S.C. § 1983, *Rev. Stat. § 1979*, that provide restitution for discrete harms. These remedies apply to all violations, including, of course, exceptional cases in which unannounced entries cause severe fright and humiliation.

Suppression is another matter. Under our precedents the causal link between a violation of the knock-and-announce requirement and a later search is too attenuated to allow suppression.... When, for example, a violation results from want of a 20–second pause but an ensuing, lawful search lasting five hours discloses evidence of criminality, the failure to wait at the door cannot properly be described as having caused the discovery of evidence.

Today's decision does not address any demonstrated pattern of knock-and-announce violations. If a widespread pattern of violations were shown, and particularly if those violations were committed against persons who lacked the means or voice to mount an effective protest, there would be reason for grave concern. Even then, however, the Court would have to acknowledge that extending the remedy of exclusion to all the evidence seized following a knock-and-announce violation would mean revising the requirement of causation that limits our discretion in applying the exclusionary rule. That type of extension also would have significant practical implications, adding to the list of issues requiring resolution at the criminal trial questions such as whether police officers entered a home after waiting 10 seconds or 20.

In this case the relevant evidence was discovered not because of a failure to knock-and-announce, but because of a subsequent search pursuant to a lawful warrant. The Court in my view is correct to hold that suppression was not required. While I am not convinced that Segura v. United States (1984), and New York v. Harris (1990), have as much relevance here as Justice Scalia appears to conclude, the Court's holding is fully supported by Parts I through III of its opinion. I accordingly join those Parts and concur in the judgment.

■ JUSTICE BREYER, with whom JUSTICE STEVENS, JUSTICE SOUTER, and JUSTICE GINSBURG join, dissenting.

In Wilson v. Arkansas (1995), a unanimous Court held that the Fourth Amendment normally requires law enforcement officers to knock and announce their presence before entering a dwelling. Today's opinion holds that evidence seized from a home following a violation of this requirement need not be suppressed

As a result, the Court destroys the strongest legal incentive to comply with the Constitution's knock-and-announce requirement. And the Court does so without significant support in precedent. At least I can find no such support in the many Fourth Amendment cases the Court has decided in the near century since it first set forth the exclusionary principle in Weeks v. United States, 232 U.S. 383, 34 S. Ct. 341, 58 L. Ed. 652, T.D. 1964 (1914). See Appendix [Appendix listing 41 Supreme Court Fourth Amendment decisions from 1914 to present requiring suppression of evidence seized (or remanding for lower court to make suppression determination) in a private home following an illegal arrest or search, omitted]

Today's opinion is thus doubly troubling. It represents a significant departure from the Court's precedents. And it weakens, perhaps destroys, much of the practical value of the Constitution's knock-and-announce protection.

I

This Court has set forth the legal principles that ought to have determined the outcome of this case in two sets of basic Fourth Amendment cases. I shall begin by describing that underlying case law.

A

The first set of cases describes the constitutional knock-and-announce requirement, a requirement that this Court initially set forth only 11 years ago Wilson v. Arkansas In *Wilson*, tracing the lineage of the knock-and-announce rule back to the 13th century, we wrote that

> "[a]n examination of the common law of search and seizure leaves no doubt that the reasonableness of a search of a dwelling may

depend in part on whether law enforcement officers announced their presence and authority prior to entering."

We noted that this "basic principle" was agreed upon by "[s]everal prominent founding-era commentators," and "was woven quickly into the fabric of early American law" via state constitutions and statutes. We further concluded that there was

> "little doubt that the Framers of the Fourth Amendment thought that the method of an officer's entry into a dwelling was among the factors to be considered in assessing the reasonableness of a search or seizure"

And we held that the "common-law 'knock and announce' principle forms a part of the reasonableness inquiry under the Fourth Amendment." Thus, "a search or seizure of a dwelling might be constitutionally defective if police officers enter without prior announcement."

B

The second set of cases sets forth certain well-established principles that are relevant here. They include:

Boyd v. United States (1886). In this seminal Fourth Amendment case, decided 120 years ago, the Court wrote, in frequently quoted language, that the Fourth Amendment's prohibitions apply

> "to all invasions on the part of the government and its employes of the sanctity of a man's home and the privacies of life. It is not the breaking of his doors, and the rummaging of his drawers, that constitutes the essence of the offence; but it is the invasion of his indefeasible right of personal security, personal liberty and private property."

Weeks. This case, decided 28 years after *Boyd*, originated the exclusionary rule. The Court held that the Federal Government could not retain evidence seized unconstitutionally and use that evidence in a federal criminal trial. The Court pointed out that "[i]f letters and private documents" could be unlawfully seized from a home "and used in evidence against a citizen accused of an offense, the protection of the Fourth Amendment declaring his right to be secure against such searches and seizures is of no value, and ... might as well be stricken from the Constitution...."

Wolf v. Colorado (1949) and Mapp v. Ohio (1961). Both of these cases considered whether *Weeks*' exclusionary rule applies to the States. In *Wolf*, the Court held that it did not. It said that "[t]he security of one's privacy against arbitrary intrusion by the police ... is ... implicit in 'the concept of ordered liberty' and as such enforceable against the States through the Due Process Clause." But the Court held that the exclusionary rule is not enforceable against the States as "an essential ingredient of the right." In *Mapp*, the Court overruled *Wolf*. Experience, it said, showed that alternative methods of enforcing the Fourth Amendment's requirements had failed. ("Experience [in California] has demonstrated, however, that neither administrative, criminal nor civil remedies are effective in suppressing lawless searches and seizures"). The Court consequently held that "all evidence obtained by searches and seizures in violation of the Constitution is, by that same authority, inadmissible in a state court." "To hold otherwise," the Court added, would be "to grant the right but in reality to withhold its privilege and enjoyment."

II

Reading our knock-and-announce cases, Part I–A, *supra*, in light of this foundational Fourth Amendment case law, Part I–B, *supra*, it is clear that the exclusionary rule should apply. For one thing, elementary logic leads to that conclusion. We have held that a court must "conside[r]" whether officers complied with the knock-and-announce requirement "in assessing the reasonableness of a search or seizure." *Wilson* (emphasis added). The Fourth Amendment insists that an unreasonable search or seizure is, constitutionally speaking, an illegal search or seizure. And ever since *Weeks* (in respect to federal prosecutions) and *Mapp* (in respect to state prosecutions), "the use of evidence secured through an illegal search and seizure" is "barred" in criminal trials.

For another thing, the driving legal purpose underlying the exclusionary rule, namely, the deterrence of unlawful government behavior, argues strongly for suppression. (purpose of the exclusionary rule is "to deter—to compel respect for the constitutional guaranty ... by removing the incentive to disregard it"). In *Weeks, Silverthorne*, and *Mapp*, the Court based its holdings requiring suppression of unlawfully obtained evidence upon the recognition that admission of that evidence would seriously undermine the Fourth Amendment's promise. All three cases recognized that failure to apply the exclusionary rule would make that promise a hollow one. Indeed, this Court in *Mapp* held that the exclusionary rule applies to the States in large part due to its belief that alternative state mechanisms for enforcing the Fourth Amendment's guarantees had proved "worthless and futile."

Why is application of the exclusionary rule any the less necessary here? Without such a rule, as in *Mapp*, police know that they can ignore the Constitution's requirements without risking suppression of evidence discovered after an unreasonable entry. As in *Mapp*, some government officers will find it easier, or believe it less risky, to proceed with what they consider a necessary search immediately and without the requisite constitutional (say, warrant or knock-and-announce) compliance. Cf. Mercli, The Apprehension of Peril Exception to the Knock and Announce Rule—Part I, 16 Search and Seizure L. Rep. 129, 130 (1989) (hereinafter Mericili) (noting that some "[d]rug enforcement authorities believe that safety for the police lies in a swift, surprising entry with overwhelming force—not in announcing their official authority")....

It is not surprising, then, that after looking at virtually every pertinent Supreme Court case decided since *Weeks*, I can find no precedent that might offer the majority support for its contrary conclusion. The Court has, of course, recognized that not every Fourth Amendment violation necessarily triggers the exclusionary rule. (application of the exclusionary rule is a separate question from whether the Fourth Amendment has been violated). But the class of Fourth Amendment violations that do not result in suppression of the evidence seized, however, is limited.

The Court has declined to apply the exclusionary rule only:

(1) where there is a specific reason to believe that application of the rule would "not result in appreciable deterrence," (exception where searching officer executes defective search warrant in "good faith"); Arizona v. Evans (1995) (exception for clerical errors by court employees); Walder v. United States (exception for impeachment purposes), or

(2) where admissibility in proceedings other than criminal trials was at issue Pennsylvania Bd. of Probation and Parole v. Scott (1998) (exception for parole revocation proceedings); INS v. Lopez–Mendoza (1984) (plurality opinion) (exception for deportation proceedings); *Janis* (exception for civil tax proceedings); United States v. Calandra (1974) (exception for grand jury proceedings); Stone v. Powell (1976) (exception for federal habeas proceedings).

Neither of these two exceptions applies here. The second does not apply because this case is an ordinary criminal trial. The first does not apply because (1) officers who violate the rule are not acting "as a reasonable officer would and should act in similar circumstances," *Leon*, (2) this case does not involve government employees other than police, *Evans*, and (3), most importantly, the key rationale for any exception, "lack of deterrence," is missing, see *Pennsylvania Bd. of Probation* (noting that the rationale for not applying the rule in noncriminal cases has been that the deterrence achieved by having the rule apply in those contexts is "minimal" *because* "application of the rule in the criminal trial context already provides significant deterrence of unconstitutional searches"); Michigan v. Tucker (1974) (noting that deterrence rationale would not be served if rule applied to police officers acting in good faith, as the "deterrent purpose of the exclusionary rule necessarily assumes that the police have engaged in willful, or at the very least negligent, conduct"). That critical latter rationale, which underlies *every* exception, does not apply here, as there is no reason to think that, in the case of knock-and-announce violations by the police, "the exclusion of evidence at trial would not sufficiently deter future errors," *Evans*, or " 'further the ends of the exclusionary rule in any appreciable way,' " *Leon*.

I am aware of no other basis for an exception. The Court has decided more than 300 Fourth Amendment cases since *Weeks*. The Court has found constitutional violations in nearly a third of them. The nature of the constitutional violation varies. In most instances officers lacked a warrant; in others, officers possessed a warrant based on false affidavits; in still others, the officers executed the search in an unconstitutional manner. But in every case involving evidence seized during an illegal search of a home (federally since *Weeks*, nationally since *Mapp*), the Court, with the exceptions mentioned, has either explicitly or implicitly upheld (or required) the suppression of the evidence at trial. See Appendix In not one of those cases did the Court "questio[n], in the absence of a more efficacious sanction, the continued application of the [exclusionary] rule to suppress evidence from the State's case" in a criminal trial. *Franks* v. *Delaware* (1978).

I can find nothing persuasive in the majority's opinion that could justify its refusal to apply the rule. It certainly is not a justification for an exception here (as the majority finds) to find odd instances in *other* areas of law that do not automatically demand suppression. (suspect confesses, police beat him up *afterwards*; suspect confesses, *then* police apparently arrest him, take him to station, and refuse to tell him of his right to counsel). Nor can it justify an exception to say that *some* police may knock at the door anyway (to avoid being mistaken for a burglar), for other police (believing quick entry is the most secure, effective entry) will not voluntarily do so.

Neither can the majority justify its failure to respect the need for deterrence, as set forth consistently in the Court's prior case law, through its claim of " 'substantial social costs' "—at least if it means that those " 'social costs' " are somehow special here. The only costs it mentions are those that typically accompany *any* use of the Fourth Amendment's exclusionary principle: (1) that where the constable blunders, a guilty defendant may be set free (consider *Mapp* itself); (2) that defendants may assert claims where Fourth Amendment rights are uncertain (consider the Court's qualified immunity jurisprudence), and (3) that sometimes it is difficult to decide the merits of those uncertain claims. In fact, the "no-knock" warrants that are provided by many States, by diminishing uncertainty, may make application of the knock-and-announce principle less " 'cost[ly]' " on the whole than application of comparable Fourth Amendment principles, such as determining whether a particular warrantless search was justified by exigency. The majority's "substantial social costs" argument is an argument against the Fourth Amendment's exclusionary principle itself. And it is an argument that this Court, until now, has consistently rejected.

III

The majority, Michigan, and the United States make several additional arguments. In my view, those arguments rest upon misunderstandings of the principles underlying this Court's precedents.

A

The majority first argues that "the constitutional violation of an illegal *manner* of entry was *not* a but-for cause of obtaining the evidence." But taking causation as it is commonly understood in the law, I do not see how that can be so. Although the police might have entered Hudson's home lawfully, they did not in fact do so. Their unlawful behavior inseparably characterizes their actual entry; that entry was a necessary condition of their presence in Hudson's home; and their presence in Hudson's home was a necessary condition of their finding and seizing the evidence. At the same time, their discovery of evidence in Hudson's home was a readily foreseeable consequence of their entry and their unlawful presence within the home.

Moreover, separating the "manner of entry" from the related search slices the violation too finely. As noted, Part I–A, *supra*, we have described a failure to comply with the knock-and-announce rule, not as an independently unlawful event, but as a factor that renders the *search* "constitutionally defective." (compliance with the knock-and-announce requirement is one of the "factors to be considered in assessing the *reasonableness of a search or seizure*" (emphasis added)); *Ker v. California* (1963) (opinion of Brennan, J.) ("[A] lawful entry is the indispensable predicate of a reasonable search").

The Court nonetheless accepts Michigan's argument that the requisite but-for-causation is not satisfied in this case because, whether or not the constitutional violation occurred (what the Court refers to as a "preliminary misstep"), "the police would have executed the warrant they had obtained, and would have discovered the gun and drugs inside the house." As support for this proposition, Michigan rests on this Court's inevitable discovery cases.

This claim, however, misunderstands the inevitable discovery doctrine....

Thus, the Court's opinion reflects a misunderstanding of what "inevitable discovery" means when it says, "[i]n this case, of course, the constitutional violation of an illegal *manner* of entry was *not* a but-for cause of obtaining the evidence." The majority rests this conclusion on its next statement: "Whether that preliminary misstep has occurred *or not*, the police ... would have discovered the gun and the drugs inside the house." *Ibid*. Despite the phrase "of course," neither of these statements is correct. It is not true that, had the illegal entry not occurred, "police ... would have discovered the guns and drugs inside the house." Without that unlawful entry they would not have been inside the house; so there would have been no discovery.

Of course, had the police entered the house lawfully, they would have found the gun and drugs. But that fact is beside the point. The question is not what police might have done had they not behaved unlawfully. The question is what they did do. Was there set in motion an independent chain of events that would have inevitably led to the discovery and seizure of the evidence despite, and independent of, that behavior? The answer here is "no."

B

The majority, Michigan, and the United States point out that the officers here possessed a warrant authorizing a search. That fact, they argue, means that the evidence would have been discovered independently or somehow diminishes the need to suppress the evidence. But I do not see why that is so. The warrant in question was not a "no-knock" warrant, which many States (but not Michigan) issue to assure police that a prior knock is not necessary. It did not authorize a search that fails to comply with knock-[*619] and-announce requirements. Rather, it was an ordinary search warrant. It authorized a search that *complied with*, not a search that *disregarded*, the Constitution's knock-and-announce rule.

Would a warrant that authorizes entry into a home on Tuesday permit the police to enter on Monday? Would a warrant that authorizes entry during the day authorize the police to enter during the middle of the night?

It is difficult for me to see how the presence of a warrant that does not authorize the entry in question has anything to do with the "inevitable discovery" exception or otherwise diminishes the need to enforce the knock-and-announce requirement through suppression.

C

The majority and the United States set forth a policy-related variant of the causal connection theme: The United States argues that the law should suppress evidence only insofar as a Fourth Amendment violation causes the kind of harm that the particular Fourth Amendment rule seeks to protect against. It adds that the constitutional purpose of the knock-and-announce rule is to prevent needless destruction of property (such as breaking down a door) and to avoid unpleasant surprise. And it concludes that the exclusionary rule should suppress evidence of, say, damage to property, the discovery of a defendant in an "intimate or compromising moment," or an excited utterance from the occupant caught by surprise, but nothing more.

The majority makes a similar argument. It says that evidence should not be suppressed once the causal connection between unlawful behavior and discovery of the evidence becomes too "attenuated." But the majority then makes clear that it is not using the word "attenuated" to mean what this Court's precedents have typically used that word to mean, namely, that the discovery of the evidence has come about long after the unlawful behavior took place or in an independent way, *i.e.*, through " 'means sufficiently distinguishable to be purged of the primary taint.' " Wong Sun v. United States (1963).

Rather, the majority gives the word "attenuation" a new meaning (thereby, in effect, making the same argument as the United States). "Attenuation," it says, "also occurs when, even given a direct causal connection, the interest protected by the constitutional guarantee that has been violated would not be served by suppression of the evidence obtained." The interests the knock-and-announce rule seeks to protect, the Court adds, are "human life" (at stake when a householder is "surprised"), "property" (such as the front door), and "those elements of privacy and dignity that can be destroyed by a sudden entrance," namely, "the opportunity to collect oneself before answering the door." Since none of those interests led to the discovery of the evidence seized here, there is no reason to suppress it.

There are three serious problems with this argument. First, it does not fully describe the constitutional values, purposes, and objectives underlying the knock-and-announce requirement. That rule does help to protect homeowners from damaged doors; it does help to protect occupants from surprise. But it does more than that. It protects the occupants' privacy by assuring them that government agents will not enter their home without complying with those requirements (among others) that diminish the offensive nature of any such intrusion. Many years ago, Justice Frankfurter wrote for the Court that the "knock at the door, ... as a prelude to a search, with-out authority of law ... [is] inconsistent with the conception of human rights enshrined in [our] history" and Constitution. How much the more offensive when the search takes place without any knock at all.

Cf. *Wilson* (knock-and-announce rule recognizes that "the common law generally protected a man's house as 'his castle of defence and asylum' " (quoting 3 W. Blackstone, Commentaries *288)); *Miller* (federal knock-and-announce statute "codif[ied] a tradition embedded in Anglo–American law" that reflected "the reverence of the law for the individual's right of privacy in his house").

Over a century ago this Court wrote that "it is not the breaking of his doors" that is the "essence of the offence," but the "invasions on the part of the government ... of the sanctity of a man's home and the privacies of life." *Boyd*. And just this Term we have reiterated that " 'it is beyond dispute that the home is entitled to special protection as the center of the private lives of our people.' " *Georgia* v. *Randolph*. The knock-and-announce requirement is no less a part of the "centuries-old principle" of special protection for the privacy of the home than the warrant requirement. The Court is therefore wrong to reduce the essence of its protection to "the right not to be intruded upon in one's nightclothes." ("[I]ndividual privacy interest[s]" protected by the rule are "not inconsequential" and "should not be unduly minimized").

Second, whether the interests underlying the knock-and-announce rule are implicated in any given case is, in a sense, beside the point. As we have explained, failure to comply with the knock-and-announce rule renders the related search unlawful. And where a search is unlawful, the law insists upon suppression of the evidence consequently discovered, even if that evidence or its possession has little or nothing to do with the reasons underlying the unconstitutionality of a search. The Fourth Amendment does not seek to protect contraband, yet we have required suppression of contraband seized in an unlawful search.... That is because the exclusionary rule protects more general "privacy values through deterrence of future police misconduct." The same is true here.

Third, the majority's interest-based approach departs from prior law. Ordinarily a court will simply look to see if the unconstitutional search produced the evidence. The majority does not refer to any relevant case in which, beyond that, suppression turned on the far more detailed relation between, say, (1) a particular materially false statement made to the magistrate who issued a (consequently) invalid warrant and (2) evidence found after a search with that warrant. And the majority's failure does not surprise me, for such efforts to trace causal connections at retail could well complicate Fourth Amendment suppression law, threatening its workability.

D

The United States, in its brief and at oral argument, has argued that suppression is "an especially harsh remedy given the nature of the violation in this case." This argument focuses upon the fact that entering a house after knocking and announcing can, in some cases, prove dangerous to a police officer. Perhaps someone inside has a gun, as turned out to be the case here. The majority adds that police officers about to encounter someone who may try to harm them will be "uncertain" as to how long to wait. It says that, "[i]f the consequences of running afoul" of the knock-

and-announce "rule were so massive," *i.e.*, would lead to the exclusion of evidence, then "officers would be inclined to wait longer than the law requires—producing preventable violence against officers in some cases."

To argue that police efforts to assure compliance with the rule may prove dangerous, however, is not to argue against evidence suppression. It is to argue against the validity of the rule itself. Similarly, to argue that enforcement means uncertainty, which in turn means the potential for dangerous and longer-than-necessary delay, is (if true) to argue against meaningful compliance with the rule.

The answer to the first argument is that the rule itself does not require police to knock or to announce their presence where police have a "reasonable suspicion" that doing so "would be dangerous or futile" or "would inhibit the effective investigation of the crime by, for example, allowing the destruction of evidence."

The answer to the second argument is that States can, and many do, reduce police uncertainty while assuring a neutral evaluation of concerns about risks to officers or the destruction of evidence by permitting police to obtain a "no-knock" search warrant from a magistrate judge, thereby assuring police that a prior announcement is not necessary. While such a procedure cannot remove all uncertainty, it does provide an easy way for officers to comply with the knock-and-announce rule.

Of course, even without such a warrant, police maintain the backup "authority to exercise independent judgment concerning the wisdom of a no-knock entry at the time the warrant is being executed." "[I]f circumstances support a reasonable suspicion of exigency when the officers arrive at the door, they may go straight in." *Banks*. And "[r]easonable suspicion is a less demanding standard than probable cause...." ...

Consider this very case. The police obtained a search warrant that authorized a search, not only for drugs, but also for *guns*. If probable cause justified a search for guns, why would it not also have justified a no-knock warrant, thereby diminishing any danger to the officers? Why (in a State such as Michigan that lacks no-knock warrants) would it not have justified the very no-knock entry at issue here? Indeed, why did the prosecutor not argue in this very case that, given the likelihood of guns, the no-knock entry was lawful? From what I have seen in the record, he would have won. And had he won, there would have been no suppression here.

That is the right way to win. The very process of arguing the merits of the violation would help to clarify the contours of the knock-and-announce rule, contours that the majority believes are too fuzzy. That procedural fact, along with no-knock warrants, back up authority to enter without knocking regardless, and use of the "reasonable suspicion" standard for doing so should resolve the government's problems with the knock-and-announce rule while reducing the "uncertain[ty]" that the majority discusses to levels beneath that found elsewhere in Fourth Amendment law (*e.g.*, exigent circumstances). Regardless, if the Court fears that effective enforcement of a constitutional requirement will have harmful consequences, it should face those fears directly by addressing the requirement itself. It should not argue, "the requirement is fine, indeed, a serious matter, just don't enforce it."

E

It should be apparent by now that the three cases upon which Justice Scalia relies—Segura v. United States, New York v. Harris, *Ramirez*— do not support his conclusion. Indeed, Justice Kennedy declines to join this section of the lead opinion because he fails to see the relevance of *Segura* and *Harris*, though he does rely on *Ramirez*.

Justice Scalia first argues that, if the "search in *Segura* could be 'wholly unrelated to the prior entry ... when the only entry was warrantless, it would be bizarre to treat more harshly the actions in this case, where the only entry was *with* a warrant.'" Then he says that, "[i]f the probable cause backing a warrant that was issued *later in time* could be an 'independent source' for a search that proceeded after the officers illegally entered and waited, a search warrant obtained *before* going in must have at least this much effect." *Ibid*. I do not understand these arguments. As I have explained, the presence of a warrant that did not authorize a search that fails to comply with knock-and-announce requirements is beside the point. See Part III–B, *supra*. And the timing of the warrant in *Segura* made no difference to the case. The relevant fact about the warrant there was that it was lawfully obtained and arguably set off an independent chain of events that led the police to seize the evidence. ("The valid warrant search was a 'means sufficiently distinguishable' to purge the evidence of any 'taint' arising from the entry"). As noted, there is no such independent event, or intervening chain of events that would purge the taint of the illegal entry, present here. The search that produced the relevant evidence here is the very search that the knock-and-announce violation rendered unlawful. There simply is no "independent source."

As importantly, the Court in *Segura* said nothing to suggest it intended to create a major exclusionary rule exception, notwithstanding the impact of such an exception on deterrence. Indeed, such an exception would be inconsistent with a critical rationale underlying the independent source and inevitable discovery rules, which was arguably available in *Segura*, and which is clearly absent here. That rationale concerns deterrence. The threat of inadmissibility deters unlawful police behavior; and the existence of an exception applicable where evidence is found through an untainted independent route will rarely undercut that deterrence. That is because the police can rarely rely upon such an exception—at least not often enough to change the deterrence calculus. See *Murray* ("We see the incentives differently. An officer with probable cause sufficient to obtain a search warrant would be foolish to enter the premises first in an unlawful manner. By doing so, he would risk suppression of all evidence on the premises ..."; *Nix* ("A police officer who is faced with the opportunity to obtain evidence illegally will rarely, if ever, be in a position to calculate whether the evidence sought would inevitably be discovered"; "If the prosecution can establish by a preponderance of the evidence that the information ultimately or inevitably would have been discovered by lawful means—here the volunteers' search—then the deterrence rationale has so little basis that the evidence should be received").

Segura's police officers would have been foolish to have entered the apartment unlawfully with the *ex ante* hope that an independent causal chain of events would later occur and render admissible the evidence they found. By way of contrast, today's holding will seriously undermine deterrence in knock-and-announce cases. Officers will almost always know *ex ante* that they can ignore the knock-and-announce requirement without risking the suppression of evidence discovered after their unlawful entry. That fact is obvious, and this Court has never before today—not in *Segura* or any other post-*Weeks* (or post-*Mapp*) case—refused to apply the exclusionary rule where its absence would so clearly and so significantly impair government officials' incentive to comply with comparable Fourth Amendment requirements....

How can Justice Scalia maintain that the evidence here—a gun and drugs seized in the home—is " 'not the fruit' " of the illegal entry? The officers' failure to knock and announce rendered the entire search unlawful, and that unlawful search led to the discovery of evidence in petitioner's home. Thus, *Harris* compels the opposite result than that reached by the Court today. Like the *Payton* rule at issue in *Harris*, the knock-and-announce rule reflects the "reverence of the law for the individual's right of privacy in his house." emphasized that our holding in that case stemmed from the "overriding respect for the sanctity of the home that has been embedded in our traditions since the origins of the Republic"). Like the confession that was "excluded, as it should have been," in *Harris* the evidence in this case was seized in the home, immediately following the illegal entry. And like *Harris*, nothing in petitioner's argument would require the suppression of evidence obtained *outside* the home following a knock-and-announce violation, precisely because officers have a remaining incentive to follow the rule to avoid the suppression of any evidence obtained from the very place they are searching. ("Even though we decline to suppress statements made outside the home following a *Payton* violation, the principal incentive to obey *Payton* still obtains: the police know that a warrantless entry will lead to the suppression of any evidence found, or statements taken, inside the home").

I concede that United States v. Ramirez offers the majority its last best hope. But not even that case can offer the majority significant support. The majority focuses on the Court's isolated statement that "destruction of property in the course of a search may violate the Fourth Amendment, *even though the entry itself is lawful and the fruits of the search are not subject to suppression*." But even if I accept this dictum, the entry here is unlawful, not lawful. It is one thing to say (in an appropriate case) that destruction of property after proper entry has nothing to do with discovery of the evidence, and to refuse to suppress. It would be quite another thing to say that improper entry had nothing to do with discovery of the evidence in this case. Moreover, the deterrence analysis for the property destruction cases (where, by definition, there will almost always be quantifiable damages) might well differ.

IV

There is perhaps one additional argument implicit in the majority's approach. The majority says, for example, that the "cost" to a defendant of "entering this lottery," *i.e.*, of claiming a "knock-and-announce" violation, "would be small, but the jackpot enormous"—namely, a potential "get-out-of-jail-free card." It adds that the "social costs" of applying the exclusionary rule here are not worth the deterrence benefits. Leaving aside what I believe are invalid arguments based on precedent or the majority's own estimate that suppression is not necessary to deter constitutional violations, one is left with a simple unvarnished conclusion, namely, that in this kind of case, a knock-and-announce case, "[r]esort to the massive remedy of suppressing evidence of guilt is unjustified." Why is that judicial judgment, taken on its own, inappropriate? Could it not be argued that the knock-and-announce rule, a subsidiary Fourth Amendment rule, is simply not important enough to warrant a suppression remedy? Could the majority not simply claim that the suppression game is not worth the candle?

The answer, I believe, is "no." That "no" reflects history, a history that shows the knock-and-announce rule is important. That "no" reflects precedent, precedent that shows there is no pre-existing legal category of exceptions to the exclusionary rule into which the knock-and-announce cases might fit. That "no" reflects empirical fact, experience that provides confirmation of what common sense suggests: without suppression there is little to deter knock-and-announce violations.

There may be instances in the law where text or history or tradition leaves room for a judicial decision that rests upon little more than an unvarnished judicial instinct. But this is not one of them. Rather, our Fourth Amendment traditions place high value upon protecting privacy in the home. They emphasize the need to assure that its constitutional protections are effective, lest the Amendment "sound the word of promise to the ear but break it to the hope." They include an exclusionary principle, which since *Weeks* has formed the centerpiece of the criminal law's effort to ensure the practical reality of those promises. That is why the Court should assure itself that any departure from that principle is firmly grounded in logic, in history, in precedent, and in empirical fact. It has not done so. That is why, with respect, I dissent.

F. FURTHER QUESTIONS ABOUT THE METHOD OF SEIZURE

The Fourth Amendment does not specify how police officers may make seizures. Tennessee v. Garner, however, established the principle that the Fourth Amendment governs the use of force permissible to make an arrest.

Tennessee v. Garner

Supreme Court of the United States, 1985.
471 U.S. 1, 105 S.Ct. 1694.

■ JUSTICE WHITE delivered the opinion of the Court.

This case requires us to determine the constitutionality of the use of deadly force to prevent the escape of an apparently unarmed suspected felon. We conclude that such force may not be used unless it is necessary to prevent the escape and the officer has probable cause to believe that the suspect poses a significant threat of death or serious physical injury to the officer or others.

I

At about 10:45 p.m. on October 3, 1974, Memphis Police Officers Elton Hymon and Leslie Wright were dispatched to answer a "prowler inside call." Upon arriving at the scene they saw a woman standing on her porch and gesturing toward the adjacent house.[1] She told them she had heard glass breaking and that "they" or "someone" was breaking in next door. While Wright radioed the dispatcher to say that they were on the scene, Hymon went behind the house. He heard a door slam and saw someone run across the backyard. The fleeing suspect, who was appellee-respondent's decedent, Edward Garner, stopped at a 6–feet–high chain link fence at the edge of the yard. With the aid of a flashlight, Hymon was able to see Garner's face and hands. He saw no sign of a weapon, and, though not certain, was "reasonably sure" and "figured" that Garner was unarmed. He thought Garner was 17 or 18 years old and about 5′5″ or 5′7″ tall.[2] While Garner was crouched at the base of the fence, Hymon called out "police, halt" and took a few steps toward him. Garner then began to climb over the fence. Convinced that if Garner made it over the fence he would elude capture, Hymon shot him. The bullet hit Garner in the back of the head. Garner was taken by ambulance to a hospital, where he died on the operating table. Ten dollars and a purse taken from the house were found on his body.

In using deadly force to prevent the escape, Hymon was acting under the authority of a Tennessee statute and pursuant to Police Department policy. The statute provides that "[if], after notice of the intention to arrest the defendant, he either flee or forcibly resist, the officer may use all the necessary means to effect the arrest." Tenn. Code Ann. § 40–7–108 (1982). 5The Department policy was slightly more restrictive than the statute, but still allowed the use of deadly force in cases of burglary. App. 140–144. The incident was reviewed by the Memphis Police Firearm's Review Board and presented to a grand jury. Neither took any action.

Garner's father then brought this action in the Federal District Court for the Western District of Tennessee, seeking damages under 42 U. S. C. § 1983 for asserted violations of Garner's constitutional rights. The complaint alleged that the shooting violated the Fourth, Fifth, Sixth, Eighth, and Fourteenth Amendments of the United States Constitution. It named as defendants Officer Hymon, the Police Department, its Director, and the Mayor and city of Memphis. After a 3–day bench trial, the District Court

1. The owner of the house testified that no lights were on in the house, but that a back door light was on. Record 160. Officer Hymon, though uncertain, stated in his deposition that there were lights on in the house.

2. In fact, Garner, an eighth-grader, was 15. He was 5′4″ tall and weighed somewhere around 100 or 110 pounds.

entered judgment for all defendants. It dismissed the claims against the Mayor and the Director for lack of evidence. It then concluded that Hymon's actions were authorized by the Tennessee statute, which in turn was constitutional. Hymon had employed the only reasonable and practicable means of preventing Garner's escape. Garner had "recklessly and heedlessly attempted to vault over the fence to escape, thereby assuming the risk of being fired upon."

The Court of Appeals for the Sixth Circuit affirmed with regard to Hymon, finding that he had acted in good-faith reliance on the Tennessee statute and was therefore within the scope of his qualified immunity....

The Court of Appeals reversed and remanded. It reasoned that the killing of a fleeing suspect is a "seizure" under the Fourth Amendment, 6and is therefore constitutional only if "reasonable." The Tennessee statute failed as applied to this case because it did not adequately limit the use of deadly force by distinguishing between felonies of different magnitudes—"the facts, as found, did not justify the use of deadly force under the Fourth Amendment." Officers cannot resort to deadly force unless they "have probable cause ... to believe that the suspect [has committed a felony and] poses a threat to the safety of the officers or a danger to the community if left at large."

The State of Tennessee, which had intervened to defend the statute, see 28 U.S.C. § 2403(b), appealed to this Court. The city filed a petition for certiorari. We noted probable jurisdiction in the appeal and granted the petition.

II

Whenever an officer restrains the freedom of a person to walk away, he has seized that person. While it is not always clear just when minimal police interference becomes a seizure, there can be no question that apprehension by the use of deadly force is a seizure subject to the reasonableness requirement of the Fourth Amendment.

A

A police officer may arrest a person if he has probable cause to believe that person committed a crime. Petitioners and appellant argue that if this requirement is satisfied the Fourth Amendment has nothing to say about *how* that seizure is made. This submission ignores the many cases in which this Court, by balancing the extent of the intrusion against the need for it, has examined the reasonableness of the manner in which a search or seizure is conducted. To determine the constitutionality of a seizure "[we] must balance the nature and quality of the intrusion on the individual's Fourth Amendment interests against the importance of the governmental interests alleged to justify the intrusion." ... We have described "the balancing of competing interests" as "the key principle of the Fourth Amendment." *Michigan v. Summers* (1981). Because one of the factors is the extent of the intrusion, it is plain that reasonableness depends on not only when a seizure is made, but also how it is carried out....

B

The same balancing process applied in the cases cited above demonstrates that, notwithstanding probable cause to seize a suspect, an officer may not always do so by killing him. The intrusiveness of a seizure by means of deadly force is unmatched. The suspect's fundamental interest in his own life need not be elaborated upon. The use of deadly force also frustrates the interest of the individual, and of society, in judicial determination of guilt and punishment. Against these interests are ranged governmental interests in effective law enforcement. It is argued that overall violence will be reduced by encouraging the peaceful submission of suspects who know that they may be shot if they flee. Effectiveness in making arrests requires the resort to deadly force, or at least the meaningful threat thereof. "Being able to arrest such individuals is a condition precedent to the state's entire system of law enforcement."

Without in any way disparaging the importance of these goals, we are not convinced that the use of deadly force is a sufficiently productive means of accomplishing them to justify the killing of nonviolent suspects.... The use of deadly force is a self-defeating way of apprehending a suspect and so setting the criminal justice mechanism in motion. If successful, it guarantees that that mechanism will not be set in motion. And while the meaningful threat of deadly force might be thought to lead to the arrest of more live suspects by discouraging escape attempts, the presently available evidence does not support this thesis. The fact is that a majority of police departments in this country have forbidden the use of deadly force against nonviolent suspects.... Petitioners and appellant have not persuaded us that shooting nondangerous fleeing suspects is so vital as to outweigh the suspect's interest in his own life.

The use of deadly force to prevent the escape of all felony suspects, whatever the circumstances, is constitutionally unreasonable. It is not better that all felony suspects die than that they escape. Where the suspect poses no immediate threat to the officer and no threat to others, the harm resulting from failing to apprehend him does not justify the use of deadly force to do so. It is no doubt unfortunate when a suspect who is in sight escapes, but the fact that the police arrive a little late or are a little slower afoot does not always justify killing the suspect. A police officer may not seize an unarmed, nondangerous suspect by shooting him dead. The Tennessee statute is unconstitutional insofar as it authorizes the use of deadly force against such fleeing suspects.

It is not, however, unconstitutional on its face. Where the officer has probable cause to believe that the suspect poses a threat of serious physical harm, either to the officer or to others, it is not constitutionally unreasonable to prevent escape by using deadly force. Thus, if the suspect threatens the officer with a weapon or there is probable cause to believe that he has committed a crime involving the infliction or threatened infliction of serious physical harm, deadly force may be used if necessary to prevent escape, and if, where feasible, some warning has been given. As applied in such circumstances, the Tennessee statute would pass constitutional muster.

III

A

It is insisted that the Fourth Amendment must be construed in light of the common-law rule, which allowed the use of whatever force was necessary to effect the arrest of a fleeing felon, though not a misdemeanant. As stated in Hale's posthumously published Pleas of the Crown:

"[If] persons that are pursued by these officers for felony or the just suspicion thereof ... shall not yield themselves to these officers, but shall either resist or fly before they are apprehended or being apprehended shall rescue themselves and resist or fly, so that they cannot be otherwise apprehended, and are upon necessity slain therein, because they cannot be otherwise taken, it is no felony."

The State and city argue that because this was the prevailing rule at the time of the adoption of the Fourth Amendment and for some time thereafter, and is still in force in some States, use of deadly force against a fleeing felon must be "reasonable." It is true that this Court has often looked to the common law in evaluating the reasonableness, for Fourth Amendment purposes, of police activity. On the other hand, it "has not simply frozen into constitutional law those law enforcement practices that existed at the time of the Fourth Amendment's passage." Because of sweeping change in the legal and technological context, reliance on the common-law rule in this case would be a mistaken literalism that ignores the purposes of a historical inquiry.

B

It has been pointed out many times that the common-law rule is best understood in light of the fact that it arose at a time when virtually all felonies were punishable by death. "Though effected without the protections and formalities of an orderly trial and conviction, the killing of a resisting or fleeing felon resulted in no greater consequences than those authorized for punishment of the felony of which the individual was charged or suspected." ... Courts have also justified the common-law rule by emphasizing the relative dangerousness of felons....

Neither of these justifications makes sense today. Almost all crimes formerly punishable by death no longer are or can be.... [T]oday the distinction [between a misdemeanor and a felony] is minor and often arbitrary ... There is an additional reason why the common-law rule cannot be directly translated to the present day. The common-law rule developed at a time when weapons were rudimentary. Deadly force could be inflicted almost solely in a hand-to-hand struggle during which, necessarily, the safety of the arresting officer was at risk. Handguns were not carried by police officers until the latter half of the last century....

One other aspect of the common-law rule bears emphasis. It forbids the use of deadly force to apprehend a misdemeanant, condemning such action as disproportionately severe.

In short, though the common-law pedigree of Tennessee's rule is pure on its face, changes in the legal and technological context mean the rule is distorted almost beyond recognition when literally applied....

It cannot be said that there is a constant or overwhelming trend away from the common-law rule. In recent years, some States have reviewed their laws and expressly rejected abandonment of the common-law rule. 21Nonetheless, the long-term movement has been away from the rule that deadly force may be used against any fleeing felon, and that remains the rule in less than half the States.

D

Actual departmental policies are important for an additional reason. We would hesitate to declare a police practice of long standing "unreasonable" if doing so would severely hamper effective law enforcement. But the indications are to the contrary . . .

Nor do we agree with petitioners and appellant that the rule we have adopted requires the police to make impossible, split-second evaluations of unknowable facts. We do not deny the practical difficulties of attempting to assess the suspect's dangerousness. However, similarly difficult judgments must be made by the police in equally uncertain circumstances. . . .

IV

The District Court concluded that Hymon was justified in shooting Garner because state law allows, and the Federal Constitution does not forbid, the use of deadly force to prevent the escape of a fleeing felony suspect if no alternative means of apprehension is available. This conclusion made a determination of Garner's apparent dangerousness unnecessary. The court did find, however, that Garner appeared to be unarmed, though Hymon could not be certain that was the case. Restated in Fourth Amendment terms, this means Hymon had no articulable basis to think Garner was armed.

In reversing, the Court of Appeals accepted the District Court's factual conclusions and held that "the facts, as found, did not justify the use of deadly force." We agree. Officer Hymon could not reasonably have believed that Garner—young, slight, and unarmed—posed any threat. Indeed, Hymon never attempted to justify his actions on any basis other than the need to prevent an escape. The District Court stated in passing that "[the] facts of this case did not indicate to Officer Hymon that Garner was 'non-dangerous.'" This conclusion is not explained, and seems to be based solely on the fact that Garner had broken into a house at night. However, the fact that Garner was a suspected burglar could not, without regard to the other circumstances, automatically justify the use of deadly force. Hymon did not have probable cause to believe that Garner, whom he correctly believed to be unarmed, posed any physical danger to himself or others.

■ Justice O'Connor, with whom The Chief Justice and Justice Rehnquist join, dissenting.

The Court today holds that the Fourth Amendment prohibits a police officer from using deadly force as a last resort to apprehend a criminal suspect who refuses to halt when fleeing the scene of a nighttime burglary. This conclusion rests on the majority's balancing of the interests of the suspect and the public interest in effective law enforcement. Notwithstanding the venerable common-law rule authorizing the use of deadly force if necessary to apprehend a fleeing felon, and continued acceptance of this rule by nearly half the States, the majority concludes that Tennessee's statute is unconstitutional inasmuch as it allows the use of such force to apprehend a burglary suspect who is not obviously armed or otherwise dangerous. Although the circumstances of this case are unquestionably tragic and unfortunate, our constitutional holdings must be sensitive both to the history of the Fourth Amendment and to the general implications of the Court's reasoning. By disregarding the serious and dangerous nature of residential burglaries and the longstanding practice of many States, the Court effectively creates a Fourth Amendment right allowing a burglary suspect to flee unimpeded from a police officer who has probable cause to arrest, who has ordered the suspect to halt, and who has no means short of firing his weapon to prevent escape. I do not believe that the Fourth Amendment supports such a right, and I accordingly dissent.

Because burglary is a serious and dangerous felony, the public interest in the prevention and detection of the crime is of compelling importance. Where a police officer has probable cause to arrest a suspected burglar, the use of deadly force as a last resort might well be the only means of apprehending the suspect. With respect to a particular burglary, subsequent investigation simply cannot represent a substitute for immediate apprehension of the criminal suspect at the scene.... Although some law enforcement agencies may choose to assume the risk that a criminal will remain at large, the Tennessee statute reflects a legislative determination that the use of deadly force in prescribed circumstances will serve generally to protect the public. Such statutes assist the police in apprehending suspected perpetrators of serious crimes and provide notice that a lawful police order to stop and submit to arrest may not be ignored with impunity....

A proper balancing of the interests involved suggests that use of deadly force as a last resort to apprehend a criminal suspect fleeing from the scene of a nighttime burglary is not unreasonable within the meaning of the Fourth Amendment. Admittedly, the events giving rise to this case are in retrospect deeply regrettable. No one can view the death of an unarmed and apparently nonviolent 15-year-old without sorrow, much less disapproval. Nonetheless, the reasonableness of Officer Hymon's conduct for purposes of the Fourth Amendment cannot be evaluated by what later appears to have been a preferable course of police action. The officer pursued a suspect in the darkened backyard of a house that from all indications had just been burglarized. The police officer was not certain whether the suspect was alone or unarmed; nor did he know what had transpired inside the house. He ordered the suspect to halt, and when the suspect refused to obey and attempted to flee into the night, the officer fired his weapon to prevent escape. The reasonableness of this action for purposes of the Fourth Amendment is not determined by the unfortunate nature of this particular case; instead, the question is whether it is constitutionally impermissible for police officers, as a last resort, to shoot a burglary suspect fleeing the scene of the crime....

III

Even if I agreed that the Fourth Amendment was violated under the circumstances of this case, I would be unable to join the Court's opinion.

The Court holds that deadly force may be used only if the suspect "threatens the officer with a weapon or there is probable cause to believe that he has committed a crime involving the infliction or threatened infliction of serious physical harm." The Court ignores the more general implications of its reasoning. Relying on the Fourth Amendment, the majority asserts that it is constitutionally unreasonable to *use* deadly force against fleeing criminal suspects who do not appear to pose a threat of serious physical harm to others. By declining to limit its holding to the use of firearms, the Court unnecessarily implies that the Fourth Amendment constrains the use of any police practice that is potentially lethal, no matter how remote the risk....

The Court's silence on critical factors in the decision to use deadly force simply invites second-guessing of difficult police decisions that must be made quickly in the most trying of circumstances.... Police are given no guidance for determining which objects, among an array of potentially lethal weapons ranging from guns to knives to baseball bats to rope, will justify the use of deadly force. The Court also declines to outline the additional factors necessary to provide "probable cause" for believing that a suspect "poses a significant threat of death or serious physical injury," when the officer has probable cause to arrest and the suspect refuses to obey an order to halt. But even if it were appropriate in this case to limit the use of deadly force to that ambiguous class of suspects, I believe the class should include nighttime residential burglars who resist arrest by attempting to flee the scene of the crime. We can expect an escalating volume of litigation as the lower courts struggle to determine if a police officer's split-second decision to shoot was justified by the danger posed by a particular object and other facts related to the crime. Thus, the majority opinion portends a burgeoning area of Fourth Amendment doctrine concerning the circumstances in which police officers can reasonably employ deadly force.

IV

The Court's opinion sweeps broadly to adopt an entirely new standard for the constitutionality of the use of deadly force to apprehend fleeing felons. Thus, the Court "lightly [brushes] aside," a longstanding police practice that predates the Fourth Amendment and continues to receive the approval of nearly half of the state legislatures. I cannot accept the majority's creation of a constitutional right to flight for burglary suspects seeking to avoid capture at the scene of the crime. Whatever the constitutional limits on police use of deadly force in order to apprehend a fleeing felon, I do not believe they are exceeded in a case in which a police officer has probable cause to arrest a suspect at the scene of a residential burglary, orders the suspect to halt, and then fires his weapon as a last resort to prevent the suspect's escape into the night. I respectfully dissent.

* * *

The Court revisited the use of force when faced with a case involving a high speed automobile chase:

Scott v. Harris

United States Supreme Court, 2007.
___ U.S. ___, 127 S.Ct. 1769.

■ JUSTICE SCALIA delivered the opinion of the Court.

We consider whether a law enforcement official can, consistent with the Fourth Amendment, attempt to stop a fleeing motorist from continuing his public-endangering flight by ramming the motorist's car from behind. Put another way: Can an officer take actions that place a fleeing motorist at risk of serious injury or death in order to stop the motorist's flight from endangering the lives of innocent bystanders?

I

In March 2001, a Georgia county deputy clocked respondent's vehicle traveling at 73 miles per hour on a road with a 55-mile-per-hour speed limit. The deputy activated his blue flashing lights indicating that respondent should pull over. Instead, respondent sped away, initiating a chase down what is in most portions a two-lane road, at speeds exceeding 85 miles per hour. The deputy radioed his dispatch to report that he was pursuing a fleeing vehicle, and broadcast its license plate number. Petitioner, Deputy Timothy Scott, heard the radio communication and joined the pursuit along with other officers. In the midst of the chase, respondent pulled into the parking lot of a shopping center and was nearly boxed in by the various police vehicles. Respondent evaded the trap by making a sharp turn, colliding with Scott's police car, exiting the parking lot, and speeding off once again down a two-lane highway.

Following respondent's shopping center maneuvering, which resulted in slight damage to Scott's police car, Scott took over as the lead pursuit vehicle. Six minutes and nearly 10 miles after the chase had begun, Scott decided to attempt to terminate the episode by employing a "Precision Intervention Technique ('PIT') maneuver, which causes the fleeing vehicle to spin to a stop. Having radioed his supervisor for permission, Scott was told to '[g]o ahead and take him out.'" Instead, Scott applied his push bumper to the rear of respondent's vehicle. As a result, respondent lost control of his vehicle, which left the roadway, ran down an embankment, overturned, and crashed. Respondent was badly injured and was rendered a quadriplegic.

Respondent filed suit against Deputy Scott and others under Rev. Stat. § 1979, 42 U.S.C. § 1983, alleging, *inter alia*, a violation of his federal constitutional rights, viz. use of excessive force resulting in an unreasonable seizure under the Fourth Amendment. In response, Scott filed a motion for summary judgment based on an assertion of qualified immunity. Taking respondent's view of the facts as given, the Court of Appeals concluded that Scott's actions could constitute "deadly force" under Tennessee v. Garner (1985), and that the use of such force in this context "would violate [respondent's] constitutional right to be free from excessive force during a seizure. Accordingly, a reasonable jury could find that Scott violated [respondent's] Fourth Amendment rights." The Court of Appeals further concluded that "the law as it existed [at the time of the incident], was sufficiently clear to give reasonable law enforcement officers 'fair notice' that ramming a vehicle under these circumstances was unlawful." The Court of Appeals thus concluded that Scott was not entitled to qualified immunity. We granted certiorari, and now reverse....

III

A

The first step in assessing the constitutionality of Scott's actions is to determine the relevant facts. As this case was decided on summary judgment, there have not yet been factual findings by a judge or jury, and respondent's version of events (unsurprisingly) differs substantially from Scott's version....

There is, however, an added wrinkle in this case: existence in the record of a videotape capturing the events in question. There are no allegations or indications that this videotape was doctored or altered in any way, nor any contention that what it depicts differs from what actually happened. The videotape quite clearly contradicts the version of the story told by respondent and adopted by the Court of Appeals. For example, the Court of Appeals adopted respondent's assertions that, during the chase, "there was little, if any, actual threat to pedestrians or other motorists, as the roads were mostly empty and [respondent] remained in control of his vehicle." Indeed, reading the lower court's opinion, one gets the impression that respondent, rather than fleeing from police, was attempting to pass his driving test:

> "[T]aking the facts from the non-movant's viewpoint, [respondent] remained in control of his vehicle, slowed for turns and intersections, and typically used his indicators for turns. He did not run any motorists off the road. Nor was he a threat to pedestrians in the shopping center parking lot, which was free from pedestrian and vehicular traffic as the center was closed. Significantly, by the time the parties were back on the highway and Scott rammed [respondent], the motorway had been cleared of motorists and pedestrians allegedly because of police blockades of the nearby intersections."

The videotape tells quite a different story. There we see respondent's vehicle racing down narrow, two-lane roads in the dead of night at speeds that are shockingly fast. We see it swerve around more than a dozen other cars, cross the double-yellow line, and force cars traveling in both directions to their respective shoulders to avoid being hit. We see it run multiple red lights and travel for considerable periods of time in the occasional center left-turn-only lane, chased by numerous police cars forced to engage in the same hazardous maneuvers just to keep up. Far from being the cautious and controlled driver the lower court depicts, what we see on the video more closely resembles a Hollywood-style car chase of the most frightening sort, placing police officers and innocent bystanders alike at great risk of serious injury....

B

Judging the matter on that basis, we think it is quite clear that Deputy Scott did not violate the Fourth Amendment. Scott does not contest that his decision to terminate the car chase by ramming his bumper into respondent's vehicle constituted a "seizure." "[A] Fourth Amendment seizure [occurs] ... when there is a governmental termination of freedom of movement through means intentionally applied." ("If ... the police cruiser had pulled alongside the fleeing car and sideswiped it, producing the crash, then the termination of the suspect's freedom of movement would have been a seizure"). It is also conceded, by both sides, that a claim of "excessive force in the course of making [a] ... 'seizure' of [the] person ... [is] properly analyzed under the Fourth Amendment's 'objective reasonableness' standard." The question we need to answer is whether Scott's actions were objectively reasonable.

1

Respondent urges us to analyze this case as we analyzed *Garner*. We must first decide, he says, whether the actions Scott took constituted "deadly force." (He defines "deadly force" as "any use of force which creates a substantial likelihood of causing death or serious bodily injury,") If so, respondent claims that *Garner* prescribes certain preconditions that must be met before Scott's actions can survive Fourth Amendment scrutiny: (1) The suspect must have posed an immediate threat of serious physical harm to the officer or others; (2) deadly force must have been necessary to prevent escape;9 and (3) where feasible, the officer must have given the suspect some warning. Since these *Garner* preconditions for using deadly force were not met in this case, Scott's actions were *per se* unreasonable.

Respondent's argument falters at its first step; *Garner* did not establish a magical on/off switch that triggers rigid preconditions whenever an officer's actions constitute "deadly force." *Garner* was simply an application of the Fourth Amendment's "reasonableness" test, to the use of a particular type of force in a particular situation. *Garner* held that it was unreasonable to kill a "young, slight, and unarmed" burglary suspect, by shooting him "in the back of the head" while he was running away on foot, and when the officer "could not reasonably have believed that [the suspect] ... posed any threat," and "never attempted to justify his actions on any basis other than the need to prevent an escape". Whatever *Garner* said about the factors that *might have* justified shooting the suspect in that case, such "preconditions" have scant applicability to this case, which has vastly different facts. "*Garner* had nothing to do with one car striking another or even with car chases in general.... A police car's bumping a fleeing car is, in fact, not much like a policeman's shooting a gun so as to hit a person." Nor is the threat posed by the flight on foot of an unarmed suspect even remotely comparable to the extreme danger to human life posed by respondent in this case. Although respondent's attempt to craft an easy-to-apply legal test in the Fourth Amendment context is admirable, in the end we must still slosh our way through the factbound morass of "reasonableness." Whether or not Scott's actions constituted application of "deadly force," all that matters is whether Scott's actions were reasonable.

2

In determining the reasonableness of the manner in which a seizure is effected, "[w]e must balance the nature and quality of the intrusion on the individual's Fourth Amendment interests against the importance of the governmental interests alleged to justify the intrusion." Scott defends his actions by pointing to the paramount governmental interest in ensuring public safety, and respondent nowhere suggests this was not the purpose motivating Scott's behavior. Thus, in judging whether Scott's actions were reasonable, we must consider the risk of bodily harm that Scott's actions posed to respondent in light of the threat to the public that Scott was trying to eliminate. Although there is no obvious way to quantify the risks on either side, it is clear from the videotape that respondent posed an actual and imminent threat to the lives of any pedestrians who might have been present, to other civilian motorists, and to the officers involved in the chase. It is equally clear that Scott's actions posed a high likelihood of serious injury or death to respondent—though not the near *certainty* of death posed by, say, shooting a fleeing felon in the back of the head, or pulling alongside a fleeing motorist's car and shooting the motorist. So how does a court go about weighing the perhaps lesser probability of injuring or killing numerous bystanders against the perhaps larger probability of injuring or killing a single person? We think it appropriate in this process to take into account not only the number of lives at risk, but also their relative culpability. It was respondent, after all, who intentionally placed himself and the public in danger by unlawfully engaging in the reckless, high-speed flight that ultimately produced the choice between two evils that Scott confronted. Multiple police cars, with blue lights flashing and sirens blaring, had been chasing respondent for nearly 10 miles, but he ignored their warning to stop. By contrast, those who might have been harmed had Scott not taken the action he did were entirely innocent. We have little difficulty in concluding it was reasonable for Scott to take the action that he did.

But wait, says respondent: Couldn't the innocent public equally have been protected, and the tragic accident entirely avoided, if the police had simply ceased their pursuit? We think the police need not have taken that chance and hoped for the best. Whereas Scott's action—ramming respondent off the road—was *certain* to eliminate the risk that respondent posed to the public, ceasing pursuit was not. First of all, there would have been no way to convey convincingly to respondent that the chase was off, and that he was free to go. Had respondent looked in his rear-view mirror and seen the police cars deactivate their flashing lights and turn around, he would have had no idea whether they were truly letting him get away, or simply devising a new strategy for capture. Perhaps the police knew a shortcut he didn't know, and would reappear down the road to intercept him; or perhaps they were setting up a roadblock in his path. Given such uncertainty, respondent might have been just as likely to respond by continuing to drive recklessly as by slowing down and wiping his brow.

Second, we are loath to lay down a rule requiring the police to allow fleeing suspects to get away whenever they drive *so recklessly* that they put other people's lives in danger. It is obvious the perverse incentives such a rule would create: Every fleeing motorist would know that escape is within his grasp, if only he accelerates to 90 miles per hour, crosses the double-yellow line a few times, and runs a few red lights. The Constitution assuredly does not impose this invitation to impunity-earned-by-recklessness. Instead, we lay down a more sensible rule: A police officer's attempt to terminate a dangerous high-speed car chase that threatens the lives of innocent bystanders does not violate the Fourth Amendment, even when it places the fleeing motorist at risk of serious injury or death.

* * *

The car chase that respondent initiated in this case posed a substantial and immediate risk of serious physical injury to others; no reasonable jury could conclude otherwise. Scott's attempt to terminate the chase by forcing respondent off the road was reasonable, and Scott is entitled to summary judgment. The Court of Appeals' decision to the contrary is reversed.

It is so ordered.

CONCUR BY: GINSBURG; BREYER

■ JUSTICE GINSBURG, concurring.

I join the Court's opinion and would underscore two points. First, I do not read today's decision as articulating a mechanical, *per se* rule. The inquiry described by the Court is situation specific. Among relevant considerations: Were the lives and well-being of others (motorists, pedestrians, police officers) at risk? Was there a safer way, given the time, place, and circumstances, to stop the fleeing vehicle? "[A]dmirable" as "[an] attempt to craft an easy-to-apply legal test in the Fourth Amendment context [may be]," the Court explains, "in the end we must still slosh our way through the factbound morass of 'reasonableness.' "

■ JUSTICE BREYER, concurring.

I join the Court's opinion with one suggestion and two qualifications. Because watching the video footage of the car chase made a difference to my own view of the case, I suggest that the interested reader take advantage of the link in the Court's opinion, and watch it. Having done so, I do not believe a reasonable jury could, in this instance, find that Officer Timothy Scott (who joined the chase late in the day and did not know the specific reason why the respondent was being pursued) acted in violation of the Constitution.

■ JUSTICE STEVENS, dissenting.

Today, the Court asks whether an officer may "take actions that place a fleeing motorist at risk of serious injury or death in order to stop the motorist's flight from endangering the lives of innocent bystanders." on the circumstances, the answer may be an obvious "yes," an obvious "no," or sufficiently doubtful that the question of the reasonableness of the officer's actions should be decided by a jury, after a review of the degree of danger and the alternatives available to the officer. A high speed chase in a desert in Nevada is, after all, quite different from one that travels through the heart of Las Vegas.

Relying on a *de novo* review of a videotape of a portion of a nighttime chase on a lightly traveled road in Georgia where no pedestrians or other "bystanders" were present, buttressed by uninformed speculation about the possible consequences of discontinuing the chase, eight of the jurors on this Court reach a verdict that differs from the views of the judges on both the District Court and the Court of Appeals who are surely more familiar with the hazards of driving on Georgia roads than we are. The Court's justification for this unprecedented departure from our well-settled standard of review of factual determinations made by a district court and affirmed by a court of appeals is based on its mistaken view that the Court of Appeals' description of the facts was "blatantly contradicted by the record" and that respondent's version of the events was "so utterly discredited by the record that no reasonable jury could have believed him."

Rather than supporting the conclusion that what we see on the video "resembles a Hollywood-style car chase of the most frightening sort," the tape actually confirms, rather than contradicts, the lower courts' appraisal of the factual questions at issue. More important, it surely does not provide a principled basis for depriving the respondent of his right to have a jury evaluate the question whether the police officers' decision to use deadly force to bring the chase to an end was reasonable.

Omitted from the Court's description of the initial speeding violation is the fact that respondent was on a four-lane portion of Highway 34 when the officer clocked his speed at 73 miles per hour and initiated the chase. More significant—and contrary to the Court's assumption that respondent's vehicle "forced cars traveling in both directions to their respective shoulders to avoid being hit"—a fact unmentioned in the text of the opinion explains why those cars pulled over prior to being passed by respondent. The sirens and flashing lights on the police cars following respondent gave the same warning that a speeding ambulance or fire engine would have provided. The 13 cars that respondent passed on his side of the road before entering the shopping center, and both of the cars that he passed on the right after leaving the center, no doubt had already pulled to the side of the road or were driving along the shoulder because they heard the police sirens or saw the flashing lights before respondent or the police cruisers approached. A jury could certainly conclude that those motorists were exposed to no greater risk than persons who take the same action in response to a speeding ambulance, and that their reactions were fully consistent with the evidence that respondent, though speeding, retained full control of his vehicle.

The police sirens also minimized any risk that may have arisen from running "multiple red lights." In fact, respondent and his pursuers went through only two intersections with stop lights and in both cases all other vehicles in sight were stationary, presumably because they had been warned of the approaching speeders. Incidentally, the videos do show that the lights were red when the police cars passed through them but, because the cameras were farther away when respondent did so and it is difficult to discern the color of the signal at that point, it is not entirely clear that he ran either or both of the red lights. In any event, the risk of harm to the stationary vehicles was minimized by the sirens, and there is no reason to believe that respondent would have disobeyed the signals if he were not being pursued.

My colleagues on the jury saw respondent "swerve around more than a dozen other cars," and "force cars traveling in both directions to their respective shoulders," but they apparently discounted the possibility that those cars were already out of the pursuit's path as a result of hearing the sirens. Even if that were not so, passing a slower vehicle on a two-lane road always involves some degree of swerving and is not especially dangerous if there are no cars coming from the opposite direction. At no point during the chase did respondent pull into the opposite lane other than to pass a car in front of him; he did the latter no more than five times and, on most of those occasions, used his turn signal. On none of these occasions was there a car traveling in the opposite direction. In fact, at one point, when respondent found himself behind a car in his own lane and there were cars traveling in the other direction, he slowed and waited for the cars traveling in the other direction to pass before overtaking the car in front of him while using his turn signal to do so. This is hardly the stuff of Hollywood. To the contrary, the video does not reveal any incidents that could even be remotely characterized as "close calls."

In sum, the factual statements by the Court of Appeals quoted by the Court were entirely accurate. That court did not describe respondent as a "cautious" driver as my colleagues imply, but it did correctly conclude that there is no evidence that he ever lost control of his vehicle. That court also correctly pointed out that the incident in the shopping center parking lot did not create any risk to pedestrians or other vehicles because the chase occurred just before 11 p.m. on a weekday night and the center was closed. It is apparent from the record (including the videotape) that local police had blocked off intersections to keep respondent from entering residential neighborhoods and possibly endangering other motorists. I would add that the videos also show that no pedestrians, parked cars, sidewalks, or residences were visible at any time during the chase. The only "innocent bystanders" who were placed "at great risk of serious injury," were the drivers who either pulled off the road in response to the sirens or passed respondent in the opposite direction when he was driving on his side of the road.

I recognize, of course, that even though respondent's original speeding violation on a four-lane highway was rather ordinary, his refusal to stop and subsequent flight was a serious offense that merited severe punishment. It was not, however, a capital offense, or even an offense that justified the use of deadly force rather than an abandonment of the chase. The Court's concern about the "imminent threat to the lives of any pedestrians who might have been present," while surely valid in an appropriate case, should be discounted in a case involving a nighttime chase in an area where no pedestrians were present.

What would have happened if the police had decided to abandon the chase? We now know that they could have apprehended respondent later because they had his license plate number. Even if that were not true, and even if he would have escaped any punishment at all, the use of deadly force in this case was no more appropriate than the use of a deadly weapon against a fleeing felon in Tennessee v. Garner. In any event, any uncertainty about the result of abandoning the pursuit has not prevented the Court from basing its conclusions on its own factual assumptions. 5The Court attempts to avoid the conclusion that deadly force was unnecessary by speculating that if the officers had let him go, respondent might have been "just as likely" to continue to drive recklessly as to slow down and wipe his brow. That speculation is unconvincing as a matter of common sense and improper as a matter of law. Our duty to view the evidence in the light most favorable to the nonmoving party would foreclose such speculation if the Court had not used its observation of the video as an excuse for replacing the rule of law with its ad hoc judgment. There is no evidentiary basis for an assumption that dangers caused by flight from a police pursuit will continue after the pursuit ends. Indeed, rules adopted by countless police departments throughout the country are based on a judgment that differs from the Court's. See, *e.g.*, App. to Brief for Georgia Association of Chiefs of Police, Inc., as *Amicus Curiae* A–52 ("During a pursuit, the need to apprehend the suspect should always outweigh the level of danger created by the pursuit. When the immediate danger to the public created by the pursuit is greater than the immediate or potential danger to the public should the suspect remain at large, then the pursuit should be discontinued or terminated.... [P]ursuits should usually be discontinued when the violator's identity has been established to the point that later apprehension can be accomplished without danger to the public").

Although *Garner* may not, as the Court suggests, "establish a magical on/off switch that triggers rigid preconditions" for the use of deadly force, it did set a threshold under which the use of deadly force would be considered constitutionally unreasonable:

> "Where the officer has probable cause to believe that the suspect poses a threat of serious physical harm, either to the officer or to others, it is not constitutionally unreasonable to prevent escape by using deadly force. Thus, if the suspect threatens the officer with a weapon or there is probable cause to believe that he has committed a crime involving the infliction or threatened infliction of serious physical harm, deadly force may be used if necessary to prevent escape, and if, where feasible, some warning has been given."

Whether a person's actions have risen to a level warranting deadly force is a question of fact best reserved for a jury. Here, the Court has usurped the jury's factfinding function and, in doing so, implicitly labeled the four other judges to review the case unreasonable. It chastises the Court of Appeals for failing to "vie[w] the facts in the light depicted by the videotape" and implies that no reasonable person could view the videotape and come to the conclusion that deadly force was unjustified. However, the three judges on the Court of Appeals panel apparently did view the videotapes entered into evidence 7and described a very different version of events:

> "At the time of the ramming, apart from speeding and running two red lights, Harris was driving in a non-aggressive fashion (i.e., without trying to ram or run into the officers). Moreover, ... Scott's path on the open highway was largely clear. The videos introduced into evidence show little to no vehicular (or pedestrian) traffic, allegedly because of the late hour and the police blockade of the nearby intersections. Finally, Scott issued absolutely no warning (e.g., over the loudspeaker or otherwise) prior to using deadly force."

If two groups of judges can disagree so vehemently about the nature of the pursuit and the circumstances surrounding that pursuit, it seems eminently likely that a reasonable juror could disagree with this Court's characterization of events. Moreover, under the standard set forth in *Garner*, it is certainly possible that "a jury could conclude that Scott unreasonably used deadly force to seize Harris by ramming him off the road under the instant circumstances."

The Court today sets forth a *per se* rule that presumes its own version of the facts: "A police officer's attempt to terminate a dangerous high-speed car chase *that threatens the lives of innocent bystanders* does not violate the Fourth Amendment, even when it places the fleeing motorist at risk of serious injury or death." Not only does that rule fly in the face of the flexible and case-by-case "reasonableness" approach applied in *Garner* and *Graham v. Connor*, but it is also arguably inapplicable to the case at hand, given that it is not clear that this chase threatened the life of any "innocent bystande[r]." In my view, the risks inherent in justifying unwarranted police conduct on the basis of unfounded assumptions are unacceptable, particularly when less drastic measures—in this case, the use of stop sticks 9or a simple warning issued from a loudspeaker—could have avoided such a tragic result. In my judgment, jurors in Georgia should be allowed to evaluate the reasonableness of the decision to ram respondent's speeding vehicle in a manner that created an obvious risk of death and has in fact made him a quadriplegic at the age of 19.

I respectfully dissent.

* * *

The above cases deal with the seizure of the individual. Are there also limits on the search of the individual and obtaining evidence from the body of the seized person?

Winston v. Lee

United States Supreme Court, 1985.
470 U.S. 753, 105 S.Ct. 1611.

■ JUSTICE BRENNAN delivered the opinion of the Court.

Schmerber v. California (1966), held, *inter alia*, that a State may, over the suspect's protest, have a physician extract blood from a person suspected of drunken driving without violation of the suspect's right secured by the Fourth Amendment not to be subjected to unreasonable searches and seizures. However, *Schmerber* cautioned: "That we today hold that the Constitution does not forbid the States['] minor intrusions into an individual's body under stringently limited conditions in no way indicates that it permits more substantial intrusions, or intrusions under other conditions." In this case, the Commonwealth of Virginia seeks to compel the respondent Rudolph Lee, who is suspected of attempting to commit armed robbery, to undergo a surgical procedure under a general anesthetic for removal of a bullet lodged in his chest. Petitioners allege that the bullet will provide evidence of respondent's guilt or innocence. We conclude that the procedure sought here is an example of the "more substantial intrusion" cautioned against in *Schmerber*, and hold that to permit the procedure would violate respondent's right to be secure in his person guaranteed by the Fourth Amendment.

I

A

At approximately 1 a. m. on July 18, 1982, Ralph E. Watkinson was closing his shop for the night. As he was locking the door, he observed someone armed with a gun coming toward him from across the street. Watkinson was also armed and when he drew his gun, the other person told him to freeze. Watkinson then fired at the other person, who returned his fire. Watkinson was hit in the legs, while the other individual, who appeared to be wounded in his left side, ran from the scene. The police arrived on the scene shortly thereafter, and Watkinson was taken by ambulance to the emergency room of the Medical College of Virginia (MCV) Hospital.

Approximately 20 minutes later, police officers responding to another call found respondent eight blocks from where the earlier shooting occurred. Respondent was suffering from a gunshot wound to his left chest area and told the police that he had been shot when two individuals attempted to rob him. An ambulance took respondent to the MCV Hospital. Watkinson was still in the MCV emergency room and, when respondent entered that room, said "[that's] the man that shot me." After an investigation, the police decided that respondent's story of having been himself the victim of a robbery was untrue and charged respondent with attempted robbery, malicious wounding, and two counts of using a firearm in the commission of a felony.

B

The Commonwealth shortly thereafter moved in state court for an order directing respondent to undergo surgery to remove an object thought to be a bullet lodged under his left collarbone. The court conducted several evidentiary hearings on the motion. At the first hearing, the Commonwealth's expert testified that the surgical procedure would take 45 minutes and would involve a three to four percent chance of temporary nerve damage, a one percent chance of permanent nerve damage, and a one-tenth of one percent chance of death. At the second hearing, the expert testified that on reexamination of respondent, he discovered that the bullet was not "back inside close to the nerves and arteries," as he originally had thought.

Instead, he now believed the bullet to be located "just beneath the skin." He testified that the surgery would require an incision of only one and one-half centimeters (slightly more than one-half inch), could be performed under local anesthesia, and would result in "no danger on the basis that there's no general anesthesia employed."

The state trial judge granted the motion to compel surgery. Respondent petitioned the Virginia Supreme Court for a writ of prohibition and/or a writ of habeas corpus, both of which were denied. Respondent then brought an action in the United States District Court for the Eastern District of Virginia to enjoin the pending operation on Fourth Amendment grounds. The court refused to issue a preliminary injunction, holding that respondent's cause had little likelihood of success on the merits.

On October 18, 1982, just before the surgery was scheduled, the surgeon ordered that X rays be taken of respondent's chest. The X rays revealed that the bullet was in fact lodged two and one-half to three centimeters (approximately one inch) deep in muscular tissue in respondent's chest, substantially deeper than had been thought when the state court granted the motion to compel surgery. The surgeon now believed that a general anesthetic would be desirable for medical reasons.

We granted certiorari to consider whether a State may consistently with the Fourth Amendment compel a suspect to undergo surgery of this kind in a search for evidence of a crime.

II

The Fourth Amendment protects "expectations of privacy,"—the individual's legitimate expectations that in certain places and at certain times he has "the right to be let alone—the most comprehensive of rights and the right most valued by civilizemen." Ohlmstead v. United States (1928) (Brandeis, J., dissenting). Putting to one side the procedural protections of the warrant requirement, the Fourth Amendment generally protects the "security" of "persons, houses, papers, and effects" against official intrusions up to the point where the community's need for evidence surmounts a specified standard, ordinarily "probable cause." Beyond this point, it is ordinarily justifiable for the community to demand that the individual give up some part of his interest in privacy and security to advance the community's vital interests in law enforcement; such a search is generally "reasonable" in the Amendment's terms.

A compelled surgical intrusion into an individual's body for evidence, however, implicates expectations of privacy and security of such magnitude that the intrusion may be "unreasonable" even if likely to produce evidence of a crime. In *Schmerber v. California*, 384 U.S. 757 (1966), we addressed a claim that the State had breached the Fourth Amendment's protection of the "right of the people to be secure in their *persons* ... against unreasonable searches and seizures" (emphasis added) when it compelled an individual suspected of drunken driving to undergo a blood test. Schmerber had been arrested at a hospital while receiving treatment for injuries suffered when the automobile he was driving struck a tree. Despite Schmerber's objection, a police officer at the hospital had directed a physician to take a blood sample from him. Schmerber subsequently objected to the introduction at trial of evidence obtained as a result of the blood test.

The authorities in *Schmerber* clearly had probable cause to believe that he had been driving while intoxicated, *id.*, at 768, and to believe that a blood test would provide evidence that was exceptionally probative in confirming this belief. Because the case fell within the exigent-circumstances exception to the warrant requirement, no warrant was necessary.... The search was not more intrusive than reasonably necessary to accomplish its goals. Nonetheless, Schmerber argued that the Fourth Amendment prohibited the authorities from intruding into his body to extract the blood that was needed as evidence....

The reasonableness of surgical intrusions beneath the skin depends on a case-by-case approach, in which the individual's interests in privacy and security are weighed against society's interests in conducting the procedure. In a given case, the question whether the community's need for evidence outweighs the substantial privacy interests at stake is a delicate one admitting of few categorical answers. We believe that *Schmerber*, however, provides the appropriate framework of analysis for such cases.

Schmerber recognized that the ordinary requirements of the Fourth Amendment would be the threshold requirements for conducting this kind of surgical search and seizure. We noted the importance of probable cause. And we pointed out: "Search warrants are ordinarily required for searches of dwellings, and, absent an emergency, no less could be required where intrusions into the human body are concerned.... The importance of informed, detached and deliberate determinations of the issue whether or not to invade another's body in search of evidence of guilt is indisputable and great."

Beyond these standards, *Schmerber*'s inquiry considered a number of other factors in determining the "reasonableness" of the blood test. A crucial factor in analyzing the magnitude of the intrusion in *Schmerber* is the extent to which the procedure may threaten the safety or health of the individual. "[For] most people [a blood test] involves virtually no risk, trauma, or pain." Moreover, all reasonable medical precautions were taken and no unusual or untested procedures were employed in *Schmerber*; the procedure was performed "by a physician in a hospital environment according to accepted medical practices." Notwithstanding the existence of probable cause, a search for evidence of a crime may be unjustifiable if it endangers the life or health of the suspect.

Another factor is the extent of intrusion upon the individual's dignitary interests in personal privacy and bodily integrity. Intruding into an individual's living room, see Payton v. New York (1980), eavesdropping upon an individual's telephone conversations, see *Katz*, or forcing an individual to accompany police officers to the police station, see Dunaway v. New York (1979), typically do not injure the physical person of the individual. Such intrusions do, however, damage the individual's sense of personal privacy and security and are thus subject to the Fourth Amendment's dictates. In noting that a blood test was "a commonplace in these days of periodic physical examinations," *Schmerber* recognized society's judgment that blood tests do not constitute an unduly extensive imposition on an individual's personal privacy and bodily integrity.[5]

Weighed against these individual interests is the community's interest in fairly and accurately determining guilt or innocence. This interest is of course of great importance. We noted in *Schmerber* that a blood test is "a highly effective means of determining the degree to which a person is under the influence of alcohol." Moreover, there was "a clear indication that in fact [desired] evidence [would] be found" if the blood test were undertaken. Especially given the difficulty of proving drunkenness by other means, these considerations showed that results of the blood test were of vital importance if the State were to enforce its drunken driving laws. In *Schmerber*, we concluded that this state interest was sufficient to justify the intrusion, and the compelled blood test was thus "reasonable" for Fourth Amendment purposes.

III

Applying the *Schmerber* balancing test in this case, we believe that the Court of Appeals reached the correct result. The Commonwealth plainly had probable cause to conduct the search. In addition, all parties apparently agree that respondent has had a full measure of procedural protections and has been able fully to litigate the difficult medical and legal questions necessarily involved in analyzing the reasonableness of a surgical incision of this magnitude. Our inquiry therefore must focus on the extent of the intrusion on respondent's privacy interests and on the State's need for the evidence.

The threats to the health or safety of respondent posed by the surgery are the subject of sharp dispute between the parties. Before the new revelations of October 18, the District Court found that the procedure could be carried out "with virtually no risk to [respondent]." On rehearing, however, with new evidence before it, the District Court held that "the risks previously involved have increased in magnitude even as new risks are being added."

The Court of Appeals examined the medical evidence in the record and found that respondent would suffer some risks associated with the surgical procedure. One surgeon had testified that the difficulty of discovering the exact location of the bullet "could require extensive probing and retracting of the muscle tissue," carrying with it "the concomitant risks of injury to the muscle as well as injury to the nerves, blood vessels and other tissue in the chest and pleural cavity." The court further noted that "the greater intrusion and the larger incisions increase the risks of infection." Moreover, there was conflict in the testimony concerning the nature and the

5. ... The degree of intrusion in *Schmerber* was minimized as well by the fact that a blood test "involves virtually no risk, trauma, or pain," and by the fact that the blood test was conducted "in a hospital environment according to accepted medical practices." *Ibid.* As such, the procedure in *Schmerber* contrasted sharply with the practice in Rochin v. California, in which police officers broke into a suspect's room, attempted to extract narcotics capsules he had put into his mouth, took him to a hospital, and directed that an emetic be administered to induce vomiting. *Rochin*, recognizing the individual's interest in "human dignity," held the search and seizure unconstitutional under the Due Process Clause.

scope of the operation. One surgeon stated that it would take 15–20 minutes, while another predicted the procedure could take up to two and one-half hours. The court properly took the resulting uncertainty about the medical risks into account.

Both lower courts in this case believed that the proposed surgery, which for purely medical reasons required the use of a general anesthetic, would be an "extensive" intrusion on respondent's personal privacy and bodily integrity. When conducted with the consent of the patient, surgery requiring general anesthesia is not necessarily demeaning or intrusive. In such a case, the surgeon is carrying out the patient's own will concerning the patient's body and the patient's right to privacy is therefore preserved. In this case, however, the Court of Appeals noted that the Commonwealth proposes to take control of respondent's body, to "drug this citizen—not yet convicted of a criminal offense—with narcotics and barbiturates into a state of unconsciousness," and then to search beneath his skin for evidence of a crime. This kind of surgery involves a virtually total divestment of respondent's ordinary control over surgical probing beneath his skin.

The other part of the balance concerns the Commonwealth's need to intrude into respondent's body to retrieve the bullet. The Commonwealth claims to need the bullet to demonstrate that it was fired from Watkinson's gun, which in turn would show that respondent was the robber who confronted Watkinson. However, although we recognize the difficulty of making determinations in advance as to the strength of the case against respondent, petitioners' assertions of a compelling need for the bullet are hardly persuasive. The very circumstances relied on in this case to demonstrate probable cause to believe that evidence will be found tend to vitiate the Commonwealth's need to compel respondent to undergo surgery. The Commonwealth has available substantial additional evidence that respondent was the individual who accosted Watkinson on the night of the robbery. No party in this case suggests that Watkinson's entirely spontaneous identification of respondent at the hospital would be inadmissible. In addition, petitioners can no doubt prove that Watkinson was found a few blocks from Watkinson's store shortly after the incident took place. And petitioners can certainly show that the location of the bullet (under respondent's left collarbone) seems to correlate with Watkinson's report that the robber "jerked" to the left. The fact that the Commonwealth has available such substantial evidence of the origin of the bullet restricts the need for the Commonwealth to compel respondent to undergo the contemplated surgery.[10]

In weighing the various factors in this case, we therefore reach the same conclusion as the courts below. The operation sought will intrude substantially on respondent's protected interests. The medical risks of the operation, although apparently not extremely severe, are a subject of considerable dispute; the very uncertainty militates against finding the

10. There are also some questions concerning the probative value of the bullet, even if it could be retrieved. The evidentiary value of the bullet depends on a comparison between markings, if any, on the bullet in respondent's shoulder and markings, if any, found on a test bullet that the police could fire from Watkinson's gun. However, the record supports some doubt whether this kind of comparison is possible....

operation to be "reasonable." In addition, the intrusion on respondent's privacy interests entailed by the operation can only be characterized as severe. On the other hand, although the bullet may turn out to be useful to the Commonwealth in prosecuting respondent, the Commonwealth has failed to demonstrate a compelling need for it. We believe that in these circumstances the Commonwealth has failed to demonstrate that it would be "reasonable" under the terms of the Fourth Amendment to search for evidence of this crime by means of the contemplated surgery.

IV

The Fourth Amendment is a vital safeguard of the right of the citizen to be free from unreasonable governmental intrusions into any area in which he has a reasonable expectation of privacy. Where the Court has found a lesser expectation of privacy, the Court has held that the Fourth Amendment's protections are correspondingly less stringent. Conversely, however, the Fourth Amendment's command that searches be "reasonable" requires that when the State seeks to intrude upon an area in which our society recognizes a significantly heightened privacy interest, a more substantial justification is required to make the search "reasonable." Applying these principles, we hold that the proposed search in this case would be "unreasonable" under the Fourth Amendment.

■ JUSTICE BLACKMUN and JUSTICE REHNQUIST concur in the judgment.

■ The concurring opinion by JUSTICE BURGER is omitted.

G. EXCEPTIONS TO THE WARRANT REQUIREMENT: THE LAW OF ARREST AND OF SEARCH INCIDENT TO ARREST

1. ARRESTS IN PUBLIC PLACES: IS A WARRANT REQUIRED?

United States v. Watson

Supreme Court of the United States, 1976.
423 U.S. 411, 96 S.Ct. 820.

[On August 17, 1972, an informant of proven reliability delivered a stolen credit card to federal postal inspectors, alleging that he had received the card from Henry Watson, who had instructed the informant to purchase airline tickets with it. Although authorities had probable cause to arrest Watson, they neither arrested him immediately nor applied for an arrest warrant. Instead they arranged for a meeting between the informant and Watson to be held on August 22. The meeting was postponed until August 23, at which time the informant signaled to postal inspectors that Watson had indicated that he presently had additional stolen credit cards in his possession. The inspectors entered the restaurant where the meeting had taken place, arrested Watson without a warrant, and searched his person, finding nothing. Watson, however, consented to a search of his near-by car; that search yielded stolen credit cards. These cards were admitted at trial, at which Watson was acquitted of the August 17 charge and convicted of August 23 charges. The United States Court of Appeals for the Ninth Circuit reversed the convictions, holding that the arrest was illegal for want of a warrant, and that the illegal arrest fatally tainted the consent to search. The Ninth Circuit held that an arrest warrant must be obtained even for a felony arrest in a public place, unless emergency circumstances necessitate an immediate arrest.]

■ JUSTICE WHITE delivered the opinion of the Court.

* * *

Contrary to the Court of Appeals' view, Watson's arrest was not invalid because executed without a warrant. Section 3061(a) of Title 18 U.S.C. expressly empowers the Board of Governors of the Postal Service to authorize Postal Service officers and employees "performing duties related to the inspection of postal matters" to

> "(3) make arrests without warrant for felonies cognizable under the laws of the United States if they have reasonable grounds to believe that the person to be arrested has committed or is committing such a felony."

* * *

... Section 3061 represents a judgment by Congress that it is not unreasonable under the Fourth Amendment for postal inspectors to arrest without a warrant provided they have probable cause to do so. This was not an isolated or quixotic judgment of the legislative branch. Other federal law enforcement officers have been expressly authorized by statute for many years to make felony arrests on probable cause but without a warrant. This is true of United States Marshals, 18 U.S.C. § 3053, and of agents of the Federal Bureau of Investigation, 18 U.S.C. § 3052; the Drug Enforcement Administration, 84 Stat. 1273, 21 U.S.C. § 878; the Secret Service, 18 U.S.C. § 3056(a); and the Customs Service, 26 U.S.C. § 7607.

... Moreover, there is nothing in the Court's prior cases indicating that under the Fourth Amendment a warrant is required to make a valid arrest for a felony. Indeed, the relevant prior decisions are uniformly to the contrary.

* * *

The cases construing the Fourth Amendment thus reflect the ancient common-law rule that a peace officer was permitted to arrest without a warrant for a misdemeanor or felony committed in his presence as well as for a felony not committed in his presence if there was reasonable grounds for making the arrest. 10 Halsbury's Laws of England 344–345 (3d ed. 1955); 4 Blackstone's Commentaries 292–293 (Lewis ed. 1902); 1 J. Stephen, A History of the Criminal Law of England 193 (1883).... This has also been the prevailing rule under state constitutions and statutes....

The balance struck by the common law in generally authorizing felony arrests on probable cause, but without warrant, has survived substantially intact. It appears in almost all of the States in the form of express statutory authorization....

This is the rule Congress has long directed its principal law enforcement officers to follow. Congress has plainly decided against conditioning warrantless arrest power on proof of exigent circumstances. Law enforcement officers may find it wise to seek arrest warrants where practicable to do so, and their judgments about probable cause may be more readily accepted where backed by a warrant issued by a magistrate.... But we decline to transform this judicial preference into a constitutional rule when the judgment of the Nation and the Congress has for so long been to authorize warrantless public arrests on probable cause rather than to encumber criminal prosecutions with endless litigation with respect to the existence of exigent circumstances, whether it was practicable to get a warrant, whether the suspect was about to flee, and the like.

Watson's arrest did not violate the Fourth Amendment, and the Court of Appeals erred in holding to the contrary.

■ JUSTICE POWELL, concurring.

.... Since the Fourth Amendment speaks equally to both searches and seizures, and since an arrest, the taking hold of one's person, is quintessentially a seizure, it would seem that the constitutional provision should impose the same limitations upon arrests that it does upon searches. Indeed, as an abstract matter an argument can be made that the restrictions upon arrest perhaps should be greater. A search may cause only annoyance and temporary inconvenience to the law-abiding citizen, assuming more serious dimension only when it turns up evidence of criminality. An arrest, however, is a serious personal intrusion regardless of whether the person seized is guilty or innocent.

.... But logic sometimes must defer to history and experience. The Court's opinion emphasizes the historical sanction accorded warrantless felony arrests. In the early days of the common law most felony arrests were made upon personal knowledge and without warrants. So established were such arrests as the usual practice that Lord Coke seriously questioned whether a justice of the peace, receiving his information secondhand instead of from personal knowledge, even could authorize an arrest by warrant. 4 E. Coke, Institutes 177 (6th ed. 1681). By the late 18th century it had been firmly established by Blackstone, with an intervening assist from Sir Matthew Hale, that magistrates could issue arrest warrants upon information supplied by others. 4 W. Blackstone, Commentaries *290; see 2 M. Hale, Pleas of the Crown *108–110. But recognition of the warrant power cast no doubt upon the validity of warrantless felony arrests, which continued to be practiced and upheld as before. 4 W. Blackstone, at 282; 1 J. Chitty, Criminal Law 14–15. There is no historical evidence that the Framers or proponents of the Fourth Amendment, outspokenly opposed to the infamous general warrants and writs of assistance, were at all concerned about warrantless arrests by local constables and other peace officers. See N. Lasson, The History and Development of the Fourth Amendment to the United States Constitution 79–105 (1937); Gerstein v. Pugh. As the Court today notes, the Second Congress' passage of an Act authorizing such arrests so soon after the adoption of the Fourth Amendment itself underscores the probability that the constitutional provision was intended to restrict entirely different practices....

■ STEWART, J., concurring.

The arrest in this case was made upon probable cause in a public place in broad daylight. The Court holds that this arrest did not violate the Fourth Amendment, and I agree. The Court does not decide, nor could it decide in this case, whether or under what circumstances an officer must obtain a warrant before he may lawfully enter a private place to effect an arrest....

* * *

■ JUSTICE MARSHALL, dissenting.

... The Court reaches its conclusion that a warrant is not necessary for a police officer to make an arrest in a public place, so long as he has probable cause to believe a felony has been committed, on the basis of its views of precedent and history.... None of the cases cited by the Court squarely confronted the issue decided today. Moreover, an examination of the history relied on by the Court shows that it does not support the conclusion laid upon it.

[JUSTICE MARSHALL then engaged in an analysis of historical developments, from which he concluded that at common law only the most serious offenses were called "felonies," and that many crimes presently deemed felonies were considered misdemeanors at common law.]

Thus the lesson of the common law, and those courts in this country that have accepted its rule, is an ambiguous one. Applied in its original context, the common-law rule would allow the warrantless arrest of some, but not all, of those we call felons today. Accordingly, the Court is simply historically wrong when it tells us that "[t]he balance struck by the common law in generally authorizing felony arrests on probable cause, but without a warrant, has survived substantially intact." ... Indeed, the only clear lesson of history is contrary to the one the Court draws: the common law considered the arrest warrant far more important than today's decision leaves it.

I do not mean by this that a modern warrant requirement should apply only to arrests precisely analogous to common-law misdemeanors, and be inapplicable to analogues of common-law felonies. Rather, the point is simply that the Court's unblinking literalism cannot replace analysis of the constitutional interests involved. While we can learn from the common law, the ancient rule does not provide a simple answer directly transferable to our system. Thus, in considering the applicability of the common-law rule to our present constitutional scheme, we must consider both of the rule's two opposing constructs: the presumption favoring warrants, as well as the exception allowing immediate arrests of the most dangerous criminals. The Court's failure to do so, indeed its failure to recognize any tension in the common-law rule at all, drains all validity from its historical analysis....

The Court has typically engaged in a two-part analysis in deciding whether the presumption favoring a warrant should be given effect in situations where a warrant has not previously been clearly required. Utilizing that approach we must now consider (1) whether the privacy of our citizens will be better protected by ordinarily requiring a warrant to be issued before they may be arrested; and (2) whether a warrant requirement would unduly burden legitimate governmental interests....

The first question is easily answered. Of course the privacy of our citizens will be better protected by a warrant requirement. We have recognized that "the Fourth Amendment protects people, not places." Katz v. United States (1967). Indeed, the privacy guaranteed by the Fourth Amendment is quintessentially personal.... Thus a warrant is required in search situations not because of some high regard for property, but because of our regard for the individual, and his interest in his possessions and person....

Not only is the Fourth Amendment directly addressed to the privacy of our citizens, but it speaks in indistinguishable terms about the freedom of both persons and property from unreasonable seizures. A warrant is required in the search situation to protect the privacy of the individual, but there can be no less invasion of privacy when the individual himself, rather than his property, is searched and seized. Indeed, an unjustified arrest that forces the individual temporarily to forfeit his right to control his person and movements and interrupts the course of his daily business may be more intrusive than an unjustified search....

A warrant requirement for arrests would, of course, minimize the possibility that such an intrusion into the individual's sacred sphere of personal privacy would occur on less than probable cause. Primarily for this reason, a warrant is required for searches. Surely there is no reason to place greater trust in the partisan assessment of a police officer that there is probable cause for an arrest than in his determination that probable cause exists for a search....

We come then to the second part of the warrant test: whether a warrant requirement would unduly burden legitimate law enforcement interests....

The Government's assertion that a warrant requirement would impose an intolerable burden stems, in large part, from the specious supposition that procurement of an arrest warrant would be necessary as soon as probable cause ripens. There is no requirement that a search warrant be obtained the moment police have probable cause to search. The rule is only that present probable cause be shown and a warrant obtained before a search is undertaken. Fed.Rule Crim.Proc. 41.... The same rule should obtain for arrest warrants, where it may even make more sense. Certainly, there is less need for prompt procurement of a warrant in the arrest situation. Unlike probable cause to search, probable cause to arrest, once formed will continue to exist for the indefinite future, at least if no intervening exculpatory facts come to light....

This sensible approach obviates most of the difficulties that have been suggested with an arrest warrant rule. Police would not have to cut their investigation short the moment they obtain probable cause to arrest, nor would undercover agents be forced suddenly to terminate their work and forfeit their covers.... Moreover, if in the course of the continued police investigation exigent circumstances develop that demand an immediate arrest, the arrest maybe made without fear of unconstitutionality, so long as the exigency was unanticipated and not used to avoid the arrest warrant requirement.... Likewise, if in the course of the continued investigation police uncover evidence tying the suspect to another crime, they may immediately arrest him for that crime if exigency demands it, and still be in full conformity with the warrant rule.... Other than where police attempt to evade the warrant requirement, the rule would invalidate an arrest only in the obvious situation: where police, with probable cause but without exigent circumstances, set out to arrest a suspect. Such an arrest must be void, even if exigency develops in the course of the arrest that would ordinarily validate it; otherwise the warrant requirement would be reduced to a toothless prescription.

In sum, the requirement that officers about to arrest a suspect ordinarily obtain a warrant before they do so does not seem unduly burdensome, at least no more burdensome than any other requirement that law enforcement officials undertake a new procedure in order to comply with the dictates of the Constitution....

It is suggested, however, that even if application of this rule does not require police to secure a warrant as soon as they obtain probable cause, the confused officer would nonetheless be prone to do so. If so, police "would risk a court decision that the warrant had grown stale by the time it was used." ... (Powell, J., concurring).... This fear is groundless. First, as suggested above, the requirement that police procure a warrant before an arrest is made is rather simple of application. Thus, there is no need for the police to find themselves in this "squeeze." Second, the "squeeze" is nonexistent. Just as it is virtually impossible for probable cause for an arrest to grow stale between the time of formation and the time a warrant is procured, it is virtually impossible for probable cause to become stale between procurement and arrest. Delay by law enforcement officers in executing an arrest warrant does not ordinarily affect the legality of the arrest....

* * *

NOTES

1. Five months after *Watson*, the Supreme Court decided United States v. Santana, 427 U.S. 38, 96 S.Ct. 2406 (1976). Police officers had probable cause to arrest Santana. As they approached her home, they observed her on its threshold. The police entered onto her property. Santana retreated into her home. The police followed her through the open door. They arrested her within, and discovered incriminating evidence incident to the arrest. In a 7–2 decision, the Court found the warrantless arrest valid and offered the following rationale:

> "While it may be true that under the common law of property the threshold of one's dwelling is 'private,' as is the yard surrounding the house, it is nonetheless clear that under the cases interpreting the Fourth Amendment Santana was in a 'public' place. She was not in an area where she had any expectation of privacy. 'What a person knowingly exposes to the public, even in his own house or office, is not a subject of Fourth Amendment protection.' Katz v. United States (1967). She was not merely visible to the public but as exposed to public view, speech, hearing and touch as if she had been standing completely outside her house. Hester v. United States (1924). Thus, when the police, who concededly had

probable cause to do so, sought to arrest her, they merely intended to perform a function which we have approved in Watson.

"The only remaining question is whether her act of retreating into her house could thwart an otherwise proper arrest. We hold that it could not. In Warden v. Hayden (1967), we recognized the right of police, who had probable cause to believe that an armed robber had entered a house a few minutes before, to make a warrantless entry to arrest the robber and to search for weapons. This case, involving a true 'hot pursuit,' is clearly governed by Warden; the need to act quickly here is even greater than in that case while the intrusion is much less.... The fact that the pursuit here ended almost as soon as it began did not render it any the less a 'hot pursuit' sufficient to justify the warrantless entry into Santana's house. Once Santana saw the police, there was likewise a realistic expectation that any delay would result in destruction of evidence. See Vale v. Louisiana, 399 U.S. 30, 35, 90 S.Ct. 1969, 1972 (1970). Once she had been arrested the search, incident to that arrest, which produced the drugs and money was clearly justified....

"We thus conclude that a suspect may not defeat an arrest which has been set in motion in a public place, and is therefore proper under *Watson*, by the expedient of escaping to a private place...."

2. Watson relied heavily on history, tradition, and the common law. Consider what role these should play in constitutional adjudication.

3. Even if an arrest warrant were never required by the Fourth Amendment, there still could be concern about whether a particular arrest warrant was valid for purposes of the Fourth Amendment. Suppose that a federal agent obtains an arrest warrant and then makes the arrest in a public place and finds evidence on the arrestee's person in a search incident to arrest. If in order to justify the arrest, the prosecutor relies solely upon the arrest warrant and makes no effort to prove through live testimony that there was probable cause for the arrest, then the validity of the arrest (and of the search incident to arrest) will depend upon the validity of the arrest warrant. This is true even though the Fourth Amendment did not mandate that an arrest warrant be obtained.

4. In view of the significant role that the *Watson* court gave to the common law in interpreting Fourth Amendment limits upon arrest powers, serious constitutional questions arose about the validity of statutes in some states which permit an officer, upon probable cause to make a warrantless arrest for a misdemeanor offense not committed in his or her presence. Compare the use of history and the common law in *Watson* with that in *Atwater* in which the Court considered the validity of a warrantless arrest for a misdemeanor:

Atwater v. City of Lago Vista

Supreme Court of the United States, 2001.
532 U.S. 318, 121 S.Ct. 1536.

JUDGES: SOUTER, J., delivered the opinion of the Court, in which REHNQUIST, C. J., and SCALIA, KENNEDY, and THOMAS, JJ., joined. O'CONNOR, J., filed a dissenting opinion, in which STEVENS, GINSBURG, and BREYER, JJ., joined.

■ JUSTICE SOUTER delivered the opinion of the Court.

The question is whether the Fourth Amendment forbids a warrantless arrest for a minor criminal offense, such as a misdemeanor seatbelt violation punishable only by a fine. We hold that it does not.

I

A

In Texas, if a car is equipped with safety belts, a front-seat passenger must wear one, Tex. Tran. Code Ann. § 545.413(a) (1999), and the driver must secure any small child riding in front, § 545.413(b). Violation of either provision is "a misdemeanor punishable by a fine not less than $25 or more than $50." § 545.413(d). Texas law expressly authorizes "any peace officer [to] arrest without warrant a person found committing a violation" of these seatbelt laws, § 543.001, although it permits police to issue citations in lieu of arrest, §§ 543.003–543.005.

In March 1997, Petitioner Gail Atwater was driving her pickup truck in Lago Vista, Texas, with her 3–year-old son and 5–year-old daughter in the front seat. None of them was wearing a seatbelt. Respondent Bart Turek, a Lago Vista police officer at the time, observed the seatbelt violations and pulled Atwater over. According to Atwater's complaint (the allegations of which we assume to be true for present purposes), Turek approached the truck and "yelled" something to the effect of "we've met before" and "you're going to jail." He then called for backup and asked to see Atwater's driver's license and insurance documentation, which state law required her to carry. When Atwater told Turek that she did not have the papers because her purse had been stolen the day before, Turek said that he had "heard that story two-hundred times."

Atwater asked to take her "frightened, upset, and crying" children to a friend's house nearby, but Turek told her, "you're not going anywhere." As it turned out, Atwater's friend learned what was going on and soon arrived to take charge of the children. Turek then handcuffed Atwater, placed her in his squad car, and drove her to the local police station, where booking officers had her remove her shoes, jewelry, and eyeglasses, and empty her pockets. Officers took Atwater's "mug shot" and placed her, alone, in a jail cell for about one hour, after which she was taken before a magistrate and released on $310 bond.

Atwater was charged with driving without her seatbelt fastened, failing to secure her children in seatbelts, driving without a license, and failing to provide proof of insurance. She ultimately pleaded no contest to the misdemeanor seatbelt offenses and paid a $50 fine; the other charges were dismissed.

B

Atwater and her husband, petitioner Michael Haas, filed suit in a Texas state court under 42 U.S.C. § 1983 against Turek and respondents City of Lago Vista and Chief of Police Frank Miller. So far as concerns us, petitioners (whom we will simply call Atwater) alleged that respondents (for simplicity, the City) had violated Atwater's Fourth Amendment "right to be free from unreasonable seizure," and sought compensatory and punitive damages....

We granted certiorari to consider whether the Fourth Amendment, either by incorporating common-law restrictions on misdemeanor arrests or otherwise, limits police officers' authority to arrest without warrant for minor criminal offenses. We now affirm.

II

The Fourth Amendment safeguards "the right of the people to be secure in their persons, houses, papers, and effects, against unreasonable searches and seizures." In reading the Amendment, we are guided by "the traditional protections against unreasonable searches and seizures afforded by the common law at the time of the framing," since "an examination of the common-law understanding of an officer's authority to arrest sheds light on the obviously relevant, if not entirely dispositive, consideration of what the Framers of the Amendment might have thought to be reasonable," Payton v. New York (1980). Thus, the first step here is to assess Atwater's claim that peace officers' authority to make warrantless arrests for misdemeanors was restricted at common law (whether "common law" is understood strictly as law judicially derived or, instead, as the whole body of law extant at the time of the framing). Atwater's specific contention is that "founding-era common-law rules" forbade peace officers to make warrantless misdemeanor arrests except in cases of "breach of the peace," a category she claims was then understood narrowly as covering only those nonfelony offenses "involving or tending toward violence." Although her historical argument is by no means insubstantial, it ultimately fails....

We thus find disagreement, not unanimity, among both the common-law jurists and the text-writers who sought to pull the cases together and summarize accepted practice. Having reviewed the relevant English decisions, as well as English and colonial American legal treatises, legal dictionaries, and procedure manuals, we simply are not convinced that Atwater's is the correct, or even necessarily the better, reading of the common-law history....

The evidence of actual practice also counsels against Atwater's position. During the period leading up to and surrounding the framing of the Bill of Rights, colonial and state legislatures, like Parliament before them, regularly authorized local peace officers to make warrantless misdemeanor arrests without conditioning statutory authority on breach of the peace....

... both the legislative tradition of granting warrantless misdemeanor arrest authority and the judicial tradition of sustaining such statutes against constitutional attack are buttressed by legal commentary that, for more than a century now, has almost uniformly recognized the constitutionality of extending warrantless arrest power to misdemeanors without limitation to breaches of the peace.... Small wonder, then, that today statutes in all 50 States and the District of Columbia permit warrantless misdemeanor arrests by at least some (if not all) peace officers without requiring any breach of the peace, as do a host of congressional enactments.

III

While it is true here that history, if not unequivocal, has expressed a decided, majority view that the police need not obtain an arrest warrant merely because a misdemeanor stopped short of violence or a threat of it, Atwater does not wager all on history. Instead, she asks us to mint a new rule of constitutional law on the understanding that when historical practice fails to speak conclusively to a claim grounded on the Fourth Amendment, courts are left to strike a current balance between individual and societal interests by subjecting particular contemporary circumstances to traditional standards of reasonableness. Atwater accordingly argues for a modern arrest rule, one not necessarily requiring violent breach of the peace, but nonetheless forbidding custodial arrest, even upon probable cause, when conviction could not ultimately carry any jail time and when the government shows no compelling need for immediate detention.

If we were to derive a rule exclusively to address the uncontested facts of this case, Atwater might well prevail. She was a known and established resident of Lago Vista with no place to hide and no incentive to flee, and common sense says she would almost certainly have buckled up as a condition of driving off with a citation. In her case, the physical incidents of arrest were merely gratuitous humiliations imposed by a police officer who was (at best) exercising extremely poor judgment. Atwater's claim to live free of pointless indignity and confinement clearly outweighs anything the City can raise against it specific to her case.

But we have traditionally recognized that a responsible Fourth Amendment balance is not well served by standards requiring sensitive, case-by-case determinations of government need, lest every discretionary judgment in the field be converted into an occasion for constitutional review. Often enough, the Fourth Amendment has to be applied on the spur (and in the heat) of the moment, and the object in implementing its command of reasonableness is to draw standards sufficiently clear and simple to be applied with a fair prospect of surviving judicial second-guessing months and years after an arrest or search is made. Courts attempting to strike a reasonable Fourth Amendment balance thus credit the government's side with an essential interest in readily administrable rules.

At first glance, Atwater's argument may seem to respect the values of clarity and simplicity, so far as she claims that the Fourth Amendment generally forbids warrantless arrests for minor crimes not accompanied by violence or some demonstrable threat of it (whether "minor crime" be defined as a fine-only traffic offense, a fine-only offense more generally, or a misdemeanor). But the claim is not ultimately so simple, nor could it be, for complications arise the moment we begin to think about the possible applications of the several criteria Atwater proposes for drawing a line between minor crimes with limited arrest authority and others not so restricted.

One line, she suggests, might be between "jailable" and "fine-only" offenses, between those for which conviction could result in commitment and those for which it could not. The trouble with this distinction, of course, is that an officer on the street might not be able to tell. It is not merely that we cannot expect every police officer to know the details of frequently complex penalty provisions. . . .

But Atwater's refinements would not end there. She represents that if the line were drawn at nonjailable traffic offenses, her proposed limitation should be qualified by a proviso authorizing warrantless arrests where "necessary for enforcement of the traffic laws or when [an] offense would otherwise continue and pose a danger to others on the road." (Were the line drawn at misdemeanors generally, a comparable qualification would presumably apply.) The proviso only compounds the difficulties. Would, for instance, either exception apply to speeding? At oral argument, Atwater's counsel said that "it would not be reasonable to arrest a driver for speeding unless the speeding rose to the level of reckless driving." But is it not fair to expect that the chronic speeder will speed again despite a citation in his pocket, and should that not qualify as showing that the "offense would . . . continue" under Atwater's rule? And why, as a constitutional matter, should we assume that only reckless driving will "pose a danger to others on the road" while speeding will not?

There is no need for more examples to show that Atwater's general rule and limiting proviso promise very little in the way of administrability. It is no answer that the police routinely make judgments on grounds like risk of immediate repetition; they surely do and should. But there is a world of difference between making that judgment in choosing between the discretionary leniency of a summons in place of a clearly lawful arrest, and making the same judgment when the question is the lawfulness of the warrantless arrest itself. It is the difference between no basis for legal action challenging the discretionary judgment, on the one hand, and the prospect of evidentiary exclusion or (as here) personal § 1983 liability for the misapplication of a constitutional standard, on the other. Atwater's rule therefore would not only place police in an almost impossible spot but would guarantee increased litigation over many of the arrests that would occur. For all these reasons, Atwater's various distinctions between permissible and impermissible arrests for minor crimes strike us as "very unsatisfactory lines" to require police officers to draw on a moment's notice.

One may ask, of course, why these difficulties may not be answered by a simple tie breaker for the police to follow in the field: if in doubt, do not arrest. The first answer is that in practice the tie breaker would boil down to something akin to a least-restrictive-alternative limitation, which is itself one of those "ifs, ands, and buts" rules. ("The logic of such elaborate less-restrictive-alternative arguments could raise insuperable barriers to the exercise of virtually all search-and-seizure powers"). Beyond that, whatever help the tie breaker might give would come at the price of a systematic disincentive to arrest in situations where even Atwater concedes that arresting would serve an important societal interest. An officer not quite sure that the drugs weighed enough to warrant jail time or not quite certain about a suspect's risk of flight would not arrest, even though it could perfectly well turn out that, in fact, the offense called for incarceration and the defendant was long gone on the day of trial. Multiplied many times over, the costs to society of such underenforcement could easily outweigh the costs to defendants of being needlessly arrested and booked, as Atwater herself acknowledges.

Just how easily the costs could outweigh the benefits may be shown by asking, as one Member of this Court did at oral argument, "how bad the problem is out there." The very fact that the law has never jelled the way Atwater would have it leads one to wonder whether warrantless misdemeanor arrests need constitutional attention, and there is cause to think the answer is no. So far as such arrests might be thought to pose a threat to the probable-cause requirement, anyone arrested for a crime without formal process, whether for felony or misdemeanor, is entitled to a magistrate's review of probable cause within 48 hours, *County of Riverside v. McLaughlin*, and there is no reason to think the procedure in this case atypical in giving the suspect a prompt opportunity to request release (persons arrested for traffic offenses to be taken "immediately" before a magistrate).... It is of course easier to devise a minor-offense limitation by statute than to derive one through the Constitution, simply because the statute can let the arrest power turn on any sort of practical consideration without having to subsume it under a broader principle. It is, in fact, only natural that States should resort to this sort of legislative regulation, for, as Atwater's own *amici* emphasize, it is in the interest of the police to limit petty-offense arrests, which carry costs that are simply too great to incur without good reason.... Finally, and significantly, under current doctrine the preference for categorical treatment of Fourth Amendment claims gives way to individualized review when a defendant makes a colorable argument that an arrest, with or without a warrant, was "conducted in an extraordinary manner, unusually harmful to [his] privacy or even physical interests."

The upshot of all these influences, combined with the good sense (and, failing that, the political accountability) of most local lawmakers and law-enforcement officials, is a dearth of horribles demanding redress. Indeed, when Atwater's counsel was asked at oral argument for any indications of comparably foolish, warrantless misdemeanor arrests, he could offer only one. 23We are sure that there are others, 24but just as surely the country is not confronting anything like an epidemic of unnecessary minor-offense arrests. That fact caps the reasons for rejecting Atwater's request for the development of a new and distinct body of constitutional law.

Accordingly, we confirm today what our prior cases have intimated: the standard of probable cause "applies to all arrests, without the need to 'balance' the interests and circumstances involved in particular situations." Dunaway v. New York (1979). If an officer has probable cause to believe that an individual has committed even a very minor criminal offense in his presence, he may, without violating the Fourth Amendment, arrest the offender.

■ JUSTICE O'CONNOR, with whom JUSTICE STEVENS, JUSTICE GINSBURG, and JUSTICE BREYER join, dissenting.

The Fourth Amendment guarantees the right to be free from "unreasonable searches and seizures." The Court recognizes that the arrest of Gail Atwater was a "pointless indignity" that served no discernible state interest, and yet holds that her arrest was constitutionally permissible. Because the Court's position is inconsistent with the explicit guarantee of the Fourth Amendment, I dissent.

I

A full custodial arrest, such as the one to which Ms. Atwater was subjected, is the quintessential seizure. When a full custodial arrest is effected without a warrant, the plain language of the Fourth Amendment requires that the arrest be reasonable. It is beyond cavil that "the touchstone of our analysis under the Fourth Amendment is always 'the reasonableness in all the circumstances of the particular governmental invasion of a citizen's personal security.' "

We have "often looked to the common law in evaluating the reasonableness, for Fourth Amendment purposes, of police activity." But history is just one of the tools we use in conducting the reasonableness inquiry. And when history is inconclusive, as the majority amply demonstrates it is in this case, we will "evaluate the search or seizure under traditional standards of reasonableness by assessing, on the one hand, the degree to which it intrudes upon an individual's privacy and, on the other, the degree to which it is needed for the promotion of legitimate governmental interests."

The majority gives a brief nod to this bedrock principle of our Fourth Amendment jurisprudence, and even acknowledges that "Atwater's claim to live free of pointless indignity and confinement clearly outweighs anything the City can raise against it specific to her case." But instead of remedying this imbalance, the majority allows itself to be swayed by the worry that "every discretionary judgment in the field [will] be converted into an occasion for constitutional review." It therefore mints a new rule that "if an officer has probable cause to believe that an individual has committed even a very minor criminal offense in his presence, he may, without violating the Fourth Amendment, arrest the offender." This rule is not only unsupported by our precedent, but runs contrary to the principles that lie at the core of the Fourth Amendment.

As the majority tacitly acknowledges, we have never considered the precise question presented here, namely, the constitutionality of a warrantless arrest for an offense punishable only by fine. . . .

Our decision in *Whren v. United States* (1996), is not to the contrary. The specific question presented there was whether, in evaluating the Fourth Amendment reasonableness of a traffic stop, the subjective intent of the police officer is a relevant consideration. We held that it is not, and stated that "the making of a traffic stop ... is governed by the usual rule that probable cause to believe the law has been broken 'outbalances' private interest in avoiding police contact."

We of course did not have occasion in *Whren* to consider the constitutional preconditions for warrantless arrests for fine-only offenses. Nor should our words be taken beyond their context. There are significant qualitative differences between a traffic stop and a full custodial arrest. While both are seizures that fall within the ambit of the Fourth Amendment, the latter entails a much greater intrusion on an individual's liberty and privacy interests. As we have said, "[a] motorist's expectations, when he sees a policeman's light flashing behind him, are that he will be obliged to spend a short period of time answering questions and waiting while the officer checks his license and registration, that he may be given a citation, but that in the end he most likely will be allowed to continue on his way." Thus, when there is probable cause to believe that a person has violated a minor traffic law, there can be little question that the state interest in law enforcement will justify the relatively limited intrusion of a traffic stop. It is by no means certain, however, that where the offense is punishable only by fine, "probable cause to believe the law has been broken [will] 'outbalance' private interest in avoiding" a full custodial arrest. Justifying a full arrest by the same quantum of evidence that justifies a traffic stop—even though the offender cannot ultimately be imprisoned for her conduct—defies any sense of proportionality and is in serious tension with the Fourth Amendment's proscription of unreasonable seizures....

The majority insists that a bright-line rule focused on probable cause is necessary to vindicate the State's interest in easily administrable law enforcement rules. Probable cause itself, however, is not a model of precision. "The quantum of information which constitutes probable cause—evidence which would 'warrant a man of reasonable caution in the belief' that a [crime] has been committed—must be measured by the facts of the particular case." The rule I propose—which merely requires a legitimate reason for the decision to escalate the seizure into a full custodial arrest—thus does not undermine an otherwise "clear and simple" rule.

While clarity is certainly a value worthy of consideration in our Fourth Amendment jurisprudence, it by no means trumps the values of liberty and privacy at the heart of the Amendment's protections. What the *Terry* rule lacks in precision it makes up for in fidelity to the Fourth Amendment's command of reasonableness and sensitivity to the competing values protected by that Amendment. Over the past 30 years, it appears that the *Terry* rule has been workable and easily applied by officers on the street.

.... Respondents also contend that the arrest was necessary to ensure Atwater's appearance in court. Atwater, however, was far from a flight risk. A 16-year resident of Lago Vista, population 2,486, Atwater was not likely to abscond. Although she was unable to produce her driver's license because it had been stolen, she gave Officer Turek her license number and address. In addition, Officer Turek knew from their previous encounter that Atwater was a local resident.

The city's justifications fall far short of rationalizing the extraordinary intrusion on Gail Atwater and her children....

III

The Court's error, however, does not merely affect the disposition of this case. The *per se* rule that the Court creates has potentially serious consequences for the everyday lives of Americans. A broad range of conduct falls into the category of fine-only misdemeanors....

To be sure, such laws are valid and wise exercises of the States' power to protect the public health and welfare. My concern lies not with the decision to enact or enforce these laws, but rather with the manner in which they may be enforced. Under today's holding, when a police officer has probable cause to believe that a fine-only misdemeanor offense has occurred, that officer may stop the suspect, issue a citation, and let the person continue on her way. Or, if a traffic violation, the officer may stop the car, arrest the driver, search the driver, search the entire passenger compartment of the car including any purse or package inside, and impound the car and inventory all of its contents. Although the Fourth Amendment expressly requires that the latter course be a reasonable and proportional response to the circumstances of the offense, the majority gives officers unfettered discretion to choose that course without articulating a single reason why such action is appropriate.

Such unbounded discretion carries with it grave potential for abuse. The majority takes comfort in the lack of evidence of "an epidemic of unnecessary minor-offense arrests." But the relatively small number of published cases dealing with such arrests proves little and should provide little solace. Indeed, as the recent debate over racial profiling demonstrates all too clearly, a relatively minor traffic infraction may often serve as an excuse for stopping and harassing an individual. After today, the arsenal available to any officer extends to a full arrest and the searches permissible concomitant to that arrest. An officer's subjective motivations for making a traffic stop are not relevant considerations in determining the reasonableness of the stop. But it is precisely because these motivations are beyond our purview that we must vigilantly ensure that officers' poststop actions—which are properly within our reach—comport with the Fourth Amendment's guarantee of reasonableness.

The Court neglects the Fourth Amendment's express command in the name of administrative ease. In so doing, it cloaks the pointless indignity that Gail Atwater suffered with the mantle of reasonableness. I respectfully dissent.

* * *

Suppose police arrest a suspect and conduct a search incident to that arrest, must any contraband discovered as a result of that search be suppressed if it is later discovered that the arrest violates state law?

Virginia v. Moore

Supreme Court of the United States, 2008.
___ U.S. ___, 128 S.Ct. 1598.

■ JUSTICE SCALIA delivered the opinion of the Court joined by JUSTICES ROBERTS, STEVENS, KENNEDY, SOUTER, THOMAS, BREYER, and ALITO.

We consider whether a police officer violates the Fourth Amendment by making an arrest based on probable cause but prohibited by state law.

I

On February 20, 2003, two City of Portsmouth police officers stopped a car driven by David Lee Moore. They had heard over the police radio that a person known as "Chubs" was driving with a suspended license, and one of the officers knew Moore by that nickname. The officers determined that Moore's license was in fact suspended, and arrested him for the misdemeanor of driving on a suspended license, which is punishable under Virginia law by a year in jail and a $2,500 fine, Va. Code Ann. §§ 18.2–11, 18.2–272, 46.2–301(C) (Lexis 2005). The officers subsequently searched Moore and found that he was carrying 16 grams of crack cocaine and $516 in cash.

Under state law, the officers should have issued Moore a summons instead of arresting him. Driving on a suspended license, like some other misdemeanors, is not an arrestable offense except as to those who "fail or refuse to discontinue" the violation, and those whom the officer reasonably believes to be likely to disregard a summons, or likely to harm themselves or others. Va. Code Ann. § 19.2–74 (Lexis 2004). The intermediate appellate court found none of these circumstances applicable, and Virginia did not appeal that determination. Virginia also permits arrest for driving on a suspended license in jurisdictions where "prior general approval has been granted by order of the general district court,"; Virginia has never claimed such approval was in effect in the county where Moore was arrested.

Moore was charged with possessing cocaine with the intent to distribute it in violation of Virginia law. He filed a pretrial motion to suppress the evidence from the arrest search. Virginia law does not, as a general matter, require suppression of evidence obtained in violation of state law. Moore argued, however, that suppression was required by the Fourth Amendment. The trial court denied the motion, and after a bench trial found Moore guilty of the drug charge and sentenced him to a 5–year prison term, with one year and six months of the sentence suspended. The conviction was reversed by a panel of Virginia's intermediate court on Fourth Amendment grounds, reinstated by the intermediate court sitting en banc, and finally reversed again by the Virginia Supreme Court. The Court reasoned that since the arresting officers should have issued Moore a citation under state law, and the Fourth Amendment does not permit search incident to citation, the arrest search violated the Fourth Amendment. We granted certiorari.

II

The Fourth Amendment protects "against unreasonable searches and seizures" of (among other things) the person. In determining whether a search or seizure is unreasonable, we begin with history. We look to the statutes and common law of the founding era to determine the norms that the Fourth Amendment was meant to preserve.

We are aware of no historical indication that those who ratified the Fourth Amendment understood it as a redundant guarantee of whatever limits on search and seizure legislatures might have enacted. The immediate object of the Fourth Amendment was to prohibit the general warrants and writs of assistance that English judges had employed against the colonists. That suggests, if anything, that founding-era citizens were skeptical of using the rules for search and seizure set by government actors as the index of reasonableness.

III

A

When history has not provided a conclusive answer, we have analyzed a search or seizure in light of traditional standards of reasonableness "by assessing, on the one hand, the degree to which it intrudes upon an individual's privacy and, on the other, the degree to which it is needed for the promotion of legitimate governmental interests." That methodology provides no support for Moore's Fourth Amendment claim. In a long line of cases, we have said that when an officer has probable cause to believe a person committed even a minor crime in his presence, the balancing of private and public interests is not in doubt. The arrest is constitutionally reasonable.

Our decisions counsel against changing this calculus when a State chooses to protect privacy beyond the level that the Fourth Amendment requires. We have treated additional protections exclusively as matters of state law....

In California v. Greenwood (1988), we held that search of an individual's garbage forbidden by California's Constitution was not forbidden by the Fourth Amendment. "[W]hether or not a search is reasonable within the meaning of the Fourth Amendment," we said, has never "depend[ed] on the law of the particular State in which the search occurs." While "[i]ndividual States may surely construe their own constitutions as imposing more stringent constraints on police conduct than does the Federal Constitution," *ibid.*, state law did not alter the content of the Fourth Amendment.

We have applied the same principle in the seizure context. Whren v. United States (1996), held that police officers had acted reasonably in stopping a car, even though their action violated regulations limiting the authority of plainclothes officers in unmarked vehicles. We thought it obvious that the Fourth Amendment's meaning did not change with local law enforcement practices—even practices set by rule. While those practices "vary from place to place and from time to time," Fourth Amendment protections are not "so variable" and cannot "be made to turn upon such trivialities."

Some decisions earlier than these excluded evidence obtained in violation of state law, but those decisions rested on our supervisory power over the federal courts, rather than the Constitution....

Later decisions did not expand the rule of *Di Re*.... And Michigan v. DeFillippo (1979), upheld a warrantless arrest in a case where compliance with state law was not at issue. While our opinion said that "[w]hether an officer is authorized to make an arrest ordinarily depends, in the first instance, on state law," it also said that a warrantless arrest satisfies the Constitution so long as the officer has "probable cause to believe that the suspect has committed or is committing a crime." We need not pick and choose among the dicta: Neither *Di Re* nor the cases following it held that violations of state arrest law are also violations of the Fourth Amendment, and our more recent decisions, discussed above, have indicated that when States go above the Fourth Amendment minimum, the Constitution's protections concerning search and seizure remain the same.

B

We are convinced that the approach of our prior cases is correct, because an arrest based on probable cause serves interests that have long been seen as sufficient to justify the seizure. *Whren*; *Atwater*. Arrest ensures that a suspect appears to answer charges and does not continue a crime, and it safeguards evidence and enables officers to conduct an in-custody investigation. See W. LaFave, Arrest: The Decision to Take a Suspect into Custody 177–202 (1965).

Moore argues that a State has no interest in arrest when it has a policy against arresting for certain crimes. That is not so, because arrest will still ensure a suspect's appearance at trial, prevent him from continuing his offense, and enable officers to investigate the incident more thoroughly. State arrest restrictions are more accurately characterized as showing that the State values its interests in forgoing arrests more highly than its interests in making them, see, *e.g.*, Dept. of Justice, National Institute of Justice, D. Whitcomb, B. Lewin, & M. Levine, Issues and Practices: Citation Release 17 (Mar. 1984) (describing cost savings as a principal benefit of citation-release ordinances); or as showing that the State places a higher premium on privacy than the Fourth Amendment requires. A State is free to prefer one search-and-seizure policy among the range of constitutionally permissible options, but its choice of a more restrictive option does not render the less restrictive ones unreasonable, and hence unconstitutional.

If we concluded otherwise, we would often frustrate rather than further state policy. Virginia chooses to protect individual privacy and dignity more than the Fourth Amendment requires, but it also chooses not to attach to violations of its arrest rules the potent remedies that federal courts have applied to Fourth Amendment violations. Virginia does not, for example, ordinarily exclude from criminal trials evidence obtained in violation of its statutes. Moore would allow Virginia to accord enhanced protection against arrest only on pain of accompanying that protection with federal remedies for Fourth Amendment violations, which often include the exclusionary rule. States unwilling to lose control over the remedy would have to abandon restrictions on arrest altogether. This is an odd consequence of a provision designed to protect against searches and seizures.

Even if we thought that state law changed the nature of the Commonwealth's interests for purposes of the Fourth Amendment, we would adhere to the probable-cause standard. In determining what is reasonable under the Fourth Amendment, we have given great weight to the "essential interest in readily administrable rules." In *Atwater*, we acknowledged that nuanced judgments about the need for warrantless arrest were desirable, but we nonetheless declined to limit to felonies and disturbances of the peace the Fourth Amendment rule allowing arrest based on probable cause to believe a law has been broken in the presence of the arresting officer. The rule extends even to minor misdemeanors, we concluded, because of the need for a bright-line constitutional standard. If the constitutionality of arrest for minor offenses turned in part on inquiries as to risk of flight and danger of repetition, officers might be deterred from making legitimate arrests. We found little to justify this cost, because there was no "epidemic of unnecessary minor-offense arrests," and hence "a dearth of horribles demanding redress."

Incorporating state-law arrest limitations into the Constitution would produce a constitutional regime no less vague and unpredictable than the one we rejected in *Atwater*. The constitutional standard would be only as easy to apply as the underlying state law, and state law can be complicated indeed. The Virginia statute in this case, for example, calls on law enforcement officers to weigh just the sort of case-specific factors that *Atwater* said would deter legitimate arrests if made part of the constitutional inquiry. It would authorize arrest if a misdemeanor suspect fails or refuses to discontinue the unlawful act, or if the officer believes the suspect to be likely to disregard a summons. *Atwater* specifically noted the "extremely poor judgment" displayed in arresting a local resident who would "almost certainly" have discontinued the offense and who had "no place to hide and no incentive to flee." It nonetheless declined to make those considerations part of the constitutional calculus. *Atwater* differs from this case in only one significant respect: It considered (and rejected) federal constitutional remedies for *all* minor-misdemeanor arrests; Moore seeks them in only that *subset* of minor-misdemeanor arrests in which there is the least to be gained—that is, where the State has already acted to constrain officers' discretion and prevent abuse. Here we confront fewer horribles than in *Atwater*, and less of a need for redress.

Finally, linking Fourth Amendment protections to state law would cause them to "vary from place to place and from time to time," *Whren*. Even at the same place and time, the Fourth Amendment's protections might vary if federal officers were not subject to the same statutory constraints as state officers. In Elkins v. United States (1960), we noted the practical difficulties posed by the "silver-platter doctrine," which had imposed more stringent limitations on federal officers than on state police acting independent of them. It would be strange to construe a constitutional provision that did not apply to the States at all when it was adopted to now restrict state officers more than federal officers, solely because the States have passed search-and-seizure laws that are the prerogative of independent sovereigns.

We conclude that warrantless arrests for crimes committed in the presence of an arresting officer are reasonable under the Constitution, and that while States are free to regulate such arrests however they desire, state restrictions do not alter the Fourth Amendment's protections.

IV

Moore argues that even if the Constitution allowed his arrest, it did not allow the arresting officers to search him. We have recognized, however, that officers may perform searches incident to constitutionally permissible arrests in order to ensure their safety and safeguard evidence. We have described this rule as covering any "lawful arrest," with constitutional law as the reference point. That is to say, we have equated a lawful arrest with an arrest based on probable cause: "A custodial arrest of a suspect based on probable cause is a reasonable intrusion under the Fourth Amendment; *that intrusion being lawful*, a search incident to the arrest requires no additional justification." Moore correctly notes that several important state-court decisions have defined the lawfulness of arrest in terms of compliance with state law.... But it is not surprising that States have used "lawful" as shorthand for compliance with state law, while our constitutional decision in *Robinson* used "lawful" as shorthand for compliance with constitutional constraints.

The interests justifying search are present whenever an officer makes an arrest. A search enables officers to safeguard evidence, and, most critically, to ensure their safety during "the extended exposure which follows the taking of a suspect into custody and transporting him to the police station." Officers issuing citations do not face the same danger, and we therefore held in Knowles v. Iowa (1998), that they do not have the same authority to search. We cannot agree with the Virginia Supreme Court that *Knowles* controls here. The state officers *arrested* Moore, and therefore faced the risks that are "an adequate basis for treating all custodial arrests alike for purposes of search justification."

The Virginia Supreme Court may have concluded that *Knowles* required the exclusion of evidence seized from Moore because, under state law, the officers who arrested Moore should have issued him a citation instead. This argument might have force if the Constitution forbade Moore's arrest, because we have sometimes excluded evidence obtained through unconstitutional methods in order to deter constitutional violations. But the arrest rules that the officers violated were those of state law alone, and as we have just concluded, it is not the province of the Fourth Amendment to enforce state law. That Amendment does not require the exclusion of evidence obtained from a constitutionally permissible arrest.

* * *

We reaffirm against a novel challenge what we have signaled for more than half a century. When officers have probable cause to believe that a person has committed a crime in their presence, the Fourth Amendment permits them to make an arrest, and to search the suspect in order to safeguard evidence and ensure their own safety. The judgment of the Supreme Court of Virginia is reversed, and the case is remanded for further proceedings not inconsistent with this opinion.

■ JUSTICE GINSBURG, concurring in the judgment.

I find in the historical record more support for Moore's position than the Court does.[1] Further, our decision in *United States v. Di Re* (1948), requiring suppression of evidence gained in a search incident to an unlaw-

1. .... Noting colonial hostility to general warrants and writs of assistance, the Court observes that "founding-era citizens were skeptical of using the rules for search and seizure set by government actors as the index of reasonableness." The practices resisted by the citizenry, however, served to invade the people's privacy, not to shield it.

ful arrest, seems to me pinned to the Fourth Amendment and not to our "supervisory power,". And I am aware of no "long line of cases" holding that, regardless of state law, probable cause renders every warrantless arrest for crimes committed in the presence of an arresting officer "constitutionally reasonable."

I agree with the Court's conclusion and its reasoning, however, to this extent. In line with the Court's decision in Atwater v. Lago Vista (2001), Virginia could have made driving on a suspended license an arrestable offense. The Commonwealth chose not to do so. Moore asks us to credit Virginia law on a police officer's arrest authority, but only in part. He emphasizes Virginia's classification of driving on a suspended license as a nonarrestable misdemeanor. Moore would have us ignore, however, the limited consequences Virginia attaches to a police officer's failure to follow the Commonwealth's summons-only instruction. For such an infraction, the officer may be disciplined and the person arrested may bring a tort suit against the officer. But Virginia law does not demand the suppression of evidence seized by an officer who arrests when he should have issued a summons.

The Fourth Amendment, today's decision holds, does not put States to an all-or-nothing choice in this regard. A State may accord protection against arrest beyond what the Fourth Amendment requires, yet restrict the remedies available when police deny to persons they apprehend the extra protection state law orders. Because I agree that the arrest and search Moore challenges violated Virginia law, but did not violate the Fourth Amendment, I join the Court's judgment.

* * *

2. Entry to Arrest: Is a Warrant Required?

Payton v. New York

Supreme Court of the United States, 1980.
445 U.S. 573, 100 S.Ct. 1371.

■ JUSTICE STEVENS delivered the opinion of the Court.

These appeals challenge the constitutionality of New York statutes that authorize police officers to enter a private residence without a warrant and with force, if necessary, to make a routine felony arrest.

* * *

On January 14, 1970, after two days of intensive investigation, New York detectives had assembled evidence sufficient to establish probable cause to believe that Theodore Payton had murdered the manager of a gas station two days earlier. At about 7:30 a.m. on January 15, six officers went to Payton's apartment in the Bronx, intending to arrest him. They had not obtained a warrant. Although light and music emanated from the apartment, there was no response to their knock on the metal door. They summoned emergency assistance and, about 30 minutes later, used crowbars to break open the door and enter the apartment. No one was there. In plain view, however, was a 30–caliber shell casing that was seized and later admitted into evidence at Payton's murder trial.

* * *

On March 14, 1974, Obie Riddick was arrested for the commission of two armed robberies that had occurred in 1971. He had been identified by the victims in June of 1973 and in January 1974 the police had learned his address. They did not obtain a warrant for his arrest. At about noon on March 14, a detective, accompanied by three other officers, knocked on the door of the Queens house where Riddick was living. When his young son opened the door, they could see Riddick sitting in bed covered by a sheet. They entered the house and placed him under arrest. Before permitting him to dress, they opened a chest of drawers two feet from the bed in search of weapons and found narcotics and related paraphernalia. Riddick was subsequently indicted on narcotics charges....

The New York Court of Appeals, in a single opinion, affirmed the convictions of both Payton and Riddick....

Although it is arguable that the warrantless entry to effect Payton's arrest might have been justified by exigent circumstances, none of the New York courts relied on any such justification. The Court of Appeals majority treated both Payton's and Riddick's cases as involving routine arrests in which there was ample time to obtain a warrant, and we will do the same. Accordingly, we have no occasion to consider the sort of emergency or dangerous situation, described in our cases as "exigent circumstances," that would justify a warrantless entry into a home for the purpose of either arrest or search.

Nor do these cases raise any question concerning the authority of the police, without either a search or arrest warrant, to enter a third party's home to arrest a suspect. The police broke into Payton's apartment intending to arrest Payton and they arrested Riddick in his own dwelling. We also note that in neither case is it argued that the police lacked probable cause to believe that the suspect was at home when they entered. Finally, in both cases we are dealing with entries into homes made without the consent of any occupant. In Payton, the police used crowbars to breakdown the door and in Riddick, although his three-year-old son answered the door, the police entered before Riddick had an opportunity either to object or to consent.

It is familiar history that indiscriminate searches and seizures conducted under the authority of "general warrants" were the immediate evils that motivated the framing and adoption of the Fourth Amendment. Indeed, as originally proposed in the House of Representatives, the draft contained only one clause, which directly imposed limitations on the issuance of warrants, but imposed no express restrictions on warrantless searches or seizures. As it was ultimately adopted, however, the Amendment contained two separate clauses, the first protecting the basic right to be free from unreasonable searches and seizures and the second requiring that warrants be particular and supported by probable cause....

It is thus perfectly clear that the evil the Amendment was designed to prevent was broader than the abuse of a general warrant. Unreasonable searches or seizures conducted without any warrant at all are condemned by the plain language of the first clause of the Amendment. . . .

The simple language of the Amendment applies equally to seizures of persons and to seizures of property. Our analysis in this case may therefore properly commence with rules that have been well established in Fourth Amendment litigation involving tangible items. As the Court unanimously reiterated just a few years ago, the "physical entry of the home is the chief evil against which the wording of the Fourth Amendment is directed." United States v. United States District Court (1970). And we have long adhered to the view that the warrant procedure minimizes the danger of needless intrusions of that sort.

It is a "basic principle of Fourth Amendment law" that searches and seizures inside a home without a warrant are presumptively unreasonable. Yet it is also well-settled that objects such as weapons or contraband found in a public place may be seized by the police without a warrant. The seizure of property in plain view involves no invasion of privacy and is presumptively reasonable, assuming that there is probable cause to associate the property with criminal activity. The distinction between a warrantless seizure in an open area and such a seizure on private premises was plainly stated in G.M. Leasing Corp. v. United States (1977):

> "It is one thing to seize without a warrant property resting in an open area or seizable by levy without an intrusion into privacy, and it is quite another thing to effect a warrantless seizure of property, even that owned by a corporation, situated on private premises to which access is not otherwise available for the seizing officer."

As the late Judge Leventhal recognized, this distinction has equal force when the seizure of a person is involved. Writing on the constitutional issue now before us for the United States Court of Appeals for the District of Columbia Circuit sitting en banc, Dorman v. United States, 140 U.S.App. D.C. 313, 435F.2d 385 (1970), Judge Leventhal first noted the settled rule that warrantless arrests in public places are valid. He immediately recognized, however, that

> "[a] greater burden is placed [ ] on officials who enter a home or dwelling without consent. Freedom from intrusion into the home or dwelling is the archetype of the privacy protection secured by the Fourth Amendment."

His analysis of this question then focused on the long-settled premise that, absent exigent circumstances, a warrantless entry to search for weapons or contraband is unconstitutional even when a felony has been committed and there is probable cause to believe that incriminating evidence will be found within.He reasoned that the constitutional protection afforded to the individual's interest in the privacy of his own home is equally applicable to a warrantless entry for the purpose of arresting a resident of the house; for it is inherent in such an entry that a search for the suspect may be required before he can be apprehended. Judge Leventhal concluded that an entry to arrest and an entry to search for and to seize property implicate the same interest in preserving the privacy and the sanctity of the home, and justify the same level of constitutional protection....

We find this reasoning to be persuasive and in accord with this Court's Fourth Amendment decisions.

The majority of the New York Court of Appeals, however, suggested that there is a substantial difference in the relative intrusiveness of an entry to search for property and an entry to search for a person. It is true that the area that may legally be searched is broader when executing a search warrant than when executing an arrest warrant in the home. See Chimel v. California. This difference may be more theoretical than real, however, because the police may need to check the entire premises for safety reasons, and sometimes they ignore the restrictions on searches incident to arrest.

But the critical point is that any differences in the intrusiveness of entries to search and entries to arrest are merely ones of degree rather than kind. The two intrusions share this fundamental characteristic: the breach of the entrance to an individual's home. The Fourth Amendment protects the individual's privacy in a variety of settings. In none is the zone of privacy more clearly defined than when bounded by the unambiguous physical dimensions of an individual's home—a zone that finds its roots in clear and specific constitutional terms: "The right of the people to be secure in their ... houses ... shall not be violated." That language unequivocally establishes the proposition that "[a]t the very core [of the Fourth Amendment] stands the right of a man to retreat into his own home and there be free from unreasonable government intrusion." Silverman v. United States (1961). In terms that apply equally to seizures of property and to seizures of persons, the Fourth Amendment has drawn a firm line at the entrance to the house. Absent exigent circumstances, that threshold may not reasonably be crossed without a warrant....

An examination of the common law understanding of an officer's authority to arrest sheds light on the obviously relevant, if not entirely dispositive,[1] consideration of what the Framers of the Amendment might have thought to be reasonable. ...

Thus, our study of the relevant common law does not provide the same guidance that was present in Watson. Whereas the rule concerning the validity of an arrest in a public place was supported by cases directly in

1. There are important differences between the common-law rules relating to searches and seizures and those that have evolved through the process of interpreting the Fourth Amendment in light of contemporary norms and conditions. For example, whereas the kinds of property subject to seizure under warrants had been limited to contraband and the fruits or instrumentalities of crime, see Gouled v. United States, 255 U.S. 298, 309, 41 S.Ct. 261, 265, 65 L.Ed. 647, the category of property that may be seized, consistent with the Fourth Amendment, has been expanded to include mere evidence. Warden v. Hayden, 387 U.S. 294, 87 S.Ct.1642, 18 L.Ed.2d 782. Also, the prohibitions of the Amendment have been extended to protect against invasion by electronic eavesdropping of an individual's privacy in a phone booth not owned by him, Katz v. United States, 389 U.S. 347, 88 S.Ct. 507, 19 L.Ed.2d 576, even though the earlier law had focused on the physical invasion of the individual's person or property interests in the course of a seizure of tangible objects. See Olmstead v. United States, 277 U.S. 438, 466, 48 S.Ct. 564.

point and by the unanimous views of the commentators, we have found no direct authority supporting forcible entries into a home to make a routine arrest and the weight of the scholarly opinion is somewhat to the contrary. Indeed, the absence of any Seventeenth or Eighteenth Century English cases directly in point, together with the unequivocal endorsement of the tenet that "a man's house is his castle," strongly suggest that the prevailing practice was not to make such arrests except in hot pursuit or when authorized by a warrant. In all events, the issue is not one that can be said to have been definitively settled by the common law at the time the Fourth Amendment was adopted....

A longstanding, widespread practice is not immune from constitutional scrutiny. But neither is it to be lightly brushed aside. This is particularly so when the constitutional standard is as amorphous as the word "reasonable," and when custom and contemporary norms necessarily play such a large role in the constitutional analysis. In this case, although the weight of state-law authority is clear, there is by no means the kind of virtual unanimity on this question that was present in United States v. Watson with regard to warrantless arrests in public places. Only 24 of the 50 States currently sanction warrantless entries into the home to arrest and there is an obvious declining trend. Further, the strength of the trend is greater than the numbers alone indicate. Seven state courts have recently held that warrantless home arrests violate the irrespective state constitutions. That is significant because by invoking a state constitutional provision, a state court immunizes its decision from review by this Court. This heightened degree of immutability underscores the depth of the principle underlying the result.

No congressional determination that warrantless entries into the home are "reasonable" has been called to our attention. None of the federal statutes cited in the Watson opinion reflects any such legislative judgment. Thus, that support for the Watson holding finds no counterpart in this case....

In this case, however, neither history nor this Nation's experience requires us to disregard the overriding respect for the sanctity of the home that has been embedded in our traditions since the origins of the Republic.[2]

The parties have argued at some length about the practical consequences of a warrant requirement as a precondition to a felony arrest in the home. In the absence of any evidence that effective law enforcement has suffered in those States that already have such a requirement, we are inclined to view such arguments with skepticism. More fundamentally, however, such arguments of policy must give way to a constitutional command that we consider to be unequivocal.

2. There can be no doubt that Pitt's address in the House of Commons in March 1763 echoed and re-echoed throughout the Colonies:

> " 'The poorest man may in his cottage bid defiance to all the forces of the Crown. It may be frail; its roof may shake; the wind may blow through it; the storm may enter; the rain may enter; but the King of England cannot enter—all his force dares not cross the threshold of the ruined tenement!' " *Miller v. United States*, 357 U.S., at 307.

Finally, we note the State's suggestion that only a search warrant based on probable cause to believe the suspect is at home at a given time can adequately protect the privacy interests at stake, and since such a warrant requirement is manifestly impractical, there need be no warrant of any kind. We find this ingenious argument unpersuasive. It is true that an arrest warrant requirement may afford less protection than a search warrant requirement, but it will suffice to interpose the magistrate's determination of probable cause between the zealous officer and the citizen. If there is sufficient evidence of a citizen's participation in a felony to persuade a judicial officer that his arrest is justified, it is constitutionally reasonable to require him to open his doors to the officers of the law. Thus, for Fourth Amendment purposes, an arrest warrant founded on probable cause implicitly carries with it the limited authority to enter a dwelling in which the suspect lives when there is reason to believe the suspect is within.

Because no arrest warrant was obtained in either of these cases, the judgments must be reversed and the cases remanded to the New York Court of Appeals for further proceedings not inconsistent with this opinion.

■ The concurring opinion of JUSTICE BLACKMUN is omitted.

■ JUSTICE WHITE, with whom THE CHIEF JUSTICE and JUSTICE REHNQUIST join, dissenting.

. . . In sum, the background, text, and legislative history of the Fourth Amendment demonstrate that the purpose was to restrict the abuses that had developed with respect to warrants; the Amendment preserved common-law rules of arrest. Because it was not considered generally unreasonable at common law for officers to break doors to effect a warrantless felony arrest, I do not believe that the Fourth Amendment was intended to outlaw the types of police conduct at issue in the present case. . . .

Today's decision ignores the carefully crafted restrictions on the common-law power of arrest entry and thereby overestimates the dangers inherent in that practice. At common law, absent exigent circumstances, entries to arrest could be made only for felony. Even in cases of felony, the officers were required to announce their presence, demand admission, and be refused entry before they were entitled to break doors. Further, it seems generally accepted that entries could be made only during daylight hours. And, in my view, the officer entering to arrest must have reasonable grounds to believe, not only that the arrestee has committed a crime, but also that the person suspected is present in the house at the time of the entry.

These four restrictions on home arrests—felony, knock and announce, daytime, and stringent probable cause—constitute powerful and complementary protections for the privacy interests associated with the home. The felony requirement guards against abusive or arbitrary enforcement and ensures that invasions of the home occur only in case of the most serious crimes. The knock and announce and daytime requirement protect individuals against the fear, humiliation and embarrassment of being aroused from the beds in states of partial or complete undress. And these requirements allow the arrestee to surrender at his front door, thereby maintaining his dignity and preventing the officers from entering other rooms of the dwelling. The stringent probable cause requirement would help ensure against the possibility that the police would enter when the suspect was not home, and, in searching for him, frighten members of the family or ransack parts of the house, seizing items in plain view. In short, these requirements, taken together, permit an individual suspected of a serious crime to surrender at the front door of his dwelling and thereby avoid most of the humiliation and indignity that the Court seems to believe necessarily accompany a house arrest entry. Such a front door arrest, in my view, is no more intrusive on personal privacy than the public warrantless arrests which we found to pass constitutional muster in Watson.

All of these limitations on warrantless arrest entries are satisfied on the facts of the present cases....

A rule permitting warrantless arrest entries would not pose a danger that officers would use their entry power as a pretext to justify an otherwise invalid warrantless search.... The policeman on his beat must now make subtle discriminations that perplex even judges in their chambers. As Mr. Justice Powell noted, concurring in Watson, police will sometimes delay making an arrest, even after probable cause is established, in order to be sure that they have enough evidence to convict. Then, if they suddenly have to arrest, they run the risk that the subsequent exigency will not excuse their prior failure to obtain a warrant. This problem cannot effectively be cured by obtaining a warrant as soon as probable cause is established because of the chance that the warrant will go stale before the arrest is made.

Further, police officers will often face the difficult task of deciding whether the circumstances are sufficiently exigent to justify their entry to arrest without a warrant. This is a decision that must be made quickly in the most trying of circumstances. If the officers mistakenly decide that the circumstances are exigent, the arrest will be invalid and any evidence seized incident to the arrest or in plain view will be excluded at trial. On the other hand, if the officers mistakenly determine that exigent circumstances are lacking, they may refrain from making the arrest, thus creating the possibility that a dangerous criminal will escape into the community. The police could reduce the likelihood of escape by staking out all possible exits until the circumstances become clearly exigent or a warrant is obtained. But the costs of such a stakeout seem excessive in an era of rising crime and scarce police resources.

The uncertainty inherent in the exigent circumstances determination burdens the judicial system as well. In the case of searches, exigent circumstances are sufficiently unusual that this Court has determined that the benefits of a warrant outweigh the burdens imposed, including the burdens on the judicial system. In contrast, arrests recurringly involve exigent circumstances, and this Court has heretofore held that a warrant can be dispensed with without undue sacrifice in Fourth Amendment values. The situation should be no different with respect to arrests in the home. Under today's decision, whenever the police have made a warrantless home arrest there will be the possibility of "endless litigation with respect to the existence of exigent circumstances, whether it was practicable to get a warrant, whether the suspect was about to flee, and the like," United States v. Watson.

Our cases establish that the ultimate test under the Fourth Amendment is one of "reasonableness." I cannot join the Court in declaring unreasonable a practice which has been thought entirely reasonable by so many for so long. It would be far preferable to adopt a clear and simple rule: after knocking and announcing their presence, police may enter the home to make a daytime arrest without a warrant when there is probable cause to believe that the person to be arrested committed a felony and is present in the house. This rule would best comport with the commonlaw background, with the traditional practice in the States, and with the history and policies of the Fourth Amendment. Accordingly, I respectfully dissent.

■ The dissenting opinion of JUSTICE REHNQUIST is opinion omitted.

NOTES

1. ***Exclusions from the* Payton *Doctrine.*** *Payton* carefully excluded exigent circumstances, entry into a third party's home, and nonconsensual entries.

2. A comparison of arrest warrants with search warrants:

As with search warrants, arrest warrants, to pass the test of the Fourth Amendment, must be supported by sworn data establishing probable cause and presented to the magistrate before issuance. Whiteley v. Warden, 401 U.S. 560, 91 S.Ct. 1031 (1971); Giordenello v. United States, 357 U.S. 480, 78 S.Ct. 1245 (1958). (In many jurisdictions sworn oral testimony rather than affidavits are used to support applications for arrest warrants.) Only a neutral judicial officer can issue a constitutionally valid arrest warrant. The arrestee must be named or described with particularity. In other words, many of the doctrines discussed earlier in this chapter are applicable in arrest warrant cases.

One key difference between arrest warrants and search warrants is that search warrants go stale while arrest warrants do not necessarily do so. For example, if there is probable cause to believe X committed a crime yesterday, in the absence of new evidence, two years later there will still be the same probable cause that X committed this crime. In contrast, a search warrant requires a showing that a crime has been committed and that evidence of the crime will be found at X location. Two years later or even ten days later, the likelihood that the evidence will still be at that location is very low. Hence search warrants generally have time limits for execution. Arrest warrants do not.

3. ***Doorway Stops***. Would the analysis in *Payton* require any different result if the suspect appeared at his door in response to a police knock and the officer merely stepped across the threshold to make the arrest? See United States v. Davis, 785 F.2d 610 (8th Cir.1986) (discussing split of authority on "doorway" warrantless arrests). Compare United States v. McCraw, 920 F.2d 224 (4th Cir.1990) (fact that suspect opens door does not justify police entry) with United States v. Berkowitz, 927 F.2d 1376 (7th Cir.1991) (if suspect opens door and submits to arrest, officers can step across the threshold to complete the arrest); United States v. Vaneaton, 49 F.3d 1423 (9th Cir.1995) (same).

Can the police validly use the tactic of tricking the suspect out of his home by, for example, telling him that his parked car has been damaged by another vehicle? If not, why not, considering that in such a case, as in Watson, the police would make an arrest in a public place without intruding against the privacy of the home?

One court has approved use of some deceit. See People v. Moore, 102 Ill.App.3d 651, 57 Ill.Dec. 949, 429 N.E.2d 1312 (1981), rev'd on other grounds 95 Ill.2d 404, 69 Ill.Dec. 640, 447 N.E.2d 1327 (1983).

Some courts have even approved the tactic of ordering a suspect out of his home. Even if the consent to leave the house is not voluntary, these courts hold that there has been no *Payton* violation because there has been no warrantless entry of the home. See People v. Trudell, 173 Cal.App.3d 1221, 219 Cal.Rptr. 679 (1985) (dicta also approving use of trickery to entice suspect out of home). People v. Graves, 135 Ill.App.3d 727, 90 Ill.Dec. 516, 482 N.E.2d 223 (1985). Is part of the Fourth Amendment protection of the home rooted in the right of an individual to be left alone while in the seclusion of his or her home? Some sense of the home as a sanctuary? Or does the Fourth Amendment only protect the secrecy provided by the home?

4. ***Police Triggering an Exigency***. Can the police go to a home of a suspect without a warrant, in the absence of exigent circumstances, in the hope of obtaining consent to enter? Suppose that, when they do, some exigency arises. Perhaps the person who answers the door cries out "Police" to alert someone else to flee or to destroy evidence. Would officers be guilty of creating the exigency? For contrasting views, see the majority and the dissenting opinions in People v. Hogan, 649 P.2d 326 (Colo.1982).

5. ***Beyond the Home.*** Does *Payton* rest upon the ground that the place entered was a home? What about a suspect's place of business? What about his hotel room? See Mowrer v. State, 447 N.E.2d 1129 (Ind.App.1983). *Payton* often is said to protect a suspect's privacy not just in the home but also in a motel or hotel room. See United States v. McCraw, 920 F.2d 224 (4th Cir.1990); United States v. Forker, 928 F.2d 365 (11th Cir.1991).

What about an office? In O'Connor v. Ortega, the United States Supreme Court held that a government employee had a Fourth Amendment privacy interest in his office, but that this privacy interest may be reduced by the practice within the office allowing work-related entries. 480 U.S. 709, 107 S.Ct. 1492 (1987).

6. ***Third Party Premises.*** In Steagald v. United States, 451 U.S. 204, 101 S.Ct. 1642 (1981), with an arrest warrant federal officers entered the home of Steagald in an effort to locate and arrest Lyons. While there the officers discovered evidence which incriminated Steagald. At Steagald's trial, Steagald claimed that the government needed a search warrant to enter a third person's home in quest of a suspect, at least where there was no hot pursuit or other emergency situation. Eventually the United States Supreme Court agreed. The Court noted that when the home is that of a third-party there is a distinct interest not present when the home is that of the individual whom authorities have probable cause to arrest. An arrest warrant addresses only the interests of the purported offender and not the interests of the third-party. Thus absent exigent circumstances a neutral judicial officer must determine that there is presently probable cause to believe that the suspected offender is in the home of the third party.

Cases like Steagald do not arise with great frequency. It is not often in such situations that the officers find evidence which incriminates the third-party homeowner or tenant. If they find evidence which incriminates the non-resident arrestee, that arrestee will lack standing to complain that the officers entered the third-party's home without a search warrant. If the arrestee has enough interest in the residence to complain of the entry, he will not be in a position to argue that the officers needed a search warrant rather than an arrest warrant. In other words, he will not be afforded more protection in someone else's house than he would have in his own home.

7. ***Is Anyone Home?*** When the police enter a suspect's home without consent to arrest him, either with an arrest warrant in the non-emergency circumstances described in *Payton*, or without a warrant in exigent circumstances, they must have reason to believe that the suspect is at home. Some language in *Payton* and in *Steagald* can be read to indicate that the officers have to have probable cause to believe that the suspect is at home rather than some lesser quantum of probability. Before these decisions there was a split of authority on the question. Older cases allowing entry on a lesser quantum of probability have not been overruled in some jurisdictions. See, e.g., People v. Sprovieri, 43 Ill.2d 223, 252 N.E.2d 531 (1969). The court there reasoned that it was natural and efficient for officers to first check a suspect's home before turning the quest elsewhere. Thus the Illinois rule emerged that officers could enter the suspect's home unless they knew he was not there. Compare United States v. Phillips, 497 F.2d 1131 (9th Cir.1974). Again remember that they always must have probable cause to believe that the suspect committed a crime and, in non-exigent circumstances, they must have a valid arrest warrant.

8. ***Entry.*** Problems concerning no-knock entries and the use of force and trickery arise in the case of entries to arrest (with or without a warrant), just as they do in the case of entries to execute a search warrant. See Section D, notes 3–4. The Supreme Court in Ker v. California, 374 U.S. 23, 83 S.Ct. 1623 (1963), a five-to-four decision, permitted a no-knock entry with a passkey to effect an arrest under emergency circumstances. The Court in Wilson v. Arkansas, 514 U.S. 927, 115 S.Ct. 1914 (1995), held that a no-knock entry to effect both search and arrest warrants required a showing that "law enforcement interests ... establish the reasonableness of an unannounced entry."

3. THE DOCTRINE OF SEARCH INCIDENT TO ARREST: IS A WARRANT REQUIRED?

(a) RIGHT TO SEARCH

United States v. Robinson

Supreme Court of the United States, 1973.
414 U.S. 218, 94 S.Ct. 467.

■ JUSTICE REHNQUIST delivered the opinion of the Court.

.... On April 23, 1968, at approximately 11 o'clock p.m., Officer Richard Jenks, a 15–year veteran of the District of Columbia Metropolitan Police Department, observed the respondent driving a 1965 Cadillac near the intersection of 8th and C Streets, Southeast, in the District of Columbia. Jenks, as a result of previous investigation following a check of respondent's operator's permit four days earlier, determined there was reason to believe that respondent was operating a motor vehicle after the revocation of his operator's permit. This is an offense defined by statute in the District of Columbia which carries a mandatory minimum jail term, a mandatory minimum fine, or both.

Jenks signaled respondent to stop the automobile, which respondent did, and all three of the occupants emerged from the car. At that point Jenks informed respondent that he was under arrest for "operating after revocation and obtaining a permit by misrepresentation." It was assumed by the majority of the Court of Appeals, and is conceded by the respondent here, that Jenks had probable cause to arrest respondent, and that he effected a full custody arrest.

In accordance with procedures prescribed in Police Department instructions, Jenks then began to search respondent. He explained at a subsequent hearing that he was "face to face" with the respondent, and "placed [his] hands on [the respondent], my right hand to his left breast like this (demonstrating)and proceeded to pat him down thus (with the right hand)." During this pat down, Jenks felt an object in the left breast pocket of the heavy coat respondent was wearing, but testified that he "couldn't tell what it was" and also that he "couldn't actually tell the size of it." Jenks then reached into the pocket and pulled out the object, which turned out to be a "crumpled up cigarette package." Jenks testified that at this point he still did not know what was in the package:

> "As I felt the package I could feel objects in the package but I couldn't tell what they were ... I knew they weren't cigarettes."

The officer then opened the cigarette pack and found 14 gelatin capsules of white powder which he thought to be, and which later analysis proved to be, heroin. Jenks then continued his search of respondent to completion, feeling around his waist and trouser legs, and examining the remaining pockets. The heroin seized from the respondent was admitted into evidence at the trial which resulted in his conviction in the District Court....

It is well settled that a search incident to a lawful arrest is a traditional exception to the warrant requirement of the Fourth Amendment. This general exception has historically been formulated into two distinct propositions. The first is that a search may be made of the person of the arrestee by virtue of the lawful arrest. The second is that a search may be made of the area within the control of the arrestee.

Examination of this Court's decisions in the area show that these two propositions have been treated quite differently. The validity of the search of a person incident to a lawful arrest has been regarded as settled from its first enunciation, and has remained virtually unchallenged until the present case. The validity of the second proposition, while likewise conceded in principle, has been subject to differing interpretations as to the extent of the area which may be searched.

Because the rule requiring exclusion of evidence obtained in violation of the Fourth Amendment was first enunciated in Weeks v. United States (1914), it is understandable that virtually all of this Court's search and seizure law has been developed since that time....

In its decision of this case, the majority of the Court of Appeals decided that even after a police officer lawfully places a suspect under arrest for the purpose of taking him into custody, he may not ordinarily proceed to fully search the prisoner. He must instead conduct a limited frisk of the outer clothing and remove such weapons that he may, as a result of that limited frisk, reasonably believe the suspect has in his possession. While recognizing that Terry v. Ohio (1968) [to be reported in the next section of this chapter], dealt with a permissible "frisk" incident to an investigative stop based on less than probable cause to arrest, the Court of Appeals felt that the principles of that case should be carried over to this probable cause arrest for driving while one's license is revoked. Since there would be no further evidence of such a crime to be obtained in a search of the arrestee, the Court held that only a search for weapons could be justified....

[Although] earlier authorities are sketchy, they tend to support the broad statement of the authority to search incident to arrest found in the successive decisions of this Court, rather than the restrictive one which was applied by the Court of Appeals in this case. The scarcity of case law before Weeks is doubtless due in part to the fact that the exclusionary rule there enunciated had been first adopted only 11 years earlier in Iowa; but it would seem to be also due in part to the fact that the issue was regarded as well-settled.

The Court of Appeals in effect determined that the only reason supporting the authority for a *full* search incident to lawful arrest was the possibility of discovery of evidence or fruits. Concluding that there could be no evidence or fruits in the case of an offense such as that with which respondent was charged, it held that any protective search would have to be limited by the conditions laid down in *Terry* for a search upon less than probable cause to arrest. Quite apart from the fact that *Terry* clearly recognized the distinction between the two types of searches, and that a different rule governed one than governed the other, we find additional reason to disagree with the Court of Appeals.

The justification or reason for the authority to search incident to a lawful arrest rests quite as much on the need to disarm the suspect in order to take him into custody as it does on the need to preserve evidence on his person for later use at trial. The standards traditionally governing a search incident to lawful arrest are not, therefore, commuted to the stricter *Terry* standards by the absence of probable fruits or further evidence of the particular crime for which the arrest is made.

Nor are we inclined, on the basis of what seems to us to be a rather speculative judgment, to qualify the breadth of the general authority to search incident to a lawful custodial arrest on an assumption that persons arrested for the offense of driving while their license has been revoked are less likely to be possessed of dangerous weapons than are those arrested for other crimes.[1] It is scarcely open to doubt that the danger to an officer is far greater in the case of the extended exposure which follows the taking of a suspect into custody and transporting him to the police station than in the case of the relatively fleeting contact resulting from the typical *Terry*

1. Such an assumption appears at least questionable in light of the available statistical data concerning assaults on police officers who are in the course of making arrests. The danger to the police officer flows from the fact of the arrest, and its attendant proximity, stress and uncertainty, and not from the grounds for arrest. One study concludes that approximately 30% of the shootings of police officers occur when the officer approaches a person seated in a car. Bristow Police Officer Shootings—A Factual Evaluation, 54 J.Crim. L.C. & P.S. 93 (1963), cited in Adams v. Williams, 407 U.S. 143, 148 (1972). The Government in its brief notes that the Uniform Crime Reports, prepared by the Federal Bureau of Investigation, indicate that a significant percentage of police officer murders occur when the officers are making traffic stops. Those reports indicate that during January–March, 1973, 35 police officers were murdered; 11 of those officers were killed while engaged in traffic stops.

[v. Ohio (1968)]. This is an adequate basis for treating all custodial arrests alike for purposes of search justification.

But quite apart from these distinctions, our more fundamental disagreement with the Court of Appeals arises from its suggestion that there must be litigated in each case the issue of whether or not there was present one of the reasons supporting the authority for a search of the person incident to a lawful arrest. We do not think the long line of authorities of this Court dating back to Weeks, nor what we can glean from the history of practice in this country and in England, requires such a case by case adjudication. A police officer's determination as to how and where to search the person of a suspect whom he has arrested is necessarily a quick ad hoc judgment which the Fourth Amendment does not require to be broken down in each instance into an analysis of each step in the search. The authority to search the person incident to a lawful custodial arrest while based upon the need to disarm and to discover evidence, does not depend on what a court may later decide was the probability in a particular arrest situation that weapons or evidence would in fact be found upon the person of the suspect. A custodial arrest of a suspect based on probable cause is a reasonable intrusion under the Fourth Amendment; that intrusion being lawful, a search incident to the arrest requires no additional justification. It is the fact of the lawful arrest which establishes the authority to search, and we hold that in the case of a lawful custodial arrest a full search of the person is not only an exception to the warrant requirement of the Fourth Amendment, but is also a "reasonable" search under that Amendment....

■ The concurring opinion of JUSTICE POWELL is omitted.

■ JUSTICE MARSHALL, with whom JUSTICE DOUGLAS and JUSTICE BRENNAN join, dissenting.

Certain fundamental principles have characterized this Court's Fourth Amendment jurisprudence over the years. Perhaps the most basic of these was expressed by Mr. Justice Butler, speaking for a unanimous Court in Go–Bart Co. v. United States, 282 U.S. 344 (1931): "There is no formula for the determination of reasonableness. Each case is to be decided on its own facts and circumstances." As we recently held, "The constitutional validity of a warrantless search is preeminently the sort of question which can only be decided in the concrete factual context of the individual case." Sibron v. New York, 392 U.S. 40, 59 (1968). And the intensive, at times painstaking, case by case analysis characteristic of our Fourth Amendment decisions bespeaks our "jealous regard for maintaining the integrity of individual rights." Mapp v. Ohio, 367 U.S. 643, 647 (1961).

In the present case, however, the majority turns its back on these principles, holding that "the fact of the lawful arrest" always establishes the authority to conduct a full search of the arrestee's person, regardless of whether in a particular case "there was present one of the reasons supporting the authority for a search of the person incident to a lawful arrest." The majority's approach represents a clear and marked departure from our long tradition of case-by-case adjudication of the reasonableness of searches and seizures under the Fourth Amendment. I continue to believe that "[t]he scheme of the Fourth Amendment becomes meaningful only when it is assured that at some point the conduct of those charged with enforcing the laws can be subjected to the more detached, neutral scrutiny of a judge who must evaluate the reasonableness of a particular search or seizure in light of the particular circumstances." Terry v. Ohio. Because I find the majority's reasoning to be at odds with these fundamental principles, I must respectfully dissent....

The majority's attempt to avoid case-by-case adjudication of Fourth Amendment issues is not only misguided as a matter of principle, but is also doomed to fail as a matter of practical application. As the majority itself is well aware, the powers granted the police in this case are strong ones, subject to potential abuse. Although, in this particular case, Officer Jenks was required by Police Department regulation to make an in-custody arrest rather than to issue a citation, in most jurisdictions and for most traffic offenses the determination of whether to issue a citation or effect a full arrest is discretionary with the officer. There is always the possibility that a police officer, lacking probable cause to obtain a search warrant, will use a traffic arrest as a pretext to conduct a search. I suggest this possibility not to impugn the integrity of our police, but merely to point out that case-by-case adjudication will always be necessary to determine whether a full arrest was effected for purely legitimate reasons or, rather, as a pretext for searching the arrestee....

NOTES

1. In the companion case of Gustafson v. Florida, 414 U.S. 260, 94 S.Ct. 488 (1973), the Supreme Court issued the following ruling (with the same three Justices dissenting as in *Robinson*):

> We hold that upon arresting petitioner for the offense of driving his automobile without a valid operator's license, and taking him into custody, Smith was entitled to make a full search of petitioner's person incident to that lawful arrest. Since it is the fact of custodial arrest which gives rise to the authority to search, it is of no moment that Smith did not indicate any subjective fear of the petitioner or that he did not himself suspect that the petitioner was armed. Having in the course of his lawful search come upon the box of cigarettes, Smith was entitled to inspect it; and when his inspection revealed the homemade cigarettes which he believed to contain an unlawful substance, he was entitled to seize them as "fruits, instrumentalities or contraband" probative of criminal conduct.

2. Several state courts, utilizing state constitutions, invalidated on state grounds searches which under Robinson comport with the Fourth Amendment. They did so in traffic cases and in cases involving other minor offenses, where a search of the arrestee is unlikely to produce "fruits" or evidence of the offense. See, e.g., State v. Caraher, 293 Or. 741, 653 P.2d 942 (1982). Such state decisions also frequently involve a situation where, although the arrest is "custodial," the suspect will be able to secure his release pending trial without ever going through complete "booking" procedures or being confined in a lock-up or jail. See e.g., Zehrung v. State, 569 P.2d 189 (Alaska 1977), mod. on reh'g, 573 P.2d 858 (1978).

B) PRETEXT: The power to arrest without warrant for misdemeanors committed in an officer's presence includes the power to stop a moving vehicle for a traffic violation. Some police officers have used traffic stops as pretexts for stopping cars they suspect may contain contraband. If the officer seizes the individual as a pretext to conduct a search incident to arrest to find evidence of an additional crime, should that additional evidence be suppressed?

Whren v. United States

Supreme Court of the United States, 1996.
517 U.S. 806, 116 S.Ct. 1769.

■ SCALIA, J., delivered the opinion for a unanimous Court.

In this case we decide whether the temporary detention of a motorist who the police have probable cause to believe has committed a civil traffic violation is inconsistent with the Fourth Amendment's prohibition against unreasonable seizures unless a reasonable officer would have been motivated to stop the car by a desire to enforce the traffic laws.

I

On the evening of June 10, 1993, plainclothes vice-squad officers of the District of Columbia Metropolitan Police Department were patrolling a "high drug area" of the city in an unmarked car. Their suspicions were aroused when they passed a dark Pathfinder truck with temporary license plates and youthful occupants waiting at a stop sign, the driver looking down into the lap of the passenger at his right. The truck remained stopped at the intersection for what seemed an unusually long time—more than 20 seconds. When the police car executed a U-turn in order to head back toward the truck, the Pathfinder turned suddenly to its right, without signaling, and sped off at an "unreasonable" speed. The policemen followed, and in a short while overtook the Pathfinder when it stopped behind other traffic at a red light. They pulled up alongside, and Officer Ephraim Soto stepped out and approached the driver's door, identifying himself as a police officer and directing the driver, petitioner Brown, to put the vehicle in park. When Soto drew up to the driver's window, he immediately observed two large plastic bags of what appeared to be crack cocaine in petitioner Whren's hands. Petitioners were arrested, and quantities of several types of illegal drugs were retrieved from the vehicle.

Petitioners were charged in a four-count indictment with violating various federal drug laws, including 21 U.S.C. §§ 844(a) and 860(a). At a pretrial suppression hearing, they challenged the legality of the stop and the resulting seizure of the drugs. They argued that the stop had not been justified by probable cause to believe, or even reasonable suspicion, that petitioners were engaged in illegal drug-dealing activity; and that Officer Soto's asserted ground for approaching the vehicle—to give the driver a warning concerning traffic violations—was pretextual. The District Court denied the suppression motion, concluding that "the facts of the stop were not controverted," and "there was nothing to really demonstrate that the actions of the officers were contrary to a normal traffic stop."

Petitioners were convicted of the counts at issue here. The Court of Appeals affirmed the convictions, holding with respect to the suppression issue that, "regardless of whether a police officer subjectively believes that the occupants of an automobile may be engaging in some other illegal behavior, a traffic stop is permissible as long as a reasonable officer in the same circumstances *could have* stopped the car for the suspected traffic violation." (cites omitted) We granted certiorari.

II

... Temporary detention of individuals during the stop of an automobile by the police, even if only for a brief period and for a limited purpose, constitutes a "seizure" of "persons" within the meaning of this provision. An automobile stop is thus subject to the constitutional imperative that it not be "unreasonable" under the circumstances. As a general matter, the decision to stop an automobile is reasonable where the police have probable cause to believe that a traffic violation has occurred.

Petitioners accept that Officer Soto had probable cause to believe that various provisions of the District of Columbia traffic code had been violated.... They argue, however, that "in the unique context of civil traffic regulations" probable cause is not enough. Since, they contend, the use of automobiles is so heavily and minutely regulated that total compliance with traffic and safety rules is nearly impossible, a police officer will almost invariably be able to catch any given motorist in a technical violation. This creates the temptation to use traffic stops as a means of investigating other law violations, as to which no probable cause or even articulable suspicion exists. Petitioners, who are both black, further contend that police officers might decide which motorists to stop based on decidedly impermissible factors, such as the race of the car's occupants. To avoid this danger, they say, the Fourth Amendment test for traffic stops should be, not the normal one (applied by the Court of Appeals) of whether probable cause existed to justify the stop; but rather, whether a police officer, acting reasonably, would have made the stop for the reason given.

A

Petitioners contend that the standard they propose is consistent with our past cases' disapproval of police attempts to use valid bases of action against citizens as pretexts for pursuing other investigatory agendas. We are reminded that in Florida v. Wells (1990), we stated that "an inventory search[1] must not be a ruse for a general rummaging in order to discover incriminating evidence"; that in Colorado v. Bertine (1987), in approving an inventory search, we apparently thought it significant that there had been "no showing that the police, who were following standardized procedures, acted in bad faith or for the sole purpose of investigation"; and that in New York v. Burger (1987), we observed, in upholding the constitutionality of a warrantless administrative inspection,[2] that the search did not appear to be "a 'pretext' for obtaining evidence of ... violation of ... penal laws." But only an undiscerning reader would regard these cases as

1. An inventory search is the search of property lawfully seized and detained, in order to ensure that it is harmless, to secure valuable items (such as might be kept in a towed car), and to protect against false claims of loss or damage. See South Dakota v. Opperman (1976).

2. An administrative inspection is the inspection of business premises conducted by authorities responsible for enforcing a pervasive regulatory scheme—for example, unannounced inspection of a mine for compliance with health and safety standards. See *Donovan v. Dewey* (1981).

endorsing the principle that ulterior motives can invalidate police conduct that is justifiable on the basis of probable cause to believe that a violation of law has occurred. In each case we were addressing the validity of a search conducted in the *absence* of probable cause. Our quoted statements simply explain that the exemption from the need for probable cause (and warrant), which is accorded to searches made for the purpose of inventory or administrative regulation, is not accorded to searches that are *not* made for those purposes.

. . .

We think these cases foreclose any argument that the constitutional reasonableness of traffic stops depends on the actual motivations of the individual officers involved. We of course agree with petitioners that the Constitution prohibits selective enforcement of the law based on considerations such as race. But the constitutional basis for objecting to intentionally discriminatory application of laws is the Equal Protection Clause, not the Fourth Amendment. Subjective intentions play no role in ordinary, probable-cause Fourth Amendment analysis.

B

Recognizing that we have been unwilling to entertain Fourth Amendment challenges based on the actual motivations of individual officers, petitioners disavow any intention to make the individual officer's subjective good faith the touchstone of "reasonableness." They insist that the standard they have put forward—whether the officer's conduct deviated materially from usual police practices, so that a reasonable officer in the same circumstances would not have made the stop for the reasons given—is an "objective" one.

But although framed in empirical terms, this approach is plainly and indisputably driven by subjective considerations. Its whole purpose is to prevent the police from doing under the guise of enforcing the traffic code what they would like to do for different reasons. Petitioners' proposed standard may not use the word "pretext," but it is designed to combat nothing other than the perceived "danger" of the pretextual stop, albeit only indirectly and over the run of cases. Instead of asking whether the individual officer had the proper state of mind, the petitioners would have us ask, in effect, whether (based on general police practices) it is plausible to believe that the officer had the proper state of mind.

Why one would frame a test designed to combat pretext in such fashion that the court cannot take into account *actual and admitted pretext* is a curiosity that can only be explained by the fact that our cases have foreclosed the more sensible option. If those cases were based only upon the evidentiary difficulty of establishing subjective intent, petitioners' attempt to root out subjective vices through objective means might make sense. But they were not based only upon that, or indeed even principally upon that. Their principal basis—which applies equally to attempts to reach subjective intent through ostensibly objective means—is simply that the Fourth Amendment's concern with "reasonableness" allows certain actions to be taken in certain circumstances, *whatever* the subjective intent. See, *e.g.*,

Robinson, supra, at 236 ("Since it is the fact of custodial arrest which gives rise to the authority to search, it is of no moment that [the officer] did not indicate any subjective fear of the [arrestee] or that he did not himself suspect that [the arrestee] was armed") (footnotes omitted) . . . But even if our concern had been only an evidentiary one, petitioners' proposal would by no means assuage it. Indeed, it seems to us somewhat easier to figure out the intent of an individual officer than to plumb the collective consciousness of law enforcement in order to determine whether a "reasonable officer" would have been moved to act upon the traffic violation. While police manuals and standard procedures may sometimes provide objective assistance, ordinarily one would be reduced to speculating about the hypothetical reaction of a hypothetical constable—an exercise that might be called virtual subjectivity.

Moreover, police enforcement practices, even if they could be practicably assessed by a judge, vary from place to place and from time to time. We cannot accept that the search and seizure protections of the Fourth Amendment are so variable, cf. *Gustafson*; United States v. Caceres (1979), and can be made to turn upon such trivialities. The difficulty is illustrated by petitioners' arguments in this case. Their claim that a reasonable officer would not have made this stop is based largely on District of Columbia police regulations which permit plainclothes officers in unmarked vehicles to enforce traffic laws "only in the case of a violation that is so grave as to pose an *immediate threat* to the safety of others." This basis of invalidation would not apply in jurisdictions that had a different practice. And it would not have applied even in the District of Columbia, if Officer Soto had been wearing a uniform or patrolling in a marked police cruiser.

Petitioners argue that our cases support insistence upon police adherence to standard practices as an objective means of rooting out pretext. They cite no holding to that effect, and dicta in only two cases. In Abel v. United States (1960), the petitioner had been arrested by the Immigration and Naturalization Service (INS), on the basis of an administrative warrant that, he claimed, had been issued on pretextual grounds in order to enable the Federal Bureau of Investigation (FBI) to search his room after his arrest. We regarded this as an allegation of "serious misconduct," but rejected Abel's claims on the ground that "[a] finding of bad faith is . . . not open to us on th[e] record" in light of the findings below, including the finding that " 'the proceedings taken by the [INS] differed in no respect from what would have been done in the case of an individual concerning whom [there was no pending FBI investigation].' " But it is a long leap from the proposition that following regular procedures is some evidence of lack of pretext to the proposition that failure to follow regular procedures *proves* (or is an operational substitute for) pretext. *Abel*, moreover, did not involve the assertion that pretext could invalidate a search or seizure for which there was probable cause—and even what it said about pretext in other contexts is plainly inconsistent with the views we later stated in *Robinson, Gustafson, Scott,* and *Villamonte-Marquez*. In the other case claimed to contain supportive dicta, United States v. Robinson (1973), in approving a search incident to an arrest for driving without a license, we noted that the arrest was "not a departure from established police department practice."

That was followed, however, by the statement that "we leave for another day questions which would arise on facts different from these." This is not even a dictum that purports to provide an answer, but merely one that leaves the question open.

III

In what would appear to be an elaboration on the "reasonable officer" test, petitioners argue that the balancing inherent in any Fourth Amendment inquiry requires us to weigh the governmental and individual interests implicated in a traffic stop such as we have here. That balancing, petitioners claim, does not support investigation of minor traffic infractions by plainclothes police in unmarked vehicles; such investigation only minimally advances the government's interest in traffic safety, and may indeed retard it by producing motorist confusion and alarm—a view said to be supported by the Metropolitan Police Department's own regulations generally prohibiting this practice. And as for the Fourth Amendment interests of the individuals concerned, petitioners point out that our cases acknowledge that even ordinary traffic stops entail "a possibly unsettling show of authority"; that they at best "interfere with freedom of movement, are inconvenient, and consume time" and at worst "may create substantial anxiety," *Prouse*. That anxiety is likely to be even more pronounced when the stop is conducted by plainclothes officers in unmarked cars.

It is of course true that in principle every Fourth Amendment case, since it turns upon a "reasonableness" determination, involves a balancing of all relevant factors. With rare exceptions not applicable here, however, the result of that balancing is not in doubt where the search or seizure is based upon probable cause. That is why petitioners must rely upon cases like *Prouse* to provide examples of actual "balancing" analysis. There, the police action in question was a random traffic stop for the purpose of checking a motorist's license and vehicle registration, a practice that—like the practices at issue in the inventory search and administrative inspection cases upon which petitioners rely in making their "pretext" claim—involves police intrusion *without the probable cause that is its traditional justification*. Our opinion in *Prouse* expressly distinguished the case from a stop based on precisely what is at issue here: "probable cause to believe that a driver is violating any one of the multitude of applicable traffic and equipment regulations." It noted approvingly that "the foremost method of enforcing traffic and vehicle safety regulations ... is acting upon observed violations," which afford the " 'quantum of individualized suspicion' " necessary to ensure that police discretion is sufficiently constrained. What is true of *Prouse* is also true of other cases that engaged in detailed "balancing" to decide the constitutionality of automobile stops, such as *Martinez-Fuerte*, which upheld checkpoint stops and *Brignoni-Ponce*, which disallowed so-called "roving patrol" stops: The detailed "balancing" analysis was necessary because they involved seizures without probable cause.

Where probable cause has existed, the only cases in which we have found it necessary actually to perform the "balancing" analysis involved searches or seizures conducted in an extraordinary manner, unusually harmful to an individual's privacy or even physical interests—such as, for example, seizure by means of deadly force, see Tennessee v. Garner (1985), unannounced entry into a home, see Wilson v. Arkansas (1995), entry into a home without a warrant, see Welsh v. Wisconsin (1984), or physical penetration of the body, see *Winston v. Lee* (1985). The making of a traffic stop out of uniform does not remotely qualify as such an extreme practice, and so is governed by the usual rule that probable cause to believe the law has been broken "outbalances" private interest in avoiding police contact.

Petitioners urge as an extraordinary factor in this case that the "multitude of applicable traffic and equipment regulations" is so large and so difficult to obey perfectly that virtually everyone is guilty of violation, permitting the police to single out almost whomever they wish for a stop. But we are aware of no principle that would allow us to decide at what point a code of law becomes so expansive and so commonly violated that infraction itself can no longer be the ordinary measure of the lawfulness of enforcement. And even if we could identify such exorbitant codes, we do not know by what standard (or what right) we would decide, as petitioners would have us do, which particular provisions are sufficiently important to merit enforcement.

For the run-of-the-mine case, which this surely is, we think there is no realistic alternative to the traditional common-law rule that probable cause justifies a search and seizure.

* * *

Here the District Court found that the officers had probable cause to believe that petitioners had violated the traffic code. That rendered the stop reasonable under the Fourth Amendment, the evidence thereby discovered admissible, and the upholding of the convictions by the Court of Appeals for the District of Columbia Circuit correct. The judgment is

Affirmed.

Beyond the Traffic Stop Context: When federal prosecutors declined to seek a search warrant for the defendant's home, an enterprising ATF agent got an arrest warrant for defendant for a minor drug offense through the state's attorney's office. He then searched areas of defendant's house incident to the arrest, finding drug manufacturing equipment. The Ninth Circuit panel, with Judge Reinhardt in dissent, held that *Whren* eliminated any inquiry into pretext. United States v. Hudson, 100 F.3d 1409 (9th Cir.1996). Judge Reinhardt would have invalidated the search on the ground that: "without regard to the officers' motives in this case . . . the overwhelmingly intrusive manner in which federal agents used their federal authority to arrest Hudson on a state charge and to collect evidence regarding a federal offense was unreasonable and therefore unconstitutional."

(b) REQUIREMENT OF PROXIMITY TO ARREST

Search Before Arrest. A search incident to arrest must, in time and place, be substantially proximate to arrest. If a search precedes the arrest by any significant span of time, it cannot be considered incident thereto. However, as long as probable cause to arrest exists before the search, the search, in the interest of the officer's safety, may slightly precede the formal arrest. See the concurring opinion of Justice Harlan in Sibron v. New York, 392 U.S. 40, 88 S.Ct. 1889 (1968).

Search After Arrest: Delayed and Second Searches. As discussed in the next subsection, searches incident to arrest include (a) searches of the arrestee's person, and (b) searches of the place within his reaching distance at the time of his arrest. With respect to the first type of search, the requirement that the search be substantially contemporaneous with the arrest has not been applied rigorously. Thus searches of the suspect conducted while he is being transported to the police station have been upheld, as have been searches of the arrestee at the police station, even when such searches are "second searches." See generally State v. Wiley, 522 S.W.2d 281 (Mo.1975); People v. Garrett, 49 Ill.App.2d 296, 200 N.E.2d 7 (1964). Compare People v. Dixon, 392 Mich. 691, 222 N.W.2d 749 (1974); People v. Bowen, 29 Ill.2d 349, 194 N.E.2d 316 (1963).

In United States v. Edwards, 415 U.S. 800, 94 S.Ct. 1234 (1974), a suspect's clothes were confiscated 12 hours after his arrest at a time when he was in jail. The Supreme Court upheld this procedure. One way of looking at the decision is to say that the requirement of contemporaneity has been made meaningless. A different view is that the Court did not use the traditional search-incident analysis, but instead, concluded that the search was reasonable under all the circumstances even if no well-recognized category precisely fit the case.

After an arrestee has been removed from a place, search of that place ordinarily may not be justified as incident to the arrest. Preston v. United States, 376 U.S. 364, 84 S.Ct. 881 (1964). Thus removing a suspect from his home may terminate an officer's right to search even the area of the home which could have been properly searched within the spatial limits of *Chimel*, discussed in the next subsection. Note, however, the *Belton* case below where a search of the interior of a car was validated as a search incident to arrest, notwithstanding the fact that the suspect had been removed from the car.

(c) SCOPE AND INTENSITY OF THE SEARCH

The Arrestee's Person. A person who is subjected to a lawful arrest can be searched even if there is no reason to expect contraband, evidence, or weapons to be on her person. Probable cause, or even reasonable suspicion, is not required. Courts, however, have generally required that more intrusive searches, such as strip searches and body cavity inspections, be based on individualized suspicion (either a *Terry*-stop standard of reasonable suspicion, or, in some jurisdictions, probable cause). See Mary Beth G. v. City of Chicago, 723 F.2d 1263 (7th Cir.1983); Fuller v. M.G. Jewelry, 950 F.2d 1437 (9th Cir.1991); Swain v. Spinney, 117 F.3d 1 (1st Cir.1997).

Beyond the Arrestee's Person. As the Supreme Court held in Chimel v. California, 395 U.S. 752, 89 S.Ct. 2034 (1969), a search incident to arrest may not exceed the area within reach of the arrestee. This limitation was said to be consonant with the rationale of the doctrine of search incident to arrest: the need to prevent the arrestee from obtaining a weapon to use against the arrestee and the need to prevent him from destroying evidence. By looking to the rationale of the rule, the Court finally resolved an issue which had seen the Court reverse its position no less than five times concerning the proper scope of a search incident to arrest. The reversals of position are treated candidly in *Chimel* and also are the subject of an excellent discussion in Moylan, The Plain View Doctrine: Unexpected Child of the Great "Search Incident," Geography Battle, 26 Mercer L.Rev. 1047 (1975). Chimel worked a radical change in the law because in the era immediately preceding that decision, following the Supreme Court lead, lower courts routinely deemed "reasonable," searches, for example, of the entire house in which a person was arrested.

Naturally some fine lines are drawn in determining the perimeter of searches permitted by *Chimel*. Concerning search of an area to which the suspect might possibly "lunge," see Application of Kiser, 419 F.2d 1134 (8th Cir.1969), and compare United States v. Mapp, 476 F.2d 67 (2d Cir.1973). Suppose that the danger of an arrestee's reaching out for a weapon or evidence has been limited by the handcuffing of the arrestee. Has the officer lost the right to search the area which was within reach at the time of the arrest? See United States v. Sholola, 124 F.3d 803 (7th Cir.1997) (no citing like cases from the 6th, 10th, and 8th Circuits); United States v. Abdul–Saboor, 85 F.3d 664 (D.C.Cir.1996) (no citing like cases from the 4th, 11th, and 3rd circuits). Compare United States v. Blue, 78 F.3d 56 (2d Cir.1996) (no likelihood cuffed suspect could reach where officers found firearm).

The police cannot move the suspect from place to place within a home to broaden the area of the permissible search under *Chimel*. United States v. Griffith, 537 F.2d 900 (7th Cir.1976). Decisions which permit the police to allow or direct the arrestee to go from place to place to gather clothing or identification preparatory to the trip to the station seem to lay the groundwork for rather crude tactics designed to broaden the area which is "within reach" of the arrestee. Naturally, however, the officer can follow the arrestee as the arrestee looks in closets or drawers. People v. Mancl, 55 Ill.App.3d 41, 12 Ill.Dec. 860, 370 N.E.2d 664 (1977).

SECURITY SWEEPS: An expansion of the scope of the search incident to arrest? Or a narrow exception based on exigency?

In Maryland v. Buie, 494 U.S. 325, 110 S.Ct. 1093 (1990), the Court upheld the concept of a protective sweep. For the majority, Justice White wrote:

> A "protective sweep" is a quick and limited search of a premises, incident to an arrest and conducted to protect the safety of police officers or others. It is narrowly confined to a cursory visual inspection of those places in which a person might be hiding....

We should emphasize that such a protective sweep, aimed at protecting the arresting officers, if justified by the circumstances, is nevertheless not a full search of the premises, but may extend only to a cursory inspection of those spaces where a person may be found. The sweep lasts no longer than is necessary to dispel the reasonable suspicion of danger and in any event no longer than it takes to complete the arrest and depart the premises....

The type of search we authorize today is far removed from the "top-to-bottom" search involved in *Chimel*; moreover, it is decidedly not "automati[c]," but may be conducted only when justified by a reasonable, articulable suspicion that the house is harboring a person posing a danger to those on the arrest scene.

We conclude that by requiring a protective sweep to be justified by probable cause to believe that a serious and demonstrable potentiality for danger existed, the Court of Appeals of Maryland applied an unnecessarily strict Fourth Amendment standard. The Fourth Amendment permits a properly limited protective sweep in conjunction with an in-home arrest when the searching officer possesses a reasonable belief based on specific and articulable facts that the area to be swept harbors an individual posing a danger to those on the arrest scene.

In a concurring opinion, Justice Stevens contended that the fact that someone may be hiding in the house, even a confederate of the arrestee, will not justify a protective sweep. He suggested, for example, that guarding a door leading to a basement might be a better way of ensuring police safety than would "sweeping" the basement. He insisted that the police must demonstrate that the sweep is truly necessary for protection.

Two dissenters argued that "police officers must have probable cause to fear that their personal safety is threatened by a hidden confederate of an arrestee before they may sweep through the entire home."

D. THE EXPANSION OF THE SCOPE OF A SEARCH INCIDENT TO ARREST IN THE CONTEXT OF AN AUTOMOBILE SEARCH

The Arrestee's Immediate Effects. In New York v. Belton, 453 U.S. 454, 101 S.Ct. 2860 (1981) the Supreme Court modified the "within reach" test of *Chimel* in situations where the search is incident to an arrest of a motor vehicle driver or passenger. A lone state trooper stopped a car for speeding. When he asked for the license and registration of the driver, he discovered that none of the occupants in the car owned the vehicle. He smelled burnt marijuana and saw an envelope on the floor of the car with the word "Supergold" which led him to believe there was marijuana in the car. He directed the occupants to leave the car and placed them under arrest. He searched each one. In addition, he searched the passenger compartment of the car, including Belton's black leather jacket on the backseat of the car. He found cocaine in the pocket. The Court stated:

> Our reading of the cases suggests the generalization that articles inside the relatively narrow compass of the passenger compartment of an automobile are in fact generally, even if not inevitably, within "the area into which an arrestee might reach in order to grab a weapon or evidentiary item." *Chimel*. In order to establish the workable rule this category of cases requires, we read Chimel's definition of the limits of the area that may be searched in light of that generalization. Accordingly, we hold that when a policeman has made a lawful custodial arrest of the occupant of an

automobile, he may, as a contemporaneous incident of that arrest, search the passenger compartment of that automobile.

The Court stated that open or closed containers found in the interior of a vehicle within the scope of a proper search incident to arrest can be searched without a warrant and without probable cause. The Court declared:

> Such a container may, of course, be searched whether it is open or closed, since the justification for the search is not that the arrestee has no privacy interest in the container, but that the lawful custodial arrest justifies the infringement of any privacy interest the arrestee may have. Thus, while the Court in *Chimel* held that the police could not search all the drawers in an arrestee's house simply because the police had arrested him at home, the Court noted that drawers within an arrestee's reach could be searched because of the danger their contents might pose to the police.
>
> It is true, of course, that these containers will sometimes be such that they could hold neither a weapon nor evidence of the criminal conduct for which the suspect was arrested. However, in United States v. Robinson, the Court rejected the argument that such a container "there a 'crumpled up cigarette package' " located during a search of Robinson incident to his arrest could not be searched: "The authority to search the person incident to a lawful custodial arrest, while based upon the need to disarm and to discover evidence, does not depend on what a court may later decide was the probability in a particular arrest situation that weapons or evidence would in fact be found upon the person of the suspect. A custodial arrest of a suspect based on probable cause is a reasonable intrusion under the Fourth Amendment; that intrusion being lawful, a search incident to the arrest requires no additional justification."
>
> ... *United States v. Chadwick* ... [did not involve] an arguably valid search incident to a lawful custodial arrest. As the Court pointed out in the *Chadwick* case, "Here the search was conducted more than an hour after federal agents had gained exclusive control of the footlocker and long after respondents were securely in custody; the search therefore cannot be viewed as incidental to the arrest or as justified by any other exigency."

The dissent responded:

... The Court's new approach leaves open too many questions and, more important, it provides the police and the courts with too few tools with which to find the answers.

Thus, although the Court concludes that a warrantless search of a car may take place even though the suspect was arrested outside the car, it does not indicate how long after the suspect's arrest that search may validly be conducted. Would a warrantless search incident to arrest be valid if conducted five minutes after the suspect left his car? Thirty minutes? Three hours? Does it matter whether the suspect is standing in close proximity to the car when the search is conducted? Does it matter whether the police formed probable cause to arrest before or after the suspect left his car? And why is the rule announced today necessarily limited to searches of cars? What if a suspect is seen walking out of a house where the police, peering in from outside, had formed probable cause to believe a crime was being committed? Could the police then arrest that suspect and enter the house to conduct a search incident to arrest? Even assuming today's rule is limited to searches of the "interior" of cars—an assumption not demanded by logic—what is meant by "interior"? Does it include locked glove compartments, the interior of door panels, or the area under the floorboards? Are special rules necessary for station wagons and hatchbacks, where the luggage compartment may be reached through the interior, or taxicabs, where a glass panel might separate the driver's compartment from the rest of the car? Are the only containers that may be searched those that are large enough to be "capable of holding another object"? Or does the new rule apply to any container, even if it "could hold neither a weapon nor evidence of the criminal conduct for which the suspect was arrested"?

> The Court does not give the police any "bright line" answers to these questions. More important, because the Court's new rule abandons the justifications underlying *Chimel, it offers no guidance to the police officer seeking to work out these answers for himself.* As we warned in *Chimel*, "No consideration relevant to the Fourth Amendment suggests any point of rational limitation, once the search is allowed to go beyond the area from which the person arrested might obtain weapons or evidentiary items."

State v. Massenburg, 66 N.C.App. 127, 310 S.E.2d 619 (1984), provided an answer to one question raised by the *Belton* dissent. The North Carolina court held that officers can search a locked glove compartment in a search incident to the arrest of a driver or passenger. The First Circuit answered another of these questions, allowing a search of a hatch area of a hatchback incident to arrest of the driver. United States v. Doward, 41 F.3d 789 (1st Cir.1994).

Courts have applied *Belton* to searches of containers in other search-incident situations. Most courts have said that under *Belton*, for example, officers can search containers found within reach of someone lawfully arrested on a public street or in his own home. See Savoie v. State, 422 So.2d 308 (Fla.1982); People v. Smith, 89 A.D.2d 549, 452 N.Y.S.2d 886 (1982). Would this apply to any container within reach? A suitcase? A large box?

Special Rules for Searches Beyond the Person of Motor Vehicle Driver or Passenger Arrestees.

In Maryland v. Wilson, 519 U.S. 408, 117 S.Ct. 882 (1997), the Court held that passengers may be routinely ordered out of the car at a traffic stop in order to protect officers from danger. Should police be permitted to search the passengers as part of a search incident to arrest because they have probable cause to arrest the driver? Drivers in the company of arrested passengers?

Can a police officer make a custodial arrest for a minor traffic violation as a pretext to search a suspicious car for drugs? Courts have held that under *Belton*, an officer may arrest for a misdemeanor committed in her presence, even though police procedures do not call for a full custodial arrest, and then may search the car incident to the arrest. United States v. Franklin, 728 F.2d 994 (8th Cir.1984) (the court found, however, that the arrest was not a pretext to search). And, the Supreme Court has held that inquiry into pretext is not appropriate or workable when a traffic stop is supported by probable cause (or reasonable suspicion under Terry v. Ohio, see infra Casebook Section K). As noted in Whren v. United States, 517 U.S. 806, 116 S.Ct. 1769 (1996), the Supreme Court resolved a circuit split over whether police officers may use minor traffic violations as justifications for stopping suspects, when the officers may suspect the occupants of more serious crimes but have no objective basis for their suspicions. Some circuits had allowed such stops whenever a reasonable officer "could" have stopped the car for the traffic infraction; other circuits had tried to employ a more stringent test, allowing stops whenever a reasonable officer "would" have stopped the car. In *Whren*, a unanimous Court held that officers may stop a car on the basis of traffic infractions, regardless of whether or not the infraction is a pretext for investigating a hunch. The Court rejected the petitioners' analogy to inventory searches, which the Court had previously cautioned should not be used as a cover for "general rummaging in order to discover incriminating evidence." Florida v. Wells, 495 U.S. 1, 4, 110 S.Ct. 1632, 1635 (1990). Inventory searches, the Court noted, occur absent probable cause, while traffic stops may be made only when the police have probable cause to believe that a traffic violation has occurred. Indeed, the Court continued, the Fourth Amendment's requirement that searches be "reasonable" makes subjective intent irrelevant. Trying to find a proxy for subjective intent, such as noncompliance with police manuals and standards, would render Fourth Amendment protections too subject to local variation.

Arguably, the sum of *Belton* and *Whren* is that pretextual arrests for minor traffic variations (speeding, failing to signal a lane change, running a red light, driving without a license) may be used to justify car searches incident to the arrest.

These concerns have led the New Jersey Supreme Court to reject *Belton* on state constitutional grounds in cases where a driver has been arrested for a minor traffic violation. State v. Pierce, 136 N.J. 184, 642 A.2d 947 (1994).

The scope of a search incident to the arrest of a car occupant was expanded in Thornton v. United States:

Thornton v. United States

Supreme Court of the United States, 2004.
541 U.S. 615, 124 S.Ct. 2127.

■ CHIEF JUSTICE REHNQUIST delivered the opinion of the Court except as to footnote 4.

In New York v. Belton (1981), we held that when a police officer has made a lawful custodial arrest of an occupant of an automobile, the Fourth

Amendment allows the officer to search the passenger compartment of that vehicle as a contemporaneous incident of arrest. We have granted certiorari twice before to determine whether *Belton*'s rule is limited to situations where the officer makes contact with the occupant while the occupant is inside the vehicle, or whether it applies as well when the officer first makes contact with the arrestee after the latter has stepped out of his vehicle. We did not reach the merits in either of those two cases. We now reach that question and conclude that *Belton* governs even when an officer does not make contact until the person arrested has left the vehicle.

Officer Deion Nichols of the Norfolk, Virginia, Police Department, who was in uniform but driving an unmarked police car, first noticed petitioner Marcus Thornton when petitioner slowed down so as to avoid driving next to him. Nichols suspected that petitioner knew he was a police officer and for some reason did not want to pull next to him. His suspicions aroused, Nichols pulled off onto a side street and petitioner passed him. After petitioner passed him, Nichols ran a check on petitioner's license tags, which revealed that the tags had been issued to a 1982 Chevy two-door and not to a Lincoln Town Car, the model of car petitioner was driving. Before Nichols had an opportunity to pull him over, petitioner drove into a parking lot, parked, and got out of the vehicle. Nichols saw petitioner leave his vehicle as he pulled in behind him. He parked the patrol car, accosted petitioner, and asked him for his driver's license. He also told him that his license tags did not match the vehicle that he was driving.

Petitioner appeared nervous. He began rambling and licking his lips; he was sweating. Concerned for his safety, Nichols asked petitioner if he had any narcotics or weapons on him or in his vehicle. Petitioner said no. Nichols then asked petitioner if he could pat him down, to which petitioner agreed. Nichols felt a bulge in petitioner's left front pocket and again asked him if he had any illegal narcotics on him. This time petitioner stated that he did, and he reached into his pocket and pulled out two individual bags, one containing three bags of marijuana and the other containing a large amount of crack cocaine. Nichols handcuffed petitioner, informed him that he was under arrest, and placed him in the back seat of the patrol car. He then searched petitioner's vehicle and found a BryCo .9–millimeter handgun under the driver's seat.

A grand jury charged petitioner with possession with intent to distribute cocaine base, possession of a firearm after having been previously convicted of a crime punishable by a term of imprisonment exceeding one year, and possession of a firearm in furtherance of a drug trafficking crime. Petitioner sought to suppress, *inter alia*, the firearm as the fruit of an unconstitutional search. After a hearing, the District Court denied petitioner's motion to suppress, holding that the automobile search was valid under New York v. Belton, and alternatively that Nichols could have conducted an inventory search of the automobile. A jury convicted petitioner on all three counts; he was sentenced to 180 months' imprisonment and 8 years of supervised release.

Petitioner appealed, challenging only the District Court's denial of the suppression motion. He argued that *Belton* was limited to situations where the officer initiated contact with an arrestee while he was still an occupant of the car. The United States Court of Appeals for the Fourth Circuit affirmed. It held that "the historical rationales for the search incident to arrest doctrine—'the need to disarm the suspect in order to take him into custody' and 'the need to preserve evidence for later use at trial,' " did not require *Belton* to be limited solely to situations in which suspects were still in their vehicles when approached by the police. Noting that petitioner conceded that he was in "close proximity, both temporally and spatially," to his vehicle, the court concluded that the car was within petitioner's immediate control, and thus Nichols' search was reasonable under *Belton* We granted certiorari, and now affirm.

We first referred to *Chimel v. California*, a case where the arrestee was arrested in his home, and we had described the scope of a search incident to a lawful arrest as the person of the arrestee and the area immediately surrounding him. This rule was justified by the need to remove any weapon the arrestee might seek to use to resist arrest or to escape, and the need to prevent the concealment or destruction of evidence. Although easily stated, the *Chimel* principle had proved difficult to apply in specific cases. We pointed out that in *United States v. Robinson* (1973), a case dealing with the scope of the search of the arrestee's person, we had rejected a suggestion that " 'there must be litigated in each case the issue of whether or not there was present one of the reasons supporting the authority' " to conduct such a search. Similarly, because "courts ha[d] found no workable definition of the 'area within the immediate control of the arrestee' when that area arguably include[d] the interior of an automobile and the arrestee [wa]s its recent occupant," we sought to set forth a clear rule for police officers and citizens alike. We therefore held that "when a policeman has made a lawful custodial arrest of the occupant of an automobile, he may, as a contemporaneous incident of that arrest, search the passenger compartment of that automobile."

In so holding, we placed no reliance on the fact that the officer in *Belton* ordered the occupants out of the vehicle, or initiated contact with them while they remained within it. Nor do we find such a factor persuasive in distinguishing the current situation, as it bears no logical relationship to *Belton*'s rationale. There is simply no basis to conclude that the span of the area generally within the arrestee's immediate control is determined by whether the arrestee exited the vehicle at the officer's direction, or whether the officer initiated contact with him while he remained in the car. We recognized as much, albeit in dicta, in Michigan v. Long (1983), where officers observed a speeding car swerve into a ditch. The driver exited and the officers met him at the rear of his car. Although there was no indication that the officers initiated contact with the driver while he was still in the vehicle, we observed that "[i]t is clear ... that if the officers had arrested [respondent] ... they could have searched the passenger compartment under *New York v. Belton*."

In all relevant aspects, the arrest of a suspect who is next to a vehicle presents identical concerns regarding officer safety and the destruction of evidence as the arrest of one who is inside the vehicle. An officer may search a suspect's vehicle under *Belton* only if the suspect is arrested. A custodial arrest is fluid and "[t]he danger to the police officer flows from *the fact of the arrest*, and its attendant proximity, stress, and uncertainty," ("Every arrest must be presumed to present a risk of danger to the arresting officer"). The stress is no less merely because the arrestee exited his car before the officer initiated contact, nor is an arrestee less likely to attempt to lunge for a weapon or to destroy evidence if he is outside of, but still in control of, the vehicle. In either case, the officer faces a highly volatile situation. It would make little sense to apply two different rules to what is, at bottom, the same situation.

In some circumstances it may be safer and more effective for officers to conceal their presence from a suspect until he has left his vehicle. Certainly that is a judgment officers should be free to make. But under the strictures of petitioner's proposed "contact initiation" rule, officers who do so would be unable to search the car's passenger compartment in the event of a custodial arrest, potentially compromising their safety and placing incriminating evidence at risk of concealment or destruction. The Fourth Amendment does not require such a gamble.

Petitioner argues, however, that *Belton* will fail to provide a "bright-line" rule if it applies to more than vehicle "occupants." But *Belton* allows police to search the passenger compartment of a vehicle incident to a lawful custodial arrest of both "occupants" and "recent occupants." Indeed, the respondent in *Belton* was not inside the car at the time of the arrest and search; he was standing on the highway. In any event, while an arrestee's status as a "recent occupant" may turn on his temporal or spatial relationship to the car at the time of the arrest and search, 2it certainly does not turn on whether he was inside or outside the car at the moment that the officer first initiated contact with him.

To be sure, not all contraband in the passenger compartment is likely to be readily accessible to a "recent occupant." It is unlikely in this case that petitioner could have reached under the driver's seat for his gun once he was outside of his automobile. But the firearm and the passenger compartment in general were no more inaccessible than were the contraband and the passenger compartment in *Belton*. The need for a clear rule, readily understood by police officers and not depending on differing estimates of what items were or were not within reach of an arrestee at any particular moment, justifies the sort of generalization which *Belton* enunciated. 3Once an officer determines that there is probable cause to make an arrest, it is reasonable to allow officers to ensure their safety and to preserve evidence by searching the entire passenger compartment.[3]

3. Justice Stevens contends that *Belton*'s bright-line rule "is not needed for cases in which the arrestee is first accosted when he is a pedestrian, because *Chimel* itself provides all the guidance that is necessary." Under Justice Stevens' approach, however, even if the car itself was within the arrestee's reaching distance under *Chimel*, police officers and courts would still have to determine whether a particular object within the passenger compartment was also within an arrestee's reaching distance under *Chimel*. This is exactly the type of unworkable and fact-specific inquiry that *Belton* rejected by holding that the entire passenger compartment may be searched when " 'the area within the

Rather than clarifying the constitutional limits of a *Belton* search, petitioner's "contact initiation" rule would obfuscate them. Under petitioner's proposed rule, an officer approaching a suspect who has just alighted from his vehicle would have to determine whether he actually confronted or signaled confrontation with the suspect while he remained in the car, or whether the suspect exited his vehicle unaware of, and for reasons unrelated to, the officer's presence. This determination would be inherently subjective and highly fact specific, and would require precisely the sort of ad hoc determinations on the part of officers in the field and reviewing courts that *Belton* sought to avoid. Experience has shown that such a rule is impracticable, and we refuse to adopt it. So long as an arrestee is the sort of "recent occupant" of a vehicle such as petitioner was here, officers may search that vehicle incident to the arrest.[4]

The judgment of the Court of Appeals is affirmed.

■ JUSTICE O'CONNOR, concurring in part.

I join all but footnote 4 of the Court's opinion. Although the opinion is a logical extension of the holding of *New York v. Belton* (1981), I write separately to express my dissatisfaction with the state of the law in this area. As Justice Scalia forcefully argues, lower court decisions seem now to treat the ability to search a vehicle incident to the arrest of a recent occupant as a police entitlement rather than as an exception justified by the twin rationales of *Chimel v. California* (1969). That erosion is a direct consequence of *Belton*'s shaky foundation. While the approach Justice Scalia proposes appears to be built on firmer ground, I am reluctant to adopt it in the context of a case in which neither the Government nor the petitioner has had a chance to speak to its merit.

■ JUSTICE SCALIA, with whom JUSTICE GINSBURG joins, concurring in the judgment.

In Chimel v. California (1969), we held that a search incident to arrest was justified only as a means to find weapons the arrestee might use or evidence he might conceal or destroy. We accordingly limited such searches to the area within the suspect's " 'immediate control' "—*i.e.*, "the area into which an arrestee might reach in order to grab a weapon or evidentiary ite[m]." In New York v. Belton (1981), we set forth a bright-line rule for arrests of automobile occupants, holding that, because the vehicle's entire passenger compartment is "in fact generally, even if not inevitably," within

immediate control of the arrestee' ... arguably includes the interior of an automobile and the arrestee is its recent occupant."

4. Whatever the merits of Justice Scalia's opinion concurring in the judgment, this is the wrong case in which to address them. Petitioner has never argued that *Belton* should be limited "to cases where it is reasonable to believe evidence relevant to the crime of arrest might be found in the vehicle," nor did any court below consider Justice Scalia's reasoning.... The question presented—"[w]hether the bright-line rule announced in *New York v. Belton* is confined to situations in which the police initiate contact with the occupant of a vehicle while that person is in the vehicle," does not fairly encompass Justice Scalia's analysis. See this Court's Rule 14.1(a) ("Only the questions set out in the petition, or fairly included therein, will be considered by the Court").... Under these circumstances, it would be imprudent to overrule, for all intents and purposes, our established constitutional precedent, which governs police authority in a common occurrence such as automobile searches pursuant to arrest, and we decline to do so at this time.

the arrestee's immediate control, a search of the whole compartment is justified in every case.

When petitioner's car was searched in this case, he was neither in, nor anywhere near, the passenger compartment of his vehicle. Rather, he was handcuffed and secured in the back of the officer's squad car. The risk that he would nevertheless "grab a weapon or evidentiary ite[m]" from his car was remote in the extreme. The Court's effort to apply our current doctrine to this search stretches it beyond its breaking point, and for that reason I cannot join the Court's opinion.

I

I see three reasons why the search in this case might have been justified to protect officer safety or prevent concealment or destruction of evidence. None ultimately persuades me.

The first is that, despite being handcuffed and secured in the back of a squad car, petitioner might have escaped and retrieved a weapon or evidence from his vehicle—a theory that calls to mind Judge Goldberg's reference to the mythical arrestee "possessed of the skill of Houdini and the strength of Hercules." The United States, endeavoring to ground this seemingly speculative fear in reality, points to a total of seven instances over the past 13 years in which state or federal officers were attacked with weapons by handcuffed or formerly handcuffed arrestees. These instances do not, however, justify the search authority claimed. Three involved arrestees who retrieved weapons concealed *on their own person*. Three more involved arrestees who seized a weapon *from the arresting officer*. Authority to search the arrestee's own person is beyond question; and of course no search could prevent seizure of the officer's gun. Only one of the seven instances involved a handcuffed arrestee who escaped from a squad car to retrieve a weapon from somewhere else: In *Plakas v. Drinski* (CA7 1994), the suspect jumped out of the squad car and ran through a forest to a house, where (still in handcuffs) he struck an officer on the wrist with a fireplace poker before ultimately being shot dead.

Of course, the Government need not document specific instances in order to justify measures that avoid obvious risks. But the risk here is far from obvious, and in a context as frequently recurring as roadside arrests, the Government's inability to come up with even a single example of a handcuffed arrestee's retrieval of arms or evidence from his vehicle undermines its claims. The risk that a suspect handcuffed in the back of a squad car might escape and recover a weapon from his vehicle is surely no greater than the risk that a suspect handcuffed in his residence might escape and recover a weapon from the next room—a danger we held insufficient to justify a search in *Chimel*.

The second defense of the search in this case is that, since the officer could have conducted the search at the time of arrest (when the suspect was still near the car), he should not be penalized for having taken the sensible precaution of securing the suspect in the squad car first. As one Court of Appeals put it: " '[I]t does not make sense to prescribe a constitutional test that is entirely at odds with safe and sensible police procedures.' " The weakness of this argument is that it assumes that, one way or another, the search must take place. But conducting a *Chimel* search is not the Government's right; it is an exception—justified by necessity—to a rule that would otherwise render the search unlawful. If "sensible police procedures" require that suspects be handcuffed and put in squad cars, then police should handcuff suspects, put them in squad cars, and not conduct the search. Indeed, if an officer leaves a suspect unrestrained nearby just to manufacture authority to search, one could argue that the search is unreasonable *precisely because* the dangerous conditions justifying it existed only by virtue of the officer's failure to follow sensible procedures.

The third defense of the search is that, even though the arrestee posed no risk here, *Belton* searches in general are reasonable, and the benefits of a bright-line rule justify upholding that small minority of searches that, on their particular facts, are not reasonable. The validity of this argument rests on the accuracy of *Belton*'s claim that the passenger compartment is "in fact generally, even if not inevitably," within the suspect's immediate control. By the United States' own admission, however, "[t]he practice of restraining an arrestee on the scene before searching a car that he just occupied is so prevalent that holding that *Belton* does not apply in that setting would . . . 'largely render *Belton* a dead letter.' " . . . Some courts uphold such searches even when the squad car carrying the handcuffed arrestee has already left the scene. . . .

The popularity of the practice is not hard to fathom. If *Belton* entitles an officer to search a vehicle upon arresting the driver despite having taken measures that eliminate any danger, what rational officer would not take those measures? . . . If it was ever true that the passenger compartment is "in fact generally, even if not inevitably," within the arrestee's immediate control at the time of the search it certainly is not true today. As one judge has put it: "[I]n our search for clarity, we have now abandoned our constitutional moorings and floated to a place where the law approves of purely exploratory searches of vehicles during which officers with no definite objective or reason for the search are allowed to rummage around in a car to see what they might find." *McLaughlin*, at 894 (Trott, J., concurring). I agree entirely with that assessment.

II

If *Belton* searches are justifiable, it is not because the arrestee might grab a weapon or evidentiary item from his car, but simply because the car might contain evidence relevant to the crime for which he was arrested. . . .

There is nothing irrational about broader police authority to search for evidence when and where the perpetrator of a crime is lawfully arrested. The fact of prior lawful arrest distinguishes the arrestee from society at large, and distinguishes a search for evidence of *his* crime from general rummaging. Moreover, it is not illogical to assume that evidence of a crime is most likely to be found where the suspect was apprehended. . . .

In short, both *Rabinowitz* and *Chimel* are plausible accounts of what the Constitution requires, and neither is so persuasive as to justify departing from settled law. But if we are going to continue to allow *Belton* searches on *stare decisis* grounds, we should at least be honest about why we are doing so. *Belton* cannot reasonably be explained as a mere application of *Chimel*. Rather, it is a return to the broader sort of search incident to arrest that we allowed before *Chimel*—limited, of course, to searches of motor vehicles, a category of "effects" which give rise to a reduced expectation of privacy....

Recasting *Belton* in these terms would have at least one important practical consequence. In *United States v. Robinson* (1973), we held that authority to search an arrestee's person does not depend on the actual presence of one of *Chimel*'s two rationales in the particular case; rather, the fact of arrest alone justifies the search. That holding stands in contrast to *Rabinowitz*, where we did not treat the fact of arrest alone as sufficient, but upheld the search only after noting that it was "not general or exploratory for whatever might be turned up" but reflected a reasonable belief that evidence would be found.... The two different rules make sense: When officer safety or imminent evidence concealment or destruction is at issue, officers should not have to make fine judgments in the heat of the moment. But in the context of a general evidence-gathering search, the state interests that might justify any overbreadth are far less compelling. A motorist may be arrested for a wide variety of offenses; in many cases, there is no reasonable basis to believe relevant evidence might be found in the car. I would therefore limit *Belton* searches to cases where it is reasonable to believe evidence relevant to the crime of arrest might be found in the vehicle.

In this case, as in *Belton*, petitioner was lawfully arrested for a drug offense. It was reasonable for Officer Nichols to believe that further contraband or similar evidence relevant to the crime for which he had been arrested might be found in the vehicle from which he had just alighted and which was still within his vicinity at the time of arrest. I would affirm the decision below on that ground.

■ JUSTICE STEVENS, with whom JUSTICE SOUTER joins, dissenting.

Prior to our decision in New York v. Belton (1981), there was a widespread conflict among both federal and state courts over the question "whether, in the course of a search incident to the lawful custodial arrest of the occupants of an automobile, police may search inside the automobile after the arrestees are no longer in it." In answering that question, the Court expanded the authority of the police in two important respects. It allowed the police to conduct a broader search than our decision in *Chimel* v. *California* (1969), would have permitted, and it authorized them to open closed containers that might be found in the vehicle's passenger compartment.

Belton's basic rationale for both expansions rested not on a concern for officer safety, but rather on an overriding desire to hew "to a straightforward rule, easily applied, and predictably enforced." 3When the case was decided, I was persuaded that the important interest in clarity and certainty adequately justified the modest extension of the *Chimel* rule to permit an officer to examine the interior of a car pursuant to an arrest for a traffic violation. But I took a different view with respect to the search of containers within the car absent probable cause, because I thought "it palpably unreasonable to require the driver of a car to open his briefcase or his luggage for inspection by the officer." I remain convinced that this aspect of the *Belton* opinion was both unnecessary and erroneous. Whether one agrees or disagrees with that view, however, the interest in certainty that supports *Belton*'s bright-line rule surely does not justify an expansion of the rule that only blurs those clear lines. Neither the rule in *Chimel* nor *Belton*'s modification of that rule would have allowed the search of petitioner's car....

The bright-line rule crafted in *Belton* is not needed for cases in which the arrestee is first accosted when he is a pedestrian, because *Chimel* itself provides all the guidance that is necessary. The only genuine justification for extending *Belton* to cover such circumstances is the interest in uncovering potentially valuable evidence. In my opinion, that goal must give way to the citizen's constitutionally protected interest in privacy when there is already in place a well-defined rule limiting the permissible scope of a search of an arrested pedestrian. The *Chimel* rule should provide the same protection to a "recent occupant" of a vehicle as to a recent occupant of a house.

Unwilling to confine the *Belton* rule to the narrow class of cases it was designed to address, the Court extends *Belton*'s reach without supplying any guidance for the future application of its swollen rule. We are told that officers may search a vehicle incident to arrest "[s]o long as [the] arrestee is the sort of 'recent occupant' of a vehicle such as petitioner was here." But we are not told how recent is recent, or how close is close, perhaps because in this case "the record is not clear." As the Court cautioned in *Belton* itself, "[w]hen a person cannot know how a court will apply a settled principle to a recurring factual situation, that person cannot know the scope of his constitutional protection, nor can a policeman know the scope of his authority." Without some limiting principle, I fear that today's decision will contribute to "a massive broadening of the automobile exception," when officers have probable cause to arrest an individual but not to search his car.

Accordingly, I respectfully dissent.

NOTES

1. How much proximity to the vehicle is required? In *Thornton*, the suspect was arrested outside his car. The United States Supreme Court has granted certiorari in case based on the following facts: the defendant was arrested on the basis of an arrest warrant about ten feet from his car. Police handcuffed him and locked him in the back of a police car before they undertook to search his vehicle pursuant to a search incident to arrest theory. The Supreme Court of Arizona distinguished *Thornton* and held that a warrantless search was not justified. Arizona v. Gant, 216 Ariz. 1, 162 P.3d 640 (2007). There was no discussion of inventory searches.

The question before the Supreme Court upon which certiorari has been granted is: "Does the Fourth Amendment require law enforcement officers to demonstrate a threat to their safety or a need to preserve evidence related to the crime of arrest in order to justify a warrantless vehicular search incident to arrest conducted after the vehicle's recent occupants have been arrested and secured?" Arizona v. Gant, ___ U.S. ___, 128 S.Ct. 1443 (2008).

How should the Court resolve this issue?

2. *Frisks and Searches of Arrestee's Companions.* If *A* is arrested in *B*'s presence *B* can be frisked for weapons if there is independent justification for such a frisk under Terry v. Ohio (Section K, infra). Some courts, however, seem to hold that such frisks are proper even though the criteria of *Terry* are not satisfied. Consider the following from United States v. Berryhill, 445 F.2d 1189 (9th Cir. 1971):

> We think that *Terry* recognizes and common sense dictates that the legality of such a limited intrusion into a citizen's personal privacy extends to a criminal's companions at the time of arrest. It is inconceivable that a peace officer effecting a lawful arrest of an occupant of a vehicle must expose himself to a shot in the back from defendant's associate because he cannot, on the spot, make the nice distinction between whether the other is a companion in crime or a social acquaintance. All companions of the arrestee within the immediate vicinity, capable of accomplishing a harmful assault on the officer, are constitutionally subjected to the cursory "pat-down" reasonably necessary to give assurance that they are unarmed.

Also consider United States v. Simmons, 567 F.2d 314 (7th Cir.1977), which held that under narrowly defined circumstances, *B* may be searched incident to the arrest of *A*. On the other hand, routine frisks or searches of companions of arrestees have been condemned. United States v. Di Re, 332 U.S. 581, 68 S.Ct. 222 (1948); United States v. Bell, 762 F.2d 495 (6th Cir.1985); Commonwealth v. Ng, 420 Mass. 236, 649 N.E.2d 157 (1995); Commonwealth v. Shiflet, 543 Pa. 164, 670 A.2d 128 (1995).

3. *Search of a Passenger's Effects*. In Wyoming v. Houghton, 526 U.S. 295, 119 S.Ct. 1297 (1999), police stopped a car and noticed a syringe in the driver's shirt pocket. The driver admitted the syringe was used to take drugs. The officer then began a search of the passenger compartment of the car for contraband. He found a purse, which a passenger, the defendant in the case, claimed was hers. Inside, the officer found two containers; both contained illegal methamphetamine. When the Supreme Court considered her argument for suppressing the drugs, it held that officer was entitled to inspect her belongings found in the car that were capable of concealing the object of the search because he had probable cause to search the car. The officer did not need any separate justification of probable cause that she had committed a crime or that even a reasonable suspicion that she possessed the drug.

4. Presumption of Probable Cause: Some jurisdictions create a presumption of probable cause to arrest all occupants of a motor vehicle if there is contraband found in the vehicle. This blurs the line between a search incident to arrest and a search of a car based on probable cause to believe there is contraband in the automobile discussed later. The Supreme Court addressed this situation in Maryland v. Pringle.

(d) LIMITATIONS UPON POWER TO SEIZE

Although under United States v. Robinson, the right to search a person who has been subject to a lawful custodial arrest does not depend upon the probability that something will turn up, the right to take and carry away the arrestee's property may depend upon a probability that such property (discovered within a proper search incident to arrest) is contraband or constitutes evidence of a crime. Suppose, for example, that within reach of the arrestee on his dresser is a bottle of pills. Can the police take and carry it away absent seizure probable cause? State v. Elkins, 245 Or. 279, 422 P.2d 250 (1966), suggests not. See also Justice Harlan's concurring opinion in Von Cleef v. New Jersey, 395 U.S. 814, 89 S.Ct. 2051 (1969), discussing Kremen v. United States, 353 U.S. 346, 77 S.Ct. 828 (1957).

In United States v. Holzman, 871 F.2d 1496 (9th Cir.1989), officers seized defendant's address book incident to his arrest for passing counterfeit bonds. The officer testified that he only realized the evidentiary importance of the book later at the station house after a closer reading. The defendant contended that because the evidentiary importance of the book was not immediately apparent, the officer had no probable cause for seizing it or searching its contents. The court rejected defendant's analogy to plain view seizures, where probable cause to believe that the item is evidence or contraband must be immediately apparent to justify a seizure or a further inspection. Should the same principle apply to the "bottle of pills" situation above?

Another limitation upon seizures incident to arrest is found in Roaden v. Kentucky, 413 U.S. 496, 93 S.Ct. 2796 (1973), which held that obscene films within reach of an arrestee cannot be seized. Because of First Amendment implications, issuance of a search warrant by a neutral judicial officer is required. Possibly Roaden would apply also to seizures of multiple copies of allegedly obscene printed matter incident to an arrest. The danger is the same: possible suppression of speech without any probable cause decision by a judicial officer.

4. EFFECT OF UNLAWFUL ARREST UPON POWER TO PROSECUTE

Although lawyers frequently speak of "quashing an arrest," the fact that an arrest is illegal does not deprive the court of jurisdiction. An illegally arrested defendant—even one who has been improperly returned to the state or country where the crime was committed—may still be subjected to trial. For instance, in the case of Adolph Eichmann, the chief executioner of millions of Jews during the Nazi regime in Germany, the Supreme Court of Israel relied heavily upon American case law to justify its right to try Eichmann, who had been kidnapped in Argentina and flown to Israel for trial. See Pearlman, The Capture and Trial of Adolph Eichmann (1963) 112. To the same effect, Frisbie v. Collins, 342 U.S. 519, 72 S.Ct. 509 (1952).

Against the weight of hundreds of precedents, a very few decisions hold that when a suspect is returned to a jurisdiction by flagrantly unlawful means, due process requires that he be released, although the re-filing of charges is not necessarily barred. See United States v. Toscanino, 500 F.2d 267 (2d Cir.1974), which, however, was sharply limited to its particular facts by several subsequent Second Circuit cases. In Toscanino the defendant had been kidnapped, drugged, and tortured. The Supreme Court called this result into question in United States v. Alvarez–Machain, 504 U.S. 655, 112 S.Ct. 2188 (1992), holding that the extradition treaty between Mexico and the U.S. did not bar kidnapping as a method of securing jurisdiction and thus no treaty violation occurred when the defendant was kidnapped in Mexico and brought to trial in the United States.

The law varies from jurisdiction to jurisdiction as to whether the illegality of an arrest prevents the prosecution from securing a conviction for resisting arrest and whether force used against an officer in resisting an unlawful arrest can be deemed justified when the arrestee is faced with a charge such as battery against the officer. What policy arguments are most persuasive in resolving these questions?

Concerning the suppression of evidence derived from an illegal arrest, see the discussion of the fruit of the poisonous tree found in Section E of Chapter 6.

H. IS A WARRANT REQUIRED FOR PLAIN VIEW SEARCHES AND SEIZURES?

Subject to some exceptions, police officers are generally allowed to seize criminal evidence or contraband which they spot in "plain view." The plain view doctrine spans several doctrines.

In one sense, items may be seized in a "pre-intrusive" mode—in other words, plain view refers to items that are seen without the benefit of a search. Thus, when an officer perceives X walk onto a public city street carrying an illegal machine gun, the officer has not conducted a search since the contraband gun is in plain view open to all. This type of "plain view" may not even rise to a level of a Fourth Amendment search under the *Katz* definition.

In the other sense, plain view deals with the scope of a search. This plain view search and seizure is "post-intrusive," it follows some prior Fourth Amendment activity. Consider this scenario: an officer enters an apartment to arrest a suspect who is within. To comply with *Payton*, the officer has an arrest warrant, but no search warrant. Once inside, she spots a pile of marijuana joints on a hallway table as she enters the apartment. In the later situation, the observations and the seizure of the contraband are lawful only if the officer gained her vantage point without violating the Fourth Amendment. In other words, the officer must legitimately be on the premises for the plain view doctrine to apply. United States v. Lewis, 910 F.2d 1367 (7th Cir.1990).

NOTES

1. ***The Implications of the Plain View Doctrine.*** The oft-repeated statement that plain view by itself does not justify a seizure has several implications. (a) It means that plain view observations and seizures are unlawful if the vantage point for the observations was gained through an intrusion which violated the Fourth Amendment. (b) It means that although plain view observations may be lawful, if a further intrusion (e.g., entering a home) is necessary before the items can be seized, the plain view doctrine does not justify the intrusion. Some other justification is required. (c) The statement means that items spotted in plain view cannot be seized and carried away absent probable cause to believe that the items are contraband or evidence of a crime. (d) The statement also suggests that plain view observations and seizures are impermissible if the original viewing violated a reasonable expectation of privacy even if there was no trespass (the *Katz* limitation). (e) Finally the

statement once may have meant, though it no longer does, that, subject to qualifications, plain view seizures are impermissible unless the discovery of evidence was inadvertent.

Consider the following hypotheticals. An officer walking down the street looks into a window and spots what she has probable cause to believe is a large quantity of marijuana resting on a kitchen table. Can she enter without a warrant? If so, on what theory? Plain view by itself does not permit an entry to seize evidence. Does it make a difference if someone is sitting at the table? What theory would justify the entry in such a case? Suppose instead the marijuana is spotted in an unoccupied car parked on a public street.

2. *Open to Public?* Under the traditional (pre-*Katz*) view, observations made from a place where the officer has a right to be are lawful plain view observations. Such observations sometimes are made from a vantage point gained without any prior Fourth Amendment intrusion; for example, from a public sidewalk or from that part of a store or a tavern or a hotel which is open to the public. Occasionally the question of what is a public area is a close one. What about the common hall of a large apartment building or the garage of a building which houses many condominium units? See State v. Bazella, 522 S.W.2d 57 (Mo.App.1975); United States v. Cruz Pagan, 537 F.2d 554 (1st Cir.1976). Compare People v. Killebrew, 76 Mich.App. 215, 256 N.W.2d 581 (1977). A most interesting case is People v. Abrams, 48 Ill.2d 446, 271 N.E.2d 37 (1971), where a home was open to general members of the public who made a small "donation" to attend an anti-war meeting. According to the court, the nature of the place changed when the hosts indicated that police officers were not welcome. If an undercover police agent attends a meeting of citizens, open to the general public, called to discuss police spying, has he violated the Fourth Amendment? Or is this a problem which calls for First Amendment analysis? The issue will arise in the context of a criminal case only if the police see or hear evidence of a crime, as in Abrams, where liquor law violations were observed.

3. *Enhanced Views.* Even if a police officer gains his or her vantage point without trespassing against a suspect's property, under the post-*Katz* approach, his or her observations still may violate the Fourth Amendment if the observations violated a "reasonable expectation of privacy." See e.g., State v. Kaaheena, 59 Haw. 23, 575 P.2d 462 (1978) (officer peeked over top of curtain). See also, People v. Triggs, 8 Cal.3d 884, 106 Cal.Rptr. 408, 506 P.2d 232 (1973) (officer peeked into stall in public washroom). An officer who with his unaided ear overhears conversations inside a motel room while stationed in the hallway or in an adjacent room probably does not violate a reasonable expectation of privacy. United States v. Jackson, 588 F.2d 1046 (5th Cir.1979); State v. Moses, 367 So.2d 800 (La.1979). Similarly, an officer who looks through an undraped window while standing in a parking lot does not violate a reasonable expectation of privacy. Gil v. Beto, 440 F.2d 666 (5th Cir.1971).

If, while standing in a place where he has a right to be, an officer looks into private property with the aid of a mechanical device, a court is more likely to find a violation of a reasonable expectation of privacy, particularly if the device is highly sophisticated like the high-power telescope in People v. Kender, 60 Haw. 301, 588 P.2d 447 (1978). On the other hand, numerous cases have upheld the use of flashlights. Observations made through the use of binoculars may present a close question which turns upon the individual circumstances. See People v. Ciochon, 23 Ill.App.3d 363, 319 N.E.2d 332 (1974). What if the police use a "startron" to look through an undraped window and make observations of activity in a darkroom? See Commonwealth v. Williams, 262 Pa.Super. 508, 396 A.2d 1286 (1978), reversed 494

Pa. 496, 431 A.2d 964 (1981) (finding violation of reasonable expectation of privacy under circumstances). Interception of a telephone conversation when one party uses a cordless phone is not a search, since users of cordless phones know that their conversations may be intercepted and thus have no reasonable expectation of privacy. In re Askin, 47 F.3d 100 (4th Cir.), cert. denied, 516 U.S. 944, 116 S.Ct. 382 (1995). The Washington Supreme Court has held that, under the Washington State privacy act, citizens do have an expectation of privacy in their cordless phone conversations. Washington v. Faford, 128 Wash.2d 476, 910 P.2d 447 (1996).

Items may be deemed to be in plain view, even though law enforcement use aerial surveillance, California v. Ciraolo, 476 U.S. 207, 106 S.Ct. 1809 (1986), or even satellite surveillance, Dow Chemical Co. v. Environmental Protection Agency, 476 U.S. 227, 106 S.Ct. 1819 (1986). These were deemed not to be searches for Fourth Amendment purposes.

NOTES: FURTHER ASPECTS OF PLAIN VIEW

1. *Pretexts.* In Coolidge v. New Hampshire, 403 U.S. 443, 91 S.Ct. 2022 (1971), a four-justice plurality declared that a plain-view seizure was unreasonable unless the officers came upon the evidence "inadvertently." One concern was that officers would use one Fourth Amendment intrusion, for example entry-to-arrest, as a pretext to seize evidence in plain view within a home. In this context, the Court condemned using a plain view search as a pretext to find evidence.

The Court abandoned the "inadvertence" requirement in Horton v. California, 496 U.S. 128, 110 S.Ct. 2301 (1990). Resolving a conflict among lower courts, the United States Supreme Court decided that there is no requirement that plain view seizures be "inadvertent." There officers had "probable cause to search petitioner's home for the proceeds of the robbery and for weapons (including a machine gun) used in the robbery." However, they obtained a warrant for the stolen property but not for the weapons. In executing the search warrant, in plain view they found the weapons, including the machine gun. They seized these weapons but did not discover the proceeds.

Writing for the majority, Justice Stevens stated:

> First, evenhanded law enforcement is best achieved by the application of objective standards of conduct, rather than standards that depend upon the subjective state of mind of the officer. The fact that an officer is interested in an item of evidence and fully expects to find it in the course of a search should not invalidate its seizure if the search is confined in area and duration by the terms of a warrant or a valid exception to the warrant requirement. If the officer has knowledge approaching certainty that the item will be found, we see no reason why he or she would deliberately omit a particular description of the item to be seized from the application for a search warrant. Specification of the additional item could only permit the officer to expand the scope of the search. On the other hand, if he or she has a valid warrant to search for one item and merely a suspicion concerning the second, whether or not it amounts to probable cause, we fail to see why that suspicion should immunize the second item from seizure if it is found during a lawful search for the first....
>
> Second, the suggestion that the inadvertence requirement is necessary to prevent the police from conducting general searches, or from converting specific warrants into general warrants, is not persuasive because that interest is already served by the requirements that no warrant issue unless it "particularly describ[es] the place to be searched and the persons or things to be seized". Scrupulous adherence to these requirements serves the interests in limiting the area and duration of the search that the

inadvertence requirement inadequately protects. Once those commands have been satisfied and the officer has a lawful right of access, however, no additional Fourth Amendment interest is furthered by requiring that the discovery of evidence be inadvertent. If the scope of the search exceeds that permitted by the terms of a validly issued warrant or the character of the relevant exception from the warrant requirement, the subsequent seizure is unconstitutional without more.

In dissent, Justice Brennan wrote:

> [T]here are a number of instances in which a law enforcement officer might deliberately choose to omit certain items from a warrant application even though he has probable cause to seize them, knows they are on the premises, and intends to seize them when they are discovered in plain view. For example, the warrant application process can often be time-consuming, especially when the police attempt to seize a large number of items. An officer interested in conducting a search as soon as possible might decide to save time by listing only one or two hard-to-find items, such as the stolen rings in this case, confident that he will find in plain view all of the other evidence he is looking for before he discovers the listed items. Because rings could be located almost anywhere inside or outside a house, it is unlikely that a warrant to search for and seize the rings would restrict the scope of the search. An officer might rationally find the risk of immediately discovering the items listed in the warrant—thereby forcing him to conclude the search immediately—outweighed by the time saved in the application process. . . .
>
> . . . It is true that the inadvertent discovery requirement furthers no privacy interests. The requirement in no way reduces the scope of a search or the number of places into which officers may look. But it does protect possessory interests. The inadvertent discovery requirement is essential if we are to take seriously the Fourth Amendment's protection of possessory interests as well as privacy interests. The Court today eliminates a rule designed to further possessory interests on the ground that it fails to further privacy interests. I cannot countenance such constitutional legerdemain.

2. ***Close Looks.*** The plain view doctrine operates on the premise that there is no "search". There is, however, a seizure and there must be probable cause to seize. Frequently the probable cause issue is intertwined with the question of how closely authorities may look before their alleged plain view observations turn into an impermissible warrantless search. If while executing a marijuana search warrant officers come across government bonds bearing the name of someone other than the resident, can the officers record the numbers and make a telephone call to determine whether the bonds are stolen? See Commonwealth v. Hawkins, 361 Mass. 384, 280 N.E.2d 665 (1972). Can they pick up and inspect shoes spotted in plain view? State v. Holloman, 197 Neb. 139, 248 N.W.2d 15 (1976). Can they smell a pipe? Gardner v. State, 32 Md.App. 629, 363 A.2d 616 (1976).Can they, in the absence of probable cause, record serial numbers of television sets or securities? Compare State v. Wilson, 279 Md. 189, 367 A.2d 1223 (1977); United States v. Clark, 531 F.2d 928 (8th Cir.1976). What about holding slides to a light? See Anderson v. State, 555 P.2d 251 (Alaska, 1976). Many of the "close look" decisions are discussed in Commonwealth v. Bond, 375 Mass. 201, 375 N.E.2d 1214 (1978).

In Arizona v. Hicks, 480 U.S. 321, 107 S.Ct. 1149 (1987), authorities were lawfully present in an apartment, having responded to reports that a bullet had been fired through the floor of that apartment, injuring a person in the apartment below. They found weapons and a stocking-cap mask. Officer Nelson "noticed two sets of expensive stereo components, which seemed out of place in the squalid and otherwise ill-appointed four-room apartment." He read and recorded the serial numbers, moving some of the stereo components in order to do so. When it developed that the numbers recorded matched those of stolen equipment, the police obtained a search warrant based on this information.

Through Justice Scalia, a six-person majority held that the conduct of Officer Nelson to gain the information to support probable cause in the warrant application had violated the Fourth Amendment and thus, had tainted the warrant. The majority declared that merely recording serial numbers was neither a search nor a seizure. It declared, however, that moving the equipment did constitute a search separate and apart from the search that was the lawful object of the officer's entry into the apartment. It was a "new invasion of privacy" to view concealed items. The distinction between observing numbers without moving anything and observing numbers after moving items a few inches was critical to Fourth Amendment analysis.

The Court held that what Officer Nelson had done was valid only if the police had full probable cause to seize the equipment before Nelson had moved it. Under such circumstances the police could have properly invoked the plain view doctrine. However, the State conceded that the police had only reasonable suspicion and not probable cause. Hence the search that yielded the numbers was unreasonable for want of a warrant. The plain view doctrine normally requires probable cause for seizure. Only under exceptional circumstances will something less suffice, as, for example, when "the seizure is minimally intrusive and operational necessities under it the only practicable means of detecting certain crimes ... United States v. Place (seizure of suspected drug dealer's luggage at airport to permit exposure to specially trained dog.)"

Dissenting justices argued that a reasonable suspicion, falling short of probable cause, can justify "cursory inspection" under circumstances such as those presented. Only if the cursory inspection yields probable cause can the officers be allowed to conduct a full search or to make a warrantless seizure, said the dissenters.

3. *Plain Feel.* A doctrine analogous to plain view is a "plain feel" rule which permits an officer who feels something incriminating during a frisk authority to seize it without a warrant. See United States v. Williams, 822 F.2d 1174 (D.C.Cir. 1987); United States v. Buchannon, 878 F.2d 1065 (8th Cir.1989).

In Minnesota v. Dickerson, 508 U.S. 366, 113 S.Ct. 2130 (1993) the Court approved a "plain feel" rule. It first noted that contraband that comes into the plain view of an officer during a frisk may be seized and then reasoned:

> "The same can be said of tactile discoveries of contraband. If a police officer lawfully pats down a suspect's outer clothing and feels an object whose contour or mass makes its identity immediately apparent, there has been no invasion of the suspect's privacy beyond that already authorized by the officer's search for weapons; if the object is contraband, its warrantless seizure would be justified by the same practical considerations that inhere in the plain view context.
>
> The Minnesota Supreme Court rejected an analogy to the plain-view doctrine on two grounds: first, its belief that "the sense of touch is inherently less immediate and less reliable than the sense of sight," and second, that "the sense of touch is far more intrusive into the personal privacy that is at the core of the [F]ourth [A]mendment." ... We have a somewhat different view. First *Terry* itself demonstrates that the sense of touch is capable of revealing the nature of an object with sufficient reliability to support a seizure. The very premise of *Terry* itself demon-

> strates that the sense of touch is capable of revealing the nature of an object with sufficient reliability to support a seizure. The very premise of *Terry*, after all, is that officers will be able to detect the presence of weapons through the sense of touch and *Terry* upheld precisely such a seizure. Even if it were true that the sense of touch is generally less reliable than the sense of sight, that only suggests that officers will less often be able to justify seizures of unseen contraband. Regardless of whether the officer detects the contraband by sight or by touch, however, the Fourth Amendment's requirement that the officer have probable cause to believe that the item is contraband before seizing it ensures against excessively speculative seizures. The court's second concern—that touch is more intrusive into privacy than is sight "is inapposite in light of the fact that the intrusion the court fears has already been authorized by the lawful search for weapons. The seizure of an item whose identity is already known occasions no further invasion of privacy...."

The Court went on to hold that "plain feel" could not be used to justify seizure of crack cocaine when the officer did not immediately detect what it was, but had to manipulate the plastic wrapped object several times before realizing it was cocaine.

I. IS A WARRANT REQUIRED FOR EXIGENT CIRCUMSTANCES: HOT PURSUIT, AND EMERGENCY SEARCHES

The Supreme Court has always recognized that there are times when it is impracticable for law enforcement to obtain a warrant. Thus, exigency is a rationale that underlies a number of the exceptions to the warrant requirement.

1. EXCEPTIONS TO THE *PAYTON* DOCTRINE

Payton held that officers must have a warrant to enter a dwelling to arrest a person, but the decision specifically excluded exigent circumstances. The Court did not decide, however, what type of special or exigent circumstances would justify a warrantless, non-consensual entry into a suspect's home for the purpose of arrest. Many of the federal and state cases which reached the "*Payton* rule" before *Payton* spelled out factors to be considered. Among the most important such early decisions were Dorman v. United States, 435 F.2d 385 (D.C.Cir.1970), and Vance v. North Carolina, 432 F.2d 984 (4th Cir.1970). The significant factors are generally said to include:

> (1) the relative peacefulness of the entry, (2) the time of day or night when the entry is made, (3) the seriousness of the crime, (4) the probability that the suspect is armed, (5) the danger of flight, (6) the delay which would be occasioned by application for a warrant, (7) the probability, beyond the minimum requirement of probable cause, that the suspect is guilty, and (8) the probability that the suspect is within the home which is to be entered.

Some commentators have observed that, after the *Payton* decision, many courts have been quick to find exigent circumstances and to excuse the absence of an arrest warrant. Nevertheless, there have been a few decisions which have rejected exigent circumstances claims.

The Supreme Court addressed a part of this issue in the per curiam decision of Welsh v. Wisconsin, 466 U.S. 740, 104 S.Ct. 2091 (1984). There the arrestee was suspected of a first-offense drunk driving violation which, under Wisconsin law, called for a fine-only penalty. After the suspect allegedly left the scene of an accident, the officers (not in hot pursuit) entered his home to make a warrantless arrest. The prosecution suggested that an emergency had been at hand because postponement of a prompt scientific test for the presence of alcohol in the suspect's system would have forever denied the police access to such evidence. The Court held that under these circumstances *Payton* did not justify a warrantless entry. It gave controlling weight to the fact that the Wisconsin legislature, through the penalty provided for, chose to treat the matter as one in which the State had no very great interest. Is that a fair characterization of a scheme which seeks to treat first-offenders by means other than heavy criminal penalties? The Court did not reach the issue, later resolved, of whether arrest warrants are always constitutionally required in the case of misdemeanors not committed in the officer's presence. The underlying assumption of the *Welsh* discussion, however, is that this common law requirement is not mandated by the Fourth Amendment.

2. WHO DECIDES WHETHER EXIGENCY EXISTS?

In Minnesota v. Olson, 495 U.S. 91, 110 S.Ct. 1684 (1990), the Supreme Court deferred to a state court decision finding inadequate exigencies to justify a warrantless entry for purposes of arresting Olson in connection with a robbery-murder that had occurred early the prior morning. The Court stated:

> The Minnesota Supreme Court applied essentially the correct standard in determining whether exigent circumstances existed. The court observed that "a warrantless intrusion may be justified by hot pursuit of a fleeing felon, or imminent destruction of evidence, or the need to prevent a suspect's escape, or the risk of danger to the police or to other persons inside or outside the dwelling." The court also apparently thought that in the absence of hot pursuit there must be at least probable cause to believe that one or more of the other factors justifying the entry were present and that in assessing the risk of danger, the gravity of the crime and likelihood that the suspect is armed should be considered. Applying this standard, the state court determined that exigent circumstances did not exist.
>
> We are not inclined to disagree with this fact-specific application of the proper legal standard. The court pointed out that although a grave crime was involved, respondent "was known not to be the murderer but thought to be the driver of the getaway car," and that the police had already recovered the murder weapon. "The police knew that Louanne and Julie were with the suspect in the upstairs duplex with no suggestion of danger to them. Three or four Minneapolis police squads surrounded the house. The time was 3 p.m., Sunday.... It was evident the suspect was going nowhere. If he came out of the house he would have

been promptly apprehended." We do not disturb the state court's judgment that these facts do not add up to exigent circumstances.

3. HOT PURSUIT

"Hot pursuit" entry into a home in search of a fleeing felon is another example of a permissible warrantless emergency intrusion. One such entry was upheld in Warden v. Hayden, 387 U.S. 294, 87 S.Ct. 1642 (1967), where the police were "on the heels" of the fleeing felon, though not in constant eyesight. The Court permitted inspection of all areas of the house where the fleeing felon could have been hiding or where he might have stashed a weapon to aid his escape. Particularly where the home is the suspect's—and not that of some innocent third person—warrantless entries into a home for arrest purposes are not always limited to true "hot pursuit" situations. In this case, the police did not find the suspect, but instead, the clothes worn by the perpetrator of the crime. Thus Warden v. Hayden, although thought of as the prime example of emergency doctrine, is more important for general theory than for its "hot pursuit" holding.

4. PROTECTIVE SWEEPS

Although the scope of a permissible search incident to a valid arrest is limited to the "grabbable area" of an arrestee, the Court has recognized that officers may make a cursory "protective sweep" of the area in order to protect themselves and others from harm. Maryland v. Buie, 494 U.S. 325, 110 S.Ct. 1093 (1990) Of course once the officers are legitimately in the area, other doctrines, such as the plain view doctrine, may apply.

5. THE EMERGENCY DOCTRINE

Exigency allows law enforcement agents to enter a home without a warrant if they have an objectively reasonable basis for believing that an occupant is seriously injured or imminently threatened with such injury.

Brigham City, Utah v. Stuart

United States Supreme Court, 2006.
547 U.S. 398, 126 S.Ct. 1943.

■ CHIEF JUSTICE ROBERTS delivered the opinion of the Court.

In this case we consider whether police may enter a home without a warrant when they have an objectively reasonable basis for believing that an occupant is seriously injured or imminently threatened with such injury. We conclude that they may.

I

This case arises out of a melee that occurred in a Brigham City, Utah, home in the early morning hours of July 23, 2000. At about 3 a.m., four police officers responded to a call regarding a loud party at a residence. Upon arriving at the house, they heard shouting from inside, and proceeded down the driveway to investigate. There, they observed two juveniles drinking beer in the backyard. They entered the backyard, and saw—through a screen door and windows—an altercation taking place in the kitchen of the home. According to the testimony of one of the officers, four adults were attempting, with some difficulty, to restrain a juvenile. The juvenile eventually "broke free, swung a fist and struck one of the adults in the face." The officer testified that he observed the victim of the blow spitting blood into a nearby sink. The other adults continued to try to restrain the juvenile, pressing him up against a refrigerator with such force that the refrigerator began moving across the floor. At this point, an officer opened the screen door and announced the officers' presence. Amid the tumult, nobody noticed. The officer entered the kitchen and again cried out, and as the occupants slowly became aware that the police were on the scene, the altercation ceased.

The officers subsequently arrested respondents and charged them with contributing to the delinquency of a minor, disorderly conduct, and intoxication. In the trial court, respondents filed a motion to suppress all evidence obtained after the officers entered the home, arguing that the warrantless entry violated the Fourth Amendment. The court granted the motion, and the Utah Court of Appeals affirmed.

Before the Supreme Court of Utah, Brigham City argued that although the officers lacked a warrant, their entry was nevertheless reasonable on either of two grounds. The court rejected both contentions and, over two dissenters, affirmed. First, the court held that the injury caused by the juvenile's punch was insufficient to trigger the so-called "emergency aid doctrine" because it did not give rise to an "objectively reasonable belief that an unconscious, semi-conscious, or missing person feared injured or dead [was] in the home." (internal quotation marks omitted). Furthermore, the court suggested that the doctrine was inapplicable because the officers had not sought to assist the injured adult, but instead had acted "exclusively in their law enforcement capacity."

The court also held that the entry did not fall within the exigent circumstances exception to the warrant requirement. This exception applies, the court explained, where police have probable cause and where "a reasonable person [would] believe that the entry was necessary to prevent physical harm to the officers or other persons." Under this standard, the court stated, the potential harm need not be as serious as that required to invoke the emergency aid exception. Although it found the case "a close and difficult call," the court nevertheless concluded that the officers' entry was not justified by exigent circumstances.

We granted certiorari, in light of differences among state courts and the Courts of Appeals concerning the appropriate Fourth Amendment standard governing warrantless entry by law enforcement in an emergency situation. Compare *In re Sealed Case 96–3167*,332 U.S. App. D.C. 84, 153 F.3d 759, 766 (CADC 1998) ("[T]he standard for exigent circumstances is an objective one"), and *People v. Hebert*, 46 P. 3d 473, 480 (Colo. 2002) (en banc) (considering the circumstances as they "would have been objectively examined by a prudent and trained police officer"), with *United States* v. *Cervantes*, 219 F.3d 882, 890 (CA9 2000) ("[U]nder the emergency doctrine, '[a] search must not be primarily motivated by intent to arrest and seize evidence' ") (quoting *People v. Mitchell*, 39 N. Y. 2d 173, 177, 347 N.E.2d 607, 609, 383 N.Y.S.2d 246 (1976)), and *State v. Mountford*, 171 Vt. 487, 492, 769 A.2d 639, 645 (2000) (*Mitchell* test "requir[es] courts to find that the primary subjective motivation behind such searches was to provide emergency aid").

II

It is a " 'basic principle of Fourth Amendment law that searches and seizures inside a home without a warrant are presumptively unreasonable.' " Groh v. Ramirez (2004) (quoting Payton v. New York (1980)). Nevertheless, because the ultimate touchstone of the Fourth Amendment is "reasonableness," the warrant requirement is subject to certain exceptions. We have held, for example, that law enforcement officers may make a warrantless entry onto private property to fight a fire and investigate its cause, to prevent the imminent destruction of evidence, or to engage in " 'hot pursuit' " of a fleeing suspect. "[W]arrants are generally required to search a person's home or his person unless 'the exigencies of the situation' make the needs of law enforcement so compelling that the warrantless search is objectively reasonable under the Fourth Amendment." Mincey v. Arizona (1978).

One exigency obviating the requirement of a warrant is the need to assist persons who are seriously injured or threatened with such injury. . . .

Respondents do not take issue with these principles, but instead advance two reasons why the officers' entry here was unreasonable. First, they argue that the officers were more interested in making arrests than quelling violence. They urge us to consider, in assessing the reasonableness of the entry, whether the officers were "indeed motivated primarily by a desire to save lives and property." The Utah Supreme Court also considered the officers' subjective motivations relevant (search under the "emergency aid doctrine" may not be "primarily motivated by intent to arrest and seize evidence.")

Our cases have repeatedly rejected this approach. An action is "reasonable" under the Fourth Amendment, regardless of the individual officer's state of mind, "as long as the circumstances, viewed *objectively*, justify [the] action." Scott v. United States (1978) (emphasis added). The officer's subjective motivation is irrelevant. See Bond v. United States (2000) ("The parties properly agree that the subjective intent of the law enforcement officer is irrelevant in determining whether that officer's actions violate the Fourth Amendment . . .; the issue is not his state of mind, but the objective effect of his actions"); Whren v. United States, (1996) ("[W]e have been unwilling to entertain Fourth Amendment challenges based on the actual motivations of individual officers"); Graham v. Connor (1989) ("[O]ur prior cases make clear" that "the subjective motivations of the individual officers . . . ha[ve] no bearing on whether a particular seizure is 'unreasonable' under the Fourth Amendment"). It therefore does not matter here—even if their subjective motives could be so neatly unraveled—whether the officers entered the kitchen to arrest respondents and gather evidence against them or to assist the injured and prevent further violence. . . .

We think the officers' entry here was plainly reasonable under the circumstances. The officers were responding, at 3 o'clock in the morning, to complaints about a loud party. As they approached the house, they could hear from within "an altercation occurring, some kind of a fight." "It was loud and it was tumultuous." The officers heard "thumping and crashing" and people yelling "stop, stop" and "get off me." As the trial court found, "it was obvious that ... knocking on the front door" would have been futile. The noise seemed to be coming from the back of the house; after looking in the front window and seeing nothing, the officers proceeded around back to investigate further. They found two juveniles drinking beer in the backyard. From there, they could see that a fracas was taking place inside the kitchen. A juvenile, fists clenched, was being held back by several adults. As the officers watch, he breaks free and strikes one of the adults in the face, sending the adult to the sink spitting blood.

In these circumstances, the officers had an objectively reasonable basis for believing both that the injured adult might need help and that the violence in the kitchen was just beginning. Nothing in the Fourth Amendment required them to wait until another blow rendered someone "unconscious" or "semi-conscious" or worse before entering. The role of a peace officer includes preventing violence and restoring order, not simply rendering first aid to casualties; an officer is not like a boxing (or hockey) referee, poised to stop a bout only if it becomes too one-sided.

The manner of the officers' entry was also reasonable. After witnessing the punch, one of the officers opened the screen door and "yelled in police." When nobody heard him, he stepped into the kitchen and announced himself again. Only then did the tumult subside. The officer's announcement of his presence was at least equivalent to a knock on the screen door. Indeed, it was probably the only option that had even a chance of rising above the din. Under these circumstances, there was no violation of the Fourth Amendment's knock-and-announce rule. Furthermore, once the announcement was made, the officers were free to enter; it would serve no purpose to require them to stand dumbly at the door awaiting a response while those within brawled on, oblivious to their presence.

Accordingly, we reverse the judgment of the Supreme Court of Utah, and remand the case for further proceedings not inconsistent with this opinion.

It is so ordered.

■ JUSTICE STEVENS, concurring.

This is an odd flyspeck of a case. The charges that have been pending against respondents for the past six years are minor offenses—intoxication, contributing to the delinquency of a minor, and disorderly conduct—two of which could have been proved by evidence that was gathered by the responding officers before they entered the home. The maximum punishment for these crimes ranges between 90 days and 6 months in jail. And the Court's unanimous opinion restating well-settled rules of federal law is so clearly persuasive that it is hard to imagine the outcome was ever in doubt.

Under these circumstances, the only difficult question is which of the following is the most peculiar: (1) that the Utah trial judge, the intermediate state appellate court, and the Utah Supreme Court all found a Fourth Amendment violation on these facts; (2) that the prosecution chose to pursue this matter all the way to the United States Supreme Court; or (3) that this Court voted to grant the petition for a writ of certiorari.

A possible explanation for the first is that the suppression ruling was correct as a matter of Utah law, and neither trial counsel nor the trial judge bothered to identify the Utah Constitution as an independent basis for the decision because they did not expect the prosecution to appeal. *The most plausible explanation for the latter two decisions is that they were made so police officers in Utah may enter a home without a warrant when they see ongoing violence—we are, of course, reversing the Utah Supreme Court's conclusion to the contrary. But that purpose, laudable though it may be, cannot be achieved in this case. Our holding today addresses only the limitations placed by the Federal Constitution on the search at issue; we have no authority to decide whether the police in this case violated the Utah Constitution.

The Utah Supreme Court, however, has made clear that the Utah Constitution provides greater protection to the privacy of the home than does the Fourth Amendment. And it complained in this case of respondents' failure to raise or adequately brief a state constitutional challenge, thus preventing the state courts from deciding the case on anything other than Fourth Amendment grounds. "[S]urpris[ed]" by "[t]he reluctance of litigants to take up and develop a state constitutional analysis," the court expressly invited future litigants to bring challenges under the Utah Constitution to enable it to fulfill its "responsibility as guardians of the individual liberty of our citizens" and "undertak[e] a principled exploration of the interplay between federal and state protections of individual rights." The fact that this admonishment and request came from the Utah Supreme Court in this very case not only demonstrates that the prosecution selected the wrong case for establishing the rule it wants, but also indicates that the Utah Supreme Court would probably adopt the same rule as a matter of state constitutional law that we reject today under the Federal Constitution.

Whether or not that forecast is accurate, I can see no reason for this Court to cause the Utah courts to redecide the question as a matter of state law. Federal interests are not offended when a single State elects to provide greater protection for its citizens than the Federal Constitution requires. Indeed, I continue to believe "that a policy of judicial restraint—one that allows other decisional bodies to have the last word in legal interpretation until it is truly necessary for this Court to intervene—enables this Court to make its most effective contribution to our federal system of government." *Michigan v. Long*, 463 U.S. 1032, 1067, 103 S. Ct. 3469, 77 L. Ed. 2d 1201 (1983) (Stevens, J., dissenting). Thus, while I join the Court's opinion, I remain persuaded that my vote to deny the State's petition for certiorari was correct.

NOTES

1. ***Civil Emergency***. Courts have sanctioned warrantless intrusions on the basis of a "civil" emergency theory, that is, by the need to preserve life, health, or property from imminent danger. The reasonableness of such intrusions depends upon a weighing of various factors, including (1) the basis for believing that an emergency exists; (2) the gravity of the situation; (3) the extent of the intrusion; (4) the availability of less intrusive alternatives; and (5) the chances that the intrusion will prove successful. See People v. Mitchell, 39 N.Y.2d 173, 383 N.Y.S.2d 246, 347 N.E.2d 607 (1976).

In Patrick v. Delaware, 227 A.2d 486 (Del. 1967) the court held confronted a fact situation in which police were called to an apartment with a report that employer had discovered the body of his employee and he could not tell if the man was alive or dead. The police entered, determined the individual dead and proceeded to conduct a homicide investigation, taking photographs and seizing bits of the brick that apparently had been used to crush the skull of the victim. Determining that the police were in the apartment legally, the state court apparently was responding to an argument made quite commonly where the police have entered a suspect's home without a warrant and have found a body: there was no true emergency because if the authorities were likely to find anything, it surely would be a corpse. The contention has been rejected and emergency theory invoked even in situations where the defense argument was more plausible than in *Stuart* See, e.g., People v. Bondi, 130 Ill.App.3d 536, 85 Ill.Dec. 773, 474 N.E.2d 733 (1984) (upholding a search which required digging up a buried body.)

Note, the Court has firmly rejected any notion of a "homicide exception" to the Fourth Amendment warrant requirement when exigency is not involved. Thompson v. Louisiana, 469 U.S. 17, 105 S.Ct. 409 (1984).

A. Civil emergency theories have been mentioned in several Supreme Court opinions. In Cady v. Dombrowski, 413 U.S. 433, 93 S.Ct. 2523 (1973), the Court upheld the warrantless search of the trunk of a car owned by an out-of-state police officer who had been arrested while intoxicated. One theory used to justify the search was that the trunk might have contained the officer's service revolver, vandals might have broken into the locked trunk, obtained the weapon, and endangered the community. In the small town where Dombrowski had been arrested, alternative means of securing the vehicle were impractical.

B. In Michigan v. Tyler, 436 U.S. 499, 98 S.Ct. 1942 (1978), the Court, in dictum, stated that even after a fire is extinguished, officials may remain or promptly reenter to determine the fire's origin so as to prevent its recurrence. Dictum in Camara v. Municipal Court, 387 U.S. 523, 87 S.Ct. 1727 (1967) (Section M), spoke of emergency health situations (rather than routine inspections) which would justify a warrantless entry. The Court cited other examples of bona fide emergency action, such as the warrantless seizure and destruction of diseased cattle.

2. ***Imminent Criminal Violence.*** The need to protect persons from being victimized by imminent criminal violence also justifies emergency intrusions. The typical case involves entry after the officer hears screams. People v. Sirhan, 7 Cal.3d 710, 102 Cal.Rptr. 385, 497 P.2d 1121 (1972), stretched the "thwarting crime" theory to its outer limits. In Sirhan the court upheld an entry into an offender's home and an exploratory search because a police officer theorized that the shooting of Senator Robert Kennedy might have been the first in a conspiracy to kill several national figures. Prompt action to learn the details was deemed proper to save other intended victims.

3. *Destruction of Evidence.* Several United States Supreme Court cases suggest that under some circumstances even a home might be entered without a warrant to prevent the imminent destruction of evidence of a crime. The Court, however, has not spelled out the limits of such a doctrine. Lower courts, however, occasionally have upheld such entries, where the threat of destruction by natural causes, by a suspect, or by a third party was very substantial and where the officers did not deliberately create the emergency which made the immediate entry necessary to prevent the destruction. See United States v. Socey, 846 F.2d 1439 (D.C.Cir.1988). In deciding whether or not officers "deliberately created an emergency," bad faith is not required, but the court must examine the reasonableness of the investigative techniques employed, while giving government agents the benefit of any doubts where reasonable minds differ. See United States v. Blount, 123 F.3d 831 (5th Cir.1997) (en banc).

Assuming that emergency entries are sometimes permissible to prevent the destruction of evidence, must the police, if they are able, "freeze" the scene after making the emergency entry and then apply for a warrant? Does the availability of telephonic warrant procedures diminish the validity of an exigent circumstances claim? United States v. Cuaron, 700 F.2d 582 (10th Cir.1983).

4. *Homicide Scene.* In the years preceding Mincey v. Arizona, 437 U.S. 385, 98 S.Ct. 2408 (1978), a number of lower courts began to recognize a "homicide scene" search exception to the warrant requirement, allowing warrantless inspections of the scene of a homicide even after the victim and the suspect had been removed from the suspect's home. In *Mincey* the Court held that there was no such exception. To justify a warrantless search of a homicide scene, law enforcement officers must show an actual "evidence emergency." Alternatively, they must obtain consent or confine their activities within the limits of one of the other recognized exceptions (e.g., search incident to arrest or plain view seizure).

In Thompson v. Louisiana, 469 U.S. 17, 105 S.Ct. 409 (1984), the Supreme Court reaffirmed Mincey under facts far less aggravated than in Mincey (where the search had occurred several days after the offense). In *Thompson* the warrantless search of the homicide scene commenced within an hour of removal of the victim. Concerning difficulties of obtaining a warrant to search a homicide scene because of the specificity requirement.

5. *Minimal Intrusions.* The Seventh Circuit held that "entry into a domicile usually requires a search warrant, which can be had only on probable cause, but quick inspections may be justified by lower degrees of suspicion." United States v. Brown, 64 F.3d 1083, 1086 (7th Cir.1995). After arresting a defendant and searching an accomplice's car, officers found the car was registered to an unknown woman who lived near where defendant was arrested. The officers asked the defendant where he lived; he pointed to a house other than the one reflected in the registration. The officers also found keys on defendant that fit in the locks of the woman's apartment. Without waiting for a warrant, officers went in the apartment and looked around, spotting some cocaine and two safes. In a rather expansive opinion that even questioned the warrant requirement itself along the way, the court held that there need not have been immediate danger in order for officers to successfully plead that exigent circumstances justified the intrusion. "The less intrusive a search, the less justification is required . . . [t]he question posed by the fourth amendment is not whether it would have been reasonable to get a warrant, but whether the search itself was reasonable." Id. at 1086. Judge Rovner dissented. The approach the Seventh Circuit takes here is consistent with its "sliding scale" approach to *Terry* stops.

6. *Searches of Persons.* Warrantless emergency intrusions against the person have been upheld in Schmerber v. California, 384 U.S. 757, 86 S.Ct. 1826 (1966), where officers took a blood sample for use in a blood-alcohol test and in Cupp v. Murphy, 412 U.S. 291, 93 S.Ct. 2000 (1973), where the police took a fingernail scraping from a homicide suspect. *Schmerber* permitted the warrantless blood test on the basis that if the police waited for a warrant, the evidence of intoxication would disappear. *Cupp* is probably more significant to emergency theory than is Schmerber because (1) in *Cupp*, unlike *Schmerber*, the doctrine of search incident to arrest could not be utilized because the suspect was not arrested; and (2) in *Cupp*, unlike *Schmerber*, it is not clear that there was full probable cause to believe that the search would yield evidence. On the other hand, in upholding the procedure in *Cupp*, the Court emphasized that the intensity of the intrusion was not as great as in *Schmerber*.

7. ***Community Caretaking***. Several cases have upheld warrantless searches where the officers were involved in community caretaking activities: stopping a car whose driver was feared suicidal, Provo v. Warden, 844 P.2d 360 (Utah App.1992); turning down a stereo, United States v. Rohrig, 98 F.3d 1506 (6th Cir.1996); after-hours security check of a building, State v. Myers, 601 P.2d 239 (Alaska 1979). For a different view, see United States v. Bute, 43 F.3d 531 (10th Cir.1994).

In United States v. McGough, 412 F.3d 1232 (11th Cir.2005), police responded to a 911 call placed accidentally by a five year old child left in an apartment alone–she dialed 911 then hung up quickly. The police responded to the location and began to forcibly enter the premises through burglar bars and a heavy door in order to remove the child for her own protection. Her father arrived in the course of this and opened the door for them. The police then arrested the father on a charge related to leaving the child unattended. The police placed the father and the child into a police car. Noticing the child was barefooted, one officer returned to the apartment to get her shoes. While doing so, he observed a bag of marijuana and a revolver. The officer used this information to obtain a warrant to search the apartment.

At the hearing on the motion to suppress, the prosecution argued that the warrantless entries that preceded the warrant were justified under the community caretaking function.

The Eleventh Circuit rejected this argument, noting that even if there is a community caretaking function, there was insufficient urgency to enter to get shoes. Thus, the community caretaking function was not applicable.

J. MOTOR VEHICLE SEARCHES

The first exception the United States Supreme Court recognized to the warrant requirement was the "automobile exception" or the "*Carroll* doctrine," [after Carroll v. United States, 267 U.S. 132, 45 S.Ct. 280 (1925)]. *Carroll*, a case involving a suspected bootleg run at the Canadian border, permitted a warrantless search reasoning that it was impractical for officers to obtain a warrant in this context. Thus, the exception began as one rooted in a form of exigency. Now, the exception has broadened in scope. Other theories of general applicability may come into play in automobile search and seizure cases (*e.g.*, abandonment or search incident to arrest). We begin with treatment of the *Carroll* doctrine.

Maryland v. Dyson

United States Supreme Court, 1999.
527 U.S. 465, 119 S.Ct. 2013.

■ PER CURIAM.

In this case, the Maryland Court of Special Appeals held that the Fourth Amendment requires police to obtain a search warrant before searching a vehicle which they have probable cause to believe contains illegal drugs. Because this holding rests upon an incorrect interpretation of the automobile exception to the Fourth Amendment's warrant requirement, we grant the petition for certiorari and reverse.

At 11 a.m. on the morning of July 2, 1996, a St. Mary's County (Maryland) Sheriff's Deputy received a tip from a reliable confidential informant that respondent had gone to New York to buy drugs, and would be returning to Maryland in a rented red Toyota, license number DDY 787, later that day with a large quantity of cocaine. The deputy investigated the tip and found that the license number given to him by the informant belonged to a red Toyota Corolla that had been rented to respondent, who was a known drug dealer in St. Mary's County. When respondent returned to St. Mary's County in the rented car at 1 a.m. on July 3, the deputies stopped and searched the vehicle, finding 23 grams of crack cocaine in a duffel bag in the trunk. Respondent was arrested, tried, and convicted of conspiracy to possess cocaine with intent to distribute. He appealed, arguing that the trial court had erroneously denied his motion to suppress the cocaine on the alternate grounds that the police lacked probable cause, or that even if there was probable cause, the warrantless search violated the Fourth Amendment because there was sufficient time after the informant's tip to obtain a warrant.

The Maryland Court of Special Appeals reversed, holding that in order for the automobile exception to the warrant requirement to apply, there must not only be probable cause to believe that evidence of a crime is contained in the automobile, but also a separate finding of exigency precluding the police from obtaining a warrant. Applying this rule to the facts of the case, the Court of Special Appeals concluded that although there was "abundant probable cause," the search violated the Fourth Amendment because there was no exigency that prevented or even made it significantly difficult for the police to obtain a search warrant. The Maryland Court of Appeals denied certiorari. We grant certiorari and now reverse.

The Fourth Amendment generally requires police to secure a warrant before conducting a search. As we recognized nearly 75 years ago in Carroll v. United States (1925), there is an exception to this requirement for searches of vehicles. And under our established precedent, the "automobile exception" has no separate exigency requirement. We made this clear in United States v. Ross (1982), when we said that in cases where there was probable cause to search a vehicle "a search is not unreasonable if based on facts that would justify the issuance of a warrant, *even though a warrant has not been actually obtained*." (Emphasis added.) In a case with virtually identical facts to this one (even down to the bag of cocaine in the trunk of the car), Pennsylvania v. Labron (1996) *(per curiam)*, we repeated that the automobile exception does not have a separate exigency requirement: "If a car is readily mobile and probable cause exists to believe it contains contraband, the Fourth Amendment ... permits police to search the vehicle without more."

In this case, the Court of Special Appeals found that there was "abundant probable cause" that the car contained contraband. This finding alone satisfies the automobile exception to the Fourth Amendment's warrant requirement, a conclusion correctly reached by the trial court when it denied respondent's motion to suppress. The holding of the Court of Special Appeals that the "automobile exception" requires a separate finding of exigency in addition to a finding of probable cause is squarely contrary to our holdings in *Ross* and *Labron*. We therefore grant the petition for writ of certiorari and reverse the judgment of the Court of Special Appeals.

NOTES

1. *Delayed Search:* In Chambers v. Maroney, 399 U.S. 42, 90 S.Ct. 1975 (1970) the police stopped a car which matched a description of one seen speeding away from at the scene of a gas station robbery. The occupants matched the description of the robbers. The arrest of the occupants was sufficiently supported by probable cause. The issue in the case, however, was whether the warrantless automobile search was valid. Instead of searching the car at the time of the arrest, police towed the car to the station and searched it there, finding weapons. Noting that "the search of an auto on the basis of probable cause is proceeds on a theory wholly different from that justifying the search incident to an arrest," the Court ruled that since the officers had probable cause to believe contraband was in the car at the spot when it was stopped, there was still probable cause to search it at the station house. Rejecting an argument that the car was secured in police custody and police should then wait for a warrant before searching the vehicle, the Court

2. *Mobility Rationale*. The rationale in *Chambers* for allowing the warrantless search of a vehicle upon probable cause was the mobility of the car. In later years, however, the Court began utilizing a second rationale: the diminished expectation of privacy one has in a vehicle (as distinguished, for example, from the expectation of privacy in a home). In the 1980's some members of the Court suggested that the mobility rationale, by itself, was inadequate because once the police have taken possession of a vehicle its mobility is no longer a threat to a successful search, yet under *Chambers* a warrantless search is even permitted in that situation.

1. THE CARROLL DOCTRINE APPLIED.

a. ***A Motor Vehicle*.** The *Carroll* doctrine applies only to motor vehicles. Sometimes this raises a definitional issue. Is a mobile home more like a home or more like a car for purposes of the *Carroll* doctrine? In California v. Carney, 471 U.S. 386, 105 S.Ct. 2066 (1985), a mobile home was used as a place from which to vend drugs and apparently not as a place of even temporary residence. It was not mounted on blocks but rather had ready access to the highway and, in fact, it was driven about. The Court characterized the mobile home as a vehicle for the purpose of applying the motor vehicle exception.

b. ***No Unlawful Stop*.** If a car is unlawfully stopped while in transit the search is unlawful. The *Carroll* doctrine itself may justify the stop, that is, the stop can be made if there is probable cause to believe that the vehicle contains contraband or criminal evidence. Alternatively, the stop preceding the *Carroll* search sometimes is justified on some other theory (e.g., reasonable suspicion for a *Terry* stop). If following a lawful stop (on what ever theory) probable cause for a search develops, then the search can be made under the *Carroll* doctrine.

c. ***Search Probable Cause***. In every case, probable cause to believe that contraband or criminal evidence is in the vehicle is a prerequisite for a valid *Carroll* search. On the other hand, the validity of the search does not depend upon a probability that somebody in the car has committed an offense.

d. ***No Requirement of an Actual Emergency.*** If a car is lawfully stopped, and if there is probable cause for a search, under *Carroll* a warrant is unnecessary even if there is no actual emergency. This was apparent from *Chambers* and from the majority per curiam opinion in the following case of Texas v. White, 423 U.S. 67, 96 S.Ct. 304 (1975):

> Respondent was arrested at 1:30 p.m. by Amarillo, Tex., police officers while attempting to pass fraudulent checks at a drive-in window of the First National Bank of Amarillo. Only 10 minutes earlier, the officers had been informed by another bank that a man answering respondent's description and driving an automobile exactly matching that of respondent had tried to negotiate four checks drawn on a non-existent account. Upon arrival at the First National Bank pursuant to a telephone call from that bank the officers obtained from the drive-in teller other checks that respondent had attempted to pass there. The officers directed respondent to park his automobile at the curb. While parking the car, respondent was observed by a bank employee and one of the officers attempting to "stuff" something between the seats. Respondent was arrested and one officer drove him to the station house while the other drove respondent's car there. At the station house, the officers questioned respondent for 30 to 45 minutes and, pursuant to their normal procedure, requested consent to search the automobile. Respondent refused to consent to the search. The officers then proceeded to search the automobile anyway. During the search, an officer discovered four wrinkled checks that corresponded to those respondent had attempted to pass at the first bank. The trial judge, relying on Chambers v. Maroney (1970), admitted over respondent's objection the four checks seized during the search of respondent's automobile at the station house. The judge expressly found probable cause both for the arrest and for the search of the vehicle, either at the scene or at the station house. Respondent was convicted after a jury trial of knowingly attempting to pass a forged instrument. The Texas Court of Criminal Appeals, in a 3–2 decision, reversed respondent's conviction on the ground that the four wrinkled checks used in evidence were obtained without a warrant in violation of respondent's Fourth Amendment rights. We reverse.
>
> In Chambers v. Maroney we held that police officers with probable cause to search an automobile at the scene where it was stopped could constitutionally do so later at the station house without first obtaining a warrant. There, as here, "[t]he probable-cause factor" that developed at the scene "still obtained at the

station house." The Court of Criminal Appeals erroneously excluded the evidence seized from the search at the station house in light of the trial judge's finding, undisturbed by the appellate court, that there was probable cause to search respondent's car.

■JUSTICE MARSHALL, with whom JUSTICE BRENNAN concurs, dissenting.

Only by misstating the holding of Chambers v. Maroney (1970), can the Court make that case appear dispositive of this one. The Court in its brief per curiam opinion today extends *Chambers* to a clearly distinguishable factual setting, without having afforded the opportunity for full briefing and oral argument. I respectfully dissent.

Chambers did not hold, as the Court suggests, that "police officers with probable cause to search an automobile at the scene where it was stopped could constitutionally do so later at the station house without first obtaining a warrant." *Chambers* simply held that to be the rule when it is reasonable to take the car to the station house in the first place.

The Supreme Court has previously acknowledged that under its application of the *Carroll–Chambers* doctrine warrantless searches were to be upheld even though "the possibilities of the vehicle's being removed or evidence in it destroyed were remote, if not non-existent." Cady v. Dombrowski, 413 U.S. 433, 93 S.Ct. 2523 (1973). In Michigan v. Thomas, 458 U.S. 259, 102 S.Ct. 3079 (1982), the Court followed White in another per curiam opinion. It declared that the justification to conduct such a warrantless search "does not vanish once the car has been immobilized; nor does it depend upon ... assessment of the likelihood in each particular case that the car would have been driven away, or that its contents would have been tampered with, during the period required for the police to obtain a warrant." To the same effect are Florida v. Meyers, 466 U.S. 380, 104 S.Ct. 1852 (1984) (per curiam), and Pennsylvania v. Labron, 518 U.S. 938, 116 S.Ct. 2485 (1996) (per curiam) (no exigent circumstances required to search car—even if parked or passengers in custody).

On state constitutional grounds, Rhode Island rejected the result of Texas v. White and held that a warrant is required for the search of a vehicle which has been stopped in transit if it is practicable to obtain one. State v. Benoit, 417 A.2d 895 (R.I.1980). New Hampshire has also rejected the view that one has a reduced expectation of privacy in a car. State v. Sterndale, 139 N.H. 445, 656 A.2d 409 (1995). Partly on the basis of its state constitution, the Oregon Supreme Court ruled that authorities cannot search an unoccupied parked car without a warrant unless they face particularized exigent circumstances. State v. Kock, 302 Or. 29, 725 P.2d 1285 (1986).

e. ***The Delayed Search.*** In United States v. Johns, 469 U.S. 478, 105 S.Ct. 881 (1985), the Court declared that interference with a privacy or a possessory interest caused by delay could render a *Carroll–Chambers* search unreasonable. It found no such violation where authorities removed packages from a vehicle and delayed their search for three days where the packages contained contraband.

f. ***Scope of the Search.*** If there is probable cause to believe that somewhere in a car there is contraband or evidence, is it proper to search each person in the vehicle without a particular reason to believe that the person has evidence? United States v. Di Re, 332 U.S. 581, 68 S.Ct. 222 (1948), indicated not; but that opinion did not state what would be required. The issue is analogous to the question of which occupants can be searched when a warrant commands the search of a certain apartment. (See Section D–5 and see also the Court's reference to the analogy between searches under warrants and warrantless searches of cars discussed in *Ross*, infra.)

* * *

What if a container, such as a briefcase, is found in a car which has been lawfully stopped under the *Carroll* doctrine. Can it be searched? As indicated in the case below, this question has received much attention from the Supreme Court in recent years.

United States v. Ross

Supreme Court of the United States, 1982.
456 U.S. 798, 102 S.Ct. 2157.

■ JUSTICE STEVENS delivered the opinion of the Court.

In Carroll v. United States (1925), the Court held that a warrantless search of an automobile stopped by police officers who had probable cause to believe the vehicle contained contraband was not unreasonable within the meaning of the Fourth Amendment. The Court in *Carroll* did not explicitly address the scope of the search that is permissible. In this case, we consider the extent to which police officers—who have legitimately stopped an automobile and who have probable cause to believe that contraband is concealed somewhere within it—may conduct a probing search of compartments and containers within the vehicle whose contents are not in plain view. We hold that they may conduct a search of the vehicle that is as thorough as a magistrate could authorize in a warrant "particularly describing the place to be searched."

In the evening of November 27, 1978, an informant who had previously proved to be reliable telephoned Detective Marcum of the District of Columbia Police Department and told him that an individual known as "Bandit" was selling narcotics kept in the trunk of a car parked at 439 Ridge Street. The informant stated that he had just observed "Bandit" complete a sale and that "Bandit" had told him that additional narcotics were in the trunk. The informant gave Marcum a detailed description of "Bandit" and stated that the car was a "purplish maroon" Chevrolet Malibu with District of Columbia license plates.

Accompanied by Detective Cassidy and Sergeant Gonzales, Marcum immediately drove to the area and found a maroon Malibu parked in front of 439 Ridge Street. A license check disclosed that the car was registered to

Albert Ross; a computer check on Ross revealed that he fit the informant's description and used the alias "Bandit." In two passes through the neighborhood the officers did not observe anyone matching the informant's description. To avoid alerting persons on the street, they left the area.

The officers returned five minutes later and observed the maroon Malibu turning off Ridge Street onto Fourth Street. They pulled alongside the Malibu, noticed that the driver matched the informant's description, and stopped the car. Marcum and Cassidy told the driver—later identified as Albert Ross, the respondent in this action—to get out of the vehicle. While they searched Ross, Sergeant Gonzales discovered a bullet on the car's front seat. He searched the interior of the car and found a pistol in the glove compartment. Ross then was arrested and handcuffed. Detective Cassidy took Ross' keys and opened the trunk, where he found a closed brown paper bag. He opened the bag and discovered a number of glassine bags containing a white powder. Cassidy replaced the bag, closed the trunk, and drove the car to Headquarters.

At the police station Cassidy thoroughly searched the car. In addition to the "lunch-type" brown paper bag, Cassidy found in the trunk a zippered red leather pouch. He unzipped the pouch and discovered $3,200 in cash. The police laboratory later determined that the powder in the paper bag was heroin. No warrant was obtained.

Ross was charged with possession of heroin with intent to distribute, in violation of 21 U.S.C. § 841(a). Prior to trial, he moved to suppress the heroin found in the paper bag and the currency found in the leather pouch. After an evidentiary hearing, the District Court denied the motion to suppress. The heroin and currency were introduced in evidence at trial and Ross was convicted.

[The en banc court of appeals reversed, rejecting an appellate panel's view that the search of the paper bag was lawful but that the search of the zippered pouch was unlawful. That view rested upon the assumption that there was a lesser expectation of privacy in the paper bag.]

[T]he exception to the warrant requirement established in *Carroll*—the scope of which we consider in this case—applies only to searches of vehicles that are supported by probable cause. In this class of cases, a search is not unreasonable if based on facts that would justify the issuance of a warrant, even though a warrant has not actually been obtained.

The rationale justifying a warrantless search of an automobile that is believed to be transporting contraband arguably applies with equal force to any movable container that is believed to be carrying an illicit substance. That argument, however, was squarely rejected in United States v. Chadwick (1977). . . .

Writing for the [unanimous] Court, The Chief Justice stated:

> "[I]f there is little evidence that the Framers intended the Warrant Clause to operate outside the home, there is no evidence at all that they intended to exclude from protection of the Clause all searches occurring outside the home. The absence of a contemporary outcry against warrantless searches in public places was because, aside from searches incident to arrest, such warrantless

searches were not a large issue in colonial America. Thus, silence in the historical record tells us little about the Framers' attitude toward application of the Warrant Clause to the search of respondents' footlocker. What we do know is that the Framers were men who focused on the wrongs of that day but who intended the Fourth Amendment to safeguard fundamental values which would far outlast the specific abuses which gave it birth."

The Court in *Chadwick* specifically rejected the argument that the warrantless search was "reasonable" because a footlocker has some of the mobile characteristics that support warrantless searches of automobiles. The Court recognized that "a person's expectations of privacy in personal luggage are substantially greater than in an automobile," and noted that the practical problems associated with the temporary detention of a piece of luggage during the period of time necessary to obtain a warrant are significantly less than those associated with the detention of an automobile. In ruling that the warrantless search of the footlocker was unjustified, the Court reaffirmed the general principle that closed packages and containers may not be searched without a warrant. In sum, the Court in *Chadwick* declined to extend the rationale of the "automobile exception" to permit a warrantless search of any movable container found in a public place.

The facts in Arkansas v. Sanders (1979), were similar to those in *Chadwick*. In *Sanders*, a Little Rock police officer received information from a reliable informant that *Sanders* would arrive at the local airport on a specified flight that afternoon carrying a green suitcase containing marijuana. The officer went to the airport. Sanders arrived on schedule and retrieved a green suitcase from the airline baggage service. Sanders gave the suitcase to a waiting companion who placed it in the trunk of a taxi. Sanders and his companion drove off in the cab; police officers followed and stopped the taxi several blocks from the airport. The officers opened the trunk, seized the suitcase, and searched it on the scene without a warrant. As predicted, the suitcase contained marijuana.

The Arkansas Supreme Court ruled that the warrantless search of the suitcase was impermissible under the Fourth Amendment, and this Court affirmed. As in *Chadwick*, the mere fact that the suitcase had been placed in the trunk of the vehicle did not render the automobile exception of *Carroll* applicable; the police had probable cause to seize the suitcase before it was placed in the trunk of the cab and did not have probable cause to search the taxi itself. Since the suitcase had been placed in the trunk, no danger existed that its contents could have been secreted elsewhere in the vehicle.... In rejecting the State's argument that the warrantless search of the suitcase was justified on the ground that it had been taken from an automobile lawfully stopped on the street, the Court broadly suggested that a warrantless search of a container found in an automobile could never be sustained as part of a warrantless search of the automobile itself. The Court did not suggest that it mattered whether probable cause existed to search the entire vehicle. It is clear, however, that in neither *Chadwick* nor *Sanders* did the police have probable cause to search the vehicle or anything within it except the footlocker in the former case and the green suitcase in the latter.

Robbins v. California (1981), however, was a case in which suspicion was not directed at a specific container. [Editor's Note: Because the Ross Court expressly overruled the plurality opinion in *Robbins*, we omit extended treatment of *Robbins*.] . . . .

Unlike *Chadwick* and *Sanders*, in this case police officers had probable cause to search respondent's entire vehicle.[1] Unlike *Robbins*, in this case the parties have squarely addressed the question whether, in the course of a legitimate warrantless search of an automobile, police are entitled to open containers found within the vehicle. We now address that question. Its answer is determined by the scope of the search that is authorized by the exception to the warrant requirement set forth in *Carroll*.

In *Carroll* itself, the whiskey that the prohibition agents seized was not in plain view. It was discovered only after an officer opened the rumble seat and tore open the upholstery of the lazyback. The Court did not find the scope of the search unreasonable. Having stopped *Carroll* and *Kiro* on a public road and subjected them to the indignity of a vehicle search—which the Court found to be a reasonable intrusion on their privacy because it was based on probable cause that their vehicle was transporting contraband—prohibition agents were entitled to tear open a portion of the roadster itself. The scope of the search was no greater than a magistrate could have authorized by issuing a warrant based on the probable cause that justified the search. Since such a warrant could have authorized the agents to open the rear portion of the roadster and to rip the upholstery in their search for concealed whiskey, the search was constitutionally permissible.

In Chambers v. Maroney the police found weapons and stolen property "concealed in a compartment under the dashboard." No suggestion was made that the scope of the search was impermissible. It would be illogical to assume that the outcome of *Chambers*—or the outcome of *Carroll* itself—would have been different if the police had found the secreted contraband enclosed within a secondary container and had opened that container without a warrant. If it was reasonable for prohibition agents to rip open the upholstery in *Carroll*, it certainly would have been reasonable for them to look into a burlap sack stashed inside; if it was reasonable to open the concealed compartment in *Chambers*, it would have been equally reasonable to open a paper bag crumpled within it. A contrary rule could produce absurd results inconsistent with the decision in *Carroll* itself.

In its application of *Carroll*, this Court in fact has sustained warrantless searches of containers found during a lawful search of an automobile. . . .

1. The en banc Court of Appeals stated that "[b]ased on the tip the police received, Ross's car was properly stopped and searched, and the pouch and bag were properly seized." 655 F.2d, at 1168 (footnote omitted). The court explained:

"[W]e believe it clear that the police had ample and reasonable cause to stop Ross and to search his car. The informer had supplied accurate information on prior occasions, and he was an eyewitness to sales of narcotics by Ross. He said he had just seen Ross take narcotics from the trunk of his car in making a sale and heard him say he possessed additional narcotics."

The court further noted that "[i]n this case, the informant told the police that Ross had narcotics in the trunk of his car. No specific container was identified."

In these cases it was not contended that police officers needed a warrant to open the whiskey bags or to unwrap the brown paper packages. These decisions nevertheless "have much weight, as they show that this point neither occurred to the bar nor the bench." Bank of the United States v. Deveaux, 5 Cranch 61, 88 (Marshall, C.J.). The fact that no such argument was even made illuminates the profession's understanding of the scope of the search permitted under *Carroll*. Indeed, prior to the decisions in *Chadwick* and *Sanders*, courts routinely had held that containers and packages found during a legitimate warrantless search of an automobile also could be searched without a warrant.

As we have stated the decision in *Carroll* was based on the Court's appraisal of practical considerations viewed in the perspective of history. It is therefore significant that the practical consequences of the *Carroll* decision would be largely nullified if the permissible scope of a warrantless search of an automobile did not include containers and packages found inside the vehicle. Contraband goods rarely are strewn across the trunk or floor of a car, since by their very nature such goods must be withheld from public view, they rarely can be placed in an automobile unless they are enclosed within some form of container. The Court in *Carroll* held that "contraband goods concealed and illegally transported in an automobile or other vehicle may be searched for without a warrant." As we noted in Henry v. United States (1959), the decision in *Carroll* "merely relaxed the requirements for a warrant on grounds of impracticability." It neither broadened nor limited the scope of a lawful search based on probable cause.

A lawful search of fixed premises generally extends to the entire area in which the object of the search may be found and is not limited by the possibility that separate acts of entry or opening may be required to complete the search. Thus, a warrant that authorizes an officer to search a home for illegal weapons also provides authority to open closets, chests, drawers, and containers in which the weapon might be found. A warrant to open a footlocker to search for marijuana would also authorize the opening of packages found inside. A warrant to search a vehicle would support a search of every part of the vehicle that might contain the object of the search. When a legitimate search is under way, and when its purpose and its limits have been precisely defined, nice distinctions between closets, drawers, and containers, in the case of a home, or between glove compartments, upholstered seats, trunks, and wrapped packages, in the case of a vehicle, must give way to the interest in the prompt and efficient completion of the task at hand.[2]

2. The practical considerations that justify a warrantless search of an automobile continue to apply until the entire search of the automobile and its contents has been completed. Arguably, the entire vehicle itself (including its upholstery) could be searched without a warrant, with all wrapped articles and containers found during that search then taken to a magistrate. But prohibiting police from opening immediately a container in which the object of the search is most likely to be found and instead forcing them first to comb the entire vehicle would actually exacerbate the intrusion on privacy interests. Moreover, until the container itself was opened the police could never be certain that the contraband was not secreted in a yet undiscovered portion of the vehicle; thus in every case in which a container was found, the vehicle would need to be secured while a warrant was obtained. Such a requirement would be directly inconsistent with the ratio-

This rule applies equally to all containers, as indeed we believe it must. One point on which the Court was in virtually unanimous agreement in *Robbins* was that a constitutional distinction between "worthy" and "unworthy" containers would be improper. Even though such a distinction perhaps could evolve in a series of cases in which paper bags, locked trunks, lunch buckets, and orange crates were placed on one side of the line or the other,[3] the central purpose of the Fourth Amendment forecloses such a distinction. For just as the most frail cottage in the kingdom is absolutely entitled to the same guarantees of privacy as the most majestic mansion, so also may a traveler who carries a toothbrush and a few articles of clothing in a paper bag or knotted scarf claim an equal right to conceal his possessions from official inspection as the sophisticated executive with the locked attaché case.

As Justice Stewart stated in *Robbins*, the Fourth Amendment provides protection to the owner of every container that conceals its contents from plain view. But the protection afforded by the Amendment varies in different settings. The luggage carried by a traveler entering the country may be searched at random by a customs officer; the luggage may be searched no matter how great the traveler's desire to conceal the contents may be. A container carried at the time of arrest often may be searched without a warrant and even without any specific suspicion concerning its contents. A container that may conceal the object of a search authorized by a warrant may be opened immediately; the individual's interest in privacy must give way to the magistrate's official determination of probable cause.

In the same manner, an individual's expectation of privacy in a vehicle and its contents may not survive if probable cause is given to believe that the vehicle is transporting contraband. Certainly the privacy interests in a car's trunk or glove compartment may be no less than those in a movable container. An individual undoubtedly has a significant interest that the upholstery of his automobile will not be ripped or a hidden compartment within it opened. These interests must yield to the authority of a search, however, which—in light of *Carroll*—does not itself require the prior approval of a magistrate. The scope of a warrantless search based on probable cause is no narrower—and no broader—than the scope of a search authorized by a warrant supported by probable cause. Only the prior approval of the magistrate is waived; the search otherwise is as the magistrate could authorize.[4]

nale supporting the decisions in *Carroll* and *Chambers*.

3. If the distinction is based on the proposition that the Fourth Amendment protects only those containers that objectively manifest an individual's reasonable expectation of privacy, however, the propriety of a warrantless search necessarily would turn on much more than the fabric of the container. A paper bag stapled shut and marked "private" might be found to manifest a reasonable expectation of privacy, as could a cardboard box stacked on top of two pieces of heavy luggage. The propriety of the warrantless search seemingly would turn on an objective appraisal of all the surrounding circumstances.

4. In choosing to search without a warrant on their own assessment of probable cause, police officers of course lose the protection that a warrant would provide to them in an action for damages brought by an individual claiming that the search was unconstitutional. Although an officer may establish that he acted in good faith in conducting the search by other evidence, a warrant issued by a magistrate normally suffices to establish it.

The scope of a warrantless search of an automobile thus is not defined by the nature of the container in which the contraband is secreted. Rather, it is defined by the object of the search and the places in which there is probable cause to believe that it may be found. Just as probable cause to believe that a stolen lawnmower may be found in a garage will not support a warrant to search an upstairs bedroom, probable cause to believe that undocumented aliens are being transported in a van will not justify a warrantless search of a suitcase. Probable cause to believe that a container placed in the trunk of a taxi contains contraband or evidence does not justify a search of the entire cab....

We hold that the scope of the warrantless search authorized by that exception is no broader and no narrower than a magistrate could legitimately authorize by warrant. If probable cause justifies the search of a lawfully stopped vehicle, it justifies the search of every part of the vehicle and its contents that may conceal the object of the search.

■ [Concurring opinions of JUSTICES BLACKMUN and POWELL omitted.]

■ [Dissenting opinion of JUSTICE WHITE omitted.]

■ JUSTICE MARSHALL, with whom JUSTICE BRENNAN joins, dissenting.

The majority today not only repeals all realistic limits on warrantless automobile searches, it repeals the Fourth Amendment warrant requirement itself. By equating a police officer's estimation of probable cause with a magistrate's, the Court utterly disregards the value of a neutral and detached magistrate....

According to the majority, whenever police have probable cause to believe that contraband may be found within an automobile that they have stopped on the highway, they may search not only the automobile but also any container found inside it, without obtaining a warrant. The scope of the search, we are told, is as broad as a magistrate could authorize in a warrant to search the automobile. The majority makes little attempt to justify this rule in terms of recognized Fourth Amendment values. The Court simply ignores the critical function that a magistrate serves. And although the Court purports to rely on the mobility of an automobile and the impracticability of obtaining a warrant, it never explains why these concerns permit the warrantless search of a container, which can easily be seized and immobilized while police are obtaining a warrant....

This "mobility" rationale is something of a misnomer, since the police ordinarily can remove the car's occupants and secure the vehicle on the spot. However, the inherent mobility of the vehicle often creates situations in which the police's only alternative to an immediate search may be to release the automobile from their possession. This alternative creates an unacceptably high risk of losing the contents of the vehicle, and is a principal basis for the Court's automobile exception to the warrant requirement.

In many cases, however, the police will, prior to searching the car, have cause to arrest the occupants and bring them to the station for booking. In this situation, the police can ordinarily seize the automobile and bring it to the station. Because the vehicle is now in the exclusive control of the authorities, any subsequent search cannot be justified by the mobility of the car. Rather, an immediate warrantless search of the vehicle is permitted because of the second major justification for the automobile exception: the diminished expectation of privacy in an automobile....

[Ed. Note: Justice Marshall then argued that there is not the same diminished expectation of privacy in containers as there is in vehicles.]

... [t]his case will have profound implications for the privacy of citizens traveling in automobiles, as the Court well understands. "For countless vehicles are stopped on highways and public streets every day and our cases demonstrate that it is not uncommon for police officers to have probable cause to believe that contraband may be found in a stopped vehicle." A closed paper bag, a tool box, a knapsack, a suitcase, and an attaché case can alike be searched without the protection of the judgment of a neutral magistrate, based only on the rarely disturbed decision of a police officer that he has probable cause to search for contraband in the vehicle. The Court derives satisfaction from the fact that its rule does not exalt the rights of the wealthy over the rights of the poor. A rule so broad that all citizens lose vital Fourth Amendment protection is no cause for celebration.

The notion of closed containers caused the Court consternation. Depending on whether there was probable cause to believe contraband was in the vehicle or whether there was probable cause to believe contraband was in a container in a vehicle, officers struggled with whether a warrant was needed or not. This came to a head with the case of United States v. Johns (1985), where the Court strained to characterize bales of marijuana in a truck. Finally the Court revisited one of the exceptions recognized in Ross: the prohibition of warrantless search of a closed container where the probable cause data is limited to the container and where there is no probable cause to believe that a search of the vehicle itself would yield evidence or contraband.

* * *

California v. Acevedo

Supreme Court of the United States, 1991.
500 U.S. 565, 111 S.Ct. 1982.

To the extent that the *Chadwick–Sanders* rule protects privacy, its protection is minimal. Law enforcement officers may seize a container and hold it until they obtain a search warrant. And the police often will be able to search containers without a warrant, despite the *Chadwick–Sanders* rule, as a search incident to a lawful arrest. New York v. Belton (1981)....

Finally, the search of a paper bag intrudes far less on individual privacy than does the incursion sanctioned long ago in *Carroll*. In that case, prohibition agents slashed the upholstery of the automobile. This Court nonetheless found their search to be reasonable under the Fourth Amendment. If destroying the interior of an automobile is not unreasonable, we cannot conclude that looking inside a closed container is. In light of the minimal protection to privacy afforded by the *Chadwick–Sanders* rule, and our serious doubt whether that rule substantially serves privacy interests, we now hold that the Fourth Amendment does not compel separate treatment for an automobile search that extends only to a container within the vehicle.

The *Chadwick–Sanders* rule not only has failed to protect privacy but it has also confused courts and police officers and impeded effective law enforcement....

■ JUSTICE SCALIA concurring:

The Fourth Amendment does not by its terms require a prior warrant for searches and seizures; it merely prohibits searches and seizures that are "unreasonable." What it explicitly states regarding warrants is by way of limitation upon their issuance rather than requirement of their use. See Wakely v. Hart, 6 Binney 316, 318 (Pa.1814). For the warrant was a means of insulating officials from personal liability assessed by colonial juries. An officer who searched or seized without a warrant did so at his own risk; he would be liable for trespass, including exemplary damages, unless the jury found that his action was "reasonable." Amar, The Bill of Rights as a Constitution, 100 Yale L.J. 1131, 1178–1180 (1991); Huckle v. Money, 95 Eng.Rep. 768 (K.B.1763). If, however, the officer acted pursuant to a proper warrant, he would be absolutely immune. See Bell v. Clapp, 10 Johns. 263 (N.Y.1813); 4 W. Blackstone, Commentaries 288 (1769). By restricting the issuance of warrants, the Framers endeavored to preserve the jury's role in regulating searches and seizures. Amar; Posner, Rethinking the Fourth Amendment, 1981 S.Ct.Rev., 49, 72–73; see also T. Taylor, Two Studies in Constitutional Interpretation 41 (1969).

Although the Fourth Amendment does not explicitly impose the requirement of a warrant, it is of course textually possible to consider that implicit within the requirement of reasonableness. For some years after the (still continuing) explosion in Fourth Amendment litigation that followed our announcement of the exclusionary rule in Weeks v. United States (1914), our jurisprudence lurched back and forth between imposing a categorical warrant requirement and looking to reasonableness alone....

The victory was illusory. Even before today's decision, the "warrant requirement" had become so riddled with exceptions that it was basically unrecognizable. In 1985, one commentator cataloged nearly 20 such exceptions, including "searches incident to arrest ... automobile searches ... border searches ... administrative searches of regulated businesses ... exigent circumstances ... search[es] incident to nonarrest when there is probable cause to arrest ... boat boarding for document checks ... welfare searches ... inventory searches ... airport searches ... school search[es]...." Bradley, Two Models of the Fourth Amendment, 83 Mich. L.Rev. 1468, 1473–1474 (1985). Since then, we have added at least two more. California v. Carney (1985) (searches of mobile homes); O'Connor v. Ortega (1987) (searches of offices of government employees). Our intricate body of law regarding "reasonable expectation of privacy" has been developed largely as a means of creating these exceptions, enabling a search to be denominated not a Fourth Amendment "search" and therefore not subject to the general warrant requirement....

There can be no clarity in this area unless we make up our minds, and unless the principles we express comport with the actions we take.

In my view, the path out of this confusion should be sought by returning to the first principle that the "reasonableness" requirement of the Fourth Amendment affords the protection that the common law afforded. I have no difficulty with the proposition that that includes the requirement of a warrant, where the common law required a warrant; and it may even be that changes in the surrounding legal rules (for example, elimination of the common-law rule that reasonable, good-faith belief was no defense to absolute liability for trespass, Little v. Barreme, 6 U.S. 170, 2 Cranch 170 (1804) (Marshall, C.J.); see generally Amar, Of Sovereignty and Federalism, 96 Yale L.J. 1425, 1486–1487 (1987)), may make a warrant indispensable to reasonableness where it once was not. But the supposed "general rule" that a warrant is always required does not appear to have any basis in the common law and confuses rather than facilitates any attempt to develop rules of reasonableness in light of changed legal circumstances, as the anomaly eliminated and the anomaly created by today's holding both demonstrate.

Three Justices dissented. Justice Stevens wrote:

In the nine years since Ross was decided, the Court has considered three cases in which the police had probable cause to search a particular container and one in which they had probable cause to search two vehicles. The decisions in all four of those cases were perfectly straightforward and provide no evidence of confusion in the state or lower federal courts....

The Court's statement that *Chadwick* and *Sanders* provide only "minimal protection to privacy," is also unpersuasive. Every citizen clearly has an interest in the privacy of the contents of his or her luggage, briefcase, handbag or any other container that conceals private papers and effects from public scrutiny. That privacy interest has been recognized repeatedly in cases spanning more than a century....

Under the Court's holding today, the privacy interest that protects the contents of a suitcase or a briefcase from a warrantless search when it is in public view simply vanishes when its owner climbs into a taxi cab. Unquestionably the rejection of the Sanders line of cases by today's decision will result in a significant loss of individual privacy.

To support its argument that today's holding works only a minimal intrusion on privacy, the Court suggests that "[i]f the police know that they may open a bag only if they are actually searching the entire car, they may search more extensively than they otherwise would in order to establish the general probable cause required by Ross." As I have already noted, this fear is unexplained and inexplicable. Neither evidence uncovered in the course of a search nor the scope of the search conducted can be used to provide post hoc justification for a search unsupported by probable cause at its inception.

The Court also justifies its claim that its holding inflicts only minor damage by suggesting that, under New York v. Belton (1981), the police could have arrested respondent and searched his bag if respondent had placed the bag in the passenger compartment of the automobile instead of the trunk. In *Belton*, however, the justification for stopping the car and arresting the driver had nothing to do with the subsequent search, which was based on the potential danger to the arresting officer.... I would not extend Belton's holding to this case, in which the container—which was protected from a warrantless search before it was placed in the car—provided the only justification for the arrest. Even accepting Belton's application to a case like this one, however, the Court's logic extends its holding to a container placed in the trunk of a vehicle, rather than in the passenger compartment. And the Court makes this extension without any justification whatsoever other than convenience to law enforcement.

* * *

K. SEARCHES OF OPEN FIELDS AND OTHER LAND EXPOSED TO PUBLIC VIEW

In a single brief paragraph, relying on common law precedent, Justice Holmes in Hester v. United States, 265 U.S. 57, 44 S.Ct. 445 (1924), recognized an "open-fields" doctrine. According to this doctrine, government agents who trespass upon open fields commit no violation against the Fourth Amendment. The area outside of the curtilage (that is, the area beyond the courtyard or equivalent space which surrounds the dwelling house) is not an area protected by the Fourth Amendment. Thus neither a warrant nor probable cause is required. Although the Supreme Court did not consider another open fields case during the half-century after Hester, some lower courts developed the doctrine to the point that even buildings not within the curtilage of a dwelling were unprotected by the Fourth Amendment. Here, the courts used a categorization approach. If the site was within the curtilage, then the Fourth Amendment offered protection; if not, and the site was an open field, then no Fourth Amendment protection was necessary. See LaFave, Search and Seizure: The Course of True Law ... Has Not ... Run Smooth, 1966 U.Ill.L.F. 255, 334, 338–340. Certainly even fenced areas posted with "No Trespass" signs were considered as open fields under this doctrine.

With Katz v. United States, 389 U.S. 347, 88 S.Ct. 507 (1967), the rejection of the notion of "protected areas," and recognition of the concept that the Fourth Amendment protects "people not places," some commentators concluded that the open-fields doctrine would not survive. In Air Pollution Variance Bd. v. Western Alfalfa Corp., 416 U.S. 861, 94 S.Ct. 2114 (1974), however, the Court, through Justice Douglas, invoked the *Hester* open-fields precedent and made no reference to *Katz*. In Western Alfalfa the Court found that the Fourth Amendment had not been violated by a trespassory entry onto land by inspectors who measured smoke against a Ringelman chart to gauge pollution.

In Oliver v. United States, 466 U.S. 170, 104 S.Ct. 1735 (1984), the Supreme Court re-affirmed the "open fields" doctrine. First, the majority declared that open fields are not within the ambit of the Fourth Amendment protection of "persons, houses, papers, and effects." (The dissent protested that *Katz* had rejected such literalism when it protected conversations.) Additionally, the majority declared that ordinarily property owners will be unable to prevent trespasses against open fields. Thus they have no reasonable expectation of privacy in such fields. Only if activities occur within the area immediately surrounding the home did the Fourth Amendment apply. Based on this generalization, the Fourth Amendment protects no open fields, not even those areas well hidden from the view of those on the public way. The majority refused to approve case-by-case analysis of expectations of privacy as to particular fields.

Of course officers who enter open fields which are posted with "no trespass" signs still may be in violation of state civil or criminal trespass laws if they enter without a warrant or some authorization justifying a warrantless entry. The Fourth Amendment does not demand exclusion of evidence obtained in violation of state law, however.

NOTES

1. ***Curtilage***. Having decided in Oliver not to resolve "open fields" issues on a case-by-case reasonable-expectation-of-privacy analysis, the Court adopted a four-part formula for determining what should be considered a part of "open fields" and what, instead, should be deemed to be "within the curtilage." See United States v. Dunn, 480 U.S. 294, 107 S.Ct. 1134 (1987). There, government agents peered into a locked barn after crossing over various sets of fences. The barn was located about fifty yards from a fence that surrounded the ranch and was about a half a mile from a public road. The entire 198 acres were encircled by a perimeter fence. Various interior fences served the purpose, according to the Court, of containing livestock, not of providing privacy.

The factors enunciated were: the proximity to the home of the area claimed to be curtilage, whether the area is included within an enclosure surrounding the home, the nature of the uses to which the area is put, and the steps taken by the resident to protect the area from observations by people passing by.

In an opinion turning upon the particular facts of the case, the Court found that the barn was outside of the curtilage. It was not called upon to decide whether the officers could have entered the barn, because the officers had not done so in the case at hand. Instead, they used their observations in support of a search warrant application. The Court concluded that even if the property owner had a reasonable expectation of privacy in the barn itself, no Fourth Amendment violation occurred because the agents were easily able to peer into the barn while standing in an area unprotected by the Fourth Amendment.

In another application of the *Dunn* factors, the Second Circuit found a cottage 375 feet from the main rural house was within the curtilage. United States v. Reilly, 76 F.3d 1271 (2d Cir.1996).

2. ***The relation of state trespass laws.*** Do decisions like Oliver put the United States Supreme Court in the position of giving tacit approval to violation of state trespass laws? Do you believe that the Kentucky State Police who trespassed in *Oliver* are likely to read *Oliver* as a license to trespass against open fields? In United States v. Burton, 894 F.2d 188 (6th Cir.1990), officers from that same agency trespassed once more and again successfully invoked the open fields doctrine.

New York has rejected the Oliver approach on state constitutional grounds in cases where owners post "No Trespassing" signs or otherwise indicate unmistakably that entry is not permitted. People v. Scott, 79 N.Y.2d 474, 583 N.Y.S.2d 920, 593 N.E.2d 1328 (1992).

3. ***The tension of the open fields doctrine and* Katz.** *Katz* can be read as expanding the open-fields doctrine so as to include certain areas within the curtilage of a home. For instance, suppose that a homeowner leaves criminal evidence within a fenced yard immediately adjacent to his home. Suppose further that the evidence is visible from a public way. A police officer makes a trespassory entry to reach the evidence. (Recall that plain view by itself does not justify the intrusion necessary to reach the evidence—Section F.) Some courts would hold that the trespassory entry did not violate the Fourth Amendment because the homeowner had no reasonable expectation of privacy as to what he exposed to public view, even though the property was on his land. City of Decatur v. Kushmer, 43 Ill.2d 334, 253 N.E.2d 425 (1969); People v. George, 49 Ill.2d 372, 274 N.E.2d 26 (1971). Other courts would disagree, asserting that *Katz* does not justify a warrantless entry onto land to seize evidence any more than it permits entry into a home to seize evidence which is visible from a public way. See State v. O'Herron, 153 N.J.Super. 570, 380 A.2d 728 (1977); United States v. Whaley, 781 F.2d 417 (5th Cir.1986).

L. Abandoned Property

When a person has abandoned property, the police can search or seize that property without violating Fourth Amendment rights. Neither a warrant nor probable cause is required. In Hester v. United States, 265 U.S. 57, 44 S.Ct. 445 (1924), the Supreme Court referred to certain jugs of moonshine liquor as "abandoned," but it provided no legal analysis of the doctrine. It did suggest that if in order to reach goods which *X* had abandoned, the police committed a Fourth Amendment intrusion in violation of *X*'s rights, *X* could complain that the seizure of the goods violated his fourth amendment rights. In Abel v. United States, 362 U.S. 217, 80 S.Ct. 683 (1960), a Soviet agent, arrested by immigration officials in his hotel room, checked out of the room and departed with the officials, leaving behind incriminating evidence in the room's wastebasket. The Court stated that nothing was wrong with the "government's appropriation of such abandoned property." As far as the Court was concerned, the Fourth Amendment was not implicated because the items were "bona vacantia" (goods without a claimant). Finally in Rios v. United States, 364 U.S. 253, 80 S.Ct. 1431 (1960), the court stated that property which a taxi passenger sought to conceal on the cab floor when police approached could not be considered abandoned. Again, there was no discussion of the elements of abandonment.

Lower courts generally agree that property can be considered abandoned for Fourth Amendment purposes even though a person retains an interest which the law of property might recognize. The key seems to be an intent to abandon, that is, to make no return to claim the property. Thus a lessee can "abandon" an apartment by fleeing the jurisdiction before her lease expires. So, also, a person who ditches his car in flight from a robbery which he has committed, under some circumstances, may have abandoned the car although he retains legal title.

After Katz v. United States, Casebook Chapter 4, some defendants argued that even if they had manifested an intent to lay no further claims to certain goods, a search and seizure of such goods could, under some circumstances, constitute an intrusion against a reasonable expectation of privacy. Thus the Fourth Amendment is implicated and a warrantless search or seizure without probable cause violates the Fourth Amendment. The argument was made most frequently in "trash" cases, largely because of a favorable decision in 1971 from the California Supreme Court in People v. Krivda, 5 Cal.3d 357, 96 Cal.Rptr. 62, 486 P.2d 1262 (1971), vacated and remanded 409 U.S. 33, 93 S.Ct. 32 (1972), affirmed 8 Cal.3d 623, 105 Cal.Rptr. 521, 504 P.2d 457 (1973). The Supreme Court considered this issue in the next principal case below.

California v. Greenwood

Supreme Court of the United States, 1988.
486 U.S. 35, 108 S.Ct. 1625.

[Local police, during the course of a narcotics investigation prompted by certain information, and following observation of activity that was consistent with drug transactions, had the municipal trash collector clean his truck bins of other refuse and then pick up trash that Greenwood had left for pick up at the curb in front of his home. The trash collector turned the bags over to the police, who found materials in the trash that were evidence of violations of drug laws. The police used this data as part of the probable cause for the issuance of search warrants. Execution of the warrants yielded drugs that were used in the successful prosecution of Greenwood and others.]

■ JUSTICE WHITE delivered the opinion of the court.

.... The Superior Court dismissed the charges against respondents on the authority of People v. Krivda, 5 Cal.3d 357, 486 P.2d 1262 (1971), which held that warrantless trash searches violate the Fourth Amendment and the California Constitution. The court found that the police would not have had probable cause to search the Greenwood home without the evidence obtained from the trash searches.

The Court of Appeal affirmed....

The California Supreme Court denied the State's petition for review of the Court of Appeal's decision....

The warrantless search and seizure of the garbage bags left at the curb outside the Greenwood house would violate the Fourth Amendment only if respondents manifested a subjective expectation of privacy in their garbage that society accepts as objectively reasonable.

It may well be that respondents did not expect that the contents of their garbage bags would become known to the police or other members of the public. An expectation of privacy does not give rise to Fourth Amendment protection, however, unless society is prepared to accept that expectation as objectively reasonable.

Here, we conclude that respondents exposed their garbage to the public sufficiently to defeat their claim to Fourth Amendment protection. It is common knowledge that plastic garbage bags left on or at the side of a public street are readily accessible to animals, children, scavengers,[1] snoops, and other members of the public. Moreover, respondents placed their refuse at the curb for the express purpose of conveying it to a third party, the trash collector, who might himself have sorted through respondents' trash or permitted others, such as the police, to do so. Accordingly, having deposited their garbage "in an area particularly suited for public inspection and, in a manner of speaking, public consumption, for the express purpose of having strangers take it," United States v. Reicherter, 647 F.2d 397, 399 (C.A.3 1981), respondents could have had no reasonable expectation of privacy in the inculpatory items that they discarded.

* * *

Our conclusion that society would not accept as reasonable respondents' claim to an expectation of privacy in trash left for collection in an area accessible to the public is reinforced by the unanimous rejection of similar claims by the Federal Courts of Appeals.

* * *

In addition, of those state appellate courts that have considered the issue, the vast majority have held that the police may conduct warrantless searches and seizures of garbage discarded in public areas. . . .[2]

We reject respondent Greenwood's alternative argument for affirmance: that his expectation of privacy in his garbage should be deemed reasonable as a matter of federal constitutional law because the warrantless search and seizure of his garbage was impermissible as a matter of California law. He urges that the state-law right of Californians to privacy in their garbage, announced by the California Supreme Court in Krivda, survived the subsequent state constitutional amendment eliminating the suppression remedy as a means of enforcing that right. See In re Lance W., 37 Cal.3d, at 886–887, 694 P.2d, at 752–753. Hence, he argues that the Fourth Amendment should itself vindicate that right.

Individual States may surely construe their own constitutions as imposing more stringent constraints on police conduct than does the Federal Constitution. We have never intimated, however, that whether or not a search is reasonable within the meaning of the Fourth Amendment depends on the law of the particular State in which the search occurs. We have emphasized instead that the Fourth Amendment analysis must turn on such factors as "our societal understanding that certain areas deserve the most scrupulous protection from government invasion." Oliver v. United States. We have already concluded that society as a whole possesses

1. Even the refuse of prominent Americans has not been invulnerable. In 1975, for example, a reporter for a weekly tabloid seized five bags of garbage from the sidewalk outside the home of Secretary of State Henry Kissinger. A newspaper editorial criticizing this journalistic "trash-picking" observed that "[e]vidently ... 'everybody does it.' " Washington Post, July 10, 1975, p. A18, col. 1. We of course do not, as the dissent implies, "bas[e] [our] conclusion" that individuals have no reasonable expectation of privacy in their garbage on this "sole incident."

2. Given that the dissenters are among the tiny minority of judges whose views are contrary to ours, we are distinctly unimpressed with the dissent's prediction that "society will be shocked to learn" of today's decision.

no such understanding with regard to garbage left for collection at the side of a public street. Respondent's argument is no less than a suggestion that concepts of privacy under the laws of each State are to determine the reach of the Fourth Amendment. We do not accept this submission....

■ JUSTICE KENNEDY took no part in the consideration or decision of this case.

■ JUSTICE BRENNAN, with whom JUSTICE MARSHALL joins, dissenting.

Every week for two months, and at least once more a month later, the Laguna Beach police clawed through the trash that respondent Greenwood left in opaque, sealed bags on the curb outside his home. Complete strangers minutely scrutinized their bounty, undoubtedly dredging up intimate details of Greenwood's private life and habits. The intrusions proceeded without a warrant, and no court before or since has concluded that the police acted on probable cause to believe Greenwood was engaged in any criminal activity.

Scrutiny of another's trash is contrary to commonly accepted notions of civilized behavior. I suspect, therefore, that members of our society will be shocked to learn that the Court, the ultimate guarantor of liberty, deems unreasonable our expectation that the aspects of our private lives that are concealed safely in a trash bag will not become public.

"A container which can support a reasonable expectation of privacy may not be searched, even on probable cause, without a warrant." United States v. Jacobsen (1984). Thus, as the Court observes, if Greenwood had a reasonable expectation that the contents of the bags that he placed on the curb would remain private, the warrantless search of those bags violated the Fourth Amendment....

Respondents deserve no less protection just because Greenwood used the bags to discard rather than to transport his personal effects. Their contents are not inherently any less private, and Greenwood's decision to discard them, at least in the manner in which he did, does not diminish his expectation of privacy....

... "[A]lmost every human activity ultimately manifests itself in waste products...." Smith v. State, 510 P.2d 793, 798 (Alaska) (renowned archaeologist Emil Haury once said, "If you want to know what is really going on in a community, look at its garbage") (quoted by W. Rathje, Archaeological Ethnography ... Because Sometimes it is Better to Give than to Receive, in Explorations in Ethnoarchaelogy 49, 54 (R. Gould ed. 1978)); Weberman, The Art of Garbage Analysis: You are What You Throw Away, 76 Esquire 113 (1971) (analyzing trash of various celebrities and drawing conclusions about their private lives). A single bag of trash testifies eloquently to the eating, reading, and recreational habits of the person who produced it. A search of trash, like a search of the bedroom, can relate intimate details about sexual practices, health, and personal hygiene. Like rifling through desk drawers or intercepting phone calls, rummaging through trash can divulge the target's financial and professional status, political affiliations and inclinations, private thoughts, personal relationships, and romantic interests. It cannot be doubted that a sealed trash bag harbors telling evidence of the "intimate activity associated with the sanctity of a man's home and the privacies of life," which the Fourth

Amendment is designed to protect. Oliver v. United States (1984) (quoting Boyd v. United States (1886))....

Most of us, I believe, would be incensed to discover a meddler—whether a neighbor, a reporter, or a detective—scrutinizing our sealed trash containers to discover some detail of our personal lives. That was, quite naturally, there action to the sole incident on which the Court bases its conclusion that "snoops" and the like defeat the expectation of privacy in trash. When a tabloid reporter examined then-Secretary of State Henry Kissinger's trash and published his findings, Kissinger was "really revolted" by the intrusion and his wife suffered "grave anguish." N.Y. Times, July 9, 1975, p. A1, col. 8. The public response roundly condemning the reporter demonstrates that society not only recognized those reactions as reasonable, but shared them as well. Commentators variously characterized his conduct as "a disgusting invasion of personal privacy," Flieger, Investigative Trash, U.S. News & World Report, July 28, 1975, p. 72 (editor's page); "indefensible ... as civilized behavior," Washington Post, July 10, 1975, p. A18, col. 1 (editorial); and contrary to "the way decent people behave in relation to each other," ibid.

Beyond a generalized expectation of privacy, many municipalities, whether for reasons of privacy, sanitation, or both, reinforce confidence in the integrity of sealed trash containers by "prohibit[ing] anyone, except authorized employees of the Town ..., to rummage into, pick up, collect, move or otherwise interfere with articles or materials placed on ... any public street for collection." United States v. Dzialak, 441 F.2d 212, 215 (C.A.2 1971) (paraphrasing ordinance for town of Cheektowaga, New York).... In fact, the California Constitution, as interpreted by the State's highest court, guarantees a right of privacy in trash vis--vis government officials. See Krivda, (recognizing right); In re Lance W., 37 Cal.3d 873, 886–887, 694 P.2d 744, 752–753 (1985) (later constitutional amendment abolished exclusionary remedy but left intact the substance of the right).

That is not to deny that isolated intrusions into opaque, sealed trash containers occur....

The mere *possibility* that unwelcome meddlers might open and rummage through the containers does not negate the expectation of privacy in its contents any more than the possibility of a burglary negates an expectation of privacy in the home; or the possibility of a private intrusion negates an expectation of privacy in an unopened package; or the possibility that an operator will listen in on a telephone conversation negates an expectation of privacy in the words spoken on the telephone.

Nor is it dispositive that "respondents placed their refuse at the curb for the express purpose of conveying it to a third party, ... who might himself have sorted through respondents' trash or permitted others, such as police, to do so." In the first place, Greenwood can hardly be faulted for leaving trash on his curb when a county ordinance commanded him to do so, ... and prohibited him from disposing of it in any other way. Unlike in other circumstances where privacy is compromised, Greenwood could not "avoid exposing personal belongings ... by simply leaving them at home." *O'Connor*. More importantly, even the voluntary relinquishment of possession or control over an effect does not necessarily amount to a relinquishment of a privacy expectation in it. Were it otherwise, a letter or package would lose all Fourth Amendment protection when placed in a mail box or other depository with the "express purpose" of entrusting it to the postal officer or a private carrier; those bailees are just as likely as trash collectors (and certainly have greater incentive) to "sor[t] through" the personal effects entrusted to them, "or permi[t] others, such as police to do so." Yet, it has been clear for at least 110 years that the possibility of such an intrusion does not justify a warrantless search by police in the first instance. See Ex parte Jackson (1878); United States v. Van Leeuwen (1970); United States v. Jacobsen (1984).

* * *

NOTES

1. ***The interplay of abandonment theory and the* Katz *expectation of privacy theory.*** Note that the majority in Greenwood responded to the defense argument on its own terms by analyzing the issue in terms of a reasonable expectation of privacy. It did not rely upon the concept of abandonment. Has the refined analysis improved upon the tersely-expressed notion of *Hester* that once goods are abandoned, no one has the right to complain about their seizure by law enforcement officials?

2. ***The interplay of the abandonment theory and the plain view theory.*** Many abandoned property cases are also plain view cases. The difference is that property which is abandoned can be seized even without seizure probable cause. Property spotted in plain view, if it has not been abandoned, can be seized only if its incriminating nature is immediately apparent, that is, only if there is probable cause to believe that it is contraband or evidence of a crime. One decision which makes this distinction is People v. Hermesch, 49 A.D.2d 587, 370 N.Y.S.2d 152 (1975).

3. ***Dropped evidence as the fruit of an illegal arrest?*** When a suspect, in response to an illegal arrest or an illegal stop, discards property, he or she typically will have no intent to retrieve the property later. Nevertheless, a majority of courts view the dropped property as evidence derived from the illegal seizure of the suspect's person, much as it would view a statement blurted out by a suspect immediately following his unlawful arrest. See Chapter 6, Section E. See, e.g., Commonwealth v. Barnett, 484 Pa. 211, 398 A.2d 1019 (1979) (property dropped after unlawful stop); People v. Severson, 39 Colo.App. 95, 561 P.2d 373 (Colo.App. 1977). See also State v. Smithers, 256 Ind. 512, 269 N.E.2d 874 (1971). There the majority declared that "where police action triggers the abandonment, that action must be lawful or the evidence will be considered obtained in an illegal search and seizure within the meaning of the Fourth Amendment." The dissent responded, "The majority opinion is an unnecessary restriction upon law enforcement activities where a guilty conscience causes the party to flee or abandon articles which are incriminating."

For a dispute similar to the one in Smithers, see People v. Boodle, 47 N.Y.2d 398, 418 N.Y.S.2d 352, 391 N.E.2d 1329 (1979), where the majority held that under the circumstances the "drop" could not be considered the product of the police illegality.

The opinion in California v. Hodari D., 499 U.S. 621, 111 S.Ct. 1547 (1991) proceeded on the assumption that if a suspect discards property after the police unlawfully stop him, the evidence should be viewed as the fruit of the unlawful stop rather than as abandoned property. Some courts, undoubtedly a minority, still disagree with this view. See Curry v. State, 576 So.2d 890 (Fla.App.1991) (unless discarding of property is in response to an illegal search, property should be deemed to be abandoned).

Some observers think that the view that discarded property is evidence derived from a seizure of the person arises out of skepticism. They believe that the police often testify that a suspect discarded property when, in fact, the police discovered such property by searching the suspect. See People v. Quinones, 61 A.D.2d 765, 402 N.Y.S.2d 196 (1978).

4. *Proving abandonment.* Often when the police come upon incriminating evidence in the vicinity of a person, that individual will deny any connection to the property. According to many courts, "A voluntary denial of ownership demonstrates sufficient intent of disassociation to prove abandonment." United States v. Lewis, 921 F.2d 1294 (D.C.Cir.1990). Does this mean that the suspect has the choice of admitting the property is hers, thus incriminating herself, or denying the property is hers, thus giving up her Fourth Amendment rights? Must she invoke her privilege against self-incrimination when asked about the property in order to preserve both her Fourth and her Fifth Amendment rights?

M. STOP-AND-FRISK AND OTHER LIMITED INVESTIGATIVE DETENTIONS

Terry v. Ohio

Supreme Court of the United States, 1968.
392 U.S. 1, 88 S.Ct. 1868.

■ CHIEF JUSTICE WARREN delivered the opinion of the Court.

This case presents serious questions concerning the role of the Fourth Amendment in the confrontation on the street between the citizen and the policeman investigating suspicious circumstances.

Petitioner Terry was convicted of carrying a concealed weapon. Following the denial of a pretrial motion to suppress, the prosecution introduced in evidence two revolvers and a number of bullets seized from Terry and a codefendant, Richard Chilton, by Cleveland Police Detective Martin McFadden. At the hearing on the motion to suppress this evidence, Officer McFadden testified that while he was patrolling in plain clothes in downtown Cleveland at approximately 2:30 in the afternoon of October 31, 1963, his attention was attracted by two men, Chilton and Terry, standing on the corner of Huron Road and Euclid Avenue. He had never seen the two men before, and he was unable to say precisely what first drew his eye to them. However, he testified that he had been a policeman for 39 years and a detective for 35 and that he had been assigned to patrol this vicinity of downtown Cleveland for shoplifters and pickpockets for 30 years. He explained that he had developed routine habits of observation over the years and that he would "stand and watch people or walk and watch people at many intervals of the day." He added: "Now, in this case when I looked over they didn't look right to me at the time."

His interest aroused, Officer McFadden took up a post of observation in the entrance to a store 300 to 400 feet away from the two men. "I get more purpose to watch them when I seen their movements," he testified. He saw one of the men leave the other one and walk southwest on Huron Road, past some stores. The man paused for a moment and looked in a store window, then walked on a short distance, turned around and walked back toward the corner, pausing once again to look in the same store window. He rejoined his companion at the corner, and the two conferred briefly. Then the second man went through the same series of motions, strolling down Huron Road, looking in the same window, walking on a short distance, turning back, peering in the store window again, and returning to confer with the first man at the corner. The two men repeated this ritual alternately between five and six times apiece—in all, roughly a dozen trips. At one point, while the two were standing together on the corner, a third man approached them and engaged them briefly in conversation. This man then left the two others and walked west on Euclid Avenue. Chilton and Terry resumed their measured pacing, peering, and conferring. After this had gone on for 10 to 12 minutes, the two men walked off together, heading west on Euclid Avenue, following the path taken earlier by the third man.

By this time Officer McFadden had become thoroughly suspicious. He testified that after observing their elaborately casual and oft-repeated reconnaissance of the store window on Huron Road, he suspected the two men of "casing a job, a stick-up," and that he considered it his duty as a police officer to investigate further. He added that he feared "they may have a gun." Thus, Officer McFadden followed Chilton and Terry and saw them stop in front of Zucker's store to talk to the same man who had conferred with them earlier on the street corner. Deciding that the situation was ripe for direct action, Officer McFadden approached the three men, identified himself as a police officer and asked for their names. At this point his knowledge was confined to what he had observed. He was not acquainted with any of the three men by name or by sight, and he had received no information concerning them from any other source. When the men "mumbled something" in response to his inquiries, Officer McFadden grabbed petitioner Terry, spun him around so that they were facing the other two, with Terry between McFadden and the others, and patted down the outside of his clothing. In the left breast pocket of Terry's overcoat Officer McFadden felt a pistol. He reached inside the overcoat pocket, but was unable to remove the gun. At this point, keeping Terry between himself and the others, the officer ordered all three men to enter Zucker's store. As they went in, he removed Terry's overcoat completely, retrieved a .38 caliber revolver from the pocket and ordered all three men to face the wall with their hands raised. Officer McFadden proceeded to pat down the outer clothing of Chilton and the third man, *Katz*. He discovered another revolver in the outer pocket of Chilton's overcoat, but no weapons were found on *Katz*. The officer testified that he only patted the men down to see whether they had weapons, and that he did not put his hands beneath the outer garments of either Terry or Chilton until he felt their guns. So far as appears from the record, he never placed his hands beneath Katz's outer garments. Officer McFadden seized Chilton's gun, asked the proprietor of the store to call a police wagon, and took all three men to the station, where Chilton and Terry were formally charged with carrying concealed weapons. . . .

After the court denied their motion to suppress, Chilton and Terry waived jury trial and pleaded not guilty. The court adjudged them guilty. . . .

I.

. . . [o]n the one hand, it is frequently argued that in dealing with the rapidly unfolding and often dangerous situations on city streets the police are in need of an escalating set of flexible responses, graduated in relation to the amount of information they possess. For this purpose it is urged that distinctions should be made between a "stop" and an "arrest" (or a "seizure" of a person), and between a "frisk" and a "search." Thus, it is argued, the police should be allowed to "stop" a person and detain him briefly for questioning upon suspicion that he may be connected with criminal activity. Upon suspicion that the person may be armed, the police should have the power to "frisk" him for weapons. If the "stop" and the "frisk" give rise to probable cause to believe that the suspect has committed a crime, then the police should be empowered to make a formal "arrest," and a full incident "search" of the person. This scheme is justified in part upon the notion that a "stop" and a "frisk" amount to a mere "minor inconvenience and petty indignity," which can properly be imposed upon the citizen in the interest of effective law enforcement on the basis of a police officer's suspicion.[1]

On the other side the argument is made that the authority of the police must be strictly circumscribed by the law of arrest and search as it has developed to date in the traditional jurisprudence of the Fourth Amendment. It is contended with some force that there is not—and cannot be—a variety of police activity which does not depend solely upon the voluntary cooperation of the citizen and yet which stops short of an arrest based upon probable cause to make such an arrest. The heart of the Fourth Amendment, the argument runs, is a severe requirement of specific justification for any intrusion upon protected personal security, coupled with a highly developed system of judicial controls to enforce upon the agents of the State the commands of the Constitution. Acquiescence by the courts in the compulsion inherent in the field interrogation practices at issue here, it is urged, would constitute an abdication of judicial control over, and indeed

1. ". . . [T]he evidence needed to make the inquiry is not of the same degree or conclusiveness as that required for an arrest. The stopping of the individual to inquire is not an arrest and the ground upon which the police may make the inquiry may be less incriminating than the ground for an arrest for a crime known to have been committed. . . .

"And as the right to stop and inquire is to be justified for a cause less conclusive than that which would sustain an arrest, so the right to frisk may be justified as an incident to inquiry upon grounds of elemental safety and precaution which might not initially sustain a search. Ultimately the validity of the frisk narrows down to whether there is or is not a right by the police to touch the person questioned. The sense of exterior touch here involved is not very far different from the sense of sight or hearing—senses upon which police customarily act." People v. Rivera, 14 N.Y.2d 441, 445, 447, 201 N.E.2d 32, 34, 35, 252 N.Y.S.2d 458, 461, 463 (1964), cert. denied, 379 U.S. 978, 85 S.Ct. 679 (1965).

an encouragement of, substantial interference with liberty and personal security by police officers whose judgment is necessarily colored by their primary involvement in "the often competitive enterprise of ferreting out crime." Johnson v. United States (1948). This, it is argued, can only serve to exacerbate police-community tensions in the crowded centers of our Nation's cities. . . .

The exclusionary rule has its limitations, however, as a tool of judicial control. It cannot properly be invoked to exclude the products of legitimate police investigative techniques on the ground that much conduct which is closely similar involves unwarranted intrusions upon constitutional protections. Moreover, in some contexts the rule is ineffective as a deterrent. Street encounters between citizens and police officers are incredibly rich in diversity. They range from wholly friendly exchanges of pleasantries or mutually useful information to hostile confrontations of armed men involving arrests, or injuries, or loss of life. Moreover, hostile confrontations are not all of a piece. Some of them begin in a friendly enough manner, only to take a different turn upon the injection of some unexpected element into the conversation. Encounters are initiated by the police for a wide variety of purposes, some of which are wholly unrelated to a desire to prosecute for crime.[2] Doubtless some police "field interrogation" conduct violates the Fourth Amendment. But a stern refusal by this Court to condone such activity does not necessarily render it responsive to the exclusionary rule. Regardless of how effective the rule may be where obtaining convictions is an important objective of the police, it is powerless to deter invasions of constitutionally guaranteed rights where the police either have no interest in prosecuting or are willing to forego successful prosecution in the interest of serving some other goal.

Proper adjudication of cases in which the exclusionary rule is invoked demands a constant awareness of these limitations. The wholesale harassment by certain elements of the police community, of which minority groups, particularly Negroes, frequently complain,[3] will not be stopped by

2. See Tiffany, McIntyre & Rotenberg, Detection of Crime: Stopping and Questioning, Search and Seizure, Encouragement and Entrapment 18–56 (1967). This sort of police conduct may, for example, be designed simply to help an intoxicated person find his way home, with no intention of arresting him unless he becomes obstreperous. Or the police may be seeking to mediate a domestic quarrel which threatens to erupt into violence. They may accost a woman in an area known for prostitution as part of a harassment campaign designed to drive prostitutes away without the considerable difficulty involved in prosecuting them. Or they may be conducting a dragnet search of all teenagers in a particular section of the city for weapons because they have heard rumors of an impending gang fight.

3. The President's Commission on Law Enforcement and Administration of Justice found that "in many communities, field interrogations are a major source of friction between the police and minority groups." President's Commission on Law Enforcement and Administration of Justice, Task Force Report: The Police1 83 (1967). It was reported that the friction caused by "misuse of field interrogations" increases "as more police departments adopt 'aggressive patrol' in which officers are encouraged routinely to stop and question persons on the street who are unknown to them, who are suspicious, or whose purpose for being abroad is not readily evident." Id., at 184. While the frequency with which "frisking" forms a part of field interrogation practice varies tremendously with the locale, the objective of the interrogation, and the particular officer, see Tiffany, McIntyre & Rotenberg, supra, n. 9, at 47–48, it cannot help but be a severely exacerbating factor in police-community tensions. This is particular-

the exclusion of any evidence from any criminal trial. Yet a rigid and unthinking application of the exclusionary rule, in futile protest against practices which it can never be used effectively to control, may exact a high toll in human injury and frustration of efforts to prevent crime. No judicial opinion can comprehend the protean variety of the street encounter, and we can only judge the facts of the case before us. Nothing we say today is to be taken as indicating approval of police conduct outside the legitimate investigative sphere. Under our decision, courts still retain their traditional responsibility to guard against police conduct which is overbearing or harassing, or which trenches upon personal security without the objective evidentiary justification which the Constitution requires. When such conduct is identified, it must be condemned by the judiciary and its fruits must be excluded from evidence in criminal trials. And, of course, our approval of legitimate and restrained investigative conduct undertaken on the basis of ample factual justification should in no way discourage the employment of other remedies than the exclusionary rule to curtail abuses for which that sanction may prove inappropriate.

II.

Our first task is to establish at what point in this encounter the Fourth Amendment becomes relevant. That is, we must decide whether and when Officer McFadden "seized" Terry and whether and when he conducted a "search." There is some suggestion in the use of such terms as "stop" and "frisk" that such police conduct is outside the purview of the Fourth Amendment because neither action rises to the level of a "search" or "seizure" within the meaning of the Constitution. We emphatically reject this notion. It is quite plain that the Fourth Amendment governs "seizures" of the person which do not eventuate in a trip to the station house and prosecution for crime—"arrests" in traditional terminology. It must be recognized that whenever a police officer accosts an individual and restrains his freedom to walk away, he has "seized" that person. And it is nothing less than sheer torture of the English language to suggest that a careful exploration of the outer surfaces of a person's clothing all over his or her body in an attempt to find weapons is not a "search." Moreover, it is simply fantastic to urge that such a procedure performed in public by a policeman while the citizen stands helpless, perhaps facing a wall with his hands raised, is a "petty indignity."[4] It is a serious intrusion upon the sanctity of the person, which may inflict great indignity and arouse strong resentment, and it is not to be undertaken lightly.[5]

ly true in situations where the "stop and frisk" of youths or minority group members is "motivated by the officers' perceived need to maintain the power image of the beat officer, an aim sometimes accomplished by humiliating anyone who attempts to undermine police control of the streets." Id., at 47–48.

4. Consider the following apt description:

"[T]he officer must feel with sensitive fingers every portion of the prisoner's body. A thorough search must be made of the prisoner's arms and armpits, waistline and back, the groin and area about the testicles, and entire surface of the legs down to the feet." Priar & Martin, Searching and Disarming Criminals, 45 J.Crim., L.C. & P.S. 481 (1954).

5. We have noted that the abusive practices which play a major, though by no means exclusive, role in creating this friction are not susceptible of control by means of the exclusionary rule, and cannot properly dictate our decision with respect to the powers of the

The danger in the logic which proceeds upon distinctions between a "stop" and an "arrest," or "seizure" of the person, and between a "frisk" and a "search" is two-fold. It seeks to isolate from constitutional scrutiny the initial stages of the contact between the policeman and the citizen. And by suggesting a rigid all-or-nothing model of justification and regulation under the Amendment, it obscures the utility of limitations upon the scope, as well as the initiation, of police action as a means of constitutional regulation....

... We therefore reject the notions that the Fourth Amendment does not come into play at all as a limitation upon police conduct if the officers stop short of something called a "technical arrest" or a "full-blown search."

In this case there can be no question, then, that Officer McFadden "seized" petitioner and subjected him to a "search" when he took hold of him and patted down the outer surfaces of his clothing. We must decide whether at that point it was reasonable for Officer McFadden to have interfered with petitioner's personal security as he did.[6] And in determining whether the seizure and search were "unreasonable" our inquiry is a dual one—whether the officer's action was justified at its inception, and whether it was reasonably related in scope to the circumstances which justified the interference in the first place.

III

... In order to assess the reasonableness of Officer McFadden's conduct as a general proposition, it is necessary "first to focus upon the governmental interest which allegedly justifies official intrusion upon the constitutionally protected interests of the private citizen," for there is "no ready test for determining reasonableness other than by balancing the need to search [or seize] against the invasion which the search [or seizure] entails." Camara v. Municipal Court (1967). And in justifying the particular intrusion the police officer must be able to point to specific and articulable facts which, taken together with rational inferences from those facts, reasonably warrant that intrusion. The scheme of the Fourth Amendment becomes meaningful only when it is assured that at some point the conduct of those charged with enforcing the laws can be subjected to the more detached, neutral scrutiny of a judge who must evaluate the reasonableness of a particular search or seizure in light of the particular circumstances.

police in genuine investigative and preventive situations. However, the degree of community resentment aroused by particular practices is clearly relevant to an assessment of the quality of the intrusion upon reasonable expectations of personal security caused by those practices.

6. We thus decide nothing today concerning the constitutional propriety of an investigative "seizure" upon less than probable cause for purposes of "detention" and/or interrogation. Obviously, not all personal intercourse between policemen and citizens involves "seizures" of persons. Only when the officer, by means of physical force or show of authority, has in some way restrained the liberty of a citizen may we conclude that a "seizure" has occurred. We cannot tell with any certainty upon this record whether any such "seizure" took place here prior to Officer McFadden's initiation of physical contact for purposes of searching Terry for weapons, and we thus may assume that up to that point no intrusion upon constitutionally protected rights had occurred.

And in making that assessment it is imperative that the facts be judged against an objective standard: would the facts available to the officer at the moment of the seizure or the search "warrant a man of reasonable caution in the belief" that the action taken was appropriate? Anything less would invite intrusions upon constitutionally guaranteed rights based on nothing more substantial than inarticulate hunches, a result this Court has consistently refused to sanction. And simple " 'good faith on the part of the arresting officer is not enough.' . . . If subjective good faith alone were the test, the protections of the Fourth Amendment would evaporate, and the people would be 'secure in their persons, houses, papers, and effects,' only in the discretion of the police."

Applying these principles to this case, we consider first the nature and extent of the governmental interests involved. One general interest is of course that of effective crime prevention and detection; it is this interest which underlies the recognition that a police officer may in appropriate circumstances and in an appropriate manner approach a person for purposes of investigating possibly criminal behavior even though there is no probable cause to make an arrest. It was this legitimate investigative function Officer McFadden was discharging when he decided to approach petitioner and his companions. He had observed *Terry, Chilton*, and *Katz* go through a series of acts, each of them perhaps innocent in itself, but which taken together warranted further investigation. There is nothing unusual in two men standing together on a street corner, perhaps waiting for someone. Nor is there anything suspicious about people in such circumstances strolling up and down the street, singly or in pairs. Store windows, moreover, are made to be looked in. But the story is quite different where, as here, two men hover about a street corner for an extended period of time, at the end of which it becomes apparent that they are not waiting for anyone or anything; where these men pace alternately along an identical route, pausing to stare in the same store window roughly 24 times; where each completion of this route is followed immediately by a conference between the two men on the corner; where they are joined in one of these conferences by a third man who leaves swiftly; and where the two men finally follow the third and rejoin him a couple of blocks away. It would have been poor police work indeed for an officer of 30 years' experience in the detection of thievery from stores in this same neighborhood to have failed to investigate this behavior further.

The crux of this case, however, is not the propriety of Officer McFadden's taking steps to investigate petitioner's suspicious behavior, but rather, whether there was justification for McFadden's invasion of Terry's personal security by searching him for weapons in the course of that investigation. We are now concerned with more than the governmental interest in investigating crime; in addition, there is the more immediate interest of the police officer in taking steps to assure himself that the person with whom he is dealing is not armed with a weapon that could unexpectedly and fatally be used against him. Certainly it would be unreasonable to require that police officers take unnecessary risks in the performance of their duties. American criminals have a long tradition of armed violence, and every year in this country many law enforcement officers are killed in the line of duty, and thousands more are wounded.

Virtually all of these deaths and a substantial portion of the injuries are inflicted with guns and knives.

In view of these facts, we cannot blind ourselves to the need for law enforcement officers to protect themselves and other prospective victims of violence in situations where they may lack probable cause for an arrest. When an officer is justified in believing that the individual whose suspicious behavior he is investigating at close range is armed and presently dangerous to the officer or to others, it would appear to be clearly unreasonable to deny the officer the power to take necessary measures to determine whether the person is in fact carrying a weapon and to neutralize the threat of physical harm.

We must still consider, however, the nature and quality of the intrusion on individual rights which must be accepted if police officers are to be conceded the right to search for weapons in situations where probable cause to arrest for crime is lacking. Even a limited search of the outer clothing for weapons constitutes a severe, though brief, intrusion upon cherished personal security, and it must surely be an annoying, frightening, and perhaps humiliating experience. Petitioner contends that such an intrusion is permissible only incident to a lawful arrest, either for a crime involving the possession of weapons or for a crime the commission of which led the officer to investigate in the first place....

There are two weaknesses in this line of reasoning, however. First, it fails to take account of traditional limitations upon the scope of searches, and thus recognizes no distinction in purpose, character, and extent between a search incident to an arrest and a limited search for weapons. The former, although justified in part by the acknowledged necessity to protect the arresting officer from assault with a concealed weapon, Preston v. United States (1964), is also justified on other grounds, ibid., and can therefore involve a relatively extensive exploration of the person. A search for weapons in the absence of probable cause to arrest, however, must, like any other search, be strictly circumscribed by the exigencies which justify its initiation. Warden v. Hayden (1967) (Mr. Justice Fortas, concurring). Thus it must be limited to that which is necessary for the discovery of weapons which might be used to harm the officer or others nearby, and may realistically be characterized as something less than a "full" search, even though it remains a serious intrusion.

A second, and related, objection to petitioner's argument is that it assumes that the law of arrest has already worked out the balance between the particular interests involved here—the neutralization of danger to the policeman in the investigative circumstance and the sanctity of the individual. But this is not so. An arrest is a wholly different kind of intrusion upon individual freedom from a limited search for weapons, and the interests each is designed to serve are likewise quite different. An arrest is the initial stage of a criminal prosecution. It is intended to vindicate society's interest in having its laws obeyed, and it is inevitably accompanied by future interference with the individual's freedom of movement, whether or not trial or conviction ultimately follows. The protective search for weapons, on the other hand, constitutes a brief, though far from inconsiderable, intrusion upon the sanctity of the person. It does not follow that because an officer may lawfully arrest a person only when he is apprised of facts sufficient to warrant a belief that the person has committed or is committing a crime, the officer is equally unjustified, absent that kind of evidence, in making any intrusions short of an arrest. Moreover, a perfectly reasonable apprehension of danger may arise long before the officer is possessed of adequate information to justify taking a person into custody for the purpose of prosecuting him for a crime. Petitioner's reliance on cases which have worked out standards of reasonableness with regard to "seizures" constituting arrests and searches incident thereto is thus misplaced. It assumes that the interests sought to be vindicated and the invasions of personal security may be equated in the two cases, and thereby ignores a vital aspect of the analysis of the reasonableness of particular types of conduct under the Fourth Amendment.

Our evaluation of the proper balance that has to be struck in this type of case leads us to conclude that there must be a narrowly drawn authority to permit a reasonable search for weapons for the protection of the police officer, where he has reason to believe that he is dealing with an armed and dangerous individual, regardless of whether he has probable cause to arrest the individual for a crime. The officer need not be absolutely certain that the individual is armed; the issue is whether a reasonably prudent man in the circumstances would be warranted in the belief that his safety or that of others was in danger. And in determining whether the officer acted reasonably in such circumstances, due weight must be given, not to his inchoate and unparticularized suspicion or "hunch," but to the specific reasonable inferences which he is entitled to draw from the facts in light of his experience.

IV.

We must now examine the conduct of Officer McFadden in this case to determine whether his search and seizure of petitioner were reasonable, both at their inception and as conducted. He had observed Terry, together with Chilton and another man, acting in a manner he took to be preface to a "stick-up." We think on the facts and circumstances Officer McFadden detailed before the trial judge a reasonably prudent man would have been warranted in believing petitioner was armed and thus presented a threat to the officer's safety while he was investigating his suspicious behavior. The actions of Terry and Chilton were consistent with McFadden's hypothesis that these men were contemplating a daylight robbery—which, it is reasonable to assume, would be likely to involve the use of weapons—and nothing in their conduct from the time he first noticed them until the time he confronted them and identified himself as a police officer gave him sufficient reason to negate that hypothesis. Although the trio had departed the original scene, there was nothing to indicate abandonment of an intent to commit a robbery at some point. Thus, when Officer McFadden approached the three men gathered before the display window at Zucker's store he had observed enough to make it quite reasonable to fear that they were armed; and nothing in their response to his hailing them, identifying himself as a police officer, and asking their names served to dispel that reasonable belief. We cannot say his decision at that point to seize Terry and pat his clothing for weapons was the product of a volatile or inventive imagination, or was undertaken simply as an act of harassment; the record evidences the tempered act of a policeman who in the course of an investigation had to make a quick decision as to how to protect himself and others from possible danger, and took limited steps to do so.

... The sole justification of the search in the present situation is the protection of the police officer and others nearby, and it must therefore be confined in scope to an intrusion reasonably designed to discover guns, knives, clubs, or other hidden instruments for the assault of the police officer.

The scope of the search in this case presents no serious problem in light of these standards. Officer McFadden patted down the outer clothing of petitioner and his two companions. He did not place his hands in their pockets or under the outer surface of their garments until he had felt weapons, and then he merely reached for and removed the guns. He never did invade Katz's person beyond the outer surfaces of his clothes, since he discovered nothing in his pat down which might have been a weapon. Officer McFadden confined his search strictly to what was minimally necessary to learn whether the men were armed and to disarm them once he discovered the weapons. He did not conduct a general exploratory search for whatever evidence of criminal activity he might find.

V.

... We merely hold today that where a police officer observes unusual conduct which leads him reasonably to conclude in light of his experience that criminal activity may be afoot and that the persons with whom he is dealing may be armed and presently dangerous; where in the course of investigating this behavior he identifies himself as a policeman and makes reasonable inquiries; and where nothing in the initial stages of the encounter serves to dispel his reasonable fear for his own or others' safety, he is entitled for the protection of himself and others in the area to conduct a carefully limited search of the outer clothing of such persons in an attempt to discover weapons which might be used to assault him. Such a search is a reasonable search under the Fourth Amendment, and any weapons seized may properly be introduced in evidence against the person from whom they were taken.

Affirmed.

■ JUSTICE HARLAN, concurring.

.... (I)f the frisk is justified in order to protect the officer during an encounter with a citizen, the officer must first have constitutional grounds to insist on an encounter, to make a forcible stop. Any person, including a policeman, is at liberty to avoid a person he considers dangerous. If and when a policeman has a right instead to disarm such a person for his own protection, he must first have a right not to avoid him but to be in his presence. That right must be more than the liberty (again, possessed by every citizen) to address questions to other persons, for ordinarily the person addressed has an equal right to ignore his interrogator and walk away; he certainly need not submit to a frisk for the questioner's protection. I would make it perfectly clear that the right to frisk in this case depends upon the reasonableness of a forcible stop to investigate a suspected crime.

Where such a stop is reasonable, however, the right to frisk must be immediate and automatic if the reason for the stop is, as here, an articulable suspicion of a crime of violence. Just as a full search incident to a lawful arrest requires no additional justification, a limited frisk incident to a lawful stop must often be rapid and routine. There is no reason why an officer, rightfully but forcibly confronting a person suspected of a serious crime, should have to ask one question and take the risk that the answer might be a bullet....

■ JUSTICE WHITE, concurring opinion omitted.

■ JUSTICE DOUGLAS, dissenting.

.... The infringement on personal liberty of any "seizure" of a person can only be "reasonable" under the Fourth Amendment if we require the police to possess "probable cause" before they seize him. Only that line draws a meaningful distinction between an officer's mere inkling and the presence of facts within the officer's personal knowledge which would convince a reasonable man that the person seized has committed, is committing, or is about to commit a particular crime....

To give the police greater power than a magistrate is to take a long step down the totalitarian path. Perhaps such a step is desirable to cope with modern forms of lawlessness. But if it is taken, it should be the deliberate choice of the people through a constitutional amendment.

NOTES

1. ***"Probable Cause" vs. "Reasonable Suspicion".*** Perhaps the most remarkable aspect of *Terry* is that it permits police action that invades the privacy of an individual without probable cause. It substitutes reasonable suspicion as the threshold requirement. Terry requires that (1) the officer's action is justified at its inception; and (2) it is reasonably related in intensity and scope to the circumstances which justified the interference in the first place.

As we saw in *Gates*, the Court treats probable cause as a "fluid concept." So too, "reasonable suspicion" does not easily reduce to a mathematical formula. Suffice it to say that "reasonable suspicion" is less than "probable cause." As you read the following cases, consider whether the concept of "reasonable suspicion" changes from case to case, or remains constant. Has it changed as the concept of probable cause has changed over time? Reasonable suspicion can be conceptualized as a lower level of probable cause.

Probable Cause ⟶ Arrest [warrant] ⟶ Search incident to arrest

Reasonable suspicion or Articulable suspicion ⟶ Stop ⟶ Frisk

Keep in mind the relationship between the two concepts. Terry is often described as a balancing test, but there is also a proportionality component. Arguably as the standards for probable cause become more relaxed, so too do the standards for reasonable suspicion. The reliance on reasonable suspicion may have caused the relaxation of the standards for probable cause. In motions to suppress, prosecutors often argue reasonable suspicion as a "back up" position, urging first that police action was based on probable cause. If not, the argument goes, then certainly it was supported by reasonable suspicion.

2. ***Terry's Companion Decision.*** In a decision handed down on the same day as *Terry*, the Supreme Court ruled on two other police-citizen encounters sub nom. Sibron v. New York, 392 U.S. 40, 88 S.Ct. 1889 (1968) and Peters v. New York (same citation). As to Sibron, the Court found that there was not probable cause for an arrest. Assuming there were *Terry*-type grounds for a stop, the Court found that there was not sufficient reason to believe that Sibron, a narcotics suspect, was armed and dangerous. Moreover, the officer's search was more intrusive than the limited pat down for a weapon permitted by *Terry*. Justice Harlan, concurring in Sibron, believed that the stop itself was improper for want of reasonable suspicion. As to the other appellant (Peters), a majority of the Court upheld the inspection as incident to a proper arrest. Justices Harlan and White concurring, believed that although there was no probable cause, there were grounds for a *Terry*-type stop of Peters. They further noted that the evidence was discovered not in a full search but rather within the confines of a proper frisk under *Terry*.

3. ***Stop-and-Frisk Statutes.*** Although stop-and-frisk has frequently been debated in legislative halls, courts generally have upheld such procedures, if within *Terry* limits, without regard to the existence or non-existence of a statute or ordinance affirmatively authorizing stop-and-frisk, and without regard to the wording of a particular stop-and-frisk statute. See e.g., State v. Hetland, 366 So.2d 831 (Fla.App. 1979). When is a state statute affirmatively authorizing an intrusion essential to a determination that the intrusion is reasonable under the Fourth Amendment?

4. ***Effect of the Exclusionary Rule.*** One judge has commented on one unusual aspect of excluding evidence in a *Terry*-stop case case:

> The exclusionary rule is designed, perhaps poorly so, to protect some of the rights guaranteed by the Constitution. One desirable consequence of the rule is that it often fosters better police work; more aggressive investigation to corroborate what the police suspect may be the case. The hardworking officer will get good warrants where the lazy officer will not.
>
> One perverse consequence of the exclusionary rule in stop and frisk cases is that it often deters only the alert, energetic and dutiful officer. The uncaring time-server who wears a star will rarely be stirred to stop and frisk anyone. It is much easier to sit and just watch even the most suspicious conduct than it is to intervene before it becomes obvious to anyone that a crime is being committed. The indifferent officer always waits until there is probable cause and perhaps even longer than that. It is always safe to wait until the failure to act might subject one to discipline.

United States v. Feliciano, 830 F.Supp. 448 (N.D.Ill.1993).

Alabama v. White

Supreme Court of the United States, 1990.
496 U.S. 325, 110 S.Ct. 2412.

■ JUSTICE WHITE delivered the opinion of the Court.

Based on an anonymous telephone tip, police stopped respondent's vehicle. A consensual search of the car revealed drugs. The issue is whether the tip, as corroborated by independent police work, exhibited sufficient indicia of reliability to provide reasonable suspicion to make the investigatory stop. We hold that it did.

On April 22, 1987, at approximately 3 p.m., Corporal B.H. Davis of the Montgomery Police Department received a telephone call from an anonymous person, stating that Vanessa White would be leaving 235–C Lynwood Terrace Apartments at a particular time in a brown Plymouth station wagon with the right taillight lens broken, that she would be going to Dobey's Motel, and that she would be in possession of about an ounce of cocaine inside a brown attaché case. Corporal Davis and his partner, Corporal P.A. Reynolds, proceeded to the Lynwood Terrace Apartments. The officers saw a brown Plymouth station wagon with a broken right taillight in the parking lot in front of the 235 building. The officers observed respondent leave the 235 building, carrying nothing in her hands, and enter the station wagon. They followed the vehicle as it drove the most direct route to Dobey's Motel. When the vehicle reached the Mobile Highway, on which Dobey's Motel is located, Corporal Reynolds requested a patrol unit to stop the vehicle. The vehicle was stopped at approximately 4:18 p.m., just short of Dobey's Motel. Corporal Davis asked respondent to step to the rear of her car, where he informed her that she had been stopped because she was suspected of carrying cocaine in the vehicle. He asked if they could look for cocaine and respondent said they could look. The officers found a locked brown attaché case in the car and, upon request, respondent provided the combination to the lock. The officers found marijuana in the attaché case and placed respondent under arrest. During processing at the station, the officers found three milligrams of cocaine in respondent's purse.

Respondent was charged in Montgomery County court with possession of marijuana and possession of cocaine. The trial court denied respondent's motion to suppress and she pleaded guilty to the charges, reserving the right to appeal the denial of her suppression motion. The Court of Criminal Appeals of Alabama held that the officers did not have the reasonable suspicion necessary under Terry v. Ohio (1968), to justify the investigatory stop of respondent's car, and that the marijuana and cocaine were fruits of respondent's unconstitutional detention. The court concluded that respondent's motion to dismiss should have been granted and reversed her conviction. The Supreme Court of Alabama denied the State's petition for writ of certiorari, two justices dissenting....

Reasonable suspicion is a less demanding standard than probable cause not only in the sense that reasonable suspicion can be established with information that is different in quantity or content than that required to establish probable cause, but also in the sense that reasonable suspicion can arise from information that is less reliable than that required to show probable cause.... Reasonable suspicion, like probable cause, is dependent upon both the content of information possessed by police and its degree of reliability. Both factors—quantity and quality—are considered in the "totality of the circumstances—the whole picture," United States v. Cortez (1981), that must be taken into account when evaluating whether there is reasonable suspicion. Thus, if a tip has a relatively low degree of reliability, more information will be required to establish the requisite quantum of suspicion than would be required if the tip were more reliable. The Gates v. Illinois (1983) Court applied its totality of the circumstances approach in this manner, taking into account the facts known to the officers from personal observation, and giving the anonymous tip the weight it deserved in light of its indicia of reliability as established through independent police work. The same approach applies in the reasonable suspicion context, the only difference being the level of suspicion that must be established. Contrary to the court below, we conclude that when the officers stopped respondent, the anonymous tip had been sufficiently corroborated to furnish reasonable suspicion that respondent was engaged in criminal activity and that the investigative stop therefore did not violate the Fourth Amendment.

It is true that not every detail mentioned by the tipster was verified, such as the name of the woman leaving the building or the precise apartment from which she left; but the officers did corroborate that a woman left the 235 building and got into the particular vehicle that was described by the caller. With respect to the time of departure predicted by the informant, Corporal Davis testified that the caller gave a particular time when the woman would be leaving, but he did not state what that time was. He did testify that, after the call, he and his partner proceeded to the Lynwood Terrace Apartments to put the 235 building under surveillance. Given the fact that the officers proceeded to the indicated address immediately after the call and that respondent emerged not too long thereafter, it appears from the record before us that respondent's departure from the building was within the time frame predicted by the caller. As for the caller's prediction of respondent's destination, it is true that the officers stopped her just short of Dobey's Motel and did not know whether she would have pulled in or continued on past it. But given that the four-mile route driven by respondent was the most direct route possible to Dobey's Motel, but nevertheless involved several turns, we think respondent's destination was significantly corroborated.

The Court's opinion in *Gates* gave credit to the proposition that because an informant is shown to be right about some things, he is probably right about other facts that he has alleged, including the claim that the object of the tip is engaged in criminal activity. Thus, it is not unreasonable to conclude in this case that the independent corroboration by the police of significant aspects of the informer's predictions imparted some degree of reliability to the other allegations made by the caller.

We think it also important that, as in *Gates*, "the anonymous [tip] contained a range of details relating not just to easily obtained facts and conditions existing at the time of the tip, but to future actions of third parties ordinarily not easily predicted." The fact that the officers found a car precisely matching the caller's description in front of the 235 building is an example of the former. Anyone could have "predicted" that fact because it was a condition presumably existing at the time of the call. What was important was the caller's ability to predict respondent's future behavior, because it demonstrated inside information—a special familiarity with respondent's affairs. The general public would have had no way of knowing that respondent would shortly leave the building, get in the described car, and drive the most direct route to Dobey's Motel. Because only a small number of people are generally privy to an individual's itinerary, it is reasonable for police to believe that a person with access to such information is likely to also have access to reliable information about that individual's illegal activities. When significant aspects of the caller's predictions were verified, there was reason to believe not only that the caller was honest but also that he was well informed, at least well enough to justify the stop.

Although it is a close case, we conclude that under the totality of the circumstances the anonymous tip, as corroborated, exhibited sufficient indicia of reliability to justify the investigatory stop of respondent's car....

■ JUSTICE STEVENS, with whom JUSTICE BRENNAN and JUSTICE MARSHALL join, dissenting.

Millions of people leave their apartments at about the same time every day carrying an attaché case and heading for a destination known to their neighbors. Usually, however, the neighbors do not know what the briefcase contains. An anonymous neighbor's prediction about somebody's time of departure and probable destination is anything but a reliable basis for assuming that the commuter is in possession of an illegal substance—particularly when the person is not even carrying the attaché case described by the tipster.

The record in this case does not tell us how often respondent drove from the Lynwood Terrace Apartments to Dobey's Motel; for all we know, she may have been a room clerk or telephone operator working the evening shift. It does not tell us whether Officer Davis made any effort to ascertain the informer's identity, his reason for calling, or the basis of his prediction about respondent's destination. Indeed, for all that this record tells us, the tipster may well have been another police officer who had a "hunch" that respondent might have cocaine in her attaché case.

Anybody with enough knowledge about a given person to make her the target of a prank, or to harbor a grudge against her, will certainly be able to formulate a tip about her like the one predicting Vanessa White's excursion. In addition, under the Court's holding, every citizen is subject to being seized and questioned by any officer who is prepared to testify that the warrantless stop was based on an anonymous tip predicting whatever conduct the officer just observed. Fortunately, the vast majority of those in our law enforcement community would not adopt such a practice. But the Fourth Amendment was intended to protect the citizen from the overzealous and unscrupulous officer as well as from those who are conscientious and truthful. This decision makes a mockery of that protection.

I respectfully dissent.

NOTES

1. The stop of a vehicle may seem relatively minor, although less so when the subsequent questioning concerns cocaine. Would the officers have had a right to frisk White on the basis of the information they had? Does reasonable suspicion of carrying an ounce of cocaine create reasonable suspicion that the individual is armed and dangerous? If so, then officers could also sweep the interior of the vehicle under Michigan v. Long. Under Whren v. United States, 517 U.S. 806, 116 S.Ct. 1769 (1996), officers may stop vehicles that they reasonably suspect of violating traffic regulations. Could the officers in White have justified the stop on the ground that White's tail light lens was broken? Once the car was stopped on this ground, what could the officers do or ask?

Presumably if the tip had alleged that White was carrying a gun in her purse, and if the officers observed a purse following the stop, officers could have inspected the purse. Does the possibility of a greater intrusion make it harder to approve White's finding of reasonable suspicion based on what seems to be so little data?

Consider the following:

A. An anonymous man called Amtrak police at 10:15 and said: A black man coming from the south on one of the arriving trains had automatic weapons, the man was "5′8″ to 5′9″, approximately twenty-five years old, very large and fat, clean shaven, with short close-cropped hair." The police tried for more information, but the caller hung up. Shortly after police inspected arrivals from Miami and found exiting the train Trevis Walker, a 23 year old, 5′11″, clean shaven, black man who had close cropped hair, weighed 470 pounds and carried two bags. The only other thing police knew was that automatic weapons are readily available in the south. Was this enough to detain Walker or his bags? The majority found the tip "unmistakenly matched" Walker. The dissent said more than "an accurate description of ... physique and whereabouts, which any observant [and mischievous] stranger could provide, should be required." United States v. Walker, 7 F.3d 26 (2d Cir.1993)

B. Police officers on patrol in an African–American neighborhood received a police radio message "16 Ruthven Street, second floor, stab victim stabbed to the back, supposed to be conscious. For a suspect we have a black male with a black 3/4 length goose known as Angelo of the Humboldt Group." Some minutes later the police saw a black male walking on a street approximately one-half mile from the stabbing scene and wearing a dark ¾ length goose down jacket. The officers approached and asked the man his name to which he responded "Zan" or "Ann." The response was not clear because the coat was zippered over the man's mouth. The man's hands were in his pockets. The officers frisked him and found a .38 caliber handgun in one of coat pockets. Is this a valid stop? What do you make of the fact that the information the police had was supplied by an anonymous tip? See Commonwealth v. Cheek, 413 Mass. 492, 597 N.E.2d 1029 (1992).

C. In Florida v. J.L., 529 U.S. 266, 120 S.Ct. 1375 (2000) the police frisked a defendant after receiving an anonymous tip that a young black male standing at a particular bus stop and wearing a plaid shirt was carrying a gun. Two officers responded to the location and saw three young black males standing at the bus stop, one of them wearing a plaid shirt. They did not observe any firearm or unusual movements prior to their action of frisking the man in the plaid shirt. The Court held that on these facts, there was insufficient information to justify the frisk and thus the gun that recovered from the defendant's pocket was the fruit of an illegal stop and frisk. The Court refrained from converting Terry into a "firearms exception" to the Fourth Amendment.

2. *White* may represent one of the "thinnest" case where the Supreme Court has upheld a *Terry* stop. In the following cases, the Court has considered several other cases posing the issue of whether authorities had such reasonable suspicion as to justify the brief detention based on an informant's tip.

A. ***Articulable Suspicion Based on Hearsay***. In Adams v. Williams, 407 U.S. 143, 92 S.Ct. 1921 (1972), the first major stop-and-frisk case before the Court after *Terry* and its companion cases. In *Adams* the Court allowed *Terry* procedures to be used when the articulable suspicion was based upon reports by a hearsay declarant. The Court acknowledged that the information known by the officer and relayed to the judge at the hearing on the motion to suppress would not have sufficed to establish probable cause. A person known to the officer approached him in the early morning hours and stated that an individual seated in a nearby vehicle was carrying narcotics and a gun at his waist. The officer went to the location, knocked on the car window, and ordered the suspect out of the car. Instead of alighting, the suspect rolled down the car's window. The officer reached through and removed a revolver from the suspect's waistband. At the hearing, the officer offered no information establishing reason to believe that he had been dealing with a tipster of established credibility.

Adams also provides an example of a case where stop-and-frisk principles lead to the discovery of data which establishes probable cause to arrest. In *Adams* the officer arrested the suspect for a gun violation once he discovered the weapon. A search incident to that arrest yielded heroin and other weapons.

B. ***Suspicious Profiles***: In Brown v. Texas, 443 U.S. 47, 99 S.Ct. 2637 (1979). Brown was convicted under a statute which made it a crime to refuse to give one's name and address "to a peace officer who has lawfully stopped him and requested the information." Without determining the validity of the statute, the Court found on the facts that the stop was unlawful under the Fourth Amendment for want of reasonable suspicion. The officer had been unable to articulate the basis of his conclusion that Brown "looked suspicious" as he entered an alley. When a "stop is not based on objective criteria, the risk of arbitrary and abusive police practice exceeds tolerable limits," wrote Chief Justice Burger for a unanimous court.

The Supreme Court has decided additional cases which apply the *Terry* test to determine if a particular stop was valid. See Reid v. Georgia, 448 U.S. 438, 100 S.Ct. 2752 (1980) (drug carrier profile inadequate on facts to justify stop of particular suspect); United States v. Cortez, 449 U.S. 411, 101 S.Ct. 690 (1981) (stop of vehicle in border vicinity adequate under *Terry* on particular facts). Some of the justices also discussed a similar issue in United States v. Mendenhall, 446 U.S. 544, 100 S.Ct. 1870 (1980).

In United States v. Sokolow, 490 U.S. 1, 109 S.Ct. 1581 (1989), the parties debated the validity of Drug Enforcement Administration agents' reliance upon a so-called "profile" of characteristics typical of persons transporting drugs. The Court responded that it would not resolve that abstract question, but instead it directed that courts examine the facts of each case to determine the presence or absence of adequate data to justify a *Terry* stop. In the view of the Sokolow majority, adequate data was present under the following circumstances:

> When respondent was stopped, the agents knew, inter alia, that (1) he paid $2,100 for two airplane tickets from a roll of $20 bills; (2) he traveled under a name that did not match the name under which his telephone number was listed; (3) his original destination was Miami, a source city for illicit drugs; (4) he stayed in Miami for only 48 hours, even though a round-trip flight from Honolulu to Miami takes 20 hours; (5) he appeared nervous during his trip; and (6) he checked none of his luggage.

Justices Marshall and Brennan dissented.

C. ***Suspicious Innocent Actions and Reliance on the "Totality of Circumstances" to Determine if There is Reasonable Suspicion***. United States v.

Arvizu, 534 U.S. 266, 122 S.Ct. 744 (2002), concerned the following facts: A border patrol agent learned that a magnetic sensor had been triggered on a back road often used to avoid a border checkpoint. He thought it was suspicious that this occurred at the time in the afternoon for border patrol agents to change shifts. He went to investigate and encountered a minivan on an isolated back road. The van was driven by a man, later identified as Arvizu. The agent described him as stiff and rigid. It seemed to the agent as if the driver were trying to pretend the agent was not there. There was a woman in the front passenger seat and three children in the back. The driver slowed dramatically as the border patrol agent approached. The agent thought the knees of some of the children in the back were unusually high, as if their feet were propped up on something. As the agent followed the minivan, the children all put their hands up at the same time and started waving at him in a mechanical, unusual way. The driver turned abruptly on the last road he could take to avoid the border patrol checkpoint, towards an area that offered no picnic or camping opportunities. A registration check revealed that the minivan was registered to an address close to the border in an area "notorious for alien and narcotics smuggling." The border patrol agent made a vehicle stop and asked the driver if he could look inside the minivan. The driver acquiesced and the border patrol agent discovered over a hundred pounds of marijuana valued at an estimated $99,080 in a black duffel bag under the feet of the children in the back seat. Arvizu was charged with possession of marijuana with intent to distribute and he moved to suppress the drugs. He argued that the border patrol agent lacked reasonable suspicion to make the vehicle stop.

The District Court denied the defendant's motion to suppress, but the Court of Appeals for the Ninth Circuit reversed. Concerned that an ad hoc weighing of the circumstances left too much uncertainly, the Court noted that many of the factors upon which the border patrol agent relied did not rise to criminality and as such, carried little weight in the determination of whether the officer had reasonable suspicion

The United States Supreme Court reversed. Chief Justice Rehnquist, joined by all the other Justices, found that on these facts, there was adequate reasonable suspicion to support the traffic stop. The Court stressed that reasonable suspicion is determined under a totality of the circumstances test that relied on the officers assessment of all the facts, even those, if taken individually, that were susceptible to innocent explanation.

D. ***Information From Another Agency.*** In United States v. Hensley, 469 U.S. 221, 105 S.Ct. 675 (1985), the Supreme Court resolved a split of authority by applying in the stop-and-frisk area principles analogous to those applied in arrest cases under Whiteley v. Warden. The *Hensley* Court declared that when a police officer makes a stop based upon directions from another police agency (in this case, pursuant to a "wanted-for questioning" flyer), the prosecutor must show that that other agency had data which created reasonable suspicion to believe that the individual stopped had committed a crime.

E. **Past Crimes.** The Court in *Terry* summarized its holding by referring to a reasonable belief "that criminal activity may be afoot." One possible reading was that the decision approves certain conduct only with regard to suspects who have just completed a crime, or are presently engaging in one, or are about to commit one. In other words, nothing in *Terry* would justify involuntary street stops to question persons suspected of crimes which occurred several days ago. The "real thrust of *Terry* is directed at instances in which there is reasonable suspicion that someone is about to commit or has just committed a crime." Anderson v. State, 282 Md. 701, 387 A.2d 281, 284 (1978).

However, in United States v. Cortez, 449 U.S. 411, 101 S.Ct. 690 (1981), in a footnote dictum the Court stated: "Of course, any officer may stop and question a suspect if there is reasonable grounds to believe that a person is wanted for past criminal conduct." Is this obvious from *Terry*? Later, in United States v. Hensley, 469 U.S. 221, 105 S.Ct. 675 (1985), this dictum became a holding. The Court declared without dissent that, at least where there is a reasonable suspicion that an individual had committed a felony, authorities can stop the individual for questioning even though there is not presently criminal activity afoot. The Court noted that such a stop is distinguishable from a stop which occurs when criminal activity is a foot. The latter type involves greater exigencies and may prevent the completion of a crime. The former type of stop may involve greater discretion in the officer as to the time or circumstances of the stop. Nevertheless, the Court did not find these distinctions sufficient to limit *Terry* stops to instances where criminal activity is afoot.

Can an officer stop someone who they believe knows where a suspect may be found? See People v. Spencer, 84 N.Y.2d 749, 622 N.Y.S.2d 483, 646 N.E.2d 785 (1995).

F. ***Frisks in Cars.*** In Michigan v. Long, 463 U.S. 1032, 103 S.Ct. 3469 (1983), the Supreme Court considered the proper scope of a frisk where an automobile has been lawfully stopped on reasonable suspicion of criminal activity and where there is a reasonable likelihood of the presence of a weapon. The Court declared that the quest for weapons need not be confined to a frisk of the suspect. Rather it may extend to areas of the vehicle where the suspect might reach to obtain a weapon. The Court defined this area as the interior of the vehicle. The search may not go beyond what would be required to discover weapons and it requires stop-and-frisk justification. These conditions met, the search can extend to the passenger compartment of the vehicle. This is so even though the suspect is out of the vehicle and thus not within reach of any weapon at the time of the search for weapons. Three justices dissented.

United States v. Peoples, 925 F.2d 1082 (8th Cir.1991), illustrates the possible breadth of a "frisk" under Michigan v. Long where there is reasonable suspicion that the suspect is armed and dangerous. After a proper stop, the police removed the suspects from a van and required them to kneel down outside the van. They then located a paper bag beneath a rear bench seat of the van and opened it up. It contained twelve individually wrapped plastic packages containing a white powdery substance later confirmed to be cocaine. The court upheld the procedure.

G. ***Length of Detention.*** In United States v. Place, 462 U.S. 696, 103 S.Ct. 2637 (1983), the Court extended the balancing of interests approach of *Terry* to the temporary detention of luggage "upon reasonable, articulable suspicion, premised on objective facts, that the luggage contained contraband or evidence of a crime." The purpose of the detention was to permit a specially trained dog to sniff the luggage in quest of the scent of narcotics. On the particular facts of the case, the Court held that the ninety-minute detention was too long, especially since the use of the dog could have been arranged more promptly and because the suspect was not told where the luggage was being taken, or for what purpose, and was not informed when or under what circumstances he could retrieve the luggage. Concurring justices protested that the balancing approach of *Terry* should not be extended to justify detention of personal property upon less than probable cause.

3. Are search and seizure cases decided on a case by case basis? Professor David Harris has posited that courts tend to analyze fact patterns involving stop and frisk cases along categorical lines:

> A look at cases applying Terry in the lower courts reveals something surprising. Even though the Court's rhetoric concerning the requirement

of particularized suspicion stands, almost unchanged, since 1968, lower courts have gradually but unmistakably eroded the force of these words. First, courts have allowed stops when individuals fit into one or perhaps two categories of entirely innocent activity: simply being in a "high crime area," for example, or exhibiting a desire to avoid the police, or both. The result is that, contrary to the Court's own repeated statements requiring particularized suspicion, police can stop based on categorical judgments, regardless of the actual individual circumstances. Second, lower courts have slowly and steadily created whole categories of cases which allow police to frisk after a stop, whatever the specific facts are. They have done this by making general declarations that crimes that need not involve weapons are, nevertheless, always dangerous enough that police can always frisk a person they suspect of involvement in such crimes. Similar cases have done the same thing with broad categories of situations that, lower courts say, always present dangers to police. Whether the particular facts indicate potential danger from weapons in an individual case, the supposed raison d'etre of the Terry frisk, becomes irrelevant. Under these cases, a frisk is automatic upon any legitimate stop, as long as the case falls into one of the "always frisk" categories.

The problem is not that these cases allow police to stop and frisk based on whether individual behavior falls into one of these categories. Rather, it is that these categories are so broad that they are far too likely to result in innocent people being stopped and frisked, and too unlikely to include the guilty. David Harris, "Terry and the Fourth Amendment: Particularized Suspicion, Categorical Judgments: Supreme Court Rhetoric Versus Lower Court Reality Under Terry v. Ohio," 72 St. John's L. Rev. 975 (1998)

4. ***The Objective Standard and the Rejection of Good Faith.*** In Terry, the Court explicitly identifies the test as an objective one. If an officer has a good faith belief that he has reasonable suspicion, but that belief is not supported objectively by the facts at hand, his actions of detaining and frisking a suspect will not be permissible under the stop and frisk doctrine.

5. ***Fear.*** Courts often inquire whether an officer was fearful of danger to himself or others as part of the examination of the validity of a stop and frisk. If the officer felt fear for his own safety, that, of course, supports the reasonableness of his actions. In order to find that a stop and frisk was valid, however, it is not necessary that the officer establish that he personally feared the suspect. The validity of the stop and frisk is not based on the existence of actual fear but rather on whether a hypothetical reasonable officer could have reasonably been suspicious and fearful. The requirement that the suspect reasonably be believed to be armed and dangerous must be fulfilled before a frisk is lawful, even though the suspect was properly stopped. Are certain persons, suspected of presently being involved in criminal activity, presumptively armed and dangerous? See Whitten v. United States, 396 A.2d 208 (D.C.App.1978) (shoplifter, no); People v. McGowan, 69 Ill.2d 73, 12 Ill.Dec. 733, 370 N.E.2d 537 (1977) (burglar, yes); Sibron v. New York, 392 U.S. 40, 88 S.Ct. 1889 (1968), Harlan, J. concurring (narcotics dealer, question left open).

6. ***Extent of Search.*** During a stop and frisk, prying into places which could not contain a weapon is not permitted. If an officer does no more than is necessary to accomplish a frisk, however, and discovers seizable material that is not a weapon, he or she may seize it. Worthy v. United States, 409 F.2d 1105 (D.C.Cir.1968) ("The need to seize weapons and the potential instruments of crime, thus indicated as relevant to the scope of a search, does not limit its admissible fruit to weapons if conducted consistently with a proper search for weapons").

Some commentators have argued for a use-exclusion rule which would allow police officers to use stop-and-frisk procedures, but which would exclude any evidence other than a weapon which was discovered through the frisk, even if the frisk did not exceed proper limits. See Amsterdam, Perspectives on the Fourth Amendment, 58 Minn.L.Rev. 349, 434 (1974). For an argument against use-exclusion, see Haddad, Well–Delineated Exceptions, Claims of Sham, and Fourfold Probable Cause, 68 J.C.L. & Crim. 198, 204–214 (1977).

* * *

How do we know if the subject is detained?

Florida v. Bostick

United States Supreme Court, 1991.
501 U.S. 429, 111 S.Ct. 2382.

[Two sheriff's department officers boarded a bus bound from Miami to Atlanta during a stopover in Fort Lauderdale. The officers had badges, insignias, and ne of them held a "recognizable zipper bag, containing a pistol." Eyeing the passengers, without reasonable suspicion, they picked out passenger Terrance Bostick. They asked to inspect his ticket and his identification. Bostick cooperated. They returned his ticket and identification when nothing remarkable appeared. They then asked Bostick's permission to search his luggage, telling him they were narcotics agents in quest of drugs, and informing Bostick of his right to refuse consent, according to the Florida trial court's finding. Bostick agreed to the search. Officers discovered cocaine in one of his suitcases.

The Florida Supreme Court held that the police conduct constituted a seizure within the meaning of the Fourth Amendment. It held the seizure unlawful for want of reasonable seizure. The illegal detention invalidated the consent to search, according to the Florida Supreme Court.

The procedure used in Bostick was a method of drug investigation used with increasing frequency. Upon further review, the United States Supreme Court said that the sole issue was "whether a police encounter on a bus of the type described above necessarily constitutes a 'seizure' within the meaning of the Fourth Amendments."]

■ JUSTICE O'CONNOR delivered the opinion of the Court:

... There is no doubt that if this same encounter had taken place before Bostick boarded the bus or in the lobby of the bus terminal, it would not rise to the level of a seizure. The Court has dealt with similar encounters in airports and has found them to be "the sort of consensual encounter[s] that implicat[e] no Fourth Amendment interest." Florida v. Rodriguez (1984). We have stated that even when officers have no basis for suspecting a particular individual, they may generally ask questions of that individual, see INS v. Delgado (1984); Rodriguez, ask to examine the individual's identification, see Delgado, Royer (plurality opinion); United States v. Mendenhall (1980); and request consent to search his or her luggage, see *Royer*, (plurality opinion)—as long as the police do not convey a message that compliance with their requests is required.

Bostick insists that this case is different because it took place in the cramped confines of a bus. A police encounter is much more intimidating in this setting, he argues, because police tower over a seated passenger and there is little room to move around.... Bostick was a passenger on a bus that was scheduled to depart. He would not have felt free to leave the bus even if the police had not been present. Bostick's movements were "confined" in a sense, but this was the natural result of his decision to take the bus; it says nothing about whether or not the police conduct at issue was coercive.

In this respect, the Court's decision in INS v. Delgado, is dispositive. At issue there was the INS' practice of visiting factories at random and questioning employees to determine whether any were illegal aliens. Several INS agents would stand near the building's exits, while other agents walked through the factory questioning workers. The Court acknowledged that the workers may not have been free to leave their worksite, but explained that this was not the result of police activity: "Ordinarily, when people are at work their freedom to move about has been meaningfully restricted, not by the actions of law enforcement officials, but by the workers' voluntary obligations to their employers." We concluded that there was no seizure because, even though the workers were not free to leave the building without being questioned, the agents' conduct should have given employees "no reason to believe that they would be detained if they gave truthful answers to the questions put to them or if they simply refused to answer."

The present case is analytically indistinguishable from Delgado. Like the workers in that case, Bostick's freedom of movement was restricted by a factor independent of police conduct—i.e., by his being a passenger on a bus. Accordingly, the "free to leave" analysis on which Bostick relies is inapplicable. In such a situation, the appropriate inquiry is whether a reasonable person would feel free to decline the officers' requests or otherwise terminate the encounter.

* * *

The facts of this case, as described by the Florida Supreme Court, leave some doubt whether a seizure occurred. Two officers walked up to Bostick on the bus, asked him a few questions, and asked if they could search his bags. As we have explained, no seizure occurs when police ask questions of an individual, ask to examine the individual's identification, and request consent to search his or her luggage—so long as the officers do not convey a message that compliance with their requests is required. Here, the facts recited by the Florida Supreme Court indicate that the officers did not point guns at Bostick or otherwise threaten him and that they specifically advised Bostick that he could refuse consent.

Nevertheless, we refrain from deciding whether or not a seizure occurred in this case. The trial court made no express findings of fact, and the Florida Supreme Court rested its decision on a single fact—that the encounter took place on a bus—rather than on the totality of the circumstances. We remand so that the Florida courts may evaluate the seizure question under the correct legal standard. We do reject, however, Bostick's argument that he must have been seized because no reasonable person would freely consent to a search of luggage that he or she knows contains drugs. This argument cannot prevail because the "reasonable person" test presupposes an innocent person. See Royer (Blackmun, J., dissenting) ("The fact that [respondent] knew the search was likely to turn up contraband is of course irrelevant; the potential intrusiveness of the officers' conduct must be judged from the viewpoint of an innocent person in [his] position")....

■ JUSTICE MARSHALL, joined by JUSTICES BLACKMUN and STEVENS, dissenting:

... The question for this Court, then, is whether the suspicionless, dragnet-style sweep of buses in intrastate and interstate travel is consistent with the Fourth Amendment. The majority suggests that this latest tactic in the drug war is perfectly compatible with the Constitution. I disagree....

These facts exhibit all of the elements of coercion associated with a typical bus sweep. Two officers boarded the Greyhound bus on which respondent was a passenger while the bus, en route from Miami to Atlanta, was on a brief stop to pick up passengers in Fort Lauderdale. The officers made a visible display of their badges and wore bright green "raid" jackets bearing the insignia of the Broward County Sheriff's Department; one held a gun in a recognizable weapons pouch. These facts alone constitute an intimidating "show of authority." Once on board, the officers approached respondent, who was sitting in the back of the bus, identified themselves as narcotics officers and began to question him. One officer stood in front of respondent's seat, partially blocking the narrow aisle through which respondent would have been required to pass to reach the exit of the bus.

As far as is revealed by facts on which the Florida Supreme Court premised its decision, the officers did not advise respondent that he was free to break off this "interview." In explicably, the majority repeatedly stresses the trial court's implicit finding that the police officers advised respondent that he was free to refuse permission to search his travel bag. This aspect of the exchange between respondent and the police is completely irrelevant to the issue before us. For as the State concedes, and as the majority purports to "accept," if respondent was unlawfully seized when the officers approached him and initiated questioning, the resulting search was likewise unlawful no matter how well advised respondent was of his right to refuse it. Consequently, the issue is not whether a passenger in respondent's position would have felt free to deny consent to the search of his bag, but whether such a passenger—without being apprised of his rights—would have felt free to terminate the antecedent encounter with the police.

Unlike the majority, I have no doubt that the answer to this question is no. Apart from trying to accommodate the officers, respondent had only two options. First, he could have remained seated while obstinately refusing to respond to the officers' questioning. But in light of the intimidating show of authority that the officers made upon boarding the bus, respondent reasonably could have believed that such behavior would only arouse the officers' suspicions and intensify their interrogation. Indeed, officers who carry out bus sweeps like the one at issue here frequently admit that this is the effect of a passenger's refusal to cooperate. The majority's observation that a mere refusal to answer questions, "without more," does not give rise to a reasonable basis for seizing a passenger, is utterly beside the point, because a passenger unadvised of his rights and otherwise unversed in constitutional law has no reason to know that the police cannot hold his refusal to cooperate against him.

Second, respondent could have tried to escape the officers' presence by leaving the bus altogether. But because doing so would have required respondent to squeeze past the gun-wielding inquisitor who was blocking the aisle of the bus, this hardly seems like a course that respondent reasonably would have viewed as available to him. The majority lamely protests that nothing in the stipulated facts shows that the questioning officer "point[ed] [his] gu[n] at [respondent] or otherwise threatened him" with the weapon. Our decisions recognize the obvious point, however, that the choice of the police to "display" their weapons during an encounter exerts significant coercive pressure on the confronted citizen. We have never suggested that the police must go so far as to put a citizen in immediate apprehension of being shot before a court can take account of the intimidating effect of being questioned by an officer with weapon in hand.

Even if respondent had perceived that the officers would let him leave the bus, moreover, he could not reasonably have been expected to resort to this means of evading their intrusive questioning. For so far as respondent knew, the bus' departure from the terminal was imminent. Unlike a person approached by the police on the street, see Michigan v. Chesternut, or at a bus or airport terminal after reaching his destination, see United States v. Mendenhall, a passenger approached by the police at an intermediate point in a long bus journey cannot simply leave the scene and repair to a safe haven to avoid unwanted probing by law-enforcement officials. The vulnerability that an intrastate or interstate traveler experiences when confronted by the police outside of his "own familiar territory" surely aggravates the coercive quality of such an encounter....

Rather than requiring the police to justify the coercive tactics employed here, the majority blames respondent for his own sensation of constraint.... The police would remain free, for example, to approach passengers whom they have a reasonable, articulable basis to suspect of criminal wrongdoing. Alternatively, they could continue to confront passengers without suspicion so long as they took simple steps, like advising the passengers confronted of their right to decline to be questioned, to dispel the aura of coercion and intimidation that pervades such encounters. There is no reason to expect that such requirements would render the Nation's buses law-enforcement-free zones.

The majority attempts to gloss over the violence that today's decision does to the Fourth Amendment with empty admonitions. "If th[e] [war on drugs] is to be fought," the majority intones, "those who fight it must respect the rights of individuals, whether or not those individuals are suspected of having committed a crime." The majority's actions, however, speak louder than its words....

NOTES

1. Does a traffic stop subject the passenger as well as the driver to a Fourth Amendment Seizure? When police stop an automobile, the driver is seized. What about passengers. In Brendlin v. California, ___ U.S. ___, 127 S.Ct. 2400 (2007) police stopped a car. They did not have an adequate provocation, either probable cause or reasonable suspicion, to do so. The state court held that the passenger lacked standing to challenge the constitutionality of the traffic stop. The Supreme Court disagreed, finding that the passenger was seized for Fourth Amendment purposes.

2. *Seizure or Conversation?*

A. Florida v. Royer, 460 U.S. 491, 103 S.Ct. 1319 (1983), indicates that there are at least three distinct categories of police-citizen encounters: (1) an encounter which does not reach the level of a seizure within the meaning of the fourth amendment, so that the prosecution need offer no justification for the encounter at all in order to satisfy the fourth amendment; (2) a "*Terry* stop" requiring reasonable suspicion; and (3) an arrest requiring full probable cause. For a good discussion of this system of categorization, see United States v. Puglisi, 723 F.2d 779 (11th Cir.1984). In applying the Royer classification system, the Royer Court found that at some point the detention became non-consensual and eventually went beyond a mere *Terry* stop.

Thus often the first question is whether an encounter constitutes a seizure. Often the issue will arise on a suppression motion where the defense urges that there was, at a minimum, a seizure requiring *Terry*-type reasonable suspicion. The defense may be seeking to suppress a statement made following what it characterizes as a seizure. Or it may seek suppression of evidence dropped or otherwise discarded after the alleged seizure. Or it may be seeking to invalidate a consent to search given after the purported seizure of the consenting party.

In United States v. Mendenhall, 446 U.S. 544, 100 S.Ct. 1870 (1980), the opinion of the Court, which was joined in, as to the following language, by only two justices, gave one view of what is required before police conduct amounts to a seizure of the person within the meaning of the Fourth Amendment and the *Terry* decision: "A person is 'seized' only when by means of physical force or a show of authority, his freedom of movement is restrained."

The plurality opinion in Royer adopted this definition of a seizure. The Court later utilized that same standard in Immigration and Naturalization Service v. Delgado.

B. Florida v. Rodriguez, 469 U.S. 1, 105 S.Ct. 308 (1984), like *Royer*, is among a line of decisions involving airport encounters between arriving passengers and narcotics enforcement agents. In a per curiam decision, the Court overturned a state court ruling finding a fourth amendment violation. On the peculiar facts, the Supreme Court characterized the initial encounter as consensual and the later detention as a *Terry* stop supported by reasonable suspicion.

C. In Michigan v. Chesternut, 486 U.S. 567, 108 S.Ct. 1975 (1988), an individual who had just been let out of a vehicle ran at the sight of a police car. The police speeded up and then drove along parallel to the individual. They did not signal him to stop, yell "Halt", turn on their flashing light, or sound a siren. Nevertheless, the individual discarded packets that the police later sought to use as evidence. The hearing magistrate held that the packets were the product of an unlawful seizure of the individual made without reasonable suspicion. A unanimous Supreme Court disagreed, concluding that officers had not seized Chesternut within the meaning of the Fourth Amendment, although the police officer who had testified had characterized the situation as a "chase." The Court held that the defendant failed to meet the test of whether, under all of the surrounding circumstances, a reasonable person would have believed that he was not free to leave. "[T]he conduct involved here would not have communicated to the reasonable person an attempt to capture or otherwise intrude upon respondent's freedom of movement." The officers did not seek to block Chesternut's course or otherwise control the direction or speed of his movement. "While the very presence of a police car driving parallel to a running pedestrian could be somewhat intimidating, this kind of police presence does not, standing alone, constitute a seizure."

Justice Kennedy, joined by Justice Scalia, would have had the Court go further by holding that, until efforts to restrain an individual resulted in actual detention, no seizure has occurred. None of the justices discussed another premise of the magistrate's decision, namely that, if the defendant were considered to have been unlawfully seized, the discarded evidence would have to be deemed a product of the seizure. Nor did the Court consider whether flight at the sight of a police officer constitutes reasonable suspicion justifying a seizure.

D. In California v. Hodari D., 499 U.S. 621, 111 S.Ct. 1547 (1991), youngsters including Hodari fled on foot at the approach of an unmarked police car occupied by officers wearing police jackets. The officers gave chase, and Hodari discarded crack cocaine shortly before an officer tackled him. Officers then recovered the cocaine from the street. Hodari argued that officers had "seized" him without reasonable suspicion at the time of the drop, so that the court should view the cocaine as the fruit of a Fourth Amendment violation. The State argued that the police had not "seized" Hodari before they had restrained him, so that the dropped cocaine was abandoned property. The Court stated: "The narrow question before us is whether, with respect to a show of authority as with respect to application of physical force, a seizure occurs even though the subject does not yield. We hold that it does not." The majority said that even if an "uncomplied-with show of authority was a common-law arrest," the Court would not stretch that far the Fourth Amendment concept of "seizure."

Under the majority's approach, even the command "Halt, police!" would not constitute a seizure within the meaning of the Fourth Amendment unless the subject complied with the command.

Two dissenters argued that because a reasonable person would not feel that he was free to leave while an officer was chasing him, the Royer–Mendenhall test indicated that a seizure had occurred. The dissenters noted that the majority was now saying that meeting the Royer–Mendenhall test was necessary but not sufficient for a police-citizen contact to constitute a seizure within the meaning of the Fourth Amendment.

The New Jersey Supreme Court has refused to follow Hodari D.'s definition of seizure for purposes of state constitutional analysis. Instead, the court will retain the rule that a seizure can occur when the actions of police would lead a reasonable person to feel not free to leave. State v. Tucker, 136 N.J. 158, 642 A.2d 401 (1994).

E. In Illinois v. Wardlow, 528 U.S. 119, 120 S.Ct. 673 (2000), the flight of the defendant was interpreted as an indication of guilt. Here, officers entered an area of Chicago known for heavy narcotics trafficking. There were several cars of officers because they anticipated encountering a crowd of people on the street. The officers were in uniform. As they pulled up, the defendant, holding an opaque bag, looked in the direction of the officers and then ran away. The officers followed in their car and stopped the defendant. In the officer's experience, it was common for there to be weapons in the vicinity of narcotics transactions. He frisked Wardlaw and recovered a loaded .38 revolver from the bag the defendant had been holding. Noting that mere presence in a high crime area by itself would not justify a pat down, the Court found that in this case the officers had reasonable suspicion for a limited intrusion based on the evasive nature of the flight plus the presence in the high crime area.

> "In allowing such detentions, *Terry* accepts the risk that officers may stop innocent people. Indeed, the Fourth Amendment accepts that risk in connection with more drastic police action; persons arrested and detained on probable cause to believe they have committed a crime may turn out to be innocent. The *Terry* stop is a far more minimal intrusion, simply allowing the officer to briefly investigate further. If the officer does not learn facts rising to the level of probable cause, the individual must be allowed to go on his way. But in this case the officers found respondent in possession of a handgun, and arrested him for violation of an Illinois firearms statute." 528 U.S. 119, 125, 120 S.Ct. 673, 677.

3. ***Low Level Street Encounters.*** Does an officer need reasonable suspicion to direct a person to "move along"? Suppose the officer wants to see the individual's indentification?

Hiibel v. Sixth Judicial District Court of Nevada, Humboldt County

Supreme Court of the United States, 2004.
542 U.S. 177, 124 S.Ct. 2451, 159 L.Ed.2d 292.

■ JUSTICE KENNEDY delivered the opinion of the Court.

The petitioner was arrested and convicted for refusing to identify himself during a stop allowed by Terry v. Ohio (1968). He challenges his conviction under the Fourth and Fifth Amendments to the United States Constitution, applicable to the States through the Fourteenth Amendment.

I

The sheriff's department in Humboldt County, Nevada, received an afternoon telephone call reporting an assault. The caller reported seeing a man assault a woman in a red and silver GMC truck on Grass Valley Road. Deputy Sheriff Lee Dove was dispatched to investigate. When the officer arrived at the scene, he found the truck parked on the side of the road. A man was standing by the truck, and a young woman was sitting inside it. The officer observed skid marks in the gravel behind the vehicle, leading him to believe it had come to a sudden stop.

The officer approached the man and explained that he was investigating a report of a fight. The man appeared to be intoxicated. The officer asked him if he had "any identification on [him]," which we understand as a request to produce a driver's license or some other form of written identification. The man refused and asked why the officer wanted to see identification. The officer responded that he was conducting an investigation and needed to see some identification. The unidentified man became agitated and insisted he had done nothing wrong. The officer explained that he wanted to find out who the man was and what he was doing there. After continued refusals to comply with the officer's request for identification, the man began to taunt the officer by placing his hands behind his back and telling the officer to arrest him and take him to jail. This routine kept up for several minutes: The officer asked for identification 11 times and was refused each time. After warning the man that he would be arrested if he continued to refuse to comply, the officer placed him under arrest.

We now know that the man arrested on Grass Valley Road is Larry Dudley Hiibel. Hiibel was charged with "willfully resist[ing], delay[ing] or obstruct[ing] a public officer in discharging or attempting to discharge any legal duty of his office" in violation of Nev. Rev. Stat. (NRS) § 199.280 (2003). The government reasoned that Hiibel had obstructed the officer in carrying out his duties under § 171.123, a Nevada statute that defines the legal rights and duties of a police officer in the context of an investigative stop. Section 171.123 provides in relevant part:

> "1. Any peace officer may detain any person whom the officer encounters under circumstances which reasonably indicate that the person has committed, is committing or is about to commit a crime.
>
> . . . . .
>
> "3. The officer may detain the person pursuant to this section only to ascertain his identity and the suspicious circumstances surrounding his presence abroad. Any person so detained shall identify himself, but may not be compelled to answer any other inquiry of any peace officer."

Hiibel was tried in the Justice Court of Union Township. The court agreed that Hiibel's refusal to identify himself as required by § 171.123 "obstructed and delayed Dove as a public officer in attempting to discharge his duty" in violation of § 199.280. App. 5. Hiibel was convicted and fined $250. The Sixth Judicial District Court affirmed, rejecting Hiibel's argument that the application of § 171.123 to his case violated the Fourth and Fifth Amendments. On review the Supreme Court of Nevada rejected the Fourth Amendment challenge in a divided opinion. Hiibel petitioned for rehearing, seeking explicit resolution of his Fifth Amendment challenge. The petition was denied without opinion. We granted certiorari.

II

NRS § 171.123(3) is an enactment sometimes referred to as a "stop and identify" statute.... Stop and identify statutes often combine elements of traditional vagrancy laws with provisions intended to regulate police behavior in the course of investigatory stops. The statutes vary from State to State, but all permit an officer to ask or require a suspect to disclose his identity. A few States model their statutes on the Uniform Arrest Act, a model code that permits an officer to stop a person reasonably suspected of committing a crime and "demand of him his name, address, business abroad and whither he is going." Other statutes are based on the text proposed by the American Law Institute as part of the Institute's Model Penal Code. The provision, originally designated § 250.12, provides that a person who is loitering "under circumstances which justify suspicion that he may be engaged or about to engage in crime commits a violation if he refuses the request of a peace officer that he identify himself and give a reasonably credible account of the lawfulness of his conduct and purposes." § 250.12 (Tent. Draft No. 13) (1961). In some States, a suspect's refusal to identify himself is a misdemeanor offense or civil violation; in others, it is a factor to be considered in whether the suspect has violated loitering laws. In other States, a suspect may decline to identify himself without penalty.

Stop and identify statutes have their roots in early English vagrancy laws that required suspected vagrants to face arrest unless they gave "a good Account of themselves," a power that itself reflected common-law rights of private persons to "arrest any suspicious night-walker, and detain him till he give a good account of himself. . . ." In recent decades, the Court has found constitutional infirmity in traditional vagrancy laws. In Papachristou v. Jacksonville (1972), the Court held that a traditional vagrancy law was void for vagueness. Its broad scope and imprecise terms denied proper notice to potential offenders and permitted police officers to exercise unfettered discretion in the enforcement of the law.

The Court has recognized similar constitutional limitations on the scope and operation of stop and identify statutes. In Brown v. Texas (1979), the Court invalidated a conviction for violating a Texas stop and identify statute on Fourth Amendment grounds. The Court ruled that the initial stop was not based on specific, objective facts establishing reasonable suspicion to believe the suspect was involved in criminal activity. Absent that factual basis for detaining the defendant, the Court held, the risk of "arbitrary and abusive police practices" was too great and the stop was impermissible. Four Terms later, the Court invalidated a modified stop and identify statute on vagueness grounds. See Kolender v. Lawson(1983). The California law in *Kolender* required a suspect to give an officer " 'credible and reliable' " identification when asked to identify himself. The Court held that the statute was void because it provided no standard for determining what a suspect must do to comply with it, resulting in " 'virtually unrestrained power to arrest and charge persons with a violation.' " *Ibid.* (quoting *Lewis v. New Orleans*, 415 U.S. 130, 135, 39 L. Ed. 2d 214, 94 S. Ct. 970 (1974) (Powell, J., concurring in result)).

The present case begins where our prior cases left off. Here there is no question that the initial stop was based on reasonable suspicion, satisfying the Fourth Amendment requirements noted in *Brown* Further, the petitioner has not alleged that the statute is unconstitutionally vague, as in *Kolender*. Here the Nevada statute is narrower and more precise. The statute in *Kolender* had been interpreted to require a suspect to give the officer "credible and reliable" identification. In contrast, the Nevada Supreme Court has interpreted NRS § 171.123(3) to require only that a suspect disclose his name. See 118 Nev., at 875, 59 P. 3d, at 1206 (opinion of Young, C. J.) ("The suspect is not required to provide private details about his background, but merely to state his name to an officer when reasonable suspicion exists"). As we understand it, the statute does not require a suspect to give the officer a driver's license or any other document. Provided that the suspect either states his name or communicates it to the officer by other means—a choice, we assume, that the suspect may make—the statute is satisfied and no violation occurs.

III

Hiibel argues that his conviction cannot stand because the officer's conduct violated his Fourth Amendment rights. We disagree.

Asking questions is an essential part of police investigations. In the ordinary course a police officer is free to ask a person for identification without implicating the Fourth Amendment. "[I]nterrogation relating to one's identity or a request for identification by the police does not, by itself, constitute a Fourth Amendment seizure." INS v. Delgado (1984). Beginning with Terry v. Ohio (1968), the Court has recognized that a law enforcement officer's reasonable suspicion that a person may be involved in criminal activity permits the officer to stop the person for a brief time and take additional steps to investigate further. To ensure that the resulting seizure is constitutionally reasonable, a *Terry* stop must be limited. The officer's action must be " 'justified at its inception, and ... reasonably related in scope to the circumstances which justified the interference in the first place.' " For example, the seizure cannot [*186] continue for an excessive period of time, see United States v. Place (1983), or resemble a traditional arrest, see Dunaway v. New York (1979).

Our decisions make clear that questions concerning a suspect's identity are a routine and accepted part of many *Terry* stops. See United States v. Hensley (1985) ("[T]he ability to briefly stop [a suspect], ask questions, or check identification in the absence of probable cause promotes the strong government interest in solving crimes and bringing offenders to justice"); Hayes v. Florida(1985) ("[I]f there are articulable facts supporting a reasonable suspicion that a person has committed a criminal offense, that person may be stopped in order to identify him, to question him briefly, or to detain him briefly while attempting to obtain additional information"); Adams v. Williams (1972) ("A brief stop of a suspicious individual, in order to determine his identity or to maintain the status quo momentarily while obtaining more information, may be most reasonable in light of the facts known to the officer at the time").

Obtaining a suspect's name in the course of a *Terry* stop serves important government interests. Knowledge of identity may inform an officer that a suspect is wanted for another offense, or has a record of violence or mental disorder. On the other hand, knowing identity may help clear a suspect and allow the police to concentrate their efforts elsewhere. Identity may prove particularly important in cases such as this, where the police are investigating what appears to be a domestic assault. Officers called to investigate domestic disputes need to know whom they are dealing with in order to assess the situation, the threat to their own safety, and possible danger to the potential victim.

Although it is well established that an officer may ask a suspect to identify himself in the course of a *Terry* stop, it has been an open question whether the suspect can be arrested and prosecuted for refusal to answer. Petitioner draws our attention to statements in prior opinions that, according to him, answer the question in his favor. In *Terry*, Justice White stated in a concurring opinion that a person detained in an investigative stop can be questioned but is "not obliged to answer, answers may not be compelled, and refusal to answer furnishes no basis for an arrest." The Court cited this opinion in dicta in Berkemer v. McCarty (1984), a decision holding that a routine traffic stop is not a custodial stop requiring the protections of Miranda v. Arizona (1966). In the course of explaining why *Terry* stops have not been subject to *Miranda*, the Court suggested reasons why *Terry* stops have a "nonthreatening character," among them the fact that a suspect detained during a *Terry* stop "is not obliged to respond" to questions. See *Berkemer*. According to petitioner, these statements establish a right to refuse to answer questions during a *Terry* stop.

We do not read these statements as controlling. The passages recognize that the Fourth Amendment does not impose obligations on the citizen but instead provides rights against the government. As a result, the Fourth Amendment itself cannot require a suspect to answer questions. This case concerns a different issue, however. Here, the source of the legal obligation arises from Nevada state law, not the Fourth Amendment. Further, the statutory obligation does not go beyond answering an officer's request to disclose a name. See NRS § 171.123(3) ("Any person so detained shall identify himself, but may not be compelled to answer any other inquiry of any peace officer"). As a result, we cannot view the dicta in *Berkemer* or Justice White's concurrence in *Terry* as answering the question whether a State can compel a suspect to disclose his name during a *Terry* stop.

The principles of *Terry* permit a State to require a suspect to disclose his name in the course of a *Terry* stop. The reasonableness of a seizure under the Fourth Amendment is determined "by balancing its intrusion on the individual's Fourth Amendment interests against its promotion of legitimate government interests." Delaware v. Prouse (1979). The Nevada statute satisfies that standard. The request for identity has an immediate relation to the purpose, rationale, and practical demands of a *Terry* stop. The threat of criminal sanction helps ensure that the request for identity does not become a legal nullity. On the other hand, the Nevada statute does not alter the nature of the stop itself: it does not change its duration, *Place*, or its location, *Dunaway*. A state law requiring a suspect to disclose his name in the course of a valid *Terry* stop is consistent with Fourth Amendment prohibitions against unreasonable searches and seizures.

Petitioner argues that the Nevada statute circumvents the probable-cause requirement, in effect allowing an officer to arrest a person for being suspicious. According to petitioner, this creates a risk of arbitrary police conduct that the Fourth Amendment does not permit. These are familiar concerns; they were central to the opinion in *Papachristou*, and also to the decisions limiting the operation of stop and identify statutes in *Kolender* and *Brown*. Petitioner's concerns are met by the requirement that a *Terry* stop must be justified at its inception and "reasonably related in scope to the circumstances which justified" the initial stop. Under these principles, an officer may not arrest a suspect for failure to identify himself if the request for identification is not reasonably related to the circumstances justifying the stop. The Court noted a similar limitation in *Hayes*, where it suggested that *Terry* may permit an officer to determine a suspect's identity by compelling the suspect to submit to fingerprinting only if there is "a reasonable basis for believing that fingerprinting will establish or negate the suspect's connection with that crime." It is clear in this case that the request for identification was "reasonably related in scope to the circumstances which justified" the stop. The officer's request was a commonsense inquiry, not an effort to obtain an arrest for failure to identify after a *Terry* stop yielded insufficient evidence. The stop, the request, and the State's requirement of a response did not contravene the guarantees of the Fourth Amendment.

IV

Petitioner further contends that his conviction violates the Fifth Amendment's prohibition on compelled self-incrimination. The Fifth Amendment states that "[n]o person . . . shall be compelled in any criminal case to be a witness against himself." To qualify for the Fifth Amendment privilege, a communication must be testimonial, incriminating, and compelled.

Respondents urge us to hold that the statements NRS § 171.123(3) requires are nontestimonial, and so outside the Clause's scope. We decline to resolve the case on that basis. "[T]o be testimonial, an accused's communication must itself, explicitly or implicitly, relate a factual assertion or disclose information." *Doe v. United States* (1988). Stating one's name may qualify as an assertion of fact relating to identity. Production of identity documents might meet the definition as well. As we noted in *Hubbell*, acts of production may yield testimony establishing "the existence, authenticity, and custody of items [the police seek]." Even if these required actions are testimonial, however, petitioner's challenge must fail because in this case disclosure of his name presented no reasonable danger of incrimination.

The Fifth Amendment prohibits only compelled testimony that is incriminating. See *Brown v. Walker*, 161 U.S. 591, 598, 40 L. Ed. 819, 16 S. Ct. 644 (1896) (noting that where "the answer of the witness will not directly show his infamy, but only *tend* to disgrace him, he is bound to answer"). A claim of Fifth Amendment privilege must establish

> " 'reasonable ground to apprehend danger to the witness from his being compelled to answer. . . . [T]he danger to be apprehended must be real and appreciable, with reference to the ordinary operation of law in the ordinary course of things,—not a danger of an imaginary and unsubstantial character, having reference to some extraordinary and barely possible contingency, so improbable that no reasonable man would suffer it to influence his conduct.' "
> *Id.*, at 599–600, 40 L. Ed. 819, 16 S. Ct. 644 (quoting *Queen v. Boyes*, 1 B. & S. 311, 330, 121 Eng. Rep. 730,738 (Q. B. 1861) (Cockburn, C. J.)).

As we stated in Kastigar v. United States (1972), the Fifth Amendment privilege against compulsory self-incrimination "protects against any disclosures that the witness reasonably believes could be used in a criminal prosecution or could lead to other evidence that might be so used." Suspects who have been granted immunity from prosecution may, therefore, be compelled to answer; with the threat of prosecution removed, there can be no reasonable belief that the evidence will be used against them.

In this case petitioner's refusal to disclose his name was not based on any articulated real and appreciable fear that his name would be used to incriminate him, or that it "would furnish a link in the chain of evidence needed to prosecute" him. Hoffman v. United States (1951). As best we can tell, petitioner refused to identify himself only because he thought his name was none of the officer's business. Even today, petitioner does not explain how the disclosure of his name could have been used against him in a criminal case. While we recognize petitioner's strong belief that he should not have to disclose his identity, the Fifth Amendment does not override the Nevada Legislature's judgment to the contrary absent a reasonable belief that the disclosure would tend to incriminate him.

The narrow scope of the disclosure requirement is also important. One's identity is, by definition, unique; yet it is, in another sense, a universal characteristic. Answering a request to disclose a name is likely to be so insignificant in the scheme of things as to be incriminating only in unusual circumstances. In every criminal case, it is known and must be known who has been arrested and who is being tried. Even witnesses who plan to invoke the Fifth Amendment privilege answer when their names are called to take the stand. Still, a case may arise where there is a substantial allegation that furnishing identity at the time of a stop would have given the police a link in the chain of evidence needed to convict the individual of a separate offense. In that case, the court can then consider whether the privilege applies, and, if the Fifth Amendment has been violated, what remedy must follow. We need not resolve those questions here.

The judgment of the Nevada Supreme Court is affirmed.

■ JUSTICE STEVENS, dissenting.

The Nevada law at issue in this case imposes a narrow duty to speak upon a specific class of individuals. The class includes only those persons detained by a police officer "under circumstances which reasonably indicate that the person has committed, is committing or is about to commit a crime" 1—persons who are, in other words, targets of a criminal investigation. The statute therefore is directed not "at the public at large," but rather "at a highly selective group inherently suspect of criminal activities." Albertson v. Subversive Activities Control Bd. (1965)....

The officer in this case told petitioner, in the Court's words, that "he was conducting an investigation and needed to see some identification." As the target of that investigation, petitioner, in my view, acted well within his rights when he opted to stand mute. Accordingly, I respectfully dissent.

■ JUSTICE BREYER, with whom JUSTICE SOUTER and JUSTICE GINSBURG join, dissenting.

Notwithstanding the vagrancy statutes to which the majority refers, this Court's Fourth Amendment precedents make clear that police may conduct a *Terry* stop only within circumscribed limits. And one of those limits invalidates laws that compel responses to police questioning.

In Terry v. Ohio (1968), the Court considered whether police, in the absence of probable cause, can stop, question, or frisk an individual at all. The Court recognized that the Fourth Amendment protects the " 'right of every individual to the possession and control of his own person.' " At the same time, it recognized that in certain circumstances, public safety might require a limited "seizure," or stop, of an individual against his will. The

Court consequently set forth conditions circumscribing when and how the police might conduct a *Terry* stop. They include what has become known as the "reasonable suspicion" standard. Justice White, in a separate concurring opinion, set forth further conditions. Justice White wrote: "Of course, the person stopped is not obliged to answer, answers may not be compelled, and refusal to answer furnishes no basis for an arrest, although it may alert the officer to the need for continued observation."

About 10 years later, the Court, in Brown v. Texas (1979), held that police lacked "any reasonable suspicion" to detain the particular petitioner and require him to identify himself. The Court noted that the trial judge had asked the following: " 'I'm sure [officers conducting a *Terry* stop] should ask everything they possibly could find out. *What I'm asking is what's the State's interest in putting a man in jail because he doesn't want to answer. . . .*' " (Appendix to opinion of the Court) (emphasis in original). The Court referred to Justice White's *Terry* concurrence. And it said that it "need not decide" the matter.

Then, five years later, the Court wrote that an "officer may ask the *[Terry]* detainee a moderate number of questions to determine his identity and to try to obtain information confirming or dispelling the officer's suspicions. *But the detainee is not obliged to respond.*" Berkemer v. McCarty (1984) (emphasis added in original). See also Kolender v. Lawson (1983) (Brennan, J., concurring) (*Terry* suspect "must be free to ... decline to answer the questions put to him"); Illinois v. Wardlow (2000) (stating that allowing officers to stop and question a fleeing person "is quite consistent with the individual's right to go about his business or to stay put and remain silent in the face of police questioning").

This lengthy history—of concurring opinions, of references, and of clear explicit statements—means that the Court's statement in *Berkemer*, while technically dicta, is the kind of strong dicta that the legal community typically takes as a statement of the law. And that law has remained undisturbed for more than 20 years.

There is no good reason now to reject this generation-old statement of the law. There are sound reasons rooted in Fifth Amendment considerations for adhering to this Fourth Amendment legal condition circumscribing police authority to stop an individual against his will. Administrative considerations also militate against change. Can a State, in addition to requiring a stopped individual to answer "What's your name?" also require an answer to "What's your license number?" or "Where do you live?" Can a police officer, who must know how to make a *Terry* stop, keep track of the constitutional answers? After all, answers to any of these questions may, or may not, incriminate, depending upon the circumstances.

Indeed, as the Court points out, a name itself—even if it is not "Killer Bill" or "Rough 'em up Harry"—will sometimes provide the police with "a link in the chain of evidence needed to convict the individual of a separate offense." The majority reserves judgment about whether compulsion is permissible in such instances. How then is a police officer in the midst of a *Terry* stop to distinguish between the majority's ordinary case and this special case where the majority reserves judgment?

The majority presents no evidence that the rule enunciated by Justice White and then by the *Berkemer* Court, which for nearly a generation has set forth a settled *Terry*-stop condition, has significantly interfered with law enforcement. Nor has the majority presented any other convincing justification for change. I would not begin to erode a clear rule with special exceptions.

I consequently dissent.

NOTES

1. A video of the events that form the basis of the Hiibel case is available on the defendant's website at http://papersplease.org/hiibel/index.html.

2. Does *Hiibel* form one more case in which the Court responds to the "needs of the day"?

> . . . with Hiibel, the Court continues its practice of manipulating the Terry rationale to reflect the needs of law enforcement officials at various points in history. For example, during the so-called "war on drugs" of the 1980s, the Court expanded Terry to allow officers to stop suspected drug couriers at airports and on buses, even though these individuals presented no safety threat to the police. However, while the Court has repeatedly loosened the requirements of the "reasonable suspicion" standard, it had not, until Hiibel, vacillated in its position that the scope of a Terry stop is limited.
>
> In the 21st century, America's focus has shifted to the "war on terrorism." Law enforcement officials now have the overwhelming burden of apprehending potential terrorists before another catastrophe like that of September 11, 2001 occurs. This Comment argues that although there was no mention of terrorism or September 11 in Hiibel, this backdrop likely played a role in the Justices' decision to grant police the authority to arrest and prosecute an individual for failing to give his name. While the information a name provides may aid police in detaining terrorists and keeping America safe, giving police the power to obtain it may narrow the already-diminished Fourth Amendment protections the Court held so dear in Terry. The decision to endorse this police power further raises the question of where the line is, and what aspect of privacy the Court may target next. (cites omitted) Comment (Stulin): "Does *Hiibel* Redefine *Terry*? The Latest Expansion of the *Terry* Doctrine and the Silent Impact of Terrorism on the Supreme Court's Decision to Compel Identification," 54 Am. U.L. Rev. 1449 (2005).

3. *Is there a search incident to a "stop"?* How far may police go to search when they stop a suspect. In *Caballes*, the case that follows, the police stopped the defendant for speeding. At the point of the stop, there was no indication that the defendant possessed contraband. Another officer appeared with a drug detection dog that alerted as it circled the defendant's car, indicating the presence of drugs. The police retrieved the drugs. Is this constitutionally permissible?

Illinois v. Caballes

Supreme Court of the United States, 2005.
543 U.S. 405, 125 S.Ct. 834.

■ JUSTICE STEVENS delivered the opinion of the Court.

Illinois State Trooper Daniel Gillette stopped respondent for speeding on an interstate highway. When Gillette radioed the police dispatcher to report the stop, a second trooper, Craig Graham, a member of the Illinois State Police Drug Interdiction Team, overheard the transmission and immediately headed for the scene with his narcotics-detection dog. When they arrived, respondent's car was on the shoulder of the road and respondent was in Gillette's vehicle. While Gillette was in the process of writing a warning ticket, Graham walked his dog around respondent's car. The dog alerted at the trunk. Based on that alert, the officers searched the trunk, found marijuana, and arrested respondent. The entire incident lasted less than 10 minutes.

Respondent was convicted of a narcotics offense and sentenced to 12 years' imprisonment and a $256,136 fine. The trial judge denied his motion to suppress the seized evidence and to quash his arrest. He held that the officers had not unnecessarily prolonged the stop and that the dog alert was sufficiently reliable to provide probable cause to conduct the search. Although the Appellate Court affirmed, the Illinois Supreme Court reversed, concluding that because the canine sniff was performed without any " 'specific and articulable facts' " to suggest drug activity, the use of the dog "unjustifiably enlarg[ed] the scope of a routine traffic stop into a drug investigation."

The question on which we granted certiorari is narrow: "Whether the Fourth Amendment requires reasonable, articulable suspicion to justify using a drug-detection dog to sniff a vehicle during a legitimate traffic stop." Thus, we proceed on the assumption that the officer conducting the dog sniff had no information about respondent except that he had been stopped for speeding; accordingly, we have omitted any reference to facts about respondent that might have triggered a modicum of suspicion.

Here, the initial seizure of respondent when he was stopped on the highway was based on probable cause and was concededly lawful. It is nevertheless clear that a seizure that is lawful at its inception can violate the Fourth Amendment if its manner of execution unreasonably infringes interests protected by the Constitution. United States v. Jacobsen (1984). A seizure that is justified solely by the interest in issuing a warning ticket to the driver can become unlawful if it is prolonged beyond the time reasonably required to complete that mission. In an earlier case involving a dog sniff that occurred during an unreasonably prolonged traffic stop, the Illinois Supreme Court held that use of the dog and the subsequent discovery of contraband were the product of an unconstitutional seizure. We may assume that a similar result would be warranted in this case if the dog sniff had been conducted while respondent was being unlawfully detained.

In the state-court proceedings, however, the judges carefully reviewed the details of Officer Gillette's conversations with respondent and the precise timing of his radio transmissions to the dispatcher to determine whether he had improperly extended the duration of the stop to enable the dog sniff to occur. We have not recounted those details because we accept the state court's conclusion that the duration of the stop in this case was entirely justified by the traffic offense and the ordinary inquiries incident to such a stop.

Despite this conclusion, the Illinois Supreme Court held that the initially lawful traffic stop became an unlawful seizure solely as a result of the canine sniff that occurred outside respondent's stopped car. That is, the court characterized the dog sniff as the cause rather than the consequence of a constitutional violation. In its view, the use of the dog converted the citizen-police encounter from a lawful traffic stop into a drug investigation, and because the shift in purpose was not supported by any reasonable suspicion that respondent possessed narcotics, it was unlawful. In our view, conducting a dog sniff would not change the character of a traffic stop that is lawful at its inception and otherwise executed in a reasonable manner, unless the dog sniff itself infringed respondent's constitutionally protected interest in privacy. Our cases hold that it did not.

Official conduct that does not "compromise any legitimate interest in privacy" is not a search subject to the Fourth Amendment. We have held that any interest in possessing contraband cannot be deemed "legitimate," and thus, governmental conduct that *only* reveals the possession of contraband "compromises no legitimate privacy interest." This is because the expectation "that certain facts will not come to the attention of the authorities" is not the same as an interest in "privacy that society is prepared to consider reasonable." In United States v. Place (1983), we treated a canine sniff by a well-trained narcotics-detection dog as "*sui generis*" because it "discloses only the presence or absence of narcotics, a contraband item." Respondent likewise concedes that "drug sniffs are designed, and if properly conducted are generally likely, to reveal only the presence of contraband." Although respondent argues that the error rates, particularly the existence of false positives, call into question the premise that drug-detection dogs alert only to contraband, the record contains no evidence or findings that support his argument. Moreover, respondent does not suggest that an erroneous alert, in and of itself, reveals any legitimate private information, and, in this case, the trial judge found that the dog sniff was sufficiently reliable to establish probable cause to conduct a full-blown search of the trunk.

Accordingly, the use of a well-trained narcotics-detection dog—one that "does not expose noncontraband items that otherwise would remain hidden from public view,"—during a lawful traffic stop, generally does not implicate legitimate privacy interests. In this case, the dog sniff was performed on the exterior of respondent's car while he was lawfully seized for a traffic violation. Any intrusion on respondent's privacy expectations does not rise to the level of a constitutionally cognizable infringement.

This conclusion is entirely consistent with our recent decision that the use of a thermal-imaging device to detect the growth of marijuana in a home constituted an unlawful search. Kyllo v. United States (2001). Critical to that decision was the fact that the device was capable of detecting lawful activity—in that case, intimate details in a home, such as "at what hour each night the lady of the house takes her daily sauna and bath." The legitimate expectation that information about perfectly lawful activity will remain private is categorically distinguishable from respondent's hopes or expectations concerning the nondetection of contraband in the trunk of his car. A dog sniff conducted during a concededly lawful traffic stop that reveals no information other than the location of a substance that no individual has any right to possess does not violate the Fourth Amendment.

The judgment of the Illinois Supreme Court is vacated, and the case is remanded for further proceedings not inconsistent with this opinion.

It is so ordered.

■ THE CHIEF JUSTICE took no part in the decision of this case.

■ JUSTICE SOUTER, dissenting.

I would hold that using the dog for the purposes of determining the presence of marijuana in the car's trunk was a search unauthorized as an incident of the speeding stop and unjustified on any other ground. I would accordingly affirm the judgment of the Supreme Court of Illinois, and I respectfully dissent.

In United States v. Place (1983) we categorized the sniff of the narcotics-seeking dog as *"sui generis"* under the Fourth Amendment and held it was not a search. The classification rests not only upon the limited nature of the intrusion, but on a further premise that experience has shown to be untenable, the assumption that trained sniffing dogs do not err. What we have learned about the fallibility of dogs in the years since *Place* was decided would itself be reason to call for reconsidering *Place*'s decision against treating the intentional use of a trained dog as a search. The portent of this very case, however, adds insistence to the call, for an uncritical adherence to *Place* would render the Fourth Amendment indifferent to suspicionless and indiscriminate sweeps of cars in parking garages and pedestrians on sidewalks; if a sniff is not preceded by a seizure subject to Fourth Amendment notice, it escapes Fourth Amendment review entirely unless it is treated as a search. We should not wait for these developments to occur before rethinking *Place*'s analysis, which invites such untoward consequences.[1]

At the heart both of *Place* and the Court's opinion today is the proposition that sniffs by a trained dog are *sui generis* because a reaction by the dog in going alert is a response to nothing but the presence of contraband.[2] ("[T]he sniff discloses only the presence or absence of narcotics, a contraband item"). Hence, the argument goes, because the sniff can

1. I also join Justice Ginsburg's dissent. Without directly reexamining the soundness of the Court's analysis of government dog sniffs in *Place*, she demonstrates that investigation into a matter beyond the subject of the traffic stop here offends the rule in *Terry v. Ohio* (1968), the analysis I, too, adopt.

2. Another proffered justification for *sui generis* status is that a dog sniff is a particularly nonintrusive procedure. United States v. Place., I agree with Justice Ginsburg that the introduction of a dog to a traffic stop (let alone an encounter with someone walking down the street) can in fact be quite intrusive.

only reveal the presence of items devoid of any legal use, the sniff "does not implicate legitimate privacy interests" and is not to be treated as a search.

The infallible dog, however, is a creature of legal fiction. Although the Supreme Court of Illinois did not get into the sniffing averages of drug dogs, their supposed infallibility is belied by judicial opinions describing well-trained animals sniffing and alerting with less than perfect accuracy, whether owing to errors by their handlers, the limitations of the dogs themselves, or even the pervasive contamination of currency by cocaine.... In practical terms, the evidence is clear that the dog that alerts hundreds of times will be wrong dozens of times.

Once the dog's fallibility is recognized, however, that ends the justification claimed in *Place* for treating the sniff as *sui generis* under the Fourth Amendment: the sniff alert does not necessarily signal hidden contraband, and opening the container or enclosed space whose emanations the dog has sensed will not necessarily reveal contraband or any other evidence of crime.... And given the fallibility of the dog, the sniff is the first step in a process that may disclose "intimate details" without revealing contraband, just as a thermal-imaging device might do, as described in *Kyllo v. United States* (2001).[3]

It makes sense, then, to treat a sniff as the search that it amounts to in practice, and to rely on the body of our Fourth Amendment cases, including *Kyllo*, in deciding whether such a search is reasonable. As a general proposition, using a dog to sniff for drugs is subject to the rule that the object of enforcing criminal laws does not, without more, justify suspicionless Fourth Amendment intrusions. Since the police claim to have had no particular suspicion that Caballes was violating any drug law, this sniff search must stand or fall on its being ancillary to the traffic stop that led up to it. It is true that the police had probable cause to stop the car for an offense committed in the officer's presence, which Caballes concedes could have justified his arrest....

In Berkemer v. McCarty (1984) we held that the analogue of the common traffic stop was the limited detention for investigation authorized by Terry v. Ohio (1968). While *Terry* authorized a restricted incidental search for weapons when reasonable suspicion warrants such a safety measure, the Court took care to keep a *Terry* stop from automatically becoming a foot in the door for all investigatory purposes; the permissible intrusion was bounded by the justification for the detention,[5] Although facts disclosed by enquiry within this limit might give grounds to go

3. *Kyllo* was concerned with whether a search occurred when the police used a thermal-imaging device on a house to detect heat emanations associated with high-powered marijuana-growing lamps. In concluding that using the device was a search, the Court stressed that the "Government [may not] us[e] a device ... to explore details of the home that would previously have been unknowable without physical intrusion.".... The justifications required by the Fourth Amendment may or may not differ as between the two practices, but if constitutional scrutiny is in order for the imager, it is in order for the dog.

5. Thus, in *Place* itself, the Government officials had independent grounds to suspect that the luggage in question contained contraband before they employed the dog sniff. (describing how Place had acted suspiciously in line at the airport and had labeled his luggage with inconsistent and fictional addresses).

further, the government could not otherwise take advantage of a suspect's immobility to search for evidence unrelated to the reason for the detention. That has to be the rule unless *Terry* is going to become an open-sesame for general searches, and that rule requires holding that the police do not have reasonable grounds to conduct sniff searches for drugs simply because they have stopped someone to receive a ticket for a highway offense. Since the police had no indication of illegal activity beyond the speed of the car in this case, the sniff search should be held unreasonable under the Fourth Amendment and its fruits should be suppressed....

The Court today does not go so far as to say explicitly that sniff searches by dogs trained to sense contraband always get a free pass under the Fourth Amendment, since it reserves judgment on the constitutional significance of sniffs assumed to be more intrusive than a dog's walk around a stopped car. For this reason, I do not take the Court's reliance on *Jacobsen* as actually signaling recognition of a broad authority to conduct suspicionless sniffs for drugs in any parked car, about which Justice Ginsburg is rightly concerned, or on the person of any pedestrian minding his own business on a sidewalk. But the Court's stated reasoning provides no apparent stopping point short of such excesses. For the sake of providing a workable framework to analyze cases on facts like these, which are certain to come along, I would treat the dog sniff as the familiar search it is in fact, subject to scrutiny under the Fourth Amendment.[7]

■ JUSTICE GINSBURG, with whom JUSTICE SOUTER joins, dissenting.

Illinois State Police Trooper Daniel Gillette stopped Roy Caballes for driving 71 miles per hour in a zone with a posted speed limit of 65 miles per hour. Trooper Craig Graham of the Drug Interdiction Team heard on the radio that Trooper Gillette was making a traffic stop. Although Gillette requested no aid, Graham decided to come to the scene to conduct a dog sniff. Gillette informed Caballes that he was speeding and asked for the usual documents—driver's license, car registration, and proof of insurance. Caballes promptly provided the requested documents but refused to consent to a search of his vehicle. After calling his dispatcher to check on the validity of Caballes' license and for outstanding warrants, Gillette returned to his vehicle to write Caballes a warning ticket. Interrupted by a radio call on an unrelated matter, Gillette was still writing the ticket when Trooper Graham arrived with his drug-detection dog. Graham walked the dog around the car, the dog alerted at Caballes' trunk, and, after opening the trunk, the troopers found marijuana.

The Supreme Court of Illinois held that the drug evidence should have been suppressed. Adhering to its decision in People v. Cox (2002), the court employed a two-part test taken from Terry v. Ohio (1968), to determine the overall reasonableness of the stop. The court asked first "whether the

7. I should take care myself to reserve judgment about a possible case significantly unlike this one. All of us are concerned not to prejudge a claim of authority to detect explosives and dangerous chemical or biological weapons that might be carried by a terrorist who prompts no individualized suspicion. Suffice it to say here that what is a reasonable search depends in part on demonstrated risk. Unreasonable sniff searches for marijuana are not necessarily unreasonable sniff searches for destructive or deadly material if suicide bombs are a societal risk.

officer's action was justified at its inception," and second "whether it was reasonably related in scope to the circumstances which justified the interference in the first place." "[I]t is undisputed," the court observed, "that the traffic stop was properly initiated"; thus, the dispositive inquiry trained on the "second part of the *Terry* test," in which "[t]he State bears the burden of establishing that the conduct remained within the scope of the stop." The court concluded that the State failed to offer sufficient justification for the canine sniff: "The police did not detect the odor of marijuana in the car or note any other evidence suggesting the presence of illegal drugs." Lacking "specific and articulable facts" supporting the canine sniff, the court ruled, "the police impermissibly broadened the scope of the traffic stop in this case into a drug investigation." supporting the canine sniff, I would affirm the Illinois Supreme Court's judgment and hold that the drug sniff violated the Fourth Amendment.

In Terry v. Ohio, the Court upheld the stop and subsequent frisk of an individual based on an officer's observation of suspicious behavior and his reasonable belief that the suspect was armed. In a *Terry*-type investigatory stop, "the officer's action [must be] justified at its inception, and ... reasonably related in scope to the circumstances which justified the interference in the first place." In applying *Terry*, the Court has several times indicated that the limitation on "scope" is not confined to the duration of the seizure; it also encompasses the manner in which the seizure is conducted. See, *e.g.*, Hiibel v. Sixth Judicial Dist. Court (2004) (an officer's request that an individual identify himself "has an immediate relation to the purpose, rationale, and practical demands of a *Terry* stop"); United States v. Hensley(1985) (examining, under *Terry*, both "the length and intrusiveness of the stop and detention"); Florida v. Royer (1983) (plurality opinion) ("[A]n investigative detention must be temporary and last no longer than is necessary to effectuate the purpose of the stop [and] ... the investigative methods employed should be the least intrusive means reasonably available to verify or dispel the officer's suspicion....").

"A routine traffic stop," the Court has observed, "is a relatively brief encounter and 'is more analogous to a so-called *Terry* stop ... than to a formal arrest.' ".... I would apply *Terry*'s reasonable-relation test, as the Illinois Supreme Court did, to determine whether the canine sniff impermissibly expanded the scope of the initially valid seizure of Caballes.

It is hardly dispositive that the dog sniff in this case may not have lengthened the duration of the stop. ("A seizure ... can become unlawful if it is prolonged beyond the time reasonably required to complete [the initial] mission."). *Terry*, it merits repetition, instructs that any investigation must be "reasonably related in *scope* to the circumstances which justified the interference in the first place." The unwarranted and nonconsensual expansion of the seizure here from a routine traffic stop to a drug investigation broadened the scope of the investigation in a manner that, in my judgment, runs afoul of the Fourth Amendment.[3]

3. The question whether a police officer inquiring about drugs without reasonable suspicion unconstitutionally broadens a traffic investigation is not before the Court. Cf. Florida v. Bostick (1991) (police questioning of a bus passenger, who might have just said "No," did not constitute a seizure).

The Court rejects the Illinois Supreme Court's judgment and, implicitly, the application of *Terry* to a traffic stop converted, by calling in a dog, to a drug search. The Court so rules, holding that a dog sniff does not render a seizure that is reasonable in time unreasonable in scope. Dog sniffs that detect only the possession of contraband may be employed without offense to the Fourth Amendment, the Court reasons, because they reveal no lawful activity and hence disturb no legitimate expectation of privacy.

In my view, the Court diminishes the Fourth Amendment's force by abandoning the second *Terry* inquiry (was the police action "reasonably related in scope to the circumstances [justifiying] the [initial] interference"). A drug-detection dog is an intimidating animal.... Injecting such an animal into a routine traffic stop changes the character of the encounter between the police and the motorist. The stop becomes broader, more adversarial, and (in at least some cases) longer. Caballes—who, as far as Troopers Gillette and Graham knew, was guilty solely of driving six miles per hour over the speed limit—was exposed to the embarrassment and intimidation of being investigated, on a public thoroughfare, for drugs. Even if the drug sniff is not characterized as a Fourth Amendment "search," the sniff surely broadened the scope of the traffic-violation-related seizure.

The Court has never removed police action from Fourth Amendment control on the ground that the action is well calculated to apprehend the guilty.... Under today's decision, every traffic stop could become an occasion to call in the dogs, to the distress and embarrassment of the law-abiding population.

The Illinois Supreme Court, it seems to me, correctly apprehended the danger in allowing the police to search for contraband despite the absence of cause to suspect its presence. Today's decision, in contrast, clears the way for suspicionless, dog-accompanied drug sweeps of parked cars along sidewalks and in parking lots. Nor would motorists have constitutional grounds for complaint should police with dogs, stationed at long traffic lights, circle cars waiting for the red signal to turn green.

Today's decision also undermines this Court's situation-sensitive balancing of Fourth Amendment interests in other contexts. For example, in Bond v. United (2000), the Court held that a bus passenger had an expectation of privacy in a bag placed in an overhead bin and that a police officer's physical manipulation of the bag constituted an illegal search. If canine drug sniffs are entirely exempt from Fourth Amendment inspection, a sniff could substitute for an officer's request to a bus passenger for permission to search his bag, with this significant difference: The passenger would not have the option to say "No."

The dog sniff in this case, it bears emphasis, was for drug detection only. A dog sniff for explosives, involving security interests not presented here, would be an entirely different matter. Detector dogs are ordinarily trained not as all-purpose sniffers, but for discrete purposes. For example, they may be trained for narcotics detection or for explosives detection or for agricultural products detection.... There is no indication in this case that the dog accompanying Trooper Graham was trained for anything other than drug detection....

This Court has distinguished between the general interest in crime control and more immediate threats to public safety. In Michigan Dep't of State Police v. Sitz (1990), this Court upheld the use of a sobriety traffic checkpoint. Balancing the State's interest in preventing drunk driving, the extent to which that could be accomplished through the checkpoint program, and the degree of intrusion the stops involved, the Court determined that the State's checkpoint program was consistent with the Fourth Amendment. Ten years after *Sitz*, in *Indianapolis v. Edmond* (2000), this Court held that a drug interdiction checkpoint violated the Fourth Amendment. Despite the illegal narcotics traffic that the Nation is struggling to stem, the Court explained, a "general interest in crime control" did not justify the stops. The Court distinguished the sobriety checkpoints in *Sitz* on the ground that those checkpoints were designed to eliminate an "immediate, vehicle-bound threat to life and limb."

The use of bomb-detection dogs to check vehicles for explosives without doubt has a closer kinship to the sobriety checkpoints in *Sitz* than to the drug checkpoints in *Edmond*. As the Court observed in *Edmond*: "[T]he Fourth Amendment would almost certainly permit an appropriately tailored roadblock set up to thwart an imminent terrorist attack...." Even if the Court were to change course and characterize a dog sniff as an independent Fourth Amendment search, the immediate, present danger of explosives would likely justify a bomb sniff under the special needs doctrine.

* * *

For the reasons stated, I would hold that the police violated Caballes' Fourth Amendment rights when, without cause to suspect wrongdoing, they conducted a dog sniff of his vehicle. I would therefore affirm the judgment of the Illinois Supreme Court.

NOTES

1. *State Court Responses to* Caballes.

Not every court agrees with the majority's reasoning in Caballes. Several state courts have relied on state constitutional grounds to reach an opposite result. See, e.g. State v. Carter, 697 N.W.2d 199 (Minn. 2005). ("Although we conclude that the dog sniff was not a 'search' within the meaning of the Fourth Amendment to the United States Constitution, we hold that the dog sniff was a 'search' within the meaning of Article I, Section 10 of the Minnesota Constitution. Because the governmental interest in the use of drug-detection dogs to aid law enforcement is significant, we hold that a dog sniff is an unreasonable search unless police have at least reasonable, articulable suspicion of criminal activity before conducting it. And because the police did not have such suspicion here, and there was no probable cause to issue the warrant without the results of the dog sniff, we reverse the appellant's conviction and grant a new trial.")

2. Terry-*stop or Arrest?*

Terry referred to a "protean" variety of street encounters between police officers and citizens, and it suggested a balancing test to determine the reasonableness of the police conduct in each instance. Frequently the police will wish to go beyond the limited detention for questioning upon reasonable suspicion approved in *Terry*. For example, authorities may wish to:

> Detain a suspect while the police determine whether there are reports of recent burglary;
>
> Detain a suspect while the police determine whether a warrant is outstanding for his arrest;
>
> Return a suspect to the scene of a crime for a prompt show-up for identification purposes;
>
> Detain a suspect, perhaps at a police station, for more than the brief interrogation contemplated under stop and frisk procedures;
>
> Secure a suspect's fingerprints or voiceprints, fingernail scrapings, a sample of his blood, his hair, or his handwriting;
>
> Require a suspect to stand in a lineup;
>
> Stop vehicles passing the scene of a hit-and-run accident which occurred on some prior day.

Dunaway v. New York, 442 U.S. 200, 99 S.Ct. 2248 (1979), held that absent a suspect's consent, the police may not take a suspect to the police station for interrogation if they lack probable cause for an arrest. Broad language in *Dunaway*, however, suggests that there are only three categories of police-citizen encounters: (1) encounters which are not seizures within the meaning of the Fourth Amendment and which require no justification; (2) *Terry* stops which require reasonable suspicion; and (3) seizures which are arrests or their equivalent and thus demand full probable cause. The majority places great emphasis on the need for certainty and suggests that a sliding-scale or balancing test will not suffice to prevent the erosion of Fourth Amendment freedoms. Justice Brennan wrote for the majority:

> "In effect, respondents urge us to adopt a multifactor balancing test of 'reasonable police conduct under the circumstances' to cover all seizures that do not amount to technical arrests. But the protections intended by the Framers could all too easily disappear in the consideration and balancing of the multifarious circumstances presented by different cases, especially when that balancing may be done in the first instance by police officers engaged in the 'often competitive enterprise of ferreting out crime.' Johnson v. United States (1948). A single, familiar standard is essential to guide police officers, who have only limited time and expertise to reflect on and balance the social and individual interests involved in the specific circumstances they confront. Indeed, our recognition of these dangers, and our consequent reluctance to depart from the proven protections afforded by the general rule, is reflected in the narrow limitations emphasized in the cases employing the balancing test. For all but those narrowly defined intrusions, the requisite 'balancing' has been performed in centuries of precedent and is embodied in the principle that seizures are 'reasonable' only if supported by probable cause."

Just three weeks later, for the unanimous court in Brown v. Texas, however, the Chief Justice wrote this dictum: "The reasonableness of seizures that are less intrusive than a traditional arrest ... depends on 'a balance between the public interest and the individual's right to personal security free from arbitrary interference by law officers.' Pennsylvania v. Mimms (1977); United States v. Brignoni–Ponce (1975). Consideration of the constitutionality of such seizures involves a weighing of the gravity of the public concerns served by the seizure, the degree to which the seizure advances the public interest, and the severity of the interference with individual liberty."

In United States v. Sharpe, 470 U.S. 675, 105 S.Ct. 1568 (1985), the Court held that a detention longer than twenty minutes at the place of the stop is consistent with *Terry* if authorities in that period pursue appropriate means to confirm or dispel the suspicion. Hayes v. Florida, 470 U.S. 811, 105 S.Ct. 1643 (1985), however, held that the warrant less transporting of a suspect to the police station even for the sole purpose of finger printing him requires full probable cause.

In the broadest interpretation of *Terry*, the Seventh Circuit adopted a "sliding scale" approach to aggravated street stops in United States v. Chaidez, 919 F.2d 1193 (7th Cir.1990). The more intrusive the detention beyond a mere *Terry* stop, the greater must be the justification, so that something greater than "reasonable suspicion" is required, although the quantum need not reach "probable cause" until the detention is characterized as an arrest. The court said that the opposite approach is no boon to suspects because courts often stretch the limits of a *Terry* stop where the quantum of justification is no more than reasonable suspicion. The court also noted that some intrusions are so great that something more than probable cause is required, citing the bullet-removal case of Winston v. Lee (Casebook p.320). Using the sliding scale approach, the Seventh Circuit in United States v. Vega, 72 F.3d 507 (7th Cir.1995), upheld a *Terry* stop that lasted a little over one hour, and involved officers' drawing weapons, holding that the length and force involved did not convert it into an arrest: "We have over the years 'witnessed a multifaceted expansion of *Terry* ... For better or worse, the trend has led to the permitting of the use of handcuffs, the placing of weapons and other measures of force more traditionally associated with arrest than with investigatory detention.' " quoting United States v. Tilmon, 19 F.3d 1221, 1224–25 (7th Cir.1994) (allowing a *Terry* stop where defendant was made to lie face down on the shoulder of the road in handcuffs, put in a squad car, and then searched.)

Similarly, in United States v. Clark, 24 F.3d 299 (D.C.Cir.1994), the court upheld a stop of defendant's car, on the basis of information that he was the "stash holder" in a drug-sale operation. The officer forced the defendant out of the car at gunpoint and made him kneel while the officer searched the car. The court observed:

> Courts today will find a permissible use of force by the police under circumstances that might have raised judicial eyebrows at the time the *Terry* decision was issued. While it was once considered necessary, in order to justify a *Terry* frisk, for a law enforcement officer to be "justified in believing that the individual whose suspicious behavior he is investigating ... is armed and presently dangerous to the officer," *Terry*, 392 U.S. at 24 (emphasis added), it now suffices, in appropriate circumstances, for the officer to be justified in believing that the individual might be armed and dangerous.... This development is a product of the times. Twenty-five years ago ... it might have been unreasonable to assume that a suspected drug dealer in a car would be armed; today, it could well be foolhardy for an officer to assume otherwise.

Many commentators have viewed the aggravation of street stops with concern, especially in light of the fact that minorities in poorer neighborhoods are often the targets of *Terry*'s "reasonable suspicion." See Tracey Maclin, Black and Blue Encounters—Some Preliminary Thoughts About Fourth Amendment Seizures: Should Race Matter?, 26 Val.U.L.Rev. 243 (1991); David A. Harris, Factors for Reasonable Suspicion: When Black and Poor Means Stopped and Frisked, 69 Ind.L.J. 659 (1994); Elizabeth A. Gaynes, The Urban Criminal Justice System: Where Young + Black + Male = Probable Cause, 20 Ford.Urb.L.J. 621 (1993).

See also, Washington v. Lambert, 98 F.3d 1181 (9th Cir.1996): "In this case we apply the Fourth Amendment's promise of security in one's being to what is, unfortunately, an all too familiar set of circumstances—an intrusive law enforcement stop and seizure of innocent persons on the basis of suspicions rooted principally in the race of 'the suspects.' On June 25, 1991, several Santa Monica police officers in police cruisers, including appellant, Skystone Lambert, followed George Washington and Darryl Hicks, two African–American men, as they drove into the parking garage of their hotel [on ground that they resembled in height two black robbery suspects wanted for robberies in another part of the city committed six days earlier]. The police shone searchlights on their car, ordered them out at gunpoint, handcuffed their hands behind their backs and placed them in separate police cars for a period of from five to 25 minutes. Only after the officers frisked the two men, searched their car and checked their identification did they release 'the suspects.' ... In balancing the interests in freedom from arbitrary government intrusion and the legitimate needs of law enforcement officers, we cannot help but be aware that the burden of aggressive and intrusive police action falls disproportionately on African–American, and sometimes, Latino, males. Not withstanding the views of some legal theoreticians, as a practical matter neither society nor our enforcement of the laws is yet colorblind. Cases, newspaper reports, books, and scholarly writings all make clear that the experience of being stopped by the police is a much more common one for black men than it is for white men.... In determining whether the use of intrusive techniques turns a stop into an arrest, we examine the reasonableness of the police conduct in light of a number of factors. Despite the absence of a bright-line rule, our cases make clear that we have only allowed the use of especially intrusive means of effecting a stop in special circumstances, such as (1) where the suspect is uncooperative or takes action at the scene that raises a reasonable possibility of danger or flight; (2) where the police have information that the suspect is currently armed; (3) where the stop closely follows a violent crime; and (4) where the police have information that a crime that may involve violence is about to occur."

3. ***Traffic Stops.*** As noted above, police officers may stop a car whenever they have probable cause or (under *Terry*) reasonable suspicion to believe the car or driver is in violation of traffic regulations. Recently, courts have become concerned that police officers were using traffic stops as pretexts for searches that would not be supported by either probable cause or reasonable suspicion. For example, in United States v. Roberson, 6 F.3d 1088 (5th Cir.1993), cert. denied, 510 U.S. 1204, 114 S.Ct. 1322 (1994), a state trooper reportedly turned traffic stops into drug arrests on 250 prior occasions by tailing "suspicious" vehicles until they committed a footfault of some technical traffic regulation—in *Roberson*, he pulled over a van for failing to signal a lane-change on a deserted highway. In Ohio v. Robinette, 519 U.S. 33, 40, 117 S.Ct. 417, 422 (1996) (Ginsburg, J., concurring), a sheriff's deputy on drug interdiction patrol requested consent to search vehicles in 786 traffic stops in 1992. Given that all of us violate some traffic rule at some time, it is fairly easy to stop a suspicious vehicle for an unrelated traffic violation, or for "reasonable suspicion" of drunken or sleepy driving. In light of this concern, some circuits began holding that an officer could not stop a vehicle for a traffic violation unless a reasonable officer "would"(not just "could") have stopped it. The Supreme Court, in a unanimous decision, disagreed, holding that officers may stop a car for a traffic violation regardless of whether or not the infraction is a pretext for a search. Whren v. United States, 517 U.S. 806, 116 S.Ct. 1769 (1996). In subsequent cases, the Court overturned Ohio's prophylactic rule (insofar as it was based on the federal, rather than the state, Constitution) that an officer must tell a driver she is free to go before asking for consent to search her car, Ohio v. Robinette, 519 U.S. 33, 117 S.Ct. 417 (1996) and held that a passenger may be routinely ordered out of the car

at such a traffic stop, in order to protect officers from danger. Maryland v. Wilson, 519 U.S. 408, 117 S.Ct. 882 (1997). This time, both decisions provoked a dissent from Justice Stevens, and in Wilson he was joined in dissent by Justice Kennedy. Justice Stevens argued that Wilson went too far in allowing police officers to order passengers out of the car in cases in which there "is not even a scintilla of evidence of any potential risk to the police officer." Justice Kennedy argued that: "The practical effect of our holding in *Whren*, of course, is to allow the police to stop vehicles in almost countless circumstances. When *Whren* is coupled with today's holding, the Court puts tens of millions of passengers at risk of arbitrary control by the police. If the command to exit were to become commonplace, the Constitution would be diminished in a most public way. As the standards suggested in dissent are adequate to protect the safety of the police, we ought not to suffer so great a loss. Since a myriad of circumstances will give a cautious officer reasonable grounds for commanding passengers to leave the vehicle, it might be thought the rule the Court adopts today will be little different in its operation than the rule offered in dissent. It does no disservice to police officers, however, to insist upon exercise of reasoned judgment. Adherence to neutral principles is the very premise of the rule of law the police themselves defend with such courage and dedication."

Like the *Terry* stop, there is substantial evidence that traffic stops fall disproportionately on minorities. See, e.g., Jeff Brazil and Steve Berry, Color of Driver is Key to Stops in I–95 Videos, Orl.Sent., Aug. 23 1992 at A11 (videotapes show that 70% of stops made by drug interdiction unit on portion of I–95 in Florida are of African–Americans or Hispanics, although they made up only 5% of the drivers on that stretch of the interstate. Only about 5% of these stops lead to arrests). As one commentator quipped: "there's a moving violation that many African–Americans know as D.W.B.: Driving While Black." Henry Louis Gates, Jr., Thirteen Ways of Looking at a Black Man, The New Yorker 56, 59 (Oct. 23, 1995). Christopher Darden, O.J. Simpson prosecutor, recently wrote that he is stopped five times a year "by some cop who is suspicious of a black man driving a Mercedes." Christopher Darden, In Contempt 110 (1996).

The Tenth Circuit in United States v. Lee, 73 F.3d 1034 (10th Cir.1996), recently held that a traffic stop/*Terry*-stop had gone too far. The officer pulled the defendant driver over after he had momentarily "straddled" the center line. The officer made sure the driver was not sleepy or drunk, confirmed his ownership of the car, but then asked to search the car. Though the initial stop was justified, the stop should have ended, the court held, when the officer cleared the suspicion that led to and justified the stop. In a similar case, the Colorado Supreme Court held that once the officer discovers that his initial observation which led to the traffic stop is erroneous, the officer may not even ask for a driver's license, car registration, or proof of insurance. People v. Redinger, 906 P.2d 81 (Colo.1995).

4. ***Seizure of Identifying Characteristics.*** Sometimes law enforcement officials will want to do something more than interrogate a suspect or hold a suspect pending further investigation. They will wish to take from his person evidence of physical characteristics which might link him to a crime: a hair sample, a blood sample, fingerprints or the like. Or they may wish to place him in a lineup. Here we assume that the search-incident method is unavailable because there is no probable cause to arrest. We also assume that there is no probable cause to issue a search warrant. Finally, we assume that the situation is not an emergency in which the evanescent nature of the evidence might allow an emergency search on something less than probable cause to believe that a search will prove fruitful. See Cupp v. Murphy, 412 U.S. 291, 93 S.Ct. 2000 (1973).

A. ***Warrants Issued Upon Less Than Probable Cause.*** Davis v. Mississippi, 394 U.S. 721, 89 S.Ct. 1394 (1969), held that the warrantless detention of a citizen without probable cause for the purpose of securing fingerprints is a violation of the Fourth Amendment. Dictum in Davis suggested that such a limited-purpose detention could be justified if prior judicial approval was secured based upon a showing of reasonableness. That showing might be sufficient even if it fell somewhat short of probable cause.

Based upon the dictum in Davis, a number of jurisdictions have enacted statutes which permit courts to issue warrants or orders for lineups or the seizure of evidence of identifying physical characteristics. Typically such statutes permit judicial authorization for such procedures where there is (1) probable cause to believe that a crime has been committed; (2) some degree of probability, less than probable cause, that the intrusion against the named person will yield evidence of the crime; and (3) reasonable limitations upon the methods and scope of the intrusion (as to time, place, etc.). See Colorado Rules of Crim. Proc. 41.1; Arizona Rev.Stat.13–3931.

Two caveats are required. Most states have no warrant or court order procedure similar to that in Arizona and Colorado. The typical warrant statute in most jurisdictions requires full probable cause and cannot be adapted, unless amended, to fit the Davis dictum. Second, Dunaway v. New York, must be considered. The Dunaway court placed great emphasis upon the lack of probable cause in Davis, not the lack of a warrant. In indicating that a detention which goes beyond a *Terry* stop requires probable cause for arrest, the Court ignored the Davis dictum that had suggested that some detentions on less than probable cause (other than *Terry* stops) would be proper if done under prior judicial approval.

B. ***The Grand Jury Alternative.*** An alternative method of securing at least some evidence of identifying physical characteristics is utilization of the grand jury. A grand jury can command the giving of a handwriting exemplar or a voice exemplar, apparently without any showing of the likelihood that the ordered intrusion will prove fruitful. See United States v. Dionisio, 410 U.S. 1, 93 S.Ct. 764 (1973); United States v. Mara, 410 U.S. 19, 93 S.Ct. 774 (1973). Whether in the case of more intensive intrusions, such as the taking of blood samples, the grand jury procedure could be utilized without a showing of reasonable grounds or probable cause has not been decided by the United States Supreme Court. Two decisions have upheld grand-jury ordered line up appearances. In re Toon, 364 A.2d 1177 (D.C.App.1976); In re Melvin, 546 F.2d 1 (1st Cir.1976). At least one court has upheld a grand jury directive that a suspect give hair samples. In re Grand Jury Proceedings (Mills), 686 F.2d 135 (3d Cir.1982), reversing 524 F.Supp. 87 (E.D.Pa. 1981).

C. ***Warrantless In-the-Field Procedures.*** Dictum in Hayes v. Florida, suggested that, where technically possible, officers in the field could seize evidence of identifying physical characteristics at the place of a stop without a warrant and without full probable cause. Concurring justices strongly objected to this dictum.

N. ADMINISTRATIVE AND "SPECIAL NEEDS" SEARCHES

Fourth Amendment intrusions which are categorized as "administrative searches" are intended to serve some governmental regulatory purpose or "special need" other than the capture of criminals or the discovery and seizure of evidence for use in a criminal trial. Thus their reasonableness must be judged by a standard different from traditional probable cause to believe that evidence of a crime will be found in the place to be searched. As with the stop and frisk doctrine, the Court will balance societal needs with the privacy interests of the individual. Even though traditional probable cause is not required, as the Court first defined the doctrine of administrative searches it toyed with the notion that the reasonableness requirement of the Fourth Amendment sometimes demanded that administrative searches be carried out only after prior judicial approval.

The administrative search doctrine can be traced back to the seminal cases of Camara v. Municipal Court of San Francisco, 387 U.S. 523, 87 S.Ct. 1727 (1967) and See v. City of Seattle, 387 U.S. 541, 87 S.Ct. 1737 (1967). In *Camara*, the Court faced a challenge to the entry of a housing inspector into a dwelling for a routine annual inspection. The Court held that the Fourth amendment applied. Since the nature of the inspection was far different from a criminal investigation, however, the accommodation between the public need and individual rights was different. The Court reasoned that the entry to inspect must be "reasonable" in light of a variety of factors, including the condition sought to be ascertained, the location, the regulatory scheme, etc. A warrant could be issued, but the Court counseled that a warrant would normally be sought only after an individual denied entry to the governmental official. In See v. City of Seattle (1967) the Court contemplated a system of issuing administrative warrants on less than probable cause. This notion that judges can issue warrants or judicial orders approving searches in the absence of traditional probable cause calls for reflection upon the interrelationship of the "reasonableness clause" and the "warrant clause" of the fourth amendment.

NOTES

1. Following *Camara* and *See* the Court considered regulatory schemes which the government sought to justify under the "licensing" power referred to in the *See* opinion:

(a) In Colonnade Catering Corp. v. United States, 397 U.S. 72, 90 S.Ct. 774 (1970), the Court excluded evidence seized by federal agents who had, without a warrant, forcibly entered a locked storeroom on the premises of a federally licensed dealer in alcoholic beverages. The court decided that the Act of Congress which authorized inspection of such premises did not authorize forcible entry. The statute took the alternative position of making it a criminal offense to refuse admission to the inspectors.

Many state statutory schemes under which a driver as a condition of his or her license is required, under specified circumstances, to take a breathalyzer or other blood-alcohol test are of the Colonnade type. If the driver refuses to take the test, in many jurisdictions he or she cannot be commanded or forced to take the test; the penalty for a refusal, however, is a suspension or revocation of the license.

(b) In Marshall v. Barlow's, Inc., 436 U.S. 307, 98 S.Ct. 1816 (1978), it became apparent that the power of government to regulate various human enterprises does not give the government the right to condition a person's or corporation's participation in those activities upon a willingness to submit to whatever fourth amendment intrusions the government deems appropriate. At issue in that case was the right of federal agents to inspect the work area of places of employment governed by the 1970 Occupational Safety and Health Act. Writing for the majority, Justice White noted that use of implied-consent regulatory schemes had been approved only in the case of "closely regulated industry of the type involved in Colonnade and Biswell." Efforts to expand this approach to justify warrantless inspections or searches in every type of industry in interstate commerce were deemed constitutionally impermissible: "The clear import of our cases is that the closely regulated industry ... is the exception. The Secretary (of Labor) would make it the rule." The court then decided that under the balancing test of *Camara* the legitimate governmental purpose of promoting safety in the work place could be safeguarded by an administrative warrant procedure available for use in cases in which the employer refused to consent to an inspection. under this scheme, "probable cause in the criminal sense is not required. ...a warrant showing that a specific business has been chosen for an OSHA search on the basis of a general administrative plan for the enforcement of the Act derived from neutral sources such as, for example, dispersion of employees in various types of industries across a given area, and the desired frequency of searches in any of the lesser divisions of the area, would protect an employer's fourth amendment rights."

In his dissent in Barlow's, Justice Stevens asserted that the majority had provided no clear guidelines for determining which industries can be subjected to warrantless inspections of the Barlow's type. Is it the longevity of the regulatory program that matters, he asked, noting that the Barlow's regulatory scheme had been enacted in 1968 and asserting that the "recent vintage" of Congressional concern for safety in the workplace ought not be determinative of the validity of the warrantless inspection scheme.

In his dissent in *Camara* and *See*, Justice Clark spoke of destroying the integrity of the warrant clause by permitting the issuance of warrants without traditional probable cause to believe that criminal evidence is in the place to be searched. In his dissent in Marshall v. Barlow's, Inc., Justice Stevens made a similar argument. He said that the "Court's approach disregards the plain language of the Warrant Clause and is unfaithful to the balance struck by the Framers of the Fourth Amendment. ..." He made the point that historically the concern of the drafters was primarily the use of general warrants absent probable cause and not the warrantless search. (Compare T. Taylor, Two Studies in Constitutional Interpretation, 21–43, with Amsterdam, Perspectives on the Fourth Amendment, 58 Minn.L.Rev. 349, 398–400.) Interestingly, Justice Stewart, who had joined in Justice Clark's attack on "new-fangled" warrants in *Camara* and *See*, sided with the majority in Marshall v. Barlow's, Inc.

Does not the Clark–Stevens position put a straitjacket upon the Court in deciding what can be required as a condition of reasonableness? If it can deem certain intrusions reasonable without either traditional probable cause or a warrant, why can it not, as a condition of reasonableness, excuse traditional probable cause but require prior judicial approval? If a traditional warrant cannot issue for want of probable cause, would not Clark and Stevens force courts into a position of approving more searches without any prior judicial approval? On the other hand, does not the warrant clause become superfluous under the majority opinions in *See* and *Marshall*?

(c) In Donovan v. Dewey, 452 U.S. 594, 101 S.Ct. 2534 (1981), the Supreme Court upheld warrantless inspections Under Section 103(a) of the Federal Mine Safety and Health Act of 1977. The Court Distinguished Marshall v. Barlow's, Inc. the Court emphasized the substantial federal interest in health and safety in the mining industry, which "is among the most hazardous in the country." It granted deference to a congressional determination that "a warrant requirement could significantly frustrate enforcement of the Act." The court upheld the warrantless inspection scheme as reasonable. It noted that the act required inspection of all mines at least twice annually and provided for additional inspections where violations of the act previously had been found. "Second, the standards with which a mine operator is required to comply are all specifically set forth . . ." finally, the Act prohibited forcible entries and required the Secretary of Labor to obtain an injunction against future refusal before carrying out inspections after a refusal.

The Court rejected the argument that the Act violated the Fourth Amendment as applied to stone quarries, which did not come under federal regulation until 1966, rejecting as "absurd" the use of the length of regulation as the "only criteria" (sic). It reasoned that under that test warrantless inspection schemes could never be applied to the nuclear power industry or to other new industries.

Only Justice Stewart dissented. He noted that he had dissented from *Camara*, but he argued that he was bound by that decision. Stewart thus impliedly provided a reason for his concurrence in Marshall v. Barlow's, Inc. He then argued that Barlow's controlled and required invalidation of the inspection scheme of the Mine Safety and Health Act as applied to stone quarries. He said that implied-consent warrantless business inspection schemes, according to Barlow's could be applied only to "businesses that are both pervasively regulated and have a long history of regulation." He noted that federal regulation of stone quarries originated long after many quarry operators entered the business and was of fairly recent origin, although quarries existed since the beginning of the Republic. Stewart concluded that the warrantless inspection of stone quarries violated the Fourth Amendment. He argued that Congress should not be able to do industry-by-industry what Barlow's prevented it from doing all at once.

(d) In New York v. Burger, 482 U.S. 691, 107 S.Ct. 2636 (1987), an unlicensed junk dealer who bought and sold used automobile parts was convicted on the basis of evidence seized by police in a warrantless inspection of his commercial premises. The search had been made pursuant to what the state called an administrative scheme regulating dealers in automobile parts. The New York statute required such dealers to be licensed. By engaging in the business, they, in effect, were deemed to have consented to other regulatory requirements. These included the keeping of a "police book" listing the automobile parts that they acquired, including the source of such acquisitions. The police (and not just some separate administrative officials) were allowed to make warrantless inspections of the records and of the commercial premises.

The defendant argued that this was no administrative search at all. Because he was unlicensed, there was no administrative action that could be taken against him. He alleged that the whole purpose of the scheme was to permit the police to search commercial premises without probable cause or a warrant in quest of evidence of stolen property. Probably more than in any other case, the defendant's arguments drew into question why the label "administrative search" can be used to justify a warrantless search for evidence of criminal activity.

The majority responded by saying that even though commercial premises are subject to Fourth Amendment protections, nevertheless there is a lesser expectation of privacy as to such types of property. Hence a search will be deemed reasonable as to such premises based upon justifications that might not suffice to justify a warrantless search of a home. The Court acknowledged that both the administrative law and the penal law may serve the same ultimate purpose, as, for example, the protection of property against theft. Neither that fact nor the possibility that a search might produce criminal evidence, however, invalidates the notion of an administrative search. The Court noted that there was a long history of state regulation of junkyards, even though, because of the relative infancy of the industry, there was not such a long history of the regulation of businesses that buy automobiles or parts and then sell the disassembled parts.

The Court then upheld as reasonable the particular regulatory scheme. It recognized the legitimate state interest in eliminating businesses that serve as purchasers of stolen automobiles. It declared that the administrative scheme was suited to serve the state interest. It added that the statute provided a constitutionally adequate substitute for a warrant. It notified operators of such businesses of the possibility of such inspection and of the authority of government to conduct such inspection. The time, place, and scope of the inspection were properly limited under the terms of the statute, which allowed such inspection only during regular business hours, and which permitted examinations only of the records and of automobiles and automobile parts.

The dissent argued that the business in question was not part of a closely regulated industry. It declared that the statute gave too much discretion to the police, providing no criteria determining which dealers should be inspected and setting no limit on the number of such inspections. Beyond this, the dissent complained that the statute authorized a search which could turn up no administrative violations and lead to no administrative action. Its purpose, plain and simple, was to permit warrantless searches in pursuit of evidence of violations of the penal law, according to the dissent. In a footnote, Justice Brennan for the dissenters observed:

> This case thus does not present the more difficult question whether a state could take any criminal conduct, make it an administrative violation, and then search without probable cause for violations of the newly created administrative rule. The increasing overlap of administrative and criminal violations creates an obvious temptation for the state to do so, and plainly toleration of this type of pretextual search would allow an end-run around the protections of the Fourth Amendment.

Skinner v. Railway Labor Executives' Association

Supreme Court of the United States, 1989.
489 U.S. 602, 109 S.Ct. 1402.

■ JUSTICE KENNEDY delivered the opinion of the Court.

... Subpart C [of the Federal Railway Administration alcohol and drug regulation] provides that railroads "shall take all practicable steps to assure that all covered employees of the railroad directly involved ... provide blood and urine samples for toxicological testing by FRA," upon the occurrence of certain specified events. Toxicological testing is required following a "major train accident," which is defined as any train accident that involves (i) a fatality, (ii) the release of hazardous material accompanied by an evacuation or a reportable injury, or (iii) damage to railroad property of $500,000. The railroad has the further duty of collecting blood and urine samples for testing after an "impact accident," which is defined as a collision that results in a reportable injury, or in damage to railroad property of $50,000 or more. Finally, the railroad is also obligated to test after "[a]ny train incident that involves a fatality to any on-duty railroad employee."

* * *

Subpart D of the regulations, which is entitled "Authorization to Test for Cause," is permissive. It authorizes railroads to require covered employees to submit to breath or urine tests in certain circumstances not addressed by Subpart C. Breath or urine tests, or both, may be ordered (1) after are portable accident or incident, where a supervisor has a "reasonable suspicion" that an employee's acts or omissions contributed to the occurrence or severity of the accident or incident; or (2) in the event of certain specific rule violations, including non-compliance with a signal and excessive speeding. A railroad also may require breath tests where a supervisor has a "reasonable suspicion" that an employee is under the influence of alcohol, based upon specific, personal observations concerning the appearance, behavior, speech, or body odors of the employee. Where impairment is suspected, a railroad, in addition, may require urine tests, but only if two supervisors make the appropriate determination, § 219.301(c)(2)(i), and, where the supervisors suspect impairment due to a substance other than alcohol, at least one of those supervisors must have received specialized training in detecting the signs of drug intoxication.

Subpart D further provides that whenever the results of either breath or urine tests are intended for use in a disciplinary proceeding, the employee must be given the opportunity to provide a blood sample for analysis at an independent medical facility.

* * *

Respondents, the Railway Labor Executives' Association and various of its member labor organizations, brought the instant suit in the United States District Court for the Northern District of California, seeking to enjoin the FRA's regulations on various statutory and constitutional grounds. In a ruling from the bench, the District Court granted summary judgment in petitioners' favor....

A divided panel of the Court of Appeals for the Ninth Circuit reversed.

* * *

We are unwilling to conclude, in the context of this facial challenge, that breath and urine tests required by private railroads in reliance on Subpart D will not implicate the Fourth Amendment.... Here, specific features of the regulations combine to convince us that the Government did more than adopt a passive position toward the underlying private conduct.

* * *

We have long recognized that a "compelled intrusio[n] into the body for blood to be analyzed for alcohol content" must be deemed a Fourth Amendment search.... Subjecting a person to a breathalyzer test, which generally requires the production of alveolar or "deep lung" breath for chemical analysis implicates similar concerns about bodily integrity and, like the blood-alcohol test we considered in Schmerber [v. California], should also be deemed a search....

[C]hemical analysis or urine, like that of blood, can reveal a host of private medical facts about an employee, including whether she is epileptic, pregnant, or diabetic. Nor can it be disputed that the process of collecting the sample to be tested, which may in some cases involve visual or aural monitoring of the act of urination, itself implicates privacy interests.[1]

* * *

Except in certain well-defined circumstances, a search or seizure in such a case is not reasonable unless it is accomplished pursuant to a judicial warrant issued upon probable cause. We have recognized exceptions to this rule, however, "when 'special needs, beyond the normal need for law enforcement, make the warrant and probable-cause requirement impracticable.'" Griffin v. Wisconsin (1987), quoting New Jersey v. T.L.O.(Blackmun, J., concurring in judgment). When faced with such special needs, we have not hesitated to balance the governmental and privacy interests to assess the practicality of the warrant and probable cause requirements in the particular context. See, e.g., Griffin v. Wisconsin, (search of probationer's home); New York v. Burger (1987) (search of premises of certain highly regulated businesses); O'Connor v. Ortega (work-related searches of employees' desks and offices); New Jersey v. T.L.O.(search of student's property by school officials); Bell v. Wolfish (1979) (body cavity searches of prison inmates).

The Government's interest in regulating the conduct of railroad employees to ensure safety, like its supervision of probationers or regulated industries, or its operation of a government office, school, or prison, "likewise presents 'special needs' beyond normal law enforcement that may justify departures from the usual warrant and probable-cause requirements." Griffin v. Wisconsin....

The FRA has prescribed toxicological tests, not to assist in the prosecution of employees but rather "to prevent accidents and casualties in railroad operations that result from impairment of employees by alcohol or drugs." 49 CFR § 219.1(a) (1987).[2] This governmental interest in ensuring

1. Taking a blood or urine sample might also be characterized as a Fourth Amendment seizure, since it may be viewed as a meaningful interference with the employee's possessory interest in his bodily fluids. Cf. United States v. Jacobsen, 466 U.S. 109, 113, 104 S.Ct. 1652, 1656, 80 L.Ed.2d 85 (1984). It is not necessary to our analysis in this case, however, to characterize the taking of blood or urine samples as a seizure of those bodily fluids, for the privacy expectations protected by this characterization are adequately taken into account by our conclusion that such intrusions are searches.

2. The regulations provide that "[e]ach sample provided under [Subpart C] is retained for not less than six months following the date of the accident or incident and may be made available to ... a party in litigation upon service of appropriate compulsory process on the custodian...." 49 CFR § 219.211(d) (1987). The Agency explained, when it promulgated this provision, that it intends to retain such samples primarily "for its own purposes (e.g., to permit reanalysis of a sample if another laboratory reported detection of a substance not tested for in the original procedure)." 50 Fed.Reg. 31545 (1985). While this provision might be read broadly to authorize the release of biological samples to law enforcement authorities, the record does not disclose that it was intended to be, or actually has been, so used. Indeed, while respondents aver generally that test results might be made available to law enforcement authorities, Brief for Respondents 24, they do not seriously contend that this provision, or any other part of the administrative scheme, was designed as "a 'pretext'

the safety of the traveling public and of the employees themselves plainly justifies prohibiting covered employees from using alcohol or drugs on duty, or while subject to being called for duty....

... A warrant assures the citizen that the intrusion is authorized by law, and that it is narrowly limited in its objectives and scope. A warrant also provides the detached scrutiny of a neutral magistrate, and thus ensures an objective determination whether an intrusion is justified in any given case. In the present context, however, a warrant would do little to further these aims. Both the circumstances justifying toxicological testing and the permissible limits of such intrusions are defined narrowly and specifically in the regulations that authorize them, and doubtless are well known to covered employees. Indeed, in light of the standardized nature of the tests and the minimal discretion vested in those charged with administering the program, there are virtually no facts for a neutral magistrate to evaluate.

We have recognized, moreover, that the Government's interest in dispensing with the warrant requirement is at its strongest when, as here, "the burden of obtaining a warrant is likely to frustrate the governmental purpose behind the search." Camara v. Municipal Court. As the Agency recognized, alcohol and other drugs are eliminated from the bloodstream at a constant rate, and blood and breath samples taken to measure whether these substances were in the bloodstream when a triggering event occurred must be obtained as soon as possible. Although the metabolites of some drugs remain in the urine for longer periods of time and may enable the Agency to estimate whether the employee was impaired by those drugs at the time of a covered accident, incident, or rule violation, the delay necessary to procure a warrant nevertheless may result in the destruction of valuable evidence.

* * *

Our cases indicate that even a search that may be performed without a warrant must be based, as a general matter, on probable cause to believe that the person to be searched has violated the law.... We made it clear, however, that a showing of individualized suspicion is not a constitutional floor, below which a search must be presumed unreasonable. In limited circumstances, where the privacy interests implicated by the search are minimal, and where an important governmental interest furthered by the intrusion would be placed in jeopardy by a requirement of individualized suspicion, a search may be reasonable despite the absence of such suspicion. We believe this is true of the intrusions in question here.

* * *

to enable law enforcement authorities to gather evidence of penal law violations." New York v. Burger, 482 U.S. 691, 716–717, n. 27, 107 S.Ct. 2636, 2651, n. 27, 96 L.Ed.2d 601 (1987). Absent a persuasive showing that the FRA's testing program is pretextual, we assess the FRA's scheme in light of its obvious administrative purpose. We leave for another day the question whether routine use in criminal prosecutions of evidence obtained pursuant to the administrative scheme would give rise to an inference of pretext, or otherwise impugn the administrative nature of the Agency's program.

The breath tests authorized by Subpart D of the regulations are even less intrusive than the blood tests prescribed by Subpart C. Unlike blood tests, breath tests do not require piercing the skin and may be conducted safely outside a hospital environment and with a minimum of inconvenience or embarrassment. Further, breath tests reveal the level of alcohol in the employee's bloodstream and nothing more. Like the blood-testing procedures mandated by Subpart C, which can be used only to ascertain the presence of alcohol or controlled substances in the bloodstream, breath tests reveal no other facts in which the employee has a substantial privacy interest. In all the circumstances, we cannot conclude that the administration of a breath test implicates significant privacy concerns.

A more difficult question is presented by urine tests. Like breath tests, urine tests are not invasive of the body and, under the regulations, may not be used as an occasion for inquiring into private facts unrelated to alcohol or drug use. We recognize, however, that the procedures for collecting the necessary samples, which require employees to perform an excretory function traditionally shielded by great privacy, raise concerns not implicated by blood or breath tests. While we would not characterize these additional privacy concerns as minimal in most contexts, we note that the regulations endeavor to reduce the intrusiveness of the collection process. The regulations do not require that samples be furnished under the direct observation of a monitor, despite the desirability of such a procedure to ensure the integrity of the sample. The sample is also collected in a medical environment, by personnel unrelated to the railroad employer, and is thus not unlike similar procedures encountered often in the context of a regular physical examination.

More importantly, the expectations of privacy of covered employees are diminished by reason of their participation in an industry that is regulated pervasively to ensure safety, a goal dependent, in substantial part, on the health and fitness of covered employees.

* * *

By contrast, the government interest in testing without a showing of individualized suspicion is compelling. Employees subject to the tests discharge duties fraught with such risks of injury to others that even a momentary lapse of attention can have disastrous consequences. Much like persons who have routine access to dangerous nuclear power facilities ... employees who are subject to testing under the FRA regulations can cause great human loss before any signs of impairment become noticeable to supervisors or others. An impaired employee, the Agency found, will seldom display any outward "signs detectable by the lay person or, in many cases, even the physician." 50 Fed.Reg. 31526 (1985).... Indeed, while respondents posit that impaired employees might be detected without alcohol or drug testing, the premise of respondents' lawsuit is that even the occurrence of a major calamity will not give rise to a suspicion of impairment with respect to any particular employee.

* * *

The testing procedures contemplated by Subpart C also help railroads obtain invaluable information about the causes of major accidents and to take appropriate measures to safeguard the general public....

A requirement of particularized suspicion of drug or alcohol use would seriously impede an employer's ability to obtain this information, despite its obvious importance. Experience confirms the Agency's judgment that the scene of a serious rail accident is chaotic. Investigators who arrive at the scene shortly after a major accident has occurred may find it difficult to determine which members of a train crew contributed to its occurrence. Obtaining evidence that might give rise to the suspicion that a particular employee is impaired, a difficult endeavor in the best of circumstances, is most impracticable in the aftermath of a serious accident. While events following the rule violations that activate the testing authority of Subpart D may be less chaotic, objective indicia of impairment are absent in these instances as well. Indeed, any attempt to gather evidence relating to the possible impairment of particular employees likely would result in the loss or deterioration of the evidence furnished by the tests....

* * *

We conclude that the compelling government interests served by the FRA's regulations would be significantly hindered if railroads were required to point to specific facts giving rise to a reasonable suspicion of impairment before testing a given employee. In view of our conclusion that, on the present record, the toxicological testing contemplated by the regulations is not an undue infringement on the justifiable expectations of privacy of covered employees, the Government's compelling interests outweigh privacy concerns.... We hold that the alcohol and drug tests contemplated by Subparts C and D of the FRA's regulations are reasonable within the meaning of the Fourth Amendment. The judgment of the Court of Appeals is accordingly reversed.

■ Opinion of JUSTICE STEVENS, concurring in part and concurring in the judgment.

■ JUSTICE MARSHALL, with whom JUSTICE BRENNAN joins,dissenting.

... For the fourth time in as many years, a majority holds that a "special nee[d], beyond the normal need for law enforcement," makes the "requirement" of probable cause "impracticable." With the recognition of "[t]he Government's interest in regulating the conduct of railroad employees to ensure safety" as such a need, the Court has now permitted "special needs" to displace constitutional text in each of the four categories of searches enumerated in the Fourth Amendment: searches of "persons"; "houses," Griffin v. Wisconsin (1987); "papers," O'Connor v. Ortega (1987); and "effects," New Jersey v. T.L.O. (1985).

* * *

Tellingly, each time the Court has found that "special needs" counseled ignoring the literal requirements of the Fourth Amendment for such full-scale searches in favor of a formless and unguided "reasonableness" balancing inquiry, it has concluded that the search in question satisfied that test.

. . . Until today, it was conceivable that, when a Government search was aimed at a person and not simply the person's possessions, balancing analysis had no place. No longer: with nary a word of explanation or acknowledgment of the novelty of its approach, the majority extends the "special needs" framework to a regulation involving compulsory blood withdrawal and urinary excretion, and chemical testing of the bodily fluids collected through these procedures. And until today, it was conceivable that a prerequisite for surviving "special needs" analysis was the existence of individualized suspicion. No longer: in contrast to the searches in T.L.O., O'Connor, and Griffin, which were supported by individualized evidence suggesting the culpability of the persons whose property was searched, the regulatory regime upheld today requires the postaccident collection and testing of the blood and urine of all covered employees—even if every member of this group gives every indication of sobriety and attentiveness. . . .

I recognize that invalidating the full-scale searches involved in the FRA's testing regime for failure to comport with the Fourth Amendment's command of probable cause may hinder the Government's attempts to make rail transit as safe as humanly possible. But constitutional rights have their consequences, and one is that efforts to maximize the public welfare, no matter how well-intentioned, must always be pursued within constitutional boundaries. Were the police freed from the constraints of the Fourth Amendment for just one day to seek out evidence of criminal wrongdoing, the resulting convictions and incarcerations would probably prevent thousands of fatalities.

* * *

NOTES

1. ***Drug Testing of Government Employees.*** On the same day that it decided *Skinner*, the Supreme Court upheld a drug-testing program instituted by the United States Customs Service. The regulations applied to employees who sought a transfer or a promotion to a position which either (1) directly involved drug interdiction or drug law enforcement, or (2) required the employee to carry a firearm.

In National Treasury Employees Union v. Von Raab, 489 U.S. 656, 109 S.Ct. 1384 (1989), the Court approved warrantless urine-testing of such employees even in the absence of particularized suspicion. The employee was allowed to produce the urine in the privacy of a bathroom stall but subject to aural monitoring by an agent of an independent contractor drug-testing company of the same gender as the Customs employee. Customs could dismiss an employee who tested positive but could not turn over the results for criminal prosecution without the consent of the employee. The Court declared "that the Government has a compelling interest in ensuring that front-line interdiction personnel are physically fit, and have unimpeachable integrity and judgment." It indicated that those employees required to carry firearms or directly involved in the interdiction of illegal drugs "have a diminished expectation of privacy in respect to the intrusions occasioned by a urine test." The Court rejected the argument that the program would not likely be effective because drug-using employees might keep clean during the period when they were seeking a transfer or promotion and were subject to testing.

Four justices dissented. In his dissenting opinion, Justice Scalia argued that there was no showing that drug use by a Customs employee had ever led to even a single instance of misuse of a firearm or of bribery or non-enforcement of drug laws. He viewed the regulations as mere "symbolism" proclaiming that the Customs Service is "clean," and he declared that such symbolism cannot justify an otherwise unreasonable search.

2. *Drug testing of Students.*

In Vernonia School District 47J v. Acton, 515 U.S. 646, 115 S.Ct. 2386 (1995), the Court allowed random, suspicionless, drug testing of student athletes. The majority opinion, authored by Justice Scalia, emphasized the lesser expectation of privacy in the school setting, due to the guardian-like position of school officials, citing New Jersey v. T.L.O., 469 U.S. 325, 105 S.Ct. 733 (1985). The opinion also stated that the way the drug testing was done was minimally intrusive, especially compared with the "communal undress" inherent in athletic participation. Finally, the Court found the school's interest in redressing drug-related sports injuries and general drug-related discipline problems well-documented and serious, if not "compelling." Justice Ginsburg concurred, on the understanding that the Court might view such a drug-testing program differently if it were imposed on all students or if the penalty for failing the test were more serious than suspension from athletics. Justice O'Connor, joined by Justices Souter and Stevens, forcefully argued that suspicionless testing was suspiciously close to the "general warrants" that the Fourth Amendment eliminated and that the school had not shown that suspicionless testing was the only feasible alternative, since school officials constantly supervised students and could easily limit drug testing to those students who were discipline problems or were obviously under the influence.

With only Justice Rehnquist in dissent, the Court circumscribed its prior drug testing opinions by striking down a Georgia statute requiring candidates for certain state offices to take drug tests. Chandler v. Miller, 520 U.S. 305, 117 S.Ct. 1295 (1997). The Court reiterated that drug testing not prompted by individualized suspicion could only be used when necessary to meet a state's "special need" other than crime detection. The Court held that the Georgia requirement did not "fit within the closely guarded category of constitutionally permissible suspicionless searches" and was justified only by a "hypothetical" and "symbolic need," not a "special need." The opinion distinguished the Court's prior rulings: there was no evidence that Georgia had ever had a problem with state officials using drugs, unlike the athletes in Vernonia; there was no imminent public safety concern as in Skinner (need to find out causes of train accidents), VonRaab (danger potentially posed by gun-carrying customs officers) and Vernonia (danger of playing field accidents); there was more day-to-day scrutiny, less access to drugs, and less danger of blackmail or bribery than for the customs officials in VonRaab; and the state was not in the role of guardian, as it is for school children in Vernonia. The symbolic nature of the drug test was underscored by the fact that candidates could choose the day of their drug test—hence, a positive result could be easily avoided.

In Board of Education v. Earls, 536 U.S. 822, 122 S.Ct. 2559 (2002), a 5–4 decision, the United States Supreme Court approved a drug policy that required all middle and high school students to submit to urinalysis as a prerequisite to participating in any extracurricular activities. Rejecting a claim for a constitutional violation brought under 42 U.S.C. § 1983, the Court held that such drug testing could be required even in the absence of a showing of any articulable suspicion of drug use. Justices O'Connor, Souter, Ginsburg, and Stevens dissented.

3. *Drug testing of pregnant patients*. When medical personnel became concerned with the number of pregnant women who were apparently using cocaine, they would order drug screening tests. Patients with positive test results were referred to a substance abuse clinic. If they continued to test positive or they did not cooperate with the clinic protocol, their case was referred to the police and they were arrested. The Court distinguished the earlier cases dealing with drug testing of governmental employees since there, the "special need" that was put forth to excuse the need for a warrant was not connected with criminal prosecution. Here, the procedure to test for drugs resulted in seizing evidence for proof in a criminal case, Thus, the cases did not fall within the administrative or special needs exception to the warrant requirement. Ferguson v. City of Charleston, 532 U.S. 67, 121 S.Ct. 1281 (2001).

4. ***Welfare Home Visits***. In Wyman v. James, 400 U.S. 309, 91 S.Ct. 381 (1971), the Court approved a state law which required welfare recipients to admit caseworkers into their homes or else face termination of benefits. The Court based its holding on several factors: the caseworkers are reasonably attempting to determine if aid is properly given to dependent children, the refusal to permit entry is not made a criminal offense, written notice of visits must be made several days in advance, forcible entry or entry under false pretenses is prohibited, visits must occur during normal working hours, the essential information secured by home visits is not available from other sources and the visit is not conducted by a law-enforcement officer looking for criminal violations. Thus, although *Camara* indicated that the Fourth Amendment protects all persons, not just those suspected of criminal activity, the "benign" purpose of the governmental intrusion was deemed relevant in James to the determination of reasonableness under the Fourth Amendment.

What about warrantless "sweeps" of public housing to react to gun violence? Does it matter if residents have signed a consent form? See Pratt v. Chicago Housing Authority, 848 F.Supp. 792 (N.D.Ill.1994).

5. ***License and Registration Check Stops.*** Even in areas in which governmental regulation is lengthy and pervasive, the power to regulate and to license does not protect government from scrutiny of the reasonableness of its warrantless inspection schemes. In Delaware v. Prouse, 440 U.S. 648, 99 S.Ct. 1391 (1979), the Court framed the issue: "The question is whether it is an unreasonable seizure under the Fourth and Fourteenth Amendments to stop an automobile, for the purpose of checking the driving license of the operator and the registration of the car, where there is neither probable cause to believe nor reasonable suspicion that the car is being driven contrary to the laws governing the operation of motor vehicles or that either the car or any of its occupants is subject to seizure or detention in connection with the violation of any other applicable law." The Court held that such random stops violate the Fourth Amendment. The Court stated that an individual who drives a car—engaging in a "basic, pervasive, and often necessary mode of transportation"—cannot be deemed to have yielded all Fourth Amendment protections. The question is resolved, said the Court, by a balancing of the intensity of the intrusion against governmental necessity. Here the Court decided the marginal contribution which a random license inspection would make to safety did not justify the intrusion involved, particularly in light of the "grave danger of abuse of discretion." The Court added that its holding did not preclude the States "from developing methods for spot checks that involve less intrusion or that do not involve the unconstrained exercise of discretion. Questioning of all oncoming traffic at roadblock-type stops is one possible alternative."

Although random stops are unconstitutional, the Court has approved roadblock searches in some cases and struck others down.

In Michigan Department of State Police v. Sitz, 496 U.S. 444, 110 S.Ct. 2481 (1990), the United States Supreme Court upheld a highway sobriety checkpoint program. Under the program all motorists were stopped at certain fixed checkpoints, with an average delay of twenty-five seconds. If the officers detected signs of intoxication, the driver would be detained for sobriety tests. While deeming the stops to be seizures within the meaning of the Fourth Amendment, the Court upheld the stops as reasonable even in the absence of particularized suspicion. The Court concluded:

> [T]he balance of the State's interest in preventing drunken driving, the extent to which this system can reasonably be said to advance this interest, and the degree of intrusion upon individual motorists who are briefly stopped, weighs in favor of the state program.

Three justices dissented. They argued that the governmental interest in the checkpoint program was minimal because the arrests for drunk driving were not shown to be more numerous than could be achieved by deployment of similar law enforcement resources in conventional patrol programs where officers would stop drivers upon reasonable suspicion of violations of the traffic code. The dissenters noted that the checkpoints are not permanent but are fixed at different places on different days, so that drivers have no advance notice or opportunity to avoid the Fourth Amendment intrusion altogether. The dissenters also complained that the procedures allowed an officer too much discretion to determine which drivers he or she would detain for sobriety checks.

In a portion of the dissent in which he spoke solely for himself, Justice Stevens called the checkpoint program "publicity stunts" that serve only a "symbolic" value like the drug testing program condemned by Justice Scalia in his Treasury Employees dissent. Not joined by his fellow dissenters, Stevens added:

> [M]y objections to random seizures or temporary checkpoints do not apply to a host of other investigatory procedures that do not depend upon surprise and are unquestionably permissible. These procedures have been used to address other threats to human life no less pressing than the threat posed by drunken drivers. It is, for example, common practice to require every prospective airline passenger, or every visitor to a public building, to pass through a metal detector that will reveal the presence of a firearm or an explosive. Permanent, nondiscretionary checkpoints could be used to control serious dangers at other publicly operated facilities. Because concealed weapons obviously represent one such substantial threat to public safety, I would suppose that all subway passengers could be required to pass through metal detectors, so long as the detectors were permanent and every passenger was subjected to the same search. Likewise, I would suppose that a State could condition access to its toll roads upon not only paying the toll but also taking a uniformly administered breathalizer test. That requirement might well keep all drunken drivers off the highways that serve the fastest and most dangerous traffic. This procedure would not be subject to the constitutional objections that control this case: the checkpoints would be permanently fixed, the stopping procedure would apply to all users of the toll road in precisely the same way, and police officers would not be free to make arbitrary choices about which neighborhoods should be targeted or about which individuals should be more thoroughly searched.

Minnesota has held DWI roadblocks unconstitutional under its state constitution. Ascher v. Commissioner of Public Safety, 519 N.W.2d 183 (Minn.1994).

In Indianapolis v. Edmond, 531 U.S. 32, 121 S.Ct. 447 (2000) the Court invalidated a checkpoint system in which the police stopped a set number of vehicles at roadblocks on city roads. An officer would approach each stopped vehicle, advise the driver of the purpose for the stop, ask the driver of his or her license and registration, look for signs of impairment and make an open view examination of the vehicle. In addition, a drug detection dog would walk around the outside of each stopped car. Finding that the roadblock's key purpose is the same as a general interest in controlling crime, the checkpoint violated the Fourth Amendment.

Illinois v. Lidster

Supreme Court of the United States, 2004.
540 U.S. 419, 124 S.Ct. 885.

■ JUSTICE BREYER delivered the opinion of the Court.

This Fourth Amendment case focuses upon a highway checkpoint where police stopped motorists to ask them for information about a recent hit-and-run accident. We hold that the police stops were reasonable, hence, constitutional.

I

The relevant background is as follows: On Saturday, August 23, 1997, just after midnight, an unknown motorist traveling eastbound on a highway in Lombard, Illinois, struck and killed a 70–year–old bicyclist. The motorist drove off without identifying himself. About one week later at about the same time of night and at about the same place, local police set up a highway checkpoint designed to obtain more information about the accident from the motoring public.

Police cars with flashing lights partially blocked the eastbound lanes of the highway. The blockage forced traffic to slow down, leading to lines of up to 15 cars in each lane. As each vehicle drew up to the checkpoint, an officer would stop it for 10 to 15 seconds, ask the occupants whether they had seen anything happen there the previous weekend, and hand each driver a flyer. The flyer said "ALERT ... FATAL HIT & RUN ACCIDENT" and requested "assistance in identifying the vehicle and driver in this accident which killed a 70 year old bicyclist."

Robert Lidster, the respondent, drove a minivan toward the checkpoint. As he approached the checkpoint, his van swerved, nearly hitting one of the officers. The officer smelled alcohol on Lidster's breath. He directed Lidster to a side street where another officer administered a sobriety test and then arrested Lidster. Lidster was tried and convicted in Illinois state court of driving under the influence of alcohol.

Lidster challenged the lawfulness of his arrest and conviction on the ground that the government had obtained much of the relevant evidence through use of a checkpoint stop that violated the Fourth Amendment. The trial court rejected that challenge. But an Illinois appellate court reached the opposite conclusion.The Illinois Supreme Court agreed with the appellate court. It held (by a vote of 4 to 3) that our decision in *Indianapolis v. Edmond*, Because lower courts have reached different conclusions about this matter, we granted certiorari.... We now reverse the Illinois Supreme Court's determination.

II

The Illinois Supreme Court basically held that our decision in *Edmond* governs the outcome of this case. We do not agree. *Edmond* involved a checkpoint at which police stopped vehicles to look for evidence of drug crimes committed by occupants of those vehicles. After stopping a vehicle at the checkpoint, police would examine (from outside the vehicle) the vehicle's interior; they would walk a drug-sniffing dog around the exterior; and, if they found sufficient evidence of drug (or other) crimes, they would arrest the vehicle's occupants. We found that police had set up this checkpoint primarily for general "crime control" purposes, *i.e.*, "to detect evidence of ordinary criminal wrongdoing." We noted that the stop was made without individualized suspicion. And we held that the Fourth Amendment forbids such a stop, in the absence of special circumstances.

The checkpoint stop here differs significantly from that in *Edmond.* The stop's primary law enforcement purpose was *not* to determine whether a vehicle's occupants were committing a crime, but to ask vehicle occupants, as members of the public, for their help in providing information about a crime in all likelihood committed by others. The police expected the information elicited to help them apprehend, not the vehicle's occupants, but other individuals.

Edmond's language, as well as its context, makes clear that the constitutionality of this latter, information-seeking kind of stop was not then before the Court. *Edmond* refers to the subject matter of its holding as "stops justified only by the generalized and ever-present possibility that interrogation and inspection may reveal that *any given motorist has committed some crime.*" *Ibid.* (emphasis added). We concede that *Edmond* describes the law enforcement objective there in question as a "general interest in crime control," but it specifies that the phrase "general interest in crime control" does not refer to every "law enforcement" objective. We must read this and related general language in *Edmond* as we often read general language in judicial opinions—as referring in context to circumstances similar to the circumstances then before the Court and not referring to quite different circumstances that the Court was not then considering.

Neither do we believe, *Edmond* aside, that the Fourth Amendment would have us apply an *Edmond*-type rule of automatic unconstitutionality to brief, information-seeking highway stops of the kind now before us. For one thing, the fact that such stops normally lack individualized suspicion cannot by itself determine the constitutional outcome. As in *Edmond*, the stop here at issue involves a motorist. The Fourth Amendment does not treat a motorist's car as his castle. And special law enforcement concerns will sometimes justify highway stops without individualized suspicion. See *Michigan Dep't of State Police v. Sitz* (1990) (sobriety checkpoint); *Martinez–Fuerte* (Border Patrol checkpoint). Moreover, unlike *Edmond*, the context here (seeking information from the public) is one in which, by definition, the concept of individualized suspicion has little role to play. Like certain other forms of police activity, say, crowd control or public safety, an information-seeking stop is not the kind of event that involves suspicion, or lack of suspicion, of the relevant individual.

For another thing, information-seeking highway stops are less likely to provoke anxiety or to prove intrusive. The stops are likely brief. The police are not likely to ask questions designed to elicit self-incriminating information. And citizens will often react positively when police simply ask for their help as "responsible citizen[s]" to "give whatever information they may have to aid in law enforcement." *Miranda v. Arizona* (1966).

Further, the law ordinarily permits police to seek the voluntary cooperation of members of the public in the investigation of a crime. "[L]aw enforcement officers do not violate the Fourth Amendment by merely approaching an individual on the street or in another public place, by asking him if he is willing to answer some questions, [or] by putting questions to him if the person is willing to listen." *Florida v. Royer* (1983). See also ALI, Model Code of Pre–Arraignment Procedure § 110.1(1) (1975) ("[L]aw enforcement officer may ... request any person to furnish information or otherwise cooperate in the investigation or prevention of crime"). That, in part, is because voluntary requests play a vital role in police investigatory work. See, *e.g., Haynes v. Washington* (1963) ("[I]nterrogation of witnesses ... is undoubtedly an essential tool in effective law enforcement"); U. S. Dept. of Justice, Eyewitness Evidence: A Guide for Law Enforcement 14–15 (1999) (instructing law enforcement to gather information from witnesses near the scene).

The importance of soliciting the public's assistance is offset to some degree by the need to stop a motorist to obtain that help—a need less likely present where a pedestrian, not a motorist, is involved. The difference is significant in light of our determinations that such an involuntary stop amounts to a "seizure" in Fourth Amendment terms. That difference, however, is not important enough to justify an *Edmond*-type rule here. After all, as we have said, the motorist stop will likely be brief. Any accompanying traffic delay should prove no more onerous than many that typically accompany normal traffic congestion. And the resulting voluntary questioning of a motorist is as likely to prove important for police investigation as is the questioning of a pedestrian. Given these considerations, it would seem anomalous were the law (1) ordinarily to allow police freely to seek the voluntary cooperation of pedestrians but (2) ordinarily to forbid police to seek similar voluntary cooperation from motorists.

Finally, we do not believe that an *Edmond*-type rule is needed to prevent an unreasonable proliferation of police checkpoints. Practical considerations—namely, limited police resources and community hostility to related traffic tie-ups—seem likely to inhibit any such proliferation.... And, of course, the Fourth Amendment's normal insistence that the stop be reasonable in context will still provide an important legal limitation on police use of this kind of information-seeking checkpoint.

These considerations, taken together, convince us that an *Edmond*-type presumptive rule of unconstitutionality does not apply here. That does not mean the stop is automatically, or even presumptively, constitutional. It simply means that we must judge its reasonableness, hence, its constitutionality, on the basis of the individual circumstances. And as this Court said in *Brown v. Texas* (1979), in judging reasonableness, we look to "the gravity of the public concerns served by the seizure, the degree to which the seizure advances the public interest, and the severity of the interference with individual liberty." See also *Sitz* (balancing these factors in determining reasonableness of a checkpoint stop)....

III

We now consider the reasonableness of the checkpoint stop before us in light of the factors just mentioned, an issue that, in our view, has been fully argued here.... We hold that the stop was constitutional.

The relevant public concern was grave. Police were investigating a crime that had resulted in a human death. No one denies the police's need to obtain more information at that time. And the stop's objective was to help find the perpetrator of a specific and known crime, not of unknown crimes of a general sort.

The stop advanced this grave public concern to a significant degree. The police appropriately tailored their checkpoint stops to fit important criminal investigatory needs. The stops took place about one week after the hit-and-run accident, on the same highway near the location of the accident, and at about the same time of night. And police used the stops to obtain information from drivers, some of whom might well have been in the vicinity of the crime at the time it occurred....

Most importantly, the stops interfered only minimally with liberty of the sort the Fourth Amendment seeks to protect. Viewed objectively, each stop required only a brief wait in line—a very few minutes at most. Contact with the police lasted only a few seconds. Cf. *Martinez–Fuerte* (upholding stops of three-to-five minutes); *Sitz* (upholding delays of 25 seconds). Police contact consisted simply of a request for information and the distribution of a flyer.... Viewed subjectively, the contact provided little reason for anxiety or alarm. The police stopped all vehicles systematically.... And there is no allegation here that the police acted in a discriminatory or otherwise unlawful manner while questioning motorists during stops.

For these reasons we conclude that the checkpoint stop was constitutional.

The judgment of the Illinois Supreme Court is reversed.

■ JUSTICE STEVENS, with whom JUSTICE SOUTER and JUSTICE GINSBURG join, concurring in part and dissenting in part.

There is a valid and important distinction between seizing a person to determine whether she has committed a crime and seizing a person to ask whether she has any information about an unknown person who committed a crime a week earlier. I therefore join Parts I and II of the Court's opinion explaining why our decision in Indianapolis v. Edmond (2000), is not controlling in this case. However, I find the issue discussed in Part III of the opinion closer than the Court does and believe it would be wise to remand the case to the Illinois state courts to address that issue in the first instance.

In contrast to pedestrians, who are free to keep walking when they encounter police officers handing out flyers or seeking information, motorists who confront a roadblock are required to stop, and to remain stopped for as long as the officers choose to detain them. Such a seizure may seem relatively innocuous to some, but annoying to others who are forced to wait for several minutes when the line of cars is lengthened—for example, by a surge of vehicles leaving a factory at the end of a shift. Still other drivers may find an unpublicized roadblock at midnight on a Saturday somewhat alarming.

On the other side of the equation, the likelihood that questioning a random sample of drivers will yield useful information about a hit-and-run accident that occurred a week earlier is speculative at best. To be sure, the sample in this case was not entirely random: The record reveals that the police knew that the victim had finished work at the Post Office shortly before the fatal accident, and hoped that other employees of the Post Office or the nearby industrial park might work on similar schedules and, thus, have been driving the same route at the same time the previous week. That is a plausible theory, but there is no evidence in the record that the police did anything to confirm that the nearby businesses in fact had shift changes at or near midnight on Saturdays, or that they had reason to believe that a roadblock would be more effective than, say, placing flyers on the employees' cars.

In short, the outcome of the multifactor test prescribed in Brown v. Texas (1979), is by no means clear on the facts of this case. Because the Illinois Appellate Court and the State Supreme Court held that the Lombard roadblock was *per se* unconstitutional under *Indianapolis v. Edmond*, neither court attempted to apply the *Brown* test.... We should be especially reluctant to abandon our role as a court of review in a case in which the constitutional inquiry requires analysis of local conditions and practices more familiar to judges closer to the scene. I would therefore remand the case to the Illinois courts to undertake the initial analysis of the issue that the Court resolves in Part III of its opinion. To that extent, I respectfully dissent.

* * *

Searches of Travelers and their Effects.

Airport Screening Searches. Anti-hijacking measures at airports provide another example of administrative searches. To some extent a "balancing" test is used. As the intensity of the search escalates from magnetometer to pat down to full search, objective data focusing suspicion may have to be present and to increase. Less intrusive measures may have to be exhausted before more intrusive ones are used. United States v. Albarado, 495 F.2d 799 (2d Cir.1974).

The airport screening search has been held to be constitutionally reasonable without reasonable suspicion and without consent. Once the search is initiated, the suspect may not change his mind to leave the search area saying he no longer wishes to board the plane. At least one court has held that allowing a person to "revoke consent" makes no sense since made little sense because such a rule would afford terrorists multiple opportunities to attempt to penetrate airport security by electing not to fly on the cusp of detection until a vulnerable portal is found. United States v. Aukai, 497 F.3d 955 (9th Cir.2007).

Maritime Screening Searches. Courts have rejected challenges by ferry passengers to the the Maritime Transportation Security Act passed after September 11, 2001. This act permits the screening of persons, baggage, and cars on the ferry, under the regulations and determinations of the Coast Guard. *See* Cassidy v. Chertoff, 471 F.3d 67 (2d Cir.2006).

Subway Screening Searches. New York City implemented a system of random searches of purses and other containers carried by subway passengers in a response to terrorist attacks on subway systems in other cities. When challenged, the Second Circuit upheld these searches on the basis of special needs. MacWade v. Kelly, 460 F.3d 260 (2d Cir.2006).

Searches of Prisoners, Probationers, and Parolees.

In Bell v. Wolfish, 441 U.S. 520, 99 S.Ct. 1861 (1979), the Supreme Court approved intensive searches of prisoners (including pre-trial detainees) even where no particular suspicion focused on a prisoner and even where other security measures had pretty well limited the opportunity of prisoners to obtain contraband items.

In Hudson v. Palmer, 468 U.S. 517, 104 S.Ct. 3194 (1984), the Supreme Court declared that a prison inmate has no reasonable expectation of privacy entitling him to the protection of the Fourth Amendment. The Court reasoned that the demands of prison security make any expectation of privacy as to the cell unreasonable and illegitimate. "A right of privacy in traditional Fourth Amendment terms is fundamentally incompatible with the close and continued surveillance of inmates and their cells required to ensure institutional security." Although not using such language, the Court seemed to be saying that even a thorough inspection of personal papers and effects in a jail cell does not constitute a search. It specifically refused to say that a prison cell inspection constitutes a search, but that ordinarily it is reasonable within the meaning of the Fourth Amendment. Rather, as in Oliver (the open-fields case), it drew a bright line: prison cells simply are not protected.

The four dissenters said that the complaint surely alleged a seizure when the plaintiff averred that prison officials had taken and destroyed his property. The dissent also condemned the denial to prisoners of any residuum of privacy.

Prison visitors retain some privacy rights. See Spear v. Sowders, 71 F.3d 626 (6th Cir.1995) (en banc), in which the court required reasonable suspicion to strip search a prison visitor as a condition of entry.

In Griffin v. Wisconsin, 483 U.S. 868, 107 S.Ct. 3164 (1987), the Supreme Court upheld a Wisconsin regulation that permitted warrantless searches of a probationer's home by probation officers when they had "reasonable grounds" to believe that evidence indicating a probation violation would be found in the home. Such "reasonable grounds" could fall short of full probable cause. The Court stressed that Wisconsin could properly determine that both a warrant requirement and a probable cause requirement would frustrate the legitimate needs of an effective probation system. The Court passed judgment only upon a system in which, as part of the probation contract, the probationer agreed to such searches. It did not rule whether, in the absence of an explicit regulation and an explicit provision in the probation agreement, probation officers could search a probationer's home without a warrant. Nor did it rule upon a system under which there was not even a requirement of "reasonable grounds" for such a search.

In United States v. Schoenrock, 868 F.2d 289 (8th Cir.1989), the court upheld a probation officer's warrantless search of a probationer's home, pursuant to the terms of probation, where there was individualized reason to believe that the probationer had violated the conditions of probation by using alcohol and drugs.

In United States v. Knights, 534 U.S. 112, 122 S.Ct. 587 (2001), the trial court sentenced the defendant to probation for a drug offense. The sentence included the condition that he submit to a search at anytime, with or without a search or arrest warrant or reasonable cause, by any probation or law enforcement officer. A sheriff's deputy searched the defendant's home and found evidence of a crime unrelated to his probationary status. At the motion to suppress, the defendant argued that under Griffin v. Wisconsin, 483 U.S. 868, 107 S.Ct. 3164, this type of "special needs" search was limited to searches bearing upon probationary status. The United States Supreme Court, in a unanimous opinion, balanced the state interests in rehabilitation and protecting society from future criminal violations against the probationers expectation of privacy. They evaluated this search under the standard of reasonableness. Finding that focus on probationers could be more intense than that on ordinary citizens, the Court held that with this condition of probation, acknowledged by Knights, the probationer's house could be searched without a warrant upon a finding of reasonable suspicion.

Samson v. California

Supreme Court of the United States, 2006.
547 U.S. 843, 126 S.Ct. 2193.

■ Justice Thomas delivered the opinion of the Court.

California law provides that every prisoner eligible for release on state parole "shall agree in writing to be subject to search or seizure by a parole officer or other peace officer at any time of the day or night, with or without a search warrant and with or without cause." Cal. Penal Code Ann. § 3067(a) (West 2000). We granted certiorari to decide whether a suspicionless search, conducted under the authority of this statute, violates the Constitution. We hold that it does not.

I

In September 2002, petitioner Donald Curtis Samson was on state parole in California, following a conviction for being a felon in possession of a firearm. On September 6, 2002, Officer Alex Rohleder of the San Bruno Police Department observed petitioner walking down a street with a woman and a child. Based on a prior contact with petitioner, Officer Rohleder was aware that petitioner was on parole and believed that he was facing an at large warrant. Accordingly, Officer Rohleder stopped petitioner and asked him whether he had an outstanding parole warrant. Petitioner responded that there was no outstanding warrant and that he "was in good standing with his parole agent." Officer Rohleder confirmed, by radio dispatch, that petitioner was on parole and that he did not have an outstanding warrant. Nevertheless, pursuant to Cal. Penal Code Ann. § 3067(a) (West 2000) and based solely on petitioner's status as a parolee, Officer Rohleder searched petitioner. During the search, Officer Rohleder found a cigarette box in petitioner's left breast pocket. Inside the box he found a plastic baggie containing methamphetamine.

The State charged petitioner with possession of methamphetamine pursuant to Cal. Health & Safety Code Ann. § 11377(a) (West 1991). The trial court denied petitioner's motion to suppress the methamphetamine evidence, finding that Cal. Penal Code Ann. § 3067(a) (West 2000) authorized the search and that the search was not "arbitrary or capricious." A jury convicted petitioner of the possession charge and the trial court sentenced him to seven years' imprisonment.

We granted certiorari to answer a variation of the question this Court left open in *United States v. Knights* (2001)—whether a condition of release can so diminish or eliminate a released prisoner's reasonable expectation of privacy that a suspicionless search by a law enforcement officer would not offend the Fourth Amendment. 1Answering that question in the affirmative today, we affirm the judgment of the California Court of Appeal.

II

"[U]nder our general Fourth Amendment approach" we "examin[e] the totality of the circumstances" to determine whether a search is reasonable within the meaning of the Fourth Amendment. Whether a search is reasonable "is determined by assessing, on the one hand, the degree to which it intrudes upon an individual's privacy and, on the other, the degree to which it is needed for the promotion of legitimate governmental interests."

We recently applied this approach in *United States v. Knights*. In that case, California law required Knights, as a probationer, to " '[s]ubmit his . . . person, property, place of residence, vehicle, personal effects, to search at anytime, with or without a search warrant, warrant of arrest or reasonable cause by any probation officer or law enforcement officer.' " Several days after Knights had been placed on probation, police suspected that he had been involved in several incidents of arson and vandalism. Based upon that suspicion and pursuant to the search condition of his probation, a police officer conducted a warrantless search of Knights' apartment and found arson and drug paraphernalia.

We concluded that the search of Knights' apartment was reasonable. In evaluating the degree of intrusion into Knights' privacy, we found Knights' probationary status "salient," . . . observing that "[p]robation is 'one point . . . on a continuum of possible punishments ranging from solitary confinement in a maximum-security facility to a few hours of mandatory community service' ". . . .

We also concluded that probation searches, such as the search of Knights' apartment, are necessary to the promotion of legitimate governmental interests. Noting the State's dual interest in integrating probationers back into the community and combating recidivism, we credited the

" 'assumption' " that, by virtue of his status, a probationer " 'is more likely than the ordinary citizen to violate the law.' " We further found that "probationers have even more of an incentive to conceal their criminal activities and quickly dispose of incriminating evidence than the ordinary criminal because probationers are aware that they may be subject to supervision and face revocation of probation, and possible incarceration, in proceedings in which the trial rights of a jury and proof beyond a reasonable doubt, among other things, do not apply." *Knights*, We explained that the State did not have to ignore the reality of recidivism or suppress its interests in "protecting potential victims of criminal enterprise" for fear of running afoul of the Fourth Amendment.

III

As we noted in *Knights*, parolees are on the "continuum" of state-imposed punishments. On this continuum, parolees have fewer expectations of privacy than probationers, because parole is more akin to imprisonment than probation is to imprisonment. As this Court has pointed out, "parole is an established variation on imprisonment of convicted criminals.... The essence of parole is release from prison, before the completion of sentence, on the condition that the prisoner abides by certain rules during the balance of the sentence." ...

California's system of parole is consistent with these observations: A California inmate may serve his parole period either in physical custody, or elect to complete his sentence out of physical custody and subject to certain conditions. Cal. Penal Code Ann. § 3060.5 (West 2000). Under the latter option, an inmate-turned-parolee remains in the legal custody of the California Department of Corrections through the remainder of his term, § 3056, and must comply with all of the terms and conditions of parole, including mandatory drug tests, restrictions on association with felons or gang members, and mandatory meetings with parole officers, Cal. Code Regs., tit. 15, § 2512 (2005); Cal. Penal Code Ann. § 3067 (West 2000).... General conditions of parole also require a parolee to report to his assigned parole officer immediately upon release, inform the parole officer within 72 hours of any change in employment status, request permission to travel a distance of more than 50 miles from the parolee's home, and refrain from criminal conduct and possession of firearms, specified weapons, or knives unrelated to employment. Cal. Code Regs., tit. 15, § 2512. Parolees may also be subject to special conditions, including psychiatric treatment programs, mandatory abstinence from alcohol, residence approval, and "[a]ny other condition deemed necessary by the Board [of Parole Hearings] or the Department [of Corrections and Rehabilitation] due to unusual circumstances." § 2513. The extent and reach of these conditions clearly demonstrate that parolees like petitioner have severely diminished expectations of privacy by virtue of their status alone.

Additionally, as we found "salient" in *Knights* with respect to the probation search condition, the parole search condition under California law—requiring inmates who opt for parole to submit to suspicionless searches by a parole officer or other peace officer "at any time," Cal. Penal Code Ann. § 3067(a) (West 2000)—was "clearly expressed" to petitioner.

He signed an order submitting to the condition and thus was "unambiguously" aware of it. In *Knights*, we found that acceptance of a clear and unambiguous search condition "significantly diminished Knights' reasonable expectation of privacy." Examining the totality of the circumstances pertaining to petitioner's status as a parolee, "an established variation on imprisonment," ... including the plain terms of the parole search condition, we conclude that petitioner did not have an expectation of privacy that society would recognize as legitimate.

The State's interests, by contrast, are substantial. This Court has repeatedly acknowledged that a State has an " 'overwhelming interest' " in supervising parolees because "parolees ... are more likely to commit future criminal offenses." Similarly, this Court has repeatedly acknowledged that a State's interests in reducing recidivism and thereby promoting reintegration and positive citizenship among probationers and parolees warrant privacy intrusions that would not otherwise be tolerated under the Fourth Amendment.

The empirical evidence presented in this case clearly demonstrates the significance of these interests to the State of California. As of November 30, 2005, California had over 130,000 released parolees. California's parolee population has a 68–to 70–percent recidivism rate. See California Attorney General, Crime in California 37 (Apr. 2001) (explaining that 68 percent of adult parolees are returned to prison, 55 percent for a parole violation, 13 percent for the commission of a new felony offense); J. Petersilia, Challenges of Prisoner Reentry and Parole in California, 12 California Policy Research Center Brief, p 2 (June 2000), available at http://www.ucop.edu/cprc/parole.pdf (as visited June 15, 2006, and available in Clerk of Court's case file) ("70% of the state's paroled felons reoffend within 18 months—the highest recidivism rate in the nation"). This Court has acknowledged the grave safety concerns that attend recidivism.

As we made clear in *Knights*, the Fourth Amendment does not render the States powerless to address these concerns *effectively*. Contrary to petitioner's contention, California's ability to conduct suspicionless searches of parolees serves its interest in reducing recidivism, in a manner that aids, rather than hinders, the reintegration of parolees into productive society.

In California, an eligible inmate serving a determinate sentence may elect parole when the actual days he has served plus statutory time credits equal the term imposed by the trial court, Cal. Penal Code Ann. §§ 2931, 2933, 3000(b)(1) (West 2000), irrespective of whether the inmate is capable of integrating himself back into productive society. As the recidivism rate demonstrates, most parolees are ill prepared to handle the pressures of reintegration. Thus, most parolees require intense supervision. The California Legislature has concluded that, given the number of inmates the State paroles and its high recidivism rate, a requirement that searches be based on individualized suspicion would undermine the State's ability to effectively supervise parolees and protect the public from criminal acts by reoffenders. This conclusion makes eminent sense. Imposing a reasonable suspicion requirement, as urged by petitioner, would give parolees greater opportunity to anticipate searches and conceal criminality. This Court concluded that the incentive-to-conceal concern justified an "intensive" system for supervising probationers in *Griffin*. That concern applies with even greater force to a system of supervising parolees. *United States v. Crawford*, 372 F.3d 1048, 1077 (CA9 2004) (Kleinfeld, J., concurring) (explaining that parolees, in contrast to probationers, "have been sentenced to prison for felonies and released before the end of their prison terms" and are "deemed to have acted more harmfully than anyone except those felons not released on parole"). . . .

Petitioner observes that the majority of States and the Federal Government have been able to further similar interests in reducing recidivism and promoting reintegration, despite having systems that permit parolee searches based upon some level of suspicion. Thus, petitioner contends, California's system is constitutionally defective by comparison. Petitioner's reliance on the practices of jurisdictions other than California, however, is misplaced. That some States and the Federal Government require a level of individualized suspicion is of little relevance to our determination whether California's supervisory system is drawn to meet its needs and is reasonable, taking into account a parolee's substantially diminished expectation of privacy.

Nor is there merit to the argument that California's parole search law permits "a blanket grant of discretion untethered by any procedural safeguards." . . . The concern that California's suspicionless search system gives officers unbridled discretion to conduct searches, thereby inflicting dignitary harms that arouse strong resentment in parolees and undermine their ability to reintegrate into productive society, is belied by California's prohibition on "arbitrary, capricious or harassing" searches. . . . The dissent's claim that parolees under California law are subject to capricious searches conducted at the unchecked "whim" of law enforcement officers, ignores this prohibition. Likewise, petitioner's concern that California's suspicionless search law frustrates reintegration efforts by permitting intrusions into the privacy interests of third parties is also unavailing because that concern would arise under a suspicion-based regime as well.

IV

Thus, we conclude that the Fourth Amendment does not prohibit a police officer from conducting a suspicionless search of a parolee. Accordingly, we affirm the judgment of the California Court of Appeal.

It is so ordered.

■ JUSTICE STEVENS, with whom JUSTICE SOUTER and JUSTICE BREYER join, dissenting.

Our prior cases have consistently assumed that the Fourth Amendment provides some degree of protection for probationers and parolees. The protection is not as robust as that afforded to ordinary citizens; we have held that probationers' lowered expectation of privacy may justify their warrantless search upon reasonable suspicion of wrongdoing, see *United States v. Knights* (2001). We have also recognized that the supervisory responsibilities of probation officers, who are required to provide " 'individualized counseling' " and to monitor their charges' progress, *Griffin v.*

Wisconsin (1987), and who are in a unique position to judge "how close a supervision the probationer requires," may give rise to special needs justifying departures from Fourth Amendment strictures. ("Although a probation officer is not an impartial magistrate, neither is he the police officer who normally conducts searches against the ordinary citizen"). But neither *Knights* nor *Griffin* supports a regime of suspicionless searches, conducted pursuant to a blanket grant of discretion untethered by any procedural safeguards, by law enforcement personnel who have no special interest in the welfare of the parolee or probationer.

What the Court sanctions today is an unprecedented curtailment of liberty. Combining faulty syllogism with circular reasoning, the Court concludes that parolees have no more legitimate an expectation of privacy in their persons than do prisoners. However superficially appealing that parity in treatment may seem, it runs roughshod over our precedent. It also rests on an intuition that fares poorly under scrutiny. And once one acknowledges that parolees do have legitimate expectations of privacy beyond those of prisoners, our Fourth Amendment jurisprudence does not permit the conclusion, reached by the Court here for the first time, that a search supported by neither individualized suspicion nor "special needs" is nonetheless "reasonable."

The suspicionless search is the very evil the Fourth Amendment was intended to stamp out.... The pre-Revolutionary "writs of assistance," which permitted roving searches for contraband, were reviled precisely because they "placed 'the liberty of every man in the hands of every petty officer.' " While individualized suspicion "is not an 'irreducible' component of reasonableness" under the Fourth Amendment, the requirement has been dispensed with only when programmatic searches were required to meet a "special need" ... divorced from the State's general interest in law enforcement

Not surprisingly, the majority does not seek to justify the search of petitioner on "special needs" grounds. Although the Court has in the past relied on special needs to uphold warrantless searches of probationers, it has never gone so far as to hold that a probationer or parolee may be subjected to full search at the whim of any law enforcement officer he happens to encounter, whether or not the officer has reason to suspect him of wrongdoing. *Griffin*, after all, involved a search *by a probation officer* that was supported by *reasonable suspicion*. The special role of probation officers was critical to the analysis; "we deal with a situation," the Court explained, "in which there is an ongoing supervisory relationship—and one that is not, or at least not entirely, adversarial—between the object of the search and the decisionmaker." The State's interest or "special need," as articulated in *Griffin*, was an interest in supervising the wayward probationer's reintegration into society—not, or at least not principally, the general law enforcement goal of detecting crime.

It is no accident, then, that when we later upheld the search of a probationer *by a law enforcement officer* (again, based on reasonable suspicion), we forwent any reliance on the special needs doctrine. Even if the supervisory relationship between a probation officer and her charge may properly be characterized as one giving rise to needs "divorced from the

State's general interest in law enforcement,'' the relationship between an ordinary law enforcement officer and a probationer unknown to him may not. ''None of our special needs precedents has sanctioned the routine inclusion of law enforcement, both in the design of the policy and in using arrests, either threatened or real, to implement the system designed for the special needs objectives.''

Ignoring just how ''closely guarded'' is that ''category of constitutionally permissible suspicionless searches,'' the Court for the first time upholds an entirely suspicionless search unsupported by any special need. And it goes further: In special needs cases we have at least insisted upon programmatic safeguards designed to ensure evenhandedness in application; if individualized suspicion is to be jettisoned, it must be replaced with measures to protect against the state actor's unfettered discretion.... Here, by contrast, there are no policies in place—no ''standards, guidelines, or procedures,''—to rein in officers and furnish a bulwark against the arbitrary exercise of discretion that is the height of unreasonableness.

The Court is able to make this unprecedented move only by making another. Coupling the dubious holding of Hudson v. Palmer (1984), with the bald statement that ''parolees have fewer expectations of privacy than probationers,'' the Court two-steps its way through a faulty syllogism and, thus, avoids the application of Fourth Amendment principles altogether. The logic, apparently, is this: Prisoners have no legitimate expectation of privacy; parolees are like prisoners; therefore, parolees have no legitimate expectation of privacy. The conclusion is remarkable not least because we have long embraced its opposite. 2It also rests on false premises. First, it is simply not true that a parolee's status, vis-a-vis either the State or the Constitution, is tantamount to that of a prisoner or even materially distinct from that of a probationer. A parolee, like a probationer, is set free in the world subject to restrictions intended to facilitate supervision and guard against antisocial behavior. As with probation, ''the State is willing to extend parole only because it is able to condition it upon compliance with certain requirements.'' Certainly, parole differs from probation insofar as parole is '' 'meted out in addition to, not in lieu of, incarceration.' '' And, certainly, parolees typically will have committed more serious crimes—ones warranting a prior term of imprisonment—than probationers. The latter distinction, perhaps, would support the conclusion that a State has a stronger interest in supervising parolees than it does in supervising probationers. But why either distinction should result in refusal to acknowledge as legitimate, when harbored by parolees, the same expectation of privacy that probationers reasonably may harbor is beyond fathom.

In any event, the notion that a parolee legitimately expects only so much privacy as a prisoner is utterly without foundation. *Hudson v. Palmer* does stand for the proposition that ''[a] right of privacy in traditional Fourth Amendment terms'' is denied individuals who are incarcerated. But this is because it ''is necessary, as a practical matter, to accommodate a myriad of 'institutional needs and objectives' '' of prison facilities, ... chief among which is internal security.... These ''institutional needs''—safety of inmates and guards, ''internal order,'' and sanitation—manifestly do not apply to parolees. As discussed above and in *Griffin, other* state interests may warrant certain intrusions into a parolee's privacy, but *Hudson*'s rationale cannot be mapped blindly onto the situation with which we are presented in this case.

Nor is it enough, in deciding whether someone's expectation of privacy is "legitimate," to rely on the existence of the offending condition or the individual's notice thereof. The Court's reasoning in this respect is entirely circular. The mere fact that a particular State refuses to acknowledge a parolee's privacy interest cannot mean that a parolee in that State has no expectation of privacy that society is willing to recognize as legitimate—especially when the measure that invades privacy is both the *subject* of the Fourth Amendment challenge and a clear outlier. With only one or two arguable exceptions, neither the Federal Government nor any other State subjects parolees to searches of the kind to which petitioner was subjected. And the fact of notice hardly cures the circularity; the loss of a subjective expectation of privacy would play "no meaningful role" in analyzing the legitimacy of expectations, for example, "if the Government were suddenly to announce on nationwide television that all homes henceforth would be subject to warrantless entry."

Threaded through the Court's reasoning is the suggestion that deprivation of Fourth Amendment rights is part and parcel of any convict's punishment. If a person may be subject to random and suspicionless searches in prison, the Court seems to assume, then he cannot complain when he is subject to the same invasion outside of prison, so long as the State still *can* imprison him. Punishment, though, is not the basis on which *Hudson* was decided. Indeed, it is settled that a prison inmate " 'retains those [constitutional] rights that are not inconsistent with his status as a prisoner or with the legitimate penological objectives of the corrections system.' " Nor, to my knowledge, have we ever sanctioned the use of any search as a punitive measure. Instead, the question in every case must be whether the balance of legitimate expectations of privacy, on the one hand, and the State's interests in conducting the relevant search, on the other, justifies dispensing with the warrant and probable-cause requirements that are otherwise dictated by the Fourth Amendment. That balance is not the same in prison as it is out. We held in *Knights*—without recourse to *Hudson*—that the balance favored allowing the State to conduct searches based on reasonable suspicion. Never before have we plunged below that floor absent a demonstration of "special needs." . . .

Respectfully, I dissent.

NOTES

1. Are there other categories of cases involving people and/or places in which the level of cause is reduced or eliminated?

A. ***Public Employees***. In O'Connor v. Ortega, 480 U.S. 709, 107 S.Ct. 1492 (1987), the Court divided four-four-one in a case where a government employer had searched a desk and file cabinet used at work by its employee. The employer was conducting an investigation into alleged work-related misconduct by a psychiatrist who had been employed at a government hospital for seventeen years.

Four justices declared that employees may have reasonable expectations of privacy in certain areas within the workplace as against police intrusions; however, some expectations of privacy in such places may be unreasonable as against intrusions by the employee's supervisor. Such expectations of privacy may be reduced by "actual office practices and procedures, or by legitimate regulation." On the facts of the case, the plurality opinion decided that Dr.Ortega had a reasonable expectation of privacy in his desks and cabinets.

Having concluded that the employer's conduct intruded upon a reasonable expectation of privacy (and thus was a search as to which the employee had a right to complain), the plurality considered whether such a search was reasonable without a warrant. It concluded that a warrantless work-related intrusion comports with the Fourth Amendment, even without probable cause, if it is reasonable under all the circumstances. Ordinarily a reasonable belief that a search will yield evidence of work-related misconduct will suffice, as will a reasonable belief that the search is necessary for a noninvestigatory work-related purpose, such as to retrieve a file. The plurality reasoned by analogy from the school search case, New Jersey v. T.L.O. (1985). It remanded for further proceedings to determine whether the searches of Dr. Ortega's desk and cabinets met this standard.

Writing separately, Justice Scalia joined in the remand order. He argued against a case-by-case analysis of whether an employee has a reasonable expectation of privacy in his business office. He also argued that a reasonable expectation of privacy does not vary depending upon who carries out the intrusion. It is the same vis-a-vis a police officer or a governmental supervisor. He argued that the Fourth Amendment provided protection against unreasonable searches in all such cases. He concluded by asserting that government searches of the workplace to retrieve work-related materials or to investigate violations of workplace rules are per se reasonable.

Four justices dissented. They argued against formulating a standard based upon assumed facts without further factual development. These justices, through Justice Blackmun, argued that many governmental investigatory searches of an employer's office are reasonable only if authorized by a magistrate based upon a finding of probable cause. Apparently the probable cause would relate to a violation of work-related rules and not to commission of an offense, under Blackmun's view.

B. ***Courthouses and Other Public Buildings.*** Judges appear more willing to approve searches and inspections of citizens entering "public" court houses and governmental office buildings than they are to approve inspections at public arenas where rock concerts are being held. See Downing v. Kunzig, 454 F.2d 1230 (6th Cir.1972) (building where Sixth Circuit sat), and compare State v. Carter, 267 N.W.2d 385 (Iowa 1978), and Gaioni v. Folmar, 460 F.Supp. 10 (M.D.Ala.1978). If it is improper to frisk a pedestrian for weapons in a high crime area absent "reasonable suspicion," how can it be reasonable to inspect purses at the entrance to a public courts complex simply because of a generalized concern for safety of the building's occupants? See Jesmore, The Courthouse Search, 21 U.C.L.A.L.Rev. 797 (1974).

C. ***Fire Scene Inspections.*** In Michigan v. Tyler, 436 U.S. 499, 98 S.Ct. 1942 (1978), the Court placed limits upon the rights of fire inspectors, absent consent, to make warrantless searches, recognizing three distinct categories of fire inspection searches:

> (1) A warrantless entry is permissible to extinguish a fire. Even after the blaze is out, officials may remain or reenter to promptly determine the fire's origin so as to prevent recurrence and to prevent intentional or accidental destruction of evidence. Evidence found in a place where officials have a right to look may be seized during this period.

(2) Subsequent entries to determine the cause of the fire, however, after a "reasonable time" for the initial investigation, necessitate, at a minimum, an administrative warrant. Traditional probable cause is not required. Rather the magistrate must balance several factors to determine the reasonableness of the proposed search: the "number of prior entries, the scope of the search, the time of day when it is proposed to be made, the lapse of time since the fire, the continued use of the building, and the owner's efforts to secure it against intruders might all be relevant factors."

(3) Once the purpose of the investigation becomes a quest for evidence of arson for use in a criminal prosecution, however, rather than the discovery of the cause of the fire as to prevent such fires from recurring, then a search is proper only upon traditional probable cause, i.e., probable cause to believe that a crime has been committed and that evidence of the crime will be found in the place to be searched. Apparently this third stage—when a traditional warrant is necessary—is reached no later than when earlier investigations have yielded probable cause to believe that a crime has been committed.

As a practical matter, probable cause to believe that arson has been committed frequently will be found during the first segment of the investigation. Apparently, under such circumstances—once the immediate danger has clearly been abated—officials would be required to apply for a traditional search warrant. Thus use of the administrative warrant provided for in time-segment two will often be bypassed.

A divided Court applied *Tyler* in Michigan v. Clifford, 464 U.S. 287, 104 S.Ct. 641 (1984), so as to invalidate a post-fire search. One justice later commented that *Tyler* created confusion about the meaning and continued viability of *Clifford*. See Michigan v. Essa, 478 U.S. 1012, 106 S.Ct. 3313 (1986) (Burger, C.J. dissenting from denial of certiorari).

2. *Purpose of the Search?* Consider again one of the puzzling things about administrative searches: some clearly have as one purpose the discovery of criminal evidence. The search at the border, the search of a probationer, and the inspection of a pharmacist's records may all have as one purpose the detection of narcotic violations. Yet this does not necessarily make the search without a traditional probable cause warrant unreasonable even in the absence of one of the other recognized exceptions. See United States v. Acklen, 690 F.2d 70 (6th Cir.1982). The case involved the use of an administrative warrant allowing Drug Enforcement Administration agents to search a pharmacy in the hope of detecting evidence of criminal law violations. Can it not be said that enforcement of all criminal laws has some public welfare purpose? Why are Fourth Amendment constraints eased in some cases under the rubric of "administrative search" and not in other cases? See William Stuntz, The Substantive Origins of Criminal Procedure, 105 Yale L.J. 393 (1995).

O. BORDER AND IMMIGRATION SEARCHES

1. *The Border Exception*. When a person is crossing into the United States at a border, he can be searched and his goods inspected. The supposed purpose of such searches is not simply to enforce the penal laws, but also to prohibit the entry into the country of substances which violate health standards. No warrant is required. Nor must the authorities possess any data suggesting that a particular person is carrying contraband before they can search such persons. Some lower court decisions held that if the intensity of the search goes beyond the "ordinary" search—as, for example, it escalates to a strip search and then to an intrusion into body cavities—an increasing amount of objective data focusing suspicion on the person is required. See, e.g., United States v. Smith, 557 F.2d 1206 (5th Cir.1977); United States v. Mastberg, 503 F.2d 465 (9th Cir.1974). Then in United States v. Montoya de Hernandez, 473 U.S. 531, 105 S.Ct. 3304 (1985), the Court upheld a court-ordered inspection by a physician of the rectum of a woman reasonably suspected of trying to smuggle into the country illicit drugs placed in balloons and then swallowed. The Court first summarized past border search decisions:

> Consistently, therefore, with Congress' power to protect the Nation by stopping and examining persons entering this country, the Fourth Amendment's balance of reasonableness is qualitatively different at the international border than in the interior. Routine searches of the persons and effects of entrants are not subject to any requirement of reasonable suspicion, probable cause, or warrant, and first-class mail may be opened without a warrant on less than probable cause. Automotive travelers may be stopped at fixed checkpoints near the border without individualized suspicion even if the stop is based largely on ethnicity, and boats on inland waters with ready access to the sea may be hailed and boarded with no suspicion whatever.
>
> These cases reflect longstanding concern for the protection of the integrity of the border. This concern is, if anything, heightened by the veritable national crisis in law enforcement caused by smuggling of illicit narcotics, and in particular by the increasing utilization of alimentary canal smuggling. This desperate practice appears to be a relatively recent addition to the smugglers' repertoire of deceptive practices, and it also appears to be exceedingly difficult to detect.

The Court then rejected use of a "clear indication" standard in connection with border detentions that are extended beyond the scope of routine custom searches and inspections, opting instead for a "reasonable suspicion" test. Here the pre-inspection detention lasted nearly twenty-four hours. The suspect was held incommunicado despite requests that she be allowed to call her family. She was denied regular toilet facilities but instead was given access to a wastebasket, while kept under the watchful eye of matrons. In obvious discomfort, she refused food and water and avoided discharge of bodily waste. The rectal inspection yielded a balloon containing cocaine and thereafter the suspect passed eighty-eight such balloons. Over a strong dissent, the Court found that the governmental conduct was reasonable within the meaning of the Fourth Amendment.

In United States v. Ramsey, 431 U.S. 606, 97 S.Ct. 1972 (1977), the Court uphold warrantless inspection of mail which is crossing into the United States from another country. It is generally agreed that border search doctrines are also applicable at first points of entry by airplane, known as "functional equivalents." See United States v. Brown, 499 F.2d 829 (7th Cir.1974) (international gate at Chicago's O'Hare Airport).

United States v. Flores–Montano

Supreme Court of the United States, 2004
541 U.S. 149, 124 S.Ct. 1582.

OPINION

■ CHIEF JUSTICE REHNQUIST delivered the opinion of the Court.

Customs officials seized 37 kilograms—a little more than 81 pounds—of marijuana from respondent Manuel Flores–Montano's gas tank at the international border. The Court of Appeals for the Ninth Circuit, relying on an earlier decision by a divided panel of that court, United States v. Molina–Tarazon, 279 F.3d 709 (2002), held that the Fourth Amendment forbade the fuel tank search absent reasonable suspicion. We hold that the search in question did not require reasonable suspicion.

Respondent, driving a 1987 Ford Taurus station wagon, attempted to enter the United States at the Otay Mesa Port of Entry in southern California. A customs inspector conducted an inspection of the station wagon, and requested respondent to leave the vehicle. The vehicle was then taken to a secondary inspection station.

At the secondary station, a second customs inspector inspected the gas tank by tapping it, and noted that the tank sounded solid. Subsequently, the inspector requested a mechanic under contract with Customs to come to the border station to remove the tank. Within 20 to 30 minutes, the mechanic arrived. He raised the car on a hydraulic lift, loosened the straps and unscrewed the bolts holding the gas tank to the undercarriage of the vehicle, and then disconnected some hoses and electrical connections. After the gas tank was removed, the inspector hammered off bondo (a putty-like hardening substance that is used to seal openings) from the top of the gas tank. The inspector opened an access plate underneath the bondo and found 37 kilograms of marijuana bricks. The process took 15 to 25 minutes.

A grand jury for the Southern District of California indicted respondent on one count of unlawfully importing marijuana, in violation of 21 U.S.C. § 952 [21 USCS § 952], and one count of possession of marijuana with intent to distribute, in violation of § 841(a)(1). Relying on *Molina-Tarazon*, respondent filed a motion to suppress the marijuana recovered from the gas tank. In *Molina–Tarazon*, a divided panel of the Court of Appeals held, *inter alia*, that removal of a gas tank requires reasonable suspicion in order to be consistent with the Fourth Amendment.

The Government advised the District Court that it was not relying on reasonable suspicion as a basis for denying respondent's suppression motion, but that it believed *Molina–Tarazon* was wrongly decided. The District Court, relying on *Molina–Tarazon*, held that reasonable suspicion was required to justify the search and, accordingly, granted respondent's motion to suppress. The Court of Appeals, citing *Molina–Tarazon*, summarily affirmed the District Court's judgment. We granted certiorari, and now reverse.

In *Molina–Tarazon*, the Court of Appeals decided a case presenting similar facts to the one at bar. It asked "whether [the removal and dismantling of the defendant's fuel tank] is a 'routine' border search for which no suspicion whatsoever is required." The Court of Appeals stated that "[i]n order to conduct a search that goes beyond the routine, an inspector must have reasonable suspicion," and the "critical factor" in determining whether a search is "routine" is the "degree of intrusiveness."

The Court of Appeals seized on language from our opinion in *United States* v. *Montoya de Hernandez* (1985), in which we used the word "routine" as a descriptive term in discussing border searches ("Routine searches of the persons and effects of entrants are not subject to any requirement of reasonable suspicion, probable cause, or warrant"); ("Because the issues are not presented today we suggest no view on what level of suspicion, if any, is required for nonroutine border searches such as strip, body-cavity, or involuntary x-ray searches"). The Court of Appeals took the term "routine," fashioned a new balancing test, and extended it to searches of vehicles. But the reasons that might support a requirement of some level of suspicion in the case of highly intrusive searches of the person—dignity and privacy interests of the person being searched—simply do not carry over to vehicles. Complex balancing tests to determine what is a "routine" search of a vehicle, as opposed to a more "intrusive" search of a person, have no place in border searches of vehicles.

The Government's interest in preventing the entry of unwanted persons and effects is at its zenith at the international border. Time and again, we have stated that "searches made at the border, pursuant to the longstanding right of the sovereign to protect itself by stopping and examining persons and property crossing into this country, are reasonable simply by virtue of the fact that they occur at the border." United States v. Ramsey (1977). Congress, since the beginning of our Government, "has granted the Executive plenary authority to conduct routine searches and seizures at the border, without probable cause or a warrant, in order to regulate the collection of duties and to prevent the introduction of contraband into this country." The modern statute that authorized the search in this case, 46 Stat. 747, 19 U.S.C. § 1581(a)[19 USCS § 1581(a)], 1derived from a statute passed by the First Congress, the Act of Aug. 4, 1790.... and reflects the "impressive historical pedigree" of the Government's power and interest. It is axiomatic that the United States, as sovereign, has the inherent authority to protect, and a paramount interest in protecting, its territorial integrity.

That interest in protecting the borders is illustrated in this case by the evidence that smugglers frequently attempt to penetrate our borders with contraband secreted in their automobiles' fuel tank. Over the past 5 1/2 fiscal years, there have been 18,788 vehicle drug seizures at the southern California ports of entry. Of those 18,788, gas tank drug seizures have accounted for 4,619 of the vehicle drug seizures, or approximately 25%. *Ibid.* In addition, instances of persons smuggled in and around gas tank compartments are discovered at the ports of entry of San Ysidro and Otay Mesa at a rate averaging 1 approximately every 10 days.

Respondent asserts two main arguments with respect to his Fourth Amendment interests. First, he urges that he has a privacy interest in his fuel tank, and that the suspicionless disassembly of his tank is an invasion of his privacy. But on many occasions, we have noted that the expectation of privacy is less at the border than it is in the interior. We have long recognized that automobiles seeking entry into this country may be searched. See Carroll v. United States (1925) ("Travellers may be so stopped in crossing an international boundary because of national self protection reasonably requiring one entering the country to identify himself as entitled to come in, and his belongings as effects which may be lawfully brought in"). It is difficult to imagine how the search of a gas tank, which should be solely a repository for fuel, could be more of an invasion of privacy than the search of the automobile's passenger compartment.

Second, respondent argues that the Fourth Amendment "protects property as well as privacy," and that the disassembly and reassembly of his gas tank is a significant deprivation of his property interest because it may damage the vehicle. He does not, and on the record cannot, truly contend that the procedure of removal, disassembly, and reassembly of the fuel tank in this case or any other has resulted in serious damage to, or destruction of, the property. 2According to the Government, for example, in fiscal year 2003, 348 gas tank searches conducted along the southern border were negative (*i.e.*, no contraband was found), the gas tanks were reassembled, and the vehicles continued their entry into the United States without incident.

Respondent cites not a single accident involving the vehicle or motorist in the many thousands of gas tank disassemblies that have occurred at the border. A gas tank search involves a brief procedure that can be reversed without damaging the safety or operation of the vehicle. If damage to a vehicle were to occur, the motorist might be entitled to recovery. While the interference with a motorist's possessory interest is not insignificant when the Government removes, disassembles, and reassembles his gas tank, it nevertheless is justified by the Government's paramount interest in protecting the border. 3

For the reasons stated, we conclude that the Government's authority to conduct suspicionless inspections at the border includes the authority to remove, disassemble, and reassemble a vehicle's fuel tank. While it may be true that some searches of property are so destructive as to require a different result, this was not one of them. The judgment of the United States Court of Appeals for the Ninth Circuit is therefore reversed, and the case is remanded for further proceedings consistent with this opinion.

It is so ordered.

■ JUSTICE BREYER, concurring.

I join the Court's opinion in full. I also note that Customs keeps track of the border searches its agents conduct, including the reasons for the searches. This administrative process should help minimize concerns that gas tank searches might be undertaken in an abusive manner.

NOTES

1. The government power to search at the border is quite broad. Suppose an individual is entering the country carrying a laptop computer. Is the computer subject to a thorough search? The flash drives? See United States v. Romm, 455 F.3d 990 (9th Cir.2006); United States v. Ickes, 393 F.3d 501 (4th Cir.2005); United States v. Arnold, 454 F. Supp. 2d 999 (C.D. Cal. 2006); NOTE (Rasha Alzahabi), "Should You Leave Your Laptop at Home When Traveling Abroad?: The Fourth Amendment and Border Searches of Laptop Computers," 41 Ind. L. Rev. 161 (2008); Note (Lindsey E. Harrell), "Down to the Last .JPEG: Addressing the Constitutionality of Suspicionless Border Searches of Computers and One Court's Pioneering Approach in United States v. Arnold," 37 Sw. U.L. Rev. 205 (2008);

Note, "Laptop Searches at the United States Borders and the Border Search Exception to the Fourth Amendment," 48 B.C. L. Rev 971 (2007);

2. *"Border Vicinity" Searches*. The Supreme Court has been very active in ruling on the validity of (1) stops and (2) searches of vehicles (3) at fixed checkpoints or (4) by roving patrols perhaps ten, twenty, or fifty miles distant from a border. In United States v. Martinez–Fuerte, 428 U.S. 543, 96 S.Ct. 3074 (1976), the Court summarized some earlier holdings. That summary is paraphrased here:

> In Almeida–Sanchez v. United States (1973), the question was whether a roving-patrol unit constitutionally could search a vehicle for illegal aliens simply because it was in the general vicinity of the border. The Court held that searches by roving patrols could be conducted without consent only if there was probable cause to believe that a car contained illegal aliens, at least in the absence of a judicial warrant authorizing random stops by roving patrols in a given area. The Court held in United States v. Ortiz (1975) that the same limitations were applied to vehicle searches conducted at a permanent checkpoint.
>
> In United States v. Brignoni–Ponce (1975), however, the Court recognized that other traffic-checking practices involve a different balance of public and private interest and appropriately are subject to less stringent constitutional safeguards. The question there was under what circumstances a roving patrol could stop motorists in the general area of the border for inquiry into their residence status. The Court said that a roving-patrol stop need not be justified by probable cause and may be undertaken if the stopping officer is "aware of specific articulable facts, together with rational inferences from those facts, that reasonably warrant suspicion" that a vehicle contains illegal aliens.

The Court in Martinez–Fuerte held that even without reasonable suspicion, vehicles may be stopped at fixed checkpoints in the vicinity of a border and the occupants briefly questioned. It rejected the argument that, at a minimum, such detentions for questioning could be considered reasonable only if done under the authority of an "area warrant" issued upon a judicial determination that it was reasonable to stop cars, in accord with certain guidelines, at that particular checkpoint. Questions thus arise as to what is a "fixed" checkpoint. Such issues are of critical importance in many drug prosecutions in certain border states.

3. *Urban I.N.S. Stops*. The procedures of the Immigration and Naturalization Service also give rise to Fourth Amendment issues in the context of the "urban stop" in quest of illegal aliens. See Illinois Migrant Council v. Pilliod, 540 F.2d 1062 (7th Cir.1976), mod. in 548 F.2d 715 (7th Cir.1977); Lee v. Immigration and Naturalization Service, 590 F.2d 497 (3d Cir.1979). Urban cases in which I.N.S. agents confront persons whom they suspect as illegal aliens often do not involve administrative search doctrines. Rather they pose the issue of (1) whether a seizure has occurred, and (2) if so, whether the known data add up to *Terry*-type reasonable suspicion justifying a detention.

In Immigration and Naturalization Service v. Delgado, 466 U.S. 210, 104 S.Ct. 1758 (1984), agents in two instances entered factories under the authority of warrants seeking illegal aliens. On a third occasion they entered a factory with the consent of the employer. Some agents stayed near the factory exits. Others approached the employees and asked them questions about their citizenship. The Supreme Court held that a request for identification or interrogation about identity does not by itself constitute a "seizure" of the person within the meaning of the Fourth Amendment: "Unless the circumstances of the encounter are so intimidating as to demonstrate that a reasonable person would have believed he was not free to leave if he had not responded, one cannot say the questioning resulted in a detention under the Fourth Amendment." The Court added that restriction on movement came from the obligations to the employer to remain at the factory during work hours, and not from the presence of the agents. The possibility that they would be questioned if they sought to leave created "no reasonable fear" in most workers that they would be detained upon leaving. The Court added that since no detention was involved, there was no need for a showing of "reasonable suspicion." It concluded that the four plaintiffs who sought to enjoin the practice had not been detained simply because they were briefly questioned and then left alone after they apparently satisfied the agents that they were not illegal aliens.

In dissent Justice Brennan wrote, it is "plain beyond cavil that the manner in which the INS conducted these surveys demonstrated a 'show of authority' of sufficient size and force to overbear the will of any reasonable person."

P. INVENTORY SEARCHES

Sometimes, as, for example, when a driver is intoxicated or becomes ill, or when an arrestee is to be placed in a jail cell, law enforcement officials may become temporary custodians of a citizen's property. In such cases they have claimed the right to conduct a warrantless "inventory search" of the property. The stated rationale is to safeguard the property, to protect against false claims of theft, and, occasionally, to prevent danger to the officers. Despite a growing trend by state and lower federal courts to limit the use of the inventory search, the United States Supreme Court gave broad approval to the inventory search doctrine in South Dakota v. Opperman, 428 U.S. 364, 96 S.Ct. 3092 (1976), a 5 to 4 decision, with Justices Marshall, Brennan, White, and Stewart dissenting. The Court held that when vehicles are lawfully impounded, routine inventorying of the vehicle, including locked components, is permissible. In Opperman there was no suggestion that the inventory was a pretext to find evidence of a crime. The car had been towed in connection with parking ordinance violations.

In Colorado v. Bertine, 479 U.S. 367, 107 S.Ct. 738 (1987), the police arrested the defendant for driving while under the influence. They inventoried his vehicle before towing it to an impoundment lot. They opened a closed backpack found in the vehicle and discovered cocaine paraphernalia, controlled substances, and a large amount of cash. The Court said that opening the backpack was legitimate in view of the three reasons said to justify the inventory search exception to the warrant requirement: preserving property, guarding against claims of theft, vandalism, or police negligence, and averting danger to the police or others. It said that the police need not give the owner the opportunity to make other arrangements for the safekeeping of the property, nor must they forego inspection if there are less intrusive means of achieving the goals of an inventory search. The Court emphasized that the police were following standard procedures and that there was no showing that the police "acted in bad faith or for the sole purpose of investigation." It added that although the police had some discretion as to whether to impound the car or lock it and park it in a public place, such a zone of discretion was not fatal, especially when the police rules spelled out standards governing the exercise of such discretion. A concurring opinion noted that the police departmental standards did require the opening of closed containers and the listing of their contents once the police had decided to impound a vehicle. Two justices dissented, largely emphasizing their view that the police decision to impound the vehicle rather than to park and lock it was the individual officer's decision, not in accord with standardized guidelines. They also said that the individual's privacy interest was greater than in Opperman and that the government interest could be served by placing the backpack in a secure storage facility.

A defendant finally won an inventory search case before the Supreme Court in Florida v. Wells, 495 U.S. 1, 110 S.Ct. 1632 (1990). There, during the course of a lawful inventory search of the trunk of the car of an intoxicated driver's vehicle, state troopers discovered a locked suitcase. They opened it and discovered "a considerable amount of marijuana." The Florida Supreme Court found that "the Florida Highway Patrol had no policy whatever with respect to the opening of closed containers encountered during an inventory search." The United States Supreme Court unanimously held "that absent such a policy, the instant search was not sufficiently regulated to satisfy the Fourth Amendment . . ."

The Court emphasized that standardized criteria are required because of the fear that an inventory search otherwise could be a "ruse for a general rummaging in order to discover incriminating evidence."

The Chief Justice's opinion for a majority of the court added that regulations can still allow the officer some latitude in deciding whether to inventory a closed container, but emphasized some policies must be in place to regulate the officer's decision. Justice Blackmun took exception to the majority's assertion that some discretion is permissible.

After Wells some courts have held that policies on inventory searches can be viewed as established even though they are not embodied in writing. State v. Weide, 155 Wis.2d 537, 455 N.W.2d 899 (1990).

May an inventory search include a page-by-page review of a notebook found in an impounded vehicle? See United States v. Andrews, 22 F.3d 1328 (5th Cir.1994).

Q. CONSENT SEARCHES AND SEIZURES

If a search of property is made by law enforcement officers under the voluntary consent of a person who has sufficient authority over the property, such a search is deemed reasonable under the Fourth Amendment even if the police have neither a warrant nor probable cause. Normally a consent to search is not so broad as to authorize the police to take and carry away any item which they come upon. If, however, looking in a place which they have a right to inspect under the authority of the consent to search, officers come upon an item which they have probable cause to believe is contraband or evidence of a crime, the officers can seize the item. The seizure in such an instance can be justified under plain view principles (discussed in the following previous section F), rather under the doctrine of consent.

Much of consent search litigation focuses upon two questions: (1) was there, in fact, a voluntary consent?, and (2) did the consenting party have sufficient authority to make it reasonable for the officers to search based upon his or her consent? We begin with the first question.

Schneckloth v. Bustamonte

Supreme Court of the United States, 1973.
412 U.S. 218, 93 S.Ct. 2041.

■ JUSTICE STEWART delivered the opinion of the Court.

* * *

While on routine patrol in Sunnyvale, California, at approximately 2:40 in the morning, Police Officer James Rand stopped an automobile when he observed that one headlight and its license plate light were burned out. Six men were in the vehicle. Joe Alcala and the respondent, Robert Bustamonte, were in the front seat with Joe Gonzales, the driver. Three older men were seated in the rear. When, in response to the policeman's question, Gonzales could not produce a driver's license, Officer Rand asked if any of the other five had any evidence of identification. Only Alcala produced a license, and he explained that the car was his brother's. After the six occupants had stepped out of the car at the officer's request and after two additional policemen had arrived, Officer Rand asked Alcala if he could search the car. Alcala replied, "Sure, go ahead." Prior to the search no one was threatened with arrest and, according to Officer Rand's uncontradicted testimony, it "was all very congenial at this time." Gonzales testified that Alcala actually helped in the search of the car, by opening the trunk and glove compartment. In Gonzales' words: "[T]he police officer asked Joe [Alcala], he goes, 'Does the trunk open?' And Joe said, 'Yes.' He went to the car and got the keys and opened up the trunk." Wadded up under the left rear seat, the police officers found three checks that had previously been stolen from a car wash.

The trial judge denied the motion to suppress, and the checks in question were admitted in evidence at Bustamonte's trial. On the basis of this and other evidence he was convicted, and the California Court of Appeal for the First Appellate District affirmed the conviction. [The California Supreme Court denied further review; Bustamonte then filed a federal habeas corpus petition which was denied by the district court. The Ninth Circuit Court of Appeals reversed and remanded for a hearing whether Joe Alcala knew he had a right to refuse to consent. The State's (Warden's) petition for certiorari was granted.]

The precise question in this case, then, is what must the prosecution prove to demonstrate that a consent was "voluntarily" given. And upon that question there is a square conflict of views between the state and federal courts that have reviewed the search involved in the case before us. The Court of Appeals for the Ninth Circuit concluded that it is an essential part of the State's initial burden to prove that a person knows he has a right to refuse consent. The California courts have followed the rule that voluntariness is a question of fact to be determined from the totality of all the circumstances, and that the state of a defendant's knowledge is only one factor to be taken into account in assessing the voluntariness of a consent.

The most extensive judicial exposition of the meaning of "voluntariness" has been developed in those cases in which the Court has had to determine the "voluntariness" of a defendant's confession for purposes of the Fourteenth Amendment. . . .

* * *

The significant fact about all of these decisions is that none of them turned on the presence or absence of a single controlling criterion; each reflected a careful scrutiny of all the surrounding circumstances. In none of them did the Court rule that the Due Process Clause required the prosecution to prove as part of its initial burden that the defendant knew he had a right to refuse to answer the questions that were put. While the state of the accused's mind, and the failure of the police to advise the accused of his rights, were certainly factors to be evaluated in assessing the "voluntariness" of an accused's responses, they were not in and of themselves determinative.

Similar considerations lead us to agree with the courts of California that the question whether a consent to a search was in fact "voluntary" or was the product of duress or coercion, express or implied, is a question of fact to be determined from the totality of all the circumstances. While knowledge of the right to refuse consent is one factor to be taken into account, the government need not establish such knowledge as the sine qua non of an effective consent. As with police questioning, two competing concerns must be accommodated in determining the meaning of a "voluntary" consent—the legitimate need for such searches and the equally important requirement of assuring the absence of coercion.

* * *

. . . But the Fourth and Fourteenth Amendments require that a consent not be coerced, by explicit or implicit means, by implied threat or covert force. For, no matter how subtly the coercion was applied, the resulting "consent" would be no more than a pretext for the unjustified police intrusion against which the Fourth Amendment is directed. . . .

* * *

The problem of reconciling the recognized legitimacy of consent searches with the requirement that they be free from any aspect of official coercion cannot be resolved by any infallible touchstone. To approve such searches without the most careful scrutiny would sanction the possibility of official coercion; to place artificial restrictions upon such searches would jeopardize their basic validity. Just as was true with confessions, the requirement of a "voluntary" consent reflects a fair accommodation of the constitutional requirements involved. In examining all the surrounding circumstances to determine if in fact the consent to search was coerced, account must be taken of subtly coercive police questions, as well as the possibly vulnerable subjective state of the person who consents. Those searches that are the product of police coercion can thus be filtered out without undermining the continuing validity of consent searches. In sum, there is no reason for us to depart in the area of consent searches, from the traditional definition of "voluntariness."

The approach of the Court of Appeals for the Ninth Circuit finds no support in any of our decisions that have attempted to define the meaning of "voluntariness." Its ruling, that the State must affirmatively prove that the subject of the search knew that he had a right to refuse consent, would, in practice, create serious doubt whether consent searches could continue to be conducted. There might be rare cases where it could be proved from the record that a person in fact affirmatively knew of his right to refuse—such as a case where he announced to the police that if he didn't sign the consent form, "you [police] are going to get a search warrant;" or a case where by prior experience and training a person had clearly and convincingly demonstrated such knowledge. But more commonly where there was no evidence of any coercion, explicit or implicit, the prosecution would nevertheless be unable to demonstrate that the subject of the search in fact had known of his right to refuse consent.

* * *

One alternative that would go far toward proving that the subject of a search did know he had a right to refuse consent would be to advise him of that right before eliciting his consent. That, however, is a suggestion that has been almost universally repudiated by both federal and state courts, and, we think, rightly so. For it would be thoroughly impractical to impose on the normal consent search the detailed requirements of an effective warning. Consent searches are part of the standard investigatory techniques of law enforcement agencies. They normally occur on the highway, or in a person's home or office, and under informal and unstructured conditions. The circumstances that prompt the initial request to search may develop quickly or be a logical extension of investigative police questioning. The police may seek to investigate further suspicious circumstances or to follow up leads developed in questioning persons at the scene of a crime. These situations are a far cry from the structured atmosphere of a trial where, assisted by counsel if he chooses, a defendant is informed of his trial rights. And, while surely a closer question, these situations are still immeasurably, far removed from "custodial interrogation" where, in Miranda v. Arizona, we found that the Constitution required certain now familiar warnings as a prerequisite to police interrogation. Indeed, in language applicable to the typical consent search, we refused to extend the need for warnings:

> "Our decision is not intended to hamper the traditional function of police officers in investigating crime. ... When an individual is in custody on probable cause, the police may, of course, seek out evidence in the field to be used at trial against him. Such investigation may include inquiry of persons not under restraint. General on-the-scene questioning as to facts surrounding a crime or other general questioning of citizens in the fact-finding process is not affected by our holding. It is an act of responsible citizenship for individuals to give whatever information they may have to aid in law enforcement."

Consequently, we cannot accept the position of the Court of Appeals in this case that proof of knowledge of the right to refuse consent is a necessary prerequisite to demonstrating a "voluntary" consent. Rather it is only by analyzing all the circumstances of an individual consent that it can be ascertained whether in fact it was voluntary or coerced. It is this careful sifting of the unique facts and circumstances of each case that is evidenced in our prior decisions involving consent searches.

* * *

The requirement of a "knowing" and "intelligent" waiver was articulated in a case involving the validity of a defendant's decision to forego a right constitutionally guaranteed to protect a fair trial and the reliability of the truth-determining process. Johnson v. Zerbst (1938) dealt with the denial of counsel in a federal criminal trial....

* * *

Almost without exception, the requirement of a knowing and intelligent waiver has been applied only to those rights which the Constitution guarantees to a criminal defendant in order to preserve a fair trial. Hence, and hardly surprisingly in view of the facts of Johnson itself, the standard of a knowing and intelligent waiver has most often been applied to test the validity of a waiver of counsel, either at trial, or upon a guilty plea. And the Court has also applied the Johnson criteria to assess the effectiveness of a waiver of other trial rights such as the right to confrontation, to a jury trial, and to a speedy trial, and the right to be free from twice being placed in jeopardy. Guilty pleas have been carefully scrutinized to determine whether the accused knew and understood all the rights to which he would be entitled at trial, and that he had intentionally chosen to forgo them. And the Court has evaluated the knowing and intelligent nature of the waiver of trial rights in trial-type situations, such as the waiver of the privilege against compulsory self-incrimination before an administrative agency or a congressional committee, or the waiver of counsel in a juvenile proceeding.

The guarantees afforded a criminal defendant at trial also protect him at certain stages before the actual trial, and any alleged waiver must meet the strict standard of an intentional relinquishment of a "known" right. But the "trial" guarantees that have been applied to the "pretrial" stage of the criminal process are similarly designed to protect the fairness of the trial itself.

Hence, in United States v. Wade (1967) and Gilbert v. California (1967), the Court held "that a post-indictment pre-trial lineup at which the accused is exhibited to identifying witnesses is a critical stage of the criminal prosecution; that police conduct of such a lineup without notice to and in the absence of his counsel denies the accused his Sixth [and Fourteenth] Amendment right to counsel. ..." Accordingly, the Court indicated that the standard of a knowing and intelligent waiver must be applied to test the waiver of counsel at such a lineup. The Court stressed the necessary interrelationship between the presence of counsel at a post-indictment lineup before trial and the protection of the trial process itself. ...

And in Miranda v. Arizona (1966) the Court found that custodial interrogation by the police was inherently coercive, and consequently held that detailed warnings were required to protect the privilege against compulsory self-incrimination. The Court made it clear that the basis for decision was the need to protect the fairness of the trial itself. ...

The standards of Johnson were, therefore, found to be a necessary prerequisite to a finding of a valid waiver.

There is a vast difference between those rights that protect a fair criminal trial and the rights guaranteed under the Fourth Amendment. Nothing, either in the purposes behind requiring a "knowing" and "intelligent" waiver of trial rights, or in the practical application of such a requirement suggests that it ought to be extended to the constitutional guarantee against unreasonable searches and seizures.

* * *

It would be unrealistic to expect that in the informal, unstructured context of a consent search, a policeman, upon pain of tainting the evidence obtained, could make the detailed type of examination demanded by Johnson. And, if for this reason a diluted form of "waiver" were found acceptable, that would itself be ample recognition of the fact that there is no universal standard that must be applied in every situation where a person foregoes a constitutional right.

* * *

Our decision today is a narrow one. We hold only that when the subject of a search is not in custody and the State attempts to justify a search on the basis of his consent, the Fourth and Fourteenth Amendments require that it demonstrate that the consent was in fact voluntarily given, and not the result of duress or coercion, express or implied. Voluntariness is a question of fact to be determined from all the circumstances, and while the subject's knowledge of a right to refuse is a factor to be taken into account, the prosecution is not required to demonstrate such knowledge as a prerequisite to establishing a voluntary consent. Because the California court followed these principles in affirming the respondent's conviction, and because the Court of Appeals for the Ninth Circuit in remanding for an evidentiary hearing required more, its judgment must be reversed.

It is so ordered.

Judgment of Court of Appeals reversed.

[Justice Blackmun concurred. In a separate concurring opinion, Justice Powell, joined by Chief Justice Burger and Justice Rehnquist agreed as to the consent search question. The thrust of Powell's opinion, however, was that the use of federal habeas corpus to litigate Fourth Amendment claims should be sharply limited. This suggestion was later accepted in Stone v. Powell. Justice Douglas dissented, arguing that a hearing should be held to determine whether Alcala knew his rights and suggesting that the issue would be moot if he did. Justice Brennan wrote a brief dissent, asserting: "It wholly escapes me how our citizens meaningfully can be said to have waived something as precious as a constitutional guarantee without ever being aware of its existence." Justice Marshall wrote a dissent calling for a requirement of a knowing consent and indicating that appropriate Fourth Amendment warnings would prima facie satisfy the prosecution's burden.]

NOTES

1. *Consent or Coercion?* In preliminary remarks in a perceptive article concerning involuntary confessions, Professor Joseph Grano points out that voluntariness, under the Supreme Court decisions, means different things in different contexts. In insisting upon voluntariness in consent search case, Grano notes, the Court has assigned little weight to the cognitive aspect: a person can voluntarily consent without knowing his rights. However, the Court has suggested "that even 'implied' or subtle coercion will render the consent involuntary." On the other hand, Grano notes, in the cases in which the Court has considered guilty pleas (see Chapter 16), the Court has insisted that the accused know his rights but has de-emphasized the volitional aspect of voluntariness by permitting significant pressures in the plea-bargaining process to influence the accused's determination of whether to plead guilty. See Grano, Voluntariness, Free Will, and The Law of Confessions, 65 Va.L.Rev.859 (1979).

When the prosecution relies upon a consent search theory, it has the burden of establishing that the consent was voluntary, Bumper v. North Carolina, 391 U.S. 543, 88 S.Ct. 1788 (1968), by a preponderance of evidence. See United States v. Hurtado, 905 F.2d 74 (5th Cir.1990) (en banc).

Although the test for consent in Schnecklothe has been criticized, the Court reaffirmed this approach in Ohio v. Robinette, 519 U.S. 33, 117 S.Ct. 417 (1996). An officer stopped a car for speeding, but then decided not to ticket the driver. Nevertheless, the officer continued the stop, ordered the driver our of the car and obtained consent to search. The Ohio court ruled that the motorist was seized because an ordinary person would not feel free to leave. Therefore, the consent was not voluntary unless the police officer told him he was free to leave. Ohio adopted a bright-line rule requiring officers completing traffic stops to warn drivers they are free to leave before asking for consent to search their cars. The Supreme Court disagreed and held that consent must be determined on a case-by-case basis under all the circumstances. On remand, the Ohio court held that, on the facts of the case, the state did not satisfy its burden to prove consent in the absence of a free-to-go advisory. 80 Ohio St.3d 234, 685 N.E.2d 762 (1997).

A. *Deception.* A false assertion that officers have the present right to search will vitiate the consent. *Bumper* (claim that officers had a warrant; warrant never produced; consent cannot be demonstrated by mere "acquiescence to a claim of lawful authority"); United States v. J. B. Kramer Grocery Co., 418 F.2d 987 (8th Cir.1969) (false assertion of right to make an administrative inspection). The mere threat to seek a warrant, however, (especially if probable cause sufficed to get a warrant) does not render a consent involuntary. See Comment, Consent to Search in Response to Police Threats to Seek or Obtain a Search Warrant, 71 J.Crim.L. & Crim. 136 (1980). United States v. Stallings, 810 F.2d 973 (10th Cir.1987). Compare Dotson v. Somers, 175 Conn. 614, 402 A.2d 790 (1978) (threat to obtain a warrant may invalidate consent absent probable cause for issuance of a warrant). And, compare Commonwealth v. Brown, 437 Pa. 1, 261 A.2d 879 (1970) (officer told defendant he would sell gun and instead had a ballistics test run) with Graves v. Beto, 424 F.2d 524 (5th Cir.1970) (defendant told blood sample was for alcohol test but it was used to type his blood for comparison with blood stains in rape case). When a government agent uses deception to gain entry to a home or other place not open to the public, the entry is illegal if the right to enter depends upon consent (and not, for example upon a valid search warrant), and if the deception consists of an assertion that the agent has come to engage in some lawful, non-law enforcement activity. Thus, posing as a meter reader will invalidate a consent. People v. Dalpe, 371 Ill. 607, 21 N.E.2d 756 (1939) ("It is the houseman. . . .") On the other hand, if the government agent through deception secures an invitation to do unlawful business, the entry is valid. On Lee v. United States, 343 U.S. 747, 72 S.Ct. 967 (1952); Lewis v. United States, 385 U.S. 206, 87 S.Ct. 424 (1966). Where an undercover officer or an informant is admitted to a home in order to purchase or deliver drugs, some courts have held that consent given to that person is also assent for the immediate entry by police into the same home to arrest and search. The issue is controversial. See the discussions in the majority and dissenting opinions in State v. Henry, 133 N.J. 104, 627 A.2d 125 (1993).

B. *Threats*. Threats or violence are likely to invalidate a consent. Waldron v. United States, 219 F.2d 37 (D.C.Cir.1955) (police told young expectant mother that they could not be responsible for the conditions of the house if they had to get a warrant); United States v. Kampbell, 574 F.2d 962 (8th Cir.1978) (threat to trash the house). But see, United States v. Wilkinson, 926 F.2d 22 (1st Cir.1991) (consent to search voluntary even though officers entered home with guns drawn, handcuffed and frisked the defendant, and threatened to "tear the place apart.")

C. *Illegal Arrest*. In Florida v. Royer, discussed earlier, the plurality held a consent search to be invalid because it was immediately preceded by an unlawful arrest. The remaining justices did not object to the proposition that if the suspect was unlawfully arrested, his consent was involuntary. Some courts invalidate consent searches following illegal arrests by declaring that the consent was the fruit of the illegal arrest. In so doing, they do not find it necessary to deem the consent involuntary. See, e.g., People v. Harris, 159 Ill.App.3d 592, 111 Ill.Dec. 176, 512 N.E.2d 80 (1987) (illegal arrest tainted consent even though consent was voluntary). See generally W. LaFave, Search and Seizure § 8.2(d) (2d Ed.1987), noting that the two tests are not identical and that a consent must be both voluntary and not the product of antecedent governmental illegality.

Consent to search given at later time, however, may not be tainted by an illegal arrest. Brown v. Illinois, 422 U.S. 590, 95 S.Ct. 2254 (1975) (considering the length of time between the illegal activity and subsequent search, whether Miranda warnings were given, intervening circumstances, and the flagrancy of the misconduct).

D. *Cognitive Impairment*. Individual characteristics of the consenting person may be relevant to a determination of voluntariness. United States v. Elrod, 441 F.2d 353 (5th Cir.1971) (incompetent individual); United States v. Williams, 544 F.2d 807 (5th Cir.1977), and White v. State, 261 Ark. 23–D, 545 S.W.2d 641 (1977) (intoxicated individual); Laasch v. State, 84 Wis.2d 587, 267 N.W.2d 278 (1978) (consent to enter granted by five-year old is invalid). But see, United States v. George, 987 F.2d 1428 (9th Cir.1993) (consent to search motel room valid even though given by defendant in emergency room recovering from drug overdose.)

E. *Conditional Consent*. Is it valid consent if the defendant agrees to an open search policy as a condition of probation? In United States v. Knights, 534 U.S. 112, 122 S.Ct. 587 (2001), the trial court sentenced the defendant to probation for a drug offense. The sentence included the condition that he submit to a search at anytime, with or without a search or arrest warrant or reasonable cause, by any probation or law enforcement officer. A sheriff's deputy searched the defendant's home and found evidence of a crime unrelated to his probationary status. At the hearing on the motion to suppress, the trial court upheld the search. The United States Supreme Court agreed, measuring the law enforcement conduct against a standard of reasonableness using a totality of the circumstances test. [The Court explicitly left open whether the acceptance of the search provision as a condition of probation constituted consent] * * *

2. *Relation to Miranda and Illegal Arrests.* In United States v. Watson, 423 U.S. 411, 96 S.Ct. 820 (1976), the United States Supreme Court held that Fourth Amendment warnings were not essential even where the consenting party was in police custody. In Watson, while there was custody, there was not police station custody with its inherently coercive atmosphere.

Many courts have upheld consent searches, in the absence of warnings, even when the consenting individual was in custody at a police station. However, where a suspect is in custody, the absence of warnings may be given significant weight in determining whether a consent is voluntary under the totality of the circumstances. United States v. Heimforth, 493 F.2d 970 (9th Cir.1974). A suspect's request to consult counsel may make it difficult for the prosecution to establish the voluntariness of a consent in the absence of counsel. United States v. McCraney, 705 F.2d 449 (5th Cir.1983); People v. Johnson, 48 N.Y.2d 565, 423 N.Y.S.2d 905, 399 N.E.2d 936 (1979).

Frequently a consent issue arises when a defendant claims that a statement which he gave while under arrest should be suppressed because the arrest was unlawful for want of probable cause. Often the prosecution responds by asserting that the defendant had voluntarily accompanied authorities to the place of detention and was not under arrest. The issue then is whether the suspect merely acquiesced to a show of authority or instead voluntarily agreed to accompany the authorities. Varying factual situations have led to some victories for the prosecution and some for the defense in state and federal reviewing courts. The prosecution's consent theory prevailed in United States v. Mendenhall, 446 U.S. 544, 100 S.Ct. 1870 (1980), but not in Dunaway v. New York, 442 U.S. 200, 99 S.Ct. 2248 (1979).

3. *Scope of the Search.* A person who consents to a search may limit the scope of the search and those limitations must be respected. United States v. Dichiarinte, 445 F.2d 126 (7th Cir.1971) (consent to search for narcotics does not confer authority to search for papers). See the excellent discussion in State v. Koucoules, 343 A.2d 860 (Me.1974). A consent to enter does not authorize a search. Gouled v. United States, 255 U.S. 298, 41 S.Ct. 261 (1921). See also Justice Marshall's dissent from the denial of certiorari in Zeigler v. Florida, 455 U.S. 1035, 102 S.Ct. 1739 (1982). Marshall contended that the court below had improperly treated a citizen's summoning of police assistance at his home as a consent to conduct a search over a period of twelve days.

In Florida v. Jimeno, 500 U.S. 248, 111 S.Ct. 1801 (1991), following a traffic stop, an officer told the driver that he believed the driver was carrying narcotics in his car. He said he was looking for narcotics and obtained consent to search the vehicle after admonishing the suspect of his right not to consent. Supposedly the suspect said he had nothing to hide. Apparently this statement was not altogether accurate: the officer found a kilogram of cocaine inside a brown paper bag on the floorboard of the car.

The Florida Supreme Court upheld a trial judge's decision to exclude the cocaine, holding that the consent to search the car did not authorize a search of the paper bag found in the car. The United States Supreme Court disagreed and overturned the suppression order. It declared:

> A reasonable person may be expected to know that narcotics are generally carried in some form of a container. "Contraband goods rarely are strewn across the trunk or floor of a car." United States v. Ross (1982). The authorization to search in this case, therefore, extended beyond the surface of the car's interior to the paper bag lying on the floor's interior.

The dissent responded:

> By the same logic a person who consents to a search of the car ... could also be deemed to consent to a search of his person or indeed of his body cavities, since a reasonable person may be expected to know that drug carriers frequently store their contraband on their persons or in their body cavities.... The majority ... never identifies a reason for conflating distinct privacy expectations that a person has in cars and in closed containers.

4. *Third–Party Consent.* In third-party consent cases, if Officer *A* obtains an involuntary consent from *B* to search the joint property of *B* and *C*, the search is illegal even as to *C*. The question of standing is not involved. Absent the voluntary consent of someone who had sufficient authority, the search of the property is illegal as to all persons who have a reasonable expectation of privacy as to the place searched. In Bumper, note 3, supra, the search and seizure was illegal as to the cotenant grandson even though it was the grandmother whose consent was deemed involuntary. Schneckloth also involved the voluntariness of consent by a third party.

The question as to who can consent usually arises where a defendant challenges the reasonableness of a search made under the purported authority of a consent granted by someone else. Rarely will a defendant claim that he himself had no authority to consent. Ordinarily, if he had an insufficient relationship to the property to authorize a consent search then he will have an insufficient relationship to the property to merit standing. In one case where the defendant attacked his own authority to consent, the court invoked an estoppel theory to defeat his claim. State v. Cole, 337 So.2d 1067 (La.1976).

When the question as to who can consent is posed, an examination is made of the person's relationship to the property to determine whether it was reasonable to conduct a search under his consent. One approach to third-party consent cases is to inquire whether *A* had the right to waive *B*'s rights. Usually this is a defense-oriented phrasing of the issue, although the Court in Amos v. United States, 255 U.S. 313, 41 S.Ct. 266 (1921), phrased the issue in precisely those terms. *A* more modern and, at the same time, more neutral posing of the issue asks whether *A* himself had a sufficient relationship to the property to make his or her consent effective. See United States v. Matlock, 415 U.S. 164, 94 S.Ct. 988 (1974), and Frazier v. Cupp, 394 U.S. 731, 89 S.Ct. 1420 (1969). Under this phrasing *A* is exercising his or her own rights over the property by consenting, not waiving someone else's rights.

Another analytical approach raises the question whether *B* had such a reasonable expectation of privacy in the property as to render *A*'s consent ineffective. A number of consent search cases utilize the reasonable expectation of privacy concept, borrowed from Katz v. United States, 389 U.S. 347, 88 S.Ct. 507 (1967). Typical is People v. Nunn, 55 Ill.2d 344, 304 N.E.2d 81 (1973). The Supreme Court of the United States, however, has never taken this approach to consent searches. Indeed, in Mancusi v. DeForte, 392 U.S. 364, 88 S.Ct. 2120 (1968), the Court noted that even though the accused had a sufficient reasonable expectation of privacy to merit standing, this expectation would not necessarily preclude a valid third-party consent. Later, in Matlock, the Court again avoided injecting *Katz* notions into consent search cases. Subsequently, the Illinois Supreme Court followed suit in People v. Stacey, 58 Ill.2d 83, 317 N.E.2d 24 (1974), where it sharply limited Nunn and the significance attributed to *Katz* in consent cases. For now it is probably safe to analyze third-party consent cases in traditional terms and without reference to *Katz*.

Following is a summary of the various situations in which third parties might have joint access or control of property to be searched:

(a) A landlord cannot consent to search of tenant's apartment. Chapman v. United States, 365 U.S. 610, 81 S.Ct. 776 (1961). The landlord may consent if the tenant has vacated the premises. A landlord may consent to search of common areas. On the same principle, a hotel manager cannot consent to the search of a hotel room during the rental period. United States v. Winsor, 846 F.2d 1569 (9th Cir.1988) (en banc).

(b) Generally a university official cannot consent to a police search of a student's dormitory room. United States v. Kress, 446 F.2d 358 (9th Cir.1971); Commonwealth v. McCloskey, 217 Pa.Super. 432, 272 A.2d 271 (1970); Piazzola v. Watkins, 442 F.2d 284 (5th Cir.1971).

(c) Co-tenants can consent to search of property they share with each other. Frazier v. Cupp, 394 U.S. 731, 89 S.Ct. 1420 (1969); United States v. Matlock, 415 U.S. 164, 94 S.Ct. 988 (1974).

(d) A spouse who is a co-tenant can consent to search of jointly occupied premises, Commonwealth v. Martin, 358 Mass. 282, 264 N.E.2d 366 (1970), even if parties are antagonistic, State v. McCarthy, 26 Ohio St.2d 87, 269 N.E.2d 424 (1971); People v. Koshiol, 45 Ill.2d 573, 262 N.E.2d 446 (1970). A lover may also consent to the search if he or she has jointly occupied the premises for a period of time. White v. United States, 444 F.2d 724 (10th Cir.1971); United States v. Wilson, 447 F.2d 1 (9th Cir.1971). But see, Illinois v. Rodriguez, 497 U.S. 177, 110 S.Ct. 2793 (1990) (no authority to consent when woman had moved herself and her children out of apartment, paid no rent, not named on lease, only spent night there occasionally, still had key, and left behind some furniture and possessions) however, some jurisdictions recognize some limits upon the authority for a particular seizure. Hawaii v. Evans, 45 Haw. 622, 372 P.2d 365 (1962) (wife cannot consent to search of husband's possessions); United States ex rel. Cabey v. Mazurkiewicz, 431 F.2d 839 (3d Cir.1970) (wife cannot consent to search of garage where husband is sole lessee and has only key); People v. Elders, 63 Ill.App.3d 554, 20 Ill.Dec. 333, 380 N.E.2d 10 (1978) (one spouse had exclusive control of car).

(e) Consent by parents or children pose knotty problems. Some courts hold that a parent can consent to the search of a child's room. State v. Schotl, 289 Minn. 175, 182 N.W.2d 878 (1971) (twenty-two-year-old son); United States v. Evans, 27 F.3d 1219 (7th Cir.1994) (defendant's father owned garage, paid utility bills, and had complete access to it, though defendant used it as place of business). Where the son or daughter has exclusive use of a particular room, however, other courts have invalidated parental consent. United States v. Whitfield, 939 F.2d 1071 (D.C.Cir.1991) (invalidating mother's consent to search adult son's room). Other relatives may have a right to consent under some circumstances. Consent by adult, married sister to search of home owned by the parents of her and her defendant brother was held proper in Garr v. Commonwealth, 463 S.W.2d 109 (Ky.1971). Consent by children may also be effective. United States v. Clutter, 914 F.2d 775 (6th Cir.1990) (12 and 14–year-old children had authority to consent because routinely left in exclusive control of house and had access to parent's bedroom). The "exclusive use" doctrine, however, may limit the scope of the search in these cases also. Thus in Shorey v. Warden, 401 F.2d 474 (4th Cir.1968), a sister who owned a home was said not to be authorized to consent to the search of her brother's bedroom in her home. In People v. Overall, 7 Mich.App. 153, 151 N.W.2d 225 (1967), a grandmother was held not authorized to consent to the search of a room occupied by her grandson.

(f) A host may permit the search of the guest's room but not the search of closed recesses and the seizure of the guest's personal property. United States v. Block, 590 F.2d 535 (4th Cir.1978) (footlocker). The exclusive use limitation may also be applied in these cases. Burge v. United States, 333 F.2d 210 (9th Cir.1964).

(g) The area of employer-employee authority to consent is not well settled. See United States v. Blok, 188 F.2d 1019 (D.C.Cir.1951) (employer's consent to search of employee's desk invalid); Braddock v. State, 127 Ga.App. 513, 194 S.E.2d 317 (1972) (truck owner may consent to search of his truck even though evidence discovered is used against employee-driver); People v. Smith, 43 Mich.App. 400, 204 N.W.2d 308 (1972) (employee cannot consent to police inspection of calculator owned by employer). Cases in which government itself is the consenting party probably lend themselves to a reasonable expectation of privacy analysis better than do cases in which a private third-party grants the consent. Concerning governmental searches of the public employee's workplace, see O'Connor v. Ortega, 480 U.S. 709, 107 S.Ct. 1492 (1987).

(h) Does a kidnap victim have actual or apparent authority to consent to a seizure of firearms in her captor's closet? A Sixth Circuit majority held no. The dissent argued that the defendant lost any expectation of privacy in his apartment when he converted it to a "prison." United States v. Johnson, 22 F.3d 674 (6th Cir.1994).

Sometimes a law enforcement officer will conduct a search pursuant to the consent of a person who, from all the facts known to the officer, clearly appears to have authority over property, but who, as it turns out, has no such authority. Is such a search reasonable? The true property owner may ask, "How can an officer derive the right to search my property from someone who had no authority over my property?" The officer might respond, "How can I be accused of making an unreasonable search when in good faith I reasonably concluded that the consenting party was the owner?" ...

In Illinois v. Rodriguez, 497 U.S. 177, 110 S.Ct. 2793 (1990), the Court validated the concept of a consent search based upon "apparent authority." The majority stated that a search is not unreasonable, within the meaning of the Fourth Amendment, "when officers enter without a warrant because they reasonably (though erroneously) believe that the person who has consented to their entry is a resident of the premises ..." It added:

> Even when the invitation is accompanied by an explicit assertion that the person lives there, the surrounding circumstances could conceivably be such that a reasonable person would doubt its truth and not act upon it without further inquiry. As with other factual determinations bearing upon search and seizure, determination of consent to enter must "be judged against an objective standard: would the facts available to the officer at the moment ... 'warrant a man of reasonable caution in the belief' " that the consenting party had authority over the premises? Terry v. Ohio (1968). If not, then warrantless entry without further inquiry is unlawful unless authority actually exists. But if so, the search is valid.

Three dissenters objected, saying:

> Our cases demonstrate that third-party consent searches are free from constitutional challenge only to the extent that they rest on consent by a party empowered to do so. The majority's conclusion to the contrary ignores the legitimate expectations of privacy on which individuals are entitled to rely. That a person who allows another joint access over his property thereby limits his expectation of privacy does not justify tram-

pling the rights of a person who has not similarly relinquished any of his privacy expectation.

Does Rodriguez apply the *Leon* good faith exception (discussed in chapter 6) to the warantless context of consent?

The Hawaii Supreme Court rejected the theory of "apparent authority" for purposes of state constitutional analysis. The court reasoned that the exclusionary rule in Hawaii is not only to deter police misconduct but also to protect the privacy rights of citizens. State v. Lopez, 78 Hawai'i 433, 896 P.2d 889 (1995).

Can a police officer seek consent from a second co-occupant even after the first has refused? See United States v. Morning, 64 F.3d 531 (9th Cir.1995) (yes); Silva v. State, 344 So.2d 559 (Fla.1977) (no).

A situation analogous to third party consent occurs when, instead of consenting to a search, the third party seizes the evidence and brings it to the police. No question of the legality of the seizure will be raised in the criminal trial because no motion to suppress lies where the search was conducted by a private citizen acting on his own. Cf. Coolidge v. New Hampshire, 403 U.S. 443, 91 S.Ct. 2022 (1971). Whenever the private citizen acts in concert with the police, state action will be found.

Georgia v. Randolph

Supreme Court of the United States, 2006.
547 U.S. 103, 126 S.Ct. 1515.

SUMMARY:

When a police officer was at a married couple's house in Georgia as a result of the wife contacting the police concerning a domestic dispute, the wife, in the presence of the husband, volunteered to the officer that there was in the house evidence of the husband's illegal drug use. The husband then unequivocally refused the officer's request for permission for a warrantless search of the house. However, the wife then consented to a search and led the officer to the evidence. The police seized this evidence and, after obtaining a search warrant, seized further evidence of drug use.

The husband was indicted under state law for cocaine possession. He moved to suppress the evidence in question on the asserted basis that it had been obtained as a result of an illegal search. However, the state trial court, ruling that the wife had common authority to consent to the search, denied the motion.

The Court of Appeals of Georgia reversed (264 Ga. App. 396, 590 S.E. 2d 834), and the Georgia Supreme Court (1) determined that the wife's consent to the search was invalid in the face of the physically-present husband's refusal, and (2) upheld the Court of Appeals' decision (278 Ga. 614, 604 S.E. 2d 835).

On certiorari, the United States Supreme Court affirmed. In an opinion by Souter, J., joined by Stevens, Kennedy, Ginsburg, and Breyer, JJ., it was held that the search was invalid under the Federal Constitution's Fourth Amendment as to the husband, as (1) for Fourth Amendment purposes, a physically present occupant's express refusal of consent to a police search of a premises was dispositive as to that occupant, regardless of the consent of a fellow occupant; (2) the husband's refusal was clear; and

(3) nothing in the record justified the search on grounds independent of the wife's consent, for the state did not argue that (a) the wife had given any indication to the police of a need for protection inside the house that might have justified entry into the area where the officer found the evidence, or (b) the entry and search should have been upheld under the rubric of exigent circumstances.

Stevens, J., concurring, said that assuming that both a husband and a wife were competent, neither one was a master possessing the power to override the other's constitutional right to deny entry to their "castle."

Breyer, J., concurring, expressed the view that (1) the reasonableness of a search under the Fourth Amendment was measured by examining the totality of the circumstances; (2) in the instant case, (a) the search was solely for evidence, (b) the objecting party was present and made his objection known clearly and directly to the police, (c) the police did not justify their search on grounds of possible evidence destruction, and (d) as far as the record revealed, the police might easily have secured the premises and sought a warrant permitting them to enter; and (3) thus, the totality of the circumstances did not suffice to justify warrantless entry.

Roberts, Ch. J., joined by Scalia, J., dissenting, said that (1) a warrantless search of premises was reasonable under the Fourth Amendment if police obtained the voluntary consent of a person authorized to give it; (2) co-occupants of premises assumed the risk that one of their number might permit a common area to be searched; (3) the Supreme Court's rule was random in its application, as that rule protected not so much privacy as the good luck of a co-owner who happened to be present at the door when the police arrived; and (4) the consequences of the Supreme Court's rule would be severe, especially in domestic-abuse situations.

Scalia, J., dissenting, expressed the view that (1) from the date of the Fourth Amendment's ratification until well into the 20th century, someone who had power to license the search of a house by a private party could authorize a police search; (2) the issue of who could give such consent generally depended on historical and legal refinements of property law; and (3) changes in the law of property to which the Fourth Amendment referred would not alter the Amendment's meaning that anyone capable of authorizing a search by a private party could consent to a warrantless search by the police.

Thomas, J., dissenting, expressed the view that (1) the Supreme Court had held in Coolidge v. New Hampshire (1971) 403 U.S. 443, 91 S. Ct. 2022, 29 L. Ed. 2d 564, that no Fourth Amendment search occurred where, as in the instant case, the spouse of an accused voluntarily led the police to potential evidence of wrongdoing by the accused; and (2) in the instant case, (a) Coolidge squarely controlled, and (b) thus, the court did not need to address whether police could permissibly have conducted a general search of the home on the basis of the wife's consent.

Alito, J., did not participate.

SYLLABUS

Respondent's estranged wife gave police permission to search the marital residence for items of drug use after respondent, who was also present, had unequivocally refused to give consent. Respondent was indicted for possession of cocaine, and the trial court denied his motion to suppress the evidence as products of a warrantless search unauthorized by consent. The Georgia Court of Appeals reversed. In affirming, the State Supreme Court held that consent given by one occupant is not valid in the face of the refusal of another physically present occupant, and distinguished *United States v. Matlock*, 415 U.S. 164, 94 S. Ct. 988, 39 L. Ed. 2d 242, which recognized the permissibility of an entry made with the consent of one co-occupant in the other's absence.

Held:

In the circumstances here at issue, a physically present co-occupant's stated refusal to permit entry renders warrantless entry and search unreasonable and invalid as to him.

(a) The Fourth Amendment recognizes a valid warrantless entry and search of a premises when the police obtain the voluntary consent of an occupant who shares, or is reasonably believed to share, common authority over the property, and no present co-tenant objects. *Matlock, supra*, at 170, 94 S. Ct. 988, 39 L. Ed. 2d 242; *Illinois v. Rodriguez*, 497 U.S. 177, 186, 110 S. Ct. 2793, 111 L. Ed. 2d 148. The constant element in assessing Fourth Amendment reasonableness in such cases is the great significance given to widely shared social expectations, which are influenced by property law but not controlled by its rules. Thus, *Matlock* not only holds that a solitary co-inhabitant may sometimes consent to a search of shared premises, but also stands for the proposition that the reasonableness of such a search is in significant part a function of commonly held understandings about the authority that co-inhabitants may exercise in ways that affect each other's interests.

(b) *Matlock*'s example of common understanding is readily apparent. The assumption tenants usually make about their common authority when they share quarters is that any one of them may admit visitors, with the consequence that a guest obnoxious to one may be admitted in his absence. *Matlock* placed no burden on the police to eliminate the possibility of atypical arrangements, absent reason to doubt that the regular scheme was in place.

(c) This Court took a step toward addressing the issue here when it held in *Minnesota v. Olson*, 495 U.S. 91, 110 S. Ct. 1684, 109 L. Ed. 2d 85, that overnight houseguests have a legitimate expectation of privacy in their temporary quarters. If that customary expectation is a foundation of a houseguest's Fourth Amendment rights, it should follow that an inhabitant of shared premises may claim at least as much. In fact, a co-inhabitant naturally has an even stronger claim. No sensible person would enter shared premises based on one occupant's invitation when a fellow tenant said to stay out. Such reticence would show not timidity but a realization that when people living together disagree over the use of their common quarters, a resolution must come through voluntary accommodation, not by appeals to authority. Absent some recognized hierarchy, *e.g.*, parent and child, there is no societal or legal understanding of superior and inferior as between co-tenants.

(d) Thus, a disputed invitation, without more, gives an officer no better claim to reasonableness in entering than the officer would have absent any consent. Disputed permission is no match for the Fourth Amendment central value of "respect for the privacy of the home," *Wilson v. Layne*, 526 U.S. 603, 610, 119 S. Ct. 1692, 143 L. Ed. 2d 818, and the State's other countervailing claims do not add up to outweigh it.

A co-tenant who has an interest in bringing criminal activity to light or in deflecting suspicion from himself can, *e.g.*, tell the police what he knows, for use before a magistrate in getting a warrant. This case, which recognizes limits on evidentiary searches, has no bearing on the capacity of the police, at the invitation of one tenant, to enter a dwelling over another tenant's objection in order to protect a resident from domestic violence. Though alternatives to disputed consent will not always open the door to search for evidence that the police suspect is inside, nothing in social custom or its reflection in private law argues for placing a higher value on delving into private premises to search for evidence in the face of disputed consent, than on requiring clear justification before the government searches private living quarters over a resident's objection.

(e) There are two loose ends. First, while *Matlock*'s explanation for the constitutional sufficiency of a co-tenant's consent to enter and search recognized a co-inhabitant's "right to permit the inspection in his own right," 415 U.S., at 171, n. 7, 94 S. Ct. 988, 39 L. Ed. 2d 242, the right to admit the police is not a right as understood under property law. It is, instead, the authority recognized by customary social usage as having a substantial bearing on Fourth Amendment reasonableness in specific circumstances. The question here is whether customary social understanding accords the consenting tenant authority to prevail over the co-tenant's objection, a question *Matlock* did not answer. Second, a fine line must be drawn to avoid undercutting *Matlock*—where the defendant, though not present, was in a squad car not far away—and *Rodriguez*—where the defendant was asleep in the apartment and could have been roused by a knock on the door; if a potential defendant with self-interest in objecting is in fact at the door and objects, the co-tenant's permission does not suffice for a reasonable search, whereas the potential objector, nearby but not part of the threshold colloquy, loses out. Such formalism is justified. So long as there is no evidence that the police have removed the potentially objecting tenant from the entrance specifically to avoid a possible objection, there is practical value in the simple clarity of complementary rules, one recognizing the co-tenant's permission when no fellow occupant is on hand, the other according dispositive weight to the fellow occupant's expressed contrary indication.

(f) Here, respondent's refusal is clear, and nothing in the record justifies the search on grounds independent of his wife's consent.

278 Ga. 614, 604 S. E. 2d 835, affirmed.

JUDGES: Souter, J., delivered the opinion of the Court, in which Stevens, Kennedy, Ginsburg, and Breyer, JJ., joined. Stevens, J., *post*, p. 123; and Breyer, J.,, *post*, p. 125, filed concurring opinions. Roberts, C. J., filed a dissenting opinion, in which Scalia, J., joined, *post*, p. 127. Scalia, J., *post*,

p. 142, and Thomas, J., *post*, p. 145, filed dissenting opinions. Alito, J., took no part in the consideration or decision of the case.

■ Justice Souter delivered the opinion of the Court.

The Fourth Amendment recognizes a valid warrantless entry and search of premises when police obtain the voluntary consent of an occupant who shares, or is reasonably believed to share, authority over the area in common with a co-occupant who later objects to the use of evidence so obtained. Illinois v. Rodriguez (1990); United States v. Matlock (1974). The question here is whether such an evidentiary seizure is likewise lawful with the permission of one occupant when the other, who later seeks to suppress the evidence, is present at the scene and expressly refuses to consent. We hold that, in the circumstances here at issue, a physically present co-occupant's stated refusal to permit entry prevails, rendering the warrantless search unreasonable and invalid as to him.

I

Respondent Scott Randolph and his wife, Janet, separated in late May 2001, when she left the marital residence in Americus, Georgia, and went to stay with her parents in Canada, taking their son and some belongings. In July, she returned to the Americus house with the child, though the record does not reveal whether her object was reconciliation or retrieval of remaining possessions.

On the morning of July 6, she complained to the police that after a domestic dispute her husband took their son away, and when officers reached the house she told them that her husband was a cocaine user whose habit had caused financial troubles. She mentioned the marital problems and said that she and their son had only recently returned after a stay of several weeks with her parents. Shortly after the police arrived, Scott Randolph returned and explained that he had removed the child to a neighbor's house out of concern that his wife might take the boy out of the country again; he denied cocaine use, and countered that it was in fact his wife who abused drugs and alcohol.

One of the officers, Sergeant Murray, went with Janet Randolph to reclaim the child, and when they returned she not only renewed her complaints about her husband's drug use, but also volunteered that there were " 'items of drug evidence' " in the house. Sergeant Murray asked Scott Randolph for permission to search the house, which he unequivocally refused.

The sergeant turned to Janet Randolph for consent to search, which she readily gave. She led the officer upstairs to a bedroom that she identified as Scott's, where the sergeant noticed a section of a drinking straw with a powdery residue he suspected was cocaine. He then left the house to get an evidence bag from his car and to call the district attorney's office, which instructed him to stop the search and apply for a warrant. When Sergeant Murray returned to the house, Janet Randolph withdrew her consent. The police took the straw to the police station, along with the Randolphs. After getting a search warrant, they returned to the house and seized further evidence of drug use, on the basis of which Scott Randolph was indicted for possession of cocaine.

He moved to suppress the evidence, as products of a warrantless search of his house unauthorized by his wife's consent over his express refusal. The trial court denied the motion, ruling that Janet Randolph had common authority to consent to the search.

The Court of Appeals of Georgia reversed and was itself sustained by the State Supreme Court, principally on the ground that "the consent to conduct a warrantless search of a residence given by one occupant is not valid in the face of the refusal of another occupant who is physically present at the scene to permit a warrantless search." The Supreme Court of Georgia acknowledged this Court's holding in *Matlock* that "the consent of one who possesses common authority over premises or effects is valid as against the absent, nonconsenting person with whom that authority is shared," and found *Matlock* distinguishable just because Scott Randolph was not "absent" from the colloquy on which the police relied for consent to make the search. The State Supreme Court stressed that the officers in *Matlock* had not been "faced with the physical presence of joint occupants, with one consenting to the search and the other objecting." It held that an individual who chooses to live with another assumes a risk no greater than " 'an inability to control access to the premises during [his] absence,' " and does not contemplate that his objection to a request to search commonly shared premises, if made, will be overlooked.

We granted certiorari to resolve a split of authority on whether one occupant may give law enforcement effective consent to search shared premises, as against a co-tenant who is present and states a refusal to permit the search. We now affirm.

II

To the Fourth Amendment rule ordinarily prohibiting the warrantless entry of a person's house as unreasonable *per se*, one "jealously and carefully drawn" exception recognizes the validity of searches with the voluntary consent of an individual possessing authority. That person might be the householder against whom evidence is sought, or a fellow occupant who shares common authority over property, when the suspect is absent, and the exception for consent extends even to entries and searches with the permission of a co-occupant whom the police reasonably, but erroneously, believe to possess shared authority as an occupant. None of our co-occupant consent-to-search cases, however, has presented the further fact of a second occupant physically present and refusing permission to search, and later moving to suppress evidence so obtained. 2The significance of such a refusal turns on the underpinnings of the co-occupant consent rule, as recognized since *Matlock*.

A

The defendant in that case was arrested in the yard of a house where he lived with a Mrs. Graff and several of her relatives, and was detained in a squad car parked nearby. When the police went to the door, Mrs. Graff admitted them and consented to a search of the house. In resolving the defendant's objection to use of the evidence taken in the warrantless search, we said that "the consent of one who possesses common authority over premises or effects is valid as against the absent, nonconsenting person with whom that authority is shared." Consistent with our prior understanding that Fourth Amendment rights are not limited by the law of property, we explained that the third party's "common authority" is not synonymous with a technical property interest:

> The authority which justifies the third-party consent does not rest upon the law of property, with its attendant historical and legal refinements, but rests rather on mutual use of the property by persons generally having joint access or control for most purposes, so that it is reasonable to recognize that any of the co-inhabitants has the right to permit the inspection in his own right and that the others have assumed the risk that one of their number might permit the common area to be searched.

.... The common authority that counts under the Fourth Amendment may thus be broader than the rights accorded by property law, although its limits, too, reflect specialized tenancy arrangements apparent to the police....

The constant element in assessing Fourth Amendment reasonableness in the consent cases, then, is the great significance given to widely shared social expectations, which are naturally enough influenced by the law of property, but not controlled by its rules.... *Matlock* accordingly not only holds that a solitary co-inhabitant may sometimes consent to a search of shared premises, but stands for the proposition that the reasonableness of such a search is in significant part a function of commonly held understanding about the authority that co-inhabitants may exercise in ways that affect each other's interests.

B

Matlock's example of common understanding is readily apparent. When someone comes to the door of a domestic dwelling with a baby at her hip, as Mrs. Graff did, she shows that she belongs there, and that fact standing alone is enough to tell a law enforcement officer or any other visitor that if she occupies the place along with others, she probably lives there subject to the assumption tenants usually make about their common authority when they share quarters. They understand that any one of them may admit visitors, with the consequence that a guest obnoxious to one may nevertheless be admitted in his absence by another. As *Matlock* put it, shared tenancy is understood to include an "assumption of risk," on which police officers are entitled to rely, and although some group living together might make an exceptional arrangement that no one could admit a guest without the agreement of all, the chance of such an eccentric scheme is too remote to expect visitors to investigate a particular household's rules before accepting an invitation to come in. So, *Matlock* relied on what was usual and placed no burden on the police to eliminate the possibility of atypical arrangements, in the absence of reason to doubt that the regular scheme was in place.

It is also easy to imagine different facts on which, if known, no common authority could sensibly be suspected. A person on the scene who identifies himself, say, as a landlord or a hotel manager calls up no customary understanding of authority to admit guests without the consent of the current occupant. A tenant in the ordinary course does not take rented premises subject to any formal or informal agreement that the landlord may let visitors into the dwelling, and a hotel guest customarily has no reason to expect the manager to allow anyone but his own employees into his room.... In these circumstances, neither state-law property rights, nor common contractual arrangements, nor any other source points to a common understanding of authority to admit third parties generally without the consent of a person occupying the premises. And when it comes to searching through bureau drawers, there will be instances in which even a person clearly belonging on premises as an occupant may lack any perceived authority to consent; "a child of eight might well be considered to have the power to consent to the police crossing the threshold into that part of the house where any caller, such as a pollster or salesman, might well be admitted," 4 LaFave § 8.4(c), at 207 (4th ed. 2004), but no one would reasonably expect such a child to be in a position to authorize anyone to rummage through his parents' bedroom.

C

Although we have not dealt directly with the reasonableness of police entry in reliance on consent by one occupant subject to immediate challenge by another, we took a step toward the issue in an earlier case dealing with the Fourth Amendment rights of a social guest arrested at premises the police entered without a warrant or the benefit of any exception to the warrant requirement. *Minnesota v. Olson* (1990), held that overnight houseguests have a legitimate expectation of privacy in their temporary quarters because "it is unlikely that [the host] will admit someone who wants to see or meet with the guest over the objection of the guest," If that customary expectation of courtesy or deference is a foundation of Fourth Amendment rights of a houseguest, it presumably should follow that an inhabitant of shared premises may claim at least as much, and it turns out that the co-inhabitant naturally has an even stronger claim.

To begin with, it is fair to say that a caller standing at the door of shared premises would have no confidence that one occupant's invitation was a sufficiently good reason to enter when a fellow tenant stood there saying, "stay out." Without some very good reason, no sensible person would go inside under those conditions. Fear for the safety of the occupant issuing the invitation, or of someone else inside, would be thought to justify entry, but the justification then would be the personal risk, the threats to life or limb, not the disputed invitation.

The visitor's reticence without some such good reason would show not timidity but a realization that when people living together disagree over the use of their common quarters, a resolution must come through voluntary accommodation, not by appeals to authority. Unless the people living together fall within some recognized hierarchy, like a household of parent and child or barracks housing military personnel of different grades, there is no societal understanding of superior and inferior, a fact reflected in a standard formulation of domestic property law, that "[e]ach cotenant ... has the right to use and enjoy the entire property as if he or she were the sole owner, limited only by the same right in the other cotenants." 7 R. Powell, Powell on Real Property § 50.03[1], p 50–14 (M. Wolf gen. ed. 2005). The want of any recognized superior authority among disagreeing tenants is also reflected in the law's response when the disagreements cannot be resolved. The law does not ask who has the better side of the conflict; it simply provides a right to any co-tenant, even the most unreasonable, to obtain a decree partitioning the property (when the relationship is one of co-ownership) and terminating the relationship. See, *e.g.*, 2 H. Tiffany, Real Property §§ 468, 473, 474, pp. 297, 307–309 (3d ed. 1939 and 2006 Cum. Supp.). And while a decree of partition is not the answer to disagreement among rental tenants, this situation resembles co-ownership in lacking the benefit of any understanding that one or the other rental co-tenant has a superior claim to control the use of the quarters they occupy together. In sum, there is no common understanding that one co-tenant generally has a right or authority to prevail over the express wishes of another, whether the issue is the color of the curtains or invitations to outsiders.

D

Since the co-tenant wishing to open the door to a third party has no recognized authority in law or social practice to prevail over a present and objecting co-tenant, his disputed invitation, without more, gives a police officer no better claim to reasonableness in entering than the officer would have in the absence of any consent at all. Accordingly, in the balancing of competing individual and governmental interests entailed by the bar to unreasonable searches, Camara v. Municipal Court of City and County of San Francisco (1967), the cooperative occupant's invitation adds nothing to the government's side to counter the force of an objecting individual's claim to security against the government's intrusion into his dwelling place. Since we hold to the "centuries-old principle of respect for the privacy of the home, it is beyond dispute that the home is entitled to special protection as the center of the private lives of our people," We have, after all, lived our whole national history with an understanding of "the ancient adage that a man's house is his castle [to the point that t]he poorest man may in his cottage bid defiance to all the forces of the Crown,"

Disputed permission is thus no match for this central value of the Fourth Amendment, and the State's other countervailing claims do not add up to outweigh it. Yes, we recognize the consenting tenant's interest as a citizen in bringing criminal activity to light. And we understand a co-tenant's legitimate self-interest in siding with the police to deflect suspicion raised by sharing quarters with a criminal ...

But society can often have the benefit of these interests without relying on a theory of consent that ignores an inhabitant's refusal to allow a warrantless search. The co-tenant acting on his own initiative may be able to deliver evidence to the police, and can tell the police what he knows, for use before a magistrate in getting a warrant. The reliance on a co-tenant's information instead of disputed consent accords with the law's general partiality toward "police action taken under a warrant [as against] searches and seizures without one," United States v. Ventresca (1965); "the informed and deliberate determinations of magistrates empowered to issue warrants as to what searches and seizures are permissible under the Constitution are to be preferred over the hurried action of officers,"[6]

Nor should this established policy of Fourth Amendment law be undermined by the principal dissent's claim that it shields spousal abusers and other violent co-tenants who will refuse to allow the police to enter a dwelling when their victims ask the police for help (opinion of Roberts, C. J.) (hereinafter the dissent). It is not that the dissent exaggerates violence in the home; we recognize that domestic abuse is a serious problem in the United States....

But this case has no bearing on the capacity of the police to protect domestic victims. The dissent's argument rests on the failure to distinguish two different issues: when the police may enter without committing a trespass, and when the police may enter to search for evidence. No question has been raised, or reasonably could be, about the authority of the police to enter a dwelling to protect a resident from domestic violence; so long as they have good reason to believe such a threat exists, it would be silly to suggest that the police would commit a tort by entering, say, to give a complaining tenant the opportunity to collect belongings and get out safely, or to determine whether violence (or threat of violence) has just occurred or is about to (or soon will) occur, however much a spouse or other co-tenant objected. And since the police would then be lawfully in the premises, there is no question that they could seize any evidence in plain view or take further action supported by any consequent probable cause.... Thus, the question whether the police might lawfully enter over objection in order to provide any protection that might be reasonable is easily answered yes.... The undoubted right of the police to enter in order to protect a victim, however, has nothing to do with the question in this case, whether a search with the consent of one co-tenant is good against another, standing at the door and expressly refusing consent....

The dissent's red herring aside, we know, of course, that alternatives to disputed consent will not always open the door to search for evidence that the police suspect is inside. The consenting tenant may simply not disclose enough information, or information factual enough, to add up to a

6. Sometimes, of course, the very exchange of information like this in front of the objecting inhabitant may render consent irrelevant by creating an exigency that justifies immediate action on the police's part; if the objecting tenant cannot be incapacitated from destroying easily disposable evidence during the time required to get a warrant, see Illinois v. McArthur (2001) (denying suspect access to his trailer home while police applied for a search warrant), a fairly perceived need to act on the spot to preserve evidence may justify entry and search under the exigent circumstances exception to the warrant requirement, cf. Schmerber v. California (1966) (warrantless search permitted when "the delay necessary to obtain a warrant ... threatened the destruction of evidence" ... Additional exigent circumstances might justify warrantless searches). See, *e.g.*, Warden, Md. Penitentiary v. Hayden (1967) (hot pursuit); Chimel v. California (1969) (protecting the safety of the police officers); Michigan v. Tyler (1978) (imminent destruction to building); Johnson v. United States (1948) (likelihood that suspect will imminently flee).

showing of probable cause, and there may be no exigency to justify fast action. But nothing in social custom or its reflection in private law argues for placing a higher value on delving into private premises to search for evidence in the face of disputed consent, than on requiring clear justification before the government searches private living quarters over a resident's objection. We therefore hold that a warrantless search of a shared dwelling for evidence over the express refusal of consent by a physically present resident cannot be justified as reasonable as to him on the basis of consent given to the police by another resident.

E

There are two loose ends, the first being the explanation given in *Matlock* for the constitutional sufficiency of a co-tenant's consent to enter and search: it "rests ... on mutual use of the property by persons generally having joint access or control for most purposes, so that it is reasonable to recognize that any of the co-inhabitants has the right to permit the inspection in his own right...." If *Matlock*'s co-tenant is giving permission "in his own right," how can his "own right" be eliminated by another tenant's objection? The answer appears in the very footnote from which the quoted statement is taken: the "right" to admit the police to which *Matlock* refers is not an enduring and enforceable ownership right as understood by the private law of property, but is instead the authority recognized by customary social usage as having a substantial bearing on Fourth Amendment reasonableness in specific circumstances. Thus, to ask whether the consenting tenant has the right to admit the police when a physically present fellow tenant objects is not to question whether some property right may be divested by the mere objection of another. It is, rather, the question whether customary social understanding accords the consenting tenant authority powerful enough to prevail over the co-tenant's objection. The *Matlock* Court did not purport to answer this question, a point made clear by another statement (which the dissent does not quote): the Court described the co-tenant's consent as good against "the absent, nonconsenting" resident. The second loose end is the significance of *Matlock* and *Rodriguez* after today's decision. Although the *Matlock* defendant was not present with the opportunity to object, he was in a squad car not far away; the *Rodriguez* defendant was actually asleep in the apartment, and the police might have roused him with a knock on the door before they entered with only the consent of an apparent co-tenant. If those cases are not to be undercut by today's holding, we have to admit that we are drawing a fine line; if a potential defendant with self-interest in objecting is in fact at the door and objects, the co-tenant's permission does not suffice for a reasonable search, whereas the potential objector, nearby but not invited to take part in the threshold colloquy, loses out.

This is the line we draw, and we think the formalism is justified. So long as there is no evidence that the police have removed the potentially objecting tenant from the entrance for the sake of avoiding a possible objection, there is practical value in the simple clarity of complementary rules, one recognizing the co-tenant's permission when there is no fellow occupant on hand, the other according dispositive weight to the fellow occupant's contrary indication when he expresses it. For the very reason that *Rodriguez* held it would be unjustifiably impractical to require the police to take affirmative steps to confirm the actual authority of a consenting individual whose authority was apparent, we think it would needlessly limit the capacity of the police to respond to ostensibly legitimate opportunities in the field if we were to hold that reasonableness required the police to take affirmative steps to find a potentially objecting co-tenant before acting on the permission they had already received. There is no ready reason to believe that efforts to invite a refusal would make a difference in many cases, whereas every co-tenant consent case would turn into a test about the adequacy of the police's efforts to consult with a potential objector. Better to accept the formalism of distinguishing *Matlock* from this case than to impose a requirement, time-consuming in the field and in the courtroom, with no apparent systemic justification. The pragmatic decision to accept the simplicity of this line is, moreover, supported by the substantial number of instances in which suspects who are asked for permission to search actually consent, 9albeit imprudently, a fact that undercuts any argument that the police should try to locate a suspected inhabitant because his denial of consent would be a foregone conclusion.

III

This case invites a straightforward application of the rule that a physically present inhabitant's express refusal of consent to a police search is dispositive as to him, regardless of the consent of a fellow occupant. Scott Randolph's refusal is clear, and nothing in the record justifies the search on grounds independent of Janet Randolph's consent. The State does not argue that she gave any indication to the police of a need for protection inside the house that might have justified entry into the portion of the premises where the police found the powdery straw (which, if lawfully seized, could have been used when attempting to establish probable cause for the warrant issued later). Nor does the State claim that the entry and search should be upheld under the rubric of exigent circumstances, owing to some apprehension by the police officers that Scott Randolph would destroy evidence of drug use before any warrant could be obtained.

The judgment of the Supreme Court of Georgia is therefore affirmed.

It is so ordered.

■ JUSTICE ALITO took no part in the consideration or decision of this case.

■ JUSTICE STEVENS, concurring.

The study of history for the purpose of ascertaining the original understanding of constitutional provisions is much like the study of legislative history for the purpose of ascertaining the intent of the lawmakers who enact statutes. In both situations the facts uncovered by the study are usually relevant but not necessarily dispositive. This case illustrates why even the most dedicated adherent to an approach to constitutional interpretation that places primary reliance on the search for original understanding would recognize the relevance of changes in our society.

At least since 1604 it has been settled that in the absence of exigent circumstances, a government agent has no right to enter a "house" or "castle" unless authorized to do so by a valid warrant.... Every occupant of the home has a right—protected by the common law for centuries and by the Fourth Amendment since 1791—to refuse entry. When an occupant gives his or her consent to enter, he or she is waiving a valuable constitutional right. To be sure that the waiver is voluntary, it is sound practice—a practice some Justices of this Court thought necessary to make the waiver voluntary—for the officer to advise the occupant of that right. The issue in this case relates to the content of the advice that the officer should provide when met at the door by a man and a woman who are apparently joint tenants or joint owners of the property.

In the 18th century, when the Fourth Amendment was adopted, the advice would have been quite different from what is appropriate today. Given the then-prevailing dramatic differences between the property rights of the husband and the far lesser rights of the wife, only the consent of the husband would matter. Whether "the master of the house" consented or objected, his decision would control. Thus if "original understanding" were to govern the outcome of this case, the search was clearly invalid because the husband did not consent. History, however, is not dispositive because it is now clear, as a matter of constitutional law, that the male and the female are equal partners.

In today's world the only advice that an officer could properly give should make it clear that each of the partners has a constitutional right that he or she may independently assert or waive. Assuming that both spouses are competent, neither one is a master possessing the power to override the other's constitutional right to deny entry to their castle.

With these observations, I join the Court's opinion.

■ JUSTICE BREYER, concurring.

If Fourth Amendment law forced us to choose between two bright-line rules, (1) a rule that always found one tenant's consent sufficient to justify a search without a warrant and (2) a rule that never did, I believe we should choose the first. That is because, as The Chief Justice's dissent points out, a rule permitting such searches can serve important law enforcement needs (for example, in domestic abuse cases), and the consenting party's joint tenancy diminishes the objecting party's reasonable expectation of privacy.

But the Fourth Amendment does not insist upon bright-line rules. Rather, it recognizes that no single set of legal rules can capture the ever changing complexity of human life. It consequently uses the general terms "unreasonable searches and seizures." And this Court has continuously emphasized that "[r]easonableness ... is measured ... by examining the totality of the circumstances." ...

The circumstances here include the following: The search at issue was a search solely for evidence. The objecting party was present and made his objection known clearly and directly to the officers seeking to enter the house. The officers did not justify their search on grounds of possible evidence destruction. Cf. Thornton v. United States (2004); Skinner v. Railway Labor Executives' Ass'n (1989); Schmerber v. California (1966). And, as far as the record reveals, the officers might easily have secured the premises and sought a warrant permitting them to enter. See Illinois v.

McArthur (2001). Thus, the "totality of the circumstances" present here do not suffice to justify abandoning the Fourth Amendment's traditional hostility to police entry into a home without a warrant.

I stress the totality of the circumstances, however, because, were the circumstances to change significantly, so should the result. The Court's opinion does not apply where the objector is not present "and object[ing]."

Moreover, the risk of an ongoing crime or other exigent circumstance can make a critical difference. Consider, for example, instances of domestic abuse. "Family disturbance calls ... constitute the largest single category of calls received by police departments each year.".... And, law enforcement officers must be able to respond effectively when confronted with the possibility of abuse.

If a possible abuse victim invites a responding officer to enter a home or consents to the officer's entry request, that invitation (or consent) itself could reflect the victim's fear about being left alone with an abuser. It could also indicate the availability of evidence, in the form of an immediate willingness to speak, that might not otherwise exist. In that context, an invitation (or consent) would provide a special reason for immediate, rather than later, police entry. And, entry following invitation or consent by one party ordinarily would be reasonable even in the face of direct objection by the other. That being so, contrary to The Chief Justice's suggestion, today's decision will not adversely affect ordinary law enforcement practices.

Given the case-specific nature of the Court's holding, and with these understandings, I join the Court's holding and its opinion.

■ CHIEF JUSTICE ROBERTS, with whom JUSTICE SCALIA joins, dissenting.

The Court creates constitutional law by surmising what is typical when a social guest encounters an entirely atypical situation. The rule the majority fashions does not implement the high office of the Fourth Amendment to protect privacy, but instead provides protection on a random and happenstance basis, protecting, for example, a co-occupant who happens to be at the front door when the other occupant consents to a search, but not one napping or watching television in the next room. And the cost of affording such random protection is great, as demonstrated by the recurring cases in which abused spouses seek to authorize police entry into a home they share with a nonconsenting abuser.

The correct approach to the question presented is clearly mapped out in our precedents: The Fourth Amendment protects privacy. If an individual shares information, papers, *or places* with another, he assumes the risk that the other person will in turn share access to that information or those papers *or places* with the government. And just as an individual who has shared illegal plans or incriminating documents with another cannot interpose an objection when that other person turns the information over to the government, just because the individual happens to be present at the time, so too someone who shares a place with another cannot interpose an objection when that person decides to grant access to the police, simply because the objecting individual happens to be present.

A warrantless search is reasonable if police obtain the voluntary consent of a person authorized to give it. Co-occupants have "assumed the risk that one of their number might permit [a] common area to be searched." Just as Mrs. Randolph could walk upstairs, come down, and turn her husband's cocaine straw over to the police, she can consent to police entry and search of what is, after all, her home, too.

I

In Illinois v. Rodriguez (1990), this Court stated that "[w]hat [a person] is assured by the Fourth Amendment ... is not that no government search of his house will occur unless he consents; but that no such search will occur that is 'unreasonable.'" One element that can make a warrantless government search of a home "'reasonable'" is voluntary consent. Proof of voluntary consent "is not limited to proof that consent was given by the defendant," but the government "may show that permission to search was obtained from a third party who possessed common authority over or other sufficient relationship to the premises." Today's opinion creates an exception to this otherwise clear rule: A third-party consent search is unreasonable, and therefore constitutionally impermissible, if the co-occupant against whom evidence is obtained was present and objected to the entry and search.

This exception is based on what the majority describes as "widely shared social expectations" that "when people living together disagree over the use of their common quarters, a resolution must come through voluntary accommodation." But this fundamental predicate to the majority's analysis gets us nowhere: Does the objecting co-tenant accede to the consenting cotenant's wishes, or the other way around? The majority's assumption about voluntary accommodation simply leads to the common stalemate of two gentlemen insisting that the other enter a room first.

Nevertheless, the majority is confident in assuming—confident enough to incorporate its assumption into the Constitution—that an invited social guest who arrives at the door of a shared residence, and is greeted by a disagreeable co-occupant shouting "'stay out,'" would simply go away. The Court observes that "no sensible person would go inside under those conditions," and concludes from this that the inviting co-occupant has no "authority" to insist on getting her way over the wishes of her co-occupant. But it seems equally accurate to say—based on the majority's conclusion that one does not have a right to prevail over the express wishes of his co-occupant—that the objector has no "authority" to insist on getting *his* way over his co-occupant's wish that her guest be admitted.

The fact is that a wide variety of differing social situations can readily be imagined, giving rise to quite different social expectations. A relative or good friend of one of two feuding roommates might well enter the apartment over the objection of the other roommate. The reason the invitee appeared at the door also affects expectations: A guest who came to celebrate an occupant's birthday, or one who had traveled some distance for a particular reason, might not readily turn away simply because of a roommate's objection. The nature of the place itself is also pertinent: Invitees may react one way if the feuding roommates share one room, differently if there are common areas from which the objecting roommate could readily be expected to absent himself. Altering the numbers might well change the social expectations: Invitees might enter if two of three co-occupants encourage them to do so, over one dissenter.

The possible scenarios are limitless, and slight variations in the fact pattern yield vastly different expectations about whether the invitee might be expected to enter or to go away. Such shifting expectations are not a promising foundation on which to ground a constitutional rule, particularly because the majority has no support for its basic assumption—that an invited guest encountering two disagreeing co-occupants would flee—beyond a hunch about how people would typically act in an atypical situation.

And in fact the Court has not looked to such expectations to decide questions of consent under the Fourth Amendment, but only to determine when a search has occurred and whether a particular person has standing to object to a search. For these latter inquiries, we ask whether a person has a subjective expectation of privacy in a particular place, and whether "the expectation [is] one that society is prepared to recognize as 'reasonable.' " Katz v. United States (1967) (Harlan, J., concurring). But the social expectations concept has not been applied to all questions arising under the Fourth Amendment, least of all issues of consent. A criminal might have a strong expectation that his longtime confidant will not allow the government to listen to their private conversations, but however profound his shock might be upon betrayal, government monitoring with the confidant's consent is reasonable under the Fourth Amendment.

The majority suggests that "widely shared social expectations" are a "constant element in assessing Fourth Amendment reasonableness," but that is not the case; the Fourth Amendment precedents the majority cites refer instead to a "legitimate expectation of *privacy*." Whatever social expectation the majority seeks to protect, it is not one of privacy. The very predicate giving rise to the question in cases of shared information, papers, containers, or places is that privacy has been shared with another. Our common social expectations may well be that the other person will not, in turn, share what we have shared with them with another—including the police—but that is the risk we take in sharing. If two

A wide variety of often subtle social conventions may shape expectations about how we act when another shares with us what is otherwise private, and those conventions go by a variety of labels—courtesy, good manners, custom, protocol, even honor among thieves. The Constitution, however, protects not these but privacy, and once privacy has been shared, the shared information, documents, or places remain private only at the discretion of the confidant.

II

.... The law acknowledges that although we might not expect our friends and family to admit the government into common areas, sharing space entails risk. A person assumes the risk that his co-occupants—just as they might report his illegal activity or deliver his contraband to the government—might consent to a search of areas over which they have access and control. See *United States v. Karo*, 468 U.S. 705, 726, 104 S. Ct. 3296, 82 L. Ed. 2d 530 (1984) (O'Connor, J., concurring in part and concurring in judgment) (finding it a "relatively easy case ... when two persons share identical, overlapping privacy interests in a particular place, container, or conversation. Here *both* share the power to surrender each other's privacy to a third party").

III

The majority states its rule as follows: "[A] warrantless search of a shared dwelling for evidence over the express refusal of consent by a physically present resident cannot be justified as reasonable as to him on the basis of consent given to the police by another resident."

Just as the source of the majority's rule is not privacy, so too the interest it protects cannot reasonably be described as such. That interest is not protected if a co-owner happens to be absent when the police arrive, in the backyard gardening, asleep in the next room, or listening to music through earphones so that only his co-occupant hears the knock on the door. That the rule is so random in its application confirms that it bears no real relation to the privacy protected by the Fourth Amendment. What the majority's rule protects is not so much privacy as the good luck of a co-owner who just happens to be present at the door when the police arrive. Usually when the development of Fourth Amendment jurisprudence leads to such arbitrary lines, we take it as a signal that the rules need to be rethought. See California v. Acevedo (1991). We should not embrace a rule at the outset that its *sponsors* appreciate will result in drawing fine, formalistic lines.

Rather than draw such random and happenstance lines—and pretend that the Constitution decreed them—the more reasonable approach is to adopt a rule acknowledging that shared living space entails a limited yielding of privacy to others, and that the law historically permits those to whom we have yielded our privacy to in turn cooperate with the government. Such a rule flows more naturally from our cases concerning Fourth Amendment reasonableness and is logically grounded in the concept of privacy underlying that Amendment.

The scope of the majority's rule is not only arbitrary but obscure as well. The majority repeats several times that a present co-occupant's refusal to permit entry renders the search unreasonable and invalid "as to him." This implies entry and search would be reasonable "as to" someone else, presumably the consenting co-occupant and any other absent co-occupants. The normal Fourth Amendment rule is that items discovered in plain view are admissible if the officers were legitimately on the premises; if the entry and search were reasonable "as to" Mrs. Randolph, based on her consent, it is not clear why the cocaine straw should not be admissible "as to" Mr. Randolph, as discovered in plain view during a legitimate search "as to" Mrs. Randolph.... This Court has rejected subjective motivations of police officers in assessing Fourth Amendment questions, see Whren v. United States (1996), with good reason: The police do not need a particular reason to ask for consent to search, whether for signs of domestic violence or evidence of drug possession.

While the majority's rule protects something random, its consequences are particularly severe.... What does the majority imagine will happen, in a case in which the consenting co-occupant is concerned about the other's criminal activity, once the door clicks shut? The objecting co-occupant may pause briefly to decide whether to destroy any evidence of wrongdoing or to inflict retribution on the consenting co-occupant first, but there can be little doubt that he will attend to both in short order. It is no answer to say that the consenting co-occupant can depart with the police; remember that it is her home, too, and the other co-occupant's very presence, which allowed him to object, may also prevent the consenting co-occupant from doing more than urging the police to enter.

Perhaps the most serious consequence of the majority's rule is its operation in domestic abuse situations, a context in which the present question often arises. While people living together might typically be accommodating to the wishes of their co-tenants, requests for police assistance may well come from co-inhabitants who are having a disagreement. The Court concludes that because "no sensible person would go inside" in the face of disputed consent, and the consenting co-tenant thus has "no recognized authority" to insist on the guest's admission, a "police officer [has] no better claim to reasonableness in entering than the officer would have in the absence of any consent at all." But the police officer's superior claim to enter is obvious: Mrs. Randolph did not invite the police to join her for dessert and coffee; the officer's precise purpose in knocking on the door was to assist with a dispute between the Randolphs—one in which Mrs. Randolph felt the need for the protective presence of the police. The majority's rule apparently forbids police from entering to assist with a domestic dispute if the abuser whose behavior prompted the request for police assistance objects.

The majority acknowledges these concerns, but dismisses them on the ground that its rule can be expected to give rise to exigent situations, and police can then rely on an exigent circumstances exception to justify entry. This is a strange way to justify a rule, and the fact that alternative justifications for entry might arise does not show that entry pursuant to consent is unreasonable....

Rather than give effect to a consenting spouse's authority to permit entry into her house to avoid such situations, the majority again alters established Fourth Amendment rules to defend giving veto power to the objecting spouse. In response to the concern that police might be turned away under its rule before entry can be justified based on exigency, the majority creates a new rule: A "good reason" to enter, coupled with one occupant's consent, will ensure that a police officer is "lawfully in the premises." ... The majority's analysis alters a great deal of established Fourth Amendment law. The majority imports the concept of "social expectations," previously used only to determine when a search has occurred and whether a particular person has standing to object to a search, into questions of consent. To determine whether entry and search are reasonable, the majority considers a police officer's subjective motive in asking for consent, which we have otherwise refrained from doing in assessing Fourth Amendment questions. And the majority creates a new exception to the warrant requirement to justify warrantless entry short of exigency in potential domestic abuse situations.

Considering the majority's rule is solely concerned with protecting a person who happens to be present at the door when a police officer asks his co-occupant for consent to search, but not one who is asleep in the next room or in the backyard gardening, the majority has taken a great deal of pain in altering Fourth Amendment doctrine, for precious little (if any) gain in privacy. Perhaps one day, as the consequences of the majority's analytic approach become clearer, today's opinion will be treated the same way the majority treats our opinions in *Matlock* and *Rodriguez*—as a "loose end" to be tied up.

One of the concurring opinions states that if it had to choose between a rule that a cotenant's consent was valid or a rule that it was not, it would choose the former. (opinion of Breyer, J.). The concurrence advises, however, that "no single set of legal rules can capture the ever changing complexity of human life," and joins what becomes the majority opinion, "[g]iven the case-specific nature of the Court's holding." What the majority establishes, in its own terms, is "*the rule* that a physically present inhabitant's express refusal of consent to a police search *is dispositive* as to him, regardless of the consent of a fellow occupant." The concurrence joins with the apparent "understandin[g]" that the majority's "rule" is not a rule at all, but simply a "case-specific" holding. The end result is a complete lack of practical guidance for the police in the field, let alone for the lower courts.

* * *

Our third-party consent cases have recognized that a person who shares common areas with others "assume[s] the risk that one of their number might permit the common area to be searched." *Matlock*, 415 U.S., at 171, n. 7, 94 S. Ct. 988, 39 L. Ed. 2d 242. The majority reminds us, in high tones, that a man's home is his castle, but even under the majority's rule, it is not his castle if he happens to be absent, asleep in the keep, or otherwise engaged when the constable arrives at the gate. Then it is his co-owner's castle. And, of course, it is not his castle if he wants to consent to entry, but his co-owner objects. Rather than constitutionalize such an arbitrary rule, we should acknowledge that a decision to share a private place, like a decision to share a secret or a confidential document, necessarily entails the risk that those with whom we share may in turn choose to share—for their own protection or for other reasons—with the police.

I respectfully dissent.

■ JUSTICE SCALIA, dissenting.

I join the dissent of The Chief Justice, but add these few words in response to Justice Stevens' concurrence.

It is not as clear to me as it is to Justice Stevens that, at the time the Fourth Amendment was adopted, a police officer could enter a married woman's home over her objection, and could not enter with only her consent. Nor is it clear to me that the answers to these questions depended solely on who owned the house. It is entirely clear, however, that *if* the matter *did* depend solely on property rights, a latter-day alteration of property rights would also produce a latter-day alteration of the Fourth Amendment outcome—without altering the Fourth Amendment itself.

Justice Stevens' attempted critique of originalism confuses the original import of the Fourth Amendment with the background sources of law to which the Amendment, on its original meaning, referred. From the date of its ratification until well into the 20th century, violation of the Amendment was tied to common-law trespass ..... On the basis of that connection, someone who had power to license the search of a house by a private party could authorize a police search.... The issue of *who* could give such consent generally depended, in turn, on "historical and legal refinements" of property law. As property law developed, individuals who previously could not authorize a search might become able to do so, and those who once could grant such consent might no longer have that power. But changes in the law of property to which the Fourth Amendment referred would not alter the Amendment's meaning: that anyone capable of authorizing a search by a private party could consent to a warrantless search by the police.

There is nothing new or surprising in the proposition that our unchanging Constitution refers to other bodies of law that might themselves change. The Fifth Amendment provides, for instance, that "private property" shall not "be taken for public use, without just compensation"; but it does not purport to define property rights. We have consistently held that "the existence of a property interest is determined by reference to 'existing rules or understandings that stem from an independent source such as state law.' ".... The same is true of the Fourteenth Amendment Due Process Clause's protection of "property." See Castle Rock v. Gonzales (2005). This reference to changeable law presents no problem for the originalist. No one supposes that the *meaning* of the Constitution changes as States expand and contract property rights. If it is indeed true, therefore, that a wife in 1791 could not authorize the search of her husband's house, the fact that current property law provides otherwise is no more troublesome for the originalist than the well-established fact that a State must compensate its takings of even those property rights that did not exist at the time of the founding.

In any event, Justice Stevens' panegyric to the *equal* rights of women under modern property law does not support his conclusion that "[a]ssuming ... both spouses are competent, neither one is a master possessing the power to override the other's constitutional right to deny entry to their castle." The issue at hand is what to do when there is a *conflict* between two equals. Now that women have authority to consent, as Justice Stevens claims men alone once did, it does not follow that the spouse who *refuses* consent should be the winner of the contest. Justice Stevens could just as well have followed the same historical developments to the opposite conclusion: Now that "the male and the female are equal partners," and women can consent to a search of their property, men can no longer obstruct their wishes. Men and women are no more "equal" in the majority's regime, where both sexes can veto each other's consent, than on the dissent's view, where both sexes cannot.

Finally, I must express grave doubt that today's decision deserves Justice Stevens' celebration as part of the forward march of women's equality. Given the usual patterns of domestic violence, how often can police be expected to encounter the situation in which a man urges them to enter the home while a woman simultaneously demands that they stay out? The most common practical effect of today's decision, insofar as the contest between the sexes is concerned, is to give men the power to stop women from allowing police into their homes—which is, curiously enough, *precisely* the power that Justice Stevens disapprovingly presumes men had in 1791.

■ JUSTICE THOMAS, dissenting.

The Court has long recognized that "[i]t is an act of responsible citizenship for individuals to give whatever information they may have to aid in law enforcement." Miranda v. Arizona (1966). Consistent with this principle, the Court held in Coolidge v. New Hampshire (1971), that no Fourth Amendment search occurs where, as here, the spouse of an accused voluntarily leads the police to potential evidence of wrongdoing by the accused. Because *Coolidge* squarely controls this case, the Court need not address whether police could permissibly have conducted a general search of the Randolph home, based on Mrs. Randolph's consent. I respectfully dissent.

In the instant case, Mrs. Randolph told police responding to a domestic dispute that respondent was using a substantial quantity of cocaine. Upon police request, she consented to a general search of her residence to investigate her statements. However, as the Court's recitation of the facts demonstrates, the record is clear that no such general search occurred. Instead, Sergeant Brett Murray asked Mrs. Randolph where the cocaine was located, and she showed him to an upstairs bedroom, where he saw the "piece of cut straw" on a dresser.... Upon closer examination, Sergeant Murray observed white residue on the straw, and concluded the straw had been used for ingesting cocaine. He then collected the straw and the residue as evidence.

Sergeant Murray's entry into the Randolphs' home at the invitation of Mrs. Randolph to be shown evidence of respondent's cocaine use does not constitute a Fourth Amendment search. Under this Court's precedents, only the action of an agent of the government can constitute a search within the meaning of the Fourth Amendment, because that Amendment "was intended as a restraint upon the activities of *sovereign authority*, and was not intended to be a limitation upon other than governmental agencies." Burdeau v. McDowell (1921) (emphasis added). See also *Coolidge*. Applying this principle in *Coolidge*, the Court held that when a citizen leads police officers into a home shared with her spouse to show them evidence relevant to their investigation into a crime, that citizen is not acting as an agent of the police, and thus no Fourth Amendment search has occurred

Review of the facts in *Coolidge* clearly demonstrates that it governs this case. While the police interrogated Coolidge as part of their investigation into a murder, two other officers were sent to his house to speak with his wife. During the course of questioning Mrs. Coolidge, the police asked whether her husband owned any guns. Mrs. Coolidge replied in the affirmative, and offered to retrieve the weapons for the police, apparently operating under the assumption that doing so would help to exonerate her husband. The police accompanied Mrs. Coolidge to the bedroom to collect the guns, as well as clothing that Mrs. Coolidge told them her husband had been wearing the night of the murder.

Before this Court, Coolidge argued that the evidence of the guns and clothing should be suppressed as the product of an unlawful search because Mrs. Coolidge was acting as an " 'instrument,' " or agent, of the police by complying with a " 'demand' " made by them. The Court recognized that, had Mrs. Coolidge sought out the guns to give to police wholly on her own initiative, "there can be no doubt under existing law that the articles would later have been admissible in evidence." That she did so in cooperation with police pursuant to their request did not transform her into their agent; after all, "it is no part of the policy underlying the Fourth and Fourteenth Amendments to discourage citizens from aiding to the utmost of their ability in the apprehension of criminals." Because the police were "acting normally and properly" when they asked about any guns, and questioning Mrs. Coolidge about the clothing was "logical and in no way coercive," the Fourth Amendment did not require police to "avert their eyes" when Mrs. Coolidge produced the guns and clothes for inspection.

This case is indistinguishable from *Coolidge*, compelling the conclusion that Mrs. Randolph was not acting as an agent of the police when she admitted Sergeant Murray into her home and led him to the incriminating evidence. Just as Mrs. Coolidge could, of her own accord, have offered her husband's weapons and clothing to the police without implicating the Fourth Amendment, so too could Mrs. Randolph have simply retrieved the straw from the house and given it to Sergeant Murray. Indeed, the majority appears to concede as much. ("The co-tenant acting on his own initiative may be able to deliver evidence to the police, *Coolidge*, *supra*, . . ., and can tell the police what he knows, for use before a magistrate in getting a warrant"). Drawing a constitutionally significant distinction between what occurred here and Mrs. Randolph's independent production of the relevant evidence is both inconsistent with *Coolidge* and unduly formalistic. 3

Accordingly, the trial court appropriately denied respondent's motion to suppress the evidence Mrs. Randolph provided to the police and the evidence obtained as a result of the consequent search warrant. I would therefore reverse the judgment of the Supreme Court of Georgia.

CHAPTER 6

EXCLUSIONARY PRINCIPLES AND ALTERNATIVE REMEDIES FOR UNLAWFUL INVESTIGATIVE PRACTICES

A. AN OVERVIEW OF EXCLUSIONARY PRINCIPLES

In previous chapters we have considered limitations, primarily of a federal constitutional dimension, upon police and prosecutorial powers to investigate crime and to effect arrests. Our attention now turns to the consequences of violations of those restrictions, particularly as they may limit the prosecution's use of evidence in a criminal trial.

The impact of exclusionary rules can be narrowed by a requirement of "standing," the principle which permits only those whose rights have been violated to obtain exclusion against them of evidence derived from unlawful police conduct. The exclusionary rule can be restricted if the law permits the use of illegally obtained evidence in certain phases of a criminal proceeding (for example, in the grand jury or at a sentencing hearing) and in other "non-criminal" proceedings (for example, at a parole revocation hearing or at a hearing to revoke a business license). It can be further limited in instances if courts apply a "good faith" exception to the exclusionary rule.

The denial of retroactive application of certain new constitutional decisions also narrows the impact of exclusionary rules, as does the admission of evidence which has been secured through the wrongdoing of private citizens without governmental participation. On the other hand, the concept of derivative evidence (the notion that suppression is proper even for evidence remotely derived from exploitation of a police illegality) expands the impact of exclusionary rules.

The debate over these subsidiary principles "such as standing, collateral use of illegally obtained evidence, and derivative evidence" requires an understanding of the rationale for exclusionary rules, and thus the cases involving these subsidiary doctrines provide insight into a court's view of exclusionary rules themselves. One's attitude toward each of the concepts discussed in the present chapter reflects his or her attitude toward the exclusionary rule itself.

We begin with the rule itself, then work through decisions involving the subsidiary principles (as applied to violations of all the types of constitutional restrictions treated in earlier chapters), and then return to a final consideration of the Fourth Amendment exclusionary rule and to suggested alternative remedies.

B. An Introduction to the Exclusionary Rule

Mapp v. Ohio

Supreme Court of the United States, 1961.
367 U.S. 643, 81 S.Ct. 1684.

■ Justice Clark delivered the opinion of the Court.

Appellant stands convicted of knowingly having had in her possession and under her control certain lewd and lascivious books, pictures, and photographs in violation of § 2905.34 of Ohio's Revised Code.**

On May 23, 1957, three Cleveland police officers arrived at appellant's residence in that city pursuant to information that "a person [was] hiding out in the home, who was wanted for questioning in connection with a recent bombing, and that there was a large amount of policy paraphernalia being hidden in the home." Miss Mapp and her daughter by a former marriage lived on the top floor of the two-family dwelling. Upon their arrival at that house, the officers knocked on the door and demanded entrance but an appellant, after telephoning her attorney, refused to admit them without a search warrant. They advised their headquarters of the situation and undertook a surveillance of the house.

The officers again sought entrance some three hours later when four or more additional officers arrived on the scene. When Miss Mapp did not come to the door immediately, at least one of the several doors to the house was forcibly opened and the policemen gained admittance. Meanwhile Miss Mapp's attorney arrived, but the officers, having secured their own entry, and continuing in their defiance of the law, would permit him neither to see Miss Mapp nor to enter the house. It appears that Miss Mapp was halfway down the stairs from the upper floor to the front door when the officers, in this high-handed manner, broke into the hall. She demanded to see the search warrant. A paper, claimed to be a warrant, was held up by one of the officers. She grabbed the "warrant" and placed it in her bosom. A struggle ensued in which the officers recovered the piece of paper and as a result of which they handcuffed appellant because she had been "belligerent" in resisting their official rescue of the "warrant" from her person. Running roughshod over appellant, a policeman "grabbed" her, "twisted

** As officially stated in the syllabus to its opinion, the Supreme Court of Ohio found that her conviction was valid though "based primarily upon the introduction in evidence of lewd and lascivious books and pictures unlawfully seized during an unlawful search of defendant's home...."

[Editors' Note: Mrs. Mapp received a seven-year sentence for possession of obscene materials. Her primary argument in her jurisdictional statement consisted of a First Amendment challenge to the statute under which she was convicted. A few years later the United States Supreme Court in Stanley v. Georgia, 394 U.S. 557, 89 S.Ct. 1243 (1969), accepted a similar argument and held that the First Amendment prohibits punishing persons for merely possessing obscene materials intended for personal use, at least where the material does not depict children.]

[her] hand," and she "yelled [and] pleaded with him" because "it was hurting." Appellant, in handcuffs, was then forcibly taken upstairs to her bedroom where the officers searched a dresser, a chest of drawers, a closet and some suitcases. They also looked into a photo album and through personal papers belonging to the appellant. The search spread to the rest of the second floor including the child's bedroom, the living room, the kitchen and a dinette. The basement of the building and a trunk found therein were also searched. The obscene materials for possession of which she was ultimately convicted were discovered in the course of that widespread search.

At the trial no search warrant was produced by the prosecution, nor was the failure to produce one explained or accounted for. At best, "There is, in the record, considerable doubt as to whether there ever was any warrant for the search of defendant's home." The Ohio Supreme Court believed a "reasonable argument" could be made that the conviction should be reversed "because the 'methods' employed to obtain the [evidence] were such as to 'offend "a sense of justice,"' " but the court found determinative the fact that the evidence had not been taken "from defendant's person by the use of brutal or offensive physical force against defendant. . . ."

The State says that even if the search were made without authority, or otherwise unreasonably, it is not prevented from using the unconstitutionally seized evidence at trial, citing Wolf v. People of State of Colorado (1949), in which this court did indeed hold "that in a prosecution in a State court for a State crime the Fourteenth Amendment does not forbid the admission of evidence obtained by an unreasonable search and seizure." On this appeal, of which we have noted probable jurisdiction, it is urged once again that we review that holding.

I.

Seventy-five years ago, in Boyd v. States (1886) considering the Fourth and Fifth Amendments as running "almost into each other" on the facts before it, this Court held that the doctrines of those Amendments

> apply to all invasions on the part of the government and its employees of the sanctity of a man's home and the privacies of life. It is not the breaking of his doors, and the rummaging of his drawers, that constitutes the essence of the offence; but it is the invasion of his indefeasible right of personal security, personal liberty and private property. . . . Breaking into a house and opening boxes and drawers are circumstances of aggravation; but any forcible and compulsory extortion of a man's own testimony or of his private papers to be used as evidence to convict him of crime or to forfeit his goods, is within the condemnation . . . [of those Amendments].

The Court noted that

> constitutional provisions for the security of person and property should be liberally construed. . . . It is the duty of courts to be watchful for the constitutional rights of the citizen, and against any stealthy encroachments thereon.

Less than 30 years after *Boyd*, this Court, in Weeks v. United States (1914).... stated that

> The 4th Amendment ... put the courts of the United States and Federal officials, in the exercise of their power and authority, under limitations and restraints [and] ... forever secure[d] the people, their persons, houses, papers, and effects, against all unreasonable searches and seizures under the guise of law ... and the duties of giving to it force and effect is obligatory upon all entrusted under our Federal system with the enforcement of the laws.

Specifically dealing with the use of the evidence unconstitutionally seized, the Court concluded:

> If letters and private documents can thus be seized and held and used in evidence against a citizen accused of an offense, the protection of the Fourth Amendment declaring his right to be secure against such searches and seizures is of no value, and, so far as those thus placed are concerned, might as well be stricken from the Constitution. The efforts of the courts and their officials to bring the guilty to punishment, praiseworthy as they are, are not to be aided by the sacrifice of those great principles established by years of endeavor and suffering which have resulted in their embodiment in the fundamental law of the land.

Finally, the Court in that case clearly stated that use of the seized evidence involved "a denial of the constitutional rights of the accused." Thus, in the year 1914, in the Weeks case, this Court "for the first time" held that "in a federal prosecution the Fourth Amendment barred the use of evidence secured through an illegal search and seizure." Wolf v. People of State of Colorado, supra. This Court has ever since required of federal law officers a strict adherence to that command which this Court has held to be a clear, specific, and constitutionally required—even if judicially implied—deterrent safeguard without insistence upon which the Fourth Amendment would have been reduced to "a form of words." Holmes, J., Silverthorne Lumber Co. v. United States (1920). It meant, quite simply, that "conviction by means of unlawful seizures and enforced confessions ... should find no sanction in the judgments of the courts ...," Weeks v. United States, supra, and that such evidence "shall not be used at all." Silverthorne Lumber Co. v. United States, supra.

There are in the cases of this Court some passing references to the Weeks rules being one of evidence. But the plain and unequivocal language of Weeks "and its later paraphrase in Wolf" to the effect that the Weeks rule is of constitutional origin, remains entirely undisturbed. In Byars v. United States, 1927, a unanimous Court declared that "the doctrine [cannot] ... be tolerated under our constitutional system, that evidences of crime discovered by a federal officer in making a search without lawful warrant maybe used against the victim of the unlawful search where a timely challenge has been interposed." (Emphasis added.) The Court, in Olmstead v. United States, 1928, in unmistakable language restated the *Weeks* rule:

> The striking outcome of the Weeks case and those which followed it was the sweeping declaration that the Fourth Amendment, although not referring to or limiting the use of evidence in court, really forbade its introduction if obtained by government officers through a violation of the amendment....

II

In 1949, 35 years after *Weeks* was announced, this Court, in Wolf v. People of State of Colorado, again for the first time, discussed the effect of the Fourth Amendment upon the States through the operation of the Due Process Clause of the Fourteenth Amendment. It said:

> [W]e have no hesitation in saying that were a State affirmatively to sanction such police incursion into privacy it would run counter to the guaranty of the Fourteenth Amendment.

Nevertheless, after declaring that the "security of one's privacy against arbitrary intrusion by the police" is "implicit in 'the concept of ordered liberty' and as such enforceable against the States through the Due Process Clause," and announcing that it "stoutly adhere[d]" to the *Weeks* decision, the Court decided that the Weeks exclusionary rule would not then be imposed upon the States as "an essential ingredient of the right." ... The Court's reasons for not considering essential to the right to privacy, as a curb imposed upon the States by the Due Process Clause, that which decades before had been posited as part and parcel of the Fourth Amendment's limitation upon federal encroachment of individual privacy, were bottomed on factual considerations.

While they are not basically relevant to a decision that the exclusionary rule is an essential ingredient of the Fourth Amendment as the right it embodies is vouchsafed against the States by the Due Process Clause, we will consider the current validity of the factual grounds upon which Wolf was based.

The Court in *Wolf* first stated that "[t]he contrariety of views of the States" on the adoption of the exclusionary rule of Weeks was "particularly impressive" ...; and, in this connection, that it could not "brush aside the experience of States which deem the incidence of such conduct by the police too slight to call for a deterrent remedy ... by overriding the [States'] relevant rules of evidence." ... While in 1949, prior to the *Wolf* case, almost two-thirds of the States were opposed to the use of the exclusionary rule, now, despite the *Wolf* case, more than half of those since passing upon it, by their own legislative or judicial decision, have wholly or partly adopted or adhered to the *Weeks* rule.... Significantly, among those now following the rule is California, which, according to its highest court, was "compelled to reach that conclusion because other remedies have completely failed to secure compliance with the constitutional provisions ..." People v. Cajan, 1955, ... In connection with this California case, we note that the second basis elaborated in *Wolf* in support of its failure to enforce the exclusionary doctrine against the States was that "other means of protection" have been afforded "the right to privacy." ... The experience of California that such other remedies have been worthless and futile is buttressed by the experience of other States. The obvious futility of relegating the Fourth Amendment to the protection of other remedies has, moreover, been recognized by this Court since *Wolf*.

Likewise, time has set its face against what *Wolf* called the "weighty testimony" of People v. Defore, 1926, 242 N.Y. 13, 150 N.E.585. There Justice (then Judge) Cardozo, rejecting adoption of the Weeks exclusionary rule in New York, had said that "[t]he Federal rule as it stands is either too strict or too lax." However, the force of that reasoning has been largely vitiated by later decisions of this Court. These include the recent discarding of the "silver platter" doctrine which allowed federal judicial use of evidence seized in violation of the Constitution by state agents, Elkins v. United States, 1960; the relaxation of the formerly strict requirements as to standing to challenge the use of evidence thus seized, so that now the procedure of exclusion, "ultimately referable to constitutional safeguards," is available to anyone even "legitimately on [the] premises" unlawfully searched, Jones v. United States, 1960; and finally, the formulation of a method to prevent state use of evidence unconstitutionally seized by federal agents, Rea v. United States, 1956. Because there can be no fixed formula, we are admittedly met with "recurring questions of the reasonableness of searches," but less is not to be expected when dealing with a Constitution, and, at any rate, "[r]easonableness is in the first instance for the [trial court] to determine." . . .

It, therefore, plainly appears that the factual considerations supporting the failure of the *Wolf* Court to include the *Weeks* exclusionary rule when it recognized the enforce ability of the right to privacy against the States in1949, while not basically relevant to the constitutional consideration, couldn't, in any analysis, now be deemed controlling.

III.

. . . Today we once again examine Wolf's constitutional documentation of the right to privacy free from unreasonable state intrusion, and, after its dozen years on our books, are led by it to close the only courtroom door remaining open to evidence secured by official lawlessness in flagrant abuse of that basic right, reserved to all persons as a specific guarantee against that very same unlawful conduct. We hold that all evidence obtained by searches and seizures in violation of the Constitution is, by that same authority, inadmissable in a state court.

IV.

Since the Fourth Amendment's right of privacy has been declared enforceable against the States through the Due Process Clause of the Fourteenth, it is enforceable against them by the same sanction of exclusion as is used against the Federal Government. Was it otherwise, then just as without the Weeks rule the assurance against unreasonable federal searches and seizures would be "a form of words," valueless and undeserving of mention in a perpetual charter of inestimable human liberties, so too, without that rule the freedom from state invasions of privacy would be so ephemeral and so neatly sever from its conceptual nexus with the freedom from all brutish means of coercing evidence as not to merit this Court's high regard as a freedom "implicit in 'the concept of ordered liberty?' " ... To hold otherwise is to grant the right but in reality to withhold its privilege and enjoyment. Only last year the Court itself recognized that the purpose of the exclusionary rule "is to deter" to compel respect for the constitutional guaranty in the only effectively available way "by removing the incentive to disregard it."

Indeed, we are aware of no restraint, similar to that rejected today, conditioning the enforcement of any other basic constitutional right. The right to privacy, no less important than any other right carefully and particularly reserved to the people, would stand in marked contrast to all other rights declared as "basic to a free society." Wolf v. People of State of Colorado, supra, ... This Court has not hesitated to enforce abstractly against the States as it does against the Federal Government the rights of free speech and of a free press, the rights to notice and to a fair, public trial, including, as it does, the right not to be convicted by use of a coerced confession, however logically relevant it be, and without regard to its reliability. And nothing could be more certain than that when a coerced confession is involved, "the relevant rules of evidence" are overridden without regard to "the incidence of such conduct by the police," slight or frequent....

V.

Moreover, our holding that the exclusionary rule is an essential part of both the Fourth and Fourteenth Amendments is not only the logical dictate of prior cases, but it also makes very good sense. Presently, a federal prosecutor may make no use of evidence illegally seized, but a State's attorney across the street may, although he supposedly is operating under the enforceable prohibitions of the same Amendment. Thus the State, by admitting evidence unlawfully seized, serves to encourage disobedience to the Federal Constitution which it is bound to uphold. Moreover, as was said in *Elkins* "the very essence of a healthy federalism depends upon the avoidance of needless conflict between state and federal courts."

* * *

There are those who say, as did Justice (then Judge) Cardozo, that under our constitutional exclusionary doctrine "[t]he criminal is to go free because the constable has blundered." People v. Defore. In some cases this will undoubtedly be the result. But, as was said in Elkins, "there is another consideration" the imperative of judicial integrity. ...The criminal goes free, if he must, but it is the law that sets him free. Nothing can destroy a government more quickly than its failure to observe its own laws, or worse, its disregard of the charter of its own existence. As Mr. Justice Brandeis, dissenting, said in Olmstead v. United States, 1928: "Our government is the potent, the omnipresent teacher. For good or for ill, it teaches the whole people by its example.... If the government becomes a lawbreaker, it breeds contempt for law; it invites every man to become a law unto himself; it invites anarchy."

* * *

The ignoble shortcut to conviction left open to the State tends to destroy the entire system of constitutional restraints on which the liberties of the people rest. Having once recognized that the right to privacy embodied in the Fourth Amendment is enforceable against the States, and that the right to be secure against rude invasions of privacy by state officers is, therefore, constitutional in origin, we can no longer permit that right to remain an empty promise. Because it is enforceable in the same manner and to like effect as other basic rights secured by the Due Process Clause, we can no longer permit it to be revocable at the whim of any police officer who, in the name of law enforcement itself, chooses to suspend its enjoyment. Our decision, founded on reason and truth, gives to the individual no more than that which the Constitution guarantees him, to the police officer no less than that to which honest law enforcement is entitled, and, to the courts, that judicial integrity so necessary in the true administration of justice. . . .

■ JUSTICE BLACK, concurring.

* * *

I am still not persuaded that the Fourth Amendment, standing alone, would be enough to bar the introduction into evidence against an accused of papers and effects seized from him in violation of its commands. For the Fourth Amendment does not itself contain any provision expressly precluding the use of such evidence, and I am extremely doubtful that such a provision could properly be inferred from nothing more than the basic command against unreasonable searches and seizures. Reflection of the problem however, in the light of cases coming before the Court since *Wolf*, has led me to conclude that when the Fourth Amendment's ban against unreasonable searches and seizures is considered together with the Fifth Amendment's ban against compelled self-incrimination, a constitutional basis emerges which not only justifies but actually requires the exclusionary rule.

The close interrelationship between the Fourth and Fifth Amendments, as they apply to this problem, has long been recognized and, indeed, was expressly made the ground for this Court's holding in Boyd v. United States. There the Court fully discussed this relationship and declared itself "unable to perceive that the seizure of a man's private books and papers to be used in evidence against him is substantially different from compelling him to be a witness against himself." . . .

* * *

. . . The Court's opinion, in my judgment, dissipates the doubt and uncertainty in this field of constitutional law and I am persuaded, for this and other reasons stated, to depart from my prior views, to accept the Boyd doctrine as controlling in this state case and to join the Court's judgment and opinion which are in accordance with that constitutional doctrine.

■ JUSTICE DOUGLAS' concurring opinion is omitted.

■ The Memorandum of JUSTICE STEWART is omitted.

■ JUSTICE HARLAN, whom JUSTICE FRANKFURTER and JUSTICE WHITTAKER join, dissenting.

In overruling the *Wolf* case the Court, in my opinion, has forgotten the sense of judicial restraint which, with due regard for stare decisis, is one element that should enter into deciding whether a past decision of this Court should be overruled. Apart from that I also believe that the *Wolf* rule represents sounder Constitutional doctrine than the new rule which now replaces it....

II.

Essential to the majority's argument against *Wolf* is the proposition that the rule of Weeks v. United States excluding in federal criminal trials the use of evidence obtained in violation of the Fourth Amendment, derives not from the "supervisory power" of this Court over the federal judicial system, but from Constitutional requirement. This is so because no one, I suppose, would suggest that this Court possesses any general supervisory power over the state courts. Although I entertain considerable doubt as to the soundness of this foundational proposition of the majority, ... I shall assume, for present purposes, that the *Weeks* rule "is of constitutional origin."

At the heart of the majority's opinion in this case is the following syllogism: (1) the rule excluding in federal criminal trials evidence which is the product of an illegal search and seizure is a "part and parcel" of the Fourth Amendment; (2) Wolf held that the "privacy" assured against federal action by the Fourth Amendment is also protected against state action by the Fourteenth Amendment; and (3) it is therefore "logically and constitutionally necessary" that the *Weeks* exclusionary rule should also be enforced against the States.

This reasoning ultimately rests on the unsound premise that because *Wolf* carried into the States, as part of "the concept of ordered liberty" embodied in the Fourteenth Amendment, the principle of "privacy" underlying the Fourth Amendment ..., it must follow that whatever configurations of the Fourth Amendment have been developed in the particularizing federal precedents are likewise to be deemed a part of "ordered liberty," and as such are enforceable against the States. For me, this does not follow at all....

I would not impose upon the States this federal exclusionary remedy. The reasons given by the majority for now suddenly turning its back on *Wolf* seem to me notably unconvincing.

First, it is said that "the factual grounds upon which *Wolf* was based" have since changed, in that more States now follow the *Weeks* exclusionary rule than was so at the time Wolf was decided. While that is true, a recent survey indicates that at present one-half of the States still adhere to the common-law non-exclusionary rule, and one, Maryland, retains the rule as to felonies. Berman and Oberst, Admissibility of Evidence Obtained by an Unconstitutional Search and Seizure, 55 N.W.L.Rev. 525, 532–533. But in any case surely all this is beside the point, as the majority itself indeed seems to recognize. Our concern here, as it was in Wolf, is not with the desirability of that rule but only with the question whether the States are Constitutionally free to follow it or not as they may themselves determine, and the relevance of the disparity of views among the States on this point lies simply in the fact that the judgment involved is a debatable one. . . .

The preservation of a proper balance between state and federal responsibility in the administration of criminal justice demands patience on the part of those who might like to see things move faster among the States in this respect. Problems of criminal law enforcement vary widely from State to State. One State, in considering the totality of its legal picture, may conclude that the need for embracing the Weeks rule is pressing because other remedies are unavailable or inadequate to secure compliance with the substantive Constitutional principle involved. Another, though equally solicitous of Constitutional rights, may choose to pursue one purpose at a time, allowing all evidence relevant to guilt to be brought into a criminal trial, and dealing with Constitutional infractions by other means. Still another may consider the exclusionary rule too rough-and-ready a remedy, in that it reaches only unconstitutional intrusions which eventuate in criminal prosecution of the victims. Further, a State after experimenting with the *Weeks* rule for a time may, because of unsatisfactory experience with it, decide to revert to a non-exclusionary rule.

* * *

Finally, it is said that the overruling of *Wolf* is supported by the established doctrine that the admission in evidence of an involuntary confession renders a state conviction Constitutionally invalid. Since such a confession may often be entirely reliable, and therefore of the greatest relevance to the issue of the trial, the argument continues, this doctrine is ample warrant in precedent that the way evidence was obtained, and not just its relevance, is Constitutionally significant to the fairness of a trial. I believe this analogy is not a true one. The "coerced confession" rule is certainly not a rule that any illegally obtained statements may not be used in evidence. I would suppose that a statement which is procured during a period of illegal detention is, as much as unlawfully seized evidence, illegally obtained, but this Court has consistently refused to reverse state convictions resting on the use of such statements. . . .

The point, then, must be that in requiring exclusion of an involuntary statement of an accused, we are concerned not with an appropriate remedy for what the police have done, but with something which is regarded as going to the heart of our concepts of fairness in judicial procedure. . . .

I regret that I find so unwise in principle and so inexpedient in policy a decision motivated by the high purpose of increasing respect for Constitutional rights. But in the last analysis I think this Court can increase respect for the Constitution only if it rigidly respects the limitations which the Constitution places upon it, and respects as well the principles inherent in its own processes. In the present case I think we exceed both, and that our voice becomes only a voice of power, not of reason.

NOTES

1. For very light reading which provides some background about Mrs. Mapp, the police "investigation" in her case, and her later encounters with the law, see L.

Stevens, Trespass! (1977). Stevens suggests that the real target of the investigation was Donald King, then a gambling suspect, but much later a highly successful boxing promoter.

2. Section 24 of the 1982 Canadian Constitution's Charter of Rights and Freedoms provides:

> (1) Anyone whose rights or freedoms, as guaranteed by this chapters, have been infringed or denied may apply to a court of competent jurisdiction to obtain such remedy as the court considers appropriate and just in the circumstances.
>
> (2) Where, in proceeding under subsection (1), a court concludes that evidence was obtained in a manner that infringed or denied any rights or freedoms guaranteed by this chapter, the evidence shall be excluded if it is established that, having regard to all the circumstances, the admission of it in proceedings would bring the administration of justice into disrepute.

3. Values underlying the Fourth Amendment Exclusionary Rule. Under Mapp, what values underlie the Fourth Amendment Exclusionary Girl? The consensus of the Court was that the Fourth amendment protected privacy. "The Fourth Amendment was meant to be a part of 'a perpetual charter of inestimable human liberties' ... and it stood on equal footing with other liberties guaranteed in the Bill of Rights." Even the dissent recognized that the *Mapp* majority opinion was "motivated by the high purpose of increasing respect for Constitutional rights." Marsh, "On Rollercoasters, Submarines, and Judicial Shipwrecks: Acoustic Separation and the Good Faith Exception to the Fourth Amendment Exclusionary Rule," 1989 U.Ill.L.Rev. 941, 953 (cites omitted)

4. Bases for Adopting the Exclusionary Rule: Consider the following as bases for the exclusionary rule: judicial integrity; deterrence, symbolic values, practicality, due process. Which of these reasons are persuasive? Which are not?

5. As the following materials will illustrate, a court's view of the purpose of the exclusionary rule may determine its attitude toward preserving or abolishing the rule, or toward broadening or narrowing its impact. To the extent that the rule's purpose and justification is to deter police misconduct, the empirical question as to its impact is of utmost importance. To the extent to which the rule's purpose has to do with the "imperative of the judicial integrity," the advocates of exclusion need not rest their case upon an empirical base. What purpose is emphasized in *Mapp*? For a view that not until Wolf, thirty-five years after *Weeks*, was deterrence offered as a justification for the exclusionary rule, see McKay, Mapp v. Ohio, The Exclusionary Rule and The Right of Privacy, 15 Ariz.L.Rev. 327 (1973).

6. The Exclusionary Rule Wars—The Case in Favor of the Exclusionary Rule. A few of the arguments in favor of the Exclusionary Rule include:

> a. If the Court does not create remedies for Fourth Amendment violations, no one will. The preservation of Fourth Amendment Rights is not a popular task for legislators trying to gain reelection.
>
> b. The Exclusionary Rule deters constitutional violations and educates and sensitizes officers to protect constitutional rights.
>
> c. If the Court did not incorporate the Exclusionary Rule to apply to the states, there would be an incentive for officers to take tainted evidence to the states where the evidence would be admis-

sible notwithstanding the constitutional violation. This is known as the "silver platter doctrine."

d. Alternative remedies are inadequate.

7. The Exclusionary Rule Wars—The Criticisms of the Exclusionary Rule. Debate over the wisdom and efficacy of the Fourth Amendment Exclusionary Rule has raged for years. A full exposition of criticisms raised against the exclusionary rule would be lengthy and unwieldy, but here is a sampling of some of the criticisms of the exclusionary rule:

a. The rule requires the sacrifice of probative evidence.

". . . it seems clear to me that the exclusionary rule has been operative long enough to demonstrate its flaws. The time has come to modify its reach, even if it is retained for a small and limited category of cases.

Over the years, the strains imposed by reality, in terms of the costs to society and the bizarre miscarriages of justice that have been experienced because of the exclusion of reliable evidence when the 'constable blunders,' have led the Court to vacillate as to the rationale for deliberate exclusion of truth from the fact-finding process. The rhetoric has varied with the rationale to the point where the rule has become a doctrinaire result in search of validating reasons.

In evaluating the exclusionary rule, it is important to bear in mind exactly what the rule accomplishes. Its function is simple—the exclusion of truth from the fact-finding process. . . . The operation of the rule is therefore unlike that of the Fifth Amendment's protection against compelled self-incrimination. A confession produced after intimidating or coercive interrogation is inherently dubious. If a suspect's will has been overborne, a cloud hangs over his custodial admissions; the exclusion of such statements is based essentially on their lack of reliability. This is not the case as to reliable evidence—a pistol, a packet of heroin, counterfeit money, or the body of a murder victim—which may be judicially declared to be the result of an 'unreasonable' search. The reliability of such evidence is beyond question; its probative value is certain." Stone v. Powell, 428 U.S. 465, 498, 96 S.Ct. 3037 (Justice Burger, concurring)

b. The rule frees the guilty. "The criminal goes free because the constable has blundered." People v. Defore, 242 N.Y. 13, 21, 150 N.E. 585, 587 (Cardozo, J.) cert. denied, 270 U.S. 657, 46 S.Ct. 353 (1926).

c. The rule frees the guilty simply on a "technicality."

d. The rule distorts the truth, undermines the integrity of the fact-finding process and intrudes on the function of the jury. See Crump, The "Tainted Evidence" Rationale: Does It Really Support the Exclusionary Rule?, 23 S. TEX. L.J. 687, 691 (1982).

e. The exclusionary rule diverts the focus of the criminal trial. As [then] California Attorney General George Deukmejian recently stated: "The nature of a criminal trial has been altered from a test of the defendant's guilt or innocence to an inquiry into the propriety of the policeman's conduct. Rather than a search for the truth, today's criminal trial is a search for error." Deukmejian, Prosecutors Attack Exclusionary Rule, 54 CAL. ST. B.J. 396 (1979).

f. The rule burdens courts with additional adjudications at the expense of resolving other matters.

g. The rule hinders police.

h. The rule encourages perjury and misconduct by police officers.

i. Criminals are able to manipulate the rule to their own benefit and to the detriment of the general public. Crump, supra, at 69 1;

j. The rule protects only the guilty, leaving the innocent without a meaningful remedy.

k. The rule forces the court to intrude unnecessarily into the powers of the executive branch and into the fact-finding process of lower courts.

l. The rule prevents the creation of alternatives and vitiates efforts to create internal police disciplinary mechanisms. See generally K.C. DAVIS, DISCRETIONARY JUSTICE: A PRELIMINARY INQUIRY (1969).

m. The rule fails to deter police illegality.

n. The rule creates a public perception that the exclusionary rule causes escalating crime rates and, as such, the legitimacy of the judicial function is undermined and the rule is actually detrimental to judicial integrity. Lesley, Is It Time for a Change in the Exclusionary Rule? United States v. Williams and the Good Faith Exception, 60 WASH. U.L.Q. 161 (1982).

o. The rule is "draconian" in its "all-or-nothing" approach that fails to account for the seriousness of the crime with which the accused is charged or the "degree" of constitutional violation by the officer. Kaplan, The Limits of the Exclusionary Rule, 26 STAN. L. REV. 1027 (1974).

See Donald Dripps, "The Case for the Contingent Exclusionary Rule," 38 Am. Crim. L. Rev. 1 (2001); Sharon Davies, "The Penalty of Exclusion—A Price or Sanction," 73 S. Cal. L. Rev. 1275 (2000); Timothy Perrin, H. Mitchell Caldwell, Carol A. Chase, Ronald W. Fagan, "If It's Broken, Fix It: Moving Beyond the Exclusionary Rule," 83 Iowa L. Rev. 669 (1998); Christopher Slobogin, "Why Liberals Should Chuck the Exclusionary Rule," 1999 U. Ill. L. Rev. 363 (1999).

C. THE GOOD-FAITH EXCEPTION

United States v. Leon

Supreme Court of the United States, 1984.
468 U.S. 897, 104 S.Ct. 3405.

■ JUSTICE WHITE delivered the opinion of the Court.

This case presents the question whether the Fourth Amendment exclusionary rule should be modified so as not to bar the use in the prosecution's case-in-chief of evidence obtained by officers acting in reasonable reliance on a search warrant issued by a detached and neutral magistrate but ultimately found to be unsupported by probable cause. To resolve this question, we must consider once again the tension between the sometimes competing goals of, on the one hand, deterring official misconduct and removing inducements to unreasonable invasions of privacy and, on the other, establishing procedures under which criminal defendants are "acquitted or convicted on the basis of all the evidence which exposes the truth." Alderman v. United States (1969).

In August 1981, a confidential informant of unproven reliability informed an officer of the Burbank Police Department that two persons known to him as "Armando" and "Patsy" were selling large quantities of cocaine and methaqualone from their residence at 620 Price Drive in

Burbank, Cal. The informant also indicated that he had witnessed a sale of methaqualone by "Patsy" at the residence approximately five months earlier and had observed at that time a shoe box containing a large amount of cash that belonged to "Patsy." He further declared that "Armando" and "Patsy" generally kept only small quantities of drugs at their residence and stored the remainder at another location in Burbank.

On the basis of this information, the Burbank police initiated an extensive investigation focusing first on the Price Drive residence and later on two other residences as well. Cars parked at the Price Drive residence were determined to belong to respondents Armando Sanchez, who had previously been arrested for possession of marihuana, and Patsy Stewart, who had no criminal record. During the course of the investigation, officers observed an automobile belonging to respondent Ricardo Del Castillo, who had previously been arrested for possession of 50 pounds of marihuana, arrive at the Price Drive residence. The driver of that car entered the house, exited shortly there after carrying a small paper sack, and drove away. A check of Del Castillo's probation records led the officers to respondent Alberto Leon, whose telephone number Del Castillo had listed as his employer's. Leon had been arrested in 1980 on drug charges, and a companion had informed the police at that time that Leon was heavily involved in the importation of drugs into this country. Before the current investigation began, the Burbank officers had learned that an informant had told a Glendale police officer that Leon stored a large quantity of methaqualone at his residence in Glendale. During the course of this investigation, the Burbank officers learned that Leon was living at 716 South Sunset Canyon in Burbank.

Subsequently, the officers observed several persons, at least one of whom had prior drug involvement, arriving at the Price Drive residence and leaving with small packages; observed a variety of other material activity at the two residences as well as at a condominium at 7902 Via Magdalena; and witnessed a variety of relevant activity involving respondents' automobiles. The officers also observed respondents Sanchez and Stewart board separate flights for Miami. The pair later returned to Los Angeles together, consented to a search of their luggage that revealed only a small amount of marihuana, and left the airport. Based on these and other observations summarized in the affidavit, App. 34, Officer Cyril Rombach of the Burbank Police Department, an experienced and well-trained narcotics investigator, prepared an application for a warrant to search 620 Price Drive, 716 South Sunset Canyon, 7902 Via Magdalena, and automobiles registered to each of the respondents for an extensive list of items believed to be related to respondents' drug-trafficking activities. Officer Rombach's extensive application was reviewed by several Deputy District Attorneys.

A facially valid search warrant was issued in September 1981 by a state superior court judge. The ensuing searches produced large quantities of drugs at the Via Magdalena and Sunset Canyon addresses and a small quantity at the Price Drive residence. Other evidence was discovered at each of the residences and in Stewart's and Del Castillo's automobiles. Respondents were indicted by a grand jury in the District Court for the

Central District of California and charged with conspiracy to possess and distribute cocaine and a variety of substantive counts.

The respondents then filed motions to suppress the evidence seized pursuant to the warrant. The District Court held an evidentiary hearing and, while recognizing that the case was a close one, granted the motions to suppress in part. It concluded that the affidavit was insufficient to establish probable cause, but did not suppress all of the evidence as to all of the respondents because none of the respondents had standing to challenge all of the searches. In response to a request from the Government, the court made clear that Officer Rombach had acted in good faith, but it rejected the Government's suggestion that the Fourth Amendment exclusionary rule should not apply where evidence is seized in reasonable, good-faith reliance on a search warrant.[1]

. . . The Court of Appeals first concluded that Officer Rombach's affidavit could not establish probable cause to search the Price Drive residence. To the extent that the affidavit set forth facts demonstrating the basis of the informant's knowledge of criminal activity, the information included was fatally stale. The affidavit, moreover, failed to establish the informant's credibility. Accordingly, the Court of Appeals concluded that the information provided by the informant was inadequate under both prongs of the two-part test established in Aguilar v. Texas (1964), and Spinelli v. United States (1969). The officers' independent investigation neither cured the staleness nor corroborated the details of the informant's declarations. The Court of Appeals then considered whether the affidavit formed a proper basis for the search of the Sunset Canyon residence. In its view, the affidavit included no facts indicating the basis for the informants' statements concerning respondent Leon's criminal activities and was devoid of information establishing the informants' reliability. Because these deficiencies had not been cured by the police investigation, the District Court properly suppressed the fruits of the search. The Court of Appeals refused the Government's invitation to recognize a good-faith exception to the Fourth Amendment exclusionary rule. . . .Although it undoubtedly is within our power to consider the question whether probable cause existed under the "totality of the circumstances" test announced last Term in Illinois v. Gates (1983), that question has not been briefed or argued; and it is also within our authority, which we choose to exercise, to take the case as it comes to us, accepting the Court of Appeals' conclusion that probable cause was lacking under the prevailing legal standards.

We have concluded that, in the Fourth Amendment context, the exclusionary rule can be modified somewhat without jeopardizing its ability to perform its intended functions. Accordingly, we reverse the judgment of the Court of Appeals.

1. "On the issue of good faith, obviously that is not the law of the Circuit, and I am not going to apply that law.

"I will say certainly in my view, there is not any question about good faith. [Officer Rombach] went to a Superior Court judge and got a warrant; obviously laid a meticulous trail. Had surveilled for a long period of time, and I believe his testimony—and I think he said he consulted with three Deputy District Attorneys before proceeding himself, and I certainly have no doubt about the fact that that is true."

Language in opinions of this Court and of individual Justices has sometimes implied that the exclusionary rule is a necessary corollary of the Fourth Amendment, Mapp v. Ohio (1961); Olmstead v. United States (1928), or that the rule is required by the conjunction of the Fourth and Fifth Amendments. Mapp v. Ohio (BLACK, J., concurring); Agnello v. United States (1925). These implications need not detain us long. The Fifth Amendment theory has not withstood critical analysis or the test of time, see Andersen v. Maryland (1976), and the Fourth Amendment "has never been interpreted to proscribe the introduction of illegally seized evidence in all proceedings or against all persons." Stone v. Powell (1976).

The Fourth Amendment contains no provision expressly precluding the use of evidence obtained in violation of its commands, and an examination of its origin and purposes makes clear that the use of fruits of a past unlawful search or seizure "work[s] no new Fourth Amendment wrong." United States v. Calandra (1974). The wrong condemned by the Amendment is "fully accomplished" by the unlawful search or seizure itself, and the exclusionary rule is neither intended nor able to "cure the invasion of the defendant's rights which he has already suffered." Stone v. Powell (WHITE, J., dissenting). The rule thus operates as "a judicially created remedy designed to safeguard Fourth Amendment rights generally through its deterrent effect, rather than a personal constitutional right of the person aggrieved." United States v. Calandra.

* * *

The substantial social costs exacted by the exclusionary rule for the vindication of Fourth Amendment rights have long been a source of concern. "Our cases have consistently recognized that unbending application of the exclusionary sanction to enforce ideals of governmental rectitude would impede unacceptably the truth-finding functions of judge and jury." United States v. Payner (1980). An objectionable collateral consequence of this interference with the criminal justice system's truth-finding function is that some guilty defendants may go free or receive reduced sentences as a result of favorable plea bargains.[2] Particularly when law

2. Researchers have only recently begun to study extensively the effects of the exclusionary rule on the disposition of felony arrests. One study suggests that the rule results in the nonprosecution or nonconviction of between 0.6% and 2.35% of individuals arrested for felonies. Davies, A Hard Look at What We Know (and Still Need to Learn) About the "Costs" of the Exclusionary Rule: The NIJ Study and Other Studies of "Lost" Arrests, 1983 A.B.F. Res. J. 611, 621. The estimates are higher for particular crimes the prosecution of which depends heavily on physical evidence. Thus, the cumulative loss due to nonprosecution or non-conviction of individuals arrested on felony drug charges is robably in the range of 2.8% to 7.1%. Id., at 680. Davies' analysis of California data suggests that screening by the police and prosecutors results in the release because of illegal searches or seizures of as many as 1.4% of all felony arrestees, id., at 650, that 0.9% of felony arrestees are released because of illegal searches or seizures at the preliminary hearing or after trial. Id., at 653, and that roughly 0.5% of all felony arrestees benefit from reversals on appeal because of illegal searches. Id., at 654. See also K. Brosi, A Cross–City comparison of Felony Case Processing 16, 18–19 (1979); Report of the Comptroller General of the United States, Impact of the Exclusionary Rule on Federal Criminal Prosecutions 10–11, 14 (1979); F. Feeney, F. Dill & A. Weir, Arrests Without Convictions: How often they Occur and why203–206 (1983); National Institute of Justice, The Effects of the Exclusionary Rule: A Study in California 1–2 (1982); Nardulli, The Societal

enforcement officers have acted in objective good faith or their transgressions have been minor, the magnitude of the benefit conferred on such guilty defendants offends basic concepts of the criminal justice system. Indiscriminate application of the exclusionary rule, therefore, may well "generat[e] disrespect for the law and the administration of justice." Accordingly, "[a]s with any remedial device, the application of the rule has been restricted to those areas where its remedial objectives are thought most efficaciously served."

Close attention to those remedial objectives has characterized our recent decisions concerning the scope of the Fourth Amendment exclusionary rule. The Court has, to be sure, not seriously questioned, "in the absence of a more efficacious sanction, the continued application of the rule to suppress evidence from the [prosecution's] case where a Fourth Amendment violation has been substantial and deliberate. . . ." Franks v. Delaware (1978); Stone v. Powell. Nevertheless, the balancing approach that has evolved in various contexts "including criminal trials" "forcefully suggest[s] that the exclusionary rule be more generally modified to permit the introduction of evidence obtained in the reasonable good-faith belief that a search or seizure was in accord with the Fourth Amendment." Illinois v. Gates (WHITE, J., concurring in the judgment). . . .

The same attention to the purposes underlying the exclusionary rule also has characterized decisions not involving the scope of the rule itself. We have not required suppression of the fruits of a search incident to an arrest made in good-faith reliance on a substantive criminal statute that subsequently is declared unconstitutional. Michigan v. DeFillippo (1979).[3] Similarly, although the Court has been unwilling to conclude that new Fourth Amendment principles are always to have only prospective effect, no Fourth Amendment decision marking a "clear break with the past" has been applied retroactively. See United States v. Peltier (1975); Desist v.

Cost of the Exclusionary Rule: An Empirical Assessment, 1983 A.B.F.Res.J. 585, 600. The exclusionary rule also has been found to effect the plea-bargaining process. S. Schlesinger, Exclusionary Injustice: The Problem of Illegally Obtained Evidence 63 (1977). But see Davies, supra, at 668–669; Nardulli, supra, at 604–606.

Many of these researchers have concluded that the impact of the exclusionary rule is insubstantial, but the small percentages with which they deal mask a large absolute number of felons who are released because the cases against them were based in part on illegal searches or seizures. "[A]ny rule of evidence that denies the jury access to clearly probative and reliable evidence must bear a heavy burden of justification, and must be carefully limited to the circumstances in which it will pay its way by deterring official unlawfulness." Illinois v. Gates (White, J., concurring in the judgment). Because we find that the rule can have no substantial deterrent effect in the sorts of situations under consideration in this case, we conclude that it cannot pay its way in those situations.

3. We have held, however, that the exclusionary rule requires suppression of evidence obtained in searches carried out pursuant to statutes, not yet declared unconstitutional, purporting to authorize searches and seizures without probable cause or search warrants. See, e.g., Ybarra v. Illinois (1979); Torres v. Puerto Rico (1979); Almeida–Sanchez v. United States (1973); Sibron v. New York (1968); Berger v. New York (1967). "Those decisions involved statutes which, by their own terms, authorized searches under circumstances which did not satisfy the traditional warrant and probable-cause requirements of the Fourth Amendment." Michigan v. DeFillippo (1979). The substantive Fourth Amendment principles announced in those cases are fully consistent with our holding here.

United States (1969); Linkletter v. Walker (1965). The propriety of retroactive application of a newly announced Fourth Amendment principle, moreover, has been assessed largely in terms of the contribution retroactivity might make to the deterrence of police misconduct.

As yet, we have not recognized any form of good-faith exception to the Fourth Amendment exclusionary rule. But the balancing approach that has evolved during the years of experience with the rule provides strong support for the modification currently urged upon us. As we discuss below, our evaluation of the costs and benefits of suppressing reliable physical evidence seized by officers reasonably relying on a warrant issued by a detached and neutral magistrate leads to the conclusion that such evidence should be admissible in the prosecution's case-in-chief.

.... To the extent that proponents of exclusion rely on its behavioral effects on judges and magistrates in these areas, their reliance is misplaced. First, the exclusionary rule is designed to deter police misconduct rather than to punish the errors of judges and magistrates. Second, there exists no evidence suggesting that judges and magistrates are inclined to ignore or subvert the Fourth Amendment or that lawlessness among these actors requires application of the extreme sanction of exclusion.[4]

Third, and most important, we discern no basis, and are offered none, for believing that exclusion of evidence seized pursuant to a warrant will have a significant deterrent effect on the issuing judge or magistrate.[5] Many of the factors that indicate that the exclusionary rule cannot provide an effective "special" or "general" deterrent for individual offending law enforcement officers apply as well to judges or magistrates. And, to the extent that the rule is thought to operate as a "systemic" deterrent on a wider audience, it clearly can have no such effect on individuals empowered

4. Although there are assertions that some magistrates become rubber stamps for the police and others may be unable effectively to screen police conduct, see, e.g., 2 W. LaFave, Search and Seizure § 4.1 (1978); Kamisar, Does (Did) (Should) the Exclusionary Rule Rest on a "Principled Basis" Rather than an "Empirical Proposition"?, 16 Creighton L.Rev. 565, 569–571 (1983); Schroeder, Deterring Fourth Amendment Violations; Alternatives to the Exclusionary Rule, 69 Geo. L.J. 1361, 1412 (1981), we are not convinced that this is a problem of major proportions. See L. Tiffany, D. McIntyre & D. Rotenberg, Detection of Crime 119 (1967); Israel, Criminal Procedure, the Burger Court, and the Legacy of the Warren Court, 75 Mich.L.Rev. 1319, 1414, n. 396 (1977); P. Johnson, New Approaches to Enforcing the Fourth Amendment 8–10 (Working Paper, Sept. 1978), quoted in Y. Kamisar, W. LaFave & J. Israel, Modern Criminal Procedure 229–230 (5th ed.1980); R. Van Duizend, L. Sutton & C. Carter, The Search Warrant Process ch. 7 (Review Draft, 1983).

5. As the Supreme Judicial Court of Massachusetts recognized in Commonwealth v. Sheppard, 387 Mass. 488, 506, 441 N.E.2d 725, 735 (1982):

"The exclusionary rule may not be well tailored to deterring judicial misconduct. If applied to judicial misconduct, the rule would be just as costly as it is when it is applied to police misconduct, but it may be ill-fitted to the job-created motivations of judges. ...[I]deally a judge is impartial as to whether a particular piece of evidence is admitted or a particular defendant convicted. Hence, in the abstract, suppression of a particular piece of evidence may not be as effective a disincentive to a neutral judge as it would be to the police. It may be that a ruling by an appellate court that a search warrant was unconstitutional would be sufficient to deter similar misconduct in the future by magistrates."

But see United States v. Karathanos, 531 F.2d 26, 33–34 (CA2), cert. denied, 428 U.S. 910, 96 S.Ct. 3221 (1976).

to issue search warrants. Judges and magistrates are not adjuncts to the law enforcement team; as neutral judicial officers, they have no stake in the outcome of particular criminal prosecutions. The threat of exclusion thus cannot be expected significantly to deter them. Imposition of the exclusionary sanction is not necessary meaningfully to inform judicial officers of their errors, and we cannot conclude that admitting evidence obtained pursuant to a warrant while at the same time declaring that the warrant was somehow defective will in any way reduce judicial officers' professional incentives to comply with the Fourth Amendment, encourage them to repeat their mistakes, or lead to the granting of all colorable warrant requests.

If exclusion of evidence obtained pursuant to a subsequently invalidated warrant is to have any deterrent effect, therefore, it must alter the behavior of individual law enforcement officers or the policies of their departments. One could argue that applying the exclusionary rule in cases where the police failed to demonstrate probable cause in the warrant application deters future inadequate presentations or "magistrate shopping" and thus promotes the ends of the Fourth Amendment. Suppressing evidence obtained pursuant to a technically defective warrant supported by probable cause also might encourage officers to scrutinize more closely the form of the warrant and to point out suspected judicial errors. We find such arguments speculative and conclude that suppression of evidence obtained pursuant to a warrant should be ordered only on a case-by-case basis and only in those unusual cases in which exclusion will further the purposes of the exclusionary rule....[6]

We conclude that the marginal or nonexistent benefits produced by suppressing evidence obtained in objectively reasonable reliance on a subsequently invalidated search warrant cannot justify the substantial costs of exclusion.[7] We do not suggest, however, that exclusion is always inappropri-

6. Our discussion of the deterrent effect of excluding evidence obtained in reasonable reliance on a subsequently invalidated warrant assumes, of course, that the officers properly executed the warrant and searched only those places and for those objects that it was reasonable to believe were covered by the warrant.

7. We emphasize that the standard of reasonableness we adopt is an objective one. Many objections to a good-faith exception assume that the exception will turn on the subjective good faith of individual officers. "Grounding the modification in objective reasonableness, however, retains the value of the exclusionary rule as an incentive for the law enforcement profession as a whole to conduct themselves in accord with the Fourth Amendment." Illinois v. Gates (White, J., concurring in the judgment); see Dunaway v. New York (Stevens, J., concurring). The objective standard we adopt, moreover, requires officers to have a reasonable knowledge of what the law prohibits. As Professor Jerold Israel has observed:

"The key to the [exclusionary] rule's effectiveness as a deterrent lies, I believe, in the impetus it has provided to police training programs that make officers aware of the limits imposed by the fourth amendment and emphasize the need to operate within those limits. [An objective good-faith exception] ... is not likely to result in the elimination of such programs, which are now viewed as an important aspect of police professionalism. Neither is it likely to alter the tenor of those programs; the possibility that illegally obtained evidence may be admitted in borderline cases is unlikely to encourage police instructors to pay less attention to fourth amendment limitations. Finally, [it] ... should not encourage officers to pay less attention to what they are taught, as the requirement that the officer act in 'good faith' is inconsistent with closing one's mind to the possibility of illegality."

ate in cases where an officer has obtained a warrant and abided by its terms. "[S]earches pursuant to a warrant will rarely require any deep inquiry into reasonableness," Illinois v. Gates, (White, J., concurring in the judgment), for "a warrant issued by a magistrate normally suffices to establish" that a law enforcement officer has "acted in good faith in conducting the search." Nevertheless, the officer's reliance on the magistrate's probable-cause determination and on the technical sufficiency of the warrant he issues must be objectively reasonable, cf. Harlow v. Fitzgerald (1982),[8] and it is clear that in some circumstances the officer[9] will have no reasonable grounds for believing that the warrant was properly issued.

Suppression therefore remains an appropriate remedy if the magistrate or judge in issuing a warrant was misled by information in an affidavit that the affiant knew was false or would have known was false except for his reckless disregard of the truth. Franks v. Delaware (1978). The exception we recognize today will also not apply in cases where the issuing magistrate wholly abandoned his judicial role in the manner condemned in Lo-Ji Sales, Inc. v. New York (1979); in such circumstances, no reasonably well-trained officer should rely on the warrant. Nor would an officer manifest objective good faith in relying on a warrant based on an affidavit "so lacking in indicia of probable cause as to render official belief in its existence entirely unreasonable." Brown v. Illinois, (POWELL, J., concurring in part); see Illinois v. Gates, (WHITE, J., concurring in the judgment). Finally, depending on the circumstances of the particular case, a warrant may be so facially deficient—i.e., in failing to particularize the place to be searched or the things to be seized—that the executing officers cannot reasonably presume it to be valid. Cf. Massachusetts v. Sheppard (1984).

In so limiting the suppression remedy, we leave untouched the probable-cause standard and the various requirements for a valid warrant. Other objections to the modification of the Fourth Amendment exclusionary rule we consider to be insubstantial. The good-faith exception for searches

8. In *Harlow*, we eliminated the subjective component of the qualified immunity public officials enjoy in suits seeking damages for alleged deprivations of constitutional rights. The situations are not perfectly analogous, but we also eschew inquiries into the subjective beliefs of law enforcement officers who seize evidence pursuant to a subsequently invalidated warrant. Although we have suggested that "[o]n occasion, the motive with which the officer conducts the illegal search may have some relevance in determining the propriety of applying the exclusionary rule," Scott v. United States (1978), we believe that "[s]ending state and federal courts into the minds of police officers would produce a grave and fruitless mis-allocation of judicial resources." Massachusetts v. Painten (1968) (White, J., dissenting). Accordingly, our good-faith inquiry is confined to the objectively ascertainable question whether a reasonably well-trained officer would have known that the search was illegal despite the magistrate's authorization. In making this determination, all of the circumstances "including whether the warrant application had previously been rejected by a different magistrate" may be considered.

9. References to "officer" throughout this opinion should not be read too narrowly. It is necessary to consider the objective reasonableness, not only of the officers who eventually executed a warrant, but also of the officers who originally obtained it or who provided information material to the probable-cause determination. Nothing in our opinion suggests, for example, that an officer could obtain a warrant on the basis of a "bare bones" affidavit and then rely on colleagues who are ignorant of the circumstances under which the warrant was obtained to conduct the search. See Whiteley v. Warden, 401 U.S. 560, 568, 91 S.Ct. 1031, 1037, 28 L.Ed.2d 306 (1971).

conducted pursuant to warrants is not intended to signal our unwillingness strictly to enforce the requirements of the Fourth Amendment, and we do not believe that it will have this effect. As we have already suggested, the good-faith exception, turning as it does on objective reasonableness, should not be difficult to apply in practice. When officers have acted pursuant to a warrant, the prosecution should ordinarily be able to establish objective good faith without a substantial expenditure of judicial time.

Nor are we persuaded that application of a good-faith exception to searches conducted pursuant to warrants will preclude review of the constitutionality of the search or seizure, deny needed guidance from the courts, or freeze Fourth Amendment law in its present state. There is no need for courts to adopt the inflexible practice of always deciding whether the officers' conduct manifested objective good faith before turning to the question whether the Fourth Amendment has been violated. Defendants seeking suppression of the fruits of allegedly unconstitutional searches or seizures undoubtedly raise live controversies which Article III empowers federal courts to adjudicate. . . .

When the principles we have enunciated today are applied to the facts of this case, it is apparent that the judgment of the Court of Appeals cannot stand. The Court of Appeals applied the prevailing legal standards to Officer Rombach's warrant application and concluded that the application could not support the magistrate's probable-cause determination. In so doing, the court clearly informed the magistrate that he had erred in issuing the challenged warrant. This aspect of the court's judgment is not under attack in this proceeding.

Having determined that the warrant should not have issued, the Court of Appeals understandably declined to adopt a modification of the Fourth Amendment exclusionary rule that this Court had not previously sanctioned. Although the modification finds strong support in our previous cases, the Court of Appeals' commendable self-restraint is not to be criticized. We have now re-examined the purposes of the exclusionary rule and the propriety of its application in cases where officers have relied on a subsequently invalidated search warrant. Our conclusion is that the rule's purposes will only rarely be served by applying it in such circumstances.

In the absence of an allegation that the magistrate abandoned his detached and neutral role, suppression is appropriate only if the officers were dishonest or reckless in preparing their affidavit or could not have harbored an objectively reasonable belief in the existence of probable cause. Only respondent Leon has contended that no reasonably well-trained police officer could have believed that there existed probable cause to search his house; significantly, the other respondents advance no comparable argument. Officer Rombach's application for a warrant clearly was supported by much more than a "bare bones" affidavit. The affidavit related the results of an extensive investigation and, as the opinions of the divided panel of the Court of Appeals make clear, provided evidence sufficient to create disagreement among thoughtful and competent judges as to the existence of probable cause. Under these circumstances, the officers' reliance on the magistrate's determination of probable cause was objectively reasonable, and application of the extreme sanction of exclusion is inappropriate.

■ Justice Blackmun, concurring.

.... As the Court's opinion in this case makes clear, the Court has narrowed the scope of the exclusionary rule because of an empirical judgment that the rule has little appreciable effect in cases where officers act in objectively reasonable reliance on search warrants. Because I share the view that the exclusionary rule is not a constitutionally compelled corollary of the Fourth Amendment itself, I see no way to avoid making an empirical judgment of this sort, and I am satisfied that the Court has made the correct one on the information before it. Like all courts, we face institutional limitations on our ability to gather information about "legislative facts," and the exclusionary rule itself has exacerbated the shortage of hard data concerning the behavior of police officers in the absence of such a rule. Nonetheless, we cannot escape the responsibility to decide the question before us, however imperfect our information may be, and I am prepared to join the Court on the information now at hand.

What must be stressed, however, is that any empirical judgment about the effect of the exclusionary rule in a particular class of cases necessarily is a provisional one. By their very nature, the assumptions on which we proceed today cannot be cast in stone. To the contrary, they now will be tested in the real world of state and federal law enforcement, and this Court will attend to the results. If it should emerge from experience that, contrary to our expectations, the good faith exception to the exclusionary rule results in a material change in police compliance with the Fourth Amendment, we shall have to reconsider what we have undertaken here. The logic of a decision that rests on untested predictions about police conduct demands no less.

If a single principle may be drawn from this Court's exclusionary rule decisions, from *Weeks* through *Mapp*, to the decisions handed down today, it is that the scope of the exclusionary rule is subject to change in light of changing judicial understanding about the effects of the rule outside the confines of the courtroom. It is incumbent on the Nation's law enforcement officers, who must continue to observe the Fourth Amendment in the wake of today's decisions, to recognize the double-edged nature of that principle.

■ Justice Brennan, with whom Justice Marshall joined, dissenting in *Leon* and in Massachusetts v. Sheppard, infra.

.... It now appears that the Court's victory over the Fourth Amendment is complete. That today's decision represents the piece de resistance of the Court's past efforts cannot be doubted, for today the Court sanctions the use in the prosecution's case-in-chief of illegally obtained evidence against the individual whose rights have been violated—a result that had previously been thought to be foreclosed.

The Court seeks to justify this result on the ground that the "costs" of adhering to the exclusionary rule in cases like those before us exceed the "benefits." But the language of deterrence and of cost/benefit analysis, if used indiscriminately, can have a narcotic effect. It creates an illusion of technical precision and ineluctability. It suggests that not only constitutional principle but also empirical data supports the majority's result. When the Court's analysis is examined carefully, however, it is clear that we have not been treated to an honest assessment of the merits of the exclusionary rule, but have instead been drawn into a curious world where the "costs" of excluding illegally obtained evidence loom to exaggerated heights and where the "benefits" of such exclusion are made to disappear with a mere waive of the hand....

For my part, "[t]he right of the people to be secure in their persons, houses, papers and effects, against unreasonable searches and seizures" comprises a personal right to exclude all evidence secured by means of unreasonable searches and seizures. The right to be free from the initial invasion of privacy and the right of exclusion are coordinate components of the central embracing right to be free from unreasonable searches and seizures.

Such a conception of the rights secured by the Fourth Amendment was unquestionably the original basis of what has come to be called the exclusionary rule when it was first formulated in Weeks v. United States (1914)....

The heart of the *Weeks* opinion, and for me the beginning of wisdom about the Fourth Amendment's proper meaning, is found in the following passage:

> "If letters and private documents can ... be seized and held and used in evidence against a citizen accused of an offense, the protection of the Fourth Amendment declaring his right to be secure against such searches and seizures is of no value, and, so far as those thus placed are concerned, might as well be stricken from the Constitution. The efforts of the courts and [federal] officials to bring the guilty to punishment, praiseworthy as they are, are not to be aided by the sacrifice of those great principles established by years of endeavor and suffering which have resulted in their embodiment in the fundamental law of the land. The United States Marshal could only have invaded the house of the accused when armed with a warrant issued as required by the Constitution. ... Instead, he acted without sanction of law, doubtless prompted by the desire to bring further proof to the aid of the Government, and under color of his office undertook to make a seizure of private papers in direct violation of the constitutional prohibition against such action.... To sanction such proceedings would be to affirm by judicial decision a manifest neglect if not an open defiance of the prohibitions of the Constitution, intended for the protection of the people against such unauthorized action."

What this passage succinctly captures is the essential recognition, ignored by the present Court, that seizures are generally executed for the purpose of bringing "proof to the aid of the Government," that the utility of such evidence in a criminal prosecution arises ultimately in the context of the courts, and that the courts therefore cannot be absolved of responsibility for the means by which evidence is obtained. As the Court in *Weeks* clearly recognized, the obligations cast upon government by the Fourth Amendment are not confined merely to the police....

.... In contrast to the present Court's restrictive reading, the Court in *Weeks* recognized that, if the Amendment is to have any meaning, police and the courts cannot be regarded as constitutional strangers to each other; because the evidence-gathering role of the police is directly linked to the evidence-admitting function of the courts, an individual's Fourth Amendment rights may be undermined as completely by one as by the other.

From the foregoing, it is clear why the question whether the exclusion of evidence would deter future police misconduct was never considered a relevant concern in the early cases from *Weeks* to *Olmstead*.[10] In those formative decisions, the Court plainly understood that the exclusion of illegally obtained evidence was compelled not by judicially fashioned remedial purposes, but rather by a direct constitutional command....

Despite this clear pronouncement, however, the Court since *Calandra* has gradually pressed the deterrence rationale for the rule back to center stage. The various arguments advanced by the Court in this campaign have only strengthened my conviction that the deterrence theory is both misguided and unworkable. First, the Court has frequently bewailed the "cost" of excluding reliable evidence. In large part, this criticism rests upon a refusal to acknowledge the function of the Fourth Amendment itself. If nothing else, the Amendment plainly operates to disable the government from gathering information and securing evidence in certain ways. In practical terms, of course, this restriction of official power means that some incriminating evidence inevitably will go undetected if the government obeys these constitutional restraints. It is the loss of that evidence that is the "price" our society pays for enjoying the freedom, and privacy safeguarded by the Fourth Amendment. Thus, some criminals will go free not, in Justice (then Judge) Cardozo's misleading epigram, "because the constable has blundered," People v. Defore, 242 N.Y. 13, 21, 150 N.E. 585, 587 (1926), but rather because official compliance with Fourth Amendment requirements makes it more difficult to catch criminals. Understood in this way, the Amendment directly contemplates that some reliable and incriminating evidence will be lost to the government; therefore, it is not the exclusionary rule, but the Amendment itself that has imposed this cost.[11]

10. See generally Kamisar, Does (Did) (Should) the Exclusionary Rule Rest On A "Principled Basis" Rather Than An "Empirical Proposition"?, 16 Creighton L.Rev. 565, 598–599 (1983); Mertens & Wasserstrom, The Good Faith Exception to the Exclusionary Rule: Deregulating the Police and Derailing the Law, 70 Geo.L.J. 365, 379–380 (1981).

11. Justice Stewart has explained this point in detail in a recent article: "Much of the criticism leveled at the exclusionary rule is misdirected; it is more properly directed at the Fourth Amendment itself. It is true that, as many observers have charged, the effect of the rule is to deprive the courts of extremely relevant, often direct evidence of the guilt of the defendant. But these same critics fail to acknowledge that, in many instances, the same extremely relevant evidence would not have been obtained had the police officer complied with the commands of the fourth amendment in the first place....

"The exclusionary rule places no limitations on the actions of the police. The fourth amendment does. The inevitable result of the Constitution's prohibition against unreasonable searches and seizures and its requirements that no warrant shall issue but upon probable cause is that police officers who obey its strictures will catch fewer criminals. ...[T]hat is the price the framers anticipated and were willing to pay to ensure the sanctity of the person, home, and property against unrestrained governmental power." Stewart, The Road to Mapp v. Ohio and Beyond: The Origins, Development and Future of the Ex-

In addition, the Court's decisions over the past decade have made plain that the entire enterprise of attempting to assess the benefits and costs of the exclusionary rule in various contexts is a virtually impossible task for the judiciary to perform honestly or accurately. Although the Court's language in those cases suggests that some specific empirical basis may support its analyses, the reality is that the Court's opinions represent inherently unstable compounds of intuition, hunches and occasional pieces of partial and often inconclusive data. . . .

* * *

[R]ecent studies have demonstrated that the "costs" of the exclusionary rule "calculated in terms of dropped prosecutions and lost convictions" are quite low. Contrary to the claims of the rule's critics that exclusion leads to "the release of countless guilty criminals," Bivens v. Six Unknown Federal Narcotics Officers, 403 U.S. 388, 416, 91 S.Ct. 1999, 2016 (Burger, C.J., dissenting), these studies have demonstrated that federal and state prosecutors very rarely drop cases because of potential search and seizure problems. For example, a 1979 study prepared at the request of Congress by the General Accounting Office reported that only 0.4% of all cases actually declined for prosecution by federal prosecutors were declined primarily because of illegal search problems. Report of the Comptroller General of the United States, Impact of the Exclusionary Rule on Federal Criminal Prosecutions 14 (1979). If the GAO data are restated as a percentage of all arrests, the study shows that only 0.2% of all felony arrests are declined for prosecution because of potential exclusionary rule problems. See Davies, A Hard Look at What We Know (and Still Need to Learn) About the "Costs" of the Exclusionary Rule: The NIJ Study and Other Studies of "Lost" Arrests, 1983 Am.Bar Found.Res.J. 611, 635.[12] Of

clusionary Rule in Search-and-Seizure Cases, 83 Colum.L.Rev. 1365, 1392–1393 (1983) (emphasis added). See also Dellinger, Of Rights and Remedies: The Constitution As A Sword, 85 Harv.L.Rev. 1532, 1563 (1972) ("Under the exclusionary rule a court attempts to maintain the status quo that would have prevailed if the constitutional requirement had been obeyed").

12. In a series of recent studies, researchers have attempted to quantify the actual costs of the rule. A recent National Institute of Justice study based on data for the four year period 1976–1979 gathered by the California Bureau of Criminal Statistics showed that 4.8% of all cases that were declined for prosecution by California prosecutors were rejected because of illegally seized evidence. National Institute of Justice, Criminal Justice Research Report—The Effects of the Exclusionary Rule: A Study in California 1 (1982). However, if these data are calculated as a percentage of all arrests that were declined for prosecution, they show that only 0.8% of all arrests were rejected for prosecution because of illegally seized evidence. See Davies, supra, at 619.

In another measure of the rule's impact—the number of prosecutions that are dismissed or result in acquittals in cases where evidence has been excluded—the available data again show that the Court's past assessment of the rule's costs has generally been exaggerated. For example, a study based on data from 9 mid-sized counties in Illinois, Michigan and Pennsylvania reveals that motions to suppress physical evidence were filed in approximately 5% of the 7,500 cases studied, but that such motions were successful in only 0.7% of all these cases. Nardulli, The Societal Cost of the Exclusionary Rule: An Empirical Assessment, 1983 Am.Bar Found. Res.J. 585, 596. The study also shows that only 0.6% of all cases resulted in acquittals because evidence had been excluded. In the GAO study, suppression motions were filed in 10.5% of all federal criminal cases surveyed, but of the motions filed, approximately 80–90% were denied. GAO Report, supra, at 8, 10. Evidence was actually excluded in only

course, these data describe only the costs attributable to the exclusion of evidence in all cases; the costs due to the exclusion of evidence in the narrower category of cases where police have made objectively reasonable mistakes must necessarily be even smaller. The Court, however, ignores this distinction and mistakenly weighs the aggregated costs of exclusion in all cases, irrespective of the circumstances that led to exclusion, against the potential benefits associated with only those cases in which evidence is excluded because police reasonably but mistakenly believe that their conduct does not violate the Fourth Amendment. When such faulty scales are used, it is little wonder that the balance tips in favor of restricting the application of the rule....

The Court has sought to turn this uncertainty to its advantage by casting the burden of proof upon proponents of the rule. "Obviously," however, "the assignment of the burden of proof on an issue where evidence does not exist and cannot be obtained is outcome determinative. [The] assignment of the burden is merely a way of announcing a predetermined conclusion."[13]

By remaining within its redoubt of empiricism and by basing the rule solely on the deterrence rationale, the Court has robbed the rule of legitimacy. A doctrine that is explained as if it were an empirical proposition but for which there is only limited empirical support is both inherently unstable and an easy mark for critics.

* * *

If the overall educational effect of the exclusionary rule is considered, application of the rule to even those situations in which individual police officers have acted on the basis of a reasonable but mistaken belief that their conduct was authorized can still be expected to have a considerable long-term deterrent effect. If evidence is consistently excluded in these circumstances, police departments will surely be prompted to instruct their officers to devote greater care and attention to providing sufficient information to establish probable cause when applying for a warrant, and to review with some attention the form of the warrant that they have been issued, rather than automatically assuming that whatever document the magistrate has signed will necessarily comport with Fourth Amendment requirements.

After today's decision, however, that institutional incentive will be lost. Indeed, the Court's "reasonable mistake" exception to the exclusionary rule will tend to put a premium on police ignorance of the law....

Finally, even if one were to believe, as the Court apparently does, that police are hobbled by inflexible and hypertechnical warrant procedures, today's decision cannot be justified. This is because, given the relaxed

1.3% of the cases studied, and only 0.7% of all cases resulted in acquittals or dismissals after evidence was excluded. See Davies, supra, at 660. And in another study based on data from cases during 1978 and 1979 in San Diego and Jacksonville, it was shown that only 1% of all cases resulting in nonconviction were caused by illegal searches. Feeney, Dill & Weir, Arrests Without Conviction: How Often They Occur and Why (1983). See generally Davies, supra, at 663.

13. Dworkin, Fact Style Adjudication and the Fourth Amendment: The Limits of Lawyering, 48 Ind.L.J. 329, 332–333 (1973).

standard for assessing probable cause established just last Term in Illinois v. Gates (1983), the Court's newly fashioned good faith exception, when applied in the warrant context, will rarely, if ever, offer any greater flexibility for police than the Gates standard already supplies. In *Gates*, the Court held that "the task of an issuing magistrate is simply to make a practical, common-sense decision whether, given all the circumstances set forth in the affidavit before him, ... there is a fair probability that contraband or evidence of a crime will be found in a particular place." The task of a reviewing court is confined to determining whether "the magistrate had a 'substantial basis' for concluding that probable cause existed." Given such a relaxed standard, it is virtually inconceivable that a reviewing court, when faced with a defendant's motion to suppress, could first find that a warrant was invalid under the new Gates standard, but then, at the same time, find that a police officer's reliance on such an invalid warrant was nevertheless "objectively reasonable" under the test announced today. Because the two standards overlap so completely, it is unlikely that a warrant could be found invalid under *Gates* and yet the police reliance upon it could be seen as objectively reasonable; otherwise, we would have to entertain the mind-boggling concept of objectively reasonable reliance upon an objectively unreasonable warrant.

* * *

■ JUSTICE STEVENS, opinion omitted—dissenting in *Leon* and concurring in Massachusetts v. Sheppard.

NOTE

1. In Massachusetts v. Sheppard, 468 U.S. 981, 104 S.Ct. 3424 (1984), decided the same day as *Leon*, the Court utilized the "good faith" exception to uphold admission of evidence which arguably had been seized unlawfully. The affidavit for a search warrant utilized in a murder investigation specified that the police sought certain named items, including a bottle of amaretto liquor and a black-grey woman's jacket. The preprinted warrant form, however, called for the seizure of a "controlled substance." The police officer pointed out to the judicial officer the problem with the form. The judicial officer assured Detective O'Malley that he would make the requisite changes and, after making some changes, assured the officer that the warrant would allow a search for the items specified in the affidavit. The judge, however, did not make the warrant incorporate the affidavit, nor did he delete the term "controlled substance." Under these circumstances, the Court concluded that O'Malley had acted in good faith in executing the warrant.

Groh v. Ramirez

Supreme Court of the United States, 2004.
540 U.S., 551, 124 S.Ct. 1284.

■ JUSTICE STEVENS delivered the opinion of the Court.

Petitioner conducted a search of respondents' home pursuant to a warrant that failed to describe the "persons or things to be seized." U.S. Const., Amdt. 4. The questions presented are (1) whether the search violated the Fourth Amendment, and (2) if so, whether petitioner nevertheless is entitled to qualified immunity, given that a Magistrate Judge (Magistrate), relying on an affidavit that particularly described the items in question, found probable cause to conduct the search.

I

Respondents, Joseph Ramirez and members of his family, live on a large ranch in Butte–Silver Bow County, Montana. Petitioner, Jeff Groh, has been a Special Agent for the Bureau of Alcohol, Tobacco and Firearms (ATF) since 1989. In February 1997, a concerned citizen informed petitioner that on a number of visits to respondents' ranch the visitor had seen a large stock of weaponry, including an automatic rifle, grenades, a grenade launcher, and a rocket launcher. Based on that information, petitioner prepared and signed an application for a warrant to search the ranch. The application stated that the search was for "any automatic firearms or parts to automatic weapons, destructive devices to include but not limited to grenades, grenade launchers, rocket launchers, and any and all receipts pertaining to the purchase or manufacture of automatic weapons or explosive devices or launchers." Petitioner supported the application with a detailed affidavit, which he also prepared and executed, that set forth the basis for his belief that the listed items were concealed on the ranch. Petitioner then presented these documents to a Magistrate, along with a warrant form that petitioner also had completed. The Magistrate signed the warrant form.

Although the application particularly described the place to be searched and the contraband petitioner expected to find, the warrant itself was less specific; it failed to identify any of the items that petitioner intended to seize. In the portion of the form that called for a description of the "person or property" to be seized, petitioner typed a description of respondents' two-story blue house rather than the alleged stockpile of firearms.[2] The warrant did not incorporate by reference the itemized list contained in the application. It did, however, recite that the Magistrate was satisfied the affidavit established probable cause to believe that contraband was concealed on the premises, and that sufficient grounds existed for the warrant's issuance.[3]

The day after the Magistrate issued the warrant, petitioner led a team of law enforcement officers, including both federal agents and members of the local sheriff's department, in the search of respondents' premises. Although respondent Joseph Ramirez was not home, his wife and children were. Petitioner states that he orally described the objects of the search to Mrs. Ramirez in person and to Mr. Ramirez by telephone. According to Mrs. Ramirez, however, petitioner explained only that he was searching for " 'an explosive device in a box.' " *Ramirez v. Butte–Silver Bow County*, 298 F.3d 1022, 1026 (CA9 2002). At any rate, the officers' search uncovered no illegal weapons or explosives. When the officers left, petitioner gave Mrs.

2. The warrant stated: "[T]here is now concealed [on the specified premises] a certain person or property, namely [a] single dwelling residence two story in height which is blue in color and has two additions attached to the east. The front entrance to the residence faces in a southerly direction." App. to Pet. for Cert. 26a.

3. The affidavit was sealed. Its sufficiency is not disputed.

Ramirez a copy of the search warrant, but not a copy of the application, which had been sealed. The following day, in response to a request from respondents' attorney, petitioner faxed the attorney a copy of the page of the application that listed the items to be seized. No charges were filed against the Ramirezes.

Respondents sued petitioner and the other officers under Bivens v. Six Unknown Fed. Narcotics Agents (1971), and Rev. Stat. § 1979, 42 USC § 1983 [42 USCS § 1983], raising eight claims, including violation of the Fourth Amendment. The District Court entered summary judgment for all defendants. The court found no Fourth Amendment violation, because it considered the case comparable to one in which the warrant contained an inaccurate address, and in such a case, the court reasoned, the warrant is sufficiently detailed if the executing officers can locate the correct house. The court added that even if a constitutional violation occurred, the defendants were entitled to qualified immunity because the failure of the warrant to describe the objects of the search amounted to a mere "typographical error."

The Court of Appeals affirmed the judgment with respect to all defendants and all claims, with the exception of respondents' Fourth Amendment claim against petitioner. On that claim, the court held that the warrant was invalid because it did not "describe with particularity the place to be searched and the items to be seized," and that oral statements by petitioner during or after the search could not cure the omission. The court observed that the warrant's facial defect "increased the likelihood and degree of confrontation between the Ramirezes and the police" and deprived respondents of the means "to challenge officers who might have exceeded the limits imposed by the magistrate." The court also expressed concern that "permitting officers to expand the scope of the warrant by oral statements would broaden the area of dispute between the parties in subsequent litigation." The court nevertheless concluded that all of the officers except petitioner were protected by qualified immunity. With respect to petitioner, the court read our opinion in United States v. Leon (1984), as precluding qualified immunity for the leader of a search who fails to "read the warrant and satisfy [himself] that [he] understand[s] its scope and limitations, and that it is not defective in some obvious way." The court added that "[t]he leaders of the search team must also make sure that a copy of the warrant is available to give to the person whose property is being searched at the commencement of the search, and that such copy has no missing pages or other obvious defects." We granted certiorari.

II

The warrant was plainly invalid. The Fourth Amendment states unambiguously that "no Warrants shall issue, but upon probable cause, supported by Oath or affirmation, and *particularly describing* the place to be searched, and *the persons or things to be seized*." (Emphasis added.) The warrant in this case complied with the first three of these requirements: It was based on probable cause and supported by a sworn affidavit, and it described particularly the place of the search. On the fourth requirement, however, the warrant failed altogether. Indeed, petitioner concedes that "the warrant ... was deficient in particularity because it provided no description of the type of evidence sought."

The fact that the *application* adequately described the "things to be seized" does not save the *warrant* from its facial invalidity. The Fourth Amendment by its terms requires particularity in the warrant, not in the supporting documents. See Massachusetts v. Sheppard (1984) ("[A] warrant that fails to conform to the particularity requirement of the Fourth Amendment is unconstitutional") ... ("The Fourth Amendment requires that the *warrant* particularly describe the things to be seized, not the papers presented to the judicial officer ... asked to issue the warrant"). And for good reason: "The presence of a search warrant serves a high function," *McDonald v. United States* (1948), and that high function is not necessarily vindicated when some other document, somewhere, says something about the objects of the search, but the contents of that document are neither known to the person whose home is being searched nor available for her inspection. We do not say that the Fourth Amendment prohibits a warrant from cross-referencing other documents. Indeed, most Courts of Appeals have held that a court may construe a warrant with reference to a supporting application or affidavit if the warrant uses appropriate words of incorporation, and if the supporting document accompanies the warrant.... But in this case the warrant did not incorporate other documents by reference, nor did either the affidavit or the application (which had been placed under seal) accompany the warrant. Hence, we need not further explore the matter of incorporation.

Petitioner argues that even though the warrant was invalid, the search nevertheless was "reasonable" within the meaning of the Fourth Amendment. He notes that a Magistrate authorized the search on the basis of adequate evidence of probable cause, that petitioner orally described to respondents the items to be seized, and that the search did not exceed the limits intended by the Magistrate and described by petitioner. Thus, petitioner maintains, his search of respondents' ranch was functionally equivalent to a search authorized by a valid warrant.

We disagree. This warrant did not simply omit a few items from a list of many to be seized, or misdescribe a few of several items. Nor did it make what fairly could be characterized as a mere technical mistake or typographical error. Rather, in the space set aside for a description of the items to be seized, the warrant stated that the items consisted of a "single dwelling residence ... blue in color." In other words, the warrant did not describe the items to be seized *at all*. In this respect the warrant was so obviously deficient that we must regard the search as "warrantless" within the meaning of our case law.... Thus, "absent exigent circumstances," a warrantless entry to search for weapons or contraband is unconstitutional even when a felony has been committed and there is probable cause to believe that incriminating evidence will be found within

We have clearly stated that the presumptive rule against warrantless searches applies with equal force to searches whose only defect is a lack of particularity in the warrant. In *Sheppard*, for instance, the petitioner argued that even though the warrant was invalid for lack of particularity, "the search was constitutional because it was reasonable within the meaning of the Fourth Amendment." In squarely rejecting that position, we explained:

> "The uniformly applied rule is that a search conducted pursuant to a warrant that fails to conform to the particularity requirement of the Fourth Amendment is unconstitutional.... That rule is in keeping with the well-established principle that 'except in certain carefully defined classes of cases, a search of private property without proper consent is "unreasonable" unless it has been authorized by a valid search warrant.' "

Petitioner asks us to hold that a search conducted pursuant to a warrant lacking particularity should be exempt from the presumption of unreasonableness if the goals served by the particularity requirement are otherwise satisfied. He maintains that the search in this case satisfied those goals—which he says are "to prevent general searches, to prevent the seizure of one thing under a warrant describing another, and to prevent warrants from being issued on vague or dubious information,"—because the scope of the search did not exceed the limits set forth in the application. But unless the particular items described in the affidavit are also set forth in the warrant itself (or at least incorporated by reference, and the affidavit present at the search), there can be no written assurance that the Magistrate actually found probable cause to search for, and to seize, every item mentioned in the affidavit. ("Absent some grave emergency, the Fourth Amendment has interposed a magistrate between the citizen and the police. This was done ... so that an objective mind might weigh the need to invade [the citizen's] privacy in order to enforce the law"). In this case, for example, it is at least theoretically possible that the Magistrate was satisfied that the search for weapons and explosives was justified by the showing in the affidavit, but not convinced that any evidentiary basis existed for rummaging through respondents' files and papers for receipts pertaining to the purchase or manufacture of such items. Or, conceivably, the Magistrate might have believed that some of the weapons mentioned in the affidavit could have been lawfully possessed and therefore should not be seized.... The mere fact that the Magistrate issued a warrant does not necessarily establish that he agreed that the scope of the search should be as broad as the affiant's request. Even though petitioner acted with restraint in conducting the search, "the inescapable fact is that this restraint was imposed by the agents themselves, not by a judicial officer." Katz v. United States (1967).[4]

4. For this reason petitioner's argument that any constitutional error was committed by the Magistrate, not petitioner, is misplaced. In Massachusetts v. Sheppard (1984), we suggested that "the judge, not the police officers," may have committed "[a]n error of constitutional dimension" id. Because the judge had assured the officers requesting the warrant that he would take the steps necessary to conform the warrant to constitutional requirements. Thus, "it was not unreasonable for the police in [that] case to rely on the judge's assurances that the warrant authorized the search they had requested." Id. In this case, by contrast, the petitioner did not alert the Magistrate to the defect in the warrant the petitioner had drafted, and we therefore cannot know whether the Magistrate was aware of the search he was authorizing. Nor would it have been reasonable for petitioner to rely on a warrant that was so patently defective, even if the Magistrate was aware of the deficiency. See United States v. Leon (1984).

We have long held, moreover, that the purpose of the particularity requirement is not limited to the prevention of general searches. A particular warrant also "assures the individual whose property is searched or seized of the lawful authority of the executing officer, his need to search, and the limits of his power to search." ...[5]

It is incumbent on the officer executing a search warrant to ensure the search is lawfully authorized and lawfully conducted. Because petitioner did not have in his possession a warrant particularly describing the things he intended to seize, proceeding with the search was clearly "unreasonable" under the Fourth Amendment. The court of appeals correctly held that the search was unconstitutional.

III

Having concluded that a constitutional violation occurred, we turn to the question whether petitioner is entitled to qualified immunity despite that violation. See *Wilson v. Layne* (1999). The answer depends on whether the right that was transgressed was " 'clearly established' "—that is, "whether it would be clear to a reasonable officer that his conduct was unlawful in the situation he confronted." *Saucier v. Katz* (2001).

Given that the particularity requirement is set forth in the text of the Constitution, no reasonable officer could believe that a warrant that plainly did not comply with that requirement was valid. ("If the law was clearly established, the immunity defense ordinarily should fail, since a reasonably competent public official should know the law governing his conduct"). Moreover, because petitioner himself prepared the invalid warrant, he may not argue that he reasonably relied on the Magistrate's assurance that the warrant contained an adequate description of the things to be seized and was therefore valid. In fact, the guidelines of petitioner's own department placed him on notice that he might be liable for executing a manifestly invalid warrant. An ATF directive in force at the time of this search warned: "Special agents are liable if they exceed their authority while executing a search warrant and must be sure that a search warrant is sufficient on its face even when issued by a magistrate." Searches and Examinations, ATF Order O 3220.1(7)(d) (Feb. 13, 1997). If any error or deficiency is discovered and there is a reasonable probability that it will invalidate the warrant, such warrant shall not be executed. The search shall be postponed until a satisfactory warrant has been obtained".[7] And

5. It is true, as petitioner points out, that neither the Fourth Amendment nor Rule 41 of the Federal Rules of Criminal Procedure requires the executing officer to serve the warrant on the owner before commencing the search. Rule 41(f)(3) provides that "[t]he officer executing the warrant must: (A) give a copy of the warrant and a receipt for the property taken to the person from whom, or from whose premises, the property was taken; or (B) leave a copy of the warrant and receipt at the place where the officer took the property." Quite obviously, in some circumstances—a surreptitious search by means of a wiretap, for example, or the search of empty or abandoned premises—it will be impracticable or imprudent for the officers to show the warrant in advance. Whether it would be unreasonable to refuse a request to furnish the warrant at the outset of the search when, as in this case, an occupant of the premises is present and poses no threat to the officers' safe and effective performance of their mission, is a question that this case does not present.

7. We do not suggest that an official is deprived of qualified immunity whenever he violates an internal guideline. We refer to the

even a cursory reading of the warrant in this case—perhaps just a simple glance—would have revealed a glaring deficiency that any reasonable police officer would have known was constitutionally fatal.

No reasonable officer could claim to be unaware of the basic rule, well established by our cases, that, absent consent or exigency, a warrantless search of the home is presumptively unconstitutional. Indeed, as we noted nearly 20 years ago in *Sheppard*: "The uniformly applied rule is that a search conducted pursuant to a warrant that fails to conform to the particularity requirement of the Fourth Amendment is unconstitutional."[8] Because not a word in any of our cases would suggest to a reasonable officer that this case fits within any exception to that fundamental tenet, petitioner is asking us, in effect, to craft a new exception. Absent any support for such an exception in our cases, he cannot reasonably have relied on an expectation that we would do so.

Petitioner contends that the search in this case was the product, at worst, of a lack of due care, and that our case law requires more than negligent behavior before depriving an official of qualified immunity. But as we observed in the companion case to *Sheppard*, "a warrant may be so facially deficient—*i.e.*, in failing to particularize the place to be searched or the things to be seized—that the executing officers cannot reasonably presume it to be valid." This is such a case.[9]

Accordingly, the judgment of the Court of Appeals is affirmed.

It is so ordered.

DISSENT

■ JUSTICE KENNEDY, with whom THE CHIEF JUSTICE joins, dissenting.

I agree with the Court that the Fourth Amendment was violated in this case. The Fourth Amendment states that "no Warrants shall issue, but upon probable cause, supported by Oath or affirmation, and particularly describing the place to be searched, and the persons or things to be seized."

ATF Order only to underscore that petitioner should have known that he should not execute a patently defective warrant.

8. Although both *Sheppard* and *Leon* involved the application of the "good faith" exception to the Fourth Amendment's general exclusionary rule, we have explained that "the same standard of objective reasonableness that we applied in the context of a suppression hearing in *Leon* defines the qualified immunity accorded an officer." *Malley v. Briggs*, 475 U.S. 335, 344, 89 L. Ed. 2d 271, 106 S. Ct. 1092 (1986) (citation omitted).

9. Justice Kennedy argues in dissent that we have not allowed " 'ample room for mistaken judgments,' " because "difficult and important tasks demand the officer's full attention in the heat of an ongoing and often dangerous criminal investigation." In this case, however, petitioner does not contend that any sort of exigency existed when he drafted the affidavit, the warrant application, and the warrant, or when he conducted the search. This is not the situation, therefore, in which we have recognized that "officers in the dangerous and difficult process of making arrests and executing search warrants" require "some latitude." Maryland v. Garrison (1987).

Nor are we according "the correctness of paper forms" a higher status than "substantive rights." As we have explained, the Fourth Amendment's particularity requirement assures the subject of the search that a magistrate has duly authorized the officer to conduct a search of limited scope. This substantive right is not protected when the officer fails to take the time to glance at the authorizing document and detect a glaring defect that Justice Kennedy agrees is of constitutional magnitude.

The warrant issued in this case did not particularly describe the things to be seized, and so did not comply with the Fourth Amendment. I disagree with the Court on whether the officer who obtained the warrant and led the search team is entitled to qualified immunity for his role in the search. In my view, the officer should receive qualified immunity.

An officer conducting a search is entitled to qualified immunity if "a reasonable officer could have believed" that the search was lawful "in light of clearly established law and the information the searching officers possessed." Anderson v. Creighton (1987). As the Court notes, this is the same objective reasonableness standard applied under the "good faith" exception to the exclusionary rule. The central question is whether someone in the officer's position could reasonably but mistakenly conclude that his conduct complied with the Fourth Amendment.

An officer might reach such a mistaken conclusion for several reasons. He may be unaware of existing law and how it should be applied. Alternatively, he may misunderstand important facts about the search and assess the legality of his conduct based on that misunderstanding. Finally, an officer may misunderstand elements of both the facts and the law. Our qualified immunity doctrine applies regardless of whether the officer's error is a mistake of law, a mistake of fact, or a mistake based on mixed questions of law and fact. (noting that qualified immunity covers "mere mistakes in judgment, whether the mistake is one of fact or one of law").

The present case involves a straightforward mistake of fact. Although the Court does not acknowledge it directly, it is obvious from the record below that the officer simply made a clerical error when he filled out the proposed warrant and offered it to the Magistrate Judge. The officer used the proper description of the property to be seized when he completed the affidavit. He also used the proper description in the accompanying application. When he typed up the description a third time for the proposed warrant, however, the officer accidentally entered a description of the place to be searched in the part of the warrant form that called for a description of the property to be seized. No one noticed the error before the search was executed. Although the record is not entirely clear on this point, the mistake apparently remained undiscovered until the day after the search when respondents' attorney reviewed the warrant for defects. The officer, being unaware of his mistake, did not rely on it in any way. It is uncontested that the officer trained the search team and executed the warrant based on his mistaken belief that the warrant contained the proper description of the items to be seized.

The question is whether the officer's mistaken belief that the warrant contained the proper language was a reasonable belief. In my view, it was. A law enforcement officer charged with leading a team to execute a search warrant for illegal weapons must fulfill a number of serious responsibilities. The officer must establish probable cause to believe the crime has been committed and that evidence is likely to be found at the place to be searched; must articulate specific items that can be seized, and a specific place to be searched; must obtain the warrant from a magistrate judge; and must instruct a search team to execute the warrant within the time allowed by the warrant. The officer must also oversee the execution of the warrant in a way that protects officer safety, directs a thorough and professional search for the evidence, and avoids unnecessary destruction of property. These difficult and important tasks demand the officer's full attention in the heat of an ongoing and often dangerous criminal investigation.

An officer who complies fully with all of these duties can be excused for not being aware that he had made a clerical error in the course of filling out the proposed warrant. See Maryland v. Garrison (1987) (recognizing "the need to allow some latitude for honest mistakes that are made by officers in the dangerous and difficult process of making arrests and executing search warrants"). An officer who drafts an affidavit, types up an application and proposed warrant, and then obtains a judge's approval naturally assumes that he has filled out the warrant form correctly. Even if the officer checks over the warrant, he may very well miss a mistake. We all tend toward myopia when looking for our own errors. Every lawyer and every judge can recite examples of documents that they wrote, checked, and doublechecked, but that still contained glaring errors. Law enforcement officers are no different. It would be better if the officer recognizes the error, of course. It would be better still if he does not make the mistake in the first place. In the context of an otherwise proper search, however, an officer's failure to recognize his clerical error on a warrant form can be a reasonable mistake.

The Court reaches a different result by construing the officer's error as a mistake of law rather than a mistake of fact. According to the Court, the officer should not receive qualified immunity because "no reasonable officer could believe that a warrant that plainly did not comply with [the particularity] requirement was valid." The majority is surely right that a reasonable officer must know that a defective warrant is invalid. This much is obvious, if not tautological. It is also irrelevant, for the essential question here is whether a reasonable officer in petitioner's position would necessarily know that the warrant had a clerical error in the first place. The issue in this case is whether an officer can reasonably fail to recognize a clerical error, not whether an officer who recognizes a clerical error can reasonably conclude that a defective warrant is legally valid.

The Court gives little attention to this important and difficult question. It receives only two sentences at the very end of the Court's opinion. In the first sentence, the Court quotes dictum from *United States v. Leon*, 468 U.S. 897, 923, 82 L. Ed. 2d 677, 104 S. Ct. 3405 (1984), to the effect that " 'a warrant may be so facially deficient—*i.e.*, in failing to particularize the place to be searched or the things to be seized—that the executing officers cannot reasonably presume it to be valid.' " In the second sentence, the Court informs us without explanation that "[t]his is such a case." This reasoning is not convincing.

To understand the passage from *Leon* that the Court relies upon, it helps to recognize that most challenges to defective search warrants arise when officers rely on the defect and conduct a search that should not have occurred. The target of the improper search then brings a civil action challenging the improper search, or, if charges have been filed, moves to suppress the fruits of the search. The inquiry in both instances is whether the officers' reliance on the defect was reasonable. See, *e.g.*, *Garrison*, *supra*, (apartment wrongly searched because the searching officers did not realize that there were two apartments on the third floor and obtained a warrant to search the entire floor); Arizona v. Evans (1995) (person wrongly arrested and searched because a court employee's clerical error led officer to believe a warrant existed for person's arrest); McLeary v. Navarro (1992) (White, J., dissenting from denial of certiorari) (house wrongly searched because informant told officers the suspect lived in the second house on the right, but the suspect lived in the third house on the right).

The language the Court quotes from *Leon* comes from a discussion of when "an officer [who] has obtained a [defective] warrant and abided by its terms" has acted reasonably. The discussion notes that there are some cases in which "no reasonably well trained officer should rely on the warrant." The passage also includes several examples, among them the one that the Court relies on in this case: "depending on the circumstances of the particular case, a warrant may be so facially deficient—*i.e.*, in failing to particularize the place to be searched or the things to be seized—that the executing officers cannot reasonably presume it to be valid."

The Court interprets this language to mean that a clerical mistake can be so obvious that an officer who fails to recognize the mistake should not receive qualified immunity. Read in context, however, the quoted language is addressed to a quite different issue. The most natural interpretation of the language is that a clerical mistake can be so obvious that the officer cannot reasonably rely on the mistake in the course of executing the warrant. In other words, a defect can be so clear that an officer cannot reasonably "abid[e] by its terms" and execute the warrant as written.

We confront no such issue here, of course. No one suggests that the officer reasonably could have relied on the defective language in the warrant. This is a case about an officer being unaware of a clerical error, not a case about an officer relying on one. The respondents do not make the usual claim that they were injured by a defect that led to an improper search. Rather, they make an unusual claim that they were injured simply because the warrant form did not contain the correct description of the property to be seized, even though no property was seized. The language from *Leon* is not on point.

Our Court has stressed that "the purpose of encouraging recourse to the warrant procedure" can be served best by rejecting overly technical standards when courts review warrants. Illinois v. Gates (1983). We have also stressed that qualified immunity "provides ample protection to all but the plainly incompetent or those who knowingly violate the law." *Malley*. The Court's opinion is inconsistent with these principles. Its analysis requires our Nation's police officers to concentrate more on the correctness of paper forms than substantive rights. The Court's new "duty to ensure that the warrant conforms to constitutional requirements" sounds laudable, but would be more at home in a regime of strict liability than within the "ample room for mistaken judgments" that our qualified immunity jurisprudence traditionally provides, *Malley*.

For these reasons, I dissent.

■ JUSTICE THOMAS, with whom JUSTICE SCALIA joins, and with whom THE CHIEF JUSTICE joins as to Part III, dissenting.

The Fourth Amendment provides: "The right of the people to be secure in their persons, houses, papers, and effects, against unreasonable searches and seizures, shall not be violated, and no Warrants shall issue, but upon probable cause, supported by Oath or affirmation, and particularly describing the place to be searched, and the persons or things to be seized." The precise relationship between the Amendment's Warrant Clause and Unreasonableness Clause is unclear. But neither Clause explicitly requires a warrant. While "it is of course textually possible to consider [a warrant requirement] implicit within the requirement of reasonableness," *California v. Acevedo* (1991) (Scalia, J., concurring in judgment), the text of the Fourth Amendment certainly does not mandate this result. Nor does the Amendment's history, which is clear as to the Amendment's principal target (general warrants), but not as clear with respect to when warrants were required, if ever. Indeed, because of the very different nature and scope of federal authority and ability to conduct searches and arrests at the founding, it is possible that neither the history of the Fourth Amendment nor the common law provides much guidance.

As a result, the Court has vacillated between imposing a categorical warrant requirement and applying a general reasonableness standard. The Court has most frequently held that warrantless searches are presumptively unreasonable, but has also found a plethora of exceptions to presumptive unreasonableness.... That is, our cases stand for the illuminating proposition that warrantless searches are *per se* unreasonable, except, of course, when they are not.

Today the Court holds that the warrant in this case was "so obviously deficient" that the ensuing search must be regarded as a warrantless search and thus presumptively unreasonable. However, the text of the Fourth Amendment, its history, and the sheer number of exceptions to the Court's categorical warrant requirement seriously undermine the bases upon which the Court today rests its holding. Instead of adding to this confusing jurisprudence, as the Court has done, I would turn to first principles in order to determine the relationship between the Warrant Clause and the Unreasonableness Clause. But even within the Court's current framework, a search conducted pursuant to a defective warrant is constitutionally different from a "warrantless search." Consequently, despite the defective warrant, I would still ask whether this search was unreasonable and would conclude that it was not. Furthermore, even if the Court were correct that this search violated the Constitution (and in particular, respondents' Fourth Amendment rights), given the confused state of our Fourth Amendment jurisprudence and the reasonableness of petitioner's actions, I cannot agree with the Court's conclusion that petitioner is not entitled to qualified immunity. For these reasons, I respectfully dissent.

I

"[A]ny Fourth Amendment case may present two separate questions: whether the search was conducted pursuant to a warrant issued in accordance with the second Clause, and, if not, whether it was nevertheless 'reasonable' within the meaning of the first." United States v. Leon (1984) (Stevens, J., dissenting). By categorizing the search here to be a "warrantless" one, the Court declines to perform a reasonableness inquiry and ignores the fact that this search is quite different from searches that the Court has considered to be "warrantless" in the past. Our cases involving "warrantless" searches do not generally involve situations in which an officer has obtained a warrant that is later determined to be facially defective, but rather involve situations in which the officers neither sought nor obtained a warrant.... By simply treating this case as if no warrant had even been sought or issued, the Court glosses over what should be the key inquiry: whether it is always appropriate to treat a search made pursuant to a warrant that fails to describe particularly the things to be seized as presumptively unreasonable.

The Court bases its holding that a defect in the particularity of the warrant by itself renders a search "warrantless" on a citation of a single footnote in Massachusetts v. Sheppard (1984). In *Sheppard*, the Court, after noting that "the sole issue ... in th[e] case is whether the officers reasonably believed that the search they conducted was authorized by a valid warrant," rejected the petitioner's argument that despite the invalid warrant, the otherwise reasonable search was constitutional. The Court recognized that under its case law a reasonableness inquiry would be appropriate if one of the exceptions to the warrant requirement applied. But the Court declined to consider whether such an exception applied and whether the search actually violated the Fourth Amendment because that question presented merely a "fact-bound issue of little importance." Because the Court in *Sheppard* did not conduct any sort of inquiry into whether a Fourth Amendment violation actually occurred, it is clear that the Court assumed a violation for the purposes of its analysis. Rather than rely on dicta buried in a footnote in *Sheppard*, the Court should actually analyze the arguably dispositive issue in this case.

The Court also rejects the argument that the details of the warrant application and affidavit save the warrant, because " '[t]he presence of a search warrant serves a high function.' " But it is not only the physical existence of the warrant and its typewritten contents that serve this high function. The Warrant Clause's principal protection lies in the fact that the " 'Fourth Amendment has interposed a magistrate between the citizen and the police.... so that an objective mind might weigh the need to invade [the searchee's] privacy in order to enforce the law.' " The Court has further explained,

> The point of the Fourth Amendment ... is not that it denies law enforcement the support of the usual inferences which reasonable men draw from evidence. Its protection consists in requiring that those inferences be drawn by a neutral and detached magistrate instead of being judged by the officer engaged in the often competitive enterprise of ferreting out crime. Any assumption that evidence sufficient to support a magistrate's disinterested determination to issue a search warrant will justify the officers in making a search without a warrant would reduce the Amendment to a

> nullity and leave the people's homes secure only in the discretion of police officers.... When the right of privacy must reasonably yield to the right of search is, as a rule, to be decided by a judicial officer, not by a policeman or government enforcement agent. Johnson v. United States (1948)

But the actual contents of the warrant are simply manifestations of this protection. Hence, in contrast to the case of a truly warrantless search, a warrant (due to a mistake) does not specify on its face the particular items to be seized but the warrant application passed on by the magistrate judge contains such details, a searchee still has the benefit of a determination by a neutral magistrate that there is probable cause to search a particular place and to seize particular items. In such a circumstance, the principal justification for applying a rule of presumptive unreasonableness falls away.

In the instant case, the items to be seized were clearly specified in the warrant application and set forth in the affidavit, both of which were given to the Judge (Magistrate). The Magistrate reviewed all of the documents and signed the warrant application and made no adjustment or correction to this application. It is clear that respondents here received the protection of the Warrant Clause, as described in *Johnson* and *McDonald*. Under these circumstances, I would not hold that any ensuing search constitutes a presumptively unreasonable warrantless search. Instead, I would determine whether, despite the invalid warrant, the resulting search was reasonable and hence constitutional.

II

Because the search was not unreasonable, I would conclude that it was constitutional. Prior to execution of the warrant, petitioner briefed the search team and provided a copy of the search warrant application, the supporting affidavit, and the warrant for the officers to review. Petitioner orally reviewed the terms of the warrant with the officers, including the specific items for which the officers were authorized to search. Petitioner and his search team then conducted the search entirely within the scope of the warrant application and warrant; that is, within the scope of what the Magistrate had authorized. Finding no illegal weapons or explosives, the search team seized nothing. Ramirez v. Butte–Silver Bow County (CA9 2002). When petitioner left, he gave respondents a copy of the search warrant. Upon request the next day, petitioner faxed respondent a copy of the more detailed warrant application. Indeed, putting aside the technical defect in the warrant, it is hard to imagine how the actual search could have been carried out any more reasonably.

The Court argues that this eminently reasonable search is nonetheless unreasonable because "there can be no written assurance that the Magistrate actually found probable cause to search for, and to seize, every item mentioned in the affidavit" "unless the particular items described in the affidavit are also set forth in the warrant itself." *Ante*, at ___, 157 L. Ed. 2d, at 1080. The Court argues that it was at least possible that the Magistrate intended to authorize a much more limited search than the one petitioner requested. *Ibid.* As a theoretical matter, this may be true. But the more reasonable inference is that the Magistrate intended to authorize everything in the warrant application, as he signed the application and did not make any written adjustments to the application or the warrant itself.

The Court also attempts to bolster its focus on the faulty warrant by arguing that the purpose of the particularity requirement is not only to prevent general searches, but also to assure the searchee of the lawful authority for the search. But as the Court recognizes, neither the Fourth Amendment nor Federal Rule of Criminal Procedure 41 requires an officer to serve the warrant on the searchee before the search. Thus, a search should not be considered *per se* unreasonable for failing to apprise the searchee of the lawful authority prior to the search, especially where, as here, the officer promptly provides the requisite information when the defect in the papers is detected. Additionally, unless the Court adopts the Court of Appeals' view that the Constitution protects a searchee's ability to "be on the lookout and to challenge officers," while the officers are actually carrying out the search, petitioner's provision of the requisite information the following day is sufficient to satisfy this interest.

III

Even assuming a constitutional violation, I would find that petitioner is entitled to qualified immunity. The qualified immunity inquiry rests on "the 'objective legal reasonableness' of the action, assessed in light of the legal rules that were 'clearly established' at the time it was taken." The outcome of this inquiry "depends substantially upon the level of generality at which the relevant 'legal rule' is . . . identified. For example, the right to due process of law is quite clearly established by the Due Process Clause, and thus there is a sense in which any action that violates that Clause . . . violates a clearly established right." To apply the standard at such a high level of generality would allow plaintiffs "to convert the rule of qualified immunity . . . into a rule of virtually unqualified liability simply by alleging violation of extremely abstract rights." The Court in *Anderson* criticized the Court of Appeals for considering the qualified immunity question only in terms of the petitioner's "right to be free from warrantless searches of one's home unless the searching officers have probable cause and there are exigent circumstances." The Court of Appeals should have instead considered "the objective (albeit fact-specific) question whether a reasonable officer could have believed Anderson's warrantless search to be lawful, in light of clearly established law and the information the searching officers possessed."

The Court errs not only by defining the question at too high a level of generality but also by assessing the question without regard to the relevant circumstances. Even if it were true that no reasonable officer could believe that a search of a home pursuant to a warrant that fails the particularity requirement is lawful absent exigent circumstances—a proposition apparently established by dicta buried in a footnote in *Sheppard*—petitioner did not know when he carried out the search that the search warrant was invalid—let alone legally nonexistent. Petitioner's entitlement to qualified immunity, then, turns on whether his belief that the search warrant was valid was objectively reasonable. Petitioner's belief surely was reasonable.

The Court has stated that "depending on the circumstances of the particular case, a warrant may be so facially deficient . . . that the executing officers cannot reasonably presume it to be valid." This language makes clear that this exception to *Leon*'s good-faith exception does not apply in every circumstance. And the Court does not explain why it should apply here. As an initial matter, the Court does not even argue that the fact that petitioner made a mistake in preparing the warrant was objectively unreasonable, nor could it. Given the sheer number of warrants prepared and executed by officers each year, combined with the fact that these same officers also prepare detailed and sometimes somewhat comprehensive documents supporting the warrant applications, it is inevitable that officers acting reasonably and entirely in good faith will occasionally make such errors.

The only remaining question is whether petitioner's failure to notice the defect was objectively unreasonable. The Court today points to no cases directing an officer to proofread a warrant after it has been passed on by a neutral magistrate, where the officer is already fully aware of the scope of the intended search and the magistrate gives no reason to believe that he has authorized anything other than the requested search. Nor does the Court point to any case suggesting that where the same officer both prepares and executes the invalid warrant, he can never rely on the magistrate's assurance that the warrant is proper. Indeed, in Massachusetts v. Sheppard (1984), the Court suggested that although an officer who is not involved in the warrant application process would normally read the issued warrant to determine the object of the search, an executing officer who is also the affiant might not need to do so

Although the Court contends that it does not impose a proofreading requirement upon officers executing warrants, I see no other way to read its decision, particularly where, as here, petitioner could have done nothing more to ensure the reasonableness of his actions than to proofread the warrant. After receiving several allegations that respondents possessed illegal firearms and explosives, petitioner prepared an application for a warrant to search respondents' ranch, along with a supporting affidavit detailing the history of allegations against respondents, petitioner's investigation into these allegations, and petitioner's verification of the sources of the allegations. Petitioner properly filled out the warrant application, which described both the place to be searched and the things to be seized, and obtained the Magistrate's signature on both the warrant application and the warrant itself. Prior to execution of the warrant, petitioner briefed the search team to ensure that each officer understood the limits of the search. Petitioner and his search team then executed the warrant within those limits. And when the error in the search warrant was discovered, petitioner promptly faxed the missing information to respondents. In my view, petitioner's actions were objectively reasonable, and thus he should be entitled to qualified immunity.

For the foregoing reasons, I respectfully dissent.

NOTES

1. Suppose the officer relied upon a search warrant where, unknown to the officer, the magistrate did not read the warrant application but simply relied upon the officer's (erroneous) judgment that probable cause existed. See United States v. Breckenridge, 782 F.2d 1317 (5th Cir.1986) (invoking *Leon* to permit use of evidence).

2. In Illinois v. Krull, 480 U.S. 340, 107 S.Ct. 1160 (1987), officers conducted a warrantless search in accordance with a statute that permitted inspection of records of persons who sell motor vehicles or motor vehicle parts. The Illinois Supreme Court had invalidated the statute on Fourth Amendment grounds shortly after the search in question, saying that the statute granted state officials too much discretion to decide who, when, and how long to search.

Assuming, without deciding, that the statutory scheme violated the Fourth Amendment, the United States Supreme Court allowed use of evidence seized in a search conducted before the Illinois Supreme Court had invalidated the statute. The United States Supreme Court recognized a good-faith exception to the exclusionary rule when an officer's reliance on the constitutionality of a statute is objectively reasonable. The Court said that exclusion of evidence under such circumstances would not deter police misconduct. It declared that the exclusionary rule is meant to shape the conduct of police officers, not legislators. Beyond that, the Court did not believe that the exclusion of evidence would effectively deter the legislature in the future, noting that the invalidated legislation might well have reasonably appeared to have comported with the Fourth Amendment.

In a footnote the Court abolished a distinction once deemed important: "For reasons of deciding whether to apply the exclusionary rule, we see no valid reason to distinguish between statutes that define substantive criminal offenses and statutes that authorize warrantless administrative searches. In either event the ... rule will not deter ... police [and] ... there is no basis for assuming that the exclusionary rule is necessary or effective in deterring the legislature from passing an unconstitutional statute."

3. For an example of a "bare bones affidavit" that requires the exclusion of evidence seized during execution of an invalid search warrant even after *Leon*, see United States v. Barrington, 806 F.2d 529 (5th Cir.1986). There the affiant police captain said only that he believed that the sought item was in the place to be searched because he had received information from a confidential informant known to him to have provided information in the past that had led to arrests and convictions. See also United States v. Wilhelm, 80 F.3d 116 (4th Cir.1996).

4. In United States v. Buck, 813 F.2d 588 (2d Cir.1987), a warrant authorized search of particular premises and seizure of anything related to a particular crime. There viewing court held that the warrant was invalid for want of particularity in describing the items to be seized. Nevertheless, it permitted use of evidence seized in a search under this warrant, utilizing the good-faith exception under Leon. Under such an approach, can you imagine any warrant lacking particularity as to the items seized that would result in the suppression of evidence after Leon? The Buck court said that its decision meant that hereafter police were on notice that such a catch-all description was invalid, and thus they could not invoke the good-faith exception as to similar warrants issued in the future.

Federal courts are split on this subject. Some have rejected Leon good faith claims where the warrant was exceedingly overbroad. See Center Art Galleries—Hawaii v. United States, 875 F.2d 747 (9th Cir.1989).

5. United States v. Vasey, 834 F.2d 782 (9th Cir.1987), holds that where evidence obtained in an unlawful warrantless search is the predicate for issuance of a search warrant, the police cannot rely upon the good-faith exception of *Leon*:

> The constitutional error was made by the officer in this case, not by the magistrate as in Leon. The Leon Court made it very clear that the

> exclusionary rule should apply (i.e., the good faith exception should not apply) if the exclusion of evidence would alter the behavior of individual law enforcement officers or the policies of their department. Officer Jensen's conduct [here] ... is an activity that the exclusionary rule was meant to deter.

For decisions to the contrary, see LaFave, Search and Seizure, § 1.3(f) (3d ed. 1996).

6. Noting a split of authority on the question, the Eleventh Circuit elaborated on the notion of *Leon* good faith. The judge on the suppression motion should view the matter from the viewpoint of a reasonable well-trained officer, not from the viewpoint of a reasonable judge, in determining whether reliance on the magistrate's decision was reasonable, according to United States v. Taxacher, 902 F.2d 867 (11th Cir.1990).

What if subjective good faith is challenged. It was in a case where a private attorney and the prosecutor's office were seriously at odds. The private attorney fired one of his associates who then reported the attorney for habitual use and possession of marijuana. It was also alleged that there was bad blood between the attorney and the magistrate who issued the warrant. An en banc court split on the merits but both majority and dissent seemed to permit consideration of a claim of actual bad faith. United States v. Czuprynski, 46 F.3d 560 (6th Cir.1995) (en banc), supplemented 65 F.3d 169 (6th Cir.1995).

7. The interesting relationship between retroactivity decisions, exclusionary principles, and deterrence of unlawful police activity has become more complex because of two relatively recent developments. On the one hand, the Court has created a good-faith exception to the Fourth Amendment exclusionary rule. On the other hand, it has chosen to apply new decisions to cases not yet final at the time of the new decision even when the relevant conduct occurred when the conduct appeared to be lawful under prevailing law (*Griffith*, Casebook, Chapter 17). In United States v. Morgan, 835 F.2d 79 (5th Cir.1987), the border patrol arguably had relied upon court decisions classifying the Sierra Blanca checkpoint as a functional equivalent of the border, thus authorizing certain conduct which otherwise would have violated the Fourth Amendment. When the Fifth Circuit changed its classification of that checkpoint, it refused to suppress the fruits of searches that were made when the older law had prevailed where the conduct was lawful under that prior law. Is this a Leon question or a retroactivity question? Can courts limit *Griffith* in Fourth Amendment cases by invoking *Leon*?

8. As a matter of state law, a number of states have rejected Leon's good faith exception to the exclusionary rule. See e.g. State v. Novembrino, 105 N.J. 95, 519 A.2d 820 (1987). And other states apply it over a smaller range of cases People v. Krueger, 175 Ill.2d 60, 675 N.E.2d 604, 221 Ill.Dec. 409 (1996).

9. Reliance on incorrect computer data as a basis for good faith was addressed in Arizona v. Evans, 514 U.S. 1, 115 S.Ct. 1185 (1995).

■ CHIEF JUSTICE REHNQUIST delivered the opinion of the Court.

> In January 1991, Phoenix police officer Bryan Sargent observed respondent Evans driving the wrong way on a one-way street in front of the police station. The officer stopped respondent and asked to see his driver's license. After respondent told him that his license had been suspended, the officer entered respondent's name into a computer data terminal located in his patrol car. The computer inquiry confirmed that respondent's license had been suspended and also indicated that there was an outstanding misdemeanor warrant for his arrest. Based upon the outstanding warrant, Officer Sargent placed respondent under arrest. While being handcuffed,

respondent dropped a hand-rolled cigarette that the officers determined smelled of marijuana. Officers proceeded to search his car and discovered a bag of marijuana under the passenger's seat.

The State charged respondent with possession of marijuana. When the police notified the Justice Court that they had arrested him, the Justice Court discovered that the arrest warrant previously had been quashed and so advised the police. Respondent argued that because his arrest was based on a warrant that had been quashed 17 days prior to his arrest, the marijuana seized incident to the arrest should be suppressed as the fruit of an unlawful arrest. Respondent also argued that "[t]he 'good faith' exception to the exclusionary rule [was] inapplicable ... because it was police error, not judicial error, which caused the invalid arrest."

At the suppression hearing, the Chief Clerk of the Justice Court testified that a Justice of the Peace had issued the arrest warrant on December 13, 1990, because respondent had failed to appear to answer for several traffic violations. On December 19, 1990, respondent appeared before a pro tem Justice of the Peace who entered a notation in respondent's file to "quash warrant."

The Chief Clerk also testified regarding the standard court procedure for quashing a warrant. Under that procedure a justice court clerk calls and informs the warrant section of the Sheriff's Office when a warrant has been quashed. The Sheriff's Office then removes the warrant from its computer records. After calling the Sheriff's Office, the clerk makes a note in the individual's file indicating the clerk who made the phone call and the person at the Sheriff's Office to whom the clerk spoke. The Chief Clerk testified that there was no indication in respondent's file that a clerk had called and notified the Sheriff's Office that his arrest warrant had been quashed. A records clerk from the Sheriff's Office also testified that the Sheriff's Office had no record of a telephone call informing it that respondent's arrest warrant had been quashed.

At the close of testimony, respondent argued that the evidence obtained as a result of the arrest should be suppressed because "the purposes of the exclusionary rule would be served here by making the clerks for the court, or the clerk for the Sheriff's Office, whoever is responsible for this mistake, to be more careful about making sure that warrants are removed from the records." The trial court granted the motion to suppress because it concluded that the State had been at fault for failing to quash the warrant. Presumably because it could find no "distinction between State action, whether it happens to be the police department or not," the trial court made no factual finding as to whether the Justice Court or Sheriff's Office was responsible for the continued presence of the quashed warrant in the police records.

* * *

Applying the reasoning of *Leon* to the facts of this case, we conclude that the decision must be reversed. The Court determined that it could not "support the distinction drawn ... between clerical errors committed by law enforcement personnel and similar mistakes by court employees," and that "even assuming ... that responsibility for the error rested with the justice court, it does not follow that the exclusionary rule should be inapplicable to these facts,".

This holding is contrary to the reasoning of *Leon*, Massachusetts v. Sheppard, and *Krull*. If court employees were responsible for the erroneous computer record, the exclusion of evidence at trial would not sufficiently deter future errors so as to warrant such a severe sanction. First, as we noted in Leon, the exclusionary rule was historically designed as a means of deterring police misconduct, not mistakes by court employees. Second, respondent offers no evidence that court employees are inclined to ignore or subvert the Fourth Amendment or that lawlessness among these actors requires application of the extreme sanction of exclusion. To the contrary, the Chief Clerk of the Justice Court testified at the suppression hearing that this type of error occurred once every three or four years.

Finally, and most important, there is no basis for believing that application of the exclusionary rule in these circumstances will have a significant effect on court employees responsible for informing the police that a warrant has been quashed. Because court clerks are not adjuncts to the law enforcement team engaged in the often competitive enterprise of ferreting out crime, see Johnson v. United States, 333 U.S. 10, 14, 68 S.Ct. 367, 369, 92 L.Ed. 436 (1948), they have no stake in the outcome of particular criminal prosecutions. The threat of exclusion of evidence could not be expected to deter such individuals from failing to inform police officials that a warrant had been quashed.

If it were indeed a court clerk who was responsible for the erroneous entry on the police computer, application of the exclusionary rule also could not be expected to alter the behavior of the arresting officer. As the trial court in this case stated: "I think the police officer [was] bound to arrest. I think he would [have been] derelict in his duty if he failed to arrest." The Chief Clerk of the Justice Court testified that this type of error occurred "on[c]e every three or four years." In fact, once the court clerks discovered the error, they immediately corrected it, and then proceeded to search their files to make sure that no similar mistakes had occurred. There is no indication that the arresting officer was not acting objectively reasonably when he relied upon the police computer record. Application of the *Leon* framework supports a categorical exception to the exclusionary rule for clerical errors of court employees.*

The judgment of the Supreme Court of Arizona is therefore reversed, and the case is remanded to that court for proceedings not inconsistent with this opinion.

It is so ordered.

■ JUSTICE O'CONNOR, with whom JUSTICE SOUTER and JUSTICE BREYER join, concurring.

The evidence in this case strongly suggests that it was a court employee's departure from established record-keeping procedures that caused the record of respondent's arrest warrant to remain in the computer system after the warrant had been quashed. Prudently, then, the Court limits itself to the question whether a court employee's departure from such established procedures is the kind of error to which the exclusionary rule should apply. The Court holds that it is not such an error, and I agree with that conclusion and join the Court's opinion. The Court's holding

* The Solicitor General, as *amicus curiae*, argues that an analysis similar to that we apply here to court personnel also would apply in order to determine whether the evidence should be suppressed if police personnel were responsible for the error. As the State has not made any such argument here, we agree that "[t]he record in this case ... does not adequately present that issue for the Court's consideration." Brief for United States as *Amicus Curiae* 13. Accordingly, we decline to address that question.

reaffirms that the exclusionary rule imposes significant costs on society's law enforcement interests and thus should apply only where its deterrence purposes are "most efficaciously served," ante, at 1191.

In limiting itself to that single question, however, the Court does not hold that the court employee's mistake in this case was necessarily the only error that may have occurred and to which the exclusionary rule might apply. While the police were innocent of the court employee's mistake, they may or may not have acted reasonably in their reliance on the recordkeeping system itself. Surely it would not be reasonable for the police to rely, say, on a recordkeeping system, their own or some other agency's, that has no mechanism to ensure its accuracy over time and that routinely leads to false arrests, even years after the probable cause for any such arrest has ceased to exist (if it ever existed).

* * *

In recent years, we have witnessed the advent of powerful, computer-based record-keeping systems that facilitate arrests in ways that have never before been possible. The police, of course, are entitled to enjoy the substantial advantages this technology confers. They may not, however, rely on it blindly. With the benefits of more efficient law enforcement mechanisms comes the burden of corresponding constitutional responsibilities.

■ JUSTICE SOUTER, with whom JUSTICE BREYER joins, concurring.

In joining the Court's opinion, I share Justice O'Connor's understanding of the narrow scope of what we hold today. To her concurrence, which I join as well, I add only that we do not answer another question that may reach us in due course, that is, how far, in dealing with fruits of computerized error, our very concept of deterrence by exclusion of evidence should extend to the government as a whole, not merely the police, on the ground that there would otherwise be no reasonable expectation of keeping the number of resulting false arrests within an acceptable minimum limit.

■ JUSTICE STEVENS, dissenting.

.... *Leon* stands for the dubious but limited proposition that courts should not look behind the face of a warrant on which police have relied in good faith. The Leon Court's exemption of judges and magistrates from the deterrent ambit of the exclusionary rule rested, consistently with the emphasis on the warrant requirement, on those officials' constitutionally determined role in issuing warrants. Taken on its own terms, *Leon*'s logic does not extend to the time after the warrant has issued; nor does it extend to court clerks and functionaries, some of whom work in the same building with police officers and may have more regular and direct contact with police than with judges or magistrates.

The Phoenix Police Department was part of the chain of information that resulted in petitioner's unlawful, warrantless arrest. We should reasonably presume that law enforcement officials, who stand in the best position to monitor such errors as occurred here, can influence mundane communication procedures in order to prevent those errors. That presumption comports with the notion that the exclusionary rule exists to deter future police misconduct systemically....

The deterrent purpose extends to law enforcement as a whole, not merely to "the arresting officer." Consequently, the Phoenix officers' good faith does not diminish the deterrent value of invalidating their arrest of petitioner.

The Court seeks to minimize the impact of its holding on the security of the citizen by referring to the testimony of the chief clerk of the East Phoenix Number One Justice Court that in her "particular court" this type of error occurred " 'maybe [once] every three or four years.' " Apart from the fact that the clerk promptly contradicted herself, this is slim evidence on which to base a conclusion that computer error poses no appreciable threat to Fourth Amendment interests. The Court overlooks the reality that computer technology has changed the nature of threats to citizens' privacy over the past half century. What has not changed is the reality that only that fraction of Fourth Amendment violations held to have resulted in unlawful arrests is ever noted and redressed. As Justice Jackson observed: "There may be, and I am convinced that there are, many unlawful searches ... of innocent people which turn up nothing incriminating, in which no arrest is made, about which courts do nothing, and about which we never hear." Moreover, even if errors in computer records of warrants were rare, that would merely minimize the cost of enforcing the exclusionary rule in cases like this.

While I agree with Justice Ginsburg that premature adjudication of this issue is particularly unwise because we have much to learn about the consequences of computer error as well as the efficacy of other preventive measures, one consequence of the Court's holding seems immediately obvious. Its most serious impact will be on the otherwise innocent citizen who is stopped for a minor traffic infraction and is wrongfully arrested based on erroneous information in a computer data base. I assume the police officer who reasonably relies on the computer information would be immune from liability in a § 1983 action. Of course, the Court has held that respondeat superior is unavailable as a basis for imposing liability on her municipality.

The dissent of Justice Ginsburg is omitted.

10. In Colorado v. Quintero, 464 U.S. 1014, 104 S.Ct. 543;, a companion case to *Leon* and *Sheppard* that was mooted by the death of the defendant, the facts indicated that an arresting officer had a good faith belief but erroneous belief that he had probable cause to arrest the defendant. Some thought the Court would address the good faith exception in a warrantless context.

In Virginia v. Moore ___ U.S. ___, 128 S.Ct. 1598 found in Chapter 5, the arresting officer believed he had the power to arrest the defendant for driving with a suspended license. In fact, Virginia law only permitted the officer to issue a citation. Is this comparable to the question in Quintero concerning a good faith but erroneous power to arrest?

D. ALTERNATIVE REMEDIES

1. CIVIL REMEDIES

In some instances in which law enforcement officers have violated the constitutional rights of a citizen or other resident, a cause of action may be present under state tort law. Typical is the action against a police officer for false arrest when the officer lacked reasonable grounds to believe that the arrestee had committed an offense. The liability of the officer's governmental employer—for example, the city, county or state—will turn upon state law. For example, the governmental employer may not be automatically liable for the officer's conduct under the principle of respondeat superior. Plaintiff may be required to show that the government was negligent in hiring or training or that the officer acted in accordance with official policy. Moreover state law may either (1) retain governmental immunity from actions for money damages or (2) set a limit upon the amount of such recoveries. Additionally an action against the state or other governmental entity (again depending upon state law) may have to be brought in a special state court such as a legislative "court of claims" where the right to trial by jury does not exist. On the other hand, many government employers make it a practice of either reimbursing the officer or paying the money judgment when an action against an individual officer is successful. Is this wise policy? What limits, if any, should be placed upon such a practice?

A cause of action may also lie against the officer under the federal civil rights act of 1871. Consider the following decision.

Monroe v. Pape

Supreme Court of the United States, 1961.
365 U.S. 167, 81 S.Ct. 473.

■ JUSTICE DOUGLAS delivered the opinion of the Court.

This case presents important questions concerning the construction of R.S. § 1979, 42 U.S.C. § 1983, which reads as follows:

> "Every person who, under color of any statute, ordinance, regulation, custom, or usage, of any State or Territory, subjects, or causes to be subjected, any citizen of the United States or other person within the jurisdiction thereof to the deprivation of any rights, privileges, or immunities secured by the Constitution and laws, shall be liable to the party injured in an action at law, suit in equity, or other proper proceeding for redress."

The complaint alleges that 13 Chicago police officers broke into petitioners' home in the early morning, routed them from bed, made them stand naked in the living room, and ransacked every room, emptying drawers and ripping mattress covers. It further alleges that Mr. Monroe was then taken to the police station and detained on "open" charges for 10 hours, while he was interrogated about a two-day-old murder, that he was not taken before a magistrate, though one was accessible, that he was not permitted to call his family or attorney, that he was subsequently released without criminal charges being preferred against him. It is alleged that the officers had no search warrant and no arrest warrant and that they acted "under color of the statutes, ordinances, regulations, customs and usages" of Illinois and of the City of Chicago....

The City of Chicago moved to dismiss the complaint on the ground that it is not liable under the Civil Rights Acts nor for acts committed in performance of its governmental functions. All defendants moved to dismiss, alleging that the complaint alleged no cause of action under those

Acts or under the Federal Constitution. The District Court dismissed the complaint. The Court of Appeals affirmed. . . .

I.

Petitioners claim that the invasion of their home and the subsequent search without a warrant and the arrest and detention of Mr. Monroe without a warrant and without arraignment constituted a deprivation of their "rights, privileges, or immunities secured by the Constitution" within the meaning of R.S. § 1979. It has been said that when 18 U.S.C. § 241 made criminal a conspiracy "to injure, oppress, threaten, or intimidate any citizen in the free exercise or enjoyment of any right or privilege secured to him by the Constitution," it embraced only rights that an individual has by reason of his relation to the central government, not to state governments. United States v. Williams, 341 U.S. 70, 71 S.Ct. 581. But the history of the section of the Civil Rights Act presently involved does not permit such a narrow interpretation.

Section 1979 came onto the books as § 1 of the Ku Klux Act of April 20, 1871. It was one of the means whereby Congress exercised the power vested in it by § 5 of the Fourteenth Amendment to enforce the provisions of that Amendment. . . . Allegation of facts constituting a deprivation under color of state authority of a right guaranteed by the Fourteenth Amendment satisfies to that extent the requirement of R.S. § 1979. See Douglas v. Jeannette, 319 U.S. 157, 161–162, 63 S.Ct. 877, 880. So far petitioners are on solid ground. For the guarantee against unreasonable searches and seizures contained in the Fourth Amendment has been made applicable to the States by reason of the Due Process Clause of the Fourteenth Amendment. . . .

II.

There can be no doubt at least since Ex parte Virginia, 100 U.S. 339, 346–347, that Congress has the power to enforce provisions of the Fourteenth Amendment against those who carry a badge of authority of a State and represent it in some capacity, whether they act in accordance with their authority or misuse it. See Home Tel. & Tel. Co. v. Los Angeles, 227 U.S. 278, 287–296, 33 S.Ct. 312, 314, 318. The question with which we now deal is the narrower one of whether Congress, in enacting § 1979, meant to give a remedy to parties deprived of constitutional rights, privileges and immunities by an official's abuse of his position.

We conclude that it did so intend.

* * *

We had before us in United States v. Classic, infra, § 20 of the Criminal Code, 18 U.S.C. § 242, which provides a criminal punishment for anyone who "under color of any law, statute, ordinance, regulation, or custom" subjects any inhabitant of a State to the deprivation of "any rights, privileges, or immunities secured or protected by the Constitution or laws of the United States." . . . The right involved in the Classic case was the right of voters in a primary to have their votes counted. The laws of Louisiana required the defendants "to count the ballots, to record the result of the count, and to certify the result of the election." United States v. Classic, supra, 313 U.S. 299, 61 S.Ct. 1031. But according to the indictment they did not perform their duty. In an opinion written by Mr. Justice (later Chief Justice) Stone, in which Mr. Justice Roberts, Mr. Justice Reed, and Mr. Justice Frankfurter joined, the Court ruled, "Misuse of power, possessed by virtue of state law and made possible only because the wrongdoer is clothed with the authority of state law, is action taken 'under color of' state law." There was a dissenting opinion; but the ruling as to the meaning of "under color of" state law was not questioned.

That view of the meaning of the words "under color of" state law, 18 U.S.C. § 242, was reaffirmed in Screws v. United States. The acts there complained of were committed by state officers in performance of their duties, viz., making an arrest effective. It was urged there, as it is here, that "under color of" state law should not be construed to duplicate in federal law what was an offense under state law (dissenting opinion). It was said there, as it is here, that the ruling in the Classic case as to the meaning of "under color of" state law was not in focus and was ill-advised (dissenting opinion). It was argued there, as it is here, that "under color of" state law included only action taken by officials pursuant to state law (dissenting opinion). We rejected that view.... it is beyond doubt that this phrase should be accorded the same construction in both statutes—in § 1979 and in 18 U.S.C. § 242.

Since the *Screws* and *Williams* decisions, Congress has had several pieces of civil rights legislation before it.

If the results of our construction of "under color of" law were as horrendous as now claimed, if they were as disruptive of our federal scheme as now urged, if they were such an unwarranted invasion of States' rights as pretended, surely the voice of the opposition would have been heard in Committee reports. Their silence and the new uses to which "under color of" law have recently been given reinforce our conclusion that our prior decisions were correct on this matter of construction.

We conclude that the meaning given "under color of" law in the Classic case and in the *Screws* and *Williams* cases was the correct one; and we adhere to it.

In the *Screws* case we dealt with a statute that imposed criminal penalties for acts "wilfully" done. We construed that word in its setting to mean the doing of an act with "a specific intent to deprive a person of a federal right." We do not think that gloss should be placed on § 1979 which we have here. The word "wilfully" does not appear in § 1979. Moreover, § 1979 provides a civil remedy, while in the *Screws* case we dealt with a criminal law challenged on the ground of vagueness. Section 1979 should be read against the background of tort liability that makes a man responsible for the natural consequences of his actions.

So far, then, the complaint states a cause of action. There remains to consider only a defense peculiar to the City of Chicago....

■ [The concurring opinion of JUSTICE HARLAN, joined by JUSTICE STEWART, is omitted.]

■ JUSTICE FRANKFURTER, dissenting.

... [All] the evidence converges to the conclusion that Congress by § 1979 created a civil liability enforceable in the federal courts only in instances of injury for which redress was barred in the state courts because some "statute, ordinance, regulation, custom, or usage" sanctioned the grievance complained of.... The jurisdiction which Article III of the Constitution conferred on the national judiciary reflected the assumption that the state courts, not the federal courts, would remain the primary guardians of that fundamental security of person and property which the long evolution of the common law had secured to one individual as against other individuals. The Fourteenth Amendment did not alter this basic aspect of our federalism.

* * *

NOTES

1. In *Monroe* the Court held that the employer of the offending police officers was not liable under 42 U.S.C. § 1983 because a city was not a "person" within the meaning of that statute. However, in Monell v. Department of Social Services, 436 U.S. 658, 98 S.Ct. 2018 (1978), the Court overturned that aspect of *Monroe* and held that a municipality was a person within the meaning of the act. The Court indicated that a city would not be automatically liable under § 1983 for the constitutional violations of its officers under the principle of respondeat superior. Rather some additional conduct on the part of the employer—such as establishing a policy pursuant to which the employee acted or engaging in faulty supervision of the employee—is required. If the employer is state government, wholly apart from the question of whether a state is a "person" within the meaning of § 1983, the state, absent a waiver, ordinarily will have immunity under the Eleventh Amendment from an action for money damages. See Edelman v. Jordan, 415 U.S. 651, 94 S.Ct. 1347 (1974).

2. For another variation on the sovereign immunity theme, see Inyo County v. Paiute–Shoshone Indians of the Bishop Community of the Bishop Colony, 538 U.S. 701, 123 S.Ct. 1887 (2003). In dicta, the Court indicated that Indian tribes, like States, are not "persons" subject to suits under 42 U.S.C. § 1983 as a claimant to argue it was immune from the execution of a search. The court determined that, in the situation presented, the Tribe did not qualify as a person within the jurisdiction of the United States under § 1983. The Tribe could not sue under § 1983 to vindicate the sovereign right it claimed. Section 1983 was designed to secure private rights against government encroachment, not to advance a sovereign's prerogative to withhold evidence relevant to a criminal investigation.

3. Suppose that an officer obtains and executes a search warrant, but later a court rules that, although the question is a close one, insufficient probable cause data existed to justify the issuance of the search warrant. Should the officer be liable under § 1983 because he engaged in a search which was unlawful under the Fourth Amendment? On the other hand, should the officer be automatically exempt from liability when a magistrate by issuing an arrest warrant or a search warrant gave prior authorization for the officer's conduct? Even if the probable cause data was woefully inadequate? In Pierson v. Ray, 386 U.S. 547, 87 S.Ct. 1213 (1967), the Court held "that the defense of good faith and probable cause, which the Court of Appeals found available to the officers in the common-law action for false arrest and imprisonment, is also available to them in the action under § 1983." Lower courts have differed widely on the interpretation of the phrase "good faith and probable cause," but it is generally agreed that "probable cause" here means something different from probable cause as used earlier in the casebook. *Pierson* must also be read in light of subsequent § 1983 decisions with respect to the liability of governmental officers and employees, other than law enforcement officers. Wood v. Strickland, 420 U.S. 308, 95 S.Ct. 992 (1975).

In Gomez v. Toledo, 446 U.S. 635, 100 S.Ct. 1920 (1980), the Court held that a § 1983 plaintiff need not allege that an individual defendant lacked good faith. Rather good faith is a defense which must be alleged and proved by the governmental agent.

For a thoughtful criticism of the defense of "good faith" in § 1983 actions against police officers, see an article authorized by an expert in the law of torts: Theis, "Good Faith" as a Defense to Suits for Police Deprivations of Individual Rights, 59 Minn.L.Rev. 991 (1975).

4. Does a defense of "good faith" in a civil rights action make more sense than use of a "good faith" exception to the exclusionary rule? On this topic, see Comment, The Proposed Good Faith Test for Fourth Amendment Exclusion Compared to the § 1983 Good Faith Defense: Problems and Prospects, 20 Ariz.L.Rev. 915 (1978).

5. Would the distinction between the civil rights context and the criminal context explain the difference in the court's approach to the facts in Massachusetts v. Sheppard, 468 U.S. 981, 104 S.Ct. 3424 (1984) as compared to the Court's approach to the facts in Groh v. Ramirez, 540 U.S. 551, 124 S.Ct. 1284 (2004).

6. After *Monell*, the Court held that if a municipality is responsible under the *Monell* principle for the violation of civil rights by a municipal agent, unlike the agent himself, the city cannot use the defense that it acted in good faith. For example, if by policy the city provides for highly intrusive searches of persons arrested on very minor charges, and if such searches are later declared to be violative of the Fourth Amendment, the city has no good faith defense even if the policy-makers had relied upon the apparently reasonable advice of legal counsel that such searches were lawful. See Owen v. City of Independence, Missouri, 445 U.S. 622, 100 S.Ct. 1398 (1980).

7. As long as the exclusionary rule remains, if a criminal defendant chooses to seek suppression of evidence in the state criminal proceedings and he loses in that forum, ordinarily he is barred by collateral estoppel from re-litigating his Fourth Amendment claim in a civil rights action. Allen v. McCurry, 449 U.S. 90, 101 S.Ct. 411 (1980). Such an individual is said to have his day in court. Does this seem proper? In such a situation has the defendant really chosen a state forum in which to litigate his federal constitutional claim? How voluntary is the choice? Consider also that if the defendant wins the motion to suppress in the state court, he will not be able to use the collateral estoppel doctrine against the police officer in a § 1983 action. This is because the police officer was not a party to the criminal case, even though he may have appeared there as a witness. Under dictum in *Allen*, collateral estoppel cannot be invoked in a second action against a person who did not have his day in court (either personally or, presumably, through a predecessor in interest).

8. In Haring v. Prosise, 462 U.S. 306, 103 S.Ct. 2368 (1983), the unanimous court held that a defendant who pleaded guilty to a criminal charge in a Virginia trial court without litigating the admissibility of evidence is not foreclosed from obtaining a federal civil rights judgment based upon an alleged violation of his Fourth Amendment rights. The court emphasized that Virginia law did not provide for collateral estoppel under these circumstances and that no overriding federal policy mandated such a result. On the contrary "Adoption of (a) rule of preclusion would threaten important interests in preserving federal courts as an available forum for the vindication of federal rights." It would require an accused to prevail in state court on a suppression motion in order to preserve a mere possibility of prevailing in a § 1983 action in federal court, according to the *Prosise* court.

In Bivens v. Six Unknown Named Agents of Federal Bureau of Narcotics, 403 U.S. 388, 91 S.Ct. 1999 (1971), the petitioner claimed that federal agents had unconstitutionally forced their way into his house, arrested him, manacled him in front of his wife and children, threatened arrest of the entire family, searched his home exhaustively, and transported him to a courthouse where he was interrogated, booked and strip searched. Section 1983 applies only to persons acting under color of state law and not to federal officers, although the Court held that a civil remedy could be based upon a Fourth Amendment violation. A federal cause of action is inherent in the Amendment and does not require Congressional action. Three dissenters (Burger, C.J., Black and Blackmun, JJ.) all agreed that only Congress could create the remedy envisioned by the Court. The Court did not deal with the claim of immunity but on remand the immunity argument was rejected. See 456 F.2d 1339 (2d Cir.1972).

7. For a summary of the debate over the exclusionary rule and alternative remedies, see the series of articles in Volume 62 of Judicature: Judge Malcolm Wilkey's article at p. 215, Professor Yale Kamisar's response at p. 337, and separate comments by Canon and by Schlesinger on empirical studies at p. 398. Rather than attempt to summarize the arguments, we strongly urge that students interested in the topic begin their further study by reading these articles. The best empirical studies are those by Thomas Davies of the American Bar Foundation cited in United States v. Leon, Casebook, p. 742, infra.

2. OTHER REMEDIES

In Bivens v. Six Unknown Named Agents of Federal Bureau of Narcotics, 403 U.S. 388, 91 S.Ct. 1999 (1971), Chief Justice Burger in dissent called for abolition of the Fourth Amendment exclusionary rule. In its place, he suggested creation of a "quasi-judicial" tribunal akin to the United States Court of Claims, vested with the power to make money damage awards in favor of victims of unreasonable searches and seizures and against the governmental employer of the offending officer.

Among other proposed "remedies" for investigative misconduct are criminal prosecutions under the federal civil rights law, as discussed in Monroe, or under state law. Concerning disciplinary actions against police officers, see Burger, Who Will Watch the Watchman?, 14 Am.U.L.Rev. 1 (1964). As to possible use of contempt of court, see McNear v. Rhay, 65 Wash.2d 530, 398 P.2d 732 (1965); Comment, 72 J.Crim.L. & E. 993 (1981). Concerning "self-help," that is, resisting unlawful police conduct, see W.LaFave, Search and Seizure (2d Ed.1987), § 1.11, and also see § 1.10 of the same volume concerning injunctions against unlawful police conduct.

E. "STANDING" TO OBTAIN EXCLUSION OF EVIDENCE

1. DEBATE OVER THE "STANDING" REQUIREMENT

People v. Martin

Supreme Court of California, 1955.
45 Cal.2d 755, 290 P.2d 855.

■ JUSTICE TRAYNOR delivered the opinion of the Court:

By information defendant was charged with two counts of horse-race bookmaking, and two counts of keeping and occupying premises for the purposes of such bookmaking. The trial court granted defendant's motion to set the information aside on the ground that all of the evidence against him had been obtained by illegal searches and seizures in violation of his constitutional rights. The People appeal.

Two of the counts were based on defendant's activities that were discovered by the arresting officers on April 20, 1955, at an office on Ventura Boulevard in Los Angeles.

* * *

The other two counts were based on defendant's activities that were discovered by the arresting officers six days later at another small office building on Ventura Boulevard....

The Attorney General contends that since defendant disclaimed any interest in the premises searched and the property seized, his constitutional rights could not have been violated and that therefore he has no standing to challenge the legality of the searches and seizures....

We cannot agree with this contention.

It is true that in Goldstein v. United States, 316 U.S. 114, 62 S.Ct. 1000, the United States Supreme Court recognized that the rule is well established in the lower federal courts that only those whose constitutional rights have been violated may object to the introduction of illegally obtained evidence against them.

Thus, the rule of the lower federal courts is based on the theory that the evidence is excluded to provide a remedy for a wrong done to the defendant, and that accordingly, if the defendant has not been wronged he is entitled to no remedy. In adopting the exclusionary rule, however, this court recognized that it could not be justified on that theory, People v. Cahan, 44 Cal.2d 434, 443, 282 P.2d 905, and based its decision on the ground that "other remedies have completely failed to secure compliance with the constitutional provisions on the part of police officers with the attendant result that the courts under the old rule have been constantly required to participate in, and in effect condone, the lawless activities of law enforcement officers." This result occurs when ever the government is allowed to profit by its own wrong by basing a conviction on illegally obtained evidence, and if law enforcement officers are allowed to evade the exclusionary rule by obtaining evidence in violation of the rights of third parties, its deterrent effect is to that extent nullified. Moreover, such a limitation virtually invites law enforcement officers to violate the rights of third parties and to trade the escape of a criminal whose rights are violated for the conviction of others by the use of the evidence illegally obtained against them.

The United States Supreme Court has clearly recognized that the purpose of the exclusionary rule is not to provide redress or punishment for a past wrong, but to deter lawless enforcement of the law. "The Government cannot violate the Fourth Amendment ... and use the fruits of such unlawful conduct to secure a conviction. Nor can the Government make indirect use of such evidence for its case, or support a conviction on evidence obtained through leads from the unlawfully obtained evidence. All these methods are outlawed, and convictions obtained by means of them are invalidated, because they encourage the kind of society that is obnoxious to free men." Walder v. United States, 347 U.S. 62, 64–65, 74 S.Ct. 354, 356.

* * *

Since all of the reasons that compelled us to adopt the exclusionary rule are applicable whenever evidence is obtained in violation of constitutional guarantees, such evidence is inadmissible whether or not it was obtained in violation of the particular defendant's constitutional rights. Accordingly, it must be determined whether the evidence was illegally obtained in this case.

[After reviewing the merits, the court found that the seizures made in this case were lawful.]

NOTES

1. Martin was very much a minority decision. Only Louisiana, through Article 1, Section 5 of its 1974 constitution, joined California in permitting a defendant at his or her criminal trial to secure exclusion of evidence derived from a violation of another person's constitutional rights. Louisiana courts have not been expansive in their interpretation of the state constitution's abolition of the standing requirement. See State v. Roach, 338 So.2d 621 (La.1976).

Martin is presented here as a good statement of the argument against the standing requirement as applied to Fourth Amendment cases and as a background for *Alderman*, the next principal case in this book, which considered and rejected this argument.

Martin is no longer the law in California. Because of the action of California voters, state courts in California cannot fashion rules which exclude evidence at criminal trials where the United States Constitution does not require such exclusion. See People v. Daan, 161 Cal.App.3d 22, 207 Cal.Rptr. 228 (1984).

2. If the police, in possession of data which fell short of justifying an emergency entry, unlawfully entered A's house and found B in the process of burglarizing that house, under Martin could B secure the exclusion of (1) B's burglary tools which the officers found within and (2) the observations of B going through drawers, which observations the officers made after illegally entering A's house? For a decision according "standing" to a burglar, see People v. Solario, 64 Cal.App.3d 532, 134 Cal.Rptr. 563 (1976). However, the California Supreme Court reversed, 19 Cal.3d 760, 139 Cal.Rptr. 725, 566 P.2d 627 (1977), but, finding the police conduct lawful, avoided the broad issue as to whether a burglar has "standing" to object to the use against him of evidence secured in violation of his victim's Fourth Amendment rights.

Alderman v. United States

Supreme Court of the United States, 1969.
394 U.S. 165, 89 S.Ct. 961.

[The Supreme Court consolidated several wiretapping cases arising out of unrelated investigations and prosecutions under the above case title. In one case the Attorney General conceded that an unlawful tap had occurred. In other cases the Court assumed, without deciding that the police conduct was unlawful. In each of the cases the Government argued that certain of the petitioners lacked standing to secure exclusion of evidence derived from the allegedly improper wiretapping.]

■ JUSTICE WHITE delivered the opinion of the Court:

The exclusionary rule fashioned in Weeks v. United States (1914) and Mapp v. Ohio (1961), excludes from a criminal trial any evidence seized from the defendant in violation of his Fourth Amendment rights. Fruits of such evidence are excluded as well. Silverthorne Lumber Co. v. United States (1920). Because the Amendment now affords protection against the uninvited ear, oral statements, if illegally overheard, and their fruits are also subject to suppression. Silverman v. United States (1967).

In *Mapp* and *Weeks* the defendant against whom the evidence was held to be inadmissible was the victim of the search. However, in the cases before us each petitioner demands retrial if any of the evidence used to convict him was the product of unauthorized surveillance, regardless of whose Fourth Amendment rights the surveillance violated. At the very least, it is urged that if evidence is inadmissible against one defendant or conspirator, because tainted by electronic surveillance illegal as to him, it is also inadmissible against his codefendant or coconspirator.

This expansive reading of the Fourth Amendment and of the exclusionary rule fashioned to enforce it is admittedly inconsistent with prior cases, and we reject it. The established principle is that suppression of the product of a Fourth Amendment violation can be successfully urged only by those whose rights were violated by the search itself, not by those who are aggrieved solely by the introduction of damaging evidence. Coconspirators and codefendants have been accorded no special standing.

Thus in Goldstein v. United States, testimony induced by disclosing to witnesses their own telephonic communications intercepted by the Government contrary to 47 U.S.C. § 605 was held admissible against their coconspirators. The Court equated the rule under § 605 with the exclusionary rule under the Fourth Amendment. Wong Sun v. United States (1963) came to like conclusions. There, two defendants were tried together; narcotics seized from a third party were held inadmissible against one defendant because they were the product of statements made by him at the time of his unlawful arrest. But the same narcotics were found to be admissible against the codefendant because "[t]he seizure of this heroin invaded no right of privacy of person or premises which would entitle [him] to object to its use at his trial."

The rule is stated in Jones v. United States (1960):

> "In order to qualify as a 'person aggrieved by an unlawful search and seizure' one must have been a victim of a search or seizure, one against whom the search was directed, as distinguished from one who claims prejudice only through the use of evidence gathered as a consequence of a search or seizure directed at someone else. . . .

"Ordinarily, then, it is entirely proper to require of one who seeks to challenge the legality of a search as the basis for suppressing relevant evidence that he allege, and if the allegation be disputed that he establish, that he himself was the victim of an invasion of privacy."[1]

* * *

We adhere to these cases and to the general rule that Fourth Amendment rights are personal rights which, like some other constitutional rights, may not be vicariously asserted. . . .

What petitioners appear to assert is an independent constitutional right of their own to exclude relevant and probative evidence because it was seized from another in violation of the Fourth Amendment. But we think there is a substantial difference for constitutional purposes between preventing the incrimination of a defendant through the very evidence illegally seized from him and suppressing evidence on the motion of a party who cannot claim this predicate for exclusion.

The necessity for that predicate was not eliminated by recognizing and acknowledging the deterrent aim of the rule. See Linkletter v. Walker (1965); Elkins v. United States (1960). Neither those cases nor any others hold that anything which deters illegal searches is thereby commanded by the Fourth Amendment. The deterrent values of preventing the incrimination of those whose rights the police have violated have been considered sufficient to justify the suppression of probative evidence even though the case against the defendant is weakened or destroyed. We adhere to that judgment. But we are not convinced that the additional benefits of extending the exclusionary rule to other defendants would justify further encroachment upon the public interest in prosecuting those accused of crime and having them acquitted or convicted on the basis of all the evidence which exposes the truth. . . .

Of course, Congress or state legislatures may extend the exclusionary rule and provide that illegally seized evidence is inadmissible against anyone for any purpose. But for constitutional purposes, we are not now inclined to expand the existing rule that unlawful wiretapping or eavesdropping, whether deliberate or negligent, can produce nothing usable against the person aggrieved by the invasion.

In these cases, therefore, any petitioner would be entitled to the suppression of government evidence originating in electronic surveillance violative of his own Fourth Amendment right to be free of unreasonable searches and seizures. Such violation would occur if the United States

1. The "person aggrieved" language is from Fed.Rule Crim.Proc. 41(e). *Jones* thus makes clear that Rule 41 conforms to the general standard and is no broader than the constitutional rule.

McDonald v. United States, 335 U.S. 451, 69 S.Ct. 191 (1948), is not authority to the contrary. It is not at all clear that the *McDonald* opinion would automatically extend standing to a codefendant. Two of the five Justices joining the majority opinion did not read the opinion to do so and found the basis for the codefendant's standing to be the fact that he was a guest on the premises searched. "But even a guest may expect the shelter of the rooftree he is under against criminal intrusion."

unlawfully overheard conversations of a petitioner himself or conversations occurring on his premises, whether or not he was present or participated in those conversations.

* * *

NOTES

1. In *Alderman*, Chief Justice Warren, Justice Brennan, and Justice Black joined in the dissenting opinion of Justice Fortas, who argued that any "target" of the investigation should have standing. This theory was later discussed and rejected in Rakas v. Illinois, Section C–2, infra. Justice Harlan joined by Justice Stewart argued for a narrower standing rule in wiretap cases, so that only persons whose conversational privacy was violated could secure exclusion of illegally obtained wiretap evidence. Under the view of these justices, even if a physical trespass was made against a homeowner's property to install the electronic device (as apparently was true in the *Alderman* and consolidated cases), he would have no standing to object to the seizure of a conversation to which he was not a party. Thus, under the views of Harlan and Stewart, if the law of evidence permitted the use against the homeowner of such conversations (under the coconspirator exception to the hearsay rule), he could not secure exclusion of evidence derived from illegal wiretaps even if the conversations occurred on his property and had been overheard through a trespass to that property.

Suppose that an unlawful wiretap occurs without any trespass. Should the homeowner who was not present when the conversation occurred on a telephone in his home be accorded standing to object to admission of the conversations to which he was not a party? To what was said by each party or only to what was said by the party who was using the homeowner's phone?

The dispute as to a nonparticipant's standing to object to admission of a conversation occurring on his premises should be reconsidered in light of *Rakas*. The problem is touched upon in what the Casebook editors have renumbered as footnote 3 in *Rakas*.

2. Under the standing requirement which was reaffirmed in *Alderman*, would standing be denied no matter how egregious the Fourth Amendment violation? Suppose that police officers, in non-emergency circumstances, without a warrant, and without knocking and announcing, broke down the door to A's apartment in the middle of the night, forced her children into the winter's cold, and ransacked the entire apartment, hoping to secure evidence against B, who lacked standing to complain of the search of A's apartment. Should B have standing? Should there be a "bad faith" exception to the standing requirement of *Alderman*?

In United States v. Payner, 447 U.S. 727, 100 S.Ct. 2439 (1980), federal officials obtained documents from A's briefcase by a very intentional and particularly offensive violation of A's rights. They then used the documents and evidence derived therefrom in building criminal cases against several other individuals as part of "Operation Trade Winds." The United States Supreme Court held that the district judge could not exclude the evidence from use in criminal cases against defendants other than A. It stated that in such a situation the district court cannot invoke the principle of "supervisory powers" as a means of avoiding the requirement of standing.

On state law grounds, one court has allowed a defendant derivative standing where authorities engaged in a grossly shocking violation of his co-defendant's rights. Waring v. State, 670 P.2d 357 (Alaska 1983).

2. "STANDING" CONCEPTS IN FOURTH AMENDMENT CASES

Rakas v. Illinois

Supreme Court of the United States, 1978.
439 U.S. 128, 99 S.Ct. 421.

■ JUSTICE REHNQUIST delivered the opinion of the Court.

Petitioners were convicted of armed robbery in the Circuit Court of Kankakee County, Ill., and their convictions were affirmed on appeal. At their trial, the prosecution offered into evidence a sawed-off rifle and rifle shells that had been seized by police during a search of an automobile in which petitioners had been passengers. Neither petitioner is the owner of the automobile and neither has ever asserted that he owned the rifle or shells seized. The Illinois Appellate Court held that petitioners lacked standing to object to the allegedly unlawful search and seizure and denied their motion to suppress the evidence....

A police officer on a routine patrol received a radio call notifying him of a robbery of a clothing store in Bourbonnais, Ill., and describing the getaway car. Shortly thereafter, the officer spotted an automobile which he thought might be the getaway car. After following the car for some time and after the arrival of assistance, he and several other officers stopped the vehicle. The occupants of the automobile, petitioners and two female companions, were ordered out of the car and after the occupants had left the car, two officers searched the interior of the vehicle. They discovered a box of rifle shells in the glove compartment, which had been locked, and a sawed-off rifle under the front passenger seat. After discovering the rifle and the shells, the officers took petitioners to the station and placed them under arrest.

Before trial petitioners moved to suppress the rifle and shells seized from the car on the ground that the search violated the Fourth and Fourteenth Amendments. They conceded that they did not own the automobile and were simply passengers; the owner of the car had been the driver of the vehicle at the time of the search. Nor did they assert that they owned the rifle or the shells seized. The prosecutor challenged petitioners' standing to object to the lawfulness of the search of the car because neither the car, the shells nor the rifle belonged to them. The trial court agreed that petitioners lacked standing and denied the motion to suppress the evidence. In view of this holding, the court did not determine whether there was probable cause for the search and seizure. On appeal after petitioners' conviction, the Appellate Court of Illinois, Third Judicial District, affirmed the trial court's denial of petitioners' motion to suppress because it held that "without a proprietary or other similar interest in an automobile, a mere passenger therein lacks standing to challenge the legality of the search of the vehicle." The court stated:

> "We believe that defendants failed to establish any prejudice to their own constitutional rights because they were not persons aggrieved by the unlawful search and seizure.... They wrongly seek to establish prejudice only through the use of evidence

gathered as a consequence of a search and seizure directed at someone else and fail to prove an invasion of their own privacy."

Petitioners first urge us to relax or broaden the rule of standing enunciated in Jones v. United States (1960), so that any criminal defendant at whom a search was "directed" would have standing to contest the legality of that search and object to the admission at trial of evidence obtained as a result of the search. Alternatively, petitioners argue that they have standing to object to the search under Jones because they were "legitimately on [the] premises" at the time of the search....

We decline to extend the rule of standing in Fourth Amendment cases in the manner suggested by petitioners.... See Simmons v. United States, supra, 390 U.S., at 389, 88 S.Ct., at 973. There is no reason to think that a party whose rights have been infringed will not, if evidence is used against him, have ample motivation to move to suppress it. Even if such a person is not a defendant in the action, he may be able to recover damages for the violation of his Fourth Amendment rights, or seek redress under state law for invasion of privacy or trespass....

In *Alderman*, Mr. Justice Fortas, in a concurring and dissenting opinion, argued that the Court should "include within the category of those who may object to the introduction of illegal evidence 'one against whom the search was directed.'" The Court did not directly comment on Mr. Justice Fortas' suggestion, but it left no doubt that it rejected this theory by holding that persons who were not parties to unlawfully overheard conversations or who did not own the premises on which such conversations took place did not have standing to contest the legality of the surveillance, regardless of whether or not they were the "targets" of the surveillance. Mr. Justice Harlan, concurring and dissenting, did squarely address Mr. Justice Fortas' arguments and declined to accept them. He identified administrative problems posed by the target theory:

> [T]he [target] rule would entail very substantial administrative difficulties. In the majority of cases, I would imagine that the police plant a bug with the expectation that it may well produce leads to a large number of crimes. A lengthy hearing would, then, appear to be necessary in order to determine whether the police knew of an accused's criminal activity at the time the bug was planted and whether the police decision to plant a bug was motivated by an effort to obtain information against the accused or some other individual. I do not believe that this administrative burden is justified in any substantial degree by the hypothesized marginal increase in Fourth Amendment protection.

When we are urged to grant standing to a criminal defendant to assert a violation, not of his own constitutional rights but of someone else's, we cannot but give weight to practical difficulties such as those foreseen by Mr. Justice Harlan in the quoted language.

Conferring standing to raise vicarious Fourth Amendment claims would necessarily mean a more widespread invocation of the exclusionary rule during criminal trials.... Each time the exclusionary rule is applied it exacts a substantial social cost for the vindication of Fourth Amendment rights. Relevant and reliable evidence is kept from the trier of fact and the search for truth at trial is deflected. Since our cases generally have held that one whose Fourth Amendment rights are violated may successfully suppress evidence obtained in the course of an illegal search and seizure, misgivings as to the benefit of enlarging the class of persons who may invoke that rule are properly considered when deciding whether to expand standing to assert Fourth Amendment violations. . . .

. . . This Court's long history of insistence that Fourth Amendment rights are personal in nature has already answered many of these traditional standing inquiries, and we think that definition of those rights is more properly placed within the purview of substantive Fourth Amendment law than within that of standing. . . .

Analyzed in these terms, the question is whether the challenged search or seizure violated the Fourth Amendment rights of a criminal defendant who seeks to exclude the evidence obtained during it. That inquiry in turn requires a determination of whether the disputed search and seizure has infringed an interest of the defendant which the Fourth Amendment was designed to protect. We are under no illusion that by dispensing with the rubric of standing used in Jones we have rendered any simpler the determination of whether the proponent of a motion to suppress is entitled to contest the legality of a search and seizure. But by frankly recognizing that this aspect of the analysis belongs more properly under the heading of substantive Fourth Amendment doctrine than under the heading of standing, we think the decision of this issue will rest on sounder logical footing.

Here petitioners, who were passengers occupying a car which they neither owned nor leased, seek to analogize their position to that of the defendant in Jones v. United States (1960). In *Jones*, petitioner was present at the time of the search of an apartment which was owned by a friend. The friend had given Jones permission to use the apartment and a key to it, with which Jones had admitted himself on the day of the search.[1] . . . He had a suit and shirt at the apartment and had slept there "maybe a night," but his home was elsewhere. At the time of the search, Jones was the only occupant of the apartment because the lessee was away for a period of several days. Under these circumstances, this Court stated that while one wrongfully on the premises could not move to suppress evidence obtained as a result of searching them, "anyone legitimately on premises where a search occurs may challenge its legality." Petitioners argue that their occupancy of the automobile in question was comparable to that of Jones in the apartment and that they therefore have standing to contest

1. The Court in *Jones* was quite careful to note that "wrongful" presence at the scene of a search would not enable a defendant to object to the legality of the search. The Court stated: "No just interest of the Government in the effective and rigorous enforcement of the criminal law will be hampered by recognizing that anyone legitimately on premises where a search occurs may challenge its legality by way of a motion to suppress, when its fruits are proposed to be used against him. *This would of course not avail those who, by virtue of their wrongful presence, cannot invoke the privacy of the premises searched.*" (emphasis added). Despite this clear statement in *Jones*, several lower courts inexplicably have held that a person present in a stolen automobile at the time of a search may object to the lawfulness of the search of the automobile. See, e.g., Cotton v. United States, 371 F.2d 385 (C.A.9 1967); Simpson v. United States, 346 F.2d 291 (C.A.10 1965).

the legality of the search—or as we have rephrased the inquiry, that they, like Jones, had their Fourth Amendment rights violated by the search.

We do not question the conclusion in *Jones* that the defendant in that case suffered a violation of his personal Fourth Amendment rights if the search in question were unlawful. Nonetheless, we believe that the phrase "legitimately on premises" coined in *Jones* creates too broad a gauge for measurement of Fourth Amendment rights.[3] For example, applied literally, this statement would permit a casual visitor who has never seen, or been permitted to visit the basement of another's house to object to a search of the basement if the visitor happened to be in the kitchen of the house at the time of the search. Likewise, a casual visitor who walks into a house one minute before a search of the house commences and leaves one minute after the search ends would be able to contest the legality of the search. The first visitor would have absolutely no interest or legitimate expectation of privacy in the basement, the second would have none in the house, and it advances no purpose served by the Fourth Amendment to permit either of them to object to the lawfulness of the search.

We think that *Jones* on its facts merely stands for the unremarkable proposition that a person can have a legally sufficient interest in a place other than his own home so that the Fourth Amendment protects him from unreasonable governmental intrusion into that place. In defining the scope of that interest, we adhere to the view expressed in *Jones* and echoed in later cases that arcane distinctions developed in property and tort law between guests, licensees, invitees, and the like, ought not to control....

... the holding in Jones can best be explained by the fact that Jones had a legitimate expectation of privacy in the premises he was using and therefore could claim the protection of the Fourth Amendment with respect to a governmental invasion of those premises, even though his "interest" in those premises might not have been a recognized property interest at common law.[4]

* * *

3. The Court in Mancusi v. DeForte, 392 U.S. 364, 88 S.Ct. 2120, 20 L.Ed.2d 1154 (1968), also must have been unsatisfied with the "legitimately on premises" statement in *Jones*. DeForte was legitimately in his office at the time of the search and if the *Mancusi* Court had literally applied the statement from *Jones*, DeForte's standing to object to the search should have been obvious. Instead, to determine whether DeForte possessed standing to object to the search, the Court inquired into whether DeForte's office was an "area was one in which there was a reasonable expectation of freedom from governmental intrusion."

Unfortunately, with few exceptions, lower courts have literally applied this language from *Jones* and have held that anyone legitimately on premises at the time of the search may contest its legality. See, e.g., Garza–Fuentes v. United States, 400 F.2d 219 (C.A.5 1968); State v. Bresolin, 13 Wash.App. 386, 534 P.2d 1394 (1975).

4. Obviously, however, a "legitimate" expectation of privacy by definition means more than a subjective expectation of not being discovered. A burglar plying his trade in a summer cabin during the off season may have a thoroughly justified subjective expectation of privacy, but it is not one which the law recognizes as "legitimate." His presence, in the words of *Jones*, is "wrongful"; his expectation is not "one that society is prepared to recognize as 'reasonable.'" Katz v. United States (1967) (Harlan, J., concurring). And it would, of course, be merely tautological to fall back on the notion that those expectations of privacy

... *Katz* held that capacity to claim the protection of the Fourth Amendment depends not upon a property right in the invaded place but upon whether the person who claims the protection of the Amendment has a legitimate expectation of privacy in the invaded place.

Our Brother White in dissent expresses the view that by rejecting the phrase "legitimately on [the] premises" as the appropriate measure of Fourth Amendment rights, we are abandoning a thoroughly workable, "bright line" test in favor of a less certain analysis of whether the facts of a particular case give rise to a legitimate expectation of privacy....

* * *

... [T]he phrase "legitimately on premises" has not shown to be an easily applicable measure of Fourth Amendment rights so much as it has proved to be simply a label placed by the courts on results which have not been subjected to careful analysis. We would not wish to be understood as saying that legitimate presence on the premises is irrelevant to one's expectation of privacy, but it cannot be deemed controlling.

Judged by the foregoing analysis, petitioners' claims must fail. They asserted neither a property nor a possessory interest in the automobile, nor an interest in the property seized. And as we have previously indicated, the fact that they were "legitimately on [the] premises" in the sense that they were in the car with the permission of its owner is not determinative of whether they had a legitimate expectation of privacy in the particular areas of the automobile searched. It is unnecessary for us to decide here whether the same expectations of privacy are warranted in a car as would be justified in a dwelling place in analogous circumstances. We have on numerous occasions pointed out that cars are not to be treated identically with houses or Apartments for Fourth Amendment purposes. But here petitioners' claim is one which would fail even in an analogous situation in a dwelling place since they made no showing that they had any legitimate expectation of privacy in the glove compartment or area under the seat of the car in which they were merely passengers. Like the trunk of an

which are legitimate depend primarily on cases deciding exclusionary rule issues in criminal cases. Legitimation of expectations of privacy by law must have a source outside of the Fourth Amendment, either by reference to concepts of real or personal property law or to understandings that are recognized and permitted by society. One of the main rights attaching to property is the right to exclude others, see W. Blackstone, Commentaries, Book II, Ch. I, and one who owns or lawfully possesses or controls property will in all likelihood have a legitimate expectation of privacy by virtue of this right to exclude. Expectations of privacy protected by the Fourth Amendment, of course, need not be based on a common-law interest in real or personal property, or on the invasion of such an interest. These ideas were rejected both in *Jones*, supra, and *Katz*, supra. But by focusing on legitimate expectations of privacy in Fourth Amendment jurisprudence, the Court has not altogether abandoned use of property concepts in determining the presence or absence of the privacy interests protected by that Amendment. No better demonstration of this proposition exists than the decision in Alderman v. United States (1969), where the Court held that an individual's property interest in his own home was so great as to allow him to object to electronic surveillance of conversations emanating from his home, even though he himself was not a party to the conversations. On the other hand, even a property interest in premises may not be sufficient to establish a legitimate expectation of privacy with respect to particular items located on the premises or activity conducted thereon.

automobile, these are areas in which a passenger qua passenger simply would not normally have a legitimate expectation of privacy.

... Katz and Jones could legitimately expect privacy in the areas which were the subject of the search and seizure they sought to contest. No such showing was made by these petitioners with respect to those portions of the automobile which were searched and from which incriminating evidence was seized.

The Illinois courts were therefore correct in concluding that it was unnecessary to decide whether the search of the car might have violated the rights secured to someone else by the Fourth and Fourteenth Amendments to the United States Constitution. Since it did not violate any rights of these petitioners, their judgment of conviction is

Affirmed.

■ JUSTICE POWELL, with whom THE CHIEF JUSTICE joins, concurring.

I concur in the opinion of the Court, and add these thoughts. I do not believe my dissenting Brethren correctly characterize the rationale of the Court's opinion when they assert that it ties "the application of the Fourth Amendment ... to property law concepts." On the contrary, I read the Court's opinion as focusing on whether there was a legitimate expectation of privacy protected by the Fourth Amendment.

The petitioners do not challenge the constitutionality of the police action in stopping the automobile in which they were riding; nor do they complain of being made to get out of the vehicle. Rather, petitioners assert that their constitutionally protected interest in privacy was violated when the police, after stopping the automobile and making them get out, searched the vehicle's interior, where they discovered a sawed-off rifle under the front seat and rifle shells in the locked glove compartment. The question before the Court, therefore, is a narrow one: Did the search of their friend's automobile after they had left it violate any Fourth Amendment right of the petitioners?

The ultimate question, therefore, is whether one's claim to privacy from government intrusion is reasonable in light of all the surrounding circumstances. As the dissenting opinion states, this standard "will not provide law enforcement officials with a bright line between the protected and the unprotected." Whatever the application of this standard may lack in ready administration, it is more faithful to the purposes of the Fourth Amendment than a test focusing solely or primarily on whether the defendant was legitimately present during the search.

* * *

■ JUSTICE WHITE, with whom JUSTICE BRENNAN, JUSTICE MARSHALL, and JUSTICE STEVENS join, dissenting.

.... The Court's holding is contrary not only to our past decisions and the logic of the Fourth Amendment, but also to the everyday expectations of privacy that we all share. Because of that, it is unworkable in all the various situations that arise in real life. If the owner of the car had not only invited petitioners to join her but had said to them "I give you a temporary possessory interest in my vehicle so that you will share the right to privacy that the Supreme Court says that I own," then apparently the majority would reverse. But people seldom say such things, though they may mean their invitation to encompass them if only they had thought of the problem. If the nonowner were the spouse or child of the owner, would the Court recognize a sufficient interest? If so, would distant relatives somehow have more of an expectation of privacy than close friends? What if the nonowner were driving with the owner's permission? Would nonowning drivers have more of an expectation of privacy than mere passengers? What about a passenger in a taxicab? Katz expressly recognized protection for such passengers. Why should Fourth Amendment rights be present when one pays a cabdriver for a ride but be absent when one is given a ride by a friend? . . .

More importantly, the ruling today undercuts the force of the exclusionary rule in the one area in which its use is most certainly justified—the deterrence of bad-faith violations of the Fourth Amendment. This decision invites police to engage in patently unreasonable searches every time an automobile contains more than one occupant. Should something be found, only the owner of the vehicle, or of the item, will have standing to seek suppression, and the evidence will presumably be usable against the other occupants. . . .

Of course, most police officers will decline the Court's invitation and will continue to do their jobs as best they can in accord with the Fourth Amendment. But the very purpose of the Bill of Rights was to answer the justified fear that governmental agents cannot be left totally to their own devices, and the Bill of Rights is enforceable in the courts because human experience teaches that not all such officials will otherwise adhere to the stated precepts. Some policemen simply do act in bad faith, even if for understandable ends, and some deterrent is needed. In the rush to limit the applicability of the exclusionary rule somewhere, anywhere, the Court ignores precedent, logic, and common sense to exclude the rule's operation from situations in which, paradoxically, it is justified and needed.

NOTES

1. Under what circumstances, if not those in *Rakas*, would a passenger have a reasonable expectation of privacy in portions of the vehicle? In *Brendlin* an officer examined a parked vehicle with expired registration tags. Upon inquiry, he learned that an application for renewal of registration was being processed. Shortly thereafter he saw the same car being driven on the road and stopped it to ascertain that the temporary operating permit matched the registration. Upon stopping the car, he recognized the passenger as "one of the Brendlin boys" and a parole violator with an outstanding warrant for his arrest. He took him into custody. In a search incident to arrest, he found a syringe on his person. The driver also possessed drugs and there were drugs and drug paraphernalia in the car. In deciding that the stop of a vehicle subjects a passenger, as well as the driver, to a Fourth Amendment seizure the Court also indicated that the passenger in the car had standing to challenge the car stop. Brendlin v. California, ___ U.S. ___, 127 S.Ct. 2400 (2007).

2. Normally, a person who is in possession of a stolen vehicle has no standing to complain about the unlawful search of the vehicle. See Palmer v. State, 14 Md.App. 159, 286 A.2d 572 (1972); People v. Henenberg, 55 Ill.2d 5, 302 N.E.2d 27 (1973).

Suppose, however, that the original stop of the car is unlawful. Can the thief-driver complain that all evidence discovered was the product of his unlawful detention and must be suppressed as the fruit of a violation of his rights? Could a passenger in a stolen vehicle make a similar argument following an unlawful stop? Could a passenger lawfully present in a vehicle complain about a search of the car's trunk following an unlawful stop? Did *Rakas* advance such an argument, contending that the items discovered should be viewed as the product of his unlawful detention? How significant is the statement in the *Rakas* concurring opinion indicating that the passengers did not claim that the stop of the car was illegal?

Some decisions have held that where the stop of the vehicle is illegal, a passenger can complain about the search of the vehicle as being the product of his illegal detention. See, e.g., United States v. Erwin, 875 F.2d 268 (10th Cir.1989); People v. Martin, 121 Ill.App.3d 196, 76 Ill.Dec. 642, 459 N.E.2d 279 (1984). The contrary view is that even if the passenger is being illegally detained, the search of the vehicle is separate from that detention, so that the passenger ordinarily has no standing as to the search even if the stop of the vehicle had been illegal. See Lewis v. State, 664 S.W.2d 345 (Tex.Crim.App.1984).

3. In Minnesota v. Olson, 495 U.S. 91, 110 S.Ct. 1684 (1990), Olson raised a Payton v. New York claim concerning the warrantless police entry of a home for the purpose of arresting Olson. The Court decided that "Olson's status as an overnight guest is alone enough to show that he had an expectation of privacy in the home that society is prepared to recognize as reasonable." This was deemed true even though Olson had no key to the duplex and was never left alone there. The majority declared:

> To hold that an overnight guest has a legitimate expectation of privacy in his host's home merely recognizes the everyday expectations of privacy that we all share. Staying overnight in another's home is a longstanding social custom that serves functions recognized as valuable by society. We stay in others' homes when we travel to a strange city for business or pleasure, when we visit our parents, children, or more distant relatives out of town, when we are in between jobs or homes, or when we house-sit for a friend. We will all be hosts and we will all be guests many times in our lives. From either perspective, we think that society recognizes that a houseguest has a legitimate expectation of privacy in his host's home.
>
> From the overnight guest's perspective, he seeks shelter in another's home precisely because it provides him with privacy, a place where he and his possessions will not be disturbed by anyone but his host and those his host allows inside. We are at our most vulnerable when we are asleep because we cannot monitor our own safety or the security of our belongings. It is for this reason that, although we may spend all day in public places, when we cannot sleep in our own home we seek out another private place to sleep, whether it be a hotel room, or the home of a friend. Society expects at least as much privacy in these places as in a telephone booth— "a temporarily private place whose momentary occupants' expectations of freedom from intrusion are recognized as reasonable," Katz v. United States (1967) (Harlan, J., concurring).
>
> That the guest has a host who has ultimate control of the house is not inconsistent with the guest having a legitimate expectation of privacy. The houseguest is there with the permission of his host, who is willing to share his house and his privacy with his guest. It is unlikely that the guest will be confined to a restricted area of the house; and when the host is away or asleep, the guest will have a measure of control over the premises. The host may admit or exclude from the house as he prefers, but it is unlikely that

he will admit someone who wants to see or meet with the guest over the objection of the guest. On the other hand, few houseguests will invite others to visit them while they are guests without consulting their hosts; but the latter, who have the authority to exclude despite the wishes of the guest, will often be accommodating. The point is that hosts will more likely than not respect the privacy interests of their guests, who are entitled to a legitimate expectation of privacy despite the fact that they have no legal interest in the premises and do not have the legal authority to determine who may or may not enter the household.

The limits of Minnesota v. Olson were tested in Minnesota v. Carter, 525 U.S. 83, 119 S.Ct. 469 (1998). In Carter, the defendants had paid the lessee of an apartment a small amount of cocaine in return for the use of the apartment to bag cocaine, and the defendants were spotted by an officer who looked through a drawn window blind. The Minnesota Supreme Court held that the defendants had a legitimate expectation of privacy in the apartment, because property owners have the right "to invite persons into the privacy of their homes to conduct a common task, be it legal or illegal activity." The Supreme Court reversed, distinguishing defendants from the "overnight guest" in Olson: "Respondents here were obviously not overnight guests, but were essentially present for a business transaction and were only in the home a matter of hours. There is no suggestion that they had a previous relationship with [the lessee], or that there was any other purpose to their visit. Nor was there anything similar to the overnight guest relationship in Olson to suggest a degree of acceptance into the household. While the apartment was a dwelling place for [the lessee], it was for these respondents simply a place to do business." The Court concluded that apartment, for defendants' purposes, was more like a commercial premises and defendants' expectation of privacy was therefore less.

Justice Scalia, joined by Justice Thomas, joined the Court's opinion, but pointed out that they eschewed the Katz "reasonable expectation of privacy" analysis as not grounded in the constitutional text, and concurred on the ground that the text and history of the Fourth Amendment made clear that one is only entitled to protection in one's own home or dwelling place ("right . . . to be secure . . . in their houses"). Justice Kennedy concurred, reasoning that while regular social guests might have a reasonable expectation of privacy in a host's home, these defendants were not social guests, but business visitors with "no meaningful tie or connection to the owner, the owner's home, or the owner's expectation of privacy." Justice Breyer concurred in the judgment, believing that even if the defendants were entitled to Fourth Amendment protection, the officer's "peek" through the blinds was made from a public area and was appropriate under the plain view doctrine. Justice Ginsburg, joined by Justices Stevens and Souter, dissented, arguing that "through the host's invitation, the guest gains a reasonable expectation of privacy in the home." She pointed out that Katz had found a legitimate expectation of privacy in a business call made from a public phone booth, and she could not distinguish the facts in this case.

4. Will there be situations in which the arrestee as a guest has enough of a reasonable expectation of privacy in a third person's home to merit standing to complain about an unlawful entry, but not so much status as to make the third person's home the equivalent of the arrestee's own home for purposes of Steagald v. United States. One court has answered this question negatively, saying that a suspect cannot be deemed to have broader Fourth Amendment rights in the home of a third person than in his own home. Thus if an arrest warrant is enough to arrest him in his own home, it is enough to arrest him in the home of a third person. United States v. Buckner, 717 F.2d 297 (6th Cir.1983). See also United States v. Underwood, 717 F.2d 482 (9th Cir.1983).

5. As noted in *Rakas*, an alternative holding in Jones v. United States (1960) provided for "automatic standing" in a certain class of cases. In that class of cases (generally interpreted as "possession" cases), a defendant did not have to allege or prove an interest in the place searched or the items seized. The Court said that it was unfair for the Government to assert the contradictory position that (a) the defendant was guilty because of his possession of certain items, but that (b) the defendant did not have sufficient interest in the place searched or the items seized so as to obtain standing. The Court also held that it was unfair to require a defendant, in order to urge a Fourth Amendment violation, to incriminate himself by testifying that he possessed or controlled the place searched or the items seized because such testimony was tantamount to a confession. Thereafter, in Simmons v. United States, 390 U.S. 377, 88 S.Ct. 967 (1968), the Court held that such testimony given by the defendant on a motion to suppress as was essential to acquire standing could not be used against the defendant at trial, at least in the prosecution's case-in-chief.

The Supreme Court abolished the doctrine of automatic standing in United States v. Salvucci, 448 U.S. 83, 100 S.Ct. 2547 (1980).

Some jurisdictions have chosen to retain the concept of automatic standing in possession cases, as a matter of state law. See State v. Settle, 141 Vt. 58, 442 A.2d 1314 (1982); State v. Alston, 88 N.J. 211, 440 A.2d 1311 (1981); State v. Sidebotham, 124 N.H. 682, 474 A.2d 1377 (1984); Commonwealth v. Sell, 504 Pa. 46, 470 A.2d 457 (1983).

6. Even ownership of the item seized may not suffice after *Rakas* to provide standing to complain of a Fourth Amendment violation. Consider this situation, which is drawn from the opinion of then Circuit Judge John Paul Stevens in United States v. Lisk, 522 F.2d 228 (7th Cir.1975), cert. denied 423 U.S. 1078, 96 S.Ct. 865 (1976). Authorities illegally open the car trunk of a car owned by an individual other than the defendant. The defendant has no reasonable expectation of privacy in the car trunk. Having acquired a vantage point for looking into the trunk illegally, but without violating the rights of the defendant, the authorities spot and seize evidence in the trunk which belongs to the defendant. The seizure would be lawful on plain view principles but for the fact that the police unlawfully acquired their vantage point in searching (opening) the car trunk. Because the defendant has no standing as to the search, the seizure is not unlawful as to him, according to Judge Stevens.

In *Salvucci* and in Rawlings v. Kentucky, 448 U.S. 98, 100 S.Ct. 2556 (1980), the Court, using an expectation-of-privacy analysis from *Rakas* and citing the *Lisk* opinion of Stevens, engaged in very similar reasoning and held that mere ownership of the property which is seized following an unlawful search will not necessarily afford the owner an opportunity to advance a Fourth Amendment claim. It also said that the legality of a search and the legality of a seizure require separate analysis.

In the *Lisk* factual situation, suppose that at the time of the seizure of the property, there was no probable cause to believe that it constituted evidence of a crime. For want of seizure probable cause, the plain view doctrine could not be invoked to justify the seizure. Under such circumstances would the property owner have standing to complain about a Fourth Amendment violation of his reasonable expectation of privacy?

7. Consider this hypothetical: A defendant contends that the police unlawfully searched his person, found nothing, but claimed to have found contraband which the prosecution seeks to use against him. He files a motion to suppress, alleging the unlawful search and alleging that officers will testify that they found the contraband while searching his person. He refuses to allege in a written motion or through his own testimony that the contraband was the product of the search. The trial court denies a hearing, saying that the accused has no standing unless he asserts that the evidence which he seeks to suppress was the product of the search. The court persists in its ruling even after, in a non-jury trial, the officers testify that they found the contraband on the defendant's person while searching him and even after the judge concludes, for innocence and guilt purposes, that such testimony is true. Is the ruling correct? Is standing derived from the claim of an unlawful search even where the defendant does not personally claim there was an unlawful seizure? In an unreported order the Seventh Circuit upheld the trial court on these facts. Application for certiorari was denied. Harris v. United States, 463 U.S. 1213, 103 S.Ct. 3550 (1983). More recently Moore v. United States, 468 A.2d 1342 (D.C.App.1983), permitted a suppression motion on facts very nearly identical to those held inadequate in Harris. See also People v. Davis, 187 Ill.App.3d 265, 134 Ill.Dec. 871, 543 N.E.2d 154 (1989).

Compare Lee v. Mississippi, 332 U.S. 742, 68 S.Ct. 300 (1948), which held that the accused who denies confessing can seek to suppress (on grounds of involuntariness) the confession which he is alleged to have given. What are the policy considerations relevant to a resolution of this issue?

8. Sometimes a suspect at the scene of an investigation will deny any connection to an object, for example, a suitcase. When that same individual later makes a motion to suppress alleging an illegal search or seizure of the object, some courts will deny him standing. Occasionally they alternatively invoke concepts of abandonment. See, e.g., United States v. Rush, 890 F.2d 45 (7th Cir.1989); United States v. Lewis, 921 F.2d 1294 (D.C.Cir.1990). Should a defendant, when asked if a suitcase is hers, have to either admit it or invoke her right to silence at the scene of the investigation in order to preserve her right to later challenge a search or a seizure? For an opposing view, see dictum in People v. Dowery, 174 Ill.App.3d 239, 123 Ill.Dec. 669, 528 N.E.2d 214 (1988), a decision which acknowledges Illinois decisions to the contrary.

9. As *Alderman* indicates in a footnote, B is not accorded standing simply because he is on trial with codefendant A, whose rights were violated, although at one time, in lower federal courts at least, the McDonald decision cited in the *Alderman* note was read to create a co-defendant standing rule. If very damning evidence is inadmissible against A but admissible against B for want of standing, in some circumstances A may be entitled to a separate trial if the case is to be tried before a jury.

3. "STANDING" CONCEPTS RESPECTING THE FRUITS OF UNLAWFUL INTERROGATION AND EYE-WITNESS IDENTIFICATION PROCEDURES

Most standing questions arise in the context of Fourth Amendment claims. Confession cases do not give rise to as many standing issues because hearsay rules normally prevent use of A's confession as substantive evidence against B. What A says on a relevant subject is admissible against A as an admission of a party opponent. As to B, however, A's confession ordinarily is inadmissible hearsay. Even if a hearsay exception is found, confrontation issues of the Sixth Amendment often preclude admissibility. Where derivative evidence questions are involved, however, standing issues can arise in a confession case. Generally, *Miranda* rights are considered personal and cannot be vicariously asserted. If a gun is discovered through custodial interrogation of A without warnings or waiver, the gun can be used against B if relevant and otherwise admissible. Similarly, if B is arrested as a result of A's confession, B cannot complain that probable cause data was acquired through a violation of A's Miranda rights. See People v. Denham, 41 Ill.2d 1, 241 N.E.2d 415 (1968). This was true even in California when Fourth Amendment rights could be vicariously asserted (see Section C–1, supra). In People v. Varnum, 66 Cal.2d 808, 59 Cal.Rptr. 108, 427 P.2d 772 (1967), the court reasoned that until the prosecutor offers A's confession (or evidence derived therefrom) against A, there is no violation of A's Miranda rights. In this view, although a constitutional violation occurs when A's house is illegally searched to obtain evidence against B, no constitutional violation occurs when A is subjected to custodial interrogation without warnings to secure information which may lead to evidence against B.

Suppose that the police obtain an involuntary confession from A and are led by it to physical evidence which helps establish B's guilt. Should B be allowed to obtain exclusion based upon a violation of A's rights? Or suppose A testifies as a defense witness for B and the prosecution seeks to impeach A by reference to A's involuntary confession. Should the standing concept bar B from raising a challenge to this use of A's confession? Should all involuntary confessions be excluded in this situation or just confessions which are, in fact, unreliable? In People v. J. Clyde K., 192 Cal.App.3d 710, 237 Cal.Rptr. 550 (1987), using California law, the court granted two defendants standing to exclude evidence derived from the involuntary confession of a third individual. The determination of involuntariness was predicated upon a promise of leniency. Consider these issues in connection with the materials on impeachment use of involuntary confessions.

An identification of A as one of the bank robbers may tend to prove B's guilt if B is proved to be an associate of A and to have been in A's company shortly before and shortly after the robbery. If the in-court identification and proof of the out-of-court identification of A are ruled to be inadmissible against A under *Stovall* and/or Manson v. Brathwaite (Chapter 3, Section B, supra), should not they also be inadmissible against B even though not the product of a violation of B's rights? Is not the court under *Manson* saying that such evidence is unreliable? Should unreliable evidence ever be utilized? Would different reasoning apply to an out-of-court identification excluded under Gilbert because of a violation of A's right to counsel? Only a few decisions treat standing questions as they relate to eyewitness identification. Compare Burton v. State, 442 S.W.2d 354 (Tex.Crim.App.1969), with State v. Isaacs, 24 Ohio App.2d 115, 265 N.E.2d 327, 53 O.O.2d 331 (1970). See also People v. Bisogni, 4 Cal.3d 582, 94 Cal.Rptr. 164, 483 P.2d 780 (1971), and United States v. Bruton, 416 F.2d 310 (8th Cir.1969).

F. COLLATERAL USE OF ILLEGALLY OBTAINED EVIDENCE

1. COLLATERAL PROCEEDINGS USAGE

United States v. Calandra

Supreme Court of the United States, 1974.
414 U.S. 338, 94 S.Ct. 613.

[Federal agents executed a search warrant at Calandra's place of business and seized an alleged loansharking record bearing the name of a

Dr. Loveland. Calandra was subpoenaed before a federal grand jury, and the government petitioned the district court to grant Calandra transactional immunity. Calandra received a postponement of a hearing on the immunity petition. He then filed a motion to suppress under Rule 41(e) of the Federal Rules of Criminal Procedure and asked that the seized items be returned and that he not be required to answer before the grand jury questions based upon illegally seized evidence. The district court found that the search warrant had been issued without probable cause and that the seizure exceeded the scope of the warrant. The district court prohibited questions based on the illegally seized evidence. The Sixth Circuit Court of Appeals affirmed. The Supreme Court granted certiorari.]

■ JUSTICE POWELL delivered the opinion of the Court.

This case presents the question whether a witness summoned to appear and testify before a grand jury may refuse to answer questions on the ground that they are based on evidence obtained from an unlawful search and seizure.

* * *

The institution of the grand jury is deeply rooted in Anglo–American history. In England, the grand jury served for centuries both as a body of accusers sworn to discover and present for trial persons suspected of criminal wrongdoing and as a protector of citizens against arbitrary and oppressive governmental action. In this country the Founders thought the grand jury so essential to basic liberties that they provided in the Fifth Amendment that federal prosecution for serious crimes can only be instituted by "a presentment or indictment of a Grand Jury." Cf. Costello v. United States . . . (1956). The grand jury's historic functions survive to this day. Its responsibilities continue to include both the determination whether there is probable cause to believe a crime has been committed and the protection of citizens against unfounded criminal prosecutions. Branzburg v. Hayes . . . (1972).

Traditionally the grand jury has been accorded wide latitude to inquire into violations of criminal law. No judge presides to monitor its proceedings. It deliberates in secret and may determine alone the course of its inquiry. The grand jury may compel the production of evidence or the testimony of witnesses as it considers appropriate, and its operation generally is unrestrained by the technical procedural and evidentiary rules governing the conduct of criminal trials. "It is a grand inquest, a body with powers of investigation and inquisition, the scope of whose inquiries is not to be limited narrowly by questions of propriety or forecasts of the probable result of the investigation, or by doubts whether any particular individual will be found properly subject to an accusation of crime." Blair v. United States . . . (1919).

The scope of the grand jury's powers reflects its special role in insuring fair and effective law enforcement. A grand jury proceeding is not an adversary hearing in which the guilt or innocence of the accused is adjudicated. Rather, it is an ex parte investigation to determine whether a crime has been committed and whether criminal proceedings should be instituted against any person. The grand jury's investigative power must be broad if its public responsibility is adequately to be discharged. Branzburg v. Hayes, supra....

* * *

Of course, the grand jury's subpoena power is not unlimited.[1] It may consider incompetent evidence, but it may not itself violate a valid privilege, whether established by the Constitution, statutes, or the common-law.... Although, for example, an indictment based on evidence obtained in violation of a defendant's Fifth Amendment privilege is nevertheless valid, Lawn v. United States, supra, the grand jury may not force a witness to answer questions in violation of that constitutional guarantee. Rather, the grand jury may override a Fifth Amendment claim only if the witness is granted immunity co-extensive with the privilege against self-incrimination. Kastigar v. United States, supra. Similarly, a grand jury may not compel a person to produce books and papers that would incriminate him. Boyd v. United States ... (1886). Cf. Couch v. United States ... (1973). The grand jury is also without power to invade a legitimate privacy interest protected by the Fourth Amendment. A grand jury's subpoena duces tecum will be disallowed if it is "far too sweeping in its terms to be regarded as reasonable" under the Fourth Amendment. Hale v. Henkel ... (1906). Judicial supervision is properly exercised in such cases to prevent the wrong before it occurs.

In the instant case, the Court of Appeals held that the exclusionary rule of the Fourth Amendment limits the grand jury's power to compel a witness to answer questions based on evidence obtained from a prior unlawful search and seizure....

The purpose of the exclusionary rule is not to redress the injury to the privacy of the search victim:

> "[T]he ruptured privacy of the victims' homes and effects cannot be restored. Reparation comes too late." Linkletter v. Walker ... (1965).

Instead, the rule's prime purpose is to deter future unlawful police conduct and thereby effectuate the guarantee of the Fourth Amendment against unreasonable search and seizures:

> "The rule is calculated to prevent, not to repair. Its purpose is to deter" to compel respect for the constitutional guaranty in the only effectively available way "by removing the incentive to disregard it." Elkins v. United States ... (1960).

Accord, Mapp v. Ohio, 367 U.S. 643, at 656; Tehan v. Shott ... (1966); Terry v. Ohio ... (1968). In sum, the rule is a judicially created remedy designed to safeguard Fourth Amendment rights generally through its

1. The grand jury is subject to the court's supervision in several respects. See Brown v. United States ... (1959); Fed.Rules Crim.Proc. 6 and 17; 1 L. Orfield, Criminal Procedure Under the Federal Rules § 6:108, pp. 475–477 (1966). In particular, the grand jury must rely on the court to compel production of books, papers, documents, and the testimony of witness, and the court may quash or modify a subpoena on motion if compliance would be "unreasonable or oppressive." Fed.Rule Crim.Proc. 17(c).

deterrent effect, rather than a personal constitutional right of the party aggrieved.

Despite its broad deterrent purpose, the exclusionary rule has never been interpreted to proscribe the use of illegally seized evidence in all proceedings or against all persons. As with any remedial device, the application of the rule has been restricted to those areas where its remedial objectives are thought most efficaciously served. The balancing process implicit in this approach is expressed in the contours of the standing requirement. . . .

In deciding whether to extend the exclusionary rule to grand jury proceedings, we must weigh the potential injury to the historic role and functions of the grand jury against the potential benefits of the rule as applied in this context.[2] It is evident that this extension of the exclusionary rule would seriously impede the grand jury. Because the grand jury does not finally adjudicate guilt or innocence, it has traditionally been allowed to pursue its investigative and accusatorial functions unimpeded by the evidentiary and procedural restrictions applicable to a criminal trial. Permitting witnesses to invoke the exclusionary rule before a grand jury would precipitate adjudication of issues hitherto reserved for the trial on the merits and would delay and disrupt grand jury proceedings. Suppression hearings would halt the orderly progress of an investigation and might necessitate extended litigation of issues only tangentially related to the grand jury's primary objective.[3] The probable result would be "protracted interruption of grand jury proceedings," Gelbard v. United States . . . (1972) (WHITE, J., concurring), effectively transforming them into preliminary trials on the merits. In some cases the delay might be fatal to the enforcement of the criminal law. Just last Term we reaffirmed our disinclination to allow litigious interference with grand jury proceedings:

> "Any holding that would saddle a grand jury with minitrials and preliminary showings would assuredly impede its investigation and frustrate the public's interest in the fair and expeditious administration of the criminal laws." United States v. Dionisio . . . (1973).

In sum, we believe that allowing a grand jury witness to invoke the exclusionary rule would unduly interfere with the effective and expeditious discharge of the grand jury's duties.

2. . . . The force of this argument is well illustrated by the facts of the present case. As of the date of this decision, almost two and one-half years will have elapsed since respondent was summoned to appear and testify before the grand jury. If respondent's testimony was vital to the grand jury's investigation in August 1971 of extortionate credit transactions, it is possible that this particular investigation has been completely frustrated.

3. In holding that the respondent had standing to invoke the exclusionary rule in a grand jury proceeding, the Court of Appeals relied on Fed.Rule Crim.Proc.41(e). . . . Rule 41(e) provides, in relevant part, that "[a] person aggrieved by an unlawful search and seizure may move the district court . . . for the return of the property and to suppress for the use as evidence anything so obtained. . . ." It further states that "[t]he motion shall be made before trial or hearing. . . ." We have recognized that Rule 41(e) is "no broader than the constitutional rule." Alderman v. United States . . . (1969). Jones v. United States . . . (1960). Rule 41(e), therefore, does not constitute a statutory expansion of the exclusionary rule.

Against this potential damage to the role and functions of the grand jury, we must weigh the benefits to be derived from this proposed extension of the exclusionary rule. ...[I]t does not follow that the Fourth Amendment requires adoption of every proposal that might deter police misconduct.

* * *

Any incremental deterrent effect which might be achieved by extending the rule to grand jury proceedings is uncertain at best. Whatever deterrence of police misconduct may result from the exclusion of illegally seized evidence from criminal trials, it is unrealistic to assume that application of the rule to grand jury proceedings would significantly further that goal. Such an extension would deter only police investigation consciously directed toward the discovery of evidence solely for use in a grand jury investigation. The incentive to disregard the requirement of the Fourth Amendment solely to obtain an indictment from a grand jury is substantially negated by the inadmissibility of the illegally seized evidence in a subsequent criminal prosecution of the search victim. For the most part, a prosecutor would be unlikely to request an indictment where a conviction could not be obtained. We therefore decline to embrace a view that would achieve a speculative and undoubtedly minimal advance in the deterrence of police misconduct at the expense of substantially impeding the role of the grand jury....

Questions based on illegally obtained evidence are only a derivative use of the product of a past unlawful search and seizure. They work no new Fourth Amendment wrong. Whether such derivative use of illegally obtained evidence by a grand jury should be proscribed presents a question, not of rights, but of remedies.

In the usual context of a criminal trial, the defendant is entitled to the suppression of, not only the evidence obtained through an unlawful search and seizure, but also any derivative use of that evidence. The prohibition of the exclusionary rule must reach such derivative use if it is to fulfill its function of deterring police misconduct. In the context of a grand jury proceeding, we believe that the damage to that institution from the unprecedented extension of the exclusionary rule urged by respondent outweighs the benefit of any possible incremental deterrent effect. Our conclusion necessarily controls both the evidence seized during the course of an unlawful search and seizure and any question or evidence derived there from (the fruits of the unlawful search).[4] The same considerations of logic and policy apply to both the fruits of an unlawful search and seizure

4. It should be noted that, even absent the exclusionary rule, a grand jury witness may have other remedies to redress the injury to his privacy and to prevent a further invasion in the future. He may be entitled to maintain a cause of action for damages against the officers who conducted the unlawful search. Bivens v. Six Unknown Federal Narcotics Agents ... (1971). He may also seek return of the illegally seized property, and exclusion of the property and its fruits from being used as evidence against him in a criminal trial. Go-Bart Importing Co. v. United States ... (1931). In these circumstances, we cannot say that such a witness is necessarily left remediless in the face of an unlawful search and seizure.

and derivative use of that evidence, and we do not distinguish between them.[5]

The judgment of the Court of Appeals is

Reversed.

■ JUSTICE BRENNAN, with whom JUSTICE DOUGLAS and JUSTICE MARSHALL join, dissenting.

* * *

This downgrading of the exclusionary rule to a determination whether its application in a particular type of proceeding furthers deterrence of future police misconduct reflects a startling misconception, unless it is a purposeful rejection, of the historical objective and purpose of the rule.

It is true that deterrence was a prominent consideration in the determination whether Mapp v. Ohio ... (1961), which applied the exclusionary rule to the States, should be given retrospective effect. Linkletter v. Walker ... (1965). But that lends no support to today's holding that the application of the exclusionary rule depends solely upon whether its invocation in a particular type of proceeding will significantly further the goal of deterrence. The emphasis upon deterrence in *Linkletter* must be understood in the light of the crucial fact that the States had justifiably relied from 1949 to 1961 upon Wolf v. Colorado ... (1949), and consequently, that application of Mapp would have required the wholesale release of innumerable convicted prisoners, few of whom could have been successfully retried. In that circumstance, *Linkletter* held not only that retrospective application of *Mapp* would not further the goal of deterrence but also that it would not further "the administration of justice and the integrity of the judicial process."

Thus, the Court seriously errs in describing the exclusionary rule as merely "a judicially created remedy designed to safeguard Fourth Amendment rights generally through its deterrent effect...." ... Rather, the exclusionary rule is "part and parcel of the Fourth Amendment's limitation

5. The dissent's reliance on Gelbard v. United States ... (1972) is misplaced. There, the Court construed 18 U.S.C.A. § 2515, the evidentiary prohibition of Tit. III of the Omnibus Crime Control and Safe Streets Act of 1968, ... as amended.... It held that § 2515 could be invoked by a grand jury witness as a defense to a contempt charge brought for refusal to answer questions based on information obtained from the witness' communications alleged to have been unlawfully intercepted through wiretapping and electronic surveillance. The Court's holding rested exclusively on an interpretation of Tit. III, which represented a congressional effort to afford special safeguards against the unique problems posed by misuse of wiretapping and electronic surveillance. There was no indication, in either Gelbard or the legislative history, that Tit. III was regarded as a restatement of existing law with respect to grand jury proceedings. As Mr. Justice White noted in his concurring opinion in Gelbard, Tit. III "unquestionably works a change in the law with respect to the rights of grand jury witnesses...." ...

The dissent also voices concern that today's decision will betray " 'the imperative of judicial integrity,' " sanction "illegal government conduct," and even "imperil the very foundation of our people's trust in their Government." ... There is no basis for this alarm. "Illegal conduct" is hardly sanctioned, nor are the foundations of the Republic imperiled, by declining to make an unprecedented extension of the exclusionary rule to grand jury proceedings where the rule's objectives would not be effectively served and where other important and historic values would be unduly prejudiced.

upon [governmental] encroachment of individual privacy," Mapp v. Ohio, supra, ... and "an essential part of both the Fourth and Fourteenth Amendments," ... that "gives to the individual no more than that which the Constitution guarantees him, to the police officer no less than that to which honest law enforcement is entitled, and, to the courts, that judicial integrity so necessary in the true administration of justice."

It is no answer, to suggest as the Court does, that the grand jury witnesses' Fourth Amendment rights will be sufficiently protected "by the inadmissibility of the illegally seized evidence in a subsequent criminal prosecution of the search victim." ... This, of course, is no alternative for Calandra, since he was granted transactional immunity and cannot be criminally prosecuted....

To be sure, the exclusionary rule does not "provide that illegally seized evidence is inadmissible against anyone for any purpose." Alderman v. United States ... (1969). But clearly there is a crucial distinction between withholding its cover from individuals whose Fourth Amendment rights have not been violated—as has been done in the "standing" cases, Alderman v. United States, supra, Jones v. United States ... (1960)—and withdrawing its cover from persons whose Fourth Amendment rights have in fact been abridged.

Respondent does not seek vicariously to assert another's Fourth Amendment rights. He himself has been the victim of an illegal search and desires "to mend no one's privacy [but his] own." Gelbard v. United States, supra ... (Douglas, J., concurring). Respondent is told that he must look to damages to redress the concededly unconstitutional invasion of his privacy. In other words, officialdom may profit from its lawlessness if it is willing to pay a price.

* * *

NOTES

1. The use of illegally seized evidence before a grand jury may be the focus of a dispute in different contexts. A target defendant might seek an order preventing presentation to the grand jury of evidence secured in violation of his rights. Alternatively, a witness might seek a suppression order prohibiting any questioning based upon data secured in violation of the rights of the witness. Or the witness might refuse to answer questions and then, in response to a contempt allegation, might assert the defense that the questioning was based upon illegally obtained data. Finally, a defendant might seek dismissal of an indictment because illegally obtained evidence was presented to the grand jury. Are different policies involved in each of these situations? Does the reasoning of Calandra apply to each?

2. Because of certain statutory provisions, the Supreme Court in Gelbard v. United States, 408 U.S. 41, 92 S.Ct. 2357 (1972), held that a grand jury witness accused of contempt can defend on the grounds that the questions he refused to answer in the grand jury were based upon information acquired by illegal interceptions of communications. Mr. Justice White, who made the majority with his concurrence, added a significant proviso to his opinion:

> "Where the Government produces a court order for the interception, however, and the witness nevertheless demands a full blown suppression

> hearing to determine the legality of the order, there may be room for striking a different accommodation between the due functioning of the grand jury system and the federal wiretap statute.... It is well, therefore, that the Court has left this issue open for consideration by the District Court on remand.... Of course, where the Government officially denies the fact of electronic surveillance of the witness, the matter is at an end and the witness must answer."

See Chapter 11, Section E, 3.

3. Does the nature of the transgression make any difference as to the use of illegally obtained evidence before a grand jury? Suppose that the only evidence connecting a suspect to a crime is an involuntary confession. Should the target defendant have a pre-indictment remedy to the presentation of that confession to the grand jury? See Kudisch v. Overbeck, 618 F.Supp. 196 (D.N.J.1985), where prosecutors used before the grand jury a co-defendant's involuntary confession without disclosing that the co-defendant had later repudiated such confession.

4. The use of illegally obtained evidence in proceedings other than the guilt-innocence phase of a criminal trial arises in many contexts in addition to the grand jury context. Normally, courts weigh various policy considerations against what they perceive to be the policies underlying the exclusionary rule. In some instances the government is allowed to have the benefit of the fruits of official wrongdoing; in other instances courts have required adherence to exclusionary principles:

(a) Preliminary Hearings. In some jurisdictions illegally obtained evidence is excluded at preliminary hearings in felony cases. Other jurisdictions, including federal courts (see Fed.R.Crim.P. 5.1), do not allow motions to suppress at this stage. Where such motions are heard, courts differ as to whether principles of res judicata make the preliminary hearing ruling binding when the motion to suppress is renewed before the trial judge.

(b) Probation Revocation Hearings. Over the years there has been a split of authority as to whether illegally seized evidence can be used to revoke probation. Compare United States v. Workman, 585 F.2d 1205 (4th Cir.1978), and Michaud v. State, 505 P.2d 1399 (Okl.Crim.App.1973), with United States v. Bazzano, 712 F.2d 826 (3d Cir.1983), and Stone v. Shea, 113 N.H. 174, 304 A.2d 647 (1973). Some jurisdictions allow for suppressions only where there is a showing of harassment of the probationer or bad faith on the part of governmental officials. See People v. Atencio, 186 Colo. 76, 525 P.2d 461 (1974); State v. Sears, 553 P.2d 907 (Alaska 1976); Chase v. State, 309 Md. 224, 522 A.2d 1348 (1987). The issue of admissibility of illegally seized evidence at probation revocation hearings should be distinguished from the question of the legality of warrantless searches of probationers by probation officers. See Chapter 5, Section N, supra. Presumably an involuntary confession or at least one which is, in fact, unreliable should not be used at a probation revocation hearing. People v. Peterson, 74 Ill.2d 478, 23 Ill.Dec. 554, 384 N.E.2d 348 (1978).

(c) Sentencing Hearings. Some courts permit illegally seized evidence to be used at sentencing hearings. See United States v. Torres, 926 F.2d 321 (3d Cir.1991); United States v. McCrory, 930 F.2d 63 (D.C.Cir.1991). Compare Verdugo v. United States, 402 F.2d 599 (9th Cir.1968).

In Estelle v. Smith, 451 U.S. 454, 101 S.Ct. 1866 (1981), the Court held that a statement secured by a psychiatrist from an incarcerated defendant was Miranda-violative. With very little discussion it then held that such a Miranda-violative statement was inadmissible at the sentencing phase of a trial which resulted in the death penalty: "We can discern no basis to distinguish between the guilt and penalty phases of respondent's capital murder trial so far as the protection of the

Fifth Amendment privilege is concerned. Given the gravity of the decision to be made at the penalty phase, the State is not relieved of the obligation to observe fundamental constitutional guarantees." Some courts have applied the principles of Estelle in non-capital cases. See Jones v. Cardwell, 686 F.2d 754 (9th Cir.1982). Compare Baumann v. United States, 692 F.2d 565 (9th Cir.1982). See also United States v. Graves, 785 F.2d 870 (10th Cir.1986) (Fourth Amendment exclusionary rule inapplicable in non-capital sentencing hearing, at least where the officers did not deliberately engage in illegal search in quest of evidence for use in enhancing sentence).

(d) Forfeiture Proceedings. In cases where the crime in which property was used is relatively minor compared to the value of the property subject to forfeiture, illegally seized evidence is not admissible at a forfeiture hearing. One 1958 Plymouth Sedan v. Pennsylvania, 380 U.S. 693, 85 S.Ct. 1246 (1965). Such a hearing, like a criminal trial itself, is viewed as penal in nature.

(e) License Revocation Proceedings. License hearings have a purpose of protecting the public in a manner which is more direct than forfeiture proceedings or criminal trials. License revocations are not simply penal proceedings. Thus some courts permit the use of illegally seized evidence at hearings to revoke licenses as long as the evidence is relevant. But see Liquor Control Bd. v. Mottola's 51 Tavern, 37 Pa.Cmwlth. 234, 389 A.2d 1213 (1978).

Suppose following an unlawful car stop, authorities direct the driver to take a breathalyzer under the state's implied consent law. The results cannot be used in a criminal prosecution, but can they be used in a proceeding to revoke or suspend the driver's license? On statutory grounds, Illinois does not allow the breathalyzer results to be used under these circumstances. People v. Krueger, 208 Ill.App.3d 897, 153 Ill.Dec. 759, 567 N.E.2d 717 (1991).

(f) Civil Cases. Normally the methods by which evidence was secured—whether by private parties or by government agents—does not affect its admissibility in a civil case. Indeed, early opponents of the exclusionary rule rested their case on the evidentiary principle that prohibited interruption of a civil case for a collateral inquiry into the source of evidence. See Wigmore, Vol. 8, § 2183 (third ed. 1940). Thus, under some decisions, even the wrongdoer may use in a civil case the evidence which he has wrongfully obtained. See, e.g., Sackler v. Sackler, 15 N.Y.2d 40, 255 N.Y.S.2d 83, 203 N.E.2d 481 (1964), involving the not infrequent divorce litigation scenario of one spouse using unlawful investigative methods to acquire evidence against the other. however, where government is both the wrongdoer and a party, the policy considerations may be different.

The issue arises most frequently in the context of civil tax litigation. For instance, in Pizzarello v. United States, 408 F.2d 579 (2d Cir.1969), evidence illegally seized by federal Treasury Department Agents was held inadmissible in a federal civil tax proceeding. In United States v. Janis, 428 U.S. 433, 96 S.Ct. 3021 (1976), however, the Supreme Court held that evidence illegally seized by state agents could be used by the federal government in a federal tax proceeding. This decision has caused some courts to consider whether evidence impermissibly seized by federal agents could be used in a federal tax proceeding, even though Janis clearly did not reach that issue. See Ryan v. Commissioner of Internal Revenue, 568 F.2d 531 (7th Cir.1977). See also Tirado v. Commissioner of Internal Revenue, 689 F.2d 307 (2d Cir.1982), where federal agents seized certain evidence which the government sought to use in a civil tax proceeding. The court held that the legality of the seizure was irrelevant, stressing that the seizure had not been made by Internal Revenue Service agents.

Over a strong dissent, one federal reviewing court had extended the exclusionary rule to exclude from civil deportation proceedings evidence derived from a violation by Immigration agents of the fourth amendment. Lopez–Mendoza v. Immigration and Naturalization Service, 705 F.2d 1059 (9th Cir.1983). The Supreme Court reversed, 5 to 4. 468 U.S. 1032, 104 S.Ct. 3479 (1984). At least one court has read Lopez–Mendoza as recognizing an exception where the governmental conduct was particularly egregious. See Arguelles–Vasquez v. Immigration and Naturalization Service, 786 F.2d 1433 (9th Cir.1986) (excluding evidence at deportation proceeding where border agents stopped individual solely because of Hispanic appearance).

(g) Parole Revocations. In Pennsylvania Board of Probation and Parole v. Scott, 524 U.S. 357, 118 S.Ct. 2014 (1998), the Supreme Court reversed the Pennsylvania Supreme Court and held that the exclusionary rule was not applicable in state parole revocation proceedings.

Respondent Scott had agreed to consent to warrantless searches as part of his parole agreement. Parole officers arrested Scott based on evidence that he had violated several conditions of his parole. He gave his house keys to the officers upon his arrest, and they searched his bedroom and adjacent sitting room, discovering several firearms and other weapons. The Pennsylvania Supreme Court held that this evidence should not have been admitted at his parole revocation hearing, because the search of the house was without reasonable suspicion. The Court further held that Scott's waiver of the warrant requirement did not waive his right to be free from "unreasonable" searches.

The Supreme Court did not address the effect of Scott's waiver, but ruled broadly that the exclusionary rule was never applicable in state parole revocation proceedings. The Court reasoned that because the exclusionary rule is "prudential rather than constitutionally mandated," it is only applicable where significant deterrence benefits outweigh its social costs. The Court argued that deterrence benefits in this context were not significant, because (1) police officers are not always aware that their suspects are on parole (and any rule to be applied only to those who are aware would generate too much collateral litigation on the issue of knowledge), (2) police officers are primarily interested in building criminal cases against suspects, not in prosecuting parole violations, and (3) parole agents are not in an adversarial relationship with parolees, so they do not need to be deterred from violating parolees' rights. The social costs of introducing the exclusionary rule into parole revocation proceedings, the Court argued, were greater than those incurred in a criminal trial, because (1) litigation over exclusion of evidence would formalize proceedings meant to be flexible, efficient, and concerned with rehabilitation, (2) security interests are keener because parolees are more likely to reoffend than average citizens, and (3) parolees have only conditional liberty at stake, since they have not yet served their full sentences.

Justices Stevens, Souter, Ginsburg, and Breyer dissented. Justice Souter's opinion found the majority's account of the deterrence/social cost balance unrealistic, pointing out that with modern data banks, police officers often know at the outset of investigation whether suspects are on parole, parole officers and police often cooperate in investigating violations, police work often does not culminate in criminal trials rather than parole revocation proceedings, and parole officers wear many hats as law enforcement officers as well as social workers and have many of the same incentives to prosecute offenders successfully as do police. Justice Stevens wrote separately to stress that the exclusionary rule was a constitutionally-mandated remedy.

(h) Warrant Applications. The Supreme Court has assumed, sometimes without discussion, that data acquired through a violation of a suspect's fourth amendment rights cannot be used to establish probable cause for issuance of a search warrant directed at the suspect's property. Such was the unspoken premise of Arizona v.

Hicks, 480 U.S. 321, 107 S.Ct. 1149 (1987). What about the fruits of a violation of the accused's Miranda rights? Can there be a violation of Miranda before a statement secured without Miranda compliance is offered at trial? For one view, read United States v. Patterson, 809 F.2d 244 (5th Cir.1987) (voluntary, but Miranda-violative statement can be used in warrant application).

Typically where part of the probable cause data has been seized in violation of the Fourth Amendment, the court will determine whether the remaining data establishes probable cause. See United States v. Johnston, 876 F.2d 589 (7th Cir.1989). In a concurring opinion, Judge Posner noted that this version of a harmless error rule cuts down on the impact of the exclusionary rule, a phenomenon which he describes as desirable.

How can a court view the issue as whether the lawfully acquired data, as a matter of law, supports probable cause, when Gates said that a magistrate has a zone of discretion in making probable cause calculations and that trial and appellate judges should defer to his or her judgment? How do we know what the magistrate would have done in the absence of the illegally acquired probable cause data?

2. IMPEACHMENT AND REBUTTAL USAGE OF ILLEGALLY OBTAINED EVIDENCE

Harris v. New York

Supreme Court of the United States, 1971.
401 U.S. 222, 91 S.Ct. 643.

■ CHIEF JUSTICE BURGER delivered the opinion of the Court.

We granted the writ in this case to consider petitioner's claim that a statement made by him to police under circumstances rendering it inadmissible to establish the prosecution's case in chief under Miranda v. Arizona (1966), may not be used to impeach his credibility.

The State of New York charged petitioner in a two-count indictment with twice selling heroin to an undercover police officer. At a subsequent jury trial the officer was the State's chief witness, and he testified as to details of the two sales. A second officer verified collateral details of the sales, and a third offered testimony about the chemical analysis of the heroin.

Petitioner took the stand in his own defense. He admitted knowing the undercover police officer but denied a sale on January 4, 1966. He admitted making a sale of contents of a glassine bag to the officer on January 6 but claimed it was baking powder and part of a scheme to defraud the purchaser.

On cross-examination petitioner was asked seriatim whether he had made specified statements to the police immediately following his arrest on January 7—statements that partially contradicted petitioner's direct testimony at trial. In response to the cross-examination, petitioner testified that he could not remember virtually any of the questions or answers recited by the prosecutor. At the request of petitioner's counsel the written statement from which the prosecutor had read questions and answers in his impeaching process was placed in the record for possible use on appeal; the statement was not shown to the jury.

The trial judge instructed the jury that the statements attributed to petitioner by the prosecution could be considered only in passing on petitioner's credibility and not as evidence of guilt. In closing summations both counsel argued the substance of the impeaching statements. The jury then found petitioner guilty on the second count of the indictment.

At trial the prosecution made no effort in its case in chief to use the statements allegedly made by petitioner, conceding that they were inadmissible under Miranda v. Arizona. The transcript of the interrogation used in the impeachment, but not given to the jury, shows that no warning of a right to appointed counsel was given before questions were put to petitioner when he was taken into custody. Petitioner makes no claim that the statements made to the police were coerced or involuntary.

Some comments in the Miranda opinion can indeed be read as indicating a bar to use of an uncounseled statement for any purpose, but discussion of that issue was not at all necessary to the Court's holding and cannot be regarded as controlling. Miranda barred the prosecution from making its case with statements of an accused made while in custody prior to having or effectively waiving counsel. It does not follow from Miranda that evidence inadmissible against an accused in the prosecution's case in chief is barred for all purposes, provided of course that the trustworthiness of the evidence satisfies legal standards.

In Walder v. United States (1954), the Court permitted physical evidence, inadmissible in the case in chief, to be used for impeachment purposes.

> "It is one thing to say that the Government cannot make an affirmative use of evidence unlawfully obtained. It is quite another to say that the defendant can turn the illegal method by which evidence in the Government's possession was obtained to his own advantage, and provide himself with a shield against contradiction of his untruths. Such an extension of the Weeks doctrine would be a perversion of the Fourth Amendment.
>
> "[T]here is hardly justification for letting the defendant affirmatively resort to perjures testimony in reliance on the Government's disability to challenge his credibility."

It is true that Walder was impeached as to collateral matters included in his direct examination, whereas petitioner here was impeached as to testimony bearing more directly on the crimes charged. We are not persuaded that there is a difference in principle that warrants a result different from that reached by the Court in Walder. Petitioner's testimony in his own behalf concerning the events of January 7 contrasted sharply with what he told the police shortly after his arrest. The impeachment process here undoubtedly provided valuable aid to the jury in assessing petitioner's credibility, and the benefits of this process should not be lost, in our view, because of the speculative possibility that impermissible police conduct will be encouraged thereby. Assuming that the exclusionary rule has a deterrent effect on proscribed police conduct, sufficient deterrence flows when the evidence in question is made unavailable to the prosecution in its case in chief.

Every criminal defendant is privileged to testify in his own defense, or to refuse to do so. But that privilege cannot be construed to include the right to commit perjury. Having voluntarily taken the stand, petitioner was under an obligation to speak truthfully and accurately, and the prosecution here did no more than utilize the traditional truth-testing devices of the adversary process.[1] Had inconsistent statements been made by the accused to some third person, it could hardly be contended that the conflict could not be laid before the jury by way of cross-examination and impeachment.

The shield provided by Miranda cannot be perverted into a license to use perjury by way of a defense, free from the risk of confrontation with prior inconsistent utterances. We hold, therefore, that petitioner's credibility was appropriately impeached by use of his earlier conflicting statements.

Affirmed.

■ The dissenting opinion of JUSTICE BLACK is omitted.

■ JUSTICE BRENNAN, with whom JUSTICE DOUGLAS and JUSTICE MARSHALL, join, dissenting.

* * *

The State's case against Harris depended upon the jury's belief of the testimony of the undercover agent that petitioner "sold" the officer heroin on January 4 and again on January 6. Petitioner took the stand and flatly denied having sold anything to the officer on January 4. He countered the officer's testimony as to the January 6 sale with testimony that he had sold the officer two glass in bags containing what appeared to be heroin, but that actually the bags contained only baking powder intended to deceive the officer in order to obtain $12. The statement contradicted petitioner's direct testimony as to the events of both days. The statement's version of the events on January 4 was that the officer had used petitioner as a middleman to buy some heroin from a third person with money furnished by the officer. The version of the events on January 6 was that petitioner had again acted for the officer in buying two bags of heroin from a third person for which petitioner received $12 and a part of the heroin. Thus, it is clear that the statement was used to impeach petitioner's direct testimony not on collateral matters but on matters directly related to the crimes for which he was on trial.

* * *

From this recital of facts it is clear that the evidence used for impeachment in Walder was related to the earlier 1950 prosecution and had no direct bearing on "the elements of the case" being tried in 1952. The evidence tended solely to impeach the credibility of the defendant's direct testimony that he had never in his life possessed heroin. But that evidence was completely unrelated to the indictment on trial and did not in

1. If, for example, an accused confessed fully to a homicide and led the police to the body of the victim under circumstances making his confession inadmissible, the petitioner would have us allow that accused to take the stand and blandly deny every fact disclosed to the police or discovered as a "fruit" of his confession, free from confrontation with his prior statements and acts. The voluntariness of the confession would, on this thesis, be totally irrelevant. We reject such an extravagant extension of the Constitution.

any way interfere with his freedom to deny all elements of that case against him. In contrast, here, the evidence used for impeachment, a statement concerning the details of the very sales alleged in the indictment, was directly related to the case against petitioner.

* * *

Thus, the accused is denied an "unfettered" choice when the decision whether to take the stand is burdened by the risk that an illegally obtained prior statement may be introduced to impeach his direct testimony denying complicity in the crime charged against him.

* * *

... The Court today tells the police that they may freely interrogate an accused incommunicado and without counsel and know that although any statement they obtain in violation of Miranda cannot be used on the State's direct case, it may be introduced if the defendant has the temerity to testify in his own defense. This goes far toward undoing much of the progress made in conforming police methods to the Constitution. I dissent.

NOTES

1. The dissent in Harris implicitly assumes that the decision is an invitation to the police to violate Miranda. Is it? Would a police officer ordinarily know at the time he first questions a suspect whether he has a legally sufficient case against the suspect and will only need the suspect's admissions for possible impeachment? Would a police officer ordinarily know that his other evidence, i.e. physical evidence and eyewitness identification will not be subject to exclusion? In short, is it likely an officer will know at the interrogation that he does not need the statements for the state's case in chief?

2. Oregon v. Hass, 420 U.S. 714, 95 S.Ct. 1215 (1975), also approved the use for impeachment purposes of a Miranda-violative statement. In that case the violation had occurred when the officer continued interrogation after the suspect had indicated a desire to consult with counsel. The majority held that Harris controlled. In dissent Justice Brennan wrote:

> "The Court's decision today goes beyond Harris in undermining Miranda. Even after Harris, police had some incentive for following Miranda by warning an accused of his right to remain silent and his right to counsel. If the warnings were given, the accused might still make a statement which could be used in the prosecution's case-in-chief. Under today's holding, however, once the warnings are given, police have almost no incentive for following Miranda's requirement that '[i]f the individual states that he wants an attorney, the interrogation must cease until an attorney is present.' If the requirement is followed there will almost surely be no statement since the attorney will advise the accused to remain silent. If, however, the requirement is disobeyed, the police may obtain a statement which can be used for impeachment if the accused has the temerity to testify in his own defense. Thus, after today's decision, if an individual states that he wants an attorney, police interrogation will doubtless now be vigorously pressed to obtain statements before the attorney arrives. I am unwilling to join this fundamental erosion of Fifth and Sixth Amendment rights and therefore dissent...."

3. The question of impeachment use of illegally obtained evidence can come up in various contexts. The defendant can create the issue by testifying on direct examination (or by volunteering an unresponsive answer on cross-exam)to a fact which is not relevant to innocence or guilt. Sometimes such testimony is admitted without objection or, erroneously, over the prosecutor's objection. This is what happened in Walder. Under the rules of evidence of most jurisdictions, the prosecutor can pursue this matter on cross-examination by confronting the defendant with questions about the contradictory evidence. Wholly apart from constitutional considerations, the rules of evidence in some jurisdictions prohibit prosecution pursuit of this "collateral" material through rebuttal testimony. The cross-examiner must "take" the response he gets on this collateral issue.

In a second situation the prosecutor seeks to impeach testimony which the defendant gave on direct (or volunteered on cross), where the testimony sought to be contradicted is directly relevant to innocence or guilt. Such was the case in Harris.

In a third situation the defendant testifies on direct but says nothing which is contradictory to the evidence which the police obtained unlawfully. The prosecution was not allowed to "open the door" in this situation by confronting the defendant with the illegally obtained evidence according to Agnello v. United States, 269 U.S. 20, 46 S.Ct. 4 (1925). Consider, however, United States v. Havens, 446 U.S. 620, 100 S.Ct. 1912 (1980), a case in which the Fifth Circuit had found a violation of the Agnello principle. In Havens the Government argued that when a defendant testifies he opens himself to cross-examination concerning details other than those which he has mentioned on direct examination. Therefore, the Government contended, the Walder rule should permit the use of illegally obtained evidence in cross-examination and rebuttal even if such material is not directly contrary to answers given on direct examination. The only limit, under the Government's theory, would be the evidentiary principle that some inquiries are beyond the scope of proper cross-examination.

The Supreme Court resolved the controversy in favor of the Government, expanded impeachment use of unlawfully obtained evidence, and strictly limited (some commentators say impliedly overruled) Agnello. The majority held that even if a defendant says nothing on direct examination which contradicts the evidence which has been derived from a Fourth Amendment violation, the prosecution can ask on cross-examination any question which is "reasonably suggested" by the testimony on direct examination, even if the questioning gets into the area of illegally obtained evidence. The dissent protested that the "reasonably suggested" standard is nothing more than the normal evidentiary limitation that exists upon cross-examination in a criminal case. Thus it argued that once a defendant testifies in his own behalf, no longer do any limitations upon cross-examination result from the fact that the authorities have unlawfully acquired evidence. Under this view, as a practical matter, where the prosecution can survive a motion for a directed verdict after Havens despite suppression of the illegally obtained evidence, the defendant has the choice of either (a) not testifying or (b) testifying but allowing the jury to learn of the illegally obtained evidence.

If the defendant testifies and denies matters which are contradicted by the illegally acquired statement or physical evidence, the latter ordinarily will be admitted subject to an instruction requiring that the contradictory evidence be used only as an aid in assessing the defendant's credibility. Is such an instruction likely to be effective? Can the jury consider the fact that the defendant was found in possession of the murder weapon only as an aid in assessing his credibility?

Suppose that a prosecutor asks a question "reasonably suggested" by the defendant's direct testimony and elicits a damaging admission (e.g., that the defendant was in possession of the murder weapon). Can that admission be used substantively (that is, for its truth) or is its use limited to discrediting the defendant's direct testimony denying a role in the crime? If the judicial admission can be used substantively despite the fact that the question was derived from illegally obtained evidence, what is left of the distinction between substantive use and use for impeachment? If such an admission can be used substantively, does the rule (a) penalize those defendants who tell the truth on cross-examination and (b) reward those who lie on cross-examination, by limiting to impeachment use any rebuttal testimony derived from the illegally obtained evidence? On the other hand, how can a defendant's in-court admission, made at his own trial, ever be limited, in theory or practice, to use for impeachment?

4. After Harris the question remained whether there was a prohibition against impeaching a defendant through the use of any involuntary confession or only through the use of confessions which were in fact unreliable. In Mincey v. Arizona, 437 U.S. 385, 98 S.Ct. 2408 (1978), however, the Court seemed to say that no involuntary confession could be used for impeachment purposes.

5. Can a statement secured in violation of Massiah (Chapter 2, Section C) be used for impeachment purposes? Does a Massiah violation cast doubt on the reliability of the statement? Is a concern for reliability the only reason for denying impeachment use of unlawfully obtained evidence?

In Michigan v. Harvey, 494 U.S. 344, 110 S.Ct. 1176 (1990), the Court permitted a voluntary statement to be used to impeach a defendant's testimony although the statement had been obtained in violation of the Massiah-based rule of Michigan v. Jackson, 475 U.S. 625, 106 S.Ct. 1404 (1986). That rule prohibits government-initiated questioning of a suspect who has invoked his Sixth Amendment right to counsel. The Court's reason arguably would not extend to all Massiah violations Harvey viewed Jackson as an extension of the Miranda-derived rule of Edwards v. Arizona, 451 U.S. 477, 101 S.Ct. 1880 (1981). It concluded that if voluntary Miranda-violative statements can be used to impeach a defendant's testimony, so can Jackson-violative statements.

People v. Harper, 228 Cal.App.3d 843, 279 Cal.Rptr. 204 (1991), holds that, despite Harvey, evidence obtained through some other Massiah violations cannot be used for purposes of impeachment. In Harper there were no warnings and no effort to obtain a Massiah waiver. The right to counsel had attached, but the suspect had not affirmatively invoked that right.

6. Concerning impeachment by reference to a defendant's silence following Miranda warnings, see Doyle v. Ohio, 426 U.S. 610, 96 S.Ct. 2240 (1976).

7. When, in order to establish standing to raise a Fourth Amendment claim, a defendant gives testimony which is incriminating on the issue of guilt, the prosecution is prevented by Simmons v. United States, 390 U.S. 377, 88 S.Ct. 967 (1968), from using such testimony in its case-in-chief at trial. The Supreme Court has not expressly resolved the question of whether a defendant's pre-trial testimony given to establish standing can be used to impeach a defendant who testifies differently at trial. In United States v. Salvucci, 448 U.S. 83, 100 S.Ct. 2547 (1980), however, the Court noted several lower court decisions which allow the prosecution to use for the limited purpose of impeachment testimony at a suppression hearing given by a defendant in order to establish "standing" or a "reasonable expectation of privacy."

8. In James v. Illinois, 493 U.S. 307, 110 S.Ct. 648 (1990), the Supreme Court refused to allow illegally obtained evidence to be used to impeach defense witnesses other than the defendant. At a murder trial, prosecution witnesses identified the shooter as having "reddish" hair, "worn shoulder length in a slicked-back 'butter' style." The defendant's hair at the time of his arrest was black and curly. However, following his arrest, James had admitted that he had his hair dyed after the date of the crime, and that it previously had been "reddish-brown, long and combed straight back." In fact, the authorities had apprehended James under a hair dryer in his mother's beauty parlor the evening after the killing.

The Cook County trial judge suppressed the defendant's statement concerning his hair color, ruling that he had been arrested without probable cause and that the statements were the fruit of the illegal arrest.

A friend of the James family named Henderson testified as a defense witness. She said that the defendant's hair had been black on the day of the crime. After determining that the defendant's statement concerning his hair color had been voluntary, the trial judge allowed the prosecution to use that statement to impeach Henderson's testimony, invoking the mode of impeachment known as "contradiction."

When the case reached the United States Supreme Court, five justices agreed that the Fourth Amendment prohibited even this limited use of the defendant's post-arrest statement. Writing for the majority, Justice Brennan stated:

> The previously recognized exception penalizes defendants for committing perjury by allowing the prosecution to expose their perjury through impeachment using illegally obtained evidence. Thus defendants are discouraged in the first instance from "affirmatively resort[ing] to perjurious testimony." Walder, supra. But the exception leaves defendants free to testify truthfully on their own behalf; they can offer probative and exculpatory evidence to the jury without opening the door to impeachment by carefully avoiding any statements that directly contradict the suppressed evidence. The exception thus generally discourages perjured testimony without discouraging truthful testimony.
>
> In contrast, expanding the impeachment exception to encompass the testimony of all defense witnesses would not have the same beneficial effects. First, the mere threat of a subsequent criminal prosecution for perjury is far more likely to deter a witness from intentionally lying on a defendant's behalf than to deter a defendant, already facing conviction for the underlying offense, from lying on his own behalf. Hence the Illinois Supreme Court's underlying premise that a defendant frustrated by our previous impeachment exception can easily find a witness to engage in "perjury by proxy" is suspect.
>
> More significantly, expanding the impeachment exception to encompass the testimony of all defense witnesses likely would chill some defendants from presenting their best defense—and sometimes any defense at all—through the testimony of others. Whenever police obtained evidence illegally, defendants would have to assess prior to trial the likelihood that the evidence would be admitted to impeach the otherwise favorable testimony of any witness they call. Defendants might reasonably fear that one or more of their witnesses, in a position to offer truthful and favorable testimony, would also make some statement in sufficient tension with the tainted evidence to allow the prosecutor to introduce that evidence for impeachment. First, defendants sometimes need to call "reluctant" or "hostile" witnesses to provide reliable and probative exculpatory testimony, and such witnesses likely will not share the defendants' concern for avoiding statements that invite impeachment through contradictory evidence. Moreover, defendants often cannot trust even "friendly" witnesses to testify without subjecting themselves to impeachment, simply due to insufficient care or attentiveness. This concern is magnified in those

occasional situations when defendants must call witnesses to testify despite having had only a limited opportunity to consult with or prepare them in advance.... As a result, an expanded impeachment exception likely would chill some defendants from calling witnesses who would otherwise offer probative evidence.

* * *

... Given the potential chill created by expanding the impeachment exception, the conceded gains to the truth seeking process from discouraging or disclosing perjured testimony would be offset to some extent by the concomitant loss of probative witness testimony. Thus, the truth seeking rationale supporting the impeachment of defendants in Walder and its progeny does not apply to other witnesses with equal force.

Moreover, the proposed expansion of the current impeachment exception would significantly weaken the exclusionary rule's deterrent effect on police misconduct. This Court has characterized as a mere "speculative possibility," Harris v. New York, the likelihood that permitting prosecutors to impeach defendants with illegally obtained evidence would encourage police misconduct. Law enforcement officers will think it unlikely that the defendant will first decide to testify at trial and will also open the door inadvertently to admission of any illegally obtained evidence. Hence, the officers' incentive to acquire evidence through illegal means is quite weak.

In contrast, expanding the impeachment exception to all defense witnesses would significantly enhance the expected value to the prosecution of illegally obtained evidence. First, this expansion would vastly increase the number of occasions on which such evidence could be used. Defense witnesses easily outnumber testifying defendants, both because many defendants do not testify themselves and because many if not most defendants call multiple witnesses on their behalf. Moreover, due to the chilling effect identified above, illegally obtained evidence holds even greater value to the prosecution for each individual witness than for each defendant. The prosecutor's access to impeachment evidence would not just deter perjury; it would also deter defendants from calling witnesses in the first place, thereby keeping from the jury much probative exculpatory evidence. For both of these reasons, police officers and their superiors would recognize that obtaining evidence through illegal means stacks the deck heavily in the prosecution's favor. It is thus far more than a "speculative possibility" that police misconduct will be encouraged by permitting such use of illegally obtained evidence.

Writing for four dissenters, JUSTICE KENNEDY wrote:

* * *

The interest in protecting the truth-seeking function of the criminal trial is every bit as strong in this case as in our earlier cases that allowed rebuttal with evidence that was inadmissible as part of the prosecution's case in chief. Here a witness who knew the accused well took the stand to testify about the accused's personal appearance. The testimony could be expected to create real doubt in the mind of jurors concerning the eyewitness identifications by persons who did not know the accused. To deprive the jurors of knowledge that statements of the defendant himself revealed the witness' testimony to be false would result in a decision by triers of fact who were not just kept in the dark as to excluded evidence, but positively misled. The potential for harm to the truth-seeking process resulting from the majority's new rule in fact will be greater than if the defendant himself had testified. It is natural for jurors to be skeptical of self-serving testimony by the defendant. Testimony by a witness said to be independent has the greater potential to deceive. And if a defense witness can present false testimony with impunity, the jurors may find the rest of the prosecution's case suspect, for ineffective and artificial cross-examination will be viewed as a real weakness in the State's case. Jurors will assume that if the prosecution had any proof the statement was false, it would make the proof known. The majority does more than deprive the prosecution of evidence. The State must also suffer the introduction of false testimony and appear to bolster the falsehood by its own silence.

The majority's fear that allowing the jury to know the whole truth will chill defendants from putting on any defense seems to me far too speculative to justify the rule here announced. No restriction on the defense results if rebuttal of testimony by witnesses other than the defendant is confined to the introduction of excludable evidence that is in direct contradiction of the testimony. If mere "tension with the tainted evidence," opened the door to introduction of all the evidence subject to suppression, then the majority's fears might be justified. But in this context rebuttal can and should be confined to situations where there is direct conflict, which is to say where, within reason, the witness' testimony and the excluded testimony cannot both be true.

* * *

It is unrealistic to say that the decision to make an illegal search turns on a precise calculation of the possibilities of rebuttal at some future trial. There is no reason to believe a police officer, unschooled in the law, will assess whether evidence already in his possession would suffice to survive a motion for acquittal following the case in chief. The officer may or may not even know the identity of the ultimate defendant. He certainly will not know anything about potential defense witnesses, much less what the content of their testimony might be. What he will know for certain is that evidence from an illegal search or arrest (which may well be crucial to securing a conviction) will be lost to the case in chief. Our earlier assessments of the marginal deterrent effect are applicable here. "Assuming that the exclusionary rule has a deterrent effect on proscribed police conduct, sufficient deterrence flows when the evidence in question is made unavailable to the prosecution in its case in chief." Harris, supra.

Suppose that the prosecution at Defendant D's trial seeks to impeach Witness W by using evidence obtained in violation of the Fourth Amendment rights of W. Normally one would assume that D would have no standing to complain about the violation of W's rights. But does the reasoning of James equally well apply in this situation?

3. ILLEGALLY OBTAINED EVIDENCE AND FEDERAL HABEAS CORPUS RELIEF

Wolff v. Rice

Supreme Court of the United States, 1976.
428 U.S. 465, 96 S.Ct. 3037.

■ JUSTICE POWELL delivered the opinion of the Court.

Respondents in these cases were convicted of criminal offenses in state courts, and their convictions were affirmed on appeal. The prosecution in each case relied upon evidence obtained by searches and seizures alleged by respondents to have been unlawful. Each respondent subsequently sought relief in a federal district court by filing a petition for a writ of federal habeas corpus under 28 U.S.C. § 2254. The question presented is whether a federal court should consider, in ruling on a petition for habeas corpus relief filed by a state prisoner, a claim that evidence obtained by an unconstitutional search or seizure was introduced at his trial, when he has previously been afforded an opportunity for full and fair litigation of his claim in the state courts. The issue is of considerable importance to the administration of criminal justice.

I.

* * *

Respondent Lloyd Powell was convicted of murder in June 1968 after trial in a California state court. At about midnight on February 17, 1968, he and three companions entered the Bonanza Liquor Store in San Bernardino, Cal., where Powell became involved in an altercation with Gerald Parsons, the store manager, over the theft of a bottle of wine. In the scuffling that followed Powell shot and killed Parson's wife. Ten hours later an officer of the Henderson, Nev., Police Department arrested Powell for violation of the Henderson vagrancy ordinance, and in the search incident to the arrest discovered a .38 caliber revolver with six expended cartridges in the cylinder.

* * *

Respondent David Rice was convicted of murder in April 1971 after trial in a Nebraska state court. At 2:05 a.m. on August 17, 1970, Omaha police received a telephone call that a woman had been heard screaming at 2867 Ohio Street. As one of the officers sent to that address examined a suitcase lying in the doorway, it exploded, killing him instantly. By August 22 the investigation of the murder centered on Duane Peak, a 15-year-old member of the National Committee to Combat Fascism ("NCCF"), and that afternoon a warrant was issued for Peak's arrest. The investigation also focused on other known members of the NCCF, including Rice, some of whom were believed to be planning to kill Peak before he could incriminate them. In their search for Peak, the police went to Rice's home at 10:30 p.m. that night and found lights and a television on, but there was no response to their repeated knocking. While some officers remained to watch the premises, a warrant was obtained to search for explosives and illegal weapons believed to be in Rice's possession.[1] Peak was not in the house but

1. The sole evidence presented to the magistrate was the affidavit in support of the warrant application. It indicated that the police believed explosives and illegal weapons were present in Rice's home because (1) Rice was an official of the NCCF, (2) a violent killing of an officer had occurred and it appeared that the NCCF was involved, and (3) police had received information in the past that Rice possessed weapons and explosives, which he had said should be used against the police.... In concluding that there existed probable cause for issuance of the warrant, although the Nebraska Supreme court found the affidavit alone sufficient, it also referred to information contained in testimony adduced at the suppression hearing but not included in the affidavit.... The District Court limited its probable cause inquiry to the face of the affidavit, see Spinelli v. United

upon entering the police discovered, in plain view, dynamite, blasting caps, and other materials useful in the construction of explosive devices. Peak subsequently was arrested, and on August 27, Rice voluntarily surrendered. The clothes Rice was wearing at that time were subjected to chemical analysis, disclosing dynamite particles.

* * *

II.

The authority of federal courts to issue the writ of habeas corpus ad subjiciendum was included in the first grant of federal court jurisdiction, made by the Judiciary Act of 1789, c. 20, § 14, 1 Stat. 81, with the limitation that the writ extend only to prisoners held in custody by the United States. The original statutory authorization did not define the substantive reach of the writ. It merely stated that the courts of the United States "shall have power to issue writs of ... habeas corpus...." The courts defined the scope of the writ in accordance with the common law and limited it to an inquiry as to the jurisdiction of the sentencing tribunal....

In 1867 the writ was extended to state prisoners.... Under the 1867 Act federal courts were authorized to give relief in "all cases where any person may be restrained of his or her liberty in violation of the constitution, or of any treaty or law of the United States...." But the limitation of federal habeas corpus jurisdiction to consideration of the jurisdiction of the sentencing court persisted.... And, although the concept of "jurisdiction" was subjected to considerable strain as the substantive scope of the writ was expanded, this expansion was limited to only a few classes of cases until Frank v. Mangum (1915). In Frank, the prisoner had claimed in the state courts that the proceedings which resulted in his conviction for murder had been dominated by a mob. After the state supreme court rejected his contentions, Frank unsuccessfully sought habeas corpus relief in the federal district court. This Court affirmed the denial of relief because Frank's federal claims had been considered by a competent and unbiased state tribunal. The Court recognized, however, that if a habeas corpus court found that the State had failed to provide adequate "corrective process" for the full and fair litigation of federal claims, whether or not "jurisdictional," the court could inquire into the merits to determine whether a detention was lawful....

In the landmark decisions in Brown v. Allen (1953), and Daniels v. Allen (1953) the scope of the writ was expanded still further. In these cases state prisoners applied for federal habeas corpus relief claiming that the trial courts had erred in failing to quash their indictments due to alleged discrimination in the selection of grand jurors and in ruling certain confessions admissible. In *Brown*, the highest court of the State had rejected these claims on direct appeal, ... and this Court had denied

States (1969); Aguilar v. Texas (1964), and concluded probable cause was lacking. Petitioner Wolff contends that police should be permitted to supplement the information contained in an affidavit for a search warrant at the hearing on a motion to suppress, a contention that we have several times rejected.

certiorari. . . . Despite the apparent adequacy of the state corrective process, the Court reviewed the denial of the writ of habeas corpus and held that *Brown* was entitled to a full reconsideration of these constitutional claims, including, if appropriate, a hearing in the Federal District Court.

* * *

III.

* * *

The exclusionary rule was a judicially created means of effectuating the rights secured by the Fourth Amendment. . . .

Decisions prior to *Mapp* advanced two principal reasons for application of the rule in federal trials. The Court in Elkins, for example, in the context of its special supervisory role over the lower federal courts, referred to the "imperative of judicial integrity," suggesting that exclusion of illegally seized evidence prevents contamination of the judicial process. . . . But even in that context a more pragmatic ground was emphasized:

> "The rule is calculated to prevent, not to repair. Its purpose is to deter 'to compel respect for the constitutional guaranty in the only effectively available way' by removing the incentive to disregard it." . . .

The *Mapp* majority justified the application of the rule to the States on several grounds, but relied principally upon the belief that exclusion would deter future unlawful police conduct. . . .

Although our decisions often have alluded to the "imperative of judicial integrity," . . . they demonstrate the limited role of this justification in the determination whether to apply the rule in a particular context. Logically extended this justification would require that courts exclude unconstitutionally seized evidence despite lack of objection by the defendant, or even over his assent. . . . It also would require abandonment of the standing limitations on who may object to the introduction of unconstitutionally seized evidence, . . . and retreat from the proposition that judicial proceedings need not abate when the defendant's person is unconstitutionally seized. . . . Similarly, the interest in promoting judicial integrity does not prevent the use of illegally seized evidence in grand jury proceedings. . . . Nor does it require that the trial court exclude such evidence from use for impeachment of a defendant, even though its introduction is certain to result in convictions in some cases. . . . While courts, of course, must ever be concerned with preserving the integrity of the judicial process, this concern has limited force as a justification for the exclusion of highly probative evidence. The force of this justification becomes minimal where federal habeas corpus relief is sought by a prisoner who previously has been afforded the opportunity for full and fair consideration of his search-and-seizure claim at trial and on direct review.

The primary justification for the exclusionary rule then is the deterrence of police conduct that violates Fourth Amendment rights. . . .

IV.

.... The costs of applying the exclusionary rule even at trial and on direct review are well known: the focus of the trial, and the attention of the participants therein, is diverted from the ultimate question of guilt or innocence that should be the central concern in a criminal proceeding. Moreover, the physical evidence sought to be excluded is typically reliable and often the most probative information bearing on the guilt or innocence of the defendant.... Application of the rule thus deflects the truth finding process and often frees the guilty. The disparity in particular cases between the error committed by the police officer and the windfall afforded a guilty defendant by application of the rule is contrary to the idea of proportionality that is essential to the concept of justice. Thus, although the rule is thought to deter unlawful police activity in part through the nurturing of respect for Fourth Amendment values, if applied indiscriminately it may well have the opposite effect of generating disrespect for the law and administration of justice. These long-recognized costs of the rule persist when a criminal conviction is sought to be overturned on collateral review on the ground that a search-and-seizure claim was erroneously rejected by two or more tiers of state courts.

Evidence obtained by police officers in violation of the Fourth Amendment is excluded at trial in the hope that the frequency of future violations will decrease. Despite the absence of supportive empirical evidence, we have assumed that the immediate effect of exclusion will be to discourage law enforcement officials from violating the Fourth Amendment by removing the incentive to disregard it. More importantly, over the long term, this demonstration that our society attaches serious consequences to violation of constitutional rights is thought to encourage those who formulate law enforcement policies, and the officers who implement them, to incorporate Fourth Amendment ideals into their value system.

We adhere to the view that these considerations support the implementation of the exclusionary rule at trial and its enforcement on direct appeal of state court convictions. But the additional contribution, if any, of the consideration of search-and-seizure claims of state prisoners on collateral review is small in relation to the costs. To be sure, each case in which such claim is considered may add marginally to an awareness of the values protected by the Fourth Amendment. There is no reason to believe, however, that the overall educative effect of the exclusionary rule would be appreciably diminished if search-and-seizure claims could not be raised in federal habeas corpus review of state convictions. Nor is there reason to assume that any specific disincentive already created by the risk of exclusion of evidence at trial or the reversal of convictions on direct review would be enhanced if there were the further risk that a conviction obtained in state court and affirmed on direct review might be overturned in collateral proceedings often occurring years after the incarceration of the defendant. The view that the deterrence of Fourth Amendment violations would be furthered rests on the dubious assumption that law enforcement authorities would fear that federal habeas review might reveal flaws in a search or seizure that went undetected at trial and on appeal. Even if one rationally could assume that some additional incremental deterrent effect would be present in isolated cases, the resulting advance of the legitimate goal of furthering Fourth Amendment rights would be outweighed by the acknowledged costs to other values vital to a rational system of criminal justice.

In sum, we conclude that where the State has provided an opportunity for full and fair litigation of a Fourth Amendment claim, a state prisoner may not be granted federal habeas corpus relief on the ground that evidence obtained in an unconstitutional search or seizure was introduced at his trial.[2] In this context the contribution of the exclusionary rule, if any, to the effectuation of the Fourth Amendment is minimal and the substantial societal costs of application of the rule persist with special force.

Accordingly, the judgments of the Courts of Appeals are reversed.

[Concurring and dissenting opinions are omitted here, but they are summarized briefly in the notes which follow.]

NOTES

1. In a concurring opinion in Stone Chief Justice Burger stated that the reach of the exclusionary rule should be modified, "even if it is retained for a small and limited category of cases." He contended that the true purpose of the exclusionary rule is deterrence and argued that empirical evidence fails to demonstrate a deterrent effect. He noted that the requirement of standing is inconsistent with the notion that the "imperative of the judicial integrity" underlies the exclusionary rule. Moreover, he asserted other common law countries, including Canada and England, uphold the integrity of the judicial system without utilizing the exclusionary rule. He concluded that the rule, by excluding relevant evidence, had become

2. The policy arguments that respondents marshal in support of the view that federal habeas corpus review is necessary to effectuate the Fourth Amendment stem from a basic mistrust of the state courts as fair and competent forums for the adjudication of federal constitutional rights. The argument is that state courts cannot be trusted to effectuate Fourth Amendment values through fair application of the rule, and the oversight jurisdiction of this Court on certiorari is an inadequate safeguard. The principal rationale for this view emphasizes the broad differences in the respective institutional setting within which federal judges and state judges operate. Despite differences in institutional environment and the unsympathetic attitude to federal constitutional claims of some state judges in years past, we are unwilling to assume that there now exists a general lack of appropriate sensitivity to constitutional rights in the trial and appellate courts of the several States. State courts, like federal courts, have a constitutional obligation to safeguard personal liberties and to uphold federal law.... Moreover, the argument that federal judges are more expert in applying federal constitutional law is especially unpersuasive in the context of search-and-seizure claims, since they are dealt with on a daily basis by trial level judges in both systems....

With all respect, the hyperbole of the dissenting opinion is misdirected. Our decision today is *not* concerned with the scope of the habeas corpus statute as authority for litigating constitutional claims generally. We do reaffirm that the exclusionary rule is a judicially created remedy rather than a personal constitutional right, ... and we emphasize the minimal utility of the rule when sought to be applied to Fourth Amendment claims in a habeas corpus proceeding. ...In sum, we hold only that a federal court need not apply the exclusionary rule on habeas review of a Fourth Amendment claim absent a showing that the state prisoner was denied an opportunity for a full and fair litigation of that claim at trial and on direct review. Our decision does not mean that the federal court lacks jurisdiction over such a claim, but only that the application of the rule is limited to cases in which there has been both such a showing and a Fourth Amendment violation.

too costly and that its very existence might dissuade legislators from experimenting with more meaningful remedies for Fourth Amendment violations.

Justice White dissented, asserting that Congressional amendments to the federal habeas corpus statute following Fay v. Noia provided for federal relief to state prisoners whose convictions were secured in violation of any federal constitutional rights, drawing no such distinction as did the Stone majority opinion. He stated that he would be willing to join in an opinion which generally limited the applicability of the exclusionary rule, one in which the good faith of the officer would be relevant. He stated, however, that as long as the rule stood in its present form, he could not approve denial of habeas corpus relief to state prisoners whose convictions were secured through the use of evidence seized in violation of their Fourth Amendment rights.

Justice Brennan, joined by Justice Marshall, strongly dissented. He stated that state prisoners convicted on the basis of evidence secured in violation of their Fourth Amendment rights are in custody in violation of the constitution and thus are entitled to relief under the plain language of 28 U.S.C. § 2254. Much of Justice Brennan's opinion concerned the interpretation of the federal habeas corpus statute, which, he asserted, like Fay v. Noia, draws no distinction between rights which are related to the integrity of the fact-finding process and other constitutional rights. He reaffirmed the principle set forth in Fay and companion decisions that federal habeas corpus should be available to state prisoners as an alternative to certiorari. He emphasized the importance of those federal constitutional rights which are not necessarily designed to improve the fact-finding process. Justice Brennan cited Wolff v. Rice as demonstrating the need for federal habeas corpus to review search and seizure claims. In Rice, he said, although the affidavit for the warrant was "clearly deficient," the search was upheld by the Nebraska Supreme Court, which, contrary to established precedent, permitted the prosecutor to sustain the warrant by proving facts which had not been presented to the issuing magistrate. Justice Brennan also suggested that, this great regret, "the groundwork is being laid today for a drastic withdrawal of federal habeas jurisdiction, if not for all grounds of alleged unconstitutional detention, then at least for claims—for example, of double jeopardy, entrapment, self-incrimination, Miranda violations, and use of invalid identification procedures—that this Court later decides are not 'guilt-related.' "

2. In Kimmelman v. Morrison, 477 U.S. 365, 106 S.Ct. 2574 (1986), the Supreme Court held that despite the restrictions of Stone v. Powell, a federal habeas corpus petitioner can obtain relief by demonstrating that his trial counsel's failure to properly pursue a Fourth Amendment motion to suppress met the test of Strickland v. Washington (Chapter 18, Section B–3.) By showing that the failure demonstrated incompetence and actually prejudiced the petitioner at his trial, the federal habeas corpus petitioner would be entitled to relief. The Court emphasized that such cases present Sixth Amendment claims and not Fourth Amendment claims. It refused to extend the rationale of Stone to such cases even though the petitioner in such instance makes no showing that counsel's default created the possibility that a factually innocent person would be convicted. Six of the justices joined an opinion which carefully limited Stone to the Fourth Amendment exclusionary rule context.

3. The question of what constitutes a full and fair hearing on a Fourth Amendment issue in state court has been the subject of conflicting federal decisions. Noting these decisions, including some that require that the state decision be "colorably correct," Justice White has urged Supreme Court attention to the issue. See Shoemaker v. Riley, 459 U.S. 948, 103 S.Ct. 266 (1982) (White, J., dissenting from denial of certiorari).

In Willett v. Lockhart, 37 F.3d 1265 (8th Cir.1994) an en banc Court of Appeals held that a federal habeas judge may not review the state court record to determine whether the state court findings are fairly supported by the evidence. Only the absence of a state court procedure or an "unconscionable breakdown" in the procedure will justify habeas review of the merits of the claim. The Court reviewed the conflicts among the circuits.

4. Stone v. Powell applies to the exclusion of statements where the request is rooted in the claim that the statements are the product of a Fourth Amendment violation. Cardwell v. Taylor, 461 U.S. 571, 103 S.Ct. 2015 (1983).

5. Suppose that a particular issue of law has been resolved one way by the highest court of a state and a different way by a federal circuit. If binding state precedent ensures an adverse rule for a defendant in state court, has he been afforded the opportunity for a full and fair hearing? Two decisions suggest that he has, even though if he could get the federal district court to reach the merits of the claim, he would be entitled to relief under applicable federal Court of Appeals Fourth Amendment precedents. See United States ex rel. Maxey v. Morris, 591 F.2d 386 (7th Cir.1979); United States ex rel. Petillo v. New Jersey, 562 F.2d 903 (3d Cir.1977). Certiorari from an adverse state rule seems the only possible remedy for such a defendant.

6. Suppose that a state reviewing court agrees that evidence was the product of a violation of the defendant's Fourth Amendment rights, but that admission of the evidence was harmless beyond a reasonable doubt. Does Stone v. Powell insulate defendant's conviction from federal habeas corpus attack? Gilmore v. Marks, 799 F.2d 51 (3d Cir.1986), answered that question affirmatively. What policies support the conclusion that a federal habeas corpus court can overturn a state harmless error determination as to other constitutional claims but not as to Fourth Amendment claims?

7. Withrow v. Williams, 507 U.S. 680, 113 S.Ct. 1745 (1993), held that Stone v. Powell should not be extended so as to bar consideration during federal habeas corpus proceedings of Miranda claims.

In an especially bitter response, Justice Marshall, joined by Justice Brennan, argued against the merits of O'Connor's position and noted that in Eagan the parties had neither briefed nor argued the appropriate scope of federal habeas corpus where Miranda claims are asserted.

G. DERIVATIVE EVIDENCE PRINCIPLES AND LIMITATIONS

Carried to their logical conclusion, exclusionary rules would deprive the prosecution of any benefit from a violation of the defendant's constitutional rights. Courts would exclude not only the immediate product of an unlawful search or interrogation, but also evidence more remotely derived from the constitutional transgression. Although all evidence obtained, directly or remotely, as a result of violations can be considered "derivative," frequently the term "derivative evidence" is used to describe the fruits of police illegality which are not the immediate product of the misconduct.

Let us begin with an example. An officer engages in custodial interrogation of a suspect without providing Miranda warnings. He obtains a confession in which the suspect indicates that he buried the murder weapon at a certain spot in a forest dozens of miles from both the suspect's home and the murder scene. Pursuant to that lead, officers find the weapon, which bears the suspect's fingerprints and which, through expert firearms identification testimony, is established as the gun which was used to fire the fatal bullet. In this hypothetical, the immediate product of the improper interrogation is the confession. Derivative evidence includes the gun and the testimony of the experts about the fingerprints and the class and individual characteristics of the gun. Relying on cases which date to Silverthorne Lumber Co. v. United States, 251 U.S. 385, 40 S.Ct. 182 (1920), where the Supreme Court said that unlawfully acquired evidence "shall not be used at all," the defendant will seek to have both the confession and the derivative evidence excluded from his criminal trial.

Absent application of one of the doctrines discussed below, if the requirement is merely a chain of causality, whether short or long, the defendant should prevail.

If, however, he or she is questioning the merits of the exclusionary rule, an opponent might argue that any deterrent effect is adequately achieved by exclusion of the confession. Exclusion of more remotely derived evidence will serve no added deterrent function.

Most disputes concern whether certain evidence should be considered to be the product of the original illegality. If the evidence is discovered independently, without any exploitation of the illegality, then the exclusionary rule need not be applied because of the "independent source" or "independent origin" limitation upon derivative evidence principles. Thus in our original hypothetical if an officer, with no knowledge of the suspect's confession, and not acting in a chain of command originating from someone who knew of the confession, found the gun on his own and linked it to the suspect, the gun, together with the expert testimony, could be received at trial.

A second commonly recognized exception is the principle of inevitable discovery. Let us suppose that following a suspect's lawful arrest, the police legally seize the murder weapon from his person. They then subject him to Miranda-violative interrogation and learn the name of the retailer from whom he had purchased the weapon two weeks earlier. To aid in proof of premeditation, the prosecution seeks to use the testimony of the dealer, who remembers the transaction. In fact the dealer has been discovered through exploitation of a violation of the defendant's Miranda rights. However, the prosecution can show that the dealer could have been easily located through readily available manufacturer's records discoverable through the serial number on the weapon, which the police had lawfully seized. Thus the prosecution claims that even without the illegal procedure the police inevitably would have discovered the retailer.

One caveat is necessary. The doctrine of inevitable discovery does not depend upon the notion that the police could have lawfully performed the very procedure which they in fact unlawfully performed and could thereby have lawfully discovered the evidence. The doctrine does not mean that because the officers easily could have secured a search warrant, therefore they will be permitted to use evidence derived from an unlawful warrantless search. Rather it means that the evidence is admissible because even apart from the challenged search (or interrogation or wiretap) the police through other available investigative techniques would inevitably have come upon the same evidence which, as it happened, was discovered, somewhat remotely, through exploitation of the challenged investigative procedure. At least this is the commonly held view of the inevitable discovery doctrine. But see the note following Nix, infra.

There are unsettled disagreements about precisely what police efforts must be shown to lead a court to believe in inevitable discovery. Compare Smith v. State, 948 P.2d 473 (Alaska 1997) (proof that predictable procedures would have been followed and lead to discovery) (review of law) United States v. Larsen, 127 F.3d 984 (10th Cir.1997) (proof of separate ongoing investigation is unnecessary) United States v. Procopio, 88 F.3d 21 (1st Cir.1996) (Police had briefcase and knew its owner was robbery suspect).

A third doctrine, "attenuation," also serves to limit exclusionary principles. The court in United States v. Ramirez–Sandoval, 872 F.2d 1392 (9th Cir.1989), summarized that doctrine:

> The "attenuated basis" exception applies when the connection between the illegality and the challenged evidence has become sufficiently weak so as to dissipate the taint caused by the illegality. Wong Sun v. United States (1963) (noting that the question is "whether, granting establishment of the primary illegality, the evidence to which instant objection is made has been come at by exploitation of that illegality or instead by means sufficiently distinguishable to be purged of the primary taint"). This exception is applied more generously when the challenged derivative evidence is live-witness testimony than when it is documentary evidence.

Nix v. Williams

Supreme Court of the United States, 1984.
467 U.S. 431, 104 S.Ct. 2501.

[Upon retrial in Brewer v. Williams (Casebook, Chapter 2. Section C,) the trial court excluded Brewer's statement but admitted evidence related to the location and the condition of the victim's body. Williams was convicted. Eventually he was granted relief by the Sixth Circuit. The Supreme Court granted certiorari.]

■ CHIEF JUSTICE BURGER delivered the opinion of the Court:

* * *

The doctrine requiring courts to suppress evidence as the tainted "fruit" of unlawful governmental conduct had its genesis in Silverthorne Lumber Co. v. United States (1920); there, the Court held that the Exclusionary Rule applies not only to the illegally obtained evidence itself, but also to other incriminating evidence derived from the primary evidence. The holding of Silverthorne was carefully limited, however, for the Court emphasized that such information does not automatically become "sacred and inaccessible."

> "If knowledge of [such facts] is gained from an independent source, they may be proved like any others. . . ." Ibid. (emphasis added).

Wong Sun v. United States (1963), extended the Exclusionary Rule to evidence that was the indirect product or "fruit" of unlawful police conduct, but there again the Court emphasized that evidence that has been illegally obtained need not always be suppressed, stating:

> "We need not hold that all evidence is 'fruit of the poisonous tree' simply because it would not have come to light but for the illegal actions of the police. Rather, the more apt question in such a case is 'whether, granting establishment of the primary illegality, the evidence to which instant objection is made has been come at by exploitation of that illegality or instead by means sufficiently distinguishable to be purged of the primary taint.' " (quoting J. Maguire, Evidence of Guilt 221 (1959)).

The Court thus pointedly negated the kind of good-faith requirement advanced by the Court of Appeals in reversing the District Court.

* * *

The core rationale consistently advanced by this Court for extending the exclusionary Rule to evidence that is the fruit of unlawful police conduct has been that this admittedly drastic and socially costly course is needed to deter police from violations of constitutional and statutory protections. This court has accepted the argument that the way to ensure such protections is to exclude evidence seized as a result of such violations notwithstanding the high social cost of letting persons obviously guilty go unpunished for their crimes. On this rationale, the prosecution is not to be put in a better position than it would have been in if no illegality had transpired.

By contrast, the derivative evidence analysis ensures that the prosecution is not put in a worse position simply because of some earlier police error or misconduct. The independent source doctrine allows admission of evidence that has been discovered by means wholly independent of any constitutional violation. That doctrine, although closely related to the inevitable discovery doctrine, does not apply here; Williams' statements to Leaming indeed led police to the child's body, but that is not the whole story. The independent source doctrine teaches us that the interest of society in deterring unlawful police conduct and the public interest in having juries receive all probative evidence of a crime are properly balanced by putting the police in the same, not a worse, position than they would have been in if no police error or misconduct had occurred.[1] . . .

It is clear that the cases implementing the Exclusionary Rule "begin with the premise that the challenged evidence is in some sense the product

1. The ultimate or inevitable discovery exception to the Exclusionary Rule is closely related in purpose to the harmless-error rule of Chapman v. California (1967). The harmless-constitutional-error rule "serve[s] a very useful purpose insofar as [it] block[s] setting aside convictions for small errors or defects that have little, if any, likelihood of having changed the result of the trial." The purpose of the inevitable discovery rule is to block setting aside convictions that would have been obtained without police misconduct.

of illegal governmental activity.'' United States v. Crews (1980) (emphasis added). Of course, this does not end the inquiry. If the prosecution can establish by a preponderance of the evidence that the information ultimately or inevitably would have been discovered by lawful means ''here the volunteers' search'' then the deterrence rational has so little basis that the evidence should be received.[2] Anything less would reject logic, experience, and common sense.

The requirement that the prosecution must prove the absence of bad faith, imposed here by the Court of Appeals, would place courts in the position of withholding from juries relevant and undoubted truth that would have been available to police absent any unlawful police activity. Of course, that view would put the police in a worse position than they would have been in if no unlawful conduct had transpired. And, of equal importance, it wholly fails to take into account the enormous societal cost of excluding truth in the search for truth in the administration of justice. Nothing in this Court's prior holdings supports any such formalistic, pointless, and punitive approach.

* * *

Exclusion of physical evidence that would inevitably have been discovered adds nothing to either the integrity or fairness of a criminal trial.... Suppression, in these circumstances, would do nothing whatever to promote the integrity of the trial process, but would inflict a wholly unacceptable burden on the administration of criminal justice.

* * *

More than a half century ago, Judge, later Justice, Cardozo speculated some court might press the Exclusionary Rule to the outer limits of its logic ''or beyond'' and suppress evidence relating to the ''body of a murdered'' victim because of the means by which it was found. Cardozo's prophecy was fulfilled in Killough v. United States, 114 U.S.App.D.C. 305, 309, 315 F.2d

2. As to the quantum of proof we have already established some relevant guidelines. In United States v. Matlock (1974), we stated that ''the controlling burden of proof at suppression hearings should impose *no greater burden* than proof by a preponderance of the evidence.'' In Lego v. Twomey (1972), we observed ''from our experience [that] no substantial evidence has accumulated that federal rights have suffered from determining admissibility by a preponderance of the evidence'' and held that the prosecution must prove by a preponderance of the evidence that a confession sought to be used at trial was voluntary. We are unwilling to impose added burdens on the already difficult task of proving guilt in criminal cases by enlarging the barrier to placing evidence of unquestioned truth before juries.

Williams argues that the preponderance of the evidence standard used by the Iowa courts is inconsistent with United States v. Wade (1967). In requiring clear and convincing evidence of an independent source for an in-court identification, the Court gave weight to the effect an uncounseled pre-trial identification has in ''crystalliz[ing] the witnesses' identification of the defendant for the future reference.'' The Court noted as well that possible unfairness at the lineup ''may be the sole means of attack upon the unequivocal courtroom identification,'' and recognized the difficulty of determining whether an in-court identification was based on independent recollection unaided by the lineup identification. By contrast, inevitable discovery involves no speculative elements but focuses on demonstrated historical facts capable of ready verification or impeachment and does not require a departure from the usual burden of proof at suppression hearings.

241, 245 (1962) (en banc). But when, as here, the evidence in question would inevitably have been discovered without reference to the police error or misconduct, there is no nexus sufficient to provide a taint and the evidence is admissible.

The Court of Appeals did not find it necessary to consider whether the record fairly supported the finding that the volunteer search party would ultimately or inevitably have discovered the victim's body. However, three courts independently reviewing the evidence have found that the body of the child inevitably would have been found by the searchers....

* * *

On this record it is clear that the search parties were approaching the actual location of the body and we are satisfied, along with three courts earlier, that the volunteer search teams would have resumed the search had Williams not earlier led the police to the body and the body inevitably would have been found....

The judgment of the Court of Appeals is reversed, and the case is remanded for further proceedings consistent with this opinion.[3]

■ The concurring opinions of JUSTICES WHITE and STEVENS are omitted (JUSTICE STEVENS, concurring in the judgment.)

■ JUSTICE BRENNAN, with whom JUSTICE MARSHALL joins, dissenting.

As has every federal Court of Appeals previously addressing this issue, I agree that in these circumstances the "inevitable discovery" exception to the exclusionary rule is consistent with the requirements of the constitution....

... The inevitable discovery exception necessarily implicates a hypothetical finding that differs in kind from the factual finding that precedes application of the independent source rule. To ensure that this hypothetical finding is narrowly confined to circumstances that are functionally equivalent to an independent source, and to protect fully the fundamental rights served by the exclusionary rule, I would require clear and convincing evidence before concluding that the government had met its burden of proof on this issue. Increasing the burden of proof serves to impress the fact finder with the importance of the decision and thereby reduces the risk that illegally obtained evidence will be admitted. Cf. Addington v. Texas (1979); Santosky v. Kramer (1982) ("Raising the standard of proof would have both practical and symbolic consequences."). Because the lower courts did not impose such a requirement, I would remand this case for application of this heightened burden of proof by the lower courts in the first instance.

NOTES

1. For one decision restricting invocation of the inevitable discovery exception to the exclusionary rule, see People v. Stith, 69 N.Y.2d 313, 514 N.Y.S.2d 201, 506 N.E.2d 911 (1987). There the court said:

3. In view of our holding that the challenged evidence was admissible under the inevitable discovery exception to the Exclusionary Rule, we find it unnecessary to decide whether Stone v. Powell (1976), should be extended to bar federal habeas corpus review of Williams' Sixth Amendment claim and we express no view on that issue.

> Although the inevitable discovery rule has for several years been established law in this state, our court has never applied the rule where, as here, the evidence was obtained in the illegal search. Our past cases have concerned secondary evidence obtained directly as a result of leads or information gained from that primary evidence.

To allow the exception to be applied as to "primary" evidence as distinguished from "derivative" evidence would be an unacceptable dilution of the exclusionary rule, according to the New York Court of Appeals.

In Stith the police had illegally searched the cab of a truck tractor after a traffic stop. The prosecutor had argued that because the police made a lawful custodial arrest in the traffic matter and took possession of the vehicle, inevitably they later would have discovered the evidence through a lawful inventory search.

Another decision which holds the doctrine of inevitable discovery inapplicable to the immediate product of an illegal search is People v. Schoondermark, 717 P.2d 504 (Colo.App.1985) reversed on other grounds, 759 P.2d 715 (1988). But compare Hayes v. State, 488 So.2d 77 (Fla.App.1986).On remand from the United States Supreme Court the court permitted the use of illegally obtained fingerprints, holding that inevitably the police would have acquired lawfully a set of the defendant's fingerprints.

One court recently rejected the argument that only the indirect or remote product of unconstitutional police conduct can be admitted under the inevitable exception doctrine, saying that there is no support in Nix for the "direct-indirect" distinction. In United States v. Whitehorn, 829 F.2d 1225 (2d Cir.1987), federal agents had engaged in an unlawful search of an apartment following the arrest and removal of one of the occupants. They observed items of evidentiary value but did not seize them. They then included reports of their observations in an affidavit for a search warrant. They then seized the items pursuant to a search warrant. The Whitehorn court agreed that the warrant was valid even when the affidavit was stripped of the reports of data observed in the earlier unlawful search. It also agreed that, on the facts of the case, federal agents inevitably would have obtained a valid warrant even if they had not engaged in the earlier unlawful search.

For another decision applying the inevitable discovery doctrine to the primary evidence discovered in an unlawful search, see United States v. Pimentel, 810 F.2d 366 (2d Cir.1987). Pimentel pointed out that some of the federal circuit decisions cited in Nix v. Williams involved application of the doctrine to the immediate product of the questioned search.

Consider a case where officers lawfully arrested a suspect, but then delayed in searching items found in his immediate possession. Later the officers searched the items in quest of evidence. Because of the delay, the search is deemed illegal because it was not a proper search incident to arrest. It also had none of the marks of a routine inventory search. Nevertheless, some courts allow use of the evidence when the prosecution can demonstrate that the officer would have inventoried the items eventually and discovered the evidence. See United States v. Andrade, 784 F.2d 1431 (9th Cir.1986). Do not such decisions sanction the use of the immediate product of an unlawful search?

Many of the cases which invoke the inevitable discovery rule so as to allow prosecution use of the primary evidence of unlawful police conduct involve a common situation: the police have unlawfully searched a car at the scene in a non-inventory procedure. Because they were in lawful possession of the vehicle, they could have and supposedly would inevitably have conducted an inventory search that would have yielded the evidence. See, e.g., State v. Milliorn, 794 S.W.2d 181 (Mo.1990); United States v. Mancera–Londono, 912 F.2d 373 (9th Cir.1990).

What principles should be used as the bases for drawing distinctions in this area? To what extent is the requirement of a search warrant diminished when law enforcement officials are allowed to argue that they could have made the seizure pursuant to a valid warrant when the seizure was not pursuant to a valid warrant? Pursuant to a valid inventory search when the search was not an inventory search.

2. In Murray v. United States, 487 U.S. 533, 108 S.Ct. 2529 (1988), federal agents unlawfully entered warehouse and spotted evidence of drug offenses in "plain view." They left without disturbing the evidence and applied for a search warrant. The warrant application made no mention of the entry and reported none of the observations made following the prior illegal entry. Instead, probable cause data was derived from independent sources antecedent to the unlawful entry.

The Murray majority, in a 4 to 3 decision, held that the evidence seized was from an independent source and was not the product of the original unlawful entry. It rejected the suggestion that the police will routinely make illegal confirmatory entries to see whether it is worth their while to apply for a search warrant even where they have antecedent probable cause. It suggested that to do so would create problems in later convincing a court that the probable cause data in the warrant application was truly derived from an independent source.

The majority limited its holding to cases where the magistrate's decision to issue the warrant was uninfluenced by any data observed pursuant to the illegal entry. The Court also held that, in order to admit the evidence, the trial judge must find that "the agents would have sought a warrant if they had not earlier entered the warehouse." It remanded for a district court determination of whether the agents would have applied for the search warrant even if they had not made the earlier illegal entry.

Justice Marshall, joined by Justices O'Connor and Stevens, declared that officers, by excluding from the search warrant all data observed in the illegal entry, would avoid problems of tainting the search. The dissent argued that officers will avoid the time and the trouble of applying for a search warrant, even when they have probable cause, until they have confirmed their suspicions by making an illegal entry. Justice Marshall noted that in Murray there had been no discussion of a warrant application until after the officers had entered illegally and had spotted evidence of drug activity.

Brown v. Illinois

Supreme Court of the United States, 1975.
422 U.S. 590, 95 S.Ct. 2254.

■ JUSTICE BLACKMUN delivered the opinion of the Court.

This case lies at the crossroads of the Fourth and the Fifth Amendments. Petitioner was arrested without probable cause and without a warrant. He was given, in full, the warnings prescribed by Miranda v. Arizona. Thereafter, while in custody, he made two inculpatory statements. The issue is whether evidence of those statements was properly admitted, or should have been excluded, in petitioner's subsequent trial for murder in state court. Expressed another way, the issue is whether the statements were to be excluded as the fruit of the illegal arrest, or were admissible because the giving of the Miranda warnings sufficiently attenuated the taint of the arrest....

I.

As petitioner Richard Brown was climbing the last of the stairs leading to the rear entrance of his Chicago apartment in the early evening of May 13, 1968, he happened to glance at the window near the door. He saw, pointed at him through the window, a revolver held by a stranger who was inside the apartment. The man said, "Don't move, you are under arrest." Another man, also with a gun, came up behind Brown and repeated the statement that he was under arrest. It was about 7:45 p.m. The two men turned out to be detectives William Nolan and William Lenz of the Chicago police force. It is not clear from the record exactly when they advised Brown of their identity, but it is not disputed that they broke into his apartment, searched it, and then arrested Brown, all without probable cause and without any warrant, when he arrived. They later testified that they made the arrest for the purpose of questioning Brown as part of their investigation of the murder of a man named Roger Corpus.

Corpus was murdered one week earlier, on May 6, with a .38 caliber revolver in his Chicago West Side second floor apartment. Shortly thereafter, Officer Lenz obtained petitioner's name, among others, from Corpus' brother. Petitioner and the others were identified as acquaintances of the victim, not as suspects.

On the day of petitioner's arrest, detectives Lenz and Nolan, armed with a photograph of Brown, and another officer arrived at petitioner's apartment about 5 p.m. While the third officer covered the front entrance downstairs, the two detectives broke into Brown's apartment and searched it. Lenz then positioned himself near the rear door and watched through the adjacent window which opened onto the back porch. Nolan sat near the front door. He described the situation at the later suppression hearing:

> "After we were there for awhile, Detective Lenz told me that somebody was coming up the back stairs. I walked out the front door through the hall and around the corner, and I stayed there behind a door leading on to the back porch. At this time I heard Detective Lenz say, 'Don't move, you are under arrest.' I looked out. I saw Mr. Brown backing away from the window. I walked up behind him, I told him he is under arrest, come back inside the apartment with us."

As both officers held him at gunpoint, the three entered the apartment. Brown was ordered to stand against the wall and was searched. No weapon was found. He was asked his name. When he denied being Richard Brown, Officer Lenz showed him the photograph, informed him that he was under arrest for the murder of Roger Corpus, handcuffed him, and escorted him to the squad car.

The two detectives took petitioner to the Maxwell Street police station.During the 20-minute drive Nolan again asked Brown, who then was sitting with him in the back seat of the car, whether his name was Richard Brown and whether he owned a 1966 Oldsmobile. Brown alternately evaded these questions or answered them falsely. Upon arrival at the station house Brown was placed in the second floor central interrogation room. The room was bare, except for a table and four chairs. He was left alone, apparently without handcuffs, for some minutes while the officers obtained the file on the Corpus homicide. They returned with the file, sat down at the table, one across from Brown and the other to his left, and spread the file on the table in front of him.

The officers warned Brown of his rights under Miranda. They then informed him that they knew of an incident that had occurred in a poolroom on May 5, when Brown, angry at having been cheated at dice, fired a shot from a revolver into the ceiling. Brown answered, "Oh, you know about that." Lenz informed him that a bullet had been obtained from the ceiling of the poolroom and had been taken to the crime laboratory to be compared with bullets taken from Corpus' body. Brown responded, "Oh, you know that, too." At this point "it was about 8:45 p.m." Lenz asked Brown whether he wanted to talk about the Corpus homicide. Petitioner answered that he did. For the next 20 to 25 minutes Brown answered questions put to him by Nolan, as Lenz typed.

This questioning produced a two-page statement in which Brown acknowledged that he and a man named Jimmy Claggett visited Corpus on the evening of May 6; that the three for some time sat drinking and smoking marijuana; that Claggett ordered him at gunpoint to bind Corpus' hands and feet with cord from the headphone of a stereo set; and that Claggett, using a .38 caliber revolver sold to him by Brown, shot Corpus three times through a pillow. The statement was signed by Brown.

About 9:30 p.m. the two detectives and Brown left the station house to look for Claggett in an area of Chicago Brown knew him to frequent. They made a tour of that area but did not locate their quarry. They then went to police headquarters where they endeavored, without success, to obtain a photograph of Claggett. They resumed their search—it was now about 11 p.m.—and they finally observed Claggett crossing at an intersection. Lenz and Nolan arrested him. All four, the two detectives and the two arrested men, returned to the Maxwell Street station about 12:15 a.m.

Brown was again placed in the interrogation room. He was given coffee and was left alone, for the most part, until 2 a.m. when Assistant State's Attorney Crilly arrived.

Crilly, too, informed Brown of his Miranda rights. After a half hour's conversation, a court reporter appeared. Once again the Miranda warnings were given: "I read him the card." Crilly told him that he "was sure he would be charged with murder." Brown gave a second statement, providing a factual account of the murder substantially in accord with his first statement, but containing factual inaccuracies with respect to his personal background. When the statement was completed, at about 3 a.m., Brown refused to sign it. An hour later he made a phone call to his mother. At 9:30 that morning, about 14 hours after his arrest, he was taken before a magistrate.

On June 20 Brown and Claggett were jointly indicted by a Cook County grand jury for Corpus' murder. Prior to trial, petitioner moved to suppress the two statements he had made. He alleged that his arrest and detention had been illegal and that the statements were taken from him in violation of his constitutional rights. After a hearing, the motion was denied.

The case proceeded to trial. The State introduced evidence of both statements. Officer Nolan testified as to the contents of the first, but the writing itself was not placed in evidence. The second statement was introduced and was read to the jury in full.... The jury found petitioner guilty of murder....

On appeal, the Supreme Court of Illinois affirmed the judgment of conviction. The court refused to accept the State's argument that Brown's arrest was lawful. "Upon review of the record, we conclude that the testimony fails to show that at the time of his apprehension there was probable cause for defendant's arrest, [and] that his arrest was, therefore, unlawful." But it went on to hold in two significant and unembellished sentences:

> "[W]e conclude that the giving of the Miranda warnings, in the first instance by the police officer and in the second by the assistant State's Attorney, served to break, the causal connection between the illegal arrest and the giving of the statements, and that defendant's act in making the statements was 'sufficiently an act of free will to purge the primary taint of the unlawful invasion' Wong Sun v. United States. We hold, therefore, that the circuit court did not err in admitting the statements into evidence."
>
> Aside from its reliance upon the presence of the Miranda warnings, no specific aspect of the record or of the circumstances was cited by the court in support of its conclusion. The court, in other words, appears to have held that the Miranda warnings in and of themselves broke the causal chain so that any subsequent statement, even one induced by the continuing effects of unconstitutional custody, was admissible so long as, in the traditional sense, it was voluntary and not coerced in violation of the Fifth and Fourteenth Amendments.

* * *

II.

In Wong Sun, the Court pronounced the principles to be applied where the issue is whether statements and other evidence obtained after an illegal arrest or search should be excluded. In that case, federal agents elicited an oral statement from defendant Toy after forcing entry at 6 a.m. into his laundry at the back of which he had his living quarters. The agents had followed Toy down the hall to the bedroom and there had placed him under arrest. The Court of Appeals found that there was no probable cause for the arrest. This Court concluded that that finding was "amply justified by the facts clearly shown on this record." Toy's statement, which bore upon his participation in the sale of narcotics, led the agents to question another person, Johnny Yee, who actually possessed narcotics. Yee stated that heroin had been brought to him earlier by Toy and another Chinese known to him only as "Sea Dog." Under questioning, Toy said that "Sea Dog" was Wong Sun. Toy led agents to a multi-family dwelling where, he said, Wong

Sun lived. Gaining admittance to the building through a bell and buzzer, the agents climbed the stairs and entered the apartment. One went into the back room and brought Wong Sun out in handcuffs. After arraignment, Wong Sun was released on his own recognizance. Several days later, he returned voluntarily to give an unsigned confession.

This Court ruled that Toy's declarations and the contraband taken from Yee were the fruits of the agents' illegal action and should not have been admitted as evidence against Toy. It held that the statement did not result from "an intervening independent act of a free will," and that it was not "sufficiently an act of free will to purge the primary taint of the unlawful invasion." With respect to Wong Sun's confession, however, the Court held that in the light of his lawful arraignment and release on his own recognizance, and of his return voluntarily several days later to make the statement, the connection between his unlawful arrest and the statement "had 'become so attenuated as to dissipate the taint.' Nardone v. United States, 308 U.S. 338, 341." The Court said:

> "We need not hold that all evidence is 'fruit of the poisonous tree' simply because it would not have come to light but for the illegal actions of the police. Rather, the more apt question in such a case is 'whether, granting establishment of the primary illegality, the evidence to which instant objection is made has been come at by exploitation of that illegality or instead by means sufficiently distinguishable to be purged of the primary taint.' Maguire, Evidence of Guilt, 221 (1959)."

The exclusionary rule thus was applied in Wong Sun primarily to protect Fourth Amendment rights. Protection of the Fifth Amendment right against self-incrimination was not the Court's paramount concern there. To the extent that the question whether Toy's statement was voluntary was considered, it was only to judge whether it "was sufficiently an act of free will to purge the primary taint of the unlawful invasion." . . .

III.

. . . . Although, almost 90 years ago, the Court observed that the Fifth Amendment is in "intimate relation" with the Fourth, Boyd v. United States (1886), the Miranda warnings thus far have not been regarded as a means either of remedying or deterring violations of Fourth Amendment rights. Frequently, as here, rights under the two Amendments may appear to coalesce since "the 'unreasonable searches and seizures' condemned in the Fourth Amendment are almost always made for the purpose of compelling a man to give evidence against himself, which in criminal cases is condemned in the Fifth Amendment." The exclusionary rule, however, when utilized to effectuate the Fourth Amendment, serves interests and policies that are distinct from those it serves under the Fifth. It is directed at all unlawful searches and seizures, and not merely those that happen to produce incriminating material or testimony as fruits. In short, exclusion of a confession made without Miranda warnings might be regarded as necessary to effectuate the Fifth Amendment, but it would not be sufficient fully to protect the Fourth. Miranda warnings, and the exclusion of a confession made without them, do not alone sufficiently deter a Fourth Amendment violation.

Thus, even if the statements in this case were found to be voluntary under the Fifth Amendment, the Fourth Amendment issue remains. In order for the causal chain, between the illegal arrest and the statements made subsequent thereto, to be broken, Wong Sun requires not merely that the statement meet the Fifth Amendment standard of voluntariness but that it be "sufficiently an act of free will to purge the primary taint." Wong Sun thus mandates consideration of a statement's admissibility in light of the distinct policies and interests of the Fourth Amendment.

If Miranda warnings, by themselves, were held to attenuate the taint of an unconstitutional arrest, regardless of how wanton and purposeful the Fourth Amendment violation, the effect of the exclusionary rule would be substantially diluted. See Davis v. Mississippi (1969). Arrests made without warrant or without probable cause, for questioning or "investigation," would be encouraged by the knowledge that evidence derived therefrom hopefully could be made admissible at trial by the simple expedient of giving Miranda warnings. Any incentive to avoid Fourth Amendment violations would be eviscerated by making the warnings, in effect, a "cure-all," and the constitutional guarantee against unlawful searches and seizures could be said to be reduced to "a form of words."

It is entirely possible, of course, as the State here argues, that persons arrested illegally frequently may decide to confess, as an act of free will unaffected by the initial illegality. But the Miranda warnings, alone and per se, cannot always make the act sufficiently a product of free will to break, for Fourth Amendment purposes, the causal connection between the illegality and the confession. They cannot assure in every case that the Fourth Amendment violation has not been unduly exploited.

While we therefore reject the per se rule which the Illinois courts appear to have accepted, we also decline to adopt any alternative per se or "but for" rule. The petitioner himself professes not to demand so much. The question whether a confession is the product of a free will under Wong Sun must be answered on the facts of each case. No single fact is dispositive. The workings of the human mind are too complex, and the possibilities of misconduct too diverse, to permit protection of the Fourth Amendment to turn on such a talismanic test. The Miranda warnings are an important factor, to be sure, in determining whether the confession is obtained by exploitation of an illegal arrest. But they are not the only factor to be considered. The temporal proximity of the arrest and the confession, the presence of intervening circumstances, see Johnson v. Louisiana (1972), and, particularly,the purpose and flagrancy of the official misconduct are all relevant. See Wong Sun v. United States. The voluntariness of the statement is a threshold requirement. And the burden of showing admissibility rests, of course, on the prosecution.

IV.

.... Brown's first statement was separated from his illegal arrest by less than two hours, and there was no intervening event of significance whatsoever. In its essentials, his situation is remarkably like that of James

Wah Toy in Wong Sun. We could hold Brown's first statement admissible only if we overrule Wong Sun. We decline to do so. And the second statement was clearly the result and the fruit of the first.[5]

The illegality here, moreover, had a quality of purposefulness. The impropriety of the arrest was obvious; awareness of that fact was virtually conceded by the two detectives when they repeatedly acknowledged, in their testimony, that the purpose of their action was "for investigation" or for "questioning." The arrest, both in design and in execution, was investigatory. The detectives embarked upon this expedition for evidence in the hope that something might turn up. The manner in which Brown's arrest was affected gives the appearance of having been calculated to cause surprise, fright, and confusion.

We emphasize that our holding is a limited one. We decide only that the Illinois courts were in error in assuming that the Miranda warnings, by themselves, under Wong Sun always purge the taint of an illegal arrest.

* * *

■ JUSTICE WHITE, concurring in the judgment.

Insofar as the Court holds (1) that despite Miranda warnings the Fourth and Fourteenth Amendments require the exclusion from evidence of statements obtained as the fruit of an arrest which the arresting officers knew or should have known was without probable cause and unconstitutional, and (2) that the statements obtained in this case were in this category, I am in agreement and therefore concur in the judgment.

■ JUSTICE POWELL, with whom JUSTICE REHNQUIST joins, concurring in part.

I join the Court insofar as it holds that the per se rule adopted by the Illinois Supreme Court for determining the admissibility of petitioner's two statements inadequately accommodates the diverse interests underlying the Fourth Amendment exclusionary rule. I would, however, remand the case for reconsideration under the general standards articulated in the Court's opinion and elaborated herein.

* * *

NOTES

Post–*Brown* Issues

1. If the effort is to decide whether, in some psychological sense, the illegal police conduct "caused" the confession, what difference does it make whether the question of probable cause was close or not? Consider the statement of Justice Stevens,

5. The fact that Brown had made one statement, believed by him to be admissible, and his cooperation with the arresting and interrogating officers in the search for Claggett, with his anticipation for leniency, bolstered the pressures for him to give the second, or at least vitiated any incentive on his part to avoid self-incrimination. Cf. Fahy v. Connecticut, 375 U.S. 85 (1963).

concurring in Dunaway v. New York, 442 U.S. 200, 99 S.Ct. 2248 (1979), a decision which applied Brown and held inadmissible a confession following an illegal arrest:

> The flagrancy of the official misconduct is relevant, in my judgment, only insofar as it has a tendency to motivate the defendant. A midnight arrest withdrawn guns will be equally frightening whether the police acted recklessly or in good faith. Conversely, a courteous command has the same effect on the arrestee whether the officer thinks he has probable cause or not.

When the law considers the flagrancy of the police conduct in determining the admissibility of derivative evidence, has it abandoned any pretext of searching for "causality" and determined that where certain facts a represent, the police conduct will be deemed to be the "legal cause" of a confession? Does causality in Brown have any more scientific or philosophical meaning than does the term "proximate cause" in tort law?

2. In his dissent from the denial of certiorari in Barry v. New Jersey, 454 U.S. 1017, 102 S.Ct. 553 (1981), Justice White (joined by Justices Brennan and Marshall), suggested that prolonged detention after an unlawful arrest may make a situation worse rather than attenuating the relationship between the unlawful arrest and the ultimate confession or admission.

3. In *Brown* the primary violation was an arrest without probable cause. Sometimes police officers, with adequate probable cause, violate the Fourth Amendment by entering the suspect's home to make a warrantless arrest in the absence of consent. See Payton v. New York, 445 U.S. 573, 100 S.Ct. 1371 (1980). In New York v. Harris, 495 U.S. 14, 110 S.Ct. 1640 (1990), the Supreme Court in dictum indicated that a statement made by the suspect in the home—during the period of unlawful police occupancy—must be suppressed as the product of the illegal entry. However, Harris held that authorities can use a statement made by a suspect later at the police station as long as they had probable cause to arrest the suspect. Payton protects the sanctity of the home. The majority in Harris did not view the police-station statement as the product of the transgression against the home, but rather as a product of an arrest upon probable cause.

Neither the Harris majority nor the dissenters addressed the question of whether the suspect's police-station statement should be viewed as the product of his earlier unlawfully obtained admission made in his home. Consider that issue after reviewing Note 7, infra.

After the United States Supreme Court remand in Harris, the New York court invoked state constitutional principles to reject the Harris result. It noted that under New York law, where the right to counsel is broader than in some places. Once an arrest warrant issues, the New York Court declares that the authorities should have a disincentive to avoid obtaining a warrant. Excluding a police-station confession after a Payton violation will provide that disincentive, according to the New York court. People v. Harris, 77 N.Y.2d 434, 568 N.Y.S.2d 702, 570 N.E.2d 1051 (1991).

4. In Taylor v. Alabama, 457 U.S. 687, 102 S.Ct. 2664 (1982), the Court, with four justices dissenting, applied Brown and Dunaway to exclude a statement made following an unlawful arrest. In Taylor six hours elapsed between the arrest and the incriminating statement. The suspect was unrepresented by counsel, was given Miranda warnings three times, and, after waiver of Miranda rights, was questioned several times. He also had been allowed to visit with his emotionally upset girl friend and with a male companion. He was confronted with the result of a fingerprint comparison, which itself was the product of evidence derived from the unlawful arrest. Based upon this same fingerprint comparison, which had made use of rolled fingerprint impressions taken following the accused's unlawful arrest, a court had issued an arrest warrant before the defendant had made his incriminating statement. The Court held that because the warrant was based upon illegally obtained evidence, it did not constitute a legally cognizable "attenuation." In suppressing the statement the Court also emphasized that the data upon which the original arrest was made fell far short of probable cause, as it had in *Brown* and Dunaway.

One post-*Brown* issue that has divided lower courts is whether confronting a suspect with untainted evidence (i.e., evidence not derived from the illegal evidence) operates to purge the taint of an unlawful arrest when the suspect makes an incriminating statement in response to the display of evidence or in response to an assertion that a fellow suspect has confessed and implicated the arrestee. See Lekas v. Illinois, 485 U.S. 942, 108 S.Ct. 1123 (1988) (White, J., dissenting from denial of certiorari). The Court has now addressed this in the case that follows:

United States v. Patane

Supreme Court of the United States, 2004.
542 U.S. 630, 124 S.Ct. 2620.

■ JUSTICE THOMAS announced the judgment of the Court and delivered an opinion, in which THE CHIEF JUSTICE and JUSTICE SCALIA join.

In this case we must decide whether a failure to give a suspect the warnings prescribed by Miranda v. Arizona 1602 (1966), requires suppression of the physical fruits of the suspect's unwarned but voluntary statements. The Court has previously addressed this question but has not reached a definitive conclusion.... Although we believe that the Court's decisions in Oregon v. Elstad (1985), and Michigan v. Tucker (1974), are instructive, the Courts of Appeals have split on the question after our decision in Dickerson v. United States (2000). See, *e.g., United States v. Villalba-Alvarado* (CA8 2003) (holding admissible the physical fruits of a *Miranda* violation); *United States v. Faulkingham* (CA1 2002) (holding admissible the physical fruits of a negligent *Miranda* violation). Because the *Miranda* rule protects against violations of the Self–Incrimination Clause, which, in turn, is not implicated by the introduction at trial of physical evidence resulting from voluntary statements, we answer the question presented in the negative.

I

In June 2001, respondent, Samuel Francis Patane, was arrested for harassing his ex-girlfriend, Linda O'Donnell. He was released on bond, subject to a temporary restraining order that prohibited him from contacting O'Donnell. Respondent apparently violated the restraining order by attempting to telephone O'Donnell. On June 6, 2001, Officer Tracy Fox of the Colorado Springs Police Department began to investigate the matter. On the same day, a county probation officer informed an agent of the Bureau of Alcohol, Tobacco and Firearms (ATF), that respondent, a convicted felon, illegally possessed a .40 Glock pistol. The ATF relayed this information to Detective Josh Benner, who worked closely with the ATF. Together, Detective Benner and Officer Fox proceeded to respondent's residence.

After reaching the residence and inquiring into respondent's attempts to contact O'Donnell, Officer Fox arrested respondent for violating the restraining order. Detective Benner attempted to advise respondent of his *Miranda* rights but got no further than the right to remain silent. At that point, respondent interrupted, asserting that he knew his rights, and neither officer attempted to complete the warning.[1]

Detective Benner then asked respondent about the Glock. Respondent was initially reluctant to discuss the matter, stating: "I am not sure I should tell you anything about the Glock because I don't want you to take it away from me." Detective Benner persisted, and respondent told him that the pistol was in his bedroom. Respondent then gave Detective Benner permission to retrieve the pistol. Detective Benner found the pistol and seized it.

A grand jury indicted respondent for possession of a firearm by a convicted felon. The District Court granted respondent's motion to suppress the firearm, reasoning that the officers lacked probable cause to arrest respondent for violating the restraining order. It therefore declined to rule on respondent's alternative argument that the gun should be suppressed as the fruit of an unwarned statement.

The Court of Appeals reversed the District Court's ruling with respect to probable cause but affirmed the suppression order on respondent's alternative theory. The court rejected the Government's argument that this Court's decisions in *Elstad* and *Tucker* foreclosed application of the fruit of the poisonous tree doctrine of Wong Sun v. United States (1963), to the present context. These holdings were, the Court of Appeals reasoned, based on the view that *Miranda* announced a prophylactic rule, a position that it found to be incompatible with this Court's decision in *Dickerson* ("*Miranda* announced a constitutional rule that Congress may not supersede legislatively").[2] The Court of Appeals thus equated *Dickerson*'s announcement that *Miranda* is a constitutional rule with the proposition that a failure to warn pursuant to *Miranda* is itself a violation of the Constitution (and, more particularly, of the suspect's Fifth Amendment rights). Based on its understanding of *Dickerson*, the Court of Appeals rejected the post-*Dickerson* views of the Third and Fourth Circuits that the fruits doctrine does not apply to *Miranda* violations. It also disagreed with the First Circuit's conclusion that suppression is not generally required in the case of negligent failures to warn, explaining that "[d]eterrence is necessary not merely to deter intentional wrongdoing, but also to ensure that officers diligently (non-negligently) protect—and properly are trained to protect—the constitutional rights of citizens." We granted certiorari.

As we explain below, the *Miranda* rule is a prophylactic employed to protect against violations of the Self–Incrimination Clause. The Self–

1. The Government concedes that respondent's answers to subsequent on-the-scene questioning are inadmissible at trial under *Miranda* v. *Arizona* (1966), despite the partial warning and respondent's assertions that he knew his rights

2. The Court of Appeals also distinguished *Oregon v. Elstad* (1985), on the ground that the second (and warned) confession at issue there was the product of the defendant's volition. For the reasons discussed below, we do not find this distinction relevant.

Incrimination Clause, however, is not implicated by the admission into evidence of the physical fruit of a voluntary statement. Accordingly, there is no justification for extending the *Miranda* rule to this context. And just as the Self–Incrimination Clause primarily focuses on the criminal trial, so too does the *Miranda* rule. The *Miranda* rule is not a code of police conduct, and police do not violate the Constitution (or even the *Miranda* rule, for that matter) by mere failures to warn. For this reason, the exclusionary rule articulated in cases such as *Wong Sun* does not apply. Accordingly, we reverse the judgment of the Court of Appeals and remand the case for further proceedings.

II

The Self–Incrimination Clause provides: "No person ... shall be compelled in any criminal case to be a witness against himself." U.S. Const., Amdt. 5. We need not decide here the precise boundaries of the Clause's protection. For present purposes, it suffices to note that the core protection afforded by the Self–Incrimination Clause is a prohibition on compelling a criminal defendant to testify against himself at trial....

To be sure, the Court has recognized and applied several prophylactic rules designed to protect the core privilege against self-incrimination....

Similarly, in *Miranda*, the Court concluded that the possibility of coercion inherent in custodial interrogations unacceptably raises the risk that a suspect's privilege against self-incrimination might be violated. See *Dickerson*; *Miranda*. To protect against this danger, the *Miranda* rule creates a presumption of coercion, in the absence of specific warnings, that is generally irrebuttable for purposes of the prosecution's case in chief....

But because these prophylactic rules (including the *Miranda* rule) necessarily sweep beyond the actual protections of the Self–Incrimination Clause, any further extension of these rules must be justified by its necessity for the protection of the actual right against compelled self-incrimination. Indeed, at times the Court has declined to extend *Miranda* even where it has perceived a need to protect the privilege against self-incrimination. See, *e.g., Quarles* (concluding "that the need for answers to questions in a situation posing a threat to the public safety outweighs the need for the prophylactic rule protecting the Fifth Amendment's privilege against self-incrimination").

It is for these reasons that statements taken without *Miranda* warnings (though not actually compelled) can be used to impeach a defendant's testimony at trial, though the fruits of actually compelled testimony cannot. More generally, the *Miranda* rule "does not require that the statements [taken without complying with the rule] and their fruits be discarded as inherently tainted," *Elstad*. Such a blanket suppression rule could not be justified by reference to the "Fifth Amendment goal of assuring trustworthy evidence" or by any deterrence rationale ... and would therefore fail our close-fit requirement.

Furthermore, the Self–Incrimination Clause contains its own exclusionary rule. It provides that "[n]o person ... shall be compelled in any criminal case to be a witness against himself." Amdt. 5. Unlike the Fourth

Amendment's bar on unreasonable searches, the Self–Incrimination Clause is self-executing. We have repeatedly explained "that those subjected to coercive police interrogations have an *automatic* protection from the use of their involuntary statements (or evidence derived from their statements) in any subsequent criminal trial." This explicit textual protection supports a strong presumption against expanding the *Miranda* rule any further.

Finally, nothing in *Dickerson,* including its characterization of *Miranda* as announcing a constitutional rule, changes any of these observations. Indeed, in *Dickerson*, the Court specifically noted that the Court's "subsequent cases have reduced the impact of the *Miranda* rule on legitimate law enforcement while reaffirming [*Miranda*]'s core ruling that unwarned statements may not be used as evidence in the prosecution's case in chief." ... This description of *Miranda,* especially the emphasis on the use of "unwarned statements ... in the prosecution's case in chief," makes clear our continued focus on the protections of the Self–Incrimination Clause. The Court's reliance on our *Miranda* precedents, including both *Tucker* and *Elstad,* further demonstrates the continuing validity of those decisions. In short, nothing in *Dickerson* calls into question our continued insistence that the closest possible fit be maintained between the Self–Incrimination Clause and any rule designed to protect it.

III

Our cases also make clear the related point that a mere failure to give *Miranda* warnings does not, by itself, violate a suspect's constitutional rights or even the *Miranda* rule. So much was evident in many of our pre-*Dickerson* cases, and we have adhered to this view since *Dickerson*. This, of course, follows from the nature of the right protected by the Self–Incrimination Clause, which the *Miranda* rule, in turn, protects. It follows that police do not violate a suspect's constitutional rights (or the *Miranda* rule) by negligent or even deliberate failures to provide the suspect with the full panoply of warnings prescribed by *Miranda*. Potential violations occur, if at all, only upon the admission of unwarned statements into evidence at trial. And, at that point, "[t]he exclusion of unwarned statements ... is a complete and sufficient remedy" for any perceived *Miranda* violation.

Thus, unlike unreasonable searches under the Fourth Amendment or actual violations of the Due Process Clause or the Self–Incrimination Clause, there is, with respect to mere failures to warn, nothing to deter. There is therefore no reason to apply the "fruit of the poisonous tree" doctrine of *Wong Sun*. See also *Nix v. Williams* (1984) (discussing the exclusionary rule in the Sixth Amendment context and noting that it applies to "*illegally* obtained evidence [and] other incriminating evidence derived from [it]" (emphasis added)). It is not for this Court to impose its preferred police practices on either federal law enforcement officials or their state counterparts.

IV

In the present case, the Court of Appeals, relying on *Dickerson*, wholly adopted the position that the taking of unwarned statements violates a suspect's constitutional rights. And, of course, if this were so, a strong deterrence-based argument could be made for suppression of the fruits.

But *Dickerson*'s characterization of *Miranda* as a constitutional rule does not lessen the need to maintain the closest possible fit between the Self–Incrimination Clause and any judge-made rule designed to protect it. And there is no such fit here. Introduction of the nontestimonial fruit of a voluntary statement, such as respondent's Glock, does not implicate the Self–Incrimination Clause. The admission of such fruit presents no risk that a defendant's coerced statements (however defined) will be used against him at a criminal trial. In any case, "[t]he exclusion of unwarned statements ... is a complete and sufficient remedy" for any perceived *Miranda* violation.... There is simply no need to extend (and therefore no justification for extending) the prophylactic rule of *Miranda* to this context.

Similarly, because police cannot violate the Self–Incrimination Clause by taking unwarned though voluntary statements, an exclusionary rule cannot be justified by reference to a deterrence effect on law enforcement, as the Court of Appeals believed/ Our decision not to apply *Wong Sun* to mere failures to give *Miranda* warnings was sound at the time *Tucker* and *Elstad* were decided, and we decline to apply *Wong Sun* to such failures now.

The Court of Appeals ascribed significance to the fact that, in this case, there might be "little [practical] difference between [respondent's] confessional statement" and the actual physical evidence. The distinction, the court said, "appears to make little sense as a matter of policy." But, putting policy aside, we have held that "[t]he word 'witness' in the constitutional text limits the" scope of the Self–Incrimination Clause to testimonial evidence.... The Constitution itself makes the distinction. And although it is true that the Court requires the exclusion of the physical fruit of actually coerced statements, it must be remembered that statements taken without sufficient *Miranda* warnings are presumed to have been coerced only for certain purposes and then only when necessary to protect the privilege against self-incrimination. See Part II, *supra*. For the reasons discussed above, we decline to extend that presumption further.

Accordingly, we reverse the judgment of the Court of Appeals and remand the case for further proceedings.

It is so ordered.

■ JUSTICE KENNEDY, with whom JUSTICE O'CONNOR joins, concurring in the judgment.

In Oregon v. Elstad (1985), New York v. Quarles (1984), and Harris v. New York (1971), evidence obtained following an unwarned interrogation was held admissible. This result was based in large part on our recognition that the concerns underlying the *Miranda v. Arizona* (1966), rule must be accommodated to other objectives of the criminal justice system. I agree with the plurality that *Dickerson v. United States* (2000), did not undermine these precedents and, in fact, cited them in support. Here, it is sufficient to note that the Government presents an even stronger case for admitting the evidence obtained as the result of Patane's unwarned statement. Admission of nontestimonial physical fruits (the Glock in this case), even more so than the postwarning statements to the police in *Elstad* and Michigan v. Tucker (1974), does not run the risk of admitting into trial an accused's coerced incriminating statements against himself. In light of the important probative value of reliable physical evidence, it is doubtful that exclusion can be justified by a deterrence rationale sensitive to both law enforcement interests and a suspect's rights during an in-custody interrogation. Unlike the plurality, however, I find it unnecessary to decide whether the detective's failure to give Patane the full *Miranda* warnings should be characterized as a violation of the *Miranda* rule itself, or whether there is "anything to deter" so long as the unwarned statements are not later introduced at trial. With these observations, I concur in the judgment of the Court.

■ JUSTICE SOUTER, with whom JUSTICE STEVENS and JUSTICE GINSBURG join, dissenting.

The plurality repeatedly says that the Fifth Amendment does not address the admissibility of nontestimonial evidence, an overstatement that is beside the point. The issue actually presented today is whether courts should apply the fruit of the poisonous tree doctrine lest we create an incentive for the police to omit *Miranda* warnings, see Miranda v. Arizona (1966), before custodial interrogation.[1] In closing their eyes to the consequences of giving an evidentiary advantage to those who ignore *Miranda*, the plurality adds an important inducement for interrogators to ignore the rule in that case.

Miranda rested on insight into the inherently coercive character of custodial interrogation and the inherently difficult exercise of assessing the voluntariness of any confession resulting from it. Unless the police give the prescribed warnings meant to counter the coercive atmosphere, a custodial confession is inadmissible, there being no need for the previous time-consuming and difficult enquiry into voluntariness. That inducement to forestall involuntary statements and troublesome issues of fact can only atrophy if we turn around and recognize an evidentiary benefit when an unwarned statement leads investigators to tangible evidence. There is, of course, a price for excluding evidence, but the Fifth Amendment is worth a price, and in the absence of a very good reason, the logic of *Miranda* should be followed: a *Miranda* violation raises a presumption of coercion, Oregon v. Elstad (1985), and the Fifth Amendment privilege against compelled self-incrimination extends to the exclusion of derivative evidence, see United States v. Hubbell (2000) (recognizing "the Fifth Amendment's protection against the prosecutor's use of incriminating information derived directly or indirectly from . . . [actually] compelled testimony) . . ." That should be the end of this case.

The fact that the books contain some exceptions to the *Miranda* exclusionary rule carries no weight here. In Harris v. New York (1971), it

1. In so saying, we are taking the legal issue as it comes to us, even though the facts give off the scent of a made-up case. If there was a *Miranda* failure, the most immediate reason was that Patane told the police to stop giving the warnings because he already knew his rights. There could easily be an analogy in this case to the bumbling mistake the police committed in Oregon v. Elstad (1985). See *Missouri v. Seibert* (2004) (plurality opinion).

was respect for the integrity of the judicial process that justified the admission of unwarned statements as impeachment evidence. But Patane's suppression motion can hardly be described as seeking to "perver[t]" *Miranda* "into a license to use perjury" or otherwise handicap the "traditional truth-testing devices of the adversary process." Nor is there any suggestion that the officers' failure to warn Patane was justified or mitigated by a public emergency or other exigent circumstance, as in New York v. Quarles (1984). And of course the premise of Oregon v. Elstad is not on point; although a failure to give *Miranda* warnings before one individual statement does not necessarily bar the admission of a subsequent statement given after adequate warnings . . . that rule obviously does not apply to physical evidence seized once and for all.[2]

There is no way to read this case except as an unjustifiable invitation to law enforcement officers to flout *Miranda* when there may be physical evidence to be gained. The incentive is an odd one, coming from the Court on the same day it decides Missouri v. Seibert. I respectfully dissent.

■ JUSTICE BREYER, dissenting.

For reasons similar to those set forth in Justice Souter's dissent and in m I would extend to this context the "fruit of the poisonous tree" approach, which I believe the Court has come close to adopting in *Seibert*. Under that approach, courts would exclude physical evidence derived from unwarned questioning unless the failure to provide *Miranda* warnings was in good faith. See *Seibert* (Breyer, J., concurring). Because the courts below made no explicit finding as to good or bad faith, I would remand for such

* * *

NOTES: OTHER DERIVATIVE EVIDENCE ISSUES

1. In United States v. Ceccolini, 435 U.S. 268, 98 S.Ct. 1054 (1978), a government agent, through the unlawful inspection of an envelope belonging to Ceccolini, discovered that Lois Hennessey, though perhaps not herself implicated, might have knowledge bearing upon Ceccolini's gambling activities. Four months later authorities interviewed Hennessey concerning her knowledge. She said she "was studying police science and would be willing to help." Later Ceccolini was indicted for perjury in connection with his sworn denials of gambling. Three years after the original search, the government called Hennessey to testify against Ceccolini. The Supreme Court approved admission of her testimony. Relevant criteria included (a) the willingness of the witness to testify, (b) the passage of time between the search and the first witness contact, on the one hand, and the date of her trial testimony on the other hand, and (c) the fact that the officer who conducted the original search had not been investigating Ceccolini or gambling activity when, in his unlawful snooping, he examined the envelope. The Court indicated that a per se rule of exclusion ought not be adopted lest a willing witness who might have come forward anyway

2. To the extent that Michigan v. Tucker (1974) (admitting the testimony of a witness who was discovered because of an unwarned custodial interrogation), created another exception to *Miranda*, it is off the point here. In *Tucker*, we explicitly declined to lay down a broad rule about the fruits of unwarned statements. Instead, we "placed our holding on a narrower ground," relying principally on the fact that the interrogation occurred before *Miranda* was decided and was conducted in good faith according to constitutional standards governing at that time.

be forever barred from testifying. Post–Ceccolini cases where the testimony of a witness discovered through unlawful means was suppressed include United States v. Cruz, 581 F.2d 535 (5th Cir.1978), and United States v. Scios, 590 F.2d 956 (D.C.Cir.1978).

2. In Harrison v. United States, 392 U.S. 219, 88 S.Ct. 2008 (1968), the Supreme Court indicated that even a defendant's own trial testimony sometimes must be viewed as the fruit of improper police investigative procedures. There a statement in which the suspect admitted a killing was secured in violation of the principles of the McNabb–Mallory rule. After the erroneous denial of a motion to suppress, the defendant testified in his own behalf, admitted the killing, but claimed that it was accident. The Supreme Court held that at the retrial the prosecution could not offer Harrison's testimony because it had not established by clear and convincing evidence that Harrison would have admitted the killing absent the erroneous admission of his post-arrest statement. Compare McMann v. Richardson, 397 U.S. 759, 90 S.Ct. 1441 (1970), where the Supreme Court held that, if a defendant had competent trial counsel, a plea of guilty will not be vacated where the defendant later claims that the reason that he entered his plea was that the police had through unconstitutional means secured evidence which the prosecution hoped to use at trial. One difference between Harrison and McMann is that in the later case the defendant made no motion to suppress, while in the former case the trial judge erroneously denied a motion to suppress. See also People v. Miller, 33 Cal.3d 545, 189 Cal.Rptr. 519, 658 P.2d 1320 (1983) (plea of guilty vacated where made following erroneous denial of motion to suppress).

3. Some of the oldest derivative evidence cases involve situations where the police have improperly secured a statement from the accused and then, hours or days later, secured a second statement. See United States v. Bayer, 331 U.S. 532, 67 S.Ct. 1394 (1947); Darwin v. Connecticut, 391 U.S. 346, 88 S.Ct. 1488 (1968) (HARLAN, J., concurring); Beecher v. Alabama, 389 U.S. 35, 88 S.Ct. 189 (1967). In Clewis v. Texas, 386 U.S. 707, 87 S.Ct. 1338 (1967), a nine day spread between the first statement and the second was deemed an inadequate break in the stream of events to render the second statement admissible.

Some of the cases pointed out that once the suspect had let the "cat out of the bag" by confessing, he might have concluded that he had nothing to lose by repeating his confession.

In the early cases, including the above-cited Supreme Court decisions, typically the original statement had been deemed involuntary under the totality of the circumstances, and therefore violative of the Due Process Clause of the Fourteenth Amendment. Later numerous reviewing court decisions expanded this derivative evidence theory to cases where the primary violation had been a Miranda violation, reasoning that the cat-out-of-the-bag rationale was equally applicable in that context.

In Oregon v. Elstad, 470 U.S. 298, 105 S.Ct. 1285 (1985), however, the Court rejected this derivative evidence theory in the Miranda context. In *Elstad* the police arguably violated *Miranda* when questioning *Elstad* in his own home without warnings, although the issue of whether Elstad was in custody was a close one. At that time Elstad said, "Yes, I was there," after being asked about a robbery. He was then transported to the police station, and, about an hour later, after a purported waiver of Miranda rights, he gave a full statement detailing his role in the robbery.

Through Justice O'Connor, the Court held that as long as the original pre-Miranda statement was voluntary and as long as the post-Miranda statement was voluntary, the authorities could use in evidence the post-Miranda statement. It said that the psychological impact of the Miranda-violative statement did not constitute compulsion within the meaning of the Fifth Amendment.

Elstad expressly rested its holding upon a view of Miranda that the Miranda majority itself might not have accepted. *Elstad* declared that not every response to custodial interrogation in the absence of warnings and waiver is compelled within the meaning of the Fifth Amendment. It said that Miranda was a judge-made prophylactic rule designed to deter the obtaining of compelled statements, which rule sometimes operates to exclude statements which in fact were not compelled. The Elstad majority thus distinguished involuntary confession cases and unreasonable search and seizure cases, which, it said, always involved actual violations of the Constitution. In the eyes of the *Elstad* majority, this distinction allowed the Court to apply a less expansive derivative evidence rule in the Miranda context.

Elstad suggested that perhaps some Miranda violations were beyond the scope of its holding. For example, *Elstad* does not necessarily apply where an officer deliberately commits a clearer *Miranda* error in an effort to obtain a statement from a suspect, intending to use that statement as a tool of further interrogation after subsequent compliance with *Miranda*. Under what circumstances could a *Miranda*-violative but voluntary statement taint a later statement that was secured in apparent compliance with *Miranda*? See State v. Madruga–Jiminez, 485 So.2d 462 (Fla.App.1986) (one and a half-hours of questioning before officer provided *Miranda* warnings).

4. Does *Elstad* apply when the Sixth Amendment has attached?

Fellers v. United States

Supreme Court of the United States, 2004.
540 U.S. 519, 124 S.Ct. 1019.

■ JUSTICE O'CONNOR delivered the opinion of the Court.

After a grand jury indicted petitioner John J. Fellers, police officers arrested him at his home. During the course of the arrest, petitioner made several inculpatory statements. He argued that the officers deliberately elicited these statements from him outside the presence of counsel, and that the admission at trial of the fruits of those statements therefore violated his Sixth Amendment right to counsel. Petitioner contends that in rejecting this argument, the Court of Appeals for the Eighth Circuit improperly held that the Sixth Amendment right to counsel was "not applicable" because "the officers did not interrogate [petitioner] at his home." We granted the petition for a writ of certiorari and now reverse.

I

On February 24, 2000, after a grand jury indicted petitioner for conspiracy to distribute methamphetamine, Lincoln Police Sergeant Michael Garnett and Lancaster County Deputy Sheriff Jeff Bliemeister went to petitioner's home in Lincoln, Nebraska, to arrest him. The officers knocked on petitioner's door and, when petitioner answered, identified themselves and asked if they could come in. Petitioner invited the officers into his living room.

The officers advised petitioner they had come to discuss his involvement in methamphetamine distribution. They informed petitioner that they had a federal warrant for his arrest and that a grand jury had indicted him for conspiracy to distribute methamphetamine. The officers told petitioner that the indictment referred to his involvement with certain individuals, four of whom they named. Petitioner then told the officers that he knew the four people and had used methamphetamine during his association with them.

After spending about 15 minutes in petitioner's home, the officers transported petitioner to the Lancaster County jail. There, the officers advised petitioner for the first time of his rights under Miranda v. Arizona (1966), and Patterson v. Illinois. (1988). Petitioner and the two officers signed a *Miranda* waiver form, and petitioner then reiterated the inculpatory statements he had made earlier, admitted to having associated with other individuals implicated in the charged conspiracy, and admitted to having loaned money to one of them even though he suspected that she was involved in drug transactions.

Before trial, petitioner moved to suppress the inculpatory statements he made at his home and at the county jail. A Magistrate Judge conducted a hearing and recommended that the statements petitioner made at his home be suppressed because the officers had not informed petitioner of his *Miranda* rights. The Magistrate Judge found that petitioner made the statements in response to the officers' "implici[t] questions," noting that the officers had told petitioner that the purpose of their visit was to discuss his use and distribution of methamphetamine. The Magistrate Judge further recommended that portions of petitioner's jailhouse statement be suppressed as fruits of the prior failure to provide *Miranda* warnings.

The District Court suppressed the "unwarned" statements petitioner made at his house but admitted petitioner's jailhouse statements pursuant to Oregon v. Elstad (1985), concluding petitioner had knowingly and voluntarily waived his *Miranda* rights before making the statements.

Following a jury trial at which petitioner's jailhouse statements were admitted into evidence, petitioner was convicted of conspiring to possess with intent to distribute methamphetamine. Petitioner appealed, arguing that his jailhouse statements should have been suppressed as fruits of the statements obtained at his home in violation of the Sixth Amendment. The Court of Appeals affirmed. With respect to petitioner's argument that the officers' failure to administer *Miranda* warnings at his home violated his Sixth Amendment right to counsel under *Patterson*, the Court of Appeals stated: "*Patterson* is not applicable here ... for the officers did not interrogate [petitioner] at his home." The Court of Appeals also concluded that the statements from the jail were properly admitted under the rule of *Elstad* (" 'Though *Miranda* requires that the unwarned admission must be suppressed, the admissibility of any subsequent statement should turn in these circumstances solely on whether it is knowingly and voluntarily made'.")

Judge Riley filed a concurring opinion. He concluded that during their conversation at petitioner's home, officers "deliberately elicited incriminating information" from petitioner. That "post-indictment conduct outside the presence of counsel," Judge Riley reasoned, violated petitioner's Sixth Amendment rights. Judge Riley nevertheless concurred in the judgment, concluding that the jailhouse statements were admissible under the rationale of *Elstad* in light of petitioner's knowing and voluntary waiver of his right to counsel.

II

The Sixth Amendment right to counsel is triggered "at or after the time that judicial proceedings have been initiated ... 'whether by way of formal charge, preliminary hearing, indictment, information, or arraignment.' " ... We have held that an accused is denied "the basic protections" of the Sixth Amendment "when there [is] used against him at his trial evidence of his own incriminating words, which federal agents ... deliberately elicited from him after he had been indicted and in the absence of his counsel." Massiah v. United States (1964); cf. Patterson v. Illinois (holding that the Sixth Amendment does not bar postindictment questioning in the absence of counsel if a defendant waives the right to counsel).

We have consistently applied the deliberate-elicitation standard in subsequent Sixth Amendment cases ... and we have expressly distinguished this standard from the Fifth Amendment custodial-interrogation standard, see Michigan v. Jackson (1986) ("[T]he Sixth Amendment provides a right to counsel ... even when there is no interrogation and no Fifth Amendment applicability"); *Rhode Island v. Innis* (1980) ("The definitions of 'interrogation' under the Fifth and Sixth Amendments, if indeed the term 'interrogation' is even apt in the Sixth Amendment context, are not necessarily interchangeable"); cf. United States v. Wade (1967) (holding that the Sixth Amendment provides the right to counsel at a postindictment lineup even though the Fifth Amendment is not implicated).

The Court of Appeals erred in holding that the absence of an "interrogation" foreclosed petitioner's claim that the jailhouse statements should have been suppressed as fruits of the statements taken from petitioner at his home. First, there is no question that the officers in this case "deliberately elicited" information from petitioner. Indeed, the officers, upon arriving at petitioner's house, informed him that their purpose in coming was to discuss his involvement in the distribution of methamphetamine and his association with certain charged co-conspirators. Because the ensuing discussion took place after petitioner had been indicted, outside the presence of counsel, and in the absence of any waiver of petitioner's Sixth Amendment rights, the Court of Appeals erred in holding that the officers' actions did not violate the Sixth Amendment standards established in *Massiah*, and its progeny.

Second, because of its erroneous determination that petitioner was not questioned in violation of Sixth Amendment standards, the Court of Appeals improperly conducted its "fruits" analysis under the Fifth Amendment. Specifically, it applied *Elstad*, to hold that the admissibility of the jailhouse statements turns solely on whether the statements were " 'knowingly and voluntarily made.' " The Court of Appeals did not reach the question whether the Sixth Amendment requires suppression of petitioner's jailhouse statements on the ground that they were the fruits of previous questioning conducted in violation of the Sixth Amendment deliberate-elicitation standard. We have not had occasion to decide whether the rationale of *Elstad* applies when a suspect makes incriminating statements after a knowing and voluntary waiver of his right to counsel notwithstanding earlier police questioning in violation of Sixth Amendment standards.

We therefore remand to the Court of Appeals to address this issue in the first instance.

Accordingly, the judgment of the Court of Appeals is reversed, and the case is remanded for further proceedings consistent with this opinion.

It is so

NOTES

1. Derivative evidence theories are as unbounded as a defense lawyer's imagination. Consider a statement made by a suspect who has been confronted with physical evidence seized in violation of his Fourth Amendment rights. And what about an incriminating statement blurted out by a suspect following a lineup identification at a proceeding which violates the principles of *Stovall* or of *Wade–Gilbert*? Or a warrant issued based upon probable cause data obtained in violation of the defendant's rights under *Miranda* or under the Fourth Amendment? Or the product of a search incident to a warrantless arrest when the arrest was based upon probable cause data which had been observed in an earlier unlawful search of the suspect's home? Reported decisions supporting each of these derivative evidence theories are readily available. The task of the defense lawyer is to determine in what fashion the evidence which the prosecutor seeks to offer—whether physical evidence, the defendant's statements, in-court or out-of-court identifications, or other testimony of prosecution witnesses—can be traced to the alleged police wrongdoing at the investigative stage. This is true whether the alleged illegality relates to arrest, search and seizure, wiretapping, *Stovall* or *Wade–Gilbert* identification principles, or *Miranda* or one of the other principles limiting police interrogation practices.

2. The most ordinary consequence of an unlawful arrest, in the context of the arrestee's criminal case, is the suppression of physical evidence derived from the arrest. If the arrest is unlawful, the prosecution is deprived of an essential predicate of the doctrine of search incident to arrest. See Chapter 5, Section E, supra. An illegal arrest may also be one factor in determining the voluntariness of a consent to search granted by the arrestee. See Chapter 5, Section G, supra.

3. In United States v. Crews, 445 U.S. 463, 100 S.Ct. 1244 (1980), the government appealed from a decision of the District of Columbia Appellate Court reported at 389 A.2d 277 (D.C.App.1978). The Appellate Court had suppressed proof on an out-of-court identification made from a photograph taken of a suspect following his arrest without probable cause. The government did not challenge that order. In dictum three of the eight participating Supreme Court justices said that this suppression order was mandated by the Fourth Amendment. The other justices made no comment on that part of the Appellate Court order.

All eight justices voted to overturn the Appellate Court order suppressing the in-court identification. Five justices, in several different opinions, seemed to say that an in-court identification of a defendant generally should not be suppressed as the fruit of an illegal arrest of the defendant. They reasoned that where, as here, the authorities' knowledge of the witness is not derived from the illegal arrest, and where the witness's knowledge of the offender's looks is not derived from the arrest, the witness will be in court prepared to make an identification. They further reasoned that an illegal arrest does not deprive the court of jurisdiction, and they asserted that it followed that the accused cannot make any Fourth Amendment claim related to his presence at trial. They concluded that, therefore, the in-court identification cannot be deemed the product of an unlawful arrest.

Three justices would have left the broader question open. They emphasized that the authorities here knew the identity of the suspect before the arrest was made. They apparently reasoned that the confrontation between witness and suspect was inevitable, perhaps because the suspect could have been compelled to appear in a lineup. They concluded that this in-court identification ought not be suppressed.

* * *

4. Justice O'Connor has suggested that courts should never suppress physical evidence derived from a *Miranda* violation. See her separate opinion in New York v. Quarles, 467 U.S. 649, 104 S.Ct. 2626 (1984). Her theory is that because the Fifth Amendment does not protect against non-testimonial disclosures, the derivative evidence of Fifth Amendment violations should be admitted.

Recent decisions have followed the suggestion, see United States v. Gonzalez-Sandoval, 894 F.2d 1043 (9th Cir.1990), United States v. Elie, 111 F.3d 1135 (4th Cir.1997), Winsett v. Washington, 130 F.3d 269 (7th Cir.1997).

Suppose that a *Miranda*-violative statement is used to supply probable cause data for the issuance of a search warrant, which, in turn, leads to discovery of evidence that the prosecution seeks to use at the confessing defendant's criminal trial. Should the physical evidence be excluded because of the *Miranda* violation? Chapter 6. Section G and United States v. Liss, 103 F.3d 617 (7th Cir.1997). Justice White has urged the Court to review the broad question of the admissibility of physical evidence derived from a *Miranda*-violative statement. See Patterson v. United States, 485 U.S. 922, 108 S.Ct. 1093 (1988) (White, J., dissenting from denial of certiorari). A narrower question presented by the hypothetical and by Patterson is whether the good-faith exception to the exclusionary rule would apply in such a situation.

5. Sometimes evidence illegally obtained in one investigation is legally relevant to a prosecution for an offense which occurs years later, for example where evidence of the earlier offense is relevant to intent or modus operandi as to the later offense. Several courts have refused to suppress the evidence, believing that the "remedy" is too far removed from the wrong to justify exclusion. See United States v. Lopez-Martinez, 725 F.2d 471 (9th Cir.1984) (evidence arguably unlawfully seized in 1974 relevant to intent issue in alleged 1982 offense).

6. "New" crimes are not ordinarily considered as the product of prior constitutional violations. Thus an officer who has illegally stopped a motorist can testify in a bribery prosecution to the motorist's efforts to bribe the officer. So also an officer can testify to a battery against her person which occurred after she had illegally entered the suspect's home.

7. If an officer, through a violation of the Fourth Amendment, discovers a person in illegal possession of drugs, the authorities might later focus their investigative efforts on that person. If the efforts prove fruitful, according to most courts, the defendant cannot exclude information discovered in that investigation absent some specific evidentiary link between the illegally acquired evidence and the new evidence. United States v. Aguilar, 883 F.2d 662 (9th Cir.1989). The issue is somewhat analogous to one that arises when individuals who have been immunized claim that their rights have been violated when immunized testimony is put to some non-evidentiary use.

H. NON-RETROACTIVITY

In Linkletter v. Walker, 381 U.S. 618, 85 S.Ct. 1731 (1965), the Supreme Court for the first time approved the practice of denying retroactive effect to new decisions which had broadened the federal constitutional rights of the accused. In so doing it relied largely upon precedents from civil cases, where the use of the "prospective only" technique was fairly well established. (For example, in abolishing sovereign tort immunity, state courts, in deference to the reliance which governmental bodies, in deciding not to obtain accident insurance, had placed upon older decisions, typically applied their new decision, except for the case at hand, only to torts occurring after the date of the new decision.) The general rule from civil cases was that as long as the older rule did not itself violate the Constitution, it was not constitutionally impermissible for a court to apply the old rule to cases arising before the new decision. See Great Northern Railway Co. v. Sunburst Oil and Refining Co., 287 U.S. 358, 53 S.Ct. 145 (1932).

Application of this technique to deny criminal defendants the benefit of a new decision of federal constitutional dimension was not free of controversy. Justices Black and Douglas consistently refused to recognize the legitimacy of the technique. Justice Fortas commented that the practice rewarded states which acted only under Supreme Court compulsion and placed a "dunce cap" on those which moved on their own in reforming their systems. Eventually Justice Harlan, an early supporter of non-retroactivity, became one of its strong critics.

In *Linkletter*, misreading the common law retroactivity decisions, the Court declared that under its cases a new decision must be applied to all cases not yet "final" as of the date when the new rule was announced. The Court defined finality as the point where the right to direct appellate review and certiorari to the United States Supreme Court has been exhausted or has expired. If such an exception for non-final matters had been applied to the non-retroactivity approach in the common law civil cases, it would have undermined the notion of reliance. If, for example, a municipality which had failed to insure itself in reliance upon the doctrine of sovereign immunity was liable for a tort committed before the date of the decision abolishing sovereign immunity, where the matter was adjudicated after the date of the new decision, the doctrine of non-retroactivity would have been of little help to the municipality. The non-retroactivity declaration would have protected the municipality only in cases that had become final before the date of the new decision. In those civil cases, however, principles of finality and res judicata already would have protected the municipality from the plaintiff's efforts to re-open the judgment to take advantage of the new decision. In cases not yet final, under the *Linkletter* exception to non-retroactivity, the municipality would have been exposed to liability even though, as of the date of the tort, it had been uninsured in reliance upon prior decisions recognizing sovereign immunity.

This theoretical limitation as to non-final adjudications quickly faded from the scene. Thus *Miranda* was held inapplicable to trials taking place before the date of *Miranda* even though the case in question had been pending on direct appeal when *Miranda* was decided. Wade was held to affect cases only where the identification procedure had occurred after the date on which Wade was decided.

In *Linkletter* and subsequent decisions the Court indicated that three criteria should determine whether a new constitutional decision is to be denied retroactive effect: (1) the extent to which the new decision has as its purpose the implementation of a value other than improvement of the integrity of the factfinding process; (2) the extent to which government justifiably relied upon the now overruled decision; and (3) the extent to which the orderly administration of justice would be impaired by retroactive application of the new decision. Most critics believe that the Court was not true to these criteria in ruling on retroactivity questions.

Although non-retroactivity criminal procedure decisions extended beyond the exclusionary rule area, in the exclusionary rule area, some justices deemed the doctrine particularly appropriate. In most of these exclusionary rule cases, the rationale for the new decision was unrelated to the goal of enhancing the integrity of the fact-finding process, so that at least one of the relevant criteria favored non-retroactivity. Moreover, in United States v. Peltier, 422 U.S. 531, 95 S.Ct. 2313 (1975), Justice Rehnquist, writing for the majority, recognized:

> We think that these cases tell us a great deal about the nature of the exclusionary rule, as well as something about the nature of retroactivity analysis ... The teaching of these retroactivity cases is that if the law enforcement officers reasonably believed that the evidence they had seized was admissible at trial, the "imperative of judicial integrity" is not offended by the introduction into evidence of that material even if decisions subsequent to the search or seizure have broadened the exclusionary rule to encompass evidence seized in that manner.

However, in Griffith v. Kentucky, 479 U.S. 314, 107 S.Ct. 708 (1987), the Court reconsidered its position and revived the distinction between final and non-final decisions. It held that even if a new constitutional criminal procedure decision is viewed as a sharp break from past precedent, courts must apply it to all cases not yet "final" as of the date of the decision even where the prosecution forces could claim reliance and even where the new decision was not designed to enhance the integrity of the fact-finding process. If the Griffith rule had been applied in the late 1960's, for example, *Miranda* would have required the overturning of thousands of convictions secured before the date of *Miranda* but not resolved on appeal until after *Miranda*. It would have required the suppression of identification testimony at trials held after Wade where the identification procedures in the absence of counsel had occurred before Wade. The Griffith majority declared that the Court must decide only "cases" and "controversies" and does not do this when it denies effect to one of its own rulings. It also said that denying the benefit of a new decision to some defendants whose cases are not yet final while granting it to the defendant who won before the Supreme Court "violates the principle of treating similarly situated defendants the same."

The Court in a constitutional civil case recently recognized one other reason for restricting the Supreme Court's power to completely deny any retroactive effect to its new decisions: a court with such power may be less inhibited in creating broad new rules if it need not live with retroactive consequences. It may function more like a legislature than an adjudicator of constitutional rights if its new decisions affect only future transactions.

See James B. Beam Distilling Co. v. Georgia, 501 U.S. 529, 111 S.Ct. 2439 (1991). If, for example, *Wade* and *Miranda* had affected all cases not yet "finally" adjudicated as of the day when those decisions were announced, would the Supreme Court have imposed such broad new obligations upon the authorities or would it have been reluctant to do so?

As to cases which had become "final" before the date of the new constitutional criminal procedure decision, the Supreme Court has effectively limited retroactivity by narrowing the scope of the federal habeas corpus remedy in such cases, beginning with Teague v. Lane, 489 U.S. 288, 109 S.Ct. 1060 (1989). For the details of those limitations, see Chapter 23, Section C.

I. NON-GOVERNMENTAL OR NON-LAW ENFORCEMENT CONDUCT

As with private citizen interrogations (e.g., by private security officers), for which *Miranda* warnings are generally held not to be required (Chapter 2, B–5), the courts have generally held that non-governmental illegal seizures of physical evidence do not invoke the exclusionary rule. The first case so holding is Burdeau v. McDowell, 256 U.S. 465, 41 S.Ct. 574 (1921). A representative later case to the same effect is: United States v. King, 55 F.3d 1193 (6th Cir.1995).

An extremely narrow exception to the rule that authorities may utilize evidence which has been turned over to them by private citizens is found in Walter v. United States, 447 U.S. 649, 100 S.Ct. 2395 (1980), where the authorities were told they should have obtained a warrant before examining certain films which had been given to them by employees of a firm to which the films had been misdirected. The holding of this complex case may turn, in part, upon the First Amendment overtones of the factual setting. The court in United States v. Jacobsen, 683 F.2d 296 (8th Cir. 1982), extended Walter beyond the first amendment context. It required use of a search warrant to inspect a package which had been opened by a private carrier, resealed, and then turned over to the government. The Supreme Court reversed that decision, however. United States v. Jacobsen, 466 U.S. 109, 104 S.Ct. 1652 (1984). It reasoned that the re-opening of the package by government agents did not constitute a search because the owner no longer had a reasonable expectation of privacy as to items already seen by the private-carrier employees. The Court went on to uphold the warrantless "field-testing" of the package.

There are at least two categories of cases, however, in which the exclusionary rule may be applied to illegal private citizen searches. First, where private security officers have been accorded full police powers, the exclusionary rule may become applicable. People v. Eastway, 67 Mich.App. 464, 241 N.W.2d 249 (1976). Contra: People v. Toliver, 60 Ill.App.3d 650, 18 Ill.Dec. 54, 377 N.E.2d 207 (1978). Second, where a private person acts in concert with or as an agent for the police, his illegal seizures are subject to the exclusionary rule. Machlan v. State, 248 Ind. 218, 225 N.E.2d 762 (1967); United States v. Newton, 510 F.2d 1149 (7th Cir.1975).

Statutory provisions may authorize both the standing and the right to suppress privately seized evidence as does the federal law regulating wiretaps and eavesdropping. See In re Grand Jury, 111 F.3d 1066 (3d Cir.1997).

The Fourth Amendment governs the conduct of governmental officials other than police officers, but a different standard of reasonableness may govern their conduct. See New Jersey v. T.L.O., 469 U.S. 325, 105 S.Ct. 733 (1985) (searches by public school teachers).

In United States v. Verdugo–Urquidez, 494 U.S. 259, 110 S.Ct. 1056 (1990), United States drug enforcement agents, working together with the Mexican Federal Judicial Police, without a warrant, searched the Mexican properties of an individual who was a resident and a citizen of Mexico. The United States and Mexican authorities seized documents which they sought to use at the individual's drug trial in a United States district court. A federal district judge suppressed the evidence, but the United States Supreme Court overturned that ruling. The Court held that the Fourth Amendment does not apply to the search and seizure of property that is owned by a nonresident alien and located in a foreign country, even when United States law enforcement officials direct the search.

CHAPTER 7

THE LIMITS OF UNDERCOVER WORK

A. OVERVIEW

Unlike other topics in this textbook, entrapment is a defense to a criminal charge. It must be raised by the defendant. Some defense counsel are reluctant to use it since it effectively requires admitting the crime before claiming that the client was entrapped. In addition, whenever predisposition is at issue, the prosecutor has a much freer hand under most systems of evidentiary principles to bring evidence of the defendant's character before the jury. Entrapment alone is not a violation of the constitution. As such, states need not recognize the defense, even though all do.

The United States Supreme Court first recognized an entrapment defense in federal cases in Sorrells v. United States, 287 U.S. 435, 53 S.Ct. 210 (1932). There, the Court adopted the so-called "subjective test" for entrapment. The line was drawn between the "unwary criminal" and the "unwary innocent." In short, if the individual was not predisposed to break the law in the absence of government inducement, then he or she can successfully make out a defense of entrapment. A minority of the Court has advocated, in contrast, an "objective test" for entrapment. The Model Penal Code adopts this position. American Law Institute, Model Penal Code and Commentaries, Comments to § 2.13. The "objective test" focuses not on the individual defendant's state of mind so much as it emphasizes the need for judicial integrity and deterrence of police misconduct. Under the "objective test," it is possible for courts to ask whether the police conduct was so outrageous that it violated due process. This prong of the entrapment debate does have constitutional dimensions, and as such, could serve to preclude a prosecution. Clearly there are some parallels between the debate over the appropriate analysis to use for entrapment and the debate over the exclusionary rules considered in earlier chapters.

More recently, with the advent of the Sentencing Guidelines, defendants have claimed a narrower type of entrapment: sentence entrapment. For example, they argue that officers induce a defendant to sell a greater quantity of drugs in order to trigger a higher level sentence.

As you read these materials, consider the underlying rationale and wisdom of each approach.

B. ENTRAPMENT—DID THE POLICE CREATE THE CRIME?

United States v. Russell

Supreme Court of the United States, 1973.
411 U.S. 423, 93 S.Ct. 1637.

■ MR. JUSTICE REHNQUIST delivered the opinion of the Court.

* * *

. . . On December 7, 1969, Joe Shapiro, an undercover agent for the Federal Bureau of Narcotics and Dangerous Drugs, went to respondent's home on Whidbey Island in the State of Washington where he met with respondent and his two codefendants, John and Patrick Connolly. Shapiro's assignment was to locate a laboratory where it was believed that methamphetamine was being manufactured illicitly. He told the respondent and the Connollys that he represented an organization in the Pacific Northwest that was interested in controlling the manufacture and distribution of methamphetamine. He then made an offer to supply the defendants with the chemical phenyl–2–propanone, an essential ingredient in the manufacture of methamphetamine, in return for one-half of the drug produced. This offer was made on the condition that Agent Shapiro be shown a sample of the drug which they were making and the laboratory where it was being produced.

During the conversation Patrick Connolly revealed that he had been making the drug since May 1969 and since then had produced three pounds of it. John Connolly gave the agent a bag containing a quantity of methamphetamine that here presented as being from "the last batch that we made." Shortly thereafter, Shapiro and Patrick Connolly left respondent's house to view the laboratory which was located in the Connolly house on Whidbey Island. At the house Shapiro observed an empty bottle bearing the chemical label phenyl–2–propanone.

By prearrangement Shapiro returned to the Connolly house on December 9, 1969, to supply 100 grams of propanone and observe the chemical reaction. When he arrived he observed Patrick Connolly and the respondent cutting up pieces of aluminum foil and placing them in a large flask. There was testimony that some of the foil pieces accidentally fell on the floor and were picked up by the respondent and Shapiro and put into the flask.[3]

About a month later Shapiro returned to the Connolly house and met with Patrick Connolly to ask if he was still interested in their "business arrangement." Connolly replied that he was interested but that he had recently obtained two additional bottles of phenyl–2–propanone and would not be finished with them for a couple of days. He provided some additional

3. Agent Shapiro did not otherwise participate in the manufacture of the drug or direct any of the work.

methamphetamine to Shapiro at that time. Three days later Shapiro returned to the Connolly house with a search warrant and, among other items, seized an empty 500–gram bottle of propanone and a 100–gram bottle, not the one he had provided, that was partially filled with the chemical.

There was testimony at the trial of respondent and Patrick Connolly that phenyl–2–propanone was generally difficult to obtain. At the request of the Bureau of Narcotics and Dangerous Drugs, some chemical supply firms had voluntarily ceased selling the chemical.

At the close of the evidence, and after receiving the District Judge's standard entrapment instruction,[4] the jury found the respondent guilty on all counts charged. On appeal the respondent conceded that the jury could have found him predisposed to commit the offenses, but argued that on the facts presented there was entrapment as a matter of law. The Court of Appeals agreed, although it did not find the District Court had misconstrued or misapplied the traditional standards governing the entrapment defense. Rather, the court in effect expanded the traditional notion of entrapment, which focuses on the predisposition of the defendant, to mandate dismissal of a criminal prosecution whenever the court determines that there has been "an intolerable degree of governmental participation in the criminal enterprise." In this case the court decided that the conduct of the agent in supplying a scarce ingredient essential for the manufacture of a controlled substance established that defense.

This Court first recognized and applied the entrapment defense in Sorrells v. United States, 287 U.S. 435, 53 S.Ct. 210 (1932). In *Sorrells*, a federal prohibition agent visited the defendant while posing as a tourist and engaged him in conversation about their common war experiences. After gaining the defendant's confidence, the agent asked for some liquor, was twice refused, but upon asking a third time the defendant finally capitulated, and was subsequently prosecuted for violating the National Prohibition Act.

Mr. Chief Justice Hughes, speaking for the Court, held that as a matter of statutory construction the defense of cntrapment should have been available to the defendant. Under the theory propounded by the Chief Justice, the entrapment defense prohibits law enforcement officers from instigating a criminal act by persons "otherwise innocent in order to lure them to its commission and to punish them." Thus, the thrust of the entrapment defense was held to focus on the intent or predisposition of the defendant to commit the crime. "[I]f the defendant seeks acquittal by reason of entrapment he cannot complain of an appropriate and searching

4. The District Judge stated the governing law on entrapment as follows:

"Where a person has the willingness and the readiness to break the law, the mere fact that the government agent provides what appears to be a favorable opportunity is not entrapment." He then instructed the jury to acquit respondent if it had a "reasonable doubt whether the defendant had the previous intent or purpose to commit the offense ... and did so only because he was induced or persuaded by some officer or agent of the government." No exception was taken by respondent to this instruction.

inquiry into his own conduct and predisposition as bearing upon that issue." Sorrells, 287 U.S. at 451, 53 S.Ct. at 216.

Mr. Justice Roberts concurred but was of the view "that courts must be closed to the trial of a crime instigated by the government's own agents." The difference in the view of the majority and the concurring opinions is that in the former the inquiry focuses on the predisposition of the defendant, whereas in the latter the inquiry focuses on whether the government "instigated the crime."

In 1958 the Court again considered the theory underlying the entrapment defense and expressly reaffirmed the view expressed by the *Sorrells* majority. Sherman v. United States, 356 U.S. 369; 78 S. Ct. 819 (1958) supra. In *Sherman* the defendant was convicted of selling narcotics to a Government informer. As in *Sorrells*, it appears that the Government agent gained the confidence of the defendant and, despite initial reluctance, the defendant finally acceded to the repeated importunings of the agent to commit the criminal act. On the basis of *Sorrells,* this Court reversed the affirmance of the defendant's conviction.

In affirming the theory underlying *Sorrells*, Mr. Chief Justice Warren for the Court, held that "[t]o determine whether entrapment has been established, a line must be drawn between the trap for the unwary innocent and the trap for the unwary criminal." Mr. Justice Frankfurter stated in an opinion concurring in the result that he believed Mr. Justice Roberts had the better view in *Sorrells* and would have framed the question to be asked in an entrapment defense in terms of "whether the police conduct revealed in the particular case falls below standards ... for the proper use of governmental power."

In the instant case respondent asks us to reconsider the theory of the entrapment defense as it is set forth in the majority opinions in *Sorrells* and *Sherman*. His principal contention is that the defense should rest on constitutional grounds. He argues that the level of Shapiro's involvement in the manufacture of the methamphetamine was so high that a criminal prosecution for the drug's manufacture violates the fundamental principles of due process. The respondent contends that the same factors that led this Court to apply the exclusionary rule to illegal searches and seizures and confessions should be considered here. But he would have the Court go further in deterring undesirable official conduct by requiring that any prosecution be barred absolutely because of the police involvement in criminal activity. The analogy is imperfect in any event, for the principal reason behind the adoption of the exclusionary rule was the government's "failure to observe its own laws." ... the government's conduct here violated no independent constitutional right of the respondent. Nor did Shapiro violate any federal statute or rule or commit any crime in infiltrating the respondent's drug enterprise.

Respondent would overcome this basic weakness in his analogy to the exclusionary rule cases by having the Court adopt a rigid constitutional rule that would preclude any prosecution when it is shown that the criminal conduct would not have been possible had not an undercover agent "supplied an indispensable means to the commission of the crime that could not have been obtained otherwise, through legal or illegal channels." Even if we were to surmount the difficulties attending the notion that due process of law can be embodied in fixed rules, and those attending respondent's particular formulation, the rule he proposes would not appear to be of significant benefit to him. For on the record presented it appears that he cannot fit within the terms of the very rule he proposes.

The record discloses that although the propanone was difficult to obtain it was by no means impossible. The defendants admitted making the drug both before and after those batches made with the propanone supplied by Shapiro. Shapiro testified that he saw an empty bottle labeled phenyl–2–propanone on his first visit to the laboratory on December 7, 1969. And when the laboratory was searched pursuant to a search warrant on January 10, 1970, two additional bottles labeled phenyl–2–propanone were seized. Thus, the facts in the record amply demonstrate that the propanone used in the illicit manufacture of methamphetamine not only *could* have been obtained without the intervention of Shapiro but was in fact obtained by these defendants.

While we may some day be presented with a situation in which the conduct of law enforcement agents is so outrageous that due process principles would absolutely bar the government from invoking judicial processes to obtain a conviction, the instant case is distinctly not of that breed. Shapiro's contribution of propanone to the criminal enterprise already in process was scarcely objectionable. The chemical is by itself a harmless substance and its possession is legal. While the government may have been seeking to make it more difficult for drug rings, such as that of which respondent was a member, to obtain the chemical, the evidence described above shows that it nonetheless was obtainable. The law enforcement conduct here stops far short of violating that "fundamental fairness, shocking to the universal sense of justice," mandated by the Due Process Clause of the Fifth Amendment.

The illicit manufacture of drugs is not a sporadic, isolated criminal incident, but a continuing, though illegal, business enterprise. In order to obtain convictions for illegally manufacturing drugs, the gathering of evidence of past unlawful conduct frequently proves to be an all but impossible task. Thus in drug-related offenses law enforcement personnel have turned to one of the only practicable means of detection: the infiltration of drug rings and a limited participation in their unlawful present practices. Such infiltration is a recognized and permissible means of apprehension; if that be so, then the supply of some item of value that the drug ring requires must, as a general rule, also be permissible. For an agent will not be taken into the confidence of the illegal entrepreneurs unless he has something of value to offer them. Law enforcement tactics such as this can hardly be said to violate "fundamental fairness" or "shocking to the universal sense of justice."

Respondent also urges, as an alternative to his constitutional argument, that we broaden the nonconstitutional defense of entrapment in order to sustain the judgment of the Court of Appeals. This Court's opinions in Sorrells v. United States, supra, and Sherman v. United States, supra, held that the principal element in the defense of entrapment was the defendant's predisposition to commit the crime. Respondent conceded in the Court of Appeals, as well he might, "that he may have harbored a predisposition to commit the charged offenses." Yet he argues that the jury's refusal to find entrapment under the charge submitted to it by the trial court should be overturned and the views of Justices Roberts and Frankfurter, concurring in *Sorrells* and *Sherman*, respectively, which make the essential element of the defense turn on the type and degree of governmental conduct, be adopted as the law.

We decline to overrule these cases. *Sorrells* is a precedent of longstanding that has already been once reexamined in *Sherman* and implicitly there reaffirmed. Since the defense is not of a constitutional dimension, Congress may address itself to the question and adopt any substantive definition of the defense that it may find desirable.

Several decisions of the United States district courts and courts of appeals have undoubtedly gone beyond this Court's opinions in *Sorrells* and *Sherman* in order to bar prosecutions because of what they thought to be, for want of a better term, "overzealous law enforcement." But the defense of entrapment enunciated in those opinions was not intended to give the federal judiciary a "chancellor's foot" veto over law enforcement practices of which it did not approve. The execution of the federal laws under our Constitution is confided primarily to the Executive Branch of the Government, subject to applicable constitutional and statutory limitations and to judicially fashioned rules to enforce those limitations. We think that the decision of the Court of Appeals in this case quite unnecessarily introduces an unmanageably subjective standard which is contrary to the holdings of this Court in *Sorrells* and *Sherman*.

Those cases establish that entrapment is a relatively limited defense. It is rooted, not in any authority of the Judicial Branch to dismiss prosecutions for what it feels to have been "overzealous law enforcement," but instead in the notion that Congress could not have intended criminal punishment for a defendant who has committed all the elements of a proscribed offense but was induced to commit them by the Government.

Sorrells and *Sherman* both recognize "that the fact that officers or employees of the Government merely afford opportunities or facilities for the commission of the offense does not defeat the prosecution." Nor will the mere fact of deceit defeat a prosecution, for there are circumstances when the use of deceit is the only practicable law enforcement technique available. It is only when the Government's deception actually implants the criminal design in the mind of the defendant that the defense of entrapment comes into play.

* * *

Reversed.

■ MR. JUSTICE DOUGLAS, with whom MR. JUSTICE BRENNAN concurs, dissenting.

A federal agent supplied the accused with one chemical ingredient of the drug known as methamphetamine ("speed") which the accused manufactured and for which act he was sentenced to prison. His defense was entrapment, which the Court of Appeals sustained and which the Court today disallows. Since I have an opposed view of entrapment, I dissent.

My view is that of Mr. Justice Brandeis expressed in Casey v. United States, 276 U.S. 413, 421, 48 S.Ct. 373, 375 (1928) (dissent), that of Mr. Justice Frankfurter stated in Sherman v. United States, 356 U.S. 369, 378, 78 S.Ct. 819, 823, 53 S.Ct. 210 (1958) (concurring in result), and that of Mr. Justice Roberts contained in Sorrells v. United States, 287 U.S. 435, 453 (concurrence).

In my view, the fact that the chemical ingredient supplied by the federal agent might have been obtained from other sources is quite irrelevant. Supplying the chemical ingredient used in the manufacture of this batch of "speed" made the United States an active participant in the unlawful activity. As stated by Mr. Justice Brandeis, dissenting in Casey v. United States, supra, at 423:

> "I am aware that courts—mistaking relative social values and forgetting that a desirable end cannot justify foul means—have, in their zeal to punish, sanctioned the use of evidence obtained through criminal violation of property and personal rights or by other practices of detectives even more revolting."
>
> But the objection here is of a different nature. It does not rest merely upon the character of the evidence or upon the fact that the evidence was illegally obtained. The obstacle to the prosecution lies in the fact that the alleged crime was instigated by officers of the Government; that the act for which the Government seeks to punish the defendant is the fruit of their criminal conspiracy to induce its commission. The Government may set decoys to entrap criminals. But it may not provoke or create a crime and then punish the criminal, its creature.

Mr. Justice Frankfurter stated the same philosophy in Sherman v. United States, supra, at 382–383: "No matter what the defendant's past record and present inclinations to criminality, or the depths to which he has sunk in the estimation of society, certain police conduct to ensnare him into further crime is not to be tolerated by an advanced society." And he added: "The power of government is abused and directed to an end for which it was not constituted when employed to promote rather than detect crime. . . ." Id., at 384.

Mr. Justice Roberts in Sorrells put the idea in the following words:

> "The applicable principle is that courts must be closed to the trial of a crime instigated by the government's own agents. No other issue, no comparison of equities as between the guilty official and the guilty defendant, has any place in the enforcement of this overruling principle of public policy." 287 U.S., at 459.

May the federal agent supply the counterfeiter with the kind of paper or ink that he needs in order to get a quick and easy arrest? The Court of Appeals in Greene v. United States, 454 F.2d 783, speaking through Judges Hamley and Hufstedler, said "no" in a case where the federal agent treated the suspects "as partners" with him, offered to supply them with a still, a still site, still equipment, and an operator and supplied them with sugar. Id., at 786.

The Court of Appeals in United States v. Bueno, 447 F.2d 903, speaking through Judges Roney, Coleman, and Simpson, held that where an informer purchased heroin for the accused who in turn sold it to a federal agent, there was entrapment because the sale was made "through the creative activity of the government." Id., at 906.

In United States v. Chisum, 312 F.Supp. 1307, the federal agent supplied the accused with the counterfeit money, the receipt of which was the charge against him. Judge Ferguson sustained the defense of entrapment saying, "When the government supplies the contraband, the receipt of which is illegal, the government cannot be permitted to punish the one receiving it." Id., at 1312.

The Court of Appeals in the instant case relied upon this line of decisions in sustaining the defense of entrapment, 459 F.2d 671. In doing so it took the view that the "prostitution of the criminal law," as Mr. Justice Roberts described it in Sorrells, 287 U.S., at 457, was the evil at which the defense of entrapment is aimed.

Federal agents play a debased role when they become the instigators of the crime, or partners in its commission, or the creative brain behind the illegal scheme. That is what the federal agent did here when he furnished the accused with one of the chemical ingredients needed to manufacture the unlawful drug.

■ MR. JUSTICE STEWART, with WHOM MR. JUSTICE BRENNAN and MR. JUSTICE MARSHALL join, dissenting.

* * *

In my view, this objective approach to entrapment advanced by [Justice Roberts and by Justice Frankfurter] is the only one truly consistent with the underlying rationale of the defense. Indeed, the very basis of the entrapment defense itself demands adherence to an approach that focuses on the conduct of the governmental agents, rather than on whether the defendant was "predisposed" or "otherwise innocent." I find it impossible to believe that the purpose of the defense is to effectuate some unexpressed congressional intent to exclude from its criminal statutes persons who committed a prohibited act, but would not have done so except for the Government's inducements. For, as Mr. Justice Frankfurter put it, "the only legislative intention that can with any show of reason be extracted from the statute is the intention to make criminal precisely the conduct in which the defendant has engaged." Since, by definition, the entrapment defense cannot arise unless the defendant actually committed the proscribed act, that defendant is manifestly covered by the terms of the criminal statute involved.

Furthermore, to say that such a defendant is "otherwise innocent" or not "predisposed" to commit the crime is misleading, at best. The very fact that he has committed an act that Congress has determined to be illegal demonstrates conclusively that he is not innocent of the offense. He may not have originated the precise plan or the precise details, but he was "predisposed" in the sense that he has proved to be quite capable of committing the crime. That he was induced, provoked, or tempted to do so by government agents does not make him any more innocent or any less predisposed than he would be if he had been induced, provoked, or tempted by a private person—which, of course, would not entitle him to cry "entrapment." Since the only difference between these situations is the identity of the tempter, it follows that the significant focus must be on the conduct of the government agents, and not on the predisposition of the defendant.

The purpose of the entrapment defense, then, cannot be to protect persons who are "otherwise innocent." Rather, it must be to prohibit unlawful governmental activity in instigating crime. As Mr. Justice Brandeis stated in Casey v. United States, "This prosecution should be stopped, not because some right of Casey's has been denied, but in order to protect the government. To protect it from illegal conduct of its officers. To preserve the purity of its courts." 276 U.S. 413, 423, 48 S.Ct. 373, 376 (1928). If that is so, then whether the particular defendant was "predisposed" or "otherwise innocent" is irrelevant; and the important question becomes whether the Government's conduct in inducing the crime was beyond judicial toleration.

Moreover, a test that makes the entrapment defense depend on whether the defendant had the requisite predisposition permits the introduction into evidence of all kinds of hearsay, suspicion, and rumor—all of which would be inadmissible in any other context—in order to prove the defendant's predisposition. It allows the prosecution, in offering such proof, to rely on the defendant's bad reputation or past criminal activities, including even rumored activities of which the prosecution may have insufficient evidence to obtain an indictment, and to present the agent's suspicions as to why they chose to tempt this defendant. This sort of evidence is not only unreliable, as the hearsay rule recognizes; but it is also highly prejudicial, especially if the matter is submitted to the jury, for, despite instructions to the contrary, the jury may well consider such evidence as probative not simply of the defendant's predisposition, but of his guilt of the offense with which he stands charged.

More fundamentally, focusing on the defendant's innocence or predisposition has the direct effect of making what is permissible or impermissible police conduct depend upon the past record and propensities of the particular defendant involved. Stated another way, this subjective test means that the Government is permitted to entrap a person with a criminal record or bad reputation, and then to prosecute him for the manufactured crime, confident that his record or reputation itself will be enough to show that he was predisposed to commit the offense anyway.

* * *

This does not mean, of course, that the Government's use of undercover activity, strategy, or deception is necessarily unlawful. Indeed, many crimes, especially so-called victimless crimes, could not otherwise be detected. Thus, government agents may engage in conduct that is likely, when objectively considered, to afford a person ready and willing to commit the crime an opportunity to do so.

But when the agents' involvement in criminal activities goes beyond the mere offering of such an opportunity and when their conduct is of a kind that could induce or instigate the commission of a crime by one not ready and willing to commit it, then—regardless of the character or propensities of the particular person induced—I think entrapment has occurred. For in that situation, the Government has engaged in the impermissible manufacturing of crime, and the federal courts should bar the prosecution in order to preserve the institutional integrity of the system of federal criminal justice.

* * *

I would affirm the judgment of the Court of Appeals.

Jacobson v. United States

Supreme Court of the United States, 1992.
503 U.S. 540, 112 S.Ct. 1535.

■ JUSTICE WHITE delivered the opinion of the Court.

On September 24, 1987, petitioner Keith Jacobson was indicted for violating a provision of the Child Protection Act of 1984, which criminalizes the knowing receipt through the mails of a "visual depiction [that] involves the use of a minor engaging in sexually explicit conduct...." Petitioner was found guilty after a jury trial.

I

In February 1984, petitioner, a 56–year–old veteran-turned-farmer who supported his elderly father in Nebraska, ordered two magazines and a brochure from a California adult bookstore. The magazines, entitled Bare Boys I and Bare Boys II, contained photographs of nude preteen and teenage boys. The contents of the magazines startled petitioner, who testified that he had expected to receive photographs of "young men 18 years or older." On cross-examination, he explained his response to the magazines:

> "[PROSECUTOR]: [Y]ou were shocked and surprised that there were pictures of very young boys without clothes on, is that correct?
>
> "[JACOBSON]: Yes, I was.
>
> "[PROSECUTOR]: Were you offended?
>
> "[JACOBSON]: I was not offended because I thought these were a nudist type publication. Many of the pictures were out in a rural or outdoor setting. There was—I didn't draw any sexual connotation or connection with that."

The young men depicted in the magazines were not engaged in sexual activity, and petitioner's receipt of the magazines was legal under both federal and Nebraska law. Within three months, the law with respect to child pornography changed; Congress passed the Act illegalizing the receipt through the mails of sexually explicit depictions of children. In the very month that the new provision became law, postal inspectors found petitioner's name on the mailing list of the California bookstore that had mailed him Bare Boys I and II. There followed over the next 2 ½ years, repeated efforts by two Government agencies, through five fictitious organizations and a bogus pen pal, to explore petitioner's willingness to break the new law by ordering sexually explicit photographs of children through the mail.

The Government began its efforts in January 1985 when a postal inspector sent petitioner a letter supposedly from the American Hedonist Society, which in fact was a fictitious organization. The letter included a membership application and stated the Society's doctrine: that members had the "right to read what we desire, the right to discuss similar interests with those who share our philosophy, and finally that we have the right to seek pleasure without restrictions being placed on us by outdated puritan morality." Petitioner enrolled in the organization and returned a sexual attitude questionnaire that asked him to rank on a scale of one to four his enjoyment of various sexual materials, with one being "really enjoy," two being "enjoy," three being "somewhat enjoy," and four being "do not enjoy." Petitioner ranked the entry "[p]reteen sex" as a two, but indicated that he was opposed to pedophilia.

For a time, the Government left petitioner alone. But then a new "prohibited mail specialist" in the Postal Service found petitioner's name in a file, and in May 1986, petitioner received a solicitation from a second fictitious consumer research company, "Midlands Data Research," seeking a response from those who "believe in the joys of sex and the complete awareness of those lusty and youthful lads and lasses of the neophite [*sic*] age." The letter never explained whether "neophite" referred to minors or young adults. Petitioner responded: "Please feel free to send me more information, I am interested in teenage sexuality. Please keep my name confidential."

Petitioner then heard from yet another Government creation, "Heartland Institute for a New Tomorrow" (HINT), which proclaimed that it was "an organization founded to protect and promote sexual freedom and freedom of choice. We believe that arbitrarily imposed legislative sanctions restricting *your* sexual freedom should be rescinded through the legislative process." The letter also enclosed a second survey. Petitioner indicated that his interest in "[p]reteen sex-homosexual" material was above average, but not high. In response to another question, petitioner wrote: "Not only sexual expression but freedom of the press is under attack. We must be ever vigilant to counter attack right wing fundamentalists who are determined to curtail our freedoms."

"HINT" replied, portraying itself as a lobbying organization seeking to repeal "all statutes which regulate sexual activities, except those laws which deal with violent behavior, such as rape. HINT is also lobbying to eliminate any legal definition of 'the age of consent'." These lobbying efforts were to be funded by sales from a catalog to be published in the future "offering the sale of various items which we believe you will find to be both interesting and stimulating." HINT also provided computer matching of group members with similar survey responses; and, although petitioner was supplied with a list of potential "pen pals," he did not initiate any correspondence.

Nevertheless, the Government's "prohibited mail specialist" began writing to petitioner, using the pseudonym "Carl Long." The letters employed a tactic known as "mirroring," which the inspector described as "reflect[ing] whatever the interests are of the person we are writing to." Petitioner responded at first, indicating that his interest was primarily in "male-male items." Inspector "Long" wrote back:

> "My interests too are primarily male-male items. Are you satisfied with the type of VCR tapes available? Personally, I like the amateur stuff better if its [sic] well produced as it can get more kinky and also seems more real. I think the actors enjoy it more."

Petitioner responded:

> "As far as my likes are concerned, I like good looking young guys (in their late teens and early 20's) doing their thing together."

Petitioner's letters to "Long" made no reference to child pornography. After writing two letters, petitioner discontinued the correspondence.

By March 1987, 34 months had passed since the Government obtained petitioner's name from the mailing list of the California bookstore, and 26 months had passed since the Postal Service had commenced its mailings to petitioner. Although petitioner had responded to surveys and letters, the Government had no evidence that petitioner had ever intentionally possessed or been exposed to child pornography. The Postal Service had not checked petitioner's mail to determine whether he was receiving questionable mailings from persons—other than the Government—involved in the child pornography industry.

At this point, a second Government agency, the Customs Service, included petitioner in its own child pornography sting, "Operation Borderline," after receiving his name on lists submitted by the Postal Service. Using the name of a fictitious Canadian company called "Produit Outaouais," the Customs Service mailed petitioner a brochure advertising photographs of young boys engaging in sex. Petitioner placed an order that was never filled.

The Postal Service also continued its efforts in the Jacobson case, writing to petitioner as the "Far Eastern Trading Company Ltd." The letter began:

> "As many of you know, much hysterical nonsense has appeared in the American media concerning 'pornography' and what must be done to stop it from coming across your borders. This brief letter does not allow us to give much comments; however, why is your government spending millions of dollars to exercise international censorship while tons of drugs, which makes yours the world's most crime ridden country are passed through easily."

The letter went on to say:

> "[W]e have devised a method of getting these to you without prying eyes of U.S. Customs seizing your mail.... After consultations with American solicitors, we have been advised that once we have posted our material through your system, it cannot be opened for any inspection without authorization of a judge."

The letter invited petitioner to send for more information. It also asked petitioner to sign an affirmation that he was "not a law enforcement officer or agent of the U.S. Government acting in an undercover capacity for the purpose of entrapping Far Eastern Trading Company, its agents or customers." Petitioner responded. A catalogue was sent, and petitioner ordered Boys Who Love Boys, a pornographic magazine depicting young boys engaged in various sexual activities. Petitioner was arrested after a controlled delivery of a photocopy of the magazine.

When petitioner was asked at trial why he placed such an order, he explained that the Government had succeeded in piquing his curiosity:

> "Well, the statement was made of all the trouble and the hysteria over pornography and I wanted to see what the material was. It didn't describe the—I didn't know for sure what kind of sexual action they were referring to in the Canadian letter. . . ."

In petitioner's home, the Government found the Bare Boys magazines and materials that the Government had sent to him in the course of its protracted investigation, but no other materials that would indicate that petitioner collected or was actively interested in child pornography.

II

There can be no dispute about the evils of child pornography or the difficulties that laws and law enforcement have encountered in eliminating it. Likewise, there can be no dispute that the Government may use undercover agents to enforce the law. "It is well settled that the fact that officers or employees of the Government merely afford opportunities or facilities for the commission of the offense does not defeat the prosecution. Artifice and stratagem may be employed to catch those engaged in criminal enterprises." Sorrells v. United States, 287 U.S. 435, 53 S.Ct. 210 (1932).

In their zeal to enforce the law, however, Government agents may not originate a criminal design, implant in an innocent person's mind the disposition to commit a criminal act, and then induce commission of the crime so that the Government may prosecute. Where the Government has induced an individual to break the law and the defense of entrapment is at issue, as it was in this case, the prosecution must prove beyond reasonable doubt that the defendant was disposed to commit the criminal act prior to first being approached by Government agents.[2]

2. Inducement is not at issue in this case. The Government does not dispute that it induced petitioner to commit the crime. The sole issue is whether the Government carried its burden of proving that petitioner was predisposed to violate the law *before* the Government intervened. The dissent is mistaken in claiming that this is an innovation in entrapment law and in suggesting that the Government's conduct prior to the moment of solicitation is irrelevant. The Court rejected these arguments five decades ago in *Sorrells*, when the Court wrote that the Government may not punish an individual "for an alleged offense which is the product of the creative activity of its own officials." Indeed, the proposition that the accused must be predisposed prior to contact with law enforcement officers is so firmly established that the Government conceded the point at oral argument, submitting that the evidence it developed during the course of its investigation was probative because it indicated petitioner's state of mind *prior* to the commencement of the Government's investigation.

This long-established standard in no way encroaches upon Government investigatory

Thus, an agent deployed to stop the traffic in illegal drugs may offer the opportunity to buy or sell drugs, and, if the offer is accepted, make an arrest on the spot or later. In such a typical case, or in a more elaborate "sting" operation involving government-sponsored fencing where the defendant is simply provided with the opportunity to commit a crime, the entrapment defense is of little use because the ready commission of the criminal act amply demonstrates the defendant's predisposition. Had the agents in this case simply offered petitioner the opportunity to order child pornography through the mails, and petitioner "who must be presumed to know the law" had promptly availed himself of this criminal opportunity, it is unlikely that his entrapment defense would have warranted a jury instruction.

But that is not what happened here. By the time petitioner finally placed his order, he had already been the target of 26 months of repeated mailings and communications from Government agents and fictitious organizations. Therefore, although he had become predisposed to break the law by May 1987, it is our view that the Government did not prove that this predisposition was independent and not the product of the attention that the Government had directed at petitioner since January 1985.

The prosecution's evidence of predisposition falls into two categories: evidence developed prior to the Postal Service's mail campaign, and that developed during the course of the investigation. The sole piece of preinvestigation evidence is petitioner's 1984 order and receipt of the Bare Boys magazines. But this is scant if any proof of petitioner's predisposition to commit an illegal act, the criminal character of which a defendant is presumed to know. It may indicate a predisposition to view sexually-oriented photographs that are responsive to his sexual tastes; but evidence that merely indicates a generic inclination to act within a broad range, not all of which is criminal, is of little probative value in establishing predisposition.

Furthermore, petitioner was acting within the law at the time he received these magazines. Receipt through the mails of sexually explicit depictions of children for noncommercial use did not become illegal under federal law until May 1984, and Nebraska had no law that forbade petitioner's possession of such material until 1988. Neb.Rev.Stat. § 28–813.01 (1989). Evidence of predisposition to do what once was lawful is not, by itself, sufficient to show predisposition to do what is now illegal, for there is a common understanding that most people obey the law even when they disapprove of it. This obedience may reflect a generalized respect for legality or the fear of prosecution, but for whatever reason, the law's

activities. Indeed, the Government's internal guidelines for undercover operations provide that an inducement to commit a crime should not be offered unless:

> "(a) there is a reasonable indication, based on information developed through informants other means, that the subject is engaging, has engaged, or is likely to engage in illegal activity of a similar type; *or*
>
> "(b) The opportunity for illegal activity has been structured so that there is reason for believing that persons drawn to the opportunity, or brought to it, are predisposed to engage in the contemplated illegal activity." Attorney General's Guidelines on FBI Undercover Operations (Dec. 31, 1980), reprinted in S.Rep. No. 97–682, p. 551 (1982).

prohibitions are matters of consequence. Hence, the fact that petitioner legally ordered and received the Bare Boys magazines does little to further the Government's burden of proving that petitioner was predisposed to commit a criminal act. This is particularly true given petitioner's unchallenged testimony was that he did not know until they arrived that the magazines would depict minors.

The prosecution's evidence gathered during the investigation also fails to carry the Government's burden. Petitioner's responses to the many communications prior to the ultimate criminal act were at most indicative of certain personal inclinations, including a predisposition to view photographs of preteen sex and a willingness to promote a given agenda by supporting lobbying organizations. Even so, petitioner's responses hardly support an inference that he would commit the crime of receiving child pornography through the mails.[3] Furthermore, a person's inclinations and "fantasies . . . are his own and beyond the reach of government. . . ." *Paris Adult Theatre I v. Slaton,* (1973).

On the other hand, the strong arguable inference is that, by waving the banner of individual rights and disparaging the legitimacy and constitutionality of efforts to restrict the availability of sexually explicit materials, the Government not only excited petitioner's interest in sexually explicit materials banned by law but also exerted substantial pressure on petitioner to obtain and read such material as part of a fight against censorship and the infringement of individual rights. For instance, HINT described itself as "an organization founded to protect and promote sexual freedom and freedom of choice" and stated that "the most appropriate means to accomplish [its]objectives is to promote honest dialogue among concerned individuals and to continue its lobbying efforts with State Legislators." These lobbying efforts were to be financed through catalogue sales. Mailings from the equally fictitious American Hedonist Society, and the correspondence from then non-existent Carl Long, endorsed these themes.

Similarly, the two solicitations in the spring of 1987 raised the specter of censorship while suggesting that petitioner ought to be allowed to do what he had been solicited to do. The mailing from the Customs Service referred to "the worldwide ban and intense enforcement on this type of material," observed that "what was legal and commonplace is now an 'underground' and secretive service," and emphasized that "[t]his environment forces us to take extreme measures" to insure delivery. The Postal Service solicitation described the concern about child pornography as "hysterical nonsense," decried "international censorship," and assured petitioner, based on consultation with "American solicitors" that an order that had been posted could not be opened for inspection without authorization of a judge. It further asked petitioner to affirm that he was not a government agent attempting to entrap the mail order company or its customers. In these particulars, both government solicitations suggested

3. We do not hold, as the dissent suggests, that the Government was required to prove that petitioner knowingly violated the law. We simply conclude that proof that petitioner engaged in legal conduct and possessed certain generalized personal inclinations is not sufficient evidence to prove beyond a reasonable doubt that he would have been predisposed to commit the crime charged independent of the Government's coaxing.

that receiving this material was something that petitioner ought to be allowed to do.

Petitioner's ready response to these solicitations cannot be enough to establish beyond reasonable doubt that he was predisposed, prior to the Government acts intended to create predisposition, to commit the crime of receiving child pornography through the mails. The evidence that petitioner was ready and willing to commit the offense came only after the Government had devoted 2½ years to convincing him that he had or should have the right to engage in the very behavior proscribed by law. Rational jurors could not say beyond a reasonable doubt that petitioner possessed the requisite predisposition prior to the Government's investigation and that it existed independent of the Government's many and varied approaches to petitioner. As was explained in *Sherman,* where entrapment was found as a matter of law, "the Government [may not] pla[y] on the weaknesses of an innocent party and beguil[e] him into committing crimes which he otherwise would not have attempted."

When the Government's quest for convictions leads to the apprehension of an otherwise law-abiding citizen who, if left to his own devices, likely would have never run afoul of the law, the courts should intervene.

Because we conclude that this is such a case and that the prosecution failed, as a matter of law, to adduce evidence to support the jury verdict that petitioner was predisposed, independent of the Government's acts and beyond a reasonable doubt, to violate the law by receiving child pornography through the mails, we reverse the Court of Appeals' judgment affirming the conviction of Keith Jacobson.

It is so ordered.

■ JUSTICE O'CONNOR, with whom THE CHIEF JUSTICE and JUSTICE KENNEDY join, and with whom JUSTICE SCALIA joins except as to Part II, dissenting.

Keith Jacobson was offered only two opportunities to buy child pornography through the mail. Both times, he ordered. Both times, he asked for opportunities to buy more. He needed no Government agent to coax, threaten, or persuade him; no one played on his sympathies, friendship, or suggested that his committing the crime would further a greater good. In fact, no Government agent even contacted him face-to-face. The Government contends that from the enthusiasm with which Mr. Jacobson responded to the chance to commit a crime, a reasonable jury could permissibly infer beyond a reasonable doubt that he was predisposed to commit the crime. I agree.

The first time the Government sent Mr. Jacobson a catalog of illegal materials, he ordered a set of photographs advertised as picturing "young boys in sex action fun." He enclosed the following note with his order: "I received your brochure and decided to place an order. If I like your product, I will order more later." For reasons undisclosed in the record, Mr. Jacobson's order was never delivered.

The second time the Government sent a catalog of illegal materials, Mr. Jacobson ordered a magazine called "Boys Who Love Boys," described as: "11 year old and 14 year old boys get it on in every way possible. Oral, anal sex and heavy masturbation. If you love boys, you will be delighted with this." Along with his order, Mr. Jacobson sent the following note: "Will order other items later. I want to be discreet in order to protect you and me."

Government agents admittedly did not offer Mr. Jacobson the chance to buy child pornography right away. Instead, they first sent questionnaires in order to make sure that he was generally interested in the subject matter. Indeed, a "cold call" in such a business would not only risk rebuff and suspicion, but might also shock and offend the uninitiated, or expose minors to suggestive materials. Mr. Jacobson's responses to the questionnaires gave the investigators reason to think he would be interested in photographs depicting preteen sex.

I believe the Court fails to acknowledge the reasonableness of the jury's inference from the evidence, redefines "predisposition," and introduces a new requirement that Government sting operations have a reasonable suspicion of illegal activity before contacting a suspect.

I

This Court has held previously that a defendant's predisposition is to be assessed as of the time the Government agent first suggested the crime, not when the Government agent first became involved. *Sherman v. United States,* (1958). Until the Government actually makes a suggestion of criminal conduct, it could not be said to have "implant[ed] in the mind of an innocent person the disposition to commit the alleged offense and induce its commission...." *Sorrells v. United States,* (1932). Even in *Sherman v. United States,* in which the Court held that the defendant had been entrapped as a matter of law, the Government agent had repeatedly and unsuccessfully coaxed the defendant to buy drugs, ultimately succeeding only by playing on the defendant's sympathy. The Court found lack of predisposition based on the Government's numerous unsuccessful attempts to induce the crime, not on the basis of preliminary contacts with the defendant.

Today, the Court holds that Government conduct may be considered to create a predisposition to commit a crime, even before any Government action to inductee commission of the crime. In my view, this holding changes entrapment doctrine. Generally, the inquiry is whether a suspect is predisposed before the Government induces the commission of the crime, not before the Government makes initial contact with him. There is no dispute here that the Government's questionnaires and letters were not sufficient to establish inducement; they did not even suggest that Mr. Jacobson should engage in any illegal activity. If all the Government had done was to send these materials, Mr. Jacobson's entrapment defense would fail. Yet the Court holds that the Government must prove not only that a suspect was predisposed to commit the crime before the opportunity to commit it arose, but also before the Government came on the scene.

The rule that preliminary Government contact can create a predisposition has the potential to be misread by lower courts as well as criminal investigators as requiring that the Government must have sufficient evidence of a defendant's predisposition *before it ever seeks to contact him.* Surely the Court cannot intend to impose such a requirement, for it would mean that the Government must have a reasonable suspicion of criminal activity before it begins an investigation, a condition that we have never before imposed. The Court denies that its new rule will affect run-of-the-mill sting operations, and one hopes that it means what it says. Nonetheless, after this case, every defendant will claim that something the Government agent did before soliciting the crime "created" a predisposition that was not there before. For example, a bribe taker will claim that the description of the amount of money available was so enticing that it implanted a disposition to accept the bribe later offered. A drug buyer will claim that the description of the drug's purity and effects was so tempting that it created the urge to try it for the first time. In short, the Court's opinion could be read to prohibit the Government from advertising the seductions of criminal activity as part of its sting operation, for fear of creating a predisposition in its suspects. That limitation would be especially likely to hamper sting operations such as this one, which mimic the advertising done by genuine purveyors of pornography. No doubt the Court would protest that its opinion does not stand for so broad a proposition, but the apparent lack of a principled basis for distinguishing these scenarios exposes a flaw in the more limited rule the Court today adopts.

The Court's rule is all the more troubling because it does not distinguish between Government conduct that merely highlights the temptation of the crime itself, and Government conduct that threatens, coerces, or leads a suspect to commit a crime in order to fulfill some other obligation. For example, in *Sorrells,* the Government agent repeatedly asked for illegal liquor, coaxing the defendant to accede on the ground that "one former war buddy would get liquor for another." In *Sherman,* the Government agent played on the defendant's sympathies, pretending to be going through drug withdrawal and begging the defendant to relieve his distress by helping him buy drugs.

The Government conduct in this case is not comparable. While the Court states that the Government "exerted substantial pressure on petitioner to obtain and read such material as part of a fight against censorship and the infringement of individual rights," one looks at the record in vain for evidence of such "substantial pressure." The most one finds is letters advocating legislative action to liberalize obscenity laws, letters which could easily be ignored or thrown away. Much later, the Government sent separate mailings of catalogs of illegal materials. Nowhere did the Government suggest that the proceeds of the sale of the illegal materials would be used to support legislative reforms. While one of the HINT letters suggested that lobbying efforts would be funded by sales from a catalog, Record, the catalogs actually sent, nearly a year later, were from different fictitious entities (Produit Outaouais and Far Eastern Trading Company), and gave no suggestion that money would be used for any political purposes. Nor did the Government claim to be organizing a civil disobedience movement, which would protest the pornography laws by breaking them. Contrary to the gloss given the evidence by the Court, the Government's suggestions of illegality may also have made buyers beware, and increased the mystique of the materials offered: "[for those of you who have enjoyed youthful material . . . we have devised a method of getting these to you without prying eyes of U.S. Customs seizing your mail.]" Mr. Jacobson's curiosity to see what

" 'all the trouble and the hysteria' " was about, is certainly susceptible of more than one interpretation. And it is the jury that is charged with the obligation of interpreting it. In sum, the Court fails to construe the evidence in the light most favorable to the Government, and fails to draw all reasonable inferences in the Government's favor. It was surely reasonable for the jury to infer that Mr. Jacobson was predisposed beyond a reasonable doubt, even if other inferences from the evidence were also possible.

II

The second puzzling thing about the Court's opinion is its redefinition of predisposition. The Court acknowledges that "[p]etitioner's responses to the many communications prior to the ultimate criminal act were ... indicative of certain personal inclinations, including a predisposition to view photographs of preteen sex...." If true, this should have settled the matter; Mr. Jacobson was predisposed to engage in the illegal conduct. Yet, the Court concludes, "petitioner's responses hardly support an inference that he would commit the crime of receiving child pornography through the mails."

The Court seems to add something new to the burden of proving predisposition. Not only must the Government show that a defendant was predisposed to engage in the illegal conduct, here, receiving photographs of minors engaged in sex, but also that the defendant was predisposed to break the law knowingly in order to do so. The statute violated here, however, does not require proof of specific intent to break the law; it requires only knowing receipt of visual depictions produced by using minors engaged in sexually explicit conduct. See 18 U.S.C. § 2252(a)(2). Under the Court's analysis, however, the Government must prove *more* to show predisposition than it need prove in order to convict.

The Court ignores the judgment of Congress that specific intent is not an element of the crime of receiving sexually explicit photographs of minors. The elements of predisposition should track the elements of the crime. The predisposition requirement is meant to eliminate the entrapment defense for those defendants who would have committed the crime anyway, even absent Government inducement. Because a defendant might very well be convicted of the crime here absent Government inducement even though he did not know his conduct was illegal, a specific intent requirement does little to distinguish between those who would commit the crime without the inducement and those who would not. In sum, although the fact that Mr. Jacobson's purchases of *Bare Boys I* and *Bare Boys II* were legal at the time may have some relevance to the question of predisposition, it is not, as the Court suggests, dispositive.

It was, however, the jury's task, as the conscience of the community, to decide whether or not Mr. Jacobson was a willing participant in the criminal activity here or an innocent dupe. The jury is the traditional "defense against arbitrary law enforcement." *Duncan v. Louisiana,* (1968). There is no dispute that the jury in this case was fully and accurately instructed on the law of entrapment, and nonetheless found Mr. Jacobson guilty. Because I believe there was sufficient evidence to uphold the jury's verdict, I respectfully dissent.

NOTES

1. *Before Jacobson.* Traditionally entrapment is a mental state defense like insanity or intoxication. See Rebecca Roiphe, "The Serpent Beguiled Me: A History of the Entrapment Defense," 33 Seton Hall L. Rev. 257 (2003). For example, an accused may admit to delivering narcotics, but claim to have done so not with the intent to commit a crime, but rather to put an end to endlessly repeated requests for narcotics from an undercover officer. People of the Territory of Guam v. Teixeira, 859 F.2d 120 (9th Cir.1988), contains a good summary of entrapment doctrine:

> Because under this subjective theory of entrapment the success of the defense depends upon a defendant's status as "otherwise innocent," a two-step test is employed in jurisdictions adopting this approach. The court first inquires as to whether there has been "inducement" by a government agent; if there has, the burden shifts to the government to show that the defendant was "predisposed" to commit the crime. Because the question of predisposition is actually one of intent and therefore bears upon the guilt or innocence of the accused, the issue is for the jury "as part of its function of determining the guilt or innocence of the accused." *Sherman.*

a. *Inducements:* In Sherman v. United States, 356 U.S. 369, 78 S.Ct. 819(1958), the Court found entrapment when an informer met Sherman at a doctor's office where both were being treated for narcotics addiction. The two met several times and had become acquainted and discussed the problems of addiction. Eventually the informer said he was not responding to treatment and required narcotics. Sherman first refused and then tried to avoid the issue but, after several repeated requests, each predicated on the claim that the informer was suffering, Sherman agreed to get narcotics and share them with the informer. He did this on several occasions and the informer paid his share of the cost. After several such times, the informer told police he had a seller for them.

The decision in *Sherman* is not typical. Entrapment defenses are presented at trial and usually rejected by triers of fact. On appeal a guilty verdict of the judge or jury is almost always sustained even when there was considerable evidence of inducement.

b. *Predisposition:* Even when the government's inducements for illegal acts are compelling, entrapment will not occur if the accused was already predisposed to commit the crime. Predisposition may be proved by showing that the accused had prior convictions for similar offenses, that he committed or indicated willingness to commit a similar, but uncharged, offense, that he displayed some criminal expertise in carrying out the offense, that he was readily able to commit the offense, i.e., the accused had quick access to a quantity of illegal drugs and so forth.

Under *traditional* entrapment rules, the police do not have to show any evidence of predisposition in order to approach an individual to ask him, say, to sell narcotics or accept a wager. Kadis v. United States, 373 F.2d 370 (1st Cir.1967). The government, under this view, does not need to disprove entrapment. United States v. DeVore, 423 F.2d 1069 (4th Cir.1970), cert. denied, 402 U.S. 950, 91 S.Ct. 1604 (1971).

Predisposition is considered in connection with inducement to arrive at a judgment of whether there was entrapment. United States v. Tobias, 662 F.2d 381 (5th Cir.1981), where the DEA established a chemical supply company and placed advertisements in High Times Magazine to sell various chemicals and equipment used in the manufacture of illegal drugs. Tobias requested and received more information from the company. Tobias then telephoned the company on numerous occasions to order supplies and to check on his orders. Within one month of placing his first order, Tobias called the company to cancel his orders because he had discovered he did not possess the knowledge or the equipment to manufacture cocaine. Before he could cancel his orders, however, a DEA agent asked him what he was trying to do. Tobias admitted his desire to manufacture cocaine and related his difficulties in trying to do so. The agent pretended to sympathize with Tobias, and stated that he too found cocaine difficult to manufacture. In response, Tobias stated that he was not interested in manufacturing cocaine per se, but that he just wanted to make some money. The agent then suggested that a number of drugs were easier to manufacture than cocaine, including amphetamines and phencyclidine (PCP). The agent explained that making PCP was as easy as "baking a cake" and offered to send Tobias everything he would need to make PCP for $500. Tobias agreed. After receiving the chemicals, Tobias called the company thirteen times for advice on how to make PCP. [His claim of entrapment was rejected because of his predisposition to commit the offense evidenced by his answering the advertisement, his expressed desire to make money, and the fact that he placed all of the thirteen calls to DEA on his own initiative.]

As the dissent in *Jacobson* points out, the *Jacobson* majority seems to take a different approach to predisposition than in earlier cases. Would *Tobias* be decided differently today?

2. *After Jacobson*. The lower courts have been working out new approaches to entrapment after *Jacobson*:

a. *"Positional"* Predisposition:

On the strength of *Jacobson,* a sharply divided en banc Court of Appeals reversed a money laundering conviction in United States v. Hollingsworth, 27 F.3d 1196, 1198 (7th Cir.1994) (en banc) (6–5). In *Hollingsworth,* an orthodontist and farmer in Arkansas were convicted of laundering money for what turned out to be a government agent. The venture began when the two defendants (Hollingsworth and Pickard) started an international banking business by buying two foreign banking licenses. Although they advertised, the two never found any customers. Finally they decided to sell one of the banking licenses and advertised it in *U.S.A. Today*. A U.S. customs agent saw the ad and decided to investigate the defendants' activities. During their first negotiations, the agent explained that his organization had a lot of cash and needed to deposit it somewhere. Defendant Pickard pointed out that the money could be deposited abroad, or divided into lots of $10,000 and deposited in the U.S. Pickard later retracted the suggestion of depositing the cash abroad, remarking that that would violate the law. (There was no evidence Pickard knew his other suggestion was also illegal). Pickard asked the agent to assure him that the cash was not from drug sales and that the agent was not a federal agent or informer. In another conversation, Pickard asked the agent whether he wanted them to "clean and polish" funds or for "extended services." Later, Pickard indicated he was interested only in a long-term banking relationship.

Nearly six months after the last unfruitful contact, at a time when the defendant's "business" was still customerless and on the verge of collapsing, the agent called Pickard again. He said he was "overwhelmed" and arranged to meet Pickard with $20,000 in sting money. The agent explained the money was from gun smuggling into South Africa. Pickard was to arrange a wire transfer of $20,000 to the agent's bank account, and then take possession of the cash for a fee of $2,405. Subsequent transactions of this sort, one carried out by Hollingsworth, brought the total transferred to $200,000.Finally, the defendants were arrested. When arrested, they were carrying false-name passports issued by the mythical "Dominion of Melchizedek." They had no other customers.

Judge Posner, writing for the majority, said that the circuits had been "drifting" toward the view that predisposition was shown by a "willingness" to commit the crime, but *Jacobson* now requires something more:

> Predisposition is not a purely mental state, the state of being willing to swallow the government's bait.... The defendant must be so situated by reason of previous training or experience or occupation or acquaintances that it is likely that if the government had not induced him to commit the crime some criminal would have done so; only then does a sting or other arranged crime take a dangerous person out of circulation. A public official is in a position to take bribes; a drug addict to deal drugs; a gun dealer to engage in illegal gun sales. For these and other traditional targets of stings all that must be shown to establish predisposition and thus defeat the defense of entrapment is willingness to violate the law without extraordinary inducements; ability can be presumed. It is different when the defendant is not in a position without the government's help to become involved in illegal activity. *Id.* at 1199.

Posner based his analysis on the language in *Jacobson* that entrapment doctrine protected against "the apprehension of an otherwise law-abiding citizen who, if left to his own devices, likely would have never run afoul of the law." The dissenters, Judges Coffey, Easterbrook, Ripple, Bauer, and Kanne, argued that Posner had read too much into the *Jacobson* opinion. Instead, they emphasized the defendants' lack of reluctance to engage in the money laundering, and pointed to Pickard's familiarity with money laundering terminology, his caution as to the agent's identity but lack of reservation about the illegality of the conduct, and the fact that Pickard often initiated contact with the agent. The entrapment doctrine should not protect the willing, though inept or disorganized criminal, regardless of his harmlessness, the dissent argued. Judge Ripple also disagreed with the majority's holding that Hollingsworth, who had not been directly contacted by the government agent but had heard of the scheme only through Pickard, could still take advantage of the entrapment doctrine.

The Circuits are split as to whether an otherwise-eager offender can claim entrapment on the ground that he or she did not have the knowledge or materials with which to commit the crime prior to the government's involvement, that is, he lacked "positional" predisposition. See United States v. Knox, 112 F.3d 802 (5th Cir.1997), cert. denied Knox v. United States, 522 U.S. 1022, 118 S.Ct. 616 (1997) A05 but issue mooted sub. nom. United States v. Brace, 145 F.3d 247 (5th Cir. 1998) cert. denied 525 U.S. 973, 119 S.Ct. 426 (1998) (following *Hollingsworth* in requiring positional predisposition in a case in which a church pastor had agreed with government agents to launder money; the court noted that the government had put forward no evidence that the naive pastor would have been approached by any "real" money launderers or that any real money launderers have ever used churches) and United States v. Thickstun, 110 F.3d 1394 (9th Cir.1997) (not following *Hollingsworth*: "We read *Jacobson* not as creating a requirement of positional readiness but as applying settled entrapment law....) It was not necessary for the court to expand the entrapment defense, nor is there language in the opinion indicating that it did so." While our reading conflicts with that of the Seventh Circuit in *Hollingsworth*, it accords with then-Judge Breyer's opinion in United States v. Gendron, 18 F.3d 955, 963 (1st Cir.1994), cert. denied 513 U.S. 1051, 115 S.Ct. 654 (1994). (Having concluded that *Jacobson* does not require "positional" predisposition, we decline to adopt such a requirement. A person's ability to commit a crime may illustrate her predisposition to do so, but should not become a separate element to be proven.... Such a rule would be especially problematic in bribery cases. A person is never "positionally" able to bribe a public official without cooperation from that official). See also United States v. Squillacote,

221 F.3d 542 (4th Cir.) (criticizing *Hollingsworth* and setting forth conflicting authorities) cert. denied, 532 U.S. 971, 121 S.Ct. 1601 (2001).

b. *Inducement Creates Predisposition*: *Jacobson* has also been read as meaning that if the government's inducements are too attractive, the inducement itself may create a predisposition. See United States v. Sandoval, 20 F.3d 134 (5th Cir.1994) (agent asked the target ten times for a bribe before the target reluctantly acceded); United States v. Gendron, 18 F.3d 955 (1st Cir.1994), cert. denied 513 U.S. 1051, 115 S.Ct. 654 (1994) (government may not confront target with circumstances different from the ordinary or typical circumstances of a private inducement.) See also, United States v. Evans, 924 F.2d 714 (7th Cir.1991) ("A person who takes advantage of an ordinary opportunity to commit criminal acts" not an extraordinary opportunity, the sort of thing that might entice an otherwise law-abiding person "is not entrapped.")

3. *State Law*. Some jurisdictions follow the "objective" approach favored by Justice Stewart in his dissent *in Russell* and do not consider the question of predisposition. See People v. Barraza, 23 Cal.3d 675, 153 Cal.Rptr. 459, 591 P.2d 947 (1979); [limited by People v. Watson, 990 P.2d 1031, 22 Cal.4th, 220 (2000)]; People v. Juillet, 439 Mich. 34, 475 N.W.2d 786 (1991).

Some states use a combination of "objective" and "subjective" tests. New Jersey has, by statute, enacted a mixed entrapment defense. For entrapment to occur, police actions must exceed permissible limits *and* the accused must not be predisposed to commit the crime. The accused must prove both of these propositions. State v. Rockholt, 96 N.J. 570, 476 A.2d 1236 (1984). See also, England v. State, 887 S.W.2d 902 (Tex.Crim.App.1994) (en banc).

In State v. Grilli, 304 Minn. 80, 230 N.W.2d 445 (1975), the Minnesota Supreme Court declared that the accused should have the option, in a jury trial, of having either the judge or the jury decide the entrapment issue. In a bifurcated proceeding, the accused would present evidence to the judge alone on the entrapment issue. The jury would hear evidence related to whether the accused did the acts alleged.

4. *Inconsistent Defenses*. May entrapment be interposed as a defense in a case where the defendant denies having committed the act charged against him or her?

In California the accused may assert entrapment and at the same time deny the acts charged (People v. Perez, 62 Cal.2d 769, 44 Cal.Rptr. 326, 401 P.2d 934 (1965)), but the accused bears the burden of proving entrapment. People v. Moran, 1 Cal.3d 755, 83 Cal.Rptr. 411, 463 P.2d 763 (1970).

In federal cases a defendant may raise entrapment even if he denies committing the crime. Mathews v. United States, 485 U.S. 58, 108 S.Ct. 883 (1988) (whenever there is sufficient evidence from which a reasonable jury could find entrapment). See United States v. Schake, 57 Fed.Appx. 523 (3d Cir.2003) (defendant seeking habeas relief alleged that his counsel was incompetent for failing to advise him of the availability of inconsistent defenses. The court did not reach the issue, since they found no prejudice to defendant) The rationale as expressed in United States v. Demma, 523 F.2d 981 (9th Cir.1975) (en banc):

> "It is well established that a defendant in a criminal prosecution may assert inconsistent defenses. The rule in favor of inconsistent defenses reflects the belief of modern criminal jurisprudence that a criminal defendant should be accorded every reasonable protection in defending himself against governmental prosecution....

* * *

"Of course, it is very unlikely that the defendant will be able to prove entrapment without testifying and, in the course of testifying, without admitting that he did the acts charged. Unless the Government's case-in-chief discloses entrapment as a matter of law (an unusual phenomenon), the defendant must come forward with evidence of his non-predisposition and of governmental inducement. A defendant can rarely produce such evidence without taking the stand—as did both defendants in the case at bar—and admitting that he did the acts to which the Government's witnesses attested. When he takes the stand,the defendant forfeits his right to remain silent, subjects himself to all the rigors of cross-examination, including impeachment, and exposes himself to prosecution for perjury. Inconsistent testimony by the defendant seriously impairs and potentially destroys his credibility. While we hold that a defendant may both deny the acts and other elements necessary to constitute the crime charged and at the same time claim entrapment, the high risks to him make it unlikely as a strategic matter that he will choose to do so."

In dissent in *Mathews,* Justice White observed "It is fundamentally inconsistent with [the search for truth] to permit a defendant to win acquittal on a rationale which he states, under oath, to be false," *Mathews* reflects a reading of federal law. States are free to reject it and some have. Wilson v. State, 577 So.2d 1300 (Fla.1991).

5. *Perjury Entrapment?* May a prosecutor call a witness before a grand jury primarily motivated by the hope that the witness will commit perjury? Suppose the prosecutor possesses a secretly-made tape recording of a conversation between an informer and the witness. Can he call the witness before the grand jury hoping that the witness will open himself to a perjury indictment by denying that the conversation occurred? Is there a legitimate investigative purpose for the inquiry if the prosecutor already has positive proof that the conversation occurred? Can the prosecutor justify such an inquiry by reference to the possibility that the witness may admit the conversation and go on to provide additional useful information? What legitimate investigative purpose is served by not disclosing to the witness the existence of the recording? For one view rejecting the entrapment claim, see United States v. Nickels, 502 F.2d 1173 (7th Cir.), cert. denied, 426 U.S. 911, 96 S.Ct. 2237 (1976) and United States v. Mandujano, 425 U.S. 564, 96 S.Ct. 1768 (1976). See Gershman, The Perjury Trap, 129 U.Pa.L.Rev. 624 (1981).

6. *Derivative Entrapment?* If the police use overreaching tactics to induce A to commit a crime, and if A then enlists the help of B to engage in the criminal activity, ordinarily B, who has not been entrapped by the authorities, will not be able to vicariously assert the defense of entrapment. Thus a principal could have an entrapment defense while her accessory might not.

A different issue arises when undercover agents are dealing with A where A's allegedly overreaching tactics induce B to participate in the criminal activities. The question is whether B can complain about the tactics of the "unwitting" middleman A. Usually the term used is "derivative entrapment." The defense of derivative entrapment is not recognized by a majority of American jurisdictions. See, e.g., United States v. Marren, 890 F.2d 924 (7th Cir.1989); People v. Wielgos, 142 Ill.2d 133, 154 Ill.Dec. 640, 568 N.E.2d 861 (1991). These cases are in line with the general proposition that no defense lies when the inducements, no matter how outrageous, are made by a private citizen unless the citizen is an informer or other agent of the police. But some courts do recognize derivative entrapment, invoking agency principles even when the inducing individual is not consciously working as an agent of the police. See Davis v. State, 570 So.2d 791 (Ala.Crim.App.1990) (noting a split among federal courts on the issue of the unwitting agent and derivative entrapment); United States v. Washington, 106 F.3d 983 (D.C.Cir.1997) (full discussion of the question, noting splits of opinion).

7. *Sentencing Entrapment?* Now that sentences for drug and money crimes under the federal sentencing guidelines depend greatly on the amounts involved, both the sentencing commission and the courts have recognized the possibility of "sentencing entrapment" in which undercover agents involved in sting operations try to manipulate the terms of the illicit bargain in order to increase the defendant's ultimate sentence. Courts have distinguished "sentencing entrapment" from "sentence manipulation," to parallel the distinction between the entrapment defense and the defense of outrageous governmental conduct, infra. See discussion in United States v. Okey, 47 F.3d 238 (7th Cir.1995).

Sentencing entrapment has been defined as "outrageous government conduct [which] overcomes the will of an individual predisposed only to dealing in small quantities for the purpose of increasing the amount of drugs." United States v. Lenfesty, 923 F.2d 1293, 1300 (8th Cir.1991). The focus of an argument of sentencing entrapment is that the defendant was not predisposed to get involved in a serious crime, but only a more minor crime. See also Leech v. Oklahoma, 66 P.3d 987, 2003 OK CR4 (2003) (Okl.Crim.App.2003) (Chapel, J. dissenting) and authorities cited therein.

The "outrageous government conduct" argument, on the other hand, relies not on the defendant's lack of predisposition, but on the Court's statement in United States v. Russell that "we may some day be presented with a situation in which the conduct of law enforcement agents is so outrageous that due process principles would absolutely bar the government from invoking judicial processes to obtain a conviction," 411 U.S. 423, 93 S.Ct. 1637 (1973). Sentence manipulation occurs when the government engages in improper or unsavory conduct designed to increase a defendant's sentence. See United States v. Cannon, 886 F.Supp. 705 (D.N.D.1995), reversed 88 F.3d 1495 (8th Cir.1996) (district court concerned that agents in a sting operation brought along a machine gun to give to defendants in addition to the handguns they asked to buy in order to raise their sentence by 25 years; circuit court held no due process violation occurred with regard to machine guns). Some courts link sentence manipulation to due process, holding that a manipulation claim could only justify a reduced sentence when there is "outrageous government conduct that offends due process." United States v. Jones, 18 F.3d 1145, 1153 (4th Cir.1994). Other courts, however, have indicated that sentence manipulation may arise from conduct which does not rise to the level of offending due process. United States v. Connell, 960 F.2d 191, 194 (1st Cir.1992).

From 1993 on, the Sentencing Commission partly acknowledged the unfairness of government undercover operations that seek to encourage defendants to commit more serious crimes. The Commission suggested that district courts might give less severe sentences than the Sentencing Guidelines prescribe in reverse sting operations in which the government sets an artificially low price for a controlled substance, thereby inducing the defendant to purchase a significantly greater quantity. U.S.S.G. § 2D1.1, comment (n. 12) (Nov. 2006).

The circuits are split as to whether to recognize entrapment-type arguments at sentencing, though the new Guidelines commentary seems to be swaying some circuits to favor some version of the theory. Compare United States v. Brewster, 1 F.3d 51 (1st Cir.1993) (recognizing such a claim might be made, but no sentence manipulation or entrapment where undercover agent's statement that he was buying a gun to use in a drug operation (thereby increasing the defendant's sentence) was made at the outset of the negotiations), United States v. Calva, 979 F.2d 119, 122–23 (8th Cir.1992) (also recognizing the potential claim, but rejecting it on the facts; government can legitimately make more than one drug buy from defendant in order to probe the organization and meet the suppliers), with United States v. Williams, 954 F.2d 668, 673 (11th Cir.1992) (refusing to recognize such a claim as a matter of law, even where government agents sold marijuana at half market price and delivered it without requiring payment). The Ninth Circuit has actually reduced a defendant's sentence on this ground. United States v. Staufer, 38 F.3d 1103, 1108 (9th Cir.1994) (finding sentencing entrapment where a defendant was persuaded to sell twice the LSD he had initially agreed to sell); United States v. McClelland, 72 F.3d 717 (9th Cir.1995) (upholding district court's downward departure from the federal sentencing guideline for murder-for-hire, on the grounds of imperfect entrapment). Defendant had hired a government informant to kill his wife. When the defendant began to get cold feet ("The thing is, what's startin' to bother me is the fact that, I don't know if ICI don't know if I like the idea, that I'm setting myself up as God"), the informant pushed him repeatedly to ("stand in the tracks.")

The Eighth Circuit has clarified that a claim of sentencing entrapment is focused on defendant's lack of predisposition and does not require a showing of outrageous government conduct. Where government informants repeatedly urged an unwilling defendant to supply crack cocaine rather than powder cocaine in order to boost his guideline sentence, the district court erred in refusing to consider a sentencing entrapment theory. United States v. Searcy, 233 F.3d 1096 (8th Cir. 2000).

See Daniel L. Abelson (Comment), "Sentencing Entrapment: An Overview and Analysis," 86 Marq. L. Rev. 773 (2003).

8. *Apprendi and Sentence Entrapment Claims?* In light of the holding in Apprendi v. New Jersey, 530 U.S. 466, 120 S.Ct. 2348 (2000), would the defendant have the right to have a jury decide the issue of sentence entrapment?

9. *"Imperfect" Entrapment?* If a defendant raises a claim of entrapment that is subsequently rejected, may it form the basis for a lower sentence nonetheless? In United States v. Takai, the Court found imperfect entrapment to be a proper factor to consider for a downward departure in sentence under the Federal Sentencing Guidelines. 941 F.2d 738 (9th Cir.1991). See Joseph M. Meadows, "The Koon Trap: Why Imperfect Entrapment Fails to Justify Departure from the Federal Sentencing Guidelines," 77 Ind. L. J. 341 (2002).

10. *Entrapment and Impossibility Defenses?* Some defendants have tried to analogize entrapment to the tradition impossibility defense. In *Recio*, police intercepted a truck loaded with drugs and then set up a sting. After the defendants took delivery of the truck, they were arrested. They argued their convictions should be overturned because they were charged with conspiracy and there was no evidence that they joined the criminal enterprise until after the government seized the drugs. Rejecting the Ninth Circuit approach to conspiracy doctrine, the Court refused to import entrapment analysis into the realm of the impossibility defense. United States v. Recio, et al., 537 U.S. 270, 123 S.Ct. 819 (2003).

11. *Cyber-entrapment?* Several popular press commentators have questioned whether officers are entrapping innocent folks when they enter chat rooms, pretending to be young children, in an effort to locate and arrest those who would prey on children to satisfy their sexual desires. Critics argue that in the separateness of cyber-space, it is unlikely that a person would act upon these statements. Jon Frank, "Cybercops Fuel Debate Over Privacy on Internet; to Fight Sex Crimes, Undercover Police Impersonate Children," The VirginianBPilot (Norfolk, Va.) Page A1, January 15, 2003. Allan Lengel, "Agents Wade in Filth to Find Predators:

Going After Online Pedophiles Not for the Squeamish, FBI Finds," The Washington Post, Metro, Page -01, January 20, 2003.

* * *

C. DUE PROCESS—"WAS THE POLICE CONDUCT 'OUTRAGEOUS' "?

Hampton v. United States

Supreme Court of the United States, 1976.
425 U.S. 484, 96 S.Ct. 1646.

■ MR. JUSTICE REHNQUIST announced the judgment of the Court in an opinion in which THE CHIEF JUSTICE and MR. JUSTICE WHITE join.

This case presents the question of whether a defendant may be convicted for the sale of contraband which he procured from a government informer or agent. The Court of Appeals for the Eighth Circuit held he could be, and we agree.

I

* * *

... The case arose from two sales of heroin by petitioner to agents of the Federal Drug Enforcement Administration (DEA) in St. Louis on February 25 and 26, 1974. The sales were arranged by one Hutton, who was a pool-playing acquaintance of petitioner at the Pud bar in St. Louis and also a DEA informant.

According to the Government's witnesses, in late February 1974, Hutton and petitioner were shooting pool at the Pud when petitioner, after observing "track" (needle) marks on Hutton's arms told Hutton that he needed money and knew where he could get some heroin. Hutton responded that he could find a buyer and petitioner suggested that he "get in touch with those people." Hutton then called DEA agent Terry Sawyer and arranged a sale for 10 p.m. on February 25.

At the appointed time, Hutton and petitioner went to a pre-arranged meeting place and were met by Agent Sawyer and DEA Agent McDowell, posing as narcotics dealers. Petitioner produced a tinfoil packet from his cap and turned it over to the agents who tested it, pronounced it "okay," and negotiated a price of $145 which was paid to petitioner. Before they parted, petitioner told Sawyer that he could obtain larger quantities of heroin and gave Sawyer a phone number where he could be reached.

The next day Sawyer called petitioner and arranged for another "buy" that afternoon. Petitioner got Hutton to go along and they met the agents again near where they had been the previous night.

They all entered the agents' car, and petitioner again produced a tinfoil packet from his cap. The agents again field-tested it and pronounced it satisfactory. Petitioner then asked for $500 which Agent Sawyer said he would get from the trunk. Sawyer got out and opened the trunk which was a signal to other agents to move in and arrest petitioner, which they did.

Petitioner's version of events was quite different. According to him, in response to petitioner's statement that he was short of cash, Hutton said that he had a friend who was a pharmacist who could produce a non-narcotic counterfeit drug which would give the same reaction as heroin. Hutton proposed selling this drug to gullible acquaintances who would be led to believe they were buying heroin. Petitioner testified that they successfully duped one buyer with this fake drug and that the sale which led to the arrest was solicited by petitioner in an effort to profit further from this ploy.

Petitioner contended that he neither intended to sell, nor knew that he was dealing in heroin and that all of the drugs he sold were supplied by Hutton. His account was at least partially disbelieved by the jury which was instructed that in order to convict petitioner they had to find that the Government proved "that the defendant knowingly did an act which the law forbids, purposely intending to violate the law." Thus the guilty verdict necessarily implies that the jury rejected petitioner's claim that he did not know the substance was heroin, and petitioner himself admitted both soliciting and carrying out sales. The only relevance of his version of the facts, then, lies in his having requested an instruction embodying that version. He did not request a standard entrapment instruction but he did request the following:

> "The defendant asserts that he was the victim of entrapment as to the crimes charged in the indictment.
>
> "If you find that the defendant's sales of narcotics were sales of narcotics supplied to him by an informer in the employ of or acting on behalf of the government, then you must acquit the defendant because the law as a matter of policy forbids his conviction in such a case.
>
> "Furthermore, under this particular defense, you need not consider the predisposition of the defendant to commit the offense charged, because if the governmental involvement through its informer reached the point that I have just defined in your own minds, then the predisposition of the defendant would not matter."

The trial court refused the instruction....

II

In United States v. Russell, 411 U.S. 423, 93 S.Ct. 1637 (1973), we held that the statutory defense of entrapment was not available where it was conceded that a government agent supplied a necessary ingredient in the manufacture of an illicit drug. We reaffirmed the principle of Sorrells v. United States, 287 U.S. 435, 53 S.Ct. 210 (1932) and Sherman v. United States, 356 U.S. 369; 78 S. Ct. 819 (1958), that the entrapment defense "focus[es] on the intent or predisposition of the defendant to commit the crime," ... rather than upon the conduct of the Government's agents. We ruled out the possibility that the defense of entrapment could ever be based upon governmental misconduct in a case, such as this one, where the predisposition of the defendant to commit the crime was established.

... In view of these holdings, petitioner correctly recognizes that his case does not qualify as one involving "entrapment" at all. He instead relies on the language in *Russell* that "we may some day be presented with a situation in which the conduct of law enforcement agents is so outrageous that due process principles would absolutely bar the government from invoking judicial processes to obtain a conviction. . . . ["]

In urging that this case involves a violation of his due process rights, petitioner misapprehends the meaning of the quoted language in *Russell*, supra. Admittedly petitioner's case is different from Russell's but the difference is one of degree, not of kind. In *Russell* the ingredient supplied by the government agent was a legal drug which the defendants demonstrably could have obtained from other sources besides the Government. Here the drug which the government informant allegedly supplied to petitioner was both illegal and constituted the *corpus delicti* for the sale of which the petitioner was convicted. The Government obviously played a more significant role in enabling petitioner to sell contraband in this case than it did *in Russell.*

But in each case the Government agents were acting in concert with the defendant, and in each case either the jury found or the defendant conceded that he was predisposed to commit the crime for which he was convicted. The remedy of the criminal defendant with respect to the acts of Government agents, which, far from being resisted, are encouraged by him, lies solely in the defense of entrapment. But, as noted, petitioner's conceded predisposition rendered this defense unavailable to him.

* * *

The limitations of the Due Process Clause of the Fifth Amendment come into play only when the Government activity in question violates some protected right of the *defendant*. Here, as we have noted, the police, the Government informant, and the defendant acted in concert with one another. If the result of the governmental activity is to "implant in the mind of an innocent person the disposition to commit the alleged offense and induce its commission . . . ," . . . the defendant is protected by the defense of entrapment. If the police engage in illegal activity in concert with a defendant beyond the scope of their duties the remedy lies, not in freeing the equally culpable defendant, but in prosecuting the police under the applicable provisions of state or federal law. . . . But the police conduct here no more deprived defendant of any right secured to him by the United States Constitution than did the police conduct in *Russell* deprive Russell of any rights.

Affirmed.

■ MR. JUSTICE POWELL, with whom MR. JUSTICE BLACKMUN joins, concurring in the judgment.

... I concur in the judgment of the Court and much of the plurality opinion directed specifically to Hampton's contention. I am not able to join the remainder of the plurality opinion, as it would unnecessarily reach and decide difficult questions not before us.

In discussing Hampton's due process contention, it enunciates a *per se* rule:

> "[In *Russell,*] [w]e ruled out the possibility that the defense of entrapment could *ever* be based upon governmental misconduct in a case, such as this one, where the predisposition of the defendant to commit the crime was established."
>
> * * *
>
> "The remedy of the criminal defendant with respect to the acts of Government agents, which ... are encouraged by him, lies *solely* in the defense of entrapment."

The plurality thus says that the concept of fundamental fairness inherent in the guarantee of due process would never prevent the conviction of a predisposed defendant, regardless of the outrageousness of police behavior in light of the surrounding circumstances.

I do not understand *Russell* or earlier cases delineating the predisposition-focused defense of entrapment to have gone so far, and there was no need for them to do so. In those cases the Court was confronted with specific claims of police "overinvolvement" in criminal activity involving contraband. Disposition of those claims did not require the Court to consider whether overinvolvement of Government agents in contraband offenses could ever reach such proportions as to bar conviction of a predisposed defendant as a matter of due process. Nor have we had occasion yet to confront Government overinvolvement in areas outside the realm of contraband offenses. In these circumstances, I am unwilling to conclude that an analysis other than one limited to predisposition would never be appropriate under due process principles.

* * *

I am not unmindful of the doctrinal and practical difficulties of delineating limits to police involvement in crime that do not focus on predisposition, as Government participation ordinarily will be fully justified in society's "war with the criminal classes." This undoubtedly is the concern that prompts the plurality to embrace an absolute rule. But we left these questions open in *Russell*, and this case is controlled completely by *Russell*. I therefore am unwilling to join the plurality in concluding that, no matter what the circumstances, neither due process principles nor our supervisory power could support a bar to conviction in any case where the Government is able to prove predisposition.

* * *

■ MR. JUSTICE BRENNAN, with whom MR. JUSTICE STEWART and MR. JUSTICE MARSHALL concur, dissenting.

* * *

I think that reversal of petitioner's conviction is compelled for those who follow the "subjective" approach to the defense of entrapment.... I agree with Mr. Justice Powell that *Russell* does not foreclose imposition of a bar to conviction—based upon our supervisory power or due process principles—where the conduct of law enforcement authorities is sufficiently offensive, even though the individuals entitled to invoke such a defense might be "predisposed." ... In my view, the police activity in this case was beyond permissible limits.

Two facts significantly distinguish this case from *Russell*. First, the chemical supplied in that case was not contraband.... In contrast, petitioner claims that the very narcotic he is accused of selling was supplied by an agent of the government....

Second, the defendant in *Russell* "was an active participant in an illegal drug manufacturing enterprise which began before the Government agent appeared on the scene, and continued after the government agent had left the scene." ... Russell was charged with unlawfully manufacturing and processing methamphetamine, ... and his crime was participation in an ongoing operation. In contrast, the two sales for which petitioner was convicted were allegedly instigated by Government agents and completed by the Government's purchase. The beginning and end of this crime thus coincided exactly with the Government's entry into and withdrawal from the criminal activity involved in this case, while the Government was not similarly involved in Russell's crime. ...

... Where the Government's agent deliberately sets up the accused by supplying him with contraband and then bringing him to another agent as a potential purchaser, the Government's role has passed the point of toleration.... The Government is doing nothing less than buying contraband from itself through an intermediary and jailing the intermediary. ... There is little, if any, law enforcement interest promoted by such conduct; plainly it is not designed to discover ongoing drug traffic. Rather, such conduct deliberately entices an individual to commit a crime. That the accused is "predisposed" cannot possibly justify the action of government officials in purposefully creating the crime. No one would suggest that the police could round up and jail all "predisposed" individuals, yet that is precisely what set-ups like the instant one are intended to accomplish. ... Thus, this case is nothing less than an instance of "the Government ... seeking to punish for an alleged offense which is the product of the creative activity of its own officials." ...

... For the reasons stated I would at a minimum hold that conviction is barred as a matter of law where the subject of the criminal charge is the sale of contraband provided to the defendant by a Government agent....

NOTES

1. *Government supplies narcotics*. In older cases, the defendant's version of events typically suggested that the undercover informer, without the knowledge of the police, provided the narcotics to the target. The police themselves then made a controlled purchase from the target, not realizing that they were buying drugs supplied by their own agent.

Today's cases approve much more direct governmental action. In the typical narcotics "reverse," an undercover police officer sells the drugs to the target and then arrests the target for possession, conspiracy, or purchase of narcotics. See United States v. Walther, 867 F.2d 1334 (11th Cir.1989) (Government supplied three thousand pounds of marijuana.); United States v. Savage, 701 F.2d 867 (11th Cir.1983). Such operations have been approved even when arrests were not made after every delivery of contraband. Sometimes the transaction is arranged to take place in the target's car, so that authorities can seek forfeiture of the vehicle as well as criminal prosecution of the target, even where the target purchased only a small amount of marijuana.

In United States v. Rogers, 701 F.2d 871 (11th Cir.1983), the Court observed:

> Appellants also point out that a DEA agent testified that some marijuana under the DEA's control may have left the DEA's warehouse in the form of samples given to brokers and prospective purchasers. Appellants argue it is intolerable that the government would allow marijuana out on the streets in violation of the law. It is apparent, however, that if the DEA's operation waste succeed, the agents had to conduct themselves as normal marijuana sellers so as not to arouse suspicion. Such conduct included distributing small samples of marijuana to potential buyers. This conduct is not even close to being outrageous and shocking. The appellants would have us believe that the government must forego confiscating huge amounts of illicit drug money and arresting numerous persons involved in illegal drug smuggling because on occasion it must provide a handful of marijuana as a sample to prospective buyers. We find this argument without logical support. Thus, we reject it.

In a similar case, the DEA believed suspect Santana was running (from prison) a large scale heroin network through Fuentes and others. Fuentes knew an undercover agent posing as a heroin supplier and asked the agent for a sample and the agent delivered 13 grams of 92% pure heroin (which equals 2,500 street sale doses). The DEA never recovered the sample and the defendants in the criminal cases asked for dismissal because the government acted outrageously in fronting so much heroin and then losing track of it so it presumably wound up in the hands of persons who were damaged by its use. Is the defense argument sound? The matter was well analyzed on both trial and appeal. United States v. Santana, 808 F.Supp. 77 (D.Mass.1992), reversed 6 F.3d 1 (1st Cir.1993). See also, United States v. Ford, 918 F.2d 1343 (8th Cir.1990) (rejecting due process claim where police supplied a targeted seller with small amounts of drugs for personal use—if court establishes rule that police cannot do so, drug sellers and buyers can use such court-imposed restrictions as a test to smoke out undercover officers).

2. *Choice of Targets*. The use of "reverse" techniques calls into question the traditional view that it matters not that police had no particular basis for approaching the defendant to propose an illegal transaction. There are inherent practical barriers—cost, embarrassment, exposure of undercover agents—which preclude widespread arbitrary acts of this sort, but there are no doctrines of law which disapprove an arbitrary approach to anyone. Of course, Justice O'Connor's dissent *in Jacobson* suggests that the danger that a court will find government inducement creates predisposition may impose a de facto requirement that investigators gather evidence of predisposition before beginning a sting. In Commonwealth v. Mance, 539 Pa. 282, 652 A.2d 299 (1995), however, the Pennsylvania Supreme Court held that *Jacobson* does not require government agents to have reasonable suspicion of wrongdoing before targeting a suspect for an undercover investigation.

3. *Agents participate in crimes*. If the law enforcement officer participates in the crime, does that guarantee a defendant a defense of entrapment?

A paid F.B.I. informant penetrated an interstate burglary ring and worked with them for over sixteen months while reporting daily to the F.B.I. During this period, he went with two ring members on forty burglaries and took part in the sale of stolen goods to fences. A claim that the police conduct was outrageous was rejected. In United States v. Brown, 635 F.2d 1207, 1212 (6th Cir.1980) the Court said:

> . . . [W]e begin our analysis with the basic proposition that the use of paid informants to infiltrate criminal enterprises is a "recognized and permissible means of investigation."
>
> This proposition remains true even though the informant or government agent engages in some criminal activity or supplies something of value to the criminal enterprise. The informant or government agent must be allowed to further the interests of the criminal enterprise in some manner to gain the confidence of the criminal elements with which he must deal.
>
> The type of criminal activity under investigation is also a relevant consideration regarding the scope of permissible government conduct. For example, the need to use paid informants to infiltrate criminal enterprises is regarded as especially necessary in the investigation of drug-related crimes. . . .
>
> Another pertinent inquiry is whether the government instigates the criminal activity in question, or whether it infiltrates a preexisting criminal enterprise. A related consideration is whether the government directs or controls the activities of the criminal enterprise or whether it merely acquiesces in its criminality. . . .
>
> We also note that the strength of the connection, or causal relationship, between the challenged government conduct and the commission of the acts for which the defendant stands convicted is an important consideration. We agree with the Tenth Circuit that "the more immediate the impact of the government's conduct upon a particular defendant, the more vigorously would be applied *Russell's* test for constitutional impropriety."
>
> On the facts presented by this record, the court finds no violation of due process. Although the individual burglars and fences might be detectable without infiltration, certainly the use of this investigative technique facilitated a more expeditious and thorough investigation. The burglary ring under investigation, like many drug rings, would have been extremely difficult to thwart without the use of Miller as an undercover agent.
>
> There is no showing of any kind that Miller, or any of the FBI agents involved in this case, instigated any criminal activity. The burglary ring was fully operative when Miller "joined" it. Even after Miller joined the ring, it appears that his participation in its criminal endeavors was limited to following the members' instructions. Miller was instructed by the FBI to participate in criminal activity only if failure to do so would endanger his life. Nothing in the record suggests that he departed from these instructions. . . .
>
> We find that, in its use of Miller, the government in no way increased the number of burglaries, or the likelihood of their success. Miller reported to the FBI on a daily basis. He revealed the location of burglaries and sometimes provided an inventory of the things taken, thus facilitating the recovery of stolen items such as those that form the basis of Brown's conviction. Although it did not materialize, Miller's presence also provided the FBI with a possible source of advance notice of burglaries. Miller also could have prevented personal injury to surprised occupants if the need had arisen. The only effect Miller's presence had on the activities of the ring was that the FBI was informed of the illegal activity in which the ring

was engaged. Nothing in the facts convinces us in the least that Miller's conduct was "shocking to the universal sense of justice."

Brown attempts to bootstrap Miller's involvement in the burglaries to the level of demonstrably outrageous conduct by dramatically emphasizing the danger of loss of property and the possibility of personal harm occasioned by the burglaries. Brown contends that after Miller accompanied Frazier and Campbell on the first burglary, they should have been arrested. If this course had been followed, argues Brown, "39 ... burglaries would have been prevented; 39 fewer homes would have been violated; 39 fewer families endangered." We find this argument unpersuasive.

Law enforcement officials are often presented with a formidable problem when they become aware of the criminal activity of individuals who are involved in a large criminal enterprise. The alternatives presented to those officials are exceedingly poor. They may arrest known criminals, thus ceasing their particular harmful effect on society; or they may allow them to continue in their violation of the law with the hope that further investigation will reveal a greater number of those involved in the criminal enterprise, the exposure and arrest of whom may effectively eliminate a much broader range and degree of criminal activity.

This is the dilemma confronted by the FBI agents in charge of the HAMFAT investigation. They were compelled to decide whether to arrest Frazier and Campbell when their criminality became known, or to delay those arrests with the prospect of casting a much larger net, and of eliminating a much broader range of criminality. This problem reasserted itself periodically as evidence accumulated sufficient to arrest and convict other members of the ring.

The difficulty of the problem was exacerbated by the fact that either alternative chosen would result in some harm to society, for the choice of either alternative results in the continuing criminality of some members of the ring. Once the burglary ring began its criminal operations, an event the government had nothing whatsoever to do with, a certain amount of harm to society was an inevitable result. Faced with this situation, the government was forced to choose an alternative that, in its judgment, would result in the least amount of harm. This type of decision is affected by a multitude of varied and subtle considerations, with which law enforcement personnel are only too familiar. Nothing in the record before us indicates that the FBI erred so dramatically in their decision in the instant case that the fundamental canons of due process were violated.

In contrast, consider the case of O'Neill. He was charged with bribing a police officer in order to prevent the paperwork for his arrest on another charge. He argued that the police officer was as guilty as he and since the officer was not advancing legitimate law enforcement objectives at the time he took the bribe, the jury instruction for entrapment was erroneous. It was erroneous because it suggested that a corrupt officer could use "reasonable persuasion." The appellate court reversed the conviction and remanded the case back to the trial court. Washington v. O'Neill, 91 Wash.App. 978, 967 P.2d 985 (1998).

4. *Government agents use sexual relationships.* In United States v. Simpson, 813 F.2d 1462 (9th Cir.1987), an undercover agent for the F.B.I., with the knowledge of federal agents, developed a sexual relationship with a target before she asked him to sell drugs to some friends. The friends turned out to be F.B.I. agents. The court held that these circumstances were not so outrageous as to have violated due process. The court said that it saw "no principled way to identify a fixed point along the continuum from casual physical contact to intense physical bonding beyond which the relationship becomes 'shocking' when entertained by an informant." It added that the police have been allowed to recruit family members as informers, citing a case where agents offered a five-year-old child five dollars to tell where mommy hid her heroin. The court also emphasized that the F.B.I. had not encouraged the sexual relationship, but rather had merely closed its eyes to the relationship after telling the informer not to continue with it. It concluded that the government sometimes can use methods that may not be judged moral if judged by "abstract" notions of decency, conceding that "many people in our society may find the deceptive use of sex in law enforcement to be morally offensive." A very similar set of facts led another court to the same conclusion where government financed abortion of pregnancy resulting from the relationship between informant and target. United States v. Shoffner, 826 F.2d 619 (7th Cir.1987).

Dictum in Simpson suggests another interesting issue. The defendant argued that the treatment by the F.B.I. of the prostitute-addict informer in his case was so shocking as to provide an outrageous conduct-due process defense to his prosecution. The court rejected the government's claim that the defendant had no standing to raise this question. It said that the target has standing to complain about any outrageous conduct occurring during the investigation.

Compare People ex rel. Difanis v. Boston, 92 Ill.App.3d 962, 48 Ill.Dec. 302, 416 N.E.2d 333 (1981) (no due process violation where individuals working for the prosecutor engaged in sexual acts as part of an effort to prove the existence of a prostitution operation), and Anchorage v. Flanagan, 649 P.2d 957 (Alaska App. 1982) (officer engaged in sexual contact with prostitute before effecting the arrest does not violate due process),with People v. Wisneski, 96 Mich.App. 299, 292 N.W.2d 196 (1980) (improper for government informer to use sex to get a physician illegally to dispense drugs); United States v. Yater, 756 F.2d 1058 (5th Cir.1985) (defendant ill with cancer; government informers allegedly promised that his eighteen month old child would be cared for by an informer after defendant's death); State v. Lively, 130 Wash.2d 1, 921 P.2d 1035 (1996) (use of romantic attachment outrageous when informer hung out at AA meetings trolling for suitable targets, pretended romantic involvement with emotionally fragile, suicidal, 21–year–old defendant, allowed her to move into his government-subsidized apartment, asked her to marry him, and then made repeated pleas for cocaine.)

In United States v. Nolan–Cooper, 155 F.3d 221 (3d Cir.1998), a case in which a government agent posing as a drug dealer had "wined and dined" his money-laundering target, and, after evidence of wrongdoing had been collected, had sexual intercourse with her, the Third Circuit established a test for determining when a government agent's use of sex or romance is "outrageous governmental conduct." The court, relying on the analysis in United States v. Cuervelo, 949 F.2d 559 (2d Cir.1991), said that the defendant must show at a minimum that (1) the government either consciously set out to use sex as an investigatory tool or acquiesced in such conduct once it knew or should have known about the agent's relationship with the target, that (2) the government agent initiated a sexual relationship or allowed it to persist in order to achieve governmental ends, and (3) the sexual relationship took place close to the period covered by the indictment and was entwined with the events charged. It held that the agent's conduct was not outrageous.

See Rachael Urbansky (Note), "Seducing the Target: Sexual Intercourse as Outrageous Government Conduct," 50 Case W. Res. L. Rev. 729 (2000).

5. *Bribery Sting Operations*. In a now famous investigation know as Abscam, FBI agents posed as officers of an investment organization. When approached with a scheme to finance equipment for Camden, New Jersey that included bribing Camden's mayor, the focus of the investigation narrowed to organized crime and political corruption. The agents posed as Arab businessmen who were worried about emigrating from Iran and sought agreements from congress members to introduce private immigration legislation on their behalf in exchange for substantial bribes. After several meetings through paid intermediaries, the agents met with Congress member Kelly. Kelly, however, refused to take any money for the services. Later, the intermediary insisted that he would receive the money and give it to Kelly indirectly. However, the FBI agent ultimately convinced Kelly to take the money himself, and he did, stuffing $25,000 into his suit pockets. The district court held that the police conduct was "outrageous" in violation of the Due Process Clause because the agents continued to press Kelly, in the face of a rejection and did not have any evidence of wrongdoing on Kelly's part before they began the investigation. The D.C. Circuit reversed, United States v. Kelly, 707 F.2d 1460 (D.C.Cir. 1983), holding:

"Abscam was indeed an elaborate hoax, involving a fictitious, FBI-created corporation purportedly representing Arabs of enormous wealth, as well as the limousines, yachts, and lavishly appointed residences necessary to make the hoax believable. Yet stripped of these trappings of wealth, Abscam was no more than an 'opportunity for the commission of crime by those willing to do so.' United States v. Myers, 692 F.2d 823, 837 (2d Cir.1982). [The FBI agents] let it be known that they would pay substantial sums of money to congressmen willing to promise to assist the wealthy Arabs with their immigration difficulties. Thereafter, the FBI operatives simply waited for the grapevine to work and to see who appeared to take bribes. No congressmen were targeted for investigation; rather Abscam pursued all who were brought to the operation by the grapevine. In essence, then, Abscam was not significantly different from an undercover drug or fencing operation offering to buy from all who appear at its door. Instead of buying stolen goods or contraband drugs, Abscam brought corrupt official influence in Congress. Such government involvement in crime does not violate principles of due process." 707 F.2d 1460, 1469–70.

Circuit Judge Ginsburg, in a concurring opinion, wrote:

> "We may not alter the contours of the entrapment defense under a due process cloak, and we lack authority, where no specific constitutional right of the defendant has been violated, to dismiss indictments as an exercise of supervisory power over the conduct of federal law enforcement agents. Precedent dictates that we refrain from applying the general due process constraint to bar a conviction except in the rare instance of '[p]olice overinvolvement in crime' that reaches 'a demonstrable level of outrageousness.' Hampton v. United States.... The requisite level of outrageousness, the Supreme Court has indicated, is not established merely upon a showing of obnoxious behavior or even flagrant misconduct on the part of the police; the broad 'fundamental fairness' guarantee, it appears from High Court decisions, is not transgressed absent 'coercion, violence or brutality to the person.' See Irvine v. California, 347 U.S. 128, 74 S.Ct. 381 (1952)." 707 F.2d 1460, 1475–76.

A general history of the Abscam cases is found in Gershman, "Abscam, The Judiciary and the Ethics of Entrapment," 91 Yale L.J. 1565 (1982). See also, United States v. Williams, 705 F.2d 603 (2d Cir.1983); United States v. Weisz, 718 F.2d 413 (D.C.Cir.1983); United States v. Jenrette, 744 F.2d 817 (D.C.Cir.1984).

6. *Physical Intimidation.* Consider the decision in People v. Isaacson, 44 N.Y.2d 511, 406 N.Y.S.2d 714, 378 N.E.2d 78 (1978). In *Isaacson* police in New York arrested J.D.B., a man with a history of inveterate drug use and sales. While under arrest for sale of drugs he was physically beaten by the police and threatened with further harm. He was eventually released on bail. In the interim the police learned the drugs he sold them most recently were not amphetamines but caffeine pills.

Upon the advice of his attorney—but still believing he still faced punishment for amphetamine sale—he agreed to act as an informer. Later J.D.B. stated he received no promises other than an improved bargaining position and that the physical violence and threats did not influence his decision to cooperate. However, he would not have aided the police if they had not deceived him about the gravity of the charges he faced. J.D.B. began his work as an informant by calling people he knew for the purpose of setting up drug sales. He reached Isaacson whom he had known for two years at State College, Pa.

Isaacson was a graduate student and teacher at Penn State, soon to receive a doctoral degree in botany. He admitted a small amount of drug use but had no criminal record. J.D.B. told Isaacson that he was facing 15 years to life, was abandoned by his parents, had been beaten by the police and needed to make a "score" or "deal" to pay a lawyer. Isaacson said, and J.D.B. denied, that J.D.B. was crying and sobbing during this talk.

Over a two week period J.D.B. made seven calls to Isaacson before arranging a sale. J.D.B. first sought heroin but Isaacson refused. As to cocaine, Isaacson first sought to put J.D.B. off by saying there was nothing worthwhile.

At the time of J.D.B.'s calls, Isaacson was living in State College with a woman who was a daily user of drugs. She said Isaacson had made two one gram sales of cocaine to J.D.B. two months before J.D.B. became an informant. Isaacson worked 12 to 14 hours a day and had no access to someone who could provide the two ounces of cocaine J.D.B. wanted, but his girl friend did and the transaction was arranged. The deal was worth $1,000 to Isaacson and his girl, but Isaacson's principal motive was to help J.D.B.

Isaacson and J.D.B. then scheduled a meeting. J.D.B. conferred with the New York police about the sale. He was advised to ask for two ounces to be sure of getting one—a statutory predicate for a higher sentence. He was told the sale must occur in New York despite the fact that Isaacson feared New York drug laws and did not want to enter the state. Isaacson chose an elaborate method of delivery of the cocaine in order, he said, to avoid a rip off. The method was suggested by the supplier his girl friend found. J.D.B. used a ruse to get Isaacson to New York—gradually negotiating to get their meeting to Lawrenceville, Pa. just south of the state boundary. Then J.D.B. designated a tavern which he said was in Lawrenceville but was, in fact, in Lindley, N.Y. Isaacson was fooled because the state line marker was damaged and hidden by vegetation. A large "Welcome to New York" sign was placed on a bridge several hundred yards past the tavern. The sale from Isaacson to J.D.B.occurred at the tavern. Isaacson was arrested and eventually sentenced to fifteen years to life.

The majority found that entrapment did not occur, as a matter of law, because Isaacson was predisposed to commit the offense. There was a due process violation arising from the police conduct at least under the due process clause of the state constitution. First, Isaacson's prior small, casual sales and lack of access to a large supplier show the more serious offense here would not have occurred without persistent instigation. Second, the abuse and deception of J.D.B., despite the fact it was directed against someone other than defendant, shows police misconduct. Third, J.D.B.'s persistence, appeals to sympathy in the face of Isaacson's refusal, goes too far. Fourth, the geographical shell game and the insistence on a specified amount display a police goal—not of cutting off a source of narcotics—but simply creating a statistic, one more conviction. "In sum this case exposes the ugliness of police brutality, upon which was imposed a cunning subterfuge employed to enlist the services of an informant who, deceived into thinking he was facing a stiff prison sentence desperately sought out any individual he could to satisfy the police thirst for conviction, even of a resident of another State possessed of no intention to enter our confines. Separately considered, the items of conduct may not rise to a level justifying dismissal but viewed in totality they reveal a brazen and continuing pattern in disregard of fundamental rights."

The dissenters argued the record showed Isaacson did deal extensively in cocaine and other drugs and used scales in his college laboratory to assist him in these sales. The police abuse of J.D.B. was not a violation of *defendant's* rights. The luring of Isaacson to New York was not misconduct especially since Isaacson knew J.D.B. intended to resell the cocaine in New York. The delay and reluctance of Isaacson was not due to his innocence but to a disruption in his line of supply and his willingness to go to New York.

Isaacson represents a fairly unique application of due process theory to police conduct in arranging the commission of crime. The dissent took little issue with the basic rule of law found by the majority. But some questions must be considered:

(1) The majority stated: "There may be those who fear that dismissal of convictions on due process grounds may portend an unmanageable subjectivity. Such apprehension is unjustified for courts by their very nature are constantly called upon to make judgments". Is the stated objection adequately answered by the court?

(2) Entrapment is a defense to a criminal charge and the issue of entrapment is tried when the case is tried on the merits. A due process claim for dismissal may be resolved in a pre-trial hearing. Does *Isaacson* allow the defendant to seek a pre-trial hearing of his claim? In *Isaacson* such a hearing would have required presentation of nearly all the evidence in the case at the pre-trial hearing. If the defendant loses his motion, all the witnesses must be recalled at trial. Should a pre-trial hearing of such claims be permitted?

(3) Is *Isaacson* consistent with principles of "standing" discussed earlier in Chapter 6, Section C, which deny defendants the right to exclude evidence obtained by virtue of violating the rights of a third party?

Courts have found few occasions to rely upon the *Isaacson* decision. One court has rejected due process claim based upon threatened legal consequences to an informer which caused him to turn against the accused. People v. Harris, 165 Cal.App.3d 324, 211 Cal.Rptr. 493 (1985).

7. *Endangering the Safety of the Target*

In United States v. Barbosa, 271 F.3d 438 (3d Cir.2001) the agents asked Barbosa to swallow about a kilogram of heroin in Aruba and then gave him an itinerary that extended his travel time to his destination. The Court wrote:

> [B]arbosa claims that the Government had orchestrated the entire narcotics transaction and had unnecessarily created an unreasonable risk of death. Citing the danger of digestive acids dissolving the packaging materials surrounding the swallowed pellets, Barbosa points to the increasing risk of a fatal mishap as more time elapses before the ingested drugs are expelled. Notwithstanding this risk of fatality, the Government purportedly solicited his assistance through its paid informants (particularly Disla) and induced him to travel to Aruba, to swallow approximately one kilogram of heroin, and then to return to the United States....
>
> * * *
>
> We recognize that Barbosa's life was arguably placed in danger by the Government's sting operation. We also recognize, however, that narcotics trafficking necessarily entails a risk of death or serious bodily harm, such

as from the use of firearms and other enforcement measures to protect or seize the contraband and money, as well as from the ancillary criminal activity that accompanies the drug trade. In fighting this "war on drugs," law enforcement personnel have needed to develop a number of sophisticated and covert investigatory techniques. One of these techniques involves the creation of what appear to be authentic drug transactions, oftentimes with the joint participation of both law enforcement personnel (or their designees) and the targets of the investigation. Such subterfuge is a well recognized and permissible means of investigation. Therefore, endangerment to the lives of the agents, informants, and targets involved, which is inherent in the drug trafficking trade, must also be permissible. It is incumbent upon the government, however, to police its own conduct and consistently revisit the parameters and constitutionality of its enforcement activities.

Smuggling narcotics into this country through swallowing or "body-packing" has unfortunately become both an effective and lucrative criminal enterprise.... Yet, this mode of conveyance is fraught with grave peril to the courier (also called a "mule," "packer," or "swallower") in the rare but potentially real situation in which the wrapped pellets burst before they can be expelled. Drug swallowing can even be fatal because acids in the digestive tract can dissolve the latex packaging materials, thereby releasing massive doses of narcotics into the body....

* * *

However cold or callous the Government's stance towards Barbosa may seem, this case does not involve the classic example of a courier (perhaps with low income, low education, and little practical skills) who was enticed, coerced, or exploited by an affluent, sophisticated drug dealer to smuggle drugs into the United States through ingestion.... On this record, Barbosa was apparently a willing participant in the operation to smuggle drugs to Philadelphia from Aruba, and he exhibited a level of professionalism concerning the activity of drug swallowing not typically found in the average courier.

At trial, the evidence revealed that Barbosa was extremely knowledgeable about packaging and swallowing drugs. He told the informants that he regularly engaged in swallowing drugs for other dealers and further claimed that he managed persons who brought drugs into the country through swallowing, even teaching them how do it....

* * *

Barbosa ... urges us to adopt a rule of law that drug swallowing is so life threatening that it is *per se* violative for the Government to place a defendant in the position of a courier who swallows drugs and transports them. However, there is nothing in the record or even general common sense notions from which to draw such a blanket rule. On the contrary, a *per se* rule would place severe restrictions on the ability of law enforcement personnel to combat narcotics trafficking.... Under the facts of this case, the Government's use of a known drug swallower in a sting operation did not rise to a level of outrageousness sufficient to offend Barbosa's due process rights.

In sum, the Government had every reason to believe in good faith that Barbosa was a willing participant in this highly dangerous form of drug trafficking, and thus, its conduct was not sufficiently "shocking, outrageous, and clearly intolerable" such that a vacatur of the conviction is warranted. Under the evidence adduced at trial, we conclude that the Government's conduct here was not fundamentally unfair and offensive to due process, and therefore, we affirm the conviction on this ground.

* * *

8. *Manufacturing Federal Jurisdiction?* Defense lawyers frequently cite United States v. Archer, 486 F.2d 670 (2d Cir.1973), for the proposition that government agents, working undercover, cannot be allowed to manufacture federal jurisdiction. There it was because of the stratagems of the agents that the illegal activities of the defendants took upon an interstate character. The court held that no federal crime occurred. The Second Circuit has carefully limited the scope of *Archer*, suggesting that it applies only to the substantive question of whether a federal basis of jurisdiction exists. United States v. Wallace, 85 F.3d 1063 (2d Cir.1996).

The desire of officers to select the place of a transaction can arise for a variety of reasons. Suppose that a sale of a small quantity of cocaine is ordinarily a Class 3, probationable felony. Suppose that, from a concern for school children, the legislature makes the sale of such a substance a Class 1 felony, with a mandatory minimum sentence of ten years, if done within one thousand feet of a school. Compare Title 21, § 845(a), of the United States Code, and see United States v. Lewin, 900 F.2d 145 (8th Cir.1990) (defendant's knowledge that school is within 1,000 feet not an element of the offense). Suppose further that, in arranging a controlled purchase of cocaine, the undercover officer arranges to meet the target at a place he knows to be 950 feet from a school, although the target's prior suspected dealings have had no nexus to schools. Some defense attorneys claim that such alleged "misuse" of the enhanced penalty statutes are the rule rather than the exception. Nevertheless, an entrapment defense is not likely to succeed under these circumstances. See generally State v. Burch, 545 So.2d 279 (Fla.App.1989). However, similar claims have been made somewhat more successfully in mitigation of punishment. See Note 7, after *Jacobson, supra,* discussing sentencing entrapment claims.

Other courts have rejected "outrageous conduct" challenges to governmental tactics designed to obtain a favorable venue. See United States v. Padilla, 869 F.2d 372 (8th Cir.1989), involving efforts to create venue in the Eastern District of Missouri rather than in the more "indulgent" Southern District of Florida. There an unsympathetic court ruled, "If it was convenient for Chappas to agree to come to St. Louis to deliver cocaine, it is convenient for him to stand trial in St. Louis on federal cocaine charges."

9. *Informant Bounties.* Courts have allowed informants to be paid on a "contingent fee" basis. United States v. Gonzales, 927 F.2d 139 (3d Cir.1991) (no Due Process violation where the compensation of the informer depended upon the amount of money that the target would forfeit when caught in the criminal activity of buying drugs); United States v. Cuellar, 96 F.3d 1179 (9th Cir.1996) (upholding a drug crime informant's fees of $50,000 for brokerage, $130,000 for time and risk, and $400,000 for a post-investigative bonus). In *Cuellar*, Judge Wiggins wrote in concurrence: "I write separately to emphasize the dangers of permitting a government agency to pay an informant, who is known to have engaged in criminal activity, over half a million dollars for little more than a year's work, primarily because the information provided led to over $7million in forfeitures.... [A]lthough I am forced to conclude under our prior cases that paying an informant $580,000, $400,000 of which is paid after the informant testifies against the defendant, is not 'so excessive, flagrant, scandalous, intolerable and offensive as to violate due process,' ... I nevertheless am personally offended by the $580,000 payment."

The Florida Supreme Court relied on *Isaacson, supra,* to overturn convictions based on the conduct and testimony of an informer whose fee payments were contingent upon positive results. State v. Glosson, 462 So.2d 1082 (Fla.1985).

10. *Governmental Direction and Control of the Illegal Operation.* Consider United States v. Twigg, 588 F.2d 373 (3d Cir.1978), another case reversing a conviction on due process grounds:

ROSENN, CIRCUIT JUDGE.

* * *

At the behest of the Drug Enforcement Agency, Kubica, a convicted felon striving to reduce the severity of his sentence, communicated with Neville and suggested the establishment of a speed laboratory. The Government gratuitously supplied about 20 percent of the glassware and the indispensable ingredient, phenyl–2–propanone. It is unclear whether the parties had the means or the money to obtain the chemical on their own. The DEA made arrangements with chemical supply houses to facilitate the purchase of the rest of the materials. Kubica, operating under the business name "Chem Kleen" supplied by the DEA, actually purchased all of the supplies with the exception of a separatory funnel. (The funnel was secured by Twigg at the direction of Kubica who was engaged in operating the laboratory.) When problems were encountered in locating an adequate production site, the Government found the solution by providing an isolated farmhouse well-suited for the location of an illegally operated laboratory. Again, there was no cost to the defendants. At all times during the production process, Kubica was completely in charge and furnished all of the laboratory expertise. Neither defendant had the know-how with which to actually manufacture methamphetamine. The assistance they provided was minimal and then at the specific direction of Kubica.

These instances of police involvement must be evaluated against the following backdrop. The only evidence that Neville was predisposed to commit the crime was his receptivity to Kubica's proposal to engage in the venture and the testimony of Kubica that he had worked with Neville in a similar laboratory four years earlier. Unlike other cases rejecting this defense, the police investigation here was not concerned with an existing laboratory, the illicit plan did not originate with the criminal defendants, and neither of the defendants were chemists—an indispensable requisite to this criminal enterprise.[9]

* * *

When Kubica, at the instance of the DEA, reestablished contact with Neville, the latter was not engaged in any illicit drug activity. Using Kubica, and actively participating with him, the DEA agents deceptively implanted the criminal design in Neville's mind. They set him up, encouraged him, provided the essential supplies and technical expertise, and when he and Kubica encountered difficulties in consummating the crime, they assisted in finding solutions. This egregious conduct on the part of government agents generated new crimes by the defendant merely for the sake of pressing criminal charges against him when, as far as the record reveals, he was lawfully and peacefully minding his own affairs. Fundamental

9. We also find it baffling that the Government would urge the reduction of the jail sentence for a man who may have run as many as 50 or 100 speed laboratories in the past in exchange for the convictions of two men with no apparent criminal designs and without the expertise required to set up a single laboratory.

fairness does not permit us to countenance such actions by law enforcement officials and prosecution for a crime so fomented by them will be barred.

* * *

Twigg did not become involved in this criminal enterprise until March 1,1977—the day the laboratory went into operation. His reason for becoming involved was to repay a debt owed to Neville. Neville introduced Twigg to Kubica, and then Twigg and Kubica went shopping for additional supplies, which Kubica purchased. There is no evidence to suggest that Twigg was aware of the ultimate purpose of these errands until informed by Kubica after returning to he farmhouse. All actions taken by Twigg from that time until his arrest were t the specific direction of Kubica, the government agent. Twigg contributed nothing in terms of expertise, money, supplies, or ideas. It also appears that Twigg would not even have shared in the proceeds from the sale of the drug. In light of these facts, we hold that Twigg's conviction is also tainted by the conduct of the DEA agents and that fundamental fairness requires its reversal.

ADAMS, CIRCUIT JUDGE, dissenting.

Under these circumstances, I am unable to join the Court in relying on the government's "instigation" of this conspiracy as support for the conclusion that the government involvement here was "outrageous."[22]

It is true, of course, that the government did more here than "suggest" the operation. Through Kubica it provided chemicals, some laboratory equipment, money, and chemical expertise. But it must be remembered that Kubica was re-creating the partnership he had had with Neville a few years earlier. He would inevitably be expected to perform the same duties he had undertaken then. If the government were unable to do as much as it in fact did, the entire operation directed against Neville would have been impossible.

Why the government was willing to use Kubica in this way in order to reach Neville is unclear. The majority appears to be of the view that Kubica, with his chemical expertise, was the more valuable catch and the more logical target for hard nosed prosecution. This may well be the case. But I am reluctant to second-guess the DEA choice of target. Neville, after all, was able to provide both money and "contacts." It cannot be said with any certainty that such a person may not ultimately prove more important than a chemist in breaking up the network of drug manufacturers and suppliers in this country.

Whatever our judgment of their wisdom may be, DEA officials chose to utilize Kubica to pursue Neville. Given this decision, as a practical matter, they had to furnish through Kubica the same skills and materials Kubica had provided in the earlier conspiracy. This they did; and Neville, and through Neville, Twigg, willingly participated in the conspiracy. Although

22. Moreover, even if I were persuaded by the majority's argument as to defendant Neville, I would reject their conclusion as to defendant Twigg. There was no government inducement of Twigg at all. He was brought into the crime by Neville. Instigation by a private person has never been a defense to criminal charges. Nor have the other facts stressed by the majority, Twigg's relative unimportance to the overall scheme, the likelihood that he would not share in the proceeds and his motives for undertaking the crime, traditionally been thought to constitute defenses to charges of criminal activity. On these facts I cannot believe that Twigg has even a colorable claim of either entrapment or overinvolvement.

there is reason to question this sort of law enforcement, I cannot say that it shocks my conscience or that it reaches a demonstrable level of outrageousness beyond my toleration. This is so in part because I recognize the difficulties faced by the DEA in combatting the spread of illegal drugs. But, more importantly, I am particularly mindful of *Russell's* warning that the federal judiciary is not to exercise " 'a Chancellor's foot' veto over law enforcement practices of which it [does] not approve." To broaden the limited exception fashioned by Mr. Justice Powell in *Hampton* may well have just such an effect. Because I believe that that opinion authorizes judicial intervention under the due process clause only in extreme cases, I must respectfully dissent from the majority's reversal of the convictions of both Neville and Twigg.

* * *

Would the defendant in this case have had an entrapment defense today, under *Jacobson*?

* * *

Another defendant used the "outrageous government conduct" argument in an attempt to aggregate other perceived police illegalities, arguing that "a campaign of illegal wiretaps, illegal searches and seizures, illegal interrogations, deception and misuse of the grand jury power" constituted a sufficient basis to dismiss the indictment. In his claims, he alleged a governmental ruse to gain jurisdiction over him (see note 7, infra) and perjury entrapment [discussed in note A(5) infra]. The court rejected all claims, noting that two circuits do not recognize the "outrageous government conduct" defense and where the defense is recognized, it rarely results in the grant of relief to the defendant. United States v. Bin Laden, 146 F.Supp.2d 373 (S.D.N.Y. 2001) (involving the terrorist bombings of United States embassies in East Africa).

11. *Decoys.* Nevada at one time condemned as entrapment certain decoy operations in which undercover officers, with money hanging from their pockets, pose as unconscious alcoholics passed out in public places. One recent opinion was especially critical of young prosecutors and police officers:

> For healthy, energetic people in the prime of life.... few pastimes would seem more enticing than to go fishing for "suckers".... who succumb to their artificial bait.... [F]ew such tyros will pause to weigh the social costs of entrapping young underclass males into manufactured crimes.... Washoe County Sheriff v. Hawkins, 104 Nev. 70, 752 P.2d 769 (1988).

Recent Nevada decisions have refused to apply *Hawkins,* rejecting defense attacks on police decoy procedures only slightly different from those utilized in *Hawkins*. See, e.g., DePasquale v. State, 104 Nev. 338, 757 P.2d 367 (1988).

12. *No due process defense?* In United States v. Miller, 891 F.2d 1265 (7th Cir.1989), the defendant argued that the government engaged in outrageous conduct "by employing a drug addict whom Miller was romantically involved to induce him to sell drugs." The court rejected the claim, partly because the defendant did not establish that the government had done what the defendant had alleged.

In a concurring opinion, Judge Easterbrook observed:

> When push comes to shove, we should reject the contention that the criminal must go free because the constable was too zealous. Why raise false hopes? Why waste litigants' and judges' time searching for and

rejecting on the facts defenses that ought not exist as a matter of law? Everyone has better things to do.

Easterbrook then analyzed Supreme Court opinions and concluded that at least five or six present United States Supreme Court justices have rejected the due-process, outrageous-conduct theory, as a matter of law. He concluded:

> Any line we draw would be unprincipled and therefore not judicial in nature. More likely there would be no line; judges would vote their lower intestines. Such a meandering, personal approach is the antithesis of justice under law, and we ought not indulge it. Inability to describe in general terms just what makes tactics too outrageous to tolerate suggests that there is no definition—and "I know it when I see it" is not a rule of any kind, let alone a command of the Due Process Clause.
>
> The kinds of prosecutions that trouble me most are not those like Operation or offers of sex in exchange for cocaine, but those that impose costs on the innocent. Take for example a sting in which the FBI sets up a fence and buys stolen goods. The money the government pumps into the business must lead people to steal things to sell to the FBI—with misery for the victims of the burglary and potential violence in the process. Stings have been upheld consistently, however, and we have concluded that the innocent victims cannot recover damages from the government. Powers v. Lightner, 820 F.2d 818 (7th Cir.1987). ... Other judges are offended by immorality (such as sponsoring an informant's use of sexual favors as currency) or by acts that endanger informants (such as supplying them with drugs for personal use) but not by a traditional sting. This shows the subjective basis of the concern—all the more reason not to have such a doctrine in our law. ... We deem it enough to support punishment that this person committed this offense, leaving to other institutions the redirection of investigative or prosecutorial resources.
>
> * * *
>
> "Outrageousness" as a defense does more than stretch the bounds of due process. It also creates serious problems of consistency. The circuits that recognize a "due process defense" can't agree on what it means. How much is "too much"? The nature of the question exposes it as (a) unanswerable, and (b) political.

The Sixth Circuit has declared that an "outrageous governmental conduct" defense, based on due process principles, simply does not exist. The court reversed a district court's dismissal of an indictment for aiding and abetting the purchase of food stamps. The district court had found outrageous conduct when a government informer, who was allowed to keep half the proceeds of each sale of food stamps, convinced her long-time friends to buy food stamps from her after she told them she was in ill health and needed to sell the stamps in order to provide "a proper Christmas" for her children.

The Sixth Circuit reasoned that *Russell* held that the basis for entrapment lies in congressional intent, not in the due process clause. Thus, if it is constitutional to convict an unpredisposed defendant, it is not "fundamentally unfair" to convict a predisposed one and the "due process" defense threatens to violate the separation of powers by giving the judiciary supervisory authority over the executive branch, and by exceeding the boundaries of the entrapment defense recognized by the legislative branch. United States v. Tucker, 28 F.3d 1420 (6th Cir. 1994)

The Seventh Circuit has agreed. United States v. Boyd, 55 F.3d 239 (7th Cir.1995). The D.C. Circuit has limited any outrageous conduct defense to conduct involving "coercion, violence, or brutality to the person." United States v. Gaviria, 116 F.3d 1498, 1533 (D.C.Cir.1997).

What all opinions make clear is that "outrageous governmental conduct" is, even if accepted, not a defense to be decided by the jury. It is more like a motion to suppress physical evidence, decided, if necessary after a hearing, by the trial judge whose ruling is subject to plenary review on appeal.

PART 2

THE JUDICIAL PROCESS

CHAPTER 8

PROSECUTORIAL DISCRETION

A. THE EXERCISE OF DISCRETION

The prosecutor is the single most powerful officer in the criminal justice system. This quality of his or her office stems from two factors: the influence he or she exercises upon the actions of other agencies within the system; and freedom from review—except in the most extraordinary circumstances—of the decisions as to whether or not to prosecute.

More than that of any other agency, the influence of a prosecutor's office is felt at every stage of the proceedings within the system. He or she is usually an advisor to, and sometimes a supervisor of, the police or other investigative agencies. The prosecutor's views, therefore, may influence the course of investigations directly; or, even if unsupervised in a particular area, the police may tailor their actions to accommodate the known preferences or prejudices of their local prosecutor. After verdict, the prosecutor's relationship to the judge, or the prosecutor's standing in the community, may influence the decision of the judge in the imposition of sentence. On appeal, the prosecutor, by virtue of his or her power to concede issues or, in some jurisdictions, to press a cross-appeal, may continue to shape the case even after it has been decided in the trial court.

After the defendant has been incarcerated, the influence of the prosecutor is still felt. Prison authorities may accept his or her view of the kind of custodial care which is required in individual cases. In many jurisdictions it is commonplace for the prosecutor to send a letter to the prison authorities giving his or her views of the nature of the charge, the evidence presented, and the character of the defendant. When parole or executive clemency is at issue, the view of the prosecutor, especially if vigorously and publicly pressed, may well be the controlling factor in determining whether the prisoner wins release or is continued in custody.

Thus, the prosecutor occupies the most powerful position in the system by virtue of control over who is prosecuted and who is not, and the fact that the influence of that office is felt at every stage from arrest to parole and pardon.

The most important factor contributing to the power of the prosecutor is his almost unbridled right, both formal and informal, to make the decision either to prosecute or not to prosecute a particular defendant. This right is largely a product of the separation of powers within our system rather than a studied determination by legislatures; and generations of acceptance by legislatures as well as the courts have endowed it with an almost unquestioned character which prosecutors are anxious to see unchanged.

This immense prosecutorial power becomes even more apparent when contrasted with that possessed by other agencies of government involved in the law enforcement process and the administration of criminal justice—the legislatures, the police, and the courts.

In contrast to the prosecutor's almost complete freedom from review by other persons or agencies, even the power of the legislature to define offenses and set punishment is subject to some controls by the executive branch of government, whose police may not arrest offenders and whose prosecutors may not initiate prosecutions. Moreover, the validity of legislative enactments is subject to judicial scrutiny.

Although the actions of the police are subject to the control of the executive branch which governs them, their power to make arrests, searches and seizures, and engage in other investigative procedures may come to naught if the prosecutor declines to process their cases through the prosecution stage. Moreover, trial judges, and later on, appellate judges may nullify as evidence the results of police investigative efforts. Then, too, there are always legislative initiatives to confine the investigative and apprehension powers and practices of the police.

Trial judges in the federal system are subject to review by federal courts of appeal as well as by the Supreme Court. The decisions of state trial judges must withstand the scrutiny, not only of the appellate courts within the state system, but, where federal constitutional rights are involved, federal trial and appellate courts are able to review the conclusions of state trial and appellate judges through federal collateral relief.

Even prison and parole authorities, historically insulated by the concept of "discretion", now find themselves checked by the recent willingness of judges, especially federal judges, to set minimum standards of prison housekeeping and disciplinary procedures within the context of civil rights or damage actions. Moreover, parole authorities, long undisputed guardians of their own procedures for determining eligibility for parole, have now been told that there are minimum due process rights with which their procedures must comply.

The prosecutor's broad discretionary power is subject to one fairly remote restriction. Under our system of checks and balances, the prosecutor may always risk rejection by the electorate at the next election or, if he or she holds office by appointment, removal for misfeasance. Removal for abuse of prosecutorial discretion is rare, however.

Control of a prosecutor's budget by the legislative authority may conceivably act as a brake in curbing prosecutorial zeal in pursuing particular cases, but the ability of the prosecutor to shift resources may neutralize such a control attempt; moreover, power over the budget cannot compel the prosecutor to act affirmatively with regard to particular case situations.

Finally, judicial control over the prosecutor is felt only with regard to those matters which the prosecutor chooses to place within the system by initiating a prosecution. Even this control is largely negative, in the sense that it operates only to curb prosecutorial misbehavior in the gathering of evidence or during the trial of a case.

From this perspective, then, we turn to a discussion of the factors which may influence the decision of the prosecutor to proceed with, or decline to bring, criminal prosecutions.

1. The Prosecutor and the Office

Who and what the prosecutor is must be taken into account in assessing how and why he or she makes his decisions. A federal prosecutor, for example, is normally subject to the control only of the President and the Attorney General. He or she may be a powerful political figure in his own right or may be politically weak and thus dependent upon the favor of the senior Senator of the President's party, who traditionally recommends both prosecutorial and judicial nominees within the federal system. On the other hand, a state prosecutor and the attorney general of a state, may be elected or appointed by the governor. A county prosecutor may be elected or appointed by the Governor or the Attorney General.

The area in which the prosecutor operates may also influence his or her decisions to some degree. Thus the problems faced by the rural prosecutor are much different than those faced by the urban or suburban prosecutor. Since priorities of law enforcement are bound to be different, so too are decisions to prosecute or not to prosecute. For example, prosecutors in rural or suburban areas tend to regard commercial offenses such as embezzlement, forgery, check "kiting", and petty theft with more seriousness than their urban counterparts who must cope with a much larger number of such offenses and who may not have such close personal relationships with community merchants.

Discretion is also affected by the quality of assistant prosecutors and the method of their selection and retention. If the office is regarded as a political stepping-stone, and if appointments are made as part of a political patronage system, political factors or favors may weigh in the balance. Sensitivity to community opinion (more precisely, the prosecutor's conception of community opinion) may be more influential. If the prosecutor, even an elected one, has served for a long time, and his or her assistants are chosen from outside the political system, or are civil service employees, less concern may be shown in this regard.

The stage of the principal prosecutor's career may also be important. If the prosecutor is young and at the beginning of a legal or political career, he or she may tend to caution in investigations and prosecutions to lessen the chances of mistakes which will adversely affect that career. Or, if the political balance is such, the prosecutor may assume the role of the "white knight" who charges forth in an aggressive manner to joust with the established order or political hierarchy. A career prosecutor will tend to steer a more even, balanced course. And an older prosecutor, perhaps one to whom a small community has turned because of the shortage of lawyers, may be less concerned with community opinion.

The size of the office is also important. In small offices discretion will remain largely with the principal prosecutor since control of the assistants and their decisions is more easily attained. In larger offices, with 50 or 100 assistants or more, control is more structured, with fewer decisions flowing to the top. The result is that initial, and often controlling, discretion rests largely with assistants who may be new, inexperienced or who do not share, to the same degree, the philosophy of enforcement of the principal prosecutor. His or her discretion is thus supervisory, rather than original, and his control of decisions depends heavily upon the ability of his supervisory staff and the formal structure of office authority. Thus, discretion in a large prosecutor's office may be that of many persons, rather than one, with review often hurried or haphazard. As a result discretion may be exercised in an internally inconsistent manner.

2. General Factors Influencing Discretion

Before examining those considerations which may influence the discretion to prosecute or decline in a particular case, some mention of *general* factors which shape a prosecutor's discretion should be made.

The first decision to be made is whether a criminal statute should be enforced at all. Though the statutory duty of prosecutors is often cast in mandatory terms, selective enforcement or nonenforcement of particular statutes is not uncommon in practice. Whether due to the personal predilections of the prosecutor, the tolerance of the local community, or the antiquity or irrationality of the statute, some laws are enforced only *pro forma* or sporadically in response to media pressure, and some laws are not enforced at all.

The second problem faced is how many criminal offenders are to be prosecuted if all cannot be. For example, if a federal prosecutor in a large urban area decided to prosecute all thefts from the mail, or all forgeries of government instruments, or all false statements on government employment applications, or all interstate auto thefts, he or she would be able to prosecute nothing else.

Third, if a particular offender has committed more than one offense, a question is raised as to whether he should be prosecuted for *all* crimes or only for the most serious. The decision on other offenses can be reserved until the disposition of the first offense charged. If one serious offense may be charged, the prosecutor may also consider filing a less serious one—an "included" or "reduced" offense.

A prosecutor must also consider the views of the police agencies with which he or she works. Some police agencies, whose abilities to win appropriations depends upon the statistics they are able to present to a budget director or a legislative body, exert pressures upon a prosecutor to maintain a high level of prosecutions in selected areas within their jurisdiction. Under other circumstances, the desires of the investigative agencies may have little effect upon the decision to prosecute, except within the framework of a prosecutor's desire to maintain "good relations". Some prosecutors, when dealing with agencies which are especially cooperative on a regular basis, may, in return, prosecute more of that agencies' cases, or go on borderline cases where the agency has a particular interest in proceeding.

The decision may also turn upon what alternative remedies are open to the prosecutor and the administrative or investigative agency. For example, if a federal prosecutor declines to prosecute a theft from interstate shipment, no alternative (other than state prosecution) is available to satisfy the FBI. But if he or she declines to prosecute a case of fraud on the Social Security Administration, the agency may recoup lost monies from future payments. The failure to prosecute food stamp violations ferreted out by agents from the Department of Agriculture does not preclude the imposition of administrative sanctions by the agency. On occasion there may be pressure from a police agency to at least initiate prosecution to protect agents from the threat of civil litigation in cases where the arrest or search techniques were questionable. And, in a related area, there may be occasional industry pressures to proceed with a weak case against an employee—a theft case against a truck driver—to forestall union demands for reinstatement in the face of management's desire to discharge the errant employee.

The kind of offense under consideration may also affect the decision to prosecute or decline. A county prosecutor, for example, would rarely decline to prosecute a crime of violence or a narcotics charge, except for insufficiency of evidence or unlawful police practices which would result in suppression and consequent acquittal. Discretion in these instances is limited to legal assessments of these two potential problems. On the other hand, when considering whether to prosecute low level visibility offenses not involving threats to life or safety, and not particularly outrageous from society's standpoint, guilt is not, ordinarily, in issue and the decision to prosecute turns upon other factors. It is, of course, a truism that the lower the visibility of the offense and the lower the visibility of the prosecution, the easier it is to exercise discretion in deciding whether to prosecute.

The particular deterrence rationale involved may also be a factor. The prosecution of a particular offense may be likely to produce a fairly effective deterrent to the commission of crimes by *others* if prosecuted vigorously and notoriously. Tax evasion, embezzlement, and other crimes involving substantial periods of contemplation and planning are viewed as offenses within this classification. On the other hand, the offense may be one which often is the product of a momentary aberration, not likely to be repeated. In such a case, the deterrence of others is of little moment. The primary concern is safeguarding society from a repetition of the acts by the *same* offender. This would be true in reckless homicide and certain marital batteries. Or the offense may simply not respond well to the criminal process: drunken and disorderly conduct, gambling, prostitution, and other crimes without complainants.

A prosecutor must also consider what kind of office he or she wants to conduct, for almost every prosecutor's office reflects the personal philosophies and priorities of the principal prosecutor. He or she may strive for a statistical result such as a high "conviction rate"; if so, the prosecutor will be inclined to be cautious and refuse to proceed with cases which are doubtful or risky. The type of community credibility he or she seeks to attain is another important consideration. If the office is used as a political lance, the prosecutor will probably seek to be aggressive, though hopefully not reckless. If the prosecutor deliberately seeks community recognition in certain high visibility areas of prosecution—public corruption, narcotics, financial frauds, civil rights, or pollution—he or she will probably be keenly aware of the difference between "winning" and "not losing".

Finally, the stage of the prosecution at which the decision is being made is a factor to consider in the exercise of prosecutorial discretion. Is the prosecutor being called upon to decide whether to proceed before arrest? Or after the decision to arrest has been made by the police without his or her concurrence, but before a complaint has been filed? Should a case in which a complaint has been filed be taken through the grand jury process? Should the case be reassessed after indictment but before trial? Is there any reason, after conviction, to acquiesce in a motion for new trial? If a case is reversed on appeal some period of time after commission of the offense, the decision to reprosecute is often made after consideration of totally different factors than those which made up the initial decision to proceed; the current state of the evidence, the current climate of community opinion, a possible change in prosecutors, the expense of a retrial, a sentence mostly served awaiting appeal, and similar considerations.

3. THE SPECIFIC FACTORS OF DISCRETION

We turn then to a consideration of some of the *specific* factors which may enter into a prosecutor's decision of whether to proceed with a charge of a criminal offense. We assume, for these purposes, the sufficiency of the evidence.

Not all of these factors may enter into the decision in every case. And a prosecutor may not consciously be aware that she is even considering some of those that do enter into the case, for, depending upon her experience, her ability to analyze summaries of evidence and the time devoted to such analysis, she may conclude very quickly that a case is worth prosecuting or it is not.

The first question to be considered is whether the case fits within the prosecution priorities of the office. Especially in large offices, many cases in which the guilt of the accused is clear are not prosecuted simply because the office resources are not sufficient to proceed in every instance. For example, in a large office, small cases of theft, embezzlement, marijuana possession and the like may be declined in order to allow the prosecutor to proceed with more serious offenses. Sometimes the potential defendants are placed in a status of "probation without conviction", which, if successfully completed, results in eventual dismissal of the charge. The federal prosecutor may decline in favor of local prosecution. If the offender is a member of the armed forces, he may be returned to the processes of military justice. A juvenile may be turned over to local juvenile authorities. Or the case may simply be declined, especially where restitution (in theft or fraud cases) has been made before the prosecutor must exercise his discretion.

In some cases, a prosecutor will decide that the arrest and temporary incarceration before release on bail was a sufficient sanction to promote deterrence. For example, the drunken business man who makes threatening remarks aboard an aircraft, and who spends the night in jail before release, is unlikely to need the additional sanction of actual prosecution to carry home the gravity of the offense. Care must be exercised in these cases, however, to prevent the concept of "trial" or "punishment" by arrest or incarceration from becoming a stated concept of law enforcement, especially one to be engaged in by investigative agencies in their discretion.

The defendant's background is also important. Prosecuting authorities tend to be more lenient with youthful and elderly offenders, with persons who have led disadvantaged lives, with people who have wretched family situations which may have been contributing factors in the commission of the offense, with defendants who have many children or whose earnings are near the poverty level, with defendants who have creditable military service records, with people who have no prior arrest or conviction records, and with defendants who have been ill or who have mental problems not amounting to insanity. Sometimes these factors may have little or nothing to do with the commission of the offense, but, since prosecutors may feel a natural sympathy for the disadvantaged, the factors weigh in the balance when the decision to prosecute or decline is made. If a prosecutor receives 100 small embezzlement cases a year and has the resources to prosecute only twenty, it is likely that he will look for extenuating factors as an excuse to rationalize declination of the eighty on grounds other than lack of resources.

The defendant's record of embroilment with the law on collateral charges is also important. If a defendant has just been convicted of another offense in the same or a sister jurisdiction, the likelihood is that a presently pending charge will not go forward, particularly if the prosecutor suspects that conviction of a second offense will simply result in the imposition of a concurrent sentence. On the other hand, if the defendant has just been acquitted of another charge, particularly in a sister jurisdiction, and there is reason to believe that the acquittal was not based upon the merits, if crucial evidence was suppressed, or, assuming conviction, if the sentence for the other offense is thought to be too lenient, the decision may well be to proceed with the pending offense.

Even though guilt of the offense is clear, the quality of the prosecution's case must be constantly scrutinized. This is especially true when the prosecutor deals with a witness to a succession of offenses, such as an accomplice in a number of prosecutions against different hijackers or "fences." While the state of the evidence in earlier prosecutions may have been convincing and convictions may have been obtained, witnesses who testify repeatedly sometimes "wear out", and their testimony may become less credible either because they or the prosecutor become careless by reason of earlier successes, or continued trials may furnish additional impeaching material. If the string of victories ends, and the prosecutor suffers several setbacks, he or she may well reconsider prosecuting the balance of the cases which looked promising a year earlier, when the indictments were obtained. On the other hand, a prior loss with the same key witness does not necessarily foreclose prosecution of a case in a new jurisdiction. The new prosecutors, jurors, community opinion, and differences in corroborating evidence may justify proceeding with an indictment in one jurisdiction even though the case is based substantially upon the testimony of a witness who has previously testified in a losing prosecution in another jurisdiction.

The age of a case may also persuade a prosecutor not to proceed. The case may be old when the offense is discovered, or the case may have lain dormant too long within the police agency or through trial delay, and the evidence may now be stale. This factor is particularly important when, following reversal for reasons other than the sufficiency of the evidence, a decision whether a case should be retried must be made. Here, the factors of cost and manpower, which may not have been considered when the initial decision to prosecute was made, may outweigh the advantages of finally achieving a verdict of guilty. This is often true when the controversial nature of a case may have stretched a trial for a lesser offense beyond the limits which ordinarily would be reached.

Even though legal guilt is clear, a prosecutor who has set prosecution goals or wishes to maintain a community posture of invincibility in priority areas may closely weigh the "winability" of a case. If there are factors upon which a jury might rest a verdict of acquittal despite the evidence of guilt, a prosecutor may fear the harmful effect of that acquittal upon the deterrence which a previous string of victories has presumably generated among potential offenders and decide that the prosecution is not worth the risk. In an analogous area, a prosecutor may also decide to delay the institution of a prosecution, even though the offense is complete at that point and there is sufficient evidence of guilt, because the case may have more "jury appeal" if subsequent conditions change. For example, if a defendant has obtained a large number of loans by means of false financial statements submitted to various lending institutions, he may be guilty of several offenses and the evidence may be sufficient to indict. But if all the loans are current and there are no losses to the banks, the case may not have the "jury appeal" necessary to obtain a conviction. Delay in the institution of prosecution until the loans go bad may appear to be a more discrete course of action on the part of the cautious prosecutor.

Prosecutors may also exercise their discretion to punish or reward defendants and, sometimes, their lawyers. Prosecution may be foregone as part of an agreement to obtain the defendant's cooperation against others. Or a case that, by application of routine standards might be declined, is pressed when a defendant refuses to cooperate with investigating or prosecuting authorities.

Occasionally, the fortuitous choice of a lawyer may work to the advantage of a defendant in his invocation of the prosecutor's discretion. If a lawyer has established a close relationship with a prosecutor, and if he or she has been of material assistance in other cases, persuading guilty clients not only to plead, but to testify against others, the prosecutor may be more inclined to deal leniently with a current client. Conversely, if a lawyer is employed who has an antagonistic relationship with the principal prosecutor or his assistants, the current client may find that his borderline case is decided in favor of prosecution.

The decision to make "new law" by instituting a criminal prosecution for the first time under a statute not previously utilized is one of the most difficult for a prosecutor. Many criminal statutes—particularly in the regulatory area—are broadly drawn and when their breadth is teamed with a prosecutor's ingenuity, practices close to the line—particularly in the business community—may be swept within the net of criminal prosecution.

When the application of the statute is clear enough, and only a new or more vigorous program of enforcement is in issue, the question is relatively easy. For example, upon the imposition of wage and price controls, the government, in order to achieve national uniformity and maximum compliance, will prosecute, with maximum public exposure, all cases brought by the investigative agency, whether large or small. When the enforcement program is well under way and a sufficient compliance has been obtained, the prosecutor will invoke her discretion only in those cases which will clear doubtful areas of the law or which, because of the visibility of the offense or the offender, will presumably serve special deterrent purposes.

When the statute has been in force for some time and the question of whether certain conduct is violative of the act is without precedent, the issues which the prosecutor must confront are somewhat different. If the conduct in question is asserted to have some claim to legitimacy—either by widespread or long time acceptance in the business community or by the assertion of industry leaders—it may well be the fairer course to publicly announce a prosecutorial conclusion that the conduct in question is viewed as unlawful. If the conduct ceases, the objectives of criminal prosecution have been accomplished. If offenders persist, then at least they have had fair warning.

Finally, a prosecutor always takes account of how a prosecution will be perceived by the defendant and his associates, by the press and public, by the court, by the investigative agency and by fellow lawyers. A case which is otherwise perfectly ripe for prosecution may be declined if, for example, a United States Attorney believes it is not "worthy" of being brought in a federal court, or, at least, suspects that a federal judge would think so. Or a case may be declined if the press or public would consider a prosecutor's priorities out of kilter if he brought it: the theft of a pair of shoes from a hospital supply room by a patient. And if cases too close to the borderline are prosecuted with sudden regularity, the investigative agencies might legitimately conclude that the prosecutor's standards have undergone unspoken adjustment and readjust their investigative priorities without consultation with the prosecutor.

Perhaps the qualities which an individual must possess in order to combine these discretionary factors into a correct and meaningful decision were best described by Mr. Justice Jackson when he was Attorney General of the United States:

> "The qualities of a good prosecutor are as elusive and as impossible to define as those which mark a gentleman. And those who need to be told would not understand it anyway. A sensitiveness to fair play and sportsmanship is perhaps the best protection against the abuse of power, and the citizen's safety lies in the prosecutor who tempers zeal with human kindness, who seeks truth and not victims, who serves the law and not factional purposes, and who approaches his task with humility."[1]

1. Jackson, The Federal Prosecutor, 31 J.Crim.L., Crim. & P.S. 3, 6 (1940). See, also Friedman, The Prosecutor: A Model for Role and Function, 1978 Wash.L.Q. 109.

NOTES

1. The United States Department of Justice in 1980 issued guidelines for the exercise of prosecutorial discretion. They are reprinted at 27 Crim.L.Rptr. 3277, and updated guidelines appear in Justice Department manuals. The guidelines purport to prevent creation of a right to be treated in accordance with the guidelines. Would a court be bound by such a declaration when a defendant claims that the authorities have violated their own standards in selecting him for prosecution? The guidelines are so general and leave so much room for subjective judgment that rarely will a defendant be able to claim that his prosecution clearly violated the standards.

2. Consider limitation upon prosecutorial discretion in connection with claims of prosecutorial vindictiveness in retaliation for a defendant's assertion of his rights within the criminal justice system. See Bordenkircher v. Hayes (Casebook, p. 1153), and Blackledge v. Perry.

3. Is there anything wrong with using the decision to charge as a kind of forum-shopping? In United States v. Schwartz, 787 F.2d 257 (7th Cir.1986), state criminal charges were assigned for trial before a judge whom the prosecution viewed as defense-minded. The state authorities then persuaded federal authorities to bring federal charges. The state prosecutors dismissed state charges. The Seventh Circuit held that the federal judiciary should not interfere with such a use of prosecutorial discretion, even if it found such forum-shopping distasteful.

United States v. Cowan

United States Court of Appeals, Fifth Circuit, 1975.
524 F.2d 504.

■ MURRAH, CIRCUIT JUDGE:

The first sentence of Rule 48(a) Fed.R.Crim.P. provides that "The Attorney General or the United States attorney may by leave of court file a dismissal of an indictment, information or complaint and the prosecution shall thereupon terminate." In our case the trial judge, the Honorable Robert M. Hill, denied the United States Attorney's motion under Rule 48(a) to dismiss pending criminal proceedings in the Northern District of Texas, and upon formal declination of the government to proceed, appointed private, special prosecutors to continue the prosecution of the case. The government took a timely appeal from the order appointing the special prosecutors. . . .

* * *

In February of 1974, a federal grand jury in the Northern District of Texas returned a seven-count indictment against Jake Jacobsen. Six of the counts charged Jacobsen and Roy Cowan with the fraudulent misapplication of funds of a federally insured savings and loan association in San Angelo, Texas. A seventh count charged Jacobsen alone with knowingly making a false statement under oath to the grand jury. The indictment was signed by the United States Attorney for the district. After rather extensive motion practice resulting in a pretrial order in April, the case was set for trial in July. On joint motion of the parties the case was continued until a day in September due to the unavailability of a government witness.

Meanwhile and in May of the same year, the Watergate Special Prosecution Force and Jacobsen's Washington counsel negotiated an agreement whereunder Jacobsen agreed to plead guilty to a one-count charge to be filed in the District of Columbia alleging violation of 18 U.S.C. § 201(f) (bribing a public official) and make a full and truthful disclosure of all relevant information and documents within Jacobsen's knowledge and possession concerning matters then under investigation by the Watergate Special Prosecution Force, and if required, be a witness on any charges arising out of any such investigation. The Special Prosecution Force agreed not to press any potential charges against Jacobsen in the District of Columbia arising out of the relevant investigation. It was also a part of the plea agreement that the government would dismiss the Texas indictment.

Apparently Jacobsen appeared before a grand jury in the District of Columbia in May giving testimony incriminating himself and others. In any event, in July the grand jury returned an indictment in the District of Columbia charging Jacobsen in one count with violation of 18 U.S.C. § 201(f) and as an unindicted co-conspirator in a conspiracy count against former Secretary of the Treasury John Connally. In August Jacobsen entered a guilty plea to the bribery count (18 U.S.C. § 201(f)). The plea was accepted and the sentence postponed. At the same time the plea agreement was filed with the clerk of the court.

In accordance with the plea agreement, the United States Attorney for the Northern District of Texas moved under Rule 48(a) to dismiss the indictment set for trial in September. A copy of the plea agreement was attached to the motion. The motion to dismiss recited that the Office of the Special Prosecutor and the Attorney General believed that Jacobsen's testimony was necessary to the investigation and prosecution of the indictment in the District of Columbia; that if it did not enter into the plea agreement, the testimony of Jacobsen in that case, or any other case in which his testimony is relevant, would be lost; that the motion to dismiss the Texas charges was made in good faith, in accordance with the plea agreement and not for purposes of harassment; and that the interest of justice will be best served by disposing of the charges against Jacobsen in this manner. A memorandum of law supporting the Attorney General's absolute discretion to dismiss the indictment even without leave of court was filed with the motion. Jacobsen's Texas counsel joined in the United States Attorney's motion to dismiss. The motion was submitted in open court without further argument or testimony. On the same day and pursuant to another plea agreement, Judge Hill accepted a guilty plea by co-defendant Cowan to two counts of the Texas indictment and the United States Attorney agreed to move to dismiss the remaining counts after sentencing. Thus, all charges against Jacobsen and Cowan not disposed of by guilty pleas were made the subject of motions to dismiss by the government with consent of the defendants in accordance with the two plea agreements.

In an exhaustive opinion, the trial court asserted its discretionary power under Rule 48(a) to grant or deny the motion for leave to dismiss the Texas indictment against Jacobsen. Upon denial of the motion to dismiss, the United States Attorney filed its notice of intention not to prosecute.

Whereupon, the court, asserting its inherent power to protect the public interest in these extraordinary circumstances, appointed private special prosecutors "with full authority to control the course of investigation and litigation related to the offenses charged in the indictment and to handle all aspects of the case to the same extent as the United States Attorney in any criminal prosecution."

The Attorney General stakes his claim to absolute power to dismiss the proceedings even without "leave of court" squarely upon the Doctrine of Separation of Powers as derived from the provisions of the Constitution establishing three separate, but co-equal branches of government, each supreme in its own sphere; and more particularly upon Article II, Section 3 which provides in material part that the President "shall take Care that the Laws be faithfully executed" and upon 28 U.S.C. §§ 516, 519, empowering the Attorney General as surrogate of the President to conduct or supervise all litigation in which the government is a party. The court-appointed prosecutors counter that the Doctrine of Separation of Powers implied in the Constitution does not cast the three branches of our government into water-tight compartments; that room is left for some commingling of responsibilities in the orderly administration of governmental affairs; that by the promulgation of Rule 48(a) as part of the Rules of Criminal Procedure, Congress intended to vest in the courts a shared responsibility for the dismissal of prosecutions once lodged in the court; and that the power to grant leave to dismiss a criminal prosecution carries with it the correlative power to exercise a discretion to deny leave to dismiss and, if necessary, to effectuate such denial by the appointment of private prosecutors.

To sustain the asserted absolute power to dismiss the proceedings without "leave of court," the Attorney General relies heavily on United States v. Cox, 342 F.2d 167 (5th Cir.1965) and its progeny. That case involved the power of the district court to require the United States Attorney, under penalty of contempt, to sign an indictment or true bill as presented by the grand jury in accordance with Rule 7(c) Fed.R.Crim.P., which provides that an indictment "shall be signed by the attorney for the government." A majority of the en banc court sustained the government's petition to prohibit the trial judge from enforcing its contempt order and from asserting jurisdiction to require the Attorney General of the United States or the United States Attorney "to institute criminal prosecution or to take any steps in regard thereto."

After delineating the powers of the Judicial Department under Article III and of the Executive Department under Article II, Section 1 of the Constitution, Judge Jones speaking for the majority of the en banc court declared:

> "Although as a member of the bar, the attorney for the United States is an officer of the court, he is nevertheless an executive official of the Government, and it is as an officer of the executive department that he exercises a discretion as to whether or not there shall be a prosecution in a particular case. It follows, as an incident of the constitutional separation of powers, that the courts are not to interfere with the free exercise of the discretionary

> powers of the attorneys of the United States in their control over criminal prosecutions. The provision of Rule 7, requiring the signing of the indictment by the attorney for the Government, is a recognition of the power of the Government counsel to permit or not to permit the bringing of an indictment. . . ." United States v. Cox, supra at 171.

This succinct and forthright statement has been quoted and applied, quite correctly we think, in a variety of situations under differing circumstances, all involving the Executive's power and authority to initiate a criminal prosecution or the power of the court to dismiss on its own motion a pending prosecution.

* * *

Though the Rule was not at issue in *Cox*, it came under the scrutiny of the court in connection with the interpretation of Rule 7(c). The majority was apparently of the view that without the discretionary power given to the United States Attorney to prevent an indictment under 7(c) by withholding his signature, the constitutionality of Rule 48(a) would be doubtful. The court accordingly justified the Rule with the observation that it was intended solely to authorize the court to protect a defendant from harassment by successive filings and dismissals. Chief Judge Brown specially concurring agreed that 48(a) "vests the unfettered discretion in the District Attorney to determine whether a prosecution is to be maintained or dismissed." He was careful, however, to acknowledge that the interpretation of 48(a) had not been directly presented and that there was no assurance the rule "might not ultimately be construed [to reserve] considerable power to the District Judge himself in determining whether to enter a dismissal on the Government's motion." See *Cox* at 183 n. 6. Judge Wisdom specially concurring was sure that "the district attorney has absolute control over criminal prosecutions [with power to] dismiss or refuse to prosecute . . . [t]he responsibility is wholly his."

* * *

The holding in *Cox* is doubtless the law on its facts, and nothing we say here is intended to derogate from it. But ours is not a *Cox* case. *Cox* involved a challenge to the power of the court to direct the commencement of a prosecution, under Rule 7(c). We are concerned with the power of the court to supervise the termination of a prosecution in being, under Rule 48(a). While the dicta in all the opinions in the *Cox* case provide a formidable preface to our inquiry, this dicta is inconclusive here because that court was not called upon to distinguish between the power to initiate and the power to terminate prosecutions.

The absolute power and discretion of the Attorney General or his subordinates to institute prosecution is conceded, as it must also be conceded that no federal appellate court has come face to face with the asserted power of the district court under 48(a) to grant or withhold leave to dismiss a criminal prosecution once begun. The question is squarely presented here for the first time as a controversy between the Executive and Judicial Branches of government involving opposing asserted powers under the Rule.

* * *

In situations like these history has its claims, and we think it is appropriate to review it. Before the adoption of 48(a), more than thirty states had, by statute or judicial decision, modified the common law to give courts a responsible role in the dismissal of a pending criminal proceeding by requiring an "order" or "leave" or "consent" of court. The state case law interpreting this change is sparse, but what there is of it consistently affirms the power and duty of the court to exercise discretion to grant or withhold leave to dismiss pending criminal prosecutions in "the public interest."

* * *

[The Advisory Committee created to propose Federal Rules of Criminal Procedure Submitted a Draft Rule to the Supreme Court which read: "The Attorney General or the United States Attorney may file a dismissal of the indictment or information with a statement of the reasons therefor and the prosecution shall thereupon terminate."]

The Supreme Court deleted the phrase "with a statement of the reasons therefor," and, in lieu thereof, inserted the phrase "by leave of court." As thus amended, 48(a) was submitted to Congress and adopted. It seems manifest that the Supreme Court intended to make a significant change in the common law rule by vesting in the courts the power and the duty to exercise a discretion for the protection of the public interest.

* * *

It seems to us that the history of the Rule belies the notion that its only scope and purpose is the protection of the defendant. ... Viewed in this light, we think it manifestly clear that the Supreme Court intended to clothe the federal courts with a discretion broad enough to protect the public interest in the fair administration of criminal justice. It is against this background that we consider the overpowering effect of the Doctrine of Separation of Powers.

In the resolution of this question, we think United States v. Nixon, [418 U.S. 683, 94 S.Ct. 3090 (1974)], both pertinent and authoritative. In that case the Chief Executive asserted the unqualified privilege of an immunity from judicial process under all circumstances as a derivative of the Doctrine of Separation of Powers. Chief Justice Burger responded:

> "The impediment that an absolute unqualified privilege would place in the way of the primary constitutional duty of the Judicial Branch to do justice in criminal prosecutions would plainly conflict with the function of the courts under Art. III. In designing the structure of our Government and dividing and allocating the sovereign power among three coequal branches, the Framers of the Constitution sought to provide a comprehensive system, but the separate powers were not intended to operate with absolute independence.

> " 'While the Constitution diffuses power the better to secure liberty, it also contemplates that practice will integrate the dispersed powers into a workable government. It enjoins upon its branches separateness but interdependence, autonomy but reciprocity.' Youngstown Sheet & Tube Co. v. Sawyer, 343 U.S. 579, 635 [72 S.Ct. 863, 870] (1952) (Jackson, J., concurring)." United States v. Nixon, supra at 707, 94 S.Ct. at 3107.

The Chief Justice, speaking for a unanimous court, went on to conclude that the legitimate needs of the judicial process may very well out weigh Executive privilege; and that it is necessary to resolve these competing interests in a manner that preserves the essential function of the Executive Branch by according high respect to its claim of privilege. Ultimately, the Court sustained the power to subpoena Executive material pertaining to the fair administration of criminal justice without affecting the national security.

That authoritative reasoning should be our guide here. We think the rule should and can be construed to preserve the essential judicial function of protecting the public interest in the evenhanded administration of criminal justice without encroaching on the primary duty of the Executive to take care that the laws are faithfully executed. The resulting balance of power is precisely what the Framers intended. As Judge Wisdom put it, quoting Montesquieu, " 'To prevent the abuse of power, it is necessary that by the very disposition of things, power should be a check to power' ... [thus] the framers wove a web of checks and balances designed to prevent abuse of power" and "were too sophisticated to believe that the three branches of government were absolutely separate, air-tight departments." United States v. Cox, supra at 190. From this, it seems altogether proper to say that the phrase "by leave of court" in Rule 48(a) was intended to modify and condition the absolute power of the Executive, consistently with the Framer's concept of Separation of Powers, by erecting a check on the abuse of Executive prerogatives. But this is not to say that the Rule was intended to confer on the Judiciary the power and authority to usurp or interfere with the good faith exercise of the Executive power to take care that the laws are faithfully executed. The rule was not promulgated to shift absolute power from the Executive to the Judicial Branch. Rather, it was intended as a power to check power. The Executive remains the absolute judge of whether a prosecution should be initiated and the first and presumptively the best judge of whether a pending prosecution should be terminated. The exercise of its discretion with respect to the termination of pending prosecutions should not be judicially disturbed unless clearly contrary to manifest public interest. In this way, the essential function of each branch is synchronized to achieve a balance that serves both practical and constitutional values.

Judge Hill was undoubtedly clothed with a discretion to determine whether the dismissal of these charges was clearly contrary to the public interest. But it is a judicial discretion subject to appellate review. And since that discretion is constitutionally sensitive, we feel bound to a closer scrutiny than in the ordinary case where such practical considerations as finality of decision, judicial economy, and trial judge's closeness to the evidentiary process dictate greater appellate court deference. If upon appraisal of all the relevant factors, the appellate court has a definite and firm conviction that the trial court committed a clear error of judgment in the conclusion it reached, the judgment must be reversed.

* * *

Judge Hill was "unable to perceive how the best interest of justice could be served by dismissing serious charges with a potential penalty of thirty-five years imprisonment and a $70,000 fine in exchange for a guilty plea in an unrelated case carrying a maximum penalty of two years and a $10,000 fine." He also referred to the fact that "the investigatory material developed by [Texas] state and federal agencies was turned over to the federal officials with the understanding that the federal government would initiate and pursue appropriate prosecution"; that the government's "bare assertion" of reasons for dismissal was unaccompanied by factual evidence. In these circumstances, he concluded, "the interest of justice would not be served by a dismissal of this case." The brief of the court-appointed prosecutors seems to impugn the good faith of the government by suggesting that the motion to continue the trial, filed jointly by the prosecution and both defendants in June 1974, was calculated to facilitate the surreptitious performance of the plea agreement negotiated one month earlier between Jacobsen and the Watergate Special Prosecution Force, and thus dispense with the trial of the Texas case.

We think this appraisal of the whole matter misapprehends the relative roles of the Executive and the Judiciary under 48(a). The considerations which prompted Judge Hill to overrule the motion to dismiss are, in our judgment, legally insufficient to overcome the presumption of the government's good faith and establish its betrayal of the public interest. We do not think the plea negotiations between the two prosecutorial arms of the government and counsel for both defendants were improper, even though not disclosed to the sentencing judges until consummation. It is not suggested that the facts recited in the joint motion for continuance were untrue, or that they were inadequate grounds for a continuance. In this situation, we can hardly say that the motion was a sham or a deception. It was not incumbent upon the government to inform the sentencing judges of the plea negotiations until after they had been consummated. The result of these negotiations was finally placed before both sentencing courts in the form of plea agreements, which themselves have a legitimate and desirable function in the effective administration of criminal justice. Nor was it clearly contrary to the public interest for the government to accept in these plea agreements a reduction in the maximum possible sentence of Cowan and Jacobsen, when, as stated in the government's motion, it served to further an investigation by an especially created and wholly autonomous arm of the Executive. We cannot agree with Judge Hill's view that this motion lacked specificity of evidentiary proof. The representations in the motion and the supporting memorandum were not merely conclusory; they specified the investigation being pursued in the District of Columbia and the necessity of obtaining Jacobsen's cooperation under the plea agreement calling for dismissal of the Texas charges. We are convinced that this is legally sufficient to justify leave of court to dismiss the Texas charges against Jacobsen in consideration of his guilty plea in the District of Columbia.

In sum, it was within the province of the two prosecutorial arms of the government to weigh the relative importance of two separate prosecutions in two separate districts and dispose of them as practical considerations seemed to dictate. Nothing in this record overcomes the presumption that they did so in good faith for substantial reasons sufficiently articulated in the motion to dismiss. As to the interest of the State of Texas in these charges, we can perceive no reason why the dismissal would bar or prejudice a state prosecution on substantially the same Texas charges. In the first place, Jacobsen was never put in jeopardy on the Texas charges. Moreover, a prosecution by one sovereign is no bar to a prosecution by another sovereign arising out of the same facts. . . .

Having concluded that the trial court exceeded the bounds of its discretion under Rule 48(a) in denying the government's motion to dismiss, we have no cause to consider the propriety of its order effectuating that denial by appointing special prosecutors. The case is reversed and remanded with directions to sustain the motion to dismiss.

NOTES

1. The authority of the prosecutor to refuse to bring a case is almost unlimited; and the authority of a court to compel a prosecution is barred by the separation of powers. In Inmates of Attica v. Rockefeller, 477 F.2d 375 (2d Cir.1973), the inmates of a prison sought to compel the United States Attorney to prosecute persons who had allegedly violated certain federal and state statutes in connection with the treatment of the inmates during and following a prison uprising. Upholding prosecutorial discretion to initiate proceedings, the court observed that "the problems inherent in the task of supervising prosecutorial decisions do not lend themselves to resolution by the judiciary." Similarly, in Powell v. Katzenbach, 359 F.2d 234 (D.C.Cir.1965), the court upheld the trial judge's dismissal of a mandamus action to require the Attorney General to initiate a criminal prosecution against a national bank and its officers on the ground that the statute relied upon disclosed no congressional intent to alter the Executive's exclusive discretion to initiate a prosecution.

In Leeke v. Timmerman, 454 U.S. 83, 102 S.Ct. 69 (1981), the Supreme Court reiterated a point made in Linda R.S. v. Richard D., 410 U.S. 614, 93 S.Ct. 1146 (1973): a private citizen "lacks a judicially cognizable interest in the prosecution or the non-prosecution of another."

In Morrison v. Olson, 487 U.S. 654, 108 S.Ct. 2597 (1988), the Court upheld the special prosecutor provision of the 1978 Ethics in Government Act. The Court held that Congress can deny to the president the power to appoint the special prosecutor because the special prosecutor is an "inferior officer." Giving the power of appointment to a specially created court did not violate separation of power requirements, according to the *Morrison* majority. The courts do not control the action of the special prosecutor, nor does the Attorney General. However, the Attorney General, whose initial request after a preliminary investigation triggers the appointment of the special prosecutor, retains the right to remove the special prosecutor.

The trend today is to hold, even though the Attorney General has mandatory duties under the Ethics in Government Act to conduct a preliminary investigation to determine whether independent counsel should be appointed to investigate allegations of criminal offenses committed by certain government officials, that members of the public, including Congressmen, have no standing to bring an action asking a court to require the Attorney General to comply with the provisions of that law. See Dellums v. Smith, 797 F.2d 817 (9th Cir.1986).

2. May a judge compel the prosecutor to treat defendants equally with respect to plea-bargaining? In Newman v. United States, 382 F.2d 479 (D.C.Cir.1967), defendant claimed that the United States Attorney violated his constitutional rights by allowing a codefendant to plead guilty to a lesser included offense under the indictment while refusing to consent to the same plea for the appellant. Chief Justice (then Judge) Burger, speaking for the court, affirmed the absolute discretion of the United States Attorney as an executive official as to whether or not there shall be a prosecution in a particular case as an incident of the constitutional separation of powers.

In United States v. Hamm, 659 F.2d 624 (5th Cir.1981) (en banc), following a defendant's plea of guilty, the government recommended leniency for the accused because of the defendant's cooperation. The district court indicated an unwillingness to be so lenient. The prosecutor then moved to dismiss the indictment lest the defendant receive a stiffer sentence than the prosecutor thought proper. The district court refused to dismiss the indictment. The Court of Appeals held that the district court erred in blocking the dismissal.

3. When criminal conduct is prohibited by two separate statutes, must the prosecution proceed on the one that carries the lesser penalty? In United States v. Batchelder, 442 U.S. 114, 99 S.Ct. 2198 (1979), the Court held that, in the absence of discrimination against a class of individuals, the prosecutor is free to elect the more severe of two overlapping statutes in bringing an indictment.

4. Fields v. Soloff, 920 F.2d 1114 (2d Cir.1990), tells the story of a New York grand juror who felt the prosecutor was not adequately investigating certain misconduct. The local court prohibited him from urging his fellow jurors to consider any matter not put before the grand jury by the prosecutor. The Second Circuit found no basis for intervention to void either that limitation or the New York requirement that validates only those indictments which the prosecutor has approved. The case illustrates that the "runaway grand jury" is largely a myth.

B. RESTRICTIONS UPON DISCRETION

Wayte v. United States

Supreme Court of the United States, 1985.
470 U.S. 598, 105 S.Ct. 1524.

■ JUSTICE POWELL delivered the opinion of the Court.

The question presented is whether a passive enforcement policy under which the Government prosecutes only those who report themselves as having violated the law, or who are reported by others, violates the First and Fifth Amendments.

On July 2, 1980, pursuant to his authority under § 3 of the Military Selective Service Act, 62 Stat. 605, as amended, 50 U.S.C.App. § 453, the President issued Presidential Proclamation No. 4771, 3 CFR 82 (1981). This proclamation directed male citizens and certain male residents born during 1960 to register with the Selective Service System during the week of July 21, 1980. Petitioner fell within that class but did not register.

Instead, he wrote several letters to Government officials, including the President, stating that he had not registered and did not intend to do so.[2]

Petitioner's letters were added to a Selective Service file of young men who advised that they had failed to register or who were reported by others a shaving failed to register. For reasons we discuss, Selective Service adopted a policy of passive enforcement under which it would investigate and prosecute only the cases of nonregistration contained in this file. In furtherance of this policy, Selective Service sent a letter on June 17, 1981 to each reported violator who had not registered and for whom it had an address. The letter explained the duty to register, stated that Selective Service had information that the person was required to register but had not done so, requested that he either comply with the law by filling out an enclosed registration card or explain why he was not subject to registration, and warned that a violation could result in criminal prosecution and specified penalties. Petitioner received a copy of this letter but did not respond.

On July 20, 1981, Selective Service transmitted to the Department of Justice, for investigation and potential prosecution, the names of petitioner and 133 other young men identified under its passive enforcement system—all of whom had not registered in response to the Service's June letter. At two later dates, it referred the names of 152 more young men similarly identified. After screening out the names of those who appeared not to be in the class required to register, the Department of Justice referred the remaining names to the Federal Bureau of Investigation for additional inquiry and to the United States Attorneys for the districts in which the nonregistrants resided. Petitioner's name was one of those referred.

Pursuant to Department of Justice policy, those referred were not immediately prosecuted. Instead, the appropriate United States Attorney was required to notify identified nonregistrants by registered mail that, unless they registered within a specified time, prosecution would be considered. In addition, an FBI agent was usually sent to interview the nonregistrant before prosecution was instituted. This effort to persuade nonregis-

2. On August 4, 1980, for example, petitioner wrote to both the President and the Selective Service System. In his letter to the President, he stated:

> "I decided to obey my conscience rather than your law. I did not register for your draft. I will never register for your draft. Nor will I ever cooperate with yours or any other military system, despite the laws I might break or the consequences which may befall me." In his letter to the Selective Service System, he similarly stated: "I have not registered for the draft. I plan never to register. I realize the possible consequences of my action, and I accept them."

Six months later, petitioner sent a second letter to Selective Service:

> "Last August I wrote to inform you of my intention not to register for the draft. Well, I did not register, and still plan never to do so, but thus far I have received no reply to my letter, much less any news about your much-threatened prosecutions.
>
> "I must interpret your silence as meaning that you are too busy or disorganized to respond to letters or keep track of us draft-age youth. So I will keep you posted of my whereabouts."

He also stated that, although he would "be traveling the nation ... encouraging resistance and spreading the word about peace and disarmament," he could be reached at his home address in Pasadena, California.

trants to change their minds became known as the "beg" policy. Under it, young men who registered late were not prosecuted, while those who never registered were investigated further by the Government. Pursuant to the "beg" policy, the United States Attorney for the Central District of California sent petition era letter on October 15, 1981 urging him to register or face possible prosecution. Again petitioner failed to respond.

On December 9, 1981, the Department of Justice instructed all United States Attorneys not to begin seeking indictments against nonregistrants until further notice. On January 7, 1982, the President announced a grace period to afford nonregistrants a further opportunity to register without penalty. This grace period extended until February 28, 1982. Petitioner still did not register.

Over the next few months, the Department decided to begin prosecuting those young men who, despite the grace period and "beg" policy, continued to refuse to register. It recognized that under the passive enforcement system those prosecuted were "liable to be vocal proponents of nonregistration" or persons "with religious or moral objections." Memorandum of March 17, 1982 from Lawrence Lippe, Chief General Litigation and Legal Advice Section, Criminal Division, Department of Justice, to D. Lowell Jensen, Assistant Attorney General, Criminal Division. It also recognized that prosecutions would "undoubtedly result in allegations that the [case was] brought in retribution for the nonregistrant's exercise of his first amendment rights." The Department was advised, however, that Selective Service could not develop a more "active" enforcement system for quite some time. Because of this, the Department decided to begin seeking indictments under the passive system without further delay. On May 21, 1982, United States Attorneys were notified to begin prosecution of nonregistrants. On June 28, 1982, FBI agents interviewed petitioner and he continued to refuse to register. Accordingly, on July 22, 1982, an indictment was returned against him for knowingly and willfully failing to register with the Selective Service in violation of sections 3 and 12(a) of the Military Selective Service Act, 62 Stat. 605 and 622, as amended, 50 U.S.C.App. §§ 453 and 462(a). This was one of the first indictments returned against any individual under the passive policy.

Petitioner moved to dismiss the indictment on the ground of selective prosecution. He contended that he and the other indicted nonregistrants[3] were "vocal" opponents of the registration program who had been impermissibly targeted (out of an estimated 647,000 nonregistrants[4]) for prosecution on the basis of their exercise of First Amendment rights.

In our criminal justice system, the Government retains "broad discretion" as to whom to prosecute. United States v. Goodwin. "[S]o long as the

3. The record indicates that only 13 of the 286 young men Selective Service referred to the Department of Justice had been indicted at the time the District Court considered this case. As of March 31, 1984, three more men had been indicted. The approximately 270 not indicted either registered, were found not to be subject of registration requirements, could not be found, or were under continuing investigation. The record does not indicate how many fell into each category.

4. On July 28, 1982, Selective Service stated that 8,365,000 young men had registered out of the estimated 9,039,000 who were required to do so.

prosecutor has probable cause to believe that the accused committed an offense defined by statute, the decision whether or not to prosecute, and what charge to file or bring before a grand jury, generally rests entirely in his discretion." Bordenkircher v. Hayes (1978). This broad discretion rests largely on the recognition that the decision to prosecute is particularly ill-suited to judicial review. Such factors as the strength of the case, the prosecution's general deterrence value, the Government's enforcement priorities, and the case's relationship to the Government's overall enforcement plan are not readily susceptible to the kind of analysis the courts are competent to undertake. Judicial supervision in this area, moreover, entails systemic costs of particular concern. Examining the basis of a prosecution delays the criminal proceeding, threatens to chill law enforcement by subjecting the prosecutor's motives and decisionmaking to outside inquiry, and may undermine prosecutorial effectiveness by revealing the Government's enforcement policy. All these are substantial concerns that make the courts properly hesitant to examine the decision whether to prosecute.

As we have noted in a slightly different context, however, although prosecutorial discretion is broad, it is not " 'unfettered.' Selectivity in the enforcement of criminal laws is ... subject to constitutional constraints." United States v. Batchelder (1979). In particular, the decision to prosecute may not be " 'deliberately based upon an unjustifiable standard such as race, religion, or other arbitrary classification,' " Bordenkircher v. Hayes, supra, quoting Oyler v. Boles (1962), including the exercise of protected statutory and constitutional rights.

It is appropriate to judge selective prosecution claims according to ordinary equal protection standards.[9] Under our prior cases, these standards require petitioner to show both that the passive enforcement system had a discriminatory effect and that it was motivated by a discriminatory purpose.[10] Personnel Administrator of Mass. v. Feeney (1979); Arlington Heights v. Metropolitan Housing Development Corp. (1977); Washington v. Davis (1976). All petitioner has shown here is that those eventually prosecuted, along with many not prosecuted, reported themselves as having violated the law. He has not shown that the enforcement policy selected nonregistrants for prosecution on the basis of their speech. Indeed, he could not have done so given the way the "beg" policy was carried out. The Government did not prosecute those who reported themselves but later registered. Nor did it prosecute those who protested registration but did not report themselves or were not reported by others. In fact, the Government did not even investigate those who wrote letters to Selective Service criticizing registration unless their letters stated affirmatively that they had refused to comply with the law. The Government, on the other hand,

9. Although the Fifth Amendment, unlike the Fourteenth, does not contain an equal protection clause, it does contain an equal protection component. "[Our] approach to Fifth Amendment equal protection claims has ... been precisely the same as to equal protection claims under the Fourteenth Amendment." Weinberger v. Wiesenfeld (1975).

10. A showing of discriminatory intent is not necessary when the equal protection claim is based on an overtly discriminatory classification. See Strauder v. West Virginia (1880). No such claim is presented here, for petitioner cannot argue that the passive policy discriminated on its face.

did prosecute people who reported themselves or were reported by others but who did not publicly protest. These facts demonstrate that the Government treated all reported nonregistrants similarly. It did not subject vocal nonregistrants to any special burden. Indeed, those prosecuted in effect selected themselves for prosecution by refusing to register after being reported and warned by the Government.

Even if the passive policy had a discriminatory effect, petitioner has not shown that the Government intended such a result. The evidence he presented demonstrated only that the Government was aware that the passive enforcement policy would result in prosecution of vocal objectors and that they would probably make selective prosecution claims. As we have noted, however, " '[d]iscriminatory purpose' ... implies more than ... intent as awareness of consequences. It implies that the decisionmaker ... selected or reaffirmed a particular course of action at least in part 'because of,' not merely 'in spite of,' its adverse effects upon an identifiable group." Personnel Administrator of Mass. v. Feeney, supra. In the present case, petitioner has not shown that the Government prosecuted him *because of* his protest activities. Absent such a showing, his claim of selective prosecution fails.

Petitioner also challenges the passive enforcement policy directly on First Amendment grounds. In particular, he claims that "[e]ven though the [Government's passive] enforcement policy did not overtly punish protected speech as such, it inevitably created a content-based regulatory system with a concomitantly disparate, content-based impact on nonregistrants."[12] This Court has held that when, as here, " 'speech' and 'nonspeech' elements are combined in the same course of conduct, a sufficiently important governmental interest in regulating the nonspeech element can justify incidental limitations on First Amendment freedoms." United States v. O'Brien (1968). Government regulation is justified

> "if it is within the constitutional power of the Government; if it furthers an important or substantial governmental interest; if the governmental interest is unrelated to the suppression of free expression; and if the incidental restriction on alleged First Amendment freedoms is no greater than is essential to the furtherance of that interest." Id., at 377, 88 S.Ct., at 1679.

In the present case, neither the first nor third condition is disputed.

There can be no doubt that the passive enforcement policy meets the second condition. Few interests can be more compelling than a nation's

12. As an initial matter, we note doubt that petitioner has demonstrated injury to his First Amendment rights. The Government's "beg" policy removed most, if not all, of any burden passive enforcement placed on free expression. Because of this policy, nonregistrants could protest registration and still avoid any danger of prosecution. By simply registering after they had reported themselves to the Selective Service, nonregistrants satisfied their obligation and could thereafter continue to protest registration. No matter how strong their protest, registration immunized them from prosecution. Strictly speaking, then, the passive enforcement system penalized continued violation of the Military Selective Service Act, not speech. The only right it burdened was the asserted "right" not to register, a "right" without foundation either in the Constitution or the history of our country.

need to ensure its own security. It is well to remember that freedom as we know it has been suppressed in many countries. Unless a society has the capability and will to defend itself from the aggressions of others, constitutional protections of any sort have little meaning. ... With these principles in mind, the three reasons the Government offers in defense of this particular enforcement policy are sufficiently compelling to satisfy the second *O'Brien* requirement—as to either those who reported themselves or those who were reported by others.

First, by relying on reports of nonregistration, the Government was able to identify and prosecute violators without further delay. Although it still was necessary to investigate those reported to make sure that they were required to register and had not, the Government did not have to search actively for the names of these likely violators. Such a search would have been difficult and costly at that time. Indeed, it would be a costly step in any "active" prosecution system involving thousands of nonregistrants. The passive enforcement program thus promoted prosecutorial efficiency. Second, the letters written to Selective Service provided strong, perhaps conclusive evidence of the nonregistrant's intent not to comply—one of the elements of the offense. Third, prosecuting visible nonregistrants was thought to be an effective way to promote general deterrence, especially since failing to proceed against publicly known offenders would encourage others to violate the law.

The passive enforcement policy also meets the final requirement of the *O'Brien* test, for it placed no more limitation on speech than was necessary to ensure registration for the national defense. Passive enforcement not only did not subject "vocal" nonregistrants to any special burden, but also was intended to be only an interim enforcement system. Although Selective Service was engaged in developing an active enforcement program when it investigated petitioner, it had by then found no practicable way of obtaining the names and current addresses of likely nonregistrants. Eventually, it obtained them by matching state driver's license records with Social Security files. It took some time, however, to obtain the necessary authorizations and to set up this system. Passive enforcement was the only effective interim solution available to carry out the Government's compelling interest.

We think it important to note as a final matter how far the implications of petitioner's First Amendment argument would extend. Strictly speaking, his argument does not concern passive enforcement but self-reporting. The concern she identifies would apply to all nonregistrants who report themselves even if the Selective Service engaged only in active enforcement. For example, a nonregistrant who wrote a letter informing Selective Service of his failure to register could, when prosecuted under an active system, claim that the Selective Service was prosecuting him only because of his "protest." Just as in this case, he could have some justification for believing that his letter had focused inquiry upon him. Prosecution in either context would equally "burden" his exercise of First Amendment rights. Under the petitioner's view, then, the Government could not constitutionally prosecute a self-reporter—even in an active enforcement system—unless perhaps it could prove that it would have prosecuted him without his letter. On principle, such a view would allow any criminal to obtain immunity from prosecution simply by reporting himself and claiming that he did so in order to "protest" the law. The First Amendment confers no such immunity from prosecution.

We conclude that the Government's passive enforcement system together with its "beg" policy violated neither the First nor Fifth Amendments.

■ JUSTICE MARSHALL, with whom JUSTICE BRENNAN joins, dissenting.

The Court decides today that petitioner "has not shown that the Government prosecuted him *because of* his protest activities," and it remands to permit his prosecution to go forward. However interesting the question decided by the Court may be, it is not necessary to the disposition of this case. Instead, the issue this Court must grapple with is far less momentous but no less deserving of thoughtful treatment. What it must decide is whether Wayte has earned the right to discover Government documents relevant to his claim of selective prosecution.

* * *

Second, and of equal importance, the Court errs in the manner in which it analyzes the merits of the equal protection claim. It simply focuses on the wrong problem when it states that "the Government treated all reported nonregistrants similarly" and that "those prosecuted in effect selected themselves for prosecution by refusing to register after being reported and warned by the Government." Those issues are irrelevant to the correct disposition of this case.

The claim here is not that the Justice Department discriminated among *known* violators of the draft registration law either in its administration of the "beg" policy, which gave such individuals the option of registering to avoid prosecution, or in prosecuting only some reported nonregistrants. Instead, the claim is that the system by which the Department defined the class of possible prosecutees—the "passive" enforcement system—was designed to discriminate against those who had exercised their First Amendment rights. Such Governmental action cannot stand if undertaken with discriminatory intent. As this Court has clearly stated, "for an agent of the State to pursue a course of action whose objective is to penalize a person's reliance on his legal rights is 'patently unconstitutional.'" Bordenkircher v. Hayes (1978). If the Government intentionally discriminated in defining the pool of potential prosecutees, it cannot immunize itself from liability merely by showing that it used permissible methods in choosing whom to prosecute from this previously tainted pool.

Under the Court's flawed approach, there would have been no equal protection violation in Yick Wo v. Hopkins, supra, this Court's seminal selective prosecution decision. In *Yick Wo*, the Court reversed a conviction under a municipal ordinance that prohibited the construction of wooden laundries without a license. The Court held that such a conviction could not stand because the municipal licensors had discriminatorily denied licenses to individuals of Chinese origin. If the Court then had focused only on the prosecutions themselves, as it does now, it would have found no discrimination in the choice, among violators of the ordinance, of the individuals to be prosecuted. Indeed, all but one of these violators were of Chinese origin. Instead, the Court properly focused on the official action that led to those prosecutions. In *Yick Wo*, that prior action was the discriminatory denial of licenses, which affected the definition of the class from which prosecutees were chosen. In this case, the referrals made by Selective Service to the Justice Department for investigation and possible prosecution played a similar role and may also have been discriminatory. It is to that issue that the Court should have directed its attention.

I do not suggest that all prosecutions undertaken pursuant to passive enforcement schemes warrant evidentiary hearings on the question of selective prosecution. But where violations of the law are so closely intertwined with political activity, where the speech at issue is so unpalatable to the Government, and where the discriminatory effect is conceded, the need for a hearing is significant and in no way opens the door to an onslaught of such hearings in less compelling contexts.[3]

Here, I believe that Wayte has raised sufficient questions about the Government's intentions to be entitled to obtain access to evidence in the Government's possession. I therefore dissent from the Court's outright dismissal of his equal protection claim.

United States v. Armstrong

Supreme Court of the United States, 1996.
517 U.S. 456, 116 S.Ct. 1480.

■ REHNQUIST, C.J., delivered the opinion of the Court.

In this case, we consider the showing necessary for a defendant to be entitled to discovery on a claim that the prosecuting attorney singled him out for prosecution on the basis of his race. We conclude that respondents failed to satisfy the threshold showing: They failed to show that the Government declined to prosecute similarly situated suspects of other races.

In April 1992, respondents were indicted in the Central District of California on charges of conspiring to possess with intent to distribute more than 50 grams of cocaine base (crack) and conspiring to distribute the same, in violation of 21 U.S.C. §§ 841 and 846 (1988 ed. and Supp. IV), and federal firearms offenses. For three months prior to the indictment, agents of the Federal Bureau of Alcohol, Tobacco, and Firearms and the Narcotics Division of the Inglewood, California, Police Department had infiltrated a suspected crack distribution ring by using three confidential informants. On seven separate occasions during this period, the informants had bought a total of 124.3 grams of crack from respondents and witnessed respondents carrying firearms during the sales. The agents searched the hotel

3. In my mind, Wayte's claim that the "passive" enforcement scheme placed a direct burden on First Amendment freedoms should not be addressed at this stage in the litigation. The materials that Wayte sought to discover, and that he well may be entitled to discover, could be relevant to that claim. The Court of Appeals should resolve the issue of access to evidence on remand; there solution of the merits of Wayte's claims should await a final determination of that issue.

room in which the sales were transacted, arrested respondents Armstrong and Hampton in the room, and found more crack and a loaded gun. The agents later arrested the other respondents as part of the ring.

In response to the indictment, respondents filed a motion for discovery or for dismissal of the indictment, alleging that they were selected for federal prosecution because they are black. In support of their motion, they offered only an affidavit by a "Paralegal Specialist," employed by the Office of the Federal Public Defender representing one of the respondents. The only allegation in the affidavit was that, in every one of the 24 §§ 841 or 846 cases closed by the office during 1991, the defendant was black. Accompanying the affidavit was a "study" listing the 24 defendants, their race, whether they were prosecuted for dealing cocaine as well as crack, and the status of each case.

The Government opposed the discovery motion, arguing, among other things, that there was no evidence or allegation "that the Government has acted unfairly or has prosecuted non-black defendants or failed to prosecute them." The District Court granted the motion. It ordered the Government (1) to provide a list of all cases from the last three years in which the Government charged both cocaine and firearms offenses, (2) to identify the race of the defendants in those cases, (3) to identify what levels of law enforcement were involved in the investigations of those cases, and (4) to explain its criteria for deciding to prosecute those defendants for federal cocaine offenses.

The Government moved for reconsideration of the District Court's discovery order. With this motion it submitted affidavits and other evidence to explain why it had chosen to prosecute respondents and why respondents' study did not support the inference that the Government was singling out blacks for cocaine prosecution. The federal and local agents participating in the case alleged in affidavits that race played no role in their investigation. An Assistant United States Attorney explained in an affidavit that the decision to prosecute met the general criteria for prosecution, because

> "there was over 100 grams of cocaine base involved, over twice the threshold necessary for a ten year mandatory minimum sentence; there were multiple sales involving multiple defendants, thereby indicating a fairly substantial crack cocaine ring; ... there were multiple federal firearms violations intertwined with the narcotics trafficking; the overall evidence in the case was extremely strong, including audio and videotapes of defendants; ... and several of the defendants had criminal histories including narcotics and firearms violations."

The Government also submitted sections of a published 1989 Drug Enforcement Administration report which concluded that "[l]arge-scale, interstate trafficking networks controlled by Jamaicans, Haitians and Black street gangs dominate the manufacture and distribution of crack." J. Featherly & E. Hill, Crack Cocaine Overview 1989; App. 103.

In response, one of respondents' attorneys submitted an affidavit alleging that an intake coordinator at a drug treatment center had told her that there are "an equal number of caucasian users and dealers to minority users and dealers." Respondents also submitted an affidavit from a criminal defense attorney alleging that in his experience many nonblacks are prosecuted in state court for crack offenses, id., at 141, and a newspaper article reporting that Federal "crack criminals ... are being punished far more severely than if they had been caught with powder cocaine, and almost every single one of them is black," Newton, Harsher Crack Sentences Criticized as Racial Inequity, Los Angeles Times, Nov. 23, 1992, p. 1; App. 208–210.

The District Court denied the motion for reconsideration. When the Government indicated it would not comply with the court's discovery order, the court dismissed the case.

A divided three-judge panel of the Court of Appeals for the Ninth Circuit reversed, holding that, because of the proof requirements for a selective-prosecution claim, defendants must "provide a colorable basis for believing that 'others similarly situated have not been prosecuted'" to obtain discovery. (quoting United States v. Wayte.) The Court of Appeals voted to rehear the case en banc, and the en banc panel affirmed the District Court's order of dismissal, holding that "a defendant is not required to demonstrate that the government has failed to prosecute others who are similarly situated."

Neither the District Court nor the Court of Appeals mentioned Federal Rule of Criminal Procedure 16, which by its terms governs discovery in criminal cases. Rule 16 provides, in pertinent part:

> "Upon request of the defendant the government shall permit the defendant to inspect and copy or photograph books, papers, documents, photographs, tangible objects, buildings or places, or copies or portions thereof, which are within the possession, custody or control of the government, and which are material to the preparation of the defendant's defense or are intended for use by the government as evidence in chief at the trial, or were obtained from or belong to the defendant." Fed.Rule Crim.Proc. 16(a)(1)(C).

Respondents argue that documents "within the possession ... of the government" that discuss the government's prosecution strategy for cocaine cases are "material" to respondents' selective-prosecution claim. Respondents argue that the Rule applies because any claim that "results in nonconviction" if successful is a "defense" for the Rule's purposes, and a successful selective-prosecution claim has that effect.

We reject this argument, because we conclude that in the context of Rule 16 "the defendant's defense" means the defendant's response to the Government's case-in-chief. While it might be argued that as a general matter, the concept of a "defense" includes any claim that is a "sword," challenging the prosecution's conduct of the case, the term may encompass only the narrower class of "shield" claims, which refute the Government's arguments that the defendant committed the crime charged. Rule 16(a)(1)(C) tends to support the "shield-only" reading. If "defense" means an argument in response to the prosecution's case-in-chief, there is a perceptible symmetry between documents "material to the preparation of the defendant's defense," and, in the very next phrase, documents "intended for use by the government as evidence in chief at the trial."

If this symmetry were not persuasive enough, paragraph (a)(2) of Rule 16 establishes beyond peradventure that "defense" in section (a)(1)(C) can refer only to defenses in response to the Government's case-in-chief. Rule 16(a)(2), as relevant here, exempts from defense inspection "reports, memoranda, or other internal government documents made by the attorney for the government or other government agents in connection with the investigation or prosecution of the case."

Under Rule 16(a)(1)(C), a defendant may examine documents material to his defense, but, under Rule 16(a)(2), he may not examine Government work product in connection with his case. If a selective-prosecution claim is a "defense," Rule 16(a)(1)(C) gives the defendant the right to examine Government work product in every prosecution except his own. Because respondents' construction of "defense" creates the anomaly of a defendant's being able to examine all Government work product except the most pertinent, we find their construction implausible. We hold that Rule 16(a)(1)(C) authorizes defendants to examine Government documents material to the preparation of their defense against the Government's case-in-chief, but not to the preparation of selective-prosecution claims.

In Wade v. United States (1992), we considered whether a federal court may review a Government decision not to file a motion to reduce a defendant's sentence for substantial assistance to the prosecution, to determine whether the Government based its decision on the defendant's race or religion. In holding that such a decision was reviewable, we assumed that discovery would be available if the defendant could make the appropriate threshold showing, although we concluded that the defendant in that case did not make such a showing. See id., at 186, 112 S.Ct., at 1844. We proceed on a like assumption here.

A selective-prosecution claim is not a defense on the merits to the criminal charge itself, but an independent assertion that the prosecutor has brought the charge for reasons forbidden by the Constitution. Our cases delineating the necessary elements to prove a claim of selective prosecution have taken great pains to explain that the standard is a demanding one. These cases afford a "background presumption," that the showing necessary to obtain discovery should itself be a significant barrier to the litigation of insubstantial claims.

A selective-prosecution claim asks a court to exercise judicial power over a "special province" of the Executive. Heckler v. Chaney (1985). The Attorney General and United States Attorneys retain " 'broad discretion' " to enforce the Nation's criminal laws. Wayte v. United States (1985). They have this latitude because they are designated by statute as the President's delegates to help him discharge his constitutional responsibility to "take Care that the Laws be faithfully executed." U.S. Const., Art. II, § 3; see 28 U.S.C. §§ 516, 547. As a result, "[t]he presumption of regularity supports" their prosecutorial decisions and "in the absence of clear evidence to the contrary, courts presume that they have properly discharged their official duties." United States v. Chemical Foundation, Inc. (1926). In the ordinary case, "so long as the prosecutor has probable cause to believe that the accused committed an offense defined by statute, the decision whether or not to prosecute, and what charge to file or bring before a grand jury, generally rests entirely in his discretion." Bordenkircher v. Hayes (1978).

Of course, a prosecutor's discretion is "subject to constitutional constraints." United States v. Batchelder (1979). One of these constraints, imposed by the equal protection component of the Due Process Clause of the Fifth Amendment, Bolling v. Sharpe (1954), is that the decision whether to prosecute may not be based on "an unjustifiable standard such as race, religion, or other arbitrary classification," Oyler v. Boles (1962). A defendant may demonstrate that the administration of a criminal law is "directed so exclusively against a particular class of persons ... with a mind so unequal and oppressive" that the system of prosecution amounts to "a practical denial" of equal protection of the law. Yick Wo v. Hopkins (1886).

Judicial deference to the decisions of these executive officers rests in part on an assessment of the relative competence of prosecutors and courts. "Such factors as the strength of the case, the prosecution's general deterrence value, the Government's enforcement priorities, and the case's relationship to the Government's overall enforcement plan are not readily susceptible to the kind of analysis the courts are competent to undertake." It also stems from a concern not to unnecessarily impair the performance of a core executive constitutional function. "Examining the basis of a prosecution delays the criminal proceeding, threatens to chill law enforcement by subjecting the prosecutor's motives and decisionmaking to outside inquiry, and may undermine prosecutorial effectiveness by revealing the Government's enforcement policy."

To establish a discriminatory effect in a race case, the claimant must show that similarly situated individuals of a different race were not prosecuted. This requirement has been established in our case law since Ah Sin v. Wittman (1905). Ah Sin, a subject of China, petitioned a California state court for a writ of habeas corpus, seeking discharge from imprisonment under a San Francisco county ordinance prohibiting persons from setting up gambling tables in rooms barricaded to stop police from entering. He alleged in his habeas petition "that the ordinance is enforced 'solely and exclusively against persons of the Chinese race and not otherwise.'" We rejected his contention that this averment made out a claim under the Equal Protection Clause, because it did not allege "that the conditions and practices to which the ordinance was directed did not exist exclusively among the Chinese, or that there were other offenders against the ordinance than the Chinese as to whom it was not enforced."

The similarly situated requirement does not make a selective-prosecution claim impossible to prove. Twenty years before Ah Sin, we invalidated an ordinance, also adopted by San Francisco, that prohibited the operation of laundries in wooden buildings. Yick Wo. The plaintiff in error successfully demonstrated that the ordinance was applied against Chinese nationals but not against other laundry-shop operators. The authorities had denied the applications of 200 Chinese subjects for permits to operate shops in wooden buildings, but granted the applications of 80 individuals who were not Chinese subjects to operate laundries in wooden buildings "under similar conditions." We explained in Ah Sin why the similarly situated requirement is necessary:

> "No latitude of intention should be indulged in a case like this. There should be certainty to every intent. Plaintiff in error seeks to set aside a criminal law of the State, not on the ground that it is unconstitutional on its face, not that it is discriminatory in tendency and ultimate actual operation as the ordinance was which was passed on in the Yick Wo case, but that it was made so by the manner of its administration. This is a matter of proof, and no fact should be omitted to make it out completely, when the power of a Federal court is invoked to interfere with the course of criminal justice of a State."

Although Ah Sin involved federal review of a state conviction, we think a similar rule applies where the power of a federal court is invoked to challenge an exercise of one of the core powers of the Executive Branch of the Federal Government, the power to prosecute.

Having reviewed the requirements to prove a selective-prosecution claim, we turn to the showing necessary to obtain discovery in support of such a claim. If discovery is ordered, the Government must assemble from its own files documents which might corroborate or refute the defendant's claim. Discovery thus imposes many of the costs present when the Government must respond to a prima facie case of selective prosecution. It will divert prosecutors' resources and may disclose the Government's prosecutorial strategy. The justifications for a rigorous standard for the elements of a selective-prosecution claim thus require a correspondingly rigorous standard for discovery in aid of such a claim.

The parties, and the Courts of Appeals which have considered the requisite showing to establish entitlement to discovery, describe this showing with a variety of phrases, like "colorable basis," "substantial threshold showing," "substantial and concrete basis," or "reasonable likelihood." However, the many labels for this showing conceal the degree of consensus about the evidence necessary to meet it. The Courts of Appeals "require some evidence tending to show the existence of the essential elements of the defense," discriminatory effect and discriminatory intent. United States v. Berrios, 501 F.2d 1207, 1211 (C.A.2 1974).

In this case we consider what evidence constitutes "some evidence tending to show the existence" of the discriminatory effect element. The Court of Appeals held that a defendant may establish a colorable basis for discriminatory effect without evidence that the Government has failed to prosecute others who are similarly situated to the defendant. We think it was mistaken in this view. The vast majority of the Courts of Appeals require the defendant to produce some evidence that similarly situated defendants of other races could have been prosecuted, but were not, and this requirement is consistent with our equal protection case law.

The Court of Appeals reached its decision in part because it started "with the presumption that people of all races commit all types of crimes—not with the premise that any type of crime is the exclusive province of any particular racial or ethnic group." 48 F.3d, at 1516–1517. It cited no authority for this proposition, which seems contradicted by the most recent statistics of the United States Sentencing Commission. Those statistics show that: More than 90% of the persons sentenced in 1994 for crack cocaine trafficking were black, United States Sentencing Comm'n, 1994 Annual Report 107; 93.4% of convicted LSD dealers were white, ibid.; and 91% of those convicted for pornography or prostitution were white. Presumptions at war with presumably reliable statistics have no proper place in the analysis of this issue.

The Court of Appeals also expressed concern about the "evidentiary obstacles defendants face." But all of its sister Circuits that have confronted the issue have required that defendants produce some evidence of differential treatment of similarly situated members of other races or protected classes. In the present case, if the claim of selective prosecution were well founded, it should not have been an insuperable task to prove that persons of other races were being treated differently than respondents. For instance, respondents could have investigated whether similarly situated persons of other races were prosecuted by the State of California, were known to federal law enforcement officers, but were not prosecuted in federal court. We think the required threshold—a credible showing of different treatment of similarly situated persons—adequately balances the Government's interest in vigorous prosecution and the defendant's interest in avoiding selective prosecution.

In the case before us, respondents' "study" did not constitute "some evidence tending to show the existence of the essential elements of" a selective-prosecution claim. The study failed to identify individuals who were not black, could have been prosecuted for the offenses for which respondents were charged, but were not so prosecuted. This omission was not remedied by respondents' evidence in opposition to the Government's motion for reconsideration. The newspaper article, which discussed the discriminatory effect of federal drug sentencing laws, was not relevant to an allegation of discrimination in decisions to prosecute. Respondents' affidavits, which recounted one attorney's conversation with a drug treatment center employee and the experience of another attorney defending drug prosecutions in state court, recounted hearsay and reported personal conclusions based on anecdotal evidence. The judgment of the Court of Appeals is therefore reversed, and the case is remanded for proceedings consistent with this opinion.

■ JUSTICE SOUTER, concurring. [omitted]

■ JUSTICE GINSBURG, concurring. [omitted]

■ JUSTICE BREYER, concurring in part and concurring in the judgment.

[N]either the alleged "symmetry" in the structure of Rule 16(a)(1)(C), nor the work product exception of Rule 16(a)(2), supports the majority's limitation of discovery under Rule 16(a)(1)(C) to documents related to the government's "case-in-chief." Rather, the language and legislative history make clear that the Rule's drafters meant it to provide a broad authorization for defendants' discovery, to be supplemented if necessary in an appropriate case. Whether or not one can also find a basis for this kind of discovery in other sources of law, Rule 16(a)(1)(C) provides one such source, and we should consider whether the defendants' discovery request satisfied the Rule's requirement that the discovery be "material to the preparation of the defendant's defense."

I believe that the defendants' request did not satisfy this threshold. Were the "selective prosecution" defense valid in this case—i.e., were there "clear evidence," United States v. Chemical Foundation, Inc. (1926), that the Federal Government's prosecutorial policy "had a discriminatory effect and was motivated by a discriminatory purpose," Wayte v. United States (1985), it should have been fairly easy for the defendants to find, not only instances in which the Federal Government prosecuted African Americans, but also some instances in which the Federal Government did not prosecute similarly situated caucasians. The defendants' failure to do so, for the reasons the Court sets forth, amounts to a failure to make the necessary threshold showing in respect to materiality.

■ JUSTICE STEVENS, dissenting.

The Court correctly concludes that in this case the facts presented to the District Court in support of respondents' claim that they had been singled out for prosecution because of their race were not sufficient to prove that defense. Moreover, I agree with the Court that their showing was not strong enough to give them a right to discovery, either under Rule 16 or under the District Court's inherent power to order discovery in appropriate circumstances. I am persuaded that the District Judge did not abuse her discretion when she concluded that the factual showing was sufficiently disturbing to require some response from the United States Attorney's Office. Perhaps the discovery order was broader than necessary, but I cannot agree with the Court's apparent conclusion that no inquiry was permissible.

The District Judge's order should be evaluated in light of three circumstances that underscore the need for judicial vigilance over certain types of drug prosecutions. First, the Anti–Drug Abuse Act of 1986 and subsequent legislation established a regime of extremely high penalties for the possession and distribution of so-called "crack" cocaine. Those provisions treat one gram of crack as the equivalent of 100 grams of powder cocaine. The distribution of 50 grams of crack is thus punishable by the same mandatory minimum sentence of 10 years in prison that applies to the distribution of 5,000 grams of powder cocaine. The Sentencing Guidelines extend this ratio to penalty levels above the mandatory minimums: for any given quantity of crack, the guideline range is the same as if the offense had involved 100 times that amount in powder cocaine. These penalties result in sentences for crack offenders that average three to eight times longer than sentences for comparable powder offenders. United States Sentencing Commission, Special Report to Congress: Cocaine and Federal Sentencing Policy 145 (Feb. 1995) (hereinafter Special Report).

Second, the disparity between the treatment of crack cocaine and powder cocaine is matched by the disparity between the severity of the punishment imposed by federal law and that imposed by state law for the same conduct. For a variety of reasons, often including the absence of mandatory minimums, the existence of parole, and lower baseline penalties, terms of imprisonment for drug offenses tend to be substantially lower in state systems than in the federal system. The difference is especially marked in the case of crack offenses. The majority of States draw no distinction between types of cocaine in their penalty schemes; of those that do, none has established as stark a differential as the Federal Government. For example, if respondent Hampton is found guilty, his federal sentence might be as long as a mandatory life term. Had he been tried in state court, his sentence could have been as short as 12 years, less worktime credits of half that amount.

Finally, it is undisputed that the brunt of the elevated federal penalties falls heavily on blacks. While 65% of the persons who have used crack are white, in 1993 they represented only 4% of the federal offenders convicted of trafficking in crack. Eighty-eight percent of such defendants were black. During the first 18 months of full guideline implementation, the sentencing disparity between black and white defendants grew from preguideline levels: blacks on average received sentences over 40% longer than whites. See Bureau of Justice Statistics, Sentencing in the Federal Courts: Does Race Matter? 6–7 (Dec. 1993). Those figures represent a major threat to the integrity of federal sentencing reform, whose main purpose was the elimination of disparity (especially racial) in sentencing. The Sentencing Commission acknowledges that the heightened crack penalties are a "primary cause of the growing disparity between sentences for Black and White federal defendants." Special Report 163.

The extraordinary severity of the imposed penalties and the troubling racial patterns of enforcement give rise to a special concern about the fairness of charging practices for crack offenses. Evidence tending to prove that black defendants charged with distribution of crack in the Central District of California are prosecuted in federal court, whereas members of other races charged with similar offenses are prosecuted in state court, warrants close scrutiny by the federal judges in that District. In my view, the District Judge, who has sat on both the federal and the state benches in Los Angeles, acted well within her discretion to call for the development of facts that would demonstrate what standards, if any, governed the choice of forum where similarly situated offenders are prosecuted.

Respondents submitted a study showing that of all cases involving crack offenses that were closed by the Federal Public Defender's Office in 1991, 24 out of 24 involved black defendants. To supplement this evidence, they submitted affidavits from two of the attorneys in the defense team. The first reported a statement from an intake coordinator at a local drug treatment center that, in his experience, an equal number of crack users and dealers were caucasian as belonged to minorities. The second was from David R. Reed, counsel for respondent Armstrong. Reed was both an active court-appointed attorney in the Central District of California and one of the directors of the leading association of criminal defense lawyers who practice before the Los Angeles County courts. Reed stated that he did not recall "ever handling a [crack] cocaine case involving non-black defendants" in federal court, nor had he even heard of one. Id., at 140. He further stated that "[t]here are many crack cocaine sales cases prosecuted in state court that do involve racial groups other than blacks." Id., at 141 (emphasis in original).

The majority discounts the probative value of the affidavits, claiming that they recounted "hearsay" and reported "personal conclusions based on anecdotal evidence." But the Reed affidavit plainly contained more than mere hearsay; Reed offered information based on his own extensive experience in both federal and state courts. Given the breadth of his background, he was well qualified to compare the practices of federal and state prosecutors. In any event, the Government never objected to the admission of either affidavit on hearsay or any other grounds. It was certainly within the District Court's discretion to credit the affidavits of two members of the bar of that Court, at least one of whom had presumably acquired a reputation by his frequent appearances there, and both of whose statements were made on pains of perjury.

The criticism that the affidavits were based on "anecdotal evidence" is also unpersuasive. I thought it was agreed that defendants do not need to prepare sophisticated statistical studies in order to receive mere discovery in cases like this one. Certainly evidence based on a drug counselor's personal observations or on an attorney's practice in two sets of courts, state and federal, can "ten[d] to show the existence" of a selective prosecution.

Even if respondents failed to carry their burden of showing that there were individuals who were not black but who could have been prosecuted in federal court for the same offenses, it does not follow that the District Court abused its discretion in ordering discovery. There can be no doubt that such individuals exist, and indeed the Government has never denied the same. In those circumstances, I fail to see why the District Court was unable to take judicial notice of this obvious fact and demand information from the Government's files to support or refute respondents' evidence. The presumption that some whites are prosecuted in state court is not "contradicted" by the statistics the majority cites, which show only that high percentages of blacks are convicted of certain federal crimes, while high percentages of whites are convicted of other federal crimes. Those figures are entirely consistent with the allegation of selective prosecution. The relevant comparison, rather, would be with the percentages of blacks and whites who commit those crimes. But, as discussed above, in the case of crack far greater numbers of whites are believed guilty of using the substance. The District Court, therefore, was entitled to find the evidence before her significant and to require some explanation from the Government.

NOTES

1. Discriminatory prosecution motions may be based upon race, religion, and the exercise of first amendment rights. Does the motion also lie for allegations of discrimination based upon sex? See City of Minneapolis v. Buschette, 307 Minn. 60, 240 N.W.2d 500 (1976), regarding the issue created by the larger number of arrests and prosecutions of females than males on charges of prostitution. The court held that this fact alone did not amount to discriminatory enforcement.

In two opinions, the Ninth Circuit addressed gender discrimination in prosecution, a claim by a man that women who committed the same offense got better terms for pleas of guilty than did men. The court relied upon the rule which accords deference to prosecutorial decisions, presumes them to be proper and requires the defendant to prove discrimination. At hearing, the prosecutors offered gender neutral reasons for its guilty plea policy in about a dozen cases. The District Judge rejected the explanations and found for defendant. This was error, said the Court of Appeals. Once the explanations were made, the defendant had to offer affirmative proof of gender discrimination. Mere disbelief of prosecutorial explanations is not proof of discrimination. See United States v. Redondo–Lemos, 955 F.2d 1296 (9th Cir.1992) and 27 F.3d 439 (9th Cir.1994).

In United States v. Maddox, 48 F.3d 791 (4th Cir.1995), an armed robbery case, the government made the following offer to the two defendants: The first defendant to plead guilty and agree to testify against the other would receive on his behalf a motion to reduce his sentence for substantial assistance. Maddox, the slower of the two, received a reduction anyway at the court's own motion because the court believed that the government's plea offer was unconstitutional. The Fourth Circuit reversed, holding that the offer was rational because it was designed to expedite plea negotiations and avoid the expense of at least one trial.

The Seventh Circuit rejected an attack on the "three strikes and out" provision of the Sentencing Guidelines. The enhanced sentence is possible only if the prosecutor serves notice of intent to ask for it. The defendant in United States v. Washington, 109 F.3d 335 (7th Cir.1997), contended that this gave the prosecutor too much power and resulted in a disparate impact on minorities. Judge Easterbrook, writing for the court, held:

> As for the contention that § 3559(c) offends principles of separation of powers by giving the prosecutor too much power over the sentence—or the due process clause of the fifth amendment by giving the judge too little—neither prosecutorial discretion nor mandatory sentences pose constitutional difficulties. If one person shoots and kills another, a prosecutor may charge anything between careless handling of a weapon and capital murder. The prosecutor's power to pursue an enhancement under § 3559(c)(1) is no more problematic than the power to choose between offenses with different maximum sentences. See United States v. Batchelder, 442 U.S. 114, 99 S.Ct. 2198, 60 L.Ed.2d 755 (1979). Section 3559(c)(1) does not specify a mandatory sentence for a crime; it sets a minimum sentence for a combination of a serious crime and a repeat violent offender. Punishment thus varies with the gravity of the offenses. Not that Congress has to allow such variation. As we discussed in United States v. Pinto, 875 F.2d 143 (7th Cir.1989), when rejecting a constitutional challenge to the Sentencing Guidelines, at the time the Constitution and Bill of Rights were adopted, mandatory sentences were the norm in federal cases. Just as in 1787, today "Congress has the power to define criminal punishments without giving the courts any sentencing discretion."

2. In a multi-defendant case, the prosecution served notice of intent to request enhanced sentences on two but not all of the defendants. in response to a charge that this was an abuse of prosecutorial discretion and resulted in "selective sentencing," Justice Thomas, in the majority opinion in United States v. LaBonte, 520 U.S. 751, 117 S.Ct. 1673 (1997), wrote:

> Second, respondents invoke the Commission's assertion that its amended commentary eliminates "unwarranted disparity associated with variations in the exercise of prosecutorial discretion in seeking enhanced penalties based on prior convictions." Ibid. As we understand it, this argument posits that if the government provides notice under § 851(a)(1) to one defendant, but not to another, the resulting difference in the maximum possible term is an "unwarranted disparity." Insofar as prosecutors, as a practical matter, may be able to determine whether a particular defendant will be subject to the enhanced

statutory maximum, any such discretion would be similar to the discretion a prosecutor exercises when he decides what, if any, charges to bring against a criminal suspect. Such discretion is an integral feature of the criminal justice system, and is appropriate, so long as it is not based upon improper factors. See United States v. Armstrong, 517 U.S. 456, 116 S.Ct. 1480, 1485–1486 (1996); Wayte v. United States, 470 U.S. 598, 607, 105 S.Ct. 1524, 1530–1531, 84 L.Ed.2d 547 (1985). Any disparity in the maximum statutory penalties between defendants who do and those who do not receive the notice is a foreseeable—but hardly improper—consequence of the statutory notice requirement.

3. In Town of Newton v. Rumery, 480 U.S. 386, 107 S.Ct. 1187 (1987), the Court refused to adopt a per se rule invalidating a release of a municipality, its officials, and the alleged crime victim from liability under federal civil right statutes, in return for a prosecutor's agreement to dismiss criminal charges brought against an arrestee. The Court held that such agreements are not inherently coercive, emphasizing that the arrestee, while not incarcerated, made a rational choice to sign the release while represented by an experienced lawyer, after considering his decision for several days. The Court refused to presume that public officials would "trump up" criminal charges in order to use the release procedure to deter civil rights suits. It further noted that some civil rights actions are meritless, so that the obtaining of a release may be in the public interest in so far as the procedures save the resources that would have to be spent defending meritless claims.

Justice O'Connor, who provided the crucial fifth vote in favor of the authorities, outlined factors she deemed of importance in deciding whether an individual release should be invalidated when it was exchanged for the dismissal of a prosecution:

> The knowledge and experience of the criminal defendant and the circumstances of the execution of the release, including, importantly, whether the defendant was counseled, are clearly relevant. The nature of the criminal charges that are pending is also important, for the greater the charge, the greater the coercive effect. The existence of a legitimate criminal justice objective for obtaining the release will support its validity. And, importantly, the possibility of abuse is clearly mitigated if the release-dismissal agreement is executed under judicial supervision.

Four justices dissented, arguing for a strong presumption against the enforceability of such agreements. It accused the majority of being less sensitive to the discouraging of valid civil rights claims than to the costs of defending invalid claims.

4. Consider this hypothetical. Police declare war on prostitution. They determine to enforce all laws violated by prostitutes. One suspected prostitute violates the law by not equipping her bicycle with a bell. Assuming that the arresting officer has overlooked every other instance of the "bell" violation by other people, does the alleged prostitute have a valid equal protection claim? If she is being singled out because she is a suspected prostitute, do prior selective enforcement decisions suggest that she has a valid constitutional claim? See People v. Kail, 150 Ill.App.3d 75, 103 Ill.Dec. 662, 501 N.E.2d 979 (1986) (divided court rules for the defendant, saying that it is irrational to enforce the bell ordinance only against suspected prostitutes).

CHAPTER 9

THE RIGHTS OF INDIGENTS IN FORMAL CRIMINAL PROCEEDINGS

A. APPELLATE ASSISTANCE: THE EQUAL PROTECTION AND DUE PROCESS APPROACHES

At various stages of formal criminal proceedings, the accused who lacks financial resources could be disadvantaged in litigating against the prosecutor, who draws upon the resources of government. By comparison to a person of wealth, an indigent defendant, caught up in the criminal process, could have the odds stacked against him or her unless government were to minimize some of the consequences which flow from a disparity of wealth.

Various legal theories have been invoked to lessen the economic-based inequities within the criminal justice system. They include the right to counsel under the sixth amendment, the due process clauses of the fifth and the fourteenth amendments, and the equal protection clause of the fourteenth amendment.[1]

In our treatment of the rights of indigents within the criminal justice system we begin by considering the rights of the indigent on appeal. If this appears strange, it can be explained by the fact that the Supreme Court's first broad-sweeping pronouncements about indigents in the formal criminal process came in a decision which treated a claim that an indigent had a right to a free transcript to assist in an appeal of a felony conviction. Griffin v. Illinois, infra. Even today it is arguable that an indigent's right to counsel in certain minor criminal cases is broader on appeal than at trial, as the materials which follow may suggest.

Griffin v. Illinois

Supreme Court of the United States, 1956.
351 U.S. 12, 76 S.Ct. 585.

■ MR. JUSTICE BLACK announced the judgment of the Court and an opinion in which THE CHIEF JUSTICE, MR. JUSTICE DOUGLAS, and MR. JUSTICE CLARK, join.

Illinois law provides that "Writs of error in all criminal cases are writs of right and shall be issued of course." The question presented here is whether Illinois may, consistent with the Due Process and Equal Protection Clauses of the Fourteenth Amendment, administer this statute so as to

1. Recall also that when a suspect is undergoing custodial interrogation, he has a right to an attorney to help protect against self-incrimination. Miranda v. Arizona, *supra* Chapter 2.

deny adequate appellate review to the poor while granting such review to all others.

The petitioners Griffin and Crenshaw were tried together and convicted of armed robbery in the Criminal Court of Cook County, Illinois. Immediately after their conviction they filed a motion in the trial court asking that a certified copy of the entire record, including a stenographic transcript of the proceedings, be furnished them without cost. They alleged that they were "poor persons with no means of paying the necessary fees to acquire the Transcript and Court Records needed to prosecute an appeal...." These allegations were not denied. Under Illinois law in order to get full direct appellate review of alleged errors by a writ of error it is necessary for the defendant to furnish the appellate court with a bill of exceptions or report of proceedings at the trial certified by the trial judge.[2] As Illinois concedes, it is sometimes impossible to prepare such bills of exceptions[3] or reports without a stenographic transcript of the trial proceedings.[4] Indigent defendants sentenced to death are provided with a free transcript at the expense of the county where convicted. In all other criminal cases defendants needing a transcript, whether indigent or not, must themselves buy it. The petitioners contended in their motion before the trial court that failure to provide them with the needed transcript would violate the Due Process and Equal Protection Clauses of the Fourteenth Amendment. The trial court denied the motion without a hearing.

Griffin and Crenshaw then filed a petition under the Illinois Post Conviction Hearing Act. Only questions arising under the Illinois or Federal Constitution may be raised in proceedings under this Act. A companion state act provides that indigent petitioners under the Post–Conviction Act may, under some circumstances, obtain a free transcript. The effect is that

2. Ill.Rev.Stat., 1953, c. 110, § 259.70A (Supreme Court Rule 70A), now Ill.Rev.Stat., 1955, c. 110, § 101.65 (Supreme Court Rule 65). A writ of error may also be prosecuted on a "mandatory record" kept by the clerk, consisting of the indictment, arraignment, plea, verdict and sentence. The "mandatory record" can be obtained free of charge by an indigent defendant. In such instances review is limited to errors on the face of the mandatory record, and there is no review of trial errors such as an erroneous ruling on the admission of evidence. See People v. Loftus, 400 Ill. 432, 81 N.E.2d 495. See also Cullen v. Stevens, 389 Ill. 35, 58 N.E.2d 456; A Study of the Illinois Supreme Court, 15 U. of Chi. L.Rev. 107, 125.

3. "A complete bill of exceptions consists of all proceedings in the case from the time of the convening of the court until the termination of the trial. It includes all of the motions and rulings of the trial court, evidence heard, instructions and other matters which do not come within the clerk's mandatory record." People ex rel. Iasello v. McKinlay, 409 Ill. 120, 124–125, 98 N.E.2d 728, 730.

4. In oral argument counsel for Illinois stated:

> "With respect to the so-called bystanders' bill of exceptions or the bill of exceptions prepared from someone's memory in condensed and narrative form and certified to by the trial judge—as to whether that's available in Illinois I can say that everybody out there understands that it is but nobody has heard of its ever being actually used in a criminal case in Illinois in recent years. I think if you went back before the days of court reporting you would find them but none today. And I will say that Illinois has not suggested in the brief that such a narrative transcript would necessarily or even generally be the equivalent of a verbatim transcript of all of the trial.
>
> There isn't any way that an Illinois convicted person in a noncapital case can obtain a bill of exceptions without paying for it."

indigents may obtain a free transcript to obtain appellate review of constitutional questions but not of other alleged trial errors such as admissibility and sufficiency of evidence. In their Post–Conviction proceeding petitioners alleged that there were manifest nonconstitutional errors in the trial which entitled them to have their convictions set aside on appeal and that the only impediment to full appellate review was their lack of funds to buy a transcript. These allegations have not been denied. Petitioners repeated their charge that refusal to afford full appellate review solely because of poverty was a denial of due process and equal protection. This petition like the first was dismissed without hearing any evidence. The Illinois Supreme Court affirmed the dismissal solely on the ground that the charges raised no substantial state or federal constitutional questions—the only kind of questions which may be raised in Post–Conviction proceedings.

Providing equal justice for poor and rich, weak and powerful alike is an age-old problem. People have never ceased to hope and strive to move closer to that goal. This hope, at least in part, brought about in 1215 the royal concessions of Magna Charta: "To no one will we sell, to no one will we refuse, or delay, right or justice.... No free man shall be taken or imprisoned, or disseised, or outlawed, or exiled, or any wise destroyed; nor shall we go upon him nor send upon him, but by the lawful judgment of his peers or by the law of the land." These pledges were unquestionably steps toward a fairer and more nearly equal application of criminal justice. In this tradition, our own constitutional guaranties of due process and equal protection both call for procedures in criminal trials which allow no invidious discriminations between persons and different groups of persons. Both equal protection and due process emphasize the central aim of our entire judicial system—all people charged with crime must, so far as the law is concerned, "stand on an equality before the bar of justice in every American court."

Surely no one would contend that either a State or the Federal Government could constitutionally provide that defendants unable to pay court costs in advance should be denied the right to plead not guilty or to defend themselves in court. Such a law would make the constitutional promise of a fair trial a worthless thing. Notice, the right to be heard, and the right to counsel would under such circumstances be meaningless promises to the poor. In criminal trials a State can no more discriminate on account of poverty than on account of religion, race, or color. Plainly the ability to pay costs in advance bears no rational relationship to a defendant's guilt or innocence and could not be used as an excuse to deprive a defendant of a fair trial. Indeed, a provision in the Constitution of Illinois of 1818 provided that every person in Illinois "ought to obtain right and justice freely, and without being obliged to purchase it, completely and without denial, promptly and without delay, conformably to the laws."

There is no meaningful distinction between a rule which would deny the poor the right to defend themselves in a trial court and one which effectively denies the poor an adequate appellate review accorded to all who have money enough to pay the costs in advance. It is true that a State is not required by the Federal Constitution to provide appellate courts or a right to appellate review at all. But that is not to say that a State that does grant appellate review can do so in a way that discriminates against some convicted defendants on account of their poverty. Appellate review has now become an integral part of the Illinois trial system for finally adjudicating the guilt or innocence of a defendant. Consequently at all stages of the proceedings the Due Process and Equal Protection Clauses protect persons like petitioners from invidious discriminations.

All of the States now provide some method of appeal from criminal convictions, recognizing the importance of appellate review to a correct adjudication of guilt or innocence. Statistics show that a substantial proportion of criminal convictions are reversed by state appellate courts. Thus to deny adequate review to the poor means that many of them may lose their life, liberty or property because of unjust convictions which appellate courts would set aside. Many States have recognized this and provided aid for convicted defendants who have a right to appeal and need a transcript but are unable to pay for it. A few have not. Such a denial is a misfit in a country dedicated to affording equal justice to all and special privileges to none in the administration of its criminal law. There can be no equal justice where the kind of trial a man gets depends on the amount of money he has. Destitute defendants must be afforded as adequate appellate review as defendants who have money enough to buy transcripts.

The Illinois Supreme Court denied these petitioners relief under the Post–Conviction Act because of its holding that no constitutional rights were violated. In view of our holding to the contrary the State Supreme Court may decide that petitioners are now entitled to a transcript, as the State's brief suggests. We do not hold, however, that Illinois must purchase a stenographer's transcript in every case where a defendant cannot buy it. The Supreme Court may find other means of affording adequate and effective appellate review to indigent defendants. For example, it may be that bystanders' bills of exceptions or other methods of reporting trial proceedings could be used in some cases. The Illinois Supreme Court appears to have broad power to promulgate rules of procedure and appellate practice. We are confident that the State will provide corrective rules to meet the problem which this case lays bare.

The judgment of the Supreme Court of Illinois is vacated and the cause is remanded to that court for further action not inconsistent with the foregoing paragraph. Mr. Justice Frankfurter joins in this disposition of the case.

Vacated and remanded.

■ MR. JUSTICE FRANKFURTER, concurring in the judgment.

The admonition of de Tocqueville not to confuse the familiar with the necessary has vivid application to appeals in criminal cases. The right to an appeal from a conviction for crime is today so established that this leads to the easy assumption that it is fundamental to the protection of life and liberty and therefore a necessary ingredient of due process of law. "Due process" is, perhaps, the least frozen concept of our law—the least confined to history and the most absorptive of powerful social standards of a progressive society. But neither the unfolding content of "due process" nor the particularized safeguards of the Bill of Rights disregard procedural ways that reflect a national historic policy. It is significant that no appeals from convictions in the federal courts were afforded (with roundabout exceptions negligible for present purposes) for nearly a hundred years; and, despite the standards of criminal justice in modern England, there was no appeal from convictions (again with exceptions not now pertinent) until 1907. Thus, it is now settled that due process of law does not require a State to afford review of criminal judgments.

Nor does the equal protection of the laws deny a State the right to make classifications in law when such classifications are rooted in reason.

* * *

Law addresses itself to actualities. It does not face actuality to suggest that Illinois affords every convicted person, financially competent or not, the opportunity to take an appeal, and that it is not Illinois that is responsible for disparity in material circumstances. Of course a State need not equalize economic conditions. A man of means may be able to afford the retention of an expensive, able counsel not within reach of a poor man's purse. Those are contingencies of life which are hardly within the power, let alone the duty, of a State to correct or cushion. But when a State deems it wise and just that convictions be susceptible to review by an appellate court, it cannot by force of its exactions draw a line which precludes convicted indigent persons, forsooth erroneously convicted, from securing such a review merely by disabling them from bringing to the notice of an appellate tribunal errors of the trial court which would upset the conviction were practical opportunity for review not foreclosed.

To sanction such a ruthless consequence, inevitably resulting from a money hurdle erected by a State, would justify a latter-day Anatole France to add one more item to his ironic comments on the "majestic equality" of the law. "The law, in its majestic equality, forbids the rich as well as the poor to sleep under bridges, to beg in the streets, and to steal bread." John Cournos, A Modern Plutarch, p. 27.

The State is not free to produce such a squalid discrimination. If it has a general policy of allowing criminal appeals, it cannot make lack of means an effective bar to the exercise of this opportunity. The State cannot keep the word of promise to the ear of those illegally convicted and break it to their hope....

* * *

■ [JUSTICE FRANKFURTER suggested that the Court's holding be denied retroactive effect as to prisoners whose time for appeal had expired.]

■ MR. JUSTICE BURTON and MR. JUSTICE MINTON, whom MR. JUSTICE REED and MR. JUSTICE HARLAN join, dissenting. [OMITTED.]

■ MR. JUSTICE HARLAN, dissenting.

* * *

According to petitioners' tabulation, no more than 29 States provide free transcripts as of right to indigents convicted of non-capital crimes. Thus the sweeping constitutional pronouncement made by the Court today will touch the laws of at least 19 States and will create a host of problems affecting the status of an unknown multitude of indigent convicts. A decision having such wide impact should not be made upon a record as obscure as this, especially where there are means read at hand to have clarified the issue sought to be presented.

... Inasmuch as the Court's decision is not—and on this record cannot be—based on any facts peculiar to this case, I consider that question to be: Is an indigent defendant who "needs" a transcript in order to appeal constitutionally entitled, regardless of the nature of the circumstances producing that need, to have the State either furnish a free transcript or take some other action to assure that he does in fact obtain full appellate review?

Equal Protection. In finding an answer to that question in the Equal Protection Clause, the Court has painted with a broad brush. It is said that a State cannot discriminate between the "rich" and the "poor" in its system of criminal appeals. That statement of course commands support, but it hardly sheds light on the true character of the problem confronting us here. Illinois has not imposed any arbitrary conditions upon the exercise of the right of appeal nor any requirements unnecessary to the effective working of its appellate system. Trial errors cannot be reviewed without an appropriate record of the proceedings below; if a transcript is used, it is surely not unreasonable to require the appellant to bear its cost; and Illinois has not foreclosed any other feasible means of preparing such a record. Nor is this a case where the State's own action has prevented a defendant from appealing. All that Illinois has done is to fail to alleviate the consequences of differences in economic circumstances that exist wholly apart from any state action.

The Court thus holds that, at least in this area of criminal appeals, the Equal Protection Clause imposes on the States an affirmative duty to lift the handicaps flowing from differences in economic circumstances. That holding produces the anomalous result that a constitutional admonition to the States to treat all persons equally means in this instance that Illinois must give to some what it requires others to pay for. Granting that such a classification would be reasonable, it does not follow that a State's failure to make it can be regarded as discrimination. It may as accurately be said that the real issue in this case is not whether Illinois *has* discriminated but whether it has a duty *to* discriminate.

I do not understand the Court to dispute either the necessity for a bill of exceptions or the reasonableness of the general requirement that the trial transcript, if used in its preparation, be paid for by the appealing party. The Court finds in the operation of these requirements, however, an invidious classification between the "rich" and the "poor." But no economic burden attendant upon the exercise of a privilege bears equally upon all, and in other circumstances the resulting differentiation is not treated as an invidious classification by the State, even though discrimination against "indigents" by name would be unconstitutional. Thus, while the exclusion of "indigents" from a free state university would deny them equal protection, requiring the payment of tuition fees surely would not, despite the resulting exclusion of those who could not afford to pay the fees. And if imposing a condition of payment is not the equivalent of a classification by the State in one case, I fail to see why it should be so regarded in another. Thus if requiring defendants in felony cases to pay for a transcript constitutes a discriminatory denial to indigents of the right of appeal available to others, why is it not a similar denial in misdemeanor cases or, for that matter, civil cases?

It is no answer to say that equal protection is not an absolute, and that in other than criminal cases the differentiation is "reasonable." The resulting *classification* would be invidious in all cases, and an invidious classification offends equal protection regardless of the seriousness of the consequences....

Due Process. Has there been a violation of the Due Process Clause? The majority of the Court concedes that the Fourteenth Amendment does not require the States to provide for any kind of appellate review. Nevertheless, Illinois, in the forefront among the States, established writs of error in criminal cases as early as 1827. In 1887, it provided for official court reporters, thereby relieving defendants of the burden of hiring reporters in order to obtain a transcript. In 1927, it provided that for indigents sentenced to death "all necessary costs and expenses" incident to a writ of error, including the cost of a transcript, would be paid by the counties. And in 1953, free transcripts were authorized for the presentation of constitutional claims. Thus Illinois has steadily expanded the protection afforded defendants in criminal cases, and in recent years has made substantial strides towards alleviating the natural disadvantages of indigents. Can it be that, while it was not unconstitutional for Illinois to afford no appeals, its steady progress in increasing the safeguards against erroneous convictions has resulted in a constitutional decline?

Of course the fact that appeals are not constitutionally required does not mean that a State is free of constitutional restraints in establishing the terms upon which appeals will be allowed. It does mean, however, that there is no "right" to an appeal in the same sense that there is a right to a trial. Rather the constitutional right under the Due Process Clause is simply the right not to be denied an appeal for arbitrary or capricious reasons. Nothing of that kind, however, can be found in any of the steps by which Illinois has established its appellate system.

We are all agreed that no objection of substance can be made to the provisions for free transcripts in capital and constitutional cases. The due process challenge must therefore be directed to the basic step of permitting appeals at all without also providing an *in forma pauperis* procedure. But whatever else may be said of Illinois' reluctance to expend public funds in perfecting appeals for indigents, it can hardly be said to be arbitrary. A policy of economy may be unenlightened, but it is certainly not capricious. And that it has never generally been so regarded is evidenced by the fact that our attention has been called to no State in which *in forma pauperis* appeals were established contemporaneously with the right of appeal. I can find nothing in the past decisions of this Court justifying a holding that the Fourteenth Amendment confines the States to a choice between allowing no appeals at all or undertaking to bear the cost of appeals for indigents, which is what the Court in effect now holds.

It is argued finally that, even if it cannot be said to be "arbitrary," the failure of Illinois to provide petitioners with the means of exercising the right of appeal that others are able to exercise is simply so "unfair" as to be a denial of due process. I have some question whether the non-arbitrary denial of a right that the State may withhold altogether could ever be so characterized. In any event, however, to so hold it is not enough that we consider free transcripts for indigents to be a desirable policy or that we would weigh the competing social values in favor of such a policy were it our function to distribute Illinois' public funds among alternative uses. Rather the question is whether some method of assuring that an indigent is able to exercise his right of appeal is "implicit in the concept of ordered liberty," Palko v. Connecticut, 302 U.S. 319, 325, 58 S.Ct. 149, so that the failure of a State so to provide constitutes a "denial of fundamental fairness, shocking to the universal sense of justice," Betts v. Brady, supra [316 U.S. 455, 62 S.Ct. 1252]. Such an equivalence between persons with the means with which to exercise a right of appeal has not, however, traditionally been regarded as an essential of "fundamental fairness," and the reforms extending such aid to indigents have only recently gained widespread acceptance. Indeed, it was not until an Act of Congress in 1944 that defendants in federal criminal cases became entitled to free transcripts, and to date approximately one-third of the States still have not taken that step. With due regard for the constitutional limitations upon the power of this Court to intervene in State matters, I am unable to bring myself to say that Illinois' failure to furnish free transcripts to indigents in all criminal cases is "shocking to the universal sense of justice."

As I view this case, it contains none of the elements hitherto regarded as essential to justify action by this Court under the Fourteenth Amendment. In truth what we have here is but the failure of Illinois to adopt as promptly as other States a desirable reform in its criminal procedure. Whatever might be said were this a question of procedure in the federal courts, regard for our system of federalism requires that matters such as this be left to the States. However strong may be one's inclination to hasten the day when *in forma pauperis* criminal procedures will be universal among the States, I think it is beyond the province of this Court to tell Illinois that it must provide such procedures.

NOTES

1. At one time some commentators believed that the United States Supreme Court would use the *Griffin* equal protection-due process rationale to alleviate many of the consequences of economic disparity which confront the poor as they go through life. As San Antonio Independent School District v. Rodriguez, 411 U.S. 1, 93 S.Ct. 1278 (1973) and Dandridge v. Williams, 397 U.S. 471, 90 S.Ct. 1153 (1970), indicate, however, the *Griffin* approach has largely been limited to addressing the consequences of poverty insofar as they affect the criminally accused. With one exception, the Court has even permitted civil litigants to be denied *access* to avenues of redress simply because of an inability to pay a filing fee. See United States v. Kras, 409 U.S. 434, 93 S.Ct. 631 (1973) (bankruptcy filing fee); Ortwein v. Schwab, 410 U.S. 656, 93 S.Ct. 1172 (1973) (administrative appeal concerning public assistance rights).

In Boddie v. Connecticut, 401 U.S. 371, 91 S.Ct. 780 (1971), where the Court held that lack of a filing fee could not bar access to divorce court, the Supreme Court extended *Griffin* beyond the formal criminal process. Rejecting equal protection analysis and a generalized due process approach, Justice Harlan wrote the majority opinion in *Boddie*. Justice Black, criticizing this due process approach to the extension of rights, drew a sharp distinction between the obligation of courts to remove the consequences of economic inequality in criminal cases and the obligation of courts as to other areas.

Similarly, in a civil case involving the permanent termination of parental rights, the Court held "that, just as a State may not block an indigent petty offender's access to an appeal afforded others (cite omitted), so Mississippi may not deny M. L. B., because of her poverty, appellate review of the sufficiency of the evidence on which the trial court found her unfit to remain a parent." M.L.B. v. S.L.J., 519 U.S. 102, 117 S.Ct. 555 (1996). The Court noted that access to justice claims involved both equal protection and due process concerns. It concluded, however, that since there is no independent due process right to appellate review, that equal protection was the linchpin of its reasoning. Once a state provides for appeals, it may not close the judicial process to those who are indigent when the case involves fundamental interests such as parental rights or marriage.

2. Justice Black's distinction between economic disparity in the criminal process and other disparities finds support in the 1963 Report of the Attorney General's Committee on Poverty and the Administration of Criminal Justice, chaired by Professor Francis Allen:

> . . . governmental obligation to deal effectively with problems of poverty in the administration of criminal justice does not rest or depend upon some hypothetical obligation of government to indulge in acts of public charity. It does not presuppose a general commitment on the part of the federal government to relieve impoverished persons of the consequences of limited means, whenever or however manifested. It does not even presuppose that government is always required to take into account the means of the citizen when dealing directly with its citizens. . . . The essential point is that the problems of poverty with which this report is concerned arise in a process initiated by government for the achievement of basic governmental purposes. It is, moreover, a process that has as one of its consequences the imposition of severe disabilities on the persons proceeded against. Duties arise from action. When a course of conduct, however legitimate, entails the possibility of serious injury to persons, a duty on the actor to avoid the reasonably avoidable injuries is ordinarily recognized. When government chooses to exert its powers in the criminal area, its obligation is surely no less than that of taking reasonable measures to eliminate those factors that are irrelevant to just administration of the law but which, nevertheless, may occasionally affect determinations of the accused's liability or penalty. While government may not be required to relieve the accused of his poverty, it may properly be required to minimize the influence of poverty on its administration of justice. . . .

Is this view consonant with the philosophy underlying American government today? Would it make sense for government to take no action while an individual, because of poverty, is denied educational and vocational opportunities, and while he or she suffers from inadequate nutrition and health care, but then to become concerned about the effects of economic disparity if and when the individual gets caught up in the criminal process?

3. Commonly by court rule, custom, or statute, indigents are permitted to proceed *in forma pauperis* in civil litigation in many jurisdictions. However, rarely does an indigent have a statutory *right* to the appointment of counsel in a civil matter. Whether counsel is available will often depend upon the extent of legal services agencies in a particular community. The limitation of the *Griffin* principles primarily to the criminal justice arena may be of increasing importance now that Congress has restricted funding available to civil legal aid agencies through the Legal Services Corporation. Many legal aid agencies depend on IOLTA money which can become scarcer in hard economic times.

4. Without mentioning equal protection, the Court in Lassiter v. Department of Social Services, 452 U.S. 18, 101 S.Ct. 2153 (1981), considered a due process claim that an indigent parent is entitled to appointed counsel in a proceeding to terminate parental rights. It declared that due process *automatically* requires that the indigent be supplied with counsel only if he or she stands to lose liberty. In other cases, whether such a right exists depends upon several factors, including the nature of the private right at stake in the litigation, the governmental interest, and the risk of an erroneous decision in the absence of counsel. On the particular facts of the case before it, the Court held that due process did not mandate the appointment of counsel. The dissent argued that the three-part test used by the Court should be employed on a category-by-category basis, rather than on a case-by-case basis. It concluded that due process mandates appointed counsel for the indigent in cases involving termination of parental rights.

5. In a 7–3 decision overturning the original panel opinion, the Fourth Circuit en banc recently upheld a Maryland statute that conditions an indigent's right to a free transcript on the use of a public defender. The felony-murder defendant wished to be represented on appeal by his trial attorney, who had taken the case pro bono. The public defender's office, defendant claimed, had a conflict of interest because the office represented defendant's co-conspirator and had taken the position that defendant was the trigger-man. But, declining defendant's Sixth Amendment and Equal Protection Clause challenges, the court held defendant could only be represented by his pro bono attorney by forgoing the chance to obtain a free trial transcript. Miller v. Smith, 115 F.3d 1136 (4th Cir.1997) (en banc). The dissent argued that the state's asserted interest in protecting its resources and reducing its administrative costs was not served in this case, creating an irrational and absurd result—encouraging defendants to be more of a burden on state resources than they otherwise would. The dissent also argued that the rule impaired the defendant's right to counsel of choice. The Second Circuit has taken the opposite view, striking down a New York law similar to Maryland's. See Fullan v. Commissioner of Corrections of N.Y., 891 F.2d 1007 (2d Cir.1989).

6. A Fourth Circuit panel overturned a Maryland rule forbidding direct-mail solicitation of criminal defendants by criminal lawyers for 30 days after arrest. The opinion, which notes that the Supreme Court had upheld a similar provision for civil actions, Florida Bar v. Went For It, Inc. (1995) points out the important differences between civil and criminal litigants: "[As] the state itself is prosecuting a defendant, it cannot lightly deprive its opponent of critical information which might assist the exercise of even a qualified right. As Maryland's Attorney General advised the Governor before the passage of this law, 'unlike the typical personal injury plaintiffs, criminal defendants are in litigation against the State. Thus, the effect of the law, if not its intent, is to make it more difficult for our opponents to get legal representation.' " Ficker v. Curran, 119 F.3d 1150 (4th Cir.1997).

Douglas v. California

Supreme Court of California, 1963.
372 U.S. 353, 83 S.Ct. 814.

■ Mr. Justice Douglas delivered the opinion of the Court.

Petitioners, Bennie Will Meyes and William Douglas, were jointly tried and convicted in a California court on an information charging them with

13 felonies. A single public defender was appointed to represent them. At the commencement of the trial, the defender moved for a continuance, stating that the case was very complicated, that he was not as prepared as he felt he should be because he was handling a different defense every day, and that there was a conflict of interest between the petitioners requiring the appointment of separate counsel for each of them. This motion was denied. Thereafter, petitioners dismissed the defender, claiming he was unprepared, and again renewed motions for separate counsel and for a continuance. These motions also were denied, and petitioners were ultimately convicted by a jury of all 13 felonies, which included robbery, assault with a deadly weapon, and assault with intent to commit murder. Both were given prison terms. Both appealed as of right to the California District Court of Appeal. That court affirmed their convictions. Both Meyes and Douglas then petitioned for further discretionary review in the California Supreme Court, but their petitions were denied without a hearing.... We granted certiorari....

Although several questions are presented in the petition for certiorari, we address ourselves to only one of them. The record shows that petitioners requested, and were denied, the assistance of counsel on appeal, even though it plainly appeared they were indigents. In denying petitioners' requests, the California District Court of Appeal stated that it had "gone through" the record and had come to the conclusion that "no good whatever could be served by appointment of counsel." ... The District Court of Appeal was acting in accordance with a California rule of criminal procedure which provides that state appellate courts, upon the request of an indigent for counsel, may make "an independent investigation of the record and determine whether it would be of advantage to the defendant or helpful to the appellate court to have counsel appointed.... After such investigation, appellate courts should appoint counsel if in their opinion it would be helpful to the defendant or the court, and should deny the appointment of counsel only if in their judgment such appointment would be of no value to either the defendant or the court." People v. Hyde, 51 Cal.2d 152, 154, 331 P.2d 42, 43.

* * *

In spite of California's forward treatment of indigents, under its present practice the type of an appeal a person is afforded in the District Court of Appeals hinges upon whether or not he can pay for the assistance of counsel. If he can the appellate court passes on the merits of his case only after having the full benefit of written briefs and oral argument by counsel. If he cannot the appellate court is forced to prejudge the merits before it can even determine whether counsel should be provided. At this stage in the proceedings only the barren record speaks for the indigent, and, unless the printed pages show that an injustice has been committed, he is forced to go without a champion on appeal. Any real chance he may have had of showing that his appeal has hidden merit is deprived him when the court decides on an *ex parte* examination of the record that the assistance of counsel is not required.

We are not here concerned with problems that might arise from the denial of counsel for the preparation of a petition for discretionary or mandatory review beyond the stage in the appellate process at which the claims have once been presented by a lawyer and passed upon by an appellate court. We are dealing only with the first appeal, granted as a matter of right to rich and poor alike (Cal.Penal Code §§ 1235, 1237), from a criminal conviction. We need not now decide whether California would have to provide counsel for an indigent seeking a discretionary hearing from the California Supreme Court after the District Court of Appeals had sustained his conviction, or whether counsel must be appointed for an indigent seeking review of an appellate affirmance of his conviction in this Court by appeal as of right or by petition for a writ of certiorari which lies within the Court's discretion. But it is appropriate to observe that a State can, consistently with the Fourteenth Amendment, provide for differences so long as the result does not amount to a denial of due process or an "invidious discrimination." ... Absolute equality is not required; lines can be and are drawn and we often sustain them.... But where the merits of the one and only appeal an indigent has as of right are decided without benefit of counsel, we think an unconstitutional line has been drawn between rich and poor.

When an indigent is forced to run this gauntlet of a preliminary showing of merit, the right to appeal does not comport with fair procedure. In the federal courts, on the other hand, an indigent must be afforded counsel on appeal whenever he challenges a certification that the appeal is not taken in good faith. Johnson v. United States, 352 U.S. 565, 77 S.Ct. 550 (1957). The federal courts must honor his request for counsel regardless of what they think the merits of the case may be; and, "representation in the role of an advocate is required." Ellis v. United States, 356 U.S. 674, 675, 78 S.Ct. 974, 975 (1958). In California, however, once the court has "gone through" the record and denied counsel, the indigent has no recourse but to prosecute his appeal on his own, as best he can, no matter how meritorious his case may turn out to be. The present case, where counsel was denied petitioners on appeal, shows that the discrimination is not between "possibly good and obviously bad cases," but between cases where the rich man can require the court to listen to argument of counsel before deciding on the merits, but a poor man cannot. There is lacking that equality demanded by the Fourteenth Amendment where the rich man, who appeals as of right, enjoys the benefit of counsel's examination into the record, research of the law, and marshalling of arguments on his behalf, while the indigent, already burdened by a preliminary determination that his case is without merit, is forced to shift for himself. The indigent, where the record is unclear or the errors are hidden, has only the right to a meaningless ritual, while the rich man has a meaningful appeal.

We vacate the judgment of the District Court of Appeals and remand the case to that court for further proceedings not inconsistent with this opinion. It is so ordered.

Judgment of the District Court of Appeal vacated and case remanded.

■ MR. JUSTICE CLARK, dissenting.

I adhere to my vote in Griffin v. Illinois [supra], but, as I have always understood that case, it does not control here. It had to do with the State's obligation to furnish a record to an indigent on appeal. There we took pains to point out that the State was free to "find other means of affording adequate and effective appellate review to indigent defendants." ... Here California has done just that in its procedure for furnishing attorneys for indigents on appeal. We all know that the overwhelming percentage of *in forma pauperis* appeals are frivolous. Statistics of this Court show that over 96% of the petitions filed here are of this variety.[1] California in the light of a like experience, has provided that upon the filing of an application for the appointment of counsel the District Court of Appeal shall make "an independent investigation of the record and determine whether it would be of advantage to the defendant or helpful to the appellate court to have counsel appointed." California's courts did that here and after examining the record certified that such an appointment would be neither advantageous to the petitioners nor helpful to the court. It, therefore, refused to go through the useless gesture of appointing an attorney. In my view neither the Equal Protection Clause nor the Due Process Clause requires more. I cannot understand why the Court says that this procedure afforded petitioners "a meaningless ritual." To appoint an attorney would not only have been utter extravagance and a waste of the State's funds but as surely "meaningless" to petitioners.

With this new fetish for indigency the Court piles an intolerable burden on the State's judicial machinery. Indeed, if the Court is correct it may be that we should first clean up our own house. We have afforded indigent litigants much less protection than has California. Last Term we received over 1,200 *in forma pauperis* applications in none of which had we appointed attorneys or required a record. Some were appeals of right. Still we denied the petitions or dismissed the appeals on the moving papers alone. At the same time we had hundreds of paid cases in which we permitted petitions or appeals to be filed with not only records but briefs by counsel, after which they were disposed of in due course. On the other hand, California furnishes the indigent a complete record and if counsel is requested requires its appellate courts either to (1) appoint counsel or (2) make an independent investigation of that record and determine whether it would be of advantage to the defendant or helpful to the court to have counsel appointed. Unlike Lane v. Brown, 372 U.S. 477, 83 S.Ct. 768 (1963), decision in these matters is not placed in the unreviewable discretion of the Public Defender or appointed counsel but is made by the appellate court, itself.

California's concern for the rights of indigents is clearly revealed in People v. Hyde, supra. There, although the Public Defender had not undertaken the prosecution of the appeal the District Court of Appeal nevertheless referred the application for counsel and the record to the Los Angeles Bar Association. One of its members reviewed these papers, after which he certified that no meritorious ground for appeal was disclosed.

1. Statistics from the office of the Clerk of this Court reveal that in the 1961 Term only 38 of 1093 *in forma pauperis* petitions for certiorari were granted (3.4%). Of 44 *in forma pauperis* appeals, all but one were summarily dismissed (2.3%).

Despite this the California District Court of Appeal made its own independent examination of the record.

There is an old adage which my good Mother used to quote to me, i.e., "People who live in glass houses had best not throw stones." I dissent.

■ [The dissenting opinion of JUSTICES HARLAN and STEWART is omitted.]

Mayer v. City of Chicago

Supreme Court of the United States, 1971.
404 U.S. 189, 92 S.Ct. 410.

■ MR. JUSTICE BRENNAN delivered the opinion of the Court.

A jury in the Circuit Court of Cook County, Illinois, convicted appellant on nonfelony charges of disorderly conduct and interference with a police officer in violation of ordinances of the city of Chicago. He was sentenced to a $250 fine on each offense; violation of each ordinance carried a maximum penalty of $500. Desiring to appeal, he petitioned the Circuit Court for a free transcript of the proceedings of his trial to support his grounds of appeal that the evidence was insufficient for conviction and that misconduct of the prosecutor denied him a fair trial.[1] The Circuit Court found that he was indigent, but denied his application, stating "that defendant was found guilty of ordinance violations and ... rule 607 of the Supreme Court applies to felony cases." The reference was to Illinois Supreme Court Rule 607(b), which in pertinent part provided: "In any case in which the defendant is convicted of a *felony*, he may petition the court in which he was convicted for a report of proceedings at his trial." (Emphasis supplied.) Other Illinois Supreme Court rules, Rules 323(c) and 323(d), provided for alternatives to a transcript in the form of a "Settled Statement" or an "Agreed Statement of Facts."[3] Without resorting to either

1. A court reporter was provided at appellant's trial pursuant to the State Court Reporters Act, I11.Rev.Stat., c. 37, § 651 et seq. (1969). It was estimated that the cost of preparing a transcript would be $300. The record refers in some places to a two-day trial and in other places to a three-day trial.

Under Illinois law at the time of appellant's convictions an appeal lay as of right either to the Illinois Supreme Court or to the Illinois Appellate Court, depending upon the nature of the case or the contentions raised. See Constitution of Illinois 1870, Art. 6, §§ 5, 7. If a case was erroneously appealed to the wrong court, it was transferred to the proper court without any loss of rights. Illinois Supreme Court Rule 365, III.Rev.Stat., c. 110A, § 365 (1969). Of course, whether an appeal is discretionary or as of right does not affect an indigent's right to a transcript, since "[i]ndigents must ... have the same opportunities to invoke the discretion of the" court as those who can afford the costs. Burns v. Ohio, 360 U.S. 252, 258 (1959).

3. These rules, III.Rev.Stat., c. 110A, § 323(c) and (d) (1969), provided:

"(c) Procedure If No Verbatim Transcript Is Available. If no verbatim transcript of the evidence or proceedings is obtainable the appellant may prepare a proposed report of proceedings from the best available sources, including recollection. It shall be served within seven days after the notice of appeal is filed. Within 21 days after the notice of appeal is filed, any other party may serve proposed amendments or his proposed report of proceedings. Within seven days thereafter, the appellant shall, upon notice, present the proposed report or reports and any proposed amendments to the trial court for settlement and approval. The court, holding hearings if necessary, shall promptly settle, certify, and order filed an accurate report of proceedings.

alternative, appellant made a motion in the Illinois Supreme Court for an order that he be furnished a transcript of proceedings without cost. The Supreme Court denied the motion in an unreported order without filing an opinion. We noted probable jurisdiction of appellant's appeal challenging the constitutionality of the limitation of Rule 607(b) to felony cases. 401 U.S. 906 (1971).

I.

... Appellee city of Chicago urges that we re-examine *Griffin*. We decline to do so. For "it is now fundamental that, once established ... avenues [of appellate review] must be kept free of unreasoned distinctions that can only impede open and equal access to the courts." Rinaldi v. Yeager, 384 U.S. 305, 310 (1966).[4] Therefore, "[i]n all cases the duty of the State is to provide the indigent as adequate and effective an appellate review as that given appellants with funds.... Draper v. Washington, 372 U.S. 487, 496 (1963). In terms of a trial record, this means that the State must afford the indigent a 'record of sufficient completeness' to permit proper consideration of [his] claims."

Washington, 372 U.S. 487, 496 (1963). In terms of a trial record, this means that the State must afford the indigent a " 'record of sufficient completeness' to permit proper consideration of [his] claims."

A "record of sufficient completeness" does not translate automatically into a complete verbatim transcript....

* * *

We emphasize, however, that the State must provide a full verbatim record where that is necessary to assure the indigent as effective an appeal as would be available to the defendant with resources to pay his own way. Moreover, where the grounds of appeal, as in this case, make out a colorable need for a complete transcript, the burden is on the State to show that only a portion of the transcript or an "alternative" will suffice for an effective appeal on those grounds. This rationale underlies our statement in *Draper*, that:

> "[T]he State could have endeavored to show that a narrative statement or only a portion of the transcript would be adequate and available for appellate consideration of petitioners' contentions. The trial judge would have complied with ... the constitutional mandate ... in limiting the grant accordingly on the basis of such a showing by the State."

> "(d) Agreed Statement of Facts. The parties by written stipulation may agree upon a statement of the facts material to the controversy and file it in lieu of and within the time for filing a report of proceedings."

These rules were also amended effective July 1, 1971, but not in ways material to this case. See 1971 Illinois Legislative Service, No. 5, p. 1690. Despite the provision limiting use of a "Settled" statement to cases where no verbatim transcript is "available" or "obtainable," the procedure of subsection (c) evidently is permissible even though the court reporter's notes are available for transcription. See Tone, New Supreme Court Rule on Expeditious and Inexpensive Appeals, 53 I11.B.J. 18, 20(1964).

4. Our decisions on the question of free transcripts for indigents include: Wade v. Wilson, 396 U.S. 282 (1970)....

II.

The distinction between felony and nonfelony offenses drawn by Rule 607(b) can no more satisfy the requirements of the Fourteenth Amendment than could the like distinction in the Wisconsin law, held invalid in Groppi v. Wisconsin, 400 U.S. 505 (1971), which permitted a change of venue in felony but not in misdemeanor trials. The size of the defendant's pocketbook bears no more relationship to his guilt or innocence in a nonfelony than in a felony case. The distinction drawn by Rule 607(b) is, therefore, an "unreasoned distinction" proscribed by the Fourteenth Amendment. That conclusion follows directly from our decision in Williams v. Oklahoma City, 395 U.S. 458, 459 (1969), rejecting the argument "that an indigent person, convicted for a violation of a city ordinance, quasi criminal in nature and often referred to as a petty offense, is [not] entitled to a case made or transcript at city expense in order to perfect an appeal. . . ."

III.

The city of Chicago urges another distinction to set this case apart from *Griffin* and its progeny. The city notes that the defendants in all the transcript cases previously decided by this Court were sentenced to some term of confinement. Where the accused, as here, is not subject to imprisonment, but only a fine, the city suggests that his interest in a transcript is outweighed by the State's fiscal and other interests in not burdening the appellate process. This argument misconceives the principle of *Griffin* no less than does the line that Rule 607(b) expressly draws. *Griffin* does not represent a balance between the needs of the accused and the interests of society; its principle is a flat prohibition against pricing indigent defendants out of as effective an appeal as would be available to others able to pay their own way. The invidiousness of the discrimination that exists when criminal procedures are made available only to those who can pay is not erased by any differences in the sentences that may be imposed. The State's fiscal interest is, therefore, irrelevant.

We add that even approaching the problem in the terms the city suggests hardly yields the answer the city tenders. The practical effects of conviction of even petty offenses of the kind involved here are not to be minimized. A fine may bear as heavily on an indigent accused as forced confinement. The collateral consequences of conviction may be even more serious, as when (as was apparently a possibility in this case) the impecunious medical student finds himself barred from the practice of medicine because of a conviction he is unable to appeal for lack of funds. Moreover, the State's long-term interest would not appear to lie in making access to appellate processes from even its most inferior courts depend upon the defendant's ability to pay. It has been aptly said:

> [F]ew citizens ever have contact with the higher courts. In the main, it is the police and the lower court Bench and Bar that convey the essence of our democracy to the people.

Justice, if it can be measured, must be measured by the experience the average citizen has with the police and the lower courts.[6]

Arbitrary denial of appellate review of proceedings of the State's lowest trial courts may save the State some dollars and cents, but only at the substantial risk of generating frustration and hostility toward its courts among the most numerous consumers of justice.

* * *

■ [CHIEF JUSTICE BURGER's concurring opinion and JUSTICE BLACKMUN's concurring opinion are omitted.]

NOTES

1. After *Griffin*, *Douglas*, and *Mayer*, can there be any doubt that an indigent convicted of a "fine-only" offense has a right to appointed counsel on appeal if appellate review of such convictions is permitted under state law? Consider this question again after reading *Ross* later in this section and *Argersinger* and *Scott* in Section B of the present chapter.

2. If counsel appointed for the first appeal concludes that the appeal is wholly without merit, he or she still must submit a brief discussing the arguable issues and defending the decision not to file a brief on the merits. Anders v. California, 386 U.S. 738, 87 S.Ct. 1396 (1967). One career public defender shortly after the *Anders* decision argued that *Anders* would place upon appointed counsel the "quixotic" requirement of "trying to find support for an appeal which he has already concluded to be without any merit whatsoever...." He concluded that *Anders* would encourage mediocrity, contribute to a backlog of unreviewed convictions, and impair the effectiveness of the *in forma pauperis* bar. Doherty, Wolf! Wolf!—The Ramifications of Frivolous Appeals, 59 J.Crim.L., C. & P.S. 1 (1968). The underlying premise of Doherty's argument was that appointed counsel, if required to file a brief, would choose to make frivolous arguments rather than briefing the case against their clients. In point of fact, the use of *Anders* briefs has varied widely from jurisdiction to jurisdiction.

In Penson v. Ohio, 488 U.S. 75, 109 S.Ct. 346 (1988), appointed appellate counsel filed a certificate of "no merit" which, without listing "colorable" arguments, recited in conclusory fashion that counsel's careful review of the record led him to conclude that the appeal was without merit. The state appellate court reviewed the record, questioned counsel's certification that the appeal was without merit, found a jury instruction error, reversed as to one count, and upheld the remaining convictions. It declared that the appellant suffered no harm from the decision to allow counsel to withdraw.

The United States Supreme Court in *Penson* found error under *Anders*. "First, the motion should have been denied because counsel's Certification of Meritless Appeal failed to draw attention to anything in the record that might arguably support the appeal." Second, the reviewing court "should not have acted on the motion to withdraw before it made its own examination of the record to determine whether counsel's evaluation of the claim was sound."

6. It is true, as the city of Chicago argues, that in *Williams* the defendant was effectively denied any right of appeal, whereas here a transcript was not a condition precedent for appeal. The constitutional infirmity in Rule 607(b) is not the less for that reason. The indigent defendant must be afforded as effective an appeal as the defendant who can pay.

The Court held that *Anders* errors were not subject to ordinary ineffectiveness of counsel standards under Strickland v. Washington (Casebook, Chapter 18). The *Anders* violation did not require a showing of prejudice because the appellant "was left completely without counsel during the appellate court's actual decisional process." Thus reversal of the state appellate decision was mandated automatically under United States v. Cronic. Presumably the appellant was entitled to a new appeal, represented by court-appointed counsel.

In McCoy v. Court of Appeals of Wisconsin, 486 U.S. 429, 108 S.Ct. 1895 (1988), by a 5–3 vote, the United States Supreme Court upheld a Wisconsin rule governing procedures where counsel appointed for an indigent appellant seeks to withdraw from an appeal that he or she deems frivolous. The rule required what *Anders* seemingly requires: the filing of a motion that states that counsel deems the appeal frivolous but that also points out arguable grounds for relief. The Wisconsin rule went further in requiring counsel to include in the motion to withdraw a statement discussing *why* the arguable issues lack merit.

The majority found no due process or equal protection violation. It held that counsel has a duty to read the record and to diligently investigate possible claims of error. Where counsel has done this and nevertheless has concluded that the appeal is without merit, he or she can withdraw as long as the court has a basis for concluding that counsel has done his or her duty. The majority viewed the Wisconsin requirement as aiding the reviewing court in determining that to allow the motion to withdraw would not violate the defendant's constitutional rights.

Three dissenting justices acknowledged that *Anders* requires appointed counsel to state the lawyer's conclusion that the appeal is wholly without merit if counsel seeks to withdraw. However, the dissenters argued that counsel should not be made to go further by briefing the case against the client. These dissenting justices noted that privately retained counsel can or must choose to decline to pursue a frivolous appeal; however, they would never file a brief telling the reviewing court why they feel the client's appeal is wholly without merit.

3. In Jones v. Barnes, 463 U.S. 745, 103 S.Ct. 3308 (1983), the Court considered a claim that court-appointed appellate counsel must raise every non-frivolous claim as a basis for reversal if his or her client wishes that to be done. The Court rejected the claim, holding that *Anders* does not preclude use of appointed counsel's best professional judgment as to how to successfully represent an appellant. The lawyer's decision that weak arguments will detract from stronger arguments must be respected. Justice Brennan dissented, emphasizing the right of the client to the *assistance* of counsel. He noted that the need to allow counsel during a trial final decision-making authority in most matters has no application on appeal, where there is more time for consultation between client and lawyer. Under these circumstances, Brennan concluded that the client should be allowed to reject his lawyer's advice while still being allowed the assistance of counsel in pursuing any non-frivolous claim which the client wishes to raise.

One solution to the Jones v. Barnes problem might be to allow the indigent to file his own brief supplementing that of court-appointed counsel and raising additional issues. Many reviewing courts allow this. However, some courts say that the appellant has to choose between representing himself and having appointed counsel, and that he or she cannot submit both counsel's brief and *a pro se* brief. See Hayes v. Hawes, 921 F.2d 100 (7th Cir.1990) (no constitutional right to hybrid representation on appeal, yet court accepts both briefs).

4. Consider the implications of Justice Brennan's statement that fiscal consequences are irrelevant to an equal protection approach. Should a legislature have no say in whether available resources go to increase the standard of living of welfare recipients or instead go to purchase free transcripts for indigents who have been convicted of fine-only ordinance violations? Under *Mayer* do the "needs" of defendants in the criminal justice system, no matter how petty their case, take economic precedence over the needs of other citizens, no matter how worthy their cause?

5. In People v. Hopping, 60 Ill.2d 246, 326 N.E.2d 395 (1975), an "official" court reporter was not present at the indigent's plea of guilty to a misdemeanor charge. Presumably a wealthy defendant could have hired a court reporter to record and transcribe the proceeding. (This is the practice in civil cases in many parts of the country. The parties, not the court, supply the reporter.) The Illinois Supreme Court rejected a claim of equal protection in *Hopping*. It declared that the bystander bill provisions of Illinois Supreme Court Rule 323 were sufficient to provide a record to be utilized in determining whether the plea admonition and waiver procedures had been adequate.

Can you see any reason not to allow a trial judge the final say when, in the absence of a court reporter, there is a dispute as to what admonitions the judge gave a defendant before accepting a plea of guilty? See also, United States ex rel. Grundset v. Franzen, 675 F.2d 870 (7th Cir.1982).

Ross v. Moffitt

Supreme Court of the United States, 1974.
417 U.S. 600, 94 S.Ct. 2437.

■ MR. JUSTICE REHNQUIST delivered the opinion of the Court.

We are asked in this case to decide whether Douglas v. California (1963), which requires appointment of counsel for indigent state defendants on their first appeal as of right, should be extended to require counsel for discretionary state appeals and for applications for review in this Court.

* * *

The case now before us has resulted from consolidation of two separate cases, North Carolina criminal prosecutions brought in the respective Superior Courts for the counties of Mecklenburg and Guilford. In both cases respondent pleaded not guilty to charges of forgery and uttering a forged instrument, and because of his indigency was represented at trial by court-appointed counsel. He then took separate appeals to the North Carolina Court of Appeals, where he was again represented by court-appointed counsel, and his convictions were affirmed. At this point the procedural histories of the two cases diverge.

* * *

The Court of Appeals reversed the two District Court judgments, holding that respondent was entitled to the assistance of counsel at state expense both on his petition for review in the North Carolina Supreme Court and on his petition for certiorari in this Court. Reviewing the procedures of the North Carolina appellate system and the possible benefits that counsel would provide for indigents seeking review in that system, the court stated:

> As long as the state provides such procedures and allows other convicted felons to seek access to the higher court with the help of retained counsel, there is a marked absence of fairness in denying

> an indigent the assistance of counsel as he seeks access to the same court.

This principle was held equally applicable to petitions for certiorari in this Court. For, said the Court of Appeals, "[t]he same concepts of fairness and equality, which require counsel in a first appeal of right, require counsel in other and subsequent discretionary appeals...."

* * *

The precise rationale for the Griffin and Douglas lines of cases has never been explicitly stated, some support being derived from the Equal Protection Clause of the Fourteenth Amendment, and some from the Due Process Clause of that Amendment. Neither clause by itself provides an entirely satisfactory basis for the result reached, each depending on a different inquiry which emphasizes different factors. "Due process" emphasizes fairness between the State and the individual dealing with the State, regardless of how other individuals in the same situation may be treated. "Equal protection," on the other hand, emphasizes disparity in treatment by a State between classes of individuals whose situations are arguably indistinguishable. We will address these issues separately in the succeeding sections.

Recognition of the due process rationale in Douglas is found both in the Court's opinion and in the dissenting opinion of Mr. Justice Harlan. The Court in Douglas stated that "[w]hen an individual is forced to run this gantlet of a preliminary showing of merit, the right to appeal does not comport with fair procedure." Mr. Justice Harlan thought that the due process issue in Douglas was the only one worthy of extended consideration, remarking: "The real question in this case, I submit, and the only one that permits of satisfactory analysis, is whether or not the state rule, as applied in this case, is consistent with the requirements of fair procedure guaranteed by the Due Process Clause."

We do not believe that the Due Process Clause requires North Carolina to provide respondent with counsel on his discretionary appeal to the State Supreme Court. At the trial stage of a criminal proceeding, the right of an indigent defendant to counsel at his trial is fundamental and binding upon the States by virtue of the Sixth and Fourteenth Amendments. But there are significant differences between the trial and appellate stages of a criminal proceeding. The purpose of the trial stage from the State's point of view is to convert a criminal defendant from a person presumed innocent to one found guilty beyond a reasonable doubt. To accomplish this purpose, the State employs a prosecuting attorney who presents evidence to the court, challenges any witnesses offered by the defendant, argues rulings of the court, and makes direct arguments to the court or jury seeking to persuade them of the defendant's guilt....

By contrast, it is ordinarily the defendant, rather than the State, who initiates the appellate process, seeking not to fend off the efforts of the State's prosecutor but rather to overturn a finding of guilt made by a judge or jury below. The defendant needs an attorney on appeal not as a shield to protect him against being "haled into court" by the State and stripped of his presumption of innocence, but rather as a sword to upset the prior determination of guilt. This difference is significant for, while no one would agree that the State may simply dispense with the trial stage of proceedings without a criminal defendant's consent, it is clear that the State need not provide any appeal at all. McKane v. Durston, supra. The fact that an appeal *has* been provided does not automatically mean that a State then acts unfairly by refusing to provide counsel to indigent defendants at every stage of the way. Douglas v. California, supra. Unfairness results only if indigents are singled out by the State and denied meaningful access to that system because of their poverty. That question is more profitably considered under an equal protection analysis.

Language invoking equal protection notions is prominent both in Douglas and in other cases treating the rights of indigents on appeal.

* * *

Despite the tendency of all rights "to declare themselves absolute to their logical extreme," there are obviously limits beyond which the equal protection analysis may not be pressed without doing violence to principles recognized in other decisions of this Court. The Fourteenth Amendment "does not require absolute equality or precisely equal advantages," San Antonio Independent School District v. Rodriquez (1973), nor does it require the State to "equalize economic conditions." Griffin v. Illinois (Frankfurter, J., concurring). It does require that the state appellate system be "free of unreasoned distinctions." Rinaldi v. Yaeger (1966), and that indigents have an adequate opportunity to present their claims fairly within the adversarial system. Griffin v. Illinois, supra; Draper v. Washington, supra. The State cannot adopt procedures which leave an indigent defendant "entirely cut off from any appeal at all," by virtue of his indigency, Lane v. Brown, supra, or extend to such indigent defendants merely a "meaningless ritual" while others in better economic circumstances have a "meaningful appeal." Douglas v. California, supra. The question is not one of absolutes, but one of degrees. In this case we do not believe that the Equal Protection Clause, when interpreted in the context of these cases, requires North Carolina to provide free counsel for indigent defendants seeking to take discretionary appeals to the North Carolina Supreme Court, or to file petitions for certiorari in this Court.

* * *

The facts show that respondent, in connection with his Mecklenburg County conviction, received the benefit of counsel in examining the record of his trial and in preparing an appellate brief on his behalf for the state Court of Appeals. Thus, prior to his seeking discretionary review in the State Supreme Court, his claims "had once been presented by a lawyer and passed upon by an appellate court." Douglas v. California, supra. We do not believe that it can be said, therefore, that a defendant in respondent's circumstances is denied meaningful access to the North Carolina Supreme Court simply because the State does not appoint counsel to aid him in seeking review in that court. At that stage he will have, at the very least, a transcript or other record of trial proceedings, a brief on his behalf in the Court of Appeals setting forth his claims of error, and in many cases an opinion by the Court of Appeals disposing of his case. These materials, supplemented by whatever submission respondent may make pro se, would appear to provide the Supreme Court of North Carolina with an adequate basis on which to base its decision to grant or deny review.

We are fortified in this conclusion by our understanding of the function served by discretionary review in the North Carolina Supreme Court. The critical issue in that court, as we perceive it, is not whether there has been "a correct adjudication of guilt" in every individual case, see Griffin v. Illinois, but rather whether "the subject matter of the appeal has significant public interest," whether "the cause involves legal principles of major significance to the jurisprudence of the state," or whether the decision below is in probable conflict with a decision of the Supreme Court. The Supreme Court may deny certiorari even though it believes that the decision of the Court of Appeals was incorrect, since a decision which appears incorrect may nevertheless fail to satisfy any of the criteria discussed above. Once a defendant's claims of error are organized and presented in a lawyer-like fashion to the Court of Appeals, the justices of the Supreme Court of North Carolina who make the decision to grant or deny discretionary review should be able to ascertain whether his case satisfies the standards established by the legislature for such review.

This is not to say, of course, that a skilled lawyer, particularly one trained in the somewhat arcane art of preparing petitions for discretionary review, would not prove helpful to any litigant able to employ him. An indigent defendant seeking review in the Supreme Court of North Carolina is therefore somewhat handicapped in comparison with a wealthy defendant who has counsel assisting him in every conceivable manner at every stage in the proceeding. But both the opportunity to have counsel prepare an initial brief in the Court of Appeals and the nature of discretionary review in the Supreme Court of North Carolina make this relative handicap far less that the handicap borne by the indigent defendant denied counsel on his initial appeal as of right in Douglas. And the fact that a particular service might be of benefit to an indigent defendant does not mean that the service is constitutionally required. The duty of the State under our cases is not to duplicate the legal arsenal that may be privately retained by a criminal defendant in a continuing effort to reverse his conviction, but only to assure the indigent defendant an adequate opportunity to present his claims fairly in the context of the State's appellate process. We think respondent was given that opportunity under the existing North Carolina system.

Much of the discussion in the preceding section is equally relevant to the question of whether a State must provide counsel for a defendant seeking review of his conviction in this Court. North Carolina will have provided counsel for a convicted defendant's only appeal as of right, and the brief prepared by that counsel together with one and perhaps two North Carolina appellate opinions will be available to this Court in order that it may decide whether or not to grant certiorari. This Court's review, much like that of the Supreme Court of North Carolina, is discretionary and depends on numerous factors other than the perceived correctness of the judgment we are asked to review.

* * *

The suggestion that a State is responsible for providing counsel to one petitioning this Court simply because it initiated the prosecution which led to the judgment sought to be reviewed is unsupported by either reason or authority. It would be quite as logical under the rationale of *Douglas* and *Griffin*, and indeed perhaps more so, to require that the Federal Government or this Court furnish and compensate counsel for petitioners who seek certiorari here to review state judgments of conviction. Yet this Court has followed a consistent policy of denying applications for appointment of counsel by persons seeking to file jurisdictional statements or petitions for certiorari in this Court.

* * *

Reversed.

■ MR. JUSTICE DOUGLAS, with whom MR. JUSTICE BRENNAN and MR. JUSTICE MARSHALL concur, dissenting.

I would affirm the judgment below because I am in agreement with the opinion of Chief Judge Haynsworth for a unanimous panel in the Court of Appeals.

* * *

Judge Haynsworth could find "no logical basis for differentiation between appeals of right and permissive review procedures in the context of the Constitution and the right to counsel." More familiar with the functioning of the North Carolina criminal justice system than are we, he concluded that "in the context of constitutional questions arising in criminal prosecutions, permissive review in the state's highest court may be predictably the most meaningful review the conviction will receive." The North Carolina Court of Appeals, for example, will be constrained in diverging from an earlier opinion of the State Supreme Court, even if subsequent developments have rendered the earlier Supreme Court decision suspect. "[T]he state's highest court remains the ultimate arbiter of the rights of its citizens."

Judge Haynsworth also correctly observed that the indigent defendant, proceeding without counsel, is at a substantial disadvantage relative to wealthy defendants represented by counsel when he is forced to fend for himself in seeking discretionary review from the State Supreme Court or from this Court. It may well not be enough to allege error in the courts below in layman's terms; a more sophisticated approach may be demanded:*

* An indigent defendant proceeding without the assistance of counsel would be attempting to satisfy one of the three statutory standards for review when seeking certiorari from the North Carolina Supreme Court:

"(1) The subject matter of the appeal has significant public interest, or

"(2) The cause involves legal principles of major significance to the jurisprudence of the State, or

"(3) The decision of the Court of Appeals appears likely to be in conflict with a decision of the Supreme Court."

N.C.Gen.Stat. § 7A–31(c). It seems likely that only the third would have been explored in a brief on the merits before the Court of Appeals, and the indigent defendant would draw little assistance from that brief in attempting to satisfy either of the first two standards.

An indigent defendant is as much in need of the assistance of a lawyer in preparing and filing a petition for certiorari as he is in the handling of an appeal as of right. In many appeals, an articulate defendant could file an effective brief by telling his story in simple language without legalisms, but the technical requirement for applications for writs of certiorari are hazards which one untrained in the law could hardly be expected to negotiate.

Certiorari proceedings constitute a highly specialized aspect of appellate work. The factors which [a court] deems important in connection with deciding whether to grant certiorari are certainly not within the normal knowledge of an indigent appellant. Boskey, The Right to Counsel in Appellate Proceedings, 45 Minn.L.Rev. 783, 797 (1961).

Furthermore, the lawyer who handled the first appeal in a case would be familiar with the facts and legal issues involved in the case. It would be a relatively easy matter for the attorney to apply his expertise in filing a petition for discretionary review to a higher court, or to advise his client that such a petition would have no chance of succeeding.

Douglas v. California was grounded on concepts of fairness and equality. The right to discretionary review is a substantial one, and one where a lawyer can be of significant assistance to an indigent defendant. It was correctly perceived below that the "same concepts of fairness and equality, which require counsel in a first appeal of right, require counsel in other and subsequent discretionary appeals."

NOTES

1. *Ross* seemed to approve "line-drawing" in determining at what point in the criminal justice system the State no longer is required to alleviate the consequences of economic disparity. Can the decision be squared with *Mayer*? After *Ross* do fiscal considerations, always relevant to a due process approach, become relevant again? What is left of an equal protection approach after *Ross*? Has the view that due process analysis is more appropriate (expressed by Justice Harlan in *Griffin*) finally prevailed?

The "line drawing" approach was followed in Halbert v. Michigan, 545 U.S. 605, 125 S.Ct. 2582 (2005). Michigan adopted, by a state constitutional amendment, a system in which there was no appeal of right from a conviction based on guilty pleas or no contest pleas. A convict could ask for the right to appeal but there was no right to counsel at this stage. The Supreme Court invalidated the Michigan practice holding (over three dissenters) that the relevant line was not to be drawn between discretionary appeals and appeals as a matter of right. The correct line was between first appeals and all those that follow. The Court reasoned that the first level appeal was one designed to correct error in the specific proceedings below as

Rule 19 of this Court provides some guidelines for the exercise of our certiorari jurisdiction, including decisions by a state court on federal questions not previously decided by this Court; but it may not be enough simply to assert that there was error in the decision of the court below. Cf.Magnum Import Co. v. Coty, 262 U.S. 159, 163, 43 S.Ct. 531. Moreover, this Court is greatly aided by briefs prepared with accuracy, brevity, and clarity in its determination of whether certiorari should be granted. See Furness, Withy & Co. v. Yang–Tsze Insurance Assn., 242 U.S. 430, 434, 37 S.Ct. 141.

opposed to discretionary second level appeals the granting of which was to be guided by the importance of the legal questions at issue. Moreover, the decision in *Ross* was based in part on the indigent defendant's ability to use the briefs and record created by counsel in the first appeal. No such materials would be available under the Michigan procedure.

2. In the federal appellate system, a convicted federal defendant represented before the Court of Appeals on direct review by an attorney appointed under the Federal Criminal Justice Act can require his attorney to file a petition for certiorari. See Doherty v. United States, 404 U.S. 28, 92 S.Ct. 175 (1971) (Douglas, J., concurring); Wilkins v. United States, 441 U.S. 468, 99 S.Ct. 1829 (1979).

3. In Pennsylvania v. Finley, 481 U.S. 551, 107 S.Ct. 1990 (1987), the Court considered the rights of an indigent, under the United States Constitution, to appointed counsel in a state post-conviction proceeding where the petitioner had already exhausted her right to direct review. The Court declared that the Constitution did not demand that a state create post-conviction procedures. If it chose to do so, it was not required to provide an indigent with the appointment of counsel, as it would be required in the first direct appeal as of right. The Court declared that Ross v. Moffitt, rather than Douglas v. California, controlled.

Finley held that where a state voluntarily chose to provide appointed counsel to indigent post-conviction petitioners, the United States Constitution did not mandate that it go further and require that such counsel comply with the requirements of Anders v. California. Instead the state could allow counsel to withdraw without filing a motion suggesting and then refuting colorable claims, and without providing the petitioner with notice of that motion to withdraw and an opportunity to respond.

In *Finley* the state trial court judge had appointed counsel to represent the petitioner on a pro se petition which seemed to raise claims that all arose from matters appearing on the face of the state record. Suppose instead petitioner's constitutional claims arose from matters not appearing entirely on the face of the record, such as then on-disclosure of evidence favorable to the accused. For want of record support, such issues could not have been litigated on direct appeal. Or suppose that, following conviction, the accused had not taken a direct appeal but now wanted to collaterally attack her conviction based upon matters not contained on the face of the record. For example, consider a petitioner who pleaded guilty but later claimed that the plea was predicated upon a promise made by the prosecutor or the trial judge, which promise was unfulfilled. Would the reasoning of *Ross* apply to such cases? *Finley* did not concern such situations.

Most state and federal courts, long before *Finley*, had declared that there is no federal constitutional right to the appointment of counsel in either state post conviction or federal habeas corpus proceedings. Federal case law typically provides for the district judge to exercise his or her discretion in ruling upon a request for counsel made by an indigent federal habeas corpus petitioner.

The district court's denial of a request for appointment of counsel for federal habeas corpus petitioners is ordinarily affirmed by the United States Court of Appeals with little discussion, even in matters where the Court of Appeals has appointed counsel to represent the habeas petitioner on appeal. For a decision which gives the matter more extended treatment, see Knaubert v. Goldsmith, 791 F.2d 722 (9th Cir.1986).

If a federal habeas corpus case goes to an evidentiary hearing, federal law requires the appointment of counsel for an indigent petitioner. See Graham v. Portuondo, 506 F.3d 105 (2d Cir.2007).

In Murray v. Giarratano, 492 U.S. 1, 109 S.Ct. 2765 (1989), a federal district judge ruled that the Virginia system of providing death-row inmates with access to the courts for the purpose of preparing post-conviction petitions was inadequate. At the penal institutions, Virginia had provided a certain number of "unit" lawyers to assist the inmates, who also had limited access to a law library. The district court declared that, under these circumstances, indigent death-row prisoners were entitled to appointed counsel to represent them in post-conviction proceedings.

When the matter came before the United States Supreme Court, the Court was badly divided. Writing for a four judge plurality, Chief Justice Rehnquist stated that the reasoning of *Finley*, note 3 supra, is equally applicable in a death-penalty setting, so that the States need not provide counsel for death-row prisoners who seek to file, in state court, collateral challenges to capital convictions. The plurality stated that, although special safeguards may be required in death-penalty cases through the trial stage, the Constitution mandates no greater rights thereafter for persons under sentences of death than it does for other convicted persons.

The plaintiffs in *Giarratano* had cited Bounds v. Smith, 430 U.S. 817, 97 S.Ct. 1491 (1977). *Bounds* had held that, where indigent prisoners do not have the right to counsel, Due Process requires that they be provided access to an adequate law library. The plurality held that, in light of *Finley*, nothing in *Bounds* could be construed as supporting the right to appointed counsel. Presumably the remedy for *a Bounds* violation would lie in providing sufficient access to an adequate library.

Providing the crucial fifth vote necessary to a holding in favor of the State, Justice Kennedy noted that, in fact, no Virginia death-row prisoner had been unable to secure a lawyer to represent him in state post-conviction proceedings, even if state law did not mandate appointment of counsel for indigent, death-row post conviction petitioners. Under these circumstances, Justice Kennedy found no violation of the plaintiff's constitutional rights. He suggested that perhaps the United States Congress should address the question of providing adequate legal assistance for death-row inmates.

Justice Stevens dissented, joined by three others. He noted that some issues can only be raised in post-conviction proceedings and cannot be urged on direct appeal because they are based upon matters outside the original trial record. He emphasized that the failure to properly raise an issue in state post-conviction proceedings can operate to preclude raising such issue in a federal habeas corpus proceeding. (Of course, both of these observations are applicable to non-capital cases as well as to capital cases.) Stevens also noted that in capital cases death-row inmates are much more likely to succeed in collateral attacks on their convictions than are non-capital petitioners, drawing on figures that suggest that very few federal habeas corpus petitions prove successful in non-capital cases, whereas, federal courts recently have often granted relief to death-row petitioners.

Justice Blackmun, dissenting from a denial of certiorari in McFarland v. Scott, 512 U.S. 1256, 114 S.Ct. 2785 (1994), found that the lack of counsel in state post-conviction proceedings was one of the principal failings of the capital punishment review process.

In the Antiterrorism and Effective Death Penalty Act, Congress provided shorter statutes of limitation in state death-penalty cases on federal habeas for states that provide death row inmates with competent and adequately compensated counsel for state habeas filings. 28 U.S.C. § 2263. States are having a difficult time, however, "opting in" to these streamlined death penalty procedures. A class action challenge to the state invoking the expedited review procedure was ultimately dismissed for lack of justiciability. Calderon v. Ashmus, 523 U.S. 740, 118 S.Ct. 1694 (1998).

B. TRIAL COUNSEL: THE SIXTH AMENDMENT APPROACH

Gideon v. Wainwright

Supreme Court of the United States, 1963.
372 U.S. 335, 83 S.Ct. 792.

■ MR. JUSTICE BLACK delivered the opinion of the Court.

Petitioner was charged in a Florida state court with having broken and entered a poolroom with intent to commit a misdemeanor. This offense is a felony under Florida law. Appearing in court without funds and without a lawyer, petitioner asked the court to appoint counsel for him, whereupon the following colloquy took place:

> The Court: Mr. Gideon, I am sorry, but I cannot appoint Counsel to represent you in this case. Under the laws of the State of Florida, the only time the Court can appoint Counsel to represent a Defendant is when that person is charged with a capital offense. I am sorry, but I will have to deny your request to appoint Counsel to defend you in this case.
>
> The Defendant: The United States Supreme Court says I am entitled to be represented by Counsel.

Put to trial before a jury, Gideon conducted his defense about as well as could be expected from a layman. He made an opening statement to the jury, cross-examined the State's witnesses, presented witnesses in his own defense, declined to testify himself, and made a short argument "emphasizing his innocence to the charge contained in the Information filed in this case." The jury returned a verdict of guilty, and petitioner was sentenced to serve five years in the state prison. Later, petitioner filed in the Florida Supreme Court this habeas corpus petition attacking his conviction and sentence on the ground that the trial court's refusal to appoint counsel for him denied him rights "guaranteed by the Constitution and the Bill of Rights by the United States Government." Treating the petition for habeas corpus as properly before it, the State Supreme Court, "upon consideration thereof" but without an opinion, denied all relief. Since 1942, when Betts v. Brady, 316 U.S.455, 62 S.Ct. 1252, 86 L.Ed. 1595, was decided by a divided Court, the problem of a defendant's federal constitutional right to counsel in a state court has been a continuing source of controversy and litigation in both state and federal courts. To give this problem another review here, we granted certiorari.... Since Gideon was proceeding *in forma pauperis*, we appointed counsel to represent him and requested both sides to discuss in their briefs and oral arguments the following: "Should this Court's holding in Betts v. Brady, ... be reconsidered?"

I.

The facts upon which Betts claimed that he had been unconstitutionally denied the right to have counsel appointed to assist him are strikingly like the facts upon which Gideon here bases his federal constitutional claim. Betts was indicted for robbery in a Maryland state court. On arraignment, he told the trial judge of his lack of funds to hire a lawyer and asked the court to appoint one for him. Betts was advised that it was not the practice in that county to appoint counsel for indigent defendants except in murder and rape cases. He then pleaded not guilty, had witnesses summoned, cross-examined the State's witnesses, examined his own, and chose not to testify himself. He was found guilty by the judge, sitting without a jury, and sentenced to eight years in prison. Like Gideon, Betts sought release by habeas corpus, alleging that he had been denied the right to assistance of counsel in violation of the Fourteenth Amendment. Betts was denied any relief, and on review this Court affirmed. It was held that a refusal to appoint counsel for an indigent defendant charged with a felony did not necessarily violate the Due Process Clause of the Fourteenth Amendment, which for reasons given the Court deemed to be the only applicable federal constitutional provision. The Court said:

> Asserted denial [of due process] is to be tested by an appraisal of the totality of facts in a given case. That which may, in one setting, constitute a denial of fundamental fairness, shocking to the universal sense of justice, may, in other circumstances, and in the light of other considerations, fall short of such denial.

Treating due process as "a concept less rigid and more fluid than those envisaged in other specific and particular provisions of the Bill of Rights," the Court held that refusal to appoint counsel under the particular facts and circumstances in the Betts case was not so "offensive to the common and fundamental ideas of fairness" as to amount to a denial of due process. Since the facts and circumstances of the two cases are so nearly indistinguishable, we think the Betts v. Brady holding if left standing would require us to reject Gideon's claim that the Constitution guarantees him the assistance of counsel. Upon full reconsideration we conclude that Bett v. Brady should be overruled.

II.

The Sixth Amendment provides, "In all criminal prosecutions, the accused shall enjoy the right . . . to have the Assistance of Counsel for his defense." We have construed this to mean that in federal courts counsel must be provided for defendants unable to employ counsel unless the right is competently and intelligently waived. Betts argued that this right is extended to indigent defendants in state courts by the Fourteenth Amendment. In response the Court stated that, while the Sixth Amendment laid down "no rule for the conduct of the states, the question recurs whether the constraint laid by the amendment upon the national courts expresses a rule so fundamental and essential to a fair trial, and so, to due process of law, that it is made obligatory upon the states by the Fourteenth Amendment." . . . In order to decide whether the Sixth Amendment's guarantee of counsel is of this fundamental nature, the Court in Betts set out and considered "[r]elevant data on the subject . . . afforded by constitutional and statutory provisions subsisting in the colonies and the states prior to the inclusion of the Bill of Rights in the national Constitution, and in the constitutional, legislative, and judicial history of the states to the present date." . . . On the basis of this historical data the Court concluded that "appointment of counsel is not a fundamental right, essential to a fair trial." ... It was for this reason the Betts Court refused to accept the contention that the Sixth Amendment's guarantee of counsel for indigent federal defendants was extended to or, in the words of that Court, "made obligatory upon the states by the Fourteenth Amendment". Plainly, had the Court concluded that appointment of counsel for an indigent criminal defendant was "a fundamental right, essential to a fair trial," it would have held that the Fourteenth Amendment requires appointment of counsel in a state court, just as the Sixth Amendment requires in a federal court.

We think the Court in Betts had ample precedent for acknowledging that those guarantees of the Bill of Rights which are fundamental safeguards of liberty immune from federal abridgment are equally protected against state invasion by the Due Process Clause of the Fourteenth Amendment. This same principle was recognized, explained, and applied in Powell v. Alabama, 287 U.S. 45, 53 S.Ct. 55 (1932), a case upholding the right of counsel, where the Court held that despite sweeping language to the contrary in Hurtado v. California, 110 U.S. 516, 4 S.Ct. 292 (1884), the Fourteenth Amendment "embraced" those " 'fundamental principles of liberty and justice which lie at the base of all our civil and political institutions,' " even though they had been "specifically dealt with in another part of the Federal Constitution." 287 U.S., at 67, 53 S.Ct., at 63. In many cases other than Powell and Betts, this Court has looked to the fundamental nature of original Bill of Rights guarantees to decide whether the Fourteenth Amendment makes them obligatory on the States. Explicitly recognized to be of this "fundamental nature" and therefore made immune from state invasion by the Fourteenth, or some part of it, are the First Amendment's freedoms of speech, press, religion, assembly, association, and petition for redress of grievances. For the same reason, though not always in precisely the same terminology, the Court has made obligatory on the States the Fifth Amendment's command that private property shall not be taken for public use without just compensation, the Fourth Amendment's prohibition of unreasonable searches and seizures, and the Eighth's ban on cruel and unusual punishment. On the other hand, this Court in Palko v. Connecticut, 302 U.S. 319, 58 S.Ct. 149 (1937), refused to hold that the Fourteenth Amendment made the double jeopardy provision of Fifth Amendment obligatory on the States. In so refusing, however, the Court, speaking through Mr. Justice Cardozo, was careful to emphasize that "immunities that are valid as against the federal government by force of the specific pledges of particular amendments have been found to be implicit in the concept of ordered liberty, and thus, through the Fourteenth Amendment, become valid as against the states" and that guarantees "in their origin ... effective against the federal government alone" had by prior cases "been taken over from the earlier articles of the Federal Bill of Rights and brought within the Fourteenth Amendment by a process of absorption."

We accept Betts v. Brady's assumption, based as it was on our prior cases, that a provision of the Bill of Rights which is "fundamental and essential to a fair trial" is made obligatory upon the States by the Fourteenth Amendment. We think the Court in Betts was wrong, however, in concluding that the Sixth Amendment's guarantee of counsel is not one of these fundamental rights. Ten years before Betts v. Brady, this Court, after full consideration of all the historical data examined in Betts, had unequivocally declared that "the right to the aid of counsel is of this fundamental character." Powell v. Alabama, 287 U.S. 45, 68, 53 S.Ct. 55, 63 (1932). While the Court at the close of its Powell opinion did by its language, as this Court frequently does, limit its holding to the particular facts and circumstances of that case, its conclusions about the fundamental nature of the right to counsel are unmistakable. Several years later, in 1936 [and in 1938], the Court re-emphasized what it had said about the fundamental nature of the right to counsel . . .

In light of these and many other prior decisions of this Court, it is not surprising that the Betts Court, when faced with the contention that "one charged with crime, who is unable to obtain counsel, must be furnished counsel by the state," conceded that "[e]xpressions in the opinions of this court lend color to the argument . . ." The fact is that in deciding as it did—that "appointment of counsel is not a fundamental right, essential to a fair trial"—the Court in Betts v. Brady made an abrupt break with its own well-considered precedents. In returning to these old precedents, sounder we believe than the new, we but restore constitutional principles established to achieve a fair system of justice. Not only these precedents but also reason and reflection require us to recognize that in our adversary system of criminal justice, any person haled into court, who is too poor to hire a lawyer, cannot be assured a fair trial unless counsel is provided for him. This seems to us to be an obvious truth. Governments, both state and federal, quite properly spend vast sums of money to establish machinery to try defendants accused of crime. Lawyers to prosecute are everywhere deemed essential to protect the public's interest in an orderly society. Similarly, there are few defendants charged with crime, few indeed, who fail to hire the best lawyers they can get to prepare and present their defenses. That government hires lawyers to prosecute and defendants who have the money hire lawyers to defend are the strongest indications of the widespread belief that lawyers in criminal courts are necessities, not luxuries. The right of one charged with crime to counsel may not be deemed fundamental and essential to fair trials in some countries, but it is in ours. From the very beginning, our state and national constitutions and laws have laid great emphasis on procedural and substantive safeguards designed to assure fair trials before impartial tribunals in which every defendant stands equal before the law. This noble ideal cannot be realized if the poor man charged with crime has to face his accusers without a lawyer to assist him. A defendant's need for a lawyer is nowhere better stated than in the moving words of Mr. Justice Sutherland in Powell v. Alabama:

> The right to be heard would be, in many cases, of little avail if it did not comprehend the right to be heard by counsel. Even the intelligent and educationed layman has small and sometimes no skill in the science of law. If charged with crime, he is incapable, generally, of determining for himself whether the indictment is good or bad. He is unfamiliar with the rules of evidence. Left without the aid of counsel he may be put on trial without a proper charge, and convicted upon incompetent evidence, or evidence

> irrelevant to the issue or otherwise inadmissible. He lacks both the skill and knowledge adequately to prepare his defense, even though he have a perfect one. He requires the guiding hand of counsel at every step in the proceedings against him. Without it, though he be not guilty, he faces the danger of conviction because he does not know how to establish his innocence.

The Court in Betts v. Brady departed from the sound wisdom upon which the Court's holding in Powell v. Alabama rested. Florida, supported by two other States, has asked that Betts v. Brady be left intact. Twenty-two States, as friends of the Court, argue that Betts was "an anachronism when handed down" and that it should now be overruled. We agree.

The judgment is reversed and the cause is remanded to the Supreme Court of Florida for further action not inconsistent with this opinion.

Reversed.

■ [The concurring opinion of JUSTICES DOUGLAS and CLARK are omitted.]

■ [MR. JUSTICE HARLAN's concurring opinion is omitted.]

Argersinger v. Hamlin

Supreme Court of the United States, 1972.
407 U.S. 25, 92 S.Ct. 2006.

■ MR. JUSTICE DOUGLAS delivered the opinion of the Court.

Petitioner, an indigent, was charged in Florida with carrying a concealed weapon, an offense punishable by imprisonment up to six months and a $1,000 fine. The trial was to a judge and petitioner was unrepresented by counsel. He was sentenced to serve 90 days in jail and brought this habeas corpus action in the Florida Supreme Court, alleging that, being deprived of his right to counsel, he was unable as an indigent layman properly to raise and present to the trial court good and sufficient defenses to the charges for which he stands convicted. The Florida Supreme Court by a four-to-three decision, in ruling on the right to counsel, followed the line we marked out in Duncan v. Louisiana (1968) as respects the right to trial by jury and held that the right to court-appointed counsel extends only to trials "for nonpetty offenses punishable by more than six months imprisonment."[1]

* * *

1. Nineteen States provide for the appointment of counsel in most misdemeanor cases. Id., pp. 124–133. One of these is Oregon whose Supreme Court said in Application of Stevenson, 254 Or. 94, 458 P.2d 414, 418, "If our objective is to insure a fair trial in every criminal prosecution, the need for counsel is not determined by the seriousness of the crime. The assistance of counsel will best avoid conviction of the innocent—an objective as important in the municipal court as in a court of general jurisdiction."

California's requirement extends to traffic violations. Blake v. Municipal Court, 242 Cal.App.2d 731, 51 Cal.Rptr. 771.

Overall, 31 States have now extended the right to defendants charged with crimes less serious than felonies. Comment, Right to Counsel, supra, at 134.

The Sixth Amendment, which in enumerated situations has been made applicable to the States by reason of the Fourteenth Amendment ... provides specified standards for "all criminal prosecutions."

One is the requirement of a "public trial." In re Oliver (1948), held that the right to a "public trial" was applicable to a state proceeding even though only a 60–day sentence was involved.

Another guarantee is the right to be informed of the nature and cause of the accusation. Still another, the right of confrontation. Pointer v. Texas (1965). And another, compulsory process for obtaining witnesses in one's favor. Washington v. Texas (1967). We have never limited these rights to felonies nor to lesser but serious offenses.

* * *

The right to trial by jury, also guaranteed by the Sixth Amendment by reason of the Fourteenth, was limited by Duncan v. Louisiana, supra, to trials where the potential punishment was imprisonment for six months or more. But, as the various opinions in Baldwin v. New York, 399 U.S. 66, 90 S.Ct. 1886, 26 L.Ed.2d 437, make plain, the right to trial by jury has a different genealogy and is brigaded with a system of trial to a judge alone. As stated in *Duncan*:

> Providing an accused with the right to be tried by a jury of his peers gave him an inestimable safeguard against the corrupt or overzealous prosecutor and against the complaint, biased, or eccentric judge. If the defendant preferred the common-sense judgment of a jury to the more tutored but perhaps less sympathetic reaction of the single judge, he was to have it. Beyond this, the jury trial provisions in the Federal and State Constitutions reflect a fundamental decision about the exercise of official power—a reluctance to entrust plenary powers over the life and liberty of the citizen to one judge or to a group of judges. Fear of unchecked power, so typical of our State and Federal Governments in other respects, found expression in the criminal law in this insistence upon community participation in the determination of guilt or innocence. The deep commitment of the Nation to the right of jury trial in serious criminal cases as a defense against arbitrary law enforcement qualifies for protection under the Due Process Clause of the Fourteenth Amendment, and must therefore be respected by the States.

While there is historical support for limiting the "deep commitment" to trial by jury to "serious criminal cases," there is no such support for a similar limitation on the right to assistance of counsel:

> Originally, in England, a person charged with treason or felony was denied the aid of counsel, except in respect of legal questions which the accused himself might suggest. At the same time parties in civil cases and persons accused of misdemeanors were entitled to the full assistance of counsel.... [It] appears that in at least twelve of the thirteen colonies the rule of the English common law, in the respect now under consideration, had been definitively rejected and the right to counsel fully recognized in all

> criminal prosecutions, save that in one or two instances the right was limited to capital offenses or to the more serious crimes.... Powell v. Alabama (1932).

The Sixth Amendment thus extended the right to counsel beyond its common-law dimensions. But there is nothing in the language of the Amendment, its history, or in the decisions of this Court, to indicate that it was intended to embody a retraction of the right in petty offenses wherein the common law previously did require that counsel be provided.

We reject, therefore, the premise that since prosecutions for crimes punishable by imprisonment for less than six months may be tried without a jury, they may always be tried without a lawyer.

The assistance of counsel is often a requisite to the very existence of a fair trial.

* * *

Both *Powell* and *Gideon* involved felonies. But the irrationale has relevance to any criminal trial, where an accused is deprived of his liberty. *Powell* and *Gideon* suggest that there are certain fundamental rights applicable to all such criminal prosecutions, even those, such as In re Oliver, supra, where the penalty is 60 days' imprisonment:

> A person's right to reasonable notice of a charge against him, and an opportunity to be heard in his defense—a right to his day in court—are basic in our system of jurisprudence; and these rights included, as a minimum, a right to examine the witnesses against him, to offer testimony, *and to be represented by counsel.* 333 U.S., at 273, 68 S.Ct., at 507 (emphasis supplied).

The requirement of counsel may well be necessary for a fair trial even in a petty offense prosecution. We are by no means convinced that legal and constitutional questions involved in a case that actually leads to imprisonment even for a brief period are any less complex than when a person can be sent off for six months or more.

* * *

The trial of vagrancy cases is illustrative. While only brief sentences of imprisonment may be imposed, the cases often bristle with thorny constitutional questions.

* * *

Beyond the problem of trials and appeals is that of the guilty plea, a problem which looms large in misdemeanor as well as in felony cases. Counsel is needed so that the accused may know precisely what he is doing, so that he is fully aware of the prospect of going to jail or prison, and so that he is treated fairly by the prosecution.

In addition, the volume of misdemeanor cases, far greater in number than felony prosecutions, may create an obsession for speedy dispositions, regardless of the fairness of the result....

* * *

"The misdemeanor trial is characterized by insufficient and frequently irresponsible preparation on the part of the defense, the prosecution, and the court. Everything is rush, rush." Hellerstein, The Importance of the Misdemeanor Case on Trial and Appeal, 38 The Legal Aid Brief Case 151, 152 (1970).

There is evidence of the prejudice which results to misdemeanor defendants from this "assembly-line justice." One study concluded that "Misdemeanants represented by attorneys are five times as likely to emerge from police court with all charges dismissed as are defendants who face similar charges without counsel." ACLU, Legal Counsel for Misdemeanants, Preliminary Report, 1 (1970).

We must conclude, therefore, that the problems associated with misdemeanor and petty offenses often require the presence of counsel to insure the accused a fair trial. Mr. Justice Powell suggests that these problems are raised even in situations where there is no prospect of imprisonment. We need not consider the requirements of the Sixth Amendment as regards the right to counsel where loss of liberty is not involved, however, for here petitioner was in fact sentenced to jail. And, as we said in Baldwin v. New York (1970): "[T]he prospect of imprisonment for however short a time will seldom be viewed by the accused as a trivial or 'petty' matter and may well result in quite serious repercussions affecting his career and his reputation."

We hold, therefore, that absent a knowing and intelligent waiver, no person may be imprisoned for any offense, whether classified as petty, misdemeanor, or felony, unless he was represented by counsel at his trial.

* * *

Under the rule we announce today, every judge will know when the trial of a misdemeanor starts that no imprisonment may be imposed, even though local law permits it, unless the accused is represented by counsel. He will have a measure of the seriousness and gravity of the offense and therefore know when to name a lawyer to represent the accused before the trial starts.

The run of misdemeanors will not be affected by today's ruling. But in those that end up in the actual deprivation of a person's liberty, the accused will receive the benefit of "the guiding hand of counsel" so necessary when one's liberty is in jeopardy.

Reversed.

■ MR. CHIEF JUSTICE BURGER, concurring in the result.

* * *

Trial judges sitting in petty and misdemeanor cases—and prosecutors—should recognize exactly what will be required by today's decision. Because no individual can be imprisoned unless he is represented by counsel, the trial judge and the prosecutor will have to engage in a predictive evaluation of each case to determine whether there is a significant likelihood that, if the defendant is convicted, the trial judge will sentence him to a jail term. The judge can preserve the option of a jail sentence only by offering counsel to any defendant unable to retain counsel on his own. This need to predict will place a new load on courts already overburdened and already compelled to deal with far more cases in one day than is reasonable and proper. Yet the prediction is not one beyond the capacity of an experienced judge, aided as he should be by the prosecuting officer. As to jury cases, the latter should be prepared to inform the judge as to any prior record of the accused, the general nature of the case against the accused, including any use of violence, the severity of harm to the victim, the impact on the community and the other factors relevant to the sentencing process. Since the judge ought to have some degree of such information after judgment of guilt is determined, ways can be found in the more serious misdemeanor cases when jury trial is not waived to make it available to the judge before trial. This will not mean a full "presentence" report on every defendant in every case before the jury passes on guilt, but a prosecutor should know before trial whether he intends to urge a jail sentence and if he does he should be prepared to aid the court with the factual and legal basis for his view on that score.

■ MR. JUSTICE BRENNAN, with whom MR. JUSTICE DOUGLAS and MR. JUSTICE STEWART join, concurring.

I join the opinion of the Court and add only an observation upon its discussion of legal resources. Law students as well as practicing attorneys may provide an important source of legal representation for the indigent. The Council on Legal Education for Professional Responsibility (CLEPR) informs us that more than 125 of the country's 147 accredited law schools have established clinical programs in which faculty supervised students aid clients in a variety of civil and criminal matters. CLEPR Newsletter, May 1972, at 2. These programs supplement practice rules enacted in 38 States authorizing students to practice law under prescribed conditions. Like the American Bar Association's Model Student Practice Rule (1969), most of these regulations permit students to make supervised court appearances as defense counsel in criminal cases. CLEPR, State Rules Permitting the Student Practice of Law: Comparisons and Comments 13 (1971). Given the huge increase in law school enrollments over the past few years, see Ruud, That Burgeoning Law School Enrollment, 58 A.B.A.J. 146 (1972), I think it plain that law students can be looked to to make a significant contribution, quantitatively and qualitatively, to the representation of the poor in many areas, including cases reached by today's decision.

[Other opinions omitted.]

NOTES

1. In Scott v. Illinois, 440 U.S. 367, 99 S.Ct. 1158 (1979), petitioner had been convicted of theft under $150, a misdemeanor which carried a possible punishment of one year in jail and a fine of $500. After a bench trial without defense counsel, Scott was convicted and sentenced to a fine of $50. By a vote of five-to-four, the Supreme Court held that Illinois was not required to provide Scott with court appointed counsel. Writing for himself and three other justices, Justice Rehnquist suggested that in *Argersinger* the Court had drawn the line in misdemeanor trials at "actual imprisonment" and had not left the question open as petitioner contended:

> "Although the intentions of the Argersinger Court are not unmistakably clear from its opinion, we conclude today that Argersinger did indeed delimit the constitutional right to appointed counsel in state criminal proceedings. Even were the matter res nova, we believe that the central premise of Argersinger—that actual imprisonment is a penalty different in kind from fines or the mere threat of imprisonment—is eminently sound and warrants adoption of actual imprisonment as the line defining the constitutional right to appointment of counsel. Argersinger has proved reasonably workable, whereas any extension would create confusion and impose unpredictable, but necessarily substantial, costs on 50 quite diverse States. We therefore hold that the Sixth and Fourteenth Amendments to the United States Constitution require only that no indigent criminal defendant be sentenced to a term of imprisonment unless the State has afforded him the right to assistance of appointed counsel in his defense. The judgment of the Supreme Court of Illinois is accordingly affirmed."

In a concurring opinion Mr. Justice Powell provided the fifth vote for affirmance:

> For the reasons stated in my opinion in Argersinger v. Hamlin (1972), I do not think the rule adopted by the Court in that case is required by the Constitution. Moreover, the drawing of a line based on whether there is imprisonment (even for overnight) can have the practical effect of precluding provision of counsel in other types of cases in which conviction can have more serious consequences. The Argersinger rule also tends to impair the proper functioning of the criminal justice system in that trial judges, in advance of hearing any evidence and before knowing anything about the case except the charge, all too often will be compelled to forego the legislatively granted option to impose a sentence of imprisonment upon conviction. Preserving this option by providing counsel often will be impossible or impracticable—particularly in congested urban courts where scores of cases are heard in a single setting, and in small and rural communities where lawyers may not be available.
>
> Despite my continuing reservations about the Argersinger rule, it was approved by the Court in the 1972 opinion and four Justices have reaffirmed it today. It is important that this Court provide clear guidance to the hundreds of courts across the country that confront this problem daily. Accordingly, and mindful of stare decisis, I join the opinion of the Court. I do so, however, with the hope that in due time a majority will recognize that a more flexible rule is consistent with due process and will better serve the cause of justice.

Justice Brennan authored a dissent, joined by Justices Stevens and Marshall. He argued that in *Argersinger* all assumed that counsel is required in any case where the possible statutory punishment exceeds six months. He noted that Justice Powell (whose vote for affirmance was necessary in *Scott*) had argued in *Argersinger* that the "right-to-counsel line must be drawn so that an indigent has a right to appointed counsel in all cases in which there is a due process right to jury trial." Brennan noted that, as a result of *Scott*, the right to trial by jury attaches in some cases in which an indigent defendant has no right to appointed counsel. He also argued that the authorized imprisonment standard is the traditional test for measuring the seriousness of the offense. He said that, as a result of *Scott*, courts, as a means of avoiding counsel, will negate the legislative judgment as to what offenses merit imprisonment. Brennan also challenged the assumption that the fiscal impact of a decision contrary to *Scott* would be intolerable. He added that "This Court's role in enforcing constitutional guarantees for criminal defendants cannot be made dependent on the budgetary decisions of state governments." Even Brennan's views left open the possibility that some "regulatory" offenses (including traffic cases), if no imprisonment is to be imposed, could be exempted from the requirement of counsel. He asserted, however, that theft, with its moral stigma, is not such an offense.

Justice Blackmun also dissented. He argued that counsel must be provided for the indigent in any case in which the statutory punishment exceeds six months *or* the actual punishment includes any period of incarceration.

In *Alabama v. Shelton*, 535 U.S. 654, 122 S.Ct. 1764 (2002), the defendant was convicted of third-degree assault. The court imposed a 30 day jail sentence, but then immediately suspended it and placed Shelton on probation for two years. Was he entitled to the Sixth Amendment right to appointed counsel under the *Argersinger* and *Scott* opinions?

The Court, in a 5–4 opinion, held that he was entitled to state appointed counsel.

Justice Ginsberg, writing for the majority, rejected the notions that this would impede a state's ability to impose probation and that it would cause states to incur additional expenses. Instead, the potential for imprisonment upon a probation violation required counsel to be provided.

Justice Scalia, writing for the dissent (joined by Chief Justice Rehnquist, and Justices Kennedy and Thomas) disagreed, urging that counsel be required only upon actual imprisonment.

In Halbert v. Michigan, 545 U.S. 605, 125 S.Ct. 2582 (2005) the defendant plead nolo contendere and then sought assistance of counsel to appeal his conviction. The state denied his request. The Supreme Court vacated his conviction on the grounds that the Due Process and Equal Protection Clauses required the appointment of counsel for defendant to access the first tier of review.

2. In Nichols v. United States, 511 U.S. 738, 114 S.Ct. 1921 (1994) the Court held that an uncounseled prior misdemeanor conviction may be used to enhance the sentence on a subsequent offense so long as the prior conviction did not result in a sentence of imprisonment. In so doing the Court overruled the contrary result of Baldasar v. Illinois, 446 U.S. 222, 100 S.Ct. 1585 (1980). The Court noted that a defendant charged with a misdemeanor has no federal constitutional right to counsel where no sentence of imprisonment is imposed, Scott v. Illinois, 440 U.S. 367, 99 S.Ct. 1158 (1979), and then reasoned that "[e]nhancement statutes ... do not change the penalty imposed for the earlier conviction." The Court, in fact, adopted Justice Powell's dissent in *Baldasar*. The Court also said:

> Petitioner contends that, at a minimum, due process requires a misdemeanor defendant to be warned that his conviction might be used for enhancement purposes should the defendant later be convicted of another crime. No such requirement was suggested in *Scott*, and we believe with good reason. In the first place, a large number of misdemeanor convictions take place in police or justice courts which are not courts of record. Without a drastic change in the procedures of these courts, there would be no way to memorialize any such warning. Nor is it at all clear exactly how expansive the warning would have to be; would a Georgia court have to warn the defendant about permutations and commutations of recidivist statutes in 49 other states, as well as the criminal history provision of the Sentencing Guidelines applicable in federal courts? And a warning at the completely general level—that if he is brought back into court on another

criminal charge, a defendant such as Nichols will be treated more harshly—would merely tell him what he must surely already know.

Concerning additional restrictions on the collateral use of convictions obtained in the absence of counsel or the waiver of counsel see chapter 21.

3. The Rules of Procedure for the Trial of Minor Offenses Before United States Magistrates, Rule 2B, following Title 18 U.S.C., provide that the indigent's right to appointed counsel depends upon the actual rather than the potential penalty. In other words the Supreme Court and Congress seems to have indicated that the rights of a federal defendant to counsel under the Sixth Amendment are no broader than the rights of state defendants under *Scott* and *Argersinger*. . . .

The rules also provide, however, that even in cases where the indigent has no right to appointed counsel, like all defendants, he must be admonished of the right to retain counsel. Does the Constitution mandate that all defendants, rich or poor, who appear without a lawyer in any criminal case, no matter how petty, be admonished of the right to retain counsel? Is it sound policy to admonish an indigent of the "right" to counsel in a case where he or she has no right to appointed counsel? Can you see any reason not to do this?

4. Does an indigent defendant's Sixth Amendment right to counsel give rise to a derivative right that appointed counsel be compensated? That he or she be fairly compensated? With rare exceptions, courts have held that, as a condition of practicing law, attorneys can be conscripted to represent indigent defendants. United States v. Bertoli, 994 F.2d 1002 (3d Cir.1993). For approval of the general rule, see Justice White's opinion in Martin County, Florida v. Makemson, 479 U.S. 1043, 107 S.Ct. 908 (1987), dissenting from the denial of certiorari, in a case where a state court had invalidated a statute that set a $3,500 limit on appointed counsel's fees in a capital case. What policy arguments support the opposing views in this controversy?

One court has held that the Constitution mandates adequate compensation for court-appointed counsel. As a matter of state law, it has prohibited trial courts from requiring lawyers to devote more than ten-percent of their work time to court appointed cases. Jewell v. Maynard, 181 W.Va. 571, 383 S.E.2d 536 (1989). See also, Arnold v. Kemp, 306 Ark. 294, 813 S.W.2d 770 (1991) (holding $1,000 cap on indigent defense fee an unconstitutional taking in a capital case).

In Mallard v. United States District Court for Southern District of Iowa, 490 U.S. 296, 109 S.Ct. 1814 (1989), the Supreme Court considered one small part of the question of whether a court can *compel* a lawyer to represent an indigent. Specifically, the Court construed 28 U.S.C. § 1915(d), which provides that in a federal civil case, "The court may request an attorney to represent [an *in forma pauperis*] litigant who is unable to employ counsel . . ." The Supreme Court held that the power to "request" does not allow a federal judge to require that counsel represent a client over the lawyer's objections. The Court did not reach policy or constitutional considerations, nor did it construe other statutes that provide for the appointment of counsel.

C. OTHER ASSISTANCE FOR THE INDIGENT

Ake v. Oklahoma

Supreme Court of the United States, 1985.
470 U.S. 68, 105 S.Ct. 1087.

■ JUSTICE MARSHALL delivered the opinion of the Court.

The issue in this case is whether the Constitution requires that an indigent defendant have access to the psychiatric examination and assistance necessary to prepare an effective defense based on his mental condition, when his sanity at the time of the offense is seriously in question.

Late in 1979, Glen Burton Ake was arrested and charged with murdering a couple and wounding their two children. He was arraigned in the District Court for Canadian County, Okla., in February 1980. His behavior at arraignment, and in other prearraignment incidents at the jail, was so bizarre that the trial judge *sua sponte* ordered him to be examined by a psychiatrist "for the purpose of advising with the Court as to his impressions of whether the Defendant may need an extended period of mental observation." The examining psychiatrist reported: "At times [Ake] appears to be frankly delusional.... He claims to be the 'sword of vengeance' of the Lord and that he will sit at the left hand of God in heaven." He diagnosed Ake as a probable paranoid schizophrenic and recommended a prolonged psychiatric evaluation to determine whether Ake was competent to stand trial.

In March, Ake was committed to a state hospital to be examined with respect to his "present sanity," i.e., his competency to stand trial. On April 10, less than six months after the incidents for which Ake was indicted, the chief forensic psychiatrist at the state hospital informed the court that Ake was not competent to stand trial. The court then held a competency hearing, at which a psychiatrist testified:

> [Ake] is a psychotic ... his psychiatric diagnosis was that of paranoid schizophrenia—chronic, with exacerbation, that is with current upset, and that in addition ... he is dangerous.... [B]ecause of the severity of his mental illness and because of the intensities of his rage, his poor control, his delusions, he requires a maximum security facility within—I believe—the State Psychiatric Hospital system.

The court found Ake to be a "mentally ill person in need of care and treatment" and incompetent to stand trial, and ordered him committed to the state mental hospital.

Six weeks later, the chief forensic psychiatrist informed the court that Ake had become competent to stand trial. At the time, Ake was receiving 200 milligrams of Thorazine, an antipsychotic drug, three times daily, and the psychiatrist indicated that, if Ake continued to receive that dosage, his condition would remain stable. The State then resumed proceedings against Ake.

At a pretrial conference in June, Ake's attorney informed the court that his client would raise an insanity defense. To enable him to prepare and present such a defense adequately, the attorney stated, a psychiatrist would have to examine Ake with respect to his mental condition at the time of the offense. During Ake's 3–month stay at the state hospital, no inquiry had been made into his sanity at the time of the offense, and, as an indigent, Ake could not afford to pay for a psychiatrist. Counsel asked the court either to arrange to have a psychiatrist perform the examination, or to provide funds to allow the defense to arrange one. The trial judge rejected counsel's argument that the Federal Constitution requires that an indigent defendant receive the assistance of a psychiatrist when that assistance is necessary to the defense, and he denied the motion for a psychiatric evaluation at state expense on the basis of this Court's decision in United States ex rel. Smith v. Baldi (1953).

Ake was tried for two counts of murder in the first degree, a crime punishable by death in Oklahoma, and for two counts of shooting with intent to kill. At the guilt phase of trial, his sole defense was insanity. Although defense counsel called to the stand and questioned each of the psychiatrists who had examined Ake at the state hospital, none testified about his mental state at the time of the offense because none had examined him on that point. The prosecution, in turn, asked each of these psychiatrists whether he had performed or seen the results of any examination diagnosing Ake's mental state at the time of the offense, and each doctor replied that he had not. As *a result, there was no expert testimony for either side on Ake's sanity at the time of the offense*. The jurors were then instructed that Ake could be found not guilty by reason of insanity if he did not have the ability to distinguish right from wrong at the time of the alleged offense. They were further told that Ake was to be presumed sane at the time of the crime unless *he* presented evidence sufficient to raise a reasonable doubt about his sanity at that time. If he raised such a doubt in their minds, the jurors were informed, the burden of proof shifted to the State to prove sanity beyond a reasonable doubt. The jury rejected Ake's insanity defense and returned a verdict of guilty on all counts.

At the sentencing proceeding, the State asked for the death penalty. No new evidence was presented. The prosecutor relied significantly on the testimony of the state psychiatrists who had examined Ake, and who had testified at the guilt phase that Ake was dangerous to society, to establish the likelihood of his future dangerous behavior. Ake had no expert witness to rebut this testimony or to introduce on his behalf evidence in mitigation of his punishment. The jury sentenced Ake to death on each of the two murder counts, and to 500 years' imprisonment on each of the two counts of shooting with intent to kill.

On appeal to the Oklahoma Court of Criminal Appeals, Ake argued that, as an indigent defendant, he should have been provided the services of a court-appointed psychiatrist. The court rejected this argument, observing: "We have held numerous times that, the unique nature of capital cases notwithstanding, the State does not have the responsibility of providing such services to indigents charged with capital crimes." Finding no error in Ake's other claims[2] the court affirmed the convictions and sentences.

2. The Oklahoma Court of Criminal Appeals also dismissed Ake's claim that the Thorazine he was given during trial rendered him unable to understand the proceedings against him or to assist counsel with his defense. The court acknowledged that Ake "stared vacantly ahead throughout the trial" but rejected Ake's challenge in reliance on a state psychiatrist's word that Ake was competent to stand trial while under the influence of the drug. Ake petitioned for a writ of certiorari on this issue as well. In light of our disposition of the other issues presented, we need not address this claim.

We hold that when a defendant has made a preliminary showing that his sanity at the time of the offense is likely to be a significant factor at trial, the Constitution requires that a State provide access to a psychiatrist's assistance on this issue, if the defendant cannot otherwise afford one. Accordingly, we reverse.

This Court has long recognized that when a State brings its judicial power to bear on an indigent defendant in a criminal proceeding, it must take steps to assure that the defendant has a fair opportunity to present his defense. This elementary principle, grounded in significant part on the Fourteenth Amendment's due process guarantee of fundamental fairness, derives from the belief that justice cannot be equal where, simply as a result of his poverty, a defendant is denied the opportunity to participate meaningfully in a judicial proceeding in which his liberty is at stake....

To implement this principle, we have focused on identifying the "basic tools of an adequate defense or appeal," Britt v. North Carolina (1971), and we have required that such tools be provided to those defendants who cannot afford to pay for them.

To say that these basic tools must be provided is, of course, merely to begin our inquiry. In this case we must decide whether, and under what conditions, the participation of a psychiatrist is important enough to preparation of a defense to require the State to provide an indigent defendant with access to competent psychiatric assistance in preparing the defense. Three factors are relevant to this determination. The first is the private interest that will be affected by the action of the State. The second is the governmental interest that will be affected if the safeguard is to be provided. The third is the probable value of the additional or substitute procedural safeguards that are sought, and the risk of an erroneous deprivation of the affected interest if those safeguards are not provided.

The private interest in the accuracy of a criminal proceeding that places an individual's life or liberty at risk is almost uniquely compelling. Indeed, the host of safeguards fashioned by this Court over the years to diminish the risk of erroneous conviction stands as a testament to that concern. The interest of the individual in the outcome of the State's effort to overcome the presumption of innocence is obvious and weighs heavily in our analysis.

We consider, next, the interest of the State. Oklahoma asserts that to provide Ake with psychiatric assistance on the record before us would result in a staggering burden to the State. We are unpersuaded by this assertion. Many States, as well as the Federal Government, currently make psychiatric assistance available to indigent defendants, and they have not found the financial burden so great as to preclude this assistance. This is especially so when the obligation of the State is limited to provision of one competent psychiatrist, as it is in many States, and as we limit the right we recognize today. At the same time, it is difficult to identify any interest of the State, other than that in its economy, that weighs against recognition of this right. The State's interest in prevailing at trial—unlike that of a private litigant—is necessarily tempered by its interest in the fair and accurate adjudication of criminal cases. Thus, also unlike a private litigant, a State may not legitimately assert an interest in maintenance of a strategic advantage over the defense, if the result of that advantage is to cast a pall on the accuracy of the verdict obtained. We therefore conclude that the governmental interest in denying Ake the assistance of a psychiatrist is not substantial, in light of the compelling interest of both the State and the individual in accurate dispositions.

Last, we inquire into the probable value of the psychiatric assistance sought, and the risk of error in the proceeding if such assistance is not offered. We begin by considering the pivotal role that psychiatry has come to play in criminal proceedings. More than 40 States, as well as the Federal Government, have decided either through legislation or judicial decision that indigent defendants are entitled, under certain circumstances, to the assistance of a psychiatrist's expertise. For example, in subsection (e) of the Criminal Justice Act, 18 U.S.C. § 3006A, Congress has provided that indigent defendants shall receive the assistance of all experts "necessary for an adequate defense." Numerous state statutes guarantee reimbursement for expert services under a like standard. And in many States that have not assured access to psychiatrists through the legislative process, state courts have interpreted the State or Federal Constitution to require that psychiatric assistance be provided to indigent defendants when necessary for an adequate defense, or when insanity is at issue.

These statutes and court decisions reflect a reality that we recognize today, namely, that when the State has made the defendant's mental condition relevant to his criminal culpability and to the punishment he might suffer, the assistance of a psychiatrist may well be crucial to the defendant's ability to marshal his defense. In this role, psychiatrists gather facts, both through professional examination, interviews, and elsewhere, that they will share with the judge or jury; they analyze the information gathered and from it draw plausible conclusions about the defendant's mental condition, and about the effects of any disorder on behavior; and they offer opinions about how the defendant's mental condition might have affected his behavior at the time in question. They know the probative questions to ask of the opposing party's psychiatrists and how to interpret their answers. Unlike lay witnesses, who can merely describe symptoms they believe might be relevant to the defendant's mental state, psychiatrists can identify the "elusive and often deceptive" symptoms of insanity, Solesbee v. Balkcom (1950), and tell the jury why their observations are relevant. Further, where permitted by evidentiary rules, psychiatrists can translate a medical diagnosis into language that will assist the trier of fact, and therefore offer evidence in a form that has meaning for the task at hand. Through this process of investigation, interpretation and testimony, psychiatrists ideally assist lay jurors, who generally have no training in psychiatric matters, to make a sensible and educated determination about the mental condition of the defendant at the time of the offense.

Psychiatry is not, however, an exact science, and psychiatrists disagree widely and frequently on what constitutes mental illness, on the appropriate diagnosis to be attached to given behavior and symptoms, on cure and treatment, and on likelihood of future dangerousness. Perhaps because there often is no single, accurate psychiatric conclusion on legal insanity in a given case, juries remain the primary factfinders on this issue, and they must resolve differences in opinion within the psychiatric profession on the basis of the evidence offered by each party. When jurors make this determination about issues that inevitably are complex and foreign, the testimony of psychiatrists can be crucial and "a virtual necessity if an insanity plea is to have any chance of success." By organizing a defendant's mental history, examination results and behavior, and other information, interpreting it in light of their expertise, and then laying out their investigative and analytic process to the jury, the psychiatrists for each party enable the jury to make its most accurate determination of the truth on the issue before them. It is for this reason that States rely on psychiatrists as examiners, consultants, and witnesses, and that private individuals do as well, when they can afford to do so. In so saying, we neither approve nor disapprove the widespread reliance on psychiatrists but instead recognize the unfairness of a contrary holding in light of the evolving practice.

The foregoing leads inexorably to the conclusion that, without the assistance of a psychiatrist to conduct a professional examination on issues relevant to the defense, to help determine whether the insanity defense is viable, to present testimony, and to assist in preparing the cross-examination of a State's psychiatric witnesses, the risk of an inaccurate resolution of sanity issues is extremely high. With such assistance, the defendant is fairly able to present at least enough information to the jury, in a meaningful manner, as to permit it to make a sensible determination.

A defendant's mental condition is not necessarily at issue in every criminal proceeding, however, and it is unlikely that psychiatric assistance of the kind we have described would be of probable value in cases where it is not. The risk of error from denial of such assistance, as well as its probable value, are most predictably at their height when the defendant's mental condition is seriously in question. When the defendant is able to make an *ex parte* threshold showing to the trial court that his sanity is likely to be a significant factor in his defense, the need for the assistance of a psychiatrist is readily apparent. It is in such cases that a defense may be devastated by the absence of a psychiatric examination and testimony; with such assistance, the defendant might have a reasonable chance of success. In such a circumstance, where the potential accuracy of the jury's determination is so dramatically enhanced, and where the interests of the individual and the State in an accurate proceeding are substantial, the State's interest in its fisc must yield.

We therefore hold that when a defendant demonstrates to the trial judge that his sanity at the time of the offense is to be a significant factor at trial, the State must, at a minimum, assure the defendant access to a competent psychiatrist who will conduct an appropriate examination and assist in evaluation, preparation, and presentation of the defense. This is not to say, of course, that the indigent defendant has a constitutional right to choose a psychiatrist of his personal liking or to receive funds to hire his own. Our concern is that the indigent defendant have access to a competent psychiatrist for the purpose we have discussed, and as in the case of the provision of counsel we leave to the State the decision on how to implement this right.

Ake also was denied the means of presenting evidence to rebut the State's evidence of his future dangerousness. The foregoing discussion compels a similar conclusion in the context of a capital sentencing proceeding, when the State presents psychiatric evidence of the defendant's future dangerousness. We have repeatedly recognized the defendant's compelling interest in fair adjudication at the sentencing phase of a capital case....

* * *

We turn now to apply these standards to the facts of this case. On the record before us, it is clear that Ake's mental state at the time of the offense was a substantial factor in his defense, and that the trial court was on notice of that fact when the request for a court-appointed psychiatrist was made. For one, Ake's sole defense was that of insanity. Second, Ake's behavior at arraignment, just four months after the offense, was so bizarre as to prompt the trial judge, *sua sponte*, to have him examined for competency. Third, a state psychiatrist shortly thereafter found Ake to be incompetent to stand trial, and suggested that he be committed. Fourth, when he was found to be competent six weeks later, it was only on the condition that he be sedated with large doses of Thorazine three times a day, during trial. Fifth, the psychiatrists who examined Ake for competency described to the trial court the severity of Ake's mental illness less than six months after the offense in question, and suggested that this mental illness might have begun many years' earlier. Finally, Oklahoma recognizes a defense of insanity, under which the initial burden of producing evidence falls on the defendant. Taken together, these factors make clear that the question of Ake's sanity was likely to be a significant factor in his defense.

In addition, Ake's future dangerousness was a significant factor at the sentencing phase. The state psychiatrist who treated Ake at the state mental hospital testified at the guilt phase that, because of his mental illness, Ake posed a threat of continuing criminal violence. This testimony raised the issue of Ake's future dangerousness, which is an aggravating factor under Oklahoma's capital sentencing scheme, Okla.Stat.Tit. 21, § 701.12(7) (1981), and on which the prosecutor relied at sentencing. We therefore conclude that Ake also was entitled to the assistance of a psychiatrist on this issue and that the denial of that assistance deprived him of due process.

■ CHIEF JUSTICE BURGER, concurring in the judgment.

This is a capital case in which the Court is asked to decide whether a State may refuse an indigent defendant "any opportunity whatsoever" to obtain psychiatric evidence for the preparation and presentation of a claim of insanity by way of defense when the defendant's legal sanity at the time of the offense was "seriously in issue."

The facts of the case and the question presented confine the actual holding of the Court. In capital cases the finality of the sentence imposed warrants protections that may or may not be required in other cases. Nothing in the Court's opinion reaches noncapital cases.

■ JUSTICE REHNQUIST, dissenting. [OPINION OMITTED]

* * *

NOTES

Experts and Other Assistance for the Indigent

1. Suppose that, on the motion of the prosecutor, the court appoints a psychiatrist to examine the defendant. Under *Ake* can the defense be required to "share" that psychiatrist? One Federal court has answered this question negatively. It reasoned that in planning an insanity defense, a defendant should have the right to work with a psychiatrist who is not also aiding the prosecution. See United States v. Sloan, 776 F.2d 926 (10th Cir.1985). Smith v. McCormick, 914 F.2d 1153 (9th Cir.1990), holds that where the *Ake* right attaches, the defendant has the right to an "adversarial" psychiatrist, one who will advise the defense. Appointment of a psychiatrist who will report to the court does not suffice. See Also, De Freece v. Texas, 848 S.W.2d 150 (Tex.Cr.App.1993) ("disinterested" expert not sufficient).

2. In Little v. Streater, 452 U.S. 1, 101 S.Ct. 2202 (1981), the Court held that the defendant in the particular paternity action could not be denied a blood test for lack of funds. The Court used a due process rather than an equal protection approach. It noted the high degree of accuracy of blood tests and commented upon the fact that the State could receive seventy-five per cent reimbursement from the Federal Government for costs incurred in the paternity action, which had been brought by a mother who received public assistance.

3. Except for *Ake* and *Little*, and except for decisions concerning an indigent defendant's right at trial to counsel and to a transcript of testimony given in an earlier proceeding (to be discussed subsequently in Note 4), the Supreme Court has generally avoided indigents' claims concerning the right to assistance at the trial level. Lower courts have frequently dealt with such issues. Generally they have refused to rule that the indigent is entitled to assistance which is the same as (or just as good as) what the defendant with funds could purchase. Normally courts have required quite a specific showing of necessity, even though the non-indigent might purchase the services in a case where necessity is not manifest. See generally State v. Sahlie, 90 S.D. 682, 245 N.W.2d 476 (1976), setting forth criteria for the granting of an indigent's request for trial assistance.

Absent statutory authority, an indigent defendant who has been denied the existence of an expert rarely succeeds in overturning a conviction on that basis. State v. Williams, 263 S.C. 290, 210 S.E.2d 298 (1974) (pathologist); Patterson v. State, 239 Ga. 409, 238 S.E.2d 2 (1977) (firearms identification expert); Harrison v. State, 644 N.E.2d 1243 (Ind.1995) (DNA expert). But see People v. Gunnerson, 74 Cal.App.3d 370, 141 Cal.Rptr. 488 (1977) (sufficient showing of uncertainty as to cause of death to require that defendant be permitted the services of a cardiologist); People v. Hatterson, 63 A.D.2d 736, 405 N.Y.S.2d 297 (1978) (defense right to services of a psychiatrist where prosecution psychotherapist had been permitted to testify that the alleged rape victim had a "compliant" or "obedient" personality); Williams v. State, 958 S.W.2d 186 (Tex.Cr.App.1997) (remanding for resentencing because defense request for expert had not been handled ex parte, prematurely revealing the defense strategy at the penalty phase).

In United States v. One Feather, 702 F.2d 736 (8th Cir.1983), the court declared that an indigent defendant is entitled to the appointment of an expert only when the facts suggest that he may benefit from such appointment. In United States v. Durant, 545 F.2d 823 (2d Cir.1976), however, the Court held that the federal district judge had erred under the Federal Criminal Justice Act, 18 U.S.C. § 3006A (1970), in denying a fingerprint expert in a case where fingerprint evidence was crucial to the defense theory of the case. In Little v. Armontrout, 835 F.2d 1240 (8th Cir.1987), an en banc court held that, under *Ake* and the particular facts of the case, an indigent state court defendant was entitled to the appointment of an expert on hypnosis in order to be able to challenge the testimony of a witness whose memory had been hypnotically refreshed. The court refused to limit *Ake* to capital cases or to cases involving requests for psychiatric assistance. In *Little*, the main issue was identification, the primary witness had been subject to hypnosis, and the prosecution had used an expert to help lay the foundation for the admission of testimony of that witness. In People v. Evans, 648 N.E.2d 964 (Ill. App. Ct. 1995) the Illinois Appellate Court reversed a conviction on the basis that the indigent defendant had been wrongfully denied an expert on the battered woman's syndrome.

In contrast to these cases, there are many instances in which funds are not granted to an indigent defendant to prepare his or her case. For example,

> The few available investigations support the view that the progeny of *Ake* have often taken a restrictive approach to the right to expert assistance. In 1990, The National Law Journal published the results of a six-month investigation on the defenses of capital murder defendants in the South. One of the key findings concerned defense experts: "Judges routinely deny lawyers' requests for expert/investigative fees." As part of this investigation, sixty death row trial lawyers were interviewed and "54.2% felt [that the] court provided inadequate investigation and expert funds." A 1992 study of indigent defense systems sponsored by the National Center for State Courts noted that the "greatest disparities occur in the areas of investigators and expert witnesses, with the prosecutors possessing more resources [than the public defenders]." In addition, a 1993 report commissioned by the State Bar of Texas concluded that "there is a serious underfunding of essential expert services and other expenses in capital trials and appeals." [cites omitted] Gianelli, *Ake v. Oklahoma: The Right to Expert Assistance in a Post–Daubert, Post–DNA World*, 89 Cornell L. Rev. 1305, 1312–13 (2004)

With increasing reliance on more complex evidentiary processes, courts will be pressed for the appointment of more experts in areas such as DNA, data mining, GPS evidence, biometric identification, genetic data, etc. Commentators have argued for a multiplicity of experts. See, for example, Comment, *A Process Right Due? Examining Whether a Capital Defendant Has a Due Process Right to a Jury Selection Expert*, 53 Am. U.L. Rev. 1143 (2004). See generally Decker, Expert Services in the Defense of Criminal Cases: The Constitutional and Statutory Rights of Indigents, 51 U.Cinn.L.R. 574 (1982).

As the cases demonstrate, some statutory rights to trial-level assistance may be broader than an indigent's rights under the Constitution. Consider again the various possible rationales for defense services: due process, equal protection, statutory right, supervisory powers, right to counsel, right to compulsory process.

4. When a prosecution witness has testified on the same subject in a former proceeding (e.g., at a preliminary hearing, a trial which resulted in a hung jury, or a co-defendant's trial), a defendant may have a constitutional right, under the *Griffin* line of cases, to a transcript of the earlier testimony if no alternative is available which would permit defense counsel to learn the content of such testimony (so as to be able to use it for discovery or impeachment purposes). See generally Roberts v. LaVallee, 389 U.S. 40, 88 S.Ct. 194 (1967); Britt v. North Carolina, 404 U.S. 226, 92 S.Ct. 431 (1971).

The Griffin Due Process–Equal Protection Ideal Revisited at Sentencing

5. The Supreme Court has held there is a Sixth Amendment right to have the jury determine the existence of "any particular fact" that the law makes essential to his punishment. United States v. Booker, 543 U.S. 220, 125 S.Ct. 738 (2005). This may lead to new questions concerning economic equality for indigent defendants at sentencing.

6. The Supreme Court has struggled with the notion of equality for the indigent in the area of sentencing, seeking to apply the due process-equal protection rationale of Griffin v. Illinois in that context. Williams v. Illinois, 399 U.S. 235, 90 S.Ct. 2018 (1970), confronted the exceedingly common practice, where the trial judge had imposed a fine as the sentence or as part of a sentence, of having an indigent (who had no funds to pay the fine) "work out" the fine by serving time in jail and receiving credit against the fine, at a statutory rate, for each day of incarceration. The judge had sentenced Williams to one year, the maximum period of incarceration set forth in the theft statute's penalty provision, and to a fine of $500, as authorized by statute. Williams was required to satisfy the $500 fine by serving an additional 100 days, getting credit of $5 for each day served.

Relying on the dual due process-equal protection rationale, the Supreme Court, through Chief Justice Burger, held that the State of Illinois could not automatically convert a fine into an additional period of incarceration—beyond the maximum statutory period of incarceration provided in the theft statute—where the failure to pay the fine was not wilful. While perhaps leaving open the possibility that at some point the State could incarcerate a defendant who had non-wilfully failed to pay the levied fine, the Court indicated that, at a minimum, the State had to try alternatives—such as use of a periodic payment schedule—in an effort to satisfy its legitimate interest in exacting a criminal punishment.

Although no justice dissented from the *Williams* result, Justice Harlan issued a concurring opinion in which he challenged the equal protection component of the *Griffin–Williams* line of decisions.

* * *

> The "equal protection" analysis of the Court is, I submit, a "wolf in a sheep's clothing," for that rationale is no more than a masquerade of a supposedly objective standard for *subjective* judicial judgment as to what state legislation offends notions of "fundamental fairness." Under the rubric of "equal protection" this Court has in recent times effectively substituted its own "enlightened" social philosophy or that of the legislature no less than did in the older days the judicial adherents of the now discredited doctrine of "substantive" due process. I, for one, would prefer to judge the legislation before us in this case in terms of due process, that is to determine whether it arbitrarily infringes a constitutionally protected interest of this petitioner....
>
> An analysis under due process standards, correctly understood is, in my view, more conducive to judicial restraint than an approach couched in slogans and ringing phrases, such as "suspect" classification or "invidious" distinctions, or "compelling" state interest, that blur analysis by shifting the focus away from the nature of the individual interest affected, the extent to which it is affected, the rationality of the connection between legislative means and purpose, the existence of alternative means for effectuating the purpose, and the degree of confidence we may have that the statute reflects the legislative concern for the purpose that would legitimately support the means chosen.

7. Williams v. Illinois gave rise to several other efforts to afford equal treatment to indigents in sentencing without exempting the indigent from punishment where the non-indigent was subject to some punishment for similar criminal conduct. In Morris v. Schoonfield, 399 U.S. 508, 90 S.Ct. 2232 (1970), the Supreme Court vacated and remanded in light of *Williams* in a situation where (a) both a fine and imprisonment were possible penalties, (b) a fine was imposed, and (c) working out of the fine did *not*, as in *Williams*, extend the period of incarceration beyond the maximum allowed by such statute. Four of the justices, concurring, expressed the view that the incarceration for inability to pay a fine was impermissible under these circumstances, arguing that the same constitutional defect condemned in *Williams* also inheres in jailing an indigent for failing to make immediate payment of any fine, whether or not the jail term of the indigent extends beyond the maximum term that may be imposed on a person willing and able to pay a fine.

In Tate v. Short, 401 U.S. 395, 91 S.Ct. 668 (1971), the maximum statutory penalty for a certain traffic offense was a fine only. Imprisonment was not a possible punishment. The Supreme Court held that requiring a defendant to work out his fine at five dollars per day ran afoul of the principles of *Williams*.

Interestingly, the majority in *Tate* cited the opinion of the four justices in *Morris*, even though *Tate* presented a narrower issue than did *Morris*.

8. The *Williams–Tate* line of decisions has had considerable impact. In State v. De Bonis, 58 N.J. 182, 276 A.2d 137 (1971), the court examined the alternatives available to the sentencing court when the defendant was unable to pay the fine immediately. Unable to pay a lump sum fine, defendant there offered to pay in installments. The trial court refused the offer and ordered him to jail at the statutory rate of five dollars a day. After studying several methods of payment, the New Jersey Supreme Court concluded that the installment system was the most practical alternative and that the defendant was therefore entitled to it by right. See also, State v. Newman, 132 N.J. 159, 623 A.2d 1355 (1993).

Justice Blackmun, concurring in *Tate*, suggested that an alternative to fines, fair to all, would be a "jail only" policy. The Hawaii Supreme Court, in State v. Tackett, 52 Haw. 601, 483 P.2d 191 (1971), rejected this idea because it would reduce sentencing flexibility and would work an inverse discrimination against "the employed man with funds".

Because of the high administrative cost involved in collecting small fines, will *Tate*, as a practical matter, force judges to impose short jail sentences rather than fines? Is this a desirable result?

9. Consider the case of an offense which is punishable by a fine only. Can an accused be held in custody before trial on such a charge if he or she is unable to post bail in the amount set by the trial judge? One court has held that such pre-trial incarceration is impermissible. See Allen v. Burke, (E.D.Va.), 29 Crim.L.Rptr. 2297; Pulliam v. Allen, 466 U.S. 522, 104 S.Ct. 1970, n. 2 (1984).

10. In Bearden v. Georgia, 461 U.S. 660, 103 S.Ct. 2064 (1983), the court sentenced the defendant to probation for burglary and theft, conditioned upon payment of a $500 fine and $250 in restitution. It set up a schedule that required completion of these payments within four months. Within a month, the defendant was laid off from his job. He had no income or assets. With the defendant still owing $550 seven months after sentencing, the court revoked probation, entered an official judgment of conviction in the case for the first time, and ordered the defendant to the penitentiary for the balance of the three-year probationary period.

Through Justice O'Connor, relying on the *Williams–Tate* line of decisions, the Supreme Court invalidated the trial court's actions. It declared:

> The decision to place the defendant on probation, however, reflects a determination by the sentencing court that the State's penological interests do not require imprisonment. A probationer's failure to make reasonable efforts to repay his debt to society may indicate that this original determination needs reevaluation, and imprisonment may now be required to satisfy the State's interests. But a probationer who has made sufficient

bona fide efforts to pay his fine and restitution, and who has complied with the other conditions of probation, has demonstrated a willingness to pay his debt to society and an ability to conform his conduct to social norms. The State nevertheless asserts three reasons why imprisonment is required to further its penal goals.

First, the State argues that revoking probation furthers its interest in ensuring that restitution be paid to the victims of crime. A rule that imprisonment may befall the probationer who fails to make sufficient bona fide efforts to pay restitution may indeed spur probationers to try hard to pay, thereby increasing the number of probationers who make restitution. Such a goal is fully served, however, by revoking probation only for persons who have not made sufficient bona fide efforts to pay. . . .

Second, the State asserts that its interest in rehabilitating the probationer and protecting society requires it to remove him from the temptation of committing other crimes. This is no more than a naked assertion that a probationer's poverty by itself indicates he may commit crimes in the future and thus that society needs for him to be incapacitated. We have already indicated that a sentencing court can consider a defendant's employment history and financial resources in setting an initial punishment. Such considerations are a necessary part of evaluating the entire background of the defendant in order to tailor an appropriate sentence for the defendant and crime. But it must be remembered that the State is seeking here to use as the *sole* justification for imprisonment the poverty of a probationer who, by assumption, has demonstrated sufficient bona fide efforts to find a job and pay the fine and whom the State initially thought it unnecessary to imprison. . . .

Third, and most plausibly, the State argues that its interests in punishing the law breaker and deterring others from criminal behavior require it to revoke probation for failure to pay a fine or restitution. The State clearly has an interest in punishment and deterrence, but this interest can often be served fully by alternative means.

* * *

For example, the sentencing court could extend the time for making payments, or reduce the fine, or direct that the probationer perform some form of labor or public service in lieu of the fine. . . . Indeed, given the general flexibility of tailoring fines to the resources of a defendant, or even permitting the defendant to do specified work to satisfy the fine, a sentencing court can often establish a reduced fine or alternate public service in lieu of a fine that adequately serves the State's goals of punishment and deterrence, given the defendant's diminished financial resources. Only if the sentencing court determines that alternatives to imprisonment are not adequate in a particular situation to meet the State's interest in punishment and deterrence may the State imprison a probationer who has made sufficient bona fide efforts to pay.

We hold, therefore, that in revocation proceedings for failure to pay a fine or restitution, a sentencing court must inquire into the reasons for the failure to pay. If the probationer willfully refused to pay or failed to make sufficient bona fide efforts legally to acquire the resources to pay, the court may revoke probation and sentence the defendant to imprisonment within the authorized range of its sentencing authority. If the probationer could not pay despite sufficient bona fide efforts to acquire the resources to do so, the court must consider alternate measures of punishment other than imprisonment. Only if alternate measures are not adequate to meet the State's interests in punishment and deterrence may the court imprison a probationer who has made sufficient bona fide efforts to pay. To do otherwise would deprive the probationer of his conditional freedom simply because, through no fault of his own, he cannot pay the fine. Such a deprivation would be contrary to the fundamental fairness required by the Fourteenth Amendment.

CHAPTER 10

THE PRELIMINARY HEARING

A. THE NATURE AND PURPOSE OF THE HEARING

Coleman v. Alabama

Supreme Court of the United States, 1970.
399 U.S. 1, 90 S.Ct. 1999, conformed to 46 Ala.App. 737, 239 So.2d 223 (1970).

■ MR. JUSTICE BRENNAN announced the judgment of the Court and delivered the following opinion.

Petitioners were convicted in an Alabama Circuit Court of assault with intent to murder in the shooting of one Reynolds after he and his wife parked their car on an Alabama highway to change a flat tire.

* * *

This Court has held that a person accused of crime "requires the guiding hand of counsel at every step in the proceedings against him," Powell v. Alabama, (1932), and that that constitutional principle is not limited to the presence of counsel at trial. "It is central to that principle that in addition to counsel's presence at trial, the accused is guaranteed that he need not stand alone against the State at any stage of the prosecution, formal or informal, in court or out, where counsel's absence might derogate from the accused's right to a fair trial." United States v. Wade [(1967)]. Accordingly, "the principle of Powell v. Alabama and succeeding cases requires that we scrutinize *any* pretrial confrontation of the accused to determine whether the presence of his counsel is necessary to preserve the defendant's basic right to a fair trial as affected by his right meaningfully to cross-examine the witnesses against him and to have effective assistance of counsel at the trial itself. It calls upon us to analyze whether potential substantial prejudice to defendant's rights inheres in the particular confrontation and the ability of counsel to help avoid that prejudice." Applying this test, the Court has held that "critical stages" include the pretrial type of arraignment where certain rights may be sacrificed or lost, Hamilton v. Alabama (1961), and the pretrial line up, United States v. Wade, supra; Cf. Miranda v. Arizona (1966), where the Court held that the privilege against compulsory self-incrimination includes a right to counsel at a pretrial custodial interrogation.

The preliminary hearing is not a required step in an Alabama prosecution. The prosecutor may seek an indictment directly from the grand jury without a preliminary hearing. The opinion of the Alabama Court of Appeals in this case instructs us that under Alabama law the sole purposes of a preliminary hearing are to determine whether there is sufficient evidence against the accused to warrant presenting his case to the grand jury, and if so to fix bail if the offense is bailable. 44 Ala.App., at 433; 211 So.2d, at 920. See Code of Alabama, Tit. 15, §§ 139, 140, 151.[3] The court continued:

> "At the preliminary hearing ... the accused is not required to advance any defenses, and failure to do so does not preclude him from availing himself of every defense he may have upon the trial of the case. Also Pointer v. State of Texas bars the admission of testimony given at a pre-trial proceeding where the accused did not have the benefit of cross-examination by and through counsel. Thus, nothing occurring at the preliminary hearing in the absence of counsel can substantially prejudice the rights of the accused on trial." 44 Ala.App., at 433; 211 So.2d at 921.

This Court is of course bound by this construction of the governing Alabama law. However, from the fact that in cases where the accused has no lawyer at the hearing the Alabama courts prohibit the State's use at trial of anything that occurred at the hearing, it does not follow that the Alabama preliminary hearing is not a "critical stage" of the State's criminal process. The determination whether the hearing is a "critical stage" requiring the provision of counsel depends, as noted, upon an analysis "whether potential substantial prejudice to defendant's rights inheres in the ... confrontation and the ability of counsel to help avoid that prejudice." United States v. Wade, supra, at 227, 87 S.Ct. at 1932. Plainly the guiding hand of counsel at the preliminary hearing is essential to protect the indigent accused against an erroneous or improper prosecution. First, the lawyer's skilled examination and cross-examination of witnesses may expose fatal weaknesses in the State's case, that may lead the magistrate to refuse to bind the accused over. Second, in any event, the skilled interrogation of witnesses by an experienced lawyer can fashion a vital impeachment tool for use in cross-examination of the State's witnesses at the trial, or preserve testimony favorable to the accused of a witness who does not appear at the trial. Third, trained counsel can more effectively discover the case the State has against his client and make possible the preparation of a proper defense to meet that case at the trial. Fourth, counsel can also be influential at the preliminary hearing in making effective arguments for the accused on such matters as the necessity for an early psychiatric examination or bail.

The inability of the indigent accused on his own to realize these advantages of a lawyer's assistance compels the conclusion that the Ala-

3. A textbook, "Criminal Procedure in Alabama," by M. Clinton McGee (University of Alabama Press 1954), at p. 41, states:

> "A preliminary hearing or examination is not a trial in its ordinary sense nor is it a final determination of guilt. It is a proceeding whereby an accused is discharged or held to answer, as the facts warrant. It seeks to determine whether there is probable cause for believing that a crime has been committed and whether the accused is probably guilty, in order that he may be informed of the nature of such charge and to allow the state to take the necessary steps to bring him to trial. Such hearing also serves to perpetuate evidence and to keep the necessary witnesses within the control of the state. It also safeguards the accused against groundless and vindictive prosecutions, and avoids for both the accused and the state the expense and inconvenience of a public trial."

bama preliminary hearing is a "critical stage" of the State's criminal process at which the accused is "as much entitled to such aid [of counsel] ... as at the trial itself." Powell v. Alabama, supra, at 57, 53 S.Ct. at 60.

There remains, then, the question of the relief to which petitioners are entitled. The trial transcript indicates that the prohibition against use by the State at trial of anything that occurred at the preliminary hearing was scrupulously observed. Cf. White v. Maryland, supra. But on the record it cannot be said whether or not petitioners were otherwise prejudiced by the absence of counsel at the preliminary hearing. That inquiry in the first instance should more properly be made by the Alabama courts. The test to be applied is whether the denial of counsel at the preliminary hearing was harmless error under Chapman v. California, 386 U.S. 18, 87 S.Ct. 824 (1967).

We accordingly vacate the petitioners' convictions and remand the case to the Alabama courts for such proceedings not inconsistent with this opinion as they may deem appropriate to determine whether such denial of counsel was harmless error ... and therefore whether the convictions should be reinstated or a new trial ordered.

■ [Omitted are the concurring opinions of JUSTICES WHITE and BLACK, the dissenting opinions of CHIEF JUSTICE BURGER and JUSTICE STEWART, the separate opinion of JUSTICE DOUGLAS, concurring, and the dissenting opinion of JUSTICE HARLAN.]

Maestas v. District Court

Supreme Court of Colorado, 1975.
189 Colo. 443, 541 P.2d 889.

■ ERICKSON, JUSTICE.

* * *

Maestas was charged in a three-count information with attempted robbery and with two enhancement of punishment counts under the Habitual Criminal Statute. He was represented by a public defender who filed a timely motion for a preliminary hearing in the county court. At this hearing, the prosecution relied solely on the testimony of one witness, a detective, whose testimony consisted of a hearsay account of a telephone conversation with the alleged victim, coupled with hearsay information the detective had gleaned from the police file.

The defendant moved to strike the detective's testimony at the preliminary hearing on the ground that it was 100% hearsay and effectively denied him the right to confront his accusers.

* * *

The purpose of a preliminary hearing is to determine whether probable cause exists to support the prosecution's charge that the accused committed a particular crime.... The preliminary hearing serves as a screening device to test the sufficiency of the prosecution's case before an impartial judge and to weed out the fatally weak case....

"The holding of a preliminary hearing is of value to the prosecution in that it offers a method for testing the complaints of prosecuting witnesses, and eliminating prosecutions actuated by prejudice or motives inconsistent with a fair administration of the criminal law. A preliminary hearing accords the defendant an opportunity to correct any misconceptions which may have arisen with respect to his conduct. An innocent defendant may be spared the ignominy resulting from a trial. (Orfield, Criminal Procedure from Arrest to Appeal pps. 72–73 (1947))." T. Borrillo, Colorado Practice, Criminal Practice and Procedure § 82.

The preliminary hearing, however, is not a mini trial, and the rules of evidence may be tempered in accordance with the sound discretion of the trial judge.... The prosecution is thus granted greater evidentiary latitude in proving the existence of probable cause. To that end, this court has held that "[h]earsay evidence, and other evidence, which would be incompetent if offered at the time of trial, may well be the bulk of the evidence at the preliminary hearing."

The parameters of [this doctrine], however, should not be extended beyond their original design. As demonstrated by the preliminary hearing in this case, the prosecution presented the testimony of peripheral, if not extraneous, witnesses who recited in a narrative fashion what others had seen, heard, or done.... Neither the key witness in this case nor the arresting officers were produced at the hearing. Instead, the sole testimony of an on perceiving witness relating second-hand information was relied upon to establish probable cause. A minimum investment of time and talent characterized this hearing. The perfunctory fashion in which it was held belies the fact that the preliminary hearing is a critical stage in the administration of criminal justice. Coleman v. Alabama (1970)....

The preliminary hearing is not a "judicial rubber stamp for prosecutorial discretion." See, K. Graham and L. Letwin, The Preliminary Hearings in Los Angeles: Some Field Findings and Legal–Policy Observations, 18 U.C.L.A.L.Rev. 636 (1971). The full potential and purpose of the preliminary hearing is only realized when it is utilized as a check on the power of the prosecution. That check assumes significance where, as in the instant case, the prosecution attempts to establish probable cause on the basis of second-hand hearsay testimony.

Where the prosecution exploits the use of hearsay on hearsay and establishes probable cause solely on the basis of second-half information, the historical function of the preliminary hearing is vitiated—that being to place before the judge evidence which establishes that probable cause exists to prove that the defendant did commit the crime charged.... By our holding here, we seek fair play and substantial justice at the preliminary hearing.

We reaffirm our previous holding that hearsay evidence is admissible at a preliminary hearing, but we admonish the courts to beware of the excessive use of hearsay in the presentation of government cases. The inordinate use of hearsay, as in the present case, foils the protective defense against unwarranted prosecutions that preliminary hearings are designed to afford to the innocent....

Unsubstantiated complaints can only be detected if a means exists by which their shaky foundations may be disclosed.... We do not require that the prosecution produce all, or even the best, witnesses at a preliminary hearing. But the evidence presented at the preliminary hearing must have some semblance of a factual foundation and must show probable cause. The process is best served when at least one witness is called whose direct perception of the criminal episode is subject to evaluation by the judge at the preliminary hearing. Establishing probable cause on the basis of hearsay alone should only be resorted to when the testimony of a perceiving witness is unavailable or when "it is demonstrably inconvenient to summon witnesses able to testify to facts from personal knowledge." ... Better prosecutorial practice entails the presentation of a residuum of competent, non-hearsay evidence at the preliminary hearing to support probable cause....

On the basis of the foregoing, we remand with the direction that the defendant be granted a new preliminary hearing in accordance with the views expressed in this opinion.

NOTES

1. In People ex rel. VanMeveren v. District Court, 195 Colo. 1, 575 P.2d 405 (1978), the court distinguished *Maestas* and reaffirmed the use of hearsay in most instances:

> "In *Maestas*, the witness was so unfamiliar with the case that an effective cross-examination could not be afforded the defendant, and the screening function of the preliminary hearing was rendered meaningless.
>
> "On the contrary, in this case the prosecution witness is the investigating officer of the case who had knowledge and information about many of the aspects of the alleged crime. Although much of his testimony was hearsay, he also testified concerning his observations of the alleged victim when she made her complaint to him. Also, he personally interviewed the defendant and witnesses whose statements he related. The transcript reflects that defendant's counsel comprehensively cross-examined the witness here."

In most jurisdictions hearsay is admissible at preliminary hearings, although frequently limitations are placed upon the use of hearsay in actual practice. See Wilson v. State, 655 P.2d 1246 (Wyo.1982); Wolke v. Fleming, 24 Wis.2d 606, 129 N.W.2d 841 (1964); United States v. Catino, 403 F.2d 491 (2d Cir.1968).

Generally the standard rules of evidence are not applicable to a preliminary hearing. See State v. Sherry, 233 Kan. 920, 667 P.2d 367 (1983); People v. Quinn, 183 Colo. 245, 516 P.2d 420 (1973). Does this mean that illegally obtained evidence may be admitted? A defense counsel may not be able to offer a well-prepared objection to such evidence at a speedy preliminary hearing. In many cases, suppression may not prevent a finding of probable cause and, if the motion is denied, defendant will likely be bound by the result for the rest of the proceedings

2. The cross-examination of witnesses designed to secure discovery of the prosecution's case rather than to refute the assertion of probable cause may be restricted. The courts have indicated that discovery may be a byproduct of the process of demonstrating probable cause, but declared that it is not a legitimate end into itself. See United States v. Hart, 526 F.2d 344 (5th Cir.1976); Coleman v. Burnett, 477 F.2d 1187 (D.C.Cir.1973).

3. In jurisdictions which do not provide for evidence depositions in criminal cases, a full adversary preliminary hearing may be the only way a party (typically the prosecutor) may preserve the testimony of a witness who later becomes unavailable. See Ohio v. Roberts, 448 U.S. 56, 100 S.Ct. 2531 (1980) (Casebook Chapter 19); California v. Green, 399 U.S. 149, 90 S.Ct. 1930 (1970) (Casebook Chapter 19).

4. In State v. Brooks, 638 P.2d 537 (Utah 1981), defendants were convicted of aggravated assault for beating fellow transients in a "hobo jungle." After testifying at a preliminary hearing where cross-examination was permissible, the victims jumped a freight car and were never heard from again. Upon conviction at a trial based upon a reading of the hearing transcripts, defendants contended on appeal that the convictions violated their confrontation rights were violated; but the convictions were affirmed:

"Defense counsel's motive and interest are the same in either setting; he acts in both situations in the interest of and motivated by establishing the innocence of his client. Therefore, cross-examination takes place at preliminary hearing and at trial under the same motive and interest. . . .

"Defendants next contend that certain omissions in cross-examination at preliminary hearing precluded them from an adequate exercise of the right to confrontation. At preliminary hearing defense counsel were unaware of some statements made to police officers by the victims since that information was unavailable under Utah's discovery rules. While it is true that they were deprived of the opportunity to cross-examine the victims concerning the statements, counsel do not claim there was any prohibition on them from presenting to the jury the inconsistency between the statements which were made to police officers and the victims' testimony at preliminary hearing.

"* * *

"While a lawyer in retrospect may often think of subjects he might have delved into more extensively, we find no error here. Defense counsel conducted extensive cross-examination in the record of the preliminary hearing. They apparently advisedly and intentionally decided to refrain from questioning concerning the victims' alcohol history and propensity for violence. In view of these facts, we hold that defendants' opportunity for cross-examination was adequate."

As a matter of federal constitutional law, denial of the right to confrontation of a witness at the preliminary hearing is of no matter where the prosecution does not later at trial offer the preliminary hearing testimony. See United States v. Andrus, 775 F.2d 825 (7th Cir.1985).

* * *

B. SCOPE OF THE HEARING REQUIREMENT

Gerstein v. Pugh

Supreme Court of the United States, 1975.
420 U.S. 103, 95 S.Ct. 854.

■ MR. JUSTICE POWELL delivered the opinion of the Court.

The issue in this case is whether a person arrested under a prosecutor's information is constitutionally entitled to a judicial determination of probable cause for pretrial restraint of liberty.

I.

In March 1971 respondents Pugh and Henderson were arrested in Dade County, Florida. Each was charged with several offenses under a prosecutor's information. Pugh was denied bail because one of the charges against him carried a potential life sentence, and Henderson remained in custody because he was unable to post a $4,500 bond.

In Florida, indictments are required only for prosecution of capital offenses. Prosecutors may charge all other crimes by information, without a prior preliminary hearing and without obtaining leave of court. . . . The only possible methods for obtaining a judicial determination of probable cause were a special statute allowing a preliminary hearing after 30 days, and arraignment, which the District Court found was often delayed a month or more after arrest. . . . As a result, a person charged by information could be detained for a substantial period solely on the decision of a prosecutor.

Pugh and Henderson filed a class action against Dade County officials in the Federal District Court, claiming a constitutional right to a judicial hearing on the issue of probable cause and requesting declaratory and injunctive relief. Respondents Turner and Faulk, also in custody under informations, subsequently intervened. Petitioner Gerstein, the State Attorney for Dade County, was one of several defendants. . . . The District Court granted the relief sought. . . . The court certified the case as a class action under Fed.Rule Civ.Proc. 23(b)(2), and held that the Fourth and Fourteenth Amendments give all arrested persons charged by information a right to a judicial hearing on the question of probable cause. . . . Before the District Court issued its findings, however, the Florida Supreme Court amended the procedural rules governing preliminary hearings statewide, and the parties agreed that the District Court should direct its inquiry to the new rules rather than the Dade County procedures.

Under the amended rules every arrested person must be taken before a judicial officer within 24 hours. Fla.Rule Crim.Proc. 3.130(b). This "first appearance" is similar to the "first appearance hearing" ordered by the District Court in all respects but the crucial one: the magistrate does not make a determination of probable cause. The rule amendments also changed the procedure for preliminary hearings, restricting them to felony charges and codifying the rule that no hearings are available to persons charged by information or indictment. Rule 3.131; see In re Rule 3.131(B), Florida Rules of Criminal Procedure, 289 So.2d 3 (Fla.1974).

In a supplemental opinion the District Court held that the amended rules had not answered the basic constitutional objection, since a defendant charged by information still could be detained pending trial without a judicial determination of probable cause. . . . Reaffirming its original ruling, the District Court declared that the continuation of this practice was unconstitutional. The Court of Appeals affirmed, . . . modifying the District Court's decree in minor particulars and suggesting that the form of preliminary hearing provided by the amended Florida rules would be acceptable, as long as it was provided to all defendants in custody pending trial. . . .

State Attorney Gerstein petitioned for review ... We affirm in part and reverse in part.

II.

As framed by the proceedings below, this case presents two issues: whether a person arrested and held for trial on an information is entitled to a judicial determination of probable cause for detention, and if so, whether the adversary hearing ordered by the District Court and approved by the Court of Appeals is required by the Constitution.

A

Both the standards and procedures for arrest and detention have been derived from the Fourth Amendment and its common-law antecedents. The standard for arrest is probable cause, defined in terms of facts and circumstances "sufficient to warrant a prudent man in believing that the [suspect] had committed or was committing an offense." Beck v. Ohio (1964).... This standard, like those for searches and seizures, represents a necessary accommodation between the individual's right to liberty and the State's duty to control crime. ...

To implement the Fourth Amendment's protection against unfounded invasions of liberty and privacy, the Court has required that the existence of probable cause be decided by a neutral and detached magistrate whenever possible. The classic statement of this principle appears in Johnson v. United States, 333 U.S. 10, 13–14 (1948):

> "The point of the Fourth Amendment, which often is not grasped by zealous officers, is not that it denies law enforcement the support of the usual inferences which reasonable men draw from evidence. Its protection consists in requiring that those inferences be drawn by a neutral and detached magistrate instead of being judged by the officer engaged in the often competitive enterprise of ferreting out crime."

See Also Terry v. Ohio (1968) [Supra Casebook, Chapter 4, Section F.][12]

Maximum protection of individual rights could be assured by requiring a magistrate's review of the factual justification prior to any arrest, but such a requirement would constitute an intolerable handicap for legitimate law enforcement. Thus, while the Court has expressed a preference for the use of arrest warrants when feasible, Beck v. Ohio, supra, it has never invalidated an arrest supported by probable cause solely because the officers failed to secure a warrant.

Under this practical compromise, a policeman's on-the-scene assessment of probable cause provides legal justification for arresting a person

12. We reiterated this principle in United States v. United States District Court, 407 U.S. 297, 92 S.Ct. 2125 (1972). In terms that apply equally to arrests, we described the "very heart of the Fourth Amendment directive" as a requirement that "where practical, a governmental search and seizure should represent both the efforts of the officer to gather evidence of wrongful acts and the judgment of the magistrate that the collected evidence is sufficient to justify invasion of a citizen's private premises or conversation." Id., at 316, 92 S.Ct., at 2136. See also Terry v. Ohio ... (1968).

suspected of crime, and for a brief period of detention to take the administrative steps incident to arrest. Once the suspect is in custody, however, the reasons that justify dispensing with the magistrate's neutral judgment evaporate. There no longer is any danger that the suspect will escape or commit further crimes while the police submit their evidence to a magistrate. And, while the State's reasons for taking summary action subside, the suspect's need for a neutral determination of probable cause increases significantly. The consequences of prolonged detention may be more serious than the interference occasioned by arrest. Pretrial confinement may imperil the suspect's job, interrupt his source of income, and impair his family relationships. See R. Goldfarb, Ransom 32–91 (1965); L. Katz, Justice Is the Crime 51–62 (1972). Even pretrial release may be accompanied by burdensome conditions that effect a significant restraint on liberty. See, e.g., 18 U.S.C. § 3146(a)(2), (5). When the stakes are this high, the detached judgment of a neutral magistrate is essential if the Fourth Amendment is to furnish meaningful protection from unfounded interference with liberty. Accordingly, we hold that the Fourth Amendment requires a judicial determination of probable cause as a prerequisite to extended restraint on liberty following arrest.

This result has historical support in the common law that has guided interpretation of the Fourth Amendment. ... At common law it was customary, if not obligatory, for an arrested person to be brought before a justice of the peace shortly after arrest. ... The justice of the peace would "examine" the prisoner and the witnesses to determine whether there was reason to believe the prisoner had committed a crime. If there was, the suspect would be committed to jail or bailed pending trial. If not, he would be discharged from custody. The initial determination of probable cause also could be reviewed by higher courts on a writ of habeas corpus. ... This practice furnished the model for criminal procedure in America immediately following the adoption of the Fourth Amendment, ... and there are indications that the Framers of the Bill of Rights regarded it as a model for a "reasonable" seizure.

B

Under the Florida procedures challenged here, a person arrested without a warrant and charged by information may be jailed or subjected to other restraints pending trial without any opportunity for a probable cause determination. Petitioner defends this practice on the ground that the prosecutor's decision to file an information is itself a determination of probable cause that furnishes sufficient reason to detain a defendant pending trial. Although a conscientious decision that the evidence warrants prosecution affords a measure of protection against unfounded detention, we do not think prosecutorial judgment standing alone meets the requirements of the Fourth Amendment. Indeed, we think the Court's previous decisions compel disapproval of the Florida procedure. In Albrecht v. United States ... (1927), the Court held that an arrest warrant issued solely upon a United States Attorney's information was invalid because the accompanying affidavits were defective. Although the Court's opinion did not explicitly state that the prosecutor's official oath could not furnish probable cause, that conclusion was implicit in the judgment that the arrest was illegal under the Fourth Amendment.[19] More recently, in Coolidge v. New Hampshire (1971), the Court held that a prosecutor's responsibility to law enforcement is inconsistent with the constitutional role of a neutral and detached magistrate. . . .

In holding that the prosecutor's assessment of probable cause is not sufficient alone to justify restraint on liberty pending trial, we do not imply that the accused is entitled to judicial oversight or review of the decision to prosecute. Instead, we adhere to the Court's prior holding that a judicial hearing is not prerequisite to prosecution by information. Beck v. Washington . . . (1962); Lem Woon v. Oregon . . . (1913). Nor do were treat from the established rule that illegal arrest or detention does not void a subsequent conviction. Frisbie v. Collins . . . (1952). . . . Thus, as the Court of Appeals noted below, although a suspect who is presently detained may challenge the probable cause for that confinement, a conviction will not be vacated on the ground that the defendant was detained pending trial without a determination of probable cause.

III.

Both the District Court and the Court of Appeals held that the determination of probable cause must be accompanied by the full panoply of adversary safeguards—counsel, confrontation, cross-examination, and compulsory process for witnesses. A full preliminary hearing of this sort is modeled after the procedure used in many States to determine whether the evidence justifies going to trial under an information or presenting the case to a grand jury. . . . The standard of proof required of the prosecution is usually referred to as "probable cause," but in some jurisdictions it may approach a prima facie case of guilt. A.L.I. Model Code of Pre-arraignment Procedure Commentary on Article 330, at 90–91 (Tent. Draft No. 5, 1972). When the hearing takes this form, adversary procedures are customarily employed. The importance of the issue to both the State and the accused justifies the presentation of witnesses and full exploration of their testimony on cross-examination. This kind of hearing also requires appointment of counsel for indigent defendants. And, as the hearing assumes increased importance and the procedures become more complex, the likelihood that it can be held promptly after arrest diminishes. . . .

These adversary safeguards are not essential for the probable cause determination required by the Fourth Amendment. The sole issue is whether there is probable cause for detaining the arrested person pending further proceedings. This issue can be determined reliably without an adversary hearing. The standard is the same as that for arrest.[21] That

19. By contrast, the Court has held that an indictment, "fair upon its face," and returned by a "properly constituted grand jury" conclusively determines the existence of probable cause and requires issuance of an arrest warrant without further inquiry. . . . The willingness to let a grand jury's judgment substitute for that of a neutral and detached magistrate is attributable to the grand jury's relationship to the courts and its historical role of protecting individuals from unjust prosecution. See United States v. Calandra . . . (1974).

21. Because the standards are identical, ordinarily there is no need for further investigation before the probable cause determination can be made.

"Presumably, whomever the police arrest they must arrest on 'probable

standard—probable cause to believe the suspect has committed a crime—traditionally has been decided by a magistrate in a nonadversary proceeding on hearsay and written testimony, and the Court has approved these informal modes of proof.

The use of an informal procedure is justified not only by the lesser consequences of a probable cause determination but also by the nature of the determination itself. It does not require the fine resolution of conflicting evidence that a reasonable-doubt or even a preponderance standard demands, and credibility determinations are seldom crucial in deciding whether the evidence supports a reasonable belief in guilt. See F. Miller, Prosecution: The Decision to Charge a Suspect with a Crime 64–109 (1969). This is not to say that confrontation and cross-examination might not enhance the reliability of probable cause determinations in some cases. In most cases, however, their value would be too slight to justify holding, as a matter of constitutional principle, that these formalities and safeguards designed for trial must also be employed in making the Fourth Amendment determination of probable cause.[23]

Because of its limited function and its nonadversary character, the probable cause determination is not a "critical stage" in the prosecution that would require appointed counsel. The Court has identified as "critical stages" those pretrial procedures that would impair defense on the merits if the accused is required to proceed without counsel. In Coleman v. Alabama, where the Court held that a preliminary hearing was a critical stage of an Alabama prosecution, the majority and concurring opinions identified two critical factors that distinguish the Alabama preliminary hearing from the probable cause determination required by the Fourth Amendment. First, under Alabama law the function of the preliminary hearing was to determine whether the evidence justified charging the suspect with an offense. A finding of no probable cause could mean that he would not be tried at all. The Fourth Amendment probable cause determination is addressed only to pretrial custody. To be sure, pretrial custody may affect to some extent the defendant's ability to assist in preparation of his defense, but this does not present the high probability of substantial harm identified as controlling in *Wade* and *Coleman*. Second, Alabama allowed the suspect to confront and cross-examine prosecution witnesses at the preliminary hearing. The Court noted that the suspect's defense on the merits could be compromised if he had no legal assistance for exploring or preserving the witnesses' testimony. This consideration does not apply when the prosecution is not required to produce witnesses for cross-examination.

cause.' It is not the function of the police to arrest, as it were at large and to use an interrogating process at police headquarters in order to determine whom they should charge before a committing magistrate on 'probable cause.' " Mallory v. United States . . . (1957).

23. Criminal justice is already overburdened by the volume of cases and the complexities of our system. The processing of misdemeanors, in particular, and the early stages of prosecution generally are marked by delays that can seriously affect the quality of justice. A constitutional doctrine requiring adversary hearings for all persons detained pending trial could exacerbate the problem of pretrial delay.

Although we conclude that the Constitution does not require an adversary determination of probable cause, we recognize that state systems of criminal procedure vary widely. There is no single preferred pretrial procedure, and the nature of the probable cause determination usually will be shaped to accord with a State's pretrial procedure viewed as a whole. While we limit our holding to the precise requirement of the Fourth Amendment, we recognize the desirability of flexibility and experimentation by the States. It may be found desirable, for example, to make the probable cause determination at the suspect's first appearance before a judicial officer, see McNabb v. United States (1943), or the determination may be incorporated into the procedure for setting bail or fixing other conditions of pretrial release. In some States, existing procedures may satisfy the requirement of the Fourth Amendment. Others may require only minor adjustment such as acceleration of existing preliminary hearings. . . . Whatever procedure a State may adopt, it must provide a fair and reliable determination of probable cause as a condition for any significant pretrial restraint on liberty,[26] and this determination must be made by a judicial officer either before or promptly after arrest.

IV.

We agree with the Court of Appeals that the Fourth Amendment requires a timely judicial determination of probable cause as a prerequisite to detention, and we accordingly affirm that much of the judgment. As we do not agree that the Fourth Amendment requires the adversary hearing outlined in the District Court's decree, we reverse in part and remand to the Court of Appeals for further proceedings consistent with this opinion.

Affirmed in part, reversed in part, and remanded.

■ MR. JUSTICE STEWART, with whom MR. JUSTICE DOUGLAS, MR. JUSTICE BRENNAN, and MR. JUSTICE MARSHALL join, concurring.

I concur in Parts I and II of the Court's opinion, since the Constitution clearly requires at least a timely judicial determination of probable cause as a prerequisite to pretrial detention. Because Florida does not provide all defendants in custody pending trial with a fair and reliable determination of probable cause for their detention, the respondents and the members of the class they represent are entitled to declaratory and injunctive relief.

Having determined that Florida's current pretrial detention procedures are constitutionally inadequate, I think it is unnecessary to go further by way of dicta. In particular, I would not, in the abstract, attempt to specify those procedural protections that constitutionally need *not* be accorded incarcerated suspects awaiting trial.

26. Because the probable cause determination is not a constitutional prerequisite to the charging decision, it is required only for those suspects who suffer restraints on liberty other than the condition that they appear for trial. There are many kinds of pretrial release and many degrees of conditional liberty. See 18 U.S.C. § 3146; ABA Standards Relating to the Administration of Criminal Justice, Pretrial Release § 5.2 (1974); Uniform Rules of Criminal Procedure, Rule 341 (Proposed Final Draft 1974). We cannot define specifically those that would require a prior probable cause determination, but the key factor is significant restraint on liberty.

Specifically, I see no need in this case for the Court to say that the Constitution extends less procedural protection to an imprisoned human being than is required to test the propriety of garnisheeing a commercial bank account, the custody of a refrigerator, . . ., the temporary suspension of a public school student, . . . or the suspension of a driver's license. . . . Although it may be true that the Fourth Amendment's "balance between individual and public interests always has been thought to define the 'process that is due' for seizures of person or property in criminal cases," . . ., this case does not involve an initial arrest, but rather the continuing incarceration of a presumptively innocent person. Accordingly, I cannot join the Court's effort to foreclose any claim that the traditional requirements of constitutional due process are applicable in the context of pretrial detention.

* * *

NOTES

1. Without benefit of a formal survey, some persons believe that the impact of *Gerstein* has not been overwhelming. In many jurisdictions, persons who have been arrested without a warrant and who have been unable to post bond quite regularly do not receive the prompt judicial determination of probable cause hearing contemplated by *Gerstein*. Under *Gerstein*, once a defendant is tried (or, perhaps, once a probable cause hearing is eventually held), the improper initial delay would seem to have no legal impact on the criminal case, and, thus, typically would not be litigated in reviewing courts. The *Gerstein* constitutionally-mandated hearing by definition serves such a limited purpose that denial of a prompt *Gerstein* hearing could not be said to prejudice the merits of the defense at trial. See United States v. Kabat, 586 F.2d 325 (4th Cir.1978) ("an accused has no constitutional right to a preliminary hearing, so long as he receives some form of 'judicial determination of probable cause as a prerequisite to extended restraint of liberty following arrest.' ") See also McKinstry, System Impact in Gerstein v. Pugh, 7 Loyola (Chi.) U.L.Rev. 901 (1976).

2. Morano v. Dillon, 746 F.2d 942 (2d Cir.1984), underscores the limited scope of *Gerstein*. Morano was charged with a drug sale, admitted to bail and, pursuant to a New York statute, requested a preliminary hearing. When the prosecution denied the request and obtained a grand jury indictment, Morano brought a civil rights action asking the federal court to enjoin the state court criminal trial because he was unconstitutionally denied the right to a preliminary hearing, with the opportunity to cross-examine witnesses. Demonstrating the minimal impact of *Gerstein*, the court upheld dismissal of the complaint: "Little or no discussion is needed. . . . [Unlike the situation in Gerstein,] Morano was not detained."

State v. Tucker, 137 N.J. 259, 645 A.2d 111 (1994). The defendant Tucker was held for 72 hours before he was given a probable cause hearing. During that time, he made several incriminating statements. On appeal, he argued that the unduly lengthy holding time was a constitutional violation and that the appropriate remedy would have been to suppress those statements.

The New Jersey Supreme Court did not buy it. After noting that the U.S.Supreme Court had not yet addressed the issue of a remedy for a violation of *Gerstein*, the court opted to examine the totality of the circumstances and to determine in retrospect what the outcome of a hearing would have been if convened in a timely manner. The court found that such a hearing would have easily yielded sufficient evidence to support a probable cause finding and, therefore, the court held that the delay did not taint the statement. This case underscores the point made in the earlier cases; essentially, *Gerstein* created a right without a remedy.

3. At a preliminary hearing, a defendant receives more than a probable cause determination. In many states he has the right to counsel, to confront and cross-examine witnesses, and to obtain early discovery. A grand jury indictment offers the defendant no similar "rights." In light of this, may a defendant indicted by a grand jury claim that he is denied equal protection compared to a similarly situated defendant prosecuted by information? If so,what is the appropriate remedy?

4. A finding of no probable cause at a pre-indictment preliminary hearing ordinarily requires that the accused be released from custody or from the requirements of bond. It does not, however, ordinarily bar a subsequent prosecution or in any way constitute "jeopardy" so as to prevent return of an indictment. See State v. Eaton, 462 A.2d 502 (Me.1983); People v. Kent, 54 Ill.2d 161, 295 N.E.2d 710 (1972).

County of Riverside v. McLaughlin

Supreme Court of the United States, 1991.
500 U.S. 44, 111 S.Ct. 1661.

■ JUSTICE O'CONNOR delivered the opinion of the Court:

In Gerstein v. Pugh, 420 U.S. 103 (1975), this Court held that the Fourth Amendment requires a prompt judicial determination of probable cause as a prerequisite to an extended pretrial detention following a warrantless arrest. This case requires us to define what is "prompt" under *Gerstein*.

* * *

This is a class action brought under 42 U.S.C. 1983 challenging the manner in which the County of Riverside, California (County), provides probable cause determinations to persons arrested without a warrant. At issue is the County's policy of combining probable cause determinations with its arraignment procedures. Under County policy, which tracks closely the provisions of Cal.Penal Code Ann. 825 (West 1985), arraignments must be conducted without unnecessary delay and, in any event, within two days of arrest. This two-day requirement excludes from computation weekends and holidays. Thus, an individual arrested without a warrant late in the week may in some cases be held for as long as five days before receiving a probable cause determination. Over the Thanksgiving holiday, a 7–day delay is possible.

The parties dispute whether the combined probable cause/arraignment procedure is available to all warrantless arrestees. Testimony by Riverside County District Attorney Grover Trask suggests that individuals arrested without warrants for felonies do not receive a probable cause determination until the preliminary hearing which may not occur until 10 days after arraignment. Before this Court, however, the County represents that its policy is to provide probable cause determinations at arraignment for all persons arrested without a warrant, regardless of the nature of the charges against them. We need not resolve the factual inconsistency here. For present purposes, we accept the County's representation.

* * *

[The Court resolved standing and mootness issues in favor of the plaintiffs.]

In *Gerstein*, this Court held unconstitutional Florida procedures under which persons arrested without a warrant could remain in police custody for 30 days or more without a judicial determination of probable cause....

... Significantly, the Court stopped short of holding that jurisdictions were constitutionally compelled to provide a probable cause hearing immediately upon taking a suspect into custody and completing booking procedures. We acknowledged the burden that proliferation of pretrial proceedings places on the criminal justice system and recognized that the interests of everyone involved, including those persons who are arrested, might be disserved by introducing further procedural complexity into an already intricate system. Accordingly, we left it to the individual States to integrate prompt probable cause determinations into their differing systems of pretrial procedures.

* * *

Inherent in *Gerstein's* invitation to the States to experiment and adapt was the recognition that the Fourth Amendment does not compel an immediate determination of probable cause upon completing the administrative steps incident to arrest. Plainly, if a probable cause hearing is constitutionally compelled the moment a suspect is finished being "booked," there is no room whatsoever for "flexibility and experimentation by the States." Incorporating probable cause determinations "into the procedure for setting bail or fixing other conditions of pretrial release"—which *Gerstein* explicitly contemplated,—would be impossible. Waiting even a few hours so that a bail hearing or arraignment could take place at the same time as the probable cause determination would amount to a constitutional violation. Clearly, *Gerstein* is not that inflexible.

Notwithstanding *Gerstein's* discussion of flexibility, the Ninth Circuit Court of Appeals held that no flexibility was permitted. It construed *Gerstein* as "requir(ing) a probable cause determination to be made as soon as the administrative steps incident to arrest were completed, and that such steps should require only a brief period." This same reading is advanced by the dissent. The foregoing discussion readily demonstrates the error of this approach. *Gerstein* held that probable cause determinations must be prompt—not immediate. The Court explained that "flexibility and experimentation" were "desirab(le)"; that "(t)here is no single preferred pretrial procedure"; and that "the nature of the probable cause determination usually will be shaped to accord with a State's pretrial procedure viewed as a whole." The Court of Appeals and the dissent disregard these statements, relying instead on selective quotations from the Court's opinion. As we have explained, *Gerstein* struck a balance between competing interests; a proper understanding of the decision is possible only if one takes into account both sides of the equation.

The dissent claims to find support for its approach in the common law. It points to several statements from the early 1800's to the effect that an arresting officer must bring a person arrested without a warrant before a judicial officer " 'as soon as he reasonably can.' " (emphasis in original).

This vague admonition offers no more support for the dissent's inflexible standard than does *Gerstein's* statement that a hearing follow "promptly after arrest." As mentioned at the outset, the question before us today is what is "prompt" under *Gerstein*. We answer that question by recognizing that *Gerstein* struck a balance between competing interests.

* * *

Given that *Gerstein* permits jurisdictions to incorporate probable cause determinations into other pretrial procedures, some delays are inevitable. For example, where, as in Riverside County, the probable cause determination is combined with arraignment, there will be delays caused by paperwork and logistical problems. Records will have to be reviewed, charging documents drafted, appearance of counsel arranged, and appropriate bail determined. On weekends, when the number of arrests is often higher and available resources tend to be limited, arraignments may get pushed back even further. In our view, the Fourth Amendment permits a reasonable postponement of a probable cause determination while the police cope with the everyday problems of processing suspects through an overly burdened criminal justice system.

But flexibility has its limits; *Gerstein* is not a blank check. A State has no legitimate interest in detaining for extended periods individuals who have been arrested without probable cause. The Court recognized in *Gerstein* that a person arrested without a warrant is entitled to a fair and reliable determination of probable cause and that this determination must be made promptly.

Unfortunately, as lower court decisions applying *Gerstein* have demonstrated, it is not enough to say that probable cause determinations must be "prompt." This vague standard simply has not provided sufficient guidance. Instead, it has led to a flurry of systemic challenges to city and county practices, putting federal judges in the role of making legislative judgments and overseeing local jailhouse operations.

* * *

Our task in this case is to articulate more clearly the boundaries of what is permissible under the Fourth Amendment. Although we hesitate to announce that the Constitution compels a specific time limit, it is important to provide some degree of certainty so that States and counties may establish procedures with confidence that they fall within constitutional bounds. Taking into account the competing interests articulated in *Gerstein*, we believe that a jurisdiction that provides judicial determinations of probable cause within 48 hours of arrest will, as a general matter, comply with the promptness requirement of *Gerstein*. For this reason, such jurisdictions will be immune from systemic challenges.

In arguing that any delay in probable cause hearings beyond completing the administrative steps incident to arrest and arranging for a magistrate is unconstitutional, the dissent, in effect, adopts the view of the Court of Appeals. Yet the dissent ignores entirely the Court of Appeals' determination of the time required to complete those procedures. That court, better situated than this one, concluded that it takes 36 hours to process arrested persons in Riverside County. In advocating a 24-hour rule, the dissent would compel Riverside County—and countless others across the Nation—to speed up its criminal justice mechanisms substantially, presumably by allotting local tax dollars to hire additional police officers and magistrates. There may be times when the Constitution compels such direct interference with local control, but this is not one. As we have explained, *Gerstein* clearly contemplated a reasonable accommodation between legitimate competing concerns. We do no more than recognize that such accommodation can take place without running afoul of the Fourth Amendment.

Everyone agrees that the police should make every attempt to minimize the time a presumptively innocent individual spends in jail. One way to do so is to provide a judicial determination of probable cause immediately upon completing the administrative steps incident to arrest—i.e., as soon as the suspect has been booked, photographed, and fingerprinted. As the dissent explains, several States, laudably, have adopted this approach. The Constitution does not compel so rigid a schedule, however. Under *Gerstein*, jurisdictions may choose to combine probable cause determinations with other pretrial proceedings, so long as they do so promptly. This necessarily means that only certain proceedings are candidates for combination. Only those proceedings that arise very early in the pretrial process—such as bail hearings and arraignments—may be chosen. Even then, every effort must be made to expedite the combined proceedings.

* * *

For the reasons we have articulated, we conclude that Riverside County is entitled to combine probable cause determinations with arraignments. The record indicates, however, that the County's current policy and practice do not comport fully with the principles we have outlined. The County's current policy is to offer combined proceedings within two days, exclusive of Saturdays, Sundays, or holidays. As a result, persons arrested on Thursdays may have to wait until the following Monday before they receive a probable cause determination. The delay is even longer if there is an intervening holiday. Thus, the County's regular practice exceeds the 48-hour period we deem constitutionally permissible, meaning that the County is not immune from systemic challenges, such as this class action.

As to arrests that occur early in the week, the County's practice is that "arraignment(s) usually tak(e) place on the last day" possible. There may well be legitimate reasons for this practice; alternatively, this may constitute delay for delay's sake. We leave it to the Court of Appeals and the District Court, on remand, to make this determination.

* * *

■ JUSTICE SCALIA, dissenting.

* * *

The Court views the task before it as one of "balanc(ing) (the) competing concerns" of "protecting public safety," on the one hand, and avoiding "prolonged detention based on incorrect or unfounded suspicion," on the other hand. It purports to reaffirm the "practical compromise" between these concerns struck in *Gerstein*. There is assuredly room for such an approach in resolving novel questions of search and seizure under the "reasonableness" standard that the Fourth Amendment sets forth. But not, I think, in resolving those questions on which a clear answer already existed in 1791 and has been generally adhered to by the traditions of our society ever since. As to those matters, the "balance" has already been struck, the "practical compromise" reached—and it is the function of the Bill of Rights to preserve that judgment, not only against the changing views of Presidents and Members of Congress, but also against the changing views of Justices whom Presidents appoint and Members of Congress confirm to this Court.

The issue before us today is of precisely that sort. As we have recently had occasion to explain, the Fourth Amendment's prohibition of "unreasonable seizures," insofar as it applies to seizure of the person, preserves for our citizens the traditional protections against unlawful arrest afforded by the common law. See California v. Hodari D. (1991). One of those—one of the most important of those—was that a person arresting a suspect without a warrant must deliver the arrestee to a magistrate "as soon as he reasonably can." 2 M. Hale, Pleas of the Crown 95, n. 13 (1st Am. ed. 1847). See also 4 W. Blackstone, Commentaries *289, *293; Wright v. Court, 107 Eng.Rep. 1182 (K.B.1825) ("(I)t is the duty of a person arresting any one on suspicion of felony to take him before a justice as soon as he reasonably can"); 1 R. Burn, Justice of the Peace 276–277 (1837) ("When a constable arrests a party for treason or felony, he must take him before a magistrate to be examined as soon as he reasonably can") (emphasis omitted). The practice in the United States was the same. It was clear, moreover, that the only element bearing upon the reasonableness of delay was, not such circumstances as the pressing need to conduct further investigation, but the arresting officer's ability, once the prisoner had been secured, to reach a magistrate who could issue the needed warrant for further detention.

We discussed and relied upon this common-law understanding in *Gerstein*, holding that the period of warrantless detention must be limited to the time necessary to complete the arrest and obtain the magistrate's review. "(A) policeman's on-the-scene assessment of probable cause provides legal justification for arresting a person suspected of crime, and for a brief period of detention to take the administrative steps incident to arrest. Once the suspect is in custody ... the reasons that justify dispensing with the magistrate's neutral judgment evaporate."

We said that "the Fourth Amendment requires a judicial determination of probable cause as a prerequisite to extended restraint of liberty," "either before or promptly after arrest,". Though how "promptly" we did not say, it was plain enough that the requirement left no room for intentional delay unrelated to the completion of "the administrative steps incident to arrest." Plain enough, at least, that all but one federal court considering the question understood *Gerstein* that way.

Today, however, the Court discerns something quite different in *Gerstein*. It finds that the plain statements set forth above (not to mention the common-law tradition of liberty upon which they were based) were trumped by the implication of a later dictum in the case which, according to the Court, manifests a "recognition that the Fourth Amendment does not compel an immediate determination of probable cause upon completing the administrative steps incident to arrest." Of course *Gerstein* did not say, nor do I contend, that an "immediate" determination is required. But what the Court today means by "not immediate" is that the delay can be attributable to something other than completing the administrative steps incident to arrest and arranging for the magistrate—namely, to the administrative convenience of combining the probable-cause determination with other state proceedings. The result, we learn later in the opinion, is that what Gerstein meant by "a brief period of detention to take the administrative steps incident to arrest" is two full days. I think it is clear that the case neither said nor meant any such thing.

* * *

The Court's holding today rests upon the statement that "we recognize the desirability of flexibility and experimentation." But in its context that statement plainly refers to the nature of the hearing and not to its timing.... It is not apparent to me, as it is to the Court, that on these terms "(i)ncorporating probable cause determinations into the 'procedure for setting bail or fixing other conditions of pretrial release' ... would be impossible," but it is clear that, if and when it is impossible, *Gerstein* envisioned that the procedural "experimentation," rather than the Fourth Amendment's requirement of prompt presentation to a magistrate, would have to yield.

Of course even if the implication of the dictum in *Gerstein* were what the Court says, that would be poor reason for keeping a wrongfully arrested citizen in jail contrary to the clear dictates of the Fourth Amendment. What is most revealing of the frailty of today's opinion is that it relies upon nothing but that implication from a dictum, plus its own (quite irrefutable because entirely value laden) "balancing" of the competing demands of the individual and the State. With respect to the point at issue here, different times and different places—even highly liberal times and places—have struck that balance in different ways. Some Western democracies currently permit the Executive a period of detention without impartially adjudicated cause. In England, for example, the Prevention of Terrorism Act 1989, 14(4), 5, permits suspects to be held without presentation and without charge for seven days. 12 Halsbury's Stat. 1294 (4th ed. 1989). It was the purpose of the Fourth Amendment to put this matter beyond time, place and judicial predilection, incorporating the traditional common-law guarantees against unlawful arrest. The Court says not a word about these guarantees, and they are determinative. *Gerstein's* approval of a "brief period" of delay to accomplish "administrative steps incident to an arrest" is already a questionable extension of the traditional formulation, though it probably has little practical effect and can perhaps be justified on de minimis grounds. To expand *Gerstein*, however, into an authorization for 48–hour detention related neither to the obtaining of a magistrate nor the administrative "completion" of the arrest seems to me utterly unjustified. Mr. McLaughlin was entitled to have a prompt impartial determination that there was reason to deprive him of his liberty—not according to a schedule that suits the State's convenience in piggy-backing various proceedings, but as soon as his arrest was completed and the magistrate could be procured.

I have finished discussing what I consider the principal question in this case, which is what factors determine whether the post arrest determination of probable cause has been (as the Fourth Amendment requires) "reasonably prompt." The Court and I both accept two of those factors, completion of the administrative steps incident to arrest and arranging for a magistrate's probable-cause determination. Since we disagree, however, upon a third factor—the Court believing, as I do not, that "combining" the determination with other proceedings justifies a delay—we necessarily disagree as well on the subsequent question, which can be described as the question of the absolute time limit. Any determinant of "reasonable promptness" that is within the control of the State (as the availability of the magistrate, the personnel and facilities for completing administrative procedures incident to arrest, and the timing of "combined procedures" all are) must be restricted by some outer time limit, or else the promptness guarantee would be worthless. If, for example, it took a full year to obtain a probable-cause determination in California because only a single magistrate had been authorized to perform that function throughout the State, the hearing would assuredly not qualify as "reasonably prompt." At some point, legitimate reasons for delay become illegitimate.

I do not know how the Court calculated its outer limit of 48 hours. I must confess, however, that I do not know how I would do so either, if I thought that one justification for delay could be the State's "desire to combine." There are no standards for "combination," and as we acknowledged in *Gerstein* the various procedures that might be combined "vary widely" from State to State. So as far as I can discern (though I cannot pretend to be able to do better), the Court simply decided that, given the administrative convenience of "combining," it is not so bad for an utterly innocent person to wait 48 hours in jail before being released.

If one eliminates (as one should) that novel justification for delay, determining the outer boundary of reasonableness is a more objective and more manageable task. We were asked to undertake it in *Gerstein*, but declined—wisely, I think, since we had before us little data to support any figure we might choose. As the Court notes, however, *Gerstein* has engendered a number of cases addressing not only the scope of the procedures "incident to arrest," but also their duration. The conclusions reached by the judges in those cases, and by others who have addressed the question, are surprisingly similar. I frankly would prefer even more information, and for that purpose would have supported reargument on the single question of an outer time limit. The data available are enough to convince me, however, that certainly no more than 24 hours is needed.

With one exception, no federal court considering the question has regarded 24 hours as an inadequate amount of time to complete arrest procedures, and with the same exception every court actually setting a limit for probable-cause determination based on those procedures has selected 24 hours.... Federal courts have reached a similar conclusion in applying Federal Rule of Criminal Procedure 5(a), which requires presentment before a federal magistrate "without unnecessary delay." And state courts have similarly applied a 24–hour limit under state statutes requiring presentment without "unreasonable delay." New York, for example, has concluded that no more than 24 hours is necessary from arrest to arraignment. Twenty-nine States have statutes similar to New York's which require either presentment or arraignment "without unnecessary delay" or "forthwith"; eight States explicitly require presentment or arraignment within 24 hours; and only seven States have statutes explicitly permitting a period longer than 24 hours. Since the States requiring a probable-cause hearing within 24 hours include both New York and Alaska, it is unlikely that circumstances of population or geography demand a longer period. Twenty-four hours is consistent with the American Law Institute's Model Code. ALI, Model Code of Pre–Arraignment Procedure 310.1 (1975). And while the American Bar Association in its proposed rules of criminal procedure initially required that presentment simply be made "without unnecessary delay," it has recently concluded that no more than six hours should be required, except at night. Uniform Rules of Criminal Procedure, 10 U.L.A.App., Criminal Justice Standard 10–4.1 (Spec.Pamph.1987).Finally, the conclusions of these commissions and judges, both state and federal, are supported by commentators who have examined the question. See, e.g., Brandes, supra, at 478–485 (discussing national 24–hour rule); Note, 74 Minn., L.Rev., at 207–209.

In my view, absent extraordinary circumstances, it is an "unreasonable seizure" within the meaning of the Fourth Amendment for the police, having arrested a suspect without a warrant, to delay a determination of probable cause for the arrest either (1) for reasons unrelated to arrangement of the probable-cause determination or completion of the steps incident to arrest, or (2) beyond 24 hours after the arrest. Like the Court, I would treat the time limit as a presumption; when the 24 hours are exceeded the burden shifts to the police to adduce unforeseeable circumstances justifying the additional delay.

* * *

. . . One hears the complaint, nowadays, that the Fourth Amendment has become constitutional law for the guilty; that it benefits the career criminal (through the exclusionary rule) often and directly, but the ordinary citizen remotely if at all. By failing to protect the innocent arrestee, today's opinion reinforces that view. The commonlaw rule of prompt hearing had as its primary beneficiaries the innocent—not those whose fully justified convictions must be overturned to scold the police; nor those who avoid conviction because the evidence, while convincing, does not establish guilt beyond a reasonable doubt; but those so blameless that there was not even good reason to arrest them. While in recent years we have invented novel applications of the Fourth Amendment to release the unquestionably guilty, we today repudiate one of its core applications so that the presumptively innocent may be left in jail. Hereafter a law-abiding citizen wrongfully arrested may be compelled to await the grace of a Dickensian bureaucratic machine, as it churns its cycle for up to two days—never once given the opportunity to show a judge that there is absolutely no reason to hold him, that a mistake has been made. In my view, this is the image of a system of justice that has lost its ancient sense of priority, a system that few Americans would recognize as our own.

* * *

■ Justice Marshall, with whom Justice Blackmun and Justice Stevens join, dissenting.

In Gerstein v. Pugh (1975), this Court held that an individual detained following a warrantless arrest is entitled to a "prompt" judicial determination of probable cause as a prerequisite to any further restraint on his liberty. I agree with Justice Scalia that a probable-cause hearing is sufficiently "prompt" under *Gerstein* only when provided immediately upon completion of the "administrative steps incident to arrest". Because the Court of Appeals correctly held that the County of Riverside must provide probable-cause hearings as soon as it completes the administrative steps incident to arrest, I would affirm the judgment of the Court of Appeals.

NOTES

1. In Powell v. Nevada, 511 U.S. 79, 114 S.Ct. 1280 (1994), the Court gave *McLaughlin's* 48–hour rule retroactive effect.

2. The Seventh Circuit held a 45–hour delay unreasonable because the delay was prolonged solely to place the defendant in lineups in the investigation of other crimes. Willis v. City of Chicago, 999 F.2d 284 (7th Cir.1993).

3. Congress may not eliminate the need for a prompt preliminary hearing or grand jury presentment by classifying those held as enemy combatants. The detained individual must be given an opportunity rebut the Government's factual allegations before a neutral fact-finder. *Hamdi v. Rumsfeld*, 542 U.S. 507, 124 S.Ct. 2633 (2004).

CHAPTER 11

GRAND JURY PROCEEDINGS

A. HISTORICAL ROLE

The evolution of the Grand Jury from its English antecedents to its contemporary function in the American criminal process was described by Justice Mosk, a critic of the use of Grand Juries, in Johnson v. Superior Court, 15 Cal.3d 248, 124 Cal.Rptr. 32, 539 P.2d 792 (1975) (concurring opinion):

> "... Most authorities date the origin of the grand jury to the Assize of Clarendon (1166) in the reign of Henry II. It was there provided that 12 knights or 'good and lawful men' of every hundred and four were to declare under oath the identities of those in the community suspected of public offenses. All persons thus "presented" were then tried by ordeal, a method undeniably more barbaric than the present ordeal of trial. Failure to demonstrate innocence at the ordeal resulted in banishment and the loss of a hand and a foot; success at the ordeal was rewarded by mere banishment.[4]
>
> " 'Slowly the character of the institution changed. Originally an important instrument of the Crown, it gradually became instead a strong independent power guarding the rights of the English people.' By 1352 the panel that accused no longer assumed responsibility for the trial itself, and the first seeds of the present bifurcated system of grand and petit jury were sown. As the age of royal absolutism developed, this body of freemen became a singularly effective deterrent to politically motivated prosecution by the crown. The return by one famous grand jury of a bill of 'ignoramus' in the attempted prosecution of the Earl of Shaftesbury in 1681 is frequently cited as demonstrating the evolution of the institution from a prosecutorial arm into an agency responsible for protecting the individual from officially sanctioned oppression.[5]

4. "There is a technical difference between an indictment and a presentment. A presentment is an accusation made by the grand jury itself, flowing from the knowledge and personal observation of the members. An indictment comes to the grand jury as a charge from without, usually from a prosecutor or the king's officer, to which the grand jury either returns a true bill or a bill of 'ignoramus.' "

5. "Thus Edwards states: 'So far as we have considered it, we have found it to be an arm of the government, acting as a public prosecutor for the purpose of ferreting out all crime, the members of the inquest being at all times bound to inform the court either singly or collectively their reasons for arriving at their verdict and the evidence upon which it was based. The seed, however, had been sown in Bracton's time, which was destined to change the grand jury from a mere instrument of the crown to a strong independent power which stood steadfast between the crown and the people in the defence of the liberty of the citizen'."

"The establishment of British hegemony in the American colonies resulted in the exportation to our shores of British legal institutions, including the grand jury. While certain of the colonies, particularly the theocracies, altered the institution to conform to religious or social predilections, the colonists themselves continued to regard the grand jury as a fundamental feature of a civilized state. Thus when in 1683 the inhabitants of New York forced the Duke of York to permit the colonial assembly to pass a 'Charter of Libertyes and Priviledges,' there was included the protection 'That in all Cases Capitall or Criminall there shall be a grand Inquest who shall first present the offence and then twelve men of the neighborhood to try the Offender who after his plea to the Indictment shall be allowed his reasonable Challenges.'

" 'By the end of the Colonial period the grand jury had become an indispensable part of government in each of the American colonies. Grand juries served as more than panels of public accusers. They acted as local representative assemblies ready to make known the wishes of the people. They proposed new laws, protested against abuses in government, and performed many administrative tasks. They wielded tremendous authority in their power to determine who should and who should not face trial. They enforced or refused to enforce laws as they saw fit and stood guard against indiscriminate prosecution by royal officials.'

"It is thus clear that a functional revolution in the grand jury occurred in the six centuries between the Assize of Clarendon and the adoption of the Fifth Amendment to the United States Constitution. By the time of the latter, the institution had evolved to its purest form: a citizen's tribunal, set resolutely between the state and the individual. Unhappily, the contemporary grand jury no longer serves that historic role and has regressed to little more than a convenient prosecutorial tool.

* * *

"... the indicting function of the grand jury has not changed in character or procedure in centuries. By contrast, in England, the country of its origin, there is no longer a need to consider reforming the grand jury to comport with modern notions of justice and due process, because the British deemed the shortcomings of the whole grand jury system compelling enough to abolish the institution in 1933.

"By contrast, California clings steadfastly to the anachronistic rules of the discarded English past. ... In this state there remains the legally tenable possibility that an individual may be compelled to undergo the trauma of a felony trial based on an ex parte proceeding from which he and all his evidence are statutorily excluded."

Despite conclusions of this nature, the Supreme Court of the United States has repeatedly stressed that the modern Grand Jury is intended to fulfill its "Historic role as a protective bulwark standing solidly between the ordinary citizen and an overzealous prosecutor." In United States v. Dionisio, 410 U.S. 1, 17, 93 S.Ct. 764, 773 (1973), the Court said:

"Under the ancient English system ... the most valuable function of the grand jury was not only to examine into the

> commission of crimes, but to stand between the prosecutor and the accused, and to determine whether the charge was founded on credible testimony or dictated by malice or personal ill will."

Nonetheless, those who have urged the abolition of the grand jury have focused upon the dominant role played by the prosecutor in the proceedings. For example, Judge Frankel has concluded that the "contemporary grand jury investigates only those whom the prosecutor asks to be investigated, and by and large indicts those whom the prosecutor wants to be indicted." Frankel & Naftalis, The Grand Jury: An Institution on Trial 100 (1977). And Judge Campbell, long a critic of the grand jury, bluntly stated in Campbell, Eliminate the Grand Jury, 64 J.Crim.L. & Crim. 174 (1973):

> Today, the grand jury is the total captive of the prosecutor who, if he is candid, will concede that he can indict anybody, at any time, for almost anything, before any grand jury.

Thus, the movement for abolishing the grand jury process springs from the notion expressed in *Dionisio*, that, "[i]t is, indeed, common knowledge that the grand jury, having been conceived as a bulwark between the citizen and the Government, is now a tool of the Executive."

In this fashion, the critical commentary has abounded. See, e.g., Antell, The Modern Grand Jury: Benighted Supergovernment, 51 A.B.A.J. 153 (1965); Comment, Grand Jury Proceedings: The Prosecutor, The Trial Judge and Undue Influence, 39 U.Chi.L.Rev. 761 (1972); Boudin, The Federal Grand Jury, 61 Geo.L.J. 1 (1972); Shannon, The Grand Jury: True Tribunal of the People or Administrative Agency of the Prosecutor?, 2 N.M.L.Rev. 141 (1972); Foster, Grand Jury Practice in the 1970's, 32 Ohio St.L.J. 701 (1971); Schwartz, Demythologizing the Historic Role of the Grand Jury, 10 Am.Crim.L.Rev. 701 (1972).

This criticism notwithstanding, the grand jury is firmly rooted in our history as a democratic institution; and, because it remains an important part of our criminal justice system, it is necessary to understand the law surrounding grand jury practice. See Sullivan & Nachman, If it ain't Broke, Don't Fix it: Why the Grand Jury's Accusatory Function Should Not Be Changed, 75 J.Crim.L. & Crim. 1047 (1984). However, it is precisely because of the criticism that the lawyer's role in the grand jury proceeding is currently emerging.

NOTES

1. For a further treatment of the historical role of the Grand Jury, see United States v. Calandra, Ch. 6, Sec. D.

2. In an article entitled Reforming the Federal Grand Jury and the State Preliminary Hearing to Prevent Conviction Without Adjudication, 78 Mich.L.Rev. 463 (1980), Professor Arenella called for a radical change in the federal grand jury function and procedures. He began with the premise that many of the defendants who enter pleas of guilty in federal court would not be convicted if they pursued their right to a trial. He argued that this is bad, even if such defendants are factually guilty, because it negates systematic values which flow from the requirement that the prosecution, using only legally admissible evidence, prove guilt beyond a reasonable doubt to the satisfaction of the trier of fact. Professor Arenella asserted that the guilty pleas are, in part, attributed to inadequate representation by appointed counsel in the federal system. As a solution he would provide for a variety of trial-like restrictions upon the use of evidence by the grand jury and for review of grand jury transcripts by federal district judges. If the defendant's motion to dismiss for violation of the new grand jury procedures were denied, Professor Arenella would provide for review of the claim only if the defendant entered a plea of guilty. The defendant who went to trial would waive his claim that proper grand jury procedures were not followed. See also Poulin, Supervision of the Grand Jury: Who Watches the Guardian, 68 Wash.U.L.Q. 885 (1990).

3. Must grand jurors who vote an indictment have been present for all of the evidence which was presented to the grand jury? If so, in prolonged grand jury investigations obtaining a majority to vote for conviction may be impossible under procedures heretofore used. It is not unusual for several members of a twenty-three person grand jury (as is used in the federal system) to be absent for a particular session. On the other hand, what kind of a safeguard is a system which permits a juror to vote without having heard all of the evidence? See United States v. Leverage Funding Systems, Inc., 637 F.2d 645 (9th Cir.1980). Are there any intermediate resolutions of the problem?

4. The grand jury, in certain types of federal criminal cases, is constitutionally mandated by the provision in the Fifth Amendment that "No person shall be held to answer for a capital, or otherwise infamous crime, unless on presentment or indictment of a Grand Jury, except in cases arising in the land and naval forces, or in the Militia, when in actual service in time of war or public danger...." The definition of "infamous" has evolved with time. See Mackin v. United States, 117 U.S. 348, 6 S.Ct. 777 (1886); United States v. Driscoll, 612 F.2d 1155 (9th Cir.1980).

5. The Fifth Amendment grand jury right has not been made applicable to the States. Hurtado v. California, 110 U.S. 516, 4 S.Ct. 111 (1884). The Constitutions of about one-half of the states prohibit a criminal trial in serious cases (typically in felony cases) unless the accused has been indicted by a grand jury or has waived that right to a grand jury proceeding. In the remaining states, the prosecutor typically bypasses the grand jury and the defendant is put to trial on an "information" signed by a prosecutor or a "complaint" signed by a police officer or another citizen. Even in these states, however, the grand jury is retained for cases whose investigation require the use of the power of subpoena. In many states where a grand jury indictment is ordinarily not required, a prosecutor may obtain an indictment following a finding of "no probable cause" by a judge at a preliminary hearing and must take this route in order to proceed with the prosecution despite the preliminary court's ruling.

6. For a balanced attempt to synthesize the views of the critics and defenders of the grand jury system, see Leipold, Why Grand Juries Do Not (And Cannot) Protect the Accused, 80 Cornell L.Rev. 260 (1995).

7. The investigation into terrorist activities following the September 11th attack brought to significance the issue of whether the government can obtain the detention of a material witness for questioning before the grand jury. The question turns on whether a grand jury appearance is a "criminal proceeding" as used in 18 U.S.C. § 344. Is it? Compare United States v. Awadallah, 202 F.Supp. 2d 55 (S.D.N.Y.2002) with In re Application for Material Witness Warrant, 213 F.Supp. 2d 287 (S.D.N.Y.2002).

B. GRAND JURY COMPOSITION

Vasquez v. Hillery

Supreme Court of the United States, 1986.
474 U.S. 254, 106 S.Ct. 617.

■ JUSTICE MARSHALL delivered the opinion of the Court.

The Warden of San Quentin State Prison asks this Court to retire a doctrine of equal protection jurisprudence first announced in 1880. The time has come, he urges, for us to abandon the rule requiring reversal of the conviction of any defendant indicted by a grand jury from which members of his own race were systematically excluded.

In 1962, the grand jury of Kings County, California, indicted respondent, Booker T. Hillery, for a brutal murder. Before trial in Superior Court, respondent moved to quash the indictment on the ground that it had been issued by a grand jury from which blacks had been systematically excluded. * * * After a hearing, the motion was denied and Hillery was thereafter convicted of murder.

For the next 16 years, respondent pursued appeals and collateral relief in the state courts, raising at every opportunity his equal protection challenge to the grand jury that indicted him. Less than one month after the California Supreme Court foreclosed his final avenue of state relief in 1978, respondent filed a petition for a writ of habeas corpus in federal court, raising that same challenge. The District Court concluded that respondent had established discrimination in the grand jury, and granted the writ.

* * *

On the merits, petitioner urges this Court to find that discrimination in the grand jury amounted to harmless error in this case, claiming that the evidence against respondent was overwhelming and that discrimination no longer infects the selection of grand juries in Kings County. Respondent's conviction after a fair trial, we are told, purged any taint attributable to the indictment process. Our acceptance of this theory would require abandonment of more than a century of consistent precedent.

In 1880, this Court reversed a state conviction on the ground that the indictment charging the offense had been issued by a grand jury from which blacks had been excluded. We reasoned that deliberate exclusion of blacks "is practically a brand upon them, affixed by the law, an assertion of their inferiority, and a stimulant to that race prejudice which is an impediment to securing to individuals of the race that equal justice which the law aims to secure to all others." Strauder v. West Virginia, 100 U.S. 303, 308 (1880).

Thereafter, the Court has repeatedly rejected all arguments that a conviction may stand despite racial discrimination in the selection of the grand jury. Only six years ago, the Court explicitly addressed the question whether this unbroken line of case law should be reconsidered in favor of a harmless-error standard, and determined that it should not. Rose v. Mitchell, 443 U.S. 545, 99 S.Ct. 2993 (1979). We reaffirmed our conviction that discrimination on the basis of race in the selection of grand jurors "strikes at the fundamental values of our judicial system and our society as a whole," and that the criminal defendant's right to equal protection of the laws has been denied when he is indicted by a grand jury from which members of a racial group purposefully have been excluded.

Petitioner argues here that requiring a State to retry a defendant, sometimes years later, imposes on it an unduly harsh penalty for a constitutional defect bearing no relation to the fundamental fairness of the trial. Yet intentional discrimination in the selection of grand jurors is a grave constitutional trespass, possible only under color of state authority, and wholly within the power of the State to prevent. Thus, the remedy we have embraced for over a century—the only effective remedy for this violation—is not disproportionate to the evil that it seeks to deter. If grand jury discrimination becomes a thing of the past, no conviction will ever again be lost on account of it.

Nor are we persuaded that discrimination in the grand jury has no effect on the fairness of the criminal trials that result from that grand jury's actions. The grand jury does not determine only that probable cause exists to believe that a defendant committed a crime, or that it does not. In the hands of the grand jury lies the power to charge a greater offense or a lesser offense; numerous counts or a single count; and perhaps most significant of all, a capital offense or a noncapital offense—all on the basis of the same facts. Moreover, "[t]the grand jury is not bound to indict in every case where a conviction can be obtained." Thus, even if a grand jury's determination of probable cause is confirmed in hindsight by a conviction on the indicted offense, that confirmation in no way suggests that the discrimination did not impermissibly infect the framing of the indictment and, consequently, the nature or very existence of the proceedings to come.

When constitutional error calls into question the objectivity of those charged with bringing a defendant to judgment, a reviewing court can neither indulge a presumption of regularity nor evaluate the resulting harm. Accordingly, when the trial judge is discovered to have had some basis for rendering a biased judgment, his actual motivations are hidden from review, and we must presume that the process was impaired. ... Similarly, when a petit jury has been selected upon improper criteria or has been exposed to prejudicial publicity, we have required reversal of the conviction because the effect of the violation cannot be ascertained. ... Like these fundamental flaws, which never have been thought harmless, discrimination in the grand jury undermines the structural integrity of the criminal tribunal itself, and is not amenable to harmless-error review.[6]

Just as a conviction is void under the Equal Protection Clause if the prosecutor deliberately charged the defendant on account of his race, a conviction cannot be understood to cure the taint attributable to a charging body selected on the basis of race. Once having found discrimination in the selection of a grand jury, we simply cannot know that the need to indict would have been assessed in the same way by a grand jury properly constituted. The overriding imperative to eliminate this systemic flaw in the charging process, as well as the difficulty of assessing its effect on any given defendant, requires our continued adherence to a rule of mandatory reversal.

* * *

6. Justice White does not join in the foregoing paragraph.

Our history does not impose any rigid formula to constrain the Court in the disposition of cases. Rather, its lesson is that every successful proponent of overruling precedent has borne the heavy burden of persuading the Court that changes in society or in the law dictate that the values served by stare decisis yield in favor of a greater objective. In the case of grand jury discrimination, we have been offered no reason to believe that any such metamorphosis has rendered the Court's long commitment to a rule of reversal out-dated, ill-founded, unworkable, or otherwise legitimately vulnerable to serious reconsideration. On the contrary, the need for such a rule is as compelling today as it was at its inception.

* * *

■ JUSTICE O'CONNOR, concurring in the judgment. [OMITTED].

■ JUSTICE POWELL, with whom THE CHIEF JUSTICE and JUSTICE REHNQUIST join, dissenting.

Respondent, a black man, was indicted by a grand jury having no black members for the stabbing murder of a 15–year–old girl. A petit jury found respondent guilty of that charge beyond a reasonable doubt, in a trial the fairness of which is unchallenged here. Twenty-three years later, we are asked to grant respondent's petition for a writ of habeas corpus—and thereby require a new trial if that is still feasible—on the ground that blacks were purposefully excluded from the grand jury that indicted him. It is undisputed that race discrimination has long since disappeared from the grand jury selection process in Kings County, California. It is undisputed that a grand jury that perfectly represented Kings County's population at the time of respondent's indictment would have contained only one black member. Yet the Court holds that respondent's petition must be granted, and that respondent must be freed unless the State is able to reconvict, more than two decades after the murder that led to his incarceration.

It is difficult to reconcile this result with a rational system of justice. The Court nevertheless finds its decision compelled by a century of precedent and by the interests of respondent and of society in ending race discrimination in the selection of grand juries. I dissent for two reasons. First, in my view, any error in the selection of the grand jury that indicted respondent is constitutionally harmless. Second even assuming that the harmless-error rule does not apply, reversal of respondent's conviction is an inappropriate remedy for the wrong that prompts this case.

* * *

In Chapman v. California, 386 U.S 18, 87 S.Ct. 824 (1967), the Court held that a trial judge's improper comment on the defendant's failure to testify—a clear violation of the Fifth and Fourteenth Amendments—was not a proper basis for reversal if harmless. Since Chapman, "the Court has consistently made clear that it is the duty of a reviewing court to consider the trial record as a whole and to ignore errors that are harmless, including most constitutional violations." This rule has been applied to a variety of constitutional violations.

* * *

In Rose v. Mitchell, 443 U.S. 545, 99 S.Ct. 2993 (1979), the Court contended that the principle of these cases is inapplicable to grand jury discrimination claims, because grand jury discrimination "destroys the appearance of justice and thereby casts doubt on the integrity of the judicial process." But *every* constitutional error may be said to raise questions as to the "appearance of justice" and the "integrity of the judicial process." Nevertheless, as the cases cited above show, the Court has required some showing of actual prejudice to the defendant as a prerequisite to reversal, even when the constitutional error directly affects the fairness of the defendant's trial.

* * *

I would dissent from the Court's decision for this reason alone. The reasoning of Chapman and its progency accords with a rational system of justice—one that fully preserves constitutional rights but recognizes that not every violation undermines the fairness of a given conviction. In this case, the grand jury error did not affect the fairness of respondent's trial or otherwise injure respondent in any cognizable way. . . .

Even assuming that now-established harmless-error principles are inapplicable, this case unjustifiably extends the "century of precedent" on which the Court relies. Those decisions do not require reversal of a decades-old conviction on the ground that it was preceded by an indictment issued by a discriminatorily selected grand jury. The purposes of the "automatic reversal" rule require otherwise.

No one questions that race discrimination in grand jury selection violates the Equal Protection Clause of the Fourteenth Amendment. The issue in this case is not whether the State erred, but what should be done about it. The question is whether reversal of respondent's conviction either is compelled by the Constitution or is an appropriate, but not constitutionally required, remedy for racial discrimination in the selection of grand jurors.

The Constitution does not compel the rule of automatic reversal that the Court applies today. In Hobby v. United States, 468 U.S. 339, 104 S.Ct. 3093 (1984), we acknowledged that discriminatory selection of grand jury foremen violated the Constitution, but we concluded that reversing the petitioner's conviction was an inappropriate remedy for the violation since grand jury foremen play a minor part in federal prosecutions. The rationale of Hobby cannot be squared with the claim that discriminatory selection of the body that charged the defendant *compels* reversal of the defendant's conviction. Rather, it is necessary to determine whether reversal of respondent's conviction is an "appropriate remedy" for the exclusion of blacks from grand juries in Kings County, California in 1962.

* * *

The scope of the remedy depends in part on the nature and degree of the harm caused by the wrong. The Court perceives two kinds of harm flowing from grand jury discrimination: harm to the respondent's interest in not being charged and convicted because of his race, and harm to society's interest in deterring racial discrimination. I consider in turn these asserted interests and the degree to which they are served in this case by the Court's automatic reversal rule.

The Court does not contend that the discriminatory selection of the grand jury that indicted respondent calls into question the correctness of the decision to indict. Such a contention could not withstand analysis. Following his indictment for murder, respondent was convicted of that charge in a trial and by a jury whose fairness are not now challenged. The conviction, affirmed on direct appeal in 1965, establishes that the grand jury's decision to indict was indisputably correct.

* * *

The Court nevertheless decides that discrimination in the selection of the grand jury potentially harmed respondent, because the grand jury is vested with broad discretion in deciding whether to indict and in framing the charges, and because it is impossible to know whether this discretion would have been exercised differently by a properly selected grand jury. The point appears to be that an all-white grand jury from which blacks are systematically excluded might be influenced by race in determining whether to indict and for what charge. Since the State may not imprison respondent for a crime if one of its elements is his race, the argument goes, his conviction must be set aside.

This reasoning ignores established principles of equal protection jurisprudence. We have consistently declined to find a violation of the Equal Protection Clause absent a finding of intentional discrimination. There has been no showing in this case—indeed, respondent does not even allege—that the Kings County grand jury indicted respondent because of his race, or that the grand jury declined to indict white suspects in the face of similarly strong evidence. Nor is it sensible to assume that impermissible discrimination might have occurred simply because the grand jury had no black members. This Court has never suggested that the racial composition of a grand jury gives rise to the inference that indictments are racially motivated, any more than it has suggested that a suspect arrested by a policeman of a different race may challenge his subsequent conviction on that basis. But the Court now holds that relief is justified in part because of the bare potential, unsupported by any evidence, that an all-white grand jury charged respondent because of his race.

* * *

In this case, due to the small number of blacks in Kings County, a random selection system could well have resulted in a grand jury identical to the one that indicted respondent. A perfectly representative grand jury—one whose composition reflected the county's racial mix—would have contained only one black member. Neither outcome would have justified an inference that respondent had been charged because of his race.

Once the inference of racial bias in the decision to indict is placed to one side, as it must be under our precedents, it is impossible to conclude that the discriminatory selection of Kings County's grand jurors caused respondent to suffer any cognizable injury. There may be a theoretical possibility that a different grand jury might have decided not to indict or to indict for a less serious charge. The fact remains, however, that the grand jury's decision to indict was *correct as a matter of law*, given respondent's subsequent, unchallenged conviction. A defendant has no right to a grand jury that errs in his favor. At most, he has an interest in not being bound over for trial in the absence of any evidence of his guilt, or based on impermissible factors such as his race. There is no allegation that those rights were violated in this case. The Court's decision cannot, therefore, be justified as a means of redressing any wrong to respondent.

As respondent suffered no prejudice from the grand jury discrimination that prompted his claim, the Court's remedy must stand or fall on its utility as a deterrent to government officials who seek to exclude particular groups from grand juries, weighed against the cost that the remedy imposes on society. The Court properly emphasized that grand jury discrimination is "a grave constitutional trespass," but it leaps from that observation to the conclusion that *no matter when the claim is raised* the appropriate response is to vacate the conviction of one indicted by a discriminatorily selected body. That conclusion is not, as the Court erroneously suggests, compelled by precedent; equally important, it seriously disserves the public interest.

* * *

This case raises the open question whether relief should be denied where the discrimination claim is pressed many years after conviction, and where the State can show that the delay prejudiced its ability to retry the defendant. Respondent first raised his grand jury discrimination claim before a federal court 16 years after his conviction. It is now almost a quarter-century since respondent was tried for murder and since the discrimination occurred. The Court finds this time lapse irrelevant. In my view, it is critically important, because it both increases the societal cost of the Court's chosen remedy and lessens any deterrent force the remedy may otherwise have.

In Rose v. Mitchell, the Court reasoned that the rule of automatic reversal imposes limited costs on society, since the State is able to retry successful petitioners, and since "the State remains free to use all the proof it introduced to obtain the conviction in the first trial." This is not the case when relief is granted many years after the original conviction. In those circumstances, the State may find itself severely handicapped in its ability to carry its heavy burden of proving guilt beyond a reasonable doubt. Where the original verdict turned on the jury's credibility judgments, long delays effectively eliminate the State's ability to reconstruct its case. Even where credibility is not central, the passage of time may make the right to retry the defendant "a matter of theory only."

* * *

Twenty-three years ago, respondent was fairly convicted of the most serious of crimes. Respondent's grand jury discrimination claim casts no doubt on the adequacy of the procedures used to convict him or on the sufficiency of the evidence of his guilt. . . . Even assuming the harmlessness of the error is irrelevant, however, reversal is still required. The Court inappropriately applies a deterrence rule in a context where it is unlikely to deter, and where its costs to society are likely to be especially high.

* * *

NOTES

1. In Castaneda v. Partida, 430 U.S. 482, 97 S.Ct. 1272 (1977), the court held that an equal protection violation presumptively exists if the defendant can show that the procedure for selecting the grand jury "resulted in substantial underrepresentation of his race or the identifiable group to which he belongs." Acknowledging that Mexican–Americans were a distinct identifiable class to which defendant belonged, the court focused on the statistical disparity:

> "The disparity proved by the 1970 Census statistics showed that the population of the county was 79.1% Mexican–American, but that, over an 11–year period, only 39% of the persons summoned for grand jury service were Mexican–American. This difference of 40% is greater than that found significant in Turner v. Fouche (1970) (60% Negroes in the general population, 37% on the grand jury lists). Since the State presented no evidence showing why the 11–year period was not reliable, we take it as the relevant base for comparison. The mathematical disparities that have been accepted by this Court as adequate for a prima facie case have all been within the range presented here. For example, in Whitus v. Georgia (1967), the number of Negroes listed on the tax digest amounted to 27.1% of the population, but only 9.1% of those on the grand jury venire. The disparity was held to be sufficient to make out a prima facie case of discrimination. See Sims v. Georgia (1967) (24.4% on tax lists, 4.7% on grand jury lists); Jones v. Georgia (1967) (19.4% on tax lists, 5.0% on jury list).
>
> * * *
>
> "... [The] facts that bear on the issue [include] the statistical disparities, the method of selection, and any other relevant testimony as to the manner in which the selection process was implemented. Under this standard, the proof offered by respondent was sufficient to demonstrate a prima facie case of discrimination in grand jury selection. Since the State failed to rebut the presumption of purposeful discrimination by competent testimony, despite two opportunities to do so, we affirm the Court of Appeals' holding of a denial of equal protection of the law in the grand jury selection process in respondent's case."

2. In Rose v. Mitchell, 443 U.S. 545, 99 S.Ct. 2993 (1979), defendants sought to quash their Tennessee murder indictments on the ground that the foreman of the grand jury which indicted them was selected in a racially discriminatory manner. To support their contention, defendants, at a hearing on the issue, called, among other witnesses, two former foremen who testified that they had never heard of a black grand jury foreman in the county and the current grand jury foreman who testified that he had no knowledge of whether a black had ever served as foreman. The Court held that claims of racial discrimination in the selection of state grand jury members are cognizable in federal habeas corpus proceedings even though the trial jury was untainted and guilt was established. However, although acknowledging that grand jury exclusion based on race was constitutionally impermissible, the Court concluded that, on the facts before it, defendants failed to make a prima facie case of improper exclusion. "Absent evidence as to the total number of foremen appointed by the judges in the county during the critical period of time, it is difficult to say that the number of Negroes appointed foreman, even if zero, is statistically so significant as to make out a case of discrimination under the 'rule of exclusion.' "

3. In Hobby v. United States, 468 U.S. 339, 104 S.Ct. 3093 (1984), the Court held that the federal grand jury foreman has no special powers other than clerical or ministerial. Accordingly, in ruling on a white male's due process challenge to discrimination against Blacks and women in selection of federal grand jury foremen, the Court held that dismissal of an indictment was not an appropriate remedy. The defendant lacked standing to raise an equal protection claim because he was not a member of a group "stigmatized" by the alleged purposeful discrimination. Compare Powers v. Ohio, Casebook p. 1215. The Court also rejected a suggestion that, in the exercise of its supervisory powers over federal grand juries, the Court should provide for dismissal of indictments to discourage purposeful discrimination. The dissenting opinion pointed out that the charge was that federal district judges had discriminated against Blacks and women. If the charge is true, said the dissenters, it diminishes confidence in the institutions of criminal justice and suggests that "racist" and "sexist" attitudes and actions may be at work elsewhere in the district judges' performance of duty.

4. In United States ex rel. Barksdale v. Blackburn, 639 F.2d 1115 (5th Cir.1981) (en banc) (1980), the court held that less than a ten-percent disparity between the number of persons of the underrepresented group in the general population and the number on grand juries does not suffice to establish a prima facie case of discrimination. See also Ellis v. Lynaugh, 873 F.2d 830 (5th Cir.1989). Can any fixed percentage be set to establish a prima facie case? Would that be mathematically sound, if the percentage did not vary according to the size of the general population and the total number of grand jurors included in the comparison? See Moultrie v. Martin, 690 F.2d 1078 (4th Cir.1982), which mandates use of a more mathematically sound method of evaluating the statistical significance of deviations between a cognizable group's percentage of the general population and that group's percentage among jurors.

5. Is there any alternative to the motion to dismiss an indictment which can be utilized to combat discrimination against minorities in grand jury selection procedures? Could a civil action be used to end underrepresentation? See Ciudadanos Unidos De San Juan v. Hidalgo County Grand Jury Commissioners, 622 F.2d 807 (5th Cir.1980).

6. The states are accorded substantial discretion in developing the proper mechanism for producing the grand jury pool. See United States v. Leonetti, 291 F.Supp. 461 (S.D.N.Y.1968). While the grand jury need not represent a mirror image of the community, the discriminatory exclusion of identifiable groups is prohibited. See United States v. Gast, 457 F.2d 141 (7th Cir.1972), cert. denied 406 U.S. 969, 92 S.Ct. 2426 (1972) (while residency requirements are constitutionally suspect, one year requirement to qualify for grand jury service does not constitute discriminatory exclusion); United States v. Dellinger, 472 F.2d 340 (7th Cir.1972), cert. denied 410 U.S. 970, 93 S.Ct. 1443 (1973) ("young alienated" not cognizable group).

7. Many jurisdictions permit various classes of individuals to be excused from grand jury service upon request. Some examples include senior citizens, women with young children, law enforcement officers, firemen, attorneys, clergymen, school teachers, doctors, nurses, and sole proprietors of business. Do exclusions of this nature rise to the level of a constitutional violation? See United States v. Grey, 355 F.Supp. 529 (W.D.Okl.1973).

8. Objections to the composition of the grand jury are generally made in the form of a motion to dismiss the indictment. However, if the statute of limitations has not run, a successful motion will not bar reindictment by another grand jury. Since reindictment is permissible, what advantages are there to a client in challenging the grand jury's composition?

9. Ordinarily a challenge to grand jury composition is waived if not raised by a pre-trial motion. Tollett v. Henderson, 411 U.S. 258, 93 S.Ct. 1602 (1973); Davis v. United States, 411 U.S. 233, 93 S.Ct. 1577 (1973).

10. Some jurisdictions, perhaps for want of resources, do not follow up on persons who eliminate themselves as possible grand or petit jurors by failing to respond to initial questionnaires or by ignoring a summons to appear for possible jury selection. Suppose that members of a minority group are eliminated in this fashion in a percentage disproportionate to their numbers in the population. Must the system compensate in some fashion? For one view, see People v. Guzman, 89 A.D.2d 14, 454 N.Y.S.2d 852 (1982). Does a negative answer to this question suggest that our real concern is not for the accused but for the persons who are denied an opportunity to serve for discriminatory reasons? See also United States v. Gometz, 730 F.2d 475 (7th Cir.1984), in which the court was highly unsympathetic to a "no follow up" claim in the context of petty jury selection even though the clerk made no effort to follow up on the seventy percent of individuals who did not respond to jury questionnaires. The defense theorized that such persons would include a disproportionate percentage of "anti-authoritarians" and a disproportionate percentage of minorities. The Seventh Circuit denied a hearing for want of statistical evidence supporting such a theory. Is a criminal defendant in a position to make such a showing before being allowed a hearing?

C. SECRECY OF THE GRAND JURY

United States v. Sells Engineering, Inc.

Supreme Court of the United States, 1983.
463 U.S. 418, 103 S.Ct. 3133.

■ JUSTICE BRENNAN delivered the opinion of the Court.

The question in this case is under what conditions attorneys for the Civil Division of the Justice Department, their paralegal and secretarial staff, and all other necessary assistants, may obtain access to grand jury materials, compiled with the assistance and knowledge of other Justice Department attorneys, for the purpose of preparing and pursuing a civil suit. We hold that such access is permissible only when the Government moves for court-ordered disclosure under Federal Rule of Criminal Procedure 6(e)(3)(C)(i) and makes the showing of particularized need required by that Rule.

I

[A grand jury indicted a company and two company officers on two counts of conspiracy to defraud the United States and nine counts of tax fraud. The defendants each pleaded guilty to one count of conspiracy to defraud the government, and all other counts were dismissed. Thereafter, the government moved for disclosure of all grand jury materials to attorneys in the Justice Department's Civil Division, their paralegal and secretarial assistants, and certain Defense Department experts, for use in preparing and conducting a possible civil suit against the defendants. The officers and company opposed the disclosure and made an allegation of grand jury misuse for civil purposes. The District Court granted the requested disclosure; and, on appeal, the Ninth Circuit vacated and remanded, holding that Civil Division attorneys could obtain disclosure only by showing particularized need under Rule 6(e)(3)(C)(i) of the Federal Rules of Criminal Procedure and that the District Court had not applied a correct standard of particularized need.]

II

A

The grand jury has always occupied a high place as an instrument of justice in our system of criminal law—so much so that it is enshrined in the Constitution. It serves the "dual function of determining if there is probable cause to believe that a crime has been committed and of protecting citizens against unfounded criminal prosecutions."

* * *

The same concern for the grand jury's dual function underlies the "long-established policy that maintains the secrecy of the grand jury proceedings in the federal courts."

> "We consistently have recognized that the proper functioning of our grand jury system depends upon the secrecy of grand jury proceedings. In particular, we have noted several distinct interests served by safeguarding the confidentiality of grand jury proceedings. First, if preindictment proceedings were made public, many prospective witnesses would be hesitant to come forward voluntarily, knowing that those against whom they testify would be aware of that testimony. Moreover, witnesses who appeared before the grand jury would be less likely to testify fully and frankly, as they would be open to retribution as well as to inducements. There also would be the risk that those about to be indicted would flee, or would try to influence individual grand jurors to vote against indictment. Finally, by preserving the secrecy of the proceedings, we assure that persons who are accused but exonerated by the grand jury will not be held up to public ridicule." Douglas Oil Co. v. Petrol Stops Northwest, 441 U.S. 211, 218–219, 99 S.Ct. 1667 (1979).

Grand jury secrecy, then, is "as important for the protection of the innocent as for the pursuit of the guilty." Both Congress and this Court have consistently stood ready to defend it against unwarranted intrusion. In the absence of a clear indication in a statute or Rule, we must always be reluctant to conclude that a breach of this secrecy has been authorized.

B

Rule 6(e) of the Federal Rules of Criminal Procedure codifies the traditional rule of grand jury secrecy. Paragraph 6(e)(2) provides that grand jurors, Government attorneys and their assistants, and other personnel attached to the grand jury are forbidden to disclose matters occurring before the grand jury. Witnesses are not under the prohibition unless they also happen to fit into one of the enumerated classes. Paragraph 6(e)(3) sets forth four exceptions to this nondisclosure rule.[7]

Subparagraph 6(e)(3)(A) contains two authorizations for disclosure as a matter of course, without any court order. First, under subparagraph 6(e)(3)(A)(i), disclosure may be made without a court order to "an attorney for the government for use in the performance of such attorney's duty" (referred to hereinafter as "(A)(i) disclosure"). "Attorney for the government" is defined in Rule 54(c) in such broad terms as potentially to include virtually every attorney in the Department of Justice. Second, under subparagraph 6(e)(3)(A)(ii), grand jury materials may likewise be provided to "government personnel . . . [who] assist an attorney for the government in the performance of such attorney's duty to enforce federal criminal law" ("(A)(ii) disclosure"). Subparagraph 6(e)(3)(B) further regulates (A)(ii) disclosure, forbidding use of grand jury materials by "government personnel" for any purpose other than assisting an attorney for the Government in his

7. Rules 6(e)(2) and (3), as presently in force, provide as follows:

"(e) Recording and Disclosure of Proceedings

* * *

"(2) General Rule of Secrecy.—A grand juror, an interpreter, a stenographer, an operator of a recording device, a typist who transcribes recorded testimony, an attorney for the government, or any person to whom disclosure is made under paragraph (3)(A)(ii) of this subdivision shall not disclose matters occurring before the grand jury, except as otherwise provided for in these rules. No obligation of secrecy may be imposed on any person except in accordance with this rule. A knowing violation of Rule 6 may be punished as a contempt of court.

"(3) Exceptions.

"(A) Disclosure otherwise prohibited by this rule of matters occurring before the grand jury, other than its deliberations and the vote of any grand juror, may be made to—

"(i) an attorney for the government for use in the performance of such attorney's duty; and

"(ii) such government personnel as are deemed necessary by an attorney for the government to assist an attorney for the government in the performance of such attorney's duty to enforce federal criminal law.

"(B) Any person to whom matters are disclosed under subparagraph (A)(ii) of this paragraph shall not utilize that grand jury material for any purpose other than assisting the attorney for the government in the performance of such attorney's duty to enforce federal criminal law. An attorney for the government shall promptly provide the district court, before which was impaneled the grand jury whose material has been so disclosed, with the names of the persons to whom such disclosure has been made.

"(C) Disclosure otherwise prohibited by this rule of matters occurring before the grand jury may also be made—

"(i) when so directed by a court preliminarily to or in connection with a judicial proceeding; or

"(ii) when permitted by a court at the request of the defendant, upon a showing that grounds may exist for a motion to dismiss the indictment because of matters occurring before the grand jury.

"If the court orders disclosure of matters occurring before the grand jury, the disclosure shall be made in such manner, at such time, and under such conditions as the court may direct."

A fifth exception has been created this Term in an amendment to Rule 6(e), to take effect August 1, 1983. 461 U.S. 1121 (1983). The amendment adds a new subparagraph 6(e)(3)(C)(iii), permitting disclosure "when the disclosure is made by an attorney for the government to another federal grand jury." The Advisory Committee's Note points out that secrecy is not thereby compromised, since the second grand jury is equally under Rule 6's requirement of secrecy.

enforcement of criminal law, and requiring that the names of such personnel be provided to the district court.

Subparagraph 6(e)(3)(C) also authorizes courts to order disclosure. Under subparagraph 6(e)(3)(C)(i), a court may order disclosure "preliminarily to or in connection with a judicial proceeding" (a "(C)(i) order"). Under subparagraph 6(e)(3)(C)(ii), a court may order disclosure under certain conditions at the request of a defendant.

The main issue in this case is whether attorneys in the Justice Department may obtain automatic (A)(i) disclosure of grand jury materials for use in a civil suit, or whether they must seek a (C)(i) court order for access. If a (C)(i) order is necessary, we must address the dependent question of what standards should govern issuance of the order.

III

The Government contends that all attorneys in the Justice Department qualify for automatic disclosure of grand jury materials under (A)(i), regardless of the nature of the litigation in which they intend to use the materials. We hold that (A)(i) disclosure is limited to use by those attorneys who conduct the criminal matters to which the materials pertain. This conclusion is mandated by the general purposes and policies of grand jury secrecy, by the limited policy reasons why Government attorneys are granted access to grand jury materials for criminal use, and by the legislative history of Rule 6(e).

A

The Government correctly contends that attorneys for the Civil Division of the Justice Department are within the class of "attorneys for the government" to whom (A)(i) allows disclosure without a court order.

* * *

It does not follow, however, that any Justice Department attorney is free to rummage through the records of any grand jury in the country, simply by right of office. Disclosure under (A)(i) is permitted only "in the performance of such attorney's duty." The heart of the primary issue in this case is whether performance of duty, within the meaning of (A)(i), includes preparation and litigation of a civil suit by a Justice Department attorney who had no part in conducting the related criminal prosecution.

Given the strong historic policy of preserving grand jury secrecy, one might wonder why Government attorneys are given any automatic access at all.

* * *

The purpose of the grand jury requires that it remain free, within constitutional and statutory limits, to operate "independently of either prosecuting attorney or judge." Nevertheless, a modern grand jury would be much less effective without the assistance of the prosecutor's office and the investigative resources it commands. The prosecutor ordinarily brings matters to the attention of the grand jury and gathers the evidence required for the jury's consideration. Although the grand jury may itself decide to investigate a matter or to seek certain evidence, it depends largely on the prosecutor's office to secure the evidence or witnesses it requires. The prosecutor also advises the lay jury on the applicable law. The prosecutor in turn needs to know what transpires before the grand jury in order to perform his own duty properly. If he considers that the law and the admissible evidence will not support a conviction, he can be expected to advise the grand jury not to indict. He must also examine indictments, and the basis for their issuance, to determine whether it is in the interests of justice to proceed with prosecution.

None of these considerations, however, provides any support for breaching grand jury secrecy in favor of Government attorneys *other than prosecutors*—either by allowing them into the grand jury room, or by granting them uncontrolled access to grand jury materials. An attorney with only civil duties lacks both the prosecutor's special role in supporting the grand jury, and the prosecutor's own crucial need to know what occurs before the grand jury.[15]

Of course, it would be of substantial help to a Justice Department civil attorney if he had free access to a storehouse of evidence compiled by a grand jury; but that is of a different order from the prosecutor's need for access. The civil lawyer's need is ordinarily nothing more than a matter of saving time and expense. The same argument could be made for access on behalf of any lawyer in another Government agency, or indeed, in private practice. We have consistently rejected the argument that such savings can justify a breach of grand jury secrecy. In most cases, the same evidence that could be obtained from the grand jury will be available through ordinary discovery or other routine avenues of investigation. If, in a particular case, ordinary discovery is insufficient for some reason, the Government may request disclosure under a (C)(i) court order.

Not only is disclosure for civil use unjustified by the considerations supporting prosecutorial access, but also it threatens to do affirmative mischief. The problem is threefold.

First, disclosure to Government bodies raises much the same concerns that underlie the rule of secrecy in other contexts. Not only does disclosure increase the number of persons to whom the information is available (thereby increasing the risk of inadvertent or illegal release to others), but also it renders considerably more concrete the threat to the willingness of witnesses to come forward and to testify fully and candidly. If a witness knows or fears that his testimony before the grand jury will be routinely available for use in governmental civil litigation or administrative action, he may well be less willing to speak for fear that he will get himself into trouble in some other forum.

Second, because the Government takes an active part in the activities of the grand jury, disclosure to Government attorneys for civil use poses a significant threat to the integrity of the grand jury itself. If prosecutors in a

15. This case involves only access by Civil Division attorneys who played no part in the criminal prosecution of respondents. It does not present any issue concerning continued use of grand jury materials, in the civil phase of a dispute, by an attorney who himself conducted the criminal prosecution. We decline to address that problem in this case.

given case knew that their colleagues would be free to use the materials generated by the grand jury for a civil case, they might be tempted to manipulate the grand jury's powerful investigative tools to root out additional evidence useful in the civil suit, or even to start or continue a grand jury inquiry where no criminal prosecution seemed likely. Any such use of grand jury proceedings to elicit evidence for use in a civil case is improper per se.

* * *

Third, use of grand jury materials by Government agencies in civil or administrative settings threatens to subvert the limitations applied outside the grand jury context on the Government's powers of discovery and investigation. While there are some limits on the investigative powers of the grand jury, there are few if any other forums in which a governmental body has such relatively unregulated power to compel other persons to divulge information or produce evidence. Other agencies, both within and without the Justice Department, operate under specific and detailed statutes, rules, or regulations conferring only limited authority to require citizens to testify or produce evidence.

* * *

If Government litigators or investigators in civil matters enjoyed unlimited access to grand jury material, though, there would be little reason for them to resort to their usual, more limited avenues of investigation. To allow these agencies to circumvent their usual methods of discovery would not only subvert the limitations and procedural requirements built into those methods, but also would grant to the Government a virtual ex parte form of discovery, from which its civil litigation opponents are excluded unless they make a strong showing of particularized need.

* * *

B

The Government argues that its reading of Rule 6 is compelled by a textual comparison of subparagraph 6(e)(3)(A)(i) with subparagraph 6(e)(3)(A)(ii). It points out that the former restricts a Government attorney's use of grand jury materials to "the performance of such attorney's duty," while the latter refers more specifically to "performance of such attorney's duty *to enforce federal criminal law*" (emphasis added). The inclusion in (A)(ii) of an express limitation to criminal matters, and the absence of that limitation in the otherwise similar language of (A)(i), the Government argues, show that Congress intended to place the limitation to criminal matters on (A)(ii) disclosure but not on (A)(i) disclosure.

* * *

[Based on the legislative history and development of Rule 6, we conclude] that Congress did not intend that "attorneys for the government" should be permitted free civil use of grand jury materials. Congress was strongly concerned with assuring that prosecutors would not be free to turn over grand jury materials to others in the Government for civil uses without court supervision, and that statutory limits on civil discovery not be subverted—concerns that apply to civil use by attorneys within the Justice Department as fully as to similar use by persons in other Government agencies. Both the Advisory Committee Notes and the testimony of the Justice Department's own representative suggested that even under the old Rule such disclosure for civil use would not have been permissible; indeed, the latter gave a hypothetical illustration closely similar to this very case. The express addition of a "criminal-use" limitation in (A)(ii) appears to have been prompted by an abundance of caution, owing to Congress' special concern that nonattorneys were the ones most likely to pose a danger of unauthorized use.

IV

Since we conclude that the Government must obtain a (C)(i) court order to secure the disclosure it seeks in this case, we must consider what standard should govern the issuance of such an order.

Rule 6(e)(3)(C)(i) simply authorizes a court to order disclosure "preliminarily to or in connection with a judicial proceeding." Neither the text of the Rule nor the accompanying commentary describes any substantive standard governing issuance of such orders. We have consistently construed the Rule, however, to require a strong showing of particularized need for grand jury materials before any disclosure will be permitted. We described the standard in detail in Douglas Oil:

> "Parties seeking grand jury transcripts under Rule 6(e) must show that the material they seek is needed to avoid a possible injustice in another judicial proceeding, that the need for disclosure is greater than the need for continued secrecy, and that their request is structured to cover only material so needed....
>
> "It is clear from Procter & Gamble and Dennis that disclosure is appropriate only in those cases where the need for it outweighs the public interest in secrecy, and that the burden of demonstrating this balance rests upon the private party seeking disclosure. It is equally clear that as the considerations justifying secrecy become less relevant, a party asserting a need for grand jury transcripts will have a lesser burden in showing justification. In sum, ... the court's duty in a case of this kind is to weigh carefully the competing interests in light of the relevant circumstances and the standards announced by this Court. And if disclosure is ordered, the court may include protective limitations on the use of the disclosed material...." 441 U.S., at 222–223, 99 S.Ct. 1667 (citations omitted).

The Government points out that Douglas Oil and its forerunners all involved private parties seeking access to grand jury materials. It contends that the Douglas Oil standard ought not be applied when Government officials seek access "in furtherance of their responsibility to protect the public weal."

* * *

[I]f we were to agree with the Government that disclosure is permissible if the grand jury materials are "relevant to matters within the duties of the attorneys for the government," Brief for United States 13, a (C)(i) court order would be a virtual rubber stamp for the Government's assertion that it desires disclosure. Thus, under the Government's argument, it would get under subparagraph (C)(i) precisely what Congress intended to deny it under subparagraphs (A) and (B)—unlimited and unregulated access to grand jury materials for civil use.

* * *

Nothing in Douglas Oil, however, requires a district court to pretend that there are no differences between governmental bodies and private parties. The Douglas Oil standard is a highly flexible one, adaptable to different circumstances and sensitive to the fact that the requirements of secrecy are greater in some situations than in others. Hence, although [we] foreclose any special dispensation from the Douglas Oil standard for Government agencies, the standard itself accommodates any relevant considerations, peculiar to Government movants, that weigh for or against disclosure in a given case. For example, a district court might reasonably consider that disclosure to Justice Department attorneys poses less risk of further leakage or improper use than would disclosure to private parties or the general public. Similarly, we are informed that it is the usual policy of the Justice Department not to seek civil use of grand jury materials until the criminal aspect of the matter is closed. And "under the particularized-need standard, the district court may weigh the public interest, if any, served by disclosure to a governmental body...." On the other hand, for example, in weighing the need for disclosure, the court could take into account any alternative discovery tools available by statute or regulation to the agency seeking disclosure.

In this case, the District Court asserted that it had found particularized need for disclosure, but its explanation of that conclusion amounted to little more than its statement that the grand jury materials sought are rationally related to the civil fraud suit to be brought by the Civil Division.

* * *

V

The Court of Appeals correctly held that disclosure to Government attorneys and their assistants for use in a civil suit is permissible only with a court order under Rule 6(e)(3)(C)(i), and that the District Court did not apply correctly the particularized-need standard for issuance of such an order. Accordingly, the judgment of the Court of Appeals is affirmed.

■ CHIEF JUSTICE BURGER, with whom JUSTICE POWELL, JUSTICE REHNQUIST, and JUSTICE O'CONNOR join, dissenting.

The Court today holds that attorneys within the Department of Justice who are not assigned to the grand jury investigation or prosecution must seek a court order on a showing of particularized need in order to obtain access, for the purpose of preparing a civil suit, to grand jury materials already in the Government's possession. In my view, this holding is contrary not only to the clear language but also to the history of Rule 6(e)(3)(A)(i) of the Federal Rules of Criminal Procedure. In addition, the Court's decision reflects an erroneous assessment of the relevant policies, and provides the courts and the Department of Justice with precious little guidance in an area of great importance. I believe that, when a grand jury is validly convened and conducted on the request of the Government for criminal investigatory purposes, it is proper and entirely consistent with the Federal Rules of Criminal Procedure for any attorney in the Department of Justice to have access to grand jury materials in pursuing inquiry into civil claims involving the same or related matters. I therefore dissent.

* * *

NOTES

1. The most often-stated reasons for protecting grand jury secrecy were articulated in United States v. Rose, 215 F.2d 617, 628–29 (3d Cir.1954), and restated with approval in United States v. Procter & Gamble, 356 U.S. 677, 681–82 n. 6, 78 S.Ct. 983, 985–86 n. 6 (1958):

> "(1) To prevent the escape of those whose indictment may be contemplated; (2) to insure the utmost freedom to the grand jury in its deliberations, and to prevent persons subject to indictment or their friends from importuning the grand jurors; (3) to prevent subornation of perjury or tampering with the witnesses who may testify before the grand jury and later appear at the trial of those indicted by it; (4) to encourage free and untrammeled disclosures by persons who have information with respect to the commission of crimes; (5) to protect innocent accused who is exonerated from disclosure of the fact that he has been under investigation, and from the expense of standing trial where there was no probability of guilt."

2. When a criminal investigation of a possible federal tax violation does not result in an indictment, should the district judge routinely grant an Internal Revenue Service request for grand jury testimony to aid a civil tax investigation? The Supreme Court has said "no" at least when the matter is at the audit stage. United States v. Baggot, 463 U.S. 476, 103 S.Ct. 3164 (1983). The same is true in connection with potential civil antitrust claims unless the materials are necessary to prevent an injustice. In re Grand Jury Proceedings, 841 F.2d 1264 (6th Cir.1988). See Comment, FRCrP 6(e) and the Disclosure of Documents Reviewed by a Grand Jury, 57 U.Chi.L.Rev. 221 (1990).

In United States v. John Doe, Inc. I, 481 U.S. 102, 107 S.Ct. 1656 (1987), the Court approved use in a civil action, without special court-approval, of materials obtained by a federal grand jury, where such use is by a Justice Department lawyer who himself conducted the criminal prosecution. Such continued use does not constitute unauthorized "disclosure" within the meaning of Rule 6(e) of the Federal Rules of Criminal Procedure. The Court did not rule on disclosure of such grand jury information by the Justice Department lawyer to others during the course of civil proceedings.

The limitation on disclosure does not apply to federal prosecutors in separate districts. Thus, prior court approval is not required in order to reveal secret grand jury information to a prosecutor in another district for use in connection with law enforcement duties. Impounded, 227 F.3d 407 (3d Cir.2002).

3. In Illinois v. Abbott & Associates, 460 U.S. 557, 103 S.Ct. 1356 (1983), a state attorney general sought federal grand jury transcripts which concerned investigations of alleged antitrust violations. He argued that provisions of the Clayton Act which encouraged cooperation between federal and state officials in antitrust matters entitled state officials to the transcripts without a showing of particularized need. The Court rejected the argument and allowed district court approval of release of transcripts only upon a showing of need on an instance-by-instance basis. In 1985 Rule 6(e) was amended to make it easier for state prosecutors to obtain federal grand jury transcripts that disclose a violation of state law.

4. What if the shoe were on the other foot? Would federal prosecutors, investigating possible federal violations, have to satisfy a state statute which required a showing of cause for release of state grand jury transcripts? Or could they simply use a federal subpoena to obtain the state transcripts, asserting that federal supremacy prohibits state interference with a federal investigation? See In re Grand Jury Proceedings, 832 F.2d 554 (11th Cir.1987). Suppose state law simply did not provide for release of grand jury transcripts to federal officials under any circumstances.

5. Does Congress have access to a judge's grand jury testimony for use in impeachment proceedings? See In re Request for Access to Grand Jury Materials, 833 F.2d 1438 (11th Cir.1987).

6. What happens when there has been a violation of the secrecy requirement by government employees? In United States v. Eisenberg, 711 F.2d 959 (11th Cir. 1983), the court held:

> "Once the court determines that Rule 6(e) has been violated, the court may properly inform the targets' counsel of the names of the violators. Targets' counsel may then play a proper role in hearings involving imposition of contempt sanctions on government employees. . . . If an indictment is issued against their clients, counsel may obtain the record of the investigation of the Rule 6(e) violations. At that time, the indicted individuals can decide whether to move for dismissal of the indictment on grounds of improper government conduct and prejudicial publicity in violation of Rule 6(e).
>
> * * *
>
> "We place no restrictions on the power of the district court to order an investigation of the government's alleged violations of Rule 6(e). We can conceive of circumstances where a district court could seek the appointment of a special counsel to assist the court in determining whether Rule 6(e) violations had occurred. We place the burden of that undertaking on the district court, however, and prohibit pre-indictment participation by counsel for targets. . . . We will not countenance violations of Rule 6(e). Nor will we authorize counsel for grand jury targets having information which would permit them to embark upon a broad scale investigation of their own."

However, violations of this type are generally viewed as harmless error when reviewed after conviction. See United States v. Alexander, 860 F.2d 508 (2d Cir.1988).

7. Does a grand jury witness have the right to a transcript of his own testimony? In re Grand Jury, 490 F.3d 978 (D.C. Cir. 2007), found that a witness' interest in reviewing his testimony outweighs the government's interest in preserving grand jury secrecy and held that the witness has a right to examine the transcripts of his own testimony in private at a place designated by the prosecutor. Although the decision contains an excellent discussion of the secrecy issue, most courts require a greater showing before they will provide a witness with his testimony. The general rule is that a witness is not automatically entitled to a transcript of his testimony before a federal grand jury and may only contain it upon a showing of a particularized need. United States v. Evans & Associates Construction Co., 839 F.2d 656 (10th Cir.1988). Other courts have indicated that the burden is on the government to show "particularized and substantial reasons" why a transcript should not be released. In re Sealed Motion, 880 F.2d 1367 (D.C.Cir.1989). See generally Comment, Grand Jury Secrecy: Should Witnesses Have Access to Their Grand Jury Testimony as a Matter of Right? 20 U.C.L.A.L.Rev. 804 (1973); Comment, Grand Jury Minutes and the Rule of Secrecy in Federal Litigation, 55 Nw.U.L.Rev. 482 (1960).

8. No secrecy obligation is imposed on the witness himself. In re Grand Jury Investigation, 610 F.2d 202 (5th Cir.1980); In re Grand Jury Subpoena, 575 F.Supp. 1219 (E.D.Pa.1983) (bank may notify customer of records subpoena it receives). Therefore, it is proper (and essential) for a lawyer to debrief his client after a grand jury appearance. However, a grand jury witness cannot be compelled to relate his testimony to third persons, including the target of the investigation. In re Swearingen Aviation Corp., 605 F.2d 125 (4th Cir.1979). It is not improper for the government to advise grand jury witnesses that they have a right not to disclose and that the government would prefer that they not do so to anyone other than their own attorneys. In re Grand Jury Proceedings, 558 F.Supp. 532 (W.D.Va.1983).

A Florida statute which prohibited a witness from revealing his or her own grand jury testimony even after the conclusion of the grand jury investigation was invalidated on First Amendment grounds in Butterworth v. Smith, 494 U.S. 624, 110 S.Ct. 1376 (1990). The Court held that an individual cannot be perpetually prohibited from revealing information which the individual knew before testifying. Many of the reasons for grand jury secrecy end once the grand jury has concluded its work, the Court said. Those which remain do not outweigh First Amendment interests, the Court concluded.

9. The preservation of grand jury secrecy is, of course, one of the reasons for excluding all other persons than those enumerated in either the federal rules or state statutes. See United States v. Gold, 470 F.Supp. 1336 (N.D.Ill.1979) (presence of EPA staff lawyers who also acted as witness required dismissal); United States v. Bowdach, 324 F.Supp. 123 (S.D.Fla.1971) (indictment invalidated because an FBI agent was present in the grand jury room to operate a tape recorder); United States v. Borys, 169 F.Supp. 366 (D.Alaska 1959) (indictment invalid because the mother of a seven-year-old witness remained in the grand jury room). Compare United States v. Computer Sciences Corp., 689 F.2d 1181 (4th Cir.1982) (presence of unauthorized persons sufficiently limited and nonprejudicial so as not to require dismissal). United States v. Mechanik, 475 U.S. 66, 106 S.Ct. 938 (1986), applied the harmless error rule to uphold a conviction after two witnesses testified in each other's presence before the grand jury. In a concurring opinion, Justice O'Connor suggested that post-conviction harmless error analysis would turn the rules governing grand jury conduct into "a dead letter." She believed dismissal warranted if the violation substantially influenced the decision to indict or raised grave doubt as to whether it had such an effect. See United States v. Kilpatrick, 821 F.2d 1456 (10th Cir.1987) (dismissal of indictment for disclosure of Grand Jury material to IRS civil auditor reversed because of the absence of evidence of an infringement on the Grand Jury's ability to exercise independent judgment).

10. When a suspect provides evidence to a grand jury as part of a broad investigation but is not thereafter indicted, may he object to disclosure of that evidence to another person who is indicted by the same grand jury and seeks the evidence through trial discovery? The issue is particularly important in criminal antitrust cases because the disclosure of documents under subpoena may affect the competitive balance between companies. In NL Industries, Inc. v. Snyder, 599 F.2d 1183 (3d

Cir.1979), the court held that an unindicted firm's objection to the disclosure of materials provided to the grand jury should make a court require the party seeking the evidence to show why it is material and why traditional secrecy policies should not prohibit disclosure. The court expressed the following view:

> Grand jury witnesses ought to be able to rely, generally, upon Rule 6(e) secrecy, with the reasonable assurance that matters not material to the Government's case or to the defense will not be disclosed in connection with the trial of an indictment. If such disclosure is actually necessary it must of course occur, but only with appropriate safeguards taken in the interest of preserving property rights in confidential business information. If the material is claimed to be confidential, and is in fact immaterial, the secrecy policies of Rule 6(e) ought to prevail.

As to the requisite showing that must be made, see In re Grand Jury Proceedings, 851 F.2d 860 (6th Cir.1988).

11. Grand jury transcripts of a federal witness who later testifies at a criminal trial may also be made available to the defendant after the witness has testified for the prosecution on direct examination at trial. Jencks Act, 18 U.S.C. § 3500(e). Federal grand jury testimony must be recorded. Federal Rule Criminal Procedure 6(e).

12. In an unusual situation in which the government released a sentencing memorandum containing secret grand jury information on its internet web site and the press sought access to additional sealed filings containing related grand jury testimony, the court in United States v. Smith, 123 F.3d 140 (3d Cir.1997), held that grand jury secrecy prevailed over first amendment claims.

D. SUBPOENAS

United States v. R. Enterprises, Inc.

Supreme Court of the United States, 1991.
498 U.S. 292, 111 S.Ct. 722.

■ JUSTICE O'CONNOR delivered the opinion of the Court.

This case requires the Court to decide what standards apply when a party seeks to avoid compliance with a subpoena *duces tecum* issued in connection with a grand jury investigation.

I

Since 1986, a federal grand jury sitting in the Eastern District of Virginia has been investigating allegations of interstate transportation of obscene materials. In early 1988, the grand jury issued a series of subpoenas to three companies—Model Magazine Distributors, Inc. (Model), R. Enterprises, Inc., and MFR Court Street Books, Inc. (MFR). Model is a New York distributor of sexually oriented paperback books, magazines, and videotapes. R. Enterprises, which distributes adult materials, and MFR, which sells books, magazines, and videotapes, are also based in New York. All three companies are wholly owned by Martin Rothstein. The grand jury subpoenas sought a variety of corporate books and records and, in Model's case, copies of 193 videotapes that Model had shipped to retailers in the Eastern District of Virginia. All three companies moved to quash the subpoenas, arguing that the subpoenas called for production of materials irrelevant to the grand jury's investigation and that the enforcement of the subpoenas would likely infringe their First Amendment rights.

The District Court, after extensive hearings, denied the motions to quash. * * * [T]he Court of Appeals quashed the business records subpoenas issued to R. Enterprises and MFR. In doing so, it applied the standards set out by this Court in *United States v. Nixon* (1974). The court recognized that *Nixon* dealt with a trial subpoena, not a grand jury subpoena, but determined that the rule was "equally applicable" in the grand jury context. Accordingly, it required the Government to clear the three hurdles that *Nixon* established in the trial context—relevancy, admissibility, and specificity—in order to enforce the grand jury subpoenas. The court concluded that the challenged subpoenas did not satisfy the *Nixon* standards, finding no evidence in the record that either company had ever shipped materials into, or otherwise conducted business in, the Eastern District of Virginia.

* * *

II

The grand jury occupies a unique role in our criminal justice system. It is an investigatory body charged with the responsibility of determining whether or not a crime has been committed. Unlike this Court, whose jurisdiction is predicated on a specific case or controversy, the grand jury "can investigate merely on suspicion that the law is being violated, or even just because it wants assurance that it is not." The function of the grand jury is to inquire into all information that might possibly bear on its investigation until it has identified an offense or has satisfied itself that none has occurred. As a necessary consequence of its investigatory function, the grand jury paints with a broad brush. "A grand jury investigation 'is not fully carried out until every available clue has been run down and all witnesses examined in every proper way to find if a crime has been committed.' "

A grand jury subpoena is thus much different from a subpoena issued in the context of a prospective criminal trial, where a specific offense has been identified and a particular defendant charged. "[T]he identity of the offender, and the precise nature of the offense, if there be one, normally are developed at the conclusion of the grand jury's labors, not at the beginning." In short, the Government cannot be required to justify the issuance of a grand jury subpoena by presenting evidence sufficient to establish probable cause because the very purpose of requesting the information is to ascertain whether probable cause exists.

This Court has emphasized on numerous occasions that many of the rules and restrictions that apply at a trial do not apply in grand jury proceedings. * * * The teaching of the Court's decisions is clear: A grand jury "may compel the production of evidence or the testimony of witnesses as it considers appropriate, and its operation generally is unrestrained by the technical procedural and evidentiary rules governing the conduct of criminal trials."

This guiding principle renders suspect the Court of Appeals' holding that the standards announced in *Nixon* as to subpoenas issued in anticipation of trial apply equally in the grand jury context. The multifactor test announced in *Nixon* would invite procedural delays and detours while courts evaluate the relevancy and admissibility of documents sought by a particular subpoena. We have expressly stated that grand jury proceedings should be free of such delays. "Any holding that would saddle a grand jury with minitrials and preliminary showings would assuredly impede its investigation and frustrate the public's interest in the fair and expeditious administration of the criminal laws." Additionally, application of the *Nixon* test in this context ignores that grand jury proceedings are subject to strict secrecy requirements. Requiring the Government to explain in too much detail the particular reasons underlying a subpoena threatens to compromise "the indispensable secrecy of grand jury proceedings." Broad disclosure also affords the targets of investigation far more information about the grand jury's internal workings than the Rules of Criminal Procedure appear to contemplate.

III

A

The investigatory powers of the grand jury are nevertheless not unlimited. Grand juries are not licensed to engage in arbitrary fishing expeditions, nor may they select targets of investigation out of malice or an intent to harass. In this case, the focus of our inquiry is the limit imposed on a grand jury by Federal Rule of Criminal Procedure 17(c), which governs the issuance of subpoenas *duces tecum* in federal criminal proceedings. The Rule provides that "the court on motion made promptly may quash or modify the subpoena if compliance would be unreasonable or oppressive."

* * *

Our task is to fashion an appropriate standard of reasonableness, one that gives due weight to the difficult position of subpoena recipients but does not impair the strong governmental interests in affording grand juries wide latitude, avoiding minitrials on peripheral matters, and preserving a necessary level of secrecy. We begin by reiterating that the law presumes, absent a strong showing to the contrary, that a grand jury acts within the legitimate scope of its authority.... Consequently, a grand jury subpoena issued through normal channels is presumed to be reasonable, and the burden of showing unreasonableness must be on the recipient who seeks to avoid compliance. Indeed, this result is indicated by the language of Rule 17(c), which permits a subpoena to be quashed only "on motion" and "if *compliance* would be unreasonable". To the extent that the Court of Appeals placed an initial burden on the Government, it committed error. Drawing on the principles articulated above, we conclude that where, as here, a subpoena is challenged on relevancy grounds, the motion to quash must be denied unless the district court determines that there is no reasonable possibility that the category of materials the Government seeks will produce information relevant to the general subject of the grand jury's investigation. Respondents did not challenge the subpoenas as being too indefinite nor did they claim that compliance would be overly burdensome. . . .

B

It seems unlikely, of course, that a challenging party who does not know the general subject matter of the grand jury's investigation, no matter how valid that party's claim, will be able to make the necessary showing that compliance would be unreasonable. After all, a subpoena recipient "cannot put his whole life before the court in order to show that there is no crime to be investigated." Consequently, a court may be justified in a case where unreasonableness is alleged in requiring the Government to reveal the general subject of the grand jury's investigation before requiring the challenging party to carry its burden of persuasion. We need not resolve this question in the present case, however, as there is no doubt that respondents knew the subject of the grand jury investigation pursuant to which the business records subpoenas were issued. In cases where the recipient of the subpoena does not know the nature of the investigation, we are confident that district courts will be able to craft appropriate procedures that balance the interests of the subpoena recipient against the strong governmental interests in maintaining secrecy, preserving investigatory flexibility, and avoiding procedural delays. For example, to ensure that subpoenas are not routinely challenged as a form of discovery, a district court may require that the Government reveal the subject of the investigation to the trial court *in camera*, so that the court may determine whether the motion to quash has a reasonable prospect for success before it discloses the subject matter to the challenging party.

Applying these principles in this case demonstrates that the District Court correctly denied respondents' motions to quash. It is undisputed that all three companies—Model, R. Enterprises, and MFR—are owned by the same person, that all do business in the same area, and that one of the three, Model, has shipped sexually explicit materials into the Eastern District of Virginia. The District Court could have concluded from these facts that there was a reasonable possibility that the business records of R. Enterprises and MFR would produce information relevant to the grand jury's investigation into the interstate transportation of obscene materials. Respondents' blanket denial of any connection to Virginia did not suffice to render the District Court's conclusion invalid. A grand jury need not accept on faith the self-serving assertions of those who may have committed criminal acts. Rather, it is entitled to determine for itself whether a crime has been committed.

* * *

The judgment is reversed insofar as the Court of Appeals quashed the subpoenas issued to R. Enterprises and MFR, and the case is remanded for further proceedings consistent with this opinion.

■ JUSTICE STEVENS, with whom JUSTICES MARSHALL and BLACKMUN join, concurring in part and concurring in the judgment. [OMITTED]

NOTES

1. The grand jury's power to subpoena witnesses derives from its investigative function and its standing as an "arm of the court." Blair v. United States, 250 U.S. 273, 39 S.Ct. 468 (1919). Subpoenas are generally prepared in blank under the seal of the relevant court clerk and filled in by the prosecutor. A subpoena may require testimony (subpoena ad testificandum) or the production of documents (subpoena duces tecum). Testimonial subpoenas may be challenged on privilege grounds, and documentary subpoenas may be contested for privilege, overbreadth or hardship.

2. Because a presumption of regularity attaches to grand jury proceedings, one who attempts to quash or modify a subpoena carries a heavy burden. Thus, objections to testimony based on relevancy, inconvenience, or fear of reprisal have been rejected. See In re Farrell, 611 F.2d 923 (1st Cir.1979) (reprisal); United States v. Weinberg, 439 F.2d 743 (9th Cir.1971) (relevancy of political affiliation).

Likewise, the fact that documents were generated or produced in a "confidential" setting does not necessarily make them privileged from production. In re Grand Jury Subpoena, 148 F.3d 487 (5th Cir.1998).

When a grand jury subpoenas materials that were produced under a protective order in a civil case, which takes priority? Compare In re Grand Jury, 286 F.3d 153 (3d Cir.2002) (a strong but rebuttable presumption in favor of a grand jury subpoena) with In re Grand Jury Subpoena, 62 F.3d 1222 (9th Cir.1995) (grand jury subpoena always prevails) with Martindell v. ITT Corp., 594 F.2d 291 (2d Cir.1979) (In the absence of extraordinary circumstances, a protective order always prevails over a grand jury subpoena).

3. Document subpoenas are subject to a rule of reasonableness. They must request materials that are relevant, specify the materials with reasonable particularity, and be limited to materials encompassing a reasonable period of time. In re Grand Jury Subpoena (Dorokee Co.), 697 F.2d 277 (10th Cir.1983); United States v. Gurule, 437 F.2d 239 (10th Cir.1970). The court may quash or modify the subpoena if compliance would be unreasonable or oppressive. Fed.R.Crim.P. 17(c); In re Grand Jury, 478 F.3d 581 (4th Cir. 2007) (grand jury subpoena of municipal police department's investigative records of inquiry into claims of excessive force properly quashed as unreasonable because it burdened city's ability to preserve confidentiality of its investigations); In re Grand Jury Investigation (General Motors Corp.), 174 F.Supp. 393 (S.D.N.Y.1959). In a motion to quash, the objecting party has the burden of proving overbreadth or unreasonableness. In re Seiffert, 446 F.Supp. 1153 (N.D.N.Y.1978).

4. The fact that a subpoena need not disclose the subject or direction of the investigation, Hale v. Henkel, 201 U.S. 43, 65, 26 S.Ct. 370, 375 (1905), makes it difficult to ascertain the scope of the grand jury's concern. However, because a grand jury cannot investigate matters beyond the jurisdiction of the court, it is conceivable that a subpoena can be quashed when counsel is able to determine that testimony is sought in relation to an area beyond the grand jury's jurisdiction. Compare Brown v. United States, 245 F.2d 549 (8th Cir.1957) (reversal of perjury conviction when grand jury investigating matters that could not have constituted crimes within district) with United States v. Nickels, 502 F.2d 1173 (7th Cir.1974) (perjury conviction upheld although questioning related to matters on which statute of limitations had run).

5. Of course, a grand jury witness may refuse to respond to grand jury inquiries on the basis of his fifth amendment privilege against self-incrimination. Counselman v. Hitchcock, 142 U.S. 547, 12 S.Ct. 195 (1892). However, once the witness invokes the privilege, the prosecutor may continue the examination by seeking information in other areas. In re Grand Jury Subpoena (Samuelson), 739 F.2d 1354 (8th Cir.1984).

The witness seeking the protection of the privilege must establish a valid claim to it by demonstrating that his reliance upon it is not a mere subterfuge. United States v. Rylander, 460 U.S. 752, 103 S.Ct. 1548 (1983); United States v. Edgerton, 734 F.2d 913 (2d Cir.1984).

6. May the government circumvent the need for a search warrant by issuing a "forthwith" subpoena for the production of records while a suspect is in custody? In United States v. Lartey, 716 F.2d 955 (2d Cir.1983), the court held that the government's use of subpoenas requiring production of certain pharmacies' records "forthwith" while defendant was under arrest was entirely lawful. The court reasoned that the federal investigators had substantial reason to believe that the pharmacist was engaged unlawfully in distributing drugs and were motivated by reasonable and good-faith concerns that the pharmacist would attempt to tamper with evidence if given the opportunity.

7. The denial of a motion to quash a subpoena is not a final, appealable order. Thus, ordinarily, a witness will have to refuse to obey the subpoena and be held in contempt in order to obtain the decision of a reviewing court. United States v. Ryan, 402 U.S. 530, 91 S.Ct. 1580 (1971); Cobbledick v. United States, 309 U.S. 323, 60 S.Ct. 540 (1940).

8. When federal regulations govern the circumstances under which a federal official or employee may give testimony, sovereign immunity bars the enforcement of a state grand jury subpoena. In re Elko County Grand Jury, 109 F.3d 554 (9th Cir.1997).

9. When materials are subpoenaed from a third party and the targets of the investigation assert that some of the documents may be privileged, the targets have a right to conduct a privilege review before the documents are submitted to the grand jury. In re Grand Jury Subpoenas, 454 F.3d 511 (6th Cir. 2006).

E. EVIDENCE BEFORE THE GRAND JURY*

1. WARNINGS

United States v. Mandujano

Supreme Court of the United States, 1976.
425 U.S. 564, 96 S.Ct. 1768.

■ MR. CHIEF JUSTICE BURGER announced the judgment of the Court in an opinion in which MR. JUSTICE WHITE, MR. JUSTICE POWELL, and MR. JUSTICE REHNQUIST join.

This case presents the question whether the warnings called for by Miranda v. Arizona, 384 U.S. 436, 86 S.Ct. 1602 (1966), must be given to a grand jury witness who is called to testify about criminal activities in which he may have been personally involved; and whether, absent such warnings, false statements made to the grand jury must be suppressed in a prosecution for perjury based on those statements.

* * *

* A substantial amount of the litigation arising in this context involves fifth amendment issues concerning witness immunity, nontestimonial evidence and the production of books and records.

Under settled principles, the Fifth Amendment does not confer an absolute right to decline to respond in a grand jury inquiry; the privilege does not negate the duty to testify but simply conditions that duty. The privilege cannot, for example, be asserted by a witness to protect others from possible criminal prosecution. Nor can it be invoked simply to protect the witness' interest in privacy. . . .

The very availability of the Fifth Amendment privilege to grand jury witnesses, recognized by this Court in Counselman v. Hitchcock, 142 U.S. 547, 12 S.Ct. 195 (1892), suggests that occasions will often arise when potentially incriminating questions will be asked in the ordinary course of the jury's investigation. Probing questions to all types of witnesses is the stuff that grand jury investigations are made of; the grand jury's mission is, after all, to determine whether to make a presentment or return an indictment. "The basic purpose of the English grand jury was to provide a fair method for instituting criminal proceedings against persons believed to have committed crimes." Costello v. United States, supra, 350 U.S., at 362, 76 S.Ct., at 408.

It is in keeping with the grand jury's historic function as a shield against arbitrary accusations to call before it persons suspected of criminal activity, so that the investigation can be complete. This is true whether the grand jury embarks upon an inquiry focused upon individuals suspected of wrongdoing, or is directed at persons suspected of no misconduct but who may be able to provide links in a chain of evidence relating to criminal conduct of others, or is centered upon broader problems of concern to society. It is entirely appropriate—indeed imperative—to summon individuals who may be able to illuminate the shadowy precincts of corruption and crime. Since the subject matter of the inquiry is crime, and often organized, systematic crime—as is true with drug traffic—it is unrealistic to assume that all of the witnesses capable of providing useful information will be pristine pillars of the community untainted by criminality.

* * *

Accordingly, the witness, though possibly engaged in some criminal enterprise, can be required to answer before a grand jury, so long as there is no compulsion to answer questions that are self-incriminating; the witness can, of course, stand on the privilege, assured that its protection "is as broad as the mischief against which it seeks to guard." Counselman v. Hitchcock, 142 U.S., at 562, 12 S.Ct., at 198. The witness must invoke the privilege, however, as the "Constitution does not forbid the asking of criminative questions." United States v. Monia, 317 U.S., at 433, 63 S.Ct., at 413 (Frankfurter, J., dissenting):

> "The [Fifth] Amendment speaks of compulsion. It does not preclude a witness from testifying voluntarily in matters which may incriminate him. If, therefore, he desires the protection of the privilege, he must claim it or he will not be considered to have been 'compelled' within the meaning of the Amendment."

Absent a claim of the privilege, the duty to give testimony remains absolute.

The stage is therefore set when the question is asked. If the witness interposes his privilege, the grand jury has two choices. If the desired testimony is of marginal value, the grand jury can pursue other avenues of inquiry; if the testimony is thought sufficiently important, the grand jury can seek a judicial determination as to the bona fides of the witness' Fifth Amendment claim, in which case the witness must satisfy the presiding judge that the claim of privilege is not a subterfuge. If in fact " 'there is reasonable ground to apprehend danger to the witness from his being compelled to answer,' " the prosecutor must then determine whether the answer is of such overriding importance as to justify a grant of immunity to the witness.

If immunity is sought by the prosecutor and granted by the presiding judge, the witness can then be compelled to answer, on pain of contempt, even though the testimony would implicate the witness in criminal activity. The reason for this is not hard to divine; Mr. Justice Frankfurter indicated as much in observing that immunity is the *quid pro quo* for securing an answer from the witness: "Immunity displaces the danger." Ullmann v. United States, 350 U.S. 422, 439, 76 S.Ct. 497, 507 (1956).

* * *

In this constitutional process of securing a witness' testimony, perjury simply has no place whatever. Perjured testimony is an obvious and flagrant affront to the basic concepts of judicial proceedings. Effective restraints against this type of egregious offense are therefore imperative. The power of subpoena, broad as it is, and the power of contempt for refusing to answer, drastic as that is—and even the solemnity of the oath—cannot insure truthful answers. Hence, Congress has made the giving of false answers a criminal act punishable by severe penalties; in no other way can criminal conduct be flushed into the open where the law can deal with it.

Similarly, our cases have consistently—indeed without exception—allowed sanctions for false statements or perjury; they have done so even in instances where the perjurer complained that the Government exceeded its constitutional powers in making the inquiry.

* * *

In this case, the Court of Appeals required the suppression of perjured testimony given by respondent, as a witness under oath, lawfully summoned before an investigative grand jury and questioned about matters directly related to the grand jury's inquiry. The court reached this result because the prosecutor failed to give *Miranda* warnings at the outset of Mandujano's interrogation. Those warnings were required, in the Court of Appeals' view, because Mandujano was a "virtual" or "putative" defendant—that is, the prosecutor had specific information concerning Mandujano's participation in an attempted sale of heroin and the focus of the grand jury interrogation, as evidenced by the prosecutor's questions, centered on Mandujano's involvement in narcotics traffic. The fundamental error of the prosecutor, in the court's view, was to treat respondent in such a way as to " 'smack' of entrapment"; as a consequence, the court concluded that "elemental fairness" required the perjured testimony to be suppressed. . . .

The court's analysis, premised upon the prosecutor's failure to give *Miranda* warnings, erroneously applied the standards fashioned by this Court in *Miranda*. Those warnings were aimed at the evils seen by the Court as endemic to police interrogation of a person in custody. *Miranda* addressed extrajudicial confessions or admissions procured in a hostile, unfamiliar environment which lacked procedural safeguards. The decision expressly rested on the privilege against compulsory self-incrimination; the prescribed warnings sought to negate the "compulsion" thought to be inherent in police station interrogation. But the *Miranda* Court simply did not perceive judicial inquiries and custodial interrogation as equivalents: "[T]he compulsion to speak in the isolated setting of the police station may well be greater than in courts or other official investigations, where there are often impartial observers to guard against intimidation or trickery."

The Court thus recognized that many official investigations, such as grand jury questioning, take place in a setting wholly different from custodial police interrogation. Indeed, the Court's opinion in *Miranda* reveals a focus on what was seen by the Court as police "coercion" derived from "factual studies [relating to] police violence and the 'third degree' . . . physical brutality—beating, hanging, whipping—and to sustained and protracted questioning incommunicado in order to extort confessions. . . ." Id., at 445–446, 86 S.Ct., at 1613. To extend these concepts to questioning before a grand jury inquiring into criminal activity under the guidance of a judge is an extravagant expansion never remotely contemplated by this Court in *Miranda*; the dynamics of constitutional interpretation do not compel constant extension of every doctrine announced by the Court.

* * *

The warnings volunteered by the prosecutor to respondent in this case were more than sufficient to inform him of his rights—and his responsibilities—and particularly of the consequences of perjury. To extend the concepts of *Miranda*, as contemplated by the Court of Appeals, would require that the witness be told that there was an absolute right to silence, and obviously any such warning would be incorrect, for there is no such right before a grand jury. Under *Miranda*, a person in police custody has, of course, an absolute right to decline to answer any question, incriminating or innocuous, whereas a grand jury witness, on the contrary, has an absolute duty to answer all questions, subject only to a valid Fifth Amendment claim. And even when the grand jury witness asserts the privilege, questioning need not cease, except as to the particular subject to which the privilege has been addressed. Other lines of inquiry may properly be pursued.

Respondent was also informed that if he desired he could have the assistance of counsel, but that counsel could not be inside the grand jury room. That statement was plainly a correct recital of the law. No criminal proceedings had been instituted against respondent, hence the Sixth Amendment right to counsel had not come into play. A witness "before a grand jury cannot insist, as a matter of constitutional right, on being represented by his counsel. . . ." Under settled principles the witness may not insist upon the presence of his attorney in the grand jury room.

Respondent, by way of further explanation, was also warned that he could be prosecuted for perjury if he testified falsely. Since respondent was already under oath to testify truthfully, this explanation was redundant; it served simply to emphasize the obligation already imposed by the oath.

* * *

In any event, a witness sworn to tell the truth before a duly constituted grand jury will not be heard to call for suppression of false statements made to that jury, any more than would be the case with false testimony before a petit jury or other duly constituted tribunal. In another context, this Court has refused to permit a witness to protect perjured testimony by proving a *Miranda* violation. In Harris v. New York, 401 U.S. 222, 91 S.Ct. 643 (1971), the Court held that notwithstanding a *Miranda* violation:

> "[The Fifth Amendment] privilege cannot be construed to include the right to commit perjury." Id., at 225.

More recently, the Court reaffirmed this salutary principle:

> "[T]he shield provided by *Miranda* is not to be perverted to a license to testify inconsistently, or even perjuriously, free from the risk of confrontation with prior inconsistent utterances." Oregon v. Hass, 420 U.S. 714, 722, 95 S.Ct. 1215, 1221 (1975).

* * *

The judgment of the Court of Appeals is therefore reversed, and the cause is remanded for further proceedings consistent with this opinion.

Reversed and remanded.

■ MR. JUSTICE STEVENS took no part in the consideration or decision of this case.

■ MR. JUSTICE BRENNAN, with whom MR. JUSTICE MARSHALL joins, concurring in the judgment. [OMITTED.]

■ MR. JUSTICE STEWART, with whom MR. JUSTICE BLACKMUN joins, concurring in the judgment. [OMITTED.]

NOTES

1. Only four justices joined in the Court's opinion in *Mandujano*. The other four participating justices concurred on the narrow ground that the failure of the prosecutor to secure an express waiver of Fifth Amendment rights was not a defense to a charge of perjury. Justices Marshall and Brennan specifically indicated that if the prosecution has probable cause to believe that a suspect has committed a crime, it cannot subpoena him before a grand jury, elicit testimony absent a knowing and intelligent waiver (such as would follow from the giving of warnings), and then use such testimony against him later at a trial on the substantive charges on which the grand jury indicted him. *Mandujano* asserts that an appearance before the grand jury is not a custodial situation under *Miranda*. See Chapter 2, Section B. Does the fact that the witness appears under the compulsion of a subpoena contain a custodial element? What about the witness who refuses to comply with a subpoena and is arrested under a material witness warrant and brought to the grand jury?

2. Is the false testimony of a witness subject to suppression when that witness is brought before a grand jury while under investigation for criminal conduct, given no effective warning of the right to silence, and later indicted for perjury? In United States v. Wong, 431 U.S. 174, 97 S.Ct. 1823 (1977), the Court held that the same general considerations applicable to a prospective witness, as identified in *Mandujano*, are applicable to a potential defendant.

3. When the prosecutor has cause to believe that a person has committed a crime, must he warn that person of his potential indictment before the grand jury in order to use the witness' testimony against him in a later trial on a substantive offense? In United States v. Washington, 431 U.S. 181, 97 S.Ct. 1814 (1977), the plurality of the Court held:

> "Because target witness status neither enlarges nor diminishes the constitutional protection against compelled self-incrimination, potential defendant warnings add nothing of value to protection of Fifth Amendment rights."

Consistent with his position in *Mandujano*, Justice Brennan, joined by Justice Marshall, dissented:

> "I would hold that a failure to warn the witness that he is a potential defendant is fatal to an indictment of him when it is made unmistakably to appear, as here, that the grand jury inquiry became an investigation directed against the witness and was pursued with the purpose of compelling him to give self-incriminating testimony upon which to indict him. I would further hold that without such prior warning and the witness' subsequent voluntary waiver of his privilege, there is such gross encroachment upon the witness' privilege as to render worthless the values protected by it unless the self-incriminating testimony is unavailable to the Government for use at any trial brought pursuant to even a valid indictment."

4. Does the *Mandujano–Wong–Washington* trilogy allow the police and the prosecutor to circumvent *Miranda* by bringing a prospective defendant before the grand jury? When the grand jury inquiry is in fact a proceeding against a witness, are there situations in which the encroachment upon the witness' fifth amendment privilege—in the absence of warnings—justify suppression of his testimony? See Newman, The Suspect and the Grand Jury: A Need for Constitutional Protection, 11 U.Rich.L.Rev. 1 (1976); Comment, The Grand Jury Witness' Privilege Against Self–Incrimination, 62 Nw.U.L.Rev. 207, 223 (1967).

5. Although warnings are not constitutionally mandated, the Department of Justice requires warnings to target witnesses as a matter of internal practice. The failure to abide by this practice, however, does not result in error unless the decision to indict was influenced by the failure to give warnings. United States v. Pacheco–Ortiz, 889 F.2d 301 (1st Cir.1989).

6. Does a potential defendant have a right to appear before the grand jury to tell his side of the story and seek to avoid indictment? In United States v. Pabian, 704 F.2d 1533 (11th Cir.1983), the court held that there was no constitutional right to appear before the grand jury when one has not been subpoenaed to do so.

2. HEARSAY

United States v. Brito

United States Court of Appeals, Second Circuit, 1990.
907 F.2d 392.

■ GEORGE C. PRATT, CIRCUIT JUDGE:

Defendants German Salcedo and Vincente Carhuapoma appeal from judgments of conviction entered against them in the United States District

Court for the Southern District of New York ... arising from their participation in narcotics trafficking in New York City.

Among their arguments, defendants claim a misuse of the grand jury process by the office of the United States Attorney for the Southern District of New York. Although this issue is troubling, we affirm the convictions because defendants have suffered no prejudice from the prosecutor's conduct before the grand jury.

* * *

[Defendants] seek reversal and dismissal of their indictments because of prosecutorial misconduct before the grand jury. In particular, Carhuapoma claims that the prosecutor misused the grand jury process ... by obtaining the indictments solely on the basis of hearsay....

Historically, the grand jury has "serve[d] the invaluable function in our society of standing between the accuser and the accused." It "provide[s] a fair method for instituting criminal proceedings against persons believed to have committed crimes", by assembling a group of citizens to assess "the likelihood of prosecutorial success" and to protect the innocent from unwarranted prosecution. Despite the "high place [the grand jury holds] as an instrument of justice", the social costs of dismissing an indictment because of an imperfect grand jury proceeding are simply too high to accept when the defendant has been convicted after a full and fair trial and no harm has been done.

Even so, pursuant to our supervisory power, we may dismiss an indictment for prosecutorial misconduct if the grand jury was misled or misinformed, or possibly if there is "a history of prosecutorial misconduct, spanning several cases, that is so systematic and pervasive as to raise a substantial and serious question about the fundamental fairness of the process".

Carhuapoma asks us to exercise our supervisory power, reverse his conviction, and dismiss his indictment because of prosecutorial misuse of the grand jury, claiming that his indictment was merely one of a series of indictments obtained through the government's policy of using a single witness to testify in grand jury proceedings. In particular, he asserts that his indictment was based solely on hearsay testimony given by an agent having no personal knowledge of the alleged acts; that the grand jury was never clearly informed that the agent's testimony was hearsay; and that the prosecutor, herself, was the "true" witness because the agent's testimony was presented through leading questions. He contends that the single-witness policy undermines the grand jury process, prevents the grand jurors from evaluating the credibility of witnesses and the strength of evidence, and shields the government's trial witnesses from cross examination based on their grand jury testimony.

The government admits to a policy of using a single witness before the grand jury in narcotics cases where the defendant is already under arrest. According to the government, the practice is simply an efficient and effective means of obtaining indictments within the required ten days of arrest, particularly because the Narcotics Special Grand Jury meets only twice a week. Thus, the government explains, the practice of presenting evidence through a single witness, usually the case agent, provides the best information quickly and accurately to the grand jury.

As to Carhuapoma, in particular, the government admits that it presented only hearsay evidence to the grand jury. It explains that the case agent was unavailable to testify at the scheduled time, so another agent, who had worked on the case and had some direct knowledge of Salcedo's participation, was used; that the grand jurors were warned, directly prior to the agent's testimony about Carhuapoma, that his testimony was hearsay; that the agent never represented to the grand jury that he had personal knowledge of Carhuapoma's conduct; and that the prosecutor reminded the grand jury that it could bring in eye witnesses if it so desired.

As we see it, there is a great deal to criticize in the government's handling of this grand jury proceeding. The single-witness policy routinely relies on hearsay, producing " 'evidence' which appears smooth, well integrated and consistent", making even weak cases appear strong. It also "prevents the defendant from utilizing grand jury testimony in cross-examining witnesses who will testify at trial".

Moreover, contrary to the government's own standard practice, it was not the case agent who testified before this grand jury. The agent who did testify had little personal knowledge of the actions of any of the defendants; no good reason was offered for the case agent's absence; and the case agent could not recall why he did not testify. In addition, the prosecutor presented many of the details of the case in the form of leading questions, while the testifying agent merely confirmed those details by answering "yes". Furthermore, prior to presenting the evidence against Carhuapoma, the prosecutor gave questionable instructions to the grand jury: she phrased the hearsay warning about the agent's testimony in the past tense, implying that the forthcoming testimony would not be hearsay; she illustrated the concept of hearsay with the agent's prior testimony, inadvertently vouching for the prior testimony; and she followed a reminder about the grand jury's right to call eye witnesses with a disclaimer that hearsay evidence was "perfectly appropriate", thus diminishing the importance of direct evidence.

We look with disfavor on all of these shortcomings. "We have previously condemned the casual attitude with respect to the presentation of evidence to a grand jury manifested by the decision * * * to rely on testimony of the law enforcement officer who knew least, rather than subject the other officers * * * to some minor inconvenience." Moreover, leading questions tend to mute one of the chief functions of the grand jury, the evaluation of the strength of the evidence and the credibility of witnesses. And careless instructions, such as those given here, tend to hamper the grand jury's understanding of the importance of evaluating the reliability of the evidence and to discourage it from demanding eye witness testimony.

Such an ill-planned presentation raises concerns that the United States Attorney's Office may again be leaning toward a casual, "anything goes", attitude with respect to grand jury proceedings. Finally, although the single-witness policy provides an efficient means for obtaining indictments in our overcrowded criminal justice system, we must be wary that we do not exalt expedience at the expense of fundamental fairness nor abandon the virtues of the grand jury process to the unreviewed control of the prosecutor.

Despite these failings, however, we cannot conclude at this time either that the single-witness policy constitutes such "systematic and pervasive" prosecutorial misconduct as would undermine fundamental fairness, or that the rights of either defendant were violated before the grand jury. The testifying agent did establish that his testimony about Carhuapoma and Salcedo was derived from conversations with other agents and from a review of the case file; the prosecutor did warn the grand jurors, however clumsily, about the hearsay nature of the agent's testimony; and most importantly, the agent's testimony to the grand jury was concededly accurate. Thus, we cannot say that the grand jury was misinformed or misled in this case, or that there was prejudice to the defendants, who were convicted after a full and fair trial. We therefore—not with great enthusiasm—decline to exercise our supervisory power in this case.

* * *

The judgments of conviction are affirmed.

NOTES

1. Almost two decades before *Brito*, in United States v. Estepa, 471 F.2d 1132 (2d Cir.1972), the court reversed a conviction and ordered dismissal of an indictment for the exclusive reliance on hearsay in the grand jury:

> The many opinions in which we have affirmed convictions despite the Government's needless reliance on hearsay before the grand jury show how loathe we have been to open up a new road for attacking convictions on grounds unrelated to the merits. We have been willing to allow ample, many doubtless think too ample, latitude in the needless use of hearsay, subject to only two provisos—that the prosecutor does not deceive grand jurors as to "the shoddy merchandise they are getting so they can seek something better if they wish," or that the case does not involve "a high probability that with eyewitness rather than hearsay testimony the grand jury would not have indicted." We had hoped that, with the clear warnings we have given to prosecutors, going back to . . . 1966, and the assurances given by United States Attorneys, a reversal for improper use of hearsay before the grand jury would not be required. Here the Assistant United States Attorney, whether wittingly or unwittingly—we prefer to think the latter, clearly violated the first of these provisos. We cannot, with proper respect for the discharge of our duties, content ourselves with yet another admonition; a reversal with instructions to dismiss the indictment may help to translate the assurances of the United States Attorneys into consistent performance by their assistants.

However, *Estepa* was either rejected outright, United States v. Barone, 584 F.2d 118 (6th Cir.1978), or limited to situations in which the prosecutor uses hearsay to deliberately deceive the grand jury or the circumstances show a high probability that the defendant would not have been indicted if eyewitness, rather than hearsay testimony, had been used. United States v. Diaz, 922 F.2d 998 (2d Cir.1990).

2. A prosecutor who provides the grand jury with nothing but hearsay evidence may have a number of reasons for so doing. He may desire to protect his witness from potential impeachment resulting from disclosure of a transcript of the witnesses' grand jury testimony when the case goes to trial. He may not have had sufficient time to develop—or find evidence to corroborate—the details of the witnesses' testimony at the grand jury stage. He may want to save the taxpayers the expense of bringing in witnesses from distant locations. He may simply want to refrain from imposing a burden on the witness who would otherwise have to miss work, come "downtown", and appear before the grand jury. Are any of these reasons sufficient to justify the exclusive use of hearsay? See Patterson, The Prosecutor's Unnecessary Use of Hearsay Evidence Before the Grand Jury, 61 Wash.U.L.Q. 191 (1983).

3. ILLEGALLY SEIZED EVIDENCE

United States v. Calandra

Supreme Court of the United States, 1974.
414 U.S. 338, 94 S.Ct. 613.

[The opinion in this case, which should be reviewed here, appears in Chapter 6, Section D, supra.]

NOTES

1. *Calandra* built upon a trilogy of earlier decisions. See United States v. Blue, 384 U.S. 251, 86 S.Ct. 1416 (1966) (indictment sustained notwithstanding compelled testimony); Lawn v. United States, 355 U.S. 339, 78 S.Ct. 311 (1958) (defendant not entitled to hearing on whether evidence before grand jury was unconstitutionally obtained); Costello v. United States, 350 U.S. 359, 76 S.Ct. 406 (1956) (hearsay before grand jury is acceptable). These cases, taken together, stand for the proposition that "[a]n indictment valid on its face cannot be challenged merely because the grand jury acted on inadequate or incompetent evidence." United States v. Morano, 697 F.2d 923, 927 (11th Cir.1983).

2. In United States v. Short, 671 F.2d 178 (6th Cir.1982), the court explained the rationale for refusing to look behind the indictment:

> Any other rule would wreak havoc, particularly in conspiracy cases. The element of agreement, which the district court found totally unsupported by the evidence before the grand jury, is nearly always established by circumstantial evidence, as conspirators seldom make records of their illegal agreements. Since direct proof of this element is usually lacking, a decision on whether it has been supplied by circumstantial evidence or permissible inferences requires an examination of all the evidence and a determination of what inferences may properly be drawn. In effect, an extensive "mini-trial" would be required in response to any motion to dismiss a conspiracy indictment on the ground relied upon by the district court in this case. Not only would such proceedings be wasteful of judicial resources; they would be contrary to the underlying assumptions of the constitutional requirement that serious criminal charges be based on a grand jury presentment or indictment. One assumption is that a grand jury will be concerned with the rights of those who may be charged with crimes as well as with determining what offenses have been committed. When a body of citizens, properly chosen and constituted as a grand jury, finds probable cause to believe that a crime has been committed within its

jurisdiction, that finding is sufficient to require a trial. The indictment is not evidence, as every petit jury in a criminal case is instructed. The prosecution must still produce evidence from which the trial jury can find every element of the offense proven beyond a reasonable doubt, or the defendant is entitled to a judgment of acquittal. However, the prosecution's evidence is tested at trial, not in a preliminary proceeding.

3. Nonetheless, there are occasional decisions in which the indictment will be dismissed because there was insufficient or improper evidence before the grand jury. See United States v. DiBernardo, 561 F.Supp. 783 (S.D.Fla.1983) (indictment tainted by FBI agent's psychological problems which cast doubt on his ability to testify truthfully); United States v. O'Shea, 447 F.Supp. 330 (S.D.Fla.1978) (no evidence, competent or otherwise, before grand jury).

4. The legislature, by statute, can avoid the effect of *Calandra* and prohibit the use of illegally seized evidence before the grand jury. The federal wire tapping statute contains a provision which the Supreme Court has construed to prohibit punishment for contempt of a witness who defends his refusal to respond to questions by asserting that the questions are the product of a violation of the rights of the witness to be free from unlawful wiretaps.

In Gelbard v. United States, 408 U.S. 41, 92 S.Ct. 2357 (1972), the Court considered the right of a grand jury witness to invoke this prohibition:

> "The purposes of [the statute] as a whole would be subverted were the plain command of [this section] ignored when the victim of an illegal interception is called as a witness before a grand jury and asked questions based upon that interception.... Contrary to the Government's assertion that the invasion of privacy is over and done with, to compel the testimony of these witnesses compounds the statutorily proscribed invasion of their privacy by adding to the injury of the interception the insult of compelled disclosure.... Hence, if the prohibition of [the section] is not available as a defense to the contempt charge, disclosure through compelled testimony makes the witness the victim, once again, of a federal crime. Finally, recognition of [the section] as a defense "relieves judges of the anomalous duty of finding a person in civil contempt for failing to cooperate with the prosecutor in a course of conduct which, if pursued unchecked, could subject the prosecutor himself to heavy civil and criminal penalties."

* * *

In their dissent in *Gelbard*, Chief Justice Burger and Justices Rehnquist, Blackmun, and Powell, had this to say:

> [W]hat was presented to the trial court in this proceeding was not a neatly stipulated question of law, but a demand by the petitioners that they be permitted to roam at will among the prosecutor's records in order to see whether they might be able to turn up any evidence indicating that the Government's overhearing of their conversations had been unauthorized by statute. In order to determine whether this particular type of remedy is open to these petitioners at this particular stage of potential criminal proceedings it is not enough to recite, as the Court does, that [the statute] prohibits the use of illegally overheard wire communications before grand juries as well as before other governmental bodies. This proposition is not disputed. The far more difficult inquiry posed by these facts is whether the granting to these petitioners at this particular stage of these proceedings of

> sweeping discovery as a prelude to a full hearing on the issue of alleged unlawful surveillance can fairly be inferred from the enactment....
>
> * * *
>
> It seems to me to be clear beyond cavil from [our prior decisions] that prior to the enactment of the Omnibus Crime and Safe Streets Act of 1968, a hearing such as that which the Court awards these petitioners was not only unauthorized by law, but completely contrary to the ingrained principles which have long governed the functioning of the grand jury.

5. *Gelbard* does not hold that a target defendant can enjoin the government from presenting evidence to the grand jury through the testimony of government agents or other witnesses even though such testimony was derived from a violation of the target's right to be free of unlawful wiretaps. Nor does it hold that an indictment based upon evidence derived from a violation of the accused's rights must be dismissed. These issues are analytically distinct. See Chapter 6, Section D, note 1, supra. Congress could have prohibited grand jury use of the fruits of illegal wiretaps. Whether it did so, however, would turn upon an interpretation of statutory provisions other than those upon which the *Gelbard* decision vacated the contempt finding.

4. ATTORNEYS

Ralls v. United States

United States Court of Appeals, Ninth Circuit, 1995.
52 F.3d 223.

■ CHOY, CIRCUIT JUDGE:

Stephen Ralls, Esq. ("Ralls"), a criminal defense attorney, appeals the district court's order denying in part his motion to quash a grand jury subpoena which required him to provide information regarding a client/fee-payer. Ralls also appeals from the district court's order holding him in contempt for failure to provide information pursuant to court orders.

* * *

Ralls was paid by a client/fee-payer to represent Philip Bonnette ("Bonnette") at his initial court appearance and at his detention hearing. Bonnette was arrested with another individual named Victor Tarrazon–Orduno ("Tarrazon") in connection with their attempt to transport approximately 300 pounds of cocaine from Arizona to California. The Government later issued a grand jury subpoena to Ralls, seeking to discover the name of the person who hired Ralls, the amount of money paid, method of payment, the existence of any retainer agreement, and conversations with the fee-payer. Ralls moved to quash the subpoena. The district court ordered Ralls to testify regarding the fee-payer's identity and the fee arrangements, but concluded that all conversations between Ralls and the fee-payer were privileged.

* * *

Generally, the attorney-client privilege does not safeguard against the disclosure of either the identity of the fee-payer or the fee arrangement. This is so because the attorney-client privilege applies only to confidential professional communications, and the payment of fees is usually incidental to the attorney-client relationship. However, a narrow exception to the general rule of disclosure [has been stated as follows:]

> An attorney may invoke the privilege to protect the identity of a client or information regarding a client's fee arrangements if disclosure would "convey[] information which ordinarily would be conceded to be part of the usual privileged communication between attorney and client."

The application of the privilege is not triggered by the fact that the disclosure of the fee-payer's identity and the fee arrangements may incriminate the fee-payer. Rather, the privilege is invoked where disclosure of the fee-payer/client identity and the fee information would infringe upon a privileged communication.

The Fifth Circuit has held that "[i]f the disclosure of the client's identity will also reveal the confidential purpose for which he consulted an attorney, we protect both the confidential communication and the client's identity as privileged." Likewise, the Seventh Circuit has stated, "[It is a] well-supported proposition that where disclosure of the unknown client would, in effect, reveal the client's motive for seeking legal advice, the privilege precludes disclosure." Both courts found significant the fact that the fee-payers had already admitted, to the subpoenaed attorneys, their involvement in the crime for which the defendants had been charged.

In contrast, the attorney-client relationship does not exist where the attorney acts as a mere conduit for the transfer of money. * * * [As the Second Circuit has observed:]

> The rule governing the unprivileged nature of client identification implicitly accepts the fact that a client might retain or consult an attorney for numerous reasons. Thus, the fact that disclosure of [the client/fee-payer's identity] might suggest the possibility of wrongdoing on his or her part does not affect analysis of whether disclosure would reveal a confidential communication.

* * *

The district court failed to apply the correct test which is whether the fee-payer's identity and the fee arrangements are so intertwined with confidential communications that revealing either the identity or the arrangements would be tantamount to revealing a privileged communication.

An examination of Ralls' sealed affidavit, leaves no doubt that the fee arrangements and the fee-payer's identity are inextricably intertwined with confidential communications and fall within the attorney-client privilege. The fee-payer sought Ralls' advice regarding his involvement in the crime for which Bonnette was arrested. Further, the fee-payer paid for Bonnette's legal fees in the very same matter which gave rise to the attorney-client relationship. "In effect, therefore, disclosure of the [fee-payer's] identity would expose the substance of a confidential communication between the attorney and the [fee-payer]."

* * *

We find that the fee-payer's identity and the fee arrangements are so intertwined with attorney-client communications that they are therefore privileged. In the interest of judicial economy, we rule that the subpoena be quashed in its entirety rather than remanding the matter to the district court.

The Government argues that there was a clear conflict of interest in Ralls' representation of both Bonnette and the fee-payer and argues that this conflict prevented the formation of an attorney-client relationship between the fee-payer and Ralls. The Government's argument is not persuasive. First, there is no evidence to indicate the existence of an actual conflict of interest. We take notice of the fact that Ralls' representation of Bonnette was limited to Bonnette's initial appearance and his detention hearing. Even if an actual conflict of interest exists, however, the proper course of action for the district court is to bar Ralls from representation.

* * *

Ralls' sealed affidavit clearly establishes that he had an attorney-client relationship with the fee-payer and that the identity of the fee-payer and the fee arrangements are inextricably intertwined with privileged communications. Therefore, the fee information is privileged, and Ralls cannot be forced to testify regarding such information. We order that the grand jury subpoena be quashed in its entirety and reverse the district court's order holding Ralls in contempt.

NOTES

1. In United States v. Zolin, 491 U.S. 554, 109 S.Ct. 2619 (1989), the Court recognized that "the purpose of the crime-fraud exception to the attorney-client privilege [is] to assure that the seal of secrecy between lawyer and client does not extend to communications made for the purpose of getting advice for the commission of a fraud or crime." Determining that allegedly privileged materials may be reviewed in camera by the trial judge to determine whether they are subject to the crime-fraud exception, the Court declared:

> We hold that in camera review may be used to determine whether allegedly privileged attorney-client communications fall within the crime-fraud exception. We further hold, however, that before a district court may engage in in camera review at the request of the party opposing the privilege, that party must present evidence sufficient to support a reasonable belief that in camera review may yield evidence that establishes the exception's applicability. Finally, we hold that the threshold showing to obtain in camera review may be met by using any relevant evidence, lawfully obtained, that has not been adjudicated to be privileged.

See also In re Grand Jury Proceedings, 492 F.3d 976 (8th Cir. 2007) (although the crime-fraud exception prevents a client from invoking the attorney-client and work product privileges, an attorney who is not complicit in his client's wrongdoing may assert the work product privilege with respect to his opinion work product); In re Grand Jury Investigation, 445 F.3d 266 (3d Cir. 2006) (crime-fraud exception required attorney to testify to conversation with client regarding grand jury subpoena when, notwithstanding the lack of impropriety on the part of counsel, certain e-mails called for by the subpoena were deleted); United States v. Doe, 429 F.3d 450 (3d Cir. 2005) (the standard for applying the crime fraud exception is whether the client sought legal counsel to further a crime, not whether the consultation assisted the client's illegal conduct);

2. When an attorney receives a grand jury subpoena for documents which the client has otherwise disclosed, the privilege will be deemed to have been waived. See In re Sealed Case, 877 F.2d 976 (D.C.Cir.1989) (disclosure of memorandum in context of defense contract audit); In re Grand Jury Proceedings Subpoena to Testify to Wine, 841 F.2d 230 (8th Cir.1988) (disclosure to bank).

3. The attorney-client privilege, as a defense to compliance with a grand jury subpoena, appears to be limited to those situations in which "the person invoking the privilege can show that a strong probability exists that disclosure of such information would implicate that client in the very criminal activity for which legal advice was sought." United States v. Hodge, 548 F.2d 1347 (9th Cir.1977).

4. The "last link" doctrine prevents an attorney from disclosing a client's identity if disclosure would be the final step in the chain of evidence to indict or prosecute that client. United States v. Gray, 876 F.2d 1411, 1415–16 (9th Cir.1989). However, the application of the "last link" doctrine has been limited to situations where disclosure of the fee-payer's identity would be tantamount to disclosure of a privileged communication. Alexiou v. United States, 39 F.3d 973 (9th Cir.1994) (the court analyzed whether the communication was privileged in order to determine that the last link exception did not apply). Therefore, the decision of whether the last link doctrine applies turns on the court's ruling on whether the attorney-client privilege prevents the disclosure of the fee-payer's identity and fee arrangements.

5. The "least intrusive means" doctrine requires the government to first exhaust all of its investigatory powers before "[it is] permitted to compel witness-attorneys to testify before a grand jury regarding matters which could be considered to be protected by the attorney-client privilege." In re Witness–Attorney Before Grand Jury No. 83–1, 613 F.Supp. 394, 398 (S.D.Fla.1984). The "least intrusive means" doctrine, however, has not gained acceptance. In United States v. Perry, 857 F.2d 1346, 1348 (9th Cir.1988), the court firmly refused to require the government to make a preindictment, preliminary showing of need before issuing a grand jury subpoena to an attorney-witness. See also In re Grand Jury Proceeding (Schofield), 721 F.2d 1221, 1222 (9th Cir.1983).

6. The fact that a law firm has provided client materials to the grand jury does not insulate them from producing the same materials in civil discovery. See In re Sunrise Securities Litigation, 130 F.R.D. 560 (E.D.Pa.1989) (rejecting claim that a "grand jury privilege" imposed an obligation of secrecy on the law firm).

7. In United States v. Edgar, 82 F.3d 499 (1st Cir.1996), defendant contended that his indictment was tainted by his business attorney's grand jury appearance. Although rejecting the contention on the facts, the court established methods to protect the attorney-client privilege:

> There may be an implicit threat to the attorney called to testify about a client to the grand jury that the attorney will become a target himself should the prosecutor think he knowingly participated in the fraud. This is particularly so where the prosecution asserts that the privilege must give way to the crime-fraud exception. The lawyer may be tempted to reveal privileged conversations in order to avoid becoming a target himself. Ideally, counsel receiving a subpoena will give notice to a client and consistently assert the privilege on behalf of a client. Ideally, a prosecutor faced with an assertion of privilege by an attorney witness will seek a judicial determination of whether the privilege is valid. But we do not live in an ideal world. We are loath to say the prosecutor here crossed over the line. But we are equally loath to say, as the government urges, that there is

no line and there is never a remedy. The first line of defense to protect [defendant's] privilege lay in the hands of his lawyer. A lawyer has an obligation not to reveal client confidences. A lawyer also has an obligation to assert privilege on behalf of a client. Generally, an attorney has an obligation to assert the privilege on behalf of the client and not to disclose confidential information until there is a judicial determination that there is no privilege. Even if there is an assertion that there is no privilege because the crime-fraud exception applies, the attorney is required to give notice to the client. If the attorney violates these duties, he is at risk at least of a malpractice suit and of professional discipline. For example, if a witness invokes the privilege against self-incrimination, the prosecutor should cease questioning as to the particular subject to which the privilege was addressed. Thus, the second line of defense is that the prosecutor will not harangue a witness, but will promptly bring the issue to a court.

The third line of defense is that there will ultimately be a disinterested judicial determination of the issue. * * * The government may obtain in camera review of the information alleged to be privileged, at the discretion of the court, upon a " 'showing of a factual basis adequate to support a good faith belief by a reasonable person' ... that in camera review of the materials may reveal evidence to establish the claim that the crime-fraud exception applies."

See also In re Grand Jury Proceedings, 43 F.3d 966 (5th Cir.1994) (reversing an order directing two attorneys to comply with a subpoena issued by a grand jury and remanding with instructions to determine whether the government could establish the requisite need to overcome the work product privilege).

8. For various proposed solutions to the problems engendered by subpoenas directed to attorneys, see Stern & Hoffman, Privileged Informers: The Attorney Subpoena Problem and a Proposal for Reform, 136 U.Pa.L.Rev. 1783 (1989); Comment, Attorney Subpoenas: The Dilemma Over a Preliminary Showing Requirement, 1991 U.Ill.L.Rev. 137.

9. An attorney is not required to reveal the identity of who is paying his fee when disclosure would reveal a client's motive for seeking legal advice. In re Subpoenaed Grand Jury Witness, 171 F.3d 511 (7th Cir.1999). Likewise, it is improper to order an attorney to testify about her missing client's understanding of his trial date. In re Grand Jury Subpoena, 425 F.3d 1221 (9th Cir. 2005).

5. EXCULPATORY EVIDENCE

United States v. Williams

Supreme Court of the United States, 1992.
504 U.S. 36, 112 S.Ct. 1735.

■ JUSTICE SCALIA delivered the opinion of the Court.

The question presented in this case is whether a district court may dismiss an otherwise valid indictment because the Government failed to disclose to the grand jury "substantial exculpatory evidence" in its possession.

* * *

Respondent does not contend that the Fifth Amendment itself obliges the prosecutor to disclose substantial exculpatory evidence in his possession to the grand jury. Instead, building on our statement that the federal courts "may, within limits, formulate procedural rules not specifically required by the Constitution of the Congress," he argues that imposition of the ... disclosure rule is supported by the courts' "supervisory power." ... That power has been applied not only to improve the truth-finding process of the trial, but also to prevent parties from reaping benefit or incurring harm from violations of substantive or procedural rules (imposed by the Constitution or laws) governing matters apart from the trial itself. Thus, *Bank of Nova Scotia v. United States* (1988), makes clear that the supervisory power can be used to dismiss an indictment because of misconduct before the grand jury, at least where that misconduct amounts to a violation of one of those "few, clear rules which were carefully drafted and approved by this Court and by Congress to ensure the integrity of the grand jury's functions."

We did not hold in *Bank of Nova Scotia*, however, that the courts' supervisory power could be used, not merely as a means of enforcing or vindicating legally compelled standards of prosecutorial conduct before the grand jury, but as a means of *prescribing* those standards of prosecutorial conduct in the first instance—just as it may be used as a means of establishing standards of prosecutorial conduct before the courts themselves. It is this latter exercise that respondent demands. Because the grand jury is an institution separate from the courts, over whose functioning the courts do not preside, we think it clear that, as a general matter at least, no such "supervisory" judicial authority exists....

* * *

The grand jury's functional independence from the judicial branch is evident both in the scope of its power to investigate criminal wrongdoing, and in the manner in which that power is exercised. "Unlike [a] [c]ourt, whose jurisdiction is predicated upon a specific case or controversy, the grand jury 'can investigate merely on suspicion that the law is being violated, or even because it wants assurance that it is not.' " It need not identify the offender it suspects, or even "the precise nature of the offense" it is investigating. The grand jury requires no authorization from its constituting court to initiate an investigation, nor does the prosecutor require leave of court to seek a grand jury indictment. And in its day-to-day functioning, the grand jury generally operates without the interference of a presiding judge. It swears in its own witnesses, and deliberates in total secrecy.

Given the grand jury's operational separateness from its constituting court, it should come as no surprise that we have been reluctant to invoke the judicial supervisory power as a basis for prescribing modes of grand jury procedure. Over the years, we have received many requests to exercise supervision over the grand jury's evidence-taking process, but we have refused them all, including some more appealing than the one presented today. In *Calandra v. United States* (1974), a grand jury witness faced questions that were allegedly based upon physical evidence the Government had obtained through a violation of the Fourth Amendment; we rejected the proposal that the exclusionary rule be extended to grand jury proceedings, because of "the potential injury to the historic role and functions of the grand jury." In *Costello v. United States* (1956), we declined to enforce the hearsay rule in grand jury proceedings, since that "would run counter to the whole history of the grand jury institution, in which laymen conduct their inquiries unfettered by technical rules."

These authorities suggest that any power federal courts may have to fashion, on their own initiative, rules of grand jury procedure is a very limited one, not remotely comparable to the power they maintain over their own proceedings. It certainly would not permit judicial reshaping of the grand jury institution, substantially altering the traditional relationships between the prosecutor, the constituting court, and the grand jury itself.

* * *

Respondent makes a generalized appeal to functional notions: Judicial supervision of the quantity and quality of the evidence relied upon by the grand jury plainly facilitates, he says, the grand jury's performance of its twin historical responsibilities, *i.e.*, bringing to trial those who may be justly accused and shielding the innocent from unfounded accusation and prosecution. We do not agree. The rule would neither preserve nor enhance the traditional functioning of the institution that the Fifth Amendment demands. To the contrary, requiring the prosecutor to present exculpatory as well as inculpatory evidence would alter the grand jury's historical role, transforming it from an accusatory to an adjudicatory body.

It is axiomatic that the grand jury sits not to determine guilt or innocence, but to assess whether there is adequate basis for bringing a criminal charge. That has always been so; and to make the assessment it has always been thought sufficient to hear only the prosecutor's side. As Blackstone described the prevailing practice in 18th-century England, the grand jury was "only to hear evidence on behalf of the prosecution[,] for the finding of an indictment is only in the nature of an enquiry or accusation, which is afterwards to be tried and determined." 4 W. Blackstone, Commentaries 300 (1769). So also in the United States. According to the description of an early American court, three years before the Fifth Amendment was ratified, it is the grand jury's function not "to enquire ... upon what foundation [the charge may be] denied," or otherwise to try the suspect's defenses, but only to examine "upon what foundation [the charge] is made" by the prosecutor. *Respublica v. Shaffer*, 1 U.S. (1 Dall.) 236, 1 L.Ed. 116 (Philadelphia Oyer and Terminer 1788). As a consequence, neither in this country nor in England has the suspect under investigation by the grand jury ever been thought to have a right to testify, or to have exculpatory evidence presented.

Imposing upon the prosecutor a legal obligation to present exculpatory evidence in his possession would be incompatible with this system. If a "balanced" assessment of the entire matter is the objective, surely the first thing to be done—rather than requiring the prosecutor to say what he knows in defense of the target of the investigation—is to entitle the target to tender his own defense. To require the former while denying (as we do) the latter would be quite absurd. It would also be quite pointless, since it would merely invite the target to circumnavigate the system by delivering his exculpatory evidence to the prosecutor, whereupon it would *have* to be passed on to the grand jury—unless the prosecutor is willing to take the chance that a court will not deem the evidence important enough to qualify for mandatory disclosure.

* * *

There is yet another respect in which respondent's proposal not only fails to comport with, but positively contradicts, the "common law" of the Fifth Amendment grand jury. Motions to quash indictments based upon the sufficiency of the evidence relied upon by the grand jury were unheard of at common law. . . .

* * *

It would make little sense, we think, to abstain from reviewing the evidentiary support for the grand jury's judgment while scrutinizing the sufficiency of the prosecutor's presentation. A complaint about the quality or adequacy of the evidence can always be recast as a complaint that the prosecutor's presentation was "incomplete" or "misleading." Our words in *Costello* bear repeating: Review of facially valid indictments on such grounds "would run counter to the whole history of the grand jury institution[,] [and] [n]either justice nor the concept of a fair trial requires [it]."

* * *

The judgment of the Court of Appeals is accordingly reversed and the cause remanded for further proceedings consistent with this opinion.

So ordered.

■ JUSTICE STEVENS, with whom JUSTICE BLACKMUN, JUSTICE O'CONNOR and JUSTICE THOMAS join.

* * *

In an opinion that I find difficult to comprehend, the Court today . . . seems to suggest that the court has no authority to supervise the conduct of the prosecutor in grand jury proceedings so long as he follows the dictates of the Constitution, applicable statutes, and Rule 6 of the Federal Rules of Criminal Procedure. The Court purports to support this conclusion by invoking the doctrine of separation of powers and citing a string of cases in which we have declined to impose categorical restraints on the grand jury. Needless to say, the Court's reasoning is unpersuasive.

Although the grand jury has not been "textually assigned" to "any of the branches described in the first three Articles" of the Constitution, it is not an autonomous body completely beyond the reach of the other branches. Throughout its life, from the moment it is convened until it is discharged, the grand jury subject to the control of the court.

* * *

Although the Court recognizes that it may invoke its supervisory authority to fashion and enforce privilege rules applicable in grand jury proceedings, and suggests that it may also invoke its supervisory authority to fashion other limited rules of grand jury procedure, it concludes that it has no authority to "*prescrib[e]* standards of prosecutorial conduct before the grand jury," *ante*, at 1741, because that would alter the grand jury's historic role as an independent, inquisitorial institution. I disagree.

We do not protect the integrity and independence of the grand jury by closing our eyes to the countless forms of prosecutorial misconduct that may occur inside the secrecy of the grand jury room. After all, the grand jury is not merely an investigatory body; it also serves as a "protector of citizens against arbitrary and oppressive governmental action."

* * *

It blinks reality to say that the grand jury can adequately perform this important historic role if it is intentionally misled by the prosecutor—on whose knowledge of the law and facts of the underlying criminal investigation the jurors will, of necessity, rely.

Unlike the Court, I am unwilling to hold that countless forms of prosecutorial misconduct must be tolerated—no matter how prejudicial they may be, or how seriously they may distort the legitimate function of the grand jury—simply because they are not proscribed by Rule 6 of the Federal Rules of Criminal Procedure or a statute that is applicable in grand jury proceedings. Such a sharp break with the traditional role of the federal judiciary is unprecedented, unwarranted, and unwise. Unrestrained prosecutorial misconduct in grand jury proceedings is inconsistent with the administration of justice in the federal courts and should be redressed in appropriate cases by the dismissal of indictments obtained by improper methods.

NOTES

1. The Williams decision has been the subject of significant criticism. See Mastrian, "Indianhead Poker in the Grand jury Room: Prosecutorial Suppression of Exculpatory Evidence," 28 Val.U.L.Rev. 1377, 1379 (1994); Bernstein, "Behind the Gray Door: Williams, Secrecy, and the Federal Grand Jury," 69 N.Y.U.L.Rev. 563, 587–591 (1994); McKendree, "United States v. Williams: Antonin's Costello—How the Grand Jury Lost the Aid of the Courts as a Check on Prosecutorial Misconduct," 37 How.L.J. 49, 81 (1993).

2. Some states have adopted a broad rule requiring a prosecutor to inform the grand jury of exculpatory evidence. See Mont.Code Ann. § 46–11–314 (requiring production of "exculpatory evidence" that will "explain away the charge"); Lay v. State, 110 Nev. 1189, 886 P.2d 448 (1994) (requiring production of exculpatory evidence that will "explain away the charge"); State v. Sandoval, 842 S.W.2d 782 (Tex.App.1992) (noting that justice would best be served by production of any information that could affect grand jury's decision whether to indict). But see Schuster v. Eighth Judicial District Court, 160 P.3d 873 (Nev. S.Ct. 2007) (statute requiring submission of known exculpatory evidence to grand jury does not mandate that the prosecutor instruct the jurors as to how the evidence is legally significant).

3. Other states require exculpatory evidence to be presented to a grand jury only if the exculpatory value of the evidence is substantial. See N.M.Stat.Ann. § 31–6–11(B) (requiring presentation of evidence that directly negates guilt of accused); Commonwealth v. LaVelle, 414 Mass. 146, 605 N.E.2d 852, 855 (1993) (evidence that would greatly undermine credibility of evidence likely to affect grand jury's decision to indict); People v. Ramjit, 203 A.D.2d 488, 612 N.Y.S.2d 600 (1994) (evidence that implicates complete legal defense or could eliminate needless or unfounded prosecution).

4. In State v. Hogan, 144 N.J. 216, 676 A.2d 533 (1996), the court rejected *Williams* and imposed what it described as "a limited duty on prosecutors, a duty that is triggered only in the rare case in which the prosecutor is informed of evidence that both directly negates the guild of the accused and is clearly exculpatory.... [T]he prosecutor's duty arises only if the evidence satisfies two requirements: it must directly negate guilt and also be clearly exculpatory." The court explained as follows:

> Confining the prosecutor's duty to the presentation of evidence that directly negates the guilt of the accused recognizes that the sole issue before the grand jury is whether the State has made out a prima facie case of the accused's guilt. Thus, unless the exculpatory evidence at issue squarely refutes an element of the crime in question, that evidence is not within the prosecutorial duty we have set forth. For example, the State is not required to inform the grand jury of evidence that indicates that the accused did not have a motive for committing the crime for which the State seeks an indictment. Similarly, the State need not impeach the credibility of the State's witnesses appearing before the grand jury by informing the grand jury of the witnesses' criminal records.
>
> The second requirement, that the evidence in question be "clearly exculpatory," requires an evaluation of the quality and reliability of the evidence. The exculpatory value of the evidence should be analyzed in the context of the nature and source of the evidence, and the strength of the State's case. For example, if the exculpatory evidence in question is eyewitness testimony, potential bias on the part of the eyewitness may affect the prosecutor's obligation to present the witness's testimony to the grand jury. Similarly, the exculpatory testimony of one eyewitness is not "clearly exculpatory" if contradicted by the incriminating testimony of a number of other witnesses. Moreover, an accused's self-serving statement denying involvement in a crime, although such a statement directly negates guilt, ordinarily would not be sufficiently credible to be "clearly exculpatory" and need not be revealed to the grand jury.
>
> On the other hand, the credible testimony of a reliable, unbiased alibi witness that demonstrates that the accused could not have committed the crime in question would be clearly exculpatory. Similarly, physical evidence of unquestioned reliability demonstrating that the defendant did not commit the alleged crime would be clearly exculpatory, and the grand jury should be informed of such evidence. In such instances, a failure to present the exculpatory evidence to the grand jury may raise questions about the prosecuting attorney's good faith, and could deprive the grand jury of the opportunity to screen out unwarranted prosecutions.
>
> We note, however, that the prosecutor need not construct a case for the accused, or search for evidence that would exculpate the accused. Only when the prosecuting attorney has actual knowledge of clearly exculpatory evidence that directly negates guilt must such evidence be presented to the grand jury. Moreover, courts should dismiss indictments on this ground only after giving due regard to the prosecutor's own evaluation of whether the evidence in question is "clearly exculpatory." Ascertaining the exculpatory value of evidence at such an early stage of the proceedings can be difficult, and courts should act with substantial caution before concluding that a prosecutor's decision in that regard was erroneous. We emphasize that it is the exceptional case in which a prosecutor's failure to present

exculpatory evidence to a grand jury will constitute grounds for challenging an indictment.

5. The grand jury need not be instructed of its right to refuse to indict even if it finds probable cause to do so. "While we may want the grand jury to refuse to indict when an oppressive government is unfairly targeting an individual, or when the laws being enforced are clearly (at least in retrospect) unjust, grand juries lose any guarantee of fairness if they have unfettered discretion to decide whether clear evidence of probable cause should be disregarded in each individual case." United States v. Marcucci, 299 F.3d 1156 (9th Cir.2002).

F. ABUSE OF THE GRAND JURY PROCESS

Bank of Nova Scotia v. United States

Supreme Court of the United States, 1988.
487 U.S. 250, 108 S.Ct. 2369.

■ JUSTICE KENNEDY delivered the opinion of the Court.

The issue presented is whether a district court may invoke its supervisory power to dismiss an indictment for prosecutorial misconduct in a grand jury investigation, where the misconduct does not prejudice the defendants.

I

In 1982, after a 20–month investigation conducted before two successive grand juries, eight defendants ... were indicted on 27 counts.

* * *

[After 10 days of hearings the trial court dismissed the indictment for, among other things, violating secrecy rules, improper disclosure of information, violations of the fifth and sixth amendments, knowing presentation of misinformation and mistreatment of witnesses]. The District Court determined that "[a]s a result of the conduct of the prosecutors and their entourage of agents, the indicting grand jury was not able to undertake its essential mission" to act independently of the prosecution.

* * *

The Government appealed ... and a divided panel of the Court of Appeals reversed the order of dismissal.

* * *

II

In the exercise of its supervisory authority, a federal court "may, within limits, formulate procedural rules not specifically required by the Constitution or the Congress." Nevertheless, it is well established that "[e]ven a sensible and efficient use of the supervisory power ... is invalid if it conflicts with constitutional or statutory provisions."

* * *

We now hold that a federal court may not invoke supervisory power to circumvent the harmless-error inquiry prescribed by Federal Rule of Criminal Procedure 52(a). Rule 52(a) provides that "[a]ny error, defect, irregularity or variance which does not affect substantial rights shall be disregarded." ... The balance struck by the Rule between societal costs and the rights of the accused may not casually be overlooked "because a court has elected to analyze the question under the supervisory power."

* * *

Having concluded that our customary harmless-error inquiry is applicable where, as in the cases before us, a court is asked to dismiss an indictment prior to the conclusion of the trial, we turn to the standard of prejudice that courts should apply in assessing such claims. We adopt for this purpose, at least where dismissal is sought for nonconstitutional error, the standard ... [that] dismissal of the indictment is appropriate only "if it is established that the violation substantially influenced the grand jury's decision to indict," or if there is "grave doubt" that the decision to indict was free from the substantial influence of such violations.

* * *

To be distinguished from the cases before us are a class of cases in which indictments are dismissed, without a particular assessment of the prejudicial impact of the errors in each case, because the errors are deemed fundamental. These cases may be explained as isolated exceptions to the harmless-error rule. We think, however, that an alternative and more clear explanation is that these cases are ones in which the structural protections of the grand jury have been so compromised as to render the proceedings fundamentally unfair, allowing the presumption of prejudice. These cases are exemplified by Vasquez v. Hillery (1986), where we held that racial discrimination in selection of grand jurors compelled dismissal of the indictment. In addition to involving an error of constitutional magnitude, other remedies were impractical and it could be presumed that a discriminatorily selected grand jury would treat defendants unfairly. The nature of the violation allowed a presumption that the defendant was prejudiced, and any inquiry into harmless error would have required unguided speculation. Such considerations are not presented here, and we review the alleged errors to assess their influence, if any, on the grand jury's decision to indict in the factual context of the cases before us.

III

* * *

The District Court found that the Government had violated Federal Rule of Criminal Procedure 6(e) by: (1) disclosing grand jury materials to Internal Revenue Service employees having civil tax enforcement responsibilities; (2) failing to give the court prompt notice of such disclosures; (3) disclosing to potential witnesses the names of targets of the investigation; and (4) instructing two grand jury witnesses, who had represented some of the defendants in a separate investigation of the same tax shelters, that they were not to reveal the substance of their testimony or that they had testified before the grand jury. The court also found that the Government had violated Federal Rule of Criminal Procedure 6(d) in allowing joint appearances by IRS agents before the grand jury for the purpose of reading transcripts to the jurors.

The District Court further concluded that one of the prosecutors improperly argued with an expert witness during a recess of the grand jury after the witness gave testimony adverse to the Government. It also held that the Government had violated the witness immunity statute, by the use of "pocket immunity" (immunity granted on representation of the prosecutor rather than by order of a judge), and that the Government caused IRS agents to mischaracterize testimony given in prior proceedings. Furthermore, the District Court found that the Government violated the Fifth Amendment by calling a number of witnesses for the sole purpose of having them assert their privilege against self-incrimination and that it had violated the Sixth Amendment by conducting postindictment interviews of several high-level employees of The Bank of Nova Scotia. Finally, the court concluded that the Government had caused IRS agents to be sworn as agents of the grand jury, thereby elevating their credibility. As we have noted, no constitutional error occurred during the grand jury proceedings. The Court of Appeals concluded that the District Court's findings of Sixth Amendment postindictment violations were unrelated to the grand jury's independence and decision-making process because the alleged violations occurred after the indictment. We agree that it was improper for the District Court to cite such matters in dismissing the indictment. The Court of Appeals also found that no Fifth Amendment violation occurred as a result of the Government's calling seven witnesses to testify despite an avowed intention to invoke their Fifth Amendment privilege. We agree that, in the circumstances of these cases, calling the witnesses was not error. The Government was not required to take at face value the unsworn assertions made by these witnesses outside the grand jury room. Once a witness invoked the privilege on the record, the prosecutors immediately ceased all questioning. Throughout the proceedings, moreover, the prosecution repeated the caution to the grand jury that it was not to draw any adverse inference from a witness' invocation of the Fifth Amendment.

* * *

We must address, however, whether ... there was any misconduct by the prosecution that otherwise may have influenced substantially the grand jury's decision to indict, or whether there is grave doubt as to whether the decision to indict was so influenced. Several instances of misconduct found by the District Court—that the prosecutors manipulated the grand jury investigation to gather evidence for use in civil audits; violated the secrecy provisions of Rule 6(e) by publicly identifying the targets and the subject matter of the grand jury investigation; and imposed secrecy obligations in violation of Rule 6(e) upon grand jury witnesses—might be relevant to an allegation of a purpose or intent to abuse the grand jury process. Here, however, it is plain that these alleged breaches could not have affected the charging decision. We have no occasion to consider them further.

We are left to consider only the District Court's findings that the prosecutors: (1) fashioned and administered unauthorized "oaths" to IRS agents in violation of Rule 6(c); (2) caused the same IRS agents to "summarize" evidence falsely and to assert incorrectly that all the evidence summarized by them had been presented previously to the grand jury; (3) deliberately berated and mistreated an expert witness for the defense in the presence of some grand jurors; (4) abused its authority by providing "pocket immunity" to 23 grand jury witnesses; and (5) permitted IRS agents to appear in tandem to present evidence to the grand jury in violation of Rule 6(d). We consider each in turn.

The Government administered oaths to IRS agents, swearing them in as "agents" of the grand jury. Although the administration of such oaths to IRS agents by the Government was unauthorized, there is ample evidence that the jurors understood that the agents were aligned with the prosecutors. At various times a prosecutor referred to the agents as "my agent(s)," and, in discussions with the prosecutors, grand jurors referred to the agents as "your guys" or "your agents." There is nothing in the record to indicate that the oaths administered to the IRS agents caused their reliability or credibility to be elevated, and the effect, if any, on the grand jury's decision to indict was negligible.

The District Court found that, to the prejudice of petitioners, IRS agents gave misleading and inaccurate summaries to the grand jury just prior to the indictment. Because the record does not reveal any prosecutorial misconduct with respect to these summaries, they provide no ground for dismissing the indictment. The District Court's finding that the summaries offered by IRS agents contained evidence that had not been presented to the grand jury in prior testimony boils down to a challenge to the reliability or competence of the evidence presented to the grand jury. We have held that an indictment valid on its face is not subject to such a challenge. To the extent that a challenge is made to the accuracy of the summaries, the mere fact that evidence itself is unreliable is not sufficient to require a dismissal of the indictment. In light of the record, the finding that the prosecutors knew the evidence to be false or misleading, or that the Government caused the agents to testify falsely, is clearly erroneous. Although the Government may have had doubts about the accuracy of certain aspects of the summaries, this is quite different from having knowledge of falsity.

The District Court found that a prosecutor was abusive to an expert defense witness during a recess and in the hearing of some grand jurors. Although the Government concedes that the treatment of the expert tax witness was improper, the witness himself testified that his testimony was unaffected by this misconduct. The prosecutors instructed the grand jury to disregard anything they may have heard in conversations between a prosecutor and a witness, and explained to the grand jury that such conversations should have no influence on its deliberations. In light of these ameliorative measures, there is nothing to indicate that the prosecutor's conduct toward this witness substantially affected the grand jury's evaluation of the testimony or its decision to indict.

The District Court found that the Government granted "pocket immunity" to 23 witnesses during the course of the grand jury proceedings. Without deciding the propriety of granting such immunity to grand jury witnesses, we conclude the conduct did not have a substantial effect on the grand jury's decision to indict, and it does not create grave doubt as to whether it affected the grand jury's decision. Some prosecutors told the grand jury that immunized witnesses retained their Fifth Amendment privilege and could refuse to testify, while other prosecutors stated that the witnesses had no Fifth Amendment privilege, but we fail to see how this could have had a substantial effect on the jury's assessment of the testimony or its decision to indict. The significant point is that the jurors were made aware that these witnesses had made a deal with the Government.

* * *

Finally, the Government permitted two IRS agents to appear before the grand jury at the same time for the purpose of reading transcripts. Although allowing the agents to read to the grand jury in tandem was a violation of Rule 6(d), it was not prejudicial. The agents gave no testimony of their own during the reading of the transcripts. The grand jury was instructed not to ask any questions and the agents were instructed not to answer any questions during the readings. There is no evidence that the agents' reading in tandem enhanced the credibility of the testimony or otherwise allowed the agents to exercise undue influence.

In considering the prejudicial effect of the foregoing instances of alleged misconduct, we note that these incidents occurred as isolated episodes in the course of a 20–month investigation, an investigation involving dozens of witnesses and thousands of documents. In view of this context, those violations that did occur do not, even when considered cumulatively, raise a substantial question, much less a grave doubt, as to whether they had a substantial effect on the grand jury's decision to charge.

Errors of the kind alleged in these cases can be remedied adequately by means other than dismissal. For example, a knowing violation of Rule 6 may be punished as a contempt of court. See Fed.Rule Crim.Proc. 6(e)(2). In addition, the court may direct a prosecutor to show cause why he should not be disciplined and request the bar or the Department of Justice to initiate disciplinary proceedings against him. The court may also chastise the prosecutor in a published opinion. Such remedies allow the court to focus on the culpable individual rather than granting a windfall to the unprejudiced defendant.

IV

We conclude that the District Court had no authority to dismiss the indictment on the basis of prosecutorial misconduct absent a finding that petitioners were prejudiced by such misconduct. The prejudicial inquiry must focus on whether any violations had an effect on the grand jury's decision to indict. If violations did substantially influence this decision, or if there is grave doubt that the decision to indict was free from such substantial influence, the violations cannot be deemed harmless. The record will not support the conclusion that petitioners can meet this standard. The judgment of the Court of Appeals is affirmed.

■ JUSTICE SCALIA, concurring. [OMITTED]

■ JUSTICE MARSHALL, dissenting.

* * *

Because of the strict protection of the secrecy of grand jury proceedings, instances of prosecutorial misconduct rarely come to light. This is especially true in the pretrial setting, because defendants' chief source of information about grand jury proceedings is governmental disclosures under the Jencks Act, 18 USC § 3500 which do not occur until trial is underway. The fact that a prosecutor knows that a Rule 6 violation is unlikely to be discovered gives the Rule little enough bite. To afford the occasional revelation of prosecutorial misconduct the additional insulation of harmless-error analysis leaves Rule 6 toothless. Moreover, "[a]ny case-by-case analysis to determine whether the defendant was actually prejudiced is simply too speculative to afford defendants meaningful protection, and imposes a difficult burden on the courts that outweighs the benefits to be derived." Given the nature of grand jury proceedings, Rule 6 violations can be deterred and redressed effectively only by a per se rule of dismissal. Today's decision reduces Rule 6 to little more than a code of honor that prosecutors can violate with virtual impunity. I respectfully dissent.

NOTES

1. What type of prosecutorial misconduct rises to the level of substantially influencing the Grand Jury's decision so as to satisfy the *Bank of Nova Scotia* standard? In United States v. Williams, 899 F.2d 898 (10th Cir.1990), the court upheld dismissal of a bank fraud indictment on the ground that the prosecution possessed exculpatory evidence that tended to negate defendant's intent and wrongfully withheld it from the Grand Jury. For the most part, however, the standard is extremely difficult to satisfy. United States v. Strouse, 286 F.3d 767 (5th Cir.2002) (the submission of perjured testimony to the grand jury does not justify dismissal of the indictment unless it was actually known to be false by the prosecutor); See United States v. Plesinski, 912 F.2d 1033 (9th Cir.1990) (Presence of unauthorized person in Grand Jury harmless); United States v. Reid, 911 F.2d 1456 (10th Cir.1990) (Failure to present impeachment evidence to Grand Jury harmless); United States v. Spillone, 879 F.2d 514 (9th Cir.1989) (Alleged perjury not sufficiently material).

2. The rationale for what appears to be a relatively loose rein on prosecutorial Grand Jury conduct was described in United States v. Fountain, 840 F.2d 509 (7th Cir.1988):

> We may assume that ... a district judge in an exceptional case may conclude that the prosecutor's use of hearsay (misleading the grand jury about the quality of the evidence) and omission to present exculpatory evidence (misleading the grand jury about the weight of the evidence) requires the government to present its case anew. The function of the grand jury is to screen out cases in which there is not even probable cause to believe a person committed the offense, and it is possible to imagine manipulations of the grand jury that prevent it from fulfilling this mission. But the people harmed by such misdeeds are the innocent, those exposed to the travail and expense of trial even though they were fated to prevail in the end. Once a person is convicted by the petit jury, we may be confident that a full presentation to the grand jury would have ended in indictment. The trial is a full, adversarial presentation, in which the live witnesses and

exculpatory evidence missing in the grand jury come to the fore. The grand jury acts by majority vote and uses a lesser burden; it is impossible to imagine evidence sufficient to produce a conviction at trial that would not also produce an indictment. So it would be silly to reverse a conviction on the ground that the evidence before the grand jury was insufficient. We know that this defendant is not a member of the class that is harmed by sloppy or overbearing conduct before the grand jury. We know that he could be reindicted in a trice (using the record of the trial as a basis), and would be tried anew in the same fashion.

3. It is improper to use a grand jury solely or dominantly to develop evidence for use at the trial of an already indicted defendant. See United States v. Doss, 563 F.2d 265 (6th Cir.1977). In State v. Burri, 87 Wash.2d 175, 550 P.2d 507 (1976), the court upheld the dismissal of an indictment when the prosecutor, following notice of an alibi defense, convened a special inquiry proceeding in order to examine the alibi witnesses in the absence of the defendant. The court found that the action of the prosecutor was "government misconduct or arbitrary action of the type historically regarded by this court as sufficient to support a dismissal of a criminal charge."

Courts are reluctant, however, to inquire into the nature and course of the grand jury's investigation to determine whether it embraces a pending indictment. In United States v. Doe, 455 F.2d 1270 (1st Cir.1972), a defendant who had been indicted in California sought a protective order banning a grand jury in Massachusetts from gathering evidence which would be relevant to the California prosecution. Although the government was represented by the same attorneys in both proceedings, the court would go only so far as to rule that the prosecutors must make available to the District Court in California the transcript of any witness who is both examined before the grand jury in Massachusetts and called to testify at the trial in California. The California court could then determine if the Government was using the Boston grand jury as a discovery device. In United States v. Braasch, 505 F.2d 139, 147 (7th Cir.1974), the court went even further, holding that "the government has every right to interrogate witnesses on subjects relevant to a continuing grand jury investigation when the evidence received may also relate to a pending indictment."

In United States v. Leung, 40 F.3d 577 (2d Cir.1994), the court held that it is improper for the government to use the grand jury for the sole or dominant purpose of preparing for trial under a pending indictment. However, when the subsequent grand jury investigation is not primarily motivated by an improper purpose, evidence obtained may be used at the trial on the initial charges. In light of the presumption of regularity which attaches to grand jury proceedings, one seeking to exclude evidence obtained by a post-indictment grand jury subpoena has the burden of showing that the use of the grand jury was improperly motivated.

4. Prosecutors frequently call alibi witnesses before the grand jury *before* indictment is returned but after the defendant has been charged on a preliminary hearing complaint or information. Suppose that they are committed to securing an indictment and are motivated by the opportunity to cross-examine the alibi witnesses in advance of trial. Or suppose prosecutors hope that a potential defense witness (other than the defendant) will invoke the privilege against self-incrimination. (In many jurisdictions, a non-defendant witness who testifies at trial can be impeached by his prior invocation of the privilege.) Has such a prosecutor acted improperly? Should he or she be required to testify as to what motivated the decision to call potential witnesses before the grand jury?

In State v. Francis, 191 N.J. 571, 926 A.2d 305 (2007), the state called certain relatives of a triple murder suspect to solicit information that likely would be used in mitigation at sentencing. At a later point, the prosecutor advised the grand jury to disregard that testimony and presented information that let to an indictment. Defendant's claim that this tactic amounted to abuse of the grand jury process was rejected. Finding that the judiciary should not hamstring the ability of the prosecutor to present evidence to the grand jury, the court distinguished the post-indictment stage, where the "dominant purpose" test applies from the pre-indictment presentation of evidence. "[T]he standard applicable to claims of pre-indictment grand jury abuse must be whether the evidence sought by the State via the grand jury was relevant to the crimes under investigation, that is, did the evidence sought have a tendency in reason to prove or disprove any fact of consequence to the determination of the action."

5. How forceful an advocate can the prosecutor be before a grand jury? Can he or she urge the importance of an indictment just as a prosecutor at trial could urge the importance of a conviction? One court has held that there are limits on a prosecutor's expression of a personal opinion before a grand jury, just as there are at trial. See United States v. McKenzie, 524 F.Supp. 186 (E.D.La.1981), vacated 678 F.2d 629 (5th Cir.1982), where the prosecutor urged the grand jury to vote again after being informed that a vote had been tied at 10–10. The *McKenzie* case represents one of those rare situations where a grand jury (at least initially) refused to provide the votes necessary for an indictment which the prosecutor sought. The case involved a civil rights investigation directed against New Orleans police officers for their conduct in an investigation following the shooting death of a fellow officer.

6. In United States v. Griffith, 756 F.2d 1244 (6th Cir.1985), the Court stated: "[The prosecutor's] comments were ... outrageous. We frankly cannot understand what makes an Assistant United States Attorney think he is justified in appearing before a grand jury and discussing ongoing plea negotiations and insinuating without one shred of evidence, that a person under investigation may have 'bugged' the grand jury room." However, the court refused to exercise its supervisory power to dismiss the indictment absent proof that misconduct before the grand jury was part of a pattern of long-standing or common misconduct and absent a showing of prejudice. How can a defendant know what goes on in grand jury hearings in which he has no involvement? Typically he has to demonstrate a particularized showing of need before he can get access to grand jury transcripts in his own case (with the exception of testimony of witnesses who have testified against him at trial). Do you believe that, upon a showing of abuse in his own case, the Sixth Circuit would allow a defendant access to transcripts of other grand jury hearings?

G. INDICTMENTS

United States v. Miller

Supreme Court of the United States, 1985.
471 U.S. 130, 105 S.Ct. 1811.

■ JUSTICE MARSHALL delivered the opinion of the Court.

The issue presented is whether the Fifth Amendment's grand jury guarantee is violated when a defendant is tried under an indictment that alleges a certain fraudulent scheme but is convicted based on trial proof that supports only a significantly narrower and more limited, though included, fraudulent scheme.

* * *

I

A

The indictment had charged Miller with various fraudulent acts in connection with a burglary at his business. Miller allegedly had defrauded his insurer both by consenting to the burglary in advance and by lying to the insurer about the value of his loss. The trial proof, however, concerned only the latter allegation, focusing on whether, prior to the burglary, Miller actually had possessed all the property that he later claimed was taken. This proof was clearly sufficient to support a jury finding that Miller's claim to his insurer had grossly inflated the value of any actual loss.

The Government moved to strike the part of the indictment that alleged prior knowledge of the burglary, and it correctly argued that even without the allegation the indictment still made out a [mail fraud] violation. Respondent's counsel opposed the change, and at his urging the entire indictment was sent to the jury. The jury found Miller guilty, and respondent appealed on the basis that the trial proof had fatally varied from the scheme alleged in the indictment.

Agreeing that Miller's Fifth Amendment right to be tried only on a grand jury indictment had been violated, the Court of Appeals vacated the conviction. It succinctly stated its rationale:

> "The grand jury may well have declined to indict Miller simply on the basis of his exaggeration of the amount of his claimed loss.... In fact it is quite possible that the grand jury would have been unwilling or unable to return an indictment based solely on Miller's exaggeration of the amount of his claimed loss even though it had concluded that an indictment could be returned based on the overall scheme involving a use of the mail caused by Miller's knowing consent to the burglary." 715 F.2d, at 1362–1363.

B

... The facts proved at trial clearly conformed to one of the theories of the offense contained within that indictment, for the indictment gave Miller clear notice that he would have to defend against an allegation that he "well knew that the amount of copper claimed to have been taken during the alleged burglary was grossly inflated for the purpose of fraudulently obtaining $150,000 from Aetna Insurance Company." Competent defense counsel certainly should have been on notice that that offense was charged and would need to be defended against. Accordingly, there can be no showing here that Miller was prejudicially surprised at trial by the absence of proof concerning his alleged complicity in the burglary; nor can there be a showing that the variance prejudiced the fairness of respondent's trial in any other way. The indictment was also sufficient to allow Miller to plead it in the future as a bar to subsequent prosecutions. Therefore, none of these "notice" related concerns—which of course are among the important concerns underlying the requirement that criminal charges be set out in an indictment—would support the result of the Court of Appeals.

The Court of Appeals did not disagree, but instead argued that Miller had been prejudiced in his right to be free from a trial for any offense other than that alleged in the grand jury's indictment. . . .

* * *

II

. . . The Court has long recognized that an indictment may charge numerous offenses or the commission of any one offense in several ways. As long as the crime and the elements of the offense that sustain the conviction are fully and clearly set out in the indictment, the right to a grand jury is not normally violated by the fact that the indictment alleges more crimes or other means of committing the same crime. Indeed, a number of long-standing doctrines of criminal procedure are premised on the notion that each offense whose elements are fully set out in an indictment can independently sustain a conviction.

* * *

. . . Convictions generally have been sustained as long as the proof upon which they are based corresponds to an offense that was clearly set out in the indictment. A part of the indictment unnecessary to and independent from the allegations of the offense proved may normally be treated as "a useless averment" that "may be ignored."

* * *

III

. . . In Stirone [v. United States (1960)] the offense proved at trial was *not* fully contained in the indictment, for trial evidence had "amended" the indictment by *broadening* the possible bases for conviction from that which appeared in the indictment. Stirone was thus wholly unlike respondent's case, which involves trial evidence that narrowed the indictment's charges without adding any new offenses. As the Stirone Court said, the issue was "whether [Stirone] was convicted of an offense *not charged in the indictment*."

* * *

Miller has shown no deprivation of his "substantial right to be tried only on charges presented in an indictment returned by a grand jury." In contrast to Stirone, Miller was tried on an indictment that clearly set out the offense for which he was ultimately convicted. His complaint is not that the indictment failed to charge the offense for which he was convicted, but that the indictment charged more than was necessary.

IV

The one decision of this Court that does offer some support to the Court of Appeals' result is Ex parte Bain (1887), for there the Court treated as an unconstitutional "amendment" the deletion from an indictment of allegations that would not have been necessary to prove the offense. This deletion, in the Court's view, did constitute a compromise of the defendant's right to be tried only on a grand jury's indictment.

* * *

Bain may best be understood in terms of two distinct propositions. Most generally, Bain stands for the proposition that a conviction cannot stand if based on an offense that is different from that alleged in the grand jury's indictment. But more specifically, Bain can support the proposition that the striking out of parts of an indictment invalidates the whole of the indictment, for a court cannot speculate as to whether the grand jury had meant for any remaining offense to stand independently, even if that remaining offense clearly was included in the original text. Under this latter proposition, the narrowing of an indictment is no different from the adding of a new allegation that had never been considered by the grand jury; both are treated as "amendments" that alter the nature of the offense charged. In evaluating the relevance of Bain to the instant case, it is necessary to examine these two aspects of Bain separately, for the Court has treated these two propositions quite differently in the years since Bain.

The proposition that a defendant cannot be convicted of an offense different from that which was included in the indictment was broadly declared in Bain:

> "If it lies within the province of a court to change the charging part of an indictment to suit its own notions of what it ought to have been, or what the grand jury would probably have made it if their attention had been called to suggested changes, the great importance which the common law attaches to an indictment by a grand jury, as a prerequisite to a prisoner's trial for a crime, and without which the Constitution says 'no person shall be held to answer,' may be frittered away until its value is almost destroyed."

* * *

But this aspect of Bain gives no support to Miller in this case, for the offense that formed the basis of Miller's conviction was clearly and fully set out in the indictment. Miller must instead rest on the second, and more specific, proposition found in Bain, that a narrowing of the indictment constitutes an amendment that renders the indictment void.

. . . [W]hen defendants have sought to rely on Bain for this point, this Court has limited or distinguished the case, sustaining convictions where courts had withdrawn or ignored independent and unnecessary allegations in the indictments. Modern criminal law has generally accepted that an indictment will support each offense contained within it. To the extent Bain stands for the proposition that it constitutes an unconstitutional amendment to drop from an indictment those allegations that are unnecessary to an offense that is clearly contained within it, that case has simply not survived. To avoid further confusion, we now explicitly reject that proposition.

Rejecting this aspect of Bain is hardly a radical step, however, given that in the years since Bain this Court has largely ignored this element of the case. Moreover, in rejecting this proposition's continued validity, we do not limit Bain's more general proposition concerning the impermissibility of actual additions to the offenses alleged in an indictment, a proposition we have repeatedly reaffirmed. That our holding today is fully consistent with prior legal understanding is apparent from an examination of the state of the law, as seen by Chief Justice Stone, more than 40 years ago:

> "An indictment is amended when it is so altered as to charge a different offense from that found by the grand jury. But here there was no alteration of the indictment, nor did the court's action, in effect, add anything to it by submitting to the jury matters which it did not charge. ... [W]here an indictment charges several offenses, or the commission of one offense in several ways, the withdrawal from the jury's consideration of one offense or one alleged method of committing it does not constitute a forbidden amendment of the indictment. Were the rule otherwise the common practice of withdrawing from the jury's consideration one count of an indictment while submitting others for its verdict, would be a fatal error."

V

The variance complained of added nothing new to the grand jury's indictment and constituted no broadening. What was removed from the case was in no way essential to the offense on which the jury convicted.... The judgment of the Court of Appeals is accordingly reversed.

NOTES

1. In most jurisdictions, "[t]he indictment or information shall be a plain, concise and definite written statement of the essential facts constituting the offense charged." Fed.R.Crim.P. 7(c)(1). The current practice was intended to put an end to "the rules of technical and formalized pleading which had characterized an earlier era." Russell v. United States, 369 U.S. 749, 762, 82 S.Ct. 1038, 1046 (1962). As a result, "[c]onvictions are no longer reversed because of minor and technical defects which did not prejudice the accused." Smith v. United States, 360 U.S. 1, 9, 79 S.Ct. 991, 996 (1959). See Scott, Fairness in Accusation of Crime, 41 Minn.L.Rev. 509 (1957).

2. The purpose of an indictment is threefold: "First, it should state all of the elements of the offense charged; second, it should inform the defendant of the nature of the charge so that he may prepare a defense; and third, it must enable the defendant to plead the judgment as a bar to any later prosecution for the same offense." United States v. Gironda, 758 F.2d 1201, 1209 (7th Cir.1985); see Hamling v. United States, 418 U.S. 87, 94 S.Ct. 2887 (1974). While older cases seem to require more detail and specifics, see United States v. Hess, 124 U.S. 483, 8 S.Ct. 571 (1888), limitations on the prosecution continue to exist. As recognized in Russell v. United States, 369 U.S. 749, 770, 82 S.Ct. 1038, 1050 (1962):

> To allow a prosecutor or court to make a subsequent guess to what was in the minds of the Grand Jury at the time that they returned the indictment would deprive the defendant of the basic protection that the Grand Jury was designed to secure. Because a defendant could not then be convicted on the basis of facts not found by, and perhaps not even presented to, the Grand Jury that indicted him.

See also United States v. Resendiz–Ponce, 549 U.S. 102, 127 S.Ct. 782 (2007) (indictment charging attempted illegal reentry following deportation on a given date near an identified location was constitutionally sufficient notice even though it did not allege an overt act that qualified as a substantial step toward completion of the offense). In essence, the test for indictment sufficiency is one of due process: "The principle of fundamental fairness, essential to the concept of due process of law, dictates that the defendant in a criminal action should not be relegated to a position from which he must speculate as to what crime he will have to meet in defense." Kreck v. Spalding, 721 F.2d 1229, 1233 (9th Cir.1983); see United States v. Peel, 837 F.2d 975 (11th Cir.1988); Note, Indictment Sufficiency, 70 Colum.L.Rev. 876 (1970).

3. The range of potential problems with pleading by indictment is quite broad. There are technical requirements pertaining to the return and filing of the indictment, the loss or destruction of indictments and the return of successive or superseding indictments. The form of the indictment is governed by detailed requirements concerning the caption, the form of accusation, the allegation of venue, the conclusion, the citation of statutes violated, the signature of the prosecutor or the grand jury foreman or both, the endorsement of the phrase "a true bill", and the names of witnesses. There are occasional problems arising from mistakes in grammar or spelling and erasures and interlineations. None of these technical concerns have a significant impact on criminal procedure. Compliance with required details usually becomes routine and even if errors occur, few courts regard them as substantial enough to require reversal.

4. On the other hand, some draftsmanship problems rise above the level of "technical" flaws and raise serious issues. For example, an indictment that fails to allege the proper mental state or words of similar import has been found defective. United States v. Pupo, 841 F.2d 1235 (4th Cir.1988). Likewise, the failure to allege a jurisdictional element, such as an effect on interstate commerce for many federal crimes, has been determined to be a material defect. United States v. Hooker, 841 F.2d 1225 (4th Cir.1988). Compare United States v. Shelton, 937 F.2d 140 (5th Cir.1991).

5. Because indictments must allege each offense in a separate count, one that alleges multiple crimes in the same count is invalid on the ground of duplicity. In Bins v. United States, 331 F.2d 390, 393 (5th Cir.1964), the court explained that the determination of whether one or several offenses are contained in a single count is contingent upon "whether identical evidence will support each of them, and if any dissimilar facts must be proved, there is more than one offense." See also United States v. Tanner, 471 F.2d 128 (7th Cir.1972) (indictment duplicitous because it contained one count, alleging the transportation of explosives in interstate commerce, which charged defendants with making successive trips, by different persons, carrying different loads of dynamite); Driscoll v. United States, 356 F.2d 324 (1st Cir.1966), vacated on other grounds 390 U.S. 202, 88 S.Ct. 899 (1968) (failure to file supplemental return under gambling tax information act is not way or means of violating initial registration requirement and, therefore, count including both was duplicitous); United States v. Kearney, 451 F.Supp. 33 (S.D.N.Y.1978) (multiple thefts from mail charged in one count is duplicitous because of dissimilar facts). However, when the same offense is carried out by a variety of means and methods, a single count is not duplicitous. United States v. Zeidman, 540 F.2d 314 (7th Cir.1976).

6. The doctrine of duplicity implicates a number of constitutional and other issues. For example, duplicitous counts conflict with the sixth amendment's guarantee than an accused be adequately informed of the nature and cause of the accusation which could result when the prosecution collects numerous charges and elements of charges together in a single confused count. The fifth amendment's interdiction against double jeopardy could be threatened by a general verdict for a defendant on a duplicitous count because it would not reveal whether the jury found the defendant not guilty of one crime or not guilty of both. Furthermore, a general verdict of guilty on a duplicitous count would not disclose whether the jury found the defendant guilty of one crime or of both, and thus could prejudice the defendant in sentencing. See United States v. Crisci, 273 F.3d 235 (2d Cir.2001) (indictment charging separate sections of bank fraud law not duplicitous because they charge two different ways of committing same offense and there is no need for jury unanimity as to which method was used to commit the offense). Finally, duplicity could prejudice the defendant with respect to evidentiary rulings during the trial, since evidence on one offense might be inadmissible on the other. United States v. Starks, 515 F.2d 112 (3d Cir.1975).

7. The opposite of duplicity is multiplicity—the allegation of one offense in multiple counts. Generally, the fact that each alleged offense contains an element that the others do not, even if there is some overlap, indicates that the legislature intended to punish them separately. United States v. Hassoun, 476 F.3d 1181 (11th Cir. 2007). United States v. Planck, 493 F.3d 501 (5th Cir. 2007) (three separate child pornography counts alleging that defendant maintained prohibited images on three different devices—a desk top computer, a lap top and diskettes—were not multiplictious). Multiplicity is not fatal to an indictment because the proper remedy is to compel an election of charges to submit to the jury. United States v. Robinson, 651 F.2d 1188 (6th Cir.1981). Moreover, courts will often defer the question to the sentencing stage and prohibit multiple sentences for the same offense. United States v. Powell, 894 F.2d 895 (7th Cir.1990) (proper remedy is to remand for resentencing). In that context, the issue is the legislative intent in permitting multiple punishment. Ball v. United States, 470 U.S. 856, 105 S.Ct. 1668 (1985) (convicted felon may not be punished twice for receipt and possession of same weapon); United States v. Woodward, 469 U.S. 105, 105 S.Ct. 611 (1985) (one who fails to report possession of over $5,000 in currency when entering country may be convicted of two offenses).

8. The accused is frequently identified in an indictment by one name and several aliases. Some courts have concluded that such a practice needlessly prejudices an accused unless the aliases are relevant to the facts of the case and will be proved. See United States v. Wilkerson, 456 F.2d 57 (6th Cir.1972). In Murzyn v. United States, 578 F.Supp. 254 (N.D.Ind.1984), the court rejected a claim that failure to move to strike an alias demonstrated ineffective assistance of counsel on the ground that defendants are usually unsuccessful in having aliases expunged.

9. The usual practice in alleging the time and place of the offense is to state the day when, and the county or district where, the offense occurred. This is generally deemed sufficient, but the accused may be entitled to a bill of particulars giving the specific time of day and the street address of the occurrence in question. See State v. Hicks, 666 S.W.2d 54 (Tenn.1984); Sparks v. State, 273 So.2d 74 (Fla.1973) ("on or about" a certain date is proper). A variance in dates is permissible so long as the statute of limitations is not implicated. United States v. Arnold, 890 F.2d 825 (6th Cir.1989).

In *State v. Wilcox*, 808 P.2d 1028 (Utah 1991), the charge was sexual abuse of a child alleged to have occurred on various instances over a 32 month period. The child was less than five years old and could not provide information about the place, date and time of the acts of abuse. Defendant demanded such data as a premise for an alibi defense. On appeal the Court said:

> The problem of young children who are unable to specify a date on which abuse occurred or a location where it occurred is exacerbated by situations in which the abuse occurred on many occasions over a long period of time,

a not uncommon occurrence.... If we were to hold that in all such circumstances, no offense could be charged because the alleged victim is too young to testify with certainty concerning the time, dates, or places where the abuse occurred, we would leave the youngest and most vulnerable children with no legal protection. An abuser could escape prosecution merely by claiming that the child's inability to remember the exact dates and places of the abuse impaired the abuser's ability to prepare an alibi defense....

... time does not become an element of an offense merely because the defendant pleads an alibi defense.... Therefore, Wilcox has no statutory or constitutional right to a charge framed so as to facilitate an alibi defense.... It is doubtful that an alibi defense is a realistic possibility because Wilcox had continual contact with the child half of the time over the thirty-two-month period....

This is not a situation in which the lack of specificity compromises the defense, as it would if Wilcox had had contact with the child only once or twice, so that specific dates and times were critical....

Once a prosecutor chooses to prosecute on such vague allegations, a necessary quid pro quo under our constitutional notice provision is that to protect the defendant from double jeopardy, the prosecutor should be precluded from bringing further charges that fall within the general description of the charging allegations....

STEWART, JUSTICE: (Dissenting) ...

Here, the majority focuses solely on the difficulties presented to the prosecution in dealing with a very young child and gives no real weight to the constitutional right of fair notice. Although the majority gives lip service to a defendant's right to notice, it holds that the right diminishes to whatever extent the exigencies of the prosecution require, and in this case, that means no notice at all in any realistic sense....

That right is not just a right of notice of the prosecution's evidence; more importantly, it is the right of a defendant not to be confronted with a case that presents a moving target....

The defendant has no realistic possibility of producing any defense—except an attack on the prosecution's case by cross-examination. The defendant will not be able to call any witnesses to testify as to his conduct on a given occasion because the prosecution will always be able to assert that the crime occurred on another occasion.

10. The jurisdictions adopt different approaches to surplus allegations in a charge. For example, it may not be necessary to allege that murder was committed by strangulation; but, if it is alleged, must it be proved? The courts split on the answer. When gratuitous language in an indictment is irrelevant to the crime charged and likely to inflame the jury, it may be stricken on motion of the defendant. See United States v. Poindexter, 725 F.Supp. 13 (D.D.C.1989).

11. The bill of particulars is a device of substantial vintage, yet there is no consistent theory concerning either its purpose or its necessity. The bill of particulars is not intended to be a discovery device, yet its purpose is to provide the accused with information about the details of the charge so that he may prepare his defense and proceed to trial without the risk of unfair surprise. United States v. Carrier, 672 F.2d 300 (2d Cir.1982); United States v. Diecidue, 603 F.2d 535 (5th Cir.1979). While anything that gives a party information about the case is a discovery device of some kind, the courts consistently hold that a bill of particulars may not be ordered solely for discovery purposes. United States v. Anderson, 799

F.2d 1438 (11th Cir.1986). The principal use of the bill is to secure a declaration of the precise date and time and place of occurrences the government will prove. In a burglary case, this would mean the time of day and the street address of the burglarized premises; in a conspiracy case, the date, time and address of the meetings of the conspirators, and the names of the persons at the meeting. United States v. Smith, 16 F.R.D. 372 (W.D.Mo.1954). Occasionally the bill concerns the names of the persons present at the occurrence. For example, in narcotics sale cases, the name of the purchaser is not, in most jurisdictions, a necessary allegation, and bills are often granted to secure this name. United States v. Orsini, 406 F.Supp. 1264 (E.D.N.Y.1976). In tax cases, the governments tax liability theory and the nature of the calculations may be compelled by the bill. United States v. Hedman, 458 F.Supp. 1384 (N.D.Ill.1978). In cases prosecuted under accountability theories, the particular acts which the government will prove in order to establish accountability for the conduct of other persons are the subjects of bills. The bill cannot be used to discover the names of the witnesses the prosecution will call or the evidence it will use, since an accusation of crime can be made sufficiently complete without resort to such matters. United States v. Dreitzler, 577 F.2d 539 (9th Cir.1978). Moreover, the trial judge has broad discretion to determine whether a request for particulars is justified. Wong Tai v. United States, 273 U.S. 77, 47 S.Ct. 300 (1927). Ultimately, the discretionary decision confronting the court must be resolved through a balancing test in which the defendant's compelling need for the information is weighted against the government's need to protect it until trial. United States v. Rosa, 891 F.2d 1074 (3d Cir.1989). See also United States v. McKinney, 53 F.3d 664 (5th Cir.1995) (finding no abuse of discretion because of defendant's failure to allege surprise of prejudice as a result of the denial of the request).

12. In some instances a response to a request for a bill of particulars that affirmatively misleads the defendant will result in reversal. For example, in United States v. Chavez, 845 F.2d 219 (9th Cir.1988), the bill requested the names of persons who had been "supervised" in connection with an indictment charging defendants with organizing and supervising a continuing criminal enterprise. The government responded by listing the names of codefendants; but in closing argument named many others who were not mentioned in the indictment or bill of particulars. The court reversed the ensuing convictions on the ground that defendants had been affirmatively misled.

13. As *Miller* makes clear, post-verdict relief on the ground that the proof varied from the indictment is difficult to obtain. See United States v. Kimberlin, 18 F.3d 1156, 1158–59 (4th Cir.1994) (strict chronological, specificity or accuracy in the indictment is not required where a particular date is not a substantive element of the crime charged); United States v. Morrow, 925 F.2d 779, 781–82 (4th Cir.1991) (in a prosecution for possession of a firearm by a convicted felon, a variance between the indictment and the proof resulting from the indictment's omission of the first digit of the firearm's serial number went only to form, not to substance, and did not reduce the government's burden of proof). However, when the trial court instructs the jury on essential elements of a crime other than the one charged, an impermissible constructive amendment of the indictment may occur. In United States v. Floresca, 38 F.3d 706 (4th Cir.1994) (en banc), a 6–5 majority of the Court found that an instruction defining the elements of a subsection of the witness tampering statute other than the subsection under which the defendant was charged resulted in a constructive amendment. The majority held that the instruction broadened the possible bases for conviction beyond those presented by the grand jury. The dissenting judges believed that the majority elevated a harmless variance into an unwarranted constructive amendment of the indictment.

See also United States v. Hoover, 467 F.3d 496 (5th Cir. 2006) (in a false statement case, when the proof does not conform to the allegation of how the statement is untruthful, the indictment is constructively amended and reversal is required). Compare United States v. Bhagat, 436 F.3d 1140 (9th Cir. 2006) (insider trading indictment charging acquisition of inside information by company e-mail was not constructively amended by proof that office was abuzz with information over the dissent of Judge Tashima who viewed the uncharged theory as "a prejudicial variance from the indictment").

United States v. Tsinhnahijinnie, 112 F.3d 988 (9th Cir.1997), is a rare example of a situation in which the date of the alleged offense, even though it was not an element of the crime charged, was found to be a fatal variance. Charged with sexual contact with a child on an Indian reservation in June or July, 1992, the evidence showed that the child lived off of the reservation until August, 1992, and the abuse did not occur until the 1994–95 school term: The court held:

> A man indicted for robbing First National Bank in Springfield on January 1, cannot be convicted on the indictment of robbing Second National Bank in Middletown on December 30, even though the elements of the crime would be exactly the same. The problem would be that the defendant was not indicted for the crime proved, had no fair notice, and would lack double jeopardy protection against an indictment for the December 30 crime if he won an acquittal. There was no evidence from which any jury could reasonably conclude beyond a reasonable doubt that Tsinhnahijinnie committed the crime charged on a date reasonably near June or July 1992.

14. For purposes of measuring the statute of limitations, is a sealed indictment returned when it is subscribed by the foreperson as a true bill or when it is opened and publicly filed? See United States v. Thompson, 287 F.3d 1244 (10th Cir.2002).

CHAPTER 12

THE RIGHT TO BAIL

A. BAIL UPON CHARGE

United States v. Salerno

Supreme Court of the United States, 1987.
481 U.S. 739, 107 S.Ct. 2095.

■ CHIEF JUSTICE REHNQUIST delivered the opinion of the Court.

The Bail Reform Act of 1984 allows a federal court to detain an arrestee pending trial if the government demonstrates by clear and convincing evidence after an adversary hearing that no release conditions "will reasonably assure ... the safety of any other person and the community." The United States Court of Appeals for the Second Circuit struck down this provision of the Act as facially unconstitutional, because, in that court's words, this type of pretrial detention violates "substantive due process." We granted certiorari because of a conflict among the Courts of Appeals regarding the validity of the Act.

* * *

I

Responding to "the alarming problem of crimes committed by persons on release," Congress formulated the Bail Reform Act of 1984 as the solution to a bail crisis in the federal courts.

* * *

To this end, § 3141(a) of the Act requires a judicial officer to determine whether an arrestee shall be detained. Section 3142(e) provides that "[i]f, after a hearing pursuant to the provisions of subsection (f), the judicial officer finds that no condition or combination of conditions will reasonably assure the appearance of the person as required and the safety of any other person and the community, he shall order the detention of the person prior to trial." Section 3142(f) provides the arrestee with a number of procedural safeguards. He may request the presence of counsel at the detention hearing, he may testify and present witnesses in his behalf, as well as proffer evidence, and he may cross-examine other witnesses appearing at the hearing. If the judicial officer finds that no conditions of pretrial release can reasonably assure the safety of other persons and the community, he must state his findings of fact in writing, § 3142(i), and support his conclusion with "clear and convincing evidence," § 3142(f).

* * *

Respondents Anthony Salerno and Vincent Cafaro were arrested on March 21, 1986, after being charged in a 29–count indictment alleging various Racketeer Influenced and Corrupt Organizations Act (RICO) violations, mail and wire fraud offenses, extortion, and various criminal gambling violations. The RICO counts alleged 35 acts of racketeering activity, including fraud, extortion, gambling, and conspiracy to commit murder. At respondents' arraignment, the Government moved to have Salerno and Cafaro detained pursuant to § 3142(e), on the ground that no condition of release would assure the safety of the community or any person. The District Court held a hearing at which the Government made a detailed proffer of evidence. The Government's case showed that Salerno was the "boss" of the Genovese Crime Family of La Cosa Nostra and that Cafaro was a "captain" in the Genovese Family. According to the Government's proffer, based in large part on conversations intercepted by a court-ordered wiretap, the two respondents had participated in wide-ranging conspiracies to aid their illegitimate enterprises through violent means. The Government also offered the testimony of two of its trial witnesses, who would assert that Salerno personally participated in two murder conspiracies. Salerno opposed the motion for detention, challenging the credibility of the Government's witnesses. He offered the testimony of several character witnesses as well as a letter from his doctor stating that he was suffering from a serious medical condition. Cafaro presented no evidence at the hearing, but instead characterized the wiretap conversations as merely "tough talk."

The District Court granted the Government's detention motion, concluding that the Government had established by clear and convincing evidence that no condition or combination of conditions of release would ensure the safety of the community or any person:

> "The activities of a criminal organization such as the Genovese Family do not cease with the arrest of its principals and their release on even the most stringent of bail conditions. The illegal businesses, in place for many years, require constant attention and protection, or they will fail. Under these circumstances, this court recognizes a strong incentive on the part of its leadership to continue business as usual. When business as usual involves threats, beatings, and murder, the present danger such people pose in the community is self-evident." 631 F.Supp. 1364, 1375 (S.D.N.Y.1986).[2]

Respondents appealed, contending that to the extent that the Bail Reform Act permits pretrial detention on the ground that the arrestee is likely to commit future crimes, it is unconstitutional on its face. Over a dissent, the United States Court of Appeals for the Second Circuit agreed. 794 F.2d 64 (1986). . . .

2. Salerno was subsequently sentenced in unrelated proceedings before a different judge. To this date, however, Salerno has not been confined pursuant to that sentence. The authority for Salerno's present incarceration remains the District Court's pretrial detention order. The case is therefore very much alive and is properly presented for our resolution.

II

A facial challenge to a legislative Act is, of course, the most difficult challenge to mount successfully, since the challenger must establish that no set of circumstances exists under which the Act would be valid. The fact that the Bail Reform Act might operate unconstitutionally under some conceivable set of circumstances is insufficient to render it wholly invalid, since we have not recognized an "overbreadth" doctrine outside the limited context of the First Amendment. We think respondents have failed to shoulder their heavy burden to demonstrate that the Act is "facially" unconstitutional.[3]

Respondents present two grounds for invalidating the Bail Reform Act's provisions permitting pretrial detention on the basis of future dangerousness. First, they rely upon the Court of Appeals' conclusion that the Act exceeds the limitations placed upon the Federal Government by the Due Process Clause of the Fifth Amendment. Second, they contend that the Act contravenes the Eighth Amendment's proscription against excessive bail.

A

. . . This Court has held that the Due Process Clause protects individuals against two types of government action. So-called "substantive due process" prevents the government from engaging in conduct that "shocks the conscience," *Rochin v. California* (1952), or interferes with rights "implicit in the concept of ordered liberty," *Palko v. Connecticut* (1937). When government action depriving a person of life, liberty, or property survives substantive due process scrutiny, it must still be implemented in a fair manner. *Mathews v. Eldridge* (1976). This requirement has traditionally been referred to as "procedural" due process.

Respondents first argue that the Act violates substantive due process because the pretrial detention it authorizes constitutes impermissible punishment before trial. The Government, however, has never argued that pretrial detention could be upheld if it were "punishment." The Court of Appeals assumed that pretrial detention under the Bail Reform Act is regulatory, not penal, and we agree that it is.

As an initial matter, the mere fact that a person is detained does not inexorably lead to the conclusion that the government has imposed punishment. To determine whether a restriction on liberty constitutes impermissible punishment or permissible regulation, we first look to legislative intent. Unless Congress expressly intended to impose punitive restrictions, the punitive/regulatory distinction turns on " 'whether an alternative purpose to which [the restriction] may rationally be connected is assignable for it, and whether it appears excessive in relation to the alternative purpose assigned [to it].' "

We conclude that the detention imposed by the Act falls on the regulatory side of the dichotomy. The legislative history of the Bail Reform Act clearly indicates that Congress did not formulate the pretrial detention

3. We intimate no view on the validity of any aspects of the Act that are not relevant to respondents' case. Nor have respondents claimed that the Act is unconstitutional because of the way it was applied to the particular facts of their case.

provisions as punishment for dangerous individuals. Congress instead perceived pretrial detention as a potential solution to a pressing societal problem. There is no doubt that preventing danger to the community is a legitimate regulatory goal.

Nor are the incidents of pretrial detention excessive in relation to the regulatory goal Congress sought to achieve. The Bail Reform Act carefully limits the circumstances under which detention may be sought to the most serious of crimes. See 18 U.S.C. § 3142(f) (detention hearings available if case involves crimes of violence, offenses for which the sentence is life imprisonment or death, serious drug offenses, or certain repeat offenders). The arrestee is entitled to a prompt detention hearing, and the maximum length of pretrial detention is limited by the stringent time limitations of the Speedy Trial Act.[4] Moreover, as in *Schall v. Martin*, the conditions of confinement envisioned by the Act "appear to reflect the regulatory purposes relied upon by the" government. As in *Schall*, the statute at issue here requires that detainees be housed in a "facility separate, to the extent practicable, from persons awaiting or serving sentences or being held in custody pending appeal." We conclude, therefore, that the pretrial detention contemplated by the Bail Reform Act is regulatory in nature, and does not constitute punishment before trial in violation of the Due Process Clause.

* * *

... We have repeatedly held that the government's regulatory interest in community safety can, in appropriate circumstances, outweigh an individual's liberty interest. For example, in times of war or insurrection, when society's interest is at its peak, the government may detain individuals whom the government believes to be dangerous. See *Ludecke v. Watkins* (1948); *Moyer v. Peabody* (1909). [W]e have found no absolute constitutional barrier to detention of potentially dangerous resident aliens pending deportation proceedings. *Carlson v. Landon* (1952); *Wong Wing v. United States* (1896). We have also held that the government may detain mentally unstable individuals who present a danger to the public, *Addington v. Texas* (1979), and dangerous defendants who become incompetent to stand trial, *Jackson v. Indiana* (1972); *Greenwood v. United States* (1956). We have approved of postarrest regulatory detention of juveniles when they present a continuing danger to the community. *Schall v. Martin*, *supra*. If the police suspect an individual of a crime, they may arrest and hold him until a neutral magistrate determines whether probable cause exists. *Gerstein v. Pugh* (1975). Finally, respondents concede and the Court of Appeals noted that an arrestee may be incarcerated until trial if he presents a risk of flight, see *Bell v. Wolfish* (1979), or a danger to witnesses.

... Given the well-established authority of the government, in special circumstances, to restrain individuals' liberty prior to or even without criminal trial and conviction, we think that the present statute providing for pretrial detention on the basis of dangerousness must be evaluated in

4. We intimate no view as to the point at which detention in a particular case might become excessively prolonged, and therefore punitive, in relation to Congress' regulatory goal.

precisely the same manner that we evaluated the laws in the cases discussed above.

The government's interest in preventing crime by arrestees is both legitimate and compelling. In *Schall*, we recognized the strength of the State's interest in preventing juvenile crime. This general concern with crime prevention is no less compelling when the suspects are adults.... The statute we upheld in *Schall* permitted pretrial detention of any juvenile arrested on any charge after a showing that the individual might commit some undefined further crimes. The Bail Reform Act, in contrast, narrowly focuses on a particularly acute problem in which the government interests are overwhelming. The Act operates only on individuals who have been arrested for a specific category of extremely serious offenses. Congress specifically found that these individuals are far more likely to be responsible for dangerous acts in the community after arrest. Nor is the Act by any means a scattershot attempt to incapacitate those who are merely suspected of these serious crimes. The government must first of all demonstrate probable cause to believe that the charged crime has been committed by the arrestee, but that is not enough. In a full-blown adversary hearing, the government must convince a neutral decisionmaker by clear and convincing evidence that no conditions of release can reasonably assure the safety of the community or any person. While the government's general interest in preventing crime is compelling, even this interest is heightened when the government musters convincing proof that the arrestee, already indicted or held to answer for a serious crime, presents a demonstrable danger to the community. Under these narrow circumstances, society's interest in crime prevention is at its greatest.

On the other side of the scale, of course, is the individual's strong interest in liberty. We do not minimize the importance and fundamental nature of this right. But, as our cases hold, this right may, in circumstances where the government's interest is sufficiently weighty, be subordinated to the greater needs of society. We think that Congress' careful delineation of the circumstances under which detention will be permitted satisfies this standard. When the government proves by clear and convincing evidence that an arrestee presents an identified and articulable threat to an individual or the community, we believe that, consistent with the Due Process Clause, a court may disable the arrestee from executing that threat. Under these circumstances, we cannot categorically state that pretrial detention "offends some principle of justice so rooted in the traditions and conscience of our people as to be ranked as fundamental." *Snyder v. Massachusetts* (1934).

Finally, we may dispose briefly of respondents' facial challenge to the procedures of the Bail Reform Act. To sustain them against such a challenge, we need only find them "adequate to authorize the pretrial detention of at least some [persons] charged with crimes," whether or not they might be insufficient in some particular circumstances. We think they pass that test. As we stated in *Schall*, "there is nothing inherently unattainable about a prediction of future criminal conduct."

Under the Bail Reform Act, the procedures by which a judicial officer evaluates the likelihood of future dangerousness are specifically designed to further the accuracy of that determination. Detainees have a right to counsel at the detention hearing. 18 U.S.C. § 3142(f). They may testify in their own behalf, present information by proffer or otherwise, and cross-examine witnesses who appear at the hearing. *Ibid.* The judicial officer charged with the responsibility of determining the appropriateness of detention is guided by statutorily enumerated factors, which include the nature and the circumstances of the charges, the weight of the evidence, the history and characteristics of the putative offender, and the danger to the community. § 3142(g). The government must prove its case by clear and convincing evidence. § 3142(f). Finally, the judicial officer must include written findings of fact and a written statement of reasons for a decision to detain. § 3142(i). The Act's review provisions, § 3145(c), provide for immediate appellate review of the detention decision.

We think these extensive safeguards suffice to repel a facial challenge. The protections are more exacting than those we found sufficient in the juvenile context, see *Schall*, and they far exceed what we found necessary to effect limited postarrest detention in *Gerstein v. Pugh* (1975). Given the legitimate and compelling regulatory purpose of the Act and the procedural protections it offers, we conclude that the Act is not facially invalid under the Due Process Clause of the Fifth Amendment.

B

Respondents also contend that the Bail Reform Act violates the Excessive Bail Clause of the Eighth Amendment. The Court of Appeals did not address this issue because it found that the Act violates the Due Process Clause. We think that the Act survives a challenge founded upon the Eighth Amendment.

The Eighth Amendment addresses pretrial release by providing merely that "Excessive bail shall not be required." This Clause, of course, says nothing about whether bail shall be available at all.... Respondents concede that the right to bail they have discovered in the Eighth Amendment is not absolute. A court may, for example, refuse bail in capital cases. And, as the Court of Appeals noted and respondents admit, a court may refuse bail when the defendant presents a threat to the judicial process by intimidating witnesses.

The Court in *Stack v. Boyle* (1952) had no occasion to consider whether the Excessive Bail Clause requires courts to admit all defendants to bail, because the statute before the Court in that case in fact allowed the defendants to be bailed. Thus, the Court had to determine only whether bail, admittedly available in that case, was excessive if set at a sum greater than that necessary to ensure the arrestees' presence at trial.

The holding of *Stack* is illuminated by the Court's holding just four months later in *Carlson v. Landon* (1952). In that case, remarkably similar to the present action, the detainees had been arrested and held without bail pending a determination of deportability. The Attorney General refused to release the individuals, "on the ground that there was reasonable cause to believe that [their] release would be prejudicial to the public interest and *would endanger the welfare and safety of the United States*." The detainees brought the same challenge that respondents bring to us today: The Eighth

Amendment required them to be admitted to bail. The Court squarely rejected this proposition:

> "The bail clause was lifted with slight changes from the English Bill of Rights Act. In England that clause has never been thought to accord a right to bail in all cases, but merely to provide that bail shall not be excessive in those cases where it is proper to grant bail. When this clause was carried over into our Bill of Rights, nothing was said that indicated any different concept. The Eighth Amendment has not prevented Congress from defining the classes of cases in which bail shall be allowed in this country. Thus, in criminal cases bail is not compulsory where the punishment may be death. Indeed, the very language of the Amendment fails to say all arrests must be bailable."

Carlson v. Landon was a civil case, and we need not decide today whether the Excessive Bail Clause speaks at all to Congress' power to define the classes of criminal arrestees who shall be admitted to bail. For even if we were to conclude that the Eighth Amendment imposes some substantive limitations on the National Legislature's powers in this area, we would still hold that the Bail Reform Act is valid. Nothing in the text of the Bail Clause limits permissible government considerations solely to questions of flight. The only arguable substantive limitation of the Bail Clause is that the government's proposed conditions of release or detention not be "excessive" in light of the perceived evil. Of course, to determine whether the government's response is excessive, we must compare that response against the interest the government seeks to protect by means of that response. Thus, when the government has admitted that its only interest is in preventing flight, bail must be set by a court at a sum designed to ensure that goal, and no more. We believe that when Congress has mandated detention on the basis of a compelling interest other than prevention of flight, as it has here, the Eighth Amendment does not require release on bail.

III

In our society liberty is the norm, and detention prior to trial or without trial is the carefully limited exception. We hold that the provisions for pretrial detention in the Bail Reform Act of 1984 fall within that carefully limited exception. The Act authorizes the detention prior to trial of arrestees charged with serious felonies who are found after an adversary hearing to pose a threat to the safety of individuals or to the community which no condition of release can dispel. The numerous procedural safeguards detailed above must attend this adversary hearing. We are unwilling to say that this congressional determination, based as it is upon that primary concern of every government—a concern for the safety and indeed the lives of its citizens—on its face violates either the Due Process Clause of the Fifth Amendment or the Excessive Bail Clause of the Eighth Amendment.

The judgment of the Court of Appeals is therefore

Reversed.

■ JUSTICE MARSHALL, with whom JUSTICE BRENNAN joins, dissenting.

This case brings before the Court for the first time a statute in which Congress declares that a person innocent of any crime may be jailed indefinitely, pending the trial of allegations which are legally presumed to be untrue, if the Government shows to the satisfaction of a judge that the accused is likely to commit crimes, unrelated to the pending charges, at any time in the future. Such statutes, consistent with the usages of tyranny and the excesses of what bitter experience teaches us to call the police state, have long been thought incompatible with the fundamental human rights protected by our Constitution. Today a majority of this Court holds otherwise. Its decision disregards basic principles of justice established centuries ago and enshrined beyond the reach of governmental interference in the Bill of Rights.

I

* * *

[Editors' Note: In Part I of his opinion, Justice Marshall argued that the case was moot. He noted that Salerno had been convicted in another federal case and had been sentenced to a term of 100 years. The Government had not moved to revoke bail in that other case, as it might have under other provisions of the 1984 Bail Act. Cafaro was cooperating with the government and had obtained his release for medical reasons. Cafaro, although still a respondent, filed no brief before the United States Supreme Court.]

II

* * *

Let us apply the majority's reasoning to a similar, hypothetical case. After investigation, Congress determines (not unrealistically) that a large proportion of violent crime is perpetrated by persons who are unemployed.[4] It also determines, equally reasonably, that much violent crime is committed at night. From amongst the panoply of "potential solutions," Congress chooses a statute which permits, after judicial proceedings, the imposition of a dusk-to-dawn curfew on anyone who is unemployed. Since this is not a measure enacted for the purpose of punishing the unemployed, and since the majority finds that preventing danger to the community is a legitimate

4. Preventing danger to the community through the enactment and enforcement of criminal laws is indeed a legitimate goal, but in our system the achievement of that goal is left primarily to the States. The Constitution does not contain an explicit delegation to the Federal Government of the power to define and administer the general criminal law. The Bail Reform Act does not limit its definition of dangerousness to the likelihood that the defendant poses a danger to others through the commission of *federal* crimes. Federal preventive detention may thus be ordered under the Act when the danger asserted by the Government is the danger that the defendant will violate state law. The majority nowhere identifies the constitutional source of congressional power to authorize the federal detention of persons whose predicted future conduct would not violate any federal statute and could not be punished by a federal court. I can only conclude that the Court's frequently expressed concern with the principles of federalism vanishes when it threatens to interfere with the Court's attainment of the desired result.

regulatory goal, the curfew statute would, according to the majority's analysis, be a mere "regulatory" detention statute, entirely compatible with the substantive components of the Due Process Clause.

The absurdity of this conclusion arises, of course, from the majority's cramped concept of substantive due process. The majority proceeds as though the only substantive right protected by the Due Process Clause is a right to be free from punishment before conviction. The majority's technique for infringing this right is simple: merely redefine any measure which is claimed to be punishment as "regulation," and, magically, the Constitution no longer prohibits its imposition. Because, as I discuss in Part III, infra, the Due Process Clause protects other substantive rights which are infringed by this legislation, the majority's argument is merely an exercise in obfuscation.

The logic of the majority's Eighth Amendment analysis is equally unsatisfactory. If excessive bail is imposed the defendant stays in jail. The same result is achieved if bail is denied altogether. Whether the magistrate sets bail at $1 billion or refuses to set bail at all, the consequences are indistinguishable. It would be mere sophistry to suggest that the Eighth Amendment protects against the former decision, and not the latter. Indeed, such a result would lead to the conclusion that there was no need for Congress to pass a preventive detention measure of any kind; every federal magistrate and district judge could simply refuse, despite the absence of any evidence of risk of flight or danger to the community, to set bail. This would be entirely constitutional, since, according to the majority, the Eighth Amendment "says nothing about whether bail shall be available at all."

But perhaps, the majority says, this manifest absurdity can be avoided. Perhaps the Bail Clause is addressed only to the judiciary.... The text of the Amendment, which provides simply that "[e]xcessive bail shall not be required, nor excessive fines imposed, nor cruel and unusual punishments inflicted," provides absolutely no support for the majority's speculation that both courts and Congress are forbidden to inflict cruel and unusual punishments, while only the courts are forbidden to require excessive bail.[5]

III

The essence of this case may be found, ironically enough, in a provision of the Act to which the majority does not refer. Title 18 U.S.C. § 3142(j) provides that "[n]othing in this section shall be construed as modifying or limiting the presumption of innocence." But the very pith and purpose of

5. The majority refers to the statement in Carlson v. Landon, 342 U.S. 524, 545 (1952) that the Bail Clause was adopted by Congress from the English Bill of Rights Act of 1689, 1 Wm. & Mary, Sess. 2, ch. II, § I(10), and that "[i]n England that clause has never been thought to accord a right to bail in all cases, but merely to provide that bail shall not be excessive in those cases where it is proper to grant bail." A sufficient answer to this meagre argument was made at the time by Justice Black: "The Eighth Amendment is in the American Bill of Rights of 1789, not the English Bill of Rights of 1689." *Carlson v. Landon*, supra, at 557 (dissenting opinion). Our Bill of Rights is contained in a written Constitution one of whose purposes is to protect the rights of the people against infringement by the Legislature, and its provisions, whatever their origins, are interpreted in relation to those purposes.

this statute is an abhorrent limitation of the presumption of innocence. The majority's untenable conclusion that the present Act is constitutional arises from a specious denial of the role of the Bail Clause and the Due Process Clause in protecting the invaluable guarantee afforded by the presumption of innocence.

"The principle that there is a presumption of innocence in favor of the accused is the undoubted law, axiomatic and elementary, and its enforcement lies at the foundation of the administration of our criminal law." Coffin v. United States, 156 U.S. 432, 453 (1895). Our society's belief, reinforced over the centuries, that all are innocent until the state has proved them to be guilty, like the companion principle that guilt must be proved beyond a reasonable doubt, is "implicit in the concept of ordered liberty," Palko v. Connecticut, 302 U.S. 319, 325 (1937), and is established beyond legislative contravention in the Due Process Clause....

The statute now before us declares that persons who have been indicted may be detained if a judicial officer finds clear and convincing evidence that they pose a danger to individuals or to the community. The statute does not authorize the government to imprison anyone it has evidence is dangerous; indictment is necessary. But let us suppose that a defendant is indicted and the government shows by clear and convincing evidence that he is dangerous and should be detained pending a trial, at which trial the defendant is acquitted. May the government continue to hold the defendant in detention based upon its showing that he is dangerous? The answer cannot be yes, for that would allow the government to imprison someone for uncommitted crimes based upon "proof" not beyond a reasonable doubt. The result must therefore be that once the indictment has failed, detention cannot continue. But our fundamental principles of justice declare that the defendant is as innocent on the day before his trial as he is on the morning after his acquittal. Under this statute an untried indictment somehow acts to permit a detention, based on other charges, which after an acquittal would be unconstitutional. The conclusion is inescapable that the indictment has been turned into evidence, if not that the defendant is guilty of the crime charged, then that left to his own devices he will soon be guilty of something else....

To be sure, an indictment is not without legal consequences. It establishes that there is probable cause to believe that an offense was committed, and that the defendant committed it. Upon probable cause a warrant for the defendant's arrest may issue; a period of administrative detention may occur before the evidence of probable cause is presented to a neutral magistrate. Once a defendant has been committed for trial he may be detained in custody if the magistrate finds that no conditions of release will prevent him from becoming a fugitive. But in this connection the charging instrument is evidence of nothing more than the fact that there will be a trial, and

> "release before trial is conditioned upon the accused's giving adequate assurance that he will stand trial and submit to sentence if found guilty. Like the ancient practice of securing the oaths of responsible persons to stand as sureties for the accused, the modern practice of requiring a bail bond or the deposit of a sum of

money subject to forfeiture serves as additional assurance of the presence of an accused." *Stack v. Boyle* (1951).[6]

The finding of probable cause conveys power to try, and the power to try imports of necessity the power to assure that the process of justice will not be evaded or obstructed.... The detention purportedly authorized by this statute bears no relation to the government's power to try charges supported by a finding of probable cause, and thus the interests it serves are outside the scope of interests which may be considered in weighing the excessiveness of bail under the Eighth Amendment.

It is not a novel proposition that the Bail Clause plays a vital role in protecting the presumption of innocence. Reviewing the application for bail pending appeal by members of the American Communist Party convicted under the Smith Act, 18 U.S.C. § 2385, Justice Jackson wrote:

> "Grave public danger is said to result from what [the defendants] may be expected to do, in addition to what they have done since their conviction. If I assume that defendants are disposed to commit every opportune disloyal act helpful to Communist countries, it is still difficult to reconcile with traditional American law the jailing of persons by the courts because of anticipated but as yet uncommitted crimes. Imprisonment to protect society from predicted but unconsummated offenses is ... unprecedented in this country and ... fraught with danger of excesses and injustice...." Williamson v. United States, 95 L.Ed. 1379, 1382 (1950) (Jackson, J., in chambers) (footnote omitted).

As Chief Justice Vinson wrote for the Court in *Stack v. Boyle*, supra: "Unless th[e] right to bail before trial is preserved, the presumption of innocence, secured only after centuries of struggle, would lose its meaning."

IV

* * *

"It is a fair summary of history to say that the safeguards of liberty have frequently been forged in controversies involving not very nice people." United States v. Rabinowitz, 339 U.S. 56, 69 (1950) (FRANKFURTER, J., dissenting). Honoring the presumption of innocence is often difficult; sometimes we must pay substantial social costs as a result of our commitment to the values we espouse. But at the end of the day the presumption of innocence protects the innocent; the shortcuts we take with those whom we believe to be guilty injure only those wrongfully accused and, ultimately, ourselves.

6. The majority states that denial of bail in capital cases has traditionally been the rule rather than the exception. And this of course is so, for it has been the considered presumption of generations of judges that a defendant in danger of execution has an extremely strong incentive to flee. If in any particular case the presumed likelihood of flight should be made irrebuttable, it would in all probability violate the Due Process Clause. Thus what the majority perceives as an exception is nothing more than an example of the traditional operation of our system of bail.

Throughout the world today there are men, women, and children interned indefinitely, awaiting trials which may never come or which may be a mockery of the word, because their governments believe them to be "dangerous." Our Constitution, whose construction began two centuries ago, can shelter us forever from the evils of such unchecked power. Over two hundred years it has slowly, through our efforts, grown more durable, more expansive, and more just. But it cannot protect us if we lack the courage, and the self-restraint, to protect ourselves. Today a majority of the Court applies itself to an ominous exercise in demolition. Theirs is truly a decision which will go forth without authority, and come back without respect.

I dissent.

■ JUSTICE STEVENS, dissenting.

There may be times when the government's interest in protecting the safety of the community will justify the brief detention of a person who has not committed any crime. To use Judge Feinberg's example, it is indeed difficult to accept the proposition that the government is without power to detain a person when it is a virtual certainty that he or she would otherwise kill a group of innocent people in the immediate future. United States v. Salerno, 794 F.2d 64, 77 (C.A.2 1986) (dissenting opinion). Similarly, I am unwilling to decide today that the police may never impose a limited curfew during a time of crisis. These questions are obviously not presented in this case, but they lurk in the background and preclude me from answering the question that is presented in as broad a manner as Justice Marshall has. Nonetheless, I firmly agree with Justice Marshall that the provision of the Bail Reform Act allowing pretrial detention on the basis of future dangerousness is unconstitutional. Whatever the answers are to the questions I have mentioned, it is clear to me that a pending indictment may not be given any weight in evaluating an individual's risk to the community or the need for immediate detention.

If the evidence of imminent danger is strong enough to warrant emergency detention, it should support that preventive measure regardless of whether the person has been charged, convicted, or acquitted of some other offense. In this case, for example, it is unrealistic to assume that the danger to the community that was present when respondents were at large did not justify their detention before they were indicted, but did require that measure the moment that the grand jury found probable cause to believe they had committed crimes in the past. It is equally unrealistic to assume that the danger will vanish if a jury happens to acquit them. Justice Marshall has demonstrated that the fact of indictment cannot, consistent with the presumption of innocence and the Eighth Amendment's Excessive Bail Clause, be used to create a special class the members of which are, alone, eligible for detention because of future dangerousness.

... But if the merits must be reached, there is no answer to the arguments made in Parts II and III of Justice Marshall's dissent. His conclusion, and not the Court's, is faithful to the "fundamental principles as they have been understood by the traditions of our people and our law." Lochner v. New York, 198 U.S. 45, 76 (1905) (Holmes, J., dissenting). Accordingly, I respectfully dissent.

United States v. Xulam

United States Court of Appeals, D.C. Circuit, 1996.
84 F.3d 441.

■ PER CURIAM:

This appeal from an order of detention pending trial under 18 U.S.C. § 3142 raises troubling issues as to the quantum of evidence necessary to detain an individual prior to trial on the ground that "no condition or combination of conditions will reasonably assure" the presence of the appellant at future court proceedings. This appellant, a Kurd from Turkey, has been an international human rights worker resident in the District of Columbia for over three years and a well-known and admired member of the national human rights community. He has no criminal record, but has been charged with making a false statement in a passport application in 1988. In short, after arriving here from Canada on a temporary student visa, he applied for and obtained an American passport under a false name. If convicted, he likely faces a maximum sentence of six months under the federal sentencing guidelines. The Immigration and Naturalization Service ("INS") has served notice that it is undertaking an investigation which may result in appellant's possible deportation and has lodged a detainer to take effect upon his release. The magistrate judge and the district court, on motion of the government, ordered his detention pending trial in the Central District of California solely as a flight risk, conceding he posed no danger to the community or any of its citizens. At the present time, a pretrial detention hearing has been scheduled before the California court.

The Bail Reform Act requires release of a defendant prior to trial unless a judicial officer determines that no conditions or combination of conditions exist which will "reasonably assure the appearance of the person." 18 U.S.C. § 3142(c) (1994). Under the Act, when the government seeks pretrial detention of an individual on the ground that he poses a risk of flight, the standard it must satisfy is a "preponderance of the evidence." That preponderance must, of course, go to the ultimate issue: that no combination of conditions—either those set out in the Bail Reform Act itself or any others that the magistrate or judge might find useful—can "reasonably" assure that the defendant will appear for trial. 18 U.S.C. § 3142(c). The Act sets out a number of conditions which may be used to ensure appearance, including, inter alia, remaining in custody of a designated person who agrees to assume supervision and to report any violation of a release condition; maintaining employment; abiding by restrictions on place of abode or travel; reporting on a regular basis to a designated law enforcement agency; complying with a curfew; executing a bail bond; and a final catch-all for any condition that the magistrate or judge deems "reasonably necessary" to assure appearance. 18 U.S.C. § 3142(c). Section 3142(g) of the Act sets out the factors to be considered by the magistrate or judge in deciding whether available conditions will reasonably assure the defendant's appearance: the nature and circumstances of the offense, particularly its nonviolent nature; the weight of the evidence; the history and characteristics of the person, including his character, family ties, employment, length of residence in the community, community ties, past conduct, criminal history, and record of court appearances; and the danger the defendant poses to the community if released.

In every category mentioned in the statute, this appellant was a prime candidate for release. His nonviolent charge carried a maximum of six months imprisonment under the sentencing guidelines; he had no criminal record or record of failure to appear; he was employed and had a wide circle of respected acquaintances and close friends in the community who testified as to his "spiritual" and "intellectual" integrity; and the government acknowledged that he posed no threat to the community. Indeed, the district court admitted that if he were facing only the criminal charge, his "chances [of appearing] might be good." Nonetheless, the magistrate and district court judge refused to release him pending trial. What militated against him, in the judge's view, was that the government witness testified that he might be facing deportation to Turkey, where as a Kurd he might be persecuted. The court also believed that "he will go to any other ends ... to address [the] cause [of Kurdish rights], especially when he now realizes there's a possibility he could be deported." For that reason, the judge concluded that there would be "no way that [a third-party custodian] can lock him up or restrain him from leaving." Obviously troubled, he added that the magistrate to whom the appellant is presented after transportation to California "may very well decide to disagree with the decision this court has made" and "nothing in my decision should suggest to [the California magistrate] that ... he does not have jurisdiction to fully consider the issue of bond." It was then clearly the appellant's alleged crime—the false identity he claimed to obtain a passport, for which he is presumed innocent—and the possibility of his deportation to Turkey that fueled the judge's decision.

There are several reasons why we do not believe those factors alone provided a legitimate ground for ordering pretrial detention. First, we are not convinced that the government satisfied its burden of showing a risk of flight. * * * Appellant's strong commitment to advocating his Kurdish cause in the United States, cited by the district court as enhancing his risk of flight, would seem to militate against, not in favor of, flight, since the only way he can pursue that cause is publicly, within the human rights community, and disappearing or fleeing would render him permanently impotent in that respect. How would he be regarded in that community, for instance, if he violated the trust of his third-party custodians, or forfeited bonds or assets they pledged for his release? On a more practical level, the government has taken away all his passports and travel documents, so it is unlikely he could go far even if he wished to. * * * Second, any or all of the conditions listed above were available in this case, but there is no indication in the record that the magistrate judge or the district court judge fully explored the commitments offered by appellant's witnesses or the appellant's proffer that he was willing to abide by whatever conditions the court imposed.

* * *

We cannot but conclude that a serious error has been made here. A first-time offender accused of a nonviolent crime with strong community ties and respected members of that community willing to supervise his release in any manner the court finds necessary, including designated residences, curfews, reporting in, is incarcerated pending trial, despite the fact that his entire lifestyle and mission strongly suggest he will stay in place, and his charged misdeed (if, indeed, he is found guilty) was to falsify information on a passport in order to remain in this country. The pretrial detention provisions of the Bail Reform Act of 1984 were not intended to apply to such an appellant. The magistrate judge and district court referred several times to the notion that if the defendant were to flee, his supervisors could not stop him. That, of course, is true of every defendant released on conditions; it is also not the standard authorized by law for determining whether pretrial detention is appropriate. Section 3142 speaks of conditions that will "reasonably" assure appearance, not guarantee it. The record here contains more than enough to satisfy the "reasonable" assurance test, and not enough to show by a preponderance of the evidence that no combination of conditions will assure the defendant's appearance.

Thus, despite the large discretion normally accorded the trial court in this area, we revoke the order of detention.

■ GINSBURG, CIRCUIT JUDGE, dissenting:

The defendant stands charged with making a false statement on a passport application in violation of 18 U.S.C. § 1542. According to the testimony of a Special Agent of the Department of State Security Service, in 1986 the defendant procured a passport in the name of a deceased person, Steven Barry Citron. In 1988, based upon a court document attesting to a change of name, he was issued a new passport, this time in the name of Sereno Citron. In 1993 he obtained yet another passport, this time in the name of Kani Xulam, again based upon a purported change of name. During a search of defendant's office, agents recovered a Turkish passport with a photograph of defendant and a Canadian social security card, both in the name of Namet Gunduez.

Because the defendant is apparently subject to deportation as an illegal alien—the INS has instituted an investigation and lodged a detainer against him—and has a demonstrated ability to obtain false travel and other documents, the Government suggested that the risk he would flee is sufficiently high that he should be detained pending trial, pursuant to 18 U.S.C. § 3142. The district court held a hearing at which the defendant made the best record he could in support of the proposition that he should be released into the custody of certain respected citizens willing to serve in that capacity. The court then granted the Government's detention request on the ground that "no condition or combination of conditions" of release could reasonably assure that the defendant would appear as required for future hearings.

* * *

Why my colleagues take it upon themselves to become advocates for the defendant—who is zealously represented by counsel of his own—is a mystery to me. One thing is clear, though: In view of the record, the district court was well within what the court acknowledges is "the large discretion normally accorded the trial court in this area."

NOTES

1. Once the trial judge resolves to admit a defendant to bail, the person so admitted must execute an appearance bond. The bond must be signed by a surety who binds himself to pay the face amount of the bond if the defendant fails to appear pursuant to the orders of the court. Generally, sureties can be divided into two classes: individual sureties and professional bondsmen. Individual sureties must go through a procedure termed justification whereby an affidavit is submitted disclosing the extent of the surety's property used to secure the bond in question. While justification is generally dispensed with where approved corporate sureties are involved, it is necessary, in the case of smaller, independent sureties, to insure that the same property is not pledged to secure a great number of individual bonds. See United States v. Nebbia, 357 F.2d 303 (2d Cir.1966) ("if the court lacks confidence in a surety's purpose or ability to secure the appearance of a bail defendant, it may refuse its approval of a bond even though the financial standing of bail is beyond question"); United States v. Melville, 309 F.Supp. 822 (S.D.N.Y. 1970) (trial judge has discretion to require justification even in the case of a professional surety).

2. Recent modernizations of the state bail systems carry few practical implications other than to suggest that counsel should be sensitive to undue pretrial incarceration. Excessive bail can almost invariably be classified as harmless error when the merits of a conviction are reviewed. See Whitty v. State, 34 Wis.2d 278, 149 N.W.2d 557 (1967). Arguments clearly delineating a risk of flight, coupled with a danger to the community, are appropriate in certain cases. Issues of importance are: (1) the defendant's proclivity toward crime through his past record; (2) the danger which he presents because of the manner in which he is alleged to have committed the offense; and (3) the high risk of flight because of either minimal ties to the community or the severity of the potential penalty. Where a defendant has previously jumped bail, that factor may clearly be taken into account. See Babb v. United States, 414 F.2d 719 (10th Cir.1968).

3. In United States v. Montalvo–Murillo, 495 U.S. 711, 110 S.Ct. 2072 (1990), a detention hearing was not held at the defendant's first judicial appearance. The defendant, who had been arrested on February 8, 1989, and who had appeared in court on February 10, finally received a detention hearing on February 21, well beyond the outer statutory period for such a hearing. The magistrate ordered the arrestee's release, finding that the Government had not made out an adequate case demonstrating risk of flight or danger to the community, although agents had found seventy-two pounds of cocaine in the defendant's truck. The magistrate required the posting of a $50,000 bond. The Government appealed. The defendant posted the bond and fled.

The Supreme Court held that the issue was not moot despite the defendant's flight. It then held that "a failure to comply with the first appearance requirement" for holding a detention hearing does not defeat the Government's authority to seek detention even when the defendant has been held in custody without bail beyond the statutory limits for such a hearing. "Although the duty is mandatory, the sanction is not loss of all power to act ... We do not agree that we should, or can, invent a remedy to satisfy some perceived need to coerce the courts into complying with the statutory time limits." It added, "The district court, the court of appeals, and this Court remain open to order immediate release of anyone detained in violation of the statute."

The Court viewed the proposed remedy for delay as too costly, permitting the release of dangerous persons or persons who are likely to flee. It added, "We have no need to consider in this case the remedies available to a person detained beyond the statutory limit and later found eligible for release."

Three justices dissented, saying that the Government should be required to suffer the consequence if it does not comply with the plain statutory command, especially because "the executive power to detain an individual is the hallmark of the totalitarian state."

4. Some courts have taken a lengthy period of pre-trial incarceration into account in mandating that an arrestee be released from preventive detention for any further period of delay. See United States v. Gonzales Claudio, 806 F.2d 334 (2d Cir.1986) (fourteen months, court used a due process analysis); United States v. Ojeda Rios, 846 F.2d 167 (2d Cir.1988).

By contrast in United States v. Quartermaine, 913 F.2d 910 (11th Cir.1990), the Court held that the prospect of lengthy pre-trial delay is irrelevant to the federal statutory preventive detentions provisions. Recognizing possible constitutional difficulties with such delay, the court found no Due Process violation would occur if the defendant were preventively detained for eight to ten months.

One might wonder how, under the federal Speedy Trial Act (Casebook 984), a defendant's trial could be delayed for such lengthy periods. Frequently, as in *Ojeda Rios*, postponements arise from various delays caused by a co-defendant. For example, there may be time consuming motions or lengthy proceedings to determine the co-defendant's competency to stand trial.

5. 18 U.S.C. § 3142(b) states that a defendant shall be released on personal recognizance or an unsecured appearance bond unless the judicial officer determines such release will not reasonably assure the defendant's appearance at trial or will endanger the safety of the community. In order to impose more restrictive conditions, the judicial officer must state his findings of fact and the reasons for his decision in writing. This applies not only to magistrates, but also to district court judges, who must consider the facts de novo. United States v. Hurtado, 779 F.2d 1467 (11th Cir.1985).

For an instance in which the district court reversed the magistrate judge's decision to permit bail, see United States v. Ippolito, 930 F.Supp. 581 (M.D.Fla. 1996), dealing with defendants who were members of an organization claiming to have the self-appointed right to punish for treason and obstruct trials in violation of a state court injunction.

In United States v. Presley, 52 F.3d 64 (4th Cir.1995), dangerousness to the community was sufficiently shown in light of defendant's previous crimes, including armed robbery, shooting into an occupied dwelling and breaking and entering with intent to commit assault, as well as the fact that he was subject to the maximum sentence of life imprisonment.

6. 18 U.S.C. § 3142(f) provides that the traditional rules of evidence do not apply at the detention hearing but the defendant has a right to counsel, the right to testify, and the right to call and cross-examine witnesses. In enacting this section, Congress intended the previous law governing the admissibility of evidence at bail hearings to apply. See United States v. Delker, 757 F.2d 1390 (3d Cir.1985). Thus, while the court may consider hearsay in deciding whether to grant bail, it cannot take evidence outside the presence of the defendant and his counsel. United States v. Wind, 527 F.2d 672 (6th Cir.1975).

7. 18 U.S.C. § 3142(c) provides that the judicial officer may not impose a financial condition that results in the pre-trial detention of the defendant. United States v. Jessup, 757 F.2d 378 (1st Cir.1985), held that this section does not require the judicial officer to release the defendant if he is unable to meet a financial condition which the officer has determined is the only form of conditional release that will reasonably assure his future appearance in court. *Jessup* concluded that the defendant was detained "not because he cannot raise the money, but because without the money, the risk of flight is too great." Compare United States v. Ferranti, 66 F.3d 540 (2d Cir.1995), where the court held that a $1 million bond was too low because it would have deterred flight, but not danger to the community. The court also held that elaborate conditions of release that depended on good faith compliance were insufficient when the defendant's violent history showed no basis for believing that good faith would be forthcoming.

8. Appellate review of pre-trial bond is not sought in the typical state case where the accused is unable to post the amount set. Often the only method of high-court review is through habeas corpus. Direct appeal is unavailable in many jurisdictions. In many states, a petition for a writ of habeas corpus can be filed in a court of review only after the reviewing court exercises its discretion to grant leave to file. The procedure can be cumbersome, and pre-trial bond issues can become moot before the reviewing court acts. Even in jurisdictions which have streamlined procedures for appellate review of pre-trial bond, appellate opinions on bond matters are rarely published. As a result, there are very few state reviewing-court opinions on the very important subject of bail.

"Review" of pre-trial bond often comes in the form of a motion to reduce bond filed in the trial court. As cases get older, and as they are passed from one judge to another in the course of the proceedings, trial court reduction of bail is not unusual.

9. In Williams v. Illinois, Casebook p. 801, the State made an *in terrorem* argument. It contended that if an indigent could not be incarcerated for failure to pay a fine after conviction, an indigent could not be held in custody for failure to post bond. An adverse decision for Illinois in *Williams*, it was contended, would require destruction of the bail system. Why has that not happened? Consider bail issues in light of *Williams*. Concerning equal protection and due process attacks made by indigents on the bail system, see a pre-*Williams* decision, Reeves v. State, 411 P.2d 212 (Alaska 1966), and a post-*Williams* opinion, Pugh v. Rainwater, 572 F.2d 1053 (5th Cir.1978) (en banc).

10. In Schall v. Martin, 467 U.S. 253, 104 S.Ct. 2403 (1984), the Supreme Court approved a statute which allowed pre-trial detention of accused juvenile delinquents upon a determination that there is a "serious risk" that the juvenile "may before the return date commit an act which if committed by an adult would constitute a crime." Using a due process analysis, the Court held that the state had a legitimate interest in protecting society and the juvenile. It noted that the statute provides a number of safeguards, so that the juvenile's interest in liberty is outweighed by the governmental purpose. The Court noted that every state permits preventive pre-trial detention for some juveniles. Under the New York scheme, the detained youth was entitled to a probable cause hearing within three or four days and a trial within, at most, fourteen days of the original appearance. In the interim he was held under "non-punitive" conditions.

The Court did not provide an Eighth Amendment analysis because the proceedings were not criminal but juvenile.

11. Upon breach of the conditions of release, the bond may be forfeited. In instances where a forfeiture is ordered, trial judges, in most jurisdictions, retain the power to set aside the forfeiture before judgment is entered. See United States v. Kirkman, 426 F.2d 747 (4th Cir.1970); United States v. Egan, 394 F.2d 262 (2d Cir.1968). A defendant who "jumps" bail subjects himself to the prosecution for such conduct; but a motion to forfeit bail is not necessarily a requirement to initiation of a subsequent charge for bail jumping. See United States v. DePugh, 434 F.2d 548 (8th Cir.1970). Where a defendant returns after an interim period of bail jumping, he may be remitted to bail under the same or new conditions of release. However, because a defendant who has once jumped bail obviously evidences a propensity toward flight, the trial judge can reconsider the conditions of bond.

B. BAIL DURING TRIAL

Bitter v. United States

Supreme Court of the United States, 1967.
389 U.S. 15, 88 S.Ct. 6.

■ PER CURIAM.

Petitioner was tried on 18 counts of violating the mail fraud statute and one count of using an assumed name. On the third day of trial, the Government rested its case. This was earlier than it had announced or than petitioner had anticipated. At recess time petitioner sought leave of the court to go to his office in order to gather additional evidence for the defense. Permission for this was granted. Forty-five minutes were allotted for the recess.

Petitioner, who had previously appeared promptly at every session of the trial, was this time tardy by 37 minutes in returning to court. Without warning, hearing, or explanation the trial judge ordered petitioner into custody for the balance of the trial. Attempts by petitioner's counsel to offer explanations for petitioner's lateness were to no avail.

Defense counsel was then advised that petitioner would be kept in custody in a county jail located some 18 miles from the court. In fact, petitioner was taken about 40 miles distant, to a different jail. Counsel's endeavors throughout the trial to obtain petitioner's release proved fruitless. Petitioner remained in custody for the duration of the trial. He was convicted on seven counts of mail fraud....

Petitioner contended that his incarceration was unjustified and that it materially interfered with his right to counsel and severely impeded his defense....

A trial judge indisputably has broad powers to ensure the orderly and expeditious progress of a trial. For this purpose, he has the power to revoke bail and to remit the defendant to custody. But this power must be exercised with circumspection. It may be invoked only when and to the extent justified by danger which the defendant's conduct presents or by danger of significant interference with the progress or order of the trial.[1] See Fernandez v. United States, 365 U.S. 397, 81 S.Ct. 642 (1961) (memorandum of Mr. Justice Harlan in chambers); Carbo v. United States, 288 F.2d 282 (C.A.9th Cir.1961); Christoffel v. United States, 89 U.S.App.D.C. 341, 196 F.2d 560 (1951).

The record in this case shows only a single, brief incident of tardiness, resulting in commitment of the defendant to custody for the balance of the trial in a jail 40 miles distant from the courtroom. In these circumstances, the trial judge's order of commitment, made without hearing or statement of reasons, had the appearance and effect of punishment rather than of an

1. It does not appear whether defendant was at large on bail at the time of the order remitting him to custody. But the same principle would apply if he had been at liberty on his own recognizance. Cf. Bail Reform Act of 1966, 18 U.S.C. § 3146.

order designed solely to facilitate the trial. Punishment may not be so inflicted. We therefore hold that the order was unjustified and that it constituted an unwarranted burden upon defendant and his counsel in the conduct of the case.

Accordingly, we grant certiorari and reverse the judgment.

Judgment reversed.

■ Mr. Justice Marshall took no part in the consideration or decision of this case.

NOTES

1. A defendant released prior to trial generally continues on bail during trial unless the trial judge, in his discretion, determines that a revision of the terms of the bail is necessary to assure presence during trial or the expeditious progress of the trial. There are two general categories of misconduct by the defendant that will warrant revocation of bail during trial. The first is his obstructive misconduct during the course of trial. See United States v. Bentvena, 288 F.2d 442 (2d Cir.1961), affirmed sub nom., Fernandez v. United States, 81 S.Ct. 642 (1961) (Harlan, J., in chambers).

2. The second category of bail revocation during trial arises where threats to government witnesses are made by a particular defendant. See Carbo v. United States, 288 F.2d 686 (9th Cir.1961). However, the defendant is entitled to an adequate hearing on the issue of whether such threats were made. Therefore, where the conduct is not within the observation of the trial judge, it is apparent that he cannot revoke bail absent a hearing on the merits. Cf. United States v. Gilbert, 425 F.2d 490 (D.C.Cir.1969).

C. Bail Pending Appeal

United States v. Miller

United States Court of Appeals for the Third Circuit, 1985.
753 F.2d 19.

■ Sloviter, Circuit Judge.

* * *

Criteria for Bail Pending Appeal Under the 1984 Act

The relevant section of the 1984 Act governing bail pending appeal, to be codified at 18 U.S.C. § 3143, provides:

(b) RELEASE OR DETENTION PENDING APPEAL BY THE DEFENDANT

> The judicial officer [of a court of original jurisdiction over an offense, or of a Federal appellate court] shall order that a person who has been found guilty of an offense and sentenced to a term of imprisonment, and who has filed an appeal or a petition for writ of certiorari, be detained, unless the judicial officer finds—

> (1) by clear and convincing evidence that the person is not likely to flee or pose a danger to the safety of any person or the community if released pursuant to sections 3142(b) or (c); and (2) that the appeal is not for purpose of delay and raises a substantial question of law or fact likely to result in reversal or an order for a new trial.
>
> If the judicial officer makes such findings, he shall order the release of the person in accordance with the provisions of sections 3142(b) or (c).

The newly enacted criteria have also been expressly incorporated in Federal Rule of Appellate Procedure 9(c). *See* Bail Reform Act of 1984, § 210.

The district court found that appellants Stanton and Robert Miller satisfied subsection (1) in that they were "not likely to flee or pose a danger to the safety of another person or community if released." The district court also found that "the appeal was not for the purpose of delay." It is not clear whether the district court found that the appeal "raises substantial questions of law or fact." The court denied bail pending appeal after stating that it could not "in good faith ... conclude that it is likely to result in a reversal or an order for a new trial."

It appears that the district court construed the statutory language to signify that it could grant bail on appeal only upon finding that its own rulings were likely to be reversed. At the hearing on the post-trial motions, the court stated that the Act "practically means that the district judge has to determine that he has probably made an error in the decision that he has rendered in the lower court...." At the sentencing hearing, the district court stated that, "it would be, I think, a very rare case that the judicial officer would make such a finding, but I think that's the intent and purpose of the statute, it seems to me rather clear they do not intend persons to remain on bail where an appeal is filed." We conclude that this is not the correct interpretation of the statutory language.

The Bail Reform Act of 1984 was enacted because Congress wished to reverse the presumption in favor of bail that had been established under the prior statute, the Bail Reform Act of 1966. Under that Act, even after conviction the defendant was entitled to bail "unless the court or judge has reason to believe that no one or more conditions of release will reasonably assure that the person will not flee or pose a danger to any other person or any other community." § 3(a), 80 Stat. 214, 215 (1966) (formerly codified at 18 U.S.C. § 3148). Congressional concern with this standard was manifest. As early as 1970, Congress enacted a much more stringent rule for bail pending appeal under its authority as the legislative body for the District of Columbia, D.C.Code Ann. § 23–1325(c), the precursor of the Bail Reform Act of 1984.

The House Report on the District of Columbia Act was explicit as to the reasons for congressional dissatisfaction with the prevailing criteria for bail pending appeal. It states:

> [O]nce a person has been convicted and sentenced to jail, there is absolutely no reason for the law to favor release pending appeal or even permit it in the absence of exceptional circumstances. First and most important, the conviction, in which the defendant's guilt of a

> crime has been established beyond a reasonable doubt, is presumably correct in law, a presumption factually supported by the low rate of reversal of criminal convictions in the Federal system. Second, the decision to send a convicted person to jail and thereby reject all other sentencing alternatives, by its very nature includes a determination by the sentencing judge that the defendant is dangerous to the person or property of others, and dangerous when sentenced, not a year later after the appeal is decided. Third, release of a criminal defendant into the community, even after conviction, destroys whatever deterrent effect remains in the criminal law. Finally, contrary to the suggestion in the *Forrest* case, [United States v. Forrest, 418 F.2d 1186 (D.C.Cir. 1969)] the purpose of the appellate process is not to give a convicted criminal, by means of release pending appeal, an opportunity to demonstrate a basis for reducing a sentence after the conviction has been affirmed.

H.Rep. No. 907, 91st Cong., 2d Sess. 186–87 (1970).

The provision governing bail on appeal in the Bail Reform Act of 1984 is identical to that in the District of Columbia Code. In the three relevant Senate Reports, that body made clear that the purpose of the Act was to reverse the presumption in favor of bail, but not to deny bail entirely to persons who appeal their convictions, as the district court believed. In the most recent report on the provision, which remained identical throughout its legislative consideration, the Senate Judiciary Committee stated, "The basic distinction between the existing provision and section 3143 is one of presumption.... It has been held that although denial of bail after conviction is frequently justified, the current statute incorporates a presumption in favor of bail even after conviction. It is the presumption that the Committee wishes to eliminate in section 3143." S.Rep. No. 225, 98th Cong., 1st Sess. at 26 (1983), *reprinted in* 1984 U.S.Code Cong. & Ad.News 1, 29 (Supp. 9A). The Senate also made it clear, however, that bail on appeal was still available. It stated that section 3143 "*statutorily permit[s]* release of a person while he is awaiting sentence or while he is appealing or filing for a writ of certiorari." Id. (emphasis added).

Our task is to give a reasonable construction to the statutory language in a manner that effectuates the congressional intent. Under the new act, after first making the findings as to flight, danger, and delay, a court must determine that the question raised on appeal is a "substantial" one, i.e. it must find that the significant question at issue is one which is either novel, which has not been decided by controlling precedent, or which is fairly doubtful. This represents a marked change in the inquiry into the merits in the context of a bail determination, since the 1966 act only required the court to determine whether the issue was "frivolous," see 18 U.S.C. § 3148 (repealed by 1984 Act).

After the court finds that the question on appeal meets the new "substantial" test, it must determine whether that issue is sufficiently important to the merits that a contrary appellate ruling is likely to require reversal or a new trial. The statutory language requiring a finding that the appeal "raises a substantial question of law or fact likely to result in reversal or an order for a new trial" cannot be read as meaning, as the district court apparently believed, that the district court must conclude that its own order is likely to be reversed.

In the first place, such a reading would render language in the statute surplusage because every question that is likely to be reversed must by definition be "substantial". In the second place, we are unwilling to attribute to Congress the cynicism that would underlie the provision were it to be read as requiring the district court to determine the likelihood of its own error. A district judge who, on reflection, concludes that s/he erred may rectify that error when ruling on post-trial motions. Judges do not knowingly leave substantial errors uncorrected, or deliberately misconstrue applicable precedent. Thus, it would have been capricious of Congress to have conditioned bail only on the willingness of a trial judge to certify his or her own error.

For a similar reason, the phrase "*likely* to result in reversal or an order for a new trial" cannot reasonably be construed to require the district court to predict the probability of reversal. The federal courts are not to be put in the position of "bookmakers" who trade on the probability of ultimate outcome. Instead, that language must be read as going to the significance of the substantial issue to the ultimate disposition of the appeal. A question of law or fact may be substantial but may, nonetheless, in the circumstances of a particular case, be considered harmless, to have no prejudicial effect, or to have been insufficiently preserved. A court may find that reversal or a new trial is "likely" only if it concludes that the question is so integral to the merits of the conviction on which defendant is to be imprisoned that a contrary appellate holding is likely to require reversal of the conviction or a new trial.

The parties are in substantial agreement with this construction of the statute. In its memorandum, the government analyzes the language as follows:

> First, the appeal must raise a "substantial question of law or fact." Second, if defendant prevails on appeal, the issue must be one that is "likely to result in reversal or an order for a new trial" on all counts on which a sentence of imprisonment was imposed. If the error would be considered harmless or reversal or new trial would otherwise not be the remedy, the Act's requirements are not satisfied.

* * *

This construction, which we accept, effectuates congressional intent in that a defendant seeking bail on appeal must now show that his or her appeal has more merit than under the discarded "frivolous" test, but preserves the court's discretion to give bail in those cases, which will consequently be considerably reduced in number, where defendant can meet the criteria discussed above. Since Congress, by its explicit language, did not deny all bail on appeal, we need not reach appellants' additional suggestion that denial of bail on appeal has "overtones of severe constitutional infirmity," nor do we express any opinion on the government's response that a concomitant of the government's right to deprive defendants of any right to appeal is the right to eliminate bail on appeal.

In summary, then, under the criteria established by the 1984 Act which the *defendant* now has the burden of proving if s/he seeks bail pending appeal, the court must find:

(1) that the defendant is not likely to flee or pose a danger to the safety of any other person or the community if released;

(2) that the appeal is not for purpose of delay;

(3) that the appeal raises a substantial question of law or fact; and

(4) that if that substantial question is determined favorably to defendant on appeal, that decision is likely to result in reversal or an order for a new trial of all counts on which imprisonment has been imposed.

NOTES

1. In United States v. Steinhorn, 927 F.2d 195 (4th Cir.1991), the court granted bond pending appeal. It said:

> We adopt the procedure first announced in United States v. Miller, 753 F.2d 19 (3d Cir.1985), and subsequently accepted by every other circuit, see United States v. Perholtz, 836 F.2d 554, 555 (D.C.Cir.1987). In applying § 3143(b)(2) the court must make two inquiries after finding that the appeal is not taken for the purpose of delay. First, whether the question presented on appeal is a "substantial" one. Second, if decided in favor of the accused, whether the substantial question is important enough to warrant reversal or a new trial on all counts for which the district court imprisoned the defendant.
>
> We adopt the definition of "substantial question" first proposed by the Eleventh Circuit in United States v. Giancola, 754 F.2d 898 (11th Cir. 1985). That court defined a "substantial question" as:
>
>> a "close" question or one that very well could be decided the other way. Further, there are no blanket categories for what questions do or do not constitute "substantial" ones. Whether a question is "substantial" must be determined on a case-by-case basis.

After conviction, the balance of interests change from protecting the innocent from an improper judgment to protecting public safety. Thus, bail pending appeal may be conditioned on factors unrelated to securing defendant's appearance. See Ex parte Anderer, 61 S.W.3d 398 (Tex.Crim.2001) (no driving condition of bail for individual convicted of negligent homicide).

2. Once a federal defendant is sentenced and incarcerated by the district judge, some defense lawyers are most reluctant to seek appellate bond from the United States Court of Appeals. They fear that their client's appeal will be "prejudged" and deemed insubstantial after the reviewing court has examined documents that necessarily have been prepared in relative haste. Once the Court of Appeals has deemed the issues "non-substantial," for purposes of appellate bond, how likely is it to later rule, when it decides the appeal, that the appellant is entitled to a reversal of his or her conviction?

3. When a person is arrested for violating the conditions of supervised released, he is entitled to a hearing on bail in accordance with the standards applicable to one convicted and awaiting sentence. United States v. Loya, 23 F.3d 1529 (9th Cir. 1994). However, once supervised release is revoked, bail pending appeal is available only upon a showing of exceptional circumstances such as the existence of substantial claims upon which the appellant has a high probability of success, a serious deterioration of health while incarcerated, and any unusual delay in the process of appeal. United States v. West, 21 F.3d 607 (5th Cir.1994).

CHAPTER 13

PRE-TRIAL MOTIONS

The modern concept of pretrial motions evolved from the common law concept of pleading to a criminal charge. Although, with the exception of the plea of guilty or not guilty, "pleadings" are generally associated with civil cases, they are particularly important to criminal cases in the pretrial setting. At common law, there were five basic challenges available to a criminal defendant:

(1) a plea to jurisdiction. See United States v. Thomas, 151 U.S. 577, 14 S.Ct. 426 (1894) (jurisdiction over Indians); (2) a plea in abatement, challenging the technical sufficiency of the indictment because of some defect in the grand jury process. See United States v. Storrs, 272 U.S. 652, 47 S.Ct. 221 (1926); (3) a motion to quash, raising defects of both form and substance in the indictment itself. See United States v. Rosenburgh, 74 U.S. (7 Wall.) 580 (1868); (4) demur to the indictment for its failure to allege an offense. Demurrers were extremely rare since they admitted the facts alleged in the indictment and the objections raised by demurrer could be argued by plea in abatement or motion to quash. See United States v. Cook, 84 U.S. (17 Wall.) 168 (1872); and (5) a plea in bar, raising claims prohibiting the action such as double jeopardy and statute of limitations concerns. See Heike v. United States, 217 U.S. 423, 30 S.Ct. 539 (1910). See generally Chitty, Criminal Law 434 (2d ed. 1826); 2 Bishop, New Criminal Procedure § 746 (4th ed. 1895).

The propriety of granting a motion to dismiss an indictment prior to trial is contingent upon whether the alleged infirmity is a question of law or involves the determination of facts. If a question of law is involved, consideration of the motion is generally proper. See United States v. Korn, 557 F.2d 1089 (5th Cir.1977). However, trial courts may make preliminary findings of fact necessary to decide questions of law. The facts may be developed at a pretrial hearing, but the court's findings on the motion cannot invade the province of the ultimate fact-finder. United States v. Jones, 542 F.2d 661 (6th Cir.1976).

As a general matter, the motions discussed in this chapter must be raised prior to trial or they will be deemed waived, and relief from waiver will not be granted in the absence of a strong showing of good cause and actual prejudice. United States v. Kaplan, 554 F.2d 958 (9th Cir.1977); United States v. Williams, 544 F.2d 1215 (4th Cir.1976). Jeopardy motions may constitute an exception to this rule. See Section A(8), infra.

The following sections dealing with specific pretrial motions is not intended to be an exhaustive list of available remedies. Certain very basic motions, such as those for discovery, bill of particulars, and grand jury challenges, are dealt with in other sections of this book. It should be noted, however, that pretrial motions range from the relatively standard, as those discussed in the following sections, to the very esoteric, as removal of a state court prosecution to federal court under the narrow circumstances set forth in 28 U.S.C. § 1443.

Under Fed.R.Crim.P. 12(b), the following motions must be raised before trial or are waived: defects in instituting the proceedings, defects in the indictment (except jurisdiction), suppression of evidence, severance of counts or defendants and discovery.

A. DISMISSAL FOR DOUBLE JEOPARDY AND RELATED PRINCIPLES

1. GENERAL INTRODUCTION

The Fifth Amendment to the United States Constitution provides, in part: "nor shall any person be subject for the same offense to be twice put in jeopardy of life or limb." The general design of the Double Jeopardy Clause of the Fifth Amendment is described in Green v. United States:

"The constitutional prohibition against 'double jeopardy' was designed to protect an individual from being subjected to the hazards of trial and possible conviction more than once for an alleged offense. . . . The underlying idea, one that is deeply ingrained in at least the Anglo–American system of jurisprudence, is that the State with all its resources and power should not be allowed to make repeated attempts to convict an individual for an alleged offense, thereby subjecting him to embarrassment, expense and ordeal and compelling him to live in a continuing state of anxiety and insecurity, as well as enhancing the possibility that even though innocent he may be found guilty." 355 U.S. 184, 187–188, 78 S.Ct. 221, 223 (1957).

On the other hand, other values militate against an expansive reading of the double jeopardy prohibition. Prominent among these is the societal interest in providing the prosecutor a single, *fair* opportunity to establish the accused's guilt.

Knowledge of the diverse policy considerations which underlie the Double Jeopardy Clause and those which underlie efforts to limit its application, while helpful, will not always aid us in predicting how the clause will be interpreted in a concrete situation. Although the student ought not abandon the effort to achieve a unified theory of double jeopardy, he or she should realize that no single theory is compatible with the various black-letter rules which now govern double jeopardy claims. Among the most difficult cases to reconcile are those which sometimes permit but sometimes prohibit the commencement of a new trial after an earlier proceeding had passed the point where jeopardy had "attached" for purposes of the Fifth Amendment. These cases are treated in subsections 3–6, infra. Theories with labels such as "waiver" or "continuing jeopardy" have been advanced, but none is entirely satisfactory.

Palko v. Connecticut

Supreme Court of the United States, 1937.
302 U.S. 319, 58 S.Ct. 149.

[Palko was charged with first degree murder, but was convicted by a jury of the lesser included offense of second-degree murder. Connecticut law permitted the prosecution to appeal to raise errors "of law." The state Supreme Court of Error reversed for a new trial on the charge of first degree murder, finding that the trial court improperly excluded a confession of the defendant and certain evidence designed to impeach the defendant's trial testimony. The reviewing court also found that the judge had erred against the prosecution in the jury instructions concerning the difference between first degree murder and second degree murder. Over objections that double jeopardy concepts barred a retrial, the defendant was retried and convicted, and that conviction was affirmed. Defendant appealed to the United States Supreme Court.]

■ Mr. Justice Cardozo delivered the opinion of the Court.

* * *

We have said that in appellant's view the Fourteenth Amendment is to be taken as embodying the prohibitions of the Fifth. His thesis is even broader. Whatever would be a violation of the original bill of rights (Amendments 1 to 8) if done by the federal government is now equally unlawful by force of the Fourteenth Amendment if done by a state. There is no such general rule.

* * *

Our survey of the cases serves, we think, to justify the statement that the dividing line between them, if not unfaltering throughout its course, has been true for the most part to a unifying principle. On which side of the line the case made out by the appellant has appropriate location must be the next inquiry and the final one. Is that kind of double jeopardy to which the statute has subjected him a hardship so acute and shocking that our polity will not endure it? Does it violate those "fundamental principles of liberty and justice which lie at the base of all our civil and political institutions"? The answer surely must be "no." What the answer would have to be if the state were permitted after a trial free from error to try the accused over again or to bring another case against him, we have no occasion to consider. We deal with the statute before us and no other. The state is not attempting to wear the accused out by a multitude of cases with accumulated trials. It asks no more than this, that the case against him shall go on until there shall be a trial free from the corrosion of substantial legal error. This is not cruelty at all, nor even vexation in any immoderate degree. If the trial had been infected with error adverse to the accused, there might have been review at his instance, and as often as necessary to purge the vicious taint. A reciprocal privilege, subject at all times to the discretion of the presiding judge (State v. Carabetta, 106 Conn. 114, 137 A. 394), has now been granted to the state. There is here no seismic innovation. The edifice of justice stands, its symmetry, to many, greater than before.

* * *

The judgment is affirmed.

■ MR. JUSTICE BUTLER dissents.

Benton v. Maryland

Supreme Court of the United States, 1969.
395 U.S. 784, 89 S.Ct. 2056.

■ MR. JUSTICE MARSHALL delivered the opinion of the Court.

In August 1965, petitioner was tried in a Maryland state court on charges of burglary and larceny. The jury found petitioner not guilty of larceny but convicted him on the burglary count. He was sentenced to 10 years in prison. Shortly after his notice of appeal was filed in the Maryland Court of Appeals, that court handed down its decision in the case of Schowgurow v. State, 240 Md. 121, 213 A.2d 475 (1965). In *Schowgurow* the Maryland Court of Appeals struck down a section of the state constitution which required jurors to swear their belief in the existence of God. As a result of this decision, petitioner's case was remanded to the trial court. Because both the grand and petit juries in petitioner's case had been selected under the invalid constitutional provision, petitioner was given the option of demanding re-indictment and retrial. He chose to have his conviction set aside, and a new indictment and new trial followed. At this second trial, petitioner was again charged with both larceny and burglary. Petitioner objected to retrial on the larceny count, arguing that because the first jury had found him not guilty of larceny, retrial would violate the constitutional prohibition against subjecting persons to double jeopardy for the same offense. The trial judge denied petitioner's motion to dismiss the larceny charge, and petitioner was tried for both larceny and burglary. This time the jury found petitioner guilty of both offenses, and the judge sentenced him to 15 years on the burglary count and 5 years for larceny, the sentences to run concurrently. On appeal to the newly created Maryland Court of Special Appeals, petitioner's double jeopardy claim was rejected on the merits. The Court of Appeals denied discretionary review.

* * *

... On the merits, we hold that the Double Jeopardy Clause of the Fifth Amendment is applicable to the States through the Fourteenth Amendment, and we reverse petitioner's conviction for larceny.

* * *

Palko represented an approach to basic constitutional rights which this Court's recent decisions have rejected. It was cut of the same cloth as Betts v. Brady, 316 U.S. 455, 62 S.Ct. 1252 (1942), the case which held that a criminal defendant's right to counsel was to be determined by deciding in each case whether the denial of that right was "shocking to the universal sense of justice." It relied upon Twining v. New Jersey (1908), which held that the right against compulsory self-incrimination was not an element of Fourteenth Amendment due process. *Betts* was overruled by Gideon v. Wainwright (1963); *Twining*, by Malloy v. Hogan (1964). Our recent cases have thoroughly rejected the *Palko* notion that basic constitutional rights can be denied by the States as long as the totality of the circumstances does not disclose a denial of "fundamental fairness." Once it is decided that a particular Bill of Rights guarantee is "fundamental to the American scheme of justice," Duncan v. Louisiana, 88 S.Ct., at 1447, the same constitutional standards apply against both the State and Federal Governments. *Palko*'s roots had thus been cut away years ago. We today only recognize the inevitable.

The fundamental nature of the guarantee against double jeopardy can hardly be doubted. Its origins can be traced to Greek and Roman times, and it became established in the common law of England long before this Nation's independence. See Bartkus v. Illinois, 359 U.S. 121, 151–155, 79 S.Ct. 676, 697 (1959) (Black, J., dissenting). As with many other elements of the common law, it was carried into the jurisprudence of this Country through the medium of Blackstone, who codified the doctrine in his Commentaries. "[T]he plea of *autrefoits acquit*, or a former acquittal," he wrote, "is grounded on this universal maxim of the common law of England, that no man is to be brought into jeopardy of his life more than once for the same offence." Today, every State incorporates some form of the prohibition in its constitution or common law. ... This underlying notion has from the very beginning been part of our constitutional tradition. Like the right to trial by jury, it is clearly "fundamental to the American scheme of justice." The validity of petitioner's larceny conviction must be judged, not by the watered-down standard enunciated in *Palko*, but under this Court's interpretations of the Fifth Amendment double jeopardy provision.

It is clear that petitioner's larceny conviction cannot stand once federal double jeopardy standards are applied. Petitioner was acquitted of larceny in his first trial. Because he decided to appeal his burglary conviction, he is forced to suffer retrial on the larceny count as well. As this Court held in Green v. United States (1957), "[c]onditioning an appeal of one offense on a coerced surrender of a valid plea of former jeopardy on another offense exacts a forfeiture in plain conflict with the constitutional bar against double jeopardy."

Judgment vacated and case remanded.

■ [Omitted are the concurring opinion of JUSTICE WHITE and the dissenting opinion of JUSTICE HARLAN, joined by JUSTICE STEWART.]

NOTES

1. At the time of *Palko* the overwhelming majority of state constitutions contained a prohibition against double jeopardy. Even in Connecticut a double jeopardy prohibition of some sort was embodied in the state's common law. No reported Connecticut decision entertained a prosecutor's claim that the jury's verdict of acquittal was manifestly against the weight of the evidence. This form of review (on what might be called a mixed question of law and fact) was apparently not available to the prosecution even in Connecticut.

2. *Palko* assumed that under the Fifth Amendment the federal government could not appeal following a jury's verdict of acquittal even if its claims related solely to errors of law which may have contributed to the verdict. This interpretation of the Fifth Amendment still prevails, although through the decades it has had its critics, including Justice Holmes, who, dissenting in Kepner v. United States, 195 U.S. 100, 24 S.Ct. 797 (1904), advanced a theory of "continuing jeopardy" which would have permitted the government an appeal so as to assure a single, error-free trial. Appeal following acquittal is treated further in subsection 5, infra.

3. One effort to offer a unified theory—though not one which purports to be consistent with what the Supreme Court has done in all the various cases—appears in Western and Drubel, Toward a General Theory of Double Jeopardy, 1979 Supreme Court Review 81. See also Thomas, An Elegant Theory of Double Jeopardy, 1988 U.Ill.L.Rev. 827.

2. WHEN DOES JEOPARDY ATTACH?

Under the United States Supreme Court decisions discussed in the notes below, jeopardy "attaches" in a non-jury trial when the first witness begins his or her testimony, and in a jury trial when the jury is empaneled and sworn. A defendant cannot properly invoke the Double Jeopardy Clause to prevent further proceedings based upon anything which has occurred before the attachment of jeopardy. Where proceedings have been aborted or terminated after jeopardy has attached, *sometimes* further proceedings in the same matter are permitted despite the protection of the Double Jeopardy Clause, but sometimes such further proceedings are barred. See Section A(3)–(5) infra.

NOTES

1. In Downum v. United States, 372 U.S. 734, 83 S.Ct. 1033 (1963), the Court held that in a federal jury trial jeopardy attaches when the jury is empaneled and sworn and, unlike a bench trial, it does not require the commencement of the testimony of the first witness. In Crist v. Bretz, 437 U.S. 28, 98 S.Ct. 2156 (1978), the Court considered the validity of the Montana rule under which, despite the swearing of the jury, jeopardy did not attach until the commencement of the evidence. Through Justice Stewart the Court struck down the Montana rule on the following grounds:

> "The reason for holding that jeopardy attaches when the jury is empaneled and sworn lies in the need to protect the interest of an accused in retaining a chosen jury. That interest was described in Wade v. Hunter, supra, as a defendant's 'valued right to have his trial completed by a particular tribunal.' 336 U.S., at 689, 69 S.Ct. 834. It is an interest with roots deep in the historic development of trial by jury in the Anglo–American system of criminal justice. Throughout that history there ran a strong tradition that once banded together a jury should not be discharged until it had completed its solemn tasks of announcing a verdict.
>
> "Regardless of its historic origin, however, the defendant's 'valued right to have his trial completed by a particular tribunal' is now within the protection of the constitutional guarantee against double jeopardy, since it is that 'right' that lies at the foundation of the federal rule that jeopardy attaches when the jury is empaneled and sworn."

Joined by Chief Justice Burger and Justice Rehnquist, Justice Powell dissented:

"The rule that jeopardy attaches in a jury trial at the moment the jury is sworn is not mandated by the Constitution. It is the product of historical accident, embodied in a Court decision without the slightest consideration of the policies it purports to serve. Because these policies would be served equally well by a rule fixing the attachment of jeopardy at the swearing of the first witness, I would uphold the Montana statute. Even if one assumed that the Fifth Amendment now requires the attachment of jeopardy at the swearing of the jury, I would view that rule as incidental to the purpose of the Double Jeopardy Clause and hence not incorporated through the Due Process Clause of the Fourteenth Amendment and not applicable to the States. I therefore dissent.

* * *

"... The federal rule of attachment in jury trials offers no basis for a double jeopardy claim if the prosecutor—dissatisfied by the jury selection process—is successful in dismissing the prosecution before the last juror is seated, or indeed before the whole panel is sworn. A defendant's protection against denial or abuse of his rights in this respect lies in the Due Process Clause."

[Similarly, Justice Powell argued, Due Process would protect against deliberate prosecution misconduct after the swearing in of the jury, but before any evidence was heard.]

2. In Serfass v. United States, 420 U.S. 377, 95 S.Ct. 1055 (1975), the defendant was charged with failure to report and submit to induction into the armed forces. In a pre-trial motion to dismiss, supported by affidavit, the defendant raised a claim which arguably constituted a defense to the merits of the charge based upon then prevailing precedent: He could not be convicted because the Selective Service Board had denied him a proper hearing on his claim for conscientious objector status. Before trial the district judge reviewed the Selective Service file, agreed that the Board had acted improperly, and dismissed the indictment. The Government appealed under 18 U.S.C. § 3731.

Serfass sought dismissal of the appeal, arguing that he had, in effect, been acquitted on the merits of the charge and pointing out that the prosecution cannot appeal from an acquittal. The Government contended that the Double Jeopardy Clause permitted the appeal because jeopardy had not yet attached at the point where the district judge dismissed the charges. The defense retorted that this contention elevated form over substance.

The Court first held that § 3731 permits a prosecution appeal wherever the Double Jeopardy Clause does not bar such an appeal. It then accepted the Government's argument that the Clause afforded Serfass no protection because jeopardy had not attached:

It is true that we have disparaged "rigid, mechanical" rules in the interpretation of the Double Jeopardy Clause. Illinois v. Somerville ... (1973). However, we also observed in that case that "the conclusion that jeopardy has attached begins, rather than ends, the inquiry as to whether the Double Jeopardy Clause bars retrial." Ibid. Cf. United States v. Sisson ... (1971). Implicit in the latter statement is the premise that the "constitutional policies underpinning the Fifth Amendment's guarantee" are not implicated before that point in the proceedings at which "jeopardy attaches." United States v. Jorn ... (1971). As we have noted above, the Court has consistently adhered to the view that jeopardy does not attach until a defendant is "put to trial before the trier of facts, whether the trier

> be a jury or a judge." ... This is by no means a mere technicality, nor is it a "rigid, mechanical" rule. It is, of course, like most legal rules, an attempt to impart content to an abstraction.
>
> When a criminal prosecution is terminated prior to trial, an accused is often spared much of the expense, delay, strain, and embarrassment which attend a trial. See Green v. United States ... (1957); United States v. Jorn.... Although an accused may raise defenses or objections before trial which are "capable of determination without the trial of the general issue," Fed.Rule Crim.Proc. 12(b)(1), and although he must raise certain other defenses or objections before trial, Fed.Rule Crim.Proc. 12(b)(2), in neither case is he "subjected to the hazards of trial and possible conviction." ... Moreover, in neither case would an appeal by the United States "allow the prosecutor to seek to persuade a second trier of fact of the defendant's guilt after having failed with the first." United States v. Wilson, 95 S.Ct. at 1026. See United States v. Jorn, 400 U.S., at 484, 91 S.Ct., at 556. Both the history of the Double Jeopardy Clause and its terms demonstrate that it does not come into play until a proceeding begins before a trier "having jurisdiction to try the question of the guilt or innocence of the accused." Kepner v. United States, 195 U.S. 100, 133 (1904) ... Without risk of a determination of guilt, jeopardy does not attach, and neither an appeal nor further prosecution constitutes double jeopardy.

3. In Smith v. Massachusetts, 543 U.S. 462, 125 S.Ct. 1129 (2005), the Court found a double jeopardy violation when the trial judge granted a motion of acquittal on one of three counts at the end of the prosecutor's case. The defense presented one witness. Before closing (and on the same day as the acquittal motion was granted) the prosecutor found precedent which caused the trial judge to reverse her ruling and send the stricken count to the jury. A five member majority found that the acquittal was final and sending it to the jury constituted double jeopardy. The Court observed that Massachusetts could avoid the re-occurrence of this result by statute or rule which barred mid trial rulings from becoming final or simply precluding mid trial acquittals. For the dissenters, Justice Ginsburg wrote:

> Smith was subjected to a single, unbroken trial proceeding in which he was denied no opportunity to air his defense before presentation of the case to the jury. I would not deny prosecutors in such circumstances, based on a trial judge's temporary error, one full and fair opportunity to present the State's case.

4. In United States v. Dionisio, 503 F.3d 78 (2d Cir. 2007), an organized crime figure pled guilty to one count of an indictment in return for the dismissal of other counts with prejudice. When the government brought a subsequent case based in part on the conduct underlying a count dismissed in the earlier case, defendant sought dismissal on double jeopardy grounds. Finding that the key issue, even in the context of a plea, was whether the disposition of an individual's indictment entailed findings of fact on the merits so as to place defendant in jeopardy, the court concluded that the dismissal of the prior count pursuant to the plea agreement did not entail a resolution of any factual elements that went to the merits of the charge. Therefore, jeopardy did not attach.

3. RETRIAL WHERE TRIAL IS TERMINATED WITHOUT VERDICT

United States v. Jorn

Supreme Court of the United States, 1971.
400 U.S. 470, 91 S.Ct. 547.

■ MR. JUSTICE HARLAN announced the judgment of the Court in an opinion joined by THE CHIEF JUSTICE, MR. JUSTICE DOUGLAS, and MR. JUSTICE MARSHALL.

The Government directly appeals the order of the United States District Court for the District of Utah dismissing, on the ground of former jeopardy, an information charging the defendant-appellee with willfully assisting in the preparation of fraudulent income tax returns, in violation of 26 U.S.C. § 7206(2).

Appellee was originally charged in February 1968 with 25 counts of violating § 7206(2). He was brought to trial before Chief Judge Ritter on August 27, 1968. After the jury was chosen and sworn, 14 of the counts were dismissed on the Government's motion. The trial then commenced, the Government calling as its first witness an Internal Revenue Service agent in order to put in evidence the remaining 11 allegedly fraudulent income tax returns the defendant was charged with helping to prepare. At the trial judge's suggestion, these exhibits were stipulated to and introduced in evidence without objection.

The Government's five remaining witnesses were taxpayers whom the defendant allegedly had aided in preparation of these returns.

After the first of these witnesses was called, but prior to the commencement of direct examination, defense counsel suggested that these witnesses be warned of their constitutional rights. The trial court agreed, and proceeded, in careful detail, to spell out the witness' right not to say anything that might be used in a subsequent criminal prosecution against him and his right, in the event of such a prosecution, to be represented by an attorney. The first witness expressed a willingness to testify and stated that he had been warned of his constitutional rights when the Internal Revenue Service first contacted him. The trial judge indicated, however, that he did not believe the witness had been given any warning at the time he was first contacted by the IRS, and refused to permit him to testify until he had consulted an attorney.

The trial judge then asked the prosecuting attorney if his remaining four witnesses were similarly situated. The prosecutor responded that they had been warned of their rights by the IRS upon initial contact. The judge, expressing the view that any warnings that might have been given were probably inadequate, proceeded to discharge the jury; he then called all the taxpayers into court, and informed them of their constitutional rights and of the considerable dangers of unwittingly making damaging admissions in these factual circumstances. Finally, he aborted the trial so the witnesses could consult with attorneys.

The case was set for retrial before another jury, but on pretrial motion by the defendant, Judge Ritter dismissed the information on the ground of former jeopardy. The Government filed a direct appeal to this Court, and we noted probable jurisdiction.

* * *

Thus the conclusion that "jeopardy attaches" when the trial commences expresses a judgment that the constitutional policies underpinning the Fifth Amendment's guarantee are implicated at that point in the proceedings. The question remains, however, in what circumstances retrial is to be precluded when the initial proceedings are aborted prior to verdict without the defendant's consent.

In dealing with that question, this Court has, for the most part, explicitly declined the invitation of litigants to formulate rules based on categories of circumstances which will permit or preclude retrial. Thus, in United States v. Perez (1824), this Court held that a defendant in a capital case might be retried after the trial judge, had, without the defendant's consent, discharged a jury that reported itself unable to agree.

* * *

But a more recent case—Gori v. United States (1961)—while adhering in the main to the *Perez* theme of a "manifest necessity" standard of appellate review—does suggest the possibility of a variation on that theme according to a determination by the appellate court as to which party to the case was the beneficiary of the mistrial ruling. In *Gori*, the Court was called upon to review the action of a trial judge in discharging the jury when it appeared to the judge that the prosecution's questioning of a witness might lead to the introduction of evidence of prior crimes. We upheld reprosecution after the mistrial in an opinion which, while applying the principle of *Perez*, appears to tie the judgment that there was no abuse of discretion in these circumstances to the fact that the judge was acting "in the sole interest of the defendant."

In the instant case, the Government, relying principally on *Gori* contends that even if we conclude the trial judge here abused his discretion, reprosecution should be permitted because the judge's ruling "benefited" the defendant and also clearly was not compelled by bad-faith prosecutorial conduct aimed at triggering a mistrial in order to get another day in court. If the judgment as to who was "benefited" by the mistrial ruling turns on the appellate court's conclusion concerning which party the trial judge was, in point of personal motivation, trying to protect from prejudice, it seems reasonably clear from the trial record here that the judge's insistence on stopping the trial until the witnesses were properly warned was motivated by the desire to protect the witnesses rather than the defendant. But the Government appears to view the question of "benefit" as turning on an appellate court's *post hoc* assessment as to which party would in fact have been aided in the hypothetical event that the witnesses had been called to the stand after consulting with their own attorneys on the course of conduct that would best serve to insulate them personally from criminal and civil liability for the fraudulent tax returns. That conception of benefit, however, involves nothing more than an exercise in pure speculation. In sum, we are unable to conclude on this record that this is a case of a mistrial made "in the sole interest of the defendant." See Gori v. United States, supra.

Further, we think that a limitation on the abuse-of-discretion principle based on an appellate court's assessment of which side benefited from the mistrial ruling does not adequately satisfy the policies underpinning the double jeopardy provision. Reprosecution after a mistrial has unnecessarily been declared by the trial court obviously subjects the defendant to the same personal strain and insecurity regardless of the motivation underlying the trial judge's action.

* * *

. . . For the crucial difference between reprosecution after appeal by the defendant and reprosecution after a *sua sponte* judicial mistrial declaration is that in the first situation the defendant has not been deprived of his option to go to the first jury and, perhaps, end the dispute then and there with an acquittal. On the other hand, where the judge, acting without the defendant's consent, aborts the proceeding, the defendant has been deprived of his "valued right to have his trial completed by a particular tribunal."

* * *

In sum, counsel for both sides perform in an imperfect world; in this area, bright-line rules based on either the source of the problem or the intended beneficiary of the ruling would only disserve the vital competing interests of the Government and the defendant. The trial judge must recognize that lack of preparedness by the Government to continue the trial directly implicates policies underpinning both the double jeopardy provision and the speedy trial guarantee. Alternatively, the judge must bear in mind the potential risks of abuse by the defendant of society's unwillingness to unnecessarily subject him to repeated prosecutions. Yet, in the final analysis, the judge must always temper the decision whether or not to abort the trial by considering the importance to the defendant of being able, once and for all, to conclude his confrontation with society through the verdict of a tribunal he might believe to be favorably disposed to his fate.

Applying these considerations to the record in this case, we must conclude that the trial judge here abused his discretion in discharging the jury. Despite assurances by both the first witness and the prosecuting attorney that the five taxpayers involved in the litigation had all been warned of their constitutional rights, the judge refused to permit them to testify, first expressing his disbelief that they were warned at all, and then expressing his views that any warnings that might have been given would be inadequate. In probing the assumed inadequacy of the warnings that might have been given, the prosecutor was asked if he really intended to try a case for willfully aiding in the preparation of fraudulent returns on a theory that would not incriminate the taxpayers. When the prosecutor started to answer that he intended to do just that, the judge cut him off in midstream and immediately discharged the jury. It is apparent from the record that no consideration was given to the possibility of a trial continuance; indeed, the trial judge acted so abruptly in discharging the jury that, had the prosecutor been disposed to suggest a continuance, or the defendant to object to the discharge of the jury, there would have been no opportunity to do so. When one examines the circumstances surrounding the discharge of this jury, it seems abundantly apparent that the trial judge made no effort to exercise a sound discretion to assure that, taking all the circumstances into account, there was a manifest necessity for the *sua sponte* declaration of this mistrial. Therefore, we must conclude that in the circumstances of this case, appellee's reprosecution would violate the double jeopardy provision of the Fifth Amendment.

Affirmed.

■ MR. CHIEF JUSTICE BURGER, concurring.

I join in the plurality opinion and in the judgement of the Court not without some reluctance, however, since the case represents a plain frustration of the right to have this case tried, attributable solely to the conduct of the trial judge. If the accused had brought about the erroneous mistrial ruling we would have a different case, but this record shows nothing to take appellee's claims outside the classic mold of being twice placed in jeopardy for the same offense.

[Omitted are the concurring opinion of JUSTICES BLACK and BRENNAN and the dissenting opinion of JUSTICE STEWART which was joined by JUSTICES WHITE and BLACKMUN.]

NOTES

1. In Arizona v. Washington, 434 U.S. 497, 98 S.Ct. 824 (1978), the prosecutor sought a mistrial because of the defense lawyer's misconduct in putting before the jury through opening statements inadmissible matter which cast the prosecutor in a bad light. Before granting the mistrial, the trial judge reminded the prosecutor that if termination of the trial over a defense objection were later deemed to be improper, jeopardy principles would forever prevent attainment of a valid conviction. (For this reason prosecutors rarely seek a mistrial. Some follow the wise policy of always seeking the detached opinion of colleagues who have not participated in the particular trial before taking the gamble entailed by a mistrial granted over defense objection.) Writing for the majority, Justice Stevens said that the requisite "high degree" of necessity for a mistrial under the "manifest necessity" test had been met. Justice Marshall dissented, arguing that perhaps a remedy short of a mistrial would have sufficed to permit the prosecution a fair trial. He noted that the trial judge had specifically not declared that a new trial was manifestly necessary.

Every year there are cases in which it is argued the trial judge has been too quick to grant a mistrial and, by doing so, has created a Double Jeopardy bar to further prosecution. In United States v. Dixon, 913 F.2d 1305 (8th Cir.1990), a jury was sworn in a major multiple-defendant drug prosecution, but before it began to hear evidence, significant prejudicial publicity, especially as to one defendant, appeared in the media. The trial judge had not instructed the jurors not to read about the case and granted a mistrial on his own motion without polling the jury to see if any had seen the publicity or considering other alternatives to a mistrial. The defendants objected, but the judge persisted. On appeal it was held the mistrial was unjustified.

In Walls v. Konteh, 490 F.3d 432 (6th Cir. 2007), a state trial judge's mid trial declaration of a mistrial over defendant's objection due to calamitous events occurring outside the courtroom based on the 9/11 terrorist attacks was necessary although other trials in the same Ohio courthouse were recessed and later continued to verdict. Judge Gilman dissented on the ground that the trial judge could not have known the impact of the external events on ongoing judicial proceedings and gave no consideration to available alternatives or the defendant's right to conclude his confrontation with society through a jury verdict.

2. Suppose that an indigent defendant's misdemeanor trial begins without either appointment of counsel or a knowing waiver. Midway through the prosecution's case the trial judge concludes that the facts are aggravated enough so that, if the defendant is found guilty, a jail sentence would be appropriate. May the judge terminate the trial, appoint counsel, and start anew? Would "manifest necessity" be present? Would it make a difference if the *pro se* defendant made no objection to the termination? Suppose the court, without explaining about *Argersinger* or *Scott* Chapter 9, (Section B) or double jeopardy principles, obtained an affirmative response to the following offer. "This is a serious matter. You need a lawyer. How about if we start all over and I appoint counsel to represent you in a new trial?"

3. In Oregon v. Kennedy, 456 U.S. 667, 102 S.Ct. 2083 (1982), the plurality opinion declared that prosecutorial misconduct which is a basis for a mistrial granted at the request of a defendant bars retrial only if "the conduct giving rise to the successful motion for a mistrial was intended to provoke the defendant into moving for a mistrial." It further declared that "prosecutorial conduct that might be viewed as harassment or overreaching," does not bar retrial absent "intent on the part of the prosecutor to subvert the protections afforded by the Double Jeopardy Clause."

Justice Powell added a separate concurrence, agreeing with the four plurality justices, that prosecutorial intent is determinative of the jeopardy issue. He emphasized that intent must be judged primarily from "objective facts and circumstances of the particular case."

The remaining four justices also concurred in the result. Through Justice Stevens they suggested that the trial court look to whether the "egregious prosecutorial misconduct has rendered meaningless the defendant's choice to continue or to abort the proceedings." Justice Stevens acknowledged that even under his test "only rarely would retrial be barred after a mistrial declared at the request of the defendant or with his consent."

Some courts on state law grounds bar re-trial even when the *Kennedy* test has not been met. See, e.g., Pool v. Superior Court, 139 Ariz. 98, 677 P.2d 261 (1984) (intentional conduct, known to be improper and not curable by means short of mistrial, bars retrial if prosecutor is indifferent to possibility that his or her conduct will necessitate a mistrial); Bauder v. State, 921 S.W.2d 696 (Tex.Crim.App.1996) (a successive prosecution is barred if the court determines the prosecutor engaging in the objectionable conduct (1) acted with the intent to induce a mistrial; or (2) was aware of, but consciously disregarded, the risk that the conduct would require a mistrial at the defendant's request). But see State v. Marti, 147 N.H. 168, 784 A.2d 1193 (2001) (retrial is barred only when the prosecutor engaged in misconduct with the specific intent to avoid a likely acquittal)

4. When a jury fails to reach agreement, the trial judge may declare a mistrial and allow the prosecution to begin anew. A retrial following a hung jury has been held not to violate the double jeopardy clause. This principle appears well settled. United States v. Sanford, 429 U.S. 14, 97 S.Ct. 20 (1976); Richardson v. United States, 468 U.S. 317, 104 S.Ct. 3081 (1984) (jury disagreement due to insufficient evidence does not "terminate" jeopardy in the way an appellate ruling on insufficient evidence would). Consider, however, the policies underlying the double jeopardy prohibition. Is retrial after a hung jury likely to increase the chances of convicting an innocent person? What about concerns for the time, money, and anxiety of the defendant. On the other hand, what policies militate against permitting a single juror to, in effect, acquit the accused? Are there any limits on how many "hung juries" the accused must suffer through before reprosecution is barred. For one view see United States v. Castellanos, 349 F.Supp. 720 (E.D.N.Y.1972) (two is enough), reversed 478 F.2d 749 (2d Cir.1973) (no bar). As this decision indicates, in the federal system the trial judge has the option, following a hung jury, of entering an acquittal rather than permitting a new trial. See Section A–4, infra, concerning the effect of such an order. See generally, Comment, Retrial after a Hung Jury, 129 U.Pa.L.Rev. 701 (1980). See also People v. Howard, 121 Ill.App.3d 938, 77 Ill.Dec. 376, 460 N.E.2d 432 (1984) (re-trial after two hung juries permissible; length of jury deliberations at earlier trial irrelevant to jeopardy issue).

5. In United States v. Scott, 437 U.S. 82, 98 S.Ct. 2187 (1978), both before and after jeopardy had attached, the defendant sought dismissal of the indictment because of alleged prejudicial pre-indictment delay. At the close of all the evidence, before submitting the case to the jury, the court (as to the count in question) granted the motion to dismiss. The government appealed and the Court had to consider whether, assuming the trial judge had erred in granting the motion to dismiss, the Double Jeopardy clause prohibited remanding for a new trial. The Court held that even though a new trial would require new evidence, a new trial was permissible. The Court emphasized that the *defendant* had sought to terminate the trial on "grounds unrelated to guilt or innocence." While rejecting a "waiver" analysis, the Court held that the "Double Jeopardy Clause, which guards against oppression, does not relieve a defendant from the consequences of his voluntary choice." It added that under the circumstances the defendant cannot be said to be "deprived" of his "valued right to go to the first jury; only the public has been deprived of its valued right to 'one complete opportunity to convict those who have violated its laws.' "

6. Suppose that a defendant makes a Fourth Amendment motion to suppress after jeopardy has attached but before verdict. If he wins, may the prosecution, consistent with the Double Jeopardy clause, have the jury discharged, take an interlocutory appeal, and then begin trial anew following the appellate decision? Is this the issue left open in *Serfass* of "a defendant who is afforded an opportunity to obtain a determination of a legal defense prior to trial and nevertheless knowingly allows himself to be placed in jeopardy before raising the defense"? Suppose that a defendant is allowed to make the belated, mid-trial motion to suppress only when, for some reason, he was not at fault in failing to make the motion earlier. Could state law still permit the prosecution an interlocutory review of an adverse decision? Some courts have permitted termination of the trial to allow the prosecution interlocutory review of a mid-trial suppression order; but they have not always fully explored the jeopardy issue. Compare People v. Young, 60 Ill.App.3d 49, 17 Ill.Dec. 566, 376 N.E.2d 712 (1978) (interlocutory appeal appropriate and its manifest necessity allowed retrial) with People v. Johnson, 113 Ill.App.3d 367, 69 Ill.Dec. 285, 447 N.E.2d 502 (1983) (interlocutory appeal on relevance ruling not appropriate; double jeopardy barred retrial).

4. RETRIAL FOLLOWING INITIAL ACQUITTAL

As already discussed, when the *initial* verdict of a jury is "not guilty" or the initial judgment of the court in a bench trial is "not guilty," the defendant cannot be tried again for the offense of which he was acquitted. Fed.R.Crim.P. 29(c) permits a district court judge to enter a judgment of acquittal after a jury has been unable to reach a verdict. In United States v. Martin Linen Supply Co., 430 U.S. 564, 97 S.Ct. 1349 (1977), the Court held that the Double Jeopardy prohibition prevents the Government from appealing such a judgment. It held that such a judgment was an acquittal in substance as well as in form. It further noted that the consequences of a successful government appeal would be a requirement that the defendant go through another trial. This, the Court found, is forbidden. The acquittal under Fed.R.Crim.P. 29(c) contemplates an end to litigation as much as does a judgment of acquittal (the federal equivalent of a directed verdict) for the defendant before the case is submitted to the jury.

In Smalis v. Pennsylvania, 476 U.S. 140, 106 S.Ct. 1745 (1986), the trial judge at the end of the prosecution's case in chief had sustained a demurrer challenging the sufficiency of the evidence. The case had been tried without a jury. The Supreme Court held that, like a directed verdict in a jury trial, a finding that the evidence is insufficient amounts to an acquittal and bars further prosecution.

Retrial following an *initial* verdict of acquittal should be carefully distinguished from the situation in which the judge or jury initially finds the defendant guilty, but the judge then vacates that finding. The latter situation is treated in subsection 5, infra.

Many "retrial following acquittal" cases involve convictions of lesser included offenses followed by retrial for the greater offense. When the jury's verdict has either expressly or impliedly acquitted the defendant of the greater offense, he can never be validly convicted of that greater offense. (Ordinarily under state law conviction of the lesser included charge is an implied acquittal of the greater charge.) See Price v. Georgia, 398 U.S. 323, 90 S.Ct. 1757 (1970), and Morris v. Mathews, 475 U.S. 237, 106 S.Ct. 1032 (1986).

Somewhat different issues arise when the defendant is tried for an offense different from (and not included in) a closely related offense of which he was previously acquitted. This raises the question of "collateral estoppel," which is the subject of the next decision.

Ashe v. Swenson

Supreme Court of the United States, 1970.
397 U.S. 436, 90 S.Ct. 1189.

■ MR. JUSTICE STEWART delivered the opinion of the Court.

* * *

Sometime in the early hours of the morning of January 10, 1960, six men were engaged in a poker game in the basement of the home of John Gladson at Lee's Summit, Missouri. Suddenly three or four masked men, armed with a shotgun and pistols, broke into the basement and robbed each of the poker players of money and various articles of personal property. The robbers—and it has never been clear whether there were three or four of them—then fled in a car belonging to one of the victims of the robbery. Shortly thereafter the stolen car was discovered in a field, and later that morning three men were arrested by a state trooper while they were walking on a highway not far from where the abandoned car had been found. The petitioner was arrested by another officer some distance away.

The four were subsequently charged with seven separate offenses—the armed robbery of each of the six poker players and the theft of the car. In May 1960 the petitioner went to trial on the charge of robbing Donald Knight, one of the participants in the poker game. At the trial the State called Knight and three of his fellow poker players as prosecution witnesses. Each of them described the circumstances of the holdup and itemized his own individual losses. The proof that an armed robbery had occurred and that personal property had been taken from Knight was unassailable. But the State's evidence that the petitioner had been one of the robbers was weak. Two of the witnesses thought that there had been only three robbers altogether, and could not identify the petitioner as one of them. Another of the victims, who was the petitioner's uncle by marriage, said that at the "patrol station" he had positively identified each of the other three men accused of the holdup, but could say only that the petitioner's voice "sounded very much like" that of one of the robbers. The fourth participant in the poker game did identify the petitioner, but only by his "size and height, and his actions."

The cross-examination of these witnesses was brief, and it was aimed primarily at exposing the weakness of their identification testimony....

The defense offered no testimony and waived final argument.

The trial judge instructed the jury that if it found that the petitioner was one of the participants in the armed robbery, the theft of "any money" from Knight would sustain a conviction. He also instructed the jury that if the petitioner was one of the robbers, he was guilty under the law even if he had not personally robbed Knight. The jury—though not instructed to elaborate upon its verdict—found the petitioner "not guilty due to insufficient evidence."

Six weeks later the petitioner was brought to trial again, this time for the robbery of another participant in the poker game, a man named Roberts. The petitioner filed a motion to dismiss, based on his previous acquittal. The motion was overruled, and the second trial began. The witnesses were for the most part the same, though this time their testimony was substantially stronger on the issue of the petitioner's identity. For example, two witnesses who at the first trial had been wholly unable to identify the petitioner as one of the robbers, now testified that his features, size, and mannerisms matched those of one of their assailants. Another witness who before had identified the petitioner only by his size and actions now also remembered him by the unusual sound of his voice. The State further refined its case at the second trial by declining to call one of the participants in the poker game whose identification testimony at the first trial had been conspicuously negative. The case went to the jury on instructions virtually identical to those given at the first trial. This time the jury found the petitioner guilty, and he was sentenced to a 35-year term in the state penitentiary. The operative facts here are virtually identical to those of Hoag v. New Jersey, [356 U.S. 464, 78 S.Ct. 829]. In that case the defendant was tried for the armed robbery of three men who, along with others, had been held up in a tavern. The proof of the robbery was clear, but the evidence identifying the defendant as one of the robbers was weak, and the defendant interposed an alibi defense. The jury brought in a verdict of not guilty. The defendant was then brought to trial again, on an indictment charging the robbery of a fourth victim of the tavern holdup. This time the jury found him guilty.

Viewing the question presented solely in terms of Fourteenth Amendment due process—whether the course that New Jersey had pursued had "led to fundamental unfairness,"—this Court declined to reverse the judgment of conviction, because "in the circumstances shown by this record, we cannot say that petitioner's later prosecution and conviction violated due process." The Court found it unnecessary to decide whether "collateral estoppel"—the principle that bars relitigation between the same parties of issues actually determined at a previous trial—is a due process requirement in a state criminal trial, since it accepted New Jersey's determination that the petitioner's previous acquittal did not in any event give rise to such an estoppel.

The doctrine of Benton v. Maryland (1969) puts the issues in a perspective quite different from that in Hoag v. New Jersey. The question is no longer whether collateral estoppel is a requirement of due process, but whether it is a part of the Fifth Amendment's guarantee against double jeopardy. And if collateral estoppel is embodied in that guarantee, then its applicability in a particular case is no longer a matter to be left for state court determination within the broad bounds of "fundamental fairness," but a matter of constitutional fact we must decide through an examination of the entire record.

"Collateral estoppel" is an awkward phrase, but it stands for an extremely important principle in our adversary system of justice. It means simply that when an issue of ultimate fact has once been determined by a valid and final judgment, that issue cannot again be litigated between the same parties in any future lawsuit. Although first developed in civil litigation, collateral estoppel has been an established rule of federal criminal law at least since this Court's decision more than 50 years ago in United States v. Oppenheimer, 242 U.S. 85, 37 S.Ct. 68.

The federal decisions have made clear that the rule of collateral estoppel in criminal cases is not to be applied with the hypertechnical and archaic approach of a 19th century pleading book, but with realism and rationality. Where a previous judgment of acquittal was based upon a general verdict, as is usually the case, this approach requires a court to "examine the record of a prior proceeding, taking into account the pleadings, evidence, charge, and other relevant matter, and conclude whether a rational jury could have grounded its verdict upon an issue other than that which the defendant seeks to foreclose from consideration." ...

Straightforward application of the federal rule to the present case can lead to but one conclusion. For the record is utterly devoid of any indication that the first jury could rationally have found that an armed robbery had not occurred, or that Knight had not been a victim of that robbery. The single rationally conceivable issue in dispute before the jury was whether the petitioner had been one of the robbers. And the jury by its verdict found that he had not. The federal rule of law, therefore, would make a second prosecution for the robbery of Roberts wholly impermissible.

The ultimate question to be determined, then, in the light of Benton v. Maryland, supra, is whether this established rule of federal law is embodied in the Fifth Amendment guarantee against double jeopardy. We do not hesitate to hold that it is. For whatever else that constitutional guarantee may embrace, it surely protects a man who has been acquitted from having to "run the gantlet" a second time.

The question is not whether Missouri could validly charge the petitioner with six separate offenses for the robbery of the six poker players. It is not whether he could have received a total of six punishments if he had been convicted in a single trial of robbing the six victims. It is simply whether, after a jury determined by its verdict that the petitioner was not one of the robbers, the State could constitutionally hale him before a new jury to litigate that issue again.

After the first jury had acquitted the petitioner of robbing Knight, Missouri could certainly not have brought him to trial again upon that charge. Once a jury had determined upon conflicting testimony that there was at least a reasonable doubt that the petitioner was one of the robbers, the State could not present the same or different identification evidence in a second prosecution for the robbery of Knight in the hope that a different jury might find that evidence more convincing. The situation is constitutionally no different here, even though the second trial related to another victim of the same robbery. For the name of the victim, in the circumstances of this case, had no bearing whatever upon the issue of whether the petitioner was one of the robbers.

In this case the State in its brief has frankly conceded that following the petitioner's acquittal, it treated the first trial as no more than a dry run for the second prosecution: "No doubt the prosecutor felt the state had a provable case on the first charge and, when he lost, he did what every good attorney would do—he refined his presentation in light of the turn of events at the first trial." But this is precisely what the constitutional guarantee forbids.

■ MR. JUSTICE BLACK, concurring. [omitted]

■ MR. JUSTICE HARLAN, concurring. [omitted]

■ MR. JUSTICE BRENNAN, whom MR. JUSTICE DOUGLAS and MR. JUSTICE MARSHALL join, concurring.

I agree that the Double Jeopardy Clause incorporates collateral estoppel as a constitutional requirement and therefore join the Court's opinion. However, even if the rule of collateral estoppel had been inapplicable to the facts of this case, it is my view that the Double Jeopardy Clause nevertheless bars the prosecution of petitioner a second time for armed robbery. The two prosecutions, the first for the robbery of Knight and the second for the robbery of Roberts, grew out of one criminal episode, and therefore I think it clear on the facts of this case that the Double Jeopardy Clause prohibited Missouri from prosecuting petitioner for each robbery at a different trial.

* * *

In my view, the Double Jeopardy Clause requires the prosecution, except in most limited circumstances, to join at one trial all the charges against a defendant that grow out of a single criminal act, occurrence, episode, or transaction. This "same transaction" test of "same offence" not only enforces the ancient prohibition against vexatious multiple prosecutions embodied in the Double Jeopardy Clause, but responds as well to the increasingly widespread recognition that the consolidation in one lawsuit of all issues arising out of a single transaction or occurrence best promotes justice, economy, and convenience. Modern rules of criminal and civil procedure reflect this recognition.

* * *

■ MR. CHIEF JUSTICE BURGER, dissenting.

* * *

The collateral-estoppel concept—originally a product only of civil litigation—is a strange mutant as it is transformed to control this criminal case. In civil cases the doctrine was justified as conserving judicial resources as well as those of the parties to the actions and additionally as providing the finality needed to plan for the future. It ordinarily applies to parties on each side of the litigation who have the same interest as or who are identical with the parties in the initial litigation. Here the complainant in the second trial is not the same as in the first even though the State is a party in both cases. Very properly, in criminal cases, finality and conservation of private, public, and judicial resources are lesser values than in civil litigation. Also, courts that have applied the collateral-estoppel concept to criminal actions would certainly not apply it to *both* parties, as is true in civil cases, i.e., here, if Ashe had been convicted at the first trial, presumably no court would then hold that he was thereby foreclosed from litigating the identification issue at the second trial.

* * *

... If the Court is today relying on a harassment concept to superimpose a new brand of collateral-estoppel gloss on the "same evidence" test, there is a short answer; this case does not remotely suggest harassment of an accused who robbed six victims and the harassment aspect does not rise to constitutional levels. Finally, the majority's opinion tells us "that the rule of collateral estoppel in criminal cases is not to be applied with the hypertechnical and archaic approach of a 19th century pleading book, but with realism and rationality." With deference I am bound to pose the question: what is reasonable and rational about holding that an acquittal of Ashe for robbing Knight bars a trial for robbing Roberts? To borrow a phrase from the Court's opinion, what could conceivably be more "hypertechnical and archaic" and more like the stilted formalisms of 17th and 18th century common-law England, than to stretch jeopardy for robbing Knight into jeopardy for robbing Roberts?

After examining the facts of this case the Court concludes that the first jury must have concluded that Ashe was not one of the robbers—that he was not present at the time. Also, since the second jury necessarily reached its decision by finding he was present, the collateral-estoppel doctrine applies. But the majority's analysis of the facts completely disregards the confusion injected into the case by the robbery of Mrs. Gladson [in the upstairs bedroom]. To me, if we are to psychoanalyze the jury, the evidence adduced at the first trial could more reasonably be construed as indicating that Ashe had been at the Gladson home with the other three men but was not one of those involved in the basement robbery. Certainly, the evidence at the first trial was equivocal as to whether there were three or four robbers, whether the man who robbed Mrs. Gladson was one of the three who robbed the six male victims, and whether a man other than the three had robbed Mrs. Gladson. Then, since the jury could have thought that the "acting together" instruction given by the trial court in both trials only applied to the actual taking from the six card players, and not to Mrs.

Gladson, the jury could well have acquitted Ashe but yet believed that he was present in the Gladson home. On the other hand, the evidence adduced at the second trial resolved issues other than identity that may have troubled the first jury. If believed, that evidence indicated that a fourth robber, Johnson, not Ashe, was with Mrs. Gladson when Ashe, Larson, and Brown were robbing the male victims. Johnson did go to the basement where the male victims were located, but only after the other three had already taken the stolen items and when the robbers were preparing for their departure in a car to be stolen from Roberts.

Accordingly, even the facts in this case, which the Court's opinion considers to "lead to but one conclusion," are susceptible of an interpretation that the first jury did not base its acquittal on the identity ground which the Court finds so compelling. The Court bases its holding on sheer "guesswork," which should have no place particularly in our review of state convictions by way of habeas corpus.

* * *

The essence of MR. JUSTICE BRENNAN's concurrence is that this was all one transaction, one episode, or, if I may so characterize it, one frolic, and, hence, only one crime. His approach, like that taken by the Court, totally overlooks the significance of there being *six entirely separate charges of robbery* against six individuals.

This "single frolic" concept is not a novel notion; it has been urged in various courts including this Court. One of the theses underlying the "single frolic" notion is that the criminal episode is "indivisible." The short answer to that is that to the victims, the criminal conduct is readily divisible and intensely personal; each offense is an offense against *a person*. For me it demeans the dignity of the human personality and individuality to talk of "a single transaction" in the context of six separate assaults on six individuals.

No court that elevates the individual rights and human dignity of the accused to a high place—as we should—ought to be so casual as to treat the victims as a single homogenized lump of human clay. I would grant the dignity of individual status to the victims as much as to those accused, not more but surely no less.

* * *

NOTES

1. In Harris v. Washington, 404 U.S. 55, 92 S.Ct. 183 (1971), the defendant allegedly sent a bomb through the mail which exploded, killing his infant son and injuring his estranged wife. He was tried for the murder of his son and acquitted. At a subsequent trial for assaulting his wife, he pleaded double jeopardy and collateral estoppel. The court rejected his defense because a threatening letter to his wife, excluded at the first trial, was admitted at the second and, thereby, the issues relating to identity had not been fully litigated so as to give rise to estoppel. The Supreme Court reversed, holding that a prior acquittal on the "ultimate issue" bars a second trial irrespective of the State's good faith in bringing successive prosecutions.

2. In civil cases some courts now allow a party to make use of the collateral estoppel effect of a former judgment even if he or she had not been a party to the first case. For example in the first case Plaintiff *A* may have established the negligence of a railroad. In the case of Plaintiff *B* versus the same defendant railroad, arising out of the same alleged negligence, Plaintiff *B* sometimes is able to estop the defendant railroad from relitigating the negligence issue. Despite *Ashe*, however, this liberal application of collateral estoppel principles has not been extended to criminal cases. If the Government prosecutes a principal and the principal is acquitted, the Government can later prosecute the alleged accessory, even though the acquittal of the principal was necessarily inconsistent with a fact essential to convict the accessory. See Standefer v. United States, 447 U.S. 10, 100 S.Ct. 1999 (1980). Ironically, at common law the prosecution of the accessory under this circumstance would have been barred. See also United States v. Sachs, 801 F.2d 839 (6th Cir.1986). It takes two to conspire, but acquittal of one alleged co-conspirator in trial *A* does not collaterally estop the prosecutor in the prosecution of the only other alleged co-conspirator when such defendant is tried in trial *B*. United States v. Mollier, 853 F.2d 1169 (5th Cir.1988), noted that Defendant *B* cannot invoke a factual finding from Defendant *A*'s trial even where a judge rather than a jury was the one who had acquitted Defendant *A*.

3. What happens when a defendant who is acquitted is later accused of having perjured himself when he testified in his own behalf? If the first trial verdict resolved a factual dispute in favor of the defendant, should the prosecutor be barred from re-litigating that issue no matter how clear the proof that defendant's testimony on that point was perjury?

For divergent views on whether it should be barred, compare United States v. Castillo–Basa, 483 F.3d 890 (9th Cir. 2007) ("Under our constitutional rule, once an issue, such as whether [defendant] told the truth, has been determined in his favor, rightly or wrongly, by a jury, he may not again be compelled to defend himself on that issue") with Id. (Trott, J., dissenting) (verdict at first trial was not necessarily determined by defendant's testimony).

4. Suppose that a new criminal charge is filed against a probationer. At a probation revocation hearing the prosecution tries but fails to prove by a preponderance of the evidence that the probationer committed the new offense. Can it nevertheless go forward with the new criminal prosecution, or is it collaterally estopped? See United States v. Miller, 797 F.2d 336 (6th Cir.1986) (probation violation not proved, yet no double jeopardy violation where defendant prosecuted for crime that had been alleged as basis of the probation violation). Compare State v. Lemmer, 736 N.W.2d 650 (Minn. 2007) (4–3 decision holding failure of administrative officials to prove a driver's license should be revoked does not bar prosecution for criminal offense that was the claimed basis for revocation)

Or suppose the prosecution seeks bail revocation because defendant has allegedly violated the conditions of bond by committing a new offense. If it fails to convince the bond court that the defendant committed the new offense, can the prosecution nevertheless go forward with prosecution of the new charge? A divided court said yes in Showery v. Samaniego, 814 F.2d 200 (5th Cir.1987). It reasoned that in a bond revocation proceeding the defendant is not in jeopardy within the meaning of the fifth amendment, because the proceeding adjudicates neither guilt nor punishment. When Ashe was on trial for robbing Knight, was he in jeopardy of being convicted of the robbery of Roberts? Did not the implicit "finding" from the trial in the Knight matter nevertheless collaterally estop the prosecution from relitigating the same matter when the Roberts matter came to trial?

The dissenting judge in *Showery* argued that, having failed to prove a fact in one proceeding, at least where liberty was at stake, the prosecution should be estopped from receiving an opportunity to prove that same fact in a subsequent criminal trial. Would the dissent's reasoning require that a finding of no probable cause at a preliminary hearing bar later prosecution for the same crime? Such is not the law.

5. RETRIAL FOLLOWING CONVICTION

Several situations may give rise to a retrial following a conviction. In evaluating the various rules governing in the different situations, as described in the notes below, consider whether the policies underlying the prohibition against double jeopardy are properly reflected in the rules of law that have emerged from the decided cases.

NOTES

1. *Successive prosecution for the same transaction or conduct.* The Double Jeopardy Clause forbids successive prosecutions for the same crime. But it is not necessarily easy to explain what is meant by "the same crime." Given any set of facts about a course of criminal conduct, there may be many ways to characterize the offense and charge it. A car crash resulting in death, for example, may be charged as murder, manslaughter, negligent homicide, reckless driving, or speeding. A drug sale involving two salespeople may be charged as possession, distribution, conspiracy to distribute, conspiracy to possess, etc.

The Court has, for the most part, adhered to the rule that "the test to be applied to determine whether there are two offenses (thus avoiding the Double Jeopardy prohibition) or one is whether each requires proof of a fact which the other does not." Blockburger v. United States, 284 U.S. 299, 52 S.Ct. 180 (1932). This very narrow test is meant to allow successive prosecutions for closely related offenses, but not to allow successive prosecutions where one of the offenses is exactly the same or is a lesser included offense of the other. See Brown v. Ohio, 432 U.S. 161, 97 S.Ct. 2221 (1977) (Double Jeopardy prohibits trial of a defendant for the greater offense after he has been convicted of a lesser "included" offense, even if he has not been previously tried for the greater offense.) This test, however, would not bar successive prosecutions for conspiracies based on the same facts but with different objects, or successive prosecutions for drunk driving and vehicular homicide.

The Court has, at other times, been tempted by an approach which looks to the underlying facts of the case, rather than to the statutory elements of the crime. Justice Brennan often dissented in *Blockburger* cases, arguing that prosecutors should be required to join all counts based on the "same transaction" in a single indictment, and could not prosecute different statutory characterizations of the same events in successive trials. He argued that only by looking at the facts underlying the indictment could double jeopardy be given any real bite or provide any real protection against repetition of trial ordeal after trial ordeal.

The Court, 5–4, tried out a variant of this approach in Grady v. Corbin, 495 U.S. 508, 110 S.Ct. 2084 (1990), holding that subsequent prosecution would be barred when "to establish an essential element of an offense charged in that prosecution, [the government] will prove conduct that constitutes an offense for which the defendant has already been prosecuted." The Court applied the test in Grady to bar prosecution for negligent homicide, where negligence was based on conduct (speeding, driving while intoxicated, failure to keep right) to which defendant had already pled guilty.

Three terms later, the Court, again 5–4, reversed itself and overruled *Grady*, returning to a *Blockburger* analysis. United States v. Dixon, 509 U.S. 688, 113 S.Ct. 2849 (1993). Subsequent cases had made the *Grady* analysis seem too broad. The Court pointed to United States v. Felix, 503 U.S. 378, 112 S.Ct. 1377 (1992), in which the Court had, despite *Grady*, allowed a subsequent prosecution for conspiracy to manufacture, possess, and distribute methamphetamine after a prior conviction for attempt to manufacture it. The five justices who voted to return to *Blockburger*, however, could not agree on how to apply it. Two justices applied *Blockburger* by asking whether the elements of the crimes as applied to the particular case were the same; three justices applied Blockburger by asking whether the generic elements of the crimes were the same. For example, Justices Scalia and Kennedy held that a defendant held in contempt for violating a court order not to engage in any criminal conduct could not be prosecuted later for the same drug offense that had brought on the contempt sanction. Rehnquist, O'Connor, and Thomas pointed out that, generically speaking, the contempt and drug offenses each required proof of an element the other did not, as the contempt offense requires knowledge of the court's prior order (not an element of drug distribution offenses), and does not require (considered in the abstract) proof of drug dealing. Chief Justice Rehnquist commented: "By focusing on the facts needed to show a violation of the specific court orders involved in this case, and not on the generic elements of the crime of contempt of court, Justice Scalia's double-jeopardy analysis bears a striking resemblance to that found in *Grady*—not what one would expect in an opinion that overrules *Grady*." See also, State v. Winningham, 958 S.W.2d 740 (Tenn.1997) (criticizing Scalia's approach because "the outcome of a case would necessarily depend upon the language of the [contempt] order at issue, and the consequence of such dependence is not easily predictable.").

Before the Double Jeopardy Clause was applied to the states, the Court upheld an Illinois case allowing three separate trials for a defendant who was charged (in four separate indictments) with shooting his wife and three children and leaving them in a burning building. The defendant was found guilty of murder in all three trials, but received the death penalty only in the third. The majority held, under the Due Process Clause, there was no fundamental unfairness in the successive prosecutions. The dissenters, however, argued that the case was "an instance of the prosecution being allowed to harass the accused with repeated trials and convictions on the same evidence, until it achieves its desired result of a capital verdict." Ciucci v. Illinois, 356 U.S. 571, 78 S.Ct. 839 (1958). How would such cases fare under Justice Brennan's "same transaction" test? Under *Grady* and *Dixon/Scalia* and *Dixon/Rehnquist*?

Some states have rejected *Dixon* under their own constitutions. In State v. Lessary, 75 Haw. 446, 865 P.2d 150 (1994), defendant pled no contest to spousal abuse charges in family court and received 5 days in jail. He was also charged with more serious offenses, including kidnapping, in circuit court. Because all charges were based on the same incident, the felony allegations were dismissed on double jeopardy grounds; and, on the state's appeal, the dismissal was affirmed. Recognizing that the state constitutional language was "virtually identical" to the federal double jeopardy clause, the court held:

> When the United States Supreme Court's interpretation of a provision present in both the United States and Hawaii Constitutions does not adequately preserve the rights and interests sought to be protected, we will not hesitate to recognize the appropriate protections as a matter of state constitutional law.

* * *

We do not believe that the State's interest in prosecuting different offenses in different courts outweighs a defendant's "paramount" interest in being free from vexatious multiple prosecutions. Moreover, the State should not be allowed to circumvent the constitutional prohibition against double jeopardy by creating a variety of courts, each having limited jurisdiction, in which to bring successive prosecutions that could not otherwise be pursued.

Thus, we are not persuaded by the State's argument and agree with the majority in *Grady* and the "dissenters" in *Dixon* that individuals should be protected against multiple prosecutions even when multiple punishments are permissible under the "same elements" test. Therefore, we conclude that the interpretation given to the double jeopardy clause by the United States Supreme Court in *Dixon* does not adequately protect individuals from being "subject for the same offense to be twice put in jeopardy."

In State v. Kurzawa, 180 Wis.2d 502, 509 N.W.2d 712, cert. denied 512 U.S. 1222, 114 S.Ct. 2712 (1994), the Wisconsin Supreme Court refused an invitation to reject *Dixon*. However, Justice Abrahamson, in a concurring opinion, called for reexamination of the issue: "When it requires a chart to determine which paragraphs of a United States Supreme Court decision constitute the law of the land, you know you are in trouble."

In Hayes v. State, 803 So.2d 695 (Fla.S.Ct. 2001), defendants broke into a residence and stole several items, including a set of keys which they used to take a vehicle parked outside. Convicted of armed robbery and auto theft, defendants contended on appeal that the multiple counts violated their double jeopardy rights because they both evolved from the same criminal episode. Reviewing the manner in which other jurisdictions have evaluated the "same criminal episode" doctrine, the court announced the following test:

> [I]n reaching a determination of double jeopardy issue in a case involving a single victim's property, courts should look to whether there was a separation of time, place, or circumstances between the initial armed robbery and the subsequent grand theft, as those factors are objective criteria utilized to determine whether there are distinct and independent criminal acts or whether there is one continuous criminal act with a single criminal intent. In making this determination of whether there is a separation of time, place, or circumstances giving rise to distinct and independent acts, the courts should consider the location of the items taken, the lapse of time taken between takings, the number of owners of the items taken, and the intervening events between the takings

In applying the test to the case before it, the court held that the armed robbery was complete when defendants left the residence and, therefore, the auto theft was sufficiently distinct as to justify separate charges. Was the court correct under its own test? See also Williams v. State, 796 A.2d 1281 (Del.2002) (simultaneous possession of drugs in car and home); State v. Mather, 264 Neb. 182, 646 N.W.2d 605 (2002) (multiple pornographic pictures of the same child).

2. *Conviction Followed by Successful Defense Claim of Procedural Error Followed by Reprosecution.* Few principles are better established than the one allowing retrial where a defendant has successfully overturned his conviction by claiming that a procedural error denied his right to a fair trial. Often the defendant is said to have "waived" his right to the jeopardy protection in such a situation. Does a waiver rationale make sense? On the other hand, would defendants generally be better off if reviewing courts had to choose between (1) affirming a conviction and (2) letting a defendant go free where the defendant has asserted that his first trial was not fair?

There may be an exception to the general rule allowing retrial. The exception would be analogous to the one prohibiting retrial following a mistrial caused by a prosecutor's conduct that had been designed to provoke a mistrial. See the discussion of Oregon v. Kennedy, section A(3) supra. See also People v. Pendleton, 75 Ill.App.3d 580, 31 Ill.Dec. 294, 394 N.E.2d 496 (1979).

3. *Conviction Overturned Because of Evidentiary Deficiencies.* When a reviewing court determines that the evidence was insufficient to sustain a conviction, a remand for a new trial is barred by the Double Jeopardy Clause. See Burks v. United States, 437 U.S. 1, 98 S.Ct. 2141 (1978); Greene v. Massey, 437 U.S. 19, 98 S.Ct. 2151 (1978). When a trial judge vacates a conviction because of insufficient evidence, unless that verdict is reinstated by a reviewing court upon an appeal by the prosecution, retrial is barred under the *Burks* principle. See Hudson v. Louisiana, 450 U.S. 40, 101 S.Ct. 970 (1981).

These decisions have no applicability where a finding of insufficiency is overturned by a higher court on further review. For example, if an intermediate appellate court of State *X* finds the evidence insufficient, upon further review the highest court of State *X* can reinstate the conviction if it finds the evidence adequate. In such an instance no further trial would be required.

Additionally in Tibbs v. Florida, 457 U.S. 31, 102 S.Ct. 2211 (1982), with four justices dissenting, the Supreme Court drew a distinction, for double jeopardy purposes, between appellate reversals based upon insufficiency of the evidence and appellate reversals based upon the weight of the evidence. Normally it is thought that a "sufficiency" reversal occurs when the reviewing court determines that, even if all the prosecution evidence is accepted as true, the evidence fails to establish one or more elements of the offense. A "weight" reversal occurs where though, if believed, the evidence would establish every element, nevertheless the evidence is deemed to lack sufficient credibility to support the verdict. (At various places in its opinion the Supreme Court seemed to be drawing this distinction, referring to "weight" reversals as involving a reviewing court's reweighing of the evidence. On the other hand, the Court said that "sufficiency" reversals are distinguished from "weight" reversals in that in the former case there is a determination that no rational finder of fact could convict. The problem is that in some courts, while recognizing the weight-sufficiency distinction, would invoke the "no rational factfinder" test when reversing on either weight or sufficiency grounds. Others would use a less stringent standard when reversing on either weight or sufficiency grounds, such as whether the record as a whole leaves an abiding doubt about guilt.) In those rare cases where the reviewing court, at the defendant's request, sets aside the jury's (or, in a bench trial, the judge's) resolution of credibility questions, the Court in *Tibbs* determined that the policies underlying the double jeopardy clause do not prohibit a second trial. The Court distinguished *Burks* and *Greene* as involving "sufficiency" questions. If the prosecution's evidence is unsatisfactory, what difference does the reason for the deficiency make in terms of double jeopardy policies?

One court has held that re-trial is not barred under *Burks* when a reviewing court determines that certain evidence was improperly admitted at trial, without which the record on appeal contains insufficient evidence to support a conviction. See Ex parte Duran, 581 S.W.2d 683 (Tex.Crim.App.1979), where the court reasoned that, in reliance upon the erroneous ruling, the prosecutor might not have introduced other evidence which would have sufficed to support a conviction. To the same effect, see State v. Wood, 596 S.W.2d 394 (Mo.1980); United States v. Tranowski, 702 F.2d 668 (7th Cir.1983).

In Lockhart v. Nelson, 488 U.S. 33, 109 S.Ct. 285 (1988), the Supreme Court declared that where an evidentiary deficiency arises, in the view of an appellate court, because of the trial judge's *erroneous* exclusion of evidence, a reviewing court does not offend the double jeopardy clause when it permits the prosecution a new chance to prove its case. Of course, if after its erroneous ruling, a *trial* court had acquitted the defendant, jeopardy would bar retrial.

In Justices of Boston Municipal Court v. Lydon, 466 U.S. 294, 104 S.Ct. 1805 (1984), the Court reviewed a system in which a defendant could elect (1) a jury trial with the normal right of appellate review upon conviction or (2) a non-jury trial with a right to a trial de novo (without need to show error). The defendant claimed that following a conviction in a non-jury trial, he must be accorded review of the sufficiency of the evidence and that double jeopardy principles would bar re-trial if the evidence were deemed insufficient.

The Court held that at the first trial the defendant was at jeopardy only in a technical sense because of his absolute right to trial de novo. Unlike the majority, Justice Brennan, in concurring, emphasized that the defendant could have avoided the two-trial system by electing trial by jury.

4. *Successful Attack Upon Plea of Guilty*. When a defendant, through action in a trial court or in an appellate court, successfully attacks his plea of guilty and is allowed to plead anew, at least two questions can arise: (1) Can the prosecution reinstate charges which have been dropped as a part of the plea negotiation process? (2) Can the trial court, if the defendant is convicted anew, impose a higher sentence than had originally been imposed?

5. *Conviction Followed by Dismissal of Prosecution for Reasons Unrelated to Sufficiency of Evidence*. In United States v. Wilson, 420 U.S. 332, 95 S.Ct. 1013 (1975), the trial judge had dismissed an indictment after a finding of guilty. The government appealed. The Supreme Court noted that if the government was correct in its argument that an erroneous interpretation of law underlay the dismissal, the error could be corrected by a reinstatement of the verdict of guilty without the necessity for a further evidentiary hearing. Under these circumstances the Court held that the government could appeal.

Consider also Ludwig v. Massachusetts, 427 U.S. 618, 96 S.Ct. 2781 (1976), upholding a statutory scheme which seemingly institutionalized multiple prosecutions. There the defendant was first tried in a proceeding in which no jury was available. An acquittal in that bench trial would be final. On the other hand, upon conviction defendant could automatically exercise the right to trial *de novo* before a jury. He could not, however, bypass the first proceedings and immediately obtain a jury trial. Although the defendant was required to undergo the time and expense of two trials in order to exercise his constitutional right to trial by jury, a majority of the Court upheld the procedure. The plurality opinion emphasized a waiver theory, asserting that it was defendant who elected the second trial. The dissenters found that the procedure violated the Sixth Amendment trial by jury right and did not dwell upon the double jeopardy claim.

6. *Effect of Prior or Subsequent Civil Penalty or Forfeiture Proceeding*. The Court has struggled over the problem of successive prosecutions for civil fines or forfeitures. In United States v. Halper, 490 U.S. 435, 109 S.Ct. 1892 (1989), the Court held that a civil action seeking $130,000 for Medicare fraud amounting to $585 was so severe as to constitute punishment, and was barred by double jeopardy because the defendant had already been convicted, sentenced to two years in prison, and fined $5,000. Following *Halper*, the Court held in Department of Revenue of Montana v. Kurth Ranch, 511 U.S. 767, 114 S.Ct. 1937 (1994), that a state tax imposed on marijuana was barred by double jeopardy, because the tax was so punitive as to constitute punishment and was conditioned on the commission of a crime.

The decisions generated a great deal of (mostly unsuccessful) litigation, challenging forfeiture statutes, prison disciplinary proceedings, license revocations, evictions, discharge and debarment proceedings, etc. In United States v. Ursery, 518 U.S. 267, 116 S.Ct. 2135 (1996), the Court backed away from *Halper*, refusing to apply *Halper's* case-by-case analysis of excessiveness to bar the drug prosecution of a defendant who had already suffered civil forfeiture of his home for the same conduct. The Court held that *Halper* applied only to civil penalties, not civil forfeitures, emphasizing that forfeiture proceeded against the property, not the person. Instead, the Court evaluated the purposes of forfeitures as a class, concluding that they "serve important nonpunitive goals" such as "encourag[ing] property owners to take care in managing their property," "abat[ing] a nuisance," and "ensuring that persons do not profit from their illegal acts." The Court also looked to whether the civil forfeiture was historically considered punishment, and whether scienter is an element of civil forfeiture. These factors also weighed against treating civil forfeitures as criminal proceedings.

The demise of *Halper* was completed in Hudson v. United States, 522 U.S. 93, 118 S.Ct. 488 (1997), in which defendants received administrative penalties and occupational debarment for violating federal banking statutes and then were later indicted for the same conduct. The Court overruled *Halper*, and confirmed its analysis in *Ursery*: a civil sanction would not be held to be punishment just because it seemed excessive as applied. Instead, the Court evaluated the civil penalties at issue on their face, applying the definition of "punishment" laid out in Kennedy v. Mendoza–Martinez, 372 U.S. 144, 83 S.Ct. 554 (1963). A penalty the legislature intended to be civil would be considered punitive, triggering the protections of the double jeopardy clause, only when a defendant provided the "clearest proof" that 1) the kind of penalty at issue had historically been viewed as punishment; 2) the penalty imposes an "affirmative disability or restraint;" 3) the sanctions come into play only on a finding of scienter; 4) the conduct sanctioned may also be criminally prosecuted; and 5) the penalty is imposed for deterrent or retributive purposes. The Court made clear that meeting even one or two of these factors would not be sufficient to provide "the clearest proof." Justices Stevens and Souter pointed out in concurring opinions that the Court need not have reached the *Halper* issue. Since the elements of the civil penalties in this case did not overlap the elements of the substantive crimes, *Blockburger* would not bar successive prosecutions, even if both proceedings were punitive. Lurking in the shadows of the opinions is the question, considered later, of to what extent the Double Jeopardy Clause protects against multiple punishments, not just multiple prosecutions. Justices Scalia and Thomas, at least, would limit protection to the latter, as they noted in concurrence.

7. *Civil Commitment After Conviction*. In Kansas v. Hendricks, 521 U.S. 346, 117 S.Ct. 2072 (1997), the Court upheld, 5–4, a Kansas statute permitting civil commitment of those charged with or convicted of a violent sexual offense and suffering from a "mental abnormality" making them likely to "engage in predatory acts of sexual violence." The Court rejected the Kansas Supreme Court's reasoning that the definition of "mental abnormality" violated substantive due process because it was essentially the equivalent of a finding of future dangerousness. ("Mental abnormality" was defined under the statute as a "congenital or acquired condition affecting the emotional or volitional capacity which predisposes the person to commit sexually violent offenses in a degree constituting such person a menace to the health and safety of others.") Emphasizing that state legislatures have great latitude in defining mental illness and need not defer to psychiatric definitions, the Court held that pedophilia was itself considered to be a mental illness and intimated that civil commitment statutes that limited confinement to those who "suffer from a volitional impairment rendering them dangerous beyond their control" would be constitutional.

The Court rejected double jeopardy and ex post facto challenges on the ground that the statute was not meant to punish or deter, but to incapacitate. The Court emphasized that the statute has no scienter requirement nor expectation of deterrence, since the population targeted is assumed to have little control over their future actions. The Court also stressed that the confinement had to be reevaluated yearly, and that the State bore a burden of proving beyond a reasonable doubt that confinement was still warranted. The Court also rejected the decision of the Kansas Supreme Court that confinement would be unconstitutional if treatment were unavailable: "While we have upheld state civil commitment statutes that aim both to incapacitate and to treat ... we have never held that the Constitution prevents a State from civilly detaining those for whom no treatment is available, but who nevertheless pose a danger to others." The Court summed up: "Where the State has 'disavowed any punitive intent'; limited confinement to a small segment of particularly dangerous individuals; provided strict procedural safeguards; directed that confined persons be segregated from the general prison population and afforded the same status as others who have been civilly committed; recommended treatment if such is possible; and permitted immediate release upon a showing that the individual is no longer dangerous or mentally impaired, we cannot say that it acted with punitive intent." Hence, the statute was "civil" not "criminal" in nature, and the ex post facto and double jeopardy challenges did not apply.

Justice Kennedy joined the Court's opinion, but added: "If the civil system is used simply to impose punishment after the State makes an improvident plea bargain on the criminal side, then it is not performing its proper function.... We should bear in mind that while incapacitation is a goal common to both the criminal and civil systems of confinement, retribution and general deterrence are reserved for the criminal system alone."

The dissenters, Justices Breyer, Stevens, Souter, and Ginsburg, argued that the fact that the statute had been invoked against Mr. Hendricks only after he had served ten years in prison proved that the state's intention was not treatment, but further punishment. The record also reflected that very little if any treatment was being provided to Hendricks after his civil commitment. Justice Breyer concluded: "a State is free to commit those who are dangerous in order to treat them. Nor does my decision preclude a State from deciding that a certain subset of people are mentally ill, dangerous, and untreatable, and that confinement of this subset is therefore necessary (again, assuming that all the procedural safeguards of Addington are in place). But when a State decides offenders can be treated and confines an offender to provide that treatment, but then refuses to provide it, the refusal to treat while a person is fully incapacitated begins to look punitive."

The dissenters, with the exception of Justice Ginsburg, agreed that the definition of "mental abnormality" as applied to this case did not violate due process.

8. *Capital Sentencing Hearing After Conviction.* The Supreme Court held in Schiro v. Farley, 510 U.S. 222, 114 S.Ct. 783 (1994), that a capital sentencing hearing is not a successive prosecution for double jeopardy purposes, even though a defendant is forced to relitigate issues for which he has just been tried. The Court left unresolved whether the government would be precluded by collateral estoppel from relitigating factual determinations resolved in defendant's favor at trial.

6. Jeopardy, Due Process, and Sentencing

Based upon Stroud v. United States, 251 U.S. 15, 40 S.Ct. 50 (1919), it was generally assumed that when a defendant through his appeal received a new trial because of trial error, the slate was wiped clean. If he or she was convicted at a second trial, any punishment permitted by statute could be imposed, including one which was greater than that imposed after the first trial. A "waiver" theory was invoked to reach this result. Thus a capital defendant who, like Stroud, had avoided a death sentence could be sentenced to death following a successful appeal, retrial, and a new conviction. Some persons chose not to appeal for this reason. See Fay v. Noia, 372 U.S. 391, 83 S.Ct. 822 (1963).

Increased sentences following retrial were made especially visible after *Gideon*, Chapter 9, Section B. Some defendants who won reversals because they had been denied counsel at their first trial received much more severe punishments following retrials. One who had been sentenced to two years, and who had won a reversal, was sentenced to ten years following reconviction. As indicated in the next case, the continuing vitality of *Stroud* was challenged, but the Supreme Court reached a solution on grounds other than the Double Jeopardy clause.

North Carolina v. Pearce

Supreme Court of the United States, 1969.
395 U.S. 711, 89 S.Ct. 2072.

■ MR. JUSTICE STEWART delivered the opinion of the Court.

When at the behest of the defendant a criminal conviction has been set aside and a new trial ordered, to what extent does the Constitution limit the imposition of a harsher sentence after conviction upon retrial? That is the question presented by these two cases.

Pearce was convicted in a North Carolina court upon a charge of assault with intent to commit rape. The trial judge sentenced him to prison for a term of 12 to 15 years. Several years later he initiated a state post-conviction proceeding which culminated in the reversal of his conviction.

... He was retried, convicted, and sentenced by the trial judge to an eight-year prison term, which, when added to the time Pearce had already spent in prison, the parties agree amounted to a longer total sentence than that originally imposed. The United States District Court held that the longer sentence imposed upon retrial was "unconstitutional and void." ... This order was affirmed by the United States Court of Appeals for the Fourth Circuit.

* * *

The respondent Rice pleaded guilty in an Alabama trial court to four separate charges of second-degree burglary. He was sentenced to prison terms aggregating 10 years. Two and one-half years later the judgments were set aside in a state *coram nobis* proceeding. ... He was retried upon three of the charges, convicted, and sentenced to prison terms aggregating 25 years. No credit was given for the time he had spent in prison on the original judgments. He then brought this habeas corpus proceeding alleging that the state trial court had acted unconstitutionally in failing to give him credit for the time he had already served in prison, and in imposing grossly harsher sentences upon retrial. Judge Johnson agreed with both contentions. While stating that he did "not believe that it is constitutionally impermissible to impose a harsher sentence upon retrial if there is recorded in the court record some legal justification for it," Judge Johnson found that Rice had been denied due process of law, because "[u]nder the evidence in this case, the conclusion is inescapable that the State of Alabama is punishing petitioner Rice for his having exercised his post-conviction right of review and for having the original sentences declared unconstitutional." 274 F.Supp. 116, 121, 122. The judgment of the District Court was affirmed by the United States Court of Appeals for the Fifth Circuit.

* * *

We turn first to the more limited aspect of the question before us—whether the Constitution requires that, in computing the sentence imposed after conviction upon retrial, credit must be given for time served under the original sentence. We then consider the broader question of what constitutional limitations there may be upon the imposition of a more severe sentence after reconviction.

I.

. . . The Fifth Amendment guarantee against double jeopardy has been said to consist of three separate constitutional protections. It protects against a second prosecution for the same offense after acquittal. It protects against a second prosecution for the same offense after conviction. And it protects against multiple punishments for the same offense.

* * *

We think it is clear that this basic constitutional guarantee is violated when punishment already exacted for an offense is not fully "credited" in imposing sentence upon a new conviction for the same offense. The constitutional violation is flagrantly apparent in a case involving the imposition of a maximum sentence after reconviction. Suppose, for example, in a jurisdiction where the maximum allowable sentence for larceny is 10 years' imprisonment, a man succeeds in getting his larceny conviction set aside after serving three years in prison. If, upon reconviction, he is given a 10–year sentence, then, quite clearly, he will have received multiple punishments for the same offense. For he will have been compelled to serve separate prison terms of three years and 10 years, although the maximum single punishment for the offense is 10 years' imprisonment. Though not so dramatically evident, the same principle obviously holds true whenever punishment already endured is not fully subtracted from any new sentence imposed.

We hold that the constitutional guarantee against multiple punishments for the same offense absolutely requires that punishment already exacted must be fully "credited" in imposing sentence upon a new conviction for the same offense. If, upon a new trial, the defendant is acquitted, there is no way the years he spent in prison can be returned to him. But if he is reconvicted, those years can and must be returned—by subtracting them from whatever new sentence is imposed.

II.

* * *

A

Long-established constitutional doctrine makes clear that, beyond the requirement already discussed, the guarantee against double jeopardy imposes no restrictions upon the length of a sentence imposed upon reconviction.

. . . at least since 1919, when Stroud v. United States, 251 U.S. 15, 40 S.Ct. 50, was decided, it has been settled that a corollary of the power to retry a defendant is the power, upon the defendant's reconviction, to impose whatever sentence may be legally authorized, whether or not it is greater than the sentence imposed after the first conviction.

* * *

Although the rationale for this "well-established part of our constitutional jurisprudence" has been variously verbalized, it rests ultimately upon the premise that the original conviction has, at the defendant's behest, been wholly nullified and the slate wiped clean. As to whatever punishment has actually been suffered under the first conviction, that premise is, of course, an unmitigated fiction, as we have recognized in Part I of this opinion. But, so far as the conviction itself goes, and that part of the sentence that has not yet been served, it is no more than a simple statement of fact to say that the slate *has* been wiped clean. The conviction *has* been set aside and the unexpired portion of the original sentence will never be served. A new trial may result in an acquittal. But if it does result in a conviction, we cannot say that the constitutional guarantee against double jeopardy of its own weight restricts the imposition of an otherwise lawful single punishment for the offense in question. To hold to the contrary would be to cast doubt upon the whole validity of the basic principle and upon the unbroken line of decisions that have followed that principle for almost 75 years. We think those decisions are entirely sound, and we decline to depart from the concept they reflect.

B

* * *

C

We hold, therefore, that neither the double jeopardy provision nor the Equal Protection Clause imposes an absolute bar to a more severe sentence upon reconviction. A trial judge is not constitutionally precluded, in other words, from imposing a new sentence, whether greater or less than the original sentence, in the light of events subsequent to the first trial that may have thrown new light upon the defendant's "life, health, habits, conduct, and mental and moral propensities." Williams v. New York, 337 U.S. 241, 245, 69 S.Ct. 1079, 1082. Such information may come to the judge's attention from evidence adduced at the second trial itself, from a new presentence investigation, from the defendant's prison record, or possibly from other sources. The freedom of a sentencing judge to consider the defendant's conduct subsequent to the first conviction in imposing a new sentence is no more than consonant with the principle that a State may adopt the "prevalent modern philosophy of penology that the punishment should fit the offender and not merely the crime."

To say that there exists no absolute constitutional bar to the imposition of a more severe sentence upon retrial is not, however, to end the inquiry. There remains for consideration the impact of the Due Process Clause of the Fourteenth Amendment.

It can hardly be doubted that it would be a flagrant violation of the Fourteenth Amendment for a state trial court to follow an announced practice of imposing a heavier sentence upon every reconvicted defendant for the explicit purpose of punishing the defendant for his having succeeded in getting his original conviction set aside. Where, as in each of the cases before us, the original conviction has been set aside because of a constitutional error, the imposition of such a punishment, "penalizing those who choose to exercise" constitutional rights, "would be patently unconstitutional." And the very threat inherent in the existence of such a punitive policy would, with respect to those still in prison, serve to "chill the exercise of basic constitutional rights." But even if the first conviction has been set aside for nonconstitutional error, the imposition of a penalty upon the defendant for having successfully pursued a statutory right of appeal or collateral remedy would be no less a violation of due process of law. "A new sentence, with enhanced punishment, based upon such a reason, would be a flagrant violation of the rights of the defendant." Nichols v. United States, 106 F. 672, 679. A court is "without right to . . . put a price on an appeal. A defendant's exercise of a right of appeal must be free and unfettered. . . . [I]t is unfair to use the great power given to the court to determine sentence to place a defendant in the dilemma of making an unfree choice."

Due process of law, then, requires that vindictiveness against a defendant for having successfully attacked his first conviction must play no part in the sentence he receives after a new trial. And since the fear of such vindictiveness may unconstitutionally deter a defendant's exercise of the right to appeal or collaterally attack his first conviction, due process also requires that a defendant be freed of apprehension of such a retaliatory motivation on the part of the sentencing judge.

In order to assure the absence of such a motivation, we have concluded that whenever a judge imposes a more severe sentence upon a defendant after a new trial, the reasons for his doing so must affirmatively appear. Those reasons must be based upon objective information concerning identifiable conduct on the part of the defendant occurring after the time of the original sentencing proceeding. And the factual data upon which the increased sentence is based must be made part of the record, so that the constitutional legitimacy of the increased sentence may be fully reviewed on appeal.

We dispose of the two cases before us in the light of [the fact] that . . . "the State of Alabama offers no evidence attempting to justify the increase in Rice's original sentences" [and] that neither at the time the increased sentence was imposed upon Pearce, nor at any stage in this habeas corpus proceeding, has the State offered any reason or justification for that sentence beyond the naked power to impose it. We conclude that in each of the cases before us, the judgment should be affirmed.

■ MR. JUSTICE BLACK, concurring in part and dissenting in part.

* * *

... Punishment based on the impermissible motivation described by the Court is, as I have said, clearly unconstitutional, and courts must of course set aside the punishment if they find, by the normal judicial process of fact-finding, that such a motivation exists. But, beyond this, the courts are not vested with any general power to prescribe particular devices "[i]n order to assure the absence of such a motivation."

* * *

■ MR. JUSTICE HARLAN, concurring in part and dissenting in part.

* * *

Given *Benton*, it is my view that the decision of this Court in Green v. United States, 355 U.S. 184, 78 S.Ct. 221 (1957), from which I dissented at the time, points strongly to the conclusion that the Double Jeopardy Clause of the Fifth Amendment governs *both* issues presently decided by the Court. ...

Green held in effect that a defendant who is convicted of a lesser offense included in that charged in the original indictment, and who thereafter secures reversal, may be retried only for the lesser included offense.

* * *

Every consideration enunciated by the Court in support of the decision in *Green* applies with equal force to the situation at bar. In each instance, the defendant was once subjected to the risk of receiving a maximum punishment, but it was determined by legal process that he should receive only a specified punishment less than the maximum. And the concept or fiction of an "implicit acquittal" of the greater offense, applies equally to the greater sentence: in each case it was determined at the former trial that the defendant or his offense was of a certain limited degree of "badness" or gravity only, and therefore merited only a certain limited punishment. Most significantly, perhaps, in each case a contrary rule would place the defendant considering whether to appeal his conviction in the same "incredible dilemma" and confront him with the same "desperate" choice. His decision whether or not to appeal would be burdened by the consideration that success, followed by retrial and conviction, might place him in a far worse position than if he remained silent and suffered what seemed to him an unjust punishment. In terms of *Green*, that the imposition of a more severe sentence on retrial is a matter of pure *chance*, rather than the result of purposeful retaliation for having taken an appeal, renders the choice no less "desperate."

I therefore conclude that, consistent with the Fifth Amendment, a defendant who has once been convicted and sentenced to a particular punishment may not on retrial be placed again in jeopardy of receiving a greater punishment than was first imposed....

■ MR. JUSTICE WHITE, concurring in part.

I join the Court's opinion except that in my view Part II–C should authorize an increased sentence on retrial based on any objective, identifiable factual data not known to the trial judge at the time of the original sentencing proceeding.

■ MR. JUSTICE DOUGLAS, whom MR. JUSTICE MARSHALL joins, concurring.

The governing principle has thus developed that a convicted man may be retried after a successful appeal; that he may run the risk, on retrial, of receiving a sentence as severe as that previously imposed; and that he may run the risk of being tried for a separate offense. But with all deference, I submit that the State does not, because of prior error, have a second chance to obtain an enlarged sentence.

Where a man successfully attacks a sentence that he has already "fully served," the State cannot create an additional sentence and send him back to prison. Similarly, where a defendant successfully attacks a sentence that he has begun to serve, the State cannot impose an added sentence by sending him to prison for a greater term.

* * *

NOTES

A. *Post–Pearce Decisions*

1. *Same Sentencer.* In Texas v. McCullough, 475 U.S. 134, 106 S.Ct. 976 (1986), following conviction and sentencing by a jury, a judge granted a defendant's motion for a new trial based upon prosecutorial misconduct. Apparently not happy about the lenient sentence, the prosecutor did not oppose the motion. Following re-conviction, the defendant elected to be sentenced by the trial judge instead of the jury. This was the same judge who had granted the motion for a new trial and who had presided over both the first and the second trial. Possibly widespread publicity and criticism concerning the first sentence led the defendant to waive his right under Texas law to be sentenced by the jury.

At re-sentencing the prosecution presented evidence of criminal conduct which had occurred before the first trial but which had been called to the prosecutor's attention after the original sentencing. The judge imposed a substantially harsher sentence than had been imposed by the jury following the first sentence.

The United States Supreme Court held that the presumption of vindictiveness only applies where the second sentence is imposed by the same judge who imposed the first sentence. The Court acknowledged that in *Pearce* the second sentence had been imposed by a judge other than the one who imposed the first sentence. However, the Court said that this fact appeared nowhere in the Court's opinion in *Pearce*. The *McCullough* Court went on to note that the trial judge there had no reason to be vindictive since she herself had granted the new trial. Moreover, she had adequately explained her reasons for imposing a greater sentence.

Along similar lines, see Chaffin v. Stynchcombe, 412 U.S. 17, 93 S.Ct. 1977 (1973) (resentencing by different juries doesn't implicate *Pearce*); Colten v. Kentucky, 407 U.S. 104, 92 S.Ct. 1953 (1972) (when two-tier court system allows misdemeanor conviction to be tried de novo by higher court, higher sentence may be imposed because different sentencer who would not be inclined to blame defendant for seeking retrial, given abbreviated procedures in lower courts).

2. *Death is Different.* In Bullington v. Missouri, 451 U.S. 430, 101 S.Ct. 1852 (1981), the Court held that after a reversal of a conviction and life sentence, a defendant could not be sentenced to death by a jury upon re-conviction. Double jeopardy principles were said to prohibit such a result. The court viewed the first jury sentencing hearing as resolving a factual issue in favor of the defendant. It likened this factual determination to one made at a trial on the question of innocence or guilt. Again the Court refused to rest its holding, even under these limited circumstances, upon the proposition that the prospect of a greater sentence after re-trial might chill a defendant's statutory right to appeal a conviction.

Bullington was extended in Arizona v. Rumsey, 467 U.S. 203, 104 S.Ct. 2305 (1984). There the trial judge refused to impose the death penalty while under the erroneous impression that state law did not define the crime in question as capital. The Supreme Court held that the trial-court resentencing of the defendant to death after a reviewing court correction of the error would constitute double jeopardy.

3. *More Serious Charges on Retrial.* In Blackledge v. Perry, 417 U.S. 21, 94 S.Ct. 2098 (1974), the Supreme Court held that a prosecutor may not bring a more serious charge based upon the same conduct after a defendant has exercised his right to a trial de novo following his conviction on a less serious charge. (This case is discussed further in Bordenkircher v. Hayes, Chapter 16.)

In Thigpen v. Roberts, 468 U.S. 27, 104 S.Ct. 2916 (1984), a defendant was convicted of several misdemeanor traffic offenses, including reckless driving and driving while intoxicated. He then claimed his right to trial de novo under Mississippi law. Instead, however, the prosecutor sought and obtained an indictment for manslaughter. Defendant was convicted and received a twenty-year sentence. The Court held that *Blackledge* controlled even though the prosecutor who obtained the felony charge had not been involved in the earlier misdemeanor prosecution. This was not enough to remove the presumption of vindictiveness. "A district attorney burdened with the retrial of an already convicted defendant might be no less vindictive because he did not bring the initial prosecution." Moreover the two attorneys (county attorney and district attorney) were not entirely independent of each other under Mississippi law. Dissenting justices thought the case was controlled by Justices of Boston and that trial in the first tier of a two-tier system does not constitute jeopardy in any meaningful sense.

4. *Justifying a Higher Sentence after Retrial.* In Wasman v. United States, 468 U.S. 559, 104 S.Ct. 3217 (1984), the Court considered whether an increased sentence upon re-trial and conviction (following an earlier successful appeal) can be justified by a conviction which (a) occurred after the original sentence but (b) was based upon conduct occurring before the original sentences. The Court approved such an increased sentence, saying that the presumption of vindictiveness was rebutted under such circumstances. The trial judge at the *original* sentencing had expressly stated that he would not consider pending charges which had not yet ripened into convictions, and the judge at the re-sentencing carefully explained that the recent conviction accounted for the increased sentence.

In United States v. Sanders, 435 F.2d 165 (9th Cir.1970), the court said:

> When resentencing Sanders the district court judge restated the comments he had made after the second trial, noting that:
>
> "(1) Sanders had committed a serious crime;
>
> "(2) Sanders had an extremely poor record as a citizen;

"(3) Sanders had obviously fabricated his defense and testified falsely at his trial, thus committing a further crime of perjury; and

"(4) It was apparent to me after studying the presentence report provided to me by the Probation Officer that Sanders had regressed rather than progressed toward rehabilitation during the time that he was in prison. I was aware of only the first two of these things at the time that I pronounced the initial sentence of fifteen years."

The stated reasons fully comply with the requirements of *Pearce*. It was appropriate for the district court judge to take Sanders' perjury into account in resentencing, Williams v. New York, 337 U.S. 241, 69 S.Ct. 1079 (1949) and the fact that he had not been favorably considered for parole.

In United States v. Saletko, 452 F.2d 193 (7th Cir.1971), the court said:

> In attempting to follow the dictates of *Pearce*, the trial judge set forth in the record the factual basis which he believed justified the longer sentence. Essentially, two factors were relied upon: first, that the defendant was impeached by his testimony at the previous trial and, second, that his testimony concerning Schang's solicitation of perjury was a fabrication on the part of the defendant. With respect to the impeachment of the defendant, we do not believe that sufficient discrepancies were revealed to warrant the additional sentence. The second trial occurred three years after the first and it is understandable that defendant was unable to recall the events in the same detail as he had at the first trial. When the defendant was confronted with his prior testimony, he acknowledged that his memory of the details was not good but admitted that if he had testified to something in the prior trial, it was correct. Similarly, the defendant's allegation of Schang's solicitation, even if perjurious, constituted no new fact upon which a more severe sentence could be predicated since that same testimony was given at the first trial. No, "identifiable conduct," subsequent to the first sentencing having been found upon which the increased sentence could be based, the mandate of *Pearce* was not complied with.

5. *Resentencing after Partial Reversal.* Occasionally a reviewing court will affirm one conviction and sentence, while overturning another conviction and sentence. Upon remand the trial judge may desire to reassess the punishment on the remaining sentence. If the judge previously imposed consecutive sentences, one of which later was overturned, the judge may feel that the original sentence on the remaining count was too light. Many federal courts routinely remand after a partial reversal to allow the trial judge to reassess the penalty. See, e.g., United States v. Handa, 122 F.3d 690 (9th Cir.1997) (reversal of one offense "unbundles" the "sentencing package" allowing resentencing on unchallenged counts). The Supreme Court seemingly approved the practice in Pennsylvania v. Goldhammer, 474 U.S. 28, 106 S.Ct. 353 (1985).

Given the availability of concurrent terms, why should a court not always be held to the term of years it deemed appropriate the first time around, absent evidence of other misconduct of the defendant which was not before the trial judge? Is not there always a potential that the trial judge will vindictively cancel out the defendant's partial appellate victory by increasing the sentence on the remaining count?

6. *Reconviction after Vacated Plea.* In Alabama v. Smith, 490 U.S. 794, 109 S.Ct. 2201 (1989), Smith pleaded guilty to burglary and rape. In exchange for the plea, the prosecution dismissed sodomy charges arising from the same incident. The trial judge sentenced Smith to concurrent terms of thirty years. Later Smith claimed that he had not knowingly and voluntarily entered his pleas of guilty. The trial judge denied relief, but an Alabama reviewing court reversed and allowed Smith to plead anew.

The prosecution then reinstated the sodomy charge. Smith was tried by a jury, presided over by the same trial judge who had accepted the pleas of guilty and who later had refused to vacate the pleas. The jury returned guilty verdicts on all three counts. The judge imposed concurrent life terms on the burglary and the sodomy convictions, to run consecutive to a term of 150 years on the rape conviction.

The United States Supreme Court held that resentencing by the trial judge after a defendant successfully petitions to vacate a bargained plea of guilty does not create the kind of presumption of vindictiveness which mandates relief under North Carolina v. Pearce.

The Court stressed that ordinarily the extent of information relevant to penalty that comes out at a full trial will be greater than that presented on a plea of guilty. The "trial judge may gather a fuller appreciation of the nature and extent of the crimes charged." The Court added that the defendant's conduct during trial may give the judge insights into his moral character and suitability for rehabilitation. It added that "after trial, the factors that may have indicated leniency as consideration for the guilty plea are no longer present." The United States Supreme Court did not reach the question of whether there was "evidence to support a finding of actual vindictiveness" on the part of the sentencing judge in the case, remanding instead for further proceedings in the Alabama courts.

Only Justice Marshall dissented. In a brief paragraph, he restated his position that whenever a conviction is vacated, double jeopardy notions prohibit imposition of a greater sentence following a new conviction.

B. *Other Sentencing—Jeopardy Claims*

7. *Prosecutor's Appeal of Sentence.* In United States v. DiFrancesco, 449 U.S. 117, 101 S.Ct. 426 (1980), the Court reviewed 18 U.S.C. § 3576, which, under specified conditions, allowed the prosecution to take an appeal in an effort to *increase* the sentence which had been imposed by a trial judge. In rejecting a double jeopardy claim, the Court said, "Historically, the pronouncement of sentence has never carried the finality that attaches to an acquittal ... The defendant's primary concern and anxiety obviously relate to the determination of innocence or guilt, and that already is behind him. The defendant is subject to no risk of being harassed and then convicted, although innocent. Furthermore, a sentence ... is purely a judicial determination, and much that goes with it is the result of inquiry that is nonadversarial in nature."

The Federal Sentencing Guidelines now allow prosecutorial appeals of sentencing decisions as a matter of course. See Koon v. United States, 518 U.S. 81, 116 S.Ct. 2035 (1996); United States v. Duso, 42 F.3d 365 (6th Cir.1994) (boost in guidelines sentence after appeal wasn't vindictive; sentence review cuts both ways).

8. *Insufficiency of Evidence at Sentencing Hearing.* Sometimes juries make factual determinations that are relevant only to the appropriate punishment. For example, state law may call upon jurors, at a separate sentencing hearing, to determine whether the defendant had prior convictions such as to make him eligible for sentencing as a recidivist. Dictum in Lockhart v. Nelson, 488 U.S. 33, 109 S.Ct. 285, 102 L.Ed.2d 265 (1988), suggests that if a reviewing court finds that the prosecution failed to provide sufficient evidence of such sentencing "facts," ordinarily double jeopardy principles will deny the prosecution a second chance to prove those essential facts at a sentencing hearing. *Nelson* held that where the reason for the evidentiary deficiency at the first sentencing proceeding was the trial court's erroneous exclusion of prosecution evidence, reviewing courts may afford the state a second sentencing hearing.

9. *Multiple Punishments for Closely Related Offenses.* The Double Jeopardy clause is said to prohibit not only multiple trials for the same offense but also multiple convictions and multiple sentences. Ex parte Lange, 85 U.S. (18 Wall.) 163 (1873); United States v. Benz, 282 U.S. 304, 51 S.Ct. 113 (1931). The limitation, however, is quite narrow. "(T)he test to be applied to determine whether there are two offenses (thus avoiding the Double Jeopardy prohibition) or one is whether each requires proof of a fact which the other does not." Blockburger v. United States, 284 U.S. 299, 52 S.Ct. 180 (1932). Thus a single act of reckless driving can result in multiple convictions and multiple sentences if the act causes death: proof of the offense of vehicular homicide requires proof of a death, which proof is not required for a conviction of reckless driving. Similarly a person who through a single act of arson kills eight people could receive eight sentences for felony-murder. The offense of murdering *X* requires proof of something not required for the offense of murdering *Y*, namely the death of *X*.

Some states have placed limits upon multiple punishments beyond those required by *Blockburger*, particularly as to sentences which are consecutive rather than concurrent. See, e.g., Ill.Rev.Stat. Ch. 730, § 5/5–8–4 (1995), which, subject to certain exceptions, prohibits consecutive sentences "for offenses which were committed as part of a single course of conduct during which there was no substantial change in the nature of the criminal objective." Compare People v. Smith, 478 Mich. 292, 733 N.W.2d 351 (2007) (Divided court overturned state precedents which provided greater double jeopardy protection than *Blockburger*)

In Missouri v. Hunter, 459 U.S. 359, 103 S.Ct. 673 (1983), the Court considered a statutory scheme which allowed consecutive sentences for two offenses (armed criminal action and robbery with a dangerous weapon) which constituted the "same offense" or the "same conduct" under the *Blockburger* test. It concluded that where, at the conclusion of a single trial, the accused is found guilty under both statutes, multiple punishments are consistent with the double jeopardy clause if the legislature so intended. The dissenting opinion in *Hunter* is directed chiefly to the imposition of multiple convictions. It declares that it is irrelevant that Missouri could have enacted a law which would have permitted a sentence for a term as great as the total of the two separate terms authorized by the two Missouri statutes under which Hunter had been convicted. "[E]ach additional conviction imposes an additional stigma...."

The principle of *Missouri v. Hunter* has been applied to allow cumulative punishment for both federal carjacking and use of a firearm during a crime of violence. Most circuits have decided that Congress intended the cumulative punishment. See, e.g., United States v. Moore, 43 F.3d 568 (11th Cir.1994). In a similar application of the doctrine, the Louisiana Supreme Court upheld double punishment for both manslaughter and feticide for defendant's strangling his pregnant girlfriend, on the ground that the legislature intended punishment for both deaths. State v. Smith, 676 So.2d 1068 (La.1996).

The Supreme Court recently held unanimously that a defendant may not be punished for both operating a continuing criminal enterprise under 21 U.S.C. § 848 and conspiracy under 21 U.S.C. § 846, since under the *Blockburger* test, conspiracy is a lesser included offense, sharing all its elements with the crime of operating a continuing criminal enterprise. Despite the fact that the sentences were to run concurrently, punishment under both statutes was double jeopardy, since a separate "special assessment" of $50 was charged for each crime and the collateral consequences of the second conviction also remained. Moreover, Congress had not made the offenses sufficiently distinct to warrant the inference that it intended double punishment. Rutledge v. United States, 517 U.S. 292, 116 S.Ct. 1241 (1996).

Justices Scalia and Thomas have stated that they do not believe the Double Jeopardy Clause protects against multiple punishments. For an acute discussion of these issues, see Nancy J. King, Portioning Punishment: Constitutional Limits on Successive and Excessive Penalties, 144 U. Penn. L. Rev. 101 (1996).

10. *Recidivist Statutes and Acquitted Conduct Used at Sentencing.* In Witte v. United States, 515 U.S. 389, 115 S.Ct. 2199 (1995), the defendant pled guilty to a federal marijuana charge, and under the Federal Sentencing Guidelines his sentence was calculated on the basis not only of the drugs involved in the counts he pled guilty to—which would have generated a sentence of 78–97 months—but also on the basis of drugs involved in uncharged conspiracies—raising the sentencing range to 292–365 months. He was then indicted for the conspiracies which had been used to increase his earlier sentence. The Court held that Double Jeopardy principles were not violated. "The relevant conduct provisions of the Sentencing Guidelines, like their criminal history counterparts and the recidivism statutes discussed above, are sentencing enhancement regimes evincing the judgment that a particular offense should receive a more serious sentence within the authorized range if it was either accompanied by or preceded by additional criminal activity. ... We hold that, where the legislature has authorized such a particular punishment range for a given crime, the resulting sentence within that range constitutes punishment only for the offense of conviction for purposes of the double jeopardy inquiry." Justice Stevens dissented, distinguishing between considering uncharged crimes as evidence of a defendant's character and considering them as aggravating the underlying offense. Because the Guidelines explicitly use them for the latter purpose rather than the former, he argued, Double Jeopardy was violated.

The Court followed up its opinion in *Witte* by explicitly overruling Ninth Circuit precedent forbidding the consideration of acquitted conduct at sentencing in a per curiam opinion: "The Court of Appeals asserted that, when a sentencing court considers facts underlying a charge on which the jury returned a verdict of not guilty, the defendant 'suffers punishment for a criminal charge for which he or she was acquitted.' ... As we explained in *Witte*, however, sentencing enhancements do not punish a defendant for crimes of which he was not convicted, but rather increase his sentence because of the manner in which he committed the crime of conviction." Justice Stevens dissented: "If Putra had been found guilty of also participating in the 5 ounce transaction ... the Guidelines would have required ... between 27 and 33 months. As the District Court applied the Guidelines, precisely the same range resulted from the acquittal as would have been dictated by a conviction. Notwithstanding the absence of sufficient evidence to prove guilt beyond a reasonable doubt, the alleged offense ... led to the imposition of a sentence six months longer than the maximum permitted for the only crime that provided any basis for punishment. In my judgment, neither our prior cases nor the text of the statute warrants this perverse result." United States v. Watts, 519 U.S. 148, 117 S.Ct. 633 (1997).

The Court's holdings in *Witte* and *Watts* presage some fairly disturbing cases: In United States v. Lombard, 102 F.3d 1 (1st Cir.1996), the court upheld a sentence of life in prison for firearms and flight charges. The long sentence was based on two murders of which defendant had been acquitted in state court. The court rejected the defendant's argument that the standard of proof at sentencing should have been higher, but stated that "that a practice is constitutional, does not make it wise." In United States v. Stokes, 947 F.Supp. 546 (D.Mass.1996), a district court dismissed a firearms case out of concern that the prosecution had indicted it only to relitigate an acquittal in a state murder case. "The procedural protections that are provided to criminal defendants by the United States Constitution are sacrosanct. ... To nullify the state court acquittal and to find defendant guilty of murder by a mere preponderance of the evidence is a practice which raises a grave constitutional question. For the Federal Sentencing Guidelines to call for a sentence of life imprisonment without the possibility of parole for a murder over which the federal court has no jurisdiction and where there has been a state court acquittal would give any sentencing judge deep concern ... The federal courts should not be used by the U.S. Attorney's office as an 'appellate court' in which to correct jury verdicts and enhance state court sentences." The *Stokes* decision was reversed on appeal, 124 F.3d 39 (1st Cir.1997), on the ground that the sentencing concerns were premature.

Does the possibility of using other-crimes evidence at sentencing eviscerate the protections provided by *Pearce* and *Blackledge*?

7. DUAL SOVEREIGNTY PROBLEMS

In situations where former jeopardy would bar a new trial (under any of the circumstances described in subsections 3–5, supra), additional considerations arise when the prosecuting entity is different from the governmental entity which brought the former prosecution. Consider the following:

NOTES

1. In Bartkus v. Illinois, 359 U.S. 121, 79 S.Ct. 676 (1959), the Court upheld a state conviction for bank robbery after an unsuccessful federal prosecution for the same offense. In Abbate v. United States, 359 U.S. 187, 79 S.Ct. 666 (1959), the Court upheld a federal conviction after a state conviction. These decisions were based upon a dual sovereignty theory which states that a citizen owes allegiance to both the United States and the state in which he resides and, if principles of federalism are to remain undisturbed, he may be prosecuted by both jurisdictions for the act. This concept has been heavily criticized. See Fisher, Double Jeopardy, Two Sovereignties, and the Intruding Constitution, 28 U. of Chi.L.R. 591 (1961); Comment, Successive State and Federal Prosecutions for the Same Offense: Bartkus v. Illinois Revisited, 62 J.Crim.L., C., & P.S. 29 (1971).

Nevertheless, in United States v. Wheeler, 435 U.S. 313, 98 S.Ct. 1079 (1978), a case involving successive prosecutions before an Indian tribal court and the United States District Court, the continuing vitality of *Bartkus* and *Abbate* was reaffirmed without extended discussion. Those who had previously distinguished these cases on the ground they had been decided before *Benton* (Section A–1, supra) made the Double Jeopardy clause applicable to the States were disappointed.

The Supreme Court considered a dual sovereignty issue in Heath v. Alabama, 474 U.S. 82, 106 S.Ct. 433 (1985). A woman was kidnapped in Alabama and killed in Georgia. Heath pleaded guilty to murder in Georgia and was sentenced to imprisonment. He was prosecuted thereafter in Alabama for murder in the course of a kidnapping. (The jurisdiction of Alabama to try an accused for murder where the death did not occur there was not before the Court in *Heath.*) The defendant was sentenced to death in Alabama. The Court held that Georgia and Alabama were separate sovereigns, each with the right to vindicate its own laws. It upheld the Alabama death sentence.

2. Do you agree with the result in *Bartkus?* Suppose that a police officer, accused of homicide, is convicted but given probation in a state court. Should he remain subject to a federal civil rights prosecution? What about the federal civil rights prosecution of Collie Lee Wilkins following his acquittal by a Loundes County,

Alabama jury in connection with the 1965 slaying of civil rights worker, Viola Liuzzo? Or the federal civil rights prosecution of officers Koon and Powell following acquittal in California in connection with the 1991 beating of Rodney King? Should federal prosecution have been barred?

Can any test be defined to indicate when the interest of the second sovereign truly is distinct so that the *Bartkus* result could be reversed without prohibiting all "same conduct" prosecutions by the second sovereign? See Amar & Marcus, Double Jeopardy Law After Rodney King, 95 Col. L. Rev. 1 (1995).

3. Following *Abbate*, under the so-called "Petite" policy, first acknowledged by the Supreme Court in Petite v. United States, 361 U.S. 529, 80 S.Ct. 450 (1960), the United States Justice Department prohibited United States Attorneys from prosecuting federally after a state prosecution except under the prior authority of Justice Department officials in Washington. Such permission was granted infrequently. When such prosecutions went forward without permission and resulted in convictions, the Justice Department, after the matter was brought to its attention, prevailed upon federal courts to vacate such perfectly valid convictions in order to implement the Petite policy. See the discussion in Rinaldi v. United States, 434 U.S. 22, 98 S.Ct. 81 (1977). The Justice Department's policy of rarely allowing a federal prosecution after an earlier state prosecution, creates no right enforceable by a defendant. Thus "the Petite policy is an internal rule (which) criminal defendants may not invoke . . . to bar prosecution by the federal government." United States v. Patterson, 809 F.2d 244 (5th Cir.1987).

The "Rodney King" case is one of the few in which DOJ has permitted federal reprosecution after a state trial. The defendants stopped King's car for speeding after a highway chase. King got down on his knees, but refused to lie prone. When officers tried to make him lie prone, he resisted and officers fired taser darts at him. When King tried to escape, he was beaten down with batons for several minutes, and it was sharply contested at both trials to what extent King was still resisting, if at all. Most of these events were serendipitously captured on videotape, and the videotape was shown during nightly news broadcasts nationwide. When the officers were acquitted in state court, racial tension ran high and riots broke out in Los Angeles, causing several deaths and extensive property damage. In United States v. Koon, 34 F.3d 1416 (9th Cir.1994), the Ninth Circuit upheld a federal civil rights reprosecution of Los Angeles police officers Koon, Powell, Briseno and Wind who were charged with using excessive force against African–American motorist Rodney King after a traffic stop. The defendants alleged unsuccessfully that the federal and state authorities had "colluded," hence, the dual sovereignty doctrine did not apply. For another example of use of the Petite policy, see United States v. Ebens, 800 F.2d 1422 (6th Cir.1986).

Some states also limit prosecution following prosecution in another jurisdiction. See, e.g., Ill.Rev.Stat. ch. 38, § 3–4 (1991) a statute passed after *Bartkus* to prevent prosecutions like the state court prosecution in Illinois following federal prosecution.

4. Several courts have applied *Abbate* to permit federal RICOprosecutions after the defendant has been acquitted in state court of the predicate criminal acts (e.g., violation of a state bribery statute) alleged as the basis of the federal racketeering charge. See United States v. Farmer, 924 F.2d 647 (7th Cir.1991), and United States v. Pungitore, 910 F.2d 1084 (3d Cir.1990); United States v. Coonan, 938 F.2d 1553 (2d Cir.1991). In one such case the accused was convicted through use of the transcript of the testimony of a witness who had appeared at the state trial but was unavailable at the time of the federal trial. The state jury had viewed the witness and had acquitted the defendant. The federal jury heard a recital of the testimony and convicted. United States v. Licavoli, 725 F.2d 1040 (6th Cir.1984).

5. Under the Federal Sentencing Guidelines, federal prosecutors may be able to obtain the same results as reprosecution would give, without Department of Justice authorization. For example, in United States v. Lombard, 102 F.3d 1 (1st Cir.1996) and United States v. Stokes, 947 F.Supp. 546 (D.Mass.1996), federal prosecutors brought firearms and conspiracy charges against defendants who had been acquitted of murders in state court. In *Lombard*, the prosecutor then brought out the state murders at sentencing as grounds for a life sentence. The district court was persuaded, by a preponderance of evidence, that the murders had in fact occurred, and sentenced the defendant to life. When a prosecutor tried something similar in *Stokes*, the district court in Stokes complained of this approach as an end-run around the Petite policy, but to no avail—its attempt to dismiss the indictment was reversed. 124 F.3d 39 (1st Cir.1997).

6. In Waller v. Florida, 397 U.S. 387, 90 S.Ct. 1184 (1970), Chief Justice Burger, for a unanimous Court, held that successive state and municipal prosecutions were barred by the double jeopardy clause. The theory is that because the city is a creature of the state, for double jeopardy purposes it must be thought of as the same sovereign. As in many multiple jurisdiction situations, the problem may be complicated because the elements of the state offense may be slightly different from those under the city ordinance. *Waller* does not on its face reach such a situation even if both prosecutions resulted from the same course of conduct. Arguably (except in the included offense situation, Section A–4, supra), a single sovereign could bring successive prosecutions where the elements are different. Thus successive city-state prosecutions may be permitted. In the case of an acquittal on the city charge, however, a combination of *Waller* and the collateral estoppel principles of *Ashe* (Section A–6, supra) may benefit the accused if the state subsequently prosecutes for a different but closely related offense.

8. JEOPARDY AND PROCEDURAL PROBLEMS

Where jeopardy claims are advanced, sometimes procedural issues must first be considered, as the following notes reflect.

NOTES

1. *Defense Waiver of Jeopardy Claim.* Until Blackledge v. Perry, 417 U.S. 21, 94 S.Ct. 2098 (1974), it was generally agreed that a pre-trial motion to dismiss was required in order to preserve a claim of former jeopardy. Such a motion might be entitled a "plea in bar" or, if common-law pleas be preserved, "*autrefois acquit*" or "*autrefois convict*." See, e.g. United States v. Hill, 473 F.2d 759 (9th Cir.1972); Haddad v. United States, 349 F.2d 511 (9th Cir.1965). *Blackledge*, however, indicated that if a defendant entered a plea of guilty without raising a claim of former jeopardy, he still could attack the plea through federal habeas corpus, and his prior procedural default would not bar a decision on the merits of his claim. See, also, Menna v. New York, 423 U.S. 61, 96 S.Ct. 241 (1975). Although *Blackledge* did not require that *state* courts entertain belated claims of former jeopardy when the issue was not raised by pre-trial motion, some state courts, noting that a federal decision on the merits lies ahead, may decide to abandon their former strict rule of forfeiture in double jeopardy matters.

It is not altogether clear that *Blackledge* would make federal habeas corpus available to a defendant who entered a plea of *not* guilty, put the state through a full trial, was convicted, and thereafter, for the first time raised a claim that the trial should have been barred because of former jeopardy. For a rather heated controversy over the meaning of *Blackledge* and other "waiver" or forfeiture decisions, see Westen, Forfeiture By Guilty Pleas—A Reply, 76 Mich.L.Rev. 1308 (1978), the earlier article by Westen, and the response by Professor Saltzburg, both cited in Westen's reply.

2. *Defense Interlocutory Appeal of Denial of Jeopardy or Related Claim.* In Abney v. United States, 431 U.S. 651, 97 S.Ct. 2034 (1977), the Supreme Court held that in the federal system, under 28 U.S.C. § 1291, an order denying the accused's motion to dismiss on double jeopardy grounds is a final decision and therefore immediately appealable. "[T]he rights conferred on a criminal accused by the Double Jeopardy Clause would be significantly undermined if appellate review of double jeopardy claims were postponed until after conviction and sentence.... It is a guarantee against being twice put to *trial* for the same offense."

Reasoning that if a criminal defendant who has been convicted has no *constitutional* right to an appeal—as the Supreme Court has often said—some state courts have concluded that there can be no federal constitutional right to an interlocutory appeal. As long as the trial judge rules on the former jeopardy motion before trial, the Constitution is not offended, according to these decisions. *Abney*, it said, in requiring interlocutory review, applies only to the federal system and is not of federal constitutional dimension. People ex rel. Mosley v. Carey, 74 Ill.2d 527, 25 Ill.Dec. 669, 387 N.E.2d 325 (1979); State v. Jones, 68 N.C.App. 514, 315 S.E.2d 491 (1984).

If there is no state procedure to obtain interlocutory review of a denial of a motion to dismiss because of former jeopardy, or if all state avenues have been exhausted, is federal habeas corpus available before the state trial commences? See Hartley v. Neely, 701 F.2d 780 (9th Cir.1983).

Some federal courts have held that a trial judge need not delay commencement of trial while a defendant pursues an appeal of the denial of a *frivolous* double jeopardy claim. United States v. Dunbar, 611 F.2d 985 (5th Cir.1980); United States v. Leppo, 634 F.2d 101 (3d Cir.1980). United States v. Salerno, 868 F.2d 524 (2d Cir.1989), also upheld the trial court's decision to proceed even though the defendant had filed an interlocutory appeal from the denial of a jeopardy motion, where the reviewing court agreed that the appeal was frivolous. What are the competing policy considerations in deciding whether the trial judge should have this power?

Concerning interlocutory appeals challenging the sufficiency of the evidence following hung juries.

Closely related to the issue of an interlocutory appeal of the denial of a jeopardy motion is the issue of such an appeal following the denial of a motion to dismiss because of a vindictive prosecution (Casebook p. 869, Note 5 and p. 1060). The Supreme Court, in a per curiam opinion, resolved a split among the federal circuits by holding that a defendant may not take an interlocutory appeal from the denial of his vindictive-prosecution motion. See United States v. Hollywood Motor Car Company, Inc., 458 U.S. 263, 102 S.Ct. 3081 (1982). The Court declared that the mere fact that a successful appeal would eliminate the necessity for a trial is not an adequate reason for federal courts to recognize the right to a pretrial appeal. A dissenting opinion in *Hollywood Motor Car* lamented the increasing trend of the Court to rule on debatable legal issues in per curiam opinions without the benefit of full briefs and without oral argument.

3. *The Prosecution's Right to Appeal.* Generally statutes or court rules permit the prosecution to appeal the dismissal of a prosecution where the ruling was based upon a finding of former jeopardy. Depending upon the jurisdiction, there might be situations where the prosecution could not appeal other jeopardy-based rulings. For example, in some jurisdictions, if a trial judge ruled that under *Blockburger* multiple sentences were improper and entered a single sentence, in many states the prosecution's right to appellate review would not be broad enough to permit a prosecution appeal on this point.

A separate issue is whether, because of jeopardy consequences of a successful government appeal, certain other rulings of the trial court are appealable by the prosecution. Many of the issues in Section (A)(1–5) arise in the context of efforts to bring a prosecution appeal. For example, can the prosecution appeal an acquittal? Can it appeal entry of a directed verdict? Can it appeal entry of a judgment of not guilty notwithstanding a jury verdict of guilty? See the previous material for answers to these questions. In the federal courts, generally the prosecution's right to appeal is as broad as jeopardy principles allow. This is not always true in state systems. For example, the Fifth Amendment no doubt would permit a prosecution appeal of an order granting a new trial following a jury conviction; some states, however, do not allow for appeal of such an order.

B. DISMISSAL FOR PLEADING DEFECTS

Concerning defective indictments, informations, and complaints, reconsider Chapter 11, Section G.

C. DISMISSAL FOR LACK OF SPEEDY TRIAL

1. AS A MATTER OF CONSTITUTIONAL RIGHT

(a) AFTER INITIATION OF CHARGES

Barker v. Wingo

Supreme Court of the United States, 1972.
407 U.S. 514, 92 S.Ct. 2182.

■ MR. JUSTICE POWELL delivered the opinion of the Court.

Although a speedy trial is guaranteed the accused by the Sixth Amendment to the Constitution, this Court has dealt with that right on frequent occasions. . . . The Court's opinion in Klopfer v. North Carolina, 386 U.S. 213, 87 S.Ct. 988 (1967), established that the right to speedy trial is "fundamental" and is imposed by the Due Process Clause of the Fourteenth Amendment on the States. See Smith v. Hooey, 393 U.S. 374, 89 S.Ct. 575 (1969); Dickey v. Florida, 398 U.S. 30, 90 S.Ct. 1564 (1970). As Mr. Justice Brennan pointed out in his concurring opinion in *Dickey*, in none of these cases have we attempted to set out the criteria by which the speedy trial right is to be judged. This case compels us to make such an attempt.

I.

On July 20, 1958, in Christian County, Kentucky, an elderly couple was beaten to death by intruders wielding an iron tire tool. Two suspects, Silas Manning and Willie Barker, the petitioner, were arrested shortly thereafter. The grand jury indicted them on September 15. Counsel was appointed on September 17, and Barker's trial was set for October 21. The Commonwealth had a stronger case against Manning, and it believed that

Barker could not be convicted unless Manning testified against him. Manning was naturally unwilling to incriminate himself. Accordingly, on October 23, the day Silas Manning was brought to trial, the Commonwealth sought and obtained the first of what was to be a series of 16 continuances of Barker's trial. Barker made no objection. By first convicting Manning, the Commonwealth would remove possible problems of self-incrimination and would be able to assure his testimony against Barker.

The Commonwealth encountered more than a few difficulties in its prosecution of Manning. The first trial ended in a hung jury. A second trial resulted in a conviction, but the Kentucky Court of Appeals reversed because of the admission of evidence obtained by an illegal search. At his third trial, Manning was again convicted, and the Court of Appeals again reversed because the trial court had not granted a change of venue. A fourth trial resulted in a hung jury. Finally, after five trials, Manning was convicted, in March 1962, of murdering one victim, and after a sixth trial, in December 1962, he was convicted of murdering the other.

The Christian County Circuit Court holds three terms each year—in February, June, and September. Barker's initial trial was to take place in the September term of 1958. The first continuance postponed it until the February 1959 term. The second continuance was granted for one month only. Every term thereafter for as long as the Manning prosecutions were in process, the Commonwealth routinely moved to continue Barker's case to the next term. When the case was continued from the June 1959 term until the following September, Barker, having spent 10 months in jail, obtained his release by posting a $5,000 bond. He thereafter remained free in the community until his trial. Barker made no objection, through his counsel, to the first 11 continuances.

When on February 12, 1962, the Commonwealth moved for the twelfth time to continue the case until the following term, Barker's counsel filed a motion to dismiss the indictment. The motion to dismiss was denied two weeks later, and the State's motion for a continuance was granted. The State was granted further continuances in June 1962 and September 1962, to which Barker did not object.

In February 1963, the first term of court following Manning's final conviction, the Commonwealth moved to set Barker's trial for March 19. But on the day scheduled for trial, it again moved for a continuance until the June term. It gave as its reason the illness of the ex-sheriff who was the chief investigating officer in the case. To this continuance, Barker objected unsuccessfully.

The witness was still unable to testify in June, and the trial, which had been set for June 19, was continued again until the September term over Barker's objection. This time the court announced that the case would be dismissed for lack of prosecution if it were not tried during the next term. The final trial date was set for October 9, 1963. On that date, Barker again moved to dismiss the indictment, and this time specified that his right to a speedy trial had been violated. The motion was denied; the trial commenced with Manning as the chief prosecution witness; Barker was convicted and given a life sentence.

* * *

II.

The right to a speedy trial is generically different from any of the other rights enshrined in the Constitution for the protection of the accused. In addition to the general concern that all accused persons be treated according to decent and fair procedures, there is a societal interest in providing a speedy trial which exists separate from and at times in opposition to the interests of the accused. The inability of courts to provide a prompt trial has contributed to a large backlog of cases in urban courts which, among other things, enables defendants to negotiate more effectively for pleas of guilty to lesser offenses and otherwise manipulate the system. In addition, persons released on bond for lengthy periods awaiting trial have an opportunity to commit other crimes. It must be of little comfort to the residents of Christian County, Kentucky, to know that Barker was at large on bail for over four years while accused of a vicious and brutal murder of which he was ultimately convicted. Moreover, the longer an accused is free awaiting trial, the more tempting becomes his opportunity to jump bail and escape. Finally, delay between arrest and punishment may have a detrimental effect on rehabilitation.

If an accused cannot make bail, he is generally confined, as was Barker for 10 months, in a local jail. This contributes to the overcrowding and generally deplorable state of those institutions. Lengthy exposure to these conditions "has a destructive effect on human character and makes the rehabilitation of the individual offender much more difficult." At times the result may even be violent rioting. Finally, lengthy pretrial detention is costly. The cost of maintaining a prisoner in jail varies from $3 to $9 per day, and this amounts to millions across the Nation. In addition, society loses wages which might have been earned, and it must often support families of incarcerated breadwinners.

A second difference between the right to speedy trial and the accused's other constitutional rights is that deprivation of the right may work to the accused's advantage. Delay is not an uncommon defense tactic. As the time between the commission of the crime and trial lengthens, witnesses may become unavailable or their memories may fade. If the witnesses support the prosecution, its case will be weakened, sometimes seriously so. And it is the prosecution which carries the burden of proof. Thus, unlike the right to counsel or the right to be free from compelled self-incrimination, deprivation of the right to speedy trial does not *per se* prejudice the accused's ability to defend himself.

Finally, and perhaps most importantly, the right to speedy trial is a more vague concept than other procedural rights. It is, for example, impossible to determine with precision when the right has been denied. We cannot definitely say how long is too long in a system where justice is supposed to be swift but deliberate.[15] As a consequence, there is no fixed

15. "[I]n large measure because of the many procedural safeguards provided an ac-

point in the criminal process when the State can put the defendant to the choice of either exercising or waiving the right to a speedy trial. If, for example, the State moves for a 60–day continuance, granting that continuance is not a violation of the right to speedy trial unless the circumstances of the case are such that further delay would endanger the values the right protects. It is impossible to do more than generalize about when those circumstances exist. There is nothing comparable to the point in the process when a defendant exercises or waives his right to counsel or his right to a jury trial. Thus, in any inquiry into a speedy trial claim necessitates a functional analysis of the right in the particular context of the case.

* * *

The amorphous quality of the right also leads to the unsatisfactorily severe remedy of dismissal of the indictment when the right has been deprived. This is indeed a serious consequence because it means that a defendant who may be guilty of a serious crime will go free, without having been tried. Such a remedy is more serious than an exclusionary rule or a reversal for a new trial, but it is the only possible remedy.

III.

Perhaps because the speedy trial right is so slippery, two rigid approaches are urged upon us as ways of eliminating some of the uncertainty which courts experience in protecting the right. The first suggestion is that we hold that the Constitution requires a criminal defendant to be offered a trial within a specified time period. The result of such a ruling would have the virtue of clarifying when the right is infringed and of simplifying courts' application of it. Recognizing this, some legislatures have enacted laws, and some courts have adopted procedural rules which more narrowly define the right.

* * *

But such a result would require this Court to engage in legislative or rulemaking activity, rather than in the adjudicative process to which we should confine our efforts. We do not establish procedural rules for the States, except when mandated by the Constitution. We find no constitutional basis for holding that the speedy trial right can be quantified into a specified number of days or months. The States, of course, are free to prescribe a reasonable period consistent with constitutional standards, but our approach must be less precise.

The second suggested alternative would restrict consideration of the right to those cases in which the accused has demanded a speedy trial. Most States have recognized what is loosely referred to as the "demand rule," although eight States reject it. It is not clear, however, precisely what is meant by that term. Although every Federal Court of Appeals that has

cused, the ordinary procedures for criminal prosecution are designed to move at a deliberate pace. A requirement of unreasonable speed would have a deleterious effect both upon the rights of the accused and upon the ability of society to protect itself." United States v. Ewell, 383 U.S. 116, 120, 86 S.Ct. 773, 776 (1966).

considered the question has endorsed some kind of demand rule, some have regarded the rule within the concept of waiver, whereas others have viewed it as a factor to be weighed in assessing whether there has been a deprivation of the speedy trial right. We shall refer to the former approach as the demand-waiver doctrine. The demand-waiver doctrine provides that a defendant waives any consideration of his right to speedy trial for any period prior to which he has not demanded a trial. Under this rigid approach, a prior demand is a necessary condition to the consideration of the speedy trial right.

Such an approach, by presuming waiver of a fundamental right from inaction, is inconsistent with this Court's pronouncements on waiver of constitutional rights. The Court has defined waiver as "an intentional relinquishment or abandonment of a known right or privilege." Courts should "indulge every reasonable presumption against waiver," and they should "not presume acquiescence in the loss of fundamental rights."

* * *

In excepting the right to speedy trial from the rule of waiver we have applied to other fundamental rights, courts that have applied the demand-waiver rule have relied on the assumption that delay usually works for the benefit of the accused and on the absence of any readily ascertainable time in the criminal process for a defendant to be given the choice of exercising or waiving his right. But it is not necessarily true that delay benefits the defendant. There are cases in which delay appreciably harms the defendant's ability to defend himself. Moreover, a defendant confined to jail prior to trial is obviously disadvantaged by delay as is a defendant released on bail but unable to lead a normal life because of community suspicion and his own anxiety.

The nature of the speedy-trial right does make it impossible to pinpoint a precise time in the process when the right must be asserted or waived, but that fact does not argue for placing the burden of protecting the right solely on defendants. Moreover, for the reasons earlier expressed society has a particular interest in bringing swift prosecutions, and society's representatives are the ones who should protect that interest.

It is also noteworthy that such a rigid view of the demand rule places defense counsel in an awkward position. Unless he demands a trial early and often, he is in danger of frustrating his client's right. If counsel is willing to tolerate some delay because he finds it reasonable and helpful in preparing his own case, he may be unable to obtain a speedy trial for his client at the end of that time. Since under the demand-waiver rule no time runs until the demand is made, the government will have whatever time is otherwise reasonable to bring the defendant to trial after a demand has been made. Thus, if the first demand is made three months after arrest in a jurisdiction which prescribes a six months rule, the prosecution will have a total of nine months—which may be wholly unreasonable under the circumstances. The result in practice is likely to be either an automatic, *pro forma* demand made immediately after appointment of counsel or delays which, but for the demand-waiver rule, would not be tolerated. Such a result is not consistent with the interests of defendants, society, or the Constitution.

We reject, therefore, the rule that a defendant who fails to demand a speedy trial forever waives his right. This does not mean, however, that the defendant has no responsibility to assert his right. We think the better rule is that the defendant's assertion of or failure to assert his right to a speedy trial is one of the factors to be considered in an inquiry into the deprivation of the right. Such a formulation avoids the rigidities of the demand-waiver rule and the resulting possible unfairness in its application. It allows the trial court to exercise a judicial discretion based on the circumstances, including due consideration of any applicable formal procedural rule. It would permit, for example, a court to attach a different weight to a situation in which the defendant knowingly fails to object from a situation in which his attorney acquiesces in long delay without adequately informing his client or from a situation in which no counsel is appointed. It would also allow a court to weigh the frequency and force of the objections as opposed to attaching significant weight to a purely *pro forma* objection.

* * *

We, therefore, reject both of the inflexible approaches—the fixed time period because it goes further than the Constitution requires; the demand-waiver rule because it is insensitive to a right which we have deemed fundamental. The approach we accept is a balancing test, in which the conduct of both the prosecution and the defendant are weighed.

IV.

A balancing test necessarily compels courts to approach speedy-trial cases on an *ad hoc* basis. We can do little more than identify some of the factors which courts should assess in determining whether a particular defendant has been deprived of his right. Though some might express them in different ways, we identify four such factors: Length of delay, the reason for the delay, the defendant's assertion of his right, and prejudice to the defendant.

The length of the delay is to some extent a triggering mechanism. Until there is some delay which is presumptively prejudicial, there is no necessity for inquiry into the other factors that go into the balance. Nevertheless, because of the imprecision of the right to speedy trial, the length of delay that will provoke such an inquiry is necessarily dependent upon the peculiar circumstances of the case. To take but one example, the delay that can be tolerated for an ordinary street crime is considerably less than for a serious, complex conspiracy charge.

Closely related to length of delay is the reason the government assigns to justify the delay. Here, too, different weights should be assigned to different reasons. A deliberate attempt to delay the trial in order to hamper the defense should be weighed heavily against the government.[32] A more neutral reason such as negligence or overcrowded courts should be weighed

32. We have indicated on previous occasions that it is improper for the prosecution intentionally to delay "to gain some tactical advantage over [defendants] or to harass them." United States v. Marion (1971).

less heavily but nevertheless should be considered since the ultimate responsibility for such circumstances must rest with the government rather than with the defendant. Finally, a valid reason, such as a missing witness, should serve to justify appropriate delay.

We have already discussed the third factor, the defendant's responsibility to assert his right. Whether and how a defendant asserts his right is closely related to the other factors we have mentioned. The strength of his efforts will be affected by the length of the delay, to some extent by the reason for the delay, and most particularly by the personal prejudice, which is not always readily identifiable, that he experiences. The more serious the deprivation, the more likely a defendant is to complain. The defendant's assertion of his speedy trial right, then, is entitled to strong evidentiary weight in determining whether the right is being deprived. We emphasize that failure to assert the right will make it difficult for a defendant to prove that he was denied a speedy trial.

A fourth factor is prejudice to the defendant. Prejudice, of course, should be assessed in the light of the interests of defendants which the speedy trial right was designed to protect. This Court has identified three such interests: (i) to prevent oppressive pretrial incarceration; (ii) to minimize anxiety and concern of the accused; and (iii) to limit the possibility that the defense will be impaired.[33] Of these, the most serious is the last, because the inability of a defendant adequately to prepare his case skews the fairness of the entire system. If witnesses die or disappear during a delay, the prejudice is obvious. There is also prejudice if defense witnesses are unable to recall accurately events of the distant past. Loss of memory, however, is not always reflected in the record because what has been forgotten can rarely be shown.

We have discussed previously the societal disadvantages of lengthy pretrial incarceration, but obviously the disadvantages for the accused who cannot obtain his release are even more serious. The time spent in jail awaiting trial has a detrimental impact on the individual. It often means loss of a job; it disrupts family life; and it enforces idleness. Most jails offer little or no recreational or rehabilitative programs. The time spent in jail is simply dead time. Moreover, if a defendant is locked up, he is hindered in his ability to gather evidence, contact witnesses, or otherwise prepare his defense. Imposing those consequences on anyone who has not yet been convicted is serious. It is especially unfortunate to impose them on those persons who are ultimately found to be innocent. Finally, even if an accused is not incarcerated prior to trial, he is still disadvantaged by restraints on his liberty and by living under a cloud of anxiety, suspicion, and often hostility.

We regard none of the four factors identified above as either a necessary or sufficient condition to the finding of a deprivation of the right of speedy trial. Rather, they are related factors and must be considered together with such other circumstances as may be relevant. In sum, these

33. In Klopfer v. North Carolina (1967), we indicated that a defendant awaiting trial on bond might be subjected to public scorn, deprived of employment, and chilled in the exercise of his right to speak for, associate with, and participate in unpopular political causes.

factors have no talismanic qualities; courts must still engage in a difficult and sensitive balancing process. But, because we are dealing with a fundamental right of the accused, this process must be carried out with full recognition that the accused's interest in a speedy trial is specifically affirmed in the Constitution.

V.

The difficulty of the task of balancing these factors is illustrated by this case, which we consider to be close. It is clear that the length of delay between arrest and trial—well over five years—was extraordinary. Only seven months of that period can be attributed to a strong excuse, the illness of the ex-sheriff who was in charge of the investigation. Perhaps some delay would have been permissible under ordinary circumstances, so that Manning could be utilized as a witness in Barker's trial, but more than four years was too long a period, particularly since a good part of that period was attributable to the Commonwealth's failure or inability to try Manning under circumstances that comported with due process.

Two counter-balancing factors, however, outweigh these deficiencies. The first is that prejudice was minimal. Of course, Barker was prejudiced to some extent by living for over four years under a cloud of suspicion and anxiety. Moreover, although he was released on bond for most of the period, he did spend 10 months in jail before trial. But there is no claim that any of Barker's witnesses died or otherwise became unavailable owing to the delay. The trial transcript indicates only two very minor lapses of memory—one on the part of a prosecution witness—which were in no way significant to the outcome.

More important than the absence of serious prejudice, is the fact that Barker did not want a speedy trial. Counsel was appointed for Barker immediately after his indictment and represented him throughout the period. Despite the fact that counsel had notice of the motions for continuances, the record shows no action whatever taken between October 21, 1958, and February 12, 1962, that could be construed as the assertion of the speedy-trial right. On the latter date, in response to another motion for continuance, Barker moved to dismiss the indictment. The record does not show on what ground this motion was based, although it is clear that no alternative motion was made for an immediate trial. Instead the record strongly suggests that while he hoped to take advantage of the delay in which he had acquiesced, and thereby obtain a dismissal of the charges, he definitely did not want to be tried. . . . The probable reason for Barker's attitude was that he was gambling on Manning's acquittal. The evidence was not terribly strong against Manning, as the reversals and hung juries suggest, and Barker undoubtedly thought that if Manning were acquitted, he would never be tried. . . . It was not until March 1963, after Manning's convictions were final, that Barker, having lost his gamble, began to object to further continuances. At that time, the Commonwealth's excuse was the illness of the ex-sheriff, which Barker has conceded justified the further delay.

We do not hold that there may never be a situation in which an indictment may be dismissed on speedy-trial grounds where the defendant has failed to object to continuances. There may be a situation in which the defendant was represented by incompetent counsel, was severely prejudiced, or even cases in which the continuances were granted *ex parte*. But barring extraordinary circumstances, we would be reluctant indeed to rule that a defendant was denied this constitutional right on a record that strongly indicates, as does this one, that the defendant did not want a speedy trial. We hold, therefore, that Barker was not deprived of his due process right to a speedy trial.

Affirmed.

■ Mr. Justice White, with whom Mr. Justice Brennan joins, concurring in the judgment and opinion of the Court. [Opinion omitted.]

Doggett v. United States

Supreme Court of the United States, 1992.
505 U.S. 647, 112 S.Ct. 2686.

■ Justice Souter delivered the opinion of the Court.

In this case we consider whether the delay of 8 years between petitioner's indictment and arrest violated his Sixth Amendment right to a speedy trial. We hold that it did.

On February 22, 1980, petitioner Marc Doggett was indicted for conspiring with several others to import and distribute cocaine. Douglas Driver, the Drug Enforcement Administration's principal agent investigating the conspiracy, told the United States Marshal's Service that the DEA would oversee the apprehension of Doggett and his confederates. On March 18, 1980, two police officers set out under Driver's orders to arrest Doggett at his parents' house in Raleigh, North Carolina, only to find that he was not there. His mother told the officers that he had left for Colombia four days earlier.

To catch Doggett on his return to the United States, Driver sent word of his outstanding arrest warrant to all United States Customs stations and to a number of law enforcement organizations. He also placed Doggett's name in the Treasury Enforcement Communication System (TECS), a computer network that helps Customs agents screen people entering the country, and in the National Crime Information Center computer system, which serves similar ends. The TECS entry expired that September, however, and Doggett's name vanished from the system.

In September 1981, Driver found out that Doggett was under arrest on drug charges in Panama and, thinking that a formal extradition request would be futile, simply asked Panama to "expel" Doggett to the United States. Although the Panamanian authorities promised to comply when their own proceedings had run their course, they freed Doggett the following July and let him go to Colombia, where he stayed with an aunt for several months. On September 25, 1982, he passed unhindered through Customs in New York City and settled down in Virginia. Since his return to the United States, he has married, earned a college degree, found a steady job as a computer operations manager, lived openly under his own name, and stayed within the law.

Doggett's travels abroad had not wholly escaped the Government's notice, however. In 1982, the American Embassy in Panama told the State Department of his departure to Colombia, but that information, for whatever reason, eluded the DEA, and Agent Driver assumed for several years that his quarry was still serving time in a Panamanian prison. Driver never asked DEA officials in Panama to check into Doggett's status, and only after his own fortuitous assignment to that country in 1985 did he discover Doggett's departure for Colombia. Driver then simply assumed Doggett had settled there, and he made no effort to find out for sure or to track Doggett down, either abroad or in the United States. Thus Doggett remained lost to the American criminal justice system until September 1988, when the Marshal's Service ran a simple credit check on several thousand people subject to outstanding arrest warrants and, within minutes, found out where Doggett lived and worked. On September 5, 1988, nearly 6 years after his return to the United States and 8 years after his indictment, Doggett was arrested.

[His motion to dismiss the indictment was denied on the ground that he failed to show how he was prejudiced by the delay. Doggett entered a conditional guilty plea to preserve the speedy trial issue; and the Court of Appeals affirmed the conviction.]

The Sixth Amendment guarantees that, "(i)n all criminal prosecutions, the accused shall enjoy the right to a speedy ... trial...." On its face, the Speedy Trial Clause is written with such breadth that, taken literally, it would forbid the government to delay the trial of an "accused" for any reason at all. Our cases, however, have qualified the literal sweep of the provision by specifically recognizing the relevance of four separate enquiries: whether delay before trial was uncommonly long, whether the government or the criminal defendant is more to blame for that delay, whether, in due course, the defendant asserted his right to a speedy trial, and whether he suffered prejudice as the delay's result.

The first of these is actually a double enquiry. Simply to trigger a speedy trial analysis, an accused must allege that the interval between accusation and trial has crossed the threshold dividing ordinary from "presumptively prejudicial" delay, since, by definition, he cannot complain that the government has denied him a "speedy" trial if it has, in fact, prosecuted his case with customary promptness. If the accused makes this showing, the court must then consider, as one factor among several, the extent to which the delay stretches beyond the bare minimum needed to trigger judicial examination of the claim. This latter enquiry is significant to the speedy trial analysis because, as we discuss below, the presumption that pretrial delay has prejudiced the accused intensifies over time. In this case, the extraordinary 8 year lag between Doggett's indictment and arrest clearly suffices to trigger the speedy trial enquiry; its further significance within that enquiry will be dealt with later.

As for Barker's second criterion, the Government claims to have sought Doggett with diligence. The findings of the courts below are to the contrary, however, and we review trial court determinations of negligence with considerable deference. The Government gives us nothing to gainsay the findings that have come up to us, and we see nothing fatal to them in the record. For six years, the Government's investigators made no serious effort to test their progressively more questionable assumption that Doggett was living abroad, and, had they done so, they could have found him within minutes. While the Government's lethargy may have reflected no more than Doggett's relative unimportance in the world of drug trafficking, it was still findable negligence, and the finding stands.

The Government goes against the record again in suggesting that Doggett knew of his indictment years before he was arrested. Were this true, Barker's third factor, concerning invocation of the right to a speedy trial, would be weighed heavily against him. But here again, the Government is trying to revisit the facts. At the hearing on Doggett's speedy trial motion, it introduced no evidence challenging the testimony of Doggett's wife, who said that she did not know of the charges until his arrest, and of his mother, who claimed not to have told him or anyone else that the police had come looking for him. . . . Thus, Doggett is not to be taxed for invoking his speedy trial right only after his arrest.

The Government is left, then, with its principal contention: that Doggett fails to make out a successful speedy trial claim because he has not shown precisely how he was prejudiced by the delay between his indictment and trial.

We have observed in prior cases that unreasonable delay between formal accusation and trial threatens to produce more than one sort of harm, including "oppressive pretrial incarceration," "anxiety and concern of the accused," and "the possibility that the (accused's) defense will be impaired" by dimming memories and loss of exculpatory evidence. Of these forms of prejudice, "the most serious is the last, because the inability of a defendant adequately to prepare his case skews the fairness of the entire system." Doggett claims this kind of prejudice, and there is probably no other kind that he can claim, since he was subjected neither to pretrial detention nor, he has successfully contended, to awareness of unresolved charges against him.

The Government answers Doggett's claim by citing language in three cases, for the proposition that the Speedy Trial Clause does not significantly protect a criminal defendant's interest in fair adjudication. In so arguing, the Government asks us, in effect, to read part of Barker right out of the law, and that we will not do. In context, the cited passages support nothing beyond the principle, which we have independently based on textual and historical grounds, that the Sixth Amendment right of the accused to a speedy trial has no application beyond the confines of a formal criminal prosecution. Once triggered by arrest, indictment, or other official accusation, however, the speedy trial enquiry must weigh the effect of delay on the accused's defense just as it has to weigh any other form of prejudice that Barker recognized.

As an alternative to limiting Barker, the Government claims Doggett has failed to make any affirmative showing that the delay weakened his ability to raise specific defenses, elicit specific testimony, or produce specific items of evidence. Though Doggett did indeed come up short in this respect, the Government's argument takes it only so far: consideration of prejudice is not limited to the specifically demonstrable, and, affirmative proof of particularized prejudice is not essential to every speedy trial claim. Barker explicitly recognized that impairment of one's defense is the most difficult form of speedy trial prejudice to prove because time's erosion of exculpatory evidence and testimony "can rarely be shown." And though time can tilt the case against either side, one cannot generally be sure which of them it has prejudiced more severely. Thus, we generally have to recognize that excessive delay presumptively compromises the reliability of a trial in ways that neither party can prove or, for that matter, identify. While such presumptive prejudice cannot alone carry a Sixth Amendment claim without regard to the other Barker criteria, it is part of the mix of relevant facts, and its importance increases with the length of delay.

This brings us to an enquiry into the role that presumptive prejudice should play in the disposition of Doggett's speedy trial claim. We begin with hypothetical and somewhat easier cases and work our way to this one.

Our speedy trial standards recognize that pretrial delay is often both inevitable and wholly justifiable. The government may need time to collect witnesses against the accused, oppose his pretrial motions, or, if he goes into hiding, track him down. We attach great weight to such considerations when balancing them against the costs of going forward with a trial whose probative accuracy the passage of time has begun by degrees to throw into question. Thus, in this case, if the Government had pursued Doggett with reasonable diligence from his indictment to his arrest, his speedy trial claim would fail. Indeed, that conclusion would generally follow as a matter of course however great the delay, so long as Doggett could not show specific prejudice to his defense.

The Government concedes, on the other hand, that Doggett would prevail if he could show that the Government had intentionally held back in its prosecution of him to gain some impermissible advantage at trial. That we cannot doubt. Barker stressed that official bad faith in causing delay will be weighed heavily against the government, and a bad-faith delay the length of this negligent one would present an overwhelming case for dismissal.

Between diligent prosecution and bad-faith delay, official negligence in bringing an accused to trial occupies the middle ground. While not compelling relief in every case where bad-faith delay would make relief virtually automatic, neither is negligence automatically tolerable simply because the accused cannot demonstrate exactly how it has prejudiced him.

Barker made it clear that "different weights (are to be) assigned to different reasons" for delay. Although negligence is obviously to be weighed more lightly than a deliberate intent to harm the accused's defense, it still falls on the wrong side of the divide between acceptable and unacceptable reasons for delaying a criminal prosecution once it has begun. And such is the nature of the prejudice presumed that the weight we assign to official negligence compounds over time as the presumption of evidentiary prejudice grows. Thus, our toleration of such negligence varies inversely with its protractedness and its consequent threat to the fairness of the accused's trial. Condoning prolonged and unjustifiable delays in prosecution would both penalize many defendants for the state's fault and simply encourage the government to gamble with the interests of criminal suspects assigned a low prosecutorial priority. The Government, indeed, can hardly complain too loudly, for persistent neglect in concluding a criminal prosecution indicates an uncommonly feeble interest in bringing an accused to justice; the more weight the Government attaches to securing a conviction, the harder it will try to get it.

To be sure, to warrant granting relief, negligence unaccompanied by particularized trial prejudice must have lasted longer than negligence demonstrably causing such prejudice. But even so, the Government's egregious persistence in failing to prosecute Doggett is clearly sufficient. The lag between Doggett's indictment and arrest was 8 years, and he would have faced trial 6 years earlier than he did but for the Government's inexcusable oversights. The portion of the delay attributable to the Government's negligence far exceeds the threshold needed to state a speedy trial claim; indeed, we have called shorter delays "extraordinary." When the Government's negligence thus causes delay six times as long as that generally sufficient to trigger judicial review, and when the presumption of prejudice, albeit unspecified, is neither extenuated, as by the defendant's acquiescence, nor persuasively rebutted, the defendant is entitled to relief.

We reverse the judgment of the Court of Appeals and remand the case for proceedings consistent with this opinion. So ordered.

■ JUSTICE O'CONNOR, dissenting. (Opinion omitted)

■ JUSTICE THOMAS, with whom THE CHIEF JUSTICE and JUSTICE SCALIA join, dissenting.

Just as "bad facts make bad law," so too odd facts make odd law. Doggett's 8–year odyssey from youthful drug dealing in the tobacco country of North Carolina, through stints in a Panamanian jail and in Colombia, to life as a computer operations manager, homeowner, and registered voter in suburban Virginia, is extraordinary. But even more extraordinary is the Court's conclusion that the Government denied Doggett his Sixth Amendment right to a speedy trial despite the fact that he has suffered none of the harms that the right was designed to prevent. I respectfully dissent.

* * *

Our constitutional law has become ever more complex in recent decades. That is, in itself, a regrettable development, for the law draws force from the clarity of its command and the certainty of its application. As the complexity of legal doctrines increases, moreover, so too does the danger that their foundational principles will become obscured. I fear that danger has been realized here. So engrossed is the Court in applying the multifactor balancing test set forth in Barker that it loses sight of the nature and purpose of the speedy trial guarantee set forth in the Sixth Amendment. The Court's error, in my view, lies not so much in its particular application of the Barker test to the facts of this case, but more fundamentally in its failure to recognize that the speedy trial guarantee cannot be violated and thus Barker does not apply at all when an accused is entirely unaware of a pending indictment against him.

I do not mean to question Barker's approach, but merely its scope. We have long recognized that whether an accused has been denied his right to a speedy trial "depends upon circumstances." By setting forth a number of relevant factors, Barker provided this contextual inquiry with at least a modicum of structure. But Barker's factors now appear to have taken on a life of their own. Instead of simply guiding the inquiry whether an individual who has been deprived of a liberty protected by the Clause is entitled to relief, Barker has become a source for new liberties under the Clause. In my view, application of Barker presupposes that an accused has been subjected to the evils against which the Speedy Trial Clause is directed and, as I have explained, neither pretrial delay nor the disruption of life is itself such an evil.

Today's opinion, I fear, will transform the courts of the land into boards of law-enforcement supervision. For the Court compels dismissal of the charges against Doggett not because he was harmed in any way by the delay between his indictment and arrest, but simply because the Government's efforts to catch him are found wanting. Indeed, the Court expressly concedes that "if the Government had pursued Doggett with reasonable diligence from his indictment to his arrest, his speedy trial claim would fail." Our function, however, is not to slap the Government on the wrist for sloppy work or misplaced priorities, but to protect the legal rights of those individuals harmed thereby. By divorcing the Speedy Trial Clause from all considerations of prejudice to an accused, the Court positively invites the Nation's judges to indulge in ad hoc and result-driven second-guessing of the government's investigatory efforts. Our Constitution neither contemplates nor tolerates such a role. I respectfully dissent.

NOTES

1. Prior to *Wingo*, the Court had considered many of the ancillary aspects of the speedy trial guarantee, but had never genuinely defined its contours. See Dickey v. Florida, 398 U.S. 30, 90 S.Ct. 1564 (1970) (defendant incarcerated for one crime has right to demand speedy trial on another pending charge); Smith v. Hooey, 393 U.S. 374, 89 S.Ct. 575 (1969) (state has obligation to attempt to bring federal prisoner to trial on state charge); Klopfer v. North Carolina, 386 U.S. 213, 87 S.Ct. 988 (1967) (Sixth Amendment speedy trial guarantee applicable to states through due process clause of Fourteenth Amendment).

2. In Strunk v. United States, 412 U.S. 434, 93 S.Ct. 2260 (1973), the lower court found that, although a speedy trial violation occurred, the fact that the defendant had received a sentence concurrent to a then pending state sentence was sufficient to relieve him of the prejudice suffered from the violation. The Supreme Court reversed, holding that outright dismissal of the indictment was the only relief available to one deprived of the federal constitutional right to a speedy trial.

3. Under the Barker v. Wingo standards, the length of delay is generally given little weight. See United States v. Scheer, 729 F.2d 164 (2d Cir.1984) (249 day delay in bringing state prisoner to trial in federal court did not violate speedy trial rights). The critical factor is prejudice to the defendant. See Gray v. King, 724 F.2d 1199 (5th Cir.1984) (gravity or seriousness of the crime and potential length of incarceration diminishes prejudice to defendant from delay); Ex parte Cofer, 440 So.2d 1121 (Ala.1983) (delay obtained by state extending trial beyond date when new law became effective so as to reduce defendant's number of preemptory challenges not prejudicial). Compare Burkett v. Cunningham, 826 F.2d 1208 (3d Cir.1987), where a "monumental" delay of five and one-half years between conviction and sentencing was deemed to violate defendant's constitutional right of itself.

4. The critical factor is the reason for delay; and a successful challenge must rest on the prosecution's deliberate procrastination, bad faith, tactical maneuvering or negligent inaction. Compare Redd v. Sowders, 809 F.2d 1266 (6th Cir.1987) (32 month delay while prosecutor sought to obtain testimony of codefendant warrants dismissal) with Flowers v. Connecticut, 853 F.2d 131 (2d Cir.1988) (17 month delay due to docket congestion, without bad faith by prosecution, insufficient). See also United States v. Doggett, 906 F.2d 573 (11th Cir.1990) ("bad faith encompasses a deliberate effort to prejudice or harass the defendant, while a dilatory purpose will include efforts made by the government to gain a tactical advantage over the accused").

5. Those claiming actual prejudice due to delay must "point quite specifically to how they were prejudiced; the defendant's showing must be concrete, not speculative." United States v. Antonino, 830 F.2d 798 (7th Cir.1987). Vague allegations of anxiety and concern are insufficient. United States v. Rein, 848 F.2d 777 (7th Cir.1988).

6. Does the delay occasioned by interlocutory appeals by either party impact on the Barker v. Wingo standards? In United States v. Loud Hawk, 474 U.S. 302, 106 S.Ct. 648 (1986), the Court, considering the *third* pretrial appeal in the same case, held:

> "The flag all litigants seek to capture is the second Barker factor, the reason for delay. In Barker, we held that 'different weights should be assigned to different reasons.' While a deliberate attempt to delay the trial in order to hamper the defense, would be weighed heavily against the Government, a delay from 'overcrowded courts'—as was the situation here—would be weighed 'less heavily.' Given the important public interests in appellate review, it hardly need be said that an interlocutory appeal by the Government ordinarily is a valid reason that justifies delay. In assessing the purpose and reasonableness of such an appeal, courts may consider several factors. These include the strength of the Government's position on the appealed issue, the importance of the issue in the posture of the case, and—in some cases—the seriousness of the crime. For example, a delay resulting from an appeal would weigh heavily against the Government if the issue were clearly tangential or frivolous. Moreover, the charged offense usually must be sufficiently serious to justify restraints that may be imposed on the defendant pending the outcome of the appeal.
>
> "Under Barker, delays in bringing the case to trial caused by the Government's interlocutory appeal may be weighed in determining whether a defendant has suffered a violation of his rights to a speedy trial. It is clear in this case, however, that respondents have failed to show a reason for according these delays any effective weight towards their speedy trial claims. There is no showing of bad faith or dilatory purpose on the Government's part. The Government's position in each of the appeals was strong, and the reversals by the Court of Appeals are prima facie evidence of the reasonableness of the Government's action. Moreover, despite the seriousness of the charged offenses, the District Court chose not to subject respondents to any actual restraints pending the outcome of the appeals.
>
> "The only remaining question is the weight to be attributed to delays caused by respondents' interlocutory appeals. In that limited class of cases where a pretrial appeal by the defendant is appropriate, delays from such an appeal ordinarily will not weigh in favor of a defendant's speedy trial claims. A defendant with a meritorious appeal would bear the heavy

burden of showing an unreasonable delay caused by the prosecution in that appeal, or a wholly unjustifiable delay by the appellate court. A defendant who resorts to an interlocutory appeal normally should not be able upon return to the district court to reap the reward of dismissal for failure to receive a speedy trial."

7. The presumption of prejudice that occurs when there is extreme pretrial delay does not extend to long delays at the appellate level. A successful criminal appellant must ordinarily "show actual trial prejudice in the event of a second prosecution in order to win outright dismissal of his indictment on the grounds of appellate delay." United States v. Mohawk, 20 F.3d 1480 (9th Cir.1994).

(b) BEFORE INITIATION OF CHARGES

United States v. Lovasco

Supreme Court of the United States, 1977.
431 U.S. 783, 97 S.Ct. 2044.

■ MR. JUSTICE MARSHALL delivered the opinion of the Court.

We granted certiorari in this case to consider the circumstances in which the Constitution requires that an indictment be dismissed because of delay between the commission of an offense and the initiation of prosecution.

I.

On March 6, 1975, respondent was indicted for possessing eight firearms stolen from the United States mail, and for dealing in firearms without a license. The offenses were alleged to have occurred between July 25 and August 31, 1973, more than 18 months before the indictment was filed. Respondent moved to dismiss the indictment due to the delay.

The District Court conducted a hearing on respondent's motion at which the respondent sought to prove that the delay was unnecessary and that it had prejudiced his defense. In an effort to establish the former proposition, respondent presented a Postal Inspector's report on his investigation that was prepared one month after the crimes were committed, and a stipulation concerning the post-report progress of the probe. The report stated, in brief, that within the first month of the investigation respondent had admitted to Government agents that he had possessed and then sold five of the stolen guns, and that the agents had developed strong evidence linking respondent to the remaining three weapons.[1] The report also stated, however, that the agents had been unable to confirm or refute respondent's claim that he had found the guns in his car when he returned to it after visiting his son, a mail handler, at work. The stipulation into

1. The report indicated that the person to whom respondent admitted selling five guns had told Government agents that respondent had actually sold him eight guns which he, in turn, had sold to one Martin Koehnken. The report also indicated that Koehnken had sold three of these guns to undercover federal agents and that a search of his house had uncovered four others. Finally the report stated that the eighth gun was sold by one David Northdruft to Government agents, and that Northdruft claimed Koehnken had sold him the gun.

At the hearing on the motion to dismiss, respondent for the first time admitted that he had possessed and sold eight guns.

which the Assistant United States Attorney entered indicated that little additional information concerning the crimes was uncovered in the 17 months following the preparation of the Inspector's report.[3]

To establish prejudice to the defense, respondent testified that he had lost the testimony of two material witnesses due to the delay. The first witness, Tom Stewart, died more than a year after the alleged crimes occurred. At the hearing respondent claimed that Stewart had been his source for two or three of the guns. The second witness, respondent's brother, died in April 1974, nine months after the crimes were completed. Respondent testified that his brother was present when respondent called Stewart to secure the guns, and witnessed all of respondent's sales. Respondent did not state how the witnesses would have aided the defense had they been willing to testify.

The Government made no systematic effort in the District Court to explain its long delay. The Assistant United States Attorney did expressly disagree, however, with defense counsel's suggestion that the investigation had ended after the Postal Inspector's Report was prepared. The prosecutor also stated that it was the Government's theory that respondent's son, who had access to the mail at the railroad terminal from which the guns were "possibly stolen," was responsible for the thefts. Finally, the prosecutor elicited somewhat cryptic testimony from the Postal Inspector indicating that the case "as to these particular weapons involves other individuals"; that information had been presented to a grand jury "in regard to this case other than ... [on] the day of the indictment itself"; and that he had spoken to the prosecutors about the case on four or five occasions.

Following the hearing, the District Court found that by October 2, 1973, the date of the postal inspector's report, "The Government had all the information relating to defendant's alleged commission of the offense charged against him," and that the 17-month delay before the case was presented to the grand jury "had not been explained or justified" and was "unnecessary and unreasonable." The Court also found that "[a]s a result of the delay defendant has been prejudiced by reason of the death of Tom Stewart, a material witness on his behalf." Accordingly, the court dismissed the indictment.

* * *

II.

In United States v. Marion, 404 U.S. 307, 92 S.Ct. 455 (1971), this Court considered the significance, for constitutional purposes, of a lengthy preindictment delay. We held that as far as the Speedy Trial Clause of the Sixth Amendment is concerned, such delay is wholly irrelevant, since our analysis of the language, history and purposes of the Clause persuaded us that only "a formal indictment or information or else the actual restraints

3. In March 1975, the Inspector learned of another person who claimed to have purchased a gun from respondent. At the hearing the parties disagreed as to whether this evidence would have been admissible since it did not involve any of the guns to which the indictment related. In any event, the Assistant United States Attorney stated that the decision to prosecute was made before this additional piece of evidence was received.

imposed by arrest and holding to answer a criminal charge ... engage the particular protections" of that provision. We went on to note that statutes of limitations which provide predictable, legislatively enacted limits on prosecutorial delay, provide "the primary guarantee, against bringing overly stale criminal charges." But we did acknowledge that the "statute of limitations does not fully define [defendants'] rights with respect to the events occurring prior to indictment," and that the Due Process Clause has a limited role to play in protecting against oppressive delay.

Respondent seems to argue that due process bars prosecution whenever a defendant suffers prejudice as a result of preindictment delay. To support that proposition respondent relies on the concluding sentence of the Court's opinion in *Marion* where, in remanding the case, we stated that "[e]vents of the trial may demonstrate actual prejudice, but at the present time appellees' due process claims are speculative and premature." But the quoted sentence establishes only that proof of actual prejudice makes a due process claim concrete and ripe for adjudication, not that it makes the claim automatically valid. Indeed, two pages earlier in the opinion we expressly rejected the argument respondent advances here:

> "[W]e need not ... determine when and in what circumstances actual prejudice resulting from preaccusation delay requires the dismissal of the prosecution. Actual prejudice to the defense of a criminal case may result from the shortest and most necessary delay; and no one suggests that every delay-caused detriment to a defendant's case should abort a criminal prosecution."

Thus *Marion* makes clear that proof of prejudice is generally a necessary but not sufficient element of a due process claim, and that the due process inquiry must consider the reasons for the delay as well as the prejudice to the accused.

... [T]he Due Process Clause does not permit courts to abort criminal prosecutions simply because they disagree with a prosecutor's judgment as to when to seek an indictment. Judges are not free, in defining "due process," to impose on law enforcement officials our "personal and private notions" of fairness and to "disregard the limits that bind judges in their judicial function." Rochin v. California, 342 U.S. 165, 170, 72 S.Ct. 205, 209 (1952). Our task is more circumscribed. We are to determine only whether the actions complained of—here, compelling respondent to stand trial after the Government delayed indictment to investigate further—violates those "fundamental conceptions of justice which lie at the base of our civil and political institutions." ...

It requires no extended argument to establish that prosecutors do not deviate from "fundamental conceptions of justice" when they defer seeking indictments until they have probable cause to believe an accused is guilty; indeed it is unprofessional conduct for a prosecutor to recommend an indictment on less than probable cause. It should be equally obvious that prosecutors are under no duty to file charges as soon as probable cause exists but before they are satisfied they will be able to establish the suspect's guilt beyond a reasonable doubt. To impose such a duty "would have a deleterious effect both upon the rights of the accused and upon the ability of society to protect itself." From the perspective of potential defendants, requiring prosecutions to commence when probable cause is established is undesirable because it would increase the likelihood of unwarranted charges being filed, and would add to the time during which defendants stand accused but untried. These costs are by no means insubstantial since, as we recognized in *Marion*, a formal accusation may "interfere with the defendant's liberty, ... disrupt his employment, drain his financial resources, curtail his associations, subject him to public obloquy, and create anxiety in him, his family and his friends." From the perspective of law enforcement officials, a requirement of immediate prosecution upon probable cause is equally unacceptable because it could make obtaining proof of guilt beyond a reasonable doubt impossible by causing potentially fruitful sources of information to evaporate before they are fully exploited. And from the standpoint of the courts, such a requirement is unwise because it would cause scarce resources to be consumed on cases that prove to be insubstantial, or that involve only some of the responsible parties or some of the criminal acts.[12] Thus, no one's interests would be well served by compelling prosecutors to initiate prosecutions as soon as they are legally entitled to do so.

It might be argued that once the Government has assembled sufficient evidence to prove guilt beyond a reasonable doubt, it should be constitutionally required to file charges promptly, even if its investigation of the entire criminal transaction is not complete. Adopting such a rule, however, would have many of the same consequences as adopting a rule requiring immediate prosecution upon probable cause.

First, compelling a prosecutor to file public charges as soon as the requisite proof has been developed against one participant on one charge would cause numerous problems in those cases in which a criminal transaction involves more than one person or more than one illegal act. In some instances, an immediate arrest or indictment would impair the prosecutor's ability to continue his investigation, thereby preventing society from bringing lawbreakers to justice. In other cases, the prosecutor would be able to obtain additional indictments despite an early prosecution, but the necessary result would be multiple trials involving a single set of facts. Such trials place needless burdens on defendants, law enforcement officials, and courts.

Second, insisting on immediate prosecution once sufficient evidence is developed to obtain a conviction would pressure prosecutors into resolving doubtful cases in favor of early—and possibly unwarranted—prosecutions. The determination of when the evidence available to the prosecution is sufficient to obtain a conviction is seldom clear-cut, and reasonable persons often will reach conflicting conclusions. In the instant case, for example, since respondent admitted possessing at least five of the firearms, the primary factual issue in dispute was whether respondent knew the guns were stolen. Not surprisingly, the Postal Inspector's report contained no direct evidence bearing on this issue. The decision whether to prosecute, therefore, required a necessarily subjective evaluation of the strength of the

12. Defendants also would be adversely affected by trials involving less than all of the criminal acts for which they are responsible, since they likely would be subjected to multiple trials growing out of the same transaction or occurrence.

circumstantial evidence available and the credibility of respondent's denial. Even if a prosecutor concluded that the case was weak and further investigation appropriate, he would have no assurance that a reviewing court would agree. To avoid the risk that a subsequent indictment would be dismissed for preindictment delay, the prosecutor might feel constrained to file premature charges, with all the disadvantages that entails.[14]

Finally, requiring the Government to make charging decisions immediately upon assembling evidence sufficient to establish guilt would preclude the Government from giving full consideration to the desirability of not prosecuting in particular cases. The decision to file criminal charges, with the awesome consequences it entails, requires consideration of a wide range of factors in addition to the strength of the Government's case, in order to determine whether prosecution would be in the public interest. Prosecutors often need more information than proof of a suspect's guilt, therefore, before deciding whether to seek an indictment. Again the instant case provides a useful illustration. Although proof of the identity of the mail thieves was not necessary to convict respondent of the possessory crimes with which he was charged, it might have been crucial in assessing respondent's culpability, as distinguished from his legal guilt. If, for example, further investigation were to show that respondent had no role in or advance knowledge of the theft and simply agreed, out of paternal loyalty, to help his son dispose of the guns once respondent discovered his son had stolen them, the United States Attorney might have decided not to prosecute, especially since at the time of the crime respondent was over 60 years old and had no prior criminal record. Requiring prosecution once the evidence of guilt is clear, however, could prevent a prosecutor from awaiting the information necessary for such a decision.

We would be most reluctant to adopt a rule which would have these consequences absent a clear constitutional command to do so. We can find no such command in the Due Process Clause of the Fifth Amendment. In our view, investigative delay is fundamentally unlike delay undertaken by the Government solely "to gain tactical advantage over the accused," United States v. Marion, supra, 404 U.S., at 324, 92 S.Ct., at 465, precisely because investigative delay is not so one-sided.[17] Rather than deviating from elementary standards of "fair play and decency," a prosecutor abides by them if he refuses to seek indictments until he is completely satisfied that he should prosecute and will be able promptly to establish guilt beyond a reasonable doubt. ... We therefore hold that to prosecute a defendant

14. In addition, if courts were required to decide in every case when the prosecution should have commenced, it would be necessary for them to trace the day-by-day progress of each investigation. Maintaining daily records would impose an administrative burden on prosecutors, and reviewing them would place an even greater burden on the courts. ...

17. In *Marion* we noted with approval that the Government conceded that a "tactical" delay would violate the Due Process Clause. The Government renews that concession here, and expands it somewhat by stating that "A due process violation might also be made out upon a showing of prosecutorial delay incurred in reckless disregard of circumstances, known to the prosecution, suggesting that there existed an appreciable risk that delay would impair the ability to mount an effective defense." As the Government notes, however, there is no evidence of recklessness here.

following investigative delay does not deprive him of due process, even if his defense might have been somewhat prejudiced by the lapse of time.

* * *

III.

In *Marion* we conceded that we could not determine in the abstract the circumstances in which preaccusation delay would require dismissing prosecutions. 404 U.S., at 324, 92 S.Ct., at 465. More than five years later, that statement remains true. Indeed, in the intervening years so few defendants have established that they were prejudiced by delay that neither this Court nor any lower court has had a sustained opportunity to consider the constitutional significance of various reasons for delay. We therefore leave to the lower courts, in the first instance, the task of applying the settled principles of due process that we have discussed to the particular circumstances of individual cases. We simply hold that in this case the lower courts erred in dismissing the indictment.

Reversed.

■ [Mr. Justice Stevens' dissenting opinion omitted.]

NOTES

1. In United States v. Marion, 404 U.S. 307, 92 S.Ct. 455 (1971), the Court held that the Sixth Amendment right to a speedy trial did not extend to delays prior to indictment when the defendant was not incarcerated. Some lower courts interpreted this to mean that pre-indictment delay is not to be counted for Sixth Amendment purposes absent an actual showing of prejudice. However, in Dillingham v. United States, 423 U.S. 64, 96 S.Ct. 303 (1975), the Court held that for purposes of determining whether the *constitutional* right to a speedy trial has been violated, the time must be calculated from the date of arrest rather than from the date of a subsequent indictment or arraignment upon the indictment.

2. In United States v. MacDonald, 456 U.S. 1, 102 S.Ct. 1497 (1982), the Court dealt with the case of an Army doctor convicted for the brutal murder of his wife and two little girls on a military base in North Carolina. The Army charged MacDonald with three murders in May, 1970; and, pursuant to military law, the Commanding General appointed an officer to investigate the charges. After hearing 56 witnesses, the officer recommended the charges be dismissed and in October, 1970, they were. However, at the request of the Justice Department, the Army continued the investigation; and, after further reports, the matter was submitted to a grand jury which returned an indictment on January, 1975. In holding that the time between dismissal of the military charges and the civilian indictment should not be considered for purposes of determining a speedy trial rights, the Court held:

> "Once charges are dismissed, the speedy trial guarantee is no longer applicable. At that point, the formerly accused is, at most, in the same position as any other subject of a criminal investigation. Certainly the knowledge of an ongoing criminal investigation will cause stress, discomfort and perhaps a certain disruption in normal life. This is true whether or not charges have been filed and then dismissed.
>
> * * *

"... But with no charges outstanding, personal liberty is certainly not impaired to the same degree as it is after arrest while charges are pending. After the charges against him have been dismissed, 'a citizen suffers no restraints on his liberty and is [no longer] the subject of public accusation: his situation does not compare with that of a defendant who has been arrested and held to answer.' United States v. Marion, supra. Following dismissal of charges, any restraint on liberty, disruption of employment, strain on financial resources, and exposure to public obloquy, stress and anxiety is no greater than it is upon anyone openly subject to a criminal investigation."

Upon remand MacDonald's remaining claims were rejected. United States v. MacDonald, 688 F.2d 224 (4th Cir.1982).

3. A problem analogous to the one not reached in *MacDonald* arises where criminal prosecutions by both state and federal authorities arise out of a single transaction. In the typical scenario state officials initiate a prosecution. The results are unsatisfactory to federal authorities who then, perhaps years after the original incident, initiate their own investigation and prosecution. As to the federal prosecution, the speedy trial clock does not start running until the federal arrest is made or until federal charges are brought. Moreover, in a due process analysis, the period between the transaction and the launching of the federal investigation is ordinarily justified by the federal policy of not authorizing federal prosecution "unless the state proceeding left substantial federal interests demonstrably unvindicated." United States v. Marler, 756 F.2d 206 (1st Cir.1985).

4. The *MacDonald* principles were further refined in United States v. Loud Hawk, 474 U.S. 302, 106 S.Ct. 648 (1986), in which the Government argued that the defendants were not under restraint because the trial judge dismissed the indictment against them and, therefore, MacDonald required that any delay flowing from the government's appeal from the dismissal should be excluded for speedy trial purposes. In a 5–4 decision, the Court upheld the government's contention:

"Respondents contend that even during the time the charges against them were dismissed, the Government was actively pursuing its case and they continued to be subjected to the possibility that bail might be imposed. This possibility, according to respondents, is sufficient to warrant counting the time towards a speedy trial claim.

* * *

"During much of the litigation, respondents were neither under indictment nor subject to bail. Further judicial proceedings would have been necessary to subject the respondents to any actual restraints. As we stated in MacDonald: 'with no charges outstanding, personal liberty is certainly not impaired to the same degree as it is after arrest while charges are pending.' After the charges against him have been dismissed, 'a citizen suffers no restraints on his liberty and is [no longer] the subject of public accusation: his situation does not compare with that of a defendant who has been arrested and held to answer.'

"Respondents argue that the speedy trial guarantee should apply to this period because the Government's desire to prosecute them was a matter of public record. Public suspicion, however, is not sufficient to justify the delay in favor of a defendant's speedy trial claim. We find that after the District Court dismissed the indictment against respondents and after respondents were freed without restraint, they were 'in the same position as any other subject of a criminal investigation.' The Speedy Trial Clause does not purport to protect a defendant from all effects flowing from a delay before trial. The clause does not, for example, limit the length of a preindictment criminal investigation even though 'the [suspect's] knowledge of an ongoing criminal investigation will cause stress, discomfort, and perhaps a certain disruption in normal life.'

"[W]e are not persuaded that respondents' need for counsel while their case was technically dismissed supports their speedy trial claim. Although the retention of counsel is frequently an inconvenience and an expense, the Speedy Trial Clause's core concern is impairment of liberty; it does not shield a suspect or a defendant from every expense or inconvenience associated with criminal defense.

"We therefore find that under the rule of MacDonald, when defendants are not incarcerated or subjected to other substantial restrictions on their liberty, a court should not weigh that time towards a claim under the Speedy Trial Clause."

Justice Marshall, on behalf of the dissenters, stated:

"There has been at all relevant times a case on a court docket captioned United States v. Loud Hawk—I can think of no more formal indication that respondents stand accused by the Government.

* * *

"The most telling difference between this case and MacDonald, however, is the fact that respondents' liberty could have been taken from them at any time during the Government's appeal. One of the primary purposes of the speedy trial right, of course, is to prevent prolonged restraints on liberty, and the absence of any possibility of such restraints was a vital part of our MacDonald holding.

* * *

"As if acknowledging that the delay in this case is more analogous to post-arrest, pre-indictment delay than to pre-arrest delay, the majority concedes that had respondents been incarcerated or forced to post bond during the Government's appeal, the automatic exclusion rule of MacDonald would not apply. Yet, inexplicably, the majority then suggests that the Speedy Trial Clause applies to post-arrest, pre-indictment delay only when the defendant has been subjected to '*actual* restraints,' * * *

* * *

"We held in ... that pre-arrest delay is not cognizable under the Speedy Trial Clause, but we certainly did not disturb the settled rule that the Government's formal institution of criminal charges, whether through arrest or indictment, always calls the speedy trial right into play. ... The majority identifies no logic or precedent supporting its novel conclusion that a defendant who is arrested and released on bail is 'accused,' while a defendant who is arrested and released without bail, on the same evidence, is not 'accused.'

* * *

"There can be no question that one who had been arrested and released ... would be entitled, under Marion, to the protections of the Speedy Trial Clause. Because respondents were by statute subject to the same restraints as that hypothetical defendant, I am at a loss to understand why they should enjoy less protection."

5. In Wilson v. McCaughtry, 994 F.2d 1228 (7th Cir.1993), the Court upheld the denial of a habeas corpus petition in a case in which the state waited sixteen years after a murder before bringing an indictment. During an investigation following the brutal murder of Wilson's stepson, the coroner who performed the autopsy testified that defendant's conduct could not be linked to the boy's death and the deceased's mother testified that Wilson did not beat her son. After both of these witnesses died and after radio reports "resurrected the case and the prosecutors felt the flush of public pressure," Wilson was indicted for murder. Holding that the witnesses deaths were not sufficient to show substantial prejudice, the majority found that, even if prejudice were shown, the right to a speedy trial, in the preindictment context, required a showing that the prejudicial delay was an intentional device on the part of the prosecution to gain a tactical advantage over the accused. What type of evidence would be necessary to satisfy so stringent a standard? Judge Cummings, in dissent, suggested a lesser burden. He would have remanded to give Wilson an opportunity to prove that the delay was incurred in "reckless disregard of his rights to speedy due process."

6. In United States v. Crouch, 51 F.3d 480 (5th Cir.1995) a majority held that a six and one-half year delay in bringing bank fraud charges violated the right to a speedy trial. The defendant's ability to demonstrate "actual prejudice" as a result of the deaths of several potential witnesses and the loss of exculpatory documentation was determinative.

The en banc court reversed in United States v. Crouch, 84 F.3d 1497 (5th Cir.1996) and adopted a standard that requires proof of the government's attempt to obtain a tactical advantage through preindictment delay in order to implicate due process:

> We ... hold that where an indictment is returned within the statute of limitations, preindictment delay does not violate due process unless that delay, in addition to prejudicing the accused, was intentionally brought about by the government for the purpose of gaining some tactical advantage over the accused in the contemplated prosecution or for some other bad faith purpose. * * *
>
> We further hold that preindictment delay does not entitle the accused to dismissal of the indictment on due process grounds unless he demonstrates that the improper delay caused actual, substantial prejudice to his defense. The requisite prejudice may not be presumed, rebuttably or otherwise, merely from the length of the delay, and the district court erred in holding to the contrary and in partially relying on presumed prejudice. Moreover, because actual, substantial prejudice to the defense at trial is required, a showing of mere potential or possible trial prejudice does not suffice. This means that dismissal on such a basis prior to trial will rarely (if ever) be appropriate. In all but the clearest and most indisputable cases, the district court, even though inclined to grant such a motion, should nevertheless normally withhold doing so until after verdict, when the assessment of actual, substantial trial prejudice can more accurately be made.

7. In United States v. Ross, 112 F.3d 422 (9th Cir.1997), the government moved to dismiss an indictment without prejudice after a mistrial was declared. Over four years later the indictment was reinstated and the defendant was convicted. At a hearing, the prosecutor testified that the delay was occasioned by the need to extradite a codefendant from Israel because a joint trial was likely to increase the odds of conviction. The court held that the time between a dismissed indictment and the issuance of a second indictment is considered preindictment delay and analyzed under due process principles. Finding that the intervening deaths of several witnesses did not prejudice the defendant because the transcripts of their testimony at the first trial could have been used at the second, the court concluded that the absence of prejudice made it unnecessary to determine whether the prosecution acted in bad faith. Accordingly, it rejected the speedy trial claim.

2. As a Matter of Statutory Right

Henderson v. United States

United States Supreme Court, 1986.
476 U.S. 321, 106 S.Ct. 1871.

■ Justice Powell delivered the opinion of the Court.

The Speedy Trial Act, 18 U.S.C. § 3161 et seq., commands that a defendant be tried within 70 days of the latest of either the filing of an indictment or information, or the first appearance before a judge or magistrate. Section 3161(h)(1)(F) excludes from this time "delay resulting from any pretrial motion, from the filing of the motion through the conclusion of the hearing on, or other prompt disposition of, such motion." This case requires us to decide the narrow questions whether that exclusion is limited to reasonably necessary delays, and whether it applies to delays occasioned by the filing of posthearing briefs on motions.

[In this case, the speedy trial clock began to run with the arraignment of the last codefendant in an alleged drug distribution scheme on September 3, 1980. Due primarily to a motion to suppress, a hearing on the motion and a number of briefs filed in connection with the motion, the trial did not begin until November 1, 1982.]

Section 3161(h)(1)(F) (subsection (F)) excludes from these 70 days certain delays occasioned by the filing of pretrial motions:

> "(h) The following periods of delay shall be excluded in computing the time within which an information or an indictment must be filed, or in computing the time within which the trial of any such offense must commence:
>
> "(1) *Any period of delay* resulting from other proceedings concerning the defendant, including but not limited to—
>
> * * *
>
> "(F) *delay resulting from any pretrial motion*, from the filing of the motion through the conclusion of the hearing on, or other prompt disposition of, such motion;" (emphasis added).

On its face, subsection (F) excludes "[a]ny period of delay" caused by "any pretrial motion," "from the filing of the motion through the conclusion of the hearing." The plain terms of the statute appear to exclude all time between the filing of and the hearing on a motion whether that hearing was prompt or not. Moreover, subsection (F) does not require that a period of delay be "reasonable" to be excluded, although Congress clearly knew how to limit an exclusion: in § 3161(h)(7), Congress provided for exclusion of a "reasonable period of delay when the defendant is joined for trial with a codefendant as to whom the time for trial has not run and no motion for severance has been granted." Apart from this single instance, every other provision in § 3161(h) provides for exclusion of "any period of delay." The provision excludes, for example, all of the time consumed by an interlocutory appeal, § 3161(h)(1)(E), by a competency examination, § 3161(h)(1)(A), and by the defendant's unavailability, § 3161(h)(3)(A).

* * *

The legislative history of the 1979 Amendments to the Act supports this reading of subsection (F). That history shows that Congress was aware of the breadth of the exclusion it was enacting in subsection (F). The Senate Judiciary Committee acknowledged "if basic standards for prompt consideration of pretrial motions are not developed," the liberalized 1979 amendments to subsection (F) "could become a loophole which could undermine the whole Act." In its subsequent consideration of subsection (F), the House of Representatives did not qualify the exclusion in any way or limit such potential abuse by statute. Instead the House adopted the Senate's version "with the intention that potentially excessive and abusive use of this exclusion be precluded by district or circuit guidelines, rules, or procedures relating to motions practice." . . .

Petitioners largely concede these arguments and advance two other contentions for limiting subsection (F)'s exclusion to time that is "reasonably necessary" for the disposition of pretrial motions. First, they contend that the phrase "other prompt disposition" within subsection (F) implies that a district court may not unreasonably delay a criminal trial by deferring a hearing on a pretrial motion. . . . But a reading of subsection (F) in connection with § 3161(h)(1)(J) (subsection (J)), which allows exclusion of up to 30 days while the district court has a motion "under advisement," i.e., 30 days from the time the court receives all the papers it reasonably expects, undermines this conclusion. The phrase "prompt disposition" was intended to prevent a district court from using subsection (F) to exclude time after a motion is taken under advisement when that time fails to qualify for exclusion under subsection (J).

Subsection (F), written in the disjunctive, excludes time in two situations. The first arises when a pretrial motion requires a hearing: subsection (F) on its face excludes the entire period between the filing of the motion and the conclusion of the hearing. The second situation concerns motions that require no hearing and that result in a "prompt disposition." There, the promptness requirement was "intended to provide a point at which time will cease to be excluded, where motions are decided on the papers filed without hearing." The "point at which time will cease to be excluded" is identified by subsection (J), which permits an exclusion of 30 days from the time a motion is actually "under advisement" by the court. Without the promptness requirement in subsection (F), a court could exclude time beyond subsection (J)'s 30–day "under advisement" provision simply by designating the additional period as time "from the filing of the motion" through its "disposition" under subsection (F). . . . We therefore conclude that for pretrial motions that require a hearing, the phrase "or other prompt disposition" in subsection (F) does not imply that only "reasonably necessary" delays may be excluded between the time of filing of a motion and the conclusion of the hearing thereon.

Petitioners' second argument rests on the sentence that immediately follows the extract quoted above: "Nor does the Committee intend that additional time be made eligible for exclusion by postponing the *hearing date* or other disposition of the motions beyond what is *reasonably necessary*."

* * *

Any qualification of subsection (F)'s exclusion based on this sentence, which appears in the paragraph discussing motions decided without a hearing, would be at odds with the plain language of the statute. ... We therefore decline to read into subsection (F) a "reasonably necessary" qualification based on this single sentence from the Senate Report. We instead hold that Congress intended subsection (F) to exclude from the Speedy Trial Act's 70–day limitation all time between the filing of a motion and the conclusion of the hearing on that motion, whether or not a delay in holding that hearing is "reasonably necessary."

The remaining issue is whether subsection (F) excludes time after a hearing on a motion but before the district court receives all the submissions by counsel it needs to decide that motion. Although the language of subsection (F) is not clear on this point, we are convinced that its structure, as well as reason, requires that such time be excluded.

The provisions of the Act are designed to exclude all time that is consumed in placing the trial court in a position to dispose of a motion. District courts often find it impossible to resolve motions on which hearings have been held until the parties have submitted posthearing briefs or additional factual materials, especially where the motion presents complicated issues. It would not have been sensible for Congress to exclude automatically all the time prior to the hearing on a motion and 30 days after the motion is taken under advisement, but not the time during which the court remains unable to rule because it is awaiting the submission by counsel of additional materials. Moreover, for motions decided solely on the papers, Congress has allowed exclusion of time during which the parties are filing their briefs. It is consistent with this exclusion to exclude time when the court awaits the briefs and materials needed to resolve a motion on which a hearing has been held—motions that the Senate Judiciary Committee recognized as typically more difficult than motions decided on the papers. We therefore hold that subsection (F) excludes time after a hearing has been held where a district court awaits additional filings from the parties that are needed for proper disposition of the motion.

We now calculate the number of nonexcludable days before petitioners' trial. The Act began to run on September 3, 1980.... On October 22, 1980, the District Court entered—with the consent of the parties—a continuance through November 12. The District Court excluded that continuance from the Speedy Trial Act's 70–day limit under § 3161(h)(8)(A) in "the interest of justice." That exclusion is not challenged in this Court.

The motion to suppress was filed during this continuance, on November 3, 1980. The hearing on this and subsequent motions was held on March 25, 1981. This time is automatically excludable under § 3161(h)(1)(F). The court declined to reach a final decision on the suppression motion at that hearing because it needed further information. The court did not receive all filings in connection with the motion until

December 15, 1981, when the Government submitted its response to petitioners' memorandum and request for an evidentiary hearing. That time is also excludable, plus 30 days for the District Court to take the matter under advisement. We therefore exclude the period from March 25, 1981, through January 14, 1982.

On January 25, 1982, the Government filed a motion to set the case for trial, noticed for February 3. We need not decide whether this time is excludable under subsection (F) as it does not affect the disposition of this case. On February 3, the court continued the case until April 21, to afford defense counsel the opportunity to file a motion to reconsider the suppression ruling. The District Court subsequently found that this time was excludable under § 3161(h)(8)(A) as a continuance necessary for the "interests of justice." Id., at 34. On March 23, petitioners filed their motion for reconsideration. Under subsection (F), an exclusion for this pending motion ran from March 23 until the disposition by hearing on May 10. At that time, the court stated that it would exclude under § 3161(h)(8)(A) the time from May 10 to September 13, the new trial date, because of the difficulty of coordinating the schedules of five defense attorneys. The court entered a similar order on September 13 that extended through the ultimate trial date of November 1, 1982. Neither of those orders is properly before us. As the case stands here, it presents 69 nonexcludable days of delay, and therefore the Speedy Trial Act was not violated.

* * *

■ JUSTICE WHITE, with whom JUSTICE BRENNAN, JUSTICE MARSHALL and JUSTICE BLACKMUN join, dissenting.

The purpose of the Speedy Trial Act of 1974, is to quantify and make effective the Sixth Amendment right to a speedy trial. To this end, the Act entitles a criminal defendant to dismissal of the charges pending against him if he is not brought to trial within 70 days of his initial appearance or indictment. In computing the running of this 70–day period, the Act permits certain periods of time to be excluded. These exclusions are designed to take account of specific and recurring periods of delay which often occur in criminal cases; they are not to be used either to undermine the time limits established by the Act, or to subvert the very purpose the Act was designed to fulfill. Nonetheless, this is precisely the result achieved by the majority's reasoning, as it allows trial judges indefinitely to delay disposing of pretrial motions. For this reason, I dissent.

As interpreted by the majority, § 3161(h)(1)(F) (subsection (F)) excludes the entire period between the filing of the pretrial motion and the date on which the motion is finally taken under advisement. For motions requiring a hearing, all time is excluded from the date the motion is filed through the conclusion of the hearing. There is no requirement that the hearing be held promptly, and the reason for the delay is irrelevant. Regardless whether a hearing is postponed due to a stipulated continuance, the sudden illness of counsel, or the trial judge's decision to play golf, until the hearing is concluded, the 70–day clock remains at a standstill. Moreover, if at the conclusion of the hearing the trial judge determines that more information would be helpful to his resolution of the motion, or if the prosecutor simply announces his intention to file supplemental papers, the period of excludable delay continues indefinitely until the court receives all of the papers it reasonably expects. Only at that point is the motion considered to be "actually under advisement," and even then, § 3161(h)(1)(J) (subsection (J)) provides for an additional 30 days before the clock begins running again.

* * *

As I see it, the majority has misread both subsection (F) and the Act as a whole. I read subsection (F) to require *all* pretrial motions, regardless of whether they require a hearing, to be disposed of promptly. There is no reason to believe that Congress did not intend the word "prompt" to mean exactly what it normally means, "done or rendered readily or immediately"; "given without delay or hesitation."

* * *

Adhering to both the plain language of the statute and its legislative history, the majority of courts considering this question have held that subsection (F) permits the exclusion of only a reasonable amount of time for the trial court to take a pretrial motion under advisement, and that any other result would defeat the purposes of the Act.

* * *

I . . . would hold that the Speedy Trial Act requires a trial court to take all pretrial motions under advisement in a prompt manner, and as a result, that only that period of delay found to be reasonably necessary to such a prompt handling of the motion is properly excludable under subsection (F). By holding that the entire period of delay from the filing of a pretrial motion until that motion is taken under advisement is excludable from the 70–day speedy trial computation, the majority allows this exception to swallow the rule and in so doing, undermines the entire Act.

* * *

NOTES

1. The Federal Speedy Trial Act, 18 U.S.C. § 3161, provides a statutory scheme dictating the time periods within which federal trials must begin. Congress intended the act "to assist in reducing crime and the danger of recidivism by requiring speedy trials. . . ." 1974 U.S.Code & Cong'l & Adm.News, 93d Cong.2d Sess. 7401. See Frase, The Speedy Trial Act of 1974, 43 U.Chi.L.Rev. 667 (1976).

1a. Under the Act, a defendant must be charged within 30 days of his initial arrest. However, § 3162(a)(1) has been held applicable only to those charges contained in the original complaint or accusatory instrument. When a subsequent charge merely "guilds" the initial charge by annotating it in more detail, the time constraint applies; but when new or different charges are added, it does not. This requires the courts to pierce the charges in order to determine whether the elements of the offenses are truly different. Compare United States v. Bailey, 111 F.3d 1229 (5th Cir.1997) (felony indictment after misdemeanor arrest does not start the clock even though same handgun is involved) with United States v. Palomba, 31

F.3d 1456 (9th Cir.1994) (dismissal required for repeated counts which were part of same criminal scheme).

2. In United States v. Brainer, 515 F.Supp. 627 (D.Md.1981), the last date on which the trial could start without violating the 70–day rule of 18 U.S.C. § 3161(c)(1) was April 10, 1981. Trial was scheduled for April 20 because of the press of other cases. The district court denied a motion to dismiss, finding the Speedy Trial Act to be invalid on separation of powers grounds, being an "unwarranted intrusion with the administration of the judicial system." Once Congress "has defined certain areas of cases arising under such provisions of the jurisdiction of the federal courts, it cannot unduly interfere with the independence of the Judiciary in fulfilling its Constitutional function." The Court of Appeals reversed at 691 F.2d 691 (4th Cir.1982), finding no violation of separation of powers principles.

3. In United States v. Rojas–Contreras, 474 U.S. 231, 106 S.Ct. 555 (1985), the Court held that the requirement that the defense be allowed at least 30 days to prepare did not apply to a superseding indictment containing only a minor technical change involving the date of a prior conviction required to be pled. When a superseding indictment contains something more than a technical change, it may be held to restart the 30 day trial preparation period. See United States v. Feldman, 761 F.2d 380 (7th Cir.1985) (second indictment was not reindictment for same offense); United States v. Guzman, 754 F.2d 482 (2d Cir.1985) (second indictment expanded scope of conspiracy). A defendant brought to trial before the 30–day period elapses must assert his right to additional time or it will be deemed to have been waived. United States v. Grosshans, 821 F.2d 1247 (6th Cir.1987).

4. If the objectives of the Speedy Trial Act are to be accomplished, is it fair to exclude delay attributable exclusively to judge from the computation? See United States v. Gonzales, 897 F.2d 1312 (5th Cir.1990) (time spent on multiple motions excludable). In United States v. Scaife, 749 F.2d 338 (6th Cir.1984), the judge conducted a voir dire on the last date under the Act, recessed the trial to attend a judicial conference and resumed the case outside of the Act's allowable period. On appeal, the court held that the trial began with the voir dire and the Act was not violated. But see United States v. Penta, 898 F.2d 815 (1st Cir.1990) (delay caused by transfer of case from one district to another not excludable); United States v. Gallardo, 773 F.2d 1496 (9th Cir.1985) (continuance granted due to general congestion of court's calendar is not excludable).

The delay between the filing of a pretrial motion and the court's decision on it is always excludable and no inquiry into whether the amount of delay was reasonably necessary for the fair processing of the motion need be made. United States v. Green, 508 F.3d 195 (5th Cir. 2007) United States v. Dorlouis, 107 F.3d 248 (4th Cir.1997). But see United States v. Scott, 270 F.3d 30 (1st Cir.2001) (speedy trial act violation when court had motions under advisement for 124 days before requesting additional filings).

5. In some instances, the government may unilaterally affect a defendant's rights under the Act. See United States v. Long, 900 F.2d 1270 (8th Cir.1990) (interlocutory appeal); United States v. May, 771 F.2d 980 (6th Cir.1985) (voluntary dismissal without prejudice of first complaint did not start period, which began to run from second indictment for similar offense); United States v. Robinson, 767 F.2d 765 (11th Cir.1985) (right did not accrue on formal arrest and charge when government dismissed complaint three days later and said that it would not proceed at that time).

6. Likewise, the right may be affected by the activities of a codefendant. As a general rule, an exclusion from the speedy trial period applicable to one defendant applies to all codefendants. United States v. Anello, 765 F.2d 253 (1st Cir.1985); see United States v. DeJesus, 887 F.2d 114 (6th Cir.1989) (delay caused by codefendant's suppression motion excludable); United States v. Cephas, 937 F.2d 816 (2d Cir.1991) (when a defendant's motion for severance is denied, the court must examine the reasonableness of any delay caused by co-defendant's motions before excluding it); Compare United States v. Khoury, 901 F.2d 948 (11th Cir.1990) (codefendant's fugitive status did not justify 18 month delay where defendant moved for severance); United States v. DeLuna, 763 F.2d 897 (8th Cir.1985) (18 month delay attributable to pretrial motions of codefendants excludable); United States v. Mejia, 82 F.3d 1032 (11th Cir.1996) (codefendant's request for extension of time to file motions excludes all time allowed for filing even if no motions are forthcoming).

7. The "ends of justice" exception which permits postponement of trial beyond 70 days after indictment has been the subject of numerous decisions. One court has held that the complexity of a case is an adequate reason for postponement of a trial, over a dissent which claims that such an "exception" could be used to eviscerate the Speedy Trial Act. United States v. Bryant, 726 F.2d 510 (9th Cir.1984). What constitutes a proper consideration under the "ends of justice" doctrine? See United States v. Amerson, 938 F.2d 116 (8th Cir.1991) (key witness broke his leg and developed complications); United States v. Blandina, 895 F.2d 293 (7th Cir.1989) (continuance requested by government to further investigate tax evasion defendant's sources of income properly excluded); United States v. Golomb, 754 F.2d 86 (2d Cir.1985) (time necessary to complete ongoing grand jury investigation may be excluded); United States v. Strong, 608 F.Supp. 188 (E.D.Pa.1985) (time for government attorney to prepare for trial not excludable); United States v. Twitty, 107 F.3d 1482 (11th Cir.1997) (open ended continuance due to illness of essential government witness). For a criticism of the lack of standards surrounding the open-ended continuance dilemma, see Ostfeld, Speedy Justice and Timeless Delays: The Validity of Open–Ended "Ends of Justice" Continuances Under the Speedy Trial Act, 64 U.Chi.L.Rev. 1037 (1997).

8. The "ends of justice" exception does not authorize a prospective waiver of rights under the Act. In Zedner v. United States, 547 U.S. 489, 126 S.Ct. 1976 (2006), defendant signed a waiver form that the court had prepared for situations in which lengthy delay was contemplated. Holding that express "end of justice" findings are necessary in each instance in which excludable delay is sought, the Court rejected the practice of prospective waivers:

> [T]he Speedy Trial Act comprehensively regulates the time within which a trial must begin. Section 3161(h) specifies in detail numerous categories of delay that are not counted in applying the Act's deadlines. Conspicuously, § 3161(h) has no provision excluding periods of delay during which a defendant waives the application of the Act, and it is apparent from the terms of the Act that this omission was a considered one. Instead of simply allowing defendants to opt out of the Act, the Act demands that defense continuance requests fit within one of the specific exclusions set out in subsection (h). Subsection (h)(8), which permits ends-of-justice continuances, was plainly meant to cover many of these requests. Among the factors that a district court must consider in deciding whether to grant an ends-of-justice continuance are a defendant's need for "reasonable time to obtain counsel," "continuity of counsel," and "effective preparation" of counsel. § 3161(h)(8)(B)(iv). If a defendant could simply waive the application of the Act whenever he or she wanted more time, no defendant would ever need to put such considerations before the court under the rubric of an ends-of-justice exclusion.
>
> The purposes of the Act also cut against exclusion on the grounds of mere consent or waiver. If the Act were designed solely to protect a

defendant's right to a speedy trial, it would make sense to allow a defendant to waive the application of the Act. But the Act was designed with the public interest firmly in mind. See e.g., 18 U.S.C. § 3161(h)(8)(A) (to exclude delay resulting from a continuance—even one "granted . . . at the request of the defendant"—the district court must find "that the ends of justice served . . . outweigh the *best interest of the public* and the defendant in a speedy trial" (emphasis added)). That public interest cannot be served, the Act recognizes, if defendants may opt out of the Act entirely.

9. If a delay violates only the Speedy Trial Act and not the Sixth Amendment, a federal judge has the option of dismissing without prejudice so as to allow the renewed filing of the same charge.

In United States v. Taylor, 487 U.S. 326, 108 S.Ct. 2413 (1988), the Court disapproved the action of a district court in dismissing "with prejudice" federal criminal charges because of a violation of the Speedy Trial Act. Trial had been scheduled in Seattle on drug conspiracy charges one day before expiration of the seventy-day period. The defendant failed to appear. After he was recaptured in California, the Government was guilty of certain unwarranted delays that were not excludable from the seventy-day period.

While stating that there was no presumption in favor of "dismissal with prejudice" and no presumption in favor of "dismissal without prejudice," the Court acknowledged that the district court has discretion in choosing the appropriate remedy. However, the Supreme Court reversed the district judge because the judge had not properly considered those factors which must play a role in the exercise of discretion, as specified in § 3162(a):

> In determining whether to dismiss the case with or without prejudice, the court shall consider, among others, each of the following factors: the seriousness of the offense, the facts and circumstances of the case which led to the dismissal, and the impact of a reprosecution on the administration of this chapter and on the administration of justice.

The Court faulted the district court for failing to make findings with respect to the statutory criteria, and it characterized the few findings as unsupported by the record. It concluded:

> Dismissal without prejudice is not a toothless sanction: it forces the Government to obtain a new indictment . . . and exposes the prosecution to the risk of dismissal on statute of limitation grounds. Given the burden borne by the prosecution . . . substantial delay well may make reprosecution, even if permitted, unlikely.

D. REQUEST FOR CONTINUANCE

Avery v. Alabama

Supreme Court of the United States, 1940.
308 U.S. 444, 60 S.Ct. 321.

■ MR. JUSTICE BLACK delivered the opinion of the Court.

Petitioner was convicted of murder in Alabama; he was sentenced to death and the State Supreme Court affirmed. The sole question presented is whether in violation of the Fourteenth Amendment, "petitioner was denied the right of counsel, with the accustomed incidents of consultation and opportunity of preparation for trial", because after competent counsel were duly appointed their motion for continuance was denied. Vigilant concern for the maintenance of the constitutional right of an accused to assistance of counsel led us to grant certiorari.

* * *

Since the Constitution nowhere specifies any period which must intervene between the required appointment of counsel and trial, the fact, standing alone, that a continuance has been denied, does not constitute a denial of the constitutional right to assistance of counsel. In the course of trial, after due appointment of competent counsel, many procedural questions necessarily arise which must be decided by the trial judge in the light of facts then presented and conditions then existing. Disposition of a request for continuance is of this nature and is made in the discretion of the trial judge, the exercise of which will ordinarily not be reviewed.

But the denial of opportunity for appointed counsel to confer, to consult with the accused and to prepare his defense, could convert the appointment of counsel into a sham and nothing more than a formal compliance with the Constitution's requirement that an accused be given the assistance of counsel. The Constitution's guarantee of assistance of counsel cannot be satisfied by mere formal appointment.

* * *

The record shows—

Petitioner was convicted on an indictment filed in the Bibb County Circuit Court for murder alleged to have occurred in 1932. He was found and arrested in Pittsburg, Pennsylvania, shortly before March 21, 1938. On that date, Monday, he was arraigned at a regular term of the Court; two practicing attorneys of the local bar were appointed to defend him; pleas of not guilty and not guilty by reason of insanity were entered and the presiding judge set his trial for Wednesday, March 23. The case was not reached Wednesday, but was called Thursday, the 24th, at which time his attorneys filed a motion for continuance, on the ground that they had not had sufficient time and opportunity since their appointment to investigate and prepare his defense. Affidavits of both attorneys accompanied the motion.

One attorney's affidavit alleged that he had not had time to investigate and prepare the defense because he had been actually engaged in another trial from the time of his appointment at 2 P.M., Monday, until 9 P.M. that evening; his presence had been required in the court room on Tuesday, March 22, due to employment in other cases set, but not actually tried; he had been detained in court Wednesday, March 23, waiting for petitioner's case to be called; but after his appointment he had talked with petitioner and "had serious doubts as to his sanity."

The affidavit by the other attorney stated that he too had not had proper time and opportunity to investigate petitioner's case because of his employment in other pending cases, some of which were not disposed of until Tuesday at 4:30 P.M.

No ruling on the motion for continuance appears in the record, but on Thursday, the 24th, the trial proceeded before a jury.

* * *

The jury returned a verdict of guilty with the death penalty. On the same day, the 24th, petitioner's counsel moved for a new trial, setting up error in the failure to grant the requested continuance. This motion for new trial was continued from time to time until June 30. In the interim, a third attorney had been employed by petitioner's sister, and on June 30, petitioner's three lawyers filed an amendment to the motion for new trial, specifically setting out that the denial of a continuance had deprived petitioner of the equal protection of the laws and due process of law guaranteed by the Fourteenth Amendment, by denying him "the right of counsel, with the accustomed incidents of consultation and opportunity of preparation for trial."

When the motion for new trial was heard the only witnesses were petitioner's three attorneys. The third attorney, employed by petitioner's sister, testified only that he had been employed after the trial and verdict. The two attorneys who had represented petitioner at the trial substantially repeated what they had set out in their original affidavits. In some detail they testified that: they had conferred with petitioner after their appointment on Monday, March 21, but he gave them no helpful information available as a defense or names of any witnesses; between their appointment and the trial they made inquiries of people who lived in the community in which the petitioner had lived prior to the crime with which he was charged and in which the killing occurred and none of those questioned, including a brother of petitioner, could offer information or assistance helpful to the defense; they (the attorneys) had not prior to the trial conferred with local doctors, of whom there were four, as to petitioner's mental condition, had neither summoned any medical experts or other witnesses nor asked for compulsory process. And in response to inquiries made by the trial judge they stated that they had not made any request for leave of absence from the court to make further inquiry or investigation.

The motion for new trial was overruled.

* * *

Under the particular circumstances appearing in this record, we do not think petitioner has been denied the benefit of assistance of counsel guaranteed to him by the Fourteenth Amendment. His appointed counsel, as the Supreme Court of Alabama recognized, have performed their "full duty intelligently and well." Not only did they present petitioner's defense in the trial court, but in conjunction with counsel later employed, they carried an appeal to the State Supreme Court, and then brought the matter here for our review. Their appointment and the representation rendered under it were not mere formalities, but petitioner's counsel have—as was their solemn duty—contested every step of the way leading to final disposition of the case. Petitioner has thus been afforded the assistance of zealous and earnest counsel from arraignment to final argument in this Court.

The offense for which petitioner was convicted occurred in a County largely rural. The County seat, where court was held, has a population of less than a thousand. Indictments in the Bibb County Circuit Court, as in most rural Counties throughout the Nation, are most frequently returned and trials had during fixed terms or sessions of court. And these rural "Court Weeks" traditionally bring grand and petit jurors, witnesses, interested persons and spectators from every part of the County into the County seat for court. Unlike metropolitan centers, people in these rural Counties know each other, and information concerning witnesses and events is more widespread and more generally known than in large cities. Because this was so, petitioner's attorneys were able to make the inquiries during Court Week at the County seat, to which they testified, and that they apparently withdrew the plea of insanity after this inquiry is significant. That the examination and preparation of the case, in the time permitted by the trial judge, had been adequate for counsel to exhaust its every angle is illuminated by the absence of any indication, on the motion and hearing for new trial, that they could have done more had additional time been granted.

Under the circumstances of this case we cannot say that the trial judge, who concluded a fairly conducted trial by carefully safeguarding petitioner's rights in a clear and fair charge, deprived petitioner of his constitutional right to assistance of counsel. The Supreme Court of Alabama having found that petitioner was afforded that right, its judgment is

Affirmed.

NOTES

1. Because the parties to an action are entitled to a prompt disposition on the merits, unreasonable delay caused by a motion for continuance is generally unwarranted. While extreme circumstances preclude a court's insistence upon expedience in the face of a justifiable request for a continuance, the determination of a continuance is within the sound discretion of the trial court. See Ungar v. Sarafite, 376 U.S. 575, 589, 84 S.Ct. 841, 849 (1964). In Morris v. Slappy, 461 U.S. 1, 103 S.Ct. 1610 (1983), the appointed public defender was hospitalized for emergency surgery shortly before trial and a senior trial attorney in the public defender's office was assigned 6 days before the scheduled trial date to represent the defendant. At the opening of the trial, defendant moved for a continuance, claiming that his attorney did not have enough time to prepare; but the court denied the motion. Defendant's newly assigned attorney stated that he was prepared and that a further continuance would not benefit him in presenting the case. The jury returned a verdict of guilty on three counts but failed to reach a verdict on two other counts. After a second trial, during which the defendant refused to co-operate with or even speak to his attorney, the jury returned a guilty verdict on the two other counts. On appeal, the convictions were reversed on the ground that the Sixth Amendment right to counsel envisioned the right to a meaningful attorney-client relationship. The Supreme Court reinstated the convictions:

> "Not every restriction on counsel's time or opportunity to investigate or to consult with his client or otherwise to prepare for trial violates a defendant's Sixth Amendment right to counsel. Trial judges necessarily require a great deal of latitude in scheduling trials. Not the least of their problems is that of assembling the witnesses, lawyers, and jurors at the same place at the same time, and this burden counsels against continu-

ances except for compelling reasons. Consequently, broad discretion must be granted trial courts on matters of continuances; only an unreasoning and arbitrary 'insistence upon expeditiousness in the face of justifiable request for delay' violates the right to be the assistance of counsel.

* * *

"No court could possibly guarantee that a defendant will develop the kind of rapport with his attorney—privately retained or provided by the public—that the Court of Appeals thought part of the Sixth Amendment guarantee of counsel. Accordingly, we reject the claim that the Sixth Amendment guarantees a 'meaningful relationship' between an accused and his counsel."

The "arbitrary insistence on expeditiousness in the face of a justifiable request for delay" is a difficult standard to meet. See United States v. Bakker, 925 F.2d 728 (4th Cir.1991) (request for five day continuance to reestablish the attorney-client relationship after competency hearing properly denied).

2. The general rule is that a court may deny a continuance, without infringing on a defendant's Sixth Amendment right to counsel, if the circumstances disclose an attempt by the defendant to engage in a dilatory course of conduct or hinder the efficient administration of justice. See United States v. Rivera, 900 F.2d 1462 (10th Cir.1990); United States v. Studley, 892 F.2d 518 (7th Cir.1989); United States v. Hughes, 891 F.2d 597 (6th Cir.1989). Under these cases, the right to counsel of choice does not support a concomitant right to a continuance where other counsel of record is present, where the motion is made close to the trial date, where an extended period for preparation has been allowed or where the trial promises to be of long duration. This is especially true where available counsel is competent and other counsel is sought merely as a matter of preference. Similarly, a defendant who seeks to discharge counsel on the eve of trial and proceed pro se is not necessarily entitled to a continuance. Barham v. Powell, 895 F.2d 19 (1st Cir.1990); United States v. Moya–Gomez, 860 F.2d 706 (7th Cir.1988). The converse is also true. United States v. Tolliver, 937 F.2d 1183 (7th Cir.1991) ("The problem is, savvy criminal defendants have learned to manipulate the system by withdrawing requests for self-representation at the eleventh hour (or, as here, in midstream) in order to cause delay").

3. Only in extreme circumstances where co-counsel is not associated with the case, has a conflict of interest, or is not given adequate opportunity to prepare will the refusal to grant a continuance constitute error. See, e.g., Glasser v. United States, 315 U.S. 60, 62 S.Ct. 457 (1942) (appointed counsel's conflict of interest was discernible from the record); United States v. Gallo, 763 F.2d 1504 (6th Cir.1985) (inadequate time to prepare); McConnell v. United States, 375 F.2d 905 (5th Cir.1967) (request for appointed counsel was refused forcing defendant to trial without counsel); United States v. Gougis, 374 F.2d 758 (7th Cir.1967) (appointed counsel had conflict of interest); Releford v. United States, 288 F.2d 298 (9th Cir.1961) (counsel who merely shared office space with unavailable chosen counsel forced to represent defendant).

4. An excellent survey of the case law in the area, and a variety of examples of the frequency with which the continuance issue is raised, is contained in United States v. Uptain, 531 F.2d 1281 (5th Cir.1976):

"The reasons for a continuance which were timely asserted in this case fall into two categories. First, Uptain through his attorney claimed that the interval between arraignment and trial was insufficient to allow proper time to prepare motions, to consult concerning the case, and to properly interview potential witnesses and subpoena them for appearance at trial.

Second, counsel for Uptain asserted at trial that he could no longer represent his client as a result of conflicts of strategy and because of nonpayment for services; because no other counsel was present, withdrawal would have necessitated a continuance.

"None of these justifications for a continuance is new to this court. To the contrary, the cases are so numerous and involve such varying factual contexts and bases for decision that merely cataloging them is a task of significant proportion. We have deemed the following factors highly relevant in assessing claims of inadequate preparation time: the quantum of time available for preparation, the likelihood of prejudice from denial, the accused's role in shortening the effective preparation time, the degree of complexity of the case, and the availability of discovery from the prosecution. We have also explicitly considered the adequacy of the defense actually provided at trial, the skill and experience of the attorney, any pre-appointment or pre-retention experience of the attorney with the accused or the alleged crime, and any representation of the defendant by other attorneys that accrues to his benefit.

"Within this general category of cases, a particularly common claim is that a continuance was necessary to interview and subpoena potential witnesses. The panels of this court that have ruled on such claims have considered the diligence of the defense in interviewing witnesses and procuring their presence, the probability of procuring their testimony within a reasonable time, the specificity with which the defense is able to describe their expected knowledge or testimony, the degree to which such testimony is expected to be favorable to the accused, and the unique or cumulative nature of the testimony. A general rule recently has emerged:

> 'A movant must show that due diligence has been exercised to obtain the attendance of the witness, that substantial favorable testimony would be tendered by the witness, that the witness is available and willing to testify, and that the denial of a continuance would materially prejudice the defendant.'

* * *

"The claim that the general lack of preparation time rendered the denial of a continuance an abuse of discretion must also be rejected. Although there was considerable time pressure on him, [counsel] in fact was able to prepare adequate pre-trial motions and received favorable consideration on the majority of them. Uptain has failed to point out to us what other motions might have been made that could have materially aided his cause, and we are inclined to believe that there are none. Similarly, we are unable to see how more preparation would have significantly changed the course of the trial. The essence of the case against Uptain was the testimony of the co-conspirators. They were effectively cross-examined and their testimony rebutted by Uptain. The jury apparently believed the co-conspirators. Nothing has been suggested to us that would indicate the possibility of a different outcome had a continuance been granted. Accordingly we find that a great number of the factors previously considered significant—likelihood or prejudice, degree of complexity of the case, the adequacy of the defense at trial, and the pre-appointment experience of the attorney with the accused and the crime—coalesce to counsel upholding the district court.

"A different issue is presented by [counsel's] attempt to withdraw from the representation of Uptain at trial. Because no other attorney was present and prepared to carry on, this necessarily would have involved a continuance as well. It too, however, is not an unfamiliar phenomenon to this court. ... In each of [the cases] which involved attempts by the defendant to change attorneys, the court noted that the freedom to have counsel of one's own choosing may not be used for the purposes of delay. ... The courts noted in each case that there was prior opportunity to bring to the court's attention any conflicts between client and counsel and that the timing of the motion gave reason to believe that it might have been imposed for purposes of delay.

"The circumstances of this case depart from these previous cases in two important particulars. First, it is not clear here that conflicts between Uptain and [his attorney] could have been brought out earlier. To the extent that the conflicts were matters of trial strategy only, it may be that they developed only in the few days prior to trial or on the first day of trial itself. Second, as well as the existence of conflict between the two, [counsel] contended that Uptain's check to him had not been honored, thus putting him in uncertainty as to whether he would be paid for his services at trial.

"We rather reluctantly conclude again that these circumstances do not warrant a finding of abuse of discretion. Here again, counsel did not specify to a significant degree the nature of any strategy conflicts which arose, and the fact that the objection was raised only on the third and last day of trial, after repeated attempts to obtain a continuance on other grounds had failed, gave some basis for a belief that the asserted conflict either was fabricated or was not a serious problem. Finally, to the extent that any specific attorney-client conflict was mentioned, the only statement made by [counsel] concerned his association with Uptain's corporation as counsel and investor. If this was the origin of the conflict, then the court properly could have concluded that it should have been discovered and brought to the attention of the court sooner, if indeed the representation of Uptain by [this attorney] should have been undertaken at all. At the least, and regardless of the origin of the conflict, the court had a right to expect [counsel] to have his co-counsel present when he sought to withdraw from the case.

"By the same token, the claim of nonpayment of services did not compel a continuance. In the first place, [counsel] did not claim that he would not eventually be paid, but only that one of Uptain's checks had been dishonored.... The fact that a single check was worthless would not alone justify an indefinite suspension of the trial, particularly with the government's case already complete and the defendant on the stand. The trial judge was entitled to take into account both the opportunity, that counsel did not take advantage of, to obtain earlier payment from Uptain, and the prejudice to Uptain in the eyes of the jury that might result if the attorney who began his direct examination suddenly disappeared. ... We therefore are unable to conclude that the court's refusal to allow withdrawal of counsel at the beginning of the second day of trial, pending arrival of co-counsel, was an abuse of discretion.

"Several lessons to defense lawyers should emerge from this case. The first is that, in cases where there is a substantial basis for a continuance, the attorney should present the claim as early as possible. Second, the attorney should exercise all reasonable diligence to prepare for trial despite the time constraints confronting him. Finally, such claims should be advanced with all the specificity and detail that is feasible under the circumstances. While some of these 'lessons' are rules of law under *Miller* with respect to continuances to interview and subpoena witnesses, they are counsels of wisdom in any continuance situation. Only with detailed information as to counsel's efforts and the legitimate justifications for extra time can the court conclude that the motion is made for reasons other than delay. Only then can it be expected to subordinate the very legitimate needs of both the criminal justice system and the defendant for speedy and economical justice.

"Finally, and without in any way disparaging the trial court, whose actions we today uphold, we must reiterate that a scheduled trial date should never become such an overarching end that it results in the erosion of the defendant's right to a fair trial. If forcing a defendant to an early trial date substantially impairs his ability to effectively present evidence to rebut the prosecution's case or to establish defenses, then pursuit of the goal of expeditiousness is far more detrimental to our common purposes in the criminal justice system than the delay of a few days or weeks that may be sought. The district courts to whom these difficult and inexact judgments are committed have, in the majority of cases, made them with a proper consideration of the rights of defendants to due process of law as well as the demands of judicial economy. Where, as here, it is possible to see how a denial of continuance resulted from a reasonable resolution of the various factors confronting a court, we will uphold its action, even if it may seem somewhat harsh."

5. The Speedy Trial Act raises special problems with respect to continuances. Under 18 U.S.C. § 3161(h)(8)(A), delay resulting from a continuance is excluded from the speedy trial computation if the court finds that the ends of justice served by the continuance outweigh the best interest of the defendant and the public in a speedy trial. A judge may not enter a retroactive continuance for reasons that were not articulated before the time period ran to justify a late trial. United States v. Brenna, 878 F.2d 117 (3d Cir.1989); United States v. Carey, 746 F.2d 228 (4th Cir.1984); United States v. Frey, 735 F.2d 350 (9th Cir.1984). However, traditional continuance motions, such as those based on the need to retain counsel, are properly excluded. United States v. Studnicka, 777 F.2d 652 (11th Cir.1985).

E. REQUEST FOR SEVERANCE

United States v. Emond

United States Court of Appeals, Seventh Circuit, 1991.
935 F.2d 1511.

■ FLAUM, CIRCUIT JUDGE.

* * *

Through the middle 1980s, Edward Emond was the village manager of Streamwood, Illinois, a northwestern suburb of Chicago. Edward used his position for personal enrichment by soliciting bribes from individuals seeking to do business with the village government. In one incident, Edward was approached by two men, Raymond Seifert and Earl Mink, who owned a used-car lot in Streamwood called Easy Auto. After selling their land to a convenience store owner, Seifert and Mink sought to purchase an adjacent unimproved lot owned by the village. The village offered to sell the land at its assessed value, $57,000, but Seifert and Mink thought that was too much to pay. Edward offered to persuade the village board to reduce the price to $37,500, and to throw in tree removal and grading, in exchange for a $10,000 bribe. The proposed sale hit a snag when Village Attorney Jay Crane advised Edward that it would violate an Illinois statute requiring sales of municipal land to be at no less than 80 percent of appraised value. Edward eliminated the problem by having the land reappraised at $43,000, thereby allowing the sale at $37,500 to proceed.

Another of Edward's deals involved John Rock and Patrick Custardo, real-estate developers who were interested in building a retirement community in Streamwood to be called Park Villas. Edward solicited a bribe from the two men, telling them that he needed the money to ensure that the project would be approved by the members of the village board. He also demanded a share of any revenues derived from the project. Rock and Custardo acceded to Edward's request, paying him $5,000.

* * *

In the last of his ventures, Edward broadened his horizons to include another target for graft, the government of Cook County. With the help of Joe Matalone, a county administrator responsible for overseeing logistical preparations for county elections, Edward began to participate in a scheme to profit from the county's need for cars to transport voting equipment repairers between polling stations. The actual supplier of cars the county leased was Econo–Car. Matalone, however, did not deal with Econo–Car directly, but rather arranged to use intermediaries. Econo–Car would send its invoices to these intermediaries, one of which was Cars–R–Us, a shell corporation controlled by Edward. Cars–R–Us, along with other dummy rental companies owned by other participants in the scheme, would then inflate the bills it received from Econo–Car and invoice the county for the inflated charges, pocketing the difference between what the county paid them and what they paid Econo–Car. They shared the overcharges with Matalone.

All these schemes generated income for Edward, but the great majority of this income went unreported on the federal income tax returns he and his wife Maxine filed with the Internal Revenue Service. The Emonds also failed to report income derived from legitimate sources, including real-estate rentals, the sale of a home, and investments.

[A] federal grand jury handed down a 46–count indictment against Edward and Maxine, as well as the people from whom Edward received bribes and the other participants in the scheme to defraud Cook County. [Edward was charged with numerous offenses, including racketeering, extortion and fraud. Maxine was charged only with tax evasion] Most of the people indicted with Edward and Maxine pled guilty and testified against Edward at trial. The only ones that did not were the two owners of Easy Auto, Raymond Seifert and Earl Mink, and the Cook County administrator, Joe Matalone.

Before trial, each of the five defendants moved for a severance. The district court granted Matalone's motion and granted Edward's motion in part, deciding that all charges relating to the Cars–R–Us scheme would be decided separately in a second proceeding involving only Edward and

Matalone. It denied Maxine's severance motion, and she proceeded to trial on the tax charges in the same proceeding in which Edward, Seifert, and Mink were tried on the various charges arising from the Easy Auto scheme, and Edward was tried for his role in the Park Villas scheme. . . .

In the first trial, the jury found Maxine guilty on all the counts of tax evasion with which she was charged. It also found Edward guilty on all charges save one count of attempted extortion.

* * *

SEVERANCE: EDWARD/SEIFERT

The first ground Edward raises on appeal concerns the district court's refusal to grant him a severance so that he and Raymond Seifert, one of the owners of Easy Auto, could be tried separately. According to Edward, Seifert's defense was that Edward coerced him into making the $10,000 bribe by threatening him with retaliation if he did not comply with Edward's demands. This defense, Edward argues, was antagonistic to his defense theory. The government responds that Seifert never fully developed the defense Edward ascribes to him, and that Seifert's efforts to shift the blame to Edward never rose beyond finger-pointing of the kind and degree this Court has held does not warrant a severance.

A district court's ruling on a ... severance motion will be overturned only upon a showing of abuse of discretion. [T]o appeal successfully a motion for severance, a defendant must demonstrate actual prejudice resulting from the denial. In reviewing severance claims based on an assertion that antagonistic defenses were presented at trial, we will reverse a district court only if the defenses conflict to the point of being irreconcilable and mutually exclusive, so that acceptance of one defendant's defense will preclude the acquittal of the other defendant. Because of the strong public interest in having persons jointly indicted tried together hostility and finger pointing during the joint trial ... alone [are] insufficient to justify granting a severance.

We conclude that the district court did not abuse its discretion in declining to sever Edward's trial from Seifert's. We observe first that Seifert never testified at trial, limiting the finger-pointing that occurred to comments made or questions posed by Seifert's trial counsel. When Seifert's lawyer commented during his opening and closing arguments that the real villain in the events surrounding Easy Auto's purchase of the village's lot was Edward, Edward objected, and the trial judge reminded the jury that the statements of counsel were neither legal instructions nor evidence. Similarly, the district court sustained objections made by Edward when Seifert's lawyer attempted to elicit testimony from others from whom Edward solicited bribes to the effect that they felt coerced into paying, and even barred Seifert's lawyer from pursuing this line of questioning in conferences with counsel held before certain witnesses appeared. When Seifert's counsel nevertheless began to question one of these witnesses about his fears, Edward's lawyer objected and the district court sustained his objections.

We agree with the government that Seifert's theory of the case was never fully developed. The various remarks by Seifert's counsel, though evincing a willful disregard for the limitations imposed on his questioning by the district court, failed to prejudice Edward to the extent of denying him his right to a fair trial. Edward supports his claim with no more than a handful of comments in the course of a four-week trial. It is possible that a defense so antagonistic as to require dispensing with the judicial economies joint trials create could be presented solely through the arguments and questions of counsel. In such a case, however, the arguments and questions establishing the antagonistic defense would have to amount to more than the isolated incidents to which Edward has pointed us.

Furthermore, the antagonism between Seifert's defense—to the extent it was developed—and Edward's was not so clear as to preclude a jury from believing the representations of Seifert's counsel that his client was coerced while still acquitting Edward. Edward's defense to the mail fraud charges stemming from the Easy Auto scheme was that in lowering the appraisal for the land he had been acting in the best interest of the village by helping business owners who offered to put an otherwise worthless—and tax exempt—piece of land to a commercial use. See Tr. 1st at 134. In other words, Edward argued that there was no fraudulent scheme furthered by mailings because there was no fraud victim. This theory of the defense was not so irreconcilable with Seifert's extortion theory as to justify a severance: a jury could have believed that Edward coerced Seifert and Mink into greasing his palm while also concluding that the village was not harmed by Edward's conduct.

* * *

Because Edward has shown neither that Seifert's defense was sufficiently developed or sufficiently antagonistic to warrant a severance, we hold that the district court did not abuse its discretion in concluding that none was required.

SEVERANCE (MAXINE & EDWARD/OTHER DEFENDANTS)

Maxine and Edward argue that they were denied a fair trial when the district court denied their motion to sever their trial on the tax counts from the trial of Edward and his codefendants on the counts arising from Edward's misuse of his official position. They argue that they were swamped by spillover from the evidence of wrongdoing introduced against Edward, Seifert, and Mink, in the Easy Auto, Park Villas, and Village Attorneys schemes. It is undisputed that Maxine did not participate in these events, and that the income the couple derived from Edward's misdeeds generated only a portion of the unreported income alleged in the tax counts. . . . A defendant is entitled to severance when the evidence against one defendant cannot be compartmentalized and the jury is likely to consider it to the prejudice of a defendant against whom it is not properly directed. Cases in which the evidence against one defendant is far more damaging than the evidence against the moving party make the process of individually assessing the weight of the evidence as to each defendant particularly difficult, increasing the risk that "the spillover may jeopardize one defendant's right to a fair trial."

* * *

[W]e [have previously] held that the joinder of tax offenses with other counts alleging illegal activity that was the source of unreported income charged in the tax counts was proper, even where the non-tax offenses were not the only source of unreported income. [J]oinder of a tax claim to another charge, when the underlying charge generated only a portion of the unreported income, does not require *automatic* reversal.

* * *

[Edward] was charged with a variety of non-tax offenses which generated income. His failure to report this income on his federal returns formed in part the basis for his convictions on the tax counts. [While] such joinder does not automatically require reversal, ... one factor to be examined was the strength of the government's case against the defendant on the non-tax counts. This factor militates against Edward's severance argument: the evidence against him on the non-tax counts was compelling. The rule of joinder in cases involving both income-generating crimes and tax evasion based on the failure to report income derived from these crimes and other income must be employed with care.... There may be cases in which income derived from the acts charged in the non-tax counts plays only a very small part in the tax charges, or where the evidence presented on the tax counts is insignificant compared to the evidence presented on the non-tax charges. In these cases, a separate trial on the tax charges may well be the most appropriate accommodation between the societal interest in judicial economy and the defendant's right to a trial in which jurors can individually assess the evidence against him on each of the charges in the indictment. Edward has not persuaded us, however, that this is such a case.

Maxine's argument that she should have been tried separately on the tax counts presents a more difficult question. [U]nlike her husband Edward, she was not named in the non-tax counts and there was no evidence introduced at trial that she played any part in the acts alleged in these counts and proven at trial. Indeed, for the great majority of the first trial her name came up only in a drumbeat of limiting instructions given during the testimony of the various prosecution witnesses who were questioned concerning their knowledge of the acts alleged in the non-tax charges against Edward Seifert, and Mink. We thus share defendants' view that the joinder of Maxine, her husband, and the other co-defendants, and the tax evasion, RICO, [extortion] and other charges, goes beyond what we allowed in [previous cases]. This case thus requires us to examine the scope of the joinder rule we adopted in that case.

We believe that in denying Maxine's motion to sever, the district court approached the outer limits of its discretion in deciding severance issues. Maxine was a bit player in a trial in which her husband and his codefendants were charged with committing a variety of offenses more serious than the tax charges lodged against her, including, as to her husband, violations of both RICO and the Hobbs Act. For the great majority of a lengthy trial she and her lawyer were spectators, watching as a parade of witnesses testified concerning the various schemes in which her husband, Seifert, and Mink were charged. We are sensitive to the concern ... that the numerous limiting instructions the district court gave to remind the jury not to consider certain testimony in determining Maxine's guilt or innocence may have lost their effect through sheer repetition, or may even have piqued the jury's curiosity as to Maxine's role in her husband's various misdeeds. Put simply, not granting Maxine's severance motion in this case tested the ability of jurors not to tar Maxine with the broad brush applied to her husband and his codefendants.

Nevertheless, we affirm Maxine's conviction despite our view that justice would have been better served by trying her on the tax counts (either alone or with her husband) in a separate proceeding. Because Maxine waived her Rule 8 objection to her joinder with Edward, Seifert, and Mink in the indictment,* she is limited to asserting a challenge under Rule 14 and must show that the joinder caused her prejudice. We believe that the risk of prejudice caused by jury confusion in this case does not require a reversal in view of the strength of the evidence against Maxine on the tax counts, the small number of codefendants with whom she was tried, and the discrete nature of the testimony against her and her husband on the tax charges, nearly all of which was presented over three consecutive days out of the twenty days of trial. We note that the jury demonstrated an ability to compartmentalize the evidence presented in the first trial when it acquitted Edward on one count of attempted extortion while finding him guilty on the other charges. Because we presume that this jury was also able to compartmentalize the evidence against Maxine, we affirm her convictions despite our discomfort with the severance ruling that allowed her joint trial.

* * *

Affirmed.

NOTES

1. In United States v. Lane, 474 U.S. 438, 106 S.Ct. 725 (1986), a father and son were jointly charged in an arson for profit scheme were making false insurance claims via the mails in connection with three fires. The father alone was charged in connection with a restaurant fire, both were charged in connection with a duplex fire and both were charged with conspiracy for a third fire. At trial, the jury was instructed to consider the evidence with respect to the restaurant fire only against the father. In a 5–4 decision, the Supreme Court, through Chief Justice Burger, held that the harmless error rule applied to misjoinder situations under Fed.R.Civ.P. 8:

> "In common with other courts, the Court has long recognized that joint trials 'conserve state funds, diminish inconvenience to witnesses and public authorities, and avoid delays in bringing those accused of crime to trial.' Rule 8 accommodates these interests while protecting against prejudicial joinder. But we do not read Rule 8 to mean that prejudice results *whenever* its requirements have not been satisfied.

* Fed.R.Crim.Pro. 8 does not allow joinder of different persons related only by fact of having committed similar offenses.

"Under Rule 52(a), the harmless-error rule focuses on whether the error 'affect[ed] substantial rights.' In Kotteakos [v. United States, 328 U.S. 750, 765, 66 S.Ct. 1239, 1248 (1946)], the Court construed a harmless-error statute with similar language, and observed:

> 'The inquiry cannot be merely whether there was enough to support the result, apart from the phase affected by the error. It is rather, even so, whether the error itself had substantial influence. If so, or if one is left in grave doubt, the conviction cannot stand.'

"Invoking the Kotteakos test, we hold that an error involving misjoinder 'affects substantial rights' and requires reversal only if the misjoinder results in actual prejudice because it 'had substantial and injurious effect or influence in determining the jury's verdict.' Only by so holding can we bring Rules 8 and 52(a) 'into substantial harmony, not into square conflict.'

"Of course, 'we are not required to review records to evaluate a harmless-error claim, and do so sparingly, [but] we plainly have the authority to do so.'

"In the face of overwhelming evidence of guilt shown here, we are satisfied that the claimed error was harmless. When evidence on misjoined Count 1 was introduced, the District Court provided a proper limiting instruction, and in the final charge repeated that instruction and admonished the jury to consider each count and defendant separately. Moreover, the same evidence on Count 1 would likely have been admissible on joint retrial of Counts 2 through 6 to show James Lane's intent under Federal Rule of Evidence 404(b). Any error therefore failed to have any 'substantial influence' on the verdict."

In dissent, Justice Stevens stated:

"In my view, harmless-error analysis is inappropriate in at least three situations: (1) when it is clear that a statute or Rule was not intended to be subject to such a rule; (2) when an independent value besides reliability of the outcome suggests that such analysis is inappropriate; and (3) when the harmlessness of an error cannot be measured with precision. In my view, misjoinder clearly falls into the first category. It also has elements of the second and third. Misjoinder implicates the independent value of individual responsibility and our deep abhorrence of the notion of 'guilt by association.' Our criminal justice system has expanded considerably in its tolerance of multiple joinders and massive conspiracy trials. The rule against misjoinder remains, however, as an ultimate safeguard of our cherished principle that one is tried for one's own deeds, and not for another's. The harmfulness of misjoinder is also the type of error that has consequences that are difficult to measure with precision. These concerns may or may not outweigh the societal interests that motivate the Court today, but they are surely strong enough to demonstrate that the draftsmen of the Federal Rules acted responsibly.... The misjoinder rule that they crafted is clear, and should be respected. Misjoinder affects 'substantial rights,' and should lead to reversal."

Harmless error is now a standard argument in appeals based on improper joinder. See, e.g., United States v. Randazzo, 80 F.3d 623 (1st Cir.1996); United States v. Weaver, 905 F.2d 1466 (11th Cir.1990); United States v. Watson, 866 F.2d 381 (11th Cir.1989).

2. "Rule 8(a), on joinder of offenses, applies only to a prosecution of a single defendant. If more than one defendant is involved, Rule 8(b) states the test for joinder." I C. Wright, Federal Practice and Procedure, § 143, at 479 (2d ed. 1982). Provisions comparable to, or specifically adopting, the Federal Rules have been enacted in a number of states. (e.g. Alaska R.Crim.P. 8; Del.R.Crim.P. 8; Ill.Rev. Stat. ch. 38, § 111–4; Ky.R.Crim.P. 6.20; Md.R.P. 716).

3. Rule 8(a) permits the joinder of multiple offenses against an individual defendant if they are based on the same act or transaction, parts of a common scheme or plan or of the same or similar character. See Decker, Joinder and Severance in Federal Criminal Cases: An Examination of Judicial Interpretations of the Federal Rules, 53 N.Dame.L.Rev. 147 (1977). State courts have adopted similar standards. See Montes v. State, 669 P.2d 961 (Alaska App.1983); Ostrowski v. State, 665 P.2d 471 (Wyo.1983).

4. Generally, the same transaction and common scheme standards are broadly applied. See United States v. Kaplan, 895 F.2d 618 (9th Cir.1990) (mail fraud and distribution of controlled substances by doctor); United States v. Whitworth, 856 F.2d 1268 (9th Cir.1988) (tax evasion and espionage); United States v. Valentine, 706 F.2d 282 (10th Cir.1983) (possession of weapons and heroin); Commonwealth v. Ellis, 12 Mass.App.Ct. 612, 427 N.E.2d 1179 (1981) (extortion and drug possession).

The "same or similar character" test is not as easy to apply. Cases involving like crimes or similar modus operandi suffice to support joinder. See United States v. Burgess, 791 F.2d 676 (9th Cir.1986) (felon in possession of firearm and drug sale); United States v. Cartwright, 632 F.2d 1290 (5th Cir.1980) (misapplication of funds and false statements both involve federally insured lending institution); State v. Abel, 104 Idaho 865, 664 P.2d 772 (1983) (assault of two women five blocks apart within 45 minutes). However, the dividing line for offenses that are not of a similar character, except when divided by time, is difficult to draw. See United States v. Halper, 590 F.2d 422 (2d Cir.1978) (medicaid fraud and tax evasion improper joinder); United States v. Graci, 504 F.2d 411 (3d Cir.1974) (sale of stolen drugs and delivery of different drugs two years later improper joinder); United States v. Quinn, 365 F.2d 256 (7th Cir.1966) (savings and loan officer charged with offenses involving two independent fraudulent transactions between financial institution and companies he personally controlled created situation in which "the most optimistic seer would hesitate to endanger his reputation by claiming that the jury could separate the proof relevant to different counts").

In United States v. Jawara, 462 F.3d 1173 (9th Cir. 2006), the court was uncomfortable with an indictment charging defendant with creating fraudulent immigration documents and conspiracy to commit marriage fraud and said the "similar character" inquiry should be decided by reference to a variety of factors, including the elements of each offense, the temporal proximity of the acts, the extent of evidentiary overlap, the physical location of the offenses, the manner in which they were committed and the identity of the victims. See also State v. Ross, 732 N.W.2d 274 (Minn. 2007) (Court refused to adopt more liberal federal standards on permissive joinder and reiterated its traditional rule that joined offenses must be part of a single behavioral incident).

5. It has been contended that it is unfair to try a defendant on a substantive count and a grand jury perjury count arising out of the defendant's testimony during the course of the investigation which led to the substantive count. What arguments support this contention? See United States v. Pacente, 503 F.2d 543 (7th Cir.1974) (en banc), which rejected the contention, overturning a panel opinion which had accepted the theory. See Comment, Joinder of Substantive Offenses and Perjury in One Indictment, 66 J.Crim.L. & C. 44 (1975).

6. Fed.R.Crim.P. 8(b) is applicable to the joinder of defendants when the alleged offenses arise out of the same series of transactions: United States v. Helms, 897 F.2d 1293 (5th Cir.1990). The "series of transactions" test does not mean that factually unrelated charges against some defendants can be joined for trial because all of the defendants are charged with one common offense or joined in a common count. See United States v. Hatcher, 680 F.2d 438 (6th Cir.1982) (improper to join one defendant charged with heroin sale with another defendant charged with same heroin offense and unrelated cocaine offense); United States v. Nettles, 570 F.2d 547 (5th Cir.1978) (three defendants charged with operating three separate gambling establishments and bribing police for protection against raids); United States v. Eagleston, 417 F.2d 11, 14 (10th Cir.1969) (joinder of two defendants in two common counts does not justify joinder of unrelated count against one codefendant); Chubet v. United States, 414 F.2d 1018, 1019 (8th Cir.1969) (one defendant common to six counts does not justify joinder of unrelated counts against other defendants). Nor will 8(b) be satisfied by joining defendants who commit similar but unrelated crimes. McElroy v. United States, 164 U.S. 76, 81, 17 S.Ct. 31, 35 (1896); Ingram v. United States, 272 F.2d 567 (4th Cir.1959). Thus, while counts of "the same or similar character" may be joined against a single defendant under Rule 8(a), the more restrictive language of Rule 8(b) demands that each count arise out of the "same series of acts or transactions constituting an offense or offenses."

On appeal, the reviewability of a misjoinder claim is limited to an examination of the indictment on its face. The trial evidence is not considered because it was unavailable to the trial judge in ruling on the motion prior to trial. United States v. Morales, 868 F.2d 1562 (11th Cir.1989).

7. Relief from prejudicial joinder is discretionary with the court under Fed. R.Civ.P. 14. Based upon the principles of judicial economy, efficiency and speed and the public interest in avoiding multiple trials, it has become axiomatic that defendants jointly indicted should be tried together except for the most compelling reasons. United States v. Kane, 887 F.2d 568 (5th Cir.1989); United States v. Wirsing, 719 F.2d 859 (6th Cir.1983). This is particularly true where a conspiracy is alleged; and, therefore, an exceptionally strong demonstration of likely prejudice is a prerequisite for severance. United States v. Davis, 809 F.2d 1194 (6th Cir.1987).

Thus a severance will be granted for only the most cogent reasons; the moving party must show prejudice, that he will be unable to obtain a fair trial without severance, not merely that a separate trial will offer a better chance of acquittal. United States v. Kane, 887 F.2d 568 (5th Cir.1989); see United States v. Bostic, 713 F.2d 401 (8th Cir.1983) (prejudice must be "real" and "clear"). The decision as to whether a joint trial will deprive a defendant of the right to a fair trial is resolved by determining whether it is within the jury's capacity to follow the trial judge's instructions to limit and separate the evidence against each defendant. The determination of severance motions rests exclusively "within the sound discretion of the trial judge. . . ." Opper v. United States, 348 U.S. 84, 95, 75 S.Ct. 158, 165 (1954).

8. In light of these considerations, requests for severance are usually denied in the absence of a strong showing of prejudice. See United States v. Perez–Garcia, 904 F.2d 1534 (11th Cir.1990) (sole defense of one defendant must be the guilt of the other); United States v. Veteto, 701 F.2d 136 (11th Cir.1983) (one defendant pro se, others represented by counsel); United States v. Walker, 720 F.2d 1527 (11th Cir.1983) (codefendant has criminal record). But see Williams v. United States, 884 A.2d 587 (D. C. App. 2005) (reversal when one codefendant confirmed that, in a separate trial, he would testify that he never saw defendant in possession of a gun found under the seat of a car in which they were riding but the trial court denied a severance on the ground that too many contingencies attached to the proposed testimony such as the codefendant being tried first and acquitted);

9. Occasionally federal prosecutors have obtained massive indictments jointly charging twenty or more defendants, and alleging hundreds of criminal acts. Management of such mega-trials is difficult. A single case may take over a year's time. Some defendants may be mentioned in the evidence pertaining to only one or a few of the counts in the indictment. Nevertheless, reviewing courts have upheld the denial of severance in such case. See, e.g., United States v. Casamento, 887 F.2d 1141 (2d Cir.1989) (twenty-one defendants jointly tried over seventeen-month period). In dictum the *Casamento* court discussed the problems of such lengthy and complex trials. The court stated:

> In those cases where the judge determines that the time for presentation of the prosecution's case will exceed four months, the judge should oblige the prosecutor to present a reasoned basis to support a conclusion that a joint trial of all the defendants is more consistent with the fair administration of justice than some manageable division of the case into separate trials for groups of defendants. In determining whether the prosecutor has made an adequate showing, the judge should weigh the interests of the prosecution, the defendants, the jurors, the court, and the public. Again, we do not contemplate a contested hearing nor precise findings on this subject. A submission by the prosecutor, a response by the defendants seeking a severance, and a conclusion by the judge will suffice. The judge should give particular attention to the feasibility of conducting separate trials for any one or more defendants as to whom a separate trial would be relatively brief, especially if such defendants are willing to stipulate, for purposes of a separate trial, to facts concerning the activities of other defendants who remain to be tried in the main trial. Such separate trials, if ordered, may, in the judge's discretion, be assigned for simultaneous trial before other judges.
>
> In considering the advisability of separate brief trials for one or more defendants, the judge should explore with the prosecutor whether the interests of justice would be adequately served by limiting the prosecution of such defendants to charges that can be proven expeditiously and that, in the event of conviction, carry exposure to adequate maximum penalties.... Even in the event that the aggregate time for separate trials would not be less than the time for a joint trial of all defendants, there are significant advantages to be achieved. The lives of each group of jurors would be imposed upon for a shorter time, there would be a smaller group of defense counsel in each trial with a consequent reduction in trial disputes, the trial judge would have a more manageable task, and the jurors' ability to focus on individual defendants would be enhanced. While the prosecution's estimate that separate trials will each require all of the evidence presented at a joint trial is often not borne out when severances occur, we note that in this case there is a striking example of an instance when a contrary estimate was made. One of the original co-defendants herein was Giuseppi Baldinucci. Instead of enduring a seventeen-month trial, he was severed at the instance of the government and brought to trial on narrower charges. He was convicted after a trial lasting just seven days.

10. In some instances, however, the nature of the separate defenses of codefendants compels a severance. See United States v. Gonzalez, 804 F.2d 691 (11th Cir.1986); United States v. Romanello, 726 F.2d 173 (5th Cir.1984); United States v. Winter, 663 F.2d 1120 (1st Cir.1981); United States v. Crawford, 581 F.2d 489 (5th Cir.1978).

11. The severance issue is often linked to an evidentiary issue. If evidence of crime *A* would be admissible in the trial of crime *B* under an exception to the general prohibition against "other crime" evidence (e.g., to show motive, intent, common scheme, *modus operandi*, etc.), the reason for holding separate trials is diminished. Conversely, if evidence of crime *A* would be inadmissible in the trial of crime *B* if that case were tried separately, then the argument for severance is stronger. See United States v. Davidson, 936 F.2d 856 (6th Cir.1991) (reversal due to failure to sever tax counts against co-defendant who was tried in absentia); United States v. Foutz, 540 F.2d 733 (4th Cir.1976) (good demonstration of the interrelationship of the severance issue and the "other crime" evidence issue).

12. Sometimes a defendant asserts that he wishes to testify as to one or more counts and to exercise his right to not testify as to the remaining count or counts. He contends that he cannot do this in a joint trial without calling attention to his silence on the latter charges. Is this argument sufficient to merit severance? See United States v. Palomino, 877 F.2d 835 (10th Cir.1989); United States v. Valentine, 706 F.2d 282 (10th Cir.1983).

13. When one defendant confesses, can he be jointly tried with a non-confessing codefendant? See Bruton v. United States, Ch. 19, Section B, and the notes following it. In some instances, in order to circumvent the *Bruton* problem, trial judges have empanelled two juries. The use of dual juries has been upheld uniformly by the federal courts. See United States v. Lewis, 716 F.2d 16 (D.C.Cir.1983); United States v. Hayes, 676 F.2d 1359 (11th Cir.1982); United States v. Rimar, 558 F.2d 1271 (6th Cir.1977). State courts, although more critical of the dual jury procedure, have upheld their use. See State v. Corsi, 86 N.J. 172, 430 A.2d 210 (1981) (the multiple jury procedure "can involve substantial risks of prejudice to a defendant's right to a fair trial. ... [T]here are too many opportunities for reversible error to take place. We do not recommend it. If it is to be used at all, it should be used in relatively uncomplicated situations"); Scarborough v. State, 50 Md.App. 276, 437 A.2d 672 (1981) ("The multiple jury system ... is precarious because all the risks inherent in the traditional jury system become twofold; as a result, courts which have sanctioned its use have done so hesitantly.") The inquiry in each case was whether the defendant could point to evidence indicating specific prejudice stemming from the dual jury procedure. In the absence of such evidence, courts have let stand the convictions of dual juries. United States v. Lewis, 716 F.2d 16 (D.C.Cir.1983).

14. A defendant, named in more than one indictment, who wants to avoid the expense, aggravation and delay involved in separate proceedings may move to consolidate the indictments for trial. See Fed.R.Crim.P. 13. The operative rules regarding the consolidation are the same concepts governing original joinder. If the separate charges could have been joined in the first instance, the court, in its discretion, may consolidate them for trial. United States v. Cannington, 729 F.2d 702 (11th Cir.1984); State v. Mitter, 168 W.Va. 531, 285 S.E.2d 376 (1981). To avoid forum shopping and venue problems, consolidation is not available to indictments brought in separate jurisdictions.

F. REQUEST FOR CHANGE OF PLACE OF TRIAL

1. THE PROBLEMS OF INNATE COMMUNITY PREJUDICE AND PREJUDICIAL NEWS MEDIA PUBLICITY

Maine v. Superior Court

Supreme Court of California, 1968.
68 Cal.2d 375, 66 Cal.Rptr. 724, 438 P.2d 372.

■ MOSK, JUSTICE.

Petitioners, Leonard E. Maine and Thomas E. Braun, seek writs of mandate directed to the Superior Court of the County of Mendocino. By grand jury indictment they are each accused of murder, two counts of kidnaping, forcible rape, and assault with intent to commit murder.

* * *

The People contend that petitioners Maine and Braun have an adequate remedy at law in that the trial court denied their motion for a change of venue without prejudice to its renewal "if the facts should so warrant." It has long been the practice, sanctioned in the decisions of this court to permit the trial court to defer its final ruling on a motion for a change of venue until the jury is empaneled. The trial court can thereby take into consideration any unanticipated difficulties encountered during *voir dire* examination of prospective jurors.

Experience shows, however, that trial courts are often reluctant to order a venue change after a jury has been empaneled. Defense counsel, moreover, is placed in an unnecessarily awkward position: unless he exhausts all his peremptory challenges he cannot claim on appeal, in the absence of a specific showing of prejudice, that the jury was not impartial. Yet, convinced that he must go to trial because his motion for a venue change was at first denied and in all likelihood will not ultimately prevail, he may fail to use every peremptory challenge sensing that the jurors he has examined may be comparatively less biased than others who might be seated were his peremptory challenges exhausted. In an antagonistic atmosphere "there will remain the problem of obtaining accurate answers on *voir dire*—is the juror consciously or subconsciously harboring prejudice against the accused resulting from widespread news coverage in the community." We can only conclude that the naked right to renew the motion for change of venue is not an adequate remedy at law to require denial of a mandamus petition.

Although we have reversed judgments of conviction on but four occasions [out of 66 cases in which the issue was raised] many cases have presented serious constitutional issues arising out of prejudicial newspaper publicity which either caused or reflected widespread hostility to a defendant in the community. ... In such cases the offenses committed were often bestial and heinous, and the discovery of the crimes as well as the unfolding of subsequent events inevitably received abundant attention in the communications media. ... In many cases that are the focus of unusual public attention, the effect of prejudicial pretrial disclosures or widespread community antagonism can be substantially overcome by a change of venue. ...

After long study the American Bar Association has tendered proposals for judicial consideration which should contribute toward freeing criminal trials from the taint of partiality.

* * *

Section 3.2(c), entitled "Standards for granting the motion," provides: "A motion for change of venue or continuance shall be granted whenever it is determined that because of the dissemination of potentially prejudicial material, there is a reasonable** likelihood that in the absence of such relief, a fair trial cannot be had. This determination may be based on such evidence as qualified public opinion surveys or opinion testimony offered by individuals, or on the court's own evaluation of the nature, frequency, and timing of the material involved. A showing of actual prejudice shall not be required."

* * *

In the case at bench petitioners are accused of crimes of the gravest consequence. They are strangers to Ukiah, a small community where they have been held for trial. On the other hand, the two victims, a popular teen-age couple from respected families in the area, were assaulted under circumstances that would compel any community's shock and indignation. Since the case has not progressed beyond the pretrial stage it would be inappropriate for us to comment on the evidence that may unfold at the trial. We confine our discussion to a few uncontradicted illustrations which demonstrate a reasonable likelihood that petitioners cannot receive a fair trial in Mendocino County.

One of the victims, the girl, was discovered on a public road nearly unconscious with bullet wounds about her neck and head. Her condition was critical and several complicated operations were performed to save her life. Local citizens immediately organized a fund to help the girl's parents defray the medical expenses, and the Ukiah Daily Journal, the local newspaper, urged every citizen to contribute. It is no small measure of the community's laudable warmth and generosity that a substantial sum was quickly raised, mostly in modest contributions. We do not hold it to be an invariable rule that sympathy for a victim demonstrates antipathy to the alleged perpetrators of an offense. But such pervasive civic involvement in the fate of a victim, particularly when the events all transpire in a relatively small community, [Ukiah (9,900); Mendocino County (51,200)] is a strong indication that the venue should be changed.

We recognize that from the outset of the investigation the local law enforcement authorities scrupulously avoided divulging any details of the crime. Both the Ukiah Daily Journal and the Santa Rosa Press Democrat, which extensively reported the case to residents of Mendocino County and vicinity, noted that the sheriff and district attorney were "extremely close-mouthed on any details." Their commendable efforts in this regard, however, were frustrated by other authorities who talked freely with representatives of the press and other news media about the crime. Principally at fault appears to be an official of the State of Washington, where petitioners are also charged with murder, who revealed that one of the petitioners had confessed and placed full responsibility on the other for the crimes. This disclosure received substantial attention in the local newspaper, and it is undoubted that the existence of a confession is now common knowledge in the community. The admissibility of the confession into evidence has not been tested in a judicial hearing, however and its premature release must be regarded as potentially prejudicial to petitioners. When such a disclosure

** [Ed.Note. In 1978 the ABA changed the word "reasonable" to the word "substantial", ABA Standards for Criminal Justice, 8–3.3 (2nd Ed.1978).]

occurs in a small community, the only effective remedy, if the defense so requests, is to change the venue. Indeed, failure to seek a change of venue may suggest to a reviewing court on appeal that no prejudice was suffered by the defendant.

Finally, this case has to some extent become involved in county politics. The district attorney disqualified Judge Winslow, an experienced trial judge, whom he is opposing on the June 1968 election ballot. The People do not deny that political factors might have influenced the district attorney's decision, but contend that since a judge from outside the county has now been assigned to hear the case, petitioners' right to a fair trial will not be infringed. The People also note that counsel for one of the petitioners has announced his candidacy for the same judgeship, but assert their belief that the assigned trial judge can exercise effective control over both the district attorney and the defense counsel. Under these circumstances, nevertheless, we harbor a gnawing fear that the campaign competition between two election adversaries might inadvertently intrude during the course of a proceeding in which they are also trial adversaries. Political factors have no place in a criminal proceeding, and when they are likely to appear, as here, they constitute an independent reason for a venue change.

* * *

The People insist that sufficient time has now elapsed since the date of petitioners' arrest that any prejudice they might have suffered has been dissipated. Under the circumstances of the case at bench this position is not persuasive. While a lengthy continuance might sufficiently protect the accused in some cases, it does not do so here. Delays may be an efficacious antidote to publicity in medium-size and large cities, but in small communities, where a major crime become embedded in the public consciousness, their effectiveness is greatly diminished. . . .

We do not assert categorically that each individual circumstance here, isolated and alone, would compel a change of venue. It may do so, or may not, depending upon the extent of the hostility engendered toward a defendant, and to some extent upon the sophistication of the community. Generally no single indicium is available as a barometer of the public mind.

We hold that where, as here, the defendants are friendless in the community, the victims prominent, the occurrence of the crime probably fortuitous as to locale, community-wide interest and generosity are expressed on behalf of the victim, newspaper publicity includes accounts of a purported confession, and two opposing counsel are also election opponents, a change of venue is clearly necessary to assure a fair trial to the defendants.

It is now incumbent upon the parties to suggest a convenient site for a fair trial. In a case of this nature it would probably be prudent to transfer the cause to a metropolitan area where comparatively little difficulty will be encountered in empaneling a jury free from any kind of prejudgment.

NOTES

1. There are few reported cases other than Maine v. Superior Court which deal strictly with the pre-trial showing required to secure a change of place of trial.

Ordinarily, if the motion is allowed, the issue is not reviewed on appeal. If the motion is denied, then trial proceeds and on review, the appeal court will consider not only the pre-trial showing but the actual voir dire of the jury to determine whether the accused was prejudiced. In a situation much like *Maine*, the court issued another mandate to require a change of place of trial. Frazier v. Superior Court, 5 Cal.3d 287, 95 Cal.Rptr. 798, 486 P.2d 694 (1971). Frazier was accused of the murder of a local physician, his wife, secretary and two small sons. The accused was generally described as a "hippie" and the court took notice of local antipathy toward hippies. The court praised the law enforcement officers for exceptional restraint in releasing news but held that "No amount of self-restraint or judicial caution ... could change ... the case. This was not an 'ordinary' homicide ... as all too often occurs in ... a robbery ... or ... family dispute; we entertain no doubt the defendants in these cases can receive unbiased trials in Santa Cruz County. Rather we deal here with an alienated member of an unpopular subculture accused of a bizarre and senseless mass murder of prominent citizens of a small community." Accord, Williams v. Superior Court, 34 Cal.3d 584, 194 Cal.Rptr. 492, 668 P.2d 799 (1983).

Where does "an alienated member of an unpopular subculture accused of a bizarre and senseless mass murder" get a fair trial? What if hostile public sentiment and wide publicity extend throughout an entire state?

The court in People v. Speck, 41 Ill.2d 177, 242 N.E.2d 208 (1968), was faced with such a problem and so was the court in State v. Thompson, 273 Minn. 1, 139 N.W.2d 490 (1966). Thompson was a lawyer, "quite successful ... in the fields of personal injury, domestic relations and criminal law" who also did some teaching in law school. He hired men to kill his wife, which they did in a particularly brutal way. The court held:

> "On an application by defendant for mandamus, we required a change of venue. In so doing, we noted:
>
> > '... Probably no case in the memory of anyone in this locality has aroused so much interest and so much discussion as this one. Over a period of several months hardly a day has elapsed when something has been said or written in a news medium of one kind or another.'
>
> "Ordinarily a defendant on motion for change of venue does not have a right to select a particular county for his trial, but it is left to the trial court to choose a county in which a fair trial can be obtained. In this case, however, defendant was granted a change to Hennepin County at his request. It cannot be denied that the case was given an unusual amount of publicity, much of which could better have been omitted. The day may come when in this country we find a way to strike a fair balance between the constitutional guaranty of a free press and the constitutional right to a fair trial. It seems that we have not yet found a solution to that problem.
>
> "It is doubtful in this case that a more fair trial could have been obtained elsewhere in this state. The same news coverage extended throughout the state as in Ramsey and Hennepin Counties. The case was one of public interest everywhere. We do not have a record of the voir dire examination of the jurors but are willing to accept counsel's statement that of some 112 jurors examined 67 expressed actual bias. That does not mean, however, that the 12 accepted were also biased. On the record before us we cannot say he was denied a fair trial, nor are we convinced that a more fair trial could have been obtained elsewhere in the state. Criminal cases must be tried somewhere and, having gone as far as we did in this case in permitting the defendant to choose his own county, we do not know what more we could have done."

2. In the case of United States v. Bakker, 925 F.2d 728 (4th Cir.1991) the Court rejected a claim of prejudicial publicity in the trial of a "well-known televangelist." It noted:

> After 1987, the level of publicity about Bakker had subsided. In fact, at the hearing, he could point to only a handful of instances in 1989 where media coverage could arguably be characterized as inflammatory. And of these few items, most occurred in January of 1989, fully seven months before trial was to begin. Under these conditions, we believe the court properly concluded that the passage of time diminished the impact of publicity upon a jury pool in the court's district.
>
> In deciding whether to presume prejudice based on pre-trial publicity, a court can consider the source of that publicity. The source of much of the publicity in this case was Bakker himself who, both before and after his indictment, engaged in a calculated media campaign to deny any wrongdoing and regain control of the PTL, following his resignation in March 1987. For example, Bakker appeared on a May 1987 *Nightline* interview during which he emphasized his desire to return to his ministry. This national program attracted an audience of approximately thirteen million viewers, its largest audience to that time. After Bakker's indictment, he appeared on the nationally syndicated *Sally Jesse Raphael Show*, and appeared on his own television show asking for money for his restructured television ministry. While Bakker had every right to protest his innocence, he must recognize that his pre-trial acts and statements invited media attention. In our view, a defendant should not be allowed to manipulate the criminal justice system by generating publicity and then using the same publicity to support his claim that the media attention surrounding his case created a presumption of prejudice.

3. What happens when one federal defendant wishes a change of venue from the district where the offense was allegedly committed, while a codefendant insists upon his or her Sixth Amendment right to be tried in that district? United States v. Stratton, 649 F.2d 1066 (5th Cir.1981), held that judicial economy arising from a joint trial does not permit denial of the co-defendant's Sixth Amendment venue right.

4. Change of place of trial has been sought because of perceived community pressure on jurors to convict. Some persons are accused of crimes so heinous and are so clearly believed to be guilty, that a juror would be reluctant to vote acquittal for fear of retaliation or ostracism by the community. A current variant upon this is the fear that acquittal will lead to riots in the jurors' community or in another community. See State v. Lozano, 616 So.2d 73 (Fla.App.1993) (vacating order of transfer designed to increase African–Americans in jury pool and decrease Hispanics).

5. Consider the comments of the trial judge in United States v. McVeigh, 955 F.Supp. 1281 (D.Colo.1997) in response to a motion to delay trial or change venue after published accounts that defendant had substantially incriminated himself in interviews with defense counsel:

> "Past experience with jurors and a general awareness of public attitudes about pretrial publicity in criminal cases strongly suggest that these stories have had neither the wide exposure nor general acceptance that the defendant's lawyers presume. Almost two years have passed since the destruction of the Murrah Building in Oklahoma City. Those who have sought to satisfy the public interest in that event and its aftermath have produced prodigious amounts of material addressing every angle of the story. The investigative efforts of law enforcement agencies have been

described, analyzed and criticized. Independent investigations have been undertaken with varying conclusions announced. Court proceedings have been extensively reported, analyzed and discussed. In sum, every possible aspect of this story has been explored in media coverage. More can be expected, with an increasing slant toward the sensational as the communicators compete for public attention before trial."

* * *

"A salient virtue of a free people in an open society is a healthy skepticism about what they are told. We have a strong tradition of civic responsibility and the great majority of our citizens consistently display a respect for fair play in all aspects of their lives.... I have full confidence that a fair minded jury can and will return a just verdict based on the law and evidence presented to them."

Mu'Min v. Virginia

Supreme Court of the United States, 1991.
500 U.S. 415, 111 S.Ct. 1899.

[This opinion concerning voir dire in high-publicity cases appears at Casebook p. 1223.]

NOTES

1. In many instances prospective jurors may not have heard of a particular case but may have been exposed to media accounts creating an unfavorable climate for a particular type of defendant, such as an alleged gang member, or for a defendant charged with a particular type of offense, such as narcotics selling or child-abuse. Sometimes the trial judge's conduct may accentuate the problem. The accused drug offenders in United States v. Thomas, 757 F.2d 1359 (2d Cir.1985), were tried by a jury whose names, addresses, and places of employment were kept secret. How would you like to be tried before such a jury? The *Thomas* court approved the practice on the particular facts of that case.

2. The problems of prejudicial publicity do not abate with jury selection. With respect to the trial judge's function when claims of mid-trial publicity arise, see Margoles v. United States, 407 F.2d 727 (7th Cir.), cert. denied 396 U.S. 833, 90 S.Ct. 89 (1969). That substantial deference will be paid a trial judge's findings with respect to the ability to proceed in light of mid-trial publicity is evidenced by United States v. Persico, 425 F.2d 1375 (2d Cir.1970). There, the government called noted crime syndicate informant Joseph Valachi as a surprise witness. The trial judge found that, notwithstanding the literal flood of publicity accompanying Valachi's appearance, a mistrial was unwarranted. His decision was affirmed.

"The publicity to which the jurors were exposed did not deal with the issues of appellants' guilt, as in Sheppard v. Maxwell, 384 U.S. 333, 86 S.Ct. 1507 (1966), and Rideau v. Louisiana, 373 U.S. 723, 83 S.Ct. 1417 (1963), but involved background information. Most of the material, save the reference to Cosa Nostra which we believe to have been dealt with effectively, was brought out at trial as competent evidence.

"The three weeks that passed before the jury was called upon to make its decision also served to blunt much of the adverse effect of the publicity.

"Appellants moved for a mistrial on the ground that the publicity prejudiced the jury, making it impossible for them to receive a fair trial.

The trial judge took prompt and effective corrective action. He held a separate voir dire of each juror, frankly and candidly discussing the problems caused by the publicity. He correctly isolated the reference to the Cosa Nostra as the most potentially prejudicial aspect of the publicity and placed that element in its proper perspective by instructing each juror that it was completely irrelevant to the case. After completing this process and carefully considering the problem, Judge Dooling concluded that, although the publicity was prejudicial, the jurors remained capable of giving the appellants a fair trial."

* * *

In Woods v. Dugger, 923 F.2d 1454 (11th Cir.1991) a conviction was reversed, Woods, a convict, was accused of murdering a correctional officer. There the trial was held in Union County, Florida. Union County is a small rural county in Northern Florida. Just over ten thousand people live in Union County, but one-third of those are prisoners. Tate Rose, What Life is Like in a Place Where Half the Residents are Behind Bars, Chicago Tribune. In the neighboring counties of Bradford and Union there are four state prisons which employ twenty-two hundred workers, and the prisons are responsible for $71 million of the local economy. ... Union County is one hundred percent rural, and that thirty-two hundred people are employed outside of the home.

Union County took note of the murder of Corrections Officer Dennard. Prior to his death, he was interviewed by the St. Petersburg Times. He told the paper that the Union Correctional Institution was dangerously understaffed and that he wanted to be transferred because he feared for his safety as a prison guard. Officer Dennard's death became a focal point for the lobbying efforts of a group called the United Correctional Employees in their demands for the government to hire more correctional officers. After Officer Dennard's death, his sister began a petition that she reported was "going like hot cakes" and had gathered hundreds of signatures. By the time of Mr. Woods' trial, defense counsel told the court that the petition had 5,000 signatures, not all of which, however, were from Union County residents. The petition stated "its [sic] time we started punishing the guilty and protecting the innocent" and demanded the death penalty for those who kill prison guards.

> ... Of thirty-five potential jurors who were eventually excused: thirty-three had relatives or close friends who worked in the prison, or the jurors had worked in the prison themselves; twenty-one of the excused jurors had heard of the case; nine knew a witness; and one was a witness who was not called by either side. Within the actual jury: four jurors and one alternate juror neither had heard of the case nor had any relatives working in the prison system; four jurors had not heard of the case, but had either worked in the prison system themselves or had relatives currently working in the system; three jurors and one alternate juror both had heard of the case and had relatives currently working in the system; and, finally, one juror had heard of the case but had no relatives or friends working in the system.
>
> In addition, the gallery of the courtroom was filled with spectators. The defense counsel raised several objections to the presence of prison guards in the gallery, and the court ordered a videotape and photographs taken of the gallery. The photos reveal that the gallery had four rows which could each seat about ten or eleven people. Virtually every seat was occupied, and several people were standing in the back of the courtroom. About half of the spectators appear to be wearing prison guard uniforms.
>
> The officers in this case were there for one reason: they hoped to show solidarity with the killed correctional officer. In part, it appears that they wanted to communicate a message to the jury. The message of the officers is clear in light of the extensive pretrial publicity. The officers wanted a

conviction followed by the imposition of the death penalty. The jury could not help but receive the message.

2. Restraints and Controls Over Prejudicial News Media Reporting

Publicity about a case might be controlled by direct means, i.e., a rule prohibiting publication by news media; however, the First Amendment leaves our courts without significant power to do so. See Craig v. Harney, 331 U.S. 367, 67 S.Ct. 1249 (1947). In Nebraska Press Association v. Stuart, 427 U.S. 539, 96 S.Ct. 2791 (1976) a state court, acting on a joint motion by prosecution and defense restrained news media from publishing or broadcasting accounts of accused's confessions or admissions and other facts "strongly implicative" of the accused. The Court, while not prohibiting per se such restraint, held that the order was invalid. Despite the certainty of intense and pervasive publicity about the accusation of the accused murdering six members of one family, the Court found that the impact of the publicity on the jury was speculative; that there was no finding that measures short of restraint would be inadequate and, in any event, where the offense occurred in a small community rapidly spreading rumors would nullify the effect of any restraint on publication. Moreover, the Court found improper any prohibition of reporting on what occurred at open hearings and found the restriction on reporting facts "strongly implicative" to be too vague and too broad. Brennan, Stewart, and Marshall, JJ. would have found publication restrictions to be impermissible under any circumstances and a fourth Justice (White) wrote that he had "grave doubt" whether such orders would ever be justifiable. Mr. Justice Powell would sustain restraining orders only on the extraordinary showing that:

> "(i) there is a clear threat to the fairness of trial, (ii) such a threat is posed by the actual publicity to be restrained, and (iii) no less restrictive alternatives are available. Notwithstanding such a showing, a restraint may not issue unless it also is shown that previous publicity or publicity from unrestrained sources will not render the restraint inefficacious."

The indirect control of publicity is achieved by closing off the sources of information about cases. In Gannett Co. v. DePasquale, 443 U.S. 368, 99 S.Ct. 2898 (1979), the accuseds moved to exclude press and public from a pretrial hearing on the admissibility of confessions and the trial judge granted the motion. The Court approved, finding that publicity concerning pretrial suppression hearings has particularly high potential to influence public opinion and to inform prospective jurors of damaging, inadmissible evidence. The majority rejected the press claim that it had a Sixth Amendment right to attend trials and, in the alternative, found that even if such a right existed, it was overcome by the accuseds' right to a fair trial, particularly in light of the fact that the denial of access was temporary, because a transcript would be provided presumably after a jury was selected and sequestered. The Court's ruling is, on its face, limited to closure of pretrial hearings.

In Richmond Newspapers Inc. v. Virginia, 448 U.S. 555, 100 S.Ct. 2814 (1980), the Court distinguished *Gannett* and held that trials, as distinguished from pre-trial hearings, must be open to the public absent "an overriding interest articulated in findings." The Court found a "right of access" to information to be a component of the First Amendment and declared that "the right to attend criminal trials is implicit in the First Amendment."

In Chandler v. Florida, 449 U.S. 560, 101 S.Ct. 802 (1981), the Court held that the televising of a criminal trial, over a defendant's objections, is not per se prejudicial or violative of due process. It expressly overturned any suggestion to the contrary found in Estes v. Texas, 381 U.S. 532, 85 S.Ct. 1628 (1965).

In Globe Newspaper Co. v. Superior Court for the County of Norfolk, 457 U.S. 596, 102 S.Ct. 2613 (1982), the Supreme Court invalidated a state rule which automatically closed the courtroom to the public during the testimony of the alleged victim in a specified class of cases involving sex offenses against persons under age eighteen. The Court left open the possibility that, under some circumstances, the public, including media members, could be excluded during the trial testimony of the young alleged victim of a sex offense.

In Press–Enterprise Co. v. Superior Court, 464 U.S. 501, 104 S.Ct. 819 (1984), the Court held that under the Constitution voir dire examination of prospective jurors must be open to the public unless it is demonstrated by the facts before the court that "closure is essential to preserving higher values and is narrowly tailored to serve that interest." On the facts before it, the Court condemned a closure which lasted six weeks and suggested that closure of limited parts of voir dire examination is more likely to receive Supreme Court approval than is complete closure in a particular case.

In Waller v. Georgia, 467 U.S. 39, 104 S.Ct. 2210 (1984), the defendant objected to closing a pre-trial hearing litigating the seizure of conversations and physical evidence pursuant to wiretap orders and a search warrant. The Government insisted that closure was necessary because some of the material related to individuals who were not indicted and other evidence related to persons indicted but not yet tried. Emphasizing the need for a public airing of complaints about law enforcement misconduct, the Court held that the Sixth Amendment requires application to a pre-trial hearing of the rule of *Press–Enterprise*. The Court found no justification for closing practically the whole seven-day hearing. The Court ordered that a new suppression hearing be held and that if the seizures be ruled lawful, the convictions be reinstated.

One might question whether the order approved in *Gannett* would again be sustained under *Waller*.

G. Request for Change of Judge

United States v. Garrison

United States District Court, Eastern District of Louisiana, 1972.
340 F.Supp. 952.

■ Christenberry, District Judge. . . .

A special federal grand jury ... returned a true bill indicting Jim Garrison and nine other persons "for conspiracy to obstruct state or local law enforcement." As part of the conspiracy it was alleged that defendant Garrison "would receive protection bribe monies contributed by the defendants who would operate the illegal gambling businesses, to permit these businesses to operate free of any substantial law enforcement interference." As a further part of the alleged conspiracy the indictment states that:

> "Perishing Gervais, a former New Orleans Police Officer and former Chief Investigator for the Orleans Parish District Attorney's Office, would receive the protection bribe monies from the principals of the illegal gambling businesses and deliver it to the District Attorney Jim Garrison."

* * *

In accordance with the requirements of Title 28 U.S.C. § 144 (1970),[2] the instant motion was accompanied by defendant Garrison's affidavit with allegations to support the motion and a certificate of his local counsel, Louis B. Merhige, stating that the defendant's affidavit was made in good faith. Because it is the focal point of this opinion, the affidavit is set forth:

> "In the latter part of 1966, my office received information which convinced me that a conspiracy to kill President John F. Kennedy was formulated in Orleans Parish. With this information in hand, I felt duty bound to conduct an investigation. As a result of this investigation, I ordered the arrest of Clay L. Shaw, for conspiracy, with others, to kill President Kennedy.
>
> "Because of the seriousness of the charge, I asked that a preliminary hearing be held in the case. This hearing resulted in all three State judges unanimously finding probable cause to bind the defendant over for trial. Still mindful of the awesome gravity of the charge, I presented the state's evidence to the Orleans Parish grand jury. After hearing the evidence, the grand jury returned an indictment against Shaw. This indictment, after much delay occasioned by defense pleadings, was finally tried. On March 1, 1969, the petit jury acquitted the defendant.
>
> "A review of the testimony in the case convinced me that Shaw had committed perjury. Consequently, a bill of information was filed against him for violating the state's perjury statute. As in the conspiracy case, the defendant sought refuge in the federal

2. "Section 144. Bias or prejudice of judge

> "Whenever a party to any proceeding in a district court makes and files a timely and sufficient affidavit that the judge before whom the matter is pending has a personal bias or prejudice either against him or in favor of any adverse party, such judge shall proceed no further therein, but another judge shall be assigned to hear such proceeding.
>
> "The affidavit shall state the facts and the reasons for the belief that bias or prejudice exists, and shall be filed not less than ten days before the beginning of the term at which the proceeding is to be heard, or good cause shall be shown for failure to file it within such time. A party may file only one such affidavit in any case. It shall be accompanied by a certificate of counsel of record stating that it is made in good faith."

court. Shaw sought an injunction preventing the state from proceeding with its perjury case, citing claimed prosecutorial bad faith as his grounds for relief.

"An evidentiary hearing was held on his complaint by this honorable court. I, members of my staff and certain state and defense witnesses on the conspiracy trial were heard. On May 27, 1971, the court rendered its decision granting the relief sought. In the course of its opinion, a copy of which is attached hereto as exhibit 'A' and made a part of this affidavit, the court launched a personal attack upon me. The opinion stated that I wrongfully used certain esoteric methods to 'implant' an otherwise untrue story in the mind of a state witness, that our prosecution was conducted in bad faith and that my sole interest in the case was financial. These conclusions, in my judgment, were totally unsupported by any evidence adduced at the hearing nor were they supportable by any form of objective reasoning.

"Feeling strongly in the matter, I caused to be issued a press release denouncing your honor's findings. A copy of this press release is annexed hereto as exhibit 'B' and made a part of this affidavit.

"Given the personal character of the court's remarks in its opinion and my equally personal remarks in my press release, it is submitted that this court cannot sit in fair judgment of me. The bias of the court, conscious or otherwise, is patent.

"/s/ Jim Garrison"

The case alluded to by Mr. Garrison, the affiant, is Shaw v. Garrison, 328 F.Supp. 390 (E.D.La.1971). As defendant states, it is this decision, rendered in the normal course of the performance of this court's judicial duties, that forms his first basis for recusal. As a second ground, Mr. Garrison asks that I recuse myself because he "issued a press release denouncing [my] findings."

Defendant Garrison's press release, which he candidly admits to having authored, represents certainly an unusual statement for an attorney to have transmitted to the media. Attorneys traditionally, occasionally pursuant to a judicial admonition, try their law suits in courts of law and not the market place. To do otherwise can be a serious reflection on a counselor's sense of propriety and, of course, can result in a finding of contempt of court. In this instance, however, nothing has transpired which would affect this court's ability to accord all litigants a fair and impartial trial. Were there any reason, apparent or otherwise, why this court could not feel assured that justice would be applied evenhandedly, then on its own volition the court would recuse itself. Affiant's contention reduces itself to the proposition that he can avoid being tried before any particular judge if he has publicly voiced disapproval of that judge or that judge's work. All the more so, affiant contends, if that judge has previously decided a case adverse to the defendant. That simply is not the law and the idea of it is counter to this court's policy against allowing a defendant to select the judge who will preside over his trial. The policy rather is that all cases should be allotted on a random basis. It should never be of any moment to a judge as to whether or not he sits on a particular case. "The court is not a party. There is nothing that affects the judges in their own persons. Their concern is only that the law should be obeyed and enforced, and their interest is no other than that they represent in every case." United States v. Shipp, 203 U.S. 563, 574, 27 S.Ct. 165, 167 (1906) (Holmes, J.). Similarly, a litigant's case must stand on its own merits and not depend on being heard by any particular judge.

In passing upon a motion to recuse on the grounds of bias or prejudice the facts alleged in the affidavit are taken as true, Berger v. United States, 255 U.S. 22, 33–35, 41 S.Ct. 230, 233 (1921), and the judge to whom the motion is presented determines only the legal sufficiency and timeliness of the affidavit and the certificate of counsel. ... Where the affidavit and certificate pass the dual tests of sufficiency and timeliness the motion to recuse must be granted though the judge knows for a certainty that the allegations of prejudice and bias are false. ... The affidavit, however, is strictly construed against the affiant, for a judge is presumed to be impartial. ...

The affidavit and certificate of counsel were timely filed. ... The sufficiency of the affidavit, however, is quite another matter. Section 144 requires a "sufficient affidavit that the judge before whom the matter is pending has a *personal* bias or prejudice...." Personal bias is defined as an attitude of extrajudicial origin. Neither prior judicial exposure to a defendant nor prior judicial rulings adverse to a defendant constitute bias or prejudice on the part of the judge sufficient to cause his recusal. ...

It follows then that Garrison's allegation of bias or prejudice founded upon the opinion in Shaw v. Garrison is insufficient as a matter of law.

Movant's second ground alleged to support the motion for recusal—his own press release denouncing the federal judiciary and this court's opinion in the *Shaw* case—is similarly inadequate. It is well settled that prior written attacks upon a judge are legally insufficient to support a charge of bias or prejudice on the part of the judge toward the author of such a statement. ...

The reasoning behind these decisions is not difficult to ascertain. As one jurist in a similar case stated:

> "Only a psychic pleader could allege that because a defendant has published uncomplimentary statements concerning a judge, the latter will be unable to give his critic a fair and impartial trial. If such a fantastic procedure were permitted, a defendant could get rid of a judge by the simple expedient of publishing a scurrilous article, *truthfully* alleging that the article was published, and clinching the matter by asserting the bald conclusion that, since the article was uncomplimentary, the judge must of necessity be prejudiced against the publisher."

United States v. Fujimoto, [101 F.Supp. 293, 296 (D.Hawai'i 1951)]. The mere fact that a defendant has made derogatory remarks about a judge is insufficient to convince a sane and reasonable mind that the attacked judge is biased or prejudiced, the standard used to test the sufficiency of an affidavit for recusal under section 144. To allow prior derogatory remarks about a judge to cause the latter's compulsory recusal would enable any defendant to cause the recusal of any judge merely by making disparaging statements about him. Such a bizarre result clearly is not contemplated in section 144.

The denial of a motion to recuse under these circumstances is in accord with the oft-stated principle that courts should not only be fair and impartial but should also appear to be fair and impartial. Indeed, the majority of circuit courts hold that it is the duty of a judge not to recuse himself where the statutory standards are not met.

* * *

Having found the reasons given in the recusal affidavit to lack the requisite legal sufficiency, the motion of defendant Jim Garrison for the recusal of this court must be and it is denied.

NOTES

1. Compare the following rulings:

(a) Defendant, Musgrave, and Bryant were jointly indicted for their conduct in connection with loans from federally insured institutions. Defendant's trial was severed because of his ill health. Musgrave and Bryant were tried and convicted. At defendant's subsequent trial before the same judge he filed an unsuccessful affidavit seeking the judge's disqualification. He won on appeal.

United States v. Womack, 454 F.2d 1337 (5th Cir.1972) said:

> We now turn to the sufficiency of the affidavits. The law on this question is extensive but we need not belabor its breadth or nuances to decide this case in which the allegations of the affidavits are clearly sufficient. During the Musgrave trial the judge referred to appellant as a man "who everybody admits was certainly a shady character," and told the jury: "If you find that Musgrave did this there is no question but that Womack was working with him hand in glove . . . he would be as culpable."
>
> The genesis of appellant's supplemental affidavit of disqualification was a June 15, 1970 pretrial conference. When appellant moved for a continuance because of his alleged ill health following a heart attack, the judge replied that appellant should have taken care of his health problems earlier and would go to trial even if he had to have a doctor in court to hold his hand. In response to appellant's motion for a change of venue to Fort Worth to put him closer to his heart specialist, the judge replied that appellant would be tried in Pecos because the judge had heard all the evidence in the Musgrave case, the Pecos jury had convicted Musgrave and Bryant, and the court was convinced appellant was guilty and would be so found by a Pecos jury. The judge said further that appellant could expect favorable treatment at his hands only if appellant saved the Government money in the trial of the cause. The motion for change of venue for convenience was denied.

The judge erred in not withdrawing from the case.

(b) Petitioners in Eaton v. United States, 458 F.2d 704 (7th Cir.1972), alleged that the sentencing judge had not been impartial, contending that he had said before the change of plea that petitioners were "shooting craps with the government only to come out losers." The record shows that the remark actually made was addressed to counsel, after inquiring as to the theory of the defense.

The judge went on:

> "I am curious as to what the theory of the defense is in the case. It doesn't mean you have to have one. You can stand trial without one. Just shoot craps with justice if you want to. That is part of your constitutional right, but I have always assumed counsel had a responsibility to advise clients that shooting craps with justice is not likely to be a profitable way to deal with a problem; that there was some theory, at least, on which the defense is predicated."

This colloquy occurred at the motion to suppress, a considerable time before the change of plea. In our opinion neither the remark quoted nor anything else in the record shows bias; certainly it does not show such probability of bias that the judge was obligated to disqualify himself from decision thereof.

(c) In United States v. Harrelson, 754 F.2d 1153 (5th Cir.1985), appellants were tried before Judge William S. Sessions, a federal judge of the Western District of Texas, on charges arising from the murder of John H. Wood, Jr., also a federal judge of that district.

"Judge Sessions had known and worked with Judge Wood for eight or nine years at the time of the latter's death and admired him. The relationship was collegial and there is no evidence of any special social relationship between the two judges or between the Wood and Sessions families. Judge Sessions was an honorary pallbearer at Judge Wood's funeral and eulogized him at several memorial ceremonies. Because of the murder, Judge Sessions was guarded 24 hours a day until December 2, 1980. The appellants contend that these facts are sufficient to render the trial court's denial of their motion for recusal reversible error.

* * *

"[The cases] uniformly support the proposition that recusal is not warranted in a criminal case absent conduct by the trial court specifically indicating personal prejudice against the defendant. See Ungar v. Sarafite (1964). More apposite to the circumstances presented here are such *a fortiori* authorities as United States v. Phillips, 664 F.2d 971 (5th Cir.1981), in which the trial judge was affirmed in declining to stand recused even in the face of evidence that certain defendants were plotting to assassinate *him*.

"Finally, appellants' contention incorporates a fundamental logical flaw: whatever the relationship between the two judges was, it can at most have served to create a degree of hostility toward the actual killers. As such, it is entirely consistent both with a desire that those not guilty be acquitted and with one that the guilty be convicted. At all stages of the trial and to this day, appellants have vigorously maintained that they are not the guilty parties; we are unwilling to presume, in the absence of a far stronger showing than has been made here, that a reasonable person would entertain doubts that the careful and seasoned trial judge who sat in this case would prejudge their guilt.

"In short, Judge Sessions' conduct advanced by appellants as a basis for his recusal demonstrates only such behavior as one might expect of a civilized and honorable man upon the death of a colleague—and that whether or not he harbored any particular affection for him. As such, it falls far short of casting his impartiality in doubt to reasonable people."

2. In Liteky v. United States, 510 U.S. 540, 114 S.Ct. 1147 (1994) a defendant had previously been tried and convicted of offenses arising out of a protest action. Nine years later before the same judge in another protest offense case the judge sought by ruling and admonitions to limit defendant's desire to try the issues underlying the protest. The judge's fairness was challenged, but the judge denied recusal because all he knew of defendant and the cases arose from the proceedings before the judge. The Supreme Court held that mandatory recusal for bias or prejudice cannot be had for judicial views formed on the basis of proceedings in court, only those based on an extrajudicial source, something learned outside the courtroom, will require recusal. Absent prejudice arising from an extrajudicial source, recusal is only appropriate when judicial comments show such deep-seated favoritism and antagonism as would make fair judgment impossible. Routine trial rulings and admonishments adverse to a party will rarely be enough for recusal even when they are legally insupportable.

3. Consider the proper result in the next two cases:

(a) "... [T]he victim returned to her apartment after dining with her mother. While standing at her mailbox, Cook, her neighbor, approached her and asked to borrow some salt. The victim entered her apartment and went into the kitchen for some salt. When she returned to her living room Cook shot her in the chest.

She began screaming and wrestled with Cook. He struck her six or eight times with the butt of the revolver, and she feigned unconsciousness. Cook pulled her along the floor into another room and left for a few moments; when he returned, he removed some of the victim's clothing, engaged in sexual deviate conduct and then raped her. The victim struggled with Cook and kicked him. Cook then left the apartment.

The victim crawled into her bathtub and attempted to hide. Cook returned with the gun and a pillow. He placed the pillow over her head and shot her through the pillow. The bullet hit the victim's forearm and grazed her forehead. She lunged forward in the tub when shot and held her breath until Cook left.

* * *

At the sentencing hearing, the victim testified about the attack. After describing Cook's action, the victim stated that she did not seek vengeance, because there was nothing the court could do to change the past. She said she was not interested in punishing Cook, but she wanted to be sure that Cook was imprisoned long enough before he was released so that he would be rehabilitated and not be a threat to others.

After these comments, the trial judge interrupted:

'I think it's appropriate for me to speak at this time because I know that—all of you know that I am crying and I want you to know the reason for that is because of [the victim's] forgiving nature, it is unusual, I believe, for a person who's been a victim of such a vicious crime to have such a forgiving attitude about her experiences. And I think that that reflects all the best that there is in human nature. And I want Mr. Glazier [Cook's counsel] and Mr. Cook to realize that, even though I'm emotional at this time and that I am crying, that you will have nothing to fear.'

After a brief recess, Cook asked the trial judge to recuse herself because he felt he could not receive an impartial adjudication from her. The trial judge denied the motion. After the cross-examination of the witness and arguments by counsel, the trial court accepted Cook's guilty plea. Cook was sentenced to a forty-year term of imprisonment for attempted murder, forty years for rape, the sentences to be served consecutively, and a ten-year sentence for confinement, to be served concurrently to the other sentences, for a total term of imprisonment of eighty years.

The trial judge articulated three aggravating circumstances to support her decision: Cook's use of subterfuge to get into a position to harm the victim; his return after the rape with the specific intent to kill the victim to evade detection and the use of the pillow to muffle the sound of the gunshot to evade detection; and her determination that Cook was in need of corrective treatment that could be found only in a prison setting. The trial judge later amended the abstract of the judgment to show that she found Cook's youth and remorse to be mitigating factors, but that the aggravating factors outweighed those mitigating circumstances."

Should the judge have been disqualified? (See Cook v. State, 612 N.E.2d 1085 (Ind.App.1993.))

(b) In United States v. Tucker, 78 F.3d 1313 (8th Cir.1996) and on denial of rehearing en banc 82 F.3d 1423 (8th Cir.1996) (2 dissents) a case in which the Governor of Arkansas was being prosecuted by the Independent Counsel. Disqualification of the trial judge was sought on the following grounds.

"The Independent Counsel relies primarily on newspaper articles to support his request. First, there are articles that connect Judge Woods and Hillary Rodham Clinton. Judge Woods appointed her as counsel for a special committee in the Pulaski County, Arkansas, school desegregation case, and was quoted as saying that he "did work with Hillary" and that he "came to admire her during that period." Rex Nelson, Road to Tucker trial full of twists for Judge Woods. In the Arkansas Democrat–Gazette article, the newspaper reported that Judge Woods said, "If anything came up regarding President Clinton, I would recuse," because of the Judge's relationship with Hillary Clinton. A column in a daily periodical with national—actually international—circulation reported that Judge Woods wrote to then Deputy White House Counsel, the late Vincent Foster, in July 1993 to ask whether he should grant an interview where the topic was to be Hillary Rodham Clinton. Finally, in a column criticizing efforts "to get federal Judge Henry Woods, a Democratic appointee, off Gov. Jim Guy Tucker's criminal case," the author acknowledged, "Indeed, the judge spent the night at the White House the night Republicans swept a majority of Congress last November.

For their part, President and Mrs. Clinton have been reported to have expressed continued support for Tucker since his indictment by the grand jury. It was reported in an article on the front page of the Arkansas Democrat–Gazette that, the day after Tucker pleaded not guilty to the charges in this case, the Clintons attended a fund-raising luncheon in Little Rock, Arkansas, where Tucker received a "sustained standing ovation." At the event, solidifying his connection with the recently indicted Tucker, the President said in a speech, "I am especially glad to see Governor and Mrs. Tucker here today and especially grateful for the reception you gave them." Tucker also acknowledged the perceived connection when he was quoted in an interview as saying of the OIC, "I think that's been much of their goal, to try and tar the [P]resident with images of wrongdoing here in his home state."

[The Independent Counsel represented] this case will as a matter of law involve matters related to the investigation of the President and Hillary Rodham Clinton."

Should Judge Woods be disqualified?

(c) See United States v. Holland, 501 F.3d 1120 (9th Cir. 2007)

Holland has a lengthy criminal record and has been incarcerated for most of his adult life for crimes ranging from armed robbery, petty theft, escape from prison, assault by a prisoner, grand theft, robbery, prisoner possession of a weapon, assault with a deadly weapon, threats against state officials, and injury to jails. At some point during the proceedings in this case, Holland obtained the sentencing judge's home telephone number, which he called, leaving more than one threatening message on an answering machine. Before sentencing, the district court revealed that he had received these threatening messages from Holland. The district court, however, dismissed them as attempts to "manipulate the system." Specifically, the judge remarked:

For the record, too, the Court is also aware that Mr. Holland did, in fact, leave voice messages at the Court's personal residence that to some people could be construed as threatening. However, in my judgment, Mr. Holland's history clearly demonstrates that these are attempts to manipulate the criminal justice system rather than threats as such and the Court is just simply not going to allow Mr. Holland to manipulate the system. So the Court has chosen to go forward with this sentencing at this time.

Later in the proceeding, the judge observed that Holland had a history of violent and assaultive crimes and "if he is given the opportunity, he has the ability to carry out his threats.... [I]t is clearly important ... that the Court impose[ ] a sentence for the protection of society." Holland did not object to the sentencing judge's decision to proceed with the hearing or request that the judge recuse himself.

[T]he security of the nation's judiciary is a serious concern. We are, unfortunately, reminded from time to time that threats against the judiciary have been carried out.[2]

The question before us, however, is different. Here we must decide when a judge *must* recuse himself sua sponte in response to threats even if he would prefer to continue his work on the case. Here, Holland contends the district judge should have recused himself sua sponte after receiving his threatening phone calls.

Applying general principles to situations where the judge receives a threat, suggests a three-step process for evaluating whether recusal is required. First, the judge must evaluate the threat itself to determine how much risk there is that it may be carried out and how much harm there

2. Despite security measures, threats against federal judges have taken a deadly turn. In 1979, Judge John H. Wood Jr., of the Western District of Texas, was shot to death outside his home by a hit man hired to prevent him from presiding over a narcotics trial. In 1988 Judge Richard J. Daronco, of the Southern District of New York, was shot outside his home by a retired police officer after the judge dismissed a sexual discrimination suit brought by the officer's daughter. Judge Robert S. Vance, of the Eleventh Circuit, was killed at his home by a pipe bomb mailed by an inmate angry that his prior conviction was not overturned. In 2005, Chicago District Court Judge Joan Lefkow's husband and mother were brutally murdered by a man whom the judge had ruled against in court. ... The wife of Judge Charles Brieant of the Southern District of New York was rushed to the hospital in 1987 after eating poisoned chocolates mailed by a former university professor jailed by Brieant for manufacturing drugs in his NYU laboratory ... We are mindful that our state counterparts are also at risk.

At the time of the Lefkow murders, the U.S. Marshal's service, tasked with providing security for the federal judiciary, logged roughly 700 threats or "inappropriate communications" against judges each year.

would be if it were. In deciding whether recusal is appropriate, the judge may wish to consider the following factors:

(1) *The defendant's capacity to carry out the threat*. Has the defendant taken concrete steps to carry out the threat? Does the defendant have a history of violence or has he previously been successful in carrying out other threats? Is he a member of a gang or does he have accomplices or contacts who could carry out the threat on his behalf?

(2) *The defendant's demeanor and the context of the threat*. Was the threat made in a fit of passion or intended as a joke? Does the judge believe that the defendant is serious in carrying out the threat? Does the judge have any prior dealings with the defendant that make the threat more or less likely to be carried out?

(3) *The perceived purpose of the threat*. Was the threat made in open court or did the judge become aware of the threat only through the fortuity of a law enforcement investigation? Does the judge believe it is an attempt to force recusal and manipulate the judicial system?

The final factor is, perhaps, the most important. Not every threat made against a judge should force recusal. If so, defendants could readily manipulate the system, threatening every jurist assigned on the "wheel" until the defendant gets a judge he preferred. Also, the defendant could force delays, perhaps making the cases against him more difficult to try, perhaps putting witnesses at greater risk. Such blatant manipulation would subvert our processes, undermine our notions of fair play and justice, and damage the public's perception of the judiciary.[6]

The second step is for the judge to determine whether he can be truly impartial when trying case. If he feels he cannot hear the case without bias, on account of the threat, then the judge has a duty to recuse himself irrespective of how it looks to the public.

The third step in evaluating whether recusal is required is to apply the "objective" standard ... if a reasonable third-party observer would perceive that there is a "significant risk" that the judge will be influenced by the threat and resolve the case on a basis other than the merits. [Yet] ... a threat to the judge's person or family necessarily involves the judge's personal sentiment. The judge must take into account his own perception of the situation and personal feelings and ask himself if there is a significant risk that the threat will influence his decision. Put differently: Would a reasonable person understanding the judge's perspective accept the judge's decision to recuse (or not to recuse) himself? If the judge cannot, in good faith, answer "yes," then he should revisit his analysis under the first two steps. If it is a close case, the balance tips in favor of recusal.

Only the judge himself, viewing the threats in context, can differentiate between threats that the author intended to be taken seriously and

6. The danger in a case where the judge has himself become the target is twofold. First, there is the risk that the judge will accede to the pressure posed by the threats. In that instance the judge is hostage to the threats and goes easy on the defendant in order to defuse the threats and protect himself and his family. But there is a second consideration that a conscientious judge should be aware of as well, namely that the judge will favor the government in a criminal case as a means of protecting himself or his family by imposing a tougher sentence on the person making the threats. Neither scenario is acceptable; we are both judges and people and cannot put our personal lives on the hanger from which we take our robes. There are situations in which it is too much to expect a judge to dispense justice faithfully and impartially, without regard for his own physical safety and the safety of his family.

those made to anger or to manipulate the system. And, only the judge can determine whether he took them seriously or dismissed them.

The precise nature of the threat is not clear from the record, but the district judge described it as a message "that to some people could be construed as threatening." The district court, however, did not consider the threats or Holland's capacity to carry them out serious enough to refer the incident to the FBI, nor did he request additional security from the U.S. Marshal's service.

The judge carefully considered Holland's extensive (and curious) history of making threats. Holland was before the district court to plead guilty of . . . "knowingly and willful" threats against the President of the United States [which] does not require proof of the defendant's capacity, or evidence that the defendant has taken any affirmative steps, to carry out such threats. Holland's current legal troubles also involved mailing threatening letters to: (1) a state court judge (he later mailed another letter apologizing for the threats); (2) to the prosecutor involved in a prior criminal proceeding; and (3) the President of the United States . . . When initially confronted with the letter to the President, Holland told an Idaho Department of Corrections lieutenant assisting the Secret Service that he did not want to remain in state custody any longer and that he wanted to go to federal prison instead. He thought he could get to federal prison by committing a federal crime. Holland also threatened a jail nurse in an apparent attempt to be transferred to the prison's medical facility and threatened his former defense lawyer in an attempt to get him to mail a second letter from Holland threatening the President. There is no evidence in the record that Holland took any steps in furtherance of any of his threats.

. . . At the beginning of the proceedings, Holland blurted out, "The detectives told me yesterday that I threatened you [the district judge] at home. Did I threaten you at home?" Later, when given an opportunity to address the court, Holland stated "I am not as bad as my paperwork says. . . . There ain't no way I am going to look for a judge. There ain't no damn way I am going to look for a President of the United States or anybody. . . . I have never hurt a victim." He attempted to explain his threats as part of the prison culture: "Maybe it's because of the lifestyle, the way prison is. Everybody threatens, 'I am going to do this, I am going to do that.' It has got to the point where it is natural to do that. . . . But as far as carrying out the threats, no. There ain't no way. Who would be stupid enough?"

Should the judge recuse?

H. REQUEST FOR SUPPRESSION OF EVIDENCE

Jackson v. Denno

Supreme Court of the United States, 1964.
378 U.S. 368, 84 S.Ct. 1774.

■ MR. JUSTICE WHITE delivered the opinion of the Court.

* * *

I.

On June 14, 1960, at about 1 a.m., petitioner, Jackson, and Nora Elliott entered a Brooklyn hotel where Miss Elliott registered for both of them. After telling Miss Elliott to leave, which she did, Jackson drew a gun and took money from the room clerk. He ordered the clerk and several other people into an upstairs room and left the hotel, only to encounter Miss Elliott and later a policeman on the street. A struggle with the latter followed, in the course of which both men drew guns. The policeman was fatally wounded and petitioner was shot twice in the body. He managed to hail a cab, however, which took him to the hospital.

A detective questioned Jackson at about 2 a.m., soon after his arrival at the hospital. Jackson, when asked for his name, said, "Nathan Jackson, I shot the colored cop. I got the drop on him." He also admitted the robbery at the hotel. According to the detective, Jackson was in "strong" condition despite his wounds.

Jackson was given 50 milligrams of demerol and 1/50 of a grain of scopolamine at 3:55 a.m. Immediately thereafter an Assistant District Attorney, in the presence of police officers and hospital personnel, questioned Jackson, the interrogation being recorded by a stenographer. Jackson, who had been shot in the liver and lung, had by this time lost about 500 cc. of blood. Jackson again admitted the robbery in the hotel, and then said "Look, I can't go on." But in response to further questions he admitted shooting the policeman and having fired the first shot. The interview was completed at 4 a.m. An operation upon petitioner was begun at 5 a.m. and completed at 8 a.m.

Jackson and Miss Elliott were indicted for murder in the first degree and were tried together. The statements made by Jackson, both at 2 and 3:55 a.m., were introduced in evidence without objection by Jackson's counsel. Jackson took the stand in his own defense. His account of the robbery and of the shooting of the policeman differed in some important respects from his confession. According to Jackson's testimony, there was a substantial interval of time between his leaving the hotel and the shooting, and the policeman attempted to draw his gun first and fired the first shot. As to the questioning at the hospital, Jackson recalled that he was in pain and gasping for breath at the time and was refused water and told he would not be let alone until the police had the answers they wanted. He knew that he had been interrogated but could remember neither the questions nor the answers.

To counter Jackson's suggestion that he had been pressured into answering questions, the State offered the testimony of the attending physician and of several other persons. They agreed that Jackson was refused water, but because of the impending operation rather than his refusal to answer questions. On cross-examination of the doctor, Jackson's counsel, with the help of the hospital records, elicited the fact that demerol and scopolamine were administered to Jackson immediately before his interrogation. But any effect of these drugs on Jackson during the interrogation was denied.

Although Jackson's counsel did not specifically object to the admission of the confession initially, the trial court indicated its awareness that Jackson's counsel was questioning the circumstances under which Jackson was interrogated.

In his closing argument, Jackson's counsel did not ask for an acquittal but for a verdict of second-degree murder or manslaughter. Counsel's main effort was to negative the premeditation and intent necessary to first-degree murder and to separate the robbery felony from the killing. He made much of the testimony tending to show a substantial interval between leaving the hotel and the beginning of the struggle with the policeman. The details of that struggle and the testimony indicating the policeman fired the first shot were also stressed.

Consistent with the New York practice where a question has been raised about the voluntariness of a confession, the trial court submitted that issue to the jury along with the other issues in the case. The jury was told that if it found the confession involuntary, it was to disregard it entirely, and determine guilt or innocence solely from the other evidence in the case; alternatively, if it found the confession voluntary, it was to determine its truth or reliability and afford it weight accordingly.

The jury found Jackson guilty of murder in the first degree, Miss Elliott of manslaughter in the first degree.

II.

In our view, the New York procedure employed in this case did not afford a reliable determination of the voluntariness of the confession offered in evidence at the trial, did not adequately protect Jackson's right to be free of a conviction based upon a coerced confession and therefore cannot withstand constitutional attack under the Due Process Clause of the Fourteenth Amendment.

III.

Under the New York rule, the trial judge must make a preliminary determination regarding a confession offered by the prosecution and exclude it if in no circumstances could the confession be deemed voluntary. But if the evidence presents a fair question as to its voluntariness, as where certain facts bearing on the issue are in dispute or where reasonable men could differ over the inferences to be drawn from undisputed facts, the judge "must receive the confession and leave to the jury, under proper instructions, the ultimate determination of its voluntary character and also its truthfulness." Stein v. New York, 346 U.S. 156, 172, 73 S.Ct. 1077, 1086. If an issue of coercion is presented, the judge may not resolve conflicting evidence or arrive at his independent appraisal of the voluntariness of the confession, one way or the other. These matters he must leave to the jury.

This procedure has a significant impact upon the defendant's Fourteenth Amendment rights. In jurisdictions following the orthodox rule, under which the judge himself solely and finally determines the voluntariness of the confession, or those following the Massachusetts procedure,[8] under which the jury passes on voluntariness only after the judge has fully and independently resolved the issue against the accused, the judge's conclusions are clearly evident from the record since he either admits the confession into evidence if it is voluntary or rejects it if involuntary. Moreover, his findings upon disputed issues of fact are expressly stated or may be ascertainable from the record. In contrast, the New York jury returns only a general verdict upon the ultimate question of guilt or innocence. It is impossible to discover whether the jury found the confession voluntary and relied upon it, or involuntary and supposedly ignored it. Nor is there any indication of how the jury resolved disputes in the evidence concerning the critical facts underlying the coercion issue. Indeed, there is nothing to show that these matters were resolved at all, one way or the other. . . .

A defendant objecting to the admission of a confession is entitled to a fair hearing in which both the underlying factual issues and the voluntariness of his confession are actually and reliably determined. But did the jury in Jackson's case make these critical determinations, and if it did, what were these determinations?

Notwithstanding these acknowledged difficulties inherent in the New York procedure, the Court in Stein v. New York, found no constitutional deprivation to the defendant. The Court proceeded to this conclusion on the basis of alternative assumptions regarding the manner in which the jury might have resolved the coercion issue. Either the jury determined the disputed issues of fact against the accused, found the confession voluntary and therefore properly relied upon it; or it found the contested facts in favor of the accused and deemed the confession involuntary, in which event it disregarded the confession in accordance with its instructions and adjudicated guilt based solely on the other evidence. On either assumption the Court found no error in the judgment of the state court.

8. We raise no question here concerning the Massachusetts procedure. In jurisdictions following this rule, the judge hears the confession evidence, himself resolves evidentiary conflicts and gives his own answer to the coercion issue, rejecting confessions he deems involuntary and admitting only those he believes voluntary. It is only the latter confessions that are heard by the jury, which may then, under this procedure, disagree with the judge, find the confession involuntary and ignore it. Given the integrity of the preliminary proceedings before the judge, the Massachusetts procedure does not, in our opinion, pose hazards to the rights of a defendant. While no more will be known about the views of the jury than under the New York rule, the jury does not hear all confessions where there is a fair question of voluntariness, but only those which a judge actually and independently determines to be voluntary, based upon all of the evidence. The judge's consideration of voluntariness is carried out separate and aside from issues of the reliability of the confession and the guilt or innocence of the accused and without regard to the fact the issue may again be raised before the jury if decided against the defendant. The record will show the judge's conclusions in this regard and his findings upon the underlying facts may be express or ascertainable from the record.

Once the confession is properly found to be voluntary by the judge, reconsideration of this issue by the jury does not, of course, improperly affect the jury's determination of the credibility or probativeness of the confession or its ultimate determination of guilt or innocence.

We disagree with the Court in Stein; for in addition to sweeping aside its own express doubts that the jury acted at all in the confession matter the Court, we think, failed to take proper account of the dangers to an accused's rights under either of the alternative assumptions.

On the assumption that the jury found the confession voluntary, the Court concluded that it could properly do so. But this judgment was arrived at only on the further assumptions that the jury had actually found the disputed issues of fact against the accused and that these findings were reliably arrived at in accordance with considerations that are permissible and proper under federal law. These additional assumptions, in our view, were unsound.

The New York jury is at once given both the evidence going to voluntariness and all of the corroborating evidence showing that the confession is true and that the defendant committed the crime. The jury may therefore believe the confession and believe that the defendant has committed the very act with which he is charged, a circumstance which may seriously distort judgment of the credibility of the accused and assessment of the testimony concerning the critical facts surrounding his confession.

In those cases where without the confession the evidence is insufficient, the defendant should not be convicted if the jury believes the confession but finds it to be involuntary. The jury, however, may find it difficult to understand the policy forbidding reliance upon a coerced, but true, confession, a policy which has divided this Court in the past, see Stein v. New York, supra, and an issue which may be reargued in the jury room. That a trustworthy confession must also be voluntary if it is to be used at all, generates natural and potent pressure to find it voluntary. Otherwise the guilty defendant goes free. Objective consideration of the conflicting evidence concerning the circumstances of the confession becomes difficult and the implicit findings become suspect.

The danger that matters pertaining to the defendant's guilt will infect the jury's findings of fact bearing upon voluntariness, as well as its conclusion upon that issue itself, is sufficiently serious to preclude their unqualified acceptance upon review in this Court, regardless of whether there is or is not sufficient other evidence to sustain a finding of guilt. In Jackson's case, he confessed to having fired the first shot, a matter very relevant to the charge of first degree murder. The jury also heard the evidence of eyewitnesses to the shooting. Jackson's testimony going to his physical and mental condition when he confessed and to the events which took place at that time, bearing upon the issue of voluntariness, was disputed by the prosecution. The obvious and serious danger is that the jury disregarded or disbelieved Jackson's testimony pertaining to the confession because it believed he had done precisely what he was charged with doing.

The failure to inquire into the reliability of the jury's resolution of disputed factual considerations underlying its conclusion as to voluntariness—findings which were afforded decisive weight by the Court in Stein—was not a mere oversight but stemmed from the premise underlying the Stein opinion that the exclusion of involuntary confessions is constitutionally required solely because of the inherent untrustworthiness of a coerced confession. It followed from this premise that a reliable or true confession need not be rejected as involuntary and that evidence corroborating the truth or falsity of the confession and the guilt or innocence of the accused is indeed pertinent to the determination of the coercion issue.

* * *

Under the New York procedure, the evidence given the jury inevitably injects irrelevant and impermissible considerations of truthfulness of the confession into the assessment of voluntariness. Indeed the jury is told to determine the truthfulness of the confession in assessing its probative value. As a consequence, it cannot be assumed, as the Stein Court assumed, that the jury reliably found the facts against the accused. This unsound assumption undermines Stein's authority as a precedent and its view on the constitutionality of the New York procedure. The admixture of reliability and voluntariness in the considerations of the jury would itself entitle a defendant to further proceedings in any case in which the essential facts are disputed, for we cannot determine how the jury resolved these issues and will not assume that they were reliably and properly resolved against the accused. And it is only a reliable determination on the voluntariness issue which satisfies the constitutional rights of the defendant and which would permit the jury to consider the confession in adjudicating guilt or innocence.

But we do not rest on this ground alone, for the other alternative hypothesized in Stein—that the jury found the confession involuntary and disregarded it—is equally unacceptable. Under the New York procedure, the fact of a defendant's confession is solidly implanted in the jury's mind, for it has not only heard the confession, but it has been instructed to consider and judge its voluntariness and is in position to assess whether it is true or false. If it finds the confession involuntary, does the jury—indeed, can it—then disregard the confession in accordance with its instructions? If there are lingering doubts about the sufficiency of the other evidence, does the jury unconsciously lay them to rest by resort to the confession? Will uncertainty about the sufficiency of the other evidence to prove guilt beyond a reasonable doubt actually result in acquittal when the jury knows the defendant has given a truthful confession?

It is difficult, if not impossible, to prove that a confession which a jury has found to be involuntary has nevertheless influenced the verdict or that its finding of voluntariness, if this is the course it took, was affected by the other evidence showing the confession was true. But the New York procedure poses substantial threats to a defendant's constitutional rights to have an involuntary confession entirely disregarded and to have the coercion issue fairly and reliably determined. These hazards we cannot ignore.[16]

* * *

16. Further obstacles to a reliable and fair determination of voluntariness under the New York procedure result from the ordinary rules relating to cross-examination.

Although not the case here, an accused may well be deterred from testifying on the voluntariness issue when the jury is present because of his vulnerability to impeachment

Expanded concepts of fairness in obtaining confessions have been accompanied by a correspondingly greater complexity in determining whether an accused's will has been overborne—facts are frequently disputed, questions of credibility are often crucial, and inferences to be drawn from established facts are often determinative. The overall determination of the voluntariness of a confession has thus become an exceedingly sensitive task, one that requires facing the issue squarely, in illuminating isolation and unbeclouded by other issues and the effect of extraneous but prejudicial evidence. Where pure factual considerations are an important ingredient, which is true in the usual case, appellate review in this Court is, as a practical matter, an inadequate substitute for a full and reliable determination of the voluntariness issue in the trial court and the trial court's determination, *pro tanto*, takes on an increasing finality. The procedures used in the trial court to arrive at its conclusions on the coercion issue progressively take on added significance as the actual measure of the protection afforded a defendant under the Due Process Clause of the Fourteenth Amendment against the use of involuntary confessions. These procedures must, therefore, be fully adequate to insure a reliable and clear-cut determination of the voluntariness of the confession, including the resolution of disputed facts upon which the voluntariness issue may depend. In our view, the New York procedure falls short of satisfying these constitutional requirements. Stein v. New York is overruled.

IV.

We turn to consideration of the disposition of this case. Since Jackson has not been given an adequate hearing upon the voluntariness of his confession he must be given one, the remaining inquiry being the scope of that hearing and the court which should provide it.

This is not a case where the facts concerning the circumstances surrounding the confession are undisputed and the task is only to judge the voluntariness of the confession based upon the clearly established facts and in accordance with proper constitutional standards. Here there are substantial facts in dispute: . . . Whether Jackson is entitled to relief depends upon how these facts are resolved, for if the State is to be believed we cannot say that Jackson's confession was involuntary, whereas if Jackson's version of the facts is accepted the confession was involuntary and inadmissible.

* * *

. . . Jackson's trial did not comport with constitutional standards and he is entitled to a determination of the voluntariness of his confession in the state courts in accordance with valid state procedures; the State is also entitled to make this determination before this Court considers the case on direct review or a petition for habeas corpus is filed in a Federal District Court. . . .

by proof of prior convictions and broad cross-examination and impeachment, both of whose prejudicial effects are familiar. The fear of such impeachment and extensive cross-examination in the presence of the jury that is to pass on guilt or innocence as well as voluntariness may induce a defendant to remain silent, although he is perhaps the only source of testimony on the facts underlying the claim of coercion. Where this occurs the determination of voluntariness is made upon less than all of the relevant evidence.

It is New York therefore, not the federal habeas corpus court, which should first provide Jackson with that which he has not yet had and to which he is constitutionally entitled—an adequate evidentiary hearing productive of reliable results concerning the voluntariness of his confession. It does not follow, however, that Jackson is automatically entitled to a complete new trial including a retrial of the issue of guilt or innocence. ... If at the conclusion of such an evidentiary hearing in the state court on the coercion issue, it is determined that Jackson's confession was voluntarily given, admissible in evidence, and properly to be considered by the jury, we see no constitutional necessity at that point for proceeding with a new trial, for Jackson has already been tried by a jury with the confession placed before it and has been found guilty. True, the jury in the first trial was permitted to deal with the issue of voluntariness and we do not know whether the conviction rested upon the confession; but if it did, there is no constitutional prejudice to Jackson from the New York procedure if the confession is now properly found to be voluntary and therefore admissible. If the jury relied upon it, it was entitled to do so. Of course, if the state court, at an evidentiary hearing, redetermines the facts and decides that Jackson's confession was involuntary, there must be a new trial on guilt or innocence without the confession's being admitted in evidence.

Obviously, the State is free to give Jackson a new trial if it so chooses, but for us to impose this requirement before the outcome of the new hearing on voluntariness is known would not comport with the interests of sound judicial administration and the proper relationship between federal and state courts. ... Accordingly, the judgment denying petitioner's writ of habeas corpus is reversed and the case is remanded to the District Court to allow the State a reasonable time to afford Jackson a hearing or a new trial, failing which Jackson is entitled to his release.

Reversed and remanded.

■ MR. JUSTICE BLACK, with whom MR. JUSTICE CLARK joins as to Part I of this opinion, dissenting in part and concurring in part. [Opinion omitted.]

■ [MR. JUSTICE CLARK's dissenting opinion is omitted]

■ MR. JUSTICE HARLAN, whom MR. JUSTICE CLARK and MR. JUSTICE STEWART join, dissenting. [Opinion omitted.]

NOTES

1. Did Jackson v. Denno indicate that the independent determination of the voluntariness had to be made upon a hearing conducted by the trial judge *outside* the presence of the jury? That was the contention made in Pinto v. Pierce, 389 U.S. 31, 88 S.Ct. 192 (1967), but it was rejected by the Court in a per curiam opinion in which the Court said:

> "This Court has never ruled that all voluntariness hearings must be held outside the presence of the jury, regardless of the circumstances.... Because a disputed confession may be found involuntary and inadmissible by the judge, it would seem prudent to hold voluntariness hearings outside the presence of the jury. In this case, however, the confession was held voluntary and admitted as evidence suitable for consideration by the jury. In addition, there is no claim that because the hearing was held in the

presence of the jury it was inadequate or had any other unfair consequences for the respondent."

In most jurisdictions, motions to suppress eye-witness identification are heard outside of the presence of the jury and resolved by the trial judge, frequently before trial commences. In Watkins v. Sowders, 449 U.S. 341, 101 S.Ct. 654 (1981), the Court held that such a procedure is not constitutionally mandated where the basis of the motion is that the out-of-court identification procedures were unnecessarily suggestive and that identification testimony must be excluded under the principles of Manson v. Brathwaite, supra, Chapter 3. The *Watkins* majority reasoned that juries can understand matters related to the reliability of identification testimony in a way that they may not be able to relate to the reasons for suppressing an involuntary confession. The *Watkins* opinion is ambiguous as to its holding. That holding is possibly either: (1) the trial court must make an independent determination of admissibility under *Manson* but can do that on the basis of evidence heard by the jury; or (2) the trial judge, as in confession cases before Jackson v. Denno, can submit the question of admissibility of identification testimony to the jury simultaneously with the question of innocence or guilt. According to the lower court Kentucky defendants Watkins and Summitt had received an independent judicial determination of the admissibility on the identification testimony, even though there was no separate suppression hearings. See Summitt v. Bordenkircher, 608 F.2d 247 (6th Cir.1979). The Sixth Circuit in *Summitt* had held that the procedure was consistent with *Pinto*. Whether the Supreme Court was going beyond *Pinto*, and, by distinguishing *Jackson*, meant to allow the jury to determine the admissibility of identification testimony is not clear from its opinion. Another possibility is that the Court was suggesting that the judge must rule on admissibility, but if he suppresses the identification testimony, he can instruct the jury to disregard the testimony and need not declare a mistrial.

2. Since Jackson the majority of jurisdictions seem to favor the orthodox rule. See Anno. 1 A.L.R.3d 1251. Some courts adopt the Massachusetts procedure and permit the jury to reconsider voluntariness after the court finds the confession to be voluntary. See People v. Huntley, 15 N.Y.2d 72, 255 N.Y.S.2d 838, 204 N.E.2d 179 (1965).

What of the other rules of suppression? Should a jury be allowed to consider Miranda compliance? The admissibility of eyewitness testimony? The legality of a search? The settled law is that search and seizure issues do not go to the jury. Can reasoned distinctions be drawn between the various types of suppressible evidence for purposes of submitting the issue to the jury? In jurisdictions where questions like these can be reargued before the jury, should the jury be told that the court has found the evidence admissible or that the lineup was not suggestive, etc.? Submission to the jury of suppression issues is not constitutionally mandated in any case. See United States v. Panepinto, 430 F.2d 613, 617–18 (3d Cir.1970).

3. The Court which decides motions to suppress must make findings. These need not be specific findings of fact. See Sims v. Georgia, 385 U.S. 538, 87 S.Ct. 639 (1967). Commonly the trial court will say "the motion to suppress is denied" or "I find the confession voluntary" or "the defendant waived his Miranda rights" or "the identification is legal". The Courts will sustain such rulings if there is evidence to support it. LaVallee v. Delle Rose, 410 U.S. 690, 93 S.Ct. 1203 (1973). The general ruling on a motion to suppress presents no problem when the hearing involves contradictory testimony by witnesses. The general finding is sometimes less than helpful when there is agreement on the facts but not upon their interpretation. Formal and detailed findings of fact should be made in complex cases, but it is doubtful that the failure to do so is grounds for reversal on appeal. Some cases have required specific findings on certain narrow issues. E.g., People v.

Brake, 191 Colo. 390, 553 P.2d 763 (1976) (whether accused requested counsel); United States v. Brown, 575 F.2d 746 (9th Cir.1978) (whether accused was intoxicated); State v. Rooks, 401 A.2d 943 (Del.1979) (whether certain promises did overbear defendant's will).

4. The motion to suppress is ordinarily made in advance of trial. The pre-trial motion is usually required regardless of the kind of evidence at issue. Some jurisdictions still do not provide for or require pre-trial suppression motions. The cases on both sides are collected in Annot. 50 A.L.R.2d 531. The policy arguments are difficult to resolve by logic alone. The use of pre-trial motions will enable the trial of the case to proceed smoothly without interruptions and delay when the jury leaves the courtroom so the judge may bear the evidence concerning admissibility. If evidence is suppressed prior to trial the prosecution may be spared the use of scarce resources in preparing for trial and the court may not have to waste time impaneling a jury, hearing opening statements and various witnesses before ending the case by suppressing evidence. On the other hand, a pretrial motion to suppress takes as much time, i.e., "delay", as a motion to suppress at any other time. Further, counsel may cause more delay by stringing out a series of suppression motions. The court will hear the evidence in the case in a piecemeal fashion. Witnesses may also be inconvenienced by having to come to court two or three times rather than once. It should be observed that trial judges may, and they often do, set motions to suppress for a given day and then set the trial for the day following resolution of the motions. In many cases, motions may be heard in the morning and trial may start in the afternoon. The prosecution will have a strong interest to have suppression issues resolved before trial if it has the right to appeal from adverse rulings.

Consider the comments in State v. Broxton, 49 N.J. 373, 230 A.2d 489 (1967):

> There are obvious advantages and disadvantages in a separate hearing either before or at trial. ... It may be well for the State and defense to know before trial whether the confessions will come in, and in some cases it may be desirable to permit interlocutory review. But on the other hand, when the issue is tried outside the presence of the jury, the issue must then be retried before the jury both under the orthodox and the Massachusetts rules. A replay is rarely as satisfactory, for there is absent the freshness of the first cross-examination. Moreover, the burden upon all concerned, principals and witnesses, is substantial, to say nothing of the burden on the judicial process which already moves at a snail's pace in criminal matters. In the case before us, the trial of the issue of voluntariness covers some 650 pages of transcript. Realistically, most confessions are admissible, and to encumber all cases with two trials of the same issue because of the danger of a mistrial in a few may be too heavy a price to exact from all concerned. Moreover, several trials of the same issue may present difficult questions. If in testifying in the absence of the jury, the defendant makes damaging admissions with respect to voluntariness, may the State prove them on the re-run before the jury? If not, the jury will be using a record different from the one the trial judge used. And what should be done if a defendant who does not testify on the preliminary hearing decides to testify before the jury, or if he offers before the jury other evidence not submitted to the trial judge alone?

Where a pre-trial suppression motion is allowed, it is often required as well. That is, failure to file a pre-trial motion operates as a waiver of the claim. The validity of this waiver rule has been the subject of much debate. Compare State v. Macon, 57 N.J. 325, 273 A.2d 1 (1971), with State v. Lemme, 104 R.I. 416, 244 A.2d 585 (1968). The constitutional validity of waiver rules generally is no longer subject to debate. Coleman v. Thompson, 501 U.S. 722, 111 S.Ct. 2546 (1991). Regardless of the debate over the abstract question of waiver, the waiver rule is applied in the overwhelming number of cases, state and federal. The corollaries to the rule requiring pre-trial suppression motions are two: (a) the ruling at the pre-trial motion is final in the absence of newly discovered evidence and the issue cannot be re-litigated at trial, (b) the filing of a pre-trial motion to suppress and the ruling thereon preserve the question for review and the defense need not object at trial. Some jurisdictions of course accept only one of these rules and others accept neither.

5. Apart from suppression of constitutionally inadmissible evidence, may a party seek pre-trial suppression of damaging evidence rendered inadmissible by ordinary rules of evidence? The right to do this may be crucial, more crucial than suppression of illegally seized evidence. Assume (and it is a fair assumption) that neither reversals on appeal nor mistrials are easy to procure even when one side acting in either good or bad faith gets inadmissible evidence before the jury. The only relief is to seek some advance ruling on the issue of admissibility at least prior to opposing counsel's opening statement. Probably every jurisdiction would permit the court discretion to entertain such a pre-trial motion (variously called motion to exclude, motion to limit proof, motion in limine, etc.). Are such motions common? Should they be and should the courts entertain them? What are the arguments for and against pre-trial motions on ordinary (as opposed to constitutional) objections to evidence and argument?

6. A number of states allow the prosecution to appeal orders suppressing evidence. The federal rule has been construed to allow prosecution appeal from any order suppressing evidence except those entered during trial. See United States v. Calandra, 455 F.2d 750 (6th Cir.1972). Could a statute provide for state appeal of an order entered during trial? See People v. Shipp, 96 Ill.App.2d 364, 239 N.E.2d 296 (1968) (allowing appeal from order entered in the course of a bench trial and effectively blocking entire prosecution—trial court had suspended trial). Would it be theoretically possible, practically feasible or desirable to allow suspension of jury trials for state appeals?

Lego v. Twomey

Supreme Court of the United States, 1972.
404 U.S. 477, 92 S.Ct. 619.

■ MR. JUSTICE WHITE delivered the opinion of the Court.

* * *

I.

Petitioner challenges the judgment of the Court of Appeals on three grounds. The first is that he was not proved guilty beyond a reasonable doubt as required by In re Winship (1970), because the confession used against him at his trial had been proved voluntary only by preponderance of the evidence. Implicit in the claim is an assumption that a voluntariness hearing is designed to enhance the reliability of jury verdicts. To judge whether that is so we must return to Jackson v. Denno (1964).

* * *

We noted in *Jackson* that there may be a relationship between the involuntariness of a confession and its unreliability. But our decision was not based in the slightest on the fear that juries might misjudge the accuracy of confessions and arrive at erroneous determinations of guilt or innocence. That case was not aimed at reducing the possibility of convicting innocent men.

Quite the contrary, we feared that the reliability and truthfulness of even coerced confessions could impermissibly influence a jury's judgment as to voluntariness. The use of coerced confessions, whether true or false, is forbidden because the method used to extract them offends constitutional principles. The procedure we established in *Jackson* was designed to safeguard the right of an individual, entirely apart from his guilt or innocence, not to be compelled to condemn himself by his own utterances. Nothing in *Jackson* questioned the province or capacity of juries to assess the truthfulness of confessions. Nothing in that opinion took from the jury any evidence relating to the accuracy or weight of confessions admitted into evidence. A defendant has been as free since *Jackson* as he was before to familiarize a jury with circumstances which attend the taking of his confession, including facts bearing upon its weight and voluntariness. In like measure, of course, juries have been at liberty to disregard confessions which are insufficiently corroborated or otherwise deemed unworthy of belief.

Since the purpose that a voluntariness hearing is designed to serve has nothing whatever to do with improving the reliability of jury verdicts, we cannot accept the charge that judging the admissibility of a confession by a preponderance of the evidence undermines the mandate of In re Winship (1970). ... *Winship* went no further than to confirm the fundamental right that protects "the accused against conviction except upon proof beyond a reasonable doubt of every fact necessary to constitute the crime with which he is charged." A high standard of proof is necessary, we said, to ensure against unjust convictions by giving substance to the presumption of innocence. A guilty verdict is not rendered less reliable or less consonant with *Winship* simply because the admissibility of a confession is determined by a less stringent standard. Petitioner does not maintain that either his confession or its voluntariness is an element of the crime with which he was charged. ... Petitioner's rights under *Winship* have not been violated.[15]

II.

Even conceding that *Winship* is inapplicable because the purpose of a voluntariness hearing is not to implement the presumption of innocence, petitioner presses for reversal on the alternative ground that evidence offered against a defendant at a criminal trial and challenged on constitutional grounds must be determined admissible beyond a reasonable doubt

15. Nothing is to be gained from restating the constitutional rule as requiring proof of guilt beyond a reasonable doubt on the basis of constitutionally obtained evidence and then arguing that rights under *Winship* are diluted unless admissibility is governed by a high standard. Transparently, this assumes the question at issue, which is whether a confession is admissible if found voluntary by a preponderance of the evidence. United States v. Schipani, 289 F.Supp. 43 (E.D.N.Y.1968), aff'd 414 F.2d 1262 (C.A.2 1969), followed this unsatisfactory course in a Fourth Amendment case but stopped short of basing the decision on the Constitution.

in order to give adequate protection to those values which exclusionary rules are designed to serve. . . .

The argument is straightforward and has appeal. But we are unconvinced that merely emphasizing the importance of the values served by exclusionary rules is itself sufficient demonstration that the Constitution also requires admissibility to be proved beyond reasonable doubt.[16] Evidence obtained in violation of the Fourth Amendment has been excluded from federal criminal trials for many years. The same is true of coerced confessions offered in either federal or state trials. But, from our experience over this period of time no substantial evidence has accumulated that federal rights have suffered from determining admissibility by a preponderance of the evidence. Petitioner offers nothing to suggest that admissibility rulings have been unreliable or otherwise wanting in quality because not based on some higher standard. . . . the exclusionary rules are very much aimed at deterring lawless conduct by police and prosecution and it is very doubtful that escalating the prosecution's burden of proof in Fourth and Fifth Amendment suppression hearings would be sufficiently productive in this respect to outweigh the public interest in placing probative evidence before juries for the purpose of arriving at truthful decisions about guilt or innocence.

To reiterate what we said in *Jackson*: when a confession challenged as involuntary is sought to be used against a criminal defendant at his trial, he is entitled to a reliable and clear-cut determination that the confession was in fact voluntarily rendered. Thus, the prosecution must prove at least by a preponderance of the evidence that the confession was voluntary. Of course, the States are free, pursuant to their own law, to adopt a higher standard. They may indeed differ as to the appropriate resolution of the values they find at stake.

III.

We also reject petitioner's final contention that, even though the trial judge ruled on his coercion claim, he was entitled to have the jury decide the claim anew. To the extent this argument asserts that the judge's determination was insufficiently reliable, it is no more persuasive than petitioner's other contentions. To the extent the position assumes that a jury is better suited than a judge to determine voluntariness, it questions the basic assumptions of Jackson v. Denno; it also ignores that *Jackson* neither raised any question about the constitutional validity of the so-called orthodox rule for judging the admissibility of confessions nor even suggested that the Constitution requires submission of voluntariness claims to a jury as well as a judge. . . . We are not disposed to impose as a constitutional requirement a procedure we have found wanting merely to afford petitioner a second forum for litigating his claim.

The decision of the Court of Appeals is affirmed.

16. It is no more persuasive to impose the stricter standard of proof as an exercise of supervisory power rather than as a constitutional rule. Cf. Ralph v. Warden, 438 F.2d 786, 793 (C.A.4 1970), clarifying United States v. Inman, 352 F.2d 954 (C.A.4 1965); Pea v. United States, 130 U.S.App.D.C. 66, 397 F.2d 627 (1967).

Affirmed.

■ MR. JUSTICE POWELL and MR. JUSTICE REHNQUIST took no part in the consideration or decision of this case.

■ MR. JUSTICE BRENNAN, with whom MR. JUSTICE DOUGLAS and MR. JUSTICE MARSHALL join, dissenting. [Opinion omitted.]

NOTES

1. Prior to Lego v. Twomey, the bare majority of jurisdictions had adopted a less than reasonable doubt standard for admitting confessions. Other jurisdictions never specifically dealt with burden of proof but it is clear that the standard is less than reasonable doubt. A substantial minority had adopted a reasonable doubt standard.

After Lego v. Twomey, most courts will apply the preponderance standard. So will some of the state courts which adopted the reasonable doubt standard because they believed the United States Supreme Court would eventually require it. State v. Johnson, 304 N.C. 680, 285 S.E.2d 792 (1982). But such state courts are free to retain the heavier burden of proof. See State v. Collins, 297 A.2d 620 (Me.1972). One state had adopted a higher burden of proof but the court rule was modified by a voter initiative. People v. Markham, 49 Cal.3d 63, 260 Cal.Rptr. 273, 775 P.2d 1042 (1989). A divided Supreme Court of Connecticut adhered to a preponderance evidence standard for proof of admissibility of confessions over a vigorous dissent which urged use of a reasonable doubt standard in light of recent proof that a significant number of confessions are false. State v. Lawrence, 282 Conn. 141, 920 A.2d 236 (2007) Would a change in the burden of proof support the reintroduction of considerations of the reliability of a confession which the Supreme Court barred in Rogers v. Richmond, 365 U.S. 534, 81 S.Ct. 735 (1961) which prohibited courts from considering probable truth of a confession is deciding whether it is admissible.

2. The rules relating to burdens of proof in motions to suppress are fitted as parts in a patchwork quilt. A summary follows:

> Under Bumper v. North Carolina, 391 U.S. 543, 548, 88 S.Ct. 1788 (1968), the prosecution bears the burden of persuasion when it relies on consent to justify a search. However, under federal rules, the defendant bears the burden of proving the illegality of a seizure of evidence pursuant to warrant and the prosecution bears the burden of proof only when the search is warrantless. See United States v. Thompson, 421 F.2d 373, 377 (5th Cir.1970).
>
> There are several federal cases seemingly holding that the burden of proof is upon defendant to establish the illegality of any challenged seizure but these cases do not seem to represent the prevailing federal rule. See United States v. Morin, 378 F.2d 472, 475 (2d Cir.1967); Wilson v. United States, 218 F.2d 754, 757 (10th Cir.1955). Under federal rules the defendant must prove that he has standing to object to an illegal seizure. United States v. Sacco, 436 F.2d 780, 784 (2d Cir.1971). A federal defendant must prove that wiretapping was unlawfully employed against him in order to secure suppression of wiretap evidence. Nardone v. United States, 308 U.S. 338, 341 (1939); Nolan v. United States, 423 F.2d 1031, 1041 (10th Cir.1969). A defendant claiming abuse of civil summons must prove that no proper civil purpose underlay the summons. United States v. Ferrone, 438 F.2d 381, 387–88 (3d Cir.1971). Where the prosecution bears the burden on motions to suppress physical evidence, the burden is not that of reasonable doubt. Manuel v. United States, 355 F.2d 344, 346 (5th Cir.1966).

Although the federal rule is widely followed, many states provide that on motions to suppress seized evidence the burden of proving illegal seizure is, in all cases, except consent search, borne by the defendant. See People v. Berrios, 28 N.Y.2d 361, 321 N.Y.S.2d 884, 887–90, 270 N.E.2d 709, 712–14 (1971).

When the suppression of eyewitness identification is sought, the basic rule seems to place upon the defendant the burden of proving that his rights were violated. In other words, the defendant must prove the primary illegality, i.e., denial of counsel or unnecessarily suggestive confrontation. If the defendant carries his burden the prosecution, if it wishes to use in court identification evidence, bears the burden of establishing by "clear and convincing evidence that the in court identifications were based upon observations of the suspect other than the line-up identification". United States v. Wade, 388 U.S. 218, 240, 87 S.Ct. 1926 (1967).

Finally, Lego v. Twomey arose in a jurisdiction where the prosecution by state law bore the burden of proof in confession questions. This is the rule in nearly every jurisdiction. Would it be constitutional to place upon the accused the burden of proof in confession cases? See Sims v. Georgia, 389 U.S. 404, 88 S.Ct. 523 (1967).

Of what significance is the burden of proof in suppression motions? It has been suggested that there is a high risk of perjury by some police officers in certain suppression hearings (a risk which is often cited by prosecutors as a ground for believing the exclusionary rule is pointless). It is then argued that placing the burden of proof on the prosecution (or placing a higher burden if the burden is already on the prosecutor) will diminish the profit in such perjury. Will it? If a police officer and an accused give diametrically opposed testimony about the seizure of evidence, the trial court must ordinarily decide to believe one or the other. This judgment does not depend upon the burden of proof but upon the credibility of the witnesses. See generally People v. Berrios, 28 N.Y.2d 361, 321 N.Y.S.2d 884, 270 N.E.2d 709 (1971). When the trier of fact chooses between two different versions of events, does it matter which burden of proof theory is applied? Doesn't the court have to decide in favor of the witness he believes in direct credibility contest cases? If the police officer (or the accused) is a successful perjurer, will he not win regardless of the burden? If he is an unsuccessful perjurer, will he not lose? Can it be argued that burden of proof assumes practical significance only in circumstantial evidence cases?

3. Lego's statement that evidence of involuntariness may be submitted to a jury to bear upon the credibility of the confession is, in fact, a rule required by the constitution. Crane v. Kentucky, 476 U.S. 683, 106 S.Ct. 2142 (1986).

Franks v. Delaware

Supreme Court of the United States, 1978.
438 U.S. 154, 98 S.Ct. 2674.

■ MR. JUSTICE BLACKMUN delivered the opinion of the Court.

This case presents an important and long-standing issue of Fourth Amendment law. Does a defendant in a criminal proceeding ever have the right, under the Fourth and Fourteenth Amendments, subsequent to the *ex parte* issuance of a search warrant, to challenge the truthfulness of factual statements made in an affidavit supporting the warrant?

. . . We hold that, where the defendant makes a substantial preliminary showing that a false statement knowingly and intentionally, or with reckless disregard for the truth, was included by the affiant in the warrant affidavit, and if the allegedly false statement is necessary to the finding of probable cause, the Fourth Amendment requires that a hearing be held at the defendant's request. In the event that at that hearing the allegation of perjury or reckless disregard is established by the defendant by a preponderance of the evidence, and, with the affidavit's false material set to one side, the affidavit's remaining content is insufficient to establish probable cause, the search warrant must be voided and the fruits of the search excluded to the same extent as if probable cause was lacking on the face of the affidavit.

The controversy over the veracity of the search warrant affidavit in this case arose in connection with petitioner Jerome Franks' state conviction for rape, kidnaping, and burglary. On Friday, March 5, 1976, Mrs. Cynthia Bailey told police in Dover, Delaware, that she had been confronted in her home earlier that morning by a man with a knife, and that he had sexually assaulted her. She described her assailant's age, race, height, build, and facial hair, and gave a detailed description of his clothing as consisting of a white thermal undershirt, black pants with a silver or gold buckle, a brown leather three-quarter length coat, and a dark knit cap that he wore pulled down around his eyes.

That same day, petitioner Franks coincidentally was taken into custody for an assault involving a 15-year-old girl, Brenda B. ______, six days earlier. After his formal arrest, and while awaiting a bail hearing in Family Court, petitioner allegedly stated to Robert McClements, the youth officer accompanying him, that he was surprised the bail hearing was "about Brenda B. ______. I know her. I thought you said Bailey. I don't know her." . . .

On the following Monday, March 8, officer McClements happened to mention the courthouse incident to a detective, Ronald R. Brooks, who was working on the *Bailey* case. On March 9, detective Brooks and detective Larry D. Gray submitted a sworn affidavit to a justice of the peace in Dover, in support of a warrant to search petitioner's apartment. In paragraph 8 of the affidavit's "probable cause page" mention was made of petitioner's statement to McClements. In paragraph 10, it was noted that the description of the assailant given to the police by Mrs. Bailey included the above-mentioned clothing. Finally, the affidavit also described the attempt made by police to confirm that petitioner's typical outfit matched that of the assailant. Paragraph 15 recited: "On Tuesday, 3/9/76, your affiant contacted Mr. James Williams and Mr. Wesley Lucas of the Delaware Youth Center where Jerome Franks is employed and did have personal conversation with both these people." Paragraphs 16 and 17 respectively stated: "Mr. James Williams revealed to your affiant that the normal dress of Jerome Franks does consist of a white knit thermal undershirt and a brown leather jacket," and "Mr. Wesley Lucas revealed to your affiant that in addition to the thermal undershirt and jacket, Jerome Franks often wears a large green knit hat."

The warrant was issued on the basis of this affidavit. Pursuant to the warrant, police searched petitioner's apartment and found a white thermal undershirt, a knit hat, dark pants, and a leather jacket, and, on petitioner's kitchen table, a single-blade knife. All these ultimately were introduced in evidence at trial.

Prior to the trial, however, petitioner's counsel filed a written motion to suppress the clothing and the knife found in the search.... At the hearing on the motion to suppress, defense counsel orally amended the challenge to include an attack on the veracity of the warrant affidavit; he also specifically requested the right to call as witnesses detective Brooks, Wesley Lucas of the Youth Center, and James D. Morrison, formerly of the Youth Center. Counsel asserted that Lucas and Morrison would testify that neither had been personally interviewed by the warrant affiants, and that, although they might have talked to another police officer, any information given by them to that officer was "somewhat different" from what was recited in the affidavit. Defense counsel charged that the misstatements were included in the affidavit not inadvertently, but in "bad faith." Counsel also sought permission to call officer McClements and petitioner as witnesses, to seek to establish that petitioner's courthouse statement to police had been obtained in violation of petitioner's *Miranda* rights, and that the search warrant was thereby tainted as the fruit of an illegally obtained confession.

In rebuttal, the State's attorney argued in detail, (a) that Del.Code Ann., Tit. 11, §§ 2306 and 2307 (1974), contemplated that any challenge to a search warrant was to be limited to questions of sufficiency based on the face of the affidavit; (b) that, purportedly, a majority of the States whose practice was not dictated by statute observed such a rule.... The State objected to petitioner's "going behind [the warrant affidavit] in any way," and argued that the court must decide petitioner's motion "on the four corners" of the affidavit.

The trial court sustained the State's objection to petitioner's proposed evidence....

On appeal, the Supreme Court of Delaware affirmed....

* * *

Whether the Fourth and Fourteenth Amendments, and the derivative exclusionary rule ..., ever mandate that a defendant be permitted to attack the veracity of a warrant affidavit after the warrant has been issued and executed, is a question that encounters conflicting values. The bulwark of Fourth Amendment protection, of course, is the Warrant Clause, requiring that, absent certain exceptions, police obtain a warrant from a neutral and disinterested magistrate before embarking upon a search. In deciding today that, in certain circumstances, a challenge to a warrant's veracity must be permitted, we derive our ground from language of the Warrant Clause itself, which surely takes the affiant's good faith as its premise: "[N]o warrants shall issue, but upon probable cause, supported by Oath or affirmation.... " Judge Frankel, in United States v. Halsey, 257 F.Supp. 1002, 1005 (S.D.N.Y.1966), put the matter simply: "[W]hen the Fourth Amendment demands a factual showing sufficient to comprise 'probable cause,' the obvious assumption is that there will be a *truthful* showing" (emphasis in original). This does not mean "truthful" in the sense that every fact recited in the warrant affidavit is necessarily correct, for probable cause may be founded upon hearsay and upon information received from informants, as well as upon information within the affiant's own knowledge that sometimes must be garnered hastily. But surely it is to be "truthful" in the sense that the information put forth is believed or appropriately accepted by the affiant as true. It is established law that a warrant affidavit must set forth particular facts and circumstances underlying the existence of probable cause, so as to allow the magistrate to make an independent evaluation of the matter. If an informant's tip is the source of information, the affidavit must recite "some of the underlying circumstances from which the informant concluded" that relevant evidence might be discovered, and "some of the underlying circumstances from which the officer concluded that the informant, whose identity need not be disclosed, ... was 'credible' or his information 'reliable.' " Because it is the magistrate who must determine independently whether there is probable cause, it would be an unthinkable imposition upon his authority if a warrant affidavit, revealed after the fact to contain a deliberately or reckless false statement, were to stand beyond impeachment.

In saying this, however, one must give cognizance to competing values that lead us to impose limitations. They perhaps can best be addressed by noting the arguments ... against allowing veracity challenges. The arguments are several:

First, respondent argues that the exclusionary rule, created in Weeks v. United States (1914), is not a personal constitutional right, but only a judicially created remedy extended where its benefit as a deterrent promises to outweigh the societal cost of its use; that the Court has declined to apply the exclusionary rule when illegally seized evidence is used to impeach the credibility of a defendant's testimony, Walder v. United States (1954), is used in a grand jury proceeding, United States v. Calandra (1974), or is used in a civil trial, United States v. Janis (1976); and that the Court similarly has restricted application of the Fourth Amendment exclusionary rule in federal habeas corpus review of a state conviction. See Stone v. Powell (1976). Respondent argues that applying the exclusionary rule to another situation—the deterrence of deliberate or reckless untruthfulness in a warrant affidavit—is not justified for many of the same reasons that led to the above restrictions; interfering with a criminal conviction in order to deter official misconduct is a burden too great to impose on society.

Second, respondent argues that a citizen's privacy interests are adequately protected by a requirement that applicants for a warrant submit a sworn affidavit and by the magistrate's independent determination of sufficiency based on the face of the affidavit. Applying the exclusionary rule to attacks upon veracity would weed out a minimal number of perjurious government statements, says respondent, but would overlap unnecessarily with existing penalties against perjury, including criminal prosecutions, departmental discipline for misconduct, contempt of court, and civil actions.

Third, it is argued that the magistrate already is equipped to conduct a fairly vigorous inquiry into the accuracy of the factual affidavit supporting a warrant application. He may question the affiant, or summon other persons to give testimony at the warrant proceeding. The incremental gain from a post-search adversary proceeding, it is said, would not be great.

Fourth, it is argued that it would unwisely diminish the solemnity and moment of the magistrate's proceeding to make his inquiry into probable cause reviewable in regard to veracity. The less final, and less deference paid to, the magistrate's determination of veracity, the less initiative will he use in that task. Denigration of the magistrate's function would be imprudent insofar as his scrutiny is the last bulwark preventing any particular invasion of primacy before it happens.

Fifth, it is argued that permitting a post-search evidentiary hearing on issues of veracity would confuse the pressing issue of guilt or innocence with the collateral question as to whether there had been official misconduct in the drafting of the affidavit. The weight of criminal dockets, and the need to prevent diversion of attention from the main issue of guilt or innocence, militate against such an added burden on the trial courts. And if such hearings were conducted routinely, it is said, they would be misused by defendants as a convenient source of discovery. Defendants might even use the hearings in an attempt to force revelation of the identity of informants.

Sixth and finally, it is argued that a post-search veracity challenge is inappropriate because the accuracy of an affidavit in large part is beyond the control of the affiant. An affidavit may properly be based on hearsay, on fleeting observations, and on tips received from unnamed informants whose identity often will be properly protected from revelation under McCray v. Illinois (1967).

None of these considerations is trivial. Indeed, because of them, the rule announced today has a limited scope, both in regard to when exclusion of the seized evidence is mandated, and when a hearing on allegations of misstatements must be accorded. But neither do the considerations cited by respondent and others have a fully controlling weight; we conclude that they are insufficient to justify an *absolute* ban on post-search impeachment of veracity. On this side of the balance, also, there are pressing considerations:

First, a flat ban on impeachment of veracity could denude the probable cause requirement of all real meaning. The requirement that a warrant not issue "but upon probable cause, supported by Oath or affirmation," would be reduced to a nullity if a police officer was able to use deliberately falsified allegations to demonstrate probable cause, and, having misled the magistrate, then was able to remain confident that the ploy was worthwhile. It is this specter of intentional falsification that, we think, has evoked such widespread opposition to the flat nonimpeachment rule from the commentators, from the American Law Institute in its Model Code of Pre-Arraignment Procedure, § SS290.3(1), from the federal courts of appeals, and from state courts. On occasion, of course, an instance of deliberate falsity will be exposed and confirmed without a special inquiry either at trial or at a hearing on the sufficiency of the affidavit. A flat nonimpeachment rule would bar re-examination of the warrant even in these cases.

Second, the hearing before the magistrate not always will suffice to discourage lawless or reckless misconduct. The presearch proceeding is necessarily *ex parte*, since the subject of the search cannot be tipped off to the application for a warrant lest he destroy or remove evidence. The usual reliance of our legal system on adversary proceedings itself should be an indication that an *ex parte* inquiry is likely to be less vigorous. The magistrate has no acquaintance with the information that may contradict the good faith and reasonable basis of the affiant's allegations. The presearch proceeding will frequently be marked by haste, because of the understandable desire to act before the evidence disappears; this urgency will not always permit the magistrate to make an extended independent examination of the affiant or other witnesses.

Third, the alternative sanctions of a perjury prosecution, administrative discipline, contempt, or a civil suit are not likely to fill the gap. Mapp v. Ohio, supra, implicitly rejected the adequacy of these alternatives. Mr. Justice Douglas noted this in his concurrence in *Mapp*: " 'Self-scrutiny is a lofty ideal, but its exaltation reaches new heights if we expect a District Attorney to prosecute himself or his associates for well-meaning violations of the search and seizure clause during a raid the District Attorney or his associates have ordered.' "

Fourth, allowing an evidentiary hearing, after a suitable preliminary proffer of material falsity, would not diminish the importance and solemnity of the warrant-issuing process. It is the *ex parte* nature of the initial hearing, rather than the magistrate's capacity, that is the reason for the review. A magistrate's determination is presently subject to review before trial as to *sufficiency* without any undue interference with the dignity of the magistrate's function. Our reluctance today to extend the rule of exclusion beyond instances of deliberate misstatements, and those of reckless disregard, leaves a broad field where the magistrate is the sole protection of a citizen's Fourth Amendment rights, namely, in instances where police have been merely negligent in checking or recording the facts relevant to a probable cause determination.

Fifth, the claim that a post-search hearing will confuse the issue of the defendant's guilt with the issue of the State's possible misbehavior is footless. The hearing will not be in the presence of the jury. An issue extraneous to guilt already is examined in any probable cause determination or review of probable cause. Nor, if a sensible threshold showing is required and sensible substantive requirements for suppression are maintained, need there be any new large-scale commitment of judicial resources; many claims will wash out at an early stage, and the more substantial ones in any event would require judicial resources for vindication if the suggested alternative sanctions were truly to be effective. The requirement of a substantial preliminary showing would suffice to prevent the misuse of a veracity hearing for purposes of discovery or obstruction. And because we are faced today with only the question of the integrity of the affiant's representations as to his own activities, we need not decide, and we in no way predetermine, the difficult question whether a reviewing court must ever require the revelation of the identity of an informant once a substantial preliminary showing of falsity has been made. *McCray v. Illinois*, the Court's earlier disquisition in this area, concluded only that the Due Process Clause of the Fourteenth Amendment did not require the State to expose an informant's identity routinely, upon a defendant's mere demand, when there was ample evidence in the probable cause hearing to show that the informant was reliable and his information credible.

Sixth and finally, as to the argument that the exclusionary rule should not be extended to a "new" area, we cannot regard any such extension really to be at issue here. Despite the deep skepticism of Members of this Court as to the wisdom of extending the exclusionary rule to collateral areas, such as civil or grand jury proceedings, the Court has not questioned, in the absence of a more efficacious sanction, the continued application of the rule to suppress evidence from the State's case where a Fourth Amendment violation has been substantial and deliberate. We see no principled basis for distinguishing between the question of the sufficiency of an affidavit, which also is subject to a post-search re-examination, and the question of its integrity.

In sum, and to repeat with some embellishment what we stated at the beginning of this opinion: There is, of course, a presumption of validity with respect to the affidavit supporting the search warrant. To mandate an evidentiary hearing, the challenger's attack must be more than conclusory and must be supported by more than a mere desire to cross-examine. There must be allegations of deliberate falsehood or of reckless disregard for the truth, and those allegations must be accompanied by an offer of proof. They should point out specifically the portion of the warrant affidavit that is claimed to be false; and they should be accompanied by a statement of supporting reasons. Affidavits or sworn or otherwise reliable statements of witnesses should be furnished, or their absence satisfactorily explained. Allegations of negligence or innocent mistake are insufficient. The deliberate falsity or reckless disregard whose impeachment is permitted today is only that of the affiant, not of any nongovernmental informant. Finally, if these requirements are met, and if, when material that is the subject of the alleged falsity or reckless disregard is set to one side, there remains sufficient content in the warrant affidavit to support a finding of probable cause, no hearing is required. On the other hand, if the remaining content is insufficient, the defendant is entitled, under the Fourth Amendment, to his hearing. Whether he will prevail at that hearing is, of course, another issue.

Because of Delaware's absolute rule, its courts did not have occasion to consider the proffer put forward by petitioner Franks. Since the framing of suitable rules to govern proffers is a matter properly left to the States, we decline ourselves to pass on petitioner's proffer. The judgment of the Supreme Court of Delaware is reversed, and the case is remanded for further proceedings not inconsistent with this opinion.

It is so ordered. [Appendix omitted.]

■ MR. JUSTICE REHNQUIST, with whom THE CHIEF JUSTICE joins, dissenting. [Omitted]

NOTES

1. To what extent may the suppression motion be used for discovery purposes? Consider that most of the facts which are developed in motions to suppress are not particularly relevant to guilt or innocence. The existence or sufficiency of a warrant and the method of executing a search will have little relation to the ultimate issue in the case. Only in jurisdictions offering very little formal discovery will the motions to suppress be useful discovery devices. There may be two exceptions to this rule, one minor and one major. The minor exception involves cases in which the crime is unlawful possession of some prohibited thing and the possession in question is that which the officer witnessed as he discovered the narcotics or weapon, etc. In such a case the testimony on a motion to suppress will include nearly everything the prosecution will prove at trial. However, the evidence in these cases is not ordinarily difficult to discover in any event and is fairly predictable. The major exception involves motions to suppress eyewitness identification. This is particularly true when the defense does establish primary illegality and the hearing turns to admissibility of in court identification. Then the defense may gain the benefit of a searching, sworn and recorded interview with the eyewitness, who may refuse to speak with defense counsel except while on the stand. The suppression hearing may not be used solely for discovery purposes and a court may limit examination. See Cefalo v. Fitzpatrick, 434 F.2d 187 (1st Cir.1970). People v. Chipp, 75 N.Y.2d 327, 553 N.Y.S.2d 72, 552 N.E.2d 608 (1990) (trial court may preclude calling the victim-witness to testify at suppression hearing to prevent harassment or abuse of victim). It is difficult to see precisely where the line may be drawn and several courts have continued to permit trial judges to allow full development of the facts.

What opportunity does the prosecution have for discovery? The answer depends largely on the degree to which the defense must offer evidence to make a case in the motion. Even so, the prosecutor is generally limited in two ways. Like the defense, he cannot examine witnesses (particularly the defendant) concerning issues outside the scope of the hearing. Rule 104(d), Fed.R.Evid. states the general rule:

> (d) Testimony by accused. The accused does not, by testifying upon a preliminary matter, subject himself to cross-examination as to other issues in the case.

Within those limits, the prosecution may get some idea of the impending defense. Apart from this, if the accused makes damaging admissions on the motion to suppress, may the prosecutor use these admissions at trial? Simmons v. United States, 390 U.S. 377, 88 S.Ct. 967 (1968), held that the admissions were inadmissible (at least in the prosecution's case-in-chief) if they were necessary in order to acquire standing. May they be used to impeach trial testimony? Compare Woody v. United States, 379 F.2d 130 (D.C.Cir.1967), and People v. Sturgis, 58 Ill.2d 211, 317 N.E.2d 545 (1974) (allowing impeachment), with People v. Luna, 37 Ill.2d 299, 226 N.E.2d 586 (1967) (forbidding impeachment). Consider the effect of Harris v. New York, 401 U.S. 222, 91 S.Ct. 643 (1971).

Both prosecution and defense do make one valuable discovery at motions to suppress; they learn a good deal about the courtroom demeanor and intelligence of the witnesses who do testify.

2. Suppose that instead of committing perjury, the officer-affiant omits from an affidavit a fact known to him which, if considered in the probable cause calculation, would weaken the case for probable cause. Does *Franks* apply in such a situation? For one decision touching on the point, see People v. Kurland, 28 Cal.3d 376, 168 Cal.Rptr. 667, 618 P.2d 213 (1980).

Some courts resolve claims of material omissions by "retesting" the affidavit after adding exculpatory information known by the affiant but omitted from the affidavit. The court did this in State v. Morris, 444 So.2d 1200 (La.1984), where the omitted data bore on the credibility of a hearsay source (a prior conviction and a strong motive to do harm to one resident of the targeted premises). But how can a trial judge or a reviewing court be sure that the issuing magistrate would have issued the warrant if he or she had known this additional information? The process of "retesting" after excluding known falsehoods or including known exculpatory data omitted from the affidavit seems to rest on the motion that whether an affidavit suffices is a question of pure law, which a reviewing court should consider de novo without deference to the issuing magistrate. That approach is fundamentally inconsistent with Illinois v. Gates, supra, Chapter 5. Compare People v. Keller, 479 Mich. 467, 739 N.W.2d 505 (2007) (Franks doctrine allows a court to suppress some seized evidence and admit others depending on what part of the warrant application remains valid).

If a citizen-informer has deceived an officer who reasonably and in good faith believed the informer, *Franks* has no application. Does it apply where the citizen rather than the officer serves as the affiant and commits perjury? For one view, see People v. Born, 113 Ill.App.3d 449, 69 Ill.Dec. 209, 447 N.E.2d 426 (1983).

In unusual circumstances, a defendant may be denied access to a search warrant and supporting documents in order to protect the identity of an informant or to safeguard future investigations. The trial court and appeal court would examine these materials and decide whether probable cause exists. Such courts must be particularly diligent to consider all possible challenges that might be raised. This result is possible only because a suppression hearing "is not aimed at safeguarding the truth-seeking process nor is its underlying purpose to redress any injury to the defendant's privacy. It is a judicially created remedy intended as a means of discouraging police misconduct." See People v. Castillo, 80 N.Y.2d 578, 592 N.Y.S.2d 945, 607 N.E.2d 1050 (1992) (5–2) and People v. Hobbs, 7 Cal.4th 948, 30 Cal.Rptr.2d 651, 873 P.2d 1246 (1994).

CHAPTER 14

COMPETENCY TO STAND TRIAL

A. SUBSTANTIVE STANDARDS AND PROCEDURES FOR DETERMINING COMPETENCY

Drope v. Missouri

Supreme Court of the United States, 1975.
420 U.S. 162, 95 S.Ct. 896.

■ MR. CHIEF JUSTICE BURGER delivered the opinion of the Court.

[The issue was whether, because of certain facts which came to the attention of the trial judge before and during trial, the United States Constitution required him to conduct an evidentiary hearing to determine whether the defendant was competent to stand trial.]

* * *

It has long been accepted that a person whose mental condition is such that he lacks the capacity to understand the nature and object of the proceedings against him, to consult with counsel, and to assist in preparing his defense may not be subjected to a trial. Thus, Blackstone wrote that one who became "mad" after the commission of an offense should not be arraigned for it "because he is not able to plead to it with that advice and caution that he ought." Similarly, if he became "mad" after pleading, he should not be tried, "for how can he make his defense?" 4 W. Blackstone Commentaries, 24. See Youtsey v. United States, 97 F. 937, 940–946 (C.A.61899). Some have viewed the common-law prohibition "as a by-product of the ban against trials *in absentia*; the mentally incompetent defendant, though physically present in the courtroom, is in reality afforded no opportunity to defend himself."

* * *

... For our purposes, it suffices to note that the prohibition is fundamental to an adversary system of justice. Accordingly, as to federal cases, we have approved a test of incompetence which seeks to ascertain whether a criminal defendant " 'has sufficient present ability to consult with his lawyer with a reasonable degree of rational understanding—and whether he has a rational as well as factual understanding of the proceedings against him.' " Dusky v. United States, 362 U.S., at 402, 80 S.Ct.788.

[The unanimous Court concluded that the trial judge erred in not holding a competency hearing either before or during trial.]

* * *

The question remains whether petitioner's due process rights would be adequately protected by remanding the case now for a psychiatric examination aimed at establishing whether petitioner was in fact competent to stand trial in 1969. Given the inherent difficulties of such a *nunc pro tunc* determination under the most favorable circumstances, see Pate v. Robinson, 383 U.S., at 386–387, 86 S.Ct. 836, 842–843; Dusky v. United States, 362 U.S., at 403, 80 S.Ct. at 789, we cannot conclude that such a procedure would be adequate here. The State is free to retry petitioner, assuming, of course, that at the time of such trial he is competent to be tried.

Pate v. Robinson

Supreme Court of the United States, 1966.
383 U.S. 375, 86 S.Ct. 836.

■ MR. JUSTICE CLARK delivered the opinion of the Court.

In 1959 respondent Robinson was convicted of the murder of his common-law wife, Flossie May Ward, and was sentenced to imprisonment for life. Being an indigent he was defended by court-appointed counsel. It was conceded at trial that Robinson shot and killed Flossie May, but his counsel claimed that he was insane at the time of the shooting and raised the issue of his incompetence to stand trial. On writ of error to the Supreme Court of Illinois it was asserted that the trial court's rejection of these contentions deprived Robinson of due process of law under the Fourteenth Amendment. His conviction was affirmed, the court finding that no hearing on mental capacity to stand trial had been requested, that the evidence failed to raise sufficient doubt as to his competence to require the trial court to conduct a hearing on its own motion, and further that the evidence did not raise a "reasonable doubt" as to his sanity at the time of the offense. We denied certiorari. Thereupon, Robinson filed this petition for habeas corpus, which was denied without a hearing by the United States District Court for the Northern District of Illinois. [The Court of Appeals reversed and remanded the case on several grounds.]

... The Court of Appeals directed that the District Court should also determine upon the hearing whether Robinson was denied due process by the state court's failure to conduct a hearing upon his competence to stand trial; and, if it were found his rights had been violated in this respect, that Robinson "should be ordered released, but such release may be delayed for a reasonable time ... to permit the State of Illinois to grant Robinson anew trial." We granted certiorari....

The State concedes that the conviction of an accused person while he is legally incompetent violates due process, Bishop v. United States, 350 U.S. 961, 76 S.Ct. 440 (1956), and that state procedures must be adequate to protect this right. It insists, however, that Robinson intelligently waived this issue by his failure to request a hearing on his competence at the trial; and further, that on the basis of the evidence before the trial judge no duty rested upon him to order a hearing *sua sponte*. A determination of these claims necessitates a detailed discussion of the conduct of the trial and the evidence touching upon the question of Robinson's competence at that time.

[The Court then reviewed the indications in the record which it believed suggested a bona fide doubt about the competency of the accused. Accurately summarized in the dissent which follows, the relevant data was found in the testimony of defense witnesses, presented as part of an insanity defense, that the accused over a period of years had behaved in an irrational manner. The Court also emphasized the testimony of witnesses who believed Robinson was insane at the time of the crime and the assertion by defense counsel that Robinson was "presently insane." Under then existing Illinois law, if a judge or jury found the defendant not guilty by reason of insanity, the trier of fact also had to decide whether the accused was "presently insane" in which case he would be committed for mental treatment. Ordinarily defense counsel urged that the client was presently insane lest the judge or jury be faced with the option of either convicting or letting the accused go free.]

* * *

The State insists that Robinson deliberately waived the defense of his competence to stand trial by failing to demand a sanity hearing as provided by Illinois law. But it is contradictory to argue that a defendant may be incompetent, and yet knowingly or intelligently "waive" his right to have the court determine his capacity to stand trial. See Taylor v. United States, 282 F.2d 16, 23 (8th Cir.1960). In any event, the record shows that counsel throughout the proceedings insisted that Robinson's present sanity was very much in issue. He made a point to elicit Mrs. Robinson's opinion of Robinson's "present sanity." And in his argument to the judge, he asserted that Robinson "should be found not guilty and presently insane on the basis of the testimony that we have heard." Moreover, the prosecutor himself suggested at trial that "we should have Dr. Haines' testimony as to his opinion whether this man is sane or insane." With this record we cannot say that Robinson waived the defense of incompetence to stand trial.[6]

We believe that the evidence introduced on Robinson's behalf entitled him to a hearing on this issue. The court's failure to make such inquiry thus deprived Robinson of his constitutional right to a fair trial. See Thomas v. Cunningham, 313 F.2d 934 (4th Cir.1963). Illinois jealously guards this right. Where the evidence raises a "*bona fide* doubt" as to a defendant's competence to stand trial, the judge on his own motion must impanel a jury and conduct a sanity hearing pursuant to Ill.Rev.Stat., c. 38, § 104–2 (1963). People v. Shrake, 25 Ill.2d 141, 182 N.E.2d 754 (1962). The Supreme Court of Illinois held that the evidence here was not sufficient to require a hearing in light of the mental alertness and understanding displayed in Robinson's "colloquies" with the trial judge. 22 Ill.2d, at 168, 174 N.E.2d, at 823. But this reasoning offers no justification for ignoring

6. Although defense counsel phrased his questions and argument in terms of Robinson's present insanity, we interpret his language as necessarily placing in issue the question of Robinson's mental competence to stand trial. Counsel was simply borrowing the terminology of the relevant Illinois statutes and decisions. The state law in effect at the time of Robinson's trial differentiated between lack of criminal responsibility and competence to stand trial, but used "insanity" to describe both concepts. Ill.Rev.Stat., c. 38, §§ 592, 593 (1963). . . .

the uncontradicted testimony of Robinson's history of pronounced irrational behavior. While Robinson's demeanor at trial might be relevant to the ultimate decision as to his sanity, it cannot be relied upon to dispense with a hearing on that very issue. . . .

Having determined that Robinson's constitutional rights were abridged by his failure to receive an adequate hearing on his competence to stand trial, we direct that the writ of habeas corpus must issue and Robinson be discharged, unless the State gives him a new trial within a reasonable time.

* * *

It has been pressed upon us that it would be sufficient for the state court to hold a limited hearing as to Robinson's mental competence at the time he was tried in 1959. If he were found competent, the judgment against him would stand. But we have previously emphasized the difficulty of retrospectively determining an accused's competence to stand trial. Dusky v. United States (1960). The jury would not be able to observe the subject of their inquiry, and expert witnesses would have to testify solely from information contained in the printed record. That Robinson's hearing would be held six years after the fact aggravates these difficulties. This need for concurrent determination distinguishes the present case from Jackson v. Denno (1964), where we held that on remand the State could discharge its constitutional obligation by giving the accused a separate hearing on the voluntariness of his confession.

If the State elects to retry Robinson, it will of course be open to him to raise the question of his competence to stand trial at that time and to request a special hearing thereon. In the event a sufficient doubt exists as to his present competence such a hearing must be held. If found competent to stand trial, Robinson would have the usual defenses available to an accused.

Case remanded to District Court with directions.

■ MR. JUSTICE HARLAN, whom MR. JUSTICE BLACK joins, dissenting.

* * *

Before turning to the facts, it is pertinent to consider the quality of the incompetence they are supposed to indicate. In federal courts—and I assume no more is asked of state courts—the test of incompetence that warrants postponing the trial is reasonably well settled. In language this Court adopted on the one occasion it faced the issue, "the 'test must be whether . . . [the defendant] has sufficient present ability to consult with his lawyer with a reasonable degree of rational understanding—and whether he has a rational as well as factual understanding of the proceedings against him.' " . . . In short, emphasis is on capacity to consult with counsel and to comprehend the proceedings, and lower courts have recognized that this is by no means the same test as those which determine criminal responsibility at the time of the crime. The question, then, is not whether the facts before the trial judge suggested that Robinson's crime was an insane act but whether they suggested he was incompetent to stand trial.

The Court's affirmative answer seemingly rests on two kinds of evidence, principally adduced by Robinson to prove an insanity defense after the State rested its main case. First, there was evidence of a number of episodes of severe irrationality in Robinson's past. Among them were the slaying of his infant son, his attempted suicide, his efforts to burn his wife's clothing, his fits of temper and of abstraction, and his seven week incarceration in a state hospital eight years before the trial. This evidence may be tempered by the State's counter arguments, for example, that Robinson was found guilty of his son's killing and that alcoholism may explain his hospitalization, but it cannot be written off entirely. The difficulty remains that while this testimony may suggest that Flossie May Ward's killing was just one more irrational act, I cannot say as a matter of common knowledge that it evidences incapacity during the trial. Indeed, the pattern revealed may best indicate that Robinson did function adequately during most of his life interrupted by periods of severe derangement that would have been quite apparent had they occurred at trial. The second class of data pertinent to the Court's theory, remarks by witnesses and counsel that Robinson was "presently insane," deserves little comment. I think it apparent that these statements were addressed to Robinson's responsibility for the killing, that is, his ability to do insane acts, and not to his general competency to stand trial.

Whatever mild doubts this evidence may stir are surely allayed by positive indications of Robinson's competence at the trial. Foremost is his own behavior in the courtroom. The record reveals colloquies between Robinson and the trial judge which undoubtedly permitted a reasonable inference that Robinson was quite cognizant of the proceedings and able to assist counsel in his defense. Turning from lay impressions to those of an expert, it was stipulated at trial that a Dr. Haines, Director of the Behavior Clinic of the Criminal Court of Cook County, had examined Robinson several months earlier and, if called, would testify that Robinson "knows the nature of the charge and is able to co-operate with his counsel." The conclusive factor is that Robinson's own lawyers, the two men who apparently had the closest contact with the defendant during the proceedings, never suggested he was incompetent to stand trial and never moved to have him examined on incompetency grounds during trial; indeed, counsel's remarks to the jury seem best read as an affirmation of Robinson's present "lucidity" which would be highly peculiar if Robinson had been unable to assist properly in his defense.

Thus, I cannot agree with the Court that the requirements of due process were violated by the failure of the trial judge, who had opportunities for personal observation of the defendant that we do not possess to halt the trial and hold a competency hearing on his own motion.

NOTES

1. *Insanity vs. Competency:* Competency to stand trial presents a different issue than insanity at the time of the crime, although courts still sometimes use the word "insanity" when speaking of incompetency. This is a vestige of the common law prohibition against trying persons who at the time of trial were "insane".... Some courts, however, believe that evidence of insanity at the time of the crime, without other data which call into question competency to stand trial, may not, by itself, suffice to require that a hearing be held to determine competency. In other words evidence that the accused was insane at the time of the alleged offense does not, by itself, create a bona fide doubt as to the defendant's ability to understand the charge or to assist in his defense. In Bryant v. State, 563 S.W.2d 37 (Mo.1978), the court held that the trial judge need not, sua sponte, hold a hearing to determine competency when a psychiatric report submitted to the judge indicates the psychiatrist's conclusion that the defendant is competent to stand trial but at the time of the crime suffered a mental disease or defect. Compare People v. Fixter, 79 A.D.2d 861, 434 N.Y.S.2d 484 (1980), where the court said that there was enough to raise the question of competence to stand trial where the defendant, two months after his plea of guilty to manslaughter, was diagnosed as having a psychosis associated with a brain tumor and where before the plea, a physician had reported the possibility of brain damage and associated emotional difficulties but no insanity. In United States v. Davis, 61 F.3d 291, 303 (5th Cir.1995), the court held that a suicide attempt alone was not sufficient to trigger the court's obligation to hold a competency hearing sua sponte.

For an argument that defendants (through counsel) should be able to waive a competency determination, see Winick, Criminal Law: Reforming Incompetency to Stand Trial and Plead Guilty: A Restated Proposal and Response to Professor Bonnie, 85 J. Crim. L. & Criminology 571 (1995).

2. *Incompetent or Unorthodox?* Should departures from the norm automatically trigger a psychiatric evaluation of a defendant for the purpose of determining competency? In some jurisdictions defendants who are clearly transsexual or transvestite are routinely subjected to competency inquiries. So, too, are persons who manifest religious beliefs substantially different from those prevalent in the community. Even if a trial judge does not believe that unorthodoxy is a sign of incompetency, he or she must be concerned about how a reviewing court will view the record. See People v. Thomas, 43 Ill.2d 328, 253 N.E.2d 431 (1969), one of a series of decisions in which the defendants, although deemed by a psychiatrist to be capable of cooperating with counsel, in fact were uncooperative with appointed counsel, stating that their attorney was "El-elohe, the Lord God of Israel." See also People v. Burson, 11 Ill.2d 360, 143 N.E.2d 239 (1957), where, in an era different from the present one, the defendant during voir dire inquired about the prospective jurors' religious beliefs, asking, for example, "Have you ever been born again?" Should a defendant who pleads guilty and seeks the death penalty be given a sua sponte competency hearing? Should a defendant who is taking psychotropic drugs be given a sua sponte competency hearing? See the discussion in State v. Kinkead, 168 Ill.2d 394, 214 Ill.Dec. 145, 660 N.E.2d 852 (1995).

3. *Use of Drugs to Achieve Competency.* In Riggins v. Nevada, 504 U.S. 127, 112 S.Ct. 1810 (1992), the Court held a defendant has a due process right to be free from the forced administration of an anti-psychotic drug prescribed after he complained of hearing voices and sleeplessness. At trial he objected to use of the drug because it denied him the ability to show jurors his true mental state when he offered an insanity defense. The Court said that before the drug use could be ordered the prosecution would have to show, and the trial court would have to find, that the drug was (1) medically appropriate, and (2) the least intrusive means to ensure the safety of defendant (or others) or to proceed to trial on the issue of guilt. The Court noted that Riggins may have been prejudiced by the effect of the drug on his appearance, the content of his testimony, his ability to follow the trial and to communicate with counsel. This prejudice *may* be outweighed by some essential state interest, but no showing of this was made. The Court did not say what that interest would be but the opinion could be read to suggest that if the use of the drug were the fairest and most reasonable way to go forward with the trial, the drug could be used over defendant's objection.

A few courts took advantage of *Riggins* language to hold that the state does have a compelling interest in medicating a dangerous person accused of murder in order to make him competent to stand trial. See State v. Garcia, 233 Conn. 44, 658 A.2d 947 (1995); Khiem v. United States, 612 A.2d 160 (D.C. 1992). In Sell v. United States, 539 U.S. 166, 123 S.Ct. 2174 (2003), the Court clarified a four-part test for determining whether a defendant may be forced to take medication in order to render him competent to stand trial. The Court held that the Government may involuntarily administer antipsychotic drugs to a mentally ill defendant in order to render that defendant competent to stand trial, but only if (1) important governmental interests are at stake, (2) the administration of the drugs is substantially likely to render the defendant competent to stand trial and substantially unlikely to have side effects that will interfere with the defendant's ability to assist counsel in conducting a defense, (3) the involuntary administration is necessary to advance the government's interests because less drastic measures will not suffice, and (4) the administration of such drugs is medically appropriate, i.e., in the defendant's best medical interest in light of his medical condition. The Court did not articulate a standard of proof to govern consideration of these factors, though the Second Circuit has suggested that the relevant findings must be supported by clear and convincing evidence. United States v. Gomes, 387 F.3d 157 (2d Cir. 2004).

Riggins does not specify what kind of pre-medication hearing would be required by due process. The Sixth Circuit recently held that an administrative hearing before a psychiatrist was inadequate, because the issue of competency, involving as it does the questions of whether the defendant can aid counsel and how defendant will appear to the jury, is beyond the expertise of a medical professional. The court specified that the defendant's physicians must be present in person at the hearing, that the defendant must be allowed to present rebuttal testimony, the government's proposal of forced medication must be reviewed under the strict scrutiny standard, and the government must make its case by clear and convincing evidence. United States v. Brandon, 158 F.3d 947 (6th Cir.1998).

4. *Procedure.* As a practical matter, the question of competency is frequently resolved without an evidentiary hearing. At the suggestion of counsel for either side, or on its own, the court may order a psychiatric evaluation of the accused. (Not infrequently where a defense of insanity is raised, the psychiatrist may examine the accused to form an opinion as to both sanity and competency.) If a psychiatric report indicates that the accused is competent, the court may declare that there is no bona fide doubt as to competency and dispense with a hearing. Such a procedure is contemplated by 18 U.S.C. §§ 4241, 4247, the statutes governing federal competency proceedings. See Pizzi, Competency to Stand Trial in Federal Courts: Conceptual and Constitutional Problems, 45 U.Chi.L.Rev. 21–71 (1977).

As *Pate* and *Drope* indicate, the failure to hold a competency hearing when a bona fide doubt exists often cannot be rectified by an appellate court remand to determine whether the defendant, at trial several years earlier, was, in fact, competent to stand trial. To avoid a retrial for want of a competency hearing, some trial judges, often at the suggestion of a prosecutor, will hold competency hearings even when everybody seems to agree that the accused is competent to stand trial.

In some jurisdictions, including United States District Courts, competency hearings are conducted by the trial judge sitting without a jury. In other jurisdictions, absent a waiver, a jury (different than the one trying the question of innocence or guilt), will decide the issue. Because there is no federal constitutional right to a jury trial on this issue, jurisdictions which provide for jury trials sometimes do allow the allegedly incompetent defendant to waive trial by jury. See People v. Brown, 43 Ill.2d 79, 250 N.E.2d 647 (1969). Does this make sense?

5. *Burden of Proof.* The Supreme Court held constitutional a state law which required a defendant claiming incompetency to prove incompetency by a preponderance of the evidence, Medina v. California, 505 U.S. 437, 112 S.Ct. 2572 (1992), but overturned a law which required defendant to prove incompetency by clear and convincing evidence. Cooper v. Oklahoma, 517 U.S. 348, 116 S.Ct. 1373 (1996) (holding that the additional risk imposed on a potentially incompetent defendant (and unaccompanied by any significant benefit to the state) violated the due process right to be tried only if competent). In Cooper, the state had argued that it had constitutional leeway to impose its own evidentiary rules, and that the clear and convincing standard was easier to administer because it was the same standard needed for civil commitment of an insane person. But the Court found that this burden transgressed due process because it had no precedent in the common law and little following among the other states.

6. *Competence to Plead Guilty.* Does entry of a plea of guilty require a higher degree of competency than does standing trial following a plea of not guilty? In Godinez v. Moran, 509 U.S. 389, 113 S.Ct. 2680 (1993), the Court held that neither pleading guilty nor waiving the right to counsel requires a higher standard of competency than that required for a defendant to go to trial. The Court reasoned that decisions to plead or to waive counsel are no more complicated than trial decisions about whether to testify, to waive a jury, to cross-examine or to offer a defense.

7. *Evidence of Competency.* Psychiatrists often are key witnesses incompetency hearings, although some psychiatrists insist that the defense lawyer, whose job it is to communicate with the defendant, is in a better position to assist the court in determining competency. The arresting officers and jail personnel may also have helpful information in competency cases. See Lingo v. State, 224 Ga. 333, 162 S.E.2d 1 (1968).

It may also be permissible to require or permit the testimony of defense counsel so long as his testimony does not repeat what his client has told him. If defense counsel testifies solely concerning his observations of defendant's conduct and ability to communicate and cooperate, and does not reveal the substance of the communications, the privilege is not violated. Tanner v. United States, 434 F.2d 260 (10th Cir.1970); United States v. Kendrick, 331 F.2d 110 (4th Cir.1964). But see Gunther v. United States, 230 F.2d 222 (D.C.Cir.1956).

One jurisdiction has sought to give statutory guidance to the sort of questions to be considered in competency hearings. See 725 ILCS 5/104–16 (1997):

> (b) Subject to the rules of evidence, matters admissible on the issue of the defendant's fitness include, but are not limited to, the following:
>
> > (1) The defendant's knowledge and understanding of the charge, the proceedings, the consequences of a plea, judgment or sentence, and the functions of the participants in the trial process;
> >
> > (2) The defendant's ability to observe, recollect and relate occurrences, especially those concerning the incidents alleged, and to communicate with counsel;
> >
> > (3) The defendant's social behavior and abilities; orientation as to time and place; recognition of persons, places and things; and performance of motor processes.

8. *Reevaluation and Review.* In some jurisdictions the accused cannot appeal a finding of incompetency to stand trial, his remedy being a "restoration" hearing in the trial court to determine whether he has regained competency. When the accused's condition is "stable" and the only issue is whether in that state he is competent, appellate review seems appropriate even if a finding of incompetency is not a "final order." See Jolley v. State, 282 Md. 353, 384 A.2d 91 (1978). To some extent, a state's failure to provide an appellate remedy has a less drastic effect because of the limits placed by Jackson v. Indiana (treated in the next section) upon holding an accused in custody solely by virtue of a finding of incompetence.

9. *Role of Counsel.* Should counsel for the defendant raise the issue of incompetency against the defendant's wishes? Is doing so ineffective assistance of counsel? A split panel of the Tenth Circuit faced these questions in United States v. Boigegrain, 155 F.3d 1181 (10th Cir.1998), cert. denied, 525 U.S. 1083, 119 S.Ct. 828 (1999). The majority held that counsel was not ineffective, arguing that requiring an attorney to take the position requested by a possibly incompetent client dis-serves both the client and the truth-seeking process. The dissenting judge looked to the practice of counsel in commitment hearings in which the decision to oppose civil commitment is the client's. He argued that counsel was constitutionally ineffective and should have asked to withdraw from representing the defendant.

B. LONG-TERM OR PERMANENT INCOMPETENCE TO STAND TRIAL

Jackson v. Indiana

Supreme Court of the United States, 1972.
406 U.S. 715, 92 S.Ct. 1845.

■ MR. JUSTICE BLACKMUN delivered the opinion of the Court.

We are here concerned with the constitutionality of certain aspects of Indiana's system for pretrial commitment of one accused of crime.

Petitioner, Theon Jackson, is a mentally defective deaf mute with a mental level of a pre-school child. He cannot read, write, or otherwise communicate except through limited sign language. In May 1968, at age 27, he was charged in the Criminal Court of Marion County, Indiana, with separate robberies of two women. The offenses were alleged to have occurred the preceding July. The first involved property (a purse and its contents) of the value of four dollars. The second concerned five dollars in money. The record sheds no light on these charges since, upon receipt of not-guilty pleas from Jackson, the trial court set in motion the Indiana procedures for determining his competency to stand trial.

As the statute requires, the court appointed two psychiatrists to examine Jackson. A competency hearing was subsequently held at which petitioner was represented by counsel. The court received the examining doctors' joint written report and oral testimony from them and from a deaf-school interpreter through whom they had attempted to communicate with petitioner. The report concluded that Jackson's almost nonexistent communication skill, together with his lack of hearing and his mental deficiency, left him unable to understand the nature of the charges against him or to participate in his defense. One doctor testified that it was extremely unlikely that petitioner could ever learn to read or write and questioned whether petitioner even had the ability to develop any proficiency in sign language. He believed that the interpreter had not been able to communicate with petitioner to any great extent and testified that petitioner's "prognosis appears rather dim." The other doctor testified that even if

Jackson were not a deaf mute, he would be incompetent to stand trial, and doubted whether petitioner had sufficient intelligence ever to develop the necessary communication skills. The interpreter testified that Indiana had no facilities that could help someone as badly off as Jackson to learn minimal communication skills.

On this evidence, the trial court found that Jackson "lack[ed] comprehension sufficient to make his defense," and ordered him committed to the Indiana Department of Mental Health until such time as that Department should certify to the court that "the defendant is sane."

Petitioner's counsel then filed a motion for a new trial, contending that there was no evidence that Jackson was "insane," or that he would ever attain a status which the court might regard as "sane" in the sense of competency to stand trial. Counsel argued that Jackson's commitment under these circumstances amounted to a "life sentence" without his ever having been convicted of a crime, and that the commitment therefore deprived Jackson of his Fourteenth Amendment rights to due process and equal protection, . . .

* * *

Petitioner's central contention is that the State, in seeking in effect to commit him to a mental institution indefinitely, should have been required to invoke the standards and procedures of Ind.Ann.Stat. § 22–1907, now Ind.Code 16–15–1–3 (1971), governing commitment of "feeble-minded" persons. That section provides that upon application of a "reputable citizen of the county" and accompanying certificate of a reputable physician that a person is "feeble-minded and is *not insane* or epileptic" (emphasis supplied), a circuit court judge shall appoint two physicians to examine such person. After notice, a hearing is held at which the patient is entitled to be represented by counsel. If the judge determines that the individual is indeed "feeble-minded," he enters an order of commitment and directs the clerk of the court to apply for the person's admission "to the superintendent of the institution for feeble-minded persons located in the district in which said county is situated." A person committed under this section may be released "at any time," provided that "in the judgment of the superintendent, the mental and physical condition of the patient justifies it." The statutes do not define either "feeble-mindedness" or "insanity". But a statute establishing a special institution for care of such persons refers to the duty of the State to provide care for its citizens who are "feeble-minded, and are therefore unable properly to care for themselves." These provisions evidently afford the State a vehicle for commitment of persons in need of custodial care who are "not insane" and therefore do not qualify as "mentally ill" under the State's general involuntary civil commitment scheme.

* * *

. . . Section 22–1201(1) defines a "mentally ill person" as one who

> "is afflicted with a psychiatric disorder which substantially impairs his mental health; and, because of such psychiatric disorder, requires care, treatment, training or detention in the interest of

the welfare of such person or the welfare of others of the community in which such person resides."

Because the evidence established little likelihood of improvement in petitioner's condition, he argues that commitment under § 9–1706a in his case amounted to a commitment for life. This deprived him of equal protection, he contends, because, absent the criminal charges pending against him, the State would have had to proceed under other statutes generally applicable to all other citizens: either the commitment procedures for feeble-minded persons, or those for mentally ill persons. He argues that under these other statutes (1) the decision whether to commit would have been made according to a different standard, (2) if commitment were warranted, applicable standards for release would have been more lenient, (3) if committed under § 22–1907, he could have been assigned to a special institution affording appropriate care, and (4) he would then have been entitled to certain privileges not now available to him.

* * *

In Baxstrom v. Herold, 383 U.S. 107, 86 S.Ct. 760 (1966), the Court held that a state prisoner civilly committed at the end of his prison sentence on the finding of a surrogate was denied equal protection when he was deprived of a jury trial that the State made generally available to all other persons civilly committed. Rejecting the State's argument that Baxstrom's conviction and sentence constituted adequate justification for the difference in procedures, the Court said that "there is no conceivable basis for distinguishing the commitment of a person who is nearing the end of a penal term from all other civil commitments." The Court also held that Baxstrom was denied equal protection by commitment to an institution maintained by the state corrections department for "dangerously mentally ill" persons, without a judicial determination of his "dangerous propensities" afforded all others so committed.

If criminal conviction and imposition of sentence are insufficient to justify less procedural and substantive protection against indefinite commitment than that generally available to all others, the mere filing of criminal charges surely cannot suffice. The *Baxstrom* principle also has been extended to commitment following an insanity acquittal, and to commitment in lieu of sentence following conviction as a sex offender.

Respondent argues, however, that because the record fails to establish affirmatively that Jackson will never improve, his commitment "until sane" is not really an indeterminate one. It is only temporary, pending possible change in his condition. Thus, presumably, it cannot be judged against commitments under other state statutes that are truly indeterminate. The State relies on the lack of "exactitude" with which psychiatry can predict the future course of mental illness, . . .

Were the State's factual premise that Jackson's commitment is only temporary a valid one, this might well be a different case. But the record does not support that premise. One of the doctors testified that in his view Jackson would be unable to acquire the substantially improved communication skills that would be necessary for him to participate in any defense. The prognosis for petitioner's developing such skills, he testified, appeared "rather dim." In answer to a question whether Jackson would ever be able to comprehend the charges or participate in his defense, even after commitment and treatment, the doctor said, "I doubt it, I don't believe so." The other psychiatrist testified that even if Jackson were able to develop such skills, he would *still* be unable to comprehend the proceedings or aid counsel due to his mental deficiency. The interpreter, a supervising teacher at the state school for the deaf, said that he would not be able to serve as an interpreter for Jackson or aid him in participating in a trial, and that the State had no facilities that could, "after a length of time," aid Jackson in so participating. The court also heard petitioner's mother testify that Jackson already had undergone rudimentary out-patient training communications skills from the deaf and dumb School in Indianapolis over a period of three years without noticeable success. There is nothing in the record that even points to any possibility that Jackson's present condition can be remedied at any future time....

... Jackson's § 9–1706a commitment is permanent in practical effect.

* * *

Under § 9–1706a, the State needed to show only Jackson's inability to stand trial. We are unable to say that, on the record before us, Indiana could have civilly committed him as mentally ill under § 22–1209 or committed him as feeble-minded under § 22–1907. The former requires at least (1) a showing of mental illness and (2) a showing that the individual is in need of "care, treatment, training or detention." § 22–1201(1). Whether Jackson's mental deficiency would meet the first test is unclear; neither examining physician addressed himself to this. Furthermore, it is problematical whether commitment for "treatment" or "training" would be appropriate since the record establishes that none is available for Jackson's condition at any state institution. The record also fails to establish that Jackson is in need of custodial care or "detention." He has been employed at times, and there is no evidence that the care he long received at home has become inadequate. The statute appears to require an independent showing of dangerousness ("requires ... detention in the interest of the welfare of such person or ... others...."). Insofar as it may require such a showing, the pending criminal charges are insufficient to establish it, and no other supporting evidence was introduced. For the same reasons, we cannot say that this record would support a feeble-mindedness commitment under § 22–1907 on the ground that Jackson is "unable properly to care for [himself]." § 22–1801.

More important, an individual committed as feeble-minded is eligible for release when his condition "justifies it," § 22–1814, and an individual civilly committed as mentally ill when the "superintendent or administrator shall discharge such person *or* [when] cured of such illness." § 22–1223 (emphasis supplied). Thus, in either case release is appropriate when the individual no longer requires the custodial care or treatment or detention that occasioned the commitment, or when the department of mental health believes release would be in his best interests. The evidence available concerning Jackson's past employment and home care strongly suggests that under these standards he might be eligible for release at almost any time, even if he did not improve. On the other hand, by the terms of his present § 9–1706a commitment, he will not be entitled to release at all, absent an unlikely substantial change for the better in his condition.

Baxstrom did not deal with the standard for release, but its rationale is applicable here. The harm to the individual is just as great if the State, without reasonable justification, can apply standards making his commitment a permanent one when standards generally applicable to all others afford him a substantial opportunity for early release.

As we noted above, we cannot conclude that pending criminal charges provide a greater justification for different treatment than conviction and sentence. Consequently, we hold that by subjecting Jackson to a more lenient commitment standard and to a more stringent standard of release than those generally applicable to all others not charged with offenses, and by thus condemning him in effect to permanent institutionalization without the showing required for commitment or the opportunity for release afforded by § 22–1209 or § 22–1907, Indiana deprived petitioner of equal protection of the laws under the Fourteenth Amendment.

For reasons closely related to those discussed above, we also hold that Indiana's indefinite commitment of a criminal defendant solely on account of his incompetency to stand trial does not square with the Fourteenth Amendment's guarantee of due process.

In the federal criminal system, the constitutional issue posed here has not been encountered precisely because the federal statutes have been construed to require that a mentally incompetent defendant must also be found "dangerous" before he can be committed indefinitely. But the decisions have uniformly articulated the constitutional problems compelling this statutory interpretation.

The federal statute, 18 U.S.C. §§ 4244 to 4246, is not dissimilar to the Indiana law.* It provides that a defendant found incompetent to stand trial may be committed "until the accused shall be mentally competent to stand trial or until the pending charges against him are disposed of according to law." Section 4247, applicable on its face only to convicted criminals whose federal sentences are about to expire, permits commitment if the prisoner is (1) "insane or mentally incompetent" and (2) "will probably endanger the safety of the officers, the property, or other interests of the United States, and ... suitable arrangements for the custody and care of the prisoner are not otherwise available," that is, in a state facility. See Greenwood v. United States, 350 U.S., at 373–374, 76 S.Ct., at 414–415. One committed under this section, however, is entitled to release when any of the three conditions no longer obtains, "whichever event shall first occur." § 4248. Thus, a person committed under § 4247 must be released when he no longer is "dangerous."

In *Greenwood*, the Court upheld the pretrial commitment of a defendant who met all three conditions of § 4247, even though there was little likelihood that he would ever become competent to stand trial. Since Greenwood had not yet stood trial, his commitment was ostensibly under

* Editor's Note: Federal competency to stand trial provisions now begin at 18 U.S.C. § 4241.

§ 4244. By the related release provision, § 4246, he could not have been released until he became competent. But the District Court had in fact applied § 4247, and found specifically that Greenwood would be dangerous if not committed. This Court approved that approach, holding § 4247 applicable before trial as well as to those about to be released from sentence. 350 U.S., at 374, 76 S.Ct., at 414. Accordingly, Greenwood was entitled to release when no longer dangerous, § 4248, even if he did not become competent to stand trial and thus did not meet the requirement of § 4246. Under these circumstances, the Court found the commitment constitutional.

Since *Greenwood*, federal courts without exception have found improper any straightforward application of §§ 4244 and 4246 to a defendant whose chance of attaining competency to stand trial is slim, thus effecting an indefinite commitment on the ground of incompetency alone.... The holding in each of these cases was grounded in an expressed substantial doubt that §§ 4244 and 4246 could survive constitutional scrutiny if interpreted to authorize indefinite commitment.

These decisions have imposed a "rule of reasonableness" upon §§ 4244 and 4246. Without a finding of dangerousness, one committed thereunder can be held only for a "reasonable period of time" necessary to determine whether there is a substantial chance of his attaining the capacity to stand trial in the foreseeable future. If the chances are slight, or if the defendant does not in fact improve, then he must be released or granted a §§ 4247–4248 hearing.

* * *

... The practice of automatic commitment with release conditioned solely upon attainment of competence has been decried on both policy and constitutional grounds. Recommendations for changes made by commentators and study committees have included incorporation into pretrial commitment procedures of the equivalent of the federal "rule of reason," a requirement of a finding of dangerousness or of full-scale civil commitment, periodic review by court or mental health administrative personnel of the defendant's condition and progress, and provisions for ultimately dropping charges if the defendant does not improve. One source of this criticism is undoubtedly the empirical data available which tend to show that many defendants committed before trial are never tried, and that those defendants committed pursuant to ordinary civil proceedings are, on the average, released sooner than defendants automatically committed solely on account of their incapacity to stand trial.[16] Related to these statistics are substantial doubts about whether the rationale for pretrial commitment—that care or treatment will aid the accused in attaining competency—is empirically valid

16. See Matthews, Mental Disability and the Criminal Law 138–140 (American Bar Foundation 1970); Morris, The Confusion of Confinement Syndrome: An Analysis of the Confinement of Mentally Ill Criminals and Ex–Criminals by the Department of Correction of the State of New York, 17 Buffalo L.Rev. 651 (1968); McGarry & Bendt, Criminal vs. Civil Commitment of Psychotic Offenders: A Seven–Year Follow–Up, 125 Am.J.Psychiatry 1387, 1391 (1969); D.C.Report 50–52.

given the state of most of our mental institutions.[17] However, very few courts appear to have addressed the problem directly in the state context.

* * *

In a 1970 case virtually indistinguishable from the one before us, the Illinois Supreme Court granted relief to an illiterate deaf mute who had been indicted for murder four years previously but found incompetent to stand trial on account of his inability to communicate, and committed. People ex rel. Myers v. Briggs, 46 Ill.2d 281, 263 N.E.2d 109 (1970). The institution where petitioner was confined had determined, "[I]t now appears that [petitioner] will never acquire the necessary communication skills needed to participate and cooperate in his trial." Petitioner, however, was found to be functioning at a "nearly normal level of performance in areas other than communication." The State contended petitioner should not be released until his competency was restored. The Illinois Supreme Court disagreed. It held:

> "This court is of the opinion that this defendant, handicapped as he is and facing an indefinite commitment because of the pending indictment against him, should be given an opportunity to obtain a trial to determine whether or not he is guilty as charged or should be released."

* * *

The States have traditionally exercised broad power to commit persons found to be mentally ill. The substantive limitations on the exercise of this power and the procedures for invoking it vary drastically among the States. The particular fashion in which the power is exercised—for instance, through various forms of civil commitment, defective delinquency laws, sexual psychopath laws, commitment of persons acquitted by reason of insanity—reflects different combinations of distinct bases for commitments ought to be vindicated. The bases that have been articulated include dangerousness to self, dangerousness to others, and the need for care or treatment or training. Considering the number of persons affected, it is perhaps remarkable that the substantive constitutional limitations on this power have not been more frequently litigated.

We need not address these broad questions here. It is clear that Jackson's commitment rests on proceedings that did not purport to bring into play, indeed did not even consider relevant, *any* of the articulated bases for exercise of Indiana's power of indefinite commitment. The state statutes contain at least two alternative methods for invoking this power. But Jackson was not afforded any "formal commitment proceedings addressed to [his] ability to function in society," or to society's interest in his restraint, or to the State's ability to aid him in attaining competency through custodial care or compulsory treatment, the ostensible purpose of the commitment. At the least, due process requires that the nature and

17. Note, supra, 81 Harv.L.Rev., at 472–473; American Bar Foundation, The Mentally Disabled and the Law 415–418 (rev. ed. 1971) (hereafter ABF Study); N.Y.Report 72–77, 102–105, 186–190.

duration of commitment bear some reasonable relation to the purpose for which the individual is committed.

We hold, consequently, that a person charged by a State with a criminal offense who is committed solely on account of his incapacity to proceed to trial cannot be held more than the reasonable period of time necessary to determine whether there is a substantial probability that he will attain that capacity in the foreseeable future. If it is determined that this is not the case, then the State must either institute the customary civil commitment proceeding that would be required to commit indefinitely any other citizen, or release the defendant. Furthermore, even if it is determined that the defendant probably soon will be able to stand trial, his continued commitment must be justified by progress toward that goal. In light of differing state facilities and procedures and a lack of evidence in this record, we do not think it appropriate for us to attempt to prescribe arbitrary time limits. We note, however, that petitioner Jackson has now been confined for three and one-half years on a record that sufficiently establishes the lack of a substantial probability that he will ever be able to participate fully in atrial.

* * *

DISPOSITION OF THE CHARGES

A. Petitioner argues that he has already made out a complete insanity defense. Jackson's criminal responsibility at the time of the alleged offenses, however, is a distinct issue from his competency to stand trial. The competency hearing below was not directed to criminal responsibility, and evidence relevant to it was presented only incidentally. Thus, in any event, we would have to remand for further consideration of Jackson's condition in the light of Indiana's law of criminal responsibility.

B. Dismissal of charges against an incompetent accused has usually been thought to be justified on grounds not squarely presented here: particularly, the Sixth–Fourteenth Amendment right to a speedy trial, or the denial of due process inherent in holding pending criminal charges indefinitely over the head of one who will never have a chance to prove his innocence. Jackson did not present the Sixth–Fourteenth Amendment issue to the state courts. Nor did the highest state court rule on the due process issue, if indeed it was presented to that court in precisely the above-described form. We think, in light of our holdings, that the Indiana courts should have the first opportunity to determine these issues.

C. Both courts and commentators have noted the desirability of permitting some proceedings to go forward despite the defendant's incompetency.[29] For instance, § 4.06(3) of the Model Penal Code would permit an incompetent accused's attorney to contest any issue "susceptible of fair determination prior to trial and without the personal participation of the

29. People ex rel. Myers v. Briggs, supra, 46 Ill.2d, at 288, 263 N.E.2d, at 113; Neely v. Hogan, 62 Misc.2d 1056, 310 N.Y.S.2d 63 (1970); N.Y.Report 115–123 (Recommendation No.13); D.C.Report 143–144 (Recommendation No. 15); Foote, supra, n. 14, at 841–845; Model Penal Code § 4.06 (alternative subsections 3, 4) (Proposed Official Draft 1962); ABF Study 423.

defendant." An alternative draft of § 4.06(4) of the Model Penal Code would also permit an evidentiary hearing at which certain defenses, not including lack of criminal responsibility, could be raised by defense counsel on the basis of which the court might quash the indictment. Some States have statutory provisions permitting pretrial motions to be made or even allowing the incompetent defendant a trial at which to establish his innocence, without permitting a conviction.[30] We do not read this Court's previous decisions to preclude the States from allowing, at a minimum, an incompetent defendant to raise certain defenses such as insufficiency of the indictment, or make certain pretrial motions through counsel. Of course, if the Indiana courts conclude that Jackson was almost certainly not capable of criminal responsibility when the offenses were committed, dismissal of the charges might be warranted. But even if this is not the case, Jackson may have other good defenses that could sustain dismissal or acquittal and that might now be asserted. We do not know if Indiana would approve procedures such as those mentioned here, but these possibilities will be open on remand.

■ MR. JUSTICE POWELL and MR. JUSTICE REHNQUIST took no part in the consideration or decision of this case.

NOTES

1. *Incompetency vs. Civil Commitment.* If an accused who is found incompetent to stand trial is committed under a state's civil commitment statutes, the narrow holding of Jackson v. Indiana has no impact. The defendant can be kept in custody on the same basis as any other civilly committed person. Problems may arise when the defendant is treated differently from other civilly committed persons. For example, the mental health authorities may, at some point, believe that a home-visit or a furlough is in the best interest of their patient. Should such furloughs be denied to patients who have murder or rape charges pending, on which they have been adjudicated incompetent to stand trial? The rights of the "mittimus patient" (one who has pending criminal charges) are often the subject of a classical institutional conflict between the mental health authorities, with paramount concern for their patient, and prosecutors, with an obligation to protect the public. Few things are as likely to generate public concern as an act of violence by an accused killer during a home-visit following a determination of incompetence to stand trial.

If the incompetent defendant is civilly committed, the holding of *Jackson* does not mandate the dismissal of charges. Even if the accused is not civilly committed, as long as he is not in custody, *Jackson* does not mandate the dropping of charges against a permanently incompetent accused. Consider, for example, a defendant on bond who suffers a permanent physical disability which renders him incompetent to stand trial. Can charges against him remain until his death, or does the right of a speedy trial at some point mandate dismissal of charges even though the state is not to be blamed for denying the accused a speedy trial? Some states mandate the termination of criminal proceedings once an incompetent accused has been in custody longer than the maximum period to which he could have been sentenced if found guilty. Such a provision benefits neither an incompetent defendant who is on

30. Wis.Stat.Ann. § 971.14(6) (1971); N.Y.Crim.Proc.Law § 730.60(5) (1971); Mass. Gen.Laws, c. 123, § 17 (Supp.1972); Mont. Rev.Code Ann. § 95–506(c) (1969); Md.Ann. Code, Art. 59, § 24(a) (1972). See Reg. v. Roberts, [1953] 3 W.L.R. 178, [1953] 2 All. E.R. 340 (Devlin, J.).

bond nor one charged with a crime for which either life or any number of years is a possible sentence.

2. *Duration of Custody after Finding of Incompetence.* How long may an accused be held in custody by virtue of a finding of incompetency if he is not civilly committed? See State ex rel. Matalik v. Schubert, 57 Wis.2d 315, 204 N.W.2d 13 (1973) (suggesting a six month limitation); Conn. Gen'l. Stat. 54–56d (I)(1) (if there is a "substantial probability" that competency can be restored, a defendant who is deemed incompetent to stand trial may be committed for a period "of the maximum sentence which the defendant could receive on conviction of the charges against him or eighteen months, whichever is less."); Cal. Penal Code 1370 (three years, or the maximum sentence defendant could receive, whichever is less, or when the superintendent of the treatment facility determines there is no substantial likelihood that defendant will regain competence).

3. *Trials to Determine Innocence Only.* As renumbered footnote 4 in *Jackson* indicates, some jurisdictions provide for an "innocent only trial" at which the prosecution is put to its proof and the incompetent defendant, aided by counsel, is allowed to advance defenses (including the insanity defense). If the trier of fact (usually a judge) finds the defendant "not guilty," the defendant is removed from the criminal justice system. If the trier of fact does not find the defendant "not guilty," the court enters no judgment of guilty. Instead the defendant's case remains in the criminal justice system and the defendant's continued incarceration is subject to the limitations of *Jackson*. Should the outer limits of incarceration tolerated by *Jackson* be extended if the system has afforded the incompetent defendant an "innocent only" trial and the prosecution has satisfied its burden of proof at such proceeding?

4. *Those Neither Competent nor Committable.* The most difficult dilemma is posed by persons who are neither competent to stand trial nor civilly committable. If state law provides for commitment of those who, because of a mental disease, are dangerous to themselves or others, some incompetent defendants may escape commitment because they have no mental disease, even though dangerous, or because their dangerousness cannot be proved. What happens to such persons after the outer limits of *Jackson* are reached? Must such persons be returned to society without ever standing trial?

In many jurisdictions the category of persons who are neither competent nor civilly committable, but nevertheless are thought dangerous by the public, is not small. Donald Lang, a deaf mute mentioned in *Jackson*, falls into that category. Although the origin of his incompetency is atypical, the problems illustrated by his case are not atypical of problems posed by persons who are neither competent nor civilly committable. Lang was accused of murdering an alleged prostitute. Because of his inability to communicate, he was found incompetent to stand trial. For many years (before *Jackson*) he was held in custody in a facility for the criminally insane. Then (before *Drope*) the Supreme Court of Illinois, on defense counsel's motion, ordered that he be tried despite his incompetency. By then, however, essential prosecution witnesses were missing and the charges were dropped. Lang was released. With in a year Lang was charged with the recent murder of a second alleged prostitute. The trial judge, believing that Lang must be tried, whether competent or not, according to the prior Illinois Supreme Court case, ordered a trial. Lang was convicted of murder on proof that was largely circumstantial. The Appellate Court reversed because the trial judge had not held a competency hearing. On remand the defendant was found to be incompetent. He was also found not to be within the civil mental commitment statute, thus creating the "limbo" status that poses the great dilemma. Should he be released without trial? The story of Donald Lang is told in a 1974 book entitled *Dummy* by Ernest Tidyman. The problem his situation has posed to the Illinois courts is updated in People v. Lang, 113 Ill.2d 407, 101 Ill.Dec. 597, 498 N.E.2d 1105 (1986) (eighth appellate opinion), in People v. Lang, 189 Ill.App.3d 384, 136 Ill.Dec. 803, 545 N.E.2d 327 (1989), and in People v. Lang, 225 Ill.App.3d 229, 167 Ill.Dec. 221, 587 N.E.2d 490 (1992). Lang remains deprived of his freedom in a secure psychiatric facility today although he does not stand convicted of murder. See Andrew Fegelman, Blind Woman Still Reaches Out to Accused Killer, Chicago Tribune, June 28, 1993, p.1. He has been found "not innocent" under an Illinois procedure akin to those described in Note 4 supra. As of 1989, he had undergone sixteen hearings at which he had been found unfit to stand trial. Following the Illinois Supreme Court's 1979 opinion, Lang has been civilly committed under the standards described in Note 6 infra.

5. *Incompetency and Dangerousness.* Does the discussion of federal practice in *Jackson* suggest that a defendant can be held permanently upon a finding of incompetency and a "special finding of dangerousness"? Under this system, although a state has no general provision for locking up citizens on the grounds of "dangerousness," a citizen who was charged with a crime and found incompetent could be held if found to be dangerous. Would this approach violate equal protection? The Illinois Supreme Court, although indirectly, seems to have approved such an approach in one of its *Lang* opinions. See People v. Lang, 76 Ill.2d 311, 29 Ill.Dec. 87, 391 N.E.2d 350 (1979). There the court found that a defendant who has been found unfit to stand trial (for any reason other than a purely physical one) is, by that very fact, mentally ill for the purposes of the Illinois civil commitment statute. To subject such a person to the civil commitment statute the government need only show that because of his condition the person is a danger to himself or another. In other words, incompetency to stand trial plus dangerousness can justify commitment even though the accused does not have a "mental disease" as psychiatrists might define that term.

In a different context, the Supreme Court held that state legislatures were not confined to traditional psychiatric categories in defining mental illness. Upholding a Kansas statute permitting the civil commitment of "sexual predators," the Court upheld a definition of mental abnormality that was nearly the equivalent of dangerousness. The statute defined mental abnormality as a "congenital or acquired condition affecting the emotional or volitional capacity which predisposes the person to commit sexually violent offenses." Kansas v. Hendricks, 521 U.S. 346, 117 S.Ct. 2072 (1997). The decision is in some tension with Foucha v. Louisiana, 504 U.S. 71, 112 S.Ct. 1780 (1992), which held that insanity acquittees may not be kept in mental institutions after they have recovered from their mental illness, even if they are still dangerous and have "antisocial personalities."

For another response to *Jackson* that seemingly involves the equivalent of a special finding of dangerousness, see Altman v. Hofferber, 28 Cal.3d 161, 167 Cal.Rptr. 854, 616 P.2d 836 (1980).

In dissenting from the denial of certiorari, in Florida v. Garrett, 454 U.S. 1004, 102 S.Ct. 544 (1981), Justice Rehnquist discussed at some length his views of Jackson v. Indiana. Among the points he made were that an improper denial of freedom need not result in the dismissal of charges under *Jackson*. He also said that a finding of "dangerousness" following a determination that an accused is incompetent to stand trial justifies further detention.

6. *Trial while Incompetent.* Should we consider the possibility of trying the permanently incompetent accused, affording him whatever special procedures may be available in an effort to remedy disadvantages which flow from incompetency? Such a solution was proposed in Burt & Morris, A Proposal for the Abolition of the Incompetency Plea, 40 U.Chi.L.Rev. 66 (1972); Winick, Criminal Law: Reforming Incompetency to Stand Trial and Plead guilty: A Restated Proposal and Response to Professor Bonnie, 85 J. Crim. L. & Criminology 571 (1995). This proposal is different from the "innocent only" procedure which, according to *Jackson*, is used in some states. (See note 4, supra.) Under the Morris–Burt proposal the result of a trial of the incompetent accused could be a finding of guilty. The proponents of the approach, however, would make it easier to vacate such a conviction based upon newly discovered evidence than is normally possible in criminal cases. In light of the subsequent *Drope* decision, must we conclude that such a scheme would be unconstitutional?

7. *Preserving Evidence.* Consider the prosecutor's problem where a defendant is found incompetent to stand trial. Is there any way a prosecutor can preserve the testimony of witnesses who may not be available to testify when the defendant many years later is found competent to stand trial? If a defendant is not competent to participate in his own trial, can evidence depositions be taken at a time when he is incompetent? If legal representation is not sufficient to permit an incompetent defendant to be tried, would the defendant's lawyers presence and participation at depositions be adequate?

8. *Amnesia.* Another kind of permanent incompetency—at least some would argue—occurs in the case of an accused who suffers permanent retrograde amnesia as a result of which he has no recollection of the time period or events alleged in the indictments. Wilson v. United States, 391 F.2d 460 (D.C.Cir.1968), is among the leading decisions confronting this problem. There Judge Wright set forth six factors for the trial court to consider in determining whether such a person is presently able to consult with counsel and to understand the charges so to be able to obtain a fair trial:

> (1) The extent to which the amnesia affected the defendant's ability to consult with and assist his lawyer.
>
> (2) The extent to which the amnesia affected the defendant's ability to testify in his own behalf.
>
> (3) The extent to which the evidence in suit could be extrinsically reconstructed in view of the defendant's amnesia. Such evidence would include evidence relating to the crime itself as well as any reasonably possible alibi.
>
> (4) The extent to which the Government assisted the defendant and his counsel in that reconstruction.
>
> (5) The strength of the prosecution's case. Most important here will be whether the Government's case is such as to negate all reasonable hypotheses of innocence. If there is any substantial possibility that the accused could, but for his amnesia, establish an alibi or other defense, it should be presumed that he would have been able to do so.
>
> (6) Any other facts and circumstances which would indicate whether or not the defendant had a fair trial.

Under Wright's opinion, charges must be dismissed if the unfairness of trying the amnesiac defendant cannot be overcome.

More recent decisions include United States v. Rinchack, 820 F.2d 1557 (11th Cir.1987); United States v. Villegas, 899 F.2d 1324 (2d Cir.1990); State v. Gilbert, 229 Conn. 228, 640 A.2d 61 (1994). See generally Hermann, Amnesia and the Criminal Law, 22 Idaho L.Rev. 257 (1985–86).

9. *Mental Retardation.* Retarded individuals may also be in a permanent state that poses questions of competence to stand trial. There seems to be no intelligence quotient which creates incompetence per se, nor one which automatically mandates a hearing. See Lewis v. State, 380 So.2d 970 (Ala.Crim.App.1979) (jury finding of competence upheld where one test showed that the defendant had IQ of 45); Hill v. State, 473 So.2d 1253 (Fla.1985) (IQ of 66 one factor which contributed to reviewing court's conclusion that the trial judge erred in not conducting a hearing to determine the defendant's competence).

CHAPTER 15

DISCLOSURE AND DISCOVERY

A. THE PROSECUTION'S CONSTITUTIONAL OBLIGATION TO DISCLOSE

Kyles v. Whitley

Supreme Court of the United States, 1995.
514 U.S. 419, 115 S.Ct. 1555.

■ JUSTICE SOUTER delivered the opinion of the Court.

After his first trial in 1984 ended in a hung jury, petitioner Curtis Lee Kyles was tried again, convicted of first-degree murder, and sentenced to death. The record indicates that, at about 2:20 p.m. on Thursday, September 20, 1984, 60–year–old Dolores Dye left the Schwegmann Brothers' store (Schwegmann's) on Old Gentilly Road in New Orleans after doing some food shopping. As she put her grocery bags into the trunk of her red Ford LTD, a man accosted her and after a short struggle drew a revolver, fired into her left temple, and killed her. The gunman took Dye's keys and drove away in the LTD.

New Orleans police took statements from six eyewitnesses, who offered various descriptions of the gunman. They agreed that he was a black man, and four of them said that he had braided hair. The witnesses differed significantly, however, in their descriptions of height, age, weight, build, and hair length. Two reported seeing a man of 17 or 18, while another described the gunman as looking as old as 28. One witness described him as 5′4″ or 5′5″, medium build, 140–150 pounds; another described the man as slim and close to six feet. One witness said he had a mustache; none of the others spoke of any facial hair at all. One witness said the murderer had shoulder-length hair; another described the hair as "short."

Since the police believed the killer might have driven his own car to Schwegmann's and left it there when he drove off in Dye's LTD, they recorded the license numbers of the cars remaining in the parking lots around the store at 9:15 p.m. on the evening of the murder. Matching these numbers with registration records produced the names and addresses of the owners of the cars, with a notation of any owner's police record. Despite this list and the eyewitness descriptions, the police had no lead to the gunman until the Saturday evening after the shooting.

At 5:30 p.m., on September 23, a man identifying himself as James Joseph called the police and reported that on the day of the murder he had bought a red Thunderbird from a friend named Curtis, whom he later identified as petitioner, Curtis Kyles. He said that he had subsequently read about Dye's murder in the newspapers and feared that the car he purchased was the victim's. He agreed to meet with the police.

A few hours later, the informant met New Orleans detective John Miller, who was wired with a hidden body microphone, through which the ensuing conversation was recorded. The informant now said his name was Joseph Banks and that he was called Beanie. His actual name was Joseph Wallace.

His story, as well as his name, had changed since his earlier call. In place of his original account of buying a Thunderbird from Kyles on Thursday, Beanie told Miller that he had not seen Kyles at all on Thursday, and had bought a red LTD the previous day, Friday. Beanie led Miller to the parking lot of a nearby bar, where he had left the red LTD, later identified as Dye's.

Beanie told Miller that he lived with Kyles's brother-in-law (later identified as Johnny Burns), whom Beanie repeatedly called his "partner." Beanie described Kyles as slim, about 6 feet tall, 24 or 25 years old, with a "bush" hairstyle. When asked if Kyles ever wore his hair in plaits, Beanie said that he did but that he "had a bush" when Beanie bought the car.

During the conversation, Beanie repeatedly expressed concern that he might himself be a suspect in the murder. He explained that he had been seen driving Dye's car on Friday evening in the French Quarter, admitted that he had changed its license plates, and worried that he "could have been charged" with the murder on the basis of his possession of the LTD. He asked if he would be put in jail. Miller acknowledged that Beanie's possession of the car would have looked suspicious, but reassured him that he "didn't do anything wrong."

Beanie seemed eager to cast suspicion on Kyles, who allegedly made his living by "robbing people," and had tried to kill Beanie at some prior time. Beanie said that Kyles regularly carried two pistols, a .38 and a .32, and that if the police could "set him up good," they could "get that same gun" used to kill Dye. Beanie rode with Miller and Miller's supervisor, Sgt. James Eaton, in an unmarked squad car to Desire Street, where he pointed out the building containing Kyles's apartment.

Beanie told the officers that after he bought the car, he and his "partner" (Burns) drove Kyles to Schwegmann's about 9 p.m. on Friday evening to pick up Kyles's car, described as an orange four-door Ford. When asked where Kyles's car had been parked, Beanie replied that it had been "[o]n the same side [of the lot] where the woman was killed at." The officers later drove Beanie to Schwegmann's, where he indicated the space where he claimed Kyles's car had been parked. Beanie went on to say that when he and Burns had brought Kyles to pick up the car, Kyles had gone to some nearby bushes to retrieve a brown purse, which Kyles subsequently hid in a wardrobe at his apartment. Beanie said that Kyles had "a lot of groceries" in Schwegmann's bags and a new baby's potty "in the car." Beanie told Eaton that Kyles's garbage would go out the next day and that if Kyles was "smart" he would "put [the purse] in [the] garbage." Beanie made it clear that he expected some reward for his help, saying at one point that he was not "doing all of this for nothing." The police repeatedly assured Beanie that he would not lose the $400 he paid for the car.

After the visit to Schwegmann's, Eaton and Miller took Beanie to a police station where Miller interviewed him again on the record, which was transcribed and signed by Beanie, using his alias "Joseph Banks." This statement, Beanie's third (the telephone call being the first, then the recorded conversation), repeats some of the essentials of the second one: that Beanie had purchased a red Ford LTD from Kyles for $400 on Friday evening; that Kyles had his hair "combed out" at the time of the sale; and that Kyles carried a .32 and a .38 with him "all the time."

Portions of the third statement, however, embellished or contradicted Beanie's preceding story and were even internally inconsistent. Beanie reported that after the sale, he and Kyles unloaded Schwegmann's grocery bags from the trunk and back seat of the LTD and placed them in Kyles's own car. Beanie said that Kyles took a brown purse from the front seat of the LTD and that they then drove in separate cars to Kyles's apartment, where they unloaded the groceries. Beanie also claimed that, a few hours later, he and his "partner" Burns went with Kyles to Schwegmann's, where they recovered Kyles's car and a "big brown pocket book" from "next to a building." Beanie did not explain how Kyles could have picked up his car and recovered the purse at Schwegmann's, after Beanie had seen Kyles with both just a few hours earlier. The police neither noted the inconsistencies nor questioned Beanie about them.

Although the police did not thereafter put Kyles under surveillance, (Dec. 6, 1984), they learned about events at his apartment from Beanie, who went there twice on Sunday. According to a fourth statement by Beanie, this one given to the chief prosecutor in November (between the first and second trials), he first went to the apartment about 2 p.m., after a telephone conversation with a police officer who asked whether Kyles had the gun that was used to kill Dye. Beanie stayed in Kyles's apartment until about 5 p.m., when he left to call Detective John Miller. Then he returned about 7 p.m. and stayed until about 9:30 p.m., when he left to meet Miller, who also asked about the gun. According to this fourth statement, Beanie "rode around" with Miller until 3 a.m. on Monday, September 24. Sometime during those same early morning hours, detectives were sent at Sgt. Eaton's behest to pick up the rubbish outside Kyles's building. As Sgt. Eaton wrote in an interoffice memorandum, he had "reason to believe the victims [sic] personal papers and the Schwegmann's bags will be in the trash."

At 10:40 a.m., Kyles was arrested as he left the apartment, which was then searched under a warrant. Behind the kitchen stove, the police found a .32 calibre revolver containing five live rounds and one spent cartridge. Ballistics tests later showed that this pistol was used to murder Dye. In a wardrobe in a hallway leading to the kitchen, the officers found a homemade shoulder holster that fit the murder weapon. In a bedroom dresser drawer, they discovered two boxes of ammunition, one containing several .32 calibre rounds of the same brand as those found in the pistol. Back in the kitchen, various cans of cat and dog food, some of them of the brands Dye typically purchased, were found in Schwegmann's sacks. No other groceries were identified as possibly being Dye's, and no potty was found. Later that afternoon at the police station, police opened the rubbish bags and found the victim's purse, identification, and other personal belongings wrapped in a Schwegmann's sack.

The gun, the LTD, the purse, and the cans of pet food were dusted for fingerprints. The gun had been wiped clean. Several prints were found on the purse and on the LTD, but none was identified as Kyles's. Dye's prints were not found on any of the cans of pet food. Kyles's prints were found, however, on a small piece of paper taken from the front passenger-side floorboard of the LTD. The crime laboratory recorded the paper as a Schwegmann's sales slip, but without noting what had been printed on it, which was obliterated in the chemical process of lifting the fingerprints. A second Schwegmann's receipt was found in the trunk of the LTD, but Kyles's prints were not found on it. Beanie's fingerprints were not compared to any of the fingerprints found.

The lead detective on the case, John Dillman, put together a photo lineup that included a photograph of Kyles (but not of Beanie) and showed the array to five of the six eyewitnesses who had given statements. Three of them picked the photograph of Kyles; the other two could not confidently identify Kyles as Dye's assailant.

Kyles was indicted for first-degree murder. Before trial, his counsel filed a lengthy motion for disclosure by the State of any exculpatory or impeachment evidence. The prosecution responded that there was "no exculpatory evidence of any nature,"

At the first trial, in November, the heart of the State's case was eyewitness testimony from four people who were at the scene of the crime (three of whom had previously picked Kyles from the photo lineup). Kyles maintained his innocence, offered supporting witnesses, and supplied an alibi that he had been picking up his children from school at the time of the murder. The theory of the defense was that Kyles had been framed by Beanie, who had planted evidence in Kyles's apartment and his rubbish for the purposes of shifting suspicion away from himself, removing an impediment to romance with Pinky Burns, and obtaining reward money. Beanie did not testify as a witness for either the defense or the prosecution.

Because the State withheld evidence, its case was much stronger, and the defense case much weaker, than the full facts would have suggested. Even so, after four hours of deliberation, the jury became deadlocked on the issue of guilt, and a mistrial was declared.

After the mistrial, the chief trial prosecutor, Cliff Strider, interviewed Beanie. Strider's notes show that Beanie again changed important elements of his story. He said that he went with Kyles to retrieve Kyles's car from the Schwegmann's lot on Thursday, the day of the murder, at some time between 5and 7:30 p.m., not on Friday, at 9 p.m., as he had said in his second and third statements. (Indeed, in his second statement, Beanie said that he had not seen Kyles at all on Thursday. He also said, for the first time, that when they had picked up the car they were accompanied not only by Johnny Burns but also by Kevin Black, who had testified for the defense at the first trial.) Beanie now claimed that after getting Kyles's car they went to Black's house, retrieved a number of bags of groceries, a child's potty, and a brown purse, all of which they took to Kyles's apartment. Beanie also stated that on the Sunday after the murder he had been at Kyles's apartment two separate times. Notwithstanding the many inconsistencies and variations among Beanie's statements, neither Strider's notes nor any of the other notes and transcripts were given to the defense.

In December 1984, Kyles was tried a second time. Again, the heart of the State's case was the testimony of four eyewitnesses who positively identified Kyles in front of the jury. The prosecution also offered a blown-up photograph taken at the crime scene soon after the murder, on the basis of which the prosecutors argued that a seemingly two-toned car in the background of the photograph was Kyles's. They repeatedly suggested during cross-examination of defense witnesses that Kyles had left his own car at Schwegmann's on the day of the murder and had retrieved it later, a theory for which they offered no evidence beyond the blown-up photograph. Once again, Beanie did not testify.

As in the first trial, the defense contended that the eyewitnesses were mistaken. Kyles's counsel called several individuals, including Kevin Black, who testified to seeing Beanie, with his hair in plaits, driving a red car similar to the victim's about an hour after the killing. Another witness testified that Beanie, with his hair in braids, had tried to sell him the car on Thursday evening, shortly after the murder. Another witness testified that Beanie, with his hair in a "Jheri curl," had attempted to sell him the car on Friday. One witness, Beanie's "partner," Burns, testified that he had seen Beanie on Sunday at Kyles's apartment, stooping down near the stove where the gun was eventually found, and the defense presented testimony that Beanie was romantically interested in Pinky Burns. To explain the pet food found in Kyles's apartment, there was testimony that Kyles's family kept a dog and cat and often fed stray animals in the neighborhood.

Finally, Kyles again took the stand. Denying any involvement in the shooting, he explained his fingerprints on the cash register receipt found in Dye's car by saying that Beanie had picked him up in a red car on Friday, September 21, and had taken him to Schwegmann's, where he purchased transmission fluid and a pack of cigarettes. He suggested that the receipt may have fallen from the bag when he removed the cigarettes.

On rebuttal, the prosecutor had Beanie brought into the courtroom. All of the testifying eyewitnesses, after viewing Beanie standing next to Kyles, reaffirmed their previous identifications of Kyles as the murderer. Kyles was convicted of first-degree murder and sentenced to death. Beanie received a total of $1,600 in reward money.

The prosecution's affirmative duty to disclose evidence favorable to a defendant can trace its origins to early 20th–century strictures against misrepresentation and is of course most prominently associated with this Court's decision in Brady v. Maryland. (1963) Brady held "that the suppression by the prosecution of evidence favorable to an accused upon request violates due process where the evidence is material either to guilt or to punishment, irrespective of the good faith or bad faith of the prosecution." In United States v. Agurs, ( ) however, it became clear that a defendant's failure to request favorable evidence did not leave the Government free of all obligation. There, the Court distinguished three situations in which a Brady claim might arise: first, where previously undisclosed evidence revealed that the prosecution introduced trial testimony that it knew or should have known was perjured, second, where the Government failed to accede to a defense request for disclosure of some specific kind of exculpatory evidence, and third, where the Government failed to volunteer exculpatory evidence never requested, or requested only in a general way. The Court found a duty on the part of the Government even in this last situation, though only when suppression of the evidence would be "of sufficient significance to result in the denial of the defendant's right to a fair trial."

In the third prominent case on the way to current Brady law, United States v. Bagley (1985), the Court disavowed any difference between exculpatory and impeachment evidence for Brady purposes, and it abandoned the distinction between the second and third Agurs circumstances, i.e., the "specific-request" and "general- or no-request" situations. Bagley held that regardless of request, favorable evidence is material, and constitutional error results from its suppression by the government, "if there is a reasonable probability that, had the evidence been disclosed to the defense, the result of the proceeding would have been different."

Four aspects of materiality under Bagley bear emphasis. Although the constitutional duty is triggered by the potential impact of favorable but undisclosed evidence, a showing of materiality does not require demonstration by a preponderance that disclosure of the suppressed evidence would have resulted ultimately in the defendant's acquittal (whether based on the presence of reasonable doubt or acceptance of an explanation for the crime that does not inculpate the defendant). Bagley's touchstone of materiality is a "reasonable probability" of a different result, and the adjective is important. The question is not whether the defendant would more likely than not have received a different verdict with the evidence, but whether in its absence he received a fair trial, understood as a trial resulting in a verdict worthy of confidence. A "reasonable probability" of a different result is accordingly shown when the Government's evidentiary suppression "undermines confidence in the outcome of the trial."

The second aspect of Bagley materiality bearing emphasis here is that it is not a sufficiency of evidence test. A defendant need not demonstrate that after discounting the inculpatory evidence in light of the undisclosed evidence, there would not have been enough left to convict. The possibility of an acquittal on a criminal charge does not imply an insufficient evidentiary basis to convict. One does not show a Brady violation by demonstrating that some of the inculpatory evidence should have been excluded, but by showing that the favorable evidence could reasonably be taken to put the whole case in such a different light as to undermine confidence in the verdict.

Third, once a reviewing court applying Bagley has found constitutional error there is no need for further harmless-error review. Assuming arguendo that a harmless error enquiry were to apply, a Bagley error could not be treated as harmless, since "a reasonable probability that, had the evidence been disclosed to the defense, the result of the proceeding would have been different," necessarily entails the conclusion that the suppression must have had " 'substantial and injurious effect or influence in determining the jury's verdict,' " Brecht v. Abrahamson (1993).

The fourth and final aspect of Bagley materiality to be stressed here is its definition in terms of suppressed evidence considered collectively, not item-by-item. As Justice Blackmun emphasized in the portion of his opinion written for the Court, the Constitution is not violated every time the government fails or chooses not to disclose evidence that might prove helpful to the defense. We have never held that the Constitution demands an open file policy (however such a policy might work out in practice), and the rule in Bagley (and, hence, in Brady) requires less of the prosecution than the ABA Standards for Criminal Justice, which call generally for prosecutorial disclosures of any evidence tending to exculpate or mitigate.

While the definition of Bagley materiality in terms of the cumulative effect of suppression must accordingly be seen as leaving the government with a degree of discretion, it must also be understood as imposing a corresponding burden. On the one side, showing that the prosecution knew of an item of favorable evidence unknown to the defense does not amount to a Brady violation, without more. But the prosecution, which alone can know what is undisclosed, must be assigned the consequent responsibility to gauge the likely net effect of all such evidence and make disclosure when the point of "reasonable probability" is reached. This in turn means that the individual prosecutor has a duty to learn of any favorable evidence known to the others acting on the government's behalf in the case, including the police. But whether the prosecutor succeeds or fails in meeting this obligation (whether, that is, a failure to disclose is in good faith or bad faith) the prosecution's responsibility for failing to disclose known, favorable evidence rising to a material level of importance is inescapable.

The State of Louisiana would prefer an even more lenient rule. It pleads that some of the favorable evidence in issue here was not disclosed even to the prosecutor until after trial, and it suggested below that it should not beheld accountable under Bagley and Brady for evidence known only to police investigators and not to the prosecutor. To accommodate the State in this manner would, however, amount to a serious change of course from the Brady line of cases. In the State's favor it may be said that no one doubts that police investigators sometimes fail to inform a prosecutor of all they know. But neither is there any serious doubt that "procedures and regulations can be established to carry [the prosecutor's] burden and to insure communication of all relevant information on each case to every lawyer who deals with it." Giglio v. United States (1972). Since, then, the prosecutor has the means to discharge the government's Brady responsibility if he will, any argument for excusing a prosecutor from disclosing what he does not happen to know about boils down to a plea to substitute the police for the prosecutor, and even for the courts themselves, as the final arbiters of the government's obligation to ensure fair trials.

Short of doing that, we were asked at oral argument to raise the threshold of materiality because the Bagley standard "makes it difficult . . .

to know" from the "perspective [of the prosecutor at] trial . . . exactly what might become important later on." The State asks for "a certain amount of leeway in making a judgment call" as to the disclosure of any given piece of evidence. Ibid.

Uncertainty about the degree of further "leeway" that might satisfy the State's request for a "certain amount" of it is the least of the reasons to deny the request. At bottom, what the State fails to recognize is that, with or without more leeway, the prosecution cannot be subject to any disclosure obligation without at some point having the responsibility to determine when it must act. Indeed, even if due process were thought to be violated by every failure to disclose an item of exculpatory or impeachment evidence (leaving harmless error as the government's only fallback), the prosecutor would still be forced to make judgment calls about what would count as favorable evidence, owing to the very fact that the character of a piece of evidence as favorable will often turn on the context of the existing or potential evidentiary record. Since the prosecutor would have to exercise some judgment even if the State were subject to this most stringent disclosure obligation, it is hard to find merit in the State's complaint over the responsibility for judgment under the existing system, which does not tax the prosecutor with error for any failure to disclose, absent a further showing of materiality. Unless, indeed, the adversary system of prosecution is to descend to a gladiatorial level unmitigated by any prosecutorial obligation for the sake of truth, the government simply cannot avoid responsibility for knowing when the suppression of evidence has come to portend such an effect on a trial's outcome as to destroy confidence in its result.

This means, naturally, that a prosecutor anxious about tacking too close to the wind will disclose a favorable piece of evidence. This is as it should be. Such disclosure will serve to justify trust in the prosecutor as "the representative ... of a sovereignty ... whose interest ... in a criminal prosecution is not that it shall win a case, but that justice shall be done." Berger v. United States (1935). And it will tend to preserve the criminal trial, as distinct from the prosecutor's private deliberations, as the chosen forum for ascertaining the truth about criminal accusations. The prudence of the careful prosecutor should not therefore be discouraged.

In this case, disclosure of the suppressed evidence to competent counsel would have made a different result reasonably probable.

As the District Court put it, "the essence of the State's case" was the testimony of eyewitnesses, who identified Kyles as Dye's killer. To begin with, the value of two of those witnesses would have been substantially reduced or destroyed.

The State rated Henry Williams as its best witness, who testified that he had seen the struggle and the actual shooting by Kyles. The jury would have found it helpful to probe this conclusion in the light of Williams's contemporaneous statement, in which he told the police that the assailant was "a black male, about 19 or 20 years old, about 5′4″ or 5′5″, 140 to 150 pounds, medium build" and that "his hair looked like it was platted." of cross-examined on this description, Williams would have had trouble explaining how he could have described Kyles, 6–feet tall and thin, as a man more than half a foot shorter with a medium build. Indeed, since Beanie was 22 years old, 5′5″ tall, and 159 pounds, the defense would have had a compelling argument that Williams's description pointed to Beanie but not to Kyles.

The trial testimony of a second eyewitness, Isaac Smallwood, was equally damning to Kyles. He testified that Kyles was the assailant, and that he saw him struggle with Dye. He said he saw Kyles take a ".32, a small black gun" out of his right pocket, shoot Dye in the head, and drive off in her LTD. When the prosecutor asked him whether he actually saw Kyles shoot Dye, Smallwood answered "Yeah."

Smallwood's statement taken at the parking lot, however, was vastly different. Immediately after the crime, Smallwood claimed that he had not seen the actual murder and had not seen the assailant outside the vehicle. "I heard a lound [sic] pop," he said. "When I looked around I saw a lady laying on the ground, and there was a red car coming toward me." Smallwood said that he got a look at the culprit, a black teenage male with a mustache and shoulder-length braided hair, as the victim's red Thunderbird passed where he was standing. When a police investigator specifically asked him whether he had seen the assailant outside the car, Smallwood answered that he had not; the gunman "was already in the car and coming toward me."

A jury would reasonably have been troubled by the adjustments to Smallwood's original story by the time of the second trial. The struggle and shooting, which earlier he had not seen, he was able to describe with such detailed clarity as to identify the murder weapon as a small black .32 calibre pistol, which, of course, was the type of weapon used. His description of the victim's car had gone from a "Thunderbird" to an "LTD"; and he saw fit to say nothing about the assailant's shoulder-length hair and moustache, details noted by no other eyewitness. These developments would have fueled a withering cross-examination, destroying confidence in Smallwood's story and raising a substantial implication that the prosecutor had coached him to give it.

Since the evolution over time of a given eyewitness's description can be fatal to its reliability, the Smallwood and Williams identifications would have been severely undermined by use of their suppressed statements. The likely damage is best understood by taking the word of the prosecutor, who contended during closing arguments that Smallwood and Williams were the State's two best witnesses. Nor, of course, would the harm to the State's case on identity have been confined to their testimony alone. The fact that neither Williams nor Smallwood could have provided a consistent eyewitness description pointing to Kyles would have undercut the prosecution all the more because the remaining eyewitnesses called to testify (Territo and Kersh) had their best views of the gunman only as he fled the scene with his body partly concealed in Dye's car. And even aside from such important details, the effective impeachment of one eyewitness can call for a new trial even though the attack does not extend directly to others.

Damage to the prosecution's case would not have been confined to evidence of the eyewitnesses, for Beanie's various statements would have raised opportunities to attack not only the probative value of crucial physical evidence and the circumstances in which it was found, but the thoroughness and even the good faith of the investigation, as well. By the State's own admission, Beanie was essential to its investigation and, indeed, "made the case" against Kyles. Contrary to what one might hope for from such a source, however, Beanie's statements to the police were replete with inconsistencies and would have allowed the jury to infer that Beanie was anxious to see Kyles arrested for Dye's murder. Their disclosure would have revealed a remarkably uncritical attitude on the part of the police.

If the defense had called Beanie as an adverse witness, he could not have said anything of any significance without being trapped by his inconsistencies. A short recapitulation of some of them will make the point. In Beanie's initial meeting with the police, and in his signed statement, he said he bought Dye's LTD and helped Kyles retrieve his car from the Schwegmann's lot on Friday. In his first call to the police, he said he bought the LTD on Thursday, and in his conversation with the prosecutor between trials it was again on Thursday that he said he helped Kyles retrieve Kyles's car. Although none of the first three versions of this story mentioned Kevin Black as taking part in the retrieval of the car and transfer of groceries, after Black implicated Beanie by his testimony for the defense at the first trial, Beanie changed his story to include Black as a participant. In Beanie's several accounts, Dye's purse first shows up variously next to a building, in some bushes, in Kyles's car, and at Black's house.

Even if Kyles's lawyer had followed the more conservative course of leaving Beanie off the stand, though, the defense could have examined the police to good effect on their knowledge of Beanie's statements and so have attacked there liability of the investigation in failing even to consider Beanie's possible guilt and in tolerating (if not countenancing) serious possibilities that incriminating evidence had been planted. See, e.g., Bowen v. Maynard, 799F.2d 593, 613 (C.A.10 1986) ("A common trial tactic of defense lawyers is to discredit the caliber of the investigation or the decision to charge the defendant, and we may consider such use in assessing a possible Brady violation"); Lindsey v. King, 769 F.2d 1034, 1042 (C.A.5 1985) (awarding new trial of prisoner convicted in Louisiana state court because withheld Brady evidence "carried within it the potential ... for the ... discrediting ... of the police methods employed in assembling the case").[15]

By demonstrating the detectives' knowledge of Beanie's affirmatively self-incriminating statements, the defense could have laid the foundation fora vigorous argument that the police had been guilty of negligence. In his initial meeting with police, Beanie admitted twice that he changed the license plates on the LTD. This admission enhanced the suspiciousness of

15. The dissent, suggests that for jurors to count the sloppiness of the investigation against the probative force of the State's evidence would have been irrational, but of course it would have been no such thing. When, for example, the probative force of evidence depends on the circumstances in which it was obtained and those circumstances raise a possibility of fraud, indications of conscientious police work will enhance probative force and slovenly work will diminish it.

his possession of the car; the defense could have argued persuasively that he was no bona fide purchaser. And when combined with his police record, evidence of prior criminal activity near Schwegmann's, and his status as a suspect in another murder, his devious behavior gave reason to believe that he had done more than buy a stolen car. There was further self-incrimination in Beanie's statement that Kyles's car was parked in the same part of the Schwegmann's lot where Dye was killed. Beanie's apparent awareness of the specific location of the murder could have been based, as the State contends, on television or newspaper reports, but perhaps it was not. Since the police admittedly never treated Beanie as a suspect, the defense could thus have used his statements to throw the reliability of the investigation into doubt and to sully the credibility of Detective Dillman, who testified that Beanie was never a suspect, and that he had "no knowledge" that Beanie had changed the license plate.

The admitted failure of the police to pursue these pointers toward Beanie's possible guilt could only have magnified the effect on the jury of explaining how the purse and the gun happened to be recovered. In Beanie's original recorded statement, he told the police that "[Kyles's] garbage goes out tomorrow," and that "if he's smart he'll put [the purse] in [the] garbage." These statements, along with the internal memorandum stating that the police had "reason to believe" Dye's personal effects and Schwegmann's bags would be in the garbage, would have supported the defense's theory that Beanie was no mere observer, but was determining the investigation's direction and success. The potential for damage from using Beanie's statement to undermine the ostensible integrity of the investigation is only confirmed by the prosecutor's admission at one of Kyles's postconviction hearings, that he did not recall a single instance before this case when police had searched and seized garbage on the street in front of a residence and by Detective John Miller's admission at the same hearing that he thought at the time that it "was a possibility" that Beanie had planted the incriminating evidence in the garbage. If a police officer thought so, a juror would have, too.

To the same effect would have been an enquiry based on Beanie's apparently revealing remark to police that "if you can set [Kyles] up good, you can get that same gun." While the jury might have understood that Beanie meant simply that if the police investigated Kyles, they would probably find the murder weapon, the jury could also have taken Beanie to have been making the more sinister suggestion that the police "set up" Kyles, and the defense could have argued that the police accepted the invitation. The prosecutor's notes of his interview with Beanie would have shown that police officers were asking Beanie the whereabouts of the gun all day Sunday, the very day when he was twice at Kyles's apartment and was allegedly seen by Johnny Burns lurking near the stove, where the gun was later found. Beanie's same statement, indeed, could have been used to cap an attack on the integrity of the investigation and on the reliability of Detective Dillman, who testified on cross-examination that he did not know if Beanie had been at Kyles's apartment on Sunday.

Next to be considered is the prosecution's list of the cars in the Schwegmann's parking lot at mid-evening after the murder. While its suppression does not rank with the failure to disclose the other evidence discussed here, it would have had some value as exculpation and impeachment, and it counts accordingly in determining whether Bagley's standard of materiality is satisfied. On the police's assumption, argued to the jury, that the killer drove to the lot and left his car there during the heat of the investigation, the list without Kyles's registration would obviously have helped Kyles and would have had some value in countering an argument by the prosecution that a grainy enlargement of a photograph of the crime scene showed Kyles's car in the background. The list would also have shown that the police either knew that it was inconsistent with their informant's second and third statements (in which Beanie described retrieving Kyles's car after the time the list was compiled) or never even bothered to check the informant's story against known fact. Either way, the defense would have had further support for arguing that the police were irresponsible in relying on Beanie to tip them off to the location of evidence damaging to Kyles.

In assessing the significance of the evidence withheld, one must of course bear in mind that not every item of the State's case would have been directly undercut if the Brady evidence had been disclosed. It is significant, however, that the physical evidence remaining unscathed would, by the State's own admission, hardly have amounted to overwhelming proof that Kyles was the murderer. Ammunition and a holster were found in Kyles's apartment, but if the jury had suspected the gun had been planted the significance of these items might have been left in doubt. The fact that pet food was found in Kyles's apartment was consistent with the testimony of several defense witnesses that Kyles owned a dog and that his children fed stray cats. The brands of pet food found were only two of the brands that Dye typically bought, and these two were common, whereas the one specialty brand that was found in Dye's apartment after her murder, was not found in Kyles's apartment. Although Kyles was wrong in describing the cat food as being on sale the day he said he bought it, he was right in describing the way it was priced at Schwegmann's market, where he commonly shopped.

Similarly undispositive is the small Schwegmann's receipt on the front passenger floorboard of the LTD, the only physical evidence that bore a fingerprint identified as Kyles's. Kyles explained that Beanie had driven him to Schwegmann's on Friday to buy cigarettes and transmission fluid, and he theorized that the slip must have fallen out of the bag when he removed the cigarettes. This explanation is consistent with the location of the slip when found and with its small size. The State cannot very well argue that the fingerprint ties Kyles to the killing without also explaining how the 2–inch–long register slip could have been the receipt for a week's worth of groceries, which Dye had gone to Schwegmann's to purchase.

The inconclusiveness of the physical evidence does not, to be sure, prove Kyles's innocence, and the jury might have found the eyewitness testimony of Territo and Kersh sufficient to convict, even though less damning to Kyles than that of Smallwood and Williams. But the question is not whether the State would have had a case to go to the jury if it had disclosed the favorable evidence, but whether we can be confident that the jury's verdict would have been the same.

Perhaps, confidence that the verdict would have been the same could survive the evidence impeaching even two eyewitnesses if the discoveries of gun and purse were above suspicion. Perhaps those suspicious circumstances would not defeat confidence in the verdict if the eyewitnesses had generally agreed on a description and were free of impeachment. But confidence that the verdict would have been unaffected cannot survive when suppressed evidence would have entitled a jury to find that the eyewitnesses were not consistent in describing the killer, that two out of the four eyewitnesses testifying were unreliable, that the most damning physical evidence was subject to suspicion, that the investigation that produced it was insufficiently probing, and that the principal police witness was insufficiently informed or candid. This is not the "massive" case envisioned by the dissent, it is a significantly weaker case than the one heard by the first jury, which could not even reach a verdict.

■ JUSTICE STEVENS, with whom JUSTICE GINSBURG and JUSTICE BREYER join, concurring.

[OMITTED]

■ JUSTICE SCALIA, with whom the CHIEF JUSTICE, JUSTICE KENNEDY, and JUSTICE THOMAS join, dissenting.

It is fundamental to the discovery rule of Brady v. Maryland, that the materiality of a failure to disclose favorable evidence "must be evaluated in the context of the entire record." United States v. Agurs. It is simply not enough to show that the undisclosed evidence would have allowed the defense to weaken, or even to "destro[y]," the particular prosecution witnesses or items of prosecution evidence to which the undisclosed evidence relates. It is petitioner's burden to show that in light of all the evidence, including that untainted by the Brady violation, it is reasonably probable that a jury would have entertained a reasonable doubt regarding petitioner's guilt. See United States v. Bagley. The Court's opinion fails almost entirely to take this principle into account. My discussion of the record will present the half of the analysis that the Court omits, emphasizing the evidence concededly unaffected by the Brady violation which demonstrates the immateriality of the violation.

In any analysis of this case, the desperate implausibility of the theory that petitioner put before the jury must be kept firmly in mind. The first half of that theory—designed to neutralize the physical evidence (Mrs. Dye's purse in his garbage, the murder weapon behind his stove)—was that petitioner was the victim of a "frame-up" by the police informer and evil genius, Beanie. Now it is not unusual for a guilty person who knows that he is suspected of a crime to try to shift blame to someone else; and it is less common, but not unheard-of, for a guilty person who is neither suspected nor subject to suspicion (because he has established a perfect alibi), to call attention to himself by coming forward to point the finger at an innocent person. But petitioner's theory is that the guilty Beanie, who could plausibly be accused of the crime but who was not a suspect any more than Kyles was (the police as yet had no leads), injected both Kyles and himself into the investigation in order to get the innocent Kyles convicted. If this were not stupid enough, the wicked Beanie is supposed to have suggested that the police search his victim's premises a full day before he got around to planting the incriminating evidence on the premises.

The second half of petitioner's theory was that he was the victim of a quadruple coincidence, in which four eyewitnesses to the crime mistakenly identified him as the murderer—three picking him out of a photo-array without hesitation, and all four affirming their identification in open court after comparing him with Beanie. The extraordinary mistake petitioner had to persuade the jury these four witnesses made was not simply to mistake the real killer, Beanie, for the very same innocent third party (hard enough to believe), but in addition to mistake him for the very man Beanie had chosen to frame—the last and most incredible level of coincidence. However small the chance that the jury would believe any one of those improbable scenarios, the likelihood that it would believe them all together is far smaller. The Court concludes that it is "reasonably probable" the undisclosed witness interviews would have persuaded the jury of petitioner's implausible theory of mistaken eyewitness testimony, and then argues that it is "reasonably probable" the undisclosed information regarding Beanie would have persuaded the jury of petitioner's implausible theory regarding the incriminating physical evidence. I think neither of those conclusions is remotely true, but even if they were the Court would still be guilty of a fallacy in declaring victory on each implausibility in turn, and thus victory on the whole, without considering the infinitesimal probability of the jury's swallowing the entire concoction of implausibility squared.

This basic error of approaching the evidence piecemeal is also what accounts for the Court's obsessive focus on the credibility or culpability of Beanie, who did not even testify at trial and whose credibility or innocence the State has never once avowed. The Court's opinion reads as if either petitioner or Beanie must be telling the truth, and any evidence tending to inculpate or undermine the credibility of the one would exculpate or enhance the credibility of the other. But the jury verdict in this case said only that petitioner was guilty of the murder. That is perfectly consistent with the possibilities that Beanie repeatedly lied, that he was an accessory after the fact, or even that he planted evidence against petitioner. Even if the undisclosed evidence would have allowed the defense to thoroughly impeach Beanie and to suggest the above possibilities, the jury could well have believed all of those things and yet have condemned petitioner because it could not believe that all four of the eyewitnesses were similarly mistaken.

Of course even that much rests on the premise that competent counsel would run the terrible risk of calling Beanie, a witness whose "testimony almost certainly would have inculpated [petitioner]" and whom "any reasonable attorney would perceive ... as a 'loose cannon.'" Perhaps because that premise seems so implausible, the Court retreats to the possibility that petitioner's counsel, even if not calling Beanie to the stand, could have used the evidence relating to Beanie to attack "the reliability of the investigation." But that is distinctly less effective than substantive evidence bearing on the guilt or innocence of the accused. In evaluating

Brady claims, we assume jury conduct that is both rational and obedient to the law. We do not assume that even though the whole mass of the evidence, both disclosed and undisclosed, shows petitioner guilty beyond a reasonable doubt, the jury will punish sloppy investigative techniques by setting the defendant free. Neither Beanie nor the police were on trial in this case. Petitioner was, and no amount of collateral evidence could have enabled his counsel to move the mountain of direct evidence against him.

Petitioner's basic theory at trial was that the State's four eyewitnesses happened to mistake Beanie, the real killer, for petitioner, the man whom Beanie was simultaneously trying to frame. Petitioner has never disputed, that three of the four eyewitnesses (Territo, Smallwood, and Williams) were shown a photo lineup of six young men four days after the shooting and, without aid or duress, identified petitioner as the murderer; and that all of them, plus the fourth eyewitness, Kersh, reaffirmed their identifications at trial after petitioner and Beanie were made to stand side-by-side.

Territo, the first eyewitness called by the State, was waiting at a red light in a truck 30 or 40 yards from the Schwegmann's parking lot. He saw petitioner shoot Mrs. Dye, start her car, drive out onto the road and pull up just behind Territo's truck. When the light turned green petitioner pulled beside Territo and stopped while waiting to make a turn. Petitioner looked Territo full in the face. Territo testified, "I got a good look at him. If I had been in the passenger seat of the little truck, I could have reached out and not even stretched my arm out, I could have grabbed hold of him." Territo also testified that a detective had shown him a picture of Beanie and asked him if the picture "could have been the guy that did it. I told him no." The second eyewitness, Kersh, also saw petitioner shoot Mrs. Dye. When asked whether she got "a good look" at him as he drove away, she answered "yes." She also answered "yes" to the question whether she "got to see the side of his face," and said that while petitioner was stopped she had driven to within reaching distance of the driver's-side door of Mrs. Dye's car and stopped there. The third eyewitness, Smallwood, testified that he saw petitioner shoot Mrs. Dye, walk to the car, and drive away. Petitioner drove slowly by, within a distance of 15 or 25 feet, and Smallwood saw his face from the side. The fourth eyewitness, Williams, who had been working outside the parking lot, testified that "the gentleman came up the side of the car," struggled with Mrs. Dye, shot her, walked around to the driver's side of the car, and drove away. Williams not only "saw him before he shot her," but watched petitioner drive slowly by "within less than ten feet." When asked "[d]id you get an opportunity to look at him good?", Williams said, "I did."

The Court attempts to dispose of this direct, unqualified and consistent eyewitness testimony in two ways. First, by relying on a theory so implausible that it was apparently not suggested by petitioner's counsel until the oral-argument-cum-evidentiary-hearing held before us, perhaps because it is a theory that only the most removed appellate court could love. This theory is, that there is a reasonable probability that the jury would have changed its mind about the eyewitness identification because the Brady material would have permitted the defense to argue that the eyewitnesses only got a good look at the killer when he was sitting in Mrs. Dye's car, and thus could identify him, not by his height and build, but only by his face. Never mind, for the moment, that this is factually false, since the Brady material showed that only one of the four eyewitnesses, Smallwood, did not see the killer outside the car. And never mind, also, the dubious premise that the build of a man six feet tall(like petitioner) is indistinguishable, when seated behind the wheel, from that of a man less than five and one-half feet tall (like Beanie). To assert that unhesitant and categorical identification by four witnesses who viewed the killer, close-up and with the sun high in the sky, would not eliminate reasonable doubt if it were based only on facial characteristics, and not on height and build, is quite simply absurd. Facial features are the primary means by which human beings recognize one another. That is why police departments distribute "mug" shots of wanted felons, rather than Ivy–League–type posture pictures; it is why bank robbers wear stockings over their faces instead of floor-length capes over their shoulders; it is why the Lone Ranger wears a mask instead of a poncho; and it is why a criminal defense lawyer who seeks to destroy an identifying witness by asking "You admit that you saw only the killer's face?" will be laughed out of the courtroom.

It would be different, of course, if there were evidence that Kyles's and Beanie's faces looked like twins, or at least bore an unusual degree of resemblance. But without evidence of facial similarity, the question "You admit that you saw only the killer's face?" draws no blood; it does not explain any witness's identification of petitioner as the killer. While the assumption of facial resemblance between Kyles and Beanie underlies all of the Court's repeated references to the partial concealment of the killer's body from view, the Court never actually says that such resemblance exists. That is because there is not the slightest basis for such a statement in the record. In fact, quite the opposite: every federal and state court that has reviewed the record photographs, or seen the two men, has found that they do not resemble each other in any respect. See 5 F.3d, at 813 ("Comparing photographs of Kyles and Beanie, it is evident that the former is taller, thinner, and has a narrower face"); ("The court examined all of the pictures used in the photographic line-up and compared Kyles' and Beanie's pictures; it finds that they did not resemble one another"); (state trial court findings on postconviction review) ("[Beanie] clearly and distinctly did not resemble the defendant in this case").

The Court's second means of seeking to neutralize the impressive and unanimous eyewitness testimony uses the same "build-is-everything" theory to exaggerate the effect of the State's failure to disclose the contemporaneous statement of Henry Williams. That statement would assuredly have permitted a sharp cross-examination, since it contained estimations of height and weight that fit Beanie better than petitioner. But I think it is hyperbole to say that the statement would have "substantially reduced or destroyed" the value of Williams' testimony. Williams saw the murderer drive slowly by less than 10feet away, and unhesitatingly picked him out of the photo lineup. The jury might well choose to give greater credence to the simple fact of identification than to the difficult estimation of height and weight.

The Court spends considerable time showing how Smallwood's testimony could have been discredited. Perhaps so, but that is all irrelevant to this appeal, since all of that impeaching material (except the "facial identification" point I have discussed above) was available to the defense independently of the Brady material. In sum, the undisclosed statements, credited with everything they could possibly have provided to the defense, leave two prosecution witnesses (Territo and Kersh) totally untouched; one prosecution witness (Smallwood) barely affected (he saw "only" the killer's face); and one prosecution witness (Williams) somewhat impaired (his description of the killer's height and weight did not match Kyles). We must keep all this in due perspective, remembering that the relevant question in the materiality inquiry is not how many points the defense could have scored off the prosecution witnesses, but whether it is reasonably probable that the new evidence would have caused the jury to accept the basic thesis that all four witnesses were mistaken. I think it plainly is not. No witness involved in the case ever identified anyone but petitioner as the murderer. Their views of the crime and the escaping criminal were obtained in bright daylight from close at hand; and their identifications were reaffirmed before the jury. After the side-by-side comparison between Beanie and Kyles, the jury heard Territo say that there was "[n]o doubt in my mind" that petitioner was the murderer; heard Kersh say "I know it was him.... I seen his face and I know the color of his skin. I know it. I know it's him," heard Smallwood say "I'm positive ... [b]ecause that's the man who I seen kill that woman," and heard Williams say "[n]o doubt in my mind." With or without the Brady evidence, there could be no doubt in the mind of the jury either.

There remains the argument that is the major contribution of today's opinion to Brady litigation; with our endorsement, it will surely be trolled past appellate courts in all future failure-to-disclose cases. The Court argues that "the effective impeachment of one eyewitness can call for a new trial even though the attack does not extend directly to others." The weakening of one witness's testimony does not weaken the unconnected testimony of another witness; and to entertain the possibility that the jury will give it such an effect is incompatible with the whole idea of a materiality standard, which presumes that the incriminating evidence that would have been destroyed by proper disclosure can be logically separated from the incriminating evidence that would have remained unaffected.

The physical evidence confirms the immateriality of the nondisclosures. In a garbage bag outside petitioner's home the police found Mrs. Dye's purse and other belongings. Inside his home they found, behind the kitchen stove, the .32 caliber revolver used to kill Mrs. Dye; hanging in a wardrobe, a homemade shoulder holster that was "a perfect fit" for the revolver, (Detective Dillman); in a dresser drawer in the bedroom, two boxes of gun cartridges, one containing only .32 caliber rounds of the same brand found in the murder weapon, another containing .22, .32, and .38 caliber rounds; in a kitchen cabinet, eight empty Schwegmann's bags; and in a cupboard underneath that cabinet, one Schwegmann's bag containing 15 cans of pet food. Petitioner's account at trial was that Beanie planted the purse, gun and holster, that petitioner received the ammunition from

Beanie as collateral for a loan, and that petitioner had bought the pet food the day of the murder. That account strains credulity to the breaking point.

The Court is correct that the Brady material would have supported the claim that Beanie planted Mrs. Dye's belongings in petitioner's garbage and (to a lesser degree) that Beanie planted the gun behind petitioner's stove. But we must see the whole story that petitioner presented to the jury. Petitioner would have it that Beanie did not plant the incriminating evidence until the day after he incited the police to search petitioner's home. Moreover, he succeeded in surreptitiously placing the gun behind the stove, and the matching shoulder holster in the wardrobe, while at least 10 and as many as 19people were present in petitioner's small apartment. Beanie, who was wearing blue jeans and either a "tank-top" shirt, or a short-sleeved shirt, would have had to be concealing about his person not only the shoulder holster and the murder weapon, but also a different gun with tape wrapped around the barrel that he showed to petitioner. Only appellate judges could swallow such a tale. Petitioner's only supporting evidence was Johnny Burns's testimony that he saw Beanie stooping behind the stove, presumably to plant the gun. Burns's credibility on the stand can perhaps best be gauged by observing that the state judge who presided over petitioner's trial stated, in a postconviction proceeding, that "[I] ha[ve] chosen to totally disregard everything that [Burns] has said," Burns, by the way, who repeatedly stated at trial that Beanie was his "best friend," has since been tried and convicted for killing Beanie.

Petitioner did not claim that the ammunition had been planted. The police found a .22 caliber rifle under petitioner's mattress and two boxes of ammunition, one containing .22, .32, and .38 caliber rounds, another containing only .32 caliber rounds of the same brand as those found loaded in the murder weapon. Petitioner's story was that Beanie gave him the rifle and the .32 caliber shells as security for a loan, but that he had taken the .22caliber shells out of the box. Put aside that the latter detail was contradicted by the facts; but consider the inherent implausibility of Beanie's giving petitioner collateral in the form of a box containing only .32 shells, if it were true that petitioner did not own a .32 caliber gun. As the Fifth Circuit wrote, "[t]he more likely inference, apparently chosen by the jury, is that [petitioner] possessed .32 caliber ammunition because he possessed a .32 caliber firearm." 5 F.3d, at 817.

We come to the evidence of the pet food, so mundane and yet so very damning. Petitioner's confused and changing explanations for the presence of 15 cans of pet food in a Schwegmann's bag under the sink must have fatally undermined his credibility before the jury (trial judge finds that petitioner's "obvious lie" concerning the pet food "may have been a crucial bit of evidence in the minds of the jurors which caused them to discount the entire defense in this case").

The full story is this. Mr. and Mrs. Dye owned two cats and a dog, for which she regularly bought varying brands of pet food, several different brands at a time. Found in Mrs. Dye's home after her murder were the brands Nine Lives, Kalkan and Puss n' Boots. Found in petitioner's home were eight cans of Nine Lives, four cans of Kalkan, and three cans of Cozy Kitten. Since we know that Mrs. Dye had been shopping that day and that the murderer made off with her goods, petitioner's possession of these items was powerful evidence that he was the murderer. Assuredly the jury drew that obvious inference. Pressed to explain why he just happened to buy 15 cans of pet food that very day (keep in mind that petitioner was a very poor man, who supported a common-law wife, a mistress, and four children), petitioner gave the reason that "it was on sale." The State, however, introduced testimony from the Schwegmann's advertising director that the pet food was not on sale that day. The sum of it is that petitioner, far from explaining the presence of the pet food, doubled the force of the State's evidence by perjuring himself before the jury, as the state trial judge observed.

I will not address the list of cars in the Schwegmann's parking lot and the receipt, found in the victim's car, that bore petitioner's fingerprints. These were collateral matters that provided little evidence of either guilt or innocence. The list of cars, which did not contain petitioner's automobile, would only have served to rebut the State's introduction of a photograph purporting to show petitioner's car in the parking lot; but petitioner does not contest that the list was not comprehensive, and that the photograph was taken about six hours before the list was compiled. Thus its rebuttal value would have been marginal at best. The receipt—although it showed that petitioner must at some point have been both in Schwegmann's and in the murdered woman's car—was as consistent with petitioner's story as with the State's.

* * *

The State presented to the jury a massive core of evidence (including four eyewitnesses) showing that petitioner was guilty of murder, and that he lied about his guilt. The effect that the Brady materials would have had in chipping away at the edges of the State's case can only be called immaterial. For the same reasons I reject petitioner's claim that the Brady materials would have created a "residual doubt" sufficient to cause the sentencing jury to withhold capital punishment.

I respectfully dissent.

NOTES

1. Kyles v. Whitley is typical of current litigation over the meaning of *Brady*, that is, the cases do not involve failure to disclose what is clearly exculpatory, i.e., confession of another to commission of the crime, but rather failure to disclose something about which one could reasonably dispute its exculpatory force. See Banks v. Dretke, 540 U.S. 668, 124 S.Ct. 1256 (2004) (To prove dangerousness prosecution called witness to show Banks provided gun for robberies without revealing that the witness was paid by police to ask Banks for a gun; found to be *Brady* violation over dissent that Banks had shot victim three times in carjacking and had severely beaten a relative). See also State v. Youngblood, 221 W.Va. 20, 650 S.E.2d 119 (2007) (5–2 split over whether evidence is exculpatory after remand from Supreme Court) (Court also notes that absence of knowledge of prosecutor is not a defense to *Brady* violation if police investigating the case were aware of the evidence).

2. Where defendant negotiates for an agreed disposition on a plea of guilty and eventually does plead guilty, has the prosecutor violated his duty by failing to disclose that the complaining witness died four days before the plea was agreed to and entered? Does the fact that the witness has died constitute exculpatory evidence? Is there an obligation to disclose information which is material to the tactical considerations which attend a determination to plead guilty? Would it make a difference if the prosecutor had affirmatively, and falsely, told defense counsel that the witness was available to testify at trial? What if the defendant gave a full, inculpatory statement at the time of his plea? What if the defendant asserts at the time of the plea that he is innocent but, in light of his assessment of the strength of the evidence against him, desires to enter a plea to a lesser offense rather than risk conviction on the greater offense? See People v. Jones, 44 N.Y.2d 76, 404 N.Y.S.2d 85, 375 N.E.2d 41 (1978).

One court held that even a classic *Brady* violation does not necessarily spoil an otherwise voluntary plea of guilty. See Campbell v. Marshall, 769 F.2d 314 (6th Cir.1985). Should a defendant be required to prove that he would not have pleaded guilty if he had known of the exculpatory evidence? See also White v. United States, 858 F.2d 416 (8th Cir.1988) (Vacation of plea proper only if court concludes that if defendant had received *Brady* material he would not have pleaded guilty). An argument for the duty to disclose is set out in McMunigal, Disclosure and Accuracy in the Guilty Plea Process, 40 Hastings L.J. 957 (1989). The Supreme Court seems to suggest that evidence of "actual innocence" must be disclosed before plea but this probably would not include failure to disclose that a crucial witness is unavailable or "impeachment information relating to any... witnesses" or affirmative defenses. See United States v. Ruiz, 536 U.S. 622, 122 S.Ct. 2450 (2002) reversing a Court of Appeals holding that any plea entered without knowledge of material information withhold by prosecutors is invalid.

3. Consider the following facts:

The principal prosecution witness (and the only one identifying the defendants) in an homicide case was Tony Malloy:

> In response to the pretrial request for *Brady* material, the prosecution acknowledged that a few days after Malloy's Grand Jury appearance it purchased airplane tickets to Virginia for Malloy and his girlfriend and paid their first month's rent there. It also paid Malloy a total of $1,500 in cash before he returned to New York for the trial about a year later. The pending charges against him were adjourned until after defendant's trial.
>
> Malloy testified at trial that he was told by the District Attorney's office at the time he returned that he would be relocated in the future, but asserted that no promises of leniency had been made with respect to his pending charges. Inasmuch as a conviction on any of the open charges would render Malloy a persistent felony offender, subject to a lengthy mandatory sentence of imprisonment, defense attorneys asked him how he could be assured of relocation unless the District Attorney contemplated a dismissal of the pending charges. Notwithstanding this apparent inconsistency, Malloy insisted no promises had been made. He acknowledged, however, that while in Virginia he had talked with McCarthy at least 25 times on the telephone and had met with him on other occasions after his return to New York and before he testified.
>
> During the trial, the defense learned that McCarthy had promised Malloy's attorney, Jonathan Latimer, that Malloy could avoid incarceration if he testified truthfully against defendants. Defendants subpoenaed Latimer who testified that he and McCarthy had negotiated such an agreement following Malloy's Grand Jury testimony. It was his "understanding, Latimer said, that no promises were made directly to Malloy, and he believed no details of the

agreement were communicated to the two trial assistants. Citing the attorney-client privilege, Latimer refused to disclose what, if anything, he told Malloy about the agreement. He also stated that he met with the trial assistants and Malloy when they prepared Malloy's trial testimony. Latimer testified that at these meetings the trial assistants instructed Malloy that if asked about promises of leniency he was to answer that none had been made to him."

Was *Brady* violated and, if so, what is the remedy? See People v. Steadman, 82 N.Y.2d 1, 603 N.Y.S.2d 382, 623 N.E.2d 509 (1993).

What if the prosecution fails to disclose the fact that one of its two principal witnesses had failed a polygraph examination on whether he had helped defendant commit the crime or had been at the scene of the crime, two points which were important to the offered defense. Would this violate Brady–Agurs if the polygraph evidence were inadmissible? One Court thought so because defense counsel could have used the polygraph results in the deposition of the witness. And because the defense counsel would have had a stronger reason to pursue investigation of his client's story. See Bartholomew v. Wood, 34 F.3d 870 (9th Cir.1994). Would the result have been different if state law permitted no deposition? The Supreme Court held there was no Brady violation with or without deposition, Wood v. Bartholomew, 516 U.S. 1, 116 S.Ct. 7 (1995).

4. Can a defense lawyer turn a general request for favorable evidence into a specific request by dividing the request into specific subcategories of evidence? How specific is specific was the subject of discussion in Brown v. Chaney, 469 U.S. 1090, 105 S.Ct. 601 (1984), Burger, C.J., dissenting from denial of certiorari.

5. When prosecutors discover material tending to exculpate a previously convicted defendant, does *Brady* require disclosure of such evidence? Suppose prosecutors and police obtain such evidence sometime after conviction, fail to disclose it, and then the prisoner or his counsel subsequently obtains the same information. If the information is not strong enough to mandate a new trial under state law procedures for newly discovered evidence, might *Brady* and *Agurs* nevertheless mandate relief under some circumstances. See Monroe v. Butler, 485 U.S. 1024, 108 S.Ct. 1582 (1988), (Marshall, J., dissenting from denial of certiorari), for an interesting discussion of this issue. See Boyle v. Johnson, 93 F.3d 180 (5th Cir.1996) (fake autopsy reports). If the material does establish the actual innocence of the convict, then it is not *Brady* that requires disclosure, it is the recognized standards of legal ethics applicable to prosecutors who may well have a duty to do more than disclose, that is, to take steps to vacate the conviction.

6. Normally perjurious testimony by a lay witness (as distinguished from a police officer or other governmental official) does not offend Due Process where the prosecutor is unaware of the testimony's falsehood. But does Due Process require a remedy where, after conviction, perjury is discovered? One court has answered this question affirmatively. See Sanders v. Sullivan, 900 F.2d 601 (2d Cir.1990).

Arizona v. Youngblood

Supreme Court of the United States, 1988.
488 U.S. 51, 109 S.Ct. 333.

■ CHIEF JUSTICE REHNQUIST delivered the opinion of the Court.

* * *

After the [sexual assault victim] made his way home, his mother took him to Kino Hospital. At the hospital, a physician ... used the swab to collect samples from the boy's rectum and mouth. He then made a microscopic slide of the samples. The doctor also obtained samples of the boy's saliva, blood, and hair. The physician did not examine the samples at any time. The police placed the kit in a secure refrigerator at the police station. At the hospital, the police also collected the boy's underwear and T–Shirt. This clothing was not refrigerated or frozen.

Nine days after the attack, on November 7, 1983, the police asked the boy to pick out his assailant from a photographic lineup. The boy identified respondent as the assailant. Respondent was not located by the police until four weeks later; he was arrested on December 9, 1983.

On November 8, 1983, Edward Heller, a police criminologist, examined the sexual assault kit. He testified that he followed standard department procedure, which was to examine the slides and determine whether sexual contact had occurred. After he determined that such contact had occurred, the criminologist did not perform any other tests, although he placed the assault kit back in the refrigerator. He testified that tests to identify blood group substances were not routinely conducted during the initial examination of an assault kit and in only about half of all cases in any event. He did not test the clothing at this time.

Respondent was indicted on charges of child molestation, sexual assault, and kidnapping. The State moved to compel respondent to provide blood and saliva samples for comparison with the material gathered through the use of the sexual assault kit, but the trial court denied the motion on the ground that the State had not obtained a sufficiently large semen sample to make a valid comparison. The prosecutor then asked the State's criminologist to perform an ABO blood group test on the rectal swab sample in an attempt to ascertain the blood type of the boy's assailant. This test failed to detect any blood group substances in the sample.

In January 1985, the police criminologist examined the boy's clothing for the first time. He found one semen stain on the boy's underwear and another on the rear of his T-shirt. The criminologist tried to obtain blood group substances from both stains using the ABO technique, but was unsuccessful. He also performed a P–30 protein molecule test on the stains, which indicated that only a small quantity of semen was present on the clothing; it was inconclusive as to the assailant's identity. The Tucson Police Department had just begun using this test, which was then used in slightly more than half of the crime laboratories in the country.

Respondent's principal defense at trial was that the boy had erred in identifying him as the perpetrator of the crime. In this connection, both a criminologist for the State and an expert witness for respondent testified as to what might have been shown by tests performed on the samples shortly after they were gathered, or by later tests performed on the samples from the boy's clothing had the clothing been properly refrigerated. The court instructed the jury that if they found the State had destroyed or lost evidence, they might "infer that the true fact is against the State's interest."

The jury found respondent guilty as charged. . . . The Court of Appeals concluded on the basis of the expert testimony at trial that timely performance of tests with properly preserved semen samples could have produced results that might have completely exonerated respondent. The Court of Appeals reached this conclusion even though it did "not imply any bad faith on the part of the State. . . ."

* * *

There is no question but that the State complied with *Brady* and *Agurs* here. The State disclosed relevant police reports to respondent, which contained information about the existence of the swab and the clothing, and the boy's examination at the hospital. The State provided respondent's expert with the laboratory reports and notes prepared by the police criminologist, and respondent's expert had access to the swab and to the clothing.

If respondent is to prevail on federal constitutional grounds, then, it must be because of some constitutional duty over and above that imposed by cases such as *Brady* and *Agurs*. Our most recent decision in this area of the law, *California v. Trombetta* (1984), arose out of a drunk driving prosecution in which the State had introduced test results indicating the concentration of alcohol in the blood of two motorists. The defendants sought to suppress the test results on the ground that the State had failed to preserve the breath samples used in the test. We rejected this argument for several reasons: first, "the officers here were acting in 'good faith and in accord with their normal practice' " second, in the light of the procedures actually used the chances that preserved samples would have exculpated the defendants were slim, and, third, even if the samples might have shown inaccuracy in the tests, the defendants had "alternative means of demonstrating their innocence." In the present case, the likelihood that the preserved materials would have enabled the defendant to exonerate himself appears to be greater than it was in *Trombetta*, but here, unlike in *Trombetta*, the State did not attempt to make any use of the materials in its own case in chief.*

* * *

The Due Process Clause of the Fourteenth Amendment, as interpreted in *Brady*, makes the good or bad faith of the State irrelevant when the State fails to disclose to the defendant material exculpatory evidence. But we think the Due Process Clause requires a different result when we deal with the failure of the State to preserve evidentiary material of which no more can be said than that it could have been subjected to tests, the results of which might have exonerated the defendant. Part of the reason for the

* . . . *Trombetta* speaks of evidence whose exculpatory value is "apparent." The possibility that the semen samples could have exculpated respondent if preserved or tested is not enough to satisfy the standard of constitutional materiality in *Trombetta*. Second, we made clear in *Trombetta* that the exculpatory value of the evidence must be apparent "*before* the evidence was destroyed." Ibid. (emphasis added). Here, respondent has not shown that the police knew the semen samples would have exculpated him when they failed to perform certain tests or to refrigerate the boy's clothing; this evidence was simply an avenue of investigation that might have led in any number of directions. The presence or absence of bad faith by the police for purposes of the Due Process Clause must necessarily turn on the police's knowledge of the exculpatory value of the evidence at the time it was lost or destroyed.

difference in treatment is found in the observation made by the Court in *Trombetta*, that "[w]henever potentially exculpatory evidence is permanently lost, courts face the treacherous task of divining the import of materials whose contents are unknown and, very often, disputed." Part of it stems from our unwillingness to read the "fundamental fairness" requirement of the Due Process Clause as imposing on the police an undifferentiated and absolute duty to retain and to preserve all material that might be of conceivable evidentiary significance in a particular prosecution. We think that requiring a defendant to show bad faith on the part of the police both limits the extent of the police's obligation to preserve evidence to reasonable bounds and confines it to that class of cases where the interests of justice most clearly require it, *i.e.*, those cases in which the police themselves by their conduct indicate that the evidence could form a basis for exonerating the defendant. We therefore hold that unless a criminal defendant can show bad faith on the part of the police, failure to preserve potentially useful evidence does not constitute a denial of due process of law.

In this case, the police collected the rectal swab and clothing on the night of the crime; respondent was not taken into custody until six weeks later. The failure of the police to refrigerate the clothing and to perform tests on the semen samples can at worst be described as negligent. None of this information was concealed from respondent at trial, and the evidence—such as it was—was made available to respondent's expert who declined to perform any tests on the samples. The Arizona Court of Appeals noted in its opinion—and we agree—that there was no suggestion of bad faith on the part of the police. It follows, therefore, from what we have said, that there was no violation of the Due Process Clause.

The Arizona Court of Appeals also referred somewhat obliquely to the State's "inability to quantitatively test" certain semen samples with the newer P–30 test. If the court meant by this statement that the Due Process Clause is violated when the police fail to use a particular investigatory tool, we strongly disagree. The situation here is no different than a prosecution for drunk driving that rests on police observation alone; the defendant is free to argue to the finder of fact that a breathalizer test might have been exculpatory, but the police do not have a constitutional duty to perform any particular tests.

The judgment of the Arizona Court of Appeals is reversed and the case remanded for further proceedings not inconsistent with this opinion.

Reversed.

■ JUSTICE STEVENS, concurring in the judgment.

Three factors are of critical importance to my evaluation of this case. First, at the time the police failed to refrigerate the victim's clothing, and thus negligently lost potentially valuable evidence, they had at least as great an interest in preserving the evidence as did the person later accused of the crime. . . .

Second, although it is not possible to know whether the lost evidence would have revealed any relevant information, it is unlikely that the defendant was prejudiced by the State's omission. In examining witnesses and in her summation, defense counsel impressed upon the jury the fact that the State failed to preserve the evidence and that the State could have conducted tests that might well have exonerated the defendant. More significantly, the trial judge instructed the jury: "If you find that the State has ... allowed to be destroyed or lost any evidence whose content or quality are in issue, you may infer that the true fact is against the State's interest." As a result, the uncertainty as to what the evidence might have proved was turned to the defendant's advantage.

Third, the fact that no juror chose to draw the permissive inference that proper preservation of the evidence would have demonstrated that the defendant was not the assailant suggests that the lost evidence was "immaterial." ... In declining defense counsel's and the court's invitations to draw the permissive inference, the jurors in effect indicated that, in their view, the other evidence at trial was so overwhelming that it was highly improbable that the lost evidence was exculpatory....

... In my opinion, there may well be cases in which the defendant is unable to prove that the State acted in bad faith but in which the loss or destruction of evidence is nonetheless so critical to the defense as to make a criminal trial fundamentally unfair. This, however, is not such a case. Accordingly, I concur in the judgment.

■ JUSTICE BLACKMUN, with whom JUSTICE BRENNAN and JUSTICE MARSHALL join, dissenting.

* * *

Brady and *Agurs* could not be more clear in their holdings that a prosecutor's bad faith in interfering with a defendant's access to material evidence is *not* an essential part of a due process violation. Nor did *Trombetta* create such a requirement. *Trombetta*'s initial discussion focused on the due process requirement "that criminal defendants be afforded a meaningful opportunity to present a complete defense," and then noted that the delivery of exculpatory evidence to the defendant "protect[s] the innocent from erroneous conviction and ensur[es] the integrity of our criminal justice system." Although the language of *Trombetta* includes a quotation in which the words "in good faith" appear, those words, for two reasons, do not have the significance claimed for them by the majority. First, the words are the antecedent part of the fuller phrase "in good faith and in accord with their normal practice." ...

Second, and more importantly, *Trombetta* demonstrates that the absence of bad faith does not end the analysis. The determination in *Trombetta* that the prosecution acted in good faith and according to normal practice merely prefaced the primary inquiry, which centers on the "constitutional materiality" of the evidence itself. There is nothing in *Trombetta* that intimates that good faith alone should be the measure.

The cases in this area clearly establish that police actions taken in bad faith are not the only species of police conduct that can result in a violation of due process. As *Agurs* points out, it makes no sense to overturn a conviction because a malicious prosecutor withholds information that he mistakenly believes to be material, but which actually would have been of no help to the defense. In the same way, it makes no sense to ignore the fact that a defendant has been denied a fair trial because the State allowed evidence that was material to the defense to deteriorate beyond the point of usefulness, simply because the police were inept rather than malicious.

I also doubt that the "bad faith" standard creates the bright-line rule sought by the majority. Apart from the inherent difficulty a defendant would have in obtaining evidence to show a lack of good faith, the line between "good faith" and "bad faith" is anything but bright, and the majority's formulation may well create more questions than it answers. What constitutes bad faith for these purposes? Does a defendant have to show actual malice, or would recklessness, or the deliberate failure to establish standards for maintaining and preserving evidence, be sufficient? Does "good faith police work" require a certain minimum of diligence, or will a lazy officer, who does not walk the few extra steps to the evidence refrigerator, be considered to be acting in good faith? While the majority leaves these questions for another day, its quick embrace of a bad faith standard has not brightened the line; it only has moved the line so as to provide fewer protections for criminal defendants.

The inquiry the majority eliminates in setting up its "bad faith" rule is whether the evidence in question here was "constitutionally material," so that its destruction violates due process. The majority does not say whether "evidentiary material of which no more can be said than that it could have been subjected to tests, the results of which might have exonerated the defendant," ante, at 337, is, for purposes of due process, material. But because I do not find the question of lack of bad faith dispositive, I now consider whether this evidence was such that its destruction rendered respondent's trial fundamentally unfair.

* * *

... To put it succinctly, where no comparable evidence is likely to be available to the defendant, police must preserve physical evidence of a type that they reasonably should know has the potential, if tested, to reveal immutable characteristics of the criminal, and hence to exculpate a defendant charged with the crime.

* * *

Due process must also take into account the burdens that the preservation of evidence places on the police. Law enforcement officers must be provided the option, as is implicit in *Trombetta*, of performing the proper tests on physical evidence and then discarding it. Once a suspect has been arrested the police, after a reasonable time, may inform defense counsel of plans to discard the evidence. When the defense has been informed of the existence of the evidence, after a reasonable time the burden of preservation may shift to the defense. There should also be flexibility to deal with evidence that is unusually dangerous or difficult to store.

NOTE

Bad faith destruction of evidence occurred when federal agents seized laboratory equipment they charged was used to manufacture methamphetamines. They found methamphetamine formulas and chemicals used in its manufacture but found no traces of the drug or precursor chemicals on the glassware and equipment which was destroyed because it might be hazardous waste. Before its destruction defendant told the agents the equipment could not be used for making the drug. An attorney repeated this assertion but, despite the absence of any immediate environmental hazard, the equipment was destroyed. When the value to the defense was promptly suggested to government agents, destruction of the equipment cannot be justified and expert testimony about the equipment and its design could not replace the missing physical evidence. See United States v. Cooper, 983 F.2d 928 (9th Cir.1993).

* * *

B. Pre-Trial Discovery

In re Di Joseph

Supreme Court of Pennsylvania, 1958.
394 Pa. 19, 145 A.2d 187.

[In a murder case the trial court required the prosecution to make available to the defendant, before trial, the gun which the prosecution alleged to be the gun used in the murder, photographs of fingerprints, if any, on the gun, the defendant's bloodstained clothing, photographs of the bedroom which was the scene of the killing, and articles of bedroom furniture seized by the police. Upon a hearing of the prosecutor's petition for a writ of prohibition regarding the order, the Supreme Court of Pennsylvania, in a per curiam opinion, affirmed the trial court's ruling except as regards the photographs of fingerprints. It was held that the prosecutor need not make the photographs available for inspection by the defendant and her counsel. Following are the concurring and dissenting opinions.]

■ Charles Alvin Jones, Chief Justice (concurring).

It is the rule in this State that a defendant in a criminal case has no absolute right to examine and inspect, prior to trial, evidence in the possession of the Commonwealth. Counsel for the present accused so conceded at bar and the Attorney General, as *amicus curiae*, so argued both orally and by brief. However, a trial court having jurisdiction of an alleged offender possesses discretionary power to permit a defendant, in appropriate circumstances, to examine and inspect in advance of trial physical or documentary evidence in the hands of the prosecution. And, this court's current action so confirms.

* * *

In [an earlier] case, we said the argument made against any such discretion is based upon a fear that the State, which is charged with the prosecution of crime, may be hampered in its duty by the disclosure of its evidence to those charged with offenses. Whatever merit that argument has as applied to a situation where it is contended that the accused has a *right* to inspect the evidence, it has no application, we think, to a situation where the trial judge in each case and on each application, determines what should be done in the interest of justice. There are cases in which it would be clearly unjust to deny such an application and, on the other hand, cases are conceivable in which it might improperly hamper the prosecution to grant such an application. We do not understand that the court below decided that the appellees were entitled to this disclosure as a "matter of right."

Likewise in the instant case, the trial court did not hold that the petitioning defendant was entitled *as a matter of right* to the disclosure ordered. And, this court in its *pro tanto* approval of the order entered by the court below is not laying down a new rule. Chief Justice Stern's quotation in Commonwealth v. Wable, 382 Pa. 80, 86, 114 A.2d 334, 338, from Wharton's Criminal Evidence that "The general rule is that the accused has no right to the inspection or disclosure before trial of evidence in the possession of the prosecution" continues to be the rule in Pennsylvania. The matter of permitting a defendant to examine and inspect evidence in the keeping of the Commonwealth depends upon an exercise of judicial discretion in any instance and our trial courts can be trusted to exercise it wisely. The justification for the discretion so reposed lies, in part, in the concept expressed by Judge Hoban in Commonwealth v. Stepper, 54 Lack. Jur. 205, 212–213,—"We would rather remove any obstacle to a fair trial, before the trial, rather than have it removed later and double the expense of difficult and protracted proceedings to the Commonwealth." Like the court in State v. Haas, supra, "We are not impressed by the fear of the prosecuting attorneys that the exercise of such discretion will change the whole practice of criminal law in this State, or will make the securing of proper convictions more difficult to obtain. It has not apparently had that effect elsewhere and we see no reason why it should have it here."

The only question before us, then, is whether the court below properly exercised its discretion. The court *en banc*, composed of the four judges of the Court of Common Pleas of Montgomery County, after reciting that it had reviewed all the evidence at its command, unanimously concluded that "... the Commonwealth has impeded and hampered defense counsel's investigation and preparation for trial by unrestrained and arbitrary power without fair co-operation and is therefore depriving the accused of that due process of law commanded by the 14th Amendment to the Constitution of the United States." Neither the record, the printed briefs, nor the oral argument has presented anything that would justify us in holding that the foregoing considered conclusion of the court below was false. Consequently, it necessarily follows that the court below, acting for the purpose of vitiating the indicated harm, exercised a sound discretion by the entry of its order as restricted by the limitation now put upon it by this court.

* * *

■ MUSMANNO, JUSTICE (concurring).

I concur in the order entered by the majority of this Court. I believe that a person who asserts his innocence of a crime of which he stands accused is entitled to examine prosecution exhibits which are reasonably associated with the theory of guilt and of which he probably may be unaware. However, where an exhibit is one of which the accused is entirely cognizant and *already knows* whether it could or could not be an item of incrimination against him, he is not entitled to its inspection if such inspection would hamper the Commonwealth in proceeding with its case. . . .

We have affirmed the action of the lower Court with regard to inspection of the weapon but have refused to the defendant an inspection of the photographs of fingerprints, if any. I believe this action to be eminently just and in no way handicaps the defendant in the preparation of her case. She is one person who knows whether she used the weapon or not and, therefore, she is not being denied anything which she needs in the ascertainment of truth. . . .

I believe the prosecution here might find itself impeded in preparing for trial if it were required to announce to the world what it found on the38–calibre revolver discovered in the culvert. . . .

■ BELL, JUSTICE (dissenting). I dissent from the majority's order which requires the Commonwealth to make available to this defendant before trial, the gun which the Commonwealth alleges is the gun used in the murder, defendant's bloodstained clothing, photographs of their bedroom which was the scene of the crime, and articles of bedroom furniture which were seized by the police. This disastrous precedent-shattering decision breaches one of the few barriers which are left to protect peaceable communities and law-abiding citizens from murderers and dangerous criminals. While the order directs the Commonwealth merely to turn over to defendant for examination before trial nearly all of its physical evidence, I believe that *the effect* of the order will be to compel the Commonwealth in the near future to turn over or disclose to a defendant in advance of trial *all* of its evidence. That this is no idle fear is clearly demonstrated by the contention of the Attorney General of Pennsylvania, who personally appeared in opposition to the Trial District Attorney and to the District Attorneys' Association of Pennsylvania.

The Attorney General orally argued that a criminal case was just like a civil case, and consequently the Commonwealth, in the interest of justice, should give or disclose to the defendant before trial *all* its evidence. It is difficult to imagine a more untenable argument or a more far-fetched analogy. A criminal trial is as different from a civil trial as day is from night. In civil trials there is pre-trial discovery and a *mutual* exchange of evidence. In a criminal trial the defendant does not have to inform the Commonwealth before or during trial or at any time his defense or any of his evidence; he does not have to take the witness stand and no unfavorable inference can be drawn therefrom; he can be convicted only if the Commonwealth proves his guilt beyond a reasonable doubt, which is defined to be a doubt which would restrain a reasonable man from acting in a matter of importance to himself; he is presumed to be innocent no matter how many terrible crimes he may have committed; if he has never been convicted of crime he can place in evidence his good reputation and that alone can be sufficient to justify his acquittal; and finally, he cannot be convicted unless all twelve of the jurors unanimously find him guilty beyond a reasonable doubt.

If we descend from ethereal theorism to the world of reality, we know that if Courts require the Commonwealth to inform each defendant of or permit him to examine its evidence, it will enable a person who commits a murder or a felony to devise, fabricate and manufacture his defense before trial—alibi, "blackout", insanity, self-defense or perpetration of the crime by someone else—and determine whether he should take the witness stand or introduce any evidence and if so, what kind. ... At the very least, a defendant should be required to present exceptional circumstances and compelling reasons to justify an exception to the general rule. No such exceptional circumstances or compelling reasons were presented by the defendant in this case. Furthermore, the contention of the Attorney General flies in the teeth of and would require us to overrule Commonwealth v. Wable and abrogate a rule which for the protection of society has existed for centuries.

In recent years the Supreme Court of the United States and this Court, in their zeal to assure a fair trial to persons accused or convicted of crime, have, in my judgment, too often forgotten that law-abiding citizens and communities likewise possess certain fundamental inalienable rights. One of these rights is that their life and property shall be protected by the State against murderers and criminals. Justice is not a one-way street—law-abiding citizens are entitled to the protection of the law, and to justice just as much as (if not more so than) criminals.

The present order goes further than this Court or, we believe, the Supreme Court of the United States, has ever gone. It permits fishing expeditions by a defendant; it sets a precedent which will make fabrication of defenses easy, and consequently (although of course unintentionally) it will make the protection of society and the conviction of dangerous criminals far more difficult than ever before. In the interest and for the protection of all law-abiding people in Pennsylvania I register this protest and dissent.

NOTE

Leaving aside material that must be disclosed under *Brady*, the accepted view is that rights of discovery may be provided by state law but are not constitutionally required. There is not much public fervor for such discovery. California's broad discovery practice was rejected by public referendum. Garcia v. Superior Court, 42 Cal.4th 63, 63 Cal.Rptr.3d 948 (2007)

Williams v. Florida

Supreme Court of the United States, 1970.
399 U.S. 78, 90 S.Ct. 1893.

■ MR. JUSTICE WHITE delivered the opinion of the Court.

Prior to his trial for robbery in the State of Florida, petitioner filed a "Motion for a Protective Order," seeking to be excused from the requirements of Rule 1.200 of the Florida Rules of Criminal Procedure, 33 F.S.A. That rule requires a defendant, on written demand of the prosecuting attorney, to give notice in advance of trial if the defendant intends to claim an alibi, and to furnish the prosecuting attorney with information as to the place where he claims to have been and with the names and addresses of the alibi witnesses he intends to use. In his motion petitioner openly declared his intent to claim an alibi, but objected to the further disclosure requirements on the ground that the rule "compels the Defendant in a criminal case to be a witness against himself" in violation of his Fifth and Fourteenth Amendment rights. The motion was denied.

Florida's notice-of-alibi rule is in essence a requirement that a defendant submit to a limited form of pretrial discovery by the State whenever he intends to rely at trial on the defense of alibi. In exchange for the defendant's disclosure of the witnesses he proposes to use to establish that defense, the State in turn is required to notify the defendant of any witnesses it proposes to offer in rebuttal to that defense. Both sides are under a continuing duty promptly to disclose the names and addresses of additional witnesses bearing on the alibi as they become available. The threatened sanction for failure to comply is the exclusion at trial of the defendant's alibi evidence—except for his own testimony—or, in the case of the State, the exclusion of the State's evidence offered in rebuttal of the alibi.

In this case, following the denial of his Motion for a Protective Order, petitioner complied with the alibi rule and gave the State the name and address of one Mary Scotty. Mrs. Scotty was summoned to the office of the State Attorney on the morning of the trial, where she gave pretrial testimony. At the trial itself, Mrs. Scotty, petitioner, and petitioner's wife all testified that the three of them had been in Mrs. Scotty's apartment during the time of the robbery. On two occasions during cross-examination of Mrs. Scotty, the prosecuting attorney confronted her with her earlier deposition in which she had given dates and times that in some respects did not correspond with the dates and times given at trial. Mrs. Scotty adhered to her trial story, insisting that she had been mistaken in her earlier testimony. The State also offered in rebuttal the testimony of one of the officers investigating the robbery who claimed that Mrs. Scotty had asked him for directions on the afternoon in question during the time when she claimed to have been in her apartment with petitioner and his wife.

We need not linger over the suggestion that the discovery permitted the State against petitioner in this case deprived him of "due process" or a "fair trial." Florida law provides for liberal discovery by the defendant against the State, and the notice-of-alibi rule is itself carefully hedged with reciprocal duties requiring state disclosure to the defendant. Given the ease with which an alibi can be fabricated, the State's interest in protecting itself against an eleventh hour defense is both obvious and legitimate. Reflecting this interest, notice-of-alibi provisions, dating at least from 1927, are now in existence in a substantial number of States. The adversary system of trial is hardly an end in itself; it is not yet a poker game in which players enjoy an absolute right always to conceal their cards until played. We find ample room in that system, at least as far as "due process" is concerned, for the instant Florida rule, which is designed to enhance the search for truth in the criminal trial by insuring both the defendant and the State ample opportunity to investigate certain facts crucial to the determination of guilt or innocence.

Petitioner's major contention is that he was "compelled . . . to be a witness against himself" contrary to the commands of the Fifth and Fourteenth Amendments because the notice-of-alibi rule required him to give the State the name and address of Mrs. Scotty in advance of trial and thus to furnish the State with information useful in convicting him. No pretrial statement of petitioner was introduced at trial; but armed with Mrs. Scotty's name and address and the knowledge that she was to be petitioner's alibi witness, the State was able to take her deposition in advance of trial and to find rebuttal testimony. Also, requiring him to reveal the elements of his defense is claimed to have interfered with his right to wait until after the State had presented its case to decide how to defend against it. We conclude, however, as has apparently every other court that has considered the issue, that the privilege against self-incrimination is not violated by a requirement that the defendant give notice of an alibi defense and disclose his alibi witnesses.

The defendant in a criminal trial is frequently forced to testify himself and to call other witnesses in an effort to reduce the risk of conviction. When he presents his witnesses, he must reveal their identity and submit them to cross-examination which in itself may prove incriminating or which may furnish the State with leads to incriminating rebuttal evidence. That the defendant faces such a dilemma demanding a choice between complete silence and presenting a defense has never been thought an invasion of the privilege against compelled self-incrimination. The pressures generated by the State's evidence may be severe but they do not vitiate the defendant's choice to present an alibi defense and witnesses to prove it, even though the attempted defense ends in catastrophe for the defendant. However "testimonial" or "incriminating" the alibi defense proves to be, it cannot be considered "compelled" within the meaning of the Fifth and Fourteenth Amendments.

Very similar constraints operate on the defendant when the State requires pretrial notice of alibi and the naming of alibi witnesses. Nothing in such a rule requires the defendant to rely on an alibi or prevents him from abandoning the defense; these matters are left to his unfettered choice. That choice must be made, but the pressures that bear on his pretrial decision are of the same nature as those that would induce him to call alibi witnesses at the trial: the force of historical fact beyond both his and the State's control and the strength of the State's case built on these facts. Response to that kind of pressure by offering evidence or testimony is not compelled self-incrimination transgressing the Fifth and Fourteenth Amendments.

In the case before us, the notice-of-alibi rule by itself in no way affected petitioner's crucial decision to call alibi witnesses or added to the legitimate pressures leading to that course of action. At most, the rule only compelled petitioner to accelerate the timing of his disclosure, forcing him to divulge at an earlier date information that the petitioner from the beginning planned to divulge at trial. Nothing in the Fifth Amendment privilege entitles a defendant as a matter of constitutional right to await the end of the State's case before announcing the nature of his defense, anymore than it entitles him to await the jury's verdict on the State's case-in-chief before deciding whether or not to take the stand himself.

Petitioner concedes that absent the notice-of-alibi rule the Constitution would raise no bar to the court's granting the State a continuance at trial on the ground of surprise as soon as the alibi witness is called. Nor would there be self-incrimination problems if, during that continuance, the State was permitted to do precisely what it did here prior to trial: take the deposition of the witness and find rebuttal evidence. But if so utilizing a continuance is permissible under the Fifth and Fourteenth Amendments, then surely the same result may be accomplished through pretrial discovery, as it was here, avoiding the necessity of a disrupted trial. We decline to hold that the privilege against compulsory self-incrimination guarantees the defendant the right to surprise the State with an alibi defense.

■ Mr. Chief Justice Burger, concurring.

I join fully in Mr. Justice White's opinion for the Court. I see an added benefit to the notice-of-alibi rule in that it will serve important functions by way of disposing of cases without trial in appropriate circumstances—a matter of considerable importance when courts, prosecution offices, and legal aid and defender agencies are vastly overworked. The prosecutor upon receiving notice will, of course, investigate prospective alibi witnesses. If he finds them reliable and unimpeachable he will doubtless re-examine his entire case and this process would very likely lead to dismissal of the charges. In turn he might be obliged to determine why false charges were instituted and where the breakdown occurred in the examination of evidence that led to a charge.

On the other hand, inquiry into a claimed alibi defense may reveal it to be contrived and fabricated and the witnesses accordingly subject to impeach mentor other attack. In this situation defense counsel would be obliged tore-examine his case and, if he found his client has proposed the use of false testimony, either seek to withdraw from the case or try to persuade his client to enter a plea of guilty, possibly by plea discussions which could lead to disposition on a lesser charge.

In either case the ends of justice will have been served and the processes expedited. These are the likely consequences of an enlarged and truly reciprocal pretrial disclosure of evidence and the move away from the "sporting contest" idea of criminal justice.

■ Mr. Justice Black, with whom Mr. Justice Douglas joins, dissenting.

* * *

... the Fifth Amendment itself clearly provides that "[n]o person ... shall be compelled in any criminal case to be a witness against himself." If words are to be given their plain and obvious meaning, that provision, in my opinion, states that a criminal defendant cannot be required to give evidence, testimony, or any other assistance to the State to aid it in convicting him of crime. The Florida notice-of-alibi rule in my opinion is a patent violation of that constitutional provision because it requires a defendant to disclose information to the State so that the State can use that information to destroy him. It seems to me at least slightly incredible to suggest that this procedure may have some beneficial effects for defendants. There is no need to encourage defendants to take actions they think will help them. The fear of conviction and the substantial cost or inconvenience resulting from criminal prosecutions are more than sufficient incentives to make defendants want to help themselves. If a defendant thinks that making disclosure of an alibi before trial is in his best interest, he will obviously do so. And the only time the State needs the compulsion provided by this procedure is when the defendant has decided that such disclosure is likely to hurt his case.

It is no answer to this argument to suggest that the Fifth Amendment as so interpreted would give the defendant an unfair element of surprise, turning atrial into a "poker game" or "sporting contest," for that tactical advantage to the defendant is inherent in the type of trial required by our Bill of Rights. The Framers were well aware of the awesome investigative and prosecutorial powers of government and it was in order to limit those powers that they spelled out in detail in the Constitution the procedure to be followed in criminal trials. A defendant, they said, is entitled to notice of the charges against him, trial by jury, the right to counsel for his defense, the right to confront and cross-examine witnesses, the right to call witnesses in his own behalf, and the right not to be a witness against himself. All of these rights are designed to shield the defendant against state power. None are designed to make convictions easier and taken together they clearly indicate that in our system the entire burden of proving criminal activity rests on the State. The defendant, under our Constitution, need not do anything at all to defend himself, and certainly he cannot be required to help convict himself. Rather he has an absolute, unqualified right to compel the State to investigate its own case, find its own witnesses, prove its own facts, and convince the jury through its own resources. Throughout the process the defendant has a fundamental right to remain silent, in effect challenging the State at every point to: "Prove it!"

* * *

This constitutional right to remain absolutely silent cannot be avoided by superficially attractive analogies to any so-called "compulsion" inherent in the trial itself that may lead a defendant to put on evidence in his own defense. Obviously the Constitution contemplates that a defendant can be "compelled" to stand trial, and obviously there will be times when the trial process itself will require the defendant to do something in order to try to avoid a conviction. But nothing in the Constitution permits the State to add to the natural consequences of a trial and compel the defendant in advance of trial to participate in any way in the State's attempt to condemn him.

A criminal trial is in part a search for truth. But it is also a system designed to protect "freedom" by insuring that no one is criminally punished unless the State has first succeeded in the admittedly difficult task of convincing a jury that the defendant is guilty. That task is made more difficult by the Bill of Rights, and the Fifth Amendment may be one of the most difficult of the barriers to surmount....

II.

On the surface this case involves only a notice-of-alibi provisions, but in effect the decision opens the way for a profound change in one of the most important traditional safeguards of a criminal defendant. The rationale of today's decision is in no way limited to alibi defenses, or any other type or classification of evidence. The theory advanced goes at least so far as to permit the State to obtain under threat of sanction complete disclosure by the defendant in advance of trial of all evidence, testimony, and tactics he plans to use at that trial. In each case the justification will be that the rule affects only the "timing" of the disclosure, and not the substantive decision itself. This inevitability is clearly revealed by the citation to Jones v. Superior Court, 58 Cal.2d 56, 22 Cal.Rptr. 879, 372 P.2d 919 (1962). The prosecutor [there] successfully obtained an order compelling the defendant to reveal the names and addresses of any doctors he consulted and the medical reports of any examinations relating to the claimed incapacity [impotency in a rape case]. The majority found no barrier to the judicial creation of pretrial discovery by the State against the defendant, least of all a barrier raised by any constitutional prohibition on compelling the defendant to be a witness against himself.

The dangerous implications of the *Jones* rationale adopted today are not, however, limited to the disclosure of evidence that the defendant has already decided he will use at trial. In State v. Grove, 65 Wash.2d 525, 398 P.2d 170 (1965), the Washington Supreme Court, relying on *Jones*, held that a defendant in a murder trial could be compelled to produce a letter he had written his wife about the alleged crime, even though he had no thought at all of using that evidence in his own behalf. These cases are sufficient evidence of the inch-by-inch, case-by-case process by which the rationale of today's decision can be used to transform radically our system of criminal justice into a process requiring the defendant to assist the State in convicting him, or be punished for failing to do so.

... In spite of the history of oppression that produced the Bill of Rights and the strong reluctance of our governments to compel a criminal defendant to assist in his own conviction, the Court today reaches out to embrace and sanctify at the first opportunity a most dangerous departure from the Constitution and the traditional safeguards afforded persons accused of crime. I cannot accept such a result and must express my most emphatic disagreement and dissent.

■ MR. JUSTICE MARSHALL, dissenting in part. [Opinion omitted.]

Taylor v. Illinois

Supreme Court of the United States, 1988.
484 U.S. 400, 108 S.Ct. 646.

[Illinois requires a defendant to disclose, in advance of trial, the names and addresses of all witnesses the defense intends to call. Taylor's lawyer sought to amend his witness list mid-trial to include Wormley. Defense counsel informed the trial court that counsel, while knowing Wormley could give exculpatory evidence, had not previously been able to locate

Wormley. At a subsequent hearing, however, Wormley acknowledged that defense counsel had visited Wormley at Wormley's home the week before trial. The trial judge, at the conclusion of a hearing outside the presence of the jury, also declared that Wormley's exculpatory evidence was not credible. Earlier the judge had expressed concern that the belated "discovery" of the witness might be part of a scheme to present manufactured exculpatory evidence. At any rate, finding a "blatant" violation of Illinois discovery rules, Judge Heyda excluded Wormley's testimony.]

■ MR. JUSTICE STEVENS delivered the opinion of the Court.

* * *

In the State's view, no Compulsory Process Clause concerns are even raised by authorizing preclusion as a discovery sanction, or by the application of the Illinois rule in this case. The State's argument is supported by the plain language of the Clause, by the historical evidence that it was intended to provide defendants with subpoena power that they lacked at common law, by some scholarly comment, and by a brief excerpt from the legislative history of the Clause. We have, however, consistently given the Clause the broader reading reflected in contemporaneous state constitutional provisions.

* * *

The right to compel a witness' presence in the courtroom could not protect the integrity of the adversary process if it did not embrace the right to have the witness' testimony heard by the trier of fact. The right to offer testimony is thus grounded in the Sixth Amendment even though it is not expressly described in so many words.

We cannot accept the State's argument that this constitutional right may never be offended by the imposition of a discovery sanction that entirely excludes the testimony of a material defense witness.

Petitioner's claim that the Sixth Amendment creates an absolute bar to the preclusion of the testimony of a surprise witness is just as extreme and just as unacceptable as the State's position that the Amendment is simply irrelevant. The accused does not have an unfettered right to offer testimony that is incompetent, privileged, or otherwise inadmissible under standard rules of evidence. The Compulsory Process Clause provides him with an effective weapon, but it is a weapon that cannot be used irresponsibly.

* * *

The principle that undergirds the defendant's right to present exculpatory evidence is also the source of essential limitations on the right. The adversary process could not function effectively without adherence to rules of procedure that govern the orderly presentation of facts and arguments to provide each party with a fair opportunity to assemble and submit evidence to contradict or explain the opponent's case. The trial process would be a shambles if either party had an absolute right to control the time and content of his witnesses' testimony. Neither may insist on the right to interrupt the opposing party's case and obviously there is no absolute right to interrupt the deliberations of the jury to present newly discovered evidence. The State's interest in the orderly conduct of a criminal trial is sufficient to justify the imposition and enforcement of firm, though not always inflexible, rules relating to the identification and presentation of evidence.

The defendant's right to compulsory process is itself designed to vindicate the principle that the "ends of criminal justice would be defeated if judgments were to be founded on a partial or speculative presentation of the facts." *United States v. Nixon*. Rules that provide for pretrial discovery of an opponent's witnesses serve the same high purpose. Discovery, like cross-examination, minimizes the risk that a judgment will be predicated on incomplete, misleading, or even deliberately fabricated testimony. The "State's interest in protecting itself against an eleventh hour defense" is merely one component of the broader public interest in a full and truthful disclosure of critical facts.

To vindicate that interest we have held that even the defendant may not testify without being subjected to cross-examination. Moreover, in *United States v. Nobles* (1975), we upheld an order excluding the testimony of an expert witness tendered by the defendant because he had refused to permit discovery of a "highly relevant" report.

* * *

Petitioner does not question the legitimacy of a rule requiring pretrial disclosure of defense witnesses, but he argues that the sanction of preclusion of the testimony of a previously undisclosed witness is so drastic that it should never be imposed. He argues, correctly, that a less drastic sanction is always available. Prejudice to the prosecution could be minimized by granting a continuance or a mistrial to provide time for further investigation; moreover, further violations can be deterred by disciplinary sanctions against the defendant or defense counsel.

It may well be true that alternative sanctions are adequate and appropriate in most cases, but it is equally clear that they would be less effective than the preclusion sanction and that there are instances in which they would perpetuate rather than limit the prejudice to the State and the harm to the adversary process. One of the purposes of the discovery rule itself is to minimize the risk that fabricated testimony will be believed. Defendants who are willing to fabricate a defense may also be willing to fabricate excuses for failing to comply with a discovery requirement. The risk of a contempt violation may seem trivial to a defendant facing the threat of imprisonment for a term of years. A dishonest client can mislead an honest attorney, and there are occasions when an attorney assumes that the duty of loyalty to the client outweighs elementary obligations to the court.

* * *

In order to reject petitioner's argument that preclusion is *never* a permissible sanction for a discovery violation it is neither necessary nor appropriate for us to attempt to draft a comprehensive set of standards to guide the exercise of discretion in every possible case. It is elementary, of course, that a trial court may not ignore the fundamental character of the defendant's right to offer the testimony of witnesses in his favor. But the mere invocation of that right cannot automatically and invariably outweigh countervailing public interests. The integrity of the adversary process, which depends both on the presentation of reliable evidence and the rejection of unreliable evidence; the interest in the fair and efficient administration of justice; and the potential prejudice to the truth-determining function of the trial process must also weigh in the balance.

A trial judge may certainly insist on an explanation for a party's failure to comply with a request to identify his or her witnesses in advance of trial. If that explanation reveals that the omission was willful and motivated by a desire to obtain a tactical advantage that would minimize the effectiveness of cross-examination and the ability to adduce rebuttal evidence, it would be entirely consistent with the purposes of the Confrontation Clause simply to exclude the witness' testimony.[20]

The simplicity of compliance with the discovery rule is also relevant. As we have noted, the Compulsory Process Clause cannot be invoked without the prior planning and affirmative conduct of the defendant. Lawyers are accustomed to meeting deadlines. Routine preparation involves location and interrogation of potential witnesses and the serving of subpoenas on those whose testimony will be offered at trial. The burden of identifying them in advance of trial adds little to these routine demands of trial preparation.

It would demean the high purpose of the Compulsory Process Clause to construe it as encompassing an absolute right to an automatic continuance or mistrial to allow presumptively perjured testimony to be presented to a jury. We reject petitioner's argument that a preclusion sanction is never appropriate no matter how serious the defendant's discovery violation may be.

Petitioner argues that the preclusion sanction was unnecessarily harsh in this case because the *voir dire* examination of Wormley adequately protected the prosecution from any possible prejudice resulting from surprise. Petitioner also contends that it is unfair to visit the sins of the lawyer upon his client. Neither argument has merit.

More is at stake than possible prejudice to the prosecution. We are also concerned with the impact of this kind of conduct on the integrity of the judicial process itself. The trial judge found that the discovery violation in this case was both willful and blatant.[22] In view of the fact that petitioner's

20. There may be cases in which a defendant has legitimate objections to disclosing the identity of a potential witness. See Note, The Preclusion Sanction—A Violation of the Constitutional Right to Present a Defense, 81 Yale L.J. 1342, 1350 (1972). Such objections, however, should be raised in advance of trial in response to the discovery request and, if the parties are unable to agree on a resolution, presented to the court. Under the Federal Rules of Criminal Procedure and under the rules adopted by most states, a party may request a protective order if he or she has just cause for objecting to a discovery request. See *e.g.*, Fed.Rule Crim.Proc. 16(d)(1); Ill.Sup.Ct.Rule 412(i). In this case, there is no issue concerning the validity of the discovery requirement or petitioner's duty to comply with it. There is also no indication that petitioner ever objected to the prosecution's discovery request.

22. The trial judge also expressed concern about discovery violations in other trials. If those violations involved the same at-

counsel had actually interviewed Wormley during the week before the trial began and the further fact that he amended his Answer to Discovery on the first day of trial without identifying Wormley while he did identify two actual eyewitnesses whom he did not place on the stand, the inference that he was deliberately seeking a tactical advantage is inescapable. Regardless of whether prejudice to the prosecution could have been avoided in this particular case, it is plain that the case fits into the category of willful misconduct in which the severest sanction is appropriate. After all, the court, as well as the prosecutor, has a vital interest in protecting the trial process from the pollution of perjured testimony. Evidentiary rules which apply to categories of inadmissible evidence—ranging from hearsay to the fruits of illegal searches—may properly be enforced even though the particular testimony being offered is not prejudicial. The pretrial conduct revealed by the record in this case gives rise to a sufficiently strong inference "that witnesses are being found that really weren't there," to justify the sanction of preclusion.[23]

The argument that the client should not be held responsible for his lawyer's misconduct strikes at the heart of the attorney-client relationship. Although there are basic rights that the attorney cannot waive without the fully informed and publicly acknowledged consent of the client, the lawyer has—and must have—full authority to manage the conduct of the trial. The adversary process could not function effectively if every tactical decision required client approval. Moreover, given the protections afforded by the attorney-client privilege and the fact that extreme cases may involve unscrupulous conduct by both the client and the lawyer, it would be highly impracticable to require an investigation into their relative responsibilities before applying the sanction of preclusion. In responding to discovery, the client has a duty to be candid and forthcoming with the lawyer, and when the lawyer responds, he or she speaks for the client. Putting to one side the exceptional cases in which counsel is ineffective, the client must accept the consequences of the lawyer's decision to forgo cross-examination, to decide not to put certain witnesses on the stand, or to decide not to disclose the identity of certain witnesses in advance of trial. In this case, petitioner has

torney, or otherwise contributed to a concern about the trustworthiness of Wormley's eleventh hour testimony, they were relevant. Unrelated discovery violations in other litigation would not, however, normally provide a proper basis for curtailing the defendant's constitutional right to present a complete defense.

23. It should be noted that in Illinois, the sanction of preclusion is reserved for only the most extreme cases. In *People v. Rayford*, the Illinois Appellate Court explained:

> "The exclusion of evidence is a drastic measure; and the rule in civil cases limits its application to flagrant violations, where the uncooperative party demonstrates a 'deliberate contumacious or unwarranted disregard of the court's authority.' (Schwartz v. Moats, 3 Ill. App.3d 596, 599, 277 N.E.2d 529, 531; Department of Transportation v. Mainline Center, Inc., 38 Ill.App.3d 538, 347 N.E.2d 837.) The reasons for restricting the use of the exclusion sanction to only the most extreme situations are even more compelling in the case of criminal defendants, where due process requires that a defendant be permitted to offer testimony of witnesses in his defense. (Washington v. Texas, 388 U.S. 14 [87 S.Ct.1920]....) 'Few rights are more fundamental than that of an accused to present witnesses in his own defense.' (Chambers v. Mississippi, 410 U.S. 284, 302 [93 S.Ct. 1038, 1049]....)" 43 Ill. App.3d, at 286–287, 1 Ill.Dec., at 944, 356 N.E.2d, at 1277.

no greater right to disavow his lawyer's decision to conceal Wormley's identity until after the trial had commenced than he has to disavow the decision to refrain from adducing testimony from the eyewitnesses who were identified in the Answer to Discovery. Whenever a lawyer makes use of the sword provided by the Compulsory Process Clause, there is some risk that he may wound his own client.

■ JUSTICE BRENNAN, with whom JUSTICE MARSHALL and JUSTICE BLACKMUN join, dissenting.

. . . I conclude that, at least where a criminal defendant is not personally responsible for the discovery violation, alternative sanctions are not only adequate to correct and deter discovery violations but are far superior to the arbitrary and disproportionate penalty imposed by the preclusion sanction. . . . I would hold that, absent evidence of the defendant's personal involvement in a discovery violation, the Compulsory Process Clause *per se* bars discovery sanctions that exclude criminal defense evidence.

* * *

NOTES

1. Like most American jurisdictions, Michigan has a "rape-shield" statute which prohibits a defendant in sexual assault cases from introducing evidence through direct testimony or cross-examination concerning the past sexual conduct or reputation of the alleged victim. The court, however, may admit relevant evidence of the past relationship between the accused and the alleged victim. The Michigan statute requires a defendant who wishes to offer such evidence to give notice of that intent by filing a written motion and an offer of proof within ten days of arraignment on the information. Although advance notice of such intent is a requirement of many rape-shield statutes, the early-notice requirement of the Michigan law is very unusual, if not unique.

In Michigan v. Lucas, 500 U.S. 145, 111 S.Ct. 1743 (1991), the defendant did not file a notice of intent at any time before trial. At the beginning of the trial, defense counsel asked the court to permit introduction of such evidence. Rather than conducting an *in camera* hearing to determine whether such evidence was relevant and admissible, as the court would have been required to do if counsel had complied with the ten-day notice provision, the trial court barred the defense evidence. As a result, the defendant, whose defense was consent, was prohibited from offering evidence of prior sexual relations with the alleged victim. The prosecution's evidence did show that the woman, who allegedly was beaten and threatened with a knife, had been the defendant's girlfriend, but the prosecution contended that she was no longer the defendant's girlfriend at the time of the incident.

The Michigan Court of Appeals reversed.

* * *

We have indicated that probative evidence may, in certain circumstances, be precluded when a criminal defendant fails to comply with a valid discovery rule. In United States v. Nobles (1975), for example, the defendant wished to put on the witness stand an investigator to testify about statements made to him during an investigation, but the defendant refused to comply with the District Court's order to submit a copy of the investigator's report to the prosecution. The District Court therefore precluded the investigator from testifying, and this Court held that the

District Court's "preclusion sanction was an entirely proper method of assuring compliance with its order."

Even more telling is Taylor v. Illinois, 484 U.S. 400, 108 S.Ct. 646 (1988)....

We did not hold in *Taylor* that preclusion is permissible every time a discovery rule is violated. Rather, we acknowledged that alternative sanctions would be "adequate and appropriate in most cases." We stated explicitly, however that there could be circumstances in which preclusion was justified because a less severe penalty "would perpetuate rather than limit the prejudice to the State and the harm to the adversary process." *Taylor* we concluded, was such a case. The trial court found that Taylor's discovery violation amounted to "willful misconduct" and was designed to obtain "a tactical advantage." Based on these findings, we determined that, "[r]egardless of whether prejudice to the prosecution could have been avoided" by a lesser penalty, "the severest sanction [wa]s appropriate."

In light of *Taylor* and *Nobles*, the Michigan Court of Appeals erred in adopting a *per se* rule that Michigan's notice-and-hearing requirement violates the Sixth Amendment in all cases where it is used to preclude evidence of past sexual conduct between a rape victim and a defendant. The Sixth Amendment is not so rigid. The notice-and-hearing requirement serves legitimate state interests in protecting against surprise, harassment, and undue delay. Failure to comply with this requirement may in some cases justify even the severe sanction of preclusion.

* * *

We express no opinion as to whether or not preclusion was justified in this case. The Michigan Court of Appeals, whose decision we review here, did not address whether the trial court abused its discretion on the facts before it. Rather, the Court of Appeals adopted a *per se* rule that preclusion is unconstitutional in all cases where the victim had a prior sexual relationship with the defendant. That judgment was error. We leave it to the Michigan courts to address in the first instance whether Michigan's rape-shield statute authorizes preclusion and whether, on the facts of this case, preclusion violated Lucas' rights under the Sixth Amendment.

2. In Wardius v. Oregon, 412 U.S. 470, 93 S.Ct. 2208 (1973), the Court dealt with the issue of reciprocal discovery as follows:

MR. JUSTICE MARSHALL delivered the opinion of the Court.

This case involves important questions concerning the right of a defendant forced to comply with a "notice of alibi" rule to reciprocal discovery.

* * *

We hold that the Due Process Clause of the Fourteenth Amendment forbids enforcement of alibi rules unless reciprocal discovery rights are given to criminal defendants. Since the Oregon statute did not provide for reciprocal discovery, it was error for the court below to enforce it against petitioner, and his conviction must be reversed.

On May 22, 1970, petitioner was indicted for unlawful sale of narcotics. The sale allegedly occurred the previous day. At trial, after the State had concluded its case, petitioner called one Colleen McFadden who testified that on the night in question, she had been with petitioner at a drive-in movie. The prosecutor thereupon brought to the judge's attention petitioner's failure to file a notice of alibi, and after hearing argument the trial judge granted the State's motion to strike McFadden's testimony because of this failure. Petitioner himself then took the stand and attempted to testify that he was at the drive-in with McFadden at the time when the State alleged the sale occurred. Once again, however, the State objected and the trial judge again refused to permit the evidence.

* * *

Notice of alibi rules, now in use in a large and growing number of States, are based on the proposition that the ends of justice will best be served by a system of liberal discovery which gives both parties the maximum possible amount of information with which to prepare their cases and thereby reduces the possibility of surprise at trial.

* * *

The growth of such discovery devices is a salutary development which, by increasing the evidence available to both parties, enhances the fairness of the adversary system. As we recognized in [Williams v. Florida], nothing in the Due Process Clause precludes States from experimenting with systems of broad discovery designed to achieve these goals.

* * *

But although the Due Process Clause has little to say regarding the amount of discovery which the parties must be afforded, it does speak to the balance of forces between the accused and his accuser. The *Williams* court was therefore careful to note that "Florida law provides for liberal discovery by the defendant against the State, and the notice-of-alibi rule is itself carefully hedged with reciprocal duties requiring state disclosure to the defendant." The same cannot be said of Oregon law. As the State conceded at oral argument, Oregon grants no discovery rights to criminal defendants, and, indeed, does not even provide defendants with bills of particulars. More significantly, Oregon, unlike Florida, has no provision which requires the State to reveal the names and addresses of witnesses it plans to use to refute an alibi defense.

We do not suggest that the Due Process Clause of its own force requires Oregon to adopt such provisions. But we do hold that in the absence of a strong showing of state interests to the contrary, discovery must be a two-way street. The State may not insist that trials be run as a "search for truth" so far as defense witnesses are concerned, while maintaining "poker game" secrecy for its own witnesses. It is fundamentally unfair to require a defendant to divulge the details of his own case while at the same time subjecting him to the hazard of surprise concerning refutation of the very pieces of evidence which he disclosed to the State.

3. Some early state opinions disapproved of discovery against defendants. Allen v. Superior Court, 18 Cal.3d 520, 134 Cal.Rptr. 774, 557 P.2d 65 (1976). In recent years this resistance has lessened. See Commonwealth v. Durham, 446 Mass. 212, 843 N.E.2d 1035 (2006) (4–3 decision permitting discovery of statements which the defense obtained from prosecution witnesses even where it could not be shown that such statements would be used by the defense).

4. The mid-twentieth century arguments over discovery were exceptionally vigorous and the statutory and court rules that emerged are now the standard. Some observations on the debate and development of the law are found in Zagel and Carr, State Criminal Discovery And The New Illinois Rules, 1971 Ill.L.F. 557 (1972):

"The arguments for both sides over criminal discovery can be summarized in a few paragraphs. The proponents of criminal discovery argue generally that pretrial discovery serves justice by ensuring that all relevant facts will be presented to the court and that the unseemly use of surprise tactics will be eliminated. These same arguments persuaded lawmakers to adopt discovery in civil cases.

"Furthermore, proponents argue that several specific aspects of the criminal process itself support the institution of discovery. First, it is only fair to give an accused, who stands to lose his liberty, the same rights given to a civil defendant. Second, the prosecution has a superior investigative force that has usually begun to act before the accused has counsel or an opportunity to commence the preparation of a defense. Third, the accused has often given the state a statement or confession. Fourth, adequate investigation by the accused may be precluded by investigating officers who usually refuse to discuss the case with defense counsel. Fifth, the late start given the accused may present defense counsel with witnesses whose memory has dimmed. Sixth, scientific evidence cannot be met effectively at trial without discovery. Finally, the accused is presumed innocent and consequently, presumed to know nothing of the crime charged.

"The opponents of discovery argue that the severity of the criminal sanction increases the likelihood that the accused will use discovery to help devise effective perjury and better fabrications in his defense. Furthermore, discovery will result in the increased intimidation of witnesses. Eventually, witnesses would be reluctant to step forward and sources of information would wither away. Discovery in criminal cases would be a one way street since the fifth amendment protects the accused from giving discovery of his case. Moreover, the defendant already has so many rights including the presumption of innocence, the right to insist on proof beyond a reasonable doubt, and the benefit of the exclusionary rule, that any additional rights would serve only to prevent the effective and just enforcement of the criminal law.

"Finally, except in rare cases, the only person who definitely knows the truth of the charge is the accused. Therefore, the most valuable source of information belongs exclusively to the defense after counsel is appointed. Indeed, if an accused consistently refuses to speak to the police, this vital source of information is totally unavailable to the prosecution.

"The advocates of discovery answer these arguments by contending that perjury is committed without discovery. With hardened criminals, the risk of intimidation exists with or without discovery, and ordinary criminals do not indulge in intimidation. Intimidation problems can be solved by provisions for protective orders. Furthermore, in the absence of discovery there is an unjustified disparity between the wealthy accused or the professional criminal, both of whom have the means to secure discovery through legitimate investigation or irregular methods, and the ordinary defendant who does not have these resources or abilities. The reply to the 'one way street' argument is that the prosecution has marvelous investigative facilities—the modern police force, the right to seize evidence and the investigative grand jury. [This argument, often cited as decisive, is only make-weight to state prosecutors in urban communities whose police forces are occupied with patrol and not investigation, and whose grand juries are of necessity used only to charge and not to investigate.] In any event, discovery against the defense is no longer the forbidden road it was once thought to be.

"The recent United States Supreme Court decision allowing prior inconsistent statements to be used as substantive evidence [California v. Green, discussed in Chapter 19] serves to reduce the incentive to intimidate witnesses. If the prior statement is admissible for its truth, an accused has little to gain by intimidation (short of killing the witness), since the prosecution will usually be able to use the witness' statement to prove its case. Furthermore, the change in the witness' testimony may lead to an adverse inference against the defendant.

"Some arguments for discovery do not rest on the merits of discovery itself, but rather emphasize the considerable collateral benefits thought to flow from discovery. These arguments, like most others, meet with significant replies.

"Brady v. Maryland requires the prosecution to produce material evidence favorable to the accused on the issues of guilt and punishment. *Brady* is not thought to require pretrial disclosure of such evidence, but arguably complete pretrial discovery would ensure both fulfillment of the prosecution's obligation under *Brady* and production of favorable evidence in time for the defense to make effective use of it. A prosecutor acting in good faith, however, will comply with *Brady* even without discovery. If the prosecutor is not acting in good faith, he can hide the evidence even if there is discovery. Compliance with *Brady* cannot be secured by courtroom procedure alone; ultimately compliance will depend upon the good faith of law enforcement personnel.

"Discovery will be valuable, it is argued, when the favorable evidence is so unobvious that even the fairest prosecutor might overlook it. This argument, however, basically supports discovery against the defense. Only when the court knows the theories of the defense can it decide what seemingly immaterial facts are relevant, material, and producible under *Brady*.

"The final argument for discovery is based on a concern for efficiency, orderliness, and finality in criminal cases. The profusion of collateral attacks upon convictions may be a direct result of the lack of discovery. Without complete discovery, a court, upon collateral review, cannot be sure that all the relevant constitutional questions were either resolved or knowingly waived at the original trial or plea of guilty. Complete discovery would help ensure the completeness of the original trial record and reveal that an adequate basis existed for a guilty plea. On the other hand, the existence of complete discovery against the prosecution may encourage defense counsel not to make an independent investigation. If this occurs, and it obviously will in some cases, courts conducting collateral proceedings will still face serious allegations which cannot be resolved on the basis of the original trial record.

* * *

"The summary of the arguments on discovery shows clearly that there are compelling arguments on both sides which cannot be satisfactorily reconciled. As Professor Wright has said: 'The arguments for each point of view may be put in balanced fashion. This is plainly an issue on which highly responsible and experienced people disagree.' [1 C. Wright, Federal Practice and Procedure § 252, at 500 (1969).] Professor Wright is also correct in that regardless of the merits of the arguments those who favor discovery are gaining support with the courts. Several jurisdictions have adopted what purport to be comprehensive discovery provisions for criminal cases.

"The new criminal discovery procedures disclose a desire to codify and clarify discovery practices. Although the new rules vary widely in substance, each one represents an expansion of criminal discovery within its own jurisdiction. Several reasons may lie behind this trend.

"Pretrial discovery never has been held to be constitutionally required. The United States Supreme Court has never gone further than to say that 'in some circumstances it may be a denial of due process for a defendant to be refused any [pretrial] discovery of his statements to the police.'

"The Court refused to require the states to provide pretrial discovery even of the defendant's own confession. [Clewis v. Texas, 386 U.S. 707, 87 S.Ct. 1338 (1967).]

"The expansion of discovery is the specific consequence of a more general condition—the wholesale dissatisfaction with the criminal process in this country. The present day administration of criminal justice satisfies no one. Justice for both society and the defendant in many cases is achieved by accident rather than by design.

"The civil law countries appear to do a better job of combining the search for truth with humane treatment of the accused. Significantly, discovery in criminal cases is present in nearly all civil law countries. But it is not admiration for continental systems of criminal law that moves us to broaden discovery. Few American lawyers have more than a passing acquaintance with these systems. Those that do realize that there are substantial cultural and social conditions essential to the success of those systems that do not exist here.

"In the final analysis, discovery is developing in this country because of two underlying assumptions. The first is that nearly all prosecutors and defense counsel are honest men who will fully comply with the discovery rules finally approved by the courts. Thus, surprise and trickery will be drastically reduced and the courts will be far more certain that the facts of the case are being fairly presented. The second, and perhaps equally important underlying assumption, is that discovery will improve a sorry state of affairs and can hardly worsen it."

5. In the federal system a defendant has had no absolute right to learn before trial the names of the government witnesses.

Amendments to Federal Rule of Criminal Procedure 16, which had been scheduled to take effect on August 1, 1975, would have provided for lists of witnesses. Just before that date, however, Congress deleted these provisions from the new version of Rule 16. The Conference report declared:

> A majority of the Conferees believe it is not in the interest of the effective administration of criminal justice to require that the government or the defendant be forced to reveal the names and addresses of its witnesses before trial. Discouragement of witnesses and improper contacts directed at influencing their testimony were deemed paramount concerns in the formulation of this policy.

H.R.Rep. No. 94–414, 94th Cong., 1st Sec. 12 (1975).

Consider the following from Haddad, Criminal Procedure and Habeas Corpus, Seventh Circuit Review, 52 Chi.-K.L.R. 294, 305 (1975):

> If Congress intended to forbid a judge from ever ordering a list of witnesses, it may have created a serious sixth amendment question ... even though (the sixth amendment) has rarely been used as a basis for developing the law of criminal discovery.

Considering the denial of mid-trial discovery (the true name of a witness), the Supreme Court in Smith v. Illinois, 390 U.S. 129, 131, 88 S.Ct. 748 in 1968 declared: "The witness' name and address open countless avenues of in-court examination and out-of-court investigation. To forbid this most rudimentary inquiry at the threshold is effectively to emasculate the right of cross-examination itself."

In the real world where efficient administration is a valued goal, mid-trial continuances are almost never granted. Accordingly, the kind of out-of-court investigation contemplated by the *Smith* decision is impossible absent a list of witnesses before trial.

Courts continue to reject arguments that confrontation or due process clause safeguards mandate pre-trial disclosure of the identity of prosecution witnesses. See United States v. McCullah, 745 F.2d 350 (6th Cir.1984). See also Pennsylvania v. Ritchie, p. 1305, note 5.

ILLINOIS SUPREME COURT RULES OF CRIMINAL DISCOVERY

Rule 411. Applicability

These rules shall be applied in all criminal cases wherein the accused is charged with an offense for which, upon conviction, he might be imprisoned in the penitentiary.... They shall become applicable following indictment or information and shall not be operative prior to or in the course of any preliminary hearing.

Rule 412. Disclosure to Accused

(a) Except as is otherwise provided in these rules as to matters not subject to disclosure and protective orders, the State shall, upon written motion of defense counsel, disclose to defense counsel the following material and information within its possession or control:

(i) the names and last known addresses of persons whom the State intends to call as witnesses, together with their relevant written or recorded statements, memoranda containing substantially verbatim reports of their oral statements, and a list of memoranda reporting or summarizing their oral statements. Upon written motion of defense counsel memoranda reporting or summarizing oral statements shall be examined by the court *in camera* and if found to be substantially verbatim reports of oral statements shall be disclosed to defense counsel;

(ii) any written or recorded statements and the substance of any oral statements made by the accused or by a codefendant, and a list of witnesses to the making and acknowledgment of such statements;

(iii) a transcript of those portions of grand jury minutes containing testimony of the accused and relevant testimony of persons whom the prosecuting attorney intends to call as witnesses at the hearing or trial;

(iv) any reports or statements of experts made in connection with the particular case, including results of physical or mental examinations and of scientific tests, experiments, or comparisons; and a statement of the qualifications of the expert;

(v) any books, papers, documents, photographs or tangible objects which the prosecuting attorney intends to use in the hearing or trial or which were obtained from or belong to the accused; and

(vi) any record of prior criminal convictions, which may be used for impeachment, of persons whom the State intends to call as witnesses at the hearing or trial.

If the State has obtained from the defendant pursuant to Rule 413(d) information regarding defenses the defendant intends to make, it shall provide to defendant not less than 7 days before the date set for the hearing or trial, or at such other time as the court may direct, the names and addresses of witnesses the state intends to call in rebuttal, together with the information required to be disclosed in connection with other witnesses by subdivisions (i), (iii), and (vi), above, and a specific statement as to the substance of the testimony such witnesses will give at the trial of the cause.

(b) The State shall inform defense counsel if there has been any electronic surveillance (including wiretapping) of conversations to which the accused was a party, or of his premises.

(c) Except as is otherwise provided in these rules as to protective orders, the State shall disclose to defense counsel any material or information within its possession or control which tends to negate the guilt of the accused as to the offense charged or would tend to reduce his punishment therefor. The State shall make a good faith effort to specifically identify by description or otherwise any material disclosed pursuant to this section based upon the information available to the State at the time the material is disclosed to the defense....

(d) The State shall perform its obligations under this rule as soon as practicable following the filing of a motion by defense counsel.

(e) The State may perform these obligations in any manner mutually agreeable to itself and defense counsel or by:

(i) notifying defense counsel that material and information, described in general terms, may be inspected, obtained, tested, copied or photographed, during specified reasonable times; and

(ii) making available to defense counsel at the time specified such material and information, and suitable facilities or other arrangements for inspection, testing, copying, and photographing of such material and information.

(f) The State should ensure that a flow of information is maintained between the various investigative personnel and its office sufficient to place within its possession or control of material and information relevant to the accused and the offense charged.

(g) Upon defense counsel's request and designation of material or information which would be discoverable if in the possession or control of the State and which is in the possession or control of other governmental personnel, the State shall use diligent good faith efforts to cause such material to be made available to defense counsel; and if the State's efforts are unsuccessful and such material or other governmental personnel are subject to the jurisdiction of the court, the court shall issue suitable subpoenas or orders to cause such material to be made available to defense counsel.

(h) *Discretionary Disclosures.* Upon a showing of materiality to the preparation of the defense, and if the request is reasonable, the court in its discretion may require disclosure to defense counsel of relevant material and information not covered by this rule.

(i) *Denial of Disclosure.* The court may deny disclosure authorized by this rule and Rule 413 if it finds that there is a substantial risk to any person of physical harm, intimidation, bribery, economic reprisals, or unnecessary annoyance or embarrassment resulting from such disclosure which outweighs any usefulness of the disclosure to counsel.

(j) *Matters Not Subject to Disclosure.*

(i) Work Product. Disclosure under this rule and Rule 413 shall not be required of legal research or of records, correspondence, reports or memoranda to the extent that they contain the opinions, theories or conclusions of the State or members of its legal or investigative staffs, or of defense counselor his staff.

(ii) Informants. Disclosure of an informant's identity shall not be required where his identity is a prosecution secret and a failure to disclose will not infringe the constitutional rights of the accused. Disclosure shall not be denied hereunder of the identity of witnesses to be produced at a hearing or trial.

(iii) National Security. Disclosure shall not be required where it involves a substantial risk of grave prejudice to national security and where a failure to disclose will not infringe the constitutional rights of the accused. Disclosure shall not thus be denied hereunder regarding witnesses or material to be produced at a hearing or trial.

Rule 413. Disclosure to Prosecution

(a) *The Person of the Accused.* Notwithstanding the initiation of judicial proceedings, and subject to constitutional limitations, a judicial officer may require the accused, among other things, to:

(i) appear in a line-up;

(ii) speak for identification by witnesses to an offense;

(iii) be fingerprinted;

(iv) pose for photographs not involving reenactment of a scene;

(v) try on articles of clothing;

(vi) permit the taking of specimens of material under his fingernails;

(vii) permit the taking of samples of his blood, hair and other materials of his body which involve no unreasonable intrusion thereof;

(viii) provide a sample of his handwriting; and

(ix) submit to a reasonable physical or medical inspection of his body.

(b) Whenever the personal appearance of the accused is required for the foregoing purposes, reasonable notice of the time and place of such appearance shall be given by the State to the accused and his counsel, who shall have the right to be present. Provision may be made for appearances for such purposes in an order admitting the accused to bail or providing for his release.

(c) *Medical and Scientific Reports.* Subject to constitutional limitations, the trial court shall, on written motion, require that the State be informed of, and permitted to inspect and copy or photograph, any reports or results, or testimony relative thereto, of physical or mental examinations or of scientific tests, experiments or comparisons, or any other reports or statements of experts which defense counsel has in his possession or control, including a statement of the qualifications of such experts, except that those portions of reports containing statements made by the defendant may be withheld if defense counsel does not intend to use any of the material contained in the report at a hearing or trial.

(d) *Defenses.* Subject to constitutional limitations and within a reasonable time after the filing of a written motion by the State, defense counsel shall inform the State of any defenses which he intends to make at a hearing or trial and shall furnish the State with the following information within his possession or control

(i) The names and last known addresses of persons he intends to call as witnesses together with their relevant written or recorded statements, including memoranda reporting or summarizing their oral statements, any record of prior criminal convictions known to him; and

(ii) any books, papers, documents, photographs, or tangible objects he intends to use as evidence or for impeachment at a hearing or trial;

(iii) and if the defendant intends to prove an alibi, specific information as to the place where he maintains he was at the time of the alleged offense.

(e) *Additional Disclosure.* Upon a showing of materiality, and if the request is reasonable, the court in its discretion may require disclosure to the State of relevant material and information not covered by this rule.

Rule 414. Evidence Depositions

(a) If it appears to the court in which a criminal charge is pending that the deposition of any person other than the defendant is necessary for the preservation of relevant testimony because of the substantial possibility it would be unavailable at the time of hearing or trial, the court may, upon motion and notice to both parties and their counsel, order the taking of such person's deposition under oral examination or written questions for use as evidence at a hearing or trial.

(b) The taking of depositions shall be in accordance with rules providing for the taking of depositions in civil cases, and the order for the taking of a deposition may provide that any designated books, papers, documents or tangible objects, not privileged, be produced at the same time and place.

(c) If a witness is committed for failure to execute a recognizance to appear to testify at a hearing or trial, the court on written motion of the witness and upon notice to the State and defense counsel may order that his deposition be taken, and after the deposition has been subscribed, the court may discharge the witness.

(d) Rule 207—Signing and Filing Depositions—shall apply to the signing and filing of depositions taken pursuant to this rule.

(e) The defendant and defense counsel shall have the right to confront and cross-examine any witness whose deposition is taken. The defendant and defense counsel may waive such right in writing, filed with the clerk of the court.

(f) If the defendant is indigent, all costs of taking depositions shall be paid by the county wherein the criminal charge is initiated. If the defendant is not indigent the costs shall be allocated as in civil cases.

Rule 415. Regulation of Discovery

(a) *Investigations Not to Be Impeded.* Except as is otherwise provided as to matters not subject to disclosure and protective orders, neither the counsel for the parties nor other prosecution or defense personnel shall advise persons having relevant material or information (except the accused) to refrain from discussing the case with opposing counsel or showing opposing counsel any relevant material, nor shall they otherwise impede opposing counsel's investigation of the case.

(b) *Continuing Duty to Disclose.* If, subsequent to compliance with the rules or orders pursuant thereto, a party discovers additional material or information which is subject to disclosure, he shall promptly notify the other party or his counsel of the existence of such additional material, and if the additional material or information is discovered during trial, the court shall also be notified.

(c) *Custody of Materials.* Any materials furnished to an attorney pursuant to these rules shall remain in his exclusive custody and be used only for the purposes of conducting his side of the case, and shall be subject to such other terms and conditions as the court may provide.

(d) *Protective Orders.* Upon a showing of cause, the court may at any time order that specified disclosures be restricted or deferred, or make such other order as is appropriate provided that all material and information to which a party is entitled must be disclosed in time to permit counsel to make beneficial use thereof.

(e) *Excision.* When some parts of certain material are discoverable under these rules, and other parts not discoverable, as much of the material should be disclosed as is consistent with the rules. Excision of certain material and disclosure of the balance is preferable to withholding the whole. Material excised pursuant to judicial order shall be sealed, impounded and preserved in the records of the court, to be made available to the reviewing court in the event of an appeal.

(f) *In Camera Proceedings.* Upon request of any person, the court may permit any showing of cause for denial or regulation of disclosures, or portion of such showing, to be made *in camera*. A record shall be made of such proceedings. If the court enters an order granting relief following a showing *in camera*, the entire record of such showing shall be sealed, impounded, and preserved in the records of the court, to be made available to the reviewing court in the event of an appeal.

(g) *Sanctions.*

(i) If at any time during the course of the proceedings it is brought to the attention of the court that a party has failed to comply with an applicable discovery rule or an order issued pursuant thereto, the court may order such party to permit the discovery of material and information not previously disclosed, grant a continuance, exclude such evidence, or enter such other order as it deems just under the circumstances.

(ii) Wilful violation by counsel of an applicable discovery rule or an order issued pursuant thereto may subject counsel to appropriate sanctions by the court.

NOTES

1. The Illinois rules are used as an example of a unified modern code of discovery for several reasons. The rules are comprehensive, expansive, and time-tested. Further, though there are important differences, the rules follow closely the pattern and substance of the American Bar Association Standards Relating To Discovery And Procedure Before Trial (3rd Edition 1996), and the A.B.A. Standards have become a focal point of debate throughout the nation over the question of discovery.

2. One distinguishing feature of the Illinois rules is the elimination of nearly all judicial discretion. Discretion in the discovery process causes two problems. First, there is a substantial difficulty in resolving questions of materiality and reasonableness of discovery requests. If "showings" by the moving party are required, much court time will be consumed in adjudicating the issues. Second, in discretionary systems there variations may exist from courtroom to courtroom depending on individual judicial predilections on discovery policy. Is the elimination of discretion wise? Is the means by which mandatory discovery can be cabined, i.e., the protective order, sufficient to meet objections to excessive discovery? Are better techniques available?

3. Consider the following questions in connection with the Illinois Rules:

(a) Discovery practice is initiated by motion. The A.B.A. Standards suggest the use of informal meetings between counsel. The Illinois practice leads to preservation of the record of the discovery process in each case. Does this justify requiring an essentially pointless filing of a formal motion which, without court action, requires the other party to give discovery? In high volume courts in Illinois, the trial judge hands each lawyer a computer generated order requiring the discovery allowed by the rules in response to motions that each side are presumed to have made.

(b) The defense is allowed the pre-trial discovery of a witness' written statements. The A.B.A. recommends this but many other jurisdictions expressly forbid it. Is it wise to permit such discovery? What are the arguments on either side? The prosecution has a similar right of discovery of defense witness statements. Would the defense counsel ordinarily take written statements from his witnesses? Would prosecutors and police and defense counsel begin to cease taking written statements or writing verbatim reports of oral statements simply to avoid discovery or to avoid creating potentially impeaching statements?

The Rules require production of prosecution memoranda of oral statements only if they are substantially verbatim reports. The Rules require production of defense documents including memoranda "summarizing ... oral statements". What accounts for the difference? Is the danger attendant upon production of "summaries", i.e., the improper attempt to contradict a witness with a prior statement he did not actually make, sufficient to justify exempting the summary from production? Would a protective order work as well? Would it make any difference if the witness had made a written statement which was produced or it there was no producible statement ever made by the witness? When the Rules are administered, the prosecution may tender a list of "summaries" which they don't intend to produce and the defense is entitled to have the court inspect them. Will this procedure strengthen or erode the limitation on production? Is it possible or likely that an overburdened trial court will simply order production of all memoranda and reserve ruling on the propriety of use at the time of trial? Discovery of witnesses and witness' statements are limited to the witnesses the party intends to call to trial. How about witnesses not to be called? Should the prosecution or defense be required to give a list of all persons they talked to or at least of all persons who were present at the time of the crime (potential occurrence witnesses)?

(c) The Illinois Rules provided for evidence depositions but not discovery depositions except in capital case. Ill.Sup.Ct. Rule 416 A few jurisdictions have provisions for discovery depositions. See Fla.R.Crim.P. 3.220(d) (deposition allowed); Tex.Code Crim.Proc.Ann., Art.39.02 (1979) (depositions in discretion of court upon showing good cause); Vt.R.Crim.P. 15 (depositions permissible if testimony may be material or relevant on the trial or of assistance in the preparation of the case recently limited for crime victims).

Vermont changed its deposition rule to prevent what was perceived as the inherently painful effect of the practice upon victims of crime. Arizona put into its Constitution a provision giving crime victims the right to refuse to give an interview or deposition to defense counsel and the right to confer with the prosecution. Ariz.Const. Article 2 § 24. The ABA Standards (3rd Ed.) propose discovery depositions under limited conditions and outside the presence of defendant. An ad hoc committee appointed by the New Jersey Supreme Court to study the question decided against discovery depositions for the following reasons:

"(1) Depositions are time consuming and costly. (2) Impartial witnesses might be unduly harassed. (3) Constitutional problems would be created by prosecutors reciprocal right to depose defense witnesses. (4) The indigent defendant might insist upon exercising his right to depose as a matter of course, apart from indications of need."

(d) Counsel are prohibited from telling or instructing a witness not to talk to the other party but may an attorney advise a witness that he has a right to talk or refuse to talk to opposing counsel as he sees fit? The witness does, of course, have this personal right but if he hears the advice from a lawyer he may infer that the lawyer does not want him to talk to opposing counsel. If the witness is to testify for one party he may think he is on that party's "team" and be unwilling to do anything against the "coach's" (lawyer's) wishes. On the other hand, how could a court today hold that an individual citizen cannot or should not be advised of his rights? Will the amount of discovery of witness statements reduce the need for personal interviews by opposing counsel?

(e) The rules adopt the exclusion sanction among others and provide an open-ended option to devise other sanctions. What of allowing counsel to prove that the opposing party failed to comply with discovery and argue unfavorable inferences from this to the jury? See, e.g., Higgins v. Wainwright, 424 F.2d 177 (5th Cir.1970) (comment on refusal to participate in lineup); United States v. Parhms, 424 F.2d 152 (9th Cir.1970) (same); People v. Hess, 10 Cal.App.3d 1071, 90 Cal.Rptr. 268 (1970) (comment on refusal to give a handwriting exemplar after court order); State v. Huson, 73 Wash.2d 660, 440 P.2d 192 (1968) (comment on refusal to participate in court-ordered mental examination).

Would this be an effective sanction? Would it be so effective as to render exclusion of evidence unnecessary except in extreme cases?

(f) Will extensive discovery provisions force attorneys on both sides to pay serious attention to their cases at an earlier stage and formulate theories of prosecution and defense? Will police be more careful in writing reports when they know that the reports are discoverable? Would such changes benefit the administration of criminal justice?

4. May the defense or the prosecution use the civil process for discovery? For example, may the defendant file a civil action for malicious prosecution or violation of civil rights and depose the prosecutor and subpoena his records? If the immunity doctrine is a barrier, may the defendant sue the individual witnesses and seek depositions from them? How do you think a court would react to such suits? May the government use civil suits to gain discovery? In United States v. Kordel, 397 U.S. 1, 90 S.Ct. 763 (1970), the government filed both criminal charges and civil proceedings against a violator of the Food and Drug Act. Information derived from civil interrogatories was used in the criminal case. The Court held that individual corporate officers could have declined to answer interrogatories on Fifth Amendment grounds and their failure to do so waives any claim of error. Further, the Court assumed that a trial court had power to order civil discovery postponed until the end of the criminal action.

In United States v. LaSalle National Bank, 437 U.S. 298, 98 S.Ct. 2357 (1978), the Supreme Court held that an IRS subpoena is proper if issued in good faith (i.e., for a valid administrative purpose) prior to a recommendation of criminal prosecution to the Department of Justice. The Second Circuit discussed the holding in LaSalle and cases ruling on the subpoena powers of other federal agencies in United States v. Gel Spice Co., Inc., 773 F.2d 427 (2d Cir.1985).

5. In Pennsylvania v. Ritchie, 480 U.S. 39, 107 S.Ct. 989 (1987), a plurality of the Court emphasized that nothing in the Sixth Amendment right of confrontation mandates that the defendant be afforded pre-trial discovery. There a defendant had been charged with rape and incest against his thirteen-year-old daughter. He sought to obtain by subpoena records of the Child and Youth Services Commission that allegedly contained information about alleged sex abuse against this daughter and other Ritchie children. The CYS resisted the subpoena on the grounds of statutory privilege. Eventually the "Pennsylvania Supreme Court held that Ritchie, through his lawyer, under the Sixth Amendment had the right to examine the full contents of the CYS records." In rejecting this conclusion, the plurality declared that it refused to transform the Confrontation Clause into a constitutionally-compelled rule of pretrial discovery. It declared that normally the right of confrontation is satisfied if the accused is permitted broad latitude in cross-examining witnesses at trial. [Discovery prior to trial is often barred by privilege even when the privilege will give way at trial when the need for the evidence becomes clear. See People v. Hammon, 15 Cal.4th 1117, 938 P.2d 986, 65 Cal.Rptr.2d 1 (1997).]

A majority of the Court went on to say that the Compulsory Process Clause allows a defendant to compel the attendance at trial of *favorable* witnesses, but it questioned whether it could be used to guarantee pre-trial discovery of the identity or *pre-trial* disclosure of exculpatory witnesses. Instead the Court embarked upon a *Brady–Agurs* Due Process analysis of the issues before it. The majority held that the defendant had a right to have the trial court examine the CYS records and to obtain a new trial if the court concluded that the information probably would have changed the outcome of his trial.

6. Every jurisdiction in the United States has provided, by statute, rule or constitutional amendment, for the rights of victims (and, sometimes, witnesses) to be notified of and participate in the prosecution of the accused victimizer and they apply, mostly, to bond hearings, guilty pleas, trial and sentencing. But, as the debate over depositions shows, there are times when victims do not want to participate, for example, in interviews by defense counsel or investigators or have their police statements turned over to the defense. While no law has been passed to allow victims to refuse participation as witnesses at trial, there have been efforts to give them the right to refuse to participate in discovery. See State v. Murtagh, 169 P.3d 602 (Alaska 2007) (Overturning legislation protecting victims from pre-trial discovery on grounds that, under the state constitution, such rules were exclusive province of the courts).

C. DISCOVERY AT TRIAL

Federal Rule of Criminal Procedure Rule 26.2 reads:

> (a) Motion for Production. After a witness other than the defendant has testified on direct examination, the court, on motion of a party who did not call the witness, shall order the attorney for the government or the defendant and the defendant's attorney to produce, for the examination and use of the moving party, any statement of the witness that is in their possession and that relates to the subject matter of the witness's testimony.
>
> (b) Production of Entire Statement. If the entire contents of the statement relate to the subject matter of the witness's testimony the court shall order that the statement be delivered to the moving party.
>
> (c) Production of Excised Statement. If the party who called the witness claims that the statement contains information that is privileged or does not relate to the subject matter of the witness's testimony, the court must inspect the statement in camera. After excising any privileged or unrelated portions, the court must order delivery of the redacted statement to the moving party. If the defendant objects to an excision, the court must preserve the entire statement with the excised portion indicated, under seal, as part of the record.
>
> (d) Recess for Examination of Statement. The court may recess the proceedings to allow time for a party to examine the statement and prepare for its use.
>
> (e) Sanction for Failure to Produce Statement. If the party who called the witness disobeys an order to produce or deliver a

statement to the moving party, the court shall order that the testimony of the witness be stricken from the record and that the trial proceed, or, if it is the attorney for the government who elects not to comply, shall declare a mistrial if required by the interest of justice.

(f) Definition. As used in this rule, a "statement" of a witness means:

(1) a written statement that the witness makes and signs, or otherwise adopts or approves.;

(2) a substantially verbatim, contemporaneously recorded recital of the witness's oral statement that is contained in any recording or transcription of a recording; or

(3) the witness's statement to a grand jury, however taken or recorded, or a transcription of such a statement.

NOTES

1. The rights created by Rule 26.2 are not constitutional in scope. See United States v. Augenblick, 393 U.S. 348, 89 S.Ct. 528 (1969). Rule 26.2 embodies and clarifies the dictates of a law widely known as the Jenck's Act which Congress enacted to control production of statements. See 18 U.S.C. § 3500.

In United States v. Nobles, 422 U.S. 225, 95 S.Ct. 2160 (1975), the Supreme Court held that a trial judge has the inherent authority to require the defense to tender statements made to a defense investigator by persons other than the defendant if the defense calls such persons as witnesses at the trial. The Court rejected claims of attorney-client and Fifth Amendment privileges because such statements do not involve client communications. The Court also narrowly construed the "work product" privilege and held that once the defense witness testified, such a privilege would not bar disclosure of his substantially verbatim statements.

In Goldberg v. United States, 425 U.S. 94, 96 S.Ct. 1338 (1976), the Supreme Court held that a statement made to a prosecutor and reduced to writing is not exempt from production after the witness has testified at trial. The Court stated that there is no "work product" exception to the Jencks Act. Any statement otherwise within the Jencks Act must be produced even though it was a lawyer rather than an investigator who took the statement.

2. Consider the tactical problem created by the dictates of Rule 26.2 described in United States v. Gardin, 382 F.2d 601 (2d Cir.1967):

■ ANDERSON, J. . . .

The appellant further objects to the fact that his trial counsel was not permitted to make his request for [statements] relating to Agent Jensen's testimony outside of the presence of the jury, although he made the request at the trial.

The Court of Appeals for the District of Columbia Circuit, in a divided panel, has held it to be reversible error for the trial judge to direct that Jencks Act material be sought in the presence of the jury. The court reasoned that the production of such material in the presence of the jury, followed by a failure to use it in cross-examining the Government's witness, implied to the jury that the witness had made prior consistent statements, which are generally not admissible.

While we are not entirely in accord with the conclusion that allowing circumstances to arise at a trial which create the possibility that a jury may draw the inference of a past consistent statement, of itself, constitutes reversible error, we are of the opinion that the fair and just administration of criminal prosecutions might well be better served if the proceeding for the production of statements or reports were to take place out of the presence of the jury when the defendant requests that this be done.

It is, of course, entirely possible, if not probable, that members of a jury may draw an inference or gain impressions scarcely helpful to a defendant who in their presence has pressed a motion for production of a statement or report made by the witness to the Government and who, after gaining possession of it, examines it with care and then makes no use of it. As this court said in United States v. Annunziato, 293 F.2d 373, 382 (2d Cir.):

"Had we been defense counsel, we would have bitterly regretted receiving it, [the witness' statement producible under the Jencks Act] since its production would have presented the dilemma, which trial lawyers strive desperately to avoid, that examination of the report would only reinforce the witness' testimony whereas failure to use it would do the same."

The Government on the other hand argues that it is entitled to have the jury know if material is used by the defense, that it has been provided by the Government. While the possible prejudice to the Government's witness resulting from nondisclosure of the statement's source is somewhat more subtle, there is no very cogent reason against letting it be known.

While we lay down no hard and fast rule, we do suggest the following which generally may meet the positions of both parties. After the completion of the witness' direct testimony and before cross-examination has been concluded, the defendant will state that he requests leave to make a motion in the absence of the jury; the trial judge will then excuse the jury, and, in its absence, the defendant will move for disclosure of Jencks Act material. Thereafter all steps through the delivery to the defendant of the statement or report, or the portions thereof, to which the defendant is found to be entitled, and including the allowance of a reasonable time to the defendant to examine the material, will take place while the jury is still absent. If, thereafter, the defendant decides to make use of any of the material for cross-examination of the witness, he will be permitted to do so only upon condition that he state preliminarily to the court and jury that he is about to question the witness on the basis of a written statement or report which the Government has made available to the defendant as required by law. This is to negative any inference that the Government had been covering something up and will precede compliance with the general rule of evidence for the protection of the witness which requires the laying of a proper foundation for the introduction of a past contradictory statement.

3. Even though a government agent testifies that a report accurately summarizes everything Witness said in an interview, the summary does not constitute the statement of X for Rule 26.2 purposes unless X had read or verbally approved the summary after the agent had prepared it. See United States v. Nathan, 816 F.2d 230 (6th Cir.1987).

Of course if the government agent who took a statement from a witness and reduced it to writing is a government witness testifying about the conversation he had with the witness, the agent's report may be viewed as the agent's statement. See United States v. Allen, 798 F.2d 985 (7th Cir.1986), a decision in which Judge Flaum provides a major exegesis of the rules, with a strong dissent by Judge Coffey.

4. Courts occasionally face the question of what constitutes a statement. In United States v. Bobadilla–Lopez, 954 F.2d 519 (9th Cir.1992) Border Patrol agents had recorded their radio transmissions made during a surveillance. These transmissions contained descriptions of what an agent had seen. The Court of Appeals held that these were not Jencks Act statements. The Court reasoned:

> Both the history of the statute and the decisions interpreting it have stressed that for production to be required, the materials should not only reflect the witness' own words, but should also be in the nature of a complete recital that eliminates the possibility of portions being selected out of context. For example, the Supreme Court in *Palermo v. United States*, (1959), stated that "the legislation was designed to eliminate the danger of distortion and misrepresentation inherent in a report which merely selects portions, albeit accurately, from a lengthy oral recital." Because the drafters did not intend to grant access to materials which take a witness' words out of context, courts have considered the nature and completeness of the alleged "statement." Thus in United States v. Bernard, 623 F.2d 551, 557–58 (9th Cir.1979), we held that an agent's rough notes jotted during surveillance were not producible under the Jencks Act due to the incomplete nature of the notes. We noted that "rough notes of an agent's surveillance activities are often sketchy and incomplete, made in a hurry, at different times, and will include the agent's own impressions and conclusions.";
>
> We believe the danger of distortion and incompleteness is especially relevant in this case. The border patrol agent's radio transmissions share the same rough, incomplete nature as notes hurriedly jotted during surveillance. They were never intended to provide a complete description of events that could serve as a basis for impeachment.
>
> Bobadilla seeks to distinguish this case from cases involving surveillance notes on the ground that this surveillance transmission was intended to communicate information to others. He relies upon our decision in United States v. Carrasco, 537 F.2d 372 (9th Cir.1976), in which we held that a diary kept by a government informant about ongoing drug transactions was Jencks Act material. In *Carrasco*, the diary became a Jencks Act statement only when the author turned the pages over to a DEA agent for use as evidence. The diary consisted of daily entries documenting the events leading up to the narcotics transaction and were signed or initialed on each page by the author as an accurate statement. In contrast, the spotty, impressionistic and incomplete on-site transmissions of the agent in this case do not amount to the same kind of narrative "statement" of a witness producible under the Jencks Act.
>
> This court has consistently recognized a clear distinction between investigative interviews with witnesses that are intended to form the basis for evidence at trial, on the one hand, and surveillance observations on the other. Records of witness interviews are Jencks Act statements. Records of surveillance activities are not Jencks Act statements, even though they may be communicated to another agent. The distinction is illustrated by our decision in U.S. v. Andersson, 813 F.2d 1450, 1459 (9th Cir.1987) where we held that a list of sites visited by suspects under surveillance, a

list which was handed over to another agent but subsequently lost, was not a Jencks Act statement required to be preserved in the event the surveillance agent testified. In contrast is our decision in United States v. Well, 572 F.2d 1383 (9th Cir.1978), which held that recorded interviews with potential witnesses were Jencks Act statements and had to be preserved. The agent's surveillance transmissions in this case did not become "statements" under section 3500(e)(2) simply because they were recorded. Neither this court nor any other court has held that by recording conversations between its agents, the government transforms the conversations into potential Jencks Act "statements." Yet that is what the dissent incorrectly declares the law to be.

We emphasize our holding is a narrow one. The recordings involved here may well have been discoverable pursuant to Fed.R.Crim.P. 16(a). In this case, however, no request for the material was made until after its routine destruction thirty days after the surveillance occurred. Indeed, at the time of the request, defense counsel was aware that the tapes had been destroyed. It is apparent that the purpose of the production request in this case was never to use the tape for impeachment purposes, but to prevent the agent who made the recording from being able to testify as to his observations on the day in question. The Jencks Act is not an appropriate tool for achieving that end.

The dissent reasoned:

Even the most talented lexicologist would have an exceedingly difficult task if asked to explain why the term "statement" does not include a verbal message communicated from one border patrol agent to another. That task would be even more difficult if the verbal transmissions were recorded on tape and the word "statement" were defined explicitly to include "a stenographic, mechanical, electrical, or other recording ... which is a substantially verbatim recital of an oral statement." The majority today nevertheless holds that a verbatim tape-recording of an oral radio transmission in which one border patrol agent reports his observations of alleged criminal activity to others does not contain a "statement" as that term is used in the Jencks Act. This remarkable interpretation contradicts the plain meaning of the text of that statute, frustrates the purpose of the law, conflicts with precedent, and needlessly raises the issue of the constitutionality of the government's destruction of potentially exculpatory evidence. I dissent.

The majority declares *ex cathedra* that all statements of government investigators regarding their investigations are exempt from discovery. That no such sweeping exception can be twisted out of the statutory language, that there is no basis for the majority's view in the legislative history [or] Ninth Circuit precedent ... appears to be of little concern to my colleagues. [They] base their unique, judicially-created exception exclusively on loose analogies to earlier but irrelevant cases. Each of these cases involves either (1) a government agent's *rough notes* concerning an investigation or surveillance operation he has performed, or (2) a government's agent's brief written *summary* of an extensive interview of another person. None of the cases relied upon by the majority involve a *recorded oral* statement—let alone a *verbatim* recorded oral statement—made by a government agent to a third person, regardless of the subject matter.

The tape recording of Agent York's radio communications clearly is a "statement" as that term is defined in 18 U.S.C. § 3500(e)(2). There is no doubt that the tape made by the government constitutes a "recording."

The tape also unquestionably contains a "substantially verbatim recital"—indeed, a *completely* verbatim recital—of Agent York's communications. Similarly, there is no doubt that Agent York's communications constitute an "oral statement" made by a witness for the government. Finally, it is undisputed that this tape was "recorded contemporaneously" with Agent York's statements. The plain language of the Jencks Act thus clearly demonstrates that the tape which recorded Agent York's oral radio transmissions to other border patrol agents contained "statements" by Agent York and hence was subject to production under the Act.

CHAPTER 16

PLEAS

One of the Federal Rules of Criminal Procedure provides:

Rule 11. Pleas

(a) Entering a Plea.

(1) In General. A defendant may plead not guilty, guilty, or (with the court's consent) nolo contendere.

(2) Conditional Plea. With the consent of the court and the government, a defendant may enter a conditional plea of guilty or nolo contendere, reserving in writing the right to have an appellate court review an adverse determination of a specified pretrial motion. A defendant who prevails on appeal may then withdraw the plea.

(3) Nolo Contendere Plea. Before accepting a plea of nolo contendere, the court must consider the parties' views and the public interest in the effective administration of justice.

(4) Failure to Enter a Plea. If a defendant refuses to enter a plea or if a defendant organization fails to appear, the court must enter a plea of not guilty.

(b) Considering and Accepting a Guilty or Nolo Contendere Plea.

(1) Advising and Questioning the Defendant. Before the court accepts a plea of guilty or nolo contendere, the defendant may be placed under oath, and the court must address the defendant personally in open court. During this address, the court must inform the defendant of, and determine that the defendant understands, the following:

(A) the government's right, in a prosecution for perjury or false statement, to use against the defendant any statement that the defendant gives under oath;

(B) the right to plead not guilty, or having already so pleaded, to persist in that plea;

(C) the right to a jury trial;

(D) the right to be represented by counsel—and if necessary have the court appoint counsel—at trial and at every other stage of the proceeding;

(E) the right at trial to confront and cross-examine adverse witnesses, to be protected from compelled self-incrimination, to testify and present evidence, and to compel the attendance of witnesses;

(F) the defendant's waiver of these trial rights if the court accepts a plea of guilty or nolo contendere;

(G) the nature of each charge to which the defendant is pleading;

(H) any maximum possible penalty, including imprisonment, fine, and term of supervised release;

(I) any mandatory minimum penalty;

(J) any applicable forfeiture;

(K) the court's authority to order restitution;

(L) the court's obligation to impose a special assessment;

(M) in determining a sentence the court's obligation to calculate the applicable sentencing guideline range and to consider that range, possible departure under the Sentencing Guidelines and other sentencing factors under 18 U.S.C. § 3553(a); and

(N) the terms of any plea-agreement provision waiving the right to appeal or to collaterally attack the sentence.

(2) Ensuring That a Plea Is Voluntary. Before accepting a plea of guilty or nolo contendere, the court must address the defendant personally in open court and determine that the plea is voluntary and did not result from force, threats, or promises (other than promises in a plea agreement).

(3) Determining the Factual Basis for a Plea. Before entering judgment on a guilty plea, the court must determine that there is a factual basis for the plea.

(c) Plea Agreement Procedure.

(1) In General. An attorney for the government and the defendant's attorney, or the defendant when proceeding pro se, may discuss and reach a plea agreement. The court must not participate in these discussions. If the defendant pleads guilty or nolo contendere to either a charged offense or a lesser or related offense, the plea agreement may specify that an attorney for the government will:

(A) not bring, or will move to dismiss, other charges;

(B) recommend, or agree not to oppose the defendant's request, that a particular sentence or sentencing range is appropriate or that a particular provision of the Sentencing Guidelines, or policy statement, or sentencing factor does or does not apply (such a recommendation or request does not bind the court); or

(C) agree that a specific sentence or sentencing range is the appropriate disposition of the case, or that a particular provision of the Sentencing Guidelines, or policy statement, or sentencing factor does or does not apply (such a recommendation or request binds the court once the court accepts the plea agreement).

(2) Disclosing a Plea Agreement. The parties must disclose the plea agreement in open court when the plea is offered, unless the court for good cause allows the parties to disclose the plea agreement in camera.

(3) Judicial Consideration of a Plea Agreement.

(A) To the extent the plea agreement is of the type specified in Rule 11(c)(1)(A) or (C), the court may accept the agreement, reject it, or defer a decision until the court has reviewed the presentence report.

(B) To the extent the plea agreement is of the type specified in Rule 11(c)(1)(B), the court must advise the defendant that the defendant has no right to withdraw the plea if the court does not follow the recommendation or request.

(4) Accepting a Plea Agreement. If the court accepts the plea agreement, it must inform the defendant that to the extent the plea agreement is of the type specified in Rule 11(c)(1)(A) or (C), the agreed disposition will be included in the judgment.

(5) Rejecting a Plea Agreement. If the court rejects a plea agreement containing provisions of the type specified in Rule 11(c)(1)(A) or (C), the court must do the following on the record and in open court (or, for good cause, in camera):

(A) inform the parties that the court rejects the plea agreement;

(B) advise the defendant personally that the court is not required to follow the plea agreement and give the defendant an opportunity to withdraw the plea; and

(C) advise the defendant personally that if the plea is not withdrawn, the court may dispose of the case less favorably toward the defendant than the plea agreement contemplated.

(d) Withdrawing a Guilty or Nolo Contendere Plea. A defendant may withdraw a plea of guilty or nolo contendere:

(1) before the court accepts the plea, for any reason or no reason; or

(2) after the court accepts the plea, but before it imposes sentence if:

(A) the court rejects a plea agreement under Rule 11(c)(5); or

(B) the defendant can show a fair and just reason for requesting the withdrawal.

(e) Finality of a Guilty or Nolo Contendere Plea. After the court imposes sentence, the defendant may not withdraw a plea of guilty or nolo contendere, and the plea may be set aside only on direct appeal or collateral attack.

(f) Admissibility or Inadmissibility of a Plea, Plea Discussions, and Related Statements. The admissibility or inadmissibility of a plea, a plea discussion, and any related statement is governed by *Federal Rule of Evidence 410*.

(g) Recording the Proceedings. The proceedings during which the defendant enters a plea must be recorded by a court reporter or by a suitable recording device. If there is a guilty plea or a nolo contendere plea, the record must include the inquiries and advice to the defendant required under Rule 11(b) and (c).

(h) Harmless Error. A variance from the requirements of this rule is harmless error if it does not affect substantial rights.

A. ADVICE TO THE DEFENDANT

Boykin v. Alabama

Supreme Court of the United States, 1969.
395 U.S. 238, 89 S.Ct. 1709.

■ MR. JUSTICE DOUGLAS delivered the opinion of the Court.

In the spring of 1966, within the period of a fortnight, a series of armed robberies occurred in Mobile, Alabama. The victims, in each case, were local shopkeepers open at night who were forced by a gunman to hand over money. While robbing one grocery store, the assailant fired his gun once, sending a bullet through a door into the ceiling. A few days earlier in a drug store, the robber had allowed his gun to discharge in such a way that the bullet, on ricochet from the floor, struck a customer in the leg. Shortly thereafter, a local grand jury returned five indictments against petitioner, a 27–year–old Negro, for common-law robbery—an offense punishable in Alabama by death.

Before the matter came to trial, the court determined that petitioner was indigent and appointed counsel to represent him. Three days later, at his arraignment, petitioner pleaded guilty to all five indictments. So far as the record shows, the judge asked no questions of petitioner concerning his plea, and petitioner did not address the court.

Trial strategy may of course make a plea of guilty seem the desirable course. But the record is wholly silent on that point and throws no light on it.

Alabama provides that when a defendant pleads guilty, "the court must cause the punishment to be determined by a jury" (except where it is required to be fixed by the court) and may "cause witnesses to be examined, to ascertain the character of the offense." Ala.Code Tit. 15, § 277 (1958). In the present case a trial of that dimension was held, the prosecution presenting its case largely through eyewitness testimony. Although counsel for petitioner engaged in cursory cross-examination, petitioner neither testified himself nor presented testimony concerning his character and background. There was nothing to indicate that he had a prior criminal record.

In instructing the jury, the judge stressed that petitioner had pleaded guilty in five cases of robbery, defined as "the felonious taking of money . . . from another against his will . . . by violence or by putting him in fear . . . [carrying] from ten years minimum in the penitentiary to the supreme penalty of death by electrocution." The jury, upon deliberation, found petitioner guilty and sentenced him severally to die on each of the five indictments.

* * *

It was error, plain on the face of the record, for the trial judge to accept petitioner's guilty plea without an affirmative showing that it was intelligent and voluntary . . .

A plea of guilty is more than a confession which admits that the accused did various acts; it is itself a conviction; nothing remains but to give judgment and determine punishment. Admissibility of a confession must be based on a "reliable determination on the voluntariness issue which satisfies the constitutional rights of the defendant." Jackson v. Denno. The requirement that the prosecution spread on the record the prerequisites of a valid waiver is no constitutional innovation. In Carnley v. Cochran, we dealt with a problem of waiver of the right to counsel, a Sixth Amendment right. We held: "Presuming waiver from a silent record is impermissible. The record must show, or there must be an allegation and evidence which show, that an accused was offered counsel but intelligently and understandingly rejected the offer. Anything less is not waiver."

We think that the same standard must be applied to determining whether a guilty plea is voluntarily made. For, as we have said, a plea of guilty is more than an admission of conduct; it is a conviction. Ignorance, incomprehension, coercion, terror, inducements, subtle or blatant threats might be a perfect cover-up of unconstitutionality. The question of an effective waiver of a federal constitutional right in a proceeding is of course governed by federal standards.

Several federal constitutional rights are involved in a waiver that takes place when a plea of guilty is entered in a state criminal trial. First, is the privilege against compulsory self-incrimination guaranteed by the Fifth Amendment and applicable to the States by reason of the Fourteenth. Second, is the right to trial by jury. Third, is the right to confront one's accusers. We cannot presume a waiver of these three important federal rights from a silent record.

What is at stake for an accused facing death or imprisonment demands the utmost solicitude of which courts are capable in canvassing the matter with the accused to make sure he has a full understanding of what the plea connotes and of its consequence. When the judge discharges that function, he leaves a record adequate for any review that may be later sought and forestalls the spin-off of collateral proceedings that seek to probe murky memories.[7] . . .

* * *

Reversed.

7. "A majority of criminal convictions are obtained after a plea of guilty. If these convictions are to be insulated from attack, the trial court is best advised to conduct an on the record examination of the defendant which should include, inter alia, an attempt to satisfy itself that the defendant understands the nature of the charges, his right to a jury trial, the acts sufficient to constitute the offenses for which he is charged and the permissible range of sentences." Commonwealth ex rel. West v. Rundle, 428 Pa. 102, 105–106, 237 A.2d 196, 197–198 (1968).

■ MR. JUSTICE HARLAN, whom MR. JUSTICE BLACK joins, dissenting.

The Court today holds that petitioner Boykin was denied due process of law, and that his robbery convictions must be reversed outright, solely, because "the record [is] inadequate to show that petitioner ... intelligently and knowingly pleaded guilty." The Court thus in effect fastens upon the States, as a matter of federal constitutional law, the rigid prophylactic requirements of Rule 11 of the Federal Rules of Criminal Procedure. It does so in circumstances where the Court itself has only very recently held application of Rule 11 to be unnecessary in the federal courts. See Halliday v. United States (1969). Moreover, the Court does all this at the behest of a petitioner who has never at any time alleged that his guilty plea was involuntary or made without knowledge of the consequences. I cannot possibly subscribe to so bizarre a result.

... The sentencing proceeding occurred some two months after petitioner pleaded guilty. During that period, petitioner made no attempt to withdraw his plea. Petitioner was present in court with his attorney when the witnesses were examined. Petitioner heard the judge state the elements of common-law robbery and heard him announce that petitioner had pleaded guilty to that offense and might be sentenced to death. Again, petitioner made no effort to withdraw his plea.

* * *

... the Court holds that the Due Process Clause of the Fourteenth Amendment requires the outright reversal of petitioner's conviction. This result is wholly unprecedented. There are past holdings of this Court to the effect that a federal habeas corpus petitioner who makes sufficiently credible allegations that his state guilty plea was involuntary is entitled to a hearing as to the truth of those allegations. These holdings suggest that if equally convincing allegations were made in a petition for certiorari on direct review, the petitioner might in some circumstances be entitled to have a judgment of affirmance vacated and the case remanded for a state hearing on voluntariness. However, as has been noted, this petitioner makes no allegations of actual involuntariness.

The Court's reversal is therefore predicated entirely upon the failure of the arraigning state judge to make an "adequate" record. In holding that this is a ground for reversal, the Court [relies on] McCarthy v. United States (1969), in which we held earlier this Term that when a *federal* district judge fails to comply in every respect with the procedure for accepting a guilty plea which is prescribed in Rule 11 of the Federal Rules of Criminal Procedure, the plea must be set aside and the defendant permitted to replead, regardless of lower-court findings that the plea was in fact voluntary. What the Court omits to mention is that in *McCarthy* we stated that our decision was based "solely upon our construction of Rule 11," and explicitly disavowed any reliance upon the Constitution. Thus *McCarthy* can provide no support whatever for today's constitutional edict.

So far as one can make out from the Court's opinion, what is now in effect being held is that the prophylactic procedures of Criminal Rule 11 are substantially applicable to the States as a matter of federal constitutional due process. If this is the basis upon which Boykin's conviction is being reversed, then the Court's disposition is plainly out of keeping with a sequel case to *McCarthy*, decided only last month. For the Court held in Halliday v. United States (1969) that "in view of the large number of constitutionally valid convictions that may have been obtained without full compliance with Rule 11, we decline to apply *McCarthy* retroactively."

The Court quite evidently found Halliday's conviction to be "constitutionally valid," for it affirmed the conviction even though Halliday's guilty plea was accepted in 1954 without any explicit inquiry into whether it was knowingly and understandingly made, as now required by present Rule 11. In justification, the Court noted that two lower courts had found in collateral proceedings that the plea was voluntary. The Court declared that:

> "[A] defendant whose plea has been accepted without full compliance with Rule 11 may still resort to appropriate post-conviction remedies to attack his plea's voluntariness. Thus, if his plea was accepted prior to our decision in *McCarthy*, he is not without a remedy to correct constitutional defects in his conviction." Id., at 833, 89 S.Ct., at 1499.

It seems elementary that the Fifth Amendment due process to which petitioner Halliday was entitled must be at least as demanding as the Fourteenth Amendment process due petitioner Boykin. Yet petitioner Halliday's federal conviction has been affirmed as "constitutionally valid," despite the omission of any judicial inquiry of record at the time of his plea, because he initiated collateral proceedings which revealed that the plea was actually voluntary. Petitioner Boykin, on the other hand, today has his Alabama conviction reversed because of exactly the same omission, even though he too "may . . . resort to appropriate post-conviction remedies to attack his plea's voluntariness" and thus "is not without a remedy to correct constitutional defects in his conviction." In short, I find it utterly impossible to square today's holding with what the Court has so recently done.

I would hold that petitioner Boykin is not entitled to outright reversal of his conviction simply because of the "inadequacy" of the record pertaining to his guilty plea. Further, I would not vacate the judgment below and remand for a state-court hearing on voluntariness. For even if it is assumed for the sake of argument that petitioner would be entitled to such a hearing if he had alleged that the plea was involuntary, a matter which I find it unnecessary to decide, the fact is that he has never made any such claim. Hence, I consider that petitioner's present arguments relating to his guilty plea entitle him to no federal relief.

NOTES

1. In McCarthy v. United States, 394 U.S. 459, 89 S.Ct. 1166 (1969), the Court held that Fed.R.Crim.P. 11 required the court to personally address the defendant to ascertain the voluntariness and basis of the plea and the defendant's understanding of its consequences. Acceptance of pleas upon the assurance of counsel that the defendant had been admonished was held to be improper. The Court did not indicate any dissatisfaction with the guidelines for admonitions contained in Rule 11. The purpose of direct inquiry is to make the court "better able to ascertain the plea's voluntariness and also to develop a more complete record to support his determination in a subsequent post-conviction attack." The holding in *McCarthy* was applicable only to federal cases, and in Halliday v. United States, 394 U.S. 831, 89 S.Ct. 1498 (1969), the Court refused to apply its requirements retroactively.

In Stano v. Dugger, 921 F.2d 1125, 1142 (11th Cir.1991) the Court approved a plea followed by a death sentence. The Court noted:

> Stano made deliberate choices in this case. He chose to have counsel, and never waived his right to counsel in any way whatsoever. He had advice from an experienced and conscientious attorney, who had represented him previously for first-degree murder pleas. Against the advice of counsel, he elected to change his pleas to guilty before Judge Foxman, who had accepted from Stano three previous guilty pleas to first-degree murder.
>
> The inquiry into whether the plea is made intelligently does not mean that the court must determine whether the defendant is making a "smart" decision by pleading guilty.

2. When *McCarthy* was decided, Rule 11 required the court to determine that the plea was made with "understanding of the nature of the charge and the consequences of the plea." In 1975, the Rule was amended to codify the requirements of *Boykin*. The amended Rule is designed to permit some flexibility in determining whether the defendant understands the nature of the charge. In run-of-the-mill cases, summarizing the indictment and explaining the elements of the offense is adequate but not necessarily for complex cases or uneducated defendants. See United States v. Kamer, 781 F.2d 1380 (9th Cir.1986) (complex financial crime where the key to the offense was material omission—judge should have fully explained the nature of the charge) United States v. Dewalt, 92 F.3d 1209 (D.C.Cir. 1996) (divided court held that trial judge must advise that gravamen of charge was that defendant knew, at the time of possession, that the shotgun was sawed off to an illegal length).

3. The specific requirements of Rule 11 are inapplicable to guilty pleas in state courts. See Roddy v. Black, 516 F.2d 1380 (6th Cir.1975); State v. Storbakken, 246 N.W.2d 78 (N.D.1976). *Boykin* stands for the principle that an adequate record must be made in state guilty plea cases but does not prescribe specific admonitions. See Hansen v. Mathews, 424 F.2d 1205 (7th Cir.1970).

All states have devised specific and detailed rules for pleas of guilty in response to *Boykin*. See Rule 402, Rules of the Supreme Court of Illinois; In re Guilty Plea Cases, 395 Mich. 96, 235 N.W.2d 132 (1975).

4. In Henderson v. Morgan, 426 U.S. 637, 96 S.Ct. 2253 (1976), the Supreme Court deemed involuntary a state court defendant's plea to second-degree murder. Defendant had been charged with first-degree murder. As is often the case, no separate charge of second-degree murder was filed. Thus the accused had no written notice of the elements of that offense. The trial court did not explain the elements of second-degree murder. Neither the defendant nor his counsel stipulated that the defendant had the necessary intent. The plurality opinion held:

> "We assume, as [the state] argues, that the prosecutor had overwhelming evidence of guilt available. We also accept [the State's] characterization of the competence of respondent's counsel and of the wisdom of their advice to plead guilty to a charge of second-degree murder. Nevertheless, such a plea cannot support a judgment of guilt unless it was voluntary in a

> constitutional sense. And clearly the plea could not be voluntary in the sense that it constituted an intelligent admission that he committed the offense unless the defendant received 'real notice of the true nature of the charge against him, the first and most universally recognized requirement of due process.'
>
> "The charge of second-degree murder was never formally made. Had it been made, it necessarily would have included a charge that respondent's assault was 'committed with a design to effect the death of the person killed.' That element of the offense might have been proved by the objective evidence even if respondent's actual state of mind was consistent with innocence or man slaughter. But even if such a design to effect death would almost inevitably have been inferred from evidence that respondent repeatedly stabbed [the victim], it is nevertheless also true that a jury would not have been required to draw that inference. The jury would have been entitled to accept defense counsel's appraisal of the incident as involving only manslaughter in the first degree. Therefore, an admission by respondent that he killed [the victim] does not necessarily also admit that he was guilty of second-degree murder.
>
> "There is nothing in this record that can serve as a substitute for either a finding after trial, or a voluntary admission, that respondent had the requisite intent. Defense counsel did not purport to stipulate to that fact; they did not explain to him that his plea would be an admission of that fact; and he made no factual statement or admission necessarily implying that he had such intent. In these circumstances it is impossible to conclude that his plea to the unexplained charge of second-degree murder was voluntary."

According to a majority of the Supreme Court, *Henderson* has no application where the plea is to a crime specified in the charging document rather than to a lesser included offense. Where a defendant who is represented by counsel enters a plea of guilty to a charge specified in an indictment, he is presumed to have adequate knowledge of the charge even where the court does not explain the elements. See Marshall v. Lonberger, 459 U.S. 422, 103 S.Ct. 843 (1983); Braxton v. United States, 500 U.S. 344, 111 S.Ct. 1854 (1991) (there must be specific stipulation to element of greater offense if that offense is to be used to fix sentence; plea to lesser offense and equivocal stipulation is not enough).

5. The consequences of a plea have to be explained but there is controversy over the amount of information the defendant needs. See Major v. State, 814 So.2d 424 (Fla.2002) (divided court holds defendant need not be warned that if he pleads and commits another crime in the future, his future sentence will be enhanced). A full catalogue of consequences would be very lengthy. Some of them matter to everyone, e.g., time in prison and some may not, e.g. inability to get a beauticians license in the future. Many of the consequences are not widely known, e.g. a person who hunts with a rifle (either for food or sport) will be barred for life from such hunting if the person pleads guilty to a felony charge. Federal law prohibits felons from possessing firearms. Rule 11 requires advice of a mandatory minimum and any possible maximum, a special parole term or supervised release (which may extend time served) and restitution. E.g. United States v. Goins, 51 F.3d 400 (4th Cir.1995). A court may, in its discretion, give further warnings about matters of particular importance. Failure to give such additional warnings is rarely error. United States v. Campusano, 947 F.2d 1 (1st Cir.1991) (plea in one case could be adverse evidence in another case) United States v. Morse, 36 F.3d 1070 (11th Cir.1994) (ineligibility for federal benefits) United States v. Del Rosario, 902 F.2d 55

(D.C.Cir.1990) (deportation) Compare People v. Pozo, 746 P.2d 523 (Colo.1987) (attorneys should warn about deportation).

Plain language explanations are permissible and sometimes mandated. United States v. Stevens, 19 F.3d 93 (2d Cir.1994) (laymans language) People v. McCracken, 3 Ill.App.3d 759, 279 N.E.2d 183 (1972) ("any number of years such as 50 or 100 years" rather than "an indeterminate number of years.")

If the details of parole eligibility need not be stated in judicial admonitions, what about a situation where defense counsel erroneously advises the defendant about the timing of parole eligibility? See Hill v. Lockhart, 474 U.S. 52, 106 S.Ct. 366 (1985) which denied relief in a case where the misinformation was not considered significant and there was no allegation of circumstances that would lead a court to believe the correct information would have affected the decision to plead.

6. In 1983 Rule 11 was amended by the addition of subsection (h), providing that errors in plea procedure not affecting substantial rights shall be disregarded.

In United States v. Vonn, 535 U.S. 55, 122 S.Ct. 1043 (2002) the defendant, charged with armed robbery, was permitted to plead guilty to an underlying firearms charge. Although the magistrate advised the defendant of his right to counsel during the earlier stages at his initial appearance and his arraignment on the indictment, when the magistrate judge allocated the defendant on his plea of guilty, the judge skipped the required advice that if he were tried, he would have the right to assistance of counsel. Eight months later, the defendant sought to withdraw his plea of guilty. He did not cite Rule 11 error, but instead claimed he was mistaken about the facts relevant to the charge. His motion was denied and he was sentenced. The Supreme Court granted *certiorari* to resolve the "conflicts among the Circuits about the legitimacy of (1) placing the burden of plain error on a defendant appealing on the basis of Rule 11 error raised for the first time on appeal, and (2) looking beyond the plea colloquy to other parts of the official record to see whether a defendant's substantial rights were affected by a deviation from Rule 11." The Court observed that the defendant had nothing to lose from failing to object to an obvious Rule 11 error when it occurred. Thus the burden properly fell on the defendant to satisfy the Rule 52(a) requirement to show that plain error had affected his substantial rights. In addition, the Court approved looking beyond the four corners of the transcript of the plea allocution to other parts of the record, such as the initial appearance and the arraignment on the indictment.

Justice Stevens concurred that a claimed Rule 11 violation should be evaluated using the entire record, but he dissented about who bore the burden. His reading of *McCarthy v. United States*, 394 U.S. 459, 89 S.Ct. 1166 (1969) placed the burden on the government.

In United States v. Kamer, 781 F.2d 1380 (9th Cir.1986), a plea was vacated in the case of an intelligent individual who may have, in the context of the whole record, be shown to have entered a proper plea after extensive personal negotiation. The court refused to consider anything other than the record of the plea procedure and found there the absence of a direct inquiry about the voluntariness of the plea and a reasonable explanation of the charge. In a separate opinion Judge Sneed observed:

> I concur while harboring the belief that the appellant has represented himself in this prosecution considerably better than he would have been served by most attorneys. That belief provides no basis for affirmance, however.
>
> Rule 11 imposes upon trial courts fairly precise formal requirements designed to reduce the opportunities for misunderstanding on the part of the defendant or the court. The price that must be paid for this benefit is

an occasional reversal solely on the basis of failure to conform to the formalities. This is the usual price that must be paid if formalities are to be taken seriously, as in the instance of Rule 11 they should be. Not to pay the price leads to forfeiture of the benefits that the formalities were intended to achieve.

Formalism in the last century or so has had harsher critics than it deserved. It is reassuring to see its beneficent aspects be recognized in a setting in which that recognition is bolstered by our more honored concern for those accused of crime.

7. The fact that a defendant is aware of the available defenses is significant and contributes to the finding of a valid plea, United States ex rel. McDonald v. Pennsylvania, 343 F.2d 447 (3d Cir.1965), but not necessary. In United States v. Broce, 488 U.S. 563, 109 S.Ct. 757 (1989), the Court noted that its "decisions have not suggested that conscious waiver is necessary with respect to each potential defense relinquished by a plea of guilty."

8. The defendant must respond affirmatively to the various judicial admonitions concerning the charge, the various waivers of rights, the desire to plead guilty, and, where appropriate, the nature of the agreement which is the basis of the plea. The failure or refusal of the defendant to respond for the record renders the plea invalid.

While the defendant is not required to state, in his own words, the facts of the offense and his detailed understanding of each consequence of the plea, United States v. Madrigal, 518 F.2d 166 (7th Cir.1975), he must acknowledge the court's admonitions. Thus, a defendant who remains mute throughout the plea procedure cannot be said to have pleaded guilty. See Williams v. State, 473 S.W.2d 97 (Mo.1971). Moreover, when co-defendants plead guilty at the same time the court must address each individually to assure that he understands his rights and the consequences of the plea. United States v. Fels, 599 F.2d 142 (7th Cir.1979).

9. Where defendant is not represented by counsel and pleads guilty, there must be both a valid waiver of counsel and an adequate plea procedure. See Smith v. United States, 238 F.2d 925 (5th Cir.1956); Lord v. United States, 412 F.2d 499 (4th Cir.1969).

The presence of counsel does not give rise to presumption that a proper plea procedure was followed. However, the presence of counsel may justify an inference that the plea was entered voluntarily. McMann v. Richardson, 397 U.S. 759, 90 S.Ct. 1441 (1970); Brady v. United States, 397 U.S. 742, 90 S.Ct. 1463 (1970); Parker v. North Carolina, 397 U.S. 790, 90 S.Ct. 1458 (1970). But that inference can be overcome by other facts of record. See Henderson v. Morgan, 426 U.S. 637, 96 S.Ct. 2253 (1976).

Defense counsel at a plea of guilty owes the same duty to his client as he would during a trial of the cause. His representation must be free from any conflict of interest. See Dukes v. Warden, 406 U.S. 250, 92 S.Ct. 1551 (1972). It is judged by the same standards of competency applied to trial counsel. Hill v. Lockhart, 474 U.S. 52, 106 S.Ct. 366 (1985).

What happens when a court gives erroneous information, i.e. overstates the maximum sentence, which causes defendant foolishly to refuse to plead guilty. Generally, the answer is nothing because such a defendant never surrenders the rights inherent in a trial. See State v. McBride, 252 Neb. 866, 567 N.W.2d 136 (1997). When bad advice is given by defense counsel the majority of courts recognize the right of defendant to challenge his conviction. See United States v. Day, 969 F.2d 39 (3d Cir.1992) (review of cases). The remedy is uncertain. If a plea bargain was offered, the prosecutor may not be required to offer it anew. If the plea was unbargained, does the judge have to impose the sentence he would have given? How does the judge know what that sentence would have been?

10. One of the major reasons for the detailed inquiry necessary to support a guilty plea is the fact that the defendant waives not only his basic right to a trial, but also many of the legal issues which attended the proceeding to the point of the plea. In Tollett v. Henderson, 411 U.S. 258, 267, 93 S.Ct. 1602, 1608 (1973), the court said: "A guilty plea represents a break in the chain of events which has preceded it in the criminal process. When a criminal defendant has solemnly admitted in open court that he is in fact guilty of the offense with which he is charged, he may not thereafter raise independent claims relating to the deprivation of constitutional rights that occurred prior to the entry of the guilty plea." Compare Haring v. Prosise, 462 U.S. 306, 103 S.Ct. 2368 (1983) (guilty plea does not waive a right to sue for civil damages for an unlawful search).

11. In some jurisdictions the alternative to reserving issues while pleading guilty is a bench trial on stipulated facts where the court enters a judgment of guilty and the defendant may appeal. Does such a procedure require the same kind of admonitions as a plea of guilty? Few courts require admonitions. A succinct review of the cases is in State v. Johnson, 104 Wash.2d 338, 705 P.2d 773 (1985) (en banc).

In Adams v. Peterson, 968 F.2d 835 (9th Cir.1992) (en banc) Adams agreed to stipulate to the facts precisely as stated in the indictment. In exchange for this, two other indictments against him were dismissed. He did this because his prior juvenile record and the more detailed facts of the case (rape and sodomy and burglary) may have resulted in a harsher sentence if the case were fully tried. The fact stipulation was entered with the specific language that "it is the expectation of the parties that the defendant will be found guilty." The court accepted the stipulation after asking the defendant whether he had discussed the matter with his attorney, and whether he was waiving a jury and agreeing to a trial on stipulated facts. He was found guilty and given forty years for rape and sodomy (a sentence much higher than he had hoped for) but no additional sentence was imposed for burglary. Adams did want to testify but he was told that if he stipulated to the facts he would not be able to testify except at sentencing. The majority said:

> In the defense's own understanding, therefore, Adams clearly did not plead guilty; he professed his innocence and pursued a trial strategy designed to avert what his attorney perceived to be potentially more damaging and perhaps prejudicial: a full-scale recitation of the evidence before the judge or jury. Perhaps wisely, the defense viewed the stipulation as (a) the most effective and least inflammatory method for presenting the facts to the trial court and (b) the most effective means of foreclosing any effort by the state to prosecute Adams to the full extent of the law. Indeed, Adams himself has admitted that a prime motivation for his agreeing to the stipulation was to have two indictments pending against him dropped. Under such circumstances—where the defense itself does not intend its actions to be construed as an admission of guilt and where it has strategic reasons to support its decision to stipulate—it would be curious indeed for the trial court to hold that the parties' stipulation does constitute a plea of guilty.
>
> From our vantage point, it may appear to us (and clearly it now appears to Adams) that the defense made an unfortunate choice. Although the stipulation prevented an "inflammatory recitation of the acts," the trial judge nevertheless sentenced Adams to the maximum period of incarceration. We decline to adopt a rule, however, that would require a state trial judge to inquire in every instance into the motive behind a stipulation, and the likelihood that the strategy pursued will succeed. There may be a variety of strategic reasons for proceeding by a stipulated facts trial, ranging from preservation of issues for

> appeal to attempting to mitigate the sentence by a partial acceptance of responsibility or by controlling the evidence presented to the sentencer.... We decline, as well, to adopt a rule applying *Boykin* to those stipulations which appear, to a federal court later presented with a habeas petition, ill-considered. We hold, instead, that a plea of not guilty in combination with a stipulated facts trial is simply not equivalent to a guilty plea for *Boykin* purposes, even if the stipulation is to all elements necessary to a conviction and even if it might appear to are viewing court that the stipulation serves little purpose.[5]

The dissent responded:

> In *Boykin*, the Supreme Court characterized a guilty plea as "more than a voluntary confession made in open court.... [A guilty plea] serves as a *stipulation* that no proof by the prosecution need be advanced.... It supplies both evidence and verdict, ending controversy."
>
> This characterization applies completely to Adams's case. Nothing remained for the trial court other than to find Adams guilty as charged, and pronounce sentence. No further evidence was needed. Adams's stipulation provided both the evidence and the verdict, and effectively ended the controversy. In these circumstances, I believe the trial court was required to ascertain on the record that Adams understood that by entering a stipulation tantamount to a guilty plea, he was in effect waiving his *Boykin* rights.
>
> * * *
>
> In this case, the trial judge could have ascertained within a few minutes whether Adams clearly understood that he was giving up important constitutional rights, including the right to testify on his own behalf, the right to confront his accusers, and the right to a jury trial. By spending a few more minutes with Adams, the trial judge could have ensured that Adams waived those constitutional rights knowingly and intelligently, and several appellate courts would have been spared countless hours of work.

12. For decades, prosecutors have rewarded defendants for quick pleas, a practice called, among other things, "pleading off the arraignment." These policies and their associated procedures were usually quite informal and valuable.

In recent years, many prosecutors have adopted formal "fast track" plea agreements. A reduced sentence is offered in exchange for a quick plea, which requires, among other things, that defendants waive the right to discovery or production of certain information, namely that which would support impeachment of prosecution witnesses or informants or which support affirmative defenses. The government does not require defendants to waive the right to disclosure of information establishing innocence. The entire Court approved this practice on grounds adopted by eight of the justices. See United States v. Ruiz, 536 U.S. 622, 122 S.Ct. 2450 (2002).

> "Justice Breyer ...
>
> ... First, impeachment information is special in relation to the *fairness of a trial*, not in respect to whether a plea is *voluntary* ("knowing,"

5. Unlike our dissenting colleagues, we do not believe our holding invites prosecutorial abuse. Prosecutors simply do not control the information available to a defendant in these circumstances. First, as we hold in Part III, a stipulation is valid only if knowingly entered. Second, defense counsel of course has an obligation to inform the defendant fully of the consequences of either a plea or a stipulation. And third, no prosecutor can prevent the trial judge from going through the *Boykin* litany. We hold only that, in the case of a stipulated facts trial, the federal constitution does not mandate a *Boykin* examination.

"intelligent," and "sufficient[ly] aware"). Of course, the more information the defendant has, the more aware he is of the likely consequences of a plea, waiver, or decision, and the wiser that decision will likely be. But the Constitution does not require the prosecutor to share all useful information with the defendant. *Weatherford v. Bursey*, 429 U.S. 545, 559, 97 S.Ct. 837 (1977) ("There is no general constitutional right to discovery in a criminal case"). And the law ordinarily considers a waiver knowing, intelligent, and sufficiently aware if the defendant fully understands the nature of the right and how it would likely apply *in general* in the circumstances—even though the defendant may not know the *specific detailed* consequences of invoking it. A defendant, for example, may waive his right to remain silent, his right to a jury trial, or his right to counsel even if the defendant does not know the specific questions the authorities intend to ask, who will likely serve on the jury, or the particular lawyer the State might otherwise provide....

It is particularly difficult to characterize impeachment information as critical information of which the defendant must always be aware prior to pleading guilty given the random way in which such information may, or may not, help a particular defendant. The degree of help that impeachment information can provide will depend upon the defendant's own independent knowledge of the prosecution's potential case—a matter that the Constitution does not require prosecutors to disclose.

Second, ... this Court has found that the Constitution, in respect to a defendant's awareness of relevant circumstances, does not require complete knowledge of the relevant circumstances, but permits a court to accept a guilty plea, with its accompanying waiver of various constitutional rights, despite various forms of misapprehension under which a defendant might labor. See *Brady v. United States*, 397 U.S., at 757 (defendant "misapprehended the quality of the State's case"); *ibid.* (defendant misapprehended "the likely penalties"); *ibid.* (defendant failed to "anticipate a change in the law regarding" relevant "punishments"); *McMann v. Richardson*, 397 U.S. 759, 770, 90 S.Ct. 1441 (1970) (counsel "misjudged the admissibility" of a "confession"); *United States v. Broce*, 488 U.S. 563, 573, 109 S.Ct. 757 (1989) (counsel failed to point out a potential defense); *Tollett v. Henderson*, 411 U.S. 258, 267, 93 S.Ct. 1602 (1973) (counsel failed to find a potential constitutional infirmity in grand jury proceedings). It is difficult to distinguish, in terms of importance, (1) a defendant's ignorance of grounds for impeachment of potential witnesses at a possible future trial from (2) the varying forms of ignorance at issue in these cases.

Third, ... [t]his Court has said that due process considerations include not only (1) the nature of the private interest at stake, but also (2) the value of the additional safeguard, and (3) the adverse impact of the requirement upon the Government's interests. *Ake v. Oklahoma*, [citation omitted] (1985). Here, as we have just pointed out, the added value of the [information] to a defendant is often limited, for it depends upon the defendant's independent awareness of the details of the Government's case. And in any case, as the proposed plea agreement at issue here specifies, the Government will provide "any information establishing the factual innocence of the defendant" regardless. That fact, along with other guilty-plea safeguards, see Fed. Rule Crim. Proc. 11, diminishes the force of Ruiz's concern that, in the absence of impeachment information, innocent individuals, accused of crimes, will plead guilty. [citation omitted]

> At the same time, a constitutional obligation to provide impeachment information during plea bargaining, prior to entry of a guilty plea, could seriously interfere with the Government's interest in securing those guilty pleas that are factually justified, desired by defendants, and help to secure the efficient administration of justice. [A disclosure] rule risks premature disclosure of Government witness information, which, the Government tells us, could "disrupt ongoing investigations" and expose prospective witnesses to serious harm. Brief for United States 25. Cf. Amendments to Federal Rules of Criminal Procedure: Hearings before the Subcommittee on Criminal Justice of the House Committee on the Judiciary, 94th Cong., 1st Sess., 92 (1975) (statement of John C. Keeney, Acting Assistant Attorney General, Criminal Div., Dept. of Justice) (opposing mandated witness disclosure three days before trial because of documented instances of witness intimidation). And the careful tailoring that characterizes most legal Government witness disclosure requirements suggests recognition by both Congress and the Federal Rules Committees that such concerns are valid . . .

Consequently, the [disclosure rule] could force the Government to abandon its "general practice" of not "disclos[ing] to a defendant pleading guilty information that would reveal the identities of cooperating informants, undercover investigators, or other prospective witnesses." Brief for United States 25. It could require the Government to devote substantially more resources to trial preparation prior to plea bargaining, thereby depriving the plea-bargaining process of its main resource-saving advantages. Or it could lead the Government instead to abandon its heavy reliance upon plea bargaining in a vast number—90% or more—of federal criminal cases. We cannot say that the Constitution's due process requirement demands so radical a change in the criminal justice process in order to achieve so comparatively small a constitutional benefit.

These considerations, taken together, lead us to conclude that the Constitution does not require the Government to disclose material impeachment evidence prior to entering a plea agreement with a criminal defendant.

In addition, we note that the "fast track" plea agreement requires a defendant to waive her right to receive information the Government has regarding any "affirmative defense" she raises at trial. . . . We do not believe the Constitution here requires provision of this information to the defendant prior to plea bargaining—for most (though not all) of the reasons previously stated. That is to say, in the context of this agreement, the need for this information is more closely related to the *fairness* of a trial than to the *voluntariness* of the plea; the value in terms of the defendant's added awareness of relevant circumstances is ordinarily limited; yet the added burden imposed upon the Government by requiring its provision well in advance of trial (often before trial preparation begins) can be serious, thereby significantly interfering with the administration of the plea bargaining process. . . .

B. VOLUNTARINESS OF THE PLEA

North Carolina v. Alford

Supreme Court of the United States, 1970.
400 U.S. 25, 91 S.Ct. 160.

■ MR. JUSTICE WHITE delivered the opinion of the Court.

On December 2, 1963, Alford was indicted for first-degree murder, a capital offense under North Carolina law.[1] The court appointed an attorney to represent him, and this attorney questioned all but one of the various witnesses who appellee said would substantiate his claim of innocence. The witnesses, however, did not support Alford's story but gave statements that strongly indicated his guilt. Faced with strong evidence of guilt and no substantial evidentiary support for the claim of innocence, Alford's attorney recommended that he plead guilty, but left the ultimate decision to Alford himself. The prosecutor agreed to accept a plea of guilty to a charge of second-degree murder, and on December 10, 1963, Alford pleaded guilty to the reduced charge.

Before the plea was finally accepted by the trial court, the court heard the sworn testimony of a police officer who summarized the State's case. Two other witnesses besides Alford were also heard. Although there was no eyewitnesses to the crime, the testimony indicated that shortly before the killing Alford took his gun from his house, stated his intention to kill the victim, and returned home with the declaration that he had carried out the killing. After the summary presentation of the State's case, Alford took the stand and testified that he had not committed the murder but that he was pleading guilty because he faced the threat of the death penalty if he did not do so.[2] In response to the questions of his counsel, he acknowledged that his counsel had informed him of the difference between second- and first-degree murder and of his rights in case he chose to go to trial.[3] The

1. At the time Alford pleaded guilty, North Carolina law provided that if a guilty plea to a charge of first-degree murder was accepted by the prosecution and the court, the penalty would be life imprisonment rather than death. The provision permitting guilty pleas in capital cases was repealed in 1969. Though under present North Carolina law it is not possible for a defendant to plead guilty to a capital charge, it seemingly remains possible for a person charged with a capital offense to plead guilty to a lesser charge.

2. After giving his version of the events of the night of the murder, Alford stated:

> "I pleaded guilty on second degree murder because they said there is too much evidence, but I ain't shot no man, but I take the fault for the other man. We never had an argument in our life and I just pleaded guilty because they said if I didn't they would gas me for it, and that is all."

In response to questions from his attorney, Alford affirmed that he had consulted several times with his attorney and with members of his family and had been informed of his rights if he chose to plead not guilty. Alford then reaffirmed his decision to plead guilty to second-degree murder:

> "Q. [by Alford's attorney]. And you authorized me to tender a plea of guilty to second degree murder before the court?
>
> "A. Yes, sir.
>
> "Q. And in doing that, that you have again affirmed your decision on that point?
>
> "A. Well, I'm still pleading that you all got me to plead guilty. I plead the other way, circumstantial evidence; that the jury will prosecute me on—on the second. You told me to plead guilty, right. I don't—I'm not guilty but I plead guilty."

3. At the state court hearing on post-conviction relief, the testimony confirmed that Alford had been fully informed by his attorney as to his rights on a plea of not guilty and as to the consequences of a plea of guilty. Since the record in this case affirmatively indicates that Alford was aware of the consequences of his plea of guilty and of the rights waived by the plea, no issues of substance under Boykin v. Alabama, 395 U.S. 238, 89 S.Ct. 1709 (1969), would be presented even if that case was held applicable to the events here in question.

trial court then asked appellee if, in light of his denial of guilt, he still desired to plead guilty to second-degree murder and appellee answered, "Yes, sir. I plead guilty on—from the circumstances that he [Alford's attorney] told me." After eliciting information about Alford's prior criminal record, which was a long one,[4] the trial court sentenced him to 30 years' imprisonment, the maximum penalty for second-degree murder.

* * *

... the Court of Appeals ruled that Alford's guilty plea was involuntary because its principal motivation was fear of the death penalty. By this standard, even if both the judge and the jury had possessed the power to impose the death penalty for first-degree murder or if guilty pleas to capital charges had not been permitted, Alford's plea of guilty to second-degree murder should still have been rejected because impermissibly induced by his desire to eliminate the possibility of a death sentence. ...

We held in Brady v. United States (1970), that a plea of guilty which would not have been entered except for the defendant's desire to avoid a possible death penalty and to limit the maximum penalty to life imprisonment or a term of years was not for that reason compelled within the meaning of the Fifth Amendment. *Jackson* established no new test for determining the validity of guilty pleas. The standard was and remains whether the plea represents a voluntary and intelligent choice among the alternative courses of action open to the defendant. ...

That he would not have pleaded except for the opportunity to limit the possible penalty does not necessarily demonstrate that the plea of guilty was not the product of a free and rational choice, especially where the defendant was represented by competent counsel whose advice was that the plea would be to the defendant's advantage. The standard fashioned and applied by the Court of Appeals was therefore erroneous.

* * *

As previously recounted after Alford's plea of guilty was offered and the State's case was placed before the judge, Alford denied that he had committed the murder but reaffirmed his desire to plead guilty to avoid a possible death sentence and to limit the penalty to the 30–year maximum provided for second-degree murder. Ordinarily, a judgment of conviction resting on a plea of guilty is justified by the defendant's admission that he committed the crime charged against him and his consent that judgment be entered without a trial of any kind. The plea usually subsumes both elements, and justifiably so, even though there is no separate, express admission by the defendant that he committed the particular acts claimed to constitute the crime charged in the indictment. ... Here Alford entered his plea but accompanied it with the statement that he had not shot the victim.

4. Before Alford was sentenced, the trial judge asked Alford about prior convictions. Alford answered that, among other things, he had served six years of a ten-year sentence for murder, had been convicted nine times for armed robbery, and had been convicted for transporting stolen goods, forgery, and carrying a concealed weapon.

If Alford's statements were to be credited as sincere assertions of his innocence, there obviously existed a factual and legal dispute between him and the State. Without more, it might be argued that the conviction entered on his guilty plea was invalid, since his assertion of innocence negatived any admission of guilt, which, as we observed in *Brady*, is normally "[c]entral to the plea and the foundation for entering judgment against the defendant...."

In addition to Alford's statement, however, the court had heard an account of the events on the night of the murder, including information from Alford's acquaintances that he had departed from his home with his gun stating his intention to kill and that he had later declared that he had carried out his intention. Nor had Alford wavered in his desire to have trial court determine his guilt without a jury trial. Although denying the charge against him, he nevertheless preferred the dispute between him and the State to be settled by the judge in the context of a guilty plea proceeding rather than by a formal trial. Thereupon, with the State's telling evidence and Alford's denial before it, the trial court proceeded to convict and sentence Alford for second-degree murder.

State and lower federal courts are divided upon whether a guilty plea can be accepted when it is accompanied by protestations of innocence and hence contains only a waiver of trial but no admission of guilt. Some courts ... require that trial judges reject such pleas. But others have concluded that they should not "force any defense on a defendant in a criminal case," particularly when advancement of the defense might "end in disaster...." They have argued that, since "guilt, or the degree of guilt, is at times uncertain and elusive," "[a]n accused, though believing in or entertaining doubts respecting his innocence, might reasonably conclude a jury would be convinced of his guilt and that he would fare better in the sentence by pleading guilty...." As one state court observed nearly a century ago, "[r]easons other than the fact that he is guilty may induce a defendant to so plead, ... [and] [h]e must be permitted to judge for himself in this respect."[7] ...

This Court has not confronted this precise issue, but prior decisions do yield relevant principles. In Lynch v. Overholser (1962), ... the Court expressly refused to rule that Lynch had an absolute right to have his guilty plea accepted, but implied that there would have been no constitutional error had his plea been accepted even though evidence before the judge indicated that there was a valid defense.

The issue in Hudson v. United States (1926), was whether a federal court has power to impose a prison sentence after accepting a plea of *nolo contendere*, a plea by which a defendant does not expressly admit his guilt, but nonetheless waives his right to a trial and authorizes the court for purposes of the case to treat him as if he were guilty.[8] The Court held that

7. A third approach has been to decline to rule definitively that a trial judge must either accept or reject an otherwise valid plea containing a protestation of innocence, but to leave that decision to his sound discretion. See Maxwell v. United States, 368 F.2d 735, 738–739 (C.A.9 1966).

8. Courts have defined the plea of *nolo contendere* in a variety of different ways, describing it, on the one hand, as "in effect, a

a trial court does have such power, and the federal courts have uniformly followed this rule, even in cases involving moral turpitude. ... Implicit in the *nolo contendere* cases is a recognition that the Constitution does not bar imposition of a prison sentence upon an accused who is unwilling expressly to admit his guilt but who, faced with grim alternatives, is willing to waive his trial and accept the sentence.

These cases would be directly in point if Alford had simply insisted on his plea but refused to admit the crime. The fact that his plea was denominated a plea of guilty rather than a plea of *nolo contendere* is of no constitutional significance with respect to the issue now before us, for the Constitution is concerned with the practical consequences, not the formal categorizations, of state law. ... Thus, while most pleas of guilty consist of both a waiver of trial and an express admission of guilt, the latter element is not a constitutional requisite to the imposition of criminal penalty. An individual accused of crime may voluntarily, knowingly, and understandingly consent to the imposition of a prison sentence even if he is unwilling or unable to admit his participation in the acts constituting the crime.

Nor can we perceive any material difference between a plea that refuses to admit commission of the criminal act and a plea containing a protestation of innocence when, as in the instant case, a defendant intelligently concludes that his interests require entry of a guilty plea and the record before the judge contains strong evidence of actual guilt. Here the State had a strong case of first-degree murder against Alford. Whether he realized or disbelieved his guilt, he insisted on his plea because in his view he had absolutely nothing to gain by a trial and much to gain by pleading. Because of the overwhelming evidence against him, a trial was precisely what neither Alford nor his attorney desired. Confronted with the choice between a trial for first-degree murder, on the one hand, and a plea of guilty to second-degree murder, on the other, Alford quite reasonably chose the latter and thereby limited the maximum penalty to a 30-year term. When his plea is viewed in light of the evidence against him, which substantially negated his claim of innocence and which further provided a means by which the judge could test whether the plea was being intelligent-

plea of guilty," and on the other, as a query directed to the court to determine the defendant's guilt. See generally Lott v. United States, 367 U.S. 421, 426–427, 81 S.Ct. 1563, 1566–1567 (1961). As a result, it is impossible to state precisely what a defendant does admit when he enters a *nolo* plea in a way that will consistently fit all the cases.

* * *

The plea may have originated in the early medieval practice by which defendants wishing to avoid imprisonment would seek to make an end of the matter (*finem facere*) by offering to pay a sum of money to the king. See 2 F. Pollock & F. Maitland, The History of English Law 517 (2d ed. 1909).

* * *

Throughout its history, that is, the plea of *nolo contendere* has been viewed not as an express admission of guilt but as a consent by the defendant that he may be punished as if he were guilty and a prayer for leniency. Fed.Rule Crim.Proc. 11 preserves this distinction in its requirement that a court cannot accept a guilty plea "unless it is satisfied that there is a factual basis for the plea"; there is no similar requirement for pleas of *nolo contendere*, since it was thought desirable to permit defendants to plead *nolo* without making any inquiry into their actual guilt.

ly entered,[10] its validity cannot be seriously questioned. In view of the strong factual basis for the plea demonstrated by the State and Alford's clearly expressed desire to enter it despite his professed belief in his innocence, we hold that the trial judge did not commit constitutional error in accepting it.[11]

Relying in United States v. Jackson, supra, Alford now argues in effect that the State should not have allowed him this choice but should have insisted on proving him guilty of murder in the first degree. The States in their wisdom may take this course by statute or otherwise and may prohibit the practice of accepting pleas to lesser included offenses under any circumstances. But this is not the mandate of the Fourteenth Amendment and the Bill of Rights. The prohibitions against involuntary or unintelligent pleas should not be relaxed, but neither should an exercise in arid logic render those constitutional guarantees counterproductive and put in jeopardy the very human values they were meant to preserve.

The Court of Appeals for the Fourth Circuit was in error to find Alford's plea of guilty invalid because it was made to avoid the possibility of the death penalty....

It is so ordered.

Vacated and remanded.

■ MR. JUSTICE BLACK, while adhering to his belief that United States v. Jackson, was wrongly decided, concurs in the judgment and in substantially all of the opinion in this case.

■ MR. JUSTICE BRENNAN, with whom MR. JUSTICE DOUGLAS and MR. JUSTICE MARSHALL join, dissenting.

Last Term, this Court held, over my dissent, that a plea of guilty may validly be induced by an unconstitutional threat to subject the defendant to the risk of death, so long as the plea is entered in open court and the defendant is represented by competent counsel who is aware of the threat,

10. Because of the importance of protecting the innocent and of insuring that guilty pleas are a product of free and intelligent choice, various state and federal court decisions properly caution that pleas coupled with claims of innocence should not be accepted unless there is a factual basis for the plea, see, e.g., Griffin v. United States, 132 U.S.App.D.C. 108, 110, 405 F.2d 1378, 1380 (1968); Bruce v. United States, supra, 126 U.S.App.D.C., at 342, 379 F.2d, at 119 (1967); Commonwealth v. Cottrell, 433 Pa. 177, 249 A.2d 294 (1969); and until the judge taking the plea has inquired into and sought to resolve the conflict between the waiver of trial and the claim of innocence. See, e.g., People v. Serrano, 15 N.Y.2d 304, 308–309, 258 N.Y.S.2d 386, 388–389, 206 N.E.2d 330, 332 (1965); State v. Branner, 149 N.C. 559, 563, 63 S.E. 169, 171 (1908). See also Kreuter v. United States, 201 F.2d 33, 36 (C.A.10 1952).

In the federal courts, Fed.Rule Crim. Proc. 11 expressly provides that a court "shall not enter a judgment upon a plea of guilty unless it is satisfied that there is a factual basis for the plea."

11. Our holding does not mean that a trial judge must accept every constitutionally valid guilty plea merely because a defendant wishes so to plead. A criminal defendant does not have an absolute right under the Constitution to have his guilty plea accepted by the court, although the States may by statute or otherwise confer such a right. Likewise, the States may bar their courts from accepting guilty pleas from any defendants who assert their innocence. Cf. Fed.Rule Crim.Proc. 11, which gives a trial judge discretion to "refuse to accept a plea of guilty...." We need not now delineate the scope of that discretion.

albeit not of its unconstitutionality. Brady v. United States (1970); Parker v. North Carolina (1970). Today the Court makes clear that its previous holding was intended to apply even when the record demonstrates that the actual effect of the unconstitutional threat was to induce a guilty plea from a defendant who was unwilling to admit his guilt.

I adhere to the view that, in any given case, the influence of such an unconstitutional threat "must necessarily be given weight in determining the voluntariness of a plea." Parker v. North Carolina (dissent). And, without reaching the question whether due process permits the entry of judgment upon a plea of guilty accompanied by a contemporaneous denial of acts constituting the crime, I believe that at the very least such a denial of guilt is also a relevant factor in determining whether the plea was voluntarily and intelligently made. With these factors in mind, it is sufficient in my view to state that the facts set out in the majority opinion demonstrate that Alford was "so gripped by fear of the death penalty" that his decision to plead guilty was not voluntary but was "the product of duress as much so as choice reflecting physical constraint."

NOTES

1. What must the record reflect to establish guilt? A prosecutor's uncontested recital of evidence or an admission of guilt by the defendant, or both, is common. Oaks v. Wainwright, 445 F.2d 1062 (5th Cir.1971). Failure to show a factual basis at the plea may require only a remand to permit the factual basis to be proven. Paulsen v. Manson, 203 Conn. 484, 525 A.2d 1315 (1987) (reviewing precedents). Some jurisdictions do not accept *Alford* and require a personal admission of guilt before acceptance of a plea. Ross v. State, 456 N.E.2d 420 (Ind.1983).

What if the accused *untruthfully* admits the crime? A plea bargain (see following section) may result in a conviction for a crime that defendant did not commit. This is to enable a lesser sentence than the one provided for the crime that he or she did commit. In many cases, all of this is clear on the record because the accused does admit perpetrating the more serious offense. See State v. Zhao, 157 Wash.2d 188, 137 P.3d 835 (2006) (accepting a plea to a hypothetical offense)

2. In McMann v. Richardson, 397 U.S. 759, 90 S.Ct. 1441 (1970), the Court held that a plea of guilty in a state court cannot be attacked on the ground that it was motivated by a coerced confession unless the defendant was incompetently advised by counsel. The Court pointed out that a plea of guilty is usually based on a wide variety of considerations, only one of which may be the question of a confession's admissibility. Furthermore, the Court set a difficult standard for proof of incompetency of counsel:

> "In our view a defendant's plea of guilty based on reasonably competent advice is an intelligent plea not open to attack on the ground that counsel may have misjudged the admissibility of the defendant's confession. Whether a plea of guilty is unintelligent and therefore vulnerable when motivated by a confession erroneously thought admissible in evidence depends as an initial matter not on whether a court would retrospectively consider counsel's advice to be right or wrong, but on whether that advice was within the range of competence demanded of attorneys in criminal cases. On the one hand, uncertainty is inherent in predicting court decisions; but on the other hand defendants facing felony charges are entitled to the effective assistance of competent counsel. Beyond this we think the

matter, for the most part, should be left to the good sense and discretion of the trial courts with the admonition that if the right to counsel guaranteed by the Constitution is to serve its purpose, defendants cannot be left to the mercies of incompetent counsel, and that judges should strive to maintain proper standards of performance by attorneys who are representing defendants in criminal cases in their courts. We hold, therefore, that a defendant who alleges that he pleaded guilty because of a prior coerced confession is not, without more, entitled to hearing on his petition for habeas corpus. ... A plea of guilty in a state court is not subject to collateral attack in a federal court on the ground that it was motivated by a coerced confession unless the defendant was incompetently advised by his attorney.

In Brady v. United States, 397 U.S. 742, 90 S.Ct. 1463 (1970), the Court held that a plea of guilty was valid although the fear of the death penalty was a prime factor in the decision to plead guilty and the statute providing for the death penalty was later ruled unconstitutional. The Court said:

> "But even if we assume that Brady would not have pleaded guilty except for the death penalty provision ..., this assumption merely identifies the penalty provision as a 'but for' cause of his plea. That the statute caused the plea in this sense does not necessarily prove that the plea was coerced and invalid as an involuntary act.... We decline to hold ... that a guilty plea is compelled and invalid under the Fifth Amendment whenever motivated by the defendant's desire to accept the certainty or probability of a lesser penalty rather than face a wider range of possibilities extending from acquittal to conviction and a higher penalty authorized by law for the crime charged."

The Court reviewed the numerous advantages to both prosecution and defense inherent in the guilty plea procedures and noted that well over three-fourths of all criminal convictions in this country are based on guilty pleas:

> "[A] great many of them no doubt motivated at least in part by the hope or assurance of a lesser penalty than might be imposed if there were a guilty verdict after a trial judge or jury. Of course, that the prevalence of guilty pleas is explainable does not necessarily validate those pleas nor the system which produces them. But we cannot hold that it is unconstitutional for the State to extend a benefit to a defendant who in turn extends a substantial benefit to the State and who demonstrates by his pleas that he is ready and willing to admit his crime and to enter the correctional system in a frame of mind which affords hope for success in rehabilitation over a shorter period of time than might otherwise be necessary. A contrary holding would require the States and Federal Government to forbid guilty pleas altogether, to provide a single invariable penalty for each crime defined by the statutes, or to place the sentencing function in a separate authority having no knowledge of the manner in which the conviction in each case was obtained. In any event, it would be necessary to forbid prosecutors and judges to accept guilty pleas to selected counts, to lesser included offenses, or to reduced charges. The Fifth Amendment does not reach so far. ..."

3. In Parker v. North Carolina, 397 U.S. 790, 90 S.Ct. 1458 (1970), a plea of guilty was held valid despite allegations that the indictment was invalid because of systematic exclusion of Blacks from the grand jury, that the plea was induced by a coerced confession, and was entered in fear of the death penalty which was provided by an unconstitutional statute. The Court, ruling on the basis of *Brady* and *McMann*, pointed out that there was an interval of one month between confession and plea, that the defendant had the advice of counsel and family before pleading and, therefore, any connection between plea and confession had become attenuated. The Court rejected the contention that the plea was invalid because counsel mistakenly thought the confession would have been admissible at trial. Even if counsel was in error, there was nothing to indicate that the advice to plead guilty was outside the range of competence required of defense counsel.

4. Do *McMann*, *Brady* and *Parker* make it extremely difficult for a defendant to attack his plea of guilty when he is represented by counsel unless counsel was grossly incompetent and the plea almost completely unreasonable? Contrast the case in which both prosecutor and defense counsel (and even the court) are mistaken about the elements of the crime. McKeever v. Warden, 486 F.3d 81 (3d Cir.2007) (defendant has absolute right to withdraw plea)

5. The defendant has the right to challenge the voluntariness of a plea when it is induced by actual threats or physical coercion. See Blackledge v. Allison, 431 U.S. 63, 97 S.Ct. 1621 (1977). State v. Frederick, 100 Wash.2d 550, 674 P.2d 136 (1983) (coercion by private persons). In Fontaine v. United States, 411 U.S. 213, 93 S.Ct. 1461 (1973), the Court, in an abbreviated per curiam opinion, held that an ostensibly voluntary plea could be subject to collateral challenge if, at an evidentiary hearing, the defendant could show that it was the product of coercion.

In People v. Adams, 836 P.2d 1045 (Colo.App.1991) the Court divided over the question of whether very rough language of defense counsel constituted coercion of a plea. Counsel repeatedly told his client that if he went to trial he would be found guilty and sent to prison. Defendant had no prior prison experience and he was told, among other things,

> So you're not tough enough for prison. You're just not tough enough for prison. That's all there is to it. So that any prison sentence is most probably for you a death sentence or very close. Because things would happen to you in prison that would cause you to wish you were dead or want to kill yourself. So that's why, you know, you have to understand the risks.
>
> * * *
>
> It is my opinion that in the two years or four years or whatever it is, awaiting for the appellate court to decide (your case) that you'll be dead.
>
> * * *
>
> And it won't do you any good because you'll be dead or your [anus] will be the size of a dinner plate ... a jury can say "you know, I'm not convinced anyone of them is telling the truth but I believe beyond a reasonable doubt that Steve Adams committed second degree murder." Ok. Then you go to prison and you're dead.

Is this plea voluntary? Does it make a difference if what was said to defendant is certainly true? likely true? possibly true? Do you think this kind of language is commonly used by defense counsel in speaking to their clients?

C. PLEA BARGAINING

Santobello v. New York

United States Supreme Court, 1971.
404 U.S. 257, 92 S.Ct. 495.

■ MR. CHIEF JUSTICE BURGER delivered the opinion of the Court.

... The State of New York indicted petitioner on two felony counts.... Petitioner first entered a plea of not guilty to both counts. After negotiations, the Assistant District Attorney in charge of the case agreed to permit petitioner to plead guilty to a lesser included offense, conviction of which would carry a maximum prison sentence of one year. The prosecutor agreed to make no recommendation as to the sentence.

On June 16, 1969, petitioner accordingly withdrew his plea of not guilty and entered a plea of guilty to the lesser charge. Petitioner represented to the sentencing judge that the plea was voluntary and that the facts of the case, as described by the Assistant District Attorney, were true. The court accepted the plea and set a date for sentencing. A series of delays followed, owing primarily to the absence of a pre-sentence report, so that by September 23, 1969, petitioner had still not been sentenced. By that date petitioner acquired new defense counsel.

Petitioner's new counsel moved immediately to withdraw the guilty plea. In an accompanying affidavit, petitioner alleged that he did not know at the time of his plea that crucial evidence against him had been obtained as a result of an illegal search. The accuracy of this affidavit is subject to challenge since petitioner had filed and withdrawn a motion to suppress, before pleading guilty. In addition to his motion to withdraw his guilty plea, petitioner renewed the motion to suppress and filed a motion to inspect the grand jury minutes.

These three motions in turn caused further delay until November 26, 1969, when the court denied all three and set January 9, 1970, as the date for sentencing. On January 9 petitioner appeared before a different judge, the judge who had presided over the case to this juncture having retired. Petitioner renewed his motions, and the court again rejected them. The court then turned to consideration of the sentence.

At this appearance, another prosecutor had replaced the prosecutor who had negotiated the plea. The new prosecutor recommended the maximum one-year sentence. In making this recommendation, he cited petitioner's criminal record and alleged links with organized crime. Defense counsel immediately objected on the ground that the State had promised petitioner before the plea was entered that there would be no sentence recommendation by the prosecution. He sought to adjourn the sentence hearing in order to have time to prepare proof of the first prosecutor's promise. The second prosecutor, apparently ignorant of his colleague's commitment, argued that there was nothing in the record to support petitioner's claim of a promise, but the State, in subsequent proceedings, has not contested that such a promise was made.

The sentencing judge ended discussion, with the following statement, quoting extensively from the pre-sentence report:

> "Mr. Aronstein [Defense Counsel], I am not at all influenced by what the District Attorney says, so that there is no need to adjourn the sentence, and there is no need to have any testimony. It doesn't make a particle of difference what the District Attorney says he will do, or what he doesn't do.

> "I have here, Mr. Aronstein, a probation report. I have here a history of along, long serious criminal record. I have here a picture of the life history of this man . . .
>
> "He is unamenable to supervision in the community. He is a 'professional criminal.' This is in quotes. 'And a recidivist. Institutionalization—'; that means, in plain language, just putting him away, 'is the only means of halting his anti-social activities,' and protecting you, your family, me, my family, protecting society. 'Institutionalization.' Plain language, put him behind bars.
>
> "Under the plea, I can only send him to the New York City Correctional Institution for men for one year, which I am hereby doing."

The judge then imposed the maximum sentence of one year.

* * *

This record represents another example of an unfortunate lapse in orderly prosecutorial procedures, in part, no doubt, because of the enormous increase in the workload of the often understaffed prosecutor's offices. The heavy workload may well explain these episodes, but it does not excuse them. The disposition of criminal charges by agreement between the prosecutor and the accused, sometimes loosely called "plea bargaining," is an essential component of the administration of justice. Properly administered, it is to be encouraged. If every criminal charge were subjected to a full-scale trial, the States and the Federal Government would need to multiply by many times the number of judges and court facilities.

Disposition of charges after plea discussions is not only an essential part of the process but a highly desirable part for many reasons. It leads to prompt and largely final disposition of most criminal cases; it avoids much of the corrosive impact of enforced idleness during pre-trial confinement for those who are denied release pending trial; it protects the public from those accused persons who are prone to continue criminal conduct even while on pre-trial release; and by shortening the time between charge and disposition, it enhances whatever may be the rehabilitative prospects of the guilty when they are ultimately imprisoned. See Brady v. United States (1970).

However, all of these considerations presuppose fairness in securing agreement between an accused and a prosecutor. It is now clear, for example, that the accused pleading guilty must be counseled absent a waiver. Moore v. Michigan (1957). Rule 11, Fed.Rule Crim.Proc., governing pleas in federal courts, now makes clear that the sentencing judge must develop, *on the record*, the factual basis for the plea, as, for example, by having the accused describe the conduct that gave rise to the charge. The plea must, of course, be voluntary and knowing and if it was induced by promises, the essence of those promises must in some way be made known. There is, of course, no absolute right to have a guilty plea accepted. Lynch v. Overholser (1962); Rule 11, Fed.Rule Crim.Proc. A court may reject a plea in exercise of sound judicial discretion.

This phase of the process of criminal justice and the adjudicative element inherent in accepting a plea of guilty, must be attended by safeguards to insure the defendant what is reasonably due in the circumstances. Those circumstances will vary, but a constant factor is that when a plea rests in any significant degree on a promise or agreement of the prosecutor, so that it can be said to be part of the inducement or consideration, such promise must be fulfilled.

On this record, petitioner "bargained" and negotiated for a particular plea in order to secure dismissal of more serious charges, but also on condition that no sentence recommendation would be made by the prosecutor. It is now conceded that the promise to abstain from a recommendation was made, and at this stage the prosecution is not in a good position to argue that its inadvertent breach of agreement is immaterial. The staff lawyers in a prosecutor's office have the burden of "letting the left hand know what the right hand is doing" or has done. That the breach of agreement was inadvertent does not lessen its impact.

We need not reach the question whether the sentencing Judge would or would not have been influenced had he known all the details of the negotiations for the plea. He stated that the prosecutor's recommendation did not influence him and we have no reason to doubt that. Nevertheless, we conclude that the interests of justice and appropriate recognition of the duties of the prosecution in relation to promises made in the negotiation of pleas of guilty will be best served by remanding the case to the state courts for further consideration. The ultimate relief to which petitioner is entitled we leave to the discretion of the state court which is in a better position to decide whether the circumstances of this case require only that there be specific performance of the agreement on the plea, in which case petitioner should be resentenced before a different judge, or whether, in the view of the state court, the circumstances require granting the relief sought by petitioner, i.e., the opportunity to withdraw his plea of guilty.[2] We emphasize that this is in no sense to question the fairness of the sentencing judge; the fault here rests on the prosecutor, not on the sentencing judge.

The judgment is vacated and the case is remanded for reconsideration not inconsistent with this opinion.

■ [MR. JUSTICE DOUGLAS' concurring opinion is omitted.]

■ MR. JUSTICE MARSHALL, with whom MR. JUSTICE BRENNAN and MR. JUSTICE STEWART join, concurring in part and dissenting in part.

I agree with much of the majority's opinion, but conclude that petitioner must be permitted to withdraw his guilty plea. This is the relief petitioner requested and, on the facts set out by the majority, it is a form of relief to which he is entitled.

There is no need to belabor the fact that the Constitution guarantees to all criminal defendants the right to a trial by judge or jury, or, put another way, the "right not to plead guilty." This and other federal rights may be waived through a guilty plea, but such waivers are not lightly presumed and, in fact, are viewed with the "utmost solicitude." Given this, I believe that where the defendant presents a reason for vacating his plea

2. If the state court decides to allow withdrawal of the plea, the petitioner will, of course, plead anew to the original charge on two felony counts.

and the government has not relied on the plea to its disadvantage, the plea may be vacated and the right to trial regained at least where the motion to vacate is made prior to sentence and judgment. In other words, in such circumstances I would not deem the earlier plea to have irrevocably waived the defendant's federal constitutional right to a trial.

Here, petitioner never claimed any automatic right to withdraw a guilty plea before sentencing. Rather, he tendered a specific reason why, in his case, the plea should be vacated. His reason was that the prosecutor had broken a promise made in return for the agreement to plead guilty. When a prosecutor breaks the bargain, he undercuts the basis for the waiver of constitutional rights implicit in the plea. This, it seems to me, provides the defendant ample justification for rescinding the plea. . . . Of course, where the prosecutor has broken the plea agreement, it may be appropriate to permit the defendant to enforce the plea bargain. But that is not the remedy sought here, and it is not a remedy I would require. Rather, it seems to me that a breach of the plea bargain provides ample reason to permit the plea to be vacated.

It is worth noting that in the ordinary case where a motion to vacate is made prior to sentencing, the government has taken no action in reliance on the previously entered guilty plea and would suffer no harm from the plea's withdrawal. More pointedly, here the State claims no such harm beyond disappointed expectations about the plea itself. At least where the government itself has broken the plea bargain, this disappointment cannot bar petitioner from withdrawing his guilty plea and reclaiming his right to a trial.

I would remand the case with instructions that the plea be vacated and petitioner given an opportunity to replead to the original charges in the indictment.

Bordenkircher v. Hayes

Supreme Court of the United States, 1978.
434 U.S. 357, 98 S.Ct. 663.

■ MR. JUSTICE STEWART delivered the opinion of the Court.

* * *

I.

The respondent, Paul Lewis Hayes, was indicted by a Fayette County, Ky., grand jury on a charge of uttering a forged instrument in the amount of $88.30, an offense then punishable by a term of two to 10 years in prison. After arraignment, Hayes, his retained counsel, and the Commonwealth's attorney met in the presence of the clerk of the court to discuss a possible plea agreement. During these conferences the prosecutor offered to recommend a sentence of five years in prison if Hayes would plead guilty to the indictment. He also said that if Hayes did not plead guilty and "save the court the inconvenience and necessity of a trial," he would return to the grand jury to seek an indictment under the Kentucky Habitual Criminal Act, which would subject Hayes to a mandatory sentence of life imprisonment by reason of his two prior felony convictions. Hayes chose not to plead guilty, and the prosecutor did obtain an indictment charging him under the Habitual Criminal Act. It is not disputed that the recidivist charge was fully justified by the evidence, that the prosecutor was in possession of this evidence at the time of the original indictment, and that Hayes' refusal to plead guilty to the original charge was what led to his indictment under the habitual criminal statute.

A jury found Hayes guilty on the principal charge of uttering a forged instrument and, in a separate proceeding, further found that he had twice before been convicted of felonies. As required by the habitual offender statute, he was sentenced to a life term in the penitentiary. The Kentucky Court of Appeals [held] ... that the prosecutor's decision to indict him as an habitual offender was a legitimate use of available leverage in the plea bargaining process.

* * *

II.

It may be helpful to clarify at the outset the nature of the issue in this case. While the prosecutor did not actually obtain the recidivist indictment until after the plea conferences had ended, his intention to do so was clearly put forth at the outset of the plea negotiations. Hayes was thus fully informed of the true terms of the offer when he made his decision to plead not guilty. This is not a situation, therefore, where the prosecutor without notice brought an additional and more serious charge after plea negotiations relating only to the original indictment had ended with the defendant's insistence on pleading not guilty. As a practical matter, in short, this case would be no different if the grand jury had indicted Hayes as a recidivist from the outset, and the prosecutor had offered to drop that charge as part of the plea bargain.

* * *

III.

We have recently had occasion to observe that "[w]hatever might be the situation in an ideal world, the fact is that the guilty plea and the often concomitant plea bargain are important components of this country's criminal justice system. Properly administered, they can benefit all concerned." Blackledge v. Allison. The open acknowledgment of this previously clandestine practice has led this Court to recognize the importance of counsel during plea negotiations, Brady v. United States, the need for a public record indicating that a plea was knowingly and voluntarily made, Boykin v. Alabama, and the requirement that a prosecutor's plea bargaining promise must be kept, Santobello v. New York....

IV.

This Court held in North Carolina v. Pearce that the Due Process Clause of the Fourteenth Amendment "requires that vindictiveness against a defendant for having successfully attacked his first conviction must play no part in the sentence he receives after a new trial." The same principle was later applied to prohibit a prosecutor from reindicting a convicted misdemeanant on a felony charge after the defendant had invoked an appellate remedy, since in this situation there was also a "realistic likelihood of 'vindictiveness.' "

In those cases the Court was dealing with the State's unilateral imposition of a penalty upon a defendant who had chosen to exercise a legal right to attack his original conviction—a situation "very different from the give-and-take negotiation common in plea bargaining between the prosecution and the defense, which arguably possess relatively equal bargaining power." The Court has emphasized that the due process violation in cases such as *Pearce* and *Perry* lay not in the possibility that a defendant might be deterred from the exercise of a legal right, but rather in the danger that the State might be retaliating against the accused for lawfully attacking his conviction.

To punish a person because he has done what the law plainly allows him to do is a due process violation of the most basic sort, and for an agent of the State to pursue a course of action whose objective is to penalize a person's reliance on his legal rights is "patently unconstitutional." . . . But in the "give-and-take" of plea bargaining, there is no such element of punishment or retaliation so long as the accused is free to accept or reject the prosecution's offer.

Plea bargaining flows from "the mutuality of advantage" to defendants and prosecutors, each with his own reasons for wanting to avoid trial. Defendants advised by competent counsel and protected by other procedural safeguards are presumptively capable of intelligent choice in response to prosecutorial persuasion, and unlikely to be driven to false self-condemnation. Indeed, acceptance of the basic legitimacy of plea bargaining necessarily implies rejection of any notion that a guilty plea is involuntary in a constitutional sense simply because it is the end result of the bargaining process. By hypothesis, the plea may have been induced by promises of a recommendation of a lenient sentence or a reduction of charges, and thus by fear of the possibility of a greater penalty upon conviction after a trial. . . .

While confronting a defendant with the risk of more severe punishment clearly may have a "discouraging effect on the defendant's assertion of his trial rights, the imposition of these difficult choices [is] an inevitable"—and permissible—"attribute of any legitimate system which tolerates and encourages the negotiation of pleas." It follows that, by tolerating and encouraging the negotiation of pleas, this Court has necessarily accepted as constitutionally legitimate the simple reality that the prosecutor's interest at the bargaining table is to persuade the defendant to forego his right to plead not guilty.

It is not disputed here that Hayes was properly chargeable under the recidivist statute, since he had in fact been convicted of two previous felonies. In our systems, so long as the prosecutor has probable cause to believe that the accused committed an offense defined by statute, the decision whether or not to prosecute, and what charge to file or bring before a grand jury, generally rests entirely in his discretion. Within the limits set by the legislature's constitutionally valid definition of chargeable offenses, "the conscious exercise of some selectivity in enforcement is not in itself a federal constitutional violation" so long as "the selection was [not] deliberately based upon an unjustifiable standard such as race, religion, or other arbitrary classification." ... To hold that the prosecutor's desire to induce a guilty plea is an "unjustifiable standard," which, like race or religion, may play no part in his charging decision, would contradict the very premises that underlie the concept of plea bargaining itself. Moreover, a rigid constitutional rule that would prohibit a prosecutor from acting forthrightly in his dealings with the defense could only invite unhealthy subterfuge that would drive the practice of plea bargaining back into the shadows from which it has so recently emerged.

There is no doubt that the breadth of discretion that our country's legal system vests in prosecuting attorneys carries with it the potential for both individual and institutional abuse. And broad though that discretion may be, there are undoubtedly constitutional limits upon its exercise. We hold only that the course of conduct engaged in by the prosecutor in this case, which no more than openly presented the defendant with the unpleasant alternatives of foregoing trial or facing charges on which he was plainly subject to prosecution, did not violate the Due Process Clause of the Fourteenth Amendment.

Accordingly, the judgment of the Court of Appeals is

Reversed.

■ MR. JUSTICE BLACKMUN, with whom MR. JUSTICE BRENNAN and MR. JUSTICE MARSHALL join, dissenting.

* * *

The Court now says, however, that concern with vindictiveness is of no import in the present case, despite the difference between five years in prison and a life sentence, because we are here concerned with plea bargaining where there is give-and-take negotiation. ...

* * *

Prosecutorial vindictiveness, it seems to me, in the present narrow context, is the fact against which the Due Process Clause ought to protect. I perceive little difference between vindictiveness after what the Court describes, as the exercise of a "legal right to attack his original conviction," and vindictiveness in the "give-and-take negotiation common in plea bargaining." Prosecutorial vindictiveness in any context is still prosecutorial vindictiveness. The Due Process Clause should protect an accused against it, however it asserts itself....

* * *

■ MR. JUSTICE POWELL, dissenting.

Although I agree with much of the Court's opinion, I am not satisfied that the result in this case is just or that the conduct of the plea bargaining met the requirements of due process.

* * *

It seems to me that the question to be asked under the circumstances is whether the prosecutor reasonably might have charged respondent under the Habitual Criminal Act in the first place. The deference that courts properly accord the exercise of a prosecutor's discretion perhaps would foreclose judicial criticism if the prosecutor originally had sought an indictment under that act, as unreasonable as it would have seemed. But here the prosecutor evidently made a reasonable, responsible judgment not to subject an individual to a mandatory life sentence when his only new offense had societal implications as limited as those accompanying the uttering of a single $88 forged check and when the circumstances of his prior convictions confirmed the inappropriateness of applying the habitual criminal statute. I think it may be inferred that the prosecutor himself deemed it unreasonable and not in the public interest to put this defendant in jeopardy of a sentence of life imprisonment.

There may be situations in which a prosecutor would be fully justified in seeking a fresh indictment for a more serious offense. The most plausible justification might be that it would have been reasonable and in the public interest initially to have charged the defendant with the greater offense. In most cases a court could not know why the harsher indictment was sought, and an inquiry into the prosecutor's motive would neither be indicated nor likely to be fruitful. In those cases, I would agree with the majority that the situation would not differ materially from one in which the higher charge was brought at the outset.

But this is not such a case. Here, any inquiry into the prosecutor's purpose is made unnecessary by his candid acknowledgment that he threatened to procure and in fact procured the habitual criminal indictment because of respondent's insistence on exercising his constitutional rights.

* * *

... Only in the most exceptional case should a court conclude that the scales of the bargaining are so unevenly balanced as to arouse suspicion. In this case, the prosecutor's actions denied respondent due process because their admitted purpose was to discourage and then to penalize with unique severity his exercise of constitutional rights. Implementation of a strategy calculated solely to deter the exercise of constitutional rights is not a constitutionally permissible exercise of discretion....

NOTES

1. Until *Santobello*, plea bargaining was thought to be questionable. The standard approach to admonitions on a plea of guilty required the court to assure itself that no promises had been made; and there was judicial language to support the reluctance to recognize plea bargaining as a valid procedure. Nonetheless, estimates placed the number of cases resolved by plea as high as 95% of all criminal charges, with a substantial number of those the result of plea negotiations. ABA Standards Relating to Pleas of Guilty 1–2 (1st Ed.1968). See Note, Guilty Plea Bargaining: Compromises by Prosecutors to Secure Guilty Pleas, 112 U.Pa.L.Rev. 865 (1964). By the time *Santobello* was decided, the criminal justice system had come to depend upon plea negotiations as an important administrative tool. See People v. West, 3

Cal.3d 595, 91 Cal.Rptr. 385, 477 P.2d 409 (1970). Following the recognition of plea bargaining, the courts began to require that the plea agreement be set forth in the record of the hearing on the plea. See Moody v. United States, 497 F.2d 359 (7th Cir.1974).

There is some dispute over the necessity for plea bargaining. One commentator, after studying the practices in Philadelphia, has concluded it may not be. Schulhofer, Is Plea Bargaining Inevitable? 97 Harv.L.Rev. 1037 (1984). Compare Abraham Goldstein Converging Criminal Justice Systems: Guilty Pleas and The Public Interest, 49 S.M.U. L.Rev. 567 (1996) (European courts adopting plea bargaining). In 1975 Alaska purportedly abolished plea-bargaining of the most usual type, that which occurs after the accused is charged with a particular offense. The Alaska experience is discussed in M. RUBENSTEIN, S. CLARKE, & T. WHITE, ALASKA BANS PLEA BARGAINING (1980).

There is a more profound concern that the prevalence of plea bargaining creates an incentive even for the innocent to plead in the face of institutional reluctance to afford a trial on the merits in a substantial number of cases. A fine study is Wright, Trial Distortion and the End of Innocence in Federal Criminal Justice, 154 U.Pa.L.Rev. 79 (2005). See also Bibas, Plea Bargaining Outside the Shadow of Trial, 117 Harv.L.Rev. 2463 (2004)

2. Fed.R.Crim.P. 11 sanctions plea negotiations and permits the prosecution to move to dismiss other charges, recommend a particular sentence, or agree not to oppose a sentence request by defendant in return for a plea of guilty. The agreement must be stated on the record, and may be accepted or rejected by the court. If the plea is rejected, must the defendant be allowed to withdraw the plea? United States v. Missouri Valley Construction Co., 704 F.2d 1026 (8th Cir.1983) (judge who does not go along with plea agreement reached by the parties must allow the defendant an opportunity to withdraw the plea if the court before the plea did not admonish the defendant that (a) it is not bound by the agreement and that, (b) nevertheless, the defendant will have no opportunity to withdraw the plea.)

If the court advises the defendant that the expected sentence may not be the actual sentence, then the plea may not be withdrawn even when there is great disparity between defense counsel's estimate of the guideline range (78–108 months) and the actual sentence (360 months). United States v. Lambey, 974 F.2d 1389 (4th Cir.1992) (en banc) (9–4) (Plea agreement stated: any estimate of the probable sentencing range "that he may have received from counsel, the government, or the probation officer, is a prediction, not a promise, and is not binding on ... the Court"). However, where defendant is (wrongly) assured that the judge will follow the recommendation the plea may be subject to attack. See United States v. Hammerman, 528 F.2d 326 (4th Cir.1975). A plea entered under the mistaken belief of all that the sentence could be lower than the law required, the plea may be withdrawn. State v. Miller, 110 Wash.2d 528, 756 P.2d 122 (1988).

Plea bargains are usually analyzed under contract law principles though most courts construe ambiguities against the prosecution. United States v. Ingram, 979 F.2d 1179 (7th Cir.1992). Like a contract, a plea agreement can be voided if either party procured it through fraud. United States v. Ballis, 28 F.3d 1399 (5th Cir.1994).

3. Under the Federal Rule, the court may not participate in plea negotiations. A judge's participation could lead the defendant to believe that he would not receive a fair trial before the judge with whom plea negotiations failed. Moreover, the power of the court may induce a defendant to plead guilty rather than risk going to trial before a judge whose plea recommendation the defendant has rejected.

In the following paragraphs the subject matter is the degree to which a court may speak to the virtues of a plea bargain in a jurisdiction where judges are barred from plea negotiations. In many states what is criticized in *O'Neill* and similar cases is permissible in many, if not most, courts.

In jurisdictions which prohibit judicial participation in the "bargaining," a judge, as in federal courts, still may indicate in advance of a plea of guilty whether the judge will go along with the terms of the agreement which has been reached by the parties. Does this allow indirect participation by a judge who indicates his refusal to concur until the parties return with an agreement which satisfies him? There is also a fine line between explaining consequences of plea and coercing a plea. Compare United States v. Johnson, 89 F.3d 778 (11th Cir.1996) (trial is a "gamble"—okay in context) with United States v. Casallas, 59 F.3d 1173 (11th Cir.1995) ("Think carefully about it—life in prison is a long time.")

There is an equally fine line between coercing a plea and explaining why the court refuses to accept an particular plea agreement. It is thoroughly explored in a case in which all three judges came to differing conclusions about the nature and effect of the comments of the trial judge who was an experienced defense counsel in criminal cases before becoming a judge. See United States v. O'Neill, 437 F.3d 654 (7th Cir. 2006)

TERENCE T. EVANS, Circuit Judge.

Mario Morales was a crooked Chicago police officer who soiled his badge by ripping off drug dealers . . . we recount just one of his brazen acts of criminality.

On a May day in 2001, Morales, cloaked in the trappings of a narcotics officer-police badge around his neck and service revolver in hand-entered the residence of a Chicago drug dealer named Jerome Carman. Morales had two nonpolice-officer cohorts with him, James O'Neill (the defendant in this case) and Gerald Cooper. Morales, O'Neill, and Cooper proceeded to relieve Carman of more than 100 kilograms of marijuana and $10,000 in cash. Morales got most of what was obtained.

Eventually, Morales, O'Neill, Cooper, and two others were charged in a superseding indictment with a bevy of charges. Morales ultimately entered a guilty plea [and]was sentenced to 210 months on the racketeering count and a consecutive 84 months on a gun charge, a total of 294 months.

The government, believing that O'Neill's substantial cooperation was critical to its case against Morales, didn't want him to receive a stiff (Morales-type) sentence. That cooperation, among other things, included wearing a wire while meeting several times with an armed Morales. Accordingly, a negotiated lock-in guilty plea under Rule 11 (c) (1) (c) . . . was agreed to . . . [for] the two same charges that Morales was convicted under, called for a total sentence of 124 months. Unfortunately for O'Neill, the judge balked. He said:

I will tell you that I am inclined not to agree to have the sentence bound by the specific sentence you have. I am not saying that I would not ultimately impose that sentence. It is possible that I might impose that sentence, and it is possible that I might be persuaded that that is the appropriate sentence. But I don't think I am willing to agree to a plea agreement that says that is the only sentence I can impose.

It is really a question—as I said, at the outset, it is really a question of—I don't have any quarrel with the proposition that Mr. O'Neill should get credit and potentially very significant credit for what he has done in assisting the government, wearing the wire and being willing to testify against the people in this case, enabling you to charge new people in the case, enabling you in part to go after other people who aren't even in this case and so on, but I object to a provision which basically says this is the exact sentence you have to impose. So I am not going to go along with that provision.

The judge then told O'Neill that he could back out of the plea deal, adding: As I said, I have no quarrel with the 5K1.1 motion [for a lesser sentence, a downward departure from a minimum provided in a guideline, based on cooperation with the prosecution], and that motion, I will tell you, unless I hear something between now and when you come back that I have not heard yet, that motion will be granted, and it is simply a question of deciding how much of a reduction that Mr. O'Neill would get as a result of that.

Should it be the approximately 100 months off ... the low end, or should it be something lesser than that? Quite frankly, I don't think it would be greater than that, but should it be 100 months or should it be something less? In fact, I can't imagine circumstances in which it would be greater than that, I will just tell you that.

But I am not ruling out the possibility that I would agree to that sentence after I, you know, gave you a chance to give me another pitch for that. But unless this is rewritten in a way that gives me leeway in making my own determination of how much of a decrease should be given, then I am not going to go along with it.

So I am—I don't know if the word is rejecting or disagreeing. I am disagreeing or rejecting the term of the particular term of the plea agreement that provides that the sentence will be 124 months. I am not rejecting the part that provides for a departure under 5K1.1, but you are going to have to decide on your end what it is you want to do at this point.

Rebuffed by the judge, the parties returned to the drawing board. Three weeks later the case was again in court, and the judge was advised that the parties were negotiating in an attempt to draft a plea agreement that would be acceptable to the court. During this proceeding, the judge observed:

I will tell you this. I know this isn't your problem, but to the extent you have a problem, I don't have a problem with there being a low end on it, okay. But what I do have a problem with is something that says that it has got to be this or this or, you know, somewhere in here.

Eventually responding, O'Neill's counsel observed:So, Judge, it leaves us between—sort of between a rock and a hard place. Mr. O'Neill desires to plead guilty, but, Judge, to put it, if I may speak freely, he is afraid of getting whacked, and basically by having an agreement that provides for—it basically would be a free-fall upward departure.

Responding to this comment, the judge remarked: There is no free-fall upward departure. I don't even know what you are talking about. You have got a—he has pled to two counts, okay. And assuming I go along with the agreement that has been made to drop the other counts, you know what the maximum is. You know what the range is. I have told you that I am willing to give some consideration under 5K1.1 to his cooperation. So the term, upward departure, doesn't really apply here.

The question is the extent of the downward departure. That is what we are talking about....

.... I am not willing to agree upfront to a specific sentence or even a range of sentences. And you already know what the range is. So like I said, it is 259 on down.

The parties next appeared in court two weeks later with a modified plea agreement in hand. The rather complicated sentencing provision ... read:

> "At the time of sentencing, the government shall make known to the sentencing judge the extent of defendant's cooperation, shall move the Court, pursuant to Sentencing Guideline 5K1.1.... to depart from the ... guidelines range and ... statutory minimum sentences provided ... and to impose the specific sentence agreed to by the parties as outlined below. Defendant understands that the decision to depart from the applicable guidelines range and the statutory minimum sentence rests solely with the Court. However, this Plea Agreement is governed, in part, by Federal Rule of Criminal Procedure 11(c)(1)(C). That is, the parties have agreed that the sentence imposed by the Court shall include a term of imprisonment in the custody of the Bureau of Prisons of between 100% and 50% of the low end of the combined sentencing range for offenses set forth in Counts One and Nine. Each party reserves the right to argue at sentencing their position as to the amount of the downward departure within this range. Other than the agreed term of incarceration, the parties have agreed that the Court remains free to impose the sentence it deems appropriate. If the Court imposes a sentence within this agreed range of incarceration, the defendant may not withdraw this plea as a matter of right ... If, however, the Court refuses to impose a sentence within this agreed range of incarceration, thereby rejecting the Plea Agreement, or otherwise refuses to accept the defendant's plea of guilty, this Agreement shall become null and void and neither party will be bound thereto.

With O'Neill's guilty plea (which, by the way, he has never asked to withdraw) in place, the judge [declared]:

> The way that the sentence will be calculated is this. I will figure out what the sentencing range is under the sentencing guidelines, including whatever mandatory minimums and consecutive things apply, which I have discussed with you on a previous occasion. That will give us a range. What this document says is that whatever the low end of the range is, that your sentence is going to be somewhere between the low end of that range and half of that.

After all was said and done, [t]he judge ... despite observing that O'Neill's cooperation "was significant in taking down Mr. Morales," opted for a stiff sentence, noting that O'Neill was a danger to the community who needed "to be incapacitated." Wrapping up, the judge said:

I am going to grant the motion for a departure, but it is not going to be a departure beyond the low end of the applicable range. I am departing off the high end of the range.

The sentence imposed was 224 months, 140 months on count one and a consecutive 84 months on count nine. O'Neill appeals his sentence, arguing, among other things, that the judge impermissibly injected himself into the plea process in several respects.

Judges, it is well-settled, may not participate in plea negotiations. This proscription against judicial intervention in plea negotiations is widely construed as categorical. *See United States v. Kraus*, 137 F.3d 447, 452 (7th Cir.1998). However, it is also certainly well-established that judges are permitted to take an active role in "evaluating the agreement" in Rule 11(c) cases. *Id.* at 452. Where to draw the line between "intervention" and "evaluating" is where the rubber meets the road in this case.

We think what the judge did here comes close to crossing the line in a Rule 11(c) case. The rule, and the better practice, is simply to reject (without a lot of editorial comment) the plea, give the defendant an opportunity to withdraw it, and advise the defendant that if the plea continues, the judge is not bound by the party's plea agreement.

That said, given that the case must go back for further proceedings under [an unrelated rule] we think it unnecessary to definitively express a view as to whether the judge crossed the permissible line ... we think it's best to send it back completely and let the parties start the sentencing process again from the go position.

We are concerned about certain statements that could have led O'Neill to believe that the recommended 124–month term still might be entered. This carrot-on-a-stick approach—"I'm not saying that I would not impose that [124 month] sentence. It is possible that I might impose that sentence and it is possible that I might be persuaded that that is the appropriate sentence"—very well could have lulled O'Neill into a false sense of comfort. Better the judge says nothing in a situation like this than give, from all appearances here, false hope.

* * *

For these reasons, we vacate O'Neill's sentence and remand the case to the district court for resentencing [by a different judge]

POSNER, Circuit Judge.

We have a three-way split. Judge Evans wants to hold O'Neill to his guilty plea, but remand for resentencing before a different judge. Judge Sykes wants to grant O'Neill just the limited remand [required for reasons unrelated to judicial conduct]. My view is that the plea should be set aside. I join Judge Evans's proposed disposition, however, because his view is nearer to mine than Judge Sykes's is, because we need to decide the case, and because Judge Evans's proposed disposition does do a kind of rough justice; for O'Neill's primary desire is just to be resentenced by another judge rather than to reopen plea negotiations. Nevertheless, at the risk of seeming a fusspot, I cannot accept Judge Evans's analysis. I know that the life of the law has not been logic, but logic does have its claims, which in this case seem to me compelling. Either O'Neill was tricked into pleading guilty or he was not. If he was, the logical remedy is to set aside the plea; if he was not, then as Judge Sykes believes he is entitled to nothing more than a [routine]remand. I think the guilty plea should be set aside, and thus that O'Neill should not be subjected to the risk that the judge to whom the case is reassigned may think Judge Kennelly got it right and sentence O'Neill to the same 224 months.

I do not agree with Judge Sykes that O'Neill "just wants to be resentenced." That is what he'd most like, all right, but as I have said it is not relief to which he is legally entitled. He preserved his (alternative) claim for vacation of the plea, stating in his brief: "Because of the manner in which and the extent to which the district court participated in the plea negotiations in this case, Mr. O'Neill should be entitled to the opportunity to negotiate a plea free of any actual or apparent intervention by the court." We pressed his lawyer at argument: "So that means," one of us asked, "it was an involuntary plea, so he should be given a chance to reconsider, right?" And the lawyer said, "Right." The judge continued, "Isn't that the logic of your position? Vacate the plea, go back to the drawing board, and if there's a new plea or if there's a trial, it will be before a different judge." The lawyer replied, "Yes, your honor."

O'Neill had been charged with nine counts of serious drug-related offenses but had negotiated a plea agreement whereby he would plead guilty to two of them and receive a sentence of 124 months, 100 months below the bottom of the guideline range applicable to his offenses, in recognition of the substantial assistance that he had given the government in rounding up his accomplices.

The agreement provided that if the judge did not agree to the 124–month sentence, the agreement was void. (That is, it was an agreement made on the authority of Rule 11(c)(1)(C) of the Federal Rules of Criminal Procedure.) The judge refused to go along, saying that he rejects as a matter of principle a plea agreement that specifies a particular sentence and hinting that he thought 124 months too lenient a sentence considering the scope of the defendant's criminal activity. The parties then submitted a new agreement which did not specify a sentence but did limit the sentencing range to between the bottom of the applicable range (224 to 259 months) and 50 percent of that bottom, that is, to between 112 and 224 months. The judge accepted the new agreement and sentenced the defendant to 224 months, the bottom of the guidelines range and therefore the top of the range authorized by the second plea agreement.

Obviously the judge thought 124 months, the sentence that the parties had agreed on, too lenient; but as an original matter one well might wonder what business it is of a judge to decide that the government has given too generous a punishment discount to the defendant (and has therefore agreed to too lenient a sentence) in exchange for the defendant's assistance to the government. The decision whether to give such a discount and if so how great a one is quintessentially an exercise of prosecutorial judgment, balancing the deterrent and incapacitative benefits to the government of a longer sentence against the benefits to the government of obtaining the defendant's assistance and encouraging other criminals to assist the government.

The exercise of prosecutorial discretion is a prerogative of the executive branch of government. *Wayte v. United States*, 470 U.S. 598, 607, 105 S.Ct. 1524, 84 L.Ed.2d 547 (1985). Judges in our system do not double as prosecutors, as we had occasion to emphasize in *In re United States*, 345 F.3d 450, 454 (7th Cir.2003), noting that "paradoxically, the plenary prosecutorial power of the executive branch safeguards liberty, for, in conjunction with the plenary legislative power of Congress, it assures that no one can be convicted of a crime without the concurrence of all three branches.... When a judge assumes the power to prosecute, the number shrinks to two." In that case we reversed the district judge's appointment of a special prosecutor to prosecute a crime that the Justice Department had decided not to prosecute. In *United States v. Zingsheim*, 384 F.3d 867, 872–73 (7th Cir.2004), we similarly reversed a standing order by a district judge that imposed various restrictions on motions by prosecutors to reduce a defendant's sentence in recognition of his assistance to the government. A judge's decision not to permit the Justice Department to reward a cooperating defendant with a lighter sentence is an equally unjustified interference with the prosecutorial function.

And when a judge does this, the adversarial method, which is fundamental to Anglo–American jurisprudence, may be compromised, as it was in this case. Although the Department of Justice is dutifully defending the judge's action, it is doing so to maintain good relations with the district court, not because it thinks that what the judge did was right. The judge upended the Department's own agreement.

There is also a futility to such judicial interventions, since the prosecution can give a defendant a sentencing discount by dropping counts or otherwise altering the charges against him, and its decision is not judicially reviewable. *Bordenkircher v. Hayes*, 434 U.S. 357, 364, 98 S.Ct. 663, 54 L.Ed.2d 604 (1978); *United States v. Smith*, 953 F.2d 1060, 1063 (7th Cir.1992). But presumably the 5K1.1 route has some advantages to the government or else it wouldn't use the device as frequently as it does.

The principle that judges in our system are not prosecutors might be thought implicit in the allocation of duties between the executive and the judiciary made by Articles II and III of the Constitution, but it exists in tension with the principle, also rooted in the Constitution, that Congress defines federal crimes and prescribes the punishments for them. Courts have therefore assumed, though perhaps with inadequate attention to the executive's prosecutorial prerogatives, that Congress can forbid all sentencing discounts for cooperation with the government and in the alternative can delegate its control over the discounts to the judiciary. E.g., *United States v. Spillman*, 924 F.2d 721, 724–25 (7th Cir.1991).

Congress followed the alternative route in the Sentencing Reform Act ... which arm[s] judges to do what the district judge did here—reject as being too lenient a sentence specified in a negotiated guilty plea.

A careful listener to what the judge said would have concluded the following: the judge as a matter of principle never accepts a stipulated sentence (a mistaken policy, by the way, as I'll point out, but that is beside the present issue); the judge accepted the government's representation that the defendant had rendered substantial assistance warranting a significant discount and thus the granting of a 5K1.1 motion; the judge might go along with the 100–month discount, but that was probably the most he would permit; probably the discount would be somewhat less.

The careful listener would have been deceived. The defendant got no discount at all. True, he was sentenced at the bottom of the guidelines range, but you can get such a sentence without filing a 5K1.1 motion. (The judge had never signaled that he might impose a sentence above the bottom of the range.) Such a motion is designed to get you *below* the guidelines range. When at the final sentencing hearing the judge said that he was granting a downward departure, only "I am departing off the high end of the range," he was either kidding or misspeaking, for that is not a departure at all. A departure is a sentencing discount or bonus that results in a sentence that is not within the guidelines range. In effect the judge denied the 5K1.1 motion, contrary to what he said he would do.

I am sure the judge was acting in good faith, but with the benefit of hindsight it is apparent that he was playing a cat and mouse game with the defendant. The defendant had a plea agreement with the government that specified a sentence that both he and the government wanted. He did not want to go to trial, possibly on more counts, and face a much higher sentence. The judge misled him by signaling that while the defendant would probably face a higher sentence if he pleaded guilty than 124 months, it would not be much higher.

Sentencing judges are placed in a quandary by being authorized on the one hand to reject a plea that specifies a sentence that the judge considers too lenient and on the other hand being forbidden to "to participate in these discussions," that is, the discussions between the prosecutor and the defense lawyer or defendant that resulted in the plea agreement. If the judge gives no explanation for why he is rejecting the agreement, the defendant is left in the dark, but if he explains the grounds of his rejection he may be thought to have initiated and participated in a discussion looking to the negotiation of a new plea agreement. Reconciling these directives is the judicial equivalent of squaring the circle, if one may judge from cases such as *United States v. Kraus, supra*, 137 F.3d at 453–54. It is another reason against the district judge's policy of refusing to accept the sentence negotiated by the parties.

But even if it would have been proper for the judge just to reject the stipulated sentence with no comment other than that he doesn't accept such stipulations, or with the comment that 100 months were much too much credit for the assistance the defendant had given the government, it was improper to create the impression that the sentence would be close to what the agreement had specified and then impose a much harsher sentence. The judge pulled the rug out from under the defendant. We should not countenance such behavior. The defendant should be allowed to withdraw his plea.

SYKES, Circuit Judge, dissenting.

Judge Kennelly did not impermissibly participate in plea negotiations in violation of Rule 11(c)(1). Rather, he explained his reasons for rejecting the parties' initial plea agreement, as *Kraus* explicitly requires. *United States v. Kraus*, 137 F.3d 447, 453 (7th Cir.1998).

The court's duty of independent evaluation extends with special force to "lock in" plea agreements. "[W]here the parties have agreed to a particular sentence pursuant to [Rule 11(c)(1)(C),] . . . the court has the power . . . and under the Sentencing Guidelines, the explicit obligation—to consider whether that sentence is adequate and to reject the plea agreement if the court finds it not to be." (*Kraus*, 137 F.3d at 453).

When a district court rejects a plea agreement, "it must be able to articulate a sound reason for doing so.". This is to prevent arbitrariness, discipline the exercise of discretion, and facilitate review. This court held in *Kraus* that when a district court rejects a plea agreement, "the court may and, under our precedent, *must* explain why it finds the agreement objectionable." *Id.* (emphasis added). Although the court's explanation "no doubt will have an effect on any future negotiations," it will not be construed as impermissible participation in plea negotiations in violation of Rule 11(c)(1) "[s]o long as the court speaks in the context of 'actively evaluating a plea agreement' . . . and its remarks are confined to the agreement before it." *Id.* (citations omitted).

Judge Kennelly was *required* under *Kraus* to explain why he was rejecting the agreement, and he did so. He confined himself to the terms of the agreement before him and spoke in the context of evaluating that agreement. O'Neill's guilty plea was not tainted by impermissible judicial participation in plea negotiations.

As Judge Posner notes, the usual remedy for impermissible judicial participation in plea negotiations is to set aside the plea, on the theory that judicial participation categorically undermines the plea's voluntariness. *See Kraus*, 137 F.3d at 458. O'Neill did not seek to withdraw his plea or otherwise object to Judge Kennelly's comments in the district court, so he is here on plain error review. Although he is claiming a Rule 11(c)(1) violation, he has not asked us to vacate his plea and conviction. He just wants to be resentenced. But there must be an error for us to grant relief, and there is no sentencing error here apart from the mandatory application of the sentencing guidelines contrary to the remedial opinion in *United States v. Booker*, 543 U.S. 220, 125 S.Ct. 738, 160 L.Ed.2d 621 (2005). The *Booker* error calls for a limited remand under *United States v. Paladino*, 401 F.3d 471 (7th Cir.2005). However, because O'Neill's sentence is within the range stipulated by the plea agreement and the district court did not impermissibly participate in plea negotiations, neither resentencing nor plea withdrawal is warranted. Accordingly, I respectfully dissent.

4. What are the perimeters within which plea negotiations must operate? In essence, what kinds of bargains are fair? Or, by another test, are there any types of promises so likely to convince an innocent defendant to enter a plea of guilty that they should be deemed improper? On policy grounds, should some types of inducements be deemed "out of bounds"? See United States v. Buckley, 847 F.2d 991 (1st Cir.1988) (permissible to include promises of leniency for defendant's brother, even when defendant was entering an *Alford*-type plea of guilty while denying factual guilt). The court noted that the original charges against relatives of the defendant had been brought in good faith and not for purposes of obtaining leverage over the defendant. See People v. Smith, 37 Mich.App. 264, 194 N.W.2d 561 (1971) (improper to promise non-prosecution of accused's wife). See Adelstein, The Negotiated Guilty Plea: A Framework for Analysis, 53 N.Y.U.L.Rev. 783 (1978). In Corbitt v. New Jersey, 439 U.S. 212, 99 S.Ct. 492 (1978), a state statute provided a mandatory sentence for a defendant convicted by a jury of first degree murder. If the accused entered a plea which made a trial unnecessary, however, the court was permitted (but not required) to impose a sentence of thirty years rather than life. The Supreme Court approved the statute, saying that it was proper for a legislature to openly provide for the possibility of leniency in return for a plea. The Court acknowledged that such a scheme might discourage an accused from exercising his rights, but it said that is an inevitable "attribute of any legitimate system which tolerates and encourages the negotiation of pleas."

5. One issue litigated with some frequency after *Santobello* is whether a prosecutor's office which enters into a plea agreement and then breaks that agreement can be required to keep its promise (for example, by reducing charges). Such cases are different from *Santobello* in that a defendant whose plea of guilty has not been accepted is seeking specific performance of the agreement. In Mabry v. Johnson, 467 U.S. 504, 104 S.Ct. 2543, the Supreme Court's holding did not reach the issue. There, after the prosecutor withdrew his "mistaken" offer before the defendant pleaded guilty, the defendant chose to plead guilty again, accepting a less lenient offer. A unanimous court held that the voluntary plea of guilty insulated the conviction from attack. In footnote dicta the Court declared that the accused had no constitutionally enforceable right to specific performance of a plea agreement, at least under the circumstances of this case. Even if his ultimate plea of guilty were vacated, the right to enter a plea of not guilty would be an adequate remedy. See United States v. Papaleo, 853 F.2d 16 (1st Cir.1988) (government may withdraw plea offer until such time as the court approves it or defendant relies upon it to his or her detriment.' In State v. Comstock, 168 Wis.2d 915, 485 N.W.2d 354 (1992), defendant was accused of sexual assault and sexual contact with a person under the age of 16. A plea agreement was reached and the trial judge accepted the plea. A presentence investigation disclosed more information about the harm done to the victim and the victim herself objected to the plea agreement. The trial judge, on his own motion, vacated the plea and reinstated more serious charges which had been dropped as a result of the agreement. On appeal the court analyzed conflicting precedents and held that acceptance of the plea constituted jeopardy and reinstatement of the original charges would violate rules against double jeopardy. The only grounds upon which an accepted plea may be vacated *sua sponte* are found in procuring the plea or deliberate withholding of material information. Two judges concurred calling the case "a perfect example of why trial judges should be very selective in accepting plea bargains." The dissent argued that jeopardy attaches upon conviction or acquittal not upon plea and that this plea agreement was void as a matter of public policy where the victim was not heard before the plea and the judge was not told all the facts.

6. Under the Federal Rule, the defendant has the burden of demonstrating a fair and just reason for withdrawal of a guilty plea once it has been made. Courts have liberally applied the "fair and just" standard to motions to withdraw pleas that are made pre-sentencing. Fair and just reasons for withdrawal include inadequate Rule 11 plea colloquies, newly discovered evidence, intervening circumstances, or any other reason for withdrawing the plea that did not exist when the defendant entered his plea. See United States v. Ortega–Ascanio, 376 F.3d 879, 883 (9th Cir. 2004) (intervening Supreme Court decision that overruled Circuit precendent and gave defendant a plausible ground for dismissal of his indictment); United States v. Davis, 428 F.3d 802 (9th Cir. 2005) (defense counsel's gross mischaracterization of defendant's possible sentence).

In United States v. Torres–Rosario, 447 F.3d 61 (1st Cir. 2006), the defendant sought to withdraw his guilty plea almost immediately after he made it, claiming that he felt pressured by his own lawyer and the government's lawyer, who pressed him very hard to plead and stated, "on my children, if you go to trial, I'm going to give you life, if you don't sign today, for each day that goes by, I'll [sic] will give you two more years." In seeking to withdraw his plea, the defendant disputed the amount of drugs, whether the firearms involved were attributable to him, and his status as a leader or organizer in the conspiracy. The Court of Appeals listed the relevant factors in evaluating a defendant's "fair and just" reason to withdraw a plea as (1) the force of the reasons given for the request, (2) its timing, (3) any assertion of actual innocence, (4) indications that the plea was less than fully informed and voluntary, and (4) possible prejudice to the government. The Court of Appeals upheld the district court's decision to refuse to allow the defendant to withdraw his guilty plea in part because there was no claim of actual innocence.

In United States v. Hyde, 520 U.S. 670, 117 S.Ct. 1630 (1997) the defendant plead guilty, the trial judge accepted the plea but deferred decision on accepting the plea agreement. Before that decision was made defendant unsuccessfully sought to withdraw his plea. The Court of Appeals said he had an absolute right to do so but the Supreme Court reversed. A unanimous Court said:

> The Court of Appeals equated acceptance of the guilty plea with acceptance of the plea agreement, and deferral of the plea agreement with deferral of the guilty plea. Nothing in the text of Rule 11 supports these conclusions. In fact, the text shows that the opposite is true: guilty pleas can be accepted while plea agreements are deferred, and the acceptance of the two can be separated in time.

If the court had decided to reject the plea agreement, it would have turned to subsection (e)(4) of Rule 11. That subsection, a critical one for our purposes, provides:

> "If the court rejects the plea agreement, the court shall ... advise the defendant personally ... that the court is not bound by the plea agreement, afford the defendant the opportunity to then withdraw the plea, and advise the defendant that if the defendant persists in a guilty plea ... the disposition of the case may be less favorable to the defendant than that contemplated by the plea agreement."

Thus, if the court rejects the agreement, the defendant can "then" withdraw his plea for any reason and does not have to comply with Rule 32(e)'s "fair and just reason" requirement. This provision implements the common sense notion that a defendant can no longer be bound by an agreement that the court has refused to sanction....

For the Court of Appeals, the rejection of the plea agreement has no significance: before rejection, the defendant is free to withdraw his plea; after rejection, the same is true. But the text of Rule 11(e)(4) gives the rejection of the agreement a great deal of significance. Only "then" is the defendant granted "the opportunity" to withdraw his plea. The necessary implication of this provision is that if the court has neither rejected nor accepted the agreement, the defendant is not granted "the opportunity to then withdraw" his plea.

Not only is the Court of Appeals' holding contradicted by the very language of the Rules, it also debases the judicial proceeding at which a defendant pleads and the court accepts his plea. After the defendant has sworn in open court that he actually committed the crimes, after he has stated that he is pleading guilty because he is guilty, after the court has found a factual basis for the plea, and after the court has explicitly announced that it accepts the plea, the Court of Appeals would allow the defendant to withdraw his guilty plea simply on a lark.

7. Sometimes the issue is the manner in which the prosecutor complies with the agreement. The opinion in United States v. Benchimol, 471 U.S. 453, 105 S.Ct. 2103 (1985) stated:

The Court of Appeals had this view of the facts:

> "Benchimol agreed to plead guilty. The government concedes that in exchange for the guilty plea it promised to recommend probation with restitution. However, at the sentencing hearing, the presentence report incorrectly stated that the government would stand silent. Benchimol's counsel informed the court that the government instead recommended probation with restitution. The Assistant United States Attorney then stated: 'That is an accurate representation.' "

The Court of Appeals concluded that the Government had breached its plea bargain because, although the Assistant United States Attorney concurred with defense counsel's statement that the Government recommended probation with restitution, it "made no effort to explain its reasons for agreeing to recommend a lenient sentence but rather left an impression with the court of less-than-enthusiastic support for leniency."

We think this holding misconceives the effect of the relevant rules and of the applicable case law. Federal Rule of Criminal Procedure 11(e) provides an elaborate formula for the negotiation of plea bargains, which allows the attorney for the Government to agree to move for dismissal of other charges and to agree that a specific sentence is the appropriate disposition of the case.

It also authorizes the Government attorney to make a recommendation for a particular sentence, or agree not to oppose the defendant's request for such a sentence, with the understanding that such recommendation or request shall not be binding upon the court.

It may well be that the Government in a particular case might commit itself to "enthusiastically" make a particular recommendation to the Court, and it may be that the Government in a particular case might agree to explain to the Court the reasons for the Government's making a particular recommendation. But respondent does not contend, nor did the Court of Appeals find, that the Government had in fact undertaken to do either of these things here. The Court of Appeals simply held that as a matter of law such an undertaking was to be implied from the Government's agreement to recommend a particular sentence. But our view of Rule 11(e) is that it speaks in terms of what the parties in fact agree to, and does not suggest that such implied-in-law terms as were read into this agreement by the Court of Appeals have any place under the Rule.

The Court of Appeals relied on cases such as United States v. Grandinetti, 564 F.2d 723 (5th Cir.1977), and United States v. Brown, 500 F.2d 375 (4th Cir.1974), for the conclusion it reached with respect to the requirement of "enthusiasm," but it appears to us that in each of these cases the Government attorney appearing personally in court at the time of the plea bargain expressed personal reservations about the agreement to which the Government had committed itself. This is quite a different proposition than an appellate determination from a transcript of the record made many years earlier that the Government attorney had "left an impression with the court of less-than-enthusiastic support for leniency." When the Government agrees pursuant to Rule 11(e) to make are commendation with respect to sentence, it must carry out its part of the bargain by making the promised recommendation; but even if Rule 11(e) allows bargaining about degrees of enthusiasm, there appears to have been none here.

Rule 11(e) may well contemplate agreement by the Government in a particular case to state to the court its reasons for making the recommendation which it agrees to make. The Government suggests that spreading on the record its reasons for agreement to a plea bargain in a particular case—for example, that it did not wish to devote scarce resources to a trial of this particular defendant, or that it wished to avoid calling the victim as a witness—would frequently harm, rather than help, the defendant's quest for leniency. These may well be reasons why the defendant would not wish to exact such a commitment from the Government, but for purposes of this case it is enough that no such agreement was made in fact. Since Rule 11(e) speaks generally of the plea bargains that the parties make, it was error for the Court of Appeals to imply as a matter of law a term which the parties themselves did not agree upon.

* * *

8. In another case, the government broke its promise to "make no specific recommendation other than to request that the sentence be within the guideline range" when the prosecutor asked "whether the community at large [had] to wonder, once [Devin's] sentence is completed and he's released back into the community, whether [he made] a genuine change or not." The court reasoned:

> The plain implication of that statement was that Devin should not be released back into the community. The prosecutor added that Devin "had his chance to be a positive influence in the community." The plain

> implication of that statement was that Devin should not be given another chance to be a positive influence in the community. The prosecutor stated that the murder victim did not get a second chance to be a positive influence in the community and urged the Court to "fashion a sentence that is fair and just to the victims in this case." The plain implication of that statement was that a fair and just sentence for Devin would deny him a second chance ... In short, "[o]nly a stubbornly literal mind would refuse to regard the Government's commentary as communicating a [specific recommendation] on sentencing." ... By recommending a "life sentence in all but name," United States v. Pollard, 959 F.2d 1011, 1024 (D.C.Cir. 1992), the government breached its agreement with Devin.

United States v. Hodge, 412 F.3d 479, 487 (3d Cir. 2005).

The government also breaches a plea agreement where it agrees not to argue for sentencing enhancing factors when it argues for those enhancements only after the district court judge's *sua sponte* suggestion. In United States v. Scott, 469 F.3d 1335 (10th Cir. 2006), the court explained that the government cannot rely upon a rigidly literal construction of the language of the agreement to circumvent its end of the bargain and that plea agreements must be construed consistently with the defendant's reasonable understanding of the agreement's terms. The court suggested the government could have responded without breaching either the plea agreement or its duty of candor to the court by providing accurate answers to the court's questions and by explaining its obligations under the plea agreement without expressly arguing for the enhancements. However, a prosecutor was not found to breach an agreement where, after agreeing not to oppose that the base offense level not be increased, the prosecutor introduced the scope of defendant's criminal activity based upon a law enforcement officer's observations. In United States v. Rodriguez–Delma, 456 F.3d 1246, 1251 (10th Cir. 2006), the Government was expressly allowed to make factual representations concerning the investigation because the agreement not to oppose the base offense level was not construed as an agreement not to comment in any fashion on the defendant's role in the conspiracy. See also, United States v. Heard, 359 F.3d 544 (D.C.C. 2004), where lack of specificity in a plea agreement with regard to consecutive versus concurrent sentencing was not construed in favor of defendant, in light of the fact that defense counsel had made clear at sentencing that both parties agreed to disagree on how the sentence was to run and had agreed to leave the matter for the district court to decide.

Sometimes the issue is whether the defendant complied with the agreement. A defendant who agrees to testify and refuses has not complied with his agreement. See Ricketts v. Adamson, 483 U.S. 1, 107 S.Ct. 2680 (1987).

* * *

9. Would the result in *Bordenkircher* have been different if the prosecutor had not advised defense counsel that the consequences of refusing the offer would be the increasing of the charge?

In United States v. Goodwin, 457 U.S. 368, 102 S.Ct. 2485 (1982), after first expressing an interest in plea bargaining, the accused had decided to exercise his right to trial by jury on the pending misdemeanor charges. The prosecutor then obtained a felony indictment. The accused claimed that this was forbidden by the rule of North Carolina v. Pearce, Casebook 945, supra even without a showing that the prosecutor acted out of a vindictive motive. The Supreme Court rejected the claim: "Both *Pearce* and *Blackledge* involved the defendant's exercise of a procedural right that caused a complete retrial after he had been once tried and convicted." In that context a presumption of vindictiveness was warranted. By contrast, "A prosecutor should remain free before trial to exercise ... broad discretion.... An initial decision should not freeze future conduct." The Court added that the "institutional bias against the retrial of a decided question that supported the decisions in *Pearce* and *Blackledge* simply had no counterpart in this case." The Court agreed with the Government's position that the "defendant is free to tender evidence ... that enhanced charges are a direct and unjustifiable penalty for the exercise of a procedural right [but that] only in a rare case would a defendant be able to overcome the presumptive validity of the prosecutor's actions through such a demonstration."

What constitutes proof of actual vindictiveness within the meaning of *Goodwin* and *Bordenkircher*? Is the test a subjective one, requiring proof of mean-spiritedness on the part of the prosecutor? See State v. Halling, 66 Or.App. 180, 672 P.2d 1386 (1983), where, after the defense rejected a plea offer and promised a prolonged litigation, the prosecutor told defense counsel "I have just thought of a way to cause further evil to poor Mr. Halling." She then obtained additional indictments against Halling. There viewing court invalidated the additional charges. Suppose the prosecutor had instead added charges after sincerely saying, "I regret that Mr. Halling has declined such favorable terms and that now I must seek additional charges against poor Halling in order to encourage other defendants to accept our generous plea offers in the future."

Cán a prosecutor, in order to facilitate cooperation of a suspect in an investigation of others, charge an offense which normally he or she would consider too minor to prosecute? See United States v. Ross, 719 F.2d 615 (2d Cir.1983), where the court approved a federal charge involving about one-third of one gram of cocaine, allegedly brought because of the suspect's refusal to cooperate.

10. Where a defendant is permitted to withdraw a guilty plea or successfully attacks a plea on direct appeal or in a collateral proceeding, can he receive greater punishment after trial than he had received following the plea which was vacated? Does it matter if the plea was "negotiated"? Can charges which were dropped be reinstated? Consider these questions in light of North Carolina v. Pearce, 395 U.S. 711, 89 S.Ct. 2072 (1969), Casebook, Chapter 13, Section A5, supra. See also Borman, The Chilled Right to Appeal from a Plea Bargain Conviction: A Due Process Cure, 69 Nw.U.L.Rev. 663 (1974); Comment, The Constitutionality of Reindicting Successful Plea–Bargain Appellants on the Original Higher Charges, 62 Cal.L.Rev. 258 (1974). Does Footnote 2, supra, indicate that the *Santobello* court resolved each of these issues? In United States v. Smith, 584 F.2d 759 (6th Cir.1978), cert. denied 441 U.S. 922, 99 S.Ct. 2030 (1979), after a successful defense attack on a plea of guilty, the prosecution was permitted to reinstate five additional charges and the trial judge was allowed to impose a much larger sentence following trial and conviction.

11. One of the main advantages of a guilty plea (judicial economy) is lost if an evidentiary hearing is later necessary to determine the validity of the plea. How can an evidentiary hearing be avoided if the defendant, sometime after incarceration, claims that he was promised (by defense counsel or prosecutor or judge) that if he entered a plea of guilty he would receive a lesser sentence than he actually received? See Blackledge v. Allison, 431 U.S. 63, 97 S.Ct. 1621 (1977), where a defendant's on-the-record statement, at the time of the plea, that he had received no promises was held *not* to conclusively bar relief under a "broken promise" theory. An increasing number of plea bargains include a waiver of the right to appeal. Are there any reasons to say that knowing appeal waivers are against public policy? Thus far, courts have not found such reasons.

12. The defendant ordinarily is not present at plea bargaining conferences. He apparently has no constitutional right to attend. See People v. Pendergraft, 45

Ill.App.3d 954, 4 Ill.Dec. 553, 360 N.E.2d 489 (1977). Some commentators have argued that "principled" plea bargaining requires that the accused, and perhaps also the victim, be present at plea conferences. See N. Morris & G. Hawkins, The Future of Imprisonment 52–57 (1974). A defendant may avoid being at plea negotiations to avoid making damaging admissions. Such admissions are privileged but a defendant's statements might adversely affect his or her standing with the prosecutor or the court.

Most jurisdictions, including the federal one, have rules which exclude from evidence any statements the defendant might make in plea bargaining. See State v. Pitt, 390 Md. 697, 891 A.2d 312 (2006) (If defendant has made a written proffer of what his testimony would be but then backs out of the agreement, the proffer can be used against him at trial; if it is the prosecution that backs out then the proffer is privileged and inadmissible). Presumably this permits a defendant to tell his side of the story in order to persuade the prosecution to accept a lesser sentence. It also helps the government which may be willing to make concessions in return for testimony and enables the government to learn what that testimony may be.

The Supreme Court recently resolved a long-standing dispute over whether such protection can be waived. Prosecutors had begun to require, as a precondition of plea negotiations, that defendants waive their right to exclusion at least to the extent of allowing impeachment use of plea negotiation statements. The prosecution was, in effect, willing to do without the statements in prosecuting the defendant unless defendant took the witness stand, then it could use the statements to impeach. The Court held that all protections of the federal rules are presumptively waivable and no legislative act or intent supports a contrary conclusion. Two dissenters thought that allowing waiver was inconsistent with the Congressional intent to promote plea negotiations. Three concurring justices emphasize that the matter might be differently decided if the government had insisted on the right to use the statements in its case in chief. See United States v. Mezzanatto, 513 U.S. 196, 115 S.Ct. 797 (1995).

The debate about the effect on plea bargaining is interesting. Justice Thomas said for the majority:

> We need not decide whether and under what circumstances substantial "public policy" interests may permit the inference that Congress intended to override the presumption of waivability, for in this case there is no basis for concluding that waiver will interfere with the Rules' goal of encouraging plea bargaining. The court below focused entirely on the *defendant's* incentives and completely ignored the other essential party to the transaction: the prosecutor. Thus, although the availability of waiver may discourage some defendants from negotiating, it is also true that prosecutors may be unwilling to proceed without it.
>
> Prosecutors may be especially reluctant to negotiate without a waiver agreement during the early stages of a criminal investigation, when prosecutors are searching for leads and suspects may be willing to offer information in exchange for some form of immunity or leniency in sentencing. In this "cooperation" context, prosecutors face "painfully delicate" choices as to "whether to proceed and prosecute those suspects against whom the already produced evidence makes a case or whether to extend leniency or full immunity to some suspects in order to procure testimony against other, more dangerous suspects against whom existing evidence is flimsy or nonexistent." Hughes, Agreements for Cooperation in Criminal Cases, 45 Vand.L.Rev. 1, 15 (1992). Because prosecutors have limited resources and must be able to answer "sensitive questions about the credibility of the testimony" they receive before entering into any sort of cooperation

agreement, id., at 10, prosecutors may condition cooperation discussions on an agreement that the testimony provided may be used for impeachment purposes.See Thompson & Sumner, Structuring Informal Immunity, 8 Crim.Just. 16, 19 (spring 1993). If prosecutors were precluded from securing such agreements,they might well decline to enter into cooperation discussions in the first place and might never take this potential first step toward a plea bargain.

Indeed, as a logical matter, it simply makes no sense to conclude that mutual settlement will be encouraged by precluding negotiation over an issue that may be particularly important to one of the parties to the transaction. A sounder way to encourage settlement is to permit the interested parties to enter into knowing and voluntary negotiations without any arbitrary limits on their bargaining chips. To use the Ninth Circuit's metaphor, if the prosecutor is interested in "buying" the reliability assurance that accompanies a waiver agreement, then precluding waiver can only stifle the market for plea bargains. A defendant can "maximize" what he has to "sell" only if he is permitted to offer what the prosecutor is most interested in buying. And while it is certainly true that prosecutors often need help from the small fish in a conspiracy in order to catch the big ones, that is no reason to preclude waiver altogether. If prosecutors decide that certain crucial information will be gained only by preserving the inadmissibility of plea statements, they will agree to leave intact the exclusionary provisions of the plea-statement Rules.

In dissent, Justice Souter said:

Whether Congress was right or wrong that unrestrained candor is necessary to promote a reasonable number of plea agreements, Congress assumed that there was such a need and meant to satisfy it by these Rules. Since the zone of unrestrained candor is diminished whenever a defendant has to stop to think about the amount of trouble his openness may cause him if the plea negotiations fall through, Congress must have understood that the judicial system's interest in candid plea discussions would be threatened by recognizing waivers under Rules 410 and 11(e)(6). See ABA Standards for Criminal Justice 14–3.4, commentary (2d ed. 1980) (a rule contrary to the one adopted by Congress "would discourage plea negotiations and agreements, for defendants would have to be constantly concerned whether, in light of their plea negotiation activities, they could successfully defend on the merits if a plea ultimately was not entered"). There is, indeed, no indication that Congress intended merely a regime of such limited openness as might happen to survive market forces sufficient to supplant a default rule of inadmissibility.

* * *

The unlikelihood that Congress intended the modest default rule that the majority sees in Rules 11(e)(6) and 410 looms all the larger when the consequences of the majority position are pursued. The first consequence is that the Rules will probably not even function as default rules, for there is little chance that they will be applied at all. Already, standard forms indicate that many federal prosecutors routinely require waiver of Rules 410 and 11(e)(6) rights before a prosecutor is willing to enter into plea discussions. Pet. for Cert. 10–11. See also United States v. Stevens, 935 F.2d 1380, 1396 (3d Cir.1991) ("Plea agreements . . . commonly contain a provision stating that proffer information that is disclosed during the course of plea negotiations is . . . admissible for purposes of impeachment"). As the Government conceded during oral argument, defendants are generally in no position to challenge demands for these waivers, and the use of waiver provisions as contracts of adhesion has become accepted practice. Today's decision can only speed the heretofore illegitimate process by which the exception has been swallowing the Rules.

The second consequence likely to emerge from today's decision is the practical certainty that the waiver demanded will in time come to function as a waiver of trial itself. It is true that many (if not all) of the waiver forms now employed go only to admissibility for impeachment. But although the erosion of the Rules has begun with this trickle, the majority's reasoning will provide no principled limit to it. The Rules draw no distinction between use of a statement for impeachment and use in the Government's case in chief. If objection can be waived for impeachment use, it can be waived for use as affirmative evidence, and if the government can effectively demand waiver in the former instance, there is no reason to believe it will not do so just as successfully in the latter. When it does, there is nothing this Court will legitimately be able to do about it. The Court is construing a congressional Rule on the theory that Congress meant to permit its waiver. Once that point is passed, as it is today, there is no legitimate limit on admissibility of a defendant's plea negotiation statements beyond what the Constitution may independently impose or the traffic may bear. Just what the traffic may bear is an open question, but what cannot be denied is that the majority opinion sanctions a demand for waiver of such scope that a defendant who gives it will be unable even to acknowledge his desire to negotiate a guilty plea without furnishing admissible evidence against himself then and there. In such cases, the possibility of trial if no agreement is reached will be reduced to fantasy. The only defendant who will not damage himself by even the most restrained candor will be the one so desperate that he might as well walk into court and enter a naked guilty plea. It defies reason to think that Congress intended to invite such a result, when it adopted a Rule said to promote candid discussion in the interest of encouraging compromise.

13. A series of new statutes has given victims of crime the right to voice their point of view during plea procedures. The practical and, particularly, the legal effect of such procedures is yet to be resolved. For a report on an experimental program in which victims and defendants were allowed to participate in the plea-negotiating session, see Heinz and Kerstetter, Pretrial Settlement Conference: Evaluation of Reform in Plea Bargaining, 13 Law and Society Review 349 (1979). See State v. McDonnell, 310 Or. 98, 794 P.2d 780 (1990) (improper to permit victims to make final decision whether to accept the plea; prosecutor may consult with victims but may not be bound by their will).

14. Pleas of guilty are always entered for very practical reasons. Even if the defendant is clearly guilty and the state has overwhelming proof and even where the sentence is perfectly just, the reasons for taking the plea are essentially practical. The plea saves the resources of the legal system. This inherent practicality underlying the plea decision is thought by some to distort the system of justice: ". . . when criminal cases are compromised, the rule of law is invariably sacrificed to the rule of convenience." Alschuler, The Prosecutor's Role in Plea Bargaining, 36 U.Chi.L.Rev. 50, 85 (1968).

Criminal laws may be passed by state legislatures; but the degree of enforcement is determined by the appropriations for courts and prosecutors—appropriations often determined by county boards.

15. Some prosecutors in multiple defendant cases will refuse to negotiate a plea with one defendant unless all defendants plead—this to insure that the time and expense of a trial is avoided completely and to avoid having the one who pleads then become an adverse witness in the trial of the others. Courts have found these prosecutorial motives to be proper and approve "package deal" plea bargains yet require special scrutiny of such bargains by the trial court. In re Ibarra, 34 Cal.3d 277, 193 Cal.Rptr. 538, 666 P.2d 980 (1983); United States v. Hodge, 412 F.3d 479 (3d Cir. 2005) Howell v. State, 185 S.W.3d 319 (Tenn. 2006) (reviewing precedents)

16. Does a defense attorney have a duty to convey a plea-agreement offer to the defendant, or can he reject the government's offer out of hand without informing the client. In dictum the court in Johnson v. Duckworth, 793 F.2d 898 (7th Cir.1986), noted that such an obligation exists and cited numerous cases that had so held, as well as various model rules and standards so providing.

CHAPTER 17

TRIAL BY JURY

A. RIGHT TO JURY TRIAL

1. SCOPE OF THE RIGHT

Duncan v. Louisiana

Supreme Court of the United States, 1968.
391 U.S. 145, 88 S.Ct. 1444.

■ MR. JUSTICE WHITE delivered the opinion of the Court.

Appellant, Gary Duncan, was convicted of simple battery in the Twenty-fifth Judicial District Court of Louisiana. Under Louisiana law simple battery is a misdemeanor, punishable by a maximum of two years' imprisonment and a $300 fine. Appellant sought trial by jury, but because the Louisiana Constitution grants jury trials only in cases in which capital punishment or imprisonment at hard labor may be imposed, the trial judge denied the request. Appellant was convicted and sentenced to serve 60 days in the parish prison and pay a fine of $150.

* * *

I.

The Fourteenth Amendment denies the States the power to "deprive any person of life, liberty, or property, without due process of law." In resolving conflicting claims concerning the meaning of this spacious language, the Court has looked increasingly to the Bill of Rights for guidance; many of the rights guaranteed by the first eight Amendments to the Constitution have been held to be protected against state action by the Due Process Clause of the Fourteenth Amendment.

* * *

The test for determining whether a right extended by the Fifth and Sixth Amendments with respect to federal criminal proceedings is also protected against state action by the Fourteenth Amendment has been phrased in a variety of ways in the opinions of this Court. The question has been asked whether a right is among those "fundamental principles of liberty and justice which lie at the base of all our civil and political institutions," whether it is "basic in our system of jurisprudence,"; and whether it is "a fundamental right, essential to a fair trial." The claim before us is that the right to trial by jury guaranteed by the Sixth Amendment meets these tests. The position of Louisiana, on the other hand, is that the Constitution imposes upon the States no duty to give a jury trial in any criminal case, regardless of the seriousness of the crime or the size of the punishment which may be imposed. Because we believe that trial by jury in criminal cases is fundamental to the American scheme of justice, we hold that the Fourteenth Amendment guarantees a right of jury trial in all criminal cases which—were they to be tried in a federal court—would come within the Sixth Amendment's guarantee. Since we consider the appeal before us to be such a case, we hold that the Constitution was violated when appellant's demand for jury trial was refused.

The history of trial by jury in criminal cases has been frequently told. It is sufficient for present purposes to say that by the time our Constitution was written, jury trial in criminal cases had been in existence in England for several centuries and carried impressive credentials traced by many to Magna Carta. Its preservation and proper operation as a protection against arbitrary rule were among the major objectives of the revolutionary settlement which was expressed in the Declaration and Bill of Rights of 1689.

* * *

Jury trial came to America with English colonists, and received strong support from them. Royal interference with the jury trial was deeply resented. Among the resolutions adopted by the First Congress of the American Colonies (the Stamp Act Congress) on October 19, 1765—resolutions deemed by their authors to state "the most essential rights and liberties of the colonists"—was the declaration:

> "That trial by jury is the inherent and invaluable right of every British subject in these colonies."

The First Continental Congress, in the resolve of October 14, 1774, objected to trials before judges dependent upon the Crown alone for their salaries and to trials in England for alleged crimes committed in the colonies; the Congress therefore declared:

> "That the respective colonies are entitled to the common law of England, and more especially to the great and inestimable privilege of being tried by their peers of the vicinage, according to the course of that law."

The Declaration of Independence stated solemn objections to the King's making "judges dependent on his will alone, for the tenure of their offices, and the amount and payment of their salaries," to his "depriving us in many cases, of the benefits of Trial by Jury," and to his "transporting us beyond Seas to be tried for pretended offenses." The Constitution itself, in Art. III. § 2, commanded:

> "The Trial of all Crimes, except in Cases of Impeachment, shall be by Jury; and such Trial shall be held in the State where the said Crimes shall have been committed."

Objections to the Constitution because of the absence of a bill of rights were met by the immediate submission and adoption of the Bill of Rights. Included was the Sixth Amendment which, among other things, provided:

"In all criminal prosecutions, the accused shall enjoy the right to a speedy and public trial, by an impartial jury of the State and district wherein the crime shall have been committed."[20]

The constitutions adopted by the original States guaranteed jury trial. Also, the constitution of every State entering the Union thereafter in one form or another protected the right to jury trial in criminal cases.

Even such skeletal history is impressive support for considering the right to jury trial in criminal cases to be fundamental to our system of justice, an importance frequently recognized in the opinions of this Court.

* * *

The guarantees of jury trial in the Federal and State Constitutions reflect a profound judgment about the way in which law should be enforced and justice administered. A right to jury trial is granted to criminal defendants in order to prevent oppression by the Government. Those who wrote our constitutions knew from history and experience that it was necessary to protect against unfounded criminal charges brought to eliminate enemies and against judges too responsive to the voice of higher authority. The framers of the constitutions strove to create an independent judiciary but insisted upon further protection against arbitrary action. Providing an accused with the right to be tried by a jury of his peers gave him an inestimable safeguard against the corrupt or overzealous prosecutor and against the compliant, biased, or eccentric judge. If the defendant preferred the common-sense judgment of a jury to the more tutored but perhaps less sympathetic reaction of the single judge, he was to have it. Beyond this, the jury trial provisions in the Federal and State Constitutions reflect a fundamental decision about the exercise of official power—a reluctance to entrust plenary powers over the life and liberty of the citizen to one judge or to a group of judges. Fear of unchecked power, so typical of our State and Federal Governments in other respects, found expression in the criminal law in this insistence upon community participation in the determination of guilt or innocence. The deep commitment of the Nation to the right of jury trial in serious criminal cases as a defense against arbitrary law enforcement qualifies for protection under the Due Process Clause of the Fourteenth Amendment, and must therefore be respected by the States.

Of course jury trial has "its weaknesses and the potential for misuse." We are aware of the long debate, especially in this century, among those who write about the administration of justice, as to the wisdom of permitting untrained laymen to determine the facts in civil and criminal proceedings. Although the debate has been intense, with powerful voices on either side, most of the controversy has centered on the jury in civil cases. Indeed,

20. Among the proposed amendments adopted by the House of Representatives in 1789 and submitted to the Senate was Article Fourteen:

> "No State shall infringe the right of trial by Jury in criminal cases, nor the rights of conscience, nor the freedom of speech, or of the press."

The Senate deleted this article in adopting the amendments which became the Bill of Rights. This relatively clear indication that the framers of the Sixth Amendment did not intend its jury trial requirement to bind the States is, of course, of little relevance to interpreting the Due Process Clause of the Fourteenth Amendment, adopted specifically to place limitations upon the States.

some of the severest critics of civil juries acknowledge that the arguments for criminal juries are much stronger. In addition, at the heart of the dispute have been express or implicit assertions that juries are incapable of adequately understanding evidence or determining issues of fact, and that they are unpredictable, quixotic, and little better than a roll of dice. Yet, the most recent and exhaustive study of the jury in criminal cases concluded that juries do understand the evidence and come to sound conclusions in most of the cases presented to them and that when juries differ with the result at which the judge would have arrived, it is usually because they are serving some of the very purposes for which they were created and for which they are now employed.

The State of Louisiana urges that holding that the Fourteenth Amendment assures a right to jury trial will cast doubt on the integrity of every trial conducted without a jury. Plainly, this is not the import of our holding. Our conclusion is that in the American States, as in the federal judicial system, a general grant of jury trial for serious offenses is a fundamental right, essential for preventing miscarriages of justice and for assuring that fair trials are provided for all defendants. We would not assert, however, that every criminal trial—or any particular trial—held before a judge alone is unfair or that a defendant may never be as fairly treated by a judge as he would be by a jury. Thus we hold no constitutional doubts about the practices, common in both federal and state courts, of accepting waivers of jury trial and prosecuting petty crimes without extending a right to jury trial. However, the fact is that in most places more trials for serious crimes are to juries than to a court alone; a great many defendants prefer the judgment of a jury to that of a court. Even where defendants are satisfied with bench trials, the right to a jury trial very likely serves its intended purpose of making judicial or prosecutorial unfairness less likely.

II.

Louisiana's final contention is that even if it must grant jury trials in serious criminal cases, the conviction before us is valid and constitutional because here the petitioner was tried for simple battery and was sentenced to only 60 days in the parish prison. We are not persuaded. It is doubtless true that there is a category of petty crimes or offenses which is not subject to the Sixth Amendment jury trial provision and should not be subject to the Fourteenth Amendment jury trial requirement here applied to the States. Crimes carrying possible penalties up to six months do not require a jury trial if they otherwise qualify as petty offenses. But the penalty authorized for a particular crime is of major relevance in determining whether it is serious or not and may in itself, if severe enough, subject the trial to the mandates of the Sixth Amendment.

* * *

In the case before us the Legislature of Louisiana has made simple battery a criminal offense punishable by imprisonment for up to two years and a fine. The question, then, is whether a crime carrying such a penalty is an offense which Louisiana may insist on trying without a jury.

We think not. So-called petty offenses were tried without juries both in England and in the Colonies and have always been held to be exempt from the otherwise comprehensive language of the Sixth Amendment's jury trial provisions. There is no substantial evidence that the Framers intended to depart from this established common-law practice, and the possible consequences to defendants from convictions for petty offenses have been thought insufficient to outweigh the benefits to efficient law enforcement and simplified judicial administration resulting from the availability of speedy and inexpensive nonjury adjudications. These same considerations compel the same result under the Fourteenth Amendment. Of course the boundaries of the petty offense category have always been ill-defined, if not ambulatory. In the absence of an explicit constitutional provision, the definitional task necessarily falls on the courts, which must either pass upon the validity of legislative attempts to identify those petty offenses which are exempt from jury trial or, where the legislature has not addressed itself to the problem, themselves face the question in the first instance. In either case it is necessary to draw a line in the spectrum of crime, separating petty from serious infractions. This process, although essential, cannot be wholly satisfactory, for it requires attaching different consequences to events which, when they lie near the line, actually differ very little.

In determining whether the length of the authorized prison term or the seriousness of other punishment is enough in itself to require a jury trial, we are counseled . . . to refer to objective criteria, chiefly the existing laws and practices in the Nation. In the federal system, petty offenses are defined as those punishable by no more than six months in prison and a $500 fine. In 49 of the 50 States crimes subject to trial without a jury, which occasionally include simple battery, are punishable by no more than one year in jail. Moreover, in the late 18th century in America crimes triable without a jury were for the most part punishable by no more than a six-month prison term, although there appear to have been exceptions to this rule. We need not, however, settle in this case the exact location of the line between petty offenses and serious crimes. It is sufficient for our purposes to hold that a crime punishable by two years in prison is, based on past and contemporary standards in this country, a serious crime and not a petty offense. Consequently, appellant was entitled to a jury trial and it was error to deny it.

The judgment below is reversed and the case is remanded for proceedings not inconsistent with this opinion.

Reversed and remanded.

■ MR. JUSTICE BLACK, with whom MR. JUSTICE DOUGLAS joins, concurring.

The Court today holds that the right to trial by jury guaranteed defendants in criminal cases in federal courts by Art. III of the United States Constitution and by the Sixth Amendment is also guaranteed by the Fourteenth Amendment to defendants tried in state courts. With this holding I agree for reasons given by the Court. I also agree because of reasons given in my dissent in Adamson v. People of State of California, 332 U.S. 46, 68, 67 S.Ct. 1672, 1683. In that dissent I took the position that the Fourteenth Amendment made all of the provisions of the Bill of Rights applicable to the States.

* * *

What I wrote there in 1947 was the product of years of study and research. My appraisal of the legislative history followed 10 years of legislative experience as a Senator of the United States, not a bad way, I suspect, to learn the value of what is said in legislative debates, committee discussions, committee reports, and various other steps taken in the course of passage of bills, resolutions, and proposed constitutional amendments.

* * *

[The dissent argues] that "due process of law requires only fundamental fairness." But the "fundamental fairness" test is one on a par with that of shocking the conscience of the Court. Each of such tests depends entirely on the particular judge's idea of ethics and morals instead of requiring him to depend on the boundaries fixed by the written words of the Constitution. Nothing in the history of the phrase "due process of law" suggests that constitutional controls are to depend on any particular judge's sense of values. The origin of the Due Process Clause is Chapter 39 of Magna Carta which declares that "No free man shall be taken, outlawed, banished, or in any way destroyed, nor will We proceed against or prosecute him, except by the lawful judgment of his peers and by the *law of the land*." (Emphasis added.) As early as 1354 the words "due process of law" were used in an English statute interpreting Magna Carta, and by the end of the 14th century "due process of law" and "law of the land" were interchangeable. Thus the origin of this clause was an attempt by those who wrote Magna Carta to do away with the so-called trials of that period where people were liable to sudden arrest and summary conviction in courts and by judicial commissions with no sure and definite procedural protections and under laws that might have been improvised to try their particular cases. Chapter 39 of Magna Carta was a guarantee that the government would take neither life, liberty, nor property without a trial in accord with the law of the land that already existed at the time the alleged offense was committed. This means that the Due Process Clause gives all Americans, whoever they are and wherever they happen to be, the right to be tried by independent and unprejudiced courts using established procedures and applying valid pre-existing laws. There is not one word of legal history that justifies making the term "due process of law" mean a guarantee of a trial free from laws and conduct which the courts deem at the time to be "arbitrary," "unreasonable," "unfair," or "contrary to civilized standards." The due process of law standard for a trial is one in accordance with the Bill of Rights and laws passed pursuant to constitutional power, guaranteeing to all alike a trial under the general law of the land.

* * *

■ MR. JUSTICE FORTAS, concurring. [OMITTED.]

■ MR. JUSTICE HARLAN, whom MR. JUSTICE STEWART joins, dissenting.

Every American jurisdiction provides for trial by jury in criminal cases. The question before us is not whether jury trial is an ancient institution, which it is; nor whether it plays a significant role in the administration of criminal justice, which it does; nor whether it will endure, which it shall. The question in this case is whether the State of Louisiana, which provides trial by jury for all felonies, is prohibited by the Constitution from trying charges of simple battery to the court alone. In my view, the answer to that question, mandated alike by our constitutional history and by the longer history of trial by jury, is clearly "no."

The States have always borne primary responsibility for operating the machinery of criminal justice within their borders, and adapting it to their particular circumstances. In exercising this responsibility, each State is compelled to conform its procedures to the requirements of the Federal Constitution. The Due Process Clause of the Fourteenth Amendment requires that those procedures be fundamentally fair in all respects. It does not, in my view, impose or encourage nationwide uniformity for its own sake; it does not command adherence to forms that happen to be old; and it does not impose on the States the rules that may be in force in the federal courts except where such rules are also found to be essential to basic fairness.

* * *

It can hardly be gainsaid, however, that the principal original virtue of the jury trial—the limitations a jury imposes on a tyrannous judiciary—has largely disappeared. We no longer live in a medieval or colonial society. Judges enforce laws enacted by democratic decision, not by regal fiat. They are elected by the people or appointed by the people's elected officials, and are responsible not to a distant monarch alone but to reviewing courts, including this one.

The jury system can also be said to have some inherent defects, which are multiplied by the emergence of the criminal law from the relative simplicity that existed when the jury system was devised. It is a cumbersome process, not only imposing great cost in time and money on both the State and the jurors themselves, but also contributing to delay in the machinery of justice. Untrained jurors are presumably less adept at reaching accurate conclusions of fact than judges, particularly if the issues are many or complex. And it is argued by some that trial by jury, far from increasing public respect for law, impairs it: the average man, it is said, reacts favorably neither to the notion that matters he knows to be complex are being decided by other average men, nor to the way the jury system distorts the process of adjudication.

* * *

... I therefore see no reason why this Court should reverse the conviction of appellant, absent any suggestion that his particular trial was in fact unfair, or compel the State of Louisiana to afford jury trial in an as yet unbounded category of cases that can, without unfairness, be tried to a court.

Indeed, even if I were persuaded that trial by jury is a fundamental right in some criminal cases, I could see nothing fundamental in the rule, not yet formulated by the Court, that places the prosecution of appellant for simple battery within the category of "jury crimes" rather than "petty crimes."

Lewis v. United States

Supreme Court of the United States, 1996.
518 U.S. 322, 116 S.Ct. 2163.

■ JUSTICE O'CONNOR delivered the opinion of the Court.

This case presents the question whether a defendant who is prosecuted in a single proceeding for multiple petty offenses has a constitutional right to a jury trial where the aggregate prison term authorized for the offenses exceeds six months. * * *

We conclude that no jury-trial right exists where a defendant is prosecuted for multiple petty offenses. The Sixth Amendment's guarantee of the right to a jury trial does not extend to petty offenses, and its scope does not change where a defendant faces a potential aggregate prison term in excess of six months for petty offenses charged. * * *

Petitioner Ray Lewis was a mail handler for the United States Postal Service. One day, postal inspectors saw him open several pieces of mail and pocket the contents. The next day, the inspectors routed "test" mail, containing marked currency, through petitioner's station. After seeing petitioner open the mail and remove the currency, the inspectors arrested him. Petitioner was charged with two counts of obstructing the mail. Each count carried a maximum authorized prison sentence of six months. Petitioner requested a jury, but the magistrate judge granted the Government's motion for a bench trial. She explained that because she would not, under any circumstances, sentence petitioner to more than six months' imprisonment, he was not entitled to a jury trial.

* * *

The Sixth Amendment guarantees that "[i]n all criminal prosecutions, the accused shall enjoy the right to a speedy and public trial, by an impartial jury of the State and district wherein the crime shall have been committed...." It is well-established that the Sixth Amendment, like the common law, reserves this jury-trial right for prosecutions of serious offenses, and that "there is a category of petty crimes or offenses which is not subject to the Sixth Amendment jury trial provision."

To determine whether an offense is properly characterized as "petty," courts at one time looked to the nature of the offense and whether it was triable by a jury at common law. Such determinations became difficult, because many statutory offenses lack common-law antecedents. Therefore, more recently, we have instead sought "objective indications of the seriousness with which society regards the offense." Now, to determine whether an offense is petty, we consider the maximum penalty attached to the offense. This criterion is considered the most relevant with which to assess the character of an offense, because it reveals the legislature's judgment about the offense's severity. "The judiciary should not substitute its judgment as to seriousness for that of a legislature, which is far better equipped to perform the task...." In evaluating the seriousness of the offense, we place primary emphasis on the maximum prison term authorized. While penalties such as probation or a fine may infringe on a defendant's freedom, the deprivation of liberty imposed by imprisonment makes that penalty the best indicator of whether the legislature considered an offense to be "petty" or "serious." An offense carrying a maximum prison term of six months or less is presumed petty, unless the legislature has authorized additional statutory penalties so severe as to indicate that the legislature considered the offense serious.

Here, the maximum authorized penalty for obstruction of mail is six months' imprisonment—a penalty that presumptively places the offense in the "petty" category. We face the question whether petitioner is nevertheless entitled to a jury trial, because he was tried in a single proceeding for two counts of the petty offense so that the potential aggregated penalty is 12 months' imprisonment.

Petitioner argues that, where a defendant is charged with multiple petty offenses in a single prosecution, the Sixth Amendment requires that the aggregate potential penalty be the basis for determining whether a jury trial is required. Although each offense charged here was petty, petitioner faced a potential penalty of more than six months' imprisonment; and, of course, if any offense charged had authorized more than six months' imprisonment, he would have been entitled to a jury trial. The Court must look to the aggregate potential prison term to determine the existence of the jury-trial right, petitioner contends, not to the "petty" character of the offenses charged.

We disagree. The Sixth Amendment reserves the jury-trial right to defendants accused of serious crimes. As set forth above, we determine whether an offense is serious by looking to the judgment of the legislature, primarily as expressed in the maximum authorized term of imprisonment. Here, by setting the maximum authorized prison term at six months, the legislature categorized the offense of obstructing the mail as petty. The fact that the petitioner was charged with two counts of a petty offense does not revise the legislative judgment as to the gravity of that particular offense, nor does it transform the petty offense into a serious one, to which the jury-trial right would apply. * * *

Petitioner nevertheless insists that a defendant is entitled to a jury trial whenever he faces a deprivation of liberty for a period exceeding six months, a proposition for which he cites our precedent establishing the six-months' prison sentence as the presumptive cut-off for determining whether an offense is "petty" or "serious." To be sure, in the cases in which we sought to determine the line between "petty" and "serious" for Sixth Amendment purposes, we considered the severity of the authorized deprivation of liberty as an indicator of the legislature's appraisal of the offense. But it is now settled that a legislature's determination that an offense carries a maximum prison terms of six months or less indicates its view that an offense is "petty." Where we have a judgment by the legislature that an offense is "petty," we do not look to the potential prison term faced by a particular defendant who is charged with more than one such petty offense. The maximum authorized penalty provides an "objective indicatio[n] of the seriousness with which society regards the offense," and it is that indication that is used to determine whether a jury trial is required, not the particularities of an individual case. Here, the penalty authorized by Congress manifests its judgment that the offense is petty, and the term of imprisonment faced by petitioner by virtue of the second count does not alter that fact.

* * *

Certainly the aggregate potential penalty faced by petitioner is of serious importance to him. But to determine whether an offense is serious for Sixth Amendment purposes, we look to the legislature's judgment, as evidenced by the maximum penalty authorized. Where the offenses charged are petty, and the deprivation of liberty exceeds six months only as a result of the aggregation of charges, the jury-trial right does not apply. As petitioner acknowledges, even if he were to prevail, the Government could properly circumvent the jury-trial right by charging the counts in separate informations and trying them separately.

The Constitution's guarantee of the right to a jury trial extends only to serious offenses, and petitioner was not charged with a serious offense. That he was tried for two counts of a petty offense, and therefore faced an aggregate potential term of imprisonment of more than six months, does not change the fact that the legislature deemed this offense petty. Petitioner is not entitled to a jury trial.

* * *

■ JUSTICE KENNEDY, with whom JUSTICE BREYER joins, concurring in the judgment.

This petitioner had no constitutional right to a jury trial because from the outset it was settled that he could be sentenced to no more than six months' imprisonment for his combined petty offenses. The particular outcome, however, should not obscure the greater consequence of today's unfortunate decision. The Court holds that a criminal defendant may be convicted of innumerable offenses in one proceeding and sentenced to any number of years' imprisonment, all without benefit of a jury trial, so long as no one of the offenses considered alone is punishable by more than six months in prison. The holding both in its doctrinal formulation and in its practical effect is one of the most serious incursions on the right to jury trial in the Court's history, and it cannot be squared with our precedents.

* * *

The primary purpose of the jury in our legal system is to stand between the accused and the powers of the State. Among the most ominous of those is the power to imprison. Blackstone expressed this principle when he described the right to trial by jury as a "strong . . . barrier . . . between the liberties of the people and the prerogative of the crown." 4 W. Blackstone, Commentaries *349–*350. * * * In more recent times we have said the right to jury trial "reflect[s] a profound judgment about the way in which law should be enforced and justice administered." Providing a defendant with the right to be tried by a jury gives "him an inestimable safeguard against the corrupt or overzealous prosecutor and against the compliant, biased, or eccentric judge." These considerations all are present when a judge in a single case sends a defendant to prison for years, whether the sentence is the result of one serious offense or several petty offenses.

On the Court's view of the case, however, there is no limit to the length of the sentence a judge can impose on a defendant without entitling him to a jury, so long as the prosecutor carves up the charges into segments punishable by no more than six months apiece. Prosecutors have broad discretion in framing charges, for criminal conduct often does not arrange itself in neat categories. In many cases, a prosecutor can choose to charge a defendant with multiple petty offenses rather than a single serious offense, and so prevent him under today's holding from obtaining a trial by jury while still obtaining the same punishment.

* * *

The significance of the Court's decision quite transcends the peculations of Ray Lewis, the petitioner here, who twice filched from the mails. The decision affects more than repeat violators of traffic laws, persons accused of public drunkenness, persons who persist in breaches of the peace, and the wide range of eccentrics capable of disturbing the quiet enjoyment of life by others. Just as alarming is the threat the Court's holding poses to millions of persons in agriculture, manufacturing, and trade who must comply with minute administrative regulations, many of them carrying a jail term of six months or less. Violations of these sorts of rules often involve repeated, discrete acts which can result in potential liability of years of imprisonment.

Still, under the Court's holding it makes no difference whether a defendant is sentenced to a year in prison or for that matter to 20 years: As long as no single violation charged is punishable by more than six months, the defendant has no right to a jury.

* * *

When a defendant's liberty is put at great risk in a trial, he is entitled to have the trial conducted to a jury. This principle lies at the heart of the Sixth Amendment. The Court does grave injury to the Amendment by allowing a defendant to suffer a prison term of any length after a single trial before a single judge and without the protection of a jury. I join only the Court's judgment.

■ JUSTICE STEVENS, with whom JUSTICE GINSBURG joins, dissenting.

The Sixth Amendment provides that the accused is entitled to trial by an impartial jury "in all criminal prosecutions." * * * I agree with Justice Kennedy to the extent he would hold that a prosecution which exposes the accused to a sentence of imprisonment longer than six months, whether for a single offense or for a series of offenses, is sufficiently serious to confer on the defendant the right to demand a jury.

Unlike JUSTICE KENNEDY, however, I believe that the right to a jury trial attaches when the prosecution begins. I do not quarrel with the established view that only defendants whose alleged misconduct is deemed serious by the legislature are entitled to be judged by a jury. But in my opinion, the legislature's determination of the severity of the charges against a defendant is properly measured by the maximum sentence authorized for the prosecution as a whole. The text of the Sixth Amendment supports this interpretation by referring expressly to "criminal prosecutions."

* * *

All agree that a judge may not strip a defendant of the right to a jury trial for a serious crime by promising a sentence of six months or less. This is so because "[o]pprobrium attaches to conviction of those crimes regardless of the length of the actual sentence imposed." In my view, the same rule must apply to prosecutions involving multiple offenses which are serious by virtue of their aggregate possible sentence. I see no basis for assuming that the dishonor associated with multiple convictions for petty offenses is less than the dishonor associated with conviction of a single serious crime. Because the right attaches at the moment of prosecution, a judge may not deprive a defendant of a jury trial by making a pretrial determination that the crimes charged will not warrant a sentence exceeding six months.

* * *

NOTES

1. In Baldwin v. New York, 399 U.S. 66, 90 S.Ct. 1886. (1970), the Court held:

> ". . . [T]he prospect of imprisonment for however short a time will seldom be viewed by the accused as a trivial or 'petty' matter and may well result in quite serious repercussions affecting his career and his reputation. Where the accused cannot possibly face more than six months' imprisonment, we have held that these disadvantages, onerous though they may be, may be outweighed by the benefits that result from speedy and inexpensive nonjury adjudications. We cannot, however, conclude that these administrative conveniences, in light of the practices that now exist in every one of the 50 States as well as in the federal courts, can similarly justify denying an accused the important right to trial by jury where the possible penalty exceeds six months' imprisonment."

When is a petty offense sufficiently serious to warrant a jury trial even though the maximum penalty is less than six months imprisonment? In Blanton v. City of North Las Vegas, 489 U.S. 538, 109 S.Ct. 1289 (1989), defendant was convicted under a Nevada law that made driving under the influence of alcohol punishable by a minimum two day to maximum six month term of imprisonment. Alternatively the defendant could receive 48 hours of work for the community while dressed in distinctive garb which identifies him as a DUI offender. The defendant also must pay a fine ranging from $200 to $1,000. In addition, the defendant automatically loses his driver's license for 90 days, and he must attend, at his own expense, an alcohol abuse education course. The Court unanimously found the circumstances insufficient to require a jury trial:

> Although we did not hold in *Baldwin* that an offense carrying a maximum prison term of six months or less automatically qualifies as a "petty" offense, and decline to do so today, we do find it appropriate to presume for purposes of the Sixth Amendment that society views such an offense as "petty." A defendant is entitled to jury trial in such circumstances only if he can demonstrate that any additional statutory penalties,

viewed in conjunction with the maximum authorized period of incarceration, are so severe that they clearly reflect a legislative determination that the offense in question is a "serious" one. This standard, albeit somewhat imprecise, should ensure the availability of a jury trial in the rare situation where a legislature packs an offense it deems "serious" with onerous penalties that nonetheless "do not puncture the 6–month incarceration line."

Applying these principles here, it is apparent that petitioners are not entitled to a jury trial. The maximum authorized prison sentence for first-time DUI offenders does not exceed six months. A presumption therefore exists that the Nevada legislature views DUI as a "petty" offense for purposes of the Sixth Amendment. Considering the additional statutory penalties as well, we do not believe that the Nevada Legislature has clearly indicated that DUI is a "serious" offense.

In the first place, it is immaterial that a first-time DUI offender may face a minimum term of imprisonment. In settling on six months' imprisonment as the constitutional demarcation point, we have assumed that a defendant convicted of the offense in question would receive the *maximum* authorized prison sentence. It is not constitutionally determinative, therefore, that a particular defendant may be required to serve some amount of jail time *less* than six months. * * * As for the 90–day license suspension, it, too, will be irrelevant if it runs concurrently with the prison sentence, which we assume for present purposes to be the maximum of six months.

We are also unpersuaded by the fact that, instead of a prison sentence, a DUI offender may be ordered to perform 48 hours of community service dressed in clothing identifying him as a DUI offender. Even assuming the outfit is the source of some embarrassment during the 48–hour period, such a penalty will be less embarrassing and less onerous than six months in jail. As for the possible $1,000 fine, it is well below the $5,000 level set by Congress in its most recent definition of a "petty" offense, 18 U.S.C. § 1, and petitioners do not suggest that this congressional figure is out of step with state practice for offenses carrying prison sentences of six months or less.

2. In criminal contempt cases, if no maximum sentence is provided by statute or rule, then the *actual* penalty that is imposed provides the benchmark for determining the right to trial by jury. See Taylor v. Hayes, 418 U.S. 488, 94 S.Ct. 2697 (1974).

3. What must a defendant do to waive his right to a jury trial? Ordinarily, a defendant and his lawyer will execute a waiver form, and he will be thereafter foreclosed from asserting his right. However, in Hawkins v. United States, 385 A.2d 744 (D.C.App.1978), the court held that even though a waiver form was signed, it was incumbent upon the court to conduct a full and complete inquiry on the record:

> "To be effective, there must be an oral inquiry of the defendant himself in open court, his replies to which indicate that he understands the nature of his right to a jury trial and that he chooses to waive the right. This oral waiver must accompany a written waiver, signed by the defendant. A written waiver signed by the defendant coupled with an oral waiver by defense counsel is not sufficient."

Is this an example of a hypertechnical theory which requires a new trial for no substantive reason? Is it asking too much to compel trial judges to take a few minutes in order to assure themselves that a defendant understands his right to a jury trial? Compare United States v. DeMichael, 692 F.2d 1059 (7th Cir.1982) (oral waiver sufficient) with United States v. Martin, 704 F.2d 267 (6th Cir.1983) (writing required).

Where the record does not establish an adequate jury waiver, ordinarily the government is not entitled to an evidentiary hearing to demonstrate that the accused knew of his right and knowingly surrendered it. United States v. Saadya, 750 F.2d 1419 (9th Cir.1985). Relate this to the requirement of an "on the record" demonstration required in guilty plea cases under Boykin v. Alabama and Federal Rule of Criminal Procedure 11 (Casebook Chapter 16).

When a trial court has reason to believe that a defendant is suffering from mental or emotional instability, it may not discharge its responsibility to determine that the defendant's waiver of his right to a jury trial was proper without an in-depth colloquy which reasonably assures the court that the signed waiver was voluntarily, knowingly, and intelligently made. In this context, the defendant should be required to express, in his own words, his understanding of the advantages and disadvantages of jury and bench trials, and the court should determine whether the defendant is under the erroneous impression that he will be rewarded, by either the court or prosecution, for waiving a jury trial. United States v. Christensen, 18 F.3d 822 (9th Cir.1994).

4. Does a defendant have a right to a bench trial? In State v. Creech, 99 Idaho 779, 589 P.2d 114 (1979), the trial judge in a murder case refused to permit the defendant to waive a jury. On review, the court held that there was no constitutional right to waive a jury trial. In a highly emotional atmosphere—for example, a multiple murder committed in a small town—should not a defendant, as an aspect of his Sixth Amendment right, have the right to waive a jury trial? In the federal system the case must be tried to a jury unless both the government and the accused assent to a bench trial. See Singer v. United States, 380 U.S. 24, 85 S.Ct. 783 (1965); United States v. Martin, 704 F.2d 267 (6th Cir.1983). Should the government have the right to demand a jury trial when the defendant seeks to waive a jury? Compare Note, Waiver of Jury Trials in Federal Criminal Cases: A Reassessment of the "Prosecutorial Veto", 51 Fordham L.Rev. 1091 (1983) with Comment, Singer v. United States and the Misapprehended Source of the Nonconsensual Bench Trial, 51 U.Chi.L.Rev. 222 (1984).

2. COMPOSITION OF THE JURY

Taylor v. Louisiana

Supreme Court of the United States, 1975.
419 U.S. 522, 95 S.Ct. 692.

■ MR. JUSTICE WHITE delivered the opinion of the Court.

When this case was tried, [Louisiana law] provided that a woman should not be selected for jury service unless she previously filed a written declaration of her desire to be subject to jury service. The constitutionality of these provisions is the issue in this case.

* * *

The Louisiana jury selection system does not disqualify women from jury service, but in operation its conceded systematic impact is that only a very few women, grossly disproportionate to the number of eligible women in the community, are called for jury service. In this case, no women were on the venire from which the petit jury was drawn. The issue we have, therefore, is whether a jury selection system which operates to exclude from jury service an identifiable class of citizens constituting 53% of eligible jurors in the community comports with the Sixth and Fourteenth Amendments.

The State first insists that Taylor, a male, has no standing to object to the exclusion of women from his jury. But Taylor's claim is that he was constitutionally entitled to a jury drawn from a venire constituting a fair cross section of the community and that the jury that tried him was not such a jury by reason of the exclusion of women. Taylor was not a member of the excluded class; but there is no rule that claims such as Taylor presents may be made only by those defendants who are members of the group excluded from jury service. In Peters v. Kiff ... (1972), the defendant, a white man, challenged his conviction on the ground that Negroes had been systematically excluded from jury service. Six Members of the Court agreed that petitioner was entitled to present the issue and concluded that he had been deprived of his federal rights. Taylor, in the case before us, was similarly entitled to tender and have adjudicated the claim that the exclusion of women from jury service deprived him of the kind of fact finder to which he was constitutionally entitled.

The background against which this case must be decided includes our holding in Duncan v. Louisiana ... (1968), that the Sixth Amendment's provision for jury trial is made binding on the States by virtue of the Fourteenth Amendment. Our inquiry is whether the presence of a fair cross section of the community on venires, panels or lists from which petit juries are drawn is essential to the fulfillment of the Sixth Amendment's guarantee of an impartial jury trial in criminal prosecutions.

The Court's prior cases are instructive. Both in the course of exercising its supervisory powers over trials in federal courts and in the constitutional context, the Court has unambiguously declared that the American concept of the jury trial contemplates a jury drawn from a fair cross section of the community. A unanimous Court stated in Smith v. Texas ... (1940), that "[i]t is part of the established tradition in the use of juries as instruments of public justice that the jury be a body truly representative of the community." To exclude racial groups from jury service was said to be "at war with our basic concepts of a democratic society and a representative government." A state jury system that resulted in systematic exclusion of Negroes as jurors was therefore held to violate the Equal Protection Clause of the Fourteenth Amendment. Glasser v. United States ... (1942), in the context of a federal criminal case and the Sixth Amendment's jury trial requirement, stated that "[o]ur notions of what a proper jury is have developed in harmony with our basic concepts of a democratic system and representative government," and repeated the Court's understanding that the jury "be a body truly representative of the community ... and not the organ of any special group or class."

A federal conviction by a jury from which women had been excluded, although eligible for service under state law, was reviewed in Ballard v. United States ... (1946). Noting the federal statutory "design to make a jury a 'cross-section of the community' " and the fact that women had been excluded, the Court exercised its supervisory powers over the federal courts and reversed the conviction. In Brown v. Allen ... (1953), the Court declared that "[o]ur duty to protect the federal constitutional rights of all does not mean we must or should impose on states our conception of the proper source of jury lists, so long as the source reasonably reflects a cross-section of the population suitable in character and intelligence for that civic duty."

Some years later in Carter v. Jury Comm'n ... (1970), the Court observed that the exclusion of Negroes from jury service because of their race "contravenes the very idea of a jury—'a body truly representative of the community....'" At about the same time it was contended that the use of six-man juries in noncapital criminal cases violated the Sixth Amendment for failure to provide juries drawn from a cross section of the community, Williams v. Florida ... (1970). In the course of rejecting that challenge, we said that the number of persons on the jury should "be large enough to promote group deliberation, free from outside attempts at intimidation, and to provide a fair possibility for obtaining a representative cross-section of the community." ... In like vein, in Apodaca v. Oregon ... (1970) (plurality opinion), it was said that "a jury will come to such a [commonsense] judgment as long as it consists of a group of laymen representative of a cross section of the community who have the duty and the opportunity to deliberate ... on the question of a defendant's guilt." Similarly, three Justices in Peters v. Kiff ... observed that the Sixth Amendment comprehended a fair possibility for obtaining a jury constituting a representative cross section of the community.

The unmistakable import of this Court's opinions is that the selection of a petit jury from a representative cross section of the community is an essential component of the Sixth Amendment right to a jury trial. We accept the fair cross section requirement as fundamental to the jury trial guaranteed by the Sixth Amendment and are convinced that the requirement has solid foundation. The purpose of a jury is to guard against the exercise of arbitrary power—to make available the commonsense judgment of the community as a hedge against the overzealous or mistaken prosecutor and in preference to the professional or perhaps overconditioned or biased response of a judge. Duncan v. Louisiana. ... This prophylactic vehicle is not provided if the jury pool is made up of only special segments of the populace or if large, distinctive groups are excluded from the pool. Community participation in the administration of the criminal law, moreover, is not only consistent with our democratic heritage but is also critical to public confidence in the fairness of the criminal justice system. Restricting jury service to only special groups or excluding identifiable segments playing major roles in the community cannot be squared with the constitutional concept of jury trial. "Trial by jury presupposes a jury drawn from a pool broadly representative of the community as well as impartial in a specific case. ... [T]he broad representative character of the jury should be maintained, partly as assurance of a diffused impartiality and partly because sharing in the administration of justice is a phase of civic responsibility."

We are also persuaded that the fair cross section requirement is violated by the systematic exclusion of women, who in the judicial district involved here amounted to 53% of the citizens eligible for jury service. This conclusion necessarily entails the judgment that women are sufficiently numerous and distinct from men that if they are systematically eliminated from jury panels, the Sixth Amendment's fair cross section requirement cannot be satisfied. This very matter was debated in Ballard v. United States, supra. Positing the fair cross-section rule—there said to be a statutory one—the Court concluded that the systematic exclusion of women was unacceptable. The dissenting view that an all-male panel drawn from various groups in the community would be as truly representative as if women were included, was firmly rejected:

> "The thought is that the factors which tend to influence the action of women are the same as those which influence the action of men—personality, background, economic status—and not sex. Yet it is not enough to say that women when sitting as jurors neither act nor tend to act as a class. Men likewise do not act as a class. But, if the shoe were on the other foot, who would claim that a jury was truly representative of the community if all men were intentionally and systematically excluded from the panel? The truth is that the two sexes are not fungible; a community made up exclusively of one is different from a community composed of both; the subtle interplay of influence one on the other is among the imponderables. To insulate the courtroom from either may not in a given case make an iota of difference. Yet a flavor, a distinct quality is lost if either sex is excluded. The exclusion of one may indeed make the jury less representative of the community than would be true if an economic or racial group were excluded."

In this respect, we agree with the Court in *Ballard*: If the fair cross-section rule is to govern the selection of juries, as we have concluded it must, women cannot be systematically excluded from jury panels from which petit juries are drawn. This conclusion is consistent with the current judgment of the country, now evidenced by legislative or constitutional provisions in every State and at the federal level qualifying women for jury service.

There remains the argument that women as a class serve a distinctive role in society and that jury service would so substantially interfere with that function that the State has ample justification for excluding women from service unless they volunteer, even though the result is that almost all jurors are men. It is true that Hoyt v. Florida (1961), held that such a system did not deny due process of law or equal protection of the laws because there was a sufficiently rational basis for such an exemption. But *Hoyt* did not involve a defendant's Sixth Amendment right to a jury drawn from a fair cross section of the community and the prospect of depriving him of that right if women as a class are systematically excluded. The right to a proper jury cannot be overcome on merely rational grounds. There must be weightier reasons if a distinctive class representing 53% of the eligible jurors is for all practical purposes to be excluded from jury service. No such basis has been tendered here.

The States are free to grant exemptions from jury service to individuals in case of special hardship or incapacity and to those engaged in particular occupations the uninterrupted performance of which is critical to the community's welfare. It would not appear that such exemptions would pose substantial threats that the remaining pool of jurors would not be representative of the community. A system excluding all women, however, is a wholly different matter. It is untenable to suggest these days that it would be a special hardship for each and every woman to perform jury service or that society cannot spare *any* women from their present duties. This may be the case with many, and it may be burdensome to sort out those who should not be exempted from those who should serve. But that task is performed in the case of men, and the administrative convenience in dealing with women as a class is insufficient justification for diluting the quality of community judgment represented by the jury in criminal trials.

* * *

Our holding does not augur or authorize the fashioning of detailed jury selection codes by federal courts. The fair cross section principle must have much leeway in application. The States remain free to prescribe relevant qualifications for their jurors and to provide reasonable exemptions so long as it may be fairly said that the jury lists or panels are representative of the community. But, as we have said, Louisiana's special exemption for women operates to exclude them from petit juries, which in our view is contrary to the command of the Sixth and Fourteenth Amendments.

It should also be emphasized that in holding that petit juries must be drawn from a source fairly representative of the community we impose no requirement that petit juries actually chosen must mirror the community and reflect the various distinctive groups in the population. Defendants are not entitled to a jury of any particular composition but the jury wheels, pools of names, panels or venires from which juries are drawn must not systematically exclude distinctive groups in the community and thereby fail to be reasonably representative thereof.

The judgment of the Louisiana Supreme Court is reversed and the case remanded to that court for further proceedings not inconsistent with this opinion.

So ordered.

Reversed and remanded.

■ (The dissenting opinion of MR. JUSTICE REHNQUIST is omitted.)

NOTES

1. In Daniel v. Louisiana, 420 U.S. 31, 95 S.Ct. 704 (1975), the Court held that *Taylor*, as a matter of federal constitutional law, need not be applied retroactively to void convictions returned by juries which had been empanelled prior to the *Taylor* decision.

2. *Taylor* involved a jury selection system in which women had to file a written declaration of their willingness to serve. But what about a system which exempts any woman who requests not to serve? At the time *Taylor* was decided, five states had just such a system: Georgia, New York, Rhode Island, Tennessee and Missouri. After *Taylor*, Georgia, New York and Rhode Island repealed their statutory exemptions for women; but the remaining two states continued the practice until Duren v.

Missouri, 439 U.S. 357, 99 S.Ct. 664 (1979), where the Court, having found that the system created a prima facie violation of the "fair cross-section" requirement, held:

> Neither the Missouri Supreme Court nor respondent in its brief have offered any substantial justification for this exemption. In response to questioning at oral argument, counsel for respondent ventured that the only state interest advanced by the exemption is safeguarding the important role played by women in home and family life. But exempting all women because of the preclusive domestic responsibilities of some women is insufficient justification for their disproportionate exclusion on jury venires. What we stated in *Taylor* with respect to the system there challenged under which women could "opt in" for jury service is equally applicable to Missouri's "opt out" exemption.
>
> * * *
>
> We recognize that a State may have an important interest in assuring that those members of the family responsible for the care of children are available to do so. An exemption appropriately tailored to this interest would, we think, survive a fair-cross-section challenge. We stress, however, that the constitutional guarantee to a jury drawn from a fair cross section of the community requires that States exercise proper caution in exempting broad categories of persons from jury service. Although most occupational and other reasonable exemptions may inevitably involve some degree of over- or under-inclusiveness, any category expressly limited to a group in the community of sufficient magnitude and distinctiveness so as to be within the cross-section requirement—such as women—runs the danger of resulting in underrepresentation sufficient to constitute a prima facie violation of that constitutional requirement.

3. Is the right to a representative cross-section violated by a statute which excuses mothers who have children under 18? See McArthur v. State, 351 So.2d 972 (Fla.1977). Is it violated by a statute which excludes convicted felons and resident aliens? See Rubio v. Superior Court, 24 Cal.3d 93, 154 Cal.Rptr. 734, 593 P.2d 595 (1979).

4. In Hamling v. United States, 418 U.S. 87, 94 S.Ct. 2887 (1974), the Court considered a claim by the defendant that the master jury list which provided the jurors in his case had not been changed in almost four years. Thus, because the master list was taken from voter registration records (which were compiled before 18 years olds were permitted to vote through the Twenty–Sixth Amendment), he claimed that he was denied a jury on which young people were represented. Rejecting this argument, the Court said "[I]f the jury wheel is not discriminatory when completely updated at the time of each refilling, a prohibited 'purposeful discrimination' does not arise near the end of the period simply because the young and other persons have belatedly become eligible for jury service by becoming registered voters."

5. There is a split of authority on the issue of whether "young persons" between the ages of 18 and 30 represent a cognizable class. Compare Barber v. Ponte, 772 F.2d 982 (1st Cir.1985) with Willis v. Zant, 720 F.2d 1212 (11th Cir.1983). In *Zant*, the court found the exclusion of young persons actionable, but tied its conclusion to the facts of the case:

> "The distinctiveness and homogeneity of a group under the sixth amendment depends upon the time and location of the trial. For example, Latins have been held to be a cognizable group in Miami, Florida. In another community, they might not be . . . [A] defendant must show: (1) that the group is defined and limited by some factor . . . (2) that a common

thread or basic similarity runs through the group; and that there is a community of interest among members of the group such that the group's interest cannot be adequately represented if the group is excluded from the jury selection process."

In Willis v. Kemp, 838 F.2d 1510 (11th Cir.1988), the petitioner failed in his efforts to show that persons between ages 18 and 29 are a distinct group for purposes of a Sixth Amendment cross-section challenge to a petit jury venire. The Black defendant, tried in a Georgia trial court, sought to establish that younger adults had different attitudes than those who lived under a system of racial segregation.

6. For other allegations of the exclusion of an "identifiable class" that have been rejected, see United States v. Gometz, 730 F.2d 475 (7th Cir.1984) ("anti-authoritarian" personalities); United States v. Clifford, 640 F.2d 150 (8th Cir.1981) (underrepresentation of Indians); United States v. De Alba–Conrado, 481 F.2d 1266 (5th Cir.1973) (Latin names); United States v. Dellinger, 472 F.2d 340 (7th Cir.1972) ("politically alienated").

7. Successful challenges to the composition of the juries generally arise from situations in which the pool is taken from an "infected" source. See Cobbs v. Robinson, 528 F.2d 1331 (2d Cir.1975) (volunteers who were sheriff's personal acquaintances); Brown v. State, 239 Ga. 435, 238 S.E.2d 21 (1977) (racially identified tax digest); Moore v. State, 427 N.E.2d 1135 (Ind.App.1981) (should not be taken from real property tax rolls, but to do so does not create cross-section violation).

8. In Alston v. Manson, 791 F.2d 255 (2d Cir.1986), the petitioners proved the statistical likelihood that the Connecticut system of selecting jury arrays would produce arrays in which small towns were overrepresented and larger urban settings were underrepresented. They also showed that the more populated urban settings had greater percentages of Black persons than did the smaller settings. Without a showing of the racial makeup of the arrays themselves, a divided court, through Judge Irving Kaufman, found that petitioners had met their burden of establishing a prima facie case of intentional discrimination in violation of the Equal Protection clause of the Fourteenth Amendment. The dissent noted that the Connecticut system, though programmed to favor smaller communities, was random, and concluded that a prima facie case of discrimination had not been made out in light of that fact and the fact that there was no actual count of the racial composition of the arrays.

9. In People v. Sanders, 51 Cal.3d 471, 273 Cal.Rptr. 537, 797 P.2d 561 (1990), prospective jurors were drawn from voter lists. The Hispanic population was 16.3 percent of the community, but only 8.3 percent of prospective jurors were Hispanic. Assuming that the statistical disparity sufficed to require the government to provide a non-discriminating reason, the court held there was no impermissible discrimination where a particular group had a lower than average voter registration. To the extent that the right involved is the right of the prospective juror and not the right of the defendant (see Powers v. Ohio, 1118, Note 2), can one find fault with this reasoning?

10. The burden of demonstrating systematic exclusion rests with the party challenging jury composition; and the satisfaction of burden is contingent on proof of a statistical disparity. Compare Machetti v. Linahan, 679 F.2d 236 (11th Cir.1982) (jury list containing 12% women in county where women are 54% of population satisfies burden) with United States ex rel. Barksdale v. Blackburn, 639 F.2d 1115 (5th Cir.1981) (en banc) (12–10 en banc decision holding burden unsatisfied when list contained 16–19% blacks out of 26% in county). See also Singleton v. Lockhart, 871 F.2d 1395 (8th Cir.1989) (36% variation does not establish systematic exclusion); United States v. Fike, 82 F.3d 1315 (5th Cir.1996) (use of the 1980 census figures for a 1993 trial fails to make out a prima facie case of a fair cross-section violation).

11. In order to prepare a challenge to the jury panel, a defendant has an unqualified right to inspect the court clerk's jury selection records. Test v. United States, 420 U.S. 28, 95 S.Ct. 749 (1975). When inspection is not provided and the defendant is convicted, reviewing courts will not reverse the conviction, but remand to provide an opportunity to make an appropriate challenge. United States v. Lawson, 670 F.2d 923 (10th Cir.1982).

12. How do the jury composition cases relate to the grand jury composition cases set in Chapter 11, Section B? Are the principles the same? Should they be? Does the answer depend on the fact that state indictments by grand juries are not constitutionally required, but jury trials are?

3. Jury Size

Ballew v. Georgia

Supreme Court of the United States, 1978.
435 U.S. 223, 98 S.Ct. 1029.

■ Mr. Justice Blackmun announced the judgment of the Court and delivered an opinion in which Mr. Justice Stevens joined.

This case presents the issue whether a state criminal trial to a jury of only five persons deprives the accused of the right to trial by jury guaranteed to him by the Sixth and Fourteenth Amendments. Our resolution of the issue requires an application of principles enunciated in Williams v. Florida, 399 U.S. 78, 90 S.Ct. 1893 (1970), where the use of a six-person jury in a state criminal trial was upheld against similar constitutional attack.

I.

[Ballew was the manager of an Atlanta movie theater which ran the motion picture, "Behind the Green Door." He was charged with distributing obscene materials, a misdemeanor under Georgia Law. Because state law permitted the trial of misdemeanor cases to proceed before five member juries, Ballew's contention that the size of the jury violated his Sixth Amendment rights was denied, and he was convicted.]

* * *

II.

The Fourteenth Amendment guarantees the right of trial by jury in all state nonpetty criminal cases. Duncan v. Louisiana (1968) [supra this chapter, A1]. The Court in *Duncan* applied this Sixth Amendment right to the States because "trial by jury in criminal cases is fundamental to the American scheme of justice." The right attaches in the present case because the maximum penalty for violating [the statute under which Ballew was convicted] exceeded six months imprisonment. . . .

In Williams v. Florida, supra the Court reaffirmed that the "purpose of the jury trial, as we noted in *Duncan*, is to prevent oppression by the

Government. 'Providing an accused with the right to be tried by a jury of his peers gave him an inestimable safeguard against the corrupt or overzealous prosecutor and against the complaint, biased, or eccentric judge.' " This purpose is attained by the participation of the community in determinations of guilt and by the application of the common sense of laymen who, as jurors, consider the case.

Williams held that these functions and this purpose could be fulfilled by a jury of six members. As the Court's opinion in that case explained at some length, common-law juries included 12 members by historical accident, "unrelated to the great purposes which gave rise to the jury in the first place." The Court's earlier cases that had *assumed* the number 12 to be constitutionally compelled were set to one side because they had not considered history and the function of the jury. Rather than requiring 12 members, then, the Sixth Amendment mandated a jury only of sufficient size to promote group deliberation, to insulate members from outside intimidation, and to provide a representative cross-section of the community. Although recognizing that by 1970 little empirical research had evaluated jury performance, the Court found no evidence that the reliability of jury verdicts diminished with six-member panels. Nor did the Court anticipate significant differences in result, including the frequency of "hung" juries. Because the reduction in size did not threaten exclusion of any particular class from jury roles, concern that the representative or cross-section character of the jury would suffer with a decrease to six members seemed "an unrealistic one." As a consequence, the six-person jury was held not to violate the Sixth and Fourteenth Amendments.

III.

When the Court in *Williams* permitted the reduction in jury size—or, to put it another way, when it held that a jury of six was not unconstitutional—it expressly reserved ruling on the issue whether a number smaller than six passed constitutional scrutiny. The Court refused to speculate when this so-called "slippery slope" would become too steep. We face now, however, the two-fold question whether a further reduction in the size of the state criminal trial jury does make the grade too dangerous, that is, whether it inhibits the functioning of the jury as an institution to a significant degree, and, if so, whether any state interest counterbalances and justifies the disruption so as to preserve its constitutionality.

Williams v. Florida and Colgrove v. Battin, 413 U.S. 149, 93 S.Ct. 2448 (1973) (where the Court held that a jury of six members did not violate the Seventh Amendment right to a jury trial in a civil case), generated a quantity of scholarly work on jury size. These writings do not draw or identify a bright line below which the number of jurors would not be able to function as required by the standards enunciated in *Williams*. On the other hand, they raise significant questions about the wisdom and constitutionality of a reduction below six. We examine these concerns:

First, recent empirical data suggest that progressively smaller juries are less likely to foster effective group deliberation. At some point, this decline leads to inaccurate fact-finding and incorrect application of the common sense of the community to the facts. Generally, a positive correlation exists between group size and both the quality of group performance and group productivity. A variety of explanations has been offered for this conclusion. Several are particularly applicable in the jury setting. The smaller the group, the less likely are members to make critical contributions necessary for the solution of a given problem. Because most juries are not permitted to take notes, memory is important for accurate jury deliberations. As juries decrease in size, then, they are less likely to have members who remember each of the important pieces of evidence or argument. Furthermore, the smaller the group, the less likely it is to overcome the biases of its members to obtain an accurate result. When individual and group decisionmaking were compared, it was seen that groups performed better because prejudices of individuals were frequently counterbalanced, and objectivity resulted. Groups also exhibited increased motivation and self-criticism. All these advantages, except, perhaps, self-motivation, tend to diminish with group size. Because juries frequently face complex problems laden with value choices, the benefits are important and should be retained. In particular, the counterbalancing of various biases is critical to the accurate application of the common sense of the community to the facts of any given case.

Second, the data now raise doubts about the accuracy of the results achieved by smaller and smaller panels. Statistical studies suggest that the risk of convicting an innocent person (Type I error) rises as the size of the jury diminishes. Because the risk of not convicting a guilty person (Type II error) increases with the size of the panel, an optimal jury size can be selected as a function of the interaction between the two risks. Nagel & Neef concluded that the optimal size, for the purpose of minimizing errors, should vary with the importance attached to the two types of mistakes. After weighing Type I error as 10 times more significant than Type II, perhaps not an unreasonable assumption, they concluded that the optimal jury size was between six and eight. As the size diminished to five and below, the weighted sum of errors increased because of the enlarging risk of the conviction of innocent defendants.[18]

Another doubt about progressively smaller juries arises from the increasing inconsistency that results from the decreases. Saks argued that the "more a jury type fosters consistency, the greater will be the proportion of juries which select the correct (i.e., the same) verdict and the fewer 'errors' will be made." M. Saks, Jury Verdicts, 86–87 (1977). From his mock trials held before undergraduates and former jurors, he computed the percentage of "correct" decisions rendered by 12–person and six-person panels. In the student experiment, 12–person groups reached correct verdicts 83% of the time; six-person panels reached correct verdicts 69% of the

18. [Nagel & Neef, Deductive Modeling to Determine an Optimum Jury Size and Fraction Required to Convict, 1975 Wash. U.L.Q. 933, 946–48, 956, 957. See also Friedman, Trial by Jury: Criteria for Convictions, Jury Size and Type I and Type II Errors, 26–2 Am.Stat. 21 (April 1972).] Friedman reached a similar conclusion. He varied the appearance of guilt in his statistical study. The more guilty the person appeared, the greater the chance that a six-member panel would convict when a 12–member panel would not. As jury size was reduced, the risk of Type I error would increase, Friedman said, without a significant corresponding advantage in reducing Type II error.

time. The results for the former juror study were 71% for the 12–person groups and 57% for the six-person groups.

* * *

... [T]hese post-*Williams* studies, therefore, raise significant doubts about the consistency and reliability of the decisions of smaller juries.

Third, the data suggest that the verdicts of jury deliberation in criminal cases will vary as juries become smaller, and that the variance amounts to an imbalance to the detriment of one side, the defense. ... [Studies have] emphasized that juries in criminal cases generally hang with only one, or more likely two jurors remaining unconvinced of guilt. Also, group theory suggests that a person in the minority will adhere to his position more frequently when he has at least one other person supporting his argument. In the jury setting the significance of this tendency is demonstrated by the following figures: If a minority viewpoint is shared by 10% of the community, 28.2% of 12–member juries may be expected to have no minority representation, but 53.1% of six-member juries would have none. Thirty-four percent of 12–percent panels could be expected to have two minority members, while only 11% of six-member panels would have two. As the numbers diminish below six, even fewer panels would have one member with the minority viewpoint and still fewer would have two. The chance for hung juries would decline accordingly.

Fourth, what has just been said about the presence of minority viewpoint as juries decrease in size foretells problems not only for jury decisionmaking, but also for the representation of minority groups in the community. The Court repeatedly has held that meaningful community participation cannot be attained with the exclusion of minorities or other identifiable groups from jury service. "It is part of the established tradition in the use of juries as instruments of public justice that the jury be a body truly representative of the community." Smith v. Texas, 311 U.S. 128, 130, 61 S.Ct. 164, 165 (1940). The exclusion of elements of the community from participation "contravenes the very idea of a jury ... composed of 'the peers or equals of the person whose rights it is selected or summoned to determine.' " Carter v. Jury Commission, 396 U.S. 320, 330, 90 S.Ct. 518, 524 (1970), quoting Strauder v. West Virginia, 100 U.S. 303, 308 (1879). Although the Court in *Williams* concluded that the six-person jury did not fail to represent adequately a cross-section of the community, the opportunity for meaningful and appropriate representation does decrease with the size of the panels. Thus, if a minority group constitutes 10% of the community, 53.1% of randomly selected six-member juries could be expected to have no minority representative among their members, and 89% not to have two. Further reduction in size will erect additional barriers to representation.

Fifth, several authors have identified in jury research methodological problems tending to mask differences in the operation of smaller and larger juries. For example, because the judicial system handles so many clear cases, decisionmakers will reach similar results through similar analyses most of the time. One study concluded that smaller and larger juries could disagree in their verdicts in no more than 14% of the cases. Disparities, therefore, appear in only small percentages. Nationwide, however, these small percentages will represent a large number of cases. And it is with respect to those cases that the jury trial right has its greatest value. When the case is close, and the guilt or innocence of the defendant is not readily apparent, a properly functioning jury system will insure evaluation by the common sense of the community and will also tend to insure accurate factfinding.

* * *

IV.

While we adhere to, and reaffirm our holding in Williams v. Florida, these studies, most of which have been made since *Williams* was decided in 1970, lead us to conclude that the purpose and functioning of the jury in a criminal trial is seriously impaired, and to a constitutional degree, by a reduction in size to below six members. We readily admit that we do not pretend to discern a clear line between six members and five. But the assembled data raise substantial doubt about the reliability and appropriate representation of panels smaller than six. Because of the fundamental importance of the jury trial to the American system of criminal justice, any further reduction that promotes inaccurate and possibly biased decision-making, that causes untoward differences in verdicts, and that prevents juries from truly representing their communities, attains constitutional significance.

* * *

... Georgia argues that its use of five-member juries does not violate the Sixth and Fourteenth Amendments because they are used only in misdemeanor cases. If six persons may constitutionally assess the felony charge in *Williams*, the State reasons, five persons should be a constitutionally adequate number for a misdemeanor trial. The problem with this argument is that the purpose and functions of the jury do not vary significantly with the importance of the crime. In Baldwin v. New York (1970), [this chapter A1], the Court held that the right to a jury trial attached in both felony and misdemeanor cases. Only in cases concerning truly petty crimes, where the deprivation of liberty was minimal, did the defendant have no constitutional right to trial by jury. In the present case the possible deprivation of liberty is substantial. ... We cannot conclude that there is less need for the imposition and the direction of the common sense of the community in this case than when the State has chosen to label an offense a felony.[33] The need for an effective jury here must be

33. We do not rely on any First Amendment aspect of this case in holding the five-person jury unconstitutional. Nevertheless, the nature of the substance of the misdemeanor charges against petitioner supports the refusal to distinguish between felonies and misdemeanors. The application of the community's standards and common sense is important in obscenity trials where juries must define and apply local standards. See Miller v. California, 413 U.S. 15, 93 S.Ct. 2607 (1973). The opportunity for harassment and overreaching by an overzealous prosecutor or a biased judge is at least as significant in an obscenity trial as in one concerning an armed robbery. This fact does not change merely because the obscenity charge may be labeled a misdemeanor and the robbery a felony.

judged by the same standards announced and applied in Williams v. Florida.

* * *

Georgia submits that the five-person jury adequately represents the community because there is no arbitrary exclusion of any particular class. We agree that it has not been demonstrated that the Georgia system violates the Equal Protection Clause by discriminating on the basis of race or some other improper classification. See Carter v. Jury Commission, 396 U.S. 320, 90 S.Ct. 518 (1970); Smith v. Texas, 311 U.S. 128, 61 S.Ct. 164 (1940). But the data outlined above raise substantial doubt about the ability of juries truly to represent the community as membership decreases below six. If the smaller and smaller juries will lack consistency, as the cited studies suggest, then the common sense of the community will not be applied equally in like cases. Not only is the representation of racial minorities threatened in such circumstances, but also majority attitude or various minority positions may be misconstrued or misapplied by the smaller groups. Even though the facts of this case would not establish a jury discrimination claim under the Equal Protection Clause, the question of representation does constitute one factor of several that, when combined, create a problem of constitutional significance under the Sixth and Fourteenth Amendments.

* * *

V.

With the reduction in the number of jurors below six creating a substantial threat to Sixth and Fourteenth Amendment guarantees, we must consider whether any interest of the State justifies the reduction. We find no significant state advantage in reducing the number of jurors from six to five.

The States utilize juries of less than 12 primarily for administrative reasons. Savings in court time and in financial costs are claimed to justify the reductions. The financial benefits of the reduction from 12 to six are substantial; this is mainly because fewer jurors draw daily allowances as they hear cases. On the other hand, the asserted saving in judicial time is not so clear. Pabst in his study found little reduction in the time for voir dire with the six-person jury because many questions were directed at the veniremen as a group. Total trial time did not diminish, and court delays and backlogs improved very little.[41] The point that is to be made, of course, is that a reduction in size from six to five or four or even three would save the States little. They could reduce slightly the daily allowances, but with a reduction from six to five the saving would be minimal. If little time is gained by the reduction from 12 to six, less will be gained with a reduction from six to five. Perhaps this explains why only three States, Georgia, Louisiana, and Virginia, have reduced the size of juries in certain nonpetty criminal cases to five. Other States appear content with six members or

41. [Pabst, Statistical Studies of the Costs of Six–Man versus Twelve–Man Juries, 14 Wm. & Mary L.Rev. 326, 328 (1972).]

more. In short the State has offered little or no justification for its reduction to five members.

Petitioner, therefore, has established that his trial on criminal charges before a five-member jury deprived him of the right to trial by jury guaranteed by the Sixth and Fourteenth Amendments.

VI.

The judgment of the Court of Appeals is reversed, and the case is remanded for further proceedings not inconsistent with this opinion.

It is so ordered.

■ MR. JUSTICE STEVENS, concurring. [Opinion omitted].

■ MR. JUSTICE WHITE, concurring in the judgment.

Agreeing that a jury of fewer than six persons would fail to represent the sense of the community and hence not satisfy the fair cross-section requirement of the Sixth and Fourteenth Amendments, I concur in the judgment of reversal.

■ MR. JUSTICE POWELL, with whom THE CHIEF JUSTICE and MR. JUSTICE REHNQUIST join, concurring in the judgment.

I concur in the judgment, as I agree that use of a jury as small as five members, with authority to convict for serious offenses, involves grave questions of fairness. As the opinion of Mr. Justice Blackmun indicates, the line between five- and six-member juries is difficult to justify, but a line has to be drawn somewhere if the substance of jury trial is to be preserved.

I do not agree, however, that every feature of jury trial practice must be the same in both federal and state courts. . . .

Because the opinion of Mr. Justicc Blackmun today assumes full incorporation of the Sixth Amendment by the Fourteenth Amendment . . . I do not join it. Also, I have reservations as to the wisdom—as well as the necessity—of Mr. Justice Blackmun's heavy reliance on numerology derived from statistical studies. Moreover, neither the validity nor the methodology employed by the studies cited was subjected to the traditional testing mechanisms of the adversary process. The studies relied on merely represent unexamined findings of persons interested in the jury system.

For these reasons I concur only in the judgment.

■ MR. JUSTICE BRENNAN, with whom MR. JUSTICE STEWART and MR. JUSTICE MARSHALL join.

■ I join MR. JUSTICE BLACKMUN's opinion insofar as it holds that the Sixth and Fourteenth Amendments require juries in criminal trials to contain more than five persons. However, I cannot agree that petitioner can be subjected to a new trial, since I continue to adhere to my belief that [the Georgia obscenity statute] is overbroad and therefore facially unconstitutional. . . .

NOTES

1. In Williams v. Florida, 399 U.S. 78, 90 S.Ct. 1893 (1970), the Supreme Court held that the states were not constitutionally prohibited from using six member juries in criminal cases. As Justice Powell's concurrence in *Ballew* recognized, the practical effects of a reduction in the jury size are difficult to measure with any degree of certainty. However, Professor Hans Zeisel, whose distinction in the field is evidenced by his co-authorship, with Harry Kalven, of the pre-eminent jury study, The American Jury (1966), has made these observations in his article "And Then There Were None: The Diminution Of The Federal Jury", 38 U.Chi.L.Rev. 710, 712–24 (1971):

> History, however, might have embodied more wisdom than the Court would allow. It might be more than an accident that after centuries of trial and error the size of the jury at common law came to be fixed at twelve. A primary function of the jury was to represent the community as broadly as possible; yet at the same time, it had to remain a group of manageable size. Twelve might have been, and might still be, the upper limit beyond which the difficulty of self-management becomes insuperable under the burdensome condition of a trial. On this view, twelve would be the number that optimizes the jury's two conflicting goals—to represent the community and to remain manageable.
>
> * * *
>
> In addition to the tendency to be less representative and to produce more varied damage verdicts, the six-member jury is likely to yield fewer examples of that treasured, paradoxical phenomenon—the hung jury. Hung juries almost always arise from situations in which there were originally several dissenters. Even if only one holds out, his having once been the member of a group is essential in sustaining him against the majority's efforts to make the verdict unanimous. Fewer hung juries can be expected in six-member juries for two reasons: first, . . . there will be fewer holders of minority positions on the jury; second, if a dissenter appears, he is more likely to be the only one on the jury. Lacking any associate to support his position, he is more likely to abandon it.
>
> * * *
>
> On grounds of economy, one might welcome any reduction in the number of hung juries. One should understand, however, that such reduction is but the combined result of less representative, more homogeneous juries and of a reduced ability to resist the pressure for unanimity.
>
> * * *
>
> Both in the short and in the long run our judicial system has many options, but every solution has its own balance sheet of advantages and costs. What is necessary is that we, and with us the United States Supreme Court, see both with equal clarity.

2. The question of jury size may arise when, after the jury has begun its deliberations, one juror is unable to continue because of illness. Some jurisdictions prohibit substitution of an alternate juror after deliberations have begun absent agreement of the parties. See State v. Lehman, 108 Wis.2d 291, 321 N.W.2d 212 (1982).

3. In United States v. Acker, 52 F.3d 509 (4th Cir.1995), on the second day of deliberations a juror called the clerk and advised that she had injured her ankle and would not be able to resume deliberations because she needed to seek medical attention. Because the court did not know when the juror was likely to return, and could not reach her and the remaining jurors were ready to resume deliberations, and the alternate jurors had been excused, the court concluded that it would have been unrealistic to require the trial judge to delay deliberations.

4. For an argument against an expansive role for social scientists in judicial resolution of issues like that posed in *Ballew*, see Lermack, No Right Number? Social Science Research and the Jury–Size Cases. 54 N.Y.U.L.Rev. 951 (1979).

4. Less–Than–Unanimous Verdicts

Johnson v. Louisiana

Supreme Court of the United States, 1972.
406 U.S. 356, 92 S.Ct. 1620.

[The defendant was tried for robbery before a 12–man jury and convicted upon a nine to three verdict, as authorized by Louisiana law in cases where the crime is necessarily punishable at hard labor. (Other state law provisions require unanimity for five-man jury trials of offenses in which the punishment may be at hard labor and for 12–man jury trials and capital cases.) The appellant's argument, according to the court, consisted of two parts: first, that nine individual jurors will be unable to vote conscientiously in favor of guilt beyond a reasonable doubt when three of their colleagues are arguing for acquittal, and second, that guilt cannot be said to have been proved beyond a reasonable doubt when one or more of a jury's members at the conclusion of deliberation still possess such a doubt. The majority of the court held that neither argument was persuasive.]

■ Mr. Justice White delivered the opinion of the Court.

* * *

... In considering the first branch of appellant's argument, we can find no basis for holding that the nine jurors who voted for his conviction failed to follow their instructions concerning the need for proof beyond such a doubt or that the vote of any one of the nine failed to reflect an honest belief that guilt had been so proved. Appellant, in effect, asks us to assume that, when minority jurors express sincere doubts about guilt, their fellow jurors will nevertheless ignore them and vote to convict even if deliberation has not been exhausted and minority jurors have grounds for acquittal which, if pursued, might persuade members of the majority to acquit. But the mere fact that three jurors voted to acquit does not in itself demonstrate that, had the nine jurors of the majority attended further to reason and the evidence, all or one of them would have developed a reasonable doubt about guilt. We have no grounds for believing that majority jurors, aware of their responsibility and power over the liberty of the defendant, would simply refuse to listen to arguments presented to them in favor of acquittal, terminate discussion and render a verdict. On the contrary it is far more likely that a juror presenting reasoned argument in favor of acquittal would either have his arguments answered or would carry enough other jurors with him to prevent conviction. A majority will cease discussion and outvote a minority only after reasoned discussion has ceased to have persuasive effect or to serve any other purpose—when a minority, that is, continues to insist upon acquittal without having persuasive reasons in support of its position. At that juncture there is no basis for denigrating the vote of so large a majority of the jury or for refusing to accept their decision as being, at least in their minds, beyond a reasonable doubt. Indeed, at this point, a "dissenting juror should consider whether his doubt was a reasonable one . . . [when it made] no impression upon the minds of so many men, equally honest, equally intelligent with himself." Allen v. United States, 164 U.S. 492, 501, 17 S.Ct. 154, 157 (1896). Appellant offers no evidence that majority jurors simply ignore the reasonable doubts of their colleagues or otherwise act irresponsibly in casting their votes in favor of conviction, and before we alter our own longstanding perceptions about jury behavior and overturn a considered legislative judgment that unanimity is not essential to reasoned jury verdicts, we must have some basis for doing so other than unsupported assumptions.

We conclude, therefore, that, as to the nine jurors who voted to convict, the State satisfied its burden of proving guilt beyond any reasonable doubt. The remaining question under the Due Process Clause is whether the vote of three jurors for acquittal can be said to impeach the verdict of the other nine and to demonstrate that guilt was not in fact proved beyond such doubt. We hold that it cannot.

Of course, the State's proof could perhaps be regarded as more certain if it had convinced all 12 jurors instead of only nine; it would have been even more compelling if it had been required to convince and had, in fact, convinced 24 or 36 jurors. But the fact remains that nine jurors—a substantial majority of the jury—were convinced by the evidence. In our view disagreement of three jurors does not alone establish reasonable doubt, particularly when such a heavy majority of the jury, after having considered the dissenters' views, remains convinced of guilt. That rational men disagree is not in itself equivalent to a failure of proof by the State, nor does it indicate infidelity to the reasonable doubt standard. Jury verdicts finding guilty beyond a reasonable doubt are regularly sustained even though the evidence was such that the jury would have been justified in having a reasonable doubt; even though the trial judge might not have reached the same conclusion as the jury; and even though appellate judges are closely divided on the issue whether there was sufficient evidence to support a conviction. That want of jury unanimity is not to be equated with the existence of a reasonable doubt emerges even more clearly from the fact that, when a jury in a federal court, which operates under the unanimity rule and is instructed to acquit a defendant if it has a reasonable doubt about his guilt, cannot agree unanimously upon a verdict, the defendant is not acquitted, but is merely given a new trial. If the doubt of a minority of jurors indicates the existence of a reasonable doubt it would appear that a defendant should receive a directed verdict of acquittal rather than a retrial. We conclude, therefore that verdicts rendered by nine out of 12 jurors are not automatically invalidated by the disagreement of the dissenting three. Appellant was not deprived of due process of law.

* * *

The judgment of the Supreme Court of Louisiana is therefore affirmed.

Affirmed.

[The concurring opinions of Justices Blackmun and Powell are omitted.]

■ MR. JUSTICE STEWART, with whom MR. JUSTICE BRENNAN and MR. JUSTICE MARSHALL join, dissenting.

... I think the Fourteenth Amendment alone clearly requires that if a State purports to accord the right of trial by jury in a criminal case, then only a unanimous jury can return a constitutionally valid verdict.

The guarantee against systematic discrimination in the selection of criminal court juries is a fundamental of the Fourteenth Amendment. That has been the insistent message of this Court in a line of decisions extending over nearly a century. The clear purpose of these decisions has been to ensure universal participation of the citizenry in the administration of criminal justice. Yet today's judgment approves the elimination of the one rule that can ensure that such participation will be meaningful—the rule requiring the assent of all jurors before a verdict of conviction or acquittal can be returned. Under today's judgment, nine jurors can simply ignore the views of their fellow panel members of a different race or class.

The constitutional guarantee of an impartial system of jury selection in a state criminal trial rests on the Due Process and Equal Protection Clauses of the Fourteenth Amendment. Only a jury so selected can assure both a fair criminal trial, and public confidence in its result. Today's decision grossly undermines those basic assurances. For only a unanimous jury so selected can serve to minimize the potential bigotry of those who might convict on inadequate evidence, or acquit when evidence of guilt was clear. And community confidence in the administration of criminal justice cannot but be corroded under a system in which a defendant who is conspicuously identified with a particular group can be acquitted or convicted by a jury split along group lines. The requirements of unanimity and impartial selection thus complement each other in ensuring the fair performance of the vital functions of a criminal court jury.

It does not denigrate the system of trial by jury to acknowledge that it is imperfect, nor does it enable that system to drape upon a jury majority the mantle of presumptive reasonableness in all circumstances. The Court has never before been so impervious to reality in this area. Its recognition of the serious risks of jury misbehavior is a theme unifying a series of constitutional decisions that may be in jeopardy if today's facile presumption of regularity becomes the new point of departure. Why, if juries do not sometimes act out of passion and prejudice, does the Constitution require the availability of a change of venue? Why, if juries do not sometimes act improperly, does the Constitution require protection from inflammatory press coverage and *ex parte* influence by court officers? Why, if juries must be presumed to obey all instructions from the bench, does the Constitution require that certain information must not go to the jury no matter how strong a cautionary charge accompanies it? Why, indeed, should we insist that no man can be constitutionally convicted by a jury from which members of an identifiable group to which he belongs have been systematically excluded?

So deeply engrained is the law's tradition of refusal to engage in after-the-fact review of jury deliberations, however, that these and other safeguards provide no more than limited protection. The requirement that the verdict of the jury be unanimous, surely as important as these other constitutional requisites, preserves the jury's function in linking law with contemporary society. It provides the simple and effective method endorsed by centuries of experience and history to combat the injuries to the fair administration of justice that can be inflicted by community passion and prejudice.

I dissent.

[The dissenting opinion of Justice Douglas is omitted.]

NOTES

1. In his concurring opinion in *Johnson*, Mr. Justice Powell expressed the view that the Sixth Amendment requires unanimous verdicts in federal prosecutions. He argued, however, that the Due Process Clause of the Fourteenth Amendment does not incorporate the unanimous verdict provision so as to make it applicable to state prosecutions. Using a generalized "fundamental right, essential to a system of ordered liberty" approach (in the mode of Cardozo and Harlan), Powell concluded that state criminal verdicts of guilt can be sustained even though the vote is less than unanimous. Powell's vote was essential to affirmance in Johnson and in the companion case of Apodaca v. Oregon, 406 U.S. 404, 92 S.Ct. 1628 (1972). The plurality in *Apodaca* said that the essential purpose of jury trial guarantee was to interpose between the accused and the accuser the commonsense judgment of a group of laymen, representative of a cross section of the community, and that this purpose is served even in the absence of a unanimity requirement. It is clear, however, that if the prosecutions under review had been federal, the Court as constituted when *Apodaca* and *Johnson* were decided would, because of Powell's position, mandate a unanimous verdict. The issue is academic now because unanimous verdicts are presently required under federal statutory law and because the Court's composition has changed since 1972.

2. In jurisdictions without statutory provisions for less-than-unanimous verdicts, may a defendant agree to such a verdict while awaiting a conclusion of the jury's deliberation?

Consider Hibdon v. United States, 204 F.2d 834 (6th Cir.1953), involving a felony prosecution, in which the jury, after twenty-seven minutes of deliberation, reported to the trial judge that they were unable to agree. The judge thereupon inquired of defense counsel and the prosecutor as to whether a majority verdict would be acceptable to them. They (as well as the defendant himself) agreed. The jury convicted the defendant on one count of the indictment by a vote of 9 to 3, and on another count by a vote of 10 to 2. Judgment was entered on the verdict and the defendant appealed. In reversing the conviction the Court of Appeals said:

> The humanitarian concept that is at the base of criminal prosecutions in Anglo–Saxon countries, and which distinguishes them from those of most continental European nations, is the presumption of innocence which can only be overthrown by proof beyond a reasonable doubt. The unanimity of a verdict in a criminal case is inextricably interwoven with the required measure of proof. To sustain the validity of a verdict by less than all of the jurors is to destroy this test of proof for there cannot be a verdict supported by proof beyond a reasonable doubt if one or more jurors remain reasonably in doubt as to guilt. It would be a contradiction in terms. We are of the view that the right to a unanimous verdict cannot under any circumstances be waived, that it is of the very essence of our traditional concept of due process in criminal cases, and that the verdict in this case is a nullity because it is not the unanimous verdict of the jury as to guilt.

3. The general rule in federal court is that a unanimous jury may not be waived. The federal courts continue to hold that a defendant cannot waive his right to a unanimous verdict. See United States v. Smedes, 760 F.2d 109 (6th Cir.1985); United States v. Morris, 612 F.2d 483, 490 (10th Cir.1979); United States v. Lopez, 581 F.2d 1338 (9th Cir.1978). The Second Circuit has indicated that waiver may be acceptable, but, when confronted with the issue, has held the waiver unacceptable under the circumstances. See United States v. Pachay, 711 F.2d 488 (2d Cir.1983) (waiver of unanimity suggested by trial court); United States v. Chavis, 719 F.2d 46 (2d Cir.1983) ("Before we could conclude that such important right had been waived, we would have to be satisfied that the trial judge had made a searching inquiry to insure that the defendant was fully aware of his right to a unanimous verdict and that he had given up that right of his own free will and not as a result of a misunderstanding, or a promise, threat or someone's suggestion"). See Note, Whose Life is it Anyway? Waiver of Unanimous Jury Verdict, 39 U.Mia.L.Rev. 369 (1985).

In United States v. Murphy, 483 F.3d 639 (9th Cir. 2007), the deliberating jury sent the court a note that one member of the panel refused to participate and the parties stipulated to the juror's removal. Before a guilty verdict was returned, it came to light that the removed juror was actually a holdout who refused to participate in a conviction. The denial of defendant's motion for a mistrial was upheld on appeal on the ground that the willing dismissal of a juror did not violate the right to a unanimous jury even though the dismissed juror turned out to be a holdout. Judge Gibson (by designation) dissented, finding the jury note created a reasonable probability that the juror was a holdout for acquittal and the defendant's non-waivable right to a unanimous verdict was violated by her dismissal.

4. An unusual unanimity claim was raised in State v. Lomagro, 113 Wis.2d 582, 335 N.W.2d 583 (1983). In a one-count sexual assault case, the complainant testified that, over the course of several hours, defendant and another forced her to engage in six separate acts of sexual intercourse. The jury found defendant guilty as charged; thereafter, defendant moved for a new trial on the ground that his right to a unanimous verdict was violated because the jury was not instructed that it must unanimously agree on the specific criminal act committed by defendant. Holding that the acts committed were part of a continuous criminal transaction and properly chargeable as one offense, the court upheld the conviction because "the jury did not have to be unanimous as to which specific act the defendant committed in order to convict the defendant, since the acts were conceptually similar."

5. Does it follow from *Johnson* (permitting less than unanimous verdicts) and *Williams* (permitting juries of less than 12 members) that a state may permit less than unanimous verdicts by a 6 member jury in criminal cases? The question was resolved in Burch v. Louisiana, 441 U.S. 130, 99 S.Ct. 1623 (1979), in which the Court held that a 5–1 vote for conviction failed to satisfy the minimum constitutional requirements.

6. For a criticism of less than unanimous verdicts based on the theory that it disenfranchises women and minorities, see Taylor–Thompson, Empty Votes in Jury Deliberations, 113 Harv.L.Rev. 1262 (2000).

B. SELECTION OF THE JURY

1. CHALLENGES

Batson v. Kentucky

Supreme Court of the United States, 1986.
476 U.S. 79, 106 S.Ct. 1712.

■ JUSTICE POWELL delivered the opinion of the Court.

This case requires us to reexamine that portion of Swain v. Alabama, 380 U.S. 202, 85 S.Ct. 824 (1965), concerning the evidentiary burden placed on a criminal defendant who claims that he has been denied equal protection through the State's use of peremptory challenges to exclude members of his race from the petit jury.

I

Petitioner, a black man, was indicted in Kentucky on charges of second-degree burglary and receipt of stolen goods. On the first day of trial in Jefferson Circuit Court, the judge conducted *voir dire* examination of the venire, excused certain jurors for cause, and permitted the parties to exercise peremptory challenges. The prosecutor used his peremptory challenges to strike all four black persons on the venire, and a jury composed only of white persons was selected. Defense counsel moved to discharge the jury before it was sworn on the ground that the prosecutor's removal of the black veniremen violated petitioner's rights under the Sixth and Fourteenth Amendments to a jury drawn from a cross-section of the community, and under the Fourteenth Amendment to equal protection of the laws. Counsel requested a hearing on his motion. Without expressly ruling on the request for a hearing, the trial judge observed that the parties were entitled to use their peremptory challenges to "strike anybody they want to." The judge then denied petitioner's motion, reasoning that the cross-section requirement applies only to selection of the venire and not to selection of the petit jury itself.

The jury convicted petitioner on both counts.

* * *

II

In *Swain v. Alabama*, this Court recognized that a "State's purposeful or deliberate denial to Negroes on account of race of participation as jurors in the administration of justice violates the Equal Protection Clause." 380 U.S., at 203–204, 85 S.Ct., at 826–27. This principle has been "consistently and repeatedly" reaffirmed, id., at 204, in numerous decisions of this Court both preceding and following *Swain*. We reaffirm the principle today.

A

More than a century ago, the Court decided that the State denies a black defendant equal protection of the laws when it puts him on trial before a jury from which members of his race have been purposefully excluded. Strauder v. West Virginia, 10 Otto 303, 100 U.S. 303 (1880).

* * *

In holding that racial discrimination in jury selection offends the Equal Protection Clause, the Court in *Strauder* recognized, however, that a defendant has no right to a "petit jury composed in whole or in part of persons of his own race." "The number of our races and nationalities stands in the way of evolution of such a conception" of the demand of equal protection. But the defendant does have the right to be tried by a jury whose members are selected pursuant to nondiscriminatory criteria. The

Equal Protection Clause guarantees the defendant that the State will not exclude members of his race from the jury venire on account of race, or on the false assumption that members of his race as a group are not qualified to serve as jurors.

* * *

The petit jury has occupied a central position in our system of justice by safeguarding a person accused of crime against the arbitrary exercise of power by prosecutor or judge. Those on the venire must be "indifferently chosen," to secure the defendant's right under the Fourteenth Amendment to "protection of life and liberty against race or color prejudice."

Racial discrimination in selection of jurors harms not only the accused whose life or liberty they are summoned to try. Competence to serve as a juror ultimately depends on an assessment of individual qualifications and ability impartially to consider evidence presented at a trial.

* * *

The harm from discriminatory jury selection extends beyond that inflicted on the defendant and the excluded juror to touch the entire community. Selection procedures that purposefully exclude black persons from juries undermine public confidence in the fairness of our system of justice. Discrimination within the judicial system is most pernicious because it is "a stimulant to that race prejudice which is an impediment to securing to [black citizens] that equal justice which the law aims to secure to all others."

B

* * *

While decisions of this Court have been concerned largely with discrimination during selection of the venire, the principles announced there also forbid discrimination on account of race in selection of the petit jury. Since the Fourteenth Amendment protects an accused throughout the proceedings bringing him to justice, the State may not draw up its jury lists pursuant to neutral procedures but then resort to discrimination at "other stages in the selection process."

Accordingly, the component of the jury selection process at issue here, the State's privilege to strike individual jurors through peremptory challenges, is subject to the commands of the Equal Protection Clause.[12]

12. We express no views on whether the Constitution imposes any limit on the exercise of peremptory challenges by defense counsel.

Nor do we express any views on the techniques used by lawyers who seek to obtain information about the community in which a case is to be tried, and about members of the venire from which the jury is likely to be drawn. Prior to *voir dire* examination, which serves as the basis for exercise of challenges, lawyers wish to know as much as possible about prospective jurors, including their age, education, employment, and economic status, so that they can ensure selection of jurors who at least have an open mind about the case. In some jurisdictions, where a pool of jurors serves for a substantial period of time, counsel also may seek to learn which members of the pool served on juries in other cases and the outcome of those cases. Counsel even may employ professional inves-

Although a prosecutor ordinarily is entitled to exercise permitted peremptory challenges "for any reason at all, as long as that reason is related to his view concerning the outcome" of the case to be tried, the Equal Protection Clause forbids the prosecutor to challenge potential jurors solely on account of their race or on the assumption that black jurors as a group will be unable impartially to consider the State's case against a black defendant.

III

The principles announced in *Strauder* never have been questioned in any subsequent decision of this Court. Rather, the Court has been called upon repeatedly to review the application of those principles to particular facts. A recurring question in these cases, as in any case alleging a violation of the Equal Protection Clause, was whether the defendant had met his burden of proving purposeful discrimination on the part of the State. That question also was at the heart of the portion of *Swain v. Alabama* we reexamine today.

A

Swain required the Court to decide, among other issues, whether a black defendant was denied equal protection by the State's exercise of peremptory challenges to exclude members of his race from the petit jury. The record in *Swain* showed that the prosecutor had used the State's peremptory challenges to strike the six black persons included on the petit jury venire. While rejecting the defendant's claim for failure to prove purposeful discrimination, the Court nonetheless indicated that the Equal Protection Clause placed some limits on the State's exercise of peremptory challenges.

The Court sought to accommodate the prosecutor's historical privilege of peremptory challenge free of judicial control, and the constitutional prohibition on exclusion of persons from jury service on account of race. While the Constitution does not confer a right to peremptory challenges, those challenges traditionally have been viewed as one means of assuring the selection of a qualified and unbiased jury. To preserve the peremptory nature of the prosecutor's challenge, the Court in *Swain* declined to scrutinize his actions in a particular case by relying on a presumption that he properly exercised the State's challenges.

The Court went on to observe, however, that a state may not exercise its challenges in contravention of the Equal Protection Clause. It was impermissible for a prosecutor to use his challenges to exclude blacks from the jury "for reasons wholly unrelated to the outcome of the particular case on trial" or to deny to blacks "the same right and opportunity to participate in the administration of justice enjoyed by the white population." Accordingly, a black defendant could make out a prima facie case of purposeful discrimination on proof that the peremptory challenge system was "being perverted" in that manner. For example, an inference of

tigators to interview persons who have served on a particular petit jury. We have had no occasion to consider particularly this practice. Of course, counsel's effort to obtain possibly relevant information about prospective jurors is to be distinguished from the practice at issue here.

purposeful discrimination would be raised on evidence that a prosecutor, "in case after case, whatever the circumstances, whatever the crime and whoever the defendant or the victim may be, is responsible for the removal of Negroes who have been selected as qualified jurors by the jury commissioners and who have survived challenges for cause, with the result that no Negroes ever serve on petit juries." Evidence offered by the defendant in *Swain* did not meet that standard. While the defendant showed that prosecutors in the jurisdiction had exercised their strikes to exclude blacks from the jury, he offered no proof of the circumstances under which prosecutors were responsible for striking black jurors beyond the facts of his own case.

A number of lower courts following the teaching of *Swain* reasoned that proof of repeated striking of blacks over a number of cases was necessary to establish a violation of the Equal Protection Clause. Since this interpretation of *Swain* has placed on defendants a crippling burden of proof, prosecutors' peremptory challenges are now largely immune from constitutional scrutiny. For reasons that follow, we reject this evidentiary formulation as inconsistent with standards that have been developed since *Swain* for assessing a prima facie case under the Equal Protection Clause.

B

* * *

The showing necessary to establish a prima facie case of purposeful discrimination in selection of the venire may be discerned in this Court's decisions. The defendant initially must show that he is a member of a racial group capable of being singled out for differential treatment. In combination with that evidence, a defendant may then make a prima facie case by proving that in the particular jurisdiction members of his race have not been summoned for jury service over an extended period of time. Proof of systematic exclusion from the venire raises an inference of purposeful discrimination because the "result bespeaks discrimination."

* * *

... [S]ince the decision in *Swain*, this Court has recognized that a defendant may make a prima facie showing of purposeful racial discrimination in selection of the venire by relying solely on the facts concerning its selection *in his case*. These decisions are in accordance with the proposition ... that "a consistent pattern of official racial discrimination" is not "a necessary predicate to a violation of the Equal Protection Clause. A single invidiously discriminatory governmental act" is not "immunized by the absence of such discrimination in the making of other comparable decisions." For evidentiary requirements to dictate that "several must suffer discrimination" before one could object, would be inconsistent with the promise of equal protection to all.

C

* * *

... [A] defendant may establish a prima facie case of purposeful discrimination in selection of the petit jury solely on evidence concerning the prosecutor's exercise of peremptory challenges at the defendant's trial. To establish such a case, the defendant first must show that he is a member of a cognizable racial group, and that the prosecutor has exercised peremptory challenges to remove from the venire members of the defendant's race. Second, the defendant is entitled to rely on the fact, as to which there can be no dispute, that peremptory challenges constitute a jury selection practice that permits "those to discriminate who are of a mind to discriminate." Finally, the defendant must show that these facts and any other relevant circumstances raise an inference that the prosecutor used that practice to exclude the veniremen from the petit jury on account of their race. This combination of factors in the empanelling of the petit jury, as in the selection of the venire, raises the necessary inference of purposeful discrimination.

In deciding whether the defendant has made the requisite showing, the trial court should consider all relevant circumstances. For example, a "pattern" of strikes against black jurors included in the particular venire might give rise to an inference of discrimination. Similarly, the prosecutor's questions and statements during *voir dire* examination and in exercising his challenges may support or refute an inference of discriminatory purpose. These examples are merely illustrative. We have confidence that trial judges, experienced in supervising *voir dire*, will be able to decide if the circumstances concerning the prosecutor's use of peremptory challenges creates a prima facie case of discrimination against black jurors.

Once the defendant makes a prima facie showing, the burden shifts to the State to come forward with a neutral explanation for challenging black jurors. Though this requirement imposes a limitation in some cases on the full peremptory character of the historic challenge, we emphasize that the prosecutor's explanation need not rise to the level justifying exercise of a challenge for cause. But the prosecutor may not rebut the defendant's prima facie case of discrimination by stating merely that he challenged jurors of the defendant's race on the assumption—or his intuitive judgment—that they would be partial to the defendant because of their shared race. Just as the Equal Protection Clause forbids the States to exclude black persons from the venire on the assumption that blacks as a group are unqualified to serve as jurors, so it forbids the States to strike black veniremen on the assumption that they will be biased in a particular case simply because the defendant is black. The core guarantee of equal protection, ensuring citizens that their State will not discriminate on account of race, would be meaningless were we to approve the exclusion of jurors on the basis of such assumptions, which arise solely from the jurors' race. Nor may the prosecutor rebut the defendant's case merely by denying that he had a discriminatory motive or "affirming his good faith in individual selections." If these general assertions were accepted as rebutting a defendant's prima facie case, the Equal Protection Clause "would be but a vain and illusory requirement." The prosecutor therefore must articulate a neutral explanation related to the particular case to be tried. The trial court then will have the duty to determine if the defendant has established purposeful discrimination.

IV

The State contends that our holding will eviscerate the fair trial values served by the peremptory challenge. Conceding that the Constitution does not guarantee a right to peremptory challenges and that *Swain* did state that their use ultimately is subject to the strictures of equal protection, the State argues that the privilege of unfettered exercise of the challenge is of vital importance to the criminal justice system.

While we recognize, of course, that the peremptory challenge occupies an important position in our trial procedures, we do not agree that our decision today will undermine the contribution the challenge generally makes to the administration of justice. The reality of practice shows that the challenge may be, and unfortunately at times has been, used to discriminate against black jurors. By requiring trial courts to be sensitive to the racially discriminatory use of peremptory challenges, our decision enforces the mandate of equal protection and furthers the ends of justice.[22] In view of the heterogeneous population of our nation, public respect for our criminal justice system and the rule of law will be strengthened if we ensure that no citizen is disqualified from jury service because of his race.

Nor are we persuaded by the State's suggestion that our holding will create serious administrative difficulties. In those states applying a version of the evidentiary standard we recognize today, courts have not experienced serious administrative burdens, and the peremptory challenge system has survived. We decline, however, to formulate particular procedures to be followed upon a defendant's timely objection to a prosecutor's challenges.[24]

V

In this case, petitioner made a timely objection to the prosecutor's removal of all black persons on the venire. Because the trial court flatly rejected the objection without requiring the prosecutor to give an explanation for his action, we remand this case for further proceedings. If the trial court decides that the facts establish, prima facie, purposeful discrimination

22. While we respect the views expressed in JUSTICE MARSHALL's concurring opinion, concerning prosecutorial and judicial enforcement of our holding today, we do not share them. The standard we adopt under the federal Constitution is designed to ensure that a State does not use peremptory challenges to strike any black juror because of his race. We have no reason to believe that prosecutors will not fulfill their duty to exercise their challenges only for legitimate purposes. Certainly, this Court may assume that trial judges, in supervising *voir dire* in light of our decision today, will be alert to identify a prima facie case of purposeful discrimination. Nor do we think that this historic trial practice, which long has served the selection of an impartial jury, should be abolished because of an apprehension that prosecutors and trial judges will not perform conscientiously their respective duties under the Constitution.

24. In light of the variety of jury selection practices followed in our state and federal trial courts, we make no attempt to instruct these courts how best to implement our holding today. For the same reason, we express no view on whether it is more appropriate in a particular case, upon a finding of discrimination against black jurors, for the trial court to discharge the venire and select a new jury from a panel not previously associated with the case, or to disallow the discriminatory challenges and resume selection with the improperly challenged jurors reinstated on the venire.

and the prosecutor does not come forward with a neutral explanation for his action, our precedents require that petitioner's conviction be reversed.[25]

It is so ordered.

■ JUSTICE WHITE, concurring. [OMITTED].

■ JUSTICE MARSHALL, concurring.

I join JUSTICE POWELL's eloquent opinion for the Court, which takes a historic step toward eliminating the shameful practice of racial discrimination in the selection of juries. The Court's opinion cogently explains the pernicious nature of the racially discriminatory use of peremptory challenges, and the repugnancy of such discrimination to the Equal Protection Clause. The Court's opinion also ably demonstrates the inadequacy of any burden of proof for racially discriminatory use of peremptories that requires that "justice ... sit supinely by" and be flouted in case after case before a remedy is available. I nonetheless write separately to express my views. The decision today will not end the racial discrimination that peremptories inject into the jury-selection process. That goal can be accomplished only by eliminating peremptory challenges entirely.

I

A little over a century ago, this Court invalidated a state statute providing that black citizens could not serve as jurors. State officials then turned to somewhat more subtle ways of keeping blacks off jury venires. Although the means used to exclude blacks have changed, the same pernicious consequence has continued.

Misuse of the peremptory challenge to exclude black jurors has become both common and flagrant.

* * *

The Court's discussion of the utter unconstitutionality of that practice needs no amplification. ... Exclusion of blacks from a jury, solely because of race, can no more be justified by a belief that blacks are less likely than whites to consider fairly or sympathetically the State's case against a black defendant than it can be justified by the notion that blacks lack the "intelligence, experience, or moral integrity," to be entrusted with that role.

II

I wholeheartedly concur in the Court's conclusion that use of the peremptory challenge to remove blacks from juries, on the basis of their race, violates the Equal Protection Clause. I would go further, however, in fashioning a remedy adequate to eliminate that discrimination. Merely allowing defendants the opportunity to challenge the racially discriminato-

25. To the extent that anything in Swain v. Alabama, 380 U.S. 202, 85 S.Ct. 824 (1965), is contrary to the principles we articulate today, that decision is overruled.

ry use of peremptory challenges in individual cases will not end the illegitimate use of the peremptory challenge.

* * *

First, defendants cannot attack the discriminatory use of peremptory challenges at all unless the challenges are so flagrant as to establish a prima facie case. This means, in those States, that where only one or two black jurors survive the challenges for cause, the prosecutor need have no compunction about striking them from the jury because of their race. ... Prosecutors are left free to discriminate against blacks in jury selection provided that they hold that discrimination to an "acceptable" level.

Second, when a defendant can establish a prima facie case, trial courts face the difficult burden of assessing prosecutors' motives. Any prosecutor can easily assert facially neutral reasons for striking a juror, and trial courts are ill-equipped to second-guess those reasons. How is the court to treat a prosecutor's statement that he struck a juror because the juror had a son about the same age as defendant, or seemed "uncommunicative," or "never cracked a smile" and, therefore "did not possess the sensitivities necessary to realistically look at the issues and decide the facts in this case." If such easily generated explanations are sufficient to discharge the prosecutor's obligation to justify his strikes on nonracial grounds, then the protection erected by the Court today may be illusory.

Nor is outright prevarication by prosecutors the only danger here. "[I]t is even possible that an attorney may lie to himself in an effort to convince himself that his motives are legal." A prosecutor's own conscious or unconscious racism may lead him easily to the conclusion that a prospective black juror is "sullen," or "distant," a characterization that would not have come to his mind if a white juror had acted identically. A judge's own conscious or unconscious racism may lead him to accept such an explanation as well supported.

* * *

III

The inherent potential of peremptory challenges to distort the jury process by permitting the exclusion of jurors on racial grounds should ideally lead the Court to ban them entirely from the criminal justice system. JUSTICE GOLDBERG, dissenting in *Swain*, emphasized that "[w]ere it necessary to make an absolute choice between the right of a defendant to have a jury chosen in conformity with the requirements of the Fourteenth Amendment and the right to challenge peremptorily, the Constitution compels a choice of the former." I believe that this case presents just such a choice, and I would resolve that choice by eliminating peremptory challenges entirely in criminal cases.

Some authors have suggested that the courts should ban prosecutors' peremptories entirely, but should zealously guard the defendant's peremptory as "essential to the fairness of trial by jury," and "one of the most important of the rights secured to the accused." I would not find that an acceptable solution. Our criminal justice system "requires not only freedom from any bias against the accused, but also from any prejudice against his prosecution. Between him and the state the scales are to be evenly held." We can maintain that balance, not by permitting both prosecutor and defendant to engage in racial discrimination in jury selection, but by banning the use of peremptory challenges by prosecutors and by allowing the States to eliminate the defendant's peremptory as well.

Much ink has been spilled regarding the historic importance of defendants' peremptory challenges. . . . But this Court has also repeatedly stated that the right of peremptory challenge is not of constitutional magnitude, and may be withheld altogether without impairing the constitutional guarantee of impartial jury and fair trial. The potential for racial prejudice, further, inheres in the defendant's challenge as well. If the prosecutor's peremptory challenge could be eliminated only at the cost of eliminating the defendant's challenge as well, I do not think that would be too great a price to pay.

I applaud the Court's holding that the racially discriminatory use of peremptory challenges violates the Equal Protection Clause, and I join the Court's opinion. However, only by banning peremptories entirely can such discrimination be ended.

■ JUSTICE STEVENS, with whom JUSTICE BRENNAN joins, concurring. [omitted].

■ JUSTICE O'CONNOR, concurring. [OMITTED]

■ CHIEF JUSTICE BURGER, joined by JUSTICE REHNQUIST, dissenting.

* * *

[P]roper resolution of this case requires more than a nodding reference to the purpose of the challenge. Long ago it was recognized that "[t]he right of challenge is almost essential for the purpose of securing perfect fairness and impartiality in a trial." The peremptory challenge has been in use without scrutiny into its basis for nearly as long as juries have existed. "It was in use amongst the Romans in criminal cases, and the *Lex Servilia* (B.C. 104) enacted that the accuser and the accused should severally propose one hundred *judices*, and that each might reject fifty from the list of the other, so that one hundred would remain to try the alleged crime."

In *Swain* JUSTICE WHITE traced the development of the peremptory challenge from the early days of the jury trial in England:

> "In all trials for felonies at common law, the defendant was allowed to challenge peremptorily 35 jurors, and the prosecutor originally had a right to challenge any number of jurors without cause, a right which was said to tend to 'infinite delays and

danger.' Coke on Littleton 156 (14th ed. 1791). Thus The Ordinance for Inquests, 33 Edw. 1, Stat. 4 (1305), provided that if 'they that sue for the King will challenge any ... Jurors, they shall assign ... a Cause certain.' So persistent was the view that a proper jury trial required peremptories on both sides, however, that the statute was construed to allow the prosecution to direct any juror after examination to 'stand aside' until the entire panel was gone over and the defendant had exercised his challenges; only if there was a deficiency of jurors in the box at that point did the Crown have to show cause in respect to jurors recalled to make up the required number. Peremptories on both sides became the settled law of England, continuing in the above form until after the separation of the Colonies." 380 U.S., at 212–213, 85 S.Ct., at 831–32 (footnotes omitted).

Peremptory challenges have a venerable tradition in this country as well:

"In the federal system, Congress early took a part of the subject in hand in establishing that the defendant was entitled to 35 peremptories in trials for treason and 20 in trials for other felonies specified in the 1790 Act as punishable by death, 1 Stat. 119 (1790). In regard to trials for other offenses without the 1790 statute, both the defendant and the Government were thought to have a right of peremptory challenge, although the source of this right was not wholly clear. ...

"The course in the States apparently paralleled that in the federal system. The defendant's right of challenge was early conferred by statute, the number often corresponding to the English practice, the prosecution was thought to have retained the Crown's common-law right to stand aside, and by 1870, most if not all, States had enacted statutes conferring on the prosecution a substantial number of peremptory challenges, the number generally being at least half, but often equal to, the number had by the defendant."

The Court's opinion, in addition to ignoring the teachings of history, also contrasts with *Swain* in its failure to even discuss the rationale of the peremptory challenge. *Swain* observed:

"The function of the challenge is not only to eliminate extremes of partiality on both sides, but to assure the parties that the jurors before whom they try the case will decide on the basis of the evidence placed for them, and not otherwise. In this way the peremptory satisfies the rule that 'to perform its high function in the best way, justice must satisfy the appearance of justice.'"

Permitting unexplained peremptories has long been regarded as a means to strengthen our jury system in other ways as well. One commentator has recognized:

"The peremptory, made without giving any reason, avoids trafficking in the core of truth in most common stereotypes. ... Common human experience, common sense, psychosociological studies, and public opinion polls tell us that it is likely that certain classes of people statistically have predispositions that would make them

> inappropriate jurors for particular kinds of cases. But to allow this knowledge to be expressed in the evaluative terms necessary for challenges for cause would undercut our desire for a society in which all people are judged as individuals and in which each is held reasonable and open to compromise. ... [For example,] [a]lthough experience reveals that black males as a class can be biased against young alienated blacks who have not tried to join the middle class, to enunciate this in the concrete expression required of a challenge for cause is societally divisive. Instead we have evolved in the peremptory challenge a system that allows the covert expression of what we dare not say but know is true more often than not." Babcock, Voir Dire: Preserving "Its Wonderful Power," 27 Stan.L.Rev. 545, 553–554 (1975).

* * *

Instead of even considering the history or function of the peremptory challenge, the bulk of the Court's opinion is spent recounting the well-established principle that intentional exclusion of racial groups from jury venires is a violation of the Equal Protection Clause. I too reaffirm that principle, which has been a part of our constitutional tradition since at least Strauder v. West Virginia, 100 U.S. (10 Otto) 303 (1880). But if today's decision is nothing more than mere "application" of the "principles announced in *Strauder*," as the Court maintains, some will consider it curious that the application went unrecognized for over a century.

* * *

Unwilling to rest solely on jury venire cases such as *Strauder*, the Court also invokes general equal protection principles in support of its holding. But peremptory challenges are often lodged, of necessity, for reasons "normally thought irrelevant to legal proceedings or official action, namely, the race, religion, nationality, occupation or affiliations of people summoned for jury duty." Moreover, in making peremptory challenges, both the prosecutor and defense attorney necessarily act on only limited information or hunch. The process can not be indicted on the sole basis that such decisions are made on the basis of "assumption" or "intuitive judgment." As a result, unadulterated equal protection analysis is simply inapplicable to peremptory challenges exercised in any particular case. A clause that requires a minimum "rationality" in government actions has no application to " 'an arbitrary and capricious right,' " a constitutional principle that may invalidate state action on the basis of "stereotypic notions," does not explain the breadth of a procedure exercised on the " 'sudden impressions and unaccountable prejudices we are apt to conceive upon the bare looks and gestures of another.' "

* * *

In short, it is quite probable that every peremptory challenge could be objected to on the basis that, because it excluded a venireman who had some characteristic not shared by the remaining members of the venire, it constituted a "classification" subject to equal protection scrutiny.

* * *

Rather than applying straightforward equal protection analysis, the Court substitutes for the holding in *Swain* a curious hybrid. The defendant must first establish a "prima facie case," of invidious discrimination, then the "burden shifts to the State to come forward with a neutral explanation for challenging black jurors." The Court explains that "the operation of prima facie burden of proof rules" is established in "[o]ur decisions in the context of Title VII 'disparate treatment'...." The Court then adds, borrowing again from a Title VII case, that "the prosecutor must give a 'clear and reasonably specific' explanation of his 'legitimate reasons' for exercising the challenges."

While undoubtedly these rules are well suited to other contexts, particularly where (as with Title VII) they are required by an act of Congress, they seem curiously out of place when applied to peremptory challenges in criminal cases. Our system permits two types of challenges: challenges for cause and peremptory challenges. Challenges for cause obviously have to be explained; by definition, peremptory challenges do not. "It is called a peremptory challenge, because the prisoner may challenge peremptorily, on his own dislike, *without showing of any cause*." Analytically, there is no middle ground: A challenge either has to be explained or it does not. It is readily apparent, then, that to permit inquiry into the basis for a peremptory challenge would force "the peremptory challenge [to] collapse into the challenge for cause."

* * *

Confronted with the dilemma it created, the Court today attempts to decree a middle ground. To rebut a prima facie case, the Court requires a "neutral explanation" for the challenge, but is at pains to "emphasize" that the "explanation need not rise to the level justifying exercise of a challenge for cause." I am at a loss to discern the governing principles here. A "clear and reasonably specific" explanation of "legitimate reasons" for exercising the challenge will be difficult to distinguish from a challenge for cause. Anything short of a challenge for cause may well be seen as an "arbitrary and capricious" challenge, to use Blackstone's characterization of the peremptory. Apparently the Court envisions permissible challenges short of a challenge for cause that are just a little bit arbitrary—but not too much. While our trial judges are "experienced in supervising *voir dire*," they have no experience in administering rules like this.

* * *

The Court does not tarry long over any of these difficult, sensitive problems, preferring instead to gloss over them as swiftly as it slides over centuries of history: "[W]e make no attempt to instruct [trial] courts on how best to implement our holding today." That leaves roughly 7,000 general jurisdiction state trial judges and approximately 500 federal trial judges at large to find their way through the morass the Court creates today. The Court essentially wishes these judges well as they begin the difficult enterprise of sorting out the implications of the Court's newly created "right." I join my colleagues in wishing the nation's judges well as they struggle to grasp how to implement today's holding. To my mind, however, attention to these "implementation" questions leads quickly to the conclusion that there is no "best" way to implement the holding, let alone a "good" way. As one apparently frustrated judge explained after reviewing a case under a rule like that promulgated by the Court today, judicial inquiry into peremptory challenges

> "from case to case will take the courts into the quagmire of quotas for groups that are difficult to define and even more difficult to quantify in the courtroom. The pursuit of judicial perfection will require both trial and appellate courts to provide speculative and impractical answers to artificial questions." Holley v. J & S Sweeping Co., 143 Cal.App.3d 588, 595–596, 192 Cal.Rptr. 74, 79 (1983) (Holmdahl, J., concurring) (footnote omitted).

The Court's effort to "further the ends of justice," and achieve hoped for utopian bliss may be admired, but it is far more likely to enlarge the evil "sporting contest" theory of criminal justice roundly condemned by Roscoe Pound almost 80 years ago to the day. Pound warned then that "too much of the current dissatisfaction has a just origin in our judicial organization and procedure." I am afraid that today's newly created constitutional right will justly give rise to similar disapproval.

* * *

■ JUSTICE REHNQUIST, with whom THE CHIEF JUSTICE joins, dissenting.

* * *

I cannot subscribe to the Court's unprecedented use of the Equal Protection Clause to restrict the historic scope of the peremptory challenge, which has been described as "a necessary part of trial by jury." In my view, there is simply nothing "unequal" about the State using its peremptory challenges to strike blacks from the jury in cases involving black defendants, so long as such challenges are also used to exclude whites in cases involving white defendants, Hispanics in cases involving Hispanic defendants, Asians in cases involving Asian defendants, and so on. This case-specific use of peremptory challenges by the State does not single out blacks, or members of any other race for that matter, for discriminatory treatment. Such use of peremptories is at best based upon seat-of-the-pants instincts, which are undoubtedly crudely stereotypical and may in many cases be hopelessly mistaken. But as long as they are applied across the board to jurors of all races and nationalities, I do not see—and the Court most certainly has not explained—how their use violates the Equal Protection Clause.

* * *

NOTES

1. After the Supreme Court held *Batson* inapplicable to cases which had become final before *Batson* was decided in Griffith v. Kentucky, 479 U.S. 314, 107 S.Ct. 708 (1987), some defendants brought Sixth Amendment cross-section challenges to prosecutorial uses of peremptory challenges against Black jurors. They argued that the question had been left open in *Batson*, so that the non-retroactivity of *Batson*'s Equal Protection holding was irrelevant. White defendants also pressed the Sixth Amendment claim even in cases not yet final as of the date of *Batson*. These contentions were considered in Holland v. Illinois, 493 U.S. 474, 110 S.Ct. 803 (1990), where the Court rejected the claim that a white defendant's sixth amendment right to a "fair possibility" of a representative jury allowed him to challenge the exclusion of blacks from his petit jury:

> We reject petitioner's fundamental thesis that a prosecutor's use of peremptory challenges to eliminate a distinctive group in the community deprives the defendant of a Sixth Amendment right to the "fair possibility" of a representative jury.... A prohibition upon the exclusion of cognizable groups through peremptory challenges has no conceivable basis in the text of the Sixth Amendment, is without support in our prior decisions, and would undermine rather than further the constitutional guarantee of an impartial jury.
>
> It has long been established that racial groups cannot be excluded from the venire from which a jury is selected. That constitutional principle was first set forth not under the Sixth Amendment but under the Equal Protection Clause.
>
> * * *
>
> Our relatively recent cases ... hold that a fair-cross-section venire requirement is imposed by the Sixth Amendment. * * * But it has never included the notion that, in the process of drawing the jury, that initial representativeness cannot be diminished by allowing both the accused and the State to eliminate persons thought to be inclined against their interests—which is precisely how the traditional peremptory-challenge system operates.
>
> * * *
>
> The Sixth Amendment requirement of a fair cross section on the venire is a means of assuring, not a *representative* jury (which the Constitution does not demand), but an *impartial* one (which it does). Without that requirement, the State could draw up jury lists in such manner as to produce a pool of prospective jurors disproportionately ill disposed towards one or all classes of defendants, and thus more likely to yield petit juries with similar disposition. The State would have, in effect, unlimited peremptory challenges to compose the pool in its favor. The fair-cross-section venire requirement assures, in other words, that in the process of selecting the petit jury the prosecution and defense will compete on an equal basis.
>
> But to say that the Sixth Amendment deprives the State of the ability to "stack the deck" in its favor is not to say that each side may not, once a fair hand is dealt, use peremptory challenges to eliminate prospective jurors belonging to groups it believes would unduly favor the other side. Any theory of the Sixth Amendment leading to that result is implausible.
>
> * * *
>
> The rule we announce today is not only the only plausible reading of the text of the Sixth Amendment, but we think it best furthers the Amendment's central purpose as well. Although the constitutional guarantee runs only to the individual and not to the State, the goal it expresses is jury impartiality with respect to both contestants: neither the defendant

> nor the State should be favored. This goal, it seems to us, would positively be obstructed by a petit jury cross section requirement which, as we have described, would cripple the device of peremptory challenge.

2. In Powers v. Ohio, 499 U.S. 400, 111 S.Ct. 1364 (1991), the Court held that a Caucasian defendant has standing to raise a *Batson* equal protection claim contesting the prosecution's peremptory challenges of Black prospective jurors. For the majority, Justice Kennedy reasoned that one of the rights at stake is the right of a citizen not to be excluded from jury service because of race. He noted that the relationship between the accused and the prospective jurors is as close as that between physician and patient in the right-to-contraceptives decision of Griswold v. Connecticut, 381 U.S. 479, 85 S.Ct. 1678 (1965). The majority said that according the accused standing may be the most meaningful way to vindicate the rights of the prospective jurors, just as according the physician standing may be the best way to vindicate the rights of the patient. Citizens on their own are not likely to litigate their racially-based dismissal from jury service, whereas the accused has substantial incentive to do so. The majority also argued that a verdict reached by a *Batson*-violative jury will not be accepted by the community as fair and that, therefore, the defendant himself will suffer real harm when "the prosecutor excludes jurors at his or her own trial on account of race."

The record in *Powers* did "not indicate that race was somehow implicated in the crime or the trial." The prosecution used seven of its ten peremptory challenges to exclude Blacks. The record did not reveal whether any Blacks served on Powers' jury or whether Powers peremptorily excused any Black prospective jurors. The State conceded that if the Supreme Court held that "the petitioner has standing to object to the prosecutor's use of the peremptory challenges, the case should be remanded." The Court so remanded for further proceedings without expressly holding that Powers had established a prima facie case under *Batson*.

Joined by Chief Justice Rehnquist, Justice Scalia dissented. He argued that according standing to members of one race to challenge the denial of the equal protection rights of members of another race was a radical departure from prior precedents in the law of standing. Scalia wrote:

> Notwithstanding history, precedent, and the significant benefits of the peremptory-challenge system, it is intolerably offensive for the State to imprison a person on the basis of a conviction rendered by a jury from which members of that person's minority race were carefully excluded. I am unmoved, however, and I think most Americans would be, by this white defendant's complaint that he was sought to be tried by an all-white jury, or that he should be permitted to press black jurors' unlodged complaint that they were not allowed to sit in judgment of him.
>
> Judging from the Court's opinion, we can expect further, wide-ranging use of the jail-house key to combat discrimination. Convictions are to be overturned, apparently, *whenever* "race is implicated in the trial"—"by casting doubt upon the credibility or dignity of a witness, or . . . upon the standing or due regard of an attorney who appears in the cause," or even by suggesting "an alleged racial motivation of the defendant or a victim." To me this makes no sense. Lofty aims do not justify every step intended to achieve them. Today's supposed blow against racism, while enormously self-satisfying, is unmeasured and misdirected. If for any reason the State is unable to reconvict Powers for the double murder at issue here, later victims may pay the price for our extravagance. Even if such a tragedy, in this or any case, never occurs, the prosecutorial efforts devoted to retrials will necessarily be withheld from other endeavors, as will the prosecutorial efforts devoted to meeting the innumerable *Powers* claims that defendants

of all races can be relied upon to present—again with the result that crime goes unpunished and criminals go free.

3. In Hernandez v. New York, 500 U.S. 352, 111 S.Ct. 1859 (1991), the Court had to determine "whether the prosecutor offered a race-neutral basis" for challenging Latino potential jurors. The prosecutor, faced with a *Batson* challenge, stated that he feared that the two challenged jurors would not accept the version of a Spanish interpreter but instead would rely on their own knowledge of Spanish in evaluating the testimony of Spanish-speaking witnesses. The Court noted that the prosecutor stated that his doubts arose from the voir dire and not merely from the fact that the prospective jurors spoke Spanish. The prosecutor also said that his four complainants were Hispanic and that he had no incentive to remove Hispanic jurors.

The plurality concluded that the prosecutor had advanced race-neutral reasons. It acknowledged that the impact of the prosecutor's reason might not be race-neutral, but the intent underlying the challenge was race-neutral and therefore not prohibited by *Batson*. The Court added that a reviewing court owed great deference to a trial judge's decision concerning discriminatory intent. Here the trial judge had accepted the prosecutor's explanation.

Justice O'Connor, concurring with Justice Scalia, also emphasized discriminatory intent rather than discriminatory effect. She stated that the opposite approach could lead to full-blown hearings involving statistical presentations concerning discriminatory impact.

On behalf of three dissenters, Justice Stevens wrote:

> The prosecutor's explanation was insufficient for three reasons. First, the justification would inevitably result in a disproportionate disqualification of Spanish-speaking venirepersons. An explanation that is "race-neutral" on its face is nonetheless unacceptable if it is merely a proxy for a discriminatory practice. Second, the prosecutor's concern could easily have been accommodated by less drastic means. As is the practice in many jurisdictions, the jury could have been instructed that the official translation alone is evidence; bilingual jurors could have been instructed to bring to the attention of the judge any disagreements they might have with the translation so that any disputes could be resolved by the court. Third, if the prosecutor's concern was valid and substantiated by the record, it would have supported a challenge for cause. The fact that the prosecutor did not make any such challenge, should disqualify him from advancing the concern as a justification for a peremptory challenge.
>
> Each of these reasons considered alone might not render insufficient the prosecutor's facially neutral explanation. In combination, however, they persuade me that his explanation should have been rejected as a matter of law.

4. In Edmonson v. Leesville Concrete Co., 500 U.S. 614, 111 S.Ct. 2077 (1991), the Court extended *Batson* to prohibit race-based peremptory challenges in civil litigation between private litigants. The majority found sufficient "state action" to invoke the Equal Protection Clause in the trial court's sustaining of peremptory challenges. "Peremptory challenges are permitted only when the government, by statute or decisional law, deems it appropriate to allow parties to exclude a given number of persons who otherwise would satisfy the requirements of service on the petit jury." The majority added, "The government summons jurors, constrains their freedom of movement, and subjects them to public scrutiny and examination. The party who exercises a challenge invokes the formal authority of the court, which must discharge the prospective juror, thus effecting the 'final and practical denial' of the excluded individual's opportunity to serve on the petit jury." Accordingly the majority concluded, "The peremptory challenge is used in selecting an entity that is a quintessential governmental body having no attributes of a private actor."

5. In Georgia v. McCollum, 505 U.S. 42, 112 S.Ct. 2348 (1992), the Court extended *Batson* to a criminal defendant's exercise of peremptory challenges:

> "Be it at the hands of the State or the defense, if a court allows jurors to be excluded because of group bias, it is a willing participant in a scheme that could only undermine the very foundation of our system of justice—our citizens' confidence in it. Just as public confidence in criminal justice is undermined by a conviction in a trial where racial discrimination has occurred in jury selection, so is public confidence undermined where a defendant, assisted by racially discriminatory peremptory strikes, obtains an acquittal."

Justice O'Connor's dissent focused on the intrinsic difficulty in perceiving a criminal defendant's conduct as the type of state action condemned by the Constitution:

> "What really seems to bother the Court is the prospect that leaving criminal defendants and their attorneys free to make racially motivated peremptory challenges will undermine the ideal of nondiscriminatory jury selection we espoused in Batson. The concept that the government alone must honor constitutional dictates, however, is a fundamental tenet of our legal order, not an obstacle to be circumvented. This is particularly so in the context of criminal trials, where we have held the prosecution to uniquely high standards of conduct."

McCollum raises a difficult question by extending the *Batson* obligation to defendants. What if a judge erroneously rejects a race neutral explanation by the defense and refuses to permit the exercise of a preemptory? In United States v. Annigoni, 96 F.3d 1132 (9th Cir.1996) (en banc), the majority answered this question by holding that automatic reversal was required and that harmless error analysis was inappropriate to the situation. On behalf of the dissenters, Judge Leavy stated:

> In my view, to subject every trial court allowance or disallowance of a preemptory challenge to automatic reversal places the trial judge in an untenable position and endangers the continued existence of the statutory right. The erroneous disallowance of a preemptory challenge only deprives a party of a statutory right, and should be reviewed for harmless error.

6. In J.E.B. v. Alabama ex rel. T.B., 511 U.S. 127, 114 S.Ct. 1419 (1994), the state used 9 of its 10 peremptory challenges to strike potential male jurors in a paternity case. In this setting, the Court again extended *Batson* to prohibit gender based peremptory challenges:

> Equal opportunity to participate in the fair administration of justice is fundamental to our democratic system. It not only furthers the goals of the jury system. It reaffirms the promise of equality under the law—that all citizens, regardless of race, ethnicity, or gender, have the chance to take part directly in our democracy. * * * When persons are excluded from participation in our democratic processes solely because of race or gender, this promise of equality dims, and the integrity of our judicial system is jeopardized.
>
> In view of these concerns, the Equal Protection Clause prohibits discrimination in jury selection on the basis of gender, or on the assumption that an individual will be biased in a particular case for no reason other than the fact that the person happens to be a woman or happens to be a man.

7. In Purkett v. Elem, 514 U.S. 765, 115 S.Ct. 1769 (1995), the Court held that a prosecutor's explanation that two black prospective jurors had long, unkempt hair and a beard, accepted by the trial judge as nonpretextual reasons striking them, sufficient to comply with Batson:

> Under our *Batson* jurisprudence, once the opponent of a peremptory challenge has made out a prima facie case of racial discrimination (step 1), the burden of production shifts to the proponent of the strike to come forward with a race-neutral explanation (step 2). If a race-neutral explanation is tendered, the trial court must then decide (step 3) whether the opponent of the strike has proved purposeful racial discrimination. The second step of this process does not demand an explanation that is persuasive, or even plausible. "At this [second] step of the inquiry, the issue is the facial validity of the prosecutor's explanation. Unless a discriminatory intent is inherent in the prosecutor's explanation, the reason offered will be deemed race neutral."
>
> * * *
>
> It is not until the *third* step that the persuasiveness of the justification becomes relevant—the step in which the trial court determines whether the opponent of the strike has carried his burden of proving purposeful discrimination. At that stage, implausible or fantastic justifications may (and probably will) be found to be pretexts for purposeful discrimination. But to say that a trial judge *may choose to disbelieve* a silly or superstitious reason at step 3 is quite different from saying that a trial judge *must terminate* the inquiry at step 2 when the race-neutral reason is silly or superstitious. The latter violates the principle that the ultimate burden of persuasion regarding racial motivation rests with, and never shifts from, the opponent of the strike.

JUSTICE STEVENS dissented:

> In my opinion, preoccupation with the niceties of a three-step analysis should not foreclose meaningful judicial review of prosecutorial explanations that are entirely unrelated to the case to be tried. I would adhere to the *Batson* rule that such an explanation does not satisfy step two. Alternatively, I would hold that, in the absence of an explicit trial court finding on the issue, a reviewing court may hold that such an explanation is pretextual as a matter of law. The Court's unnecessary tolerance of silly, fantastic, and implausible explanations, together with its assumption that there is a difference of constitutional magnitude between a statement that "I had a hunch about this juror based on his appearance," and "I challenged this juror because he had a mustache," demeans the importance of the values vindicated by our decision in *Batson*.

Does *Purkett*'s acceptance of a facially neutral explanation, even if implausible or fantastic, sound the death knell for *Batson* in all but the most flagrant cases? *Compare* United States v. Bishop, 959 F.2d 820 (9th Cir.1992) (pre-*Purkett* decision finding a *Batson* violation in a strike based on juror's residence in a poor and violent area where people are anesthetized to violence) *with* United States v. Fike, 82 F.3d 1315 (5th Cir.1996) (striking of a black juror because of his distrust for the past practices of the U.S. Justice System found acceptable under *Batson* in light of *Purkett*'s "great deference" standard of review). See also United States v. Perkins, 105 F.3d 976 (5th Cir.1997) (disgusted look on juror's face sufficient reason under "great deference" standard).

These types of cases have led to a "dual motivation" analysis. In Guzman v. State, 85 S.W.3d 242 (Tex.Crim.App.2002), a prospective juror was excluded in a case involving the death of a young child because he was a single male and fell asleep during the voir dire. In a 5–4 decision, the majority found that, when the motives for striking a juror are mixed, the striking party must show that it would have struck the juror based solely on the neutral reasons and the trial judge must make explicit findings that the neutral reasons are sufficient. The dissent relied upon a bright line test in which any non-neutral justification taints the strike. See Wilkerson v. Texas, 493 U.S. 924, 110 S.Ct. 292 (1989) (Marshall, J., dissenting from denial of certiorari); State v. Lucas, 199 Ariz. 366, 18 P.3d 160 (2001); Payton v. Kearse, 329 S.C. 51, 495 S.E.2d 205 (1998).

8. *Batson* and its progeny have spawned litigation over procedural and substantive issues concerning the use of protected-class based peremptories:

a. Who has standing to complain? Because *Batson* was decided on equal protection grounds, members of a number of minority groups have sought to challenge the exercise of peremptories. Gender-based claims have generally failed. See United States v. De Gross, 913 F.2d 1417 (9th Cir.1990); United States v. Hamilton, 850 F.2d 1038 (4th Cir.1988); United States v. Dennis, 804 F.2d 1208 (11th Cir.1986) (exclusion of Black males, but not females); State v. Levinson, 71 Haw. 492, 795 P.2d 845 (1990); State v. Culver, 233 Neb. 228, 444 N.W.2d 662 (1989) (exclusion of males in purse-snatching case).

Ethnic based challenges have been given some credence, but have not successfully risen to the level of *Batson* because of the judicially imposed requirement that the proponent prove that a clearly identifiable group shares a common thread of attitudes, ideas or experiences, and that a community of interests exists among its members such that the group's interests cannot be adequately represented if the group is excluded. See United States v. Watson, 483 F.3d 828 (D.C.Cir. 2007) ("we find no basis for applying heightened scrutiny to preemptory challenges of blind jurors"); United States v. Sgro, 816 F.2d 30 (1st Cir.1987) (Italian–American failed to satisfy standard); United States v. Bucci, 839 F.2d 825 (1st Cir.1988) (whether Italian–Americans comprise a group needing protection from community prejudice is a question of fact). How can this standard be met? By a sociological survey of attitudes? By an appeal to history? Was such a showing made in *Batson* with respect to blacks? Was it presumed? Another difficulty is identifying the group in which a prospective juror is properly placed. For example, are surnames an inadequate basis for determining who is Italian–American? See United States v. Di Pasquale, 864 F.2d 271 (3d Cir.1988). Compare United States v. Gelb, 881 F.2d 1155 (2d Cir.1989) (Jewish persons a cognizable subgroup but use of surnames an inadequate method of identifying such persons). See also State v. Alen, 616 So.2d 452 (Fla.1993) (setting forth criteria for determining whether a prospective juror belonged to a cognizable ethnic group).

b. What constitutes a sufficient prima-facie showing of improper exercise of a challenge so as to require an explanation? In Johnson v. California, 545 U.S. 162, 125 S.Ct. 2410 (2005), the Court held that the states may not create barriers to impose the obligation to explain the reasons for the exercise of a preemptory. While the party of objecting to the opponent's exercise of the challenge bears the ultimate burden of showing purposeful discrimination, he need not show that discrimination was "more likely than not" (as California required) but need only raise any circumstance that gives rise to an inference of discrimination. In certain situations, the striking of a single juror may establish a *Batson* showing even though members of the same group are seated on the jury. *See* United

States v. Johnson, 873 F.2d 1137 (8th Cir.1989); United States v. Hughes, 880 F.2d 101 (8th Cir.1989). The courts generally recognize that numbers alone are not controlling, but look to the questions and statements of the prosecutor during voir dire to determine whether discriminatory intent can be inferred. United States v. Dawn, 897 F.2d 1444 (8th Cir.1990). The following factors have been viewed as examples of discriminatory intent. "(1) alleged group bias not shown to be shared by the juror in question, (2) failure to examine the juror or perfunctory examination, assuming neither the trial court nor opposing counsel had questioned the juror, (3) singling the juror out for special questioning to evoke a certain response, (4) the prosecutor's reason is unrelated to the facts of the case, and (5) a challenge based on reasons equally applicable to jurors who were not challenged." State v. Slappy, 522 So.2d 18 (Fla.1988). See State v. Butler, 731 S.W.2d 265 (Mo.App.1987), focusing on the race of the victim, a comparison of excluded jurors and those seated and the prosecutor's past practices as factors. Compare People v. Johnson, 210 Cal.App.3d 316, 258 Cal.Rptr. 347 (1989), suggesting that a comparison of the characteristics of minority jurors challenged by the prosecution to non-minority jurors accepted by the prosecution should not be dispositive because an attorney might accept a prospective juror late in jury selection, after most peremptories have been used, even though the lawyer would have challenged the same juror earlier in the process.

c. What is a racially neutral, nonpretextual reason for striking a particular juror? For examples of acceptable justifications, see United States v. Mitchell, 877 F.2d 294 (4th Cir.1989) (Black jurors struck because they resided in congressional district of a popular congressman slated to be a defense witness); United States v. Clemons, 843 F.2d 741 (3d Cir.1988) (Black jurors struck were included within group of unmarried single persons under the age of 35, all of whom were struck); Wallace v. State, 507 So.2d 466 (Ala.1987). (One Black was too grandmotherly, another had a beard, a third was too close in age to the parents of the deceased, one did not have necessary experience, another might tend to be irresponsible). For examples of insufficient justifications, see Snyder v. Louisiana, 128 S.Ct. 1203 (2008) (claim that black prospective juror would opt for a lesser included offense. To avoid death penalty hearing so that he could return to student teaching obligations was a pretreat when white jurors who revealed conflicting obligations were accepted); Miller–El v. Dretke, 545 U.S. 231, 125 S.Ct. 2317 (2005) (when prosecutor struck ten of eleven qualified black jurors and its reasons for so doing appeared to apply equally to white jurors it seated, sufficient evidence of pretext was shown to demonstrate purposeful discrimination);United States v. Wilson, 884 F.2d 1121 (8th Cir.1989) (defendant's friends were more likely to contact a Black than a White juror); United States v. Horsley, 864 F.2d 1543 (11th Cir.1989) ("I just got a feeling about him"); James v. Commonwealth, 247 Va. 459, 442 S.E.2d 396 (1994) (prosecutor's statement that he struck Juror wearing a crucifix because it reflected an undesirable "sympathetic disposition" was found an acceptable race neutral explanation over a dissent arguing that the strike violated freedom of religion considerations); Devose v. Norris, 53 F.3d 201 (8th Cir.1995) (justification offered for striking two black prospective jurors and one black prospective alternate juror on ground that the jurors had previous jury experience and therefore suffered from jury burnout was unacceptable). For a dispute over whether the claim that a juror lived in a "high crime area" was sufficient, compare the majority and dissenting opinions in Gray v. Commonwealth, 203 S.W.3d 679 (Ky. S. Ct. 2006).

d. What may a defendant do to contest the prosecutor's explanation? Courts have reached different results as to whether, once a defendant makes a prima facie showing of race-based peremptory challenges, the defendant has a right to participate in an adversary hearing concerning the prosecution's explanations. See United States v. Alcantar, 832 F.2d 1175 (9th Cir.1987) (upholding the right, at least when the trial judge does not find that prosecution strategy precludes an open hearing). Compare United States v. Tucker, 836 F.2d 334 (7th Cir.1988) (allowing an in camera hearing, out of the presence of the defendant and his lawyer, when the prosecution's explanation was offered during the voir dire itself, and not after-the-fact, and the Government claimed its strategy would be compromised if it had to make disclosure to the defendant). See also United States v. Davis, 809 F.2d 1194 (6th Cir.1987); United States v. Tindle, 860 F.2d 125 (4th Cir.1988). Other procedural issues concern whether the prosecutor should be placed under oath when explaining the reason, and whether the defense should be allowed access to the prosecutor's notes pertaining to prospective jurors? Illinois courts have resolved these issues in favor of the prosecution. People v. Hope, 137 Ill.2d 430, 148 Ill.Dec. 252, 560 N.E.2d 849 (1990); People v. Brisbon, 129 Ill.2d 200, 135 Ill.Dec. 801, 544 N.E.2d 297 (1989).

e. When must the claim be raised? The *Batson* issue must be raised prior to commencement of trial or it may be deemed waived. McCrory v. Henderson, 82 F.3d 1243 (2d Cir.1996); United States v. Romero–Reyna, 867 F.2d 834 (5th Cir.1989). Waiver will also occur when defense counsel accepts the prosecutor's explanation. United States v. Rudas, 905 F.2d 38 (2d Cir.1990). However, the failure to raise the issue, in certain circumstances, may result in ineffective assistance of counsel. Virgin Islands v. Forte, 865 F.2d 59 (3d Cir.1989) (exclusion of White males in trial of White man for raping Black female).

9. When a judge erroneously refuses to excuse a juror for cause and thereby forces the defendant to exercise a peremptory challenge, reversible error may result even though the juror did not sit in the case. See United States v. Amerson, 938 F.2d 116 (8th Cir.1991) (four jurors who indicated that they would give greater credence to testimony of law enforcement officers); United States v. Allsup, 566 F.2d 68 (9th Cir.1977) (bank employee in bank robbery case); State v. Singletary, 156 N.J.Super. 303, 383 A.2d 1151 (1978), reversed on other grounds 80 N.J. 55, 402 A.2d 203 (1979) (juror was an armed robbery victim 17 days before armed robbery); Commonwealth v. Jones, 477 Pa. 164, 383 A.2d 874 (1978) (juror was a Philadelphia policeman; all police who testified in case were from same force).

10. Some jurisdictions, however, require that a defendant completely exhaust all peremptory challenges in order to preserve for appeal a claim of error in the overruling of a peremptory challenge. Other forms of waiver include failure to raise the grounds of the challenge before the panel is chosen, United States v. Franklin, 700 F.2d 1241 (10th Cir.1983) (prior jury service in similar case); United States v. Cepeda Penes, 577 F.2d 754 (1st Cir.1978), and acceptance of the panel notwithstanding the judge's express willingness to exclude a juror for cause. United States v. Renfro, 620 F.2d 569 (6th Cir.1980).

In some jurisdictions, even when a trial judge has erroneously denied a challenge for cause, the defendant has then exercised a peremptory challenge against the juror in question, and the defendant eventually has exhausted all of his or her peremptory challenges, the defendant still may not be entitled to relief on appeal. See Ross v. Oklahoma, 487 U.S. 81, 108 S.Ct. 2273 (1988), where the Court held that the erroneous refusal to sustain the challenge for cause is not necessarily reversible error even when the defendant is forced to use a peremptory challenge to eliminate the juror in question, and even when the defendant eventually exhausts all of his or her peremptory challenges. The Court noted that under Oklahoma law, a party who has a peremptory challenge left must use such challenge to remedy an erroneous challenge for cause. Only if a party is forced to accept such a juror, and the juror actually sits, does the party have a right to complain on appeal under Oklahoma law. The United States Supreme Court, noting that there is no federal constitutional right to peremptory challenges, held that the Oklahoma approach does not violate the Constitution. As long as there is no reason to believe that the jury that actually sat was unfair, the defendant is not entitled to relief.

11. Challenges for cause are limited to situations in which bias is admitted or clearly implied from the relationship of the prospective juror to the parties or the case. The trial judge's decision to exclude for cause is subject to an abuse of discretion standard on review; and the challenging party has a "heavy burden" to demonstrate that the juror's prejudice was "manifest." United States v. Jones, 608 F.2d 1004 (4th Cir.1979); United States v. Gullion, 575 F.2d 26 (1st Cir.1978).

12. When a prospective juror articulates his lack of impartiality, the court may excuse him for cause without infringing on the defendant's rights. See United States v. Jimenez–Diaz, 659 F.2d 562 (5th Cir.1981) (two jurors stated that they could not serve fairly and impartially); United States v. Pappas, 639 F.2d 1 (1st Cir.1980) (juror, due to religious beliefs, said he could not "serve in judgment of his fellow man"); United States v. Gonzalez, 483 F.2d 223 (2d Cir.1973) ("I don't know if I can honestly send the man to jail").

13. The mere fact that a juror knows something about the case or the defendant is not sufficient to excuse him for cause so long as he indicates that he can be impartial. See Murphy v. Florida, 421 U.S. 794, 95 S.Ct. 2031 (1975) (pretrial publicity); United States v. Hueftle, 687 F.2d 1305 (10th Cir.1982) (juror knew of case involving trespassing at nuclear plant site); United States v. Barber, 668 F.2d 778 (4th Cir.1982) (juror stated that he was inclined toward finding of guilt, but could put inclination aside); United States v. Gullion, 575 F.2d 26 (1st Cir.1978) (juror knew defendant's name). See also People v. Porter, 111 Ill.2d 386, 95 Ill.Dec. 465, 489 N.E.2d 1329 (1986), where the Illinois Supreme Court, in a 4–3 decision, held that it was not error to refuse to excuse for cause a juror who attended the same church as the victim's mother.

14. Bias or prejudice will not be presumed from the fact that the prospective juror is or has been connected with law enforcement. See United States v. Apodaca, 666 F.2d 89 (5th Cir.1982) (both juror and retired husband worked for FBI); United States v. Le Pera, 443 F.2d 810 (9th Cir.1971) (wife of police officer); Mikus v. United States, 433 F.2d 719 (2d Cir.1970) (membership on police force is not presumptively disqualifying).

15. Jurors who participated in prior trial in which the same defendant was convicted must be excused for cause. Virgin Islands v. Parrott, 551 F.2d 553 (3d Cir.1977). The mere exposure to the fact that defendant has a prior conviction requires disqualification. Leonard v. United States, 378 U.S. 544, 84 S.Ct. 1696 (1964). However, prior exposure to the same witnesses or the same type of crime does not afford a basis for challenge unless the defendant is on trial for an offense arising out of the same transactions. See Johnson v. United States, 484 F.2d 309 (8th Cir.1973) (same witnesses); United States v. Salazar, 480 F.2d 144 (5th Cir.1973) (jurors rejected similar alibi defense in prior case); Virgin Islands v. Hendricks, 476 F.2d 776 (3d Cir.1973) (same informant witness); United States v. Palumbo, 401 F.2d 270 (2d Cir.1968) (same prosecutor).

16. What happens when the court improperly excludes for cause, over defense objections, members of a particular group? Under *Lockhart v. McCree*, 476 U.S. 162, 106 S.Ct. 1758 (1986), improper challenges during the voir dire do not necessarily give rise to valid Sixth Amendment cross-section claims. See United States v. Salamone, 800 F.2d 1216 (3d Cir.1986), where the court held that the trial judge, in a weapons violation case, improperly sustained challenges for cause to National Rifle Association members without determining that the challenged jurors would be unwilling or unable to follow the law. Although finding the error not to be of constitutional dimension, the Third Circuit granted relief. In dictum it noted that if only one such person had been improperly disqualified, it might have held the error harmless. Because six such potential jurors were disqualified improperly, it granted relief.

17. For an interesting take on what prosecutors should ask themselves before exercising a challenge and what trial judges should ask of prosecutors to assure Batson compliance, see Johnson, Batson Ethics for Prosecutors and Trial Court Judges, 73 Chi–Kent L.Rev. 475 (1998).

2. VOIR DIRE

Mu'Min v. Virginia

Supreme Court of the United States, 1991.
500 U.S. 415, 111 S.Ct. 1899.

■ CHIEF JUSTICE REHNQUIST delivered the opinion of the Court.

Petitioner Dawud Majid Mu'Min was convicted of murdering a woman in Prince William County, Virginia, while out of prison on work detail, and was sentenced to death. The case engendered substantial publicity, and 8 of the 12 venirepersons eventually sworn as jurors answered on *voir dire* that they had read or heard something about the case. None of those who had read or heard something indicated that they had formed an opinion based on the outside information, or that it would affect their ability to determine petitioner's guilt or innocence based solely on the evidence presented at trial. Petitioner contends, however, that his Sixth Amendment right to an impartial jury and his right to due process under the Fourteenth Amendment were violated because the trial judge refused to question further prospective jurors about the specific contents of the news reports to which they had been exposed.

* * *

About three months before trial, petitioner submitted to the trial court, in support of a motion for a change of venue, 47 newspaper articles relating to the murder. One or more of the articles discussed details of the murder and investigation, and included information about petitioner's prior criminal record, the fact that he had been rejected for parole six times, accounts of alleged prison infractions, details about the prior murder for which Mu'Min was serving his sentence at the time of this murder, a comment that the death penalty had not been available when Mu'Min was convicted for this earlier murder, and indications that Mu'Min had confessed.... Several articles focused on the alleged laxity in the supervision of work gangs, and argued for reform of the prison work-crew system. The trial judge deferred ruling on the venue motion until after making an attempt to seat a jury.

Shortly before the date set for trial, petitioner submitted to the trial judge 64 proposed *voir dire* questions* and filed a motion for individual *voir dire*. The trial court denied the motion for individual *voir dire*; it ruled that *voir dire* would begin with collective questioning of the venire, but the venire would be broken down into panels of four, if necessary, to deal with issues of publicity. The trial court also refused to ask any of petitioner's proposed questions relating to the content of news items that potential jurors might have read or seen.

Twenty-six prospective jurors were summoned into the courtroom and questioned as a group. When asked by the judge whether anyone had acquired any information about the alleged offense or the accused from the news media or from any other source, 16 of the potential jurors replied that they had. The prospective jurors were not asked about the source or content of prior knowledge, but the court then asked the following questions:

> "Would the information that you heard, received, or read from whatever source, would that information affect your impartiality in this case?
>
> "Is there anyone that would say what you've read, seen, heard, or whatever information you may have acquired from whatever the source would affect your impartiality so that you could not be impartial?
>
> * * *
>
> "Considering what the ladies and gentlemen who have answered in the affirmative have heard or read about this case, do you believe that you can enter the Jury box with an open mind and wait until the entire case is presented before reaching a fixed opinion or conclusion as to the guilt or innocence of the accused?
>
> * * *

"... In view of everything that you've seen, heard, or read, or any information from whatever source that you've acquired about this case, is there anyone who believes that you could not become a Juror, enter the Jury box with an open mind and wait until the entire case is presented

* The court approved 24 of the proposed questions, but did not allow the following questions regarding the content of what jurors had read or heard about the case:

> "31. Have you acquired any information about this case from the newspapers, television, conversations, or any other source?"
>
> "32. What have you seen, read or heard about this case?
>
> "33. From whom or what did you get this information?
>
> "34. When and where did you get this information?"
>
> "35. Have you discussed this case with anyone?
>
> "36. With whom?
>
> "37. When and where?"
>
> "38. What did you discuss?"
>
> "41. Has anyone expressed any opinion about this case to you?

The trial court did ask several of the requested questions concerning prior knowledge of the case:

> "42. Who? What? When? Where?"

before reaching a fixed opinion or a conclusion as to the guilt or innocence of the accused?''

One of the 16 panel members who admitted to having prior knowledge of the case answered in response to these questions that he could not be impartial, and was dismissed for cause. Petitioner moved that all potential jurors who indicated that they had been exposed to pretrial publicity be excused for cause. This motion was denied, as was petitioner's renewed motion for a change of venue based on the pretrial publicity.

The trial court then conducted further *voir dire* of the prospective jurors in panels of four. Whenever a potential juror indicated that he had read or heard something about the case, the juror was then asked whether he had formed an opinion, and whether he could nonetheless be impartial. None of those eventually seated stated that he had formed an opinion, or gave any indication that he was biased or prejudiced against the defendant. All swore that they could enter the jury box with an open mind and wait until the entire case was presented before reaching a conclusion as to guilt or innocence.

If any juror indicated that he had discussed the case with anyone, the court asked follow-up questions to determine with whom the discussion took place, and whether the juror could have an open mind despite the discussion. One juror who equivocated as to whether she could enter the jury box with an open mind was removed *sua sponte* by the trial judge. One juror was dismissed for cause because she was not ''as frank as she could [be]'' concerning the effect of her feelings toward members of the Islamic Faith and toward defense counsel. One juror was dismissed because of her inability to impose the death penalty, while another was removed based upon his statement that upon a finding of first-degree murder, he could not consider a penalty less than death. The prosecution and the defense each peremptorily challenged 6 potential jurors, and the remaining 14 were seated and sworn as jurors (two as alternates). Petitioner did not renew his motion for change of venue or make any other objection to the composition of the jury. Of the 12 jurors who decided petitioner's case, 8 had at one time or another read or heard something about the case. None had indicated that he had formed an opinion about the case or would be biased in any way.

The jury found petitioner guilty of first-degree murder and recommended that he be sentenced to death. After taking the matter under advisement and reviewing a presentence report, the trial judge accepted the jury's recommendation and sentenced Mu'Min to death.

* * *

Our cases dealing with the requirements of *voir dire* are of two kinds: those that were tried in federal courts, and are therefore subject to this Court's supervisory power, and those that were tried in state courts, with respect to which our authority is limited to enforcing the commands of the United States Constitution.

* * *

In *Aldridge v. United States* (1931), counsel for a black defendant sought to have the Court put a question to the jury as to whether any of them might be prejudiced against the defendant because of his race. We held that it was reversible error for the Court not to have put such a question, saying "[t]he Court failed to ask any question which could be deemed to cover the subject." More recently, in *Rosales–Lopez v. United States* [1981], we held that such an inquiry as to racial or ethnic prejudice need not be made in every case, but only where the defendant was accused of a violent crime and the defendant and the victim were members of different racial or ethnic groups. We said:

> "Because the obligation to empanel an impartial jury lies in the first instance with the trial judge, and because he must rely largely on his immediate perceptions, federal judges have been accorded ample discretion in determining how best to conduct the *voir dire*."

Three of our cases dealing with the extent of *voir dire* examination have dealt with trials in state courts. The first of these was *Ham v. South Carolina* [1973]. In that case, the defendant was black and had been active in the civil rights movement in South Carolina; his defense at trial was that enforcement officers were "out to get him" because of his civil rights activities, and that he had been framed on the charge of marijuana possession of which he was accused. He requested that two questions be asked regarding racial prejudice and one question be asked regarding prejudice against persons, such as himself, who wore beards. We held that the Due Process Clause of the Fourteenth Amendment required the court to ask "either of the brief, general questions urged by the petitioner" with respect to race, but rejected his claim that an inquiry as to prejudice against persons with beards be made, "[g]iven the traditionally broad discretion accorded to the trial judge in conducting *voir dire*. . . ."

In *Ristaino v. Ross* [1976], we held that the Constitution does not require a state court trial judge to question prospective jurors as to racial prejudice in every case where the races of the defendant and the victim differ, but in *Turner v. Murray* [1986], we held that in a capital case involving a charge of murder of a white person by a black defendant such questions must be asked.

We enjoy more latitude in setting standards for *voir dire* in federal courts under our supervisory power than we have in interpreting the provisions of the Fourteenth Amendment with respect to *voir dire* in state courts. But, two parallel themes emerge from both sets of cases: first, the possibility of racial prejudice against a black defendant charged with a violent crime against a white person is sufficiently real that the Fourteenth Amendment requires that inquiry be made into racial prejudice; second, the trial court retains great latitude in deciding what questions should be asked on *voir dire*.

* * *

Petitioner asserts that the Fourteenth Amendment requires more in the way of *voir dire* with respect to pretrial publicity than our cases have held that it does with respect to racial or ethnic prejudice. Not only must the Court "cover the subject," but it must make precise inquiries about the contents of any news reports that potential jurors have read. Petitioner argues that these "content" questions would materially assist in obtaining a jury less likely to be tainted by pretrial publicity than one selected without such questions. There is a certain common sense appeal to this argument.

Undoubtedly, if counsel were allowed to see individual jurors answer questions about exactly what they had read, a better sense of the juror's general outlook on life might be revealed, and such a revelation would be of some use in exercising peremptory challenges. But, since peremptory challenges are not required by the Constitution, this benefit cannot be a basis for making "content" questions about pretrial publicity a constitutional requirement. Such questions might also have some effect in causing jurors to re-evaluate their own answers as to whether they had formed any opinion about the case, but this is necessarily speculative.

Acceptance of petitioner's claim would require that each potential juror be interrogated individually; even were the interrogation conducted in panels of four jurors, as the trial court did here, descriptions of one juror about pretrial publicity would obviously be communicated to the three other members of the panel being interrogated, with the prospect that more harm than good would be done by the interrogation. Petitioner says that the questioning can be accomplished by juror questionnaires submitted in advance at trial, but such written answers would not give counsel or the court any exposure to the demeanor of the juror in the course of answering the content questions. The trial court in this case expressed reservations about interrogating jurors individually because it might make the jurors feel that they themselves were on trial. While concern for the feelings and sensibilities of potential jurors cannot be allowed to defeat inquiry necessary to protect a constitutional right, we do not believe that "content" questions are constitutionally required.

Whether a trial court decides to put questions about the content of publicity to a potential juror or not, it must make the same decision at the end of the questioning: is this juror to be believed when he says he has not formed an opinion about the case? Questions about the content of the publicity to which jurors have been exposed might be helpful in assessing whether a juror is impartial. To be constitutionally compelled, however, it is not enough that such questions might be helpful. Rather, the trial court's failure to ask these questions must render the defendant's trial fundamentally unfair.

* * *

[O]ur own cases have stressed the wide discretion granted to the trial court in conducting *voir dire* in the area of pretrial publicity and in other areas of inquiry that might tend to show juror bias. Particularly with respect to pretrial publicity, we think this primary reliance on the judgment of the trial court makes good sense. The judge of that court sits in the locale where the publicity is said to have had its effect, and brings to his evaluation of any such claim his own perception of the depth and extent of news stories that might influence a juror. The trial court, of course, does not impute his own perceptions to the jurors who are being examined, but these perceptions should be of assistance to it in deciding how detailed an inquiry to make of the members of the jury venire.

Petitioner relies heavily on our opinion in *Irvin v. Dowd* [1961], to support his position. In that case, we held that pretrial publicity in connection with a capital trial had so tainted the jury pool in Gibson County, Indiana, that the defendant was entitled as a matter of federal constitutional law to a change of venue to another county.

* * *

A trial court's findings of juror impartiality may "be overturned only for 'manifest error.'" "[A]dverse pretrial publicity can create such a presumption of prejudice in a community that the jurors' claims that they can be impartial should not be believed," but this is not such a case. Had the trial court in this case been confronted with the "wave of public passion" engendered by pretrial publicity that occurred in connection with Irvin's trial, the Due Process Clause of the Fourteenth Amendment might well have required more extensive examination of potential jurors than it undertook here. But the showings are not comparable; the cases differ both in the kind of community in which the coverage took place and in extent of media coverage. Unlike the community involved in *Irvin*, the county in which petitioner was tried, Prince William, had a population in 1988 of 182,537, and this was one of nine murders committed in the county that year. It is a part of the metropolitan Washington statistical area, which has a population of over 3 million, and in which, unfortunately, hundreds of murders are committed each year. In *Irvin*, news accounts included details of the defendant's confessions to 24 burglaries and six murders, including the one for which he was tried, as well as his unaccepted offer to plead guilty in order to avoid the death sentence. They contained numerous opinions as to his guilt, as well as opinions about the appropriate punishment. While news reports about Mu'Min were not favorable, they did not contain the same sort of damaging information. Much of the pretrial publicity was aimed at the Department of Corrections and the criminal justice system in general, criticizing the furlough and work release programs that made this and other crimes possible. Any killing that ultimately results in a charge of capital murder will engender considerable media coverage, and this one may have engendered more than most because of its occurrence during the 1988 Presidential campaign, when a similar crime committed by a Massachusetts inmate became a subject of national debate. But, while the pretrial publicity in this case appears to have been substantial, it was not of the same kind or extent as that found to exist in *Irvin*.

Petitioner also relies on the Standards for Criminal Justice 8–3.5 (2d ed. 1980), promulgated by the American Bar Association. These standards require interrogation of each juror individually with respect to "what the prospective juror has read and heard about the case," "[i]f there is a substantial possibility that individual jurors will be ineligible to serve because of exposure to potentially prejudicial material." These standards, of course, leave to the trial court the initial determination of whether there is such a substantial possibility. But, more importantly, the standards relating to *voir dire* are based on a substantive rule that renders a potential juror subject to challenge for cause, without regard to his state of mind, if he has been exposed to and remembers "highly significant information" or "other incriminating matters that may be inadmissible in evidence." That is a stricter standard of juror eligibility than that which we have held the Constitution to require. Under the ABA standard, answers to questions about content, without more, could disqualify the juror from sitting. Under the constitutional standard, on the other hand, "[t]he relevant question is not whether the community remembered the case, but whether the jurors ... had such fixed opinions that they could not judge impartially the guilt of the defendant." *Patton, supra.* Under this constitutional standard, answers to questions about content alone, which reveal that a juror remembered facts about the case, would not be sufficient to disqualify a juror. "It is not required ... that the jurors be totally ignorant of the facts and issues involved."

* * *

The *voir dire* examination conducted by the trial court in this case was by no means perfunctory. The court asked the entire venire of jurors four separate questions about the effect on them of pretrial publicity or information about the case obtained by other means. One juror admitted to having formed a belief as to petitioner's guilt, and was excused for cause. The trial court then conducted further *voir dire* in panels of four, and each time an individual juror indicated that he had acquired knowledge about the case from outside sources, he was asked whether he had formed an opinion; none of the jurors seated indicated that he had formed an opinion. One juror who equivocated as to her impartiality was excused by the trial court on its own motion. Several other jurors were excused for other reasons. It is quite possible that if *voir dire* interrogation had revealed one or more jurors who had formed an opinion about the case, the trial court might have decided to question succeeding jurors more extensively.

Voir dire examination serves the dual purposes of enabling the court to select an impartial jury and assisting counsel in exercising peremptory challenges. In *Aldridge* and *Ham* we held that the subject of possible racial bias must be "covered" by the questioning of the trial court in the course of its examination of potential jurors, but we were careful not to specify the particulars by which this could be done. We did not, for instance, require questioning of individual jurors about facts or experiences that might have led to racial bias. Petitioner in this case insists, as a matter of constitutional right, not only that the subject of possible bias from pretrial publicity be covered—which it was—but that questions specifically dealing with the content of what each juror has read be asked. For the reasons previously stated, we hold that the Due Process Clause of the Fourteenth Amendment does not reach this far, and that the *voir dire* examination conducted by the trial court in this case was consistent with that provision. The judgment of the Supreme Court of Virginia is accordingly

Affirmed.

■ JUSTICE O'CONNOR, concurring. [OMITTED]

■ JUSTICE MARSHALL, with whom JUSTICE BLACKMUN and JUSTICE STEVENS join, dissenting.

Today's decision turns a critical constitutional guarantee—the Sixth Amendment's right to an impartial jury—into a hollow formality.

* * *

The question before us is whether, in light of the charged atmosphere that surrounded this case, the trial court was constitutionally obliged to ask the eight jurors who admitted exposure to pretrial publicity to identify precisely *what* they had read, seen, or heard. The majority answers this question in the negative. According to the majority, the trial court need ask no more of a prospective juror who has admitted exposure to pretrial publicity than whether that prospective juror views himself as impartial. Our cases on juror-bias, the majority asserts, have never gone so far as to require trial courts to engage in so-called "content questioning," and to impose such a requirement would prove unduly burdensome to the administration of justice. I cannot accept this analysis.

* * *

In my view, once a prospective juror admits exposure to pretrial publicity, content questioning must be part of the *voir dire* for at least three reasons. First, content questioning is necessary to determine whether the type and extent of the publicity to which a prospective juror has been exposed would disqualify the juror as a matter of law.

* * *

Second, even when pretrial publicity is not so extreme as to make a juror's exposure to it *per se* disqualifying, content questioning still is essential to give legal depth to the trial court's finding of impartiality.

* * *

Third, content questioning facilitates accurate trial court factfinding. As this Court has recognized, the impartiality "determination is essentially one of credibility." Where a prospective juror acknowledges exposure to pretrial publicity, the precise content of that publicity constitutes contextual information essential to an accurate assessment of whether the prospective juror's profession of impartiality is believable.

* * *

Eight of the twelve jurors who voted to strip Dawud Majid Mu'Min of his life may well have been rendered incapable of reaching any other verdict after reading of the grisly accusations against Mu'Min and the succession of stories indicating that he was guilty. The majority holds that the trial court was entitled to seat those jurors—entirely blind to what they in fact already knew about the case—based solely upon their assertions of impartiality. Far from "tak[ing] strong measures to ensure that the balance [was not] weighed against the accused," the procedures undertaken in this case amounted to no more than the trial court going through the motions. I cannot accept that a defendant's Sixth Amendment right to an impartial jury means so little. I dissent.

■ JUSTICE KENNEDY, dissenting. [OMITTED]

NOTES

1. The efficacy of asking very detailed questions on voir dire to uncover latent juror prejudice was analyzed by Learned Hand in United States v. Dennis, 183 F.2d 201, 227 (2d Cir.1950), affirmed 341 U.S. 494, 71 S.Ct. 857 (1951):

> "It is of course true that any examination on the *voir dire* is a clumsy and imperfect way of detecting suppressed emotional commitments to which all of us are to some extent subject, unconsciously or subconsciously. It is of the nature of our deepest antipathies that often we do not admit them even to ourselves; but when that is so, nothing but an examination, utterly impracticable in a courtroom, will disclose them, an examination extending at times for months, and even then unsuccessful. No such examination is required; indeed, it was exactly the purpose of Criminal Rule 24(a), which allows the judge to frame questions on the *voir dire* if he thinks best, to avoid the interminable examinations sometimes extending for weeks on end that had frequently resulted from the former method. If trial by jury is not to break down by its own weight, it is not feasible to probe more than the upper levels of a juror's mind. The judge's questions ... were indeed limited to the flat inquiry whether he was aware of any bias, but it is by no means unusual for a juror to admit as much, as anyone accustomed to jury trials knows."

In line with Judge Hand's psychological analysis of the *voir dire*, one might well question whether the propounding of detailed questions concerning the veniremen's life styles would be self-defeating of the primary goal of securing an impartial jury. If the juror's life style, the magazines and newspapers they read, or the music they listen to is relevant to the inquiry on *voir dire*, then the jurors cannot fail to appreciate the implication that the defendant may be tried on some other basis than the evidence submitted in court. It may well be a psychological truth that, if the prospective jurors are treated as if they are expected to decide on the basis of legally impermissible criteria, the jurors who successfully run the *voir dire* gauntlet may be more inclined to decide on the basis of legally irrelevant and impermissible criteria. The *voir dire* may be more effective in securing an impartial jury if this goal is not obscured in the minds of the veniremen by reference to factors which every person knows to be irrelevant to legal guilt.

2. Whatever persuasive qualities Judge Hand's position may have, it represents only one viewpoint. Another view seems to favor an elaborate voir dire with penetrating questions seeking to elicit juror attitudes with regard to issues likely to arise in the trial. The rationale underlying this conception of the voir dire was well stated in United States v. Lewin, 467 F.2d 1132, 1137 (7th Cir.1972):

> While trial lawyers devote much cogitation and intraprofessional discussion to the matter of selecting a proper jury—propriety presumably being equated with fairness and disinterestedness—nevertheless, because of the uncertainty of human reactions to often unknown or unanticipated motivating factors, the entire voir dire procedure is fraught with precariousness as to whether the desired resultant jury will be realized. Character

qualities derivable from interrogation are often elusive and the answers to questions may frequently be illusory as a firm basis for any type of challenge.

> Prejudice and bias are deep running streams more often than not concealed by the calm surface stemming from an awareness of societal distaste for their existence. Extended and trial-delaying interrogation may not pierce the veil, yet a few specific associational questions as a maieutic process may indicate the dormant seeds of prejudice, preconceived and unalterable concepts or other nonfairness disqualifications. The result may not reach the stage of being a basis for cause challenge but could well, because of an abundance of counsel caution, bring about a peremptory challenge which an omniscient eye would have known should have been exercised.
>
> We are told that the British courts quickly secure their juries, and criticism is directed at time-consuming trials within trials in this country when prospective members of the jury may wonder, as their lives are being probed, who is being tried. We think the criticism of too extended voir dire is justified but we are not ready to say that the person who has his liberty or, indeed, his property, at stake must be compelled to accept a jury on a strictly cursory, generality interrogation basis.
>
> At some happy mesne point, there must be permitted sufficient questioning to produce, in the light of the factual situation involved in the particular trial, some basis for a reasonably knowledgeable exercise of the right of challenge.

3. Pursuant to the modern view, the courts have generally accorded the defendant a right to seek detailed information from prospective jurors in general categories:

a. *Racial Bias:* The general standard was articulated in Rosales–Lopez v. United States, 451 U.S. 182, 101 S.Ct. 1629 (1981), where the trial judge's refusal to ask whether defendant's Mexican descent would affect the jury's evaluation of the evidence in a case involving a plan to bring three Mexican aliens into the country illegally was upheld:

> Only when there are more substantial indications of the likelihood of racial or ethnic prejudice affecting the jurors in a particular case does the trial court's denial of a defendant's request to examine the jurors' ability to deal impartially with this subject amount to an unconstitutional abuse of discretion.
>
> Absent such circumstances, the Constitution leaves it to the trial court, and the judicial system within which that court operates, to determine the need for such questions.
>
> * * *
>
> In our judgment, it is usually best to allow the defendant to resolve this conflict by making the determination of whether or not he would prefer to have the inquiry into racial or ethnic prejudice pursued. Failure to honor his request, however, will only be reversible error where the circumstances of the case indicate that there is a reasonable possibility that racial or ethnic prejudice might have influenced the jury.

Compare Ham v. South Carolina, 409 U.S. 524, 93 S.Ct. 848 (1973) (must inquire into potential racial prejudice) with Ristaino v. Ross, 424 U.S. 589, 96 S.Ct. 1017 (1976) (but only if there is a significant possibility that racial prejudice may affect the jury's decision). See also United States v. Dickens, 695 F.2d 765 (3d Cir.1982) (when Black Muslim defendants charged with conspiracy embracing bank robbery felony murder of nine white police officers did not request specific inquiries into racial bias, general voir dire adequate); United States v. Groce, 682 F.2d 1359 (11th Cir.1982) (drug conspiracy was not an interracial crime and no special circumstances existed to warrant specific inquiry into bias).

b. *Pretrial Publicity:* While inflammatory adverse pretrial publicity on the eve of trial is highly relevant to whether defendant received a fair jury trial, so long as all potential jurors with fixed opinions are excluded for cause and others are examined in detail to demonstrate impartiality, an impartial jury can be secured through a detained voir dire. Patton v. Yount, 467 U.S. 1025, 104 S.Ct. 2885 (1984); Murphy v. Florida, 421 U.S. 794, 95 S.Ct. 2031 (1975); Irvin v. Dowd, 366 U.S. 717, 81 S.Ct. 1639 (1961). When a substantial number of the venire have been exposed to pervasive inflammatory publicity, each prospective juror must be examined individually, out of the presence of the others, to assure that he does not have a fixed opinion of guilt based on the publicity. See United States v. Hawkins, 658 F.2d 279 (5th Cir.1981). When there are mere allegations of adverse pretrial publicity and less than a majority of the venire indicate that they have been exposed to it, a collective voir dire is sufficient. United States v. Whitt, 718 F.2d 1494 (10th Cir.1983).

c. *Connection to Law Enforcement:* Although mere connection to law enforcement agencies is not an appropriate basis for a challenge for cause, detailed voir dire is required to permit a knowledgeable exercise of peremptories. See United States v. Evans, 917 F.2d 800 (4th Cir.1990); United States v. Anagnos, 853 F.2d 1 (1st Cir.1988) (error to deny voir due as to whether jurors would give special weight to the testimony of police officers or special agents); United States v. Scott, 854 F.2d 697 (5th Cir.1988) (juror's brother was a deputy sheriff); United States v. Verkuilen, 690 F.2d 648 (7th Cir.1982) (IRS employees in tax case); United States v. Corey, 625 F.2d 704 (5th Cir.1980) (bias in favor of government); United States v. Baldwin, 607 F.2d 1295 (9th Cir.1979) (error to refuse to ask whether greater credibility would be given to testimony of law enforcement agents).

d. *Relationship to Class of Persons to which Victim Belongs:* United States v. Shavers, 615 F.2d 266 (5th Cir.1980) (whether juror ever suffered lacerations and, if so, from what source in assault case); United States v. Jones, 608 F.2d 1004 (4th Cir.1979) (whether family member works at victim bank); Sims v. United States, 405 F.2d 1381 (D.C.Cir.1968) (relationship to cab drivers in case involving murder of cab driver).

e. *Prior Jury Service:* While not necessarily a basis for a challenge for cause, detailed inquiries into prior jury service are relevant. See United States v. Franklin, 700 F.2d 1241 (10th Cir.1983); United States v. Capua, 656 F.2d 1033 (5th Cir.1981). But see United States v. Hurley, 746 F.2d 725 (11th Cir.1984) (necessary only when there is a pronounced likelihood of prejudice). In United States v. Parmley, 108 F.3d 922 (8th Cir.1997), the district court refused to strike the jury panel although 18 members participated in the voir dire, but did not serve as jurors, at defendant's earlier trial for the same offense that ended in a mistrial. The decision was upheld on the ground that defendant failed to show that the overlapping jurors brought prior knowledge to the second trial that would have tainted their view of the evidence. Judge McMillian dissented, finding the fact that one juror discussed the evidence of the first trial with a juror who had served on the mistrial jury sufficient to pose a significant risk of prejudice.

f. *Moral Scruples Concerning Crime Charged:* See Commonwealth v. Ellison, 902 A.2d 419 (Pa. Sup. Ct. 2006) (sharply divided court upheld adequacy of voire dire in case involving violent sex crime although trial judge refused to ask submitted questions designed to elicit juror attitudes on sexual violence); United States v. Napoleone, 349 F.2d 350 (3d Cir.1965) (questions concerning moral repugnance to lying in impersonating government investigator case); State v. Barnett, 251 Or. 234, 445 P.2d 124 (1968) (religious affiliations in abortion case). State v. Thomas, 369 Md. 202, 798 A.2d 566 (2002) (strong feelings regarding violations of the narcotics laws).

4. Can a prospective juror's bias be determined by simply asking: "Can you be fair?" In the trial of the former governor of Tennessee, despite massive pre-trial publicity, potential federal jurors were merely asked this question or its equivalent en masse with no individual questioning. The Court of Appeals reversed the conviction on this ground. United States v. Blanton, 697 F.2d 146 (6th Cir.1983). However, the en banc court overruled the panel decision and reinstated the conviction, over a strong dissent. 719 F.2d 815 (6th Cir.1983). In dissent Judge Engel wrote: "The new rule is that where inflammatory pretrial publicity is pervasive, inquiry into an individual's knowledge and predisposition is superfluous. The only necessary inquiry, according to the majority, is whether the juror believes in his own mind that he can lay aside such knowledge and preconceived notions and decide the case only upon the evidence presented."

5. Some states take a more restrictive approach toward jury selection. In Davis v. State, 333 Md. 27, 633 A.2d 867 (1993), where the critical issue for trial was the credibility of a police officer, the trial court refused to ask prospective jurors whether they were law enforcement officers or related to, or associated with, law enforcement offices. On appeal, the court found this refusal proper under Maryland law:

> This Court initially adopted the rules concerning the scope of *voir dire* because allowing more extensive inquiry would unduly tax the efficiency of Maryland's judicial system. Although some litigants might benefit from broader mandatory *voir dire*, a greater number of citizens would be hindered due to the accompanying decline in their ability to gain prompt resolution of their litigation.
>
> * * *
>
> Although it was within the trial judge's discretion to allow the line of questioning, he was not required to do so. The trial judge did not abuse his discretion by refusing to propound Davis's question to the prospective jurors.

6. The manner in which a trial judge interacts with jurors during voir dire in attempting to ferret out bias is subject to scrutiny. For an example of a situation in which the judge was so abusive in her response to juror statements so as to cut off the vital flow of information from other prospective jurors, see United States v. Rowe, 106 F.3d 1226 (5th Cir.1997).

7. Must the judge inquire as to whether the prospective jurors agree with the law governing the case? Compare United States v. Brunty, 701 F.2d 1375 (11th Cir.1983) (no need to inquire since jurors are not free to disregard law) with Gold, Voir Dire: Questioning Prospective Jurors on Their Willingness to Follow the Law, 60 Ind.L.J. 163 (1985) (juror who cannot decide a case according to the law is not impartial and, therefore, such questions are legitimate and essential). The courts have generally avoided inquiry on matters of law. See King v. Lynaugh, 850 F.2d 1055 (5th Cir.1988) (no right to question jurors on their views of parole procedures in capital case).

Similarly "commitment questions" seeking to commit a juror to a particular position on a hypothetical fact situation are generally deemed improper lines of inquiry. See Standefer v. State, 59 S.W.3d 177 (Tex.Crim.App.2001).

8. It is clear that a judge need not ask the specific questions submitted by the defense so long as its examination is sufficient to test the qualifications and competency of the prospective jurors. In Hamling v. United States, 418 U.S. 87, 94

S.Ct. 2887 (1974), the defendants, in an obscenity case, requested the court to ask specific and detailed questions as to whether the jurors' educational, political and religious beliefs might affect their views on obscenity. The Court upheld the trial judge's refusal to ask the specific questions: "... the trial judge made a general inquiry into the jurors' general views concerning obscenity. Failure to ask specific questions as to the possible effect of educational, political, and religious biases did 'not reach the level of a constitutional violation,' nor was it error requiring the exercise of our supervisory authority over the administration of justice in the federal courts."

9. For voire dire purposes, prospective jurors are sometimes asked to complete questionnaires with their names, addresses, occupations, prior criminal records, relationships to law enforcement, other jury service and questions suggested by counsel and permitted by the trial court. What happens when a prospective juror answers a question falsely? In McDonough Power Equipment, Inc. v. Greenwood, 464 U.S. 548, 104 S.Ct. 845 (1984), the Court held that an inaccurate answer on a jury questionnaire discovered after verdict could require a new trial only if a correct response would have provided a valid basis for a challenge for cause. This standard was employed to excuse jurors who lied about their prior criminal records when the information came to light during deliberations in United States v. Warner, 498 F.3d 666 (7th Cir. 2007), a criminal prosecution involving the former Governor of Illinois. The court concluded that the McDonough standards were applied properly to excuse each of the jurors with undisclosed criminal histories. Judge Kanne dissented in part because of the structural error arising from "the jurors' irreconcilable conflicts of interest that resulted from the jury questionnaire situation."

10. In some cases, special precautions are taken on motion of the prosecution to protect jurors from potential harassment or intimidation. In trials relating to organized crime, street gang activity or narcotics enterprises, courts have acted to protect potential jurors and their families by withholding identifying information such as names, addresses, occupations and places of employment about each juror, both before and during the voir dire. In United States v. Paccione, 949 F.2d 1183, 1192 (2d Cir.1991), the court held that trial judges "should not order the empaneling of an anonymous jury without (a) concluding that there is strong reason to believe the jury needs protection, and (b) taking reasonable precautions to minimize any prejudicial effects on the defendant and to ensure that his fundamental rights are protected." See also United States v. Crockett, 979 F.2d 1204, 1215–16 (7th Cir.1992) (murder of cooperating potential witness and threats to intimidate other witnesses).

Compare United States v. Edwards, 303 F.3d 606 (5th Cir.2002) (in trial of Louisiana governor the intense media interest and highly charged emotional and political fervor surrounding the case were sufficient to justify anonymous jury) *with* United States v. Mansoori, 304 F.3d 635 (7th Cir.2002) (in trial of street gang drug distribution ring, the need for jury protection is not simply the means of intimidation but some evidence that intimidation is likely). For an argument in favor of the routine use of anonymous juries, see King, Nameless Justice: The Case for the Routine Use of Anonymous Juries in Criminal Trials, 49 Vand.L.Rev 123 (1996).

11. In light of the important role that the court plays during the voir dire, must a federal defendant personally waive his right to have a district judge rather than a magistrate preside at jury selection? In Gonzales v. United States, 128 S.Ct. 1765 (2008), the Court held that a magistrate may preside without the defendant's personal consent because the decision is a tactical consideration well-suited for the attorney's discretion.

12. Mark Twain supposedly said, "We have a criminal jury system which is superior to any in the world, and its efficiency is marred only by the difficulty of finding twelve men every day who don't know anything and can't read." To what extent does our method of jury selection support this conclusion? See Minow & Cate, Who is an Impartial Juror in an Age of Mass Media, 40 Am.U.L.Rev. 631 (1991).

CHAPTER 18

Quality of Representation by Counsel

A. Limits of Prosecutorial Zeal

1. American Bar Association Standards

(For Criminal Justice: Prosecution Function and Defense Function, 3d ed., 1993)

Standard 3–1.2 The Function of the Prosecutor

(a) The office of prosecutor is charged with responsibility for prosecutions in its jurisdiction.

(b) The prosecutor is an administrator of justice, an advocate, and an officer of the court; the prosecutor must exercise sound discretion in the performance of his or her functions.

(c) The duty of the prosecutor is to seek justice, not merely to convict.

(d) It is an important function of the prosecutor to seek to reform and improve the administration of criminal justice. When inadequacies or injustices in the substantive or procedural law come to the prosecutor's attention, he or she should stimulate efforts for remedial action.

(e) It is the duty of the prosecutor to know and be guided by the standards of professional conduct as defined by applicable professional traditions, ethical codes, and law in the prosecutor's jurisdiction. The prosecutor should make use of the guidance afforded by an advisory council of the kind described in standard 4–1.5.

Standard 3–3.1 Investigative Function of Prosecutor

(a) A prosecutor ordinarily relies on police and other investigative agencies for investigation of alleged criminal acts, but the prosecutor has an affirmative responsibility to investigate suspected illegal activity when it is not adequately dealt with by other agencies.

(b) A prosecutor should not invidiously discriminate against or in favor of any person on the basis of race, religion, sex, sexual preference, or ethnicity in exercising discretion to investigate or to prosecute. A prosecutor should not use other improper considerations in exercising such discretion.

(c) A prosecutor should not knowingly use illegal means to obtain evidence or to employ or instruct or encourage others to use such means.

(d) A prosecutor should not discourage or obstruct communication between prospective witnesses and defense counsel. A prosecutor should not advise any person or cause any person to be advised to decline to give to the defense information which such person has the right to give.

(e) A prosecutor should not secure the attendance of persons for interviews by use of any communication which has the appearance or color of a subpoena or similar judicial process unless the prosecutor is authorized by law to do so.

* * *

Standard 3–3.9 Discretion in the Charging Decision

(a) A prosecutor should not institute, or cause to be instituted, or permit the continued pendency of criminal charges when the prosecutor knows that the charges are not supported by probable cause. A prosecutor should not institute, cause to be instituted, or permit the continued pendency of criminal charges in the absence of sufficient admissible evidence to support a conviction.

(b) The prosecutor is not obliged to present all charges which the evidence might support. The prosecutor may in some circumstances and for good cause consistent with the public interest decline to prosecute, notwithstanding that sufficient evidence may exist which would support a conviction. Illustrative or the factors which the prosecutor may properly consider in exercising his or her discretion are:

(i) the prosecutor's reasonable doubt that the accused is in fact guilty;

(ii) the extent of the harm caused by the offense;

(iii) the disproportion of the authorized punishment in relation to the particular offense or the offender;

(iv) possible improper motives of a complainant;

(v) reluctance of the victim to testify;

(vi) cooperation of the accused in the apprehension or conviction of others; and

(vii) availability and likelihood of prosecution by another jurisdiction.

(c) A prosecutor should not be compelled by his or her supervisor to prosecute a case in which he or she has a reasonable doubt about the guilt of the accused.

(d) In making the decision to prosecute, the prosecutor should give no weight to the personal or political advantages or disadvantages which might be involved or to a desire to enhance his or her record of convictions.

(e) In cases which involve a serious threat to the community, the prosecutor should not be deterred from prosecution by the fact that in the jurisdiction juries have tended to acquit persons accused of the particular kind of criminal act in question.

(f) The prosecutor should not bring or seek charges greater in number of degree than can reasonably be supported with evidence at trial or than are necessary to fairly reflect the gravity of the offense.

(g) The prosecutor should not condition a dismissal of charges, nolle prosequi, or similar action on the accused's relinquishment of the right to seek civil redress unless the accused has agreed to the action knowingly and intelligently, freely and voluntarily, and where such waiver is approved by the court.

Standard 3–3.11 Disclosure of Evidence by the Prosecutor

(a) A prosecutor should not intentionally fail to make timely disclosure to the defense, at the earliest feasible opportunity, of the existence of all evidence or information which tends to negate the guilt of the accused or mitigate the offense charged or which would tend to reduce the punishment of the accused.

(b) A prosecutor should not fail to make a reasonably diligent effort to comply with a legally proper discovery request.

(c) A prosecutor should not intentionally avoid pursuit of evidence because he or she believes it will damage the prosecution's case or aid the accused.

Standard 3–5.6 Presentation of Evidence

(a) A prosecutor should not knowingly offer false evidence, whether by documents, tangible evidence, or the testimony of witnesses, or fail to seek withdrawal thereof upon discovery of its falsity.

(b) A prosecutor should not knowingly and for the purpose of bringing inadmissible matter to the attention of the judge or jury offer inadmissible evidence, ask legally objectionable questions, or make other impermissible comments or arguments in the presence of the judge or jury.

(c) A prosecutor should not permit any tangible evidence to be displayed in the view of the judge or jury which would tend to prejudice fair consideration by the judge or jury until such time as a good faith tender of such evidence is made.

(d) A prosecutor should not tender tangible evidence in the view of the judge or jury if it would tend to prejudice fair consideration by the judge or jury unless there is a reasonable basis for its admission in evidence. When here is any substantial doubt about the admissibility of such evidence, it should be tendered by an offer of proof and a ruling obtained.

Standard 3–5.7 Examination of Witnesses

(a) The interrogation of all witnesses should be conducted fairly, objectively, and with due regard for the dignity and legitimate privacy of the witness, and without seeking to intimidate or humiliate the witness unnecessarily.

(b) The prosecutor's belief that the witness is telling the truth does not preclude cross-examination, but may affect the method and scope of cross-examination. A prosecutor should not use the power of cross-examination to discredit or undermine a witness if the prosecutor knows the witness is testifying truthfully.

(c) A prosecutor should not call a witness in the presence of the jury who the prosecutor knows will claim a valid privilege not to testify.

(d) A prosecutor should not ask a question which implies the existence of a factual predicate for which a good faith belief is lacking.

Standard 3–6.1 Role in Sentencing

(a) The prosecutor should not make the severity of sentences the index of his or her effectiveness. To the extent that the prosecutor becomes involved in the sentencing process, he or she should seek to assure that a fair and informed judgment is made on the sentence and to avoid unfair sentence disparities.

* * *

2. CASE ILLUSTRATION OF PROSECUTORIAL ZEAL

In re Friedman

Supreme Court of Illinois, 1979.
76 Ill.2d 392, 30 Ill.Dec. 288, 392 N.E.2d 1333.

■ MR. CHIEF JUSTICE GOLDENHERSH delivered the decision of the court and the following opinion in which MR. JUSTICE KLUCZYNSKI joins:

The Review Board of the Attorney Registration and Disciplinary Commission recommended that respondent ... be censured. The two-count complaint filed by the Administrator of the attorney discipline system charged that respondent, while serving as chief of the criminal division of the Cook County State's Attorney's office, was guilty of conduct tending to bring the legal profession into disrepute and violative of four Disciplinary Rules of the Code of Professional Responsibility: Disciplinary Rule 7–102(A)(6) (creation of false evidence), Disciplinary Rule 7–102(A)(4) (knowing use of false evidence), Disciplinary Rule 7–109(B) (secreting of a witness), and Disciplinary Rule 1–102(A)(4). The Hearing Board of the Attorney Registration and Disciplinary Commission found that respondent did not violate the Code of Professional Responsibility and recommended that the complaint be dismissed with prejudice. The Administrator filed exceptions with the Review Board.

* * *

[T]he Review Board issued a report and recommendation in which a five-member majority recommended that respondent be censured while three members, with a written dissent, voted that the complaint be dismissed with prejudice.

* * *

Charles Graber was arrested by Officer Jerry Maculitis and charged with driving while under the influence of alcohol. Respondent was informed that Officer Maculitis believed he had been solicited to receive a bribe from Graber's attorney, Lee Howard. Respondent met with Officer Maculitis and directed him to follow Howard's instructions even if those instructions included testifying falsely in favor of Graber. Howard told Maculitis that the defense would not be ready to proceed if the breathalyzer operator were present. Maculitis was instructed by respondent to arrange for the absence of the breathalyzer operator, who, however, on the day of the trial, appeared in court to testify. Following respondent's instructions, Maculitis falsely advised the court that the breathalyzer operator was unavailable. The charges against Graber were dismissed. In a washroom adjacent to the courtroom Maculitis was given $50 by Howard, who was later indicted for bribery.

During the first recess of court after the disposition of the Graber case, an assistant State's Attorney, acting upon the respondent's instructions, advised the associate circuit judge of the circumstances surrounding the case.

The charge contained in count II of the Administrator's complaint arose from [these] facts. ... Juanita Guevara was arrested by Chicago police officer Jose Martinez and charged with the aggravated battery of Awilda Torres.... [R]espondent was told that Martinez had been approached by Guevara's attorney, Paul Powell, and was solicited to receive a bribe. Respondent instructed Martinez to give the appearance of cooperating with Powell. After meeting with Powell, Martinez told respondent that Powell had offered to pay him if he would arrest Ms. Torres and use the threat of prosecution to persuade her to drop the charges. Respondent instructed Martinez to tell Powell that the complaining witness had been persuaded to drop the charges. Martinez was also told that if he were called as a witness at the preliminary hearing, he should advise the court that Torres did not wish to appear. Although Torres and her mother appeared in court ready to testify at the preliminary hearing, they were advised of the pending investigation concerning Powell's conduct and escorted to the State's Attorney's office, where they remained until the preliminary hearing was concluded. The assistant State's Attorney in charge moved that the case be stricken with leave to reinstate. Before ruling on the motion the court asked that Martinez be placed under oath in order to verify the reason for the request, and Martinez testified falsely that he had spoken to Torres and her mother and had been advised that they did not wish to prosecute. The court then granted the State's motion to strike with leave to reinstate. After the preliminary hearing Martinez met Powell in the latter's car and was paid $250. Powell was later indicted and convicted of bribery. Immediately following the preliminary hearing the court was advised of the reasons for Martinez's testimony. The charges against Guevara were later reinstated.

This case presents the questions whether disciplinary action is merited and, if so, the nature of the sanction to be imposed when a prosecutor admittedly engages in conduct violative of the Code of Professional Responsibility for the purpose of developing evidence to be used in a subsequent prosecution. The parties have not been cited nor has our research disclosed any analogous cases previously considered by either a court or disciplinary committee.

Analogizing to the court-tolerated deceit employed in narcotics investigations ..., respondent argues that "the courtroom is not immunized by the Code of Professional Responsibility from investigation methods otherwise lawful and ethical" and that perjury and the secreting of witnesses are necessary methods for the successful investigation and prosecution of corrupt attorneys, whose stealth makes less deceptive investigatory techniques ineffective. He contends, too, that motive and intent must be considered in judging the ethics of respondent's conduct, and that respondent's lofty motive negates any technical violation of the Code of Professional Responsibility. Any intent to subvert the judicial processes in the two cases, respondent argues, originated not with him, but with attorneys Howard and Powell.

The Administrator contends that deceit and deception, although permissible in drug investigations, may not be employed to mislead or deceive a court while hearing one matter in order to develop evidence to be used in another proceeding, and that motive is not relevant to the question whether there has been professional misconduct and should be considered only in determining the appropriate sanction to be imposed.

ABA Standards, The Prosecution Function, section 1.1(d) (1971), states that "It is the duty of the prosecutor to know and be guided by the standards of professional conduct as defined in codes and canons of the legal profession, and in this report." It provides, too, that it is "unprofessional conduct for a prosecutor knowingly to offer false evidence, whether by documents, tangible evidence, or the testimony of witnesses." (ABA Standards, The Prosecution Function sec. 5.6(a) (1971).) Although this court has not formally approved the Code of Professional Responsibility adopted by the American Bar Association, it frequently serves as a guide for standards of professional conduct. ... The complaint charged the violation of Disciplinary Rule 1–102(A)(4), which generally proscribes "conduct involving dishonesty, fraud, deceit, or misrepresentation," and violations of Disciplinary Rule 7–102(A)(4), Disciplinary Rule 7–102(A)(6), and Disciplinary Rule 7–109(B), which provide:

"DR 7–102(A) In his representation of a client a lawyer shall not:

* * *

(4) Knowingly use perjured testimony or false evidence.

* * *

(6) Participate in the creation or preservation of evidence when he knows or it is obvious that the evidence is false."

"DR 7–109

* * *

(B) A lawyer shall not advise or cause a person to secrete himself or to leave the jurisdiction of a tribunal for the purpose of making him unavailable as a witness therein."

That respondent's conduct has deviated from these rules is apparent; respondent himself admits that were it not for his motives he would be in violation. He argues that to impose discipline for his conduct would give more emphasis to the abstract concept of a courtroom's sanctity than to the substances of an honest legal system. While respondent asserts that he is not arguing that the end justifies the means, we so construe his argument and find it unacceptable. The integrity of the courtroom is so vital to the health of our legal system that no violation of that integrity, no matter what its motivation, can be condoned or ignored. Although arising out of a different context, we find apposite the words of Mr. Justice Brandeis in Olmstead v. United States (1928) (dissenting opinion):

> "Decency, security and liberty alike demand that government officials shall be subjected to the same rules of conduct that are commands to the citizen. In a government of laws, existence of the government will be imperilled if it fails to observe the law scrupulously. Our Government is the potent, the omnipresent teacher. For good or for ill, it teaches the whole people by its example. Crime is contagious. If the Government becomes a law-breaker, it breeds contempt for law; it invites every man to become a law unto himself; it invites anarchy. To declare that in the administration of the criminal law the end justifies the means—to declare that the Government may commit crimes in order to secure the conviction of a private criminal—would bring terrible retribution. Against that pernicious doctrine this Court should resolutely set its face."

Respondent's contention that no alternative methods were available to insure the successful prosecution of corrupt attorneys is also unpersuasive. As the above-quoted language indicates, even if no other ways existed to ferret out bribery, the respondent would still not be privileged to engage in unethical (and perhaps illegal) conduct. Moreover, in the present case alternatives were available to investigate and prosecute the suspected attorneys. They could, for example, have been charged with solicitation of perjury, or attempted bribery. Respondent maintains that as a practical matter convictions are virtually impossible to obtain unless the crime has been consummated and the money has been paid, that even when these circumstances are present conviction is still very difficult. Such factors cannot, however, justify respondent's conduct.

Because respondent acted without the guidance of precedent or settled opinion and because there is apparently considerable belief (as evidenced by the letters and affidavit supporting respondent) that he acted properly in conducting the investigations, we conclude that no sanction should be imposed. It appears that respondent has otherwise served the public diligently and with integrity and acted in the present matter not out of self-interest, but from a sincere, if misguided, desire to bring corrupt attorneys to justice. In light of all these considerations, we hold that no discipline will be imposed.

Respondent discharged.

■ MR. JUSTICE UNDERWOOD, concurring in the decision:

* * *

[W]hile I do not join in the finding of impropriety contained in the Chief Justice's opinion, I do join in discharging respondent, rather than dismissing the complaint, so that we may have the constitutionally required concurrence of four members in the action to be taken (Ill. Const.1970, art. VI, sec. 3).

The Administrator's case against respondent consisted solely of a statement of facts stipulated to by respondent. In contrast, respondent, after testifying fully and candidly that he accepted full responsibility for the conduct now alleged to be improper, introduced [expert testimony] and some 35 affidavits, statements and letters from both Federal and State judges and prosecutors, the Governor of Illinois, a law school dean and professors, criminal defense attorneys, and others. Many of these, in addition to attesting to respondent's excellent character and impeccable integrity, viewed the undisputed facts as involving no professional impropriety. Notable among them is Dean Monroe H.Freedman of Hofstra University Law School, a former faculty member at Harvard and George Washington law schools who specializes in the field of lawyers' ethics and has written extensively on the subject. His book *Lawyers' Ethics in an Adversary System* has been characterized as the best in the field of legal ethics. Dean Freedman, who was serving as chairman of the Committee on Professional Responsibility of the Society of American Law Teachers, has also served or is serving in many other positions of responsibility in the professional ethics field. He indicated that "[m]otive is, of course, a primary consideration in making judgments regarding the ethical quality of conduct." (M. Freedman, Lawyers' Ethics in an Adversary System 83 (1975).) In his statement in this case, submitted in affidavit form, he indicates his opinion that the proper construction of the ABA-approved Code of Professional Responsibility Rules proscribing the knowing use of false evidence, deceit and misrepresentation restricts the application of those rules to situations in which the responsible attorney engages in such conduct with the intent not to reveal the fraud and deception to the affected person or tribunal. In Dean Freedman's opinion, the complaint in this case should be dismissed for respondent was carrying out his express ethical obligation as a prosecutor to "improve the administration of criminal justice." ABA Standards, The Prosecution Function sec. 1.4 (1971).

* * *

[Based on other affidavits submitted] it is apparent that the pernicious activities of some police officers and some court personnel were either eliminated or substantially reduced by procedural changes suggested by, or inaugurated by, respondent.

* * *

In the *amicus* brief filed in his individual capacity by Thomas P.Sullivan, an able lawyer who formerly argued both criminal and civil cases in this court and now serves the Northern District of Illinois as United States District Attorney, Mr. Sullivan succinctly portrays the difficulty faced by law-enforcement personnel in cases like these. He states:

> "From time to time, prosecutors receive what appear to be reliable allegations that defense attorneys in criminal cases are engaged in suborning perjury, or bribing witnesses, bailiffs, clerks, prosecutors or judges, or the like. The prosecutor to whom such allegations are made has a duty to investigate, and to prosecute those found to be corrupting the criminal process.

> Usually, the hard evidence to prove these crimes is the payment of money by the defense lawyer to the witness, policeman, prosecutor, clerk, bailiff, or judge.
>
> Usually, to obtain the hard evidence of payment, it is necessary to have one or more of the participants in the case pretend to abet the scheme. Payment usually occurs *after* the policeman, witness, prosecutor, clerk or judge has done whatever he is supposed to do; usually, the payment is made *after* the defendant is acquitted, the evidence is suppressed, the case is dismissed, or the like.
>
> The Hearing Board's ruling recognizes the practical problems faced by the prosecutor who wishes to investigate these kinds of allegations. Contrariwise, the ruling of the majority of the Review Board, if sustained by this Court, will seriously impair investigations in cases of this kind in Illinois. The unfortunate result may well be cessation of meaningful investigations of corrupt conduct by defense lawyers, witnesses, clerks, bailiffs, and judges in Illinois.
>
> It is respectfully submitted that this Court should not hold an Illinois prosecutor guilty of unethical conduct when, in good faith, he carefully seeks evidence to ferret out and prosecute lawyers who are engaged in corrupting the criminal process. Surely Mr. Friedman should not be censured for doing that which he honestly believed to be a proper and ethical exercise of his sworn duty."

In an attempt to answer, my colleagues suggest that respondent had alternatives available—the suspect lawyers could have been charged with solicitation of perjury or attempted bribery. The weakness of that naive answer lies in the demonstrated fact that a prosecution of either of those charges, based upon the testimony of a single, uncorroborated witness as to the ambiguous language in which such offers are customarily made, will rarely succeed against the lawyer's vigorous denial of any criminal intent. . . .

The situation before us is analogous to that visualized by section 7 13 of the Criminal Code of 1961.

> "Conduct which would otherwise be an offense is justifiable by reason of necessity if the accused was without blame in occasioning or developing the situation and reasonably believed such conduct was necessary to avoid a public or private injury greater than the injury which might reasonably result from his own conduct."

Certainly respondent was without blame in connection with the original bribe offers, and there is no doubt he believed his own conduct necessary to avoid a greater injury—the continued corruption of the judicial process by the two attorneys. That belief was, in my judgment, not only reasonable—it was correct. The fact is that no one, other than the dishonest lawyers, was injured by respondent's conduct. The courts were promptly informed. One case was reinstated, and the other could have been. And respondent created a substantial and obviously needed deterrent to similar misconduct by other attorneys.

I should make clear that I abhor the thought of intentionally deceiving a judge—even temporarily—by the presentation of false testimony. But I abhor even more those members of my profession who seek to prostitute our courts. Since corrupt lawyers will not make payment of the bribe until that which they seek has been done, and payment is, in my judgment, a practical necessity to conviction of the lawyer, some form of misrepresentation to the judge is required if the evidence of payment is to be secured. What was done here, much as I dislike it, seems to me preferable to informing the judge in advance, thereby making him a participant, or immunizing the corrupt lawyer from investigation and prosecution which, I fear, will inevitably result if respondent's conduct is held ethically impermissible.

In short, it is undisputed that respondent was a conscientious prosecutor dedicated to improving the administration of criminal justice. Both defendants and prosecutors benefited from his efforts as Professor Haddad's statement illustrates. At no time did respondent intend to permanently deceive anyone, and the necessary, temporary deception practiced upon the court was corrected immediately after it had served its purpose. No authority is cited by my colleagues indicating that the proscriptions in the disciplinary rules of fraud, misrepresentation, deceit and the use of false evidence were intended to embrace the factual situation involved here, and I agree with Dean Freedman and the hearing panel that they were not so intended.

While I believe respondent's conduct, motivated and circumscribed as it was, did not breach the disciplinary rules, for the reasons earlier noted I concur in respondent's discharge.

■ MR. JUSTICE RYAN joins in this concurrence.

■ MR. JUSTICE WARD took no part in the consideration or decision of this case.

■ MR. JUSTICE CLARK and MR. JUSTICE MORAN's dissents omitted.

* * *

NOTES

1. The issue of whether prosecutors or police officers are guilty of wrong doing must be distinguished from the question of whether their investigative techniques prevent a valid conviction of the target of the investigation. The latter issue is touched upon in Chapter 7 of the Casebook. Although the Illinois court deemed improper the conduct of the prosecutor in the *Friedman* case, it upheld the bribery conviction of the corrupt criminal defense lawyer based upon evidence secured through use by Prosecutor Friedman of the tactic in question. People v. Powell, 72 Ill.2d 50, 18 Ill.Dec. 318, 377 N.E.2d 803 (1978), cert. denied 440 U.S. 907, 99 S.Ct. 1214 (1979).

2. Federal prosecutors in all of their cases are to be guided by the following principles stated by Mr. Justice Sutherland in Berger v. United States, 295 U.S. 78, 88, 55 S.Ct. 629, 633 (1935).

"The United States Attorney is the representative not of an ordinary party to a controversy, but of a sovereignty whose obligation to govern impartially is as compelling as its obligation to govern at all; and whose interest, therefore, in a criminal prosecution is not that it shall win a case, but that justice shall be done. As such, he is in a peculiar and very definite sense the servant of the law, the twofold aim of which is that guilt shall not escape or innocence suffer. He may prosecute with earnestness and vigor—indeed, he should do so. But, while he may strike hard blows, he is not at liberty to strike foul ones. It is as much his duty to refrain from improper methods calculated to produce a wrongful conviction as it is to use every legitimate means to bring about a just one."

3. In 1972, working together to combat corruption, federal and New York officials went much further than would Prosecutor Friedman the next year. In order to get a case in the system so as to test the honesty of lawyers and other criminal justice system participants, they staged an arrest of an undercover agent, in effect manufacturing a crime and using false court documents, false statements to judges, and false grand jury testimony. The story of subsequent litigation is told in Gershman, Entrapment, Shocked Consciences, and the Staged Arrest, 66 Minn. L.Rev. 567 (1982). While the account is from the perspective of defenses to criminal charges brought against persons who, indeed, were proved to be corrupt through the use of the government tactics, the article and the cases discussed therein give insight into varying views of the ethics of such prosecution tactics.

Somewhat similar tactics, though not involving grand jury perjury, were used in the so-called "Greylord investigation" conducted by federal authorities in Chicago. Undercover agents swore to numerous false criminal complaints and often testified falsely in state court as part of criminal prosecutions "created" by federal authorities. United States v. Murphy, 768 F.2d 1518 (7th Cir.1985), declared that officers who knowingly gave false testimony only "appeared" to commit perjury, lacking "criminal intent" and harming no litigant while using "necessary" means to root out corruption.

One federal prosecutor who deceived a (non-target) federal judge in obtaining a writ as part of an investigation was severely chastised in United States v. Gjieli, 717 F.2d 968 (6th Cir.1983). Because the deception did not violate the rights of the target, the Court of Appeals refused him relief in the case which culminated from the investigation. A case condemning sham use of subpoena as a tool of an undercover investigation is United States v. Caputo, 633 F.Supp. 1479 (E.D.Pa. 1986).

The Second Circuit reversed the District Court's ruling in *Caputo*, in a case captioned United States v. Martino, 825 F.2d 754 (3d Cir.1987).The court noted that the use of a "sham" subpoena did not involve deception of a grand jury or of a court, but only of persons suspected of criminal activity. In that sense, it was little different from other forms of deception utilized in undercover investigations:

> If government officials may pose as nonexistent sheiks in an elaborately concocted scheme, supply a necessary ingredient for a drug operation, and utilize landing strips, docking facilities, and other accoutrements of an organized smuggling operation [citations omitted], all in order to catch criminals, then their use of a subpoena in the name of an undercover agent to enable him to retain his credibility with suspected criminals seems innocuous by comparison.

The *Martino* court not only refused to grant relief to the defendant—which was the issue at hand in *Martino* and in the decisions it cited—it declared that the governmental conduct was not improper. Recall that these are two distinct questions.

Finally, *Martino* declared that the "sham" subpoena technique was far less objectionable than the false swearing and the deception of state judges in the Greylord investigation approved by the Seventh Circuit in *Murphy*. *Martino*, in emphasizing that no grand jury or court was deceived in the investigation under consideration, reserved judgment on the propriety of such deception as occurred in *Murphy*.

* * *

4. In Imbler v. Pachtman, 424 U.S. 409, 96 S.Ct. 984 (1976), the Supreme Court held that for purposes of the federal civil rights statute, 42 U.S.C. § 1983, a state prosecutor is immune from an action for money damages even where the complaint alleges that he knowingly utilized perjured testimony. What policy can possibly justify such a result?

In Burns v. Reed, 500 U.S. 478, 111 S.Ct. 1934 (1991), the Court distinguished Imbler v. Pachtman and refused to grant absolute immunity to a prosecutor for his or her conduct in giving legal advice to the police. The prosecutor had advised police that they could interrogate a suspect under hypnosis. Later the prosecutor gave the officers his opinion that they probably had probable cause. Still later he participated in a judicial hearing which sought a search warrant and allegedly elicited misleading testimony that led the judge to issue the warrant.

While upholding absolute immunity for the prosecutor's conduct in the judicial proceeding (the warrant application), Justice White for the majority noted that at American common law, there was no absolute immunity for a prosecutor who gave advice to the police even though the public prosecutor's office did exist at American common law. He added that vexatious litigation for legal advice was less likely, absent absolute immunity, based upon legal advice, as distinguished from conduct in a judicial proceeding. The majority reasoned that a potential plaintiff was less likely to be aware of a prosecutor's role in advising the police. But even if a prosecutor's role in giving advice to the police "does carry with it some risks of burdensome litigation, the concern with litigation in our immunity cases in not merely a generalized concern with interference with an official's duties, but rather a concern with interference with the conduct closely related to the judicial process."

The majority added that other judicial remedies for prosecutorial misconduct in giving advice "will not necessarily restrain out-of-court activities by a prosecutor that occur prior to the initiation of a prosecution, such as providing legal advice to the police." The majority added that the police do not have absolute immunity when they rely on the legal advice of the police, and that it would be anomalous to allow trained lawyers absolute immunity forgiving legal advice no matter how erroneous.

Justice Scalia, joined by Justices Blackmun and Marshall, unlike the majority, believed that *Burns* also presented the issue of whether a prosecutor was immune for approving a search warrant application. These justices stated that absolute immunity should not attach to such prosecutorial conduct, although it noted some tension between its view and the *Imbler* decision that a prosecutor's seeking of a grand jury indictment is cloaked by absolute immunity.

In Buckley v. Fitzsimmons, 509 U.S. 259, 113 S.Ct. 2606 (1993), the Court found that a prosecutor's actions obtaining (during the investigation of a crime and before charges were filed) an expert to identify a boot print were not protected by absolute immunity. Nor were the prosecutor's statements at a press conference. It was alleged that the prosecutor sought out a witness whom he knew to be willing to fabricate unreliable expert testimony and that the prosecutor defamed defendant at pre-election day press conference held after indictment was returned. The Court was unanimous in deciding there was no immunity for press conference statements. Four justices voted to grant immunity on the false expert witness claim. While the majority found the actions to be "investigative," the dissenters thought they were "preparation for trial".

In Houston v. Partee, 978 F.2d 362 (7th Cir.1992), the court held that prosecutors who had failed to disclose exculpatory evidence *after* convictions had been secured were not entitled to absolute immunity in the convicted's civil rights suit.

United States v. Boyd

United States Court of Appeals, Seventh Circuit, 1995.
55 F.3d 239.

■ POSNER, CHIEF JUDGE. * * * The defendants, six leaders and one close associate of the "El Rukns," a notorious Chicago street gang formerly known as the "Blackstone Rangers" and the "Black P Stone Nation," were convicted by a jury after a four-month trial of a variety of very serious federal crimes. The judge sentenced five of the defendants to life in prison and the other two to fifty years. The evidence showed that during the 1980s the El Rukns had trafficked in heroin and cocaine on a large scale in the southern and western areas of the city and to protect their lucrative turf had committed many murders, attempted murders, kidnappings, and acts of intimidation. Their targets had included not only rivals in the drug trade but also potential witnesses.

The government's case depended heavily on the testimony of six former gang leaders, including Harry Evans and Henry Harris. The ground for the motion for a new trial was that the government had knowingly allowed Evans and Harris to perjure themselves at the trial and had withheld from the defense evidence that during the trial all six, who were being held at the Metropolitan Correctional Center (near the federal courthouse where the trial was held), had used illegal drugs and received unlawful favors from government prosecutors and their staffs. The district judge granted the motion for a new trial—in an opinion that occupies 90 pages of small print in the *Federal Supplement*—after he had taken testimony at a post-trial evidentiary hearing from 29 witnesses. The testimony convinced him that prosecutors and staff in the office of the U.S. Attorney for the Northern District of Illinois had engaged in misconduct far more serious than anything involved in typical cases in which a prosecutor is accused of the knowing use of perjured testimony or of the violation of a defendant's right under Brady v. Maryland, 373 U.S. 83 (1963), to be shown exculpatory evidence that is in the prosecution's possession. The government does not challenge the district judge's finding of gross prosecutorial misconduct, and we have no reason to suppose the finding flawed. But the Supreme Court has told us that we are not to reverse convictions in order to punish prosecutors. United States v. Hasting, 461 U.S. 499, 506–07 (1983). Prosecutorial misconduct may precipitate a reversible error, but it is never in itself a reversible error. United States v. Van Engel, 15 F.3d 623, 631 (7th Cir.1993). In great tension with this principle, there are intimations that "outrageous governmental misconduct" is an independent ground for ordering a new trial in a federal criminal case; but we agree with the First Circuit that "the doctrine [of outrageous governmental misconduct] is moribund." United States v. Santana, 6 F.3d 1, 4 (1st

Cir.1993). "Stillborn" might be a better term, for it never had any life; and it certainly has no support in the decisions of this court, which go out of their way to criticize the doctrine.United States v. Okey, 47 F.3d 238, 240 n. 2 (7th Cir.1995). Today we let the other shoe drop, and hold that the doctrine does not exist in this circuit. The gravity of the prosecutors' misconduct is relevant only insofar as it may shed light on the materiality of the infringement of the defendants' rights; it may support, but it can never compel, an inference that the prosecutors resorted to improper tactics because they were justifiably fearful that without such tactics the defendants might be acquitted. If the prosecutors did not think their case airtight (and so they tried to bolster it improperly), this is some indication that it was indeed not airtight.

Although the government intimates that Judge Aspen's real motive for granting the motion for a new trial was to punish the U.S. Attorney's office for its misbehavior, there is no evidence of such a motive and we think it unlikely that, having just sat through a four-month trial and sentenced five of the defendants to life in prison and the other two to fifty years apiece, Judge Aspen would have been predisposed to grant a motion that might require him to sit through another four-month trial of the same defendants.

* * *

We are not fetishistic about standards of appellate review. We acknowledge that there are more verbal formulas for the scope of appellate review (plenary or de novo, clearly erroneous, abuse of discretion, substantial evidence, arbitrary and capricious, some evidence, reasonable basis, presumed correct, and maybe others) than there are distinctions actually capable of being drawn in the practice of appellate review. Morales v. Yeutter, 952 F.2d 954, 957 (7th Cir.1991). But even if, as we have sometimes heretically suggested, there are operationally only two degrees of review, plenary (that is, no deference given to the tribunal being reviewed) and deferential, *that* distinction at least is a feasible, intelligible, and important one. Yet apart from a parenthetical acknowledgment that the standard of review of denial of a motion for a new trial is abuse of discretion, the issue of the proper standard was ignored by the government until its reply brief, which acknowledged that appellate review of an order granting a new trial in a criminal case is indeed deferential—a concession that the government then evaded at the oral argument.

Appellate review of these orders is not deferential *t out court*. If the judge in the course of his analysis has occasion to resolve a pure issue of law, our review of that resolution is plenary. United States v. Adebayo, 985 F.2d 1333, 1341 (7th Cir.1993). But the other judgments that the district judge makes, signally here the judgment whether some piece (or pieces) of evidence wrongfully withheld by the government might if disclosed have changed the outcome of the trial, are to be reviewed deferentially. This is not only the rule; it is the dictate of common sense, especially in a case such as this. Forget the 29 witnesses at the evidentiary hearing; forget there *was* an evidentiary hearing on the motion for a new trial. Before then, during the trial, Judge Aspen had for months on end listened to witnesses—had heard, had not merely read, their testimony, and had watched them as they gave it. And he had observed the jurors as they listened to the witnesses. A trial judge of long experience, he would have developed a feel for the impact of the witnesses on the jury—and how that impact might have been different had the government played by the rules—that an appellate court, confined to reading the transcript, cannot duplicate. Judge Aspen may have been mistaken; we might suspect that he *was* mistaken; but unless we are *convinced* that he was mistaken, we have no warrant to reverse. That is what it means to say that appellate review is deferential. It is not abject, Carr v. Allison Gas Turbine Division, 32 F.3d 1007, 1008 (7th Cir.1994), but it is deferential.

We consider first whether Judge Aspen committed clear error in finding that the government had made knowing use of perjured testimony at the trial. Witness Evans, jailed in 1988 on numerous charges, had been held in the Metropolitan Correctional Center ever since. He thus was there throughout the trial of the defendants, which was held in 1991, except of course when he was testifying or meeting with prosecutors or prosecution staff in the courthouse or in the federal building across the street. Throughout the entire period Evans used illegal drugs and the prosecutors knew it. The question of his drug use came up at trial. He was asked by the prosecutor, "[Y]ou used and abused drugs from the seventies until the time you went to jail in 1988, isn't that correct?" "Yes, sir," replied Evans. The prosecutor then asked, "[H]ow many years would you say you have been using and abusing drugs?" Answer: "You just said it." "From '74 to '88, or earlier?" "That's a good figure." Judge Aspen interpreted Evans's last answer to mean that he had stopped using drugs in 1988. This is not an inevitable interpretation, but we cannot call it unreasonable; and so interpreted Evans's answer was a lie, and the government knew it. Whether the question was precise enough that Evans could actually be convicted of perjury may be doubted; but the wrong of knowing use by prosecutors of perjured testimony does not require a determination that the witness could have been successfully prosecuted. Successful prosecution would require proof beyond a reasonable doubt not only that the witness's testimony had been false but also that it had been knowingly false (and hence perjury). The wrong of knowing use by prosecutors of perjured testimony is different, and misnamed—it is knowing use of *false* testimony. It is enough that the jury was likely to understand the witness to have said something that was, as the prosecution knew, false. Hamric v. Bailey, 386 F.2d 390, 394 (4th Cir.1967); Ronald L. Carlson, "False or Suppressed Evidence: Why a Need for the Prosecutorial Tie?" 1969 *Duke L.J.* 1171, 1186 n. 42; David Wolf, Note, "I Cannot Tell a Lie: The Standard for New Trial in False Testimony Cases," 83 *Mich.L.Rev.* 1925, 1926 n. 7, 1943 (1985). We cannot find any recent cases that enunciate this principle clearly, but it is implicit in the frequent use of "false" as a synonym for "perjured" in cases in which prosecutors are claimed to have knowingly used perjured testimony. E.g., United States v. Agurs, 427 U.S. 97, 103 (1976).

Shortly after the exchange that we just quoted, Evans said, "But I'm not on drugs now." We do not *know* whether he was high when he said this, so probably, again, he could not be successfully prosecuted for perjury. But given the context, Judge Aspen was entitled to infer that Evans would have been understood by the jury to have meant that he was no longer using drugs, which was false. Evans also answered "No" to the question, "You are not dealing drugs anymore?" The evidence is that he was. He was heard to admit this in a phone conversation a year later, while before the trial he not only had been using drugs but had had in his possession large, unexplained quantities of cash. The suspicious circumstances bracketed the trial and there was no basis for supposing that he had behaved himself during the trial. The government knew all this. Judge Aspen was entitled to infer that Evans had lied when he testified that he was not dealing in drugs any more, and that the government had known that he had lied.

The knowing use of perjured testimony is not an automatic ground for a new trial. There must be some likelihood that it made a difference. But of course the impact of the testimony need not be considered apart from the impact of other improprieties committed by the government. So we consider the other improprieties first, and return to the issue of impact, of "prejudice," later.

The other improprieties are the alleged violations of the *Brady* rule. The prisoner witnesses, not only Harris and Evans but the four other ex-El Rukns, received a continuous stream of unlawful, indeed scandalous, favors from staff at the U.S. Attorney's office while jailed at the MCC awaiting the trial of the defendants. Disclosure of these benefits, of course known to the prosecution (the *source* of the benefits), would have helped the defendants by undermining the credibility of key witnesses against them. The rule of *Brady* applies to evidence usable only to impeach the credibility of the prosecution's witnesses, and not just to direct evidence of innocence. This means that, quite apart from either the favors or the perjured testimony, the fact, known to the government, that the witnesses were using drugs throughout the period of the trial and its preparation should have been disclosed to the defendants because it was a fact they could have used to challenge the witnesses' credibility.

The favors must not be ignored, however. In the MCC itself, visitors are forbidden to make physical contact with prisoners; the primary fear is that the visitors will pass drugs to the prisoners. Bizarrely, the prosecutors permitted the prisoner witnesses—hardened and dangerous criminals all—to entertain their visitors in the U.S. Attorney's office in the federal courthouse and in the office of the Bureau of Alcohol, Tobacco, and Firearms in the federal building across the street from the courthouse. Security for these visits was so lax that the visitors, almost always women, were able not only to pass drugs to the witnesses but also to have sexual intercourse with them. Evans's most frequent visitor was a woman politely described as his "common law wife" (there is no common law marriage in Illinois). Evans had been caught having sex with her in the MCC and had been disciplined for this violation of the MCC's rules, as the prosecutors well knew. The prosecutors nevertheless allowed her to visit him in the government offices in circumstances in which a repetition of his offense was certain. Evans's "common law wife" also appears to have been the principal source for the drugs that he obtained and used—and sold—throughout the period of the trial. The government, while not aware of the details of these visits, was well aware of the opportunity that the visits afforded for shenanigans involving sex and drugs. It also knew that the witnesses used their opportunity to roam about in government offices unsupervised to steal numerous documents (some highly confidential), later found back in the MCC whither they had carried them.

The prosecutors also gave the witnesses unlimited and unsupervised telephone privileges available to no other federal prisoners. Members of the prosecution team would routinely accept collect calls from the witnesses at the MCC and then at the witness's request would forward the calls to outside numbers. The telephoning was incessant, reaching a point at which two of the prosecutors complained to the head of the prosecution team about the cost to the government. Some witnesses, on their visits to the office of the Bureau of Alcohol, Tobacco, and Firearms, were permitted to answer the phones in the office, and they would often answer "ATF." Some of the calls they answered were from other inmates, and they would forward these calls to outside numbers at the request of the caller. The witnesses also used their phone privileges to order drugs. On occasion the witnesses drank beer in the government offices, although it is unclear whether the prosecutors knew about this.

A government paralegal named Luchetta, a member of the prosecution team, developed personal relationships with the prisoner witnesses. These relationships involved phone sex and assistance in smuggling contraband into the MCC. Luchetta gave witness Harris a number of presents: a U.S. flag, a thesaurus, two maps of the world, one emphasis pointer, two pairs of pants, two shirts, one sweatshirt, and a pair of gym shoes. In addition she threw two birthday parties for him. Harris and other witnesses received presents from other members of the prosecution team as well. The head of the team, Hogan, developed a personal relationship with Harris. Hogan accepted gifts from Harris, who in turn made Hogan a legatee in his will. Harris took a fancy to a female paralegal (not Luchetta), and apparently told Hogan about this, for Hogan approached the paralegal's supervisor and asked her whether the paralegal would accept phone calls from Harris. (The supervisor replied, "Absolutely not.")

The government did not disclose any of these goings-on to the defendants. A few of the shenanigans, it is true, such as the naming of Hogan in Harris's will, occurred after the trial and strictly, therefore, were relevant only to a motion for a new trial on the basis of newly discovered evidence, which is not before us. Judge Aspen knew this, but remarked, properly we think, that even the later-occurring events gave an insight into the character of the relationship between the prosecutorial team and the prisoner witnesses. The events in question occurred shortly after trial and were obviously the culmination of an unprofessionally, indeed scandalously, close relationship between prosecutors and criminals that had started before the trial and had continued through it.

The difficult question is that of the impact on the trial's outcome. We agree with the government that a unitary standard guides our inquiry into the prejudicial impact of all the alleged improprieties, and that it is whether there is a reasonable probability that, had it not been for the improprieties, the defendants would have been acquitted. But the precise question for us is not whether *we* think the combination of perjured testimony and concealing exculpatory evidence is likely to have affected the outcome of the trial but whether we are convinced that Judge Aspen's answer to the question was wrong. As the perjured testimony and the concealed evidence went only to the credibility of the prisoner witnesses, the question of prejudicial impact can be further decomposed into two questions: Is there some reasonable probability that the jury would have acquitted the defendants on at least some of the counts against them had the jury disbelieved the essential testimony of these witnesses? And might the jury have disbelieved that testimony if the witnesses hadn't perjured themselves about their continued use of drugs and (or) if the government had revealed to the defense the witnesses' continued use of drugs and the favors that the prosecution had extended to them?

The answer to the first question is clearly "yes." Although the testimony of the six prisoner witnesses for the prosecution was corroborated, had their testimony been disbelieved the defendants would have had to be acquitted on most counts. It is true that the government introduced a number of taped conversations that were highly incriminating of the defendants, but these tapes were translated by witness Harris and their meaning was thus conveyed to the jury through his testimony. If the jury hadn't believed him, it would not have been impressed by the tapes. And without the tapes, the testimony of the prisoner witnesses was essential on most of the counts of which the defendants were convicted.

So the case comes down to whether Judge Aspen abused his discretion in finding that there was a reasonable probability that the jury would have disbelieved the essential testimony of the prisoner witnesses had the defendants been able to impeach them without the impediments created by the government's improprieties. The government argues that the witnesses had already been so thoroughly impeached that additional impeachment could have made no difference. United States v. Derr, 990 F.2d 1330, 1336 (D.C.Cir.1993). The witnesses were cross-examined extensively about their criminal activities while they were members of the El Rukns. These activities covered the full gamut of the El Rukns' crimes and thus included drug trafficking and murder, not to mention the intimidation of witnesses. The jury could not have doubted that the witnesses would lie if they thought it in their interest and that their only hope of avoiding life imprisonment or, in the case of one witness, capital punishment lay with the prosecution. The argument is that if the jury believed that such scoundrels notwithstanding such pressures were telling the truth, additional impeachment could not have shaken that belief. Merely cumulative evidence is excludable, as having little probative value, Fed.R.Evid. 403; merely cumulative impeachment evidence likewise. And obviously it need not be inadmissible in order to lack sufficient weight to require acquittal on the ground that its exclusion was a prejudicial error; not all admissible evidence is strongly probative of the proposition for which it is introduced.

If the evidence that was not revealed had consisted of one more crime, or for that matter ten more crimes, committed by each of the witnesses when he was an El Rukn, we have no doubt that Judge Aspen would have denied the motion for a new trial; for extending the list of past crimes would not have made a difference to the jury's evaluation of the witnesses' credibility. The reason the concealed evidence might well have made a difference was that the witnesses had claimed to have "seen the light" when, having been arrested and sentenced or threatened with severe punishment for their activities as El Rukns, they had decided to cooperate with the government. That had been in 1985. Six years later they were still dealing drugs, stealing, smuggling, violating jail rules, and lying on the stand. Had these things been known to the jury it might have doubted their testimony that they had "seen the light." Knowing that they were lying under oath about their using and dealing in drugs, the jury might reasonably have supposed that they were lying about the criminal activities of the defendants as well. And this is not all. Had the jury known that the prisoner witnesses were receiving favors, including sexual favors, the equivalent of a free telephone credit card, and illegal drugs, all with the permission or connivance of the U.S. Attorney's office, the jury might have wondered whether the witnesses were not receiving implicit assurances of compensation for their testimony going far beyond anything promised in their plea agreements, the terms of which had been revealed to the jury. If a prisoner is treated by officers of the United States Government as if he had the sexual and other privileges of a free man, treated indeed as a *friend* (even as a potential lover), may it not occur to him that if he plays ball with his powerful friend the friend will not just get his death sentence reduced to natural life or his natural-life sentence reduced to thirty years but will somehow arrange to restore his freedom to him in the near future? Do you throw a birthday party for a man who you think deserves to spend his life behind bars? Might not a reasonable jury have concluded, had they known all the facts, that the prosecution team must have had *desperate* doubts about the testimonial reliability of these witnesses to have lavished such extraordinary personal attentions upon them? In short, might not the prosecution's case have collapsed *entirely* had the truth come out about the behavior and the treatment of these witnesses?

We do not know, of course. An alternative hypothesis is that the witnesses were simply very good bargainers, who obtained more consideration from the prosecution in exchange for their testimony than most witnesses do. The issue is judgmental. The responsibility for the exercise of the requisite judgment is the district judge's and we are to intervene only if strongly convinced that he judged wrong. We are not strongly convinced. The grant of the new trial must therefore stand.

AFFIRMED.

B. THE DILEMMA OF DEFENSE COUNSEL

1. AMERICAN BAR ASSOCIATION STANDARDS

For Criminal Justice: Prosecution Function and Defense Function, 3d Ed., 1993 (approved 1994)

Standard 4–1.2 The Function of Defense Counsel

(a) Counsel for the accused is an essential component of the administration of criminal justice. A court properly constituted to hear a criminal case must be viewed as a tripartite entity consisting of the judge (and jury, where appropriate), counsel for the prosecution, and counsel for the accused.

(b) The basic duty defense counsel owes to the administration of justice and as an officer of the court is to serve as the accused's counselor and advocate with courage and devotion and to render effective, quality representation.

* * *

(e) Defense counsel, in common with all members of the bar, is subject to standards of conduct stated in statutes, rules, decisions of courts, and codes, canons, or other standards of professional conduct. Defense counsel has no duty to execute any directive of the accused which does not comport with law or such standards. Defense counsel is the professional representative of the accused, not the accused's alter ego.

(f) Defense counsel should not intentionally misrepresent matters of fact or law to the court.

(g) Defense counsel should disclose to the tribunal legal authority in the controlling jurisdiction known to defense counsel to be directly adverse to the position of the accused and not disclosed by the prosecutor.

(h) It is the duty of defense counsel to know and be guided by the standards of professional conduct as defined in codes and canons of the legal profession applicable in defense counsel's jurisdiction. Once representation has been undertaken, the functions and duties of defense counsel are the same whether defense counsel is assigned, privately retained, or serving in a legal aid or defender program.

Standard 4–1.3 Delays; Punctuality; Workload

(a) Defense counsel should act with reasonable diligence and promptness in representing a client.

(b) Defense counsel should avoid unnecessary delay in the disposition of cases. Defense counsel should be punctual in attendance upon court and in the submission of all motions, briefs, and other papers. Defense counsel should emphasize to the client and all witnesses the importance of punctuality in attendance in court.

(c) Defense counsel should not intentionally misrepresent facts or otherwise mislead the court in order to obtain a continuance.

(d) Defense counsel should not intentionally use procedural devices for delay for which there is no legitimate basis.

(e) Defense counsel should not carry a workload that, by reason of its excessive size, interferes with the rendering of quality representation, endangers the client's interest in the speedy disposition of charges, or may lead to the breach of professional obligations. Defense counsel should not accept employment for the purpose of delaying trial.

Standard 4–3.1 Establishment of Relationship

(a) Defense counsel should seek to establish a relationship of trust and confidence with the accused and should discuss the objectives of the representation and whether defense counsel will continue to represent the accused if there is an appeal. Defense counsel should explain the necessity of full disclosure of all facts known to the client for an effective defense, and defense counsel should explain the extent to which counsel's obligation of confidentiality makes privileged the accused's disclosures.

Standard 4–3.2 Interviewing the Client

(a) As soon as practicable, defense counsel should seek to determine all relevant facts known to the accused. In so doing, defense counsel should probe for all legally relevant information without seeking to influence the direction of the client's responses.

(b) Defense counsel should not instruct the client or intimate to the client in any way that the client should not be candid in revealing facts so as to afford defense counsel free rein to take action which would be precluded by counsel's knowing of such facts.

Standard 4–3.3 Fees

(a) Defense counsel should not enter into an agreement for, charge, or collect an illegal or unreasonable fee.

(b) In determining the amount of the fee in a criminal case, it is proper to consider the time and effort required, the responsibility assumed by counsel, the novelty and difficulty of the questions involved, the skill requisite to proper representation, the likelihood that other employment will be precluded, the fee customarily charged in the locality for similar services, the gravity of the charge, the experience, reputation, and ability of defense counsel, and the capacity of the client to pay the fee.

(c) Defense counsel should not imply that his or her compensation is for anything other than professional services rendered by defense counsel or by others for defense counsel.

(d) Defense counsel should not divide a fee with a nonlawyer, except as permitted by applicable ethical codes of conflict.

(e) Defense counsel not in the same firm should not divide fees unless the division is in proportion to the services performed by each counsel or, by written agreement with the client, each counsel assumes joint responsibility for the representation, the client is advised of and does not object to the participation of all counsel involved, and the total fee is reasonable.

(f) Defense counsel should not enter into an arrangement for, charge, or collect a contingent fee for representing a defendant in a criminal case.

(g) When defense counsel has not regularly represented he client, defense counsel should communicate the basis or rate of the fee to the client, preferably in writing, before or within a reasonable time after commencing the representation.

Standard 4–3.5 Conflicts of Interest

(a) Defense counsel should not permit his or her professional judgment or obligations to be affected by his or her own political, financial, business, property, or personal interests.

(b) Defense counsel should disclose to the defendant at the earliest feasible opportunity any interest in or connection with the case or any other matter that might be relevant to the defendant's selection of counsel to represent him or her or counsel's continuing representation. Such disclosure should include communication of information reasonably sufficient to permit the client to appreciate the significance of any conflict or potential conflict of interest.

(c) Except for preliminary matters such as initial hearings or applications for bail, defense counsel who are associated in practice should not undertake to defend more than one defendant in the same criminal case if the duty to one of the defendants may conflict with the duty to another. The potential for conflict of interest in representing multiple defendants is so grave that ordinarily defense counsel should decline to act for more than one of several codefendants except in unusual situations when, after careful investigation, it is clear either that no conflict is likely to develop at trial, sentencing, or at any other time in the proceeding or that common representation will be advantageous to each of the codefendants represented and, in either case, that:

(i) the several defendants give an informed consent to such multiple representation; and

(ii) the consent of the defendants is made a matter of judicial record. In determining the presence of consent by the defendants, the trial judge should make appropriate inquiries respecting actual or potential conflicts of interest of counsel and whether the defendants fully comprehend the difficulties that defense counsel sometimes encounters in defending multiple clients.

(d) Defense counsel who has formerly represented a defendant should not thereafter use information related to the former representation to the disadvantage of the former client unless the information has become generally known or the ethical obligation of confidentiality otherwise does not apply.

(e) In accepting payment of fees by one person for the defense of another, defense counsel should be careful to determine that he or she will not be confronted with a conflict of loyalty since defense counsel's entire loyalty is due the accused. Defense counsel should not accept such compensation unless:

(i) the accused consents after disclosure;

(ii) there is no interference with defense counsel's independence of professional judgment or with the client-lawyer relationship; and

(iii) information relating to the representation of the accused is protected from disclosure as required by defense counsel's ethical obligation of confidentiality.

Defense counsel should not permit a person who recommends, employs, or pays defense counsel to render legal services for another to direct or regulate counsel's professional judgment in rendering such legal services.

(f) Defense counsel should not defend a criminal case in which counsel's partner or other professional associate is or has been the prosecutor in the same case.

(g) Defense counsel should not represent a criminal defendant in a jurisdiction in which he or she is also a prosecutor.

(h) Defense counsel who formerly participated personally and substantially in the prosecution of a defendant should not thereafter represent any person in the same or a substantially related matter. Defense counsel who was formerly a prosecutor should not use confidential information about a person acquired when defense counsel was a prosecutor in the representation of a client whose interests are adverse to that person in a matter.

(i) Defense counsel who is related to a prosecutor as parent, child, sibling or spouse should not represent a client in a criminal matter where defense counsel knows the government is represented in the matter by such a prosecutor. Nor should defense counsel who has a significant personal or financial relationship with a prosecutor represent a client in a criminal matter where defense counsel knows the government is represented in the matter by such prosecutor, except upon consent by the client after consultation regarding the relationship.

(j) Defense counsel should not act as surety on a bond either for the accused represented by counsel or for any other accused in the same or a related case.

(k) Except as law may otherwise expressly permit, defense counsel should not negotiate to employ any person who is significantly involved as an attorney or employee of the government in a matter in which defense counsel is participating personally and substantially.

Standard 4–3.7 Advice and Service on Anticipated Unlawful Conduct

(a) It is defense counsel's duty to advise a client to comply with the law, but counsel may advise concerning the meaning, scope, and validity of a law.

(b) Defense counsel should not counsel a client in or knowingly assist a client to engage in conduct which defense counsel knows to be illegal or fraudulent but defense counsel may discuss the legal consequences of any proposed course of conduct with a client.

(c) Defense counsel should not agree in advance of the commission of a crime that he or she will serve as counsel for the defendant, except as part of a bona fide effort to determine the validity, scope, meaning, or application of the law, or where the defense is incident to a general retainer for legal services to a person or enterprise engaged in legitimate activity.

(d) Defense counsel should not reveal information relating to representation of a client unless the client consents after consultation, except for disclosures that are impliedly authorized in order to carry out the representation and except that defense counsel may reveal such information to the extent he or she reasonably believes necessary to prevent the client from committing a criminal act that defense counsel believes is likely to result in imminent death or substantial bodily harm.

Standard 4–4.1 Duty to Investigate

(a) Defense counsel should conduct a prompt investigation of the circumstances of the case and explore all avenues leading to facts relevant to the merits of the case and the penalty in the event of conviction. The investigation should include efforts to secure information in the possession of the prosecution and law enforcement authorities. The duty to investigate exists regardless of the accused's admissions or statements to defense counsel of facts constituting guilt or the accused's stated desire to plead guilty.

(b) Defense counsel should not seek to acquire possession of physical evidence personally or through use of an investigator where defense counsel's sole purpose is to obstruct access to such evidence.

Standard 4–4.2 Illegal Investigation

Defense counsel should not knowingly use illegal means to obtain evidence or information or to employ, instruct, or encourage others to do so.

Standard 4–4.3 Relations With Prospective Witnesses

(a) Defense counsel, in representing an accused, should not use means that have no substantial purpose other than to embarrass, delay, or burden a third person, or use methods of obtaining evidence that violate the legal rights of such a person.

(b) Defense counsel should not compensate a witness, other than an expert, for giving testimony, but it is not improper to reimburse a witness for the reasonable expenses of attendance upon court, including transportation and loss of income, attendance for depositions pursuant to statute or court rule, or attendance for pretrial interviews, provided there is no attempt to conceal the fact of reimbursement.

(c) It is not necessary for defense counsel or defense counsel's investigator, in interviewing a prospective witness, to caution the witness concerning possible self-incrimination and the need for counsel.

(d) Defense counsel should not discourage or obstruct communication between prospective witnesses and the prosecutor. It is unprofessional conduct to advise any person other than a client, or cause such person to be advised, to decline to give to the prosecutor or defense counsel for codefendants information which such person has a right to give.

(e) Unless defense counsel is prepared to forgo impeachment of a witness by counsel's own testimony as to what the witness stated in an interview or to seek leave to withdraw from the case in order to present such impeaching testimony, defense counsel should avoid interviewing a prospective witness except in the presence of a third person.

Standard 4–4.6 Physical Evidence

(a) Defense counsel who receives a physical item under circumstances implicating a client in criminal conduct should disclose the location of or should deliver that item to law enforcement authorities only: (1) if required by law or court order, or (2) as provided in paragraph (d).

(b) Unless required to disclose, defense counsel should return the item to the source from whom defense counsel received it, except as provided in paragraph (c) and (d). In returning the item to the source, defense counsel should advise the source of the legal consequences pertaining to possession or destruction of the item. Defense counsel should also prepare a written record of these events for his or her file, but should not give the source a copy of such record.

(c) Defense counsel may receive the item for a reasonable period of time during which defense counsel: (1) intends to return it to the owner; (2) reasonably fears that return of the item to the source will result in destruction of the item; (3) reasonably fears that return of the item to the source will result in physical harm to anyone; (4) intends to test, examine, inspect, or use the item in any way as part of defense counsel's representation of the client; or (5) cannot return it to the source. If defense counsel tests or examines the item, he or she should thereafter return it to the source unless there is reason to believe that the evidence might be altered or destroyed or used to harm another or return is otherwise impossible. If defense counsel retains the item, he or she should retain it in his or her law office in a manner that does not impede the lawful ability of law enforcement authorities to obtain the item.

(d) If the item received is contraband, i.e., an item possession of which is in and of itself a crime such as narcotics, defense counsel may suggest that the client destroy it where there is no pending case or investigation relating to this evidence and where such destruction is clearly not in violation of any criminal statute. If such destruction is not permitted by law or if in defense counsel's judgment he or she cannot retain the item, whether or not it is contraband, in a way that does not pose an unreasonable risk of physical harm to anyone, defense counsel should disclose the location of or should deliver the item to law enforcement authorities.

(e) If defense counsel discloses the location of or delivers the item to law enforcement authorities under paragraphs (a) or (d), or to a third party under paragraph (c)(1), he or she should do so in the way best designed to protect the client's interests.

Standard 4–5.1 Advising the Accused

(a) After informing himself or herself fully on the facts and the law, defense counsel should advise the accused with complete candor concerning all aspects of the case, including a candid estimate of the probable outcome.

(b) Defense counsel should not intentionally understate or overstate the risks, hazards, or prospects of the case to exert undue influence on the accused's decision as to his or her plea.

(c) Defense counsel should caution the client to avoid communication about the case with witnesses, except with the approval of counsel, to avoid any contact with jurors or prospective jurors, and to avoid either the reality or the appearance of any other improper activity.

Standard 4–5.2 Control and Direction of the Case

(a) Certain decisions relating to the conduct of the case are ultimately for the accused and others are ultimately for defense counsel. The decisions which are to be made by the accused after full consultation with counsel include:

(i) what pleas to enter;

(ii) whether to accept a plea agreement;

(iii) whether to waive jury trial;

(iv) whether to testify in his or her own behalf; and

(v) whether to appeal.

(b) Strategic and tactical decisions should be made by defense counsel after consultation with the client where feasible and appropriate. Such decisions include what witnesses to call, whether and how to conduct cross-examination, what jurors to accept or strike, what trial motions should be made, and what evidence should be introduced.

(c) If a disagreement on significant matters of tactics or strategy arises between defense counsel and the client, defense counsel should make a record of the circumstances, counsel's advice and reasons, and the conclusion reached. The record should be made in a manner which protects the confidentiality of the lawyer-client relationship.

Standard 4–6.1 Duty to Explore Disposition Without Trial

(a) Whenever the law, nature, and circumstances of the case permit, defense counsel should explore the possibility of an early diversion of the case from the criminal process through the use of other community agencies.

(b) Defense counsel may engage in plea discussions with the prosecutor. Under no circumstances should defense counsel recommend to a defendant acceptance of a plea unless appropriate investigation and study of the case has been completed, including an analysis of controlling law and the evidence likely to be introduced at trial.

Standard 4–6.2 Plea Discussions

(a) Defense counsel should keep the accused advised of developments arising out of plea discussions conducted with the prosecutor.

(b) Defense counsel should promptly communicate and explain to the accused all significant plea proposals made by the prosecutor.

(c) Defense counsel should not knowingly make false statements concerning the evidence in the course of plea discussions with the prosecutor.

(d) Defense counsel should not seek concessions favorable to one client by any agreement which is detrimental to the legitimate interests of a client in another case.

(e) Defense counsel representing two or more clients in the same or related cases should not participate in making an aggregated agreement as to guilty or nolo contendere pleas, unless each client consents after consultation, including disclosure of the existence and nature of all the claims or pleas involved.

Standard 4–7.5 Presentation of Evidence

(a) Defense counsel should not knowingly offer false evidence, whether by documents, tangible evidence, or the testimony of witnesses, or fail to take reasonable remedial measures upon discovery of its falsity.

(b) Defense counsel should not knowingly and for the purpose of bringing inadmissible matter to the attention of the judge or jury offer inadmissible evidence, ask legally objectionable questions, or make other impermissible comments or arguments in the presence of the judge or jury.

(c) Defense counsel should not permit any tangible evidence to be displayed in the view of the judge or jury which would tend to prejudice fair consideration of the case by the judge or jury until such time as a good faith tender of such evidence is made.

(d) Defense counsel should not tender tangible evidence in the presence of the judge or jury if it would tend to prejudice fair consideration of the case, unless there is a reasonable basis for its admission in evidence. When there is any substantial doubt about the admissibility of such evidence, it should be tendered by an offer of proof and a ruling obtained.

Standard 4–7.6 Examination of Witnesses

(a) The interrogation of all witnesses should be conducted fairly, objectively, and with due regard for the dignity and legitimate privacy of the witness, and without seeking to intimidate or humiliate the witness unnecessarily.

(b) Defense counsel's belief or knowledge that the witness is telling the truth does not preclude cross-examination.

(c) Defense counsel should not call a witness in the presence of the jury who the lawyer knows will claim a valid privilege not to testify.

(d) Defense counsel should not ask a question which implies the existence of a factual predicate for which a good faith belief is lacking.

NOTE

There is controversy over the degree to which a defendant who decides to plead not guilty may control his lawyer's decision about the nature of the defense. A typical case in Chapman v. State, 273 Ga. 348, 541 S.E.2d 634 (2001). There, a defendant who was found in possession of incriminating evidence and gave a tape-recorded confession wanted to deny his presence at the murder, deny that the voice on the police tape was his and claim that the real killer planted evidence on him. Defense counsel, who knew these things to be untrue, refused and offered a defense of guilty but mentally ill, a course of conduct sustained on appeal. In contrast, a defendant who wanted to deny his presence at the scene of the murder was found to have the right to do so in State v. Carter, 270 Kan. 426, 14 P.3d 1138 (2000). Defense counsel in that case conceded that his client was present at the killing but lacked intent to kill. One difference between the cases is that the evidence in State v. Carter while strong was not overwhelming.

Under ordinary conditions, defense counsel is the one who decides tactics. In order to prevail against counsel's judgment, a defendant has to argue that the counsel's decisions had the effect of changing a plea of not guilty to one of guilty a choice which only defendant can make. Chapman and Carter are typical because both involved defenses that conceded an important prosecution fact.

* * *

2. CASE ILLUSTRATION OF DEFENSE COUNSEL'S DILEMMA

In re January 1976 Grand Jury (Genson)

United States Court of Appeals, Seventh Circuit, 1976.
534 F.2d 719.

■ PELL, CIRCUIT JUDGE.

This is an appeal from an order of the district court dated January 15, 1976, adjudging appellant, an attorney, in civil contempt and ordering him to be remanded to the custody of the Attorney General "until such time as he shall purge himself of this contempt or the discharge of the January 1976 Grand Jury, whichever comes first."

* * *

I. Statement of Facts

On December 30, 1975, between 9:00 and 9:30 A.M., the Bellwood Savings and Loan Association of Bellwood, Illinois, was robbed of approximately $6,120.00 by a man and a woman. Investigators from the Federal Bureau of Investigation uncovered information leading to the identification of two suspects, Paul Bijeol and Sharon Kay Holloway, and a complaint and warrant were sworn and issued on December 31, 1975, naming these two suspects.

Investigation and interview disclosed that Bijeol had been in the employ of Edward Genson, attorney at law, prior to the commission of the robbery. Investigation also disclosed that Bijeol and his alleged female accomplice were in the Chicago office of Mr. Genson and one of his associates, Mr. Barry Goodman, between 10:00 A.M. and 12:00 noon on December 30, 1975, approximately one to three hours after the commission of the robbery. Further, Government investigators learned that the male suspect had transferred $200.00 in cash to Mr. Goodman at this time. It was also learned that Bijeol met with Genson at approximately 1:30 P.M. and again at approximately 5:30 P.M. on the day of the robbery.

At approximately 10:00 A.M. on December 31, 1975, Genson was notified by an agent of the FBI that any monies which he had received or would receive as fees for his legal services for the two suspects might constitute proceeds of the robbery. In response to an inquiry of an FBI agent, Genson stated that he received "something" from the male suspect, but he refrained from disclosing what the "something" was. In response to a subsequent inquiry whether he had in fact received any monies or any firearms from either of the two suspects at the time of or subsequent to their meetings on the day of the robbery, Genson asserted the attorney-client privilege as a basis for refusing to respond to the questions.

On January 7, 1976, Genson was served with a subpoena duces tecum requesting the production of

> "[a]ny and all monies paid or delivered to you or into your care, custody, and control by Paul Bijeol or Sharon K. Holloway, ... or their agents, subsequent to 9:00 A.M. on Tuesday, December 30, 1975."

[Genson's motion to quash the subpoena was denied; and following his refusal to comply with the subpoena before the grand jury, he was held in contempt].

* * *

II. The Fifth Amendment Testimonial Privilege

The major issue in this appeal is whether a subpoena duces tecum requiring an attorney to produce for a grand jury investigation monies turned over to him by his clients and believed to be proceeds of a bank robbery infringes his clients' Fifth Amendment privilege against compelled self-incrimination....

The Fifth Amendment privilege against self-incrimination does not merely encompass evidence which may lead to a criminal conviction, but also includes information which would furnish a "link in the chain of evidence" that could lead to prosecution as well as evidence which an individual reasonably believes could be used against him in a criminal prosecution. ... One of the important policies underlying the testimonial privilege is the protection of an individual's "private enclave". ... In order to promote the basic policy objectives which it was believed the framers sought to achieve, the Supreme Court has recognized that the Fifth Amendment privilege respects a private inner sanctum which "necessarily includes an individual's papers and *effects* to the extent that the privilege *bars their compulsory production and authentication*." ...

A series of recent Supreme Court decisions has established, however, that compulsion which makes a suspect or accused the source of real or physical evidence does not violate the testimonial privilege. ... The Government relies upon this series of decisions to bolster its contention that Genson's production of the monies, which it characterizes as mere physical evidence, would not be equatable with any self-incriminatory disclosures of a testimonial or communicative nature.

More precisely, the Government contends that Genson's compliance with the subpoena duces tecum would not represent an impermissible authentication of the physical evidence. The only arguable testimonial disclosure which would accompany Genson's production of the subpoenaed monies would be the implied admission that the currency had been transferred to him from one or both of his clients. The appellant meets this argument by observing that the challenged subpoena seeks not just items, but items that were allegedly obtained from the attorney's clients after a specified time on a specified day. Appellant thus argues that because the wording of the subpoena contains references to the "who" and the "when" of the alleged transfer of monies, it necessarily involves assertive conduct which, as such, might well be interpreted to constitute an admission by Genson's clients.

The question of whether the monies constitute mere physical evidence or represent a testimonial utterance is not one to be categorically or easily answered. At oral argument, the appellant insisted that he stood in such a special relationship to his clients that the Government could not enforce a subpoena duces tecum against him. In sum, the Government could demand from Genson only what it might legitimately demand from his clients. Appellant insists that no one could fail to agree that the Government could not enforce a subpoena duces tecum against the robbery suspects demanding production of the monies.

* * *

... Here, the subpoena is not being served directly upon the suspects. The clients allegedly transferred monies to Genson, their attorney. He is the witness who has been ordered to appear before the grand jury. His implied admission that he received the monies from his clients on the very day of the bank robbery is not the direct testimony of the suspects themselves. ...

... [It] has been recently established that a lawyer is not subject to the penalty of contempt for *advising* his client to refuse on Fifth Amendment grounds to produce materials demanded by a subpoena duces tecum where the lawyer believes in good faith that the material may tend to incriminate his client. Maness v. Meyers, [419 U.S. 449, 95 S.Ct. 584(1975)]. In this appeal, however, the court confronts not the situation where the attorney advises his client to refuse production but rather one where the attorney himself, now the alleged possessor of the demanded item, declines to produce.

Unless the relationship of attorney and client is completely *sui generis*, as appellant argues, the author of this opinion finds no precedents supporting Genson's refusal to produce what may possibly be the fruits of a violent crime. ...

* * *

The attorney-client relationship is not so close or special as to create some form of mystical identity between the two natural persons. No reason exists to obliterate the distinction between the person of the attorney and that of the client. The Fifth Amendment explicitly prohibits compelling an accused to bear witness against himself; it does not proscribe incriminating statements elicited from another. ... In the present case, the compulsion of the subpoena is directly exerted on Genson and not upon his clients. Unless he has standing to invoke on their behalf the Fifth Amendment privilege, the appellant has shown no just cause for failing to comply with the subpoena or the order of the court.

* * *

In this appeal, the court is concerned not with the compelled production, either by IRS summons or grand jury subpoena, of personal papers or documents but rather with the demand for monies which may have been stolen from a federally insured savings institution. The important testimonial communication in this case is that the suspects have had at a point in time subsequent to the armed robbery possession of the stolen monies. Such an evidentiary fact would appear to the author of this opinion to be an important link in the chain of evidence. . . .

. . . The recognition that an attorney need not produce stolen monies in response to a subpoena would provide a mechanism by which a member of a learned profession could become the privileged repository of the fruits of a violent crime. There is no reason for thinking that the policy of respecting the private enclave of individual citizens reaches that far.

. . . [T]he majority of the panel is of the opinion that the money itself is non-testimonial and that its delivery was not assertive conduct. In this situation, the attorney is simply a witness to a criminal act. The fact that the attorney is also a participant in the act is irrelevant since he is not asserting his own privilege against self-incrimination. The author of this opinion rests his opinion upon the lack of standing on the part of the lawyer to assert the Fifth Amendment claim on behalf of his clients. Whatever implied testimony arises from the act of production is that of the lawyer. This remains true even if the wording of the subpoena contains implied questions regarding the "who" and the "when" of the alleged transfer.

III. The Attorney–Client Privilege

Genson also based his refusal on the attorney-client privilege. Analytically, of course, this privilege is not identical with the Fifth Amendment right, even though closely-related concepts of privacy and confidentiality play an important role in determining the scope of the two privileges. Nor is there a similarity of analysis as regards the issue of standing. The attorney-client privilege arose in the days of Elizabeth I from a consideration of the oath and the honor of the attorney rather than for the apprehensions of his client, and only in the middle of the nineteenth century did the privilege become substantially recognized as that of the client. . . .

The basis for the privilege is to afford the client a reasonable expectation of privacy and confidentiality with regard to disclosures made during the course of consultation with his attorney. The general rule is that, barring unusual circumstances, matters involving the receipt of fees from a client are not privileged.

* * *

Assuming that the alleged transfer of monies represented a retainer or a prepayment of fees, the fact of payment and the money itself would fall outside the scope of the privilege. Assuming that the monies were transferred not as a fee payment but as a bailment for the purposes of safekeeping, the appellant finds himself in a position closely analogous to the attorney in the case of In re Ryder, 263 F.Supp. 360 (E.D.Va.) aff'd, 381 F.2d 713 (4th Cir.1967).

... Genson contends that he was under an ethical responsibility not to produce the demanded monies or to answer questions regarding them. The ethical obligation of a lawyer to guard the confidences and secrets of his client is broader than the attorney-client privilege. See A.B.A. Code of Professional Responsibility, EC 4–4 (1974).[18] Accordingly, our focus on the attorney-client privilege proceeds on narrower terms than appellant recognizes as appropriate.

* * *

In Ryder, supra, an attorney secreted in his own safety deposit box the greater portion of the proceeds of a bank robbery as well as the sawed-off shotgun used in the crime. When Ryder asserted the attorney-client privilege in defense of his actions, the Fourth Circuit, in affirming an 18–month suspension from the practice of law, stated:

> "Viewed in any light, the facts furnished no basis for the assertion of an attorney-client privilege. It is an abuse of a lawyer's professional responsibility knowingly to take possession of and secrete the fruits and instrumentalities of a crime. Ryder's acts bear no reasonable relation to the privilege and duty to refuse to divulge a client's confidential communication."

We are aware that the *Ryder* case was decided at a time when an earlier formulation of the canons of legal ethics was in force. The code of conduct then in force did not attempt to distinguish between aspirational provisions labelled as Ethical Considerations and minimum standards of conduct regulated by Disciplinary Rules. We do not think that the format change initiated in 1969 has any bearing on the scope of the evidentiary privilege.

Ethical Consideration 7–27 states that "[b]ecause it interferes with the proper administration of justice, a lawyer should not suppress evidence that he or his client has a legal obligation to reveal or produce." Our holding that Genson, under the circumstances of this case, cannot avoid compliance with the subpoena because of a claim of Fifth Amendment protection leads us to conclude that he is under a legal obligation to reveal or produce the monies which we have assumed arguendo that he has. Failure to comply with the subpoena and the subsequent court order to produce and testify effects the practical suppression of the sought after evidence.

18. Canon 4 of the Code is captioned, "A Lawyer Should Preserve the Confidences and Secrets of a Client." Each canon is divided into Ethical Considerations (EC) which in the Preamble of the Code are referred to as aspirational in character, representing objectives toward which every member of the profession should strive, and Disciplinary Rules (DR) which, unlike the Ethical Considerations, are mandatory in character. The first two sentences of EC 4–4 read: "The attorney-client privilege is more limited than the ethical obligation of a lawyer to guard the confidences and secrets of his client. This ethical precept, unlike the evidentiary privilege, exists without regard to the nature or source of information or the fact that others share the knowledge."

We think that the *Ryder* conclusion is persuasive authority that the appellant cannot assert the privilege. We hold that Genson's refusal to testify or to produce does not bear a reasonable relation to the privilege and duty to refuse to divulge a client's confidential communications.

We express no opinion as to the extent, if any, to which the conduct of Genson does or does not equate with that of *Ryder* in the aforementioned disciplinary proceedings. The Supreme Court has consistently held that the necessity for expedition in the administration of the criminal law justifies putting one who seeks to resist the production of desired information to a choice between compliance with a court's order to produce prior to any review of that order, and resistance to that order with the concomitant possibility of an adjudication of contempt if his claims are rejected on appeal. ... We conclude that the appellant's risk of a contempt citation was an appropriate means of achieving pre-compliance review....

IV. The Sixth Amendment Right to Counsel

A third contention in this appeal is that the subpoena duces tecum violated the clients' Sixth Amendment right to counsel. The appellant argues that the attempt of the Government to subpoena the known attorney of the two suspects and to make him the source of evidence against his clients impermissibly infringes upon their right to counsel. The Government insists that defendants have no right to *particular* counsel and that there is no reason why appellant could not be replaced by equally able counsel. The Government cites several cases from other circuits in support of its assertion that the Sixth Amendment argument is without merit.

It may well be that eventually the appellant's compliance with the subpoena duces tecum and his testimonial response to questions regarding the alleged transfer of monies may place him in the position of being a source of evidence against either or both of his clients. We express no opinion as to whether the suspects having chosen to make the appellant a witness to their crime, if such should subsequently prove to be the fact, may properly invoke the Sixth Amendment to bar his eyewitness testimony at trial. For the purposes of this appeal, we deem any reliance upon a claim of deprivation of right of counsel in violation of the Sixth Amendment is too premature to merit further consideration.

* * *

Affirmed.

NOTES

1. After the Seventh Circuit opinion, attorney Genson obtained a waiver of the attorney-client privilege from his client. Genson revealed that after allegations about the source of the funds had arisen, he opened a safety deposit box specially for those funds and left them untouched until he turned them over to the government. His client was later acquitted of participation in the robbery. See generally, Comment, Ethics, Law and Loyalty: the Attorney's Duty to Turn Over Incriminating Physical Evidence, 32 Stan.L.Rev.977 (1980).

The attorney who receives, from someone other than his client, evidence of a crime may be required to turn over such evidence and give testimony about it even when he discovered the evidence while investigating his client's case. See Arizona State Bar Committee on Rules of Professional Conduct 85–4, excerpted at 37 Crim.L.Rptr. 2151.

1(a). The Ninth Circuit in Alexiou v. United States, 39 F.3d 973 (9th Cir.1994), the district court denied a motion to quash a subpoena by a lawyer seeking to invoke attorney-client privilege. The lawyer had deposited a counterfeit $100 bill in his law firm account but refused to reveal the identity of the client who had given him the money. On appeal, the Ninth Circuit affirmed.

Starting out with the general rule that a client's identity is not typically protected by the privilege, the court went on to determine whether this case fell within the exception to that rule: namely, where identification of the client automatically acknowledges that the client is guilty. In this case, identification of the client would not automatically lead to a finding of guilt because the government would still have to prove that the client knowingly used the counterfeit money. The likelihood that identification of the client could be equated to a finding of guilt was further eviscerated by the fact that the attorney was retained for assistance in a traffic dispute and nothing remotely connected to counterfeiting.

2. What should counsel do if, prior to trial, his client advises him that he intends to testify falsely at trial? In a famous article, Professor Monroe Freedman argued that counsel owes a greater responsibility to his client than to the court, and, therefore, should put the client on the stand and vigorously argue the validity of the false testimony. Freedman, The Three Hardest Questions, 64 Mich.L.Rev. 1469 (1966). This unorthodox view generated heated criticism. See Burger, Standards of Conduct for Prosecution and Defense Personnel: A Judge's Viewpoint, 5 Am.Crim. L.Q. 11 (1966); Braun, Ethical Crisis in Criminal Law, 4 Trial 35 (1967).

See Nix v. Whiteside, 475 U.S. 157, 106 S.Ct. 988 (1986), for a discussion of the constitutional (Sixth Amendment right to counsel) implications of one possible approach to the attorney's dilemma where the client wishes to perjure himself. Defense counsel had threatened to testify against the client or to inform the court if the client testified perjuriously. The Court of Appeals held that such conduct contravened the right to the effective assistance of counsel and to due process. The Eighth Circuit opinion at 744 F.2d 1323 (8th Cir.1984) contains a listing of numerous authorities which discuss the client-perjury problem. The opinion concluded that a threat to withdraw as counsel, with or without informing the court of the client's intention to commit perjury, might or might not be proper. A threat to testify against the client, however, was deemed improper.

The Court of Appeals reached this result even though the defendant ultimately had testified in accordance with his original version of events rather than the one which the lawyer had concluded was false. The Supreme Court reversed. In the course of deciding that the lawyer's actions were consistent with competent representation of a client, the Court observed:

> Although counsel must take all reasonable lawful means to attain the objectives of the client, counsel is precluded from taking steps or in any way assisting the client in presenting false evidence or otherwise violating the law. This principle has consistently been recognized in most unequivocal terms by expositors of the norms of professional conduct since the first Canons of Professional Ethics were adopted by the American Bar Association in 1908.
>
> * * *
>
> Both the Model Code of Professional Conduct and the Model Rules of Professional Conduct also adopt the specific exception from the attorney-client privilege for disclosure of perjury that his client intends to commit or

has committed. DR 4–101(C)(3) (intention of client to commit a crime); Rule 3.3 (lawyer has duty to disclose falsity of evidence even if disclosure compromises client confidences). Indeed, both the Model Code and the Model Rules do not merely *authorize* disclosure by counsel of client perjury; they *require* such disclosure. See Rule 3.3(a)(4); DR 7–102(B)(1); *Committee on Professional Ethics and Conduct of Iowa State Bar Association v. Crary*, 245 N.W.2d 298 (Iowa 1976).

It is universally agreed that at a minimum the attorney's first duty when confronted with a proposal for perjurious testimony is to attempt to dissuade the client from the unlawful course of conduct. Model Rules of Professional Conduct, Rule 3.3, Comment; Wolfram, Client Perjury, 50 S.Cal.L.Rev. 809, 846 (1977). A statement directly in point is found in the Commentary to the Model Rules of Professional Conduct under the heading "False Evidence":

"When false evidence is offered by the client, however, a conflict may arise between the lawyer's duty to keep the client's revelations confidential and the duty of candor to the court. Upon ascertaining that material evidence is false, the lawyer *should seek to persuade the client that the evidence should not be offered* or, if it has been offered, that its false character should immediately be disclosed." Model Rules of Professional Conduct, Rule 3.3, Comment (1983) (emphasis added).

Without disagreeing with the rejection of the sixth amendment claim, concurring justices asserted that the majority went beyond what was necessary to the decision when it suggested what it believed was the preferred method of handling the client whom the lawyer suspects would perjure himself if allowed to testify.

In Jackson v. United States, 928 F.2d 245 (8th Cir.1991), the court approved the conduct of an attorney who told the judge that the client intended to commit perjury. It said that where there is a firm basis for believing that the defendant will perjure himself, the trial judge may give the defendant the choice of either not testifying or testifying in narrative form without the aid of counsel. Compare Nichols v. Butler, 917 F.2d 518 (11th Cir.1990), where defense counsel, without claiming that she feared perjury, threatened to withdraw as counsel if the defendant insisted upon testifying.

3. Effective Assistance

United States v. Cronic

Supreme Court of the United States, 1984.
466 U.S. 648, 104 S.Ct. 2039.

■ Justice Stevens delivered the opinion of the Court.

Respondent and two associates were indicted on mail fraud charges involving the transfer of over $9,400,000 in checks between banks in Tampa, Florida, and Norman, Oklahoma, during a four-month period in 1975. Shortly before the scheduled trial date, respondent's retained counsel withdrew. The court appointed a young lawyer with a real estate practice to represent respondent, but allowed him only 25 days for pretrial preparation, even though it had taken the Government over four and one-half years to investigate the case and it had reviewed thousands of documents during that investigation. The two codefendants agreed to testify for the

Government; respondent was convicted on 11 of the 13 counts in the indictment and received a 25–year sentence.

The Court of Appeals reversed the conviction because it concluded that respondent did not "have the Assistance of Counsel for his defence" that is guaranteed by the Sixth Amendment to the Constitution. This conclusion was not supported by a determination that respondent's trial counsel had made any specified errors, that his actual performance had prejudiced the defense, or that he failed to exercise "the skill, judgment, and diligence of a reasonably competent defense attorney"; instead the conclusion rested on the premise that no such showing is necessary "when circumstances hamper a given lawyer's preparation of a defendant's case." The question presented by the Government's petition for certiorari is whether the Court of Appeals has correctly interpreted the Sixth Amendment.

The indictment alleged a "check kiting" scheme. At the direction of respondent, his codefendant Cummings opened a bank account in the name of Skyproof Manufacturing, Inc. (Skyproof), at a bank in Tampa, Florida, and codefendant Merritt opened two accounts, one in his own name and one in the name of Skyproof, at banks in Norman, Oklahoma. Knowing that there were insufficient funds in either account, the defendants allegedly drew a series of checks and wire transfers on the Tampa account aggregating $4,841,073.95, all of which were deposited in Skyproof's Norman bank account during the period between June 23, 1975, and October 16, 1975; during approximately the same period they drew checks on Skyproof's Norman account for deposits in Tampa aggregating $4,600,881.39. The process of clearing the checks involved the use of the mails. By "kiting" insufficient funds checks between the banks in those two cities, defendants allegedly created false or inflated balances in the accounts. After outlining the overall scheme, count I of the indictment alleged the mailing of two checks each for less than $1,000 early in May. Each of the additional 12 counts realleged the allegations in Count I except its reference to the two specific checks, and then added an allegation identifying other checks issued and mailed at later dates.

At trial the Government proved that Skyproof's checks were issued and deposited at the times and places, and in the amounts, described in the indictment. Having made plea bargains with defendants Cummings and Merritt, who had actually handled the issuance and delivery of the relevant written instruments, the Government proved through their testimony that respondent had conceived and directed the entire scheme, and that he had deliberately concealed his connection with Skyproof because of prior financial and tax problems.

After the District Court ruled that a prior conviction could be used to impeach his testimony, respondent decided not to testify. Counsel put on no defense. By cross-examination of Government witnesses, however, he established that Skyproof was not merely a sham, but actually was an operating company with a significant cash flow, though its revenues were not sufficient to justify as large a "float" as the record disclosed. Cross-examination also established the absence of written evidence that respondent had any control over Skyproof, or personally participated in the withdrawals or deposits.

The four-day jury trial ended on July 17, 1980, and respondent was sentenced on August 28, 1980. His counsel perfected a timely appeal, which was docketed on September 11, 1980. Two months later respondent filed a motion to substitute a new attorney in the Court of Appeals, and also filed a motion in the District Court seeking to vacate his conviction on the ground that he had newly discovered evidence of perjury by officers of the Norman bank, and that the Government knew or should have known of that perjury. In that motion he also challenged the competence of his trial counsel.[6] The District Court refused to entertain the motion while the appeal was pending. The Court of Appeals denied the motion to substitute the attorney designated by respondent, but did appoint still another attorney to handle the appeal. Later it allowed respondent's motion to supplement the record with material critical of trial counsel's performance.

The Court of Appeals reversed the conviction because it inferred that respondent's constitutional right to the effective assistance of counsel had been violated. That inference was based on its use of five criteria: "(1) [T]he time afforded for investigation and preparation; (2) the experience of counsel; (3) the gravity of the charge; (4) the complexity of possible defenses; and (5) the accessibility of witnesses to counsel." Under the test employed by the Court of Appeals, reversal is required even if the lawyer's actual performance was flawless. By utilizing this inferential approach, the Court of Appeals erred.

An accused's right to be represented by counsel is a fundamental component of our criminal justice system. Lawyers in criminal cases "are necessities, not luxuries." Their presence is essential because they are the means through which the other rights of the person on trial are secured. Without counsel, the right to a trial itself would be "of little avail," as this Court has recognized repeatedly. "Of all the rights that an accused person has, the right to be represented by counsel is by far the most precious, for it affects his ability to assert any other right he may have."

The special value of the right to the assistance of counsel explains why "[i]t has long been recognized that the right to counsel is the right to the effective assistance of counsel." McMann v. Richardson (1970). The text of the Sixth Amendment itself suggests as much. The amendment requires not merely the provision counsel to the accused, but "Assistance," which is to be "for his defence." Thus, "the core purpose of the counsel guarantee was to assure 'Assistance' at trial, when the accused was confronted with both the intricacies of the law and the advocacy of the prosecutor." United States v. Ash (1973). If no actual "Assistance" "for" the accused's "defence" is provided, then the constitutional guarantee has been violated.[11] To hold otherwise

6. During trial, in response to questions from the bench, respondent expressed his satisfaction with counsel's performance. However, in his motion for new trial, respondent attacked counsel's performance and explained his prior praise of counsel through an affidavit of a psychologist who indicated that he had advised respondent to praise trial counsel in order to ameliorate the lawyer's apparent lack of self-confidence.

11. "The Sixth Amendment, however, guarantees more than the appointment of competent counsel. By its terms, one has a right to 'Assistance of Counsel [for] his defence.' Assistance begins with the appointment of counsel, it does not end there. In

"could convert the appointment of counsel into nothing more than a formal compliance with the Constitution's requirement that an accused be given the assistance of counsel. The Constitution's guarantee of assistance of counsel cannot be satisfied by mere formal appointment. Avery v. Alabama (1940)."

* * *

The substance of the Constitution's guarantee of the effective assistance of counsel is illuminated by reference to its underlying purpose. "Truth," Lord Eldon said, "is best discovered by powerful statements on both sides of the question." This dictum describes the unique strength of our system of criminal justice. "The very premise of our adversary system of criminal justice is that partisan advocacy on both sides of a case will best promote the ultimate objective that the guilty be convicted and the innocent go free." Herring v. New York. It is that "very premise" that underlies and gives meaning to the Sixth Amendment. . . .

Thus, the adversarial process protected by the Sixth Amendment requires that the accused have "counsel acting in the role of an advocate," Anders v. California (1967). The right to the effective assistance of counsel is thus the right of the accused to require the prosecution's case to survive the crucible of meaningful adversarial testing. When a true adversarial criminal trial has been conducted—even if defense counsel may have made demonstrable errors—the kind of testing envisioned by the Sixth Amendment has occurred. But if the process loses its character as a confrontation between adversaries, the constitutional guarantee is violated. As Judge Wyzanski has written: "While a criminal trial is not a game in which the participants are expected to enter the ring with a near match in skills, neither is it a sacrifice of unarmed prisoners to gladiators." United States ex rel. Williams v. Twomey, 510 F.2d 634, 640 (CA7).

While the Court of Appeals purported to apply a standard of reasonable competence, it did not indicate that there had been an actual breakdown of the adversarial process during the trial of this case. Instead it concluded that the circumstances surrounding the representation of respondent mandated an inference that counsel was unable to discharge his duties.

In our evaluation of that conclusion, we begin by recognizing that the right to the effective assistance of counsel is recognized not for its own sake, but because of the effect it has on the ability of the accused to receive a fair trial. Absent some effect of challenged conduct on the reliability of the trial process, the Sixth Amendment guarantee is generally not implicated. Moreover, because we presume that the lawyer is competent to provide the guiding hand that the defendant needs, see Michel v. New York (1955), the burden rests on the accused to demonstrate a constitutional violation.[23]

some cases the performance of counsel may be so inadequate that, in effect, no assistance of counsel is provided. Clearly, in such cases, the defendant's Sixth Amendment right to 'have Assistance of Counsel' is denied." United States v. Decoster, 624 F.2d 196, 219 (C.A.D.C.) (MacKinnon, J., concurring).

23. "Whenever we are asked to consider a charge that counsel has failed to discharge his professional responsibilities, we start with a presumption that he was conscious of his duties to his clients and that he sought conscientiously to discharge those duties. The burden of demonstrating the con-

There are, however, circumstances that are so likely to prejudice the accused that the cost of litigating their effect in a particular case is unjustified.

Most obvious, of course, is the complete denial of counsel. The presumption that counsel's assistance is essential requires us to conclude that a trial is unfair if the accused is denied counsel at a critical stage of his trial. Similarly, if counsel entirely fails to subject the prosecution's case to meaningful adversarial testing, then there has been a denial of Sixth Amendment rights that makes the adversary process itself presumptively unreliable. No specific showing of prejudice was required in Davis v. Alaska, 415 U.S. 308, 94 S.Ct. 1105 (1974) because the petitioner had been "denied the right of effective cross-examination" which " 'would be constitutional error of the first magnitude and no amount of showing of want of prejudice would cure it.' " (citing Smith v. Illinois (1968), and Brookhart v. Janis (1965)).[26]

Circumstances of that magnitude may be present on some occasions when although counsel is available to assist the accused during trial, the likelihood that any lawyer, even a fully competent one, could provide effective assistance is so small that a presumption of prejudice is appropriate without inquiry into the actual conduct of the trial. Powell v. Alabama (1932), was such a case.

The defendants had been indicted for a highly publicized capital offense. Six days before trial, the trial judge appointed "all the members of the bar" for purposes of arraignment. "Whether they would represent the defendants thereafter if no counsel appeared in their behalf, was a matter of speculation only, or, as the judge indicated, of mere anticipation on the part of the court." On the day of trial, a lawyer from Tennessee appeared on behalf of persons "interested" in the defendants, but stated that he had not had an opportunity to prepare the case or to familiarize himself with local procedure, and therefore was unwilling to represent the defendants on such short notice. The problem was resolved when the court decided that the Tennessee lawyer would represent the defendants, with whatever help the local bar could provide.

* * *

This Court held that "such designation of counsel as was attempted here was either so indefinite or so close upon the trial as to amount to a denial of effective and substantial aid in that regard." The Court did not examine the actual performance of counsel at trial, but instead concluded that under these circumstances the likelihood that counsel could have performed as an effective adversary was so remote as to have made the trial inherently unfair. *Powell* was thus a case in which the surrounding circumstances made it so unlikely that any lawyer could provide effective

trary is on his former clients." Matthews v. United States, 518 F.2d 1245, 1246 (7th Cir. 1975.)

26. Apart from circumstances of that magnitude, however, there is generally no basis for finding a Sixth Amendment violation unless the accused can show how specific errors of counsel undermined the reliability of the finding of guilt. See Strickland v. Washington (1984) Casebook, p. 1470.

assistance that ineffectiveness was properly presumed without inquiry into actual performance at trial.

But every refusal to postpone a criminal trial will not give rise to such a presumption. In Avery v. Alabama (1940), counsel was appointed in a capital case only three days before trial, and the trial court denied counsel's request for additional time to prepare. Nevertheless, the Court held that since evidence and witnesses were easily accessible to defense counsel, the circumstances did not make it unreasonable to expect that counsel could adequately prepare for trial during that period of time. Similarly, in Chambers v. Maroney, 399 U.S. 42, 90 S.Ct. 1975 (1970), the Court refused "to fashion a *per se* rule requiring reversal of every conviction following tardy appointment of counsel." Thus, only when surrounding circumstances justify a presumption of ineffectiveness can a Sixth Amendment claim be sufficient without inquiry into counsel's actual performance at trial.[31]

The Court of Appeals did not find that respondent was denied the presence of counsel at a critical stage of the prosecution. Nor did it find, based on the actual conduct of the trial, that there was a breakdown in the adversarial process that would justify a presumption that respondent's conviction was insufficiently reliable to satisfy the Constitution. The dispositive question in this case therefore is whether the circumstances surrounding respondent's representation—and in particular the five criteria identified by the Court of Appeals—justified such a presumption.

The five factors listed in the Court of Appeals' opinion are relevant to an evaluation of a lawyer's effectiveness in a particular case, but neither separately nor in combination do they provide a basis for concluding that competent counsel was not able to provide this respondent with the guiding hand that the Constitution guarantees.

Respondent places special stress on the disparity between the duration of the Government's investigation and the period the District Court allowed to newly appointed counsel for trial preparation. The lawyer was appointed to represent respondent on June 12, 1980, and on June 19, filed a written motion for a continuance of the trial that was then scheduled to begin on June 30. Although counsel contended that he needed at least 30 days for preparation, the District Court reset the trial for July 14—thus allowing 25 additional days for preparation.

Neither the period of time that the Government spent investigating the case, nor the number of documents that its agents reviewed during that investigation, is necessarily relevant to the question whether a competent lawyer could prepare to defend the case in 25 days. The Government's task of finding and assembling admissible evidence that will carry its burden of

31. The Government suggests that a presumption of prejudice is justified when counsel is subject to "external constraints" on his performance. In this case the Court of Appeals identified an "external" constraint—the District Court's decision to give counsel only 25 days to prepare for trial. The fact that the accused can attribute a deficiency in his representation to a source external to trial counsel does not make it any more or less likely that he received the type of trial envisioned by the Sixth Amendment, nor does it justify reversal of his conviction absent an actual effect on the trial process or the likelihood of such an effect.

proving guilt beyond a reasonable doubt is entirely different from the defendant's task in preparing to deny or rebut a criminal charge. Of course, in some cases the rebuttal may be equally burdensome and time consuming, but there is no necessary correlation between the two. In this case, the time devoted by the Government to the assembly, organization, and summarization of the thousands of written records evidencing the two streams of checks flowing between the banks in Florida and Oklahoma unquestionably simplified the work of defense counsel in identifying and understanding the basic character of the defendants' scheme. When a series of repetitious transactions fit into a single mold, the number of written exhibits that are needed to define the pattern may be unrelated to the time that is needed to understand it.

The significance of counsel's preparation time is further reduced by the nature of the charges against respondent. Most of the Government's case consisted merely of establishing the transactions between the two banks. A competent attorney would have no reason to question the authenticity, accuracy or relevance of this evidence—there could be no dispute that these transactions actually occurred. As respondent appears to recognize, the only *bona fide* jury issue open to competent defense counsel on these facts was whether respondent acted with intent to defraud. When there is no reason to dispute the underlying historical facts, the period of 25 days to consider the question whether those facts justify an inference of criminal intent is not so short that it even arguably justifies a presumption that no lawyer could provide the respondent with the effective assistance of counsel required by the Constitution.

That conclusion is not undermined by the fact that respondent's lawyer was young, that his principal practice was in real estate, or that this was his first jury trial. Every experienced criminal defense attorney once tried his first criminal case. Moreover, a lawyer's experience with real estate transactions might be more useful in preparing to try a criminal case involving financial transactions than would prior experience in handling, for example, armed robbery prosecutions. The character of a particular lawyer's experience may shed light in an evaluation of his actual performance, but it does not justify a presumption of ineffectiveness in the absence of such an evaluation.

The three other criteria—the gravity of the charge, the complexity of the case, and the accessibility of witnesses—are all matters that may affect what a reasonably competent attorney could be expected to have done under the circumstances, but none identifies circumstances that in themselves make it unlikely that respondent received the effective assistance of counsel.

This case is not one in which the surrounding circumstances make it unlikely that the defendant could have received the effective assistance of counsel. The criteria used by the Court of Appeals do not demonstrate that counsel failed to function in any meaningful sense as the Government's adversary. Respondent can therefore make out a claim of ineffective assistance only by pointing to specific errors made by trial counsel.[41] In this

41. Since counsel's overall performance was the only question on which the Court of Appeals passed, and is the primary focus of respondent's arguments in this court, we

Court, respondent's present counsel argues that the record would support such an attack, but we leave that claim—as well as the other alleged trial errors raised by respondent which were not passed upon by the Court of Appeals—for the consideration of the Court of Appeals on remand.[42]

The judgment is reversed and the case is remanded for further proceedings consistent with this opinion.

■ JUSTICE MARSHALL concurs in the judgment.

NOTE

In Martin v. McCotter, 796 F.2d 813 (5th Cir.1986), the Court found no *Cronic* violation where, in bifurcated proceedings, defense counsel made no closing argument at all to the jury at sentencing. It noted that at the guilt-innocence phase the defense lawyer participated vigorously and brought out matters that could be viewed as mitigating if not as exculpatory. Applying *Strickland*, the court determined on the facts of the case, even if no tactical decision justified the defense lawyer's silence at sentencing, the defendant had not established prejudice, although the jury sentenced him to life imprisonment for a non-capital crime.

In People v. Hattery, 109 Ill.2d 449, 94 Ill.Dec. 514, 488 N.E.2d 513 (1985), cert. denied 478 U.S. 1013, 106 S.Ct. 3314 (1986), the court granted relief without a showing of prejudice where, in the absence of judicial admonitions to the defendant, defense counsel in opening statements to the jury conceded the defendant's guilt even though the defendant had pleaded not guilty.

Strickland v. Washington

Supreme Court of the United States, 1984.
466 U.S. 668, 104 S.Ct. 2052.

■ JUSTICE O'CONNOR delivered the opinion of the Court.

* * *

During a ten-day period in September 1976, respondent planned and committed three groups of crimes, which included three brutal stabbing murders, torture, kidnapping, severe assaults, attempted murders, attempted extortion, and theft. After his two accomplices were arrested, respondent

have confined our analysis to a claim challenging counsel's overall performance, and not one based on particular errors or omissions. Should respondent pursue claims based on specified errors made by counsel on remand, they should be evaluated under the standards enunciated in Strickland v. Washington (1984).

42. The Government argues that a defendant can attack the actual performance of trial counsel only through a petition for post-conviction relief under 28 U.S.C. § 2255 (1982 ed.), and not through direct appeal, because ineffective assistance claims are generally not properly raised in the District Court nor preserved for review on appeal. Whatever the merits of this position as a general matter, in this case respondent did raise his claim in the District Court through his motion for new trial under Fed.Rule Crim.Proc. 33. The District Court denied that motion for lack of jurisdiction because the case was pending on direct appeal at the time, but that ruling was erroneous. The District Court had jurisdiction to entertain the motion and either deny the motion on its merits, or certify its intention to grant the motion to the Court of Appeals, which could then entertain a motion to remand the case....

surrendered to police and voluntarily gave a lengthy statement confessing to the third of the criminal episodes. The State of Florida indicted respondent for kidnapping and murder and appointed an experienced criminal lawyer to represent him.

Counsel actively pursued pretrial motions and discovery. He cut his efforts short, however, and he experienced a sense of hopelessness about the case, when he learned that, against his specific advice, respondent had also confessed to the first two murders. By the date set for trial, respondent was subject to indictment for three counts of first degree murder and multiple counts of robbery, kidnapping for ransom, breaking and entering and assault, attempted murder, and conspiracy to commit robbery. Respondent waived his right to a jury trial, again acting against counsel's advice, and pleaded guilty to all charges, including the three capital murder charges.

In the plea colloquy, respondent told the trial judge that, although he had committed a string of burglaries, he had no significant prior criminal record and that at the time of his criminal spree he was under extreme stress caused by his inability to support his family. He also stated, however, that he accepted responsibility for the crimes. The trial judge told respondent that he had "a great deal of respect for people who are willing to step forward and admit their responsibility" but that he was making no statement at all about his likely sentencing decision.

Counsel advised respondent to invoke his right under Florida law to an advisory jury at his capital sentencing hearing. Respondent rejected the advice and waived the right. He chose instead to be sentenced by the trial judge without a jury recommendation.

In preparing for the sentencing hearing, counsel spoke with respondent about his background. He also spoke on the telephone with respondent's wife and mother, though he did not follow up on the one unsuccessful effort to meet with them. He did not otherwise seek out character witnesses for respondent. Nor did he request a psychiatric examination, since his conversations with his client gave no indication that respondent had psychological problems.

Counsel decided not to present and hence not to look further for evidence concerning respondent's character and emotional state. That decision reflected trial counsel's sense of hopelessness about overcoming the evidentiary effect of respondent's confessions to the gruesome crimes. It also reflected the judgment that it was advisable to rely on the plea colloquy for evidence about respondent's background and about his claim of emotional stress: the plea colloquy communicated sufficient information about these subjects, and by foregoing the opportunity to present new evidence on these subjects, counsel prevented the State from cross-examining respondent on his claim and from putting on psychiatric evidence of its own.

Counsel also excluded from the sentencing hearing other evidence he thought was potentially damaging. He successfully moved to exclude respondent's "rap sheet." Because he judged that a presentence report might prove more detrimental than helpful, as it would have included respondent's criminal history and thereby undermined the claim of no significant history of criminal activity, he did not request that one be prepared.

At the sentencing hearing, counsel's strategy was based primarily on the trial judge's remarks at the plea colloquy as well as on his reputation as a sentencing judge who thought it important for a convicted defendant to own up to his crime. Counsel argued that respondent's remorse and acceptance of responsibility justified sparing him from the death penalty. Counsel also argued that respondent had no history of criminal activity and that respondent committed the crimes under extreme mental or emotional disturbance, thus coming within the statutory list of mitigating circumstances. He further argued that respondent should be spared death because he had surrendered, confessed, and offered to testify against a co-defendant and because respondent was fundamentally a good person who had briefly gone badly wrong in extremely stressful circumstances. The State put on evidence and witnesses largely for the purpose of describing the details of the crimes. Counsel did not cross-examine the medical experts who testified about the manner of death of respondent's victims.

The trial judge found several aggravating circumstances with respect to each of the three murders. He found that all three murders were especially heinous, atrocious, and cruel, all involving repeated stabbings. All three murders were committed in the course of at least one other dangerous and violent felony, and since all involved robbery, the murders were for pecuniary gain. All three murders were committed to avoid arrest for the accompanying crimes and to hinder law enforcement. In the course of one of the murders, respondent knowingly subjected numerous persons to a grave risk of death by deliberately stabbing and shooting the murder victim's sisters-in-law, who sustained severe—in one case, ultimately fatal—injuries.

With respect to mitigating circumstances, the trial judge made the same findings for all three capital murders. First, although there was no admitted evidence of prior convictions, respondent had stated that he had engaged in a course of stealing. In any case, even if respondent had no significant history of criminal activity, the aggravating circumstances "would still clearly far outweigh" that mitigating factor. Second, the judge found that, during all three crimes, respondent was not suffering from extreme mental or emotional disturbance and could appreciate the criminality of his acts. Third, none of the victims was a participant in, or consented to, respondent's conduct. Fourth, respondent's participation in the crimes was neither minor nor the result of duress or domination by an accomplice. Finally, respondent's age (26) could not be considered a factor in mitigation, especially when viewed in light of respondent's planning of the crimes and disposition of the proceeds of the various accompanying thefts.

In short, the trial judge found numerous aggravating circumstances and no (or a single comparatively insignificant) mitigating circumstance. With respect to each of the three convictions for capital murder, the trial judge concluded: "A careful consideration of all matters presented to the court impels the conclusion that there are insufficient mitigating circumstances ... to outweigh the aggravating circumstances. ..." He therefore sentenced respondent to death on each of the three counts of murder and to prison terms for the other crimes. The Florida Supreme Court upheld the convictions and sentences on direct appeal.

Respondent subsequently sought collateral relief in state court on numerous grounds, among them that counsel had rendered ineffective assistance at the sentencing proceeding. Respondent challenged counsel's assistance in six respects. He asserted that counsel was ineffective because he failed to move for a continuance to prepare for sentencing, to request a psychiatric report, to investigate and present character witnesses, to seek a presentence investigation report, to present meaningful arguments to the sentencing judge and to investigate the medical examiner's reports or cross-examine the medical experts. In support of the claim, respondent submitted fourteen affidavits from friends, neighbors, and relatives stating that they would have testified if asked to do so. He also submitted one psychiatric report and one psychological report stating that respondent, though not under the influence of extreme mental or emotional disturbance, was "chronically frustrated and depressed because of his economic dilemma" at the time of his crimes.

The trial court denied relief without an evidentiary hearing, finding that the record evidence conclusively showed that the ineffectiveness claim was meritless. Four of the assertedly prejudicial errors required little discussion. First, there were no grounds to request a continuance, so there was no error in not requesting one when respondent pleaded guilty. Second, failure to request a presentence investigation was not a serious error because the trial judge had discretion not to grant such a request and because any presentence investigation would have resulted in admission of respondent's rap sheet and thus undermined his assertion of no significant history of criminal activity. Third, the argument and memorandum given to the sentencing judge were "admirable" in light of the overwhelming aggravating circumstances and absence of mitigating circumstances. Fourth, there was no error in failure to examine the medical examiner's reports or to cross-examine the medical witnesses, testifying on the manner of death of respondent's victims, since respondent admitted that the victims died in the ways shown by the unchallenged medical evidence.

The trial court dealt at greater length with the two other bases for the ineffectiveness claim. The court pointed out that a psychiatric examination of respondent was conducted by state order soon after respondent's initial arraignment. That report states that there was no indication of major mental illness at the time of the crimes. Moreover, both the reports submitted in the collateral proceeding state that, although respondent was "chronically frustrated and depressed because of his economic dilemma," he was not under the influence of extreme mental or emotional disturbance. All three reports thus directly undermine the contention made at the sentencing hearing that respondent was suffering from extreme mental or emotional disturbance during his crime spree. Accordingly, counsel could reasonably decide not to seek psychiatric reports; indeed, by relying solely on the plea colloquy to support the emotional disturbance contention, counsel denied the State an opportunity to rebut his claim with psychiatric testimony. In any event, the aggravating circumstances were so overwhelming that no substantial prejudice resulted from the absence at sentencing of the psychiatric evidence offered in the collateral attack.

The court rejected the challenge to counsel's failure to develop and to present character evidence for much the same reasons. The affidavits submitted in the collateral proceeding showed nothing more than that certain persons would have testified that respondent was basically a good person who was worried about his family's financial problems. Respondent himself had already testified along those lines at the plea colloquy. Moreover, respondent's admission of a course of stealing rebutted many of the factual allegations in the affidavits. For those reasons, and because the sentencing judge had stated that the death sentence would be appropriate even if respondent had no significant prior criminal history, no substantial prejudice resulted from the absence at sentencing of the character evidence offered in the collateral attack.

Applying the standard for ineffectiveness claims articulated by the Florida Supreme Court in Knight v. State, 394 So.2d 997(Fla.1981), the trial court concluded that respondent had not shown that counsel's assistance reflected any substantial and serious deficiency measurably below that of competent counsel that was likely to have affected the outcome of the sentencing proceeding. The court specifically found that, "as a matter of law, the record affirmatively demonstrates beyond any doubt that even if [counsel] had done each of the ... things [that respondent alleged counsel had failed to do] at the time of sentencing, there is not even the remotest chance that the outcome would have been any different. The plain fact is that the aggravating circumstances proved in this case were completely *overwhelming*. ..."

The Florida Supreme Court affirmed the denial of relief.

* * *

Respondent next filed a petition for a writ of habeas corpus in the United States District Court for the Southern District of Florida. He advanced numerous grounds for relief, among them ineffective assistance of counsel based on the same errors, except for the failure to move for a continuance, as those he had identified in state court. The District Court held an evidentiary hearing to inquire into trial counsel's efforts to investigate and to present mitigating circumstances. Respondent offered the affidavits and reports he had submitted in the state collateral proceedings; he also called his trial counsel to testify. The State of Florida, over respondent's objection, called the trial judge to testify.

The District Court disputed none of the state court factual findings concerning trial counsel's assistance and made findings of its own that are consistent with the state court findings. The account of trial counsel's actions and decisions given above reflects the combined findings. On the legal issue of ineffectiveness, the District Court concluded that, although trial counsel made errors in judgment in failing to investigate nonstatutory mitigating evidence further than he did, no prejudice to respondent's sentence resulted from any such error in judgment. Relying in part on the trial judge's testimony but also on the same factors that led the state courts to find no prejudice, the District Court concluded that "there does not appear to be a likelihood, or even a significant possibility," that any errors of trial counsel had affected the outcome of the sentencing proceeding. ... The court accordingly denied the petition for a writ of habeas corpus. ... The full Court of Appeals developed its own framework for analyzing ineffective assistance claims and reversed the judgment of the District Court and remanded the case for new factfinding under the newly announced standards.

* * *

Petitioners, who are officials of the State of Florida, filed a petition for a writ of certiorari seeking review of the decision of the Court of Appeals.... Thus, a fair trial is one in which evidence subject to adversarial testing is presented to an impartial tribunal for resolution of issues defined in advance of the proceeding. The right to counsel plays a crucial role in the adversarial system embodied in the Sixth Amendment, since access to counsel's skill and knowledge is necessary to accord defendants the "ample opportunity to meet the case of the prosecution" to which they are entitled.

That a person who happens to be a lawyer is present at trial alongside the accused, however, is not enough to satisfy the constitutional command. The Sixth Amendment recognizes the right to the assistance of counsel because it envisions counsel's playing a role that is critical to the ability of the adversarial system to produce just results. An accused is entitled to be assisted by an attorney, whether retained or appointed, who plays the role necessary to ensure that the trial is fair.

For that reason, the Court has recognized that "the right to counsel is the right to the effective assistance of counsel." McMann v. Richardson (1970). Government violates the right to effective assistance when it interferes in certain ways with the ability of counsel to make independent decisions about how to conduct the defense. See, e.g., Geders v. United States (1976) (bar on attorney-client consultation during overnight recess); Herring v. New York (1975) (bar on summation at bench trial); Brooks v. Tennessee (1972) (requirement that defendant be first defense witness); Ferguson v. Georgia (1961) (bar on direct examination of defendant). Counsel, however, can also deprive a defendant of the right to effective assistance, simply by failing to render "adequate legal assistance," Cuyler v. Sullivan (actual conflict of interest adversely affecting lawyer's performance renders assistance ineffective).

The Court has not elaborated on the meaning of the constitutional requirement of effective assistance in the latter class of cases—that is, those presenting claims of "actual ineffectiveness." In giving meaning to the requirement, however, we must take its purpose—to ensure a fair trial—as the guide. The benchmark for judging any claim of ineffectiveness must be whether counsel's conduct so undermined the proper functioning of the adversarial process that the trial cannot be relied on as having produced a just result.

The same principle applies to a capital sentencing proceeding such as that provided by Florida law. We need not consider the role of counsel in an ordinary sentencing, which may involve informal proceedings and standardless discretion in the sentencer, and hence may require a different approach to the definition of constitutionally effective assistance. A capital sentencing proceeding like the one involved in this case, however, is sufficiently like a trial in its adversarial format and in the existence of standards for decision, that counsel's role in the proceeding is comparable to counsel's role at trial—to ensure that the adversarial testing process works to produce a just result under the standards governing decision. For purposes of describing counsel's duties, therefore, Florida's capital sentencing proceeding need not be distinguished from an ordinary trial.

A convicted defendant's claim that counsel's assistance was so defective as to require reversal of a conviction or death sentence has two components. First, the defendant must show that counsel's performance was deficient. This requires showing that counsel made errors so serious that counsel was not functioning as the "counsel" guaranteed the defendant by the Sixth Amendment. Second, the defendant must show that the deficient performance prejudiced the defense. This requires showing that counsel's errors were so serious as to deprive the defendant of a fair trial, a trial whose result is reliable. Unless a defendant makes both showings, it cannot be said that the conviction or death sentence resulted from a breakdown in the adversary process that renders the result unreliable.

As all the Federal Courts of Appeals have now held, the proper standard for attorney performance is that of reasonably effective assistance. The Court indirectly recognized as much when it stated in McMann v. Richardson, that a guilty plea cannot be attacked as based on inadequate legal advice unless counsel was not "a reasonably competent attorney" and the advice was not "within the range of competence demanded of attorneys in criminal cases." When a convicted defendant complains of the ineffectiveness of counsel's assistance, the defendant must show that counsel's representation fell below an objective standard of reasonableness.

More specific guidelines are not appropriate. The Sixth Amendment refers simply to "counsel," not specifying particular requirements of effective assistance. It relies instead on the legal profession's maintenance of standards sufficient to justify the law's presumption that counsel willful fill the role in the adversary process that the Amendment envisions. The proper measure of attorney performance remains simply reasonableness under prevailing professional norms.

Representation of a criminal defendant entails certain basic duties. Counsel's function is to assist the defendant, and hence counsel owes the client a duty of loyalty, a duty to avoid conflicts of interest. From counsel's function as assistant to the defendant derive the overarching duty to advocate the defendant's cause and the more particular duties to consult with the defendant on important decisions and to keep the defendant informed of important developments in the course of the prosecution. Counsel also has a duty to bring to bear such skill and knowledge as will render the trial a reliable adversarial testing process.

These basic duties neither exhaustively define the obligations of counsel nor form a checklist for judicial evaluation of attorney performance. In any case presenting an ineffectiveness claim, the performance inquiry must be whether counsel's assistance was reasonable considering all the circumstances. Prevailing norms of practice as reflected in American Bar Association standards and the like, e.g., ABA Standards for Criminal Justice 4–1.1 to 4–8.6 (2d ed. 1980) ("The Defense Function"), are guides to determining what is reasonable, but they are only guides. No particular set of detailed rules for counsel's conduct can satisfactorily take account of the variety of circumstances faced by defense counsel or the range of legitimate decisions regarding how best to represent a criminal defendant. Any such set of rules would interfere with the constitutionally protected independence of counsel and restrict the wide latitude counsel must have in making tactical decisions. Indeed, the existence of detailed guidelines for representation could distract counsel from the overriding mission of vigorous advocacy of the defendant's cause. Moreover, the purpose of the effective assistance guarantee of the Sixth Amendment is not to improve the quality of legal representation, although that is a goal of considerable importance to the legal system. The purpose is simply to ensure that criminal defendants receive a fair trial.

Judicial scrutiny of counsel's performance must be highly deferential. It is all too tempting for a defendant to second-guess counsel's assistance after conviction or adverse sentence, and it is all too easy for a court, examining counsel's defense after it has proved unsuccessful, to conclude that a particular act or omission of counsel was unreasonable. A fair assessment of attorney performance requires that every effort be made to eliminate the distorting effects of hindsight, to reconstruct the circumstances of counsel's challenged conduct, and to evaluate the conduct from counsel's perspective at the time. Because of the difficulties inherent in making the evaluation, a court must indulge a strong presumption that counsel's conduct falls within the wide range of reasonable professional assistance; that is, the defendant must overcome the presumption that, under the circumstances, the challenged action "might be considered sound trial strategy." There are countless ways to provide effective assistance in any given case. Even the best criminal defense attorneys would not defend a particular client in the same way.

The availability of intrusive post-trial inquiry into attorney performance or of detailed guidelines for its evaluation would encourage the proliferation of ineffectiveness challenges. Criminal trials resolved unfavorably to the defendant would increasingly come to be followed by a second trial, this one of counsel's unsuccessful defense. Counsel's performance and even willingness to serve could be adversely affected. Intensive scrutiny of counsel and rigid requirements for acceptable assistance could dampen the ardor and impair the independence of defense counsel, discourage the acceptance of assigned cases, and undermine the trust between attorney and client.

Thus, a court deciding an actual ineffectiveness claim must judge the reasonableness of counsel's challenged conduct on the facts of the particular case, viewed as of the time of counsel's conduct. A convicted defendant making a claim of ineffective assistance must identify the acts or omissions of counsel that are alleged not to have been the result of reasonable professional judgment. The court must then determine whether, in light of all the circumstances, the identified acts or omissions were outside the wide range of professionally competent assistance. In making that determination, the court should keep in mind that counsel's function, as elaborated in prevailing professional norms, is to make the adversarial testing process work in the particular case. At the same time, the court should recognize that counsel is strongly presumed to have rendered adequate assistance and made all significant decisions in the exercise of reasonable professional judgment.

These standards require no special amplification in order to define counsel's duty to investigate, the duty at issue in this case. As the Court of Appeals concluded, strategic choices made after thorough investigation of law and facts relevant to plausible options are virtually unchallengeable; and strategic choices made after less than complete investigation are reasonable precisely to the extent that reasonable professional judgments support the limitations on investigation. In other words counsel has a duty to make reasonable investigations or to make a reasonable decision that makes particular investigations unnecessary. In any ineffectiveness case, a particular decision not to investigate must be directly assessed for reasonableness in all the circumstances, applying a heavy measure of deference to counsel's judgments.

The reasonableness of counsel's actions may be determined or substantially influenced by the defendant's own statements or actions. Counsel's actions are usually based, quite properly, on informed strategic choices made by the defendant and on information supplied by the defendant. In particular, what investigation decisions are reasonable depends critically on such information. For example, when the facts that support a certain potential line of defense are generally known to counsel because of what the defendant has said, the need for further investigation may be considerably diminished or eliminated altogether. And when a defendant has given counsel reason to believe that pursuing certain investigations would be fruitless or even harmful, counsel's failure to pursue those investigations may not later be challenged as unreasonable. In short, inquiry into counsel's conversations with the defendant may be critical to a proper assessment of counsel's investigation decisions, just as it may be critical to a proper assessment of counsel's other litigation decisions.

An error by counsel, even if professionally unreasonable, does not warrant setting aside the judgment of a criminal proceeding if the error had no effect on the judgment. The purpose of the Sixth Amendment guarantee of counsel is to ensure that a defendant has the assistance necessary to justify reliance on the outcome of the proceeding. Accordingly, any deficiencies in counsel's performance must be prejudicial to the defense in order to constitute ineffective assistance under the Constitution.

In certain Sixth Amendment contexts, prejudice is presumed. Actual or constructive denial of the assistance of counsel altogether is legally presumed to result in prejudice. So are various kinds of state interference with counsel's assistance.... Prejudice in these circumstances is so likely that case by case inquiry into prejudice is not worth the cost. Moreover such circumstances involve impairments of the Sixth Amendment right that are easy to identify and, for that reason and because the prosecution is directly responsible, easy for the government to prevent.

One type of actual ineffectiveness claim warrants a similar, though more limited, presumption of prejudice. In Cuyler v. Sullivan, the Court held that prejudice is presumed when counsel is burdened by an actual conflict of interest. In those circumstances, counsel breaches the duty of loyalty, perhaps the most basic of counsel's duties. Moreover, it is difficult to measure the precise effect on the defense of representation corrupted by conflicting interests. Given the obligation of counsel to avoid conflicts of interest and the ability of trial courts to make early inquiry in certain situations likely to give rise to conflicts, see e.g., Fed.Rule Crim.Proc. 44(c), it is reasonable for the criminal justice system to maintain a fairly rigid rule of presumed prejudice for conflicts of interest. Even so, the rule is not quite the *per se* rule of prejudice that exists for the Sixth Amendment claims mentioned above. Prejudice is presumed only if the defendant demonstrates that counsel "actively represented conflicting interests" and "that an actual conflict of interest adversely affected his lawyer's performance." Cuyler v. Sullivan.

Conflict of interest claims aside, actual ineffectiveness claims alleging a deficiency in attorney performance are subject to a general requirement that the defendant affirmatively prove prejudice. The government is not responsible for, and hence not able to prevent, attorney errors that will result in reversal of a conviction or sentence. Attorney errors come in an infinite variety and are as likely to be utterly harmless in a particular case as they are to be prejudicial. They cannot be classified according to likelihood of causing prejudice. Nor can they be defined with sufficient precision to inform defense attorneys correctly just what conduct to avoid. Representation is an art, and an act or omission that is unprofessional in one case may be sound or even brilliant in another. Even if a defendant shows that particular errors of counsel were unreasonable, therefore, the defendant must show that they actually had an adverse effect on the defense.

It is not enough for the defendant to show that the errors had some conceivable effect on the outcome of the proceeding. Virtually every act or omission of counsel would meet that test, and not every error that conceivably could have influenced the outcome undermines the reliability of the result of the proceeding. Respondent suggests requiring a showing that the errors "impaired the presentation of the defense." That standard, however, provides no workable principle. Since any error, if it is indeed an error, "impairs" the presentation of the defense, the proposed standard is inadequate because it provides no way of deciding what impairments are sufficiently serious to warrant setting aside the outcome of the proceeding.

On the other hand, we believe that a defendant need not show that counsel's deficient conduct more likely than not altered the outcome in the case. This outcome-determinative standard has several strengths. It defines the relevant inquiry in a way familiar to courts, though the inquiry, as is inevitable, is anything but precise. The standard also reflects the profound importance of finality in criminal proceedings. Moreover, it comports with the widely used standard for assessing motions for new trial based on newly discovered evidence. Nevertheless, the standard is not quite appropriate.

Even when the specified attorney error results in the omission of certain evidence, the newly discovered evidence standard is not an apt source from which to draw a prejudice standard for ineffectiveness claims. The high standard for newly discovered evidence claims presupposes that all the essential elements of a presumptively accurate and fair proceeding were present in the proceeding whose result is challenged. An ineffective assistance claim asserts the absence of one of the crucial assurances that the result of the proceeding is reliable, so finality concerns are somewhat weaker and the appropriate standard of prejudice should be somewhat lower. The result of a proceeding can be rendered unreliable, and hence the proceeding itself unfair, even if the errors of counsel cannot be shown by a preponderance of the evidence to have determined the outcome.

Accordingly, the appropriate test for prejudice finds its roots in the test for materiality of exculpatory information not disclosed to the defense by the prosecution, United States v. Agurs, and in the test for materiality of testimony made unavailable to the defense by Government deportation of a witness, United States v. Valenzuela–Bernal. The defendant must show that there is a reasonable probability that, but for counsel's unprofessional errors, the result of the proceeding would have been different. A reasonable probability is a probability sufficient to undermine confidence in the outcome.

In making the determination whether the specified errors resulted in the required prejudice, a court should presume, absent challenge to the judgment on grounds of evidentiary insufficiency, that the judge or jury acted according to law. An assessment of the likelihood of a result more favorable to the defendant must exclude the possibility of arbitrariness, whimsy, caprice, "nullification," and the like. A defendant has no entitlement to the luck of a lawless decisionmaker, even if a lawless decision cannot be reviewed. The assessment of prejudice should proceed on the assumption that the decisionmaker is reasonably, conscientiously, and impartially applying the standards that govern the decision. It should not depend on the idiosyncracies of the particular decisionmaker, such as unusual propensities toward harshness or leniency. Although these factors may actually have entered into counsel's selection of strategies and, to that limited extent, may thus affect the performance inquiry, they are irrelevant to the prejudice inquiry. Thus, evidence about the actual process of decision, if not part of the record of the proceeding under review, and evidence about, for example, a particular judge's sentencing practices, should not be considered in the prejudice determination.

The governing legal standard plays a critical role in defining the question to be asked in assessing the prejudice from counsel's errors. When a defendant challenges a conviction the question is whether there is a reasonable probability that, absent the errors, the factfinder would have had a reasonable doubt respecting guilt. When a defendant challenges a death sentence such as the one at issue in this case, the question is whether there is a reasonable probability that, absent the errors, the sentencer—including an appellate court, to the extent it independently reweighs the evidence—would have concluded that the balance of aggravating and mitigating circumstances did not warrant death.

In making this determination, a court hearing an ineffectiveness claim must consider the totality of the evidence before the judge or jury. Some of the factual findings will have been unaffected by the errors, and factual findings that were affected will have been affected in different ways. Some errors will have had a pervasive effect on the inferences to be drawn from the evidence, altering the entire evidentiary picture, and some will have had an isolated, trivial effect. Moreover, a verdict or conclusion only weakly supported by the record is more likely to have been affected by errors than one with overwhelming record support. Taking the unaffected findings as a given, and taking due account of the effect of the errors on the remaining findings, a court making the prejudice inquiry must ask if the defendant has met the burden of showing that the decision reached would reasonably likely have been different absent the errors.

A number of practical considerations are important for the application of the standards we have outlined. Most important, in adjudicating a claim of actual ineffectiveness of counsel, a court should keep in mind that the principles we have stated do not establish mechanical rules. Although those principles should guide the process of decision, the ultimate focus of inquiry must be on the fundamental fairness of the proceeding whose result is being challenged. In every case the court should be concerned with whether, despite the strong presumption of reliability, the result of the particular proceeding is unreliable because of a breakdown in the adversarial process that our system counts on to produce just results.

To the extent that this has already been the guiding inquiry in the lower courts, the standards articulated today do not require reconsideration of ineffectiveness claims rejected under different standards. Cf. Trapnell v. United States, 725 F.2d, at 153 (in several years of applying "farce and mockery" standard along with "reasonable competence" standard, court "never found that the result of a case hinged on the choice of a particular standard"). In particular, the minor differences in the lower courts' precise formulations of the performance standard are insignificant: the different formulations are mere variations of the overarching reasonableness standard. With regard to the prejudice inquiry, only the strict outcome-determinative test, among the standards articulated in the lower courts, imposes a heavier burden on defendants than the tests laid down today. The difference, however, should alter the merit of an ineffectiveness claim only in the rarest case.

Although we have discussed the performance component of an ineffectiveness claim prior to the prejudice component, there is no reason for a court deciding an ineffective assistance claim to approach the inquiry in the same order or even to address both components of the inquiry if the defendant makes an insufficient showing on one. In particular, a court need not determine whether counsel's performance was deficient before examining the prejudice suffered by the defendant as a result of the alleged deficiencies. The object of an ineffectiveness claim is not to grade counsel's performance. If it is easier to dispose of an ineffectiveness claim on the ground of lack of sufficient prejudice, which we expect will often be so, that course should be followed. Courts should strive to ensure that ineffectiveness claims not become so burdensome to defense counsel that the entire criminal justice system suffers as a result.

The principles governing ineffectiveness claims should apply in federal collateral proceedings as they do on direct appeal or in motions for a new trial. As indicated by the "cause and prejudice" test for overcoming procedural waivers of claims of error, the presumption that a criminal judgment is final is at its strongest in collateral attacks on that judgment. An ineffectiveness claim, however, as our articulation of the standards that govern decision of such claims makes clear, is an attack on the fundamental fairness of the proceeding whose result is challenged. Since fundamental fairness is the central concern of the writ of habeas corpus, no special standards ought to apply to ineffectiveness claims made in habeas proceedings.

Finally, in a federal habeas challenge to a state criminal judgment, a state court conclusion that counsel rendered effective assistance is not a finding of fact binding on the federal court to the extent stated by 28 U.S.C. § 2254(d). Ineffectiveness is not a question of "basic, primary, or historical fact[ ]," Townsend v. Sain (1963). Rather, like the question whether multiple representation in a particular case gave rise to a conflict of interest, it is a mixed question of law and fact. Although state court findings of fact made in the course of deciding an ineffectiveness claim are subject to the deference requirement of § 2254(d), and although District Court findings are subject to the clearly erroneous standard of Fed.Rules Civ.Proc.52(a), both the performance and prejudice components of the ineffectiveness inquiry are mixed questions of law and fact.

Having articulated general standards for judging ineffectiveness claims, we think it useful to apply those standards to the facts of this case in order to illustrate the meaning of the general principles. The record makes it possible to do so. There are no conflicts between the state and federal courts over findings of fact, and the principles we have articulated are sufficiently close to the principles applied both in the Florida courts and in the District Court that it is clear that the factfinding was not affected by erroneous legal principles.

Application of the governing principles is not difficult in this case. The facts as described above make clear that the conduct of respondent's counsel at and before respondent's sentencing proceeding cannot be found unreasonable. They also make clear that, even assuming the challenged conduct of counsel was unreasonable, respondent suffered insufficient prejudice to warrant setting aside his death sentence.

With respect to the performance component, the record shows that respondent's counsel made a strategic choice to argue for the extreme emotional distress mitigating circumstance and to rely as fully as possible on respondent's acceptance of responsibility for his crimes. Although counsel understandably felt hopeless about respondent's prospects nothing in the record indicates, as one possible reading of the District Court's opinion suggests, that counsel's sense of hopelessness distorted his professional judgment. Counsel's strategy choice was well within the range of professionally reasonable judgments, and the decision not to seek more character or psychological evidence than was already in hand was likewise reasonable.

The trial judge's views on the importance of owning up to one's crimes were well known to counsel. The aggravating circumstances were utterly overwhelming. Trial counsel could reasonably surmise from his conversations with respondent that character and psychological evidence would be of little help. Respondent had already been able to mention at the plea colloquy the substance of what there was to know about his financial and emotional troubles. Restricting testimony on respondent's character to what had come in at the plea colloquy ensured that contrary character and psychological evidence and respondent's criminal history, which counsel had successfully moved to exclude, would not come in. On these facts, there can be little question, even without application of the presumption of adequate performance, that trial counsel's defense, though unsuccessful, was the result of reasonable professional judgment.

With respect to the prejudice component, the lack of merit of respondent's claim is even more stark. The evidence that respondent says his trial counsel should have offered at the sentencing hearing would barely have altered the sentencing profile presented to the sentencing judge. As the state courts and District Court found, at most this evidence shows that numerous people who knew respondent thought he was generally a good person and that a psychiatrist and a psychologist believed he was under considerable emotional stress that did not rise to the level of extreme disturbance. Given the overwhelming aggravating factors, there is no reasonable probability that the omitted evidence would have changed the conclusion that the aggravating circumstances outweighed the mitigating circumstances and, hence, the sentence imposed. Indeed, admission of the evidence respondent now offers might even have been harmful to his case: his "rap sheet" would probably have been admitted into evidence, and the psychological reports would have directly contradicted respondent's claim that the mitigating circumstance of extreme emotional disturbance applied to his case.

Our conclusions on both the prejudice and performance components of the ineffectiveness inquiry do not depend on the trial judge's testimony at the District Court hearing. We therefore need not consider the general admissibility of that testimony, although, as noted, that testimony is irrelevant to the prejudice inquiry. Moreover, the prejudice question is resolvable, and hence the ineffectiveness claim can be rejected, without regard to the evidence presented at the District Court hearing. The state courts properly concluded that the ineffectiveness claim was meritless without holding an evidentiary hearing.

Failure to make the required showing of either deficient performance or sufficient prejudice defeats the ineffectiveness claim. Here there is a double failure. More generally, respondent has made no showing that the justice of his sentence was rendered unreliable by a breakdown in the adversary process caused by deficiencies in counsel's assistance. Respondent's sentencing proceeding was not fundamentally unfair.

We conclude, therefore, that the District Court properly declined to issue a writ of habeas corpus.

■ JUSTICE BRENNAN, concurring in part and dissenting in part.

I join the Court's opinion but dissent from its judgment. Adhering to my view that the death penalty is in all circumstances cruel and unusual punishment forbidden by the Eighth and Fourteenth Amendments I would vacate respondent's death sentence and remand the case for further proceedings.

* * *

I join the Court's opinion because I believe that the standards it sets out today will both provide helpful guidance to courts considering claims of actual ineffectiveness of counsel and also permit those courts to continue their efforts to achieve progressive development of this area of the law.

* * *

■ JUSTICE MARSHALL, dissenting. [OMITTED.]

Bellamy v. Cogdell

United States Court of Appeals, Second Circuit, 1992.
974 F.2d 302.

(An *en banc* court of the Second Circuit affirmed a murder conviction where the appeal centered entirely on a claim of ineffective assistance of counsel. Defendant claimed a *per se* denial of his Sixth Amendment rights under the following set of facts:)

Altimari, *Circuit Judge*. The facts in this case are largely undisputed. In January 1987, Bellamy went on trial in New York Supreme Court, Queens County, for his charged participation in the murder of State Parole Officer Brian Rooney. Lorenzo "Fat Cat" Nichols, a notorious Queens drug dealer, ordered Rooney's murder from Nichols' jail cell. This "hit" was a revenge killing for Rooney's efforts in placing Nichols behind bars. The state's evidence at trial showed that, in exchange for $5,000, Bellamy lured Rooney to a park in Queens where associates of Nichols shot Rooney repeatedly as Rooney sat in his car. After almost three weeks of trial, including five days of jury deliberations, a jury convicted Bellamy of second degree murder and second degree criminal possession of a weapon. Bellamy was eventually sentenced to fifteen years to life for the murder conviction and five to fifteen years for the weapon possession conviction, the sentences to run concurrently.

Over one year prior to the start of Bellamy's trial, Bellamy's mother contacted Attorney Sidney Guran to represent Bellamy. Although Guran was then retired and living in Florida, he had represented Bellamy numerous times in the past and agreed to represent him again. At that time, Guran was seventy-one years old and had been a duly admitted and successful member of the bar for almost fifty years.

In the months preceding and during Bellamy's trial, Guran was the subject of disciplinary proceedings in the Appellate Division, First Department. In October 1986, the Departmental Disciplinary Committee alleged that Guran had converted client funds in 1976 and had negligently handled a real estate transaction in 1977. The Committee scheduled a hearing on these charges for December 11, 1986. On November 10, 1986, Guran's attorney, Richard L. Baltimore, Jr., requested that the hearing be adjourned because more time was needed to compile documents for the hearing and because Guran was then "not mentally capable of preparing for the hearing." Baltimore based his evaluation of Guran's capacity on phone conversations with Guran in which he found "a certain amount of disorientation" and on a letter, dated October 29, 1986, from Guran's physician, Dr. Richard P. Cohen.

According to Dr. Cohen, Guran suffered from a variety of physiological ailments, including a recently diagnosed polyneuropathy, a condition "characterized by peripheral motor weakness [and] unsteadiness" on one's feet. Dr. Cohen had been treating Guran for that condition for the preceding six weeks. During that time, as a result of the "physical and emotional stress" associated with Guran's recently discovered illness and of certain medications, Guran had been "virtually incapacitated." Dr. Cohen also noted that as a result of that condition, Guran "at times" had "an inability to concentrate." The prognosis for Guran's newly discovered condition was uncertain at that time, but Dr. Cohen "anticipated" that evaluation and treatment of the polyneuropathy would take three to six months, and that Guran would be "effectively incapacitated during that time."

Based on these communications, and on the underlying charges, the Disciplinary Committee filed a note of petition with the First Department on November 21, 1986 seeking to have Guran suspended immediately and indefinitely from the practice of law. The accompanying petition recounted, among other things, the substance of the letters that Guran's attorney and physician had submitted to the Committee. In response, Guran submitted an affidavit to the First Department dated December 12, 1986, in which he admitted his medical problems, but stated that a suspension, with its attendant stigma, was unnecessary. According to Guran, he had been essentially retired since 1984, having taken on no new work except for Bellamy's case. Because of his prior representation of Bellamy and because of his familiarity with the case, Guran requested that he be permitted to represent Bellamy, stating:

> I, of course, will not attempt to try this case by myself. I will have a competent attorney, but I must be present to assist him. Bellamy relies on, and strictly trusts only me and his mother has paid me. It would be a complete disservice to this defendant and jeopardize his right to a fair trial if I were not permitted to assist in his trial and defense.

Neither the Disciplinary Committee nor the First Department ever responded to Guran's affidavit.

On December 11, 1986, Guran also advised the trial judge, John T. Gallagher, in an *ex parte* submission, about the pending disciplinary charges and his attendant health problems. Among other things, Guran informed Judge Gallagher:

> You might remember that I had a Dr. [sic] appointment ... at N.Y. Hospital at which time a tentative diagnosis of [a form of polio commonly known as Lou Gehrig's Disease] was made. Needing time to prepare [for the disciplinary hearing scheduled for December 11, 1986], feeling miserable, [and] discouraged, I returned home and, through my lawyer, sent a copy of my medical statement to the Committee. Immediately they moved to suspend me pending my recovery....
>
> I am feeling better and have secured the services of Marvin D. Skedelsky, Esq. [to assist me with the trial].

Jury selection in Bellamy's trial began on January 6, 1987. Although Skedelsky told Guran that he would be available to assist Guran at trial, Skedelsky was unexpectedly occupied with another case when Bellamy's trial commenced. As a result, Guran represented Bellamy alone. At no time was Bellamy informed of Guran's disciplinary or health problems. On January 24, 1987, after almost three weeks of trial including five days of deliberations, the jury convicted Bellamy of second degree murder and second degree criminal possession of a weapon.

On March 26, 1987, more than two months after Bellamy's conviction, the First Department—without a hearing—suspended Guran from the further practice of law. The First Department chose to suspend Guran based on his representation made over three months earlier in December 1986 that his then-existing state of health prevented him from preparing for his disciplinary hearing.

Having learned that Guran had been suspended, Bellamy, represented by pro bono counsel, moved in June 1987 pursuant to N.Y.Crim. Proc.L. Art. 440 (McKinney 1983) to vacate his judgment of conviction. Among other things, Bellamy claimed that he was not afforded effective representation due to Guran's alleged incapacity and his subsequent suspension on that ground....

(The state trial court heard the original competency matter and found that Bellamy's counsel at the time of trial "was mentally and physically capable to try the defendant's case and did so in a competent manner.")

Because Bellamy had a full, fair and adequate Art. 440 hearing, and because the district court concluded that the state court's factual determination regarding Guran's competence was supported by the record, the district court properly deferred to the state court's factual finding, see 28 U.S.C. § 2254(d); Sumner v. Mata, 455 U.S. 591, 598, 102 S.Ct. 1303, 1307, 71 L.Ed.2d 480 (1982) (per curiam) (§ 2254(d) "requires the federal courts to show a high measure of deference to the factfindings made by the state courts."); Ventura v. Meachum, 957 F.2d 1048, 1054 (2d Cir.1992), and was well within its discretion not to hold an evidentiary hearing on this same issue. See, e.g., Townsend v. Sain, 372 U.S. 293, 318, 83 S.Ct. 745, 759, 9 L.Ed.2d 770 (1963), overruled on other grounds, Keeney v. Tamayo–Reyes, 112 S.Ct. 1715,

118 L.Ed.2d 318 (1992); Tate v. Wood, 963 F.2d 20, 24 (2d Cir.1992). Under these circumstances, Bellamy's reliance on Guran's alleged incapacity as a ground for applying the *per se* rule is, as a factual matter, unwarranted.

Feinberg, *Circuit Judge*, dissenting. We note that it is undisputed that at the time of trial, Bellamy knew nothing about the charges against Guran, Guran's admission of incapacity or Guran's representation that he would not attempt to try the case alone. Bellamy has sworn in an affidavit that he would not have allowed Guran to represent him at trial had he known of the facts stated above, and that contention is not disputed. Indeed, according to the affidavit, Bellamy got his first inkling of Guran's situation only at sentencing on April 8, 1987, when the trial judge would not allow Guran to represent Bellamy due to Guran's suspension on March 26.

Contrary to the majority's claim that it is "unclear" what effect Guran's misrepresentations had on his suspension, the only reasonable inference is that the Appellate Division would have suspended Guran immediately or prevented him from trying Bellamy's case if it had known he would not be honoring his promise. Guran admitted his incompetence and falsely promised to take preventive actions for the express purpose of avoiding a suspension. Without making full disclosure, he prevailed upon the trial court to allow him to try the case. It is unrealistic to assume that Guran's course of conduct did not bring about the desired result, i.e., no suspension and no need to hire another attorney as lead counsel ... I would therefore reverse the judgment of the district court, as the panel did. At the very least, I would remand for a *Strickland* hearing.

NOTES

1. Should the issue of effective assistance of counsel, as commonly happens today, be decided on direct review of a conviction? Would not a post-conviction petition filed in the trial court present a better avenue for reviewing the issue, at least initially? Should the lawyer who is accused of incompetency be given an opportunity to explain his actions? Consider the following hypothetical based upon an actual occurrence. The appellate record reflected that in voir dire examination defense counsel, presumably to lessen the impact, gave jurors advance knowledge that after the accused had testified, the prosecution would be allowed to prove that the defendant had previously been convicted of armed robbery. However, the defendant did not testify, so that the prosecution was not allowed to introduce the "provable" conviction for impeachment purposes. But for the defense lawyer's statements in voir dire the jury never would have known that the accused armed robber had previously been convicted of the same crime. On this record what judgments would you make about the lawyer's competence? Would your view change if you had before you the testimony of the defense lawyer in a post-conviction proceeding to this effect: Although the client had repeatedly been admonished to tell his lawyer the truth before trial, only mid-trial did the client tell the lawyer that he was guilty and that his alibi was fabricated. At that point the lawyer and client agreed that the client would not testify. What would you have done if you were the lawyer? After sentencing would you have explained for the record what had happened? Does a lawyer have a right to protect himself against a charge of incompetency at the risk of diminishing his client's chances on appeal? How would it look to an appellate court if the last statement by defense counsel in the trial court was that the client had privately admitted his guilt to the lawyer? Would ethical principles permit such a disclosure *before* the client has accused the lawyer of incompetency?

See United States v. Reiswitz, 941 F.2d 488 (7th Cir.1991), where the court stated:

> Reiswitz has a final go at it by raising the inevitable ineffective assistance of counsel claim. This appeal marks the first time this issue has been raised. In direct appeals of criminal convictions, ineffective assistance of counsel claims are best dealt with at the district court level, either through a motion or a new trial, see Fed.R.Crim.P. 33, or through the collateral relief available under 28 U.S.C. § 2255. See United States v. Lang, 644 F.2d 1232, 1240 (7th Cir.), cert. denied, 454 U.S. 870, 102S.Ct. 338 (1981). It is not our province as an appellate court to make findings regarding counsel's performance when, unlike the district court, we have not had the benefit of actually having observed it. However, we have the discretion to resolve an attorney incompetence issue when, as here, both parties ask us to resolve the matter, the question has been briefed and argued, and we have the entire trial record before us. United States v. Williams, 934 F.2d 847, 851 (7th Cir.1991); United States v. Asubonteng, 895 F.2d 424, 428 (7th Cir.), cert. denied, 494 U.S. 1089, 110 S.Ct. 1830 (1990).

2. A major theme of the ineffectiveness cases has been whether *per se* rules ought to be adopted. Arguably, the Court did so in Rompilla v. Beard, 545 U.S. 374, 125 S.Ct. 2456 (2005), a capital case in which defense counsel failed to examine a file pertaining to a prior conviction. While defense counsel were vigorous in their defense, it did appear that the file might well have opened a different and promising line of defense. The issue was whether the defense counsel had been reasonable in stopping their investigation at the point they did. Consider the following excerpts from the 5–4 decision and note that the facts are stated in the dissent.

"Justice Souter . . ."

> A standard of reasonableness applied as if one stood in counsel's shoes spawns few hard-edged rules, and the merits of a number of counsel's choices in this case are subject to fair debate. This is not a case in which defense counsel simply ignored their obligation to find mitigating evidence, and their workload as busy public defenders did not keep them from making a number of efforts, including interviews with Rompilla and some members of his family, and examinations of reports by three mental health experts who gave opinions at the guilt phase. None of the sources proved particularly helpful.
>
> Rompilla's own contributions to any mitigation case were minimal. Counsel found him uninterested in helping, as on their visit to his prison to go over a proposed mitigation strategy, when Rompilla told them he was "bored being here listening" and returned to his cell. To questions about childhood and schooling, his answers indicated they had been normal, save for quitting school in the ninth grade. There were times when Rompilla was even actively obstructive by sending counsel off on false leads.
>
> The lawyers also spoke with five members of Rompilla's family (his former wife, two brothers, a sister-in-law, and his son), and counsel testified that they developed a good relationship with the family in the course of their representation. The state postconviction court found that counsel spoke to the relatives in a "detailed manner," attempting to

unearth mitigating information, although the weight of this finding is qualified by the lawyers' concession that "the overwhelming response from the family was that they didn't really feel as though they knew him all that well since he had spent the majority of his adult years and some of his childhood years in custody," Defense counsel also said that because the family was "coming from the position that [Rompilla] was innocent ... they weren't looking for reasons for why he might have done this."

The third and final source tapped for mitigating material was the cadre of three mental health witnesses who were asked to look into Rompilla's mental state as of the time of the offense and his competency to stand trial. but their reports revealed "nothing useful" to Rompilla's case, and the lawyers consequently did not go to any other historical source that might have cast light on Rompilla's mental condition.

When new counsel entered the case to raise Rompilla's postconviction claims, however, they identified a number of likely avenues the trial lawyers could fruitfully have followed in building a mitigation case. School records are one example, which trial counsel never examined in spite of the professed unfamiliarity of the several family members with Rompilla's childhood, and despite counsel's knowledge that Rompilla left school after the ninth grade. Others examples are records of Rompilla's juvenile and adult incarcerations, which counsel did not consult, although they were aware of their client's criminal record. And while counsel knew from police reports provided in pretrial discovery that Rompilla had been drinking heavily at the time of his offense, and although one of the mental health experts reported that Rompilla's troubles with alcohol merited further investigation, counsel did not look for evidence of a history of dependence on alcohol that might have extenuating significance.

Before us, trial counsel and the Commonwealth respond to these unexplored possibilities by emphasizing this Court's recognition that the duty to investigate does not force defense lawyers to scour the globe on the off-chance something will turn up; reasonably diligent counsel may draw a line when they have good reason to think further investigation would be a waste. See *Wiggins v. Smith*, (further investigation excusable where counsel has evidence suggesting it would be fruitless); *Strickland v. Washington*, (counsel could "reasonably surmise ... that character and psychological evidence would be of little help"); *Burger v. Kemp*, (1987) (limited investigation reasonable because all witnesses brought to counsel's attention provided predominantly harmful information). The Commonwealth argues that the information trial counsel gathered from Rompilla and the other sources gave them sound reason to think it would have been pointless to spend time and money on the additional investigation espoused by postconviction counsel, and we can say that there is room for debate about trial counsel's obligation to follow at least some of those potential lines of enquiry. There is no need to say more, however, for a further point is clear and dispositive: the lawyers were deficient in failing to examine the court file on Rompilla's prior conviction.

* * *

There is an obvious reason that the failure to examine Rompilla's prior conviction file fell below the level of reasonable performance. Counsel knew that the Commonwealth intended to seek the death penalty by proving Rompilla had a significant history of felony convictions indicating the use or threat of violence, an aggravator under state law. Counsel further knew that the Commonwealth would attempt to establish this history by proving

Rompilla's prior conviction for rape and assault, and would emphasize his violent character by introducing a transcript of the rape victim's testimony given in that earlier trial. There is no question that defense counsel were on notice, since they acknowledge that a "plea letter," written by one of them four days prior to trial, mentioned the prosecutor's plans. *Ibid.* It is also undisputed that the prior conviction file was a public document, readily available for the asking at the very courthouse where Rompilla was to be tried.

With every effort to view the facts as a defense lawyer would have done at the time, it is difficult to see how counsel could have failed to realize that without examining the readily available file they were seriously compromising their opportunity to respond to a case for aggravation. The prosecution was going to use the dramatic facts of a similar prior offense, and Rompilla's counsel had a duty to make all reasonable efforts to learn what they could about the offense. Reasonable efforts certainly included obtaining the Commonwealth's own readily available file on the prior conviction to learn what the Commonwealth knew about the crime, to discover any mitigating evidence the Commonwealth would downplay and to anticipate the details of the aggravating evidence the Commonwealth would emphasize. n4 Without making reasonable efforts to review the file, defense counsel could have had no hope of knowing whether the prosecution was quoting selectively from the transcript, or whether there were circumstances extenuating the behavior described by the victim. The obligation to get the file was particularly pressing here owing to the similarity of the violent prior offense to the crime charged and Rompilla's sentencing strategy stressing residual doubt. Without making efforts to learn the details and rebut the relevance of the earlier crime, a convincing argument for residual doubt was certainly beyond any hope.

* * *

At argument the most that Pennsylvania (and the United States as *amicus*) could say was that defense counsel's efforts to find mitigating evidence by other means excused them from looking at the prior conviction file. And that, of course, is the position taken by the state postconviction courts. Without specifically discussing the prior case file, they too found that defense counsel's efforts were enough to free them from any obligation to enquire further.

We think this conclusion of the state court fails to answer the considerations we have set out, to the point of being an objectively unreasonable conclusion. It flouts prudence to deny that a defense lawyer should try to look at a file he knows the prosecution will cull for aggravating evidence, let alone when the file is sitting in the trial courthouse, open for the asking. No reasonable lawyer would forgo examination of the file thinking he could do as well by asking the defendant or family relations whether they recalled anything helpful or damaging in the prior victim's testimony. Nor would a reasonable lawyer compare possible searches for school reports, juvenile records, and evidence of drinking habits to the opportunity to take a look at a file disclosing what the prosecutor knows and even plans to read from in his case. Questioning a few more family members and searching for old records can promise less than looking for a needle in a haystack, when a lawyer truly has reason to doubt there is any needle there.... But looking at a file the prosecution says it will use is a sure bet: whatever may be in that file is going to tell defense counsel something about what the prosecution can produce.

The dissent thinks this analysis creates a "rigid, *per se*" rule that requires defense counsel to do a complete review of the file on any prior conviction introduced (opinion of KENNEDY, J.), but that is a mistake. Counsel fell short here because they failed to make reasonable efforts to review the prior conviction file, despite knowing that the prosecution intended to introduce Rompilla's prior conviction not merely by entering a notice of conviction into evidence but by quoting damaging testimony of the rape victim in that case. The unreasonableness of attempting no more than they did was heightened by the easy availability of the file at the trial courthouse, and the great risk that testimony about a similar violent crime would hamstring counsel's chosen defense of residual doubt. It is owing to these circumstances that the state courts were objectively unreasonable in concluding that counsel could reasonably decline to make any effort to review the file. Other situations, where a defense lawyer is not charged with knowledge that the prosecutor intends to use a prior conviction in this way, might well warrant a different assessment.

* * *

If the defense lawyers had looked in the file on Rompilla's prior conviction, it is uncontested they would have found a range of mitigation leads that no other source had opened up. In the same file with the transcript of the prior trial were the records of Rompilla's imprisonment on the earlier conviction, which defense counsel testified she had never seen ... The prison files pictured Rompilla's childhood and mental health very differently from anything defense counsel had seen or heard. An evaluation by a corrections counselor states that Rompilla was "reared in the slum environment of Allentown, Pa. vicinity. He early came to the attention of juvenile authorities, quit school at 16, [and] started a series of incarcerations in and out Penna. often of assaultive nature and commonly related to over-indulgence in alcoholic beverages." The same file discloses test results that the defense's mental health experts would have viewed as pointing to schizophrenia and other disorders, and test scores showing a third grade level of cognition after nine years of schooling.

* * *

The accumulated entries would have destroyed the benign conception of Rompilla's upbringing and mental capacity defense counsel had formed from talking with Rompilla himself and some of his family members, and from the reports of the mental health experts. With this information, counsel would have become skeptical of the impression given by the five family members and would unquestionably have gone further to build a mitigation case. Further effort would presumably have unearthed much of the material postconviction counsel found, including testimony from several members of Rompilla's family, whom trial counsel did not interview. Judge Sloviter summarized this evidence:

"Rompilla's parents were both severe alcoholics who drank constantly. His mother drank during her pregnancy with Rompilla, and he and his brothers eventually developed serious drinking problems. His father, who had a vicious temper, frequently beat Rompilla's mother, leaving her bruised and black-eyed, and bragged about his cheating on her. His parents fought violently, and on at least one occasion his mother stabbed his father. He was abused by his father who beat him when he was young with his hands, fists, leather straps, belts and sticks. All of the children lived in terror. There were no expressions of parental love, affection or approval.

Instead, he was subjected to yelling and verbal abuse. His father locked Rompilla and his brother Richard in a small wire mesh dog pen that was filthy and excrement filled. He had an isolated background, and was not allowed to visit other children or to speak to anyone on the phone. They had no indoor plumbing in the house, he slept in the attic with no heat, and the children were not given clothes and attended school in rags."

The jury never heard any of this and neither did the mental health experts who examined Rompilla before trial. While they found "nothing helpful to [Rompilla's] case," *Rompilla*, their postconviction counterparts, alerted by information from school, medical, and prison records that trial counsel never saw, found plenty of " 'red flags' " pointing up a need to test further. (Sloviter, J., dissenting). When they tested, they found that Rompilla "suffers from organic brain damage, an extreme mental disturbance significantly impairing several of his cognitive functions.". They also said that "Rompilla's problems relate back to his childhood, and were likely caused by fetal alcohol syndrome [and that] Rompilla's capacity to appreciate the criminality of his conduct or to conform his conduct to the law was substantially impaired at the time of the offense. . . ."

These findings in turn would probably have prompted a look at school and juvenile records, all of them easy to get, showing, for example, that when Rompilla was 16 his mother "was missing from home frequently for a period of one or several weeks at a time." ... The same report noted that his mother "has been reported ... frequently under the influence of alcoholic beverages, with the result that the children have always been poorly kept and on the filthy side which was also the condition of the home at all times." *Ibid.* School records showed Rompilla's IQ was in the mentally retarded range. . . .

This evidence adds up to a mitigation case that bears no relation to the few naked pleas for mercy actually put before the jury, and although we suppose it is possible that a jury could have heard it all and still have decided on the death penalty, that is not the test.

Pennsylvania must either retry the case on penalty or stipulate to a life sentence.

It is so ordered.

JUSTICE O'CONNOR, concurring.

I write separately to put to rest one concern. The dissent worries that the Court's opinion "imposes on defense counsel a rigid requirement to review all documents in what it calls the 'case file' of any prior conviction that the prosecution might rely on at trial." But the Court's opinion imposes no such rule. Rather, today's decision simply applies our longstanding case-by-case approach to determining whether an attorney's performance was unconstitutionally deficient under *Strickland v. Washington* ... In particular, there were three circumstances which made the attorneys' failure to examine Rompilla's prior conviction file unreasonable.

First, Rompilla's attorneys knew that their client's prior conviction would be at the very heart of the *prosecution's* case. The prior conviction went not to a collateral matter, but rather to one of the aggravating circumstances making Rompilla eligible for the death penalty. The prosecutors intended not merely to mention the fact of prior conviction, but to read testimony about the details of the crime. That crime, besides being quite violent in its own right, was very similar to the murder for which Rompilla was on trial, and Rompilla had committed the murder at issue a mere three months after his release from prison on the earlier conviction. In other words, the prosecutor clearly planned to use details of the prior crime as powerful evidence that Rompilla was a dangerous man for whom the death penalty would be both appropriate punishment and a necessary means of incapacitation. This was evidence the defense should have been prepared to meet: A reasonable defense lawyer would have attached a high importance to obtaining the record of the prior trial, in order to anticipate and find ways of deflecting the prosecutor's aggravation argument.

Second, the prosecutor's planned use of the prior conviction threatened to eviscerate one of the *defense's* primary mitigation arguments. Rompilla was convicted on the basis of strong circumstantial evidence. His lawyers structured the entire mitigation argument around the hope of convincing the jury that residual doubt about Rompilla's guilt made it inappropriate to impose the death penalty. In announcing an intention to introduce testimony about Rompilla's similar prior offense, the prosecutor put Rompilla's attorneys on notice that the prospective defense on mitigation likely would be ineffective and counterproductive. The similarities between the two crimes, combined with the timing and the already strong circumstantial evidence, raised a strong likelihood that the jury would reject Rompilla's residual doubt argument. Rompilla's attorneys' reliance on this transparently weak argument risked damaging their credibility. Such a scenario called for further investigation, to determine whether circumstances of the prior case gave any hope of saving the residual doubt argument, or whether the best strategy instead would be to jettison that argument so as to focus on other, more promising issues.

Third, the attorneys' decision not to obtain Rompilla's prior conviction file was not the result of an informed tactical decision about how the lawyers' time would best be spent. Although Rompilla's attorneys had ample warning that the details of Rompilla's prior conviction would be critical to their case, their failure to obtain that file would not necessarily have been deficient if it had resulted from the lawyers' careful exercise of judgment about how best to marshal their time and serve their client. But Rompilla's attorneys did not ignore the prior case file in order to spend their time on other crucial leads. They did not determine that the file was so inaccessible or so large that examining it would necessarily divert them from other trial-preparation tasks they thought more promising. They did not learn at the 11th hour about the prosecution's intent to use the prior conviction, when it was too late for them to change plans. Rather, their failure to obtain the crucial file "was the result of inattention, not reasoned strategic judgment." *Wiggins v. Smith*, 539 U.S. 510, 534, 123 S.Ct. 2527, 156 L.Ed.2d 471 (2003).

Because the Court's opinion is consistent with the " 'case-by-case examination of the evidence' " called for under our cases . . .

JUSTICE KENNEDY, with whom THE CHIEF JUSTICE, JUSTICE SCALIA, and JUSTICE THOMAS join, dissenting.

Today the Court brands two committed criminal defense attorneys as ineffective—"outside the wide range of professionally competent counsel," *Strickland v. Washington*, (1984)—because they did not look in an old case file and stumble upon something they had not set out to find. By implication the Court also labels incompetent the work done by the three mental health professionals who examined Ronald Rompilla. To reach this result, the majority imposes on defense counsel a rigid requirement to review all documents in what it calls the "case file" of any prior conviction that the prosecution might rely on at trial. The Court's holding, a mistake under any standard of review, is all the more troubling because this case arises under the Antiterrorism and Effective Death Penalty Act of 1996. In order to grant Rompilla habeas relief the Court must say, and indeed does say, that the Pennsylvania Supreme Court was objectively unreasonable in failing to anticipate today's new case file rule.

* * *

Rompilla's attorneys recognized from the outset that building an effective mitigation case was crucial to helping their client avoid the death penalty. Rompilla stood accused of a brutal crime. In January 1988, James Scanlon was murdered while he was closing the Cozy Corner Cafe, a bar he owned in Allentown, Pennsylvania. Scanlon's body was discovered later the next morning, lying in a pool of blood. Scanlon had been stabbed multiple times, including 16 wounds around the neck and head. Scanlon also had been beaten with a blunt object, and his face had been gashed, possibly with shards from broken liquor and beer bottles found at the scene of the crime. After Scanlon was stabbed to death his body had been set on fire.

Substantial evidence linked Rompilla to the crime ... He was at the Cozy Corner Cafe near closing time on the night of the murder and was observed going to the bathroom approximately 10 times during a 1–hour period. A window in that bathroom, the police later determined, was the probable point of entry used by Scanlon's assailant. A pair of Rompilla's sneakers seized by the police matched a bloody footprint found near the victim's body, and blood on the sneakers matched the victim's blood type. Rompilla's fingerprint was found on one of the two knives used to commit the murder. Sometime after leaving the bar on the night of the murder, Rompilla checked into a nearby motel under a false name. Although he told the police he left the bar with only two dollars, Rompilla had paid cash for the room and flashed a large amount of money to the desk clerks. The victim's wallet was discovered in the bushes just outside of Rompilla's motel room. When the police questioned Rompilla about the murder, his version of events was inconsistent with the testimony of other witnesses.

Rompilla was represented at trial by Fredrick Charles, the chief public defender for Lehigh County at the time, and Maria Dantos, an assistant public defender. Charles and Dantos were assisted by John Whispell, an investigator in the public defender's office. Rompilla's defense team sought to develop mitigating evidence from various sources. First, they questioned Rompilla extensively about his upbringing and background. ... To make these conversations more productive they provided Rompilla with a list of the mitigating circumstances recognized by Pennsylvania law.... Second, Charles and Dantos arranged for Rompilla to be examined by three experienced mental health professionals, experts described by Charles as "the best forensic psychiatrist around here, [another] tremendous psychiatrist and a fabulous forensic psychologist." Finally, Rompilla's attorneys questioned his family extensively in search of any information that might help spare Rompilla the death penalty. Dantos, in particular, developed a "very close" relationship with Rompilla's family, which was a "constant source of information.". Indeed, after trial Rompilla's wife sent Dantos a letter expressing her gratitude. The letter referred to Charles and Dantos as "superb human beings" who "fought and felt everything [Rompilla's] family did."

The Court acknowledges the steps taken by Rompilla's attorneys in preparation for sentencing but finds fault nonetheless. "The lawyers were deficient," the Court says, "in failing to examine the court file on Rompilla's prior conviction."

* * *

A *per se* rule requiring counsel in every case to review the records of prior convictions used by the State as aggravation evidence is a radical departure from *Strickland* and its progeny. We have warned in the past against the creation of "specific guidelines" or "checklists for judicial evaluation of attorney performance." See also *Wiggins v. Smith*, (2003); *Roe v. Flores–Ortega*, (2000). "No particular set of detailed rules for counsel's conduct can satisfactorily take account of the variety of circumstances faced by defense counsel or the range of legitimate decisions regarding how best to represent a criminal defendant. Any such set of rules would interfere with the constitutionally protected independence of counsel and restrict the wide latitude counsel must have in making tactical decisions. Indeed, the existence of detailed guidelines for representation could distract from the overriding mission of vigorous advocacy of the defendant's cause."

* * *

While the Court disclaims any intention to create a bright-line rule, this affords little comfort. The Court's opinion makes clear it has imposed on counsel a broad obligation to review prior conviction case files where those priors are used in aggravation—and to review every document in those files if not every single page of every document, regardless of the prosecution's proposed use for the prior conviction.... The Court also protests that the exceptional weight Rompilla's attorneys at sentencing placed on residual doubt required them to review the prior conviction file, (O'CONNOR, J., concurring). In fact, residual doubt was not central to Rompilla's mitigation case. Rompilla's family members did testify at sentencing that they thought he was innocent, but Dantos tried to draw attention away from this point and instead use the family's testimony to humanize Rompilla and ask for mercy.

* * *

Even with the benefit of hindsight the Court struggles to explain how the file would have proved helpful, offering only the vague speculation that Rompilla's attorneys might have discovered "circumstances that extenuated the behavior described by the [rape] victim." What the Court means by "circumstances" is a mystery. If the Court is referring to details on Rompilla's mental fitness or upbringing, surely Rompilla's attorneys were more likely to discover such information through the sources they consulted: Rompilla; his family; and the three mental health experts that examined him.

Perhaps the circumstances to which the majority refers are the details of Rompilla's 1974 crimes. Charles and Dantos, however, had enough information about the prior convictions to determine that reviewing the case file was not the most effective use of their time. Rompilla had been convicted of breaking into the residence of Josephine Macrenna, who lived in an apartment above the bar she owned. After Macrenna gave him the bar's receipts for the night, Rompilla demanded that she disrobe. When she initially resisted, Rompilla slashed her left breast with a knife. Rompilla then held Macrenna at knifepoint while he raped her for over an hour. Charles and Dantos were aware of these circumstances of the prior conviction and the brutality of the crime. It did not take a review of the case file to know that quibbling with the Commonwealth's version of events was a dubious trial strategy. At sentencing Dantos fought vigorously to prevent the Commonwealth from introducing the details of the 1974 crimes, *id.*, at 16–40, but once the transcript was admitted there was nothing that could be done. Rompilla was unlikely to endear himself to the jury by arguing that his prior conviction for burglary, theft, and rape really was not as bad as the Commonwealth was making it out to be. Recognizing this, Rompilla's attorneys instead devoted their limited time and resources to developing a mitigation case. That those efforts turned up little useful evidence does not make the *ex ante* strategic calculation of Rompilla's attorneys constitutionally deficient.

One of the primary reasons this Court has rejected a checklist approach to effective assistance of counsel is that each new requirement risks distracting attorneys from the real objective of providing vigorous advocacy as dictated by the facts and circumstances in the particular case. The Court's rigid requirement that counsel always review the case files of convictions the prosecution seeks to use at trial will be just such a distraction. Capital defendants often have a history of crime. For example, as of 2003, 64 percent of inmates on death row had prior felony convictions.... If the prosecution relies on these convictions as aggravators, the Court has now obligated defense attorneys to review the boxes of documents that come with them.

In imposing this new rule, the Court states that counsel in this case could review the "entire file" with "ease." There is simply no support in the record for this assumption. Case files often comprise numerous boxes. The file may contain, among other things, witness statements, forensic evidence, arrest reports, grand jury transcripts, testimony and exhibits relating to any pretrial suppression hearings, trial transcripts, trial exhibits, post-trial motions and presentence reports. Full review of even a single prior conviction case file could be time consuming, and many of the documents in a file are duplicative or irrelevant. The Court, recognizing the flaw in its analysis, suggests that cases involving "warehouses of records" "will call for greater subtlety." Yet for all we know, this is such a case. As to the time component, the Court tells us nothing as to the number of hours counsel had available to prepare for sentencing or why the decisions they made in allocating their time were so flawed as to constitute deficient performance under *Strickland*.

Today's decision will not increase the resources committed to capital defense. (At the time of Rompilla's trial, the Lehigh County Public Defender's Office had two investigators for 2,000 cases.... If defense attorneys dutifully comply with the Court's new rule, they will have to divert resources from other tasks. The net effect of today's holding in many cases—instances where trial counsel reasonably can conclude that reviewing old case files is not an effective use of time—will be to diminish the quality of representation. We have "consistently declined to impose mechanical rules on counsel—even when those rules might lead to better representation," *Roe v. Flores–Ortega*, I see no occasion to depart from this approach in order to impose a requirement that might well lead to worse representation).

It is quite possible defense attorneys, recognizing the absurdity of a one-size-fits-all approach to effective advocacy, will simply ignore the Court's new requirement and continue to exercise their best judgment about how to allocate time and resources in preparation for trial. While this decision would be understandable—and might even be required by state ethical rules, cf. Pa. Rules of Professional Conduct, Preamble, and Rule 1.1 (2005)—it leaves open the possibility that a defendant will seek to overturn his conviction based on something in a prior conviction case file that went unreviewed. This elevation of needle-in-a-haystack claims to the status of constitutional violations will benefit undeserving defendants and saddle States with the considerable costs of retrial and/or resentencing.

Today's decision is wrong under any standard, but the Court's error is compounded by the fact that this case arises on federal habeas.... Rompilla must show that the Pennsylvania Supreme Court decision was not just "incorrect or erroneous," but "objectively unreasonable." *Lockyer v. Andrade*, (citing *Williams v. Taylor*, (2000)). He cannot do so.

The Court pays lipservice to the *Williams* standard, but it proceeds to adopt a rigid, *per se* obligation that binds counsel in every case and finds little support in our precedents. Indeed, *Strickland*, the case the Court purports to apply, is directly to the contrary: "Most important, in adjudicating a claim of actual ineffectiveness of counsel, a court should keep in mind that the principles we have stated do not establish mechanical rules."

* * *

The Court's theory of prejudice rests on serendipity. Nothing in the old case file diminishes the aggravating nature of the prior conviction. The only way Rompilla's attorneys could have minimized the aggravating force of the earlier rape conviction was through Dantos' forceful, but ultimately unsuccessful, fight to exclude the transcript at sentencing. The Court, recognizing this problem, instead finds prejudice through chance. If Rompilla's attorneys had reviewed the case file of his prior rape and burglary conviction, the Court says, they would have stumbled across "a range of mitigation leads."

The range of leads to which the Court refers is in fact a handful of notations within a single 10–page document. The document, an "Initial Transfer Petition," appears to have been prepared by the Pennsylvania Department of Corrections after Rompilla's conviction to facilitate his initial assignment to one of the Commonwealth's maximum-security prisons.

Rompilla cannot demonstrate prejudice because nothing in the record indicates that Rompilla's trial attorneys would have discovered the transfer petition, or the clues contained in it, if they had reviewed the old file. The majority faults Rompilla's attorneys for failing to "learn what the Commonwealth knew about the crime," "discover any mitigating evidence the Commonwealth would downplay," and "anticipate the details of the aggravating evidence the Commonwealth would emphasize." Yet if Rompilla's attorneys had reviewed the case file with these purposes in mind, they almost surely would have attributed no significance to the transfer petition following only a cursory review. The petition, after all, was prepared by the Bureau of Correction after Rompilla's conviction for the purpose of determining Rompilla's initial prison assignment. It contained no details regarding the circumstances of the conviction. Reviewing the prior conviction file for information to counter the Commonwealth, counsel would have looked first at the transcript of the trial testimony, and perhaps then to probative exhibits or forensic evidence. There would have been no reason for counsel to read, or even to skim, this obscure document.

The Court claims that the transfer petition would have been discovered because it was in the "same file" with the transcript, but this characterization is misleading and the conclusion the Court draws from it is accordingly fallacious. The record indicates only that the transfer petition was a part of the same case file, but Rompilla provides no indication of the size of the file, which for all we know originally comprised several boxes of documents. By the time of Rompilla's state postconviction hearing, moreover, the transfer petition was not stored in any "file" at all—it had been transferred to microfilm.

* * *

The majority thus finds itself in a bind. If counsel's alleged deficiency lies in the failure to review the file for the purposes the majority has identified, then there is no prejudice: for there is no reasonable probability that review of the file for those purposes would have led counsel to accord the transfer petition enough attention to discover the leads the majority cites. Prejudice could only be demonstrated if the deficiency in counsel's performance were to be described not as the failure to perform a purposive review of the file, but instead as the failure to accord intense scrutiny to every single page of every single document in that file, regardless of the purpose motivating the review ... Surely, however, the Court would not require defense counsel to look at every document, no matter how tangential, included in the prior conviction file on the off chance that some notation therein might provide a lead, which in turn might result in the discovery of useful information. The Constitution does not mandate that defense attorneys perform busy work. This rigid requirement would divert counsel's limited time and energy away from more important tasks. In this way, it would ultimately disserve the rationale underlying the Court's new rule, which is to ensure that defense counsel counter the State's aggravation case effectively.

If the Court does intend to impose on counsel a constitutional obligation to review every page of every document included in the case file of a prior conviction, then today's holding is even more misguided than I imagined.

* * *

Today, the Court succumbs to the very temptation that *Strickland* warned against. In the process, the majority imposes on defense attorneys a rigid requirement that finds no support in our cases or common sense.

3. In Florida v. Nixon, 543 U.S. 175, 125 S.Ct. 551 (2004), a unanimous Court held that a defense counsel may make, without the client's consent, a decision to admit guilt at trial in order to improve the chances of avoiding the death penalty.

* * *

Justice Ginsburg delivered the opinion of the Court.

This capital case concerns defense counsel's strategic decision to concede, at the guilt phase of the trial, the defendant's commission of murder, and to concentrate the defense on establishing, at the penalty phase, cause for sparing the defendant's life. Any concession of that order, the Florida Supreme Court held, made without the defendant's express consent—however gruesome the crime and despite the strength of the evidence of guilt—automatically ranks as prejudicial ineffective assistance of counsel necessitating a new trial. We reverse the Florida Supreme Court's judgment.

* * *

On Monday, August 13, 1984, near a dirt road in the environs of Tallahassee, Florida, a passing motorist discovered Jeanne Bickner's charred body. Bickner had been tied to a tree and set on fire while still alive.Her left leg and arm, and most of her hair and skin, had been burned away. The next day, police found Bickner's car, abandoned on a Tallahassee street corner, on fire. Id., at 2520. Police arrested 23–year–old Joe Elton Nixon later that morning, after Nixon's brother informed the sheriff's office that Nixon had confessed to the murder.

Questioned by the police, Nixon described in graphic detail how he had kidnaped Bickner, then killed her. He recounted that he had approached Bickner, a stranger, in a mall, and asked her to help him jump-start his car. Bickner offered Nixon a ride home in her 1973 MG sports car. Once on the road, Nixon directed Bickner to drive to a remote place; en route, he overpowered her and stopped the car. Nixon next put Bickner in the MG's trunk, drove into a wooded area, removed Bickner from the car, and tied her to a tree with jumper cables. Bickner pleaded with Nixon to release her, offering him money in exchange. Concerned that Bickner might identify him, Nixon decided to kill her. He set fire to Bickner's personal belongings and ignited her with burning objects. Nixon drove away in the MG, and later told his brother and girlfriend what he had done. He burned the MG on Tuesday, August 14, after reading in the newspaper that Bickner's body had been discovered.

The State gathered overwhelming evidence establishing that Nixon had committed the murder in the manner he described. A witness saw Nixon approach Bickner in the mall's parking lot on August 12, and observed Bickner taking jumper cables out of the trunk of her car and giving them to Nixon. Several witnesses told police they saw Nixon driving around in the MG in the hours and days following Bickner's death. Nixon's palm print was found on the trunk of the car. Nixon's girlfriend, Wanda Robinson, and his brother, John Nixon, both stated that Nixon told them he had killed someone and showed them two rings later identified as Bickner's. According to Nixon's brother, Nixon pawned the rings, and attempted to sell the car. At a local pawnshop, police recovered the rings and a receipt for them bearing Nixon's driver's license number; the pawnshop owner identified Nixon as the person who sold the rings to him.

... Assistant public defender Michael Corin, assigned to represent Nixon, filed a plea of not guilty, and deposed all of the State's potential witnesses. Corin concluded, given the strength of the evidence, that Nixon's guilt was not "subject to any reasonable dispute." Corin thereupon commenced plea negotiations, hoping to persuade the prosecution to drop the death penalty in exchange for Nixon's guilty pleas to all charges. Negotiations broke down when the prosecutors indicated their unwillingness to recommend a sentence other than death.

Faced with the inevitability of going to trial on a capital charge, Corin turned his attention to the penalty phase, believing that the only way to save Nixon's life would be to present extensive mitigation evidence centering on Nixon's mental instability. Experienced in capital defense, Corin feared that denying Nixon's commission of the kidnaping and murder during the guilt phase would compromise Corin's ability to persuade the jury, during the penalty phase, that Nixon's conduct was the product of his mental illness. Corin concluded that the best strategy would be to concede guilt, thereby preserving his credibility in urging leniency during the penalty phase.

Corin attempted to explain this strategy to Nixon at least three times. Although Corin had represented Nixon previously on unrelated charges and the two had a good relationship in Corin's estimation, Nixon was generally unresponsive during their discussions. He never verbally approved or protested Corin's proposed strategy. Overall, Nixon gave Corin very little, if any, assistance or direction in preparing the case, and refused to attend pretrial dispositions of various motions. Corin eventually exercised his professional judgment to pursue the concession strategy. As he explained: "There are many times lawyers make decisions because they have to make them because the client does nothing."

When Nixon's trial began on July 15, 1985, his unresponsiveness deepened into disruptive and violent behavior. On the second day of jury selection, Nixon pulled off his clothing, demanded a black judge and lawyer, refused to be escorted into the courtroom, and threatened to force the guards to shoot him. An extended on-the-record colloquy followed Nixon's bizarre behavior, during which Corin urged the trial judge to explain Nixon's rights to him and ascertain whether Nixon understood the significance of absenting himself from the trial. Corin also argued that restraining Nixon and compelling him to be present would prejudice him in the eyes of the jury. When the judge examined Nixon on the record in a holding cell, Nixon stated he had no interest in the trial and threatened to misbehave if forced to attend. The judge ruled that Nixon had intelligently and voluntarily waived his right to be present at trial.

The guilt phase of the trial thus began in Nixon's absence. In his opening statement, Corin acknowledged Nixon's guilt and urged the jury to focus on the penalty phase:

"In this case, there won't be any question, none whatsoever, that my client, Joe Elton Nixon, caused Jeannie Bickner's death.... [T]hat fact will be proved to your satisfaction beyond any doubt.

"This case is about the death of Joe Elton Nixon and whether it should occur within the next few years by electrocution or maybe its natural expiration after a lifetime of confinement.

...

"Now, in arriving at your verdict, in your penalty recommendation, for we will get that far, you are going to learn many facts ... about Joe Elton Nixon. Some of those facts are going to be good. That may not seem clear to you at this time. But, and sadly, most of the things you learn of Joe Elton Nixon are not going to be good. But, I'm suggesting to you that when you have seen all the testimony, heard all the testimony and the evidence that has been shown, there are going to be reasons why you should recommend that his life be spared."

During its case in chief, the State introduced the tape of Nixon's confession, expert testimony on the manner in which Bickner died, and witness testimony regarding Nixon's confessions to his relatives and his possession of Bickner's car and personal effects. Corin cross-examined these witnesses only when he felt their statements needed clarification, and he did not present a defense case. Corin did object to the introduction of crime scene photographs as unduly prejudicial, and actively contested several aspects of the jury instructions during the charge conference. In his closing argument, Corin again conceded Nixon's guilt, and reminded the jury of the importance of the penalty phase: "I will hope to ... argue to you and give you reasons not that Mr. Nixon's life be spared one final and terminal confinement forever, but that he not be sentenced to die." The jury found Nixon guilty on all counts.

At the start of the penalty phase, Corin argued to the jury that "Joe Elton Nixon is not normal organically, intellectually, emotionally or educationally or in any other way." Corin presented the testimony of eight witnesses. Relatives and friends described Nixon's childhood emotional troubles and his erratic behavior in the days preceding the murder. A psychiatrist and a psychologist addressed Nixon's antisocial personality, his history of emotional instability and psychiatric care, his low IQ, and the possibility that at some point he suffered brain damage. The State presented little evidence during the penalty phase, simply incorporating its guilt-phase evidence by reference, and introducing testimony, over Corin's objection, that Nixon had removed Bickner's underwear in order to terrorize her.

In his closing argument, Corin emphasized Nixon's youth, the psychiatric evidence, and the jury's discretion to consider any mitigating circumstances. Corin urged that, if not sentenced to death, "Joe Elton Nixon would [n]ever be released from confinement." The death penalty, Corin maintained, was appropriate only for "intact human being[s]," and "Joe Elton Nixon is not one of those. He's never been one of those. He never will be one of those." Corin concluded: "You know, we're not around here all that long. And it's rare when we have the opportunity to give or take life. And you have that opportunity to give life. And I'm going to ask you to do that. Thank you." After deliberating for approximately three hours, the jury recommended that Nixon be sentenced to death.

In accord with the jury's recommendation, the trial court imposed the death penalty. Notably, at the close of the penalty phase, the court commended Corin's performance during the trial, stating that "the tactic employed by trial counsel ... was an excellent analysis of [the] reality of his case." The evidence of guilt "would have persuaded any jury ... beyond all doubt," and "[f]or trial counsel to have inferred that Mr. Nixon was not guilty ... would have deprived [counsel] of any credibility during the penalty phase."

* * *

Observing that "no competent, substantial evidence ... establish[ed] that Nixon affirmatively and explicitly agreed to counsel's strategy," the Florida Supreme Court reversed and remanded for a new trial. Nixon v. State, 857 So.2d 172, 176 (Fla. 2003) (Nixon III) (emphasis in original)....

An attorney undoubtedly has a duty to consult with the client regarding "important decisions," including questions of overarching defense strategy. Strickland, 466 U.S., at 688, 104 S.Ct. 2052, 80 L.Ed.2d 674. That obligation, however, does not require counsel to obtain the defendant's consent to "every tactical decision." Taylor v. Illinois, 484 U.S. 400, 417418, 108 S.Ct. 646, 98 L.Ed.2d 798 (1988) (an attorney has authority to manage most aspects of the defense without obtaining his client's approval). But certain decisions regarding the exercise or waiver of basic trial rights are of such moment that they cannot be made for the defendant by a surrogate. A defendant, this Court affirmed, has "the ultimate authority" to determine "whether to plead guilty, waive a jury, testify in his or her own behalf, or take an appeal." Jones v. Barnes, 463 U.S. 745, 751, 103 S.Ct. 3308, 77 L.Ed.2d 987 (1983). Concerning those decisions, an attorney must both consult with the defendant and obtain consent to the recommended course of action.

A guilty plea, we recognized in Boykin v. Alabama, is an event of signal significance in a criminal proceeding. By entering a guilty plea, a defendant waives constitutional rights that inhere in a criminal trial, including the right to trial by jury, the protection against self-incrimination, and the right to confront one's accusers. While a guilty plea may be tactically advantageous for the defendant, the plea is not simply a strategic choice; it is "itself a conviction," and the high stakes for the defendant require "the utmost solicitude," Accordingly, counsel lacks authority to consent to a guilty plea on a client's behalf, Brookhart v. Janis; moreover, a defendant's tacit acquiescence in the decision to plead is insufficient to render the plea valid

The Florida Supreme Court ... deemed Corin's statements to the jury "the functional equivalent of a guilty plea." We disagree with that assessment.

Despite Corin's concession, Nixon retained the rights accorded a defendant in a criminal trial.... The State was obliged to present during the guilt phase competent, admissible evidence establishing the essential elements of the crimes with which Nixon was charged. That aggressive evidence would thus be separated from the penalty phase, enabling the defense to concentrate that portion of the trial on mitigating factors. Further, the defense reserved the right to cross-examine witnesses for the prosecution and could endeavor, as Corin did, to exclude prejudicial evidence. In addition, in the event of errors in the trial or jury instructions, a concession of guilt would not hinder the defendant's right to appeal.

* * *

Corin was obliged to, and in fact several times did, explain his proposed trial strategy to Nixon. Given Nixon's constant resistance to answering inquiries put to him by counsel and court. Corin was not additionally required to gain express consent before conceding Nixon's guilt.

* * *

The Florida Supreme Court's erroneous equation of Corin's concession strategy to a guilty plea led it to apply the wrong standard in determining whether counsel's performance ranked as ineffective assistance. The court first presumed deficient performance, then applied the presumption of prejudice that United States v. Cronic, reserved for situations in which counsel has entirely failed to function as the client's advocate. The Florida court therefore did not hold Nixon to the standard prescribed in Strickland v. Washington, (1984), which would have required Nixon to show that counsel's concession strategy was unreasonable.

* * *

Cronic recognized a narrow exception to Strickland's holding that a defendant who asserts ineffective assistance of counsel must demonstrate not only that his attorney's performance was deficient, but also that the deficiency prejudiced the defense. Cronic instructed that a presumption of prejudice would be in order in "circumstances that are so likely to prejudice the accused that the cost of litigating their effect in a particular case is unjustified." The Court elaborated: "[I]f counsel entirely fails to subject the prosecution's case to meaningful adversarial testing, then there has been a denial of Sixth Amendment rights that makes the adversary process itself presumptively unreliable." see Bell v. Cone, (for Cronic's presumed prejudice standard to apply, counsel's "failure must be complete"). We illustrated just how infrequently the "surrounding circumstances [will] justify a presumption of ineffectiveness" in Cronic itself. In that case, we reversed a Court of Appeals ruling that ranked as prejudicially inadequate the performance of an inexperienced, under-prepared attorney in a complex mail fraud trial.

On the record thus far developed, Corin's concession of Nixon's guilt does not rank as a "fail[ure] to function in any meaningful sense as the Government's adversary." Although such a concession in a run-of-the-mine trial might present a closer question, the gravity of the potential sentence in a capital trial and the proceeding's two-phase structure vitally affect counsel's strategic calculus. Attorneys representing capital defendants face daunting challenges in developing trial strategies, not least because the defendant's guilt is often clear. Prosecutors are more likely to seek the death penalty, and to refuse to accept a plea to a life sentence, when the evidence is overwhelming and the crime heinous. See Goodpaster, The Trial for Life: Effective Assistance of Counsel in Death Penalty Cases, 58 N. Y. U. L. Rev. 299, 329 (1983). In such cases, "avoiding execution [may be] the best and only realistic result possible." ABA Guidelines for the Appointment and Performance of Defense Counsel in Death Penalty Cases 10.9.1, Commentary (rev. ed. 2003).

* * *

Counsel therefore may reasonably decide to focus on the trial's penalty phase, at which time counsel's mission is to persuade the trier that his client's life should be spared. Unable to negotiate a guilty plea in exchange for a life sentence, defense counsel must strive at the guilt phase to avoid a counterproductive course. See Lyon, Defending the Death Penalty Case: What Makes Death Different?, 42 Mercer L. Rev. 695, 708 (1991) ("It is not good to put on a 'he didn't do it' defense and a 'he is sorry he did it' mitigation. This just does not work. The jury will give the death penalty to the client and, in essence, the attorney."); Sundby, The Capital Jury and Absolution: The Intersection of Trial Strategy, Remorse, and the Death Penalty, 83 Cornell L. Rev. 1557, 15891591 (1998) (interviews of jurors in capital trials indicate that juries approach the sentencing phase "cynically" where counsel's sentencing-phase presentation is logically inconsistent with the guilt-phase defense); id., at 1597 (in capital cases, a "run-of-the-mill strategy of challenging the prosecution's case for failing to prove guilt beyond a reasonable doubt" can have dire implications for the sentencing phase). In this light, counsel cannot be deemed ineffective for attempting to impress the jury with his candor and his unwillingness to engage in "a useless charade." See Cronic, 466 U.S., at 656657, n. 19, 80 L. Ed. 657 104 S. Ct. 2039. Renowned advocate Clarence Darrow, we note, famously employed a similar strategy as counsel for the youthful, cold-blooded killers Richard Loeb and Nathan Leopold. Imploring the judge to spare the boys' lives, Darrow declared: "I do not know how much salvage there is in these two boys.... I will be honest with this court as I have tried to be from the beginning. I know that these boys are not fit to be at large." Attorney for the Damned: Clarence Darrow in the Courtroom 84 (A. Weinberg ed. 1989); see Tr. of Oral Arg. 4041 (Darrow's clients) "did not expressly consent to what he did. But he saved their lives."

To summarize, in a capital case, counsel must consider in conjunction both the guilt and penalty phases in determining how best to proceed. When counsel informs the defendant of the strategy counsel believes to be in the defendant's best interest and the defendant is unresponsive, counsel's strategic choice is not impeded by any blanket rule demanding the defendant's explicit consent. Instead, if counsel's strategy, given the evidence bearing on the defendant's guilt, satisfies the Strickland standard, that is the end of the matter; no tenable claim of ineffective assistance would remain.

* * *

For the reasons stated, the judgment of the Florida Supreme Court is reversed, and the case is remanded for further proceedings not inconsistent with this opinion.

It is so ordered.

4. In Commonwealth v. Pavao, 39 Mass.App.Ct. 490, 658 N.E.2d 175 (1995), the court held that a defense lawyer had the duty to bring to the court's attention an omission to engage the defendant in the required colloquy when a written waiver of jury was presented.

After being convicted in a bench trial for indecent assault, the defendant raised the absence of the colloquy as the sole grounds for reversal. The court acknowledged the "clear error" of not implementing colloquy but found in "the unique circumstances of this case, no reversible error occurred." The defense counsel acknowledged that he did not call the court's attention to the lapse deliberately in anticipation that the oversight would afford him grounds for reversible error.

"We, however, deem such tactical silence to have exceeded the bounds of acceptably zealous representation. '[I]t is not consistent with the purposes of justice, for a party knowing of a secret defect, to proceed and take his chance for a favorable verdict, with the power and intent to annul it, as erroneous and void, if it should be against him.' Commonwealth v. Cancel,394 Mass. 567, 571–572, 476 N.E.2d 610 (1985), quoting from Cady v. Norton, 31 Mass. 236, 14 Pick. 236, 237 (1833) (Shaw, C.J.)...."

And "[s]uch limits upon advocacy are essential to preserve the adversary system itself, since it is a process in which the courts are almost wholly dependent on counsel to marshal and proffer the true facts and the accurate applicable law, so that correct conclusions that most closely approximate justice will emerge from the crucible of contending presentations."

5. What happens when counsel fails to file a notice of appeal because his client did not ask her to do so? In Roe v. Flores–Ortega, 528 U.S. 470, 120 S.Ct. 1029 (2000), the Court held:

> In those cases where the defendant neither instructs counsel to file an appeal nor asks that an appeal not be taken, we believe the question whether counsel has performed deficiently by not filing a notice of appeal is best answered by first asking a separate, but antecedent, question: whether counsel in fact consulted with the defendant about an appeal. We employ the term "consult" to convey a specific meaning advising the defendant about the advantages and disadvantages of taking an appeal, and making a reasonable effort to discover the defendant's wishes. If counsel has consulted with the defendant, the question of deficient performance is easily

answered: Counsel performs in a professionally unreasonable manner only by failing to follow the defendant's express instructions with respect to an appeal. If counsel has not consulted with the defendant, the court must in turn ask a second, and subsidiary, question: whether counsel's failure to consult with the defendant itself constitutes deficient performance. That question lies at the heart of this case: Under what circumstances does counsel have an obligation to consult with the defendant about an appeal?

* * *

We ... reject a bright-line rule that counsel must always consult with the defendant regarding an appeal.

We instead hold that counsel has a constitutionally-imposed duty to consult with the defendant about an appeal when there is reason to think either (1) that a rational defendant would want to appeal (for example, because there are nonfrivolous grounds for appeal), or (2) that this particular defendant reasonably demonstrated to counsel that he was interested in appealing. In making this determination courts must take into account all the information counsel knew or should have known (focusing on the totality of the circumstances). Although not determinative, a highly relevant factor in this inquiry will be whether the conviction follows a trial or a guilty plea, both because a guilty plea reduces the scope of potentially appealable issues and because such a plea may indicate that the defendant seeks an end to judicial proceedings. Even in cases when the defendant pleads guilty, the court must consider such factors as whether the defendant received the sentence bargained for as part of the plea and whether the plea expressly reserved or waived some or all appeal rights. Only by considering all relevant factors in a given case can a court properly determine whether a rational defendant would have desired an appeal or that the particular defendant sufficiently demonstrated to counsel an interest in an appeal.

Addressing the "prejudice" prong of the Strickland analysis, the Court held that, "to show prejudice in these circumstances, a defendant must demonstrate that there is a reasonably probability that, but for counsel's deficient failure to consult with him about an appeal, he would have timely appealed."

4. CONFLICTS OF INTEREST

Holloway v. Arkansas

Supreme Court of the United States, 1978.
435 U.S. 475, 98 S.Ct. 1173.

■ MR. CHIEF JUSTICE BURGER delivered the opinion of the Court.

Petitioners, codefendants at trial, made timely motions for appointment of separate counsel, based on the representations of their appointed counsel that, because of confidential information received from the codefendants, he was confronted with the risk of representing conflicting interests and could not, therefore, provide effective assistance for each client. We granted certiorari to decide whether petitioners were deprived of the effective assistance of counsel by the denial of those motions. ...

I.

[Harold Hall, a public defender, was appointed to represent three defendants charged with robbery and rape. Twice prior to trial, Hall moved to have separate counsel appointed because the confidential communications which he had received from individual defendants indicated that a conflict of interest might arise if the defendants elected to testify.]

* * *

On the second day of trial, after the prosecution had rested its case, Hall advised the court that, against his recommendation, all three defendants had decided to testify. He then stated:

> "Now, since I have been appointed, I had previously filed a motion asking the Court to appoint a separate attorney for each defendant because of a possible conflict of interest. This conflict will probably be now coming up since each one of them wants to testify.
>
> "THE COURT: That's all right; let them testify. There is no conflict of interest. Every time I try more than one person is this court each one blames it on the other one.
>
> "MR. HALL: I have talked to each one of these defendants, and I have talked to them individually, not collectively.
>
> "THE COURT: Now talk to them collectively."

The court then indicated satisfaction that each petitioner understood the nature and consequences of his right to testify on his own behalf, whereupon Hall observed:

> "I am in a position now where I am more or less muzzled as to any cross-examination.
>
> "THE COURT: You have no right to cross-examine your own witness.
>
> "MR. HALL: Or to examine them.
>
> "THE COURT: You have a right to examine them, but have no right to cross-examine them. The prosecuting attorney does that.
>
> "MR. HALL: If one [defendant] takes the stand, somebody needs to protect the other two's interest while that one is testifying, and I can't do that since I have talked to each one individually.
>
> "THE COURT: Well, you have talked to them, I assume, individually and collectively, too. They all say they want to testify. I think it's perfectly alright for them to testify if they want to, or not. It's their business.
>
> * * *
>
> "Each defendant said he wants to testify, and there will be no cross-examination of these witnesses, just a direct examination by you.

"MR. HALL: Your Honor, I can't even put them on direct examination because if I ask them—

"THE COURT: (interposing) You can just put them on the stand and tell the Court that you have advised them of their rights and they want to testify; then you tell the man to go ahead and relate what he wants to. That's all you need to do."[4]

Holloway then took the stand on his own behalf, testifying that during the time described as the time of the robbery he was at his brother's home. His brother had previously given similar testimony. When Welch took the witness stand, the record shows Hall advised him, as he had Holloway, that "I cannot ask you any questions that might tend to incriminate any one of the three of you.... Now, the only thing I can say is tell these ladies and gentlemen of the jury what you know about this case...." Welch responded that he did not "have any kind of speech ready for the jury or anything. I thought I was going to be questioned." When Welch denied, from the witness stand, that he was at the restaurant the night of the robbery, Holloway interrupted, asking:

"Your Honor, are we allowed to make an objection?

"THE COURT: No, sir. Your counsel will take care of any objections.

"MR. HALL: Your Honor, that is what I am trying to say. I can't cross-examine them.

"THE COURT: You proceed like I tell you to, Mr. Hall. You have no right to cross-examine your own witnesses anyhow."

Welch proceeded with his unguided direct testimony, denying any involvement in the crime and stating that he was at his home at the time it occurred. Campbell gave similar testimony when he took the stand. He also denied making any confession to the arresting officers.

The jury rejected the versions of events presented by the three defendants and the alibi witness, and returned guilty verdicts on all counts.

* * *

II.

More than 35 years ago, in Glasser v. United States, 315 U.S. 60, 62 S.Ct.457 (1942), this Court held that by requiring an attorney to represent two codefendants whose interests were in conflict the District Court had denied one of the defendants his Sixth Amendment right to the effective assistance of counsel.

* * *

One principle applicable here emerges from *Glasser* without ambiguity. Requiring or permitting a single attorney to represent codefendants, often

4. The record reveals that both the trial court and defense counsel were alert to defense counsel's obligation to avoid assisting in the presentation of what counsel had reason to believe was false testimony, or, at least, testimony contrary to the version of facts given to him earlier and in confidence. Cf. ABA, Standards Relating to the Administration of Criminal Justice—The Defense Function § 7.7(c), at 133 (1974).

referred to as joint representation, is not *per se* violative of constitutional guarantees of effective assistance of counsel. This principle recognizes that in some cases multiple defendants can appropriately be represented by one attorney; indeed, in some cases, certain advantages might accrue from joint representation. In Mr. Justice Frankfurter's view: "Joint representation is a means of insuring against reciprocal recrimination. A common defense often gives strength against a common attack." Glasser v. United States, supra, 315 U.S., at 92, 62 S.Ct., at 475 (dissenting).[5]

* * *

Here trial counsel, by the pretrial motions ... and by his accompanying representations, made as an officer of the court, focused explicitly on the probable risk of a conflict of interests. The judge then failed either to appoint separate counsel or to take adequate steps to ascertain whether the risk was too remote to warrant separate counsel. We hold that the failure, in the face of the representations made by counsel weeks before trial and again before the jury was empanelled, deprived petitioners of the guarantee of "assistance of counsel."

This conclusion is supported by the Court's reasoning in *Glasser*:

> "Upon the trial judge rests the duty of seeing that the trial is conducted with solicitude for the essential rights of the accused. ... The trial court should protect the right of an accused to have the assistance of counsel. ...
>
> * * *
>
> "Of equal importance with the duty of the court to see that an accused has the assistance of counsel is its duty to refrain from embarrassing counsel in the defense of an accused *by insisting, or indeed, even suggesting, that counsel undertake to concurrently represent interests which might diverge from those of his first client, when the possibility of that divergence is brought home to the court*." (Emphasis added).

This reasoning has direct applicability in this case where the "possibility of [petitioners'] inconsistent interests" were "brought home to the court" by formal objections, motions, and defense counsel's representations.

* * *

Additionally, since the decision in *Glasser*, most courts have held that an attorney's request for the appointment of separate counsel, based on his representations as an officer of the court regarding a conflict of interests, should be granted. ... In so holding, the courts have acknowledged and given effect to several interrelated considerations. An "attorney representing two defendants in a criminal matter is in the best position professionally and ethically to determine when a conflict of interest exists or will probably develop in the course of a trial." Second, defense attorneys have

5. By inquiring in *Glasser* whether there had been a waiver, the Court also confirmed that a defendant may waive his right to the assistance of an attorney unhindered by a conflict of interests. 315 U.S., at 70, 62 S.Ct., at 464. In this case, however, Arkansas does not contend that petitioners waived that right.

the obligation, upon discovering a conflict of interests, to advise the court at once of the problem.[8] Finally, attorneys are officers of the court, and " 'when they address the judge solemnly upon a matter before the court, their declarations are virtually made under oath.' " We find these considerations persuasive.

The State argues, however, that to credit Hall's representations to the trial court would be tantamount to transferring to defense counsel the authority of the trial judge to rule on the existence or risk of a conflict and to appoint separate counsel. In the State's view, the ultimate decision on those matters must remain with the trial judge; otherwise unscrupulous defense attorneys might abuse their "authority," presumably for purposes of delay or obstruction of the orderly conduct of the trial.[10]

The State has an obvious interest in avoiding such abuses. But our holding does not undermine that interest. When an untimely motion for separate counsel is made for dilatory purposes, our holding does not impair the trial court's ability to deal with counsel who resort to such tactics. ... Nor does our holding preclude a trial court from exploring the adequacy of the basis of defense counsel's representations regarding a conflict of interests without improperly requiring disclosure of the confidential communications of the client.[11] In this case the trial court simply failed to take adequate steps in response to the repeated motions, objections and representations made to it, and no prospect of dilatory practices was present to justify that failure.

III.

The issue remains whether the error committed at petitioners' trial requires reversal of their convictions. It has generally been assumed that *Glasser* requires reversal, even in the absence of a showing of specific prejudice to the complaining codefendant, whenever a trial court improperly permits or requires joint presentation.... Some courts and commentators have argued, however, that appellate courts should not reverse automatically in such cases but rather should affirm unless the defendant can demonstrate prejudice. ... This argument rests on two aspects of the

8. The American Bar Association in its Standards Relating to the Administration of Criminal Justice—The Defense Function § 3.5(b), at 123 (1974) cautions:

> "Except for preliminary matters such as initial hearings or applications for bail, a lawyer or lawyers who are associated in practice should not undertake to defend more than one defendant in the same criminal case if the duty to one of the defendants may conflict with the duty to another. The potential for conflict of interest in representing multiple defendants is so grave that ordinarily a lawyer should decline to act for more than one of several co-defendants except in unusual situations when, after careful investigation, it is clear that no conflict is likely to develop and when the several defendants give an informed consent to such multiple representation."

10. Such risks are undoubtedly present; they are inherent in the adversary system. But courts have abundant power to deal with attorneys who misrepresent facts.

11. This case does not require an inquiry into the extent of a court's power to compel an attorney to disclose confidential communications that he concludes would be damaging to his client. Cf. ABA, Code of Professional Responsibility, DR 4–101(C)(2). Such compelled disclosure creates significant risks of unfair prejudice, especially when the disclosure is to a judge who may be called upon later to select sentences for the attorney's clients.

Court's decision in *Glasser*. First, although it had concluded that Stewart was forced to represent conflicting interests, the Court did *not* reverse the conviction of Kretske, Stewart's other client, because Kretske failed to "show that the denial of Glasser's constitutional rights *prejudiced* [him] in some manner." (Emphasis added). Second, the Court justified the reversal of Glasser's conviction, in part, by emphasizing the weakness of the Government's evidence against him; with guilt a close question, "error, which under some circumstances *would not be ground for reversal*, cannot be brushed aside as immaterial, since there is a real chance that it might have provided the slight impetus which swung the scales toward guilt." (Emphasis added). Assessing the strength of the prosecution's evidence against the defendant is, of course, one step in applying a harmless error standard. . . .

We read the Court's opinion in *Glasser*, however, as holding that whenever a trial court improperly requires joint representation over timely objection reversal is automatic. The *Glasser* Court stated:

> "To determine the precise degree of prejudice sustained by Glasser as a result of the [District] Court's appointment of Stewart as counsel for Kretske is at once difficult and unnecessary. The right to have the assistance of counsel is too fundamental and absolute to allow courts to indulge in nice calculations as to the amount of prejudice arising from its denial. . . ."

This language presupposes that the joint representation, over his express objections, prejudiced the accused in some degree. But from the cases cited it is clear that the prejudice is presumed regardless of whether it was independently shown.

* * *

. . . The Court's refusal to reverse Kretske's conviction is not contrary to this interpretation of *Glasser*. Kretske did *not* raise his own Sixth Amendment challenge to the joint representation. As the Court's opinion indicates, some of the codefendants argued that the denial of Glasser's right to the effective assistance of counsel prejudiced them as alleged coconspirators. In that context, the Court required a showing of prejudice; finding none, it affirmed the convictions of the codefendants, including Kretske.

Moreover, this Court has concluded that the assistance of counsel is among those "constitutional rights so basic to a fair trial that their infraction can never be treated as harmless error." . . . Accordingly, when a defendant is deprived of the presence and assistance of his attorney, either throughout the prosecution or during a critical stage in, at least, the prosecution of a capital offense, reversal is automatic. . . .

That an attorney representing multiple defendants with conflicting interests is physically present at pretrial proceedings, during trial, and at sentencing does not warrant departure from this general rule. Joint representation of conflicting interests is suspect because of what it tends to prevent the attorney from doing. For example, in this case it may well have precluded defense counsel for [one defendant] from exploring possible plea negotiations and the possibility of an agreement to testify for the prosecution, provided a lesser charge or a favorable sentencing recommendation would be acceptable. Generally speaking, a conflict may also prevent an attorney from challenging the admission of evidence prejudicial to one client but perhaps favorable to another, or from arguing at the sentencing hearing the relative involvement and culpability of his clients in order to minimize the culpability of one by emphasizing that of another. Examples can be readily multiplied. The mere physical presence of an attorney does not fulfill the Sixth Amendment guarantee when the advocate's conflicting obligations has effectively sealed his lips on crucial matters.

Finally, a rule requiring a defendant to show that a conflict of interests—which he and his counsel tried to avoid by timely objections to the joint representation—prejudiced him in some specific fashion would not be susceptible to intelligent, evenhanded application. In the normal case where a harmless error rule is applied, the error occurs at trial and its scope is readily identifiable. Accordingly, the reviewing court can undertake with some confidence its relatively narrow task of assessing the likelihood that the error materially affected the deliberations of the jury. ... But in a case of joint representation of conflicting interests the evil—it bears repeating—is in what the advocate finds himself compelled to *refrain* from doing, not only at trial but also as to possible pretrial plea negotiations and in the sentencing process. It may be possible in some cases to identify from the record the prejudice resulting from an attorney's failure to undertake certain trial tasks, but even with a record of the sentencing hearing available it would be difficult to judge intelligently the impact of a conflict on the attorney's representation of a client. And to assess the impact of a conflict of interests on the attorney's options, tactics and decisions in plea negotiations would be virtually impossible. Thus, an inquiry into a claim of harmless error here would require, unlike most cases, unguided speculation.

Accordingly, we reverse and remand for further proceedings not inconsistent with this opinion.

■ MR. JUSTICE POWELL with whom MR. JUSTICE BLACKMUN and MR. JUSTICE REHNQUIST join, dissenting.

While disavowing a *per se* rule of separate representation, the Court holds today that the trial judge's failure in this case "either to appoint separate counsel or take adequate steps to ascertain whether the risk was too remote to warrant separate counsel" worked a violation of the guarantee of "assistance of counsel" embodied in the Sixth and Fourteenth Amendments.

* * *

... Because I cannot agree that, in the particular circumstances of this case, the court's failure to inquire requires reversal of petitioners' convictions and because the Court's opinion contains seeds of a *per se* rule of separate representation merely upon the demand of defense counsel, I respectfully dissent.

I.

* * *

The Court's approach in this case is not premised on an ultimate finding of conflict of interest or ineffective assistance of counsel. Rather, it presumes prejudice from the failure to conduct an inquiry, equating that failure with a violation of the Sixth Amendment guarantee. The justification for this approach appears to be the difficulty of a *post-hoc* reconstruction of the record to determine whether a different outcome, or even a different defense strategy, might have obtained had the trial court engaged in the requisite inquiry and ordered separate representation. Although such difficulty may be taken into account in the allocation of the burden of persuasion on the questions of conflict and prejudice, I am not convinced of the need for a prophylactic gloss on the requirements of the Constitution in this area of criminal law. . . .

Several other aspects of the Court opinion suggest a rule of separate representation upon demand of defense counsel. The Court leaves little room for maneuver for a trial judge who seeks to inquire into the substantiality of the defense counsel's representations. Apparently, the trial judge must order separate representation unless the asserted risk of conflict "was too remote to warrant separate counsel," a formulation that suggests a minimal showing on the part of defense counsel. The Court also offers the view that defense counsel in this case could not be expected to make the kind of specific proffer that was present in *Glasser* because of "a risk of violating, by more disclosure, his duty of confidentiality to his clients." Although concededly not necessary to a decision in this case, the Court then states that the trial court's inquiry must be conducted "without improperly requiring disclosure of the confidential communications of the client." When these intimations are coupled with the Court's policy of automatic reversal, the path may have been cleared for potentially disruptive demands for separate counsel predicated solely on the representations of defense counsel.

II.

Recognition of the limits of this Court's role in adding protective layers to the requirements of the Constitution does not detract from the Sixth Amendment obligation to provide separate counsel upon a showing of reasonable probability of need. In my view, a proper accommodation of the interests of defendants in securing effective assistance of counsel and that of the State in avoiding the delay, potential for disruption and costs inherent in the appointment of multiple counsel,[2] can be achieved by means which sweep less broadly than the approach taken by the Court. I would follow the lead of the several Courts of Appeals that have recognized the trial court's duty of inquiry in joint representation cases without minimizing the constitutional predicate of "conflicting interests."

2. Each addition of a lawyer in the trial of multiple defendants presents increased opportunities for delay in setting the trial date, in disposing of pretrial motions, in selecting the jury, and in the conduct of the trial itself. Additional lawyers also may tend to enhance the possibility of trial errors. Moreover, in light of professional canons of ethics, cf. ABA, Code of Professional Responsibility, DR 5–105(D), . . . a rule requiring separate counsel virtually upon demand may disrupt the operation of public defender offices.

Ordinarily defense counsel has the obligation to raise objections to joint representation as early as possible before the commencement of the trial.[4] When such a motion is made, supported by a satisfactory proffer, the trial court is under a duty to conduct "the most careful inquiry to satisfy itself that no conflict of interest would be likely to result and that the parties involved had no valid objection." At that hearing, the burden is on defense counsel, because his clients are in possession of the relevant facts, to make a showing of a reasonable likelihood of conflict or prejudice. Upon such a showing, separate counsel should be appointed. "If the court has carried out this duty of inquiry, then to the extent a defendant later attacks his conviction on grounds of conflict of interest arising from joint representation he will bear a heavy burden indeed of persuading" the reviewing court "that he was, for that reason, deprived of a fair trial." If, however, a proper and timely motion is made, and no hearing is held, "the lack of satisfactory judicial inquiry shifts the burden of proof on the question of prejudice to the Government."

Since the trial judge in this case failed to inquire into the substantiality of defense counsel's representations, ... the burden shifted to the State to establish the improbability of conflict or prejudice. I agree that the State's burden is not met simply by the assertion that the defenses of petitioners were not mutually inconsistent, for that is not an infrequent consequence of improper joint representation. Nevertheless, the record must offer some basis for a reasonable inference that "conflicting interests" hampered a potentially effective defense. Because the State has demonstrated that such a basis cannot be found in the record of this case,[5] I would affirm the judgment of the Supreme Court of Arkansas.

NOTES

1. What is the trial judge's role in determining whether a conflict of interest will work to a defendant's detriment? See ABA, Standards Relating to the Administration of Criminal Justice—The Function of the Trial Judge § 3.4(b), at 171 (1974):

> "Whenever two or more defendants who have been jointly charged, or whose cases have been consolidated, are represented by the same attorney, the trial judge should inquire into potential conflicts which may jeopardize the right of each defendant to the fidelity of his counsel."

2. In Cuyler v. Sullivan, 446 U.S. 335, 100 S.Ct. 1708 (1980), the Court held that the Constitution does not require the trial judge to admonish defendants who have

4. Since a proper, timely objection was interposed in this case, there is no occasion to identify the circumstances which might trigger a duty of inquiry in the absence of such a motion.

Of course, a later motion may be appropriate if the conflict is not known or does not become apparent before trial proceeds. To guard against strategic disruption of the trial, however, the court may require a substantial showing of justification for such midtrial motions.

5. It is unlikely that separate counsel would have been able to develop an independent defense in this case because of the degree of overlap in the identification testimony by the State's witnesses and because of the consistency of the alibis advanced by petitioners. ... Moreover, petitioners do not argue in this Court that joint representation impeded effective cross-examination of the State's witnesses. In sum, this is not a case where an inquiry into the possibility of "conflicting interests" reasonably might have revealed a basis for separate representation.

the same lawyer as their codefendants of the right to separate representation. The Court noted that such warnings were a good idea and were scheduled to become mandatory in Federal District Courts under amendments to Federal Rule of Criminal Procedure 44(c), effective December 1, 1980. The Court also held that if a defendant has not complained of multiple representation in the trial court, he cannot later obtain relief based upon a claim of conflict unless he can demonstrate an actual conflict which adversely affected his interests. The Court added that once such a showing is made, the defendant need not demonstrate prejudice in order to gain relief.

Apparently the various federal circuits are unanimous in holding that a violation of Federal Rule 44(c), concerning the obligation of a United States District Court to warn jointly-represented defendants of their right to separate counsel, is not *per se* reversible error. See United States v. Crespo de Llano, 838 F.2d 1006 (9th Cir.1987).

In Hamilton v. Ford, 969 F.2d 1006 (11th Cir.1992), cert. denied, 507 U.S. 1000, 113 S.Ct. 1625 (1993), the Eleventh Circuit held that when defendants make timely objection to joint representation, they need not show actual conflict of interest to secure reversal of conviction on grounds of ineffective assistance of counsel when the trial court failed to adequately inquire into the basis of the objection. Such lack of action by the trial court is a failure to discharge the constitutional duty of the court to determine whether the defendants are receiving adequate assistance of counsel. The court reversed the felony-murder conviction, saying such action was "automatic" in such cases.

3. In People v. Macerola, 47 N.Y.2d 257, 417 N.Y.S.2d 908, 391 N.E.2d 990 (1979), two defendants, charged with burglary and assault, were jointly represented. In reversing the conviction, the majority held:

> "... we have charged the trial court, in cases where codefendants are represented by a single attorney, with the weighty responsibility of determining whether 'the defendant's decision to proceed with his attorney is an informed decision.' ... The rationale for imposing such duty is obvious. It is all too apparent that the respective interests of each defendant which must be zealously safeguarded are oftentimes at odds, making crucial decisions by defense counsel during the entire criminal proceeding all the more difficult, and, at times, precluding certain defense strategies. For example, an attorney may be less than willing to engage fervently in plea negotiations to obtain a lesser charge for one defendant if to do so would require that defendant to testify against the other defendants, or to call a defendant to testify on his own behalf when his testimony may be detrimental to other defendants whom the attorney represents.
>
> * * *
>
> "... [T]he record is devoid of any indication that the Trial Judge, by proper inquiry, took the necessary precautions to ensure that the defendants perceived the potential risks inherent in joint representation. Thus, because of this absence of a proper inquiry on the record, we are unable to ascertain whether the defendants' decision to proceed with their attorney was knowingly and intelligently made, or whether they merely acquiesced out of ignorance to their joint representation.
>
> * * *
>
> "In this case, the record reveals that there was indeed a conflict of interest which endangered each defendant's right to receive advice and assistance from an attorney whose paramount responsibility is to that

defendant alone. Defense counsel found himself in a very awkward position at trial in that by attempting to establish a separate defense for each defendant, he was, by implication, incriminating the other defendant. Thus, to establish [one's] defense to the assault charges, it was necessary for counsel to attribute the responsibility for the physical injuries to [the second defendant]. Further, to establish [the second's] defense to the burglary charge, defense counsel had to stress that only [the other defendant entered the place where the burglary was alleged to have occurred]."

JUDGE GABRIELLI dissented:

"The record in this case does not indicate that either defendant was in any way prejudiced by the joint representation. They merely intimate how their interests *might* have conflicted *if a different theory of defense was used*. This was not a case where a defendant testified and made statements shifting the blame to his codefendant. Nor is it a case where evidence was admissible against only one codefendant but was nevertheless not objected to on behalf of the other. Counsel was not precluded from cross-examining any defense witnesses because he was privy to their secrets. It is, pure and simple, a case where the defendants agreed totally on their story, so access to another attorney would not have changed matters.

* * *

"Mere speculation of what might have been is not enough. Actual, not imagined, conflict of interest must be shown before a defendant may successfully claim that he was denied the right to effective assistance of counsel."

4. With increased frequency prosecutors are filing motions to disqualify defense counsel, alleging a conflict of interest. This often happens while a case is under investigation and the prosecution is hoping to get one of an attorney's clients to testify against another of the same attorney's clients. On occasion it happens just before trial.

One court has warned against too-free disqualification of a defense lawyer initiated by a prosecutor who claims that a conflict may exist. See In re Special Investigation No. 231, 295 Md. 366, 455 A.2d 442 (1983). See also United States v. Curcio, 680 F.2d 881 (2d Cir.1982) (allowing joint representation despite conflict). Compare United States v. Flanagan, 679 F.2d 1072 (3d Cir.1982) (permitting disqualification). The Court of Appeals in *Flanagan* distinguished the question of whether an informed waiver would insulate a conviction from attack (it would), from the issue of whether an individual has the right to insist upon representation by a lawyer where a conflict exists or is very likely to arise. The Supreme Court granted certiorari but did not reach the substantive issues. Instead it held that the accused in the federal system has no statutory or constitutional right to an interlocutory appeal from a pre-trial order disqualifying counsel. His remedy is an appeal if he ultimately is convicted. Without resolving the issue, the Court left open the possibility that an improper disqualification of counsel of the defendant's choosing could constitute per se reversible error mandating a new trial without regard to the evidence or to the competence demonstrated by substitute defense counsel. 465 U.S. 259, 104 S.Ct. 1051 (1984).

5. A per se rule of reversal emerged from People v. Jackson, 167 Cal.App.3d 829, 213 Cal.Rptr. 521 (1985), where, without the defendant's knowledge, the defense lawyer at the time of trial had been dating the prosecutor. They had not been living together, but they continued to date regularly during the course of the trial.

6. Can a single attorney effectively represent co-defendants in a case where the prosecution seeks the death penalty? Are there any special problems for a single lawyer at the sentencing phase of a death case that are not present when one lawyer represents codefendants at a sentencing hearing in a non-death penalty case? For one view, see Fleming v. State, 246 Ga. 90, 270 S.E.2d 185 (1980), where the court used its supervisory powers to prevent multiple representation in a death penalty case.

7. Normally where one attorney is disqualified from representing clients with conflicting interests, the disqualification extends to other members of the attorney's firm. Several courts have held, however, that different assistant public defenders from a single office sometimes may separately represent clients with conflicting interests. The decisions are reviewed in State v. Rogers, 177 N.J.Super. 365, 426 A.2d 1035 (1981).

Courts are divided on whether an outside attorney must be called upon to replace an assistant public defender where a convicted defendant raises a colorable claim of ineffective assistance by a different assistant public defender from the same office. Compare McCall v. Twenty–First Judicial District Court (Mesa County), 783 P.2d 1223 (Colo.1989), with People v. Banks, 121 Ill.2d 36, 117 Ill.Dec. 266, 520 N.E.2d 617 (1987).

8. In Wood v. Georgia, 450 U.S. 261, 101 S.Ct. 1097 (1981), an attorney argued before the Supreme Court that it would be impermissible for his clients (employees of a book store who had been convicted on obscenity charges) to have their probation revoked for non-payment of a fine. The Court on its own initiative, on the peculiar facts of the case, determined that the attorney in the trial court *might* have been pursuing the interests of the employer to the detriment of the employees. It remanded for further proceedings.

9. One state has now provided that ordinarily separate counsel will be appointed in all instances involving multiple indigent defendants. See People v. Mroczko, 35 Cal.3d 86, 197 Cal.Rptr. 52, 672 P.2d 835 (1983).

10. In Burger v. Kemp, 483 U.S. 776, 107 S.Ct. 3114 (1987), two co-defendants were tried separately for capital crimes. The attorney for one defendant was the partner of the attorney for the co-defendant. The two lawyers cooperated with each other to some extent, although in the separate trials the defense sought to shift primary blame to the defendant who was not currently on trial. One of the attorneys had the primary role in preparing the appeal for both defendants. On that appeal, the defense dropped the tactic that earlier had seen each defendant blaming the other.

The Supreme Court held that even if the two partner attorneys be viewed as one, there is no presumption of a conflict, even in a capital case, simply because co-defendants receive joint representation. The Court examined the facts of the case and found no actual conflict. It rejected the notion that the defendant was deprived of an opportunity to offer cooperation to the State against his co-defendant in return for leniency. The record showed that the prosecutor from the outset had rebuffed all defense efforts to plea-bargain for something less than the death penalty. It also showed that the evidence was strong against each defendant, so that the prosecution did not need the cooperation of either defendant. The Court viewed the decision to abandon the blame-shifting tactic as reasonable on the facts that had been developed in a post-conviction evidentiary hearing.

11. In a 5–4 opinion, Mickens v. Taylor, 535 U.S. 162, 122 S.Ct. 1237 (2002) the Court addressed the question of what a defendant must show to demonstrate a Sixth Amendment violation in cases where the trial court fails to inquire into a potential conflict of interest about which it knew or reasonably should have known. The defendant had been convicted of premeditated murder and sentenced to death. Prior to the murder, the lead defense counsel had been appointed counsel for the murder victim on assault charges. The defense counsel did not reveal this to the court, his co-counsel or to the defendant. Federal habeas counsel discovered this information and alleged ineffective assistance of counsel based on the conflict.

In an opinion by Justice Scalia, the Court rejected a rule of automatic reversal where a conflict existed, but concluded that in this case, the trial judge did not make the necessary inquiry. Thus, the Court distinguished this case from Holloway v. Arkansas, 435 U.S. 475, 98 S.Ct. 1173 (1978). Instead, the defendant must show that the conflict of interest actually adversely affected his counsel's performance before a Sixth Amendment violation will be found when the trial court fails to make inquiry. The Court distinguished this from the inquiry required under Strickland, 466 U.S. 668, 104 S.Ct. 2052 (1984) where a defendant must establish "a reasonable probability that, but for counsel's unprofessional errors, the result of the proceeding would have been different."

Justice Stevens, joined by Justice Souter and Justice Breyer, issued a strong dissent emphasizing the defendant's constitutional right to the services of an attorney devoted solely to his interests. Justice Breyer, joined by Justice Ginsburg, emphasized that the Commonwealth created the conflict, and, as such, the error was of a greater magnitude and would diminish the public confidence in the criminal justice system.

Wheat v. United States

Supreme Court of the United States, 1988.
486 U.S. 153, 108 S.Ct. 1692.

■ CHIEF JUSTICE REHNQUIST delivered the opinion of the Court.

* * *

Petitioner Mark Wheat, along with numerous codefendants, was charged with participating in a far-flung drug distribution conspiracy....

Also charged in the conspiracy were Juvenal Gomez–Barajas and Javier Bravo, who were represented in their criminal proceedings by attorney Eugene Iredale. Gomez–Barajas was tried first and was acquitted on drug charges overlapping with those against petitioner. To avoid a second trial on other charges, however, Gomez–Barajas offered to plead guilty to tax evasion and illegal importation of merchandise. At the commencement of petitioner's trial, the District Court had not accepted the plea; he was thus free to withdraw his guilty plea and proceed to trial.

Bravo, evidently a lesser player in the conspiracy, decided to forgo trial and plead guilty to one count of transporting approximately 2400 pounds of marijuana from Los Angeles to a residence controlled by Victor Vidal. At the conclusion of Bravo's guilty plea proceedings on August 22, 1985, Iredale notified the District Court that he had been contacted by petitioner and had been asked to try petitioner's case as well. In response, the Government registered substantial concern about the possibility of conflict in there presentation. After entertaining some initial discussion of the substitution of counsel, the District Court instructed the parties to present more detailed arguments the following Monday, just one day before the scheduled start of petitioner's trial.

At the Monday hearing, the Government objected to petitioner's proposed substitution on the ground that Iredale's representation of Gomez–

Barajas and Bravo created a serious conflict of interest. The Government's position was premised on two possible conflicts. First, the District Court had not yet accepted the plea and sentencing arrangement negotiated between Gomez–Barajas and the Government; in the event that arrangement were rejected by the court, Gomez–Barajas would be free to withdraw the plea and stand trial. He would then be faced with the prospect of representation by Iredale, who in the meantime would have acted as petitioner's attorney. Petitioner, through his participation in the drug distribution scheme, was familiar with the sources and size of Gomez–Barajas' income, and was thus likely to be called as a witness for the Government at any subsequent trial of Gomez–Barajas. This scenario would pose a conflict of interest for Iredale, who would be prevented from cross-examining petitioner and thereby from effectively representing Gomez–Barajas.

Second, and of more immediate concern, Iredale's representation of Bravo would directly affect his ability to act as counsel for petitioner. The Government believed that a portion of the marijuana delivered by Bravo to Vidal's residence eventually was transferred to petitioner. In this regard, the Government contacted Iredale and asked that Bravo be made available as a witness to testify against petitioner, and agreed in exchange to modify its position at the time of Bravo's sentencing. In the likely event that Bravo were called to testify, Iredale's position in representing both men would become untenable, for ethical proscriptions would forbid him from cross-examining Bravo in any meaningful way. By failing to do so, he would also fail to provide petitioner with effective assistance of counsel. Thus, because of Iredale's prior representation of Gomez–Barajas and Bravo and the potential for serious conflict of interest, the Government urged the District Court to reject the substitution of attorneys.

In response, petitioner emphasized his right to have counsel of his own choosing and the willingness of Gomez–Barajas, Bravo, and petitioner to waive the right to conflict-free counsel. Petitioner argued that the circumstances posited by the Government that would create a conflict for Iredale were highly speculative and bore no connection to the true relationship between the co-conspirators. If called to testify, Bravo would simply say that he did not know petitioner and had no dealings with him; no attempt by Iredale to impeach Bravo would be necessary. Further, in the unlikely event that Gomez–Barajas went to trial on the charges of tax evasion and illegal importation, petitioner's lack of involvement in those alleged crimes made his appearance as a witness highly improbable. Finally, and most importantly, all three defendants agreed to allow Iredale to represent petitioner and to waive any future claims of conflict of interest. In petitioner's view, the Government was manufacturing implausible conflicts in an attempt to disqualify Iredale, who had already proved extremely effective in representing Gomez–Barajas and Bravo.

After hearing argument from each side, the District Court noted that it was unfortunate that petitioner had not suggested the substitution sooner, rather than two court days before the commencement of trial. The Court then ruled:

"[B]ased upon the representation of the Government in [its] memorandum that the Court really has no choice at this point other than to find that an irreconcilable conflict of interest exists. I don't think it can be waived, and accordingly, Mr. Wheat's request to substitute Mr. Iredale as attorney of record is denied."

Petitioner proceeded to trial with his original counsel and was convicted of conspiracy to possess more than 1000 pounds of marijuana with intent to distribute, in violation of 21 U.S.C. § 846, and five counts of possessing marijuana with intent to distribute, in violation of § 841(a)(1).

The Court of Appeals for the Ninth Circuit affirmed....

* * *

The Sixth Amendment right to choose one's own counsel is circumscribed in several important respects. Regardless of his persuasive powers, an advocate who is not a member of the bar may not represent clients (other than himself) in court.[3] Similarly, a defendant may not insist on representation by an attorney he cannot afford or who for other reasons declines to represent the defendant. Nor may a defendant insist on the counsel of an attorney who has a previous or ongoing relationship with an opposing party, even when the opposing party is the Government. The question raised in this case is the extent to which a criminal defendant's right under the Sixth Amendment to his chosen attorney is qualified by the fact that the attorney has represented other defendants charged in the same criminal conspiracy.

In previous cases, we have recognized that multiple representation of criminal defendants engenders special dangers of which a court must be aware.

* * *

Petitioner insists that the provision of waivers by all affected defendants cures any problems created by the multiple representation. But no such flat rule can be deduced from the Sixth Amendment presumption in favor of counsel of choice. Federal courts have an independent interest in ensuring that criminal trials are conducted within the ethical standards of the profession and that legal proceedings appear fair to all who observe them. Both the American Bar Association's Model Code of Professional Responsibility and its Model Rules of Professional Conduct, as well as the rules of the California Bar Association (which governed the attorneys in this case), impose limitations on multiple representation of clients. Not only the interest of a criminal defendant but the institutional interest in the rendition of just verdicts in criminal cases may be jeopardized by unregulated multiple representation.

For this reason, the Federal Rules of Criminal Procedure direct trial judges to investigate specially cases involving joint representation. In pertinent part, Rule 44(c) provides:

3. Our holding in Faretta v. California, 422 U.S. 806, 95 S.Ct. 2525 (1975), that a criminal defendant has a Sixth Amendment right to represent *himself* if he voluntarily elects to do so, does not encompass the right to choose any advocate if the defendant wishes to be represented by counsel.

> "[T]he court shall promptly inquire with respect to such joint representation and shall personally advise each defendant of his right to the effective assistance of counsel, including separate representation. Unless it appears that there is good cause to believe no conflict of interest is likely to arise, the court shall take such measures as may be appropriate to protect each defendant's right to counsel."
>
> Although Rule 44(c) does not specify what particular measures may be taken by a district court, one option suggested by the Notes of the Advisory Committee is an order by the court that the defendants be separately represented in subsequent proceedings in the case. This suggestion comports with our instructions in *Holloway* and in Glasser v. United States, 315 U.S. 60, 62 S.Ct. 457 (1942), that the trial courts, when alerted by objection from one of the parties, have an independent duty to ensure that criminal defendants receive a trial that is fair and does not contravene the Sixth Amendment.

To be sure, this need to investigate potential conflicts a rises in part from the legitimate wish of District Courts that their judgments remain intact on appeal. As the Court of Appeals accurately pointed out, trial courts confronted with multiple representations face the prospect of being "whipsawed" by assertions of error no matter which way they rule. If a district court agrees to the multiple representation, and the advocacy of counsel is thereafter impaired as a result, the defendant may well claim that he did not receive effective assistance. On the other hand, a district court's refusal to accede to the multiple representation may result in a challenge such as petitioner's in this case. Nor does a waiver by the defendant necessarily solve the problem, for we note, without passing judgment on, the apparent willingness of Courts of Appeals to entertain ineffective assistance claims from defendants who have specifically waived the right to conflict-free counsel....

Thus, where a court justifiably finds an actual conflict of interest, there can be no doubt that it may decline a proffer of waiver, and insist that defendants be separately represented. As the Court of Appeals for the Third Circuit stated in United States v. Dolan, 570 F.2d 1177, 1184 (C.A.31978):

> "[W]hen a trial court finds an actual conflict of interest which impairs the ability of a criminal defendant's chosen counsel to conform with the ABA Code of Professional Responsibility, the court should not be required to tolerate an inadequate representation of a defendant. Such representation not only constitutes a breach of professional ethics and invites disrespect for the integrity of the court, but it is also detrimental to the independent interest of the trial judge to be free from future attacks over the adequacy of the waiver or the fairness of the proceedings in his own court and the subtle problems implicating the defendant's comprehension of the waiver."

Unfortunately for all concerned, a district court must pass on the issue of whether or not to allow a waiver of a conflict of interest by a criminal defendant not with the wisdom of hindsight after the trial has taken place, but in the murkier pretrial context when relationships between parties are seen through a glass, darkly. The likelihood and dimensions of nascent conflicts of interest are notoriously hard to predict, even for those thoroughly familiar with criminal trials. It is a rare attorney who will be fortunate enough to learn the entire truth from his own client, much less be fully apprised before trial of what each of the Government's witnesses will say on the stand. A few bits of unforeseen testimony or a single previously unknown or unnoticed document may significantly shift the relationship between multiple defendants. These imponderables are difficult enough for a lawyer to assess, and even more difficult to convey by way of explanation to a criminal defendant untutored in the niceties of legal ethics. Nor is it amiss to observe that the willingness of an attorney to obtain such waivers from his clients may bear an inverse relation to the care with which he conveys all the necessary information to them.

For these reasons we think the District Court must be allowed substantial latitude in refusing waivers of conflicts of interest not only in those rare cases where an actual conflict may be demonstrated before trial, but in the more common cases where a potential for conflict exists which may or may not burgeon into an actual conflict as the trial progresses. In the circumstances of this case, with the motion for substitution of counsel made so close to the time of trial, the District Court relied on instinct and judgment based on experience in making its decision. We do not think it can be said that the court exceeded the broad latitude which must be accorded it in making this decision. Petitioner of course rightly points out that the government may seek to "manufacture" a conflict in order to prevent a defendant from having a particularly able defense counsel at his side; but trial courts are undoubtedly aware of this possibility, and must take it into consideration along with all of the other factors which inform this sort of a decision.

Here the District Court was confronted not simply with an attorney who wished to represent two coequal defendants in a straightforward criminal prosecution; rather, Iredale proposed to defend three conspirators of varying stature in a complex drug distribution scheme. The Government intended to call Bravo as a witness for the prosecution at petitioner's trial.[4] The Government might readily have tied certain deliveries of marijuana by Bravo to petitioner, necessitating vigorous cross-examination of Bravo by petitioner's counsel. Iredale, because of his prior representation of Bravo, would have been unable ethically to provide that cross-examination.

Iredale had also represented Gomez–Barajas, one of the alleged kingpins of the distribution ring, and had succeeded in obtaining a verdict of acquittal for him. Gomez–Barajas had agreed with the Government to plead guilty to other charges, but the District Court had not yet accepted the plea arrangement. If the agreement were rejected, petitioner's probable testimony at the resulting trial of Gomez–Barajas would create an ethical dilemma for Iredale from which one or the other of his clients would likely suffer.

4. Bravo was in fact called as a witness at petitioner's trial. His testimony was elicited to demonstrate the transportation of drugs that the prosecution hoped to link to petitioner.

Viewing the situation as it did before trial, we hold that the District Court's refusal to permit the substitution of counsel in this case was within its discretion and did not violate petitioner's Sixth Amendment rights. Other district courts might have reached differing or opposite conclusions with equal justification, but that does not mean that one conclusion was "right" and the other "wrong." The District Court must recognize a presumption in favor of petitioner's counsel of choice, but that presumption may be overcome not only by a demonstration of actual conflict but by a showing of a serious potential for conflict. The evaluation of the facts and circumstances of each case under this standard must be left primarily to the informed judgment of the trial court.

■ JUSTICE MARSHALL, with whom JUSTICE BRENNAN joins, dissenting.

This Court today concludes that the District Court did not commit reversible error by denying the motion of petitioner Mark Wheat to add or substitute counsel of his choice. In the course of discussing the District Court's ruling, the Court sets forth several principles with which I agree. The Court acknowledges, as it must, that the Sixth Amendment's guarantee of assistance of counsel comprehends the right to select one's own attorney. The Court also states that, although this constitutional right is not absolute, it mandates a presumption in favor of accepting a criminal defendant's choice of counsel. Having articulated these principles, however, the Court unaccountably grants broad discretion to the trial court to decide whether this presumption has been overcome. As a consequence of this unwarranted deference to a trial court's decision respecting a constitutional right, the Court countenances a ruling that is patently incorrect. Because I believe that the potential for a conflict of interest in this case did not overcome petitioner's right to choose his own counsel, I dissent.

* * *

I do disagree, however, with the Court's suggestion that the trial court's decision as to whether a potential conflict justifies rejection of a defendant's chosen counsel is entitled to some kind of special deference on appeal....

The trial court's decision as to whether the circumstances of a given case constitute grounds for rejecting a defendant's chosen counsel—that is, as to whether these circumstances present a substantial potential for a serious conflict of interest—is a mixed determination of law and fact. The decision is properly described in this way because it requires and results from the application of a legal standard to the established facts of a case. Appellate courts traditionally do not defer to such determinations. For this reason, the Court in Cuyler v. Sullivan, 446 U.S. 335, 100 S.Ct. 1708 (1980), held that a trial court's determination as to whether an attorney had represented conflicting interests at trial was not entitled to any deference. The determination at issue here, which focuses on the potential for a conflict of interest, is not different in any relevant respect.[2]

* * *

2. It is true that a trial court, in making a determination regarding the potential for a conflict of interest, must make a prediction as to future events, which frequently is a

... The propriety of the District Court's order thus depends on whether the Government showed that the particular facts and circumstances of the multiple representation proposed in this case were such as to overcome the presumption in favor of petitioner's choice of counsel. I believe it is clear that the Government failed to make this showing. Neither Eugene Iredale's representation of Juvenal Gomez–Barajas nor Iredale's representation of Javier Bravo posed any threat of causing a conflict of interest.

At the time of petitioner's trial, Iredale's representation of Gomez–Barajas was effectively completed. As the Court notes, Iredale had obtained an acquittal for Gomez–Barajas on charges relating to a conspiracy to distribute marijuana. Iredale also had negotiated an agreement with the Government under which Gomez–Barajas would plead guilty to charges of tax evasion and illegal importation of merchandise, although the trial court had not yet accepted this plea arrangement. Gomez–Barajas was not scheduled to appear as a witness at petitioner's trial; thus, Iredale's conduct of that trial would not require him to question his former client. The only possible conflict this Court can divine from Iredale's representation of both petitioner and Gomez–Barajas rests on the premise that the trial court would reject the negotiated plea agreement and that Gomez–Barajas then would decide to go to trial. In this event, the Court tells us, "petitioner's probable testimony at the resulting trial of Gomez–Barajas would create an ethical dilemma for Iredale."

This argument rests on speculation of the most dubious kind. The Court offers no reason to think that the trial court would have rejected Gomez–Barajas's plea agreement; neither did the Government posit any such reason in its argument or brief before this Court. The most likely occurrence at the time petitioner moved to retain Iredale as his defense counsel was that the trial court would accept Gomez–Barajas's plea agreement, as the court in fact later did. Moreover, even if Gomez–Barajas had gone to trial, petitioner probably would not have testified. The record contains no indication that petitioner had any involvement in or information about crimes for which Gomez–Barajas might yet have stood trial. The only alleged connection between petitioner and Gomez–Barajas sprang from the conspiracy to distribute marijuana, and a jury already had acquitted Gomez–Barajas of that charge. It is therefore disingenuous to say that representation of both petitioner and Gomez–Barajas posed a serious potential for a conflict of interest.

Similarly, Iredale's prior representation of Bravo was not a cause for concern. The Court notes that the prosecution intended to call Bravo to the stand at petitioner's trial and asserts that Bravo's testimony could well have "necessitat[ed] vigorous cross-examination ... by petitioner's coun-

difficult task. This aspect of the decision, however, does not call for a lax standard of review. The question on review is whether the trial court was correct in holding that the facts and circumstances apparent *at the time of its decision* demonstrated a substantial potential for a serious conflict of interest. Appellate courts are fully capable of posing and resolving this question. A deferential standard of review therefore is not necessary to generate appellate decisions that take into account and appropriately reflect the uncertainties existing at the time of the trial court's ruling.

sel." The facts, however, belie the claim that Bravo's anticipated testimony created a serious potential for conflict. Contrary to the Court's inference, Bravo could not have testified about petitioner's involvement in the alleged marijuana distribution scheme. As all parties were aware at the time, Bravo did not know and could not identify petitioner; indeed, prior to the commencement of legal proceedings, the two men never had heard of each other. Bravo's eventual testimony at petitioner's trial related to a shipment of marijuana in which petitioner was not involved; the testimony contained not a single reference to petitioner. Petitioner's counsel did not cross-examine Bravo, and neither petitioner's counsel nor the prosecutor mentioned Bravo's testimony in closing argument. All of these developments were predictable when the District Court ruled on petitioner's request that Iredale serve as trial counsel; the contours of Bravo's testimony were clear at that time. Given the insignificance of this testimony to any matter that petitioner's counsel would dispute, the proposed joint representation of petitioner and Bravo did not threaten a conflict of interest.[3]

Moreover, even assuming that Bravo's testimony might have "necessitat[ed] vigorous cross-examination," the District Court could have insured against the possibility of any conflict of interest without wholly depriving petitioner of his constitutional right to the counsel of his choice. Petitioner's motion requested that Iredale either be substituted for petitioner's current counsel or be added to petitioner's defense team. Had the District Court allowed the addition of Iredale and then ordered that he take no part in the cross-examination of Bravo, any possibility of a conflict would have been removed. Especially in light of the availability of this precautionary measure, the notion that Iredale's prior representation of Bravo might well have caused a conflict of interest at petitioner's trial is nothing short of ludicrous.

The Court gives short shrift to the actual circumstances of this case in upholding the decision below. These circumstances show that the District

3. The very insignificance of Bravo's testimony, combined with the timing of the prosecutor's decision to call Bravo as a witness, raises a serious concern that the prosecutor attempted to manufacture a conflict in this case. The prosecutor's decision to use Bravo as a witness was an 11th–hour development. Throughout the course of plea negotiations with Bravo, the prosecutor never had suggested that Bravo testify at petitioner's trial. At Bravo's guilty-plea proceedings, when Iredale notified the District Court of petitioner's substitution motion, the prosecutor conceded that he had made no plans to call Bravo as a witness. Only after the prosecutor learned of the substitution motion and decided to oppose it did he arrange for Bravo's testimony by agreeing to recommend to the trial court a reduction in Bravo's sentence. Especially in light of the scarce value of Bravo's testimony, this prosecutorial behavior very plausibly may be viewed as a maneuver to prevent Iredale from representing petitioner at trial. Iredale had proved to be a formidable adversary; he previously had gained an acquittal for the alleged kingpin of the marijuana distribution scheme. As the District Court stated in considering petitioner's motion, "Were I in [petitioner's] position I'm sure I would want Mr. Iredale representing me, too. He did a fantastic job in that [Gomez–Barajas] trial...." The prosecutor's decision to call Bravo as a witness may well have stemmed from a concern that Iredale would do an equally fantastic job at petitioner's trial. As the Court notes, governmental maneuvering of this kind is relevant to a trial court's decision as to whether to accept a criminal defendant's chosen counsel. The significant possibility that the prosecutor was engaging in such bad-faith conduct provides yet another reason to dispute the Court's resolution of this case.

Court erred in denying petitioner's motion to substitute or add Iredale as defense counsel. The proposed representation did not pose a substantial risk of a serious conflict of interest. The District Court therefore had no authority to deny petitioner's Sixth Amendment right to retain counsel of his choice. This constitutional error demands that petitioner's conviction be reversed. I accordingly dissent.

■ JUSTICE STEVENS, with whom JUSTICE BLACKMUN joins, dissenting.

... But even under the Court's paternalistic view of the citizen's right to select his or her own lawyer, its analysis of this case is seriously flawed. As Justice Marshall demonstrates, the Court exaggerates the significance of the potential conflict. Of greater importance, the Court gives inadequate weight to the informed and voluntary character of the clients' waiver of their right to conflict-free representation. Particularly, the Court virtually ignores the fact that additional counsel representing petitioner had provided him with sound advice concerning the wisdom of a waiver and would have remained available during the trial to assist in the defense. Thus, this is not the case in which the District Judge faced the question whether one counsel should be substituted for another; rather the question before him was whether petitioner should be permitted to have *additional* counsel of his choice. I agree with Justice Marshall that the answer to that question is perfectly clear.

Accordingly, although I agree with the Court's premise that district judges must be afforded wide latitude in passing on motions of this kind;* in this case it is abundantly clear to me that the District Judge abused his discretion and deprived this petitioner of a constitutional right of such fundamental character that reversal is required.

NOTES

1. Where a reviewing court rules that the trial court impermissibly disqualified counsel of the defendant's choice, should it deem the error per se reversible? Or should it examine the quality of the performance of the attorney who substituted for the disqualified lawyer? Is there anything left of the right to counsel of one's choice if, in order to prevail, an appellant must demonstrate that substitute counsel was incompetent? Or is it improper to look at the issue solely from an appellate perspective, without assuming that most trial judges will deny a defendant counsel of his or her choice only where disqualification is constitutionally permissible? In United States v. Diozzi, 807 F.2d 10 (1st Cir.1986), the court held that when the trial court, over defense objection, improperly disqualifies counsel of the defendant's choice, the prosecution will not be heard to argue that new counsel performed satisfactorily so that the error was harmless.

2. Many prosecutorial efforts to disqualify attorneys occur at the stage of a grand jury investigation. The Sixth Amendment right to counsel has not attached at that stage because formal adversary judicial proceedings have not yet commenced. Nevertheless some reviewing courts have used *Wheat* as a standard in determining

* In my view, deference to the trial judge is appropriate in light of his or her greater familiarity with such factors as the ability of the defendant knowingly and voluntarily to waive a potential conflict (including the possibility that a codefendant may be exerting undue influence over the defendant), the character of the lawyers, the particular facts of the case, and the availability of alternative counsel of a like caliber.

counsel-disqualification issues at the investigatory stage. See In re Grand Jury Proceedings, Appeal of John Doe, 859 F.2d 1021 (1st Cir.1988).

C. THE RIGHT OF SELF-REPRESENTATION

Although courts ordinarily are obligated to ensure an accused competent representation (however that term be defined), the Supreme Court has held that a defendant has a right to represent himself or herself in a criminal prosecution. Faretta v. California, 422 U.S. 806, 95 S.Ct. 2525 (1975). Recently the Court held that the presence of standby counsel did not interfere with this right of self-representation where the defendant was allowed to control the defense. The error, if any, was harmless. McKaskle v. Wiggins, 465 U.S. 168, 104 S.Ct. 944 (1984).

The *McKaskle* issue is to be carefully distinguished from the question of whether appointment of counsel (and the denial of self-representation) over the objections of a defendant who has been advised of his right to counsel and has made a knowing waiver, can ever be deemed harmless error. Ordinarily, it will be impossible to prove that the appointment of counsel harmed the accused's chance of acquittal. *Faretta*, however, is designed to protect values that are largely unrelated to affording the accused a fair trial. *Faretta* heavily emphasizes recognition of an individual's autonomy.

On the other hand, most decisions hold that a defendant who chooses to represent himself does not have a right to the appointment of an attorney to assist him in representing himself. He must choose between self-representation and representation by an attorney. The latter contemplates that counsel will have the final word on most matters of strategy. See, e.g., People v. Williams, 97 Ill.2d 252, 73 Ill.Dec. 360, 454 N.E.2d 220 (1983).

Does a defendant who exercises his right to defend himself have a Sixth Amendment right to change his mind mid-trial? Does it matter whether "stand-by" counsel has been present to assist the pro se defendant, and so is familiar with what has transpired at trial? What if the defendant changes his mind after trial but before a separate sentencing hearing? See Grandison v. Maryland, 479 U.S. 873, 107 S.Ct. 38 (1986) (Marshall, J., dissenting from denial of certiorari).

In Martinez v. Court of Appeal of California, 528 U.S. 152, 120 S.Ct. 684 (2000), the court held that the right to self-representation does not extend to proceedings on appeal. Because there was no right to appeal criminal judgments at common law and the right is strictly a statutory creation, the constitutional considerations present in Faretta did not apply. Moreover, "[t]he status of the accused defendant, who retains a presumption of innocence throughout the trial process, changes dramatically when a jury returns a guilty verdict." Although the right to self-representation on appeal was not compelled, the court noted that the states are free to recognize such a right.

NOTE

1. What if a decision to represent oneself is not only figuratively suicidal, it is literally suicidal?

In the "Unabomber" case, United States v. Kaczynski, 239 F.3d 1108 (9th Cir.2001) the defendant sought to vacate his pleas of guilty on the ground that the made them because his counsel intended to present evidence of his abnormal mental condition at trial. This tactic went against his express wishes. During jury selection, he sought (in fits and starts) to proceed as his own counsel. The trial court refused on the ground that permitting him to do so would forego "the only defense that is likely to prevent his conviction and execution." To forfend evidence of a serious mental illness, he plead guilty in exchange for a prosecution withdrawal of its request for the death penalty. The plea, he said, was involuntary because it was precipitated by a wrongful denial of his right to defend himself. The trial court and a majority of the Court of Appeals refused to vacate the pleas because (1) the defendant had declared in open court that his plea was voluntary, (2) the plea was rationale, and (3) the request to represent himself was made "as a tactic to delay trial proceedings so the denial of the request was not wrongful."

Consider the dissent of Judge Reinhardt:

> "The case of Ted Kaczynski not only brings together a host of legal issues basic to our system of justice, it also presents a compelling individual problem: what should be the fate of a man, undoubtedly learned and brilliant, who determines, on the basis of a pattern of reasoning that can only be described as perverse, that in order to save society he must commit a series of horrendous crimes? What is the proper response of the legal system when such an individual demands that he be allowed to offer those perverse theories to a jury as his only defense in a capital case—a defense that obviously has no legal merit and certainly has no chance of success? What should the response be when he also insists on serving as his own lawyer, not for the purpose of pursuing a proper legal defense, but in order to ensure that no evidence will be presented that exposes the nature and extent of his mental problems? The district judge faced these questions and, understandably, blinked. He quite clearly did so out of compassionate and humanitarian concerns. Nevertheless, in denying Kaczynski's request to represent himself, the district court unquestionably failed to follow the law. Notwithstanding the majority's arguments in defense of the district judge's actions, they simply cannot be supported on the ground he offered, or on any other ground available under the law as it now stands....
>
> Kaczynski maintains that from December 22 through January 4, he believed that (1) his attorneys would not be permitted to introduce any mental-state evidence during the guilt phase of his trial, and (2) attorney J. Tony Serra—who had written to Kaczynski and offered to represent him without employing a mental-health defense but had subsequently withdrawn the offer of representation—was unwilling to serve as his counsel at trial. Kaczynski first learned of his attorneys' intention to present non-expert mental-state testimony at the guilt phase of his trial on the evening of January 4, 1998—the day before trial was to begin. Denvir and Clarke visited him at the jail that evening and read him their opening statement. Kaczynski declares that he was "horrified to learn that his attorneys planned to present extensive nonexpert evidence of severe mental illness in the guilt phase."
>
> On the morning of January 5, Kaczynski informed Judge Burrell of his continuing conflict with counsel, and the judge appointed attorney Kevin

Clymo as "conflicts counsel" to represent Kaczynski's interests. Proceedings were postponed until January 7. On that day, Judge Burrell ruled that Kaczynski's counsel could present mental-state testimony even if Kaczynski objected. Judge Burrell then offered Kaczynski the option of self-representation, warning: "I don't advise it, but if you want to, I've got to give you certain rights." At the time of the court's offer, Kaczynski declined to accept it, explaining that he was "too tired . . . [to] take on such a difficult task," and that he did not feel "up to taking that challenge at the moment." . . .

On January 8, Kaczynski decided to accept the court's offer of the previous day and informed the court that he wished to represent himself. Kaczynski's counsel conveyed his request to the court with great reluctance:

Your Honor, if I may address the Court, Mr. Kaczynski had a request that we alert the Court to, on his behalf—it is his request that he be permitted to proceed in this case as his own counsel. This is a very difficult position for him. He believes that he has no choice but to go forward as his own lawyer. It is a very heartfelt reaction, I believe, to the presentation of a mental illness defense, a situation in which he simply cannot endure. Kaczynski's attorneys made clear that he was not seeking any delay in proceedings and that he was prepared to proceed pro se immediately. On that day, as before, Judge Burrell did not intimate that he perceived any bad-faith motive on Kaczynski's part. To the contrary, he made numerous comments demonstrating his belief that Kaczynski sought self-representation solely because of the conflict over control of the mental-health defense—in other words, solely because of his desire to prevent the introduction of evidence regarding his mental health. . . .

[In response to defendant's request, the trial court ordered an examination to determine whether he was competent to waive his right to counsel. The examiners concluded he was.]

It stretches the imagination to believe that at some point during the two weeks in which Kaczynski was undergoing mental competency tests, initially suggested by Judge Burrell, the judge suddenly came to believe that he had been hoodwinked by Kaczynski from the start. Rather, as some of his later comments on the subject indicate (e.g., the trial would become a "suicide forum"), Judge Burrell became more and more appalled at the grotesque and one-sided spectacle over which he would be forced to preside were Kaczynski to conduct his own defense. He understandably developed a strong desire to avoid the chaos, legal and otherwise, that would have ensued had Kaczynski been allowed to present his twisted theories to a jury as his defense to a capital murder charge. Not only would such a trial have had a circus atmosphere but, in light of Kaczynski's aversion to mitigating evidence, it would in all likelihood have resulted in his execution. It is not difficult to appreciate, therefore, how the denial of Kaczynski's request for self-representation—regardless of the unquestionable legitimacy of the request—must have seemed the lesser evil. . . .

There can be no doubt that Judge Burrell's admirable desire to prevent an uncounseled, and seriously disturbed, defendant from confronting, on his own, the "prosecutorial forces of organized society"—in this case, three experienced federal prosecutors aggressively seeking that defendant's execution—lay at the heart of his denial of Kaczynski's request for self-representation. A fair reading of the record provides no support for the finding that Kaczynski's purpose was delay. Instead, it leads to the inexorable conclusion that Kaczynski requested self-representation on January 8, 1998, not because he wished to manipulate the trial process, but because Judge Burrell's rulings of the previous day had ensured that his lawyers would present the mental-health defense that he found so abhorrent. Yet it is easy to appreciate why, as one commentator has suggested, "[t]he judicial system breathed a collective sigh of relief when the Unabomber pled guilty." Indeed, all the players in this unfortunate drama—all except Kaczynski, that is—had reason to celebrate Kaczynski's unconditional guilty plea. His attorneys had achieved their principal and worthy objective by preventing his execution. The government had been spared the awkwardness of pitting three experienced prosecutors against an untrained, and mentally unsound, defendant, and conducting an execution following a trial that lacked the fundamental elements of due process at best, and was farcical at worst. Judge Burrell, as noted, had narrowly avoided having to preside over such a debacle and to impose a death penalty he would have considered improper in the absence of a fair trial. It is no wonder that today's majority is not eager to disturb so delicate a balance.

The problem with this "happy" solution, of course, is that it violates the core principle of Faretta v. California—a defendant who objects to his counsel's strategic choices has the option of going to trial alone. Personally, I believe that the right of self-representation should in some instances yield to the more fundamental constitutional guarantee of a fair trial. Here, the district court understood that giving effect to Faretta's guarantee would likely result in a proceeding that was fundamentally unfair. However, Faretta does not permit the courts to take account of such considerations. Under the law as it now stands, there was no legitimate basis for denying Kaczynski the right to be his own lawyer in his capital murder trial."

CHAPTER 19

PRESENTING THE CASE—PROBLEMS ENCOUNTERED

A. GETTING THE EVIDENCE BEFORE THE TRIER OF FACTS

Introduction

A problem common to all who defend or prosecute is a material witness who is unavailable to whoever needs the witness's evidence. A witness might be deceased or otherwise beyond the reach of a court order. The witness might be unwilling to testify and able to assert privilege to refuse to testify, or, if willing, unable to testify because legal privilege bars the witness from telling what he knows. Or the witness may have lost memory. The witness may have changed his or her testimony over time for reasons which might be good or bad.

The next best thing for a lawyer who can no longer get that desired testimony at trial is to introduce the witness's prior statements into evidence. The rules of hearsay and the Confrontation Clause of the Constitution will govern the lawyer's ability to do so. The courts have especially struggled with this issue over the last over the past forty years.

In 2004, the Supreme Court made a major change in its doctrine in Crawford v. Washington. Just before its decision the landmarks were these. Pointer v. Texas, 380 U.S. 400, 85 S.Ct. 1065 (1965) held that testimony of a missing witness given at a preliminary hearing could not be introduced against Pointer, who had no counsel at the hearing, had no effective opportunity to cross-examine (and thus confront) the victim of the charged offense. When prior cross-examination was adequate, the prior testimony was admissible. Mancusi v. Stubbs, 408 U.S. 204, 92 S.Ct. 2308 (1972) (testimony at first trial). Ohio v. Roberts, 448 U.S. 56, 100 S.Ct. 2531 (1980) held that the preliminary hearing testimony of a *defense* witness—surprisingly damaging testimony—whom the prosecutor did not cross-examine was admissible because it bore "particularized guarantees of trustworthiness" which was the applicable standard when the evidence did not fall under a "firmly rooted hearsay exception." United States v. Owens, 484 U.S. 554, 108 S.Ct. 838 (1988) allowed evidence that the victim of a crime had identified his attacker by name and by photographic array although he had no memory of defendant attacking him.*

* The Court's opinion noted that it was adopting the view that what is guaranteed is " 'an *opportunity* for effective cross-examination, not [one] that is effective in whatever way and to whatever extent, the defense might wish' . . . the opportunity is not denied when a witness testifies as to his current belief but is unable to recollect the reason for that belief. It is sufficient that the defendant has the opportunity to bring out such mat-

1. The Confrontation Clause and Its General Application

Crawford v. Washington

Supreme Court of the United States, 2004.
541 U.S. 36, 124 S.Ct. 1354.

■ Justice Scalia delivered the opinion of the Court.

Petitioner Michael Crawford stabbed a man who allegedly tried to rape his wife, Sylvia. At his trial, the State played for the jury Sylvia's tape-recorded statement to the police describing the stabbing, even though he had no opportunity for cross-examination. The Washington Supreme Court upheld petitioner's conviction after determining that Sylvia's statement was reliable....

* * *

The State charged petitioner with assault and attempted murder. At trial, he claimed self-defense. Sylvia did not testify because of the state marital privilege, which generally bars a spouse from testifying without the other spouse's consent. In Washington, this privilege does not extend to a spouse's out-of-court statements admissible under a hearsay exception, so the State sought to introduce Sylvia's tape-recorded statements to the police as evidence that the stabbing was not in self-defense. Noting that Sylvia had admitted she led petitioner to Lee's apartment and thus had facilitated the assault, the State invoked the hearsay exception for statements against penal interest, Wash. Rule Evid. 804(b)(3) (2003).

* * *

II

Ohio v. Roberts says that an unavailable witness's out-of-court statement may be admitted so long as it has adequate indicia of reliability *i.e.*, falls within a "firmly rooted hearsay exception" or bears "particularized guarantees of trustworthiness." Petitioner argues that this test strays from the original meaning of the Confrontation Clause and urges us to reconsider it.

The Constitution's text does not alone resolve this case. One could plausibly read "witnesses against" a defendant to mean those who actually testify at trial, cf. *Woodsides v. State*, 3 Miss. 655, 664665 (1837), those whose statements are offered at trial, see 3 J. Wigmore, Evidence 1397, p. 104 (2d ed.1923) (hereinafter Wigmore), or something in-between. We must therefore turn to the historical background of the Clause to understand its meaning.

* * *

ters as the witness's bias, his lack of care and attentiveness, his poor eyesight, and even (what is often a prime objective of cross-examination) the very fact that he has a bad memory."

III

History supports two inferences about the meaning of the Sixth Amendment.

First, the principal evil at which the Confrontation Clause was directed was the civil-law mode of criminal procedure, and particularly its use of *ex parte* examinations as evidence against the accused. It was these practices that the Crown deployed in notorious treason cases like Raleigh's; that the Marian statutes invited; that English law's assertion of a right to confrontation was meant to prohibit; and that the founding-era rhetoric decried. . . .

Accordingly, we once again reject the view that the Confrontation Clause applies of its own force only to in-court testimony, and that its application to out-of-court statements introduced at trial depends upon "the law of Evidence for the time being." 3 Wigmore § 1397, at 101. Leaving the regulation of out-of-court statements to the law of evidence would render the Confrontation Clause powerless to prevent even the most flagrant inquisitorial practices. . . .

* * *

The text of the Confrontation Clause reflects this focus. It applies to "witnesses" against the accused—in other words, those who "bear testimony." 1 N. Webster, An American Dictionary of the English Language (1828). "Testimony," in turn, is typically "[a] solemn declaration or affirmation made for the purpose of establishing or proving some fact." *Ibid.* An accuser who makes a formal statement to government officers bears testimony in a sense that a person who makes a casual remark to an acquaintance does not. The constitutional text, like the history underlying the common-law right of confrontation, thus reflects an especially acute concern with a specific type of out-of-court statement.

* * *

Statements taken by police officers in the course of interrogations are also testimonial under even a narrow standard. . . .

* * *

The historical record also supports a second proposition: that the Framers would not have allowed admission of testimonial statements of a witness who did not appear at trial unless he was unavailable to testify, and the defendant had had a prior opportunity for cross-examination. The text of the Sixth Amendment does not suggest any open-ended exceptions from the confrontation requirement to be developed by the courts. Rather, the "right . . . to be confronted with the witnesses against him," Amdt. 6, is most naturally read as a reference to the right of confrontation at common law, admitting only those exceptions established at the time of the founding. See *Mattox v. United States*, 156 U.S. 237, 243, 15 S.Ct. 337, 39 L.Ed. 409 (1895). . . .

We do not read the historical sources to say that a prior opportunity to cross-examine was merely a sufficient, rather than a necessary, condition for admissibility of testimonial statements. They suggest that this requirement was dispositive, and not merely one of several ways to establish reliability. This is not to deny, as THE CHIEF JUSTICE notes, that "[t]here were always exceptions to the general rule of exclusion" of hearsay evidence. Several had become well established by 1791. See 3 Wigmore § 1397, at 101. But there is scant evidence that exceptions were invoked to admit *testimonial* statements against the accused in a *criminal* case. Most of the hearsay exceptions covered statements that by their nature were not testimonial—for example, business records or statements in furtherance of a conspiracy. We do not infer from these that the Framers thought exceptions would apply even to prior testimony. Cf. *Lilly v. Virginia*, 527 U.S. 116, 134, 119 S.Ct. 1887, 144 L.Ed.2d 117 (1999) (plurality opinion) ("[A]ccomplices' confessions that inculpate a criminal defendant are not within a firmly rooted exception to the hearsay rule").

* * *

Even our recent cases, in their outcomes, hew closely to the traditional line. *Ohio v. Roberts*, ..., admitted testimony from a preliminary hearing at which the defendant had examined the witness. *Lilly v. Virginia*, *supra*, excluded testimonial statements that the defendant had had no opportunity to test by cross-examination....

V

Although the results of our decisions have generally been faithful to the original meaning of the Confrontation Clause, the same cannot be said of our rationales. *Roberts* conditions the admissibility of all hearsay evidence on whether it falls under a "firmly rooted hearsay exception" or bears "particularized guarantees of trustworthiness." ... This test departs from the historical principles identified above in two respects. First, it is too broad: It applies the same mode of analysis whether or not the hearsay consists of *ex parte* testimony. This often results in close constitutional scrutiny in cases that are far removed from the core concerns of the Clause. At the same time, however, the test is too narrow: It admits statements that *do* consist of *ex parte* testimony upon a mere finding of reliability. This malleable standard often fails to protect against paradigmatic confrontation violations.

* * *

Where testimonial statements are involved, we do not think the Framers meant to leave the Sixth Amendment's protection to the vagaries of the rules of evidence, much less to amorphous notions of "reliability." Certainly none of the authorities discussed above acknowledges any general reliability exception to the common-law rule. Admitting statements deemed reliable by a judge is fundamentally at odds with the right of confrontation. To be sure, the Clause's ultimate goal is to ensure reliability of evidence, but it is a procedural rather than a substantive guarantee. It commands, not that evidence be reliable, but that reliability be assessed in a particular manner: by testing in the crucible of cross-examination. The Clause thus reflects a judgment, not only about the desirability of reliable evidence (a point on which there could be little dissent), but about how reliability can best be determined....

The *Roberts* test allows a jury to hear evidence, untested by the adversary process, based on a mere judicial determination of reliability. It thus replaces the constitutionally prescribed method of assessing reliability with a wholly foreign one. In this respect, it is very different from exceptions to the Confrontation Clause that make no claim to be a surrogate means of assessing reliability....

* * *

Dispensing with confrontation because testimony is obviously reliable is akin to dispensing with jury trial because a defendant is obviously guilty. This is not what the Sixth Amendment prescribes.

B

The legacy of *Roberts* in other courts vindicates the Framers' wisdom in rejecting a general reliability exception. The framework is so unpredictable that it fails to provide meaningful protection from even core confrontation violations.

Reliability is an amorphous, if not entirely subjective, concept. There are countless factors bearing on whether a statement is reliable; the nine-factor balancing test applied by the Court of Appeals below is representative. See, *e.g.*, *People v. Farrell*, 34 P.3d 401, 406–407 (Colo.2001) (eight-factor test). Whether a statement is deemed reliable depends heavily on which factors the judge considers and how much weight he accords each of them. Some courts wind up attaching the same significance to opposite facts. For example, the Colorado Supreme Court held a statement more reliable because its inculpation of the defendant was "detailed," *id.*, at 407, while the Fourth Circuit found a statement more reliable because the portion implicating another was "fleeting," *United States v. Photogrammetric Data Servs., Inc.*, 259 F.3d 229, 245 (C.A.4 2001). The Virginia Court of Appeals found a statement more reliable because the witness was in custody and charged with a crime (thus making the statement more obviously against her penal interest), see *Nowlin v. Commonwealth*, 40 Va.App. 327, 335–338, 579 S.E.2d 367, 371–372 (2003), while the Wisconsin Court of Appeals found a statement more reliable because the witness was *not* in custody and *not* a suspect, see *State v. Bintz*, 2002 WI App. 204, ¶ 13, 257 Wis.2d 177, 187, 650 N.W.2d 913, 918. Finally, the Colorado Supreme Court in one case found a statement more reliable because it was given "immediately after" the events at issue, *Farrell*, *supra*, at 407, while that same court, in another case, found a statement more reliable because two years had elapsed, *Stevens v. People*, 29 P.3d 305, 316 (Colo.2001).

The unpardonable vice of the *Roberts* test, however, is not its unpredictability, but its demonstrated capacity to admit core testimonial statements that the Confrontation Clause plainly meant to exclude. Despite the plurality's speculation in *Lilly*, 527 U.S., at 137, 119 S.Ct. 1887, that it was "highly unlikely" that accomplice confessions implicating the accused could survive *Roberts*, courts continue routinely to admit them.... One recent study found that, after *Lilly*, appellate courts admitted accomplice statements to the authorities in 25 out of 70 cases—more than one-third of the time. Kirst, Appellate Court Answers to the Confrontation Questions in

Lilly v. Virginia, 53 Syracuse L.Rev. 87, 105 (2003). Courts have invoked *Roberts* to admit other sorts of plainly testimonial statements despite the absence of any opportunity to cross-examine.

To add insult to injury, some of the courts that admit untested testimonial statements find reliability in the very factors that *make* the statements testimonial.... One court relied on the fact that the witness's statement was made to police while in custody on pending charges—the theory being that this made the statement more clearly against penal interest and thus more reliable. Other courts routinely rely on the fact that a prior statement is given under oath in judicial proceedings. That inculpating statements are given in a testimonial setting is not an antidote to the confrontation problem, but rather the trigger that makes the Clause's demands most urgent. It is not enough to point out that most of the usual safeguards of the adversary process attend the statement, when the single safeguard missing is the one the Confrontation Clause demands.

Roberts' failings were on full display in the proceedings below. Sylvia Crawford made her statement while in police custody, herself a potential suspect in the case. Indeed, she had been told that whether she would be released "depend[ed] on how the investigation continues." In response to often leading questions from police detectives, she implicated her husband in Lee's stabbing and at least arguably undermined his self-defense claim. Despite all this, the trial court admitted her statement, listing several reasons why it was reliable. In its opinion reversing, the Court of Appeals listed several *other* reasons why the statement was *not* reliable. Finally, the State Supreme Court relied exclusively on the interlocking character of the statement and disregarded every other factor the lower courts had considered. The case is thus a self-contained demonstration of *Roberts'* unpredictable and inconsistent application.

Each of the courts also made assumptions that cross-examination might well have undermined. The trial court, for example, stated that Sylvia Crawford's statement was reliable because she was an eyewitness with direct knowledge of the events. But Sylvia at one point told the police that she had "shut [her] eyes and ... didn't really watch" part of the fight, and that she was "in shock." The trial court also buttressed its reliability finding by claiming that Sylvia was "being questioned by law enforcement, and, thus, the [questioner] is ... neutral to her and not someone who would be inclined to advance her interests and shade her version of the truth unfavorably toward the defendant." The Framers would be astounded to learn that *ex parte* testimony could be admitted against a criminal defendant because it was elicited by "neutral" government officers. But even if the court's assessment of the officer's motives was accurate, it says nothing about Sylvia's perception of her situation. Only cross-examination could reveal that.

* * *

We readily concede that we could resolve this case by simply reweighing the "reliability factors" under *Roberts* and finding that Sylvia Crawford's statement falls short. But we view this as one of those rare cases in which the result below is so improbable that it reveals a fundamental failure on our part to interpret the Constitution in a way that secures its intended constraint on judicial discretion. Moreover, to reverse the Washington Supreme Court's decision after conducting our own reliability analysis would perpetuate, not avoid, what the Sixth Amendment condemns. The Constitution prescribes a procedure for determining the reliability of testimony in criminal trials, and we, no less than the state courts, lack authority to replace it with one of our own devising.

We have no doubt that the courts below were acting in utmost good faith when they found reliability. The Framers, however, would not have been content to indulge this assumption. They knew that judges, like other government officers, could not always be trusted to safeguard the rights of the people; the likes of the dread Lord Jeffreys were not yet too distant a memory. They were loath to leave too much discretion in judicial hands. Cf. U.S. Const., Amdt. 6 (criminal jury trial); Amdt. 7 (civil jury trial); By replacing categorical constitutional guarantees with open-ended balancing tests, we do violence to their design. Vague standards are manipulable, and, while that might be a small concern in run-of-the-mill assault prosecutions like this one, the Framers had an eye toward politically charged cases like Raleigh's—great state trials where the impartiality of even those at the highest levels of the judiciary might not be so clear. It is difficult to imagine *Roberts'* providing any meaningful protection in those circumstances.

* * *

Where nontestimonial hearsay is at issue, it is wholly consistent with the Framers' design to afford the States flexibility in their development of hearsay law—as does *Roberts*, and as would an approach that exempted such statements from Confrontation Clause scrutiny altogether. Where testimonial evidence is at issue, however, the Sixth Amendment demands what the common law required: unavailability and a prior opportunity for cross-examination. We leave for another day any effort to spell out a comprehensive definition of "testimonial." Whatever else the term covers, it applies at a minimum to prior testimony at a preliminary hearing, before a grand jury, or at a former trial; and to police interrogations. These are the modern practices with closest kinship to the abuses at which the Confrontation Clause was directed.

In this case, the State admitted Sylvia's testimonial statement against petitioner, despite the fact that he had no opportunity to cross-examine her. That alone is sufficient to make out a violation of the Sixth Amendment. *Roberts* notwithstanding, we decline to mine the record in search of indicia of reliability. Where testimonial statements are at issue, the only indicium of reliability sufficient to satisfy constitutional demands is the one the Constitution actually prescribes: confrontation.

The judgment of the Washington Supreme Court is reversed, and the case is remanded for further proceedings not inconsistent with this opinion.

It is so ordered.

■ CHIEF JUSTICE REHNQUIST, with whom JUSTICE O'CONNOR joins, concurring in the judgment.

I dissent from the Court's decision to overrule *Ohio v. Roberts*, 448 U.S. 56, 100 S.Ct. 2531, 65 L.Ed.2d 597 (1980). I believe that the Court's adoption of a new interpretation of the Confrontation Clause is not backed by sufficiently persuasive reasoning to overrule long-established precedent. Its decision casts a mantle of uncertainty over future criminal trials in both federal and state courts, and is by no means necessary to decide the present case.

The Court's distinction between testimonial and nontestimonial statements, contrary to its claim, is no better rooted in history than our current doctrine. Under the common law, although the courts were far from consistent, out-of-court statements made by someone other than the accused and not taken under oath, unlike *ex parte* depositions or affidavits, were generally not considered substantive evidence upon which a conviction could be based. See, *e.g.*, *King v. Brasier*, 1 Leach 199, 200, 168 Eng. Rep. 202 (K.B.1779); see also J. Langbein, Origins of Adversary Criminal Trial 235–242 (2003); G. Gilbert, Evidence 152 (3d ed. 1769). Testimonial statements such as accusatory statements to police officers likely would have been disapproved of in the 18th century, not necessarily because they resembled *ex parte* affidavits or depositions as the Court reasons, but more likely than not because they were not made under oath. See *King v. Woodcock*, 1 Leach 500, 503, 168 Eng. Rep. 352, 353 (1789) (noting that a statement taken by a justice of the peace may not be admitted into evidence unless taken under oath). Without an oath, one usually did not get to the second step of whether confrontation was required.

* * *

Thus, while I agree that the Framers were mainly concerned about sworn affidavits and depositions, it does not follow that they were similarly concerned about the Court's broader category of testimonial statements. See 1 N. Webster, An American Dictionary of the English Language (1828) (defining "Testimony" as "[a] solemn declaration or affirmation made for the purpose of establishing or proving some fact. *Such affirmation in judicial proceedings, may be verbal or written, but must be under oath*" (emphasis added)). As far as I can tell, unsworn testimonial statements were treated no differently at common law than were nontestimonial statements, and it seems to me any classification of statements as testimonial beyond that of sworn affidavits and depositions will be somewhat arbitrary, merely a proxy for what the Framers might have intended had such evidence been liberally admitted as substantive evidence like it is today.

I therefore see no reason why the distinction the Court draws is preferable to our precedent. Starting with Chief Justice Marshall's interpretation as a Circuit Justice in 1807, 16 years after the ratification of the Sixth Amendment, *United States v. Burr*, 25 F.Cas. 187, 193 (No. 14,694) (CC Va. 1807), continuing with our cases in the late 19th century, *Mattox v. United States*, 156 U.S. 237, 243–244, 15 S.Ct. 337, 39 L.Ed. 409 (1895); *Kirby v. United States*, 174 U.S. 47, 54–57, 19 S.Ct. 574, 43 L.Ed. 890 (1899), and through today, *e.g.*, *White v. Illinois*, 502 U.S. 346, 352–353, 112 S.Ct. 736, 116 L.Ed.2d 848 (1992), we have never drawn a distinction between testimonial and nontestimonial statements. And for that matter, neither has any other court of which I am aware. I see little value in trading our precedent for an imprecise approximation at this late date.

I am also not convinced that the Confrontation Clause categorically requires the exclusion of testimonial statements. Although many States had their own Confrontation Clauses, they were of recent vintage and were not interpreted with any regularity before 1791. State cases that recently followed the ratification of the Sixth Amendment were not uniform; the Court itself cites state cases from the early 19th century that took a more stringent view of the right to confrontation than does the Court, prohibiting former testimony even if the witness was subjected to cross-examination. See *ante*, at 1363 (citing *Finn v. Commonwealth*, 26 Va. 701, 708 (1827); *State v. Atkins*, 1 Tenn. 229 (1807) *(per curiam)*).

* * *

Between 1700 and 1800 the rules regarding the admissibility of out-of-court statements were still being developed. There were always exceptions to the general rule of exclusion, and it is not clear to me that the Framers categorically wanted to eliminate further ones. It is one thing to trace the right of confrontation back to the Roman Empire; it is quite another to conclude that such a right absolutely excludes a large category of evidence. It is an odd conclusion indeed to think that the Framers created a cut-and-dried rule with respect to the admissibility of testimonial statements when the law during their own time was not fully settled.

* * *

Exceptions to confrontation have always been derived from the experience that some out-of-court statements are just as reliable as cross-examined in-court testimony due to the circumstances under which they were made. We have recognized, for example, that co-conspirator statements simply "cannot be replicated, even if the declarant testifies to the same matters in court." *United States v. Inadi*, 475 U.S. 387, 395, 106 S.Ct. 1121, 89 L.Ed.2d 390 (1986). Because the statements are made while the declarant and the accused are partners in an illegal enterprise, the statements are unlikely to be false and their admission "actually furthers the 'Confrontation Clause's very mission' which is to 'advance the accuracy of the truth-determining process in criminal trials.' " *Id.*, at 396, 106 S.Ct. 1121 (quoting *Tennessee v. Street*, 471 U.S. 409, 415, 105 S.Ct. 2078, 85 L.Ed.2d 425 (1985) (some internal quotation marks omitted)). Similar reasons justify the introduction of spontaneous declarations, see *White*, 502 U.S., at 356, 112 S.Ct. 736, statements made in the course of procuring medical services, see *ibid.*, dying declarations, see *Kirby*, *supra*, at 61, 19 S.Ct. 574, and countless other hearsay exceptions. That a statement might be testimonial does nothing to undermine the wisdom of one of these exceptions.

* * *

In choosing the path it does, the Court of course overrules *Ohio v. Roberts* (1980), a case decided nearly a quarter of a century ago. *Stare decisis* is not an inexorable command in the area of constitutional law, see *Payne v. Tennessee*, 501 U.S. 808, 828, 111 S.Ct. 2597, 115 L.Ed.2d 720

(1991), but by and large, it "is the preferred course because it promotes the evenhanded, predictable, and consistent development of legal principles, fosters reliance on judicial decisions, and contributes to the actual and perceived integrity of the judicial process," *id.* And in making this appraisal, doubt that the new rule is indeed the "right" one should surely be weighed in the balance. Though there are no vested interests involved, unresolved questions for the future of everyday criminal trials throughout the country surely counsel the same sort of caution. The Court grandly declares that "[w]e leave for another day any effort to spell out a comprehensive definition of 'testimonial,' " But the thousands of federal prosecutors and the tens of thousands of state prosecutors need answers as to what beyond the specific kinds of "testimony" the Court lists ..., is covered by the new rule. They need them now, not months or years from now. Rules of criminal evidence are applied every day in courts throughout the country, and parties should not be left in the dark in this manner.

To its credit, the Court's analysis of "testimony" excludes at least some hearsay exceptions, such as business records and official records. To hold otherwise would require numerous additional witnesses without any apparent gain in the truth-seeking process. Likewise to the Court's credit is its implicit recognition that the mistaken application of its new rule by courts which guess wrong as to the scope of the rule is subject to harmless-error analysis.

But these are palliatives to what I believe is a mistaken change of course. It is a change of course not in the least necessary to reverse the judgment of the Supreme Court of Washington in this case. The result the Court reaches follows inexorably from *Roberts* and its progeny without any need for overruling that line of cases....

NOTE

Crawford is applicable only to those cases still on direct appeal and thus not fully retroactive. Whorton v. Bockting, ___ U.S. ___, 127 S.Ct. 1173 (2007)

Davis v. Washington

Supreme Court of the United States, 2006.
547 U.S. 813, 126 S.Ct. 2266.

■ JUSTICE SCALIA delivered the opinion of the Court.

These cases require us to determine when statements made to law enforcement personnel during a 911 call or at a crime scene are "testimonial" and thus subject to the requirements of the Sixth Amendment's Confrontation Clause.

I

A

The relevant statements in *Davis v. Washington*, No. 05–5224, were made to a 911 emergency operator on February 1, 2001. When the operator answered the initial call, the connection terminated before anyone spoke.

She reversed the call, and Michelle McCottry answered. In the ensuing conversation, the operator ascertained that McCottry was involved in a domestic disturbance with her former boyfriend Adrian Davis, the petitioner in this case:

"911 Operator: Hello.

"Complainant: Hello.

"911 Operator: What's going on?

"Complainant: He's here jumpin' on me again.

"911 Operator: Okay. Listen to me carefully. Are you in a house or an apartment?

"Complainant: I'm in a house.

"911 Operator: Are there any weapons?

"Complainant: No. He's usin' his fists.

"911 Operator: Okay. Has he been drinking?

"Complainant: No.

"911 Operator: Okay, sweetie. I've got help started. Stay on the line with me, okay?

"Complainant: I'm on the line.

"911 Operator: Listen to me carefully. Do you know his last name?

"Complainant: It's Davis.

"911 Operator: Davis? Okay, what's his first name?

"Complainant: Adran

"911 Operator: What is it?

"Complainant: Adrian.

"911 Operator: Adrian?

"Complainant: Yeah.

"911 Operator: Okay. What's his middle initial?

"Complainant: Martell. He's runnin' now." App. in No. 05–5224, pp. 8–9.

As the conversation continued, the operator learned that Davis had "just run out the door" after hitting McCottry, and that he was leaving in a car with someone else. McCottry started talking, but the operator cut her off, saying, "Stop talking and answer my questions." She then gathered more information about Davis (including his birthday), and learned that Davis had told McCottry that his purpose in coming to the house was "to get his stuff," since McCottry was moving. McCottry described the context of the assault, after which the operator told her that the police were on their way. "They're gonna check the area for him first," the operator said, "and then they're gonna come talk to you."

The police arrived within four minutes of the 911 call and observed McCottry's shaken state, the "fresh injuries on her forearm and her face," and her "frantic efforts to gather her belongings and her children so that they could leave the residence."

The State charged Davis with felony violation of a domestic no-contact order. "The State's only witnesses were the two police officers who responded to the 911 call. Both officers testified that McCottry exhibited injuries that appeared to be recent, but neither officer could testify as to the cause of the injuries." McCottry presumably could have testified as to whether Davis was her assailant, but she did not appear. Over Davis's objection, based on the Confrontation Clause of the Sixth Amendment, the trial court admitted the recording of her exchange with the 911 operator, and the jury convicted him. The Supreme Court of Washington, with one dissenting justice, also affirmed, concluding that the portion of the 911 conversation in which McCottry identified Davis was not testimonial, and that if other portions of the conversation were testimonial, admitting them was harmless beyond a reasonable doubt. We granted certiorari.

B

In *Hammon v. Indiana*, police responded late on the night of February 26, 2003, to a "reported domestic disturbance" at the home of Hershel and Amy Hammon ... They found Amy alone on the front porch, appearing "somewhat frightened," but she told them that "nothing was the matter." She gave them permission to enter the house, where an officer saw "a gas heating unit in the corner of the living room" that had "flames coming out of the ... partial glass front. There were pieces of glass on the ground in front of it and there was flame emitting from the front of the heating unit."

Hershel, meanwhile, was in the kitchen. He told the police "that he and his wife had 'been in an argument' but 'everything was fine now' and the argument 'never became physical.' " By this point Amy had come back inside. One of the officers remained with Hershel; the other went to the living room to talk with Amy, and "again asked [her] what had occurred." Hershel made several attempts to participate in Amy's conversation with the police, but was rebuffed. The officer later testified that Hershel "became angry when I insisted that [he] stay separated from Mrs. Hammon so that we can investigate what had happened." After hearing Amy's account, the officer "had her fill out and sign a battery affidavit." Amy handwrote the following: "Broke our Furnace & shoved me down on the floor into the broken glass. Hit me in the chest and threw me down. Broke our lamps & phone. Tore up my van where I couldn't leave the house. Attacked my daughter."

The State charged Hershel with domestic battery and with violating his probation. Amy was subpoenaed, but she did not appear at his subsequent bench trial. The State called the officer who had questioned Amy, and asked him to recount what Amy told him and to authenticate the affidavit. Hershel's counsel repeatedly objected to the admission of this evidence. At one point, after hearing the prosecutor defend the affidavit because it was made "under oath," defense counsel said, "That doesn't give us the opportunity to cross examine [the] person who allegedly drafted it. Makes me mad." Nonetheless, the trial court admitted the affidavit as a "present sense impression," and Amy's statements as "excited utterances" that "are expressly permitted in these kinds of cases even if the declarant is not available to testify." The officer thus testified that Amy "informed me that she and Hershel had been in an argument. That he became irrate [sic] over the fact of their daughter going to a boyfriend's house. The argument became . . . physical after being verbal and she informed me that Mr. Hammon, during the verbal part of the argument was breaking things in the living room and I believe she stated he broke the phone, broke the lamp, broke the front of the heater. When it became physical he threw her down into the glass of the heater."

. . .

"She informed me Mr. Hammon had pushed her onto the ground, had shoved her head into the broken glass of the heater and that he had punched her in the chest twice I believe."

The trial judge found Hershel guilty on both charges. The Indiana Supreme Court affirmed, concluding that Amy's statement was admissible for state-law purposes as an excited utterance; that "a 'testimonial' statement is one given or taken in significant part for purposes of preserving it for potential future use in legal proceedings," where "the motivations of the questioner and declarant are the central concerns"; and that Amy's oral statement was not "testimonial" under these standards. It also concluded that, although the affidavit was testimonial and thus wrongly admitted, it was harmless beyond a reasonable doubt, largely because the trial was to the bench. We granted certiorari.

II

In *Crawford v. Washington*, 541 U.S. 36, 53–54 (2004), we held that this provision bars "admission of testimonial statements of a witness who did not appear at trial unless he was unavailable to testify, and the defendant had had a prior opportunity for cross-examination." A critical portion of this holding, and the portion central to resolution of the two cases now before us, is the phrase "testimonial statements." Only statements of this sort cause the declarant to be a "witness" within the meaning of the Confrontation Clause. It is the testimonial character of the statement that separates it from other hearsay that, while subject to traditional limitations upon hearsay evidence, is not subject to the Confrontation Clause.

Our opinion in *Crawford* set forth "various formulations" of the core class of "testimonial" . . . [a]mong those, we said, were "statements taken by police officers in the course of interrogations." The questioning that generated the deponent's statement in *Crawford*—which was made and recorded while she was in police custody, after having been given *Miranda* warnings as a possible suspect herself "qualifies under any conceivable definition" of an "interrogation." . . . The character of the statements in the present cases is not as clear, and these cases require us to determine more precisely which police interrogations produce testimony.

Without attempting to produce an exhaustive classification of all conceivable statements—or even all conceivable statements in response to police interrogation—as either testimonial or nontestimonial, it suffices to decide the present cases to hold as follows: Statements are nontestimonial when made in the course of police interrogation under circumstances objectively indicating that the primary purpose of the interrogation is to enable police assistance to meet an ongoing emergency. They are testimonial when the circumstances objectively indicate that there is no such ongoing emergency, and that the primary purpose of the interrogation is to establish or prove past events potentially relevant to later criminal prosecution.[1]

III

A

In *Crawford* ... the facts of that case spared us the need to define what we meant by "interrogations." The *Davis* case today does not permit us this luxury of indecision. The inquiries of a police operator in the course of a 911 call[2] are an interrogation in one sense, but not in a sense that "qualifies under any conceivable definition." We must decide, therefore, whether the Confrontation Clause applies only to testimonial hearsay; and, if so, whether the recording of a 911 call qualifies.

The answer to the first question was suggested in *Crawford*, even if not explicitly held:

> "The text of the Confrontation Clause reflects this focus [on testimonial hearsay]. It applies to 'witnesses' against the accused—in other words, those who 'bear testimony.' 1 N. Webster, An American Dictionary of the English Language (1828). 'Testimony,' in turn, is typically 'a solemn declaration or affirmation made for the purpose of establishing or proving some fact.' An accuser who makes a formal statement to government officers bears testimony in a sense that a person who makes a casual remark to an acquaintance does not." (cite omitted)

A limitation so clearly reflected in the text of the constitutional provision must fairly be said to mark out not merely its "core," but its perimeter.

We are not aware of any early American case invoking the Confrontation Clause or the common-law right to confrontation that did not clearly

1. Our holding refers to interrogations because, as explained below, the statements in the cases presently before us are the products of interrogations—which in some circumstances tend to generate testimonial responses. This is not to imply, however, that statements made in the absence of any interrogation are necessarily nontestimonial. The Framers were no more willing to exempt from cross-examination volunteered testimony or answers to open-ended questions than they were to exempt answers to detailed interrogation. (Part of the evidence against Sir Walter Raleigh was a letter from Lord Cobham that was plainly not the result of sustained questioning. *Raleigh's Case*, 2 How. St. Tr. 1, 27 (1603).) And of course even when interrogation exists, it is in the final analysis the declarant's statements, not the interrogator's questions, that the Confrontation Clause requires us to evaluate.

2. If 911 operators are not themselves law enforcement officers, they may at least be agents of law enforcement when they conduct interrogations of 911 callers. For purposes of this opinion (and without deciding the point), we consider their acts to be acts of the police. As in *Crawford v. Washington*, 541 U.S. 36, 124 S.Ct. 1354, 158 L.Ed.2d 177 (2004), therefore, our holding today makes it unnecessary to consider whether and when statements made to someone other than law enforcement personnel are "testimonial."

involve testimony as thus defined. Well into the 20th century, our own Confrontation Clause jurisprudence was carefully applied only in the testimonial context. See, *e.g.*, *Reynolds v. United States*, 98 U.S. 145, 158 (1879) (testimony at prior trial was subject to the Confrontation Clause, but petitioner had forfeited that right by procuring witness's absence); *Mattox v. United States*, 156 U.S. 237, 240–244 (1895) (prior trial testimony of deceased witnesses admitted because subject to cross-examination); *Kirby v. United States*, 174 U.S. 47, 55–56 (1899) (guilty pleas and jury conviction of others could not be admitted to show that property defendant received from them was stolen); *Motes v. United States*, 178 U.S. 458, 467, 470–471 (1900) (written deposition subject to cross-examination was not admissible because witness was available); *Dowdell v. United States*, 221 U.S. 325, 330–331 (1911) (facts regarding conduct of prior trial certified to by the judge, the clerk of court, and the official reporter did not relate to defendants' guilt or innocence and hence were not statements of "witnesses" under the Confrontation Clause)....

Most of the American cases applying the Confrontation Clause or its state constitutional or common-law counterparts involved testimonial statements of the most formal sort—sworn testimony in prior judicial proceedings or formal depositions under oath—which invites the argument that the scope of the Clause is limited to that very formal category. But the English cases that were the progenitors of the Confrontation Clause did not limit the exclusionary rule to prior court testimony and formal depositions. In any event, we do not think it conceivable that the protections of the Confrontation Clause can readily be evaded by having a note-taking policeman *recite* the unsworn hearsay testimony of the declarant, instead of having the declarant sign a deposition. Indeed, if there is one point for which no case—English or early American, state or federal—can be cited, that is it.

The question before us in *Davis*, then, is whether, objectively considered, the interrogation that took place in the course of the 911 call produced testimonial statements. When we said in Crawford that "interrogations by law enforcement officers fall squarely within [the] class" of testimonial hearsay, we had immediately in mind (for that was the case before us) interrogations solely directed at establishing the facts of a past crime, in order to identify (or provide evidence to convict) the perpetrator. The product of such interrogation, whether reduced to a writing signed by the declarant or embedded in the memory (and perhaps notes) of the interrogating officer, is testimonial. It is ... "[a] solemn declaration or affirmation made for the purpose of establishing or proving some fact." The solemnity of even an oral declaration of relevant past fact to an investigating officer is well enough established by the severe consequences that can attend a deliberate falsehood.... A 911 call, on the other hand, and at least the initial interrogation conducted in connection with a 911 call, is ordinarily not designed primarily to "establish or prove" some past fact, but to describe current circumstances requiring police assistance.

In *Davis*, McCottry was speaking about events *as they were actually happening*, rather than "describing past events," (emphasis in original). Sylvia Crawford's interrogation, on the other hand, took place hours after the events she described had occurred. Moreover, any reasonable listener would recognize that McCottry (unlike Sylvia Crawford) was facing an ongoing emergency. Although one *might* call 911 to provide a narrative report of a crime absent any imminent danger, McCottry's call was plainly a call for help against bona fide physical threat. Third, the nature of what was asked and answered in *Davis*, again viewed objectively, was such that the elicited statements were necessary to be able to *resolve* the present emergency, rather than simply to learn (as in *Crawford*) what had happened in the past. That is true even of the operator's effort to establish the identity of the assailant, so that the dispatched officers might know whether they would be encountering a violent felon. And finally, the difference in the level of formality between the two interviews is striking. Crawford was responding calmly, at the station house, to a series of questions, with the officer-interrogator taping and making notes of her answers; McCottry's frantic answers were provided over the phone, in an environment that was not tranquil, or even (as far as any reasonable 911 operator could make out) safe.

We conclude from all this that the circumstances of McCottry's interrogation objectively indicate its primary purpose was to enable police assistance to meet an ongoing emergency. She simply was not acting as a *witness*; she was not *testifying*. What she said was not "a weaker substitute for live testimony" at trial, like Lord Cobham's statements in *Raleigh's Case*, 2 How. St. Tr. 1 (1603), or Jane Dingler's *ex parte* statements against her husband in *King v. Dingler*, 2 Leach 561, 168 Eng. Rep. 383 (1791), or Sylvia Crawford's statement in *Crawford*. In each of those cases, the *ex parte* actors and the evidentiary products of the *ex parte* communication aligned perfectly with their courtroom analogues. McCottry's emergency statement does not. No "witness" goes into court to proclaim an emergency and seek help....

This is not to say that a conversation which begins as an interrogation to determine the need for emergency assistance cannot, as the Indiana Supreme Court put it, "evolve into testimonial statements," once that purpose has been achieved. In this case, for example, after the operator gained the information needed to address the exigency of the moment, the emergency appears to have ended (when Davis drove away from the premises). The operator then told McCottry to be quiet, and proceeded to pose a battery of questions. It could readily be maintained that, from that point on, McCottry's statements were testimonial, not unlike the "structured police questioning" that occurred in *Crawford* ... his presents no great problem. Just as, for Fifth Amendment purposes, "police officers can and will distinguish almost instinctively between questions necessary to secure their own safety or the safety of the public and questions designed solely to elicit testimonial evidence from a suspect," *New York v. Quarles*, 467 U.S. 649, 658–659 (1984), trial courts will recognize the point at which, for Sixth Amendment purposes, statements in response to interrogations become testimonial. Through *in limine* procedure, they should redact or exclude the portions of any statement that have become testimonial, as they do, for example, with unduly prejudicial portions of otherwise admissible evidence. Davis's jury did not hear the *complete* 911 call, although it may well have heard some testimonial portions. We were asked to classify only McCottry's early statements identifying Davis as her assailant, and we agree with the Washington Supreme Court that they were not testimonial. That court also concluded that, even if later parts of the call were testimonial, their admission was harmless beyond a reasonable doubt. Davis does not challenge that holding, and we therefore assume it to be correct.

B

Determining the testimonial or nontestimonial character of the statements that were the product of the interrogation in *Hammon* is a much easier task, since they were not much different from the statements we found to be testimonial in *Crawford*. It is entirely clear from the circumstances that the interrogation was part of an investigation into possibly criminal past conduct—as, indeed, the testifying officer expressly acknowledged, There was no emergency in progress; the interrogating officer testified that he had heard no arguments or crashing and saw no one throw or break anything. When the officers first arrived, Amy told them that things were fine, and there was no immediate threat to her person. When the officer questioned Amy for the second time, and elicited the challenged statements, he was not seeking to determine (as in *Davis*) "what is happening," but rather "what happened." Objectively viewed, the primary, if not indeed the sole, purpose of the interrogation was to investigate a possible crime—which is, of course, precisely what the officer *should* have done.

It is true that the *Crawford* interrogation was more formal. It followed a *Miranda* warning, was tape-recorded, and took place at the station house. While these features certainly strengthened the statements' testimonial aspect—made it more objectively apparent, that is, that the purpose of the exercise was to nail down the truth about past criminal events—none was essential to the point. It was formal enough that Amy's interrogation was conducted in a separate room, away from her husband (who tried to intervene), with the officer receiving her replies for use in his "investigation." What we called the "striking resemblance" of the *Crawford* statement to civil-law *ex parte* examinations, is shared by Amy's statement here. Both declarants were actively separated from the defendant—officers forcibly prevented Hershel from participating in the interrogation. Both statements deliberately recounted, in response to police questioning, how potentially criminal past events began and progressed. And both took place some time after the events described were over. Such statements under official interrogation are an obvious substitute for live testimony, because they do precisely *what a witness does* on direct examination; they are inherently testimonial.

Both Indiana and the United States as *amicus curiae* argue that this case should be resolved much like *Davis*. For the reasons we find the comparison to *Crawford* compelling, we find the comparison to *Davis* unpersuasive. The statements in *Davis* were taken when McCottry was alone, not only unprotected by police (as Amy Hammon was protected), but apparently in immediate danger from Davis. She was seeking aid, not telling a story about the past. McCottry's present-tense statements showed immediacy; Amy's narrative of past events was delivered at some remove in time from the danger she described. And after Amy answered the officer's questions, he had her execute an affidavit, in order, he testified, "to establish events that have occurred previously."

Although we necessarily reject the Indiana Supreme Court's implication that virtually any "initial inquiries" at the crime scene will not be testimonial, we do not hold the opposite—that *no* questions at the scene will yield nontestimonial answers. We have already observed of domestic disputes that "officers called to investigate ... need to know whom they are dealing with in order to assess the situation, the threat to their own safety, and possible danger to the potential victim." *Hiibel*, 542 U.S., at 186. Such exigencies may *often* mean that "initial inquiries" produce nontestimonial statements. But in cases like this one, where Amy's statements were neither a cry for help nor the provision of information enabling officers immediately to end a threatening situation, the fact that they were given at an alleged crime scene and were "initial inquiries" is immaterial.

Police investigations themselves are, of course, in no way impugned by our characterization of their fruits as testimonial. Investigations of past crimes prevent future harms and lead to necessary arrests. While prosecutors may hope that inculpatory "nontestimonial" evidence is gathered, this is essentially beyond police control. Their saying that an emergency exists cannot make it be so. The Confrontation Clause in no way governs police conduct, because it is the trial *use* of, not the investigatory *collection* of, *ex parte* testimonial statements which offends that provision. But neither can police conduct govern the Confrontation Clause; testimonial statements are what they are.

IV

Respondents in both cases, joined by a number of their *amici*, contend that the nature of the offenses charged in these two cases—domestic violence—requires greater flexibility in the use of testimonial evidence. This particular type of crime is notoriously susceptible to intimidation or coercion of the victim to ensure that she does not testify at trial. When this occurs, the Confrontation Clause gives the criminal a windfall. We may not, however, vitiate constitutional guarantees when they have the effect of allowing the guilty to go free.... But when defendants seek to undermine the judicial process by procuring or coercing silence from witnesses and victims, the Sixth Amendment does not require courts to acquiesce. While defendants have no duty to assist the State in proving their guilt, they *do* have the duty to refrain from acting in ways that destroy the integrity of the criminal-trial system. We reiterate what we said in *Crawford*: that "the rule of forfeiture by wrongdoing ... extinguishes confrontation claims on essentially equitable grounds." 541 U.S., at 62 (citing *Reynolds*, 98 U.S., at 158–159). That is, one who obtains the absence of a witness by wrongdoing forfeits the constitutional right to confrontation.

We take no position on the standards necessary to demonstrate such forfeiture, but federal courts using Federal Rule of Evidence 804(b)(6), which codifies the forfeiture doctrine, have generally held the Government to the preponderance-of-the-evidence standard.... Moreover, if a hearing on forfeiture is required, *Edwards*, for instance, observed that "hearsay evidence, including the unavailable witness's out-of-court statements, may be considered." The *Roberts* approach to the Confrontation Clause undoubtedly made recourse to this doctrine less necessary, because prosecutors could show the "reliability" of *ex parte* statements more easily than they could show the defendant's procurement of the witness's absence. *Crawford*, in overruling *Roberts*, did not destroy the ability of courts to protect the integrity of their proceedings.

We have determined that, absent a finding of forfeiture by wrongdoing, the Sixth Amendment operates to exclude Amy Hammon's affidavit. The Indiana courts may (if they are asked) determine on remand whether such a claim of forfeiture is properly raised and, if so, whether it is meritorious.

We affirm the judgment of the Supreme Court of Washington in No. 05–5224. We reverse the judgment of the Supreme Court of Indiana in No. 05–5705, and remand the case to that Court for proceedings not inconsistent with this opinion.

It is so ordered.

JUSTICE THOMAS, concurring in the judgment in part and dissenting in part.

In *Crawford* ... we abandoned the general reliability inquiry we had long employed to judge the admissibility of hearsay evidence under the Confrontation Clause, describing that inquiry as "*inherently*, and therefore *permanently*, unpredictable...." Today, a mere two years after the Court decided *Crawford*, it adopts an equally unpredictable test, under which district courts are charged with divining the "primary purpose" of police interrogations. Besides being difficult for courts to apply, this test characterizes as "testimonial," and therefore inadmissible, evidence that bears little resemblance to what we have recognized as the evidence targeted by the Confrontation Clause. Because neither of the cases before the Court today would implicate the Confrontation Clause under an appropriately targeted standard, I concur only in the judgment in *Davis v. Washington*, and dissent from the Court's resolution of *Hammon v. Indiana*.

I

A

The Confrontation Clause provides that "in all criminal prosecutions, the accused shall enjoy the right ... to be confronted with the witnesses against him...." U.S. Const., Amdt. 6. We have recognized that the operative phrase in the Clause, "witnesses against him," could be interpreted narrowly, to reach only those witnesses who actually testify at trial, or more broadly, to reach many or all of those whose out-of-court statements are offered at trial. ... Because the narrowest interpretation of the Clause would conflict with both the history giving rise to the adoption of the Clause and this Court's precedent, we have rejected such a reading.

Rejection of the narrowest view of the Clause does not, however, require the broadest application of the Clause to exclude otherwise admissible hearsay evidence. The history surrounding the right to confrontation supports the conclusion that it was developed to target particular practices that occurred under the English bail and committal statutes passed during the reign of Queen Mary, namely, the "civil-law mode of criminal procedure, and particularly its use of *ex parte* examinations as evidence against the accused." which the Framers proposed the Confrontation Clause to prevent....

In *Crawford*, we recognized that this history could be squared with the language of the Clause, giving rise to a workable, and more accurate, interpretation of the Clause.... Admittedly, we did not set forth a detailed framework for addressing whether a statement is "testimonial" and thus subject to the Confrontation Clause. But the plain terms of the "testimony" definition we endorsed necessarily require some degree of solemnity before a statement can be deemed "testimonial."

Although the Court concedes that the early American cases invoking the right to confrontation or the Confrontation Clause itself all "clearly involved testimony" as defined in *Crawford*, it fails to acknowledge that all of the cases it cites fall within the narrower category of formalized testimonial materials I have proposed. Interactions between the police and an accused (or witnesses) resemble Marian proceedings—and these early cases—only when the interactions are somehow rendered "formal." In *Crawford*, for example, the interrogation was custodial, taken after warnings given pursuant to *Miranda v. Arizona*, 384 U.S. 436. *Miranda* warnings, by their terms, inform a prospective defendant that " 'anything he says can be used against him in a court of law.' " *Dickerson v. United States*, 530 U.S. 428, 435. This imports a solemnity to the process that is not present in a mere conversation between a witness or suspect and a police officer.

The Court all but concedes that no case can be cited for its conclusion that the Confrontation Clause also applies to informal police questioning under certain circumstances. Instead, the sole basis for the Court's conclusion is its apprehension that the Confrontation Clause will "readily be evaded" if it is only applicable to formalized testimonial materials. But the Court's proposed solution to the risk of evasion is needlessly overinclusive. Because the Confrontation Clause sought to regulate prosecutorial abuse occurring through use of *ex parte* statements as evidence against the accused, it also reaches the use of technically informal statements when used to evade the formalized process.... That is, even if the interrogation itself is not formal, the production of evidence by the prosecution at trial would resemble the abuses targeted by the Confrontation Clause if the prosecution attempted to use out-of-court statements as a means of circumventing the literal right of confrontation, see *Coy v. Iowa*, 487 U.S. 1012, 108 S. Ct. 2798, 101 L. Ed. 2d 857 (1988). In such a case, the Confrontation Clause could fairly be applied to exclude the hearsay statements offered by the prosecution, preventing evasion without simultaneously excluding evidence offered by the prosecution in good faith.

The Court's standard is not only disconnected from history and unnecessary to prevent abuse; it also yields no predictable results to police officers and prosecutors attempting to comply with the law.... In many, if not most, cases where police respond to a report of a crime, whether pursuant to a 911 call from the victim or otherwise, the purposes of an interrogation, viewed from the perspective of the police, are *both* to respond to the emergency situation *and* to gather evidence. See *New York v.*

Quarles, 467 U.S. 649, 656 (1984) ("Undoubtedly most police officers [deciding whether to give *Miranda* warnings in a possible emergency situation] would act out of a host of different, instinctive, and largely unverifiable motives—their own safety, the safety of others, and perhaps as well the desire to obtain incriminating evidence from the suspect"). Assigning one of these two "largely unverifiable motives," primacy requires constructing a hierarchy of purpose that will rarely be present—and is not reliably discernible. It will inevitably be, quite simply, an exercise in fiction.

The Court's repeated invocation of the word "objective" to describe its test, however, suggests that the Court may not mean to reference purpose at all, but instead to inquire into the function served by the interrogation. Certainly such a test would avoid the pitfalls that have led us repeatedly to reject tests dependent on the subjective intentions of police officers.[4] It would do so, however, at the cost of being even more disconnected from the prosecutorial abuses targeted by the Confrontation Clause. Additionally, it would shift the ability to control whether a violation occurred from the police and prosecutor to the judge, whose determination as to the "primary purpose" of a particular interrogation would be unpredictable and not necessarily tethered to the actual purpose for which the police performed the interrogation.

B

Neither the 911 call at issue in *Davis* nor the police questioning at issue in *Hammon* is testimonial under the appropriate framework. Neither the call nor the questioning is itself a formalized dialogue. n5 Nor do any circumstances surrounding the taking of the statements render those statements sufficiently formal to resemble the Marian examinations; the statements were neither Mirandized nor custodial, nor accompanied by any similar indicia of formality. Finally, there is no suggestion that the prosecution attempted to offer the women's hearsay evidence at trial in order to evade confrontation.... Accordingly, the statements at issue in both cases are nontestimonial and admissible under the Confrontation Clause.

The Court's determination that the evidence against Hammon must be excluded extends the Confrontation Clause far beyond the abuses it was intended to prevent. When combined with the Court's holding that the evidence against Davis is perfectly admissible, however, the Court's *Hammon* holding also reveals the difficulty of applying the Court's requirement that courts investigate the "primary purposes" of the investigation. The Court draws a line between the two cases based on its explanation that *Hammon* involves "no emergency in progress," but instead, mere questioning as "part of an investigation into possibly criminal past conduct," and its explanation that *Davis* involves questioning for the "primary purpose" of "enabling police assistance to meet an ongoing emergency," But the fact

4. See *New York v. Quarles*, 467 U.S. 649, 655656 (1984) (subjective motivation of officer not relevant in considering whether the public safety exception to *Miranda v. Arizona*, 384 U.S. 436 (1966), is applicable); *Rhode Island v. Innis*, 446 U.S. 291, 301 (1980) (subjective intent of police officer to obtain incriminatory statement not relevant to whether an interrogation has occurred); *Whren v. United States*, 517 U.S. 806, 813 (1996) (refusing to evaluate Fourth Amendment reasonableness in light of the officers' actual motivations).

that the officer in *Hammon* was investigating Mr. Hammon's past conduct does not foreclose the possibility that the primary purpose of his inquiry was to assess whether Mr. Hammon constituted a continuing danger to his wife, requiring further police presence or action. It is hardly remarkable that Hammon did not act abusively towards his wife in the presence of the officers, and his good judgment to refrain from criminal behavior in the presence of police sheds little, if any, light on whether his violence would have resumed had the police left without further questioning, transforming what the Court dismisses as "past conduct" back into an "ongoing emergency." Nor does the mere fact that McCottry needed emergency aid shed light on whether the "primary purpose" of gathering, for example, the name of her assailant was to protect the police, to protect the victim, or to gather information for prosecution. In both of the cases before the Court, like many similar cases, pronouncement of the "primary" motive behind the interrogation calls for nothing more than a guess by courts.

II

Because the standard adopted by the Court today is neither workable nor a targeted attempt to reach the abuses forbidden by the Clause, I concur only in the judgment in *Davis v. Washington*, and respectfully dissent from the Court's resolution of *Hammon v. Indiana*.

NOTES

1. An example of forfeiture of confrontation is found in United States v. White, 116 F.3d 903 (D.C.Cir.1997) where defendant murdered the witness and the court admitted the statements made by the witness during debriefings before and after drug transactions. See pp. 1316–1321, infra.

2. The Supreme Court has always rejected Confrontation Clause challenges to the use of hearsay against criminal defendants, as it did in where the hearsay fits within a "well rooted" exception to the rule against hearsay, a standard approved in *Crawford*.

The courts may re-examine the very large number of exceptions to determine if they allow "testimonial" evidence and, if so, whether they are "deeply rooted." Consider the modern "catchall" hearsay exception which admits hearsay which, while not fitting into traditional exception categories, is reliable (Federal Rule of Evidence 804 (24)). This exception was found not to be deeply rooted. Idaho v. Wright, 497 U.S. 805, 110 S.Ct. 3139 (1990) (statements by two-and-a-half year old about sexual abuse made to a pediatrician)

The two most prominent exceptions used in criminal cases have been statements made by coconspirators and statements against penal interest but there is little expectation that co-conspirator statements or those against penal interest are likely to be excluded under *Crawford*. On the co-conspirator rule see Bourjaily v. United States, infra Ch. 19, Section B.

The ambit of the penal interest exception is considered in two pre-*Crawford* cases.

In Williamson v. United States, 512 U.S. 594, 114 S.Ct. 2431 (1994) a witness, Harris, refused to testify at Williamson's trial so the court permitted a law officer to testify that Harris had twice confessed his own involvement in moving drugs and accused Williamson of owning the drugs. This was permitted because Harris' confessions were against his penal interest.

Justice O'Connor spoke for the Court in approving the notion that statements against penal interest are reliable because "even ... people who are not specially honest, tend not to make self-inculpatory statements unless they believe them to be true." But, she noted, the "fact that a person is making a broadly self-inculpatory statement does not make more credible the confession's non-self-inculpatory parts. One of the most effective ways to lie is to mix falsehood with truth that seems particularly persuasive because of its self-inculpatory nature." Indeed, in this case some of the first confession had been proved false. The Court then said that Congress could, subject to the limits of the Confrontation Clause, make admissible statements like those of Harris about Williamson solely because "of their proximity to self-inculpatory statements," but neither the text nor the history of Federal Rules of Evidence 804(b)(3) leads to the conclusion that Congress did this. The rule to be applied then is whether any particular statement was sufficiently against the declarant's penal interest "that a reasonable person in the declarant's position would not have made the statement unless believing it to be true." In this reasoning Justice O'Connor was joined by Justices Blackmun, Stevens, Scalia, Souter and Ginsburg.

Only Justice Scalia joined her in her conclusion that the matter should be remanded for a "fact-intensive" inquiry on whether the out-of-court accusations of Williamson were self-inculpatory, in light of the fact that Harris might have been a small fish trying to incriminate not himself but a bigger fish, in which case there might be no indicia of reliability of those statements.

Justice Ginsburg, joined by Justices Blackmun, Stevens and Souter, would simply hold that the Harris statements about Williamson were not declarations against penal interest but simply self-serving declarations of one trying to lessen the personal consequences of being caught with 19 kilograms of cocaine.

Justice Kennedy, with the Chief Justice and Justice Thomas, read Rule 804(b)(3) to apply to the accusations of Williamson made in the course of a clearly self-inculpatory confession. He noted that the statements against Williamson did nothing to diminish the legal guilt of Harris. He, too, agreed that a further analysis of the statements (and a remand for that purpose) was necessary. The standard he proposed was whether the particular statement was so motivated by self-interest that it is unreliable.

In Lilly v. Virginia, 527 U.S. 116, 119 S.Ct. 1887 (1999), defendant's brother, Mark, gave a statement to police implicating himself and his brother in a two-day crime spree. When the brother exercised his fifth amendment right and declined to testify at Lilly's separate trial, the court admitted the tape of the statement into evidence under the statement against penal interest exception to the hearsay rule. The Court held that the admission of the tape violated the Confrontation Clause:

> It is clear that our cases consistently have viewed an accomplice's statements that shift or spread the blame to a criminal defendant as falling outside the realm of those "hearsay exception[s] [that are] so trustworthy that adversarial testing an be expected to add little to [the statements'] reliability."
>
> * * *
>
> The decisive fact, which we make explicit today, is that accomplices' confessions that inculpate a criminal defendant are not within a firmly

rooted exception to the hearsay rule as that concept has been defined in our Confrontation Clause jurisprudence.

* * *

It is abundantly clear that neither the words that Mark spoke nor the setting in which he was questioned provides any basis for concluding that his comments regarding petitioner's guilt were so reliable that there was no need to subject them to adversarial testing in a trial setting. Mark was in custody for his involvement in, and knowledge of, serious crimes and made his statements under the supervision of governmental authorities. He was primarily responding to the officer's leading questions, which were asked without any contemporaneous cross-examination by adverse parties. Thus, Mark had a natural motive to attempt to exculpate himself as much as possible. Mark also was obviously under the influence of alcohol. Each of these factors militates against finding that his statements were so inherently reliable that cross examination would have been superfluous.

3. The defense, as well as the prosecution, will want use the exceptions to the hearsay rule. See Chambers v. Mississippi, supra. Section A. 3. The defense does not have to cope with the Confrontation Clause because it is a right not accorded to the prosecution; it has only to surmount the rule against hearsay. Statements against penal interest i.e., someone else confessing to the crime, is the most crucial to the defense of the standard hearsay exceptions. See United States v. Paguio, 114 F.3d 928 (9th Cir.1997) (statement against penal interest); People v. Robinson, 89 N.Y.2d 648, 679 N.E.2d 1055, 657 N.Y.S.2d 575 (1997) (Witness testified before grand jury where prosecutor had a chance to test her exculpatory statements.)

4. Some commentators argue that it is a mistake to bend the confrontation clause to fit existing hearsay exceptions. See Jonakait, Restoring The Confrontation Clause to The Sixth Amendment, 35 U.C.L.A. L.Rev. 557 (1988):

In interpreting the confrontation clause, the Supreme Court has misunderstood the purpose of the provision. As a result, evidence law now controls the content of the confrontation clause, and the clause now offers an accused little protection. Correctly interpreted, the confrontation clause is not a minor adjunct of evidence law, but is one of a bundle of rights that assures the accused the protection of our adversary system. It assures the accused the right to the adversarial testing of the prosecution's evidence. This is granted to assure that the jury will not overvalue the evidence against the defendant. The confrontation clause gives the accused the right to exclude all out-of-court statements when the declarant is not produced except when the prosecutor establishes the lack of a reasonable probability that the accused's cross-examination of the declarant would have led the jury to weigh the evidence more favorably to the accused.

Professor Graham argues that hearsay exceptions to the confrontation clause are not defensible when the prior statement was accusatory in nature when it was made. See Graham, "The Confrontation Clause, the Hearsay Rule, and Child Sexual Abuse Prosecutions" 72 Minn.L.Rev. 523 (1988).

2. The Privileged Witness

United States v. Fallon

United States Court of Appeals, Seventh Circuit, 1985.
776 F.2d 727.

■ Bauer, Circuit Judge.

[Fallon was convicted of federal crimes arising from the systematic practice of rolling back odometers on used cars and altering title certificates to conceal the roll back. Several witnesses testified that many cars sold by Fallon's enterprise had higher mileage readings on purchase than when resold. One employee testified Fallon discussed a particular method of altering odometer readings on title certificates].

The government also presented the testimony of another employee, Richard Huebner, an indicted co-conspirator who pled guilty prior to trial. On Fallon's motion the district court judge later struck Huebner's testimony on the ground that Huebner had made a "performance deal" with the government; as the district court phrased it, "it would be Huebner's performance at trial which would be the determining factor in whether he would be prosecuted." Immediately after striking Huebner's testimony, the court instructed the jury to disregard the testimony. Huebner was the only witness to testify that Fallon directed him to roll back odometers, saw him perform the work, and paid him for it.

* * *

Even if the jury considered Huebner's testimony, Fallon received a fair trial. The trial judge was not required to exclude Huebner's testimony merely because that testimony was given as a result of a "performance deal" with the government. Consideration of that testimony by the jury could not have given Fallon an unfair trial.

Accomplices and co-conspirators who have been granted immunity from prosecution are generally competent to testify. They are competent under the Federal Rules of Evidence, Fed.R.Ev. 601, and under long-standing case law. Washington v. Texas (1967); Hoffa v. United States (1966); Rosen v. United States (1918); Benson v. United States (1892).

Huebner's performance deal presents no special considerations that convince us to deviate from the general rule of accepting his testimony as the testimony of an accomplice who has made a favorable deal with the prosecution. Huebner's deal conditions lenient treatment upon his "complete and truthful cooperation." It indicates that there would be at most three charges brought, that these charges would be delayed until Huebner "had completed his cooperation with the government," and that "if the level of cooperation would materialize as represented, ... the government would, at the time of sentencing, recommend that the client not be incarcerated." The agreement further states that only upon completion of Huebner's cooperation would the government "be in the best posture to evaluate the witness' efforts." The agreement concludes that "the government could decide to charge Huebner with less than the three aforesaid counts if in the considered opinion of the responsible Assistant U.S. Attorney he, in his sole judgment, decided the level of cooperation so warranted."

Courts have upheld agreements similar to Huebner's. In United States v. Dailey, 759 F.2d 192 (1st Cir.1985), the court allowed the testimony of three co-conspirators who had made performance deals with the prosecution. The agreement reached with two co-conspirators provided that "depending principally upon the value to the Government of the defendant's cooperation, the Government, in its sole discretion, may recommend [a reduced sentence]". The agreement of the other co-conspirator conditioned a stay of sentencing and government support for the co-conspirator's motion for a reduced sentence upon "the value or 'benefit' of his information to the government." Although expressing "concern and uneasiness ... over the coercive potential of these plea agreements", the *Dailey* court held that "the risk of perjury created by the agreements is not so great that Dailey's due process rights will be violated by the admission of the accomplice's testimony at trial." Many cases have allowed the testimony of informers whose payment, whether it be leniency or cash, was contingent upon the beneficial results obtained by their testimony. United States v. Valle–Ferrer, 739 F.2d 545, 546–47 (11th Cir.1984) (allowing testimony of informant who would receive $1,000 only if testimony resulted in conviction); United States v. Jones, 575 F.2d 81, 85–86 (6th Cir.1978) (allowing testimony of informant who would receive $1,000 only if investigation "successful"); United States v. Edwards, 549 F.2d 362, 365 (5th Cir.1977), (allowing testimony of informant whose payment was contingent upon "final results"); United States v. Dickens, 524 F.2d 441, 446 (5th Cir.1975), (allowing testimony of informants "paid on the basis of what they produce"); United States v. Grimes, 438 F.2d 391, 395–96 (6th Cir.1971), (generally allowing testimony obtained under contingency deals). Courts also routinely allow the testimony of accomplices who have been promised leniency conditioned upon adequate cooperation. [Citations omitted] It requires no extension of these authorities to allow Huebner's testimony.

In our legal system, the danger of perjured or unreliable testimony from immunized accomplices is minimized not by excluding that testimony but through the use of procedural safeguards. The Supreme Court discussed these safeguards in connection with the testimony of an informant who had been rewarded for his information with leniency and money:

> [This informer], perhaps even more than most informers, may have had motives to lie. But it does not follow that his testimony was untrue, nor does it follow that his testimony was constitutionally inadmissible. The established safeguards of the Anglo–American legal system leave the veracity of a witness to be tested by cross-examination, and the credibility of his testimony to be determined by a properly instructed jury.

Hoffa v. United States (1966). The adequacy of these procedures is also recognized in the circuits. [Citations omitted]

Fallon's rights of due process would be adequately protected by informing the jury of the terms of Huebner's deal, subjecting Huebner to vigorous cross-examination, and properly instructing the jury. The lower court went beyond this and instructed the jury to totally disregard Huebner's testimony. This instruction was favorable to Fallon and could not have denied him due process. Fallon thus has no grounds upon which to base a motion for mistrial.

We also note that there are factors besides the Due Process clause which limit the government's use of performance deals based on results or vesting large amounts of discretion in the prosecution. As the deal becomes more discretionary or based on results, the accused becomes less likely to accept it because it is less favorable to him or her. The government must also balance the benefit from testimony obtained under a performance deal against that testimony's decreased credibility. Although these factors do not provide the immutable guarantee of the Due Process clause against outrageous deals or against testimony not adequately qualified by procedural safeguards, they provide some assurance that even well within the bounds of due process the government is constrained from freely dictating the terms of leniency deals to co-conspirators and accomplices.

Affirmed.

NOTES

1. On the issue of accomplices, consider the comments of a judge who had along and distinguished career as both a federal and state prosecutor. United States v. Bernal–Obeso, 989 F.2d 331 (9th Cir.1993)

■ TROTT, CIRCUIT JUDGE:

I

Bernal–Obeso's conviction was based in large measure on the testimony of a confidential informant named Cabrera–Diaz. Cabrera–Diaz, a Mexican citizen, had worked undercover for the Drug Enforcement Administration (DEA) for three to four years and was instrumental in the investigation resulting in Bernal–Obeso's conviction. For his work related to this case, Cabrera–Diaz was paid (1) $1,000 on the day Bernal–Obeso was arrested, (2) $1,000 a few days later when debriefed by the government, and (3) $10,000 shortly before the appellant's indictment. Cabrera–Diaz's relationship with the DEA also permitted him to travel freely throughout the United States for the DEA, even though he had only a border crossing card.

The trouble leading to this appeal started when ... five days late, and only five days before the trial was scheduled to begin, the government advised the defense in a written memorandum that Cabrera–Diaz had killed two people in1982, but had not been charged with any crimes pertaining to their deaths ... [I]mmediately before the trial began, defense counsel [moved] for a continuance, advising the court that the government's memorandum was wrong in almost all respects: (1) Cabrera–Diaz had been charged with two counts of murder and two counts of attempted murder for his involvement in the 1982 killings; (2) he had not raised a claim of self-defense; and (3) he had pleaded guilty to two felony counts of voluntary manslaughter with a firearm enhancement ... [D]efense counsel requested a preliminary ruling from the court allowing him to attempt to impeach Cabrera–Diaz with what counsel believed were lies to the DEA concerning his prior record. Both requests were denied. The court permitted impeachment of the informant with his prior manslaughter convictions, but allowed no questions about the possibility of lies to the DEA.

[1] The vexing hitch in this case is that the government has created the impression that Cabrera–Diaz lied to the DEA before the trial about his impeach able criminal history. The difference between the government's memorandum regarding Cabrera–Diaz's criminal history and the facts relating to his pleas of guilty to manslaughter is responsible for this impression.

II

The use of informants to investigate and prosecute persons engaged in clandestine criminal activity is fraught with peril. This hazard is a matter "capable of accurate and ready determination by resort to sources whose accuracy cannot reasonably be questioned" and thus of which we can take judicial notice.... By definition, criminal informants are cut from untrustworthy cloth and must be managed and carefully watched by the government and the courts to prevent them from falsely accusing the innocent, from manufacturing evidence against those under suspicion of crime, and from lying under oath in the courtroom ... A prosecutor who does not appreciate the perils of using rewarded criminals as witnesses risks compromising the truth-seeking mission of our criminal justice system. See United States v. Wallach, 935 F.2d 445 (2d Cir.1991) (convictions reversed because government should have known witness was committing perjury).Because the government decides whether and when to use such witnesses, and what, if anything, to give them for their service, the government stands uniquely positioned to guard against perfidy. By its actions, the government can either contribute to or eliminate the problem. Accordingly, we expect prosecutors and investigators to take all reasonable measures to safeguard the system against treachery. This responsibility includes the duty as required by Giglio to turn over to the defense in discovery all material information casting a shadow on a government witness's credibility.

Our judicial history is speckled with cases where informants falsely pointed the finger of guilt at suspects and defendants, creating the risk of sending innocent persons to prison. As an example from our own circuit, one need only recall the widely publicized Leslie Vernon White saga in Los Angeles, California, which resulted in the reinvestigation of over 100 felony cases by the Office of the District Attorney of Los Angeles County involving alleged jailhouse confessions brought to the attention of the authorities by cell mates. White, a frequent witness for state prosecutors, is now in state prison for perjury. The White revelations also triggered an investigation of the use of such informants by the Los Angeles County Grand Jury which issued an eye-opening report on June 26, 1990. In this report, the Grand Jury makes this telling observation:

> Informants do not tend to follow mores. According to one informant, "in the old days" informants abided by a rule not to act as an informant against other informants, but presently informants "will even book their own mother."

This disinclination to follow societal rules extends to their willingness to defile an oath. Informants testified before the Grand Jury to repeated instances of perjury and providing false information to law enforcement. With one exception, each informant who testified claimed he himself had committed perjury or provided false information incriminating another inmate one or more times.

Criminals caught in our system understand they can mitigate their own problems with the law by becoming a witness against someone else. Some of these informants will stop at nothing to maneuver themselves into a position where they have something to sell. It is no accident that some federal jury instructions regarding an immunized witness warn jurors [about] such a witness.... A pattern jury instruction puts it this way:

ACCOMPLICE–INFORMER–IMMUNITY

The testimony of some witnesses must be considered with more caution than the testimony of other witnesses.

> For example, a paid informer, or a witness who has been promised that he or she will not be charged or prosecuted, or a witness who hopes to gain more favorable treatment in his or her own case, may have a reason to make a false statement because he wants to strike a good bargain with the Government.

So, while a witness of that kind may be entirely truthful when testifying, you should consider that testimony with more caution than the testimony of other witnesses.

Pattern Jury Instructions of the District Judges Association of the Eleventh Circuit, Criminal Cases, Special Instruction No. 1.1 (1985).

It is also true, however, that our criminal justice system could not adequately function without information provided by informants and without their sworn testimony in certain cases. This need is created by our rules permitting persons accused of crime to confront the witnesses against them, measures that elevate the hearsay rule to Constitutional dimensions. Moreover, it is a well-known phenomena that the higher-ups in criminal enterprises attempt to insulate themselves from detection and exposure by having their unlawful schemes carried out by others. Without informants, law enforcement authorities would be unable to penetrate and destroy organized crime syndicates, drug trafficking cartels, bank frauds, telephone solicitations cams, public corruption, terrorist gangs, money launderers, espionage rings, and the likes. In the words of Judge Learned Hand, "Courts have countenanced the use of informers from time immemorial; in cases of conspiracy, or in other cases when the crime consists of preparing for another crime, it is usually necessary to rely upon them or upon accomplices because the criminals will almost certainly proceed covertly." United States v. Dennis, 183 F.2d 201, 224 (2d Cir.1950), aff'd, 341 U.S. 494, 71 S.Ct. 857, 95 L.Ed. 1137 (1951); On Lee v. United States, 343 U.S. at 756, 72 S.Ct. at 973 ("Certainly no one would foreclose the turning of state's evidence by denizens of the underworld."). Innumerable important convictions have been appropriately attained using informants' testimony.

Thus, we have decided on balance not to prohibit, as some have suggested, the practice of rewarding self-confessed criminals for their cooperation, or to outlaw the testimony in court of those who receive something in return for their testimony. Instead, we have chosen to rely on (1) the integrity of government agents and prosecutors not to introduce untrustworthy evidence into the system ... (2) trial judges and stringent discovery rules to subject the process to close scrutiny, ... (3) defense counsel to test such evidence with vigorous cross examination, Davis v. Alaska, ... (1974) ("Cross examination is the principle means by which the believability of a witness and the truth of his testimony are tested."), and (4) the wisdom of a properly instructed jury whose duty it is to assess each witness's credibility and not to convict unless persuaded beyond a reasonable doubt of the accused's guilt.... See also United States v. Cervantes–Pacheco, 826 F.2d 310, 315 (5th Cir.1987), ... ("[A]n informant who is promised a contingent fee by the government is not disqualified from testifying in a federal criminal trial.") Because we have made this choice, it is essential that relevant evidence bearing on the credibility of an informant-witness be timely revealed (1) to defense counsel as required by

Giglio, and (2) to the ultimate trier of fact, unless clearly cumulative or attenuated.

Turning to the present case, we simply do not know what it is that floats menacingly into our waters. The unseen part of the iceberg as to Cabrera–Diaz's credibility may be benign, or it may spell trouble for the government's case. It is clear in the abstract, however, that a lie to the authorities paying for his services by an informant-witness about his felony criminal record would be relevant evidence as to the informant's credibility. See Fed.R.Evid. 608(b). The usefulness of an informant as a witness depends in large measure on the degree to which he both is and can be presented to a fact finder as a reliable person. As any trial lawyer knows, felony convictions trench heavily upon such a person's credibility. Prior felony convictions frequently convince defense attorneys not to call their clients to the witness stand for fear that a jury might be swayed by such a background to disregard the defendant's testimony. Prosecutors confront the same problem in evaluating the usefulness of an informant as a witness: a serious felony record could cause a jury completely to disregard his testimony and possibly to conclude from it that the government's entire case is suspect. For reasons not yet brought to the light of day, the government did not bring the existence of Cabrera–Diaz's felony convictions to the attention of the defense; the defense discovered the convictions on its own initiative.

Moreover, an informant who attempted to conceal his felony criminal record either from an investigating agency or a prosecutor could well be seen by a jury as someone whose testimony should be flatly rejected. If he would lie to the DEA to get his well-paying job, why would he not lie to a jury about the activities of his quarry to keep it, or so goes the argument. This is especially true of an informant such as Cabrera–Diaz who appears from the record to have been on the payroll of the DEA, as compared to someone only involved in a single case or episode. To demonstrate this point, we need look no farther than Cabrera–Diaz's answers on cross-examination:

> Q. And you've come to learn that the more information you give them the more money you can make?
>
> A. Yes.
>
> Q. You've come to learn that the bigger the case the more money you're able to make?
>
> A. Well, yes.
>
> Q. The more drugs, the more money?
>
> A. Yes.
>
> Q. The more people, the more money?
>
> A. Yes.

As the government conceded at oral argument, such a material lie by a critical informant-witness about his prior record would be exculpatory and thus discoverable Brady information which the government would be under a Constitutional duty to disclose. Evidence of such a lie might be equivalent to the proverbial smoking gun. All the other evidence used by the defense to punch holes in Cabrera–Diaz's credibility amounted only to circumstantial reasons why Cabrera–Diaz might alter the truth to continue to feather his own nest. A lie would be direct proof of this concern, eliminating the need for inferences.

III

Ordinarily, "we review the district court's limitation on the extent of the cross-examination for an abuse of discretion." United States v. Guthrie, 931 F.2d 564, 568 (9th Cir.1991). Because neither we nor the trial court know what it is we are attempting to review, however, we cannot fulfill this responsibility on this record. Notwithstanding the government's liability for this quandary, we will not presume under these circumstances that the government has intentionally deprived the defendant of evidence that would erode the informant's credibility. On the other hand, we will not assume an innocent explanation from a silent record. The appropriate step is to vacate the defendant's conviction and remand to the district court for an evidentiary hearing to determine what happened and why, with respect to the government's miscommunication to the defense about Cabrera–Diaz's criminal record....

Our intent in ordering an evidentiary hearing is to restore the parties to the position in which they found themselves pretrial, but with counsel for the defendant and the court fully enlightened as to the facts surrounding the issue of Cabrera–Diaz's communications with the government, if any, about his felony record. In that posture, the court shall determine under the usual standards if admissible evidence exists in connection with Cabrera–Diaz's behavior that would impeach his credibility. See Fed. R.Evid. 608(b). If the court determines that "a threshold level of evidence [exists] to show that the defendant's allegations of misconduct have some grounding in reality," United States v. Ray, 731 F.2d 1361, 1364 (9th Cir.1984), the court shall order a new trial. To avoid this outcome, in essence the government shall have to demonstrate to the satisfaction of the court that there is no grounding in reality for the claim that Cabrera–Diaz lied. This procedure should most closely approximate the manner in which the decision regarding admissibility should have been made in the first place. If the court determines that a new trial is not in order, the court may reinstate the judgment of conviction. Should the court uncover egregious wrongdoing by the government, however, nothing in this opinion forecloses consideration by the court of dismissing the indictment for outrageous government conduct. See ... United States v. Barrera–Moreno,951 F.2d 1089 (9th Cir.1991). This panel retains appellate jurisdiction over this matter.[3]

VACATED and REMANDED.

2. In the federal courts and in most state jurisdictions, accomplice testimony alone, if believed by the trier of fact, is sufficient to sustain a conviction. See Caminetti v. United States, 242 U.S. 470, 37 S.Ct. 192 (1917); Green v. State, 241 Ind. 96, 168 N.E.2d 345 (1960). Several state jurisdictions require independent corroboration. See People v. MacEwing, 45 Cal.2d 218, 45 Cal.2d 218, 288 P.2d 257 (1955); Stein v. New York, 346 U.S. 156, 73 S.Ct. 1077 (1953). See 7 Wigmore, Evidence, § 2059.

The question of what constitutes corroboration is, in those jurisdictions which require it, often an extremely complicated one to resolve. The difficulty of defining what is adequate corroboration as well as the belief that juries and courts will not readily accept uncorroborated accomplice evidence is a significant factor in deter-

3. Bernal–Obeso raises other issues pertaining to (1) the exclusion of evidence explaining why he could afford two motel rooms on the evening of May 30, and (2) statements by the prosecutor during closing argument regarding his economic status. We have examined his contentions in this regard and conclude they have no merit.

ring the majority of jurisdictions from adopting formal corroboration requirements and in causing those states with such requirements to lower the bar on what might be adequate corroboration. See Castillo v. State, 221 S.W.3d 689 (Tex.Crim. App. 2007) (explaining that only slight corroboration is required)

United States v. Taylor

United States Court of Appeals, Seventh Circuit, 1984.
728 F.2d 930.

■ Flaum, Circuit Judge.

[The charge was bank robbery and there was testimony that Taylor and Neff were friends and had discussed pulling an armed robbery, that Neff had borrowed a weapon and owned another weapon and a car of the type used in the offense and that Taylor and Neff had large amounts of money but only after the date of the offense.]

* * *

On the second day of the three-day trial, prior to the close of the government's case, a conference took place outside the presence of the jury, during which the court discussed the defendant's intention to call David Neff as a witness. The prosecutor informed the court that, although the government had granted Neff use immunity to testify before the grand jury in this case, the government had revoked that immunity in a letter that was mailed to Neff's attorney earlier in the day. The prosecutor stated that the government had evidence that Neff "perhaps perjured himself" and that he was the subject o fa grand jury investigation for bank robbery, perjury, and cocaine distribution. Trial Transcript at 463. The following day, another conference took place outside the presence of the jury, at which Neff's attorney appeared and indicated that Neff would assert his rights under the fifth amendment if he were called to testify at the defendant's trial. The defendant's attorney charged that the government had revoked Neff's immunity only to frustrate the defendant's defense, and he asked the court to compel the government to extend immunity to Neff. The prosecutor, on the other hand, represented to the court that the government had every intention of indicting Neff. Ruling that it had not heard anything that would indicate bad faith on the part of the government, the court refused to compel the government to extend immunity to Neff. However, in view of Neff's intention to invoke the fifth amendment, the court found Neff to be unavailable, pursuant to rule 804(a)(1) of the Federal Rules of Evidence, and it allowed excerpts of Neff's grand jury testimony, in which Neff denied involvement in the robbery, to be read to the jury at the close of the government's case.

* * *

The defendant claims that the government violated his fifth amendment right to due process and his sixth amendment right to compulsory process when it revoked Neff's use immunity on the second day of the trial. According to this claim, "unfairness to the defendant resulted from the fact that the government alone was able to determine whether it was to its immediate advantage to continue or revoke the grant of immunity to Mr.

Neff." The defendant argues that, in light of this unfairness, the trial court should have compelled the government to grant immunity to Neff. ...

The government replies that the trial court did not err in refusing to order the government to grant immunity to Neff—"[n]either the courts nor defense counsel have a legal or constitutional right to use the immunity statute to compel the testimony of defense witnesses." Moreover, the government contends that the defendant was not prejudiced by the revocation of Neff's immunity because the government did not use any testimony by Neff in its case. In fact, the defense counsel was allowed to read Neff's exonerating grand jury testimony to the jury. According to the government, there is no duty to provide immunity where, as here, evidence exists that the witness perjured himself and did not meet his immunity obligations.

It is clear that use immunity is a statutory creation, United States v. Lenz, 616 F.2d 960, 962 (6th Cir.), and that Congress has delegated the authority to grant use immunity solely to the executive branch of government. 18 U.S.C. § 6003 (1982). In exercising this authority, the executive must balance "the public need for the particular testimony or documentary information in question against the social cost of granting immunity and thereby precluding the possibility of criminally prosecuting an individual who has violated the criminal law." In re Daley, 549 F.2d 469, 478–79 (7th Cir.). Both the exclusive nature of Congress's delegation and the fact that the balancing process is wholly within the expertise of the executive branch foreclose the federal courts from taking more than a ministerial role in prosecutorial immunity decisions that are made properly under 18 U.S.C. § 6003. Id. at 479. The sixth amendment right to compulsory process does not mandate otherwise. This provision ensures that a defendant has subpoena power to summon witnesses so that the jury may hear the defendant's version of the facts. See Washington v. Texas (1967). It "does not suggest a right to supercede [sic] a witness' invocation of his own fifth amendment privilege or the right to demand that the government shield a witness from the consequences of his own testimony." United States v. Chagra, 669 F.2d 241, 260 (5th Cir.). . . .

The government's authority to request immunity under 18 U.S.C. § 6003 is not unlimited. Prosecutors must exercise this authority within the bounds of the due process clause of the fifth amendment. Thus, this circuit has held that it"will not review a prosecutor's immunization decisions in the absence of substantial evidence showing that the prosecutor's actions amounted to a clear abuse of discretion violating the due process clause." United States v. Wilson, 715 F.2d 1164, 1173 (7th Cir.1983). Such an abuse of discretion occurs when a prosecutor intends to use his authority under the immunity statute to distort the judicial fact-finding process. United States v. Frans, 697 F.2d 188, 191 (7th Cir.).

In the present case, the prosecutor explained to the trial court that, less than a week before the commencement of trial, the government had received information indicating that Neff had lied when he testified before the grand jury under a grant of immunity. The prosecutor identified this new information by referring to certain facts elicited from Ken Tudor, a prosecution witness. The district court found no bad faith on the part of the government. We also can find no basis in the record for not believing that the prosecutor, while preparing for trial, learned information from one witness that contradicted Neff's grand jury testimony. Since Neff's immunity agreement required him to give truthful testimony, it was within the prosecutor's discretion, under 18 U.S.C. § 6003, to determine that Neff had broken the agreement and to revoke his immunity as a consequence. In addition, the record does not show that the government's decision to grant immunity to Tudor and to Dallas Manns, another government witness who testified at trial, was related to the decision to revoke Neff's immunity. Thus, the granting of immunity to both Tudor and Manns is not indicative of prosecutorial bad faith in revoking Neff's immunity. See United States v. Herman, 589 F.2d 1191, 1204 (3d Cir.1978). Cf. United States v. Thevis, 665 F.2d 616, 641 n. 28 (5th Cir.1982) ("a trial is not a 'symmetrical proceeding' which requires a court to grant the defendant's witnesses immunity because the government uses immunized witnesses"). Based on our review of the record, we conclude that there is not substantial evidence showing that the prosecutor intended to distort the fact-finding process by revoking Neff's immunity on the second day of trial. We therefore hold that due process did not require the trial court to order the government to grant immunity to Neff.

* * *

NOTES

1. Assume a defendant is charged with possessing narcotics and he claims that his mistress, who was the only other person with access to the apartment, planted the narcotics in his overcoat lining. She may be the only witness who can exonerate him but she claims privilege. The prosecution has no intention of prosecuting her, but could a court require the prosecution to grant immunity? Should it?

May a defendant at trial ever obtain immunity for a witness who would exculpate the defendant and inculpate himself? Does due process demand that the trial judge be permitted to grant such a request under specified circumstances. See Comment, Defense Witness Immunity and the Right to a Fair Trial, 129 U.Pa. L.Rev. 377 (1980). People v. Sapia, 41 N.Y.2d 160, 391 N.Y.S.2d 93, 359 N.E.2d 688 (1976).

Some have advocated immunity under certain circumstances for defense witnesses, cases mandating such grants of immunity are far fewer. For one, see People v. Owens, 97 A.D.2d 855, 469 N.Y.S.2d 249 (1983), reversed 63 N.Y.2d 824, 482 N.Y.S.2d 250, 472 N.E.2d 26 (1984). Except for the Third Circuit the federal courts have generally rejected claims that the court has either statutory or inherent power to grant immunity to defense witnesses. See United States v. Pennell, 737 F.2d 521 (6th Cir.1984) (review of cases and policy); United States v. Mendia, 731 F.2d 1412 (9th Cir.1984). The First Circuit recognizes "two theories ... under the 'effective defense theory' a court has power to immunize witnesses whose testimony is essential to an effective defense ... under the 'prosecutorial misconduct theory' courts [can] require ... immunity ... if the government has deliberately attempted to distort the fact finding process." United States v. Pratt, 913 F.2d 982 (1st Cir.1990) (dictum).

2. Assume the defense can not secure immunity for a witness who refuses to testify for it without immunity. May the defense call the witness to the stand for the purpose of having the fifth amendment privilege asserted in the presence of the trier of fact and then argue the assertion is evidence the witness (not the accused) is guilty?

3. In New Jersey v. Portash, 440 U.S. 450, 99 S.Ct. 1292 (1979), the Supreme Court held that testimony which was given under a grant of immunity cannot be used to impeach the witness who at trial tells a version of events different from that included in his immunized testimony. The Court held that immunized testimony is coerced in a "classical" sense and upon that basis distinguished the use for impeachment purposes of a Miranda-violative statement. Compare Harris v. New York, Chapter 6, Section D–2, supra. Of course a defendant who changes his story from the version he gave under immunity may be setting himself up for a perjury indictment.

4. While the court must issue the immunity order, this function has been described as "ministerial". The court may not review the prosecutor's decision to grant immunity; the primary purpose of a hearing on the question is to permit technical objections to compliance requirements. See In re Lochiatto, 497 F.2d 803 (1st Cir.1974). For an argument that the judge should have a meaningful role in the decision, see Wolfson, Immunity: How it Works in Real Life, 69 J.Crim. L & C. 322 (1978). Moreover, a defendant has no standing to object to the granting of immunity to a witness against him. United States v. Braasch, 505 F.2d 139, 146 (7th Cir.1974); United States v. Neal, 743 F.2d 1441 (10th Cir.1984).

5. United States v. Jones, 703 F.2d 473 (10th Cir.1983), provides a good review of standards for determining when a claim of possible self-incrimination ought to be upheld in the absence of a grant of immunity. It indicates that the test is *not* whether authorities are likely to bring a prosecution, but rather whether the individual's responses or evidence derived from them could, viewed realistically, *if* a prosecutor so chose, be used in a prosecution of an offense within the applicable statute of limitations and not barred by double jeopardy principles. See State v. Whitt, 220 W.Va. 685, 649 S.E.2d 258 (2007) (claim of privilege invalid where witness had already been acquitted of the crime about which she was to testify).

Washington v. Texas

Supreme Court of the United States, 1967.
388 U.S. 14, 87 S.Ct. 1920, on remand 417 S.W.2d 278 (Tex.Crim.App.1967).

■ MR. CHIEF JUSTICE WARREN delivered the opinion of the Court.

* * *

Petitioner, Jackie Washington, was convicted of murder with malice and was sentenced by a jury to 50 years in prison. The prosecution's evidence showed that petitioner, an 18–year–old youth, had dated a girl named Jean Carter until her mother had forbidden her to see him. The girl thereafter began dating another boy, the deceased. Evidently motivated by jealousy, petitioner with several other boys began driving around the City of Dallas on the night of August 29, 1964, looking for a gun. The search eventually led to one Charles Fuller, who joined the group with his shotgun. After obtaining some shells from another source, the group of boys proceeded to Jean Carter's home, where Jean, her family and the deceased were having supper. Some of the boys threw bricks at the house and then ran back to the car, leaving petitioner and Fuller alone in front of the house with the shotgun. At the sound of the bricks the deceased and Jean Carter's mother rushed out on the porch to investigate. The shotgun was fired by either petitioner or Fuller, and the deceased was fatally wounded. Shortly afterward petitioner and Fuller came running back to the car where the other boys waited, with Fuller carrying the shotgun.

Petitioner testified in his own behalf. He claimed that Fuller, who was intoxicated, had taken the gun from him, and that he had unsuccessfully tried to persuade Fuller to leave before the shooting. Fuller had insisted that he was going to shoot someone, and petitioner had run back to the automobile. He saw the girl's mother come out of the door as he began running, and he subsequently heard the shot. At the time, he had thought that Fuller had shot the woman. In support of his version of the facts petitioner offered the testimony of Fuller. The record indicates that Fuller would have testified that petitioner pulled at him and tried to persuade him to leave, and that petitioner ran before Fuller fired the fatal shot.

It is undisputed that Fuller's testimony would have been relevant and material, and that it was vital to the defense. Fuller was the only person other than petitioner who knew exactly who had fired the shotgun and whether petitioner had at the last minute attempted to prevent the shooting. Fuller, however, had been previously convicted of the same murder and sentenced to 50years in prison. Two Texas statutes provided at the time of the trial in this case that persons charged or convicted as co-participants in the same crime could not testify for one another, although there was no bar to their testifying for the State. On the basis of these statutes the trial judge sustained the State's objection and refused to allow Fuller to testify....

I.

We have not previously been called upon to decide whether the right of an accused to have compulsory process for obtaining witnesses in his favor, guaranteed in federal trials by the Sixth Amendment, is so fundamental and essential to a fair trial that it is incorporated in the Due Process Clause of the Fourteenth Amendment. ...

... This Court had occasion In re Oliver, to describe what it regarded as the most basic ingredients of due process of law. It observed that:

> "A person's right to reasonable notice of a charge against him, and an opportunity to be heard in his defense—a right to his day in court—are basic in our system of jurisprudence; and these rights include, as a minimum, aright to examine the witnesses against him, to offer testimony, and to be represented by counsel."

The right to offer the testimony of witnesses, and to compel their attendance, if necessary, is in plain terms the right to present a defense, the right to present the defendant's version of the facts as well as the prosecution's to the jury so it may decide where the truth lies. Just as an accused has the right to confront the prosecution's witnesses for the purpose of challenging their testimony, he has the right to present his own witnesses to establish a defense. This right is a fundamental element of due process of law.

II.

Since the right to compulsory process is applicable in this state proceeding, the question remains whether it was violated in the circumstances of this case. The testimony of Charles Fuller was denied to the defense not because the State refused to compel his attendance, but because a state statute made his testimony inadmissible whether he was present in the courtroom or not....

Joseph Story, in his famous Commentaries on the Constitution of the United States, observed that the right to compulsory process was included in the Bill of Rights in reaction to the notorious common-law rule that in cases oft reason or felony the accused was not allowed to introduce witnesses in his defense at all. ...

Despite the abolition of the rule generally disqualifying defense witnesses, the common law retained a number of restrictions on witnesses who were physically and mentally capable of testifying. To the extent that they were applicable, they had the same effect of suppressing the truth that the general proscription had. Defendants and codefendants were among the large class of witnesses disqualified from testifying on the ground of interest. A party to a civil or criminal case was not allowed to testify on his own behalf for fear that he might be tempted to lie. Although originally the disqualification of a codefendant appears to have been based only on his status as a party to the action, and in some jurisdictions co-indictees were allowed to testify for or against each other if granted separate trials, other jurisdictions came to the view that accomplices or co-indictees were incompetent to testify at least in favor of each other even at separate trials, and in spite of statutes making a defendant competent to testify in his own behalf. It was thought that if two persons charged with the same crime were allowed to testify on behalf of each other, "each would try to swear the other out of the charge." This rule, as well as the other disqualifications for interest, rested on the unstated premises that the right to present witnesses was subordinate to the court's interest in preventing perjury, and that erroneous decisions were best avoided by preventing the jury from hearing any testimony that might be perjured, even if it were the only testimony available on a crucial issue.[18]

The federal courts followed the common-law restrictions for a time, despite the Sixth Amendment. ... The holding in United States v. Reid was not satisfactory to later generations, however, and in 1918 this Court expressly overruled it, refusing to be bound by the "the dead hand of the common-law rule of 1789," and taking note of "the conviction of our time that the truth is more likely to be arrived at by hearing the testimony of all persons of competent understanding who may seem to have knowledge of the facts involved in a case, leaving the credit and weight of such testimony to be determined by the jury or by the court...." Rosen v. United States. In light of the common-law history, and in view of the recognition that the Sixth Amendment was designed in part to make the testimony of a defendant's witnesses admissible on his behalf in court, it could hardly be argued that a State would not violate the clause if it made all defense

18. "Indeed, the theory of the common law was to admit to the witness stand only those presumably honest, appreciating the sanctity of an oath, unaffected as a party by the result, and free from any of the temptations of interest. The courts were afraid to trust the intelligence of jurors." Benson v. United States, 146 U.S. 325, 336, 13 S.Ct. 60, 63 (1892).

testimony inadmissible as a matter of procedural law. It is difficult to see how the Constitution is any less violated by arbitrary rules that prevent whole categories of defense witnesses from testifying on the basis of *a priori* categories that presume them unworthy of belief.

The rule disqualifying an alleged accomplice from testifying on behalf of the defendant cannot even be defended on the ground that it rationally sets apart a group of persons who are particularly likely to commit perjury. The absurdity of the rule is amply demonstrated by the exceptions that have been made to it. For example, the accused accomplice may be called by the prosecution to testify against the defendant. Common sense would suggest that he often has a greater interest in lying in favor of the prosecution rather than against it, especially if he is still awaiting his own trial or sentencing. To think that criminals will lie to save their fellows but not to obtain favors from the prosecution for themselves is indeed to clothe the criminal class with more nobility than one might expect to find in the public at large. Moreover, under the Texas statutes, the accused accomplice is no longer disqualified if he is acquitted at his own trial. Presumably, he would then be free to testify on behalf of his comrade, secure in the knowledge that he could incriminate himself as freely as he liked in his testimony, since he could not again be prosecuted for the same offense. The Texas law leaves him free to testify when he has a great incentive to perjury, and bars his testimony in situations where he has a lesser motive to lie.

We hold that the petitioner in this case was denied his right to have compulsory process for obtaining witnesses in his favor because the State arbitrarily denied him the right to put on the stand a witness who was physically and mentally capable of testifying to events that he had personally observed, and whose testimony would have been relevant and material to the defense.[21] The Framers of the Constitution did not intend to commit the futile act of giving to a defendant the right to secure the attendance of witnesses whose testimony he had no right to use. The judgment of conviction must be reversed. It is so ordered.

Reversed.

■ MR. JUSTICE HARLAN [omitted].

NOTES

1. The concluding footnote of the Court's opinion in Washington v. Texas states that "nothing in this opinion should be construed as disapproving testimonial privileges, such as the privilege against self-incrimination or the lawyer-client or husband-wife privileges. . . ." The Court's examples are not exhaustive. There are numerous statutory privileges and their number has increased in recent years. There is the priest-penitent or clergyman privilege, the physician-patient privilege,

21. Nothing in this opinion should be construed as disapproving testimonial privileges, such as the privilege against self-incrimination or the lawyer-client or husband-wife privileges, which are based on entirely different considerations from those underlying the common-law disqualifications for interest. Nor do we deal in this case with nonarbitrary state rules that disqualify as witnesses persons who, because of mental infirmity or infancy, are incapable of observing events or testifying about them.

and the psychologist-patient privilege. Some jurisdictions have an accountant-client privilege. Recently there has been the use of the news media informant privilege.

The nature and scope of these privileges varies from jurisdiction to jurisdiction. A thorough dissertation of privilege law is found in 8 Wigmore, Evidence (McNaughton Rev.1961). The privilege against self-incrimination is usually limited to communications, that is, evidence of what the person says as opposed to evidence of what he has done or evidence about his physical characters. This limitation was explored in United States v. Dionisio, supra Chapter 11. Similar forms of limitations usually apply to the husband-wife, psychiatrist-patient and psychologist-patient and clergyman privileges. In most but not all jurisdictions, such privileges preclude only evidence concerning statements made by spouse, patient or penitent. Thus a wife may usually testify as to what her husband did but not what he said, i.e., she may reveal that when he came home his clothes were bloody and that he burned his clothes but she may not reveal that he said "I just killed a child with my hunting knife." See United States v. Archer, 733 F.2d 354 (5th Cir.1984). Another example is encountered occasionally in modern criminal cases. An attorney may attend a line-up on his client's behalf. What he observes at the line-up is not privileged and the prosecution often is entitled to his testimony if it helps establish their case. See People v. Dozier, 22 Mich.App. 528, 177 N.W.2d 694 (1970). Similarly, counsel may be compelled to testify as to his observations of his client's physical condition at the police station if there is claim that a confession was physically coerced. State v. Funicello, 49 N.J. 553, 231 A.2d 579 (1967). But in some jurisdictions, privilege extends to "information" acquired as a result of the privileged relationship as well as communications. The physician-patient, accountant-client, and news media-informant privileges usually cover more than communications. The physician-patient privilege is often at issue in welfare fraud cases when the government needs patient names so that it can determine whether the services billed were provided. See Commonwealth v. Kobrin, 395 Mass. 284, 479 N.E.2d 674 (1985). Generally such privileges apply to all information acquired by virtue of the privileged relationship.

Finally, the various privileges are subject to statutory exceptions. A court is often given power to disregard privilege in the interests of justice; for instance, physician-patient privileges are sometimes inapplicable in homicide cases.

2. Is there any method to determine effect of these privileges on criminal cases? There is simply no way to measure the amount of privileged communication and information that is relevant to criminal cases from the frequency with which the privilege is asserted. The privilege is asserted when one party to the privileged communication has improperly revealed its contents and the prosecution or defense counsel learns of the contents and attempts to introduce it into evidence. The attorneys may, of course, guess without knowing that privileged information may be of value, but usually this involves an accomplice or participant in the crime and the privilege against self-incrimination is claimed. We suspect that some relevant information simply never surfaces at all. Most legally privileged relationships correspond to relationships which society would generally consider confidential even without sanction of law. Those who receive confidential communications will often feel a personal compulsion or distaste for public revelation even when they are legally free to do so. A husband may confess a crime to his wife and she may never repeat his confession to anyone, not because of legal restraint, but rather because she loves her husband and does not wish to damage her own family.

Are we in a position to judge whether privileges or any given privilege should restrict access to evidence when we cannot judge how great a price we pay in terms of the loss of relevant information?

If we cannot judge the price we pay for privilege, is it proper to assume that privileges should exist and place the burden of proof upon those who would abolish privilege or any given privilege?

If privileged information is seldom uncovered because of social rather than legal pressures, would any purpose be served by abolishing socially endorsed privileges? For example, would repeal of a marital privilege statute really lessen the number of hidden communications? Assume that prosecutors and defense counsel would, after repeal, regularly interview and perhaps subpoena the spouses of the accused, his accomplices, other suspects and key witnesses. Would not the spouse who is willing to keep silent also be willing to commit perjury? If most persons were aware that the privilege had no legal sanction, would they confide in their spouses to the degree they do now? Would the answers be different if a different privilege were involved, e.g., lack of candor with one's physician even where there is no privilege may well have disagreeable or even fatal effects?

3. Consider the effect of privilege on the factual situation presented in Chambers v. Mississippi, infra, Section 2. Assume McDonald confessed not to Chambers' lawyer but to his own lawyer, or to his wife, or to his priest, and Chambers' lawyer learned of the confession. Would the Court adhere to its position in Washington v. Texas and reject Chambers' appeal? From the viewpoint of Chambers himself, does not a ruling sustaining the privilege have precisely the same effect as one sustaining the witness voucher and hearsay arguments that Mississippi offered to defend the conviction? What would the Court say the difference was and would their answer satisfy you?

Suppose that McDonald did not confess to anyone but that Chambers' lawyer suspects (say from physical evidence) that he committed the crime and then he interviews McDonald, but McDonald refuses to answer on grounds of self-incrimination. What can Chambers' lawyer do? McDonald can exonerate his client but the privilege is a barrier. (And cases can be conceived in which the only possible exonerating witness, other than the defendant, may claim the privilege.) Can the prosecution be compelled to grant immunity to McDonald? If this is done, the prosecution will either never be able to prosecute McDonald (if transactional immunity is granted) or will probably be unable to prosecute (if use immunity is granted). It may be said that the policy of the law is to prefer acquittal of the innocent over conviction of the guilty and that it is better to have both McDonald and Chambers escape. But this assumes that McDonald is guilty and Chambers is innocent, an assumption which generally cannot be made in advance of trial. Perhaps McDonald is falsely claiming privilege or he claims privilege because he did not commit murder but was committing robbery or shooting at the other officer at the time of the incident? Perhaps McDonald is operating under a mistaken belief of guilt, i.e., McDonald fires his gun at the officer not knowing the powder was stale and bullet was spent before reaching the target.

4. The privileges thus far mentioned belong to private individuals. The state has its own set of privileges, the most common of which is the informer privilege. Law enforcement officers frequently use informers and are entitled generally to keep their names secret. In McCray v. Illinois, 386 U.S. 300, 87 S.Ct. 1056 (1967), the petitioner was arrested, searched, and successfully prosecuted for possession of heroin found in the course of the search. The officers justified the arrest and search on the basis of information from an informer, not present at the arrest, whose reliability was adequately established but whose identity the officers refused to disclose. The Court sustained the informer privilege for the following reasons:

"... When the issue is not guilt or innocence, but, as here, the question of probable cause for an arrest or search, the Illinois Supreme Court has held that police officers need not invariably be required to disclose an informant's identity if the trial judge is convinced, by evidence submitted in open court and subject to cross-examination, that the officers did rely in good faith upon credible information supplied by a reliable informant. . . ."

"The reasoning of the Supreme Court of New Jersey in judicially adopting the same basic evidentiary rule was instructively expressed by Chief Justice Weintraub in State v. Burnett, 42 N.J. 377, 201 A.2d 39:

> 'If a defendant may insist upon disclosure of the informant in order to test the truth of the officer's statement that there is an informant or as to what the informant related or as to the informant's reliability, we can be sure that every defendant will demand disclosure. He has nothing to lose and the prize may be the suppression of damaging evidence if the State cannot afford to reveal its source, as is so often the case. And since there is no way to test the good faith of a defendant who presses the demand, we must assume the routine demand would have to be routinely granted. The result would be that the State could use the informant's information only as a lead and could search only if it could gather adequate evidence of probable cause apart from the informant's data. Perhaps that approach would sharpen investigatorial techniques, but we doubt that there would be enough talent and time to cope with crime upon that basis. Rather we accept the premise that the informer is a vital part of society's defensive arsenal. The basic rule protecting his identity rests upon that belief. . . .
>
> 'We must remember also that we are not dealing with the trial of the criminal charge itself. There the need for a truthful verdict outweighs society's need for the informer privilege. Here, however, the accused seeks to avoid the truth. The very purpose of a motion to suppress is to escape the inculpatory thrust of evidence in hand, not because its probative force is diluted in the least by the mode of seizure, but rather as a sanction to compel enforcement officers to respect the constitutional security of all of us under the Fourth Amendment. . . . If the motion to suppress is denied, defendant will still be judged upon the untarnished truth. . . .'

* * *

". . . In the exercise of supervisory jurisdiction the Court had occasion 10 years ago, in Roviaro v. United States, to give thorough consideration to one aspect of the informer's privilege, the privilege itself having long been recognized in the federal judicial system.

"The *Roviaro* case involved the informer's privilege, not at a preliminary hearing to determine probable cause for an arrest or search, but at the trial itself where the issue was the fundamental one of innocence or guilt. The petitioner there had been brought to trial upon a two-count federal indictment charging sale and transportation of narcotics. According to the prosecution's evidence, the informer had been an active participant in the crime. He 'had taken a material part in bringing about the possession of certain drugs by the accused, had been present with the accused at the occurrence of the alleged crime, and might be a material witness as to whether the accused knowingly transported the drugs as charged.'

'This Court held that where, in an actual trial of a federal criminal case,

> 'the disclosure of an informer's identity . . . is relevant and helpful to the defense of an accused, or is essential to a fair determination of a cause, the privilege must give way. In these situations the trial court may require disclosure and, if the Government withholds the information, dismiss the action. . . .

'We believe that no fixed rule with respect to disclosure is justifiable. The problem is one that calls for balancing the public interest in protecting the flow of information against the individual's right to prepare his defense. Whether a proper balance renders nondisclosure erroneous must depend on the particular circumstances of each case, taking into consideration the crime charged, the possible defenses, the possible significance of the informer's testimony, and other relevant factors.'

"The Court's opinion then carefully reviewed the particular circumstances of Roviaro's trial, pointing out that the informer's 'possible testimony was highly relevant ...,' that he 'might have disclosed an entrapment ... ,' 'might have thrown doubt upon petitioner's identity or on the identity of the package ...,' 'might have testified to petitioner's possible lack of knowledge of the contents of the package that he "transported" ...,' and that the 'informer was the sole participant, other than the accused, in the transaction charged.' The Court concluded 'that, under these circumstances, the trial court committed prejudicial error in permitting the Government to withhold the identity of its undercover employee in the face of repeated demands by the accused for his disclosure.' "

* * *

Now that the Supreme Court has permitted evidentiary hearings under limited circumstances to test the truthfulness of an affidavit in support of a warrant application, Franks v. Delaware, Casebook, p. 1038, the issue frequently arises as to what sort of a showing a defendant must make in order to force the disclosure of the identity of the alleged informer referred to in the affidavit. The defense claim is that without such knowledge, ordinarily it will be impossible to prove (as is required for relief under *Franks*) that the affiant (and not just the informant) deliberately lied or acted with reckless disregard of the truth. So far courts have held that *McCray* remains good law after *Franks* and have disapproved routine disclosure of the identity of sources referred to in warrant applications. See United States v. Kiser, 716 F.2d 1268 (9th Cir.1983).

5. In *McCray* there is a dichotomy set forth between the assertion of privilege which affects the validity of the acquisition of evidence and the assertion of privilege which affects the trial on the merits. In the first situation, the privilege may be validly asserted; in the second it generally may not.

The premise that the government may not assert its privileges when they preclude defense access to material evidence on the merits is the traditional rule. The courts do not say that the privilege may not be asserted and preserved; the government is given a choice between preserving confidentiality and abandoning the prosecution or pursuing the prosecution and abandoning the privilege. See United States v. Andolschek, 142 F.2d 503, 506 (2d Cir.1944).

The government may be entitled to have a court examine the privileged material outside the presence of the defense at least to determine if the material does have any arguable relevance to the case on trial. Palermo v. United States, 360 U.S. 343, 79 S.Ct. 1217 (1959); but see Alderman v. United States, 394 U.S. 165, 89 S.Ct. 961 (1969).

A serious question may arise when a state government institutes prosecution and the defense seeks access to evidence which is in the possession of the federal government and protected by federal privilege. Presumably the state government would have no more right to the evidence than the defendant and the matter would be treated as any case in which a witness (as opposed to a party) asserts the privilege. The nature of the material covered by traditional federal privileges is likely to have relevance to only the rarest of state prosecutions. See Zagel, The State Secrets Privilege, 50 Minn.L.Rev. 875 (1966).

The government may waive any of its privileges and use the evidence if it so chooses. The government may use the informer or reveal the state secret if it regards the prosecution as sufficiently important. In this regard the defendant is in a similar position when he must decide whether exercising his right to take the stand is worth the sacrifice of his self-incrimination privilege on cross-examination. Brown v. United States, 356 U.S. 148, 78 S.Ct. 622 (1958).

6. There are literally hundreds of other pockets of privilege in American law. These privileges nearly all pertain to government records and are found in either statutes or administrative regulations. Common examples are rules insuring confidentiality of tax returns, accident reports, juvenile delinquency records, unemployment compensation, police reports, and welfare records. Some rules merely prohibit public inspection, while allowing production of records in response to subpoena. These records are sometimes available to the government if it wishes to use them in a prosecution and, if it does so, the defense will presumably be allowed access to them. If the records are not available to the prosecution, the problems which arise are identical to those occurring when the husband-wife privilege is asserted. These privileges have not created many controversies in the administration of criminal justice, but difficulties have arisen particularly with respect to impeachment of witnesses with their otherwise confidential records of juvenile misconduct.

In Davis v. Alaska, 415 U.S. 308, 94 S.Ct. 1105 (1974), the issue was whether the statutory privilege for juvenile court adjudications could preclude cross-examination of a juvenile witness about his current status on probation. The Court said:

> "The claim is made that the State has an important interest in protecting the anonymity of juvenile offenders and that this interest outweighs any competing interest this petitioner might have in cross-examining Green about his being on probation. The State argues that exposure of a juvenile's record of delinquency would likely cause impairment of rehabilitative goals of the juvenile correctional procedures. This exposure, it is argued, might encourage the juvenile offender to commit further acts of delinquency, or cause the juvenile offender to lose employment opportunities or otherwise suffer unnecessarily for his youthful transgression.
>
> "We do not and need not challenge the State's interest as a matter of its own policy in the administration of criminal justice to seek to preserve the anonymity of a juvenile offender. Here, however, petitioner sought to introduce evidence of Green's probation for the purpose of suggesting that Green was biased and, therefore, that his testimony was either not to be believed in his identification of petitioner or at least very carefully considered in that light. Serious damage to the strength of the State's case would have been a real possibility had petitioner been allowed to pursue this line of inquiry. In this setting we conclude that the right of confrontation is paramount to the State's policy of protecting a juvenile offender. Whatever temporary embarrassment might result to Green or his family by disclosure of his juvenile record—if the prosecution insisted on using him to make its case—is outweighed by petitioner's right to probe into the influence of possible bias in the testimony of a crucial identification witness.
>
> "In Alford v. United States, we upheld the right of defense counsel to impeach a witness by showing that because of the witness' incarceration in federal prison at the time of trial, the witness' testimony was biased as 'given under promise or expectation of immunity, or under the coercive effect of his detention by officers of the United States.' 282 U.S., at 693, 51

S.Ct., at 220. In response to the argument that the witness had a right to be protected from exposure of his criminal record, the Court stated:

> "[N]o obligation is imposed on the court, such as that suggested below, to protect a witness from being discredited on cross-examination, short of an attempted invasion of his constitutional protection from self incrimination, properly invoked. There is a duty to protect him from questions which go beyond the bounds of proper cross-examination merely to harass, annoy or humiliate him.

"As in *Alford*, we conclude that the State's desire that Green fulfill his public duty to testify free from embarrassment and with his reputation unblemished must fall before the right of petitioner to seek out the truth in the process of defending himself.

"The State's policy interest in protecting the confidentiality of a juvenile offender's record cannot require yielding of so vital a constitutional right as the effective cross-examination for bias of an adverse witness. The State could have protected Green from exposure of his juvenile adjudication in these circumstances by refraining from using him to make out its case; the State cannot, consistent with the right of confrontation, require the petitioner to bear the full burden of vindicating the State's interest in the secrecy of juvenile criminal records."

Compare People v. Knight, 139 Ill.App.3d 188, 93 Ill.Dec. 521, 486 N.E.2d 1356 (1985) (statements made by victim to civil lawyer she retained to file damage suit are privileged and the attorney client privilege—one deemed to promote the judicial process—is not secondary to accused's trial rights under Davis v. Alaska).

The sexual assault counselor's privilege was determined to be absolute and, over dissent, to be constitutional in Commonwealth v. Wilson, 529 Pa. 268, 602 A.2d 1290 (1992) (extensive discussion of the issue). A sharply divided en banc Court of Appeals upheld application of the Indiana Rape Shield Statute which excluded from evidence two statements he allegedly made during the course of the incident. One referred to a sexual practice and defendant allegedly said, "don't you like it like this? . . . Tim Hall said you did." The other was a remark about switching partners. The theory of defense was consent and defendant wanted to testify that his remarks angered the complainant who told him to stop. He did stop but her anger also led her to fabricate the charge. The evidence was excluded because it was evidence of her past sexual conduct. The trial court permitted only evidence that defendant said "something" which angered the complainant. See Stephens v. Miller, 13 F.3d 998 (7th Cir.1994). A more recent federal decision found that a victim's diary could not be excluded under the Ohio rape shield law if it provided evidence of consent to sexual acts and evidence of improper motive to make the charge of rape. Lewis v. Wilkinson, 307 F.3d 413 (6th Cir.2002) (denial of right of confrontation).

7. A discussion of the problems of privilege is found in Welsh White, Evidentiary Privileges And The Defendant's Constitutional Right To Introduce Evidence, 80 J.Crim.L. & Crim. 377 (1989). White concludes that one must first decide whether a "privilege, either in general or in the context of its specific application, . . . favors the government." The informer privilege favors the government, physician-patient or attorney-client does not .Professor White concludes,

> 1) the defendant should have a constitutional right to introduce evidence that is protected by a privilege designed to assist the government in performing one of its essential functions when the evidence is reasonably likely to affect the outcome at trial; 2) barring extraordinary circumstances, the defendant should have a constitutional right to introduce evidence that is protected by a privilege when the privilege would not

exclude comparable evidence offered by the government; and 3) no privilege should be invoked to deprive the defendant of an opportunity to effectively cross-examine a government witness, where effective cross-examination is defined as the type of cross-examination that is expected in view of the norms of the adversary process.

3. THE TURNCOAT WITNESS

California v. Green

Supreme Court of the United States, 1970.
399 U.S. 149, 90 S.Ct. 1930.

■ MR. JUSTICE WHITE delivered the opinion of the Court.

Section 1235 of the California Evidence Code, provides that "[e]vidence of a statement made by a witness is not made inadmissible by the hearsay rule if the statement is inconsistent with his testimony at the hearing and is offered in compliance with Section 770."[1] The California Supreme Court held that prior statements of a witness that were not subject to cross-examination when originally made, could not be introduced under this section to prove the charges against a defendant without violating the defendant's right of confrontation guaranteed by the Sixth Amendment and made applicable to the States by the Fourteenth Amendment. In the case now before us the California Supreme Court applied the same ban to a prior statement of a witness made at a preliminary hearing, under oath and subject to full cross-examination by an adequately counseled defendant. We cannot agree with the California court.

I.

In January 1967, one Melvin Porter, a 16–year–old minor, was arrested for selling marihuana to an undercover police officer. Four days after his arrest, while in the custody of juvenile authorities, Porter named respondent Green as his supplier. Porter claimed that Green had called him earlier that month, had asked him to sell some "stuff" or "grass," and had that same afternoon personally delivered a shopping bag containing 29 "baggies" of marihuana. It was from this supply that Porter had made his sale to the undercover officer. A week later, Porter testified at respondent's preliminary hearing. He again named respondent as his supplier, although he now claimed that instead of personally delivering the marihuana, Green had showed him where to pick up the shopping bag, hidden in the bushes at Green's parents' house. Porter's story at the preliminary hearing was subjected to extensive cross-examination by respondent's counsel—the same counsel who represented respondent at his subsequent trial....

Respondent's trial took place some two months later before a court sitting without a jury. The State's chief witness was again young Porter. But this time Porter, in the words of the California Supreme Court, proved to be "markedly evasive and uncooperative on the stand." He testified that

1. Cal.Evid.Code, § 1235 (1966). Section 770 merely requires that the witness be given an opportunity to explain or deny the prior statement at some point in the trial. See Cal.Evid.Code, § 770 (1966).

respondent had called him in January 1967, and asked him to sell some unidentified "stuff." He admitted obtaining shortly thereafter 29 plastic "baggies" of marihuana, some of which he sold. But when pressed as to whether respondent had been his supplier, Porter claimed that he was uncertain how he obtained the marihuana, primarily because he was at the time on"acid" (LSD), which he had taken 20 minutes before respondent phoned. Porter claimed that he was unable to remember the events that followed the phone call, and that the drugs he had taken prevented his distinguishing fact from fantasy.

At various points during Porter's direct examination, the prosecutor read excerpts from Porter's preliminary hearing testimony. This evidence was admitted under § 1235 for the truth of the matter contained therein. With his memory "refreshed" by his preliminary hearing testimony, Porter "guessed" that he had indeed obtained the marihuana from the backyard of respondent's parents' home, and had given the money from its sale to respondent. On cross-examination, however, Porter indicated that it was his memory of the preliminary testimony which was "mostly" refreshed, rather than his memory of the events themselves, and he was still unsure of the actual episode. Later in the trial, Officer Wade testified, relating Porter's earlier statement that respondent had personally delivered the marihuana. This statement was also admitted as substantive evidence. Porter admitted making the statement, and insisted that he had been telling the truth as he then believed it both to Officer Wade and at the preliminary hearing; but he insisted that he was also telling the truth now in claiming inability to remember the actual events.

Respondent was convicted. . . .

II.

* * *

Section 1235 of the California Evidence Code represents a considered choice by the California Legislature between two opposing positions concerning the extent to which a witness' prior statements may be introduced at trial without violating hearsay rules of evidence. The orthodox view, adopted in most jurisdictions, has been that the out-of-court statements are inadmissible for the usual reasons that have led to the exclusion of hearsay statements: the statement may not have been made under oath; the declarant may not have been subjected to cross-examination when he made the statement; and the jury cannot observe the declarant's demeanor at the time he made the statement. Accordingly, under this view, the statement may not be offered to show the truth of the matters asserted therein, but can be introduced under appropriate limiting instructions to impeach the credibility of the witness who has changed his story at trial.

In contrast, the minority view adopted in some jurisdictions and supported by most legal commentators and by recent proposals to codify the law of evidence[6] would permit the substantive use of prior inconsistent

6. Dean Wigmore was the first noted commentator to adopt this position, abandoning his earlier approval, in the first edition of his Treatise, of the orthodox view. See 3

statements on the theory that the usual dangers of hearsay are largely nonexistent where the witness testifies at trial. "The whole purpose of the Hearsay rule has been already satisfied [because] the witness is present and subject to cross-examination [and] [t]here is ample opportunity to test him as to the basis for his former statement."

Our task in this case is not to decide which of these positions, purely as a matter of the law of evidence, is the sounder. The issue before us is the considerably narrower one of whether a defendant's constitutional right "to be confronted with the witnesses against him" is necessarily inconsistent with a State's decision to change its hearsay rules to reflect the minority view described above. While it may readily be conceded that hearsay rules and the Confrontation Clause are generally designed to protect similar values, it is quite a different thing to suggest that the overlap is complete and that the Confrontation Clause is nothing more or less than a codification of the rules of hearsay and their exceptions as they existed historically at common law. Our decisions have never established such a congruence; indeed, we have more than once found a violation of confrontation values even though the statements in issue were admitted under an arguably recognized hearsay exception. See Barber v. Page (1968); Pointer v. Texas (1965). The converse is equally true: merely because evidence is admitted in violation of along-established hearsay rule does not lead to the automatic conclusion that confrontation rights have been denied.

Given the similarity of the values protected, however, the modification of a State's hearsay rules to create new exceptions for the admission of evidence against a defendant, will often raise questions of compatibility with the defendant's constitutional right to confrontation....

[T]he particular vice that gave impetus to the confrontation claim was the practice of trying defendants on "evidence" which consisted solely of *ex parte* affidavits or depositions secured by the examining magistrates, thus denying the defendant the opportunity to challenge his accuser in a face-to-face encounter in front of the trier of fact. Prosecuting attorneys "would frequently allege matters which the prisoner denied and called upon them to prove. The proof was usually given by reading depositions, confessions of accomplices, letters, and the like; and this occasioned frequent demands by the prisoner to have his 'accusers,' i.e. the witnesses against him, brought before him face to face...."

But objections occasioned by this practice appear primarily to have been aimed at the failure to call the witness to confront personally the defendant at his trial. So far as appears, in claiming confrontation rights no objection was made against receiving a witness' out-of-court depositions or statements, so long as the witness was present at trial to repeat his story and to explain or repudiate any conflicting prior stories before the trier of fact.

* * *

Wigmore § 1018 n. 2. Both the Model Code and the Uniform Rules have since followed the Wigmore position, see Model Code of Evidence Rule 503(b) (1942); Uniform Rule of Evidence 63(1) (1953), as has the recent preliminary draft of the rules of evidence for the lower federal courts.

Viewed historically, then, there is good reason to conclude that the Confrontation Clause is not violated by admitting a declarant's out-of-court statements, as long as the declarant is testifying as a witness and subject to full and effective cross-examination.

This conclusion is supported by comparing the purposes of confrontation with the alleged dangers in admitting an out-of-court statement. Confrontation: (1)insures that the witness will give his statements under oath—thus impressing him with the seriousness of the matter and guarding against the lie by the possibility of a penalty for perjury; (2) forces the witness to submit to cross-examination, the "greatest legal engine ever invented for the discovery of truth"; (3) permits the jury that is to decide the defendant's fate to observe the demeanor of the witness in making his statement, thus aiding the jury in assessing his credibility.

It is, of course, true that the out-of-court statement may have been made under circumstances subject to none of these protections. But if the declarant is present and testifying at trial, the out-of-court statement for all practical purposes regains most of the lost protections. If the witness admits the prior statement is his, or if there is other evidence to show the statement is his, the danger of faulty reproduction is negligible and the jury can be confident that it has before it two conflicting statements by the same witness. Thus, as far as the oath is concerned, the witness must now affirm, deny, or qualify the truth of the prior statement under the penalty of perjury; indeed, the very fact that the prior statement was not given under a similar circumstance may become the witness' explanation for its inaccuracy—an explanation a jury may be expected to understand and take into account in deciding which, if either, of the statements represents the truth.

Second, the inability to cross-examine the witness at the time he made his prior statement cannot easily be shown to be of crucial significance as long as the defendant is assured of full and effective cross-examination at the time of trial. The most successful cross-examination at the time the prior statement was made could hardly hope to accomplish more than has already been accomplished by the fact that the witness is now telling a different, inconsistent story, and—in this case—one that is favorable to the defendant. We cannot share the California Supreme Court's view that belated cross-examination can never serve as a constitutionally adequate substitute for cross-examination contemporaneous with the original statement. The main danger in substituting subsequent for timely cross-examination seems to lie in the possibility that the witness' "[f]alse testimony is apt to harden and become unyielding to the blows of truth in proportion as the witness has opportunity for reconsideration and influence by the suggestions of others whose interest may be, and often is, to maintain falsehood rather than truth." State v. Saporen, 205 Minn. 358, 362, 285 N.W. 898, 901 (1939). That danger, however, disappears when the witness has changed his testimony so that, far from "hardening," his prior statement has softened to the point where he now repudiates it.

The defendant's task in cross-examination is, of course, no longer identical to the task that he would have faced if the witness had not changed his story and hence had to be examined as a "hostile" witness giving evidence for the prosecution. This difference, however, far from lessening, may actually enhance the defendant's ability to attack the prior statement. For the witness, favorable to the defendant, should be more than willing to give the usual suggested explanations for the inaccuracy of his prior statement, such as faulty perception or undue haste in recounting the event. Under such circumstances, the defendant is not likely to be hampered in effectively attacking the prior statement, solely because his attack comes later in time.

Similar reasons lead us to discount as a constitutional matter the fact that the jury at trial is foreclosed from viewing the declarant's demeanor when he first made his out-of-court statement. The witness who now relates a different story about the events in question must necessarily assume a position as to the truth value of his prior statement, thus giving the jury a chance to observe and evaluate his demeanor as he either disavows or qualifies his earlier statement. The jury is alerted by the inconsistency in the stories, and its attention is sharply focused on determining either that one of the stories reflects the truth or that the witness who has apparently lied once, is simply too lacking in credibility to warrant its believing either story. The defendant's confrontation rights are not violated, even though some demeanor evidence that would have been relevant in resolving this credibility issue is forever lost.

It may be true that a jury would be in a better position to evaluate the truth of the prior statement if it could somehow be whisked magically back in time to witness a grueling cross-examination of the declarant as he first gives his statement. But the question as we see it must be not whether one can somehow imagine the jury in "a better position," but whether subsequent cross-examination at the defendant's trial will still afford the trier of fact a satisfactory basis for evaluating the truth of the prior statement. On that issue, neither evidence nor reason convinces us that contemporaneous cross-examination before the ultimate trier of fact is so much more effective than subsequent examination that it must be made the touchstone of the Confrontation Clause.

Finally, we note that none of our decisions interpreting the Confrontation Clause requires excluding the out-of-court statements of a witness who is available and testifying at trial. The concern of most of our cases has been focused on precisely the opposite situation—situations where statements have been admitted in the absence of the declarant and without any chance to cross-examine him at trial.... In Pointer v. Texas, for example, the State introduced at defendant's trial the transcript of a crucial witness' testimony from a prior preliminary hearing. The witness himself, one Phillips, had left the jurisdiction and did not appear at trial. "Because the transcript of Phillips' statement offered against petitioner at his trial had not been taken at a time and under circumstances affording petitioner through counsel an adequate opportunity to cross-examine Phillips," we held that its introduction violated the defendant's confrontation rights. Similarly, in Barber v. Page, the State introduced the preliminary hearing testimony of an absent witness, incarcerated in a federal prison, under an "unavailability" exception to its hearsay rules. We held that exception would not justify the denial of confrontation where the State had not made a good-faith effort to obtain the presence of the allegedly "unavailable" witness.

We have no occasion in the present case to map out a theory of the Confrontation Clause that would determine the validity of all such hearsay "exceptions" permitting the introduction of an absent declarant's statements. For where the declarant is not absent, but is present to testify and to submit to cross-examination, our cases, if anything, support the conclusion that the admission of his out-of-court statements does not create a confrontation problem. Thus, in Douglas v. Alabama (1965), decided on the same day as *Pointer*, we reversed a conviction in which the prosecution read into the record an alleged confession of the defendant's supposed accomplice, Loyd, who refused to testify on self-incrimination grounds. The confrontation problem arose precisely because Loyd could not be cross-examined as to his prior statement; had such cross-examination taken place, the opinion strongly suggests that the confrontation problem would have been nonexistent.

* * *

III.

We also think that Porter's preliminary hearing testimony was admissible as far as the Constitution is concerned wholly apart from the question of whether respondent had an effective opportunity for confrontation at the subsequent trial. For Porter's statement at the preliminary hearing had already been given under circumstances closely approximating those that surround the typical trial. Porter was under oath; respondent was represented by counsel—the same counsel in fact who later represented him at the trial; respondent had every opportunity to cross-examine Porter as to his statement; and the proceedings were conducted before a judicial tribunal, equipped to provide a judicial record of the hearings. Under these circumstances, Porter's statement would, we think, have been admissible at trial even in Porter's absence if Porter had been actually unavailable, despite good-faith efforts of the State to produce him. That being the case, we do not think a different result should follow where the witness is actually produced.

This Court long ago held that admitting the prior testimony of an unavailable witness does not violate the Confrontation Clause. Mattox v. United States (1895). That case involved testimony given at the defendant's first trial by a witness who had died by the time of the second trial, but we do not find the instant preliminary hearing significantly different from an actual trial to warrant distinguishing the two cases for purposes of the Confrontation Clause.... In the present case respondent's counsel does not appear to have been significantly limited in any way in the scope or nature of his cross-examination of the witness Porter at the preliminary hearing. If Porter had died or was otherwise unavailable, the Confrontation Clause would not have been violated by admitting his testimony given at the preliminary hearing—the right of cross-examination then afforded provides substantial compliance with the purposes behind the confrontation requirement, as long as the declarant's inability to give live testimony is in no way the fault of the State.

But nothing in other cases in this Court indicates that a different result must follow where the State produces the declarant and swears him as a witness at the trial. It may be that the rules of evidence applicable in state or federal courts would restrict resort to prior sworn testimony where the declarant is present at the trial. But as a constitutional matter, it is untenable to construe the Confrontation Clause to permit the use of prior testimony to prove the State's case where the declarant never appears, but to bar that testimony where the declarant is present at the trial, exposed to the defendant and the trier of fact, and subject to cross-examination.[16] As in the case where the witness is physically unproducible, the State here has made every effort to introduce its evidence through the live testimony of the witness; it produced Porter at trial, swore him as a witness, and tendered him for cross-examination. Whether Porter then testified in a manner consistent or inconsistent with his preliminary hearing testimony, claimed a loss of memory, claimed his privilege against compulsory self-incrimination, or simply refused to answer, nothing in the Confrontation Clause prohibited the State from also relying on his prior testimony to prove its case against Green.[17]

IV.

There is a narrow question lurking in this case concerning the admissibility of Porter's statements to Officer Wade. In the typical case to which the California court addressed itself, the witness at trial gives a version of the ultimate events different from that given on a prior occasion. In such a case, as our holding in Part II makes clear, we find little reason to distinguish among prior inconsistent statements on the basis of the circumstances under which the prior statements were given. The subsequent

16. The explanation advanced for the contrary conclusion seems to be that where the witness is dead or otherwise unavailable, the State may in good faith assume he would have given the same story at trial, and may introduce the former testimony as reasonably reliable and as prompted by the factor of "necessity." On the contrary, it is argued, where the witness is present to testify but does not relate the same story, "necessity," "reliability," and the assumption that the story would be the same are all destroyed. But the only "necessity" that exists in either case is the State's "need" to introduce relevant evidence that through no fault of its own cannot be introduced in any other way. And the "assumption" that the witness would have given the same story if he had been available at trial, is little more than another way of saying that the testimony was given under circumstances that make it reasonably reliable—there is nothing in a witness' death by itself, for example, which would justify assuming his story would not have changed at trial. Finally, the "reliability" of the statement is based on the circumstances under which it was given—circumstances that remain unaffected regardless of whether the witness is present or absent at the later trial. Surely in terms of protecting the defendant's interests, and the jury's ability to assess the reliability of the evidence it hears, it seems most unlikely that respondent in this case would have been better off, as the dissent seems to suggest, if Porter had died, and his prior testimony were admitted, than he was in the instant case where Porter's conduct on the stand cast substantial doubt on his prior statement. As long as the State has made a good-faith effort to produce the witness, the actual presence or absence of the witness cannot be constitutionally relevant for purposes of the "unavailability" exception.

17. The hearsay exception itself has generally recognized that a witness is "unavailable" for purposes of the exception where through lapse of memory or a plea of the Fifth Amendment privilege, the State cannot secure his live testimony. See 5 Wigmore §§ 1408, 1409.

opportunity for cross-examination at trial with respect to both present and past versions of the event, is adequate to make equally admissible, as far as the Confrontation Clause is concerned, both the casual, off-hand remark to a stranger, and the carefully recorded testimony at a prior hearing. Here, however, Porter claimed at trial that he could not remember the events that occurred after respondent telephoned him and hence failed to give any current version of the more important events described in his earlier statement.

Whether Porter's apparent lapse of memory so affected Green's right to cross-examine as to make a critical difference in the application of the Confrontation Clause in this case[18] is an issue which is not ripe for decision at this juncture.... Its resolution depends much upon the unique facts in this record, and we are reluctant to proceed without the state court's views of what the record actually discloses relevant to this particular issue. What is more, since we hold that the admission of Porter's preliminary hearing testimony is not barred by the Sixth Amendment despite his apparent lapse of memory, the reception into evidence of the Porter statement to Officer Wade may pose a harmless-error question which is more appropriately resolved by the California courts in the first instance.

* * *

We therefore vacate the judgment of the California Supreme Court and remand the case to that court for further proceedings not inconsistent with this opinion. It is so ordered.

■ Mr. Justice Marshall took no part in the decision of this case.

■ Mr. Justice Blackmun took no part in the consideration or decision of this case.

■ [Chief Justice Burger's concurring opinion is omitted.]

■ Mr. Justice Harlan, concurring.

The California decision that we today reverse demonstrates, however, the need to approach this case more broadly than the Court has seen fit to do, and, to confront squarely the Confrontation Clause because the holding of the California Supreme Court is the result of an understandable misconception, as I see things, of numerous decisions of this Court, old and recent,

18. Even among proponents of the view that prior statements should be admissible as substantive evidence, disagreement appears to exist as to whether to apply this rule to the case of a witness who disclaims all present knowledge of the ultimate event. Commentators have noted that in such a case the opportunities for testing the prior statement through cross-examination at trial may be significantly diminished. While both the Model Code and the Uniform Rules would apparently admit prior inconsistent statements even where the witness claims to have no present knowledge or recollection of the event, the preliminary draft of proposed rules of evidence for lower federal courts seems to limit admissibility to the case where the witness actually testifies concerning the substance of the event at issue. The latter position accords with the common-law practice of not permitting prior inconsistent statements to be introduced even for impeachment purposes until and unless the witness has actually given "inconsistent" testimony concerning the substance of the event described in the prior statement.

that have indiscriminately equated "confrontation" with "cross-examination."

* * *

From the scant information available it may tentatively be concluded that the Confrontation Clause was meant to constitutionalize a barrier against flagrant abuses, trials by anonymous accusers, and absentee witnesses. That the Clause was intended to ordain common law rules of evidence with constitutional sanction is doubtful, notwithstanding English decisions that equate confrontation and hearsay. Rather, having established a broad principle, it is far more likely that the Framers anticipated it would be supplemented, as a matter of judge-made common law, by prevailing rules of evidence.

* * *

Notwithstanding language that appears to equate the Confrontation Clause with a right to cross-examine, and, by implication, exclude hearsay, the early holdings and dicta can, I think, only be harmonized by viewing the confrontation guarantee as being confined to an availability rule, one that requires the production of a witness when he is available to testify. This view explains the recognition of the dying declaration exception, which dispenses with any requirement of cross-examination, and the refusal to make an exception for prior recorded statements, taken subject to cross-examination by the accused, when the witness is still available to testify.

* * *

I turn finally to the question of whether this conviction stands on such unreliable evidence that reversal is required. I cannot conclude that the preliminary hearing testimony was obtained under circumstances, as such, so unreliable that its admission requires reversal as a matter of due process, even though it was crucial to the central issue in the case....

■ MR. JUSTICE BRENNAN, dissenting.

* * *

The evidence on which respondent was found guilty consisted of two pretrial statements by Porter. The first was the account given Officer Wade. It was unsworn and not subject to defense cross-examination. Porter's demeanor while making the statement was not observed by the trial fact finder. The statement was made under unreliable circumstances—it was taken four days after Porter's arrest for selling marihuana to an undercover agent and while he was still in custody. No written transcript of the statement was introduced at trial. Officer Wade recounted it simply as he remembered Porter's words. The second statement was given by Porter during respondent's preliminary hearing. It was sworn and subject to cross-examination. Defense counsel, however, did not engage in a searching examination.[4] Again, Porter's demeanor while he made this statement was unobserved by the trial fact finder. The statement was put before this fact

4. No question, for example, was asked Porter by either the defense or prosecution as to whether he was under the influence of drugs at the time of the alleged offense.

finder, of course, when at various points during Porter's direct examination at trial the prosecutor read excerpts from his preliminary hearing testimony.

* * *

I.

* * *

There is no way to test the recollection and sift the conscience of a witness regarding the facts of an alleged offense if he is unwilling or unable to be questioned about them; defense counsel cannot probe the story of a silent witness and attempt to expose facts that qualify or discredit it. The impetus to truth inherent in the oath sworn by the witness, in a penalty for perjury, and in the serious purpose of the courtroom have no effect on him so far as the facts of the alleged offense are concerned. Nor, obviously, can the factfinder view his demeanor while he recounts the facts. If the witness claims that he is unable to remember the pertinent events, it is true that this assertion can be challenged, and that in making and defending it the witness will be affected by his oath, the penalty for perjury, and the courtroom atmosphere. It is equally true that the trial fact finder can observe and weigh the witness' demeanor as he makes and defends such a claim. But a decision by the fact finder that the witness is lying sheds no direct light on the accuracy of any pretrial statement made by him; that statement remains without the support or discredit that can come only from the probing of its factual basis while the witness stands face to face with the accused and the factfinder. If the fact finder decides that the witness is honestly unable to remember the events in question, that conclusion may or may not directly guide the factfinder in assessing the reliability of the pretrial statement. If, for example, the witness were unable to remember the pertinent facts because he was under the influence of drugs at the time they occurred, the factfinder might reasonably disregard any pretrial account of these events given by the witness.

* * *

For purposes of the Confrontation Clause, there is no significant difference between a witness who fails to testify about an alleged offense because he is unwilling to do so and a witness whose silence is compelled by an inability to remember. Both are called to the stand to testify. The jury may view the demeanor of each as he indicates why he will not discuss the crucial events. But in neither instance are the purposes of the Confrontation Clause satisfied, because the witness cannot be questioned at trial concerning the pertinent facts. In both cases, if a pretrial statement is introduced for the truth of the facts asserted, the witness becomes simply a conduit for the admission of stale evidence, whose reliability can never be tested before the trial factfinder by cross-examination of the declarant about the operative events, and by observation of his demeanor as he testifies about them.

Unlike the Court, I see no reason to leave undecided the inadmissibility of Porter's statements to Officer Wade. We have before us the transcript of Porter's trial testimony. He could not remember the operative events. Whether he feigned loss of memory is irrelevant to respondent's confrontation claim. His statement to Officer Wade must be excluded as substantive evidence.[6]

II.

The question remains whether the fact that a pretrial statement was obtained at a preliminary hearing under oath and subject to cross-examination, distinguishes that statement for confrontation purposes from an extrajudicial statement. . . .

* * *

Preliminary hearings in California are not atypical in their nature and objectives:

> "In most California criminal prosecutions the preliminary examination is conducted as a rather perfunctory uncontested proceeding with only one likely denouement—an order holding the defendant for trial. Only television lawyers customarily demolish the prosecution in the magistrate's court. The prosecution need show only 'probable cause,' a burden vastly lighter than proof beyond a reasonable doubt."

It follows that the purposes of the Confrontation Clause cannot be satisfied by a face-to-face encounter at the preliminary hearing. Cross-examination at the hearing pales beside that which takes place at trial. This is so for a number of reasons. First, as noted, the objective of the hearing is to establish the presence or absence of probable cause, not guilt or innocence proved beyond a reasonable doubt; thus, if evidence suffices to establish probable cause, defense counsel has little reason at the preliminary hearing to show that it does not conclusively establish guilt—or, at least, he had little reason before today's decision. Second, neither defense nor prosecution is eager before trial to disclose its case by extensive examination at the preliminary hearing; thorough questioning of a prosecution witness by defense counsel may easily amount to a grant of gratis discovery to the State. Third, the schedules of neither court nor counsel, can easily accommodate lengthy preliminary hearings. Fourth, even were the judge and lawyers not concerned that the proceedings be brief, the defense and prosecution have generally had inadequate time before the hearing to prepare for extensive examination. Finally, though counsel were to engage in extensive questioning, a part of its force would never reach the trial factfinder, who would know the examination only second hand.

* * *

If cross-examination at the preliminary hearing rarely approximates that at trial, observation by the trial factfinder of the witness' demeanor as

6. The fact that in appropriate circumstances such a statement may be admitted to impeach a witness is not as anomalous as the Court suggests. If, for example, Porter's pretrial statements had been admitted at respondent's trial solely for impeachment purposes, they would not have provided substantive proof of his guilt, and, as noted, there would then very likely have been insufficient evidence to sustain his conviction.

he gives his prior testimony is virtually nonexistent. Unless the committing magistrate is also the trial factfinder, the demeanor purpose of the Confrontation Clause is wholly negated by substituting confrontation at the preliminary hearing for confrontation at trial. And yet, in the words of the California court, "[i]t is because demeanor—attitude and manner—is a significant factor in weighing testimonial evidence, that it is axiomatic the trier of fact, before whom the witness testified and was cross-examined . . ., is the sole judge of the credibility of a witness and of the weight to be given his testimony." No such determination of credibility is possible when the witness comes before the trial factfinder by the reading of a cold transcript.

It appears, then, that in terms of the purposes of the Confrontation Clause, an equation of face-to-face encounter at the preliminary hearing with confrontation at trial must rest largely on the fact that the witness testified at the hearing under oath, subject to the penalty for perjury, and in a courtroom atmosphere. These factors are not insignificant, but by themselves they fall far short of satisfying the demands of constitutional confrontation. Moreover, the atmosphere and stakes are different in the two proceedings. In the hurried, somewhat *pro forma* context of the average preliminary hearing, a witness may be more careless in his testimony than in the more measured and searching atmosphere of a trial. Similarly, a man willing to perjure himself when the consequences are simply that the accused will stand trial may be less willing to do so when his lies may condemn the defendant to loss of liberty. In short, it ignores reality to assume that the purposes of the Confrontation Clause are met during a preliminary hearing. Accordingly, to introduce preliminary hearing testimony for the truth of the facts asserted, when the witness is in court and either unwilling or unable to testify regarding the pertinent events, denies the accused his Sixth Amendment right to grapple effectively with incriminating evidence.

* * *

In sum, I find that Porter's real or pretended lapse of memory about the pertinent events casts serious doubt upon the reliability of his preliminary hearing testimony. It is clear that so long as a witness, such as Porter, cannot or will not testify about these events at trial, the accused remains unable to challenge effectively that witness' prior assertions about them. The probable unreliability of the prior testimony, coupled with the impossibility of its examination during trial, denies the accused his right to probe and attempt to discredit incriminating evidence. Accordingly, I would hold California Evidence Code, § 1235 in violation of the Confrontation Clause to the extent that it permits the substantive use at trial of prior statements, whether extrajudicial or testimonial, when the declarant is present at trial but unable or unwilling to be questioned about the events with which the prior statements dealt. I would therefore affirm the reversal of respondent's conviction.

Chambers v. Mississippi

Supreme Court of the United States, 1973.
410 U.S. 284, 93 S.Ct. 1038.

■ MR. JUSTICE POWELL delivered the opinion of the Court.

Petitioner, Leon Chambers, was tried by a jury in a Mississippi trial court and convicted of murdering a policeman. The jury assessed punishment at life imprisonment and the Mississippi Supreme Court affirmed, one justice dissenting....

I.

The events that led to petitioner's prosecution for murder occurred in the small town of Woodville in southern Mississippi. On Saturday evening, June 14,1969, two Woodville policemen, James Forman and Aaron "Sonny" Liberty, entered a local bar and pool hall to execute a warrant for the arrest of a youth named C.C. Jackson. Jackson resisted and a hostile crowd of some 50 or60 persons gathered. The officers' first attempt to handcuff Jackson was frustrated when 20 or 25 men in the crowd intervened and wrestled him free. Forman then radioed for assistance and Liberty removed his riot gun, a 12–gauge sawed-off shotgun, from the car. Three deputy sheriffs arrived shortly thereafter and the officers again attempted to make their arrest. Once more the officers were attacked by the onlookers and during the commotion five or six pistol shots were fired. Forman was looking in a different direction when the shooting began, but immediately saw that Liberty had been shot several times in the back. Before Liberty died he turned around and fired both barrels of his riot gun into an alley in the area from which the shots appeared to have come. The first shot was wild and high and scattered the crowd standing at the face of the alley. Liberty appeared, however, to take more deliberate aim before the second shot and hit one of the men in the crowd in the back of the head and neck as he ran down the alley. That man was Leon Chambers.

Officer Forman could not see from his vantage point who shot Liberty or whether Liberty's shots hit anyone. One of the deputy sheriffs testified at trial that he was standing several feet from Liberty and that he saw Chambers shoot him. Another deputy sheriff stated that, although he could not see whether Chambers had a gun in his hand, he did see Chambers "break his arm down" shortly before the shots were fired. The officers who saw Chambers fall testified that they thought he was dead but they made no effort at that time either to examine him or to search for the murder weapon. Instead they attended to Liberty, who was placed in the police car and taken to the hospital where he was declared dead on arrival. A subsequent autopsy showed that he had been hit with four bullets from a .22–caliber revolver.

Shortly after the shooting, three of Chambers' friends discovered that he was not yet dead. James Williams, Berkley Turner, and Gable McDonald loaded him into a car and transported him to the same hospital. Later that night, when the county sheriff discovered that Chambers was still alive, a guard was placed outside his room. Chambers was subsequently charged with Liberty's murder. He pleaded not guilty and has asserted his innocence throughout.

The story of Leon Chambers is intertwined with the story of another man, Gable McDonald. McDonald, a lifelong resident of Woodville, was in the crowd on the evening of Liberty's death. Sometime shortly after that day he left his wife in Woodville and moved to Louisiana and found a job at a sugar mill. In November of that same year he returned to Woodville when his wife informed him that an acquaintance of his, known as Reverend Stokes, wanted to see him. Stokes owned a gas station in Natchez, Mississippi, several miles north of Woodville, and upon his return McDonald went to see him. After talking to Stokes, McDonald agreed to make a statement to Chambers' attorneys, who maintained offices in Natchez. Two days later he appeared at the attorneys' offices and gave a sworn confession that he shot Officer Liberty. He also stated that he had already told a friend of his, James Williams, that he shot Liberty. He said that he used his own pistol, a nine-shot .22–caliber revolver, which he had discarded shortly after the shooting. In response to questions from Chambers' attorneys, McDonald affirmed that his confession was voluntary and that no one had compelled him to come to them. Once the confession had been transcribed, signed and witnessed, McDonald was turned over to the local police authorities and was placed in jail.

One month later, at a preliminary hearing, McDonald repudiated his prior sworn confession. He testified that Stokes had persuaded him to confess that he shot Liberty. He claimed that Stokes had promised that he would not go to jail and that he would share in the proceeds of a lawsuit that Chambers would bring against the town of Woodville. On examination by his own attorney and on cross-examination by the State, McDonald swore that he had not been on the scene when Liberty was shot but had been down the street drinking beer in a cafe with a friend, Berkley Turner. When he and Turner heard the shooting he testified that they walked up the street and found Chambers lying in the alley. He, Turner and Williams took Chambers to the hospital. McDonald further testified at the preliminary hearing that he did not know what had happened, that there was no discussion about the shooting either going to or coming back from the hospital, and that it was not until the next day that he learned that Chambers had been felled by a blast from Liberty's riot gun. In addition, McDonald stated that while he once owned a .22–caliber pistol he had lost it many months before the shooting and did not own or possess a weapon at that time. The local justice of the peace accepted McDonald's repudiation, released him from custody, and the local authorities undertook no further investigation of his possible involvement.

Chambers' case came on for trial in October of the next year. At trial he endeavored to develop two grounds of defense. He first attempted to show that he did not shoot Liberty. Only one officer testified that he actually saw Chambers fire the shots. Although three officers saw Liberty shoot Chambers and testified that they assumed he was shooting his attacker, none of them examined Chambers to see whether he was still alive or whether he possessed a gun. Indeed, no weapon was ever recovered from the scene and there was no proof that Chambers had ever owned a .22–caliber pistol. One witness testified that he was standing in the street near where Liberty was shot, that he was looking at Chambers when the shooting began, and that he was sure that Chambers did not fire the shots.

Petitioner's second defense was that Gable McDonald had shot Officer Liberty. He was only partially successful, however, in his efforts to bring before the jury the testimony supporting this defense. Sam Hardin, a lifelong friend of McDonald's, testified that he saw McDonald shoot Liberty. A second witness, one of Liberty's cousins, testified that he saw McDonald immediately after the shooting with a pistol in his hand. In addition to the testimony of these two witnesses, Chambers endeavored to show the jury that McDonald had repeatedly confessed to the crime. Chambers attempted to prove that McDonald had admitted responsibility for the murder on four separate occasions, once when he gave the sworn statement to Chambers' counsel and three other times prior to that occasion in private conversations with friends.

In large measure, he was thwarted in his attempt to present this portion of his defense by the strict application of certain Mississippi rules of evidence....

II.

... At trial, after the State failed to put McDonald on the stand, Chambers called McDonald, laid a predicate for the introduction of his sworn out-of-court confession, had it admitted into evidence, and read it to the jury. The State, upon cross-examination, elicited from McDonald the fact that he had rejected his prior confession. McDonald further testified, as he had at the preliminary hearing, that he did not shoot Liberty, and that he confessed to the crime only on the promise of Reverend Stokes that he would not go to jail and would share in a sizeable tort recovery from the town. He also retold his own story of his actions on the evening of the shooting, including his visit to the cafe down the street, his absence from the scene during the critical period, and his subsequent trip to the hospital with Chambers.

At the conclusion of the State's cross-examination, Chambers renewed his motion to examine McDonald as an adverse witness. The trial court denied the motion, stating: "He may be hostile, but he is not adverse in the sense of the word, so your request will be overruled." On appeal, the State Supreme Court upheld the trial court's ruling, finding that "McDonald's testimony was not adverse to appellant" because "[n]owhere did he point the finger at Chambers."

Defeated in his attempt to challenge directly McDonald's renunciation of his prior confession, Chambers sought to introduce the testimony of the three witnesses to whom McDonald had admitted that he shot the officer. The first of these, Sam Hardin, would have testified that, on the night of the shooting, he spent the late evening hours with McDonald at a friend's house after their return from the hospital and that, while driving McDonald home later that night, McDonald stated that he shot Liberty. The State objected to the admission of this testimony on the ground that it was hearsay. The trial court sustained the objection.[4]

Berkley Turner, the friend with whom McDonald said he was drinking beer when the shooting occurred, was then called to testify. In the jury's presence, and without objection, he testified that he had not been in the cafe that Saturday and had not had any beers with McDonald. The jury was

4. Hardin's testimony, unlike the testimony of the other two men who stated that McDonald had confessed to them, was actually given in the jury's presence. After the State's objection to Hardin's account of McDonald's statement was sustained, the trial court ordered the jury to disregard it.

then excused. In the absence of the jury, Turner recounted his conversations with McDonald while they were riding with James Williams to take Chambers to the hospital. When asked whether McDonald said anything regarding the shooting of Liberty, Turner testified that McDonald told him that he "shot him." Turner further stated that one week later, when he met McDonald at a friend's house, McDonald reminded him of their prior conversation and urged Turner not to "mess him up." Petitioner argued to the court that, especially where there was other proof in the case that was corroborative of these out-of-court statements, Turner's testimony as to McDonald's self-incriminating remarks should have been admitted as an exception to the hearsay rule. Again, the trial court sustained the State's objection.

The third witness, Albert Carter, was McDonald's neighbor. They had been friends for about 25 years. Although Carter had not been in Woodville on the evening of the shooting, he stated that he learned about it the next morning from McDonald. That same day he and McDonald walked out to a well near McDonald's house and there McDonald told him that he was the one who shot Officer Liberty. Carter testified that McDonald also told him that he had disposed of the .22–caliber revolver later that night. He further testified that several weeks after the shooting he accompanied McDonald to Natchez where McDonald purchased another .22 pistol to replace the one he had discarded.[5] The jury was not allowed to hear Carter's testimony. Chamber surged that these statements were admissible, the State objected, and the court sustained the objection. On appeal, the State Supreme Court approved the lower court's exclusion of these witnesses' testimony on hearsay grounds.

In sum, then, this was Chambers' predicament. As a consequence of the combination of Mississippi's "party witness" or "voucher" rule and its hearsay rule, he was unable either to cross-examine McDonald or to present witnesses in his own behalf who would have discredited McDonald's repudiation and demonstrated his complicity. Chambers had, however, chipped away at the fringes of McDonald's story by introducing admissible testimony from other sources indicating that he had not been seen in the cafe where he says he was when the shooting started, that he had not been having beer with Turner, and that he possessed a .22 pistol at the time of the crime. But all that remained from McDonald's own testimony was a single written confession countered by an arguably acceptable renunciation. Chambers' defense was far less persuasive than it might have been had he been given an opportunity to subject McDonald's statements to cross-examination or had the other confessions been admitted.

III.

... The rights to confront and cross-examine witnesses and to call witnesses in one's own behalf have long been recognized as essential to due process....

* * *

5. A gun dealer from Natchez testified that McDonald had made two purchases. The witness' business records indicated that McDonald purchased a nine-shot .22–caliber revolver about a year prior to the murder. He purchased a different style .22 three weeks after Liberty's death.

Both of these elements of a fair trial are implicated in the present case.

A

* * *

In this case, petitioner's request to cross-examine McDonald was denied on the basis of a Mississippi common law rule that a party may not impeach his own witness. The rule rests on the presumption—without regard to the circumstances of the particular case—that a party who calls a witness "vouches for his credibility." Although the historical origins of the "voucher" rule are uncertain, it appears to be a remnant of primitive English trial practice in which "oath-takers" or "compurgators" were called to stand behind a particular party's position in any controversy. Their assertions were strictly partisan and, quite unlike witnesses in criminal trials today, their role bore little relation to the impartial ascertainment of the facts.

Whatever validity the "voucher" rule may have once enjoyed, and apart from whatever usefulness it retains today in the civil trial process, it bears little present relationship to the realities of the criminal process. It might have been logical for the early common law to require a party to vouch for the credibility of witnesses he brought before the jury to affirm his veracity. Having selected them especially for that purpose, the party might reasonably be expected to stand firmly behind their testimony. But in modern criminal trials defendants are rarely able to select their witnesses: they must take them where they find them. Moreover, as applied in this case, the "voucher" rule's impact was doubly harmful to Chambers' efforts to develop his defense. Not only was he precluded from cross-examining McDonald, but, as the State conceded at oral argument, he was also restricted in the scope of his direct examination by the rule's corollary requirement that the party calling the witness is bound by anything he might say. He was, therefore, effectively prevented from exploring the circumstances of McDonald's three prior oral confessions and from challenging the renunciation of the written confession.

In this Court Mississippi has not sought to defend the rule or explain its underlying rationale. Nor has it contended that its rule should override the accused's right of confrontation. Instead, it argues that there is no incompatibility between the rule and Chambers' rights because no right of confrontation exists unless the testifying witness is "adverse" to the accused. The State's brief asserts that the "right of confrontation is limited to witnesses *against* the accused." Relying on the trial court's determination that McDonald was not "adverse," and on the State Supreme Court's holding that McDonald "did not point the finger at Chambers," the State contends that Chambers' constitutional right was not involved.

The argument that McDonald's testimony was not "adverse" to, or "against," Chambers is not convincing. The State's proof at trial excluded the theory that more than one person participated in the shooting of Liberty. To the extent that McDonald's sworn confession tended to incriminate him, it tended also to exculpate Chambers. And, in the circumstances of this case, McDonald's retraction inculpated Chambers to the same extent that it exculpated McDonald. It can hardly be disputed that McDonald's testimony was in fact seriously adverse to Chambers. The availability of the right to confront and to cross-examine those who give damaging testimony against the accused has never been held to depend on whether the witness was initially put on the stand by the accused or by the State. We reject the notion that a right of such substance in the criminal process may be governed by that technicality or by any narrow and unrealistic definition of the word "against." The "voucher" rule, as applied in this case, plainly interfered with Chambers' right to defend against the State's charges.

B

We need not decide, however, whether this error alone would occasion reversal since Chambers' claimed denial of due process rests on the ultimate impact of that error when viewed in conjunction with the trial court's refusal to permit him to call other witnesses. The trial court refused to allow him to introduce the testimony of Hardin, Turner and Carter. Each would have testified to the statements purportedly made by McDonald, on three separate occasions shortly after the crime, naming himself as the murderer. The State Supreme Court approved the exclusion of this evidence on the ground that it was hearsay.

The hearsay rule, which has long been recognized and respected by virtually every State, is based on experience and grounded in the notion that untrustworthy evidence should not be presented to the triers of fact. Out-of-court statements are traditionally excluded because they lack the conventional indicia of reliability: they are usually not made under oath or other circumstances that impress the speaker with the solemnity of his statement; the declarant's word is not subject to cross-examination; and he is not available in order that his demeanor and credibility may be assessed by the jury. A number of exceptions have developed over the years to allow admission of hearsay statements made under circumstances that tend to assure reliability and thereby compensate for the absence of the oath and opportunity for cross-examination. Among the most prevalent of these exceptions is the one applicable to declarations against interest—an exception founded on the assumption that a person is unlikely to fabricate a statement against his own interest at the time it is made. Mississippi recognizes this exception but applies it only to declarations against pecuniary interest. It recognizes no exceptions for declarations like McDonald's in this case, that are against the penal interest of the declarant.

This materialistic limitation on the declaration-against-interest hearsay exception appears to be accepted by most States in their criminal trial processes, although a number of States have discarded it. Declarations against penal interest have also been excluded in federal courts under the authority of Donnelly v. United States (1913), although exclusion would not be required under the newly proposed Federal Rules of Evidence. Exclusion, where the limitation prevails, is usually premised on the view that admission would lead to the frequent presentation of perjured testimony to the jury. It is believed that confessions of criminal activity are often motivated by extraneous considerations and, therefore, are not as inherently reliable as statements against pecuniary or proprietary interest. While that rationale has been the subject of considerable scholarly criticism, we need not decide in this case whether, under other circumstances, it might serve some valid state purpose by excluding untrustworthy testimony.

The hearsay statements involved in this case were originally made and subsequently offered at trial under circumstances that provided considerable assurance of their reliability. First, each of McDonald's confessions was made spontaneously to a close acquaintance shortly after the murder had occurred. Second, each one was corroborated by some other evidence in the case—McDonald's sworn confession, the testimony of an eyewitness to the shooting, the testimony that McDonald was seen with a gun immediately after the shooting, and proof of his prior ownership of a .22–caliber revolver and subsequent purchase of a new weapon. The sheer number of independent confessions provided additional corroboration for each. Third, whatever may be the parameters of the penal-interest rationale, each confession here was in a very real sense self-incriminatory and unquestionably against interest. McDonald stood to benefit nothing by disclosing his role in the shooting to any of his three friends and he must have been aware of the possibility that disclosure would lead to criminal prosecution. Indeed, after telling Turner of his involvement, he subsequently urged Turner not to "mess him up." Finally, if there was any question about the truthfulness of the extrajudicial statements, McDonald was present in the courtroom and had been under oath. He could have been cross-examined by the State, and his demeanor and responses weighed by the jury. The availability of McDonald significantly distinguishes this case from the prior Mississippi precedent, Brown v. State, and from the *Donnelly*-type situation, since in both cases the declarant was unavailable at the time of trial.[21]

... Although perhaps no rule of evidence has been more respected or more frequently applied in jury trials than that applicable to the exclusion of hearsay, exceptions tailored to allow the introduction of evidence which in fact is likely to be trustworthy have long existed. The testimony rejected by the trial court here bore persuasive assurances of trustworthiness and thus was well within the basic rationale of the exception for declarations against interest. That testimony also was critical to Chambers' defense. In these circumstances, where constitutional rights directly affecting the ascertainment of guilt are implicated, the hearsay rule may not be applied mechanistically to defeat the ends of justice.

21. McDonald's presence also deprives the State's argument for retention of the penal-interest rule of much of its force. In claiming that "[t]o change the rule would work a travesty of justice," the State posited the following hypothetical:

> "If the rule were changed, A could be charged with the crime; B could tell C and D that he committed the crime; B *could go into hiding* and at A's trial C and D would testify as to B's admission of guilt; A could be acquitted and B would return to stand trial; B could then provide several witnesses to testify as to his whereabouts at the time of the crime. The testimony of those witnesses along with A's statement that he really committed the crime would result in B's acquittal. A would be barred from further prosecution because of the protection against double jeopardy. No one could be convicted of perjury as A did not testify at his first trial, B did not lie under oath, and C and D were truthful in their testimony." Respondent's Brief, at 7 n. 3 (emphasis supplied).

Obviously, "B's" absence at trial is critical to the success of the justice-subverting ploy.

We conclude that the exclusion of this critical evidence, coupled with the State's refusal to permit Chambers to cross-examine McDonald, denied him atrial in accord with traditional and fundamental standards of due process. In reaching this judgment we establish no new principles of constitutional law. Nor does our holding signal any diminution in the respect traditionally accorded to the States in the establishment and implementation of their own criminal trial rules and procedures. Rather, we hold quite simply that under the facts and circumstances of this case the rulings of the trial court deprived Chambers of a fair trial.

* * *

■ [The concurring opinion of MR. JUSTICE WHITE is omitted].

■ MR. JUSTICE REHNQUIST, dissenting.

Were I to reach the merits in this case, I would have considerable difficulty in subscribing to the Court's further constitutionalization of the intricacies of the common law of evidence. I do not reach the merits, since I conclude that petitioner failed to properly raise in the Mississippi courts the constitutional issue that he seeks to have this Court decide.

NOTES

1. In Rock v. Arkansas, 483 U.S. 44, 107 S.Ct. 2704 (1987), the Court invalidated a state rule which prohibited in all cases any use of hypnotically refreshed testimony.

2. Prosecutors in jurisdictions which prohibit the use of prior inconsistent statements as substantive evidence may seek to have the turncoat witness called as a hostile witness, or as a court's witness, and then will try to get the out-of-court statement before the jury under the guise of refreshing his memory, quickening his conscience, or impeaching his testimony. See People v. Bailey, 60 Ill.2d 37, 322 N.E.2d 804 (1975) (Divided court disapproved the practice.) Federal rules allow prior inconsistent statements as substantive evidence only where the original statement was given under oath at a hearing or in a deposition. Fed.Rule of Evid. 801(d)(1)(A). However, Rule 607 permits a party to impeach his own witness. See United States v. Leighton Lee Fay, 668 F.2d 375 (8th Cir.1981), which cautions against the use of Rule 607 as a subterfuge to place otherwise inadmissible hearsay before the jury. For a most thoughtful article which would support the result later reached in *Leighton Lee Fay*, see Graham, Examination of a Party's Own Witness Under the Federal Rules of Evidence: A Promise Unfulfilled, 54 Tex.L.Rev. 914 (1976). Professor Graham's critics contend that the net result of his approach is to read back into the Federal Rules of Evidence the requirement that a party be allowed to impeach the testimony of his own witness only if the testimony of that witness is surprising and damaging—which requirements were deliberately omitted from Rule 607.

3. Several states adopted the rule which permits the substantive use of prior inconsistent statements. See State v. Fields, 115 Haw. 503, 168 P.3d 955 (2007) Gibbons v. State, 248 Ga. 858, 286 S.E.2d 717 (1982); Commonwealth v. Daye, 393 Mass. 55, 469 N.E.2d 483 (1984); Commonwealth v. Brady, 510 Pa. 336, 508 A.2d 286 (1986); State v. Whelan, 200 Conn. 743, 513 A.2d 86 (1986). Highly experienced attorneys often disagree with Chief Justice Burger's position that the cross-examiner could not be in a better position than when questioning a witness who has changed his position and, at the time of trial, is siding with the cross-examiner. For a professor's fine analysis of the deficiencies of cross-examination in such a situation, see Bein, Prior Inconsistent Statements and the Hearsay Rule: 801(d)(1)(A) and 803(24), 26 U.C.L.A.L.Rev. 967 (1979). Compare United States v. Thomas, 987 F.2d 1298 (7th Cir.1993) (court allowed prosecutor "to lay all of Adams" relevant testimony—both favorable and unfavorable—before the jury ... far from being a violation of due process, this is precisely how the trial process is supposed to work.)

4. The Federal Rules of Evidence, Rule 801(d)(1)(C) provides "[a]statement is not hearsay if the declarant testifies at the trial or hearing and is subject to cross-examination concerning the statement and the statement is ... one of identification of a person made after perceiving him." Applying this rule the Court held that substantive use of pre-trial statements is constitutional where the witness has no present knowledge of the event about which the statement was made. See United States v. Owens, 484 U.S. 554, 108 S.Ct. 838 (1988) (Victim of the offense eventually lost memory as a result of injuries). In United States v. O'Malley, 796 F.2d 891 (7th Cir.1986) an F.B.I. agent's testimony that a witness previously identified a man as an extorter was admissible substantively where the witness admitted at trial that he had made the identification but then recanted the identification.

4. The Intimidated Witness

Webb v. Texas

Supreme Court of the United States, 1972.
409 U.S. 95, 93 S.Ct. 351.

■ Per Curiam.

The petitioner was convicted of burglary in the Criminal District Court of Dallas County, Texas....

The record shows that, after the prosecution had rested its case, the jury was temporarily excused. During this recess, the petitioner called his only witness, Leslie Max Mills, who had a prior criminal record and was then serving a prison sentence. At this point, the trial judge, on his own initiative, undertook to admonish the witness as follows:

> "Now you have been called down as a witness in this case by the Defendant. It is the Court's duty to admonish you that you don't have to testify, that anything you say can and will be used against you. If you take the witness stand and lie under oath, the Court will personally see that your case goes to the grand jury and you will be indicted for perjury and the liklihood [sic] is that you would get convicted of perjury and that it would be stacked onto what you have already got, so that is the matter you have got to make up your mind on. If you get on the witness stand and lie, it is probably going to mean several years and at least more time that you are going to have to serve. It will also be held against you in the penitentiary when you're up for parole and the Court wants you to thoroughly understand the chances you're taking by getting on that witness stand under oath. You may tell the truth and if you do, that is all right, but if you lie you can get into real trouble. The court wants you to know that. You don't owe anybody anything to testify and it must be done freely and voluntarily and

with the thorough understanding that you know the hazard you are taking."

The petitioner's counsel objected to these comments, on the ground that the judge was exerting on the mind of the witness such duress that the witness could not freely and voluntarily decide whether or not to testify in the petitioner's behalf, and was thereby depriving the petitioner of his defense by coercing the only defense witness into refusing to testify. Counsel pointed out that none of the witnesses for the State had been so admonished. When the petitioner's counsel then indicated that he was nonetheless going to ask the witness to take the stand, the judge interrupted: "Counsel, you can state the facts, nobody is going to dispute it. Let him decline to testify." The witness then refused to testify for any purpose and was excused by the court. The petitioner's subsequent motion for a mistrial was overruled.

On appeal, the petitioner argued that the judge's conduct indicated a bias against the petitioner and deprived him of due process of law by driving his sole witness off the witness stand. The Court of Criminal Appeals rejected this contention, stating that, while it did not condone the manner of the admonition, the petitioner had made no objection until the admonition was completed, and there was no showing that the witness had been intimidated by the admonition or had refused to testify because of it.

We cannot agree. The suggestion that the petitioner or his counsel should have interrupted the judge in the middle of his remarks to object is, on this record, not a basis to ground a waiver of the petitioner's rights. The fact that Mills was willing to come to court to testify in the petitioner's behalf, refusing to do so only after the judge's lengthy and intimidating warning, strongly suggests that the judge's comments were the cause of Mills' refusal to testify.

The trial judge gratuitously singled out this one witness for a lengthy admonition on the dangers of perjury. But the judge did not stop at warning the witness of his right to refuse to testify and of the necessity to tell the truth. Instead, the judge implied that he expected Mills to lie, and went onto assure him that if he lied, he would be prosecuted and probably convicted for perjury, that the sentence for that conviction would be added on to his present sentence, and that the result would be to impair his chances for parole. At least some of these threats may have been beyond the power of this judge to carry out. Yet in light of the great disparity between the posture of the presiding judge and that of a witness in these circumstances, the unnecessarily strong terms used by the judge could well have exerted such duress on the witness' mind as to preclude him from making a free and voluntary choice whether or not to testify.

* * *

In the circumstances of this case, we conclude that the judge's threatening remarks, directed alone at the single witness for the defense, effectively drove that witness off the stand, and thus deprived the petitioner of due process of law under the Fourteenth Amendment. The admonition by the Texas Court of Criminal Appeals might well have given the trial judge guidance for future cases, but it did not serve to repair the infringement of the petitioner's due process rights under the Fourteenth Amendment.

Reversed.

■ MR. JUSTICE BLACKMUN, with whom MR. JUSTICE REHNQUIST joins, dissenting.

The facts before us do not, in my opinion, justify the Court's summary disposition. Petitioner Webb (who, on a prior occasion, had been convicted on still another burglary charge) was apprehended by the owner of a lumber business. The owner, armed with his shotgun, had driven to his office at three o'clock in the morning upon the activation of a burglar alarm. When he entered the building, the owner observed a broken window and an assortment of what he regarded as burglary tools on his desk. When men emerged from an adjacent room, a gun fight ensued. Two intruders escaped, but the owner, despite his having been shot twice, succeeded in holding the petitioner at gun point until police arrived.

Although the admonition given by the state trial judge to the sole witness proffered by the defense is obviously improper, sufficient facts have not been presented to this Court to demonstrate the depth of prejudice that requires a summary reversal. The admonition might prove far less offensive, and the conduct of the trial judge understandable, if, for example, as is indicated in petitioner's brief, filed with the Texas Court of Criminal Appeals, the witness were known to have been called for the purpose of presenting an alibi defense. Against the backdrop of being caught on the premises and of apparently overwhelming evidence of guilt, offset only by a bare allegation of prejudice, I would deny the petition for certiorari and, as the Court so often has done, I would remit the petitioner to the relief available to him by way of a post-conviction proceeding with a full evidentiary hearing.

NOTES

1. Consider People v. Carradine, 52 Ill.2d 231, 287 N.E.2d 670 (1972):

"MR. CHIEF JUSTICE UNDERWOOD delivered the opinion of the court.

> The Cook County circuit court found Georgia Carradine to be in direct contempt of court for her refusal to testify [as a witness to a homicide] and sentenced her to imprisonment for six months in the Cook County jail. . . .
>
> * * *
>
> "The more difficult question is the contemnor's request, predicated upon the extenuating circumstances surrounding her refusal to testify, that her punishment be reduced to the two weeks already spent in jail. Those circumstances include the fact that Mrs. Carradine had been separated from her husband for some four years, had six children aged 5 to 18 at home, and was supported by payments from her husband and supplemental welfare funds; that there seems little reason to doubt her refusal to testify resulted solely from her fear of harm to herself and her children if she testified against the defendants who apparently were members of the Blackstone Rangers, a youth gang; that she believed she had been 'tricked' and lied to by the assistant State's Attorney to whom she had given a statement, because, as she stated, he told her she would not have to appear and testify and that, absent this assurance, she never would have given

him the statement; that she did not believe the law enforcement authorities could protect her from the 'Stones' for, as she put it:

"THE WITNESS: Well, look, Judge, I am going to tell you, I live in the middle of the slums, down in the slums. Where I live the police don't even come in there even if we call. I called the police one night about a fight. You'd think they were going to kill one another. But the police don't even come up in there where I live. So, how are they going to protect me and my family when they don't even come up in the building where we live?"

Nor does she believe that relocating her family would solve the problems, for the "Stones" were "everywhere."

"It is completely clear from the record that Mrs. Carradine understood the likely results of her refusal to testify and deliberately chose to incur imprisonment rather than expose herself and her family to what she considered to be the certainty of serious physical harm or death. The conscientious trial judge appointed counsel for her and patiently, clearly and repeatedly explained the situation, urging her to change her mind and reiterating the offers of protection and relocation; the proceedings were continued on several occasions in order that she might have an opportunity to reconsider her decision.

"No useful purpose would be served by prolonged discussion. The reluctance of witnesses to testify is not an uncommon problem, although the circumstances here are particularly distressing. The contempt proceedings were conducted with eminent fairness, and, in our opinion, the judgment and sentence must be affirmed. The fundamental reason therefore was stated by the trial court: '... one of the problems that the Court has is that unless we receive the cooperation of the citizens who see certain alleged events take place these events are not going to be rooted out, nor are perpetrators of these acts going to be brought before the bar of justice unless citizens stand up to be counted, and I think this [fear] is not a valid reason for not testifying. If it's a valid reason then we might as well close the doors.'

"The judgment of the Cook County circuit court is affirmed."

2. The scope of Webb v. Texas was considered in United States v. Vavages, 151 F.3d 1185 (9th Cir.1998) In this case an officer stopped a vehicle for speeding and crossing the center line of the roadway. He discovered large amounts of marijuana in the car and the four occupants ran away. He later identified Vavages as one of the persons who ran away.

The alleged misconduct in this case concerns comments made by the prosecutor in Vavages' criminal case to counsel for witness Manuel (Vavages' spouse). When Vavages filed his notice of intention to offer an alibi defense, Manuel's name was included on the list of witnesses he would call. A government agent subsequently interviewed Manuel about Vavages' alibi. Manuel told the agent that she and Lavages were at home at the time of his alleged offense, and Lavages undoubtedly intended to call Manuel to testify in his defense at trial.

Approximately a month and a half after this initial interview, the prosecutor learned that Manuel had herself been arrested earlier the same year in a marijuana transportation case, pled guilty, and agreed to cooperate fully with the government. Notwithstanding Manuel's potential alibi testimony, the prosecutor believed that similarities between Lavages' alleged drug activities and the drug offense for which Manuel had pled guilty would bolster the government's case against Lavages. Accordingly, the prosecutor considered calling Manuel as part of the government's case-in-chief.

Just before Vavages' trial was scheduled to begin, the prosecutor contacted Manuel's attorney about the possibility of Manuel testifying. The basic content of the conversation is not disputed. The prosecutor warned Manuel's attorney that he did not believe Vavages' alibi defense and that if Manuel testified falsely, the government could bring perjury charges against her and withdraw from the plea agreement in Manuel's own criminal case. The prosecutor had a total of three or four face-to-face and telephone exchanges with Manuel's attorney concerning the possibility of Manuel testifying. Neither the prosecutor nor Manuel's attorney suggests that any of the exchanges were unprofessional in tone, and Manuel's attorney admits that he did not feel personally intimidated by the conversations. Nonetheless, the undisputed consequence of the exchanges was that Manuel's attorney advised his client to assert her Fifth Amendment privilege against self-incrimination to avoid a perjury prosecution for what the prosecutor clearly believed would be false alibi testimony. The court recognized Manuel's blanket invocation of the Fifth Amendment, and she did not testify at trial.

Unnecessarily strong admonitions against perjury aimed at discouraging defense witnesses from testifying have been held to deprive a criminal defendant of his Sixth Amendment right to compulsory process for obtaining witnesses in his favor. The seminal case is Webb v. Texas.

A number of post-Webb cases reveal that the trial judge is not the only person whose admonitions against perjury can deprive a criminal defendant of his right to compulsory process. In United States v. Morrison, 535 F.2d 223 (3d Cir.1976), for instance, the court held that a criminal defendant in a federal drug prosecution had been deprived of due process where the prosecutor told a potential witness that federal perjury charges were possible if she testified. Far from simply warning the defense witness about the dangers of perjury, the prosecutor in that case subjected the witness to a "barrage of warnings" that her testimony might result in a perjury prosecution and could be used against her in the event she was prosecuted for federal drug charges. Three warnings were delivered through defense counsel, while one was delivered directly to the witness during a personal interview. Though noting that the prosecutor was "a figure somewhat lower in the hierarchy than the trial judge," the court held that he was a potent "symbol of the Government's power to prosecute offenders" and that his conduct violated Webb.

The substantial interference inquiry is extremely fact specific. Among the factors courts consider in determining the coercive impact of perjury warnings are the manner in which the prosecutor or judge raises the issue, the language of the warnings, and the prosecutor's or judge's basis in the record for believing the witness might lie.

In the present case, there is no question that the prosecutor was justified in contacting Manuel's counsel, cautioning him against his client's testifying falsely, and informing him of the possible consequences of perjurious testimony. Though there is no intimation that the prosecutor berated or badgered Manuel or her counsel with admonishments against perjury, three aspects of the prosecutor's conduct give us serious pause.

We are first concerned by the prosecutor's articulation of his belief that Manuel's alibi testimony would be false. The prosecutor combined a standard admonition against perjury—that Manuel could be prosecuted for perjury in the event she lied on the stand—with an unambiguous statement of his belief that Manuel would be lying if she testified in support of Vavages' alibi. The prosecutor contends that there was nothing wrong with the latter statement, and the statement indeed can be viewed simply as an articulation of the obvious. After all, it should be evident to a defense witness and her counsel that the government does not believe testimony that contradicts its case-in-chief, and the threat of a perjury prosecution does not seem especially greater simply because the prosecutor articulates this belief. We cannot disregard this prosecutor's conduct, however, where the additional statement served as no more than a thinly veiled attempt to coerce a witness off the stand. It does not require much of an interpretative gloss on the prosecutor's warning to conclude that unless Manuel changed her testimony or refused to testify at all, she would be prosecuted for perjury and suffer any attendant consequences. As the district court found, "[the prosecutor's] warnings were intimidating and were intended to stifle testimony which he believed would be perjurious in the defense of Mr. Vavages."

We do not mean to suggest that a prosecutor should never articulate his belief that a witness is lying. Rather, we disapprove of such conduct where the prosecutor lacks any substantial basis in the record for believing the witness is lying. That Manuel's testimony would have contradicted the testimony of the government's own witnesses does not form a sufficient basis for the prosecutor's warning. Rather, unusually strong admonitions against perjury are typically justified only where the prosecutor has a more substantial basis in the record for believing the witness might lie—for instance, a direct conflict between the witness' proposed testimony and her own prior testimony. See United States v. Smith, 997 F.2d 674, 680–81 (10th Cir.1993) ("[W]e are cognizant that [the court] was faced with a more real possibility of perjury than in some cases, in that the witness seemed to be preparing to give testimony in direct contradiction of her prior trial testimony, making a government charge of perjury apparently easy to establish."); Davis, 974 F.2d at 188 (finding no coercion where defendant's testimony would conflict with his own statements in presentence report). Because Manuel's alibi testimony would have been entirely consistent with her own prior statements and would not have conflicted with any past testimony, the prosecutor lacked this substantial basis for believing Manuel would perjure herself.

Even more troubling than the threatened perjury prosecution was the prosecutor's threat to withdraw Manuel's plea agreement in her own unrelated criminal prosecution if she testified in support of Vavages' alibi. See Blackwell, 694 F.2d at 1333–34 (citing cases involving threats of prosecution for other crimes, reindictment on dropped charges, and revocation of probation). Because Manuel's plea agreement remains under seal, we cannot ascertain just how easily the government could have withdrawn the agreement had Manuel testified in Vavages' defense. If the government could have withdrawn from the plea agreement without successfully prosecuting Manuel for perjury, the prosecutor's additional threat was especially coercive. Even if withdrawal from the plea agreement would have required a perjury conviction, the threat rendered the prosecutor's warning considerably more intimidating.

The prosecutor attempts to justify his conduct by emphasizing that the government was itself considering calling Manuel as a witness. Whether or not Webb applies to prosecution witnesses, see Griffin v. Davies, 929 F.2d 550, 554 (10th Cir.1991) (describing this as an open question), we decline to grant significantly more leeway to the prosecutor when the potential government witness has already been listed as a critical alibi witness for the defense.

Our concerns are heightened by the prosecutor's emphasis during his closing argument on Vavages' failure to present anyone but his "cute[ ] ... little kids" to support his alibi defense. The prosecutor emphasized that "[y]ou have in this case an alibi in which not one adult steps forward." He accused the defense of "every manipulation," calling the children's testimony "the shabbiest ploy in this case." He used an analogy in which the wife confronts a lying husband. He pointed out that Manuel was in the courtroom by noting that the testifying children "never looked at Dad," that they "had to look over at Mother, to make sure they're not getting into trouble." He concluded by arguing, "And you could ask, why didn't he bring other witnesses? ... They could have brought other people, other than little cute children." Even if the prosecutor did not intend his comments to refer to Manuel's absence from the stand, the implication was plain. The inference can easily be drawn that the prosecutor intimidated a witness into refusing to testify, then capitalized on his misconduct during his closing argument by emphasizing that witness' failure to appear.

The strongest factor in the government's favor is that the prosecutor never directly admonished Manuel. The prosecutor instead admonished only Manuel's counsel, and admonishments that are threatening or intimidating to a lay witness might not be threatening or intimidating to the witness' counsel. See Viera, 839 F.2d at 1115. In other words, a defendant may not be prejudiced by a prosecutor's improper warnings where counsel for a witness strips the warnings of their coercive force. In the present case, however, there is no question that the prosecutor's warnings were a "but for" cause of Manuel's refusal to testify. Manuel's counsel clearly believed that the prosecutor would file perjury charges against Manuel and seek to withdraw her plea agreement if she testified in support of Vavages' alibi—whether truthfully or not—and the prosecutor's admonitions were "a very determining factor" in counsel's decision to advise Manuel not to testify. We are thus persuaded that the prosecutor substantially interfered with Manuel's decision whether to testify.

In Smith v. Baldwin, 466 F.3d 805 (9th Cir. 2006), a divided court said it might be proper to require state prosecutors to grant immunity if witness for defense was threatened by them with death penalty if he testified consistent with his exculpatory affidavits.

5. THE DEPARTED WITNESS

People v. Wilson

Supreme Court of Illinois, 1962.
24 Ill.2d 425, 182 N.E.2d 203.

■ MR. JUSTICE SCHAEFER delivered the opinion of the court:

The defendants, Cladie B. Wilson and Louis Washington, were [convicted] for the unlawful sale of narcotic drugs to Inez Anderson. Cladie Wilson was sentenced to the penitentiary for a term of ten to eleven years and Louis Washington was sentenced to life imprisonment as an habitual criminal. The defendant Wilson asserts that the State's failure to produce Ruth Killingsworth, an informer for the Federal bureau of narcotics, deprived her of a fair trial, and that the evidence establishes her defense of entrapment....

* * *

In response to the defendants' inquiries as to the whereabouts of Ruth Killingsworth, the State had replied by giving her address as the local office of the Federal bureau of narcotics. Before the trial the attorney for the defendants moved for the entry of an order directing the prosecution to produce Ruth Killingsworth so that he might interview her in order to prepare his defense, to prepare for cross-examination of the State's witnesses, and to call, or request the court to call, Ruth Killingsworth as a witness. The prosecution resisted the motion, and the court reserved his ruling until the evidence had been heard.

At the trial one of the Federal agents testified that on or about September 14, 1958, he went to Ruth Killingsworth's apartment, and drove her, and a man named Fred Stein whom he described as her "husband," to a railroad station in a government car. There he watched them buy tickets, and put them on a train for Fort Worth, Texas. He further testified that he gave her $60 at this time and had given her $700 a few days earlier. He acknowledged that he was acting in his official capacity and that he used official funds. At the conclusion of the testimony the defendants' motion was renewed, and it was then denied upon the ground that the court did not see "how the production of this witness could help either defendant."

To the defendants' contention that the conduct of the Federal agents deprived her of a fair trial, the State replies that it is not required to call all material witnesses to the commission of a crime. That is true, but there is more here than a determination to call, or not to call, a particular witness. Here a crucial witness was deliberately sent beyond the jurisdiction of the court, and where, as here, all of the evidence is secured by or under the direction of Federal agents, the State can not divorce itself from their conduct when it undertakes a prosecution.

The fact that the prosecution itself brought about the absence of the witness makes it unnecessary to consider the State's contention that the defendant did not show that it could compel her return. We may point out, however, that in a case in which Federal narcotic agents deliberately deferred the prosecution until an informer had voluntarily left the jurisdiction, the Supreme Court of California set aside the conviction, saying: "The record does indicate that the police did not arrange for Stough's absence. The critical question, however, is not necessarily one of improper conduct in bringing about Stough's absence, but rather, whether the defendant's conviction resulted from some form of trial in which his essential rights were disregarded or denied."

* * *

Entrapment is a recognized defense to a criminal prosecution, and the defendant was entitled to a fair hearing on that defense. Moreover, the testimony of Killingsworth as to what was said during the defendants' visits to her apartment was critical.

We hold, therefore, that the conduct of the Federal agents in sending her out of the jurisdiction, and the ruling of the trial court in denying the defendants' motion to compel her production, deprived them of a fair trial....

The judgment of the criminal court of Cook County is reversed, and the cause is remanded for a new trial.

NOTES

1. The police must make reasonable efforts to retain or obtain information which can be used to locate informers. People v. Goliday, 8 Cal.3d 771, 106 Cal.Rptr. 113, 505 P.2d 537 (1973). See Freeman v. Georgia, 599 F.2d 65 (5th Cir.1979) (police concealed location of a witness).

2. For many years courts have struggled with defense claims that the United States Government has deported alleged illegal aliens who may have given testimony favorable to the accused. The prosecution's response has been that such persons were routinely excluded from the country in the normal course of enforcing immigration laws. In United States v. Valenzuela–Bernal, 458 U.S. 858, 102 S.Ct. 3440 (1982), a typical case, the defendant was arrested with three illegal aliens he was transporting. One was placed in custody to provide non-hearsay evidence of the violation, the other two were sent home. The Court found first that "Congress has determined that prompt deportation, such as occurred in this case, constitutes the most effective method for curbing the enormous flow of illegal aliens across our southern border" and then that retaining all witnesses was too great a burden: "During fiscal year 1979, almost one-half of the more than 11,000 inmates incarcerated in federal facilities in the Southern District of California were material witnesses who had neither been charged with nor convicted of a criminal offense. The average period of detention for such witnesses exceeded 5 days, and many were detained for more than 20 days. Thus, the detention of alien eyewitnesses imposes substantial financial and physical burdens upon the Government, not to mention the human cost to potential witnesses who are incarcerated though charged with no crime." The Court believed that even under present practices valid and appropriate prosecutions are foregone. The Court then analyzed *Washington v. Texas* as providing a compulsory process to an accused to secure witnesses "in his favor" and further found that all its cases dealing with access to evidence required that the evidence be favorable and material. The Court also analyzed rules dealing with speedy trial, disclosure of favorable evidence, disclosure of informants and discovery of witness statements. The Court stated:

> To summarize, the responsibility of the Executive Branch faithfully to execute the immigration policy adopted by Congress justifies the prompt deportation of illegal-alien witnesses upon the Executive's good-faith determination that they possess no evidence favorable to the defendant in a criminal prosecution. The mere fact that the Government deports such witnesses is not sufficient to establish a violation of the Compulsory Process Clause of the Sixth Amendment or the Due Process Clause of the Fifth Amendment. A violation of these provisions requires some showing that the evidence lost would be both material and favorable to the defense.
>
> Because prompt deportation deprives the defendant of an opportunity to interview the witnesses to determine precisely what favorable evidence they possess, however, the defendant cannot be expected to render a detailed description of their lost testimony. But this does not, as the Court of Appeals concluded, relieve the defendant of the duty to make some showing of materiality. Sanctions may be imposed on the Government for deporting witnesses only if the criminal defendant makes a plausible showing that the testimony of the deported witnesses would have been material and favorable to his defense, in ways not merely cumulative to the testimony of available witnesses. In some cases such a showing may be based upon agreed facts, and will be in the nature of a legal argument rather than a submission of additional facts. In other cases the criminal defendant may advance additional facts, either consistent with facts already known to the court or accompanied by a reasonable explanation for

their inconsistency with such facts, with a view to persuading the court that the testimony of a deported witness would have been material and favorable to his defense. Because in the latter situation the explanation of materiality is testimonial in nature, and constitutes evidence of the prejudice incurred as a result of the deportation, it should be verified by oath or affirmation of either the defendant or his attorney. See Fed.R.Evid. 603; Fed.R.Crim.P. 47.

As in other cases concerning the loss of material evidence, sanctions will be warranted for deportation of alien witnesses only if there is a reasonable likelihood that the testimony could have affected the judgment of the trier off act. In making such a determination, courts should afford some leeway for the fact that the defendant necessarily proffers a description of the material evidence rather than the evidence itself. Because determinations of materiality are often best made in light of all of the evidence adduced at trial, judges may wish to defer ruling on motions until after the presentation of evidence.

In this case the respondent made no effort to explain what material, favorable evidence the deported passengers would have provided for his defense. Under the principles set forth today, he therefore failed to establish a violation of the Fifth or Sixth Amendment, and the District Court did not err in denying his motion to dismiss the indictment.

Concurring in the result, Justice O'Connor suggested use of a procedure which would briefly delay deportation until defense counsel had a chance to interview the witness. A magistrate would then decide, if the defense so requested, whether there were valid reasons for deferring deportation until after the accused's trial. In dissent, Justice Brennan, joined by Justice Marshall, called for use of somewhat similar procedures, akin to those used in the Ninth Circuit for about the last decade.

3. In Lee v. Kemna, 534 U.S. 362, 122 S.Ct. 877 (2002), the defendant was on trial for murder and planned to present an alibi defense. His alibi witnesses (his mother, stepfather, and sister) voluntarily came from California to Missouri to testify on his behalf, but on the day the defense case began, they were unexplainably missing from the court. The defendant requested a continuance to gain time to find the witnesses. The trial court denied this motion, the trial proceeded, and the defendant was convicted. Later, when Lee filed for postconviction relief, he asserted that the witnesses had left the courthouse because an employee of the prosecutor's office had told them they were not needed any more. The state argued that his failure to present a written motion foreclosed this attack. The Supreme Court permitted review of the defendant's due process claim on habeas review, notwithstanding the general rule that the violation of firmly established state rules are normally adequate to foreclose review of a federal claim.

B. MULTIPLE DEFENDANT TRIALS

1. STATEMENTS OF CO-DEFENDANTS

Bruton v. United States

Supreme Court of the United States, 1968.
391 U.S. 123, 88 S.Ct. 1620, appeal after remand, 416 F.2d 310 (8th Cir.1969), certiorari denied 397 U.S. 1014, 90 S.Ct. 1248 (1970).

■ MR. JUSTICE BRENNAN delivered the opinion of the Court.

* * *

A joint trial of petitioner and one Evans resulted in the conviction of both by a jury on a federal charge of armed postal robbery. A postal inspector testified that Evans orally confessed to him that Evans and petitioner committed the armed robbery. The postal inspector obtained the oral confession, and another in which Evans admitted he had an accomplice whom he would not name, in the course of two interrogations of Evans. Both petitioner and Evans appealed their convictions to the Court of Appeals. That court set aside Evans' conviction on the ground that his oral confessions to the postal inspector should not have been received in evidence against him. However, the court affirmed petitioner's conviction because the trial judge instructed the jury that although Evans' confession was competent evidence against Evans it was inadmissible hearsay against petitioner and therefore had to be disregarded in determining petitioner's guilt or innocence.

* * *

We hold that, because of the substantial risk that the jury, despite instructions to the contrary, looked to the incriminating extrajudicial statements in determining petitioner's guilt, admission of Evans' confession in this joint trial violated petitioner's right of cross-examination secured by the Confrontation Clause of the Sixth Amendment. We overrule *Delli Paoli* [*v. United States*, 352 U.S. 232, 77 S.Ct.294] and reverse.

The basic premise of *Delli Paoli* was that it is "reasonably possible for the jury to follow" sufficiently clear instructions to disregard the confessor's extrajudicial statement that his codefendant participated with him in committing the crime. If it were true that the jury disregarded the reference to the codefendant no question would arise under the Confrontation Clause, because by hypothesis the case is treated as if the confessor made no statement inculpating the non-confessor. But since *Delli Paoli* was decided this Court has effectively repudiated its basic premise....

* * *

Here Evans' oral confessions were in fact testified to, and were therefore actually in evidence. That testimony was legitimate evidence against Evans and to that extent was properly before the jury during its deliberations. Even greater, then, was the likelihood that the jury would believe Evans made the statements and that they were true—not just the self-incriminating portions but those implicating petitioner as well. Plainly, the introduction of Evans' confession added substantial, perhaps even critical, weight to the Government's case in a form not subject to cross-examination, since Evans did not take the stand. Petitioner thus was denied his constitutional right of confrontation.

Delli Paoli assumed that this encroachment on the right to confrontation could be avoided by the instruction to the jury to disregard the inadmissible hearsay evidence.[3] But, as we have said, that assumption has

3. We emphasize that the hearsay statement inculpating petitioner was clearly inadmissible against him under traditional rules of evidence, the problem arising only because the statement was admissible against the declarant Evans. There is not before us, therefore, any recognized exception to the hearsay rule insofar as petitioner is con-

since been effectively repudiated. True, the repudiation was not in the context of the admission of a confession inculpating a codefendant but in the context of a New York rule which submitted to the jury the question of the voluntariness of the confession itself. Jackson v. Denno. Nonetheless the message of *Jackson* for *Delli Paoli* was clear. We there held that a defendant is constitutionally entitled at least to have the trial judge first determine whether a confession was made voluntarily before submitting it to the jury for an assessment of its credibility. More specifically, we expressly rejected the proposition that a jury, when determining the confessor's guilt, could be relied on to ignore his confession of guilt should it find the confession involuntary.

[The *Delli Paoli* dissenters] challenged the basic premise that a properly instructed jury would ignore the confessor's inculpation of the nonconfessor in determining the latter's guilt. "The fact of the matter is that too often such admonition against misuse is intrinsically ineffective in that the effect of such a nonadmissible declaration cannot be wiped from the brains of the jurors. The admonition therefore becomes a futile collocation of words and fails of its purpose as a legal protection to defendants against whom such a declaration should not tell." "The government should not have the windfall of having the jury be influenced by evidence against a defendant which, as a matter of law, they should not consider but which they cannot put out of their minds." To the same effect is the statement of Mr. Justice Jackson in his concurring opinion in Krulewitch v. United States: "The naive assumption that prejudicial effects can be overcome by instructions to the jury ... all practicing lawyers know to be unmitigated fiction...."

* * *

Those who have defended reliance on the limiting instruction in this area have cited several reasons in support. Judge Learned Hand, a particularly severe critic of the proposition that juries could be counted on to disregard inadmissible hearsay,[8] wrote the opinion for the Second Circuit which affirmed Delli Paoli's conviction, 229 F.2d 319. In Judge Hand's view the limiting instruction, although not really capable of preventing the jury from considering the prejudicial evidence, does as a matter of form provide a way around the exclusionary rules of evidence that is defensible because it "probably furthers, rather than impedes, the search for truth...." Nash v. United States, 54 F.2d 1006, 1007. Insofar as this implies the prosecution

cerned and we intimate no view whatever that such exceptions necessarily raise questions under the Confrontation Clause.

8. Judge Hand addressed the subject several times. The limiting instruction, he said, is a "recommendation to the jury of a mental gymnastic which is beyond, not only their powers, but anybody else's," Nash v. United States, 54 F.2d 1006, 1007: "Nobody can indeed fail to doubt whether the caution is effective, or whether usually the practical result is not to let in hearsay," United States v. Gottfried, 165 F.2d 360, 367; "it is indeed very hard to believe that a jury will, or for that matter can, in practice observe the admonition," United States v. Delli Paoli, 229 F.2d 319, 321.Judge Hand referred to the instruction as a "placebo," medically defined as "a medicinal lie." Judge Jerome Frank suggested that its legal equivalent "is a kind of 'judicial lie': It undermines a moral relationship between the courts, the jurors, and the public; like any other judicial deception, it damages the decent judicial administration of justice." United States v. Grunewald, 233 F.2d 556, 574.

ought not to be denied the benefit of the confession to prove the confessor's guilt, however, it overlooks alternative ways of achieving that benefit without at the same time infringing the non-confessor's right of confrontation. Where viable alternatives do exist, it is deceptive to rely on the pursuit of truth to defend a clearly harmful practice.

Another reason cited in defense of *DelliPaoli* is the justification for joint trials in general, the argument being that the benefits of joint proceedings should not have to be sacrificed by requiring separate trials in order to use the confession against the declarant. Joint trials do conserve state funds, diminish inconvenience to witnesses and public authorities, and avoid delays in bringing those accused of crime to trial. But the answer to this argument was cogently stated by Judge Lehman of the New York Court of Appeals, dissenting in People v. Fisher, 249 N.Y. 419, 432, 164 N.W. 336, 341:

> ". . . . We destroy the age-old rule which in the past has been regarded as a fundamental principle of our jurisprudence by a legalistic formula, required of the judge, that the jury may not consider any admissions against any party who did not join in them. We secure greater speed, economy and convenience in the administration of the law at the price of fundamental principles of constitutional liberty. That price is too high."

Finally, the reason advanced by the majority in *Delli Paoli* was to tie the result to maintenance of the jury system. "Unless we proceed on the basis that the jury will follow the court's instructions where those instructions are clear and the circumstances are such that the jury can reasonably be expected to follow them, the jury system makes little sense." We agree that there are many circumstances in which this reliance is justified. Not every admission of inadmissible hearsay or other evidence can be considered to be reversible error unavoidable through limiting instructions; instances occur in almost every trial where inadmissible evidence creeps in, usually inadvertently. "A defendant is entitled to a fair trial but not a perfect one." It is not unreasonable to conclude that in many such cases the jury can and will follow the trial judge's instructions to disregard such information. Nevertheless, as was recognized in *Jackson* there are some contexts in which the risk that the jury will not, or cannot, follow instructions is so great, and the consequences of failure so vital to the defendant, that the practical and human limitations of the jury system cannot be ignored. Such a context is presented here, where the powerfully incriminating extrajudicial statements of a codefendant, who stands accused side-by-side with the defendant, are deliberately spread before the jury in a joint trial. Not only are the incriminations devastating to the defendant but their credibility is inevitably suspect, a fact recognized when accomplices do take the stand and the jury is instructed to weigh their testimony carefully given the recognized motivation to shift blame onto others. The unreliability of such evidence is intolerably compounded when the alleged accomplice, as here, does not testify and cannot be tested by cross-examination. It was against such threats to a fair trial that the Confrontation Clause was directed.

We, of course, acknowledge the impossibility of determining whether in fact the jury did or did not ignore Evans' statement inculpating petitioner in determining petitioner's guilt. But that was also true in the analogous situation in *Jackson* and was not regarded as militating against striking down the New York procedure there involved. It was enough that the procedure posed "substantial threats to a defendant's constitutional rights to have an involuntary confession entirely disregarded and to have the coercion issue fairly and reliably determined. These hazards we cannot ignore." Here the introduction of Evans' confession posed a substantial threat to petitioner's right to confront the witnesses against him, and this is a hazard we cannot ignore. Despite the concededly clear instructions to the jury to disregard Evans' inadmissible hearsay evidence inculpating petitioner, in the context of a joint trial we cannot accept limiting instructions as an adequate substitute for petitioner's constitutional right of cross-examination. The effect is the same as if there had been no instruction at all.

Reversed.

■ MR. JUSTICE BLACK concurs in the result for the reasons stated in the dissent in Delli Paoli v. United States, 352 U.S. 232, 246, 77 S.Ct. 294, 302.

■ MR. JUSTICE MARSHALL took no part in the consideration or decision of this case.

■ [MR. JUSTICE STEWART'S concurring opinion is omitted.]

■ MR. JUSTICE WHITE, dissenting.

* * *

The rule which the Court announces today will severely limit the circumstances in which defendants may be tried together for a crime which they are both charged with committing. Unquestionably, joint trials are more economical and minimize the burden on witnesses, prosecutors and courts. They also avoid delays in bringing those accused of crime to trial. This much the Court concedes. It is also worth saying that separate trials are apt to have varying consequences for legally indistinguishable defendants. The unfairness of this is confirmed by the common prosecutorial experience of seeing codefendants who are tried separately strenuously jockeying for position with regard to who should be the first to be tried.

In view of the practical difficulties of separate trials and their potential unfairness, I am disappointed that the Court has not spelled out how the federal courts might conduct their business consistent with today's opinion. I would suppose that it will be necessary to exclude all extrajudicial confessions unless all portions of them which implicate defendants other than the declarant are effectively deleted. Effective deletion will probably require not only omission of all direct and indirect inculpations of codefendants but also of any statement that could be employed against those defendants once their identity is otherwise established. Of course, the deletion must not be such that it will distort the statements to the substantial prejudice of either the declarant or the Government. If deletion is not feasible, then the Government will have to choose either not to use the confession at all or to try the defendants separately. To save time, money, and effort, the Government might best seek a ruling at the earliest possible stage of the trial proceedings as to whether the confession is admissible once offending portions are deleted. The failure of the Government to adopt and follow proper procedures for insuring that the inadmissible portions of confessions are excluded will be relevant to the question of whether it was harmless error for them to have gotten before the jury. Oral statements, such as that involved in the present case, will present special problems, for there is a risk that the witness in testifying will inadvertently exceed permissible limits. Except for recommending that caution be used with regard to such oral statements, it is difficult to anticipate the issues which will arise in concrete factual situations.

I would hope, but am not sure, that by using these procedures the federal courts would escape reversal under today's ruling. Even so, I persist in believing that the reversal of *Delli Paoli* unnecessarily burdens the already difficult task of conducting criminal trials, and therefore I dissent in this case.

■ MR. JUSTICE HARLAN joins this opinion without abandoning his original disagreement with Jackson v. Denno, 378 U.S. 368, 427, 84 S.Ct. 1774, 1807, expressed in his dissenting opinion in that case.

NOTES ON POST-*BRUTON* DEVELOPMENTS

Frequently *Bruton* issues are treated with severance materials because the *Bruton* "problem" can be solved by severance. Other problems arise, nevertheless. See, generally, Haddad, Post–Bruton Developments: a Reconsideration of the Confrontation Rationale, and a Proposal For a Due Process Evaluation of Limiting Instructions, 18Am.Cr.L.Rev. 1 (1980).

1. *Burden of Raising Issue.* When the defendant before trial knows that a co-defendant made a statement implicating the defendant, must the defendant make a pre-trial request for severance? United States v. Marks, 585 F.2d 164 (6th Cir.1978), noted that in *Bruton* neither a severance motion nor a request for redaction had been made by defense counsel. *Marks*, therefore, placed the burden on the prosecution to seek pre-trial solution of *Bruton* problems. Compare People v. McGautha, 70 Cal.2d 770, 76 Cal.Rptr. 434, 452 P.2d 650 (1969). See also Commonwealth v. Johnson, 474 Pa. 410, 378 A.2d 859 (1977); State v. Barnett, 53 N.J. 559, 252 A.2d 33 (1969); Ortiz v. State, 265 Ind. 549, 356 N.E.2d 1188 (1976).

2. *Other Mechanical Solutions.* Severance may not be the only way to prevent the jury in a defendant's case from hearing a co-defendant's out-of-court accusations before deciding the defendant's fate. On probably at least one hundred occasions trial judges have impanelled separate juries for each defendant, excluded the defendant's jury during testimony about the co-defendant's confession (and during opening and closing statements), but otherwise seated both juries in a single courtroom at the same time. Reviewing courts have avoided flat condemnation or wholehearted approval of such single-trial, multiple-juries solution. See, e.g., United States v. Sidman, 470 F.2d 1158 (9th Cir.1972); People v. Hernandez, 163 N.J.Super. 283, 394 A.2d 883 (1978). They typically find no harm in use of the procedure. See People v. Harris, 47 Cal.3d 1047, 255 Cal.Rptr. 352, 767 P.2d 619 (1989); People v. Greenberg, 176 Mich.App. 296, 439 N.W.2d 336 (1989); Smith v. DeRobertis, 758 F.2d 1151 (7th Cir.1985) (review of federal cases). Compare State v. Lambright, 138 Ariz. 63, 673 P.2d 1 (1983) (finding procedure "unauthorized" under Arizona law but not reversing in the case at hand). See also Morris and Savitt, Bruton Revisited:

One Trial/Two Juries, 12 Prosecutor 92 (1976). See also 72 ALR FED 522. What dangers are there in this procedure? What about allowing a single jury to (1) hear all the evidence except the co-defendant's confession, (2) decide the fate of the defendant, (3) return to hear the confession of the co-defendant, and (4) retire again to deliberate the fate of the co-defendant? Such a procedure was used in United States v. Crane, 499 F.2d 1385 (6th Cir.1974). It may originally have been the idea of a Columbia University law student. See 3 Columbia Journal of Law and Social Problems 80 (1967). Is it fair to the co-defendant? Would a prosecutor like the idea? Compare United States v. McIver, 688 F.2d 726 (11th Cir.1982) (condemning similar bifurcation but not in the *Bruton* context).

3. *Inapplicability to Non–Jury Trials.* Most courts view the *Bruton* problem as arising from the ineffectiveness of jury instructions. A trial judge, however, is presumed to be able to hear *C*'s confession in a joint trial of *C* and *D* without considering *C*'s confession in deciding *D*'s fate. Hence most courts have held that severance is not required in bench trials. See, e.g., Rogers v. McMackin, 884 F.2d 252 (6th Cir.1989); State v. Gleason, 359 A.2d 308 (Me.1976); People v. Vinson, 49 Ill.App.3d 602, 7 Ill.Dec. 203, 364 N.E.2d 364 (1977); Cockrell v. Oberhauser, 413 F.2d 256 (9th Cir.1969). This seems consistent with dictum in Lee v. Illinois, 476 U.S. 530, 106 S.Ct. 2056 (1986). If we are worried about a judge making improper use of a co-defendant's confession, would the defendant in a bench trial have to be tried by a judge who did not know that the co-defendant had implicated the defendant? Of course, if in a multiple-defendant bench trial the judge indicates that he or she has used *C*'s confession to convict *D*, the judge has rebutted the presumption of propriety; in effect, the judge has made a hearsay blunder by using as evidence an out-of-court statement which, as to *D*, is inadmissible hearsay. See, e.g., In re Appeal No. 977, 22 Md.App. 511, 323 A.2d 663 (1974); United States v. Longee, 603 F.2d 1342 (9th Cir.1979).

4. *Inapplicable When Statement is Admissible Against Both Defendants.* When the co-defendant's statement is admissible against the defendant (either under a hearsay exception or as relevant non-hearsay evidence), the statement will be admitted at *D*'s trial even if he is tried separately from *C*. Hence there is no *Bruton* problem. Lee v. Illinois, 476 U.S. 530, 106 S.Ct. 2056 (1986) (dictum). In a joint trial there would be no limiting instruction as to the evidence being admissible against both *C* and *D*. See, for example, United States v. Apollo, 476 F.2d 156 (5th Cir.1973) (statement was non-hearsay resgestae evidence, relevant against both defendants); Dutton v. Evans, 400 U.S. 74, 91 S.Ct. 210 (1970) (co-conspirator exception); McLaughlin v. Vinzant, 522 F.2d 448 (1st Cir.1975) (excited utterance); Miller v. Cardwell, 448 F.2d 186 (6th Cir.1971), and Commonwealth v. Bethea, 214 Pa.Super. 253, 251 A.2d 727 (1969) (adopted admission). Of course, use of *C*'s out-of-court statement as evidence against *D* will not only have to be permissible under local rules of evidence; as in *Dutton*, supra, it may also face an argument that such use violates *D*'s right to confront witnesses. This is not a *Bruton* problem, however. *Lee*, supra. The same issue would be presented even if *D* were tried separately. Moreover, *Dutton* indicates that *Bruton* might require severance if local law made a certain statement by *C* inadmissible against *D*; but, also, that if local law were changed to allow use of that same statement against *D*, such use of *C*'s out-of-court accusation would not necessarily violate the confrontation clause guarantee. Does it make sense to say that *D*'s Sixth Amendment rights are violated if the jury is told not to consider *C*'s statement as evidence against *D* whereas his Sixth Amendment rights are not violated if the jury is told that it should consider that statement as evidence against *D*? Would "due process" provide a better rationale than confrontation? At no stage of his case, neither before the Supreme Court nor earlier, did George Bruton ever raise a Sixth Amendment claim. Instead, he urged that the procedure was unfair. Why, then, did the Supreme Court use a confrontation analysis?

With increasing frequency, some courts have held *A*'s confession to be substantively admissible against *B* as a declaration against interest under Fed.R.Evid. 804(b)(3) or a state court counterpart, reliable enough to satisfy the Confrontation Clause even in the absence of an opportunity for *B* to cross-examine *A*. More often such inculpatory statements were allegedly made by *A* to a friend or to an undercover informer, but sometimes they were made in a typical post-arrest interrogation situation. See United States v. Garcia, 897 F.2d 1413 (7th Cir.1990); United States v. Fields, 871 F.2d 188 (1st Cir.1989); United States v. Holland, 880 F.2d 1091 (9th Cir.1989); State v. Earnest, 106 N.M. 411, 744 P.2d 539 (1987); State v. St. Pierre, 111 Wash.2d 105, 759 P.2d 383 (1988).

See generally Haddad and Agin, A Potential Revolution in Bruton Doctrine: Is Bruton Applicable Where Domestic Evidence Rules Prohibit Use of Codefendant's Confession as Evidence Against a Defendant Although the Confrontation Clause Would Allow Such Use, 81 J.Crim.L. & C. 235 (1990).

5. *Inapplicable When Statement Does Not Implicate Co–Defendant.* Unless the co-defendant's statement implicates the defendant, either as originally given, or as edited, *Bruton* has been held not to require severance. State v. Cross, 32 Wash.App. 193, 646 P.2d 171 (1982); State v. Smith, 15 Conn.App. 122, 543 A.2d 301 (1988); Smith v. State, 516 N.E.2d 1055 (Ind.1987); United States v. Belle, 593 F.2d 487 (3d Cir.1979); Commonwealth v. Clark, 5 Mass.App. 673, 369 N.E.2d 468(1977). Courts vary greatly on how direct the implication must be. See United States v. Trudo, 449 F.2d 649 (2d Cir.1971); Fox v. State, 179 Ind.App. 267, 384 N.E.2d 1159 (1979).

Consider this situation. *C* and *D* are jointly charged with arson. The prosecution's theory is that *D* hired *C* to burn a building. *C* has confessed to setting a fire but all references to his having been hired by anyone have been edited out of the confession. At trial both *C* and *D* contend that no arson occurred, contending that the fire was not of human origin. *C*'s statement (not implicating *D*) is admitted, subject to a limiting instruction directing the jury not to consider the statement as evidence in deciding *D*'s fate. Have *D*'s Sixth Amendment rights been violated? Has *D* any less right to confront *C* concerning the corpus delicti than concerning *D*'s alleged involvement? Is the jury any less likely to misuse the confession in this case than in *Bruton*?

In Richardson v. Marsh, 481 U.S. 200, 107 S.Ct. 1702 (1987), Justice Scalia, for a six-person majority, held that in deciding whether admission of a co-defendant's statement at a joint jury trial is error, the court need look only to the text of the statement itself and not to the statement in the context of the rest of the evidence.

Scalia reviewed other instances where the law has relied upon the use of limiting instructions, for example, where the accused's inadmissible *Miranda*—violative statement is admitted for the limited purpose of impeachment. Viewing *Bruton* as a narrow exception to the general rule that the use of limiting instructions is constitutionally permissible, he declared that practical concerns support the narrow interpretation of the exception.

The majority declared that where the incriminating nature of the statement does not appear on the face of the statement but rather involves "linkage," then "it is a less valid generalization that the jury will not likely obey the instructions to disregard the evidence." In the latter case, "there does not exist the overwhelming probability of their inability to do so that is the foundation of *Bruton*'s exception to the general rule."

The Court said that "[e]ven more significantly," the opposite holding would have significant practical effect. Trial judges would not be in a position to assess a

Bruton claim at the time they were ruling on a pre-trial severance request. The defense might manipulate the trial evidence so that they would have a claim, at the conclusion of a joint trial, that, in context, the co-defendant's statement inculpated the defendant. Justice Scalia noted that almost one third of federal trials involve multiple defendants, and many are conspiracy cases involving numerous co-defendants. Expanding the *Bruton* rule would require the expenditure of scarce federal trial resources.

The majority added that it was not considering the admissibility of a confession "in which the defendant's name has been replaced with a symbol or neutral pronoun." Subject to that limitation, the Court held "the Confrontation Clause is not violated by the admission of a nontestifying co-defendant's confession with a proper limiting instruction when, as here, the confession is redacted to eliminate not only the defendant's name, but any reference to her existence."

Finally, the Court noted that it remained constitutionally improper for the prosecutor "to undo the effect of the limiting instruction by urging the jury to use the co-defendant's confession in evaluating the defendant's case." Because the prosecutor had done that in Marsh's case, the Court remanded for consideration of the question of whether the federal district court was empowered to grant habeas corpus relief where defense counsel had not objected to such argument in the state trial court.

Justice Stevens, joined by Justice Marshall and by the author of *Bruton*, Justice Brennan, dissented, saying the "result demeans the values protected by the Confrontation Clause." The dissent explained how, on the particular facts of the case, the jury would be certain to link a co-defendant's confession to a critical question of the defendant's intent even though the confession did not refer to the defendant. "Viewed in the total context of the trial evidence, this confession was of critical importance because it was the only evidence directly linking respondent with the specific intent, expressed before the robbery, to kill the victim afterwards."

The dissent argued that the efficiencies achieved by joint trial had been deemed inadequate to prevent adoption of the *Bruton* rule in the first instance. The dissent would find a *Bruton* error where the co-defendant's confession, in context, was "powerfully incriminating." The dissent did not seem to articulate a standard for determining whether *Bruton* "linkage" likely occurred in a case where the defendant's claim rested upon an assertion that the rest of the evidence would create a risk that the jury would use the co-defendant's confession as evidence of the defendant's guilt.

In Gray v. Maryland, 523 U.S. 185, 118 S.Ct. 1151 (1998), the Court, in a 5–4 vote, held that *Bruton* prohibited the introduction of a statement that was redacted in such a way as to replace the name of the defendant with an obvious indication of deletion such as a blank space, the word "deleted" or a similar symbol.

6. *Applicable When Defendants Have Both Given Similar Confessions.* In the decade following *Bruton* many courts declared that severance is not required if both defendants have given similar confessions. The theory seemed to be that a co-defendant's confession is not as "powerfully incriminating" if the defendant has also confessed. For the exception to apply, various courts said that the two had to be "reciprocal," "dovetailing," "interlocking," or "substantially similar."

In Parker v. Randolph, 442 U.S. 62, 99 S.Ct. 2132 (1979), the four justices who made up the prevailing plurality recognized the "similar confessions" exception. The other four participating justices, including one who would have invoked the harmless error doctrine, refused to recognize an exception.

However, Cruz v. New York, 481 U.S. 186, 107 S.Ct. 1714 (1987), rejected the *Parker* plurality opinion approach to interlocking confessions. Through Justice

Scalia, the Court held that, even if the prosecution introduces the accused's own confession, admission of the co-defendant's similar confession implicating the defendant still constitutes *Bruton* error where the defendant has no opportunity to confront the confessing co-defendant. Justice Scalia's majority opinion noted that "(w)hile devastating practical effect was one of the factors that *Bruton* considered in assessing whether the Confrontation Clause might require some departure from the general rule that jury instructions suffice to exclude improper testimony, it did not suggest that the existence of such an effect should be assessed on a case-by-case basis. Rather that was one of the justifications for excepting from the general rule the entire category of co-defendant confessions that implicate the defendant in the crime."

Moreover, the majority noted that where the co-defendant has told the same story allegedly told by the defendant, the effect often will be devastating."Having decided *Bruton*, we must face the consequences of what it holds."

The *Cruz* majority acknowledged that where a co-defendant's interlocking confession improperly was presented to the defendant's jury, the prosecution, in seeking to preserve a conviction, may argue on the particular facts of the case that the error was harmless beyond a reasonable doubt. Harmless error is a matter for reviewing courts, however. *Cruz* makes it clear that the *Bruton* principles prohibit admission at a joint trial, subject to limiting instructions, of unredacted interlocking confessions, if the confession of one defendant is inadmissible against the other. Four justices dissented, adopting the views of the Parker v. Randolph plurality opinion.

7. *Inapplicable When Confessing Co–Defendant Takes the Stand and is Available for Cross–Examination by Defendant.* In *Bruton* the Supreme Court said that the procedures utilized by the trial court were constitutionally deficient because the defendant had no opportunity to cross-examine the co-defendant. Subsequently, in California v. Green, Chapter 19, Section A, supra, (a case not concerned with *Bruton* problems) the Court held that use of an earlier out-of-court statement does not violate the confrontation guarantee if the defendant at the time of trial has the opportunity to cross-examine the declarant. From these two premises, the Court concluded in Nelson v. O'Neil, 402 U.S. 622, 91 S.Ct. 1723 (1971), that any *Bruton* error is cured if the confessing co-defendant takes the stand in a joint trial and is available for cross-examination by the defendant. See also Commonwealth v. Parker, 402 Mass. 333, 522 N.E.2d 924 (1988); People v. Ainsworth, 45 Cal.3d 984, 248 Cal.Rptr. 568, 755 P.2d 1017 (1988). (Presumably, however, the two must be represented by separate attorneys for *Nelson* to apply). Because it is not known before trial whether the accused will testify, *Nelson* may be of little help in avoiding severance. On certain occasions, prosecutors have avoided severance by pledging not to use the co-defendant's confession unless the co-defendant testifies and contradicts what he said in the confession.

When *Nelson* applies, *C*'s references to *D* need not be edited out of the confession, since *D* has an opportunity to cross-examine *C*. However (except in those jurisdictions such as California which allow prior inconsistent statements as substantive evidence), *C*'s out-of-court statement remains inadmissible hearsay as to *D*. *D* is still entitled to a limiting instruction even though he had an opportunity to cross-examine *C*. State v. Slate, 38 N.C.App. 209, 247 S.E.2d 430 (1978).

2. ANTAGONISTIC DEFENSES

Zafiro v. United States

Supreme Court of the United States, 1993.
506 U.S. 534, 113 S.Ct. 933.

■ JUSTICE O'CONNOR delivered the opinion of the Court.

Rule 8(b) of the Federal Rules of Criminal Procedure provides that defendants may be charged together "if they are alleged to have participated in the same act or transaction or in the same series of acts or transactions constituting an offense or offenses." Rule 14 of the Rules, in turn, permits a district court to grant a severance of defendants if "it appears that a defendant or the government is prejudiced by a joinder." In this case, we consider whether Rule 14 requires severance as a matter of law when codefendants present "mutually antagonistic defenses."

[Defendants were charged in a drug distribution conspiracy in the Chicago area. Two men were observed placing a large box in the trunk of a car and driving to a woman's suburban apartment. As they were carrying the box up the stairs to the apartment two agents approached and identified themselves. The men dropped the box and ran into the apartment and the agents followed in pursuit. The box contained 55 pounds of cocaine and a search of the apartment, pursuant to a warrant subsequently obtained, revealed substantial cocaine, heroin and marijuana in a suitcase in the closet and a nearby sack containing $22,960 in cash.

At trial, the woman and one of the men sought a severance on the ground of antagonistic defenses. She claimed that the man was her boyfriend, occasionally stayed in her apartment and kept some clothes and a suitcase in her closet, but she had no idea that the suitcase contained illegal drugs. The man claimed that he was merely visiting his girlfriend and did not know that she was involved in distributing drugs. The district court denied the motion, the defendants were convicted, and the convictions were affirmed on appeal.]

* * *

There is a preference in the federal system for joint trials of defendants indicted together. Joint trials ... promote efficiency and "serve the interests of justice by avoiding the scandal and inequity of inconsistent verdicts." For these reasons, we repeatedly have approved of joint trials. But Rule 14 recognizes that joinder, even when proper under Rule 8(b), may prejudice either a defendant or the Government. Thus, the Rule provides,"(i)f it appears that a defendant or the government is prejudiced by a joinder of ... defendants ... for trial together, the court may order an election or separate trials of counts, grant a severance of defendants or provide whatever other relief justice requires." In interpreting Rule 14, the Courts of Appeals frequently have expressed the view that "mutually antagonistic" or "irreconcilable" defenses may be so prejudicial in some circumstances as to mandate severance. Notwithstanding such assertions, the courts have reversed relatively few convictions for failure to grant a severance on grounds of mutually antagonistic or irreconcilable defenses. The low rate of reversal may reflect the inability of defendants to prove a risk of prejudice in most cases involving conflicting defenses.

Nevertheless, petitioners urge us to adopt a bright-line rule, mandating severance whenever codefendants have conflicting defenses. We decline to do so. Mutually antagonistic defenses are not prejudicial per se. Moreover, Rule 14 does not require severance even if prejudice is shown; rather, it leaves the tailoring of the relief to be granted, if any, to the district court's sound discretion.

We believe that, when defendants properly have been joined under Rule 8(b), a district court should grant a severance under Rule 14 only if there is a serious risk that a joint trial would compromise a specific trial right of one of the defendants, or prevent the jury from making a reliable judgment about guilt or innocence. Such a risk might occur when evidence that the jury should not consider against a defendant and that would not be admissible if a defendant were tried alone is admitted against a codefendant. For example, evidence of a codefendant's wrongdoing in some circumstances erroneously could lead a jury to conclude that a defendant was guilty. When many defendants are tried together in a complex case and they have markedly different degrees of culpability, this risk of prejudice is heightened. Evidence that is probative of a defendant's guilt but technically admissible only against a codefendant also might present a risk of prejudice. Conversely, a defendant might suffer prejudice if essential exculpatory evidence that would be available to a defendant tried alone were unavailable in a joint trial. The risk of prejudice will vary with the facts in each case, and district courts may find prejudice in situations not discussed here. When the risk of prejudice is high, a district court is more likely to determine that separate trials are necessary, but, . . . less drastic measures, such as limiting instructions, often will suffice to cure any risk of prejudice.

Turning to the facts of this case, we note that petitioners do not articulate any specific instances of prejudice. Instead they contend that the very nature of their defenses, without more, prejudiced them. Their theory is that when two defendants both claim they are innocent and each accuses the other of the crime, a jury will conclude (1) that both defendants are lying and convict them both on that basis, or (2) that at least one of the two must be guilty without regard to whether the Government has proved its case beyond a reasonable doubt.

As to the first contention, it is well settled that defendants are not entitled to severance merely because they may have a better chance of acquittal in separate trials. Rules 8(b) and 14 are designed "to promote economy and efficiency and to avoid a multiplicity of trials, (so long as) these objectives can be achieved without substantial prejudice to the right of the defendants to a fair trial." While "(a)n important element of a fair trial is that a jury consider only relevant and competent evidence bearing on the issue of guilt or innocence," a fair trial does not include the right to exclude relevant and competent evidence. A defendant normally would not been titled to exclude the testimony of a former codefendant if the district court did sever their trials, and we see no reason why relevant and competent testimony would be prejudicial merely because the witness is also a codefendant.

As to the second contention, the short answer is that petitioners' scenario simply did not occur here. * * * [E]ven if there were some risk of prejudice, here it is of the type that can be cured with proper instructions, and "juries are presumed to follow their instructions." The District Court properly instructed the jury that the Government had "the burden of proving beyond a reasonable doubt" that each defendant committed the crimes with which he or she was charged. The court then instructed the jury that it must"give separate consideration to each individual defendant and to each separate charge against him. Each defendant is entitled to have his or her case determined from his or her own conduct and from the evidence (that) maybe applicable to him or to her." * * * These instructions sufficed to cure any possibility of prejudice.

Rule 14 leaves the determination of risk of prejudice and any remedy that maybe necessary to the sound discretion of the district courts. Because petitioners have not shown that their joint trial subjected them to any legally cognizable prejudice, we conclude that the District Court did not abuse its discretion in denying petitioners' motions to sever. The judgment of the Court of Appeals is affirmed.

■ JUSTICE STEVENS, concurring in the judgment.

When two people are apprehended in possession of a container filled with narcotics, it is probable that they both know what is inside. The inference of knowledge is heightened when, as in this case, both people flee when confronted by police officers, or both people occupy the premises in which the container is found.

* * *

In my view, the defenses presented in this case did not rise to the level of mutual antagonism.

* * *

The burden of overcoming any individual defendant's presumption of innocence, by proving guilt beyond a reasonable doubt, rests solely on the shoulders of the prosecutor. Joinder is problematic in cases involving mutually antagonistic defenses because it may operate to reduce the burden on the prosecutor, in two general ways. First, joinder may introduce what is in effect a second prosecutor into a case, by turning each codefendant into the other's most forceful adversary. Second, joinder may invite a jury confronted with two defendants, at least one of whom is almost certainly guilty, to convict the defendant who appears the more guilty of the two regardless of whether the prosecutor has proven guilt beyond a reasonable doubt as to that particular defendant. Though the Court is surely correct that this second risk may be minimized by careful instructions insisting on separate consideration of the evidence as to each codefendant, the danger will remain relevant to the prejudice inquiry in some cases.

Given these concerns, I cannot share the Court's enthusiastic and unqualified "preference" for the joint trial of defendants indicted together. * * * There will, however, almost certainly be multi defendant cases in which a series of separate trials would be not only more reliable, but also more efficient and manageable than some of the mammoth conspiracy cases which the Government often elects to prosecute. And in all cases, the Court should be mindful of the serious risks of prejudice and overreaching that are characteristic of joint trials, particularly when a conspiracy count is included in the indictment.

* * *

I agree with the Court that a "bright-line rule, mandating severance whenever codefendants have conflicting defenses" is unwarranted. For the reasons discussed above, however, I think district courts must retain their traditional discretion to consider severance whenever mutually antagonistic defenses are presented. Accordingly, I would refrain from announcing a preference for joint trials, or any general rule that might be construed as a limit on that discretion.

Because I believe the District Court correctly decided the severance motions in this case, I concur in the Court's judgment of affirmance.

NOTES

1. The standards for a severance are the same whether sought prior to trial or after the defense presents antagonistic defenses during the course of trial. Consult casebook ch. 13E (p. 998).

2. A severance because of "antagonistic defenses" espoused by different defendants is extraordinarily rare. According to United States v. Sandoval, 847 F.2d 179 (5th Cir.1988), the defenses must be so irreconcilable that for the jury to believe the core of one defendant's defense, it must disbelieve the core of the other defendant's defense. Usually, as in Sandoval, that strict standard is not met. In Sandoval, one defendant said he was not associated with any criminal enterprise; the other claimed entrapment.

Noting that a federal trial judge's decision is "virtually unreviewable" where the judge has rejected an antagonistic defense-severance request, the court nevertheless reversed in United States v. Serpoosh, 919 F.2d 835 (2d Cir.1990). It said:

> We have described the decision to deny a severance as " 'virtually unreviewable,' " because appellants must show prejudice so severe as to amount to a denial of a constitutionally fair trial. Mere antagonism between the defenses is not enough. "The mere fact that codefendants seek to place the blame on each other is not the sort of antagonism that requires a severance." Appellants must show "the conflict is so irreconcilable" that acceptance of one defendant's defense will lead the jury to convict the other. Severance is required only when " 'the jury, in order to believe the core of testimony offered on behalf of [one] defendant, must necessarily disbelieve the testimony offered on behalf of his codefendant.' " Alternatively, appellants must show that "the jury will infer that both defendants are guilty solely due to the conflict." [citations omitted]

3. Following *Zafiro*, some lower courts believe that the rationale supporting a severance based on antagonistic defenses has been so severely undercut that, if proper limiting instructions are given, the sole question is whether the prosecution offered sufficient evidence as to each defendant. See United States v. Talley, 108 F.3d 277 (11th Cir.1997). However, the right to a severance still exists in exceptional cases such as United States v. Breinig, 70 F.3d 850 (6th Cir.1995), in which a husband and his ex-wife were jointly tried for income tax violations. The wife raised a diminished capacity defense which was supported by testimony from her psychiatrist that her husband was an adulterous, mentally abusive and manipulating spouse. Because the husband's credibility was at issue and the evidence clearly would have been inadmissible in a tax prosecution of him alone, the court concluded that the facts presented a rare situation in which a severance should have been granted.

4. Although defense counsel's comment on a co-defendant's failure to testify has been deemed sufficient to warrant a severance, De Luna v. United States, 324 F.2d 375 (5th Cir.1963), that situation is now solved, as a practical matter, by an order directing counsel to refrain from comment. Only where one defendant's sole defense is to discredit and impose blame on a co-defendant will a severance be warranted. See United States v. Odom, 888 F.2d 1014 (4th Cir.1989).

5. The need to call a co-defendant as a witness at trial is another situation in which a severance may be necessary. See Byrd v. Wainwright, 428 F.2d 1017 (5th Cir.1970).

It has been uniformly held that a defendant's bare assertion that a joint trial would deprive him of the testimony of his codefendant, without a showing as to the likelihood of testimony being given in separate trials, without a showing that his codefendant would be willing to waive his privilege against self-incrimination and testify, and without a showing that such testimony will tend to exculpate the moving party, is insufficient to support a motion for severance. See, e.g., United States v. Ford, 870 F.2d 729 (D.C.Cir.1989); United States v. Williams, 809 F.2d 1072 (5th Cir.1987); United States v. Voss, 787 F.2d 393 (8th Cir.1986). An interesting theory based upon this rationale was used to support a motion fora continuance in United States v. Haldeman, 559 F.2d 31 (D.C.Cir.1976). There, defendants argued that they should be able to obtain a continuance because of the unavailability of President Nixon to testify. The court held that the trial judge "must assess the likelihood—again based primarily on defendants' showing—that the evidence will be favorable to the defense and, if so, that it will be significant." It concluded that the trial judge did not abuse his discretion because of the absence of a "verifiable representation" of what the President would say.

6. The trial judge has an obligation to monitor the evidence and order severance when the massive and complex nature of the evidence makes it impossible for a jury to compartmentalize the evidence against each defendant or where there is a "gross" disparity in the weight of evidence against the defendants. However, the matter is invariably left to the trial court's discretion. See United States v. Morales, 868 F.2d 1562 (11th Cir.1989); United States v. Garner, 837 F.2d 1404 (7th Cir.1987).

7. One method that has been devised to avoid the impact of antagonistic defenses or the taint of a *Bruton* problem is the use of multiple juries. See United States v. Lebron–Gonzalez, 816 F.2d 823 (1st Cir.1987); People v. Harris, 47 Cal.3d 1047, 255 Cal.Rptr. 352, 767 P.2d 619 (1989). This approach, however, has been subjected to recent criticism. See Ewish v. State, 110 Nev. 221, 871 P.2d 306 (1994):

> The case at hand illustrates that the device can become a breeding ground for confusion in process and results alike. What should have been a relatively simple trial took four weeks to conduct in the lower court. Much of the time, expense, and confusion complained of on appeal was the natural result of having three different defense lawyers practicing law in front of three different juries. The length of the trial, the curious results of the verdicts, and the length of this appeal indicate that the multiple jury process should be engaged with great caution.
>
> In addition to these administrative concerns, the Nevada Rules of Criminal Procedure do not authorize empaneling multiple juries. This situation contrasts with that in some federal courts and the courts of other states.[Nevada law] merely states that the trial court may grant separate trials and "provide whatever relief justice requires." This language cannot mean that atrial judge has the authority to empanel 36 jurors and alternates to hear the joint trial of three co-defendants.

Our skepticism is further enhanced by the fact that this court has not approved any guidelines for steering the district court through such an ambitious and complicated process. Again, our trepidation has been solidified by the facts of the instant appeal. The threat of prejudice and impropriety was multiplied by three. The procedure is administratively cumbersome with two juries present, and it appears nearly unworkable ushering 36 individuals plus alternates in and out of the courtroom.

We therefore conclude that the trial court's maiden voyage with the multiple jury device was unauthorized by Nevada's Rules of Criminal Procedure and this court. In accord with the great weight of authority in other jurisdictions, however, we conclude that novelty alone is not enough to reverse defendants' respective convictions.

3. CONSPIRACY CASES

United States v. Inadi

Supreme Court of the United States, 1986.
475 U.S. 387, 106 S.Ct. 1121.

■ JUSTICE POWELL delivered the opinion of the Court.

* * *

I

Following a jury trial, respondent Joseph Inadi was convicted of conspiring to manufacture and distribute methamphetamine, and related offenses. [At trial, legal wiretaps, played to the jury, contained the statements of Inadi's alleged co-conspirators, including one Lazaro.]

* * *

Respondent sought to exclude the recorded statements of Lazaro and the other unindicted co-conspirators on the ground that the statements did not satisfy the requirements of Federal Rule of Evidence 801(d)(2)(E), governing admission of co-conspirator declarations.[1] After listening to the tapes the trial court admitted the statements, finding that they were made by conspirators during the course of and in furtherance of the conspiracy, and thereby satisfied Rule 801(d)(2)(E).

Respondent also objected to admission of the statements on Confrontation Clause grounds, contending that the statements were inadmissible absent a showing that the declarants were unavailable. The court suggested that the prosecutor bring Lazaro to court in order to demonstrate unavailability. The court also asked defense counsel whether she wanted the prosecution to call Lazaro as a witness, and defense counsel stated that she would discuss the matter with her client. The co-conspirators' statements were admitted, conditioned on the prosecution's commitment to produce Lazaro. The Government subpoenaed Lazaro, but he failed to appear,

1. Federal Rule of Evidence 801(d)(2)(E) provides that a statement is not hearsay if it is offered against a party and is "a statement by a co-conspirator of a party during the course and in furtherance of the conspiracy."

claiming car trouble. The record does not indicate that the defense made any effort on its own part to secure Lazaro's presence in court.

Respondent renewed his Confrontation Clause objections, arguing that the Government had not met its burden of showing that Lazaro was unavailable to testify. The trial court overruled the objection, ruling that Lazaro's statements were admissible because they satisfied the co-conspirator rule.

* * *

II

* * *

There are good reasons why the unavailability rule, developed in cases involving former testimony, is not applicable to co-conspirators' out-of-court statements. Unlike some other exceptions to the hearsay rules, or the exemption from the hearsay definition involved in this case, former testimony often is only a weaker substitute for live testimony. It seldom has independent evidentiary significance of its own, but is intended to replace live testimony. If the declarant is available and the same information can be presented to the trier of fact in the form of live testimony, with full cross-examination and the opportunity to view the demeanor of the declarant, there is little justification for relying on the weaker version. When two versions of the same evidence are available, longstanding principles of the law of hearsay, applicable as well to Confrontation Clause analysis, favor the better evidence. But if the declarant is unavailable, no "better" version of the evidence exists, and the former testimony may be admitted as a substitute for live testimony on the same point.

Those same principles do not apply to co-conspirator statements. Because they are made while the conspiracy is in progress, such statements provide evidence of the conspiracy's context that cannot be replicated, even if the declarant testifies to the same matters in court. When the Government—as here—offers the statement of one drug dealer to another in furtherance of an illegal conspiracy, the statement often will derive its significance from the circumstances in which it was made. Conspirators are likely to speak differently when talking to each other in furtherance of their illegal aims than when testifying on the witness stand. Even when the declarant takes the stand, his in-court testimony seldom will reproduce a significant portion of the evidentiary value of his statements during the course of the conspiracy.

In addition, the relative positions of the parties will have changed substantially between the time of the statements and the trial. The declarant and the defendant will have changed from partners in an illegal conspiracy to suspects or defendants in a criminal trial, each with information potentially damaging to the other. The declarant himself may be facing indictment or trial, in which case he has little incentive to aid the prosecution, and yet will be equally wary of coming to the aid of his former partners in crime. In that situation, it is extremely unlikely that in-court testimony will recapture the evidentiary significance of statements made when the conspiracy was operating in full force.

These points distinguish co-conspirators' statements from the statements involved in . . . our other prior testimony cases. Those cases rested in part on the strong similarities between the prior judicial proceedings and the trial. No such strong similarities exist between co-conspirator statements and live testimony at trial. To the contrary, co-conspirator statements derive much of their value from the fact that they are made in a context very different from trial, and therefore are usually irreplaceable as substantive evidence. Under these circumstances, "only clear folly would dictate an across the board policy of doing without" such statements. The admission of co-conspirators' declarations into evidence thus actually furthers the "Confrontation Clause's very mission" which is to "advance 'the accuracy of the truth-determining process in criminal trials.' "

C

There appears to be little, if any, benefit to be accomplished by the . . . unavailability rule. First, if the declarant either is unavailable, or is available and produced by the prosecution, the statements can be introduced anyway. Thus, the unavailability rule cannot be defended as a constitutional "better evidence" rule, because it does not actually serve to exclude anything, unless the prosecution makes the mistake of not producing another wise available witness.

* * *

Second, an unavailability rule is not likely to produce much testimony that adds anything to the "truth-determining process" over and above what would be produced without such a rule. Some of the available declarants already will have been subpoenaed by the prosecution or the defense, regardless of any Confrontation Clause requirements. Presumably only those declarants that neither side believes will be particularly helpful will not have been subpoenaed as witnesses. There is much to indicate that Lazaro was in that position in this case. Neither the Government nor the defense originally subpoenaed Lazaro as a witness.[7] When he subsequently failed to show, alleging car trouble, respondent did nothing to secure his testimony. If respondent independently wanted to secure Lazaro's testimony, he had several options available, particularly under Federal Rule of Evidence 806, which provides that if the party against whom a co-conspirator statement has been admitted calls the declarant as a witness, "the party is entitled to examine him on the statement as if under cross-examination." Rule 806 would not require respondent to make the showing necessary to have Lazaro declared a hostile witness, although presumably that option also was available to him. The Compulsory Process Clause would have aided respondent in obtaining the testimony of any of these declarants. If the Government has no desire to call a co-conspirator declarant as a witness, and if the defense has not chosen to subpoena such a declarant, either as a witness favorable to the defense, or as a hostile

7. In fact, the actions of the parties in this case demonstrate what is no doubt a frequent occurrence in conspiracy cases—neither side wants a co-conspirator as a witness. . . . [T]he interests of the prosecution and the co-conspirator seldom will run together. Nor do the co-conspirator's interests coincide with his former partners, since each is in a position that is potentially harmful to the others.

witness, or for cross-examination under Federal Rule of Evidence 806, then it is difficult to see what, if anything, is gained by a rule that requires the prosecution to make that declarant "available."

While the benefits seem slight, the burden imposed by the unavailability rule is significant. A constitutional rule requiring a determination of availability every time the prosecution seeks to introduce a co-conspirator's declaration automatically adds another avenue of appellate review in these complex cases. The co-conspirator rule apparently is the most frequently used exception to the hearsay rule. A rule that required each invocation of Rule 801(d)(2)(E) to be accompanied by a decision on the declarant's availability would impose a substantial burden on the entire criminal justice system.

Moreover, an unavailability rule places a significant practical burden on the prosecution. In every case involving co-conspirator statements, the prosecution would be required to identify with specificity each declarant, locate those declarants, and then endeavor to ensure their continuing availability for trial. Where declarants are incarcerated there is the burden on prison officials and marshals of transporting them to and from the courthouse, as well as the increased risk of escape. For unincarcerated declarants the unavailability rule would require that during the sometimes lengthy period before trial the Government must endeavor to be aware of the whereabouts of the declarant or run the risk of a court determination that its efforts to produce the declarant did not satisfy the test of "good faith."

An unavailability rule would impose all of these burdens even if neither the prosecution nor the defense wished to examine the declarant at trial. Any marginal protection to the defendant by forcing the government to call as witnesses those co-conspirator declarants who are available, willing to testify, hostile to the defense and yet not already subpoenaed by the prosecution, when the defendant himself can call and cross-examine such declarants, cannot support an unavailability rule. We hold today that the Confrontation Clause does not embody such a rule.

III

To some degree, respondent's arguments in this case require us to revisit this Court's resolution of this question in Dutton v. Evans (1970). Although *Dutton* involved a state co-conspirator rule instead of Federal Rule of Evidence 801, the state rule actually admitted a broader category of coconspirator statements. Nevertheless, a plurality of this Court found that the rule did not violate the Confrontation Clause and a fifth Member of the Court, Justice Harlan, reasoned that the Confrontation Clause was not applicable at all. In *Dutton* the plurality stated that "we do not question the validity of the co-conspirator exception applied in the federal courts." Upon close rexamination today, we continue to affirm the validity of the use of co-conspirator statements, and we decline to require a showing of the declarant's unavailability as a prerequisite to their admission.

* * *

■ JUSTICE MARSHALL, with whom JUSTICE BRENNAN joins, dissenting.

* * *

I

The majority is quite right to suggest that "[c]onspirators are likely to speak differently when talking to each other in furtherance of their illegal aims than when testifying on the witness stand." However, the differences between an accomplice's conspiratorial utterances and his testimony in court are not merely those of diction and demeanor. That a statement was truly made "in furtherance" of a conspiracy cannot possibly be a guarantee, or even an indicium, of its reliability. As one commentator "Conspirators' declarations are good to prove that some conspiracy exists but less trustworthy to show its aims and membership. The conspirator's interest is likely to lie in misleading the listener into believing the conspiracy stronger with more members (and different members) and other aims than in fact it has. It is no victory for common sense to make a belief that criminals are notorious for their veracity the basis for law." Levie, Hearsay and Conspiracy, 52 Mich.L.Rev. 1159, 1165–1166 (1954).

The unreliability of co-conspirator declarations as trial evidence is not merely a product of the duplicity with which criminals often conduct their business. It also stems from the ambiguities that so often appear in all casual conversations, not just those of outlaws. And the difficulties one has in making sense of slang and dialect can be compounded where conspirators use private codes, as indeed they did in this case. Because of these problems, trained case agents are often hard pressed to piece together the facts of a criminal conspiracy from the confused tangle of conversations they have intercepted. The appearance of a co-conspirator declarant in court will allow the elimination of ambiguity that neither side has a right to profit from.

Consideration of the reasons why co-conspirator declarations have been exempted from the rule against hearsay only confirms doubts as to there liability of the truth asserted in those statements. In contrast to other types of statements excepted from the rule, the co-conspirator declarations have not been admitted because of a belief in their special reliability. Rather, the root of the exemption lies in substantive law. Under the agency theory that supports conspiracy law, "once the conspiracy or combination is established, the act of one conspirator, in the prosecution of the enterprise, is considered the act of all, and is evidence against all." Every statement of co-conspirators in furtherance of their illegal scheme is thus a verbal act admissible against each conspirator as if it had been his own.

This agency theory, which even the Advisory Committee on the proposed Federal Rules of Evidence labelled "at best a fiction," might justify the exemption conferred upon co-conspirator declarations from the traditional rule against hearsay. But it speaks not at all to the Confrontation Clause's concern for reliable fact finding.

* * *

I truly cannot understand the majority's fear that a rule requiring the prosecution to do its best to produce a co-conspirator declarant in court would somehow deprive triers of fact of valuable evidence. Under this rule, if the prosecution could not in all good faith produce the declarant, the extrajudicial statements could come in, so long as they could be shown to have "adequate 'indicia of reliability.' " The majority's fear must therefore stem from a notion that if the prosecution is able to produce the declarant in court, his presence will somehow prevent the jury from hearing the truth. This conclusion overlooks the critical importance of cross-examination in the truth-seeking process.

If a declarant takes the stand, his out-of-court statements will still be admitted as evidence, so long as they are sufficiently reliable and there are no other grounds for their exclusion. And cross-examination will only enhance their value to the jury. The defendant will have a chance to inquire into the circumstances under which the statements were made and the motives that might have led the declarant to color their truth at the time. Cross-examination also may force the declarant to clarify ambiguous phrases and coded references. If anything he says is inconsistent with his prior statement, the declarant will no doubt advance some explanation for the inaccuracy of the extrajudicial statement—"an explanation a jury may be expected to understand and take into account in deciding which, if either, of the statements represents the truth."

Whether or not a co-conspirator produced in court affirms, denies, or qualifies the truth of his out-of-court statement, his presence will contribute to the accuracy of the fact-finding enterprise, the accuracy that is the primary concern of the Confrontation Clause. Whatever truth is contained in his extrajudicial declarations cannot be lost. It can only be supplemented by additional information of no less use to the triers of fact.

* * *

At bottom, today's decision rests upon the Court's judgment that a defendant's constitutional interest in subjecting the extrajudicial declarations of co-conspirators to the cross-examination that has traditionally been the primary guarantee of reliability in trials must be subordinated to considerations of prosecutorial efficiency. I do not believe the concerns of the Confrontation Clause should be so easily disregarded. The plight of Sir Walter Raleigh, condemned on the deposition of an alleged accomplice who had since recanted, may have loomed large in the eyes of those who drafted that constitutional guarantee. But the Framers, had they the prescience, would surely have been as apprehensive of the spectacle of a defendant's conviction upon the testimony of a handful of surveillance technicians and a very large box of tapes recording the boasts, faulty recollections, and coded or ambiguous utterances of outlaws. The Court's decision helps clear the way for this spectacle to become a common occurrence. I dissent.

NOTES

1. Any act or declaration by a co-conspirator, committed in furtherance of the conspiracy and during its pendency, is admissible against each member of the conspiracy if, by way of foundation, independent evidence of a conspiracy and an individual defendant's participation in it are shown. See Krulewitch v. United States, 336 U.S. 440, 69 S.Ct. 716 (1949); Glasser v. United States, 315 U.S. 60, 62 S.Ct. 457 (1942). The question is when and under what circumstances, the Act's and statements of a nontestifying coconspirator will be attributable to his alleged coconspirators on trial.

2. Fed.R.Evid. 801(d)(2)(E) indicates that evidence is not hearsay if it is "a statement made by a coconspirator or a party during the course and in furtherance of the conspiracy."

In Bourjaily v. United States, 483 U.S. 171, 107 S.Ct. 2775 (1987), the Court declared that under the Federal Rules of Evidence, in determining whether the defendant and the declarant are parties to the conspiracy (one of the prerequisites for invocation of the co-conspirator exception), the trial court under Rule 104(a)can use the alleged co-conspirator declaration itself. The court need not rely wholly upon evidence independent of the statement in determining whether the co-conspirator declaration exception is applicable in the case at hand. The Court also held that the preliminary facts essential to use of the exception need only be established by a preponderance of the evidence. Finally, the Court declared that where a hearsay exception, such as the co-conspirator exception, is "firmly rooted," the exception can be used, consistent with the Confrontation Clause, even though the court has made no assessment of the reliability of the statement under the circumstances of the individual case. If the statement properly fits under the exception embodied in Federal Rule 801(d)(2)(E), the trial court need engage in no further Confrontation Clause-reliability analysis.

The dissent, among other things, argued that the co-conspirator exception evolved not because of belief in the general reliability of co-conspirator declarations, but rather from notions of *respondeat superior*. Accordingly, the dissenters strongly objected to the notion that a trial judge should admit co-conspirator declarations without any analysis of their reliability under the circumstances of the case.

3. Admissible declarations in furtherance of the conspiracy include statements made to keep coconspirators informed about the progress of the conspiracy, to recruit others, or to control damage to the conspiracy. However, idle chatter and narrative declarations are not. Only a reasonable basis need exist for concluding that statements furthered a conspiracy. United States v. Stephenson, 53 F.3d 836 (7th Cir.1995).

4. To prove that a conspiracy existed, it is incumbent upon the prosecution to show an agreement to violate the law and one overt act, in furtherance of that agreement—"to effect the object of the conspiracy". United States v. Bayer, 331 U.S. 532, 542, 67 S.Ct. 1394, 1399 (1947). See also Ingram v. United States, 360 U.S. 672, 677, 79 S.Ct. 1314, 1318–1319 (1959). The existence of a conspiracy need not be demonstrated by direct evidence, but, rather, a common plan may be inferred from circumstantial evidence. See Glasser v. United States, 315 U.S. 60, 80, 62 S.Ct. 457, 469–70 (1942). In most cases of its nature, because of the secretiveness and complexity of contemporary conspiracies, proof of an agreement is possible only by circumstantial evidence. United States v. Galvan, 693 F.2d 417 (5th Cir.1982).

5. Once the conspiracy is established, it is necessary that the independent evidence in the record show that a defendant, by virtue if his knowledge of the purpose of the conspiracy and intent to further it, was personally connected with the conspiracy charged. See Ingram v. United States, 360 U.S. 672, 678, 79 S.Ct. 1314, 1319 (1959). However, because a defendant need not have knowledge of each and every detail in order to be a member of the conspiracy, the cases uniformly hold that each defendant need not know the identity or number of all of his coconspirators. See Blumenthal v. United States, 332 U.S. 539, 557, 68 S.Ct. 248, 256–57 (1947); United States v. Escalante, 637 F.2d 1197 (9th Cir.1980). This showing is not contingent upon proof of a defendant's awareness of every detail of the conspiratorial plan; it is satisfactory if the independent evidence indicates that the defendant knew of the conspiracy's essential objective and acted to further it. As with proof of the conspiratorial agreement itself, an individual defendant's knowledge and intent may be shown by circumstantial evidence. However, a defendant cannot be convicted of conspiracy if he lacks intent to further its aims or knowledge of its existence. United States v. Tyler, 758 F.2d 66 (2d Cir.1985) (defendant merely helped willing buyer of drugs find willing seller and was not shown to be part of conspiracy); United States v. Fitzharris, 633 F.2d 416 (5th Cir.1980); United States v. Soto, 716 F.2d 989 (2d Cir.1983).

6. Taking into account all cognizable independent evidence, the trial judge must determine whether the prosecution has proved a conspiracy and each defendant's connection with it. In evaluating the evidence of a defendant's participation in a conspiracy, the criterion employed is the slight evidence test "Once the existence of a common scheme is established, very little is required to show that a defendant became a party—'slight evidence may be sufficient to connect the defendant with it'." United States v. Robinson, 470 F.2d 121, 123 (7th Cir.1972); United States v. Hartman, 627 F.2d 7 (6th Cir.1980). Because the repeated invocation of the slight evidence rule led to concern over whether the government was being held to its burden of proof, some courts have abandoned it in favor of the following: "a defendant may be convicted for even a minor role in a conspiracy, so long as the government proves beyond a reasonable doubt that he or she was a member of the conspiracy." United States v. Lopez, 443 F.3d 1026 (8th Cir. 2006) (en banc)

7. Based upon the "slight evidence test" the courts have recognized that a single act may be the foundation for drawing the actor within the ambit of a conspiracy if the act is such that one may reasonably infer from it an intent to participate in an unlawful venture. See United States v. Battaglia, 394 F.2d 304, 311 (7th Cir.1968), vacated on other grounds 394 U.S. 310, 89 S.Ct. 1163 (1969) (defendant made one statement; he said "he liked Lakey and they could use him in other things because he was clean"); United States v. McGann, 431 F.2d 1104, 1107 (5th Cir.1970) (defendant agreed to purchase television sets); Lopez v. United States, 414 F.2d 909, 911 (5th Cir.1969) (defendant agreed to haul certain goods). But see United States v. Fiorito, 499 F.2d 106 (7th Cir.1974) (single ambiguous act—telephone call—held insufficient to connect defendant to conspiracy).

8. What happens when, after all of its evidence has been introduced, the government has failed to prove a conspiracy? In Schaffer v. United States, 362 U.S. 511, 80 S.Ct. 945 (1960), five defendants were tried on substantive and conspiracy counts of transporting stolen goods in interstate commerce. Before sending the case to the jury the trial judge dismissed the conspiracy count and, in his charge to the jury, meticulously set out the separate evidence against each of the defendants and admonished the jury that they were not to take into consideration any proof against one defendant and apply it by inference to another. After the conviction on the substantive counts was affirmed by the Second Circuit, defendants argued, before the Supreme Court, that, despite the cautionary instructions, prejudice was implicit in the continuation of the joint trial after dismissal of the conspiracy count. The Court, finding joinder to have been originally proper, examined the facts of the case to determine whether any of the defendants were prejudiced by the failure of the trial judge to order a severance after the dismissal of the conspiracy count. The majority of the Court concluded that no prejudice was shown. See also United States v. Morales, 868 F.2d 1562 (11th Cir.1989).

Under what circumstances are limiting instructions so confusing that a mistrial must be declared on the non conspiracy counts of an indictment?

9. Sometimes a defendant whose fellow defendant's co-conspirator statements implicating the defendant have been admitted, will claim a desire to take advantage of the rule which allows a party to impeach a hearsay declarant. Perhaps the claim is sincere, perhaps it is a desire to mandate severance. In United States v. Lenfesty, 923 F.2d 1293 (8th Cir.1991), the district judge simply refused to allow the defendant to introduce, as impeachment, evidence of his codefendant's prior conviction even though such evidence would have been admissible if the defendant's trials were separate. The reviewing court approved the district judge's ruling.

C. The Accused as a Witness

Brooks v. Tennessee

Supreme Court of the United States, 1972.
406 U.S. 605, 92 S.Ct. 1891.

■ MR. JUSTICE BRENNAN delivered the opinion of the Court.

Petitioner was tried and convicted ... on charges of armed robbery and unlawful possession of a pistol. During the trial, at the close of the State's case, defense counsel moved to delay petitioner's testimony until after other defense witnesses had testified. The trial court denied this motion on the basis of Tenn.Code Ann. § 40–2403, which requires that a criminal defendant "desiring to testify shall do so before any other testimony for the defense is heard by the court trying the case." Although the prosecutor agreed to waive the statute, the trial court refused, stating that "the law is, as you know it to be, that if a defendant testifies he has to testify first." The defense called two witnesses, but petitioner himself did not take the stand.

I.

The rule that a defendant must testify first is related to the ancient practice of sequestering prospective witnesses in order to prevent their being influenced by other testimony in the case. See 6 Wigmore, Evidence § 1837 (3d ed. 1940). Because the criminal defendant is entitled to be present during trial, and thus cannot be sequestered, the requirement that he precede other defense witnesses was developed by court decision and statute as an alternative means of minimizing this influence as to him. According to Professor Wigmore, "The reason for this rule is the occasional readiness of the interested person to adapt his testimony, when offered later, to victory rather than veracity, so as to meet the necessities as laid open by prior witnesses...." 6 Wigmore, supra, § 1869.

Despite this traditional justification, the validity of the requirement has been questioned in a number of jurisdictions as a limitation upon the defendant's freedom to decide whether or not to take the stand. Two federal courts have rejected the contention, holding that a trial court does not abuse its discretion by requiring the defendant to testify first....

* * *

... we are persuaded that the rule embodied in § 40–2403 is an impermissible restriction on the defendant's right against self-incrimination,"to remain silent unless he chooses to speak in the unfettered exercise of his own will, and to suffer no penalty ... for such silence." Malloy v. Hogan (1964).... a defendant's choice to take the stand carries with it serious risks of impeachment and cross-examination; it "may open the door to otherwise inadmissible evidence which is damaging to his case," McGautha v. California (1971), including, now, the use of some confessions for impeachment purposes that would be excluded from the State's case in chief because of constitutional defects. Harris v. New York (1971). Although "it is not thought inconsistent with the enlightened administration of criminal justice to require the defendant to weigh such pros and cons in deciding whether to testify," none would deny that the choice itself may pose serious dangers to the success of an accused's defense.

Although a defendant will usually have some idea of the strength of his evidence, he cannot be absolutely certain that his witnesses will testify as expected or that they will be effective on the stand. They may collapse under skillful and persistent cross-examination, and through no fault of their own they may fail to impress the jury as honest and reliable witnesses. In addition, a defendant is sometimes compelled to call a hostile prosecution witness as his own. Unless the State provides for discovery depositions of prosecution witnesses, which Tennessee apparently does not, the defendant is unlikely to know whether this testimony will prove entirely favorable.

Because of these uncertainties, a defendant may not know at the close of the State's case whether his own testimony will be necessary or even helpful to his cause. Rather than risk the dangers of taking the stand, he might prefer to remain silent at that point, putting off his testimony until its value can be realistically assessed. Yet, under the Tennessee rule, he cannot make that choice "in the unfettered exercise of his own will." Section 40–2403 exacts a price for his silence by keeping him off the stand entirely unless he chooses to testify first. This, we think, casts a heavy burden on a defendant's otherwise unconditional right not to take the stand. The rule, in other words, "cuts down on the privilege [to remain silent] by making its assertion costly."

Although the Tennessee statute does reflect a state interest in preventing testimonial influence, we do not regard that interest as sufficient to override the defendant's right to remain silent at trial. This is not to imply that there may be no risk of a defendant's coloring his testimony to conform to what has gone before. But our adversary system reposes judgment of the credibility of all witnesses in the jury. Pressuring the defendant to take the stand, by foreclosing later testimony if he refuses, is not a constitutionally permissible means of ensuring his honesty. It fails to take into account the very real and legitimate concerns that might motivate a defendant to exercise his right of silence. And it may compel even a wholly truthful defendant, who might otherwise decline to testify for legitimate reasons, to subject himself to impeachment and cross-examination at a time when the strength of his other evidence is not yet clear. For these reasons we hold that § 40–2403 violates an accused's constitutional right to remain silent insofar as it requires him to testify first for the defense or not at all.

II.

For closely related reasons we also regard the Tennessee rule as an infringement on the defendant's right of due process as defined in Ferguson v. Georgia (1961). There the Court reviewed a Georgia statute providing that a criminal defendant, though not competent to testify under oath, could make an unsworn statement at trial. The statute did not permit defense counsel to aid the accused by eliciting his statement through questions. The Court held that this limitation deprived the accused of " 'the guiding hand of counsel at every step in the proceedings against him,' within the requirement of due process in that regard as imposed upon the States by the Fourteenth Amendment." The same may be said of § 40–2403. Whether the defendant is to testify is an important tactical decision as well as a matter of constitutional right. By requiring the accused and his lawyer to make that choice without an opportunity to evaluate the actual worth of their evidence, the statute restricts the defense—particularly counsel—in the planning of its case. Furthermore, the penalty for not testifying first is to keep the defendant off the stand entirely, even though as a matter of professional judgment his lawyer might want to call him later in the trial. The accused is thereby deprived of the "guiding hand of counsel" in the timing of this critical element of his defense. While nothing we say here otherwise curtails in any way the ordinary power of a trial judge to set the order of proof, the accused and his counsel may not be restricted in deciding whether, and when in the course of presenting his defense, the accused should take the stand.

Petitioner, then, was deprived of his constitutional rights when the trial court excluded him from the stand for failing to testify first. The State makes no claim that this was harmless error.

■ MR. JUSTICE STEWART joins Part II of the opinion, and in the judgment of the Court.

■ MR. CHIEF JUSTICE BURGER, with whom MR. JUSTICE BLACKMUN and MR. JUSTICE REHNQUIST, join, dissenting.

This case is an example of the Court confusing what it does not approve with the demands of the Constitution. As a matter of choice and policy—if I were a legislator, for example—I would not vote for a statute like that the Court strikes down today. But I cannot accept the idea that the Constitution forbids the States to have such a statute.

Of course it is more convenient for a lawyer to defer the decision to have the accused take the stand until he knows how his other witnesses fare. By the same token it is helpful for an accused to be able to adjust his testimony to what his witnesses have had to say on the matter. No one has seriously challenged the absolute discretion of a trial judge to exclude witnesses, other than the accused, from the courtroom until they are called to the stand. The obvious purpose is to get honest testimony and minimize the prospect that a witness will adjust and "tailor" his version to fit what others have said; it seems somewhat odd to say the Constitution forbids all States to require the accused to give his version before his other witnesses speak, since it is not possible to exclude him from the courtroom, as is the common rule on witnesses who are not parties.

The Court's holding under the Fifth Amendment is admittedly unsupported by any authority and cannot withstand analysis. The Constitution provides only that no person shall "be compelled in any criminal case to be a witness against himself." It is undisputed that petitioner was not in fact compelled to be a witness against himself, as he did not take the stand. Nor was the jury authorized or encouraged to draw perhaps unwarranted inferences from his silence, as in Griffin v. California (1965). Petitioner was clearly not subjected to the obvious compulsion of being held in contempt for his silence, as in Malloy v. Hogan (1964), nor did the Tennessee procedure subject him to any other significant compulsion to testify other than the compulsion faced by every defendant who chooses not to take the stand—the knowledge that in the absence of his testimony the force of the State's evidence may lead the jury to convict. Cases such as Spevack v. Klein (1967), and Gardner v. Broderick (1968), involving loss of employment or disbarment are therefore clearly inapposite. That should end the matter.

However, the Court distorts both the context and content of Malloy v. Hogan, by intimating that the Fifth Amendment may be violated if the defendant is forced to make a difficult choice as to whether to take the stand at some point in time prior to the conclusion of a criminal trial. But, as the Court pointed out only last Term in McGautha v. California (1971), "although a defendant may have a right, even of constitutional dimensions, to follow whichever course he chooses, the Constitution does not by that token always forbid requiring him to choose." Indeed, the "choice" we sustained in *McGautha* was far more difficult than that here, as the procedure there clearly exerted considerable force to compel the defendant to waive the privilege and take the stand in order to avoid the possible imposition of the death penalty. There is no such pressure here. The majority's rationale would lead to the absurd result that the State could not even require the defendant to finally decide whether he wishes to take the stand prior to the time the jury retires for deliberations, for, even at that point, he "may not know . . . whether his own testimony will be necessary or even helpful to his cause." Even then, he might "prefer to remain silent . . . putting off his testimony until its value can be realistically assessed." In short, even at the close of the defense case, his decision to take the stand is not unfettered by the difficulty to make the hard choice to waive the privilege. Perhaps the defendant's decision will be easier at the close of all the evidence. Perhaps not. The only "burden" cast on the defendant's choice to take the stand by the Tennessee procedure is the burden to make the choice at a given point in time. That the choice might in some cases be easier if made later is hardly a matter of constitutional dimension.

The Court's holding that the Tennessee rule deprives the defendant of the "guiding hand of counsel" at every stage of the proceedings fares no better. It amounts to nothing more than the assertion that counsel may not be restricted by ordinary rules of evidence and procedure in presenting an accused's defense if it might be more advantageous to present it in some other way. A rule forbidding defense counsel to ask leading questions of the defendant when he takes the stand may restrict defense counsel in his options and may in many cases bear only remote relationship to the goal of truthful testimony. Yet no one would seriously question that such a universal rule of procedure is prohibited by the Constitution. The rule that the defendant waives the Fifth Amendment privilege as to any and all relevant matters when he decides to take the stand certainly inhibits the choices and options of counsel, yet this Court has never questioned such a rule and reaffirmed its validity only last Term. Countless other rules of evidence and procedure of every State may interfere with the "guiding hand of counsel." The Court does not explain why the rule here differs from those other rules.

Perhaps this reflects what is the true, if unspoken, basis for the Court's decision. That is, that in the majority's view the Tennessee rule is invalid because it is followed presently by only two States in our federal system. But differences in criminal procedures among our States do not provide an occasion for judicial condemnation by this Court.

This is not a case or an issue of great importance, except as it erodes the important policy of allowing diversity of method and procedure to the States to the end that they can experiment and innovate, and retreat if they find they have taken a wrong path. Long ago, Justice Brandeis spoke of the need to let "a single courageous state" try what others have not tried or will not try. In the faltering condition of our machinery of justice this is a singularly inappropriate time to throttle the diversity so essential in the search for improvement.

■ MR. JUSTICE REHNQUIST, with whom THE CHIEF JUSTICE and MR. JUSTICE BLACKMUN join, dissenting. [Opinion omitted.]

* * *

Portuondo v. Agard

Supreme Court of the United States, 2000.
529 U.S. 61, 120 S.Ct. 1119.

■ JUSTICE SCALIA delivered the opinion of the Court. . . .

Respondent's trial on 19 sodomy and assault counts and 3 weapons counts ultimately came down to a credibility determination. The alleged victim, Nessa Winder, and her friend, Breda Keegan, testified that respondent physically assaulted, raped, and orally and anally sodomized Winder, and that he threatened both women with a handgun. Respondent testified that he and Winder had engaged in consensual vaginal intercourse. He further testified that during an argument he had with Winder, he struck her once in the face. He denied raping her or threatening either woman with a handgun.

During summation, defense counsel charged Winder and Keegan with lying. The prosecutor similarly focused on the credibility of the witnesses. She stressed respondent's interest in the outcome of the trial, his prior felony conviction, and his prior bad acts. She argued that respondent was a "smooth slick character . . . who had an answer for everything," and that part of his testimony "sound[ed] rehearsed." Finally, over defense objection, the prosecutor remarked:

"You know, ladies and gentlemen, unlike all the other witnesses in this case the defendant has a benefit and the benefit that he has, unlike all the other witnesses, is he gets to sit here and listen to the testimony of all the other witnesses before he testifies....

"That gives you a big advantage, doesn't it. You get to sit here and think what am I going to say and how am I going to say it? How am I going to fit it into the evidence?....

"He's a smart man. I never said he was stupid.... He used everything to his advantage."

The trial court rejected defense counsel's claim that these last comments violated respondent's right to be present at trial. The court stated that respondent's status as the last witness in the case was simply a matter of fact, and held that his presence during the entire trial, and the advantage that this afforded him, "may fairly be commented on."

Respondent was convicted of one count of anal sodomy and two counts of third-degree possession of a weapon....

A divided panel of the Second Circuit reversed, holding that the prosecutor's comments violated respondent's Fifth, Sixth, and Fourteenth Amendment rights....

Respondent's argument boils down to a request that we extend to comments of the type the prosecutor made here the rationale of Griffin v. California (1965), which involved comments upon a defendant's refusal to testify. In that case, the trial court instructed the jury that it was free to take the defendant's failure to deny or explain facts within his knowledge as tending to indicate the truth of the prosecution's case. This Court held that such a comment, by "solemniz[ing] the silence of the accused into evidence against him," unconstitutionally "cuts down on the privilege [against self-incrimination] by making its assertion costly."

We decline to extend Griffin to the present context. As an initial matter, respondent's claims have no historical foundation, neither in 1791, when the Bill of Rights was adopted, nor in 1868 when, according to our jurisprudence, the Fourteenth Amendment extended the strictures of the Fifth and Sixth Amendments to the States. The process by which criminal defendants were brought to justice in 1791 largely obviated the need for comments of the type the prosecutor made here. Defendants routinely were asked (and agreed) to provide a pretrial statement to a justice of the peace detailing the events in dispute. See Moglen, The Privilege in British North America: The Colonial Period to the Fifth Amendment, in The Privilege Against Self-Incrimination 109, 112, 114 (R. Helmholz et al. eds.1997). If their story at trial—where they typically spoke and conducted their defense personally, without counsel, see J. Goebel & T. Naughton, Law Enforcement in Colonial New York: A Study in Criminal Procedure (1664–1776), p. 574 (1944); A. Scott, Criminal Law in Colonial Virginia 79 (1930)—differed from their pretrial statement, the contradiction could be noted. See Levy, Origins of the Fifth Amendment and Its Critics, 19 Cardozo L.Rev. 821, 843 (1997). Moreover, what they said at trial was not considered to be evidence, since they were disqualified from testifying under oath. See 2 J. Wigmore, Evidence § 579 (3d ed.1940).

The pretrial statement did not begin to fall into disuse until the 1830s, see Alschuler, A Peculiar Privilege in Historical Perspective, in The Privilege Against Self–Incrimination, supra, at 198, and the first State to make defendants competent witnesses was Maine, in 1864, see 2 Wigmore, supra, § 579, at 701. In response to these developments, some States attempted to limit a defendant's opportunity to tailor his sworn testimony by requiring him to testify prior to his own witnesses. See 3 J. Wigmore, Evidence § 1841, 1869 (1904); Ky. Stat., ch. 45, § 1646 (1899); Tenn.Code Ann., ch. 4, § 5601 (1896). Although the majority of States did not impose such a restriction, there is no evidence to suggest they also took the affirmative step of forbidding comment upon the defendant's opportunity to tailor his testimony. The dissent faults us for "call[ing] up no instance of an eighteenth- or nineteenth-century prosecutor's urging that a defendant's presence at trial facilitated tailored testimony." We think the burden is rather upon respondent and the dissent, who assert the unconstitutionality of the practice, to come up with a case in which such urging was held improper. They cannot even produce one in which the practice was so much as challenged until after our decision in Griffin. This absence cuts in favor of respondent (as the dissent asserts) only if it is possible to believe that after reading Griffin prosecutors suddenly realized that commenting on a testifying defendant's unique ability to hear prior testimony was a good idea. Evidently, prosecutors were making these comments all along without objection; Griffin simply sparked the notion that such commentary might be problematic.

Lacking any historical support for the constitutional rights that he asserts, respondent must rely entirely upon our opinion in Griffin. That case is a poor analogue, however, for several reasons. What we prohibited the prosecutor from urging the jury to do in Griffin was something the jury is not permitted to do. The defendant's right to hold the prosecution to proving its case without his assistance is not to be impaired by the jury's counting the defendant's silence at trial against him—and upon request the court must instruct the jury to that effect. See Carter v. Kentucky (1981). It is reasonable enough to expect a jury to comply with that instruction since, as we observed in Griffin, the inference of guilt from silence is not always "natural or irresistible." A defendant might refuse to testify simply out of fear that he will be made to look bad by clever counsel, or fear " 'that his prior convictions will prejudice the jury.' " Ibid. By contrast, it is natural and irresistible for a jury, in evaluating the relative credibility of a defendant who testifies last, to have in mind and weigh in the balance the fact that he heard the testimony of all those who preceded him. It is one thing (as Griffin requires) for the jury to evaluate all the other evidence in the case without giving any effect to the defendant's refusal to testify; it is something else (and quite impossible) for the jury to evaluate the credibility of the defendant's testimony while blotting out from its mind the fact that before giving the testimony the defendant had been sitting there listening to the other witnesses. Thus, the principle respondent asks us to adopt here differs from what we adopted in Griffin in one or the other of the following respects: It either prohibits inviting the jury to do what the jury is perfectly entitled to do; or it requires the jury to do what is practically impossible.[1]

Second, Griffin prohibited comments that suggest a defendant's silence is "evidence of guilt." ... The prosecutor's comments in this case, by contrast, concerned respondent's credibility as a witness, and were therefore in accord with our longstanding rule that when a defendant takes the stand, "his credibility may be impeached and his testimony assailed like that of any other witness." Brown v. United States (1958).

. . .

Respondent and the dissent also contend that the prosecutor's comments were impermissible because they were "generic" rather than based upon any specific indication of tailoring. Such comment, the dissent claims, is unconstitutional because it "does not serve to distinguish guilty defendants from innocent ones." But this Court has approved of such "generic" comment before. In Reagan v. United States, for example, the trial court instructed the jury that "[t]he deep personal interest which [the defendant] may have in the result of the suit should be considered ... in weighing his evidence and in determining how far or to what extent, if at all, it is worthy of credit." The instruction did not rely on any specific evidence of actual fabrication for its application; nor did it, directly at least, delineate the guilty and the innocent. Like the comments in this case, it simply set forth a consideration the jury was to have in mind when assessing the defendant's credibility, which, in turn, assisted it in determining the guilt of the defendant. We deemed that instruction perfectly proper. Thus, that the comments before us here did not, of their own force, demonstrate the guilt of the defendant, or even distinguish among defendants, does not render them infirm.[2]

1. The dissent seeks to place us in the position of defending the proposition that inferences that the jury is free to make are inferences that the prosecutor must be free to invite. Of course we say no such thing. We simply say (in the sentence to which this note is appended) that forbidding invitation of a permissible inference is one of two alternative respects in which this case is substantially different from respondent's sole source of support, Griffin. Similarly, the dissent seeks to place us in the position of defending the proposition that it is more natural to infer tailoring from presence than to infer guilt from silence. The quite different point we do make is that inferring opportunity to tailor from presence is inevitable, and prohibiting that inference (while simultaneously asking the jury to evaluate the veracity of the defendant's testimony) is demanding the impossible—producing the other alternative respect in which this case differs from Griffin. The dissent seeks to rebut this point by asserting that in the present case the prosecutorial comments went beyond pointing out the opportunity to tailor and actually made an accusation of tailoring. It would be worth inquiring into that subtle distinction if the dissent proposed to permit the former while forbidding the latter. It does not, of course; nor, as far as we know, does any other authority. Drawing the line between pointing out the availability of the inference and inviting the inference would be neither useful nor practicable. Thus, under the second alternative described above, the jury must be prohibited from taking into account the opportunity of tailoring.

2. The dissent's stern disapproval of generic comment (it "tarnishes the innocent no less than the guilty," it suffers from an "incapacity to serve the individualized truth-finding function of trials," so that "when a defendant's exercise of a constitutional fair trial right is 'insolubly ambiguous' as between innocence and guilt, the prosecutor may not urge the jury to construe the bare invocation of the right against the defendant,") hardly comports with its praising the

Finally, the Second Circuit held, and the dissent contends, that the comments were impermissible here because they were made, not during cross-examination, but at summation, leaving the defense no opportunity to reply. 117 F.3d, at 708, and n. 6. That this is not a constitutionally significant distinction is demonstrated by our decision in Reagan. There the challenged instruction came at the end of the case, after the defense had rested, just as the prosecutor's comments did here. . . .

Our trial structure, which requires the defense to close before the prosecution, regularly forces the defense to predict what the prosecution will say. Indeed, defense counsel in this case explained to the jury that it was his job in "closing argument here to try and anticipate as best [he could] some of the arguments that the prosecution [would] be making." What Reagan permitted—a generic interested-witness instruction, after the defense has closed—is in a long tradition that continues to the present day. 2 C. Wright, Federal Practice and Procedure § 501, and n. 1 (1982). Indeed, the instruction was given in this very case. [citations omitted] . . .

In sum, we see no reason to depart from the practice of treating testifying defendants the same as other witnesses. A witness's ability to hear prior testimony and to tailor his account accordingly, and the threat that ability presents to the integrity of the trial, are no different when it is the defendant doing the listening. Allowing comment upon the fact that a defendant's presence in the courtroom provides him a unique opportunity to tailor his testimony is appropriate—and indeed, given the inability to sequester the defendant, sometimes essential—to the central function of the trial, which is to discover the truth. . . .

Respondent contends, however, that because New York law required him to be present at his trial, the prosecution violated his right to due process by commenting on that presence. He asserts that our decision in Doyle v. Ohio, (1976), requires such a holding. In Doyle, the defendants, after being arrested for selling marijuana, received their Miranda warnings and chose to remain silent. At their trials, both took the stand and claimed that they had not sold marijuana, but had been "framed." To impeach the defendants, the prosecutors asked each why he had not related this version of events at the time he was arrested. We held that this violated the defendants' rights to due process because the Miranda warnings contained an implicit "assurance that silence will carry no penalty."

Although there might be reason to reconsider Doyle, we need not do so here. "[W]e have consistently explained Doyle as a case where the government had induced silence by implicitly assuring the defendant that his silence would not be used against him." Fletcher v. Weir (1982) (per

Court of Appeals for its "carefully restrained and moderate position" in forbidding this monstrous practice only on summation and allowing it during the rest of the trial. The dissent would also allow a prosecutor to remark at any time even at summation on the convenient "fit" between specific elements of a defendant's testimony and the testimony of others. It is only a "general accusation of tailoring" that is forbidden. But if the dissent believes that comments which "invite the jury to convict on the basis of conduct as consistent with innocence as with guilt" should be out of bounds, ibid. or at least should be out of bounds in summation comments focusing on such "fit" must similarly be forbidden. As the dissent acknowledges, "fit" is as likely to result from the defendant's "sheer innocence" as from anything else.

curiam). The Miranda warnings had, after all, specifically given the defendant both the option of speaking and the option of remaining silent—and had then gone on to say that if he chose the former option what he said could be used against him. It is possible to believe that this contained an implicit promise that his choice of the option of silence would not be used against him. It is not possible, we think, to believe that a similar promise of impunity is implicit in a statute requiring the defendant to be present at trial.

Respondent contends that this case contains an element of unfairness even worse than what existed in Doyle: Whereas the defendant in that case had the ability to avoid impairment of his case by choosing to speak rather than remain silent, the respondent here (he asserts) had no choice but to be present at the trial. Though this is far from certain, see, e.g., People v. Aiken, 45 N.Y.2d 394, 397, 408 N.Y.S.2d 444, 380 N.E.2d 272, 274 (1978) ("[A] defendant charged with a felony not punishable by death may, by his voluntary and willful absence from trial, waive his right to be present at every stage of his trial"), we shall assume for the sake of argument that it is true. There is, however, no authority whatever for the proposition that the impairment of credibility, if any, caused by mandatory presence at trial violates due process. If the ability to avoid the accusation (or suspicion) of tailoring were as crucial a factor as respondent contends, one would expect criminal defendants—in jurisdictions that do not have compulsory attendance requirements—frequently to absent themselves from trial when they intend to give testimony. But to our knowledge, a criminal trial without the defendant present is a rarity. Many long established elements of criminal procedure deprive a defendant of advantages he would otherwise possess—for example, the requirement that he plead to the charge before, rather than after, all the evidence is in. The consequences of the requirement that he be present at trial seem to us no worse.

For the foregoing reasons, the judgment of the Court of Appeals for the Second Circuit is reversed, and the case is remanded for further proceedings consistent with this opinion. [citations omitted] . . .

■ JUSTICE GINSBURG with JUSTICE SOUTER, dissenting.

The Court today transforms a defendant's presence at trial from a Sixth Amendment right into an automatic burden on his credibility. . . .

The same principle should decide this case. Ray Agard attended his trial, as was his constitutional right and his statutory duty, and he testified in a manner consistent with other evidence in the case. One evident explanation for the coherence of his testimony cannot be ruled out: Agard may have been telling the truth. It is no more possible to know whether Agard used his presence at trial to figure out how to tell potent lies from the witness stand than it is to know whether an accused who remains silent had no exculpatory story to tell. . . .

New York law requires defendants to be present when tried. It follows that every defendant who testifies is equally susceptible to a generic accusation about his opportunity for tailoring. The prosecutorial comment at issue, tied only to the defendant's presence in the courtroom and not to his actual testimony, tarnishes the innocent no less than the guilty. Nor can a jury measure a defendant's credibility by evaluating the defendant's response to the accusation, for the broadside is fired after the defense has submitted its case. An irrebuttable observation that can be made about any testifying defendant cannot sort those who tailor their testimony from those who do not, much less the guilty from the innocent.

The Court of Appeals took a carefully restrained and moderate position in this case. It held that a prosecutor may not, as part of her summation, use the mere fact of a defendant's presence at his trial as the basis for impugning his credibility. A prosecutor who wishes at any stage of a trial to accuse a defendant of tailoring specific elements of his testimony to fit with particular testimony given by other witnesses would, under the decision of the Court of Appeals, have leave to do so. Moreover, on cross-examination, a prosecutor would be free to challenge a defendant's overall credibility by pointing out that the defendant had the opportunity to tailor his testimony in general, even if the prosecutor could point to no facts suggesting that the defendant had actually engaged in tailoring. The Court of Appeals held only that the prosecutor may not launch a general accusation of tailoring on summation. Thus, the decision below would rein in a prosecutor solely in situations where there is no particular reason to believe that tailoring has occurred and where the defendant has no opportunity to rebut the accusation.

The Court of Appeals' judgment was correct in light of Griffin and Doyle. Those decisions instruct that when a defendant's exercise of a constitutional fair trial right is "insolubly ambiguous" as between innocence and guilt, the prosecutor may not urge the jury to construe the bare invocation of the right against the defendant. See Doyle, 426 U.S., at 617, 96 S.Ct. 2240. To be sure, defendants are not categorically exempt from some costs associated with the assertion of their constitutional prerogatives. The Court is correct to say that the truth-seeking function of trials places demands on defendants. In a proper case, that central function could justify a particular burden on the exercise of Sixth Amendment rights. But the interests of truth are not advanced by allowing a prosecutor, at a time when the defendant cannot respond, to invite the jury to convict on the basis of conduct as consistent with innocence as with guilt. Where burdening a constitutional right will not yield a compensating benefit, as in the present case, there is no justification for imposing the burden.

The truth-seeking function of trials may be served by permitting prosecutors to make accusations of tailoring—even wholly generic accusations of tailoring—as part of cross-examination. Some defendants no doubt do give false testimony calculated to fit with the testimony they hear from other witnesses. If accused on cross-examination of having tailored their testimony, those defendants might display signals of untrustworthiness that it is the province of the jury to detect and interpret. But when a generic argument is offered on summation, it cannot in the slightest degree distinguish the guilty from the innocent. It undermines all defendants equally and therefore does not help answer the question that is the essence of a trial's search for truth: Is this particular defendant lying to cover his guilt or truthfully narrating his innocence?

In addition to its incapacity to serve the individualized truth-finding function of trials, a generic tailoring argument launched on summation entails the simple unfairness of preventing a defendant from answering the charge. This problem was especially pronounced in the instant case. Under New York law, defendants generally may not bolster their own credibility by introducing their prior consistent statements but may introduce such statements to rebut claims of recent fabrication. Had the prosecution made its tailoring accusations on cross-examination, Agard might have been able to prove that his story at trial was the same as it had been before he heard the testimony of other witnesses. A prosecutor who can withhold a tailoring accusation until summation can avert such a rebuttal. [citations omitted] . . .

The Court offers two arguments in support of its conclusion that a prosecutor may make the generic tailoring accusations at issue in this case. First, it suggests that such comment has historically not been seen as problematic. Second, it contends that respondent Agard's case is readily distinguishable from Griffin. The Court's historical excursus does not even begin to prove that comments like those in this case have ever been accepted as constitutional, and the attempt to distinguish Griffin relies on implausible premises that this Court has previously rejected.

The Court's historical narrative proceeds as follows: In the early days of the Republic, prosecutors had no "need" to suggest that defendants might use their presence at trial to tailor their testimony, because defendants' (unsworn) statements at trial could be compared with pretrial statements that defendants gave as a matter of course. Later, some States instituted rules requiring defendants to testify before the other witnesses did, thus obviating once again any need to make arguments about tailoring. There is no evidence, the Court says, that any State ever prohibited the kind of generic argument now at issue until recent times. So it must be the case that generic tailoring arguments have traditionally been thought unproblematic.

I do not comprehend why the Court finds in this account any demonstration that the prosecutorial comment at issue here has a long history of unchallenged use. If prosecutors in times past had no need to make generic tailoring arguments, it is likely such arguments simply were not made. Notably, the Court calls up no instance of an 18th– or 19th–century prosecutor's urging that a defendant's presence at trial facilitated tailored testimony. And if prosecutors did not make such arguments, courts had no occasion to rule them out of order. The absence of old cases prohibiting the comment that the Court now confronts thus scarcely indicates that generic accusations of tailoring have long been considered constitutional.

The Court's discussion of Griffin is equally unconvincing. The Court posits that a ban on inviting juries to draw adverse inferences from a defendant's silence differs materially from a ban on inviting juries to draw adverse inferences from a defendant's presence, because the inference from silence "is not . . . 'natural or irresistible.' " This is a startling statement. It fails to convey what the Court actually said in Griffin, which was that the inference from silence to guilt is "not always so natural or irresistible." The statement that an inference is not always natural or irresistible implies that the inference is indeed natural or irresistible in many, perhaps most, cases. And so it is. See Mitchell v. United States (1999) (SCALIA, J., dissenting) (The Griffin rule "runs exactly counter to normal evidentiary inferences: If I ask my son whether he saw a movie I had forbidden him to watch, and he remains silent, the import of his silence is clear."); Lakeside v. Oregon (1978) (It is "very doubtful" that jurors, left to their own devices, would not draw adverse inferences from a defendant's failure to testify.). It is precisely because the inference is often natural (but nonetheless prohibited) that the jury, if a defendant so requests, is instructed not to draw it. Carter v. Kentucky, 450 U.S. 288, 301–303, 101 S.Ct. 1112, 67 L.Ed.2d 241 (1981) (An uninstructed jury is likely to draw adverse inferences from a defendant's failure to testify, so defendants are entitled to have trial courts instruct juries that no such inference may be drawn.)

The inference involved in Griffin is at least as "natural" or "irresistible" as the inference the prosecutor in Agard's case invited the jury to draw. There are, to be sure, reasons why an innocent defendant might not want to testify. Perhaps he fears that his convictions for prior crimes will generate prejudice against him if placed before the jury; perhaps he has an unappealing countenance that could produce the same effect; perhaps he worries that cross-examination will drag into public view prior conduct that, though not unlawful, is deeply embarrassing. For similar reasons, an innocent person might choose to remain silent after arrest. But in either the Griffin scenario of silence at trial or the Doyle scenario of silence after arrest, something beyond the simple innocence of the defendant must be hypothesized in order to explain the defendant's behavior.

Not so in the present case. If a defendant appears at trial and gives testimony that fits the rest of the evidence, sheer innocence could explain his behavior completely. The inference from silence to guilt in Griffin or from silence to untrustworthiness in Doyle is thus more direct than the inference from presence to tailoring. Unless one has prejudged the defendant as guilty, or unless there are specific reasons to believe that particular testimony has been altered, the possibility that the defendant is telling the truth is surely as good an explanation for the coherence of the defendant's testimony as any that involves wrongful tailoring. I therefore disagree with the Court's assertion, that the Court of Appeals' decision in Agard's case differs from our decision in Griffin by "requir[ing] the jury to do what is practically impossible." It makes little sense to maintain that juries able to avoid drawing adverse inferences from a defendant's silence would be unable to avoid thinking that only a defendant's opportunity to spin a web of lies could explain the seamlessness of his testimony.

The Court describes the inference now at issue as one not from presence to tailoring but merely from presence to opportunity to tailor. The proposition that Agard simply had the opportunity to tailor, we note, is not what the prosecutor urged upon the jury. She encouraged the jury to draw, from the fact of Agard's opportunity, the inference that he had actually tailored his testimony. (Defendant was able "to sit here and listen to the testimony of all the other witnesses before he testifie[d]. . . . [He got] to sit here and think what am I going to say and how am I going to say it? How am I going to fit it into the evidence? ... He's a smart man.... He used everything to his advantage.")

The Court states in the alternative that if proscribing generic accusations of tailoring at summation does not require the jury to do the impossible, then it prohibits prosecutors from "inviting the jury to do what the jury is perfectly entitled to do." The Court offers no prior authority, however, for the proposition that a jury may constitutionally draw the inference now at issue. The Second Circuit thought the matter open, and understandably so in light of Griffin and Carter. But even if juries were permitted to draw the inference in question, it would not follow that prosecutors could urge juries to draw it. Doyle prohibits prosecutors from urging juries to draw adverse inferences from a defendant's choice to remain silent after receiving Miranda warnings, but the Court today shows no readiness to say that juries may not draw that inference themselves. It therefore seems unproblematic to hold that a prosecutor's latitude for argument is narrower than a jury's latitude for assessment.

In its final endeavor to distinguish the two inferences, the Court maintains that the one in Griffin goes to a defendant's guilt but the one now at issue goes merely to a defendant's credibility as a witness. But it is dominantly in cases where the physical evidence is inconclusive that prosecutors will concentrate all available firepower on the credibility of a testifying defendant. Argument that goes to the defendant's credibility in such a case also goes to guilt. Indeed, the first sentence of the Court's account of the trial in this case acknowledges that the questions of guilt and credibility were coextensive.

The distinction between cross-examination and summation is critical. Cross-examination is the criminal trial's primary means of contesting the credibility of any witness, and a defendant who is also a witness may of course be cross-examined. Jenkins supports the proposition that cross-examination is of sufficient value as an aid to finding truth at trial that prosecutors may sometimes question defendants even about matters that may touch on their constitutional rights, and Brooks suggests that cross-examination can expose a defendant who tailors his testimony. Thus the prosecutor's tactics in Jenkins and our own counsel in Brooks are entirely consistent with the moderate restriction on prosecutorial license that the Court today rejects.

In the end, we are left with a prosecutorial practice that burdens the constitutional rights of defendants, that cannot be justified by reference to the trial's aim of sorting guilty defendants from innocent ones, and that is not supported by our case law. The restriction that the Court of Appeals placed on generic accusations of tailoring is both moderate and warranted. That court declared it permissible for the prosecutor to comment on "what the defendant testified to regarding pertinent events"—"the fit between the testimony of the defendant and other witnesses." What is impermissible, the Second Circuit held, is simply and only a summation "bolstering ... the prosecution witnesses' credibility vis-a-vis the defendant's based solely on the defendant's exercise of a constitutional right to be present during the trial." I would affirm that sound judgment and therefore dissent from the Court's disposition. [Citations omitted]

NOTES

1. Consider the state's interest in the rule which requires that a defendant whose motion for directed verdict is denied must choose between resting on his motion or offering evidence. The defendant who decides to offer evidence waives any future claim (trial or appeal) that his motion should have been granted and he bears the risk that his evidence may supply a missing element of the state's case or strengthen in the jury's eyes a technically sufficient but unpersuasive presentation by the prosecution.

2. In Rock v. Arkansas, 483 U.S. 44, 107 S.Ct. 2704 (1987) the Supreme Court for the first time declared unequivocally that a criminal defendant has a constitutional right to testify in his or her own behalf, even though at common law parties, in civil and criminal cases, were deemed incompetent to testify by virtue of their interest in the outcome. The Court then went on to consider a state rule of law that completely barred testimony of any witness (including a defendant) from memory that had been refreshed through hypnosis. The state court had ruled that a witness could only testify to events that she had remembered and described before the session with the hypnotist. The ban as to post-hypnotic recollections was absolute, without regard to an analysis of the reliability of such testimony or the methods used by the hypnotist. The United States Supreme Court held that such a broad rule violated the defendant's right to testify in her own behalf. It said that, at least as to the proposed testimony of a criminal defendant, a rule of exclusion must depend upon an analysis of the reliability of the proposed testimony in the individual circumstances of the case. Dissenting justices declared that in formulating a general rule of evidence, applicable to all cases, a state should be free to engage in the generalization that hypnotically refreshed testimony is too fraught with dangers to be admissible.

The majority's ruling in *Rock* did not deal with the more common situation in which a defendant is complaining about the prosecution's use of testimony of a witness who has been subjected to hypnosis.

The decision whether to testify, like the decision to plead guilty or not guilty, is ultimately the defendant's to make. It is not one of those areas of trial strategy within the province of defense counsel. See Nichols v. Butler, 917 F.2d 518 (11th Cir.1990), condemning defense counsel who, without stating that she feared perjury, threatened to withdraw if her client insisted upon testifying. Many courts have rejected the argument that the trial judge is obligated to admonish the defendant of his or her right to testify. See United States v. Martinez, 883 F.2d 750 (9th Cir.1989) (2–1). The issue may not arise often because it is common practice for the court to make personal inquiry of defendant to ensure that it is the defendant's personal decision. Defense counsel (with a view to later attacks on their competency) will also seek confirmation from their clients in open court.

3. In Lee v. Kemna, 534 U.S. 362, 122 S.Ct. 877 (2002), the defendant was on trial for murder and planned to present an alibi defense. His alibi witnesses (his mother, stepfather, and sister) voluntarily came from California to Missouri to testify on his behalf, but on the day the defense case began, they were unexplainably missing from the court. The defendant requested a continuance to gain time to find the witnesses. The trial court denied this motion, the trial proceeded, and the defendant was convicted. Later, when Lee filed for postconviction relief, he asserted that the witnesses had left the courthouse because an employee of the prosecutor's office had told them they were not needed any more. If true, the Court said, this would be a violation of the accused's rights.

D. Other Crimes Evidence

United States v. DeCastris

United States Court of Appeals, Seventh Circuit, 1986.
798 F.2d 261.

■ Easterbrook, Circuit Judge.

A former Chicago police officer collected disability benefits while working full time. For more than two years he mailed monthly affidavits representing that he had not "resume[d] employment for compensation while in receipt of disability benefit". One who "resumes" employment (in the language of the affidavit) or "assumes" employment (in the language of the state statute)has his disability benefits reduced one dollar for every dollar of earnings, once the combination of disability benefits and earnings exceeds the officer's former salary.

DeCastris had not exactly "assumed" or "resumed" employment, however. For five years before he left the police force, he had held a full-time job managing the nationwide trucking operation for Zenith Electronics Corp. The job with Zenith paid more than the job with the police. Holding two full-time jobs is forbidden by Zenith. Zenith learned of the police job in 1978 and demanded that DeCastris quit one or the other. DeCastris left the police job with disability benefits, which led to this case. The police did not learn of the Zenith job until DeCastris had collected benefits for 27 months, the maximum to which an officer with DeCastris's nine years of service is entitled. Had he disclosed that he was making more than $2,500 a month from Zenith (which he was in 1979), disability officials testified, he would not have received disability benefits. The crime is mail fraud, (the affidavits went by mail); the sentence is two years' imprisonment, five years' probation, and a fine of $5,000.

* * *

If DeCastris knew that he had to disclose his employment, that his earnings may have mattered no matter when he started working at Zenith, then there was a scheme to defraud, and if not, not.

* * *

The evidence, now taken in the light most favorable to the prosecution, supports an affirmative answer. DeCastris had received a letter from the disability officials stating: "in the event disability benefit payments and regular employment compensation exceed Civil Service salary, a reduction in payment of disability benefits shall be made the following month." This letter, coupled with the evident purport of an affidavit seeking information about employment, could lead a reasonable juror to conclude that DeCastris—a police officer, the supervisor of 90 employees at Zenith, and therefore aware of the nature of bureaucratic forms in general—knew that he had to reveal information about all earnings from employment.

The prosecutor bolstered the inference by showing that DeCastris lied in response to clear questions as well as cloudy ones. The judge allowed the prosecutor to introduce ten documents containing lies. One was DeCastris's application for employment at Zenith, which claimed more education than DeCastris possessed and omitted information about his job as a police officer. DeCastris claimed to be self-employed. Most of the rest were annual questionnaires filed with the police claiming nonexistent educational credentials. The judge excluded from evidence another form in which DeCastris told the police department that he lived in Chicago (which is legally required of a Chicago police officer); DeCastris did not live in Chicago, and the judge thought this particular lie would be unduly prejudicial. See Fed.R.Evid. 403.

DeCastris's counsel put his intent in issue by emphasizing the ambiguity of "assume" and "resume". (DeCastris did not testify, so we do not have his own account of his mental state.) Fed.R.Evid. 404(b) allows the introduction of "other wrong" evidence to show intent, although not to show the defendant's character. "Intent" and "character" may merge in a case such as this, however, making the application of the rule difficult. DeCastris says that the forms were used to portray him as a bad actor, likely to lie again in filling out the next form. No doubt there is something to this concern. Evidence of this type invites the inference that he who lies often ought to be damned as a liar without regard to the crime in question. On the other hand, a demonstration that DeCastris lied repeatedly in response to clear questions on other forms shows something about his intent in filling out the affidavits for the disability officials. Did he omit the information because of confusion or even a genuine belief that pre-existing jobs need not be revealed? Or did he omit the information in order to befuddle the officials and obtain benefits to which he knew he was not entitled? Evidence that DeCastris had sought to mislead through the use of other forms influences the proper understanding of his intent in filling out the affidavits.

The "bad character" inference is inseparable from the "bad intent" inference. We do not pretend that a jury can keep one inference in mind without thinking about the other. An instruction told the jury to do this,[3] but this is like telling someone not to think about a hippopotamus. To tell someone not to think about the beast is to assure at least a fleeting mental image. So it is here. Each juror must have had both the legitimate and the forbidden considerations somewhere in mind, if only in the subconscious.

Yet this unwelcome consequence of using "other wrong" evidence does not make the evidence inadmissible. It is relevant to the outcome of the case. The risks of error are not one-sided. A jury forced to assess DeCastris's claim of mistaken interpretation without being able to examine his history of filling out forms may have been led to error. The prosecutor could not stop with a single incorrect form. That, too, may have been

3. "You have heard evidence of acts of the defendant other than those charged in the indictment relating to employment and a credit application. You may consider this evidence only on the question of intent. The evidence is to be considered by you only for this limited purpose. It would be improper for the jury to consider this evidence for any other purpose."

chalked up to error or mistake. The relevant evidence is the *pattern* of lies in response to questions on forms. It is the pattern, and not an isolated episode, that helps the jury to assess DeCastris's intent in returning the affidavits month upon month. Naturally the pattern will span a course of years (otherwise it's not much of a pattern), so the fact that the forms introduced here go as much as ten years before the first affidavit does not count against them.

When the "other wrong" evidence is relevant to a legitimate subject such as intent, the district judge must decide how much is too much. This delicate balance of probative force against undue prejudice calls for all of the judge's skills. The judge must enter the mind of the jurors and appreciate how a piece of evidence fits. How the evidence fills out the picture drawn at trial, how well the jurors can suppress their natural inclinations to use the information for forbidden as well as legitimate purposes, and even more factors require an assessment of imponderables. In this case there are no clear answers, and reasonable judges could come to different conclusions. When there is no clear right and wrong, we review the decision under a deferential standard.

The evidence of prior lies had great potential to produce condemnation of character, which could lead to an emotional rather than reasoned conviction, but this potential was not so powerful (in relation to the legitimate value of the lies) that the district judge's decision is beyond the pale. The judge approached the job thoughtfully, and she eliminated evidence of a lie about residence to which she thought jurors would react improperly. The line must be drawn somewhere, and when the line is drawn with care, as it was here, an appellate court may not substitute its judgment for that of the district judge. The district judges, specialists in applying rules to facts, generally have the last word in drawing lines where surveyors do not go. The line drawn in this case was tenable.

Affirmed

■ Ripple, Circuit Judge, dissenting.

* * *

The government's theory of this prosecution was that Mr. DeCastris had a duty under section 5–157 of the Illinois Policeman's Annuity and Benefit Fund Act to report the income which he earned from his employment with Zenith Electronics Corporation. It further alleged that he knowingly breached that duty by filing with the Fund affidavits which failed to disclose that income. Neither proposition is established in the record.

First, although the district judge held that, as a matter of law, the statute required the disclosure of the Zenith employment, the statutory language hardly supports that reading. The statute requires a reduction of payments for those individuals who earned income from jobs which they *assumed* during the disability period (or *resumed*, to use the exact language of the affidavits which the Disability Board sent to potential recipients). . . . In essence, the Policeman's Annuity and Benefit Fund specifically asked Mr. DeCastris to report all of the income which he had earned from jobs that he either *assumed* or *resumed* during the disability period. He reported no such income. That statement was the truth. Consequently, he cannot be guilty of knowingly making misstatements to the Fund.

Furthermore, even if the statute had placed such an obligation upon him, there is no real evidence that he should—or could—have understood such an obligation and, therefore, could have intended to violate it. . . . Mr. DeCastris, like an increasingly large number of people today, held two jobs at the same time. The government offered no evidence to indicate that the police department prohibited that type of "moonlighting." Mr. DeCastris' disability payments were the consequence of an actual injury and replaced that portion of his total income formerly attributable to his police salary. It would have been quite understandable for Mr. DeCastris to interpret the Fund's communication and affidavits as expressing a concern as to whether he had taken on civilian work to replace his police income.

* * *

One may fairly wonder, then, how Mr. DeCastris was convicted. The answer can be found in the trial court's wholesale admission into evidence of almost a dozen documents in which Mr. DeCastris had allegedly lied about other matters. Most of these documents contained misstatements about his educational background. These documents did more than—as the majority puts it—"bolster" the government's case. They were, as a practical matter, the government's entire case. Through the admission of this material, the government was able to expand the trial into a general review of the defendant's moral life and to convey to the jury a single, potent message: the defendant was a very bad man who should be punished because he had been "getting away with things" for along time. This litigation tactic is explicitly forbidden by Fed.R.Evid. 404.

The majority asserts that this evidence is tightly intertwined with evidence of Mr. DeCastris' intent to defraud. Thus, according to the majority's analysis, if the appellant's intent was put in issue in this case, the evidence must be admissible. The majority then concludes that "DeCastris's counsel put his intent in issue by emphasizing the ambiguity of 'assume' and 'resume.' . . . The relevant evidence is the *pattern* of lies in response to questions on forms." This argument must fail. Whatever relevance the evidence might have had on the issue of intent to defraud was drastically outweighed by the possibility of prejudice. Given the absence of any other evidence tending to show that Mr. DeCastris intended to defraud the Fund by his statements, the admission of this evidence could only have confused the jury with respect to the actual issue before it. Some of the alleged misstatements had occurred in substantially different time frames and involved substantially different matters. Moreover, the trial judge showed little selectivity in determining what information to admit and what to exclude.

In this case, the government had to prove a very precise allegation. Although it specifically charged the defendant with breaching a duty imposed by a specific state statute, it failed to prove that he had such a duty or, if he had such a duty, that he knew or could have known of it. Instead, it simply established that, in his lifetime, he had done other things which were dishonest. This is hardly, under the rule of law, a basis for a federal mail fraud conviction. Accordingly, I respectfully dissent.

NOTES

1. The landmark opinions, both majority and dissent, about other crimes evidence are in People v. Molineux, 168 N.Y. 264, 61 N.E. 286 (1901), which stated:

> "The general rule of evidence applicable to criminal trials is that the state cannot prove against a defendant any crime not alleged in the indictment, either as a foundation for a separate punishment, or as aiding the proofs that he is guilty of the crime charged."

The opinion went on to say:

> "The exceptions to the rule cannot be stated with categorical precision. Generally speaking, evidence of other crimes is competent to prove the specific crime charged when it tends to establish (1) motive; (2) intent; (3) the absence of mistake or accident; (4) a common scheme or plan embracing the commission of two or more crimes so related to each other that proof of one tends to establish the others; (5) the identity of the person charged with the commission of the crime on trial."

An alternative formulation is stated in People v. Peete, 28 Cal.2d 306, 315–16, 169 P.2d 924, 929–30 (1946):

> "... except when it shows merely criminal disposition [citations omitted], evidence that is relevant is not excluded because it reveals the commission of an offense other than that charged. 'The general tests of the admissibility of evidence in a criminal case are: ... does it tend logically, naturally, and by reasonable inference to establish any fact material for the people, or to overcome any material matter sought to be proved by the defense? If it does, then it is admissible, whether it embraces the commission of another crime or does not, whether the other crime be similar in kind or not, whether it be part of a single design or not.'[citations omitted] 'It is true that in trying a person charged with one offense it is ordinarily inadmissible to offer proof of another and distinct offense, but this is only because the proof of a distinct offense has ordinarily no tendency to establish the offense charged; But, whenever the case is such that proof of one crime tends to prove any fact material in the trial of another, such proof is admissible, and the fact that it may tend to prejudice the defendant in the minds of jurors is no ground for its exclusion.' "

A very careful analysis of other crimes evidence is found in State v. Johns, 301 Or. 535, 725 P.2d 312 (1986) (in spouse murder case, prior attempt to murder a previous wife admissible); Commonwealth v. Foy, 394 Pa.Super. 442, 576 A.2d 366 (1990) (cessation of signature crimes upon defendant's arrest is admissible). A comprehensive treatise in the matter is found in Imwinkelried, Uncharged Misconduct Evidence (1984).

2. Where the prosecution seeks permission to use "other crime" evidence to link a defendant to the presently charged offense, the question arises as to the quantum of proof necessary with respect to that other crime. Some courts have required proof by clear and convincing evidence that the defendant committed that other crime. Other jurisdictions have required proof by a preponderance of the evidence. In Huddleston v. United States, 485 U.S. 681, 108 S.Ct. 1496 (1988), the trial court concluded that the prosecution need pass no special burden-of-proof hurdle before the court admits other-crime evidence which otherwise qualifies under Federal Rule of Evidence 404(b). As long as there is evidence from which the jury can find that the defendant was responsible for the other acts, the judge can admit the evidence without making an independent judgment that the evidence, in fact, establishes by a preponderance or by some higher standard that the defendant committed the other crime.

3. The Supreme Court has held that where a defendant has been acquitted at an earlier trial of the "other crime," the Double Jeopardy provision of the Fifth Amendment does not prohibit evidence of the same conduct when offered by the prosecution in a subsequent prosecution under an exception to the general prohibition against other crime evidence. See Dowling v. United States, 493 U.S. 342, 110 S.Ct. 668 (1990).

4. A due process attack on other crimes evidence was rejected in Estelle v. McGuire, 502 U.S. 62, 112 S.Ct. 475 (1991) where prior injuries were proved to show that the child-victim was "battered" and was killed intentionally and not accidentally. The jury was told to use the evidence to determine guilt only if it believed the accused had inflicted the prior injuries.

5. In Commonwealth v. McGowan, 535 Pa. 292, 635 A.2d 113 (1993) the Court was faced with a defendant who wanted to introduce evidence of other crimes:

> On December 20, 1988, at approximately 7:15 p.m., a man entered Kramer's Pharmacy in White Oak, Pennsylvania, and, at gunpoint, ordered the pharmacist and a clerk to "give me all your Dilaudid." The perpetrator then ran from the pharmacy with a cigar box containing drugs. Appellant was later arrested and charged with the robbery after the pharmacist and the clerk identified him as the perpetrator.
>
> During cross-examination of one of the arresting officers, defense counsel attempted to elicit testimony relating to a string of similar prior robberies wherein appellant had been misidentified as the perpetrator. The trial court refused to hear evidence of these prior misidentifications, ruling that the evidence was irrelevant to the instant charge. Defense counsel was not given ample opportunity to set forth the relevant similarities. Rather, it is apparent from a reading of the following excerpt from the trial, that the trial court ordered defense counsel to terminate all argument as to the admissibility of this evidence:
>
> Q. [by defense counsel]: Sir, the individual who you arrested that day was also wanted by the police for other acts, wasn't he?
>
> MS. NECESSARY [for the prosecution]: Objection. Irrelevant.
>
> A. [arresting officer]: I can't answer that, not by our department, no.
>
> Q. Weren't you aware also of his being wanted for several other drugstore robberies in that area?
>
> A. I believe he was arrested by the city police for robbery. I don't know how many.
>
> Q. There was also, were you aware of a robbery at the Medicine Shoppe and also a robbery at John's Drugstore, John's Drugstore and the Medicine Shoppe? Are you aware of that?
>
> A. I don't know. I am not aware of the specific places. I know that they were located throughout the city.
>
> Q. Well, were you also aware, sir, that Mr. McGowan was dismissed on all those counts?
>
> THE COURT: What's the relevancy of that case to this?

MR. MARCUS: The relevance, Your Honor, is this: Mr. McGowan had been arrested on several drugstore robberies, and all those robberies, it turned out same type of identification, same type of description was given in each of those cases also.

A search warrant was executed for his house with an affidavit for probable cause which I was given in discovery on this case, and the search warrant alleges that it's the same actor that's committing the robberies all around.

In other words, same MO, same description, and the reason it's relevant is because in each of those cases, Mr. McGowan was not the person who did it, and was at work at the time that it happened. It's relevant, Your Honor, because they keep arresting this guy for the same thing.

THE COURT: Well, I have heard all I intend to hear about that.

Defense counsel was clearly trying to establish the similarities between the prior robberies and the robbery of Kramer's Pharmacy in an effort to support the defense theory of misidentification when the trial court refused to allow him to continue. To hold, as did the Superior Court, that appellant failed to establish these similarities, when in fact he had been precluded by the trial court from elaborating on the alleged similarities, is error.

E. CROSS EXAMINATION AND IMPEACHMENT

1. THE WITNESS

Delaware v. Fensterer

Supreme Court of the United States, 1985.
474 U.S. 15, 106 S.Ct. 292.

■ PER CURIAM.

* * *

I

Respondent was convicted of murdering his fiance, Stephanie Ann Swift. The State's case was based on circumstantial evidence, and proceeded on the theory that respondent had strangled Swift with a cat leash. To establish that the cat leash was the murder weapon, the State sought to prove that two hairs found on the leash were similar to Swift's hair, and that one of those hairs had been forcibly removed. To prove these theories, the State relied on the testimony of Special Agent Allen Robillard of the Federal Bureau of Investigation.

At trial, Robillard testified that one of the hairs had been forcibly removed. He explained that, in his opinion, there are three methods of determining that a hair has forcibly been removed: (1) if the follicular tag is present on the hair, (2) if the root is elongated and misshaped, or (3) if a sheath of skin surrounds the root. However, Robillard went on to say that "I have reviewed my notes, and I have no specific knowledge as to the particular way that I determined the hair was forcibly removed other than the fact that one of those hairs was forcibly removed." On cross-examination, Agent Robillard was again unable to recall which method he had employed to determine that the hair had forcibly been removed. He also explained that what he meant by "forcibly removed" was no more than that the hair could have been removed by as little force as is entailed in " 'brushing your hand through your head or brushing your hair.' " The trial court overruled respondent's objection that the admission of Robillard's testimony precluded adequate cross-examination unless he could testify as to which of the three theories he relied upon, explaining that in its view this objection went to the weight of the evidence rather than its admissibility.

The defense offered its own expert in hair analysis, Dr. Peter DeForest, who agreed with Agent Robillard that the hairs were similar to Swift's. Dr. DeForest testified that he had observed that one of the hairs had a follicular tag. He also testified that he had spoken by telephone with Robillard, who advised him that his conclusion of forcible removal was based on the presence of the follicular tag. Dr. DeForest then proceeded to challenge the premise of Robillard's theory—that the presence of a follicular tag indicates forcible removal. According to Dr. DeForest, no adequate scientific study supported that premise, and a follicular tag could be attached to hairs that naturally fall out.

* * *

II

This Court's Confrontation Clause cases fall into two broad categories: cases involving the admission of out-of-court statements and cases involving restrictions imposed by law or by the trial court on the scope of cross-examination.

This case falls in neither category. It is outside the first category, because the State made no attempt to introduce an out-of-court statement by Agent Robillard for any purpose, let alone as hearsay.

The second category is also inapplicable here, for the trial court did not limit the scope or nature of defense counsel's cross-examination in any way. The Court has recognized that "the cross-examiner is not only permitted to delve into the witness' story to test the witness' perceptions and memory, but [also] . . . allowed to impeach, i.e., discredit, the witness." Davis, [v. Alaska]. But it does not follow that the right to cross-examine is denied by the State whenever the witness' lapse of memory impedes one method of discrediting him. Quite obviously, an expert witness who cannot recall the basis for his opinion invites the jury to find that his opinion is as unreliable as his memory. That the defense might prefer the expert to embrace a particular theory, which it is prepared to refute with special vigor, is irrelevant. " 'The main and essential purpose of confrontation is *to secure for the opponent the opportunity of cross-examination.*' " (Emphasis in original). Generally speaking, the Confrontation Clause guarantees an *opportunity* for effective cross-examination, not cross-examination that is effective in whatever way, and to whatever extent, the defense might wish. See [Ohio v.] Roberts, (even where the only opportunity the defense has to cross-examine the declarant is at a preliminary hearing, except in "extraordinary cases" where defense counsel provided ineffective re presentation at the earlier proceeding, "no inquiry into 'effectiveness' is required"). This conclusion is confirmed by the fact that the assurances of reliability our cases have found in the right of cross-examination are fully satisfied in cases such as this one, notwithstanding the witness' inability to recall the basis for his opinion; the factfinder can observe the witness' demeanor under cross-examination, and the witness is testifying under oath and in the presence of the accused.

We need not decide whether there are circumstances in which a witness' lapse of memory may so frustrate any opportunity for cross-examination that admission of the witness' direct testimony violates the Confrontation Clause. In this case, defense counsel's cross-examination of Agent Robillard demonstrated to the jury that Robillard could not even recall the theory on which his opinion was based. Moreover, through its own expert witness, the defense was able to suggest to the jury that Robillard had relied on a theory which the defense expert considered baseless. The Confrontation Clause certainly requires no more than this.

* * *

Under the Court's cases, then, Agent Robillard's inability to recall on the stand the basis for his opinion presents none of the perils from which the Confrontation Clause protects defendants in criminal proceedings. The Confrontation Clause includes no guarantee that every witness called by the prosecution will refrain from giving testimony that is marred by forgetfulness, confusion, or evasion. To the contrary, the Confrontation Clause is generally satisfied when the defense is given a full and fair opportunity to probe and expose these infirmities through cross-examination, thereby calling to the attention of the factfinder the reasons for giving scant weight to the witness' testimony. Accordingly, we hold that the admission into evidence of Agent Robillard's opinion did not offend the Confrontation Clause despite his inability to recall the basis for that opinion.

The Delaware Supreme Court appears to have believed that the prosecution breached its "serious obligation not to obstruct a criminal defendant's cross-examination of expert testimony," seemingly because the prosecution knew in advance that Agent Robillard would be unable to recall the basis for his opinion when he testified at trial. While we would agree that Robillard's testimony at the *voir dire* examination must be taken to have alerted both the prosecution and the defense to his lapse of memory, we do not think the prosecution was obliged to refrain from calling Robillard unless it could somehow refresh his recollection. Whether or not, under state law,* Robillard's opinion should have been admitted into evidence, nothing in the Federal Constitution forbids the conclusion reached by the trial court in this case: that the expert's inability to recall the basis for his opinion went to the weight of the evidence, not its admissibility. See United States v. Bastanipour, 697 F.2d 170, 176–177 (C.A.7 1982).That being so,

* Ed. Note: On remand Delaware held that state law precluded admission of opinion evidence when the expert cannot establish a basis for it. Fensterer v. State, 509 A.2d 1106 (Del.1986).

the prosecution's foreknowledge that its expert would be unable to give the precise basis for his opinion did not impose an obligation on it, as a matter of due process, to refrain from introducing the expert's testimony unless the basis for that testimony could definitely be ascertained. We need not decide whether the introduction of an expert opinion with no basis could ever be so lacking in reliability, and so prejudicial, as to deny a defendant a fair trial. The testimony of Dr. DeForest, suggesting the actual basis for Robillard's opinion and vigorously disputing its validity, utterly dispels any possibility of such a claim in this case.

The petition for certiorari is granted, the judgment of the Delaware Supreme Court is reversed, and the case is remanded to that court for further proceedings not inconsistent with this opinion.

It is so ordered.

■ JUSTICE MARSHALL dissents from this summary disposition, which has been ordered without affording the parties prior notice or an opportunity to file briefs on the merits.

■ JUSTICE BLACKMUN would grant certiorari and give this case plenary consideration.

■ JUSTICE STEVENS, concurring in the judgment.

[Omitted]

United States v. Owens

Supreme Court of the United States, 1988.
484 U.S. 554, 108 S.Ct. 838.

■ JUSTICE SCALIA delivered the opinion of the Court.

On April 12, 1982, John Foster, a correctional counselor at the federal prison in Lompoc, California, was attacked and brutally beaten with a metal pipe. His skull was fractured, and he remained hospitalized for almost a month. As a result of his injuries, Foster's memory was severely impaired. When Thomas Mansfield, an FBI agent investigating the assault, first attempted to interview Foster, on April 19, he found Foster lethargic and unable to remember his attacker's name. On May 5, Mansfield again spoke to Foster, who was much improved and able to describe the attack. Foster named respondent as his attacker and identified respondent from an array of photographs.

Respondent was tried in Federal District Court for assault with intent to commit murder under 18 U.S.C. § 113(a). At trial, Foster recounted his activities just before the attack, and described feeling the blows to his head and seeing blood on the floor. He testified that he clearly remembered identifying respondent as his assailant during his May 5th interview with Mansfield. On cross-examination, he admitted that he could not remember seeing his assailant. He also admitted that, although there was evidence that he had received numerous visitors in the hospital, he was unable to remember any of them except Mansfield, and could not remember whether any of these visitors had suggested that respondent was the assailant. Defense counsel unsuccessfully sought to refresh his recollection with hospital records, including one indicating that Foster had attributed the assault to someone other than respondent. Respondent was convicted and sentenced to 20 years' imprisonment to be served consecutively to a previous sentence.

* * *

This Court has never held that a Confrontation Clause violation can be founded upon a witness's loss of memory, but in two cases has expressly left that possibility open.... *California v. Green* [and] *Delaware v. Fensterer* (1985).

Here that question is squarely presented, and we agree with the answer suggested 18 years ago by Justice Harlan. "[T]he Confrontation Clause guarantees only 'an *opportunity* for effective cross-examination, not cross-examination that is effective in whatever way, and to whatever extent, the defense might wish.' " As *Fensterer* demonstrates, that opportunity is not denied when a witness testifies as to his current belief but is unable to recollect the reason for that belief. It is sufficient that the defendant has the opportunity to bring out such matters as the witness's bias, his lack of care and attentiveness, his poor eyesight, and even (what is often a prime objective of cross-examination) the very fact that he has a bad memory. If the ability to inquire into these matters suffices to establish the constitutionally requisite opportunity for cross-examination when a witness testifies as to his current belief, the basis for which he cannot recall, we see no reason why it should not suffice when the witness's past belief is introduced and he is unable to recollect the reason for that past belief. In both cases the foundation for the belief (current or past) cannot effectively be elicited, but other means of impugning the belief are available. Indeed, if there is any difference in persuasive impact between the statement "I believe this to be the man who assaulted me, but can't remember why" and the statement "I don't know whether this is the man who assaulted me, but I told the police I believed so earlier," the former would seem, if anything, more damaging and hence give rise to a greater need for memory-testing, if that is to be considered essential to an opportunity for effective cross-examination. We conclude with respect to this latter example, as we did in *Fensterer* with respect to the former, that it is not. The weapons available to impugn the witness's statement when memory loss is asserted will of course not always achieve success, but successful cross-examination is not the constitutional guarantee. They are, however, realistic weapons, as is demonstrated by defense counsel's summation in this very case, which emphasized Foster's memory loss and argued that his identification of respondent was the result of the suggestions of people who visited him in the hospital.

Our constitutional analysis is not altered by the fact that the testimony here involved an out-of-court identification that would traditionally be categorized as hearsay. This Court has recognized a partial (and somewhat indeterminate) overlap between the requirements of the traditional hearsay rule and the Confrontation Clause. The dangers associated with hearsay inspired the Court of Appeals in the present case to believe that the Constitution required the testimony to be examined for "indicia of reliability," *Dutton v. Evans* (1970), or"particularized guarantees of trustworthiness," *Roberts*, supra. We do not think such an inquiry is called for when a hearsay declarant is present at trial and subject to unrestricted cross-examination. In that situation, as the Court recognized in *Green*, the traditional protections of the oath, cross-examination, and opportunity for the jury to observe the witness's demeanor satisfy the constitutional requirements. We do not think that a constitutional line drawn by the Confrontation Clause falls between a forgetful witness's live testimony that he once believed this defendant to be the perpetrator of the crime, and the introduction of the witness's earlier statement to that effect.

... Respondent has not ... argued that the identification procedure used here was in any way suggestive. There does not appear in our opinions, and we decline to adopt today, the principle that, because of the mere possibility of suggestive procedures, out-of-court statements of identification are inherently less reliable than other out-of-court statements.

* * *

■ JUSTICE KENNEDY took no part in the consideration or decision of this case.

■ JUSTICE BRENNAN, with whom JUSTICE MARSHALL joins, dissenting.

* * *

The principal witness against respondent was not the John Foster who took the stand in December 1983—that witness could recall virtually nothing of the events of April 12, 1982, and candidly admitted that he had no idea whether respondent had assaulted him. Instead, respondent's sole accuser was the John Foster who, on May 5, 1982, identified respondent as his attacker. This John Foster, however, did not testify at respondent's trial: the profound memory loss he suffered during the approximately 18 months following his identification prevented him from affirming, explaining, or elaborating upon his out-of-court statement just as surely and completely as his assertion of a testimonial privilege, or his death, would have. Thus, while the Court asserts that defense counsel had "realistic weapons" with which to impugn Foster's prior statement, it does not and cannot claim that cross-examination could have elicited any information that would have enabled a jury to evaluate the trustworthiness or reliability of the identification.

* * *

Fensterer worked no change in our Confrontation Clause jurisprudence, yet the Court purports to discern in it a principle under which all live testimony as to a witness's past belief is constitutionally admissible, provided the defendant is afforded an opportunity to question the witness. From this the Court derives the corollary that prior statements as to past belief are equally admissible, again given the requisite opportunity for questioning the declarant at trial. Accordingly, the Court asserts, the Confrontation Clause draws no line "between a forgetful witness's live testimony that he once believed this defendant to be the perpetrator of the crime, and the introduction of the witness's earlier statement to that effect." The obvious shortcoming in this reasoning, of course, is that *Fensterer* announced no such blanket rule: while the expert's memory lapse in that case was self-impeaching, it does not follow—and we have therefore never held—that all forgetfulness may be so characterized. Certainly in the present case, Foster's inability in December 1983 to remember the events of April 1982 in no way impugned or otherwise cast doubt upon the accuracy or trustworthiness of his memory in May 1982, particularly in light of the uncontradicted medical testimony explaining that his forgetfulness was the result of the head injuries he sustained. Under our prior cases, then, the constitutional admissibility of Foster's prior statement, and the testimony of the Court's hypothetical witness who cannot recall the basis for his past belief, should depend on whether the memory loss so seriously impedes cross-examination that the factfinder lacks an adequate basis upon which to assess the truth of the proffered evidence. Whatever may be said of the Court's hypothetical, it is clear in the case before us that Foster's near total loss of memory precluded any meaningful examination or assessment of his out-of-court statement and thus should have barred the admission of that statement.

* * *

I agree with the Court that the Confrontation Clause does not guarantee defendants the right to confront only those witnesses whose testimony is not marred by forgetfulness, confusion, or evasion, and that the right of confrontation " 'is generally satisfied when the defense is given a full and fair opportunity to probe and expose these infirmities through cross-examination.' " But as we stressed just last Term, this right to cross-examination "is essentially a 'functional' right designed to promote reliability in the truth-finding functions of a criminal trial." *Kentucky v. Stincer*. In the present case, respondent Owens was afforded no opportunity to probe and expose the infirmities of Foster's May 5, 1982 recollections, for here cross-examination, the "greatest legal engine ever invented for the discovery of truth," *California v. Green* stood as helpless as current medical technology before Foster's profound memory loss. In concluding that respondent's Sixth Amendment rights were satisfied by Foster's mere presence in the courtroom, the Court reduces the right of confrontation to a hollow formalism. Because I believe the Confrontation Clause guarantees more than the right to ask questions of a live witness, no matter how dead that witness's memory proves to be, I dissent.

NOTES

1. In Delaware v. Van Arsdall, 475 U.S. 673, 106 S.Ct. 1431 (1986), the trial court refused to allow defense counsel to cross-examine a prosecution witness about an agreement to talk about the murder at issue in exchange for dismissal of an unrelated charge against him. The Court found the restriction to be a clear violation of the right to explore the bias of a witness. But, it ruled, such an error does not require reversal in every case as would denial of counsel. The Court said:

> Accordingly, we hold that the constitutionally improper denial of a defendant's opportunity to impeach a witness for bias, like other Confrontation Clause errors, is subject to harmless-error analysis. The correct inquiry is whether, assuming that the damaging potential of the cross-examination were fully realized, a reviewing court might nonetheless say that the error was harmless beyond a reasonable doubt. Whether such an error is harmless in a particular case depends upon a host of factors, all readily

accessible to reviewing courts. These factors include the importance of the witness' testimony in the prosecution's case, whether the testimony was cumulative, the presence or absence of evidence corroborating or contradicting the testimony of the witness on material points, the extent of cross-examination otherwise permitted, and, of course, the overall strength of the prosecution's case.

Justice White concurred but thought that the restriction on cross-examination did not violate the confrontation clause. Justice Marshall rejected the harmless error rule in confrontation clause cases.

In Olden v. Kentucky, 488 U.S. 227, 109 S.Ct. 480 (1988), the Supreme Court invoked the confrontation clause to invalidate limits on defense cross-examination and impeachment of a male prosecution witness, imposed by a state trial court. The defense contended that the female complainant in a sexual assault case had constructed her story to deceive her male friend as a means of explaining her presence in the company of the defendant. According to the defense, the male friend of the victim had been living with the complainant. When the male friend testified as a prosecution witness, the trial judge prevented the jury from learning that the two lived together. The judge believed that whatever value the evidence would have for impeachment was outweighed by the possibility of undue prejudice arising from the fact that the complainant was White and her lover was Black. The United States Supreme Court held that the Confrontation Clause required that the defense be able to explore the relationship between the complainant and her friend when he testified for the prosecution.

2. McCormick offers the following observations on the value of cross-examination. Kenneth S. Broun, McCormick on Evidence § 31, at 139–41 (6th ed.2006).

Cross–Examination Revalued

Early Victorian writers on advocacy exaggerated the strategic importance of cross-examination. One wrote, "There is never a cause contested, the result of which is not mainly dependent upon the skill with which the advocate conducts his cross-examination." This romanticism contrasts with the realism of Scarlett, a great "leader" of a later day. Scarlett remarked, "I learned by much experience that the most useful duty of an advocate is the examination of witnesses, and that much more mischief than benefit generally results from cross-examination. I therefore rarely allowed that duty to be performed by my colleagues. I cross-examined in general very little, and more with a view to enforce the facts I meant to rely upon than to affect the witness's credit,—for the most part a vain attempt." Reed, one of the most sensible early 20th century writers on trial tactics, observed, "Sometimes a great speech bears down the adversary, and sometimes a searching cross-examination turns a witness inside out and shows him up to be a perjured villain. But ordinarily cases are not won by either speaking or cross-examining." Even today most lawyers who write concerning the art of cross-examination believe that failure to use this tool effectively can lose a case. That belief often holds true for criminal defense counsel.

However, to the contemporary advocate, cross-examination is more important as a means of gleaning additional facts on the merits to support the cross-examiner's theory of the case; in the real world—as opposed to movies—the cross-examiner rarely destroys the credibility of an opposing witness. It is true that cross-examination of experts is critical in many cases. Federal Rule of Evidence 705 makes the opportunity to cross-examine particularly important when, as the rule permits, on direct examination an expert states only her opinion and the theoretical reasons for the opinion. In that situation, Rule 705 places the burden on the cross-examiner to expose the facts or data about the specific case on which the opinion is based. However, even in this context, the focus is ordinarily on the validity of the expert's reasoning process rather than the expert witness's personal credibility. In summary, while cross-examination can be an important tool at some trials, realistically it does not loom large as a determinant of victory in most cases.

An evaluation of cross-examination as an engine for discovering truth should factor into any discussion of the reform of American evidence law. The traditional assumption is that if there is no opportunity for cross-examination, the statement of an out-of-court declarant or witness is so lacking in reliability that it is not even worth hearing at trial. The traditional mindset is that the opportunity for cross-examination is indispensable. Obviously, cross-examination is a useful device to ensure greater accuracy and completeness in the witness's testimony. In the hands of a skillful advocate, it will sometimes expose fraud or honest error. But it has its own potential for producing errors. The litigator can use cross-examination to expose perjury; but it may be the honest, timid witness, rather than the liar, who more often goes down under the fire of cross-examination. Every witness in judicial proceedings should in fairness be made available for cross-examination wherever feasible. However, where cross-examination is impossible, as in the case of an out-of-court statement or a witness who dies before cross-examination, it is dubious to insist that the statement or testimony normally be excluded for that reason alone. Cross-examination ought to be considered useful, but not indispensable, as a means of discovering truth. The absence of opportunity to cross-examine should be only one relevant factor in determining whether the statement or testimony ought to be received. A modern, reformist approach to hearsay problems might lead us to conclude that when opportunity to cross-examine a witness is permanently cut off without either party's fault, the direct testimony should nevertheless be admissible. It might also prompt us to conclude that hearsay statements ought to be admitted if (1) the statement was made by the declarant on personal knowledge and reported by the witness at first hand, and if the declarant is now dead or unavailable for cross-examination or, (2) the declarant is alive and still available for cross-examination. Perhaps written statements ought to be admitted wherever production for cross-examination can fairly be dispensed with.

Although this reformist viewpoint is defensible, there are special constitutional concerns in criminal cases. The source of those concerns, of course, is the accused's right of cross-examination under the Fifth, Sixth, and Fourteenth Amendments. Those constitutional guarantees may constrain the liberalization of cross-examination practice and the hearsay rule.

3. In Kentucky v. Stincer, 482 U.S. 730, 107 S.Ct. 2658 (1987), a defendant claimed that he had aright, under the Sixth Amendment's Confrontation Clause and under the Fourteenth Amendment's Due Process Clause, to be present when the trial court determined whether the defendant's alleged youthful victims were competent to testify as witnesses against him. Defense counsel, but not the defendant, had been allowed to be present at such hearing. The majority upheld the exclusion. It emphasized that the defendant had been afforded a full right to cross-examine the witnesses once they had been deemed competent. He was present throughout such cross-examination and available to consult with his counsel as necessary. No bar was placed on the repetition during cross-examination of the questions previously asked by the trial judge during the voir dire of the witnesses. The majority emphasized that in the case at hand, the competency questions did not go into the events that were the subject of the trial testimony. Rather they were limited to such matters as the ability to remember and narrate facts, and to the obligation to tell the truth. There was no reason to believe that the defendant's absence from the hearing undermined the integrity of the fact-finding process. The majority refused to draw a line between pre-trial proceedings, on the one hand, and trial proceedings, on the other hand, for the purpose of deciding when a defendant has the right to be present.

Three dissenting justices viewed the competency proceeding as a crucial phase of the proceedings at which the defendant had the right to be present. They noted that a defendant who represented himself would stand in the place of defense counsel and thus would have a right to be present at such a hearing. Thus the defendant was placed in the position of having to waive the right to counsel in order to be allowed to enjoy the right to be present at the hearing held to determine the competency of a witness. The defense declared that it was impermissible to put the defendant to such a choice.

4. Efforts to spare children from traditional cross-examination in the presence of the defendant and a jury in sex-abuse prosecutions have generated a variety of statutory schemes and numerous challenges under the Confrontation Clause of the Sixth Amendment. Some schemes permit pre-trial depositions in lieu of trial testimony. Others use televised testimony beamed "live" to the courtroom from some other room. Still others utilize traditional trial procedures except that the defendant is excluded from the courtroom and views the child's testimony on closed-circuit television. According to Miller v. State, 517 N.E.2d 64 (Ind.1987):

> Legislation allowing the videotaped testimony of a child abuse victim is intended to reduce trauma to the child and to facilitate successful prosecution of child molestors. Thirty-four states allow videotaped testimony, and twenty-three allow testimony by closed circuit TV. Nearly all explicitly require that the defendant have an opportunity for cross-examination either at trial or when the statement is made.

In Coy v. Iowa, 487 U.S. 1012, 108 S.Ct. 2798 (1988), the Supreme Court invalidated a procedure in which, without any particularized showing of necessity, young alleged victims of sex abuse were allowed to testify against the alleged offender while testifying behind a screen. The defendant could see dimly the young teenage accusers, but they could not see him at all.

The Court held that the right of a "face-to-face" meeting is part of the Confrontation Clause protection. Citing President Eisenhower's reflections upon Kansas justice in his youth, the Court noted that the right of the accused to stand face to face with his accuser serves both the appearance and the reality of fair procedure. The very trauma that flows from a face-to-face meeting may make it more difficult for someone to accuse another falsely. The Court said that nothing can actually compel the accuser to look the accused in the eye, but if the accuser looks away, the jury can assess such conduct in evaluating credibility. The Court said that while some strong interest might create an exception to the right to face-to-face confrontation, the Court would not approve the 1985 Iowa statute that created a presumption that in sex abuse cases, the alleged young victim would always be so traumatized so as to permit use of the Iowa "screening" procedure.

Coy did not specify under what circumstances the videotaping of a victim's testimony would be permissible. It held only that the Iowa procedure—in the absence of a showing of necessity that met some not-yet-defined standard—the Iowa procedure violated the Sixth Amendment. The Court held that under some circumstances the error could be deemed harmless beyond a reasonable doubt, and it remanded for a determination of the harmless error issue without giving a clue as to how the lower court should divine whether in the particular case use of the screen was harmless beyond a reasonable doubt.

Justice Blackmun's dissent argued that Dean Wigmore's position—that the value of confrontation lies solely in the right to cross-examine one's accuser—was more persuasive than were the views of President Eisenhower.

Two years later, in Maryland v. Craig, 497 U.S. 836, 110 S.Ct. 3157 (1990), the Supreme Court rejected a Confrontation Clause challenge to the use of a closed circuit television procedure where a showing of necessity is made on a case-by-case basis. There a child who was alleged to be the victim of abuse was allowed to testify out of the presence of the defendant and the jury. Only the child, the judge, the prosecutor, and one of the defense attorneys were present during the testimony of the child. The defendant and her second attorney remained in the courtroom and were in telephonic contact with the first defense attorney as the child's testimony was televised into the courtroom. The Maryland judge permitted the procedure only after finding, based upon expert testimony, that the statutory prerequisite for the procedure was met, namely that:

> The judge determines that the testimony of the child victim in the courtroom will result in the child suffering serious emotional distress such that the child cannot reasonably communicate.

Justice O'Connor wrote for the majority:

> In sum, our precedents establish that "the Confrontation Clause reflects a *preference* for face-to-face confrontation at trial," a preference that must occasionally give way to considerations of public policy and the "necessities of the case."
>
> * * *
>
> We likewise conclude today that a State's interest in the physical and psychological well-being of child abuse victims may be sufficiently important to outweigh, at least in some cases, a defendant's right to face his or her accusers in court.
>
> * * *
>
> The requisite finding of necessity must of course be a case-specific one: the trial court must hear evidence and determine whether use of the one-way closed circuit television procedure is necessary to protect the welfare of the particular child witness who seeks to testify.

Four justices dissented in an opinion by Justice Scalia, who had authored the majority opinion in Coy v. Iowa:

> Seldom has this Court failed so conspicuously to sustain a categorical guarantee of the Constitution against the tide of prevailing current opinion.
>
> * * *
>
> Because of this subordination of explicit constitutional text to currently favored public policy, the following scene can be played out in an American courtroom for the first time in two centuries: A father whose young daughter has been given over to the exclusive custody of his estranged wife, or a mother whose young son has been taken into custody by the State's child welfare department, is sentenced to prison for sexual abuse on the basis of testimony by a child the parent has not seen or spoken to for many months; and the guilty verdict is rendered without giving the parent so much as the opportunity to sit in the presence of the

child, and to ask, personally or through counsel, "it is really not true, is it, that I—your father (or mother) whom you see before you—did these terrible things?" Perhaps that is a procedure today's society desires; perhaps (though I doubt it) it is even a fair procedure; but it is assuredly not a procedure permitted by the Constitution.

Because the text of the Sixth Amendment is clear, and because the Constitution is meant to protect against, rather than conform to, current "widespread belief," I respectfully dissent.

5. In Commonwealth v. Amirault, 424 Mass. 618, 677 N.E.2d 652 (1997), accused child abusers were present in court when eight children testified against them. Each child witness sat at a small table with a microphone placed in its center. The defendants were at a table which was behind and to the side of the witness. At best the defendants could see almost a profile. To make eye contact the witness would have to turn toward defendants. The Court held that such an arrangement might survive a challenge based on the federal constitution but could not be used in light of the specific provision of the Massachusetts Declaration of Rights which says "every subject shall have a right ... to meet the witnesses against him face to face".

American Bar Association Standards Relating To The Prosecution Function And The Defense Function (3d Ed. 1993)

3–5.7 and 4–7.6 Examination of Witnesses

(a) The interrogation of all witnesses should be conducted fairly, objectively and with due regard for the dignity and legitimate privacy of the witness, and without seeking to intimidate or humiliate the witness unnecessarily.

3–5.7 [Prosecution]

(b) The prosecutor's belief that the witness is telling the truth does not preclude cross-examination, but may affect the method and scope of cross-examination. A prosecutor should not use the power of cross-examination to discredit or undermine a witness if the prosecutor knows the witness is testifying truthfully.

4–7.6 [Defense]

(b) A defense counsel's belief or knowledge that the witness is telling the truth does not preclude cross-examination.

* * *

Commentary on The Prosecution Standard [Footnotes Omitted]

Undermining a Truthful Witness

A question of long standing is whether a prosecutor, in cross-examining a witness, should be restrained by the belief that the witness has testified truthfully. Generally, a lawyer is not required to substitute personal opinion for the available fact-finding processes of the trial and may, therefore, properly invoke the usual cross-examination techniques to test the witness's capacity and opportunity for observation and the witness's ability to recall. However, it is sometimes argued that the manner and tenor of cross-examination ought to be restricted where examining counsel believes in the truthfulness of the testimony given by the witness.

Where the prosecutor knows that the testimony of the witness is accurate, paragraph (b) adopts the view that the power of cross-examination may not be invoked to destroy or undermine the truth. In this regard, it is believed that the duty of the prosecutor differs from that of the defense lawyer, who on occasion may be required to challenge known truthful witnesses of the prosecution in order to put the state to its proof.

Commentary on Defense Standard [Footnotes Omitted]

Undermining a Truthful Witness

Justice White, in a 1967 Supreme Court opinion, addressed the sometimes professional obligation of defense counsel to impeach truthful witnesses:

> [A]bsent a voluntary plea of guilty, we . . . insist that [defense counsel] defend his client whether he is innocent or guilty. The State has the obligation to present the evidence. Defense counsel need present nothing, even if he knows what the truth is. He need not furnish any witnesses to the police, or reveal any confidences of his client, or furnish any other information to help the prosecution's case. If he can confuse a witness, even a truthful one, or make him appear at a disadvantage, unsure or indecisive, that will be his normal course. Our interest in not convicting the innocent permits counsel to put the State to its proof, to put the State's case in the worst possible light, regardless of what he thinks or knows to be the truth. Undoubtedly there are some limits which defense counsel must observe but more often than not, defense counsel will cross-examine a prosecution witness, and impeach him if he can, even if he thinks the witness is telling the truth, just as he will attempt to destroy a witness who he thinks is lying. In this respect, as part of our modified adversary system and as part of the duty imposed on the most honorable defense counsel, we countenance or require conduct which in many instances has little, if any, relation to the search for truth.
>
> There unquestionably are many cases where defense counsel cannot provide the accused with a defense at all if counsel is precluded from engaging in vigorous cross-examination of witnesses either believed or known to have testified truthfully. For example, where the defendant has admitted guilt to the lawyer and does not plan to testify, and the lawyer simply intends to put the state to its proof and raise a reasonable doubt, skillful cross-examination of the prosecution's witnesses is essential. Indeed, were counsel in this circumstance to forgo vigorous cross-examination of the prosecution's witnesses, counsel would violate the clear duty of zealous representation that is owed to the client.

> Nonetheless, the mere fact that defense counsel can, by use of impeachment, impair or destroy the credibility of an adverse witness does not impose upon counsel the duty to do so. Such impeachment is not always in the client's best interest. . . .

Another example of a situation where restraint may be called for is where a witness whose testimony the lawyer believes to be truthful is subject to impeachment by revealing to the jury that the witness was convicted of a crime many years earlier. The use of this conventional method of impeachment against a witness who has testified truthfully should be avoided if it is possible for defense counsel to do so without jeopardizing the defense of the accused. In deciding whether to use such impeachment, counsel undoubtedly will want to consider the tactical implications, since the jury may recognize the undue humiliation to the witness and thus react adversely to the lawyer.

There also is a public policy factor underlying restraint in use of impeachment powers vested in a lawyer. The policy of the law is to encourage witnesses to come forward and give evidence in litigation. If witnesses are subjected to needless humiliation when they testify, the existing human tendency to avoid "becoming involved" will be increased.

[Editors' note: The original defense standard closely resembled the prosecution standard. The rationale for change was expressed thusly:

> Original paragraph (b) provided that defense counsel "should not misuse the power of cross-examination or impeachment by employing it to discredit or undermine a witness if he knows the witness is testifying truthfully." This standard has been changed to make clear that it is permissible, if necessary, for defense counsel to cross-examine vigorously witnesses who are believed or known to be testifying truthfully. There are some cases where, unless counsel challenges the prosecution's known truthful witnesses, there will be no opposition to the prosecution's evidence and the defendant will be denied an effective defense. However, lawyers are encouraged in paragraph (b) to take into consideration in conducting cross-examination the fact that the state's witness is testifying truthfully.]

NOTES

1. Are the A.B.A. Standards "practical" in the sense that lawyers may be expected to follow them? What of the overworked prosecutor and public defender in a large urban jurisdiction without much time to prepare or to consult with witnesses? Can these lawyers fairly be expected to make delicate judgments about whether cross examination is "unnecessarily" intimidating or humiliating? Public defenders with large caseloads often have cross examination as their only defense tool; can they worry about its overuse? Is the potential penalty of alienating the trier of fact by abusive cross examination a sufficient check on the overly aggressive lawyer?

The A.B.A. Commentary recites the case of a lawyer who agreed not to use an old conviction against a crucial opposition witness even though the use of the conviction would cause the witness's memory to "fail". Did the lawyer fulfil his duty to his client? Does the lawyer have any other duty? The previous edition of the

Commentary spoke also of the high reputation of a lawyer who exercises restraint and of the benefit his clients will accrue from his stature. Is it a proper function of an attorney to use his personal reputation to benefit his client? What value does this reputation have when the case is tried before a jury from which, in most cases, people who know the lawyers are excluded?

On the other hand, in revising the defense standard in 1978, the A.B.A. said it is "permissible, if necessary" to use the power of cross-examination against witnesses known to be testifying truthfully. Is this a defensible principle? Is there any tactic whose use could not be defended on the ground that it was "necessary" ?

There is precedent for judicial control of both the length and substance of cross-examination. United States v. Vest, 116 F.3d 1179 (7th Cir.1997); United States v. Pulido, 69 F.3d 192 (7th Cir.1995).

2. When the government calls an informer as a witness, the defense is entitled to cross-examination concerning the informer's true name and address at least where the testimony is uncorroborated. Smith v. Illinois, 390 U.S. 129, 88 S.Ct. 748 (1968). The rationale is that the defense is entitled to the "identification of the witness with his environment". Presumably defense counsel may make investigation into the witness' reputation, character, etc. The rule in *Smith* is not absolute and several courts have upheld the refusal to allow inquiries, particularly as to the witness' present home address, where there is some basis for believing the witness would be endangered if his present whereabouts are learned by the accused. McGrath v. Vinzant, 528 F.2d 681 (1st Cir.1976). See Comment, "The Informer Privilege: What's In A Name?", 64 J.Crim.L.C. 56 (1973). Of what value to the defense is an informer's address at the time of trial or his new name if the informer has moved from the address where he resided at the time of the crime and assumed a new name? If the witness has moved recently will the defense be able to make meaningful inquiries as to character and reputation in a new neighborhood? Assume defense counsel has no intention of making investigations but knows that pressing for the information may shake the composure of the witness, is it proper for counsel to cross-examine the witness about his present address? If it is proper to do so, will the witness' reluctance to reveal his address or the prosecution's objections to the question lead the jury to believe the prosecution is improperly hiding something or that the accused is a dangerous man?

2. THE ACCUSED

Doyle v. Ohio

Supreme Court of the United States, 1976.
426 U.S. 610, 96 S.Ct. 2240.

■ MR. JUSTICE POWELL delivered the opinion of the Court.

* * *

I.

Petitioners Doyle and Wood were arrested together and charged with selling 10 pounds of marihuana to a local narcotics bureau informant. They were convicted in ... separate trials held about one week apart. The evidence at their trials was identical in all material respects.

The State's witnesses sketched a picture of a routine marihuana transaction. William Bonnell, a well-known "street person" with a long criminal record, offered to assist the local narcotics investigation unit in setting up drug"pushers" in return for support in his efforts to receive lenient treatment in his latest legal problems. The narcotics agents agreed. A short time later, Bonnell advised the unit that he had arranged a "buy" of 10 pounds of marihuana and needed $1,750 to pay for it. Since the banks were closed and time was short, the agents were able to collect only $1,320. Bonnell took this money and left for the rendezvous, under surveillance by four narcotics agents in two cars. As planned, he met petitioners in a bar in Dover, Ohio. From there, he and petitioner Wood drove in Bonnell's pick-up truck to the nearby town of New Philadelphia, Ohio, while petitioner Doyle drove off to obtain the marihuana and then meet them at a prearranged location in New Philadelphia. The narcotics agents followed the Bonnell truck. When Doyle arrived at Bonnell's waiting truck in New Philadelphia, the two vehicles proceeded to a parking lot where the transaction took place. Bonnell left in his truck, and Doyle and Wood departed in Doyle's car. They quickly discovered that they had been paid some $430 less than the agreed-upon price, and began circling the neighborhood looking for Bonnell. They were stopped within minutes by New Philadelphia police acting on radioed instructions from the narcotics agents. One of those agents, Kenneth Beamer, arrived on the scene promptly, arrested petitioners, and gave them *Miranda* warnings. A search of the car, authorized by warrant, uncovered the $1,320.

At both trials, defense counsel's cross-examination of the participating narcotics agents was aimed primarily at establishing that due to a limited view of the parking lot, none of them had seen the actual transaction but had seen only Bonnell standing next to Doyle's car with a package under his arm, presumably after the transaction.[2] Each petitioner took the stand at his trial and admitted practically everything about the State's case except the most crucial point: who was selling marihuana to whom. According to petitioners, Bonnell had framed them. The arrangement had been for Bonnell to sell Doyle 10 pounds of marihuana. Doyle had left the Dover bar for the purpose of borrowing the necessary money, but while driving by himself had decided that he only wanted one or two pounds instead of the agreed-upon 10pounds. When Bonnell reached Doyle's car in the New Philadelphia parking lot, with the marihuana under his arm, Doyle tried to explain his change of mind. Bonnell grew angry, threw the $1,320 into Doyle's car, and took all 10 pounds of marihuana back to his truck. The ensuing chase was the effort of Wood and Doyle to catch Bonnell to find out what the $1,320 was all about.

Petitioners' explanation of the events presented some difficulty for the prosecution, as it was not entirely implausible and there was little if any direct evidence to contradict it. As part of a wide-ranging cross-examination for impeachment purposes, and in an effort to undercut the explanation the

2. Defense counsel's efforts were not totally successful. One of the four narcotics agents testified at both trials that he had seen the package passed through the window of Doyle's car to Bonnell. In an effort to impeach that testimony, defense counsel played a tape of the preliminary hearing at which the same agent had testified only to seeing the package under Bonnell's arm. The agent did not retract his trial testimony, and both he and the prosecutor explained the apparent inconsistency by noting that the examination at the preliminary hearing had not focused upon whether anyone had seen the package pass to Bonnell.

prosecutor asked each petitioner at his respective trial why he had not told the frame-up story to agent Beamer when he arrested petitioners. In the first trial, that of petitioner Wood, the following colloquy occurred:

> "Q. [by the prosecutor] Mr. Beamer did arrive on the scene?
>
> "A: [by Wood] Yes, he did.
>
> "Q: And I assume you told him all about what happened to you?
>
> * * *
>
> "A: No.
>
> "Q: You didn't tell Mr. Beamer?
>
> * * *
>
> "A: No.
>
> "Q: You didn't tell Mr. Beamer this guy put $1,300 in your car?
>
> * * *
>
> "A: No, sir.
>
> "Q: And we can't understand any reason why anyone would put money in your car and you were chasing him around town and trying to give it back?
>
> * * *
>
> "A: I didn't understand that.
>
> "Q. You mean you didn't tell him that?
>
> * * *
>
> "A: Tell him what?
>
> * * *
>
> "Q: Mr. Wood, if that is all you had to do with this and you are innocent, when Mr. Beamer arrived on the scene why didn't you tell him?
>
> * * *
>
> "Q: But in any event you didn't bother to tell Mr. Beamer anything about this?
>
> "A: No, sir."

Defense counsel's timely objections to each of the prosecutor's questions were overruled. The cross-examination of petitioner Doyle at his trial contained a similar exchange, and again defense counsel's timely objections were overruled.

* * *

II.

The State pleads necessity as justification for the prosecutor's action in these cases. It argues that the discrepancy between an exculpatory story at trial and silence at time of arrest gives rise to an inference that the story was fabricated somewhere along the way, perhaps to fit within the seams of the State's case as it was developed at pretrial hearings. Noting that the prosecution usually has little else with which to counter such an exculpatory story, the State seeks only the right to cross-examine a defendant as to post-arrest silence for the limited purpose of impeachment. In support of its position the State emphasizes the importance of cross-examination in general ... and relies upon those cases in which this Court has permitted use for impeachment purposes of post-arrest statements that were inadmissible as evidence of guilt because of an officer's failure to follow *Miranda*'s dictates. Harris v. New York (1971).... Thus, although the State does not suggest petitioners' silence could be used as evidence of guilt, it contends that the need to present to the jury all information relevant to the truth of petitioners' exculpatory story fully justifies the cross-examination that is at issue.

Despite the importance of cross-examination,[7] we have concluded that the *Miranda* decision compels rejection of the State's position. The warnings mandated by that case, as a prophylactic means of safeguarding Fifth Amendment rights, ... require that a person taken into custody be advised immediately that he has the right to remain silent, that anything he says maybe used against him, and that he has a right to retained or appointed counsel before submitting to interrogation. Silence in the wake of these warnings maybe nothing more than the arrestee's exercise of these *Miranda* rights. Thus, every post-arrest silence is insolubly ambiguous because of what the State is required to advise the person arrested. ... Moreover, while it is true that the *Miranda* warnings contain no express assurance that silence will carry no penalty, such assurance is implicit to any person who receives the warnings. In such circumstances, it would be fundamentally unfair and a deprivation of due process to allow the arrested person's silence to be used to impeach an explanation subsequently offered at trial. Mr. Justice White, concurring in the judgment in United States v. Hale, put it very well:

> "... when a person under arrest is informed as *Miranda* requires, that he may remain silent, that anything he says may be used against him, and that he may have an attorney if he wishes, it seems to me that it does not comport with due process to permit the prosecution during the trial to call attention to his silence at the time of arrest and to insist that because he did not speak about the facts of the case at that time, as he was told he need not do, an unfavorable inference might be drawn as to the truth of his trial testimony. ... Surely Hale was not informed here that his silence, as well as his words, could be used against him at trial. Indeed,

7. We recognize, of course, that unless prosecutors are allowed wide leeway in the scope of impeachment cross-examination some defendants would be able to frustrate the truth-seeking function of a trial by presenting tailored defenses insulated from effective challenge. ...

anyone would reasonably conclude from *Miranda* warnings that this would not be the case."

We hold that the use for impeachment purposes of petitioners' silence, at the time of arrest and after receiving *Miranda* warnings, violated the Due Process Clause of the Fourteenth Amendment.[11] The State has not claimed that such use in the circumstances of this case might have been harmless error. Accordingly, petitioners' convictions are reversed.

* * *

■ MR. JUSTICE STEVENS, with whom MR. JUSTICE BLACKMUN and MR. JUSTICE REHNQUIST join, dissenting.

* * *

I.

The Court's due process rationale has some of the characteristics of an estoppel theory. If (a) the defendant is advised that he may remain silent, and (b) he does remain silent, then we (c) presume that his decision was made in reliance on the advice, and (d) conclude that it is unfair in certain cases, ... to use his silence to impeach his trial testimony. The key to the Court's analysis is apparently a concern that the *Miranda* warning, which is intended to increase the probability that a person's response to police questioning will be intelligent and voluntary, will actually be deceptive unless we require the State to honor an unstated promise not to use the accused's silence against him.

In my judgment there is nothing deceptive or prejudicial to the defendant in the *Miranda* warning. Nor do I believe that the fact that such advice was given to the defendant lessens the probative value of his silence, or makes the prosecutor's cross-examination about his silence any more unfair than if he had received no such warning.

This is a case in which the defendants' silence at the time of their arrest was graphically inconsistent with their trial testimony that they were the unwitting victims of a "frame" in which the police did not participate. If defendants had been framed, their failure to mention that fact at the time of their arrest is almost inexplicable; for that reason, under accepted rules of evidence, their silence is tantamount to a prior inconsistent statement and admissible for purposes of impeachment.

Indeed, there is irony in the fact that the *Miranda* warning provides the only plausible explanation for their silence. If it were the true explanation, I should think that they would have responded to the questions on cross-examination about why they had remained silent by stating that they relied on their understanding of the advice given by the arresting officers. Instead, however, they gave quite a different jumble of responses.[4] Those

11. It goes almost without saying that the fact of post-arrest silence could be used by the prosecution to contradict a defendant who testifies to an exculpatory version of events and claims to have told the police the same version upon arrest. In that situation the fact of earlier silence would not be used to impeach the exculpatory story, but rather to challenge the defendant's testimony as to his behavior following arrest. ...

4. Petitioner Doyle gave the following testimony on direct and cross-examination at his trial:

responses negate the Court's presumption that their silence was induced by reliance on deceptive advice.

Since the record requires us to put to one side the Court's presumption that the defendants' silence was the product of reliance on the *Miranda* warning, the Court's entire due process rationale collapses. For without reliance on the waiver, the case is no different than if no warning had been given, and nothing in the Court's opinion suggests that there would be any unfairness in using petitioners' prior inconsistent silence for impeachment purposes in such a case.

Indeed, as a general proposition, if we assume the defendant's silence would be admissible for impeachment purposes if no *Miranda* warning had been given, I should think that the warning would have a tendency to salvage the defendant's credibility as a witness. If the defendant is a truthful witness, and if his silence is the consequence of his understanding of the *Miranda* warning, he may explain that fact when he is on the stand. Even if he is untruthful, the availability of that explanation puts him in a better position than if he had received no warning. In my judgment, the risk that a truthful defendant will be deceived by the *Miranda* warning and also will be unable to explain his honest misunderstanding is so much less

"Q. [By defense counsel.] And you were placed under arrest at that time?

"A. [By Doyle.] Yes. I asked what for and he said,—'For the sale of marijuana.' I told him,—I didn't know what he was talking about.

* * *

"Q. [By the prosecutor.] As a matter of fact, if I recall your testimony correctly, you said instead of protesting your innocence, as you do today, you said in response to a question of Mr. Beamer,—'I don't know what you are talking about.'

"A. [By Doyle.] I believe what I said,—'What's this all about?' If I remember, that's the only thing I said.

"Q. You testified on direct.

"A. If I did, then I didn't understand.

"Q. [sic] I was questioning, you know, what it was about. That's what I didn't know. I knew that I was trying to buy, which was wrong, but I didn't know what was going on. I don't know that Bill Bonnell was trying to frame me, or what-have-you."

* * *

At Wood's trial, Doyle gave a somewhat different explanation of his silence at the time of arrest:

* * *

"A. The police officers said they stopped us for a red light. I wanted to get my hands on Bill Bonnell.

* * *

"Q. Why didn't you tell the police that Bill Bonnell just set you up?

"A. Because I would rather have my own hands on him.

* * *

"Q. So on the night of April 29 you felt that you were being framed like you are being framed today?

"A. I was so confused that night, the night of the arrest.

* * *

"Q. You didn't talk to a soul about how rotten it was because you were framed?

* * *

"A. I will answer the question, sir, the best I can. I didn't know what to say. I was stunned about what was going on and I was asked questions and I answered the questions as simply as I could because I didn't have nobody thereto help me answer the questions."

* * *

than the risk that exclusion of the evidence will merely provide a shield for perjury that I cannot accept the Court's due process rationale.

Accordingly, if we assume that the use of a defendant's silence for impeachment purposes would be otherwise unobjectionable, I find no merit in the notion that he is denied due process of law because he received a *Miranda* warning.

II.

Petitioners argue that the State violated their Fifth Amendment privilege against self-incrimination by asking the jury to draw an inference of guilt from their constitutionally protected silence. They challenge both the prosecutor's cross-examination and his closing argument.

Petitioners claim that the cross-examination was improper because it referred to their silence at the time of their arrest, to their failure to testify at the preliminary hearing, and to their failure to reveal the "frame" prior to trial. Their claim applies to the testimony of each defendant at his own trial....

In support of their objections to the cross-examination about their silence at the time of arrest, petitioners primarily rely on the statement in Miranda v. Arizona, that the prosecution may not use at trial the fact that the defendant stood mute or claimed the privilege in the face of accusations during custodial interrogation. There are two reasons why that statement does not adequately support petitioners argument.

First, it is not accurate to say that the petitioners "stood mute or claimed the privilege in the face of accusations." Neither petitioner claimed the privilege and petitioner Doyle did not even remain silent. The case is not one in which a description of the actual conversation between the defendants and the police would give rise to any inference of guilt if it were not so flagrantly inconsistent with their trial testimony. Rather than a claim of privilege, we simply have a failure to advise the police of a "frame" at a time when it most surely would have been mentioned if petitioners' trial testimony were true. That failure gave rise to an inference of guilt only because it belied their trial testimony.

* * *

Although I have no doubt concerning the propriety of the cross-examination about petitioners' failure to mention the purported "frame" at the time of their arrest, a more difficult question is presented by their objection to the questioning about their failure to testify at the preliminary hearing and their failure generally to mention the "frame" before trial.[10]

10. Under Ohio law, the preliminary hearing determines only whether the defendant should be held for trial. The prosecution need establish, at most, that a crime has been committed and that there is "probable and reasonable cause" to hold the defendant for trial, and the court need only find "substantial credible evidence" of the charge against the defendant. Defense counsel thus will have no incentive to divulge the defendant's case at the preliminary hearing if the prosecution has presented substantial evidence of guilt. Since that was the case here, no significant impeaching inference maybe drawn from petitioners' silence at that proceeding.

Petitioners' failure to refer to the "frame" at any time between arrest and trial is somewhat more probative; for if the

Unlike the failure to make the kind of spontaneous comment that discovery of a "frame" would be expected to prompt, there is no significant inconsistency between petitioners' trial testimony and their adherence to counsel's advice not to take the stand at the preliminary hearing; moreover, the decision not to divulge their defense prior to trial is probably attributable to counsel rather than to petitioners. Nevertheless, unless and until this Court overrules Raffel v. United States, I think a state court is[11] free to regard the defendant's decision to take the stand as a waiver of his objection to the use of his failure to testify at an earlier proceeding or his failure to offer his version of the events prior to trial.

Jenkins v. Anderson

Supreme Court of the United States, 1980.
447 U.S. 231, 100 S.Ct. 2124.

■ MR. JUSTICE POWELL delivered the opinion of the Court.

* * *

... The petitioner stabbed and killed Doyle Redding. The petitioner was not apprehended until he turned himself in to governmental authorities about two weeks later. At his state trial for first-degree murder, the petitioner contended that the killing was in self-defense.

The petitioner testified that his sister and her boyfriend were robbed by Redding and another man during the evening of August 12, 1974. The petitioner, who was nearby when the robbery occurred, followed the thieves a short distance and reported their whereabouts to the police. According to the petitioner's testimony, the next day he encountered Redding, who accused him of informing the police of the robbery. The petitioner stated that Redding attacked him with a knife, that the two men struggled briefly, and that the petitioner broke away. On cross-examination, the petitioner admitted that during the struggle he had tried "[t]o push that knife into

"frame" story were true, one would have expected counsel to try to persuade the prosecution to dismiss the charges in advance of trial.

11. *Raffel* was the last decision of this Court to address the constitutionality of admitting evidence of a defendant's prior silence to impeach his testimony upon direct examination. Raffel had been charged with conspiracy to violate the National Prohibition Act. An agent testified at his first trial that he had admitted ownership of a drinking place; Raffel did not take the stand. The trial ended in a hung jury, and upon retrial, the agent testified as before. Raffel elected to testify and denied making the statement, but he was cross-examined on his failure to testify in the first trial. This Court held that the evidence was admissible because Raffel had completely waived the privilege against self-incrimination by deciding to testify.

Subsequent cases, decided in the exercise of this Court's supervisory powers, have diminished the force of *Raffel* in the federal courts. United States v. Hale. Stewart v. United States. Grunewald v. United States. All three of these cases held that the defendant's prior silence or prior claim of the privilege was inadmissible for purposes of impeachment; all three distinguished *Raffel* on the ground that the Court there assumed that the defendant's prior silence was significantly inconsistent with his testimony on direct examination. Two of the three cases relied upon the need to protect the defendant's exercise of the privilege against self-incrimination from unwarranted inferences of guilt, a rationale that is not easily reconciled with the reasoning in *Raffel* that the decision to testify constitutes a complete waiver of the protection afforded by the privilege.

[Redding] as far as [he] could," but maintained that he had acted solely in self-defense.

During the cross-examination, the prosecutor questioned the petitioner about his actions after the stabbing:

> "Q. And I suppose you waited for the Police to tell them what happened?
>
> "A. No, I didn't.
>
> "Q. You didn't?
>
> "A. No.
>
> "Q. I see.
>
> "And how long was it after this day that you were arrested, or that you were taken into custody?"
>
> After some discussion of the date on which petitioner surrendered, the prosecutor continued:
>
> "Q. When was the first time that you reported the things that you have told us in Court today to anybody?
>
> "A. Two days after it happened.
>
> "Q. And who did you report it to?
>
> "A. To my probation officer.
>
> "Q. Well, apart from him?
>
> "A. No one.
>
> "Q. Who?
>
> "A. No one but my—
>
> "Q. (Interposing) Did you ever go to a Police Officer or to anyone else?
>
> "A. No, I didn't.
>
> "Q. As a matter of fact, it was two weeks later, wasn't it?
>
> "A. Yes."

In closing argument to the jury, the prosecutor again referred to the petitioner's prearrest silence. The prosecutor noted that petitioner had "waited two weeks, according to the testimony—at least two weeks before he did anything about surrendering himself or reporting [the stabbing] to anybody." The prosecutor contended that the petitioner had committed murder in retaliation for the robbery the night before.

The petitioner was convicted of manslaughter. . . .

* * *

This Court's decision in Raffel v. United States (1926), recognized that the Fifth Amendment is not violated when a defendant who testifies in his own defense is impeached with his prior silence.

It can be argued that a person facing arrest will not remain silent if his failure to speak later can be used to impeach him. But the Constitution does not forbid "every government-imposed choice in the criminal process that has the effect of discouraging the exercise of constitutional rights." Chaffin v. Stynchcombe (1973).

The " 'threshold question is whether compelling the election impairs to an appreciable extent any of the policies behind the rights involved.' " Chaffin v. Stynchcombe, supra. The *Raffel* Court explicitly rejected the contention that the possibility of impeachment by prior silence is an impermissible burden upon the exercise of Fifth Amendment rights. "We are unable to see that the rule that [an accused who] testified ... must testify fully, adds in any substantial manner to the inescapable embarrassment which the accused must experience in determining whether he shall testify or not."

This Court similarly defined the scope of the Fifth Amendment protection in *Harris v. New York* (1971). There the Court held that a statement taken in violation of *Miranda* may be used to impeach a defendant's credibility. Rejecting the contention that such impeachment violates the Fifth Amendment, the Court said:

> "Every criminal defendant is privileged to testify in his own defense, or to refuse to do so. But that privilege cannot be construed to include the right to commit perjury. ... Having voluntarily taken the stand, petitioner was under an obligation to speak truthfully and accurately, and the prosecution here did not more than utilize the traditional truth-testing devices of the adversary process."

In determining whether a constitutional right has been burdened impermissibly, it also is appropriate to consider the legitimacy of the challenged governmental practice. Attempted impeachment on cross-examination of a defendant, the practice at issue here, may enhance the reliability of the criminal process. Use of such impeachment on cross-examination allows prosecutors to test the credibility of witnesses by asking them to explain prior inconsistent statements and acts. A defendant may decide not to take the witness stand because of the risk of cross-examination. But this is a choice of litigation tactics.

Thus, impeachment follows the defendant's own decision to cast aside his cloak of silence and advances the truth finding function of the criminal trial. We conclude that the Fifth Amendment is not violated by the use of prearrest silence to impeach a criminal defendant's credibility.

The petitioner also contends that use of prearrest silence to impeach his credibility denied him the fundamental fairness guaranteed by the Fourteenth Amendment. We do not agree. Common law traditionally has allowed witnesses to be impeached by their previous failure to state a fact in circumstances in which that fact naturally would have been asserted.

Only in Doyle v. Ohio (1976), did we find that impeachment by silence violated the Constitution. In that case, a defendant received the warnings required by Miranda v. Arizona, when he was arrested for selling marihuana.

* * *

In this case, no governmental action induced petitioner to remain silent before arrest. The failure to speak occurred before the petitioner was taken into custody and given *Miranda* warnings. Consequently, the fundamental unfairness present in *Doyle* is not present in this case. We hold that impeachment by use of prearrest silence does not violate the Fourteenth Amendment.

Our decision today does not force any state court to allow impeachment through the use of prearrest silence. Each jurisdiction remains free to formulate evidentiary rules defining the situations in which silence is viewed as more probative than prejudicial. We merely conclude that the use of prearrest silence to impeach a defendant's credibility does not violate the Constitution. The judgment of the Court of Appeals is

Affirmed.

■ MR. JUSTICE STEWART concurs in the judgment.

■ MR. JUSTICE STEVENS, concurring in the judgment.

[Opinion Omitted]

■ MR. JUSTICE MARSHALL, with whom MR. JUSTICE BRENNAN joins, dissenting.

* * *

The Court's holding that a criminal defendant's testimony may be impeached by his prearrest silence has three patent—and, in my view, fatal—defects. First, the mere fact of prearrest silence is so unlikely to be probative of the falsity of the defendant's trial testimony that its use for impeachment purposes is contrary to the Due Process Clause of the Fourteenth Amendment. Second, the drawing of an adverse inference from the failure to volunteer incriminating statements impermissibly infringes the privilege against self-incrimination. Third, the availability of the inference for impeachment purposes impermissibly burdens the decision to exercise the constitutional right to testify in one's own defense.

The use of prior silence for impeachment purposes depends, as the majority recognizes ... on the reasonableness of an inference that it is inconsistent with the statements that are to be impeached. If the defendant's prior silence does not make it more likely that his trial testimony was false, the evidence is simply irrelevant. Such an inference cannot fairly be drawn from petitioner's failure to go to the police before any charges were brought, admit that he had committed a homicide, and offer an exculpatory explanation.

In order for petitioner to offer his explanation of self-defense, he would necessarily have had to admit that it was he who fatally stabbed the victim, thereby supplying against himself the strongest possible proof of an essential element of criminal homicide. It is hard to imagine a purer case of self-incrimination. Since we cannot assume that in the absence of official warnings individuals are ignorant of or oblivious to their constitutional rights, we must recognize that petitioner may have acted in reliance on the constitutional guarantee. In fact, petitioner had most likely been informed previously of his privilege against self-incrimination, since he had two prior felony convictions. One who has at least twice before been given the *Miranda* warnings, which carry the implied promise that silence will not be penalized by use for impeachment purposes, Doyle v. Ohio (1976), may well remember the rights of which he has been informed, and believe that the promise is still in force. Accordingly, the inference that petitioner's conduct was inconsistent with his exculpatory trial testimony is precluded.

Moreover, other possible explanations for silence spring readily to mind. It is conceivable that a person who had acted in self-defense might believe that he had committed no crime and therefore had no call to explain himself to the police. Indeed, all the witnesses agreed that after the stabbing the victim ran across the street and climbed a flight of stairs before collapsing. Initially, at least, then, petitioner might not have known that there was a homicide to explain. Moreover, petitioner testified that he feared retaliation if he went to the police. One need not be persuaded that any of these possible explanations represents the true reason for petitioner's conduct to recognize that the availability of other plausible hypotheses vitiates the inference on which the admissibility of the evidence depends.

* * *

Since petitioner's failure to report and explain his actions prior to his arrest was not probative of the falsity of his testimony at trial, it was fundamentally unfair and a deprivation of due process to allow the jury to draw from that silence an inference that his trial testimony was false.

The use of prearrest silence for impeachment purposes also violates the privilege against self-incrimination secured by the Fifth and Fourteenth Amendments. The privilege prohibits the government from imposing upon citizens any duty to present themselves to the authorities and report their own wrongdoing. As I have explained, in order to offer his exculpatory explanation petitioner would inevitably have had to incriminate himself as to facts that would be crucial in any subsequent prosecution. To penalize him for failing to relinquish his privilege against self-incrimination by permitting the jury to draw an adverse inference from his silence is to place an impermissible burden on his exercise of the privilege. In practical effect, it replaces the privilege against self-incrimination with a duty to incriminate oneself. The Court attempts to avoid this conclusion by asserting that the burden does not threaten the purposes underlying the Fifth Amendment. But it is hard to see how the burden could be more substantial or direct.

* * *

Finally, impeachment by prearrest silence impermissibly burdens the constitutionally protected decision to testify in one's own defense.

Under today's decision a defendant who did not report his conduct to the police at the first possible moment must, in deciding whether to testify in his own defense, take into account the possibility that if he does testify the jury may be permitted to add that omission to the reasons for disbelieving his defense. This means that a person who thinks he may have done something wrong must immediately decide, most likely without the assistance of counsel, whether, if he is ever charged with an offense and brought to trial, he may wish to take the stand. For if he may later want to take the stand, he had better go to the police station right away to preserve his exculpatory explanation of the events—even though in so doing he must incriminate himself and provide evidence which may be crucial to his eventual conviction. But if he decides not to incriminate himself, he may anticipate that his right to testify in his own defense will be undetermined by the argument that his story is probably untrue because he did not volunteer it to the police at the earliest opportunity. All of these strategic decisions must be made before the individual even knows if he will be charged and of what offense he will be accused.

To force persons to make this kind of choice between two fundamental rights places an intolerable burden on the exercise of those rights. "It cuts down on the privilege [of testifying in one's own defense] by making its assertion costly," Griffin v. California and is therefore forbidden.

* * *

NOTES

1. A defendant may, of course, open the door to inquiry about his failure to tell his story the first time he had a chance to do so.

In one case the defendant himself brought out his refusal on direct examination and it was held that the prosecution could then cross-examine as to why he did not turn himself in or assert self defense then. People v. Shugar, 29 Mich.App. 139, 185 N.W.2d 178 (1970). See United States v. Mitchell, 457 F.2d 513 (6th Cir.1972) (defense asked why there was not further investigation after arrest, explanation was lack of exculpatory statement). Or defendant claims that he tried to tell the police his story and was not allowed to do so. See United States v. Shue, 766 F.2d 1122 (7th Cir.1985) (claim of cooperation with police opens the door to impeachment with fact of refusal to speak but not to claim that silence is evidence of guilt); United States v. Blalock, 564 F.2d 1180 (5th Cir.1977) (claim by accused that he cooperated with the police opens him to inquiry about prior refusal to speak).

2. What if the defendant did make a statement to the police and he testifies in a similar fashion at trial but gives additional, important information he omitted from his police statement. May he be impeached by his omission. An omission from a statement is not equated with silence in the face of an accusation. Anderson v. Charles, 447 U.S. 404, 408, 100 S.Ct. 2180, 2182 (1980). Silence may also be admissible when it is part of a larger occurrence, i.e. failure, as opposed to refusal, to answer one question out of several asked and answered. United States v. Lorenzo, 570 F.2d 294 (9th Cir.1978); People v. Chriswell, 133 Ill.App.3d 458, 88 Ill.Dec. 568, 478 N.E.2d 1176 (1985). But see Younie v. State, 272 Md. 233, 322 A.2d 211 (1974).

3. A troublesome question has been whether certain evidence implies that defendant exercised his right to silence.

In United States v. Cook, 432 F.2d 1093 (7th Cir.1970), the court rejected an argument that, after completion of a lengthy interrogation, evidence that defendant asked and was allowed to leave constituted a reference to an assertion of the right to silence. In State v. Finn, 111 Ariz. 271, 528 P.2d 615 (1974), it was held that the phrase "I would be crazy to tell you that" was not an assertion of rights. Compare Commonwealth v. Cobb, 374 Mass. 514, 373 N.E.2d 1145 (1978) (improper to show accused said "what can I say?" in response to inquiry about location of a weapon).

In United States v. Davenport, 929 F.2d 1169 (7th Cir.1991), the Court dealt with the admissibility of the refusal to answer some questions among many they did answer. The Court said:

> "The Davenports were told that they didn't have to answer the agent's questions. As they were not in custody, there was no implicit threat if they kept mum. They decided to answer the agent's questions, no doubt hoping that they could satisfy him and ward off further investigation. As an original matter, we would incline to the view that once they started down this path of self-exculpation, any statement they made—including" I won't tell you"—was fair game.
>
> * * *
>
> What about the questions the Davenports *didn't* answer, such as the question asked Mrs. Davenport what her father-in-law's name was? The agent did not compel her to answer. But at trial the prosecution used her refusal to answer against her. Did the government by doing so break the agent's promise that she didn't have to answer his questions, implying that her silence would not be a subject of comment at trial? If she had said she wouldn't answer his questions, that would have been the end of it; and having told her that she didn't have to answer his questions, the agent could not have commented on her silence at the trial. But had she a privilege to weave a tapestry of evasions? Or, once she began answering questions about the offense, was it too late to rewind the tape? The agent had not said, "If you answer my questions and when you're through repent your decision to talk to me, I won't testify about our conversation." He gave her the option not to answer his questions and it is arguable that when she declined it, all bets were off; that no understanding was violated when he testified to the full range of her answers, including refusals to answer.

4. Is there any difference between the introduction of post-warning silence as probative of defendant's conduct and the introduction of post-warning silence as probative of the defendant's sanity? The Supreme Court held such use of silence constitutionally impermissible as evidence of sanity. See Wainwright v. Greenfield, 474 U.S. 284, 106 S.Ct. 634 (1986).

5. In Fletcher v. Weir, 455 U.S. 603, 102 S.Ct. 1309 (1982), in a per curiam opinion, the Supreme Court reached the issue of whether an accused can be cross-examined about his "failure" to give his exculpatory version of events after his arrest during a custodial period in which he was not given *Miranda* warnings. The Court held that his silence under these circumstances could be used for impeachment. It emphasized that the rationale of *Doyle* depended upon implicit governmental assurance, through warnings, that the suspect's silence would not be used against him:

> In the absence of the sort of affirmative assurance embodied in the Miranda warnings, we do not believe that it violates due process of law for a State to permit cross-examination as to post-arrest silence when a defendant chooses to take the stand.

Justices Marshall and Brennan dissented from the summary reversal, but neither wrote an opinion.

On remand both a federal magistrate and a district judge criticized the Supreme Court's reasoning in *Weir* but reluctantly accepted the result. The Court of Appeals reconciled itself to the decision by noting that the case involved only situations where defendants have testified and observing that in such cases the defendants always have the option of explaining why they contend that silence was not probative of guilt. See Weir v. Wilson, 744 F.2d 532 (6th Cir.1984). See also State v. Robinson, 496 A.2d 1067 (Me.1985) (admissible even though one not in custody is given unnecessary warnings).

6. When a suspect has consulted with counsel before his arrest and later is put on trial, may the prosecutor draw the jury's attention to that fact at trial? Does proof of consultation with counsel have any probative value? Does it create the possibility of unfair prejudice? Would any provision of the United States Constitution prohibit such comment? See People v. Collins, 140 A.D.2d 186, 528 N.Y.S.2d 41 (1988). *Collins* condemned extensive focus by the prosecutor on the suspect's consultation with counsel, resting its opinion largely upon state law grounds.

In 1972, a woman either was pushed or hurled herself through a sturdy glass window and fell to her death from an upper floor of a Chicago high-rise. It was alleged that, within a very few minutes, the man whose apartment the woman had departed telephoned the most prestigious criminal defense attorney in town. If the man had been prosecuted, would the fact of that call have been probative of guilt? Is it probative in your own mind? In somewhat an analogous situation, one court has held that a prosecutor cannot use consultation with an attorney as evidence of guilt. See Sizemore v. Fletcher, 921 F.2d 667 (6th Cir.1990).

Gordon v. United States

United States Court of Appeals, District of Columbia Circuit, 1967.
127 U.S.App.D.C. 343, 383 F.2d 936, cert.denied 390 U.S. 1029, 88 S.Ct. 1421 (1968).

■ BURGER, CIRCUIT JUDGE.

Appellant was convicted of robbery and assault with a dangerous weapon....

... Appellant claims that the District Court Judge abused the discretion vested in him by Luck v. United States, 348 F.2d 763 (1965), when he permitted the government to impeach Appellant's testimony by showing prior convictions. ...

Because of the direct conflict in the evidence the verdict necessarily turned on how the jury resolved the credibility contest between the complainant and the defendant. Appellant's argument now is that while it was appropriate for him to impeach the complaining witness with a prior criminal record [for larceny] it was improper to allow impeachment of his own credibility by asking him about his criminal convictions. ...

The rationale of our *Luck* opinion is important; it recognized that a showing of prior convictions can have genuine probative value on the issue of credibility, but that because of the potential for prejudice, the receiving of such convictions as impeachment was discretionary. The defendant who has a criminal record may ask the court to weigh the probative value of the convictions as to the credibility against the degree of prejudice which the revelation of his past crimes would cause; and he may ask the court to consider whether it is more important for the jury to hear his story than to know about prior convictions in relation to his credibility. We contemplated the possibility of allowing some convictions to be shown and some excluded; examples are to be found in those which are remote and those which have no direct bearing on veracity, and those which because of the peculiar circumstances at hand might better be excluded. The *Luck* opinion contemplated an on-the-record consideration by the trial judge whose action would be reviewable only for abuse of discretion, and that once the exercise of discretion appeared, the trial court's action be "accorded a respect appropriately reflective of the inescapable remoteness of appellate review." This is a recognition that the cold record on appeal cannot present all facets and elements which the trial judge must weigh in striking the balance.

Luck also contemplated that it was for the defendant to present to the trial court sufficient reasons for withholding past convictions from the jury in the face of a statute which makes such convictions admissible. The underlying assumption was that prior convictions would ordinarily be admissible unless this burden is met. "The trial court is not *required* to allow impeachment by prior conviction every time a defendant takes the stand in his own defense."

The standard to be applied by the District Judge was stated in terms of whether he "believes the prejudicial effect of impeachment far outweighs the probative relevance of the prior conviction to the issue of credibility." The impact of criminal convictions will often be damaging to an accused and it is admittedly difficult to restrict its impact, by cautionary instructions, to the issue of credibility. The test of *Luck*, however, is that to bar them as impeachment the court must find that the prejudice must "far outweigh" the probative relevance to credibility, or that even if relevant the "cause of truth would be helped more by letting the jury hear the defendant's story than by the defendant's foregoing that opportunity because of the fear of prejudice founded upon a prior conviction."

The burden of persuasion in this regard is on the accused; and, once the issue is raised, the District Court should make an inquiry, allowing the accused an opportunity to show why judicial discretion should be exercised in favor of exclusion of the criminal record.[8] This, admittedly, places a very difficult burden on trial judges and some added guidelines are needed even at risk of adding to the burdens of the trial courts.

In considering how the District Court is to exercise the discretionary power we granted, we must look to the legitimate purpose of impeachment which is, of course, not to show that the accused who takes the stand is a "bad" person but rather to show background facts which bear directly on whether jurors ought to believe him rather than other and conflicting witnesses. In common human experience acts of deceit, fraud, cheating, or stealing, for example, are universally regarded as conduct which reflects adversely on a man's honesty and integrity. Acts of violence on the other hand, which may result from a short temper, a combative nature, extreme provocation, or other causes, generally have little or no direct bearing on

8. It must be remembered that the prior conviction involved in *Luck* was a guilty plea. The relevance of prior convictions to credibility may well be different as between a case where the conviction of the accused was by admission of guilt by a plea and on the other hand a case where the accused affirmatively contested the charge and testified, for example, that he was not present and did not commit the acts charged. In the latter situation the accused affirmatively puts his own veracity in issue when he testifies so that the jury's verdict amounted to rejection of his testimony; the verdict is in a sense a de facto finding that the accused did not tell the truth when sworn to do so. Exploration of this area risks a diversion which may well be time consuming; hence use of this inquiry should be limited.

honesty and veracity. A "rule of thumb" thus should be that convictions which rest on dishonest conduct relate to credibility whereas those of violent or assaultive crimes generally do not; traffic violations, however serious, are in the same category. The nearness or remoteness of the prior conviction is also a factor of no small importance. Even one involving fraud or stealing, for example, if it occurred long before and has been followed by a legally blameless life, should generally be excluded on the ground of remoteness.

A special and even more difficult problem arises when the prior conviction is for the same or substantially the same conduct for which the accused is on trial. Where multiple convictions of various kinds can be shown, strong reasons arise for excluding those which are for the same crime because of the inevitable pressure on lay jurors to believe that "if he did it before he probably did so this time." As a general guide, those convictions which are for the same crime should be admitted sparingly; one solution might well be that discretion be exercised to limit the impeachment by way of a similar crime to a single conviction and then only when the circumstances indicate strong reasons for disclosure, and where the conviction directly relates to veracity.

Of course, there are many other factors that may be relevant in deciding whether or not to exclude prior convictions in a particular case. One important consideration is what the effect will be if the defendant does not testify out of fear of being prejudiced because of impeachment by prior convictions. Even though a judge might find that the prior convictions are relevant to credibility and the risk of prejudice to the defendant does not warrant their exclusion, he may nevertheless conclude that it is more important that the jury have the benefit of the defendant's version of the case than to have the defendant remain silent out of fear of impeachment.[11]

We recognize the undesirability of prolonging the trial unduly when the court is already confronted with requirements which work to that end, but in many cases the best way for the District Judge to evaluate the situation is to have the accused take the stand in a nonjury hearing and elicit his testimony and allow cross examination before resolving the *Luck* issue. Not only the trial judge, but both counsel, would then be in a better position to make decisions concerning the impeachment issue. Of course, the defendant could not be compelled to give testimony in the non-jury

11. This weighing process would occur only where it has been determined that the prior convictions are otherwise admissible. Having made that determination, the judge would then consider whether the defendant's testimony is so important that he should not be forced to elect between staying silent—risking prejudice due to the jury's going without one version of the facts—and testifying—risking prejudice through exposure of his criminal past. In this regard, the judge may want to evaluate just how relevant to credibility the prior convictions are; for example, a recent perjury conviction would be difficult to ignore even where the defendant's testimony would be of great importance. This could well be true as to a multiplicity of convictions for crimes of dishonesty referred to earlier. On the other hand, where an instruction relative to inferences arising from unexplained possession of recently stolen property is permissible, the importance of the defendant's testimony becomes more acute. See Smith v. United States, 123 U.S.App.D.C. 259, 359 F.2d 243 (1966).

hearing and his testimony taken at the non-jury hearing would not be admissible in evidence except for impeachment.

We are well aware that these are not firm guidelines which can be applied readily as though they were part of the structure of the Federal Rules of Criminal Procedure; the very nature of judicial discretion precludes rigid standards for its exercise; we seek to give some assistance to the trial judge to whom we have assigned the extremely difficult task of weighing and balancing these elusive concepts. Surely, it would be much simpler if prior convictions of an accused were totally admissible or totally excludable as impeachment; but in the face of an explicit, unambiguous statute allowing use of prior convictions and the holding in *Luck* we have little choice. The lesser step has been taken in *Luck* saying that the statute is to be read as permitting a discretion in the trial judge.

Even though we need not go beyond Appellant's failure to raise the issue he now relies on, we note that the admission of Appellant's criminal record here, along with the criminal record of the complaining witness, was not in a vindictive or "eye for an eye" sense, as Appellant argues. Rather it was received because the case had narrowed to the credibility of two persons—the accused and his accuser—and in those circumstances there was greater, not less, compelling reason for exploring all avenues which would shed light on which of the two witnesses was to be believed. The jurors saw and heard both and we are able to see and hear neither. None of the other contentions urged by Appellant affords a basis for disturbing the judgment.

Affirmed.

NOTES

1. The general rule among the states allowing for impeachment by prior conviction is derived from the ancient common law rule that conviction of a person of treason or any felony, or of a misdemeanor involving dishonesty, or the obstruction of justice rendered the person totally incompetent as a witness. Wigmore, Evidence (Chadbourn rev. 1961) §§ 980, 980a, 985–987. By statutes everywhere, disqualification was eliminated and by specific provision or decision, conviction for a crime was reduced to grounds for impeachment of credibility. The definitions of crimes for which a conviction became grounds for impeachment varied widely among the states. People v. Birdette, 22 Ill.2d 577, 177 N.E.2d 170 (1961) (infamous crimes); West's Ann.Cal.Evid.Code, § 788 (only felonies); Sims v. Callahan, 269 Ala. 216, 112 So.2d 776 (1959) (offenses involving moral turpitude); State v. Hurt, 49 N.J. 114, 228 A.2d 673 (1967) (any felony or misdemeanor). The Uniform Rules of Evidence, Rule 21, limit impeachment to conviction of crimes "involving dishonesty or false statement."

One court reversed its judicially created rule allowing impeachment by prior conviction. In State v. McAboy, 160 W.Va. 497, 236 S.E.2d 431 (1977), the Court said:

* * *

> "Even if the relevancy issue were conceded, there are unquestionable prejudicial consequences flowing from the practice of allowing prior conviction impeachment. One of the most significant is that it has a chilling

effect as it keeps the defendant with a prior conviction from becoming a witness in his own behalf.

"Statistical evidence supporting the theory that the threat of the use of prior convictions operates to keep the defendant from taking the witness stand is found in Kalvin & Zeizel, The American Jury, Table 43, page 160 (1966). The cases sampled were ranked in three categories: clear for acquittal, close, and clear for conviction. In the average of all categories the defendant with no record testified in 91% of the cases, while the defendant with a record testified in 74% of the cases. Of even more significance was the category where the case was clear for acquittal. The defendant without a record testified 90% of the time, while the defendant with a record testified only 53% of the time.

"As to the prejudicial effect on the jury, Table 52 in The American Jury, supra, at page 160, reveals that in the cases sampled where the defendant had no record and took the stand, the acquittal rate was 65%. In contrast with cases sampled of the same quality of evidence where the defendant did not take the stand, the acquittal rate was 38%.

* * *

... In returning the law in this area to its status before *Friedman*, we believe that we attain a more harmonious result with the general law as to impeachment of a defendant's character and reputation. This also follows a settled trend in the law to remove the common law restrictions that bar the accused criminal from effectively asserting his defenses.

"Thus far, we have discussed generally the reasons for re-establishing the earlier rule followed by this Court up to the *Friedman* case. We have noted that this rule prohibited the use of evidence of prior criminal convictions to impeach the defendant's credibility. It has been pointed out that under this rule, there was the recognized exception that if the defendant elected to place his good character in issue, evidence of prior convictions could then be introduced along with other relevant evidence bearing on bad character.

"Another exception to the general prohibition against impeachment of the defendant by evidence of his prior convictions which we believe is appropriate is a prior conviction of perjury or false swearing. Conviction of these crimes goes directly to the credibility of the defendant and, in our judgment, their relevancy has a priority over their possible prejudicial effect.

"What has been said about the use of prior criminal convictions to impeach the defendant if he elects to testify is not meant to alter our existing law in regard to other witnesses. As to such other witnesses, the rule is that it rests within the sound discretion of the trial court whether a prior conviction may be shown to impeach his credibility.

"The difference between the two rules is measured by the ultimate penalty arising from the possible prejudice. With a witness, the use of a prior conviction to impeach credibility may result in some loss of credibility in the eyes of the jury and attendant personal embarrassment. With the defendant, the prejudicial effect of a prior conviction may result in an unwarranted conviction."

2. In Loper v. Beto, 405 U.S. 473, 92 S.Ct. 1014 (1972), the Court held that prior convictions could not be used for impeachment of defendant if the defendant had not been represented by counsel at the time of prior conviction.

3. *Federal Rule of Evidence 609* now controls the use of impeachment evidence prosecuting limits on use of certain types of convictions and of convictions more than ten years past. The rule still permits a broad range of uses.

Suppose that the court rules that it will admit the conviction if the accused testifies and thereafter the accused declines to testify. If the court erred in its ruling that the conviction would have been admissible, is the accused entitled to an automatic reversal? Must he make an offer if proof as to what his testimony would have been so that the court can assess a prosecution claim of harmless error? Should the court speculate as to whether the trial judge's ruling was the real reason why the accused declined to testify. The United States Supreme Court resolved the issue in so far as the federal courts are concerned. In Luce v. United States, 469 U.S. 38, 105 S.Ct. 460 (1984), the unanimous Court held that the claim of error is not preserved unless the defendant testifies. It suggested that a reviewing court cannot possibly make the required harmless error calculation in the absence of actual testimony by the defendant. Moreover, the Court expressed fears of "planting error" by defendants who really had no intention of testifying even if not subject to impeachment use of their prior convictions.

F. COURTROOM CONDUCT

American Bar Association Standards (3d Ed. 1993)

Section 3–5.2 Courtroom Decorum (Prosecution Function)

(a) As an officer of the court, the prosecutor should support the authority of the court and the dignity of the trial courtroom by strict adherence to the rules of decorum and by manifesting an attitude of professional respect toward the judge, opposing counsel, witnesses, defendants, jurors and others in the courtroom.

(b) When court is in session the prosecutor should address the court, not opposing counsel, on all matters relating to the case.

(c) A prosecutor should comply promptly with all orders and directives of the court, but the prosecutor has a duty to have the record reflect adverse rulings or judicial conduct which the prosecutor considers prejudicial. He has a right to make respectful requests for reconsideration of adverse rulings.

(d) Prosecutors should cooperate with courts and the organized bar in developing codes of professionalism for each jurisdiction.

Section 4–7.1 Courtroom Decorum (Defense Function)

(a) As an officer of the court, defense counsel should support the authority of the court and the dignity of the trial courtroom by strict adherence to the codes of professionalism and by manifesting a professional attitude toward the judge, opposing counsel, witnesses, jurors, and others in the courtroom.

(b) Defense counsel should not engage in unauthorized ex parte discussions with or submission of material to a judge relating to a particular case which may or may not come before the judge.

(c) When court is in session defense counsel should address the court and should not address the prosecutor directly on any matter relating to the case.

(d) Defense counsel should comply promptly with all orders and directives of the court, but he has a duty to have the record reflect adverse rulings or judicial conduct which he considers prejudicial to his client's legitimate interests. Defense counsel has a right to make respectful requests for reconsideration of adverse rulings.

(e) Lawyers should cooperate with courts and the organized bar in developing codes of professionalism for each jurisdiction.

Section 3–5.4(b) [4–7.3(b)] Attitudes Toward the Jury

(b) The prosecutor [defense counsel] should treat jurors with deference and respect, avoiding the reality or appearance of currying favor by a show of undue solicitude for their comfort or convenience.

Section 3–5.6 [4–7.5] Presentation of Evidence

(a) A prosecutor [defense counsel] should not knowingly offer false evidence, whether by documents, tangible evidence, or the testimony of witnesses, or fail to seek withdrawal thereof [take reasonable remedial measures] upon discovery of its falsity.

(b) A prosecutor [defense counsel] should not knowingly and for the purpose of bringing inadmissible matter to the attention of the judge or jury offer inadmissible evidence, ask legally objectionable questions, or make other impermissible comments or arguments in the presence of the judge or jury.

(c) A prosecutor [defense counsel] should not permit any tangible evidence to be displayed in the view of the judge or jury which would tend to prejudice fair consideration by the judge or jury until such time as a good faith tender of such evidence is made.

(d) A prosecutor [defense counsel] should not tender tangible evidence in the view of the judge or jury if it would tend to prejudice fair consideration by the judge or jury unless there is a reasonable basis for its admission in evidence. When there is any substantial doubt about the admissibility of such evidence, it should be tendered by an offer of proof and a ruling obtained.

NOTE

What would occur if one attorney followed the rules and the other did not? Should the attorney following the rules continue to do so? Of course, an attorney who is blatant in his violation of the accepted standards of courtroom conduct will alienate both court and jury and his opponent need not worry. But subtle evasions of the rules may damage the opposition and the court may not be strong enough or determined enough to stop the culpable lawyer.

The most commonly effective, but improper, tactics are those which are designed to annoy opposing counsel, those which are designed to convey to the jury the unfavorable impression arising from adverse court rulings and from the court's personal bias toward the attorney or his client, and those which are designed to show less than a respectful attitude toward opposing counsel or his witnesses. If these tactics are used by one lawyer, should the other lawyer respond in kind? Further, a lawyer who is too dispassionate in his courtroom practices may run the risk of impressing the jury that he does not care about his case or he has no confidence in its merits. One generally accepted principle among criminal lawyers is that counsel must adopt a courtroom demeanor fairly consistent with his out-of-court personality. A volatile man will appear artificial in court if he keeps too tight a rein on himself and so will a methodical man who tries a flamboyant style. Do the A.B.A. Standards ignore these facts of life?

G. ADDRESSING THE JURY

1. OPENING STATEMENTS

Gladden v. Frazier

United States Court of Appeals, Ninth Circuit, 1968.
388 F.2d 777, affirmed 394 U.S. 731, 89 S.Ct. 1420 (1969).

■ MADDEN, JUDGE.

The appellee Frazier was convicted in 1965 of second degree murder....

Frazier and Rawls, a cousin of Frazier, were jointly indicted by the Oregon authorities for the murder of one Marleau. Rawls made a confession to the Oregon authorities, first orally and then in a writing signed by him, which confession deeply implicated Frazier in the killing. Rawls later pleaded guilty to second degree murder and when Frazier's trial took place, had not yet been sentenced on his plea of guilty.

In Frazier's trial, the Oregon prosecutor, in his opening statement to the jury, stated in considerable detail the evidence which he intended to present, naming the witness or witnesses who would testify to the several items of evidence. He stated that he expected Rawls to testify to the commission of the crime, and recited what Rawls' testimony would be. He did not say that Rawls had confessed. When the prosecutor had completed his opening statement, Frazier's defense counsel moved for a mistrial. The court denied the motion. The prosecutor had subpoenaed Rawls, and called him to the witness stand. When questioned, Rawls claimed the privilege against self-incrimination and refused to answer the prosecutor's questions. The trial judge sustained Rawls' claim of privilege, and Rawls left the witness stand. Frazier's defense counsel again moved for a mistrial, and the motion was again denied. The prosecuting attorney, in the course of a lengthy trial, made no other reference to any statement made by Rawls.

The events above recited constituted one of the grounds on which the district court based his grant of Frazier's application for the writ of habeas corpus. The court held that the prosecutor's recital, in his opening statement, of what testimony he expected from Rawls, while the prosecutor held in his hand several papers, one of which was Rawls' signed confession, and read several times from that paper, was, in effect, the introduction before the jury of Rawls' statement, as to which Frazier's counsel had no opportunity to cross-examine Rawls.

In any case in which counsel for a litigant elects to make an opening statement outlining to the jury the substance of what he expects to prove, and naming the witnesses by which he hopes to prove it, rather than leaving it to the jury to pick up the thread of the continued story from the succession of incidents, each incident testified to by a separate witness, there is the possibility that the testimony which counsel has spoken of will never materialize on the witness stand. The expected witness may die or disappear or may effectively claim a privilege not to testify, or some person who has the right to prevent the witness from testifying may assert that right. If it happens that counsel does not get the expected testimony, he has to do the best he can without it. If he can prove his case without it, he may still win. But a rule that a mistrial must be declared because the expected testimony outlined in the opening statement is never given from the witness stand, and consequently the adversary never has a chance to test its truth by cross-examination, would be a wasteful and mischievous rule. The controlling question should be the good faith or lack of good faith of counsel in saying what he said in his opening statement and the likelihood that the opening statement was unfairly prejudicial to the defendant.

In the instant case, at the beginning of the trial and before the jury was selected, Frazier's lawyer, in the presence of the prosecutor, said he had information that Rawls, if called as a witness, would claim his privilege against self-incrimination. He did not say what the source of his information was. Some days before Frazier's trial, the prosecutor had telephoned to Rawls' lawyer, Mr. Jacobs, to get permission to talk to Rawls. Permission was not immediately given, Jacobs saying that he himself had not talked to Rawls yet. The next day the prosecutor's assistant, Thomas, picked up Jacobs and transported him to the jail, where Jacobs talked to Rawls, then told Thomas that Rawls was going to refuse to testify, and gave permission to Thomas to talk to Rawls, saying, "All right, you talk to him. This is what he tells me. This is his own decision." Between that time and the trial, a deputy sheriff had talked to Rawls and had reported to the prosecutor that he felt sure that Rawls would testify and that Rawls' brothers, who had conversed with Rawls, had told the deputy that he wanted to testify and they thought he would testify, in spite of the advice of his lawyer. Rawls' probation officer told the prosecutor that he thought Rawls would testify.

In addition to the foregoing reasons for the prosecutor to believe that Rawls would, if called to the stand, testify, there was of course the fact that Rawls had pleaded guilty and was awaiting sentence, and would feel under strong compulsion not to refuse to cooperate with the prosecutor.

The Oregon trial judge, who was in the best position to determine whether the prosecutor had acted in good faith in calling Rawls to the witness stand, and whether this incident, when coupled with the opening statement, was prejudicial to the defendant, held that the prosecutor had acted in good faith and denied a motion for mistrial. We have before us the same cold record which the United States District Court had before it in this habeas corpus case, and we are in as good a position as was the district court to determine whether the Oregon court's implied findings were supported by the evidence. The district court's position in the habeas corpus case may well have been that good faith and prejudice were not the issues, but that counsel acts subject to the risk that the expected testimony which he recites in his opening statement, if it does not materialize, will require a mistrial. If that was the view of the district court, it was erroneous.

The fact that Rawls' expected testimony, once it became unavailable, was never again mentioned in the extended trial is of some significance on the question of the prosecutor's good faith, and of great significance on the question of the prejudicial effect of the opening statement and the calling of Rawls to the stand.

The Oregon trial judge said, in denying Frazier's second motion for a mistrial, that he would instruct the jury not to give any weight to what the prosecutor had said in his opening statement about Rawls' expected testimony. He did not give a specific instruction on that point. He either forgot his earlier statement or, more probably, thought better of it. Such an instruction, if given, would have recalled the incident to the minds of the jurors. Counsel for Frazier apparently for the same reason did not desire such an instruction or he would have reminded the court of its earlier statement. The court did give a general instruction that statements of counsel are not evidence.

Counsel for Frazier rely heavily upon the Supreme Court's decision in Douglas v. State of Alabama, supra. In Douglas, after the witness had claimed the privilege against self-incrimination, the prosecutor read the confession to him, a few sentences at a time, asking the witness after the reading of each few sentences, "Did you make that statement?" Each time the witness refused to answer, claiming the privilege. Thus the prosecutor, knowing that he was not going to get any testimony from the witness, deliberately placed every word of the inadmissible hearsay before the jury, compelling the witness to repeatedly claim his right to keep silent, and thus impressing the jury with the probable truth of the statement. The prosecutor could not possibly claim that he acted in a good faith expectation that the witness would testify. Douglas was a flagrant case of purposely and in bad faith placing before the jury in the most impressive possible manner inadmissible evidence the truth of which could not be tested by cross-examination. The "evidence" thus offered was the only evidence relating to a crucial element of the prosecution's case. Counsel for Frazier does not cite any case in which an appellate court has reversed a judgment for the reason relied upon by the district court in this phase of the instant case.

In the case before us, there is no problem of lack of opportunity to confront a witness who had given testimony, either directly or, as in Douglas v. State of Alabama, supra, indirectly by having his extra-judicial statements read to him and to the jury while he refused to confirm or deny his having made the statements attributed to him. Rawls was on the witness stand only momentarily, and neither by question nor answer was anything which was contained in his confession brought to the attention of the jury. Our problem then, is whether the references to Rawls in the opening statement, followed by the calling of Rawls to the witness stand, was prosecutorial misconduct. We hold that it was not. We have shown above that it was done in a good faith expectation that Rawls would testify. . . .

* * *

The judgment of the district court is reversed, and the court is directed to dismiss the petition for a writ of habeas corpus.

NOTES

1. In Commonwealth v. Bearse, 358 Mass. 481, 265 N.E.2d 496 (1970), the defendant was convicted of the murder of his son. The killing was admitted and the issue was whether the act was deliberate (murder) or reckless (involuntary manslaughter). The case was close and on appeal the Court commented on the prosecution's opening statement:

> The prosecutor told the jury that he would prove that the defendant said to Mrs. Bearse on the evening of the fatal event, "I'm going to kill that kid." That proof was never forthcoming. It is of no avail retrospectively to surmise that if made, it was excluded because it was uttered in the course of a private conversation between husband and wife. The statement should never have been included in the opening unless there was no doubt of its admissibility. Having been made, although never proved, it was irretrievably and fatally prejudicial to the defendant in the circumstances, and especially so when the prosecutor in his closing argument repeatedly asserted that the killing was by "design."

Despite the ruling in Commonwealth v. Bearse, reversals based on improper opening statements are not common.

For collected cases, see 16 A.L.R.2d 810 (1982). One court found an improper opening statement more egregious than a bad closing argument because it is planned, not provoked. United States v. Johnson, 767 F.2d 1259, 1274 (8th Cir.1985).

2. Apart from the possibility of reversal on appeal (which is meaningful only to the prosecutor), there is a more significant restraint on an advocate tempted to overstate his opening. An advocate who says that he will prove something and then fails to do so may pay a significant tactical penalty of loss of credibility. Most jurisdictions permit opposing counsel to comment on the failure to keep the "promises" made in the opening statement. See State v. McGonigle, 103 Ariz. 267, 440 P.2d 100 (1968). Contra, People v. Levy, 28 Mich.App. 339, 184 N.W.2d 325 (1970).

3. The defense has a particularly difficult dilemma regarding the opening statement. Most jurisdictions require the defense, subject to the court's discretion, to give its opening statement immediately after the prosecution makes its opening statement. If the defense gives a full opening statement, in those jurisdictions denying discovery to the prosecution, it has the effect of giving the prosecution advance discovery of the defense case. Further, in order to make a detailed opening, the defense usually has to commit itself to a particular defense and perhaps to calling the defendant to the stand. On the other hand, a general, vague opening statement may present an unfavorable contrast to a detailed and moving prosecution statement. Then, too, if the defense opening can be delayed until after the prosecution closes its case, the jury may become suspicious about the delay. State law may allow the prosecutor to attack the belated declaration of the defense, although some jurisdictions prohibit such an attack.

2. CLOSING ARGUMENTS

Griffin v. California

Supreme Court of the United States, 1965.
380 U.S. 609, 85 S.Ct. 1229, rehearing denied 381 U.S. 957, 85 S.Ct. 1797 (1965).

■ MR. JUSTICE DOUGLAS delivered the opinion of the Court.

Petitioner was convicted of murder in the first degree after a jury trial in a California court. He did not testify at the trial on the issue of guilt, though he did testify at the separate trial on the issue of penalty. The trial court instructed the jury on the issue of guilt, stating that a defendant has a constitutional right not to testify. But it told the jury:

> "As to any evidence or facts against him which the defendant can reasonably be expected to deny or explain because of facts within his knowledge, if he does not testify or if, though he does testify, he fails to deny or explain such evidence, the jury may take that failure into consideration as tending to indicate the truth of such evidence and as indicating that among the inferences that may be reasonably drawn therefrom those unfavorable to the defendant are the more probable."

It added, however, that no such inference could be drawn as to evidence respecting which he had no knowledge. It stated that failure of a defendant to deny or explain the evidence of which he had knowledge does not create a presumption of guilt nor by itself warrant an inference of guilt nor relieve the prosecution of any of its burden of proof.

Petitioner had been seen with the deceased the evening of her death, the evidence placing him with her in the alley where her body was found. The prosecutor made much of the failure of petitioner to testify:

> "The defendant certainly knows whether Essie Mae had this beat up appearance at the time he left her apartment and went down the alley with her.
>
> "What kind of a man is it that would want to have sex with a woman that beat up if she was beat up at the time he left?
>
> "He would know that. He would know how she got down the alley. He would knowhow the blood got on the bottom of the concrete steps. He would know how long he was with her in that box. He would know how her wig got off. He would know whether he beat her or mistreated her. He would know whether he walked away from that place cool as a cucumber when he saw Mr. Villase nor because he was conscious of his own guilt and wanted to get away from that damaged or injured woman.
>
> "These things he has not seen fit to take the stand and deny or explain.
>
> "And in the whole world, if anybody would know, this defendant would know.
>
> "Essie Mae is dead, she can't tell you her side of the story. The defendant won't."

The case is here on a writ of certiorari to consider whether comment on the failure to testify violated the Self–Incrimination Clause of the Fifth Amendment.[3]

We think it does. It is in substance a rule of evidence that allows the State the privilege of tendering to the jury for its consideration the failure of the accused to testify. No formal offer of proof is made as in other situations; but the prosecutor's comment and the court's acquiescence are the equivalent of an offer of evidence and its acceptance. The Court in Wilson [v. United States, 149 U.S. 60, 13 S.Ct. 765] stated:

> "... the act was framed with a due regard also to those who might prefer to rely upon the presumption of innocence which the law gives to every one, and not wish to be witnesses. It is not every one who can safely venture on the witness stand, though entirely innocent of the charge against him. Excessive timidity, nervousness when facing others and attempting to explain transactions of a suspicious character, and offenses charged against him, will often confuse and embarrass him to such a degree as to increase rather than remove prejudices against him. It is not every one, however, honest, who would therefore willingly be placed on the witness stand. The statute, in tenderness to the weakness of those who from the causes mentioned might refuse to ask to be witnesses, particularly when they may have been in some degree compromised by their association with others, declares that the failure of a defendant in a criminal action to request to be a witness shall not create any presumption against him."

If the words "Fifth Amendment" are substituted for "act" and for"statute" the spirit of the Self–Incrimination Clause is reflected. For comment on the refusal to testify is a remnant of the "inquisitorial system of criminal justice" which the Fifth Amendment outlaws. It is a penalty imposed by courts for exercising a constitutional privilege. It cuts down on the privilege by making its assertion costly. It is said, however, that the inference of guilt for failure to testify as to facts peculiarly within the accused's knowledge is in any event natural and irresistible, and that comment on the failure does not magnify that inference into a penalty for asserting a constitutional privilege. What the jury may infer, given no help from the court, is one thing. What it may infer when the court solemnizes the silence of the accused into evidence against him is quite another. ...

* * *

3. The overwhelming consensus of the States is opposed to allowing comment on the defendant's failure to testify. The legislatures or courts of 44 States have recognized that such comment is, in light of the privilege against self-incrimination, "an unwarrantable line of argument." Of the six States which permit comment, two, California and Ohio, give this permission by means of an explicit constitutional qualification of the privilege against self-incrimination. New Jersey permits comment but its constitution contains no provision embodying the privilege against self-incrimination. The absence of an express constitutional privilege against self-incrimination also puts Iowa among the six. Connecticut permits comment by the judge but not by the prosecutor. New Mexico permits comment by the prosecutor but holds that the accused is then entitled to an instruction that "the jury shall indulge no presumption against the accused because of his failure to testify".

... We ... hold that the Fifth Amendment, ... forbids either comment by the prosecution on the accused's silence or instructions by the court that such silence is evidence of guilt.

Reversed.

■ THE CHIEF JUSTICE took no part in the decision of this case.

■ [MR. JUSTICE HARLAN's concurring opinion is omitted.]

■ MR. JUSTICE STEWART, with whom MR. JUSTICE WHITE joins, dissenting.

* * *

No claim is made that the prosecutor's argument or the trial judge's instructions to the jury in this case deprived the petitioner of due process of law as such. This Court long ago decided that the Due Process Clause of the Fourteenth Amendment does not of its own force forbid this kind of comment on a defendant's failure to testify. The Court holds, however, that the California constitutional provision violates the Fifth Amendment's injunction that no person "shall be compelled in any criminal case to be a witness against himself," an injunction which the Court less than a year ago for the first time found was applicable to trials in the courts of the several States.

With both candor and accuracy, the Court concedes that the question before us is one of first impression here. It is a question which has not arisen before, because until last year the self-incrimination provision of the Fifth Amendment had been held to apply only to federal proceedings, and in the federal judicial system the matter has been covered by a specific Act of Congress which has been in effect ever since defendants have been permitted to testify at all in federal criminal trials.

We must determine whether the petitioner has been "compelled ... to be a witness against himself." Compulsion is the focus of the inquiry. ...

... I think that the Court in this case stretches the concept of compulsion beyond all reasonable bounds, and that whatever compulsion may exist derives from the defendant's choice not to testify, not from any comment by court or counsel. In support of its conclusion that the California procedure does compel the accused to testify, the Court has only this to say:"It is a penalty imposed by courts for exercising a constitutional privilege. It cuts down on the privilege by making its assertion costly." Exactly what the penalty imposed consists of is not clear. It is not, as I understand the problem, that the jury becomes aware that the defendant has chosen not to testify in his own defense, for the jury will, of course, realize this quite evident fact, even though the choice goes unmentioned. Since comment by counsel and the court does not compel testimony by creating such an awareness, the Court must be saying that the California constitutional provision places some other compulsion upon the defendant to incriminate himself, some compulsion which the Court does not describe and which I cannot readily perceive.

It is not at all apparent to me, on any realistic view of the trial process, that a defendant will be at more of a disadvantage under the California practice than he would be in a court which permitted no comment at all on his failure to take the witness stand. How can it be said that the inferences drawn by a jury will be more detrimental to a defendant under the limiting and carefully controlling language of the instruction here involved than would result if the jury were left to roam at large with only its untutored instincts to guide it, to draw from the defendant's silence broad inferences of guilt? The instructions in this case expressly cautioned the jury that the defendant's failure to testify "does not create a presumption of guilt or by itself warrant an inference of guilt"; it was further admonished that such failure does not "relieve the prosecution of its burden of proving every essential element of the crime," and finally the trial judge warned that the prosecution's burden remained that of proof "beyond a reasonable doubt." Whether the same limitations would be observed by a jury without the benefit of protective instructions shielding the defendant is certainly open to real doubt.

Moreover, no one can say where the balance of advantage might lie as a result of the attorneys' discussion of the matter. No doubt the prosecution's argument will seek to encourage the drawing of inferences unfavorable to the defendant. However, the defendant's counsel equally has an opportunity to explain the various other reasons why a defendant may not wish to take the stand, and thus rebut the natural if uneducated assumption that it is because the defendant cannot truthfully deny the accusations made.

I think the California comment rule is not a coercive device which impairs the right against self-incrimination, but rather a means of articulating and bringing into the light of rational discussion a fact inescapably impressed on the jury's consciousness. The California procedure is not only designed to protect the defendant against unwarranted inferences which might be drawn by an uninformed jury; it is also an attempt by the State to recognize and articulate what it believes to be the natural probative force of certain facts. Surely no one would deny that the State has an important interest in throwing the light of rational discussion on that which transpires in the course of a trial, both to protect the defendant from the very real dangers of silence and to shape a legal process designed to ascertain the truth.

The California rule allowing comment by counsel and instruction by the judge on the defendant's failure to take the stand is hardly an idiosyncratic aberration. The Model Code of Evidence, and the Uniform Rules of Evidence both sanction the use of such procedures. The practice has been endorsed by resolution of the American Bar Association and the American Law Institute, and has the support of the weight of scholarly opinion.

The formulation of procedural rules to govern the administration of criminal justice in the various States is properly a matter of local concern. We are charged with no general supervisory power over such matters; our only legitimate function is to prevent violations of the Constitution's commands. California has honored the constitutional command that no person shall "be compelled in any criminal case to be a witness against himself." The petitioner was not compelled to testify, and he did not do so. But whenever in a jury trial a defendant exercises this constitutional right, the members of the jury are bound to draw inferences from his silence. No constitution can prevent the operation of the human mind. Without limiting instructions, the danger exists that the inferences drawn by the jury may be unfairly broad. Some States have permitted this danger to go unchecked, by forbidding any comment at all upon the defendant's failure to take the witness stand. Other States have dealt with this danger in a variety of ways. Some might differ, as a matter of policy, with the way California has chosen to deal with the problem or even disapprove of the judge's specific instructions in this case. But, so long as the constitutional command is obeyed, such matters of state policy are not for this Court to decide.

I would affirm the judgment.

NOTES

1. The *Griffin* rule is not absolute. If the accused testifies, but refuses to answer certain questions, it is proper for the prosecutor to comment upon the failure to answer these questions. Dyson v. United States, 283 F.2d 636 (9th Cir.1960); United States ex rel. Irwin v. Pate, 357 F.2d 911 (7th Cir.1966). Occasionally, an accused wishes to perform some demonstration in court without taking the stand, say, to try on an article of clothing belonging to the perpetrator. The extent to which he may do this without waiving his Fifth Amendment privilege (and thus subject himself to adverse comment on his failure to give fuller testimony) is subject to some disagreement. See United States ex rel. Mitchell v. Pinto, 438 F.2d 814 (3d Cir.1971) (defendant did not waive privilege by rising and standing next to witness to demonstrate similarity of appearance); State v. Fioravanti, 46 N.J. 109, 215 A.2d 16 (1965) (trying on criminal's trousers to show lack of fit is testimonial appearance sufficient to justify comment on failure to deny other evidence). See also People v. Harris, 46 Ill.2d 395, 263 N.E.2d 35 (1970), denial of habeas corpus 457 F.2d 191 (7th Cir.1972) (accused who wishes to display absence of teeth to jury may not do so without submitting to cross-examination at least as to circumstances and timing of loss of teeth).

2. In United States v. Robinson, 485 U.S. 25, 108 S.Ct. 864 (1988), the Court held that a prosecutor's comment on the defendant's silence at trial sometimes may be a fair response to a defense argument. In *Robinson* the defense lawyer invited the response by claiming that the defendant had no chance to tell his side of the story.

United States v. Young

Supreme Court of the United States, 1985.
470 U.S. 1, 105 S.Ct. 1038.

■ CHIEF JUSTICE BURGER delivered the opinion of the Court.

* * *

I

Respondent Billy G. Young, as vice president and general manager of the Compton Petroleum Corporation in Abilene, Texas, contracted in 1976 and 1977 to deliver monthly supplies of "sweet" crude oil to the Apco Oil Corporation refinery in Cyril, Oklahoma. Some 205,000 barrels of oil were delivered under the contract between January and September 1977, but more than half of the oil delivered to Apco, approximately 117,250 barrels, consisted of fuel oil, an already refined product less valuable than crude oil. Compton's invoices accompanying those deliveries falsely certified that all of the oil was crude. Apco relied on those false certifications and reported to the Federal Energy Administration, in compliance with government regulations, the amount of crude oil it thought it was refining each month. The Federal Energy Administration in turn relied on Apco's reports to determine the national averages of tier categories of refined oil for purposes of equalizing the cost of crude oil under its entitlement program.

Respondent's scheme to deceive Apco by selling it cheaper fuel oil masquerading as "sweet" crude oil was relatively simple. Respondent arranged with an oil brokerage firm, owned by a longtime friend, to procure fuel oil from another source and sell it to Compton under the false certification that it was crude oil. Compton would then pay the brokerage firm 10 cents per barrel commission as a fee for the "recertification." Once in Compton's storage tanks, respondent had the fuel oil disguised as crude oil before delivering it to Apco by blending condensate, a high gravity liquid taken from the wellheads of natural gas wells, with the fuel oil.[1] In September 1977,after an Apco technician performed a distillation test on one of Compton's deliveries, Apco discovered that it had not been receiving crude oil as required by the contract, but rather a mixture of fuel oil and condensate. This discovery prompted the FBI to launch an investigation which resulted in this prosecution.

On December 1, 1980, respondent and Compton were charged with 11 counts of mail fraud, three counts of willfully and knowingly making false statements to a government agency, one count of interstate transportation of stolen property, and with aiding and abetting in the commission of all 15 counts. A jury trial was held in the District Court for the Western District of Oklahoma. In his own defense, respondent testified that he had knowingly purchased fuel oil and delivered it to Apco, but he claimed that he thought such fuel oil could legitimately be certified as crude oil. He also believed that if condensate were blended with fuel oil, the result would be the equivalent of crude oil. Because Apco had not complained about the deliveries before September 1977, respondent thought that Apco was satisfied with the quality of oil he was supplying.

At the close of the case, the prosecutor summarized the evidence against respondent. Defense counsel began his own summation by arguing that the case against respondent "has been presented unfairly by the prosecution," and that "[f]rom the beginning" to "this very moment the [prosecution's] statements have been made to poison your minds unfairly." He intimated that the prosecution deliberately withheld exculpatory evidence, and proceeded to charge the prosecution with "reprehensible" conduct in purportedly attempting to cast a false light on respondent's activities. Defense counsel also pointed directly at the prosecutor's table and stated, "I submit to you that there's not a person in this courtroom including those sitting at this table who think that Billy Young intended to

1. Apco wanted a high gravity crude oil for gasoline production. A high gravity crude oil yields greater quantities of gasoline and diesel fuels after refining than does a lower gravity crude oil, which yields more fuel oil and asphalt. Fuel oil, on the other hand, has a low gravity and was neither what Apco needed nor thought it was buying.

defraud Apco." Finally, defense counsel stated that respondent had been "the only one in this whole affair that has acted with honor and with integrity" and that "[t]hese complex [Department of Energy] regulations should not have any place in an effort to put someone away."

The prosecutor did not object to defense counsel's summation, but in rebuttal argument he responded to defense counsel's claim that the Government did not believe in its own case:

> "I think [defense counsel] said that not anyone sitting at this table thinks that Mr. Young intended to defraud Apco. Well, I was sitting there and I think he was. I think he got 85 cents a barrel for every one of those 117,250.91 barrels he hauled and every bit of the money they made on that he got one percent of. So, I think he did. If we are allowed to give our personal impressions *since it was asked of me*." (Emphasis added.)

Continuing with a review of portions of the evidence against respondent, the prosecutor responded to defense counsel's statement that Apco was not defrauded:

> "I don't know what you call that, I call it fraud.
>
> "You can look at the evidence and remember the testimony, you remember what [the witnesses] said and what [respondent] admitted they said. I think it's a fraud."

Finally, the prosecutor addressed defense counsel's claim that respondent had acted with honor and integrity. The prosecutor briefly recapped some of respondent's conduct and stated:

> "I don't know whether you call it honor and integrity, I don't call it that,[defense counsel] does. If you feel you should acquit him for that it's your pleasure. I don't think you're doing your job as jurors in finding facts as opposed to the law that this Judge is going to instruct you, you think that's honor and integrity then stand up here in Oklahoma courtroom and say that's honor and integrity; I don't believe it."

In turn, defense counsel did not object to the prosecutor's statements. Nor did he request any curative instructions and none were given.

The jury returned a verdict of guilty as to each of the mail fraud and false statement counts. Respondent was acquitted of interstate transportation of stolen property. . . .

On appeal, respondent alleged that he was unfairly prejudiced by the prosecutor's remarks made during closing rebuttal argument. In a *per curiam* opinion, the Court of Appeals, one judge dissenting without opinion, reversed the conviction and remanded for retrial. The Court of Appeals held that the prosecutor's statements constituted misconduct and were sufficiently egregious to constitute plain error. In short, respondent's failure to object at trial was held not to preclude appellate review. Rejecting the Government's contention that the statements were invited by the defense counsel's own closing argument, the Court of Appeals stated that "the rule is clear in this Circuit that improper conduct on the part of opposing counsel should be met with an objection to the court, not a similarly improper response."

II

The principal issue to be resolved is not whether the prosecutor's response to defense counsel's misconduct was appropriate, but whether it was "plain error" that a reviewing court could act on absent a timely objection.

Nearly a half century ago this Court counselled prosecutors "to refrain from improper methods calculated to produce a wrongful conviction...." Berger v. United States (1935). The Court made clear, however, that the adversary system permits the prosecutor to "prosecute with earnestness and vigor." In other words, "while he may strike hard blows, he is not at liberty to strike foul ones."

The line separating acceptable from improper advocacy is not easily drawn; there is often a gray zone. Prosecutors sometimes breach their duty to refrain from overzealous conduct by commenting on the defendant's guilt and offering unsolicited personal views on the evidence. Accordingly, the legal profession, through its Codes of Professional Responsibility, and the federal courts, have tried to police prosecutorial misconduct. In complementing these efforts, the American Bar Association's Standing Committee on Standards for Criminal Justice has promulgated useful guidelines, one of which states that

> "[i]t is unprofessional conduct for the prosecutor to express his or her personal belief or opinion as to the truth or falsity of any testimony or evidence or the guilt of the defendant." ABA Standards for Criminal Justice 3–5.8(b) (2d ed. 1980).

It is clear that counsel on both sides of the table share a duty to confine arguments to the jury within proper bounds. Just as the conduct of prosecutors is circumscribed, "[t]he interests of society in the preservation of courtroom control by the judges are no more to be frustrated through unchecked improprieties by defenders." Sacher v. United States (1952). Defense counsel, like the prosecutor, must refrain from interjecting personal beliefs into the presentation of his case. See, e.g., ABA Code of Professional Responsibility DR 7–106(C)(3) and (4), ABA Model Rules of Professional Conduct, Rule 3.4(e) (1983). Defense counsel, like his adversary, must not be permitted to make unfounded and inflammatory attacks on the opposing advocate.[6]

The kind of advocacy shown by this record has no place in the administration of justice and should neither be permitted nor rewarded; a trial judge should deal promptly with any breach by either counsel. These considerations plainly guided the ABA Standing Committee on Standards for Criminal Justice in laying down rules of trial conduct for counsel that

6. Of course, when defense counsel employs tactics which would be reversible error if used by a prosecutor, the result may be an unreviewable acquittal. The prosecutor's conduct and utterances, however, are always reviewable on appeal, for he is "both an administrator of justice and an advocate." ABA Standards for Criminal Justice 3–1.1(b) (2d ed. 1980).

quite properly hold all advocates to essentially the same standards. Indeed, the accompanying commentary points out that "[i]t should be accepted that both prosecutor and defense counsel are subject to the same general limitations in the scope of their argument," ABA Standards for Criminal Justice 4–7.8, p. 4.97, and provides the following guideline:

> "The prohibition of personal attacks on the prosecutor is but a part of the larger duty of counsel to avoid acrimony in relations with opposing counsel during trial and confine argument to record evidence. It is firmly established that the lawyer should abstain from any allusion to the personal peculiarities and idiosyncrasies of opposing counsel. A personal attack by the prosecutor on defense counsel is improper, and the duty to abstain from such attacks is obviously reciprocal."

These standards reflect a consensus of the profession that the courts must not lose sight of the reality that "[a] criminal trial does not unfold like a play with actors following a script." Geders v. United States (1976). It should come as no surprise that "in the heat of argument, counsel do occasionally make remarks that are not justified by the testimony, and which are, or may be, prejudicial to the accused." Dunlop v. United States, (1897).[8]

We emphasize that the trial judge has the responsibility to maintain decorum in keeping with the nature of the proceeding; "the judge is not a mere moderator, but is the governor of the trial for the purpose of assuring its proper conduct." Quercia v. United States (1933). The judge "must meet situations as they arise and [be able] to cope with ... the contingencies inherent in the adversary process." Geders v. United States, supra. Of course, "hard blows" cannot be avoided in criminal trials; both the prosecutor and defense counsel must be kept within appropriate bounds.

III

The situation brought before the Court of Appeals was but one example of an all too common occurrence in criminal trials—the defense counsel argues improperly, provoking the prosecutor to respond in kind, and the trial judge takes no corrective action. Clearly two improper arguments—two apparent wrongs—do not make for a right result. Nevertheless, a criminal conviction is not to be lightly overturned on the basis of a prosecutor's comments standing alone, for the statements or conduct must be viewed in context; only by so doing can it be determined whether the prosecutor's conduct affected the fairness of the trial. To help resolve this problem, courts have invoked what is sometimes called the "invited response" or "invited reply" rule, which the Court treated in Lawn v. United States (1958).

The petitioners in *Lawn* sought to have the Court overturn their criminal convictions for income tax evasion on a number of grounds, one of

8. Learned Hand observed: "It is impossible to expect that a criminal trial shall be conducted without some showing of feeling; the stakes are high, and the participants are inevitably charged with emotion." United States v. Wexler, 79 F.2d 526, 529–530 (C.A.2 1935).

which was that the prosecutor's closing argument deprived them of a fair trial. In his closing argument at trial, defense counsel in *Lawn* had attacked the Government for "persecuting" the defendants. He told the jury that the prosecution was instituted in bad faith at the behest of federal revenue agents and asserted that the Government's key witnesses were perjurers. The prosecutor in response vouched for the credibility of the challenged witnesses, telling the jury that the Government thought those witnesses testified truthfully. In concluding that the prosecutor's remarks, when viewed within the context of the entire trial, did not deprive petitioners of a fair trial, the Court pointed out that defense counsel's "comments clearly invited the reply."

This Court's holding in *Lawn* was no more than an application of settled law. Inappropriate prosecutorial comments, standing alone, would not justify are viewing court to reverse a criminal conviction obtained in an otherwise fair proceeding. Instead, as *Lawn* teaches, the remarks must be examined within the context of the trial to determine whether the prosecutor's behavior amounted to prejudicial error. In other words, the Court must consider the probable effect the prosecutor's response would have on the jury's ability to judge the evidence fairly. In this context, defense counsel's conduct, as well as the nature of the prosecutor's response, is relevant. See United States v. Socony–Vacuum Oil Co. (1940); Crumpton v. United States (1891). Indeed most Courts of Appeals, applying these holdings, have refused to reverse convictions where prosecutors have responded reasonably in closing argument to defense counsel's attacks, thus rendering it unlikely that the jury was led astray.

In retrospect, perhaps the idea of "invited response" has evolved in a way not contemplated. *Lawn* and the earlier cases cited above should not be read as suggesting judicial approval or—encouragement—of response-in-kind that inevitably exacerbate the tensions inherent in the adversary process. As *Lawn* itself indicates, the issue is not the prosecutor's license to make otherwise improper arguments, but whether the prosecutor's "invited response," taken in context, unfairly prejudiced the defendant.

In order to make an appropriate assessment, the reviewing court must not only weigh the impact of the prosecutor's remarks, but must also take into account defense counsel's opening salvo. Thus the import of the evaluation has been that if the prosecutor's remarks were "invited," and did no more than respond substantially in order to "right the scale," such comments would not warrant reversing a conviction.

Courts have not intended by any means to encourage the practice of zealous counsel's going "out of bounds" in the manner of defense counsel here, or to encourage prosecutors to respond to the "invitation." Reviewing courts ought not to be put in the position of weighing which of two inappropriate arguments was the lesser. "Invited responses" can be effectively discouraged by prompt action from the bench in the form of corrective instructions to the jury, and when necessary, an admonition to the errant advocate.

Plainly, the better remedy in this case, at least with the accurate vision of hindsight, would have been for the District Judge to deal with the improper argument of the defense counsel promptly and thus blunt the need for the prosecutor to respond. Arguably defense counsel's misconduct could have warranted the judge to interrupt the argument and admonish him, thereby rendering the prosecutor's response unnecessary. Similarly, the prosecutor at the close of defense summation should have objected to the defense counsel's improper statements with a request that the court give a timely warning and curative instruction to the jury. Defense counsel, even though obviously vulnerable, could well have done likewise if he thought that the prosecutor's remarks were harmful to his client. Here neither counsel made a timely objection to preserve the issue for review. However, interruptions of arguments, either by an opposing counsel or the presiding judge, are matters to be approached cautiously. At the very least, a bench conference might have been convened out of the hearing of the jury once defense counsel closed, and an appropriate instruction given.

IV

Here the Court of Appeals was not unaware of our holdings and those of other Circuits, but seemingly did not undertake to weigh the prosecutor's comments in context. The court acknowledged defense counsel's obvious misconduct, but it does not appear that this was given appropriate weight in evaluating the situation.

We share the Court of Appeals' desire to minimize "invited responses"; and we agree that the prosecutor's response constituted error. In addition to departing from the Tenth Circuit's "rule" prohibiting such remarks, the prosecutor's comments crossed the line of permissible conduct established by the ethical rules of the legal profession, as did defense counsel's argument, and went beyond what was necessary to "right the scale" in the wake of defense counsel's misconduct. Indeed the prosecutor's first error was in failing to ask the District Judge to deal with defense counsel's misconduct.

As we suggested earlier, the dispositive issue under the holdings of this Court is not whether the prosecutor's remarks amounted to error, but whether they rose to the level of "plain error" when he responded to defense counsel. . . .

The plain error doctrine of Federal Rule Criminal Procedure 52(b) tempers the blow of a rigid application of the contemporaneous objection requirement. The Rule authorizes the Courts of Appeals to correct only "particularly egregious errors," United States v. Frady (1982), those errors that "seriously affect the fairness, integrity or public reputation of judicial proceedings," United States v. Atkinson. In other words, the plain error exception to the contemporaneous objection rule is to be "used sparingly, solely in those circumstances in which a miscarriage of justice would otherwise result." United States v. Frady.

Especially when addressing plain error, a reviewing court cannot properly evaluate a case except by viewing such a claim against the entire record. We have been reminded:

> "In reviewing criminal cases, it is particularly important for appellate courts to relive the whole trial imaginatively and not to extract from episodes in isolation abstract questions of evidence

> and procedure. To turn a criminal trial into a quest for error no more promotes the ends of justice than to acquiesce in low standards of criminal prosecution." Johnson v. United States, 318 U.S. 189, 202, 63 S.Ct. 549, 555, 87 L.Ed. 704 (1943) (Frankfurter, J., concurring).

It is simply not possible for an appellate court to assess the seriousness of the claimed error by any other means. As the Court stated in United States v. Socony–Vacuum Oil Co., "each case necessarily turns on its own facts."

The prosecutor responded with his "personal impression[ ]," that respondent intended to commit a fraud to answer defense counsel's accusation that no member of the prosecution team believed that respondent intended to defraud Apco. Indeed, the prosecutor made a point to preface his statement by summarizing defense counsel's acerbic charge and candidly told the jury that he was giving his "personal impressions" because defense counsel had asked for them.

Notwithstanding the defense counsel's breach of ethical standards, the prosecutor's statement of his belief that the evidence showed Apco had been defrauded should not have been made; it was an improper expression of personal opinion and was not necessary to answer defense counsel's improper assertion that no one on the prosecution team believed respondent intended to defraud Apco. Nevertheless, we conclude that any potential harm from this remark was mitigated by the jury's understanding that the prosecutor was countering defense counsel's repeated attacks on the prosecution's integrity and defense counsel's argument that the evidence established no such crime.

Finally, the prosecutor's comments that respondent had not acted with "honor and integrity," and his calling attention to the jury's responsibility to follow the court's instructions were in response to defense counsel's rhetoric that respondent alone was the sole honorable actor in "this whole affair," and that the jury should not find respondent guilty simply because he could not understand applicable, but complex, federal regulations. The prosecutor was also in error to try to exhort the jury to "do its job"; that kind of pressure, whether by the prosecutor or defense counsel, has no place in the administration of criminal justice. Given the context of the prosecutor's remarks and defense counsel's broadside attack, however, we conclude that the jury was not influenced to stray from its responsibility to be fair and unbiased.[15]

The concerns underlying our reactions against improper prosecutorial arguments to the jury are implicated here, but not to the extent that we conclude that the jury's deliberations were compromised. The prosecutor's vouching for the credibility of witnesses and expressing his personal opinion concerning the guilt of the accused pose two dangers: such comments can convey the impression that evidence not presented to the jury, but known to the prosecutor, supports the charges against the defendant and

15. The jury acquitted respondent of the most serious charge he faced, interstate transportation of stolen property. This reinforces our conclusion that the prosecutor's remarks did not undermine the jury's ability to view the evidence independently and fairly.

can thus jeopardize the defendant's right to be tried solely on the basis of the evidence presented to the jury; and the prosecutor's opinion carries with it the imprimatur of the Government and may induce the jury to trust the Government's judgment rather than its own view of the evidence. See Berger v. United States.

The prosecutor's statement of his belief that respondent intended to commit a fraud contained no suggestion that he was relying on information outside the evidence presented at trial. He supported his comment by referring to respondent's own testimony that Compton received 85 cents a barrel for its deliveries to Apco and that respondent personally received a bonus of one percent of Compton's net profits, he then summarized portions of the evidence adduced at trial before suggesting to the jury that the record established the fraud charged. Although it was improper for the prosecutor to express his personal opinion about respondent's guilt, see Berger v. United States, ABA Standards for Criminal Justice, at 3–5.8(b), when viewed in context, the prosecutor's remarks cannot be read as implying that the prosecutor had access to evidence outside the record. The jury surely understood the comment for what it was—a defense of his decision and his integrity—in bringing criminal charges on the basis of the very evidence the jury had heard during the trial.

Finally, the overwhelming evidence of respondent's intent to defraud Apco and submit false oil certifications to the Government eliminates any lingering doubt that the prosecutor's remarks unfairly prejudiced the jury's deliberations or exploited the Government's prestige in the eyes of the jury. Not a single witness supported respondent's asserted defense that fuel oil mixed with condensate could be certified and sold as crude oil, and several witnesses flatly rejected such a proposition. Indeed, respondent's crude oil trader testified that he had never heard of a firm legally blending fuel oil with condensate and stating that the mixture was crude oil. It was undisputed that respondent failed to advise Apco of what he was actually supplying and that the oil supplied did not meet the contract requirements. See id., at 358–359.

Moreover, the evidence established beyond any doubt whatever that respondent deliberately concealed his scheme to defraud Apco. Apart from enlisting the aid of an oil brokerage firm to "recertify" the fuel oil as crude oil, respondent on three separate occasions, when questioned by two Apco officials and by FBI agents, falsely denied that he was supplying fuel oil instead of crude oil. Under these circumstances, the substantial and virtually uncontradicted evidence of respondent's willful violation provides an additional indication that the prosecutor's remarks, when reviewed in context, cannot be said to undermine the fairness of the trial and contribute to a miscarriage of justice.

V

On this record, we hold that the argument of the prosecutor, although error, did not constitute plain error warranting the Court of Appeals to overlook the failure of the defense counsel to preserve the point by timely objection; nor are we persuaded that the challenged argument seriously affected the fairness of the trial. Accordingly, the judgment of the Court of

Appeals, ordering anew trial based on the prosecutor's argument, is reversed.

It is so ordered.

■ JUSTICE BRENNAN, with whom JUSTICE MARSHALL and JUSTICE BLACKMUN join, concurring in part and dissenting in part.

* * *

I

This Court only infrequently gives plenary consideration to cases involving standards of prosecutorial conduct. When we do, it is important that we attempt to set forth with clarity the standards by which federal prosecutors must guide their trial conduct.

A

The Court granted the Government's petition for a writ of certiorari to resolve, *inter alia*, the question "[w]hether a prosecutor may rebut [improper] closing defense argument ... by responsive argument that would be inappropriate in the absence of such provocation." The Government contends that we should recognize "a prosecutor's right to respond" to improper defense arguments and that, in light of this "right," we should hold that such responses "are not improper" even if standing alone they would be impermissible.

Today the Court rejects this asserted "right" of reply, emphasizing instead that prosecutors have no "license to make otherwise improper arguments" in response to defense rhetoric, and holding that the prosecutor's responses in this case "constituted error." As the Court observes, "[c]learly two improper arguments—two apparent wrongs—do not make for a right result." Instead, the Court instructs, the proper recourse is an objection to the trial judge and "prompt action from the bench in the form of corrective instructions to the jury, and when necessary, an admonition to the errant advocate."

The Court today also reaffirms the authority of lower courts to define and enforce reasonable rules of prosecutorial conduct. As the Court notes, the prosecutor in this case departed from Tenth Circuit precedents requiring prosecutors to object to defense misconduct rather than respond in kind; this action in and of itself "constituted error."

B

I fully agree with these conclusions. The Court goes on to suggest, however, that courts should apply an "invited error" analysis in determining the consequences of prosecutorial violations of these standards. Under this analysis, courts not only should determine the possible effect of the misconduct "on the jury's ability to judge the evidence fairly," but also should consider (1) "[d]efense counsel's conduct," and (2) whether the prosecutor "responded reasonably" under the circumstances. The conclusion is that prosecutorial misconduct, if "invited" by defense misconduct, will be excused if it "did no more than respond substantially in order to 'right the scale.' "

I believe the Court's "invited error" analysis is critically flawed: it overlooks the ethical responsibilities of federal prosecutors and threatens to undercut the prohibition of prosecutorial misconduct in the first place. In addition, the Court's analysis is misapplied to the facts of this case.

To begin with, while the Court correctly observes that both sides are subject to ethical rules of rhetorical conduct, it fails completely to acknowledge that we have long emphasized that a representative of the United States Government is held to a *higher* standard of behavior:

> "The United States Attorney is the representative not of an ordinary party to a controversy, but of a sovereignty whose obligation to govern impartially is as compelling as its obligation to govern at all; and whose interest, therefore, in a criminal prosecution is not that it shall win a case, but that justice shall be done....
>
> "... Consequently, improper suggestions, insinuations and, especially, assertions of personal knowledge are apt to carry much weight against the accused when they should properly carry none." Berger v. United States (1935).
>
> ... I believe the Court trivializes these high standards by suggesting that a violation may be overlooked merely because the prosecutor decided *sua sponte* that he had to "right the scale."

Moreover, the Court's suggestion that lower courts should evaluate prosecutorial misconduct to determine whether it was "reasonabl[e]" and "necessary to 'right the scale,'" is palpably inconsistent with the Court's conclusion that such misconduct "constitute[s] error." As the Court observes, prosecutorial rhetoric of the sort in this case has "no place in the administration of justice and should neither be permitted nor rewarded." Such errors in appropriate cases might be determined to be harmless, but it is a contradiction in terms to suggest they might be "reasonabl[e]" or "necessary to 'right the scale.'"

There was certainly nothing "reasonabl[e]" in this case about the prosecutor's responses to the concededly improper defense arguments. The defense counsel's most serious assertion was that the prosecutor did not believe Young had intended to defraud Apco. The prosecutor's initial statement that he personally believed that Young had indeed intended to defraud Apco, while itself error, might be characterized as falling within the bounds of restrained reply. But the prosecutor was not content to leave matters there. First, he repeatedly emphasized his personal opinion that Young was guilty of fraud. Second, he made predictions about the continuing effects of Young's conduct based on his prosecutorial "experience in these matters." Third, he warned the jurors that they would not be "doing your job as jurors" if they failed to convict Young.

These arguments, which separately and cumulatively so clearly violated the disciplinary rules of our profession, deserve stern and unqualified judicial condemnation. Yet the Court reserves the force of its ire for criticism of the *defense* counsel's behavior: the Court castigates the defense counsel's "attacks," "opening salvo," "going 'out of bounds,'" "misconduct," "obviously vulnerable" position, "obvious misconduct," "accusation[s]," "acerbic charge[s]," "breach of ethical standards," "improper assertion[s]," "repeated attacks," and "broadside attack[s]." In comparison, the Court appears only reluctantly to concede that "we agree that the prosecutor's response constituted error" because his remarks were "inappropriate," "should not have been made," and were "not necessary." This disparity of tone illustrates one of the major abuses of the "invited error" doctrine, an abuse often noted by the commentators.[11] Rather than apply the doctrine as a limited corrective, courts frequently employ it as a rule of unclean hands that altogether prevents a defendant from successfully challenging prosecutorial improprieties. Such use of the doctrine results, as it has today, in minimizing the gravity of virtually unchecked prosecutorial appeals going far beyond a "fair" response to the defense counsel's arguments.[12]

In further support of its analysis, the Court contends that while the underlying "concerns" of the legal and ethical strictures against improper prosecutorial arguments "are implicated here," they are not implicated in a serious way. The Court maintains, for example, that the prosecutor's arguments "contained no suggestion that he was relying on information outside the evidence presented at trial." I doubt very much, however, that the prosecutor ever testified or presented evidence about "my experience in these matters." Moreover, the proscription against prosecutorial assertions of personal belief is obviously not concerned solely with references to nonrecord evidence. As the Court itself recognizes, "the prosecutor's opinion carries with it the imprimatur of the Government and may induce the jury to trust the Government's judgment rather than its own view of the evidence." Thus "improper suggestions, insinuations and, especially, assertions of personal knowledge are apt to carry much weight against the accused when they should properly carry none." Berger v. United States. The Court today acknowledges these risks, but then decrees that the prosecutor's assertions in this case cannot be construed as having "exploited the Government's prestige in the eyes of the jury." This cavalier assertion is wholly at odds with a longstanding presumption to the contrary, see Berger v. United States, supra, and the Court should at least provide a more reasoned basis for this striking departure.

Similarly, the prosecutor's admonition that the jurors would not be "doing your job as jurors" if they voted to acquit was neither invited nor excusable, as the Court concedes. Many courts historically have viewed such warnings about not "doing your job" as among the most egregious forms of prosecutorial misconduct. See, e.g., Annot., 85 A.L.R.2d 1132 (1962 and Supp.1979). How possibly, then, can the Court characterize remarks

11. See, e.g., J. Stein, Closing Argument—The Art and the Law § 88 (1982); Alschuler, Courtroom Misconduct by Prosecutors and Trial Judges, 50 Texas L.Rev. 629, 657–658 (1972); Crump, The Function and Limits of Prosecution Jury Argument, 28 Sw. L.Rev. 505, 531–533 (1974).

12. Under this sort of application of the invited-response rule, "[t]he prosecutor may deduce ... that he would do well to watch carefully for certain mistakes that the defense counsel may make, and, instead of objecting if that course is open to him, attempt to take advantage of that mistake...." Comment, Limitations Upon the Prosecutor's Summation to the Jury, 42 J.Crim.L., C. & P.S. 73, 81 (1951).

such as these as a "defense" by the prosecutor "of his decision and his integrity in bringing criminal charges"?

II

* * *

When we detect legal error in a lower court's application of the plain-error or harmless-error rules, as here, the proper course is to set forth the appropriate standards and then remand for further proceedings. We have followed this procedure in countless cases. But the Court today reaches out without explanation and inappropriately decides the issue itself. Its analysis is flawed in several respects, and these flaws demonstrate the wisdom of leaving such inquiries in the first instance to the lower courts.

First, the Court's conclusion that the prosecutor's arguments could not have prejudiced Young rests in large part on its "invited error" analysis. The gravamen of its reasoning apparently is that, since the defense misconduct supposedly canceled out much of the prosecutor's excesses, the prosecutor's remarks were tied to the record evidence, and the jurors "surely understood" the prosecutor's rhetoric "for what it was," the prosecutor's unethical behavior could not likely have had a prejudicial impact on the jurors' deliberations. I have already demonstrated the fallacy of these underlying premises.

Second, the plain-error inquiry necessarily requires a careful review of the entire record to determine the question of possible prejudice. The Court in two brief paragraphs summarizes its review of the record and proclaims that the evidence of Young's guilt was "overwhelming" and supported the conviction "beyond any doubt whatever." The Court invokes a curious analysis in support of this pronouncement: the fact that the jury acquitted Young on"the most serious charge he faced . . . reinforces our conclusion that the prosecutor's remarks did not undermine the jury's ability to view the evidence independently and fairly." If the evidence against Young was so"overwhelming," it is difficult to perceive why the jury would have returned a partial acquittal. The jury's decision can just as naturally be interpreted to suggest that the evidence was close and the verdict a compromise, thus supporting a belief that the prosecutor's assertion of personal knowledge and his exhortation to "do your job" did in fact have a prejudicial impact. Moreover, the Court minimizes the fact that mail fraud and the making of false statements are specific-intent crimes and that good faith therefore stands as a complete defense. The question of Young's specific intent to defraud necessarily turned on witness credibility, and in this context the prosecutor's misconduct may well have had a prejudicial impact on the jurors' deliberations. Although the Court is surely correct in emphasizing the impropriety of the crude oil condensate blending scheme that Young participated in, there was significant evidence that, if believed, might well have suggested Young's innocent though ignorant motives.

Third, the Court altogether fails to consider whether the prosecutor's gross misconduct and flouting of the professional canons "seriously affect[ed] the . . . integrity or public reputation of [the] judicial proceedings." United States v. Atkinson. From the citations in the Tenth Circuit's opinion, see 736 F.2d, at 570, it would appear that prosecutorial improprieties of the sort committed in this case may present a recurring problem. This Court is in no position at this time to pass judgment on the gravity of the problem and the panel's apparent concern that the prosecutor's misconduct in this case compromised the integrity and public reputation of the Circuit's administration of justice. Clearly a remand to address the question is necessary.

These deficiencies in the Court's plain-error analysis reinforce the conviction that it was poor judicial administration for the Court to embark on its inquiry in the first place. Our traditional practice has been to leave fact-bound questions of possible prejudicial error to the lower courts on remand. . . .

* * *

Surely the Court's time could have been better spent than on familiarizing ourselves in this case with the details of crude-oil refining and blending processes; the relative gravities and qualities of sweet crude, crude oil condensate, and Number 4 fuel oil; long-rescinded Government regulations; various oil-industry testing procedures; and the complex of companies and individuals with whom Billy G. Young interacted—matters that are all important to a fair evaluation of Young's defense, but that necessarily are limited to the facts of this isolated case.

■ JUSTICE STEVENS, dissenting. [OMITTED]

NOTES

1. With regard to the limitations on defense argument, the A.B.A. Standard for Closing Argument of the defense is similar to the Standard for the prosecution:

4–7.7 Argument to the jury

> (a) In closing argument to the jury, defense counsel may argue all reasonable inferences from the evidence in the record. Defense counsel should not intentionally misstate evidence or mislead the jury as to the inferences it may draw.
>
> (b) Defense counsel should not express his personal belie for opinion in his or her client's innocence or personal belief or opinion in the truth or falsity of any testimony or evidence.
>
> (c) Defense counsel should not make arguments calculated to appeal to the prejudices of the jury.
>
> (d) Defense counsel should refrain from argument which would divert the jury from its duty to decide the case on the evidence.

The Commentary to this Standard specifically condemns, under 7.8(c), arguments containing personal attacks on the prosecutor. Presumably defense counsel has some leeway to condemn prosecutorial tactics if justified by the record that the prosecution has when defense tactics are at issue. The value of such an attack, unless based on the evidence, is doubtful. The usual prosecution response is fairly effective i.e., "every lawyer in the criminal court knows that when the facts are against you, tell the jury about the law. If the law is against you, stress the facts to the jury. If both the law and the facts are against you, attack the prosecutor."

2. Some prosecutors comment upon the demeanor of the defendant at trial even when he has not testified, i.e., a prosecutor might argue to a jury that the defendant sat laughing and smirking during the victim's testimony. With increasing frequency courts have ruled that such comment is impermissible because such facts are not in evidence, saying that the jury is allowed to consider the demeanor of only those witnesses who testify. See, e.g., United States v. Schuler, 813 F.2d 978 (9th Cir.1987), where a dissenting judge argued that a defendant's demeanor at trial, even when he does not testify, is a proper consideration for the jury.

3. A witness testified that during trial defendant Gatto glared angrily at him while the witness was on the stand. The witness knew the defendant well enough to characterize the look as threatening. The prosecutor used this testimony in closing argument. On appeal, defendant said that a prosecutor may not comment on a non-testifying defendant's courtroom demeanor citing United States v. Schuler, 813 F.2d 978 (9th Cir.1987) (laughter during testimony); United States v. Wright, 489 F.2d 1181 (D.C.Cir.1973) (amusement at murder charge); United States v. Pearson, 746 F.2d 787 (11th Cir.1984) (constant leg movements showed fear). The Court distinguished all these cases on the ground that there was no testimony about defendant's demeanor in the prior cases as there was in Gatto's case and that Gatto's threats were admissible non-testimonial evidence(as threats generally are) on which a prosecutor could comment without transgressing Griffin v. California. United States v. Gatto, 995 F.2d 449 (3d Cir.1993) (distinguishing also cases of defendant's laughter or tears because these involve proof of character inadmissible to prove guilt).

4. In Herring v. New York, 422 U.S. 853, 95 S.Ct. 2550 (1975), the Court held that Due Process prohibits the total denial of an opportunity for the defense to make a closing argument in a non-jury trial.

5. In general, the prosecution has effective responses to make to nearly every improper defense tactic either by entering the door opened by the defense and responding in kind, or by pointing out the impropriety of the argument (i.e., appeals to sympathy or prejudice, relies on his personal reputation) and telling the jury why the argument is improper and then stating that no lawyer as able as defense counsel would rely on such desperation tactics if he did not know his case was hopeless. Accordingly, though the prosecution has no right to appeal even from a grossly improper but effective defense argument (i.e., one causing acquittal), the right of the prosecution to the last word may deter much potential abuse of defense argument. (It should be noted, however, that in some jurisdictions the defense is allowed to close, at least when the defense offers no evidence.) The risk of judicial admonition may also temper extreme defense arguments.

The prosecutor is not allowed to attack defense counsel by accusing defense counsel (as opposed to defendant) of trying to deceive the jury. Whether such arguments matter is the subject of countless judicial disagreements about the judgment to be made. Consider United States v. Holmes, 413 F.3d 770 (8th Cir. 2005).

MELLOY, CIRCUIT JUDGE

> . . . Mr. Holmes objected to a statement the government made at the beginning of its rebuttal argument: "Mr. Moss is a good defense attorney, tries to get you to focus your attention over here when what really is important is right in front of you. It's all smoke and mirrors." (Mr. Moss was Mr. Holmes's trial counsel.) The district court overruled Mr. Holmes's objection that this comment was "improper." The government continued to make similar comments about Mr. Moss later in its rebuttal argument, stating that "Mr. Moss wants to distract you and tell you about all this other evidence that's not important," and that issues that Mr. Moss had

raised about who had owned the gun in question were a "ed herring." The government also commented that "r. Moss needs to make sure that they get their stories straight" ("hey" presumably referred to Mr. Moss and Mr. Holmes), and that the jury should "look at Mr. Moss's story. That's why I said he's got to get his stories straight."

We think that these various comments referring personally to Mr. Moss and the necessity for Mr. Moss to "et his stories straight," taken as a whole and in the context of the rebuttal argument, show that the government attorney was accusing defense counsel of conspiring with the defendant to fabricate testimony. These types of statements are highly improper because they improperly encourage the jury to focus on the conduct and role of Mr. Holmes's attorney rather than on the evidence of Mr. Holmes's guilt. Such personal, unsubstantiated attacks on the character and ethics of opposing counsel have no place in the trial of any criminal or civil case.

* * *

Here, ... the prosecutor's improper comment came in the rebuttal phase of closing arguments. Defense counsel was left with no opportunity to rebut the allegations and the jury heard the remark immediately before deliberations. The potential for prejudice is great during closing arguments, especially when the defense has no opportunity for rebuttal.

* * *

Here, the government's case was less than overwhelming. This is a case where one police officer, Officer Snyder, presented a version of the facts that conflicted with the defendant's version of the facts. A second police officer, Officer Le Moine, offered testimony that could have supported either explanation.

* * *

MORRIS SHEPPARD ARNOLD, CIRCUIT JUDGE, dissenting.

I would not reverse this conviction based on the remarks that the government's counsel made during closing arguments. The court indulges every presumption against a benign construction of those remarks and its characterization of their purport is harsh. In my judgment, the statements objected to did not directly implicate defense counsel's honesty.

I see no reason, moreover, to believe that the statements had a substantially injurious effect on the outcome of the case. Juries know that argument is not evidence; it is just talk. For all that we can know, the argument may well have gotten the jury's back up and prejudiced the government rather than the defendant. The court presumes that juries are a lot more impressionable than experience will allow for, and gives them too little credit for a common sense ability to discount vituperation and hyperbole and to restrict themselves to a consideration of the evidence adduced at trial.

There is nothing in this case to differentiate it from the scores, perhaps hundreds of cases that have routinely come before us in the last thirty or forty years in which an identical argument has been rejected out of hand. This counsels more caution than the court employs in the present circumstances.

I would uphold this judgment and therefore respectfully dissent.

6. In many jurisdictions, the prosecutor begins, is followed by defense counsel, and then is allowed rebuttal. Often a tradition has grown in which the so-called rebuttal is really the primary closing argument. For an account of one judge's effort to curb this practice, see United States v. Sarmiento, 744 F.2d 755 (11th Cir.1984), and especially the dissenting opinion; United States v. Taylor, 728 F.2d 930, 936–38 (7th Cir.1984). Allowing the defense sur-rebuttal is one option a judge has when the prosecutor exceeds the proper limits of rebuttal.

7. The absence of the sanction of appeal from improper defense tactics must leap to mind whenever a study of final argument is made. One can literally read hundreds of cases on jury arguments without ever encountering a discussion of defense arguments except for a handful of cases dealing with prosecutorial responses in kind. For reasons we have suggested, the practical consequences of this lack of sanction are probably not particularly serious. However, at the point of any consideration, it is worthwhile to consider the absence of the appeal sanction in relation to the defense view of the rules discussed in each of the sections of this Chapter. Is it reasonable to expect defense counsel who are often under financial and emotional pressures(resulting from the individual's need to win contests and gratitude from clients) to gain favorable verdicts, to be punctilious about observing the rules of the game? Reconsider particularly the standards and decisions dealing with perjured testimony, attempting to place probative but inadmissible evidence before the jury, dealing with witnesses who may claim privilege, and putting the defendant on the stand. In these areas are there meaningful sanctions other than appeal (as in the case of closing arguments)?

What are these sanctions and are they effective? Is the appeal sanction itself an adequate and effective check on the one party to whom it does apply, the prosecutor?

In People v. Butler, 58 Ill.2d 45, 317 N.E.2d 35 (1974), the Supreme Court of Illinois stated that a reviewing court should refer to the appropriate disciplinary body instances of improper argument by counsel which come to the court's attention during the course of an appeal. It noted that often prosecutorial misconduct, though great, is properly held harmless error because of the overwhelming nature of the evidence. Accordingly the Illinois high court concluded that some alternative penalty must be exacted.

Rarely does a reviewing court opinion identify by name the attorney who has utilized improper argument. Would identification be a meaningful sanction? Would there be anything wrong with naming the attorney in the appellate opinion?

8. In Darden v. Wainwright, 477 U.S. 168, 106 S.Ct. 2464 (1986), in the context of a capital case, the Supreme Court indicated that for a state prosecutor's closing argument to be deemed violative of the defendant's due process right to a fair trial, that argument must be exceedingly improper. The Court found no due process violation even though the prosecutor clearly and repeatedly expressed his personal opinion that the defendant was guilty. He also stated that he regretted that one of the victims had not blown the defendant's face off, so that the defendant would be sitting in the courtroom with no face. Referring to the fact that Darden was on furlough at the time of his alleged crime, the prosecutor called him an animal who shouldn't be out of a cell without a leash. To a large extent, without approving the argument, the majority relied upon the doctrine of "invited error" in finding no due process violation.

The war on drugs has engendered occasional prosecutorial slurs directed at folks from whatever country the defendant emigrated, blaming those people for America's drug problem. See United States v. Doe, 903 F.2d 16 (D.C.Cir.1990), where the prosecutor opined that Jamaicans controlled the drug traffic in Washington, D.C., and where the court condemned such argument.

9. Note on Arguments That Evidence Is Uncontradicted

(A)

People v. Hughes, 27 Cal.4th 287, 116 Cal.Rptr.2d 401, 39 P.3d 432 (2002) is a typical expression of the view that if the prosecution evidence characterized as uncontradicted is such that only the defendant himself could contradict it, the comment constitutes an improper reference to the defendant's failure to testify. There are jurisdictions, however, which approve the argument even when defendant could logically be the only possible witness. People v. Stanbeary, 126 Ill.App.2d 244, 261 N.E.2d 765 (1970).

Most courts hold that if a particular comment that prosecution evidence is uncontradicted refers to testimony which persons other than the defendant could have contradicted, the comment is not an improper reference to defendant's failure to testify. Shea v. United States, 251 Fed. 440 (6th Cir.1918), cert. denied 248 U.S. 581, 39 S.Ct. 132 (1918); Morrison v. United States, 6 F.2d 809 (8th Cir.1925). For collected state and federal cases see 14 A.L.R.3d 723. Some courts simply construe such statements as reference to the evidence adduced by the state, as by estimating its weight or persuasiveness, and not as improper comments on defendant's refusal to testify. Bary v. United States, 248 F.2d 201 (10th Cir.1957).

(B)

A particular problem is presented by a defendant who represents himself. If the defendant confines himself to conventional argument, the prosecutor is entitled only to the standard instruction that the arguments of counsel are not evidence. If the accused makes persistent use of his right to address court and jury to make statements amounting to the offering of testimony, the prosecutor may comment on his failure to testify. State v. Schultz, 46 N.J. 254, 216 A.2d 372 (1966).

(C)

There is one further limited exception to *Griffin*. In cases where inference of guilt arises from some unexplained act, i.e., unexplained possession of recently stolen property, the prosecutor may comment on the absence of explanation (which of course need not, but usually is, given only by defendant). United States v. Davis, 437 F.2d 928 (7th Cir.1971); State v. DiRienzo, 53 N.J. 360, 251 A.2d 99 (1969).

10. Note on Arguments That The Failure of the Opposition To Produce Evidence Justifies An Inference That The Evidence Would Weigh Against The Opposing Party

(A)

In the leading case of United States v. Young, 463 F.2d 934 (D.C.Cir.1972), the rule was stated thus: "when the judge concludes that the witness was not peculiarly available to a party or that his testimony would not be such as to elucidate the transaction, comment of opposing counsel arguing for an inference from his absence is contrary to law and unfair and cannot be permitted in argument to the jury." The Court suggested a model instruction to the jury in cases where such argument is proper:

Specimen Instruction on Absent Witnesses

> Counsel have argued that you should draw an inference from the absence of certain witnesses. The court has determined that each side had the ability to produce the witnesses. If you conclude that the testimony of a witness would have cast significant light on the issues, and that it would have been natural for one of the parties to have called that witness in support of his presentation if the facts known by the witness had been favorable to the position of that party, you may infer that if the witness

had been called he would have given testimony that would have been unfavorable to that party which failed to call him. But you are not required to draw that inference. And if you think that it would have been equally natural for each of the parties to have called the witness, and that each might equally have been expected to do so, then you may rightly conclude that since an equal inference could be drawn against each party, they cancel each other out. And if the matter seems doubtful, then you may rightly decide that no inference should be drawn from the absence of the witness. In that event, your verdict should be based on the evidence that was presented in court, and should not be affected by the witnesses who were not called.

(B)

Prosecution comment on the failure to produce witnesses is logically similar to the comment that the state's evidence is uncontradicted. The comment on missing witnesses is, of course, more specific than the use of the general "uncontradicted". Furthermore, the missing witness is an argument that the defense may have more use for than the prosecution.

Occasionally the courts decide that the defense may use the missing witness argument freely when the absence of the witness is unexplained, because the government has the burden of proof. People v. Gonzales, 125 Ill.App.2d 225, 260 N.E.2d 234 (1970). The prosecutor may usually respond by asserting that the defense did not use its right to subpoena, a right which is as great as the prosecution's. United States v. Panepinto, 430 F.2d 613 (3d Cir.1970).

The more common rule is to apply the general principles announced in United States v. Young to both parties. Many courts adopt the rule that comment by either party is prohibited when the witness is equally available to both parties. Maine flatly forbids prosecution comment upon the defendant's failure to call a witness as an improper burden on defendant to prove his innocence. State v. Brewer, 505 A.2d 774 (Me.1985). The question of equal accessibility depends upon more than mere amenability to subpoena or absence of privilege as United States v. Young points out. Relationships arising from family and business ties as well as friendship are significant factors in determining equality of access.

(C)

Occasionally, counsel wish to comment on the absence of material evidence. A common defense tactic is to ask, in closing argument, "where are the guns, jewels, fingerprints, bloody shirt, hair samples, fingernail scrapings, etc.?" *If* a prosecutor has established that evidence technicians made appropriate efforts to secure such evidence but failed to do so, he may argue an inference that the defendant is responsible for the absence of such evidence. People v. Williams, 40 Ill.2d 522, 240 N.E.2d 645 (1968)—accused could not afford to allow weapon to turn up and be submitted to ballistic analysis; State v. Wrose, 463 S.W.2d 792 (Mo.1971)—absence of fingerprints shows professionalism. In United States v. Latimer, 511 F.2d 498 (10th Cir.1975), defense counsel argued that the film from the bank's security camera was not introduced because his client, accused of robbing the bank, was not in the film. The prosecutor argued in response that the camera had malfunctioned and not even filmed the crime—in fact—filming only the arrival of the F.B.I. after the robbery. A divided court found the prosecutor's argument wrong in citing matters out side the record. The dissent argued defense counsel was "out of bounds" and "the prosecutor should be permitted to set the record straight".

An improper commenting on missing witnesses, when promptly admonished by the trial judge, who specifically instructs the jury to disregard prosecutor's comments, does not justify reversal. Dunlop v. United States, 165 U.S. 486, 17 S.Ct. 375 (1897). As the Supreme Court said very early in *Dunlop*: "If every remark made by counsel outside of the testimony were ground for reversal, comparatively few verdicts would stand".

(D)

Where evidence has been suppressed on defense motion, how far can defense counsel go in urging the jury to draw inferences from the absence of such testimony? Suppose that an out-of-court identification was suppressed because the accused's right to counsel at a lineup was violated. Suppose further that an in-court identification was permitted after a finding that such an identification had origins independent of the lineup. (See Casebook, ch. 3, § A.) Can defense counsel argue that the evidence shows that the first post-crime identification occurred at trial when he knows that is not true? If he did, could the prosecutor respond by telling the jury about the lineup? Should the prosecutor be permitted to re-open his case at this point? Can a prosecutor ever respond to a defense argument by referring to matters not in evidence?

3. Consistency in Argument Among Multiple Defendants

In re Peter Sakarias on Habeas Corpus
In re Tauno Waidla on Habeas Corpus

Supreme Court of California, 2005.
35 Cal.4th 140, 106 P.3d 931, 25 Cal.Rptr.3d 265.

■ Werdegar, J. In 1990, petitioners Peter Sakarias and Tauno Waidla were each, in separate trials, convicted of first degree murder with special circumstances and sentenced to death in the killing of Viivi Piirisild. We affirmed each of their convictions and sentences on automatic appeal, but issued orders to show cause in response to their petitions for writs of habeas corpus, on claims the prosecutor, in each trial, had presented factual theories inconsistent with those presented at the codefendant's trial.... On receipt of the returns and traverses, we consolidated the two causes for consideration and decision and appointed a referee to hear evidence and make factual findings. The referee has now issued his report, and the parties have filed briefs on the merits.

The evidence at petitioners' trials showed they both participated in the fatal attack on Viivi Piirisild, which was perpetrated with a hatchet and a knife. But both petitioners contend their joint prosecutor, Los Angeles County Deputy District Attorney Steven Ipsen, inconsistently and falsely portrayed their respective roles in the attack, attributing to each, in their respective trials, a series of three blows struck to the victim's head with the blade of the hatchet.... We agree with Sakarias that the prosecutor violated his due process rights by intentionally and without good faith justification arguing inconsistent and irreconcilable factual theories in the two trials, attributing to each petitioner in turn culpable acts that could have been committed by only one person. We also agree this violation prejudiced Sakarias, entitling him to relief. We do not decide whether the prosecutor's conduct was a due process violation as to Waidla, as we conclude any such violation was harmless in his case.

* * *

I. Factual and Procedural Background

A. Facts of the Crime

Waidla and Sakarias were both born in Estonia while that nation was part of the Soviet Union. They met as conscripts in the Soviet Army, from which they defected together, coming in 1987 to Los Angeles. There, they were taken under the wing of an Estonian–American couple, Avo and Viivi Piirisild, who offered to help them obtain jobs and education. For a period in 1987 to 1988, Waidla lived in the Piirisilds' guest house, performing remodeling work and other chores in exchange for his room and board.

Relations soon soured between petitioners and the Piirisilds. In May 1988, Waidla demanded the Piirisilds give him money or a sports car they had promised him for his work and threatened, otherwise, to report them for doing construction without a permit. When the Piirisilds told Waidla to leave their home, Waidla threatened to hurt or kill Avo. Later, Viivi received a postcard with a rattlesnake on it from Sakarias and Waidla, who were traveling together. Sakarias later told police he believed Viivi had been spreading harmful rumors about him and Waidla within the Estonian community, damaging their prospects for help from other Estonians around North America.

During early July 1988, petitioners broke into the Piirisilds' unoccupied cabin in Crestline. They stayed for several days, leaving only when they ran out of food and taking with them various items of the Piirisilds' property, including a hatchet. On July 12, angry, hungry, and in need of money, they went to the Piirisilds' North Hollywood home and broke in through the back door. They ate food from the kitchen and took some jewelry while waiting for Viivi to return home. Sakarias later told the police he and Waidla were planning to get money for food and to confront Viivi and frighten her into giving them the sports car; he also said that having contemplated killing themselves because of their poor situation, they decided to kill Viivi first so " 'she is not gonna see my funeral' " or, with her husband, " 'laugh on us for the rest of their lives.' "

When Viivi entered the house through the front door, petitioners immediately attacked her, using a knife and the hatchet they had taken from the Crestline cabin. They bludgeoned her with the blunt end of the hatchet, stabbed her with the knife, and chopped at her with the hatchet blade. Overall, the medical examiner found five blunt force impacts to Viivi's head (which fractured her skull and facial bones, knocked out her teeth, and broke her larynx), four stab wounds to her chest (two of which passed through vital organs), and three chopping wounds to her upper head. One of this last group of injuries, inflicted before death, was struck with "tremendous" force, penetrating Viivi's skull completely. The other two chopping wounds were inflicted with somewhat less force, after or around the time of death. The medical examiner attributed Viivi's death to the combination of wounds, several of which could have been fatal individually. After the attack in the entryway, petitioners dragged Viivi down the hall to a bedroom, where her body was found. According to the medical examiner's testimony at Waidla's trial, an abrasion on Viivi's lower back, caused by rubbing of her skin against another surface (which could have been incurred when she was dragged to the bedroom), was inflicted after her death.

Sakarias told police that during the initial attack he wielded the knife while Waidla used the hatchet. Sometime later, at Waidla's direction, he went to the bedroom and chopped Viivi's head twice with the hatchet. Waidla gave a statement admitting only a single bludgeoning blow, with the back of the hatchet at the outset of the attack, and denying any memory of how the rest of the attack proceeded. He recanted even that confession at his trial, testifying he had left Los Angeles three days before Viivi Piirisild was killed.

Petitioners sold the jewelry they took and used Viivi's credit cards for airline tickets, telephone calls, and other purchases. They were arrested more than a month later near the United States–Canada border in New York State.

B. The Inconsistent Factual Theories

Petitioners were jointly charged with Viivi Piirisild's murder, but their cases were severed after Sakarias was found incompetent to stand trial....

As reflected in the summary above, the evidence at petitioners' trials, taken as a whole, strongly suggests Waidla (who first wielded the hatchet, according to both petitioners' statements) struck the first, antemortem blow with the hatchet blade in the entryway, while Sakarias (who admitted doing so) inflicted the two postmortem or perimortem chopping wounds in the bedroom. (There was no evidence in either trial to suggest the perpetrators switched weapons during the initial attack.) But the prosecutor, Ipsen, did not argue at either trial the version of the attack best supported by all the evidence. Instead, at each defendant's trial he maintained the defendant on trial had inflicted *all* the chopping wounds.

In Waidla's trial, Ipsen introduced Waidla's admission that he, rather than Sakarias, had initially used the hatchet against Viivi Piirisild. (Sakarias's confession to police, in which he admitted striking two blows with the hatchet in the bedroom, was not introduced at Waidla's trial.) Although Waidla only admitted hitting Viivi with the back of the hatchet, Ipsen argued the jury should find Waidla actually used the hatchet throughout, "choosing ... the more devastating of the instruments," while Sakarias "accept[ed]" the knife, "the lesser implement." With the hatchet, Ipsen argued, Waidla first inflicted the blunt force injuries, then, "turning the hatchet blade so it was more effective ... [he] was now able to chop through the top of her skull." Ipsen suggested Waidla simply did not want to acknowledge his role in the attack, "his repeated striking of Viivi Piirisild, and swinging with the sharp end of the hatchet ... until she was dead." He emphasized the extended and repeated efforts both assailants made to ensure Viivi's death, "as Mr. Waidla indicated, himself with the hatchet, Mr. Sakarias who came up later with the knife." Waidla's use of the hatchet blade continued, Ipsen argued, even after Viivi was dead: " '[S]he's alive, she's alive, she's alive.' Sharp end, 'she's dead,' and then further blows indicating further blows were struck after she was dead, the non-hemorrhagic chop wounds to the head."

Having elicited, in the Waidla trial, the opinion of Dr. James Ribe, the medical examiner, that the abrasion on Viivi's lower back was incurred postmortem, Ipsen emphasized that the initial attack in the living room was fatal: "At the point that she was dragged into the back room, we know that Viivi Piirisild was already dead by the facts as the coroner testified. So, we know it was in that front room that the attack occurred, and that Viivi Piirisild was bludgeoned, chopped and stabbed until life left her body." Finally, in penalty argument, Ipsen urged a death sentence, in part because Waidla, after hitting Viivi repeatedly with the hatchet's blunt end, "chose to change the angle of the blade. ... Although he felt her head and her flesh against the back of his hatchet numerous times, he knew his mission wasn't accomplished, and that's when he changed and switched and used the sharp edge of the hatchet to give that death blow."

In Sakarias's trial, the prosecutor asked the medical examiner, Dr. Ribe, about each stabbing, chopping, or blunt force injury shown in the autopsy photographs, in many instances asking whether the wounds were antemortem or postmortem, but he did not examine Dr. Ribe about the lower back abrasion at all. He thus avoided eliciting Dr. Ribe's opinion, expressed in Waidla's earlier trial, that the abrasion had occurred after death and could have been caused by dragging Viivi's body along the carpeted hallway to the bedroom.

Due to this omission, no evidence was before Sakarias's jury that Viivi Piirisild was dead by the time Sakarias, as he admitted, struck her with the hatchet in the bedroom. The prosecutor was thus able to, and did, argue that Sakarias had, in the bedroom, inflicted all three chopping injuries, including the first, antemortem one. Thus Ipsen, in his guilt phase argument, told the jury that Sakarias, in the bedroom, inflicted "three ... sharp hatchet wounds to the top of Viivi's head with a tremendous force. ... [P] ... [P] We know that there are in fact three hatchet wounds; the first penetrating the top of the skull, and I know it was the first because it was a hemorrhagic wound, the one in the hairline, the one that chopped the top of her head completely off with the exception of some of the scalp that kept it completely on. [P] We know that when it's hemorrhagic it means that Viivi, whether conscious or not, still suffered that blow while alive, and we know that the last two in the forehead area being non-hemorrhagic were at a time when her body had ceased to live, or unfortunately actually possibly that the blood flow was not great enough to cause hemorrhage. [P] ... [P] Again, Mr. Sakarias indicates he believes he hit her two times with the hatchet when he used the hatchet. Again, by the evidence, he was off by only one blow."

In the penalty phase argument at Sakarias's trial, the prosecutor again portrayed Sakarias as having inflicted the antemortem hatchet-blade wound, which he characterized as finally causing Viivi's death. Sakarias's participation in the crime could not be considered minor, Ipsen argued; he was "as involved in the murder of Viivi Piirisild as one could ask, swinging what I suggest were the blows that actually ended her life." Referring to Sakarias in the second person, Ipsen argued that if, after the attack in the living room, "you had called 911, realizing what you had done and attempted to save her life, ... perhaps you would deserve the pity, the sympathy, perhaps the scales of justice would lean in your direction. [P] ... [P] If, when you walked back to the back room with that hatchet and thought Viivi Piirisild is still alive, and you must have, otherwise you wouldn't have gone back there with that hatchet, and if you just simply didn't chop the top of her head off, as the evidence indicated you did in that back room, thus finally ending her life."

In addition to the prosecutorial arguments just recited, petitioners also complain of inconsistency in the prosecutor's penalty phase arguments relating to domination. (See *Pen. Code, 190.3, factor (g)* ["substantial domination" by another may be considered in mitigation].) At Waidla's trial, Ipsen argued Waidla "is not one who is dominated by another, but instead the facts indicate that he was the dominate [*sic*] person between himself and Mr. Sakarias, that he was the planner, he was the one who knew of the Piirisild home and knew of the facts surrounding the burglary, the robbery of Mrs. Piirisild." At Sakarias's trial, in contrast, Ipsen argued Sakarias was "in no way" dominated by Waidla: "They were separate individuals joined by a common plan, a common hatred, common goals." Petitioners' actions in killing Viivi and escaping were those of "a partnership like a right hand and a left hand," with "absolutely no evidence of domination."

C. The Habeas Corpus Proceedings

* * *

II. Discussion

A. Review of Referee's Findings

... Upon review, we find each of the referee's findings supported by substantial evidence and, like the parties, we accept them.

1. *Ipsen's use of divergent factual theories was intentional*

Ipsen testified at the reference hearing, as he stated in his earlier declaration, that his presentation of inconsistent theories was "not intentional." He noted that in the interval between the trials he probably handled other cases and described himself as an "instinct[ive]" litigator who did not typically follow detailed notes or a script in his examination of witnesses. When he made his closing argument in the Sakarias case, he did not have in mind what he had argued to the Waidla jury: "the last thing I'm thinking about when I'm arguing in one trial is trying to remember what I argued in another trial."

The referee found Ipsen's claim of inadvertence "unconvincing": "Despite a lapse of eight months between trials, it is unlikely that a competent and committed prosecutor like Ipsen, handling the severed trials of two defendants jointly charged with capital murder, would simply forget at the second trial what specific factual theory of the gruesome murder he presented at the first. ... [T]he Waidla and Sakarias trials were Ipsen's first murder cases, his first death penalty cases. He was depressed about the death verdict in Waidla for approximately two weeks. It is improbable that his factual depiction of the killing in Waidla would have totally escaped his notice in Sakarias. Moreover, the assertion of inadvertence in presenting the inconsistent theories implies a level of carelessness that is simply not present in Ipsen's prosecution of Sakarias."

* * *

2. *Ipsen had strong reason to believe, while prosecuting Sakarias, that the victim was already dead when moved to the bedroom*

Although there were slight grounds for doubt, the referee found, "the great weight of the available evidence" supported the view that Viivi Piirisild died in the living room. The postmortem abrasion, in particular, was best explained as the result of Viivi's body being dragged across the carpet to the bedroom. While the abrasion could conceivably have had other causes, "[t]he dragging explained the size, nature, and location of the abrasion" and was also consistent with the condition of Viivi's clothing.

* * *

3. *Ipsen deliberately refrained from asking Dr. Ribe about the postmortem abrasion in Sakarias's trial*

The referee, observing that in Sakarias's trial Ipsen had introduced virtually all the same autopsy photographs as in Waidla's trial but had omitted exhibit 59K, which showed the abrasion on Viivi Piirisild's back, concluded Ipsen's omissions of this exhibit and of questioning regarding the abrasion were deliberate, designed to avoid the presentation of evidence "inconvenient" to his new and different theory of the attack, evidence "much easier to omit than to explain."

4. *Ipsen did not offer Sakarias's confession at Waidla's trial because he believed it would be inadmissible*

Ipsen testified he would have liked to introduce Sakarias's confession, which implicated Waidla equally, in Waidla's trial, but assumed it would be subject to a successful objection. "My understanding of the law at the time and still today, is that when I'm prosecuting Mr. Waidla and charging him with murder, I can't use the statement of his accomplice against him." At trial before a judge he knew to be highly experienced in criminal law, "If I had tried to get in evidence, which everyone knows is inadmissible and is wrong, I'd look like an idiot to say I'd like to offer the codefendant's statement."

The referee accepted Ipsen's testimony on this point, stating the confession would have been inadmissible under *People v. Aranda* (1965) and *Bruton v. United States* (1968). The prosecutor's failure to offer the statement, the referee found, "did not relate to its inconsistency with the factual theory he intended to present at Waidla's trial."

* * *

B. The People's Bad Faith Use of Inconsistent Theories Deprived Sakarias of Due Process, Requiring Vacation of His Death Sentence

. . . The Attorney General contends the use of inconsistent arguments at separate trials "is permissible provided a prosecutor does not argue something that the prosecutor knows to be false." For reasons explained below, we conclude that fundamental fairness does not permit the People, without a good faith justification, to attribute to two defendants, in separate trials, a criminal act only one defendant could have committed. By doing so, the state necessarily urges conviction or an increase in culpability in one of the cases on a false factual basis, a result inconsistent with the goal of the criminal trial as a search for truth. At least where, as in Sakarias's case, the change in theories between the two trials is achieved partly through deliberate manipulation of the evidence put before the jury, the use of such inconsistent and irreconcilable theories impermissibly undermines the reliability of the convictions or sentences thereby obtained.

We also conclude, however, that where, as here, the available evidence points clearly to the truth of one theory and the falsity of the other, only the defendant against whom the false theory was used can show constitutionally significant prejudice. For that reason, we conclude that Sakarias, but not Waidla, is entitled to relief on his petition.

1. *The People may not convict two individuals of a crime only one could have committed or obtain harsher sentences against two individuals by unjustifiably attributing to each a culpable act only one could have committed*

Judicial disapproval of the state's use of inconsistent and irreconcilable theories in separate trials for the same crimes was first articulated in opinions by individual Supreme Court and lower federal court judges. (See *Jacobs v. Scott* (1995) 513 U.S. 1067 [130 L. Ed. 2d 618, 115 S. Ct. 711] (dis. opn. of Stevens, J., from denial of stay) [fundamentally unfair to execute a person "on the basis of a factual determination that the State has formally disavowed" in coperpetrator's later trial]; *Drake v. Kemp* (11th Cir. 1985) 762 F.2d 1449, 1479 (conc. opn. of Clark, J.) [prosecutor's "flip flopping of theories of the offense was inherently unfair"].) Drawing on these separate opinions, several federal courts have since held that a prosecutor's inconsistent argument in two defendants' separate trials attributing the same criminal or culpability-increasing act to each defendant denies the defendants fundamentally fair trials.

In *Thompson v. Calderon* (9th Cir. 1997) 120 F.3d 1045 (*Thompson*), a majority of the en banc court held that inconsistent prosecutorial theories may present a due process violation. There, Leitch and Thompson were both charged with raping and killing Ginger Fleischli. At their joint preliminary hearing and at Leitch's trial, the prosecutor introduced and relied on evidence, including testimony by jailhouse informants recounting statements by Thompson, that indicated the two defendants had acted together, killing Fleischli because she was interfering with Leitch's efforts to reconcile with his ex-wife. (*Thompson*, (plur. opn. of Fletcher, J.).) At Thompson's trial (held before Leitch's), however, the same prosecutor had introduced and relied upon other evidence, to the effect that Thompson alone killed Fleischli to prevent her reporting that he had raped her. The prosecutor thus "asserted as the truth before Thompson's jury the story he subsequently labeled absurd and incredible in Leitch's trial."

The *Thompson* plurality concluded that "when no new significant evidence comes to light a prosecutor cannot, in order to convict two defendants at separate trials, offer inconsistent theories and facts regarding the same crime." Three of the 11 judges participating fully joined with Judge Fletcher in her opinion on this point. Two more, in a concurring opinion by Judge Tashima, agreed that prosecutorial use of wholly inconsistent theories violates due process, but believed that Thompson's entitlement to relief depended on whether he was prejudiced, which in turn required a determination "which of the two inconsistent theories pursued by the prosecutor represents the true facts and which is false."

In *Smith v. Groose* (8th Cir. 2000) 205 F.3d 1045 (*Smith*), members of two criminal groups who had separately burglarized the same house during overlapping periods of the same day were tried separately for the murder of the occupants. At the trials of both Cunningham, a member of the first group of burglars, and Smith, a member of the second, Lytle, also a member of the second group, testified the occupants were killed by Cunningham's group. In one prior statement to police, Lytle had attributed the killings to a member of his own group, Bowman, while in another he said, consistently with his trial testimony, that Cunningham's group had killed the occupants. At Smith's trial, the prosecutor used Lytle's prior statement implicating Bowman in the killings, arguing to the jury that Smith, Bowman's accomplice in burglary, was guilty of felony murder. Later, at Cunningham's trial, the prosecutor relied on Lytle's testimony, introduced his prior consistent statement to police, did not introduce his prior inconsistent statement, and objected to defense efforts to impeach him ... In short, what the State claimed to be true in Smith's case it rejected in Cunningham's case, and vice versa.

The *Smith* court concluded, "the use of inherently ... contradictory theories violates the principles of due process", for "[t]he State's duty to its citizens does not allow it to pursue as many convictions as possible without regard to fairness and the search for truth" (*id.* at p. 1051; see also *United States v. Butner* (W.D.Mo. 2000) 2000 WL 1842410, *1517 [following *Smith*]).

Recently, the Sixth Circuit Court of Appeals reached the same conclusion in *Stumpf v. Mitchell* (6th Cir. 2004) 367 F.3d 594, ... Stumpf and his accomplice, Wesley, robbed and killed a couple, the Stouts, in their home. That Stumpf shot Mr. Stout was undisputed, but whether he also shot Mrs. Stout or Wesley did so with Stumpf's handgun was unclear. At Stumpf's plea hearing, the prosecutor argued that since both victims were shot with the same weapon, the evidence showed Stumpf must have killed both victims " 'in order not to leave anyone available to identify him.' " But at Wesley's later trial, the prosecutor introduced a jail informant's testimony that Wesley had confessed to picking up Stumpf's handgun and shooting Mrs. Stout. On that basis, the prosecutor argued Stumpf had left the room after shooting Mr. Stout, whereupon Wesley, " 'whose own gun was jammed, picked that chrome colored Raven up and as Mrs. Stout sat helplessly on her bed, shot her four times in order to leave no witnesses to the crime.' "

The appellate court concluded, "the use of inconsistent, irreconcilable theories to convict two defendants for the same crime is a due process violation." The vice rests in the fact that of two inconsistent and irreconcilable theories, one must be false: "Because inconsistent theories render convictions unreliable, they constitute a violation of the due process rights of any defendant in whose trial they are used." In *Stumpf*, the state had clearly used such irreconcilable theories, for "[a]t each proceeding, the prosecutor argued that the defendant had been the one to pull the trigger, resulting in the fatal shots to [Mrs.] Stout."

These courts and judges have found a prosecutor's 180degree change in theory "deeply troubling" in part because by taking a formal position inconsistent with the guilt or culpability of at least one convicted defendant, the government, through the prosecutor, has cast doubt on the factual basis for the conviction. "If the prosecutor's statements at the Hogan trial were correct, then Jacobs is innocent of capital murder." "The conclusion seems inescapable that the prosecutor obtained Henry Drake's conviction through the use of testimony he did not believe...." "The prosecutor ... at Leitch's trial essentially ridiculed the theory he had used to obtain a conviction and death sentence at Thompson's trial." As both of two irreconcilable theories of guilt cannot be true, "inconsistent theories render convictions unreliable."

Because it undermines the reliability of the convictions or sentences, the prosecution's use of inconsistent and irreconcilable theories has also been criticized as inconsistent with the principles of public prosecution and the integrity of the criminal trial system. A criminal prosecutor's function "is not merely to prosecute crimes, but also to make certain that the truth is honored to the fullest extent possible during the course of the criminal prosecution and trial." (*United States v. Kattar* (1st Cir.1988) 840 F.2d 118, 127.) His or her goal must be "not simply to obtain a conviction, but to obtain a fair conviction." (*Brown v. Borg* (9th Cir. 1991) 951 F.2d 1011, 1015, italics omitted.) "Although the prosecutor must prosecute with earnestness and vigor and 'may strike hard blows, he is not at liberty to strike foul ones.'" (*Smith, supra*, 205 F.3d at p. 1049, quoting *Berger v. United States* (1935) 295 U.S. 78, 88 [79 L.Ed. 1314, 55 S.Ct. 629]; see also ABA Model Code Prof. Responsibility, EC 713 ["The responsibility of a public prosecutor differs from that of the usual advocate; his duty is to seek justice, not merely to convict"].)

* * *

We have previously indicated that an inconsistent prosecutorial argument "made in bad faith" could be misconduct, and conversely that such argument was not improper if "based on the record and made in good faith" (*People v. Farmer* (1989) 47 Cal.3d 888, 923 [254 Cal. Rptr. 508, 765 P.2d 940] (*Farmer*)), though we did not have occasion in that case to deal more definitively with the problem. With the issue more squarely before us here, we hold that the People's use of irreconcilable theories of guilt or culpability, unjustified by a good faith justification for the inconsistency, is fundamentally unfair, for it necessarily creates the potential for—and, where prejudicial, actually achieves—a false conviction or increased punishment on a false factual basis for one of the accuseds. "The criminal trial should be viewed not as an adversarial sporting contest, but as a quest for truth." (*United States v. Kattar*, supra, 840 F.2d at p. 127.)

By intentionally and in bad faith seeking a conviction or death sentence for two defendants on the basis of culpable acts for which only one could be responsible, the People violate "the due process requirement that the government prosecute fairly in a search for truth...." (*Smith, supra*, 205 F.3d at p. 1053.) In such circumstances, the People's conduct gives rise to a due process claim (under both the *United States* and *California Constitutions*) similar to a claim of factual innocence. Just as it would be impermissible for the state to punish a person factually innocent of the charged crime, so too does it violate due process to base criminal punishment on unjustified attribution of the same criminal or culpability-increasing acts to two different persons when only one could have committed them. In that situation, we *know* that *someone* is factually innocent of the culpable acts attributed to both. (See *Prosecutorial Inconsistency, supra*, 89 Cal. L.Rev. at p. 1425 ["When the prosecution advances a position in the trial of one defendant and then adopts an inconsistent position in the trial of another on the same facts, the prosecution is relying on a known falsity"].)

2. *The People unjustifiably used inconsistent and irreconcilable theories to obtain a death sentence against Sakarias*

Prosecutor Ipsen attributed first to Waidla alone and later to Sakarias alone, in their respective trials, a series of blows to the victim's head with the hatchet blade. These two theories are irreconcilable; that Waidla alone inflicted each of these wounds, as the prosecutor maintained at his trial, and that Sakarias alone also did so, as the prosecutor maintained at his trial, is not possible. One or the other theory (or both, if each man inflicted some but not all of the wounds) must be false.

(6) The acts attributed to both Waidla and Sakarias in turn were not necessary to establish their guilt of first degree murder (*Pen. Code, 189*) or the truth of the charged robbery- and burglary-murder special circumstances (*id., 190.2, subd. (a)(17)*). But the prosecutor attributed the three hatchet-edge blows to each defendant in turn in order to establish an aggravating circumstance of the crime (*id., 190.3*) on the basis of which the jury was urged to sentence each defendant to death. At least where the punishment involved is death, due process is as offended by the People's inconsistent and irreconcilable attribution of culpability-increasing acts as by the inconsistent and irreconcilable attribution of crimes.

* * *

Because Ipsen used different attributions of the chopping wounds to argue each petitioner should receive the death penalty, his factual theories were significantly inconsistent and irreconcilable. The present case is thus critically distinguishable from those in which the prosecutor's theories were held fundamentally consistent because any variation did not concern a fact used to convict the defendant or increase his or her punishment. (See *Nguyen v. Lindsey* (9th Cir. 2000) 232 F.3d 1236, 12401241 [variation in prosecutorial argument as to which of two gangs fired the first shot in a gun battle that killed a bystander not significant where prosecutor at both trials pursued the same "underlying theory" that all participants in the gang battle were equally responsible for the death].) Unlike those cases, here Ipsen's underlying theory of why petitioners each deserved the death penalty was not the same in the two cases; in Waidla's case, it included Waidla's supposed striking of all three blows with the hatchet blade, while in Sakarias's case it included Sakarias's striking the same three blows.

We turn to the question of justification. . . .

. . . We agree a significant change in the available evidence might, under some circumstances, warrant the use of an inconsistent prosecutorial theory in a subsequent trial. Here, one difference in evidence between the two trials was the introduction at Waidla's trial, but not at Sakarias's, of Dr. Ribe's testimony that the abrasion on the victim's back was non-hemorrhagic and therefore appeared to have been inflicted after death. But Ipsen's deliberate strategic choice in Sakarias's trial not to examine Dr. Ribe regarding the abrasion on the victim's lower back, as he had done a few months earlier at Waidla's trial, plainly cannot establish Ipsen's good faith or otherwise justify the use of irreconcilable theories. To the contrary, such manipulation of the evidence for the purpose of pursuing inconsistent theories establishes the prosecutor's *bad* faith. . . .

The referee found, on substantial evidence, that Ipsen omitted questioning about the back abrasion in order to avoid presenting evidence "inconvenient" to his new theory that Sakarias had inflicted all three chopping wounds to the victim's head. Such intentional manipulation of the evidence was instrumental to, and cannot justify, the prosecutor's use of irreconcilable theories. . . .

The dissenting opinion finds no indication of bad faith in Ipsen's conduct because, where the information available to the prosecutor is of public record or has been disclosed to the defense. . . . We agree no due process violation arises simply from a prosecutor's failure to introduce evidence favorable to the defense. But where, as here, a prosecutor who seeks convictions or death sentences against two individuals through inconsistent and irreconcilable factual theories deliberately omits in one trial evidence used in the other, so as to make possible the argument of the inconsistent theories, the prosecutor's manipulation of evidence does show that the inconsistent theories were not pursued in good faith. . . . Whether that conduct was prejudicial must still be determined.

* * *

3. *The People's use of inconsistent and irreconcilable theories was prejudicial as to Sakarias*

* * *

We need not decide here what result obtains when the likely truth of the prosecutor's inconsistent theories *cannot* be determined, for the case at bench is not one of ambiguous or inconclusive evidence. As the referee found, the great weight of available evidence indicates that Viivi Piirisild was dead or near death when dragged into the bedroom and thus that

Waidla, rather than Sakarias, struck the antemortem, hemorrhagic hatchet-blade blow. True, *some* evidence—blood spatters in the bedroom—suggests the possibility of an antemortem blow being struck in that room. But that evidence is overwhelmed by other evidence that Viivi's hemorrhagic wounds, including the hemorrhagic chopping wound Ipsen characterized as the "death blow," were inflicted during petitioners' initial attack on her in the living room, including the large pool of blood in the living room, the minimum quantity of blood on the bedroom walls and ceiling, the lack of blood on the bedroom floor, Sakarias's statement that petitioners felled Viivi in the living room before eventually dragging her into the bedroom, and the nonhemorrhagic character of the abrasion on Viivi's back. As both petitioners' statements have Waidla using the hatchet during that initial attack and Sakarias the knife, and as no evidence at all suggests the two exchanged weapons during the initial attack, the inescapable inference from all the available evidence is that Waidla inflicted the hemorrhagic chopping wound to Viivi's head.

To the extent the false attribution of the antemortem hatchet-blade blow to Sakarias was potentially material to the penalty decision, it deprived Sakarias of a fair penalty trial and entitles him to relief....

Aside from attributing the hemorrhagic chopping wound to Sakarias, the prosecutor introduced and relied upon other significant aggravating circumstances. Sakarias undisputedly played a direct role in the brutal, unprovoked killing of Viivi Piirisild. The uncontroverted evidence showed that Sakarias stabbed Viivi four times in the chest, including two potentially fatal wounds passing through vital organs, and that he later took the hatchet, went to the bedroom, and struck her at least twice in the head with the hatchet blade. Sakarias had a loaded handgun when arrested and later was found in possession of shanks in the county jail (for use, he said, against gang members who had robbed him). He also made statements during trial indicating a lack of remorse for killing Viivi and suggesting that he and Waidla had intended to kill Avo Piirisild as well.

Other considerations, however, make it impossible for us to conclude *beyond a reasonable doubt* that the prosecutorial argument that Sakarias struck all the hatchet-blade blows, including the first, antemortem one, played no role in the penalty decision. The first hatchet-blade wound was especially severe and was described in gruesome detail by the medical examiner on direct examination by the prosecutor. The path of the blade was parallel to the top of the head, straight up and down as if the victim was lying on the floor. The blade entered on the upper forehead, penetrated through the scalp and the skull bone, then hit the inside of the skull. Dr. Ribe believed the blade then "bounced" off the bone and continued to the rear and right of the victim's head, leaving another incision. The blow's force not only penetrated the front of the skull but fractured the back as well, pushing it backward. As a result, a portion of the upper skull and scalp were partially detached from the rest of the head, forming a flap that could be easily folded back. Because of the strength of an adult human's skull, Dr. Ribe believed a "tremendous amount of force," as much as an average man could exert swinging the hatchet "very hard," was needed to cause this wound.

In the guilt phase argument, the prosecutor discussed in detail Sakarias's attack on Viivi Piirisild with the hatchet, stating he went into the bedroom "to strike a few more blows, to make sure that Viivi was dead in case the stabbing and the bludgeoning weren't enough. [P] We know that there were three, in this series of blows, sharp hatchet wounds to the top of Viivi's head with a tremendous force. . . . [P] And it was with this strength that Peter Sakarias swung this hatchet to penetrate this skull, to reach that most vital organ . . . [P] . . . [P] We know that there are in fact three hatchet wounds; the first penetrating the top of the skull, and I know it was the first because it was a hemorrhagic wound, the one in the hairline, the one that chopped the top of her head completely off with the exception of some of the scalp that kept it completely on. [P] . . . [P] We know that this last series of chop wounds . . . was consistent with the last three blows she received." In the penalty argument, the prosecutor twice again asserted that Sakarias had inflicted all the chopping wounds, "swinging what I suggest were the blows that actually ended her life." Sakarias, according to Ipsen, "simply . . . chop[ped] the top of her head off, as the evidence indicated you did in that back room, thus finally ending her life."

As to mitigation, Sakarias was young (21 years old) at the time of the offense, had no record of violence, and had suffered persecution in the Soviet Army. He was diagnosed with schizo-affective disorder, characterized by paranoia and bipolar affect; the jury was informed that he had been found incompetent to stand trial in May 1990 and spent almost a year in a state hospital. The defense also played tapes of Sakarias's mother, father, and friends, recorded in Estonia, describing his childhood and youth. (*Sakarias*, *supra*, 22 Cal.4th at pp. 614616.)

Some aspect or aspects of the case evidently gave one or more jurors considerable pause in the sentencing decision, as the penalty jury deliberated for more than 10 hours over three days and, at one point, declared itself unable to reach a unanimous verdict, before finally returning a verdict of death.

In light of the prominence the prosecutor gave the antemortem chopping wound, treating it as the final, fatal wound, and the likely impact the medical examiner's description of that wound and the force necessary to inflict it would have had, that the prosecutor's attribution of that blow to Sakarias had an effect on the penalty verdict is reasonably likely. Though Sakarias's undisputed conduct in stabbing Viivi Piirisild and stealing her property played, no doubt, a major role in the jury's decision, we cannot conclude beyond a reasonable doubt that the jury's decision would have been the same had it not also been told that Sakarias finally ended Viivi's life by swinging a hatchet with all his strength, nearly cutting off the top of her head. The prosecutor's intentional and unjustified argument, inconsistent with the factual theory and evidence he had presented at Waidla's trial, that Sakarias struck the antemortem hatchet-blade blow was therefore prejudicial to Sakarias as to penalty.

4. *The People's use of inconsistent and irreconcilable theories was harmless as to Waidla*

Our conclusion is necessarily different as to Waidla. As discussed earlier, and as the referee found, the great weight of the evidence available—the statements of both petitioners, the physical crime scene evidence, and the medical examiner's expert testimony—tended to show that Waidla wielded the hatchet in the initial attack, that the first chopping wound was inflicted before Viivi Piirisild's death, and that Viivi died in her living room from the initial attack before being dragged to the back bedroom. Ipsen's argument in Waidla's trial that Waidla struck the first, antemortem blow with the hatchet blade, therefore, was likely true.

Waidla points to Sakarias's statement that he struck Viivi with the hatchet in the bedroom. But Sakarias confessed to hitting Viivi with the hatchet only *twice*, which left open the possibility—a probability under the other evidence—that the first of the three chopping wounds was inflicted by Waidla during the initial attack. To be sure, in his arguments to the Waidla jury Ipsen suggested that Waidla had inflicted *all* the chop wounds, including the two postmortem or perimortem wounds that Ipsen had strong reason to believe were actually attributable to Sakarias. But this apparently false argument, inconsistent with the arguments made in Sakarias's trial, was not prejudicial to Waidla as to penalty, even under the reasonable likelihood standard of *United States v. Agurs*. To the extent he focused on particular blows, the impact of the prosecutor's arguments derived from the hemorrhagic hatchet-blade wound, the chop "through the top of her skull" or "death blow," rather than from the fact that "further blows were struck after she was dead."

Waidla admitted that after burglarizing the home of Viivi Piirisild, an older woman who had been his benefactor, he hit her with the back of a hatchet he had stolen from her vacation cabin. The medical examiner opined that these blunt force wounds, which fractured several bones and knocked out Viivi's teeth, contributed to her death. The evidence, moreover, was strong that Waidla, during this attack, turned the hatchet around and struck Viivi with the sharp blade with such force as to penetrate her skull and cut a flap of skull and scalp from the top of her head. Even balanced against Waidla's youth, lack of a violent criminal record, and personal history of brutalization in the Soviet Army (*Waidla*, *supra*, 22 Cal.4th at pp. 706, 712), the circumstances of the crime offered a compelling case in aggravation. More to the point, the case would not have been made significantly less compelling by a prosecutorial concession that Sakarias may have inflicted the two later chop wounds, after Viivi had expired. As the Attorney General remarks, "Under the circumstances, it would have made no difference to the jury whether Waidla inflicted the nonhemorrhagic chopping wounds or handed the weapon to Sakarias so he could inflict them, particularly since the wounds were likely postmortem." We conclude beyond a reasonable doubt that the prosecutor's attribution of these two wounds to Waidla, though likely false, did not affect Waidla's penalty and does not entitle him to relief.

* * *

The order to show cause as to Waidla's petition is discharged.

Sakarias's petition for a writ of habeas corpus is granted insofar as it claims prosecutorial inconsistency material to the penalty verdict, and the judgment of the Los Angeles County Superior Court in *People v. Peter*

Sakarias, No. A711340, therefore is vacated insofar as it imposes a sentence of death....

■ Concur by: BAXTER

■ Dissent by: BAXTER

■ Dissent: BAXTER, J., concurring and dissenting.I concur in the judgment except insofar as it orders vacation of petitioner Sakarias's death judgment. As to Sakarias, I respectfully dissent.

* * *

... [T]he majority say Sakarias's due process rights were prejudicially violated as to penalty when, in their separate trials, Prosecutor Ipsen, acting in "bad faith," sought to enhance each petitioner's culpability by attributing the same *single* antemortem hatchet-chopping wound to each killer. Ipsen's bad faith is demonstrated, the majority assert, because (1) the available evidence pointed strongly to Waidla, not Sakarias, as the perpetrator of this act, and (2) Ipsen "manipulated" the evidence at Sakarias's trial by failing to elicit certain medical testimony he had earlier used to attribute the same act to Waidla. The majority insist that the misimpression thus conveyed to Sakarias's jury may have influenced its penalty decision. I disagree.

At the outset, I discern no bad faith in Ipsen's conduct. Our referee was never asked to make such a finding, and he did not do so. In my view, there is no basis for a bad faith determination. Ipsen adhered to the well-established rule against the knowing presentation of *false* evidence. Moreover, he presumably discharged his obligation to *give the defense* any otherwise unavailable evidence he possessed that materially undermined the prosecution's case against Sakarias. Nor was there any secret, at the time of Sakarias's trial, about Ipsen's case against Waidla. Because Sakarias's trial followed Waidla's, this information was by then a matter of public record.

Under such circumstances, the People would not generally be required to *introduce*, in their own case, evidence *helpful to the defense*. Instead, the prosecution could properly rely on the defense to expose the gaps and weaknesses in its proof. I see no reason why a different rule should apply in Sakarias's case simply because the omitted evidence was earlier presented against Waidla.

Further, I believe Ipsen demonstrated no bad faith by theorizing, in each defendant's trial, that the antemortem hatchet chop was inflicted by that defendant. I have two reasons for this conclusion. First, the law governing inconsistent prosecutorial arguments is complex and unsettled; indeed, a case presenting such issues is currently under review by the United States Supreme Court. (*Stumpf v. Mitchell* (6th Cir.2004) 367 F.3d 594 (*Stumpf*), cert. granted *sub nom. Mitchell v. Stumpf* (2005) 543 U.S. 1042 [160 L.Ed. 2d 610, 125 S.Ct. 824].) Because appellate judges significantly disagree about what a prosecutor may and may not do in this regard, there seems little basis to conclude that Ipsen's strategy constituted bad faith. Second, the evidence of who delivered the antemortem chopping blow is hardly as clear as the majority suggest. Our referee found that Ipsen himself was sincerely uncertain which of the two murderers had committed this particular act. Under these circumstances, I cannot find bad faith in Ipsen's efforts to make a plausible case against each petitioner.

* * *

Here, Ipsen did not use inconsistent theories to obtain capital murder judgments against two defendants, where only one could be guilty or death-eligible. There is no doubt that Sakarias and Waidla together committed the first degree murder of Viivi Piirisild with special circumstances, and that both men were enthusiastic participants in the gruesome attack. The only dispute in this case relates to a particular *detail* which a jury *could* consider in deciding whether death was the appropriate penalty for each killer. Under these circumstances, and given the uncertain state of the law, I cannot find in Ipsen's conduct an act of bad faith amounting to a constitutional violation.

. . . Ipsen was not an eyewitness to Viivi's murder. Neither Waidla nor Sakarias confessed to delivering the disputed blow. Evidence on that point was entirely circumstantial. In my view, it was not so clear as to preclude Ipsen from reserving personal judgmentas he didand presenting the plausible case against each man.

As the majority notes, the case against Waidla is as follows: When the attack began in the Piirisilds' living room, Sakarias was using a knife, while Waidla was using the blunt edge of the hatchet to bludgeon the victim. At some point, she was moved from the living room to the bedroom. There is evidence she was already dead by that time, and the two hatchet chops to which Sakarias admitted were, he said, inflicted in the bedroom. Hence, the earlier, antemortem chopping blow must have been inflicted in the living room, and by Waidla.

This is a plausible scenario, but a substantial case could be made against Sakarias as well. After all, neither Sakarias nor Waidla ever attributed *any* hatchet chops to Waidla. On the other hand, Sakarias conceded that he did use the hatchet to deliver such blows. Indeed, Sakarias admitted inflicting *two of the three* hatchet chops disclosed by the evidence, all of which were in relatively close proximity on the victim's head. As Ipsen implied in Sakarias's trial, one could infer that Sakarias had simply understated by one the number of chops he delivered. Moreover, while most of the bloodstains and spatters were found in the living room, there were significant spatters in the bedroom as well. In one place in the bedroom, a detective testified at Sakarias's trial, there was enough blood "to actually start to trickle down the wall." This was some, if not conclusive, evidence that the victim bled in the bedroom, and was thus still alive.

The majority claim Waidla must have inflicted the antemortem wound because the medical examiner testified at Waidla's trial that an abrasion on Viivi's back was probably caused by dragging, and that the "nonhemorrhagic" nature of the abrasion suggested it was sustained postmortem. Thus, the majority infer, the abrasion must have occurred when the victim, already dead, was dragged to the bedroom. Because Sakarias admitted only two chop wounds in the bedroom, the majority reason he must have inflicted the two postmortem wounds, and none other.

But this analysis is hardly conclusive. Expert opinions are often subject to debate and interpretation. Moreover, even if we credit an inference that the victim was already dead when she was moved to the bedroom, that does not prove Sakarias wielded the hatchet only thereafter. We know this weapon was transferred from Waidla to Sakarias at some point, but we do not know exactly when. Given the uncertain evidence, I conclude that so long as Ipsen did not introduce false evidence, he acted in good faith by presenting alternative theories about this detail of the attack. Having satisfied his discovery obligations, Ipsen could properly rely, in each case, on the due diligence of the defense to expose weaknesses in the People's proof.

By concluding that Ipsen could only present the case they think is stronger, the majority intrude much too far into matters which, for good reason, have traditionally been left to prosecutorial discretion. I cannot join the majority's attempt to second-guess the prosecution's strategy in this way.

In any event, I do not accept the majority's conclusion that Sakarias suffered prejudice on the issue of penalty. The undisputed details of Sakarias's role in this brutal murder are aggravated in the extreme. Though the Piirisilds had bestowed many kindnesses on Sakarias and Waidla, the two men decided they had been slighted by their benefactors. Filled with hate and greed, Sakarias and Waidla hatched a plan to burglarize and rob the couple. But once in the Piirisild home, they did not simply take property and leave. Instead, they "started waiting for Viivi" with murderous intent.

As the majority recite, Sakarias personally used his knife to stab Viivi at least four times in the chest. Two of these wounds were potentially fatal. Sakarias ceased his attack with the knife only when its handle broke off. He also inflicted at least two chopping wounds to Viivi's head with the hatchet. His jury must have understood that, regardless of whether Viivi was then still alive, Sakarias administered these blows for the purpose of ensuring her death.

Far from horrified at their bloody work, the murderers stayed for a snack, and Sakarias calmly ate liverwurst from the Piirisilds' refrigerator. Later, he made clear to the police his only regretthat they had not killed Avo Piirisild as well.

Thus, the uncontroverted evidence demonstrates Sakarias's full, remorseless involvement in the murder plot, and details the many grievous blows and wounds he administered during the joint attack on the victim. Under these circumstances, it stretches credulity to suggest that the issue whether he inflicted a single additional blowgruesome as it wascould alone have tipped the jury's penalty determination.

The majority note that Ipsen made Sakarias's responsibility for the antemortem hatchet chop a significant theme of his argument. But such references occurred, for the most part, at the guilt phase of Sakarias's trial, where they could have caused no prejudice. As the majority concede, Ipsen gave this subject only two brief references at the penalty phase. The bulk of Ipsen's penalty argument was devoted to rebutting the defense case in mitigation, including Sakarias's claims of extreme mental disorder. In my view, this further reduces any chance that the penalty outcome was affected.

* * *

I would discharge the order to show cause as to both Waidla and Sakarias.

CHAPTER 20

SUBMITTING THE CASE TO THE JURY

A. JURY INSTRUCTIONS: AN INTRODUCTION

Arthur Anderson LLP v. United States

Supreme Court of the United States, 2005.
544 U.S. 696, 125 S.Ct. 2129.

■ CHIEF JUSTICE REHNQUIST delivered the opinion of the Court.

As Enron Corporation's financial difficulties became public in 2001, petitioner Arthur Andersen LLP, Enron's auditor, instructed its employees to destroy documents pursuant to its document retention policy. A jury found that this action made petitioner guilty of violating 18 U. S. C. §§ 1512(b)(2)(A) and (B). These sections make it a crime to "knowingly us[e] intimidation or physical force, threate[n], or corruptly persuad[e] another person ... with intent to ... cause" that person to "withhold" documents from, or "alter" documents for use in, an "official proceeding." The Court of Appeals for the Fifth Circuit affirmed. We hold that the jury instructions failed to convey properly the elements of a "corrup[t] persuas[ion]" conviction under § 1512(b), and therefore reverse.

Enron Corporation, during the 1990's, switched its business from operation of natural gas pipelines to an energy conglomerate, a move that was accompanied by aggressive accounting practices and rapid growth. Petitioner audited Enron's publicly filed financial statements and provided internal audit and consulting services to it.

* * *

On August 28, an article in the Wall Street Journal suggested improprieties at Enron, and the SEC opened an informal investigation. By early September, petitioner had formed an Enron "crisis-response" team....

On October 10, [an Anderson supervising partner] spoke at a general training meeting attended by 89 employees, including 10 from the Enron engagement team. He urged everyone to comply with the firm's document retention policy.[4] He added: "[I]f it's destroyed in the course of [the]

4. The firm's policy called for a single central engagement file, which "should contain only that information which is relevant to supporting our work." The policy stated that, "in cases of threatened litigation, ... no related information will be destroyed." It also separately provided that, if petitioner is "advised of litigation or subpoenas regarding a particular engagement, the related information should not be destroyed. [It] set forth 'notification' procedures for whenever 'professional practice litigation against [petition-

normal policy and litigation is filed the next day, that's great.... [W]e've followed our own policy, and whatever there was that might have been of interest to somebody is gone and irretrievable."

On October 16, Enron announced its third quarter results. That release disclosed a $1.01 billion charge to earnings. The following day, the SEC notified Enron by letter that it had opened an investigation in August and requested certain information and documents. On October 19, Enron forwarded a copy of that letter to petitioner.

[Thereafter, the document retention policy was e-mailed to Anderson's internal group of accounting experts, conference calls were held with Enron crisis-response team instructing participants to follow the policy and meetings were held at which Anderson partners on the Enron engagement were urged to make sure that the policy was being followed.] These, and other smaller meetings, were followed by substantial destruction of paper and electronic documents.

In March 2002, [after Enron had filed for bankruptcy] petitioner was indicted in the Southern District of Texas on one count of violating § 151 2(b)(2)(A) and (B). The indictment alleged that, between October 10 and November 9, 2001, petitioner "did knowingly, intentionally and corruptly persuade ... other persons, to wit: [petitioner's] employees, with intent to cause" them to withhold documents from, and alter documents for use in, "official proceedings, namely: regulatory and criminal proceedings and investigations." [After ten days of deliberations, the jury returned a verdict of guilty and the Court of Appeals for the Fifth Circuit affirmed].

Sections 1512(b)(2)(A) and (B), part of the witness tampering provisions, provide in relevant part:

> "Whoever knowingly uses intimidation or physical force, threatens, or corruptly persuades another person, or attempts to do so, or engages in misleading conduct toward another person, with intent to ... cause or induce any person to ... withhold testimony, or withhold a record, document, or other object, from an official proceeding [or] alter, destroy, mutilate, or conceal an object with intent to impair the object's integrity or availability for use in an official proceeding ... shall be fined under this title or imprisoned not more than ten years, or both."

In this case, our attention is focused on what it means to "knowingly ... corruptly persuad[e]" another person "with intent to ... cause" that person to "withhold" documents from, or "alter" documents for use in, an "official proceeding."

We have traditionally exercised restraint in assessing the reach of a federal criminal statute, both out of deference to the prerogatives of Congress, and out of concern that a fair warning should be given to the world in language that the common world will understand, of what the law intends to do if a certain line is passed.

er] or any of its personnel has been commenced, has been threatened or is judged likely to occur, or when governmental or professional investigations that may involve [petitioner] or any of its personnel have been commenced or are judged likely.' "

Such restraint is particularly appropriate here, where the act underlying the conviction—"persua[sion]"—is by itself innocuous. Indeed, "persuad[ing]" a person "with intent to . . . cause" that person to "withhold" testimony or documents from a Government proceeding or Government official is not inherently malign. Consider, for instance, a mother who suggests to her son that he invoke his right against compelled self-incrimination, see U.S. Const., Amdt. 5, or a wife who persuades her husband not to disclose marital confidences.

* * *

"Document retention policies," which are created in part to keep certain information from getting into the hands of others, including the Government, are common in business. It is, of course, not wrongful for a manager to instruct his employees to comply with a valid document retention policy under ordinary circumstances.

Acknowledging this point, the parties have largely focused their attention on the word "corruptly" as the key to what may or may not lawfully be done in the situation presented here. Section 1512(b) punishes not just "corruptly persuad[ing]" another, but "knowingly . . . corruptly persuad[ing]" another. The Government suggests that "knowingly" does not modify "corruptly persuades," but that is not how the statute most naturally reads. It provides the mens rea—"knowingly"—and then a list of acts—"uses intimidation or physical force, threatens, or corruptly persuades." We have recognized with regard to similar statutory language that the mens rea at least applies to the acts that immediately follow, if not to other elements down the statutory chain. The Government suggests that it is questionable whether Congress would employ such an inelegant formulation as knowingly . . . corruptly persuades. Long experience has not taught us to share the Government's doubts on this score, and we must simply interpret the statute as written.

"[K]nowledge" and "knowingly" are normally associated with awareness, understanding, or consciousness. "Corrupt" and "corruptly" are normally associated with wrongful, immoral, depraved, or evil. "Corrupt" and "corruptly" are normally associated with wrongful, immoral, depraved, or evil. Joining these meanings together here makes sense both linguistically and in the statutory scheme. Only persons conscious of wrongdoing can be said to "knowingly . . . corruptly persuad[e]." And limiting criminality to persuaders conscious of their wrongdoing sensibly allows § 1512(b) to reach only those with the level of "culpability . . . we usually require in order to impose criminal liability."

The outer limits of this element need not be explored here because the jury instructions at issue simply failed to convey the requisite consciousness of wrongdoing. Indeed, it is striking how little culpability the instructions required. For example, the jury was told that, "even if [petitioner] honestly and sincerely believed that its conduct was lawful, you may find [petitioner] guilty." The instructions also diluted the meaning of "corruptly" so that it covered innocent conduct.

The parties vigorously disputed how the jury would be instructed on "corruptly." The District Court based its instruction on the definition of that term found in the Fifth Circuit Pattern Jury Instruction for § 1503. This pattern instruction defined "corruptly" as "knowingly and dishonestly, with the specific intent to subvert or undermine the integrity" of a proceeding. The Government, however, insisted on excluding "dishonestly" and adding the term "impede" to the phrase "subvert or undermine." The District Court agreed over petitioner's objections, and the jury was told to convict if it found petitioner intended to "subvert, undermine, or impede" governmental fact-finding by suggesting to its employees that they enforce the document retention policy.

These changes were significant. No longer was any type of "dishonest[y]" necessary to a finding of guilt, and it was enough for petitioner to have simply "impede[d]" the Government's factfinding ability. As the Government conceded at oral argument, "impede" has broader connotations than "subvert" or even "undermine," and many of these connotations do not incorporate any "corrupt[ness]" at all. The dictionary defines "impede" as "to interfere with or get in the way of the progress of" or "hold up" or "detract from." By definition, anyone who innocently persuades another to withhold information from the Government "get[s] in the way of the progress of" the Government. With regard to such innocent conduct, the "corruptly" instructions did no limiting work whatsoever.

The instructions also were infirm for another reason. They led the jury to believe that it did not have to find any nexus between the "persua[sion]" to destroy documents and any particular proceeding. In resisting any type of nexus element, the Government relies heavily on § 1512(e)(1), which states that an official proceeding "need not be pending or about to be instituted at the time of the offense." It is, however, one thing to say that a proceeding "need not be pending or about to be instituted at the time of the offense," and quite another to say a proceeding need not even be foreseen. A "knowingly ... corrup[t] persuade[r]" cannot be someone who persuades others to shred documents under a document retention policy when he does not have in contemplation any particular official proceeding in which those documents might be material.

* * *

For these reasons, the jury instructions here were flawed in important respects. The judgment of the Court of Appeals is reversed, and the case is remanded for further proceedings consistent with this opinion.

NOTES

1. In defining the element of the alleged offense, jury instructions raise the issues of substantive criminal law, statutory construction and, on occasion, constitutional dimension. Substantive analysis of the elements of an offense must be clearly defined. Compare United States v. Harrill, 877 F.2d 341 (5th Cir.1989) (instruction improperly expanded charges of indictment) with United States v. Asher, 854 F.2d 1483 (3d Cir.1988) (instructions did not broaden charges).

2. The primary object of the judge's charge to the jury is to explain the law, point out the essential elements that must be proved to sustain the allegations made by each side and bring into perspective the relationship of the evidence to the issues on trial. See White, Some Approaches to the Instructional Problem, 40 Neb.L.Rev. 413

(1961); Soper, The Charge to the Jury, 1 F.R.D. 540 (1941). On a somewhat different level, jury instructions have been viewed as performing the "theoretical" function of enlightening the jury on the law, the function by which appellate courts control judges and juries, the function, from counsel's viewpoint, of trapping the court into reversible error and the function by which trial judges maintain their integrity. Farley, Instruction to Juries—Their Role in the Judicial Process, 42 Yale L.J. 194 (1932).

3. Instructions have been looked upon as the single most important aspect of the trial judge's role. Mr. Justice Frankfurter in Andres v. United States, 333 U.S. 740, 68 S.Ct. 880, 886, 92 L.Ed. 1055 (1948), stated:

> Charging a jury is not a matter of abracadabra. No part of the conduct of a criminal trial lays a heavier task upon the presiding judge. The charge is that part of the whole trial which probably exercises the weightiest influence upon jurors. It should guide their understanding after jurors have been subjected to confusion and deflection from the relevant by the stiff partisanship of counsel.

It is obligatory upon the judge to give instructions that are "clear, concise, accurate and impartial statements of the law written in understandable language and delivered in a conversational tone which will be of helpful guidance to the jurors". Devitt, Ten Practical Suggestions About Federal Jury Instructions, 38 F.R.D. 75 (1966). Because of the difficulties in phrasing unimpeachable statements of law in a comprehensible manner, there is a growing trend toward developing and employing pattern jury instructions. "The reasons given for the adoption of pattern jury instructions vary from state to state, and in order of importance; but generally there are five: accuracy, time savings, impartiality, intelligibility, uniformity". Note, 40 N.Dak.L.Rev. 164 (1964). Variations in standardized instructions are closely scrutinized. United States v. MacDonald, 455 F.2d 1259 (1st Cir.1972).

4. As a procedural matter, the federal practice, followed in several states, is governed by Fed.R.Crim.P. 30. Under this rule the parties are permitted, but not required, to file suggested instructions "at the close of the evidence or at such earlier time during the trial as the court reasonably directs". See United States v. Johnson, 713 F.2d 633 (11th Cir.1983) (proper to refuse to give instructions not submitted prior to trial in accordance with local rule). The instructions tendered must be clear, accurate, nonpartisan statements of law, for a prolix, imprecise charge that intertwines evidentiary assumptions with a partisan statement of the law can justifiably be rejected outright by the court. United States v. Barham, 595 F.2d 231 (5th Cir.1979); United States v. Bessesen, 445 F.2d 463 (7th Cir.1971). Defense counsel is advised to tender a proper, intelligible charge to avoid total rejection and the loss of a valuable ground for appeal; and the prosecution should do so to avoid generating reversible error.

5. Although the trial judge must rule on each instruction submitted and advise counsel of his decision prior to closing argument, Rule 30 does not guarantee advance knowledge of all instructions. United States v. Newson, 531 F.2d 979 (10th Cir.1976). What happens when the court changes its mind after the instruction conference? Compare United States v. McCown, 711 F.2d 1441 (9th Cir.1983) (no prejudice when judge gave entrapment instruction after indicating that he would not), with United States v. Gaskins, 849 F.2d 454 (9th Cir.1988) (failure to inform defendant, prior to summation, of proposed instruction was reversible error). See also United States v. Pena, 897 F.2d 1075 (11th Cir.1990) (supplemental instruction appropriate when counsel made blatant misstatement of law in closing argument).

6. As a predicate to appellate review of a particular instruction, defense counsel must make a specific objection to the instruction involved and briefly state the basis of his complaint. Compare United States v. Verkuilen, 690 F.2d 648 (7th Cir.1982) (failure to object) with United States v. Sloan, 811 F.2d 1359 (10th Cir.1987) (court failed to permit objection outside jury's presence). This is generally done after the full charge is given and the jury temporarily excused in order to permit the court to recall the jury to modify its charge if counsel's argument proves persuasive. See United States v. Phillips, 869 F.2d 1361 (10th Cir.1988) (defendant had opportunity to object after instructions were read, but failed to do so). In some jurisdictions, it is necessary to object *and* submit a proposed alternative instruction to preserve the issue. See United States v. Lewis, 671 F.2d 1025 (7th Cir.1982); United States v. Parisien, 574 F.2d 974 (8th Cir.1978).

7. Absent a specific objection, an instruction will be reviewed only where it generates "plain error" under Fed.R.Crim.P. 52(b). See United States v. Torres, 901 F.2d 205 (2d Cir.1990); United States v. Wharton, 433 F.2d 451, 456–57 (D.C.Cir. 1970):

> Our function does not end with recognition of these instructional miscues; there remains the question whether, in the circumstances presented by this litigation, they warrant reversal. That task, one often fraught with difficulty, is compounded here by the absence of protest to the instructions in the trial court, where possibly the mistakes, upon identification, could have been corrected. Appellant can survive the omission of appropriate objections only if we should exert our authority, which he invokes, to notice "[p]lain errors or defects affecting substantial rights."
>
> * * *
>
> The inquiry here ... is the probable impact, appraised realistically, of the particular instructional mistakes upon the jury's factfinding function. [We have therefore, examined] the faulty instruction, not in isolation but, as always, against the backdrop of related segments of the trial judge's charge, and concluded that it was unlikely that in context the single misstatement led the jury astray.

8. Is a defendant who fails to object to a jury instruction at his state trial entitled to federal habeas corpus relief when a change in the law later invalidates the instruction? Compare Reed v. Ross, 468 U.S. 1, 104 S.Ct. 2901 (1984), with Engle v. Isaac, 456 U.S. 107, 102 S.Ct. 1558 (1982). See Chapter 23, p. 1525.

9. A defendant is entitled to an instruction on any theory of defense that is supported by the evidence. United States v. Prieskorn, 658 F.2d 631 (8th Cir.1981). This is particularly significant in specific intent crimes when the defendant may concede the act but contend that it was done with a good faith misunderstanding of the law. See Cheek v. United States, 498 U.S. 192, 111 S.Ct. 604 (1991); United States v. Morris, 20 F.3d 1111 (11th Cir.1994). However, when there is no basis in the evidence for theory of defense instruction, it need not be given. United States v. Bailey, 444 U.S. 394, 100 S.Ct. 624 (1980). The issue of whether the instruction proposed by the defendant accurately states the law and finds support in the evidence often present seriously disputed questions. See United States v. Kayser, 488 F.3d 1070 (9th Cir. 2007) (Kozinski, J., dissenting) (stating that reversal of tax conviction for failure to give defendant's theory instruction "eviscerates the evidentiary standard for proposed jury instructions by forcing a district court to give an instruction that's only supported by generalities and hypothetical possibilities"). Conversely, if no instruction is presented on a particular prosecution theory, a reviewing court cannot uphold a conviction on the basis of that theory. Chiarella v. United States, 445 U.S. 222, 100 S.Ct. 1108 (1980).

10. In determining whether a requested instruction was improperly refused, reviewing courts examine whether it (1) was a correct statement of the law; (2) was substantially given in the charge as a whole; and (3) concerned an important point in the trial so that the failure to give it seriously impaired the defendant's ability to effectively present a defense. United States v. Sanchez–Sotelo, 8 F.3d 202 (5th Cir.1993); see also United States v. Lewis, 53 F.3d 29 (4th Cir.1995) (reversing for failure to give defendant's proposed instruction).

11. Erroneous instructions "are the greatest single source of reversible error." Skidmore v. Baltimore & Ohio R. Co., 167 F.2d 54, 65 (2d Cir.1948). Because there is rarely a case where technical error cannot be found in a single, isolated instruction, appellate courts focus upon whether the charge as a whole, not a specific instruction, either given or refused, comports with legal requirements. Cupp v. Naughten, 414 U.S. 141, 94 S.Ct. 396 (1973); United States v. Figueroa, 900 F.2d 1211 (8th Cir.1990).

12. The concept of "jury nullification" refers to a jury's decision to depart from established principles of law, as reflected in the court's instructions, in order to do what it deems the just or merciful thing in the case at hand. In criminal cases, jury nullification ordinarily refers to the jury's acquittal of a defendant where application of the law to the facts would require conviction. The power exists de facto. Some issues arise as to whether defense lawyers may properly argue for nullification and whether the court should instruct the jury in any regard as to the possibility of nullification. In United States v. Krzyske, 836 F.2d 1013 (6th Cir. 1988), the court held that a defendant was not entitled to an instruction informing the jury of its power of nullification. "To have given an instruction on nullification would have undermined the impartial determination of justice based on law."

On the other hand, is it error for the court to instruct the jury that it must not engage in nullification? The trial judge did something like that in People v. Douglas, 208 Ill.App.3d 664, 153 Ill.Dec. 586, 567 N.E.2d 544 (1991), after the jury made an inquiry about the possibility of lenity. The judge told the jury just to follow the instructions. The reviewing court approved, reiterating that the defense is not entitled to an instruction informing the jury of the possibility of its exercising lenity.

California had a pattern instruction directing jurors to inform the court if any member refuses to deliberate or expresses an intention to disregard the law. In People v. Engelman, 28 Cal.4th 436, 121 Cal.Rptr.2d 862, 49 P.3d 209 (2002), the court upheld the instruction against a constitutional challenge but opted to abandon it as a matter of policy:

> The threat that the contents of the jury's deliberations might be reported to the judge could chill the free exchange of ideas that lies at the center of the deliberative process. Additionally, jurors entering into deliberations should be tolerant of and patient with the differences of opinion that may arise, and should remain open to persuasion.... Jurors should not be led to believe that disagreement during deliberations constitutes misconduct, nor should self-confident jurors be furnished with a means to short circuit discussions by threatening to call upon the court to arbitrate normal disagreements.

For differing views on the value of nullification instructions, compare King, Silencing Nullification Advocacy Inside the Jury Room and Outside the Courtroom, 65 U.Chi.L.Rev. 443 (1998) with Brown, Jury Nullification Within the Rule of Law, 81 Minn.L.Rev. 1149 (1997).

13. When the indictment alleges one offense and some evidence is before the jury which, if believed, would be a basis for concluding that the defendant is guilty of a less serious offense, the issue arises as to whether a defendant, if he or she so elects, is entitled to instruction defining the lesser offense and allowing the jury to consider such an alternative verdict. In many jurisdictions, unless all of the elements of the less serious offense are included in the offense charged, so that the lesser offense is "included" in the offense charged in the traditional sense, a defendant is not entitled to an instruction on the lesser charge. A minority of jurisdictions allow an instruction on the less serious offense when there is "an inherent relationship" between the two offenses and when the evidence could support a finding on the less serious offense. Of course, a jury can never be instructed on a lesser offense over the defendant's objections unless the lesser offense is "included" in the greater offense. This is a matter of "fair notice."

In Schmuck v. United States, 489 U.S. 705, 109 S.Ct. 1443 (1989), the Court determined that, in federal courts, the "elements" test is to be used in determining when a lesser offense instruction is appropriate under Fed.R.Crim.P. 31(c). Only in a case where proof sufficient to establish every element of the greater offense would necessarily establish every element of the lesser offense can a federal court instruct on a lesser offense that has not been alleged in the indictment or the information. Because the less serious offense of odometer tampering includes at least one element that is not an element of mail fraud, where the defendant has been charged only with the more serious offense of mail fraud, the defendant is not entitled to an odometer tampering instruction no matter what the evidence shows. The Court said that the elements test is rooted in history and is easier to apply than is a test that asks whether the two offenses bear an "inherent relationship."

As interpreted, *Schmuck* requires a two step analysis before a lesser included offense instruction is given. First, the offense on which the instruction is sought must be lesser included in the one charged. Second, the evidence must allow the jury to rationally conclude that the defendant was guilty of the lesser offense, but not the greater one. United States v. Torres, 937 F.2d 1469 (9th Cir.1991).

14. Jury instructions in capital-sentencing are often subjected to constitutional scrutiny. In Simmons v. South Carolina, 512 U.S. 154, 114 S.Ct. 2187 (1994), the defendant's request for a parole-ineligibility instruction to combat the state's claim of future dangerousness was refused. The trial judge later responded to the jury's inquiry as to whether life imprisonment carried the possibility of parole with the statement, "you are not to consider parole or parole eligibility in reaching your verdict." The ensuing death penalty verdict was overturned in a plurality opinion finding that the "refusal to apprise the jury of information so crucial to its sentencing determination, particularly when the prosecution alluded to the defendant's future dangerousness in its argument to the jury, cannot be reconciled with our well-established precedents interpreting the Due Process Clause."

15. For an interesting argument in favor of greater clarity in jury instructions, enhanced judicial review, and a proposal that judges use the defendant's proposed instruction in a critical subset of jury charges, see Brown, Regulating Decision Effects of Legally Sufficient Jury Instructions, 73 U.S.C.L.Rev. 1105 (2000).

B. JUDGE'S COMMENT ON THE EVIDENCE

United States v. Neumann

United States Court of Appeals, Eighth Circuit (en banc), 1989.
887 F.2d 880.

■ MAGILL, CIRCUIT JUDGE.

Steven Earl Neumann appeals from his conviction for bank robbery by the use of a dangerous weapon and use of a firearm during the robbery. Neumann alleges error in the judge's ... comments on the evidence.

* * *

Neumann takes issue with the following portion of the trial court's instruction:

> I have the feeling, from the arguments of both lawyers and from listening to the evidence—and I kept pretty good notes—that there really isn't much question about these four requirements in one case and two in the other being satisfied, if this is the defendant who did the robbery. And, of course, that is the principal defense of the defendant—that he didn't do it and the government hasn't proved that he did it. So I think that, probably, may turn out to be the principal issue that you have for decision; not the satisfaction of these requirements, because it doesn't seem to be disputed that somebody came into the bank with a rifle and threatened people and shot up on the wall. And the three tellers told us how frightened and apprehensive they were. And money was gone, no question about it. Some $16,000.00.
>
> So these somewhat technical requirements for bank robbery and using a dangerous weapon in a crime of violence, it seems to me, are satisfied if, if this is the man who did it.

Although Neumann concedes that his counsel made no objection to these comments at trial, he contends that the plain error rule mandates a reversal of his conviction because in effect the trial judge expressed his opinion on his guilt as to some of the elements of the crime charged, and thereby impermissibly usurped the jury's function.

Given the great deference the jury may give the words and actions of the trial judge, we recognize the possibility of prejudice when the trial judge's comments display one-sidedness or the prejudgment of disputed issues. The jury might take such comments as a direction to find against the defendant.... The propriety of the judge's comments must be viewed in the context of the complete charge to the jury. Here, the jury was informed that the government must prove each element of the charged offenses beyond a reasonable doubt, and that determination of guilt lay with the jury. The trial judge's comments on the evidence were prefaced with caution: "Now, these comments I make about the evidence are not intended to substitute the facts as you find them to be, but these are some comments I'm going to make to try to assist you in getting the point of it all and what the issue is."

Neumann contends that his plea of not guilty put each element of the charged offenses at issue, and therefore it was improper for the judge to comment that, apart from identity, the "somewhat technical requirements" of each offense seemed to be satisfied. In the context of the complete jury charge and the evidence presented at trial, we find that the trial judge's comments were a fair summary of the evidence, and did not relieve the jury of its duty to find that each element of the charged offenses was satisfied. The government put on a case which included direct evidence of the armed robbery of a federally insured bank. The trial judge correctly noted that this evidence was not contradicted. Neumann's counsel conceded at the pretrial status conference and the jury charge conference that identification was the basic factual issue. The trial judge also properly focused the jury's attention on the "principal issue"—circumstantial evidence establishing that Neumann was the bank robber. We hold that the judge's comments on the evidence did not constitute plain error.

Neumann also claims that the court's summary of the evidence was one-sided because it did not include several aspects of the evidence that were favorable to his defense. We find no merit in this claim. Neumann did not make a timely request at trial for the summary of his defense which he now claims should have been given. Furthermore, the comments suggested by Neumann on appeal were not supported by the evidence.

* * *

Accordingly, we affirm the conviction.

■ MCMILLIAN, CIRCUIT JUDGE, dissenting.

I respectfully dissent. I cannot agree that the district court's summary of and comments upon the evidence in this case are not plain error. Accordingly, I would reverse and remand for a new trial.

If the analysis of the majority ... is correct, then in every criminal case in which identity is the "principal" issue, that is, when the defendant asserts that he or she did not commit the offense charged, it is proper for the trial judge to direct a verdict against the defendant on all of the elements of the offense but identity. In my opinion, this analysis improperly diminishes the jury's role, limiting it to that of determining only identity. As I understand the law, directed verdicts against criminal defendants are not permissible. In a jury-tried case, whether or not the elements of the offense are disputed and regardless of the quantum of evidence presented against a criminal defendant, each element of the offense must be submitted to the jury, not the trial judge, for decision.

In the present case, the district court's summary of and comments upon the evidence amounted, in my opinion, to a directed verdict against appellant on each element of the offenses charged except that of identity. Trial judges may summarize fairly and comment upon the evidence and focus the jury's attention on the "principal" issues in a case. The comments here simply went too far.

NOTES

1. While there is no requirement that the judge review or marshal the evidence, he or she may do so as long as the charge is fair to both sides. United States v. GAF Corp., 928 F.2d 1253 (2d Cir.1991); United States v. Glasser, 750 F.2d 1197 (3d Cir.1984).

2. The general rule regarding the judge's authority to comment on the evidence was stated in United States v. Tourine, 428 F.2d 865 (2d Cir.1970):

> The trial judge in a federal court may summarize and comment upon the evidence and inferences to be drawn therefrom, in his discretion. This

does not mean that he must include every scrap of evidence as if the jury were dependent upon the court's summation alone as the basis for its deliberations. The purpose of such summation and comment is to assist the jury in winnowing out the truth from the mass of evidence, much of it conflicting, and perhaps placed out of focus by different claims concerning its meaning and interpretation by the arguments of the parties. So long as the trial judge does not by one means or another try to impose his own opinions and conclusions as to the facts on the jury and does not act as an advocate in advancing factual findings of his own, he may in his discretion decide what evidence he will comment upon. His fairness in doing so must be judged in the context of the whole trial record, particularly the evidence and the arguments of the parties. So examined and considered in the present case, we are satisfied that the court did not step outside of its legitimate province in commenting on the evidence. Although most of what he had to say concerned the Government's, rather than the defendants' evidence, there was a great deal more of the former, which ran over three hundred pages, than the latter, which covered less than one hundred pages of the trial transcript.

Although a charge which usurps the function of the jury will not be saved from error by simply repeating in it from time to time that the jury and not the court is the finder of the facts, such a statement does serve to remind the jury, in the usual case where the court makes no more than fair comment for clarification and to aid the jury in its deliberations, that it must exercise its own judgment and not take what the court has said without further deliberation of its own.

3. Some judges like to humanize their instructions with examples. See State v. Williams, 337 N.W.2d 689 (Minn.1983), where defendant was charged with attempted murder and assault in instructing the jury on the attempt charges, the judge explained the meaning of taking a "substantial step" by citing the contrasting examples of someone who thinks about shooting someone but stays at home and someone who, having thought about shooting someone, goes to that person's house to look for him. On appeal from the ensuing conviction, the court noted the "danger of using an example that fits too closely," but upheld the conviction on the ground that intent and not "substantial step" was the real issue in the case.

4. Appellate review of a judge's comments on the evidence will be dependent upon the facts of the case and the extent to which the judge's commentary impartially reflects the evidence. Some comments are plainly erroneous. See Malaga v. United States, 57 F.2d 822 (1st Cir.1932) ("Do you believe that story, gentlemen? To me it is perfectly plain that it is a lie."); Blunt v. United States, 244 F.2d 355 (D.C.Cir. 1957) (psychiatrist's opinion is just a "feeling" and not based on fact). Some present more difficult decisions. See Hance v. United States, 299 F.2d 389 (8th Cir.1962) (no reversal despite instruction that government witness was a brave dedicated public servant who did not deserve to be labeled as a liar by defense counsel); People v. Easley, 34 Cal.3d 858, 196 Cal.Rptr. 309, 671 P.2d 813 (1983) (death penalty reversed when court said, "As jurors, you must not be influenced by mere sentiment, conjecture, sympathy, passion, prejudice, public opinion or public feeling.")

5. The reason why there is no black letter rule regarding judicial comment was provided by Judge Learned Hand in United States v. Allied Stevedoring Corp., 241 F.2d 925 (2d Cir.1957):

It is indeed impossible to lay down any general rule that will help to define the limits beyond which a judge may not stop in his dealing with a jury. That there are such everyone agrees, and we have so held; but the occasion must be one where it is apparent that he has assumed an attitude

> which goes further than to express his personal opinion. He must give them to suppose that he is more than an impartial observer; and that what he says has the backing of legal authority.

6. For one decision where the trial judge's instructions to the jury were characterized as impermissibly directing a finding as to one of the elements of the offense charged, see United States v. Mentz, 840 F.2d 315 (6th Cir.1988). There the prosecution was required to prove that funds in a certain financial institution were insured by the Federal Deposit Insurance Corporation at the time of the alleged offense. The court instructed the jury that the funds were so insured. See also Wheeler v. United States, 930 A.2d 232 (D.C. Ct. App. 2007) (while trial judge enjoys a common law privilege to comment on the evidence, an instruction that the lack of fingerprint evidence, as a matter of law, cannot constitute reasonable doubt impermissibly invaded the province of the jury).

C. PARTICULAR JURY INSTRUCTION PROBLEMS

1. ALLOCATION OF THE BURDEN OF PROOF

Victor v. Nebraska

Supreme Court of the United States, 1994.
511 U.S. 1, 114 S.Ct. 1239.

■ JUSTICE O'CONNOR delivered the opinion of the Court.*

The government must prove beyond a reasonable doubt every element of a charged offense. *In re Winship* (1970). Although this standard is an ancient and honored aspect of our criminal justice system, it defies easy explication. In these cases, we consider the constitutionality of two attempts to define "reasonable doubt."

I

The beyond a reasonable doubt standard is a requirement of due process, but the Constitution neither prohibits trial courts from defining reasonable doubt nor requires them to do so as a matter of course. Indeed, so long as the court instructs the jury on the necessity that the defendant's guilt be proven beyond a reasonable doubt, the Constitution does not require that any particular form of words be used in advising the jury of the government's burden of proof. Rather, "taken as a whole, the instructions [must] correctly conve[y] the concept of reasonable doubt to the jury." *Holland v. United States* (1954).

In only one case have we held that a definition of reasonable doubt violated the Due Process Clause. *Cage v. Louisiana* (1990) (*per curiam*). There, the jurors were told:

> " '[A reasonable doubt] is one that is founded upon a real tangible substantial basis and not upon mere caprice and conjecture. *It must be such doubt as would give rise to a grave uncertainty*, raised

* Justices Blackmun and Souter join only Part II of this opinion. Justice Ginsburg joins only Parts II, III–B, and IV.

> in your mind by reasons of the unsatisfactory character of the evidence or lack thereof. A reasonable doubt is not a mere possible doubt. *It is an actual substantial doubt.* It is a doubt that a reasonable man can seriously entertain. What is required is not an absolute or mathematical certainty, but a *moral certainty.*' "

We held that the highlighted portions of the instruction rendered it unconstitutional:

> "It is plain to us that the words 'substantial' and 'grave,' as they are commonly understood, suggest a higher degree of doubt than is required for acquittal under the reasonable doubt standard. When those statements are then considered with the reference to 'moral certainty,' rather than evidentiary certainty, it becomes clear that a reasonable juror could have interpreted the instruction to allow a finding of guilt based on a degree of proof below that required by the Due Process Clause."

In a subsequent case, we made clear that the proper inquiry is not whether the instruction "could have" been applied in unconstitutional manner, but whether there is a reasonable likelihood that the jury *did* so apply it. *Estelle v. McGuire* (1991). The constitutional question in the present cases, therefore, is whether there is a reasonable likelihood that the jury understood the instructions to allow conviction based on proof insufficient to meet the *Winship* standard.

* * *

II

On October 14, 1984, petitioner Sandoval shot three men, two of them fatally, in a gang-related incident in Los Angeles. About two weeks later, he entered the home of a man who had given information to the police about the murders and shot him dead; Sandoval then killed the man's wife because she had seen him murder her husband. Sandoval was convicted on four counts of first degree murder. The jury found that Sandoval personally used a firearm in the commission of each offense, and found the special circumstance of multiple murder. He was sentenced to death for murdering the woman and to life in prison without possibility of parole for the other three murders. The California Supreme Court affirmed the convictions and sentences.

The jury in Sandoval's case was given the following instruction on the government's burden of proof:

> "A defendant in a criminal action is presumed to be innocent until the contrary is proved, and in case of a reasonable doubt whether his guilt is satisfactorily shown, he is entitled to a verdict of not guilty. This presumption places upon the State the burden of proving him guilty beyond a reasonable doubt.
>
> "Reasonable doubt is defined as follows: It is *not a mere possible doubt*; because everything relating to human affairs, and *depending on moral evidence*, is open to some possible or imaginary doubt. It is that state of the case which, after the entire

> comparison and consideration of all the evidence, leaves the minds of the jurors in that condition that they cannot say they feel an abiding conviction, *to a moral certainty*, of the truth of the charge."

The California Supreme Court rejected Sandoval's claim that the instruction, particularly the highlighted passages, violated the Due Process Clause.

The instruction given in Sandoval's case has its genesis in a charge given by Chief Justice Shaw of the Massachusetts Supreme Judicial Court more than a century ago:

> "[W]hat is reasonable doubt? It is a term often used, probably pretty well understood, but not easily defined. It is not mere possible doubt; because every thing relating to human affairs, and depending on moral evidence, is open to some possible or imaginary doubt. It is that state of the case, which, after the entire comparison and consideration of all the evidence, leaves the minds of jurors in that condition that they cannot say they feel an abiding conviction, to a moral certainty, of the truth of the charge. The burden of proof is upon the prosecutor. All the presumptions of law independent of evidence are in favor of innocence; and every person is presumed to be innocent until he is proved guilty. If upon such proof there is reasonable doubt remaining, the accused is entitled to the benefit of it by an acquittal. For it is not sufficient to establish a probability, though a strong one arising from the doctrine of chances, that the fact charged is more likely to be true than the contrary; but the evidence must establish the truth of the fact to a reasonable and moral certainty; a certainty that convinces and directs the understanding, and satisfies the reason and judgment, of those who are bound to act conscientiously upon it. This we take to be proof beyond reasonable doubt." *Commonwealth v. Webster*, 59 Mass. 295, 320 (1850).

The *Webster* charge is representative of the time when "American courts began applying [the beyond a reasonable doubt standard] in its modern form in criminal cases." In [1866], the California Supreme Court characterized the *Webster* instruction as "probably the most satisfactory definition ever given to the words 'reasonable doubt' in any case known to criminal jurisprudence." And in 1927, the state legislature adopted the bulk of the *Webster* instruction as a statutory definition of reasonable doubt.

* * *

A

Sandoval's primary objection is to the use of the phrases "moral evidence" and "moral certainty" in the instruction. As noted, this part of the charge was lifted verbatim from Chief Justice Shaw's *Webster* decision; some understanding of the historical context in which that instruction was written is accordingly helpful in evaluating its continuing validity.

By the beginning of the Republic, lawyers had borrowed the concept of "moral evidence" from the philosophers and historians of the 17th and

18th centuries. James Wilson, who was instrumental in framing the Constitution and who served as one of the original Members of this Court, explained in a 1790 lecture on law that "evidence ... is divided into two species—demonstrative and moral." Wilson went on to explain the distinction thus:

"Demonstrative evidence has for its subject abstract and necessary truths, or the unchangeable relations of ideas. Moral evidence has for its subject the real but contingent truths and connections, which take place among things actually existing....

"In moral evidence, there not only may be, but there generally is, contrariety of proofs: in demonstrative evidence, no such contrariety can take place.... [T]o suppose that two contrary demonstrations can exist, is to suppose that the same proposition is both true and false: which is manifestly absurd. With regard to moral evidence, there is, for the most part, real evidence on both sides. On both sides, contrary presumptions, contrary testimonies, contrary experiences must be balanced."

* * *

Thus, when Chief Justice Shaw penned the *Webster* instruction in 1850, moral certainty meant a state of subjective certitude about some event or occurrence. As the Massachusetts Supreme Judicial Court subsequently explained:

> "Proof 'beyond a reasonable doubt' ... is proof 'to a moral certainty,' as distinguished from an absolute certainty. As applied to a judicial trial for crime, the two phrases are synonymous and equivalent; each has been used by eminent judges to explain the other; and each signifies such proof as satisfies the judgment and consciences of the jury, as reasonable men, and applying their reason to the evidence before them, that the crime charged has been committed by the defendant, and so satisfies them as to leave no other reasonable conclusion possible." Commonwealth v. Costley, 118 Mass. 1, 24 (1875).

* * *

We recognize that the phrase "moral evidence" is not a mainstay of the modern lexicon, though we do not think it means anything different today than it did in the 19th century. The few contemporary dictionaries that define moral evidence do so consistently with its original meaning. * * *

Moreover, the instruction itself gives a definition of the phrase. The jury was told that "everything relating to human affairs, and depending on moral evidence, is open to some possible or imaginary doubt"—in other words, that absolute certainty is unattainable in matters relating to human affairs. Moral evidence, in this sentence, can only mean empirical evidence offered to prove such matters—the proof introduced at trial.

This conclusion is reinforced by other instructions given in Sandoval's case. The judge informed the jurors that their duty was "to determine the facts of the case from the evidence received in the trial and not from any other source." The judge continued: "Evidence consists of testimony of witnesses, writings, material objects, or anything presented to the senses and offered to prove the existence or non-existence of a fact." The judge also told the jurors that "you must not be influenced by pity for a defendant or by prejudice against him," and that "[y]ou must not be swayed by mere sentiment, conjecture, sympathy, passion, prejudice, public opinion or public feeling." These instructions correctly pointed the jurors' attention to the facts of the case before them, not (as Sandoval contends) the ethics or morality of Sandoval's criminal acts. Accordingly, we find the reference to moral evidence unproblematic.

We are somewhat more concerned with Sandoval's argument that the phrase "moral certainty" has lost its historical meaning, and that a modern jury would understand it to allow conviction on proof that does not meet the beyond a reasonable doubt standard. Words and phrases can change meaning over time: a passage generally understood in 1850 may be incomprehensible or confusing to a modern juror. And although some contemporary dictionaries contain definitions of moral certainty similar to the 19th century understanding of the phrase, ... we are willing to accept Sandoval's premise that "moral certainty," standing alone, might not be recognized by modern jurors as a synonym for "proof beyond a reasonable doubt." But it does not necessarily follow that the California instruction is unconstitutional.

Sandoval first argues that moral certainty would be understood by modern jurors to mean a standard of proof lower than beyond a reasonable doubt. In support of this proposition, Sandoval points to contemporary dictionaries that define moral certainty in terms of probability. But the beyond a reasonable doubt standard is itself probabilistic. "[I]n a judicial proceeding in which there is a dispute about the facts of some earlier event, the factfinder cannot acquire unassailably accurate knowledge of what happened. Instead, all the factfinder can acquire is a belief of what *probably* happened." *In re Winship*, (Harlan, J., concurring). The problem is not that moral certainty may be understood in terms of probability, but that a jury might understand the phrase to mean something less than the very high level of probability required by the Constitution in criminal cases.

Although in this respect moral certainty is ambiguous in the abstract, the rest of the instruction given in Sandoval's case lends content to the phrase. The jurors were told that they must have "an abiding conviction, to a moral certainty, of the truth of the charge." An instruction cast in terms of an abiding conviction as to guilt, without reference to moral certainty, correctly states the government's burden of proof. And the judge had already informed the jury that matters relating to human affairs are proven by moral evidence, giving the same meaning to the word moral in this part of the instruction, moral certainty can only mean certainty with respect to human affairs. As used in this instruction, therefore, we are satisfied that the reference to moral certainty, in conjunction with the abiding conviction language, "impress[ed] upon the factfinder the need to reach a subjective state of near certitude of the guilt of the accused." Accordingly, we reject Sandoval's contention that the moral certainty element of the California instruction invited the jury to convict him on proof below that required by the Due Process Clause.

Sandoval's second argument is a variant of the first. Accepting that the instruction requires a high level of confidence in the defendant's guilt, Sandoval argues that a juror might be convinced to a moral certainty that the defendant is guilty even though the government has failed to *prove* his guilt beyond a reasonable doubt. A definition of moral certainty in a widely used modern dictionary lends support to this argument, see The American Heritage Dictionary of the English Language 1173 (3d ed. 1992) ("Based on strong likelihood or firm conviction, rather than on the actual evidence"), and we do not gainsay its force. As we have noted, "[t]he constitutional standard recognized in the *Winship* case was expressly phrased as one that protects an accused against a conviction except on '*proof* beyond a reasonable doubt.' "

But the moral certainty language cannot be sequestered from its surroundings. The jury in Sandoval's case was told that a reasonable doubt is "that state of the case which, *after the entire comparison and consideration of all the evidence*, leaves the minds of the jurors in that condition that they cannot say they feel an abiding conviction, to a moral certainty, of the truth of the charge." The instruction thus explicitly told the jurors that their conclusion had to be based on the evidence in the case. Other instructions reinforced this message. The jury was told "to determine the facts of the case from the evidence received in the trial and not from any other source." The judge continued that "you must not be influenced by pity for a defendant or by prejudice against him.... You must not be swayed by mere sentiment, conjecture, sympathy, passion, prejudice, public opinion or public feeling." Accordingly, there is no reasonable likelihood that the jury would have understood moral certainty to be disassociated from the evidence in the case.

We do not think it reasonably likely that the jury understood the words moral certainty either as suggesting a standard of proof lower than due process requires or as allowing conviction on factors other than the government's proof. At the same time, however, we do not condone the use of the phrase. As modern dictionary definitions of moral certainty attest, the common meaning of the phrase has changed since it was used in the *Webster* instruction, and it may continue to do so to the point that it conflicts with the *Winship* standard. Indeed, the definitions of reasonable doubt most widely used in the federal courts do not contain any reference to moral certainty. But we have no supervisory power over the state courts, and in the context of the instructions as a whole we cannot say that the use of the phrase rendered the instruction given in Sandoval's case unconstitutional.

B

Finally, Sandoval objects to the portion of the charge in which the judge instructed the jury that a reasonable doubt is "not a mere possible doubt." * * * "[A] 'reasonable doubt,' at a minimum, is one based upon 'reason.' " A fanciful doubt is not a reasonable doubt. As Sandoval's defense attorney told the jury: "[A]nything can be possible.... [A] planet could be made out of blue cheese. But that's really not in the realm of what we're talking about." That this is the sense in which the instruction uses "possible" is made clear from the final phrase of the sentence, which notes that everything "is open to some possible or imaginary doubt." We therefore reject Sandoval's challenge to this portion of the instruction as well.

III

On December 26, 1987, petitioner Victor went to the Omaha home of an 82-year-old woman for whom he occasionally did gardening work. Once inside, he beat her with a pipe and cut her throat with a knife, killing her. Victor was convicted of first degree murder. A three-judge panel found the statutory aggravating circumstances that Victor had previously been convicted of murder, and that the murder in this case was especially heinous, atrocious, and cruel. Finding none of the statutory mitigating circumstances, the panel sentenced Victor to death. The Nebraska Supreme Court affirmed the conviction and sentence.

At Victor's trial, the judge instructed the jury that "[t]he burden is always on the State to prove beyond a reasonable doubt all of the material elements of the crime charged, and this burden never shifts." The charge continued:

> " 'Reasonable doubt' is such a doubt as would cause a reasonable and prudent person, in one of the graver and more important transactions of life, to pause and hesitate before taking the represented facts as true and relying and acting thereon. It is such a doubt as will not permit you, after full, fair, and impartial consideration of all the evidence, to have an abiding conviction, *to a moral certainty*, of the guilt of the accused. At the same time, absolute or mathematical certainty is not required. You may be convinced of the truth of a fact beyond a reasonable doubt and yet be fully aware that possibly you may be mistaken. You may find an accused guilty upon the *strong probabilities of the case*, provided such probabilities are strong enough to exclude any doubt of his guilt that is reasonable. A reasonable doubt is an *actual and substantial doubt* arising from the evidence, from the facts or circumstances shown by the evidence, or from the lack of evidence on the part of the state, as distinguished from a doubt arising from mere possibility, from bare imagination, or from fanciful conjecture."

* * *

The instruction given in Victor's case can be traced to two separate lines of cases. Much of the charge is taken from Chief Justice Shaw's *Webster* instruction. The rest derives from a series of decisions approving instructions cast in terms of an "actual doubt" that would cause a reasonable person to hesitate to act. In 1968, a committee appointed by the Nebraska Supreme Court developed model jury instructions; a court rule in effect at the time Victor was tried directed that those instructions were to be used where applicable. The model instruction on reasonable doubt, is the one given at Victor's trial. (Since Victor was tried, a revised reasonable-doubt instruction, has been adopted, although the prior version may still be used.)

A

Victor's primary argument is that equating a reasonable doubt with a "substantial doubt" overstated the degree of doubt necessary for acquittal. We agree that this construction is somewhat problematic. On the one hand, "substantial" means "not seeming or imaginary"; on the other, it means "that specified to a large degree." The former is unexceptionable, as it informs the jury only that a reasonable doubt is something more than a speculative one; but the latter could imply a doubt greater than required for acquittal under *Winship*. Any ambiguity, however, is removed by reading the phrase in the context of the sentence in which it appears: "A reasonable doubt is an actual and substantial doubt ... *as distinguished from* a doubt arising from mere possibility, from bare imagination, or from fanciful conjecture."

* * *

In any event, the instruction provided an alternative definition of reasonable doubt: a doubt that would cause a reasonable person to hesitate to act. This is a formulation we have repeatedly approved, and to the extent the word substantial denotes the quantum of doubt necessary for acquittal, the hesitate to act standard gives a common-sense benchmark for just how substantial such a doubt must be. We therefore do not think it reasonably likely that the jury would have interpreted this instruction to indicate that the doubt must be anything other than a reasonable one.

B

Victor also challenges the "moral certainty" portion of the instruction. * * *

Instructing the jurors that they must have an abiding conviction of the defendant's guilt does much to alleviate any concerns that the phrase moral certainty might be misunderstood in the abstract. The instruction also equated a doubt sufficient to preclude moral certainty with a doubt that would cause a reasonable person to hesitate to act. In other words, a juror morally certain of a fact would not hesitate to rely on it; and such a fact can fairly be said to have been proven beyond a reasonable doubt. The jurors were told that they must be convinced of Victor's guilt "after full, fair, and impartial consideration of all the evidence." The judge also told them: "In determining any issues of fact presented in this case, you should be governed solely by the evidence introduced before you. You should not indulge in speculation, conjectures, or inferences not supported by the evidence." There is accordingly no reasonable likelihood that the jurors understood the reference to moral certainty to allow conviction on a standard insufficient to satisfy *Winship*, or to allow conviction on factors other than the government's proof. Though we reiterate that we do not countenance its use, the inclusion of the moral certainty phrase did not render the instruction given in Victor's case unconstitutional.

C

Finally, Victor argues that the reference to "strong probabilities" in the instruction unconstitutionally understated the government's burden.

But in the same sentence, the instruction informs the jury that the probabilities must be strong enough to prove the defendant's guilt beyond a reasonable doubt. We upheld a nearly identical instruction in *Dunbar v. United States* (1895): "While it is true that [the challenged instruction] used the words 'probabilities' and 'strong probabilities,' yet it emphasized the fact that those probabilities must be so strong as to exclude any reasonable doubt, and that is unquestionably the law". That conclusion has lost no force in the course of a century, and we therefore consider *Dunbar* controlling on this point.

IV

The Due Process Clause requires the government to prove a criminal defendant's guilt beyond a reasonable doubt, and trial courts must avoid defining reasonable doubt so as to lead the jury to convict on a lesser showing than due process requires. In these cases, however, we conclude that "taken as a whole, the instructions correctly conveyed the concept of reasonable doubt to the jury." There is no reasonable likelihood that the jurors who determined petitioners' guilt applied the instructions in a way that violated the Constitution. The judgments in both cases are accordingly

Affirmed.

■ JUSTICE KENNEDY, concurring. [OPINION OMITTED]

■ JUSTICE GINSBURG, concurring in part and concurring in the judgment.

I agree with the Court that the reasonable doubt instructions given in these cases, read as a whole, satisfy the Constitution's due process requirement. As the Court observes, the instructions adequately conveyed to the jurors that they should focus exclusively upon the evidence, and that they should convict only if they had an "abiding conviction" of the defendant's guilt. I agree, further, with the Court's suggestion that the term "moral certainty," while not in itself so misleading as to render the instructions unconstitutional, should be avoided as an unhelpful way of explaining what reasonable doubt means.

Similarly unhelpful, in my view, are two other features of the instruction given in Victor's case. That instruction begins by defining reasonable doubt as "such a doubt as would cause a reasonable and prudent person, in one of the graver and more important transactions of life, to pause and hesitate before taking the represented facts as true and relying and acting thereon." A committee of distinguished federal judges, reporting to the Judicial Conference of the United States, has criticized this "hesitate to act" formulation

> "because the analogy it uses seems misplaced. In the decisions people make in the most important of their own affairs, resolution of conflicts about past events does not usually play a major role. Indeed, decisions we make in the most important affairs of our lives—choosing a spouse, a job, a place to live, and the like—generally involve a very heavy element of uncertainty and risk-

> taking. They are wholly unlike the decisions jurors ought to make in criminal cases."

* * *

Even less enlightening than the "hesitate to act" formulation is the passage of the *Victor* instruction counseling: "[The jury] may find an accused guilty upon the strong probabilities of the case, *provided such probabilities are strong enough to exclude any doubt of his guilt that is reasonable.*" If the italicized words save this part of the instruction from understating the prosecution's burden of proof, they do so with uninstructive circularity. Jury comprehension is scarcely advanced when a court "defines" reasonable doubt as "doubt . . . that is reasonable."

These and similar difficulties have led some courts to question the efficacy of any reasonable doubt instruction. At least two of the Federal Courts of Appeals have admonished their District Judges not to attempt a definition. This Court, too, has suggested on occasion that prevailing definitions of "reasonable doubt" afford no real aid. * * * But we have never held that the concept of reasonable doubt is undefinable, or that trial courts should not, as a matter of course, provide a definition. Nor, contrary to the Court's suggestion, have we ever held that the Constitution does not require trial courts to define reasonable doubt.

Because the trial judges in fact defined reasonable doubt in both jury charges we review, we need not decide whether the Constitution required them to do so. Whether or not the Constitution so requires, however, the argument for defining the concept is strong. While judges and lawyers are familiar with the reasonable doubt standard, the words "beyond a reasonable doubt" are not self-defining for jurors. Several studies of jury behavior have concluded that "jurors are often confused about the meaning of reasonable doubt," when that term is left undefined. Thus, even if definitions of reasonable doubt are necessarily imperfect, the alternative—refusing to define the concept at all—is not obviously preferable.

Fortunately, the choice need not be one between two kinds of potential juror confusion—on one hand, the confusion that may be caused by leaving "reasonable doubt" undefined, and on the other, the confusion that might be induced by the anachronism of "moral certainty," the misplaced analogy of "hesitation to act," or the circularity of "doubt that is reasonable." The Federal Judicial Center has proposed a definition of reasonable doubt that is clear, straightforward, and accurate. That instruction reads:

> "[T]he government has the burden of proving the defendant guilty beyond a reasonable doubt. Some of you may have served as jurors in civil cases, where you were told that it is only necessary to prove that a fact is more likely true than not true. In criminal cases, the government's proof must be more powerful than that. It must be beyond a reasonable doubt.
>
> "Proof beyond a reasonable doubt is proof that leaves you firmly convinced of the defendant's guilt. There are very few things in this world that we know with absolute certainty, and in criminal cases the law does not require proof that overcomes every possible doubt. If, based on your consideration of the evidence, you are

> firmly convinced that the defendant is guilty of the crime charged, you must find him guilty. If on the other hand, you think there is a real possibility that he is not guilty, you must give him the benefit of the doubt and find him not guilty." Federal Judicial Center, Pattern Criminal Jury Instructions 17–18 (1987) (instruction 21).

This instruction plainly informs the jurors that the prosecution must prove its case by more than a mere preponderance of the evidence, yet not necessarily to an absolute certainty. The "firmly convinced" standard for conviction, repeated for emphasis, is further enhanced by the juxtaposed prescription that the jury must acquit if there is a "real possibility" that the defendant is innocent. This model instruction surpasses others I have seen in stating the reasonable doubt standard succinctly and comprehensibly.

I recognize, however, that this Court has no supervisory powers over the state courts, and that the test we properly apply in evaluating the constitutionality of a reasonable doubt instruction is not whether we find it exemplary; instead, we inquire only whether there is a "reasonable likelihood that the jury understood the instructio[n] to allow conviction based on proof insufficient to meet" the reasonable doubt standard. On that understanding, I join Parts II, III–B, and IV of the Court's opinion and concur in its judgment.

■ JUSTICE BLACKMUN, with whom JUSTICE SOUTER joins in all but Part II, concurring in part and dissenting in part.

* * *

Our democracy rests in no small part on our faith in the ability of the criminal justice system to separate those who are guilty from those who are not. This is a faith which springs fundamentally from the requirement that unless guilt is established beyond all reasonable doubt, the accused shall go free. It was not until 1970, however, in *In re Winship*, that the Court finally and explicitly held that "the Due Process Clause protects the accused against conviction except upon proof beyond a reasonable doubt of every fact necessary to constitute the crime with which he is charged."

In *Winship*, the Court recounted the long history of the reasonable doubt standard, noting that it "dates at least from our early years as a Nation." The Court explained that any "society that values the good name and freedom of every individual should not condemn a man for commission of a crime when there is a reasonable doubt about his guilt."

Despite the inherent appeal of the reasonable-doubt standard, it provides protection to the innocent only to the extent that the standard, in reality, is an enforceable rule of law. To be a meaningful safeguard, the reasonable-doubt standard must have a tangible meaning that is capable of being understood by those who are required to apply it. It must be stated accurately and with the precision owed to those whose liberty or life is at risk. Because of the extraordinarily high stakes in criminal trials, "[i]t is critical that the moral force of the criminal law not be diluted by a standard of proof that leaves people in doubt whether innocent men are being condemned."

When reviewing a jury instruction that defines "reasonable doubt," it is necessary to consider the instruction as a whole and to give the words their common and ordinary meaning. It is not sufficient for the jury instruction merely to be susceptible to an interpretation that is technically correct. The important question is whether there is a "reasonable likelihood" that the jury was misled or confused by the instruction, and therefore applied it in a way that violated the Constitution. Any jury instruction defining "reasonable doubt" that suggests an improperly high degree of doubt for acquittal or an improperly low degree of certainty for conviction, offends due process. Either misstatement of the reasonable-doubt standard is prejudicial to the defendant, as it "vitiates all of the jury's findings," and removes the only constitutionally appropriate predicate for the jury's verdict.

* * *

In my view, the predominance of potentially misleading language in Victor's instruction made it likely that the jury interpreted the phrase "substantial doubt" to mean that a "large" doubt, as opposed to a merely reasonable doubt, is required to acquit a defendant. It seems that a central purpose of the instruction is to minimize the jury's sense of responsibility for the conviction of those who may be innocent. The instruction goes out of its way to assure jurors that "[y]ou may be convinced of the truth of a fact beyond a reasonable doubt and yet be fully aware that possibly you may be mistaken"; and then, after acquainting jurors with the possibility that their consciences will be unsettled after convicting the defendant, the instruction states that the jurors should feel free to convict based on the "strong probabilities of the case." Viewed as a whole, the instruction is geared toward assuring jurors that although they may be mistaken, they are to make their decision on those "strong probabilities," and only a "substantial doubt" of a defendant's guilt should deter them from convicting.

The majority dismisses the potentially harmful effects of the "strong probabilities" language on the grounds that a "nearly identical instruction" was upheld by the Court a century ago. *Dunbar v. United States* (1895). But the instruction in *Dunbar* did not equate reasonable doubt with "substantial doubt," nor did it contain the phrase "moral certainty." As the majority appreciates elsewhere in its opinion, challenged jury instructions must be considered in their entirety. Rather than examining the jury instruction as a whole, the majority parses it, ignoring the relationship between the challenged phrases as well as their cumulative effect.

Considering the instruction in its entirety, it seems fairly obvious to me that the "strong probabilities" language increased the likelihood that the jury understood "substantial doubt" to mean "to a large degree." Indeed, the jury could have a reasonable doubt about a defendant's guilt but still find that the "strong probabilities" are in favor of conviction. Only when a reasonable doubt is understood to be a doubt "to a large degree" does the "strong probabilities" language begin to make sense. * * * A jury could have a large and reasonable doubt about a defendant's guilt but still find the defendant guilty on "the strong probabilities of the case," believing it "likely" that the defendant committed the crime for which he was charged.

To be sure, the instruction does qualify the "strong probabilities" language by noting that "the strong probabilities of the case" should be "strong enough to exclude any doubt of his guilt that is reasonable." But this qualification is useless since a "doubt of his guilt that is reasonable" is immediately defined, in the very next sentence, as a "substantial doubt." Thus, the supposed clarification only compounds the confusion, by referring the jury to the "substantial doubt" phrase as a means of defining the "strong probabilities" language.

Finally, the instruction issued in Victor's case states that a reasonable doubt "is such a doubt as will not permit you, after full, fair, and impartial consideration of all the evidence, to have an abiding conviction, *to a moral certainty*, of the guilt of the accused." * * * The risk that jurors would understand "moral certainty" to authorize convictions based in part on value judgments regarding the defendant's behavior is particularly high in cases where the defendant is alleged to have committed a repugnant or brutal crime. [The] "moral certainty" phrase in Victor's instruction is particularly dangerous because it is used in conjunction with language that overstates the degree of doubt necessary to convict. This relationship between the "moral certainty" language, which potentially understates the degree of certainty required to convict, and the "substantial doubt," "strong probabilities," and "possibly you may be mistaken" language which, especially when taken together, overstates the degree of doubt necessary to acquit,. . . .

* * * [A]ll of the misleading language is mutually reinforcing, both overstating the degree of doubt necessary to acquit and understating the degree of certainty required to convict.

This confusing and misleading state of affairs leads me ineluctably to the conclusion that, in Victor's case, there exists a reasonable likelihood that the jury believed that a lesser burden of proof rested with the prosecution. * * * Where, as here, a jury instruction attempts but fails to convey with clarity and accuracy the meaning of reasonable doubt, the reviewing court should reverse the conviction and remand for a new trial. * * *

Francis v. Franklin

United States Supreme Court, 1985.
471 U.S. 307, 105 S.Ct. 1965.

■ JUSTICE BRENNAN delivered the opinion of the Court.

[A state prisoner seized an officer's gun while receiving dental care at a local dentist's office, forced the dentist's assistant to accompany him as a hostage, and managed to escape. They fled to a nearby home. As the prisoner demanded the resident's car keys, the front door was slammed and the prisoner's gun went off. The bullet traveled through the wooden door and into the resident's chest killing him. The prisoner was subsequently tried in a state court on a charge of malice murder. His sole defense to the charge was a lack of the requisite intent to kill. On the dispositive issue of intent, the trial judge instructed the jury as follows: "The acts of a person of sound mind and discretion are presumed to be the product of the person's will, but the presumption may be rebutted. A person of sound mind and discretion is presumed to intend the natural and probable consequences of his acts, but the presumption may be rebutted. A person will not be presumed to act with criminal intention but the trier of facts, that is, the Jury, may find criminal intention upon a consideration of the words, conduct, demeanor, motive and all other circumstances connected with the act for which the accused is prosecuted." The jury was also instructed that the defendant was presumed innocent and that the state was required to prove every element of the offense beyond a reasonable doubt. The jury returned a verdict of guilty and the prisoner was sentenced to death. He unsuccessfully appealed the conviction and sentence, and exhausted state postconviction remedies. An application for federal habeas corpus was denied by the district court; but the Eleventh Circuit reversed, holding that the jury instructions violated Franklin's fourteenth amendment rights.]

The Due Process Clause of the Fourteenth Amendment "protects the accused against conviction except upon proof beyond a reasonable doubt of every fact necessary to constitute the crime with which he is charged." In re Winship. This "bedrock, 'axiomatic and elementary' " [constitutional] principle, prohibits the State from using evidentiary presumptions in a jury charge that have the effect of relieving the State of its burden of persuasion beyond a reasonable doubt of every essential element of a crime. The prohibition protects the "fundamental value determination of our society," given voice in Justice Harlan's concurrence in Winship, "that it is far worse to convict an innocent man than to let a guilty man go free." The question before the Court in this case is . . .: "whether the challenged jury instruction had the effect of relieving the State of the burden of proof on the critical question of . . . state of mind," by creating a mandatory presumption of intent upon proof by the State of other elements of the offense.

The analysis is straightforward. "The threshold inquiry in ascertaining the constitutional analysis applicable to this kind of jury instruction is to determine the nature of the presumption it describes." The court must determine whether the challenged portion of the instruction creates a mandatory presumption, or merely a permissive inference. A mandatory presumption instructs the jury that it must infer the presumed fact if the State proves certain predicate facts.[2] A permissive inference suggests to the jury a possible conclusion to be drawn if the State proves predicate facts, but does not require the jury to draw that conclusion.

2. A mandatory presumption may be either conclusive or rebuttable. A conclusive presumption removes the presumed element from the case once the State has proven the predicate facts giving rise to the presumption. A rebuttable presumption does not remove the presumed element from the case but nevertheless requires the jury to find the presumed element unless the defendant persuades the jury that such a finding is unwarranted.

Mandatory presumptions ... violate the Due Process Clause if they relieve the State of the burden of persuasion on an element of an offense. ...

A permissive inference does not relieve the State of its burden of persuasion because it still requires the State to convince the jury that the suggested conclusion should be inferred based on the predicate facts proven. A permissive inference violates the Due Process Clause only if the suggested conclusion is not one that reason and common sense justify in light of the proven facts before the jury.

Analysis must focus initially on the specific language challenged, but the inquiry does not end there. If a specific portion of the jury charge, considered in isolation, could reasonably have been understood as creating a presumption that relieves the State of its burden of persuasion on an element of an offense, the potentially offending words must be considered in the context of the charge as a whole. Other instructions might explain the particular infirm language to the extent that a reasonable juror could not have considered the charge to have created an unconstitutional presumption. This analysis "requires careful attention to the words actually spoken to the jury ..., for whether a defendant has been accorded his constitutional rights depends upon the way in which a reasonable juror could have interpreted the instruction."

Franklin levels his constitutional attack at the following two sentences in the jury charge: "The acts of a person of sound mind and discretion are presumed to be the product of a person's will, but the presumption may be rebutted. A person of sound mind and discretion is presumed to intend the natural and probable consequences of his acts, but the presumption may be rebutted." The Georgia Supreme Court has interpreted this language as creating no more than a permissive inference that comports with ... constitutional standards.... The question, however, is not what the State Supreme Court declares the meaning of the charge to be, but rather what a reasonable juror could have understood the charge as meaning. ... The federal constitutional question is whether a reasonable juror could have understood the two sentences as a mandatory presumption that shifted to the defendant the burden of persuasion on the element of intent once the State had proved the predicate acts.

The challenged sentences are cast in the language of command. They instruct the jury that "acts of a person of sound mind and discretion *are presumed* to be the product of the person's will," and that a person "*is presumed* to intend the natural and probable consequences of his acts." ... The jurors "were not told that they had a choice, or that they *might* infer that conclusion; they were told only that the law presumed it. It is clear that a reasonable juror could easily have viewed such an instruction as mandatory." The portion of the jury charge challenged in this case directs the jury to presume an essential element of the offense—intent to kill—upon proof of other elements of the offense—the act of slaying another. In this way the instructions "undermine the factfinder's responsibility at trial, based on evidence adduced by the State, to *find* the ultimate facts beyond a reasonable doubt."

... [T]he jury in this case was explicitly informed that the presumptions "may be rebutted." The State makes much of this additional aspect of the instruction.

* * *

An irrebuttable or conclusive presumption relieves the State of its burden of persuasion by removing the presumed element from the case entirely if the State proves the predicate facts. A mandatory rebuttable presumption does not remove the presumed element from the case if the State proves the predicate facts, but it nonetheless relieves the State of the affirmative burden of persuasion on the presumed element by instructing the jury that it must find the presumed element unless the defendant persuades the jury not to make such a finding. A mandatory rebuttable presumption is perhaps less onerous from the defendant's perspective, but it is no less unconstitutional. Our cases make clear that "[s]uch shifting of the burden of persuasion with respect to a fact which the State deems so important that it must be either proved or presumed is impermissible under the Due Process Clause."

* * *

When combined with the immediately preceding mandatory language, the instruction that the presumptions "may be rebutted" could reasonably be read as telling the jury that it was required to infer intent to kill as the natural and probable consequence of the act of firing the gun unless the defendant persuaded the jury that such an inference was unwarranted. The very statement that the presumption "may be rebutted" could have indicated to a reasonable juror that the defendant bore an affirmative burden of persuasion once the State proved the underlying act giving rise to the presumption. Standing alone, the challenged language undeniably created an unconstitutional burden-shifting presumption with respect to the element of intent.

The jury, of course, did not hear only the two challenged sentences. The jury charge taken as a whole might have explained the proper allocation of burdens with sufficient clarity that any ambiguity in the particular language challenged could not have been understood by a reasonable juror as shifting the burden of persuasion. The State argues that sufficient clarifying language exists in this case. In particular, the State relies on an earlier portion of the charge instructing the jurors that the defendant was presumed innocent and that the State was required to prove every element of the offense beyond a reasonable doubt.[6] The State also points to the sentence immediately following the challenged portion of the

6. These portions of the instructions read:

> "... I charge you that before the State is entitled to a verdict of conviction of this defendant at your hands ... the burden is upon the State of proving the defendant's guilt as charged ... beyond a reasonable doubt."
>
> "Now ... the defendant enters upon his trial with the presumption of innocence in his favor and this presumption ... remains with him throughout the trial, unless it is overcome by evidence sufficiently strong to satisfy you of his guilt ... beyond a reasonable doubt."

charge, which reads: "[a] person will not be presumed to act with criminal intention...."

[G]eneral instructions on the State's burden of persuasion and the defendant's presumption of innocence are not "rhetorically inconsistent with a conclusive or burden-shifting presumption," because "[t]he jury could have interpreted the two sets of instructions as indicating that the presumption was a means by which proof beyond a reasonable doubt as to intent could be satisfied." In light of the instructions on intent given in this case, a reasonable juror could thus have thought that, although intent must be proved beyond a reasonable doubt, proof of the firing of the gun and its ordinary consequences constituted proof of intent beyond a reasonable doubt unless the defendant persuaded the jury otherwise. These general instructions as to the prosecution's burden and the defendant's presumption of innocence do not dissipate the error in the challenged portion of the instructions.

Nor does the more specific instruction following the challenged sentences—"A person will not be presumed to act with criminal intention but the trier of facts, that is, the Jury, may find criminal intention upon a consideration of the words, conduct, demeanor, motive and all other circumstances connected with the act for which the accused is prosecuted,"—provide a sufficient corrective. It may well be that this "*criminal* intention" instruction was not directed to the element of intent at all, but to another element of the Georgia crime of malice murder. ... Under state law malice aforethought comprises two elements: intent to kill and the absence of provocation or justification. ... At another point in the charge in this case, the trial court, consistently with this understanding of Georgia law, instructed the jury that malice is "the unlawful, deliberate intention to kill a human being without justification or mitigation or excuse."

The statement "*criminal* intention may not be presumed" may well have been intended to instruct the jurors that they were not permitted to presume the absence of provocation or justification but that they could infer this conclusion from circumstantial evidence. Whatever the court's motivation in giving the instruction, the jury could certainly have understood it this way. A reasonable juror trying to make sense of the juxtaposition of an instruction that "a person of sound mind and discretion is presumed to intend the natural and probable consequences of his acts," and an instruction that "[a] person will not be presumed to act with criminal intention," may well have thought that the instructions related to different elements of the crime and were therefore not contradictory—that he could presume intent to kill but not the absence of justification or provocation.

Even if a reasonable juror could have understood the prohibition of presuming "criminal intention" as applying to the element of intent, that instruction did no more than contradict the instruction in the immediately preceding sentence. A reasonable juror could easily have resolved the contradiction in the instruction by choosing to abide by the mandatory presumption and ignore the prohibition of presumption. Nothing in these specific sentences or in the charge as a whole makes clear to the jury that one of these contradictory instructions carries more weight than the other.

Language that merely contradicts and does not explain a constitutionally infirm instruction will not suffice to absolve the infirmity. A reviewing court has no way of knowing which of the two irreconcilable instructions the jurors applied in reaching their verdict. Had the instruction "[a] person ... is presumed to intend the natural and probable consequences of his acts," been followed by the instruction "*this means that* a person will not be presumed to act with criminal intention but the jury may find criminal intention upon consideration of all circumstances connected with the act for which the accused is prosecuted," a somewhat stronger argument might be made that a reasonable juror could not have understood the challenged language as shifting the burden of persuasion to the defendant. ... Whether or not such explanatory language might have been sufficient, however, no such language is present in this jury charge. If a juror thought the "criminal intention" instruction pertained to the element of intent, the juror was left in a quandary as to whether to follow that instruction or the immediately preceding one it contradicted.

Because a reasonable juror could have understood the challenged portions of the jury instruction in this case as creating a mandatory presumption that shifted to the defendant the burden of persuasion on the crucial element of intent, and because the charge read as a whole does not explain or cure the error, we hold that the jury charge does not comport with the requirements of the Due Process Clause.

* * *

... [T]he Due Process Clause of the Fourteenth Amendment prohibits the State from making use of jury instructions that have the effect of relieving the State of the burden of proof on the critical question of intent in a criminal prosecution. Today we reaffirm [this] wellspring due process principle.... The Court of Appeals faithfully and correctly applied this rule and the court's judgment is therefore affirmed.

■ Justice Powell, dissenting. [Omitted]

■ Justice Rehnquist, with whom The Chief Justice and Justice O'Connor join, dissenting.

* * *

Today the Court sets aside Franklin's murder conviction, but not because either the trial judge or the trial jury found that his guilt had not been proven beyond a reasonable doubt. The conviction is set aside because this Court concludes that one or two sentences out of several pages of instructions given by the judge to the jury could be read as allowing the jury to return a guilty verdict in the absence of proof establishing every statutory element of the crime beyond a reasonable doubt. The Court reaches this result even though the judge admonished the jury at least four separate times that they could convict only if they found guilt beyond a reasonable doubt. The Court, instead of examining the charge to the jury as a whole, seems bent on piling syllogism on syllogism to prove that someone *might* understand a few sentences in the charge to allow conviction on less than proof beyond a reasonable doubt. Such fine parsing of the jury instructions given in a state court trial is not required by anything in the United States Constitution.

* * *

It should be clear that the instructions at issue here—which provide that the challenged presumptions "may be rebutted"—are very different from ... conclusive language.... The conclusive presumption eliminates an element of the crime altogether; the rebuttable presumption here indicates that the particular element is still relevant, and may be shown not to exist.

* * *

In Cupp v. Naughten (1973), we dealt with a constitutional challenge to an instruction that "every witness is presumed to speak the truth," in the context of a criminal trial where the defense presented no witnesses. We there reaffirmed "the well-established proposition that a single instruction to a jury may not be judged in artificial isolation, but must be viewed in the context of the overall charge." We noted that if a particular instruction was erroneous a reviewing court still must ask "whether the ailing instruction by itself so infected the entire trial that the resulting conviction violates due process." In reaching our conclusion that the instruction at issue in Cupp did not violate due process, we noted that the jury had been fully informed of the State's burden to prove guilt beyond a reasonable doubt. We also pointed out that the instruction concerning the presumption of truthfulness had been accompanied by an instruction that in assessing a witness's credibility the jury should be attentive to the witness's own manner and words. We concluded that these instructions sufficiently allowed the jury to exercise its own judgment on the question of a witness's truthfulness; we also found no undue pressure on the defendant to take the stand and rebut the State's testimony, since the instruction indicated that such rebuttal could be founded on the State's own evidence.

I see no meaningful distinction between Cupp and the case at bar. Here the jury was instructed no less than four times that the State bore the burden of proof beyond a reasonable doubt. This language was accompanied early in the charge by a detailed discussion indicating that the jurors were the judges of their own reasonable doubt, that this doubt could arise after taking into account all the circumstances surrounding the incident at issue, and that where such doubt existed it was the jurors' duty to acquit. Four sentences prior to the offending language identified by the Court the jury was explicitly charged that "there is no burden on the defendant to prove anything." Immediately following that language the jury was charged that a person "will not be presumed to act with criminal intention," but that the jury could find such intention based upon the circumstances surrounding the act. The jury was then charged on Georgia's definition of malice, an essential element of murder which includes (1) deliberate intent to kill (2) without justification or mitigation or excuse. Again, the jury was explicitly charged that "it is not incumbent upon the accused to prove an absence of malice, if the evidence for the prosecution shows facts which may excuse or justify the homicide."

The Court nevertheless concludes, upon reading the charge in its entirety, that a "reasonable juror" could have understood the instruction to mean (1) that the State had satisfied its burden of proving intent to kill by introducing evidence of the defendant's acts—drawing, aiming and firing the gun—the "natural and probable consequences" of which were the death in question; (2) that upon proof of these acts the burden shifted to the defendant to disprove that he had acted with intent to kill; and (3) that if the defendant introduced no evidence or the jury was unconvinced by his evidence, the jury was *required* to find that the State had proved intent to kill even if the State's proof did not convince them of the defendant's intent.

The reasoning which leads to this conclusion would appeal only to a lawyer, and it is indeed difficult to believe that "reasonable jurors" would have arrived at it on their own. It runs like this. First, the Court states that a "reasonable juror" could understand the particular offending sentences, considered in isolation, to shift the burden to the defendant of disproving his intent to kill. The Court then proceeds to examine other portions of the charge, to determine whether they militate against this understanding. It casually dismisses the "general instructions on the State's burden of persuasion."

* * *

Since in this case the presumption was "rebuttable," the obvious question is: "rebuttable by what?" The Court's analysis must assume that a "reasonable juror" understood the presumption to be a means for satisfying the State's burden unless rebutted *by the defendant*. The italicized words, of course, are not included in the charge in this case, but if the jurors reasonably believed that the presumption could be rebutted by other means—for example, by the circumstances surrounding the incident—then the Court's analysis fails. But I find the Court's assumption unrealistic in any event, because if the jurors understood the charge as the Court posits then that conclusion was reached in the face of the contradictory preceding statement that *the defendant had no burden to prove anything*.

* * *

It may well be that the Court's technical analysis of the charge holds together from a legal standpoint, but its tortured reasoning is alone sufficient to convince me that no "reasonable juror" followed that path. It is not that I think jurors are not conscientious, or that I believe jurors disregard troublesome trial court instructions; I agree with the Court that we generally must assume that jurors strive to follow the law as charged. Rather, I simply do not believe that a "reasonable juror," upon listening to the above charge, could have interpreted it as shifting the burden to the defendant to disprove intent, and as requiring the juror to follow the presumption *even if he was not satisfied with the State's proof on that element.*

* * *

Thus, even accepting the Court's reasonable juror test, I cannot agree that the charge read as a whole was constitutionally infirm. But quite apart from that, I would take a different approach than the Court does with respect to the applicable legal standard. It appears that under the Court's approach it will reverse a conviction if a "reasonable juror" hypothetically *might* have understood the charge unconstitutionally to shift a burden of proof, even if it was unlikely that a single juror had such an understanding. I believe that it must at least be *likely* that a juror so understood the charge before constitutional error can be found. Where as here a Sandstrom error is alleged involving not a conclusive presumption, but a rebuttable presumption, language in the charge indicating the State's general burden of proof and the jury's duty to examine all surrounding facts and circumstances generally should be sufficient to dissipate any constitutional infirmity. Otherwise we risk finding constitutional error in a record such as this one, after finely parsing through the elements of state crimes that are really far removed from the problems presented by the burden of proof charge. I do not believe that the Court must inject itself this far into the state criminal process to protect the fundamental rights of criminal defendants. I dissent and would reverse the judgment of the Court of Appeals.

NOTES

1. The burden of proof analysis begins with the proposition that a defendant must be convicted by evidence that satisfies the jury of his guilt beyond a reasonable doubt. In In re Winship, 397 U.S. 358, 90 S.Ct. 1068 (1970), the Court said: "... we explicitly hold that the Due Process Clause protects the accused against conviction except upon proof of guilt beyond a reasonable doubt of every fact necessary to constitute the crime with which he is charged". The Court then went on to hold that the reasonable doubt standard was a constitutional requirement in the adjudicatory stage of state juvenile court proceedings where the allegation underlying the delinquency petition is the alleged violation of a criminal statute.

2. Despite the constitutional imperative of the "beyond a reasonable doubt" standard, the courts have struggled with its definition. "Attempts to explain the term 'reasonable doubt' do not usually result in making it any clearer to the minds of the jury." Miles v. United States, 103 U.S. (13 Otto) 304 (1880). The standard definition, derived from Holland v. United States, 348 U.S. 121, 75 S.Ct. 127 (1954), suggests that a reasonable doubt is a doubt that would cause prudent men to hesitate before acting in a matter of importance to themselves. See United States v. Jones, 663 F.2d 567 (5th Cir.1981). However, the variations are endless. See United States v. DeVincent, 632 F.2d 147 (1st Cir.1980) (a doubt based on reason and common sense); Tsoumas v. New Hampshire, 611 F.2d 412 (1st Cir.1980) (not frivolous or fanciful doubt nor one that can be easily explained away); State v. Butler, 277 S.C. 452, 290 S.E.2d 1 (1982) (substantial doubt); Commonwealth v. Conceicao, 388 Mass. 255, 446 N.E.2d 383 (1983) (persuasion to a reasonable or a moral certainty is acceptable but not the best definition). Occasionally, the definition given by the judge has warranted reversal. See United States v. Wosepka, 757 F.2d 1006 (9th Cir.1985), modified 787 F.2d 1294 (9th Cir.1985); Dunn v. Perrin, 570 F.2d 21 (1st Cir.1978); United States v. Cummings, 468 F.2d 274 (9th Cir.1972); McCullough v. State, 99 Nev. 72, 657 P.2d 1157 (1983) (beyond a reasonable doubt is about "7½ on a scale of 10"); State v. Moss, 189 Conn. 364, 456 A.2d 274 (1983) (reasonable doubt standard is met when scales of justice are substantially out of equipoise). For this reason, certain courts prohibit trial judges from attempting to define reasonable doubt. United States v. Regilio, 669 F.2d 1169 (7th Cir.1981).

3. Additional cases suggest that efforts to define the term reasonable doubt "inevitably lead to constitutional challenges," so that judges might be wise to give no definition of the term. United States v. Jorge, 865 F.2d 6 (1st Cir.1989). See also United States v. Hall, 854 F.2d 1036 (7th Cir.1988). There the court suggested that a proper definition should be possible, but that what usually results in a formulation which, at best, is unhelpful, and often creates risk of error.

For one discussion of instructions on the topic of reasonable doubt, see United States v. Nolasco, 926 F.2d 869 (9th Cir.1991) (en banc):

> The challenge confronting a court that would define reasonable doubt is to avoid language that may "mislead the jury into finding no reasonable doubt when in fact there was some." Numerous attempts to define reasonable doubt have resulted in reversible error or otherwise unacceptable deviations from the "hesitate to act" language. See Cage v. Louisiana (1990) (reversing conviction equating reasonable doubt with "grave uncertainty" and "actual substantial doubt", note 4 infra); Monk v. Zelez, 901 F.2d 885, 889–90 (10th Cir.1990) (reversing conviction where reasonable doubt defined as "a substantial honest, conscientious doubt"); United States v. Campbell, 874 F.2d 838, 843 (1st Cir.1989) (warning that defining reasonable doubt as " 'a fair doubt' could impose a lesser burden on the prosecution"). We have generally warned against significant departure from the "hesitate to act" language, see United States v. Robinson, 546 F.2d 309, 313–14 (9th Cir.1976), although we have upheld the use of other definitions. E.g., id. (not reversible error to define burden as evidence upon which juror would be "willing to act" on vital matters); United States v. Bustillo, 789 F.2d 1364, 1368 (9th Cir.1986) ("firmly convinced" and "real possibility" language did not constitute plain error). Cf. Ninth Circuit Model Criminal Jury Instructions No. 3.03 (1989) (adopting "firmly convinced" language).
>
> * * *
>
> We recognize that several circuits discourage or even condemn the use of reasonable doubt definitions. See United States v. Ricks, 882 F.2d 885, 894 (4th Cir.1989); Thompson v. Lynaugh, 821 F.2d 1054, 1061 (5th Cir.1987); United States v. Marquardt, 786 F.2d 771, 784 (7th Cir.1986). But see Friedman v. United States, 381 F.2d 155, 160 (8th Cir.1967) (trial courts are required to define reasonable doubt); Blatt v. United States, 60 F.2d 481 (3d Cir.1932) (same). However, a substantial number of state jurisdictions within the confines of the Ninth Circuit take a contrary view. In these jurisdictions an instruction defining reasonable doubt is constitutionally required, or simply provided as a matter of practice or statute. See, e.g., State v. McHenry, 88 Wash.2d 211, 558 P.2d 188, 190 (1977) ("constitutional failure" not to define); State v. Cotton, 100 Idaho 573, 602 P.2d 71, 74 (1979); State v. Robinson, 235 Or. 524, 385 P.2d 754, 756 (1963) ("practice prevails" for jury to be instructed on definition of reasonable doubt); see also Nev.Rev.Stat. § 175.211 (1986) (specifying language of acceptable definition of reasonable doubt). We therefore refuse to preclude the giving of a supplemental instruction since counsel experienced in preparing such instructions in state courts will in all probability request them in federal cases. Moreover, a supplemental instruction may be helpful or even necessary in a few cases where, for example, the jury through questions submitted to the judge suggests it may be confused or uncertain as to the meaning of "reasonable doubt," or where counsel in argument or the court through other instructions may have invoked uncertainty or

confusion as to its meaning. We therefore hold that an appropriate instruction defining reasonable doubt is permissible but not necessarily required.

See Diamond, Reasonable Doubt: To Define or not to Define, 90 Columb.L.Rev. 1716 (1990).

4. In Cage v. Louisiana, 498 U.S. 39, 111 S.Ct. 328 (1990), the Supreme Court found that one judge's definition of reasonable doubt diluted the standard required by *Winship*. The Court said:

* * *

The instruction provided in relevant part:

> If you entertain a reasonable doubt as to any fact or element necessary to constitute the defendant's guilt, it is your duty to give him the benefit of that doubt and return a verdict of not guilty. Even where the evidence demonstrates a probability of guilt, if it does not establish such guilt beyond a reasonable doubt, you must acquit the accused. This doubt, however, must be a reasonable one; that is one that is founded upon a real tangible substantial basis and not upon mere caprice and conjecture. *It must be such doubt as would give rise to a grave uncertainty*, raised in your mind by reasons of the unsatisfactory character of the evidence or lack thereof. A reasonable doubt is not a mere possible doubt. *It is an actual substantial doubt.* It is a doubt that a reasonable man can seriously entertain. What is required is not an absolute or mathematical certainty, but a *moral certainty*.

The Court held:

> In construing the instruction, we consider how reasonable jurors could have understood the charge as a whole. The charge did at one point instruct that to convict, guilt must be found beyond a reasonable doubt; but it then equated a reasonable doubt with a "grave uncertainty" and an "actual substantial doubt," and stated that what was required was a "moral certainty" that the defendant was guilty. It is plain to us that the words "substantial" and "grave," as they are commonly understood, suggest a higher degree of doubt than is required for acquittal under the reasonable doubt standard. When those statements are then considered with the reference to "moral certainty," rather than evidentiary certainty, it becomes clear that a reasonable juror could have interpreted the instruction to allow a finding of guilt based on a degree of proof below that required by the Due Process Clause.

5. Following Cage v. Louisiana, 498 U.S. 39, 111 S.Ct. 328 (1990), the Court unanimously found that a constitutionally inadequate definition of reasonable doubt can never amount to harmless error. In Sullivan v. Louisiana, 508 U.S. 275, 113 S.Ct. 2078 (1993), the Court held:

> In Chapman v. California (1967), we rejected the view that all federal constitutional errors in the course of a criminal trial require reversal. We held that the Fifth Amendment violation of prosecutorial comment upon the defendant's failure to testify would not require reversal of the conviction if the State could show "beyond a reasonable doubt that the error complained of did not contribute to the verdict obtained." The *Chapman* standard recognizes that "certain constitutional errors, no less than other errors, may have been 'harmless' in terms of their effect on the factfinding process at trial." Although most constitutional errors have been held amenable to harmless-error analysis, some will always invalidate the con-

viction. The question in the present case is to which category the present error belongs.

Chapman itself suggests the answer. Consistent with the jury-trial guarantee, the question it instructs the reviewing court to consider is not what effect the constitutional error might generally be expected to have upon a reasonable jury, but rather what effect it had upon the guilty verdict in the case at hand. Harmless-error review looks, ... to the basis on which "the jury *actually rested* its verdict." The inquiry, in other words, is not whether, in a trial that occurred without the error, a guilty verdict would surely have been rendered, but whether the guilty verdict actually rendered in *this* trial was surely unattributable to the error. That must be so, because to hypothesize a guilty verdict that was never in fact rendered—no matter how inescapable the findings to support that verdict might be—would violate the jury-trial guarantee.

Once the proper role of an appellate court engaged in the *Chapman* inquiry is understood, the illogic of harmless-error review in the present case becomes evident. Since ... there has been no jury verdict within the meaning of the Sixth Amendment, the entire premise of *Chapman* review is simply absent. There being no jury verdict of guilty-beyond-a-reasonable-doubt, the question whether the *same* verdict of guilty-beyond-a-reasonable-doubt would have been rendered absent the constitutional error is utterly meaningless. There is no *object*, so to speak, upon which harmless-error scrutiny can operate. The most an appellate court can conclude is that a jury *would surely have found* petitioner guilty beyond a reasonable doubt—not that the jury's actual finding of guilty beyond a reasonable doubt *would surely not have been different* absent the constitutional error. That is not enough. The Sixth Amendment requires more than appellate speculation about a hypothetical jury's action, or else directed verdicts for the State would be sustainable on appeal; it requires an actual jury finding of guilty.

6. For examples of lower courts attempting to come to grips with the definitional problems inherent in reasonable doubt instructions in light of Supreme Court precedent, see Brown v. Cain, 104 F.3d 744 (5th Cir.1997) (doubt equated to "grave uncertainty" does not taint instruction in the context given); United States v. Campbell, 61 F.3d 976 (1st Cir.1995) (a fair doubt based on reason and common sense); Adams v. Aiken, 41 F.3d 175 (4th Cir.1994) (substantial doubt as contrasted with whimsical, imaginary weak and slight doubt); United States v. Oreto, 37 F.3d 739 (1st Cir.1994) (a real doubt, based upon reason and common sense after careful and impartial consideration of all the evidence in the case ... it does not mean beyond all doubt, but rather, a doubt based upon reason); Commonwealth v. James, 424 Mass. 770, 678 N.E.2d 1170 (1997) (use of the phrase "moral certainty" is acceptable if it is linked with language that lends content to it).

7. Given the constitutional stature of the reasonable doubt standard, the court began to apply it to the related question of the allocation of the burden of proof. In so doing, it considered a number of state substantive law provisions embodied in jury instructions. In Mullaney v. Wilbur, 421 U.S. 684, 95 S.Ct. 1881 (1975), the court invalidated a Maine law which required the defendant to establish, by a preponderance of the evidence, that he acted in the heat of passion on sudden provocation to reduce murder to manslaughter. In Patterson v. New York, 432 U.S. 197, 97 S.Ct. 2319 (1977), the court limited *Mullaney* to situations in which the defendant had a burden to establish an essential element of the state's case; but refused to eliminate the defendant's obligation to establish an affirmative defense.

Accordingly, a state may place the burden of proving an affirmative defense, such as self-defense, on the defendant.

These decisions formed the basis of Sandstrom v. Montana, 442 U.S. 510, 99 S.Ct. 2450 (1979), in which the court invalidated a then fairly standard instruction indicating that "the law presumes that a person intends the ordinary consequences of his voluntary acts":

> [A] reasonable jury could well have interpreted the presumption as "conclusive," that is, not technically as a presumption at all, but rather as an irrebuttable direction by the court to find intent once convinced of the facts triggering the presumption. Alternatively, the jury may have interpreted the instruction as a direction to find intent upon proof of the defendant's voluntary actions (and their "ordinary" consequences), unless *the defendant* proved the contrary by some quantum of proof which may well have been considerably greater than "some" evidence—thus effectively shifting the burden of persuasion on the element of intent. Numerous federal and state courts have warned that instructions of the type given here can be interpreted in just these ways. . . .
>
> It is clear that under Montana law, whether the crime was committed purposely or knowingly is a fact necessary to constitute the crime of deliberate homicide. Indeed, it was the lone element of the offense at issue in Sandstrom's trial, as he confessed to causing the death of the victim, told the jury that knowledge and purpose were the only questions he was controverting, and introduced evidence solely on those points. Moreover, it is conceded that proof of defendant's "intent" would be sufficient to establish this element. Thus, the question before this Court is whether the challenged jury instruction had the effect of relieving the State of the burden of proof enunciated in *Winship* on the critical question of petitioner's state of mind. We conclude that under either of the two possible interpretations of the instruction set out above, precisely that effect would result, and that the instruction therefore represents constitutional error.
>
> * * *
>
> [A] conclusive presumption in this case would "conflict with the overriding presumption of innocence with which the law endows the accused and which extends to every element of the crime," and would "invade [the] factfinding function" which in a criminal case the law assigns solely to the jury. The instruction announced to David Sandstrom's jury may well have had exactly these consequences. Upon finding proof of one element of the crime (causing death), and of facts insufficient to establish the second (the voluntariness and "ordinary consequences" of defendant's action), Sandstrom's jurors could reasonably have concluded that they were directed to find against defendant on the element of intent. The State was thus not forced to prove "beyond a reasonable doubt . . . every fact necessary to constitute the crime . . . charged."

In Connecticut v. Johnson, 460 U.S. 73, 103 S.Ct. 969 (1983), a four justice plurality held that a conclusive presumption on the issue of intent in a jury instruction was tantamount to a directed verdict and could (almost) never be "harmless error."

8. In Carella v. California, 491 U.S. 263, 109 S.Ct. 2419 (1989), the Court invalidated an instruction which stated that a person who has leased a vehicle and who fails to return it within five days after the lease expires "shall be presumed to have embezzled the vehicle." The Court applied the test of whether the presumption is mandatory and therefore unconstitutional, "that is whether the specific instruction, both alone and in the context of the overall charge, could have been understood by reasonable jurors to require them to find the presumed fact if the State proves certain predicate facts." The Court concluded that the instruction violated due process.

The five-judge majority then held that such an error could be deemed harmless, depending upon the facts, and did not constitute per se reversible error. Four concurring justices stated that, although such errors could be deemed harmless, normal harmless error analysis is inappropriate. These justices noted that a mandatory conclusive presumption invades the province of the jury. Thus, these justices concluded, a harmless error analysis in the type of situation should not involve a review of the evidence as a whole. The issue is not whether the evidence as a whole overwhelmingly establishes guilt, according to the four concurring justices. They suggested that such an improper instruction may be harmless when "the predicate facts relied upon in the instruction, or other facts necessarily found by the jury, are so closely related to the ultimate fact to be presumed that no rational jury could find those facts without also finding that ultimate fact, making those findings functionally equivalent to finding the element required to be presumed."

See also Yates v. Evatt, 500 U.S. 391, 111 S.Ct. 1884 (1991):

> In charging the jurors on the issue of malice in this case, the trial judge instructed them on two mandatory presumptions.... The jury was told that "malice is implied or presumed" from the "willful, deliberate, and intentional doing of an unlawful act" and from the "use of a deadly weapon." With respect to the unlawful act presumption, the jury was told that the "presumption is rebuttable, that is, it is not conclusive on you, but it is rebuttable by the rest of the evidence." Following the description of the deadly weapon presumption, the jurors were told that it was their responsibility "under all the evidence to make a determination as to whether malice existed in the mind and heart of the killer."
>
> We think a reasonable juror would have understood the unlawful act presumption to mean that upon introduction of evidence tending to rebut malice, the jury should consider all evidence bearing on the issue of malice, together with the presumption, which would still retain some probative significance. A reasonable juror would have understood the deadly weapon presumption to mean that its probative force should be considered along with all other evidence tending to prove or disprove malice. Although the presumptions were rebuttable in these ways, the mandate to apply them remained, as did their tendency to shift the burden of proof on malice from the prosecution to petitioner.

9. Another series of instruction cases deals with the issue of statutory and common law inferences and presumptions designed to facilitate proof of the defendant's knowledge. See County Court of Ulster County v. Allen, 442 U.S. 140, 99 S.Ct. 2213 (1979):

> A New York statute provides that, with certain exceptions, the presence of a firearm in an automobile is presumptive evidence of its illegal possession by all persons then occupying the vehicle. The United States Court of Appeals for the Second Circuit held ... that the statute is "unconstitutional on its face." ...
>
> Four persons, three adult males (respondents) and a 16–year–old girl (Jane Doe, who is not a respondent here), were jointly tried on charges that they possessed two loaded handguns, a loaded machinegun, and over a pound of heroin found in a Chevrolet in which they were riding when it was stopped for speeding on the New York Thruway shortly after noon on

March 28, 1973. The two large-caliber handguns, which together with their ammunition weighed approximately six pounds, were seen through the window of the car by the investigating police officer. They were positioned crosswise in an open handbag on either the front floor or the front seat of the car on the passenger side where Jane Doe was sitting. Jane Doe admitted that the handbag was hers. The machinegun and the heroin were discovered in the trunk after the police pried it open.

* * *

At the close of the trial, the judge instructed the jurors that they were entitled to infer possession from the defendants' presence in the car. He did not make any reference to the "upon the person" exception in his explanation of the statutory presumption, nor did any of the defendants object to this omission or request alternative or additional instructions on the subject.

As applied to the facts of this case, the presumption of possession is entirely rational. ... The argument against possession by any of the respondents was predicated solely on the fact that the guns were in Jane Doe's pocketbook. But several circumstances ... made it highly improbable that she was the sole custodian of those weapons.

Even if it was reasonable to conclude that she had placed the guns in her purse before the car was stopped by police, the facts strongly suggest that Jane Doe was not the only person able to exercise dominion over them. The two guns were too large to be concealed in her handbag. The bag was consequently open, and part of one of the guns was in plain view, within easy access of the driver of the car and even, perhaps, of the other two respondents who were riding in the rear seat.

* * *

Under these circumstances, the jury would have been entirely reasonable in rejecting the suggestion ... that the handguns were in the sole possession of Jane Doe. Assuming that the jury did reject it, the case is tantamount to one in which the guns were lying on the floor or the seat of the car in the plain view of the three other occupants of the automobile. In such a case it is surely rational to infer that each of the respondents was fully aware of the presence of the guns and had both the ability and the intent to exercise dominion and control over the weapons. The application of the statutory presumption in this case therefore comports with the standard [of prior cases because] there is a "rational connection" between the basic facts that the prosecution proved and the ultimate fact presumed, and the latter is "more likely than not to flow from" the former.

Respondents argue, however, that the validity of the New York presumption must be judged by a "reasonable doubt" test rather than the "more likely than not" standard.... Under the more stringent test, it is argued that a statutory presumption must be rejected unless the evidence necessary to invoke the inference is sufficient for a rational jury to find the inferred fact beyond a reasonable doubt. Respondents' argument again overlooks the distinction between a permissive presumption on which the prosecution is entitled to rely as one not-necessarily-sufficient part of its proof and a mandatory presumption which the jury must accept even if it is the sole evidence of an element of the offense.

In the latter situation, since the prosecution bears the burden of establishing guilt, it may not rest its case entirely on a presumption unless

> the fact proved is sufficient to support the inference of guilt beyond a reasonable doubt. But in the former situation, the prosecution may rely on all of the evidence in the record to meet the reasonable doubt standard. There is no more reason to require a permissive statutory presumption to meet a reasonable doubt standard before it may be permitted to play any part in a trial than there is to require that degree of probative force for other relevant evidence before it may be admitted.

* * *

The judgment is reversed.

Prior cases defined the test applied in *Allen* in a two stage process. First, the factual basis for the inference must be sound. Compare Leary v. United States, 395 U.S. 6, 89 S.Ct. 1532 (1969) (presumption of knowledge of importation from possession of marijuana invalid because, given the significant amount of domestically grown marijuana, "it would be no more than speculation" to conclude that one who possessed automatically "knew" the source) with Turner v. United States, 396 U.S. 398, 90 S.Ct. 642 (1970) (same presumption is valid for heroin but not cocaine since a sizeable quantity of cocaine is lawfully produced in this country for medicinal purposes, and consequently, there is the very real possibility that cocaine in a defendant's possession may have been stolen from a legal source.) Second, "where there is a rational connection between the facts proved and the fact presumed or inferred, it is permissible to shift the burden of going forward to the defendant. Where an inference satisfies the reasonable doubt standard ... there will certainly be a rational connection between the fact presumed or inferred (in this case, knowledge) and the facts the Government must prove in order to shift the burden of going forward (possession of recently stolen property)." Barnes v. United States, 412 U.S. 837, 93 S.Ct. 2357 (1973) (upholding instruction that possession of recently stolen property, if not satisfactorily explained, is ordinarily a circumstance from which you may reasonably draw the inference and find, in the light of the surrounding circumstances shown by the evidence in the case, that the person in possession knew the property had been stolen).

10. In Martin v. Ohio, 480 U.S. 228, 107 S.Ct. 1098 (1987), the Court upheld an Ohio law which requires the defendant, in order to prevail on a theory of self-defense, to establish by a preponderance of the evidence facts that constitute justification under Ohio law. It said that the Ohio scheme did not shift to the defendant the burden of disproving the existence of any element of the offense of murder. Moreover, "The State did not exceed its authority by defining the crime of murder as purposely causing the death of another with prior calculation or design." It noted that historically affirmative defenses, such as self-defense and insanity, required the defendant to bear the burden of proof. Even though forty-eight states now require the prosecution to bear the burden (by some quantum of evidence) of disproving the claim of self-defense once there is sufficient evidence to put the matter in issue, the Court refused to utilize the Constitution to impose such a burden upon the prosecution in the remaining states of Ohio and South Carolina.

Three dissenting justices protested that the Court should not give complete discretion to state legislators in deciding what constitute the elements of an offense and what constitutes an affirmative defense. They suggested that the legislature may not use the affirmative defense approach of shifting the burden of proof to the defendant on an issue which makes a substantial difference to guilt or innocence, or to punishment, if in the Anglo–American legal tradition "such factor in question has historically held that level of importance." Applying that standard, Justices Powell, Brennan, and Marshall would have invalidated any scheme which required the defendant to bear the burden of proof on the question of self-defense.

A narrower issue in *Martin* was whether, in fact, under Ohio law, the jury might have believed that the defense had the burden of negating an element of the offense where there was an overlap between proof of the element of "prior calculation" and proof negating a claim of self-defense. By a vote of five-to-four, the majority ruled that the instructions adequately provided that the prosecution had the burden of proof beyond a reasonable doubt as to every element of the offense.

11. The Constitution does not require the prosecution to negate beyond a reasonable doubt the facts that constitute an affirmative defense. See Dixon v. United States, 548 U.S. 1, 126 S.Ct. 2437 (2006) (defendant is not entitled to a jury instruction requiring the government to disprove a duress defense beyond a reasonable doubt). Nevertheless, a particular statute may establish such a burden. For example, state law may require, once insanity is in issue, that the prosecution, in order to merit a conviction, prove beyond a reasonable doubt that the defendant was sane at the time of the offense. However, as Dixon held, in the absence of legislative intent to the contrary the court will presume that the burden of proving an affirmative defense rests with the party asserting it.

12. Especially in the federal system, the "ostrich" instruction is fairly common. Where the prosecution has to prove the defendant's knowledge of certain facts as an element of an offense, judges often instruct juries that an individual cannot keep himself or herself deliberately ignorant of facts to escape the knowledge requirement. For cases providing guidance on the circumstances in which these instructions may be used, see United States v. Carrillo, 435 F.3d 767 (7th Cir. 2006); United States v. Alston–Graves, 435 F.3d 331 (D. C. Cir. 2006). For some fairly rare criticism of this type of instruction, see United States v. Heredia, 483 F.3d 913 (9th Cir. 2007) (en banc) (Graber, J., dissenting) ("If Congress wants to criminalize willful ignorance, it is free to amend the statute to say so ...."); United States v. Sanchez–Robles, 927 F.2d 1070 (9th Cir.1991) (instruction should be used sparingly), and United States v. Giovannetti, 928 F.2d 225 (7th Cir.1991). See Chinni, Whose Head is in the Sand: Problems With the Use of the Ostrich Instruction in Conspiracy Cases, 13 Western N.E.L. Rev 35 (1991).

13. Several courts have invalidated an instruction advising the jury that a .10 blood alcohol level gives rise to a presumption that the defendant is intoxicated. Sturgeon v. State, 575 N.E.2d 679 (Ind.App.1991); Wilhelm v. State, 568 So.2d 1 (Fla.1990); State v. Leverett, 245 Mont. 124, 799 P.2d 119 (1990). The *Leverett* Court suggested that the solution to the due process problem is not to make the presumption rebuttable, but to make it "unambiguously permissive."

14. For an excellent effort to provide a unified framework on which to analyze evidentiary inferences and presumptions, see Allen, Structuring Jury Decision–Making in Criminal Cases: A Unified Constitutional Approach to Evidentiary Devices, 94 Harv.L.Rev. 321 (1980).

2. PRESUMPTION OF INNOCENCE

Taylor v. Kentucky

Supreme Court of the United States, 1978.
436 U.S. 478, 98 S.Ct. 1930.

■ MR. JUSTICE POWELL delivered the opinion of the Court.

* * *

I.

Petitioner was tried for robbery in 1976, allegedly having forced his way into the home of James Maddox and stolen a house key and a billfold containing $10 to $15. During *voir dire* of the jury, defense counsel questioned the panel about their understanding of the presumption of innocence, the burden of proof beyond a reasonable doubt, and the fact that an indictment is not evidence. The prosecutor then read the indictment to the jury.

* * *

[Following the trial, defense] counsel requested the trial court to instruct the jury that "[t]he law presumes a defendant to be innocent of a crime,"[5] and that the indictment, previously read to the jury, was not evidence to be considered against the defendant.[6] The court declined to give either instruction, and did not convey their substance in its charge to the jury. It did instruct the jury as to the Commonwealth's burden of proving petitioner's guilt beyond a reasonable doubt.[7] Petitioner was found guilty.

* * *

5. Petitioner's requested instruction on this point read as follows:

> "The law presumes a defendant to be innocent of a crime. Thus a defendant, although accused, begins the trial with a 'clean slate.' That is, with no evidence against him. The law permits nothing but legal evidence presented before a jury to be considered in support of any charge against the accused. So the presumption of innocence alone is sufficient to acquit a defendant, unless you are satisfied beyond a reasonable doubt of the defendant's guilt after careful and impartial consideration of all the evidence in the case."

6. Petitioner's proposed instruction on this point read as follows:

> "The jury is instructed that an indictment is in no way any evidence against the defendant and no adverse inference can be drawn against the defendant from a finding of the indictment. The indictment is merely a written accusation charging the defendant with the commission of a crime. It has no probative force and carries with it no implication of guilt."

7. The trial court's instructions, in their entirety, were as follows:

> "All right. These are your instructions as to the law applicable to the facts you've heard in evidence from the witness stand in this case.
>
> "Number one, you will find the defendant guilty under this instruction if and only if you believe from the evidence beyond a reasonable doubt all of the following: A. That in this county on or about February 16, 1976 and before the finding of the indictment herein, he the defendant stole a sum of money and a house key from James Maddox, 249 Rosewood, Frankfort, Kentucky; and B. in the course of so doing he used physical force on James Maddox. If you find the defendant guilty under this instruction you will fix his punishment at confinement in the penitentiary for not less than five nor more than ten years in your discretion.
>
> "Number two, if upon the whole case you have a reasonable doubt as to the defendant's guilt you will find him not guilty. The term 'reasonable doubt' as used in these instructions means a substantial doubt, a real doubt, in that you must ask yourself not whether a better case might have been proved but whether after hearing all the evidence you actually doubt that the defendant is guilty.
>
> "Number three, the verdict of the jury must be unanimous and be signed by one of you as foreman. You may use the form provided at the end of these instructions for writing your verdict.
>
> "There is appended to these instructions a form with alternate verdicts, one

II.

"The principle that there is a presumption of innocence in favor of the accused is the undoubted law, axiomatic and elementary, and its enforcement lies at the foundation of the administration of our criminal law." Coffin v. United States, 156 U.S. 432, 453, 15 S.Ct. 394, 403 (1895). The *Coffin* Court traced the venerable history of the presumption from Deuteronomy through Roman law, English common law, and the common law of the United States. While *Coffin* held that the presumption of innocence and the equally fundamental principle that the prosecution bears the burden of proof beyond a reasonable doubt were logically separate and distinct, sharp scholarly criticism demonstrated the error of that view, see e.g., J. Thayer, A Preliminary Treatise on Evidence 551–576 (1898) (hereafter Thayer); 9 J. Wigmore, Evidence § 2511 (3d ed.1940) (hereafter Wigmore); C. McCormick, Evidence 805–806 (2d ed.1972).[12]

Nevertheless, these same scholars advise against abandoning the instruction on the presumption of innocence, even when a complete explanation of the burden of proof beyond a reasonable doubt is provided. This admonition derives from a perceived salutary effect upon lay jurors. While the legal scholar may understand that the presumption of innocence and the prosecution's burden of proof are logically similar, the ordinary citizen well may draw significant additional guidance from an instruction on the presumption of innocence. Wigmore described this effect as follows:

> "[I]n a criminal case the term [presumption of innocence] does convey a special and perhaps useful hint over and above the other form of the rule about the burden of proof, in that it cautions the jury to put away from their minds all the suspicion that arises from the arrest, the indictment, and the arraignment, and to reach their conclusion solely from the legal evidence adduced. In other

of which you will use: A. We the jury find the defendant not guilty; B. We the jury find the defendant guilty under instruction number one and fix his punishment at blank years in the penitentiary."

12. The *Coffin* Court viewed the presumption of innocence as "an instrument of proof created by the law in favor of one accused, whereby his innocence is established until sufficient evidence is introduced to overcome the proof which the law has created." As actual "evidence in favor of the accused," it was distinguished from the reasonable-doubt standard, which merely described "the condition of mind produced by the proof resulting from the evidence in the cause." Ibid. Professor Thayer ably demonstrated the error of this distinction, pointing out that the so-called "presumption" is not evidence—not even an inference drawn from a fact in evidence—but instead is a way of describing the prosecution's duty both to produce evidence on guilt and to convince the jury beyond a reasonable doubt. Thayer 560–563. Shortly after the appearance of Thayer's criticism, the Court, in a case in which the presumption-of-innocence instruction was given, retreated from its conclusion that the presumption of innocence is evidence to be weighed by the jury. See Agnew v. United States, 165 U.S. 36, 51–52, 17 S.Ct. 235, 241 (1897).

It is now generally recognized that the "presumption of innocence" is an inaccurate, shorthand description of the right of the accused to "remain inactive and secure, until the prosecution has taken up its burden and produced evidence and effected persuasion; i.e., to say in this case, as in any other, that the opponent of a claim or charge is presumed not to be guilty is to say in another form that the proponent of the claim or charge must evidence it." Wigmore 407. The principal inaccuracy is the fact that it is not technically a "presumption"—a mandatory inference drawn from a fact in evidence. Instead, it is better characterized as an "assumption" that is indulged in the absence of contrary evidence.

> words, the rule about burden of proof requires the prosecution by evidence to convince the jury of the accused's guilt; while the presumption of innocence, too, requires this, but conveys for the jury a special and additional caution (which is perhaps only an implied corollary to the other) to consider, in the material for their belief, *nothing but the evidence*, i.e., no surmises based on the present situation of the accused. This caution is indeed particularly needed in criminal cases." Wigmore 407.

This Court has declared that one accused of a crime is entitled to have his guilt or innocence determined solely on the basis of the evidence introduced at trial, and not on grounds of official suspicion, indictment, continued custody, or other circumstances not adduced as proof at trial. And it long has been recognized that an instruction on the presumption is one way of impressing upon the jury the importance of that right. While use of the particular phrase "presumption of innocence"—or any other form of words—may not be constitutionally mandated, the Due Process Clause of the Fourteenth Amendment must be held to safeguard "against dilution of the principle that guilt is to be established by probative evidence and beyond a reasonable doubt." The "purging" effect of an instruction on the presumption of innocence simply represents one means of protecting the accused's constitutional right to be judged solely on the basis of proof adduced at trial.

III.

Petitioner argues that in the circumstances of this case, the purging effect of an instruction on the presumption of innocence was essential to a fair trial. He points out that the trial court's instructions were themselves skeletal, placing little emphasis on the prosecution's duty to prove the case beyond a reasonable doubt and none at all on the jury's duty to judge petitioner only on the basis of the testimony heard at trial.

Against the background of the court's rather Spartan instructions, the prosecutor's closing argument ranged far and wide, asking the jury to draw inferences about petitioner's conduct from "facts" not in evidence, but propounded by the prosecutor. For example, he described the reasonable-doubt standard by declaring that petitioner, "*like every other defendant* who's ever been tried who's in the penitentiary or in the reformatory today, has this presumption of innocence until proved guilty beyond a reasonable doubt." (Emphasis added). This statement linked petitioner to every defendant who turned out to be guilty and was sentenced to imprisonment. It could be viewed as an invitation to the jury to consider petitioner's status as a defendant as evidence tending to prove his guilt. Similarly, in responding to defense counsel's rhetorical query as to the whereabouts of the items stolen from Maddox, the prosecutor declared that "[o]ne of the first things *defendants do after they rip someone off*, they get rid of the evidence as fast and as quickly as they can." (Emphasis added). This statement also implied that all defendants are guilty and invited the jury to consider that proposition in determining petitioner's guilt or innocence.[14]

14. We do not suggest that such prosecutorial comments, standing alone, would rise to the level of reversible error, an issue not raised in this case. But they are relevant

Additionally, the prosecutor observed in his opening statement that Maddox "took out" a warrant against petitioner and that the grand jury had returned an indictment which the prosecutor read to the jury. Thus, the jury not only was invited to consider the petitioner's status as a defendant, but also was permitted to draw inferences of guilt from the fact of arrest and indictment.[15] The prosecutor's description of those events was not necessarily improper, but the combination of the skeletal instructions, the possible harmful inferences from the references to the indictment, and the repeated suggestions that petitioner's status as a defendant tended to establish his guilt created a genuine danger that the jury would convict petitioner on the basis of those extraneous considerations, rather than on the evidence introduced at trial. That risk was heightened because the trial essentially was a swearing contest between victim and accused.[16]

IV.

Against the need for a presumption-of-innocence instruction, the Commonwealth argues first that such an instruction is not required where, as here, the jury is instructed as to the burden of proof beyond a reasonable doubt. The trial court's truncated discussion of reasonable doubt, however, was hardly a model of clarity. It defined reasonable doubt as "a substantial doubt, a real doubt." This definition, though perhaps not in itself reversible error, often has been criticized as confusing. And even if the instruction on reasonable doubt had been more clearly stated, the Commonwealth's argument ignores both the special purpose of a presumption-of-innocence instruction and the particular need for such an instruction in this case.

The Commonwealth also contends that no additional instructions were required, because defense counsel argued the presumption of innocence in both his opening and closing statements. But arguments of counsel cannot substitute for instructions by the court. Petitioner's right to have the jury deliberate solely on the basis of the evidence cannot be permitted to hinge upon a hope that defense counsel will be a more effective advocate for that proposition than the prosecutor will be in implying that extraneous circumstances may be considered. It was the duty of the court to safeguard petitioner's rights, a duty only it could have performed reliably. . . .

to the need for carefully framed instructions designed to assure that the accused be judged only on the evidence.

15. As noted above, the trial court also refused petitioner's request for an instruction that the indictment was not evidence. This permitted the prosecutor's reference to the indictment to serve as one more extraneous, negative circumstance which may have influenced the jury's deliberations. Because of our conclusion that the cumulative effect of the potentially damaging circumstances of this case violated the due process guarantee of fundamental fairness in the absence of an instruction as to the presumption of innocence, we do not reach petitioner's further claim that the refusal to instruct that an indictment is not evidence independently constituted reversible error.

16. While we do not necessarily approve of the presumption-of-innocence instruction requested by petitioner, it appears to have been well suited to forestalling the jury's consideration of extraneous matters, that is, to performing the purging function described in Part II, above. The requested instruction noted that petitioner, "although accused, [began] the trial with a 'clean slate.'" It emphasized that the law would permit "nothing but legal evidence presented before a jury to be considered in support of any charge against the accused."

V.

We hold that on the facts of this case the trial court's refusal to give petitioner's requested instruction on the presumption of innocence resulted in a violation of his right to a fair trial as guaranteed by the Due Process Clause of the Fourteenth Amendment. The judgment of conviction is reversed and the case is remanded.

So ordered.

■ [MR. JUSTICE BRENNAN's concurring opinion omitted.]

■ MR. JUSTICE STEVENS, with whom MR. JUSTICE REHNQUIST joins, dissenting.

In a federal court it is reversible error to refuse a request for a proper instruction on the presumption of innocence. That is not, however, a sufficient reason for holding that such an instruction is constitutionally required in every criminal trial.

The function of the instruction is to make it clear that the burden of persuasion rests entirely on the prosecutor. The same function is performed by the instruction requiring proof beyond a reasonable doubt. One standard instruction adds emphasis to the other. Neither should be omitted, but an "omission, or an incomplete instruction, is less likely to be prejudicial than a misstatement of the law." In some cases the omission may be fatal, but the Court wisely avoids a holding that this is always so.

In this case the omission did not violate a specific constitutional guarantee, such as the privilege against compulsory self-incrimination. Nor did it deny the defendant his fundamental right to a fair trial. An instruction on reasonable doubt, admittedly brief, was given. The *voir dire* had made clear to each juror the defendant's right to be presumed innocent despite his indictment. The prosecutor's closing argument did not precipitate any objection from defense counsel who listened to it; it may not, therefore, provide the basis for a reversal. Although the Court's appraisal is not unreasonable, for this was by no means a perfect trial, I do not believe that constitutional error was committed. Accordingly, I respectfully dissent.

NOTES

1. As indicated in *Taylor*, Coffin v. United States requires the court to give a presumption of innocence instruction, upon defendant's request in federal cases. Does *Taylor* impose the same requirement upon state courts? In Kentucky v. Whorton, 441 U.S. 786, 99 S.Ct. 2088 (1979), the Court indicated that *Taylor* does not stand for that proposition:

> While this Court in *Taylor* reversed a conviction resulting from a trial in which the judge had refused to give a requested instruction on the presumption of innocence, the Court did not there fashion a new rule of constitutional law requiring that such an instruction be given in every criminal case. Rather, the Court's opinion focused on the failure to give the instruction as it related to the overall fairness of the trial considered in its entirety.
>
> * * *
>
> In short, the failure to give a requested instruction on the presumption of innocence does not in and of itself violate the Constitution. Under

> *Taylor*, such a failure must be evaluated in light of the totality of the circumstances—including all the instructions to the jury, the arguments of counsel, whether the weight of the evidence was overwhelming, and other relevant factors—to determine whether the defendant received a constitutionally fair trial.

2. Based on *Whorton*, the courts have taken the position that, although a presumption of innocence instruction should be given, its absence does not amount to a constitutional infirmity in all cases. See People v. Layhew, 139 Ill.2d 476, 151 Ill.Dec. 570, 564 N.E.2d 1232 (1990); United States v. DeJohn, 638 F.2d 1048 (7th Cir.1981). The words "presumption of innocence" need not be used precisely so long as the instruction otherwise communicates the intent. See City of Bucyrus v. Fawley, 50 Ohio App.3d 25, 552 N.E.2d 676 (1988).

3. Does reversible error occur when the court, in its initial explanation of a criminal case to the prospective jury panel, explains the presumption of innocence to the jury, but does not repeat it in the final instructions after closing argument? Compare United States v. Dilg, 700 F.2d 620 (11th Cir.1983) (yes), with United States v. Ruppel, 666 F.2d 261 (5th Cir.1982) (no).

4. In Cupp v. Naughten, 414 U.S. 141, 94 S.Ct. 396 (1973), the jury was instructed as follows:

> Every witness is presumed to speak the truth. This presumption may be overcome by the manner in which the witness testifies, by the nature of his or her testimony, by evidence affecting his or her character, interest, or motives, by contradictory evidence or by a presumption.

The majority responded to defendant's claim that this instruction diluted the presumption of innocence by holding:

> Certainly the instruction by its language neither shifts the burden of proof nor negates the presumption of innocence accorded under Oregon law. It would be possible perhaps as a matter of abstract logic to contend that any instruction suggesting that the jury should believe the testimony of a witness might in some tangential respect "impinge" upon the right of the defendant to have his guilt proved beyond a reasonable doubt. But instructions bearing on the burden of proof, just as those bearing on the weight to be accorded different types of testimony and other familiar subjects of jury instructions, are in one way or another designed to get the jury off dead center and to give it some guidance by which to evaluate the frequently confusing and conflicting testimony which it has heard.
>
> * * *
>
> The jury here was charged fully and explicitly about the presumption of innocence and the State's duty to prove guilt beyond a reasonable doubt. Whatever tangential undercutting of these clearly stated propositions may, as a theoretical matter, have resulted from the giving of the instruction on the presumption of truthfulness is not of constitutional dimension.

JUSTICE BRENNAN, joined by JUSTICES DOUGLAS and MARSHALL, dissented:

> The reduction of the prosecution's burden of persuasion to a preponderance clearly conflicts with the Due Process Clause guarantee that an accused shall not be convicted "except upon proof beyond a reasonable doubt of every fact necessary to constitute the crime with which he is charged."
>
> * * *

> In the instant case, common sense does not dictate that a prosecution witness who has sworn or affirmed to tell the truth will *inevitably* do so, and there is surely a *reasonable possibility* that he will fail to do so. Since here no defense witnesses were called, the practical effect of the presumption of truthfulness was to permit the jury to find each and every element of the crimes charged without requiring that the elements be proved beyond a reasonable doubt.

5. Other events during the course of trial may raise presumption of innocence claims. See Norris v. Risley, 918 F.2d 828 (9th Cir.1990) (presumption of innocence impermissibly affected by spectators at rape trial who wore "Women Against Rape" buttons); Mahorney v. Wallman, 917 F.2d 469 (10th Cir.1990) (habeas corpus granted over a strong dissent due to prosecutor's argument that the "presumption has been removed by evidence and he is standing before you now guilty. That presumption is not there anymore"); United States v. Samuel, 431 F.2d 610, 614–15 (4th Cir.1970) (fact that defendant was handcuffed during testimony did not intrude on presumption because "the accused's right to the indicia of innocence before the jury must bow to the competing rights of participants in the courtroom and society at large").

6. A most unusual, or, as the Court of Appeals said, "inexplicable" incident involving a presumption of innocence problem arose in Armstead v. United States, 347 F.2d 806 (D.C.Cir.1965). The prosecutor, while cross-examining the defendant, referred to him as "Mr. Armstead"; the judge instructed him to discontinue doing so, saying that although he thought witnesses and counsel should be addressed as "Mister", "Mrs.", or "Miss", that should not be done as regards the defendant. In reversing the defendant's conviction the reviewing court said: "When a defendant takes the stand he is a witness; he is entitled to the same form of address, the same courtesies and consideration as all others involved in the proceeding. The presumption of innocence, apart from other factors, requires no less than that nothing be permitted to trench on that presumption."

7. In United States v. Doyle, 130 F.3d 523 (2d Cir.1997), the court reversed a conviction because the instructions included the following observation:

> It is the sworn duty of Courts and jurors to safeguard the rights of persons charged with a crime by respecting the presumption of innocence which the law imputes to every person so charged, but the law is made to protect innocent persons and not to protect guilty ones.

Focusing on the comment that the presumption of innocence is not intended to protect guilty parties, the court held:

> A natural inclination of some jurors may be to assume that, because the defendant has been selected for prosecution, he must be guilty. One of the greatest responsibilities of the trial judge is her duty to overcome that inclination by impressing upon the jury the importance of the presumption of innocence and of the Government's burden to prove guilt beyond a reasonable doubt.
>
> * * *
>
> In order to reduce those risks, then, the jurors must be made to see that the case against the defendant begins as a tabula rasa, a slate upon which may be written only such marks as derive from the evidence admitted at trial. Unless and until the Government meets its burden of proof beyond a reasonable doubt, the presumption of innocence remains with the accused regardless of the fact that he has been charged with the crime, regardless of what is said about him at trial, regardless of whether the jurors believe that he is likely guilty, regardless of whether he is

actually guilty. The presumption attaches to those who are actually innocent and to those who are actually guilty alike throughout all stages of the trial and deliberations unless and until that burden is met. A jury charge which implies otherwise creates a serious risk of undermining that vital protection.

3. DEFENDANT'S FAILURE TO TESTIFY

Carter v. Kentucky

United States Supreme Court, 1981.
450 U.S. 288, 101 S.Ct. 1112.

■ JUSTICE STEWART delivered the opinion of the Court.

In this case a Kentucky criminal trial judge refused a defendant's request to give the following jury instruction: "The [defendant] is not compelled to testify and the fact that he does not cannot be used as an inference of guilt and should not prejudice him in any way." The Supreme Court of Kentucky found no error.[2]

* * *

The constitutional question presented by this case ... [was resolved as a matter of federal statutory law] over 40 years ago in Bruno v. United States, 308 U.S. 287, 60 S.Ct. 198. The petitioner in Bruno was a defendant in a federal criminal trial who had requested a jury instruction similar to the one requested by the petitioner in this case. The Court, addressing the question whether Bruno "had the indefeasible right" that his proffered instruction be given to the jury, decided that a federal statute, which prohibits the creation of any presumption from a defendant's failure to testify, required that the "substance of the denied request should have been granted.... "[9]

* * *

In Lakeside v. Oregon, 435 U.S. 333, 98 S.Ct. 1091, the question was whether the giving of a "no-inference" instruction over defense objection violates the Constitution. Despite trial counsel's complaint that his strategy was to avoid any mention of his client's failure to testify, a no-inference instruction[13] was given by the trial judge. The petitioner contended that

2. Kentucky is one of at least five States that prohibit giving such an instruction to the jury.

9. At common law, defendants in criminal trials could not be compelled to furnish evidence against themselves, but they were also not permitted to testify. In the context of the original enactment of the federal statute found dispositive in the Bruno case, this Court commented on the alteration of this common-law rule: "This rule, while affording great protection to the accused against unfounded accusation, in many cases deprived him from explaining [incriminating] circumstances.... To relieve him from this embarrassment the law was passed. ... [H]e is by the act in question permitted ... to testify...."

13. The Lakeside trial judge gave the following instruction to the jury:

> "Under the laws of this State a defendant has the option to take the witness stand in his or her own behalf. If a defendant chooses not to testify, such a circumstance gives rise to no inference or presumption against the defendant, and this must not be considered by you in

when a trial judge in any way draws the jury's attention to a defendant's failure to testify, unless the defendant acquiesces, the court invades the defendant's privilege against compulsory self-incrimination. This argument was rejected.

The Lakeside Court reasoned that the Fifth and Fourteenth Amendments bar only *adverse* comment on a defendant's failure to testify, and that "a judge's instruction that the jury must draw *no* adverse inferences of any kind from the defendant's exercise of his privilege not to testify is 'comment' of an entirely different order." The purpose of such an instruction, the Court stated, "is to remove from the jury's deliberations any influence of unspoken adverse inferences," and "cannot provide the pressure on a defendant found impermissible in Griffin."

The Court observed in Lakeside that the petitioner's argument there rested on "two very doubtful assumptions:"

> "First, that the jurors have not noticed that the defendant did not testify and will not, therefore, draw adverse inferences on their own. Second, that the jurors will totally disregard the instruction, and affirmatively give weight to what they have been told not to consider at all. Federal constitutional law cannot rest on speculative assumptions so dubious as these."

Finally, the Court stressed that "[t]he very purpose" of a jury instruction is to direct the jurors' attention to important legal concepts "that must not be misunderstood, such as reasonable doubt and burden of proof," and emphasized that instruction "in the meaning of the privilege against compulsory self-incrimination is no different."

* * *

... Jurors are not experts in legal principles; to function effectively, and justly, they must be accurately instructed in the law. Such instructions are perhaps nowhere more important than in the context of the Fifth Amendment privilege against compulsory self-incrimination, since "[t]oo many, even those who should be better advised, view this privilege as a shelter for wrongdoers. They too readily assume that those who invoke it are ... guilty of crime...." And, as the Court has stated, "we have not yet attained that certitude about the human mind which would justify us in ... a dogmatic assumption that jurors, if properly admonished, neither could nor would heed the instructions of the trial court...."[20]

A trial judge has a powerful tool at his disposal to protect the constitutional privilege—the jury instruction—and he has an affirmative constitutional obligation to use that tool when a defendant seeks its employment. No judge can prevent jurors from speculating about why a defendant stands mute in the face of a criminal accusation, but a judge can,

determining the question of guilt or innocence."

20. "It is obvious that under any system of jury trials the influence of the trial judge on the jury is necessarily and properly of great weight, and that his lightest word or intimation is received with deference, and may prove controlling." ...

and must, if requested to do so, use the unique power of the jury instruction to reduce that speculation to a minimum.[21]

The only state interest advanced by Kentucky in refusing a request for such a jury instruction is protection of the defendant: "the requested 'no inference' instruction ... would have been a direct 'comment' by the court and would have emphasized the fact that the accused had not testified in his own behalf." This purported justification was specifically rejected in the Lakeside case, where the Court noted that "[i]t would be strange indeed to conclude that this cautionary instruction violates the very constitutional provision it is intended to protect."

Kentucky also argues that in the circumstances of this case the jurors knew they could not make adverse inferences from the petitioner's election to remain silent because they were instructed to determine guilt "from the evidence alone," and because failure to testify is not evidence. The Commonwealth's argument is unpersuasive. Jurors are not lawyers; they do not know the technical meaning of "evidence." They can be expected to notice a defendant's failure to testify, and, without limiting instruction, to speculate about incriminating inferences from a defendant's silence.

The other trial instructions and arguments of counsel that the petitioner's jurors heard at the trial of this case were no substitute for the explicit instruction that the petitioner's lawyer requested.

* * *

... The failure to limit the jurors' speculation on the meaning of that silence, when the defendant makes a timely request that a prophylactic instruction be given, exacts an impermissible toll on the full and free exercise of the privilege. Accordingly, we hold that a state trial judge has the constitutional obligation, upon proper request, to minimize the danger that the jury will give evidentiary weight to a defendant's failure to testify.

... the judgment is reversed, and the case is remanded....

It is so ordered.

■ JUSTICE POWELL, concurring. [Omitted]

■ JUSTICE STEVENS, with whom JUSTICE BRENNAN joins, concurring.

While I join the Court's opinion, I add this comment to emphasize that today's holding is limited to cases in which the defendant has requested that the jury be instructed not to draw an inference of guilt from the defendant's failure to testify. I remain convinced that the question whether such an instruction should be given in any specific case—like the question whether the defendant should testify on his own behalf—should be answered by the defendant and his lawyer, not by the State.

21. The importance of a no-inference instruction is underscored by a recent national public opinion survey conducted for the National Center for State Courts, revealing that 37% of those interviewed believed that it is the responsibility of the accused to prove his innocence. 64 ABAJ 653 (1978).

■ JUSTICE REHNQUIST, dissenting.

* * *

If we begin with the relevant provisions of the Constitution, which is where an unsophisticated lawyer or layman would probably think we should begin, we find the provision in the Fifth Amendment stating that "[n]o person ... shall be compelled in any criminal case to be a witness against himself.... " Until the mysterious process of transmogrification by which this Amendment was held to be "incorporated" and made applicable to the States by the Fourteenth Amendment the provision itself would not have regulated the conduct of criminal trials in Kentucky. But even if it did, no one here claims that the defendant was forced to take the stand against his will or to testify against himself inconsistently with the provisions of the Fifth Amendment.

* * *

The Court's opinion states that "[t]he Griffin case stands for the proposition that a defendant must pay no court-imposed price for the exercise of his constitutional privilege not to testify." Such Thomistic reasoning is now carried from the constitutional provision itself, to the Griffin case, to the present case, and where it will stop no one can know. The concept of "burdens" and "penalties" is such a vague one that the Court's decision allows a criminal defendant in a state proceeding virtually to take from the trial judge any control over the instructions to be given to the jury in the case being tried.

* * *

NOTES

1. The right to a no adverse inference instruction does not entitle the defendant to specific language so long as the subject is adequately covered. See Commonwealth v. Feroli, 407 Mass. 405, 553 N.E.2d 934 (1990) (defendant has the absolute right to remain passive); United States v. Adams, 914 F.2d 1404 (10th Cir.1990) (use of "failure to testify" instruction did not suggest that defendant was guilty of neglect or omission).

2. In Hunter v. Clark, 934 F.2d 856 (7th Cir.1991) (en banc), one defendant requested that a "no adverse inference" instruction be given and another asked that it not be. The trial judge offered to sever the cases; but the defendants declined the offer. In a sharply divided opinion the en banc plurality held that the failure to give the instruction was harmless error under the circumstances. Two judges concurred because the issue arose on Federal habeas corpus and "*Carter* establishes a prophylactic rule, and there is much less need to enforce such rules on collateral attack than there is to enforce the core constitutional rules." Five judges dissented on the ground that the evidence against defendant was not so overwhelming that the failure to give the "no adverse evidence instruction" could be viewed as harmless. Both the concurring and dissenting opinions, a majority of the court, found the severance alternative inadequate because a trial judge may not compel the accused to choose between his double jeopardy right "to get things over in a single trial" and the *Carter* instruction.

3. Contrary to federal law, several states hold that it is reversible error to give the no adverse inference instruction if the defendant, as part of his trial strategy, objects to it. See Commonwealth v. Garcia, 888 A.2d 633 (Pa. Sup. Ct. 2005).

4. Credibility of Witnesses

(a) The Defendant

Reagan v. United States

Supreme Court of the United States, 1895.
157 U.S. 301, 15 S.Ct. 610.

■ Mr. Justice Brewer delivered the opinion of the court.

... the defendant was found guilty by ... of a jury of a violation of unlawfully, fraudulently, wilfully, knowingly and with intent to defraud the United States, receiving into his possession and concealing forty head of cattle which had been with like intent smuggled and introduced into the United States from the Republic of Mexico.

* * *

[Defendant's principal claim of error is that the court gave this instruction: "You should especially look to the interest which the respective witnesses have in the suit or in its result. Where the witness has a direct personal interest in the result of the suit the temptation is strong to color, pervert, or withhold the facts. The law permits the defendant, at his own request, to testify in his own behalf. The defendant here has availed himself of this privilege. His testimony is before you and you must determine how far it is credible. The deep personal interest which he may have in the result of the suit should be considered by the jury in weighing his evidence and in determining how far or to what extent, if at all, it is worthy of credit."]

* * *

[If the defendant testifies in his own behalf] his credibility may be impeached, his testimony may be assailed, and is to be weighed as that of any other witness. Assuming the position of a witness, he is entitled to all its rights and protections, and is subject to all its criticisms and burdens. ... The privileges and limitations are those which inhere in the witness as a witness, and which affect the testimony voluntarily given. As to that, he may be fully cross-examined. It may be assailed by contradictory testimony. His credibility may be impeached, and by the same methods as are pursued in the case of any other witness. The jury may properly consider his manner of testifying, the inherent probabilities of his story, the amount and character of the contradictory testimony, the nature and extent of his interest in the result of the trial, and the impeaching evidence in determining how much of credence he is entitled to.

It is within the province of the court to call the attention of the jury to any matters which legitimately affect his testimony and his credibility. This does not imply that the court may arbitrarily single out his testimony and denounce it as false. The fact that he is a defendant does not condemn him as unworthy of belief, but at the same time it creates an interest greater than that of any other witness, and to that extent affects the question of credibility. It is, therefore, a matter properly to be suggested by the court to the jury. But the limits of suggestion are the same in respect to him as to others. It is a familiar rule that the relations of a witness to the matter to be decided are legitimate subjects of consideration in respect to the weight to be given to his testimony. The old law was that interest debarred one from testifying, for fear that such interest might tend to a perversion of the truth. A more enlightened spirit has thrown down this barrier, and now mere interest does not exclude one from the witness stand, but the interest is to be considered as affecting his credibility. This rule is equally potent in criminal as in civil cases, and in neither is it error for the trial court to direct the attention of the jury to the interest which any witness may have in the result of the trial as a circumstance to be considered in weighing his testimony and determining the credence that shall be given to his story.

* * *

[T]he court is not at liberty to charge the jury directly or indirectly that the defendant is to be disbelieved because he is a defendant, for that would practically take away the benefit which the law grants when it gives him the privilege of being a witness. On the other hand, the court may, and sometimes ought, to remind the jury that interest creates a motive for false testimony; that the greater the interest the stronger is the temptation, and that the interest of the defendant in the result of the trial is of a character possessed by no other witness, and is therefore a matter which may seriously affect the credence that shall be given to his testimony. The court should be impartial between the government and the defendant. On behalf of the defendant it is its duty to caution the jury not to convict upon the uncorroborated testimony of an accomplice. Indeed, according to some authorities, it should peremptorily instruct that no verdict of guilty can be founded on such uncorroborated testimony, and this because the inducements to falsehood on the part of an accomplice are so great. And if any other witness for the government is disclosed to have great feeling or large interest against the defendant, the court may, in the interests of justice, call the attention of the jury to the extent of that feeling or interest as affecting his credibility. In the same manner in behalf of the government, the court may charge the jury that the peculiar and deep interest which the defendant has in the result of the trial is a matter affecting his credibility, and to be carefully considered by them.

Tested by these rules we see in the instruction objected to nothing of which complaint can reasonably be made. In the first part it lays down a general rule, applicable to all circumstances, and then in the latter part simply calls attention to the fact that the defendant has a deep personal interest in the result of the suit, and that that should be considered by the jury. There is no declaration nor intimation that the defendant has been untruthful in his testimony. There is only a reference to the jury of the matter of credibility coupled with the declaration that interest in the result is a circumstance to be weighed in its determination. This clearly is unobjectionable.

* * *

The judgment is affirmed.

NOTES

1. In Johnson v. United States, 157 U.S. 320, 15 S.Ct. 614 (1895), a companion to *Reagan*, the Court upheld the following instruction in the context of the overall charge:

> The defendant goes upon the stand before you and he makes his statement; tells his story. Above all things, in a case of this kind you are to see whether that statement is corroborated substantially and reliably by the proven facts; if so, it is strengthened to the extent of its corroboration. If it is not strengthened in that way, you are to weigh it by its own inherent truthfulness, its own inherent proving power that may belong to it.

2. The *Reagan–Johnson* doctrine remains good law in the federal courts today. The standard instruction reads as follows:

> A defendant in a criminal trial is permitted to become a witness in his own behalf. His testimony should not be disbelieved merely because he is the defendant. However, in weighing his testimony, you have a right to consider the fact that he does have a vital interest in the outcome of the case. But, again, you should give his testimony such weight as in your very good judgment that testimony is fairly entitled to receive.

This instruction has been routinely upheld. United States v. Sullivan, 919 F.2d 1403 (10th Cir.1990); United States v. Walker, 710 F.2d 1062 (5th Cir.1983); United States v. Raper, 676 F.2d 841 (D.C.Cir.1982). However, the current trend is to avoid the "interest in the outcome" instruction and inform the jury that a defendant's testimony should be evaluated by the jury in the same way that it judges the testimony of other witnesses. See United States v. Brutus, 505 F.3d 80 (2d. Cir. 2007) (overruling prior precedent and invalidating instruction on the ground that "an instruction that the defendant's interest in the outcome of the case creates a motive to testify falsely impermissibly undermines the presumption of innocence because it presupposes the defendant's guilt").

3. Several state courts have rejected "interest in the outcome" instruction on the ground that it constitutes judicial comment on the evidence, a practice forbidden in some states, and unduly singles out the testimony of a single witness—the defendant. See State v. Bester, 167 N.W.2d 705 (Iowa 1969). Other states permit, but do not require, the judge to instruct the jury that the defendant's testimony should be considered on the same basis and given the same weight as the testimony of any other witness. Marbley v. State, 461 N.E.2d 1102 (Ind.1984). However, the majority of states sanction the federal rule and permit both instruction and jury argument on the defendant's interest in the outcome. E.g., People v. Barney, 176 Ill.2d 69, 223 Ill.Dec. 30, 678 N.E.2d 1038 (1997).

(b) THE EYE–WITNESS

United States v. Hodges

United States Court of Appeals, Seventh Circuit, 1975.
515 F.2d 650.

■ GRANT, SENIOR DISTRICT JUDGE.

Appellant was charged in a one-count indictment with possession of a check stolen from the mail, with knowledge that it was stolen.... After a trial by jury, he was convicted and sentenced to probation for a period of three years. The check in question was an Illinois Public Assistance check payable to the order of one Paul Watkins in the amount of $144.12. With the check, appellant first attempted to purchase a bottle of whisky at Angelo's Liquors, a store in Wilmington, Illinois. However, an employee of the store, Charles Toncrey, refused to cash the check after consulting with the owner, Angelo Aggelopoulous. Appellant then proceeded to go to a Western Auto Store in Coal City, Illinois, where he used the check to purchase a child's bicycle. Clarence A. Rolando, the owner of the store, honored the check but then alerted police after the transaction because of appellant's activities subsequent to the purchase. Shortly thereafter appellant was arrested. The government's case rested almost entirely upon the three eyewitness identifications of Toncrey, Aggelopoulous, and Rolando. Each of these persons positively identified appellant as the man who had attempted to cash the check. At appellant's trial, nevertheless, the court refused to give an identification instruction tendered by appellant's counsel because the court considered the instruction to be argumentative as well as a comment on the evidence. . . .

Appellant contends that an instruction telling the jury that identification was the sole issue in the case was required in the court below because: (1) there was a 15–month delay between the crime and the in-court identifications; (2) a show-up instead of a line-up was used at the Coal City police station to identify him; and (3) two of the witnesses, Toncrey and Aggelopoulous, were not able to identify, immediately before trial, the picture which showed what appellant looked like on the day of the arrest. Under these circumstances, appellant argues that the instruction which he tendered was neither argumentative nor a comment on the evidence. Rather, it served to focus the jury's attention on the true issue before them. Further, appellant maintains that an identification instruction must be given where, as here, it is supported by the evidence and requested by the defense. Finally, appellant cites the Court to the tendency of many Circuits to give such an instruction for the reason that "testimony tending to prove identity is to be scrutinized with extreme care." . . .

In response, appellee maintains that, although there are some factual situations which would compel an instruction which warns the jury to closely scrutinize identification testimony, the factual circumstances of the instant case do not require such an instruction. In this regard, appellee emphasizes that in the present case there is neither the uncorroborated testimony of a single eyewitness nor a situation where a conviction has resulted from an identification during a confusing affray of short duration involving a number of participants. Instead, in the instant case, appellee notes that there were three positive identifications made from direct observation which were, in turn, corroborated by the identification of the arresting officer. . . . Since the witnesses here, argues appellee, had the opportunity to observe the accused, were positive in their identifications, were not weakened by prior misidentification, and remained unqualified after cross-examination, an instruction on the dangers of identification testimony was not warranted by the facts. It is appellee's position, then, that the likelihood of misidentification in the present case was virtually nonexistent.

In any event, appellee notes that many Circuits have left the matter of giving an identification instruction to the trial judge's discretion. In this regard, some courts have found such an instruction to be superfluous in light of adequate cross-examination, summation, and appropriate burden of proof and credibility instructions. In the instant case, appellee maintains that cross-examination focused on the possibility of mistaken identification and that counsel's summation plainly apprised the jury that the identification made by the witnesses was the underlying issue in the case. Therefore, appellee argues that the identification issue was fully aired and argued before the jury, and that the jury was clearly aware of its duty to find beyond a reasonable doubt that appellant was properly identified as the person who attempted to cash the check. . . .

Although it has been recognized that the giving of instructions on identification is largely within the discretion of the trial judge, . . . it has also been stated that trial courts should, as a matter of routine, in cases where identification is a key issue, include an identification instruction which emphasizes to the jury the need for finding that the circumstances of the identification are convincing beyond a reasonable doubt. United States v. Telfaire, 469 F.2d 552, 555 (1972). In *Telfaire*, the District of Columbia Circuit adopted generally for judges within the district a model instruction, but permitting variation and adaptation to suit the proof and contentions of a particular case. . . . Moreover, we stated in United States v. Napue, 401 F.2d 107, 112 (7th Cir.1968), that the "better practice" would be to give some instruction on mistaken identity even though the instruction given need not necessarily be in the exact form as offered by the defense. We now adopt what we labeled to be the better practice in *Napue*, as the required practice in this Circuit; and although it is not our intention to require that the *Telfaire* model be given verbatim, we hereby publish notice that we shall in the future view with grave concern the failure to give the substantial equivalent of such an instruction.

. . . First and foremost, although we realize, on the basis of our careful review of the record herein, that the subject of identification was explored by counsel at appellant's trial on cross-examination as well as in final argument, and that the court's instructions to the jury were indeed accurate as to the burden of proof required in criminal cases and concerning the credibility of witnesses, and that the existence of these circumstances has induced some courts to decline to give a detailed charge on eyewitness identification, we are not persuaded to say that the existence of such circumstances necessarily obviates the giving of such an instruction to the jury. Further, we are not completely satisfied that in the instant case the existence of such circumstances served to focus the jury's attention on the issue of identity. In this regard, we are mindful of what the court stated in United States v. Evans, 484 F.2d 1178 (2d Cir.1973), with respect to the trial court's failure to give a specific charge to the jury on the dangers of eyewitness identification:

> There is no question that identification testimony is notably fallible, and the result of it can be, and sometimes has been, "the greatest single injustice that can arise out of our system of criminal law," namely the conviction of the wrong man through a

> mistake in identity. The dangers in this area have been well chronicled, and have been the proper subject of careful attention in this and many other courts. . . .

. . . We are convinced that neither summation of counsel at the close of the evidence, however prolonged or explicit, nor cross-examination as to the matter of identification by defense counsel adequately protects a defendant against the dangers of misidentification which are inherent in eyewitness testimony. Nor do we believe that such summation and cross-examination by counsel may substitute for proper instructions to the jury by the court. In cases where the issue of identification is paramount, we define proper instructions to include an identification instruction, when it is tendered to the court, in addition to accurate instructions as to burden of proof and the credibility of witnesses. As the District of Columbia Circuit stated in Salley v. United States, 353 F.2d 897, 899 (1965): It is the obligation of the trial judge "to instruct the jury that if there was a reasonable doubt as to the identification of the defendant as the person who [committed the crime], then the jury should acquit."

We believe that the *Salley* decision lays down the correct rule of law and that the *Telfaire* case propounds an appropriate model instruction to be applied in cases where, as here, the crucial issue involved is the defendant's identification, and where an instruction specifically bringing the identity issue to the jury's attention is requested by counsel and tendered to the court. . . . The judgment of conviction in the court below is hereby reversed, and the cause is remanded for a new trial. . . .

NOTES

1. In United States v. Telfaire, 469 F.2d 552 (D.C.Cir.1972), the principal case cited in *Hodges*, the court affirmed a conviction for a $10 robbery secured through the uncorroborated testimony of the victim who briefly had observed defendant in a dimly lighted hotel hallway. Finding cross-examination of the witness, arguments of counsel, and the standard burden of proof instructions insufficient to focus the jury's attention on the identification issue, the court concluded that the absence of a special identification was not prejudicial. However, under its supervisory powers, the court promulgated the following, rather elaborate, instruction for use in future cases:

> One of the most important issues in this case is the identification of the defendant as the perpetrator of the crime. The Government has the burden of providing identity, beyond a reasonable doubt. It is not essential that the witness himself be free from doubt as to the correctness of his statement. However, you, the jury, must be satisfied beyond a reasonable doubt of the accuracy of the identification of the defendant before you may convict him. If you are not convinced beyond a reasonable doubt that the defendant was the person who committed the crime, you must find the defendant not guilty.
>
> Identification testimony is an expression of belief or impression by the witness. Its value depends on the opportunity the witness had to observe the offender at the time of the offense and to make a reliable identification later.

In appraising the identification testimony of a witness, you should consider the following:

(1) Are you convinced that the witness had the capacity and an adequate opportunity to observe the offender?

Whether the witness had an adequate opportunity to observe the offender at the time of the offense will be affected by such matters as how long or short a time was available, how far or close the witness was, how good were lighting conditions, whether the witness had had occasion to see or know the person in the past.

[In general, a witness bases any identification he makes on his perception through the use of his senses. Usually the witness identifies an offender by the sense of sight—but this is not necessarily so, and he may use other senses.]

(2) Are you satisfied that the identification made by the witness subsequent to the offense was the product of his own recollection? You may take into account both the strength of the identification, and the circumstances under which the identification was made.

If the identification by the witness may have been influenced by the circumstances under which the defendant was presented to him for identification, you should scrutinize the identification with great care. You may also consider the length of time that lapsed between the occurrence of the crime and the next opportunity of the witness to see defendant, as a factor bearing on the reliability of the identification.

[You may also take into account that an identification made by picking the defendant out of a group of similar individuals is generally more reliable than one which results from the presentation of the defendant alone to the witness.]

[(3) You make take into account any occasions in which the witness failed to make an identification of defendant, or made an identification that was inconsistent with his identification at trial.]

(4) Finally, you must consider the credibility of each identification witness in the same way as any other witness, consider whether he is truthful, and consider whether he had the capacity and opportunity to make a reliable observation on the matter covered in his testimony.

I again emphasize that the burden of proof on the prosecutor extends to every element of the crime charged, and this specifically includes the burden of proving beyond a reasonable doubt the identity of the defendant as the perpetrator of the crime with which he stands charged. If after examining the testimony, you have a reasonable doubt as to the accuracy of the identification, you must find the defendant not guilty.

2. Because of the dangers of eyewitness testimony, many other courts require a form of this instruction. See United States v. Cueto, 628 F.2d 1273 (10th Cir.1980); United States v. Cain, 616 F.2d 1056 (8th Cir.1980); United States v. Masterson, 529 F.2d 30 (9th Cir.1976). United States v. Holley, 502 F.2d 273 (4th Cir.1974); United States v. Barber, 442 F.2d 517 (3d Cir.1971). In the majority of jurisdictions, trial judges are given broad discretion to determine whether the circumstances require a special identification instruction. See United States v. Luis, 835 F.2d 37 (2d Cir.1987); United States v. Ramirez–Rizo, 809 F.2d 1069 (5th Cir.1987); Clark v. State, 498 N.E.2d 918 (Ind.1986). When the identification issue is raised in cross-examination and there is independent evidence of guilt, a special eyewitness instruction need not be given. See United States v. Montelbano, 605 F.2d 56 (2d

Cir.1979); United States v. Kavanagh, 572 F.2d 9 (1st Cir.1978). However, it should be given "when the issue of identity is crucial, *i.e.*, either where no corroboration of the testimony exists, or where the witness' memory has faded by the time of trial, or where there was a limited opportunity for observation." United States v. Tipton, 11 F.3d 602 (6th Cir.1993); see also United States v. Smith, 41 F.3d 1565 (D.C.Cir. 1994).

3. Based on empirical evidence that people have greater difficulty in identifying members of a different race, one defendant sought an instruction advising the jury to take race into account when evaluating eyewitness testimony. The trial court's refusal to give the instruction was upheld on appeal. People v. Bias, 131 Ill.App.3d 98, 86 Ill.Dec. 256, 475 N.E.2d 253 (1985).

State v. Cromedy

Supreme Court of New Jersey, 1999.
158 N.J. 112, 727 A.2d 457.

■ Coleman, J.

* * *

The novel issue presented is whether a cross-racial identification jury instruction should be required in certain cases before it is established that there is substantial agreement in the scientific community that cross-racial recognition impairment of eyewitnesses is significant enough to warrant a special jury instruction. Our study of the recommendations of a Court-appointed Task Force, judicial literature, and decisional law from other jurisdictions persuades us that there exists a reliable basis for a cross-racial identification charge. We hold that the trial court's failure to submit to the jury an instruction similar to the one requested by defendant requires a reversal of defendant's convictions.

On the night of August 28, 1992, D.S., a white female student then enrolled at Rutgers University in New Brunswick, was watching television in her basement apartment. While she was relaxing on the couch, an African–American male entered the brightly-lit apartment and demanded money from D.S., claiming that he was wanted for murder and that he needed funds to get to New York. After D.S. told the intruder that she had no money, he spotted her purse, rifled through it, and removed money and credit cards.

The intruder then placed his hand on D.S.'s leg, demanded that she be quiet and closed the window blinds. He led her by the arm into the brightly-lit kitchen and ordered her to remove her shorts. The intruder then vaginally penetrated D.S. from behind. Throughout the sexual assault, D.S. was facing the kitchen door with her eyes closed and hand over her mouth to avoid crying loudly.

Once the assault was over, D.S. faced her attacker who, after threatening her again, turned around and left the apartment. At the time of the second threat, D.S. was standing approximately two feet away from her assailant. The attacker made no attempt to conceal his face at any time.

D.S. immediately called the New Brunswick Police Department after the intruder left the apartment.

* * *

[A]lmost eight months after the crimes were committed, D.S. saw an African–American male across the street from her who she thought was her attacker. She spotted the man while she was standing on the corner of a street in New Brunswick waiting for the light to change. As the two passed on the street, D.S. studied the individual's face and gait. Believing that the man was her attacker, D.S. ran home and telephoned the police, giving them a description of the man she had just seen. Defendant was picked up by the New Brunswick police and taken to headquarters almost immediately.

Within fifteen minutes after seeing defendant on the street, D.S. viewed defendant in a "show-up" from behind a one-way mirror and immediately identified him as the man she had just seen on the street and as her attacker. Defendant was then arrested and, with his consent, saliva and blood samples were taken for scientific analysis.

No forensic evidence linking defendant to the offenses was presented during the trial. The police did not lift any fingerprints belonging to defendant from the apartment.

* * *

Because of the nature of the crimes, the races of the victim and defendant, and the inability of the victim to identify defendant from his photograph, and because defendant was not positively identified until almost eight months after the date of the offenses, defense counsel sought a cross-racial identification jury charge. The following language was proposed:

[Y]ou know that the identifying witness is of a different race than the defendant. When a witness who is a member of one race identifies a member who is of another race we say there has been a cross-racial identification. You may consider, if you think it is appropriate to do so, whether the cross-racial nature of the identification has affected the accuracy of the witness's original perception and/or accuracy of a subsequent identification.

In support of that request, defendant cited the June 1992 New Jersey Supreme Court Task Force on Minority Concerns Final Report, 131 N.J.L.J. 1145 (1992) (Task Force Report).

The trial court denied the request because this Court had not yet adopted the Task Force Report and because there had been no expert testimony with respect to the issue of cross-racial identification.

The trial court instead provided the jury with the Model Jury Charge on Identification. The jury convicted defendant of first-degree aggravated sexual assault, second-degree robbery, second-degree burglary, and third-degree terroristic threats.

* * *

A cross-racial identification occurs when an eyewitness is asked to identify a person of another race.

* * *

For more than forty years, empirical studies concerning the psychological factors affecting eyewitness cross-racial or cross-ethnic identifications have appeared with increasing frequency in professional literature of the behavioral and social sciences. One study finds that jurors tend to place great weight on eyewitness identifications, often ignoring other exculpatory evidence. Others have concluded that eyewitnesses are superior at identifying persons of their own race and have difficulty identifying members of another race. This phenomenon has been dubbed the "own-race" effect or "own-race" bias. Its corollary is that eyewitnesses experience a "cross-racial impairment" when identifying members of another race. Studies have consistently shown that the "own-race effect" is "strongest when white witnesses attempt to recognize black subjects."

Although researchers generally agree that some eyewitnesses exhibit an own-race bias, they disagree about the degree to which own-race bias affects identification. A snap-shot of the literature reveals that although many scientists agree that witnesses are better at identifying suspects of their own race, they cannot agree on the extent to which cross-racial impairment affects identification.

The research also indicates disagreement about whether cross-racial impairment affects all racial groups. Four studies have found that African–American eyewitnesses do not experience cross-racial impairment at all. Other studies have concluded that white eyewitnesses experience cross-racial impairment more often than African–American eyewitnesses.

Many studies on cross-racial impairment involve subjects observing photographs for a few seconds. Because the subjects remembered the white faces more often than they recalled the African–American faces, researchers concluded that they were biased towards their own-race. Yet, there is disagreement over whether the results of some of the tests can be generalized to real-world situations in which a victim or witness confronts an assailant face-to-face and experiences the full range of emotions that accompany such a traumatic event.

The debate among researchers did not prevent the Supreme Court of the United States, in the famous school desegregation case of Brown v. Board of Education of Topeka (1954), from using behavioral and social sciences to support legal conclusions without requiring that the methodology employed by those scientists have general acceptance in the scientific community. The ultimate holding in Brown that segregation is harmful "was not only a nomological statement but a sociological observation as well." The Court's finding that segregation was harmful "was not based simply on [intuition] or common-sense, ... [but] was attributed to ... seven social science studies." Thus, Brown v. Board of Education is the prototypical example of an appellate court using modern social and behavioral sciences as legislative evidence to support its choice of a rule of law.

* * *

Although there have been no reported decisions in our own State addressing the propriety of requiring a cross-racial identification jury instruction, decisions have been rendered by courts in other jurisdictions. The majority of courts allowing cross-racial identification charges hold that the decision to provide the instruction is a matter within the trial judge's discretion. Omission of such a cautionary instruction has been held to be prejudicial error where identification is the critical or central issue in the case, there is no corroborating evidence, and the circumstances of the case raise doubts concerning the reliability of the identification.

* * *

Courts typically have refused the instruction where the eyewitness or victim had an adequate opportunity to observe the defendant, there was corroborating evidence bolstering the identification, and/or there was no evidence that race affected the identification. * * * Those courts have determined that the cross-racial instruction requires expert guidance, and that cross-examination and summation are adequate safeguards to highlight unreliable identifications.

Other jurisdictions have denied the instruction, finding that the results of empirical studies on cross-racial identification are questionable.

* * *

The defense in the present case did not question whether the victim had been sexually assaulted. Rather, the defense asserted that the victim's identification of defendant as the perpetrator was mistaken. It is well-established in this State that when identification is a critical issue in the case, the trial court is obligated to give the jury a discrete and specific instruction that provides appropriate guidelines to focus the jury's attention on how to analyze and consider the trustworthiness of eyewitness identification.

* * *

What defendant sought through the requested charge in the present case was an instruction that informed the jury that it could consider the fact that the victim made a cross-racial identification as part of the "attendant circumstances" when evaluating the reliability of the eyewitness identification.

* * *

The Court-appointed Task Force discussed and debated the issue of the need for a cross-racial and cross-ethnic identification jury instruction for more than five years. That Task Force was comprised of an appellate judge, trial judges, lawyers representing both the prosecution and defense, social scientists, and ordinary citizens. * * * Except for the view expressed by a county prosecutor, the Task Force was unanimously convinced that a problem exists respecting cross-racial identifications and that the Court should take corrective action. Ultimately, in 1992 the Task Force submitted its final report to the Court in which it recommended, among other things, that the Court develop a special jury charge regarding the unreliability of cross-racial identifications.

The Court referred that recommendation to the Criminal Practice Committee. The Criminal Practice Committee reviewed the recommendation and created a subcommittee to draft a cross-racial identification charge for consideration by the full Committee. The subcommittee drafted and submitted to the Criminal Practice Committee [a proposed instruction almost identical to the one sought in this case].

The Criminal Practice Committee, however, decided against recommending a charge to the Court. Development of a cross-racial charge was deemed to be premature because the issue of admissibility of evidence to support the charge had not been decided by case law.

* * *

We reject the State's contention that we should not require a cross-racial identification charge before it has been demonstrated that there is substantial agreement in the relevant scientific community that cross-racial recognition impairment is significant enough to support the need for such a charge. This case does not concern the introduction of scientific evidence to attack the reliability of the eyewitness's identification. Defendant's requested jury instruction was not based upon any "scientific, technical, or other specialized knowledge" to assist the jury. He relied instead on ordinary human experience and the legislative-type findings of the Task Force because the basis for his request did not involve a matter that was beyond the ken of the average juror.

This case requires us to focus on the well-established differences between adjudicative or hard evidence, argument, and jury instructions. The hard evidence revealed a cross-racial identification and the circumstances under which that identification was made. The State argued to the jury that the identification was credible based on the evidence. Counsel for defendant, on the other hand, argued that there was a mistaken identification based on the totality of the circumstances. Defendant requested a cross-racial identification jury instruction that would treat the racial character of the eyewitness identification as one of the factors bearing on its reliability in much the same way as lighting and proximity to the perpetrator at the time of the offense.

A national review of the use of cross-racial identification jury instructions reveals that only a small minority of jurisdictions have declined such an instruction because studies finding unreliability in cross-racial identifications lack general acceptance in the relevant scientific community. The majority of jurisdictions that have rejected the instruction did so based on judicial discretion. Those discretionary rulings were influenced by factors such as the nature and quality of the eyewitness identification, the existence of strong corroborating evidence, the fact that the eyewitness had an adequate opportunity to observe the perpetrator, or a combination of those reasons. * * *

[W]e hold that a cross-racial identification, as a subset of eyewitness identification, requires a special jury instruction in an appropriate case.

Indeed, some courtroom observers have commented that the ordinary person's difficulty of "cross-racial recognition is so commonplace as to be the subject of both cliche and joke: 'they all look alike.'" Although laboratory studies concerning the reliability of cross-racial identifications have not been validated in actual courtroom atmospheres, the results of many of those experiments suggest that "decreased accuracy in the recognition of other-race faces is not within the observer's conscious control, and that seriousness of criminal proceedings would not improve accuracy." Moreover, the stress associated with the courtroom atmosphere, based on human experience, is likely to diminish rather than enhance recognition accuracy.

* * *

We conclude that the empirical data encapsulate much of the ordinary human experience and provide an appropriate frame of reference for requiring a cross-racial identification jury instruction. Under the jurisprudence of this Court, in a prosecution "in which race by definition is a patent factor[, race] must be taken into account to assure a fair trial."

At the same time, we recognize that unrestricted use of cross-racial identification instructions could be counter-productive. Consequently, care must be taken to insulate criminal trials from base appeals to racial prejudice. An appropriate jury instruction should carefully delineate the context in which the jury is permitted to consider racial differences. The simple fact pattern of a white victim of a violent crime at the hands of a black assailant would not automatically give rise to the need for a cross-racial identification charge. More is required.

A cross-racial instruction should be given only when, as in the present case, identification is a critical issue in the case, and an eyewitness's cross-racial identification is not corroborated by other evidence giving it independent reliability. Here, the eyewitness identification was critical; yet it was not corroborated by any forensic evidence or other eyewitness account. The circumstances of the case raise some doubt concerning the reliability of the victim's identification in that no positive identification was made for nearly eight months despite attempts within the first five days following the commission of the offenses. Under those circumstances, turning over to the jury the vital question of the reliability of that identification without acquainting the jury with the potential risks associated with such identifications could have affected the jurors' ability to evaluate the reliability of the identification. We conclude, therefore, that it was reversible error not to have given an instruction that informed the jury about the possible significance of the cross-racial identification factor, a factor the jury can observe in many cases with its own eyes, in determining the critical issue—the accuracy of the identification.

NOTES

1. The Cromedy rationale has not been examined in other jurisdictions. However, when the instruction that it mandates is not requested by the defense, the failure to give it is not plain error requiring reversal. See State v. Murray, 338 N.J.Super. 80, 768 A.2d 221 (2001); State v. Gaskin, 325 N.J.Super. 563, 740 A.2d 157 (1999).

2. Some courts have upheld the refusal to give the instruction in the absence of a showing that there exists a specific risk that the eyewitness may have been mistaken due to cross-racial factors. See Miller v. State, 759 N.E.2d 680 (Ind.App.

2001). Others have simply stated that the refusal to instruct in this manner does not violate due process. See Lenoir v. State, 77 Ark.App. 250, 72 S.W.3d 899 (2002).

3. In State v. Valentine, 345 N.J.Super. 490, 785 A.2d 940 (2001) the court refused to require the instruction in a cross-ethnic, as opposed to cross-racial, identification in a case in which a Hispanic victim testified that he was robbed by a black man.

5. Consequences of Verdict

Shannon v. United States

Supreme Court of the United States, 1994.
512 U.S. 573, 114 S.Ct. 2419.

■ Justice Thomas delivered the opinion of the Court.

In this case, we consider whether a federal district court is required to instruct the jury regarding the consequences to the defendant of a verdict of "not guilty by reason of insanity," either under the Insanity Defense Reform Act of 1984 or as a matter of general federal practice. We conclude that such an instruction is not required, and therefore affirm.

I

A

Prior to the enactment of the Insanity Defense Reform Act of 1984 (IDRA or Act) federal courts generally did not recognize a verdict of "not guilty by reason of insanity" (NGI). Defendants who mounted a successful insanity defense—that is, those who raised a reasonable doubt as to their sanity at the time of the offense—were simply found "not guilty." In addition, there was no general federal civil commitment procedure available to ensure that an insanity acquittee would receive proper care and treatment. Only in the District of Columbia was a defendant who successfully presented an insanity defense to a federal criminal charge subject to a federal commitment process—a process governed by a 1955 congressional enactment. Elsewhere, federal authorities were forced to rely on the willingness of state authorities to institute civil commitment proceedings. Reliance on state cooperation was "at best a partial solution to a serious problem," however, and federal courts "[t]ime and again ... decried this gaping statutory hole."

Before the IDRA was enacted, the Federal Courts of Appeals generally disapproved of instructing the jury concerning the post-trial consequences of an insanity acquittal. Thus, jurors typically were given no information with regard to what would happen to a defendant acquitted by reason of insanity. The courts in general gave two reasons for disapproving such instructions. First, they pointed out that, given the absence of a federal commitment procedure, the consequences of an insanity acquittal were far from certain. Second, they concluded that such instructions would run afoul of the well-established principle that a jury is to base its verdict on the evidence before it, without regard to the possible consequences of the verdict.

The only Court of Appeals to endorse the practice of instructing the jury regarding the consequences of an insanity acquittal was the District of

Columbia Circuit. See Lyles v. United States, 254 F.2d 725 (1957) (en banc). In Lyles, the D.C. Circuit addressed the jury instruction question in the context of D.C.Code Ann. § 24–301, which, unlike generally applicable federal law, provided for a special verdict of NGI and, as noted above, a civil commitment procedure. The Lyles court recognized the "well established and sound" doctrine "that the jury has no concern with the consequences" of a verdict, but stated that the doctrine "d[id] not apply" to the situation before it. According to the court, although jurors generally were "aware of the meanings of verdicts of guilty and not guilty," they were unfamiliar with the meaning of an NGI verdict. The court concluded that jurors had "a right to know" the meaning of an NGI verdict "as accurately as [they] kno[w] by common knowledge the meaning of the other two possible verdicts." Ibid.

The acquittal of John Hinckley on all charges stemming from his attempt on President Reagan's life, coupled with the ensuing public focus on the insanity defense, prompted Congress to undertake a comprehensive overhaul of the insanity defense as it operated in the federal courts. The result of this effort was the IDRA. In the IDRA, Congress made insanity an affirmative defense to be proved by the defendant by clear and convincing evidence, and created a special verdict of "not guilty only by reason of insanity." In addition, Congress filled the "statutory hole" that had been identified by federal courts by creating a comprehensive civil commitment procedure. Under that procedure, a defendant found NGI is held in custody pending a court hearing, which must occur within 40 days of the verdict. At the conclusion of the hearing, the court determines whether the defendant should be hospitalized or released.

B

At about 4 a.m. on August 25, 1990, a police officer stopped petitioner Terry Lee Shannon, a convicted felon, on a street in Tupelo, Mississippi. For reasons not explained in the record before us, the officer asked Shannon to accompany him to the station house to speak with a detective. After telling the officer that he did not want to live anymore, Shannon walked across the street, pulled a pistol from his coat, and shot himself in the chest.

Shannon survived his suicide attempt and was indicted for unlawful possession of a firearm by a felon. At trial, he raised the insanity defense, and asked the District Court to instruct the jury that he would be involuntarily committed if the jury returned an NGI verdict. The District Court refused to give Shannon's proposed charge. Instead, it instructed the jury "to apply the law as [instructed] regardless of the consequence," and that "punishment ... should not enter your consideration or discussion." The jury returned a guilty verdict.

II

It is well established that when a jury has no sentencing function, it should be admonished to "reach its verdict without regard to what sentence might be imposed." Rogers v. United States, 422 U.S. 35, 40 (1975). The principle that juries are not to consider the consequences of their verdicts is a reflection of the basic division of labor in our legal system between judge and jury. The jury's function is to find the facts and to decide whether, on those facts, the defendant is guilty of the crime charged. The judge, by contrast, imposes sentence on the defendant after the jury has arrived at a guilty verdict. Information regarding the consequences of a verdict is therefore irrelevant to the jury's task. Moreover, providing jurors sentencing information invites them to ponder matters that are not within their province, distracts them from their factfinding responsibilities, and creates a strong possibility of confusion.

A

To determine whether Congress intended courts to depart from the principle that jurors are not to be informed of the consequences of their verdicts, we turn first, as always, to the text of the statute. The IDRA refers to the subject of jury instructions only once, and that reference occurs in its description of the possible verdicts a jury may return. Under the Act, "the jury shall be instructed to find . . . the defendant—(1) guilty; (2) not guilty; or (3) not guilty only by reason of insanity." The text of the Act gives no indication that jurors are to be instructed regarding the consequences of an NGI verdict. As the court below observed, the Act "leaves the jury solely with its customary determination of guilt or innocence." The Act's text thus gives no support to Shannon's contention that an instruction informing the jury of the consequences of an NGI verdict is required.

Shannon asserts, however, that an express statutory directive is not necessary because, by modeling the IDRA on D.C.Code Ann. § 24–301 (1981), Congress impliedly adopted the D.C. Circuit's decision in Lyles and the practice endorsed by that decision of instructing the jury as to the consequences of an NGI verdict. For this argument he relies on Capital Traction Co. v. Hof, 174 U.S. 1, 36 (1899), in which we stated:

"By a familiar canon of interpretation, heretofore applied by this court whenever Congress . . . has borrowed from the statutes of a State provisions which had received in that State a known and settled construction before their enactment by Congress, that construction must be deemed to have been adopted by Congress together with the text which it expounded, and the provisions must be construed as they were understood at the time in the State."

The canon of interpretation upon which Shannon relies, however, is merely a "presumption of legislative intention" to be invoked only "under suitable conditions." We believe that the "conditions" are not "suitable" in this case. Indeed, although Congress may have had the D.C. Code in mind when it passed the IDRA, it did not, in the language of Hof, "borrow" the terms of the IDRA from the D.C. Code. Rather, Congress departed from the scheme embodied in D.C. Code Ann. § 24–301 in several significant ways.

The IDRA, for example, requires a defendant at trial to prove insanity by clear and convincing evidence; the D.C. statute, by contrast, employs a preponderance standard. A commitment hearing must be held under the IDRA within 40 days of an NGI verdict; the period is 50 days under the D.C. scheme. Under the IDRA, a defendant whose offense involved bodily injury to another or serious damage to another's property, or the substantial risk thereof, must demonstrate at the hearing by clear and convincing evidence that he is entitled to release, under the D.C. scheme, an acquittee, regardless of the character of his offense, need only meet the preponderance standard. The IDRA provides that an acquittee, once committed, may be released when he no longer presents a substantial risk of harm to others or to their property; an acquittee under the D.C. system may be released from commitment when he "will not in the reasonable future be dangerous to himself or others."

Finally, in the IDRA, Congress rejected the broad test for insanity that had been utilized under the D.C. provision, and instead adopted a more restrictive formulation under which a person is deemed insane if he is unable "to appreciate the nature and quality or the wrongfulness of his acts." We believe that these significant differences between the IDRA and D.C.Code Ann. render the canon upon which Shannon relies inapplicable in this case.

Alternatively, Shannon contends that a provision explicitly requiring the instruction is unnecessary for a different reason: namely, that Congress made its intention to adopt the Lyles practice crystal clear in the IDRA's legislative history. In particular, Shannon points to the following statement in the Senate Report:

> "The Committee endorses the procedure used in the District of Columbia whereby the jury, in a case in which the insanity defense has been raised, may be instructed on the effect of a verdict of not guilty by reason of insanity. If the defendant requests that the instruction not be given, it is within the discretion of the court whether to give it or not." S.Rep. No. 98–225, p. 240 (1983).

Members of this Court have expressed differing views regarding the role that legislative history should play in statutory interpretation. Compare County of Washington v. Gunther, 452 U.S. 161, 182 (1981) (Rehnquist, J., dissenting) ("[I]t [is] well settled that the legislative history of a statute is a useful guide to the intent of Congress"), with Wisconsin Public Intervenor v. Mortier, 501 U.S. 597, 617 (1991) (Scalia, J., concurring in judgment) (legislative history is "unreliable ... as a genuine indicator of congressional intent"). We are not aware of any case, however (and Shannon does not bring one to our attention), in which we have given authoritative weight to a single passage of legislative history that is in no way anchored in the text of the statute. On its face, the passage Shannon identifies does not purport to explain or interpret any provision of the IDRA. Rather, it merely conveys the Committee's "endorsement" of the Lyles "procedure"—a procedure that Congress did not include in the text of the Act. To give effect to this snippet of legislative history, we would have to abandon altogether the text of the statute as a guide in the interpretative process. We agree with the D.C. Circuit that "courts have no authority to enforce [a] principl[e] gleaned solely from legislative history that has no statutory reference point." International Brotherhood of Elec. Workers, Local Union No. 474, AFL–CIO v. NLRB, 814 F.2d 697, 712

(1987). We thus conclude that there is no support in the Act for the instruction Shannon seeks.

B

Setting the Act aside, Shannon argues that the instruction he proposes is required as a matter of general federal criminal practice. Presumably, Shannon asks us to invoke our supervisory power over the federal courts. According to Shannon, the instruction is necessary because jurors are generally unfamiliar with the consequences of an NGI verdict, and may erroneously believe that a defendant who is found NGI will be immediately released into society. Jurors who are under this mistaken impression, Shannon continues, may also fear that the defendant, if released, would pose a danger to the community. Shannon concludes that such jurors, in order to ensure that the defendant will not be released, may be tempted to return a guilty verdict in a case in which an NGI verdict would be appropriate.

Even assuming Shannon is correct that some jurors will harbor the mistaken belief that defendants found NGI will be released into society immediately—an assumption that is open to debate—the jury in his case was instructed "to apply the law as [instructed] regardless of the consequence," and that "punishment . . . should not enter your consideration or discussion." That an NGI verdict was an option here gives us no reason to depart from "the almost invariable assumption of the law that jurors follow their instructions." Richardson v. Marsh, 481 U.S. 200, 206 (1987). Indeed, although it may take effort on a juror's part to ignore the potential consequences of the verdict, the effort required in a case in which an NGI defense is raised is no different from that required in many other situations. For example, if the Government fails to meet its burden of proof at trial, our judicial system necessarily assumes that a juror will vote to acquit, rather than to convict, even if he is convinced the defendant is highly dangerous and should be incarcerated. We do not believe that the situation involving an NGI verdict should be treated any differently.

We also are not persuaded that the instruction Shannon proposes would allay the fears of the misinformed juror about whom Shannon is concerned. "[I]f the members of a jury are so fearful of a particular defendant's release that they would violate their oaths by convicting [the defendant] solely in order to ensure that he is not set free, it is questionable whether they would be reassured by anything short of an instruction strongly suggesting that the defendant, if found NGI, would very likely be civilly committed for a lengthy period." United States v. Fisher, 10 F.3d 115, 122 (C.A.3 1993). An accurate instruction about the consequences of an NGI verdict, however, would give no such assurance. Under the IDRA, a postverdict hearing must be held within 40 days to determine whether the defendant should be released immediately into society or hospitalized. Thus, the only mandatory period of confinement for an insanity acquittee is the period between the verdict and the hearing. Instead of encouraging a juror to return an NGI verdict, as Shannon predicts, such information might have the opposite effect—that is, a juror might vote to convict in order to eliminate the possibility that a dangerous defendant could be released after 40 days or less. Whether the instruction works to the advantage or disadvantage of a defendant is, of course, somewhat beside the point. Our central concern here is that the inevitable result of such an instruction would be to draw the jury's attention toward the very thing—the possible consequences of its verdict—it should ignore.

Moreover, Shannon offers us no principled way to limit the availability of instructions detailing the consequences of a verdict to cases in which an NGI defense is raised. Jurors may be as unfamiliar with other aspects of the criminal sentencing process as they are with NGI verdicts. But, as a general matter, jurors are not informed of mandatory minimum or maximum sentences, nor are they instructed regarding probation, parole, or the sentencing range accompanying a lesser included offense. See United States v. Thigpen, 4 F.3d 1573, 1578 (C.A.11 1993) (en banc); United States v. Frank, 956 F.2d 872, 879 (C.A.9 1991), cert. denied, 506 U.S. (1992). Because it is conceivable that some jurors might harbor misunderstandings with regard to these sentencing options, a district court, under Shannon's reasoning, might be obligated to give juries information regarding these possibilities as well. In short, if we pursue the logic of Shannon's position, the rule against informing jurors of the consequences of their verdicts would soon be swallowed by the exceptions.

Finally, Congress' recent action in this area counsels hesitation in invoking our supervisory powers. As noted above, the IDRA was the product of a thorough and exhaustive review of the insanity defense as used in the federal courts. Given the comprehensive nature of the task before it, Congress certainly could have included a provision requiring the instruction Shannon seeks. For whatever reason, Congress chose not to do so. Under these circumstances, we are reluctant to depart from well-established principles of criminal practice without more explicit guidance from Congress.

III

Although we conclude that the IDRA does not require an instruction concerning the consequences of an NGI verdict, and that such an instruction is not to be given as a matter of general practice, we recognize that an instruction of some form may be necessary under certain limited circumstances. If, for example, a witness or prosecutor states in the presence of the jury that a particular defendant would "go free" if found NGI, it may be necessary for the district court to intervene with an instruction to counter such a misstatement. The appropriate response, of course, will vary as is necessary to remedy the specific misstatement or error. We note this possibility merely so that our decision will not be misunderstood as an absolute prohibition on instructing the jury with regard to the consequences of an NGI verdict. Our observations in this regard are not applicable to Shannon's situation, however, for there is no indication that any improper statement was made in the presence of the jury during his trial.

* * *

Because the District Court properly refused to give the instruction Shannon requested, we affirm.

So ordered.

■ JUSTICE STEVENS, with whom JUSTICE BLACKMUN joins, dissenting.

A rule that has minimized the risk of injustice for almost 40 years should not be abandoned without good reason. In 1957, shortly after Congress enacted the statute providing for civil commitment of persons found not guilty by reason of insanity in trials conducted in the District of Columbia, the Court of Appeals, sitting in banc, considered whether juries should be instructed about the significance of that provision. Recognizing that an uninformed jury might erroneously find an insane defendant guilty to avoid the risk that a dangerous individual would otherwise go free, the court held that such an instruction should be given. Lyles v. United States, 254 F.2d 725 (C.A.D.C.1957).

* * *

When Congress enacted the Insanity Defense Reform Act of 1984 it established a civil commitment process for the entire federal system, thus making the basis for the D.C. Circuit's holding in Lyles applicable to all federal courts. The Act's legislative history unmistakably demonstrates that the Act's sponsors assumed that the Lyles precedent would thereafter be followed nationwide. That assumption does not have the force of a statutory mandate, but it verifies that thoughtful legislators familiar with the issue believed that precedent to be entirely sound. That this Court should now decide to change an established rule that Congress accepted and that protects defendants meaningfully against an obvious risk of injustice is startling—particularly when that change is for no reason other than a perceived inconsistency with another rule that is generally protective of defendants' rights. A far wiser disposition would allow the defendant to choose between the two rules, rather than tilt the scales to favor the prosecutor in every case.

NOTE

Where the jury has responsibility for sentencing, the Supreme Court has held that, under some circumstances, the jury must be told of the penal consequences of its verdict. In Simmons v. South Carolina, 512 U.S. 154, 114 S.Ct. 2187 (1994) four justices concluded that where "future dangerousness" is at issue in a capital case, the jury must be told that the alternative to the death penalty is life imprisonment without possibility of parole. The plurality did not hold that such information must be given where the prosecution does not argue future dangerousness. Three justices (and perhaps a fourth) concurred at least to the extent of agreeing that either the court (in instruction) or defense counsel (in argument) should inform the jury that defendant would not be paroled. Except for Justices Souter and Stevens, all these opinions were grounded on a due process analysis, not upon the cruel and unusual punishment provisions of the Eighth Amendment. Two dissenters saw no reason to impose this information requirement in all cases and particularly in a case where "future dangerousness" while argued was not emphasized and the prosecutor never referred to dangerousness outside of prison. Moreover, they noted, under state law parole is prohibited but furlough, work release and pardon are not.

D. DELIBERATION AND VERDICT

1. JURY DELIBERATIONS

Parker v. Gladden

Supreme Court of the United States, 1966.
385 U.S. 363, 87 S.Ct. 468.

■ PER CURIAM.

Petitioner, after his conviction for second degree murder, filed a petition for post-conviction relief. At a hearing on the petition the trial court found that a court bailiff assigned to shepherd the sequestered jury, which sat for eight days, stated to one of the jurors in the presence of others while the jury was out walking on a public sidewalk: "Oh that wicked fellow [petitioner], he is guilty"; and on another occasion said to another juror under similar circumstances, "If there is anything wrong [in finding petitioner guilty] the Supreme Court will correct it." Both statements were overheard by at least one regular juror or an alternate. The trial court found "that the unauthorized communication was prejudicial and that such conduct materially affected the rights of the [petitioner]." The Supreme Court of Oregon reversed, finding that "the bailiff's misconduct did not deprive [petitioner] of a constitutionally correct trial."

* * *

We believe that the statements of the bailiff to the jurors are controlled by the command of the Sixth Amendment, made applicable to the States through the Due Process Clause of the Fourteenth Amendment. It guarantees that "the accused shall enjoy the right to a ... trial, by an impartial jury ... [and] be confronted with the witnesses against him...." As we said in Turner v. Louisiana (1965), "the 'evidence developed' against a defendant shall come from the witness stand in a public courtroom where there is full judicial protection of the defendant's right of confrontation, of cross-examination, and of counsel." Here there is dispute neither as to what the bailiff, an officer of the State, said nor that when he said it he was not subjected to confrontation, cross-examination or other safeguards guaranteed to the petitioner. Rather, his expressions were "private talk," tending to reach the jury by "outside influence."

* * *

The State suggests that no prejudice was shown and that no harm could have resulted because 10 members of the jury testified that they had not heard the bailiff's statements and that Oregon law permits a verdict of guilty by 10 affirmative votes. This overlooks the fact that the official character of the bailiff—as an officer of the court as well as the State—beyond question carries great weight with a jury which he had been shepherding for eight days and nights. Moreover, the jurors deliberated for 26 hours, indicating a difference among them as to the guilt of petitioner. Finally, one of the jurors testified that she *was* prejudiced by the statements, which supports the trial court's finding "that the unauthorized communication was prejudicial and that such conduct materially affected the rights of the defendant." ... Aside from this, we believe that the unauthorized conduct of the bailiff "involves such a probability that prejudice will result that it is deemed inherently lacking in due process," Estes v. State of Texas, (1965). As we said in Turner "it would be blinking reality not to recognize the extreme prejudice inherent" in such statements that reached at least three members of the jury and one alternate member. The State says that 10 of the jurors testified that they had not heard the statements of the bailiff.

* * *

In any event, petitioner was entitled to be tried by 12, not 9 or even 10, impartial and unprejudiced jurors.

Reversed.

■ MR. JUSTICE HARLAN, dissenting.

By not setting forth the background of this proceeding the Court has put seriously out of focus the constitutional issue involved in this case.

Parker was convicted of second degree murder on May 19, 1961, and sentenced to life imprisonment. On September 7, 1961, he addressed a letter to several jurors protesting his innocence, condemning his attorneys for incompetence, intimating that witnesses were coerced into lying, and chiding the jurors for being duped into finding him guilty. After affirmance of his conviction by the Supreme Court of Oregon on September 15, 1963—some two years after the jury verdict—Parker again set out to take his case to the jury. He furnished his wife with a tape recording in which he propounded a series of questions designed to uncover possible improprieties in the jury's deliberations. The jury had deliberated a long time and Parker had been told that their discussion was heated. Although unaware of any irregularities he commenced "shooting in the dark." Mrs. Parker then acquired a jury list and discovered those jurors who had been most sympathetic to her husband. She invited two regular jurors and an alternate to her home to listen to the recording and discuss the case. An attorney was then retained to prepare affidavits detailing the allegations before us and to institute this post-conviction proceeding. The statements before this Court were found to have been made by this apparently Elizabethan-tongued bailiff, but, contrary to this Court's assertion, the trial court found that these statements were only prejudicial in nature and not that they had a prejudicial effect. The Oregon Supreme Court did not find the trial proceedings fundamentally unfair.

* * *

As to the confrontation problem here asserted, I know of no case in which this Court has held that jurors must have been absolutely insulated from all expressions of opinion on the merits of the case or the judicial process at the risk of declaration of a new trial. Even where this Court has acted in its supervisory capacity it has refused to hold that jury contact with outside information is always a cause for overthrowing a verdict, wisely preferring to allow "each case [to] turn on its special facts." The

Court notes that these remarks were made by a state officer, but does not explain why the bailiff's official capacity would in this instance make him any more a "witness" than any other person able to communicate with the jury. Thus, though I believe unintentionally, the Court's opinion leaves open the possibility of automatically requiring a mistrial on constitutional grounds whenever any juror is exposed to any potentially prejudicial expression of opinion.

* * *

The occurrences before us seem inconsequential to me in light of the eight-day trial and twenty-six-hour jury deliberation. And my feeling is confirmed by the extremely trivial evidence of prejudice amounting to no more than an assertion by one obviously highly emotional and "guilt-ridden" juror that she might have been influenced without realizing it. "[I]t is an impossible standard to require that tribunal [the jury] to be a laboratory, completely sterilized and freed from any external factors." Rideau v. Louisiana, 373 U.S. 723, 733, 83 S.Ct. 1417, 1423, (Clark, J., dissenting).

The potentialities of today's decision may go far beyond what, I am sure, the Court intends. Certainly the Court does not wish to encourage convicted felons to "intimidate, beset and harass," a discharged jury in an effort to establish possible grounds for a new trial. Our courts have always been alert to protect the sanctity of the jury process. But in allowing Parker to overturn his conviction on the basis of what are no more than inconsequential incidents in an otherwise constitutionally flawless proceeding, the Court encourages others to follow his example in pursuing the jury and may be thought by some to commit federal courts in habeas corpus proceedings to interrogate the jury upon the mere allegation that a prejudicial remark has reached the ears of one of its members. To any such result I cannot subscribe.

NOTES

1. In United States v. United States Gypsum Co., 438 U.S. 422, 98 S.Ct. 2864 (1978), the jury foreman, after seven days of deliberations, informed the judge that he wanted to discuss the health condition of some jurors. The judge's ex parte meeting with the foreman was held with the parties' consent; but the foreman came away with the impression that the judge wanted a verdict one way or the other. A guilty verdict was returned the following morning. Upholding the reversal of the conviction, the Court said:

> [I]t is not simply the action of the judge in having the private meeting with the jury foreman, standing alone,—undesirable as that procedure is—which constitutes the error; rather, it is the fact that the *ex parte* discussion was inadvertently allowed to drift into what amounted to a supplemental instruction to the foreman relating to the jury's obligation to return a verdict, coupled with the fact that counsel were denied any chance to correct whatever mistaken impression the foreman might have taken from this conversation, that we find most troubling.

Compare Rushen v. Spain, 464 U.S. 114, 104 S.Ct. 453 (1983), where the court reversed the Ninth Circuit's holding that an unrecorded ex parte judge-juror communication can never be harmless error. In a 5–4 per curiam opinion decided summarily without oral argument, the court held that an ex parte communication between the trial judge and a juror, in which the juror told the judge of her personal acquaintance with a crime that was unrelated to the crimes at issue in the trial, was harmless error because it was innocuous, they did not discuss any fact in the controversy or any law applicable to the case, and the jury's deliberations, as a whole, were not biased by the undisclosed communication.

2. Fed.R.Evid. 606(b) provides:

> Upon an inquiry into the validity of a verdict or indictment, a juror may not testify as to any matter or statement occurring during the course of the jury's deliberations or to the effect of anything upon his or her or any other juror's mind or emotions as influencing the juror to assent to or dissent from the verdict or indictment or concerning the juror's mental processes in connection therewith, except that a juror's mental processes in connection therewith, except that a juror may testify on the question whether extraneous prejudicial information was improperly brought to the jury's attention or whether any outside influence was improperly brought to bear upon any juror. Nor may the juror's affidavit or evidence of any statement by the juror concerning a matter about which the juror would be precluded from testifying be received for these purposes.

Juror testimony regarding unauthorized juror views of crime scenes and other "experiments" do not fall within the rule. See, e.g., In re Beverly Hills Fire Litigation, 695 F.2d 207, 213 (6th Cir.1982) (juror experiment is extraneous information); United States v. Williams–Davis, 821 F.Supp. 727, 740 (D.D.C.1993), affirmed 90 F.3d 490 (D.C.Cir.1996) (juror's unauthorized visit to crime scene is extraneous information).

3. Because a court may not inquire of a juror what effect extraneous information had on the deliberative process, a defendant can never objectively prove actual prejudice. Under Remmer v. United States, 347 U.S. 227, 74 S.Ct. 450 (1954), any private communication, contact or tampering, directly or indirectly with a juror about the pending case is presumptively prejudicial unless done by the court with knowledge of the parties or otherwise consistent with court rules. The presumption may be rebutted by a showing by the prosecution that the contact was harmless to defendant. An inquiry into extraneous influences must strike a balance between protecting against prejudicial interference and allowing deliberations to proceed unimpeded.

Prejudice is determined by, among other things, the nature and extent of the unauthorized contact, the answers that individual jurors give to the court's questions and the ability of curative instructions to remedy the problem. United States v. Aguirre, 108 F.3d 1284 (10th Cir. 1997) (jurors use of dictionary to finding the meaning of certain words was harmless); United States v. Sanders, 962 F.2d 660 (7th Cir. 1992) (juror testified that she could put incident behind her and continue to serve impartially).

In United States v. Vasquez–Ruiz, 502 F.3d 700 (7th Cir. 2007), an unidentified third party wrote "GUILTY" in a juror's notebook. The trial judge interviewed the juror to assure that she could remain impartial and gave a cautionary instruction regarding the presumption of innocence and the jurors' obligation to keep an open mind until instructed to deliberate. The court refused to interview other jurors and denied defendant's motion for a mistrial. Finding the mysterious appearance of the "GUILTY" suggestion to be presumptively prejudicial, the court of appeals reversed. Noting that the presumption of prejudice can be rebutted, the court held that, in the absence of additional attempts by the trial judge to learn what happened, the presumption could not be overcome. "Here, where a mysterious note simply appears in a juror's notebook, and where we cannot even say with assurance that it was another juror who wrote the note in the first place, there was a need to make a greater effort to find out what had happened before declaring that it did not make any difference."

4. In Lawson v. Borg, 60 F.3d 608 (9th Cir.1995), one juror solicited information from neighbors who knew the defendant and reported to his fellow jurors that the defendant was a violent person with a bad reputation. After his murder conviction was upheld by the state courts, a writ of habeas corpus was granted:

> Several factors are relevant to determining whether the alleged introduction of extrinsic evidence constitutes reversible error:
>
> > (1) whether the extrinsic material was actually received, and if so, how; (2) the length of time it was available to the jury; (3) the extent to which the jury discussed and considered it; (4) whether the material was introduced before a verdict was reached, and if so, at what point in the deliberations it was introduced; and (5) any other matters which may bear on the issue of ... whether the introduction of extrinsic material [substantially and injuriously] affected the verdict.
>
> When assessing prejudice claims in juror misconduct cases, this court also places great weight on the nature of the extrinsic evidence introduced.
>
> Here, juror Scott introduced the extrinsic evidence on the second of five days of protracted guilt-phase deliberations, well before a verdict was rendered.
>
> Furthermore, the extrinsic information directly related to a material issue in the case: intent.
>
> * * *
>
> This court has observed that "reversible error commonly occurs where there is a direct and rational connection between the extrinsic material and a prejudicial jury conclusion, and where the misconduct relates directly to a material aspect of the case." Such a direct connection is present here.

Judge Trott dissented:

> [T]he jury in this case did not decide the verdict in the abstract. It decided the verdict with all the evidence in mind—record evidence that included several violent acts on the part of petitioner. In comparing the admissible evidence of petitioner's violence with the extraneous evidence, ... the effect of the reputation evidence describing an extraneous propensity for violence [was] diluted to the point where it did not have a substantial and injurious effect on the verdict.

5. Where the judge gives additional substantive instructions to the jury without notice to counsel, reversal is generally mandated. United States v. Schor, 418 F.2d 26 (2d Cir.1969); Jones v. United States, 308 F.2d 307 (D.C.Cir.1962). A mid-deliberation instruction, which counsel had no opportunity to address in closing argument is not erroneous if it is in keeping with the thrust of the trial issues. United States v. Civelli, 883 F.2d 191 (2d Cir.1989). Messages to continue deliberations, conveyed through a marshal or bailiff, are generally regarded as harmless absent a strong showing of prejudice. Walsh v. United States, 371 F.2d 135 (9th Cir.1967). Similarly, innocuous communications with regard to documentary information have been held inconsequential. United States v. Arriagada, 451 F.2d 487 (4th Cir.1971) (grant of request to rehear testimony). Ferrari v. United States, 244 F.2d 132 (9th Cir.1957) (denial of request to hear recording). Compare Harrison v. State, 575 N.E.2d 642 (Ind.App.1991) (reversal required when, in response to jury's request, bailiff gave them written definitions of theft).

When the trial judge responds to an open-ended jury question by rereading a select portion of a witness' testimony, it may have the effect of encouraging the jury to believe the witness and discredit alternative accounts of the events. If the manner in which the judge culls the evidence suggests that he is becoming a fact-finder, reversal is required. United States v. Rivera–Santiago, 107 F.3d 960 (1st Cir.1997).

Indiana has a unique procedure that requires the trial court, after consulting with counsel, to provide specific information if the jury informs it that there is disagreement among them as to any part of the testimony or point of law. In Perry v. State, 867 N.E.2d 638 (Ind. 2007), the jury asked whether a state witness responded to an inquiry as to how many times the defendant fired shots with the answer "maybe a couple." After the parties stipulated that the court could answer the question in the affirmative, the court committed a scrivener's error in restating the question by inserting the defendant's name, rather than that of the witness, in its written response. Accepting defendant's contention that the response made it appear that he fired the shots, the court reversed the conviction because it could not determine that the trial judge's error did not influence the verdict. Judge Crone dissented on the ground that the court's typographical error was not so egregious as to warrant reversal.

6. When contact with the deliberating jury is made by someone other than the trial judge, the courts have been more sensitive to claims of prejudicial error. See Turner v. Louisiana, 379 U.S. 466, 85 S.Ct. 546 (1965) (deliberating jury in custody of sheriffs who had served as key prosecution witnesses); United States v. Freeman, 634 F.2d 1267 (10th Cir.1980) (government agent to operate tape recorder requires reversal); United States v. Dellinger, 472 F.2d 340 (7th Cir.1972) (authorized communication by marshal); United States v. Pittman, 449 F.2d 1284 (9th Cir.1971) (government agent in jury room during deliberations). However, when the contact is nothing more than an off-hand remark or casual non-specific comment unrelated to factual evidence not developed at trial, no presumption of prejudice arises. See United States v. Wallingford, 82 F.3d 278 (8th Cir.1996) (cashier at restaurant said she hoped that jury would not find them guilty). The question, in each instance, is whether the contact was so inherently prejudicial as to transgress due process rights; and the correlative issue is the extent of the showing that must be made by a defendant before a court must adjudicate the larger question.

7. Where it is determined that "foreign" objects were present in the jury room during deliberations, the courts assess prejudice by measuring the nature of the object and its likely effect on the jury's deliberations. See United States v. Navarro–Garcia, 926 F.2d 818 (9th Cir.1991) (some jurors engaged in improper experiments during the course of deliberations); United States v. Hill, 688 F.2d 18 (6th Cir.1982) (affirmance despite presence of law book); United States v. Bassler, 651 F.2d 600 (8th Cir.1981) (copy of *Robert's Rules of Order*); United States v. Shafer, 455 F.2d 1167 (5th Cir.1972) (documents not admitted into evidence requires reversal); United States v. Siragusa, 450 F.2d 592 (2d Cir.1971) (affirmance despite presence of I.R.S. tax booklet).

8. In United States v. Olano, 507 U.S. 725, 113 S.Ct. 1770 (1993), the Court held that a trial judge's decision to allow alternate jurors to sit in on jury deliberations under an instruction not to participate, to which the defense did not object, was not "plain error" warranting reversal:

> The presence of alternate jurors during jury deliberations is no doubt a deviation from Rule 24(c). The Rule explicitly states: "An alternate juror who does not replace a regular juror shall be discharged after the jury retires to consider its verdict." It is a separate question whether such deviation amounts to "error" when the defendant consents to the alter-

nates' presence. The Government supposes that there was indeed an "error" in this case, on the premise that Rule 24(c) is nonwaivable, and we assume without deciding that this premise is correct. The Government also essentially concedes that the "error" was "plain."

We therefore focus our attention on whether the error "affect[ed] substantial rights" within the meaning of Rule 52(b), and conclude that it did not. The presence of alternate jurors during jury deliberations is not the kind of error that "affect[s] substantial rights" independent of its prejudicial impact. Nor have respondents made a specific showing of prejudice. Finally, we see no reason to presume prejudice here.

On behalf of the three dissenters, Justice Stevens disagreed:

At least some defects bearing on the jury's deliberative function are subject to reversal regardless of whether prejudice can be shown, not only because it is so difficult to measure their effects on a jury's decision, but also because such defects "undermin[e] the structural integrity of the criminal tribunal itself." Whether or not they harm the defendant, errors that call into question the integrity of the jury's deliberations may harm the system as a whole. In that sense, they may be said to "seriously affect the fairness, integrity or public reputation of judicial proceedings," making them candidates for reversal under Rule 52.

9. In two companion cases, the California Supreme Court dealt with circumstances of a "lone holdout" juror situation. In People v. Williams, 25 Cal.4th 441, 106 Cal.Rptr.2d 295, 21 P.3d 1209 (2001), a juror refused to follow the court's instructions on the offense of sexual intercourse with a minor because he disagreed with the criminalization of that conduct between an 18 year old boy and his 16 year old girl friend (although the girl contended that it was forced by threats). In People v. Cleveland, 25 Cal.4th 466, 106 Cal.Rptr.2d 313, 21 P.3d 1225 (2001), other jurors claimed that one juror was refusing to deliberate and prejudging the evidence. In both cases the trial judge excused the juror, replaced him with an alternate and a conviction followed.

Under California law, the trial court has discretion to replace a juror for death, illness or other good cause to show the juror's inability to perform his duty. Although acknowledging that the sanctity of deliberations must be protected to the extent possible, allegations of misconduct during deliberations warrant limited inquiry and, if necessary, corrective action.

In Williams, the court viewed the issue as a question of jury nullification and found that a juror who is unwilling to follow the law as articulated in the judge's instructions may be excluded:

Jury nullification is contrary to our idea of equal justice for all and permits both the prosecution's case and the defendant's fate to depend upon the whims of a particular jury, rather than upon the equal application of settled rules of law. . . . "When jurors enter a verdict in contravention of what the law authorizes and requires, they subvert the rule of law and subject citizens—defendants, witnesses, victims, and everyone affected by criminal justice administration—to power based on the subject predilections of twelve individuals. They affect the rule of men, not law." A nullifying jury is essentially a lawless jury.

We reaffirm, therefore, the basic rule that jurors are required to determine the facts and render a verdict in accordance with the court's instructions on the law. A juror who is unable or unwilling to do so is "unable to perform his [or her] duty" as a juror and may be discharged.

In Cleveland, the court found that the record did not reveal a demonstrable reality that the juror refused to deliberate, but only that he viewed the evidence differently:

> A refusal to deliberate consists of a juror's unwillingness to engage in the deliberative process; that is, he or she will not participate in discussions with fellow jurors by listening to their views and by expressing his or her own views. Examples of refusal to deliberate include, but are not limited to, expressing a fixed conclusion at the beginning of deliberations and refusing to consider other points of view, refusing to speak to other jurors, and attempting to separate oneself physically from the remainder of the jury. The circumstance that a juror does not deliberate well or relies upon faulty logic or analysis does not constitute a refusal to deliberate and is not a ground for discharge. Similarly, the circumstance that a juror disagrees with the majority of the jury as to what the evidence shows, or how the law should be applied to the facts or the manner in which deliberations should be conducted does not constitute a refusal to deliberate and is not a ground for discharge. A juror who has participated in deliberations for a reasonable period of time may not be discharged for refusing to deliberate, simply because the juror expresses the belief that further discussion will not alter his or her views.
>
> * * *
>
> [In this case, it is possible that the juror] employed faulty logic and reached an "incorrect" result, but it cannot properly be said that he refused to deliberate. [The juror] participated in deliberations, attempting to explain, however inarticulately, the basis for his conclusion that the evidence was insufficient to prove an attempted robbery, and he listened, even if less than sympathetically, to the contrary views of his fellow jurors.
>
> Under these circumstances, we conclude that the trial court abused its discretion in excusing [the juror]. This error is prejudicial and requires reversal of the judgment.

The federal courts agree that if there is no "substantial possibility" that a juror is basing his or her decision on the sufficiency of the evidence, the deliberating juror may be dismissed. United States v. Abbell, 271 F.3d 1286 (11th Cir.2001).

2. "DEADLOCKED" ("HUNG") JURIES

Lowenfield v. Phelps

Supreme Court of the United States, 1988.
484 U.S. 231, 108 S.Ct. 546.

[Louisiana law, like the law of some other states, provides that if jurors, in the sentencing phase of a capital case, do not unanimously agree upon a sentence of death, the court shall impose a sentence of imprisonment. In other words, under Louisiana law, a "hung jury" on the question of the death penalty does not result in a new sentencing hearing.]

Having earlier found Lowenfield guilty, the jury heard further evidence and arguments as to penalty.

■ MR. JUSTICE REHNQUIST delivered the opinion of the Court.

* * *

[The trial judge's instructions] included the familiar admonition that the jurors should consider the views of others with the objective of reaching a verdict, but that they should not surrender their own honest beliefs in doing so. The court also charged the jury that if it were unable to reach a unanimous recommendation, the court would impose a sentence of life imprisonment without the possibility of probation, parole, or suspension of sentence.

The jury was allowed to retire late in the evening, and reconvene the next day. During the afternoon of that day a note came from the foreman of the jury stating that the jury was unable to reach a decision at that time, and requesting that the court again advise the jury as to its responsibilities. The jury was called back. The court provided a piece of paper to each juror and asked each to write on the paper his or her name and the answer to the question whether "further deliberations would be helpful in obtaining a verdict." The jurors complied, and were asked to retire to the jury room. The papers revealed eight answers in the affirmative—that more deliberation would be helpful—and four in the negative. Defense counsel renewed a previously-made motion for a mistrial, arguing that the jury was obviously hung. The trial court denied the motion, noting that this was the first sign that the jury was having trouble reaching a verdict in the penalty phase. The court directed that as previously agreed upon the jury would return to the courtroom and be instructed again as to its obligations in reaching a verdict.

When the jurors returned to the courtroom a new note from them was given to the judge. This note stated that some of the jurors had misunderstood the question previously asked. The judge polled the jury again using the same method but changing the question slightly; the judge asked, "Do you feel that any further deliberations will enable you to arrive at a verdict?" This time 11 jurors answered in the affirmative and 1 in the negative. The court then reinstructed the jury:

> "Ladies and Gentlemen, as I instructed you earlier if the jury is unable to unanimously agree on a recommendation the Court shall impose the sentence of Life Imprisonment without benefit of Probation, Parole, or Suspension of Sentence.
>
> "When you enter the jury room it is your duty to consult with one another to consider each other's views and to discuss the evidence with the objective of reaching a just verdict if you can do so without violence to that individual judgment.
>
> "Each of you must decide the case for yourself but only after discussion and impartial consideration of the case with your fellow jurors. You are not advocates for one side or the other. Do not hesitate to reexamine your own views and to change your opinion if you are convinced you are wrong but do not surrender your honest belief as to the weight and effect of evidence solely because of the opinion of your fellow jurors or for the mere purpose of returning a verdict."

Defense counsel did not object to either poll, to the manner in which the polls were conducted, or to the supplemental instruction. The jury resumed its deliberations and in 30 minutes returned with a verdict sentencing petitioner to death on all three counts of first-degree murder. In support of all three sentences, the jury found the statutory aggravating circumstance of "knowingly creat[ing] a risk of death or great bodily harm to more than one person." One death sentence was additionally supported by the aggravating circumstance that "the victim was a witness in a prosecution against the defendant. . . ." Art. 905.4(h).

On direct appeal, the Louisiana Supreme Court upheld the convictions and sentences.

* * *

Subsequently petitioner sought habeas corpus from the United States District Court for the Eastern District of Louisiana. * * * The District Court denied relief and a divided panel of the United States Court of Appeals for the Fifth Circuit affirmed. 817 F.2d 285 (C.A.5 1987).

* * *

Our review of petitioner's contention that the jury was improperly coerced requires that we consider the supplemental charge given by the trial court "in its context and under all the circumstances." *Jenkins v. United States* (1965). The use of a supplemental charge has long been sanctioned. Nearly a century ago in *Allen v. United States* (1896), this Court reviewed a charge similar but by no means identical to that given to the Louisiana jury here, and concluded that it was not reversible error even within the federal system. The defendant in that case had been sentenced to death by Judge Parker in the Western District of Arkansas, exercising a jurisdiction unique among federal courts. The judge's charge is not set out verbatim in the opinion of this Court, but it differed from the charge given in the present case in that the *Allen* charge urged the minority to consider the views of the majority, and ask themselves whether their own views were reasonable under the circumstances. This Court upheld the conviction and sentence against the defendant's claim of coercion, saying:

> "The very object of the jury system is to secure unanimity by a comparison of views, and by arguments among the jurors themselves. It certainly cannot be the law that each juror should not listen with deference to the arguments and with a distrust of his own judgment, if he finds a large majority of the jury taking a different view of the case from what he does himself. It cannot be that each juror should go to the jury room with a blind determination that the verdict shall represent his opinion of the case at that moment; or, that he should close his ears to the arguments of men who are equally honest and intelligent as himself."

The continuing validity of this Court's observations in *Allen* are beyond dispute, and they apply with even greater force in a case such as this, where the charge given, in contrast to the so-called "traditional *Allen* charge," does not speak specifically to the minority jurors.[1] But in this case

1. All of the Federal Courts of Appeals have upheld some form of a supplemental jury charge. . . .

one of the purposes served by such a charge—the avoidance of the societal costs of a retrial—is not present because Louisiana law provides that if the jury hangs, the court shall impose a sentence of life imprisonment. Petitioner naturally urges that this difference makes the charge here impermissible under the Due Process Clause and the Eighth Amendment. The difference between the division of function between the jury and judge in this case and the division in *Allen* obviously weighs in the constitutional calculus, but we do not find it dispositive.... Surely if the jury had returned from its deliberations after only one hour and informed the court that it had failed to achieve unanimity on the first ballot, the court would incontestably have had the authority to insist that they deliberate further. This is true even in capital cases such as this one and *Allen*, even though we are naturally mindful in such cases that the "qualitative difference between death and other penalties calls for a greater degree of reliability when the death sentence is imposed." Lockett v. Ohio (1978).

Petitioner relies on this Court's decision in Jenkins v. United States, supra,[2] but we think that case affords him no help. There the jury had sent a note to the judge to the effect that it was unable to agree upon a verdict; the judge then gave additional instructions to the jury, in the course of which he said: " 'You have got to reach a decision in this case.' " This Court concluded that "in its context and under all the circumstances the judge's statement had the coercive effect attributed to it." The difference between the language used there and the language used in the present case is sufficiently obvious to show the fallacy of petitioner's reliance.

Petitioner argues, however, that the coercive effect of the supplemental charge was exacerbated by inquiries made to the jury by the trial court. In *Brasfield v. United States* (1926), the trial court had, after deliberations stalled, inquired as to how the jury was divided, and was informed simply that the jury stood nine to three. The jury resumed deliberations and subsequently found the defendants guilty. This Court concluded that the inquiry into the jury's numerical division necessitated reversal because it was generally coercive and almost always brought to bear "in some degree, serious although not measurable, an improper influence upon the jury." Although the decision in *Brasfield* was an exercise of this Court's supervisory powers,[3] it is nonetheless instructive as to the potential dangers of jury polling.

Petitioner's attempt to fit the instant facts within the holding of *Brasfield* is, however, unavailing. Here the inquiry as to the numerical division of the jury was not as to how they stood on the merits of the verdict, but how they stood on the question of whether further deliberations might assist them in returning a verdict. There is no reason why those who may have been in the minority on the merits would necessarily conclude that further deliberation would not be helpful, or that those in the

2. We note that our ruling in Jenkins v. United States (1965), was based on our supervisory power over the federal courts, and not on constitutional grounds....

3. Our decision in *Brasfield* makes no mention of the Due Process Clause or any other constitutional provision. The Circuit Courts of Appeals have uniformly rejected the notion that *Brasfield's per se* reversal approach must be followed when reviewing state proceedings on habeas corpus....

majority would necessarily conclude otherwise. The two questions are clearly independent of one another. We believe the type of question asked by the trial court in this case is exactly what the Court in *Brasfield* implicitly approved when it stated: "[An inquiry as to numerical division] serves no useful purpose that cannot be attained by questions not requiring the jury to reveal the nature or extent of its division."

We are mindful that the jury returned with its verdict soon after receiving the supplemental instruction, and that this suggests the possibility of coercion. We note, however, that defense counsel did not object to either the polls or the supplemental instruction. We do not suggest that petitioner thereby waived this issue, but we think such an omission indicates that the potential for coercion argued now was not apparent to one on the spot.

We hold that on these facts the combination of the polling of the jury and the supplemental instruction was not "coercive" in such a way as to deny petitioner any constitutional right. By so holding we do not mean to be understood as saying other combinations of supplemental charges and polling might not require a different conclusion. Any criminal defendant, and especially any capital defendant, being tried by a jury is entitled to the uncoerced verdict of that body. For the reasons stated we hold there was no coercion here.

* * *

■ Justice Marshall, with whom Justice Brennan joins, and Justice Stevens joins as to Part I, dissenting.

* * *

The Court's most significant analytical failure, however, lies in its refusal to consider petitioner's charge of coercion in other than a piecemeal fashion. Content that the polling procedures did not contravene *Brasfield* and that the verdict-urging charge satisfied *Allen*, the Court never considers the two practices in tandem. Other federal courts have recognized that an *Allen* charge given on the heels of a jury poll poses special risks of coercion. These courts have noted that when a jury poll is followed by an *Allen* charge, "the impression is inherently conveyed to the jury that the revelation of their division prompted the giving of the subsequent verdict-urging instruction and that it is, therefore, directed toward the minority jurors." *Cornell v. Iowa*, 628 F.2d 1044, 1048 n. 2 (C.A.8 1980). In this case, the charge was given after the polling had pared down the minority to a single juror, identified to the court by name. That juror could not help feeling that the verdict-urging charge was directed at him and him alone. The polling and the charge in this case together created an atmosphere far more charged with coercion than either practice alone possibly could have engendered. Such coercion is strongly evidenced by the fact that the jury returned a verdict of death a mere 30 minutes after the Court gave the verdict-urging charge.[3]

3. The Court argues that the failure of petitioner's counsel to object to the polling or the *Allen* charge suggests that their coercive potential was not "apparent." Ante, at 552. The Court fails to acknowledge, however, that at the time of the polling and charge,

It is an open and a far closer question whether the practices challenged in this case should be deemed coercive in an ordinary criminal context. We have recognized often and reiterated last Term that practices entirely appropriate in other contexts may be improper in capital sentencing proceedings. The Court in this case, however, fails to recognize this principle and makes no attempt to assess how the capital sentencing context affects the legitimacy of the challenged practices. This failure is troubling not only because we require greater reliability in capital sentencings, but also because the nature of the capital sentencing process makes the practices challenged here more dangerous. The capital sentencing jury is asked to make a moral decision about whether a particular individual should live or die. Despite the objective factors that are introduced in an attempt to guide the exercise of the jurors' discretion, theirs is largely a subjective judgment. Given the amorphous and volatile nature of their inquiry, capital sentencing juries that have reached an impasse in their deliberations may be particularly prone to coercion from the court. This concern leads me to conclude that the jury polling and *Allen* charge used in this case created an unacceptable risk of jury coercion and thus were "inconsistent with the reasoned decisionmaking we require in capital cases."

* * *

NOTES

1. The *Allen* or "dynamite" charge to deadlocked juries has been the subject of intensive criticism from both the courts and commentators alike. See United States v. Smith, 635 F.2d 716 (8th Cir.1980) (McMillian, J.) ("It is my opinion, based upon sixteen years of experience as a state trial judge and six years' experience as a state appellate judge, that the Allen charge in all its forms, whether given as part of the original charge or as a supplemental charge, is inherently coercive."); Andrews v. United States, 309 F.2d 127, 129 (5th Cir.1962) (Wisdom, J., dissenting), ("The *Allen* charge causes more trouble in the administration of justice than it is worth.... 'Like Banquo's ghost it will not remain at rest.' "). See United States v. Young, 702 F.2d 133 (8th Cir.1983) (method to determine if the charge is coercive). Note, Deadlocked Juries and the Allen Charge, 37 Me.L.Rev. 167–185 (1985); Allen Instruction in Criminal Cases: Is the Dynamite Charge About to be Permanently Defused?, 43 Mo.L.Rev. 613 (1978). Note, Supplemental Jury Charges Urging a Verdict—The Answer Is Yet To Be Found, 56 Minn.L.Rev. 1199, 1210 (1972); Comment, The Allen Charge: Recurring Problems and Recent Developments, 47 N.Y.U.L.Rev. 296, 315 (1972).

For an extensive discussion and criticism of the *Allen* charge, together with a survey of recent *Allen* charge decisions, see United States v. Rey, 811 F.2d 1453 (11th Cir.1987). There, the court affirmed use of such an instruction because the

defense counsel had already moved three separate times for a mistrial during the sentencing phase: once when the jury had been out for more than five hours, again when the jury sent a note indicating its deadlock, and again after the first polling revealed an 8 to 4 division as to whether further deliberations would be helpful. Defense counsel may well have reasoned that renewing his motions during the second polling or the *Allen* charge would be unavailing. In any case, counsel's repeated mistrial motions clearly demonstrate his awareness of the jury's confusion and distress.

Eleventh Circuit (like many federal circuits) only overrules earlier precedent through en banc decisions. The panel observed, however:

> This instruction can intimidate individual jurors. After hearing this confusing instruction, a juror will likely remember only that the judge wants them to reach a verdict and they should reconsider their opinions. Practically, the pressure to change position will fall most heavily on the minority.

Compare United States v. Rodriguez–Mejia, 20 F.3d 1090 (10th Cir.1994) where the Allen charge was found not to be coercive even though given without evidence of jury deadlock and after only two hours of deliberation. The fact that the jury deliberated for three more hours after the court gave the instruction, recessing for the evening and returning the next morning to continue deliberations was found determinative.

In State v. O'Neil, 261 Conn. 49, 801 A.2d 730 (2002), the court upheld a dynamite charge but adopted a revised version in which jurors are informed not to acquiesce in others' views merely for the sake of arriving at a unanimous verdict.

2. In People v. Pankey, 58 Ill.App.3d 924, 16 Ill.Dec. 339, 374 N.E.2d 1114 (1978), the trial judge read to a deadlocked jury from the "New Judge's Creed" which stated, in part, "I hope I shall have the strength to make the hard decisions and the composure to stick to them." Is this language likely to coerce a verdict?

3. In United States v. Graham, 758 F.2d 879 (3d Cir.1985), the trial court gave a modified *Allen* charged under some unusual circumstances. Earlier in the trial jurors asked that they be dismissed at 4 p.m. on Friday, September 16, in order that Jewish jurors could make it home by sundown to observe Yom Kippur. The judge did not respond to the request. At 11 a.m. on September 16 the jury informed the court that, after seventeen hours of deliberation, it had "no doubt" it would be unable to reach a verdict. The trial court, at defense counsel's request, promised to inform the jury that they would be recessed at 4 p.m. even if they had not reached verdicts. Instead, however, the judge made no mention of this fact in his supplemental deadlocked jury instruction. Defense counsel renewed the request for instructions about the 4 p.m. recess. The court declined, apparently believing he had already told the jury about the recess. The jurors reached a verdict at 3:20 p.m. as to some but not all of the counts on which it had previously declared itself deadlocked. Over a strong dissent, the majority affirmed, noting that the defense had not objected to the supplemental charge itself but only to the absence of reference to the 4 p.m. recess.

* * *

4. May the judge ask a deadlocked jury what its numerical division is? In Brasfield v. United States, 272 U.S. 448, 47 S.Ct. 135 (1926), the court held: "We deem it essential to the fair and impartial conduct of the trial, that the inquiry itself should be regarded as grounds for reversal." See also United States v. Webb, 816 F.2d 1263 (8th Cir.1987) (reversal required when trial court inquired into numerical division, declared a mistrial, withdrew the mistrial order and gave an incomplete *Allen* charge). In Ellis v. Reed, 596 F.2d 1195 (4th Cir.1979), a habeas corpus proceeding arising from a North Carolina trial, the trial judge, upon inquiry, was told that the jury was divided eleven to one. He then gave a modified *Allen* charge; and, eight minutes later, a guilty verdict was returned. The Fourth Circuit majority sustained the verdict, holding that "under the principles of federalism, the decision whether to allow the inquiry is best left to the supervising state court." Judge Winter, dissenting, found the *Brasfield* rule constitutionally mandated, and, therefore, applicable to the states. See also United States ex rel. Kirk v. Director, Dept. of Corrections, 678 F.2d 723 (7th Cir.1982) (*Brasfield* rule prohibiting inquiry into numerical division of deliberating jurors is not of federal constitutional dimension, so that states remain free to permit such inquiries); State v. Fowler, 312 N.C. 304, 322 S.E.2d 389 (1984) (*Brasfield* rule not followed in North Carolina).

5. In United States v. Ianniello, 866 F.2d 540 (2d Cir.1989), certain jurors claimed that, a week into deliberations, after a thirteen month trial, a federal district judge entered the jury room, out of the presence of the parties, and told the jurors she wanted a verdict one way or the other and did not want a hung jury. Somewhat incredulous that a federal judge would do such a thing, the reviewing court ordered a hearing to determine whether such judicial misconduct had occurred and, if so, whether the error might be deemed harmless. Presumably the judge who would conduct a hearing would try to assess the impact of the trial judge's statements upon the jurors' deliberations.

3. Inconsistent Verdicts

United States v. Powell

Supreme Court of the United States, 1984.
469 U.S. 57, 105 S.Ct. 471.

■ JUSTICE REHNQUIST delivered the opinion of the Court.

In Dunn v. United States (1932), this Court held that a criminal defendant convicted by a jury on one count could not attack that conviction because it was inconsistent with the jury's verdict of acquittal on another count. We granted certiorari in this case to determine whether the Court of Appeals for the Ninth Circuit correctly enunciated an exception to Dunn when it overturned respondent's convictions.

In 1982, respondent Betty Lou Powell's husband, Ron Powell, aided by his 17–year–old son Jeff and others, was operating a lucrative cocaine and methaqualone distributorship from the Powell home near San Diego, Cal. Federal authorities tapped the Powell's telephone pursuant to a court order, and many conversations were recorded, including at least four which indicated that respondent was playing a minor role in the drug distributorship. Three of these conversations indicated that respondent was helping her husband and son to distribute drugs and to collect money owed for drugs sold. The fourth involved a conversation with a travel agent in which respondent booked an airline ticket for her husband in an assumed name. In April 1982, Ron Powell learned of the wiretap and notified his son, who called respondent and told her to leave home and drive to Los Angeles. Respondent was followed by FBI agents, who after some difficulty managed to stop respondent and arrest her. A search of the car uncovered, inter alia, 2 kilograms of cocaine, 2,700 methaqualone tablets, a pistol, a machine gun, 2 silencers, and $30,000 cash.

Respondent was indicted by a grand jury [on a multicount indictment. To the extent relevant,] Count 1 ... charged respondent with conspiring with her husband and 17–year–old son, and others, "to knowingly and intentionally possess with intent to distribute cocaine." Four of the "overt acts" listed in support of this conspiracy were the above-mentioned telephone conversations. Count 9 charged respondent with possession of a specific quantity of cocaine with intent to distribute it. The jury acquitted respondent of Counts 1 and 9. Counts 3, 4, 5 and 6 charged respondent with the compound offenses of using the telephone in "committing and in causing and facilitating" certain felonies—"conspiracy to possess with intent to distribute and possession with intent to distribute cocaine". The jury convicted her of Counts 3, 4, and 5, and acquitted her of Count 6.

On appeal respondent argued that the verdicts were inconsistent, and that she therefore was entitled to reversal of the telephone facilitation convictions. She contended that proof that she had conspired to possess cocaine with intent to distribute, or had so possessed cocaine, was an element of each of the telephone facilitation counts; since she had been acquitted of these offenses in Counts 1 and 9, respondent argued that the telephone facilitation convictions were not consistent with those acquittals. The United States Court of Appeals for the Ninth Circuit agreed.

* * *

The defendant in Dunn was tried pursuant to a three-count indictment charging violations of the federal liquor laws. The first count alleged that the defendant had maintained a common nuisance by keeping intoxicating liquor for sale at a specified place; the second and third counts charged unlawful possession, and unlawful sale, of such liquor. The jury convicted defendant of the first count and acquitted him of the second and third. On review, this Court rejected the claim that the defendant was entitled to discharge because the verdicts were inconsistent. Speaking through Justice Holmes, the Court stated:

> "Consistency in the verdict is not necessary. Each count in an indictment is regarded as if it was a separate indictment. If separate indictments had been presented against the defendant for possession and for maintenance of a nuisance, and had been separately tried, the same evidence being offered in support of each, an acquittal on one could not be pleaded as res judicata of the other. Where the offenses are separately charged in the counts of a single indictment the same rule must hold. As was said in Steckler v. United States, 7 F.2d 59, 60:
>
> " 'The most that can be said in such cases is that the verdict shows that either in the acquittal or the conviction the jury did not speak their real conclusions, but that does not show that they were not convinced of the defendant's guilt. We interpret the acquittal as no more than their assumption of a power which they had no right to exercise, but to which they were disposed through lenity.' "

Fifty-three years later most of what Justice Holmes so succinctly stated retains its force. Indeed, although not expressly reaffirming Dunn this Court has on numerous occasions alluded to its rule as an established principle. ... This Court noted [in 1981 its cases] establish "the unreviewable power of a jury to return a verdict of not guilty for impermissible reasons."

These decisions indicate that this is not a case where a once-established principle has gradually been eroded by subsequent opinions of this Court. Nevertheless, recent decisions in the Courts of Appeals have begun to carve exceptions out of the Dunn rule. ... In addition to evidencing a general displeasure with allowing inconsistent verdicts to stand under some circumstances, these courts have distinguished Dunn on the ground that, where the predicate felony count and the telephone facilitation count are each submitted to the jury, the counts are "interdependent" and each count cannot be regarded as "as if it [were] a separate indictment."

In so stating, these courts may be attempting to distinguish Dunn on its facts, or they may mean to take issue with Dunn's statement that "[i]f separate indictments had been presented against the defendant . . . and had been separately tried . . . an acquittal on one could not be pleaded as res judicata of the other." The latter statement, if not incorrect at the time, . . . can no longer be accepted in light of cases . . . which hold that the doctrine of collateral estoppel would apply under those circumstances. Respondent argues that this defect in Dunn's rationale precludes the rule's application in this case; indeed, respondent urges that principles of res judicata or collateral estoppel should apply to verdicts rendered by a single jury, to preclude acceptance of a guilty verdict on a telephone facilitation count where the jury acquits the defendant of the predicate felony.

We believe that the Dunn rule rests on a sound rationale that is independent of its theories of res judicata, and that it therefore survives an attack based upon its presently erroneous reliance on such theories. As the Dunn Court noted, where truly inconsistent verdicts have been reached, "[t]he most that can be said . . . is that the verdict shows that either in the acquittal or the conviction the jury did not speak their real conclusions, but that does not show that they were not convinced of the defendant's guilt." The rule that the defendant may not upset such a verdict embodies a prudent acknowledgement of a number of factors. First, as the above quote suggests, inconsistent verdicts—even verdicts that acquit on a predicate offense while convicting on the compound offense—should not necessarily be interpreted as a windfall to the Government at the defendant's expense. It is equally possible that the jury, convinced of guilt, properly reached its conclusion on the compound offense, and then through mistake, compromise, or lenity, arrived at an inconsistent conclusion on the lesser offense. But in such situations the Government has no recourse if it wishes to correct the jury's error; the Government is precluded from appealing or otherwise upsetting such an acquittal by the Constitution's Double Jeopardy Clause.

Inconsistent verdicts therefore present a situation where "error," in the sense that the jury has not followed the court's instructions, most certainly has occurred, but it is unclear whose ox has been gored. Given this uncertainty, and the fact that the Government is precluded from challenging the acquittal, it is hardly satisfactory to allow the defendant to receive a new trial on the conviction as a matter of course. Nothing in the Constitution would require such a protection, and we therefore address the problem only under our supervisory powers over the federal criminal process. For us, the possibility that the inconsistent verdicts may favor the criminal defendant as well as the Government militates against review of such convictions at the defendant's behest. This possibility is a premise of Dunn's alternative rationale—that such inconsistencies often are a product of jury lenity. Thus, Dunn has been explained by both courts and commentators as a recognition of the jury's historic function, in criminal trials, as a check against arbitrary or oppressive exercises of power by the Executive Branch.

The burden of the exercise of lenity falls only on the Government, and it has been suggested that such an alternative should be available for the difficult cases where the jury wishes to avoid an all-or-nothing verdict. Such an act is, as the Dunn Court recognized, an "assumption of a power which [the jury has] no right to exercise," but the illegality alone does not mean that such a collective judgment should be subject to review. The fact that the inconsistency may be the result of lenity, coupled with the Government's inability to invoke review, suggests that inconsistent verdicts should not be reviewable.

We also reject, as imprudent and unworkable, a rule that would allow criminal defendants to challenge inconsistent verdicts on the ground that in their case the verdict was not the product of lenity, but of some error that worked against them. Such an individualized assessment of the reason for the inconsistency would be based either on pure speculation, or would require inquiries into the jury's deliberations that courts generally will not undertake. Jurors, of course, take an oath to follow the law as charged, and they are expected to follow it. To this end trials generally begin with voir dire, by judge or counsel, seeking to identify those jurors who for whatever reason may be unwilling or unable to follow the law and render an impartial verdict on the facts and the evidence. But with few exceptions, once the jury has heard the evidence and the case has been submitted, the litigants must accept the jury's collective judgment. Courts have always resisted inquiring into a jury's thought processes; through this deference the jury brings to the criminal process, in addition to the collective judgment of the community, an element of needed finality.

Finally, we note that a criminal defendant already is afforded protection against jury irrationality or error by the independent review of the sufficiency of the evidence undertaken by the trial and appellate courts. This review should not be confused with the problems caused by inconsistent verdicts. Sufficiency of the evidence review involves assessment by the courts of whether the evidence adduced at trial could support any rational determination of guilt beyond a reasonable doubt. This review should be independent of the jury's determination that evidence on another count was insufficient. The Government must convince the jury with its proof, and must also satisfy the courts that given this proof the jury could rationally have reached a verdict of guilt beyond a reasonable doubt. We do not believe that further safeguards against jury irrationality are necessary.

Respondent contends, nevertheless, that an exception to the Dunn rule should be made where the jury acquits a defendant of a predicate felony, but convicts on the compound felony. Such an "exception" falls almost of its own weight. First, the acceptability of this exception is belied by the facts of Dunn itself. In Dunn, the defendant was acquitted of unlawful possession, and unlawful sale, of liquor, but was convicted of maintaining a nuisance by keeping unlawful liquor for sale at a specified place. The same evidence was adduced for all three counts, and Justice Butler's dissent persuasively points out that the jury could not have convicted on the nuisance count without finding that the defendant possessed, or sold, intoxicating liquor. Respondent's exception therefore threatens to swallow the rule.

Second, respondent's argument that an acquittal on a predicate offense necessitates a finding of insufficient evidence on a compound felony count simply misunderstands the nature of the inconsistent verdict problem. Whether presented as an insufficient evidence argument, or as an argument that the acquittal on the predicate offense should collaterally estop the Government on the compound offense, the argument necessarily assumes that the acquittal on the predicate offense was proper—the one the jury "really meant." This, of course, is not necessarily correct; all we know is that the verdicts are inconsistent. The Government could just as easily—and erroneously—argue that since the jury convicted on the compound offense the evidence on the predicate offense must have been sufficient. The problem is that the same jury reached inconsistent results; once that is established principles of collateral estoppel—which are predicated on the assumption that the jury acted rationally and found certain facts in reaching its verdict—are no longer useful.

This problem is not altered when the trial judge instructs the jury that it must find the defendant guilty of the predicate offense to convict on the compound offense. Although such an instruction might indicate that the counts are no longer independent, if inconsistent verdicts are nevertheless reached those verdicts still are likely to be the result of mistake, or lenity, and therefore are subject to the Dunn rationale. Given this impasse, the factors detailed above—the Government's inability to invoke review, the general reluctance to inquire into the workings of the jury, and the possible exercise of lenity—suggest that the best course to take is simply to insulate jury verdicts from review on this ground.

* * *

The rule established in Dunn v. United States has stood without exception in this Court for 53 years. If it is to remain that way, and we think it should, the judgment of the Court of Appeals must be reversed.

NOTES

1. In Harris v. Rivera, 454 U.S. 339, 102 S.Ct. 460 (1981), the Court held that inconsistent verdicts in a bench trial were not proper grounds for habeas corpus relief:

> Although [our cases] preclude a holding that inconsistency in a verdict is intolerable in itself, inconsistency nevertheless might constitute evidence of arbitrariness that would undermine confidence in the quality of the judge's conclusion. In this case, the Court of Appeals suggested the possibility that the trial judge might have relied on impermissible considerations such as the fact that neither respondent nor his wife testified, or knowledge of adverse information not contained in the record. Undeniably, these possibilities exist, but they also would have existed if Robinson had been convicted or if he had been tried separately. . . . We are not persuaded that an apparent inconsistency in a trial judge's verdict gives rise to an inference of irregularity in his finding of guilt that is sufficiently strong to

overcome the well-established presumption that the judge adhered to basic rules of procedure.

Other explanations for an apparent inconsistency are far more likely. Most apparent is the likelihood that the judge's actual observation of everything that transpired in the courtroom created some doubt about the guilt of one defendant that he might or might not be able to articulate in a convincing manner. In this case, if the judge was convinced beyond a reasonable doubt that respondent and his wife were both guilty, it would be most unfortunate if a concern about the plausibility of a lingering doubt about Robinson should cause him to decide to convict all three rather than to try to articulate the basis for his doubt.

It is also possible that the judge may have made an error of law and erroneously assumed, for example, that Robinson should not be found guilty without evidence that he was to share in the proceeds of the larceny. There is no reason—and surely no constitutional requirement—that such an error pertaining to the case against Robinson should redound to the benefit of respondent.

Even the unlikely possibility that the acquittal is the product of a lenity that judges are free to exercise at the time of sentencing but generally are forbidden to exercise when ruling on guilt or innocence, would not create a constitutional violation. We are aware of nothing in the Federal Constitution that would prevent a State from empowering its judges to render verdicts of acquittal whenever they are convinced that no sentence should be imposed for reasons that are unrelated to guilt or innocence. The Constitution does not prohibit state judges from being excessively lenient.

2. In conspiracy cases, some courts had imposed a "rule of consistency" prohibiting the conviction of one defendant if all of his coconspirators were acquitted on the theory that he could not have had anyone with whom to conspire. See United States v. Morales, 677 F.2d 1 (1st Cir.1982). That rule has now been abandoned in light of *Powell*. See United States v. Bucuvalas, 909 F.2d 593 (1st Cir.1990); State v. Johnson, 367 Md. 418, 788 A.2d 628 (2002) (rule of consistency inapplicable to separate trials of coconspirators).

In a related vein, a general guilty verdict on a multi-object conspiracy charge is sufficient to sustain a conviction even if the evidence fails to support a conviction on one of the objects. Griffin v. United States, 502 U.S. 46, 112 S.Ct. 466 (1991).

3. For other interesting applications of the rule in *Powell*, see United States v. Scurlock, 52 F.3d 531 (5th Cir.1995) (although elements of mail fraud scheme and conspiracy are the same, acquittal of conspiracy charge did not require reversal of mail fraud conviction); United States v. Liebo, 923 F.2d 1308 (8th Cir.1991) (reviewing court could consider evidence admitted on counts on which defendant was acquitted to determine sufficiency of evidence on the one count on which he was convicted); United States v. Williams, 923 F.2d 115 (8th Cir.1991) (acquittal of conspiracy did not prohibit conviction on substantive count even though sole defense was entrapment); United States v. Clemmer, 918 F.2d 570 (6th Cir.1990) (trial judge erred in granting post trial motion for acquittal based on conclusion that not guilty finding on bribery charge precluded conviction for failing to pay tax of funds).

4. For a criticism of the courts' approach to inconsistent verdicts and a suggestion of how to heed the red flags that they raise, see Muller, The Hobgoblin of Little Minds? Our Foolish Law on Inconsistent Verdicts, 111 Harv.L.Rev. 771 (1998).

5. The ancient practice of "polling the jury", carried over from the common law, exists to determine "before it is too late, whether the jury's verdict reflects the conscience of each of the jurors or whether it was brought about through the coercion or domination of one of them by some of his fellow jurors or resulted from sheer physical or mental exhaustion of a juror." Commonwealth v. Martin, 379 Pa. 587, 593, 109 A.2d 325, 328 (1954). After the verdict is read, each juror is asked if that verdict "was then and is now" his verdict.

6. In virtually all jurisdictions, either by statute or decision, the jury must be polled upon the defendant's request. See Fed.R.Crim.P. 31(d); N.Y.Code Crim.P. § 450; Ohio Rev.Code Ann. § 2945.77. However, in some states, notably Connecticut and Rhode Island, a poll is not mandatory, but rests within the discretion of the trial judge. Under what circumstances should a judge be permitted to deny a request to poll the jury? While, in the majority of jurisdictions, the court may conduct a poll *sua sponte*, it is never a requirement absent a specific request. The right to poll is waived if it is not exercised before the jury has "dispersed" and come into contact with outside elements. Compare Miranda v. United States, 255 F.2d 9 (1st Cir.1958).

7. The court or the clerk, not counsel, conducts the poll; and jurors are not to be asked for the reasons underlying their verdict. State v. Bounds, 74 Idaho 136, 258 P.2d 751 (1953); State v. Brown, 110 Ohio App. 57, 168 N.E.2d 419 (1953). If counsel consents to a sealed verdict, does he automatically waive the right to have the jury polled? Compare Vaughan v. State, 9 Ga.App. 613, 71 S.E. 945 (1911) (yes) with State v. Callahan, 55 Iowa 364, 7 N.W. 603 (1880) (no).

8. If a juror during the course of polling indicates that he does not subscribe to the verdict, must the court declare a mistrial or can it direct the jury to retire to continue deliberations? Some statutes compel the court to order continued deliberations while others give the trial judge discretion to do either. Which form of statutory language is preferable? One case State v. Gullette, 3 Conn.Cir. 153, 209 A.2d 529 (1964), has indicated, by way of dictum, that a mistrial must be declared.

9. In the federal courts, the trial judge has discretion to discharge the jury or send them back for further deliberations when the poll shows a lack of unanimity. Fed.R.Crim.P. 31(d). See United States v. Rastelli, 870 F.2d 822 (2d Cir.1989) (when the foreman registers confusion over the verdict when delivering it, no polling is warranted and jury must be sent back to deliberate); United States v. Williams, 873 F.2d 1102 (8th Cir.1989) (further deliberations ordered when one juror expressed view that each offense had not been proven beyond a reasonable doubt); United States v. Freedson, 608 F.2d 739 (9th Cir.1979). In response to the poll, one juror responded weeping "I voted yes to man, but no to God" and that she wished to say not guilty. On appeal, the court held that the trial judge was within the bounds of discretion in directing further deliberations since the court could well have concluded that further deliberations might clarify the undecided juror's state of mind and produce either clear argument or clear disagreement.

10. Do double jeopardy implications flow from a poll requested by the prosecution following an acquittal? See United States v. Chinchic, 655 F.2d 547, 548 (4th Cir.1981) (defendant was not "acquitted" at a first trial and retrial was not barred by double jeopardy concerns, where, following announcement of an acquittal verdict in the first trial, one juror changed his or her mind and a deadlock was declared.)

11. The trial court may not attempt to coerce an assenting vote from a juror. See United States v. Nelson, 692 F.2d 83 (9th Cir.1982):

> Nothing in the rule permits the judge to ask the juror why he or she does not concur. Indeed such questioning would constitute an "undue intrusion" into the "exclusive province" of the jury.

When the lack of unanimity is established by any juror's response, does continued polling constitute reversible error because it amounts to inquiry into the jury's numerical division and can be viewed as coercive? Compare United States v. Fiorilla, 850 F.2d 172 (3d Cir.1988), with United States v. Spitz, 696 F.2d 916 (11th Cir.1983).

12. In United States v. Varela–Andujo, 746 F.2d 1046 (5th Cir.1984), defense counsel received a call from a juror after the trial indicating that the guilty verdict was not truly his own. The denial of a motion for a new trial was upheld on appeal on the ground that the evidence did not support a claim that the jury engaged in any misconduct or based its verdict on matters outside the record or other improper considerations. The court noted that only where there is a showing of illegal or prejudicial intrusion into the jury process will the court sanction an inquiry.

4. IMPEACHMENT OF VERDICTS

Smith v. Phillips

United States Supreme Court, 1982.
455 U.S. 209, 102 S.Ct. 940.

■ JUSTICE REHNQUIST delivered the opinion of the Court.

[After being convicted of murder at a jury trial in a New York court, respondent moved to vacate his conviction on the ground that a juror in his case submitted during the trial an application for employment as an investigator in the District Attorney's Office. At a hearing on the motion before the same judge who had presided at the trial, the motion was denied, the judge finding "beyond a reasonable doubt" that the events giving rise to the motion did not influence the verdict. After his conviction was upheld by the state courts, respondent sought Federal habeas corpus relief. While finding insufficient evidence to demonstrate that the juror was actually biased, the District Court nevertheless imputed bias to him and, accordingly, ordered respondent released unless the State granted him a new trial. The decision was affirmed by the Second Circuit.]

* * *

This Court has long held that the remedy for allegations of juror partiality is a hearing in which the defendant has the opportunity to prove actual bias. For example, in Remmer v. United States, 347 U.S. 227, 74 S.Ct. 450 (1954), a juror in a federal criminal trial was approached by someone offering money in exchange for a favorable verdict. An FBI agent was assigned to investigate the attempted bribe, and the agent's report was reviewed by the trial judge and the prosecutor without disclosure to defense counsel. When they learned of the incident after trial, the defense attorneys moved that the verdict be vacated, alleging that "they would have moved for a mistrial and requested that the juror in question be replaced by an alternate juror" had the incident been disclosed to them during trial.

This Court recognized the seriousness not only of the attempted bribe, which it characterized as "presumptively prejudicial," but also of the undisclosed investigation, which was "bound to impress the juror and [was] very apt to do so unduly." Despite this recognition, and a conviction that "[t]he integrity of jury proceedings must not be jeopardized by unauthorized invasions," ibid., the Court did not require a new trial like that ordered in this case. Rather, the Court instructed the trial judge to "determine the circumstances, the impact thereof upon the juror, and whether or not [they were] prejudicial, in a *hearing* with all interested parties permitted to participate."

Even before the decision in Remmer, this Court confronted allegations of implied juror bias in Dennis v. United States, 339 U.S. 162, 70 S.Ct. 519 (1950). Dennis was convicted of criminal contempt for failure to appear before the Committee on Un–American Activities of the House of Representatives. He argued that the jury which convicted him, composed primarily of employees of the United States Government, was inherently biased because such employees were subject to ... discharge upon reasonable grounds for belief that they were disloyal to the Government. Dennis contended that such employees would not risk the charge of disloyalty or the termination of their employment which might result from a vote for acquittal. The Court rejected this claim of implied bias, noting that Dennis was "free to show the existence of actual bias" but had failed to do so. The Court thus concluded: "A holding of implied bias to disqualify jurors because of their relationship with the Government is no longer permissible. ... Preservation of the opportunity to prove actual bias is a guarantee of a defendant's right to an impartial jury."

* * *

These cases demonstrate that due process does not require a new trial every time a juror has been placed in a potentially compromising situation. Were that the rule, few trials would be constitutionally acceptable. The safeguards of juror impartiality, such as voir dire and protective instructions from the trial judge, are not infallible; it is virtually impossible to shield jurors from every contact or influence that might theoretically affect their vote. Due process means a jury capable and willing to decide the case solely on the evidence before it, and a trial judge ever watchful to prevent prejudicial occurrences and to determine the effect of such occurrences when they happen. Such determinations may properly be made at a hearing like that ordered in Remmer and held in this case.*

The District Court and the Court of Appeals disregarded this doctrine: they held that a post-trial hearing comporting with our decisions in Remmer and other cases prosecuted in the *federal* courts was constitutionally insufficient in a state court under the Due Process Clause of the Fourteenth Amendment. It seems to us to follow "as the night the day" that if in the federal system a post-trial hearing such as that conducted here is sufficient to decide allegations of juror partiality, the Due Process Clause of the Fourteenth Amendment cannot possibly require more of a state court system.

* * *

* Respondent correctly notes that determinations made in Remmer-type hearings will frequently turn upon testimony of the juror in question, but errs in contending that such evidence is inherently suspect. As we said in Dennis, "[o]ne may not know or altogether understand the imponderables which cause one to think what he thinks, but surely one who is trying as an honest man to live up to the sanctity of his oath is well qualified to say whether he has an unbiased mind in a certain matter."

A federally issued writ of habeas corpus, of course, reaches only convictions obtained in violation of some provision of the United States Constitution. . . . Absent such a constitutional violation, it was error for the lower courts in this case to order a new trial. . . . Federal courts hold no supervisory authority over state judicial proceedings and may intervene only to correct wrongs of constitutional dimension. No such wrongs occurred here. Accordingly, the judgment of the Court of Appeals is reversed.

■ JUSTICE O'CONNOR, concurring.

I concur in the Court's opinion, but write separately to express my view that the opinion does not foreclose the use of "implied bias" in appropriate circumstances.

Determining whether a juror is biased or has prejudged a case is difficult, partly because the juror may have an interest in concealing his own bias and partly because the juror may be unaware of it. The problem may be compounded when a charge of bias arises from juror misconduct, and not simply from attempts of third parties to influence a juror.

Nevertheless, I believe that in most instances a postconviction hearing will be adequate to determine whether a juror is biased. A hearing permits counsel to probe the juror's memory, his reasons for acting as he did, and his understanding of the consequences of his actions. A hearing also permits the trial judge to observe the juror's demeanor under cross-examination and to evaluate his answers in light of the particular circumstances of the case.

I am concerned, however, that in certain instances a hearing may be inadequate for uncovering a juror's biases, leaving serious question whether the trial court had subjected the defendant to manifestly unjust procedures resulting in a miscarriage of justice. While each case must turn on its own facts, there are some extreme situations that would justify a finding of implied bias. Some examples might include a revelation that the juror is an actual employee of the prosecuting agency, that the juror is a close relative of one of the participants in the trial or the criminal transaction, or that the juror was a witness or somehow involved in the criminal transaction. Whether or not the state proceedings result in a finding of "no bias," the Sixth Amendment right to an impartial jury should not allow a verdict to stand under such circumstances.

* * *

Because there may be circumstances in which a postconviction hearing will not be adequate to remedy a charge of juror bias, it is important for the Court to retain the doctrine of implied bias to preserve Sixth Amendment rights. I read the Court's opinion as not foreclosing the use of implied bias in appropriate situations, and, therefore, I concur.

■ JUSTICE MARSHALL, with whom JUSTICE BRENNAN and JUSTICE STEVENS join, dissenting.

* * *

When a juror vigorously and actively pursues employment in the prosecutor's office throughout the course of a trial, the probability of bias is substantial. This bias may be conscious, part of a calculated effort to obtain a job. The juror may believe that his application will be viewed favorably if the defendant is found guilty. Thus, he may decide to vote for a verdict of guilty regardless of the evidence, and he may attempt to persuade the other jurors that acquittal is not justified. There is also a very serious danger of unconscious bias. Only individuals of extraordinary character would not be affected in some way by their interest in future employment. Subconsciously, the juror may tend to favor the prosecutor simply because he feels some affinity with his potential employer. Indeed, the juror may make a sincere effort to remain impartial, and yet be unable to do so.

Not only is the probability of bias high, it is also unlikely that a post-trial evidentiary hearing would reveal this bias.

* * *

I believe that in cases like this one, where the probability of bias is very high, and where the evidence adduced at a hearing can offer little assurance that prejudice does not exist, the juror should be deemed biased as a matter of law. Specifically, where a juror pursues employment with the office of the prosecutor, under circumstances highly suggestive of misconduct or conflict of interest, bias should be "implied," and he should be automatically disqualified, despite the absence of proof of actual bias. If the juror's efforts to secure employment are not revealed until after the trial, the conviction must be set aside. The right to a trial by an impartial jury is too important, and the threat to that right too great, to justify rigid insistence on actual proof of bias. Such a requirement blinks reality.

Adoption of a conclusive presumption of bias in these limited circumstances would not be without precedent; such presumptions of juror bias have ancient historical roots. . . .

* * *

The States also employ rules of implied bias. Most jurisdictions have statutes that set forth conduct or status that will automatically disqualify prospective jurors, without regard to whether that person is actually biased. These statutes frequently exclude persons related to the prosecution, defense counsel, a witness, or the defendant.

* * *

Of course, the fact that many States employ rules of implied bias in situations similar to those presented here does not necessarily imply that such rules are constitutionally mandated. The widespread state practice does, however, support that conclusion. The States would not adopt such rules at the expense of their strong interest in efficiently procuring convictions if they were not committed to safeguarding the right to trial by an impartial jury, and if they did not believe that this right was seriously threatened.

* * *

The majority adopts a completely unrealistic view of the efficacy of a post-trial hearing, and thus fails to accord any meaningful protection to the right to an impartial jury, one of the most valuable rights possessed by criminal defendants. I would affirm the judgment of the Court of Appeals on the ground that a juror who applies for employment with the office of the prosecutor and vigorously pursues that employment throughout the course of the trial is impliedly biased.

* * *

If due process really does mean a full and fair opportunity to be tried by an unbiased jury, "capable and willing to decide the case solely on the evidence"—then in this case, due process has been denied.

NOTES

1. In Tanner v. United States, 483 U.S. 107, 107 S.Ct. 2739 (1987), the Court interpreted Fed. R.Evi. 606(b) to forbid attacks on jury verdicts through the use of the affidavits or testimony by jurors to the effect that jurors had been drinking during the course of the proceedings and that some had slept through parts of the testimony. The Court did not prohibit proof of such juror misconduct, under certain circumstances, from voiding a juror verdict. It held, however, that jurors were disqualified from giving such testimony because this amounted to the use of juror testimony as to the course of the jury's deliberations. It added that jurors were free to report to the court before verdict whatever conduct of their fellow jurors that they deemed improper. The dissenters construed the federal rule more narrowly, so that it would prohibit jury testimony about the substance of what fellow jurors had said during the course of the deliberation, but not about their use of alcohol or about their sleeping during the course of the trial.

2. The challenged conduct must relate to extraneous factors and not arise out of the contact between jurors. Thus, attempts to impeach the verdict in the following cases were rejected because they did not involve outside influence. See United States v. Marrero, 904 F.2d 251 (5th Cir.1990) (two regretful jurors asserted that some fellow jurors had told them that they had to vote with the majority no matter how they personally believed); United States v. Bassler, 651 F.2d 600 (8th Cir.1981) (one juror, contrary to judge's instructions, summarized testimony in notes following each trial day); United States v. Edwards, 696 F.2d 1277 (11th Cir.1983) (excused alternate juror indicated that, contrary to instructions, jurors discussed case during trial); United States v. Vannelli, 595 F.2d 402 (8th Cir.1979) (juror sent note to judge indicating that she had made wrong decision); United States v. Dioguardi, 492 F.2d 70 (2d Cir.1974) (juror sent letter to defendant claiming clairvoyance).

3. In Dickson v. Sullivan, 849 F.2d 403 (9th Cir.1988), a murder case, the deputy sheriff responsible for escorting the jurors to and from the courtroom made a statement to two jurors indicating that defendant "had done something like this before." In ordering a new trial on federal habeas corpus, the court held:

> A defendant is entitled to a new trial when the jury obtains or uses evidence that has not been introduced during trial if there is "a reasonable possibility that the extrinsic material *could* have affected the verdict."

* * *

When a jury is exposed to facts that have not been introduced into evidence, a defendant has effectively lost the rights of confrontation, cross-examination, and the assistance of counsel with regard to the extraneous information. In the present case, both parties agree that the exposure of the two jurors to the deputy sheriff's remarks violated Dickson's constitutional rights. The parties disagree, however, about whether the state met its burden of proving that the constitutional error was harmless beyond a reasonable doubt.

* * *

In the case before us ... it is clear that the deputy's comment was both directly related to a material issue in the case and highly inflammatory. There is a direct and rational connection between the statement that Dickson had "done something like this before" and the conclusion that Dickson had done "this" again.... Although we ordinarily assume that instructing the jury to disregard extraneous evidence sufficiently ensures that inadmissible evidence will not influence the jury, ... where the extrajudicial statement concerns a defendant's prior criminal acts, the efficacy of such instructions is subject to serious doubt.

Compare United States v. Zelinka, 862 F.2d 92 (6th Cir.1988) (burden is on defendant to demonstrate that statement to juror disclosed actual bias rather than on prosecution to show that contact was harmless).

4. In order to avoid impeachment of verdict problems, may the court order the jurors not to communicate with the media following return of their verdict? See Note, Public Disclosures of Jury Deliberations, 96 Harv.L.Rev. 886 (1983). In United States v. Sherman, 581 F.2d 1358 (9th Cir.1978), following a controversial bank robbery trial, the trial judge forbade the jurors from discussing the case with anyone, and ordered everyone, including the news media, to stay away from the jurors. On a petition for mandamus filed by the *Seattle Times*, the court held that the order operated as a restraint on the media which could not be justified by competing interests. Accordingly, it found that the order, "by depriving the media the opportunity to ask the jurors if they wished to be interviewed, was clearly erroneous as a matter of law." However, the trial judge does have the authority to control abuses of the interviewing process, particularly when the ethical conduct of attorney is implicated. Compare United States v. Moten, 582 F.2d 654 (2d Cir.1978) ("[I]n order to insure that jurors are protected from harassment, a district judge has the power, and sometimes the duty, to order that all post-trial investigation of jurors shall be under his supervision.")

CHAPTER 21

SENTENCING

A. INTRODUCTION

Traditional penalties for crime included execution, exile, fines, indentured servitude, whipping, branding, public stocks and public apologies. Jail in the colonial period and early days of the nation had been reserved primarily for civil debtors, political prisoners and persons awaiting trial. When legislatures provided for terms of imprisonment as penalties for crime, this was a significant change. See Adam Hirsch, The Rise of the Penitentiary (1992); The Oxford History of the Prison: The Practice of Punishment in Western Society (Morris & Rothman, eds. 1998).

The early sentencing laws imposed specific terms for specific offenses. With the rise of the social sciences and the rehabilitative ideal at the turn of this century, this method was attacked as excessively rigid, and eventually legislatures began to set more expansive ranges within which sentence was to be imposed—some of the most serious offenses might carry terms of zero years to, say, twenty years or life. Judges would and did exercise unlimited discretion within these broad ranges, imposing a sentence that reflected the judge's prediction about the likelihood that the offender could be rehabilitated. Sentences could be shortened by parole boards, who reevaluated a prisoner's rehabilitative progress periodically. See generally United States v. Grayson, 438 U.S. 41, 98 S.Ct. 2610 (1978).

The excessive rigidity of the early law was repaired, but the repair work came under criticism. Over the years judges exercised the discretion given them and it became clear that essentially similar cases were being treated quite differently within a single jurisdiction, within a single courthouse and even within a single courtroom. These differences could be attributed in theory to differences in the defendants, but this theory was not proven (and, even if true, may be unprovable). Even more sinister were racial and ethnic disparities in sentences given for similar crimes. There came to be a consensus that the differences were not so much due to a difference in defendants as they were to differences in judges; judges were "hard", "soft", "harsh", "lenient", "stern", "forgiving", "average", "somewhere in the middle", and, worst of all, "erratic." This state of affairs was attacked as "lawless." See Frankel, Lawlessness In Sentencing, 41 Cincinnati L.Rev. 1 (1972).

Legislatures reacted by narrowing the range of discretion given judges and by abolishing parole. New laws set mandatory minimums. Several jurisdictions, notably California and Minnesota, adopted systems which required sentences to be imposed within a narrow range determined by the mechanical application of rules assigning weight (often numerical in nature) to the offense of conviction, aggravating and mitigating factors, and prior criminal history. See Schulhofer, Due Process of Sentencing, 128 U.Pa.L.Rev 733 (1980); Frase, Sentencing Reform in Minnesota, 75 Minn. L.Rev. 727 (1991). The United States Congress enacted the Sentencing Reform Act of 1984 which resulted in sentences specified by offense levels and prior criminal history, each calculated by specific and elaborate methods. An initial challenge to the guidelines on separation of powers and impermissible delegation grounds was rejected in Mistretta v. United States, 488 U.S. 361, 109 S.Ct. 647 (1989). For the modern history of mandatory, or "guideline," sentencing, see Michael Tonry, Sentencing Matters (1996).

In either discretionary or guideline-based sentencing systems, there are a wide variety of criminal sentences other than death and imprisonment. Probation, fines and restitution are the principal alternatives, though home detention, electronic monitoring, and intermittent confinement are being used more frequently. Probation always requires that the probationer commit no offense and usually requires reporting to a probation officer. If probation is violated, it may be continued as is or with new conditions, it may be terminated unsatisfactorily, or it may be revoked and a prison term imposed in its place. Before revoking probation a defendant must be given notice and a hearing at which defendant has the right to counsel. See generally Gagnon v. Scarpelli, 411 U.S. 778, 93 S.Ct. 1756 (1973). There is no need to prove violation of probation beyond a reasonable doubt nor is there a right to jury trial.

There are a wide variety of conditions that can be affixed to a term of probation, such as community service. The condition imposed, however, must be reasonable. Compare Higdon v. United States, 627 F.2d 893 (9th Cir.1980) (forfeiture of all assets, including home, to government and charitable work for three years unreasonable) with United States v. Arthur, 602 F.2d 660 (4th Cir.1979) (two years of unpaid work for approved charity reasonable). There are other conditions tailored to the individual defendant which may be imposed absent abuse of discretion, e.g., giving up alcohol, drugs, gambling, political activity or associating with certain persons, keeping employment, paying taxes. "Shaming" sanctions have also had a mild popularity in state courts. See, e.g., People v. Meyer, 176 Ill.2d 372, 223 Ill.Dec. 582, 680 N.E.2d 315 (1997) (striking down a trial court's decision to require a sign reading: "Warning! A Violent Felon lives here. Enter at your own Risk!" as a condition of probation); State v. Burdin, 924 S.W.2d 82 (Tenn.1996) (striking down a trial court's decision to require a sign reading: "Warning, all children. Wayne Burdin is an admitted and convicted child molester. Parents beware" as a condition of probation); Lindsay v. State, 606 So.2d 652 (Fla.Ct.App.1992) (upholding a requirement that a defendant place a Driving–While–Intoxicated ad in the local paper with his name and picture). For arguments for and against the use of shaming sanctions, see Kahan, What Do Alternative Sanctions Mean? 63 U. Chi. L. Rev. 591 (1996), and Massaro, Shame, Culture, and American Criminal Law, 89 Mich. L. Rev. 1880 (1991).

Fines may be imposed either by themselves or as a condition of probation. The limits are those set by statute. There is debate over the efficacy of fines. See Kadish, Some Observations on the Use of Criminal

Sanctions in Enforcing Economic Regulations, 30 U.Chi.L.Rev. 423, 434–35 (1963). Often when a defendant can pay a fine but the offense also injured a victim, a court may wish to require restitution to the victim. Most jurisdictions permit restitution to be ordered in lieu of or in addition to a fine; some require restitution. See 18 U.S.C. § 3556. The limits on restitution are the defendant's financial capacity, and the loss to the victim.

Other alternatives to traditional incarceration include victim-offender mediation, a procedure in which victims negotiate with offenders for restitution or some other sanction. In some jurisdictions, victims participate directly, in others, citizen boards determine the sanction. For an explanation and critical discussion, see Brown, The Use of Mediation to Resolve Criminal Cases: A Procedural Critique, 43 Emory L.J. 1247 (1994).

Absent statutory direction to consider alternative sanctions (and many statutes do so direct) there is no constitutional duty to do so. In Black v. Romano, 471 U.S. 606, 105 S.Ct. 2254 (1985), the Court held that due process does not require a judge to indicate on the record that he has considered alternatives to incarceration before sentencing a defendant to the penitentiary after finding that the defendant had violated the conditions of probation. The Court noted the desirability of considering alternatives to imprisonment but it rejected the notion that (at least in the revocation of probation situation) incarceration can be imposed only when it represents the sole means of promoting the State's interest in punishment and deterrence.

All of this is part of criminal law, not criminal procedure. And there are few federal constitutional limits on what a legislature may impose as punishment. In Solem v. Helm, 463 U.S. 277, 103 S.Ct. 3001 (1983), Helm was put in prison for life without parole. His crime was uttering a "no account" check. It was also his seventh conviction, the prior six were also for non-violent offenses and his life sentence was imposed under an habitual offender statute. By a vote of 5–4 the Court found the extraordinary disproportion between the offense and the sentence to constitute a violation of the Eighth Amendment, but its opinion made clear that such rulings were not easily secured. And they are not.[1] In Harmelin v. Michigan, 501 U.S. 957, 111 S.Ct. 2680 (1991), the sentence was life without parole and its imposition was required for any conviction of possession of more than 650 grams of cocaine. The Court rejected the notion that mandatory sentences are improper because they preclude consideration of mitigating factors.

> "... this claim has no support in the text and history of the Eighth Amendment. Severe, mandatory penalties may be cruel, but they are not unusual in the constitutional sense, having been employed in various forms throughout our Nation's history. As noted earlier, mandatory death sentences abounded in our first Penal Code. They were also common in the several states ...

1. The decided cases are discussed in Justice White's dissent in *Harmelin* (only four cases in which sentences were declared so disproportionate as to violate the Constitution).

> "It is true that petitioner's sentence is unique in that it is the second most severe known to the law; but life imprisonment *with* possibility of parole is also unique in that it is the third most severe. And if petitioner's sentence forecloses some 'flexible techniques' for later reducing sentence, it does not foreclose all of them, since there remain the possibilities of retroactive legislative reduction and executive clemency. In some cases, moreover, there will be negligible difference between life without parole and other sentences of imprisonment—for example, a life sentence with eligibility for parole after 20 years, or even a lengthy term sentence without eligibility for parole, given to a 65–year–old man. But even where the difference is the greatest, it cannot be compared with death. We have drawn the line of required individualized sentencing at capital cases, and see no basis for extending it further."

Justice Scalia and Chief Justice Rehnquist further stated that the Eighth Amendment does not require that sentence be proportionate to the crime and that Solem v. Helm ought to be overruled.

Justice Kennedy with Justices O'Connor and Souter wrote that "stare decisis counsels our adherence to the narrow proportionality principle that has existed in our Eighth Amendment jurisprudence for 80 years", but he concluded the principle was satisfied. Harmelin's crime was "far more grave" than Helm's no account check. The cocaine had a yield of 30 to 60 thousand doses. The crime was neither victimless nor non-violent—there is "a direct nexus between illegal drugs and crimes of violence ... 57 percent of a national sample of males arrested in 1989 for homicide tested positive for illegal drugs ... comparable statistics for assault, robbery and weapons arrests were 55, 73 and 63 percent respectively. ... In Detroit ... in 1988, 68 percent of a sample of male arrestees and 81 percent of a sample of female arrestees tested positive for illegal drugs ... last year an estimated 60 percent of the homicides in Detroit were drug related, primarily cocaine related." He concluded that it was unnecessary to compare sentences imposed on criminals in the same jurisdiction or the sentences imposed on the same crime in other jurisdictions—this is only to be done where "a threshold comparison of the crime committed and the sentence imposed leads to an inference of gross disproportionality."

> "The severity of petitioner's crime brings his sentence within the constitutional boundaries established by our prior decisions. In Hutto v. Davis (1982), we upheld against proportionality attack a sentence of 40 years' imprisonment for possession with intent to distribute nine ounces of marijuana. Here, Michigan could with good reason conclude that petitioner's crime is more serious than the crime in *Davis*. . . .
>
> "In asserting the constitutionality of this mandatory sentence, I offer no judgment on its wisdom. Mandatory sentencing schemes can be criticized for depriving judges of the power to exercise individual discretion when remorse and acknowledgment of guilt, or other extenuating facts, present what might seem a compelling case for departure from the maximum. On the other hand, broad

and unreviewed discretion exercised by sentencing judges leads to the perception that no clear standards are being applied, and that the rule of law is imperiled by sentences imposed for no discernible reason other than the subjective reactions of the sentencing judge. The debate illustrates that arguments for and against particular sentencing schemes are for legislatures to resolve."

The four dissenters rejected the reasoning of both the Scalia and Kennedy opinions and found the sentence disproportionate because (1) Harmelin was punished as severely as one who possessed with intent to deliver and his crime was not as serious, (2) Harmelin was a first time offender, (3) Michigan *may* punish second degree murder, rape and armed robbery less severely, and (4) no other jurisdiction provides as severe a penalty.

Besides prohibiting cruel and unusual punishment, the Eighth Amendment also forbids excessive fines. In United States v. Bajakajian, 524 U.S. 321, 118 S.Ct. 2028 (1998), the Court undertook to decide whether a criminal forfeiture of $357,144 was an "excessive fine" for the crime of trying to take this amount of unreported cash out of the country. Five justices declared the fine was excessive, because it was "grossly disproportional" to the underlying crime. The majority took pains to distinguish "civil forfeitures" which it had declared not "punishment" for purposes of double jeopardy analysis a few Terms back. See page 871. Justice Kennedy, joined by Rehnquist, O'Connor and Scalia, dissented. The dissent charged the majority with downplaying the seriousness of the crime, given the connection between smuggling cash and drug trafficking, money laundering, and organized crime. The dissent was also concerned that the majority's bright-line distinction between *in rem* forfeitures and *in personam* forfeitures created doctrinal anomalies and distinctions without a difference, treating differently, for example, a forfeiture for failure to declare currency from a forfeiture of smuggled goods. Finally, the dissent argued that "[t]he Court's holding may in the long run undermine the purpose of the Excessive Fines Clause. One of the main purposes of the ban on excessive fines was to prevent the King from assessing unpayable fines to keep his enemies in debtor's prison. ... Under the Court's holding, legislators may rely on mandatory prison sentences in lieu of fines. Drug lords will be heartened by this, knowing the prison terms will fall upon their couriers while leaving their own wallets untouched."

The absence of constitutional restraint over substantive sentencing law was, for many years, accompanied by a similar lack of constitutional or statutory restraint on sentencing procedure. It is safe to say, for many years, a treatise could be written on the mores and customs of sentencing hearings while the law governing sentencing hearings could be summarized in the same way legend says Lincoln wrote the Gettysburg address—on the back of an envelope.

This has changed and will continue to change. A concomitant of the efforts to control judicial discretion through change in substantive law is the effort to control discretion by the imposition of required procedures.

At times the question arises as to whether the civil commitment of an offender violates due process. The Court has expressed concern that a civil commitment might become a hidden criminal punishment. In Kansas v. Hendricks, 521 U.S. 346, 117 S.Ct. 2072 (1997), the United States Supreme Court upheld the constitutionality of the Kansas Sexually Violate Predator Act which provided for the forcible commitment of a previously convicted sexual offender. In Kansas v. Crane, 534 U.S. 407, 122 S.Ct. 867 (2002), the Supreme Court, in a 6–2 opinion, held that the offender need not lack total or complete control, but that the state must prove that the offender did lack some self control.

B. SENTENCING PROCEDURES

1. OVERVIEW

a. Notice. The sentence procedure (in cases where the jury plays no role in sentencing) usually begins with a presentence investigation by a probation officer. The officer will compile a presentence report describing the personal history of the defendant. The report is often quite comprehensive, informing the judge in detail of family background, work record, education, financial status, prior criminal history, intelligence, attitude, physical condition and character. In some jurisdictions the probation officer evaluates the defendant as a person, discusses the crime and recommends a sentence.

The right of the defendant to see this report has been debated for many years. Those opposed contended that disclosure would prevent the free flow of information, reveal confidences and create unnecessary disruption of the sentencing process. Those in favor contended that, without disclosure, there was a risk of an enhanced sentence based on misinformation. See Fennell & Hall, Due Process at Sentencing: An Empirical and Legal Analysis of Disclosure of Presentence Reports in Federal Courts, 93 Harv.L.Rev. 1613 (1980).

In Gardner v. Florida, 430 U.S. 349, 97 S.Ct. 1197 (1977), a jury returned a verdict recommending mercy. Before sentencing the judge reviewed the presentence report which was not made available to the accused—and, as permitted by Florida law, imposed the death sentence. The Supreme Court disapproved this procedure, at least in capital cases. In 1983 the federal rules were amended to require disclosure. Fed.R.Crim.P. 32. Most courts have permitted redaction or summary of reports in order to protect confidential sources. United States v. Scalzo, 716 F.2d 463 (7th Cir.1983).

In Burns v. United States, 501 U.S. 129, 111 S.Ct. 2182 (1991), the Court found that Congress intended that notice of a judge's intent to impose a sentence outside a set range along with the grounds for the action must be given to defendant. The Court suggested that if this were not the intent of Congress, it might be required by due process. Four dissenters argued that the intent of Congress could not be inferred from its silence on the subject. Three dissenters asserted that, absent a need to introduce evidence, due process does not require notice that the judge may adopt a view of the law which allows a higher sentence. The right to argue at the hearing and the right to appeal as a matter of right are adequate safeguards.

Now that the sentencing guidelines are no longer mandatory, however, *Burns* has been limited to pre-Booker cases:

Irizarry v. United States

United States Supreme Court, 2008.
___ U.S. ___, 128 S.Ct. 2198.

■ JUSTICE STEVENS delivered the opinion of the Court.

Rule 32(h) of the Federal Rules of Criminal Procedure, promulgated in response to our decision in *Burns v. United States*, 501 U.S. 129, 111 S. Ct. 2182 (1991), states that "[b]efore the court may depart from the applicable sentencing range on a ground not identified for departure either in the presentence report or in a party's prehearing submission, the court must give the parties reasonable notice that it is contemplating such a departure." The question presented by this case is whether that Rule applies to every sentence that is a variance from the recommended Federal Sentencing Guidelines range even though not considered a "departure" as that term was used when Rule 32(h) was promulgated.

I

Petitioner, Richard Irizarry, pleaded guilty to one count of making a threatening interstate communication, in violation of 18 U.S.C. § 875(c). Petitioner made the following admissions in the factual resume accompanying his plea: (1) On November 5, 2003, he sent an e-mail threatening to kill his ex-wife and her new husband; (2) he had sent "dozens" of similar e-mails in violation of a restraining order; (3) he intended the e-mails to "convey true threats to kill or injure multiple persons"; and (4) at all times he acted knowingly and willfully.

The presentence report (PSR), in addition to describing the threatening e-mails, reported that petitioner had asked another inmate to kill his ex-wife's new husband. The PSR advised against an adjustment for acceptance of responsibility and recommended a Guidelines sentencing range of 41–to–51 months of imprisonment, based on enhancements for violating court protective orders, making multiple threats, and intending to carry out those threats. As possible grounds for a departure, the probation officer stated that petitioner's criminal history category might not adequately reflect his " 'past criminal conduct or the likelihood that [petitioner] will commit other crimes.' "

The Government made no objection to the PSR, but advised the court that it intended to call petitioner's ex-wife as a witness at the sentencing hearing. Petitioner objected to the PSR's application of the enhancement based on his intention to carry out the threats and its rejection of an adjustment for acceptance of responsibility.

Four witnesses testified at the sentencing hearing. Petitioner's ex-wife described incidents of domestic violence, the basis for the restraining order against petitioner, and the threats petitioner made against her and her family and friends. She emphasized at some length her genuine concern that petitioner fully intended to carry out his threats. A special agent of the Federal Bureau of Investigation was called to describe documents recovered from petitioner's vehicle when he was arrested; those documents indicated he intended to track down his ex-wife and their children. Petitioner's cellmate next testified that petitioner "was obsessed with the idea of getting rid of" his ex-wife's husband. Finally, petitioner testified at some length, stating that he accepted responsibility for the e-mails, but that he did not really intend to carry out his threats. Petitioner also denied speaking to his cellmate about killing his ex-wife's husband.

After hearing from counsel, the trial judge delivered a thoughtful oral decision, which included findings resolving certain disputed issues of fact. She found that petitioner had deliberately terrorized his ex-wife, that he intended to carry out one or more of his threats, "that he still intends to terrorize Ms. Smith by whatever means he can and that he does not accept responsibility for what he has done." After giving both petitioner and counsel an opportunity to make further comment, the judge concluded:

> "I've considered all of the evidence presented today, I've considered everything that's in the presentence report, and I've considered the statutory purpose of sentencing and the sentencing guideline range. I find the guideline range is not appropriate in this case. I find Mr. Irizarry's conduct most disturbing. I am sincerely convinced that he will continue, as his ex-wife testified, in this conduct regardless of what this court does and regardless of what kind of supervision he's under. And based upon that, I find that the maximum time that he can be incapacitated is what is best for society, and therefore the guideline range, I think, is not high enough.
>
> "The guideline range goes up to 51 months, which is only nine months shorter than the statutory maximum. But I think in Mr. Irizarry's case the statutory maximum is what's appropriate, and that's what I'm going to sentence him."

The court imposed a sentence of 60 months of imprisonment to be followed by a 3–year term of supervised release.

Defense counsel then raised the objection that presents the issue before us today. He stated, "We didn't have notice of [the court's] intent to upwardly depart. What the law is on that now with—," to which the Court responded, "I think the law on that is out the window.... You had notice that the guidelines were only advisory and the court could sentence anywhere within the statutory range."

The Court of Appeals for the Eleventh Circuit affirmed petitioner's sentence, reasoning that Rule 32(h) did not apply because "the above-guidelines sentence imposed by the district court in this case was a variance, not a guidelines departure." The Court of Appeals declined to extend the rule to variances. "After [*United States v. Booker* (2005),] parties are inherently on notice that the sentencing guidelines range is advisory.... Given *Booker*, parties cannot claim unfair surprise or inability to present informed comment."

Because the Courts of Appeals are divided with respect to the applicability of Rule 32(h) to Guidelines variances, we granted certiorari. We now affirm.

II

At the time of our decision in *Burns*, the Guidelines were mandatory; the Sentencing Reform Act of 1984, § 211 *et seq.*, 98 Stat. 1987, prohibited district courts from disregarding "the mechanical dictates of the Guidelines" except in narrowly defined circumstances. Confronted with the constitutional problems that might otherwise arise, we held that the provision of Rule 32 that allowed parties an opportunity to comment on the appropriate sentence—now Rule 32(i)(1)(C)—would be "render[ed] meaningless" unless the defendant were given notice of any contemplated departure. Justice Souter disagreed with our conclusion with respect to the text of Rule 32 and conducted a due process analysis.

Any expectation subject to due process protection at the time we decided *Burns* that a criminal defendant would receive a sentence within the presumptively applicable guideline range did not survive our decision in United States v. Booker, 543 U.S. (2005), which invalidated the mandatory features of the Guidelines. Now faced with advisory Guidelines, neither the Government nor the defendant may place the same degree of reliance on the type of "expectancy" that gave rise to a special need for notice in *Burns*. Indeed, a sentence outside the Guidelines carries no presumption of unreasonableness. Gall v. United States (2007) see also Rita v. United States (2007).

It is, therefore, no longer the case that "were we to read Rule 32 to dispense with notice [of a contemplated non-Guidelines sentence], we would then have to confront the serious question whether [such] notice in this setting is mandated by the Due Process Clause." *Burns*. The due process concerns that motivated the Court to require notice in a world of mandatory Guidelines no longer provide a basis for this Court to extend the rule set forth in *Burns* either through an interpretation of Rule 32(h) itself or through Rule 32(i)(1)(C). And contrary to what the dissent argues (opinion of BREYER, J.), the rule does not apply to § 3553 variances by its terms. "Departure" is a term of art under the Guidelines and refers only to non-Guidelines sentences imposed under the framework set out in the Guidelines.

The notice requirement set out in *Burns* applied to a narrow category of cases. The only relevant departures were those authorized by 18 U.S.C. § 3553(b) (1988 ed.), which required "an aggravating or mitigating circumstance of a kind, or to a degree, not adequately taken into consideration by the Sentencing Commission in formulating the guidelines that should result in a sentence different from that described." That determination could only be made based on "the sentencing guidelines, policy statements, and official commentary of the Sentencing Commission." And the notice requirement only applied to the subcategory of those departures that were based on "a ground not identified as a ground for ... departure either in the presentence report or in a pre-hearing submission." *Burns*; see also Fed. Rule Crim. Proc. 32(h). Although the Guidelines, as the "starting point and the initial benchmark," continue to play a role in the sentencing determination, there is no longer a limit comparable to the one at issue in *Burns* on the variances from Guidelines ranges that a District Court may find justified under the sentencing factors set forth in 18 U.S.C. § 3553(a) (2000 ed. and Supp. V).

Rule 32(i)(1)(C) requires the district court to allow the parties to comment on "matters relating to an appropriate sentence," and given the scope of the issues that may be considered at a sentencing hearing, a judge will normally be well-advised to withhold her final judgment until after the parties have had a full opportunity to present their evidence and their arguments. Sentencing is "a fluid and dynamic process and the court itself may not know until the end whether a variance will be adopted, let alone on what grounds." Adding a special notice requirement whenever a judge is contemplating a variance may create unnecessary delay; a judge who concludes during the sentencing hearing that a variance is appropriate may be forced to continue the hearing even where the content of the Rule 32(h) notice would not affect the parties' presentation of argument and evidence. In the case before us today, even if we assume that the judge had contemplated a variance before the sentencing hearing began, the record does not indicate that a statement announcing that possibility would have changed the parties' presentations in any material way; nor do we think it would in most cases. The Government admits as much in arguing that the error here was harmless.

Sound practice dictates that judges in all cases should make sure that the information provided to the parties in advance of the hearing, and in the hearing itself, has given them an adequate opportunity to confront and debate the relevant issues. We recognize that there will be some cases in which the factual basis for a particular sentence will come as a surprise to a defendant or the Government. The more appropriate response to such a problem is not to extend the reach of Rule 32(h)'s notice requirement categorically, but rather for a district judge to consider granting a continuance when a party has a legitimate basis for claiming that the surprise was prejudicial. As Judge Boudin has noted,

> "In the normal case a competent lawyer . . . will anticipate most of what might occur at the sentencing hearing—based on the trial, the pre-sentence report, the exchanges of the parties concerning the report, and the preparation of mitigation evidence. Garden variety considerations of culpability, criminal history, likelihood of re-offense, seriousness of the crime, nature of the conduct and so forth should not generally come as a surprise to trial lawyers who have prepared for sentencing."

The fact that Rule 32(h) remains in effect today does not justify extending its protections to variances; the justification for our decision in *Burns* no longer exists and such an extension is apt to complicate rather than to simplify sentencing procedures. We have confidence in the ability of district judges and counsel—especially in light of Rule 32's other procedural protections 2—to make sure that all relevant matters relating to a sentencing decision have been considered before the final sentencing determination is made.

Rule 32 requires that a defendant be given a copy of his PSR at least 35 days before sentencing, Fed. Rule Crim. Proc. 32(e)(2). Further, each party has 14 days to object to the PSR, Rule 32(f)(1), and at least 7 days before sentencing the probation officer must submit a final version of the PSR to the parties, stating any unresolved objections, Rule 32(g). Finally, at sentencing, the parties must be allowed to comment on "matters relating to an appropriate sentence," Rule 32(i)(1)(C), and the defendant must be given an opportunity to speak and present mitigation testimony, Rule 32(i)(4)(A)(ii).

The judgment of the Court of Appeals is affirmed.

It is so ordered.

■ JUSTICE THOMAS, concurring.

Earlier this Term, I explained that because "there is no principled way to apply the *Booker* remedy," it is "best to apply the statute as written, including 18 U.S.C. § 3553(b), which makes the [Federal Sentencing] Guidelines mandatory." Kimbrough v. United States, (dissenting opinion) (referencing United States v. Booker (2005)); see also Gall v. United States (2007) (Thomas, J., dissenting) (applying the Guidelines as mandatory). Consistent with that view, I would hold that the District Court committed statutory error when it imposed a sentence at "variance" with the Guidelines in a manner not authorized by the text of the Guidelines, which permit sentences outside the Guidelines, or "departures," only when certain aggravating or mitigating circumstances are present. See United States Sentencing Commission, Guidelines Manual § 1B1.1 (Nov. 2007). But the issue whether such post-*Booker* "variances" are permissible is not currently before us. . . .

Rather, we are presented with the narrow question whether Federal Rule of Criminal Procedure 32(h) requires a judge to give notice before he imposes a sentence outside the Guidelines on a ground not identified in the presentence report or in a prehearing submission by the Government. I agree with the Court that neither Rule 32(h) nor Burns v. United States (1991), compels a judge to provide notice before imposing a sentence at "variance" with the post-*Booker* advisory Guidelines. Each addresses only "departures" under the mandatory Guidelines and does not contemplate the drastic changes to federal sentencing wrought by the *Booker* remedy. For this reason, I join the Court's opinion.

■ JUSTICE BREYER, with whom JUSTICE KENNEDY, JUSTICE SOUTER, and JUSTICE GINSBURG join, dissenting.

Federal Rule of Criminal Procedure 32(h) says:

> "Before the court may depart from the applicable sentencing range on a ground not identified for departure either in the presentence report or in a party's prehearing submission, the court must give the parties reasonable notice that it is contemplating such a departure."

The question before us is whether this Rule applies when a sentencing judge decides, pursuant to 18 U.S.C. § 3553(a) (2000 ed. and Supp. V), to impose a sentence that is a "variance" *from* the advisory Guidelines, but is not a "departure" *within* the Guidelines. The Court says that the Rule does not apply. I disagree.

The Court creates a legal distinction without much of a difference. The Rule speaks specifically of "departure[s]," but I see no reason why that term should not be read to encompass what the Court calls § 3553(a) "variances." The Guidelines define "departure" to mean "imposition of a sentence outside the applicable guideline range or of a sentence that is otherwise different from the guideline sentence." United States Sentencing Commission, Guidelines Manual (USSG), § 1B1.1, comment., n. 1(E) (Nov. 2007). So-called variances fall comfortably within this definition. Variances are also consistent with the ordinary meaning of the term "departure." See, *e.g.*, Webster's Third New International Dictionary 604 (1993) (defining "departure" to mean a "deviation or divergence esp. from a rule" (def. 5a)). And conceptually speaking, the substantive difference between a "variance" and a "departure" is nonexistent, as this Court's opinions themselves make clear. See, *e.g.*, Gall v. United States (2007) (using the term "departure" to describe any non-Guideline sentence); Rita v. United States (2007) (stating that courts "may depart (either pursuant to the Guidelines or, since *Booker*, by imposing a non-Guidelines sentence)").

Of course, when Rule 32(h) was written, its drafters had *only* Guidelines-authorized departures in mind: Rule 32(h) was written after the Guidelines took effect but before this Court decided United States v. Booker (2005). Yet the language of a statute or a rule, read in light of its purpose, often applies to circumstances that its authors did not then foresee.

And here, the purpose behind Rule 32(h) requires that the Rule be construed to apply to variances. That Rule was added to "reflect" our decision in Burns v. United States (1991). See Advisory Committee's Notes on Fed. Rule Crim. Proc. 32, 18 U.S.C. App., p. 1141 (2000 ed., Supp. II). (2002 Amendments). In *Burns*, the Court focused upon "the extraordinary case in which the district court, on its own initiative and contrary to the expectations both the defendant and the Government, decides that the factual and legal predicates for a departure are satisfied." The Court held that "before a district court can depart upward on a ground not identified as a ground for upward departure either in the presentence report or in a prehearing submission by the Government ... the district court [must] give the parties reasonable notice that it is contemplating such a ruling."

Our holding in *Burns* was motivated, in part, by a desire to avoid due process concerns. ("[W]ere we to read Rule 32 to dispense with notice, we would then have to confront the serious question whether notice in this setting is mandated by the Due Process Clause"). That is perhaps why the majority today suggests that "[a]ny expectation subject to due process protection at the time we decided *Burns*" failed to survive *Booker*. But the due process concern was not the only reason for our holding in *Burns*, nor was it even the primary one. Rather, the Court principally based its decision upon Rule 32's requirement that parties be given " 'an opportunity to comment upon ... matters relating to the appropriate sentence.' " "Obviously," the Court said, whether a *sua sponte* departure was warranted was a "matter relating to the appropriate sentence." To deprive the parties of notice of such a departure would thus "rende[r] meaningless" their right to comment on "matters relating to the appropriate sentence." Notice, the Court added, was "essential to assuring procedural fairness."

The Court's decision in *Burns* also relied on what the Court described as Rule 32's overall purpose of "provid[ing] for focused, adversarial development of the factual and legal issues" related to sentencing. This could be gleaned, *inter alia*, from the requirement that parties be given an opportunity to file responses or objections to the presentence report and from the requirement that parties be given an opportunity to speak at the sentencing proceeding. Construing Rule 32 not to require notice of *sua sponte* departures, the Court reasoned, would be "inconsistent with Rule 32's purpose of promoting focused, adversarial resolution" of sentencing issues.

The primary grounds for the Court's decision in *Burns* apply with equal force to the variances we consider here. Today, Rule 32(i)(1)(C) provides a virtually identical requirement that the district court "allow the parties' attorneys to comment on the probation officer's determinations *and other matters relating to an appropriate sentence.*" (Emphasis added.) To deprive the parties of notice of previously unidentified grounds for a variance would *today* "rende[r] meaningless" the parties' right to comment on "matters relating to [an] appropriate sentence." *Burns.* To deprive the parties of notice would *today* subvert Rule 32's purpose of "promoting focused, adversarial resolution" of sentencing issues. In a word, it is not fair.

Seeking to overcome the fact that text, purpose, and precedent are not on its side, the majority makes two practical arguments in its defense. First, it says that notice is unnecessary because "there is no longer a limit comparable to the one at issue in *Burns*" as to the number of reasons why a district court might *sua sponte* impose a sentence outside the applicable range. Is that so? Courts, while now free to impose sentences that vary from a Guideline-specified range, have *always* been free to depart from such a range. See USSG ch. 1, pt. A, § 4(b) (Nov. 1987), reprinted in § 1A1.1 comment., editorial note (Nov. 2007) (suggesting broad departure authority). Indeed, even *Burns* recognized that "the Guidelines place essentially no limit on the number of potential factors that may warrant a departure." (citing USSG ch. 1, pt. A, § 4(b) (1990)). Regardless, if *Booker* expanded the number of grounds on which a district court may impose a non-Guideline sentence, that would seem to be an additional argument *in favor of*, not *against*, giving the parties notice of the district court's intention to impose a non-Guideline sentence for some previously unidentified reason. Notice, after all, would promote "focused, adversarial" litigation at sentencing. *Burns.*

Second, the majority fears that a notice requirement would unnecessarily "delay" and "complicate" sentencing. But this concern seems exaggerated. Rule 32(h) applies only where the court seeks to depart on a ground *not* previously identified by the presentence report or the parties' presentencing submissions. And the Solicitor General, after consulting with federal prosecutors, tells us that "in the vast majority of cases in which a district court imposes a sentence outside the Guidelines range, the grounds for the variance have previously been identified by the [presentence report] or the parties."

In the remaining cases, notice does not necessarily mean delay. The parties may well be prepared to address the point and a meaningful continuance of sentencing would likely be in order only where a party would adduce additional evidence or brief an unconsidered legal issue. Further, to the extent that district judges find a notice requirement to complicate sentencing, those judges could make use of Rule 32(d)(2)(F), which enables them to require that presentence reports address the sentence that would be appropriate in light of the § 3553(a) factors (including, presumably, whether there exist grounds for imposing a non-Guidelines sentence). If a presentence report includes a section on whether a variance would be appropriate under § 3553(a), that would likely eliminate the possibility that the district court would wind up imposing a non-Guidelines sentence for some reason *not previously identified*.

Finally, if notice *still* produced some burdens and delay, fairness justifies notice regardless. Indeed, the Government and the defendant here—the parties most directly affected by sentencing—both urge the Court to find a notice requirement. Clearly they recognize, as did the Court in *Burns*, that notice is "essential to assuring procedural fairness" at sentencing.

I believe that Rule 32(h) provides this procedural safeguard. And I would vacate and remand to the Court of Appeals so that it could determine whether the petitioner received the required notice and, if not, act accordingly.

I respectfully dissent.

* * *

b. Hearing and Resolution. The obvious companion of disclosure of a presentence report is the opportunity to rebut incorrect information. Indeed, even before the rule permitted disclosure it was clear that the defendant had a right to correct adverse information. See United States v. Charmer Industries, Inc., 711 F.2d 1164 (2d Cir.1983). In most cases defense counsel knew what the prosecution or judge would regard as damaging information and these matters were often discussed at the hearing. If there were particularly aggravating or mitigating circumstances in a case, it is not uncommon for either side to call witnesses to establish facts, e.g., that defendant defrauded a dozen other persons, that the victim had provoked the defendant for many years. The opponent could test or refute this evidence. Indeed, failure to challenge misinformation is a waiver of the point. United States v. Plisek, 657 F.2d 920 (7th Cir.1981). It has been generally understood that a sentence clearly based upon incorrect information is a violation of due process. United States v. Jackson, 649 F.2d 967 (3d Cir.1981); United States v. Jones, 640 F.2d 284 (10th Cir.1981).

The federal statute is explicit on the question of hearing and a resolution by the court of disputed, material matters:

> In pre-guidelines practice, factors relevant sentencing were often determined in an informal fashion. The informality was to some

> extent explained by the fact that particular offense and offender characteristics rarely had a highly specific or required sentencing consequence. This situation will no longer exist under sentencing guidelines. The court's resolution of disputed sentencing factors will usually have a measurable effect on the applicable punishment. More formality is therefore unavoidable if the sentencing process is to be accurate and fair.... When a dispute exists about any factor important to the sentencing determination, the court must ensure that the parties have an adequate opportunity to present relevant information. U.S. Sentencing Comm'n, Guidelines Manual § 6A1.3, official commentary (2002).
>
> Guideline § 6A1.3(b) states:
>
> The court shall resolve disputed sentencing factors in accordance with Rule 32(a)(1), Fed.R.Crim.P.

Though there is a right to a hearing, the decision to allow a full adversarial evidentiary hearing is within the trial court's discretion. The court need not afford others an opportunity to testify on defendant's behalf at sentencing. See United States v. Jackson, 700 F.2d 181 (5th Cir.1983) (defendant's wife); United States v. Pino, 608 F.2d 1001 (4th Cir.1979) (character witnesses). Because hearsay and confrontation rules do not apply at sentencing, many matters of disputed fact are resolved by statements of counsel, hearsay testimony by the probation officer, or affidavits. See U.S.S.G. § 6A1.3; United States v. Brown, 133 F.3d 917 (4th Cir.1997) (trial court did not abuse discretion in refusing to require evidentiary hearing so defense counsel could cross-examine grand jury witnesses whose testimony formed basis of facts found at sentencing); United States v. Beltran, 109 F.3d 365 (7th Cir.1997) (no right to subpoena or cross-examine witnesses).

c. Allocution and Argument. One convicted of a crime has the right to address the court personally before sentence is imposed, called allocution. The rationale of this common law right is "that the defendant might be identified by the court as the real party adjudged guilty; that he might have a chance to plead a pardon ... that he might have an opportunity to say why judgment should not be given up against him; and that the example of being brought up for the animadversion of the court and the open denunciation of punishment might tend to deter others from the commission of similar offenses." Ball v. United States, 140 U.S. 118, 11 S.Ct. 761 (1891).

In Green v. United States, 365 U.S. 301, 81 S.Ct. 653 (1961), the trial judge asked "Do you want to say something?" At that point, defense counsel made a detailed argument in mitigation of sentence. In a 5–4 decision, the Court upheld the sentence for the following reason:

> "A record, certainly this record, unlike a play, is unaccompanied with stage directions which may tell the significant cast of the eye or the nod of the head. It may well be that the defendant himself was recognized and sufficiently apprised of his right to speak and chose to exercise this right through his counsel. Especially is this conclusion warranted by the fact that the defendant

has raised this claim seven years after the occurrence. The defendant has failed to meet his burden of showing that he was not accorded the personal right ... and we therefore find that his sentence was not illegal.

"However, to avoid litigation arising out of ambiguous records in order to determine whether the trial judge did address himself to the defendant personally, we think that the problem should be, as it readily can be, taken out of the realm of controversy. This is easily accomplished. Trial judges before sentencing should, as a matter of good judicial administration, unambiguously address themselves to the defendant. Hereafter trial judges should leave no room for doubt that the defendant has been issued a personal invitation to speak prior to sentencing."

When the judge asks to defendant if she has any comment before sentence, the right of allocution will generally be deemed satisfied. See United States v. Meyers, 646 F.2d 1142 (6th Cir.1981); What is remedy for the denial of allocution? See United States v. Navarro–Flores, 628 F.2d 1178 (9th Cir.1980) (remand for resentencing at which allocution is provided). See generally Barrett, Allocution, 9 Mo.L.Rev. 115 (1944).

Counsel for defendant has the right to speak at sentencing. Counsel for the prosecution also has a right, under Fed. R. Crim. P. 32(a)(1), to state her position with respect to the sentence and make such recommendations as she deems appropriate. United States v. Santarelli, 729 F.2d 1388 (11th Cir.1984): United States v. Garcia, 694 F.2d 294 (1st Cir.1982).

d. Sentencing. In jurisdictions with indeterminate sentencing, the trial judge is free to set the sentence at any level between a statutory minimum and a statutory maximum. She is usually aided in this determination by the probation officer's sentencing recommendation, as well as defense counsel's and the state's recommendations. The sentencing hearing often involves a tense and at times emotionally charged interchange between the judge and the defendant, punctuated by argument from counsel. Family members of both the defendant and the victim may be present, sitting across the courtroom aisle from each other. In many jurisdictions, victims or victims' families have a right to be heard at the time of sentence. The Justice for All Act of 2004, 18 U.S.C. § 3771(a), establishes victims' rights in the federal system and insures the right to be reasonably heard at any public proceeding in the district court involving sentencing. Usually the judge pronounces the sentence at the end of the hearing and the defendant is immediately remanded to custody, though a judge may, in rare instances, allow the defendant to turn himself in at a later time for service of the sentence.

In a guideline sentencing jurisdiction, the sentencing hearing may be more like a miniature trial, and may include presentation of witnesses or evidence and legal argument by counsel. Sentences are computed in accordance with a set method, see Frankel & Orland, Sentencing Commissions and Guidelines, 73 Geo.L.J. 225 (1984), at the end of which is a guideline range expressed in terms of months (minimum and maximum). The probation officer prepares the initial application of the guidelines, which is subject to dispute and argument by counsel.

When the federal sentencing guidelines first went into effect, the procedure worked as follows (in simplified summary). The court identified the offense and, consulted a list approved by Congress to determine an offense level, expressed as a number. After deriving this number the court must consider in turn a series of adjustments:

> Two or more levels were added for hate crime or if the victim is vulnerable or was physically restrained or was a police officer.
>
> Two to four levels were added if defendant led criminal activity. Two to four levels were subtracted if defendant was a minor or minimal participant.
>
> Two levels were added if there was abuse of trust or use of special skill.
>
> Two levels were added for obstructing justice or endangering others during flight.
>
> Up to five levels may have been added for multiple offense counts and an elaborate weighting system was used to determine these levels.
>
> Two to three levels were subtracted if defendant accepted responsibility for the offense.

After the offense level was computed a Criminal History Category was derived by assigning points to various prior convictions (dependent upon the length of prior sentences) and adding to those points a further number if the offense was committed while on probation or parole or within two years of release from prison. Those points were then compared to a table and a Criminal History Category of I to VI is affixed.

Special methods to increase offense levels and Criminal History Categories were provided for terrorism career offenders, armed career offenders and those whose livelihood is criminal.

Computation under the guidelines was often simple but not invariably so. While elaborate definitions and rules were set forth, some cases present difficult questions of application.

When the computation was complete, the court looked at a grid to find the intersection of the offense level column with the criminal history category. At the intersection is the sentencing range—the ranges are set so that the maximum sentence did not exceed the minimum sentence by more than six months or 25%, whichever was greater.

Under the sentencing guidelines as initially applied, a court could depart from the prescribed guideline range and impose a sentence greater or lesser than provided in the guideline but its right to do so was constrained. Departure may have occurred if substantial assistance had been given to authorities and the government moved for departure. Otherwise departure might be granted only when the court found "that there exists an aggravating or mitigating circumstance of a kind, or to a degree, not adequately taken into consideration by the Sentencing Commission in formulating the guidelines [and] that should result in a [different] sentence", 18 U.S.C. § 3553(b). The guidelines give examples: if the offense resulted in death, physical or extreme psychological injury, abduction, disruption of government, etc., an upward departure might be appropriate. Wrongful conduct by the victim and offenses committed under duress may justify a downward departures.

One preliminary study concluded that the guidelines were working to reduce sentence disparity without affecting plea bargaining but also exacerbated prison crowding. Disparity still occurred wherever guidelines are ambiguous. Sager, Are The Federal Sentencing Guidelines Meeting Congressional Goals?, 40 Emory L.J. 393 (1991). Later studies found various degrees of remaining disparity, including racial and gender disparities. See Gelacak, Nagel, and Johnson, Departures Under the Guidelines: An Empirical and Jurisprudential Analysis, 88 Minn. L. Rev. 299 (1996), Yellen, Illusion, Illogic, and Injustice: Real Offense Sentencing and the Federal Sentencing Guidelines, 78 Minn. L. Rev. 403 (1995); Symposium on the Federal Sentencing Guidelines, 91 Nw. U. L. Rev. 1231 (1997).

Now, the sentencing guidelines procedures are no longer mandatory, though judges often still use the guidelines to arrive at a presumptively valid sentence.

e. Appeals. In an indeterminate sentencing system, the judge's sentence is for all practical purposes unreviewable, except for limited constitutional defects considered below. Some jurisdictions allow proportionality review, but rarely overturn sentences on this ground. See Zalman, Appellate Review of Sentences and the Antinomy of Law Reform, 1983 Det. C.L.Rev. 1513. However, a parole board will usually reconsider the offender's sentence periodically, in light of progress and good behavior in prison and prison resources.

Guidelines sentencing usually involves the abolition of parole, but more extensive appellate review of sentences—allowing appeals by both defendants and prosecutors to review the accuracy of the trial court's guideline application. Legal questions of guideline application are, like all legal questions, reviewed de novo. But the standard of review for discretionary departures from the guidelines is a more difficult question.

In Koon v. United States, 518 U.S. 81, 116 S.Ct. 2035 (1996), the Court held that the standard of review for district court departures from the federal guidelines was an abuse of discretion standard. In Koon, the district court sentenced Stacy Koon and Laurence Powell, the police officers convicted of violating Rodney King's constitutional rights, to 30 months in prison, even though the applicable Guideline sentence was in the range of 70–87 months. The Ninth Circuit had reversed, reviewing de novo the legitimacy of the district court's reasons for the downward departure. The district court had departed downward on the ground that the victim had contributed to the offense, and on the grounds that petitioners were unusually subject to abuse in prison, that they would lose their jobs, that they had been subject to both state and federal prosecutions, and that they posed a low risk of recidivism. The Ninth Circuit found all of these factors impermissible. The Supreme Court, using an abuse of discretion standard of review, rejected only the job loss and recidivism factors on the ground that these factors would be no different for other offenders and thus did not take the case "out of the heartland" of the guidelines. Other factors were permissible, as long as they were not ruled out by the Sentencing

Commission. The Commission, not the appellate courts, should decide which departure factors should be foreclosed. Justices Souter, Ginsburg, and Breyer (a former member of the Sentencing Commission that drafted the guidelines) argued that the district court also abused its discretion in considering potential abuse in prison and the double prosecution as grounds for departure. Justice Souter argued: "the District Court concluded that petitioners would be subject to abuse not simply because they were former police officers, but in large part because of the degree of publicity and condemnation surrounding their crime.... To allow a departure on this basis is to reason, in effect, that the more serious the crime, and the more widespread its consequent publicity and condemnation, the less one should be punished; the more egregious the act, the less culpable the offender. This moral irrationality cannot be attributed to the heartland scheme ... reading the guidelines to suggest that those who profit from state court malfunctions should get the benefit of a downward departure would again attribute a normative irrationality to the heartland concept." Justice Breyer argued that double prosecution was already considered in framing the Guideline for civil rights violations, and that "differences in prison treatment are fairly common—to the point where too frequent use of this factor as a basis for departure could undermine the uniformity that the Guidelines seek."

The Koon standard has been altered by statute. Now, under the PROTECT Act, appellate courts review departures de novo. Section 401 of the PROTECT Act "amends 18 U.S.C. § 3742(e), which now provides:

> (e) *Consideration.*—Upon review of the record, the court of appeals shall determine whether the sentence—
>
> . . .
>
> (3) is outside the applicable guideline range, and
>
> (A) the district court failed to provide the written statement of reasons required by section 3553(c)(B) the sentence departs from the applicable guideline range based on a factor that—
>
> (i) does not advance the objectives set forth in section 3553(a)(2); or
>
> (ii) is not authorized under section 3553(b); or
>
> (iii) is not justified by the facts of the case; or
>
> (C) the sentence departs to an unreasonable degree from the applicable guidelines range, having regard for the factors to be considered in imposing a sentence, as set forth in section 3553(a) of this title and the reasons for the imposition of the particular sentence, as stated by the district court pursuant to the provisions of section 3553(c);....
>
> . . .
>
> The court of appeals shall give due regard to the opportunity of the district court to judge the credibility of the witnesses, and shall accept the findings of fact of the district court unless they are clearly erroneous and, *except with respect to determinations under*

subsection (3)(A) or (3)(B), shall give due deference to the district court's application of the guidelines to the facts. *With respect to determinations under* subsection (3)(A) or (3)(B), *the court of appeals shall review de novo the district court's application of the guidelines to the facts.* (emphasis added)."

"This changed the law. Under Koon v. United States (1996), the courts of appeals were not to review a departure decision de novo, but were to ask whether the sentencing court abused its discretion in granting the departure. In appeals from sentencing departures, we had, before the PROTECT Act, engaged in a three-part review:" (1) we determined whether the stated ground for departure [was] theoretically permissible under the guidelines; (2) if so, we examined the record to assess whether there [was] adequate factual support; and (3) we determined the appropriateness of the degree of departure. *United States v. Bogdan*, 302 F.3d 12, 16 (1st Cir.2002). Whether the stated ground for departure was theoretically permissible—the first part—was a question of law reviewed de novo. United States v. Bradstreet, 207 F.3d 76, 81 (1st Cir.2000); see also United States v. Diaz, 285 F.3d 92, 97–98 (1st Cir.2002). Under *Koon*, our review under the remaining two parts was for abuse of discretion only. *See Koon*, 518 U.S. 81 at 96 at 96–100, 135 L. Ed. 2d 392; United States v. Lujan, 324 F.3d 27, 31 n.5 (1st Cir.2003); United States v. Martin, 221 F.3d 52, 55 (1st Cir.2000).

"After the PROTECT Act, the statute requires de novo review not merely of the ultimate decision to depart, but also of 'the district court's application of the guidelines to the facts.' § 3742(e). If this court agrees that the decision to depart was justified under the guidelines, however, the *extent* of the departure granted by the district court is reviewed deferentially, just as it was prior to the PROTECT Act." Id.; United States v. Frazier, 340 F.3d 5, 14 n.4 (1st Cir.2003); *see also* United States v. Mallon, 345 F.3d 943, 946 (7th Cir.2003); United States v. Thurston, 358 F.3d 51 (1st Cir.2004), *certiorari granted*, 543 U.S. 1097, 125 S.Ct. 984 (2005) [On petition for writ of certiorari to the United States Court of Appeals for the First Circuit granted. Judgment vacated, and case remanded to the United States Court of Appeals for the First Circuit for further consideration in light of United States v. Booker, 543 U.S. 220, 125 S. Ct. 738 (2005).]

2. Rules of Evidence

Williams v. New York

United States Supreme Court, 1949.
337 U.S. 241, 69 S.Ct. 1079.

■ Justice Black delivered the opinion of the Court.

* * *

About five weeks after the verdict of guilty with recommendation of life imprisonment, and after a statutory pre-sentence investigation report to the judge, the defendant was brought to court to be sentenced. Asked what he had to say, appellant protested his innocence. After each of his three lawyers had appealed to the court to accept the jury's recommendation of a life sentence, the judge gave reasons why he felt that the death sentence should be imposed. He narrated the shocking details of the crime as shown by the trial evidence, expressing his own complete belief in appellant's guilt. He stated that the pre-sentence investigation revealed many material facts concerning appellant's background which though relevant to the question of punishment could not properly have been brought to the attention of the jury in its consideration of the question of guilt. He referred to the experience appellant "had had on thirty other burglaries in and about the same vicinity" where the murder had been committed. The appellant had not been convicted of these burglaries although the judge had information that he had confessed to some and had been identified as the perpetrator of some of the others. The judge also referred to certain activities of appellant as shown by the probation report that indicated appellant possessed "a morbid sexuality" and classified him as a "menace to society." The accuracy of the statements made by the judge as to appellant's background and past practices were not challenged by appellant or his counsel, nor was the judge asked to disregard any of them or to afford appellant a chance to refute or discredit any of them by cross-examination or otherwise.

The case presents a serious and difficult question. The question relates to the rules of evidence applicable to the manner in which a judge may obtain information to guide him in the imposition of sentence upon an already convicted defendant. Within limits fixed by statutes, New York judges are given a broad discretion to decide the type and extent of punishment for convicted defendants. Here, for example, the judge's discretion was to sentence to life imprisonment or death. To aid a judge in exercising this discretion intelligently the New York procedural policy encourages him to consider information about the convicted person's past life, health, habits, conduct, and mental and moral propensities. The sentencing judge may consider such information even though obtained outside the courtroom from persons whom a defendant has not been permitted to confront or cross-examine....

Appellant urges that the New York statutory policy is in irreconcilable conflict with the underlying philosophy of a second procedural policy grounded in the due process of law clause of the Fourteenth Amendment. That policy ... is in part that no person shall be tried and convicted of an offense unless he is given reasonable notice of the charges against him and is afforded an opportunity to examine adverse witnesses.

* * *

Tribunals passing on the guilt of a defendant always have been hedged in by strict evidentiary procedural limitations. But ... a sentencing judge could exercise a wide discretion in the sources and types of evidence used to assist him in determining the kind and extent of punishment to be imposed within limits fixed by law. Out-of-court affidavits have been used frequently, and of course in the smaller communities sentencing judges naturally have in mind their knowledge of the personalities and backgrounds of convicted offenders....

... In a trial before verdict the issue is whether a defendant is guilty of having engaged in certain criminal conduct of which he has been specifically accused. Rules of evidence have been fashioned for criminal trials which narrowly confine the trial contest to evidence that is strictly relevant to the particular offense charged. These rules rest in part on a necessity to prevent a time consuming and confusing trial of collateral issues. They were also designed to prevent tribunals concerned solely with the issue of guilt of a particular offense from being influenced to convict for that offense by evidence that the defendant had habitually engaged in other misconduct. A sentencing judge, however, is not confined to the narrow issue of guilt. His task within fixed statutory or constitutional limits is to determine the type and extent of punishment after the issue of guilt has been determined. Highly relevant—if not essential—to his selection of an appropriate sentence is the possession of the fullest information possible concerning the defendant's life and characteristics. And modern concepts individualizing punishment have made it all the more necessary that a sentencing judge not be denied an opportunity to obtain pertinent information by a requirement of rigid adherence to restrictive rules of evidence properly applicable to the trial.

Undoubtedly the New York statutes emphasize a prevalent modern philosophy of penology that the punishment should fit the offender and not merely the crime. The belief no longer prevails that every offense in a like legal category calls for an identical punishment without regard to the past life and habits of a particular offender. This whole country has traveled far from the period in which the death sentence was an automatic and commonplace result of convictions—even for offenses today deemed trivial. Today's philosophy of individualizing sentences makes sharp distinctions for example between first and repeated offenders. Indeterminate sentences, the ultimate termination of which are sometimes decided by nonjudicial agencies have to a large extent taken the place of the old rigidly fixed punishments. The practice of probation which relies heavily on nonjudicial implementation has been accepted as a wise policy....

Modern changes in the treatment of offenders make it more necessary now than a century ago for observance of the distinctions in the evidential procedure in the trial and sentencing processes. For indeterminate sentences and probation have resulted in an increase in the discretionary powers exercised in fixing punishments. In general, these modern changes have not resulted in making the lot of offenders harder. On the contrary a strong motivating force for the changes has been the belief that by careful study of the lives and personalities of convicted offenders many could be less severely punished and restored sooner to complete freedom and useful citizenship. This belief to a large extent has been justified.

Under the practice of individualizing punishments, investigational techniques have been given an important role. Probation workers making reports of their investigations have not been trained to prosecute but to aid offenders. Their reports have been given a high value by conscientious judges who want to sentence persons on the best available information rather than on guesswork and inadequate information. To deprive sentencing judges of this kind of information would undermine modern penological procedural policies that have been cautiously adopted throughout the nation after careful consideration and experimentation. We must recognize that most of the information now relied upon by judges to guide them in the intelligent imposition of sentences would be unavailable if information were restricted to that given in open court by witnesses subject to cross-examination. And the modern probation report draws on information concerning every aspect of a defendant's life.[1] The type and extent of this information make totally impractical if not impossible open court testimony with cross-examination. Such a procedure could endlessly delay criminal administration in a retrial of collateral issues.

... In determining whether a defendant shall receive a one-year minimum or a twenty-year maximum sentence, we do not think the Federal Constitution restricts the view of the sentencing judge to the information received in open court. The due-process clause should not be treated as a device for freezing the evidential procedure of sentencing in the mold of trial procedure. So to treat the due-process clause would hinder if not preclude all courts—state and federal—from making progressive efforts to improve the administration of criminal justice.

* * *

... We hold that appellant was not denied due process of law.[2]

Affirmed.

■ The dissent of JUSTICE RUTLEDGE is omitted.

■ JUSTICE MURPHY dissenting.

A combination of factors in this case impels me to dissent.

Petitioner was convicted of murder by a jury, and sentenced to death by the judge. The jury which heard the trial unanimously recommended life imprisonment as a suitable punishment for the defendant. They had observed him throughout the trial, had heard all the evidence adduced against him, and in spite of the shocking character of the crime of which they found him guilty, were unwilling to decree that his life should be taken. In our criminal courts the jury sits as the representative of the community; its voice is that of the society against which the crime was

1. A publication circulated by the Administrative Office of the United States Courts contains a suggested form for all United States probation reports and serves as an example of the type of information contained in the reports. This form consists of thirteen "marginal headings." (1) Offense; (2) Prior Record; (3) Family History; (4) Home and Neighborhood; (5) Education; (6) Religion; (7) Interests and Activities; (8) Health (physical and mental); (9) Employment; (10) Resources; (11) Summary; (12) Plan; and (13) Agencies Interested. Each of the headings is further broken down into sub-headings. The form represents a framework into which information can be inserted to give the sentencing judge a composite picture of the defendant. Administrative Office of the United States Courts, The Presentence Investigation Report, Pub. No. 101 (1943).

2. What we have said is not to be accepted as a holding that the sentencing procedure is immune from scrutiny under the due-process clause. See Townsend v. Burke, 334 U.S. 736, 68 S.Ct. 1252.

committed. A judge even though vested with statutory authority to do so, should hesitate indeed to increase the severity of such a community expression.

He should be willing to increase it, moreover, only with the most scrupulous regard for the rights of the defendant. The record before us indicates that the judge exercised his discretion to deprive a man of his life, in reliance on material made available to him in a probation report, consisting almost entirely of evidence that would have been inadmissible at the trial. Some, such as allegations of prior crimes, was irrelevant. Much was incompetent as hearsay. All was damaging, and none was subject to scrutiny by the defendant.

Due process of law includes at least the idea that a person accused of crime shall be accorded a fair hearing through all the stages of the proceedings against him. I agree with the Court as to the value and humaneness of liberal use of probation reports as developed by modern penologists, but, in a capital case, against the unanimous recommendation of a jury, where the report would concededly not have been admissible at the trial, and was not subject to examination by the defendant, I am forced to conclude that the high commands of due process were not obeyed.

NOTES

1. Justice Black's view of the efficacy of indeterminate sentences and individualized sentencing would draw much dissent today, in the era of guideline sentencing. The tenor of *Williams* is that, in sentencing proceedings there are few, if any, rules. In the 1990s, the *Williams* opinion would not be written the same way and its result in a capital case would not be the same, but its holding regarding rules of evidence still holds sway and the idea that sentencing a defendant is different from trying a defendant remains a central tenet of the law.

On the question of considering in sentence hearings that which would be inadmissible at trial, *see* United States v. Query, 928 F.2d 383 (11th Cir.1991) (hearsay); United States v. Tejada, 956 F.2d 1256 (2d Cir.1992) (illegally obtained evidence); United States v. McCrory, 930 F.2d 63 (D.C.Cir.1991) (same); United States v. Ochoa, 659 F.2d 547 (5th Cir.1981) (state conviction pending on appeal); Smith v. United States, 551 F.2d 1193 (10th Cir.1977) (prior arrests); U.S.S.G. § 4A1.3,1B1.3 ("a prior arrest record itself shall not be considered" in computing criminal history, but may be evidence of "relevant conduct" if underlying conduct proved by preponderance of evidence); United States v. Metz, 470 F.2d 1140 (3d Cir.1972) (pending indictments); United States v. Doyle, 348 F.2d 715 (2d Cir.1965) (dismissed charges); U.S.S.G. § 1B1.4 commentary (same).

The rule permitting a broad range of factors to be considered has been criticized in Nemerson, "Coercive Sentencing", 64 Minn.L.Rev. 699 (1980). However, Congress explicitly endorsed the rule when it enacted the Sentencing Reform Act of 1984 providing "No limitation shall be placed on the information concerning the background, character, and conduct of a person convicted of an offense which a court of the United States may receive and consider for the purpose of imposing an appropriate sentence." 18 U.S.C. § 3577. Moreover, the Sentencing Guidelines reiterate: "In determining the sentence to impose within the guidelines range, or whether a departure from the guidelines is warranted, the court may consider without limitation, any information concerning the background, character and conduct of the defendant, unless otherwise prohibited by law." See 18 U.S.C. § 3661.

2. A legislature may choose to limit the scope of evidence at sentencing. This may be done by explicit language or by making sentences mandatory. There are limitations to this in capital cases.

3. In death penalty cases, Eighth Amendment principles prevent legislatures from restricting the fact-finder's ability to consider mitigating circumstances. In Woodson v. North Carolina, 428 U.S. 280, 96 S.Ct. 2978 (1976), the Court held that, in a capital case, a statute which imposed a *mandatory* death sentence—and, thus, preempted the judge's sentencing function—was unconstitutional. Several states had enacted mandatory execution statutes to avoid the effect of Furman v. Georgia, 408 U.S. 238, 92 S.Ct. 2726 (1972), which voided all pending death sentences because, according to the plurality, the imposition of those sentences was "pregnant with discrimination." Nonetheless, *Woodson* concluded that, in a capital case, the respect for humanity underlying the eighth amendment required the court to consider the character and record of the individual and the circumstances of the offense. The Ohio capital punishment statute, enacted in the wake of *Furman*, required the imposition of the death penalty in the absence of a finding that any of three statutory mitigating factors was present: (1) the victim induced or facilitated the offense; (2) the crime was committed under duress or provocation; or (3) the defendant was operating under a mental deficiency that did not rise to the level of an insanity defense. In Lockett v. Ohio, 438 U.S. 586, 98 S.Ct. 2954 (1978), the Court held the statute too restrictive to permit a full consideration of all factors in mitigation before a death sentence was imposed. In Eddings v. Oklahoma, 455 U.S. 104, 102 S.Ct. 869 (1982), the sentencing judge refused to hear evidence of defendant's troubled youth, beatings by his father and severe emotional disturbance, and the Court remanded, holding that the Eighth Amendment required consideration of the defendant's character and record as well as the circumstances of the offense. This concept was carried further in Skipper v. South Carolina, 476 U.S. 1, 106 S.Ct. 1669 (1986), where the Court held that testimony of two prison officials and a regular visitor of defendant during his incarceration between arrest and trial should have been admitted to show his adaptability to prison life, and in Penry v. Lynaugh, 492 U.S. 302, 109 S.Ct. 2934 (1989), where the Court held that evidence of mental retardation and childhood abuse had to be considered for its mitigating value, not just for its bearing on "future dangerousness."

Several members of the Court (Justices Scalia, Thomas, and Rehnquist), however, believe that the result in *Woodson* is open to question. Concurring in Graham v. Collins, 506 U.S. 461, 113 S.Ct. 892 (1993), Justice Thomas argued: "To withhold the death penalty out of sympathy for a defendant who is a member of a favored group is no different from a decision to impose the penalty on the basis of negative bias, and it matters not how narrow the class of death-eligible defendants or crimes. Surely that is exactly what the petitioners and the Legal Defense Fund argued in Woodson and Roberts. ... It is manifest that 'the power to be lenient [also] is the power to discriminate.' " (citations omitted).

The strain between mercy and discrimination led Justice Blackmun to declare categorical opposition to the death penalty in Callins v. Collins, 510 U.S. 1141, 114 S.Ct. 1127 (1994) (dissent from denial of certiorari):

> To be fair, a capital sentencing scheme must treat each person convicted of a capital offense with that "degree of respect due the uniqueness of the individual." Lockett v. Ohio (1978) (plurality opinion). That means affording the sentencer the power and discretion to grant mercy in a particular case, and providing avenues for the consideration of any and all relevant mitigating evidence that would justify a sentence less than death.

> Reasonable consistency, on the other hand, requires that the death penalty be inflicted evenhandedly, in accordance with reason and objective standards, rather than by whim, caprice, or prejudice.
>
> * * *
>
> [I]n the death penalty area, this Court, in my view, has engaged in a futile effort to balance these constitutional demands, and now is retreating not only from the Furman promise of consistency and rationality, but from the requirement of individualized sentencing as well. ... From this day forward, I no longer shall tinker with the machinery of death. For more than 20 years I have endeavored—indeed, I have struggled—along with a majority of this Court, to develop procedural and substantive rules that would lend more than the mere appearance of fairness to the death penalty endeavor. ... I feel morally and intellectually obligated simply to concede that the death penalty experiment has failed. ... The basic question—does the system accurately and consistently determine which defendants "deserve" to die?—cannot be answered in the affirmative.

Which is the preferable way out of this dilemma—a mandatory death penalty or the abolition of it? Or is the dilemma a dilemma at all? Should these principles be applied to all sentences? See infra Section 2(d).

4. In capital cases and others there are an increasing number of statutes which permit or mandate the right of a victim to testify as to the harm done. Such testimony is often heard, in any event, at trial, and many courts allowed it at sentencing when the victims had something more to say. In Booth v. Maryland, 482 U.S. 496, 107 S.Ct. 2529 (1987) the Court held that such testimony is inadmissible in capital cases. See also South Carolina v. Gathers, 490 U.S. 805, 109 S.Ct. 2207 (1989). Both opinions were overruled in Payne v. Tennessee, 501 U.S. 808, 111 S.Ct. 2597 (1991). The Court regarded its holding as an extension of the principle in *Lockett v. Ohio* which mandates full consideration of all factors. The Court said:

> We are now of the view that a State may properly conclude that for the jury to assess meaningfully the defendant's moral culpability and blameworthiness, it should have before it at the sentencing phase evidence of the specific harm caused by the defendant. "[T]he State has a legitimate interest in counteracting the mitigating evidence which the defendant is entitled to put in, by reminding the sentencer that just as the murderer should be considered as an individual, so too the victim is an individual whose death represents a unique loss to society and in particular to his family." *Booth* (White, J., dissenting). By turning the victim into a "faceless stranger at the penalty phase of a capital trial," *Gathers* (O'Connor, J., dissenting), *Booth* deprives the State of the full moral force of its evidence and may prevent the jury from having before it all the information necessary to determine the proper punishment for a first-degree murder.
>
> The present case is an example of the potential for such unfairness. The capital sentencing jury heard testimony from Payne's girlfriend that they met at church, that he was affectionate, caring, kind to her children, that he was not an abuser of drugs or alcohol, and that it was inconsistent with his character to have committed the murders. Payne's parents testified that he was a good son, and a clinical psychologist testified that Payne was an extremely polite prisoner and suffered from a low IQ. None of this testimony was related to the circumstances of Payne's brutal crimes. In contrast, the only evidence of the impact of Payne's offenses during the sentencing phase was Nicholas' grandmother's description—in response to a single question—that the child misses his mother and baby sister. Payne argues that the Eighth Amendment commands that the jury's death

sentence must be set aside because the jury heard this testimony. But the testimony illustrated quite poignantly some of the harm that Payne's killing had caused; there is nothing unfair about allowing the jury to bear in mind that harm at the same time as it considers the mitigating evidence introduced by the defendant. The Supreme Court of Tennessee in this case obviously felt the unfairness of the rule pronounced by *Booth* when it said "[i]t is an affront to the civilized members of the human race to say that at sentencing in a capital case, a parade of witnesses may praise the background, character and good deeds of Defendant (as was done in this case), without limitation as to relevancy, but nothing may be said that bears upon the character of, or the harm imposed, upon the victims." 791 S.W.2d, at 19.

In *Gathers*, as indicated above, we extended the holding of *Booth* barring victim impact evidence to the prosecutor's argument to the jury. Human nature being what it is, capable lawyers trying cases to juries try to convey to the jurors that the people involved in the underlying events are, or were, living human beings, with something to be gained or lost from the jury's verdict. Under the aegis of the Eighth Amendment, we have given the broadest latitude to the defendant to introduce relevant mitigating evidence reflecting on his individual personality, and the defendant's attorney may argue that evidence to the jury. Petitioner's attorney in this case did just that. For the reasons discussed above, we now reject the view—expressed in *Gathers*—that a State may not permit the prosecutor to similarly argue to the jury the human cost of the crime of which the defendant stands convicted. We reaffirm the view expressed by Justice Cardozo in *Snyder v. Massachusetts* (1934): "justice, though due to the accused, is due to the accuser also. The concept of fairness must not be strained till it is narrowed to a filament. We are to keep the balance true."

We thus hold that if the State chooses to permit the admission of victim impact evidence and prosecutorial argument on that subject, the Eighth Amendment erects no *per se* bar. A State may legitimately conclude that evidence about the victim and about the impact of the murder on the victim's family is relevant to the jury's decision as to whether or not the death penalty should be imposed. There is no reason to treat such evidence differently than other relevant evidence is treated.

C. THE PRE-*BLAKELY/BOOKER* TRANSFORMATION

McMillan v. Pennsylvania

Supreme Court of the United States, 1986.
477 U.S. 79, 106 S.Ct. 2411.

■ JUSTICE REHNQUIST delivered the opinion of the Court.

[Pennsylvania law provided that, if during the course of certain felonies, the offender "visibly possessed a firearm" the trial court must impose a sentence of at least five years. Visible possession of a firearm was not an element of the crime but a factor of aggravation. Under law, the state had to and did provide notice that it intended to invoke this law. One of the issues on appeal was whether the prosecution had to prove the "visible possession of a firearm" beyond a reasonable doubt.]

Section 9712 "ups the ante" for the defendant only by raising to five years the minimum sentence which may be imposed within no impression of having been tailored to permit the visible possession finding to be a tail which wags the dog of the substantive offense. Petitioners' claim that visible possession under the Pennsylvania statute is "really" an element of the offenses for which they are being punished—that Pennsylvania has in effect defined a new set of upgraded felonies—would have at least more superficial appeal if a finding of visible possession exposed them to greater or additional punishment, cf. 18 U. S. C. § 2113(d) (providing separate and greater punishment for bank robberies accomplished through "use of a dangerous weapon or device"), but it does not.

* * *

Having concluded that States may treat "visible possession of a firearm" as a sentencing consideration rather than an element of a particular offense, we now turn to petitioners' subsidiary claim that due process nonetheless requires that visible possession be proved by at least clear and convincing evidence. Like the court below, we have little difficulty concluding that in this case the preponderance standard satisfies due process.... There is, after all, only one Due Process Clause in the Fourteenth Amendment. Furthermore, petitioners do not and could not claim that a sentencing court may never rely on a particular fact in passing sentence without finding that fact by "clear and convincing evidence." Sentencing courts have traditionally heard evidence and found facts without any prescribed burden of proof at all. See *Williams v. New York* (1949). Pennsylvania has deemed a particular fact relevant and prescribed a particular burden of proof. We see nothing in Pennsylvania's scheme that would warrant constitutionalizing burdens of proof at sentencing.[1]

Petitioners apparently concede that Pennsylvania's scheme would pass constitutional muster if only it did not remove the sentencing court's discretion, i.e., if the legislature had simply directed the court to *consider* visible possession in passing sentence. We have some difficulty fathoming why the due process calculus would change simply because the legislature has seen fit to provide sentencing courts with additional guidance. Nor is there merit to the claim that a heightened burden of proof is required because visible possession is a fact "concerning the crime committed" rather than the background or character of the defendant. Sentencing courts necessarily consider the circumstances of an offense in selecting the

1. *Addington v. Texas* (1979), and *Santosky v. Kramer* (1982), which respectively applied the "clear and convincing evidence" standard where the State sought involuntary commitment to a mental institution and involuntary termination of parental rights, are not to the contrary. Quite unlike the situation in those cases, criminal sentencing takes place only after a defendant has been adjudged guilty beyond a reasonable doubt. Once the reasonable-doubt standard has been applied to obtain a valid conviction, "the criminal defendant has been constitutionally deprived of his liberty to the extent that the State may confine him." *Meachum v. Fano* (1976). As noted in text, sentencing courts have always operated without constitutionally imposed burdens of proof; embracing petitioners' suggestion that we apply the clear-and-convincing standard here would significantly alter criminal sentencing, for we see no way to distinguish the visible possession finding at issue here from a host of other express or implied findings sentencing judges typically make on the way to passing sentence.

appropriate punishment, and we have consistently approved sentencing schemes that mandate consideration of facts related to the crime, e.g., Proffitt v. Florida (1976), without suggesting that those facts must be proved beyond a reasonable doubt. The Courts of Appeals have uniformly rejected due process challenges to the preponderance standard under the federal "dangerous special offender" statute ... See United States v. Davis, 710 F.2d 104 (C.A.3) (collecting cases)....

NOTES

1. *Dog–Wagging Tails?* The enhancement in *McMillan* was only five years, but much greater enhancements may be proved at sentencing under the Federal Sentencing Guidelines. For example, the Third Circuit in United States v. Kikumura, 918 F.2d 1084 (3d Cir.1990), addressed the burden of proof issue in a case in which evidence brought forward at the sentencing hearing altered defendant's sentence from 27–33 months to 30 years imprisonment. The court held that a clear and convincing standard of proof was appropriate, distinguishing *McMillan:* "This is perhaps the most dramatic example imaginable of a sentencing hearing that functions as 'a tail which wags the dog of the substantive offense.' McMillan, 477 U.S. at 88. In this extreme context, we believe, a court cannot reflexively apply the truncated procedures that are perfectly adequate for all of the more mundane, familiar sentencing determinations."

The Seventh Circuit recently remanded a case in which information about drug quantities proved at sentencing through police investigative reports of an interview with a coconspirator provided the basis for a six-level increase in the defendant's offense level. The out-of court statements "considering the gravity of their consequences, give us pause" especially in light of the fact that the prices per quantity given by the coconspirator "defie[d] common sense." Though a judge need not hear direct testimony from witnesses to establish sentencing factors and relevant conduct, the court said "we think it's not a terribly bad idea to do so when the witness is going to provide the basis for, as here, 97 percent of the defendant's relevant conduct." United States v. Robinson, 164 F.3d 1068 (7th Cir.1999).

The Supreme Court reaffirmed *McMillan* in United States v. Watts, 519 U.S. 148, 117 S.Ct. 633 (1997), but noted: "We acknowledge a divergence of opinion among the Circuits as to whether, in extreme circumstances, relevant conduct that would dramatically increase the sentence must be based on clear and convincing evidence. The cases presented before us today do not present such exceptional circumstances, and we therefore do not address that issue."

For a case presenting the mirror-image of *McMillan*, in which gun possession was proved at trial and a murder at sentencing, see United States v. Lombard, 102 F.3d 1 (1st Cir.1996) (reluctantly upholding life sentence imposed for firearms violation based on murders proved at sentencing) and United States v. Stokes, 947 F.Supp. 546 (1996) (dismissing same sort of prosecution for "constitutional concerns"), reversed on appeal, 124 F.3d 39 (1st Cir.1997). Despite affirming the sentence in *Lombard*, the First Circuit panel commented: "In the past, uncharged conduct was merely a background fact, like the defendant's criminal record or his habit of kicking his dog, that a judge might consider in making the highly discretionary, and largely ad hoc, decision as to sentence. The guidelines have altered matters in at least one significant respect. We now have a regime that, aiming to provide equal treatment, requires the sentencing judge to make findings as to relevant uncharged conduct and absent a departure requires the judge to sentence on that basis within a very narrow range. ... Thus a finding of an uncharged crime at sentencing, and the compulsory fixing of the sentence on that basis, makes the sentencing itself now look somewhat more like a conviction for that uncharged crime—but without the benefit of the criminal standard of proof beyond a reasonable doubt or, for that matter, an indictment or jury trial on that crime." See United States v. Restrepo, 946 F.2d 654 (9th Cir.1991) (en banc) (Norris J., dissenting, arguing that mandatory guidelines create a "liberty interest" in baseline sentence, which cannot be changed without heightened procedural safeguards).

For opposing commentary, compare Herman, The Tail that Wagged the Dog: Bifurcated Fact–Finding Under the Federal Sentencing Guidelines and the Limits of Due Process, 66 S. Cal. L. Rev. 289 (1992), ABA Criminal Justice Sentencing Standards, 18–3.6 (1994) (restricting consideration at sentencing to crime of conviction), with Wilkins, Jr. & Steer, Relevant Conduct: The Cornerstone of the Federal Sentencing Guidelines, 41 S. Cal. L. Rev. 495, 496 (1990) and Breyer, The Federal Guidelines and the Key Compromises on which They Rest, 17 Hofstra L. Rev. 1 (1988).

The Court has recently struggled with the argument that McMillan's holding was limited to sentencing enhancements that did not raise the statutory maximum for the crime. In Almendarez–Torres v. United States, 523 U.S. 224, 118 S.Ct. 1219 (1998), the Court held that it was constitutionally unproblematic to treat recidivism as a sentencing factor rather than as an element of the offense, despite the fact that proof of the prior crimes at sentencing by only a preponderance of evidence allowed the defendant to be sentenced to serve a term longer than the maximum sentence prescribed for the crime of which he was convicted. Justice Scalia wrote a strong dissent in both *Torres* and Monge v. California, 524 U.S. 721, 118 S.Ct. 2246 (1998) a case raising similar issues about whether double jeopardy principles applied to sentencing hearings. In *Monge*, Justice Scalia posed the following hypothetical: "Suppose that a State repealed all of the violent crimes in its criminal code and replaced them with only one offense, 'knowingly causing injury to another,' bearing a penalty of 30 days in prison, but subject to a series of 'sentencing enhancements' authorizing additional punishment up to life imprisonment or death on the basis of various levels of mens rea, severity of injury and other surrounding circumstances. Could the state then grant the defendant a jury trial, with requirement of proof beyond a reasonable doubt, solely on the question whether he 'knowingly caused injury to another,' but leave it for the judge to determine by a preponderance of the evidence whether the defendant acted intentionally or accidentally, whether he used a deadly weapon, and whether the victim ultimately died from the injury the defendant inflicted?" He concluded that any sentencing enhancement that would raise the statutory maximum sentence of the crime of conviction should be considered an element of the crime itself, requiring proof at trial by a reasonable doubt standard. He was joined by Justices Souter and Ginsburg.

In Jones v. United States, 526 U.S. 227, 119 S.Ct. 1215 (1999), however, the Court took a different view in reading a federal carjacking statute. In Jones, the Court held that the increase in the statutory maximum sentence for cases involving death or serious bodily injury could not be made at sentencing, instead, death or serious bodily injury was an element of the offense to be proved at trial.

Though relying in part on the legislative history of the provision as well as background practice in other statutes, the Court decided to read the statute to require proof of death or serious bodily injury beyond a reasonable doubt in order to avoid "grave and doubtful" constitutional questions: "*McMillan*, then, recognizes a question under both the Due Process Clause of the Fourteenth Amendment and the jury guarantee of the Sixth: when a jury determination has not been waived, may judicial factfinding by a preponderance support the application of a provision that increases the potential severity of the penalty for a variant of a given crime?. . . .

The terms of the carjacking statute illustrate very well what is at stake. If serious bodily injury were merely a sentencing factor under § 2119(2) (increasing the authorized penalty by two thirds, to 25 years), then death would presumably be nothing more than a sentencing factor under subsection (3) (increasing the penalty range to life). If a potential penalty might rise from 15 years to life on a nonjury determination, the jury's role would correspondingly shrink from the significance usually carried by determinations of guilt to the relative importance of low-level gatekeeping: in some cases, a jury finding of fact necessary for a maximum 15—year sentence would merely open the door to a judicial finding sufficient for life imprisonment. It is therefore no trivial question to ask whether recognizing an unlimited legislative power to authorize determinations setting ultimate sentencing limits without a jury would invite erosion of the jury's function to a point against which a line must necessarily be drawn." The Court distinguished *Almendarez-Torres* on the ground that recidivism was traditionally a sentencing factor and relied on prior convictions which themselves had to be established "through procedures satisfying the fair notice, reasonable doubt, and jury trial guarantees."

Justices Stevens and Scalia concurred, Stevens on the ground that any factor which increased either the minimum or maximum sentence would require proof at trial, and Scalia on the ground that any factor which increased the maximum sentence would require proof at trial. Justice Kennedy, joined by Rehnquist, O'Connor, and Breyer, dissented. The dissent argued that the Court's interpretation of the statute was contrary to its plain meaning, and that the opinion conflicted with *Almendarez-Torres'* analysis. The dissent also pointed out that if the rule established by the majority's opinion were merely that a factor proved at sentencing could not raise the statutory maximum, Congress could comply with the Court's opinion by minor redrafting—making clear that the statutory maximum for the offense is life, and adding that if no death or bodily injury resulted, the penalty would be only 15 years. "If so, the Court's principle amounts to nothing more than chastising Congress for failing to use the approved phrasing in expressing its intent ... No constitutional values are served by so formalistic an approach." If, on the other hand, the Court's principle has more substantive bite, forbidding certain kinds of factors to be proved at sentencing, it would call into question much of guideline sentencing, both at the state and federal levels.

For recent academic commentary, see Kate Stith & Jose A. Cabranes, Fear of Judging: Sentencing Guidelines in the Federal Courts (1998).

The Supreme Court finally limited the practice of proving other criminal conduct at sentencing on a preponderance standard, rather than at jury trial on a beyond-a-reasonable-doubt standard in Apprendi v. New Jersey, 530 U.S. 466, 120 S.Ct. 2348 (2000). Relying on In re Winship, 397 U.S. 358, 90 S.Ct. 1068 (1970) and Jones v. United States, 526 U.S. 227, 119 S.Ct. 1215 (1999), the Court held that any fact that increases the penalty for a crime beyond the statutory maximum sentence, except a prior conviction, must be submitted to a jury and proved beyond a reasonable doubt. The Court pointed out that without such a restriction, states could redefine crimes to place much of the critical fact-finding at sentencing, circumventing the procedural protections of trial guaranteed in the Fifth and Sixth Amendments. The Court therefore struck down a New Jersey statute that increased the sentence for possession of a firearm from 5–10 years to 10–20 years if a judge finds at sentencing that the defendant's purpose was to intimidate others because of race, color, gender, handicap, religion, sexual orientation, or ethnicity.

A concurring opinion by Justice Thomas, based on sentencing practice around the time of the adoption of the Fourteenth Amendment due process clause, suggested a willingness to go further; arguing that any fact increasing a sentence must be considered an element of the crime to be proved to a jury beyond a reasonable doubt.

Dissents by Justices O'Connor and Breyer (one of the authors of the Federal Sentencing Guidelines), joined by The Chief Justice and Justice Kennedy, pointed out the "watershed" nature of this new constitutional rule and the danger it potentially posed for determinate sentencing schemes like the federal sentencing guidelines and many states'. Justice O'Connor pointed out that prior decisions had allowed sentencing judges absolute discretion within broad statutory ranges without any procedural protections or restrictions on fact-finding—so why should legislative direction for that discretion, designed to reduce inter-judge disparities, be more problematic or unfair? While the majority pointed out that the decision is limited to sentencing schemes in which the findings at sentencing change the statutory maximum for the offense, the dissents criticized this rule for being unprincipled, because states could easily rewrite their statutory maxima to make room for the enhancements, and because this "no exceeding the statutory maximum rule" fails to address itself to mandatory minimum penalties imposed for conduct proved only at sentencing. Justice Breyer suggested in his dissent that "the solution to the problem lies, not in prohibiting legislatures from enacting sentencing factors, but in sentencing rules that determine punishments on the basis of properly defined relevant conduct, with sensitivity to the need for procedural protections where sentencing factors are determined by a judge (for example, use of a 'reasonable doubt' standard), and invocation of the Due Process Clause where the history of the crime at issue, together with the nature of the facts to be proved, reveals unusual and serious procedural unfairness."

Justice Scalia, concurring with the majority, had a rejoinder for Justice Breyer: "The jury trial guarantee ... has never been efficient; but it has always been free."

The Court has been trying to sort out the implications of *Apprendi* in a trio of cases in the 2001–2002 term ... *Apprendi*, a hate crime case, held that an element of the crime that increased the sentence, must be submitted to the jury

In Ring v. Arizona, 536 U.S. 584, 122 S.Ct. 2428 (2002), the defendant was charged and convicted of and related crimes stemming from the shooting of a guard during the robbery of an armored car. Arizona followed a capital sentencing system in which the jury determines guilt and the judge alone weighs aggravating and mitigating factors. The judge in the *Ring* trial weighed the factual showings in the sentencing phase and condemned Ring to death. The defendant appealed, claiming that the Arizona capital sentencing scheme violated the Sixth Amendment because it left it to the judge rather than the jury to make the finding of fact required to raise the defendant's maximum penalty. The defendant argued that this violated the principles set forth in *Apprendi.* Although an earlier case upholding this system, Walton v. Arizona, 497 U.S. 639, 110 S.Ct. 3047 (1990), was cited approvingly in the *Apprendi* opinion, the Supreme Court overruled *Walton* in the *Ring* decision. The jury must make the death penalty decision.

In United States v. Cotton, 535 U.S. 625, 122 S.Ct. 1781 (2002), the defendant was charged with a conspiracy to distribute and to possess a "detectable amount" of cocaine. The indictment did not allege the amount of cocaine, a fact that potentially enhanced the maximum sentence the defendant could have received. The trial jury was instructed that the drug weight was not important, but the trial judge used the drug weight to raise the defendant's sentence. The Court of Appeals for the Fourth Circuit treated the cocaine amount as a jurisdictional element. Since the amount was not alleged in the indictment, the Court of Appeals vacated the trial sentence and imposed a sentence for the crime that did not depend on the drug amount. The Supreme Court reversed and remanded the case. The Sixth Amendment requires that the question of the drug weight must be alleged in the indictment and submitted to a jury. Nevertheless, the failure of the indictment to specify the drug quantity in this case did not deprive the court of the power to hear the case and impose sentence. The defendant did not properly object before the trial court and thus, the error did not threaten the fairness and integrity of the proceedings. The Court of Appeals was not justified in vacating the trial court's sentence. There was sufficient evidence adduced at trial to support the enhanced sentence. Justice O'Connor, joined by Chief Justice Rehnquist, dissented. Justice Kennedy wrote a separate concurring opinion, reiterating some of his earlier disagreement with the *Apprendi* holding.

The case was remanded.

Finally, in Harris v. United States, 536 U.S. 545, 122 S.Ct. 2406 (2002), the defendant was charged with drug and firearm offenses, including a charge that made it a crime to possess a firearm in connection with drug trafficking. The statute, 18 U.S.C. § 924 (c)(1)(A)(ii) provided that the minimum sentence of five years could be raised to seven years if the firearm was brandished during the crime. Justice Kennedy, in a plurality opinion, noted that not every fact that affects sentence is an element. Looking to the structure of section 924, Justice Kennedy found that the structure of the statute indicated the factor of brandishing was a sentencing factor and not an element of the crime. Thus the sentence, which was within the range provided by the statute, stood.

The Sentencing Guidelines Commentary states: "The Commission believes that use of a preponderance of the evidence standard is appropriate to meet due process requirements and policy concerns in resolving disputes regarding application of the guidelines to the facts of a case." § 6A1.3. The Sentencing Commission explains the dilemma: "The Commission recognized that a charge offense system [in which sentencing is based solely on the elements of the crimes proved or pled to] has drawbacks of its own. One of the most important is the potential it affords prosecutors to influence sentences by increasing or decreasing the number of counts in an indictment." On the other hand, "[t]he Commission found no practical way to combine and account for the large number of diverse harms arising in different circumstances; nor did it find a practical way to reconcile the need for a fair adjudicatory procedure with the need for a speedy sentencing process given the potential existence of hosts of adjudicated 'real harm' facts in many typical cases." In the end, the Commission wrote "guidelines that are descriptive of generic conduct rather than guidelines that track purely statutory language ... [and they] take account of a number of important, commonly occurring real offense elements such as role in the offense, the presence of a gun, or the amount of money actually taken, through alternative base offense levels, specific offense characteristics, cross references, and adjustments." Guidelines Manual, Ch. 1 Pt.A (4)(a) (2002).

2. The federal rule is fairly typical in requiring the prosecution to prove factors in aggravation and the defense to prove factors in mitigation. See United States v. Howard, 894 F.2d 1085 (9th Cir.1990); United States v. Kirk, 894 F.2d 1162 (10th Cir.1990).

3. Few courts have addressed the problem of applying a standard of proof—whether preponderance, clear and convincing, reasonable doubt—in a context where no rules of evidence apply. See, e.g., United States v. Simmons, 964 F.2d 763 (8th Cir.1992) (remanding for resentencing because could not determine basis for facts found—whether hearsay interview with probation officer, trial testimony, or co-defendant's statements). There are some statutory rules regarding proof. In Braxton v. United States, 500 U.S. 344, 111 S.Ct. 1854 (1991), four marshals came to arrest Braxton who fired shots which hit no one. He was charged with attempting to kill a marshal, assaulting a marshal and unlawfully using a firearm. He pled guilty without a plea agreement to the last two charges and stipulated that what the government says it could prove happened, happened. The court sentenced Braxton as though he had been convicted of attempting to kill (the charge to which he did not plead guilty). Federal law said the court could do this if the plea contained a stipulation that specifically establishes a more serious offense. The Supreme Court held that "a stipulation that at best supports two reasonable readings—one that Braxton shot across the room at the marshals when they entered, and one that he shot across the room before they entered to frighten them off—is [not] a stipulation that 'specifically establishes' that Braxton attempted to murder one of the marshals."

D. THE *BLAKELY/BOOKER* TRANSFORMATION

In 2000, the United States Supreme Court held Due Process requires that factors that lead to an extended sentence, in that case whether or not the crimes were committed with a biased, hate motive, must be submitted to a jury. "Other than the fact of a prior conviction, any fact that increases the penalty for a crime beyond the prescribed statutory maximum must be submitted to a jury, and proved beyond a reasonable doubt." Apprendi v. New Jersey, 530 U.S. 466, 493, 120 S.Ct. 2348, 2362 (2000). This worked a significant change, ultimately invalidating the mandatory nature of sentencing guidelines.

The Court first addressed the mandatory sentencing guidelines of the Washington State sentencing system. Applying the rule in *Apprendi*, the Court held that allowing judges to determine whether or not factors that increased the sentence range existed violated the Sixth Amendment.

Blakely v. Washington

United States Supreme Court, 2004.
542 U.S. 296, 124 S.Ct. 2531.

■ JUSTICE SCALIA delivered the opinion of the Court.

Petitioner Ralph Howard Blakely, Jr., pleaded guilty to the kidnaping of his estranged wife. The facts admitted in his plea, standing alone, supported a maximum sentence of 53 months. Pursuant to state law, the court imposed an "exceptional" sentence of 90 months after making a judicial determination that he had acted with "deliberate cruelty." We consider whether this violated petitioner's Sixth Amendment right to trial by jury.

I

Petitioner married his wife Yolanda in 1973. He was evidently a difficult man to live with, having been diagnosed at various times with psychological and personality disorders including paranoid schizophrenia. His wife ultimately filed for divorce. In 1998, he abducted her from their orchard home in Grant County, Washington, binding her with duct tape and forcing her at knifepoint into a wooden box in the bed of his pickup truck. In the process, he implored her to dismiss the divorce suit and related trust proceedings.

When the couple's 13–year–old son Ralphy returned home from school, petitioner ordered him to follow in another car, threatening to harm Yolanda with a shotgun if he did not do so. Ralphy escaped and sought help when they stopped at a gas station, but petitioner continued on with Yolanda to a friend's house in Montana. He was finally arrested after the friend called the police.

The State charged petitioner with first-degree kidnaping, Wash. Rev. Code Ann. § 9A.40.020(1) (2000). Upon reaching a plea agreement, however, it reduced the charge to second-degree kidnaping involving domestic violence and use of a firearm, see §§ 9A.40.030(1), 10.99.020(3)(p), 9.94A.125. 2Petitioner entered a guilty plea admitting the elements of second-degree kidnaping and the domestic-violence and firearm allegations, but no other relevant facts.

The case then proceeded to sentencing. In Washington, second-degree kidnaping is a class B felony. § 9A.40.030(3). State law provides that "[n]o person convicted of a [class B] felony shall be punished by confinement . . . exceeding . . . a term of ten years." § 9A.20.021(1)(b). Other provisions of state law, however, further limit the range of sentences a judge may impose. Washington's Sentencing Reform Act specifies, for petitioner's offense of second-degree kidnaping with a firearm, a "standard range" of 49 to 53 months. See § 9.94A.320 (seriousness level V for second-degree kidnaping); App. 27 (offender score 2 based on § 9.94A.360); § 9.94A.310(1), box 2–V (standard range of 13–17 months); § 9.94A.310(3)(b) (36–month firearm enhancement).[3] A judge may impose a sentence above the standard range if he finds "substantial and compelling reasons justifying an exceptional sentence." § 9.94A.120(2). The Act lists aggravating factors that justify such a departure, which it recites to be illustrative rather than exhaustive. § 9.94A.390. Nevertheless, "[a] reason offered to justify an exceptional sentence can be considered only if it takes into account factors other than those which are used in computing the standard range sentence for the offense." When a judge imposes an exceptional sentence, he must set forth findings of fact and conclusions of law supporting it. § 9.94A.120(3). A reviewing court will reverse the sentence if it finds that "under a clearly erroneous standard there is insufficient evidence in the record to support the reasons for imposing an exceptional sentence."

Pursuant to the plea agreement, the State recommended a sentence within the standard range of 49 to 53 months. After hearing Yolanda's description of the kidnaping, however, the judge rejected the State's recommendation and imposed an exceptional sentence of 90 months—37 months beyond the standard maximum.[4] He justified the sentence on the ground

3. The domestic-violence stipulation subjected petitioner to such measures as a "no-contact" order, see § 10.99.040, but did not increase the standard range of his sentence.

4. The judge found other aggravating factors, but the Court of Appeals questioned their validity under state law and their independent sufficiency to support the extent of the departure. See 111 Wn. App. 851, 868–870, and n 3, 47 P.3d 149, 158–159, and n 3 (2002). It affirmed the sentence solely on the finding of domestic violence with deliberate cruelty. We therefore focus only on that factor.

that petitioner had acted with "deliberate cruelty," a statutorily enumerated ground for departure in domestic-violence cases. § 9.94A.390(2)(h)(iii).

Faced with an unexpected increase of more than three years in his sentence, petitioner objected. The judge accordingly conducted a 3-day bench hearing featuring testimony from petitioner, Yolanda, Ralphy, a police officer, and medical experts. After the hearing, he issued 32 findings of fact, concluding:

> "The defendant's motivation to commit kidnapping was complex, contributed to by his mental condition and personality disorders, the pressures of the divorce litigation, the impending trust litigation trial and anger over his troubled interpersonal relationships with his spouse and children. While he misguidedly intended to forcefully reunite his family, his attempt to do so was subservient to his desire to terminate lawsuits and modify title ownerships to his benefit.
>
> "The defendant's methods were more homogeneous than his motive. He used stealth and surprise, and took advantage of the victim's isolation. He immediately employed physical violence, restrained the victim with tape, and threatened her with injury and death to herself and others. He immediately coerced the victim into providing information by the threatening application of a knife. He violated a subsisting restraining order."

The judge adhered to his initial determination of deliberate cruelty.

Petitioner appealed, arguing that this sentencing procedure deprived him of his federal constitutional right to have a jury determine beyond a reasonable doubt all facts legally essential to his sentence. The State Court of Appeals affirmed, relying on the Washington Supreme Court's rejection of a similar challenge in *Gore*, *supra*. The Washington Supreme Court denied discretionary review. We granted certiorari.

II

This case requires us to apply the rule we expressed in *Apprendi v. New Jersey* (2000): "Other than the fact of a prior conviction, any fact that increases the penalty for a crime beyond the prescribed statutory maximum must be submitted to a jury, and proved beyond a reasonable doubt." This rule reflects two longstanding tenets of common-law criminal jurisprudence: that the "truth of every accusation" against a defendant "should afterwards be confirmed by the unanimous suffrage of twelve of his equals and neighbours," 4 W. Blackstone, Commentaries on the Laws of England 343 (1769), and that "an accusation which lacks any particular fact which the law makes essential to the punishment is ... no accusation within the requirements of the common law, and it is no accusation in reason," 1 J. Bishop, Criminal Procedure § 87, p 55 (2d ed. 1872).[5] These principles have

5. Justice Breyer cites Justice O'Connor's *Apprendi* dissent for the point that this Bishop quotation means only that indictments must charge facts that trigger statutory aggravation of a common-law offense. (dissenting opinion). Of course, as he notes, Justice O'Connor was referring to an entirely different quotation, from *Archbold's* treatise (citing J. Archbold, Pleading and Evidence in Criminal Cases 51, 188 (15th ed.

been acknowledged by courts and treatises since the earliest days of graduated sentencing; we compiled the relevant authorities in *Apprendi*, and need not repeat them here.[6]

.... In this case, petitioner was sentenced to more than three years above the 53–month statutory maximum of the standard range because he had acted with "deliberate cruelty." The facts supporting that finding were neither admitted by petitioner nor found by a jury. The State nevertheless contends that there was no *Apprendi* violation because the relevant "statutory maximum" is not 53 months, but the 10–year maximum for class B felonies in § 9A.20.021(1)(b). It observes that no exceptional sentence may exceed that limit. See § 9.94A.420. Our precedents make clear, however, that the "statutory maximum" for *Apprendi* purposes is the maximum sentence a judge may impose *solely on the basis of the facts reflected in the jury verdict or admitted by the defendant.* ... In other words, the relevant "statutory maximum" is not the maximum sentence a judge may impose after finding additional facts, but the maximum he may impose *without* any additional findings. When a judge inflicts punishment that the jury's verdict alone does not allow, the jury has not found all the facts "which the law makes essential to the punishment," and the judge exceeds his proper authority.

The judge in this case could not have imposed the exceptional 90–month sentence solely on the basis of the facts admitted in the guilty plea. Those facts alone were insufficient because, as the Washington Supreme Court has explained, "[a] reason offered to justify an exceptional sentence can be considered only if it takes into account factors other than those which are used in computing the standard range sentence for the offense," ... which in this case included the elements of second-degree kidnaping and the use of a firearm, see §§ 9.94A.320, 9.94A.310(3)(b).[7] Had the judge imposed the 90–month sentence solely on the basis of the plea, he would have been reversed. See § 9.94A.210(4). The "maximum sentence" is no more 10 years here than it was 20 years in *Apprendi* (because that is what

1862)). Justice Breyer claims the two are "similar,", but they are as similar as chalk and cheese. Bishop was not "addressing" the "problem" of statutes that aggravate common-law offenses. Rather, the entire chapter of his treatise is devoted to the point that "every fact which is legally essential to the punishment" 1 Criminal Procedure § 81, at 51, must be charged in the indictment and proved to a jury ... As one "example" of this principle (appearing several pages before the language we quote in text above), he notes a statute aggravating common-law assault. But nowhere is there the slightest indication that his general principle was *limited* to that example. Even Justice Breyer's academic supporters do not make *that* claim

6. As to Justice O'Connor's criticism of the quantity of historical support for the *Apprendi* rule, (dissenting opinion): It bears repeating that the issue between us is not *whether* the Constitution limits States' authority to reclassify elements as sentencing factors (we all agree that it does); it is only which line, ours or hers, the Constitution draws. Criticism of the quantity of evidence favoring our alternative would have some force if it were accompanied by *any* evidence favoring hers. Justice O'Connor does not even provide a coherent alternative meaning for the jury-trial guarantee, unless one considers "whatever the legislature chooses to leave to the jury, so long as it does not go too far" coherent.

7. The State does not contend that the domestic-violence stipulation alone supports the departure. That the statute lists domestic violence as grounds for departure only when combined with some other aggravating factor suggests it could not. See §§ 9.94A.390(2)(h)(i)–(iii).

the judge could have imposed upon finding a hate crime) or death in *Ring* (because that is what the judge could have imposed upon finding an aggravator).

The State defends the sentence by drawing an analogy to those we upheld in McMillan v. Pennsylvania (1986), and Williams v. New York (1949). Neither case is on point. *McMillan* involved a sentencing scheme that imposed a statutory *minimum* if a judge found a particular fact. We specifically noted that the statute "does not authorize a sentence in excess of that otherwise allowed for [the underlying] offense.". *Williams* involved an indeterminate-sentencing regime that allowed a judge (but did not compel him) to rely on facts outside the trial record in determining whether to sentence a defendant to death. The judge could have "sentenced [the defendant] to death giving no reason at all." Thus, neither case involved a sentence greater than what state law authorized on the basis of the verdict alone.

Finally, the State tries to distinguish *Apprendi* and *Ring* by pointing out that the enumerated grounds for departure in its regime are illustrative rather than exhaustive. This distinction is immaterial. Whether the judge's authority to impose an enhanced sentence depends on finding a specified fact (as in *Apprendi*), one of several specified facts (as in *Ring*), or *any* aggravating fact (as here), it remains the case that the jury's verdict alone does not authorize the sentence. The judge acquires that authority only upon finding some additional fact.[8]

Because the State's sentencing procedure did not comply with the Sixth Amendment, petitioner's sentence is invalid.[9]

III

Our commitment to *Apprendi* in this context reflects not just respect for longstanding precedent, but the need to give intelligible content to the right of jury trial. That right is no mere procedural formality, but a fundamental reservation of power in our constitutional structure. Just as suffrage ensures the people's ultimate control in the legislative and executive branches, jury trial is meant to ensure their control in the judiciary.... *Apprendi* carries out this design by ensuring that the judge's authority to sentence derives wholly from the jury's verdict. Without that restriction, the jury would not exercise the control that the Framers intended.

Those who would reject *Apprendi* are resigned to one of two alternatives. The first is that the jury need only find whatever facts the legislature

8. Nor does it matter that the judge must, after finding aggravating facts, make a judgment that they present a compelling ground for departure. He cannot make that judgment without finding some facts to support it beyond the bare elements of the offense. Whether the judicially determined facts *require* a sentence enhancement or merely *allow* it, the verdict alone does not authorize the sentence.

9. The United States, as *amicus curiae*, urges us to affirm. It notes differences between Washington's sentencing regime and the Federal Sentencing Guidelines but questions whether those differences are constitutionally significant. See Brief for United States as *Amicus Curiae* 25–30. The Federal Guidelines are not before us, and we express no opinion on them.

chooses to label elements of the crime, and that those it labels sentencing factors—no matter how much they may increase the punishment—may be found by the judge. This would mean, for example, that a judge could sentence a man for committing murder even if the jury convicted him only of illegally possessing the firearm used to commit it—or of making an illegal lane change while fleeing the death scene. Not even *Apprendi*'s critics would advocate this absurd result.... The jury could not function as circuitbreaker in the State's machinery of justice if it were relegated to making a determination that the defendant at some point did something wrong, a mere preliminary to a judicial inquisition into the facts of the crime the State *actually* seeks to punish. 10

The second alternative is that legislatures may establish legally essential sentencing factors *within limits*—limits crossed when, perhaps, the sentencing factor is a "tail which wags the dog of the substantive offense." What this means in operation is that the law must not go *too far*—it must not exceed the judicial estimation of the proper role of the judge.

The subjectivity of this standard is obvious. Petitioner argued below that second-degree kidnaping with deliberate cruelty was essentially the same as first-degree kidnaping, the very charge he had avoided by pleading to a lesser offense. The court conceded this might be so but held it irrelevant. Petitioner's 90-month sentence exceeded the 53-month standard maximum by almost 70%; the Washington Supreme Court in other cases has upheld exceptional sentences 15 times the standard maximum.... Did the court go *too far* in any of these cases? There is no answer that legal analysis can provide. With *too far* as the yardstick, it is always possible to disagree with such judgments and never to refute them.

Whether the Sixth Amendment incorporates this manipulable standard rather than *Apprendi*'s bright-line rule depends on the plausibility of the claim that the Framers would have left definition of the scope of jury power up to judges' intuitive sense of how far is *too far*. We think that claim not plausible at all, because the very reason the Framers put a jury-trial guarantee in the Constitution is that they were unwilling to trust government to mark out the role of the jury.

IV

By reversing the judgment below, we are not, as the State would have it, "find[ing] determinate sentencing schemes unconstitutional." This case is not about whether determinate sentencing is constitutional, only about how it can be implemented in a way that respects the Sixth Amendment. Several policies prompted Washington's adoption of determinate sentencing, including proportionality to the gravity of the offense and parity among defendants. Nothing we have said impugns those salutary objectives....

But even assuming that restraint of judicial power unrelated to the jury's role is a Sixth Amendment objective, it is far from clear that *Apprendi* disserves that goal. Determinate judicial-factfinding schemes entail less judicial power than indeterminate schemes, but more judicial power than determinate *jury*-factfinding schemes. Whether *Apprendi* increases judicial power overall depends on what States with determinate judicial-factfinding schemes would do, given the choice between the two alternatives. Justice O'Connor simply assumes that the net effect will favor judges, but she has no empirical basis for that prediction. Indeed, what evidence we have points exactly the other way: When the Kansas Supreme Court found *Apprendi* infirmities in that State's determinate-sentencing regime in *State v. Gould*, 271 Kan. 394, 404–414, 23 P.3d 801, 809–814 (2001), the legislature responded not by reestablishing indeterminate sentencing but by applying *Apprendi*'s requirements to its current regime. The result was less, not more, judicial power.

Justice Breyer argues that *Apprendi* works to the detriment of criminal defendants who plead guilty by depriving them of the opportunity to argue sentencing factors to a judge. But nothing prevents a defendant from waiving his *Apprendi* rights. When a defendant pleads guilty, the State is free to seek judicial sentence enhancements so long as the defendant either stipulates to the relevant facts or consents to judicial factfinding. If appropriate waivers are procured, States may continue to offer judicial factfinding as a matter of course to all defendants who plead guilty. Even a defendant who stands trial may consent to judicial factfinding as to sentence enhancements, which may well be in his interest if relevant evidence would prejudice him at trial. We do not understand how *Apprendi* can possibly work to the detriment of those who are free, if they think its costs outweigh its benefits, to render it inapplicable.

Nor do we see any merit to Justice Breyer's contention that *Apprendi* is unfair to criminal defendants because, if States respond by enacting "17–element robbery crime[s]," prosecutors will have more elements with which to bargain. Bargaining already exists with regard to sentencing factors because defendants can either stipulate or contest the facts that make them applicable. If there is any difference between bargaining over sentencing factors and bargaining over elements, the latter probably favors the defendant. Every new element that a prosecutor can threaten to charge is also an element that a defendant can threaten to contest at trial and make the prosecutor prove beyond a reasonable doubt. Moreover, given the sprawling scope of most criminal codes, and the power to affect sentences by making (even nonbinding) sentencing recommendations, there is already no shortage of *in terrorem* tools at prosecutors' disposal.

Any evaluation of *Apprendi*'s "fairness" to criminal defendants must compare it with the regime it replaced, in which a defendant, with no warning in either his indictment or plea, would routinely see his maximum potential sentence balloon from as little as five years to as much as life imprisonment, see 21 U.S.C. §§ 841(b)(1)(A), (D), [21 USCS §§ 841(b)(1)(A), (D)][13] based not on facts proved to his peers beyond a reasonable doubt, but on facts extracted after trial from a report compiled

13. To be sure, Justice Breyer and the other dissenters would forbid those increases of sentence that violate the constitutional principle that tail shall not wag dog. The source of this principle is entirely unclear. Its precise effect, if precise effect it has, is presumably to require that the ratio of sentencing-factor add-on to basic criminal sentence be no greater than the ratio of caudal vertebrae to body in the breed of canine with the longest tail. Or perhaps no greater than the average such ratio for all breeds. Or perhaps the median. Regrettably, *Apprendi* has prevented full development of this line of jurisprudence.

by a probation officer who the judge thinks more likely got it right than got it wrong. We can conceive of no measure of fairness that would find more fault in the utterly speculative bargaining effects Justice Breyer identifies than in the regime he champions. Suffice it to say that, if such a measure exists, it is not the one the Framers left us with.

The implausibility of Justice Breyer's contention that *Apprendi* is unfair to criminal defendants is exposed by the lineup of *amici* in this case. It is hard to believe that the National Association of Criminal Defense Lawyers was somehow duped into arguing for the wrong side. Justice Breyer's only authority asking that defendants be protected from *Apprendi* is an article written not by a criminal defense lawyer but by a law professor and former prosecutor. (citing Bibas, *supra*); Association of American Law Schools Directory of Law Teachers 2003–2004, p 319.

Justice Breyer also claims that *Apprendi* will attenuate the connection between "real criminal conduct and real punishment" by encouraging plea bargaining and by restricting alternatives to adversarial factfinding. The short answer to the former point (even assuming the questionable premise that *Apprendi* does encourage plea bargaining ...) is that the Sixth Amendment was not written for the benefit of those who choose to forgo its protection. It guarantees the *right* to jury trial. It does not guarantee that a particular number of jury trials will actually take place. That more defendants elect to waive that right (because, for example, government at the moment is not particularly oppressive) does not prove that a constitutional provision guaranteeing *availability* of that option is disserved.

Justice Breyer's more general argument—that *Apprendi* undermines alternatives to adversarial factfinding—is not so much a criticism of *Apprendi* as an assault on jury trial generally. His esteem for "non-adversarial" truth-seeking processes supports just as well an argument against either. Our Constitution and the common-law traditions it entrenches, however, do not admit the contention that facts are better discovered by judicial inquisition than by adversarial testing before a jury. Justice Breyer may be convinced of the equity of the regime he favors, but his views are not the ones we are bound to uphold.

Ultimately, our decision cannot turn on whether or to what degree trial by jury impairs the efficiency or fairness of criminal justice. One can certainly argue that both these values would be better served by leaving justice entirely in the hands of professionals; many nations of the world, particularly those following civil-law traditions, take just that course. There is not one shred of doubt, however, about the Framers' paradigm for criminal justice: not the civil-law ideal of administrative perfection, but the common-law ideal of limited state power accomplished by strict division of authority between judge and jury. As *Apprendi* held, every defendant has the *right* to insist that the prosecutor prove to a jury all facts legally essential to the punishment. Under the dissenters' alternative, he has no such right. That should be the end of the matter.

* * *

Petitioner was sentenced to prison for more than three years beyond what the law allowed for the crime to which he confessed, on the basis of a disputed finding that he had acted with "deliberate cruelty." The Framers would not have thought it too much to demand that, before depriving a man of three more years of his liberty, the State should suffer the modest inconvenience of submitting its accusation to "the unanimous suffrage of twelve of his equals and neighbours," 4 Blackstone, Commentaries, *supra* at 343, rather than a lone employee of the State.

The judgment of the Washington Court of Appeals is reversed, and the case is remanded for further proceedings not inconsistent with this opinion.

■ JUSTICE O'CONNOR, with whom JUSTICE BREYER joins, and with whom THE CHIEF JUSTICE and JUSTICE KENNEDY join as to all but Part IV–B, dissenting.

The legacy of today's opinion, whether intended or not, will be the consolidation of sentencing power in the State and Federal Judiciaries. The Court says to Congress and state legislatures: If you want to constrain the sentencing discretion of judges and bring some uniformity to sentencing, it will cost you—dearly. Congress and States, faced with the burdens imposed by the extension of Apprendi v. New Jersey (2000), to the present context, will either trim or eliminate altogether their sentencing guidelines schemes and, with them, 20 years of sentencing reform. It is thus of little moment that the majority does not expressly declare guidelines schemes unconstitutional, for, as residents of "*Apprendi*-land" are fond of saying, "the relevant inquiry is one not of form, but of effect." (2000); *Ring v. Arizona*, (2002) (Scalia, J., concurring). The "effect" of today's decision will be greater judicial discretion and less uniformity in sentencing. Because I find it implausible that the Framers would have considered such a result to be required by the Due Process Clause or the Sixth Amendment, and because the practical consequences of today's decision may be disastrous, I respectfully dissent.

I

One need look no further than the history leading up to and following the enactment of Washington's guidelines scheme to appreciate the damage that today's decision will cause. Prior to 1981, Washington, like most other States and the Federal Government, employed an indeterminate sentencing scheme. Washington's criminal code separated all felonies into three broad categories: "class A," carrying a sentence of 20 years to life; "class B," carrying a sentence of 0 to 10 years; and "class C," carrying a sentence of 0 to 5 years. Wash. Rev. Code Ann. § 9A.20.020 (2000); see also Sentencing Reform Act of 1981, 1981 Wash. Laws, ch. 137, p 534. Sentencing judges, in conjunction with parole boards, had virtually unfettered discretion to sentence defendants to prison terms falling anywhere within the statutory range, including probation—*i.e.*, no jail sentence at all. Wash. Rev. Code Ann. §§ 9.95.010–.011; Boerner & Lieb, Sentencing Reform in the Other Washington, 28 Crime and Justice 71, 73 (M. Tonry ed. 2001) (hereinafter Boerner & Lieb) ("Judges were authorized to choose between prison and probation with few exceptions, subject only to review for abuse of discretion"). See also D. Boerner, Sentencing in Washington § 2.4, pp. 2–27 to 2–28 (1985).

This system of unguided discretion inevitably resulted in severe disparities in sentences received and served by defendants committing the same offense and having similar criminal histories.... ("[E]very day Federal judges mete out an unjustifiably wide range of sentences to offenders with similar histories, convicted of similar crimes, committed under similar circumstances.... These disparities, whether they occur at the time of the initial sentencing or at the parole stage, can be traced directly to the unfettered discretion the law confers on those judges and parole authorities responsible for imposing and implementing the sentence"). Indeed, rather than reflect legally relevant criteria, these disparities too often were correlated with constitutionally suspect variables such as race. Boerner & Lieb 126–128. See also Breyer, The Federal Sentencing Guidelines and the Key Compromises Upon Which They Rest, 17 Hofstra L. Rev. 1, 5 (1988) (elimination of racial disparity one reason behind Congress' creation of the Federal Sentencing Commission).

To counteract these trends, the state legislature passed the Sentencing Reform Act of 1981. The Act had the laudable purposes of "mak[ing] the criminal justice system accountable to the public," and "[e]nsur[ing] that the punishment for a criminal offense is proportionate to the seriousness of the offense ... [and] commensurate with the punishment imposed on others committing similar offenses." Wash. Rev. Code Ann. § 9.94A.010 (2000). The Act neither increased any of the statutory sentencing ranges for the three types of felonies (though it did eliminate the statutory mandatory minimum for class A felonies), nor reclassified any substantive offenses. 1981 Wash. Laws ch. 137, p. 534. It merely placed meaningful constraints on discretion to sentence offenders within the statutory ranges, and eliminated parole. There is thus no evidence that the legislature was attempting to manipulate the statutory elements of criminal offenses or to circumvent the procedural protections of the Bill of Rights. Rather, lawmakers were trying to bring some much-needed uniformity, transparency, and accountability to an otherwise " 'labyrinthine' sentencing and corrections system that 'lack[ed] any principle except unguided discretion.' " Boerner & Lieb 73 (quoting F. Zimring, Making the Punishment Fit the Crime: A Consumers' Guide to Sentencing Reform, Occasional Paper No. 12, p 6 (1977)).

II

Far from disregarding principles of due process and the jury trial right, as the majority today suggests, Washington's reform has served them. Before passage of the Act, a defendant charged with second degree kidnaping, like petitioner, had no idea whether he would receive a 10–year sentence or probation. The ultimate sentencing determination could turn as much on the idiosyncracies of a particular judge as on the specifics of the defendant's crime or background. A defendant did not know what facts, if any, about his offense or his history would be considered relevant by the sentencing judge or by the parole board. After passage of the Act, a defendant charged with second degree kidnaping knows what his presumptive sentence will be; he has a good idea of the types of factors that a sentencing judge can and will consider when deciding whether to sentence him outside that range; he is guaranteed meaningful appellate review to protect against an arbitrary sentence. Boerner & Lieb 93 ("By consulting one sheet, practitioners could identify the applicable scoring rules for criminal history, the sentencing range, and the available sentencing options for each case"). Criminal defendants still face the same statutory maximum sentences, but they now at least know, much more than before, the real consequences of their actions.

Washington's move to a system of guided discretion has served equal protection principles as well. Over the past 20 years, there has been a substantial reduction in racial disparity in sentencing across the State. (Racial disparities that do exist "are accounted for by differences in legally relevant variables—the offense of conviction and prior criminal record"). ("[J]udicial authority to impose exceptional sentences under the court's departure authority shows little evidence of disparity correlated with race"). The reduction is directly traceable to the constraining effects of the guidelines—namely, its "presumptive range[s]" and limits on the imposition of "exceptional sentences" outside of those ranges. For instance, sentencing judges still retain unreviewable discretion in first-time offender cases and in certain sex offender cases to impose alternative sentences that are far more lenient than those contemplated by the guidelines. To the extent that unjustifiable racial disparities have persisted in Washington, it has been in the imposition of such alternative sentences: "The lesson is powerful: racial disparity is correlated with unstructured and unreviewed discretion."

The majority does not, because it cannot, disagree that determinate sentencing schemes, like Washington's, serve important constitutional values. Thus, the majority says: "[t]his case is not about whether determinate sentencing is constitutional, only about how it can be implemented in a way that respects the Sixth Amendment." But extension of *Apprendi* to the present context will impose significant costs on a legislature's determination that a particular fact, not historically an element, warrants a higher sentence. While not a constitutional prohibition on guidelines schemes, the majority's decision today exacts a substantial constitutional tax.

The costs are substantial and real. Under the majority's approach, any fact that increases the upper bound on a judge's sentencing discretion is an element of the offense. Thus, facts that historically have been taken into account by sentencing judges to assess a sentence within a broad range—such as drug quantity, role in the offense, risk of bodily harm—all must now be charged in an indictment and submitted to a jury, *In re Winship* (1970), simply because it is the legislature, rather than the judge, that constrains the extent to which such facts may be used to impose a sentence within a pre-existing statutory range.

While that alone is enough to threaten the continued use of sentencing guidelines schemes, there are additional costs. For example, a legislature might rightly think that some factors bearing on sentencing, such as prior bad acts or criminal history, should not be considered in a jury's determination of a defendant's guilt—such "character evidence" has traditionally been off limits during the guilt phase of criminal proceedings because of its tendency to inflame the passions of the jury. See, *e.g.*, Fed. Rule Evid. 404; 1 E. Imwinkelried, P. Giannelli, F. Gilligan, & F. Lederer, Courtroom Criminal Evidence 285 (3d ed. 1998). If a legislature desires uniform consideration of such factors at sentencing, but does not want them to impact a jury's initial determination of guilt, the State may have to bear the additional expense of a separate, full-blown jury trial during the penalty phase proceeding.

Some facts that bear on sentencing either will not be discovered, or are not discoverable, prior to trial. For instance, a legislature might desire that defendants who act in an obstructive manner during trial or post-trial proceedings receive a greater sentence than defendants who do not.... In such cases, the violation arises too late for the State to provide notice to the defendant or to argue the facts to the jury. A State wanting to make such facts relevant at sentencing must now either vest sufficient discretion in the judge to account for them *or* bring a separate criminal prosecution for obstruction of justice or perjury. And, the latter option is available only to the extent that a defendant's obstructive behavior is so severe as to constitute an already-existing separate offense, unless the legislature is willing to undertake the unlikely expense of criminalizing relatively minor obstructive behavior.

Likewise, not all facts that historically have been relevant to sentencing always will be known prior to trial. For instance, trial or sentencing proceedings of a drug distribution defendant might reveal that he sold primarily to children. Under the majority's approach, a State wishing such a revelation to result in a higher sentence within a pre-existing statutory range either must vest judges with sufficient discretion to account for it (and trust that they exercise that discretion) *or* bring a separate criminal prosecution. Indeed, the latter choice might not be available—a separate prosecution, if it is for an aggravated offense, likely would be barred altogether by the Double Jeopardy Clause. Blockburger v. United States (1932) (government cannot prosecute for separate offenses unless each offense has at least one element that the other does not).

The majority may be correct that States and the Federal Government will be willing to bear some of these costs. But simple economics dictate that they will not, and cannot, bear them all. To the extent that they do not, there will be an inevitable increase in judicial discretion with all of its attendant failings.[1]

III

Washington's Sentencing Reform Act did not alter the statutory maximum sentence to which petitioner was exposed.... Petitioner was informed in the charging document, his plea agreement, and during his plea hearing that he faced a potential statutory maximum of 10 years in prison. As discussed above, the guidelines served due process by providing notice to petitioner of the consequences of his acts; they vindicated his jury trial right by informing him of the stakes of risking trial; they served equal protection by ensuring petitioner that invidious characteristics such as race would not impact his sentence.

1. The paucity of empirical evidence regarding the impact of extending *Apprendi v. New Jersey* (2000), to guidelines schemes should come as no surprise to the majority.... Thus, there is no map of the uncharted territory blazed by today's unprecedented holding.

Given these observations, it is difficult for me to discern what principle besides doctrinaire formalism actually motivates today's decision. The majority chides the *Apprendi* dissenters for preferring a nuanced interpretation of the Due Process Clause and Sixth Amendment jury trial guarantee that would generally defer to legislative labels while acknowledging the existence of constitutional constraints—what the majority calls "the law must not go too far" approach. If indeed the choice is between adopting a balanced case-by-case approach that takes into consideration the values underlying the Bill of Rights, as well as the history of a particular sentencing reform law, and adopting a rigid rule that destroys everything in its path, I will choose the former . . .

But even were one to accept formalism as a principle worth vindicating for its own sake, it would not explain *Apprendi*'s, or today's, result. A rule of deferring to legislative labels has no less formal pedigree. . . .

The majority is correct that rigid adherence to such an approach *could conceivably* produce absurd results, but, as today's decision demonstrates, rigid adherence to the majority's approach *does and will continue* to produce results that disserve the very principles the majority purports to vindicate. The pre-*Apprendi* rule of deference to the legislature retains a built-in political check to prevent lawmakers from shifting the prosecution for crimes to the penalty phase proceedings of lesser included and easier-to-prove offenses—*e.g.*, the majority's hypothesized prosecution of murder in the guise of a traffic offense sentencing proceeding. There is no similar check, however, on application of the majority's " 'any fact that increases the upper bound of judicial discretion' " by courts.

The majority claims the mantle of history and original intent. But as I have explained elsewhere, a handful of state decisions in the mid–19th century and a criminal procedure treatise have little if any persuasive value as evidence of what the Framers of the Federal Constitution intended in the late 18th century. Because broad judicial sentencing discretion was foreign to the Framers, *id.*, at 478–479, 147 L. Ed. 2d 435, 120 S. Ct. 2348 (citing J. Archbold, Pleading and Evidence in Criminal Cases 44 (15th ed. 1862)), they were never faced with the constitutional choice between submitting every fact that increases a sentence to the jury or vesting the sentencing judge with broad discretionary authority to account for differences in offenses and offenders.

IV

A

The consequences of today's decision will be as far reaching as they are disturbing. Washington's sentencing system is by no means unique. Numerous other States have enacted guidelines systems, as has the Federal Government11. . . . Today's decision casts constitutional doubt over them all and, in so doing, threatens an untold number of criminal judgments. Every sentence imposed under such guidelines in cases currently pending on direct appeal is in jeopardy. And, despite the fact that we hold in Schriro v. Summerlin that *Ring* (and *a fortiori Apprendi*) does not apply retroactively on habeas review, all criminal sentences imposed under the federal and state guidelines since *Apprendi* was decided in 2000 arguably remain open to collateral attack. See *Teague v. Lane* (1989) (plurality opinion) ("[A] case announces a new rule if the result was not *dictated* by precedent existing at the time the defendant's conviction became final").[2]

The practical consequences for trial courts, starting today, will be equally unsettling: How are courts to mete out guidelines sentences? Do courts apply the guidelines as to mitigating factors, but not as to aggravating factors? Do they jettison the guidelines altogether? The Court ignores the havoc it is about to wreak on trial courts across the country.

B

It is no answer to say that today's opinion impacts only Washington's scheme and not others, such as, for example, the Federal Sentencing Guidelines....

The structure of the Federal Guidelines likewise does not, as the Government half-heartedly suggests, provide any grounds for distinction.... If anything, the structural differences that do exist make the Federal Guidelines more vulnerable to attack. The provision struck down here provides for an increase in the upper bound of the presumptive sentencing range if the sentencing court finds, "considering the purpose of [the Act], that there are substantial and compelling reasons justifying an exceptional sentence." The Act elsewhere provides a nonexhaustive list of aggravating factors that satisfy the definition. § 9.94A.390. The Court flatly rejects respondent's argument that such soft constraints, which still allow Washington judges to exercise a substantial amount of discretion, survive *Apprendi*. This suggests that the hard constraints found throughout chapters 2 and 3 of the Federal Sentencing Guidelines, which require an increase in the sentencing range upon specified factual findings, will meet the same fate. See, *e.g.*, USSG § 2K2.1 (increases in offense level for firearms offenses based on number of firearms involved, whether possession was in connection with another offense, whether the firearm was stolen); § 2B1.1 (increase in offense level for financial crimes based on amount of money involved, number of victims, possession of weapon); § 3C1.1 (general increase in offense level for obstruction of justice).

Indeed, the "extraordinary sentence" provision struck down today is as inoffensive to the holding of *Apprendi* as a regime of guided discretion could possibly be. The list of facts that justify an increase in the range is nonexhaustive. The State's "real facts" doctrine precludes reliance by sentencing courts upon facts that would constitute the elements of a different or aggravated offense. If the Washington scheme does not comport with the Constitution, it is hard to imagine a guidelines scheme that would.

* * *

2. The numbers available from the federal system alone are staggering. On March 31, 2004, there were 8,320 federal criminal appeals pending in which the defendant's sentence was at issue.... Between June 27, 2000, when *Apprendi* was decided, and March 31, 2004, there have been 272,191 defendants sentenced in federal court. Given that nearly all federal sentences are governed by the Federal Sentencing Guidelines, the vast majority of these cases are Guidelines cases.

What I have feared most has now come to pass: Over 20 years of sentencing reform are all but lost, and tens of thousands of criminal judgments are in jeopardy. I respectfully dissent.

■ JUSTICE KENNEDY, with whom JUSTICE BREYER joins, dissenting.

The majority opinion does considerable damage to our laws and to the administration of the criminal justice system for all the reasons well stated in Justice O'Connor's dissent, plus one more: The Court, in my respectful submission, disregards the fundamental principle under our constitutional system that different branches of government "converse with each other on matters of vital common interest." *Mistretta v. United States*, (1989). As the Court in *Mistretta* explained, the Constitution establishes a system of government that presupposes, not just " 'autonomy' " and " 'separateness,' " but also " 'interdependence' " and " 'reciprocity.' " (quoting *Youngstown Sheet & Tube Co. v. Sawyer*, 343 U.S. 579, 635, 96 L. Ed. 1153, 72 S. Ct. 863 (1952) (Jackson, J., concurring)). Constant, constructive discourse between our courts and our legislatures is an integral and admirable part of the constitutional design. Case-by-case judicial determinations often yield intelligible patterns that can be refined by legislatures and codified into statutes or rules as general standards. As these legislative enactments are followed by incremental judicial interpretation, the legislatures may respond again, and the cycle repeats. This recurring dialogue, an essential source for the elaboration and the evolution of the law, is basic constitutional theory in action.

Sentencing guidelines are a prime example of this collaborative process. Dissatisfied with the wide disparity in sentencing, participants in the criminal justice system, including judges, pressed for legislative reforms. In response, legislators drew from these participants' shared experiences and enacted measures to correct the problems, which, as Justice O'Connor explains, could sometimes rise to the level of a constitutional injury. As *Mistretta* recognized, this interchange among different actors in the constitutional scheme is consistent with the Constitution's structural protections.

To be sure, this case concerns the work of a state legislature, and not of Congress. If anything, however, this distinction counsels even greater judicial caution. Unlike *Mistretta*, the case here implicates not just the collective wisdom of legislators on the other side of the continuing dialogue over fair sentencing, but also the interest of the States to serve as laboratories for innovation and experiment. With no apparent sense of irony that the effect of today's decision is the destruction of a sentencing scheme devised by democratically elected legislators, the majority shuts down alternative, nonjudicial, sources of ideas and experience. It does so under a faintly disguised distrust of judges and their purported usurpation of the jury's function in criminal trials. It tells not only trial judges who have spent years studying the problem but also legislators who have devoted valuable time and resources "calling upon the accumulated wisdom and experience of the Judicial Branch ... on a matter uniquely within the ken of judges," that their efforts and judgments were all for naught. Numerous States that have enacted sentencing guidelines similar to the one in Washington State are now commanded to scrap everything and start over.

If the Constitution required this result, the majority's decision, while unfortunate, would at least be understandable and defensible. As Justice O'Connor's dissent demonstrates, however, this is simply not the case. For that reason, and because the Constitution does not prohibit the dynamic and fruitful dialogue between the judicial and legislative branches of government that has marked sentencing reform on both the state and the federal levels for more than 20 years, I dissent.

■ JUSTICE BREYER, with whom JUSTICE O'CONNOR joins, dissenting.

The Court makes clear that it means what it said in Apprendi v. New Jersey (2000). In its view, the Sixth Amendment says that " 'any fact that increases the penalty for a crime beyond the prescribed statutory maximum must be submitted to a jury.' " ... " '[P]rescribed statutory maximum' " means the penalty that the relevant statute authorizes "solely on the basis of the facts reflected in the jury verdict." Thus, a jury must find, not only the facts that make up the crime of which the offender is charged, but also all (punishment-increasing) facts about the *way* in which the offender carried out that crime.

It is not difficult to understand the impulse that produced this holding. Imagine a classic example—a statute (or mandatory sentencing guideline) that provides a 10–year sentence for ordinary bank robbery, but a 15–year sentence for bank robbery committed with a gun. One might ask why it should matter for jury trial purposes whether the statute (or guideline) labels the gun's presence (a) a *sentencing fact* about the way in which the offender carried out the *lesser* crime of ordinary bank robbery, or (b) a factual *element* of the *greater* crime of bank robbery with a gun? If the Sixth Amendment requires a jury finding about the gun in the latter circumstance, why should it not also require a jury to find the same fact in the former circumstance? The two sets of circumstances are functionally identical. In both instances, identical punishment follows from identical factual findings (related to, *e.g.*, a bank, a taking, a thing-of-value, force or threat of force, and a gun). The only difference between the two circumstances concerns a legislative (or Sentencing Commission) decision about which *label* ("sentencing fact" or "element of a greater crime") to affix to one of the facts, namely, the presence of the gun, that will lead to the greater sentence. Given the identity of circumstances apart from the label, the jury's traditional factfinding role, and the law's insistence upon treating like cases alike, why should the legislature's labeling choice make an important Sixth Amendment difference?

The Court in *Apprendi*, and now here, concludes that it should not make a difference. The Sixth Amendment's jury trial guarantee applies similarly to both. I agree with the majority's analysis, but not with its conclusion. That is to say, I agree that, classically speaking, the difference between a traditional sentencing factor and an element of a greater offense often comes down to a legislative choice about which label to affix. But I cannot jump from there to the conclusion that the Sixth Amendment always requires identical treatment of the two scenarios. That jump is fraught with consequences that threaten the fairness of our traditional criminal justice system; it distorts historical sentencing or criminal trial practices; and it upsets settled law on which legislatures have relied in designing punishment systems.

The Justices who have dissented from *Apprendi* have written about many of these matters in other opinions.... At the risk of some repetition, I shall set forth several of the most important considerations here. They lead me to conclude that I must again dissent.

I

The majority ignores the adverse consequences inherent in its conclusion. As a result of the majority's rule, sentencing must now take one of three forms, each of which risks either impracticality, unfairness, or harm to the jury trial right the majority purports to strengthen. This circumstance shows that the majority's Sixth Amendment interpretation cannot be right.

A

A first option for legislators is to create a simple, pure or nearly pure "charge offense" or "determinate" sentencing system. See Breyer, The Federal Sentencing Guidelines and the Key Compromises upon Which They Rest, 17 Hofstra L. Rev. 1, 8–9 (1988). In such a system, an indictment would charge a few facts which, taken together, constitute a crime, such as robbery. Robbery would carry a single sentence, say, five years' imprisonment. And every person convicted of robbery would receive that sentence—just as, centuries ago, everyone convicted of almost any serious crime was sentenced to death.

Such a system assures uniformity, but at intolerable costs. First, simple determinate sentencing systems impose identical punishments on people who committed their crimes in very different ways. When dramatically different conduct ends up being punished the same way, an injustice has taken place. Simple determinate sentencing has the virtue of treating like cases alike, but it simultaneously fails to treat different cases differently. Some commentators have leveled this charge at sentencing guideline systems themselves. See, *e.g.*, Schulhofer, Assessing the Federal Sentencing Process: The Problem Is Uniformity, Not Disparity, 29 Am. Crim. L. Rev. 833, 847 (1992) (arguing that the "most important problem under the Guidelines system is not too much disparity, but rather excessive uniformity" and arguing for adjustments, including elimination of mandatory minimums, to make the Guidelines system more responsive to relevant differences). The charge is doubly applicable to simple "pure charge" systems that permit no departures from the prescribed sentences, even in extraordinary cases.

Second, in a world of statutorily fixed mandatory sentences for many crimes, determinate sentencing gives tremendous power to prosecutors to manipulate sentences through their choice of charges. Prosecutors can simply charge, or threaten to charge, defendants with crimes bearing higher mandatory sentences. Defendants, knowing that they will not have a chance to argue for a lower sentence in front of a judge, may plead to charges that they might otherwise contest. Considering that most criminal cases do not go to trial and resolution by plea bargaining is the norm, the rule of *Apprendi*, to the extent it results in a return to determinate sentencing, threatens serious unfairness. See Bibas, Judicial Fact–Finding and Sentence Enhancements in a World of Guilty Pleas, 110 Yale L. J. 1097, 1100–1101 (2001) (explaining that the rule of *Apprendi* hurts defendants by depriving them of sentencing hearings, "the only hearings they were likely to have"; forcing defendants to surrender sentencing issues like drug quantity when they agree to the plea; and transferring power to prosecutors).

B

A second option for legislators is to return to a system of indeterminate sentencing, such as California had before the recent sentencing reform movement. See *Payne v. Tennessee* (1991) ("With the increasing importance of probation, as opposed to imprisonment, as a part of the penological process, some States such as California developed the 'indeterminate sentence,' where the time of incarceration was left almost entirely to the penological authorities rather than to the courts"); Thompson, Navigating the Hidden Obstacles to Ex–Offender Reentry, 45 Boston College L. Rev. 255, 267 (2004) ("In the late 1970s, California switched from an indeterminate criminal sentencing scheme to determinate sentencing"). Under indeterminate systems, the length of the sentence is entirely or almost entirely within the discretion of the judge or of the parole board, which typically has broad power to decide when to release a prisoner.

When such systems were in vogue, they were criticized, and rightly so, for producing unfair disparities, including race-based disparities, in the punishment of similarly situated defendants. The length of time a person spent in prison appeared to depend on "what the judge ate for breakfast" on the day of sentencing, on which judge you got, or on other factors that should not have made a difference to the length of the sentence. And under such a system, the judge could vary the sentence greatly based upon his findings about how the defendant had committed the crime—findings that might not have been made by a "preponderance of the evidence," much less "beyond a reasonable doubt." See *McMillan* ("Sentencing courts have traditionally heard evidence and found facts without any prescribed burden of proof at all" (citing Williams v. New York (1949))).

Returning to such a system would diminish the " 'reason' " the majority claims it is trying to uphold. It also would do little to "ensur[e] [the] control" of what the majority calls "the peopl[e,]" *i.e.*, the jury, "in the judiciary," since "the peopl[e]" would only decide the defendant's guilt, a finding with no effect on the duration of the sentence. While "the judge's authority to sentence" would formally derive from the jury's verdict, the jury would exercise little or no control over the sentence itself. It is difficult to see how such an outcome protects the structural safeguards the majority claims to be defending.

C

A third option is that which the Court seems to believe legislators will in fact take. That is the option of retaining structured schemes that attempt to punish similar conduct similarly and different conduct differently, but modifying them to conform to *Apprendi*'s dictates. Judges would be able to depart *downward* from presumptive sentences upon finding that mitigating factors were present, but would not be able to depart *upward* unless the prosecutor charged the aggravating fact to a jury and proved it beyond a reasonable doubt. The majority argues, based on the single example of Kansas, that most legislatures will enact amendments along these lines in the face of the oncoming *Apprendi* train. It is therefore worth exploring how this option could work in practice, as well as the assumptions on which it depends.

1

This option can be implemented in one of two ways. The first way would be for legislatures to subdivide each crime into a list of complex crimes, each of which would be defined to include commonly found sentencing factors such as drug quantity, type of victim, presence of violence, degree of injury, use of gun, and so on. A legislature, for example, might enact a robbery statute, modeled on robbery sentencing guidelines, that increases punishment depending upon (1) the nature of the institution robbed, (2) the (a) presence of, (b) brandishing of, (c) other use of, a firearm, (3) making of a death threat, (4) presence of (a) ordinary, (b) serious, (c) permanent or life threatening, bodily injury, (5) abduction, (6) physical restraint, (7) taking of a firearm, (8) taking of drugs, (9) value of property loss, etc. Cf. United States Sentencing Commission, Guidelines Manual § 2B3.1 (Nov. 2003) (hereinafter USSG).

This possibility is, of course, merely a highly calibrated form of the "pure charge" system discussed in Part I–A, And it suffers from some of the same defects. The prosecutor, through control of the precise charge, controls the punishment, thereby marching the sentencing system directly away from, not toward, one important guideline goal: rough uniformity of punishment for those who engage in roughly the same *real* criminal conduct. The artificial (and consequently unfair) nature of the resulting sentence is aggravated by the fact that prosecutors must charge all relevant facts about the way the crime was committed before a presentence investigation examines the criminal conduct, perhaps before the trial itself, *i.e.*, before many of the facts relevant to punishment are known.

This "complex charge offense" system also prejudices defendants who seek trial, for it can put them in the untenable position of contesting material aggravating facts in the guilt phases of their trials. Consider a defendant who is charged, not with mere possession of cocaine, but with the specific offense of possession of more than 500 grams of cocaine. Or consider a defendant charged, not with murder, but with the new crime of murder using a machete. Or consider a defendant whom the prosecution wants to claim was a "supervisor," rather than an ordinary gang member. How can a Constitution that guarantees due process put these defendants, as a matter of course, in the position of arguing, "I did not sell drugs, and if I did, I did not sell more than 500 grams," or, "I did not kill him, and if I did, I did not use a machete," or "I did not engage in gang activity, and certainly not as a supervisor" to a single jury? The system can tolerate this kind of problem up to a point (consider the defendant who wants to argue innocence, and, in the alternative, second-degree, not first-degree, murder). But a rereading of the many distinctions made in a typical robbery guideline suggests that an effort to incorporate any real set of guidelines in a complex statute would reach well beyond that point.

The majority announces that there really is no problem here because "States may continue to offer judicial factfinding as a matter of course to all defendants who plead guilty" and defendants may "stipulat[e] to the relevant facts or consen[t] to judicial factfinding." The problem, of course, concerns defendants who do not want to plead guilty to those elements that, until recently, were commonly thought of as sentencing factors. As to those defendants, the fairness problem arises because States may very well decide that they will *not* permit defendants to carve subsets of facts out of the new, *Apprendi*-required 17–element robbery crime, seeking a judicial determination as to some of those facts and a jury determination as to others. Instead, States may simply require defendants to plead guilty to all 17 elements or proceed with a (likely prejudicial) trial on all 17 elements.

The majority does not deny that States may make this choice; it simply fails to understand *why* any State would want to exercise it. The answer is, as I shall explain in a moment, that the alternative may prove too expensive and unwieldy for States to provide. States that offer defendants the option of judicial factfinding as to some facts (*i.e.*, sentencing facts), say, because of fairness concerns, will also have to offer the defendant a second sentencing jury—just as Kansas has done. I therefore turn to that alternative.

2

The second way to make sentencing guidelines *Apprendi*-compliant would be to require at least two juries for each defendant whenever aggravating facts are present: one jury to determine guilt of the crime charged, and an additional jury to try the disputed facts that, if found, would aggravate the sentence. Our experience with bifurcated trials in the capital punishment context suggests that requiring them for run-of-the-mill sentences would be costly, both in money and in judicial time and resources.... In the context of noncapital crimes, the potential need for a second indictment alleging aggravating facts, the likely need for formal evidentiary rules to prevent prejudice, and the increased difficulty of obtaining relevant sentencing information, all will mean greater complexity, added cost, and further delay. See Part V, *infra*. Indeed, cost and delay could lead legislatures to revert to the complex charge offense system described in Part I–C–1.The majority refers to an *amicus curiae* brief filed by the Kansas Appellate Defender Office, which suggests that a two-jury system has proved workable in Kansas. And that may be so. But in all likelihood, any such workability reflects an uncomfortable fact, a fact at which the majority hints, but whose constitutional implications it does not seem to grasp. The uncomfortable fact that could make the system seem workable—even desirable in the minds of some, including defense attorneys—is called "plea bargaining." ... The Court can announce that the Constitution requires at least two jury trials for each criminal defendant—one for guilt, another for sentencing—but only because it knows full well that more than 90% of defendants will not go to trial even once, much less insist on two or more trials.

What will be the consequences of the Court's holding for the 90% of defendants who do not go to trial? The truthful answer is that we do not know. Some defendants may receive bargaining advantages if the increased cost of the "double jury trial" guarantee makes prosecutors more willing to cede certain sentencing issues to the defense. Other defendants may be hurt if a "single-jury-decides-all" approach makes them more reluctant to risk a trial—perhaps because they want to argue that they did not know what was in the cocaine bag, that it was a small amount regardless, that they were unaware a confederate had a gun, etc. See Bibas, 110 Yale L. J., at 1100 ("Because for many defendants going to trial is not a desirable option, they are left without any real hearings at all"); ("The trial right does little good when most defendants do not go to trial").

At the least, the greater expense attached to trials and their greater complexity, taken together in the context of an overworked criminal justice system, will likely mean, other things being equal, fewer trials and a greater reliance upon plea bargaining—a system in which punishment is set not by judges or juries but by advocates acting under bargaining constraints. At the same time, the greater power of the prosecutor to control the punishment through the charge would likely weaken the relation between real conduct and real punishment as well. . . . Even if the Court's holding does not further embed plea-bargaining practices (as I fear it will), its success depends upon the existence of present practice. I do not understand how the Sixth Amendment could *require* a sentencing system that will work in practice only if no more than a handful of defendants exercise their right to a jury trial.

The majority's only response is to state that "bargaining over elements . . . probably favors the defendant," adding that many criminal defense lawyers favor its position. But the basic problem is not one of "fairness" to defendants or, for that matter, "fairness" to prosecutors. Rather, it concerns the greater fairness of a sentencing system that a more uniform correspondence between real criminal conduct and real punishment helps to create. At a minimum, a two-jury system, by preventing a judge from taking account of an aggravating fact without the prosecutor's acquiescence, would undercut, if not nullify, legislative efforts to ensure through guidelines that punishments reflect a convicted offender's real criminal conduct, rather than that portion of the offender's conduct that a prosecutor decides to charge and prove.

Efforts to tie real punishment to real conduct are not new. They are embodied in well-established preguidelines sentencing practices—practices under which a judge, looking at a presentence report, would seek to tailor the sentence in significant part to fit the criminal conduct in which the offender actually engaged. For more than a century, questions of *punishment* (not those of guilt or innocence) have reflected determinations made, not only by juries, but also by judges, probation officers, and executive parole boards. Such truth-seeking determinations have rested upon both adversarial and nonadversarial processes. The Court's holding undermines efforts to reform these processes, for it means that legislatures cannot *both* permit judges to base sentencing upon real conduct *and* seek, through guidelines, to make the results more uniform.

In these and other ways, the two-jury system would work a radical change in pre-existing criminal law. It is not surprising that this Court has never previously suggested that the Constitution—outside the unique context of the death penalty—might require bifurcated jury-based sentencing. And it is the impediment the Court's holding poses to legislative efforts to achieve that greater systematic fairness that casts doubt on its constitutional validity.

D

Is there a fourth option? Perhaps. Congress and state legislatures might, for example, rewrite their criminal codes, attaching astronomically high sentences to each crime, followed by long lists of mitigating facts, which, for the most part, would consist of the absence of aggravating facts. But political impediments to legislative action make such rewrites difficult to achieve; and it is difficult to see why the Sixth Amendment would require legislatures to undertake them.

It may also prove possible to find combinations of, or variations upon, my first three options. But I am unaware of any variation that does not involve (a) the shift of power to the prosecutor (weakening the connection between real conduct and real punishment) inherent in any charge offense system, (b) the lack of uniformity inherent in any system of pure judicial discretion, or (c) the complexity, expense, and increased reliance on plea bargains involved in a "two-jury" system. The simple fact is that the design of any fair sentencing system must involve efforts to make practical compromises among competing goals. The majority's reading of the Sixth Amendment makes the effort to find those compromises—already difficult—virtually impossible.

II

The majority rests its conclusion in significant part upon a claimed historical (and therefore constitutional) imperative. According to the majority, the rule it applies in this case is rooted in "longstanding tenets of common-law criminal jurisprudence," that every accusation against a defendant must be proved to a jury and that " 'an accusation which lacks any particular fact which the law makes essential to the punishment is . . . no accusation within the requirements of the common law, and it is no accusation in reason.' " The historical sources upon which the majority relies, however, do not compel the result it reaches. The quotation from Bishop, to which the majority attributes great weight, stands for nothing more than the "unremarkable proposition" that where a legislature passes a statute setting forth heavier penalties than were available for committing a common-law offense and specifying those facts that triggered the statutory penalty, "a defendant could receive the greater statutory punishment only if the indictment expressly charged and the prosecutor proved the facts that made up the statutory offense, as opposed to simply those facts that made up the common-law offense."

This is obvious when one considers the problem that Bishop was addressing. He provides as an example "statutes whereby, when [a common-law crime] is committed with a particular intent, or with a particular weapon, or the like, it is subjected to a particular corresponding punishment, heavier than that for" the simple common-law offense....

Neither Bishop nor any other historical treatise writer, however, disputes the proposition that judges historically had discretion to vary the sentence, within the range provided by the statute, based on facts not proved at the trial. K. Stith & J. Cabranes, Fear of Judging: Sentencing Guidelines in the Federal Courts 9 (1998). The modern history of preguidelines sentencing likewise indicates that judges had broad discretion to set sentences within a statutory range based on uncharged conduct. Usually, the judge based his or her sentencing decision on facts gleaned from a presentence report, which the defendant could dispute at a sentencing hearing. In the federal system, for example, Federal Rule of Criminal Procedure 32 provided that probation officers, who are employees of the Judicial Branch, prepared a presentence report for the judge, a copy of which was generally given to the prosecution and defense before the sentencing hearing....

Given history's silence on the question of laws that structure a judge's discretion within the range provided by the legislatively labeled maximum term, it is not surprising that our modern, pre-*Apprendi* cases made clear that legislatures could, within broad limits, distinguish between "sentencing facts" and "elements of crimes." See *McMillan*. By their choice of label, legislatures could indicate whether a judge or a jury must make the relevant factual determination. History does not preclude legislatures from making this decision. And, as I argued in Part I, *supra*, allowing legislatures to structure sentencing in this way has the dual effect of enhancing and giving meaning to the Sixth Amendment's jury trial right as to core crimes, while affording additional due process to defendants in the form of sentencing hearings before judges—hearings the majority's rule will eliminate for many.

Is there a risk of unfairness involved in permitting Congress to make this labeling decision? Of course. As we have recognized, the "tail" of the sentencing fact might "wa[g] the dog of the substantive offense." *McMillan*. Congress might permit a judge to sentence an individual for murder though convicted only of making an illegal lane change. But that is the kind of problem that the Due Process Clause is well suited to cure. *McMillan* foresaw the possibility that judges would have to use their own judgment in dealing with such a problem; but that is what judges are there for. And, as Part I, *supra*, makes clear, the alternatives are worse—not only practically, but, although the majority refuses to admit it, constitutionally as well.

Historic practice, then, does not compel the result the majority reaches. And constitutional concerns counsel the opposite.

III

The majority also overlooks important institutional considerations. Congress and the States relied upon what they believed was their constitutional power to decide, within broad limits, whether to make a particular fact (a) a sentencing factor or (b) an element in a greater crime. They relied upon *McMillan* as guaranteeing the constitutional validity of that proposition. They created sentencing reform, an effort to change the criminal justice system so that it reflects systematically not simply upon guilt or innocence but also upon what should be done about this now-guilty offender. Those efforts have spanned a generation. They have led to state sentencing guidelines and the Federal Sentencing Guideline system. These systems are imperfect and they yield far from perfect results, but I cannot believe the Constitution forbids the state legislatures and Congress to adopt such systems and to try to improve them over time. Nor can I believe that the Constitution hamstrings legislatures in the way that Justice O'Connor and I have discussed.

IV

Now, let us return to the question I posed at the outset. Why does the Sixth Amendment permit a jury trial right (in respect to a particular fact) to depend upon a legislative labeling decision, namely, the legislative decision to label the fact a *sentencing fact*, instead of an *element of the crime?* The answer is that the fairness and effectiveness of a sentencing system, and the related fairness and effectiveness of the criminal justice system itself, depends upon the legislature's possessing the constitutional authority (within due process limits) to make that labeling decision. To restrict radically the legislature's power in this respect, as the majority interprets the Sixth Amendment to do, prevents the legislature from seeking sentencing systems that are consistent with, and indeed may help to advance, the Constitution's greater fairness goals.

To say this is not simply to express concerns about fairness to defendants. It is also to express concerns about the serious practical (or impractical) changes that the Court's decision seems likely to impose upon the criminal process; about the tendency of the Court's decision to embed further plea bargaining processes that lack transparency and too often mean nonuniform, sometimes arbitrary, sentencing practices; about the obstacles the Court's decision poses to legislative efforts to bring about greater uniformity between real criminal conduct and real punishment; and ultimately about the limitations that the Court imposes upon legislatures' ability to make democratic legislative decisions. Whatever the faults of guidelines systems—and there are many—they are more likely to find their cure in legislation emerging from the experience of, and discussion among, all elements of the criminal justice community, than in a virtually unchangeable constitutional decision of this Court.

V

Taken together these three sets of considerations, concerning consequences, concerning history, concerning institutional reliance, leave me where I was in *Apprendi, i.e.*, convinced that the Court is wrong. Until now, I would have thought the Court might have limited *Apprendi* so that its underlying principle would not undo sentencing reform efforts. Today's case dispels that illusion. At a minimum, the case sets aside numerous state efforts in that direction. Perhaps the Court will distinguish the Federal Sentencing Guidelines, but I am uncertain how. As a result of today's decision, federal prosecutors, like state prosecutors, must decide what to do next, how to handle tomorrow's case.

Consider some of the matters that federal prosecutors must know about, or guess about, when they prosecute their next case: (1) Does today's decision apply in full force to the Federal Sentencing Guidelines? (2) If so, must the initial indictment contain all sentencing factors, charged as "elements" of the crime? (3) What, then, are the evidentiary rules? Can the prosecution continue to use, say presentence reports, with their conclusions reflecting layers of hearsay? Cf. *Crawford v. Washington* (2004) (clarifying the Sixth Amendment's requirement of confrontation with respect to testimonial hearsay) . . . (4) How are juries to deal with highly complex or open-ended Sentencing Guidelines obviously written for application by an experienced trial judge? . . .

Ordinarily, this Court simply waits for cases to arise in which it can answer such questions. But this case affects tens of thousands of criminal prosecutions, including federal prosecutions. Federal prosecutors will proceed with those prosecutions subject to the risk that all defendants in those cases will have to be sentenced, perhaps tried, anew. Given this consequence and the need for certainty, I would not proceed further piecemeal; rather, I would call for further argument on the ramifications of the concerns I have raised. But that is not the Court's view.

For the reasons given, I dissent.

NOTES

1. The debate among members of the Court in *Blakeley* concerning whether or not that decision would affect the Federal Sentencing Guidelines was resolved in *Booker*:

United States v. Booker

United States Supreme Court, 2005.
543 U.S. 220, 125 S.Ct. 738.

■ **OPINION BY:** STEVENS (IN PART), BREYER (IN PART)

JUSTICE STEVENS delivered the opinion of the Court in part. JUSTICE SCALIA, JUSTICE SOUTER, JUSTICE THOMAS, and JUSTICE GINSBURG join this opinion.

The question presented in each of these cases is whether an application of the Federal Sentencing Guidelines violated the Sixth Amendment. In each case, the courts below held that binding rules set forth in the Guidelines limited the severity of the sentence that the judge could lawfully impose on the defendant based on the facts found by the jury at his trial. In both cases the courts rejected, on the basis of our decision in Blakely v. Washington, the Government's recommended application of the Sentencing Guidelines because the proposed sentences were based on additional facts that the sentencing judge found by a preponderance of the evidence. We hold that both courts correctly concluded that the Sixth Amendment as construed in *Blakely* does apply to the Sentencing Guidelines. In a separate opinion authored by Justice Breyer, the Court concludes that in light of this holding, two provisions of the Sentencing Reform Act of 1984 (SRA) that have the effect of making the Guidelines mandatory must be invalidated in order to allow the statute to operate in a manner consistent with congressional intent.

I

Respondent Booker was charged with possession with intent to distribute at least 50 grams of cocaine base (crack). Having heard evidence that he had 92.5 grams in his duffel bag, the jury found him guilty of violating 21 U.S.C. § 841(a)(1) [21 USCS § 841(a)(1)]. That statute prescribes a minimum sentence of 10 years in prison and a maximum sentence of life for that offense. § 841(b)(1)(A)(iii).

Based upon Booker's criminal history and the quantity of drugs found by the jury, the Sentencing Guidelines required the District Court Judge to select a "base" sentence of not less than 210 nor more than 262 months in prison. The judge, however, held a post-trial sentencing proceeding and concluded by a preponderance of the evidence that Booker had possessed an additional 566 grams of crack and that he was guilty of obstructing justice. Those findings mandated that the judge select a sentence between 360 months and life imprisonment; the judge imposed a sentence at the low end of the range. Thus, instead of the sentence of 21 years and 10 months that the judge could have imposed on the basis of the facts proved to the jury beyond a reasonable doubt, Booker received a 30–year sentence.

Over the dissent of Judge Easterbrook, the Court of Appeals for the Seventh Circuit held that this application of the Sentencing Guidelines conflicted with our holding in Apprendi v. New Jersey (2000), that "[o]ther than the fact of a prior conviction, any fact that increases the penalty for a crime beyond the prescribed statutory maximum must be submitted to a jury, and proved beyond a reasonable doubt." 375 F.3d 508, 510 (2004). The majority relied on our holding in *Blakely*, that "the 'statutory maximum' for *Apprendi* purposes is the maximum sentence a judge may impose *solely on the basis of the facts reflected in the jury verdict or admitted by the defendant.*" The court held that the sentence violated the Sixth Amendment, and remanded with instructions to the District Court either to sentence respondent within the sentencing range supported by the jury's findings or to hold a separate sentencing hearing before a jury.

Respondent Fanfan was charged with conspiracy to distribute and to possess with intent to distribute at least 500 grams of cocaine in violation of 21 USC §§ 846, 841(a)(1), and 841(b)(1)(B)(ii) [21 USCS §§ 846, 841(a)(1), and 841(b)(1)(B)(ii)]. He was convicted by the jury after it answered "Yes" to the question "Was the amount of cocaine 500 or more grams?" Under the Guidelines, without additional findings of fact, the maximum sentence authorized by the jury verdict was imprisonment for 78 months.

A few days after our decision in *Blakely*, the trial judge conducted a sentencing hearing at which he found additional facts that, under the Guidelines, would have authorized a sentence in the 188–to–235–month range. Specifically, he found that respondent Fanfan was responsible for 2.5 kilograms of cocaine powder, and 261.6 grams of crack. He also concluded that respondent had been an organizer, leader, manager, or supervisor in the criminal activity. Both findings were made by a preponderance of the evidence. Under the Guidelines, these additional findings would have required an enhanced sentence of 15 or 16 years instead of the 5 or 6 years authorized by the jury verdict alone. Relying not only on the majority opinion in *Blakely*, but also on the categorical statements in the dissenting opinions and in the Solicitor General's brief in *Blakely*, the judge concluded that he could not follow the particular provisions of the Sentencing Guidelines "which involve drug quantity and role enhancement." Expressly refusing to make "any blanket decision about the federal guidelines," he followed the provisions of the Guidelines that did not implicate the Sixth Amendment by imposing a sentence on respondent "based solely upon the jury verdict in this case." *Ibid*. . . .

In both petitions, the Government asks us to determine whether our *Apprendi* line of cases applies to the Sentencing Guidelines, and if so, what portions of the Guidelines remain in effect.

The questions presented are:

> "1. Whether the Sixth Amendment is violated by the imposition of an enhanced sentence under the United States Sentencing Guidelines based on the sentencing judge's determination of a fact (other than a prior conviction) that was not found by the jury or admitted by the defendant.
>
> "2. If the answer to the first question is 'yes,' the following question is presented: whether, in a case in which the Guidelines would require the court to find a sentence-enhancing fact, the Sentencing Guidelines as a whole would be inapplicable, as a matter of severability analysis, such that the sentencing court must exercise its discretion to sentence the defendant within the maximum and minimum set by statute for the offense of conviction."

In this opinion, we explain why we agree with the lower courts' answer to the first question. In a separate opinion for the Court, Justice Breyer explains the Court's answer to the second question.

II

. . . . In *Bla*kely v. Washington (2004), we dealt with a determinate sentencing scheme similar to the Federal Sentencing Guidelines. . . .

As the dissenting opinions in *Blakely* recognized, there is no distinction of constitutional significance between the Federal Sentencing Guidelines and the Washington procedures at issue in that case. . . . This conclusion rests on the premise, common to both systems, that the relevant sentencing rules are mandatory and impose binding requirements on all sentencing judges.

If the Guidelines as currently written could be read as merely advisory provisions that recommended, rather than required, the selection of particular sentences in response to differing sets of facts, their use would not implicate the Sixth Amendment.We have never doubted the authority of a judge to exercise broad discretion in imposing a sentence within a statutory range. See *Apprendi;* Williams v. New York (1949). Indeed, everyone agrees that the constitutional issues presented by these cases would have been avoided entirely if Congress had omitted from the SRA the provisions that make the Guidelines binding on district judges; it is that circumstance that makes the Court's answer to the second question presented possible. For when a trial judge exercises his discretion to select a specific sentence within a defined range, the defendant has no right to a jury determination of the facts that the judge deems relevant.

The Guidelines as written, however, are not advisory; they are mandatory and binding on all judges. While subsection (a) of § 3553 of the sentencing statute lists the Sentencing Guidelines as one factor to be considered in imposing a sentence, subsection (b) directs that the court "*shall* impose a sentence of the kind, and within the range" established by the Guidelines, subject to departures in specific, limited cases. (Emphasis added.) Because they are binding on judges, we have consistently held that the Guidelines have the force and effect of laws. See, *e.g.*, Mistretta v. United States.

The availability of a departure in specified circumstances does not avoid the constitutional issue, just as it did not in *Blakely* itself. The Guidelines permit departures from the prescribed sentencing range in cases in which the judge "finds that there exists an aggravating or mitigating circumstance of a kind, or to a degree, not adequately taken into consideration by the Sentencing Commission in formulating the guidelines that should result in a sentence different from that described." ... Importantly, however, departures are not available in every case, and in fact are unavailable in most. In most cases, as a matter of law, the Commission will have adequately taken all relevant factors into account, and no departure will be legally permissible. In those instances, the judge is bound to impose a sentence within the Guidelines range....

.... Booker's is a run-of-the-mill drug case, and does not present any factors that were inadequately considered by the Commission. The sentencing judge would therefore have been reversed had he not imposed a sentence within the level 32 Guidelines range.

Booker's actual sentence, however, was 360 months, almost 10 years longer than the Guidelines range supported by the jury verdict alone. To reach this sentence, the judge found facts beyond those found by the jury: namely, that Booker possessed 566 grams of crack in addition to the 92.5 grams in his duffel bag. The jury never heard any evidence of the additional drug quantity, and the judge found it true by a preponderance of the evidence. Thus, just as in *Blakely*, "the jury's verdict alone does not authorize the sentence. The judge acquires that authority only upon finding some additional fact." There is no relevant distinction between the sentence imposed pursuant to the Washington statutes in *Blakely* and the sentences imposed pursuant to the Federal Sentencing Guidelines in these cases....

It is quite true that once determinate sentencing had fallen from favor, American judges commonly determined facts justifying a choice of a heavier sentence on account of the manner in which particular defendants acted. In 1986, however, our own cases first recognized a new trend in the legislative regulation of sentencing when we considered the significance of facts selected by legislatures that not only authorized, or even mandated, heavier sentences than would otherwise have been imposed, but increased the range of sentences possible for the underlying crime. See McMillan v. Pennsylvania (1986). Provisions for such enhancements of the permissible sentencing range reflected growing and wholly justified legislative concern about the proliferation and variety of drug crimes and their frequent identification with firearms offences.

The effect of the increasing emphasis on facts that enhanced sentencing ranges, however, was to increase the judge's power and diminish that of the jury. It became the judge, not the jury, who determined the upper limits of sentencing, and the facts determined were not required to be raised before trial or proved by more than a preponderance.

As the enhancements became greater, the jury's finding of the underlying crime became less significant. And the enhancements became very serious indeed.... Respondent Booker's case (from 262 months to a life sentence); respondent Fanfan's case (from 78 to 235 months); United States v. Rodriguez, 73 F.3d 161, 162–163 (CA7 1996) (Posner, C.J., dissenting from denial of rehearing en banc) (from approximately 54 months to a life sentence); *United States v. Hammoud*, 381 F.3d 316, 361–362 (CA4 2004) (en banc) (Motz, J., dissenting) (actual sentence increased from 57 months to 155 years).

.... The new sentencing practice forced the Court to address the question how the right of jury trial could be preserved, in a meaningful way guaranteeing that the jury would still stand between the individual and the power of the government under the new sentencing regime. And it is the new circumstances, not a tradition or practice that the new circumstances have superseded, that have led us to the answer first considered in *Jones* and developed in *Apprendi* and subsequent cases culminating with this one. It is an answer not motivated by Sixth Amendment formalism, but by the need to preserve Sixth Amendment substance.

* * *

IV

... We recognize, as we did in ... *Apprendi*, and *Blakely*, that in some cases jury factfinding may impair the most expedient and efficient sentencing of defendants. But the interest in fairness and reliability protected by the right to a jury trial—a common-law right that defendants enjoyed for centuries and that is now enshrined in the Sixth Amendment—has always outweighed the interest in concluding trials swiftly.

* * *

Accordingly, we reaffirm our holding in *Apprendi:* Any fact (other than a prior conviction) which is necessary to support a sentence exceeding the maximum authorized by the facts established by a plea of guilty or a jury verdict must be admitted by the defendant or proved to a jury beyond a reasonable doubt.

* * *

■ JUSTICE BREYER delivered the opinion of the Court in part. THE CHIEF JUSTICE, JUSTICE O'CONNOR, JUSTICE KENNEDY, and JUSTICE GINSBURG join this opinion.

The first question that the Government has presented in these cases is the following:

> "Whether the Sixth Amendment is violated by the imposition of an enhanced sentence under the United States Sentencing Guidelines based on the sentencing judge's determination of a fact (other than a prior conviction) that was not found by the jury or admitted by the defendant."

The Court, in an opinion by Justice Stevens, answers this question in the affirmative.... the Court holds that, in the circumstances mentioned, the Sixth Amendment requires juries, not judges, to find facts relevant to sentencing.

We here turn to the second question presented, a question that concerns the remedy. We must decide whether or to what extent, "as a matter of severability analysis," the Guidelines "as a whole" are "inapplicable ... such that the sentencing court must exercise its discretion to sentence the defendant within the maximum and minimum set by statute for the offense of conviction."

We answer the question of remedy by finding the provision of the federal sentencing statute that makes the Guidelines mandatory, incompatible with today's constitutional holding. We conclude that this provision must be severed and excised, as must one other statutory section, which depends upon the Guidelines' mandatory nature. So modified, the federal sentencing statute, makes the Guidelines effectively advisory. It requires a sentencing court to consider Guidelines ranges, but it permits the court to tailor the sentence in light of other statutory concerns as well.

I

We answer the remedial question by looking to legislative intent. We seek to determine what "Congress would have intended" in light of the Court's constitutional holding....

One approach, that of Justice Stevens' dissent, would retain the Sentencing Act (and the Guidelines) as written, but would engraft onto the existing system today's Sixth Amendment "jury trial" requirement. The addition would change the Guidelines by preventing the sentencing court from increasing a sentence on the basis of a fact that the jury did not find (or that the offender did not admit).

The other approach, which we now adopt, would ... make the Guidelines system advisory while maintaining a strong connection between the sentence imposed and the offender's real conduct—a connection important to the increased uniformity of sentencing that Congress intended its Guidelines system to achieve.

Both approaches would significantly alter the system that Congress designed. But today's constitutional holding means that it is no longer possible to maintain the judicial factfinding that Congress thought would underpin the mandatory Guidelines system that it sought to create and that Congress wrote into the Act. Hence we must decide whether we would deviate less radically from Congress' intended system (1) by superimposing the constitutional requirement announced today or (2) through elimination of some provisions of the statute.

To say this is not to create a new kind of severability analysis. Rather, it is to recognize that sometimes severability questions (questions as to how, or whether, Congress would intend a statute to apply) can arise when a legislatively unforeseen constitutional problem requires modification of a statutory provision as applied in a significant number of instances....

* * *

In today's context—a highly complex statute, interrelated provisions, and a constitutional requirement that creates fundamental change—we cannot assume that Congress, if faced with the statute's invalidity in key applications, would have preferred to apply the statute in as many other instances as possible. Neither can we determine likely congressional intent mechanically. We cannot simply approach the problem grammatically, say, by looking to see whether the constitutional requirement and the words of the Act are linguistically compatible.

Nor do simple numbers provide an answer. It is, of course, true that the numbers show that the constitutional jury trial requirement would lead to additional decisionmaking by juries in only a minority of cases. Prosecutors and defense attorneys would still resolve the lion's share of criminal matters through plea bargaining, and plea bargaining takes place without a jury. Many of the rest involve only simple issues calling for no upward Guidelines adjustment. And in at least some of the remainder, a judge may find adequate room to adjust a sentence within the single Guidelines range to which the jury verdict points, or within the overlap between that range and the next highest.

But the constitutional jury trial requirement would nonetheless affect every case. It would affect decisions about whether to go to trial. It would affect the content of plea negotiations. It would alter the judge's role in sentencing. Thus we must determine likely intent not by counting proceedings, but by evaluating the consequences of the Court's constitutional requirement in light of the Act's language, its history, and its basic purposes.

While reasonable minds can, and do, differ about the outcome, we conclude that the constitutional jury trial requirement is not compatible with the Act as written and that some severance and excision are necessary.... That is to say, in light of today's holding, we compare maintaining the Act as written with jury factfinding added (the dissenters' proposed remedy) to the total invalidation of the statute, and conclude that Congress would have preferred the latter. We then compare our own remedy to the total invalidation of the statute, and conclude that Congress would have preferred our remedy.

II

Several considerations convince us that, were the Court's constitutional requirement added onto the Sentencing Act as currently written, the requirement would so transform the scheme that Congress created that Congress likely would not have intended the Act as so modified to stand. First, the statute's text states that "[t]he court" when sentencing will consider "the nature and circumstances of the offense and the history and characteristics of the defendant." In context, the words "the court" mean "the judge without the jury," not "the judge working together with the jury." A further statutory provision, by removing typical "jury trial" evidentiary limitations, makes this clear. See § 3661 (ruling out any "limitation ... on the information concerning the [offender's] background, character, and conduct" that the "court ... may receive").

* * *

Second, Congress' basic statutory goal—a system that diminishes sentencing disparity—depends for its success upon judicial efforts to determine, and to base punishment upon, the *real conduct* that underlies the crime of conviction. That determination is particularly important in the federal system where crimes defined as, for example, "obstruct[ing], delay[ing], or affect[ing] commerce or the movement of any article or commodity in commerce, by ... extortion," or, say, using the mail "for the purpose of executing" a "scheme or artifice to defraud," can encompass a vast range of very different kinds of underlying conduct. But it is also important even in respect to ordinary crimes, such as robbery, where an act that meets the statutory definition can be committed in a host of different ways. Judges have long looked to real conduct when sentencing. Federal judges have long relied upon a presentence report, prepared by a probation officer, for information (often unavailable until *after* the trial) relevant to the manner in which the convicted offender committed the crime of conviction.

* * *

To engraft the Court's constitutional requirement onto the sentencing statutes, however, would destroy the system. It would prevent a judge from relying upon a presentence report for factual information, relevant to sentencing, uncovered after the trial. In doing so, it would, even compared to pre-Guidelines sentencing, weaken the tie between a sentence and an offender's real conduct. It would thereby undermine the sentencing statute's basic aim of ensuring similar sentences for those who have committed similar crimes in similar ways.

Several examples help illustrate the point. Imagine Smith and Jones, each of whom violates the Hobbs Act in very different ways.... Smith threatens to injure a co-worker unless the co-worker advances him a few dollars from the interstate company's till; Jones, after similarly threatening the co-worker, causes far more harm by seeking far more money, by making certain that the co-worker's family is aware of the threat, by arranging for deliveries of dead animals to the co-worker's home to show he is serious, and so forth. The offenders' behavior is very different; the known harmful consequences of their actions are different; their punishments both before, and after, the Guidelines would have been different. But, under the dissenters' approach, unless prosecutors decide to charge more than the elements of the crime, the judge would have to impose similar punishments.

Now imagine two former felons, Johnson and Jackson, each of whom engages in identical criminal behavior: threatening a bank teller with a gun, securing $50,000, and injuring an innocent bystander while fleeing the bank. Suppose prosecutors charge Johnson with one crime (say, illegal gun possession), and Jackson with another (say, bank robbery). Before the Guidelines, a single judge faced with such similar real conduct would have been able (within statutory limits) to impose similar sentences upon the two similar offenders despite the different charges brought against them. The Guidelines themselves would ordinarily have required judges to sentence the two offenders similarly. But under the dissenters' system, in these circumstances the offenders likely would receive different punishments.

Consider, too, a complex mail fraud conspiracy where a prosecutor may well be uncertain of the amount of harm and of the role each indicted individual played until after conviction—when the offenders may turn over financial records, when it becomes easier to determine who were the leaders and who the followers, when victim interviews are seen to be worth the time. In such a case the relation between the sentence and what actually occurred is likely to be considerably more distant under a system with a jury trial requirement patched onto it than it was even prior to the Sentencing Act, when judges routinely used information obtained after the verdict to decide upon a proper sentence.

This point is critically important. Congress' basic goal in passing the Sentencing Act was to move the sentencing system in the direction of increased uniformity. That uniformity does not consist simply of similar sentences for those convicted of violations of the same statute—a uniformity consistent with the dissenters' remedial approach. It consists, more importantly, of similar relationships between sentences and real conduct, relationships that Congress' sentencing statutes helped to advance and that Justice Stevens' approach would undermine....

Third, the sentencing statutes, read to include the Court's Sixth Amendment requirement, would create a system far more complex than Congress could have intended. How would courts and counsel work with an indictment and a jury trial that involved not just whether a defendant robbed a bank but also how? Would the indictment have to allege, in addition to the elements of robbery, whether the defendant possessed a firearm, whether he brandished or discharged it, whether he threatened death, whether he caused bodily injury, whether any such injury was ordinary, serious, permanent or life threatening, whether he abducted or physically restrained anyone, whether any victim was unusually vulnerable, how much money was taken, and whether he was an organizer, leader, manager, or supervisor in a robbery gang? If so, how could a defendant mount a defense against some or all such specific claims should he also try simultaneously to maintain that the Government's evidence failed to place him at the scene of the crime? Would the indictment in a mail fraud case have to allege the number of victims, their vulnerability, and the amount taken from each? How could a judge expect a jury to work with the

Guidelines' definitions of, say, "relevant conduct," which includes "all acts and omissions committed, aided, abetted, counseled, commanded, induced, procured, or willfully caused by the defendant; and [in the case of a conspiracy] all reasonably foreseeable acts and omissions of others in furtherance of the jointly undertaken criminal activity"? How would a jury measure "loss" in a securities fraud case—a matter so complex as to lead the Commission to instruct judges to make "only . . . a reasonable estimate"? How would the court take account, for punishment purposes, of a defendant's contemptuous behavior at trial—a matter that the Government could not have charged in the indictment?

Fourth, plea bargaining would not significantly diminish the consequences of the Court's constitutional holding for the operation of the Guidelines. Rather, plea bargaining would make matters worse. Congress enacted the sentencing statutes in major part to achieve greater uniformity in sentencing, *i.e.*, to increase the likelihood that offenders who engage in similar real conduct would receive similar sentences. The statutes reasonably assume that their efforts to move the trial-based sentencing process in the direction of greater sentencing uniformity would have a similar positive impact upon plea-bargained sentences, for plea bargaining takes place *in the shadow of* (*i.e.*, with an eye toward the hypothetical result of) a potential trial.

That, too, is why Congress, understanding the realities of plea bargaining, authorized the Commission to promulgate policy statements that would assist sentencing judges in determining whether to reject a plea agreement after reading about the defendant's real conduct in a presentence report (and giving the offender an opportunity to challenge the report). This system has not worked perfectly; judges have often simply accepted an agreed-upon account of the conduct at issue. But compared to pre-existing law, the statutes try to move the system in the right direction, *i.e.*, toward greater sentencing uniformity.

The Court's constitutional jury trial requirement, however, if patched onto the present Sentencing Act, would move the system backwards in respect both to tried and to plea-bargained cases. In respect to tried cases, it would effectively deprive the judge of the ability to use post-verdict-acquired real-conduct information; it would prohibit the judge from basing a sentence upon any conduct other than the conduct the prosecutor chose to charge; and it would put a defendant to a set of difficult strategic choices as to which prosecutorial claims he would contest. The sentence that would emerge in a case tried under such a system would likely reflect real conduct less completely, less accurately, and less often than did a pre-Guidelines, as well as a Guidelines, trial.

Because plea bargaining inevitably reflects estimates of what would happen at trial, plea bargaining too under such a system would move in the wrong direction. That is to say, in a sentencing system modified by the Court's constitutional requirement, plea bargaining would likely lead to sentences that gave greater weight not to real conduct, but rather to the skill of counsel, the policies of the prosecutor, the caseload, and other factors that vary from place to place, defendant to defendant, and crime to crime. Compared to pre-Guidelines plea bargaining, plea bargaining of this kind would necessarily move federal sentencing in the direction of diminished, not increased, uniformity in sentencing. It would tend to defeat, not to further, Congress' basic statutory goal.

Such a system would have particularly troubling consequences with respect to prosecutorial power. Until now, sentencing factors have come before the judge in the presentence report. But in a sentencing system with the Court's constitutional requirement engrafted onto it, any factor that a prosecutor chose not to charge at the plea negotiation would be placed beyond the reach of the judge entirely. Prosecutors would thus exercise a power the Sentencing Act vested in judges: the power to decide, based on relevant information about the offense and the offender, which defendants merit heavier punishment.

In respondent Booker's case, for example, the jury heard evidence that the crime had involved 92.5 grams of crack cocaine, and convicted Booker of possessing more than 50 grams. But the judge, at sentencing, found that the crime had involved an additional 566 grams, for a total of 658.5 grams. A system that would require the jury, not the judge, to make the additional "566 grams" finding is a system in which the prosecutor, not the judge, would control the sentence. That is because it is the prosecutor who would have to decide what drug amount to charge. He could choose to charge 658.5 grams, or 92.5, or less. It is the prosecutor who, through such a charging decision, would control the sentencing range. And it is different prosecutors who, in different cases—say, in two cases involving 566 grams—would potentially insist upon different punishments for similar defendants who engaged in similar criminal conduct involving similar amounts of unlawful drugs—say, by charging one of them with the full 566 grams, and the other with 10. As long as different prosecutors react differently, a system with a patched-on jury factfinding requirement would mean different sentences for otherwise similar conduct, whether in the context of trials or that of plea bargaining.

Fifth, Congress would not have enacted sentencing statutes that make it more difficult to adjust sentences *upward* than to adjust them *downward*. As several United States Senators have written in an *amicus* brief, "the Congress that enacted the 1984 Act did not conceive of—much less establish—a sentencing guidelines system in which sentencing judges were free to consider facts or circumstances not found by a jury or admitted in a plea agreement for the purpose of adjusting a base-offense level *down*, but not *up*, within the applicable guidelines range. Such a one-way lever would be grossly at odds with Congress's intent." Brief for Sen. Orrin G. Hatch et al. as *Amici Curiae* 22. Yet that is the system that the dissenters' remedy would create....

For all these reasons, Congress, had it been faced with the constitutional jury trial requirement, likely would not have passed the same Sentencing Act. It likely would have found the requirement incompatible with the Act as written. Hence the Act cannot remain valid in its entirety. Severance and excision are necessary.

III

We now turn to the question of *which* portions of the sentencing statute we must sever and excise as inconsistent with the Court's constitutional requirement. Although, as we have explained, we believe that Congress would have preferred the total invalidation of the statute to the dissenters' remedial approach, we nevertheless do not believe that the entire statute must be invalidated. Most of the statute is perfectly valid.... And we must "refrain from invalidating more of the statute than is necessary." Indeed, we must retain those portions of the Act that are (1) constitutionally valid, (2) capable of "functioning independently," and (3) consistent with Congress' basic objectives in enacting the statute.

Application of these criteria indicates that we must sever and excise two specific statutory provisions: the provision that requires sentencing courts to impose a sentence within the applicable Guidelines range (in the absence of circumstances that justify a departure), and the provision that sets forth standards of review on appeal, including *de novo* review of departures from the applicable Guidelines range. With these two sections excised (and statutory cross-references to the two sections consequently invalidated), the remainder of the Act satisfies the Court's constitutional requirements.

As the Court today recognizes in its first opinion in these cases,[without] ... the provision that makes "the relevant sentencing rules ... mandatory and impose[s] binding requirements on all sentencing judges"—the statute falls outside the scope of *Apprendi's* requirement.

The remainder of the Act "function[s] independently." Without the "mandatory" provision, the Act nonetheless requires judges to take account of the Guidelines together with other sentencing goals. The Act nonetheless requires judges to consider the Guidelines "sentencing range established for ... the applicable category of offense committed by the applicable category of defendant," the pertinent Sentencing Commission policy statements, the need to avoid unwarranted sentencing disparities, and the need to provide restitution to victims. And the Act nonetheless requires judges to impose sentences that reflect the seriousness of the offense, promote respect for the law, provide just punishment, afford adequate deterrence, protect the public, and effectively provide the defendant with needed educational or vocational training and medical care.

Moreover, the Act continues to provide for appeals from sentencing decisions irrespective of whether the trial judge sentences within or outside the Guidelines range in the exercise of his discretionary power ... We concede that the excision of [mandatory sentences] requires the excision of a different, appeals-related section, which sets forth standards of review on appeal....

[This] excision ... does not pose a critical problem for the handling of appeals. That is because, as we have previously held, a statute that does not *explicitly* set forth a standard of review may nonetheless do so *implicitly*. ... And in this instance those factors, in addition to the past two decades of appellate practice in cases involving departures, imply a practical standard of review already familiar to appellate courts: review for "unreasonable[ness]."

[W]e share the dissenters' doubts about the practicality of a "reasonableness" standard of review. "Reasonableness" standards are not foreign to sentencing law. The Act has long required their use in important sentencing circumstances—both on review of departures, and on review of sentences imposed where there was no applicable Guideline. Together, these cases account for about 16.7% of sentencing appeals. See United States Sentencing Commission, 2002 Sourcebook of Federal Sentencing Statistics 107, n 1, 111 (at least 711 of 5,018 sentencing appeals involved departures), 108 (at least 126 of 5,018 sentencing appeals involved the imposition of a term of imprisonment after the revocation of supervised release). That is why we think it fair (and not, in Justice Scalia's words, a "gross exaggeratio[n]," to assume judicial familiarity with a "reasonableness" standard). And that is why we believe that appellate judges will prove capable of facing with greater equanimity than would Justice Scalia what he calls the "daunting prospect," of applying such a standard across the board.

Neither do we share Justice Scalia's belief that use of a reasonableness standard "will produce a discordant symphony" leading to "excessive sentencing disparities," and "wreak havoc" on the judicial system. The Sentencing Commission will continue to collect and study appellate court decisionmaking. It will continue to modify its Guidelines in light of what it learns, thereby encouraging what it finds to be better sentencing practices. It will thereby promote uniformity in the sentencing process.

Regardless, in this context, we must view fears of a "discordant symphony," "excessive disparities," and "havoc" (if they are not themselves "gross exaggerations") with a comparative eye. We cannot and do not claim that use of a "reasonableness" standard will provide the uniformity that Congress originally sought to secure. Nor do we doubt that Congress wrote the language of the appellate provisions to correspond with the mandatory system it intended to create.... But, as by now should be clear, that mandatory system is no longer an open choice. And the remedial question we must ask here is, which alternative adheres more closely to Congress' original objective: (1) retention of sentencing appeals, or (2) invalidation of the entire Act, including its appellate provisions? The former, by providing appellate review, would tend to iron out sentencing differences; the latter would not. Hence we believe Congress would have preferred the former to the latter—even if the former means that some provisions will apply differently from the way Congress had originally expected. But, as we have said, we believe that Congress would have preferred even the latter to the system the dissenters recommend, a system that has its own problems of practicality.

* * *

The system remaining after excision, while lacking the mandatory features that Congress enacted, retains other features that help to further these ... [Congressional] objectives.

As we have said, the Sentencing Commission remains in place, writing Guidelines, collecting information about actual district court sentencing decisions, undertaking research, and revising the Guidelines accordingly. The district courts, while not bound to apply the Guidelines, must consult those Guidelines and take them into account when sentencing.... The courts of appeals review sentencing decisions for unreasonableness. These features of the remaining system, while not the system Congress enacted, nonetheless continue to move sentencing in Congress' preferred direction, helping to avoid excessive sentencing disparities while maintaining flexibility sufficient to individualize sentences where necessary. We can find no feature of the remaining system that tends to hinder, rather than to further, these basic objectives. Under these circumstances, why would Congress not have preferred excision of the "mandatory" provision to a system that engrafts today's constitutional requirement onto the unchanged pre-existing statute—a system that, in terms of Congress' basic objectives, is counterproductive?

* * *

Ours, of course, is not the last word: The ball now lies in Congress' court. The National Legislature is equipped to devise and install, long term, the sentencing system, compatible with the Constitution, that Congress judges best for the federal system of justice.

* * *

In respondent Booker's case, the District Court applied the Guidelines as written and imposed a sentence higher than the maximum authorized solely by the jury's verdict. The Court of Appeals held *Blakely* applicable to the Guidelines, concluded that Booker's sentence violated the Sixth Amendment, vacated the judgment of the District Court, and remanded for resentencing. We affirm the judgment of the Court of Appeals and remand the case. On remand, the District Court should impose a sentence in accordance with today's opinions, and, if the sentence comes before the Court of Appeals for review, the Court of Appeals should apply the review standards set forth in this opinion.

In respondent Fanfan's case, the District Court held *Blakely* applicable to the Guidelines. It then imposed a sentence that was authorized by the jury's verdict—a sentence lower than the sentence authorized by the Guidelines as written. Thus, Fanfan's sentence does not violate the Sixth Amendment. Nonetheless, the Government (and the defendant should he so choose) may seek resentencing under the system set forth in today's opinions. Hence we vacate the judgment of the District Court and remand the case for further proceedings consistent with this opinion.

The opinion of Justice Stevens, with whom Justice Souter joings, and with whom Justice Scalia joins except for Part III and footnote 17, dissent in part, is omitted.

■ The opinion of JUSTICE SCALIA, dissenting in part, is omitted

■ The opinion of JUSTICE THOMAS, dissenting in part, is omitted.

■ The opinion of JUSTICE BREYER, with whom THE CHIEF JUSTICE, JUSTICE O'CONNOR, and JUSTICE KENNEDY join, dissenting in part, is omitted.

NOTES

1. Would Booker undercut efforts at uniformity? What of factors other than race? See Raeder, "Gender–Related Issues in a Post–Booker Federal Guidelines World." 37 McGeorge Law Review 691 (2006).

2. Once the guidelines became advisory, the court struggled with the appropriate standard under which to assess sentences imposed at the trial level

Rita v. United States

United States Supreme Court, 2007.
551 U.S. ___, 127 S.Ct. 2456.

■ JUSTICE BREYER delivered the opinion of the Court.

The federal courts of appeals review federal sentences and set aside those they find "unreasonable." Several Circuits have held that, when doing so, they will presume that a sentence imposed within a properly calculated United States Sentencing Guidelines range is a reasonable sentence. The most important question before us is whether the law permits the courts of appeals to use this presumption. We hold that it does.

I

A

The basic crime in this case concerns two false statements which Victor Rita, the petitioner, made under oath to a federal grand jury. The jury was investigating a gun company called InterOrdnance. Prosecutors believed that buyers of an InterOrdnance kit, called a "PPSH 41 machinegun 'parts kit,' " could assemble a machinegun from the kit, that those kits consequently amounted to machineguns, and that InterOrdnance had not secured proper registrations for the importation of the guns.

Rita had bought a PPSH 41 machinegun parts kit. Rita, when contacted by the Bureau of Alcohol, Tobacco, and Firearms and Explosives (ATF), agreed to let a federal agent inspect the kit. But before meeting with the agent, Rita called InterOrdnance and then sent back the kit. He subsequently turned over to ATF a different kit that apparently did not amount to a machinegun.

The investigating prosecutor brought Rita before the grand jury, placed him under oath, and asked him about these matters. Rita denied that the Government agent had asked him for the PPSH kit, and also denied that he had spoken soon thereafter about the PPSH kit to someone at InterOrdnance. The Government claimed these statements were false, charged Rita with perjury, making false statements, and obstructing justice, and, after a jury trial, obtained convictions on all counts.

B

The parties subsequently proceeded to sentencing. Initially, a probation officer, with the help of the parties, and after investigating the background both of the offenses and of the offender, prepared a presentence report. The completed report describes "offense characteristics," "offender characteristics," and other matters that might be relevant to the sentence, and then calculates a Guidelines sentence. The report also sets forth factors potentially relevant to a departure from the Guidelines or relevant to the imposition of an other-than-Guidelines sentence. It ultimately makes a sentencing recommendation based on the Guidelines. In respect to "offense characteristics," for example, the report points out that the five counts of conviction all stem from a single incident. Hence, pursuant to the Guidelines, the report, in calculating a recommended sentence, groups the five counts of conviction together, treating them as if they amounted to the single most serious count among them (and ignoring all others). The single most serious offense in Rita's case is "perjury." The relevant Guideline instructs the sentencing court (and the probation officer) to calculate the Guidelines sentence for "perjury ... in respect to a criminal offense" by applying the Guideline for an "accessory after the fact," as to that criminal offense. And that latter Guideline says that the judge, for calculation purposes, should take as a base offense level, a level that is "6 levels lower than the offense level for the *underlying offense*," Here the "underlying offense" consisted of InterOrdnance's possible violation of the machinegun registration law. The base offense level for the gun registration crime is 26. See USSG § 2M5.2. Six levels less is 20. And 20, says the presentence report, is the base offense level applicable to Rita for purposes of Guidelines sentence calculation.

The presentence report next considers Rita's "Criminal History." Rita was convicted in May 1986, and sentenced to five years' probation for making false statements in connection with the purchase of firearms. Because this conviction took place more than 10 years before the present offense, it did not count against Rita. And because Rita had no other relevant convictions, the Guidelines considered him as having no "criminal history points." The report consequently places Rita in criminal history category I, the lowest category for purposes of calculating a Guidelines' sentence.

The report goes on to describe other "Offender Characteristics." The description includes Rita's personal and family data, Rita's physical condition (including a detailed description of ailments), Rita's mental and emotional health, the lack of any history of substance abuse, Rita's vocational and nonvocational education, and Rita's employment record. It states that he served in the Armed Forces for over 25 years, on active duty and in the Reserve. During that time he received 35 commendations, awards, or medals of different kinds. The report analyzes Rita's financial condition.

Ultimately, the report calculates the Guidelines sentencing range. The Guidelines specify for base level 20, criminal history category I, a sentence of 33–to–41 months' imprisonment. The report adds that there "appears to be no circumstance or combination of circumstances that warrant a departure from the prescribed sentencing guidelines."

C

At the sentencing hearing, both Rita and the Government presented their sentencing arguments. Each side addressed the report. Rita argued for a sentence outside (and lower than) the recommended Guidelines 33–to–41 month range.

The judge made clear that Rita's argument for a lower sentence could take either of two forms. First, Rita might argue *within the Guidelines' framework*, for a departure from the applicable Guidelines range on the ground that his circumstances present an "atypical case" that falls outside the "heartland" to which the United States Sentencing Commission intends each individual Guideline to apply. Second, Rita might argue that, independent of the Guidelines, application of the sentencing factors warrants a lower sentence.

Thus, the judge asked Rita's counsel, "Are you going to put on evidence to show that [Rita] should be getting a downward departure, or under 3553, your client would be entitled to a different sentence than he should get under sentencing guidelines?" And the judge later summarized:

"You're asking for a departure from the guidelines or a sentence under 3553 that is lower than the guidelines, and here are the reasons:

> "One, he is a vulnerable defendant because he's been involved in [government criminal justice] work which has caused people to become convicted criminals who are in prison and there may be retribution against him.
>
> "Two, his military experience...."

Counsel agreed, while adding that Rita's poor physical condition constituted a third reason. And counsel said that he rested his claim for a lower sentence on "just [those] three" special circumstances, "physical condition, vulnerability in prison and the military service." Rita presented evidence and argument related to these three factors. The Government, while not asking for a sentence higher than the report's recommended Guidelines range, said that Rita's perjury had interfered with the Government's potential "obstruction of justice" claim against InterOrdnance and that Rita, as a former Government criminal justice employee, should have known better than to commit perjury. The sentencing judge asked questions about each factor.

After hearing the arguments, the judge concluded that he was "unable to find that the [report's recommended] sentencing guideline range ... is an inappropriate guideline range for that ... the public needs to be protected if it is true, and I must accept as true the jury verdict." The court concluded: "So the Court finds that it is appropriate to enter" a sentence at the bottom of the Guidelines range, namely a sentence of imprisonment "for a period of 33 months."

D

On appeal, Rita argued that his 33–month sentence was "unreasonable" because (1) it did not adequately take account of "the defendant's history and characteristics," and (2) it "is greater than necessary to comply with the purposes of sentencing set forth in 18 U.S.C. § 3553(a)(2)." The Fourth Circuit observed that it must set aside a sentence that is not "reasonable." The Circuit stated that "a sentence imposed within the properly calculated Guidelines range ... is presumptively reasonable." It added that "while we believe that the appropriate circumstances for imposing a sentence outside the guideline range will depend on the facts of individual cases, we have no reason to doubt that most sentences will continue to fall within the applicable guideline range." The Fourth Circuit then rejected Rita's arguments and upheld the sentence.

E

Rita petitioned for a writ of certiorari. He pointed out that the Circuits are split as to the use of a presumption of reasonableness for within-Guidelines sentences.... We consequently granted Rita's petition. We agreed to decide whether a circuit court may afford a "presumption of reasonableness" to a "within-Guidelines" sentence. We also agreed to decide whether the District Court properly analyzed the relevant sentencing factors and whether, given the record, the District Court's ultimate choice of a 33–month sentence was "unreasonable."

II

The first question is whether a court of appeals may apply a presumption of reasonableness to a district court sentence that reflects a proper application of the Sentencing Guidelines. We conclude that it can.

A

For one thing, the presumption is not binding. It does not, like a trial-related evidentiary presumption, insist that one side, or the other, shoulder a particular burden of persuasion or proof lest they lose their case. Nor does the presumption reflect strong judicial deference of the kind that leads appeals courts to grant greater factfinding leeway to an expert agency than to a district judge. Rather, the presumption reflects the fact that, by the time an appeals court is considering a within-Guidelines sentence on review, *both* the sentencing judge and the Sentencing Commission will have reached the *same* conclusion as to the proper sentence in the particular case. That double determination significantly increases the likelihood that the sentence is a reasonable one.

Further, the presumption reflects the nature of the Guidelines-writing task that Congress set for the Commission and the manner in which the Commission carried out that task. In instructing both the *sentencing judge* and the *Commission* what to do, Congress referred to the basic sentencing objectives ... which instruct ... the *sentencing judge* to consider (1) offense and offender characteristics; (2) the need for a sentence to reflect the basic aims of sentencing, namely (a) "just punishment" (retribution), (b) deterrence, (c) incapacitation, (d) rehabilitation; (3) the sentences legally available; (4) the Sentencing Guidelines; (5) Sentencing Commission policy statements; (6) the need to avoid unwarranted disparities; and (7) the need for restitution. The provision also tells the sentencing judge to "impose a sentence sufficient, but not greater than necessary, to comply with" the basic aims of sentencing as set out above.

Congressional statutes then tell the *Commission* to write Guidelines that will carry out these same objectives. Thus, ... one of the Commission's basic objectives is to "assure the meeting of the purposes of sentencing" ... the Commission must seek to "provide certainty and fairness" in sentencing, to "avoid unwarranted sentencing disparities," to "maintain sufficient flexibility to permit individualized sentences when warranted by mitigating or aggravating factors not taken into account in the establishment of general sentencing practices," and to "reflect, to the extent practicable [sentencing-relevant] advancement in [the] knowledge of human behavior."

The upshot is that the sentencing statutes envision both the sentencing judge and the Commission as carrying out the same basic objectives, the one, at retail, the other at wholesale.

The Commission has made a serious, sometimes controversial, effort to carry out this mandate. The Commission, in describing its Guidelines-writing efforts, refers to these same statutory provisions. It says that it has tried to embody in the Guidelines the factors and considerations.... The Commission's introductory statement recognizes that Congress "foresees guidelines that will further the basic purposes of criminal punishment, *i.e.*, deterring crime, incapacitating the offender, providing just punishment, and rehabilitating the offender." It adds that Congress "sought *uniformity* in sentencing by narrowing the wide disparity in sentences imposed by different federal courts for similar criminal conduct," as well as "*proportionality* in sentencing through a system that imposes appropriately different sentences for criminal conduct of different severity."

The Guidelines commentary explains how, despite considerable disagreement within the criminal justice community, the Commission has gone about writing Guidelines that it intends to embody these ends. It says, for example, that the goals of *uniformity* and *proportionality* often conflict. The commentary describes the difficulties involved in developing a practical sentencing system that sensibly reconciles the two ends. It adds that a "philosophical problem arose when the Commission attempted to reconcile the differing perceptions of the purposes of criminal punishment." Some would emphasize moral culpability and "just punishment"; others would emphasize the need for "crime control." Rather than choose among differing practical and philosophical objectives, the Commission took an "empirical approach," beginning with an empirical examination of 10,000 presentence reports setting forth what judges had done in the past and then modifying and adjusting past practice in the interests of greater rationality, avoiding inconsistency, complying with congressional instructions, and the like.

The Guidelines as written reflect the fact that the Sentencing Commission examined tens of thousands of sentences and worked with the help of many others in the law enforcement community over a long period of time in an effort to fulfill this statutory mandate. They also reflect the fact that different judges (and others) can differ as to how best to reconcile the disparate ends of punishment.

The Commission's work is ongoing. The statutes and the Guidelines themselves foresee continuous evolution helped by the sentencing courts and courts of appeals in that process. The sentencing courts, applying the Guidelines in individual cases may depart (either pursuant to the Guidelines or, since *Booker*, by imposing a non-Guidelines sentence). The judges will set forth their reasons. The Courts of Appeals will determine the reasonableness of the resulting sentence. The Commission will collect and examine the results. In doing so, it may obtain advice from prosecutors, defenders, law enforcement groups, civil liberties associations, experts in penology, and others. And it can revise the Guidelines accordingly....

The result is a set of Guidelines that seek to embody the considerations, both in principle and in practice. Given the difficulties of doing so, the abstract and potentially conflicting nature of general sentencing objectives, and the differences of philosophical view among those who work within the criminal justice community as to how best to apply general sentencing objectives, it is fair to assume that the Guidelines, insofar as practicable, reflect a rough approximation of sentences that might achieve these objectives.

An individual judge who imposes a sentence within the range recommended by the Guidelines thus makes a decision that is fully consistent with the Commission's judgment in general. Despite Justice Souter's fears to the contrary, the courts of appeals' "reasonableness" presumption, rather than having independent legal effect, simply recognizes the real-world circumstance that when the judge's discretionary decision accords with the Commission's view of the appropriate application of § 3553(a) in the mine run of cases, it is probable that the sentence is reasonable. Indeed, even the Circuits that have declined to adopt a formal presumption also recognize that a Guidelines sentence will usually be reasonable, because it reflects both the Commission's and the sentencing court's judgment as to what is an appropriate sentence for a given offender.

We repeat that the presumption before us is an *appellate* court presumption. Given our explanation in *Booker* that appellate "reasonableness" review merely asks whether the trial court abused its discretion, the presumption applies only on appellate review. The sentencing judge, as a matter of process, will normally begin by considering the presentence report and its interpretation of the Guidelines. He may hear arguments by prosecution or defense that the Guidelines sentence should not apply, perhaps because (as the Guidelines themselves foresee) the case at hand falls outside the "heartland" to which the Commission intends individual Guidelines to apply, perhaps because the Guidelines sentence itself fails properly to reflect § 3553(a) considerations, or perhaps because the case warrants a different sentence regardless. Thus, the sentencing court subjects the defendant's sentence to the thorough adversarial testing contemplated by federal sentencing procedure.... In determining the merits of these arguments, the sentencing court does not enjoy the benefit of a legal presumption that the Guidelines sentence should apply.

B

Rita and his supporting *amici* make two further arguments against use of the presumption. First, Rita points out that many individual Guidelines apply higher sentences in the presence of special facts, for example, brandishing a weapon. In many cases, the sentencing judge, not the jury, will determine the existence of those facts. A pro-Guidelines "presumption of reasonableness" will increase the likelihood that courts of appeals will affirm such sentences, thereby increasing the likelihood that sentencing judges will impose such sentences. For that reason, Rita says, the presumption raises Sixth Amendment "concerns."

In our view, however, the presumption, even if it increases the likelihood that the judge, not the jury, will find "sentencing facts," does not violate the Sixth Amendment. This Court's Sixth Amendment cases do not automatically forbid a sentencing court to take account of factual matters not determined by a jury and to increase the sentence in consequence. Nor do they prohibit the sentencing judge from taking account of the Sentencing Commission's factual findings or recommended sentences.

The Sixth Amendment question, the Court has said, is whether the law *forbids* a judge to increase a defendant's sentence *unless* the judge finds facts that the jury did not find (and the offender did not concede) .....

A nonbinding appellate presumption that a Guidelines sentence is reasonable does not *require* the sentencing judge to impose that sentence. Still less does it *forbid* the sentencing judge from imposing a sentence higher than the Guidelines provide for the jury-determined facts standing alone. As far as the law is concerned, the judge could disregard the Guidelines and apply the same sentence (higher than the statutory minimum or the bottom of the unenhanced Guidelines range) in the absence of the special facts (say, gun brandishing) which, in the view of the Sentencing Commission, would warrant a higher sentence within the statutorily permissible range. Thus, our Sixth Amendment cases do not forbid appellate court use of the presumption.

Justice Scalia concedes that the Sixth Amendment concerns he foresees are not presented by this case. And his need to rely on *hypotheticals* to make his point is consistent with our view that the approach adopted here will not "raise a multitude of constitutional problems." Similarly, Justice Scalia agrees that we have never held that "the Sixth Amendment prohibits judges from ever finding any facts" relevant to sentencing. In sentencing, as in other areas, district judges at time make mistakes that are substantive. At times, they will impose sentences that are unreasonable. Circuit courts exist to correct such mistakes when they occur. Our decision in *Booker* recognized as much. *Booker* held unconstitutional that portion of the Guidelines that made them mandatory. It also recognized that when district courts impose discretionary sentences, which are reviewed under normal appellate principles by courts of appeals, such a sentencing scheme will ordinarily raise no Sixth Amendment concern.... That being so, our opinion in *Booker* made clear that today's holding does not violate the Sixth Amendment.

Rita may be correct that the presumption will encourage sentencing judges to impose Guidelines sentences. But we do not see how that fact could change the constitutional calculus. Congress sought to diminish unwarranted sentencing disparity. It sought a Guidelines system that would bring about greater fairness in sentencing through increased uniformity. The fact that the presumption might help achieve these congressional goals does not provide cause for holding the presumption unlawful as long as the presumption remains constitutional. And, given our case law, we cannot conclude that the presumption itself violates the Sixth Amendment.

The fact that we permit courts of appeals to adopt a presumption of reasonableness does not mean that courts may adopt a presumption of unreasonableness. Even the Government concedes that appellate courts may not presume that every variance from the advisory Guidelines is unreasonable. Several courts of appeals have also rejected a presumption of unreasonableness. However, a number of circuits adhere to the proposition that the strength of the justification needed to sustain an outside-Guidelines sentence varies in proportion to the degree of the variance. We will consider that approach next Term in United States v. Gall.

Second, Rita and his *amici* claim that use of a pro-Guidelines presumption on appeal conflicts with Congress' insistence that sentencing judges apply the factors set forth in [the guidelines] .... We have explained above, however, why we believe that, where judge and Commission *both* determine that the Guidelines sentences is an appropriate sentence for the case at hand, that sentence likely reflects the factors (including its "not greater than necessary" requirement). See *supra*, at 8. This circumstance alleviates any serious general conflict between § 3553(a) [*2468] and the Guidelines, for the purposes of appellate review.

III

We next turn to the question whether the District Court properly analyzed the relevant sentencing factors. In particular, Rita argues that the court took inadequate account of ... a provision that requires a sentencing judge, "at the time of sentencing," to "state in open court the reasons for its imposition of the particular sentence." In our view, given the straightforward, conceptually simple arguments before the judge, the judge's statement of reasons here, though brief, was legally sufficient.

The statute does call for the judge to "state" his "reasons." And that requirement reflects sound judicial practice. Judicial decisions are reasoned decisions. Confidence in a judge's use of reason underlies the public's trust in the judicial institution. A public statement of those reasons helps provide the public with the assurance that creates that trust.

That said, we cannot read the statute (or our precedent) as insisting upon a full opinion in every case. The appropriateness of brevity or length, conciseness or detail, when to write, what to say, depends upon circumstances. Sometimes a judicial opinion responds to every argument; sometimes it does not; sometimes a judge simply writes the word "granted," or "denied" on the face of a motion while relying upon context and the parties' prior arguments to make the reasons clear. The law leaves much, in this respect, to the judge's own professional judgment.

In the present context, a statement of reasons is important. The sentencing judge should set forth enough to satisfy the appellate court that he has considered the parties' arguments and has a reasoned basis for exercising his own legal decisionmaking authority. Nonetheless, when a judge decides simply to apply the Guidelines to a particular case, doing so will not necessarily require lengthy explanation. Circumstances may well make clear that the judge rests his decision upon the Commission's own reasoning that the Guidelines sentence is a proper sentence ... in the typical case, and that the judge has found that the case before him is typical....

Where the defendant or prosecutor presents nonfrivolous reasons for imposing a different sentence, however, the judge will normally go further and explain why he has rejected those arguments. Sometimes the circumstances will call for a brief explanation; sometimes they will call for a lengthier explanation. Where the judge imposes a sentence outside the Guidelines, the judge will explain why he has done so. To our knowledge, an ordinary explanation of judicial reasons as to why the judge has, or has not, applied the Guidelines triggers no Sixth Amendment "jury trial" requirement. Cf. *Booker* ("For when a trial judge exercises his discretion to select a specific sentence within a defined range, the defendant has no right to a jury determination of the facts that the judge deems relevant")....

By articulating reasons, even if brief, the sentencing judge not only assures reviewing courts (and the public) that the sentencing process is a reasoned process but also helps that process evolve. The sentencing judge has access to, and greater familiarity with, the individual case and the individual defendant before him than the Commission or the appeals court. That being so, his reasoned sentencing judgment, resting upon an effort to filter the Guidelines' general advice through ... [the] list of factors, can provide relevant information to both the court of appeals and ultimately the Sentencing Commission. The reasoned responses of these latter institutions to the sentencing judge's explanation should help the Guidelines constructively evolve over time, as both Congress and the Commission foresaw. See generally *supra*, at 11.

In the present case the sentencing judge's statement of reasons was brief but legally sufficient. Rita argued for a downward departure from the 33–to–41 month Guidelines sentence on the basis of three sets of special circumstances: health, fear of retaliation in prison, and military record. See App. 40–47. He added that, in any event, these same circumstances warrant leniency beyond that contemplated by the Guidelines.

The record makes clear that the sentencing judge listened to each argument. The judge considered the supporting evidence. The judge was fully aware of defendant's various physical ailments and imposed a sentence that takes them into account. The judge understood that Rita had previously worked in the immigration service where he had been involved in detecting criminal offenses. And he considered Rita's lengthy military service, including over 25 years of service, both on active duty and in the Reserve, and Rita's receipt of 35 medals, awards, and nominations.

The judge then simply found these circumstances insufficient to warrant a sentence lower than the Guidelines range of 33 to 45 months. He said that this range was not "inappropriate." (This, of course, is not the legal standard for imposition of sentence, but taken in context it is plain that the judge so understood.) He immediately added that he found that the 33–month sentence at the bottom of the Guidelines range was "appropriate." He must have believed that there was not much more to say.

We acknowledge that the judge might have said more. He might have added explicitly that he had heard and considered the evidence and argument; that (as no one before him denied) he thought the Commission in the Guidelines had determined a sentence that was proper in the minerun of roughly similar perjury cases; and that he found that Rita's personal circumstances here were simply not different enough to warrant a different sentence. But context and the record make clear that this, or similar, reasoning, underlies the judge's conclusion. Where a matter is as conceptually simple as in the case at hand and the record makes clear that the sentencing judge considered the evidence and arguments, we do not believe the law requires the judge to write more extensively.

IV

We turn to the final question: Was the Court of Appeals, after applying its presumption, legally correct in holding that Rita's sentence (a sentence that applied, and did not depart from, the relevant sentencing Guideline) was not "unreasonable"? In our view, the Court of Appeals' conclusion was lawful.

As we previously said, the crimes at issue are perjury and obstruction of justice. In essence those offenses involved the making of knowingly false, material statements under oath before a grand jury, thereby impeding its criminal investigation. The Guidelines provide for a typical such offense a base offense level of 20, 6 levels below the level provided for a simple violation of the crime being investigated (here the unlawful importation of machineguns). The offender, Rita, has no countable prior offenses and consequently falls within criminal history category I. The intersection of base offense level 20 and criminal history category I sets forth a sentencing range of imprisonment of 33 to 45 months.

Finally, Rita and supporting *amici* here claim that the Guidelines sentence is not reasonable ... because it expressly declines to consider various personal characteristics of the defendant, such as physical condition, employment record, and military service, under the view that these factors are "not ordinarily relevant." Rita did not make this argument below, and we shall not consider it.

* * *

For the foregoing reasons, the judgment of the Court of Appeals is

Affirmed.

■ JUSTICE STEVENS, with whom JUSTICE GINSBURG joins as to all but Part II, concurring.

It is no secret that the Court's remedial opinion in United States v. Booker was not unanimous. But *Booker* is now settled law and must be accepted as such. See B. Cardozo, The Nature of the Judicial Process 149 (1921) ("The labor of judges would be increased almost to the breaking point if every past decision could be reopened in every case, and one could not lay one's own course of bricks on the secure foundation of the courses laid by others who had gone before him"). Therefore, our task today is to apply *Booker*'s "reasonableness" standard to a District Judge's decision to impose a sentence within the range recommended by United States Sentencing Guidelines that are now advisory, rather than binding.

I

Simply stated, *Booker* replaced the *de novo* standard of review ... with an abuse-of-discretion standard that we called " 'reasonableness' " review. We noted in *Booker* that the *de novo* standard was a recent addition to the law. Prior to 2003, appellate courts reviewed sentencing departures for abuse of discretion under our decision in *Koon v. United States.* In 2003, however, Congress overruled *Koon* and added the *de novo* standard. Recognizing that "the reasons for this revision—to make Guidelines sentencing even more mandatory than it had been—. . . ceased to be relevant" in light of the Court's constitutional holding, *Booker* excised the portion of § 3742(e) that directed courts of appeals to apply the *de novo* standard. Critically, we did not touch the portions of § 3742(e) requiring appellate courts to "give due regard to the opportunity of the district court to judge the credibility of the witnesses," to "accept the findings of fact of the district court unless they are clearly erroneous," and to "give due deference to the district court's application of the guidelines to the facts." By leaving those portions of the statute intact while severing the portion mandating a *de novo* standard of review, *Booker* restored the abuse-of-discretion standard. . . .

These basic considerations about the nature of sentencing have not changed in a post-*Booker* world. While the specific holding in *Koon* concerned only the scope of the trial judge's discretion on whether to depart from the Guidelines, now that the Guidelines are no longer mandatory, our reasoning applies with equal force to the sentencing judge's decision " 'as to the appropriateness of a particular sentence.' "

. . . Guided by these . . . factors, *Booker*'s abuse-of-discretion standard directs appellate courts to evaluate what motivated the District Judge's individualized sentencing decision. While reviewing courts may presume that a sentence within the advisory Guidelines is reasonable, appellate judges must still always defer to the sentencing judge's individualized sentencing determination. As we stated in *Koon*, "it has been uniform and constant in the federal judicial tradition for the sentencing judge to consider every convicted person as an individual and every case as a unique study in the human failings that sometimes mitigate, sometimes magnify, the crime and the punishment to ensue." The Commission has not developed any standards or recommendations that affect sentencing ranges for many individual characteristics. Matters such as age, education, mental or emotional condition, medical condition (including drug or alcohol addiction), employment history, lack of guidance as a youth, family ties, or military, civic, charitable, or public service are not ordinarily considered under the Guidelines. These are, however, matters that [the guidelines authorize] the sentencing judge to consider. As such, they are factors that an appellate court must consider under *Booker*'s abuse-of-discretion standard.

My disagreement with Justice Scalia and Justice Souter rests on the above understanding of *Booker*'s standard of appellate review. I do not join Justice Scalia opinion because I believe that the purely procedural review he advocates is inconsistent with our remedial opinion in *Booker*, which plainly contemplated that reasonableness review would contain a substantive component. After all, a district judge who gives harsh sentences to Yankees fans and lenient sentences to Red Sox fans would not be acting reasonably even if her procedural rulings were impeccable. Moreover, even if some future unusually harsh sentence might violate the Sixth Amendment because it exceeds some yet-to-be-defined judicial standard of reasonableness, Justice Scalia correctly acknowledges this case does not present such a problem . . .

As to Justice Souter's opinion, I think he overestimates the "gravitational pull" towards the advisory Guidelines that will result from a presumption of reasonableness . . .

Applying this standard, I would affirm the sentence imposed by the District Court. Although I would have imposed a lower sentence had I been the District Judge, I agree that he did not abuse his discretion in making the particular decision that he did. I also agree with the Court that his decision is entitled to added respect because it was consistent with the advice in the Guidelines.

II

That said, I do believe that there was a significant flaw in the sentencing procedure in this case. The petitioner is a veteran who received significant recognition for his service to his country. That aspect of his background is not taken into consideration in the sentencing guidelines and was not mentioned by the District Judge in his explanation of his choice of the sentence that defendant received. I regard this as a serious omission because I think the judge's statement to the defendant, made at the time of sentencing, is an especially important part of the criminal process. If the defendant is convinced that justice has been done in his case—that society has dealt with him fairly—the likelihood of his successful rehabilitation will surely be enhanced. Nevertheless, given the importance of paying appropriate respect to the exercise of a sentencing judge's discretion, I join the Court's opinion and judgment.

■ JUSTICE SCALIA, with whom JUSTICE THOMAS joins, concurring in part and concurring in the judgment.

In *United States v. Booker* (2005), five Justices of this Court, I among them, held that our previous decision in *Blakely* v. *Washington*(2004), applied to sentences imposed under the Federal Sentencing Guidelines because those Guidelines were mandatory and binding on judges. . . . I disagreed with the Court's remedial choice, believing instead that the proper remedy was to maintain the mandatory character of the Guidelines and simply to require, for that small category of cases in which a fact was legally essential to the sentence imposed, that the fact be proved to a jury beyond a reasonable doubt or admitted by the defendant.

I do not mean to reopen that debate. As a matter of statutory *stare decisis*, I accept *Booker*'s remedial holding that district courts are no longer bound by the Guidelines and that appellate courts should review the sentences imposed for reasonableness. As should be clear from our need to decide the case today, however, precisely what "reasonableness" review entails is not dictated by *Booker*. As I lamented then, "the worst feature of the scheme is that no one knows—and perhaps no one is meant to know—how advisory Guidelines and 'unreasonableness' review will function in practice."

Earlier this Term, the Court intensified its silence when it declined to flesh out what it had in mind in the face of an argument that the form of reasonableness review had constitutional implications. In *Cunningham* v. *California* (2007), Justice Alito defended the constitutionality of California's sentencing system in part by arguing that, even post-*Booker*, some federal sentences will be upheld as reasonable only if the judge makes additional findings of fact beyond those encompassed by the jury verdict or guilty plea. The *Cunningham* majority's response, much like the *Booker* remedial opinion, was cryptic. While the Court did not explain *why* Justice Alito was incorrect, it strongly intimated that his premise was wrong: that he had erroneously "anticipated" how "reasonableness review operates in practice." Because that question is squarely presented in this case that was then pending, the Court found it "neither necessary nor proper . . . to join issue with Justice Alito on this matter," suggesting that all would be revealed in the opinion we issue today.

Today has arrived, and the Court has broken its promise. Nothing in the Court's opinion explains why, under the advisory Guidelines scheme, judge-found facts are *never* legally necessary to justify the sentence. By this I mean the Court has failed to establish that every sentence which will be imposed under the advisory Guidelines scheme could equally have been imposed had the judge relied upon no facts other than those found by the jury or admitted by the defendant. In fact, the Court implicitly, but quite plainly, acknowledges that this will not be the case, by treating as a permissible post-*Booker* claim petitioner's challenge of his within-Guidelines sentence as substantively excessive.... The Court does not even attempt to explain how this is consistent with the Sixth Amendment.

No explanation is given because no explanation is possible. The Court has reintroduced the constitutional defect that *Booker* purported to eliminate. I cannot acquiesce in this course. If a sentencing system is permissible in which some sentences cannot lawfully be imposed by a judge unless the judge finds certain facts by a preponderance of the evidence, then we should have left in place the compulsory Guidelines that Congress enacted, instead of imposing this jerry-rigged scheme of our own. In order to avoid the possibility of a Sixth Amendment violation, which was the object of the *Booker* remedy, district courts must be able, without finding any facts not embraced in the jury verdict or guilty plea, to sentence to the maximum of the *statutory* range. Because, therefore, appellate courts cannot reverse within-range sentences for being too high; and because no one would contend that Congress intended that sentences be reviewed only for being too low; I would hold that reasonableness review cannot contain a substantive component at all. I believe, however, that appellate courts can nevertheless secure some amount of sentencing uniformity through the procedural reasonableness review made possible by the *Booker* remedial opinion....

I

A

The Sixth Amendment requires that "any fact (other than a prior conviction) which is necessary to support a sentence exceeding the maximum authorized by the facts established by a plea of guilty or a jury verdict must be admitted by the defendant or proved to a jury beyond a reasonable doubt." *Booker*. Two hypotheticals will suffice to reveal why the notion of excessive sentences within the statutory range, and the ability of appellate courts to reverse such sentences, inexorably produces, in violation of the Sixth Amendment, sentences whose legality is premised on a judge's finding some fact (or combination of facts) by a preponderance of the evidence.

First, consider two brothers with similar backgrounds and criminal histories who are convicted by a jury of respectively robbing two banks of an equal amount of money. Next assume that the district judge finds that one brother, fueled by racial animus, had targeted the first bank because it was owned and operated by minorities, whereas the other brother had selected the second bank simply because its location enabled a quick getaway. Further assume that the district judge imposes the statutory maximum upon both brothers, basing those sentences primarily upon his perception that bank robbery should be punished much more severely than the Guidelines base level advises, but explicitly noting that the racially biased decisionmaking of the first brother further justified his sentence. Now imagine that the appellate court reverses as excessive only the sentence of the nonracist brother. Given the dual holdings of the appellate court, the racist has a valid Sixth Amendment claim that his sentence was reasonable (and hence lawful) only because of the judicial finding of his motive in selecting his victim. 1

Second, consider the common case in which the district court imposes a sentence *within* an advisory Guidelines range that has been substantially enhanced by certain judge-found facts. For example, the base offense level for robbery under the Guidelines is 20, which, if the defendant has a criminal history of I, corresponds to an advisory range of 33–41 months. If, however, a judge finds that a firearm was discharged, that a victim incurred serious bodily injury, and that more than $5 million was stolen, then the base level jumps by 18, producing an advisory range of 235–293 months. When a judge finds all of those facts to be true and then imposes a within-Guidelines sentence of 293 months, those judge-found facts, or some combination of them, are not merely facts that the judge finds relevant in exercising his discretion; they are the legally essential predicate for his imposition of the 293–month sentence. His failure to find them would render the 293–month sentence unlawful. That is evident because, were the district judge explicitly to find *none* of those facts true and nevertheless to impose a 293–month sentence (simply because he thinks robbery merits seven times the sentence that the Guidelines provide) the sentence would surely be reversed as unreasonably excessive.

These hypotheticals are stylized ways of illustrating the basic problem with a system in which district courts lack full discretion to sentence within the statutory range. Under such a system, for every given crime there is some maximum sentence that will be upheld as reasonable based only on the facts found by the jury or admitted by the defendant. *Every* sentence higher than that is legally authorized only by some judge-found fact, in violation of the Sixth Amendment. Appellate courts' excessiveness review will explicitly or implicitly accept those judge-found facts as justifying sentences that would otherwise be unlawful. The only difference between this system and the pre-*Booker* mandatory Guidelines is that the maximum sentence based on the jury verdict or guilty plea was specified under the latter but must be established by appellate courts, in case-by-case fashion, under the former. This is, if anything, an additional constitutional disease, not a constitutional cure.

To be clear, I am not suggesting that the Sixth Amendment prohibits judges from ever finding any facts. We have repeatedly affirmed the proposition that judges can find facts that help guide their discretion *within* the sentencing range that is authorized by the facts found by the jury or admitted by the defendant. But there is a fundamental difference, one underpinning our entire *Apprendi* jurisprudence, between facts that *must* be found in order for a sentence to be lawful, and facts that individual judges *choose* to make relevant to the exercise of their discretion. The former, but not the latter, must be found by the jury beyond a reasonable doubt in order "to give intelligible content to the right of jury trial."

I am also not contending that there is a Sixth Amendment problem with the Court's affirmation of a presumption of reasonableness for within-Guidelines sentences. I agree with the Court that such a presumption never itself makes judge-found facts legally essential to the sentence imposed, since it has no direct relevance to whether the sentence would have been *unreasonable* in the *absence* of any judge-found facts. Nor is my claim that the Sixth Amendment was violated in this case, for petitioner cannot demonstrate that his relatively low sentence would have been unreasonable if the District Court had relied on nothing but jury-found or admitted facts.

Rather, my position is that there will inevitably be *some* constitutional violations under a system of substantive reasonableness review, because there will be some sentences that will be upheld as reasonable only because of the existence of judge-found facts. *Booker* itself reveals why that reality dooms the construct of reasonableness review established and applied by today's opinion. *Booker* made two things quite plain. First, reasonableness is the standard of review implicitly contained within the Sentencing Reform Act of 1984 (SRA). Second, Congress wanted a uniform system of sentencing review, rather than different schemes depending on whether there were Sixth Amendment problems in particular cases. Thus, if the contours of reasonableness review must be narrowed in *some* cases because of constitutional concerns, then they must be narrowed in *all* cases in light of Congress's desire for a uniform standard of review. The Justices composing today's Court were in total agreement with this principle of statutory interpretation the day *Booker* was decided:

> "When deciding which of two plausible statutory constructions to adopt, a court must consider the necessary consequences of its choice. If one of them would raise a multitude of constitutional problems, the other should prevail—whether or not those constitutional problems pertain to the particular litigant before the Court." *Clark v. Martinez* (2005) (opinion for the Court by SCALIA, J., joined by, *inter alios*, STEVENS, KENNEDY, GINSBURG, and BREYER, JJ.).

Yet they now adopt substantive reasonableness review without offering any rebuttal to my charge of patent constitutional flaw inherent in such review. The one comfort to be found in the Court's opinion—though it does not excuse the failure to apply *Martinez*'s interpretive principle—is that it does not rule out as-applied Sixth Amendment challenges to sentences that would not have been upheld as reasonable on the facts encompassed by the jury verdict or guilty plea

Had the Court bothered to frame objections to the constitutional analysis undertaken above, there are four conceivable candidates.

1

The most simplistic objection is that the Sixth Amendment is not violated because the judge-found facts are made legally necessary by the decision of appellate courts rather than the decision of Congress. This rebuttal errs both in premise and in conclusion....

2

The next objection minimizes the extent to which excessiveness review makes judge-found facts legally essential to punishment. If appellate courts will uphold, based only on the facts found by the jury, a district court's decision to impose all but the lengthiest sentences, then the number of sentences that are legally dependent on judge-found facts will be quite small....

3

Proponents of substantive reasonableness review could next argue that actual sentencing involves the consideration of dozens of different facts in order to make an individualized determination about each defendant. In the real world, they would contend, it is difficult, if not impossible, to determine whether any given fact was legally essential to the punishment imposed. But identifying the particular fatal fact is not necessary to identifying a constitutional violation. In the second hypothetical given above, for example, it is not possible to say which single fact, or which combination of facts, sufficed to bring the sentence within the bounds of the "reasonable." But it *is* possible to say (indeed, it *must* be said) that *some* judge-found fact or combination of facts had that effect—and that suffices to establish a Sixth Amendment violation....

4

The last conceivable defense of the Guidelines-light would be to wrap them in the mantle of history and tradition.

> "When a practice not expressly prohibited by the text of the Bill of Rights bears the endorsement of a long tradition of open, widespread, and unchallenged use that dates back to the beginning of the Republic, we have no proper basis for striking it down. Such a venerable and accepted tradition is not to be laid on the examining table and scrutinized for its conformity to some abstract principle of [constitutional] adjudication devised by this Court...."

This consideration has no application here.... It would be an exaggeration to say that history reflects an established understanding that appellate review of excessive sentences conflicts with the Sixth Amendment. But it would also be an exaggeration to say that the historical pedigree of substantive appellate review of sentencing is so strong and clear as to overcome the basic principle underlying the jury-trial right applied by this Court in *Apprendi*, *Blakely*, *Booker*, and *Cunningham*.

C

A final defense of substantive reasonableness review would be to invoke the intent of Congress or of the *Booker* remedial opinion. As for congressional intent: *Of course* Congress intended that judge-found facts be legally essential to the punishment imposed; that was the whole reason the mandatory Guidelines violated the Sixth Amendment. If we are now to indulge a newfound respect for unconstitutional congressional intent, we should reimpose the mandatory Guidelines system. The quasi-Guidelines system the Court creates today manages to contravene *both* congressional intent *and* the Sixth Amendment.

As for the "intent" of the Booker remedial opinion: That opinion purported to be divining congressional intent *in light of what the Sixth Amendment compelled*. Absent some explanation of why substantive reasonableness review does not cause judge-found facts to justify greater punishment than the jury's verdict or the defendant's guilty plea would sustain, I fail to understand how such review could possibly have been intended by all five Justices who composed the *Booker* remedial majority....

The Court's decision today leaves unexplained why the mandatory Guidelines were unconstitutional, but the Court-created substantive-review system that contains the same potential for Sixth Amendment violation is not. It is irresponsible to leave this patent inconsistency hanging in the air, threatening in the future yet another major revision of Guidelines practices to which the district courts and courts of appeals will have to adjust. Procedural review would lay the matter to rest, comporting with both parts of the *Booker* opinion and achieving the maximum degree of sentencing uniformity on the basis of judge-found facts that the Constitution permits.

■ JUSTICE SOUTER, dissenting.

Applying the Sixth Amendment to current sentencing law has gotten complicated, and someone coming cold to this case might wonder how we reached this point. A very general overview of the course of decisions over the past eight years may help to put today's holding in perspective.

Members of a criminal jury are guaranteed to be impartial residents of the State and district of the crime, but the Sixth Amendment right to trial by jury otherwise relies on history for details, and the practical instincts of judges and legislators for implementation in the courts.

One additional issue of both detail and implementation is the line between judge and jury in determining facts, and in particular the legitimate extent of factfinding by a judge when sentencing a defendant after a guilty plea or a jury's verdict of guilty. Since the very inception of judicial discretion in determining a sentence, judges have acted on what they learn in the course of a trial (and later what they gather from a presentence report or other evidence at time of sentencing), including details a trial jury may not have found to be true when it returned the guilty verdict or answered a special question. But historically, also, the customary judicial use of these extraverdict facts has been in deciding on a sentence within a range set in advance by the statute defining the crime in question. See Williams v. New York (1949). Thus, traditionally when a judge imposed a sentence at some point in the range, say, of 0–to–5 years specified by statute for some offense, every fact necessary to go as high as five years had been found by the jury (or admitted), even though the jury had not made particular or implicit findings of the facts the judge might consider in exercising discretion to set the sentence higher or lower within the 5–year range.

It was against this background, in Jones v. United States (1999), that we called attention to a serious threat to the practical value of a criminal defendant's jury right. Jones had been prosecuted under a statute that exemplified a growing practice of providing a definition and penalty for some basic crime subject to the right of jury trial, but then identifying variants carrying higher ranges of penalties depending on facts that arguably might be found by a judge sitting alone. Thus, Jones was convicted solely of carjacking, but if the further fact of causing " 'serious bodily injury' " was shown, the maximum penalty jumped from 15 years to 25. The Government's position was that the extra fact of serious bodily injury raising the penalty range required no jury finding because it was only a condition for imposing an enhanced sentence, up to a judge, not an element of a more serious crime, subject to the right to a jury's determination.

It was an unsettling argument, because in prosecutions under these statutory schemes the most serious issue in the case might well be not guilt or innocence of the basic offense, but liability to the substantially enhanced penalty. If, for example, the judge found that Jones had caused not just serious bodily injury, but death, such extraverdict factfinding could have made the difference between 15 years and life imprisonment. In a case like that, giving judges the exclusive power to find the facts necessary to sentence in the higher range would make the jury a mere gatekeeper to the more important trial before a judge alone. The Sixth Amendment does not, of course, speak expressly to such a scheme, but that is not a sufficient reason to give it constitutional approval. For if judicial factfinding necessary for an enhanced sentencing range were held to be adequate in the face of a defendant's objection, a defendant's right to have a jury standing between himself and the power of the government to curtail his liberty would take on a previously unsuspected modesty.

Jones accordingly treated this practice as suspect enough to call for applying the doctrine of constitutional avoidance when the Court interpreted the statute in question. What the Government called a mere condition for imposing a sentencing enhancement was treated as an element of a more serious offense and made subject to a jury's factfinding. This interpretation obviated the constitutional decision whether subjecting an unwilling defendant to a more onerous range of sentence on facts found solely by a judge would violate the Sixth Amendment.

The issue did not go away with *Jones*, and the constitutional challenge was soon presented inescapably, in *Apprendi v. New Jersey* (2000). We held that exposing a defendant to an increased penalty beyond the range for a basic crime, based on facts determined exclusively by a judge, violated the Sixth Amendment, in the absence of a jury waiver; a defendant could not be subjected to a penalty more serious than one authorized by the facts found by the jury or admitted by the defendant. . . .

From the moment *Apprendi* drew that line, however, its holding carried apparent implications. The general object of Guidelines sentencing was the eminently laudable one of promoting substantial consistency in exercising judicial discretion to sentence within the range set by statute for a given crime. Thus, at the elementary level, the Guidelines law limits the sentence that a judge may impose even within the sentencing range provided by the statute creating a particular offense. In effect, it divides a basic sentencing range into subranges and assigns an offender to a subrange based on the particular facts of the case and the offender's criminal history. A judge may depart from the assigned subrange only if the case presents a circumstance "not adequately taken into consideration by the Sentencing Commission in formulating the guidelines." . . .

In *Blakely v. Washington* (2004), considering a state sentencing system similar to the federal scheme, we decided that the latter way of looking at it made more sense, if *Apprendi* was going to mean something in preserving the historical significance of the jury. We held that the additional factfinding necessary for a judge to sentence within a high subrange was comparable to the finding of additional fact required for a judge to impose an enhanced sentence under the law considered in *Apprendi*. If *Blakely* had come out the other way, the significance of *Apprendi* itself would be in jeopardy: a legislature would be free to bypass *Apprendi* by providing an abnormally spacious sentencing range for any basic crime (theoretically exposing a defendant to the highest sentence just by the jury's guilty verdict), then leaving it to a judge to make supplementary findings not only appropriate but necessary for a sentence in a subrange at the high end. That would spell the end of *Apprendi* and diminish the real significance of jury protection that *Apprendi* had shored up.

In *United States v. Booker* (2005), a majority of the Court applied *Blakely*'s reasoning and held that the Federal Guidelines, too, subjected defendants to unconstitutional sentences in upper subranges, absent a jury finding or waiver. So far, so good for the Sixth Amendment, but there was the further issue of remedy, and at that step consistency began to falter. If statutory Guidelines were to survive, there were two serious alternatives. One was already in place in courts with the foresight to apply *Apprendi* to the Guidelines: require any additional facts necessary for a possible high subrange sentence to be charged and submitted to the jury. True, the Government would have to think ahead (and could not charge relevant facts that emerged unexpectedly at trial). But the mandatory character of the Guidelines would be preserved, the goal of consistency would continue to be served, and the practical value of the jury right would not face erosion.

The second remedial alternative was a declaration by the Court that the Guidelines were not mandatory but discretionary, so that finding extraverdict facts was not strictly necessary for sentencing in a high subrange under the Guidelines. On this alternative, a judge who found a subsidiary fact specified as a condition for a high subrange sentence might decide to impose a low sentence (independently of the Guidelines' own provisions for downward departure), and a judge who found no such fact might sentence within the high subrange for other reasons that seemed sufficient. If the Guidelines were not mandatory, the subsidiary fact merely provided one reasoned basis for a traditional exercise of discretion to sentence at the high end of the sentencing range provided by the statute defining the crime.

But that second alternative could not be so simple: it raised yet further issues, and the reconfigured majority of the Court that in fact adopted it, guaranteed that we would have the case now before us. If district judges treated the now-discretionary Guidelines simply as worthy of consideration but open to rejection in any given case, the *Booker* remedy would threaten a return to the old sentencing regime and would presumably produce the apparent disuniformity that convinced Congress to adopt Guidelines sentencing in the first place. But if sentencing judges attributed substantial gravitational pull to the now-discretionary Guidelines, if they treated the Guidelines result as persuasive or presumptively appropriate, the *Booker* remedy would in practical terms preserve the very feature of the Guidelines that threatened to trivialize the jury right. For a presumption of Guidelines reasonableness would tend to produce Guidelines sentences almost as regularly as mandatory Guidelines had done, with judges finding the facts needed for a sentence in an upper subrange. This would open the door to undermining *Apprendi* itself, and this is what has happened today.

Without a powerful reason to risk reversal on the sentence, a district judge faced with evidence supporting a high subrange Guidelines sentence will do the appropriate factfinding in disparagement of the jury right and will sentence within the high subrange. This prediction is weakened not a whit by the Court's description of within-Guidelines reasonableness as an "appellate" presumption. What works on appeal determines what works at trial, and if the Sentencing Commission's views are as weighty as the Court says they are, a trial judge will find it far easier to make the appropriate findings and sentence within the appropriate Guideline, than to go through the unorthodox factfinding necessary to justify a sentence outside the Guidelines range. The upshot is that today's decision moves the threat to the practical value of the Sixth Amendment jury right closer to what it was when this Court flagged it in *Jones*, and it seems fair to ask just what has been accomplished in real terms by all the judicial labor imposed by *Apprendi* and its associated cases.

Taking the *Booker* remedy (of discretionary Guidelines) as a given, however, the way to avoid further risk to *Apprendi* and the jury right is to hold that a discretionary within-Guidelines sentence carries no presumption of reasonableness. Only if sentencing decisions are reviewed according to the same standard of reasonableness whether or not they fall within the Guidelines range will district courts be assured that the entire sentencing range set by statute is available to them.... I would therefore reject the presumption of reasonableness adopted in this case, not because it is pernicious in and of itself, but because I do not think we can recognize such a presumption and still retain the full effect of *Apprendi* in aid of the Sixth Amendment guarantee. But I would not stop at rejecting the presumption. Neither my preferred course nor the choice of today's majority can avoid being at odds to some degree with the intent of Congress; there is no question that Congress meant to impose mandatory Guidelines as the means of bringing greater uniformity to sentencing. So I point out that the congressional objective can still be attained, but that *Booker*'s remedial holding means that only Congress can restore the scheme to what it had in mind, and in a way that gives full measure to the right to a jury trial. If Congress has not had a change of heart about the value of a Guidelines system, it can reenact the Guidelines law to give it the same binding force it originally had, but with provision for jury, not judicial, determination of any fact necessary for a sentence within an upper Guidelines subrange. At this point, only Congress can make good on both its enacted policy of mandatory Guidelines sentencing and the guarantee of a robust right of jury trial.

I respectfully dissent.

* * *

In the case that follows, the Court applies the reasonableness standard set forth in *Rita*:

Gall v. United States

United States Supreme Court, 2007.
552 U.S. ___, 128 S.Ct. 586.

■ JUSTICE STEVENS delivered the opinion of the Court.

In two cases argued on the same day last Term we considered the standard that courts of appeals should apply when reviewing the reasonableness of sentences imposed by district judges. The first, *Rita v. United States* (2007), involved a sentence *within* the range recommended by the Federal Sentencing Guidelines; we held that when a district judge's discretionary decision in a particular case accords with the sentence the United States Sentencing Commission deems appropriate "in the mine run of cases," the court of appeals may presume that the sentence is reasonable.

The second case, *Claiborne v. United States*, involved a sentence *below* the range recommended by the Guidelines, and raised the converse question whether a court of appeals may apply a "proportionality test," and require that a sentence that constitutes a substantial variance from the Guidelines be justified by extraordinary circumstances. We did not have the opportunity to answer this question because the case was mooted by Claiborne's untimely death. We granted certiorari in the case before us today in order to reach that question, left unanswered last Term. We now hold that, while the extent of the difference between a particular sentence and the recommended Guidelines range is surely relevant, courts of appeals must review all sentences—whether inside, just outside, or significantly outside the Guidelines range—under a deferential abuse-of-discretion standard. We also hold that the sentence imposed by the experienced District Judge in this case was reasonable.

I

In February or March 2000, petitioner Brian Gall, a second-year college student at the University of Iowa, was invited by Luke Rinderknecht to join an ongoing enterprise distributing a controlled substance popularly known as "ecstasy." Gall—who was then a user of ecstasy, cocaine, and marijuana—accepted the invitation. During the ensuing seven months, Gall delivered ecstasy pills, which he received from Rinderknecht, to other conspirators, who then sold them to consumers. He netted over $30,000.

A month or two after joining the conspiracy, Gall stopped using ecstasy. A few months after that, in September 2000, he advised Rinderknecht and other co-conspirators that he was withdrawing from the conspiracy. He has not sold illegal drugs of any kind since. He has, in the words of the District Court, "self-rehabilitated." He graduated from the University of Iowa in 2002, and moved first to Arizona, where he obtained a job in the construction industry, and later to Colorado, where he earned $18 per hour as a master carpenter. He has not used any illegal drugs since graduating from college.

After Gall moved to Arizona, he was approached by federal law enforcement agents who questioned him about his involvement in the ecstasy distribution conspiracy. Gall admitted his limited participation in the distribution of ecstasy, and the agents took no further action at that time. On April 28, 2004—approximately a year and a half after this initial interview, and three and a half years after Gall withdrew from the conspiracy—an indictment was returned in the Southern District of Iowa charging him and seven other defendants with participating in a conspiracy to distribute ecstasy, cocaine, and marijuana, that began in or about May 1996 and continued through October 30, 2002. The Government has never questioned the truthfulness of any of Gall's earlier statements or contended that he played any role in, or had any knowledge of, other aspects of the conspiracy described in the indictment. When he received notice of the indictment, Gall moved back to Iowa and surrendered to the authorities. While free on his own recognizance, Gall started his own business in the construction industry, primarily engaged in subcontracting for the installation of windows and doors. In his first year, his profits were over $2,000 per month.

Gall entered into a plea agreement with the Government, stipulating that he was "responsible for, but did not necessarily distribute himself, at least 2,500 grams of [ecstasy], or the equivalent of at least 87.5 kilograms of marijuana." In the agreement, the Government acknowledged that by "on or about September of 2000," Gall had communicated his intent to stop distributing ecstasy to Rinderknecht and other members of the conspiracy. The agreement further provided that recent changes in the Guidelines that enhanced the recommended punishment for distributing ecstasy were not applicable to Gall because he had withdrawn from the conspiracy prior to the effective date of those changes.

In her presentence report, the probation officer concluded that Gall had no significant criminal history; that he was not an organizer, leader, or manager; and that his offense did not involve the use of any weapons. The report stated that Gall had truthfully provided the Government with all of the evidence he had concerning the alleged offenses, but that his evidence was not useful because he provided no new information to the agents. The report also described Gall's substantial use of drugs prior to his offense and the absence of any such use in recent years. The report recommended a sentencing range of 30 to 37 months of imprisonment.

The record of the sentencing hearing held on May 27, 2005includes a "small flood" of letters from Gall's parents and other relatives, his fiance, neighbors, and representatives of firms doing business with him, uniformly praising his character and work ethic. The transcript includes the testimony of several witnesses and the District Judge's colloquy with the Assistant United States Attorney (AUSA) and with Gall. The AUSA did not contest any of the evidence concerning Gall's law-abiding life during the preceding five years, but urged that "the Guidelines are appropriate and should be followed," and requested that the court impose a prison sentence within the Guidelines range. He mentioned that two of Gall's co-conspirators had been sentenced to 30 and 35 months, respectively, but upon further questioning by the District Court, he acknowledged that neither of them had voluntarily withdrawn from the conspiracy.

The District Judge sentenced Gall to probation for a term of 36 months. In addition to making a lengthy statement on the record, the judge filed a detailed sentencing memorandum explaining his decision, and provided the following statement of reasons in his written judgment:

> "The Court determined that, considering all the factors ... the Defendant's explicit withdrawal from the conspiracy almost four years before the filing of the Indictment, the Defendant's post-offense conduct, especially obtaining a college degree and the start of his own successful business, the support of family and friends, lack of criminal history, and his age at the time of the offense conduct, all warrant the sentence imposed, which was sufficient, but not greater than necessary to serve the purposes of sentencing."

At the end of both the sentencing hearing and the sentencing memorandum, the District Judge reminded Gall that probation, rather than "an act of leniency," is a "substantial restriction of freedom." In the memorandum, he emphasized:

> "[Gall] will have to comply with strict reporting conditions along with a three-year regime of alcohol and drug testing. He will not be able to change or make decisions about significant circumstances in his life, such as where to live or work, which are prized liberty interests, without first seeking authorization from his Probation Officer or, perhaps, even the Court. Of course, the

Defendant always faces the harsh consequences that await if he violates the conditions of his probationary term."

Finally, the District Judge explained why he had concluded that the sentence of probation reflected the seriousness of Gall's offense and that no term of imprisonment was necessary:

> "Any term of imprisonment in this case would be counter effective by depriving society of the contributions of the Defendant who, the Court has found, understands the consequences of his criminal conduct and is doing everything in his power to forge a new life. The Defendant's post-offense conduct indicates neither that he will return to criminal behavior nor that the Defendant is a danger to society. In fact, the Defendant's post-offense conduct was not motivated by a desire to please the Court or any other governmental agency, but was the pre-Indictment product of the Defendant's own desire to lead a better life."

II

The Court of Appeals reversed and remanded for resentencing. Relying on its earlier opinion in *United States v. Claiborne* (CA8 2006), it held that a sentence outside of the Guidelines range must be supported by a justification that " 'is proportional to the extent of the difference between the advisory range and the sentence imposed.' " Characterizing the difference between a sentence of probation and the bottom of Gall's advisory Guidelines range of 30 months as "extraordinary" because it amounted to "a 100% downward variance," the Court of Appeals held that such a variance must be—and here was not—supported by extraordinary circumstances.

Rather than making an attempt to quantify the value of the justifications provided by the District Judge, the Court of Appeals identified what it regarded as five separate errors in the District Judge's reasoning: (1) He gave "too much weight to Gall's withdrawal from the conspiracy"; (2) given that Gall was 21 at the time of his offense, the District Judge erroneously gave "significant weight" to studies showing impetuous behavior by persons under the age of 18; (3) he did not "properly weigh" the seriousness of Gall's offense; (4) he failed to consider whether a sentence of probation would result in "unwarranted" disparities; and (5) he placed "too much emphasis on Gall's post-offense rehabilitation." As we shall explain, we are not persuaded that these factors, whether viewed separately or in the aggregate, are sufficient to support the conclusion that the District Judge abused his discretion. As a preface to our discussion of these particulars, however, we shall explain why the Court of Appeals' rule requiring "proportional" justifications for departures from the Guidelines range is not consistent with our remedial opinion in *United States v. Booker*

III

In *Booker* we invalidated both the statutory provision, which made the Sentencing Guidelines mandatory, and which directed appellate courts to apply a *de novo* standard of review to departures from the Guidelines. As a result of our decision, the Guidelines are now advisory, and appellate review of sentencing decisions is limited to determining whether they are "reasonable." Our explanation of "reasonableness" review in the *Booker* opinion made it pellucidly clear that the familiar abuse-of-discretion standard of review now applies to appellate review of sentencing decisions.

It is also clear that a district judge must give serious consideration to the extent of any departure from the Guidelines and must explain his conclusion that an unusually lenient or an unusually harsh sentence is appropriate in a particular case with sufficient justifications. For even though the Guidelines are advisory rather than mandatory, they are, as we pointed out in *Rita*, the product of careful study based on extensive empirical evidence derived from the review of thousands of individual sentencing decisions.

In reviewing the reasonableness of a sentence outside the Guidelines range, appellate courts may therefore take the degree of variance into account and consider the extent of a deviation from the Guidelines. We reject, however, an appellate rule that requires "extraordinary" circumstances to justify a sentence outside the Guidelines range. We also reject the use of a rigid mathematical formula that uses the percentage of a departure as the standard for determining the strength of the justifications required for a specific sentence.

As we explained in *Rita*, a district court should begin all sentencing proceedings by correctly calculating the applicable Guidelines range. As a matter of administration and to secure nationwide consistency, the Guidelines should be the starting point and the initial benchmark. The Guidelines are not the only consideration, however. Accordingly, after giving both parties an opportunity to argue for whatever sentence they deem appropriate, the district judge should then consider all of the ... factors to determine whether they support the sentence requested by a party.[6] In so doing, he may not presume that the Guidelines range is reasonable. He must make an individualized assessment based on the facts presented. If he

6. Section 3553(a) lists seven factors that a sentencing court must consider. The first factor is a broad command to consider "the nature and circumstances of the offense and the history and characteristics of the defendant." 18 U.S.C. § 3553(a)(1). The second factor requires the consideration of the general purposes of sentencing, including:

"the need for the sentence imposed—

"(A) to reflect the seriousness of the offense, to promote respect for the law, and to provide just punishment for the offense;

"(B) to afford adequate deterrence to criminal conduct;

"(C) to protect the public from further crimes of the defendant; and

"(D) to provide the defendant with needed educational or vocational training, medical care, or other correctional treatment in the most effective manner." § 3553(a)(2).

The third factor pertains to "the kinds of sentences available," § 3553(a)(3); the fourth to the Sentencing Guidelines; the fifth to any relevant policy statement issued by the Sentencing Commission; the sixth to "the need to avoid unwarranted sentence disparities," § 3553(a)(6); and the seventh to "the need to provide restitution to any victim," § 3553(a)(7). Preceding this list is a general directive to "impose a sentence sufficient, but not greater than necessary, to comply with the purposes" of sentencing described in the second factor. The fact that § 3553(a) explicitly directs sentencing courts to consider the Guidelines supports the premise that district courts must begin their analysis with the Guidelines and remain cognizant of them throughout the sentencing process.

decides that an outside-Guidelines sentence is warranted, he must consider the extent of the deviation and ensure that the justification is sufficiently compelling to support the degree of the variance. We find it uncontroversial that a major departure should be supported by a more significant justification than a minor one. After settling on the appropriate sentence, he must adequately explain the chosen sentence to allow for meaningful appellate review and to promote the perception of fair sentencing.

Regardless of whether the sentence imposed is inside or outside the Guidelines range, the appellate court must review the sentence under an abuse-of-discretion standard. It must first ensure that the district court committed no significant procedural error, such as failing to calculate (or improperly calculating) the Guidelines range, treating the Guidelines as mandatory, failing to consider the § 3553(a) factors, selecting a sentence based on clearly erroneous facts, or failing to adequately explain the chosen sentence—including an explanation for any deviation from the Guidelines range. Assuming that the district court's sentencing decision is procedurally sound, the appellate court should then consider the substantive reasonableness of the sentence imposed under an abuse-of-discretion standard. When conducting this review, the court will, of course, take into account the totality of the circumstances, including the extent of any variance from the Guidelines range. If the sentence is within the Guidelines range, the appellate court may, but is not required to, apply a presumption of reasonableness. But if the sentence is outside the Guidelines range, the court may not apply a presumption of unreasonableness. It may consider the extent of the deviation, but must give due deference to the district court's decision that the § 3553(a) factors, on a whole, justify the extent of the variance. The fact that the appellate court might reasonably have concluded that a different sentence was appropriate is insufficient to justify reversal of the district court.

Practical considerations also underlie this legal principle. "The sentencing judge is in a superior position to find facts and judge their import under § 3553(a) in the individual case. The judge sees and hears the evidence, makes credibility determinations, has full knowledge of the facts and gains insights not conveyed by the record." "The sentencing judge has access to, and greater familiarity with, the individual case and the individual defendant before him than the Commission or the appeals court." Moreover, "district courts have an institutional advantage over appellate courts in making these sorts of determinations, especially as they see so many more Guidelines sentences than appellate courts do."

"It has been uniform and constant in the federal judicial tradition for the sentencing judge to consider every convicted person as an individual and every case as a unique study in the human failings that sometimes mitigate, sometimes magnify, the crime and the punishment to ensue." The uniqueness of the individual case, however, does not change the deferential abuse-of-discretion standard of review that applies to all sentencing decisions. As we shall now explain, the opinion of the Court of Appeals in this case does not reflect the requisite deference and does not support the conclusion that the District Court abused its discretion.

IV

As an initial matter, we note that the District Judge committed no significant procedural error. He correctly calculated the applicable Guidelines range, allowed both parties to present arguments as to what they believed the appropriate sentence should be, considered all of the § 3553(a) factors, and thoroughly documented his reasoning. The Court of Appeals found that the District Judge erred in failing to give proper weight to the seriousness of the offense, as required by § 3553(a)(2)(A), and failing to consider whether a sentence of probation would create unwarranted disparities, as required by § 3553(a)(6). We disagree.

Section 3553(a)(2)(A) requires judges to consider "the need for the sentence imposed . . . to reflect the seriousness of the offense, to promote respect for the law, and to provide just punishment for the offense." The Court of Appeals concluded that "the district court did not properly weigh the seriousness of Gall's offense" because it "ignored the serious health risks ecstasy poses." Contrary to the Court of Appeals' conclusion, the District Judge plainly did consider the seriousness of the offense. ("The Court, however, is bound to impose a sentence that reflects the seriousness of joining a conspiracy to distribute MDMA or ecstasy"); It is true that the District Judge did not make specific reference to the (unquestionably significant) health risks posed by ecstasy, but the prosecutor did not raise ecstasy's effects at the sentencing hearing. Had the prosecutor raised the issue, specific discussion of the point might have been in order, but it was not incumbent on the District Judge to raise every conceivably relevant issue on his own initiative.

The Government's legitimate concern that a lenient sentence for a serious offense threatens to promote disrespect for the law is at least to some extent offset by the fact that seven of the eight defendants in this case have been sentenced to significant prison terms. Moreover, the unique facts of Gall's situation provide support for the District Judge's conclusion that, in Gall's case, "a sentence of imprisonment may work to promote not respect, but derision, of the law if the law is viewed as merely a means to dispense harsh punishment without taking into account the real conduct and circumstances involved in sentencing."

Section 3553(a)(6) requires judges to consider "the need to avoid unwarranted sentence disparities among defendants with similar records who have been found guilty of similar conduct." The Court of Appeals stated that "the record does not show that the district court considered whether a sentence of probation would result in unwarranted disparities." As with the seriousness of the offense conduct, avoidance of unwarranted disparities was clearly considered by the Sentencing Commission when setting the Guidelines ranges. Since the District Judge correctly calculated and carefully reviewed the Guidelines range, he necessarily gave significant weight and consideration to the need to avoid unwarranted disparities.

Moreover, as we understand the colloquy between the District Judge and the AUSA, it seems that the judge gave specific attention to the issue of disparity when he inquired about the sentences already imposed by a different judge on two of Gall's codefendants. The AUSA advised the District Judge that defendant Harbison had received a 30–month sentence and that Gooding had received 35 months. The following colloquy then occurred:

> "THE COURT: ... You probably know more about this than anybody. How long did those two stay in the conspiracy, and did they voluntarily withdraw?
>
> "MR GRIESS: They did not.
>
> "THE COURT: They did not?
>
> "MR. GRIESS: They did not voluntarily withdraw. And they were in the conspiracy, I think, for a shorter period of time, but at the very end.
>
> "THE COURT: Okay. Thank you.
>
> "MR. GRIESS: A significant difference there, Your Honor, is that they were in the conspiracy after the guidelines changed and, therefore, were sentenced at a much higher level because of that."

A little later Mr. Griess stated: "The last thing I want to talk about goes to sentencing disparity.... Obviously, the Court is cognizant of that and wants to avoid any unwarranted sentencing disparities." He then discussed at some length the sentence of 36 months imposed on another codefendant, Jarod Yoder, whose participation in the conspiracy was roughly comparable to Gall's. Griess voluntarily acknowledged three differences between Yoder and Gall: Yoder was in the conspiracy at its end and therefore was sentenced under the more severe Guidelines, he had a more serious criminal history, and he did not withdraw from the conspiracy.

From these facts, it is perfectly clear that the District Judge considered the need to avoid unwarranted disparities, but also considered the need to avoid unwarranted *similarities* among other co-conspirators who were not similarly situated. The District Judge regarded Gall's voluntary withdrawal as a reasonable basis for giving him a less severe sentence than the three codefendants discussed with the AUSA, who neither withdrew from the conspiracy nor rehabilitated themselves as Gall had done. We also note that neither the Court of Appeals nor the Government has called our attention to a comparable defendant who received a more severe sentence.

Since the District Court committed no procedural error, the only question for the Court of Appeals was whether the sentence was reasonable—*i.e.*, whether the District Judge abused his discretion in determining that the § 3553(a) factors supported a sentence of probation and justified a substantial deviation from the Guidelines range. As we shall now explain, the sentence was reasonable. The Court of Appeals' decision to the contrary was incorrect and failed to demonstrate the requisite deference to the District Judge's decision.

V

The Court of Appeals gave virtually no deference to the District Court's decision that the § 3553(a) factors justified a significant variance in this case. Although the Court of Appeals correctly stated that the appropriate standard of review was abuse of discretion, it engaged in an analysis that more closely resembled *de novo* review of the facts presented and determined that, in its view, the degree of variance was not warranted.

The Court of Appeals thought that the District Court "gave too much weight to Gall's withdrawal from the conspiracy because the court failed to acknowledge the significant benefit Gall received from being subject to the 1999 Guidelines." This criticism is flawed in that it ignores the critical relevance of Gall's voluntary withdrawal, a circumstance that distinguished his conduct not only from that of all his codefendants, but from the vast majority of defendants convicted of conspiracy in federal court. The District Court quite reasonably attached great weight to the fact that Gall voluntarily withdrew from the conspiracy after deciding, on his own initiative, to change his life. This lends strong support to the District Court's conclusion that Gall is not going to return to criminal behavior and is not a danger to society. Compared to a case where the offender's rehabilitation occurred after he was charged with a crime, the District Court here had greater justification for believing Gall's turnaround was genuine, as distinct from a transparent attempt to build a mitigation case.

The Court of Appeals thought the District Judge "gave significant weight to an improper factor" when he compared Gall's sale of ecstasy when he was a 21–year–old adult to the "impetuous and ill-considered" actions of persons under the age of 18. The appellate court correctly observed that the studies cited by the District Judge do not explain how Gall's "specific behavior in the instant case was impetuous or ill-considered."

In that portion of his sentencing memorandum, however, the judge was discussing the "character of the defendant," not the nature of his offense. He noted that Gall's criminal history included a ticket for underage drinking when he was 18 years old and possession of marijuana that was contemporaneous with his offense in this case. In summary, the District Judge observed that all of Gall's criminal history "including the present offense, occurred when he was twenty-one-years old or younger" and appeared "to stem from his addictions to drugs and alcohol." The District Judge appended a long footnote to his discussion of Gall's immaturity. The footnote includes an excerpt from our opinion in Roper v. Simmons (2005), which quotes a study stating that a lack of maturity and an undeveloped sense of responsibility are qualities that " 'often result in impetuous and ill-considered actions.' "....

Given the dramatic contrast between Gall's behavior before he joined the conspiracy and his conduct after withdrawing, it was not unreasonable for the District Judge to view Gall's immaturity at the time of the offense as a mitigating factor, and his later behavior as a sign that he had matured and would not engage in such impetuous and ill-considered conduct in the future. Indeed, his consideration of that factor finds support in our cases....

Finally, the Court of Appeals thought that, even if Gall's rehabilitation was dramatic and permanent, a sentence of probation for participation as a middleman in a conspiracy distributing 10,000 pills of ecstasy "lies outside the range of choice dictated by the facts of the case." If the Guidelines were still mandatory, and assuming the facts did not justify a Guidelines-based downward departure, this would provide a sufficient basis for setting aside Gall's sentence because the Guidelines state that probation alone is not an appropriate sentence for comparable offenses. But the Guidelines are not mandatory, and thus the "range of choice dictated by the facts of the case" is significantly broadened. Moreover, the Guidelines are only one of the factors to consider when imposing sentence, and § 3553(a)(3) directs the judge to consider sentences other than imprisonment.

We also note that the Government did not argue below, and has not argued here, that a sentence of probation could never be imposed for a crime identical to Gall's. Indeed, it acknowledged that probation could be permissible if the record contained different—but in our view, no more compelling—mitigating evidence . . .

The District Court quite reasonably attached great weight to Gall's self-motivated rehabilitation, which was undertaken not at the direction of, or under supervision by, any court, but on his own initiative. This also lends strong support to the conclusion that imprisonment was not necessary to deter Gall from engaging in future criminal conduct or to protect the public from his future criminal acts.

The Court of Appeals clearly disagreed with the District Judge's conclusion that consideration of the § 3553(a) factors justified a sentence of probation; it believed that the circumstances presented here were insufficient to sustain such a marked deviation from the Guidelines range. But it is not for the Court of Appeals to decide *de novo* whether the justification for a variance is sufficient or the sentence reasonable. On abuse-of-discretion review, the Court of Appeals should have given due deference to the District Court's reasoned and reasonable decision that the § 3553(a) factors, on the whole, justified the sentence. Accordingly, the judgment of the Court of Appeals is reversed.

It is so ordered.

■ Justice Scalia, concurring.

I join the opinion of the Court.

In Rita v. United States (2007), I wrote separately to state my view that any appellate review of sentences for substantive reasonableness will necessarily result in a sentencing scheme constitutionally indistinguishable from the mandatory Guidelines struck down in United States v. Booker (2005). Whether a sentencing scheme uses mandatory Guidelines, a "proportionality test" for Guidelines variances, or a deferential abuse-of-discretion standard, there will be some sentences upheld only on the basis of additional judge-found facts.

Although I continue to believe that substantive-reasonableness review is inherently flawed, I give *stare decisis* effect to the statutory holding of *Rita*. The highly deferential standard adopted by the Court today will result in far fewer unconstitutional sentences than the proportionality standard employed by the Eighth Circuit. Moreover, as I noted in *Rita*, the Court has not foreclosed as-applied constitutional challenges to sentences. The door therefore remains open for a defendant to demonstrate that his sentence, whether inside or outside the advisory Guidelines range, would not have been upheld but for the existence of a fact found by the sentencing judge and not by the jury.

■ JUSTICE SOUTER, concurring.

I join the Court's opinion here, as I do in today's companion case of Kimbrough v. United States, which follow United States v. Booker, and Rita v. United States (2007). My disagreements with holdings in those earlier cases are not the stuff of formally perpetual dissent, but I see their objectionable points hexing our judgments today. After *Booker*'s remedial holding, I continue to think that the best resolution of the tension between substantial consistency throughout the system and the right of jury trial would be a new Act of Congress: reestablishing a statutory system of mandatory sentencing guidelines (though not identical to the original in all points of detail), but providing for jury findings of all facts necessary to set the upper range of sentencing discretion.

■ JUSTICE THOMAS, dissenting.

Consistent with my dissenting opinion in Kimbrough v. United States I would affirm the judgment of the Court of Appeals because the District Court committed statutory error when it departed below the applicable Guidelines range.

■ JUSTICE ALITO, dissenting.

The fundamental question in this case is whether, under the remedial decision in United States v. Booker, a district court must give the policy decisions that are embodied in the Sentencing Guidelines at least some significant weight in making a sentencing decision. I would answer that question in the affirmative and would therefore affirm the decision of the Court of Appeals.

I

In *Booker*, a bare majority held that the Sentencing Reform Act of 1984 (Sentencing Reform Act), violated the Sixth Amendment insofar as it required district judges to follow the United States Sentencing Guidelines, but another bare majority held that this defect could be remedied by excising the two statutory provisions, 18 U.S.C. §§ 3553(b)(1) and 3742(e) that made compliance with the Guidelines mandatory. As a result of these two holdings, the lower federal courts were instructed that the Guidelines must be regarded as "effectively advisory," and that individual sentencing decisions are subject to appellate review for " 'reasonableness.' " The *Booker* remedial opinion did not explain exactly what it meant by a system of "advisory" guidelines or by "reasonableness" review, and the opinion is open to different interpretations....

It is unrealistic to think this goal can be achieved over the long term if sentencing judges need only give lip service to the Guidelines. The other sentencing factors set out in § 3553(a) are so broad that they impose few real restraints on sentencing judges. Thus, if judges are obligated to do no more than consult the Guidelines before deciding upon the sentence that is, in their independent judgment, sufficient to serve the other § 3553(a) factors, federal sentencing will not "move ... in Congress' preferred direction." On the contrary, sentencing disparities will gradually increase.

Appellate decisions affirming sentences that diverge from the Guidelines (such as the Court's decision today) will be influential, and the sentencing habits developed during the pre-*Booker* era will fade.

Finally, in reading the *Booker* remedial opinion, we should not forget the decision's constitutional underpinnings. *Booker* and its antecedents are based on the Sixth Amendment right to trial by jury. The Court has held that (at least under a mandatory guidelines system) a defendant has the right to have a jury, not a judge, find facts that increase the defendant's authorized sentence. It is telling that the rules set out in the Court's opinion in the present case have nothing to do with juries or factfinding and, indeed, that not one of the facts that bears on petitioner's sentence is disputed. What is at issue, instead, is the allocation of the authority to decide issues of substantive sentencing policy, an issue on which the Sixth Amendment says absolutely nothing. The yawning gap between the Sixth Amendment and the Court's opinion should be enough to show that the *Blakely–Booker* line of cases has gone astray.

In *Blakely*, the Court drew a distinction—between judicial factfinding under a guidelines system and judicial factfinding under a discretionary sentencing system,—that, in my judgment, cannot be defended as a matter of principle. It would be a coherent principle to hold that any fact that increases a defendant's sentence beyond the minimum required by the jury's verdict of guilt must be found by a jury. Such a holding, however, would clash with accepted sentencing practice at the time of the adoption of the Sixth Amendment. By that time, many States had enacted criminal statutes that gave trial judges the discretion to select a sentence from within [* * *47] a prescribed range, 1and the First Congress enacted federal criminal statutes that were cast in this mold. See An Act for the Punishment of certain Crimes against the United States.

Under a sentencing system of this type, trial judges inevitably make findings of fact (albeit informally) that increase sentences beyond the minimum required by the jury's verdict. For example, under a statute providing that the punishment for burglary is, say, imprisonment for up to *x* years, the sentencing court might increase the sentence that it would have otherwise imposed by some amount based on evidence introduced at trial that the defendant was armed or that, before committing the crime, the defendant had told a confederate that he would kill the occupants if they awakened during the burglary. The only difference between this sort of factfinding and the type that occurs under a guidelines system is that factfinding under a guidelines system is explicit and the effect of each critical finding is quantified. But in both instances, facts that cause a defendant to spend more time in prison are found by judges, not juries, and therefore no distinction can be drawn as a matter of Sixth Amendment principle.

The Court's acceptance of this distinction also produced strange collateral consequences. A sentencing system that gives trial judges the discretion to sentence within a specified range not only permits judicial factfinding that may increase a sentence, such a system also gives individual judges discretion to implement their own sentencing policies. This latter feature, whether wise or unwise, has nothing to do with the concerns of the Sixth

Amendment, and a principal objective of the Sentencing Reform Act was to take this power out of the hands of individual district judges.

The *Booker* remedy, however, undid this congressional choice. In curing the Sentencing Reform Act's perceived defect regarding judicial factfinding, *Booker* restored to the district courts at least a measure of the policymaking authority that the Sentencing Reform Act had taken away. (How much of this authority was given back is, of course, the issue here.)

I recognize that the Court is committed to the *Blakely–Booker* line of cases, but we are not required to continue along a path that will take us further and further off course. [Because] the *Booker* remedial opinion may be read to require sentencing judges to give weight to the Guidelines, I would adopt that interpretation and thus minimize the gap between what the Sixth Amendment requires and what our cases have held.

II

A

Read fairly, the opinion of the Court of Appeals holds that the District Court did not properly exercise its sentencing discretion because it did not give sufficient weight to the policy decisions reflected in the Guidelines. Petitioner was convicted of a serious crime, conspiracy to distribute "ecstasy." He distributed thousands of pills and made between $30,000 and $40,000 in profit. Although he eventually left the conspiracy, he did so because he was worried about apprehension. The Sentencing Guidelines called for a term of imprisonment of 30 to 37 months, but the District Court imposed a term of probation.

Compelled to interpret the *Booker* remedial opinion, the District Court, it appears, essentially chose the interpretation outlined in Justice Stevens' and Justice Scalia's dissents. The District Court considered the sentence called for by the Guidelines, but I see no evidence that the District Court deferred to the Guidelines to any significant degree. Rather, the court determined what it thought was appropriate under the circumstances and sentenced petitioner accordingly.

If the question before us was whether a reasonable jurist could conclude that a sentence of probation was sufficient in this case to serve the purposes of punishment set out in 18 U.S.C. § 3553(a)(2), the District Court's decision could not be disturbed. But because I believe that sentencing judges must still give some significant weight to the Guidelines sentencing range, the Commission's policy statements, and the need to avoid unwarranted sentencing disparities, § 3553(a)(3), (4), and (5) (2000 ed. and Supp. V), I agree with the Eighth Circuit that the District Court did not properly exercise its discretion.

Appellate review for abuse of discretion is not an empty formality. A decision calling for the exercise of judicial discretion "hardly means that it is unfettered by meaningful standards or shielded from thorough appellate review." And when a trial court is required by statute to take specified factors into account in making a discretionary decision, the trial court must be reversed if it "ignored or slighted a factor that Congress has deemed pertinent."

Here, the District Court "slighted" the factors set out in 18 U.S.C. §§ 3553(a)(3), (4), and (5) (2000 ed. and Supp. V)—namely, the Guidelines sentencing range, the Commission's policy statements, and the need to avoid unwarranted sentencing disparities. Although the Guidelines called for a prison term of at least 30 months, the District Court did not require any imprisonment—not one day. The opinion of the Court makes much of the restrictions and burdens of probation, but in the real world there is a huge difference between imprisonment and probation. If the District Court had given any appreciable weight to the Guidelines, the District Court could not have sentenced petitioner to probation without very strong countervailing considerations.

The court listed five considerations as justification for a sentence of probation: (1) petitioner's "voluntary and explicit withdrawal from the conspiracy," (2) his "exemplary behavior while on bond," (3) "the support manifested by family and friends," (4) "the lack of criminal history, especially a complete lack of any violent criminal history," (5) and his age at the time of the offense, 21.

Two of the considerations that the District Court cited—"the support manifested by family and friends" and his age, *ibid.*—amounted to a direct rejection of the Sentencing Commission's authority to decide the most basic issues of sentencing policy. In the Sentencing Reform Act, Congress required the Sentencing Commission to consider and decide whether certain specified factors—including "age," "education," "previous employment record," "physical condition," "family ties and responsibilities," and "community ties"—"have any relevance to the nature [and] extent ... of an appropriate sentence." These factors come up with great frequency, and judges in the pre-Sentencing Reform Act era disagreed regarding their relevance. Indeed, some of these factors were viewed by some judges as reasons for increasing a sentence and by others as reasons for decreasing a sentence. For example, if a defendant had a job, a supportive family, and friends, those factors were sometimes viewed as justifying a harsher sentence on the ground that the defendant had squandered the opportunity to lead a law-abiding life. Alternatively, those same factors were sometimes viewed as justifications for a more lenient sentence on the ground that a defendant with a job and a network of support would be less likely to return to crime. If each judge is free to implement his or her personal views on such matters, sentencing disparities are inevitable.

In response to Congress' direction to establish uniform national sentencing policies regarding these common sentencing factors, the Sentencing Commission issued policy statements concluding that "age," "family ties," and "community ties" are relevant to sentencing only in unusual cases. See United States Sentencing Commission, Guidelines Manual §§ 5H1.1 (age), 5H1.6 (family and community ties) (Nov. 2006). The District Court in this case did not claim that there was anything particularly unusual about petitioner's family or community ties or his age, but the court cited these factors as justifications for a sentence of probation. Although the District Court was obligated to take into account the Commission's policy statements and the need to avoid sentencing disparities, the District Court rejected Commission policy statements that are critical to the effort to reduce such disparities.

The District Court relied on petitioner's lack of criminal history, but criminal history (or the lack thereof) is a central factor in the calculation of the Guidelines range. Petitioner was given credit for his lack of criminal history in the calculation of his Guidelines sentence. Consequently, giving petitioner additional credit for this factor was nothing more than an expression of disagreement with the policy determination reflected in the Guidelines range.

The District Court mentioned petitioner's "exemplary behavior while on bond," but this surely cannot be regarded as a weighty factor.

Finally, the District Court was plainly impressed by petitioner's "voluntary and explicit withdrawal from the conspiracy." *Ibid.* As the Government argues, the legitimate strength of this factor is diminished by petitioner's motivation in withdrawing. He did not leave the conspiracy for reasons of conscience, and he made no effort to stop the others in the ring. He withdrew because he had become afraid of apprehension. While the District Court was within its rights in regarding this factor and petitioner's "self-rehabilitation," as positive considerations, they are not enough, in light of the Guidelines' call for a 30– to 37–month prison term, to warrant a sentence of probation.

B

In reaching the opposite conclusion, the Court attacks straw men. The Court unjustifiably faults the Eighth Circuit for using what it characterizes as a "rigid mathematical formula.".... Taking this language literally as requiring a mathematical computation, the Court has an easy time showing that mathematical precision is not possible:

> "The mathematical approach assumes the existence of some ascertainable method of assigning percentages to various justifications. Does withdrawal from a conspiracy justify more or less than, say, a 30% reduction? ... What percentage, if any, should be assigned to evidence that a defendant poses no future threat to society, or to evidence that innocent third parties are dependent on him?" *Ante*, at 10.

This criticism is quite unfair. It is apparent that the Seventh and Eighth Circuits did not mean to suggest that proportionality review could be reduced to a mathematical equation, and certainly the Eighth Circuit in this case did not assign numbers to the various justifications offered by the District Court. All that the Seventh and Eighth Circuits meant, I am convinced, is what this Court's opinion states, *i.e.*, that "the extent of the difference between a particular sentence and the recommended Guidelines range" is a relevant consideration in determining whether the District Court properly exercised its sentencing discretion.

This Court's opinion is also wrong in suggesting that the Eighth Circuit's approach was inconsistent with the abuse-of-discretion standard of appellate review. The abuse-of-discretion review is not toothless; and it is entirely proper for a reviewing court to find an abuse of discretion when important factors—in this case, the Guidelines, policy statements, and the need to avoid sentencing disparities—are "slighted." The mere fact that the Circuit reversed is hardly proof that the Eighth Circuit did not apply the correct standard of review.

Because I believe that the Eighth Circuit correctly interpreted and applied the standards set out in the *Booker* remedial opinion, I must respectfully dissent.

* * *

Kimbrough v. United States

United States Supreme Court, 2007.
552 U.S. ___, 128 S.Ct. 558.

■ JUSTICE GINSBURG delivered the opinion of the Court.

This Court's remedial opinion in United States v. Booker (2005), instructed district courts to read the United States Sentencing Guidelines as "effectively advisory." In accord with 18 U.S.C. § 3553(a), the Guidelines, formerly mandatory, now serve as one factor among several courts must consider in determining an appropriate sentence. *Booker* further instructed that "reasonableness" is the standard controlling appellate review of the sentences district courts impose.

Under the statute criminalizing the manufacture and distribution of crack cocaine, 21 U.S.C. § 841, and the relevant Guidelines prescription, § 2D1.1, a drug trafficker dealing in crack cocaine is subject to the same sentence as one dealing in 100 times more powder cocaine. The question here presented is whether, as the Court of Appeals held in this case, "a sentence ... outside the guidelines range is per se unreasonable when it is based on a disagreement with the sentencing disparity for crack and powder cocaine offenses." We hold that, under *Booker*, the cocaine Guidelines, like all other Guidelines, are advisory only, and that the Court of Appeals erred in holding the crack/powder disparity effectively mandatory. A district judge must include the Guidelines range in the array of factors warranting consideration. The judge may determine, however, that, in the particular case, a within-Guidelines sentence is "greater than necessary" to serve the objectives of sentencing. In making that determination, the judge may consider the disparity between the Guidelines' treatment of crack and powder cocaine offenses.

I

In September 2004, petitioner Derrick Kimbrough was indicted in the United States District Court for the Eastern District of Virginia and charged with four offenses: conspiracy to distribute crack and powder cocaine; possession with intent to distribute more than 50 grams of crack cocaine; possession with intent to distribute powder cocaine; and possession of a firearm in furtherance of a drug-trafficking offense. Kimbrough pleaded guilty to all four charges.

Under the relevant statutes, Kimbrough's plea subjected him to an aggregate sentence of 15 years to life in prison: 10 years to life for the three drug offenses, plus a consecutive term of 5 years to life for the firearm offense.[1] In order to determine the appropriate sentence within this statutory range, the District Court first calculated Kimbrough's sentence under the advisory Sentencing Guidelines. Kimbrough's guilty plea acknowledged that he was accountable for 56 grams of crack cocaine and 92.1 grams of powder cocaine. This quantity of drugs yielded a base offense level of 32 for the three drug charges. Finding that Kimbrough, by asserting sole culpability for the crime, had testified falsely at his codefendant's trial, the District Court increased his offense level to 34. In accord with the presentence report, the court determined that Kimbrough's criminal history category was II. An offense level of 34 and a criminal history category of II yielded a Guidelines range of 168 to 210 months for the three drug charges. The Guidelines sentence for the firearm offense was the statutory minimum, 60 months. Kimbrough's final advisory Guidelines range was thus 228 to 270 months, or 19 to 22.5 years.

A sentence in this range, in the District Court's judgment, would have been "greater than necessary" to accomplish the purposes of sentencing.... As required by § 3553(a), the court took into account the "nature and circumstances" of the offense and Kimbrough's "history and characteristics." The court also commented that the case exemplified the "disproportionate and unjust effect that crack cocaine guidelines have in sentencing." In this regard, the court contrasted Kimbrough's Guidelines range of 228 to 270 months with the range that would have applied had he been accountable for an equivalent amount of powder cocaine: 97 to 106 months, inclusive of the 5-year mandatory minimum for the firearm charge. Concluding that the statutory minimum sentence was "clearly long enough" to accomplish the objectives listed in § 3553(a), the court sentenced Kimbrough to 15 years, or 180 months, in prison plus 5 years of supervised release.

In an unpublished *per curiam* opinion, the Fourth Circuit vacated the sentence. Under Circuit precedent, the Court of Appeals observed, a sentence "outside the guidelines range is per se unreasonable when it is based on a disagreement with the sentencing disparity for crack and powder cocaine offenses."

We granted certiorari, to determine whether the crack/powder disparity adopted in the United States Sentencing Guidelines has been rendered "advisory" by our decision in *Booker*.[4]

II

We begin with some background on the different treatment of crack and powder cocaine under the federal sentencing laws. Crack and powder cocaine are two forms of the same drug. Powder cocaine, or cocaine

1. The statutory range for possession with intent to distribute more than 50 grams of crack is ten years to life. The same range applies to the conspiracy offense. The statutory range for possession with intent to distribute powder cocaine is 0 to 20 years. Finally, the statutory range for possession of a firearm in furtherance of a drug-trafficking offense is five years to life. The sentences for the three drug crimes may run concurrently, but the sentence for the firearm offense must be consecutive.

4. This question has divided the Courts of Appeals....

hydrochloride, is generally inhaled through the nose; it may also be mixed with water and injected. See United States Sentencing Commission, Special Report to Congress: Cocaine and Federal Sentencing Policy 5, 12 (Feb. 1995), available at http://www.ussc.gov/crack/exec.htm (hereinafter 1995 Report). (All Internet materials as visited Dec. 7, 2007, and included in Clerk of Court's case file.) Crack cocaine, a type of cocaine base, is formed by dissolving powder cocaine and baking soda in boiling water. The resulting solid is divided into single-dose "rocks" that users smoke. The active ingredient in powder and crack cocaine is the same. The two forms of the drug also have the same physiological and psychotropic effects, but smoking crack cocaine allows the body to absorb the drug much faster than inhaling powder cocaine and thus produces a shorter, more intense high.

Although chemically similar, crack and powder cocaine are handled very differently for sentencing purposes. The 100–to–1 ratio yields sentences for crack offenses three to six times longer than those for powder offenses involving equal amounts of drugs. See United States Sentencing Commission, Report to Congress: Cocaine and Federal Sentencing Policy iv (May 2002), available at http://www.ussc.gov/r_congress/02crack/2002 crackrpt.pdf (hereinafter 2002 Report). This disparity means that a major supplier of powder cocaine may receive a shorter sentence than a low-level dealer who buys powder from the supplier but then converts it to crack.

A

The crack/powder disparity originated in the Anti–Drug Abuse Act of 1986 The 1986 Act created a two-tiered scheme of five-and ten-year mandatory minimum sentences for drug manufacturing and distribution offenses. Congress sought "to link the ten-year mandatory minimum trafficking prison term to major drug dealers and to link the five-year minimum term to serious traffickers." 1995 Report 119. The 1986 Act uses the weight of the drugs involved in the offense as the sole proxy to identify "major" and "serious" dealers. For example, any defendant responsible for 100 grams of heroin is subject to the five-year mandatory minimum, and any defendant responsible for 1,000 grams of heroin is subject to the ten-year mandatory minimum.

Crack cocaine was a relatively new drug when the 1986 Act was signed into law, but it was already a matter of great public concern: "Drug abuse in general, and crack cocaine in particular, had become in public opinion and in members' minds a problem of overwhelming dimensions." Congress apparently believed that crack was significantly more dangerous than powder cocaine in that: (1) crack was highly addictive; (2) crack users and dealers were more likely to be violent than users and dealers of other drugs; (3) crack was more harmful to users than powder, particularly for children who had been exposed by their mothers' drug use during pregnancy; (4) crack use was especially prevalent among teenagers; and (5) crack's potency and low cost were making it increasingly popular.

Based on these assumptions, the 1986 Act adopted a "100–to–1 ratio" that treated every gram of crack cocaine as the equivalent of 100 grams of powder cocaine. The Act's five-year mandatory minimum applies to any defendant accountable for 5 grams of crack or 500 grams of powder; its ten-year mandatory minimum applies to any defendant accountable for 50 grams of crack or 5,000 grams of powder.

While Congress was considering adoption of the 1986 Act, the Sentencing Commission was engaged in formulating the Sentencing Guidelines. In the main, the Commission developed Guidelines sentences using an empirical approach based on data about past sentencing practices, including 10,000 presentence investigation reports.

The Commission did not use this empirical approach in developing the Guidelines sentences for drug-trafficking offenses. Instead, it employed the 1986 Act's weight-driven scheme. The Guidelines use a drug quantity table based on drug type and weight to set base offense levels for drug trafficking offenses. In setting offense levels for crack and powder cocaine, the Commission, in line with the 1986 Act, adopted the 100–to–1 ratio. The statute itself specifies only two quantities of each drug, but the Guidelines "go further and set sentences for the full range of possible drug quantities using the same 100–to–1 quantity ratio."

B

Although the Commission immediately used the 100–to–1 ratio to define base offense levels for all crack and powder offenses, it later determined that the crack/powder sentencing disparity is generally unwarranted. Based on additional research and experience with the 100–to–1 ratio, the Commission concluded that the disparity "fails to meet the sentencing objectives set forth by Congress in both the Sentencing Reform Act and the 1986 Act." In a series of reports, the Commission identified three problems with the crack/powder disparity.

First, the Commission reported, the 100–to–1 ratio rested on assumptions about "the relative harmfulness of the two drugs and the relative prevalence of certain harmful conduct associated with their use and distribution that more recent research and data no longer support." For example, the Commission found that crack is associated with "significantly less trafficking-related violence . . . than previously assumed." It also observed that "the negative effects of prenatal crack cocaine exposure are identical to the negative effects of prenatal powder cocaine exposure." The Commission furthermore noted that "the epidemic of crack cocaine use by youth never materialized to the extent feared."

Second, the Commission concluded that the crack/powder disparity is inconsistent with the 1986 Act's goal of punishing major drug traffickers more severely than low-level dealers. Drug importers and major traffickers generally deal in powder cocaine, which is then converted into crack by street-level sellers. But the 100–to–1 ratio can lead to the "anomalous" result that "retail crack dealers get longer sentences than the wholesale drug distributors who supply them the powder cocaine from which their crack is produced."

Finally, the Commission stated that the crack/powder sentencing differential "fosters disrespect for and lack of confidence in the criminal justice system" because of a "widely-held perception" that it "promotes unwarranted disparity based on race." Approximately 85 percent of defendants convicted of crack offenses in federal court are black; thus the severe sentences required by the 100–to–1 ratio are imposed "primarily upon black offenders."

Despite these observations, the Commission's most recent reports do not urge identical treatment of crack and powder cocaine. In the Commission's view, "some differential in the quantity-based penalties" for the two drugs is warranted, because crack is more addictive than powder, crack offenses are more likely to involve weapons or bodily injury, and crack distribution is associated with higher levels of crime. But the 100–to–1 crack/powder ratio, the Commission concluded, significantly overstates the differences between the two forms of the drug. Accordingly, the Commission recommended that the ratio be "substantially" reduced.

C

The Commission has several times sought to achieve a reduction in the crack/powder ratio. In 1995, it proposed amendments to the Guidelines that would have replaced the 100–to–1 ratio with a 1–to–1 ratio. Complementing that change, the Commission would have installed special enhancements for trafficking offenses involving weapons or bodily injury. See Amendments to the Sentencing Guidelines for United States Courts. Congress rejected the amendments. Simultaneously, however, Congress directed the Commission to "propose revision of the drug quantity ratio of crack cocaine to powder cocaine under the relevant statutes and guidelines."

In response to this directive, the Commission issued reports in 1997 and 2002 recommending that Congress change the 100–to–1 ratio prescribed in the 1986 Act. The 1997 Report proposed a 5–to–1 ratio. The 2002 Report recommended lowering the ratio "at least" to 20 to 1. Neither proposal prompted congressional action.

The Commission's most recent report, issued in 2007, again urged Congress to amend the 1986 Act to reduce the 100–to–1 ratio. This time, however, the Commission did not simply await congressional action. Instead, the Commission adopted an ameliorating change in the Guidelines. The alteration, which became effective on November 1, 2007, reduces the base offense level associated with each quantity of crack by two levels. This modest amendment yields sentences for crack offenses between two and five times longer than sentences for equal amounts of powder. Describing the amendment as "only . . . a partial remedy" for the problems generated by the crack/powder disparity, the Commission noted that "any comprehensive solution requires appropriate legislative action by Congress."

III

With this history of the crack/powder sentencing ratio in mind, we next consider the status of the Guidelines tied to the ratio after our decision in United States v. Booker (2005). In *Booker*, the Court held that the mandatory Sentencing Guidelines system violated the Sixth Amendment. The *Booker* remedial opinion determined that the appropriate cure was to sever and excise the provision of the statute that rendered the Guidelines mandatory. This modification of the federal sentencing statute, we explained, "makes the Guidelines effectively advisory."

The statute, as modified by *Booker*, contains an overarching provision instructing district courts to "impose a sentence sufficient, but not greater than necessary" to accomplish the goals of sentencing, including "to reflect the seriousness of the offense," "to promote respect for the law," "to provide just punishment for the offense," "to afford adequate deterrence to criminal conduct," and "to protect the public from further crimes of the defendant." The statute further provides that, in determining the appropriate sentence, the court should consider a number of factors, including "the nature and circumstances of the offense," "the history and characteristics of the defendant," "the sentencing range established" by the Guidelines, "any pertinent policy statement" issued by the Sentencing Commission pursuant to its statutory authority, and "the need to avoid unwarranted sentence disparities among defendants with similar records who have been found guilty of similar conduct." In sum, while the statute still requires a court to give respectful consideration to the Guidelines ... *Booker* "permits the court to tailor the sentence in light of other statutory concerns as well,"

The Government acknowledges that the Guidelines "are now advisory" and that, as a general matter, "courts may vary [from Guidelines ranges] based solely on policy considerations, including disagreements with the Guidelines." ... But the Government contends that the Guidelines adopting the 100–to–1 ratio are an exception to the "general freedom that sentencing courts have to apply the [§ 3553(a)] factors." That is so, according to the Government, because the ratio is a "specific policy determination that Congress has directed sentencing courts to observe." The Government offers three arguments in support of this position. We consider each in turn.

A

As its first and most heavily pressed argument, the Government urges that the 1986 Act itself prohibits the Sentencing Commission and sentencing courts from disagreeing with the 100–to–1 ratio.[13] The Government acknowledges that the "Congress did not *expressly* direct the Sentencing Commission to incorporate the 100:1 ratio in the Guidelines." Nevertheless, it asserts that the Act "implicit[ly]" requires the Commission and sentencing courts to apply the 100–to–1 ratio. Any deviation, the Government urges, would be "logically incoherent" when combined with mandatory minimum sentences based on the 100–to–1 ratio.

This argument encounters a formidable obstacle: It lacks grounding in the text of the 1986 Act. The statute, by its terms, mandates only maximum and minimum sentences: A person convicted of possession with intent to distribute 5 grams or more of crack cocaine must be sentenced to a minimum of 5 years and the maximum term is 40 years. A person with 50 grams or more of crack cocaine must be sentenced to a minimum of 10

13. The Government concedes that a district court may vary from the 100–to–1 ratio if it does so "based on the individualized circumstances" of a particular case. But the Government maintains that the 100–to–1 ratio is binding in the sense that a court may not give any weight to its own view that the ratio itself is inconsistent with the § 3553(a) factors.

years and the maximum term is life. The statute says nothing about the appropriate sentences within these brackets, and we decline to read any implicit directive into that congressional silence ... Drawing meaning from silence is particularly inappropriate here, for Congress has shown that it knows how to direct sentencing practices in express terms. For example, Congress has specifically required the Sentencing Commission to set Guidelines sentences for serious recidivist offenders "at or near" the statutory maximum.

Our cautious reading of the 1986 Act draws force from Neal v. United States (1996). That case involved different methods of calculating lysergic acid diethylamide (LSD) weights, one applicable in determining statutory minimum sentences, the other controlling the calculation of Guidelines ranges. The 1986 Act sets mandatory minimum sentences based on the weight of "a mixture or substance containing a detectable amount" of LSD. Prior to *Neal*, we had interpreted that language to include the weight of the carrier medium (usually blotter paper) on which LSD is absorbed even though the carrier is usually far heavier than the LSD itself. Until 1993, the Sentencing Commission had interpreted the relevant Guidelines in the same way. That year, however, the Commission changed its approach and "instructed courts to give each dose of LSD on a carrier medium a constructive or presumed weight of 0.4 milligrams." The Commission's change significantly lowered the Guidelines range applicable to most LSD offenses, but defendants remained subject to higher statutory minimum sentences based on the combined weight of the pure drug and its carrier medium. The defendant in *Neal* argued that the revised Guidelines and the statute should be interpreted consistently and that the "presumptive-weight method of the Guidelines should also control the mandatory minimum calculation." We rejected that argument, emphasizing that the Commission had not purported to interpret the statute and could not in any event overrule our decision in *Chapman*.

If the Government's current position were correct, then the Guidelines involved in *Neal* would be in serious jeopardy.... Yet our opinion in *Neal* never questioned the validity of the altered Guidelines. To the contrary, we stated: "Entrusted within its sphere to make policy judgments, the Commission may abandon its old methods in favor of what it has deemed a more desirable 'approach' to calculating LSD quantities." If the 1986 Act does not require the Commission to adhere to the Act's method for determining LSD weights, it does not require the Commission—or, after *Booker*, sentencing courts—to adhere to the 100–to–1 ratio for crack cocaine quantities other than those that trigger the statutory mandatory minimum sentences.

B

In addition to the 1986 Act, the Government relies on Congress' disapproval of the Guidelines amendment that the Sentencing Commission proposed in 1995. Congress "not only disapproved of the 1:1 ratio," the Government urges; it also made clear "that the 1986 Act required the Commission (and sentencing courts) to take drug quantities into account, and to do so in a manner that respects the 100:1 ratio."

It is true that Congress rejected the Commission's 1995 proposal to place a 1–to–1 ratio in the Guidelines, and that Congress also expressed the view that "the sentence imposed for trafficking in a quantity of crack cocaine should generally exceed the sentence imposed for trafficking in a like quantity of powder cocaine." But nothing in Congress' 1995 reaction to the Commission-proposed 1–to–1 ratio suggested that crack sentences must exceed powder sentences by a ratio of 100 to 1. To the contrary, Congress' 1995 action required the Commission to recommend a "revision of the drug quantity ratio of crack cocaine to powder cocaine."

The Government emphasizes that Congress required the Commission to propose changes to the 100–to–1 ratio in *both* the 1986 Act and the Guidelines. This requirement, the Government contends, implicitly foreclosed any deviation from the 100–to–1 ratio in the Guidelines (or by sentencing courts) in the absence of a corresponding change in the statute. But it does not follow as the night follows the day that, by calling for recommendations to change the statute, Congress meant to bar any Guidelines alteration in advance of congressional action. The more likely reading is that Congress sought proposals to amend both the statute and the Guidelines because the Commission's criticisms of the 100–to–1 ratio, concerned the exorbitance of the crack/powder disparity in both contexts....

C

Finally, the Government argues that if district courts are free to deviate from the Guidelines based on disagreements with the crack/powder ratio, unwarranted disparities of two kinds will ensue. First, because sentencing courts remain bound by the mandatory minimum sentences prescribed in the 1986 Act, deviations from the 100–to–1 ratio could result in sentencing "cliffs" around quantities that trigger the mandatory minimums. For example, a district court could grant a sizable downward variance to a defendant convicted of distributing 49 grams of crack but would be required by the statutory minimum to impose a much higher sentence on a defendant responsible for only 1 additional gram. Second, the Government maintains that, if district courts are permitted to vary from the Guidelines based on their disagreement with the crack/powder disparity, "defendants with identical real conduct will receive markedly different sentences, depending on nothing more than the particular judge drawn for sentencing."

Neither of these arguments persuades us to hold the crack/powder ratio untouchable by sentencing courts. As to the first, the LSD Guidelines we approved in *Neal* create a similar risk of sentencing "cliffs." An offender who possesses LSD on a carrier medium weighing ten grams is subject to the ten-year mandatory minimum, but an offender whose carrier medium weighs slightly less may receive a considerably lower sentence based on the Guidelines' presumptive-weight methodology. Concerning the second disparity, it is unquestioned that uniformity remains an important goal of sentencing. As we explained in *Booker*, however, advisory Guidelines combined with appellate review for reasonableness and ongoing revision of the Guidelines in response to sentencing practices will help to "avoid excessive sentencing disparities." These measures will not eliminate variations between district courts, but our opinion in *Booker* recognized that some departures from uniformity were a necessary cost of the remedy we adopted. And as to crack cocaine sentences in particular, we note a congressional control on disparities: possible variations among district courts are constrained by the mandatory minimums Congress prescribed in the 1986 Act.

Moreover, to the extent that the Government correctly identifies risks of "unwarranted sentence disparities" within the meaning of 18 U.S.C. § 3553(a)(6), the proper solution is not to treat the crack/powder ratio as mandatory.... Under this instruction, district courts must take account of sentencing practices in other courts and the "cliffs" resulting from the statutory mandatory minimum sentences. To reach an appropriate sentence, these disparities must be weighed against the other § 3553(a) factors and any unwarranted disparity created by the crack/powder ratio itself.

IV

While rendering the Sentencing Guidelines advisory, United States v. Booker, we have nevertheless preserved a key role for the Sentencing Commission. As explained in *Rita* and *Gall*, district courts must treat the Guidelines as the "starting point and the initial benchmark." Congress established the Commission to formulate and constantly refine national sentencing standards. Carrying out its charge, the Commission fills an important institutional role: It has the capacity courts lack to "base its determinations on empirical data and national experience, guided by a professional staff with appropriate expertise."

We have accordingly recognized that, in the ordinary case, the Commission's recommendation of a sentencing range will "reflect a rough approximation of sentences that might achieve § 3553(a)'s objectives." The sentencing judge, on the other hand, has "greater familiarity with ... the individual case and the individual defendant before him than the Commission or the appeals court." He is therefore "in a superior position to find facts and judge their import under § 3553(a)" in each particular case. In light of these discrete institutional strengths, a district court's decision to vary from the advisory Guidelines may attract greatest respect when the sentencing judge finds a particular case "outside the 'heartland' to which the Commission intends individual Guidelines to apply." On the other hand, while the Guidelines are no longer binding, closer review may be in order when the sentencing judge varies from the Guidelines based solely on the judge's view that the Guidelines range "fails properly to reflect § 3553(a) considerations" even in a mine-run case.

The crack cocaine Guidelines, however, present no occasion for elaborative discussion of this matter because those Guidelines do not exemplify the Commission's exercise of its characteristic institutional role. In formulating Guidelines ranges for crack cocaine offenses, as we earlier noted, the Commission looked to the mandatory minimum sentences set in the 1986 Act, and did not take account of "empirical data and national experience." Indeed, the Commission itself has reported that the crack/powder disparity produces disproportionately harsh sanctions, *i.e.*, sentences for crack cocaine offenses "greater than necessary" in light of the purposes of sentencing. Given all this, it would not be an abuse of discretion for a district court to conclude when sentencing a particular defendant that the crack/powder disparity yields a sentence "greater than necessary" to achieve § 3553(a)'s purposes, even in a mine-run case.

V

Taking account of the foregoing discussion in appraising the District Court's disposition in this case, we conclude that the 180–month sentence imposed on Kimbrough should survive appellate inspection. The District Court began by properly calculating and considering the advisory Guidelines range. It then addressed the relevant § 3553(a) factors. First, the court considered "the nature and circumstances" of the crime, which was an unremarkable drug-trafficking offense. ("This defendant and another defendant were caught sitting in a car with some crack cocaine and powder by two police officers—that's the sum and substance of it—[and they also had] a firearm."). Second, the court considered Kimbrough's "history and characteristics." The court noted that Kimbrough had no prior felony convictions, that he had served in combat during Operation Desert Storm and received an honorable discharge from the Marine Corps, and that he had a steady history of employment.

Furthermore, the court alluded to the Sentencing Commission's reports criticizing the 100–to–1 ratio, noting that the Commission "recognizes that crack cocaine has not caused the damage that the Justice Department alleges it has." Comparing the Guidelines range to the range that would have applied if Kimbrough had possessed an equal amount of powder, the court suggested that the 100–to–1 ratio itself created an unwarranted disparity within the meaning of § 3553(a). Finally, the court did not purport to establish a ratio of its own. Rather, it appropriately framed its final determination in line with § 3553(a)'s overarching instruction to "impose a sentence sufficient, but not greater than necessary" to accomplish the sentencing goals advanced in § 3553(a)(2). Concluding that "the crack cocaine guidelines [drove] the offense level to a point higher than is necessary to do justice in this case," the District Court thus rested its sentence on the appropriate considerations and "committed no procedural error,"

The ultimate question in Kimbrough's case is "whether the sentence was reasonable—*i.e.*, whether the District Judge abused his discretion in determining that the § 3553(a) factors supported a sentence of [15 years] and justified a substantial deviation from the Guidelines range." The sentence the District Court imposed on Kimbrough was 4.5 years below the bottom of the Guidelines range. But in determining that 15 years was the appropriate prison term, the District Court properly homed in on the particular circumstances of Kimbrough's case and accorded weight to the Sentencing Commission's consistent and emphatic position that the crack/powder disparity is at odds with § 3553(a). Indeed, aside from its claim that the 100–to–1 ratio is mandatory, the Government did not attack the District Court's downward variance as unsupported by § 3553(a). Giving due respect to the District Court's reasoned appraisal, a reviewing court could not rationally conclude that the 4.5–year sentence reduction Kimbrough received qualified as an abuse of discretion.

* * *

For the reasons stated, the judgment of the United States Court of Appeals for the Fourth Circuit is reversed, and the case is remanded for further proceedings consistent with this opinion.

It is so ordered.

■ JUSTICE SCALIA, concurring.

The Court says that "closer review may be in order when the sentencing judge varies from the Guidelines based solely on the judge's view that the Guidelines range 'fails properly to reflect § 3553(a) considerations' even in a mine-run case," but that this case "presents no occasion for elaborative discussion of this matter." I join the opinion only because I do not take this to be an unannounced abandonment of the following clear statements in our recent opinions....

These statements mean that the district court is free to make its own reasonable application of the § 3553(a) factors, and to reject (after due consideration) the advice of the Guidelines. If there is any thumb on the scales; if the Guidelines *must* be followed even where the district court's application of the § 3553(a) factors is entirely reasonable; then the "advisory" Guidelines would, over a large expanse of their application, *entitle* the defendant to a lesser sentence *but for* the presence of certain additional facts found by judge rather than jury. This, as we said in *Booker*, would violate the Sixth Amendment.

■ JUSTICE THOMAS, dissenting.

I continue to disagree with the remedy fashioned in United States v. Booker. The Court's post-*Booker* sentencing cases illustrate why the remedial majority in *Booker* was mistaken to craft a remedy far broader than necessary to correct constitutional error. The Court is now confronted with a host of questions about how to administer a sentencing scheme that has no basis in the statute. Because the Court's decisions in this area are necessarily grounded in policy considerations rather than law, I respectfully dissent.

In *Booker*, the Court held that the Federal Sentencing Guidelines violate the Sixth Amendment insofar as they permit a judge to make findings that raise a sentence beyond the level justified by the " 'facts reflected in the jury verdict or admitted by the defendant.' In my view, this violation was more suitably remedied by requiring any such facts to be submitted to the jury." *Booker*, (Thomas, J., dissenting in part). That approach would have been consistent with our longstanding presumption of the severability of unconstitutional applications of statutory provisions. And it would have achieved compliance with the Sixth Amendment while doing the least amount of violence to the mandatory sentencing regime that Congress enacted. The Court, however, chose a more sweeping remedy. Despite acknowledging that under the mandatory Guidelines not "every sentence gives rise to a Sixth Amendment violation," the Court rendered the Guidelines advisory in their entirety and mandated appellate review of all sentences for "reasonableness." Because the Court's "solution failed to tailor the remedy to the wrong," I dissented from the remedial opinion.

As a result of the Court's remedial approach, we are now called upon to decide a multiplicity of questions that have no discernibly legal answers. Last Term, in *Rita* (2007), the Court held that a Court of Appeals may treat sentences within the properly calculated Guidelines range as presumptively reasonable. Today, in *Gall* the Court holds that a Court of Appeals may not require sentences that deviate substantially from the Guidelines range to be justified by extraordinary circumstances. And here the Court holds that sentencing courts are free to reject the Sentencing Guidelines' 100–to–1 crack-to-powder ratio.

These outcomes may be perfectly reasonable as a matter of policy, but they have no basis in law. Congress did not mandate a reasonableness standard of appellate review—that was a standard the remedial majority in *Booker* fashioned out of whole cloth. The Court must now give content to that standard, but in so doing it does not and cannot rely on any statutory language or congressional intent. We are asked here to determine whether, under the new advisory Guidelines regime, district courts may impose sentences based in part on their disagreement with a categorical policy judgment reflected in the Guidelines. But the Court's answer to that question necessarily derives from something other than the statutory language or congressional intent because Congress, by making the Guidelines mandatory, quite clearly intended to bind district courts to the Sentencing Commission's categorical policy judgments. By rejecting this statutory approach, the *Booker* remedial majority has left the Court with no law to apply and forced it to assume the legislative role of devising a new sentencing scheme.

Although I joined Justice Scalia's dissent in *Rita* accepting the *Booker* remedial opinion as a matter of "statutory *stare decisis*," I am now convinced that there is no principled way to apply the *Booker* remedy—certainly not one based on the statute.

Applying the statute as written, it is clear that the District Court erred by departing below the mandatory Guidelines range. I would therefore affirm the judgment of the Court of Appeals vacating petitioner's sentence and remanding for resentencing.

■ JUSTICE ALITO, dissenting.

For the reasons explained in my dissent in Gall v. United States, I would hold that, under the remedial decision in United States v. Booker (2005), a district judge is still required to give significant weight to the policy decisions embodied in the Guidelines. The *Booker* remedial decision, however, does not permit a court of appeals to treat the Guidelines' policy decisions as binding. I would not draw a distinction between the Guideline at issue here and other Guidelines. Accordingly, I would vacate the decision of the Court of Appeals and remand for reconsideration.

* * *

The above cases all concern cases in which a sentence below the guideline level was imposed. Given the Court's struggle with nonmandatory sentencing guidelines, does a reviewing court have the power to raise a defendant's sentence? If so, when?

Greenlaw v. United States

United States Supreme Court, 2008.
___ U.S. ___, 128 S.Ct. 2559.

■ JUSTICE GINSBURG delivered the opinion of the Court.

This case concerns the role of courts in our adversarial system. The specific question presented: May a United States Court of Appeals, acting on its own initiative, order an increase in a defendant's sentence? Petitioner Michael J. Greenlaw was convicted of various offenses relating to drugs and firearms, and was sentenced to imprisonment for 442 months. He appealed urging, *inter alia*, that his sentence was unreasonably long. After rejecting all of Greenlaw's arguments, the Court of Appeals determined, without Government invitation, that the applicable law plainly required a prison sentence 15 years longer than the term the trial court had imposed. Accordingly, the appeals court instructed the trial court to increase Greenlaw's sentence to 622 months. We hold that, absent a Government appeal or cross-appeal, the sentence Greenlaw received should not have been increased. We therefore vacate the Court of Appeals' judgment.

I

Greenlaw was a member of a gang that, for years, controlled the sale of crack cocaine in a southside Minneapolis neighborhood. To protect their drug stash and to prevent rival dealers from moving into their territory, gang members carried and concealed numerous weapons. For his part in the operation, Greenlaw was charged, in the United States District Court for the District of Minnesota, with eight offenses; after trial, he was found guilty on seven of the charges.

Among Greenlaw's convictions were two for violating 18 U.S.C. § 924(c)(1)(A), which prohibits carrying a firearm during and in relation to a crime of violence or a drug trafficking crime: His first § 924(c) conviction was for carrying a firearm in connection with a crime committed in 1998; his second, for both carrying and discharging a firearm in connection with a crime committed in 1999. A first conviction for violating § 924(c) carries a mandatory minimum term of 5 years, if the firearm is simply carried. If the firearm is also discharged, the mandatory minimum increases to 10 years. For "a second or subsequent conviction," however, whether the weapon is only carried or discharged as well, the mandatory minimum jumps to 25 years. Any sentence for violating § 924(c), moreover, must run consecutively to "any other term of imprisonment," including any other conviction under § 924(c).

At sentencing, the District Court made an error. Over the Government's objection, the court held that a § 924(c) conviction does not count as "second or subsequent" when it is "charged in the same indictment" as the defendant's first § 924(c) conviction. The error was plain because this Court had held ... that when a defendant is charged in the same indictment with more than one offense qualifying for punishment under § 924(c), all convictions after the first rank as "second or subsequent."

As determined by the District Court, Greenlaw's sentence included 262 months (without separately counting sentences that ran concurrently) for all his convictions other than the two under § 924(c). For the first § 924(c) offense, the court imposed a 5–year sentence in accord with § 924(c)(1)(A)(i). As to the second § 924(c) conviction, the District Court rejected the Government's request for the 25–year minimum prescribed in § 924(c)(1)(C) for "second or subsequent" offenses; instead, it imposed the 10–year term prescribed in § 924(c)(1)(A)(iii) for first-time offenses.[1] The total sentence thus calculated came to 442 months.

Greenlaw appealed to the United States Court of Appeals for the Eighth Circuit, urging, *inter alia*, that the appropriate total sentence for all his crimes was 15 years. The Court of Appeals found no merit in any of Greenlaw's arguments. Although the Government did not appeal or cross-appeal, it did note, on brief and at oral argument, the District Court's error: Greenlaw's sentence should have been 15 years longer than the 442 months imposed by the District Court, the Government observed, because his second § 924(c) conviction called for a 25–year (not a 10–year) mandatory minimum consecutive sentence.

The Government made the observation that the sentence was 15 years too short only to counter Greenlaw's argument that it was unreasonably long. See App. 84–86; Recording of Oral Arg. in *United States v. Carter*, No. 05–3391, (CA8, Sept. 26, 2006), at 16:53–19:04, available at http://www.ca8.uscourts.gov/oralargs/oaFrame.html (as visited June 13, 2008). Having refrained from seeking correction of the District Court's error by pursuing its own appeal, the Government simply urged that Greenlaw's sentence should be affirmed.

The Court of Appeals acknowledged that the Government, while objecting at sentencing to the trial court's erroneous reading of § 924(c)(1)(C), had elected to seek no appellate court alteration of Greenlaw's sentence. Relying on the "plain-error rule" stated in Federal Rule of Criminal Procedure 52(b), however, the appeals court held that it had discretion to raise and correct the District Court's error on its own initiative. The Court of Appeals therefore vacated the sentence and instructed the District Court "to impose the [statutorily mandated] consecutive minimum sentence of 25 years."

... Greenlaw asked the Eighth Circuit to adopt the position advanced by the Seventh Circuit. "By deciding not to take a cross-appeal," the Seventh Circuit stated, "the United States has ensured that [the defendant's] sentence cannot be increased." The Eighth Circuit denied rehearing without an opinion. On remand, as instructed by the Court of Appeals, the District Court increased Greenlaw's sentence by 15 years, yielding a total prison term of 622 months ...

1. The court added 10 years rather than 5 based on the jury's finding that the firearm Greenlaw carried in connection with the second § 924(c) offense had been discharged.

Greenlaw petitioned for certiorari noting a division among the Circuits on this question: When a defendant unsuccessfully challenges his sentence as too high, may a court of appeals, on its own initiative, increase the sentence absent a cross-appeal by the Government? In response, the Government "agree[d] with [Greenlaw] that the court of appeals erred in *sua sponte* remanding the case with directions to enhance petitioner's sentence." We granted review and invited Jay T. Jorgensen to brief and argue this case, as *amicus curiae*, in support of the Court of Appeals' judgment. Mr. Jorgensen accepted the appointment and has well fulfilled his assigned responsibility.

II

In our adversary system, in both civil and criminal cases, in the first instance and on appeal, we follow the principle of party presentation. That is, we rely on the parties to frame the issues for decision and assign to courts the role of neutral arbiter of matters the parties present. To the extent courts have approved departures from the party presentation principle in criminal cases, the justification has usually been to protect a *pro se* litigant's rights.[2] But as a general rule, "[o]ur adversary system is designed around the premise that the parties know what is best for them, and are responsible for advancing the facts and arguments entitling them to relief." As cogently explained:

> "[Courts] do not, or should not, sally forth each day looking for wrongs to right. We wait for cases to come to us, and when they do we normally decide only questions presented by the parties. Counsel almost always know a great deal more about their cases than we do, and this must be particularly true of counsel for the United States, the richest, most powerful, and best represented litigant to appear before us."

The cross-appeal rule, pivotal in this case, is both informed by, and illustrative of, the party presentation principle. Under that unwritten but longstanding rule, an appellate court may not alter a judgment to benefit a nonappealing party. This Court, from its earliest years, has recognized that it takes a cross-appeal to justify a remedy in favor of an appellee. We have called the rule "inveterate and certain."

Courts of Appeals have disagreed, however, on the proper characterization of the cross-appeal rule: Is it "jurisdictional," and therefore exceptionless, or a "rule of practice," and thus potentially subject to judicially created exceptions? . . .

Congress has eased our decision by specifying the instances in which the Government may seek appellate review of a sentence, and then adding this clear instruction: Even when a United States Attorney files a notice of appeal with respect to a sentence qualifying for review, "[t]he Government may not further prosecute [the] appeal without the personal approval of the Attorney General, the Solicitor General, or a deputy solicitor general

2. Because this case does not present the issue, we take no position on whether correction of an error prejudicial to a nonappealing criminal defendant might be justified as a measure to obviate the need for a collateral attack.

designated by the Solicitor General." Congress thus entrusted to named high-ranking officials within the Department of Justice responsibility for determining whether the Government, on behalf of the public, should seek a sentence higher than the one imposed. It would severely undermine Congress' instruction were appellate judges to "sally forth" on their own motion, to take up errors adverse to the Government when the designated Department of Justice officials have not authorized an appeal from the sentence the trial court imposed.

This Court has recognized that "the Executive Branch has exclusive authority and absolute discretion to decide whether to prosecute a case." We need not decide whether comparable authority and discretion are lodged in the Executive Branch with respect to the pursuit of issues on appeal. We need only recognize that Congress, in § 3742(b), has accorded to the top representatives of the United States in litigation the prerogative to seek or forgo appellate correction of sentencing errors, however plain they may be. That measure should garner the Judiciary's full respect.

III

A

In ordering the District Court to add 15 years to Greenlaw's sentence, despite the absence of a cross-appeal by the Government, the Court of Appeals identified Federal Rule of Criminal Procedure 52(b) as the source of its authority. Rule 52(b) reads: "A plain error that affects substantial rights may be considered even though it was not brought to the court's attention." Nothing in the text or history of Rule 52(b) suggests that the rulemakers, in codifying the plain-error doctrine, meant to override the cross-appeal requirement.

Nor do our opinions support a plain-error exception to the cross-appeal rule. This Court has indeed noticed, and ordered correction of, plain errors not raised by defendants, but we have done so only to benefit a defendant who had himself petitioned the Court for review on other grounds. In no case have we applied plain-error doctrine to the detriment of a petitioning party. Rather, in every case in which correction of a plain error would result in modification of a judgment to the advantage of a party who did not seek this Court's review, we have invoked the cross-appeal rule to bar the correction.

In Chittenden v. Brewster (1865), for example, the appellants asserted that an award entered in their favor was too small. A prior decision of this Court, however, made it plain that they were entitled to no award at all. But because the appellee had not filed a cross-appeal, the Court left the award undisturbed. Strunk v. United States (1973), decided over a century later, is similarly illustrative. There, the Court of Appeals had determined that the defendant was denied his right to a speedy trial, but held that the proper remedy was reduction of his sentence as compensation for the delay, not dismissal of the charges against him. As petitioner in this Court, the defendant sought review of the remedial order. The Court suggested that there may have been no speedy trial violation, as "it seem[ed] clear that [the defendant] was responsible for a large part of the . . . delay." But because the Government had not raised the issue by cross-petition, we considered the case on the premise that the defendant had been deprived of his Sixth Amendment right, and ruled that dismissal of the indictment was the proper remedy.

Even if there might be circumstances in which it would be proper for an appellate court to initiate plain-error review, sentencing errors that the Government refrained from pursuing would not fit the bill. Heightening the generally applicable party presentation principle, Congress has provided a dispositive direction regarding sentencing errors that aggrieve the Government. In § 3742(b), as earlier explained, see *supra*, at 7, Congress designated leading Department of Justice officers as the decisionmakers responsible for determining when Government pursuit of a sentencing appeal is in order. Those high officers, Congress recognized, are best equipped to determine where the Government's interest lies. Rule 52(b) does not invite appellate court interference with their assessment.

B

Amicus supporting the Eighth Circuit's judgment links the argument based on Rule 52(b) to a similar argument based on 28 U.S.C. § 2106. Section 2106 states that federal appellate courts "may affirm, modify, vacate, set aside or reverse any judgment . . . lawfully brought before it for review." For substantially the same reasons that Rule 52(b) does not override the cross-appeal requirement, § 2106 does not do so either. Section 2106 is not limited to plain errors, much less to sentencing errors in criminal cases—it applies to all cases, civil and criminal, and to all errors. Were the construction *amicus* offers correct, § 2106 would displace the cross-appeal rule cross-the-board. The authority described in § 2106, we have observed, "must be exercised consistent with the requirements of the Federal Rules of Civil Procedure as interpreted by this Court." No different conclusion is warranted with respect to the "inveterate and certain" cross-appeal rule.

C

In defending the Court of Appeals judgment, *amicus* places heavy weight on an argument pinned not to Rule 52(b) or 28 U.S.C. § 2106, but to the text of 18 U.S.C. § 3742, the Criminal Code provision governing appellate review of criminal sentences. As *amicus* reads § 3742, once either party appeals a sentence, the Court of Appeals must remand "any illegal sentence regardless of whether the remand hurts or helps the appealing party." Congress so directed, *amicus* argues, by instructing that, upon review of the record, a court of appeals "*shall determine* . . . whether the sentence was imposed in violation of law," § 3742(e) (emphasis added), and "*shall remand*" if it so determines, § 3742(f)(1) (2000 ed., Supp. V) (emphasis added).

Amicus makes a further text-based observation. He notes that § 3742(f)(2)—the provision covering sentences "outside the applicable [G]uideline range"—calls for a remand only where a departure from the Federal Sentencing Guidelines harms the appellant. In contrast, *amicus* emphasizes, § 3742(f)(1)—the provision controlling sentences imposed "in violation of law" and Guideline application errors—contains no such appellant-linked limitation. The inference *amicus* draws from this distinction is that Congress intended to override the cross-appeal rule for sentences controlled by § 3742(f)(1), *i.e.*, those imposed "in violation of law" (or incorrectly applying the Guidelines), but not for Guideline departure errors, the category covered by § 3742(f)(2).

This novel construction of § 3742, presented for the first time in the brief *amicus* filed in this Court, is clever and complex, but ultimately unpersuasive. Congress enacted § 3742 in 1984. At that time, the cross-appeal requirement was a solidly grounded rule of appellate practice. The inference properly drawn, we think, is that Congress was aware of the cross-appeal rule, and framed § 3742 expecting that the new provision would operate in harmony with the "inveterate and certain" bar to enlarging judgments in favor of an appellee who filed no cross-appeal....

Amicus' reading of § 3742, moreover, would yield some strange results. We note two, in particular. Under his construction, § 3742 would give with one hand what it takes away with the other: § 3742(b) entrusts to certain Government officials the decision whether to appeal an illegally low sentence; but according to *amicus*, §§ 3742(e) and (f) would instruct appellate courts to correct an error of that order on their own initiative, thereby trumping the officials' decision. We resist attributing to Congress an intention to render a statute so internally inconsistent ... Further, the construction proposed by *amicus* would draw a puzzling distinction between incorrect applications of the Sentencing Guidelines, controlled by § 3742(f)(1), and erroneous departures from the Guidelines, covered by § 3742(f)(2). The latter would be subject to the cross-appeal rule, the former would not. We do not see why Congress would want to differentiate Guidelines decisions this way....

D

In increasing Greenlaw's sentence by 15 years on its own initiative, the Eighth Circuit did not advert to the procedural rules setting deadlines for launching appeals and cross-appeals. Unyielding in character, these rules may be seen as auxiliary to the cross-appeal rule and the party presentation principle served by that rule. Federal Rule of Appellate Procedure 3(a)(1) provides that "[a]n appeal permitted by law ... may be taken *only by filing a notice of appeal* ... within the [prescribed] time." Complementing Rule 3(a)(1), Rule 4(b)(1)(B)(ii) instructs that, when the Government has the right to cross-appeal in a criminal case, its notice "*must be filed* ... within 30 days after ... the filing of a notice of appeal by any defendant." The filing time for a notice of appeal or cross-appeal, Rule 4(b)(4) states, may be extended "for a period not to exceed 30 days." Rule 26(b) bars any extension beyond that time.

The firm deadlines set by the Appellate Rules advance the interests of the parties and the legal system in fair notice and finality. Thus a defendant who appeals but faces no cross-appeal can proceed anticipating that the appellate court will not enlarge his sentence. And if the Government files a cross-appeal, the defendant will have fair warning, well in advance of briefing and argument, that pursuit of his appeal exposes him to the risk of a higher sentence. Given early warning, he can tailor his arguments to take account of that risk. Or he can seek the Government's agreement to voluntary dismissal of the competing appeals before positions become hardened during the hours invested in preparing the case for appellate court consideration.

The strict time limits on notices of appeal and cross-appeal would be undermined, in both civil and criminal cases, if an appeals court could modify a judgment in favor of a party who filed no notice of appeal. In a criminal prosecution, moreover, the defendant would appeal at his peril, with nothing to alert him that, on his own appeal, his sentence would be increased until the appeals court so decreed. In this very case, Greenlaw might have made different strategic decisions had he known soon after filing his notice of appeal that he risked a 15–year increase in an already lengthy sentence.

E

We note that nothing we have said in this opinion requires courts to modify their current practice in so-called "sentencing package cases." Those cases typically involve multicount indictments and a successful attack by a defendant on some but not all of the counts of conviction. The appeals court, in such instances, may vacate the entire sentence on all counts so that, on remand, the trial court can reconfigure the sentencing plan to assure that it remains adequate to satisfy the sentencing factors in 18 U.S.C. § 3553(a). In remanded cases, the Government relates, trial courts have imposed a sentence on the remaining counts longer than the sentence originally imposed on those particular counts, but yielding an aggregate sentence no longer than the aggregate sentence initially imposed. Thus the defendant ultimately may gain nothing from his limited success on appeal, but he will also lose nothing, as he will serve no more time than the trial court originally ordered.

The practice the Government describes is not at odds with the cross-appeal rule, which stops appellate judges from adding years to a defendant's sentence on their own initiative. It simply ensures that the sentence " 'will suit not merely the offense but the individual defendant.' " And the assessment will be made by the sentencing judge exercising discretion, not by an appellate panel ruling on an issue of law no party tendered to the court.

This is not a "sentencing package" case. Greenlaw was unsuccessful on all his appellate issues. There was no occasion for the Court of Appeals to vacate his sentence and no warrant, in the absence of a cross-appeal, to order the addition of 15 years to his sentence.

* * *

For the reasons stated, the judgment of the United States Court of Appeals for the Eighth Circuit is vacated, and the case is remanded for further proceedings consistent with this opinion.

■ Justice Breyer, concurring in the judgment.

I agree with Justice Alito that the cross-appeal requirement is simply a rule of practice for appellate courts, rather than a limitation on their power, and I therefore join Parts I–III of his opinion. Moreover, as a general matter, I would leave application of the rule to the courts of appeals, with our power to review their discretion "seldom to be called into action." But since this case is now before us, I would consider whether the Court of Appeals here acted properly. Primarily for the reasons stated by the majority in footnote 9 of its opinion, I believe that the court abused its discretion in *sua sponte* increasing petitioner's sentence. Our precedent precludes the creation of an exception to the cross-appeal requirement based solely on the obviousness of the lower court's error. And I cannot see how the interests of justice are significantly disserved by permitting petitioner's release from prison at roughly age 62, after almost 37 years behind bars, as opposed to age 77.

■ JUSTICE ALITO, with whom JUSTICE STEVENS joins, and with whom JUSTICE BREYER joins as to Parts I, II, and III, dissenting.

I respectfully dissent because I view the cross-appeal requirement as a rule of appellate practice. It is akin to the rule that courts invoke when they decline to consider arguments that the parties have not raised. Both rules rest on premises about the efficient use of judicial resources and the proper role of the tribunal in an adversary system. Both are sound and should generally be followed. But just as the courts have made them, the courts may make exceptions to them, and I do not understand why a reviewing court should enjoy less discretion to correct an error *sua sponte* than it enjoys to raise and address an argument *sua sponte*. Absent congressional direction to the contrary, and subject to our limited oversight as a supervisory court, we should entrust the decision to initiate error correction to the sound discretion of the courts of appeals.

I

Before laying out my view in more detail, I must first address the question whether federal courts have subject-matter jurisdiction to enlarge an appellee's judgment in the absence of a cross-appeal. Because the Court would not recognize any exceptions to the cross-appeal requirement when the defendant appeals his sentence, it does not decide that question. I must confront it, though I do not regard it as a substantial question. The cross-appeal requirement seems to me a prime example of a " 'rule of practice,' subject to exceptions, not an unqualified limit on the power of appellate courts." While a court should generally enforce the cross-appeal requirement, a departure from it would not divest the court of jurisdiction.

This Court has never addressed whether an appellate court's jurisdiction to enlarge a judgment in favor of an appellee is contingent on a duly filed cross-appeal. The majority's contention that "[o]ur own opinions contain statements supporting" the " 'jurisdictional' " characterization of the requirement relies on a misreading of that precedent. A court may lack the power to do something for reasons other than want of jurisdiction, and a rule can be inflexible without being jurisdictional.

The jurisdiction of the courts of appeals is fixed by Congress. If Congress wants to withhold from the courts of appeals the power to decide questions that expand the rights of nonappealing parties, it may do so. See U.S. Const., Art. III, § 1 (authorizing Congress to establish the lower courts and, by corollary, to fix their jurisdiction); The jurisdictional question thus reduces to whether Congress intended to make a cross-appeal a condition precedent to the appellate court's jurisdiction to enlarge a judgment in favor of a nonappealing party.

As always with such questions, the text of the relevant statute provides the best evidence of congressional intent. The relevant statute in this case is 18 U.S.C. § 3742 Section 3742(a) authorizes a criminal defendant to "file a notice of appeal" to review a sentence that was, among other possibilities, "imposed in violation of law." Section 3742(b) provides parallel authority for the Government to "file a notice of appeal" to review unlawful sentences. *E.g.*, § 3742(b)(1). The statute conditions the Government's authority to further prosecute its appeal on "the personal approval of the Attorney General, the Solicitor General, or a deputy solicitor general designated by the Solicitor General." § 3742(b).

Nothing in this language remotely suggests that a court of appeals lacks subject-matter jurisdiction to increase a defendant's sentence in the absence of a cross-appeal by the Government. In fact, the statute does not even mention cross-appeals. It separately authorizes either party to "file a notice of appeal," but it never suggests that the reviewing court's power is limited to correcting errors for the benefit of the appealing party. If anything, it suggests the opposite. Without qualifying the appellate court's power in any way, § 3742(e) instructs the court to determine, among other things, whether the sentence was "imposed in violation of law." § 3742(e)(1). And while § 3742(f)(2) limits the action that a court of appeals can take depending on which party filed the appeal, compare § 3742(f)(2)(A) (sentences set aside as "too high" if defendant filed) with § 3742(f)(2)(B) (sentences set aside as "too low" if Government filed), no such limitation appears in § 3742(f)(1). That paragraph requires a court of appeals simply to set aside any sentence "imposed in violation of law or imposed as a result of an incorrect application of the sentencing guidelines."

II

Since a cross-appeal has no effect on the appellate court's subject-matter jurisdiction, the cross-appeal requirement is best characterized as a rule of practice. It is a rule created by the courts to serve interests that are important to the Judiciary. The Court identifies two of these interests: notice to litigants and finality. One might add that the cross-appeal requirement also serves a third interest: the appellate court's interest in being adequately briefed on the issues that it decides. Although these are substantial interests in the abstract, I question how well an inflexible cross-appeal requirement serves them.

Notice. With respect to notice, the benefits of an unyielding cross-appeal requirement are insubstantial. When the Government files a notice of cross-appeal, the defendant is alerted to the possibility that his or her sentence may be increased as a result of the appellate decision. But if the cross-appeal rule is, as I would hold, a strong rule of practice that should be followed in all but exceptional instances, the Government's failure to file a notice of cross-appeal would mean in the vast majority of cases that the defendant thereafter ran little risk of an increased sentence. And the rare cases where that possibility arose would generally involve errors so plain that no conceivable response by the defendant could alter the result. It is not unreasonable to consider an appealing party to be on notice as to such serious errors of law in his favor. And while there may be rare cases in which the existence of such a legal error would come as a complete surprise to the defendant or in which argument from the parties would be of assistance to the court, the solution to such a problem is not to eliminate the courts of appeals' authority to correct egregious errors. Rather, the appropriate response is for the court of appeals to request supplemental briefing or—if it deems that insufficient—simply to refuse to exercise its authority. Cf. *Irizarry v. United States*, 553 U.S. (2008). In short, the Court's holding does not increase the substance of the notice that a defendant receives; it merely accelerates that notice by at most a few weeks in a very small number of cases. . . .

Finality. An inflexible cross-appeal rule also does little to further the interest of the parties and the Judiciary in the finality of decisions. An appellate court's decision to grant a nonappealing party additional relief does not interrupt a long, undisturbed slumber. The error's repose begins no earlier than the deadline for filing a cross-appeal, and it ends as soon as the reviewing court issues its opinion—and often much sooner. Here, for example, the slumber was broken when the Government identified the error in its brief as appellee.

Orderly Briefing. I do not doubt that adversarial briefing improves the quality of appellate decisionmaking, but it hardly follows that appellate courts should be denied the authority to correct errors that seriously prejudice nonappealing parties. Under my interpretation of the cross-appeal rule, a court of appeals would not be obligated to address errors that are prejudicial to a nonappealing party; a court of appeals would merely have the authority to do so in appropriate cases. If a court of appeals noticed such an error and concluded that it was appropriate to address the issue, the court could, if it wished, order additional briefing. If, on the other hand, the court concluded that the issue was not adequately addressed by the briefs filed by the parties in the ordinary course and that additional briefing would interfere with the efficient administration of the court's work, the court would not be required to decide the issue. Therefore, I do not see how the courts of appeals' interest in orderly briefing is furthered by denying those courts the discretionary authority to address important issues that they find it appropriate to decide.

Indeed, the inflexible cross-appeal rule that the Court adopts may disserve the interest in judicial efficiency in some cases. For example, correcting an error that prejudiced a nonappealing defendant on direct review might obviate the need for a collateral attack. Because the reviewing court is in the best position to decide whether a departure from the cross-appeal rule would be efficient, rigid enforcement of that rule is more likely to waste judicial resources than to conserve them.

In sum, the Court exaggerates the interests served by the cross-appeal requirement. At the same time, it overlooks an important interest that the rule disserves: the interest of the Judiciary and the public in correcting grossly prejudicial errors of law that undermine confidence in our legal system. We have repeatedly stressed the importance of that interest, and it has justified departures from our traditional adversary framework in other contexts. The Court mentions one of those contexts, (*pro se* litigation), but there are others that deserve mention.

The most well-known is plain-error review. Federal Rule of Criminal Procedure 52(b) authorizes reviewing courts to correct "[a] plain error that affects substantial rights ... even though it was not brought to the court's attention." Although I agree with the Court that this Rule does not independently justify the Eighth Circuit's decision, I believe that the Rule's underlying policy sheds some light on the issue before us. We have explained that courts may rely on Rule 52(b) to correct only those plain errors that " 'seriously affec[t] the fairness, integrity or public reputation of judicial proceedings.' " We have thus recognized that preservation of the "fairness, integrity or public reputation of judicial proceedings" may sometimes justify a departure from the traditional adversarial framework of issue presentation.

Perhaps the closest analogue to the cross-appeal requirement is the rule of appellate practice that restrains reviewing courts from addressing arguments that the parties have not made. Courts typically invoke this rule to avoid resolving a case based on an unaired argument, even if the argument could change the outcome. But courts also recognize that the rule is not inflexible,

A reviewing court will generally address an argument *sua sponte* only to correct the most patent and serious errors.... Because the prejudicial effect of the error and the impact of error correction on judicial resources are matters best determined by the reviewing court, the court's decision to go beyond the arguments made by the parties is committed to its sound discretion....

This authority provides a good model for our decision in this case. The Court has not persuaded me that the interests at stake when a reviewing court awards a nonappealing party additional relief are qualitatively different from the interests at stake when a reviewing court raises an issue *sua sponte*. Authority on the latter point recognizes that the interest of the public and the Judiciary in correcting grossly prejudicial errors of law may sometimes outweigh other interests normally furthered by fidelity to our adversarial tradition. I would recognize the same possibility here. And just as reviewing courts enjoy discretion to decide for themselves when to raise and decide arguments *sua sponte*, I would grant them substantial latitude to decide when to enlarge an appellee's judgment in the absence of a cross-appeal.

III

The approach I advocate is not out of step with our precedent. The Court has never decided whether the cross-appeal requirement is "subject to exceptions [or] an unqualified limit on the power of appellate courts." That question was reserved in *Neztsosie*, even as the Court recognized that lower courts had reached different conclusions. I would simply confirm what our precedent had assumed: that there are exceptional circumstances when it is appropriate for a reviewing court to correct an error for the benefit of a party that has not cross-appealed the decision below.

Indeed, the Court has already reached the very result that it claims to disavow today. We have long held that a sentencing court confronted with new circumstances may impose a stiffer sentence on remand than the defendant received prior to a successful appeal.... The Court makes no effort to explain the analytical difference between those cases and this one. If a sentencing court may rely on new circumstances to justify a longer sentence on remand, why cannot one of the new circumstances be the court's discovery (by dint of appellate review) that its first sentence was based on an error of law?

Even today, the Court refuses to decide whether the cross-appeal requirement admits of exceptions in appropriate cases. While calling the rule " 'inveterate and certain,' " the Court allows that "there might be circumstances in which it would be proper for an appellate court to initiate plain-error review," The Court's mandate is limited to a single class of cases—sentencing appeals, and then only when the appeal is brought by the Government.

The Court justifies the asymmetry in its decision by pointing to 18 U.S.C. § 3742(b), which provides that "[t]he Government may not further prosecute [the] appeal without the personal approval of the Attorney General, the Solicitor General, or a deputy solicitor general designated by the Solicitor General." According to the majority, "[i]t would severely undermine Congress' instruction were appellate judges to 'sally forth' on their own motion to take up errors adverse to the Government when the designated Department of Justice officials have not authorized an appeal from the sentence the trial court imposed."

The problem with this argument is that § 3742(b) does not apportion authority over sentencing appeals between the Executive and Judicial Branches. By its terms, § 3742(b) simply apportions that authority *within* an executive department. It provides that the "[t]he Government" may not "prosecute" the appeal without approval from one of the listed officials. It says nothing about the power of the courts to correct error in the absence of a Government appeal. Had Congress intended to restrict the power of the courts, the statute would not stop "[t]he Government" from "prosecut[ing]" unauthorized appeals; instead, it would stop "the Court of Appeals" from "deciding" them.

The design that the Court imputes to the drafters of § 3742(b) is inconsistent with the text in another important respect. Suppose that the District Court imposes a sentence below the range set forth in the Federal Sentencing Guidelines, and the Government files an authorized appeal on the ground that the sentence is unreasonable. Suppose further that the reviewing court discovers, to the surprise of both parties, that the District Court made a further error by overlooking a mandatory minimum to which the defendant was subject. The mandatory minimum would raise the defendant's sentence beyond what even the Government had wanted. Under the majority's theory, the reviewing court should not remand for imposition of the mandatory minimum, since the decision to seek the higher sentence belonged to the Government alone. But that conclusion is plainly at odds with the text of the statute, which imposes no limits on sentencing review once the named officials have signed off on the appeal.

Section 3742(b)'s limited effect on sentencing review implies that the statute was not designed to prevent judicial encroachment on the prerogatives of the Executive. It is more likely that Congress wanted to withhold from the Executive the power to force the courts of appeals to entertain Government appeals that are not regarded as sufficiently important by the leadership of the Department of Justice. Allowing the courts of appeals, in their discretion, to remedy errors not raised in a cross-appeal in no way trenches on the authority of the Executive. Section 3742(b) may have also been designed to serve the Executive's institutional interests. Congress may have wanted to ensure that the Government maintained a consistent legal position across different sentencing appeals. Or perhaps Congress wanted to maximize the impact of the Government's sentencing appeals by giving high-level officials the authority to nix meritless or marginal ones. These institutional interests of the Executive do not undermine the Judiciary's authority to correct unlawful sentences in the absence of a Government appeal, and they do not justify the Court's decision today.

IV

For the reasons given above, I would hold that the courts of appeals enjoy the discretion to correct error *sua sponte* for the benefit of nonappealing parties. The Court errs in vacating the judgment of the Eighth Circuit, and I respectfully dissent.

E. DUE PROCESS AND SENTENCING FACTORS

1. OTHER CRIMES

United States v. Tucker

Supreme Court of the United States, 1972.
404 U.S. 443, 92 S.Ct. 589.

■ JUSTICE STEWART delivered the opinion of the Court.

In 1953 Tucker, was brought to trial in a federal district court in California upon a charge of armed bank robbery. He pleaded not guilty. Four female employees of the bank were called as witnesses for the prosecution, and they identified the respondent as the robber. He testified in his own behalf, denying participation in the robbery and offering an alibi defense. To impeach the credibility of his testimony, the prosecution was permitted on cross-examination to ask him whether he had previously been convicted of any felonies. He acknowledged three previous felony convictions, one in Florida in 1938, another in Louisiana in 1946, and a third in Florida in 1950. At the conclusion of the trial the jury returned a verdict of guilty. In the ensuing sentencing proceeding the District Judge conducted an inquiry into the respondent's background, and, the record shows, gave explicit attention to the three previous felony convictions the respondent had acknowledged. The judge then sentenced him to serve 25 years in prison—the maximum term authorized by the applicable federal statute.

Several years later it was conclusively determined that the respondent's 1938 conviction in Florida and his 1946 conviction in Louisiana were constitutionally invalid. ... [Because] the respondent had been unrepresented by counsel, ... we deal here not with a sentence imposed in the informed discretion of a trial judge, but with a sentence founded at least in part upon misinformation of constitutional magnitude. As in Townsend v. Burke, "this prisoner was sentenced on the basis of assumptions concerning his criminal record which were materially untrue." The record in the present case makes evident that the sentencing judge gave specific consideration to the respondent's previous convictions before imposing sentence upon him. Yet it is now clear that two of those convictions were wholly unconstitutional under Gideon v. Wainwright.

* * *

... if the trial judge in 1953 had been aware of the constitutional infirmity of two of the previous convictions, the factual circumstances of the respondent's background would have appeared in a dramatically different light at the sentencing proceeding. Instead of confronting a defendant who had been legally convicted of three previous felonies, the judge would then have been dealing with a man who, beginning at age 17, had been unconstitutionally imprisoned for more than ten years, including five and one-half years on a chain gang. We cannot agree with the government that a re-evaluation of the respondent's sentence by the District Court even at this late date will be either "artificial" or "unrealistic."

... In *Burgett* we said that "[t]o permit a conviction obtained in violation of Gideon v. Wainwright to be used against a person either to support guilt or enhance punishment for another offense ... is to erode the principle of that case." Erosion of the *Gideon* principle can be prevented here only by affirming the judgment of the Court of Appeals remanding this case to the trial court for reconsideration of the respondent's sentence.

■ JUSTICE POWELL and JUSTICE REHNQUIST took no part in the consideration or decision of this case.

■ JUSTICE BLACKMUN, with whom THE CHIEF JUSTICE joins, dissenting.

The Court's opinion, of course, is a fine and acceptable exposition of abstract law. If I felt that it fit Tucker's case, I would join it. The Court, however, fails to mention and to give effect to certain facts that, for me, are controlling:

1. At his armed bank robbery trial in May 1953 Tucker was no juvenile. He was 32 years of age and was represented by counsel. A reading of his trial testimony discloses that he was very knowledgeable indeed. Tucker testified on cross-examination at that trial not only as to the fact of three prior state felony convictions, but, as well, as to his engaging in the proscribed conduct underlying two of those convictions. He stated flatly (a) that in 1938 he broke into a garage and took a man's automobile, and (b) that in 1946 he broke into a jewelry store at night. He also acknowledged that, while waiting for transportation to prison in Florida after the third conviction, he escaped and went to California using an assumed name. Thus, wholly apart from formal convictions, Tucker conceded criminal conduct on his part on three separate prior occasions.

2. The judge who presided at Tucker's pre-*Gideon* trial for armed bank robbery in 1953 was the Honorable George B. Harris of the United States District Court for the Northern District of California. After Tucker's conviction by a jury Judge Harris imposed the 25–year maximum sentence. Despite the interim passage of 16 years, Tucker's present petition, filed pursuant to 28 U.S.C. § 2255, also came before the very same Judge Harris, then Chief Judge of the Northern District. The judge denied relief on the ground that the error in the use, for impeachment purposes, of two constitutionally invalid prior convictions was harmless beyond a reasonable doubt (a) because the issue of guilt or innocence was not at all close, (b) because Tucker's testimony "had been successfully impeached by prior inconsistent statements made to the Federal Bureau of Investigation agents, and by rebuttal testimony which demonstrated that portions of [his] testimony [were] improbable and untrue," and (c) because his "testimony was successfully impeached, and, in fact, demolished by additional items." Tucker v. United States, 299 F.Supp. 1376, 1378 (N.D.Cal.1969).

Chief Judge Harris' § 2255 ruling translates for me into something completely inescapable, namely, that in 1953, wholly apart from the 1938 and 1946 convictions, he would have imposed the 25–year maximum sentence anyway. Surely Judge Harris, of all people, is the best source of knowledge as to the effect, if any, of those two convictions in his determination of the sentence to be imposed. Yet the Court speculates that, despite his identity and despite his obvious disclaimer, Judge Harris might have been influenced in his sentencing by the fact of the two prior convictions, rather than by the three criminal acts that Tucker himself acknowledged.

On remand the case presumably will go once again to Judge Harris, and undoubtedly the same sentence once again will be imposed. Perhaps this is all worthwhile and, if so, I must be content with the Court's disposition of the case on general principles. I entertain more than a mild suspicion, however, that this is an exercise in futility, that the Court is merely marching up the hill only to march right down again, and that it is time we become just a little realistic in the face of a record such as this one.

NOTES

1. In Tucker, a pre-guidelines case, judges had a very wide discretion in fashioning sentences.

2. When a defendant challenges information in a presentence report, the court must make findings concerning the accuracy of the information *or* state that the disputed information is not being relied upon. United States v. Stewart, 770 F.2d 825 (9th Cir.1985).

3. In Custis v. United States, 511 U.S. 485, 114 S.Ct. 1732 (1994) the Court construed the Armed Career Criminal Act (which increases sentences for those with prior convictions) to preclude defendants from challenging prior conviction at their sentencing hearing except when there was a complete denial of counsel in the prior proceeding. In so doing it limited the constitutional rule in Tucker to cases in which defendant was utterly without counsel in the prior proceeding. The Court did say that Custis could attack his prior convictions either in state or federal court and, if successful, may apply for reopening of the federal sentence. The Court did not express any view on whether or not the sentence should or would be reopened.

3. The Federal sentencing scheme allows the defendant, subject to a statute of limitations, to attack prior convictions which federal prosecutors seek to use for enhancement purposes. The defendant need not first attempt to use post-conviction remedies to vacate the convictions in the court of origin. He or she can ask the federal judge to adjudicate the validity of such convictions for the limited purposes of deciding whether such convictions can be considered in the federal sentencing proceedings. See 21 U.S.C. § 851; U.S.S.G. § 4A1.2 application note 6.

4. The Guidelines require the trial court to take into account not only the facts of the offense of which a defendant is convicted, but also any other "relevant conduct," defined as including all acts committed or aided by the defendant, all reasonably foreseeable criminal activity of coconspirators, and for certain crimes, all acts that were "part of the same course of conduct or common scheme or plan." U.S.S.G. § 1B1.3. If the defendant contests them, the prosecution bears the burden of proving these other offenses at the sentencing hearing by a preponderance of evidence (See Section B2, supra). Although judges have been considering such information for years, the explicit findings and formalized process required by the Guidelines have made the constitutional and practical difficulties with such hearings more apparent. For example: (1) Can the government, consistent with double jeopardy principles, prosecute the defendant for a crime already proven and taken into account to enhance a prior sentence? Witte v. United States, 515 U.S. 389, 115 S.Ct. 2199 (1995) (yes). (2) Can the government prove at sentencing crimes it dropped from its indictment as part of a plea agreement or crimes it never charged? United States v. Patten, 40 F.3d 774 (5th Cir.1994) (yes). (3) Can the government, consistent with due process and the Confrontation Clause, prove crimes at sentencing by a preponderance standard of proof and hearsay evidence that it failed to prove at trial by proof beyond a reasonable doubt? United States v. Watts, 519 U.S. 148, 117 S.Ct. 633 (1997) (yes) (The Court left open the question whether a higher standard of proof should be required where the acquitted conduct is more important to the sentence than the offense for which defendant is convicted). (4) Can a defendant, consistent with 5th Amendment principles, be required to admit uncharged crimes in order to merit a sentence reduction for acceptance of responsibility? See United States v. Piper, 918 F.2d 839 (9th Cir.1990) (no); United States v. Rutledge, 28 F.3d 998 (9th Cir.1994) (silence is protected, not perjury); United States v. Johns, 27 F.3d 31 (2d Cir.1994) (under Guidelines, defendant's sentence cannot be increased for obstruction of justice for denying guilt).(5) Can the government, consistent with Fourth Amendment principles, use evidence of other criminal conduct at sentencing that was suppressed at trial as the fruit of an unlawful search? United States v. Kim, 25 F.3d 1426 (9th Cir.1994) (yes); United States v. Tejada, 956 F.2d 1256 (2d Cir.1992) ("a sentencing judge should consider illegally obtained evidence where it was not seized expressly to enhance the sentence"). (6) Can a defendant's sentence been enhanced, consistent with the Fifth Amendment, if a judge finds by a preponderance of evidence that defendant committed perjury at trial? United States v. Dunnigan, 507 U.S. 87, 113 S.Ct. 1111 (1993) (yes); (7) Can the government, consistent with the Sixth Amendment, seek to enhance a defendant's prison sentence based on prior, uncounseled misdemeanor convictions? See Nichols v. United States, 511 U.S. 738, 114 S.Ct. 1921 (1994) (yes, as long as no term of confinement was required for the prior conviction, overruling Baldasar v. Illinois, 446 U.S. 222, 100 S.Ct. 1585 (1980)).

Compare ABA Criminal Justice Sentencing Standards 18–3.6 (1994) (restricting consideration at sentencing to offense of conviction, because "infliction of punishment for a given crime ought to be preceded by conviction for that crime" and "real-offense sentencing gives the government 'two bites at the apple' for proof of criminal conduct."); Lear, Is Conviction Irrelevant? 40 U.C.L.A. L. Rev. 1179 (1993); Alschuler, *The Failure of Sentencing Guidelines; A Plea for Less Aggrega-*

tion, 58 U.Chi.L.Rev. 901 (1991); United States v. Galloway, 976 F.2d 414, 436–44 (8th Cir.1992) (Bright, Arnold, Lay and MacMillan, JJ., dissenting).

Can the government, consistent with double jeopardy principles, re-prove relevant conduct against a defendant at a second sentencing hearing even if an appellate court held the government's case to be insufficient at the first sentencing hearing? Monge v. California, 524 U.S. 721, 118 S.Ct. 2246 (1998) (suggests the answer is yes). May a defendant, consistent with the 5th Amendment, who seeks a sentence below the mandatory minimum be required to disclose any uncharged acts qualifying as relevant conduct? United States v. Cruz, 156 F.3d 366 (2d Cir.1998).

5. The Supreme Court, in a 5–4 decision, held that a defendant who has pled guilty still retains a Fifth Amendment right to remain silent at the sentencing hearing, and the sentencing judge may not draw any adverse inferences from the defendant's failure to rebut testimony proffered by the prosecutor concerning the details of the crime. Mitchell v. United States, 526 U.S. 314, 119 S.Ct. 1307 (1999). In *Mitchell*, the defendant pled guilty to a drug trafficking offense, but the amount of drugs involved was determined at the sentencing hearing. The defense attorney challenged the testimony of the prosecutor's witnesses, but the defendant herself did not testify. The judge explicitly said that he was drawing an adverse inference from her failure to take the stand and rebut the testimony. The Court, in an opinion by Justice Kennedy, held that the defendant retained her Fifth Amendment privilege, even though she had pled guilty, and even though the case involved a sentencing proceeding rather than a trial. Relying on Estelle v. Smith, 451 U.S. 454, 101 S.Ct. 1866, the Court held it "well-established" that a defendant retains a Fifth Amendment privilege at sentencing. The Court declined the government's theory that a guilty plea (in which defendant admits certain facts about the crime) amounted to the same thing as defendant's taking the stand, waiving privilege as in Rogers v. United States, 340 U.S. 367, 71 S.Ct. 438 (1951):

> "There is no convincing reason why the narrow inquiry at the plea colloquy should entail such an extensive waiver of the privilege. Unlike the defendant taking the stand, who 'cannot reasonably claim that the Fifth Amendment gives him ... an immunity from cross-examination on the matters he has himself put in dispute,' [citation omitted], the defendant who pleads guilty puts nothing in dispute regarding the essentials of the offense. Rather, the defendant takes those matters out of dispute, often by making a joint statement with the prosecution or confirming the prosecution's version of the facts. Under these circumstances, there is little danger that the court will be misled by selective disclosure. In this respect a guilty plea is more like an offer to stipulate than a decision to take the stand. Here, petitioner's statement that she had done 'some of' the proffered conduct did not pose a threat to the integrity of factfinding proceedings, for the purpose of the District Court's inquiry was simply to ensure that petitioner understood the charges and that there was a factual basis for the Government's case."

The Court asserted the importance of retaining the Fifth Amendment privilege at sentencing:

> "Treating a guilty plea as a waiver of the privilege at sentencing would be a grave encroachment on the rights of defendants. At oral argument, we asked counsel for the United States whether, on the facts of this case, if Government had no reliable evidence of the amount of drugs involved, the prosecutor 'could say, well, we can't prove it, but we'd like to put her on the stand and cross-examine her and see if we can't get her to admit it.' Tr. of Oral Arg. 45. Counsel answered: 'The waiver analysis that we have put forward suggests that at least as to the facts surrounding the conspiracy to

which she admitted, the Government could do that.' Ibid. Over 90% of federal criminal defendants whose cases are not dismissed enter pleas of guilty or nolo contendere.... Were we to accept the Government's position, prosecutors could indict without specifying the quantity of drugs involved, obtain a guilty plea, and then put the defendant on the stand at sentencing to fill in the drug quantity. The result would be to enlist the defendant as an instrument in his or her own condemnation, undermining the long tradition and vital principle that criminal proceedings rely on accusations proved by the Government, not on inquisitions conducted to enhance its own prosecutorial power."

The majority left open the question whether a defendant's failure to testify could be relevant to her "contrition" or "acceptance of responsibility."

Justice Scalia, joined by the Chief Justice, Justice O'Connor, and Justice Thomas, dissented. He called into question the historic pedigree of the rule in Griffin v. California, 380 U.S. 609, 85 S.Ct. 1229 (1965), that the prosecutor or judge could not ask the jury to draw an adverse inference from the defendant's failure to testify. Given the fact that this was not the rule at common law, Justice Scalia argued that *Griffin* should not be extended to the sentencing context. He also asserted that, given the wide-ranging nature of the evidence which can be considered in sentencing proceedings, it would be impossible to separate impermissible adverse inferences from defendant's silence as to the facts of the offense from permissible adverse inferences from the defendant's silence as to the defendant's character or remorse:

> "Which brings me to the greatest—the most bizarre—inconsistency of all: the combination of the rule that the Court adopts today with the balance of our jurisprudence relating to sentencing in particular. 'Courts in this country and in England,' we have said, have 'practiced a policy under which a sentencing judge [can] exercise a wide discretion in the sources and types of evidence used to assist him in determining the kind and extent of punishment to be imposed within limits fixed by law.' " Williams v. New York, at 246. "[A] sentencing judge 'may appropriately conduct an inquiry broad in scope, largely unlimited either as to the kind of information he may consider, or the source from which it may come.' " Nichols v. United States, 511 U.S. 738, 747 (1994) (quoting United States v. Tucker, 404 U.S. 443, 446 (1972)). "Few facts available to a sentencing judge," we have observed, "are more relevant to 'the likelihood that [a defendant] will transgress no more, the hope that he may respond to rehabilitative efforts to assist with a lawful future career, [and] the degree to which he does or does not deem himself at war with his society' " than a defendant's willingness to cooperate. Roberts v. United States, 445 U.S. 552, 558 (1980). See also 18 U.S.C. § 3661 ("No limitation shall be placed on the information concerning the background, character, and conduct of a person convicted of an offense which a court of the United States may receive and consider to the purpose of imposing an appropriate sentence.") Today's opinion states, in as inconspicuous a manner as possible at the very end of its analysis (one imagines that if the statement were delivered orally it would be spoken in a very low voice, and with the Court's hand over its mouth), that its holding applies only to inferences drawn from silence "in determining facts of the offense." Ante, at 15. "Whether silence bears upon the determination of a lack of remorse, or upon acceptance of responsibility for purposes of the downward adjustment provided in § 3E1.1 of the United States Sentencing Guidelines (1998) is a separate question" on which the majority expresses no view. Ibid. Never mind that we have said before, albeit in dicta, that "we doubt that a principled distinction may be

drawn between 'enhancing' the punishment imposed upon the petitioner and denying him the 'leniency' he claims would be appropriate if he had cooperated." Roberts, supra, at 557, n. 4.

Of course the clutter swept under the rug by limiting the opinion to "determining facts of the offense" is not merely application of today's opinion to § 3E1.1, but its application to all determinations of acceptance of responsibility, repentance, character, and future dangerousness, in both federal and state prosecutions—that is to say, to what is probably the bulk of what most sentencing is all about. If the Court ultimately decides—in the fullness of time and after a decent period of confusion in the lower courts—that the "no inference" rule is indeed limited to "determining facts of the offense," then we will have a system in which a state court can increase the sentence of a convicted drug possessor who refuses to say how many ounces he possessed—not because that suggests he possessed the larger amount (to make such an inference would be unconstitutional!) but because his refusal to cooperate suggests he is unrepentant. Apart from the fact that there is no logical basis for drawing such a line within the sentencing phase (whereas drawing a line between guilt and sentencing is entirely logical), the result produced provides new support for Mr. Bumble's renowned evaluation of the law. Its only sensible feature is that it will almost always be unenforceable, since it will ordinarily be impossible to tell whether the sentencer has used the silence for either purpose or for neither.

If, on the other hand, the Court ultimately decides—in the fullness of time and after a decent period of confusion in the lower courts—that the extension of Griffin announced today is not limited to "determining facts of the offense," then it will have created a system in which we give the sentencing judge access to all sorts of out-of-court evidence, including the most remote hearsay, concerning the character of the defendant, his prior misdeeds, his acceptance of responsibility and determination to mend his ways, but declare taboo the most obvious piece of first-hand evidence standing in front of the judge: the defendant's refusal to cooperate with the court. Such a rule orders the judge to avert his eyes from the elephant in the courtroom when it is the judge's job to size up the elephant.

The patent inadequacy of both of these courses with regard to determining matters other than the "facts of the offense" is not finessed by simply resolving, for the time being, not to choose between them. Sooner or later the choice must be made, and the fact that both alternatives are unsatisfactory cries out that the Court's extension of Griffin is a mistake.

Justice Thomas wrote separately to agree that *Griffin* had been wrongly decided and to suggest that he would be amenable to overruling it.

2. THE DEFENDANT'S WORDS AND ACTIONS

(a) REFUSING TO COOPERATE WITH AUTHORITIES

Roberts v. United States

Supreme Court of the United States, 1980.
445 U.S. 552, 100 S.Ct. 1358.

■ JUSTICE POWELL delivered the opinion of the Court.

I

Petitioner Winfield Roberts accompanied Cecilia Payne to the office of the United States Attorney for the District of Columbia one day in June of

1975. Government surveillance previously had revealed that a green Jaguar owned by Payne was used to transport heroin within the District. Payne told investigators that she occasionally lent the Jaguar to petitioner, who was waiting outside in the hall. At Payne's suggestion the investigators asked petitioner if he would answer some questions. Although petitioner was present voluntarily, the investigators gave him the warnings required by Miranda v. Arizona (1966). They also told him that he was free to leave. When petitioner indicated that he would stay, the investigators asked whether he knew "Boo" Thornton, then the principle target of the heroin investigation. Petitioner admitted that he had delivered heroin to Thornton on several occasions. Confessing also that he had discussed drug transactions with Thornton in certain intercepted telephone conversations, petitioner explained the meaning of code words used in the conversations. When asked to name suppliers, however, petitioner gave evasive answers. Although the investigators warned petitioner that the extent of his cooperation would bear on the charges brought against him, he provided no further information.

* * *

[Roberts eventually pleaded guilty to two counts of using a telephone to facilitate the distribution of heroin]. The District Court imposed consecutive sentences of one to four years on each count and a special parole term of three years, but it declined to impose a fine. The Court explained that these sentences were appropriate because petitioner was on parole from a bank robbery conviction at the time of the offenses, and because he was a dealer who had refused to cooperate with the Government.

* * *

II

No misinformation was present in this case. The sentencing court relied upon essentially undisputed facts. There is no question that petitioner rebuffed repeated requests for his cooperation over a period of three years. Nor does petitioner contend that he was unable to provide the requested assistance.... Unless a different explanation is provided, a defendant's refusal to assist in the investigation of ongoing crimes gives rise to an inference that these laudable attitudes are lacking.

It hardly could be otherwise. Concealment of crime has been condemned throughout our history. The citizen's duty to "raise the 'hue and cry' and report felonies to the authorities," ... Although the term "misprision of felony" now has an archaic ring, gross indifference to the duty to report known criminal behavior remains a badge of irresponsible citizenship.

This deeply rooted social obligation is not diminished when the witness to crime is involved in illicit activities himself. Unless his silence is protected by the privilege against self-incrimination, the criminal defendant no less than any other citizen is obliged to assist the authorities. The petitioner, for example, was asked to expose the purveyors of heroin in his own community in exchange for a favorable disposition of his case. By declining to cooperate, petitioner rejected an "obligatio[n] of community life" that should be recognized before rehabilitation can begin. Moreover, petitioner's refusal to cooperate protected his former partners in crime, thereby preserving his ability to resume criminal activities upon release.

* * *

III

Petitioner does not seriously contend that disregard for the obligation to assist in a criminal investigation is irrelevant to the determination of an appropriate sentence. He rather contends that his failure to cooperate was justified by legitimate fears of physical retaliation and self-incrimination. In view of these concerns, petitioner asserts that his refusal to act as an informer has no bearing on his prospects for rehabilitation. He also believes that the District Court punished him for exercising his Fifth Amendment privilege against self-incrimination.

These arguments would have merited serious consideration if they had been presented properly to the sentencing judge. But the mere possibility of unarticulated explanations or excuses for anti-social conduct does not make that conduct irrelevant to the sentencing decision. The District Court had no opportunity to consider the theories that petitioner now advances, for each was raised for the first time in petitioner's appellate brief. Although petitioner knew that his intransigency would be used against him, neither he nor his lawyer offered any explanation to the sentencing court. Even after the prosecutor observed that the failure to cooperate could be viewed as evidence of continuing criminal intent, petitioner remained silent.

Petitioner insists that he had a constitutional right to remain silent and that no adverse inferences can be drawn from the exercise of that right. We find this argument singularly unpersuasive. The Fifth Amendment privilege against compelled self-incrimination is not self-executing. At least where the government has no substantial reason to believe that the requested disclosures are likely to be incriminating, the privilege may not be relied upon unless it is invoked in a timely fashion....

* * *

Petitioner has identified nothing that might have impaired his " 'free choice to admit, to deny, or to refuse to answer.' " His conduct bears no resemblance to the "insolubly ambiguous" post-arrest silence that may be induced by the assurances contained in *Miranda* warnings. If we were to invalidate petitioner's sentence on the record before us, we would sanction an unwarranted interference with a function traditionally vested in the trial courts.

■ JUSTICE BRENNAN, concurring.

I join the Court's opinion.

I agree with the Court that the trial judge cannot be faulted for drawing a negative inference from petitioner's noncooperation when petitioner failed to suggest that other, neutral, inferences were available.

* * *

Nevertheless, the problem of drawing inferences from an ambiguous silence is troubling. As a matter of due process, an offender may not be sentenced on the basis of mistaken facts or unfounded assumptions.... It is of comparable importance to assure that a defendant is not penalized on the basis of groundless inferences. At the least, sentencing judges should conduct an inquiry into the circumstances of silence where a defendant indicates before sentencing that his refusal to cooperate is prompted by constitutionally protected, or morally defensible, motives. Furthermore, especially where conviction is based upon a guilty plea, it may be advisable for trial judges to raise the question of motive themselves when presented with a prosecutorial recommendation for severity due to an offender's noncooperation. During the allocution before sentencing, the defendant could be asked on the record whether he has a reasonable explanation for his silence; if a justification were proffered, the judge would then proceed to determine its veracity and reasonableness. Such an allocution procedure would reduce the danger of erroneous inference and provide a record to support sentencing against subsequent challenge....

■ JUSTICE MARSHALL, dissenting.

* * *

There can be no doubt that a judge would be barred from increasing the length of a jail sentence because of a defendant's refusal to cooperate based on the constitutional privilege against self-incrimination. In such a case, the threat of a longer sentence of imprisonment would plainly be compulsion within the meaning of the Fifth Amendment. Such an aggravation of sentence would amount to an impermissible penalty imposed solely because of the defendant's assertion of the Fifth Amendment privilege.

I also believe that it would be an abuse of discretion for a judge to use a defendant's refusal to become an informer to increase the length of a sentence when the refusal was motivated by a fear of retaliation. In such a case, the failure to identify other participants in the crime is irrelevant to the defendant's prospects for rehabilitation, and bears no relation to any of the legitimate purposes of sentencing.

* * *

The enhancement of petitioner's sentence, then, was impermissible because it may have burdened petitioner's exercise of his constitutional rights or been based on a factor unrelated to the permissible goals of sentencing. In addition, it represented an improper involvement of the judicial office in the prosecutorial function that should be corrected through our supervisory power over the federal courts.

* * *

I find disturbing the majority's willingness to brush aside these serious objections to the propriety of petitioner's sentence on the strength of "the duty to report known criminal behavior."

* * *

American society has always approved those who own up to their wrong doing and vow to do better, just as it has admired those who come to the aid of the victims of criminal conduct. But our admiration of those who inform on others has never been as unambiguous as the majority suggests. The countervailing social values of loyalty and personal privacy have prevented us from imposing on the citizenry at large a duty to join in the business of crime detection. If the Court's view of social mores were accurate, it would be hard to understand how terms such as "stoolpigeon," "snitch," "squealer," and "tattletale" have come to be the common description of those who engage in such behavior.

I do not, of course, suggest that those who have engaged in criminal activity should refuse to cooperate with the authorities. The informer plays a vital role in the struggle to check crime, especially the narcotics trade. We could not do without him. In recognition of this role, it is fully appropriate to encourage such behavior by offering leniency in exchange for "cooperation." Cooperation of that sort may be a sign of repentance and the beginning of rehabilitation. But our government has allowed its citizens to decide for themselves whether to enlist in the enterprise of enforcing the criminal laws; it has never imposed a duty to do so, as the Court's opinion suggests. I find no justification for creating such a duty in this case and applying it only to persons about to be sentenced for a crime.

* * *

NOTE

Under 1987 federal sentencing law a defendant's refusal to assist authorities in the investigation of other persons may not be considered as an aggravating sentencing factor. U.S.S.G. § 5K1.2

(b) PERJURY

United States v. Grayson

Supreme Court of the United States, 1978.
438 U.S. 41, 98 S.Ct. 2610.

■ Chief Justice Burger delivered the opinion of the Court.

Grayson was confined in a federal prison camp. He escaped but was apprehended two days later by FBI agents in New York City. He was indicted for prison escape.

During its case in chief, the United States proved the essential elements of the crime, including his lawful confinement and the unlawful escape. In addition, it presented the testimony of the arresting FBI agents that Grayson, upon being apprehended, denied his true identity.

Grayson testified in his own defense. He admitted leaving the camp but asserted that he did so out of fear: "I had just been threatened with a large stick with a nail protruding through it by an inmate that was serving time at Allenwood, and I was scared, and I just ran." He testified that the threat was made in the presence of many inmates by prisoner Barnes who sought to enforce collection of a gambling debt and followed other threats and physical assaults made for the same purpose. Grayson called one inmate, who testified: "I heard [Barnes] talk to Grayson in a loud voice one day, but that's all. In ever seen no harm, no hands or no shuffling whatsoever."

Grayson's version of the facts was contradicted by the Government's rebuttal evidence and by cross-examination on crucial aspects of his story. For example, Grayson stated that after crossing the prison fence he left his prison jacket by the side of the road. On recross, he stated that he also lef this prison shirt but not his trousers. Government testimony showed that on the morning after the escape, a shirt marked with Grayson's number, a jacket, and a pair of prison trousers were found outside a hole in the prison fence. Grayson also testified on cross-examination: "I do believe that I phrased the rhetorical question to Captain Kurd, who was in charge of [the prison], and I think I said something if an inmate was being threatened by somebody, what would ... he do? First of all he said he would want to know who it was." On further cross-examination, however, Grayson modified his description of the conversation. Captain Kurd testified that Grayson had never mentioned in any fashion threats from other inmates. Finally, the alleged assailant, Barnes, by then no longer an inmate, testified that Grayson had never owed him any money and that he had never threatened or physically assaulted Grayson.

The jury returned a guilty verdict, whereupon the District Judge ordered the United States Probation Office to prepare a presentence report. At the sentencing hearing, the judge stated: ...

> *it is my view that your defense was a complete fabrication without the slightest merit whatsoever. I feel it is proper for me to consider that fact in the sentencing, and I will do so.* (Emphasis added.)

In his due process argument, Grayson does not contend directly that the District Court had an impermissible purpose in considering his perjury and selecting the sentence. Rather, he argues that this Court, in order to preserve due process rights, not only must prohibit the impermissible sentencing practice of incarcerating for the purpose of saving the Government the burden of bringing a separate and subsequent perjury prosecution but also must prohibit the otherwise *permissible* practice of considering a defendant's untruthfulness for the purpose of illuminating his need for rehabilitation and society's need for protection. He presents two interrelated reasons. The effect of both permissible and impermissible sentencing practices may be the same: additional time in prison. Further, it is virtually impossible, he contends, to identify and establish the impermissible practice. We find these reasons insufficient justification for prohibiting what the Court and the Congress have declared appropriate judicial conduct.

... The "parlous" effort to appraise "character," *United States v. Hendrix* degenerates into a game of chance to the extent that a sentencing judge is deprived of relevant information concerning "every aspect of a defendant's life." *Williams v. New York.* The Government's interest, as well as the offender's, in avoiding irrationality is of the highest order. That interest more than justifies the risk that Grayson asserts is present when a sentencing judge considers a defendant's untruthfulness under oath.

Second, in our view, *Williams* fully supports consideration of such conduct in sentencing. There the Court permitted the sentencing judge to consider the offender's history of prior anti social conduct, including burglaries for which he had not been duly convicted. This it did despite the risk that the judge might use his knowledge of the offender's prior crimes for an improper purpose.

Third, the efficacy of Grayson's suggested "exclusionary rule" is open to serious doubt. No rule of law, even one garbed in constitutional terms, can prevent improper use of firsthand observations of perjury. The integrity of the judges, and their fidelity to their oaths of office, necessarily provide the only, and in our view adequate, assurance against that.

Grayson's argument that judicial consideration of his conduct at trial impermissibly "chills" a defendant's statutory right, and perhaps a constitutional right to testify on his own behalf is without basis. The right guaranteed by law to a defendant is narrowly the right to testify truthfully in accordance with the oath—unless we are to say that the oath is mere ritual without meaning. This view of the right involved is confirmed by the unquestioned constitutionality of perjury statutes, which punish those who willfully give false testimony. Further support for this is found in an important limitation on a defendant's right to the assistance of counsel: Counsel ethically cannot assist his client in presenting what the attorney has reason to believe is false testimony. Assuming, *arguendo*, that the sentencing judge's consideration of defendants' untruthfulness in testifying has any chilling effect on a defendant's decision to testify falsely, that effect is entirely permissible. There is no protected right to commit perjury.

Grayson's further argument that the sentencing practice challenged here will inhibit exercise of the right to testify truthfully is entirely frivolous. That argument misapprehends the nature and scope of the practice we find permissible. Nothing we say today requires a sentencing judge to enhance, in some wooden or reflex fashion, the sentences of all defendants whose testimony is deemed false. Rather, we are reaffirming the authority of a sentencing judge to evaluate carefully a defendant's testimony on the stand, determine—with a consciousness of the frailty of human judgment—whether that testimony contained willful and material falsehoods, and, if so, assess in light of all the other knowledge gained about the defendant the meaning of that conduct with respect to his prospects for rehabilitation and restoration to a useful place in society. Awareness of such a process realistically cannot be deemed to affect the decision of an accused but unconvicted defendant to testify truthfully in his own behalf.

■ JUSTICE STEWART, with whom JUSTICE BRENNAN and JUSTICE MARSHALL join, dissenting.

The Court begins its consideration of this case, with the assumption that the respondent gave false testimony at his trial. But there has been no determination that his testimony was false. This respondent was given a greater sentence than he would otherwise have received—how much greater we have no way of knowing—solely because a single judge *thought* that he had not testified truthfully. In essence, the Court holds today that *whenever* a defendant testifies in his own behalf and is found guilty, he opens himself to the possibility of an enhanced sentence. Such a sentence is nothing more or less than a penalty imposed on the defendant's exercise of his constitutional and statutory rights to plead not guilty and to testify in his own behalf.

It does not change matters to say that the enhanced sentence merely reflects the defendant's "prospects for rehabilitation" rather than an additional punishment for testifying falsely. The fact remains that all defendants who choose to testify, and only those who do so, face the very real prospect of a greater sentence based upon the trial judge's unreviewable perception that the testimony was untruthful. The Court prescribes no limitations or safeguards to minimize a defendant's rational fear that his truthful testimony will be perceived as false. Indeed, encumbrance of the sentencing process with the collateral inquiries necessary to provide such assurance would be both pragmatically unworkable and theoretically inconsistent with the assumption that the trial judge is merely considering one more piece of information in his overall evaluation of the defendant's prospects for rehabilitation. But without such safeguards I fail to see how the Court can dismiss as "frivolous" the argument that this sentencing practice will "inhibit exercise of the right to testify truthfully."

A defendant's decision to testify may be inhibited by a number of considerations, such as the possibility that damaging evidence not otherwise admissible will be admitted to impeach his credibility. These constraints arise solely from the fact that the defendant is quite properly treated like any other witness who testifies at trial. But the practice that the Court approves today actually places the defendant at a disadvantage, as compared with any other witness at trial, simply because he is the defendant. Other witnesses risk punishment for perjury only upon indictment and conviction in accord with the full protections of the Constitution. Only the defendant himself, whose testimony is likely to be of critical importance to his defense, faces the additional risk that the disbelief of a single listener will itself result in time in prison.

The minimal contribution that the defendant's possibly untruthful testimony might make to an overall assessment of his potential for rehabilitation, seen. 3, *supra*, cannot justify imposing this additional burden on his right to testify in his own behalf.

NOTE

The Supreme Court later unanimously reaffirmed that a defendant who testifies falsely at trial may have her sentence increased upon a sentencing judge's finding that perjury was committed; this does not undermine the right to testify since a defendant may testify and be convicted without necessarily committing perjury, i.e., confusion, mistake or faulty memory may be the cause of untrue testimony. United States v. Dunnigan, 507 U.S. 87, 113 S.Ct. 1111 (1993). Based on Guidelines commentary that "in respect to alleged false testimony or statements by the defendant, such testimony or statements should be evaluated in a light most favorable to the defendant," § 3C1.1, the D.C. Circuit (among others) required that trial judges be convinced of defendants' perjury by clear and convincing evidence before factoring it into the sentence. United States v. Montague, 40 F.3d 1251 (D.C.Cir.1994). However, the Sentencing Commission amended the guidelines in 1997 "so that it no longer suggests the use of a heightened standard of proof." U.S.S.G. Amendment 566 (1997).

(c) ACCEPTANCE OF RESPONSIBILITY

The federal law accords a reduction of sentence to one who accepts responsibility. This rule has been attacked as violative of the Fifth Amendment by forcing defendant to admit guilt in part or whole or even to plead guilty. The arguments have been uniformly rejected. United States v. Mondello, 927 F.2d 1463 (9th Cir.1991); United States v. Cordell, 924 F.2d 614 (6th Cir.1991) (rule not facially invalid but might be invalid in some applications). Courts have construed the rule to avoid constitutional conflict. One need not plead guilty to accept responsibility. United States v. Thomas, 870 F.2d 174 (5th Cir.1989). The arguments that the defense of entrapment is inconsistent with acceptance of responsibility have been rejected. United States v. Fleener, 900 F.2d 914 (6th Cir.1990). One court, on non-constitutional grounds, held that acceptance of responsibility could not be denied where a defendant refused to be interviewed by the probation officer without an attorney—the court said the attorney should be present if defendant so requests. United States v. Herrera–Figueroa, 918 F.2d 1430 (9th Cir.1990).

A tougher issue implicating 5th Amendment concerns is presented when a trial judge requires a defendant to admit to uncharged or acquitted conduct in order to qualify for an acceptance of responsibility reduction. See United States v. Piper, 918 F.2d 839 (9th Cir.1990) (defendant cannot be required to admit to uncharged or acquitted conduct in order to quality for reduction); United States v. Rutledge, 28 F.3d 998 (9th Cir.1994) (court may deny the reduction when defendant has falsely denied involvement in relevant conduct); United States v. Johns, 27 F.3d 31 (2d Cir.1994) (court may not enhance sentence for obstruction of justice merely because defendant has denied involvement in relevant conduct).

The Second Circuit, which had previously held that a defendant could not be required to admit to other crimes in order to qualify for an acceptance of responsibility reduction, United States v. Oliveras, 905 F.2d 623 (2d Cir.1990), recently decided that a defendant could be required to admit to other crimes in order to qualify for a reduction below the mandatory minimum under special "safety valve" legislation for first-time offenders. United States v. Cruz, 156 F.3d 366 (2d Cir.1998). The court called into doubt its *Oliveras* reasoning, and characterized *Oliveras*' comments on Fifth Amendment requirements as dicta (the holding resting only on statutory interpretation, not constitutional grounds): "Contrary to the reasoning in *Oliveras* that a defendant will feel compelled to provide incriminating information to earn a reduction in his or her sentence, we hold that the choice confronting the defendant gives rise to no more compulsion than that present in a typical plea bargain."

(d) OTHER FACTORS

United States v. Bakker

United States Court of Appeals, Fourth Circuit, 1991.
925 F.2d 728.

■ Wilkinson, Circuit Judge:

This appeal stems from the trial and sentencing of a well-known televangelist, James O. Bakker....

In 1974, James Bakker formed a corporation known as the PTL. PTL stands for "Praise the Lord" and "People that Love." The PTL's activities soon expanded from their initial focus on televised religious broadcasting. For example, in the late 1970s PTL began construction on "Heritage USA," described by PTL officials as a Christian retreat center for families. The concept of the center became increasingly ambitious. In 1983, Bakker announced plans to enlarge the center by adding a vacation park, "Heritage Village," that would include the 500–room Grand Hotel. Between 1984 and 1986, appellant announced further proposals to expand the Village by constructing the Towers Hotel, 50 bunkhouses, and several additional facilities.

Bakker planned to finance these projects by selling lifetime partnerships. He offered eleven different partnership programs ranging in cost from $500 to $10,000. Eight of the partnerships promised benefits that included annual lodging in one of the Heritage Village facilities. In January 1984, appellant began using the mail to solicit lifetime partners. Also, from February 1984 through May 1987, Bakker used broadcasts carried on the PTL Television Network and various commercial affiliates to solicit lifetime partners. Many of these partners drew on meager incomes to purchase Heritage Village lodging benefits. Appellant raised at least $158 million through the sale of approximately 153,000 partnerships with lodging benefits.

Bakker promised television viewers that he would limit the sale of partnerships to ensure that each partner would be able to use the facilities annually. Appellant, however, oversold the partnerships. He promised, for instance, to limit the sale of Grand Hotel partnerships to 25,000 but actually sold 66,683. In addition, Bakker used relatively few of the funds solicited from the partners to construct promised facilities. In fact, of the proposed Heritage Village facilities, only the Grand Hotel and one bunkhouse were actually completed. Instead, Bakker used partnership funds to pay operating expenses of the PTL and to support a lavish lifestyle. This extravagant living included gold-plated fixtures and a $570 shower curtain in his bathroom, transportation in private jets and limousines, an air-conditioned treehouse for his children and an air-conditioned doghouse for his pets. This combination of overselling partnerships and diverting partnership proceeds meant that the overwhelming majority of the partners never received the lodging benefits Bakker promised them.

In response to these activities, a grand jury on December 5, 1988 indicted Bakker on counts of fraud ... Bakker's trial lasted five weeks. The jury found him guilty on all 24 counts. The court sentenced him to 45 years imprisonment and fined him $500,000.... During sentencing, the judge stated of Bakker: "He had no thought whatever about his victims and those of us who do have a religion are ridiculed as being saps from money-grubbing preachers or priests." Bakker contends that these comments reveal that the trial judge abused his discretion and violated due process by factoring his own sense of religiosity and victimization into the sentence he imposed on Bakker.

In contrast, the government argues that the phrase "those of us" reflects the judge speaking not for himself but for society as a whole. The governmental so contends that the trial court was simply considering the impact of Bakker's crimes on society and was well within its discretion in doing so. We recognize that a sentencing court can consider the impact a defendant's crimes have had on a community and can vindicate that community's interests in justice. See, e.g., United States v. Torres, 901 F.2d 205, 246–47 (2d Cir.1990). To a considerable extent a sentencing judge is the embodiment of public condemnation and social outrage. See, e.g., United States v. Madison, 689 F.2d 1300, 1314–15 (7th Cir.1982). As the community's spokesperson, a judge can lecture a defendant as a lesson to that defendant and as a deterrent to others.[1] If that were all that occurred here, the court would have been properly exercising its discretion, and we would be loathe to disturb what surely is an integral part of the sentencing process.

Sentencing discretion, however, must be exercised within the boundaries of due process. In this case, the trial judge exceeded those boundaries. Courts have held that sentences imposed on the basis of impermissible considerations, such as a defendant's race or national origin, violate due process. See, e.g., United States v. Borrero–Isaza, 887 F.2d 1349, 1352–57 (9th Cir.1989); United States v. Gomez, 797 F.2d 417, 419 (7th Cir.1986) (sentencing more harshly based on nationality or alienage "obviously would be unconstitutional.") While these cases focused on a defendant's characteristics, we believe that similar principles apply when a judge impermissibly takes his own religious characteristics into account in sentencing.

Our Constitution, of course, does not require a person to surrender his or her religious beliefs upon the assumption of judicial office. Courts, however, cannot sanction sentencing procedures that create the perception of the bench as a pulpit from which judges announce their personal sense of religiosity and simultaneously punish defendants for offending it. Whether or not the trial judge has a religion is irrelevant for purposes of sentencing. Regrettably, we are left with the apprehension that the imposition of a lengthy prison term here may have reflected the fact that the court's own sense of religious propriety had somehow been betrayed. In this way, we believe that the trial court abused its discretion in sentencing Bakker.... This resentencing will be carried out by a different district judge to ensure that the ends of due process are achieved.

We remand this case with genuine reluctance because Bakker's assignments of error at the trial phase only underscore a proceeding which was fairly conducted in the face of trying circumstances....

Yet, the fact remains that this case involves the explicit intrusion of personal religious principles as the basis of a sentencing decision; at least,

1. For example, many of the comments the district court made reflect an appropriate exercise of the sentencing function. The court faulted Bakker for believing that he "deserves all of his gain received from the little people who sent in their savings," noted that where "the top management of any organization ... is deceitful and untruthful, it gradually filters down to the lower echelons," and concluded that "there was massive fraud here and I feel like it's going to have to be punished." We find no fault in any of these statements, and believe the court acted well within its discretion in making them.

that is not an unfair reading of the trial court's comments in this case. We recognize that a trial judge on occasion will misspeak during sentencing and that every ill-advised word will not be the basis for reversible error. In this case, however, our review of the sentencing transcript reveals comments that are, in the end, too intemperate to be ignored. Because an impermissible consideration was injected into the sentencing process, we must remand the case.

NOTES

1. There are similar cases overturning sentences for reliance upon improper factors but they are few. See United States v. Messer, 785 F.2d 832 (9th Cir.1986) (refusal to admit uncharged crime); United States v. Lemon, 723 F.2d 922 (D.C.Cir. 1983) (association with a group known to aid fugitives).

The federal guidelines specify that the following are *not* relevant in the determination of a sentence: race, sex, national origin, creed, religion, socio-economic status, lack of guidance as a youth, disadvantaged upbringing. According to the Sentencing Commission, drug and alcohol dependence are not reasons for imposing a sentence below the guidelines. The guidelines also "discourage" courts from factoring in a defendant's mental and emotional conditions, physical condition or appearance, age, education and vocational skills, employment record, family ties and responsibilities, and prior good works.

We have come a long way from sentencing based on rehabilitation. Compare Bazelon, The Morality of the Criminal Law, 49 S. Cal. L. Rev. 385 (1976) (describing cases in which "rotten social background" played an important role in mitigating a sentence).

Given evidence that women are far more likely to have sole responsibility for children than are men, does refusing to take into account family ties and responsibilities disadvantage women relative to men? See Myrna Raeder, Gender and Sentencing: Single Moms, Battered Women and Other Sex–Based Anomalies in the Gender–Free World of the Federal Sentencing Guidelines, 20 Pepp. L. Rev. 905 (1993). On this issue, compare the approaches of United States v. Pozzy, 902 F.2d 133 (1st Cir.1990) (reversing a downward departure for pregnant woman, commenting, "it has been recognized since time immemorial that the sins of parents are visited upon their children"); and United States v. Johnson, 964 F.2d 124 (2d Cir.1992) (allowing downward departure for single mother of four young children, commenting, "we are reluctant to wreak extraordinary destruction on dependents who rely solely on the defendant for their upbringing.").

In Jackson v. State, 364 Md. 192, 772 A.2d 273 (2001), the court remanded for resentencing by a different judge, because the sentencing judge commented: "people moved to Howard County to get away from people like petitioner, who come to Howard County from Baltimore City and act like they are animals living in the jungle."

Should a court allow a victim's close relative to testify at sentencing that she forgives the defendant? The court in Greene v. State, 343 Ark. 526, 37 S.W.3d 579 (2001), said no. The testimony wasn't relevant as mitigating evidence because it did not speak to the character or deeds of the defendant. Neither was it relevant as "victim-impact" evidence: "We conclude that penalty recommendations from family members of the victim are not relevant as victim-impact evidence. Certainly, the penalty recommendation from Edna Burnett that Greene proposes would not counteract mitigating evidence or show the human cost of the murder on the victim's family. But in addition, if this court permitted forgiveness and penalty recommendations as victim-impact evidence, then it stands to reason that it must also allow any evidence of nonforgiveness by the victim's family and any recommendation of a harsher sentence such as death. We cannot condone either brand of testimony as both would interfere with and be irrelevant to a jury's decision on punishment. Indeed, such testimony would have the potential of reducing a trial to 'a contest of irrelevant opinions.' "

2. The ABA has taken issue with the Guidelines approach in its own sentencing standards: "the Standards allow for greater consideration by sentencing courts of the personal characteristics of offenders, even when unrelated to culpability, than the current federal guidelines. There was great concern among the drafters that the federal guidelines were too rigid, not only in structure, but in limiting the 'human' factors permitted to influence sentence decisions. Certainly among federal judges there have been frequent complaints that the federal law institutes 'sentencing by computer.' Standard 18–3.4 was created expressly to deal with such issues. Recognizing the danger that class and racial biases can be imported with the consideration of social and economic characteristics of offenders, the Standards provide that such characteristics should be consulted only as factors in mitigation of sentence, or as having bearing on the choice of sanctions to be imposed." ABA Standards for Criminal Justice Sentencing xxv–xxvi (3rd Ed. 1994). See also, Alschuler, *The Failure of Sentencing Guidelines; A Plea for Less Aggregation*, 58 U.Chi.L.Rev. 901 (1991).

> "Standard 18–3.4: (c) Except as provided in (b), the legislature and the agency should provide that sentencing courts may take into account personal characteristics of offenders not material to their culpability to determine the appropriate types of sanctions to impose or, if the characteristics are indicative of circumstances of hardship, deprivation, or handicap, to lessen the severity of sentences that would have been imposed."

Standard 18–3.4 (d) forbids consideration of race, gender or sexual orientation, national origin, religion or creed, marital status, or political affiliation or belief. Note that some of these factors (sexual orientation, political affiliation) are not forbidden by the Guidelines.

What about "the power to be lenient is also the power to discriminate"?

* * *

CHAPTER 22

POST-TRIAL MOTIONS

United States v. Miller

United States Court of Appeals, Second Circuit, 1969.
411 F.2d 825.

■ FRIENDLY, CIRCUIT JUDGE.

... We affirmed the conviction [for conspiring to import heroin] in an opinion noting that the appeal was "rather unusual these days in that Miller claims he was innocent of the crime charged". ... After holding a petition for certiorari for many months, the Supreme Court denied this on the last day of its 1967 Term. Meanwhile the district court had entered an order, denying a motion for a new trial. ... We are constrained to reverse so much of the order as refused a new trial on the ground of the Government's failure to disclose to the defense the pre-trial hypnosis of its principal witness, in part by the attorney who examined him at trial. ...

* * *

In May 1968, at the request of defense counsel, the Government arranged to have Caron attend at the New York City office of Dr. Herbert Walker for a psychiatric interview including hypnosis in the presence of counsel for both sides. Just before being placed under hypnosis, Caron disclosed he had been hypnotized while in custody in Texas....

Caron had been brought to the Southern District of Texas shortly before the trial of Miller's codefendants in September 1965 and had been extensively interviewed by the prosecutors, including Butler. Caron had then gone into some detail about the car used by the recipients of the second Bridgeport delivery that Butler had not previously heard; he identified the car as an old Buick and indicated that he had taken particular note of the license number. Since the identity of the recipients at Bridgeport was of no great importance in the Texas trial, the prosecutors had not pressed him on that point.

After the Texas trial Butler heard that Caron was threatening not to cooperate in the separate Miller trial, the continuance and prospective transfer of which to Connecticut had apparently become known to him. Butler went to see Caron in jail on February 16, 1966, "to assure him I would do the best I could to help him with his problems," and also to revive the question of his memory of the license number of the Buick. The best Caron could do was to recall that the number included 26. Having "a slight knowledge of hypnotism," Butler asked Caron "whether he would be willing to submit to hypnotism to see whether he could recall the license plate." Caron agreed.

Butler was back on February 21 with Edward B. Cushing whom he regarded as an expert in hypnosis. Cushing got the subject into hypnosis quickly. Caron remembered that the car was a green Buick and that the plates were black on yellow. He muttered the letters AM and then some numbers Butler thought were 526 but Cushing identified as 1826, as Caron confirmed. Since Caron was manifesting some distress, Cushing brought him out of hypnosis. After an interval, a second attempt by Cushing failed to produce hypnosis. Butler decided to take over, thinking that despite his "very limited knowledge of hypnotic techniques," he might have more success because of Caron's confidence in him. He asked Caron to reconstruct the early part of his second trip to Bridgeport in his mind and to tell what he recalled. Caron began this recital substantially as in his interviews with the prosecutors but when he reached the point of being in the restaurant for lunch with his family, Butler's questions became more searching and Caron gave details Butler had not heard before. He described that the Buick would not start, that Frankie and the other man had to raise the hood, and that one of them complained over the choice of the car. There were six digits on the license plates but, while Caron put forward a considerable number of letters and numbers, he was uncertain about them. After suggesting that Caron dream about the license plates that night, Butler brought Caron out of hypnosis.

Butler and Cushing did not let go that easily. After lunch, Cushing again put Caron into hypnosis, and Butler took over the interrogation, this time proceeding to the license plates rather swiftly; Caron was now quite sure about "AM 1826." Cushing sought a description of the second man and got one consistent with what Caron had previously given.

Once the initial surprise over use of hypnosis has subsided, the incident seems rather colorless. Butler appears to have acted in entire good faith in subjecting Caron to hypnosis. He was endeavoring to revive Caron's memory about the license number, and a correct recollection of this could have tended to lead away from Miller as much as toward him. Neither Butler nor Cushing suggested anything to Caron he had not already said. The Government made no use of Caron's dim recollection of the license number at the trial, and the defense does not assert it would have been assisted by this. To the contrary, the one point on which Caron was clear, namely, the colors of the plates, points away from the defense's current theory.

Naturally the defense did not leave the matter in this stance. It adduced, through affidavit or testimony, the evidence of three psychiatrists expert in hypnosis. They claimed in the first instance that repetition under hypnosis of the story Caron had already told tended to imprint this on his mind; ... After the hypnosis, they contended, Caron would always behold Miller as Frank and would be immune to defense suggestions that he had picked the wrong man. Still more damage was wrought in their view by Butler's having acted as hypnotist. This, they said, increased the influence Butler already possessed as the man who could help to relieve Caron of the many problems besetting him, and further reduced the reliability of Caron's testimony at the Connecticut trial, where Butler interrogated Caron and acted for the Government during the protracted cross-examination....

While the expert called by the Government regarded many of these claims as exaggerated, he conceded on cross-examination that if the hypnosis was not conducted according to expert techniques, what happened "could have had an effect" on Caron's subsequent ability to correct a mistake.

Whatever the rights and wrongs of the expert testimony may be, it is undeniable that disclosure of the hypnosis would have added another arrow to the rather large quiver trial counsel for the defense shot at Caron—limited opportunity for observation; initial alleged misdescription and picking the photograph of another man; a suggestion through the inclusion of three photographs of Miller in the dozen initially exhibited; knowledge that the prosecution was pleased with his identification; a lengthy criminal record; a letter written from jail telling his wife he had lied in identifying Frank; the Government's failure to place any charge against his wife, or any charge against him for the Bridgeport crimes; the Government's maintenance of his family during his incarceration; his fear of deportation; and his hope for pardon or commutation of sentence on the charge of smuggling heroin from Mexico to which he had pleaded guilty. It is not difficult to hear the ringing tones in which defense counsel would have told the jury that, not satisfied with "buying" Caron with money for his family and promises of leniency, the Government had blocked the door to repentance under cross-examination and the sanctity of the oath by hypnotism carried out by none other than the examining prosecutor himself. It is altogether plain that if the defense had known of the hypnosis incident and the court had refused to allow its use at the trial, the amount of other impeaching evidence against Caron would not have avoided a reversal.

The issue here differs since the request is for a new trial on the ground of newly discovered evidence. We have noted, the two classical formulations of the criterion—whether the new evidence "is so material that it would probably produce a different verdict, if the new trial were granted," and whether it might have produced a different verdict, a test that has been stated to be limited to cases of "recantation or where it has been proved that false testimony was given at the trial." We think developments during the trial placed a duty on the Government to disclose the hypnosis; that, where such a duty has not been discharged, a motion for a new trial must be granted if there is a significant possibility that the undisclosed evidence might have led to an acquittal or a hung jury; and that such a possibility exists here.

* * *

Repeatedly during several days of cross-examination, Caron was questioned about the license number of the green Buick.

Defense counsel had earlier requested notes of all interviews with Caron in the Galveston jail.... When the court asked whether "everything that was conceivably Jencks Act material in this case had been furnished to defense counsel or to the Court," Mr. Butler had answered in the affirmative, adding "We made a special effort to search the files." But his special effort had not unearthed his memorandum describing the hypnosis, although admittedly it was there....

After full allowance for the problems confronting counsel in the stress of a long and heated trial, the prodding furnished by these episodes must be taken to have served the "valuable office" of "flagging" the pretrial hypnosis, thus placing upon Mr. Butler a duty of disclosure he did not discharge. Even if he did not recall the hypnosis or remember or locate his memorandum of it, he should have, and negligence of the prosecutor in failing to make evidence available to the defense reduces the standard of materiality needed to require the granting of a new trial below the formulations applicable where no prosecutorial misconduct exists.

Negligent or even intentional failure of the prosecutor to disclose an additional item of impeaching evidence would not invariably require that a verdict be set aside. Here, as we have noted, the defense already possessed an abundance of impeaching material, the hypnosis incident seems without much force apart from the elaboration by the defense's psychiatric experts, and we have our own views how seriously a jury of Connecticut Yankees would have been likely to regard that. Still, as the record stands, the hypnosis had arguably placed at least some obstacle in the way of one of the most valuable protections accorded Miller by the Sixth Amendment—the possibility that the sanctity of the oath and effective cross-examination might lead Caron to recant his identification or at least to admit doubt. The defense could and very likely would have made this the capstone of its attack on the crucial witness for the prosecution—with what effect we cannot confidently say. Under all the circumstances, as Judge Swan wrote in Consolidated Laundries, "we are content to rest our decision on our conviction that the denial of a new trial here is inconsistent with the correct administration of criminal justice in the federal courts, which it is our duty as an appellate court to supervise."

We have reached this conclusion with some reluctance, particularly in light of the considered belief of the able and conscientious district judge, who has lived with this case for years, that review of the record in light of all the defense new trial motions left him "convinced of the correctness of the jury's verdict." We, who also have had no small exposure to the facts, are by no means convinced otherwise. The test, however, is not how the newly discovered evidence concerning the hypnosis would affect the trial judge or ourselves but whether, with the Government's case against Miller already subject to serious attack, there was a significant chance that this added item, developed by skilled counsel as it would have been, could have induced a reasonable doubt in the minds of enough jurors to avoid a conviction. We cannot conscientiously say there was not. With the panoply of rules that our legal system has devised to insure fairness in criminal trials, the least appropriate instance for a grudging attitude in applying them would be one where a defendant supposedly leading a blameless life has steadfastly asserted that the prosecution got the wrong man and the proof consisted almost wholly of an identification by an accomplice in the conspiracy and the latter's wife and other testimony by the former. If the price of our decision should be the ultimate escape of a guilty man rather than the vindication of an innocent one, this is the kind of case where that price is worth paying.

■ MOORE, CIRCUIT JUDGE (concurring in the result):

Although I concur in the result reached by the majority, I cannot adopt the hypotheses or philosophies of the opinion except the one ground on which we place common reliance, namely, disclosure of the hypnosis....

The privilege of dealing with the problem in an abstract way is not afforded us here. We are confronted with actual facts: Caron was a key witness; identification of Miller was all-important; Caron was hypnotized and interrogated by the government in advance of trial (and I assume for purposes of developing the truth); defense counsel were not notified of the hypnosis and had no opportunity by examination or cross-examination to explore whatever might have been found at that time in Caron's subconscious mind or memory; defense counsel were not aware of the pre-trial hypnosis before or during the trial or that the prosecuting attorney had participated therein.

Specifically, I do not join in the majority's reference to the defendant's claim that he had led a blameless life and that because he asserted that "the prosecution got the wrong man," we should be willing to pay the price of "the ultimate escape of a guilty man." Any such philosophy strikes at the heart of our jury system. They saw, heard and convicted. It is what they saw and heard that is crucial. Of course no innocent man should be convicted. And this is no time or place to debate the philosophy, at odds with society's experience in most other fields, that it were better that ninety-nine guilty escape rather than one innocent man be convicted. If mistakes there have been, they have been the mistakes of the judgments of the defendants' fellow men.

Thus the only question open here in my opinion is: did the jury have all the facts before them essential to a fair appraisal of Caron's testimony? With full knowledge of the hypnosis incident, the jury might well have been satisfied with Caron's testimony. But this question is for the jury—not for our speculation. On this subject, I add my complete concurrence with the majority's statement that this "decision is not to be taken as implying any view that Caron's hypnosis disqualifies him from testifying on a new trial."

Lastly a word about Butler's supposed influence over Caron. Naturally, to capitalize on the incident to the maximum, the defense would depict Butler as a modern Svengali and Caron (to up-date the simile) as merely his Charlie McCarthy-like puppet. Here again is a jury question. Very few criminal jury cases are tried by equally-matched counsel. A few highly gifted members of the Bar in that field seem to possess extraordinary talents in eliciting testimony that their less talented brethren, fail to develop. This disparity may be countered—and usually is in jury summation—by comment on this very disparity in counsel's abilities. Many a David has overcome a courtroom Goliath. Whether such an appeal has been the cause or not must be kept securely locked in the jury room. Therefore, despite the interesting statistics and speculations of Messrs. Kalven & Zeisel, I prefer to leave to the future jury here their own appraisal of the effectiveness or influence of such counsel as may appear before them. And with similar thoughts in mind, I would refrain from comment on any evidence adduced on the former trial or on any language in our previous opinions relating thereto.

Thus, because the use of hypnosis as a means of attempting to ascertain the truth is, to say the least, novel and apparently subject to differing medical opinions, I believe that under the circumstances of this particular case, the jury should have had this fact before it in weighing Caron's testimony.

NOTES

1. The *Miller* case is unusual in two regards. It extended over an unusually long period of time and the defendant finally prevailed. The general rule (stated in *Miller*) is that motions for new trial on grounds of newly discovered evidence are generally disfavored and only granted with great caution. See United States v. Thornbrugh, 962 F.2d 1438, 1443 (10th Cir.1992). As the Illinois Supreme Court noted in People v. Holtzman, 1 Ill.2d 562, 116 N.E.2d 338 (1953):

> Applications for a new trial on the ground of newly discovered evidence are not looked upon with favor by the courts, and in order to prevent, so far as possible, fraud and imposition which defeated parties may be tempted to practice, as a last resort, to escape the consequence of an adverse verdict, such application should always be subjected to the closest scrutiny by the court, and the burden is upon the applicant to rebut the presumption that the verdict is correct and to show there has been no lack of diligence. The matter is largely discretionary with the trial court, and the exercise of its discretion will not be disturbed except in case of manifest abuse.

See State v. Talbot, 408 So.2d 861 (La.1980) (new trial granted where eyewitness was inconsistent about a crucial point of identification; where another person was proved to have committed other very similar crimes in the area and to have lied about a significant fact when he denied committing this crime—all discovered after trial). The general principle disapproving new trials for newly discovered evidence has very few exceptions. And the trial court can deny them by deciding, on the merits, that the new evidence is not credible. See Adams v. State, 259 Conn. 831, 792 A.2d 809 (2002). Motions for new trial based on prosecution's knowingly withholding or concealing evidence favorable to the accused are not so disfavored. United States v. Garner, 507 F.3d 399 (6th Cir.2007)

Motions for new trial based on improper influence of the jury are rarely filed or granted. Jurors are not commonly subjected to improper influence and, if they are, the matter is usually brought to the court's attention before the end of trial (except when a bailiff makes improper remarks to a jury during deliberation, Parker v. Gladden, 385 U.S. 363, 87 S.Ct. 468 (1966)). Finally, because of the strictures against questioning jurors and their reluctance to answer questions and their ignorance of what is improper, the fact of unauthorized contact by some outsider with the jury is not readily uncovered.

2. Most courts have changed the old rule that motion for new trial was necessary to preserve trial objections for appeal. United States v. Cook, 432 F.2d 1093 (7th Cir.1970) (1971): ("Under federal procedure, it is not necessary to file motion for new trial in order to have reviewed on appeal questions properly preserved at trial"); People v. McCabe, 49 Ill.2d 338, 275 N.E.2d 407 (1971).

If written motions for new trial are or must be filed, several courts deem waived any errors not specifically alleged therein. See Thompson v. State, 257 Ga. 386, 359 S.E.2d 664 (1987); People v. Thomas, 116 Ill.App.3d 216, 219–21, 72 Ill.Dec. 145, 452 N.E.2d 77, 80–81 (1983).

Motions for new trial cover both errors of law and sufficiency of the evidence. The scope of evidence review on motions for new trial is, theoretically at least, broader than the motions for a directed verdict of acquittal. The usual standard in directed verdict motions is whether, if believed, the stated case is sufficient. The motion for new trial allows (as the *Miller* case shows) a certain latitude to the court to act as the thirteenth juror and make credibility judgments.

Ordinarily, post-trial motions are a very unexciting matter. Defense counsel files form motions raising legal questions or simply states his motions orally. The prosecution seldom replies and the court routinely denies them.

3. In considering the *Miller* case it ought to be noted that motions for new trial based on newly discovered evidence are often, but not always, subject to time limits. The Federal Rule (Fed.R.Crim.P. 33) provides a three-year limitation for motions made on the basis of new evidence (other new trial motions must be filed within 7 days of the jury verdict). Few jurisdictions allow such a long period. Consider also what the result in *Miller* would have been if government counsel or the witness Caron had not consented to have Caron examined by a defense psychiatrist? Of course, if a convict discovers strong exculpatory evidence after his conviction is final, he may seek post-conviction relief, i.e. state or federal habeas corpus, if he can establish government suppression of the evidence. If this is not the case, his only official recourse will usually be the pursuit of executive clemency since, without proof of a *Brady* violation (see Chapter 15–A), newly discovered evidence does not provide grounds for federal habeas corpus relief. Unofficially, he may persuade the prosecutor and the court of his innocence and file a motion for new trial, the lateness of which will not be "noticed" by court or prosecutor and which will be granted by agreement.

Federal Rule 29(c) allows a defendant to move for a judgment of acquittal within 7 days of the jury verdict unless, before the time expires, the court grants an extension. This limit is strictly enforced but it is not jurisdictional and can be waived. Eberhart v. United States, 546 U.S. 12, 126 S.Ct. 403 (2005)

Traditional constraints on time and manner of new trial motions are being modified, by statute and court rule, to permit DNA evidence which, in some cases, may establish the wrongful nature of convictions. See Note, Post Conviction DNA Evidence, 50 Drake L.Rev 695 (2002).

4. Consider United States v. Williams, 233 F.3d 592 (D.C.Cir.2000):

> "Randolph, Circuit Judge:
>
> When arrested, Williams had 10.5 grams of heroin in 87 small plastic "baggies" in his coat pocket, and was storing another 75.3 grams of heroin, packaged in 638 small plastic "baggies," in an automobile. One government expert, a forensic chemist, testified about the tests he performed to establish that the material in the "baggies" was heroin.
>
> Another government witness, Detective Johnny St. Valentine–Brown, answered a question about his qualifications, stating that he had been a narcotics expert for more than twenty years and had served as a senior narcotics policy analyst in the Reagan and Bush administrations. At the end of his lengthy response, he added: "I am also a Board-certified pharmacist. I receive, maintain compound and dispense narcotic, as well as non-narcotic substances per prescription." Without objection, the court accepted Brown as an expert in the "distribution and use of narcotics, the packaging of narcotics for street-level distribution, the manner in which narcotic dealers distribute narcotic substances in the District of Columbia, the price for which narcotics are sold, both the wholesale and the street value ... [and] ... the Metropolitan Police Department and Drug Enforcement Administration procedures for the safeguarding of narcotics evidence." Brown went on to testify about the procedures the Police Depart-

ment used to store narcotic substances and to give his opinion, in light of Williams' large collection of small "baggies" of heroin, that "[h]eroin users don't buy this amount of dope broken down and packaged like this for their own personal use. It just does not happen."

After Williams' conviction, his attorney learned that Brown was not a pharmacist and had no degree in pharmacology, facts unknown to the prosecution during the trial. Williams then moved for a new trial pursuant to Federal Rule of Criminal Procedure 33, which the district court denied.

What is the standard for ordering a new trial when the newly discovered evidence is that perjury occurred? Rule 33 says only: "the court may grant a new trial ... if the interests of justice so require." An ancient opinion from another circuit lays down this test: a defendant is entitled to a new trial if, without the perjured testimony, "the jury might have reached a different conclusion." Larrison v. United States, 24 F.2d 82, 87 (7th Cir.1928). Notice that the Larrison formulation focuses on the importance of the perjured testimony to the prosecution's case. It does not ask whether the jury would have reached a different conclusion had the perjury been revealed at trial, although the Seventh Circuit has now modified the test to take this into account. See United States v. Mazzanti, 925 F.2d 1026, 1030 & n. 6 (7th Cir.1991). Notice too that Larrison puts the test in terms of what "might" have happened rather than what likely would have occurred.

Under our usual Rule 33 standard, a defendant is not entitled to a retrial on the basis of newly discovered evidence unless he can show that "a new trial would probably produce an acquittal." Thompson v. United States, 188 F.2d 652, 653 (D.C.Cir.1951) (emphasis added). This formulation, common throughout the federal courts, has been used for nearly a century and a half. We have consistently followed the Thompson standard in evaluating motions for a new trial under Rule 33. The difference between Larrison and Thompson is not just in the use of "might" versus "probably." Thompson looks ahead and evaluates the outcome of a new trial; Larrison looks back and evaluates the impact of the perjury on the jury in the original trial.

This circuit has never adopted Larrison. In the past we have managed to avoid choosing between it and the standard of Thompson because the defendant was not entitled to a new trial under either formulation. See United States v. Stofsky, 527 F.2d 237, 246 (2d Cir.1975).

This is not to say that the Larrison test is difficult to satisfy. It is not. The Second Circuit's Stofsky opinion put the matter well: "the test, if literally applied, should require reversal in cases of perjury with respect to even minor matters, especially in light of the standard jury instruction that upon finding that a witness had deliberately proffered false testimony in part, the jury may disregard his entire testimony." 527 F.2d at 245–46. That is reason enough to reject Larrison.

If not Larrison, what should the standard be? One possibility is the standard laid down in Thompson for other types of newly discovered evidence. This would mean that, when perjury by a prosecution witness is discovered after trial and when the prosecution did not know of the perjury until then, a defendant would be entitled to a new trial only if he can establish that he would probably be acquitted on retrial. History provides a reason for adhering to the Thompson formulation. Rule 33's current text was adopted in 1944. The accompanying Advisory Committee note stated that the rule "substantially continues existing practice." Fed.R.Crim.P. 33, advisory committee's note. The widely-accepted practice in 1944, a practice derived from a mid–19th century state court decision, required a defendant seeking a new trial to demonstrate a likelihood of success in a future retrial.

Another reason for adhering to the Thompson standard is that newly discovered evidence of perjury is not distinguishable from other newly discovered evidence. One author disagrees, arguing that perjury is different because it creates "an error at trial" whereas in the case of other types of newly discovered evidence, "the evidence at trial may have been incomplete, but it was all true." Note, I Cannot Tell A Lie: The Standard for New Trial in False Testimony Cases, 83 MICH. L. REV. 1925, 1945 (1985). The difference is illusory. Newly discovered evidence may often tend to prove that the evidence before the jury was not "true." A third party may confess to the crime; it may turn out that the main government witness has a string of felony convictions; proof positive of the defendant's alibi might surface. Any one of these items of newly discovered evidence, in various degrees, throws doubt on the accuracy of the trial evidence pointing to the defendant's guilt. Yet the district court, faced with Rule 33 motions in such cases, will evaluate the motions by using the Thompson test.

We recognize that the Second Circuit in Stofsky, while refusing to follow Larrison, may have devised a variation of it. Rather than asking whether the outcome of the trial might have been different had the jury known of the witness's lie, the Second Circuit asks whether the defendant probably would have been acquitted. This differs from our Thompson standard because, like Larrison, it looks at the matter retrospectively. The retrospective-prospective difference may not matter in the mine run of cases. But we can imagine situations in which it would matter, situations in which Stofsky would command a new trial that in all probability would not produce a difference outcome. Because we can see no good reason to treat newly discovered evidence of perjury differently than other types of newly discovered evidence, we reject Stofsky and adhere to our original formulation under Thompson.

If Williams were retried, the government would have at its disposal any number of experts who could testify that the amount of heroin in his possession was inconsistent with personal use. Or the government could decide not to call an expert on this subject. Any rational juror could infer from the fact that Williams was carrying 725 individual "baggies" of heroin that he was intending to sell them. So too the fact that drugs were segregated into "baggies" supports an inference of intent to distribute. In either event—a different expert or no expert—it is most unlikely that a jury would acquit Williams in a new trial.

Affirmed. [Citations omitted]

CHAPTER 23

APPELLATE AND OTHER POST-TRIAL REMEDIES

A. APPEALS

1. APPEALS FROM CONVICTIONS

Though the Court has never declared a constitutional right to an appeal, some form of appellate review is provided in every state. See Arkin, Rethinking the Constitutional Right to A Criminal Appeal, 39 U.C.L.A. L. Rev. 503 (1992). In the vast majority of jurisdictions a state court defendant who has been convicted of a serious offense has a right to take a direct appeal to a state reviewing court. In a very few states a defendant must petition for leave to appeal. If the state has a two-tiered appellate system, normally appeal as of right is taken to the intermediate appellate court. The losing party, whether that be the defendant or the prosecution, then can petition the state's highest court to exercise its discretion to further review the case.

Some jurisdictions retain a trial *de novo* system in minor criminal cases. Under that system, a defendant convicted in the lowest level trial court, without a showing of error, can obtain a new trial as of right in a trial court of broader jurisdiction. Often the latter court can impose a heavier penalty than the maximum permissible in the lowest level trial court. See Chapter 13, Section A–6 concerning jeopardy and due process question arising from imposition of a greater sentence following a trial *de novo*.

Once all avenues of direct review are exhausted within the state system, a convicted defendant may petition the United States Supreme Court for certiorari to review any federal constitutional claim which the state reviewing courts rejected. 28 U.S.C. § 1257. In the past, a state court defendant who unsuccessfully challenged a state statute upon federal constitutional grounds had a *right* to have his or her case heard on appeal by the Supreme Court. Congress, however, amended § 1257 to eliminate that right and to give the Supreme Court more control of its own docket.

NOTES

1. *Rights of Indigent Appellants.* Issues concerning the rights of indigents have been discussed previously in Chapter 9, Section A.

2. *Waiver Principle.* In both federal and state reviewing court, normally an issue will not be considered on direct appeal unless it has been presented to the trial court (in the form of a timely offer of proof, objection, motion to suppress, etc.). This is true even of claims which are of federal constitutional dimension. If a state reviewing court, in accordance with a fairly administered waiver rule, rejects a claim because it had not been properly preserved, an "adequate, independent" state basis for the decision will prevent review by the Supreme Court on certiorari from the state reviewing court. Henry v. Mississippi, 379 U.S. 443, 85 S.Ct. 564 (1965).

Occasionally an appellate court, in reviewing a conviction, will take notice of a "plain error" even though the defense did not properly preserve the issue in the trial court. Normally such an error must be both blatant and particularly prejudicial. Johnson v. United States, 520 U.S. 461, 117 S.Ct. 1544 (1997) (showing of prejudice for "plain error" must be greater than for harmless error review). Sometimes such errors are noted to avoid defendant's claim on appeal that defense counsel at trial was incompetent. Although a "plain error" is far more likely to be noticed in an appeal from a criminal conviction than in a civil appeal, even in criminal cases, in the vast majority of situations, a claim of error not properly preserved in the trial court will be deemed waived for appellate purposes.

3. *Harmless Error.* Not every error in a criminal trial requires reversal of a conviction. States remain free to apply their own harmless error rules where the error consists of a violation of state law. However, where the error is of federal constitutional dimension, a federal standard governs.

In recent years there has been substantial discussion of which federal constitutional errors are per se grounds for reversal and not subject to harmless error analysis. For example, denial of the right to trial counsel, denial of the right to an impartial judge, denial of the right to trial by jury, trial of a defendant who is incompetent, denial of the right to self-representation, improper grand jury selection procedures, and erroneous reasonable-doubt instructions so completely infest the proceedings as to be per se reversible error. See Sullivan v. Louisiana, 508 U.S. 275, 113 S.Ct. 2078 (1993); Vasquez v. Hillery, 474 U.S. 254, 106 S.Ct. 617 (1986), Casebook Chapter 11, B, supra. Excessive and prejudicial pre-trial and trial publicity may also generate a "pervasive" error that cannot be evaluated through harmless error analysis. Woods v. Dugger, 923 F.2d 1454 (11th Cir.1991).

However, "trial errors," the effects of which are somewhat contained, or which taint only part of the evidence, may be subjected to harmless error analysis. In Satterwhite v. Texas, 486 U.S. 249, 108 S.Ct. 1792 (1988), the trial judge had erred by admitting at a death-penalty sentencing hearing the testimony of a psychiatrist who opined that Satterwhite was a sociopath who was beyond the possibility of rehabilitation. The psychiatrist, at the State's request, and arguably pursuant to a court order, had interviewed Satterwhite while Satterwhite was under indictment. Defense counsel was not notified of the proposed examination, which was for the purpose of determining whether "defendant would commit criminal acts of violence that would constitute a threat to society." Absent such a probability, under Texas law, the defendant could not be sentenced to death.

Admission of the psychiatrist's testimony constituted a Sixth Amendment violation under the rule of Estelle v. Smith (supra, p. 1959), which itself was based upon right to counsel principles of Massiah v. United States (Casebook, Chapter 2, C). A majority of the Court declared that admission of such constitutionally-flawed testimony was not *per se* reversible error. Rather, a new penalty hearing was mandated unless the prosecution, in accordance with Chapman v. California, established that the error was harmless beyond a reasonable doubt. The Court limited *per se* reversals to cases where the deprivation of the right to counsel affected—and contaminated—the entire proceedings, such as in Gideon v. Wainwright (Casebook, Chapter 9, B) and Holloway v. Arkansas (Casebook, Chapter 18, B). Applying the *Chapman* test, the Court found that the facts of *Satterwhite* did *not* support a conclusion that admission of the testimony was harmless beyond a reasonable doubt.

Concurring justices argued that a Sixth Amendment error, as in *Satterwhite*, should automatically entitle the defendant to a new sentencing hearing because of the special character of capital sentencing.

In Arizona v. Fulminante, 499 U.S. 279, 111 S.Ct. 1246 (1991), a majority of the Supreme Court declared that admission of an involuntary confession could be deemed harmless error. The Court said that such admission is a classical trial error and, as such, is not subject to a *per se* rule of reversal. The *Fulminante* majority noted that whether the source of the error is rooted in the Due Process Clause, which underlies the voluntariness doctrine, or, for example, in the Sixth Amendment, which underlies the *Massiah* doctrine, the impact of an erroneously admitted confession can be the same. It is possible to assess that impact in the context of other evidence to determine whether the error was harmless beyond a reasonable doubt. The majority distinguished structural errors, such as the denial of trial counsel, or trial conducted by a judge who is not impartial. Those constitutional errors still require automatic reversal of a conviction.

Four dissenting justices (White, Marshall, Blackmun, Stevens) argued against the Court's abandoning its oft-repeated declaration that the admission of an involuntary confession can never be deemed harmless. They argued that the Court's decisions concerning harmless error and *per se* error do not support the trial error-structural error dichotomy. The dissenters also contended that the "deeply-rooted feeling" against police methods that yield involuntary confession make a rule of automatic reversal important in involuntary confession cases.

On the facts of *Fulminante*, a majority of the Court found that admission of the involuntary confession was not harmless beyond a reasonable doubt and reversed the conviction.

Over the years, one issue which has divided reviewing courts is whether a court's failure to instruct a jury on a material element of a crime can ever be deemed harmless error. The difficulty, as Justice Scalia pointed out in a concurring opinion in Carella v. California, 491 U.S. 263, 109 S.Ct. 2419 (1989), is that allowing an appellate court to decide that there was "overwhelming evidence" of the missing element of the crime usurps the defendant's right to have a jury, rather than a judge, decide whether that element is proved beyond a reasonable doubt. In Yates v. Evatt, 500 U.S. 391, 111 S.Ct. 1884 (1991), the Court considered the question in the context of an erroneous instruction to presume malice from use of a deadly weapon, which it found not to be harmless error:

> Before reaching such a judgment [of harmlessness under Chapman], a court must take two quite distinct steps. First, it must ask what evidence the jury actually considered in reaching its verdict. If, for example, the fact presumed is necessary to support the verdict, a reviewing court must ask what evidence the jury considered as tending to prove or disprove that fact. Did the jury look at only the predicate facts, or did it consider other evidence bearing on the fact subject to the presumption? In answering this question, a court does not conduct a subjective enquiry into the jurors' minds. The answer must come, instead, from analysis of the instructions given to the jurors and from application of that customary presumption that jurors follow instructions and, specifically, that they consider relevant evidence on a point in issue when they are told that they may do so. Once a court has made the first enquiry into the evidence considered by the jury, it must then weigh the probative force of that evidence as against the probative force of the presumption standing alone. To satisfy Chapman's reasonable-doubt standard, it will not be enough that the jury considered evidence from which it could have come to the verdict without reliance on the presumption. Rather, the issue under Chapman is whether the jury

> actually rested its verdict on evidence establishing the presumed fact beyond a reasonable doubt, independently of the presumption. Since that enquiry cannot be a subjective one into the jurors' minds, a court must approach it by asking whether the force of the evidence presumably considered by the jury in accordance with the instructions is so overwhelming as to leave it beyond a reasonable doubt that the verdict resting on that evidence would have been the same in the absence of the presumption. It is only when the effect of the presumption is comparatively minimal to this degree that it can be said, in Chapman's words, that the presumption did not contribute to the verdict rendered.

Justice Scalia disagreed with this approach, reiterating his position in *Carella*.

> Given the nature of the instruction here, then, to determine from the "entire record" that the error is "harmless" would be to answer a purely hypothetical question, viz., whether, if the jury had been instructed correctly, it would have found that the State proved the existence of malice beyond a reasonable doubt. Such a hypothetical inquiry is inconsistent with the harmless-error standard announced in Chapman v. California (1967), and reiterated by the Court today. "The issue under Chapman is whether the jury actually rested its verdict on evidence establishing the presumed fact beyond a reasonable doubt, independently of the presumption." Ante, at 404 (emphasis added). See also Bollenbach v. United States (1946) ("The question is not whether guilt may be spelt out of a record, but whether guilt has been found by a jury according to the procedure and standards appropriate for criminal trials"). While such a hypothetical inquiry ensures that the State has, in fact, proved malice beyond a reasonable doubt, it does not ensure that it has proved that element beyond a reasonable doubt to the satisfaction of a jury.

Even after Yates, the issue remains clouded. The Court struck down the Ninth Circuit's attempt to apply Justice Scalia's views in *Carella* in a habeas case involving a missing-element jury instruction, but the opinion skirted the question whether Justice Scalia's approach, or something like it, would be appropriate on direct review. California v. Roy, 519 U.S. 2, 117 S.Ct. 337 (1996) (per curiam). A later opinion also left the question open. Johnson v. United States, 520 U.S. 461, 117 S.Ct. 1544 (1997).

If the error is subject to a harmless error analysis, a federal constitutional standard governs where the error is of federal constitutional dimension.

In Chapman v. California, 386 U.S. 18, 87 S.Ct. 824 (1967), the Supreme Court held that reversal was required unless the constitutional error was "harmless beyond a reasonable doubt". Although not expressly disavowing that standard, the Supreme Court has, in the eyes of some observers, deemed error harmless according to a standard more favorable to the prosecution.

In Harrington v. California, 395 U.S. 250, 89 S.Ct. 1726 (1969), the Supreme Court assumed arguendo a violation of the rule announced in Bruton v. United States, 391 U.S. 123, 88 S.Ct. 1620 (1968), in that confessions by two co-defendants apparently implicating Harrington were admitted into evidence at a joint trial. The respondent state of California argued that the erroneous admission of these statements was harmless under the *Chapman* standard. An amicus brief argued that reviewing courts must be "freed from the bonds of the dictum in Chapman which seems to suggest that other overwhelming evidence is not to be an important factor in determining whether a particular constitutional error should be deemed harmless."

A majority of the Court, asserting that it was not departing from *Chapman*, held the error in question to be harmless, noting that the remaining evidence was "overwhelming." Justice Brennan, joined by Chief Justice Warren and Justice Marshall, dissented, declaring that the Court, purporting to apply *Chapman*, in fact overruled it by holding that "constitutional error in the trial of a criminal offense may be held harmless if there is 'overwhelming' untainted evidence to support the conviction". Note that application of a less stringent harmless error rule is one method of reducing the number of convictions overturned by retroactive application of new constitutional decisions such as *Bruton*. Is this a healthy compromise?

In Chambers v. Maroney, 399 U.S. 42, 90 S.Ct. 1975 (1970), the Supreme Court upheld lower court determinations that the admission into evidence of ammunition allegedly unlawfully seized in a robbery suspect's home, if erroneous, was harmless beyond a reasonable doubt. The Court cited *Harrington* and omitted reference to *Chapman*.

Should a harmless error rule protect a deliberate wrongdoer? Suppose that a prosecutor in closing argument repeatedly violates a well established principle, for example, by personally vouching for the credibility of witnesses or by commenting adversely on the defendant's decision not to testify. Should there be a per se rule of reversal for some prosecutorial misconduct without regard to the overwhelming nature of the prosecution's evidence? Or do other avenues of redress against the prosecutor provide a sufficient remedy for such misconduct?

In United States v. Hasting, 461 U.S. 499, 103 S.Ct. 1974 (1983), the Supreme Court reviewed a reversal reported at 660 F.2d 301 (7th Cir.1981). One view of the Seventh Circuit opinion was that the court had exercised its supervisory powers to reverse a conviction without considering the overwhelming evidence. Supposedly it had done so to deter prosecutors from deliberately violating clear principles of law in questioning witnesses and in making closing arguments. The Supreme Court reversed the Seventh Circuit and upheld the conviction, applying the "harmless beyond a reasonable doubt" standard applicable to errors of a federal constitutional dimension. The Court suggested that rarely, if ever, should a court exercise supervisory powers to reverse when the error is "harmless beyond a reasonable doubt." The Court noted that on the facts before it the prosecutor's alleged misconduct was not as clear as the Seventh Circuit suggested. It also referred to alternative remedies of discipline against the offending prosecutor and chastisement through identification, in the published opinion, of the prosecutor.

Dictum in *Hasting* suggests that the "harmless beyond a reasonable doubt" standard is a stringent one, applicable only when "the conviction would have been obtained notwithstanding" the error with "no reasonable possibility" that the practice complained of may have contributed to the conviction. In practice many courts have been rather quick to find that such a standard has been met.

For a critical discussion of the Court's harmless error jurisprudence, especially the distinction between "pervasive errors" and "trial errors," see Ogletree, *Arizona v. Fulminante*: The Harm of Applying Harmless Error to Coerced Confessions, 105 Harv. L. Rev. 152 (1991).

2. DEFENSE INTERLOCUTORY APPEALS

In most jurisdictions, a defendant who loses a pre-trial ruling (e.g., through the denial of a motion to suppress), has no right to a review of that decision before trial. He or she must go through trial and, if convicted, can present the claim on appeal. One exception in the federal system is that a defendant who loses a motion to dismiss for former jeopardy has a right to interlocutory review. See Chapter 13, Section A8.

Some state jurisdictions, either through appeal as a matter of right, or through the use of discretionary writs such as mandamus, prohibition, or habeas corpus, more frequently allow a defendant access to a court of review before trial.

3. THE PROSECUTION'S RIGHT TO APPEAL

In many jurisdictions the prosecution has the right to an interlocutory appeal from a pre-trial order suppressing evidence, as was discussed briefly in Chapter 13, Section H. Once jeopardy has attached the prosecution's right to appeal is much more limited. Constitutional limitations upon this right have been treated in various cases and notes found within Chapter 13, Section A.

B. STATE COLLATERAL REMEDIES

Each state provides a defendant with one or more methods of initiating an attack upon a conviction by filing a petition in the trial court after he or she has been sentenced.* Some of these remedies were created specifically to permit post-conviction attacks, for example, the Illinois Post Conviction Hearing Act, Ill.Rev.Stat. ch. 38, § 122 (1991). Others, such as coram nobis and state habeas corpus, have come to serve as post-conviction remedies through the evolution of case law or statutory changes. The scope of each post-conviction remedy varies, but some general principles always determine the availability and the limitations of each remedy. The important questions remain the same.

1. What kind of issues can be raised? Can a particular remedy be used to litigate non-jurisdictional issues? Is it designed to remedy wrongs only of a constitutional dimension? Is its use limited to cases where the trial court was under a critical misapprehension of the facts?

2. Is there an exhaustion of remedies requirement? Suppose no direct appeal was taken or suppose a direct appeal is pending; does that mean that a particular collateral remedy is not presently available?

3. Is there a statute of limitations? If so, when does it commence and when is it tolled?

* Sometimes these remedies are called "collateral" to distinguish them from direct appellate review. The term is something of a misnomer because, if successful, the post-conviction attack voids the conviction just as does a reversal on direct review. Elsewhere in the law the term "collateral attack" refers to efforts in Proceeding *B* to prevent Judgment *A* from being given collateral effect. Thus, for example, a plaintiff seeking child custody in State B may try to get the court in State B to deny effect to an earlier decree in State A, arguing that the court in State A lacked jurisdiction when it awarded custody to plaintiff's spouse. Similarly, a defendant who argues against the use of Conviction *A* in sentencing him in Trial *B* because he was denied counsel in Trial *A* is collaterally attacking Conviction *A*, as that term is usually used outside the criminal law.

4. Is there a custody requirement? If so, what constitutes custody? Does release from custody *pendente lite* moot the proceedings?

5. Is the use of the remedy restricted to certain types of convictions? Does it matter whether the petitioner is a misdemeanant or a felon? Must the sentence under attack have commenced to run before a petitioner serving consecutive sentences is eligible to complain about that sentence?

6. What is the effect of a prior direct appeal or the previous use of the same or a different collateral remedy? How strictly are doctrines of *res judicata* and waiver applied?

State post-conviction proceedings ordinarily are initiated by the filing of a written petition in the trial court. Frequently the warden who has custody is the named respondent. Where matters outside the original trial record are alleged, typically there is a requirement of supporting affidavits. The trial court is required to decide whether sufficient cause is shown to justify an evidentiary hearing.

Frequently post-conviction proceedings are deemed civil in nature, although just as often ordinary civil discovery rules are held inapplicable. The United States Supreme Court has held that the indigent state post-conviction petitioner or the federal habeas corpus petitioner has no absolute right to counsel at the trial level. Thus unless state law provides the right to counsel, appointment of counsel for the post-conviction petitioner is a matter of judicial discretion. See Casebook, Chapter 9, B.

Generally the losing party, whether the petitioner or the respondent, can appeal the state trial court's decision in the post-conviction proceedings. The indigent has no absolute constitutional right to appellate counsel in post-conviction proceedings under current decisions. However he or she does have the right to proceed in *forma pauperis* and the right to a free transcript of the post-conviction proceedings. See Lane v. Brown, 372 U.S. 477, 83 S.Ct. 768 (1963).

The primary post-conviction remedy for attacking a *federal* conviction is 28 U.S.C. § 2255, which is sometimes called an analog to federal habeas corpus for state prisoners (28 U.S.C. §§ 2241–2254).

C. FEDERAL HABEAS CORPUS FOR STATE PRISONERS

A defendant who has been convicted of a state crime may at some point be barred from making effective use of any and all state remedies as a means of raising a particular issue. In such an instance, if the question is of federal constitutional dimension, petitioner may be entitled to a decision on the merits of the claim from a federal district judge where a federal habeas corpus petition has been filed.

Early habeas corpus cases limited federal review to the question whether a state court had "jurisdiction" over the petitioner. Gradually, "jurisdiction" came to include the idea of a "fair hearing," and hence, due process. Finally, through a series of decisions, including Brown v. Allen, 344 U.S. 443, 73 S.Ct. 397 (1953), and Fay v. Noia, 372 U.S. 391, 83 S.Ct. 822 (1963), federal habeas corpus evolved to the point where it could serve as a post-conviction remedy for almost any state prisoner whose trial had involved constitutional error and who had exhausted presently available state remedies. In an extremely influential article, Finality in Criminal Law and Federal Habeas Corpus for State Prisoners, 76 Harv. L. Rev. 441 (1963), Professor Paul Bator argued that federal habeas should not be available to state prisoners whose claims had been "fully and fairly litigated" in state courts. Otherwise, federal district courts were essentially serving as appellate courts for the states, a perversion of federalist principles.

Under Chief Justices Burger and Rehnquist, the Supreme Court began to agree. Given the revival of the death penalty, the lack of finality in habeas litigation meant that executions were delayed indefinitely, causing consternation among the states and among death penalty proponents. So, the Court began reversing prior decisions that had expanded habeas review, especially those that had allowed litigants to overcome easily state court procedural bars, such as contemporary objection rules, and those that had allowed petitioners to file successive habeas petitions. See Wainwright v. Sykes, 433 U.S. 72, 97 S.Ct. 2497 (1977) (greatly limiting Fay v. Noia and requiring a petitioner to show cause for failing to failing to raise an issue at the appropriate time in state proceedings, and prejudice from the default); McCleskey v. Zant, 499 U.S. 467, 111 S.Ct. 1454 (1991) (greatly limiting Sanders v. United States (1963) and requiring a petitioner to show cause and prejudice in order to file a second or successive habeas petition raising new claims); Keeney v. Tamayo–Reyes, 504 U.S. 1, 112 S.Ct. 1715 (1992) (cause and prejudice showing required to excuse failure to develop factual record in state court).

The Court also limited the substance and scope of constitutional claims that might be brought on habeas. In Stone v. Powell, Chapter 6, Section D3, supra, the Supreme Court traced the history of the Twentieth Century expansion of federal habeas corpus whereby habeas became a tool for federal post-conviction review of federal constitutional claims previously adjudicated in state court. It then excluded Fourth Amendment claims from the scope of federal habeas corpus relief. (The Court refused, however, to exclude Miranda claims from the scope of habeas relief. Withrow v. Williams, 507 U.S. 680, 113 S.Ct. 1745 (1993)). The Court also barred (except in rare cases) retroactive application to habeas cases of "new rules" of constitutional law that did not exist when the case was on direct appeal, Teague v. Lane, 489 U.S. 288, 109 S.Ct. 1060 (1989). Even if the substance of a claim is reviewable, the Court established a rule of deference to state court findings of fact, Sumner v. Mata, 449 U.S. 539, 101 S.Ct. 764 (1981), and limited harmless error review to whether a constitutional error "had substantial and injurious effect or influence in determining the jury's verdict," Brecht v. Abrahamson, 507 U.S. 619, 113 S.Ct. 1710 (1993), instead of the more searching "harmless beyond reasonable doubt" standard of *Chapman*.

Although habeas corpus relief is governed by statute, Congress had, for decades, failed to reach consensus on habeas reform, and the Court was left to expand and contract the "Great Writ" by judicial decision (most decisions do not even refer to the statutory language). However, in 1996,

Congress enacted a comprehensive habeas reform, entitled the Antiterrorism and Effective Death Penalty Act (AEDPA), that both codified some of the Supreme Court's cutbacks and added some new ones. Because AEDPA does not follow the Court's decisions exactly, however, it has already been the source of much litigation. The Supreme Court held that the new law was not an unconstitutional "suspension of the Writ" in Felker v. Turpin, 518 U.S. 651, 116 S.Ct. 2333 (1996), but would be applied only to cases filed after its enactment. Lindh v. Murphy, 521 U.S. 320, 117 S.Ct. 2059 (1997). An extremely brief analysis of AEDPA's major provisions follows. For more extended discussion, see, Yackle, A Primer on the New Habeas Corpus Statute, 44 Buffalo L. Rev. 381 (1996); Tushnet & Yackle, Symbolic Statutes and Real Laws: The Pathologies of the Antiterrorism and Effective Death Penalty Act and the Prison Litigation Reform Act, 47 Duke L.J. 1 (1997).

28 U.S.C. § 2241. Power to grant writ

a) Writs of habeas corpus may be granted by the Supreme Court, any justice thereof, the district courts and any circuit judge within their respective jurisdictions....

* * *

c) The writ of habeas corpus shall not extend to a prisoner unless—

1) He is in custody ...

Discussion:

"Custody" is a prerequisite for federal habeas corpus, but the concept has been expanded to permit habeas corpus for individuals on parole, Jones v. Cunningham, 371 U.S. 236, 83 S.Ct. 373 (1963), probation, Benson v. California, 328 F.2d 159 (9th Cir.1964), and, in some instances, for convicted defendants free on bond or recognizance before serving their sentences, Hensley v. Municipal Court, 411 U.S. 345, 93 S.Ct. 1571 (1973).

If the petition is filed while the petitioner is in custody, as long as "collateral consequences" flow from the conviction, a habeas corpus petition attacking a conviction cannot be dismissed as moot even though the petitioner has been completely discharged *pendente lite.* Carafas v. LaVallee, 391 U.S. 234, 88 S.Ct. 1556 (1968). A petition arguing that parole was wrongfully revoked, however, may become moot if the petitioner cannot point to any particular collateral consequences likely to follow from the revocation. "Speculative or remote" collateral consequences, such as the use of the revocation to increase a future sentence, are held insufficient. Spencer v. Kemna, 523 U.S. 1, 118 S.Ct. 978 (1998).

§ 2254. State custody; remedies in State courts

a) The Supreme Court, a Justice thereof, a circuit judge, or a district court shall entertain an application for a writ of habeas corpus on behalf of a person in custody pursuant to the judgment of a State court only on the ground that he is in custody in violation or the Constitution or laws or treaties of the United States.

b)(1) An application for a writ of habeas corpus on behalf of a person in custody pursuant to the judgment of a State court shall not be granted unless it appears that—

A) the applicant has exhausted the remedies available in the courts of the States; or

B)(i) there is an absence of available State corrective process; or

(ii) circumstances exist that render such process ineffective to protect the rights of the applicant.

(2) An application for a writ of habeas corpus may be denied on the merits, notwithstanding the failure of the applicant to exhaust the remedies available in the courts of the State.

(3) A State shall not be deemed to have waived the exhaustion requirement or be estopped from reliance upon the requirement unless the State, through counsel, expressly waives the requirement.

c) An applicant shall not be deemed to have exhausted the remedies available in the courts of the State, within the meaning of this section, if he has the right under the law of the State to raise, by any available procedure, the question presented.

d) An application for a writ of habeas corpus on behalf of a person in custody pursuant to the judgment of a State court shall not be granted with respect to any claim that was adjudicated on the merits in State court proceedings unless the adjudication of the claim—

(1) resulted in a decision that was contrary to, or involved an unreasonable application of, clearly established Federal law, as determined by the Supreme Court of the United States; or

(2) resulted in a decision that was based on an unreasonable determination of the facts in light of the evidence presented in the State court proceeding.

e)(1) In a proceeding instituted by an application for a writ of habeas corpus by a person in custody pursuant to the judgment of a State court, a determination of a factual issue made by a State court shall be presumed to be correct. The applicant shall have the burden of rebutting the presumption of correctness by clear and convincing evidence.

(2) If the applicant has failed to develop the factual basis of a claim in State court proceedings, the court shall not hold an evidentiary hearing on the claim unless the applicant shows that—

(A) the claim relies on—

i) a new rule of constitutional law, made retroactive to cases on collateral review by the Supreme Court, that was previously unavailable; or

ii) a factual predicate that could not have been previously discovered through the exercise of due diligence; and

(B) the facts underlying the claim would be sufficient to establish by clear and convincing evidence that but for constitutional error, no reasonable factfinder would have found the applicant guilty of the underlying offense.

* * *

i) The ineffectiveness or incompetence of counsel during Federal or State collateral post-conviction proceedings shall not be a ground for relief in a proceeding arising under section 2254.

Discussion:

Exhaustion and Waiver: § 2254(b)–(c) basically codified existing Supreme Court precedent requiring petitioners to exhaust state remedies. See Duckworth v. Serrano, 454 U.S. 1, 102 S.Ct. 18 (1981); Strickland v. Washington, 466 U.S. 668, 104 S.Ct. 2052 (1984); Granberry v. Greer, 481 U.S. 129, 107 S.Ct. 1671 (1987).

The statute does not expressly address the question whether a petitioner should be able to litigate issues in federal court that a state court held were waived because of a procedural footfault. However, existing Supreme Court precedent requires federal courts to respect state procedural bar rules and refuse to address on the merits any questions that have been waived, unless "the prisoner can demonstrate cause for the default and actual prejudice as a result of the alleged violation of federal law, or demonstrate that failure to consider the claims will result in a fundamental miscarriage of justice." Coleman v. Thompson, 501 U.S. 722, 111 S.Ct. 2546 (1991) (refusing to hear claim because petitioner's attorney—Arnold & Porter—had filed state petition 3 days late). "Fundamental miscarriage of justice" may include the execution of a petitioner who is actually innocent. The showing of innocence required depends on how the claim is framed:

1) Defendants who claim that a constitutional defect in their trials resulted in mistaken convictions must show that the constitutional flaw "probably has caused the conviction of one innocent of the crime." Schlup v. Delo, 513 U.S. 298, 115 S.Ct. 851 (1995). The claim of innocence serves as a way to overcome the procedural bar, but the petitioner must still prevail on the constitutional claim.

2) Defendants who claim that they are actually innocent of aggravating circumstances that led to the imposition of the death penalty must show by "clear and convincing evidence that but for a constitutional error, no reasonable juror would have imposed the death penalty." Sawyer v. Whitley, 505 U.S. 333, 112 S.Ct. 2514 (1992).

3) Defendants who claim that they received a constitutionally adequate trial, but are actually innocent must make a showing of innocence strong enough to make an execution "constitutionally intolerable." Herrera v. Collins, 506 U.S. 390, 113 S.Ct. 853 (1993). There are strong indications that federal courts will now determine issues of fact with respect to innocence claims as opposed to the more conventional method of deciding questions of law on a state court record. Courts of Appeals and the supreme Court will conduct fact intensive reviews of District Court decisions both with respect to "innocence excusing waiver" and "free standing innocence

claims'' as found in House v. Bell, 545 U.S. 1151, 125 S.Ct. 2991 (2005). See also, In re Lott, 424 F.3d 446 (6th Cir.2005) (discussing whether actual innocence claim waives attorney-client privilege.)

Scope of Review: Section (d) may be even less forgiving than the Supreme Court's previous jurisprudence. Section (d)(1) essentially bars retroactive application of ''new rules'' of constitutional law, as did Teague v. Lane, *supra*. However, the statute uses the broadest formulation of *Teague*, see Butler v. McKellar, 494 U.S. 407, 110 S.Ct. 1212 (1990), that a majority of the Court rejected as too deferential to state courts in Wright v. West, 505 U.S. 277, 112 S.Ct. 2482 (1992) (O'Connor, concurring in the judgment) and Thompson v. Keohane, 516 U.S. 99, 116 S.Ct. 457 (1995). See Meyer, ''Nothing We Say Matters'': *Teague* and New Rules, 61 U. Chi. L. Rev. 423 (1994). Indeed, AEDPA almost appears to require federal courts to defer to the ''reasonable'' constitutional rulings of state courts, rather than giving questions of law or application of law *de novo* review. But see, Yackle, A Primer on the New Federal Habeas Corpus Statute, 44 Buffalo L. Rev. 381, 384 (1996) (''For section 2254(d) establishes no general rule of deference to 'reasonable' state court decisions on questions of federal law or on mixed questions of law and fact. Previous attempts to establish such a rule of deference to the state courts were unsuccessful. Accordingly, proponents made a calculated decision to drop those attempts in order to win passage of a general habeas bill in this Congress.'') For discussion of the appropriate standard of review, see Drinkard v. Johnson, 97 F.3d 751 (5th Cir.1996) (overruled on other grounds); Spreitzer v. Peters, 114 F.3d 1435 (7th Cir.1997).

The provision also goes farther than the *Teague* cases in confining ''clearly established'' law to that set forth by the Supreme Court. See Long v. Krenke, 138 F.3d 1160 (7th Cir.1998) (rejecting under AEDPA claim based on circuit, rather than Supreme Court, precedent).

States however may give broader effect to new rules of criminal procedure than *Teague* requires. ''New constitutional rules announced by this Court that place certain kinds of primary individual conduct beyond the power of the States to proscribe, as well as 'watershed' rules of criminal procedure, must be applied in all future trials, all cases pending on direct review, and all federal habeas corpus proceedings. All other new rules of criminal procedure must be applied in future trials and in cases pending on direct review, but may not provide the basis for a federal collateral attack on a state-court conviction. This is the substance of the '*Teague* rule' described by Justice O'Connor in her plurality opinion in Teague v. Lane, (1989). The question in this case is whether *Teague* constrains the authority of state courts to give broader effect to new rules of criminal procedure than is required by that opinion. We have never suggested that it does, and now hold that it does not.'' Danforth v. Minnesota, ___ U.S. ___, 128 S.Ct. 1029 (2008).

Fact-finding: Section (e)(1) codifies existing law regarding deference to state court findings of fact, though adding a ''clear and convincing evidence'' burden of proof. See Sumner v. Mata, 455 U.S. 591, 102 S.Ct. 1303 (1982).

Section (e)(2) codifies, to some extent, the Court's ruling in Keeney v. Tamayo–Reyes, 504 U.S. 1, 112 S.Ct. 1715 (1992), that a petitioner must show cause and prejudice for failing to develop the factual basis of a claim in state court. However, (e)(2) goes farther than a traditional cause and prejudice standard in requiring that the factual predicate "could not have been previously discovered through the exercise of due diligence," making ineffective assistance of counsel seem not to be adequate "cause." Section (e)(2) also requires a much tougher showing of actual innocence than "probable innocence" as required in *Schlup*. It does not appear on its face to recognize a stand-alone claim of actual innocence, as in *Herrera*. No doubt subsequent litigation will clarify whether the Eighth Amendment requires the Court to "read in" the *Herrera* exception. See Washington v. Mazurkiewicz, 1997 WL 83771 (E.D.Pa.1997) (reserving question); Bush v. Singletary, 99 F.3d 373 (11th Cir.1996).

The exception stated in (e)(2)(A)(i) for new rules made retroactive by the Supreme Court refers to *Teague v. Lane*'s exceptions. New rules of constitutional law will not be retroactively applied to habeas cases unless they place a category of conduct beyond the reach of the criminal law, prohibit "imposition of a certain type of punishment for a class of defendants because of their status or offense"; or alter "our understanding of the bedrock procedural elements" essential to the fairness of a proceeding. See Sawyer v. Smith, 497 U.S. 227, 110 S.Ct. 2822 (1990). The Court has never invoked any of these exceptions.

What should a court do under AEDPA in a case like Bracy v. Gramley, 520 U.S. 899, 117 S.Ct. 1793 (1997), in which a habeas petitioner sought (and received) discovery to determine whether a corrupt judge had used his case to "cover up" bribery in other cases?

Harmless Error. The statute does not address what standard of harmless error is appropriate on habeas. Should courts use the standard articulated in Brecht v. Abrahamson, 507 U.S. 619, 113 S.Ct. 1710 (1993), that non-structural errors must have had "substantial or injurious effect or influence in determining the jury's verdict" in order to justify relief on habeas? Or the standard that is more favorable to petitioners that the error is "harmless beyond a reasonable doubt" formulated in *Chapman* for direct review. In O'Neal v. McAninch, 513 U.S. 432, 115 S.Ct. 992 (1995), the Court rejected the view that the habeas petitioner bore the burden of proving an error not harmless. Instead, a court in equipoise must rule in petitioner's favor, because liberty is at stake.

In Fry v. Pliler, ___ U.S. ___, 127 S.Ct. 2321 (2007), *reh.denied* ___ U.S. ___, 128 S.Ct. 19 (2007), a defendant convicted of two murders filed a writ of habeas corpus claiming, *inter alia*, that the trial court's exclusion of a witness's testimony deprived him of a fair opportunity to defend himself in violation of Chambers v. Mississippi (1973). The Supreme Court affirmed the denial of habeas corpus stating: "We hold that in § 2254 proceedings a court must assess the prejudicial impact of constitutional error in a state-court criminal trial under the 'substantial and injurious effect' standard set forth in *Brecht*, whether or not the state appellate court recognized the error and reviewed it for harmlessness under the 'harmless beyond a reasonable doubt' standard set forth in *Chapman* Since the Ninth Circuit correctly applied the *Brecht* standard rather than the *Chapman* standard, we affirm the judgment below." Fry, 127 S.Ct. at 2328.

Incompetence of counsel. Section (i) codifies existing law. Because there is no right to assistance of counsel in collateral proceedings, the Court has held that incompetence of counsel does not raise a constitutional issue. See Coleman v. Thompson, 501 U.S. 722, 111 S.Ct. 2546 (1991). *Coleman* held that attorney error short of constitutionally ineffective counsel could not even serve as "cause" for failing to meet a state procedural requirement.

§ 2244. Finality of determination

a) No circuit or district judge shall be required to entertain an application for a writ of habeas corpus to inquire into the detention of a person pursuant to a judgment of a court of the United States if it appears that the legality of such detention has been determined by a judge or court of the United States on a prior application for a writ of habeas corpus, except as provided in section 2255.

b)(1) A claim presented in a second or successive habeas corpus application under section 2254 that was presented in a prior application shall be dismissed.

(2) A claim presented in a second or successive habeas corpus application under section 2254 that was not presented in a prior application shall be dismissed unless—

A) the applicant shows that the claim relies on a new rule of constitutional law, made retroactive to cases on collateral review by the Supreme Court, that was previously unavailable; or

B)(i) the factual predicate for the claim could not have been discovered previously through the exercise of due diligence; and

(ii) the facts underlying the claim, if proven and viewed in light of the evidence as a whole, would be sufficient to establish by clear and convincing evidence that, but for constitutional error, no reasonable factfinder would have found the applicant guilty of the underlying offense.

(3)(A) Before a second or successive application permitted by this section is filed in the district court, the applicant shall move in the appropriate court of appeals for an order authorizing the district court to consider the application.

* * *

(E) The grant or denial of an authorization by a court of appeals to file a second or successive application shall not be appealable and shall not be the subject of a petition for rehearing or for a writ of certiorari.

* * *

(1) A 1-year period of limitation shall apply to an application for a writ of habeas corpus by a person in custody pursuant to the judgment of a State court. . . .

Discussion:

Before enactment of AEDPA, the Supreme Court had barred successive habeas petitions, except where a petitioner could show cause and prejudice for failing to raise a claim in a prior petition, or where the petitioner demonstrated actual innocence of the crime. McCleskey v. Zant, 499 U.S. 467, 111 S.Ct. 1454 (1991). AEDPA limits successive petitions still more—even cause and prejudice is not sufficient. Instead, a petitioner must bring forward new evidence, previously unavailable (and poor representation is no excuse), show constitutional error, *and* must make a very tough showing of actual innocence. As with § 2254's provision concerning evidentiary hearings, it is open to question whether the Court must read in a "miscarriage of justice" exception. See discussion of § 2254, *supra*.

The statute also includes a new one-year statute of limitations for the bringing of habeas claims. Prior law limited the time within which a habeas petition could be brought only when the state had been prejudiced. Lonchar v. Thomas, 517 U.S. 314, 116 S.Ct. 1293 (1996). A few courts have held that the statute is subject to equitable tolling.

The Supreme Court held in Felker v. Turpin, 518 U.S. 651, 116 S.Ct. 2333 (1996), that § 2244(b)(3)(E) does not prevent a petitioner from seeking habeas relief from the Court directly through its original jurisdiction under § 2241 and § 2254; it merely forecloses the court's appellate habeas jurisdiction.

§ 2261. Prisoners in State custody subject to capital sentence; appointment of counsel; requirement of rule of court or statute; procedures for appointment

[omitted]

Discussion:

If a state passes legislation providing death row inmates with counsel for state habeas filings (not constitutionally required, see Pennsylvania v. Finley, 481 U.S. 551, 107 S.Ct. 1990 (1987)), the state may take advantage of the streamlined procedures for capital cases set forth in §§ 2261–66. If the state qualifies, its death row petitioners must file their federal habeas petitions within 180 days of final state court (or Supreme Court) action. § 2263. The federal district court must, on pain of mandamus, act on the petition within 180 days of receiving it. § 2266. The statute also includes stricter limits on review of procedurally defaulted claims. § 2264.

A state must ensure that counsel is competent and adequately compensated in order for the state to take advantage of the short limitations periods, although the definitions of these parameters are left for the states to determine. If a petitioner fails to meet the deadlines or "fails to make a substantial showing of the denial of a Federal right or is denied relief in the district court or at any subsequent stage of review . . . no Federal court thereafter shall have the authority to enter a stay of execution in the case, unless the court of appeals approves the filing of a second or successive application under section 2244(b)." § 2262(b), (c). So far, courts have held that no state has yet ensured competent and adequately compensated counsel for collateral review in order to "opt-in" to the streamlined death penalty review procedures.*

Given the strict rules concerning procedural defaults and successive claims, shouldn't the states also be required to adequately compensate and train *trial* counsel? For some disturbing case studies, see Bright, Counsel for the Poor: The Death Sentence Not for the Worst Crime But for the Worst Lawyer, 103 Yale L.J. 1835 (1994) (citations omitted):

> After years in which she and her children were physically abused by her adulterous husband, a woman in Talladega County, Alabama, arranged to have him killed. Tragically, murders of abusive spouses are not rare in our violent society, but seldom are they punished by the death penalty. Yet this woman was sentenced to death. Why?
>
> It may have been in part because one of her court-appointed lawyers was so drunk that the trial had to be delayed for a day after he was held in contempt and sent to jail. The next morning, he and his client were both produced from jail, the trial resumed, and the death penalty was imposed a few days later. It may also have been in part because this lawyer failed to find hospital records documenting injuries received by the woman and her daughter, which would have corroborated their testimony about abuse. And it may also have been because her lawyers did not bring their expert witness on domestic abuse to see the defendant until 8 p.m. on the night before he testified at trial.
>
> The woman in Talladega, like any other person facing the death penalty who cannot afford counsel, is entitled to a court-appointed lawyer under the Supreme Court's decision in Powell v. Alabama. But achieving competent representation in capital and other criminal cases requires much more than the Court's recognition, in Powell and in Gideon v. Wainwright, of the vital importance of counsel and of "thoroughgoing investigation and preparation." Providing better representation today than the defendants had in Scottsboro in 1931 requires money, a structure for providing indigent defense that is independent of the judiciary and prosecution, and skilled and dedicated lawyers.
>
> * * *
>
> Quality legal representation also made a difference for Gary Nelson and Frederico Martinez–Macias, but they did not receive it until years after they were wrongly convicted and sentenced to death. Nelson was represented at his capital trial in Georgia in

* In Calderon v. Ashmus, 523 U.S. 740, 118 S.Ct. 1694 (1998), the Supreme Court held that potential habeas petitioners could not seek a declaratory judgment against the state to determine whether or not the new statute of limitations would apply. How could a petitioner challenge the state's counsel requirements then? Justices Souter and Breyer suggest one possibility in their concurrence.

1980 by a sole practitioner who had never tried a capital case. The court-appointed lawyer, who was struggling with financial problems and a divorce, was paid at a rate of only $15 to $20 per hour. His request for co-counsel was denied. The case against Nelson was entirely circumstantial, based on questionable scientific evidence, including the opinion of a prosecution expert that a hair found on the victim's body could have come from Nelson. Nevertheless, the appointed lawyer was not provided funds for an investigator and, knowing a request would be denied, did not seek funds for an expert. Counsel's closing argument was only 255 words long. The lawyer was later disbarred for other reasons.

Nelson had the good fortune to be represented pro bono in postconviction proceedings by lawyers willing to spend their own money to investigate Nelson's case. They discovered that the hair found on the victim's body, which the prosecution expert had linked to Nelson, lacked sufficient characteristics for microscopic comparison. Indeed, they found that the Federal Bureau of Investigation had previously examined the hair and found that it could not validly be compared. As a result of such inquiry, Gary Nelson was released after eleven years on death row.

Frederico Martinez–Macias was represented at his capital trial in ElPaso, Texas, by a court-appointed attorney paid only $11.84 per hour. Counsel failed to present an available alibi witness, relied upon an incorrect assumption about a key evidentiary point without doing the research that would have corrected his erroneous view of the law, and failed to interview and present witnesses who could have testified in rebuttal of the prosecutor's case. Martinez–Macias was sentenced to death.

Martinez–Macias received competent representation for the first time when a Washington, D.C., firm took his case pro bono. After a full investigation and development of facts regarding his innocence, Martinez–Macias won federal habeas corpus relief. An El Paso grand jury refused to re-indict him and he was released after nine years on death row.

How will cases like these be treated after AEDPA?

D. FEDERAL HABEAS CORPUS FOR ENEMY COMBATANTS

In *Hamdi v. Rumsfeld*, 542 U.S. 507, 124 S.Ct. 2633 (2004) the Court upheld the right of the federal government to detain enemy combatants. However, the Court held that such a detainee would retain the right of habeas corpus 28 U.S.C. § 2241.

The statute governing habas corpus allowed aliens detained in Guantanamo Bay Naval Base ini Cuba, a territory over which the United States government exercised plenary and exclusive jurisdiction to pursue petitions for writs of habas corpus. The statute conferred jurisdiction over these cases in United States courts. *Rasul v. Bush*, 542 U.S. 466, 124 S.Ct. 2686 (2004).

Later, in a plurality opinion, the Court did not reach the issue of whether Congress had unconstitutionally suspended the writ of habeas corpus as to Guantanamo detainees. It did deny the Government's motion to dismiss and ruled that the military commissions established to try the detainees were invalid. *Hamdan v. Rumsfeld*, 548 U.S. 557, 126 S.Ct. 2749 (2006).

APPENDIX

PROVISIONS OF THE CONSTITUTION OF THE UNITED STATES

Provisions of the Constitution of the United States, and certain Amendments thereto, of particular significance in the administration of criminal justice:

Preamble

We the People of the United States, in Order to form a more perfect Union, establish Justice, insure domestic Tranquility, provide for the common defense, promote the general Welfare, and secure the Blessings of Liberty to ourselves and our Posterity, do ordain and establish this Constitution for the United States of America.

Article I.

* * *

Section 8. The Congress shall have Power To lay and collect Taxes, Duties, Imposts and Excises, to pay the Debts and provide for the common Defence and general Welfare of the United States; but all Duties, Imposts and Excises shall be uniform throughout the United States; . . .

To regulate Commerce with foreign Nations, and among the several States and with the Indian Tribes; . . .

To provide for the Punishment of counterfeiting the Securities and current Coin of the United States; . . .

To constitute Tribunals inferior to the supreme Court;

To define and punish Piracies and Felonies committed on the high Seas, and Offences against the Law of Nations;

To declare War, grant Letters of Marque and Reprisal, and make Rules concerning Captures on Land and Water; . . .;

To make Rules for the Government and Regulation of the land and naval forces;

To provide for calling forth the Militia to execute the Laws of the Union, suppress Insurrections and repel Invasions;

To provide for organizing, arming, and disciplining, the Militia, and for governing such Part of them as may be employed in the Service of the United States, reserving to the States respectively, the Appointment of the Officers, and the Authority of training the Militia according to the discipline prescribed by Congress;

To exercise exclusive Legislation in all Cases whatsoever, over such District (not exceeding ten Miles square) as may, by Cession of particular States, and the Acceptance of Congress, become the Seat of the Government of the United States, and to exercise like Authority over all Places purchased by the Consent of the Legislature of the State in which the Same shall be, for the Erection of Forts, Magazines, Arsenals, dock-Yards, and other needful Buildings;—And

To make all Laws which shall be necessary and proper for carrying into Execution the foregoing Powers, and all other Powers vested by this Constitution in the Government of the United States, or in any Department or Officer thereof.

Section 9.

* * *

No Bill of Attainder or ex post facto Law shall be passed.

Article III.

Section 1. The judicial Power of the United States, shall be vested in one supreme Court, and in such inferior Courts as the Congress may from time to time ordain and establish. The Judges, both of the supreme and inferior Courts, shall hold their Offices during good Behaviour, and shall, at stated Times, receive for their Services, a Compensation, which shall not be diminished during their Continuance in Office.

Section 2.

... the supreme Court shall have appellate Jurisdiction, both as to Law and Fact, with such Exceptions, and under such Regulations as the Congress shall make.

The Trial of all Crimes, except in Cases of Impeachment, shall be by Jury; and such Trial shall be held in the State where the said Crimes shall have been committed; but when not committed within any State, the Trial shall be at such Place or Places as the Congress may by Law have directed.

Section 3. Treason against the United States, shall consist only in levying War against them, or in adhering to their Enemies, giving them Aid and Comfort. No Person shall be convicted of Treason unless on the Testimony of two Witnesses to the same overt Act, or on Confession in open Court.

The Congress shall have Power to declare the Punishment of Treason, but no Attainder of Treason shall work Corruption of Blood, or Forfeiture except during the Life of the Person attainted.

Article VI.

* * *

This Constitution, and the Laws of the United States which shall be made in Pursuance thereof; and all Treaties made, or which shall be made, under the Authority of the United States, shall be the supreme Law of the

Land; and the Judges in every State shall be bound thereby, any Thing in the Constitution or Laws of any State to the Contrary notwithstanding.

* * *

Amendments

Amendment I.

Congress shall make no law respecting an establishment of religion, or prohibiting the free exercise thereof; or abridging the freedom of speech, or of the press; or the right of the people peaceably to assemble, and to petition the Government for a redress of grievances.

Amendment II.

A well regulated militia, being necessary to the security of a free State, the right of the people to keep and bear arms, shall not be infringed.

Amendment III.

No Soldier shall, in time of peace be quartered in any house, without the consent of the owner, nor in time of war, but in a manner to be prescribed by law.

Amendment IV.

The right of the people to be secure in their persons, houses, papers, and effects, against unreasonable searches and seizures, shall not be violated, and no warrants shall issue, but upon probable cause, supported by oath or affirmation, and particularly describing the place to be searched, and the persons or things to be seized.

Amendment V.

No person shall be held to answer for a capital, or otherwise infamous crime, unless on a presentment or indictment of a Grand Jury, except in cases arising in the land or naval forces, or in the militia, when in actual service in time of war or public danger; nor shall any person be subject for the same offence to be twice put in jeopardy of life or limb; nor shall be compelled in any criminal case to be a witness against himself, nor be deprived of life, liberty, or property, without due process of law; nor shall private property be taken for public use, without just compensation.

Amendment VI.

In all criminal prosecutions, the accused shall enjoy the right to a speedy and public trial, by an impartial jury of the State and district wherein the crime shall have been committed, which district shall have been previously ascertained by law, and to be informed of the nature and cause of the accusation; to be confronted with the witnesses against him; to have compulsory process for obtaining witnesses in his favor, and to have the assistance of Counsel for his defence.

Amendment VII.

In Suits at common law, where the value in controversy shall exceed twenty dollars, the right of trial by jury shall be preserved, and no fact tried by a jury, shall be otherwise re-examined in any Court of the United States, than according to the rules of the common law.

Amendment VIII.

Excessive bail shall not be required, nor excessive fines imposed, nor cruel and unusual punishments inflicted.

Amendment IX.

The enumeration in the Constitution, of certain rights, shall not be construed to deny or disparage others retained by the people.

Amendment X.

The powers not delegated to the United States by the Constitution, nor prohibited by it to the States, are reserved to the States respectively, or to the people.

* * *

Amendment XIII.

Section 1. Neither slavery nor involuntary servitude, except as a punishment for crime whereof the party shall have been duly convicted, shall exist within the United States, or any place subject to their jurisdiction.

Section 2. Congress shall have power to enforce this article by appropriate legislation.

Amendment XIV.

Section 1. All persons born or naturalized in the United States, and subject to the jurisdiction thereof, are citizens of the United States and of the State wherein they reside. No State shall make or enforce any law which shall abridge the privileges or immunities of citizens of the United States; nor shall any State deprive any person of life, liberty, or property, without due process of law; nor deny to any person within its jurisdiction the equal protection of laws. . . .

Section 5. The Congress shall have power to enforce, by appropriate legislation, the provisions of this article.

Amendment XV.

Section 1. The right of citizens of the United States to vote shall not be denied or abridged by the United States or by any State on account of race, color, or previous condition of servitude.

Section 2. The Congress shall have power to enforce this article by appropriate legislation.

Amendment XVI.

The Congress shall have power to lay and collect taxes on incomes, from whatever source derived, without apportionment among the several States, and without regard to any census or enumeration. . . .

INDEX

References are to Pages.

†